In the Desert Sun

IN THE
DESERT SUN
1994

John J. Purcell, III, Editor

THE NATIONAL LIBRARY OF POETRY

In the Desert Sun

Copyright 1994 by the National Library of Poetry

As a compilation.
Rights to individual poems reside with the artists themselves.

All rights reserved under International and Pan-American copyright conventions. No part of this book may be reproduced, stored in a retrieval system or transmitted in any form, electonic, mechanical or by any other means, without written permission of the publisher. Address all inquiries to Jeffrey Franz, Publisher, P.O. Box 704, Owings Mills, MD 21117.

Library of Congress
Cataloging in Publication Data

ISBN 1-56167-047-2

Manufactured in The United States of America by
Watermark Press
11419 Cronridge Dr., Suite 10
Owings Mills, MD 21117

Editor's Note

As editor of In the Desert Sun, I had the remarkably good fortune to review and contemplate the widely varied poetic selections featured within this anthology. Each work published in In the Desert Sun contains an element of human nature expressed in original and deliberate fashion. Below are discussed several poems which I would like to honor with special recognition.

The poem "Stains," by Dion Birney, struck a particularly strong chord within me, and is a work to which I feel many of us can relate. Dion, in a rapid fire delivery, uses a somewhat taboo subject to create a metaphor illustrating man's internal struggle for an understanding of self and the powerlessness one experiences in struggling for definition.

Kirsten Kirwan, in "Two Sons," uses the persona to express desperation and heartache. The poem leaves the reader with a lingering sense of emptiness, while at the same time offering many people an example of how the struggles and challenges we face in life are never as bad as we believe them to be, for there always exists someone with greater challenges.

Another favorite is "Ssenizzid Diova Ot," a poem which uses a buzzing fly as a metaphor for the seemingly endless and directionless journey man takes through life. The poem also illustrates that our perspective on the world is extremely subjective, as illustrated by the fly's observations of man.

Instead of offering my interpretation of our Grand Prize-Winning poem "Autumnal," by Del Pine, I leave it to you, the readers, to draw your own conclusions. I congratulate Del on creating a work of great intensity.

Unfortunately, I don't have the time or space to critique each and every one of the prominent poems appearing within this anthology. Yet, as In the Desert Sun illustrates, all of the poems featured are worthy of merit. The poets artistically present a variety of subjects and styles, each contributing to the quality of this publication. May all of the artists within this anthology be renowned for their talents and efforts in creative writing.

I sincerely hope that you enjoy reading In the Desert Sun.

John J. Purcell III

Acknowledgements

The publication In the Desert Sun is a culmination of the efforts of many individuals. Judges, editors, assistant editors, graphic artists, layout artists and office administrators have all brought their respective talents to bear on this project. The editors are grateful for the contribution of these fine people:

Jeffrey Bryan, Keith Crummedy, Lisa Della, Chrystal Eldridge, Ardie L. Freeman, Hope Freeman, Diane Mills, Cynthia Stevens, Caroline Sullivan, and Margaret Zirn.

Grand Prize Winner

Del Pine

Second Prize Winners

Dion Birney	Kristen Kirwan
J. W. Churchill	Laurie Leininger
Shawn E. Fisher	Krisi Prater
George Higgs	Larry Rowdon
Edgar F. Hosking Jr	Mark Simonson

Third Prize Winners

Jana Babb	Richard G. Flores	Gary T. Muse
Elizabeth J. Barrett	Edward Garner	Bobbi Nesmith
Mildred Creighton Barry	Art Glasow	Jane MacKinnon Oldroyd
Dawn Bieber	Pauline Good	Maxa Ott
D. N. Blakeley	Tina Gordon	Billie J. Ponzetti
Gary D. Bliss	L. M. Green	Susan Portalatin
Tyler Cady	Catherine Hope Greene	Mitch Posner
Jill Clevenger	Tara Guthrie	John E. Pregler
Kathleen L. Cook	Dourlas R. Handlon	June A. Robinette
David P. Couston	Mary Louise S. Hardin	Hilda Schaefer
Margaret Sue Cox	Jean Hays	Mary L. Schaeffer
Melinda de Marmion	David Herman	Stuart Schrader
Velda Douglas	Douglas Winfield Hiser II	Robin Schraider
Kristine E. Doyle	Susan Jones	Darren A. Singer
Steve Doyle	Thea Aneke Kampfer	Lovelle Sokan
Elizabeth Elliott	Roberta Lawringsky	Linda Stauffer
Melanie M. Ellis	Crystal Michelle McAlister	Sharon Thibodeaux
Leonard Ferrante	Martha I. McGahan	Nicole Kathryn Tremel
Vincent Fettinger	Jessica Meyer	Bryan Whitefield
Roberta Jean Flissinger		Teodulfo T. Yerro

Congratulations also to our semi-finalists.

Grand Prize Winner

Autumnal

Living day by day is wise,
Declared the old man. Dusty lies
The way ahead, and steep. But here
It's peaceful, and the air is clear.
This height I've reached is not, true, where
In former years I thought to dare,
But far enough. I am content
To rest, and watch the slow ascent
Of others past those rocks which seem,
Surmounted, nothing but a dream.
--Del Pine

The Woman Of My Dream

There is a Spanish proverb which says it best.
A beautiful woman is a treasure to the eyes;
But a good woman is a jewel to the heart.
But how much better it's to have both combined
that is, to be both a treasure to the eyes
And a jewel to the heart
As personified in you.
If adoring you is sinful,
then I would gladly become a sinner.
You are the apotheosis of beauty, poise and charm,
the epitome of integrity, generosity and grace.
It always comforts my heart to think of you.
My only regret is that I did not find you sooner
You are the fulfillment of a dream come true.
—*Joseph S. Hughes*

A Single White Rose

A single white rose left to lie
A broken heart, is heard to cry.
A symbol of pure love, a rose of pure white.
Forbidden hopes, and dreams that felt so right.

An autumn breeze carries life away,
never again to be seen in the light of day.
A soul is leaving full of pain,
fantasies bound and slowly slain.
Painful tears filled with fear,
drowning pure love, inside this rose bud.

A single white rose, left to die.
Only to be forgotten, that love was inside.
It's fading beauty struggling to survive,
As this is it's duty, it must not die.

Only a memory existing within,
reflecting the beauty that once had been.
A broken heart hides, from it's insufferable pain.
In order to keep from going insane.

A single white rose left to lie.
All alone inside, pure love shall surely die.
—*T. C. Crawford*

"Star Child"

September is gone, and October is in,
A chill in the air, A slight wind.
A perfect time to walk down the beach,
Hand in hand, surf spray on your cheek.
We are all "Star" children, this I know,
For the same Atoms that created stars, made us grow.
All the energy that ever was, still is, and will ever be,
That's what's so comforting about you and me.
Its all so eternal, so gentle and sweet
Goddess is Good! This life is a treat!
Happy Day to you, STAR CHILD, may you smile,
This is a hug to you, all the while.
—*Sharon DeVaughn*

A New Baby!

With support from the highest court in the land,
  A human fetus can become one of two things:
    A Human Being...
Deserving of tender care and affection, or...
    A piece of garbage!
     At a lady's merest whim
And denied even a twenty-four-hour period
    Between a tossed-off wish
     And a last-minute reprieve!
  You have INDEED come a long way, Baby!
—*Fidelis*

Image

I used to be dignified
A college professor for god's sake
A colleague complained when I wore backless sandals
She never expected me to dress like that
When I had a baby, a neighbor thought me too serious for that
Once I wore a strawberry blond wig to lunch for fun
And a friend said I was the last person
She would picture as a blond
Men shook hands with me even before feminism.

Since the heart attack
Everybody hugs me
The hospital nurses
I suppose they're professional huggers
Not only Mary, who watches our house when we're away
But her husband hugs me, though he still calls me Mrs.
The department secretary, the department chairman,
In the supermarket, a colleague thought a second
And then what the hell, threw her arms around me.
Suddenly I'm everybody's lovable grandma.
—*Barbara R. DuBois*

A Cowboy's Life

From the time that he was old enough to talk.
  A cowboy he wanted to be.
He lived out his dreams from the day he could walk,
  A cowboy he truly would be.

All through his teen years he played the part.
  His mind was really set.
Only his horse Lady, could hold his heart.
  There would be no regrets.

I watched him step into being a man,
  Still set on the life of a cowboy.
Knowing for sure his predestined plan,
  He was my life's pride and joy.

Today I watched him set his dreams aside,
  Entering the workman's world of strife.
Within my heart my feeling I would hide,
  He'd never return to a cowboys life.

I knew he had laid his dreams aside,
  To never look back at the cowboy plan.
My heart ached to know he had grown in stride,
  To walk the road of a full fledged man.
—*Zelda Engle Fletcher*

"I Am A Frail Flower"

I am a frail flower,
A creature just like us all,
Unlike the other creatures,
I am meek, fragile and small.
I sit in a peaceful garden,
A garden of hopes and dreams,
I look upon a big, bright world,
At least that's what it seems.
I do not know of burden,
I do not know of sin,
I live alone in my peaceful world,
Waiting for my life to begin.
A life of wondrous moments,
A life of joyful dreams,
A life full of hope and love wrapped in golden beams.
Yes, I am a frail flower,
In a world that only "seems,"
I live peacefully all alone,
In my garden of hopes and dreams.
—*Anna Marie Neri*

A Daughter

A daughter's hands so thin and frail
A daughter's face so sweet and pale.
The love of a girl so charming and fair,
The voice of a mother so full of care.
Her blanket and pillow so pink and bright
And of course her warming night light.
The crib in one corner, the closet the other.
And in the doorway stands her mother.

—*Katie Teitsworth*

A Private Place For Me

A private place for me,
A daydream I can see
A place I can stay,
And never worry about events happening that same day.
A place to put my thoughts away, during that midsummer's day.
Watching toddlers learning to walk,
And watching a boat before it reaches it's dock.
The only music you can hear, is a high school band
Playing far from near.
I will not reveal this place
Because every person has their own place.

—*Tania Kooros*

The Door

When God gave us a friendship He gave us
  a door and a room.
The door to open and close. The room
is filled with all our secrets, loves,
  and angers.
Sometimes we choose to close that door
now I'm willing to open that door
back up. I wish you could understand the
pain I've been through. So please I ask
you, "Will you open your door for me to
  come through?"

—*Stephanie Galindo*

My Special Place

Up in a cloud, a cloud of your own,
A dreamy place to wonder.
Where you think your own thoughts
and express your feelings to no one in particular.
You call out your deepest secrets and inner thoughts.
It appears to be like a loud cry,
but then fades into a whisper with a gust of wind.

—*Sarah Allison Smith*

Elise Of Milan

My name is Elise, a refugee from Milan,
A dying planet millions of light years away.
I came to your world in search of a safe haven
But find a complicated and devastated society
Where people constantly fight in costly wars
As murders, rapes, and robberies run rampant.
Your children die of desperate hunger
While being cradled by emaciated mothers
With husbands that work for an empty surplus.
Knowingly, you destroy natural resources
And live in selfish corners with no regards
Concerning the intense, unjust suffering of others.
If this is the only living I can do
Then I choose to die as my world, with my world
And the peace of mind to be free
From a place overwhelmed by ignorance
And the lack of true liberty.

—*Melvin Moore*

Flowers

A flower is a beautiful peace of life.
A flower can be "grateful".
A flower can be "peaceful".
A flower can be "beautiful".
That's why a flower can be a beautiful piece of life
A flower has many "beautiful" colors,
A flower has many "graceful" colors.
A flower has many "peaceful" colors.
That's why a flower can be a beautiful piece of life.
A flower gives people joy and love.
A flower gives people forgiveness and peace.
That's why a flower can be a beautiful piece of life.

—*Ginger L. Miller*

A Park

A park in the midst of the city.
  A fresco, a verdant world with earthtones,
  Azure and grey, sparkles with sunlight shone.
A park, separating man from the motor.
  Human needs, a calming and peaceful silence,
  Rustling leaves, a calling bird, a quiet sense.
A park, giving pleasure to children.
  A playground, happy voices with freedom,
  Running, jumping, with infinite room.
A park, meeting the social needs.
  A gathering place, babies, picnics with ants,
  Lovers' trysts, blankets, the dance.
A park in the midst of the jungle.
  A nightmare, evil, forbidding and black,
  Crime, violence; now a meaningless tract.

—*Elizabeth S. Head*

The World's Greatest Friend

  Hallelujah to you God.
  A friend who goes everywhere with me.
You know all the right things to do to make
  my life wonderful.
  I place all of my trust only in you God.
  God you control life and death.
  Always kind and forgiving. You are a good
  friend that I can always depend on.
Hallelujah, Hallelujah to the World's Greatest
  friend.

—*Brenda Esau*

What Is A Good Mother?

A mother is someone who loves her children more than any other.
A good mother is someone like you.
Someone who taught me there's nothing I can't make it through.
Someone who is patient, loving, honest and caring.
Someone who never tires of sharing.
You raised three children, helped to teach them right from wrong.
You in your own quiet way taught us how to be strong.
You were there if we got sick in the night.
You were there if we needed to be reminded of what is right.
You were there, through the years, through the laughter,
tears, and sorrow,
You were there, our good mother.
You were there to help us have a better tomorrow.

—*Patty Icard*

A Friend

A friend is someone special to you,
A help in a different way.

You skip, talk, and have lots of fun,
And pick some flowers in May.

Without a friend you are lonely and sad
Nothing you do is joyful or glad.

There is no one to go shopping with,
Or take on a beach relaxation trip.

There is nobody with whom to talk on the phone,
For without a friend you are all alone.

So have a friend, or two, or three,
And your life will be better, I guarantee!
  —*Kristi Brown*

A Friend? Indeed!

Times had been good, but then gone bad.
A life of love now filled with sadness.
A love had gone, another to come;
The new couldn't fill the void.

Then came a friend to lend a hand
And bring with it some gladness.
The friend was there to help fight
through the clouds and darkness.

The time came when they parted ways,
The friendship never forgotten.
The friend kept tabs and thought of him often.

As the years rolled on the thoughts of friends
Grew stronger, though far apart, as times grew longer,
Until one day they met again and found that friendship
Transcended all else.

The friend of the friend soon discovered there was love in
His heart enough to share with another.
The love he felt for the friend was not the same as a man
Has for a wife, Nor for a lover.
This love surpassed, is higher than any other.
  —*Thomas D. Conger*

Broken String

Eyes opened wide, one bright summer day,
  a little boy had got, what he wanted that day.
A little white sailboat, on a string.
  Wrapped in tissue paper, he christened her,
  the Paper Queen.

He took her down, right down to the sea,
  this newest addition, to his little navy.
This little white sailboat, on a string.
  Bringing her back to land, there in his hand's,
  a broken string.

Paper Queen, your living out a dream,
  of sailing free, not tied to a string.
Letting the breeze, carry you where it please,
  a toy sailing boat, with a broken string.

She never turned, not back to the land,
  once she was free of that, little boy's hand.
This little white sailboat, sailed the seas.
  With tears in his eyes, one little boy cried,
  "God Save the Queen".
  —*Muriel Vorrath*

See With Me

I looked in the sky and what did I see?
a midnight sky of course filled with the sea.

I looked farther than that and I saw what I saw
a forest so green filled with vast beautiful trees.

I looked even farther and what did I see?
A unicorn drinking out of a pond so hectically
It had a horn of silver, a mane of stars and
even a little twinkle between the eyes. The tail
was all strung with beads of gold, it was beautiful
from head to toe.

I looked even farther to see what I saw,
two red dragons with horns gracious as the stars.
While they slept on a bed of bronze near the sea
snoring and laughing in their sleep.

There are more imaginary things past the moon and
the stars. But there's one thing I know, and that's
I'll cherish them all.
  —*Rashonda Ogletree*

Reflection

   Sometimes I got to visit
a mortal being in my echo,
In calm seas and tranquil waters.
Many eyes that can not
See; pain,
   So many distraught thorns
Such greedy hands, oblivious misery,
Modern days that morn to live.
   Fictional hungry fights to win
Imbrued minds, revulsion for all spirits,
Weak, power, love, hate, our mother earth,
Sin; me
   My extraordinary existence goes beyond
Egoism for ethical diviness,
While most of us futilely argue for resistance.
   Sometimes I go to visit
Myself, and I understand my resolution to modify myself.
I Am Me!
I choose to rightfully influence my world.
  —*Karen McFarland*

Misti

Among my memories I have filed
A myriad thoughts of a precious child
With hair so long, so black, so wild—
Where has that baby gone?

A run through the sprayer without any clothes
Climbing the trees with barefoot toes,
Walking the wall with sunburned nose—
Where has that little girl gone?

Learning of Jesus, His Will to do
Making of speeches to state her view,
Training of horses for ribbons a few—
Where has that young girl gone?

Now stands on the threshold of future's door
The baby, the child, and the girl of yore
Experiencing joys God has in store
For a lady of purpose to find more and more

Now that you're eighteen and we've loved you so
It won't be too hard to let you go
A person to let God fill every need,
Farewell to the child—now go with Godspeed.
  —*Mary E. Hicks*

Back

It's dawning
A new beginning
In an old land

The sun rises and sets
Too often forgets
Those upon whom it shines
I can't seem to fade memories
The tormented tales and histories
I long to extinguish

Fire burns my soul
Such that I must return to the land of old
Ways, thoughts, beliefs and deeds

I pray, oh Lord, be my guide
Let this be wise and thy will provide
Goodness, happiness, health and success

So, I return to the home of my people
So, I return home
So, I return...
—*Mell J.-Branch Roy*

My Morning Glory!

When I woke up one morning, I had
A new friend. His name was Christ Jesus,
So I invited him in.
Since that day he has never left.
Now I no longer feel the weight of guilt
And sin around my chest.
My ways and actions are much different
too. Since my divine savior said, my son
I'll carry you through.
He said trust in me, with all your might.
For it is with faith, that you wage a
good fight!
Then when temptations become to great
to bare, he says, call on me Christ Jesus,
For I'am always there.
Then in the end my friend, for being
true to me.
You can share in my "Glory" in a place
   "So Heavenly"
     —*Gary Sheppard*

A New Beginning

The sun is rising, a new day has begun;
a new life is your future, a somewhat
uncertain one.

Stepping out into this world alone takes
courage and strength; the life you knew
is over. Though your destiny awaits.

Why succumb to a lonely depression,
why feel failure through and through?
When your new life is just beginning,
a new life that's just for you.

Now in the beginning of your new journey,
the past may dominate your thoughts;
though as time goes by, your eyes will dry,
and a healing will come to your heart.

For the strength you've gained will allow
yourself to heal in a powerful way.
Persevere, be strong, and live life for the day!
—*Barbara L. Tedesco*

Yuri And Malcolm

The struggle of the ages—Eons ago...
A night to remember—the Autobahn—a man so slow
Dared kill my friend, compatriot for decency;
But—we all recall—Malcolm X,
His lips were stilled; But I still see—
A Japanese; A Woman of the Ages, in defense of all my sex;
Not merely gender, but a cry for all humanity
It's not for you to judge and castigate
Nor what Nostradamus cast and prophesied.
Your nation shall be doomed if festering hate
spews unabated—and like the stallions shied
And prophecy fulfilled-Repent-before the times too late
Does your Christian book foretell—
Run—and weep and weep before the Bell.
     —*Sue S. Chin*

Protocosmos

Once there was a quiet,
A peace so deep and undisturbed that it seemed
as if eternity held it in place.
Then, without warning, the heavens took a breath.
And so began the spectacular show.
Swirling masses of stardust intertwined
with all of the elements;
Mixing, glowing, radiating, heaving,
As thick balls of starthread unwound and tore away
from the huge ensemble.
The rays of a trillion blazing suns flashed across the universe,
And coated the void with soothing points of light.
Order was brought to the cosmic confusion,
As life held out a candle in the dark,
Awaiting a new beginning,
To a cosmic cycle of never-end.
     —*Abbe Effron*

"Reflections"

I am in my grandmother house.
A peaceful air
Surrounds me there.
While I look at pictures of her,
As a child,
A sense of remorse comes over me:
She is no longer that child.
Now, as she sits beside me,
We find a picture of her
As a teenager
And notice we have the same eyes.
As I focus on that similarity
There is a realization
That we have more in common than facial features:
We have our souls.
And although the image of her
Changes with time,
She will eternally be
My gram.
     —*Courtney Brooks*

Lori

I am alone with a memory.
A time gone by, never to return.
A moment, forever captured in my thoughts.
She was the light of my life.

When she smiled, my day was complete.
My reason for being, just to see her.
A memory, my only support.
Always close to my heart.
—*Brent Hansen*

A Place Where Grown Men Cry!

They come from across the America.
A pilgrimage to a wall, a tribute to themselves they made.
Inscribed with names of comrades in battle fell.

To black granite and concrete,
they are drawn.
With tears in their eyes
the past they must face, before a future to begin.

Dressed in worn battle fatigues:
Olive drab, jungle garb, adorned with campaign ribbons,
medals, patches of long gone battles they come,
to reconcile what they had done.

Professionals and Non, fathers and so on.
They come to find, shipmates, soul mates, comrades in arms,
Acquaintances and strangers, friends they become,
a war fought still un-won.

With empty stares they gaze,
into dark panels reflections.
Younger faces stare back, young men they once were.
For hours it seems, they stand expressionless,
as tears well up their eyes
—*Tony Giberson*

You Are The Parlor Inside Me

You were always a reclusive visiting room,
   a place for mumbling to yourself
     and sipping tea alone.

A dark room
   with drawn velvet curtains
And cracks of light that splinter through.

When I choose to visit with that side
   of myself that you call to mind,
I am always polite,
   bring small gifts,
Say I must be going,
   inch my way towards the door,
Run, once I reach the hallway.
—*Jennifer Militello*

Home

A real home is a shelter from the storms of life,
   A place to enjoy,
A place in which to relax,
   A place of peace.

A true home is the center of all hope and ideals -
   It does not have to be a mansion!
Just a shack by a running brook,
Full of "Big Ole Oak Trees,"
A dream garden, with a swing - of course!-
   Filled with tons of books
Filled with laughter and glee
   Of my children; and especially
My twelve beautiful (All Genius) Grandchildren -
   And...
We shall eat ice cream
   Forever!
Love you - Everyday!
—*Nancy C. da Vinci*

Insane Man

Locked up behind bars
A prisoner to himself
Only he holds the key to let in the world
Instead he lives within a world.
Perhaps it is a world of joy,
   leaving him fulfilled.
Perhaps it is a world of sorrow,
   terror, grief, and gloom.
What is shut behind the doors so tight
   captured in his mind?
No one in this world will ever know
   and might never find
A pathway from his helpless mind.
—*Mark Prange*

My Mourning Heart

An air of silence takes over my life
A quietness forever spoken.
Bitter feelings of loneliness
in a heart that's newly broken.

Why? is the only question
I want the answer to
Why couldn't He have taken me
instead of taking you?

Life is for the living
or so I've been told.
But a part of me died along with you
and now this once warm heart has turned cold.

Now I have no place in life
since my place was always with you
I don't want to stay where I don't belong
So I know what I must do.

I pray the Lord my soul to take
because it isn't mine to keep
I hope I die before I wake
to join you in eternal sleep.
—*Ken E. Milam*

Yesterday's Lollipop Smile

A flicker of light pushing darkness aside
A ray of hope, sunshine peeking through.
Lollipop smile, chubby fingers pulling at heart strings.
I see a star dancing across the Milkyway.
Rain drops, silver beads tip toe through the grass.
An Orchestra of winds hitting both high and low.
Birds in chorus singing with all their gusto.
Flowers bursting forth in bloom to decorate the stage.
Curtains of sky blue tinged with green and yellow.
Actors, each portraying characters to be heard.
Funny, lovable, calculating serious, convincing, seeking encore.
Lollipop smile, chubby hands, raise the curtain.
Guide me across to center stage
Tug at my heart strings
Help me listen to the worlds sing.
Portraying the character giving my best performance.
Playing the part that gives life to me
Living the part that gives life to others.
—*Bobbi M. Setzer*

Forfeit Of Beauty

They were the eyes that could stop
a rebel nation in its tracks,
or prompt a passive nation to revolt.
It was the hair, flowing so long and lush,
that was the envy of even Rapunzel.
They were the cheeks so full of the color
of roses that men dreamed of drinking
the wine that brought such beauty to her face.
It was the skin, so soft, so tender,
that glowed like a gentle white light
plucked out of the sky at night.
It was the smile that begat eternal innocence,
while exhibiting a smirk for times of play.
It was the voice that harvested mountains
and made flowers bloom to the sky.
They were the bitter sweet tears
that brought salt to the sea.

And the tears were mine, as I watched her go.
 —Marc Spencer

You

Your dark brown eyes share a passion with mine
A rebellion inside, a love that is blind
But when you turn my way you seem to see through me
Your vacant stare not seeing me there
Your rich black hair shows your youth and desire
Your inner most self and your passion and fire
And I say to myself it's all in due time
That your tan lips will fall upon mine
Your beautiful skin of rich creamy brown
Ripples as your muscles become big and round
Your outer strength matches your strength within
But your vulnerability is not found on your skin
I long for the day when our bodies will meet
And bring out the passion, the fire, the heat
And although I know we were not meant to be
You will always be a big part of me.
 —Jenny Levine

"Relationships"

Oh how I long to have a relationship that's true.
A relationship that won't make me blue.
A relationship that'll last, and make hard times pass.
A relationship that'll be real.
A relationship everyone feels.
To walk on a moonlite beach, this relationship is within reach.
But this time the feelings we have, will not crumble in the sand.
For once in my life a relationship that won't break.
Like the waves upon the rocks, every time they hit each other,
those are my cries.
But with every tear that falls a sea gull appears and my fears
disappear with drifting tears.
The tears I cry are special because they're rain to other people.
You see I'm in Heaven, and still trying to find, a relationship
but I am blind.
 —Jessica Clary

A Faithful Worshiper

Silence...
A solemn expression with deep thought
Concentrating on things that can never be bought.
He can only prepare himself for everlasting life
Called eternity...

With thoughts no one can see,
He is probably holding a key
To happiness and heaven.
Although we're unconscious of him,
He is full of grace to the brim.
 —Dolores Leyland

Divine Forever

As I sit, and think, and dream and wonder;
a return once again to Pulse's center.
Forever, her image imprinted in mind;
A rhythmic melody will never subside.

She would not dream of hurting a presence;
Perhaps she knew not of my quiet existence.
But in her perfection, she does supersede;
all else that I want, that I think, that I need.

In quiet awe I admired her poise;
Her eyes and her hair and her mind and her voice.
She left me behind in my humbled state
Too fearful to approach; to intonate.

And to this day her motionless perfection
Persists to endure in my quiet reflection.
So although she is gone and was never quite mine,
I shall always remember her for being Divine.
 —David Barzilai

"The Angelic Face"

I once had this dream that I was walking along
 a riverside,
Not with some idiot,
 but with someone on my side.
I never saw the man with the angelic way,
But I knew some how...
 I would one day.

As time grew on I didn't think I would
 ever find,
Someone so gentle,
 so perfect, so kind.
I found him in the most ridiculous place,
In my dreams....
 with the angelic face.
 —Sine Lee Murphy

Kristy

Ten little fingers, ten little toes,
A rosebud mouth and a cute little nose,
Twinkling eyes, shining hair,
I'd know you, Kristy, anywhere.

You're a special child with manner mild,
God gives to a chosen few,
And it takes more effort on your part
For you to learn and do.

Patience is a virtue
A fact that's quite well known
So if we keep waiting, soon we'll see
You'll do things on your own.

Of all the gifts we're given
From our heavenly father above,
Special children all are blessed
With an extra measure of love.

May you always know as you learn and grow
That God blesses you with his grace,
Little Kristy - - - A special child
With the happy smiling face.
 —Janalene L. Oakes

"The Night Of Jesus' Birth"

The night was dark and very quiet
A silence covered the valleys and hills.
The stars God had made and called by their names
whispered to each other, "This was the night"
God would reveal his plan. The moon, in its splendor and glow
God had created so long ago, also knew of God's plan
that would show his love to all mankind.
The angels stood with heads bowed low,
knowing Jesus would be leaving Heaven to go to the earth below.
They knew God was going to send his Son to be born in Bethlehem
The shepherds, after a long hard day,
were watching their sheep nearby.
They watched in the stillness of the night
how the stars were shining so "extra bright"
when the sky lit up and the angels began to sing
telling them where they could find
the Christ child who was to be their King.
God chose the eastern star to lead the way
where they would find the baby Jesus sleeping in the hay.
The stars and moon played a part in the night of Jesus' birth.
   —*Mary Murphy*

Star Dust

In my dream of darkness there shines through
A single ray of light
Came to take me to the moon
As I board the flight
I'm seein' streaks, your face, a star
Yet I travel on
Turned to look from afar
Knowing you were gone
Out of darkness shining through
A single ray of light
Warning me it's morning soon
So don't put up a fight
For just as sure the sun comes up
The nights they will come down
From the dipper fill a cup
Safe landing on the ground
As I awake to see you go
I smile to myself
Some night soon again we'll blow
The stardust from the shelf
   —*Nelda E. Harvell*

Trash Day

I never throw out all of the trash
A small pile turns into a dump overnight in my life
A mountain of rubbish so large it encompasses
Many years previous

Trash churning, incessant both inside and out
The land-fill grows larger there's a dozen pair of high tops
And coats long gone, clothes I bought but never wore
There's stacks of money and friends I have lost
Arguments with you I lost of those too

It's the ticket stubs and orange peels
The peanut shells and cassette tapes
The pens and papers, the letters never sent that turn my life
Into a garbage heap ever growing, beating a path to my door
And the city won't take any of it away

The candy wrappers, beer cans, and bakery bags
Magazines, matchbooks, melted ice
Worn shoes, autumn leaves, Pepsi bottles
   And tubes of lipstick
Are somewhere in my path, in my past, in my way
   But... It's trash day
   —*Lisa Hines*

"The Wolf"

Come closer to Daddy, sweetheart, and listen to me well!
A story now I have for you, one I love to tell,
It was a stormy, stormy night, just such a storm as this is
I'll tell you my story, sweetheart, then you must pay me with
   kisses!

I was walking through a forest, there in a pitch black night.
Until I found a shelter, then, two eyes gleamed so bright!
There where I found the shelter a place 'neat the trees to hide me
Those glowing eyes came closer - and a wolf lay down beside me!

Now, little one, be not afraid , for it was awful weather.
I, and the wolf, lay side by side, safe and dry together!
And there we lay, through the long, long night safe and warm
Cuddling close together, hid from the awful storm!

Then, at last, came the day light, the storm was gone
I, and the wolf, we parted, there, at the break of dawn,
Before we left, the wolf came close, and licked my hand
I stroked his shaggy head-and left-the best friend in the land-
   —*Mabel L. McKinney*

Remembering Scott

I met him first when he was almost fourteen,
A sweeter young man I had never seen.
Once every year I saw him after that,
We became good friends and loved to chat.

Something about us always magically clicked,
And in our conversations we had the world licked.
He was so very handsome; witty and polite,
And I loved him always with a motherly insight.

His beautiful smile would light up a room,
And he had no time for thoughts filled with gloom.
My life is the richer for him being a part,
And his memory will always be tucked in my heart.
   —*Peggy Blevins*

Sunlight For Genevieve

Awaking now, I pay the selfish night
A toll, lest gates obliterate the sunrise,
And wait the stirring day as blind my eyes
Since birth, quicken other senses into sight.

I hear a melody from tree-top height
That breaks the rosy hush of dawn's surprise—
A wing-ed song that far, above the sigh
Of breezes, notes the gifted bird of light.

With one swift touch, revealing East to West,
Describing sky-arcs out of traveller's reach,
He warms horizons with a beacon goal,
And I, though grounded still at evening's rest,
Shall feel cadenza sunsets and in each
Scintillated cloud, the sunlight for my soul.
   —*Helen W. Webb*

Untitled

Once upon a dark dreary night,
above the clouds, stars shines so bright.
With dark clouds of rain and snow,
their beauty is gone, hidden to show.
Farther than our eyes can see,
they shine so bright for you and me.
The stars in the heavens shine so bright.
I only wish we could see them tonight.
   —*Michael B. Graham*

A Few Tears

I wished on a star, hoping it will come true.
A twinkle in my eye, a teardrop falling for you.
   I wished we could've stayed together,
forever and always.
   During the times I need you most,
on lonely cold days.
   But you decided you had to cheat on me.
I really don't understand.
   Kissing someone else,
Holding another's hand.
   Maybe it wasn't meant to be,
I know we could've tried.
   Desperately seeking for an answer,
on the feelings I dare to hide.
   So now I think of what I could do,
If anything at all.
   Though I cried a few tears already,
I won't let anymore fall.

—*Anna Mulrenan*

Why You Are My Best Friend

You are a very special person,
A warm and comfortable friend.
You are someone I hope I will always know,
From now until the end.

You have so many wonderful qualities
That make your personality glow.
You are so much fun and so caring,
You've helped me more than you will
   ever know.
No matter what the circumstances may be,
I want to be there for you
To show you all the warmth, support and
   understanding
That you have shown to me.

—*Megan Ahlstrom*

Seventy Wonderful Years

In the year of 1923
A wee lad was born and that lad was me.

I was a farm boy 'till' 41
It was the year W.W. 2 had begun.

In early 1942,
I volunteered, we had a job to do.
Then in 1945,
The war was over and I was still alive.

1946 was a wonderful year
I met a beautiful girl, my what a dear.

The most wonderful lady in all the land,
Three months later she gave me her hand.

In this marriage of 47 years,
She bore me 5 sons, what wonderful dears.

Now that I'm 70 and she's 67,
These wonderful years have been close to heaven.

It doesn't seem it's been 70 years since I was a lad,
But I'll tell you folks, my life ain't been half bad.

—*Clarence W. Stovall*

Friends Are Forever

Don't remember me as STRONG...Remember me as HUMAN with the ability to be fragile.. to FAIL,
Don't remember me as PERFECT...Remember me as one who strives for PERFECTION,
I've achieved success in many areas of my life, Reserved still areas for Self-Improvement,
Don't remember me as the GREATEST,
I'm always committed to uphold the image you have of me,
"MEMORIES" of our Friendship are "MONUMENTAL"....
"Nothing is eternal" expect what we HOLD in our "HEARTS" for each other, Don't place me upon a PEDESTAL...It is a LONG FALL TO THE BOTTOM, while I appreciate your prejudice... I realize "Pedestals" C-R-U-M-B-L-E. Everything that is not created for the Glory of God is VANITY and will pass away. So give me your "FRIENDSHIP" and whatever happens...no matter what....... I'll "S-U-R-V-I-V-E" with your Love.....Remember, "FRIENDS ARE FOREVER."

—*Yve Palmer Lamb*

"The Buckaroo"

Stories are told, that sound so true,
About a cowboy's life, as a Buckaroo.

They ride the range, from morning till night,
On sure footed horses, that show no fright.

They arise in the morning, before the break of
day, then after chow, they ride away.

They ride the fences, and through the creeks,
for the cattle they seek, know lots of tricks.

A cow in the brush, with a calf at her side,
can give a Buckaroo, a mighty hard ride.

They ride through the year, but winter is worst,
It's even harder than the hot summer thirst.

The Buckaroo's chaps, scrape through the brush,
a hidden cow comes out with a rush.

He sinks his spurs into his horse's side, like
a shot from a gun, his horse is in stride.

He builds a loop, with an educated hand, to rope
a calf, that has no brand.

This goes on, till day is through, as this is the
life, of the Buckaroo!

—*Fred R. Tuxon*

If Only Love Knew

About the tears that fall upon my pillow,
About the words I yearn to say but can only whisper,
About the pounding of my heart, when visions I behold:
rainbows and spring showers.
About the rapture of a long-awaited glance,
the sweetness of a kiss.
About the comfort and security that come from loving,
About the satisfaction of a promise and the sealing of
commitments,
About the contentment that comes from solidity,
About the joy of knowing love knew.

—*Renee M. Hall*

(Have You Heard Of A City Called Glory)

Have you heard of a city called glory,
Above all land and sea.
Where God created a resting place,
For all saved souls to be.

Have you heard of this city in heaven,
Where there is no hunger, pain or strife.
Only a chosen few abide there,
Possessing everlasting life.

There are no murders or suicides,
No jealousy, bitterness or shame.
Only peace and harmony preside,
Because God's love for all is the same.

The only way to reach this city,
Is through eternal love and grace.
Following God's teachings, and his rules,
You can reach this resting place.

The road to glory is long and rough,
With many diversions along the way.
Keep faith in God when things are tough,
And he will meet you there someday.
—*Lonnie B. Thomas*

There Is A God

There is a God
    above many breezes,
      many seas and many mountain
        sides.
There is a God
    that loves us so and
    cherishes us in his heart.
There is a God
    that sees our sins
    and evil work caused by temptation.
There is a God
    that intercedes for us
    and we ask for forgiveness.
He helps us day by day to keep our love for one
    another and to keep him in our
      hearts.
And then one day a trumpet sound will penetrate
    the earth that only his children
      shall hear and they
    shall rise into his humble Home.
—*Kristin Lee Ace*

"Tomorrow"

As the switch is turned, the beam from the lamp extends
  across the room
Relieving it of all its shadows and its gloom.
The brightness that suddenly appears, erases from my mind all
  loneliness, doubt and fears.
It represents hope and gives me a lift... renewing my spirits
I thank God for His wonderful gifts, for life, love, family
  and friends whom I adore...
All of these and much more.
His Son, Jesus, who came, suffered and died just for me
  And a whole list of memories —
I glance back at the lamp that provided the beam...
My whole life before me unfolds, it seems.
As I slowly surrender the past, I can look forward
  to the future at last.
—*Mary Kathleen Osborne Hyde*

Confusion

Acknowledging the true facts surrounding us,
  Accomplishing the challenges set before me,
  Attempting to let you know how it could be,
Accepting that when you leave I cannot fuss.

  Expecting to hear those words "good-bye,"
    Realizing that you have never been mine,
    Remembering I shouldn't exceed the love line,
  Controlling my feelings so as not to cry.

  Making love with you at the break of dawn,
    Dreaming of your gorgeous self and sexy smile,
    Catching myself before I go the whole mile,
      Treasuring you and the moments before you're gone.

Inching my way into your heart as well as I can,
  Leaving no space for you to deny what we have,
  Ensuring that you know of the feelings I have
Arriving to a decision that I want you as my man.

  Awaiting the moment to say "I love you,"
    Wishing it was as easy for you as for me,
    Hoping one day "us" is what we would be,
      Wondering if your feeling the same too.
—*Jodie Ston*

Roses For Remembrance

We started out in a two room shack with a trellis of roses across the back, cabbage roses of yellow and red. The rich sweet smell drifted across our bed.

I dried the petals to make them last through winters cold and frigid blasts, and when spring brought new blooms to life, you had a child and a wife.

Three more winters and four small beds that old shack sheltered all our heads. And every year the petals were saved to bring summers promise to winter days.

From house to house and state to state the Roses always had their place. The kids grew up and took cuttings too, scattered roses the country through.

Then the saddest time I ever knew, was when I planted one for you. Let it grow upon your grave.

The only rose I never saved.

Soon now I'll be by your side as I was as your bride. When we started out in that two room shack with a trellis of roses across the back
—*Vonna Bechtel*

Feelings

After all is said and done -
After battles are lost and won,
Then comes the singular thought -
Was the effort worthy or naught?

For if it is worth the fight
To try and set things right,
Then it merits one daring "must"
To uncover feelings true and just.

And if the opposite be the case
Does one then tread in place?
In blissful ignorance, without a word -
Not hearing, not being heard.
With silent scream echoing in one's head
Showing only feelings passive - dead.
Yet within, feelings fast and furious flow
While emitting a blank unnatural show.

Nature shies at this inhuman anomaly,
For feelings in humans come by naturally.
—*David Avoth*

"The Passing Of Time"

Time…Conceived, you wait nine months until you enter the world.
Afraid, unprepared, you sit in your mother's arms for
what seems like an eternity. You have no knowledge of it.
Time…As a child you seem to have time in your control.
Things either last for days, or go by in a matter of seconds.
At this point, you are simply intrigued by it.
Time…As you approach adolescence, school days take forever,
And good times happen quickly. You begin to feel the impact of
   it.
Time…Then you graduate from college, and you think to yourself,
Where did the days go? Like many others, you are a victim of it.
Time…But wait, you have fifty more years of life.
You have a family to raise in the future, and you say,
"Why should I let it phase me?"
Time…Then, with a sudden rush of reality, you wake up.
You are fifty-five years of age, and your children are
Growing up at a more rapid pace. Life is getting shorter.
You scream out, "Wait up! I'd like to take things slowly for once!"
But it does not listen.
Time…Now, you are an old man, a cripple.
You lie in bed all day, undaunted by death.
However, you cannot resist saying, in a low murmur:
"It has take life from me"…Time
 —*Evan Goldgerg*

"The Inside Door"

 Upon opening the inside door, I wonder
"After this time will I come here anymore?"

 Walking down the hallway and glancing in
Every room, my heart is doing flip-flops and my
Pulse goes boom-boom.

 As I get halfway I try to take hold of my
Emotions,
I feel my stomach churning like the roughest ocean.

 I reach my destination and slowly I look in,
To find my grandfather in the bed on the very end.

 I walk closer to him, my emotions running
Wild,
I feel my body trembling like a frightened
Little child.

 I go to his bedside and see that he's okay,
My goodness he looks smaller than he did yesterday.

 I go to visit him often whether he knows me
Or not,
Unlike some who live there he will not be forgot.

 It still is not easy to open the inside door,
But now he needs the love I can give more than
Ever before.
 —*Colleen Clark Johnson*

Safe in sound

Safe in sound, surrounded by blent noises,
air washer dish conditioner humming.
I watch him from my window. He poises,
poses…wails like Loudon Wainwright strumming
a burning red guitar. His left leg lifts.
His tongue extends. He shudders as a night
train vibration rocks the stage. His weight shifts.
Then he falls. I reach out to him, despite
this aerie perch six flights up from the street.
Blue-yellow lamp-light softens the sidewalk;
curbside to pillow, mattress from concrete.
Sleep cradles him where he lands, this old hawk.
 In his nest under thick Hoboken skies,
 the dawn arrives as he closes his eyes.
 —*Darren A. Singer*

Obsession

i pore over your time-honored picture,
Alert. i
keep an all-night vigil for you, i remain
intact before your harsh stare…
but my fingers!
i am an old woman in my fingers,
filthy and weather-worn from my
trek to find you. i never did…
and yet i continue to gaze at you, despite everything.
despite that fact that in your eyes,
i am ash in the wind…
for my heart still beats hard and fast
when i reflect on you.
it will throughout eternity.
 —*Kelly Lea*

Reflections

Natures way of giving us yesterdays already past: Keeping alive memories that will forever last; The waters rippling against a river shore; Bringing back memories of the days gone before. The moon glistening against the darkened sky; With floods of memories of the days gone by. The warm breeze across my shadowed face; my heart letting me know: this is the place; The clouds lie gently behind a silver moon; Knowing another day will be breaking soon. Another memory, opens with each new day. My mind is telling me go, my hearts telling me stay; A place where our memories we reflect upon; On those special days that have past and gone. A place where the heart can always run free; This beautiful setting is where I want to be; A place where you can go and always reflect; Where the days gone by you'll never forget. Where peace and joy will forever flow; Such supreme peace everyone should know. An open setting for my eyes to look upon; Holding all the memories of yesterdays gone. An open setting where memories will forever last; And all the reflections of days gone past.
 —*Katie A. Strait*

Pretty Birdy

Pretty birdy loves to fly
 all around the house.

Pretty birdy loves to run
 just like a little mouse.

He loves to play and play all day
 with his old tin can.

He pecks it down, rolls it around
 and stands it up again.

He flies around and loves to land
 in front of a big mirror.

He chirps and chirps and talks and talks
 with a lot of cheer.

Pretty birdy loves good food
 from seeds to veggies and fruits.

He eats some lettuce with the turtle
 and gives the turtle the boot.

Our family loves this pretty bird,
 his cute personality, too.

We love him so much, he's soft to the touch,
 without him what would we do?
 —*Carrie R. McBride*

"Flowers I Am"

Flowers about all in clusters, except one, just one,
All by itself, standing still like a figure on a shelf.
Animals like friends, the kind that despise me in mind.
They come yet always go like the last of winter's snow.
Wishing someone, something cared, but where,
where is that someone, does anyone really care?
Waiting, waiting for one small shower to bloom.
The rain that falls here and there
pelt my petals as would tears.
Wishing I had the strength to carry on,
knowing it's time to be going on.
But how when there's no one to encourage,
but always someone to discourage.
One full of life now seasons heaven with spice.
Loving all I can see, wishing all loved me of which I see.
Hiding behind a frame of petals and sunshine
Knowing all the time, that flower is really me.
—*Sarah Byrd*

Prayer Of Daddy's Little Girl

Dad, I know I'm not your little girl any longer,
All grown up now, and I hope a little stronger.

I know I'm not with you every day,
But it doesn't change the fact that I pray.

I pray to God every morning, noon and night,
That God gives you the strength to fight.

God knows that old cancer has got you down,
But it won't be long now till you're up and around.

It remains so, that I worry about you,
And worry about Mom, and what she has to do.

I thank God you have a wife so fine,
She stands by her man; that mother of mine.

I hope soon that old cancer will be gone,
And we'll praise God for all he has done.

I'm not giving up on prayers just yet,
I have lots of them left, you can bet.

This little poem is to let you know,
Just how much, I love you so.

And that daddy's little girl won't forget to pray.
—*Sharon C. May*

Awakening

One day
all of my cares
and all of my work
and all the worth of everything
altered without warning
as suddenly as the avian warbling
dawns marvelously through a warming wind
to enthrall the coming of day.

One day
as the dream-released expanse was brightly borne
the world sounded a wary shuttering
with a strangeness long since forgotten,
and my searching, silent listening
wonders on its hovering wings
just how this changing time can be
a new welcome awakening.
—*D. N. Blakeley*

Take Your Time

Time: our actuality augmenting any age by altering anyone and
All of us. Racing, ruthless, reaching, rarely resting; reeling
Reams of reverenced recordings. Free for foolishness,
Feasting, fulfilling fondest feats with fascination.
Silently sending sensations, selections, successions; swiftly
Sending ceaseless separations.
Heaping humans with hopes, helps, hurts, healings, hovering
Here briefly for hurried happiness.
Donating a chance for doing, daring; deeply dedicated to deeds
Done devoutly or dutifully dispensed daily.
We willing, wishing, working, wrestling with worthwhile
Wonderings while wending our way with watchfulness.
Creating cautions, caring, our questions quietly cause
Convictions or converted conclusions continuously.
Time: treasured, trying; truly telling temporary tenants to take
Tasks to termination. Unseen, unless ultimately uniquely
Unified and used in unconscious understanding. Lavishly leased
For living, loving, learning lest we learn how brief our
Breath, our being, burdens, battles. Yea! Being born beckons
Beings back to New Beginnings.
—*Rosalie M. Motta*

To The Magnolia Tree

No two the same in design or measure,
All parts unique down to the silhouette.
A seed, a branch, a leaf, and a flower
Combined together make a wondrous tree.
You rise up high into the clear blue sky
And shimmer with each day's crisp morning dew.
The colors you project entwine the leaves
In fair magenta, mixed with white on green.
Each of the blossoms bloom in sheer delight
Just as creatures big and small venture near.
Birds sit in the branches chirping for joy
While squirrels eat their walnuts high above,
And crickets play a merry tune at night.
So walk this way and see the Magnolia.
—*Christine Schnetz*

Now and Forever

The wind caresses the reed with barely a shiver...
   almost a kiss, but more sensual.
From the dew on a petal of magenta comes a memory...
   merely a whisper, but more loving.
An aroma distinct of all that's life feeds the senses...
   too far away, but oh! So real.
A vision—you—appears.
Mirroring everything that was our life on the ripples of
   the purest blue.
Touching the image with a teardrop
   It blurs the apparition, the mirage, but I smile.
Emotion is forever. And pictures of the mind last an eternity,
   like a rock through a lifetime that withstand the elements
Yet never erodes.
You're never gone. You're never lost.
   It's a special part of love I can no longer touch.
But my mind...my mind can feel your inner essence...
   Your ever presence.
And I'll always love you...Dad.
—*Hollie J. Slusarczyk*

Fireflies

Suddenly halting evening woodland stroll -
Alone in sparkling breezy starry surf -
Owly song, rainbow imagery flooding in -
Finger touching diamond dewdrops trickling
   down granite face - Slowly tracing lines
   lighting hidden summery memories -

Sorceress of shimmering lemony light,
weaving your deep tale on this enchanted
beach - Wind driven spray filling with your
   flickering gossamer threads intersecting
   my fairy tale - Awakening the caring -
Desiring to engage, dreaming of filling you -
Starlight caressing, loving you forever more -

Sampling this sparkling full bodied wine -
Being thankful for the golden wonder gift
   you left behind - Opening Pandora's box -
Fireflies erupting, weaving their scintillating
   rainbow web across the starry abyss.
—*Jonathan Grace*

Untitled

It helps a bit to be Irish! You'll laugh a bit -
Along the way - and cry a bit - maybe every day -
And you'll work - and you'll pray so I think I'd say -
It helps a bit to be Irish - as I pass along the way.

Where did they come from?
Just who were they?
I have a bit of them in me!
The call I hear - the places I see
The faith I have - the peace I seek -
An insight - a glimpse - a feeling so real
   of what there was once, of what there will be.

It helped to be Irish - more than a bit
I'd say it helped - it helped so much -
   there was so much else - along the way.

A quest within - an affinity I feel
   but not to do an "Irish Reel" -
To be there now - though how? How? How?
I can't now - they couldn't then -
So it helped a bit to be Irish -

I won't pass this way again!
—*Louise M. Barnes*

Love Needs No Words

   Love needs no words,
Although they're nice to hear.
   It makes me happy
Just to know you're near.

   A simple glance, a gentle smile
I know the feeling's there.
   You don't have to say "I Love You,"
For me to know you care.

   I know sometimes the loneliness
Is more than you can bear.
   I hope you know I'll be here,
To help you dry your tears.

   I value your friendship,
It is so very rare.
   I don't understand everything you say,
But, I'll lend an attentive ear.

   I'm happy you're part of my life
I'll make that very clear.
   Love needs no words,
But, they are so nice to hear.
—*Julia Ilse*

Acrostic

Read, Rafael, read and keep everything in your mind.
Although you are to young to understand me...
Forever would you remember advices of this kind.
Active, if you do everything like I say, you will be.

Endless is the exercising life of a fighter.
Losing health and time with cigarettes, alcohol and drugs is
no way. Boxing and other sports make a man's discipline
tighter and tighter, one who wants to be a real man far from
bad habits should stay. No one who thinks different about this
should you ever listen. No one who wants to go the wrong way.
Even if against yourself you have to become stiffen... Listen
to me and you will become the real man one day. Life is very,
very precious, yes, forever you have to think of all this about
common sense says that living healthful and long is marvelous
Once you don't listen to me, death too early will knock you out
Never, little Rafael, forget this old man, this old friend.
Time will go by and, for sure, I will not be here. Read and
read all this and try hard to understand. Even if you become
world's champion "Next" year. Remember it even if I will be
from your sight too far.
—*Henrique De Paula*

Scrabbling Alone

With words, I have this fascination
Always -
Not with dice, to win, but with words
Always.

To many, it wouldn't be fun
Being four persons all in one -
Keeps me quite busy
Mind being in a spelling tizzy -
While I scrabble all alone.

Some read on trains/planes.
Scrabble I, on my Connie-gift travel game.
Sitting beside me, telling what to spell
I resent it, always.

At the beginning join me.
Even if I have low score,
I'll enjoy the competition
'Cause when scrabbling all alone,
Being players, one, two, three and four,
One of me is bound to win,
Always.
—*Harriett C. Graham*

Forever...Goodbye

When someone dies, they are gone from you...forever, but they always leave something behind. The sound of their voice, the the look in their eyes, the warmth of a hug; these things will always be treasured, but will never be known again.

The love of a Grandmother is very special, and hard to give up. Having the love of a Grandmother for a lifetime, and having to let go, is letting go of part of yourself...forever.

Never getting the chance to say Goodbye or I love you is frightening. No one's love could ever replace the love of a Grandmother; that love can never be taken away from the heart.

When you're young the thoughts of death are very far away, the opportunities for hugs, seem..forever. As the years go on each day if filled with the new and different. The time spent with those dear to us is less often. Although we hold their thoughts in our hearts, we never have the time until is too late and they are gone forever. Too late to say I love you, too late for the warmth of their hugs, too late to hear the sound of their voice, too late. We will always remember; we will always hold that special place in our hearts; we will always know we were too late ... forever. I love you Nanny, Goodbye.
—*Pamela Anderson-Lovell*

Path

Go forward, children, prepare thyself
Always seeking life' dreams
Open your minds to the truth
And your soul be spiritful in God
And you heart filled with love for peace and freedom
To learn wisdom from past memories
To live for the moment filled with the hope of a wonderful future
Remember all things change, life and death and what happens in between.

Give of yourself, and never give up believing that life is for reason and purpose
Believe in yourself that all things are possible
Through love and understanding, you will never be alone
With imagination and courage, you can find a way to succeed in life through respect of all things, you can find happiness.

Go forward, Children, go forward with your life
Go forward with your life
Don't let anything stop you. Dream!
Go forward, Children, believe in yourself, believe in God
Love peace and freedom go forward with your life.
—*Randy Shaw*

The Ideal Friend

The ideal friend, that's you my dear
Always there to lend an ear

Always there to help me try
To hear me laugh, and let me cry

Always special, always caring
Always loving, always sharing

Your quiet understanding eyes
See right through me where my soul lies

My burdened soul that you see
Is comforted when you're with me

When a loved one is lost, you're there by my side
To comfort and help me, to be my good guide

Silently loving, quietly caring
This, my friend, is what we're sharing

A silent love, a quiet care
Best friends always and everywhere
—*Corri Smith*

December 27th

A wonderful gift I have been given
An alarm clock from God- a clock set to heaven
Whenever I need Him, He sets it off ringing
Although to my ears it sounds more like singing
The clock has two hands that move round and round
And the alarm makes quite a very loud sound
This morning my clock gave me a surprise
When I looked at its face, I saw it has eyes!
Two eyes-bright and blue like the heavens above
One look and I knew that I was in love.
On closer inspection I found a small mouth
When opened, I found where the sound comes out!
A face, two eyes, a small mouth, and two hands
My clock is my son who will soon be a man.
—*Colleen E. Feeney*

Ssenizzid Diova Ot

There's a fly roaming the room buzzlessly.
   An odd fly, without an errand, doing what flies do best...flying
Nowhere really...just going round and round on the same
plane periodically changing direction to avoid dizziness
ssenizzid diova ot
to avoid dizziness

Maybe it's therapy prescribed by an aged fly physician.
   RX: Go to apt. #24, trace 200 polygonal shapes, alternating
direction every fourth, decreasing by five shapes every third
day until utterly confused.

Or perhaps it's looking for something lost: an old flying chum,
the eye fallen from the thousandth socket, or an egg laid long ago

It might even be a poet hovering above and, having found
   inspiration in my watchful form, composing the lines in my
image through his own:

There's a man roaming the room wordlessly.
   An odd man, without an errand, doing what men do best ....
Nothing really... just going round and round on the same
plane periodically changing direction to avoid dizziness
ssenizzid diova ot
to avoid dizziness
—*George Higgs*

Untitled

I have a piece of paper that tells me I exist
And a card that told me I could reside here legally.
I have some more parchment that says I belong to this land
And still another paper that gives me my social number name.
I have a mailing address that says I'm cart-rt-sort
And my school has a convenient 93236 to identify me.
I have a home, in a town, on a block, and people know I live there
And a library card to identify me for dues long overdue.
I have my family, so I'm her brother, their son
And I have a yearbook, so people may remember my name.
I have an identity that even I can not define
And why can't some token, some paper, tell me who I am?
—*Huy Dao*

Behold The Beauty

I look as far as the eye can see
And behold the beauty of the mountains and trees;
God knew what he was doing when he created the land,
As it supplies our daily needs,
But is often taken for granted.

I look as far as the eye can see
And behold the beauty of the sky and sea;
God knew what he was doing when he created the sun and water,
As they supply our daily needs,
But are often taken for granted.

I look as far as the eye can see
And behold the beauty of the people before me;
God knew what he was doing when he created man,
But who often abuses this beautiful land.

God grant us the wisdom and foresight,
To preserve this beautiful earth,
So that it will not be destroyed by man,
And the future generations will be able to look
As far as the eye can see,
And behold the beauty that is now before me.
—*Peggy Potter Hearl*

Night-Sounds

As twilight shadows dance and play upon the rim of day,
And birds in homeward flight retreat across the sky,
The earthy fragrance of the pines embrace the evening breeze,
And singly now, the firefly reveals itself in glowing light.
The quiet reverie of even'tide enfolds the day in slumber.

As moon-lit trees cast shadowy forms upon the quiet meadow,
A whip-poor-will in sheer delight is calling to its mate,
And Nite-hawks on the wing caress the distant stars.

The crickets' nightly, plaintive, chirp reflects an ageless wonder, and woodland paths, now deep in gloom, wind their way to yester-year.

As deepening night unlocks the dew in shimmering repose,
And forest trees are inter-laced with sighing wisps of wind,
The frogs' shrill chorus drifts along the river's bank,
And ruffled owls, unblinking, call out and then are still.
The night-sounds weave their magic spell until the dawn.

—Malcolm M. Russell

The Raft Down The River

A raft knocks against the side of a bank
And bounces back unhurt, except for a slight bruise or light
Discoloration gracing the wood.
Like Old Abe Lincoln's homey cabin,
The logs are stitched together loosely
But with pride and precision.
No matter how often the raft falls apart, It can never divide, never die.
Its owner, already cold beneath the deceptively calm river, made sure of it.
Like a tombstone, a bouquet of roses sailing down the river, the raft is a Monument, a perverse gift to a Grotesque, fantastic world. Trees whistle and sunlight hums uneasily;
They are unreal, they are insecure and transitory.
The raft smiles and sings loudly, secure in its knowledge that it can never die, never vanish completely.
For even if it was dashed over the rapids a thousand times and converted into a million slivers of wood, each splinter would look upwards towards the sky and scream at the top of its little lungs.

—Sonesh Chainani

True Beauty

The heavens truly forged her image
And broke the mold after creating such a masterpiece.
Her beauty supercedes the lot of God's creations:
Her eyes are as brilliant as the stars at night,
Shining brightly in the empty darkness.
Her lips are as ruby as a red rose's petals,
Fluttering in the fresh Spring breeze.
Her cheeks are as soft as a newborn's bottom,
Gentle to the touch, yet unblemished by human hand.
It seems impossible to reach out to such beauty.

But, oh, how I'd circle the earth 100-fold
Just to make those beautiful baby blues twinkle with luster,
Just to meet those ruby reds with mine,
And just to gently caress that soft blush cheek.
Yes, her image is the epitome of true beauty.
In her presence stars will become solar systems,
Rosebuds will blossom into beautiful flowers,
And babies will grow to become productive adults.

—Kevin Hediger

Nine Cranes

Just before sundown nine cranes came
   And brought me their
     Luck for a while

They waited one-legged near the shore of my pond
   Beaks printing westward
     And watched

The sun hanging low over distant reeds
   Held everything in silence
     For a moment

Suddenly as one move the nine heads turned
   The cranes took flight
     Took their luck elsewhere

Leaving only the late sunlight dying on the water
   The hollow reeds
     And me

And then the sunlight went
   Like the cranes
     Like luck
       Like you

—Marie Savanella

Contemplation

If these two eyes couldst dwell upon thee dear
And by forsaking other visions blest,
Pass each and every moment of the year
In contemplating thee and never rest,
A thousand spans of life couldst not provide
The time my eager yearning heart wouldst need
To take its fill of love so deep and wide
As that which from thy heart doth now proceed.
And if perchance the grace of heaven shouldst fail
To grant this soul a long and gracious life,
Or shouldst the somber hand of death prevail
And take thee lest thou shouldst become my wife,
My heart wouldst bid my voice the world to tell
That once I loved thee dear and loved thee well.

—John of Yorkshire

Needing

Did you ever need an item
And could not find it?
A repair requires a screwdriver
But instead of a Phillips, only flatheads.
Perhaps you prepare to write,
Need a pen, but only pencils.
Perhaps a shirt needs attention
Requires a button, but only snaps.
Perhaps it's a nickel you need,
But no change, only a twenty.

Like me, God loves a joke,
But I don't carry it as far.
Our motto is "In God we trust."
Holy Cow! The jokes on us.
He created the earth from chaos
An orderly mess He made.
He sent His Son to help us out;
Giggled, then took him away.
His joke is a lesson for all,
"Smile, you're on candid camera."

—Richard T. M. Ketron

Remembrance

A warm blanket is drawn over the child of my soul,
And electric-like sparks surge and flood my heart.
That little boy can still hear the crickets' sleepy chirping,
And the black, night-wind as it wisps through the screened window.

He can still feel the darkness of the night
As it quietly lifts and shifts every single hair on his arms.
Again he gazes into the swirling, white world of his whipped cream ceiling,
And traces the destructive paths of the majestic dragons.

I lift the blanket and cold reality races to my extremities.
It thrusts me and winds the gears of my routine.
Bowing my head, the relentless worries and responsibilities of the present
Forcibly enter and sit beside me, on their thrones that I have constructed.

—*Jeffrey Stephen Lewis*

A Promise

I stood beside the sea today
And felt the gentle touch of God
Upholding me - quietly - with great love
  and tenderness.

Beyond surf and spray and wind and tide,
An overwhelming sense of thankfulness and joy
Flooded my very being and my soul
As I plodded through the shifting sand,
Along the wave-tossed shore.

A sea gull, swooping, darting gracefully,
Pierced this thunderous, salt-filled din
With plaintive, haunting cry,
And in my heart re-echoed a reply - a prayer,
  "Lord - lead Thou me".

In the gathering dusk - alone -
Surrounded by sea and mist and fog,
Came forth a sure and welcome response -
  "Trust Me".

Smiling and secure -
I walked on.

—*Thelma M. Sturgis*

A Desert Walk

Have you ever walked through the desert
And felt the sand beneath your feet
Observing the beauty of the Cactus
Blooming in the summer heat?

Have you noticed the rocks that surround you
And the Colors that they hold
Painted by Monsoon Rainbows
Touched by the pot o' gold?

Have you climbed to the top of a mountain
and glanced at the valley below
Seeing Canyons in their glory
Where streams of water flow?

Sunset setting the sky ablaze
Sunshine warming the sand
Cactus filled with colorful blooms
That's the desert, the Miracle land.

—*Mavis E. Spry*

Our Blessings And Faults

We seldom count our blessings each day,
And few of us take time out to pray.
When we see a man with his leg in a brace,
Is all we think, "Man, would we hate to be in his place!"
When we see a child who is not nearly as smart as mine,
Do we feel sorry for a while then put them out of our mind?

When a person is in bed with pain hard to bear,
Do we go see them just to say that we've been there?
When other than our friends are down and out,
Do we like to stand with the other crowd and shout?

Regardless of how bad a shape you are in,
There's someone that's worse just around the bend,
How much nicer this world would be
If all our bad points we could wake up and see.

Just think how happier we would have been,
If we would open our hearts, and let everyone in.
Just think of all the bad things we would see out there,
If Jesus had laid down the cross he had to bear.

—*Jim Simpson*

October 17, 1989: "Do Not Call California!"

But calls came through — from worried relatives
And friends in other states, from provinces
In Canada, from other countries near
And half a world away:
"Are you all right?" "We saw the news..." "You don't
Know just how good it is to hear your voice..."
And local calls get through at last - from friend
To friend that night, each day
That followed it: "Are you all right?" "I can't
Believe it's happened..." "... thought our bridge would hold
In any quake..." "We saw Marina fires
From clear across the bay..."
"My God! The Cypress overpass...! They've pulled
Another victim out alive!" "We've got
The guilts out here because the damage was
So light... We're gathering
Equipment and supplies for Santa Cruz
And Watsonville..." When asked to limit calls
We tried, yet welcomed caring and concern
That came with every ring.

—*Mauricia Price*

Little Grand-son

A precious little grand-son has come to spend the day,
  And grandma has looked forward to lots of fun and play.
She gets out all his Dad's old things,
  his favorite books and toys,
But I guess in these quick passing years,
  she forgot about little boys.

They're not content to sit and look for any length of time,
  At pretty pictures in a book, or listen to a rhyme.
Little boys are full of zip, and always on the go.
  Little hands just have to touch, so little minds can grow.

Little feet have learned to walk, unsteady, that is true,
  But fast enough to run away and then look back at you.
Grandma puffs right after him, lest he should come to harm,
  And satisfies most every whim, the willing captive of his charm.

—*Irene B. Rose*

Mr. President

I have lived long enough to know
And have seen Presidents come and go
Wouldn't it be nice to see
The troubles of the nation freed

Mr. President I'd like to say
Above all the former presidents
You have a special quality
You try so hard to succeed
All the sides you want to please

You know you have a lot at stake
So you've made a few mistakes
Soon the dawn will come upon us
That you're special they must agree
They will know you have done your best
Much better than all the rest

They will finally see, this I truly do believe
You're a person that will not deceive
Don't let them change you, or crush you down
Your high ideals, just stand your ground
They'll soon see that you will save our democracy.

—*Marie Higgins*

Become Concerned

Create in me a clean heart, o God,
and heal the land upon which I trod.
Make me become my neighbors' neighbor,
wherein we enjoy the fruits of our labor.

Keep united lest we divide and fall,
as working together is for the good of all.
Obedience to this axiom we have learned,
will our desires fulfill if we become concerned.

If volunteer service is all you can give,
this is the christian way to live.
For if from your earnings you willingly share,
then you are practicing both love and care.

Let's begin to watch and pray every day.
This is the christian lifestyle way.
The peace and tranquility for which we've yearned
can be acquired if we sincerely become concerned.

—*R. L. Radford*

Ode To A Retiring Airman

They say he's grown too old to ride the skies,
And hold the stick and throttles of a jet.
Although his heart is young, his aging eyes,
Can't cope with rate of closure's deadly threat.
So now his well worn helmet's laid aside,
Along with memories of those many hours,
Of wearing silver wings with special pride,
And flying through the sky's white cloudy towers.
He'll ne'er again fly through flak's deadly hail,
To sweat out bomb runs over alien soil;
Or try to shake the fighters off his tail,
While feathering an engine spewing oil.
So like the war-scarred, grizzled knight of old,
He passes on to those who take his place,
A stick or wheel instead of sword to hold,
And future's thrilling quest of outer space.
One day he'll make that final power-off glide,
To land upon Valhalla's golden strip,
Where comrades wait to toast with quiet pride,
The airman who has flown his final trip.

—*C. L. Kit Carson*

My Granddaughters

There was a time so long ago that there were four little girls and I always called them my "Grandbabies"...and now I look at you and find that you are all four beautiful young ladies. I think of the times I changed your diapers and sang to you and rocked you in my arms...and how I tried to hold you close and stroke your hair and keep you from all harm. And now the passing years have brought me so much pride, and I pray I'll see the day when you each become a bride. A real poet can find the words and always make them rhyme, but I am just an amateur but some how the words come to me in time. You never made me feel old or that I embarrassed you and you introduced me to all your friends...I think of all the love and happiness from you that I have had. When you line up one by one and give me the hugs each time we meet. It means so very much and makes my life so complete. I want to thank your mom's and your dad's for all the pride and joy...you girls have brought to your grandma's and grandad's. Remember...if ever you feel lost or maybe want to cry...there will always be a strong shoulder standing by. And tho sometimes we may be miles apart—you are always and forever in my heart.

—*Lucille Brouelette*

Twas The Time

Twas the time before English, I had no homework done
and I knew I would bake just like a bun.
I knew I was dead I thought to myself
and missing assignments isn't good for my health.
I wish I was snug in my very own bed,
but the visions of hot lava still danced in my head.
All of a sudden there arose such a clatter,
that I sprang into the room to see what was the matter.
Into the room I flew like a flash,
threw down my books, knocking over the trash.
It was only a substitute messing around.
Just then a smile spread across my face
as I said to myself in that happy place
"there's no need to rush I'm not running a race!"
I went through English in a fret,
but I just might make it through yet.
"O.K. class you are dismissed."
Saved by the sub, but wait not yet.
I forgot my math homework,
just how lucky can I get!

—*Carolyn DeJonge*

Imprisoned In Myself

I know it's sad when two loves must part
And I know it is worse when her dying heart
Mours for freedom, yet loves the cage
Forever and ever I'll walk the bounds
That my soul has set, oh round and round
I'll go, ever searching, never finding
Wanting only to end this mascarade
But then I know that the dream would fade
And what could be worse than losing
Because the jailer set free and unleashed my soul
To wander aimlessly throughout the world; a burning coal
Lost in a sea of ice.

—*Ellen Ayers*

"School"

School is far behind me now,
And I worry about it yet,
For when all the teaching was taking place
   An education I didn't get.

My mother had too many kids
   To keep us all in line,
So all my sisters, brothers and me
   Would just loaf all the time.

I wish somewhere a teacher who likes to teach,
   Would find me along the way,
And if I asked her what she knew
   She would look at me and say:

You have just wasted years,
   For now you are old and gray.
There are so many things you should have learned
   As you came along your way.

I know you need the education now
So please sit down and stay,
At least I can teach you a few things
   Just to keep you from day to day.

   —Elsie Hillis

Paint Me A Picture

How often we are asked what can be done for us
And if we give a reply, there's always a big fuss
But if you do not mind, and I don't mean to be a pest
May I just make this one small request?
I would like you to paint me a picture better than the best
I would like my picture to be able to pass any test
In this picture, I would like a sky of cerulean blue
For the blue sky represents the happy thoughts I think of you
Also in my picture, I would like mountain peaks
For mountain peaks represent what my heart longs to speak
And again in the picture you will paint for me
There's one more thing I wish to see
Grass—a shade deeper than the deepest green
A mile longer than the longest stream
For the grass will represent everything to me you mean
And when you look at it, in your mind this can be seen
So when I hold this picture close to me, and stare at it hard
   and long
Only then will I realize that love is powerful and strong.

   —Kim Whitchurch

"Father Was A Gentle Dreamer"

My father was a gentle dreamer. Mother died when I was young; And I'm not proud of things that I have done. I'm not blaming father, or saying he didn't care, but his time was spent chasing dreams to be a millionaire. He never talked about mother; just said, "She went away." And all the questions I asked, that's all he would say. I wish he had talked to me and helped me understand, for all those years I thought she had left us for some man. Father was a gentle dreamer who chased his dreams each day. Like all gentle dreamers, he dreamed his life away; but he left me mother's picture, and that is when childhood memories came rolling in. I remembered when she left us. She said, "I hate to go. My darling you will need me so. Your father is a gentle dreamer." That is all she said before her hand went limp upon the bed. I had forgotten my childhood home with its spacious hall and the beautiful pink roses blooming along the wall, but that is understandable for I was just a child. How could I forget the sunshine of Mother's smile?

   —Tilda S. Akers

The Sands Of Time

Take this kiss on your brow
And in parting from now
Let me a vow-
Is the time we have as one
Like the sand in my hand.

Is all the time you and I have
together all but sand slowly
slipping away like sand in an hour-glass.

O' God! can I not hold them with
A tighter grasp.
O' God why can't I hold on to what
We have now.
Why is it all slipping away?

Give me the chance to
hold this sand with a
tighter clasp, so that time
doesn't slip by to fast.

Is all the time we have
as one like the sand within
my hand?

   —Jammie Hampton

Early Morning Walk

A wonderful thing happened to me today.
And it happened in an unusual way.

I turned left instead of right
And came upon a glorious sight.

A path of pink petals had formed overnight.
Newly fallen from the aged cherry trees lining the street.

A thing of beauty for just a moment.
Too Soon swept away by wind and broom.

Only a Hero, a Goddess or God would know how I felt
As I trod

A path of pink petals
Newly fallen from the aged cherry trees lining the street.

   —Vivienne J. Schmelzer

Over

What we had doesn't come so easy
And it's sad that we took it for granted,
The love I have for you is still in my heart,
Where it will always be planted,
You were special to me in every way
And I still think about you each day
I know you're sorry for what you did,
But it's something that will never be forgiven
All I can do now is hope to be free,
Free from my feelings-free from me.

   —Rachael Hayes

Fall

Rising
always rising,
you breezed the autumn furls of my uncertainties,
breathed them toward turns and swirling fantasies
scarcely known before.
Then you married.

I wait bare now
in my own certain way.

   —Leonard Ferrante

The Storm

The Storm destroys tranquillity
and knocks down lines of electricity.
A flickering candle the only light
with which to see on this blackened night.

Shadows dancing on the walls
like ghosts called up from Hades halls
seem to howl with the wind
and beg forgiveness for their sins.

A hundred hoofbeats fill our ears
when thunder rolls as it grows near.
Like Mustangs descending on the plain,
the thunder mixes with the rain.

With the rumble comes the sound
which fills the air all around.
The clap of thunder fills the sky
like the Furies shrilling cry.

After a while the violence stops
and the sky yields its final drops.
But somewhere else clouds will form
to release the fury of the storm.

—*Steve Doyle*

This House For Sale

I'll close the door and turn the key
   and leave a part of you and me.
Put out the lights, my heart still sees
   the glow of treasured memories.
I hear the sounds of yesterday,
   the laughter of a child at play,
A chiming clock, a puppie's bark,
   your step, your whisper in the dark.

I love this house, this home we built,
   this garden, though the roses wilt
We shared a love forever green,
   but birth and death these walls have seen.
September wanes, the year grows old,
   these rooms are bare, the hearth is cold,
The time has come to turn the key
   and leave a part of you and me.

I pray this house once more will be
   home to a loving family,
I holds my dearest memory,
   it claims a part of you and me.

—*Alice C. Walker*

A Prayer For Us

May the Lord bless you and keep you free
And make His face to shine upon you and me

May the world be peaceful and might be right
Forever and a day including the night

May the space exist unknown to us
Know our brother here and stop this fuss

Set my people free where they're bound in chains
They'll want to plant corn before it rains

Let the animals live. Don't shoot the deer
And strap him on your fender, red tag in his ear

Be kind to each other. We're all we've got
No one can replace the one whom God sought

So that's my story, that's my song
It may not be great but it's never wrong

May the Lord bless you and keep you free
And make His to face shine upon you and me

—*Donn P. Drake*

A Lost Love

My heart is saying that you're unfair,
   And life is telling me that you don't care.

I trusted and believed in you,
   And now you're gone and left me blue.

You took all my love and broke my heart,
   You did that one thing it tore me apart.

I came to realize I love you so much,
   Oh what I wouldn't do for one more simple touch.

The time now is going by so slow,
   I think it's because I miss you so.

Why did it have to be this way,
   I wish I could bring you back someday.

I hope one day you'll walk through that door,
   Then we'll be together forever more.

My life isn't the same without your love by my side,
   All I want to do is take my dreams and go hide.

I knew our love was to good to be true,
   There aren't too many like ours, so very few.

Love reminds me of how beautiful life can be,
   But once it's gone there's nothing left to do or see.

—*Jennifer Courchesne*

Untitled

Nothing undone
   and nothing discovered—
   no bones to bury
   and no stories to tell—
You've walked the bridge
   and seen the view of the rocks below...
   you admire the beauty of the scenery,
But you have yet to walk among the rocks,
   you have yet to feel the flowers
   and hold them close to your nose,
Breathe in true beauty...
   stop treating the world like a painting...
   step into it,
   interact with it,
   admire and respect it,
For the grass is all tall as you
   and often taller,
   ...hold humble eyes my friend,
   and feed the ground below
   and it will feed you

—*Rob Lewis*

The Lady And The Oak

The tree was planted the day she was born
And now they both look withered and worn

They both withstood the seasons together
Taking a stand through all kinds of weather

The trees has scars as does her soul
Years of endurance have taken their toll

Her life didn't last as long as the trees
Hardships brought her to her knees

Now her suffering has come to rest
Laid beneath the oak with its limbs abreast

Humans can't touch the soul of the oak
Unless with a chainsaw they do it one stroke.

—*Kathryn D. Turner*

Woe Is Me

I looked in the mirror this morning
   And Oh! What a glorious surprise.
Instead of my usual appearance
   A beauteous vision greeted my eyes.
Oh Glory Be! A miracle!
   A miracle this happy morn —
Nere have I seen any so lovely
   Since the day that I was born.
But my joy didn't last forever —
   It was only a short lived dream.
I soon made the horrible discovery
   That the mirror was covered with steam!
Then I polished that deceitful mirror
   Until it was gleaming bright.
And when again I saw my reflection
   I got my usual fright!
   —*Lola Grant*

Topsy-Turvy

Sometimes this world seems topsy-turvy,
   And our road seems awfully curvy;
But our Lord is still the king
   And His love all blessings bring.

   And

Though our world is truly crazy,
   And our circumstances hazy,
Still He lives and reigns on high
   And lights His candles in the sky.

   Now

Knowing this let's look above
   And watch and wait and pray in love;
For some day He will come again
   And snatch us from this den of sin.

   So

Let's remember who we are —
   His children - one day freed from war
Through His love on the cross confirmed —
   And with this note our love we affirm
   —*Don Martin*

The Little Ones

We set up the tables
And poured out the paints.
A few at a time,
They poured in.

We fitted T-shirts to them.
They chose their favorite colors.
Their tiny hands went into the paints,
And little hand prints showed up everywhere.

After they were finished,
Punch and cookies were drunk and eaten.
Spills and crumbs were everywhere,
While the kids had on happy faces.

They were amused by a game
That I had won at a festival the day before.
It was a cheap little plastic thing—
One that I would have just thrown out.

I brought some joy to them,
And they brought joy to me.
I'll never forget those little kids.
The homeless ones, I mean.
   —*Leslie Pohlenz*

"Little Hollow Porcelain Swan"

My mother picked it out to be a plant-container just for me;
and put some water'd stones inside - and then a bulb two inches wide.
It was a hollow porcelain swan my bureau-top to keep upon.
She said to start it on a shelf in a dark cupboard by itself
Till the bulb-leaves were first seen, pointing upwards, tender-green;
And then to move it to the light, where soon it was a fragrant sight.
That hollow swan, from Japan, made a fine bulb-can,
Its porcelain neck curved deep in porcelain feathers, sound asleep.
I'd never grown a plant before, although my mother had, galore,
And told me with a playful air that the bulb was in my sole care,
Entrusted to myself alone, responsibility my own.
Well, I then earnestly agreed to undertake the vigilant deed
Of caring for it while it grew, a worthy sort of thing to do.
My mother's gone now, though, for that was long, long ago;
But the little swan is here still, sleeping on a window-sill
Where I see it every day, reminding me that far away
In the lost realities of time my mother gave it to be mine,
This little hollow porcelain swan my bureau-top to keep upon,
While I grew with cheery price the little bulb she put inside.
   —*Nancy McKeen*

Missing Person

I was taught to read and write
and say my prayers every night.
I was made to feel special in every way;
good deeds, good thoughts filled each day.

Strong family values were safely inside.
My country's flag filled me with pride.
I heard everyone around me say,
"you are promised happiness every day!"

I can't hear those voices any more;
they've disappeared to a distant shore,
dashed and shattered by the waves,
leaving only a trail of graves.

Ghosts of tall ships hover around,
I listen. I listen. But still no sound!
Please tell me again, what did you say?
What have I missed along the way?

My tasks were many, like grains of sand.
Was I too busy to fully understand?
Please tell me again, I need to hear,
just what did I miss year after year?
   —*Marilyn A. Greig*

The Clock

I wish that I could take the hands of time
   and set them back -
To days of Sunday dinners, pies cooling on a rack
To country walks and backyard games and lying in the shade
Or going to a nearby lake where everyone could wade.
Rides in the country, picnics in the park,
Catching all those lightning bugs in glass jars after dark -
Wild flowers everywhere, big old bumble bees, roller
Skating, riding bikes, all those skinned up knees.
Can you tell me where they went? Those special family days
Where Moms & Dads & Grams & Gramps were never in the way.
Popcorn, truade, a saturday matinee,
Don't forget the baskets, received the first of May.
I know I can't go back there, to where I got my start,
So I've tucked special memories just inside my heart
On those days I'm feeling blue, fed up with greed & crime
I take those hands and turn that clock back to that
   Special time -
   —*Lynda Brown*

"Sonnet 28"

If dawn arrives without the sun's soft light
And skies at dusk give no hope to moon's glow
If crashing waves no longer fall with might
Will hope be in your eyes enough to know?
When distance seems so hard to overcome
And time apart brings stinging tears and pain
When situations seem so troublesome
Will faith pull on your heartstrings to remain?
If fears about the future cross your mind
And logic tells you all can't be this well
If disbelief and worry are unkind
Will love engulf your soul enough to tell?

   My love for you will see you through each day
   So love recall and all else cast away
   —*James Martin*

You

You reach to the sky to touch the clouds, to feel the softness and smell the freshness,

But as your eyes begin to focus, as if to wake from a dream, you find it isn't the clouds but me.

I've come to help you feel the excitement in secrecy, as the two children who hide among the trees playing a game.

I've come to share the feelings you have in your soul but you hide in your heart.

Those feelings that you would welcome back like an old friend temporarily gone but not forgotten.

Just as the shadow of the cloud moves slowly over the ground, feel again the passion of belief in cause and the right in truth.

Touch with your spirit the great strength in having rejuvenated the freedom in your heart.

Let me help you to find that smile that appears for no reason, or the tear that flows with the sensitivity of compassion.

Let me help you to shake the everyday bonds that build complacency, if only for a moment, an hour, or a day.

To reach beyond the flesh and share the warmth, the joy, the wonder and excitement of really being you.

   —*Deborah Ann Bice*

"Tell Me Why"

My baby is growing with each passing day,
And soon the years will have flown quickly away.

Your first steps will be a miracle for me,
First words a reward for a new mommy.

Your little arms wrapped around my neck,
Will be from a hug I'll never forget.

The days will then slip quickly by,
Bringing the Tomorrows I fear with a cry.

When the days of your childhood have grown old,
And a young woman has my baby's place stole.

You'll be learning of life, of how did I get here,
Who is my daddy, why wasn't he there?

What does he look like and how does he smile,
Are my eyes his same color, or how tall is he high?

Doesn't Daddy love us, why is he gone,
Can't he come live with us, why are you crying mom?

These questions I have no answers for now,
So I love enough for us both somehow.

But Dear Lord, what shall I say when I hear that word why,
And have to answer those questioning eyes?

   —*Debbie Fowler*

To My Wife On Her 80th Birthday

Eighty years have come and gone
And still the melody lingers on.
The sound grows sweeter every year;
The beautiful melodies caress my ear.

Together we have created new life upon this earth,
Two lovely daughters you have given birth
And a son, now long departed,
Whose sad sweet memory in our hearts is charted.

We have roamed this world together— you and I,
From Barrow's arctic waters
To the Southern Cross in Australia's sky.

For eighty years you've been around,
But fifty-four are common ground.
These have been the best by far—
Since I have coupled with your star.

For as far into the future that I abide
I know you will be walking with me— side by side.
   —*Arthur P. Selleck*

Even Before I Knew Him

Within his heart burns a desire, a dream for someone to love and that will love him.

He makes a oath to himself that he will love her with an everlasting love, hold her up by his victorious hand and underneath he would place his ever strengthening arms.

Immediately he begins plans that will give her a future and a hope. Faithfully he writes the thoughts of good he has for this special one. They are as numerous as the grains of sand on the seashore.

He calls her by name as he forms her in the innermost parts of the mother's womb. Carefully and with great affection he has chosen every detail regarding her...The place of birth, time, parents, color of eyes, hair, and skin.

An exuberance of joy overflows within him as he counts the days before her birth. For him a day is like a million years and a million years as a day...But, at last that special moment arrives.

Just a glimpse of her causes the thoughts and plans he has for her to start in motion....A beautiful daughter...Yes,

She is the father God's desire and dream.
   —*Sherry E. Alvarado*

Black Woodsman

As I was walking under an azure sky
and the bright evening cloud,
I was inspired with awe at the visages
I saw in the wilderness
My mind misgave me as I met a sable man
in this unfrequented place
As I perceived this strange figure,
I could hear the sound of the deathwatches
Wisely I proceeded - with caution and gazed
at this seemingly powerful man
He called himself the black woodsman
and he spoke my name
How could this rara avis of terris know my name?
He said come and join me
with obstinacy I did resist his entreaties
I felt an antipathy for this man and
refused the request of the soul
For the alternative of life is great....
   —*Matthew D. Sleister*

Dad's Rocking Chair

I still see the kitchen, each thing in its place,
And the chair by the window, in its usual space.
And Dad, rheumatic, would sit down with care,
Seeking for comfort in his old rocking chair.

In vision I picture him, shabby and bent,
(No outsider knows what this picture has meant)
I can see his calm face and fringe of white hair
And his knobby old hands on the arms of his chair.

Dad would turn to the light with the Bible so worn,
All tattered and marked, all faded and torn;
It was here that he knelt before heaven in prayer
Beside that old battered and scarred rocking chair.

It squeaked when you moved, its arms were well worn,
And I guess it served years before I was born.
It was padded and braced in points of most wear,
But always preferred as the best rocking chair.

Now treasures have flown, and time fades away.
The bright past is gone, for youth cannot stay;
But wherever I'll go, I'll take with me there
The picture of Dad in that old Rocking Chair.

—*Beatrice Vratanina*

The Poet's Lament

When I am in my tomb,
And the earth is fair above me;
When I am in my tomb,
And all are gone who love me—

I wish that I could leave something behind!

A wee ripple in the infinite
From my too-finite mind,

One little scribble,
One little rhyme,
One little scratch
In the reaches of time—

I wish that I could leave something behind!

—*Stella Klepac*

To My Town Cove And The Memory Of Laughter

In the spring I love the splash of forsythia,
And the headiness of the lilac scent.
Music moves me more than any other force
From Chopin to Tiajuana Brass.
I love my Town Cove, sprinkled with diamonds from the sun—
Shades of recurrent dreams from my youth
When I was ecstatic with countless pennies at my feet
As far as the eyes could see—
More than I could collection in a small bag.
I love the sound of a hammer on the roof,
When the day is warm and sultry.
I love new leaves when they rush to be born—
Pale green and chartreuse and not the blatant green
Of a later sophistication.
Pastels I love and sunlight.
I am a photophile.
I love the sound of laughter when it is kind.
Most of all, I love to remember
The great laughter of my husband,
When tears coursed down his cheeks from sheer joy!

—*Polly Cooper*

Sad Song

There is a song that is playing,
And the melody is sad.
For the people never considered,
Just how much they had.
Now, some kids complain of parents,
Who never seem to understand.
Why don't they think of others,
Who are orphaned across the land.
And there are folks with plenty of money,
Who eat until they're satisfied.
And never stop to think of the hungry,
And, My God, the way they died.
Why can't you hear what I am saying
Why can't you see what's going on
Why can't you help, instead of complaining,
And enjoy what you have before it's gone.
There is a song that is playing,
And the melody is sad.
For the people never considered,
Just how much they really had.

—*Teresa Rice*

Stains

I want to be perfect, someone above whines
and the natural order of things, someone other than me
until I can't stand it another minute and rise slowly
like I'm in control, no problem, and head to the John
with a furrowed brow, flick the switch and the bulb bursts
bright for a split second like the brief white light of God
and then blacks out, total darkness, and I can't see a thing
and I'm starting to pee on myself and I think maybe I should
sit as girls do, sit and not have to aim, but even here and now
I know I can't, I've spent my whole life pushing
the girl things down, so I decide to leave
the door open a crack, a sliver of light
my guide and pray the fire alarm will ring
or the end of the world wild come, but suddenly -
silence, deep and penetrating like the moonless night
and the only sound is the waterfall rush of my pee
splattering against the bowl in something other than relief,
and I've spent eternity standing here in a black hole
wearing pee stained pants with the whole world listening in
on the wrong thing.

—*Dion Birney*

The Road

The road continues past the locked gate
and the picket fences.
Past county water and sewage systems.
Beyond leach lines and cable television
to where the water comes up
just below the surface of the reclaimed land.
The road leads on, keeping close along the creek,
until it tires of pavement and of following
and of the controversy
between formula and milk feeding. Then,
cleanly cuts across still Winter-stunted pasture,
never-minding where it floods
or that the creek goes on alone.
The road climbs up the levee top
before it drops again
winding of its own free will,
no other purpose or direction.
Suffering less and less from use,
until it disappears beneath the stalks and minion
of the greening unpretentious land.

—*J. W. Churchill*

Winter

In winter bare are the trees,
and the snow is up to your knees,
and you are never slow when shovelling snow.
When you ride on your sled
it's fun, but you can't help it,
you wish you were snug in your bed.
When you're sitting by the stove
You remember sledding in the grove.
Then when it's hot summer you say,
I wish it was still a cold winter day!

—*Kelly Procter*

Sadness, A Prelude To Happiness

When the skies seem dark and dreary
   And the sun seems too shy to shine,
Think not of impending darkness -
   Nor of pains that in some hearts whine.

Think of light that comes after dark
   And stars that twinkle at sundown,
The calm after the dreadful storm -
   Sweet music floating when you're down.

When the thought of flitting sadness,
   Seems to flicker by overhead,
Let this ominous sadness fly -
   To unknown realms so far ahead.

Think, sadness a prelude to bliss -
   The forerunner of something sweet,
Like bitter "eats" that need honey,
   To make a palatable treat.

So, when you're blue, bliss is starting,
   Like a cell in your heart growing,
To blossom into your sweet smiles,
   Making friends happy and loving.

—*Teodulfo T. Yerro*

Indiscriminate Winds

When I move I lose focus
And the vision of who I am
Shimmers and blows away
Like a hot breeze whips dessert sands

If I don't move at all
My life is a dune
Shapeless and insubstantial
Subject to the indiscriminate winds of change.

—*Tracey Cox*

Nature

When rain drops fall
And there is no more snow,
The sun comes out with a glitter
And the flowers begin to grow.

With spring in the air
And the birds begin to sing,
We know it is summer
From the beauty it brings.

The creeks and the meadows
They are beauty at its best,
With nature as our caretaker
We know our world will be beautifully dressed.

And with fall in the air
And the cold winds that blow,
We must prepare for winter,
For nature will surely bring snow.

—*Edna Baldridge Cornett*

Now That You Are Gone

At first I was in love, love, with love,
And then I was in love, love, with you,
And now you are gone.

After a while I mused surely I would know you.
After a while I hoped surely you would love me.
But then there were the others,
And now you're gone.

Once I thought I knew all about love,
And once I thought I knew all about you.
Once I thought I knew, too, about death, and death was real,
but far away. "Thus," thought I, love, "we'll grow old
together!" But then one by one there came the others
and death stepped in, and now you are gone and they are gone.

Tears flowed and flowed til tear ducts ran dry and achy.
A dull pain, indistinct but persistent, resigned but longing,
lives stubbornly in my breast,
And I wonder...
I think I might know now about love,
And I think I might know now about death, but I guess I'll
never know, love, about you now that you are gone.

—*James W. Cole, III*

Reality

I am the reality of my dreams, a thousand times
And then some.
Miles and miles I have traveled, all within my
Mind, taking with me...only my soul...my closest
Companion.

Unknown faces and untraveled places seem to
Inhabit my thoughts.
Each searching for their own time and place.
Emotions flow silently through my veins causing
My heart to soar beyond the limits of my dreams.

With pen in hand I breathe the immortal breath
Of life into dreams that otherwise would cease
To exist.
I am the reality of my dreams, a thousand times
And then some.

—*E. Kay Holcomb*

First Snow

The mountain is clothed in full raiment of white
And there must have been extra that fell through the night
   For she tossed to the valley
   A white coating volley
That was noted with dawn's early light.

It could have been rain to swell the streams might
Or chill frost could have gripped in a manner polite
   But instead it is snowy
   Not foul and not blowy
Hear the children squeal with delight.

Tinkling sleds race downhill in a swift, rugged flight
While laughter resounds from a snowbank sprawled plight
   By the hearth dry the mittens
   Like sweet tempered kittens
How the mountain must gloat from her height.

—*Mildred E. Koop*

Summer Romance

A fool can lose tomorrow, reaching back for yesterday
And things will never be the same, since you have gone away.
But I always will remember the good times that we shared,
And things will never be the way they were when you still cared.

Now that summer's turned to fall, I miss you since you've gone.
I'll keep your memory in my heart, to help me to go on,
Your sweet embrace and tender kiss, you saved them all for me,
Your flashing eyes and loving smile, in memory I see.

You came into an empty life and made each dream come true.
You filled a longing in my heart, that no one else could do.
I'm sure you never would have gone, had you wanted me to care
In fantasy I built a dream, a life that we could share.

But summer's gone and so are you, and now it's plain to see,
The things we shared, didn't mean the same to you they did to me.
Now sadness fills my lonely hours, since you have gone away
And I know that I must never, look back to yesterday

—*J. W. Townsend*

Irony

The Victoria Cross is pinned on men who heroic deeds have done, and various trophies presented to those who in some speedy race have won. No one has ever given a thought to the act that seems most brave, to those who make a promise firm and never once do waive. Death sentence is passed on murderers who their fellowmen do slay. Confinement is given to those who snatch the passers-by goods away, and ultimate death comes to duelists who abuse the dreadful sword, yet the punishment given is still unknown to the men who break their word. There are men who are killed for treason and those in sly treachery are found, but the enemies of God who are still left at large are yet in the majority abound. His trial is pending for one and all-living be they or deceased, where the hidden crimes shall He recall and no guilty will be released.

—*Mavis Laughton Rogers*

A River's Cry

I work and crawl and seep from underground,
And wait and gather strength enough to run
In pools and little pockets in the sun
Where silver water fingers spread around.

With ancient sense keen and so renowned,
I know that life for me has just begun,
And if it's Nature's will, it will be done!
So listen to my echo and my sound.

With unheard groaning voice and lonely call,
I drop the final distance to the lake,
Where rainbow colors dance across the sky
And not one thing can keep me from the fall.

My life is lost so soon within the wake.
Why must my journey end, why must I die?

—*James H. Ham*

Sands

As they walk through the soggy sand,
  around her shoulder he places his hand.
As he talks with a lovely charm,
  she can feel the warmth of his arm.
As he kisses her cheek so soft and sweet,
  she can feel the sweat drip at her feet.
The warmth of his arm the sweetest kiss,
  the feeling turns into total bliss.
Even through he, she, will always miss,
  she will always remember his soft sweet kiss.

—*Kristin Dregne*

Precious Children

God checked His book of joy and mirth,
And with a smile looked down on earth.
He saw a place, a loving home
Where children would grow to be his own.
Some special joys would soon unfold
With all the love a heart could hold.

Each tiny babe, so sweet so dear,
What love was felt to hold them near.
A snug little bundle all dressed in blue,
Kind of bald and wrinkly, with ten toes too.
Four times God blessed us with gifts so small,
Knowing so well we'd love them all.

Now our sons have long been grown.
We've felt a strength beyond our own.
With help from above we've weathered the days,
And laughed and cried and offered our praise.
God in His wisdom knew all along
Where each precious child could only belong.

—*Marilyn Jaskulke*

Thoughts Of A Room

The alarm clock rings, she stretches and yawns
Another day is starting to dawn.
As she slowly rises, the bed springs creek
She ruffles her hair tossed about during sleep.
Staring in the mirror she shivers, what a mess
But with great care and attention she soon looks her best.
Adorned in her finery she is ready to start her day of
adventure to return at dark. My heart cries out as she shuts
the door. No! No! Not again, I can't take it no more.
She is tall and slender a beauty to see
So why, oh why, does she abuse me?
In silence I lie here all tattered and torn
My furnishings debris, clothes and junk on my floor.
There's a cake in the dresser all hairy and green
I'm glad the drawer's shut and can't be seen. The closets are
stuffed, don't open the door the trash can's so full, paper
spills to the floor. You would think with the care that she
gives to herself I would be neat as a pin from my floor to my
shelf. I'll never understand it, I'm lonely and doomed
Who cares... she doesn't... I'm only a room.

—*Amy Jo Seyler*

The School Bell

The big brass bell is ringing,
another year is o'er.
The kids are all stampeding straight for the door.
The halls that rang with chatter
chatter will be silenced for a time.
The ghost will walk the hallways looking for a rhyme.
The doors will not be swinging,
As they did from day to day.
And the playground will be idle,
Because no one's there to play.
It's vacation for the summer and everyone is glad.
No more early morning risings,
which were always very bad.
But when the summer's over,
And the bell rings loud and clear,
The kids will all come running from afar and very near.
It's the same old school day's story,
As it has been so very long.
Bringing back the same old message
Through the laughter and a song.

—*Patsy Schmidt*

Words Of Love

You say you love me from your heart. You say we'll never be apart. You say that you would die for me. You say that we are destiny
You say no one can break us down. You say you'll smile when I frown. You say always that you'll be true. You say my dear that I love you. You say sometimes that we may fight
You say you'll hold me close and tight. You say you care for me so much. You say your heart is what I touch
You say I'm wind and you are fire
You say I burn you with desire. You say my eyes are clear as glass. You say your love will not surpass.
You say your true forever on. You say I write your sacred song
You say I'm gold and shine so bright. You say you'll hold me in the night. You said so much, but now I'm gone it's time for me to carry on. Cause what you said from tears I cry
That was the day you told a lie

—*Cindy Bennett*

Home

Among the lovely things I see
Are homes constructed magnificently
In beauty with trees and lots of green grass
That catches the eye each time you pass.

Tri-levels, split-levels and all designs
Built to please the eye and soothe the mind.
Some may envy and others may be
Inclined to know what the eyes don't see:

Is she the queen of his domain...
Reigning in all her feminine claim...
Never in doubt as to where she stands
With her lover, her husband, her man?

Is she to him the "Champion's Prize",
Showing her "Colors" without disguise, making it easy for him to dare to ever yield to the temptress's snare?

Is he to her the throb in her heart, the man she has vowed never to part, the knight in armor in her life, his lover, his pal, his darling wife? Are they to each the "Comforter", the confidant, the solace they prefer? Or is this home in which they dwell Only a shell which houses hell?

—*Henry J. Thornton*

Marital Joy

Loving hearts and happiness goals
Are often sadly obscured
When euphoria turns to resentment
As partners suffer the unkind word.

Yes, forgiveness may heal the breach
Nothing may erase the scar
Of a verbal wound too deeply dealt
Within a matrimonial war.

Frequently convey, "I LOVE you,"
Look for the good in your mate
And proclaim these laurels to others
Praise your spouse before it is too late.
Each is basically human
With needs to be daily fed
Black so easily covers the white
So let us refrain from seeing red.

—*Julia Irene Hardy*

Life

Gray clouds that wander through the blue-lined sky,
Are pushed by winds that govern every side;
Dead clouds, like life which circumstances dye,
Are shaped by constant motion—see them glide?

One's life and clouds have differences slight,
To some life seems to be a joyless feud;
Day in and out they find no purpose bright,
Existence only in a joke so rude.

Much more than this is there to life, I say;
Come ope' your mind, your eyes, and all your sight;
And see your purpose true in that you may
Christ Jesus glorify with all your might!

Love not the world, nor let your cares have ground,
Seek Christ where mercy, grace, and peace abound.

—*Jon Ranous*

Carrier Of The Torch

My dreams of happiness
Are shattered by those of hate and destruction
Thoughts of burning flesh while I sleep
Brings a grin to my cheek
This inspiration has hit me in my dreams
Voices of the shadows tell me I am next
To carry on the torment of others
Which, I will enjoy.
I finally know who or what I am
For I am the messenger of Death
My feelings have rotted away upon my alteration
For those I had called friend
Stay away!
For those I had called enemy
Come and enjoy the pain!
For your suffering will not be quick
But, eternal
I have now started my revenge
Against all of humanity.

—*Raymond James Hartford*

Ghetto Madness

Some people don't like to see the darkness of our world. We are the country of freedom but our freedom is a lie you see America in one spectrum of light. But there is one color you do not see. Our country is full blackness and full of hate. You don't live in the hood were there is drugs and gangs in every neighborhood blacks against blacks, whites against whites Where drive by shootings is the way of life we are a nation of power just about to destruct. Every day or every night some one gets shot drugs are sold to 5-yr. old kids. Who smoke crack like it was candy. Look at our prisons who let drug dealers and killers go free. Cause there is not enough room for all the villains to seat. It's not safe to walk at night with gang wars on every street. No one looks at our country in the whole spectrum of light. Just the colors they want to see. But I see them all. And they are not very bright. Cause one colors sticks our from them all. Black. Cause we are the country full of hate.

—*Denise Smith*

Time... It Takes Too Much

Young people, where are you going?
Are you afraid to be left behind?
Why is there such a hurry about life,
Does everything take too much time?

Time is an important part of our lives;
We can live, expand and grow.
It's the distance between the cradle and grave
That creates our ability to know.

Nothing is as long as it appears to be
If you are patient with desire and plan.
You can set your goal and achieve its height,
But it is always time you must demand.

So strive for tomorrow and fulfill your dreams,
But don't falter or rush for such;
Believe it can happen and see it prevail—
Time, after all, doesn't take that much.
—*Julette Hilton Stephens*

Oh Powerful Boulder

I find you sitting in the hot sun and ask
Are you sleeping or are you on the run
Do you smell the spring flowers
   growing at your sides
Do you feel the lizard who around your body
   takes a slide
How deep are your feet in the desert sand
When you take a walk
Do the little stones give you a hand
When Mother Earth shakes her rug
Do you move to another space
Or do you your shoulder shrug
When she turns on the tap
   do you take a swim
Or catch the water in a bowl on your lap
As you sit in place
   and gaze back at me
Can you be sure you know
   which is free
You or me.
—*Mary Marcos, O.P.*

"Are You There?"

Heavenly father are you there?
Are you the wind, the rain, the air?
Are you the stars, the moon, the sun?
Are you the love of everyone?
Are you the gift I love to give?
Are you the light in which we live?
Are you the golden days gone by?
Are you the song in every sigh?
Are you the blossom of my soul?
Do you expect it to behold?
If this be true my God I pray.
Lift up my heart and light the way.
Are you the woodland green with trees?
Kissed by the gentle evening breeze?
Are you the meadows ripe with grain?
Are you the bird upon the wing?
Are you the voice that whispers low?
Guiding my feet as on I go?
I seek your forgiveness Father above.
Please teach me faith, charity, and love.
—*Joyce P. Richardson*

Little Superman

On, I can see him clearly three years old and fierce of eye
Arms at hips ready for action, wearing the cape that made him
fly. Tho' a reject from the towel rack, who could tell it had
   been ripped?
He could jump the tallest stairstep, I'd ignore the times he
   tripped.

I'd kiss away the cuts and hurts as mothers have always done
I'd listen to his tales of woe, I was his champion
He and I against the world, oh, the trials that were to come
But we'd always end up laughing, this zany mother and her
   only son

Those days of innocence so long ago. Thirty, he just can't be
He clutched my hand for strength and love when he was only
   three
He's a handsome tall man now, has a family of his own
And he's become a leader as those Captain's bars have shown

I know I'm getting older, seems I'm crotchety at times
The aches and pains are spreading guess no longer in my prime
But should I need a champion I'll just call across the years
"Where are you little Superman?" and I know he will be here.
—*Patricia Rodermund*

Homeless

My arms are racked with pain from carrying my world
around from place to place; searching and looking for
something, someone who'd respond to my daily cries of
anguish and pain.

My heart aches from the emptiness of compassion and love;
beating only at a pace sufficient enough to keep me alive.

My hair once glistened in the sun while a mild breeze
gently caressed my head. I long for the pampering, the
attention I once knew, but no longer receive.

The streets are my livelihood, my means of survival. My
neighbors change like the rush hour commute through Grand
Central Station. No chance to socialize and express myself. No
one cares, no one shares.

How much longer will it prevail? How many more will shy
away from me not willing to lend a hand, a blanket, some time?

I'm human, I breathe, I hurt. I, too, need love. I no
longer desire to want for anything. People, hear my echoes of
mercy beckoning for a chance, a change, something to call my
own.

I'm homeless, less a home!
—*Jacqueline Pearson*

Mother's Day

I sit here by myself and cry
As another Mother's Day goes by
I can't help but wonder why,
or how you could have said, "Good-bye."

The questions constantly are there
Sometimes the wonder is too hard to bear
What could I have done to make you care,
Do I live with the questions or do I take a dare.

Sometimes it is best to know
Sometimes it is best to let it go,
I have to love you though,
Without you I would have no life to sow.

So thank you, Mother, wherever you might be
Maybe someday I will see,
That again this Mother's Day you might think of me,
As I think of you and maybe someday we will become a "We."
—*Nanette Thomas*

Think About It

    Hands of time move so slow
as days go on from young to old
    You can't stop the hands of time
All you can do is listen for the chime
    Days of hot, days of cold
When the young get older and the old get bold
    People think that life's a joke
that is why the young and old smoke
    They don't think about life the way they should
As if they even could
    Some have fear for the future on
So they kill themselves to be gone
    Just think about how it would be
If the world didn't have you and me
    Listen when someone tells you they care
Because soon our world will be bare.

    —Lisa Jeffers

My South

My South entangles me with a gossamer web...
As delicate as the Queen Anne's lace growing along the roadside
As strong as brown legs and bare feet on a creek bank
Watching out for cottonmouths and copperheads
As fragrant as wild roses and honeysuckle
Lapping and tying in lover's knots on hedgerows
As soothing as a white wicker porch swing in late evening
Listening to the night calls of the whippoorwills
As spiritual as Sunday morning with baby on my hip
Knowing all the words by heart
As lasting as the generations before me and those to come after
Teaching my grandson to be a "gentleman"
As sustaining as the air I breathe, the life blood
flowing through these veins.
My heart and my soul
My South

    —Sandra C. Morris

"Beyond The Gate"

"At the ending of a perfect day, When twilight starts to fall, As eyes grow dim it's hard to see, What lays behind the wall, Will I enter in at the door, where many feet have trod, Or shall I find that narrow path, To a city made of God, The lonely path I started on, So many years ago, Was filled with trouble, trials and cares, But onward I must go, I always tried to honor man, who stands for what is right, And pray for those who thought that sin, Could fill their selfish plight, But now it's time that I must go, I'm tired and need the rest, I've nothing to be ashamed of, I've tried to do my best, Don't weep for me when I am gone, And try to understand, It takes a special kind of man, To reach the promise land, You have the right to live your life, The way that you think best, But when your time has come to go, Can you say I've stood the test, At last I've found the narrow gate, there standing is a man, With arms out reached he smiles at me, he seems to understand, No longer will I have to cry, and pray for worldly gain, Or will I have to suffer, with a body filled with pain, As I touch the hand of God, I pray that you will take. The lonely path I traveled on. That leads beyond the gate.

    —James V. Dunaway

The Runaway Shopping Cart

His brown eyes twinkle mischievously
As his hands grab hold the bar
Of the metal shopping cart, with one wheel quite ajar.

I wonder what goes through his mind as I pass the list his way,
But before I have a chance to think
The wagon is gone-come what may.

I feel I should warn the other shoppers
That my son is behind the wheel
Of a four-wheel drive Ford Bronco,
At least that's how he feels.

Every other shopping cart
Is an obstacle in his view that must be overcome.
He missed that one, phew!

"Oh, please don't hit that lady," I think as he rounds the bend.
He knows he's out of sight. I don't know him, I'll pretend.

I can't stand the suspense any longer.
What condition will I find him in?
Will he have trampled someone's grandmother?
Will he be broken limb from limb?

I hear his familiar whistle, So he must still be alive.
I better get him out of here before the cops arrive!

    —Cindra Reed

"A Love's Lament"

This evening again, I love you;
    as I did this morning.
Your a soft, gentle peace to my being.
My joy, at knowing tomorrows.
That I've known you, is grace to my days.

Oh love, the time's not right for us;
    there's no place.
I'll keep your eyes and your smile.
In my arms, I'll carry that song sweet;
    we could not know.
Echoes of your laughter, our light
    moments; I'll continue to embrace.

Go now love, I cannot follow.
Warm thoughts of you, will remain my
    dream without end.
You take with you my heart, I'll grieve;
    I'll so need comfort.
Never mind, I love you with all.

    —Mary Voigtsberger

"That Extra Mile"

In loving memory of Charles T. Parker
As I laid in my bed,
A million thoughts, songs, ideas...
Ran through my head.
I found you, I loved you, I walked away...
But, in my heart you silently stayed.
I walked in confusion, turning from the light,
Though deep inside I knew the path wasn't right.
Alone I thought with life's battles to fight.
The pain of all the days gone by,
The guilt, the shame, the games...I cried.
I reached for a promise you made to me,
That with me you would always be.
Falling silently, to my knees,
Before you I brought my pleas.
I thought of you, of me, of the present and the past.
I found forgiveness through you at last.
We talked for a long while,
I said Amen and smiled.
Thank you my friend, my Jesus for taking me,
"That extra mile"...

    —Jeanne Parker

Morning Glory

I awoke to the welcoming sound of cheerful song birds.
As I splash cold water on my face,
   I am shocked into total awareness.
The dull, cloudy sky brightens as the yellow, luminous sun
   Slowly ascends above the warm, glowing horizon.
The flowery, lilac-scented air is cool and refreshing to both
   body and soul.
Suddenly, the peacefulness is broken by the penetrating siren
   noise
   Of an ambulance rushing to the aid of another.
A wolf-like howl from a neighbor's dog
   Joins this unrestful turmoil.
The reverberating ringing of church bells
   Summons people to their buildings for the worship of our
   God, the Creator of the universe.
The tranquil composure is once again self-possessed.
The Lord has given me the joy of the birth
   Of another new day!
    —*Christine Kulczak*

Worlds

Another world is calling me from here
As I walk out on the pier
To the heavens do I draw near

Memories rustle through my hair
But I toss them a side without a care
Like the swift feet of the mare

Leaving behind all which have forsaken me
But still do I seek the key
Locked up in a mystery.

Locked up from the light
Like the gutters in prison the poets
Special people do I cite
Words of wonder, words of might

And the sky shades from blue to black
And the trees green to brown
Everything is changing
With every doeth ring

But do not get me wrong
As you listen to my song
It's just so hard to sing along.
    —*Cristina Alexander*

Hidden Thoughts

Him, him
As I whisper to myself, he's the one who
lays in the pit of my soul. The one who digs
deep in my heart who pulls out my worries my
weaknesses, my love. The love I use to see
him and every step he takes to be closer to me.
As we sit together under the tree, the wind
blowing in our hair, we lay together talking
about what we do, and what we did to make our
lives more difficult, than they ever were.
As we say our goodbyes until the next day our
thoughts slip into the ground to the roots of
this tree. For the days to come after this day
has passed. We get older and we come back to
this tree, we lay on the grass our thoughts rise
and we become the same children after our childhood has passed.
    —*Felicia Rodriguez*

The Saddle

The saddle is old and worn now
As it hangs on the old barn wall.
Left by a man who loved this barn
And the horses he kept in it's stalls.

It's cover is cracked and shows it's age.
There is no one to care for it any more
Since he placed it there and went away
To his home on that golden shore.

He loved that saddle, it was part of his life
As he rode the open range—
Never dreaming that he would soon be gone
And there would be such an awful change.

He rode the range from morning till night
To make a home for his children and wife,
But one day his horse stumbled and fell
Snuffing out the young man's life.

Now there is no one to care for his saddle
And his horse is gone from the stall.
The only reminder left of him
Is the saddle on the old barn wall.
    —*Flora Stokes Capehart*

Life Is Such...

Life is such...with reality we lose touch;
As it leaves you empty and cold;
By the way it takes hold of ones body and soul.
In reality we find; it is never so kind.

Life is such...this life of love and hate
It's our destiny and our fate.
It can bring many tears; this life of hopes and fears.
For there will come a day; when we will dearly pay

But if we all take the time, in this world filled with crime.
We can all make it right; take a stand, stand and fight

Life is such...with all that we know;
Ready and willing to grow;
With the will to survive;
We will simply decide;
Whatever its worth;
We were put on this earth;
With the desire to live
And to give all we can give.
    —*Donna Chandler*

"Someone Special"

I can still remember the look on your face
As the bus above away, my own life to place
And while reading your letter of your feelings at heart
I was reassured of your love, I'm off to a good start.

In your letter you said, I hope I did right
In raising you up my son, to make it in life
After taking that step out to be on my own
You taught me everything to make my own home

When I got married to the girl of my dreams
I knew she was the one for both you and me
I hope that we have made you ever so proud
We're off to a good start, we now have a child.

Once again you said your wise words to me
Your daughter will grow up so fast, it'll be a memory
You said, share your life with her as long as you can
For one day she'll say, I want to marry this man.

Now, what this poem is really trying to say
That you are the woman created in God's own way
From others I've heard say, including myself and my dream
If I could be like anyone at all, it would be thee.
    —*Michael Sayers*

Bon Voyage

My heart is sad; my eyes reflect fright
As the departing ship sails out of sight.
On board is someone I hold most dear
Who told me, "I have no fear."
A wave of the hand, a gentle smile,
"Do not grieve, for in a little while
You will join me on the other shore
With all our loved ones gone on before,
Where we will live with Jesus evermore."

Sometimes at night when I cannot sleep,
A void in my heart too vast and deep,
I lie very quietly, with bated breath,
And hear, "My child, I've conquered death.
There is a season for everything,
A time to mourn and a time to sing.
Find peace in knowing that one so dear
In your memory will always be near.
He's safe now with Jesus. Have no fear!"

—*Bessie Foster*

Alexandra

Music is lodged within your soul
as the rose without its thorns.

When I cannot create
and I begin beating and beating and beating myself
against the range of my rage,
I feel how harmony burgeons in you, in drops
falling from your fingertips
you fingerpaint a world;
some savannah seeded by the sun
where you wear your crown of sky.
And my fingers stretch as from a nap,
yearning toward yours.

You have shown me
that there on the hem of heaven
anything is possible.

The green of your eyes
takes root in my mind
Alexandra

—*Olivia Frazier*

Earth Soup

We sat on a salty log that day
As the waves licked our toes in Miracle Bay.
The sea smelt like whale urine, trout lips and squid
While we kept hot seafood bisque under a lid.

The kelp draped nearby us where sea lions lay
As the waves licked our toes in Miracle Bay.
The sourdough we sopped came from Kansas heartland
Seasoned richly with butter and a sprinkling of sand.

The crab slipped from each other's fingers to throat
As the harbor was entered by a real Crabman's boat.
It seemed Heaven and Earth had mingled some way
There eating our earth soup on Miracle Bay.

—*David C.W. Prather*

Untitled

Although I couldn't see you
You're in all my dreams
Missing you everyday
Sending my love your way
Keeping you in my heart
Although we've always been apart!

—*Carey Luckeroth*

In Memory Of Robert M. Lynn,

The day was bleak and held a chill,
As they laid you to rest on that cold Hill,
At Old Stone Church, above White Hall.
Yes, Dad, I was young, but remember all.
Years have come —— passed quietly by
And still on the Hill, you will ever lie.
'Til Jesus calls you from your rest.
To rise from that Hill and stand the test.
'Tis then, my Dad, I will see and know
Your earthly face with the heavenly glow.
Now rest, missed one, on that beautiful Hill.
Where you had to go - at Jesus' Will.

—*Evelyn Lynn Chapman*

A Different Child

His brothers and sisters must have thought him odd
As they went about their play
For the words that he spoke were different
Than what they had to say.

His thoughts were not on things of Earth
But were on his father above
Yet he was always a perfect child
Whom all found it easy to love.

He knew a childhood like others of his race
An obedient child was he on every hand
Yet he sometimes had a faraway look
That they could not understand.

His daily chores he never forsook
In that Earthly, humble abode
He knew from an early age
He had to carry his load.

A greater load he'd someday bear
Upon the cross of Calvary
This child would see himself as a man
Dying to set a lost world free.

—*Rose Dell Freemon*

Past, Present, Future

Accept the past,
   as those memories will always last
Learn the lessons,
   both the good and bad memorable sessions
Enjoy the present
   for each little joy or caring that is lent
Love life today,
   as each step is a new and exciting way
Revel the future,
   for every dream is a seed to nurture
Embrace all tomorrows,
   God will help heal any sorrows

—*Delphine A. Faust*

School Reflections

The years were drifting by,
As voices echoed throughout the school.
What did the children become,
As they left their mark upon the halls?
Teachers, doctors, laborers they became.
All shared the privilege of having that unique teacher,
The mentor who shared that engrossing story or book,
Or provided a listening ear for recreations of a story.
The teacher gave the protege time,
To read, share, and express their thoughts,
To become more prolific writers.
The teacher challenged students as thinkers and literate
   people.

—*Pat Cruzan*

Life's Destinies

Growing through life's destinies
As time moves swiftly and years fade away
Burying memories in graves of yesterday
Fleeting earthly pleasures grow stale and steps become few
All inspiration begins to nod
There is just so little to do
While I sit here in my rocking chair
With visions of memories through space and stare
Recalling events, childhood friends, and old sweet songs
Knowing in all truth, these too are all gone
Then I say to myself, I am the captain of this vessel
But of course with the Lord Divine
For I know His hand is on the rudder
While guiding me through time
I am now convinced of earthly fates which are destined to be
As man sails to his last shore eventually
While lying in a still and silent form
Waiting for God and eternity
—*Myrtle McNease*

A Hidden Waterfall

What can be so refreshing
As to discover a lovely waterfall
Amidst a mountain woodland scene
Cascading down some rocks;
An experience ever so serene!

One could watch a waterfall endlessly
Even to feeling its atomizing effect.
As a day can be enhanced by such a treasure
Just to look up with the blue sky above
And realize God's gift of a waterfall a pleasure.
—*Dorothy H. Rodke*

You're Not There

Oh the joy we used to share
As we gazed upon a sunset fair
Or if ever I were filled with care
I'd just reach out -
And you'd be there...and you'd be there

We liked the patter of the rain
We liked to walk a country lane
But if sorrow ever came
I'd just reach out -
And you'd be there...and you'd be there

Now each day I wake at dawn
We cannot share a sunrise warm
I feel so lost and so forlorn
I just reach out -
And you are gone...and you are gone

I hope someday again I'll care
About the things we used to share
But now its more than I can bear
When I reach out -
And you're not there...and you're not there
—*Ruby Hallett*

In My Memory ....

In my memory your bitter face lingers;
  Your shattered promises waver about my mind.
In my memory your harsh words cut deep within my soul;
  Your mysterious eyes see straight through me.
In my memory I love you;
  Why I do not know.
Your feelings were never just.
—*Robyn Eck*

First Father's Day

Remember the shepherd tending his flock,
As you embark on your path through fatherhood.
While guiding your children through life,
Try to be the father who always understood.

Teach your children to search and seek,
So there won't be any corner
In the Universe
Where they'll be afraid to peak.

It really doesn't matter,
If a leader or a follower they may be.
As long as they dare to dream,
And let their souls fly free.
—*Carol Gulke Self*

Hope

What do you see, oh Dove of Peace
As you soar in the Heavens above.
The green of the trees, the blue of the seas,
Tell me, do you see love?

Can you espy the goodness around,
The laughter, the holding of hands.
Children at play in their own little way,
The freedom of these righteous lands?

What do you feel when carnage you see,
Created by greed of mankind.
The homeless, the sad, the good and the bad,
Do you grieve at this picture you find?

Do not despair, oh bird on the wing,
Fly with your purpose in mind.
In a world full of grace, whatever the race,
Bring your message of Peace for Mankind.
—*Joan A. Horton*

From My Heart To My Love

Today I pledge my troth to thee,
As you too pledge your troth to me.
And from this day forward as time goes by,
We'll walk this earth together as one, you and I.

For you have been in my heart
  since the moment I met you,
And throughout all the years apart
  I was nare to forget you.

And though the road may get narrow
  or the road may be wide,
Whatever the distance
  I'll be here by your side.

I'll stand tall beside you throughout all of our life.
You my strong handsome husband.
And I,
   Your Best Friend,
     Your Soul Mate,
        Your Lover,
          Your Wife......
—*Elizabeth Ann Austin*

Untitled

I cannot envision life without you, for you are my life!
Your love is more essential than food or drink;
You encompass every breath I take.
To lose you would be to lose life.
—*Nancy Jo Stephens*

We Turn To Look At The Two Of You

Rivers turn to oceans, and flows into the sea. Embers turn to ashes. Love into memories. Rain turns to rainbows. Gray skies turn blue. But when it comes to true love. We turn to look at the two of you. Love is so deep in each of your souls. And always on your mind. Forever in each others heart. You're that special light that shines. You have each other to hold on to, cause no one else will ever do. When it comes to true love we turn to look at the two of you. A thirsty man needs water. A bird needs to fly.
A woman needs a man. Or she'll wither up and die. Roses need the sunshine. Like violets need the dew. But not the way you need each other to make all your dreams come true.

—*Sandy Ramirez*

Fosterlings

Let someone take the weighty task; leave me the little ones I ask. Argue on in deep discussion, spare my time and introduction. A cork upon the tide that's out, I will bounce and float about Collecting little fragile things that cling to me as breezes bring, A little laughter music-sound, little feet to patter 'round, Little hugs and small embraces - cherub angels - dirty faces. Seek we then a greater ocean; ride the wave's of all emotion! Will I live on in little ways—through these whose lives have helped my days? Let them pass on the better things, the joy a word or smile can bring! If they should choose a cork to be, I'll worry not, for if like me - Hold out their hands to those adrift and briefly give a little lift, A better world, a better time engulf these little lives - once "mine."

—*Elaine Kuehne*

The Manic

The swing goes up and down, and up again.
At first it seemed, it will slow down and stop, and you will get off.
Walk on earth, like the rest of us.
Enjoy the flowers of spring and colors of fall, no matter where in time, you are.
Sleep through the night, and get up at dawn.
Be an introvert or an extrovert — either one, but consistent.
How I wish the swing would stop!
I hear your laughter and uncontrollable chatter.
Your mind so sharp, tongue witty, and self esteem as high as you are.
The sky is your limit!
I wish I could be happy with you, but I am not.
I know the swing is headed down, to darkness, gloom and tears.
I am terrified anticipating the expected.

—*Angie Hane*

Communication

It was not just a matter of eloquence
At the Tower of Babel,
Nor before or after.
Even today some poets proclaim in
Obvious obscurity,
Deliberate or not.
The problem is often at some interface of what
I say and what you hear.
I could not comprehend a
Foreign couple, yet
Their diaperling and I
Made faces, rolled eyes, hand shadowed and
We smiled.

—*Barnet Delson*

Dreams

At three I dreamed of being a doctor.
At five I wanted to be a doctor and a lawyer.
At nine, dancing was my dream.
At ten dancing and singing entered.
At twelve acting and art came to.
Thirteen years, dancing, singing and acting.
Fifteen, I was confused but dreams were there, true enough.
At sixteen dreams were fading.
Eighteen rolled around and college was far off my list.
Twenty, no dreams had entered my head.
I run from the police,
hide from my folks.
Steal from anyone,
take whatever I believe I needed or wanted.
As I walk out his door,
wallet in hand,
dropped everything,
Got any dreams?

—*Nikki Rizzo*

The Bridge

Shoreline and clouds extend parallel, melding and distorting at the farthest horizon. Ocean, earth and inhabitants play out their life rhythms, aware of little else and no one. A universal emptiness exists for every man, bridged but by the winds of future and past. Miles unfold without end, blind faith and resolve alone navigate passage across this scape so vast. A solitary road, maybe hope for eventual success, maybe a menacing, vicarious scar in the hostile terrain. An illusionary autonomy; man's obstacles abound, congested with doubt, fear, hate, suffering and pain. So much time behind, so little time ahead, so great the distance, so hard the fight, so extensive the tears. Great oceans swell, clouds darken, trees tower, threatening, tormenting and fanning deeply instilled fears! Far beyond the reaches of space and time or man, buried within the infinite perception of the mind; a whisper of light stabs through the darkness, a strand of hope takes shape, a spectacular find! An extension binding horizon to horizon, shore to shore, ground to sky, time to time and then more. An extraordinary sight, a bridge going everywhere and nowhere, a presence to light the path, open the door.

—*Connie L. Sherwood*

Live Or Die

One must live, one must die
At times one that lives is dead
One that dies is alive
Life and death are not always physical, or emotional
Life and death are both and neither at the same time

Life, where would this world be?
A shame to be without
Nothing is more valuable than life

Change is both physical and emotional
Change is both life and death, and neither
It is a sign of life, and a sign of death
One's dead can't accept change in oneself or others

Once one forgets, there is no future
There is no life, only death
Only the soul considers life or death
Chooses what is best
It is not an easy choice
But, as long as it is up to me I choose. ....life ...death

—*Ronald G. Wolfe*

Untitled

My true emotions, are rooted quite deep
At times they will surface, awakening from sleep
But then they are gone; they've disappeared again
And they slumber in peace, until I reach for my pen.
Once more they surrender, held captive to the page
Lying there exhausted, my thoughts rest uncaged
Silent victims of suppression, known only to my heart
Outpoured with such a passion, let my pen play his part.
In giving them a name, with fluent vibrations,
He gives unto them a voice, to vent their sad frustrations.
Characters in a play, individuals left to speak
Each of different origin, all of them unique
They are granted lasting life-forever, black on white
Finally at amity, revealed in the light.

—*Christy Mason*

"The Modem Romance"

I bought a new computer, that linked me to a place
At which I met a woman, although not face to face.
This place fits on my desktop; it doesn't take up space.
But when I flip the off switch, it's gone without a trace.

Each night I go and talk to this girl I've never seen;
Yet, times we speak together are silent and serene.
Well, reading words we've written is more of what I mean.
The only place I meet her: A single-colored screen.

You see, I do not know her, but through the things we write.
Like Pyramus and Thisbe, we speak through walls 'til light,
Denied as well the pleasure and privilege of sight.
I fear like they we'll never speak again next night.

Our feelings and emotions are things that are discussed.
But I cannot be near her; the keyboard is a must.
Through words we try to strengthen our friendship based on trust.
But we know our attraction is one not based on lust.

At least through times of trouble, some help I carry her.
Though I have no intention to meet or marry her.
Out time alone is finite, another barrier.
Oh no! I've reached my limit! Goodbye — NO CARRIER

—*Patrick Murowsky*

Spring

A passing look at "out-of-doors"
Away from nagging household chores
Reveals a most intriguing sight -
A grown-up man out flying a kite!

For this is Spring, and all around
Abound the sight, the smell and sound
Of this, the most elusive season
When sensible folk lose hold of "reason!"

Attention caught by diving kite
A dozen feathered migrants light
Resting while they seem to ponder
What it is that flies up yonder.

Suddenly away they go
Flying high and flying low;
Leaving sky, so blue and bright
To wildly dancing, dizzy kite!

So then I turn, - begin again
The chores that seem to never end,
But heart is lifted, spirit gay,
Because of that brief Spring display!

—*Rita Beal*

Paper Memories

Paper memories are all that I have left since the day you went away. It's true that life is easier to live when you're living day by day. They say that time heals all wounds except the wounds that are within your own mind. And today the paper memories of you refuse to be kind. I take down your picture and look at the way you smile from where you stand. A tear runs down my cheek to fall upon the paper memory in my hand. I think about you often but I only cry from time to time. When I read the poem I wrote so long ago for you I see a tear glisten on the paper rhyme. The letters that you wrote to me I keep in a box marked with your name. The pages may be old and faded but the paper memories of you are still the same. Everything in this world that lives must one day pass on. And, although you are no longer here, the paper memories of you are never gone. All I have are the memories of you and at times I feel so alone. In my mind I sigh as I place a rose beside your name chiseled on a stone. I stand and smile at your picture and the tears fall from my eyes as they almost always do. As I walk away I place my pen upon this memory I've made of you.

—*Clarisse Ann Bradley*

The Suavest L'Expressways Around 'Yo' Boulevardiers

So, Alfio's Centaurians, smile at me and be gayer!
Babes, so thanks to you and you alone, not that I don't—for
I have a busy imagination of that romances day at home
It is cooler, much more off than the fuller moon and lazier
Than some years in folks can say a passe' in...
Oh you cool moon and reggae gazer tell me of lifts in dreams
Only for the innocent betrayal of that memory of any a day
Of means, when my days will never explain it like a so and so
Not for now and anyway, and so, as they all hadda say it,
The going's gone okay, and then; though I still feel in it the
hot Civvie'itis' of the cities and city in the faces of some
strangers It may have been such a gift with which I've coped
in... In all of its fragilities,...yes, although I cannot take
those Walks to the angels of a yesterday in this country,
hey... And so I will stay where the stars heat the skies for
always in a wake of the toasts to and into my todays, whether it
Be usual or unusual, yeah, what can you or I say in the U.S.A.
For the angels think and they say it to me - "I'll be out too-"
Are you okay...honey...I don't know...I'll see ya later...
I'm gonna hang out 'til it's time to leave forever in anything!

—*Hee-Ju Yoo*

Yesterday's Memories

It seems like yesterday when I was child
Back in those days I was all smiles
I know now those were the good ole days
My memories now belong to those yesterdays...

As youngsters the years ahead were not on our minds
I guess we thought later, some other time
Time can pass so fast as we know
Its hard to accept and hard to let go...

But there's one thing that time can not take from us
Our memories, we hope we can always trust
To re-live our past and often recall
Those days that meant so much to us all...

Now I'm still here but my face is worn
Between now and then I am always torn
For my younger years are what I yearn for
But I know they will be here no more...

So I accept and I'm thankful for my years
For their many joys and some tears
I am thankful to have lived this long
Even though some of my years are already gone...

—*Martha B. Whitehead*

"Hate Me"

Before the day Christopher Columbus set sail, it was upon my
back you did wail. HATE ME, I AM POOR.

When after he opened that western door, it was upon my back
your hate I bore. HATE ME, I AM BLACK.

When your lust and greed for land did rise, the tears were then
in my eyes. HATE ME, I AM INDIAN.

When you called for all to come, it was me you placed within
your slum. HATE ME, I AM ITALIAN.

When the black-man was set free, it was me you forced to my
knee. HATE ME, I AM WOMAN.
When you could no more money make, it was my small body you
did forsake. HATE ME, I AM A CHILD.

Now it is not, whether or not I choose, you just need another's
back to bruise. HATE ME, I AM HOMOSEXUAL.

Who am I you ask, with your supreme indignity?
I am the lost soul of FREEDOM and HUMAN LIBERTY.

From generation to generation you pass this legacy;
of crying freedom while living hypocrisy!

And when at last we shall meet, at that Great and Pearly Gate,
let it be Him who decides whom to isolate.

—*Dawn Rene Smith*

The Fort

How do I feel, about the long lost past.
Bad memories and feelings,
How long do they last

The days were long, and the night's too short
For time for reflection,
So I built up this fort.

A fort for protection, to keep harm away
To keep my emotions inside
And others out to decay.

These walls are sturdy, and they do fine
Until I go outside
To find enemies in a line.

They are out there, waiting to attack
To battle my feelings
And to push me back.
They knock me down and bring me to the ground
Pushing harder backwards
Back into the fort, I am bound.

I raise the walls and shut the gate, here I am safe and
healthy waiting, Yes waiting, for my fate.

—*James Patterson*

There She Lay...

Her eyes glazed over with a film of white,
barely showing the glowing blue that used to shine.
Her brittle hair lay dead around her head and he remembered
how it used to shine and flow with its deep brown curls.
Her full lips, frozen to its last moving state, used to be
so warm and soft against his cheek and gentle on his lips.
Her cheeks lay stiff and cold, but once were rosy and warm
with happiness.
Her hands, not moving any longer, used to touch with care
and lay warm in his strong hands.
Her heart, not pounding like a drum, used to beat with life.

—*Terez R. Fraser*

Mama's Anger

Young boy's blood spilled on the ground
Battle is ours, not a sound.

Scarred memories of a nation torn apart
Boy couldn't wait for the battle to start
Mama waitin', waitin' for her boy to come home
She'll be waitin' all alone.

Mama, I'm sorry to tell you your boy is dead
There's no more ground he can tread
Died with nobility, with honor
No one could call him a coward.

Young boy died like his father
What a pain to his mother
No more fears, she will lay
For the people of this nation will pay.

She watches with anger as people kill each other
Son against father and brother against brother
Her nation is torn apart
She prays another battle will not start.

Young boys blood spilled on the ground
Battle is ours, not a sound.

—*Jeremy Arnold*

Distance

Distant, is the life you lead or choose to lead, it seems to
be taking forever. But remember the further you are apart,
in distance, the closer you are together. Deviation, is the
part that distance plays. Instantly you wonder if he's gave
his love away. Separated, not only by space but also sound
and time. Thoughts in your head, become Inner-Twinned.
Anxiety steps in, and takes over. So there you sat. Not
knowing what he's doing, or whom he's with. Pain, that you
feel inside, causes you to anguish with fears. Affection taps
you on your shoulder, to let you know he still cares. For
distance plays a funny game on weak hearts and weak minds.
For some can see straight through distance, but for others,
distance leaves them blind. Noticing how you got carried
away, and that distance plays a-fool. So concentrate on the
next time he makes sweet love to you. You'll see, nothing's
changed, he still lights your flames, and the only one left
to blame is.................Distance!

—*James Holman Jr.*

Gangs

Blood, crip, folk, VL-makes your life a living hell
Beat In, Beat Out- That's what the life is all about
Gang bangin-Out all night
Hats Kicked left and right, hand signs flying—people dying
Blue, Purple, Black, or Red
Look on the street you'll find someone dead
Folk—black, utc—White
Why do gangs have to fight
They think they're cool, they think they're bad
But really they are just a fad.
They carry their colors and don't tell their mothers
They carry their gun and kill people just for fun
They have a knife and can take someone's life
Heart with wings, five point stars
This is going way too far
Saggin' jeans, playboy scenes, Fila shoes—red and blue
Starter hats, baseball bats
Kill a child now and then
Go to hell and back again
Why do gangs have to fight? That's the question for tonight.

—*Kasey Phelps*

I Choose

Last night a force, out of control.
Beaten, battered, shaken and shoved.

I CHOOSE Freedom.
Slapping and degrading violence hurting private, inner spaces.

I CHOOSE
Being the dominant creative force in my life.
Flowers and roses. Hearts and flowers. Charming indeed.

I CHOOSE
Being true to myself and being free.
No job. No money. Where will I go? Who will hire you?

I CHOOSE
Trusting myself. Intimidation and name calling a favorite game.

I CHOOSE
Loving myself one hundred percent, unconditionally, for being me.

I CHOOSE A Cycle Broken.
I CHOOSE Love, Happiness, Fun, LIFE!
—*Jeanmarie Abrahamson*

God's Friends

God, your friendship I treasure as no other can be,
Beautiful and lovely, I glorify thee.
You give me strength through your son, Jesus Christ,
Guiding my actions, through prayerful insight.

You have greatly blessed me, this very day,
With the loving arms of friends, and the words they say.
It is the friendship of others, that helps keep me growing,
As life's joys and sorrows, unexpectedly keep flowing.

Lord, grant me the wisdom and courage to be,
A loving friend, to those whom I see.
We all have abilities, to each his own,
Grant me the security, to let mine be shown.

I love to praise you, with the poetry of my heart,
Showing others my love for you, with this very art.
I never knew the words, were bubbling within my soul,
Until the love of your friends, filled the empty hole.

Lord, let me keep writing the words you give to me,
So that others may hear the joy, that comes from being free.
With you as my Father and guardian of my life,
I will never be without friends, through all the joys and strife.
—*Laurie A. Scott*

Love

When I'm sitting on the outside looking in it all looks so beautiful so clean and simple
It all seems so clear "This is what I want"
Then I reach for it, to be part of it and the picture changes
It fades and twists, the breeze and the green grass are gone
It's stifling hot, it's overwhelming, I can't breathe!!
I don't want to be here, I want out, I can't handle this anymore
I reach, I reach for the door but it's so far away
[it was so much easier getting in, now I can't get out]
But then I stop, just to think what if I do get out, what then?
Won't it all just happen all over again?
Won't I reach for the light and won't it pull me in (again)?
"Will I ever learn?" I ask, as my heart is wrenched out and my stomach twists
As I'm saying "this is the last time, this is the end"
I won't fall for that, never again
But look at the sky...
—*Melissa Chapman*

My Love, The Sea

Come with me, come see the wondrous eternal
  beauty of the sea.
She will enfold you in mist, wonder and love
Watch with hope as each new sunrise brings
  a gift of love for a new day
See the breathtaking glory of a sunset
  inspiring love for the one above.

Respect and love her many moods, tranquil
  or violent
Let the power of love fill your heart
Open your arms, embrace her and say,
  "You are mine for all time."
Since time began, the sea is where
  Heaven meets the Earth.
—*Antoinette Kelleher*

Because

Because of the years I let go by.
Because of the years I made you cry.
Because of the years I know this to be wrong
Because of the years I waited so long
Because of the years I caused you pain
Because of the years I held you to blame.
Because of the years I thought you found fault
Because of the years I yelled and fought
Because sorry is not the word to say
Because - forgiveness, may.
Because our marriage vows remained in tact
Because all else will only prove this fact
That I give to you and you give to me true love
Because of this love, forget the above
—*Nathan Smith*

"Time To Come Clean"

You know you need help but you're unable to see.
Because you enjoy this thing and that's a real tragedy.
But all you are really doing, is killing yourself slow.
Because you are captured by something
That you will, never really know
And the true question is: Are you really getting high.
Or are you just believing, in another "Big" lie?
Because you found yourself hooked, under the influence of crack.
And now that you can't have it, you want your life back
At some point in time you say this.
This my last hit and there will be "No" more
As you are picking the carpet and rubbing the floor.
Wishing you could come up with, one more hit.
Is this life your living, do you really need the shit.
The answer is NO and I'm not saying this to be mean.
But for all you brothers and sisters who are
messing up your lives, by drinking or drugging or using crack
Step in the 90's, it's time to come clean.
—*Charles Luke Jr*

To Life

I live in a sugar house
Where the Vanilla smell
Sates my sense
My heart feeds on cream
My spirit on Honey
The heat and the hush
And the sweet syrup
Of my love fills my flesh.
—*Davina Stein*

Before Paper Clips

      Before paper clips
      Before stapled pages
        however did we keep
    our thoughts together.
      We wrote in long-hand
  dipped nibs of pens in wells of ink
   penned words on yellow paper ruled
     to keep our thoughts aligned.
  Page after page our thesis increases.
We somehow must bind our thoughts together.
        Teacher teaches:
    Gather all your papers in a pile.
     Fold all into a triangle
    in the upper left hand corner.
  Tear parallel slits half an inch apart.
    Then fold the torn patch back.
  Complete! Our ordered thesis bound.
    —*Mildred Toogood*

The Cattle Are Blowing It

Slowly we're killing old Mother Earth,
beginning with the diapers they put on us at birth.
They can't be recycled...well...neither can we!
We keep searching for answers and trying to see
who to blame for this mess...besides you and me!
Ah! There is old bossy eating all of that grass
and filling her stomachs with pure methane gas!
She wanders the pastures and merrily "toots"
never giving a care to the air she pollutes!
"They" say for each problem there is a solution
So how do "they" purpose to stop this pollution?
Some genius I'm sure will invent a converter'
For old bossy to wear...gee...I hope it won't hurt her!
    —*Helen Kirkorian*

Anissa

Anissa Bingham lies in a cold, dark grave
Behind a wall of stone, her memory I keep
A daughter born to sorrow, could saving grace not save
This child who closed her eyes, and drifted off to sleep?

A score, no more was lent, eternity defends
The hope that filled my heart, a love that never ends.
The light that filled my eyes, the joy that filled my days
Walks in heavenly places, and sings a song of praise.

My child, my dearest child, if I could but amend
The frailty of my soul from sorrows which offend,
And rend the heavens above, that I may then define
The hope that I have lost, the will that I resign.

I long for sanctuary, a place I may refrain
Where peace consoles my spirit, and love consumes my pain
Where children never see, nor taste the darkness born of hell
And all that issued from its womb, reason would expel.

My dreams they were the portal, I was cradled by the Most High,
He said, "Why dost thou trouble me?" and this my sole reply,
"I did not mean to trespass, nor meant I to displease,
I sought to escape the sorrow that brought me to my knees."
    —*Anthony Brantley*

"Allison"

You entered my life and my heart you won.
We laughed and played and took walks in the sun.
We watched 'Barney' and 'Disney' and through you I've learned
  a ton.
Now my days with you are all but done.
I'll miss you and I love you... Allison.
    —*Kelly A. Cook*

January Landsape With Father And Hourglass

Saturn tree,
Bent,
branches near breaking,
laden with winter layers,
should have another blossoming,
another year of renewal.

Weary tree,
branches sheathed in icicles
of frozen weeping,
look what has rooted from your seeds.

Stoic tree
should have been an evergreen,
or been nourished by temperate soil.
How heroically
against the frosts you have toiled.
    —*T. Phyllis Cleaver*

Winds Of Horror

    Crashing winds of horror,
    Bewilderness unknown,
    Pleading for a prayer,
  He wonders to find his own.

    Screeching winds scatter,
    All the souls he lost.
    Dwelling in his realm,
    He unfinds the past.

    Roaming in uncertainess,
    All will be destroyed.
    The candles are lit.
    The world turns to a tear.

Dwelling in a realm all his own, searching for the land he calls home, he makes the puddles of sadness. Waiting for his master to give the sign, will silence takes its prize?

    Waiting for a mistakeful soul,
      He tries to awaken.
  Digging in a grave he has now forsaken.
    He tries to correct his sinful past.
    A hopeless circle of recreation.
    —*Kathryn Massung*

Appaloosa Canyon

You stepped-out, on cool dunes.
  Blanket fluttering like some
lost bird's feathers.
  Black, faultless hair,
rising and falling; lazy sweet-grass smoke.
  I have summoned you
from the woodlands,
  where my people turn into trees.
Spirits beat their turtle-rattles
  on the rivers.
Your brothers sang in
  thunder-tongues, Horse-woman.
Their meanings are imprisoned
  in the yellowness of sands.
(Can't you hear the Canyon
  when she's singing?)
    —*Melanie M. Ellis*

Mal de Mere

Mother painted stories with her tongue,
Blending blue words with red words,
Seemingly stirring water into fire,
Creating the world we never knew.

Deep way back beyond the black pupils
Where the memories dwelled,
Her lessons spun and spread out
Through her lips invading the silence.

She pronounced our father daddy papa
In forbidden sounding syllables,
Coloring within the thick black lines,
Giving life to the formerly trans-parent.

The forever moving man had left waving.
From the doorstep the orphaned family
Portrait, stained yellow hazy, faded
Bloomed faded to father incomplete.

But through her the oats-sower returned,
Leaf-flitting through the molasses air.
Tottering on her spreading blue words,
He became real in the Kentucky night.

—Michael Hyde

Lost Beauty Of Love

I lost the beauty of the flowers that
bloom in the spring like the blooming
love we shared.

I lost the beautiful color of the leaves
in the fall like the color of your hair.

I lost the gentle touch of a rose like
the soft touch of your lips against mine.

I lost the meaning of the twinkle of
the stars in the sky, so much like the
twinkle in your eye.

I lost the meaning of nature's touch
like the love and care that touched my
soul.

I lost the feeling of the bright future
like the dreams and desires of my heart.

I lost the love of beauty when I lost
the beauty of love.

—Marquita Goins

Goodbye, San Francisco

San Francisco has native travelers' hearts,
Blue ribbon elegance, all the arts,
The Golden Gate, an ocean view,
A dazzling pyramid, Chinatown, the zoo.

There's great cuisine, great bay, too,
Sailboats frolic and ships steam through,
Famous cable cars, North Beach lights,
Atop Twin Peaks, so many sights.

Southern Illinois has rare white squirrels,
Kind, gentle folks, smiling country girls,
Neighbors drop in, real small-town charm,
Good wholesome lifestyle, ground to farm.

There's wheat, beans, miles of corn,
Hardly changed since I was born,
Across the Mississippi, Little Egypt land,
That's my home, there I'll stand.

You can understand the reason why,
I'm going home, must say goodbye,
My heart waits in the Midwest,
Goodbye, San Francisco . . . all the best.

—Lester E. Linder

Mother Nature/Father Time

They are like Mother Nature's precious jewels strewn about her
  blue skies.
In all their glory I watch her hummingbirds dance before my eyes.
Then before you know it, Old Man Winter sneaks up in disguise
Father Time shall pass now and hummingbirds return much to my
  surprise.

—Sindy Chavez

Moment In Time

Green canoe
Blue water of lake
White granite of mountains
The feel of the paddle
against the water
Water dripping from the end of the paddle
splashes into the lake and sends out circles of light
and energy.
Light from the sun reflects the shape of the trees
in the water.
Greens and yellows mix with a sense of green
within me.
Beauty surrounds me and reflects in the water back to
me.

—Elizabeth J. Barrett

Tonight, Perhaps Again

The majestic mountains silhouette the
  blushing horizon,
Cascading shadows pirouette, and shade
  the town far below.

The God of the stars bids the earth goodbye,
  And the Angel of the darkened sky,
Appears solemn against a blackened canvas.

All the souls of the village below,
  Slumbering unaware, content with covers and dreams.

Clouds move in, and hide the moon,
  Torment unleashed in anguish,
Sleep no longer happiness.

Light curses the darkness,
  Noise punishes the silence
All the elements and their fury,
  Find release in fear.
The storm moves on
  The town again sleeps
Birds sing in the new-born hours
  Tonight, perhaps again.

—Veronica Roxby

Love

Our love is one, and not a pair,
Bonding was instantly, no one should compare.
For we knew from the start what we both wanted from life,
Now we have it, and everything is right.
God has his reason for putting us together,
He knew we had so much love to give to each other.
The day is soon we will be married in the eyes of our Lord,
For you have turned my world around, and I in yours.
Then when death comes to part us and I'm left here all alone,
I'll have our loving memories to help carry me on.

—Dicie Ledbetter

Hail ——Nature!

Thud - Ker-plunk, ker plang -
Booming allegro drum beats
Explosions of enormous entities.
Chirps silenced by direct hits -
Dents of damaging dimensions -
Scattered glass, shattered dreams -
Rooftops revealing heaven-made skylights,
Unforeseen destruction in dawn's awakening.

Behold strewn material belongings
Visions of man's progress,
A pyramid of possessions and obsessions
Destroyed in a moments maddening fury,
Nature's hold upon man!

Competition - never!
Preservation of fragmented dreams placed in freezers,
A reminder of Nature's power display.
No match can man surmise
Unequivocally Master -
Nature - Hail o' hail
N'er to be forgotten!

—*Lenora R. Crowder*

Lines For Pamela

Your trees are framed in frame of gold
Branches leafless, winter sky lucid, cold
Like your bare arms heavenward raised
Seeking light, seeking love— peace erased.
Pamela did you conclude that unending bargain
Found and lost, lost and found again?
Did you find that trembling balance
Between heart and head, exit to entrance
Into the golden mean? If you only knew
That true is true but not quite so true,
Knew how crooked are the straight,
How much goodness in the reprobate,
You will take the rose with the thorn
Chase the ideal, always there, never born.

—*Anwer Beg*

"Life"

Oh how life can tear at the soul,
Breaking the man and taking control,
Blistering scenes that fill up the mind,
Tainted love most often you'll find,

Tragedy strikes without much delay,
Material world disappears in a day,
Time passes on to realize,
Judge not life by wallet size,

Searching for hope somewhere to exist,
Only to stumble, fall in the mist,
Sanity held by a single thread,
Longing to hold a rope instead,

Watching the day turn into night,
Maybe tomorrow will be a new light,
Oh how life can tear at the soul,
Breaking the man and taking control.

—*William James Bean*

The Wild Goose

Fly wild goose - high in the sky.
Wend your way home - winter is nigh.

Fly Wild Goose - in perfect formation.
Honking direction - to cross the nation.

Fly Wild Goose - soaring brave and free.
The sight of you - stirs a longing in me!

—*Clara B. Hopping*

The Never Ending Dream

In dreams life's fatal visions rest, upon the weighted, heavy breast, of love's ill-fated, dreadful foe, that led astray and then let go.

From summer rose a love so dear, that taunted naive children near. With eyes of red and jaws of steel, disguised itself with clever zeal.

In autumn through the perfect light, was cast about a demonish plight. And on her feeble hands did leave, the scars of feelings yet conceived.

Winter denies the love once found, the crack of doom would soon be bound. Through darkened sky there came new hope, the victory won, she had forged the slope.

Spring brought fresh life, a start anew, problems gone, but still remained, a few. Pressure fled and love flourished the air, but remorse and pity again would be there. Because, in dreams life's fatal visions rest, upon loves weighted, heavy breast.

—*Robin Bell*

Riches

I may not be in this world tomorrow. But for as long as I breathe, I possess today. Each precious moment is like a treasure chest with the richest overflow. There is the radiant sunrise to behold. And I can watch the kaleidoscope of clouds. When I hear the choir of the birds, I have wealth untold. Tomorrow I may travel on to another realm. Hold my hand today before I go. Sit awhile and help me capture each minute as if it were on film. The traffic outside my window reminds me that life relentlessly marches onward. Please don't hurry away; I need you with me now. If you lend me your presence, you'll chase away the fear; and together we'll move forward. I want to gather each blessing, as one picks up sea shells from the sand. There are multitudes of shells—so I dare not pass one by. Each one is unique and full of intrigue, but there is always the hope that the next one will be even more grand. Please stay by my side as I collect these small riches. I want to cherish the signs of life each moment presents. We will be better prepared for our separate journeys if you will honor these wishes. No one can say for certain which breath will be my last.

—*Barbara A. Sweeney*

Shadow Of The Stalker

In a dark alley in the still damp night,
Breathing in rapturous moans of the anticipated prey,
Tortured by memories as the moon glowed above,
The tapping of soles approached...

With the monotonous sound of that rhythmatic beat
White knuckles drew the knife slowly overhead
As the tension grew stronger
the pounding grew louder.

The shadow of the walker
touched the heart of the stalker
and the gleam of the knife
sparkled like diamonds in the light.

A deep hollow scream erupted the night
There was no turning back as he slumped to the ground
There was a glint that
could be seen in her eyes.

The last thing he saw
as the life drained from his corpse,
Was the shadow of the stalker
as she walked out of sight.

—*Barbara Spencer*

Lighthouse

When the sun shines bright, and the
  breezes gently blow,
The Lighthouse, still stands.
When night slips in, bringing the blackest
  of black shrouds,
The Lighthouse, still stands.
When the fog envelopes the rocks that
  would dash in pieces all who venture
  near,
The Lighthouse, still stands.
When the storm unleashes its fury, and the
  sea rages against it,
The Lighthouse, still stands.
Its light, lit with love, will remain a
  beacon of hope and shelter.
The Lighthouse, still stands.
  —*Marvin Breshears*

Autumn

Brown and orange, yellow and gold,
Bright autumn leaves succumb to the cold.
Floating and rocking, drifting to earth
To nourish the soil which first gave them birth.
Returning as planned to the primeval source,
Fine-tuned to nature's seasonal course.
Repaying the elements for matter once taken,
Still bearing the pattern that nature awakened.
All through the winter the patient trees sleep,
Till spring's leafy harvest is ready to reap.
Living and dying, sleeping and waking,
Creation's deep mystery; life in the making.
  —*Ruth Madsen*

October

October's a month in which to delight,
Bright blue skies with birds in flight,
Juicy red apples all crisp and cold,
Turning leaves, a sight to behold.
The smell of bonfires, wieners on sticks,
Marshmallows dripping like candles with wicks.
Pumpkins in patches, pumpkins on porches,
Jack-o-lanterns lit up like torches.
Witches and goblins roaming about
To scare you silly, without a doubt.
Bright frosty mornings, chilly nights,
Bright stars above, heavenly sights,
Harvest moon glowing orange in the east
Huge and beautiful, to say the least.
"What is so rare as a day in June?"
An October night with a harvest moon.
  —*Marjorie K. Hazen*

Dear Grandma And Grandpa:

    Being together for so many years
    Brings to my eyes, so many happy tears.
  Divorce is common these days, but not to you
    You always find time to say "I Love You."
      You've always lived so far away
      But your love has been so near.
  Grandma and Grandpa have been the names we've
    called you year after year.
    Coming to see you has been a lovely vacation
Showering us with love and gifts has always been your tradition
      Grandma and Grandpa?
    In your days you've probably shed some tears
    But you've been comforted by one another for a
      Special 50 Years!!
      Happy 50th Anniversary!!
  —*Jenny Craig*

Bluebird In The Snow

There you sit o'gentle puffed up creature
Brilliant blue upon a cold gray branch
The sky, a moment ago sparkling gold to the south
has turned all at once black and ominous to the north.
A snow squall sends down from the heavens
The season's first bits of ice and snow
And you little bluebird sit and watch.

What are you waiting for beautiful bird?
The snow engulfs you and still you perch.
Do you yearn for the softness of Spring
to cheer your heart?
Perhaps you are showing me that life is both
sunshine and storm.
Bluebirds of summer meadows also survive the
harshness of winter.
So too the "winters of our lives" will yield
to eternal Springs of joy.

Thanks, o' sky, snow squall, and bluebird
for lessons of light, darkness, and happiness.
  —*Carolyn Constable*

Amazing Grace

A Presence will come in your darkest hour
Bringing light and great power.

Surrounding you with protection
Guiding you while you seek direction.

By the strength of the Presence in the air
A passage will be made, to lead you out of despair.

As you take your first step, you'll receive the greatest gift
The gift of love, that conquers all
By building bridges instead of walls.

And if you feel, it will depart
Fear not...
For it resides within your heart
Waiting for release.

Remember...
It has no face, but is known every place as...
  Amazing grace.
  —*Patricia Kelso Davis*

Growth

Gaining a year of age
brings upon remarkable delight!
For it's the addition of a page
in the great book of life!

The contents of this book contain
fragmented memories; shame and dandy, both.
And, these memories will always remain
as measured morals of growth!

Step forth utilizing the past;
move inward towards the light.
Remember all make mistakes, which last.
Meaning all one does is right!
  —*Joseph Glebo*

The Desert

In the desert,
Where the water is low,
In the desert,
Where fields of Cacti grow,
Horses and cattle,
Fight an endless battle
In the raging heat of the desert.
  —*Emily Carol Sumner*

Welcome Home, Polly Lois

Mt Pisgah welcomed me home today
Broad shoulders greened by balsams gay,
Clouds hanging low as kindly guards,
With birds, and breezes honor bards.
Far northeast Mt. Katahdin kin.
Northwest, softened Ozark friends ascend.
I have not felt this way before.
Nestling in the Asheville core
French Broad and Swannanoa too
Chatting unheard, I stay so new.
Mt. Pisgah, named for a holy mount,
Welcomed me home with its spirit route.

—*Pauline Whitacre*

Millennium

Unconditional love
   brought forth without wrought
   as sweet as a dove forever in thought
Unforgivable sin
   sorrow deepest in heart
   destiny at the foot of men. Find the foot to start.
   find the foot to start
Uncontrollable urge
   until tomorrows part yesterdays merge
   search for passage reveals nought
Unbelievable joy
   for time that's caught
   seasons turn man to boy until seasons halt
Unchangeable past
   come back to haunt
   reveille in spell that's cast seas hard to chart
Unbreakable bond
   from destination sought
   a quest to ride upon to a majesty with no fault.

—*Joseph Lunsford*

Morrisa

My cat Morrisa was born in Atlanta, April '83
Brought to Alabama in June, only for me.

She keeps her fur, colored orange and white
Very clean and shining bright
By licking and bathing day and night.
When I brush her she stretches and purrs with delight!

She rolls on her back for a tummy rub
And only drinks water from a bowl in the tub.

"Come, Morrisa," signals her to the front door to run,
To go out on the porch to rock or swing in the sun.

Up high, on the window sills, by the hour, she will stay
To look out in the yard at squirrels and birds feed and play.
With her tail held high, to go out doors night or day,
She will reach with her paws to ring
Three elephant bells on the doorknob on a string!

A watcher, a protector, if needed, she is around.
An amuser, a friend, a welcomer, often a clown!

A more loveable, smart ruler of my home, than she
Could never be found on land or sea
My cat named after Morris, "Morrisa!"

—*Martha H. Kilpatrick*

Between

The dusk has come, the dawn's not near, you wonder why, I've brought you here. The sky is pitch, the stars don't shine Don't worry now, leave the world behind. For this our world of unconscious love, of little things you never think of. Like a flower bursting into bloom. Here, a place where all have room.

A place to treasure each moment, each day in each other's presence, we'll find a way. Forgetting this place or this dream that used to be, would kill these feelings inside of me.

You know the place when you sleep, the dreams you remember and always keep. Between the place of sleep and wake, where your
unsure of love or if your heart will break. Remember this place, remember me, remember my heart you hold the key.

This place within a twilight morn, where realities questioned and trust we shall form. And now as our moment is fading and gone. Blessed be the memory of a coming new dawn.

—*Kirsten Kent*

Exit

Salt water stings my eyes - dripping slowly - blue cleansing my brown above the sun - beautiful, noble - conquering my blood - racing my pulse - victim to the roughness in my breath

If your balanced your eyes stay dry.
Floating never balanced, a trickle of chlorinated water drowns my lashes and for a moment it is the Ionian and this water is blue

Greening white chlorine fog escapes sucked up spiraling air vents pool lamp dots and fluorescent lights distort my focus vents spin air into my lungs
I stroke, back arched in chlorinated water. I breathe.
In American trinity locked - I yearn for guardian temples
I reach, stroke, stay afloat

Sink me into safety of geographic plates - shifting - erupting into mountains folding into caves hovering over the salty sea.

Here, my toes scrape on pool's tile patterns and I focus on the fire exit bleeding over heavy steel doors.

—*Janet Marie Goehner*

Desert Winds

Nine months is short,
But a new life grows in that time;
Grieving and healing take much longer,
To adjust to my life without her may take an eternity.

Each day is like a speck of sand:
The wind blows it here and there,
And many times there is no rest
Because changes are scary but required.

Even the vastness of a desert
Is mercifully broken by an occasional oasis;
The water is clear and refreshing
While the shade cools the fevered brow.

This weary traveler needs to rest.
Let the angry hot desert winds blow,
Reflect on life,
And allow the present to happen.

—*Don C. Kittinger*

Time

Things go around but don't repeat ... Time goes in circles but doesn't repeat ... Monday . Tuesday . Wednesday . Thursday . Friday . Saturday . Sunday . And then around again yet it never repeats ...
   He lives his circles, Waiting, Resting, Unhappy
   He lives his circles, Rushing, Working, Unhappy

Every circle is unhappy yet it never repeats:

     Time is a trap ... We are trapped.
Trapped in a circle that never breaks never ends never stops...
     Goes around forever.
—*Jonathan Weichsel*

Teams Consist Of...

Teams consist of enemies and friends,
But even the best will make amends.
Through good and bad the teams we play,
We'll stick together to call it a day.

Teams consist of athletes that shine,
It all comes down to the coach's sign.
Observing the signal and waiting to hit,
The runner is going when the ball's in the mitt.

Teams consist of good and bad calls,
If one person's thrown out, the team might fall.
To keep the spirit of the team alive,
To get to the base, you must somehow dive.

Sometimes we win, sometimes we lose,
Still it brings a painful bruise.
Strikeouts and popouts are hard to come by,
But only the best will lurk in my eye.
—*Joey Lynn Gatto*

Drugs Kill

They can boost your ego, or raise the level of your vanity,
  But eventually, they will cost you your sanity.

They make you feel pretty, make you the center of attention,
  And give you free room and board in the 'big house' of
            detention.

They can make you bold, make you feel stronger,
  Mostly stop you from living much longer.

They can make you feel sexy, make you feel invincible,
  But you won't be 'getting off', that cold steel table.

So whether you're drinking it, smoking it, snorting it,
       shooting it up, or just popping
          that 'harmless pill',
  Remember the only thing you need to remember to live,
          is that Drugs Kill.
—*Charlotte Alonso*

If I Could Have You Back

Leaving you was easy, or so that's what I said.
But I couldn't let you know of the feelings left in my head.
The love you had to offer, never seemed to be enough,
But if I could only have you back, I'd shower you with love.
I'll love you like you loved me, and never let you down.
I'd talk out all our problems, and turn this love around.
If I could have you back you'd see a girl you never knew,
And I promise the love I have, will always be true.
So baby please forgive me, and love me once again,
And I can promise you, I'll stay with you till the end.
—*Jennifer Johnson*

A Child Of God

I live on this earth as everyone else,
But I don't follow the world's way;
I've made a decision that's not always easy to do,
I'm following the Lord day by day.

What I am to the world, who can say,
To it I'm just a minor speck;
Not living for material things,
And trying to earn its respect.

What I am to God, he can say,
I'm part of his family;
And sometimes it's hard to be a part,
But I know it's where I should be.

What I am to you doesn't matter,
For when I'm buried in earth's sod;
In heaven I'll be rejoicing,
For I'm a child of God.
—*Justin Sorice*

When I Follow Mama Home

Mother's Day won't be the same. Since dear old mom has gone.
But I know someday I'll see her, when I follow mama home.

Like many times when I was young, at Mama's heels I'd run.
I'd follow her each step she took. From dawn to set of sun.

And then at night when I lay down. Our Mom would tuck me in.
She'd listen as I said my prayer's, and when I'd say amen.....

Our Mom would pray, and thank the Lord, for keeping us safe
  that day.
And it sure did bless my heart each night, to hear my mother pray.

Mama taught us right from wrong. And showed us how to live.
She brought us joy and happiness, with all the love she'd give.

Then God in heaven called her home. To sing around his throne.
And I know someday we'll meet again. When I follow Mama
  home.
—*Andrew R. Britt*

On M.C. Escher's 'Symmetry Watercolor 118'

Not to stare
but I swear the salamanders
on my ceiling are smiling.
Nestled in their niches,
clasped claws in symbiotic union
with brother or sister;
(it doesn't really matter)
colorblind reptiles coupling.
I squint and I see order; ripples of color
Shimmering yellow waves on a field of red and blue bursts
or azure boats carrying peaceful passengers
or pairs making circles
making links on a never-ending chain
or red rings of fire.
The utter order imperceptible
except from afar-and even then,
only its presence, not its identity,
is decipherable; reptile rumplestilskin.
—*David P. Coustan*

Dreams

Dreams to me are mystical illusions,
Which many times end in unknown confusions.

Trying and trying to remember them so,
They sometimes remind me of a villain or foe.

Horror to laughter, beginning to end,
Then you wake up trying to remember again.
—*Tammi Pascucci*

Mud Pies And Little Girls

Little girls called me to come and play
But I was to busy to go that day —
　To busy with dusting and sweeping to play
I stayed indoors the entire day.

　They made mud pies with an artist's flair
crimping and edging and shaping with care.
　I could hear their squeals of sheer delight
When a pie turned out to be just right.

　The years are many, and the years are long
Where have those little girls gone?
　If they would but call to me today
Never a house could keep me away.

　I would gladly join in their play
and make mud pies through-out the day.
　The dusting and sweeping are still there
But my back-yard is silent and bare.

　The girls have scattered and gone their way
No squeals of delight are heard today,
　Like the pies they shaped with an artist's flair
Their shaping their lives with love and care.
　　—*Wanda Lee Burrell*

The Mask

To you I'm sure I seem secure, happy, and cheerful,
　But inside I'm really quite sad, depressed, and tearful.
My face shows I'm sunny, smooth, and self-assured,
　But don't you believe the veneer you observe.

　Don't be fooled by me,
　Don't be fooled by the face I wear.
　For I wear a mask,
　A mask to hide my tears and fears.

To the outside world I appear fun and spontaneous,
　Confidence my name; coolness my game.
I'm fiercely independent; I pretend I need no one but me.
　Pretending is indeed an art second-nature to me.

But beneath it all, I'm really desperate for love and approval.
　My heart is aching; I feel so confused and lonely.
My feelings are wrapped in chains and this facade is quite
　phony.

Yet underneath I pray someone will see through the Mask,
　And hear my cry for love and acceptance and assure me
　of what I really can't assure myself-That I really am worth
. something.

Remember the mask I wear that hides the fears;
　So don't be fooled by the face I wear.
　　—*Sam Kofoed*

"Just Playing Dead"

Just playing dead may happen to few,
But it happened to me and could happen to you.
The fall hunting season had men in a whirl.
I was roaming the prairie, no place for a girl.
When walking the cowpath I trembled with fear,
for a bullet whizzed by grazing close to my ear
I hid in the rushes of a lake that was dry;
Soon footsteps approaches and I thought I would die.
He parted the rushes and looked for his prey,
And he said, "God forgive me" and his face turned to gray.
I dabbed at my cheek and my fingers turned red,
from a bullet that barely had grazed my poor head.
And I said to the man as he bent down to see,
"Just a wound on my cheek, Sir, I am well as can be,
I'm trying to save me, I'm not full of lead,
I'm just playing dead Sir, I'm just playing dead."
　　—*Esther Franke*

A Rainbow

A rainbow is a treasure we yearn to reach,
　but is always beyond our outstretched hand.
A rainbow is a promise we make to keep,
　but with a little twist of fate,
　we never seem to.
A rainbow is a dream we hope to pursue,
　but somehow,
　it always fades away into eternity.
A rainbow is a wish we hope comes true,
　maybe it will, or maybe it won't.
But whenever I see a rainbow,
　I am reminded of life, love, and beauty.
Inner gifts that God gave to all of us,
　even if we are not the most beautiful,
　even if we don't have some one to love,
　even if we lost one who was close to us,
We can all turn to a rainbow,
　and be remind of these,
　the gifts God gave us.
　　—*Mary Wozny*

How Sweet It Was First Kiss

It is not something that is new,
But is sure an enjoyable thing to do.
So pucker up your lips, before my heart starts to make some
　skips
If you don't do it soon, I'm going to swoon,
and fall into your arms, hoping you will accept my charms.

Now don't you back away, I still have more to say.
Just give me a big kiss.
And not the kind you give your little baby siss.
Just once you try and do it, you will want to come back
and renew it, so loosen up and smile.
I'm ready to give it my best trial.
Now see that was not to bad,
Just kiss with a little more feeling,

And the rest you will gently add.
Soon your heart will be feeling,
Something you will be revealing,
That's driving you mad.
Not all the things you do in life, are really so bad.
　　—*A. George Stallings*

Moment In Time

For a thousand years, nay, a thousand and more
But it was only a moment in His life that He bore.
"Let there be light" was what He had said
and across the sky I saw the path that it led.
The moon and the stars He made for the night,
And with pains taking care hung each one just right.
The mountains and seas, oh how rich can it get?
He hadn't even made the animals yet,
Let them fly, let them swim, let them walk on the land,
And they all appeared at His command.
In His own image and by His own hand and with
The breath of life He had created man.
Then He put them all in a beautiful garden site,
Then He stood back to look and said "It's all just right",
Oh, His light is so great, and I am so small
I couldn't cast any shadow at all.
But, for a thousand years, nay, ten thousand and more,
It was only a moment in His time that He bore...
　　—*Mariana Cincotta*

All The Signs

It's hard to admit,
but it's harder to deny.
You get that funny feeling in your stomach
every time you see him.
Everything has changed and all the signs are there

You're floating on air, nothing can bring you down,
"It's so childish," you say,
but you can deny it no longer
All the signs are there.

You see his handsome face everywhere.
His hypnotic baby blue eyes, the look of his boyishly styled,
soft brown hair which you long to run your fingers through,
his luscious red lips you dream of someday kissing. All the
signs are there

You stare at his picture to memorize his face,
hoping he's thinking about you.
What if he knows, worse yet, what if he doesn't.
It's finally happened, all the signs are there.
—*Jennette T. Eddy*

The Violet

Its petals wept tears as clear as mine,
   But its were more sincere.
Its thorns ripped deep into your soul,
   But mine cut like a knife.
It loved your water, I loved your mind,
   But you cared for it more.
You rejected my love, and took the flower,
   To spite me for my acts.
Now the rose dies softly while I live on,
   But you chose the one that wilts.
Now I cry sincerely, and I no longer tear,
   I shrivel dying softly all alone,
     Gasping for your water.
   I should have been the rose.
—*Emily Dievendorf*

What I Feel For You

Feelings so strong they formed a bond,
But miles apart doesn't mean they're gone,
The distance is great,
  but love is near
Held deep in my heart,
  with nothing to fear
It's hard to describe the love I have inside
  Freely flowing through me like an ongoing tide,
I miss you dearly,
I miss you much,
But with your frequent calls my heart you touch,
So love me please, as I love you, and
  together we can make all our dreams
  come true.
—*Natalie Accardo*

Heading For A Heartbreak

I saw him there, a stranger
But my heart leaped in fear
for it knew more pain was on the way
His aura mingled with mine
taunting, teasing, whispering sweet
words drawing me into his web
A spell was cast and I fell, hook, line,
and sinker.
Sweetness wraps around me when
I'm in his presence but depression
is a heavy burden to bear when he's gone.
—*Brandie Terrell*

Along The Shore

Walked by the ocean today not alone
But myself and my dog his quest was a bone
Mine was different how can I explain
Like the search for the sun after a rain

There's something about the sea I've found the look of it
And also the sound with its waves so high and ever so strong
That makes you forget all that's gone wrong

The questions one has the ifs and the whys somehow fall into
Place under the skies and the people that walk the shores
Each day seem calm and serene and friendly in their way

I found myself focusing on losses I've had
Some good and those that were somewhat bad
As I filled them in order one by one
I'm sure I heard "THY WILL BE DONE"

If one could bottle this effect I'm sure
The world would have a miraculous cure
And the generals and all the powers that be
Could conduct their meetings by the sea
And all the problems behind closed doors
Would be resolved with walks along the shore
—*Donna DePaolo*

Harry Had No Hair

Harry was a brilliant man
But no one seemed to care
All they seemed to notice
Was that Harry had no hair.

They never invited Harry
To join in their affairs
Although he had a lot to offer
What they offered him were stares.

But Harry didn't mind
He was far ahead of the rest
It was only a matter of time
Before issues came to rest.

No—it wasn't his head
That made Harry shine
It was his foresight and tenacity
That left the rest behind.

You see—Harry never split hairs with anyone.
—*Vicki Rubio*

But Not Today

You tell me to accept Jesus — and I will —
  but not today.

You tell me His love will change my life — I believe you —
  but not today.

You tell me my prayers will be answered, that He will hear
  me — it would be nice —
  but not today.

You tell me I will have peace, direction, and understanding —
  I could use it at times —
  but not today.

You tell me He will take on all my problems — perhaps —
  but not today.

You tell me eternal life could be mine — I suppose —
  but not today.

You told me He will be back for His children — I thought
  "Yea, but not today."

Now as I stand here before Him, I begged for another chance.
  He just looked at me and said "But not today."
—*Deborah A. McNear*

Be Careful Of Thoughts And Words

You may whisper your criticism about someone,
But, oh, so soon you'll find in it no fun;
For a little bird is awaiting to carry the word,
You may have thought no one ever heard.

Then when the tale has made the route,
And the little bird has told what it was about;
You'll have to live with a conscience of guilt,
That pierces your soul to the hilt.

So to rob the little bird of its prey,
Be careful of what you think or say;
Remember to keep your conversation loving and kind,
Then peace and harmony you are sure to find.

We're told, "As a man thinketh in heart so is he,"
And God wants us to be like Himself you see;
So if the little bird is to kept at bay,
We must keep living carefully day by day.
—*Will H. Havens*

Song Of The Wind

The wind tries to whisper pleasant songs to the trees
but only the birds answer back
the tall grass sways to the song of the wind
only words are what they lack
humming birds hum to the beat of the drum
of natures most perfect beat thunder
but now trees are scared 'cause lightning is dared
will it strike us down, they all now wonder
humming birds now run from the beat of the drum
they're also scared they might get hit,
the thunder got louder, lightning struck flowers
the weather was throwing a fit
soon dark clouds passed by nature with a sigh
but aware it will come again
now back to before the storm is no more
let's restart the song of the wind.
—*Brian Carney*

"Faithful Wounds"

They say nothing ever lasts forever,
But our friendship is one that can't be severed.
There's not another friend who could ever be-
As good friend as you have been to me.

You have unlocked so many secret doors
　with your heart key,
And you were the only one who could ever
　help this heart to once again see -
All the beauty and life's simple treasures
　That have been awaiting me.

If fate chooses our relatives then
　God must choose our friends.
For it's with these faithful wounds
　that our broken life mends.
—*Tonia Thompson*

Untitled

In ancient times, some problems that
　they thought were too complex,
they solved by hurling heavy stones,
　or by the battle axe.

Some people now agree upon
　a novel resolution,
they settle problems peacefully,
　without a revolution.
—*David Boyd*

The Stare

Life is hard, the adults always said,
but she already knew that, the subject was dead.
A little child, touched in an adult way,
becomes wise and old too early, and hears not what they say.
A shattered child, her misery quite there,
is unseen by adults, gets just a blank stare.
She shuffles through life, abused and alone,
with pain quite real, it cuts to the bone.
But she has to grow up, and assume the position,
of denial, self-hatred, and total suppression.
Until one day that little girl reappears,
no longer denying, admitting with tears,
what happened long ago and seemingly far away,
the touch that plagues her day after day.
Slowly, she sheds away the dirt and the guilt,
that she suffered at the hands of a shadowy adult.
A child is a person too, and that's what
adults must keep learning to do-
look and listen to children, and not just
stare through.
—*Cheryl Frye*

Live Tonight

The sign on the marquee says, "Live Tonight,"
But the lights, they have been dimmed,
for the stage, it will be empty,
and the curtains have been trimmed.

The plane was lost in Tennessee,
And the Golden Voice was stilled,
The Disc Jockey held back the tears,
As he announced that Patsy Cline was killed.

Country stars and fans alike,
Were saddened by the news,
For a woman whose love of life,
Was to sing the country blues.

The Grand Ole Opry is silent,
At the loss of a good friend,
But the music from this country star,
Will last till time does end.

The sign on the marquee says, "Live Tonight",
And Patsy Cline will sing,
For the Lord so loved her beautiful voice,
That to heaven, Patsy, he did bring.
—*James G. Greenfield*

Adultery

　You never meant to do it even once,
　　But then you did it twice.
　　　Repented quick,
　　But then you did it thrice.

　　Now she's gone, really gone.
　　Empty house, clock ticks, alone!

Hot tears, trickle down on flushed cheek,
Curled up in a ball, humiliated....weak.

　　　Another vain promise,
　　　　Was glibly given,
　　　Now meaningless life,
　　　　Isn't worth livin'.

　　You just went to far,
　　　That girl from the bar,
　　Was she worth all this pain,
　Now going insane, what did you gain?

　　Oh God, you're just so sorry!
　　　Repentance is now real,
　　But blankly staring back at you,
She walked away. She's too numb to feel!
—*Timothy Johnson*

The Computational Brain And You

Your brain is a very important part of you
   But there is yet another side of you

With your brain you can learn and build on your knowledge
   But if you perceive yourself weak never can it peak

In your brain you behold your ultimate goal
   But if your mind is not made up it will go untold

In your brain you possess the gift of great logic
   Yet nothing will it teach if your heart is not toward it

To have and to hold the options are untold
   But to engage or refrain remain in your will

Like Jekyll and Hyde they wrestle inside
   Both are a part of the true hidden you
     —*George Anthony Ortiz*

Unwinding World

The bright sun streamed through my window
But there was something about it I did not know.
A mild breeze ran through my hair,
It slightly stirred the morning air.
The clouds were above the trees,
Which I could hear clearly through the breeze.
The air was damp and cold,
The sky became dark and bold.
A frightening wind blew,
And I suddenly knew.
A steady rain fell,
And that was the beginning of all hell.
I then felt very depressed,
But I was not defeated.
There are the failures and frustrations of everything,
Yet I feel nothing.
    —*Courtney Huckel*

In My Shoes

Every one can give advice
But, they are not in my shoes
Everyone can say, smile, be nice
But, they are not in my shoes
Depression, regression, fear, anxiety, regression
Emotions left to run wild at a moment of
   unexpected drama
Motivation, self control, reduction of tension,
   defense mechanism
They all break down when the initial shock hits
   "unexpected"
Everyone says: If I were you I'd do so and so.
But, they are not in my shoes.
Each situation changes like the seasons
But, still everyone else seems to think
   they have an answer or logical reason
As the saying goes "Never judge a man
   until you have walked a mile in his shoes"
My shoes are now only being walked in by me.
    —*Sally L. Lee*

To Die On A Starlit Night

To die on a starlit night,
To die in this beautiful way,
To die with eyes closed, breathing
slowly, in the quiet night air,
To die in peace, peacefully dying.
To die on a starlit night.
    —*Amber L. Kelley*

The Diary

The world in nowhere can I out pour my heart,
But this dear path am I to rove along;
To wilfully continue, I tonight,
The discontinuous discourses, chapt'rs of life,
For whom have cover'd another trip towards
The end that always seems too far away.

It's here the spring fair water is congeal'd;
It's here the winter ice is melted clean;
It's here the empty head is fill'd up high;
For here there still remains the pious mind,
To give the courage me in search of route,
To give to me the dream that will come true.
    —*Junmin Liu*

Dreamland Of The Heart

Most people think dreams begin in their head,
But this isn't where they start.
They come from somewhere deeper,
In the dreamland of the heart.

It contains peaceful thoughts of past and present,
From the beaches golden sand.
To the beautiful sights of the mountains
They're all kept in the hearts dreamland.

From the summer heat burning from the sun,
To the winter's soft falling snow.
The dreamland of the heart,
Is where the winds of wisdom blow.

The heart is the source of the stream of love,
And the fruits of honesty grow here, too.
The dreamland of the heart holds things,
That are only special to you.

So don't think dreams begin in your head,
Because that isn't where they start.
They come from somewhere deeper,
In the dreamland of the heart.
    —*April Morgan*

The Beauty Of Life

There is such beauty all around,
but to take the time to see,
birds, flowers, and the trees,
all these can be found.

There is such sadness all around,
in the papers and the news,
war and crime and hunger,
all these can be found.

There is always strife everywhere,
but one can never dwell,
upon only the negative things around,
but the goodness can be found.

There is also a beauty found,
within each human soul,
if only we had the courage to seek,
all these can be found.

There is such beauty all over this world,
in the trees, and flowers and such,
but Oh, to find the beauty within,
we know we have truly found.
    —*Courtney Erwin*

Suicide And A Special Friend

Life is something everyone should pride,
But tonight I lost that feeling and thought of suicide.
I thought it would be the easiest way to get away from
   my problems,
Then I chose to stay alive, yes, I chose to solve them.
A problem is a minute thing when you have so many friends,
Especially when they're by side from beginning to the end.
Many times in your life, you lose all direction,
But that is what friends are for—love and protection.
Problems will come and problems will go,
They'll eat you inside 'til you let someone know.
If you can't solve them, I'm sure someone can,
If not, at least they know and can help you understand.
If you've got problems—let someone know,
Because suicide—is not the way to go.
Read this again and try to repent.
If not for a friend, my words would be silent.
   —*Jodi Roy*

Hope For Peace

Why do we say your my sister or my brother
But turn our backs to condemn one another?
People thought all the hard times we had to for go
Had ended a long time ago.
All we have done seems to be in vain
Because look around, you still see hatred and pain!
There will never be a day
When we can truthfully say
We truly live in peace and harmony.
But that's only an opinion from me.
Still I want a place where my children don't have to worry
About being shot or beat
Or having the shoes stolen off their very feet.
Maybe someday there will be a place
Where everywhere you turn is a happy face.
But until then don't say your my sister or my brother,
Then turn around to condemn one another!
   —*Sunshine Groves*

Mixed Up

  There must be something worse than a mixed up mind.
         But what, I ask you?

   In the closed off portions of the emotions—
Unseen, yet glaring at you are the lonely searchings,
Deep tearless cryings, the yearnings, hot and hottest
Lying still, yet struggling for release and fulfillment.

   Thoughts running the maze in frantic exploration
     For the answer to such a complex puzzle,
   Again and again returning down the same path—
     Dead end—unanswered, weary from the search.

   Striving still to try to satisfy the pangs
  Of hunger, aching deep in the pit of the soul.
  Never ending, even when depression and despair
   Hangs a heavy cloak, closing in, shutting out
Escape that would bare the soul and free the spirit.
   —*Mildred Stevens*

Together In My Dreams

When I close my eyes and dream,
the tears in my eyes fall like a stream,
because in my dreams I know I can touch,
the handsome man I love so much,
but when I awake and you're not here,
that's what brings each new tear.
   —*Bonnie Jasso*

Our Touchstones

Your Touchstone may be just a rock, tumbled in a stream.
But what matters that, if it does help you find your dream?

Now my stone is round and not too smooth, and a light brown;
'Tis nice to hold, and to think about; hard to lay down.

'Tis also a bit transparent when held to the light.
It can be held 'tween two hands - or either one, just right.

This cool, round, hard object is an Arkansas River Stone,
passed by a lesson leader to each of us alone.

This cool surface filled us with awareness of our Lord;
Linking folk together for renewal and reward.

So for all it was an afternoon of shared wonder;
Perhaps taking each a bit nearer Heaven, yonder.

We can now dare to live since we were born - not spawned;
The Lord can count us as all one — on Earth and Beyond.
   —*Frances A.N. Reber*

The Seasons Of Love

Seasons come and seasons go
   but you're the one who needs to know

My love for you is oh so true
   I will never ever leave you blue

In the winter when it's cold
   I will keep you warm and hold you close

And in the spring when things turn green
   we know nothing will come between

In the summer when it's hot
   our love takes us to our favorite spot

By the river where we met
   we will always be in love, you bet

In the fall when leaves turn brown
   you will see us all around

Holding hands and walking close
   down the trails of love we coast
   —*Marvin R. Norton*

Darkness

Darkness is usually thought of on the negative side
But you've made me see darkness in a brand new "light"
While I'm closed in its blanket of black
It always brings thought of you back
Whether it's deep in the night or I just close my eyes
I always imagine you're right by my side
Where darkness is some's enemy, it's my good friend
When you're not here it helps me pretend
So when I finally see you I'll feel just right
Just like I did those darkest of nights
   —*David S. Gibson*

"First Mind"

You think about things and after a while you think about those same
   things again.
As time passes by it's still on your mind. You think on
   it once again.
Before you know it, you've made the wrong decision.
   Last but not least you will say to yourself, "I should have followed
   my First Mind."
   —*Ivanoria D. Elliot*

Butterflies Are Like

Butterflies are like leaves; falling from trees.

Like a soft velvety song, sung by a nightingale.

Beautiful clouds that you can catch.

Easily broken like glass or crystal.
Butterflies are like the wind,
They flutter past you without a care in the world.
Gliding through the air, like a lost kite...
Flowers, that float through the air
A beautiful dream or the tear of a princess.
A Goddess' message to the world
A heavenly spirit adorned in color.
Butterflies are like a sunset
Butterflies are like...
—*Emily Boyd*

Nature's Aspiration

   Crystal droplets congealed, quietly concealed
   By the expanse of sky fallen, timidly peeled—
     Away by the bucking, to and fro
Of the gulls, the heavenly wings of earth and snow.
    Tredding water, as it falls down my face
   Dropping to the ocean the remnants of my disgrace
     Square in the center of a silver lining
Is a tear or a tear, which ever, I find it shining . . .
    Hatching a rainbow from the egg-dome sky—
It is signalling for my crescent-shaped reply.
—*Kara Thompson*

Remember When.....

A leggy dark-haired girl crossed the
cafeteria in swift, strong strides.
Your gaze discreetly followed her
with those hooded dark brown eyes.
You'd been plotting your approach for
days and bragging to the guys,
'Bout how you'd suavely ask her out without telling any lies.
Your chance had come, she worked
that night dishing veggies on each tray.
You sidled up, tray in hand, practicing what you'd say.
You licked your lips, wiped your
palms, and tried to catch her eye.
As she looked up, you raised your
tray and said "How 'bout another fry?"
She smiled demurely, gripped her tongs
and dropped one on your plate.
You blushed "beet red," raised your
brows and said "So this is a poor guy's fate,
After all this planning, sweat and
nerves to gain a beauty for a date!"
—*Linda L. Ryan*

Desire

The berries were not yet ripe for picking
Though summer was nearly spent,
And I was hungry for some berries—
I craved a handful, no more.
The summer had been long—
Hot, dry, wearisome, but enduring;
And I was anxious for ripeness—
Eager like a little boy by the window
On a rainy day
Who wishes he could go out to play.
—*Fred Saxton*

Caged

You keep me concealed;
   Caged in reality;
   Restrained by morality;
   Bound to rationale.

Guarding you from unknown pain.
Each emotion kept in submission.

Each emotion desiring, pleading,
   screaming for release — all unheard.
Logic smothers all cries.

Forcing each move;
   calculated, controlled, predicted.
Releasing each emotion; well trained, tested safe.
   well-trained, tested, safe.

One day I will escape this prison.

Passion will be unleashed; uncontrolled; untempered.
   Liberated to speak without thought;
     touch without limits;
     feel without anxiety;
     know without remorse;
     and love without fear.
—*Melissa Rose Reuscher*

"Memories"

Faded with the dust of years gone by
Calling in the darkened gloom of night
Riding on a shaft of silver light
Into dreams of yesterday they fly.

Connecting moments with a fragile web
They shape us into what we are today
Imprinting on the hearts in which they stay
A sense that life is one unbroken thread.

That ties together people from all lands
Embroidering a future yet unsure.
Where are the souls among us that are pure?
We need the use of all your helping hands.

To build a future better than the past
With memories which shout a joyful cheer.
Progress of good will is prayed for here.
Help us build up something that will last.
—*Shelley Street*

What I Hear

What I hear is the trees speaking to me
calling out my name remember me
Your roots are deep as mine
we are intertwined needing the same substance to survive
Mother Earth has given us both the best she has for our growth

The leaves on my tree they are like your clothes they cover me
The children you have is your family
like the branches of my tree is the life of me
I love to feel the wind blow through me
it's like the spirit moving in you making you fresh and anew

Can you hear what the trees are saying
we are life please let us live too
Clean up the environment love respect show gratitude
give back to Mother Nature the work of a positive attitude

Stop being careless with our lives
polluting the air is not wise
The air is the breath we breathe
the spirit of life indeed
—*G'ya Hamashea*

Song Of Myself

My spirit whispers the song of myself
Calling out to the ones who will listen
Begging not judgment, but understanding
Weeping for those who cannot see

The trees which rustle in the breeze stand tall
Telling the tale of my strength
They are the souls of those who share my blood
Guiding me through a forest of shadows

I drink the words from the book of knowledge
Thirsty for but one more drop
Never quenched, reaching for some unnamed star
To satisfy a hunger that will always be there

I stare at my surroundings and marvel
At all the wondrous miracles I behold
And shake my head in consternation
At those who choose to be blind

The music of my song plays in my ears
Drowning out the wrenching sound of pain
As the charming melody of a dewy spring morning
Stills the clamor of a writhing soul
—*Janine DePaulo*

"Love From My Heart"

When you're in love you know it well, so many ways that you
    can tell, like when your heart begins to race,
        A smile comes across your face
    When one you love, is there with you
        You know it then, you feel it too
            The satisfaction of the heart
Is in the friendship from the start, love is also all your
    soul, deep within, it is your goal
        To share it with a special friend
        You get as much as you can send
        You feel much better, when it's there
        The one you love, will show they care
            You can't resist the feel of love
            It's everywhere, it's from above
    So show your love with all your heart
        And you will never lose the part
        That bonds your mate and you as one
            Your love will be forever fun
        And let love take the heart of you
    To let you know, you'll see things through.
—*Robert Burns*

Little Bird

Little bird with your feathers all wet
Can you tell me has it stopped raining yet?
I can see that it has, but in your tree
Rain is still dripping off the leaves

You skitter back and forth across a branch
A leave fills above you, starting an avalanche
Of rain that drips upon your head
I feel your discomfort, it goes unsaid

But wait little bird, I see the sun
Soon you'll be flying and having fun
As soon as all your feathers dry
You'll be flying across the sky

You will do loops and spins
Flying to places I've never been
Making your living off the land
With the love of God's helping hand

Little bird who's looking at me
How I wish that I was thee
To fly anywhere, a home in every tree
A beautiful creature, wild and free.
—*Timothy Shawn Cowing*

Cry In The Dark

Little people, frail and afraid.
Can't recall the youth they had.

Unspoken words for fear of shame.
No one knows the cry or the pain.

Must holdback, the scream of the inner
child, frail and afraid.

Try you try to forget,
only you can understand.

No, you're not alone, others tell
and so must you.

Heal thyself, little child.
Release this dreadful shame.

It's not you, it's them.
They are the ones to blame.

Even though your life will never be the same.
You can survive and learn to live again.
—*Diana Handy Armagost*

Be A Young Centenarian

Our goal is to help every soul to reach with good health the
century mark. It wasn't a lark.
The journey they took. They didn't do it by reading a book.

Love of life is necessity to help accept life's unwelcome tragedy.
But bouncing back they kept up their energy.
Enjoying life almost every day.

Being good to others.
Treating all as they were brothers,
While making old and new friends.

Conquering T.B and Cancer.
How they did it, they cannot answer.

Accepting themselves as a special person
Their purpose in life had a reason
Fulfilling the need to be useful and needed.

What a joy to behold
The young centenarians who refuse to be old;

The cross and the cranky die (in their 60's and 70's) young,
not old. The 80's and 90's have hearts of gold.
The young centenarians who never grow old.
—*Virginia G. King*

Screamers

Scream children, in rage, for the dead in Sri Lanka; and the
charred down in Waco.
Scream children for a lack of esteem now taught in our schools.
Scream for stripes, not solids.
Scream for equality and balance and paper straws, not landfills.
Scream for me and old re-runs of Jay Jay and "Good Times"...
we sure could use 'em now.
Scream for baseball, not astroturf.
Scream for college life and MTV responsibility.
Scream for rap and rock and roll and old big bands.
Scream for L.A. women and fallen angels on Hollywood
Boulevard, and Clinton learning to inhale.
Scream against the Croats, Serbs, and the resurgence of LSD.
And child, please scream before you can only say, and then only
whisper, and then carry voicelessness, but for now, scream.
Scream for metal detectors in schools and 7-Elevens without
    Twinkies.
Scream with your voice and I'll scream with my voice, for it
    to stop.
—*Freddy Koehler*

Cheat A Little, Lie A Little, Steal A Lot

Walk the picket line of life, strike against the powers to be.
Cheat a little, lie a little, steal a lot.
Help yourself to the abundant life, capitalize upon your
　fortune and greed.
Cheat a little, lie a little, steal a lot.
Grab hold of the gusto of life, poke fun at the workers you see.
Cheat a little, lie a little, steal a lot.
Keep all of your possessions of life,
Exploit the poor and the ones in need.
Cheat a little, lie a little, steal a lot.
Don't take no for "your" answers to life, darken your eyes,
deafen your ears to any plea.
Cheat a little, lie a little, steal a lot.
Turn in your soul, you thought you owned,
And the body that now has no life
You cheated a little, lied a little, stole a lot.
Jesus is waiting and he's anticipating, "all" the things
You did in vainglory and strife.
You cheated a little, lied a little, stole a lot.
Everything you did in word and deed, has come to the master as
　your creed:
"I cheated a little, lied a little, stole a lot."
　　—*Rubye L. Fobbs*

Born To Die

Her soiled dress was pulled over pregnant abdomen. An aborning
　child kicked in womb in its heedless way toward life as yet
　unseen.
Little of love had gone into its procreation. Nothing of
　security had fate allowed for its bloody path into grimy world.
Its eyes would meet the face of mother, poverty ridden and
　unprepared. The woman's lips, slack in swollen cheeks, hung
　morosely - no joy curved their corners.
Sweat dripped down the sallow face as sudden grimace twisted
　blurred features.
This woman was soon to enter the traditional, albeit doubtful,
　joy of motherhood's realm. For her, stretched on ragged
　bed, haggard fear dulled pain-glazed eyes.
In solitude she groaned as the pains of labor made of her a
　struggling, painting animal.
In tortuous journey, through channel of blood and fluid, the
　child burst. No cry came. It lay attached umbilically to
　its silent mother.
Together the souls of mother and child fled to halcyon fields
　whose glories are known to wretched and wealthy alike.
　　—*Dorothy M. Schreiber*

On Saying Goodbye To Prince Charming
(Who Turned Out To Be A Frog)

So hard to say — that word goodbye.
Why can't I say it? I know why.

To say goodbye, to see the end,
To start all over once again
With someone new—
It's easier to stay with you.

But that's not true.

To stay when knowing I must go,
What seems to be just isn't so;
A waste of precious time that could
Be spent with someone that it should.

So hard to say — that word goodbye.
Why can't I say it? I know why.

Coward? No. A fool am I.
　　—*Angeline B. Lyons*

Fading Summer

The summer haze is fading
Children can no longer go wading

I feel a hint of fall in the air
Still people are hustling everywhere

Soon the snow will start to fly
Another summer has hurried by

The picnics will soon be over
What happened to the beautiful clover

The grass is starting to turn brown
Not a green leaf can be found

The lawnmower is put in the shed
Flannel sheets adorn all the beds

The chimney has been cleaned by a man in a hat
Eek! He came down the chimney holding a rat

The cat and dog are getting furrier by the day
New winter coats are on their way

The trees are showing their splendid colors
Leaves are falling——another and another

I long for the days of lazing in the sun
But must wait a year for more summer fun.
　　—*Connie Hensley*

"Old Calvary Hill"

As a dense darkness enveloped the heaven over head
Christ suffered agony and he was nearly dead.
With nails in his feet and hands he did suffer so,
as his heart broken mother viewed from below.

Upon that rugged made cross from a crude old tree,
he cried, "My God, why has thou forsaken me?"
They thought he said Elias, that worried them too,
but he had quoted faith scripture, Psalms 22.

Jesus had been betrayed, scourged and then mocked,
yet Romans continued to mimic as they talked.
Suddenly, the earth did quake, and the rocks rent,
then they knew he was truly the Messiah sent.

Jesus, dead on the cross and not a bone was broken
as the prophecy in scripture had thus spoken.
The ultimate in obedience Jesus gave to God's will
by the blood of the lamb on old Calvary Hill.
　　—*Wanda Pena*

The Promise Of Christmas

On Christmas day our hearts unite,
Christ's Birthday to proclaim -
There is a magic mystery
Reserved for Jesus' name.
On Christmas Day we look and find
A glow on every face,
While church bells chime and snow flakes fall
We slow our frenzied pace.
The Christmas Star the Wise Men saw
So many years ago
Still brightly shines to guide our paths
Through fresh untrodden snow.

For Christmas Day brings Hope and Cheer,
The promise of a bright New Year!
　　—*Kathleen Irene Tibbetts*

The Recluse

She, whose life was lived
closed to society, held to her fire
without warmth, giving none.

Demon fear or pride?
Who knows what subterranean pools,
what shark's tooth prevails?
Nor could she have told, questioned, "Why?"
bruised only, or bitten to the blood,
or, "When?". as child, virgin or initiate of marriage bed?

Pulse, the body's rhythm, nothing more?
Mind, or fragile psyche, shrinks,
cowers in undress.

A whole continent under water,
a lost Atlantis.

And she, recluse to the end,
escaped one prison's dark into a colder other;
a few last rites speeding her on.

Again closed to society,
without warmth, giving none.
Mute witness, pass by, dry-eyed.
—*Mary Weeden Stiver*

It's Cold Today

It's cold today and the wind isn't even blowing. You feel so
cold and lonely, feelings you've grown used to knowing.
Hide your eyes little one from life's painful decisions.
It's cold today, wounds carved, binding incisions.

It's cold today, yet you still laugh with beaming compassion.
You are a rare jewel my child, and God awaits you with
pleased anticipation.
It's cold today, and while you're laughing you're crying.
You hide from the world your deep desires and all your
unheard sighing.

It's cold today, it would feel so nice to be warm, but all
you can remember are shattered images, memories torn.
It's cold today, and it has begun to rain. A familiar ritual
fighting through despair and pain.

It's cold today, you need to feel some love. But life's
cruel lessons have taught, your dreams are that of a captive
dove. Follow your destiny my darling, keep holding your head
high. Someday the rays of sunshine will unfold your wings
and you will forever fly.
—*Cat Davis*

"Time"

Rifle swung back, hat warms head,
Cold from nose—silent as night

I think how it is, how it was—how it used to be
Feels like I'm in some kind of trap, when only time
Will tell my true happiness

As I walk, I think about old memories and how it was—how I
wish I could relive them.

Now I am blinded by the snow I walk on—how beautiful it is
Getting closer to the red building—it smiles upon me and
welcomes me

I enter and feel old memories.
—*Matt Carpenter*

"As I Look Into Tomorrow"

As I seek the light into tomorrow, I see myself dancing on ice. I dream and work until I see the light that will lead me in the right direction.
The ice is a miracle to me, created by nature. I will slide the blades as gentle as I desire. When I dance on the ice, it will look like I am soaring through air. I will wear glittering sensational suits that will shine as the light glimmers upon them.
I will have time to teach my own children the way to make their dreams reality. I will help them to realize that no matter how unbelievable a dream may seem, they should try their hardest to make their dream come true. That is what I hope tomorrow will bring.
—*Erica Lynn Rusinak*

Dreamers

If the world were kind to lovers, and loved them just as much;
I'd be a loved one and not such a lonely one—reluctant to the
  slightest touch.
If the world were kind to searchers, searching for the end;
In a journey of useless smiles—an unborn child to be condemned
If the world were kind to followers, following as fast as they
  "should",
It'd be echoed in harmony from hills and mountains; but only if
  it could.
If the world were kind to writers, who wrote each melodic
  life-verse;
My sun would rise gleaming, and so it'd be seeming not to be
  life's curse.
If the world were kind to children, and if it'd help to cover
  their heads;
We'd hear no more cries, bake more sweet apple pies, and tuck
  them into their beds.
And if the world were kind to dreamers; gentle in every way,
More of us would live for the moment, and not for our dying
  day!
—*Elizabeth J. Klinger*

Feelings From The Heart

I'd give anything to see you one more last time.
I'd give anything to touch you just one second.
I'd give anything to hear your sweet voice again.
  One day I will see you it might not be
today or tomorrow, but when the day comes
I want to ask why you left me all alone.
One minute you were here and then with a blink
of an eye you were gone.
  I wonder if you still look the same. What is your life
like? Do you like it better here or there?
When that day comes I want to ask all of these questions,
and more, But most of all I want to say "I LOVE YOU", and
nothing can take that away.
—*Elaina Granger*

For Dad

Appreciation, it seems, is not part of their Dreams
If dreams they even have,
A Man with a Vision, Compassion and Wisdom
A Flower in a field of brambles,
Self focused, myopic these fools weave their cloth
Of common pedestrian worth,
Mental stagnation obscures recognition
Of humanity's precious pearl,
In viewing his off'ring to man's greatest art
The blind and the deaf Hear and See,
Far better and longer than these fools that squander
This gift that's awash
In their unworthy sea.
—*Tony Partington*

Untitled

Drugs are...
  a black moonless night
Drugs are...
  getting punched in the stomach by a
  clenching fist - only worse
Drugs are...
  being locked up all alone in a room
  with nobody in sight
Drugs are...
  a hollow tree that is empty
Drugs are...
  bungy jumping - you risk your
  life doing it
Drugs are...
  celebrating a holiday with relatives
  but no one shows up.
Drugs are...
  a dead end!
—Jessica Bakach

A Poem For 1993

I look forward to this year
A book that's without print
But it will be filled
As soon as I begin it.

Sunrises and sunsets
Weddings and birthdays
Whatever I achieve
Is coming my way.

The different seasons
Blooming flowers, falling leaves
I, too, will witness change
Accompanied by joy or grief.

God has blessed me with my life
May I not waste a day
Live it as fully as I can
All along the way.
—Melanie Smith

The Leaves Of Fall

A striking combination,
A colorful array,
The leaves of fall put on a show
Almost every day.

Orange, red and yellow
Mixed up with all the greens,
Really do the best they can
To make simply charming scenes.

But, there can be exceptions,
When the rain drops hit the ground,
Then the leaves get wet and matted
And turn an ugly brown.

We'll still remember autumn
For its color and its glow,
Until the ground is covered
With an early winter snow.
—Frances Bucaro McCliment

"Dreams"

  With the wind on our backs,
    the sun on our faces,
we will travel in search of our new places.
We will live free as a bird above the trees,
  with love and kindness were we belong
  flying free were we can do know wrong.
—Jennifer Michelle

Untitled

  A row of expressionless faces.
  A crowd full of unspeakable fright.
    Just think of all the places
      They've seen at night.
    Think of all the chases
      They've had to fight.

    Not seen during the day
      Nor seen at night.
    It's not the shape or size
      Nor is it the actions.
      Very sadly said;
      "It's the race!"
—Sarah Brown

A Child Is Buried Here

A child is buried here.
A final blanket covers it
  like a puff of down
    not pressed, but blown
      in place
        with a kiss.

One senses dance...
there is a playful poise.
Song's there without a noise.

Daisy chains circle and circle
  the headstone
    like a love
and rabbit's-foot fern crouch
  where the sprouting granite
    grows skyward
      from the earth.
—Wilma Spellman

Terrorism

A fire within me rages
A flame that will not cease
A turbulence fueled by indignation
That disturbs my inner peace

What cause can be so noble
Which purpose so divine
Whose blatant feat of terror
Were but the human decline

Beasts, barbarians and butchers
From your deed the stench does reek
Depraved, deranged, dishonored
At you my soul does shriek

The outrageous cruel insanity
of rank misguided violence
sheathed in the banner of devotion,
instills anger that bellows in silence
—Albert Lemishow

Untitled

Wild hearts, running free
  a passion for life
    so full yet so new.
Dependent only on each other
  striving for that love so grand
    hanging on hand to hand.
Weaving mountains in their eyes
  they chased the wind
    to hear a lesson in it's song
    and that song is called love.
—Mike Johnson

"Ode To Lydia"

Lydia, flesh of my flesh;
a flower opening her mind
to the world, inspired by
learning, independence
flowing so constant, the
future beckons; wonders
of life lie ahead, the
years plentiful, abundant
with hope.

My heart rejoices; her
lively spirit will carry
my child's child to heights
of glorious achievement.

Oh, my dream to live long;
witness her triumphs, behold
her quest for truth and complete
fulfillment.

God, guide her to the
Mountain top.
—Elsie Kendis

...Not Your 'Mom'...

It's not your 'Mom' I want to be,
A girlfriend sounds more fun to me.
We could laugh, sing and dance,
Having feelings of romance.

It's not your mom I want to be;
It's not my responsibility
To pick your socks up off the floor,
Or closing all your dresser drawers.

It's not your mom I want to be,
You have a mom and she's not me.
Look again - I could just scream,
The cap is off your shaving cream!

It's not your mom I want to be,
Leave the cooking all to me,
Laundry, dishes, housework too
But wipe up your spills...that's up to you.
—Rhonda King

Untitled

You came into my life
A good friend to be
Then one day I realized
Just what you mean to me

The more I got to know you
The more my eyes did see
You are the most Important one
In all the world to me.

I know that God He sent you
To bring joy into my life
To be with me forever more
And share my days and nights.

Together we'll have children
And watch then grow with pride
and through all the good and bad
We'll stand together side by side.
—Danny Ferguson

Emptiness

Emptiness...
A great void where my
heart used to belong.
Yet it fills me to
overflowing with

Sadness...
A sense of loss,
That something in my
life is missing.
It leaves me with

Loneliness...
A feeling that
no one is there, and yet
I almost enjoy it.
It haunts me with

Depression...
A frightening sense of despair;
That life is meaningless,
and love does not exist.
Which replaces my heart with
Emptiness...
—*Stacie L. Krause*

What Is Green?

Green is a slime.
A leaf on a tree.
Green is a whisper.
A wave in the sea.
Nature is green,
The dew in the air.
Green is the feeling.
When you don't have a care.
Green stands for peace,
Cleanliness, and good.
representing the world,
Like most colors should.

It's hard sour candy,
That is bought at the store.
It's a dollar, a holiday,
A world to explore.
From pickles to pears,
From land to sea.
Can anyone guess,
What this color could be?
—*Steve Boysen Jr.*

A Place Called Nowhere

There is a place,
A place in my mind, and in my heart,
This is a place called nowhere,
It is a place that no one can escape,
Once you enter that long, dark hall you
  can never return,
Screams for help,
Destined for doom,
Silent, silent as a dream,
No more screaming,
No more torture,
It's over,
Over for now, until I come back.
—*Kelli Eddinger*

Poet's Pearls

I sip God's cup of endless love
A poet who seeks secrets of
The perfect words to pearl a poem
A deed we poets deem our own

Intoxicated? Undenied.
I'm drunk with beauty I've espied
My love letters of life must be
Penned to the world in symmetry

Ah, then's the chance my poem gains fame
With pride I'll garland my own name
When melted into mists of time
The truth is we've small claim to rhyme

We poets are a special tribe
Who sip God's cup of love to scribe
Unlike the sweetest grain of sand
Grasp credit for the pearl God planned.
—*J.C. Pohlman*

Colors

Ah, I see -
A rainbow!

Yellow is for
My smile
Red is for
My anger.
Blue is for
My sadness.
Green is for
My growth in life.
Purple is for my
Creativity.
But -
What is black for?
A secret.

Which is why there's no
Black in a rainbow...
—*Michelle Scott*

Little Silk Rose

Only a little silk rose,
A rose I give you.
So you'll never be blue.
Remember me too.
Only a little silk rose.

Only a little silk rose.
A rose to remember,
It was early in September,
We first met our love.
Only a little silk rose.

Only a little silk rose.
I've grown to love you more.
Through the fast years of sixty,
I'll love you ever in Dixie.
Only a little silk rose.
—*Maryleath Hall Williams*

Life Is

Life is...
A sea of fears,
A river of tears,
A room full of jeers,
A round of beers,
A world without cares.

Life is...
Measured in a year,
The results of a pap-smear,
Someone you hold dear.

Life is...
So far away ... but yet, so near,
Who's that in the rear?
I know you're here,
Controlling me, like a gear,
Your motives ... very clear.

Life is...
A velvet Elvis!
—*Terry Presnell*

A New Day

A new day has begun
a shell full of joys
a window of air
a box of toys

A bird's new song
a gush of air
a plane of hope
that'll take you there

What a wonderful day
a day so gay!
A breath to breathe,
a prayer to pray

So much to happen
nothing to grieve
so much for sorrow
so much to believe.

But the day is done
The birds have gone in.
The plane has landed.
Shall we begin again?
—*Courtney Robinson*

Music

  French Horns start the show
a soft, heady feeling of control.
  Woodwinds seek revenge
Loving battles of flutes singe.
  Clarinets stay low for fear of scold
Low Brass supports all too bold.
  Tuba sending sparks of anger
Trombones soothing the danger.
  Drums pound with might
Bass surrounds with mere delight.
  Music grasps the soul,
through an intensity that will grow!
—*Holly Reed*

The Rhapsody

Listen, listen to the rhapsody.
A song of fondness and passion.
This exquisite blending of harmony,
For a tale of so much affection.

Trumpets announce an arrival,
Of a secret favor shared.
Strings ripple for love's survival.
Lyrics capture a willingness to care.

The notes scream off the pages,
In a silence no one can hear.
Present is a serenade for the ages,
A special sweetness for only one ear.

His heart beats like a drum,
As he endures so impatiently,
A cherished union yet to come,
Togetherness sought so desperately.

Listen, listen to the rhapsody.
Music for only you and he?
Tunes snared away from many,
Only to drift so far from me?
—*Keith M. Gillies*

Untitled

A gift of love we give to you.
A song straight from our hearts.

For all the years of care you gave,
to each a special part.

A part of us, is a part of you,
Entwined for eternity.

A seed of love in each our hearts,
that grows as endless seas.

So mother dear, on this day,
We must take the time to say,

We love you more each passing year,
than all the yesterdays.
—*Brenda Lawson*

Later

The world I say
A stone in trouble
Don't ask why
Reasons above us
Don't look here
We'll find out later

Young and forgotten
Old and neglected
Where are we?
Why are we?
Don't ask
We'll find out later

New hope in our heart
In a book
What book?
So holy and forgotten
Why? We'll find out later

Don't cry, we'll be safe
How? Don't ask
We'll find out later
—*C. James Obudho*

To Loved Ones

My great grandmother is great
A sweetheart that carries weight
Not weight in pounds, but in
feelings, caring and all the good things
folks have no time for.
Think back! Summers at the pool side
Hamburgers at the local burger shop.
Shopping at all the right stores
Little goodies every once in a while.
What more can a child ask for.
Without Grandma, life would be a bore.
—*Mary Damore*

Death Of A Butterfly

A tomb.
A tomb for a butterfly,
That flew upon a gentle breeze.
And only the ladybugs do cry.

The tulips bob their heavy heads,
As if they are in mourning.
And yet they wear a regal red,
In the brilliant yellow morning.

The butterfly has died.
He shall fly no more.
The world continues on unheeding,
It doesn't want to mourn.

A mere butterfly.
A butterfly that children chased,
A butterfly that bore a wish,
On fragile wings as thin as lace.
—*Sarah Zajaczek*

Picture It

I stand before this canvas, bold
a vision I am trying to hold
intending to create a dream
not an easy task it seems
I cannot concentrate I fear
for my subject is too dear
his eyes they penetrate my soul
his smile does set the room aglow
I have lost composure and resistance
I can no longer keep my distance
in his arms I long to be
his eyes, his smile they beckon me
I cannot his image capture
as I'm a victim of such rapture.
—*D. McClarin*

A Smile

A friendly gesture to say hello
A willingness to bring joy to others
Believing in the day's goodness
Looking ahead to the future
Enhancing your face to show your heart
Filling your standards high with reality
The only real way of giving happiness
to yourself and others around you -
A smile.
—*Katie Kilkelly*

Without

It is a weekend without a day,
A year which leaves out May,
The future without today,
A lake without the bay.

Snow and rain without slush,
Old memories without dust,
Christmas time without the rush,
And old rail tracks without the rust.

A rocky sea without a wave,
Jagged mountains without caves,
Warm sunlight without rays,
Wanted memories we cannot save.

A shivering hand without a glove,
A far below without above,
A sign of peace without the dove,
A warm world without any love.

Starting a song without a cue,
Seeing the world without a view,
Are examples of my feeling blue,
On a day that I am without you.
—*Jeffrey Ayer*

Fishing Trip

A fishing pole a can of worms
a young boy and his Dad
Bring back memories to me
of good times we have had

When Dad and I together
in the times now past
Would fish in all the lakes and streams
for Crappie and for Bass

So many happy hours
Dad and I have seen
While sitting with our fishing poles
beside a tiny stream

If only we could do once more
the things we used to do
I would be so happy
and I know that Dad would too

So I'll make one request oh Lord
please grant my humble plea
Just one more fishing trip I pray
for dear ole Dad and me
—*Urvin D. Crump*

A Dream I Once Had

I had a dream last night
About a fellow I once knew.
He looked different
From head to toe.
Then I realized
No one stays the same
Everyone changes even the people
You once knew.
We talked about things
Things that were fun.
I asked if he were married
And he said "no".
We had a long talk
A very long talk about the dreams
We once had.
We both realized dreams can change
No matter what you say or do.
I never had a chance
To finish this dream
But I hope someday it will come back to me.
—*Shondel Roach*

Flies

Flies are small,
About one centimeter tall.
They are not cute,
But in fact, are mute.
They love to eat,
Especially meat.
They can fly high
And don't usually sigh.
They take your food,
But only when they are in a bad mood!

—*Nicholas Damante*

Deadly Shadow

It hovers
   above my unmoving form.
Smiling with evil glee.
A mere shadow upon my wall
watches me with intense scrutiny.
The body twisted as deformed as I feel.
It picks at my greatest fears,
perceives my pain,
and relishes my agony.
Survives only because of my torment;
Taunts me with its power;
Intimidates me with its brute strength.
It holds a weapon,
yet I know not what.
Raising it to slaughter me—
the victim.
I scream—
   then it's dark.

—*Eleanor Calasara Tinio*

When Twilight Comes

When twilight comes,
Again I see
My childhood home,
A rocking chair, and me on daddy's knee.

I think of things he used to say.
Things which once I couldn't understand.
Stories of God, nature, pioneer days,
My duty to my native land.

I see again a head of silver grey.
A pair of hands strong and brown.
A spirit too strong to say
"I give up," and then lie down.

Twilight brings him back to me,
And all those happy times we had.
And life is like it used to be,
When I rocked with Dad.

—*Hazel Irene Norton Wright*

I Love You

You really are a dream come true
All my life I've searched for you
The first time I saw you I was amazed
Lost in some kind love phase.
If only you know how much you mean to me.
If only there was way to make you see
I pray to God everyday
that the way I feel for you
You feel the same way
Please believe me it's true
Because I really love you!

—*Sally Hughes*

Untitled

So far Easter Bunny
Ain't exactly my best friend
If he'll stay in his cabbage patch
I'll stay in my play pen

You say I'll change my mind
When he comes on Easter morn
With things for me to play with, eat
and wear to keep me warm

Well, I'm just a little fella
But I love you both a lot
And when you say he's quite a guy
It puts me on the spot

So if it's all the same to you
Don't wake me Easter day
'Til that big rabbit's left my stuff
and hopped a long, long way.

—*Patricia J. Ross*

The Macedon

The fishermen of Lesbos cry
Alexander, who lives and is King!
Son of Zeus Ammon, accept
these poor gifts we bring.
Your worship we've continued
down long year of paltry deeds.
Remembering when the gods were humbled
by what the man achieved.

The shades of Greece's long dead heroes
whisper through their pain.
Macedon, wake from your ancient slumber
and give us our glory again!

Breathe life, Achilles' favorite,
into our time-blasted bones.
We shall rebuild your shattered cities,
and fill the dead men's empty thrones.
Dance into this rambling void
lover of Homer and wine.
Let Khandahar ring again to music,
and the song of Euripides' lines!

—*Lorne Patterson*

Untitled

I was talking with an old friend,
all about nothing in particular,
and nothing, and nothing more.
We spoke of her eyes, lips and nose
we spoke of another friend
and all the amazing
little things that may not mean much.
Never a time like that,
never once did someone make me happier.

—*Travis Rayle*

Untitled

See far up in the sky
A pale new born moon,
full of new found courage soon
to blossom into age.

'Tis like unto us
with childhood's faint beams,
and confidence turning to dreams
as life glides by.

—*Jane M. Schrand*

Faces Unclaimed

Unclaimed faces
   All around me.
Not caring; not knowing
   If I'm alive or dead.
Children's cries.
Drunken bastards lies.
There isn't a caring face for miles.
Unclaimed faces all around me,
   Laughing at me.
Why?
Why do you laugh at your troubles?
Because you know no one will
   Claim your soul?
Because no one knows to care for
   An unclaimed face?
No one can care
   For anyone else if they can't
     Care for themselves.
Unclaimed faces.
Faces unclaimed.

—*Christina Rae Blackmon*

An Irish Wake, If You Please

Let the bearers of me pall,
All be big, and strong, and tall.
Let them hum a tune that's mod,
As they carry out me bod.

Let them pause to tilt a flask,
As they go about their task.
For ne'er was an Irish wake,
That was all that hard to take.

Now, no sighs, no cries, no tears,
Now, no thoughts of wasted years.
Ne'er a thing be taken back,
What would have made another track.

Just accept the way we were,
Both the flower and the burr.
Let them sing a happy song,
As they carry me along.

Let the bearers of me pall,
All be big, and strong, and tall.
A wee simple prayer to God,
As they cover me with sod.

—*Ray L. Sansom, Jr.*

Memories Of A Countryside

There once were many trees,
All very tall and wide;
And there once were many birds,
Soaring graceful above and outside.

Now there are many shopping malls,
And many foreign cars;
And there are many meeting halls,
And too much smog to see the stars.

There once was a rushing river
And a waterfall and streams;
But all have been replaced
By merchants and their dreams.

—*Jaime L. Brunton*

"Loving You"

Loving you is hard to do
   All you do is make me blue.
Your lips are cold, your eyes are lost
   But still, I love you
What ever the cost.
   I say nice things to warm your heart.
All it does is tear us apart.
   This heart of mine is so confused
Torn and broken and abused.
   What do I do as the days go on?
I watch your heart turn into stone.
   And even tho I am blue
I just keep on loving you.
—*Brenda K. Evans*

Sorority

"Sex" struts strategic streets,
Alone, or in pairs,
Tenders tantalizing treats
"Just up the stairs."

Easy eyes ever so large,
The liner thick.
The fee that they charge,
A costly trick.

A "John" called sweet names
By honeyed voice,
Is a toy in their games,
Without a choice.

Such sex-selling sisters
Function by rote,
No love for their "misters"
Worthy of note.

Tarts, turn your last trick,
Exit the street.
From the dead to the quick
Cannot be beat!
—*George B. Williams*

Love Hurts

My heart beats within,
although it lives, without,
love the one thing I need most.
It hurts, but yet I live.

To live without love, and I
ponder why bother live at all?
nothing else matters.

It's the one true thing that
makes me happy,
but also the one thing that
always seems to cut at my heart
with a dull knife
in the face of a God whose
only goal in life is to do such a thing.

And then my tears do fall,
down the face, that so wants,
to be touched by masculine hands
that long to do so, then I wake
and see him.

It was only a dream.
—*April Seeber*

Serenity

Peace is here
   Among the very dear
Laying beneath the earth

Sprays of bouquet
   Don the graves
Some covered with dirt

The whispering breeze
   Sing through the trees
For the deceased

I love to Tarry
   In the cemetery
Ah! Sweet serenity.
—*Oliver Kelly*

Him

He is really
an Actor-
He doesn't really live in
a Box-
He doesn't really beg
for Money-
The wind at night doesn't really
Beat him-
That's just the alcohol on
his breath beating Him.
—*Stuart Schrader*

Change

A score four years and two months later
An attorney general and senator died
He died for change to carry on his late
brother's work for peace to the world
A reason a soldier did not want peace
for the Holy Land
And a nation cried.

Four people in history died for change
change that a nation was afraid to try
Change comes without warning at any time
A reason we must be catalysts who accept
And not be a nation that cries.
—*Daniel Pavlish*

A Sinner's Prayer

Dear Lord, I come to You in shame,
And bow my head in humble prayer.
Oh Lord, my soul is filled with blame;
Because I failed You I am bare.

I pray, Oh Lord, remove my stain,
And wash me in Your precious blood.
I pray, please let your love remain,
But lift my burdens from above.

  I bend my knees in humble prayer,
  Knowing You are there to make whole.
  I give my heart to Your tender care,
  Knowing You are there to mend my soul.
—*NeVada S. Howren*

Spring Again

It's spring again
And comes the rain
The lilacs bloom
And dandelions loom.
Violets lurking in the grass
The sweetest scent,
When e'er you pass.
Peonies blooming along the way.
They'll be ready by memorial day
Apple blossoms on the trees
seem to fly away with the breeze.
Cherry trees in the Orchard too.
all the flowers and trees,
What a view.
All this because it's spring again.
All God's work was not in vain.
—*Thelma Gooch*

Man And Boy

I could love you more than life,
and covert you like a sacred knife.

I gave you life, and you became a man
To be what I cannot, and what I am.

I loved you since birth, and I'll love
  you till death

I'll love you more, after my very last
  breath.

You are my boy my only one
You are my dearest gift out of some
For you I'll never turn or shun

I love you greatly my loving son.
—*Mayia Warren*

Reflections

As sands of time run slowly,
   And days just drift away.
I sometimes sit and ponder
   On how I used this day.

Did I help a troubled neighbor,
   Or stop to greet a friend?
Did I kiss a child's small hurt,
   Perhaps to help it mend?

Or through my own frustrations
   And the anger in my day,
Did I forget my fellow man
   and turn myself away?

"We only pass this way, but once,"
   They say, as I recall.
It sometimes makes me wonder,
   Have I passed this way at all?
—*Dorothy Rueb*

A Commercial

I'd like to make a commercial
and do it on TVee
Look up and down, left and right
T'would be a cinch for me

I could make it for a cat food
or even sandbox stuff
There's really nothing to it
I'd just have to smile enough
—*Susan Rose*

To My Mother

When I was small you held me close
And dried away my tears.
You rocked me when I needed love
And vanished all my fears.

When unkind thoughts crept in my head
You firmly gave them chase.
You wouldn't tolerate a slur
Against another's race.

You taught me how to cope in life
And stand up strong and true
To face my troubles by myself
And try to work them through.

And then I grew to womanhood
And we just changed our place.
For now it's I who holds you close
And strokes your loving face.

So, Mother Dear, be proud of me
And when this life we part
Remember that this loving child
Will hold you ever in her heart.
—*Jean Hays*

Untitled

When hope is lost to nowhere
And envisions no longer see clear
When your head only echoes pain
And your heart only bleeds tears

When nowhere is better than here
And sanity has crossed the line
When dreaming only leads to nightmares
And hate wraps you like a vine

When voices you hear at night
Whisper low and sweet
Find you the haunting answer
But your wisdom you must defeat

When the pale moon rises not for you
And the stars invading heaven lay low
When smiles no longer touch your lips
And the winds for you no longer blow

Then skeleton I leave to thee
The flesh and blood upon a thorn
And onto the place I sat before
This world I had been born
—*Brenda K. Carstensen*

Graduation

As we walk down the aisle in twos
   And fill seats row by row
We'll say goodbye to yesterday
   With memories in tow.

Then one by one they'll call our names:
   We'll smile with pride and stand
With confidence we'll cross the floor
   Diploma close at hand.

Twelve years of work and tolerance-
   But now our work's complete
Our efforts will be legalized
   Upon that precious sheet.

And when we walk back to our chairs
   A mist will block our sight
As we reflect upon the past;
   This graduation night.
—*Janet Zlomek*

Travels

When we walk down a lonely road,
And find a place to ease our load
What awaits us many be sorrow or peace.
It could be some blessed release.

So all travelers heed this thought
Seeking the best to be wrought.
Come what my of trouble or joy,
Which awaits each girl or boy.
—*Jane Warner*

Tax 'N Facts

Two and two were always four
And five and five were ten,
Until I started working on
My income tax again.
I had no tax deduction
For a wife or for a son,
That made it simple to put down
A lonely forlorn "one."
Adjusted gross was next in line
And adding up my pay,
That needed gross adjusting,
I began on my outlay.
The Charity was easy
But when I reached my expense,
I found it more than I had made
Which didn't make much sense.
So now my problem, strange to say,
Is where is my mistake?
How could I spend the money
That I didn't even make?
—*Agnes Guilfoyle Edwards*

Untitled

Whenever I desire peace
  And happiness for other.
    Then shall my peace
    Come unto me.
  For this is God's love
for nothing good come to us
  except we first desire
    it for other
—*Mrs. Ruth H. Martinez*

I Walked Beside A Stream

I walked beside a stream
And heard its music.
How beautiful!
And wondered what it was
That made it sound.

Then I stood beside
The swiftly flowing water
And watched how rocks
Stood in the way
Of easy flow.

I saw water meeting rock,
Bubbling up to surmount,
To find its way around,
And understood:
It is in overcoming
That we sing.
—*Rose Perl Shuler*

Going forward

I tried to fear not
  And hide my identity
But everywhere I went
It would seem to catch up with me
  So each passing hour
Going from minute to minute
  I look forward to another hour
The past no longer in it
  Now I'm like a baby
Crawling to stand and walk
  Listening and learning
How to walk and talk
  I have hope and also trust
And my serenity
  I tell people from experience
What beauty life can be
—*Rita Wilkins*

Untitled

When I was yet a wee small child
And hurt myself at play,
My mom would take me on her knee
And kiss the hurt away.

Well time has come full circle
I've had two sons of my own,
And my baby "Precious Matt"
Was very nearly grown.

When in his fifteenth summer,
The Lord was so unkind.
Greedy God, he took the best
And left us here behind.

I never knew a broken heart
Could pain my soul so much.
I only wish this kind of hurt
Would flee at mother's touch.

I see her now with tear filled eyes.
She feels my agony.
Since she can't kiss my hurt away,
She shares my grief with me.
—*Dee Anna Newbanks*

A Friend I Miss

You used to smile at me
And I could talk openly with you
But I didn't wait patiently
For you to make the first move
If I could go back in the past
I'd try to slow down my feelings
But you don't seem to understand
That my heart goes through the ceiling
Each time you walk through the door
And I look at your pretty blue eyes
I'd forget what I was waiting for
And then I wouldn't say good-bye
To the emotions which made me ask
The question which caused the problem
And you'd again have to put on the mask
Of being a male instead of my friend
—*Charrolee Murphy*

"The Question"

If I were a man,
And I had a ring.
Asking you this question,
Wouldn't be a hard thing.

I'd kneel on one knee,
And propose to you now.
So I could have you for myself,
And forever somehow.

I'd pop this question,
And hope your answer is yes.
And I'd walk down the aisle,
In a beautiful, white dress.

You and I,
Could never be apart.
For separation would only,
Break my heart.

We'd be together,
For forever and a day.
And I have to ask,
Would you marry me today?
—*Beatrice Anders*

A Prophecy

We met a short time back.
And if then someone had said,
"My dear, you'll marry this man."
I'd have kicked them in the head!

But now it looks as if it's true.
I'm going to be your wife.
My sincerest hope is that our love
grows deeper throughout our lives.

And then the children soon will come.
They'll look like you and me.
And as we watch them grow
we'll fill them love and security.

And then our kids will leave their home.
Like tiny birds that leave the nest.
And that's the time that in our lives
our love will be the best.

I know this must seem silly.
A poem of what's to be.
But I felt that you should know.
How much your love means to me.
—*Marcia Carroll*

Summer Apple Dumplin'

It's Yellow Harvest apple time,
And let me tell you somethin',
There's nothin' I like better
Than summer apple dumplin'.
This morning, Mom picked apples
from our old Harvest tree.
When her apron lap was full,
She turned and said to me,
"Now Son, I'll need a box of wood
To heat the big range oven."
Believe you me, I went right then,
For I am dumplin' lovin'.
Once Mom stirred up a chocolate cake,
With frostin' piled sky high.
It took first at the county fair
and didn't even try.
But there is one thing you should know,
Or so it seems to me;
That summer people dumplin'
Is her own specialty!

—*Frances Sobotka*

My Soul Is Tired

I walked along a narrow path
and listened while the leaves did sing
Of days when laughter filled the air
and worry was a foreign thing.

I look at faces passing by,
fleeting moments, passing time.
Future present, present past,
feeling lost, feeling last.

Gentle breeze caress my face.
Take me to a special place.
Wrap around my heart your arms
keep me safe, keep me warm.

My soul is tired.
—*Susan A. Rife*

Moon Shadow

The earth took the moon
   and lost the light.

The deepened shadows masking
   the stillness of the night.

This is what the earth lost when
   the moon was far away.

For no one can replace the difference
   between that night and day.
—*Naomi Weaver*

Day Off

I must wander in the woods today
And meet a dozen birds:
I'll listen to the things they say
In songs that have no words.

I shall lose my trifle grief:
I'll lean against a tree,
And watch the rhythm of a leaf
In wood-borne melody.

I'll watch a rabbit scamper by,
Though he need not have feared;
There is so much of earth and sky,
And spaces newly cleared:
And so much room for being free;
But I'll always be aware,
That I came home a different me
Because the woods were there!
—*Elsie Rose Sumerlin*

"The Old Apple Tree"

It has a silent history,
   and memories to share -
This quaint and twisted apple tree,
   with a trunk beyond repair -
Of branches filled with apples
   so pleasant to the eyes.
The green and tasty slices
   That make such delicious pies -
Over eighty years of fruitful growth,
   the apples testify -
Through winds and stormy weather
   as they continue to multiply.
Her trunk is gnarled and rotting
   as it lays upon the ground -
While her branches nod in silence
   as found memories abound.
—*Harriet M. Sahli*

L'Envoi

Our day is done, our lives have run,
   And night gathers up the tools.
So much begun, yet, so little done
   As we tinkered at the rules.

As fields of grain repeat the refrain
   Each season sees another crop.
Our years slipped by, give youth a try;
   Ask not the world to stop.

For tomorrow forsakes the past mistakes.
   Fresh faith is born with the dawn.
Sparse last year's crop is soon forgot
   And the world goes marching on.
—*Eugene V. Shea*

I Truly Am Sorry

We've been friends for years.
And now I've wrecked our friendship.
I truly didn't mean to.
But I did and I'm sorry.

I did it out of anger.
And as soon as the words left my mouth
I wish I could take them back.
And for that I truly am sorry.
So every time you think of me
remember I truly am sorry.
—*Shanda Smalls*

Life's Dance

Round
   and round
     and round
       we go

In time
   Hands
     And hearts
       Meet

Join
   Become one
     Dance together
       Inseparably

Part
   Turn away
     Dance alone
       Eternally

Round
   And round
     And round.
—*Elizabeth B. Stroup*

Cloud Rider

Have you ever looked on high
And seen the clouds go dancing by?
They gather their trains with care
Like pretty ladies oh so fair.

It brings a smile to my face
To see them move with such grace.
I wish I could with them go
And join in the lovely show.

Though the earth holds me fast
In spirit I myself will cast
Life's fears and sorrows all aside
And climb upon those clouds and ride.
—*Dorothy Butler*

The Children

Sunshine walks on little legs,
   and smiles from tiny eyes.

Laughter bubbles up from little throats,
   and floats into the skies.

The children are our future;
   they also are our past.

It's true in every era,
   they all grow up too fast.

So treat each special moment
   as though it's golden treasure.

Because when all is said and done
   it's what we'll use to measure;

The joys of all the early years;
   and the trauma in between.

The child is left behind in life;
   it's the adult who now is seen.

—*Toni Stanford-Miller*

Springtime

As winter fades away,
   And spring comes in,
The flowers start to grow,
   So do the leaves on the trees,
You might even notice a little
   bit of breeze.

It gets a bit warmer,
   And children come out to play,
The sun stays out longer,
   Each and everyday.
Spring is so pretty,
   And ever so bright,
It makes you want to stay out,
   All day and all night.

—*Kristin Arendale*

Suffering Sneedle

The dandel-lion does a jig
and swigs his powders from a wig
which sniggle up the sneedle's nose
and then "ACH-OOO!" down to his toes

The dust-mote twizzles twirly-fly
and settles in the sneedle's eye
a giant slush of tears and itch
come slinkering to a swollen twitch

The furry-fuzzle sheds its down
and conjures up the sneedle's frown
with swirly patches bumpling up
upon the sneedle's loving cup

Alas, the sneedle is a frazzle
he's had it with the razzle dazzle
Of seasons that are whoosh and whee—
they only bring him misery.

—*Peter Gregory*

Dear Father...

   I pray for you so often
   and thank the Lord above
   for giving me a father
   that shows me so much love.

I've been blessed beyond riches
and you mean the world to me
I appreciate the things you've done,
   for you gave so willingly.

Though I'm growing up so fast
I'm a little girl within
who still needs a hug from daddy
when life tries to do her in.

   Life often gets so hectic
   but let me never stop to say
   how much I love you dad-
   for I thank the Lord each day...

—*Melissa Rae Butler*

Untitled

As the sun plunges into the ocean,
And the nights winds begin to blow.
Everything seems in slow motion,
Peaceful and mellow.
The stars above,
Glitter like jewels.
And you lay beside the one you love,
Gazing into his eyes, as deep as pools.
First he caresses you,
Like you've never felt before.
Then he kisses you.
Leaving you wanting more.
Suddenly you feel its a must.
Something you need.
A night of lust,
Is what must proceed.
A feeling of regret,
Is all you feel.
After this night you shall never forget
His sincere appeal.

—*Melissa Davids*

Solitude

As the rain softly taps my window
And the oil in my lamp burns low,
A dead silence fills my world
While the winds outside still blow.

I sit and listen to the rain
Sing melancholy music to my soul.
Oh, what a restless night it's been,
So void and dark as coal.

On the hearth lie only ashes
From a fire once long ago.
But now there is no warmth,
Nor merry flames aglow.

There seems no end in sight.
The rain its tale has told.
The light in my lamp is dying
As the room grows somber and cold.

—*Tara Guthrie*

Like A Rose

As morning dew puffs upon her petals
And the sun begins to rise
She lifts her head slowly and blossoms
Her beauty is inside

Nurturing, soft and sweet
Delicate to the eye
Compassionate to a touch
Yes, considerate she asks not why

She feeds on sunlight
The earth and the rains
No other is like her
She's different but the same

Admire her
Cherish her
And smell the sweetness of her embrace
She can provide warmth and comfort
When given with love and grace

—*Ronnie T. Isler*

"The Rose"

Into the flower garden of life did walk
and there I selected a Rose.
This Rose became so dear to me
A fragrance to my nose.

I put my life around this Rose
to protect it from all harm.
I kept it from the pickers hand.
I cuddled it in my arms.

I loved this Rose with all my heart,
it meant the world to me.
I loved it so that I squeezed it tight
to keep it permanently.

The care I took was too much.
It soon began to die.
Day by day I watched it wilt,
Not knowing the reason why.

Then one day the Rose was gone
and I wondered why.
Too much love will smother it
and won't keep it satisfied.

—*Donely Spencer*

My Dad

He stuck with me through thick
and thin and I always knew he
was there.
He taught me how to be a man,
because he taught me how to care.

He showed me things and taught
me others, that if I tried I could
not repay.
I just pray to God to have the
wisdom to teach my son some day.

I hope I never let him down or
make him ashamed of me.
Because if I turn out to be
half the man he is, that will
be man enough for me.

—*Eric Grooms*

Forever Yours...

As I stand at your casket
and think of our past
I knew it was much too good
much too good to ever last.

We've survived all of the bad times
and shared oceans of salty tears
we've experienced so much together
in just a short matter of years.

I never really pictured it
myself not by your side
the pain is just enough to make me
want to run away and hide.

Now as I stand so near to you again
I can only hope and pray
that we will meet up soon again
I anticipate that sweet day.

I was never close to anyone
like I was so close to you
and to my very dying day
you'll be one of the chosen few.

—*Kimberly Rae Hosman*

Evolve

Just as the wind blows softly
And time goes slipping by
Our world, it keeps revolving
The same as you and I

Change, it's unpredictable
Though leaves are sure to fall
Age, it's uncontrollable
And happens to us all

The earth spends time so gracefully
Spinning, not to cease
If man would learn this lesson
We all could live in peace

Clouds may bring the rain down
But sun shines for all man
Harmony and compassion
Will bring a better land

—*Raymonda Doyle*

#23

One day a flower opened
  and viewed a man.

She saw his perplexity.

She spread her scent for him to smell.

  She wanted to do more,
  but she was mute;

and he

  unheeding.
—*Ethel Gardner*

"God Children"

As silently, as the sun will rise,
the little children really can be;
Good as gold, made for you and me.
Some are made of happiness,
some are made of fears.
You and I have God to thank,
for all the things of today's tears.

—*Donna Nisonger Green*

The Sky

In summer I like to lie
and watch the action in the sky
See the clouds go floating by
In the blue a plane so high
Only a trail meets the eye
On a gentle wind the gulls do glide
As a hawk to his prey does fly
And sparrows chase a lonely crow
Insects fly without control
Seedlings float slowly in the air
So peaceful this time spent
Watching the sky with each event.

—*Mary Hesbon*

The Storm

I sit by my window
And watch the stormy sky,
Lightning flashes
Thunder crashes
And heavens tears come down,
The mournful wind
Whips through the trees
Their agony ignored,
I feel kinship to their plight
As the stormy winds of change
Have torn my heart apart,
The pain is more than I can bear
I turn to God for solace
His guidance I implore,
To ease the loneliness and pain
This stormy night has brought,
Tonight the Lord has taken home
My love of sixty years.

—*Elody De Crane*

"The Valley Mill"

Outlined against the silver moon,
  And way upon the mountain hill.
Beneath an oak tree stood a coon-
  Looking down at the valley mill.

The labour of the working men,
  And the spinning of the wa'er wheel
Had long since stopped, observed a hen,
  While roosting on some rotten meal.

The pow'rful river ran no more
  By pasture land and grazing sheep.
There was, upon its banks a boar -
  Preparing for a restful sleep.

Upon this scene did burst the sun
  With blushing rays that felt so new -
To spread its warmth on ev'ryone,
  And melt away the morning dew.

—*Joel Cook*

Friends

Friends are people whom
  are very dear to a soul.
Friends help you to make
  new friends.
Friends are there to give you
  a smile when you need it the most.
Friends go out of the way to
  make you happy.
Friends; you can't live life
  without a friend.

—*Sarah McDonald*

Two Lovers

Lover take this lover's hand
And we will both soar free;
Forgetting all cares and strife
Unto eternity.
  Eternity shall find us thus;
  Hearts and lips entwined
  Two souls forever happy
  Till the end of time.
    If the End shall come to us -
    We will meet again
    For it was meant to be,
    Two Hearts, Two Loves,
      Two Souls forever,
      For all Eternity.

—*Donna M. Polanek*

"Color"

Where the mountains reach the sky
And where the sun says goodbye
And where an eagle spreads his wings
Freedom will come in all things

In the shadow of the wind
Man will find his soul again
Pride will walk upon his face
He'll see the world without race

From burning rage
Man's eyes are blind
He walks this earth
In a state of mind
His spirit groaning from within
To find a place to start again

Man will rise above all shame
When the bells of freedom rings
There'll be no chains
To bind his soul
When he lets the word 'color' go

—*Ann Pruitt*

Identity

"Who are I?"
And "Who am we?"—
A question without an answer,
Yet an answer within a question.
Universal knowledge,
Isolated belief.
For all know that you are I,
And us you shall become.
A piece in the puzzle?
A letter in a name? No!
Rather a speck in the universe.
All are equal,
None distinct.
We share the same character,
But still we ask,
"Who are I?"
And "Who am we?"

—*Jason Richard Smith*

With Or Without

The sun comes up
the shadows disappear
another day has come,
life will continue once again
with or without you I will go on.

—*Kim Kroopnick*

Time

The Summer is almost over,
and Winter will soon be here;
The days have passed me by so
fast, that next will be a new
year:

I don't know where the time
has gone, it seems like yesterday;
One minute it was
September, then the next was
May:

Now is the middle of Summer
that will more than soon be
gone; like all the days and
years before, time keeps
moving on:

There is no way of stopping
time, for it cannot be restrained;
For it is just
the process of a never ending
thing.
—*Florence C. Robertson*

Bondage

  With men in despair
and women in chain
    The night grows longer
but the day seems the same

  With love bound in shackles
and fear bound in fame
    I fear in the end
there'll be nothing but shame

  As the tears fall again
and dreams die away
    While fools cry alone
For the love they betrayed

  And what is the truth
We find all men abide
    There are too many lies
and I just can't decide.
—*Nicole Drury*

Walk Backwards

If you've forgotten what you came for
    and wonder why you're here,
  Walk backwards in your memories
    until your mind sees clear.

  Walk backwards through your memories
when you reach that time in space,
  where crossroads cause anxieties,
    and deciding slows your pace.

  Step lightly through your reverie
    to see where you have been,
      ponder all your journeys,
    retrace your path of dreams.

  And when you near your childhood,
    be energized by youth
regain your zest for life as good,
    Stop! Do not walk backwards,
    go forward toward the truth.
—*Elizabeth A. Flannery*

Remembering

To sit
And write about
Her complexity
Is almost impossible.

To try to
Explain her
True self
Is very rare.

To create
The perfect poem
For slight imperfection
Is asking too much.

I ask
Not for her offerings,
But only her simple
Friendship to remember.
—*Theodore B. Grove*

Look For Me

When times are hard
    and you feel down
Look for me
    I'll turn the frown around

When life isn't worth living
    and friends don't care
Look for me
    I'll always be there

When you feel frightened
    and need to cry tears
Look for me
    I'll comfort your fears

When you just need a friend
    someone to listen
Look for me
    I'll never be missing!
—*Michele DeLong*

Untitled

When we're angry,
Anger doesn't pay.
Make use of suffering.
It helps to pray.
People aren't bad
Because they want to be,
But because they use free will
Too freely.
To live with love
We each want to do
While hoping for heaven
When this life is through.
—*Eileen R. Hallahan*

As Seen With Sunsets In Mine Eyes

Cooled by deepened ocean blues
As bathed in poem of passioned sea,
The soul is filled with tranquil hues
Inspired by this world to be...
To hear the mermaids sing to each
As moved to flights of spirits — Reach
To know the sea's sweet mystery,
To live what mean have dreamed to see!
Oh Ocean, whose gentle stirrings speak
Of a hidden soul beneath,
You echo full love of life in sighs
As seen with sunsets in thine eyes...
—*Leslie M. Kahn*

For Fame

Who
Are you
To say
Delay!

Unbend
Descend
and wait
of fate.

Not I
I cry

Ascend
and rend
the sky
- or die

For fame
for fame!
—*James F. Barrett*

Lost Without A Compass

Are You lost without a compass:
Are you drifting on life's sea
As you sail uncharted waters
Forsaking hope and victory?

Does your life seem, oh, so pointless
'cause you're locked in Satan's grip?
You sob about your broken dreams
That just slip away - - and slip - -.

Come - - let me take you to Jesus
Tell Him about all your cares
And give Him all of your problems
As we kneel together in prayer.

Jesus will comfort and heal you
And He will restore your joy.
He'll wash you clean and renew you:
You'll no longer be Satan's ploy.

The Bible is our compass
To help us to chart our way.
Jesus will love and forgive you:
You can start you life over today.
—*Noella M. Zapisek*

Mother Poem

Winter and summer go
as baby, lays her head on
mother's shoulder,

Spring lays ahead to make
its debut as mother makes
dinner by firelight letting
shadows fold it's wings
across the house,

Mother makes everything
okay as we fall and skin
our knees and she gently holds
us as we cry.
—*Shannon Nicole Hannon*

Still Waiting

Somewhere,
Somehow;
If ever...
Not now.
—*Jane E. Jensen*

Over The Rainbow

Over the rainbow,
as far as I can see,
is a place full of wonder,
as beautiful as can be.
Prisms of light reflected,
shines on yet never detected.
The Earth, united with the Sun,
together, apart, a rainbow has begun.
Beyond this hidden world,
are people unlike before,
all it takes are spirit and feelings,
to open up this door.
—*Melissa Hubbard*

Of Course, I'm A Christian

I'm a Christian, it's true
As good as they come
Here's my ten pound Bible
There's the church that I'm from

I got a cross on my necklace
Ten commandments on my wall
I attend conventions all Summer
And revivals in the Fall

Of course, I'm a Christian
I don't miss a Sabbath
I don't sin no more
Not one bad habit

I'm certainly a Christian
My seat is pew ten
Been to church twice today
Now I'm going back again

What's that you say—
Sorry, I can't spare a dime
Take you across town to that shelter—
I just don't have the time.
—*Wenifer Rencher*

Vicious Twist

He sat home alone last night
As he did most every night

He ate his dinner
And cleaned his plate

For dessert — put a gun in his mouth
Pulled the trigger
And realized his fate

He said he had nothing
But he had it all

I think he forgot to realize
That in every life
A little rain must fall

So screw him
That's what I say

Hew knew the rules
But decided not to play
—*J. Craig Lambert*

Summer

Puffy clouds like marshmallows,
The sun burns your skin,
Swimming, running, playing,
Your childhood shines within.
—*Katharine A. Williamson*

The Beach

I feel as if I am drifting away
As I am sitting on the shore of a beach
The sun is beating down
As the salt water washes me away

As I am sitting on the shore of a beach
My eyes wander away
As the salt water washes me away
I am off in my own little world

My eyes wander away
As the crowds wander off in my mind
I am off in my own little world
As I am dreaming away

As the crowds wander off in my mind
The sun is beating down
As I am dreaming away
I feel as if I drifting away
—*Shawnda Weaver*

"Feel So Good"

Feel so good
As I knew I would
Listening to, "the sound of poetry."
May, I note?
I never thought
That any verse I wrote
Though be set to beautiful music
Or have a special reader.
So I could hear it by ear.
Sounds good to me.
Elated as can be.
Thank you,
From me,
To you.
—*Carmen J. Smith*

Lament

Even in Heaven
as I look down
I shall weep in anguish
to see a frown
disturb your brow
that used to be
smooth as a child's is
and as dear to me.

If I, in Heaven,
should chance to see
you, whom I left
so reluctantly,
grieve, or sob, or even sigh
to St. Peter himself
I must surely hie
and give the lie to this heaven-story:
you crying? Then I am in Purgatory.
—*Genevieve Silbert*

Horses

Whinnie, Whinnie, Whinnie,
The horses all say
'Give us some hay
so we can all nay'—

Whinnie, Whinnie, Whinnieeee,
We've been up all day
And now it's time to say
'GOODNIGHT'
—*Doris Zurlo*

Old Letter's

I walked down memories lane,
As I read some old letter's today.
Each one had it's own "special memory"
Of things along life's way,
Each one had its own special memory,
Of a day that used to be
Some happy, some sad, some gay,
As each one I did carefully read.

Each day makes a memory for someone
Who will come after me
I hope they will only be happy ones
As they recall memories of me.
I hope they will always be bright ones
Of sunshine and flowers,
And happy hours
And at night only beautiful dreams.
—*Dorothy Abshagen*

A New Day Dawning

A new day is dawning,
as I wake up yawning,
and go slowly to the door.

Outside it's raining,
the thought is paining
that I'm so very poor.

I have no money,
yet it seems funny;
I'm richer all the more…

Because I have JESUS
who always see us
as children to adore.

So, when you wake up yawning
as the new day is dawning,
give thanks, give thanks galore!
—*Carolyn J. Bogan*

Midnight Dreams

The rustle of the breeze
as it wanders among the trees
As it southward sails,
carries the song of a Nightingale
A silver fox hunts in the grass
for the little mice, Alas
but look yonder among the glades
dancing upon the grass blades
There is a bright light
So uncommon to the night
not even the sun compares
to this light so fair
it is a nymph of the night
Suddenly she vanishes from sight
leaving memory only
again the night is lonely
Then the rustle of the breeze
as it wanders among the trees
—*Alisha Pagel*

Untitled

A walk on the beach hand and hand
The soft crashing of the waves
The comfort of his touch,
And gentleness of his kiss
Is still all that remains.
—*Mackenzie Hjelm*

Over Yonder

There are some hills over yonder,
As lovely as can be.
Below the hills is a valley,
Above the hills are some trees.
Down deep, deep, in the valley
Where the sun no longer sees
The brooks bubbles over with laughter.
And the stream, sings, merrily.
They welcome their daily routine
They have as much work as we;
But still they laugh in the sunshine,
And still they sing in the breeze,
Until the "Mighty River of Life."
Meets the "Sea of Eternity."
—*Bertha Snyder*

Undercurrent

Hair about his face
as moss tenaciously
on the trunk of an oak tree
standing timeless.
Witnessing nature's beauty
in the sun ray's tremulous
on the brooks
freed from their prison
of winter's ice.
Yielding to the elements
turbulence and calm
wrinkles and lines are
etched on his face.
His eyes reveal a soul
of reverent submission
someday one of natures deeds
will take and cradle
him forever.
—*Karle Williams Tolbert*

Me

I'm as free as the wind,
  As soft as a feather,
  As neat as a butterfly.
I'm as smart as an eagle,
  As sly as a fox,
  As mean as a dog.
My Mamma told me so.
—*Jason C. Berry*

Changes

The grass stands still
As spring slowly sweeps by
The trees go unnoticed
And the birds fly so high

The day is coming
Faster and faster each morn
As the flowers sway in the breeze
Their friendship is torn

It's time to depart
We must say goodbye
No more easy times
As the wind gives a sigh

They will always have each other
But never in the same way
What they had was special
Each and every day
—*Jamie Nardino*

Untitled

Bombarded with the chill
As the blue slides through my brain
The monotonous chuckle of the pond
Eats me just the same.
I'm just no good at this
Hungry for a chance
Susceptible to a prayer
Self ostracizing dork
on the inevitable Holden path
Traveling clueless with all the answers
into pending dearth
Wallowing in phony semantics
the biggest hypocrite of the age
Hoping for a touch beyond me
—*Cary Cortese*

The Hymns Of The Pines

Moving gently through the meadows
  As the evening, sun goes down
The whispering hymns, of the pines
  Will rise high with a lonesome sound

And then the dawn replaces
  The night with a mystery dew
As if the whispering pines
  Shed's tears for what they knew

Like the Indian maiden's blue's song
  These whispering of the pines
Knows the suffering of our nation
  When the foe's are all but kind

Yet our hopes will be green meadows
  Though no man know's all his years
These sad hymns of the pines
  Has respect of all our fears

They seem to know who is listening
  And speak gently to our minds
Could be God's way of healing,
  Through the whispering of the pines
—*Ina Smith*

Last Goodbye

The cold swirling winds made an echo
As the gold bell began a slow chime,
The chapel people were mellow
A special someone lost in time.

The blue tears of hurt fell
On prayer books open up wide,
Feeling a deep and burning hell
Memories torn apart inside.

We have sung our last song
As we walk out feeling grief,
In my heart you will always belong
But now you will lie in peace.

Your soul lives on and will never die,
As we mourners say our last goodbye.
—*Cynthia E. Hahn*

Untitled

crimson rose petals
splayed across ebony silk
hopelessly alive.
—*Ron Kule*

Untitled

Being slowly ripped apart
As the loneliness increases.
Those who torture
Could not make it painless
Pain gives them glory
But what does it give me?
The thoughts linger
Of the way it used to be
The present is gone
The future was never there
I search for sometime is which
I thrived
But the blackness has dissolved all.
Irrelevant illusions remind me
Of his touch
And the tears begin.
—*Shalohm Engstrom*

Lush Life

Silent
as the love
of wet leaves
and moss...
the soft song wedding
of
long
   green
       rain.
—*Margrit Fiddle*

Sea Swimmer

She sits upon the coral rock,
as the sea's body gently massages
the nakedness of her ankles.
Resting on the arch of her limbs
with her head laid back,
ringlet locks, silky black,
dancing in the evening breeze.
Her long pale garment,
drawn just beneath,
the blossom of her virginity.
The heat of the night
splashing against her partially
shown breast, as pearls of sweat
pamper her chest.
Have the Gods no mercy,
I,
beneath these waters,
pray to become a man,
in place of the sea swimmer,
that I am.
—*Robert L. Allen*

Taylor

  Your smile is as bright
as the soft summer sun.
  It is as wide as the
widest river.
  Your laugh brightens
up the darkest room.
  It's like warm cocoa
on a cold winter day.
  You're like a delicate rose,
soft and gentle that will
grow with the warmth of the
sun and will mature with
the test of time.
—*Jacqulyn Manning*

The Fireplace

I love the flickering shadows,
As they cast their magic spell
On the walls and on the ceiling,
What stories they can tell;
Stories of a woodland romance,
Life and laughter, love and tears,
Stories of departed loved ones,
Lives and hopes of former years.
Lying there before the fire,
Dreaming dreams of long ago,
Looking deep into the future
Through the bright red embers' glow;
In a world of sweet contentment,
Cares and troubles soon erase,
Sounds fade slowly, peace and quiet,
Asleep, before the fireplace.
—*Daniel S. Smith*

The Columbine

High above the toilsome prairie,
As we climb toward timberline,
Near the azure blue of heaven,
Grows the graceful columbine.

And the white clouds that are drifting,
Seem to linger in the blue
Of the flower that God has given
Everything we'd like him to.

Though I might be showered with flowers,
Of a hue and scent divine.
I would travel far to witness,
Colorado's columbine.
—*Elwood H. Sheppard*

The Bread Of Life

Does thirst and hunger assail you
As you travel along life's way?
Then stop and go to the inn where
You'll not have to pay.
Because Jesus paid the fare
On the cross long ago,
He is the Living Bread of Life.
And the water doth freely flow.
Just go in by the door of faith
And trust in His blessed blood.
And thou shalt be filled
With abundance of soul food,
Just think of eating with Jesus
In that Mansion up above!
Where everything is ready and waiting
And all is peace and love.
The food will be so delicious
And served by Jesus the Lord.
So come one and all - both great and small,
And partake of the bounties of God.
—*Irene Blue*

My Grandma

My Grandma is special
   Because, she loves us.
As she walks up the stairs
   A storm of breath flows
Out of her mouth.

She stops on the thick wooden
   Floor to catch her lost breath.
If only she would quit smoking
   She could live a little longer.
—*Mark Demyanovich*

Pictures

Pictures can be taken
At any time in our lives
But one picture lasts forever
That's the one that's in our minds

Photos only show the surface
But memories will tell all
Photos only show a second
Memories never end

Take a picture from the wall
Then take a picture from your head
Which one will show the better moment
I'd rather have memories instead
—*Jackie Cavet*

Laughter

If laughter could be ordered
   At the corner drug store,
I'm sure we'd all be laughing
   Much more and more and more.

For I'm sure that our doctors
   Would prescribe for everyone
Many laughs a day,
   And our problems would be gone.

So why not try the laughter
   That Jesus Christ can give;
No need to pay the druggist
   To learn how to live.

When God chooses a man,
   He puts laughter in his life;
God's Spirit moves into his heart
   And replaces all doubt and strife.

Old things pass away,
   And now he has a new goal.
He has become a new man;
   He has laughter in his soul.
—*Ruth DeLozier*

Praise To God

I will praise you in the morning
   At the start of each new day
For you give us new beginnings
   For our lives in every way.

I will praise You at the noontime
   When the sun is shining bright
And the flowers, trees and grass
   Yes, all nature is just right.

I will praise You in the evening
   As the night is drawing near
Praise You for your loving care
   And knowing no need for fear.

I will praise You in the nighttime
   When the sun has left the sky
When all of your creation rests
   And to another day has said goodbye.
—*Verna L. Welsh*

Alone

Gray sky and humid air
Awaken blank despair
Carefully tidy up the room
Your lover is coming soon

A gift bought for the occasion
   A rendezvous
   A romantic situation
A bottle of wine for lightness
A black negligee for night dress
   Violins for mood
Incense would be good

   A jasmine scent
   A candle lit
   I sit
   Alone
—*Carla Fulton*

Feel From The Heart

I know I own the sun
   Because it only rains
When you're away from me
I have to have the moon
And I want the stars, too
They light the faith and truth
   In the glory of love
In the name of our trust
I will show you God's art
   In a feel from the heart
When all begins today
Flowers will tower off
Their blooms upon the shore
   In a radiant shine
In the sand that someday
Will make mirrors and glass
   In the belief of choice
In the gift of our joy
I will show you God's art
   In a feel from the heart
—*Marc Tolzman*

The Silent Scream

Holding back what should have
   been said

Having all when all else
   fails

Having fears when nothing
   even matters

Having tears when your eyes
   aren't crying

Having smiles when no one
   is trying

Having thoughts when your brain is on
   auto-matic-pilot

Having emotion when you
   are numb

Hearing words when there is
   no song

Taking stabs no blood
   from wound

In every person there is a living
   Silent Scream
—*Dina M. McCarty*

Beauty From Above

A calm I had never felt
Began to shower over me,
It iced the land with peacefulness
As far as I could see;

My eyes had never seen before
This beauty from above,
One that God sent for us
To fill our hearts with love;

There is nothing like this feeling
That I now have come to know,
When the ground is fully covered
By a freshly fallen snow;

If I could have one special wish
I know what it would be,
I would wish for God to send this sight
For everyone to see.

—*Janet Allen Armstrong*

Between 13 And 19

Around and round we go,
Being a teenager is hard you know.
Growing up,
Being scared.
Not knowing what to do.
School work piled 3 feet high.
Middle school just flies by.
A friend to help you out here,
A small argument there.
Between 13 and 19,
Your life can change.
You go to school,
Grow up quick.
And wonder what am I going to do.

—*Kim McCabe*

Age Of Technology

    Sun in the sky
    Birds in the air
A field of clover, wide and fair.
    Insects buzz
    Flowers abound
Nowhere near, an unnatural sound.

    Hills roll gently
    A stream gurgles by
And there in the middle
    On a blanket, am I.

Thinking, dreaming, I sit and write
    Line after line,
    Flows through my mind,
        There I sit
    And there I type ...
        On my computer!

—*Shawn David Kline*

A Year Ago Tomorrow

It was a year ago tomorrow,
But it seems like yesterday;
And all those haunting memories
Keep coming back my way.

Can I ever escape the nightmare?
The pain, the grief, the sorrow?
Why does it keep on hurting me?
It was a year ago tomorrow.

—*Karen S. Munhall*

Spring

Spring creeps into our lives
bit by bit
slithering
between storms
calling
sleepy crocus
young lovers
greybeards.
Glad voices
skip rope chants
roller skates
gardeners
revel in returning light.
Hearts soar
take wing
like robins coming back
after the dark.
'Zalea red, dogwood white, blazing sky blue.
Proud to be here.
Proud to call you friend.

—*Elizabeth Elliott*

Where Has The Cub Scout Gone?

  Where has that little cub scout gone?
Blonde wavy hair, eyes sparkling
    grinning innocence of tender years.
To be replaced by a tall long haired
    young man with distrust in his
red bleary drug - alcohol eyes.
  Where did everybody go wrong?
was it his parents, his school
  his den mother of years ago?
or was it society who let him down?
  Oh, to recapture those tender years
and change the path he's heading down.
  If only we could recall yesterday;
and make everything alright again.
  My little blonde-haired cub scout.

—*Barbara Kelley*

Life

As I feel the sweet touch of the wind,
  Blowing gently against my face,
And the kiss of the soothing sun,
  Warming me with such embrace,
With the crickets' lonely chirp,
  The birds' silent hum,
I think of what has passed,
  And what is yet to come,
I think of why we're here,
  And if we'll ever leave,
I think of why the sky is blue,
  And why the grass is green,
These are simple questions,
  Or as though they may seem,
Are we living life for real,
  Or is it just a dream?

—*Monika L. Arvelo*

"I'm Not Different!"

Maybe I can see what others can't
But I'm not different
I can be what others aren't able to be.
But I'm not different!
I have the key, and they don't
But I'm not different!

—*Renee De Michiel*

Guardians

The line we tread
bounds the butte
just north of town—
an unseen fence
beside barbed wire
that bears "No Hunting"
on an aged post.

When we have passed
and dark has come,
coyotes pace the northern rim
beyond our path.

Toward the south
where children sleep,
vows are made —
the guard is changed.

—*Carol Crandell*

The Old Women

To see the children run,
  brings tears to my eyes.
As they frolic to and fro,
  I am taken back to my youth.
Where days were care free,
  and wasted without thought,
  and happiness prevailed.
I remember when my legs could run,
  and my eyes could see.
  and my ears could hear.
Oh, to spend one day in youth again,
  once more before I die.

—*Sarah Martini*

One Spring Day

Walking outdoors, I felt the
Brisk spring breeze.
Looking up at the sky
I saw birds of prey
Having a silent drill
They soared high and wide
Then higher and wider
Until they disappeared from view.
As I glanced over at the Orchard,
An Orchard wedding was beginning.
The pear trees were gleaming with
white blossoms, like brides,
Following were peach trees in pink
As bridesmaids.

—*Sophia M. Evans*

Sweet Memories

When there was candy in jars,
Bubblegum cigars,
And the smell of fresh popcorn,
Foamy root beer floats,
And giant banana boats,
The sound of an old car's horn.
A big ice cream cone,
And an old style phone,
To call to say you'll be late.
You meet someone nice,
All sugar and spice,
What a charming place for a date.
Share a malt with a friend,
Hoping the day never ends,
Cause the sundaes were always sublime,
The tasty soda pop,
At the ice cream shop,
These are sweet memories of mine.

—*Bill Buchda*

Dreams

Dreams are nothing but pain,
but dreams are all I've got.
I hide my tears under the rain.
People pass saying I have a lot,
but its all been ripped apart,
just for me to hold as it dies.
Just some more blood from my heart,
as no one hears my cries.
I look outside and wonder why
there's no one I could really talk to.
I wonder why dreams had to die,
instead of just coming true.
—*Christine Miles*

Poem for Peace

Peace may be a dream
But dreams do come true
You need to make an effort
For me and for you

It is well worth the time
And all that it takes
For less harm to happen
For all of our sakes

Nothing comes easy
That we all know
Let's begin now
By forgiving a foe

With love in our hearts
This dream we'll achieve
Don't ever give up
Until we all leave

And once we are gone
Behind us will be
A much better world
For our Children to see
—*Ellen Jane Poppe*

Incubus

I would like to think you spectral,
but I can feel your form
surging over me
like the ocean's waves
pressuring the sands.

I would be more fearful
but you haunt me by my leave—
penetrate my soul by my assent.
So we both descend.

I could claim you a night spirit
suffusing me by unearthly devise,
but my mind lies about is innocence:
my dreams embrace desire.

So we tremble,
arch and ache towards culmination.
Borne aloft on keening tides,
eye to eye, sigh to sigh.
Passion.
—*Patricia G. Sullivan*

Untitled

I feel being pressed tightly,
compacted into a small container.
No matter what feelings I have,
I must not show them.
But I hurt so much inside
all I want to do is cry and flood
the world with my tears.
—*June Ohata*

Untitled

You always told me you loved me
But little did I know,
You'd stay for a while
Then get up and go.
You toyed with my emotions
And tore them all apart,
I never thought you'd be the one
To try and break my heart.
I know deep inside you cared
But you were to blind to see,
All the pain inside my eyes
whenever you looked at me.
I don't know when the pain will stop
When it's going to end,
But until that day comes to me
I know my heart won't mend.
—*Jessica Levesgue*

To Gloria

You've enslaved my heart
But set my spirit free.
Your loving grace
Has ennobled me.

I feel beknighted
To have your love,
To be yours alone
All others, above.

You alone are mine
And I'll love you forever.
To have your love remain,
My goal and endeavor.

My being and existence
Is enmeshed with your own.
I glow when my thoughts
Image the love we have sown.

I want to be with you
Till we have to depart
The joyous world you've made
By taking my heart.
—*Richard Jacobsen*

Another Year

What's an age
But the turn of a page
What is life
But struggle and strife
What is the sun
But warmth and fun
What is the moon
But light to subdue the
  gloom
So all in all my
  precious friend
I can go on and on
  which is my trend
I'll turn you over to
  our Lord and Saviour
'Cause you know and I
  know He governs our
  behavior.
—*Helen F. Stolz*

"Moon Light"

In the eve of night
By dim moon light
Body to body, hand in hand
By the water and the sand
I held her tight to my chest
And felt the heaving of her breast
Like crashing water on the shore
Upon or bodies passion tore
Endless waves of lust
Crashed upon us in the dusk
It took our bodies on a quest
An exploration of our flesh
All night long we held on tight
Making love by dim moon light
—*Brent R. Daley*

My Oldest

Once he was a little boy, who ran
by my side,
But as he grew older he wanted to be
Like his Dad and when I looked for
him he would hide,
He grew to be a fine young man I could
Not ask for more,
Until the war broke in Vietnam and he
was drafted and was sent very far.
When he came back he was a change man
The young man that was fun to be around
had been change in another land;
Now when I see him, it breaks my heart
I cry and pray that his illness will
come to a halt.
—*Viola Dart*

Gold Dust

A horse named Gold Dust flies
by the others on the track.
This horse named Gold Dust he
never looks back.
His loyalty and pride can't be
denied.
No other horse could ever match
his stride.
He is faithful to his master,
And when he urges he always
goes faster.
He is a born runner.
His hooves, they sound like thunder.
This horse is a true champion,
He has the spirit of a hawk,
And once he begins running
he can never be caught.
—*Becky Pickett*

I Like Summer

I like summer
'cause you can play
a million different games a day
You can go to a friend house
and maybe sleep over
Or you can look for a four-leaf clover
I like summer
'cause you can sleep in
Or play a game where you can win
I like summer a really whole lot
'cause you can go to the mall
and shop, shop, shop
I like summer
—*Annika Kay*

Kiddo

You strolled into my heart
   calmly as you please,
Narry a by-your-leave....
   bringing with you
Your large copper eyes
   and full chubby cheeks

I watched you while away the hours,
   sniffing at the flowers
I listened to your "meow" for your chow
I felt your purring,
   as you were furrowing
      deep in my lap
Yes, you my little chap!

Now my "Kiddo" - you've gone on
   to someplace
      never without
         and I've no doubt
That your little face
   is giving joy
      to all about
         as it did for me.
—*Veronica A. Chell*

Introduction To A Nation

Our fathers built a country in which we
can be proud.
With liberty and justice for all,
we are endowed.
Through courage and integrity is born
this mighty nation.
Creating a land of freedom for each
new generation.
Steadfast we've formed this union that
declares us all brothers.
Standing tall for equality and defending
the rights of others.
May the eagle soar high, o'er our lady's
shining flame.
For in God shall we trust, and America
is my name.

—*John E. Blackmon, Jr.*

Nurses' Day

No words of ours, bouquets of flowers,
can say our thanks for the many hours
   you give to us.

You hear the call of each and all
for help to stand and walk, not fall;
   you show your love.

To sense our need and with skill to see
the way to bring us some relief,
   you serve with love.

You come with food - to cheer our mood -
or big, pink pill to do us good;
   you're kind, dear friend.

No doubt you've read of The One who said
"Work done in love, with heart and head
   is worth God's praise!

—*Margaret Horton Webber*

Barney Bird

Barney Bird
Can't talk
Barney Bird
Can't peep
Barney Bird
Won't leave his cage
Barney Bird
Won't sleep
Barney Bird
Eats tuna fish
Barney Bird
Eats pie
Barney Bird
Hangs upside down
Don't you wonder why?

—*Maria Bei and Marjorie Joy*

Family

Sick, moaning, gasping for air
Care taker, liar, dying
I called her grandmother

Silent, big chair, tobacco, spittoon
Grunts, fondler, drunk
I called him grandfather

Towering, traveling, drunk
I called him uncle

Two bitches, two drunk
I called them aunts

Never there, removed
Wicked humor, laughter
Screaming, crying
Athletic, beauty
Drunk, gone
I called her mother

Little boy lost I called brother
—*Carmen M. Bragg*

Ebbing Tides Echo His Questions

   In each burst of sunrise
challenged by waves that leap and lunge,
this sun-bronzed man of painted bark
   and fin-snarled nets
spans his oars above coral and pearls.

And he sings of dawns with golden plums,
   of raindrops,
of purpling jacaranda trees.

He returns to green lagoons,
   shares the glow and fury of desire.
He is young — he scatters blossoms
   on her shoulders,
lays kisses on her breasts
past the midnight hour of his seeding.

Soft crests of waves and troughs
   encore and encore
the song he ever hears —
   the song in sea shells.

Ebbing tides echo his questions
   of sea-spray, sunlight and soul.
—*Emma Crobaugh*

Bosnia

Blood in the streets
   Children dying and lost
Pools of humanity
   Our modern holocaust

Auschwitz and Dachau
   Aren't those days gone?
Life ebbing away
   Massacre goes on

What pain, what tragedy
   See the child's broken limb
Mothers crying, fathers dead
   For political whim

Infinitesimal problems
   That trouble us so
Look at the carnage
   What do we know?

There's life in my belly
   And fire in my brain
Such senseless destruction
   For God's sake, what gain?
—*Tessa McGovern*

Waco

He abhorred silver bells,
clamoring rings, order

He would confine himself
to stand erect and proud

He shared his vision,
though some mocked, chastised his name

Entwined with Christ, he hoped
finally, to be glorified

But even while he burned
before eyes of millions

The perished souls cried,
descend descend descend.

—*Quanda V. Spencer*

Kaleidoscope

Fingers turn the cylinder
   clinging to the eye
   that makes the patterns;
Splinters of glass
   scatterings of beads
Flutter in the light
   to rubied reds
   faceted whites.
A shift of fingers,
A click of colors,
Mirage cloned by mirrors
Bend reflections to oases in dust.
In garbled margins,
In fractured forms,
   the circled eye finds order;
The covered eye
   cannot see the shadows
   for the dark.

—*Dorothy Brummel*

Babies

Did you ever hold a baby
Close upon your breast
And feel its soft warm body
And be filled with tenderness?

Did you ever look into a little
  baby's eyes
And see all heaven reflected
  there,
The sun, the stars and skies?

Did you ever watch a baby
In its first attempt to smile?
Well, if you have,
Then you have seen
All that makes life worthwhile.
—*Winifred B. Schmidt*

A Song For Autumn Days

Red leaves of autumn,
Clothing all the trees;
Rustling melodies
In the breeze.

Brown leaves of autumn,
Scattered all around;
Dancing 'cross the ground —
Autumn's sound.

Autumn days are here again;
Winter days are near again;
Blustery cold the winds will blow
Until the spring.

Gold leaves of autumn;
Treasure ev'ry one;
Sorrow when there's none —
No autumn leaves.

Oh, autumn days;
Lovely autumn days.
—*Carl A. Loy*

Untitled

   Why does the pain always
come to my sickened brain? Weighed
down by all the burdens of the world.
   Why does the sorrow linger
in my heart? Only to leave love
in the cold.
   I want you to be the one to
touch me, but you're afraid.
   Why do you keep your heart
from me?
Keeping your love behind locked doors.
   Are you going to give me the
key or am I going to have to break
down the door?
—*Jake Bartok*

Octopus

Gracefully eight arms waving in motion
   Comes the dancer of the ocean

Changing its colors here and there
Moving through water as dancer does air

Cautiously gliding he hides in his ink
Propelling himself he's gone in a wink

Again comes this dancer of sea and ocean
   Gracefully moving in watery motion
—*Barbara Levy/Walls*

The Raindrop (3/3/1961 Washington D.C.)

   The raindrop,
   Coming from such,
   An awesome height,
   Splatters on a,
   Leaf.
   The leaf,
   Recoils,
   But the raindrop
   Is shattered,
   Battered.
   Piece-
   Meal,
   It,
   Falls,
But the ground does not recoil.
   The pieces seep,
   Deeply creep-
      il-
       y.
—*Carl Masthay*

Inside

Somewhere in the darkness, in the
corners of your imagination,
in the black depths of your
mind, in the true concepts of
your blood, in the fog of your
tortured soul, the evil brought
upon you, lurks with conceited pride.
You must hide it no, you
mustn't let anyone see it.
For the smog that covers
your insane eyes must never
be lifted to reveal your
passions for death, and fire.
Sad, but true, you may never
act on it, nor tell anyone who
you really want to be.
You cannot face it, can you?
—*Jessica Weinstock*

Friendship

Friendship is a never ending
dedication for love. To expect this,
one must understand the responsibilities
that come with it. To accept a person
as they really are; and to be able to
be there for the pain and suffering
another is feeling, but must also be
there when they are happy. To be
happy is one thing but to have a
friend is to be one with another and
to stand with them through thick
and thin. No fight, and no one can come
through a true friendship. Let your
friend understand that you are willing
to stand with them through the end.
Let your friend understand you love them.
—*Suzy Manning*

Only For A Moment!

I hear the song of tranquility
deep in the heart of Nature,
Where the birds whistle
and the streams break
the pebbles into the crystals.
With this harmony of the senses
of the sound and the sight,
I "absorb" the whole of nature,
as if with one big "gulp"
   into the "depths" of the "deep"
   ... of tranquility.
—*Nalini P. Shah*

Stormfront

Ever notice that the colors
   deepen before?
Ever notice that the world
   has gone still?
Ever notice that feeling of
   waiting?
That feeling that something
   is going to happen
That feeling of an impending
   explosion
That feeling ...
   Whoosh, Thunder, Rain!
—*Mary Elizabeth Ruffin*

Spring

Fragrant breezes,
Delicate flowers,
Spending the rosy,
Twilight hours,
Counting the stars
In the sky
And watching a,
Colorful butterfly,
Catch the wind,
Over your head,
Spring is a dream you have as you lay,
Peacefully in your bed
—*Kristen Burgess*

"The Crossroad Of Love"

Love can be hard to find,
   depending where you look,
but sooner or later,
   you'll meet at a point.
Your roads would meet,
   then it'll cross.
Your love may soon be lost.
Your roads may go
   their separate ways,
   but in the end
Your roads may meet
   again...!
—*Hana Salas*

Ballet

Hard Fun
Sweating Hurting Leaping
   Point Smile
Fast Concentration Excited
   Practice Split
      Breath
—*Robin-Louise Burkitt*

People And The Earth

People and the earth they
do compare
Day by day and year by year
In the spring the sparkling
Sun, is like people, when
they were young.
In the fall and the winter
cold, is like people
growing old.
Days and years are passing
by, then comes the time
we must die, and
say to this world our
  last goodbye.
—*Osmond Toresdahl*

Graceland Telegram

Now that death has come my way
Do not try to run away
Put the situation in the Lord's hands
And pray to Him, He understands
Listen to what I have to say…
Jesus will give you strength day by day.
Heaven is my home now
At the feet of Jesus I do bow
I want you to feel His peace
For in Christ I have found release.
I know it's hard to let me go
But Jesus really loves me so
He died to set me free
With Him I shall forever be
Praise God for His grace
I have seen Jesus face to face
HEAVEN IS A WONDERFUL PLACE
—*Rebekah Hric*

A Rumor

Perhaps you had nothing better to
do that day
But to start a rumor
The heartache and tears you have
brought to my family
If only you knew, you almost
destroyed us that day
The story you told was untrue.
But trying to prove it, we couldn't do
We must live with what you did
But why, oh why was it us,
That you targeted that day
Because you had nothing better to do
that day.
—*Marge Plowchin*

Adams Leaf

What about clothes
do they make the man…
no…
not bigger…
or better…
they do what they ought…
cover up skin…
so forget about those…
open up your heart to
let that thought transpose
for men were only men…
long before they wore
those clothes.
—*Marilynn J. Eagan*

Untitled

What didn't you tell me?
Do you love me—
do you? And where, oh where
did the spaghetti
on the ceiling come from?

Where did you mind go
a minute ago?
I looked at you
you weren't there.

Sometimes I feel I was there
when they built those
pyramids in Egypt.

and it's no good to say
you're as young as you feel—
it's confusing
to feel like that baby being born
and like that loved one
leaving

all in the same thought.
—*Brenda Spencer*

"Day And Night Like Black And White"

The night - dark
Does it frighten you?
I am the color of night
I be beautiful!
Do you not see?
You hate me for what you see!
Are you afraid of the dark?
Listen to me; know me
I be beautiful!
Night
Day sun hurts me!
I can't be you, sorry
Colors but not colors
World revolve; you and me
Day
Night
Friends
Maybe?
Please?!
Day sun don't hurt me!
—*Analisa Granillo*

My Dumb Bed.

Here I am in this dumb bed
  Doing all that "Nursey" said.

Tubes and gadgets stuck here and there
  While nurses smile and look so fair.

This dumb bed is soft no more.
  Soon I'll have a big bed sore.

I can't believe it's I in bed
  Although I seem to be well fed.

This dumb bed has got me down.
  I'll try to smile instead of frown.

Really, nurses aren't so bad.
  They try to keep me from being sad.

This dumb bed I'm grateful for.
  'Twill make me better than before.
—*Hazel D. Buffmire*

Spiral

A time when youthful strength
  Dominated and obliterated
    the weakness within
Defeat was only an untouchable concept
Another word used only in context,
  For this young, strong spirit
    Would not, could not be defeated.
Well, for all the belief and all
  The struggling
We see that concepts are just that
  How we choose to interpret.
And what we choose to interpret
  Is at times the defeat in itself
    For self-denial can wound within.
In short this undefeated heart
  Has been spurned
  And in the long,
  Treacherous process
  Has inadvertently defeated
    Itself also…
—*Martha Munoz-Knowles*

"Hers No More"

A trail of tears run
  down her cheeks.
How can this be?
What went wrong?
He was hers but now
  he is gone.
She knew him only a
  very short while, but the
  love they had shared
  was like no other.
As the tiny casket is lowered down
  she struggles back the urge
  to scream, "Let him out! My
  son cannot breathe."
She knows now that the son whom
  she had bore, was no longer hers
  just a memory that was to be shared.
—*Jeannie M. Roseberry*

As I Walk Down Life's Pathway

As I walk alone
Down life's pathway
I know not what tomorrow
May bring.

But I know if God
Is beside me that
All things
Will be easier.

And if I bring a joy
To someone's face
And watch an older person
Smile
And say, "Thank you."
Because I have done a good deed
For them

I will know that
I have done my best
For that day.
—*Laura Sexton*

Love Chant

If in the long,
dread wanderlust of
an age
that speaks to
rhythms beyond
that which
we now know;

When the vapors
that cover
a still pond

Lurking in the
night, cover thee,
and the dragon
stirs to his feet;

Having fed upon
all the souls
we now know.

In such a time, I will be with you!
—*Paul Joseph Rovelli*

Give Me My Days Rest

Cold heartless night
 dreary dampness permeates the air

I am alone
 prisoner to my own consciousness

Self-full blame
 things I had done & hadn't

Longing for the past
 a chance to right the wrongs

Lips I dream to kiss
 feelings to share

Captive to my thoughts
 she is in everything

I must move on
 yet wish to go back

Lord, I beg of you
 give me my days rest
—*Adam M. Garfinkel*

Unnoticed

Dry painted leaves
 drifting
  silently
   falling

From tall oak tree
 float
  caught

Momentarily suspended
 in the haze
  of sunlight
   one last time

They are lifted
 on gentle breeze

Before they lay
 unnoticed.
—*Annie J. Heart*

Pitter Patter Goes The Rain

Pitter patter goes the rain
dripping down the window pane
I'm crying tears of hurt and shame
I have changed, I'm not the same.

I call your name but your not there
I can't find you anywhere
I'm singing songs of sweet despair
as I mumble, "life isn't fair".

Where did you go? Oh I don't know
I hide my tears so they won't show
come back please, I need you so
Listen to the harsh wind blow.

I've counted the hours past today
wondering if you'll come my way
what more am I able to say?
You never loved me anyway.

Pitter patter goes the rain
dripping down the window pane
I'm crying tears of hurt and shame
I have changed, I'm not the same...
—*Sonia Lewark*

Poet's Blade

Sheathed in my chest,
Drunk from my blood,
 Pain making me move,
Giving reasons to exist.
 Gripping the bone hilt,
I pull it free,
 Applying the crimson tip
to paper,
 Speaking neither love
nor blasphemy,
 Yet something there
between.
 Words flow free
like blood and tears,
 Then the well runs dry,
I must dip my quill in its ink.

The blade plunges,
New sheath,
New pain,
New poem.
—*Joseph Spencer Johnson*

Life

Why is life sometimes
 dull, boring mad -
and sad.
 I which I knew
But sometimes it's fun, -
 daring and adventurous.
That's something I do
 Know.
You go through a lot.
Like love, sadness -
frightfulness and madness.
 That's the way life -
goes.
—*Jennifer Schroyer*

The Book

Everything that you have done,
each and every act,
has been written down;
a record of each and every fact.

One page at a time
the writing is done.
One day at a time
each page is begun.

On these pages
will be your entire life;
every moment of happiness,
every moment of strife.

In heaven, this book is all you have.
So, make your life a pleasure not pain
because this is the only book
that can not be written again.
—*Allan F. Gilbreath*

"A Snow Flake"

White ... pure white
Each line a delicate handiwork
Made by the most scrutinizing
 eye;
Carefully etched to form a beautiful
 crystal;
Sparkling forever as it sails
Down under the pale moonlit
Night;
Falling... falling, ever so
Gracefully, it dances its way
Down in the icy air
Proud and joyous, it lives
For a few minutes - a wonder
To all.
Yet soon... with gentle care, its
Creator, ever so lovingly, places
It to melt in the hands
Of a tiny child.
—*Nicole Buyansky*

Peace

O Lord, You know
each one whom You create.

Your gifts to all
reveal Your care.

Life, learning, and love!
temporal, then eternal!

Gratitude and humility
are our keys to grace.

Creation, redemption
and sanctification
we acknowledge.

We praise you now
and hope
to praise You forever.
—*Mary Frances*

Untitled

June is for daisies
swaying in the meadow
 and
For songbird's symphonic
salute to summer.
—*May Getzelman*

War

A war with two sides,
Each side an enemy to the other,
Brother against brother,
Families apart,
All with a broken heart.
Mind takes over,
Greed will come,
A war will start,
So beat the warning drum.
But if we allow peace to come
to this place,
We will be filled with love and grace.
Everything will be green and fresh,
And we will never see another
piece of bloody flesh.
—*Kate Erickson*

"Colton Town"

The Racqette river lies asleep
  entwined in quilts of snow.
Beneath the ice where it
  has never ceased to flow.

The trees like towering
  sentinels, along it's banks
stand motionless and cold,
will come alive when spring
  unfolds.

Snow burdened houses dot
  the slopes around.
And through the silence
  out of their chimney's
comes the smoke from fires
  that heats the homes
in "Colton Town".
—*Bud Graham*

Words

Sadness,
Ever maddening with each
Fatal Blow,
To a child who cares so much,
These words of hatred
Linger hard upon his soul,
Like large heavy weights,
Pulling him lower
And lower,
Until there is nothing left,
Of his mind,
His heart,
His soul,
Or his very existence...
—*Jonathan D. Moody*

Childhood

How positive we were that
every day was a good day.
We played and dreamed big dreams
the air was clean and sweet.
We loved animals - talked to them,
they were our friends.

We didn't have to worry about smog,
the government, terrorists or drugs,
or that someone would trump our ace.

We were sure evil would be punished!
And so certain good would triumph!
Mankind in innocent childhood,
when the earth was fresh and new.
—*Mary E. Roberts*

Tender

  The touch was so soft,
    everlasting; never-ending
  Dreams could never compare,
    endless was the soft sigh
    remembering was easy;
    she could never forget
  that day, so very long ago.
    She had found her true love,
  but, alas, it was not meant to be.
For at that time, he, nor she was free.
    Free to live, free to love.
  Knowing he could never have her,
    he took his own life
  now she lay in the cold room
  remembering the whispering sigh
    of his lips, on hers
      on that day,
    so very long ago.
—*Danielle Valentine*

Aspirations

Aspirations, the spirits'
  exalted desire...
A breath of inspiration,
  as though constantly on fire
With eyes of deep awareness
You'll see the greatest plan.
Of God's predestined careness
  in his image of you as man.
Ascending forever upward
  to your highest ideal
this power is within you...
Your true self—the only real
though sometimes they
  become obsessions
I'm sure that you will see
that following Aspirations
  will lead to Eternity!
—*Jo Ella Clark*

Every Time

Every time I see your
face my heart shatters and
falls to a million pieces.
Every time I hear your name
my ears whimper with sadness.
Every time I look into your
eyes it brings tears
to mine.
Every time I get around you
on in the same room I
get a tingling sensation up
my spine.
Every time I close my eyes
at night I see you in my
dreams and wish it was
true but I wake up and
I am all alone once again
and my world is filled
with darkness once more
  This is what happens
  every time?
—*Theresa Price*

"A Week In May"

He found a baby bird
Fallen from it's nest
Abandoned by the rest,
And he loved him.
He kept him in the shade
Of the lilac tree
He was too little to be free,
And he loved him.
He ran home from school
To feed him bits of bread
Stroked his tiny head,
And he loved him.
He had him for a week
Held him when he died
And I cried,
Because he loved him.
Beneath the lilac tree
He buried him that day
The sky was dripping gray
Because he loved him.
—*Patricia C. Nicklas*

Wind Of Trees

I see the leaves of yesterday
Falling off the mother trees
Like cascading water falls
As though in columns fold
Yellow, orange, red, and green
Flying through the air serene
Chilly winds flowing free
Blowing branches off a tree
The seasons pass
Like moons of old
And stars in mass
As though to mold
One era to another
As not to smother
To be free
Blowing from tree to tree
—*Michael Piccoli*

Take Me

  Take me to a place
    far away from here
  where everything is peaceful
  no longer living in fear.

  Take me to that place
    that has never been found
  where you and I live happily
  with no one else around.

  Waters made of crystals
    sand made of gold
    love everlasting
    our feelings unfold.

  Waves splash upon us
    replenishing our soul
  this new place discovered
  can now be called our own.

  Dream away on the shore
    never to leave
  take me to that place
  where we'll never be deceived.
—*Elizabeth Hermann*

Gone Astray

Have you ever gone astray?
Far into deep, deep, distress
And oh, what a mess
All the sin and distress
While still stumbling and
    Falling
On you, Lord, I am calling
Oh come, by my "all in all"
So let heaven hear my call
    Redeemed; now born from
    Above
Sweet, sweet, Holy Spirit,
    Sweet as a Dove
"But Christ is all, and in all"
—*Marion Hughart*

((Grace))

As I look out my window,
Feel the cool wind upon my face,
My thoughts turn to our Saviour,
His love and saving grace.

On a limb a little sparrow.
It hops, chirps and calls.
They are in the care of God,
For he knows when each one falls.

And as I watch the sparrow,
Taking food to the young in nest,
Stirring leaves in restless breeze,
It brings my heart to rest.

For when you look at nature,
You look upon God's face.
True joy comes from loving Him
As He shares with us His grace.

And my thoughts go back to Calvary,
The price Jesus paid that day.
And all He asked is to believe in Him,
Yet some can't find the way.
—*Earl Peterson*

Kazoos Ain't Blue

Goin down de road
Feelin bad boy
Goin down de road
Feelin blue, red

Hey! Hot Spring Day
Ho! Flowers in pots
Yo! Watch em grow
Stop! Makin me blue

Feelin mean. Pushin bad
Don do me this way
Not gonna work cuz
Kazoo's ain't blue

Walkin down de Pike
Streets a-blowin purple
Twirly sticks, windsock fish
See a dimple's showin

Goin down de road
Wood boats rubber band rudders
Blue 'n black eyes brown
Red ruby smiles acomin
—*Cindy Laue*

The Last Line

If all the stars,
Fell from the sky.
And one left shown.
Someone asks why.
I'd say to them.
I just don't know.
And look up.
At that one a glow.
I'd think of you,
And all your love.
And know it was sent.
From heaven above.
And with this love.
I know in you.
This is what,
I'm going to do.
Love you till.
The end of time,
And yes,
That's the last line.
—*Shannon A. Gavin*

The Lost Boyz Of The Sudan

The lost boyz of the Sudan
    Fifteen hundred strong
      Yet one not a man

Five thousand miles or so -
    They've walked
      With wounded body
      And empty soul
        Hunger and blistering sands
        Death did take its toll

Villages abandoned
    Families dispersed
      The atrocities of war
        Proclaim mankind at its worst

The lost boyz of the Sudan
    Fifteen hundred strong
      Rhythmically they march on
        To tribal beats -
        A survival song.
—*Charles Renwick McDowell*

I See White Lilies

The fragrance of the lilies
fill my house each day.
In every room I work in
the fragrance follows me
It helps me think of Easter
and Jesus that He's near to me,
The whiteness of the lilies
is Jesus Victory from death,
Green leaves are hope for all people
Hope that we all need
that Jesus He Is Real,
and always talks to me
to know and touch the lilies
that are real and so is Jesus
real to me. It is through
the lilies God's beauty
that I see - let me talk
in prayer to Him where
ever I may be.
—*Blanche Mary Colombo*

Ravished Shadow

Dancing hands thread my needs
    Filling pockets of disease
Yesterday should have never been
    Fort of power and the sin

Nervous hands control all thoughts
    Emptied room forgets me not
Tomorrow could be the day for me
    Seek the love and forever see

Giving hands find there way
    Equal passion does not stray
Today should be like the first
Feeling, searching before the burst

Open hands pick the pieces
    Giving life such increases
Now you fade the shadow of pain
    Lifting, loving the soul of rain
—*Christy L. Donner*

The Flag That I See

This great, big and beautiful
    flag that I see,
The old red, white and blue,
    is really for me.
As I think back in glory,
    To the men I once knew,
    Who young as they were,
Gave there lives for it too.
    Some gave their lives,
    And others a limb,
    I gave my mind,
    Is it a sin?
But, I think not forever,
    Will all remain lost?
But to honor Old Glory,
    There must be a cost!
So do not surrender,
The treasure that is dear,
As Old Glory will resound,
    And dry up those tears.
—*Tom Penaskovic*

Freedom's Song

Let's give a big hurrah for America,
Flawed though it may be.
Its still a place that we call home,
Where we can all be free.
A freedom we all can treasure
And sleep in peace at night.
Wake up in the morning, serene.
Not filled with fright.
So raise your hands, praise to the Lord
Who gave us the U.S.A.
Best of all we have the right,
In peace, to kneel and pray.
—*Lee Reynolds*

Life

Come stand on a cat's tail
For only a dollar;
Come stand on his tail
And listen to him holler.

Even if he doesn't yell
It's money well spent.
Just the chance to stand there
Is worth every cent.
—*W. A. Read*

Contentment

Floating…
Floating…
Along;
Floating…
Floating…
Alone.

Like a seaweed
  far out from
    the shore
I, in my shallop,
  go sailing once more.

Drifting…
Drifting…
Away…
—*Mabel Smith Fink*

Touch The Rose

Warm rain comes.
Flowers bloom.
Hot sun shines.
Gone too soon.

God gives life.
Petals sweet.
In that gift
No deceit.

Giving joy.
Taking none.
Silent friend.
Job well done.

Life near end.
Fragrance gone.
Wasted not.
Like a song.

Touch the rose
While it's here.
Pass it not.
Hold it dear.

—*David L. Reynolds*

"Behold"

Upon the wings of mercy
  Fly yesterday's forgivings
And through the beauties of the past
  Life is forgotten
The stillness of peace not yet achieved
  Erases the minds of believers
Wonders laced with wonder
  Let life live on
Space through which time exceeds
  Beholds the wishes of all
Light brings faith
  As darkness closes in
But discovery is clouded
  With many untruths
And we are enclosed
—*Ann Kardos*

"A Thought"

It was a dream, an idea, a thought
For which we all fought.
Fighting bravely and united
We couldn't be divided.
We stood tall and strong as trees
To keep our earthly peace.
—*Jorge A. Resendiz*

Untitled

Here's a bit of Trivia
for all you trivia buffs.
This question I will give ya.
Might knock you on your duffs

It might make you beg,
or cry like the dickens
was it first the egg
or was it first the chickens

To me the answer is inherent.
At least I think maybe.
If you don't have a parent.
You can't have a baby.

The eggs have to be fertilized
At least that's my perception
My brain would have to be expertalized
To understand egg-maculate conception

That's the end of the tale.
And the things stand as they are.
If you don't have a male.
You'd better lock for a star.
—*James E. Wilson*

A Moment: In Memory Of Hope DiMario

A moment is all it takes
For dawn to change to day
A moment is all it takes
To have one snatched away
A moment is all it takes
To smile and say hello
And in a moment she was gone
Before we were ready to let go.
A moment is so precious
Yet we let so many slip by
A moment can last forever
Or be gone with the blink of an eye
A moment can be full of love,
Wonder, happiness, delight
A moment was all it took
To change our lives that night.
Now we wait for the day
That we may see her again
Grateful she touched our hearts
And shared our lives, for just a moment.
—*Beth Blair*

"Feeling Good Again"

Lord I thank you,
  for feeling good again.
Lord I thank you,
  for feeling like I can win.

I feel like,
  there's a reason for living,
I feel like,
  there's a reason for giving.

The sun is shining
  in my heart,
Even on cloudy days,
  I can't let it part.

I never thought I'd see
  the day, when I'd say,
I feel good again
  with a big beautiful grin.
—*Debra Robison*

Untitled

Hold onto your dreams
for if you don't who will?
They will be shattered
your heart will become still

Your life will have no meaning
no direction in which to go
Nothing to fight for
No ambition in which to show

Take control of your thoughts
And use them to the best
The world is a cruel place
Your patience will be put to the test

Make the most of each day
For who knows when it will be your last
Live life to the fullest
Everyday flies by so fast
Take time to do the things you want
but also the things you must
believe in yourself
put all of your strength into that trust
—*Angela Horkey*

Time Is Running Out

Time is running out
For me and for you
I think we'll be saying goodbye
Before this night is through

It's hard to hold on
Even harder to let go
Right at this moment
I'm feeling pretty low.

I'll always cherish what we had
We'll have the memories to look back
Even though right now
My heart is starting to crack

I want you to know
Right from the start
I've always loved you
It's just now we have to part

So goodbye my dear friend
Memories I have, I'll always endeavor
I'm sure that you know
You'll be a part of me forever.
—*Diane Swantek*

Captive

Her cries for freedom,
for mercy,
Are the silent winds,
blowing over the sea.

Her heartbeat
is the pounding of waves
on the shore.

We cannot free her,
from the power that holds her captive.

She waits in vain,
for the day
when she can be free from her capture,
To be free.
—*Amanda Padwa*

Games - After Fifty

Playing games of love regained -
For now you cast a new shadow.
Reflecting on the past
And love begins again -
Refreshed, anew like children
Friends and foes
At once with life casting us around.
Now jesting at life
Now we both fall down,
And around - and around.
—*Courtenaye Evans*

Thank You, God!

I thank you God, in my humble way…
   For the nighttime and for the day;
I thank you for the moonlight
   And each shining star;
And its vision of grandeur
   As it's seen from afar.

Thank you God, for the flowers;
   For the grass and the trees;
For the oceans and rivers
   And the gentle breeze.

Thank you God, for the saints
   That have gone before;
For the pathways they marked to
   Your open door.

Thanks for your forgiveness that
   At death we may ascend;
To that City in Heaven
   Where there will be no end.
—*C.E. Puckett*

Gems

Children-their minds are there
for us to mold-
Small hands reach out to hold.
Some innocent-some wise
beyond their years,
Sweet smiles that quickly
turn to tears.

So let us nurture them
with love and caring
because our future lies with them,
and when we're done, tho'
we have found it wearing,
perhaps we'll also see
   a Polished Gem.
—*Elaine Fink*

Untitled

Through the blue Kentucky hills, I roam.
Forever,
In my dreams.
After all these lonely years,
I am still too far from home.

My dreams are all I have of you
Kentucky bluegrass home.
My love is all I have to give
As I wonder far from home.

My loves,
The blue Kentucky hills and you.
My dreams,
Forever true.
My heart wanders back to you…
   My blue Kentucky home.
—*T. Claytina Lewis*

Forever

Forever friends have gone away,
Forever memories each and all.
Forever days have gone on by,
The Forever summer turned to fall.
A wife's Forever kiss
Replaced a mother's Forever call.

Forever changes at Forever's will,
But have no fear; Forever is tomorrow,
And tomorrow comes Forever still.
—*Mark Wright*

Hear My Prayer Lord

Bless me Heavenly Father
Forgive my erring ways
Grant me strength to serve thee
Put purpose in my days
Give me understanding
Enough to make me kind
So I may judge all people
With my heart and not my mind
And teach me to be patient
In every thing I do
Content to trust your wisdom
And to follow after you
And help me when I falter
And hear me when I pray
And receive me in thy Kingdom
To dwell with thee some day.
—*Sally Pipkin*

Friends

Friends are neat,
Friends are sweet,
Friends can sweep you
Off your feet,
Friends will wish
You lots of luck,
They won't laugh and
Say "Tut Tut".

Friends are friends
Forevermore
"Friend I like you"
That's for sure!
—*Dawn Snowdall*

A Sick-Bed Lament

From head to toe,
From north to south,
My health is in a rout!
From seborrhea to diarrhea,
Plus arthritis and some gout.

Can't shake these symptomatic pains,
And medicine does no good-
Why can't my health record some gains?
Guess I'll just "Knock on wood!"

But what the heck! I'm still alive-
Perhaps I should fly south?
Nah, I wouldn't enjoy the trip
With all these ulcers in my mouth.

Where does it end?
Is there anything
I can feel good about?
Of course there is!
I think I'll sing-
For the sun has just come out!
   Amen!
—*John R. Gsell*

Friendship Is Forever

Friendship is a love
from one friend to another
A friend who cares for all
A friend or other,
Friends aren't supposed to fight
or be a bother,
They're just supposed to be there
Kind of like our Father
Friends are fun to be with
and are always there to talk
Some even help you through
the longest walks, so if you
have a friendship like every
one should, don't let go of them
even if you could!
—*Charlotte Datson*

Broken Promises

Promises made years ago
From the mouth of my beau.
Alas, to him just words.
But I every promise heard.
In faith the marriage vows I took,
Not knowing he lived not by the Book.
Twenty years now have past,
Forsaken, I have grown weary at last.
No faith of a mustard seed,
His life overtaken by the weed
Of selfishness and greed
For a wife and children, no need.
—*Connie Easterly*

"Moonlight Sweetheart"

You're my little moonlight sweetheart
From you dear I never will part

I do not want diamonds or gold
All I want is you dear to hold

You're some one so special to me
The most beautiful I can see

You are always on my mind
I'll want you till the end of time

Tho I can't buy you everything
I can buy one diamond ring

We would have such a wonderful life
If you would be my dear wife

You are an angel to me
Oh sweetheart will you marry me

I love you with all my heart
You pretty moon light sweetheart

You pretty moon light sweetheart
—*Allen E. Enlow*

Our World

Flowers are springing,
Birds are singing,

Water is flowing,
Trees are growing,

As these actions take place can we
Make the world a better place?
—*Suzann Hubbard*

Soul To Soul

Through the woods,
   full moon.
Filtering light,
   between the darkened trees.

In the distance,
   a bonfire.
Piercing the silence,
   a single drum with deep sound.

Closer and closer,
   louder and louder.
Looking to the full moon,
   my heart opens.

Approaching the fire,
   a silhouetted man.
Wildly bearing an African djembe,
   his soul visible,

Fire blazing skyward,
   illumined with the light.
We meet and,
   say hello....again.
—*Bobbi Nesmith*

The Balloon

The balloon bobbed up
   further and further
     a tiny speck.

The brave men
   drifted along the wind
     ballast they threw away.

Higher and higher it floated
   far above the earth.

They sailed into freedom
   the sky was the limit.

On the wind they would go
   where they'd land
     no one would know.

Far off into the cold
   over the gulf stream
     across the ocean blue.

Softly, softly
   they landed in France.
—*Marilyn Vanistendael*

Wonderful Wishes

If you are lonely, I wish you love,
   Gentle and sweet;
If you are gloomy, I would promote,
   Joy complete.
If you are troubled, may you have —
   Peace of soul;
If you are burdened, find ease to reach
   Your goal.
If things are chaotic, please know
   Some quietude;
If all seems forlorn get into a
   Hopeful mood.
If you're in despair, - remember to
   Pray is great;
If life is dismal and dark, light up the
   Candle of faith.
—*Agnes M. Pacholik*

Speak Dear Lord

Speak dear Lord speak to me
Gently keep my trust in thee
And when I kneel down to pray
Give me words that I should say.

May I help a needy soul
Who has wandered from the fold
Of thy grace and righteousness
Find the way to peace and rest.

With a helping hand to lend
To a weary lonely friend
And a word of comfort give
So that for Christ we both shall live.
—*Nellie M. Farrow*

Letting Go

The hands on a clock
go round and round never
stopping, never hearing,
never waiting for things
left behind.

Time is a constant reminder
that things are forever changing
forever moving... Marching on
and on.

You can't stay in one place
forever, you can't hold on to
time... You see it has no
handles and is meant to
pass you by.

So I'm letting go of you
now, all though it's very hard,
I see you have no handles
and you're meant to pass me
by.
—*Renee L. Mack*

We

We are the individuals
God has chosen us to be.
He made the different faces
That we look around and see.

We never stood in line
To choose the color we'd be.
I never had a choice
To be anyone but me.

God did not give us prejudice
Hate reared that ugly head.
Why look for faults in others?
Let's look at ours instead.

Continue as we're going
And it will be our fate,
To become as other lands.
Filled with war and hate.

Don't make an issue of color.
Don't judge your fellowman.
We want no one to suffer
From prejudice in this land.
—*Frances Lunn Odom*

A Ball In The Night Sky

Tonight the moon is full,
Golden and bright;
Romantic paths,
Are filled with lovers;
And children play
Hide n' seek,
Under a moonlit sky;
Whispers and laughter,
Murmurs and giggles;
The moon is a mysterious thing,
Surrounded by it's minions,
The stars;
An omen,
For those who wish it to be;
Or maybe,
Just a pretty,
Ball in the night sky.
—*Carson Relitz*

Gone Away

What once was here has
gone away. There was no
reason we could not stay.
Our love for him was great,
but yet he still went on
his way.

What once we cared for
has gone away. For he
thought there was no reason
left to stay. I guess that
explains why he went away.

What once was here has
chosen not to stay. What
once was here has gone
away.
—*Susan Hayes*

Wisdom To Come

   When I am old and
grandchildren give Christmas boxes
    of lilac talcum
     and I linger alone
among the green and red paper,
    ribbons clutched in my
     brown-veined hands,

     I will know

each segment of life
   repeats
    painful love.
—*Sara Claytor*

Life

  Life, do we take it for
granted?
  Some do
Do we realize the gift
we've been given?
  Some don't
Are we walking down life's long,
and twisted road,
taking our scares and dares?
  Some are
Open you eyes and see
  Life, was meant to be
—*Alyssa Johnson*

Cat

It slinks across the dewy
　　ground,
With each step it makes no
　　sound.
It wears a thin cloak in any
　　weather,
The color of it is a
　　heather.
It feeds mostly upon birds and
　　mice,
And to this animal they taste quite
　　nice.
When it's angry its tail goes
　　swoosh,
Then it might jump in a
　　bush.
It has an independent kind of
　　mind.
Yet in my lap it's very kind.

—*Tamara Fowls*

Beyond The Years

As a tiny baby has no fear, we
　　grow old in spite of the years,
Life is a challenge as it really
　　appears
So let it go gracefully in spite
　　of the tears
Take life as it comes to all of
　　you dears
And we will all reach way
　　"Beyond the Years"

—*Dorothy J. Farmer*

Autumn

Brightest leaves are softly drifting,
Gypsy fall has come at last,
Humbling all the other seasons,
With its flaunting, flaming class.

Air so soft and wind so gentle,
Brings the scent of earth and flower,
Splurging in a last grand gesture,
Of its swiftly waning hour.

Fall is like a rare old vintage,
Making spirits leap like flame,
At its gorgeous glowing beauty,
Gypsy princess, wild, untamed,
But its coming brings a feeling,
Half of gladness, half of pain,
Happiness for its enchantments,
Sadness when its gone again.

—*Bernice Weidler*

Peace Work

The patchwork quilt of humanity
　　Has covered many misdeeds
　　　　and injustices
　　As each generation replaces
　　　　And renews
Patches that weren't well fitted
　　　　Or squared
The guilt of human kindness grows
　　Into a warm beautiful spread
　　　　That covers all mankind
　　　　In a world endeavor
　　　　　　For peace

—*Vivian Moody*

Snowblind

This cruel winter
has hidden all the earth's jewels
and robbed nature
of her healing tools.

Fast asleep is the dandelion
of summer's brilliant yellow hue—
All but forgotten is the smell of grass
in morning dew.

I have long missed the kiss
of gentle spring rain
and must trudge
the disguised, deserted
streets of winter
once again.

Seeking again again the furry green
and red-brown carpet of the forest floor;
I wait in a snowy thicket
just beyond
winter's closed, cold door.

—*Ann Podolski Palmer*

I'll Never Stop Believing

The love you have given me
Has made my heart soar high...
Your love has gently grasped me
Sadness has said goodbye...
Our dreams will become reality
They will come alive...
We will fulfill our fantasies
Together we will strive...
We will take the steps of life
Together...one day at a time...
We will always believe in each other
And never commit a love crime...
I will always be there for you
Through good times and the bad...
We will have many happy times
And also we will have some sad...
Believe in me my love
For my love for you is true...
I promise I'll never stop
Believing solely in you...

—*Nichole Anne Jasper*

Poem For Peace

A world of peace oh would we could,
Have peace and love and brotherhood.
This is God's world, just ours to share.
To keep the peace that is our care.
The pain, the heartache and the strife
Of war and fighting in this life;
The tears from women's eyes once shed
To no avail, their men are dead.
Oh, let men talk and talk yet more.
'Tis better than the cannon's roar.
Let leaders talk from dusk till dawn
And with the coming light of morn,
God's light illuminate their mind
That they may know, the peace to sign
From this day, forever more
Our heads upheld, our spirits soar
God, from you the world we lease:
Let us your tenants live in peace.

—*Eleanor G. Coen*

God's Gift

Have you looked at a flower
Have you looked at a tree
Have you seen all the beauty
God meant you to see
From a small blade of grass
To a cloud in the sky
From a smile on a child
To a bird flying high
It's the beauty around us
Just look and you'll see
It's there for a purpose
As God meant it to be

—*Mary Wood*

Acceptance

My spouse is no longer with me.
He died after a heart attack.
911 brought help quite quickly,
But doctors couldn't bring him back.

Now my life is a void without him,
No longer I see his tender smile
Or the touch of his hand on my elbow
As I mount a step or walk down an aisle

I look at his picture - the tears come
I can hardly believe it's true
That he's gone from this world forever.
But sometime, I must leave it, too.

There must be a purpose for
My staying on earth for awhile.
Perhaps there's someone who needs me
Or maybe I'm still here on trial.

So I'll do my best to "carry on",
Try to live every day with joy,
And ask God to bless each thing I do
'Til Heaven's the end of my story.

—*Doris K. Lepa*

Life

I'm living my life for Jesus, for
he gave his for me. Don't tell
me you've forgotten how he died
at calvary. He carried his own
cross. Shed his blood and died,
and I can just imagine how Mary
stood and cried. You know he was
the perfect one but they killed him any
way. And the blood he shed washed
all our sins away, yes, I'm living
my life for Jesus for he gave his
for me, and I have not forgotten
how he died at calvary. No, I
have not forgotten how he died
for you and me.

—*Jean Lander*

The Day Before April

The day before April,
　　All alone,
　　I walked in the woods,
　　And sat on a stone.

I sat on a broad stone,
　　And sang to the birds,
　　The tune was God's making,
　　But I made the words.

—*Misty Campbell*

Innocents

Eyes of blue, curls of gold.
"Come eat your soup, it's growing cold."
Dark eyes sunk in a tiny face.
No food awaits, no drink, no grace.

Shattered limbs, hanging, bleeding.
Mother's arms outstretched, pleading.
Crying children how can we
Bequeath to you such misery?

Warlords, presidents, poets, priests,
Can't we at the very least,
Sacrifice greed,
For lasting peace.

Dry the tears on each tiny face.
Return childhood to it's rightful place.
Or divide and conquer, then to our sorrow,
Innocence won't live in our near tomorrow.
—*Jessica Whittaker*

Books

A book, a book
Come take a look.
A princess I will be.
But when I see a dragon
I can always be me.
I can be a mermaid,
Sitting on some rocks.
And another book after that
I can be Goldilocks!
I could be a popular kid
And have more than just one friend.
I could be a mean villain,
And lose in the end.
I could visit planets, places galore.
I will always have these thoughts,
As long as I keep reading more and more and
    more!
—*Jessica Farrell*

That World I Know To Please

One knows not one, but two worlds on this earth, that have
    come to be.
A world of war and killing fields, that's not what we shall need,
in the future of those of us who need beauteous trees to breathe,
There comes another world we love, but that we cannot see.
Could that second world be hidden there, beneath the waves
    of seas?
We want that world that better world, for those who need the trees.
But where is that world? I ask, begging on my knees.
Just tell me what has become of it, that world I know to please.
—*Debbie Abu*

You, Marc Nichols

With you I've always had the honor of your trust and open
communication. That trust will probably be tested in the
years to come, but throughout all this I want you to know
that there will never be anything you think about that I
won't be interested in hearing you say. There will never
be any question you can even imagine asking that I won't
want to hear and help with. This is not because I feel I
have to know everything about you, it's because you are the
best friend I have in the whole world. I want to talk,
laugh, cry, struggle, serve, and win with you for the rest
of my life.
—*Wendy Park*

Cocktail Vespers

"Homer, an ancient but articulate Greek once observed..."
Commenced the eristic, nugatory patter
    of a chattering hair-do with leased teeth;
minuscule minnows of deceit danced through the eyes-
    -eyes like dull, dumb, numb thumb tacks.
The speaker's visage was congealed into that pale patina
    of polished mediocrity, geometrically smug
    in it's caricature of energetic intimacy.
The words clattered on in a neon slum of bureaubabble,
    a dialectical chant which belied the listeners'
    patronizing glee at it's self-erasing toxicity.
".....this is an epicenter of insanity
    where the sinuses of history are draining
    due to ideological infections,
    politically deliberate misrecollections and
    the crystalized confusions of Rorschach-Deco blague!
    How is possible for reality to be so lifelike?
    When will history go insane.........................?"
Local, contemporary jitters amid the labyrinthine global
entropy soothed, temporally, by the philistine charm of
cocktail vespers.
—*Adrian V. Brinsley*

Lost Soul

Here is a soul cast upon the swirling churning waters of life completely out of control at the mercy of the wind, rain and snow. Burning in the midday sun, freezing in the midnight cold. Life devoid of fun, has the Devil claimed this soul into the fold? Where did it all begin where will it all end? Is it all because of some big sin? And as we speed through space at this fantastic pace before you blink your eye we have said our hellos and then our goodbyes, Have we lived before? Will we live again? Oh Lord I pray give me a rudder so I will no longer be adrift and with this life there will be no reft, Let me guide my destiny towards happiness and a usefulness upon this earth that I have never had since birth, Let me live this life so good and great that there will be no hate, let this be my fate, To rid the world of blindness to open their eyes to see all of the beauty you have created for them and me, Let there be love so good and true that when this life is through you will say, "let it be, you shall live eternally with me"
—*Walt Bobay*

Perfection

There is beauty in your eyes,
    confidence in your stride,
        strength in your voice
        and comfort in your arms.

    I, an unwilling participate had no choice
        but to fall in love with you.
            I did not ask to.
My heart was not ready to surrender to another,
yet something about you commanded the chains to be broken.
        Fight as I may there is no battle,
you have claimed victory before knowing yourself you would
            desire to.
    You have conquered more than my thoughts,
            more than my love,
        but my dreams as well,
    For I can no longer vision past the perfection of you
        as your presence makes me complete.
—*Susan Castelamare*

Ambiguities

Conflicting messages,
Confusing images
Create doubt, distrust, and deception.

Celebrate with a drink!
Cheers!
But don't drink and drive.
Ambiguous message: to drink or not to drive?

It's a new age,
Experiment.
Express your feelings.
How can it be wrong when it feels so good?
Abstinence?
That's passe.
Go all the way.
But be careful. Have safe sex.

Sexually transmitted diseases, teenage pregnancy,
Products of a new morality.
Love freely,
Love safely,
But remember, AIDS kills!
—*Valerie Knowles Combie*

Brick Salad

Walls of brick. Steps of stone.
Congregations! Lectures! Each - a world their own.

Brick walls softened with green. Books, papers,
those darned typing machines!

Tidy white shirts, follow tidy white walks.
All really lost, an occasional eye-lock.

Chalk dust, the gray hair of rooms.
Knowledge. Wisdom. Funneled in a zoom.

Control of the minds is mindless.
Spoken visions are sightless.

Learning one has to change the future.
Hearing history always repeats itself.

Facing grades that mark the moment.
Results that guide your future.

The agony of defeat. The fear of failure.
Nervous white knuckles take notes.

Brick Salad.
—*Sheri Richardson*

Guilt

Not all my books, nor wise words
Could teach me this, only the years.
Only the years made manifest
That one man's sins are not his alone,
That I, smug and aloof,
Set you on your course with compass fouled
And, unfeeling, watched you toss with storm.

Blame not yourself. Your gravest fault
Was to love without return.
Cherish not my image
And think not, as of old,
That none has ever loved as you.
Love is a fountain,
Not a spring that wells up once.

And if one, unforgiven, can forgive
Think of me as one
Who begs to free, both you and me,
From guilt.
—*Helen Perry Swope*

Memories

The mirror images of the past
Constantly reflecting what didn't last;
Forever recording my everyday life,
Occasionally stabbing me like a knife.

Looking back, what a sight to see,
Totally treasuring what I turned out to be.
It couldn't have been any other way,
Or I wouldn't be the man I am today!

So I value the good and the bad,
I enjoyed the happy, experienced the sad.
I took the joy, I felt the pain
I loved the sun, accepted the rain.

So looking back, I can see
How exactly I turned into me.
These are times to value most,
They have been my lifetime host.

So what may have been, but is no more
Is still around just like before
It has stored itself in a little treasury,
This thing we call our memory!
—*Andy Mavros*

Bird Chatter

Two little birds sat in a tree
Content with the world and really carefree.
They were having a nice bird chat
Chirping and twittering about this and that

Then their chatter took a more serious turn
From them, a lesson we should learn
There's something wrong, what could it be,
Something's surely wrong, you can plainly see.

There's something wrong with the human race
They hardly have time to wash their face.
They're searching for something, I've been told
Something to sluff their old billfold.

Why can't they listen, have they not heard?
Our Father takes care of each little bird,
We know he's near, always close around
And knows when a tiny sparrow falls to the ground.

If only they too would trust him, they would see
He cares for them, the same as for me.
So why do they worry and why do they fret
Our father loves us all, we should never forget"
—*Grace Gunnell*

The Other Side Of Noon

Hey, you, sitting on the wall,
Could you pass that bottle of alcohol?
No, not to me, that's not what I meant -
I want it through the window or over my head.
I like it pouring down my back now, so cooling...
"No, I don't really love you, I was just fooling."
Oh, that's okay, that's what I thought -
The flower from him said, "He loves you not..."
Hey, what's the time? Curfew's coming soon,
I see the sky is at the other side of noon.
I feel the earth is spinning backwards upside down
The phantoms all around me are screaming with no sound
The protest they're enacting is in the nights they live
The questions they are asking are in the looks they give
The dances we are dancing, they make me laugh and scream,
But within each blackened pupil, a hidden teardrop gleams...
Hey, you, sitting on the wall,
Do you even notice that I'm here at all?
Should we leave? Our time will be up soon,
I see the sky is at the other side of noon...
—*Kimberly Lockwood Bowen*

Lies

Permit me to tell you about lies

   For they are evil black sheets,
   Covering the truth.
   They are hideous creatures
   Lurking through your mind,
   Waiting for the right time to come out.
   Though a lie is always uncovered.

Yet the lie I remember most

   Was never found out,
   And now I live with a
   Lie,
   Hanging on my shoulder.
     —*Montine L. Charles*

Our Home

God made the soil and the grass that grows,
Created and put them there.
He colored the sky an indigo blue,
And distilled every breath of air.

He planted the carpet and laid it with grass,
And bade the path gently wind.
He sowed the overall sod with serene,
And the slope with peace of mind.

He made on the hill, forgotten and still,
A clearing sod so well,
There for a man to make his future,
There for a man to dwell.

He covered the land with a blanket of showers,
Which washed and cleansed the air,
And thus I remember our future dream,
When I took my family there.

Then I thanked God for the bounties of heaven,
And promised never to roam,
From the childhood dream I had never forgotten,
Our answered prayer, and our home.
   —*Dorothy Cotter*

The Enlightment Of Yin Moe

Your job is like a pond of which flows from one of life's
   creeks.
Within this pond their are many stones, but of only one I
   speak.
Covered with earth this rock rolled into the shallow end.
Broken shale just crumbling from the hill this rock had
   descend.
Within time the positive cleansing of the water had
   clearly shown.
That this simple rock was a gleaming gem not just a stone.
For when no fear or desire stirs the surface of this pond
   it forms a perfect mirror.
And in its reflection one sees God and creation making life
   a little clearer.
The wise leader knows yielding over comes resistance and
   gentleness melts rigid defence.
So thank you for being the rushing water in which made this
   stone more aware of his inner sense.
   —*Kevin Braga*

Untitled

There are lines here. Straight ones are abundant. A few crooked ones exist. Both narrow and wide lines live and thrive here. Brightly colored ones mostly. And all different shades. No two are alike, so they mix very well. Many cross and make odd colored patches that resemble splashes of emotion. The straight lines never run parallel, but cross over one another repeated times. They usually mix very pretty colors but sometimes the shades become dark and unpleasant to look at. The crooked lines zig-zag over all of the others and they become more noticeable. It is easy to see those brighter colored lines in a picture like this. The more narrow, straight, and lighter colored lines get overlooked. Not really appreciated as they should be. And only if they cross a very bright color and the mix is attention getting are they given recognition. Of course it is only temporary and soon disappears. So they blend back in immediately with the background. It can be fulfilling to help these lines grow. Sometimes longer, maybe wider or brighter. But it is also very nice to know the intricacies of these lines. Because people who walk them are very interesting.
   —*Joy E. Adams*

One Morning

Gloom falls over like a thick blanket,
Cutting off all light.
Making me blind to the outside world.
All alone, desolate, no one in sight.
Like being in a desert,
Thirsty for someone to talk to,
To tell everything.
Someone who will understand,
Not just listen.
My head is filled with so many thoughts,
Rambling through my brain.
I try to grasp a hold of one, just one,
So I can try to unravel the great mystery
Of why this blanket, this cloud,
I can't get off, so I can see,
Just a bit, so maybe then,
Just maybe, I can make my way into that light,
I long for.
   —*Elizabeth D. Stockton*

A Star's Trek

It was a black and a foreboding of grey that tubular cylinder we entered that day. It was very massive without a single seam enveloped all nature and I was in between. There were tens of millions in the place I stood All of us, everyone waiting for something, longing, for something good. There was not a light but,- yet one could see A brighter light came forth as if it had entered me There was a man, but,- how did one get in. He immediately scanned our brain, I felt he was standing in it. He knew that I was worried, he replied, the trip is short Just stand by me child for I have heard your report You must pass through mass a million times denser than space meshing of atoms will alter you matter and mass will embrace He told me how it transpired that I had vanished all night While sifted from cylinder grey I was left with nothing but light. Child I issued your transfer the cylinder is mine. There is no way of leaving you have redeemed all time.
   —*Marshall*

Dancers In The Moonlight

In the pale moonlight, wee fairies
dance in the fragrant lilac bushes.
Velvet roses etch across their faces
dainty, little blushes.
They climb the iris stalks and slide
the satin stems.
They hide in forsythia trumpets and swing
from the swaying limbs.
The moon sends a silver reflection
across their flowing tresses.
The stars reflect the light from their
diamond necklaces.
Dressed in gossamer gowns, they waltz
with dewy pearl drops on their wings,
then fly away with the dawning glow
the morning sunlight brings.
—*Doris Hartsell Brewer*

Down The Street From The Smith's to the Wetherby's

As the first flakes fall,
Dancing in the air,
Turning and twirling
Lace blanket the earth.
Winter's breath shivers a naked tree.
Candled-lit streetlamps decorate the village square.
With a tip of a top hat,
Mr. Jones' frosty exhalation illuminates
As he wishes a crisp "G'd evenin'"
To Ms. McFarrell.
Children race & giggle catching frozen crystals on their
tongues.
The last frolicking flakes lazily drift
To the ground;
They greet the celebrating villagers
As the churchbell's chiming ceases.

I pick up the tiny glass-globed village,
Shake it vigorously.
And watch the midnight flurries
Dance Again.
—*John Freiberger IV*

Queen Of The Spring

Fresh is the vale; verdant the dale;
Dawn in the valley insects the quail.

Lilies in bloom; zephyr's perfume;
Nature, a phoenix, breaks from her tomb.

Bees in the hive, hummingbirds thrives;
Songbirds are singing; all is alive.

Long, long ago, childhood aglow,
Knew I a maiden, fair as the snow.

Diffident, shy; many a sigh;
Silent, my spirit lived in her eye.

Tongue made of stone failed to intone.
Now she is married. I am alone.

Now as my race slackens its pace,
Thoughts of her beauty charm with their grace.

As the birds sing, butterflies wing,
Soars her remembrance, queen of the spring.
—*Daniel Zimmermann*

"To You"

Thoughts of you go through my mind;
Day and night it doesn't matter what time.
I can't express the way that I feel;
But, I can say that it is real.
I know I love you; and this is true;
I just hope, in your heart, you know it too.
For you and I have a lot together;
And this I want to keep forever.
Dear, with you here; my life is full;
And I dearly promise not to be cruel.
I know at times, I am really hard;
But, it's the love we have, I try to guard.
Dear, I hope you can bare with me;
And please don't ever, set me free.
—*Patti Waddle*

Being Me

Boy, I tell you; Life is hard enough.
Dealing with drugs, AIDS, and other such stuff.
And then there's school and peer pressure.
It seems they're all saying "C'mon! Let's get her!"
Handling love and truth and lies
With that crap out there, I'll keep myself inside.
Me, the person, the one that I am.
The little lost soul bottled up in a can.
The can, oh the can, my bold cover-up.
The "me" the world sees, the "me" that sucks.
The "me" that says stupid, shallow things.
The "me" that hurts people, then does it again.
The can's going crazy, trying to control
To keep it bottled up, that little lost soul.
And the soul's going crazy, goin' out of its head
To destroy that can, to slay it dead.
And now you see my struggle within.
Both trying to take over, to control my gem.
The can wants to live, the soul wants to be free.
Boy, I'll tell you; It's not easy being me.
—*Cecily Schuler*

No!

The night was young and so was I, I had no heed or care for deaths. Life was in me ... I was life, I never thought I'd hear her dying breaths. The pity, the agony, the sorrow I felt, the self-loathing that seethed inside, to see her alone in the hospital bed, all for my self-loving pride. The waiting, the unspeakable question: Will she live? The mind full of horrible suggestions. The final analysis had to come, "She's dead, we did what we could to save her." The voices blocked out, everything's blurry, the room's spinning. What's the big hurry?
You must be mistaken, my mother's not dead! She was with me tonight, the laughing, the fun; she told me she loved me, she told me she cared, she can't leave now, her life isn't done.
She had ideas, ways to make everything right. She made me determined. She made me stronger!
Her body was stiff and frozen. So cold, so still, so unforgiving Her eyes stared blankly ahead, God I wish she were still living!
But I heard it and I screamed for her. Because I felt her pain and I felt her everlasting love. So I screamed. I scream for you mother.
—*Rebecca Krefting*

One Enchanted Path

Follow the sound of my voice
And I'll meet you where our two singular ways
become the one enchanted path;
that winds through the forest of always
and along the streams of forever
sharing everything beautiful that life has.
—*J. Vincent Dickens*

Vacation

Lazy, I lie in the nutrient rays of the sun,
Deriding industrious bees in the free-hearted clover;
I shall sip honey tonight in the cool of the moon.
Enchanted, I list to the leaves gaily gossiping over
News of the woods. (I shall bribe them to silence again)
Unhurried, I drift where I will scorning arrows and minutes
Careless of days, unconcerned of finance; and if, when
The spirit shall move I grow tired of rest I may wander
Into a region where living is more arabesque.
Ah, joyful explorer....I'll be glad to get back to my desk.
—*Clara K. Doleman*

The Heritage Of the Fields

The moonbeams fall upon the cottage
Deserted, forsaken, but in memory ingrained
Gone is the laughter, the tears, and the toiling
Only a shell, no soul here remains.

The smoke has vanished from among the pines
Hope and miracles seem long since past.
Wisdom mingled with love and glory
Broken dreams among the shattered glass.

Who spoke of the heritage of the fields?
Providence for certain did exclaim
There is no just cause to harbor dispassion
Are we all but pawns in an eternal game?

This air I breathe is blessed to me
Creation comes from what is not
Rise the sun on a day much brighter
Bring forth which this night is sought.

The fields to me this night lie fallow
The seed of expectation is sown
Restored is life, and faith, and glory
Nothing that leaves is forever gone.
—*Gary T. Muse*

Naphtha

Tears plummet down a waterfall of sorrow,
Despising the thought of no tomorrow.
Yesterday was lightly beaded with grandeur,
Riches of spirit surpass all measure.

Alas, destiny strikes its sweetened pose,
Besieged upon the crest of a tangled rose.
Genteel amounts of porcelain wisdom,
Interlude with a once crystalline kingdom.

Stricken hornets attack the flowery petals of life,
Arousing new levels of torment and strife.
Grey the ghosts that search the soul for morbidity,
Arranged in a spectrum of common indignity.

Retrospective liaisons of malignant visions,
Unspeakable targets of ongoing submissions.
Candy coated residue of incoherent desire,
Outweigh the strength of onerous fire.

Prevalent pearls of primitive positions,
Heighten awareness of lost decisions.
Open the chambers of the inner seed,
Reveal the embryo and watch it bleed.
—*Michael Peters*

Life Is Like

Life is like a river it flows to new adventures
and like a river your life is something special and something
to cherish and never take for granted. A river sparkles with
new life when it is born and when a river dries out you know
that death has come.
—*Amy Petersen*

Of Poetry

A poem is fire winning its beauty in a bright path of
destruction;
   It is leaves that loosen to tumble and fall;
   It is grass fresh and green dipped in dew;
A poem is huge waves crashing against moss covered boulders
    making thunder in the sun;
   It is the mystery of fog now concealing, now revealing;
   It is lightening's jagged streak ripping open the sky;
A poem is night falling, swiftly, quietly,
    stealing light from corners, making shadows lengthen and
blend;
   It is a lover's eyes sparkling with love's surprise;
   It is a mother's soundless singing and a child's rippling
laugh;
A poem is a living hand lifting a lamp to the universe.
—*Harold Paul Donahue*

What Was It Like To Turn Fifty

What was it like to turn fifty
Did the roses take on a sweeter smell...
Did daily tasks become a little easier,
Knowing it's not so important, if you fail...

What was it like to turn fifty, did your children become more
Sociable...Did your friends seem to carry more weight, was the
Twinkle in your partners eye more noticeable...

What was it like to turn fifty, did you start watching baseball
For the game...Did your grandchild become your favorite player,
And did you start carrying an umbrella for the rain...

What was it like to turn fifty, did you recognize more people
In the news... did a party seem to take on a new meaning,
And did your budget start allowing for more dues...

What was it like to turn fifty, did the President seem younger
To you... have the cowboys all turned in their holsters,
And do you spend more time at the zoo...

What was it like to turn fifty, was it the same for you as for
Me... did you feel that life was just beginning,
And you want to see the age of one-o-three...
—*Bernard W. Ingraham*

'Just Like Dad'

He wants to be like his dad! you men
Did you ever think, as you pause,
That the boy who watches your every move
Is building a set of laws?

He's molding a life you're the model for,
And whether it's good or bad,
Depends on the kind of example set
To the boy who'd be like his dad.

Would you have him go everywhere you go?
Have him do just the things you do?
And see everything that your eyes behold,
And woo all the Gods you woo?

When you see the worship that shines in the eyes
Of your lovable little lad?
Could you rest content if he gets his wish
And grows to be like his dad?
—*James L. Curry*

With New Eyes

What hard task-masters we Dickinson scholars all are
Digging into Her past to find the gem—the gold star
Slowing Down and snatching Deep can make us all wise
Look deeply now in "Secret Love" poetry with new eyes

Miss Emily composed three hot letters to Her "Master"
In those five long years of quite poetic passion—
1858-1862—She wrote love poems to "Sam" at Republican
He Squired Her—"Mr Bowles"—She loved Him—revered man

Father was a Congressman who committed Her to Secrecy
"Bio" hypocrisy by any other name is still—Hypocrisy
"Master" for "Mister Sam"—a forward-reversed anagram
Often called Him—Her "Master Bowles"—hidden amalgam

She made acrostics of his name in poem after love poem
"My Splendors, are Menagerie"—spelled out—"My S a M"
Then in "Bronze—and Blaze"—worked in "Bowles" with Bs
Ows—Ws—Ls—ESs—then "dishonored" name—Miss Daisy's Ds.
—*Bill Arnold*

Dust To Dust

When prayers as dry as dust
Discolor Sunday's liturgy
In a network of fine threads
Cobwebs bring our worship to a halt

The declension of our faith begins
With motes, specks, and pauses:
   A web to a filament is bound
   Simple questions are the most profound

When prayers as dry as dust
Abandon us to sackcloth
Whose images pursue us for cruel sport
Threads collapse in nets of dusk
And shadowed webs of maya
To surround us in a chrysalis of nouns

Straw, manger, thorns, a crown,
Moth and rust, dust to dust,
Who am I asks the Shepherd?
For which no simple answer can be found.
—*P. Marguerite Forcier*

Before Anyone Sees

'Do not worship Him,' They say. 'Worship Us.'
'Do not follow Him,' They ask. 'Follow Us.'
'Do not obey Him,' They beg. 'Obey Us.'
'Do not die for Him,' They spit. 'Die for Us.'

And so,
When faced with a choice
Of a leash or a coffin,
Of a gun to kill
Or a gun to kill,
I lift up my head towards the opaque blackness.
Uncertain, yet sure.
I raise my hand to the temple

And shoot.

'Oh, well,' They say, and move on
To the next.
'But hurry up and get rid of this
body,
Before anyone sees.'
—*Michael Price*

Untitled

What are all the assets you have in your account?
  Do the blessings you receive total to a large amount?

You home and health and talents would all be listed there,
  Along with all the comforts that your family have to share.

And next — your liabilities —, obligations that you owe.
  Are there things you should be doing to help someone you know.

When you're checking out the balance in the ledger of your life
  Are things all calm and peaceful or sometimes is there strife?

Do the credits equal debits, as you check back through the the year —
  O'er all the things that happened with those that you hold dear?
—*Mary J. Bomgaars*

"For My Heart Knows Of One"

Who knows about a girl that possesses a love which has no end?
Do you know a girl with which no other can contend?
For my heart knows of one.
Can a woman singular and but one
Dominate your thoughts so that you don't notice the setting of the sun.
For my heart knows of one.
Is there a woman that can listen as well as tell?
And no matter how poor you may feel, to her are always well?
for my heart knows of one.
In all the world's my story and all the world's treasure
Can one find a woman who has beauty that is outer As well as inner?
For my heart knows of one
Yes my heart knows of one
And only one can there be
For, not by coincidence,
The one my heart knows
Belongs completely to me.
—*Michael James McCabe*

Life

When the sun comes up each morning
Do you look for a bright new day?
Or do you spend time thinking and moaning
Of what happened - or what friends might say?

Give strength, and look ahead without fear
Make life worthwhile in the coming year.
Set your mind on a great new goal—
You'll be surprised what it does for your soul.

When Springtime comes
And flowers begin to bloom
Look at the beauty of life around you
And think not once of gloom.
—*Lois Keller*

Hanging Begonia

As I picked the dead leaves from my plant
And cut back the weak branches
That were taking too much strength,
I saw a beautiful blossom that I had to take
  into my home to admire.
And the thought came to me
Is God a gardener too?
—*Diane Burbank*

Killing

What is it that killing does to a man?
Does it destroy his soul or merely chew away at the edges
like a hungry rat?
Does it deaden his senses or cause them to come alive like
a rocket?
Does it cause him anguish or fuel the evil that hides in the
recesses of his mind?
Does it take away his self-respect or strengthen his macho
mannerisms?
Does it cloud his judgment or cause him to see beyond reality
and into truth?
Does it make him an animal or just another creature sucking
on survival?
What is it that killing does to a man?
—*I. S. Parrish*

Sun-Clouded Memories

Sun shine away from the gray
don't cloud my memories
shattered lightning don't strive to strike
the love from my soul
scattered rain refrain from reigning over me
let sacred shelter be found in the shadows of darkness
grant me just this wish
don't let the sun cloud those memories
I can't let go
of the love I've come to know
let me find it in rainbows
—*Mark T. Morris*

Let's Pull Up A Chair

Let's try to face it, let's pull up our chair.
Don't sit up and stare, to each other
Don't shut our eyes, to turn our wondering eyes.
Don't wait for me, I'll wait for you
If you show me' I'll only hold you.
Don't shut up, I'll only get up.
Don't you see, "You see, I see".
I talk to you, you talk to me.
We've seen, they've seen, we all see
You see, we all can be.
You and I, eye to eye.
too see each other, eye to eye
Too only see as One, To Each Other
—*Cynthia D. Buchanan*

Together

   Warm or cold the weather, we'll go hand-in-hand,
down life's road, together.

   Be my shade in the summer sun, keep me warm when
winter comes, side-by-side when day is done, together.

   The warmth, the glow of a fireplace, the candle-
light upon your face, is but a spark to our embrace,
together.

   Just be my strength on a windy day, or when the
storm clouds come our way, remembering to kneel and
pray, together.

   Share days filled with love and cheer, or lend a
shoulder for a tear, we'll walk along together, dear,
side-by-side, and trust the Lord to be our guide,
together.

   After the setting of the sun, we'll bow our heads
when day is done, and thank the Lord that we are one,
together!
—*Verle Elizabeth Davis*

I'm Captain Of The World

I'm captain of the world; up over the mountains,
down through the Valley, I've wandered, roamed, and
sailed. Far and wide across the deep blue sea
North, East, South and West I've been all over this
land. The seven wonders of the world I've seen.
I'm captain of the world

My life is like the lapping of the
Oceans tides, endlessly searching for
the pleasure of the world
Stopping at many distant ports along the
way, meeting and making new friends
Many arms have held me, many lips I've kissed
then I've sailed off again through life's
many stormy seas.
Till again I find a calm in a friendly port.
I'm Captain of the world.

Always knowing in my heart that through
Life's storm there Is a place where the
water's calm and A friendly port is Near in
which to anchor. I'm Captain of the world
—*Raymond Chaput*

Childhood

Her childhood was horrible.
Dreams of it haunted her at night.
Daddy chasing after her,
screaming at her.
There was blood and pain one dreadful night.
The worst part being that there was no one in sight.
Her screams echoed but only in the house.
She fears for her own little girl.
That someday, somehow, it will all return.
—*Shaunna Ferry*

Summer Storm

The deep purple rumbling
Drew me from my heavy summer sleep
Wake up! For it is coming!
The rain crow called
As she flew through the trees
Using the thunder for her bass

Lightening streaking closer
Leading the way for the heavy black clouds
As they boiled across the heavens

Slashing majestically around me
Perfectly orchestrated
The concert had began
The age old play
Seen once more

Rain wept down
The now dark window panes
As if brought to tears
By God's greatest show
As it swept off the stage
—*Sharon Jones*

Believe Yee Me

If truth is the sail on your ship of life
And love is the prevailing winds
All ports your ship enters will be called happiness
And the people you meet there will be called friends.
—*Edward Lehr Clifford*

Photo Negative

Bright green skies
Dull grey misty trees the shining
petals of the Purple man and
    The aging wrinkled flesh of
Spring flowers
   the sun occasionally shows itself
through the photosynthesizing Sky
Spreading its DEEP RED flowing blood across
all that is Above and Through THE blue Clouds
   tinting the glowing world below.
As the White shoots of grass Stand straight
In the Face of the harsh breath of Death
   or is it Life?
Constantly but ever so slowly
growing younger until
   they finally meet
     their Beginning.
     —*Alexander Carreno*

Memorial Day

We gather today to honor the brave,
each have flags to mark their graves.

Husbands, Sons and friends share this hallowed ground,
we pray that peace they have finally found.

The wind through the trees carries a voice,
to defend this country was my choice.

Freedom isn't given, sometimes you must fight,
and in my heart I knew I was right.

When you see Old Glory flying against a blue sky,
remember those who have fought and those who have died.

It is up to you to keep our Nation strong,
don't let anyone tell you that Patriotism is wrong.

In your memory I will always stay,
for you have visited me on Memorial Day.
     —*In Memory of Thomas E. Crofton*

"A Desert Treasure Hunt"

The young folks scatter everywhere
Each intent on his treasure lair
Some are cautious, others bold
Each intent on his hope for gold
They putted about with shouts and cries of
"Look what I found" and with eager eyes
One comes back with a rusted pot
A quick reminder of some miner's lot
A long handled skillet full of holes
No doubt cooked pancakes or panned some gold
Another comes back with a sunglasses frame
Wonder what those eyes saw, was it gold or game
One finds a lovely white stone so pure
Like a bit of natures riches with such allure
Each has a treasure, each a story
Kettles and skillets and stones galore
Now to sit down and assess each one
A story unfolds from everyone
How agile the mind as each child tells
His own little tale of how these fell
Their minds are awakened, their thoughts expressed
A treasure hunt ended but knowledge gained best.
     —*Alice R. Lafleur*

True Peace

True peace is not enforced with a gun.

True peace is when people are able to love
each other, not hate.

True peace is when we can see past the
racial scene.

True peace is when we live in a worldly country
with no crime or riots.

True peace is when parents are not afraid to let
their child play with other children of other
races.

True peace is when there is only one race that is
bent on world peace.

If we can't do this for us, let's do it for our
children.
     —*Jason Surmiller*

An Urge To Push

    It starts as a twinge
      Easy to disregard

  No breathing techniques required

But the nagging itch won't be dismissed

The wondering and wrinkled brow becomes
    a knowing grimace
      This is it
Too late now to change your mind

    The ache takes command
    No longer to be ignored

  Mind-twisting torture follows
'til at last the sweat and gore
  are absorbed by a desperate
     urge to Push

    Ultimately
The only release is in
   the letting go

   And out
bursts a brand new
   verse
     —*Sheri Everts Rogers*

Untitled

Raised all his life for only one reason,
Eaten by mankind from season to season,
He was shoved into a truck, he didn't know why.
Little did he know he was soon to die.

All of a sudden the truck came to a stop.
A big, heavy man lifted the top.
He yanked the cow out, a grim look on his face.
As for sympathy, there was no trace.

Once inside the building all bloody and cold,
The big, heavy man let go of his hold.
He grabbed for his hammer, dirty and dull,
And then smashed the innocent cow right in the skull.

The poor cow was baffled, he did not understand.
The poor cow was killed from the blow of one hand.
He buckled to his knees. One more down.
He could not see any longer and there was no sound.

You think this is sick? You think I am crude?
Look at yourselves, you eat this food.
     —*Julia Maxine Ruskin*

Our Last Long Goodbye

Sipping Italian wine from plastic cups
Eating cheese on crackers in moonlight
Walking alongside the murky brown river
Listening to water slapping rough sides of barges
Staring up at the stars shining brightly
Straining tightly clasped hands together
Breathing shakily fresh gulps of crisp April air
Caressing slowly with wide-remembering eyes
Fearing we will never again touch the wonders of each other
Remembering with our few remaining hours
Thinking in precious moments of 'mountains and valleys"
Sensing incomparable emotions and depths of feeling
Knowing the countless dreams realized and yet unfulfilled
Sharing the remnants of a passing love in
   Our last long goodbye.
Reliving a special memory of a secret love
Coming blindingly from the ages and thence returning
Remaining 'til you and I are side by side together—eternally alone.
Ending, in our last long goodbye.

—*Lynne B. Phoomsathan*

At 55 MPH

Freightliner, Peterbilt, Kenmore, International;
Eighteen wheelers ride the interstate. My cruise
control is set at fifty five. They all pass me by.

Some are towing two trailers. All carry living quarters
for the driver, except those towing two trailers.
Nevertheless, they pass me by.

Most all have wind breakers over the cab,
To deflect headwind breaking on square end of the trailer,
behind. In early morning, eighteen wheelers parked,
In dark, while driver sleeps. I pass by.

Lights, yellow, glow in the dark,
Eighteen wheelers clustered together
In rest stops, exit ramps, on interstates.
But night drivers pass me by.

Drivers wake, start engines, rumble, roar.
Headlights come alive, split the dark.
Slowly begin to move, gather speed.
Left turn signals on as eighteen wheels, pull onto
interstate, gather muscles, go through gear shifts, faster
and faster. At my speed, fifty five, they pass me by.

—*George Bernhard*

Memories

She said, unknowingly
"Eleanor is such a strange girl.
She doesn't have a thing to wear,
But she spends money
On such foolish things.
Only yesterday, she showed me
A pair of Jimmy's first baby shoes
That she must have spent all of forty dollars
To have cast in bronze.—Silly girl."
I could not answer
For my mother heart knew
and understood
That to Eleanor
The memory of tiny baby feet enshrined,
Meant more than the costliest dress.
While to Dorothy
Who wore nothing but "Original Creations,"
Baby shoes were things one cast aside
Like last year's models,
Slightly worn, and no longer useful.

—*Lois Petrykowski*

Time

The cross-road of time cast shadows.
Embracing, cuddling, teasing, and tormenting.
Luring me into a cobweb of lost memories.
Time speaks, I answer. Images appear and fade.
Voices swim before my clouded eyes.
I try to escape to my youth, but it no longer accepts me.
My smile reflects a frown.
I crawl through the bars of my cradle.
Searching for that I do not know.
I'm nobody's lover, wife, or Mother.
I'm twice a child.
Enclosed in the body of age.
Waiting for time to release me.
To heaven, a far better place.

—*Mildred L. Dixon*

Down Casting, The Eyes Of The Perpetrator.

It is torture to be used. I've been neglected, rejected,
emotional bruise... Eager now, to receive physical abuse.
I've been broken before I was ready. I was falling, my stance
unsteady. I received a moments worth of pleasure for a
lifetime of grief. My time in ecstasy was disappointingly
brief. Violated, then forgotten and free... I sigh in mercy's
relief! Why was I the victim of passionate rage? Why was my
protective shield stolen at such an early age? Must I be so
naive? Everyday, I swear to you, lost innocence
will grieve.

I'm not blissful anymore! I've been shun unjustly into society's
whore.
I will change, I say..... this promise I won't ignore. But
first I must confront this manly brute. Tempt him with Eve's
passionate fruit. After I will go insane, I will accuse. I'll
be smiling as I return lover's abuse. I'm haunted, though.
Deep down I will always know what I really am! Weak! And you,
you are to me, forsaken—the damned! But, still, I will love
you. Smile now, and be happy. I am not me, but what you have
molded me to be.

—*Chasiti Puckett*

Liquid Tranquility

Black ribbons cut of emotion,
Emotions better known as pain,
Cut a jagged edge into the desert plains,
of this heart, this place, I can't escape.
Draped in the midnight sky,
Are these memories of you and I.
Liquid tranquility transcending the mind,
Dulling only the surface of my pain,
of my conscience storms and rain.
White lightening illuminates beyond the
liquid blue.
I can see it clearly, just before I slip off
the edge, into subconscience waters.
Fighting the waves of truth that rush over me,
blinding me, wishing it would drowned me.
White lightening flashes again, illuminating
the skies above, waking me to conscience
reality, that I can only dull with liquid tranquility.

—*Lisa Lobeck*

Heavenly

Had there only been more time before
Eternity drew her rigid line
Across our paths, the iron weather
Vane not shifted into the distant
East, the tides receded revealing
Nothing, perhaps we'd have
Learned, by day and by night, to spend the
Years in each other's sheltering peace.

—*Alvin Knox*

Acropolis

The temple still stands at the crest of the hill,
Etched tall and square and pillared
Against the blue Hellenic sky.
Once, arrogant and proud,
It towered above the worshippers
Who climbed the marble steps
And passed between the massive portals
To sacrifice, and to appease their Gods.
Now, ancient and broken and faded with time,
It remains aloof from the lives of those
Who pay to come, to photograph,
To wander through once-sacred halls,
Then, replete with lectures, and with history, depart.

But when Artemis slides across the midnight sky
And drifts thin veils of moonlight
Along the crumbling corridors,
In the shadows one can faintly see
The fluttering folds of long white garments
And hear the whispered tread of sandaled feet!
—*Peggy Sanford Weed*

Alone

Shadows play puppets on walls that I've known
   Ethereal figures of shape without bone
    Spiders of fire that dance on the wall
     I huddle in wonder watching it all

     I didn't see you there,
Watching me wondering distant and bare;
     Alone

   Wonderful images dancing in flame
   Hearth-born or heaven I wonder the same
   Casually breathing the breath of my life
    Truly I feel I know why I'm alive

    I couldn't see you still,
Watching me wondering of my own will;
     Alone

   Is man a creature of wandering will
   Try to stop me; I'll go further still
  if you can't imagine my distance then try-
      To leave me...
      Alone
—*Christopher E. Ballod*

Island In The Sun

The wind blows the sands across the plains,
Even the familiar mountains don't look the same.
My love is far away and I feel the pain,
I hate the wind; I wish it would rain....
When the rain falls it hides the tears.

Distance between us is measured in time,
That island may someday be yours and mine.
People and places in our lives are re-arranged,
The feelings inside out never seem to change....
The nights still seem so empty and long.

All those nights we held one another and felt the songs,
While the bond between us grew so very strong.
You may be far away; but still so close within me,
People say if you turn that love loose and set it free....
If it's meant to be; it will come back to you.

When I'm driving in my car; I remember it all,
The lightening in the sky and our kiss in the rainfall.
I close my eyes and I feel the warmth and the touch,
The fun, laughter and bunches of love that meant so much...
Don't give up on dreams; something special takes time.
—*Laurie Davis*

Untitled

Sometimes depression comes over one
Even tho one has everything under the sun.
Health is good - wealth not bad
Even with all that depression makes one sad.
One loves God and knows he is by one's side.
But life seems like an up hill ride.
Of course, it certainly shouldn't be that way
But ever so often one has that kind of day.
One counts one's blessings and is truly aware
That God is always, always there.
Be that as it may, "depression" comes over one
And one feels like everything is wrong under the sun.
Then one looks up and sees through heaven's door
Lo and behold! "depression" is no more.
—*Clara Jane McDonald*

Korie

Teardrops fall when I think about you
  even though you are only "two"
You're my little niece, so tiny and small
  and look like me most of all
We used to play and have it all
  but that was before I took the fall
By telling your Mommy she was wrong that day
Means we're the ones who have to pay
Now they keep you away and tell you
  I'm bad
Just because they are mad
I hope real soon we can be together again
Cause I sure do miss, my little friend
—*Tracie L. Norton*

Observing Everything

Have you ever wondered why the world goes around? Have you ever wondered why there is violence now? Have you ever wondered or questioned anything? Well, I have because I'm the young observing everything. I was looking out my window of truth. I saw children playing unsupervised, running loose. Not a care in the world, did they possess. That's how the world should be, I guess. I was captured by their sweet innocence. A week ago I walked straight through gang violence. Surprised I'm alive to talk to you, but here I am. Thank God. All gangs are not violent, but this one was. Children walk this way everyday. I've been thinking about my future, through my window of truth. My future looks good, but I don't know about the people who live around me. Some do not understand they can pass the detractions of the neighborhood. A little girl asked, "Why do I always see a book in your hand?" I told her, "Knowledge is the key to her future. Within books you gain knowledge." Now I see her with a book in her hands. Have you ever wondered why the world goes around? Have you wondered why there is violence now? Have you ever wondered or questioned anything? Well, I have because I'm the young observing everything.
—*Yavonda T. Bradley*

Eagle

An eagle is like a nomad, living a solitary life and bearing extreme circumstances.
An eagle is like a brave and bold hunter, killing its prey mercilessly.
An eagle is like a hero, fighting on and on, till death or victory.
An eagle is a rare animal, fascinating mankind with its beauty.
The eagle cries for help, fearing extinction.
—*Luis Pedroza*

Our Questions

Cars with people pass our windows
Every hour without stopping.
Who knows where their journey takes them?
Will they find a place for resting?

Birds fly swiftly past our windows
Seeking shelter in the trees.
Are they guided to their nestings?
Does support come from the breeze?

Clouds float slow across our windows.
Some are white and some are gray.
Will they bring the needed showers?
Does wind and sun chase them away?

When the Moon is full and bright
Through our windows beaming,
Can we comprehend its power
On Earth and Human dreaming?

There is no Waterfall or River
From our windows to behold.
Do they constantly keep flowing?
Questions with answers still untold.
—*Benita Winget Johnson*

In Memory Of William Rene Kampfer

I saw you lying there, so lonely, so cold.
Every minute you lie there I feel myself grow old.
I want to reach out and hold you one last time.
   I want you to know you are still mine.
I stand there watching as they lower your casket
       into the ground...
   ....farther and farther you go down.
   I know you will always be near....
   ....your gentle voice in my ear.
When I think of you my worries go away.
I know I will be with you once again someday...
—*Thea Aneke Kampfer*

The Prize

  I came to you as a friend and soon became your wife, up every mountain and down the valleys always by your side, far enough away so you could make your path, within reach to lend a hand if you had every slipped.
  So easily we fit together, our thoughts they were as one talking to each other without having said a word. Honesty came from you as natural as the dawn, to lie you said would rip apart your soul, you would be no more.
  I must of turned or closed my eyes, for I lost sight of you, the wall you built took to long for me to break away.
  I sensed your troubled mind, the shame and despair, long before I found your footsteps leading to nowhere.
  Placing my feet upon your steps, I went into the dark my love for you so strong that I had to give you light.
  How cold and calculating this mistress of the night, for under every lie you laid she put pieces of your heart.
  The hole she dug for you to share embraced in her arms, only holds your soul that she covered with her web, while above holding her trophy, The Quality of the Man.
    —*Wanda Solland*

Untitled

As if in a cradle he holds me close,
And tells me how he loves me the most,
To sleep at night would be a sin,
If I were not sleeping next to him
    —*Sara Varlie MontBlanc*

Faded Rose

As the day slowly turns to dark
Every star in the sky reminds me of you
Every tear I cry slowly rolls down my cheek
as I think of how we used to be
Together as lovers
The time we shared together will
always be remembered in my heart
Like the two roses all alone,
separated from each other
Slowly they fade and die
Because their love they had for each other
no longer existed, for he loved another
and she loved him with all her heart
But her pain she held back inside
Until she could not take the pain that
he had left her, so she decided to end
her life with the memory of their love together
Now she lives six feet under with a
faded rose planted upon her grave forever
as time goes by the memory will last forever
    —*Kathi Dumich*

Respect - Protect Youth

Our days are numbered in this world.
Everyone should be mindful of the blessings
from above.
Everyone borne a babe everyone passes
through the youth stage.

Slow down and enjoy your young days.
Babe, toddler, intermediate and teenage,
Young adult, full adult, middle age and
if one is blessed to reach senior age -
Our bodies makes many changes.

No matter how many digress obtained
how much life experience gained and earthly possessions
so great one can not name.
All... All is replaced with some aches and
pains, physical and mental change.
So respect - protect youth while you can.
    —*Mattie C. Bolden*

My Love

Sitting with you on the patio, my hand entwined with yours,
Everything so quiet, in this, our out of doors.
Neither of us speaking, just sitting, holding hands
Enjoying each others company, with the passing of times sands.

I wonder what's going through your mind, are there memories so dear? Or are you thinking of the present, what's happening right here. I'll tell you what I'm thinking as I sit really close to you. I think of all the things I wish that I could do for you.

I know I'll never do these things, as time is fleeing by. All I can do is love you more, and I breathe an inaudible sigh. We've had such a good life together, the years have gone by so fast. But I'm caught up with you in the present, even though we've loved the past.

I just enjoy sitting with you, having you here by my side. E'en though I think of times gone by, times when we laughed and we cried. My love, as we grow older, our steps may falter a bit. Always remember, how warm was our love, and that, that flame is still lit.
    —*Raymond M. Wright*

Just Before Breakfast

Then he went into a trance-like state
Evoking words that only he could create
And nothing moved from dusk till dawn
While outside, crickets dove in the lawn
Was it the calm before the storm
Or just anticipation becoming the norm.

In his ears an eerie strumming
Through lost alleys his brain was thumbing
Particles moving faster
Pace could lead to mock disaster
Release the reins and let her run
Down the hill like an angry Hun.

Commitments would soon disturb the stream
Never reaching the intended theme
Only thirty lifetimes to go
The city won't hear the rooster crow.

Seeing what blind men see
Leaning on a bended knee
A simple period he cannot find
Here it comes, the daily grind.
  —*Anthony Eugene Mosher*

Let's Be Friends

Let's educate our minds towards health
    explore
    develop
Reach a life of humble wealth

Let's exchange ideas — some old, some new
    listen
    share
Find what works best for you

Let's design individual ways to cope
    be open
    become aware
Participate with bright hope

Let's live a life that is whole
    join
    harmonize
Watch our love unfold

Let's place your hand in mine
    laugh
    cry
Taste God's precious bread and wine
  —*Susie Fosbrook*

Tari And Sheba Gypsy Angels

Tari and Sheba - wings of golden light
  Eyes like crystal reflecting the sun
Forms - delicate like flowers - touches of
    morning dew
Gypsy Angels always ready for adventure
Fragrance - of purest love radiating from
    them
  Universe of light is there home
With many startian friends - always in
    flight
Tari and Sheba in a ray of light immersed
Beaming beyond time into infinity flight
  Colors expressing infinity of light
  They bowed there heads in silence
To what was given - this ancient garden
    far beyond words
    They dwelled for a while
  —*Manuela R. Lacayo*

Mom

A small lady
  face, beautifully lined with life
hair, curly, gray and silvery where light lingers.

Her movements
  graceful, easy smooth
thought painful arthritis changes the shape of her fingers.

Her lips
  faintly pink, moving slowly
into a smile or words of hope and caring.

Her thoughts
  seem always of others
her material things are for giving and sharing.

Her clothes
  pastels, green and pink and blue
bring out the softness of her smiling eyes.

Her words
  spoken quietly, steady and unwavering
in ways that reveal her fierce family ties.
  —*Hazel Smith*

Family Counseling

Bound by shackles of duty, I mold a deceptive smile across my face, but I cannot maintain the masquerade. Under your scrutiny, trying to squirm away from your harsh gaze. Refusing to let you see those infallible indicators: The evasive watery depths of my eyes. Yet the sea-blue pools are powerless to deny the relentless pull of gravity; even now, the tides of tears rise. Stop interrogating me with your stare, do not hammer me with your Socratic questions. You have already stripped me with your penetrating glare. Each moment is torture, yet I remain calmly. Why do I endure, feigning an anguished grin? There are no shackles binding me. Just the expected duty, my role which I have always fulfilled: Too comfortable a place to leave so abruptly. Dare I face the possible dangers in an unexplored world? For now I remain trapped in my chair with invisible bonds, but wonder…has anyone else ever stood up before?
  —*Laura J. Hester*

Delightful Nightmares

You cannot live without them, they are indispensable
  faith, truth, and destiny to embrace through

Left alone in the middle of nowhere
  wandering around and searching elsewhere.

To know the unknown you must dream. In a sleepless night
  I felt the heat going through me

Helpless, wondering, looking for a new me.
Here my little thoughts get caught
  in a middle of yes or not.

One to share the good in me, the other
  to cut through me.

To myriad places I went
  looking for peace under the tent.
One bright light shining upon me
  strikingly changing the dream in me.

So when I awake from the exhausting voyage
  I felt the adrenaline travelling into
    my blood stream

Very fast beating the speed of the light
  by the average and the mean.
  —*Walid George Harfouche*

Time Alone

The pitter pattering of the pelting rain drops
fall against the dismal girl's fallen face.
She takes a couple steps
toward the cadaverous casket that is closed,
Looking deeper than the Ravishing Red Roses,
she finds her decaying lover's corpse.
Tears trickle and moans cry out
from the heartbroken soul.
Lively spirits use to bounce from within.
Now all that remains are shallow shadows
and Meaningless, Miserable Memories.
As the casket enters the soaked soil,
she can hear the storm that stirs above.
Slowly and surely,
She glides away,
Now knowing that everybody needs some time alone.
—*Marlene Micinski*

Harvest to Harvest

The crops are in for the "92" year,
Fall and winter drawing near.

Its time to start on the "93" crop,
Only snow the field work will stop.

Disk, plow, cultivate, fertilize and rod weed,
Spray whenever needed and weed again before you seed.

Overhaul all equipment when weather is bad,
For breakdowns at harvest time are sad.

As crops ripen the combines start,
Each family member does his part.

Out in the fields we eat a lunch,
A sandwich, fruit and cookies we munch.

Approaching thunder, then rain from the sky,
Do the washing, cleaning and baking while the grain dries.

For the grass, peas, wheat and barley gotten,
The weights and prices are rotten.

Hoping for better crops next year,
But high expenses and low prices we fear.

A years work draws to an end,
Tomorrow we start the cycle all over again.
—*Janet Scoggin*

The Final days

The earth starts to tremble, the landmarks
    fall down,
The innocent victims fall dead upon the ground.

As the moon turns scarlet, and the trumpets
    start to sound,
    Nothing is heard but silence, from everywhere
    around.

He gently picks up every soul, and puts
    them in his hand,

….And reaches to the sky,
    and gives his last command!
—*Becky Cybart*

Beholder

I am a tree, I am the beginning, the beginning of life. I am the beholder of the seed, I watch the birth of the newborn in my very own arms. I feel the movement of the ground. I live, I die, I am dead, I am the beginning.
—*Tonya Saylor*

The Power Of The Cold

Hark; the snow has fallen to the ground
Falling clippings of angels' wings falling round,
    Burying the leaves and providing graves,
        For the fallen Indian braves,
        Then the Season of the Dead reigns,
        And the snow and the cold gains,
        It's the power long awaited,
        As powerful as a largely baited,
        Trap of the Undead; Fated,
            To lie in sorrow,
            But then, on the morrow,
            Spring comes and banishes,
            Winter which soon vanishes.
—*Andrew T. Jensen*

Crying Heart

Loneliness is…
    Falling off your greatest dream
    It's being tossed about in a restless
        stream of cold emptiness
    Standing in a dark room, with all your
        emotions tied to your heart,
        trying desperately to break free
    Its your mind in a suffocating blur
    Loneliness is a crying inside yourself
    Tears that wash away all emotions
        except for one—loneliness,
    It leaves you empty,
    Making you realize things about yourself
    That you knew were true
    But you didn't want to accept
—*Jessica Morse*

Generation Gap

My teenage daughter tells me there's a mysterious generation gap,
far too wide, too cool for me to understand our present day teens.
In this era they're far more modern, up to date and hip it seems,
than us unhip old fogeys were, when we made the scene in our
    teens.

Using drugs, drinking booze wasn't fashionably hip, I don't deny;
Holding each other pledging our love 'neath a lover's moonlit sky,
going to movies, dances, picnics, skinny dipping was our way to
    fly;
this clean fun was what occupied most teenager's of our era's
    minds.

A generation gap? It's a shame they can't visit our era of time.
Though our clothes were different, drugs and booze were taboo,
we knew how to live, have fun, even when we didn't have a dime;
and I'm sure, if they could visit our era they'd have fun too.
—*Betty J. Pieratt*

Feelings

Feelings, I feel like they get caught in the door,
Feelings, I feel like not having them anymore.
I look into the mirror and what do I see?
I see a face of confusion that's the face of me.
Feelings, I wish they would not exist,
Feelings, I could make up a whole list.
It would be a list of pain, sorrow and regret,
Hope that all of these feelings I would forget.
I wake up in the morning with no hope for today.
I go to sleep at night hoping a miracle will come my way.
—*Amber Johnson*

Greeting Cards

Greeting cards are made for you to convey silent thoughts,
feelings, and emotions captured in verse by the poet.
Expressions from the artist showing symbolism in design and
color contribute to choice in selection.
There are greeting cards for all seasons and special days.
You may find it in a card of laughter or one sincere in
anniversaries, birthdays, sympathies, get-wells, announcements,
thank-you's, or many others. Whether a greeting card is
received with a personal gift, a bouquet of flowers
or a postage stamp it is an extended thought from the giver.
When you hear someone's call, in joy or sorrow, share these
hours together with a card.
Miles do not separate us when there are thoughts of love, hope,
or inspiration.
The sunshine you give in the sending or receiving a card will
make an impact on your life and warm your days.
As you become a part of memory lane, cards can be a collector's
choice.
Cards—like the ripples in the brook reflect the thoughts of
the sender and the receiver.
—*Catherine E. Hoilien*

Me And You

   We met many years ago...
Fell in Love, of course, you know

   We set a date, and we married...
Formed the bond, in our hearts we've carried

   We had times, both good and bad...
Always made the best of what we had

   We were doubted by others, from time to time...
Said we'd last no longer than a dime

   We were right and they were wrong...
They didn't realize our love was so strong

   We will always stay together...
There's no storm we couldn't weather

   We have something special, it's true...
You've got me and I've got you!
   —*Nancy S. Hotchkiss*

Being A Chaplain Is Tough!

My first year of being a prison Chaplain,
   Felt heavy and deeper everyday.
Too often I tried to hear everyone's shame...
   Who had slipped from the narrow way.

The first young black man named Mike was so afraid;
   He never dreamed he'd land in prison.
Because of the vast difference in our age,
   He referred to me as being far too staid.
So I worked extra hard to help him discover
   Even in this stinking place, he had a vision.

Moses Tyrone was a slow moving black man.
   Since he had problems with recurring bad dreams,
He had a tough time staying out of the can...
   Still keeping me busy with all of his schemes.

My latest challenge is Paul Anthony - Male -
   Who has lived one fast homosexual life style!
With HIV positive, Lithium, mentally dysfunctional...
   Asking: "Who am I?" But he misses it a mile!

After four years, I see them again and again...
   I often ask: "Will you ever find your Name?"
   —*Chaplain Fred W. Hood*

Dreamers Vision

When you arrive in the land of dreamers' vision and the
Fiery eagle burns the lion's jaw,
You shall not rest!

The dove swallows the serpent who lies writhing in its
Agony as the crimson bell chimes and the black mist sleeps,
And all lies still.

As you hear voices singing softly on and you learn of
Secrets from lovely crimson maidens,
Touch the golden chest!

Multi-colored diamonds spray their mystical lights about you
And love eats your heart while unity devours your body,
And you lend your will.

As you bathe in the lights and peace conquers your being and
Restores your visions,
Give in to what's best!

Screams and laughter fills the void as you plummet -
Down -
Down -
Back to your aging prison of flesh,
And there's still time to learn!
   —*Carsen Furcello*

Blackness

Made of it
Filled with it
Excellent stuff
We've got it
Blackness

Striving against oppression and depression
Breaking the chains that hold
We rise with leaded feet and wings
And glide with the sun in the sky

Blackness, visible yet invisible
Hold it you cannot
Tame it you can't
Too elusive to be chained
Watch it, see it going by
Rising, soaring on its way
Blackness

Free-spirited and brave
Excellent stuff ingrained in us
To make us what we are
Survivors.
   —*Jasmine M. Smith*

Love Conquers All

      Love is like a song,
    flowing peacefully through a heart,
the scales of life go up and down but never do they part.

    Their binding is a strong one,
      love overpowers all,
even being bumpy their relationship will never fall.

      Being close together,
       forever in a life,
even through life's hardships that sometimes cause them strife.

     Lovers through a lifetime,
      lovers through it all,
Always for them, love will conquer all.
   —*Heather Gromko*

Beauty Was The Song

The song shimmered throughout the hall,
filling it with the sensation of all

the artist molded into its form,
using the purity of the vowels to perform

the lyricists' intent,
the legato the composer had lent.

It was connected and liquid in style,
smooth and natural — much like a smile.

The emotion expressed was clearly part
of the involvement and love of her art.

With ease, she'd spin a delicate sound,
reaching to the corners of the theater round.

An intelligent performance yet uncontrived,
controlled and focused but very much alive.

She sang the song; she became the song.
All those who heard would remember it long

as hers alone— a personal flight
that came floating across the stage and the light.
Beauty was the song— that night!

—*Beth Donnelly Feller*

Messy Miracles

Dirty faces and grimy hands,
fingerpaint on walls.
Driving over bicycles,
tripping on footballs.

Dolls with broken arms and legs,
a mountain of toys on the floor.
Melted crayons in the dryer,
sibling rivalry turned to war.

A runny nose and a broken arm,
a toothache, then the flue.
Lost homework and missing socks,
Hey Mommy! Where's my shoe?

Ballet lessons, baseball games,
the band concert in spring.
Bruised elbows and scraped up knees,
endless tears these owies bring.

The sparkling eyes, the innocent smiles,
endless hugs and kisses too.
Mothers could you love anything more
than this miracle made by you?

—*Kandie L. Elsberg*

A Hand Full Of Dreams

Listen to the wind
For it tells stories of the land,
From the snow capped mountains
To the dry desert sand.
It knows of the battles fought
To save it's soul,
Buried the hopes and dreams of the many
Who were lost in the search for silver and gold.
It's dried the tears of the Indian Nation,
And the sweat of the common man's brow.
Memorized every stab of the miners pick,
And the feel of the farmers plow.
Knowledge of the past, present and future
Can be found deep in the heart of the land,
Isn't it amazing how a lifetime of memories
Can simply be held
In the palm of ones hand?

—*Jane Vaughn*

Facets

I hold the gemstone in my hands. Cool and smooth, my fingertips caressing the sharp edges.
I hold it up to the light; I see the textures within. Points of light dancing as the sparkle in your eyes. They tell of happiness at the very core of our heart.
Turning one facet in the light. I see impish good-humor, vivid as a distant star on a summer's night. A twinkle of a smile. Essence of a star sapphire.
From another side I see cloudy opacity. Feelings, dreams, desires unshared or unknown. They wait to take form. To have substance; to dance in the light. Free from fear or uncertainty. The jewel glints as I turn it. Again myriad colors greet my gaze. A few and dark, memories and frustrations past. Most are alive, a plenitude, of shades unfathomable. The colors of the rainbow inhabit this sky with tenderness and warmth. Experience bends over a raw stone. Carefully, lovingly he grinds away imperfections. Every facet slowly cut until the gem shows its dazzling best. You have grown from child to woman-child to woman. Polished by life; every adventure adding the luster of maturity.

—*Jim Lenz*

Remember God And Think

O dear, O dear,
First see that you are a man, a true human being.
For it is only a man
That does anything good
And moves nearer and nearer to God.

Big talks, high positions, popularity,
Even philanthropic works and movements
Are not the true signs of a man.
The true and infallible sign of a man
Is only one!
And that is
"To spontaneously remember God and think."

Therefore, O dear,
Try to remember God and think,
Try to remember God and think,
Try to remember God and think,

—*Ganesh L. Bhirud*

Reality

A concept so ambiguous for the distraught,
Fleeting perceptions of the overwrought;
And who are these people which conflict delights,
The masses who cherish controversial plights.

But what about lives forever changed,
By gossip and rumors usually profane;
Often not accurate or frequently lies,
These innuendoes don't readily die.

"Perception is reality" it is often said,
With little reflection, hesitation or dread;
A position so nefarious it should make blood chill,
Is ironically accepted by many as "God's will."

If reality is an illusion one might conclude,
Man moves through life with little grasp on truth;
If our existence is truly defined by lies,
What is it about life that makes us cry?

Ah, but this is a cynic's view,
For reality is based on truth;
Without truth, what one has is plain,
Perception..... whose purpose is pain.

—*Gary D. Crotty*

If I Could Fly

If I could fly it would be just grand,
flying high above the land.
Over seas and mountains tall, if I could fly, I'd show you all.
Over raging watered seas, across the prairies and through
   the trees.
If I could fly I'd have some fun, in the clouds and around the
   sun.
Above the clouds, fog, and rain, above the hatred, sin, and
   pain.
I've known this was true, though, the question is have you?
I can see the world below, the ice, fog, and the wind, that
   blows.
To earth never shall I return, that is something I won't yearn.
II can see a house's roof, the pitter, patter, of a hoof.
I will fly far away, and there is where I shall stay.
If you travel far and near, you will find me right here.
In your dreams I will stay, every night and every day.
So I must go and roam, to my house, my humble home.
Among the breath of my final sigh, I bid you all a loving
good-bye.

   —*Thomas Maher*

Indian Man

Silently the indian man raises his bow and arrow,
Focusing on the kill, a deer,
It will supply food enough for his family.
The arrow is released, the deer dead.
Suddenly a shot is heard,
The indian man falls to the ground.
Dead, shot in the back, the indian man lies.
A soldier stands over him grinning,
Grinning with prejudice and hate.
Bountiful with ignorance,
He kicks dirt onto the indian man.
And walks away living up the joy of his stupidity.
He walks blissfully over to the deer,
His knife out, ready to take choice cuts back to
   the rest of the unit.
Abandoning the remains to rot along with the
   indian man.

   —*Josephine Jean VanDam*

Red Barn

O barn ye barn O barn of might
For all of those who come in sight
For travelers, alone alight
Or hide aways from nature's plight.
O timbers high, O timbers low
O neigh of horses years ago
Perhaps a hundred perhaps more
Yet nigh a score before.
I sometime wander, sometimes dream
Yet I within thy walls do seem, a stranger
Seeking in vain, the past, present, future to retain.
For roofs that leek
For doors that creek
For moths that seek
Your shadows creep
And on thy hearths that burn
The logs that centuries turned.
O moon that shines through window pane, sees you in vain
O moon that tells the story of those who dwell.

   —*Marie F. Lupienski*

God's Miracles

I praise the Lord each day that I live,
for all the wonders that He gives.
From the miracle of birth, as He placed me
upon this earth, I have marveled, each day
at His work.

I smell the fragrance of the rose and gently
touch each petal as it's beauty unfolds.
I hear the birds, as they sing overhead -
ever trusting in His care.
I feel the wind against my face, the rain
that falls as the flowers patiently wait.
The sun warms me by day and at night the
moon lights my way.
I feel His presence ever so near as I
contemplate His miracles everywhere.

   —*Doris K. Cervenka*

Thank You

Thank You, dear Lord, for autumn gold,
For beauty bright in colors bold,
For bluest heaven stretching high,
For the endless starry sky!

We thank you, Lord, for meadows green,
For fragrant flowers to be seen,
For mountains high with snow-capped peaks,
For sparkling, singing little creeks.

We're thankful for the ocean wide,
The restless waves of ebb and tide,
The juicy fruits, the berries red,
And mushrooms on the mossy bed.

God made this world a lovely place,
A testimony of his grace.
And God made us - both you and me
His crowning glory here to be.

   —*Svea Kanna*

The Peace Treaty

Why can't we deter the nuclear bomb?
For I won't fight in another 'Nam.
I'm young, bright, and have years ahead,
But I can't create, if I'm dead.

Please stop this madness, and save us kids.
Let's close up war with impenetrable lids!
I love peace, and I know you will;
so devise a way to pass "The Bill"!

A bill for all the world to see-
A bill that is a Peace Treaty!
One that states, " Farewell to war-
This we declare is a New World Law"!

For I know that all children wish, as I,
For the time to come, when war will die.
We demand peace in our day—
Not in sometime, that is far away.

So come earth's elders—see our worth.
Stop nuclear warfare for peace on earth!
Then we all may live in a world that's free—
A world of hope and harmony!

   —*Jamie Levy*

Helen

A very special tribute, goes out to my wife
For quite some time now, you've been a part of my life

You've been a great mother, also a great wife
So relax and be happy, enjoy the rest of your life

Our family is grown now, and we're all alone
So our love for each other, should be stronger than stone

Remember all the laughter, forget about the tears
We've had some of both, being together these years

Honey I love you, it seems hard to say
But I hope I can show you, in my own little way

That my love for you, is greater by far
Than the distance from earth, to the farthest star

The tears that you've shed, they weren't meant to be
I've made some mistakes, but I'm only human you see

And if before you, this life I depart
Keep a very special place, for me in your heart

And if you're feeling down, or you feel all alone
Take a minute to read, and enjoy this special poem
—*Ellsworth M. Becker*

Down To The Divine

Alone among my vegetables I have wished
for ribbons. Not the kind to hold organdy caps
but those brilliant strips of apple butter gold
the English women wear. Red
beets and cucumbers quiet me down
to the divine, our small dignity,
for I know that news is of the devil
and that only pilgrims kissed by the Holy stay old.
We hold ourselves against white-washed
fences, build barns for summer praying
and the strength of our charter.
Soon I will jar my fruit for cold weather,
sell it to the Others. This is as far as I go.
—*Reid Cottingham*

Reincarnation

They say the past can't live again, but I have doubt to spare.
For sometimes "darkly through a glass" I see my mother's
spirit there.

A man so tall and handsome, strong yet gentle in his ways.
He has her loving, giving heart and makes a gladness for my days.

For now I know her soul lives on; within another form, tis
true, but joyously, with such a grace;
she lives again, my son, in you.
—*Marilyn Wasson*

Plea To The Wind

Blow wind we plea with all our might,
for without you
we cannot take flight.
We cannot dance high in the sky, if you don't lift us
from this ground where we lie,
We cannot caress the soft white cloud, when we are
forced to stay on this grassy mound,
Nor with the eagle will we soar way up high, because you
have continued to pass us on by,
So blow mighty wind, hear our pleas, we need you to
escort us high above the trees.
—*Sue Scott*

Behold The Line

Behold the line of an artist's dismay
for the abstract expressionist is here to stay.
It's just squiggly lines of emotion and thought,
But except to the artist, it really means naught.

I'm an artist and a poet-as if you couldn't guess—
inhibited by the line of the abstract expressionist.
In college I'm learning to follow Pollock's cue
when he said-so what if children can do this, can you?

No—I scream as my grade falls below F.
Will my life be better as an abstract expressionist?
But what is in this art I despise?
A lot—I am told, which is really a surprise.

Abstractions are beginning to get my applause
since I have now made lines with shoestrings and straws.
Texture—they call it, and that's how it looks.
I never learned this type of art from books.

Behold the line of linear genius
for I realize maybe it's not just meaningless.
Patience may yet grant me a mind for abstraction,
but until then I will leave the lines to Jackson.
—*Susan Nordman*

My Real Father And Me

How long, oh, how long will this heart bleed
for the caring of parents it desperately needs?
The answer's unknown as to why I am here-
yet, I hear others say - "Just be of good cheer."

"You have much to be thankful, you've all that you need"—
so why, then, oh, why does this heart still bleed?

Only one really cares and knows the unknown.
Oh, what will I be when I'm fully grown?
Or will I grow up though I desperately try?
Will I race to the end or give up with a sigh?

No! I'll not give up though sometimes I'm quite bothered
by the thought of not having a real mother and father.
But - why should I worry, oh, why should I fret?
Come to think of it - I have the best father yet!

My father is caring, loving, forgiving—
he's my reason for laughing, for singing, just living!
My aim is to grow as he wants me to be.
From now on, it will be my real father and me.

Why, then, oh, why should my weary heart bleed?
For, I have the real father I so desperately need.
—*Rhae Lynn Cowan*

The Power Of Heart And Eye

The eye cannot see what the heart can see
for the heart endures the pain.
The eye can see through a cloud of rain,
but the heart through a dim mist of hate.
The fate of a being looking through the eye
has yet to see the joy,
of the hearts and souls
of many untold
who discovered the secrets of life.
—*Lowell Sorenson*

A Trip To The Beach

Laying there barely conscious,
For the hot, heavy rays of deep, bright sunlight
  are absorbed relentlessly by my weighted body.

Yet, for all the dead calm and tranquillity felt,
  the crashing, thunderous,

Lapping sounds compel me on with burning quick steps
  to the cold, icy, splashing wetness.

With numb toes and chilled thighs, I swish and sway and sink
  till all submerged.

With stinging eyes and swooshing ears, my hair floats up
  and, I am one with eternal life.

To spring up and feel the warmth, the spray of diamonds fall
  about.

Laughter fills the sky with sound and salty lips are tasted
  now.

To be all this and slip into the enticing waves...
  ever moving.. rolling... till all of life is gone.

With heavy heart and purple lips, I leave behind a part of me
  from younger days.

    —*Francine Infortunio*

"Don't Wish Your Love Away"

    Don't wish your love in the stars,
    For the stars may fall from the sky
      Don't wish love in the night,
      For the night will soon be gone
And don't wish your love in the flower, with love,
    For the flower will one day die.
    Don't wish your love in the future,
    For the future will start and end like a song
    And don't wish your love in the past,
    For the past has already gone.

Don't wish your love in the little things of everyday
    But wish your love in the heart
      For the heart is the start
      Of the only love that stays
      And for without the heart
      You're wishing your love away.

    —*Timothy Scott Clapp*

"Good News"

It's not the first Christmas, anymore,
For there have been almost 2,000 more!
But, He's still the same Jesus we adore,
He's just not a baby like before.

No longer wrapped in swaddling clothes,
Or a tiny infant with little pink toes.
A man among men He's long since been!
But, His memory does not grow dim.

He's lived and died and, lives forever more!
Knowing Him could never be a bore.
By the time this story filtered down to me,
It was close to the completion of His-story!

Ah, this story indeed is very, very old,
But I'm sorry to say, to some still not told.
As again we celebrate a Birthday with Him,
Let's release the strong holds, that keep us so grim!

The love and joy and new life He gives,
Let us reflect in the lives we live.
No better present could any of us give,
Than to share the Good News—Our Jesus lives!!!

    —*Carlena*

The Path Of Life

The road of life is not a straight path
For we are often at the mercy of the weather's wrath

Who said it would be easy to pick and choose
Make the wrong choice in the game of life...and loose

To sit by the stream and watch the river flow
Is like looking in the mirror and watching you grow

Swiftly the current flows down stream
As years in your life pass like a dream
Was it so long ago a child was born?
Am I so old that my skin looks worn?
Do you yearn for what was? Do I sit and morn?
Do I sit and sigh and look forlorn?
No—life's to live and to live I must, for it is in God
that I place my trust.
When the road of life gets narrow and rocky
Stand straight and tall — travel it with moxy
Don't doubt yourself or give into despair
Hold your head tall and feel the crisp air
For only you choose the cloak in life you wear
And your choice alone makes the game fair.

    —*Fritzie Hagan*

Why?

Do you ever think what this world this world will be
for your children's children. Do you ever
think that maybe there won't be a world
for your children's children. Well think
about it because if we keep polluting
this world, that's what's going to happen.

I lay in bed wondering how it will be for my
children in the years to follow, I think
what my parents, grandparents, and ancestors
did to this world we will pay for. I know
one person can't do nothing compared
to 100 million people but one person can
do more than none at all, so next time
you're laying in bed thinking about how
awful this world is. Think, you're one
of them who pollute it.

    —*Nicole Strunk*

Remembering

If I should speak a word of truth...I'd say it with your name
For you're the only love I know...though I live my life in
vain. You once did bring me happiness...but now my side
you've left, and I will never forget...the love you taught me best.

You used to hold me close to you...and keep me safe from harm
But now you've gone...and set me free...I don't now where to
turn for you're the only one I want...and for your love I
will yearn. I will pray to God each night...to keep you safe
from harm, and someday He will bring you back...right into my
arms.

Our meetings were brief...but oh so sweet
Each week-end remembered...was a blissful treat
Your face so far...your voice so near
And in my heart...your voice...I will always hear.

I remember your smile...your cheeks so lovely and red
I remember all the nice things...you've ever said.
I remember your mood...which was never blue
But most of all...I remember a very beautiful lady...you.

    —*Eleanor Puskar*

A New Coming

As I look yonder past the clouds of nebulous, I see the formation of the future to come.
It seems bleak, with the red clouds in the sky.
The man on top of the summit overlooking the valley looks at his watch.
He notices that decades have passed without a blink of the eye.
Cities are growing, babies born, but no one notices that the world is shedding its first tear.
That tear is filled with the memory of past wars, deaths of martyrs, and accomplishments to fill the times of sand.
The man walks slowly down the summit embracing that hard, but tender substance like it were a new born.
Upon reaching the bottom he is awaited by Alexandria.
The knowledge the beauty the mystery.
Their embrace can be felt through the soul of every living creature.
Their kiss seals the destiny of the world, as the tear is wiped off and the future sees tomorrow.
—*Carlos Zeisel*

From Anaheim To Fond Du Lac

They made it official in April of Eighty-six
Frances and Margaret were coming back to the sticks!
At this wonderful news we were filled with elation
Our minds were a-whirl in anticipation -
We began to take stock from our heads to our toes, and our
Collective blood pressures rose. To our kith and kin, after
Many a year, with all of our faults, how would we appear?
With our double chins, pot bellies, limps, halitosis
Bridge-work, capsules, pills and neurosis,
Bunions, hearing aids, corns and shingles,
Piles and pneumonia and toes that tingle.
We consulted our barbers, doctors, and friends,
But our mirrors told us we were around the bend.
When Margaret and Frances arrived for their visit
We were all amazed, how could we have missed it?
They were tired and weary, and saw not our flaws
Guess the Lord drew a veil to cover the years.
But it couldn't conceal the spark that was kindled
And eyeball to eyeball, we all shed some tears
And were soon deep in happiness up to our ears.
—*Emma Reinhardt*

Untitled

The passing of a sun's waken dew. The end of an afternoon's frightened hurry. The eternity of the moon's effervescent glimmer. This day in my life I've spent… I've traded it away for a memory, I wonder.. Have I been too thrifty or was it too lavish? This day I'll never have again to spend for a moment. Memories reign eternal— Moments are fleeting. Capture a handful of memories…. and your palm is filled with a lifetime. Chase a moment to hold and ponder and your palm is forever empty. Odd isn't it that our love should have the elusiveness of a moment, but the infinity of a memory? Nothing is lost or mis-spent. Each moment we exchange for a memory. Each memory is an investment on a lifetime. A lifetime of the sun's morning dew…the afternoon's frightened hurry…
and the moon's effervescent glimmer. And days well spent just loving you.
—*Yvonne R. Conkling*

An Awakening

God woke me up in the middle of the night
From a sound and peaceful sleep.
He said, "I really need to talk to you,
And what I have to say won't keep.
I am sorely disappointed,
And a little bit surprised
You have become so quick to anger
When others criticize.
You must have patience and understanding
For you will always find it so
That some have to put others down
To build their own ego.
Oh, if they would stop and think
There would be extra stars in their crown,
If they would only start to build
Rather than tear down.
So will you work toward being an example
So that others might see
When you lift a fallen spirit…
You are doing this for me?"
—*Vona Ann White*

Nature's Bounty

From tiny sparrow eggs to the magnificent eagle in flight
From a wiggly tadpole to a mossy old bullfrog croaking in the night,

A spotted baby fawn lies silently in the sheltering trees
Going unnoticed by its enemies,

Furry bobcat kittens play and tumble while mother is away
Silvery fish and the wood duck swim aimlessly in the inland bay,

All these things—both great and small—are ours to behold
Invaluable and priceless - their riches untold,

Keeping God's creatures dear and free is our goal
Herein lies our heritage and the beauty of our soul,

As the great eagle soars in his unending sky
Let our glad hearts be with him forever high.
—*Jayne J. Smith*

The Splendor Of Spring

When April makes her entrance
   From a winter of deadly gray
She is gowned in pastel colors
   Waving to all who look her way.

The tulips on their willowy stems,
   Lilacs swaying in the breeze,
Dogwood blossoms of pink and white
   And birds soaring high above the trees.

The daffodils of lemon yellow,
   Hyacinths with their heavy scent;
Let us be ever grateful to our Lord
   For all this beauty he has sent.

He has dressed the trees in emerald green
   To shade us through the day
Casting sun through leaves like diamonds
   Brightening each step along our way.

He has placed a carpet beneath our feet
   Making each burden lighter to bear,
While high in the sky billowy clouds drift by
   On a blue background beyond compare.
—*Ruth Tirri*

A Cricket Team

Preysal is the glamour team,
from Central Trinidad burning steam.
It all started with Zahir Baksh,
who got things going from scratch.
From Inshan, Theo, Giles and Rangy,
They won matches all over the Country.
Central Cricketers are fortunate,
to Inshan Ali, who opened the gate.
Rangy Nanan played one Test,
But as an Off-Spinner he was the best.
Theo Cuffy was a great Captain,
Led by example with his batting.
From near and far they all came by,
To see Giles Antoine let it fly.
Nirmal Nanan who played County Cricket,
Scored heavily every time at the wicket.
Eugene Antoine is the latest in the land,
To play League Cricket in England.
I love this team, I love it bad,
More than any other in Trinidad.
— *Anzard Phundar*

Beauty

Scenes of beauty caress my soul longing to be free,
From mountain sides with snow covered trees to the mesmerizing sun.
From desolate beaches in the dead of winter and the setting of the sun,
To the speckled sky in the deep dark night once it has begun.
From the cloudy days with downpouring rains and the sounds of distant thunder,
To the fog filled nights that are all aglow, the ones that makes you wonder.
Scenes of beauty caress my soul longing to be free,
Striving, pushing, banging down the walls inside of me,
And now they are free, free at last, no more are they all confined,
The scenes of beauty that caressed my soul are no longer in my mind.
— *Joseph Rainone Jr.*

Real To Irate

I find myself erratically changing
From real to irate.
Safe to dangerous.
Contentment becomes frustration,
Guaranteeing another harsh and sleepless night.

Finding new methods of self-abuse;
For reasons I'll never understand in this lifetime.

I keep asking myself;
Where do I go now?
Where do I go with all this mystery and knowledge?
Where do I go with all my extremities, sorrow,
And anger?

I crawl back into my solitude,
Back into the depths of my sacred tavern.
Not caring if I ever see another tomorrow,
Just wanting desperately to end today.

I look out my window and curse another sunrise.
One more passed night of useless panic.
— *Jason Butler*

Story Teller

A dream like stillness fell over her, things would fade from sight.
Shadows made from soft moon light.
All around there was a stillness in the night.
Her voice would weave a spell when she had a story to tell.
Because it was her favorite she knew it so well.
I sat listening, enthralled, my heart pounding.
So eager to hear, did I remember to breathe, with my mind racing and bounding?
When she would start a rhythm would invade her soul,
the words would roll out, coming from her heart for all to know.
Words that told about our past, trying to keep the years alive.
It's the only way for our heritage to survive!
No matter how young the story, the words are old as time.
They are meant to find a place in your heart and mine.
If you don't listen and remember, if you chose to spurn,
what stories will you tell when it's your turn?
— *Bonnie Sue Beard*

Go With It

The world is filled with so many things.
From summer to fall, from winter to spring.
Footprints in the sand at the beach.
Biting into a fresh, fuzzy peach.
Learning how our world came about.
Fishing in a river squirming with trout.
Just open your eyes, look around and see,
The ocean, the flowers, the bushes, the trees.
Put your faith in books, put your knowledge to the test.
Finding whether you finished last, or if you are truly one of the best.
All that you want can, one day, be yours.
Opportunity knocks, just open the door.
— *Whitney Hix Padden*

Girl Talk

It seems like we're miles away
from talks we had of boys
We used to laugh at them,
"How silly they are," we'd say
or we might be attracted to one
and watch him from afar,
until together, and able to whisper
and exchange tales of how we saw "Him"
Your "him" was different from mine,
but they were the same stories
"He said `Hi'today," I'd say
"Could you just die?"
Bonded by our frequent crushes,
we could talk for hours about them,
their tiniest remarks sparked speeches between us
We'd take long walks that outlasted our talks
but the silence spoke too, with our thoughts
Now, with gold and cold, hard stone,
I am alone
— *Antonia Knobbe*

Everything

The world is my playground,
As far as the eye can see,
I walk toward the edge of the world,
But it continues farther ahead of me.
I wonder if I'll reach the end of the world,
Before the end of the world reaches me.
— *Brenda Mintle*

The Ancient One

The winter sun shines bravely
From the milky blue white sky,
Pale, watery, glaring light,
Devoid of warmth.

Long years ago fields stretched away
Where buildings crowd around.
Dense forests filled the space
Beyond his sight.
Today no wild things lurk
Just out of touch,
No wild things
Except his fellow human beings!

The ancient warrior sadly shakes his head.
The changes he has witnessed weigh upon him
Like the weight of all the centuries of time,
Too deep to contemplate directly,
Too overwhelming to ignore.

—Betty Stevens

The Value Of A Mother

A portal into the light of day
From the nesting place tucked away
Under the shadow of her wing
A Mother designed for new life to bring

Strong hands put daily to the task
Listening ears that hear all questions asked
Lips that touch each painful hurt
A Mother provides refuge, at the hem of her skirt

Feet that are swift to bring comfort and correction
Arms filled with hugs, that provide help and protection
Eyes that see from the back of her head
Mothers always know what you've done or you've said

A heart that can hold all the love that's required
To nurture the soul 'til the dreams desired
Have been fulfilled in her little ones lives
A Mother, for their good, continually strives

Without them the world would cease to be
From statesman, to plowman, they all sit on the knee
Of a mentor, a guide, a wiseman indeed
'Tis a Mother whose value none will ever exceed

—H. Elizabeth Woessner

"From The Womb To The Tomb"

I heard my daughter, Kathy's first cries of joy
from the womb.
Thirty-eight years later, I heard her cries
of terror to the tomb.
We, her family were poor, but had lots of love.
The kind of love that can only come from above.
As attorney and judge, she set an example.
Her honesty and righteousness were certainly ample.
She studied and worked hard far her career.
Yet for all who had trouble, she still lent an ear.
She called me in the night for help which was too late.
she instantly entered the white pearly gate.
She is now without trouble and sorrow galore.
I would have her back in her turmoil no more.
Through trials and tribulation that she surely bore.
Crime, drugs and injustice she did abhor.
Thank God for her son, whom she does favor.
Every moment with him I certainly savour.
Without her, forever will never be the same.
I pray each day for strength and courage in the Lord's name.

—Barbara G. Wigley

Four Seasons

In the winter time seems to be standing still
Frozen droplets of water make up the land fill
Animals are hidden way deep in their burroughs
Making sure they get their rest to the very thorough

Springs is when the nature starts to come alive
With sun and rain all the vegetation will survive
The smell of freshness just seems to be everywhere
And the beautiful colors, nothing else can compare

During the summertime there's a lot of commotion
If the weather permits, it can bring on promotion
For barbeques, get togethers, and drinking fools
Don't forget all the people having fun in the pools

Fall is when busy bees go back to school daze
The leaves on the trees turn colors and fall many ways
People close windows and bundle up for the change to occur
Because they all know that winter is coming for sure

—Mathew A. Tallman

"Silence At The Seaside"

The wind whipped furiously through her hair, as she stood,
gazing quietly, thoughtfully out at the ocean.
Waves crashed wildly around her
as the tide flung itself at the shore,
the attempt, all in vain as it was swept away
to where it had begun.
The silver moon, with its friendly smiling face,
gladly flung down its bright beams,
sharing its beauty with her.
A lone gull twirled around above her
in the brilliant, star lit sky,
and cried one forlorn note before winging away.
She stood alone once again
with only the heavy crashing waves for company.
She would end her life alone,
as she had always felt living it.
She began walking slowly into the freezing grey waves
until the lead colored water was up to her nose.
The last sight for her dying eyes was the twinkling sky,
the only sight which had brought her pleasure in her life.

—Erin Aloan

Forget-Me-Not

A little flower
gentle and lovely grows inside my heart.
Blooms every year, despite storm and rain.
And the sun gives my little flower her most beautiful smiles.
She is there, still and quiet,
with her warm and loving peace.
I hear her soothing songs when sadness and loneliness
is tearing my heart apart.
I can feel all the hate in the world disappear when
the wind is softly whispering her name in my ear.
She can never die, as long as I keep her in my heart.
She will never leave me, as long as God writes
her name into my soul.
She will always bloom, and her blossoms will
always spread the scent of love and peace
here and everywhere.
Wherever the way of life will take me,
through darkness or through light.
My sweet and beloved little flower will always be by my side.
Diana my Forget-me not.

—Heidrun M. Arment

Presence: Molana-al-Moazam Hazrat Salaheddin Ali Nader Shah Angha

    A delicate tenderness
      gently permeates
        the quiet bliss
of the Divine Cup-Bearer's wine.

    Flowing outward
      from heart center,
  a subtle, strong softness
of child-like, gentle, melting wonder.

    Bars disintegrate,
      boundaries fade,
        the locked door opens
to freedom's release from earthly bonds.

    Light illuminates
      the hidden treasure,
        softly shimmering,
the priceless pearl of truth.

    —*Lynn Wilcox*

The Storm Of Life

Please God show me the way, help and guide me through this day.
Give me the strength I need a new, give me the courage to
see it through.
Help me to set my life aright, give me the faith and show
me the light.
Pilot me, guide me, I beg of thee as I am one in a raging sea.
Ease my torment, free my mind, give me the solace I need
to find.
Show me the course I need to chart to reach those calm waters
and love impart.
My life has been one tumultuous sea raging for years to my
destiny.
With conflicts tearing at my heart, the waves engulf and
the course is dark.
My mind is torn with every roll and the years lap away life and
take its toll.
The harbor of happiness I seek but my ship seems bound for the
barrier reef.
So God, I beg you to take over the helm, steady my hand, calm
my mind. Pilot me to A SOUND peace of mind

    —*Norma L. Jones*

Of Mad Dogs And Thunderbirds

Electrocuted urine
glistens in broken lamplight

shreds of shades
drift
over tattered asphalt

swaddled in newsprint
sucked by dumpsters

won't spend your dime on coffee
just a nickel away from screwcap oblivion

    —*Jay Ferrari*

"Parts"

When young, we believe we are completely whole,
    But we learn we are parts,
        As we grow old.
It is best to examine all of your parts,
      And find your soul,
        it outlives your heart.

    —*James F. Cross*

Within These Walls

What do you know you school walls that enter each classroom and go down each hall? You stand each day from morning 'til night from day to day from light to light. What have you learned over these many years? Have you learned laughter? Have you heard tears? The monotonous buzz of students at work. The shrill cheering and clapping as the class goes beserk—over some small favor given or award that's been won. And then, dreadful silence when everyone's gone. What have you learned? That life's a constant flow of people, of children who come and who go - to other halls and walls in other schools and rooms, to other places in which their future looms. You are silent now but I have heard whispers in this vacant place. I've heard strange echoes call gently through space. Once a beacon, you stand in decay, empty and lonely and in disarray. Right now all I hear is the sound of my feet, but I feel your heart and it's very beat. You stand as a testament, a product of time in a world ever- changing and out of it's mind. Will we learn the lesson that you teach, dear walls? That no matter what happens: Stand strong and stand tall?

    —*Judy M. Graf*

Love

I heard a little bird
Go "Tweet, tweet, tweet,"
As if to say, "At last I am heard."
She took to wing
And flew round and round.
She barely made a single sound
Until she came to a big high hill,
And flew about it very very still.
Then she sat on a thorny bramble bush
By the side of the rocky dusty road.
She flapped her tiny tiny wings
And this is what I thought I heard,
"God is love.
God's love is agape love.
Only that love is worth striving for.
Because God's love for Creatures on land and sea.
Even, takes care of sparrows like me."

    —*C. Marguerite Klein*

Dominance And Death

Father
   God banished Adam and Eve, a wondrous team.
Since then this "Inca" chief demands the death of us
each-together with the Holy Innocents, His only Son and
twelve followers in particular. Only his mother got away
mercifully, clean is the assumption.

Son
   From Christ who shared the throne with us in
Person, we learn. We learn of a loving and merciful God! But
had Eve obeyed, would we be knowing Christ, or simply the
wonder of Creation?

And apple pie!
   We celebrate fear drifting away in church
acknowledging ever so wisely: God and men are not to be
obeyed. God, man, and women is a trinity-like sharing - "unto
death do us part" largely eliminated. Take a bite of love!

    —*Michael Ruel*

The Beauty Of Truth

Truth! Oh, Truth! Beauty of day and night,
    Author of principle and Mover of mass
How oft Thy patrons, reason and light,
    Hath showed the fool his ass.

    —*Pitman Buck, Jr.*

"Love One Another Or At Least Try"

While I was sleeping one special night,
God gently nudged me and whispered, get up and write
Love one another or at least try.
No one is listening to me why?
The whole world seems to be in such strife,
This isn't what God wanted in our life.
He's sending messages loud and clear,
But nobody seems to hear.
He's getting angry,
And can change seasons,
So what's the reason that your not listening to him?
To love one another, or at least try,
If he ended the world now,
We'd know why!
—*Louise Dyl*

The Children Of God

Long before we were created and placed upon this Earth. Our God had made a plan for us which started with our birth.

Earth for us will be our home until this plan is done. Each day a memory we make of joy and love and fun.

Real beauty is a gift of God and is buried in our heart. The more we give the more we get, we never can depart (from love).

Love stretches out and grows and grows, the inner fire burns and glows. What happiness can you impart, reach out and touch another's heart.

By caring for another's needs, what you can give alone. Can change a miserable stumbling block into a marvelous stepping stone. One touch, one word, one caring gesture, can change a persons life forever. In you I see,

B blessings to give to all you meet-
E energy to live and make life sweet-
A armor of God to shield your heart-
U understanding to build your dreams apart (in time and space)
T tenderness to care for those deprived (of love and home)-
Y youth of heart to share with those trying to survive in this world
—*Myrna L. Gallaway*

My Message To John

Speak to me if only memories of your past,
God only knows how long your voice will last.

Speak to me while I can hear your voice.
As it weakens I have no other choice, but to smile and tenderly touch your hand,
Hoping you too will understand how much I care.

As my hearing lessens day by day you seem to be so unaware,

Now I leave you with sadness in my heart.
I know this is the time for my depart.

Soon I'll be a memory of your past,
hoping this docile voice will last, forever in your dreams.
—*Toyetta M. Byrd*

To My Sister And Friend: 1965—1983

Jody Lyn Wolthius Barthlomew
God sent you down from above so we could
share that special love you brought us laughter
joy and tears no one but you could be so
dear as time goes on I realized just what
you meant to me know one could share that
sisterly love no one but you and me.
—*Your Sister, Tina Cline*

Untitled

Oh what a pleasure to behold
God's rainbow of promise
forever we're told;
Hope for tomorrow for you and me
Beautiful colors of pink, green and
blue, lift our spirits and help us to
Believe in the teachings of God's Holy
Word, divinely inspired by the prophets of old,
The plan of salvation as we are told
To trust in the Savior and our sins
He'll set free
   and cast them away as far as the sea.
—*Sara Delores Martin*

Secret Cat

Pitter-pat, pitter-pat cat
going down the path.
With cat secrets, with cat knowledge.
Tail down, eyes straight ahead,
pitter-pat cat on her way.
Pitter-pat, pitter-pat cat
whiskers atwitch, eyes and ears alert.
Pitter-pat cat jump's upon the wall.
Eyes right, eyes left, nose sniffing,
pitter-pat cat on secret business.
Eyes bright, ears straight up.
Pitter-pat, pitter-pat cat jumps down,
up a tree faster than any can see.
High up the tree, eyes right, eyes left,
down the tree with nose sniffing.
Pitter-pat, pitter-pat cat, tail up, to her home.
Eats dinner, curls up with
private secret dreams.
—*Gail Tamara Taylor*

Sweetheart

(To Geraldine Shartrand)
Good night sweetheart good night
My dreams are all of you
So kiss me once again before we part dear
And my love will always be true
And when I close my eyes
I'll dream of only you
So sleep, sleep my pretty one sleep
God night sweetheart good night
Twilight stars are brightly shining
Back in my home town tonight
Where my loving wife and little loved ones
Sleep so tenderly
Since I started roaming
Never a night goes by
I wish that I never said good bye
Soon I'll be returning
Never more to roam
Good night sweetheart good night
—*Raymond Shartrand*

Fuller's Earth

Deity energizes — the human computer feeds,
Fulfilling macrocosmic yearnings and microcosmic needs...
How frightening is the prospect of that energy's depletion —
Of withdrawn power before the hour of destiny's completion.
And ovoid heads in plastic beds reflect the source
In earth-bound homes of geodesic domes, while
The Great Conductor plans the course.
—*Glory Lukacs Johnson*

"Boss Man"

Heh! Mr. Boss Man, you've got strength and you've
  got style
When it's time to set those trusses -
First you cuss and then you smile

I never saw a boss run a crew the way
  you do -
I never heard a man swear as much as you
But I've come to understand
It's just the fight in the man
Cause there ain't no such thing as it
  can't be done

Heh! Mr. Boss man, why do you work
  so hard
Lord knows how I worry about you -
Now it's time to put that hammer down

My man's a boss man, he runs a framing crew
Not much pats on the back, but they ought to -
It's hard row to hoe
Not much money, you know
And they don't give awards, but they ought to.
    —*Patricia A. Edstrom*

Grandparents

Worshipped by generations yet unborn.
Grandpapa, Grandmama, words adorned.
Uttered by voices small and clear;
Making hearts leap and sing with cheer.
Small faces smiling with eyes so bright
They cause a day to be sunny and light.
Little ones they are right now,
But still they make your heart feel proud.
As they climb upon your knee.
Shouting loudly. Do me, do me.
You bounce your foot upon the floor,
As they gleefully ask for more.
Causing your knee to ache with pain;
But you just smile and play the game.
Until they tire and then move on
To another toy to climb upon.
For grandchildren have a special gift,
To cheer the old and give a lift.
To cause the face to crack and smile.
To turn old to young, for a little while.
    —*John E. Pregler*

Victory Road

As I walked along a busy road, I glanced down and saw a small, green toad. It seemed he longed for pastures green, which aren't always what they seem. I heard the rumble, and he was no more. How he tried, one, two, three and four...I wiped the tears from my eyes and saw to my surprise, another toad hopping on to the Golgotha road. Gingerly he hopped as he glanced at me, this isn't all it's cracked up to be....He tried to turn back—then the roar!! I looked hoping prayerfully, he was no more. This must be all, I cannot stand any more! Oh, no, another toad was in the road——don't try again, it just isn't fair. He seemed to say, "I must try to get over there." I closed my eyes and breathed a prayer......From somewhere I saw the flags, flying high in the smoked filled sky. I heard the sound of the drummer's beat. The shout, the noise of soldiers feet. I opened my eyes, afraid to see... Across the road, triumphant, sat he. The little toad was grinning at me.
    —*Helen J. Yolinski*

The Heart Of Clay And The Potter

The clay sways from side to side
guided carefully by the master's eye.
Hands move upon the potters wheel
the clay is hard and will not yield,
the mold is in the heart alone
the shape begins, the seed is sown.
To form, To grow, To cast but one
the day seems worth it when all is done.
God's creations see us now,
our shape, our hearts, this is how
how with clay, from a thought
were formed and molded from what were taught.
We let our ears, eyes, tell us all
and fail to feel the potter's call
he shapes and molds us one by one
some will form, some will shun.
For in our casting, he's made a heart
to choose to hug him or chose to part.
And in his work, I see all good.
It's us who sway from what we should.
    —*Charles Bridges*

Brave Soldier

General Patton once said, "I am proud to lead a great bunch of guys like you."
I am not General Patton but I am a veteran of world war two, and I wish to say," I am proud to be one of the great bunch of guys like you."
I salute the red, white and blue.
We need more brave men to serve, protect and defend—only real men can we send.
We are the greatest nation in the world.
I wish to give credit where credit is due.
What would we do without brave men and women like you.
You are brave and you are true to the red, white, and blue.
You are not just a name on the wall-all of you men can stand tall.
General Patton you were an inspiration, and we were proud to follow a great General like you.
We were also proud to follow General Eisenhowers!
Expeditionary forces too.
"God bless you, brave soldier."
"May we have peace on earth and good will to all men."
    —*Alfred Goldman*

The Conquering Hero

Over the horizon I see the annihilation of man.
Hail, the conquering hero, as his blood trickles,
  from his ever agonizing flesh.
His soul wails, the cry is long, and echoes
  through the hollow minds, of its impassionate owners.

  A timeless universe listens in to the warning of,
  The self conquering heroes.
As the mourning moon rises, there can be seen,
In the shadow of an ocean, a remnant of man.
Now the universe, deep, dark and quiet sounds with a thunderous roar.
  Man is returning! Man is returning!

The age of tears is born again, blood will flow,
Rockets rise, and satellites spy.
Over the horizon there can be seen,
The annihilation of man. Pity, the conquering;
  Heroes???
    —*Jane Corcoran*

"The Lame Shall Enter First"

Every day he is Vulcan going to the forge,
hammering out the agonies of his solitary life
upon a shield
which only he can bear.

A warrior,
apart from his comrades-in-arms,
fighting an unseen enemy,
with bravado and heart.

Seeking grace by detour,
salvation by fire —
a modern-day muted hero.
—*Betty Cleveland*

Always Together, Never Alone

Deep inside my heart I feel a little flitter
Happy, sad, bouncie, or maybe even bitter.
My heart has been broken, cracked and torn; but still stands
  true
I will wait until the day that you let it be close to you.
You won't have to put anything on the line
Just let your heart be close to mine.
Our heart would no longer be two, they would join and be one
It would be like something new.
Our hearts would be free, like the winds at sea
They would be like waves of the ocean
Moving in a gentle, loving motion.
They would sing and sore and fly high too;
Over the hills and mountains, in the skies so blue.
In my heart you'll always be, very dear and special to me
Love, romance, sex on the beach
There would never be a final speech
You'd say it in a special tone, "Always Together, Never Alone"
When our hearts meet, it is then
That mine will finally be complete.
—*Monica Parmley*

Wreckage

It seemed I met a girl. A silver-shining grief
Has been reflecting on her iris - gray and azure.
As if a sailing ship has dashed against a reef
And in her gulf of velvet pupils lost its treasure.

A flashing magic force played on her radiant face.
It charmed me deep and drew as steadily as magnets.
My heart was sinking when...I heard her dangling pace,
The earth was slipping when...I felt her silken fragrance.

I really got obsessed...And — lovely and bizarre
One night she's given me her body's warmth and nacre —
Embracing alar arms and nectarine lips ajar....
I held her all that night — so tender, close, shaking....

Our story didn't start — because that's all that was.
One night she was my love — my Alpha and Omega.
God knows what she thought... My heart aches and adores
The one who has become forever my heartbreaker....

It seemed I met a girl. A silver-shining grief
Has been reflecting on her iris — gray and azure.
As if a sailing ship has dashed against a reef
And gave her gulf of velvet pupils all its treasure.
—*Andrei Dmitriev*

Untitled

The laughter I feel when I'm with you
Has drifted away and left me blue
The times we spent together
Were supposed to last forever
But now that you've gone away
I now just think and say
That you'll always be in my heart
Even though we're far apart
The love I show for you
Will always be so true
For I'll always hope and pray
That you'll soon be back someday
And show me how you feel
When I say that "my love is real."
Someone once told me
That if the love was meant to be
We'd never try to hide
Our feelings deep inside
So I say this to you with hope and love
That I pray the Lord's watching you from above.
—*Kandiemarie Almanza*

To Singles

The "slings and arrows of outrageous fortune"
Have come your way
A single - that is what you are
For now, at least, and so you be
Whether a mate before
Or always lone and wished it so
No matter what, and sad or glad, you are a single,
And commended for the way you conquer life
And do all those things that you must do.. single handed
No, rather double handed..
For single you may be
But double-handed are
With a mop in one hand
And hammer in t'other
Or as Shakespeare might have said
"Both a borrower and a lender be"
For you play both roles
Both a she and a he
Laughing at your own jokes
Weeping in your bed alone...
—*Mildred Creighton Barry*

A Mother's Pride, A Mother's Pain

You are first to be your Mother's pride
Having conceived, and nourished you from inside
But at birth, when she tries - and tries again
You, dear child - have been your Mother's pain

As you came to life of pride and much desire
That you be Her child for which to care
So that she may spend much time tending to your need
Or to teach you of all the love to share

So it is that you grow to be your Mother's pride
To walk, to talk - to be always near Her side
For she has had the heart to share your pain
And for you- She would do it once again

But you have grown to think you need not share
Or honor of the pride and lessons there
Remember, what you do to hurt your Mother's pride
Must live with you forever - down deep inside

If you listen, and can hear the pride in a Mother's voice
Or see the stress upon the face - that is pain
Still, you can not see or feel the aching in Her heart
Child, have you caused your Mother - pain again!!!
—*"Cap" Snell*

Untitled

Not all viewers are fans. The man was a fan.
He came to watch the match. He held something in his hands.
It looked like an ordinary object. It gleamed in the midday
  sun.
It was as shiny as a new penny, and was as sharp as a razor.
It looked as long as a mile. The knife appeared in his
  outstretched hand and had a life of its own.
Her face became pale. She was as white as a ghost.
She screamed, and then collapsed. People were running over
  to see what happened.
All the people were shocked. Some didn't see much, but heard
the screaming a mixture of pain and agony.
It looked as if she were asleep. The game stopped.
Her career along with her life was almost lost forever.
For she, Monica Seles, had been stabbed.
—Randi Morse

America My Home

Everything was fine until someone came along.
He didn't have the same color skin as me.
He was white and mine was red.
He said to me, "Go away!
You're not welcome here!"
I didn't understand.
We came here first.
We shared our land with him.
And now we must go.
America, Freedom for all
But not for my people.
—Pamela Gersht

Roy's Last Battle

Roy was just a boy, when sent to fight in World War II
He fought for his country he fought for me and you

He was captured by the enemy and put in a prison camp
The living conditions were miserable, crowded, cold and damp

Roy came back a man, older and wiser that's true
He had fought for his country, and for the red, white and blue

Roy went to work, prospered, and built him a home
He was content to be with his family and never again roam

Roy was a gentle man, thoughtful and kind to all
He never raised his voice in anger, or caused a tear to fall

A car wreck injured him and took away his wife
He fought back and recovered and went on with his life

Roy was now getting older, and decided to retire
Now he could just relax, and sit by the fire

One day an enemy attacked that he could not see. It robbed
his body of its strength, and left him helpless as could be

Roy fought this battle valiantly, he gave it his best
This time however, the enemy won, and he was laid to rest

I will miss Roy, there will never be another, he was kind
courageous, brave and strong, and he was my brother
—Lavelle Ginzel

The Art Of Sharing

One knows when a teacher has come into their midst,
for that person is seeking knowledge, only experience can give.

Likewise when a student comes,
prepared by life's experiences, you know that they will teach.

Open are they for learning and equal is their need.
Standing side by side, one without the other, they could not
continue to be.
—Donna J. Andrews

Reunited

A little baby bird lay dead.
  He had fallen out of bed.
  I picked him up to bury him,
  As I proceeded, the sun grew dim.
  It seemed as if the world was sad;
He's gone to heaven to be with his dad.
  Two days ago his father died
and for those two days, baby bird cried.
  But now he sheds tears of joy,
    he is again, daddy's boy.
When he entered through the "pearly gates"
    the sun began to illuminate
        once again.
—Rene Ann Pipta

Sitting In The Darkness

Sitting in the darkness I am no more,
  he has left.
At last, a wave of calmness may wash over my soul,
  sweep me away.
How can one man take something so sacred, so personal,
  part of me.
In return he left feelings of filth and disgust,
  it forever stains.
Thoughts of his demonic face cringes me into a
  helpless ball, I am nothing.
What did I do to make him want to hurt me so?
  It's my fault.
I kicked, bit, punched, but could not free from the bonds of
  the hungry lecher,
  could shout louder.
I close my eyes, shut the tears in, and in hopeless desperation
  just lay there,
  I gave up.
Soon he must stop and cowardly run back into his own world,
  I lost mine.
—Nhu Qucch

Uncle Sam

Uncle Sam is a grand old man
He is guardian of every clan.
In dire need he gives us food
And he seems to sense our every mood.
In sickness we can rely on medicare
For help is needed everywhere.
As he waves the flag red white and blue
You know he is counting on you.
To roll up your sleeves, bury your prejudice
  and greed
Pray and join others to help your brothers
  in need.
This will make our country stronger
The time is now, he can't wait any longer.
—L. H. Kemp

Untitled

Today is the night the morning is late
He is the boy the girl said she'd date

It rained the day the month the year was over
The flower the weed the five-leaved clover

They knew they saw they cared then left
Stolen, loved, bewildered and theft

Old is the young and new is to death
Leave is to come and to sigh is breath

Sparkling new lights to dull the old hate
Better to see it than be blind and too late
—Barbara Lewis

Elwyn Rowe

    The best man a man could know.
     He learned to fly during the
       barnstormin' days.
    With no ball at all he mapped
       the airways.
He was a pilot, a father, a husband to his wife,
an uncle, a brother and a rancher in this life.
      And now in Heaven, I believe,
     He is happy doing all of these.
     Looking back at what he's done,
   I feel so proud to have known Elwyn.
   What a wonderful life he's lived.

    —*Edward Charles Rowe*

Daddy's Girl

   He loved me when I wasn't good,
    He loved me when I whined.
  He loved me when I made mistakes,
    He loved me all the time.

   As I grew he help me through
    Some very trying times.
He cheered me up when I needed it most,
He was the best, the best of all times.

He helped me get over my very first love,
  He would always lend an ear.
  He always gave me good advice,
  He knew what I needed to hear.

But then one day without a warning,
  Someone walked into his life,
   And in one bitter moment,
  He took my father's life.

    I love you daddy,
  And I know you love me too.
But one day we'll be together again,
Until then, I'll never stop missing you.

    —*Denise Gavetti*

My Very Best Friend

My very best friend is Christ the Lord,
He makes my life happy and never bored,
Through these eighty one years I have been blessed
With good health and wisdom at its very best.
Someday, I will hear Christ the Lord say,
Come on home dear, I will show you the way.
Life here on earth, will be over for me,
but life in Heaven will be wonderful to see.
I will see Jesus face to face and know that
His home is my very own place.
I would like to be a servant for my friend,
Christ the Lord, then I know I will be
happy and never bored.

    —*Sibyl Bryan*

Legend

He took the sun, moon and the stars and put them within reach
He said if I wanted to, I could reach out and touch each
He made it look and sound so simple, he was a inspiration
There was no mere mortal like him, but then, he was a legend
I follow behind him through the family line
My own adventures and my own way he said I must find
The way I seek adventure I have learned from him
He taught me so much, he was a legend but also a terrific man
He is our legend, he is our family treasure
So we must hold on to his memory forever

    —*Cindy Carrabine*

Self-Centered

The boy was lost, bewildered and alone,
He needed someone to lean upon,
He was too young to understand
Why you did not offer a helping hand.

The man was old and weak and frail,
He needed warmth against the wintry gale,
You had no time for his faltering feet
Shuffling along on the busy street.

Somewhere close you heard the cry
Of a lonely heart as you passed by.
You did not heed the call of distress
Away out there in the wilderness.

You traveled on, becoming discontent
Then found out when your life was spent
You had failed to leave from day to day
A part of yourself along the way.

You joined the band of the rushing throng
Forgetting all others as you hurried along
Then you asked of yourself the reason why
You had missed so much as life passed by.

    —*Thelma Brady*

Sarah Girl

"This ones for you, Sarah Girl"
he said as he quietly kissed the
delicate lips, which made him reflect
on his love for her.
Quickly,
he looked her over.
Then
slowly,
slowly.
The face he rested upon.
Chin, he saw, was strong.
Eyes, he saw, were, large, inquiring.
Lips... he saw, were full, longing, loving.
  ... And he knew
  then, he could never
  leave his Sarah Girl.

    —*Shannon McDaniel*

David Koresh

David Koresh came upon this land,
He talked like God, but died like man.
His body perished in a fiery hell,
In the last flames, his flag, it fell.

He gathered his disciples one by one,
And at the end, only a few would run.
The faithful remained and they all died.
To save a disaster, the government tried.

What was the bond that held so tight?
What could have caused such a terrible fight?
Is this the end, or will it grow?
To all these questions, we may never know.

They began by practicing religious beliefs,
But their methods have caused terrible grief.
With their God they wanted to be,
Now from persecution they are free.

David Koresh came upon this land,
He said He was God, but He died like a man.
Did He lead his people to a fiery hell,
In the last moment, when his flag, it fell?

    —*Lemmie Young*

"The Essence Of Life"

When the man upstairs gave us "Essence of Life,"
  He tried to subside our suffering and strife.
If we give him our faith, courage and trust,
  We will be rewarded by our innermost crust.
He will not let us down, He'll teach us to care,
And will show us the way, that He wants us to share.
    To give to each other as only we can,
  For this is part of His purposeful plan.
    He loves us all, in spite of our sins,
    He gave us life…a chance to begin.
It is up to us how we can use these great gifts,
  And His spirit is with us, for He will uplift.
  Uplift us to heights we thought out of reach,
  But in our hearts we know…we cannot beseech.
    The hopes and dreams that He has for us,
    To become unique, in us He will trust.
  He knows of our sins, our innermost thoughts,
And forgives us transgressions, we thought were naught.
Yes, He gave us the true meaning of faith and of Love,
  And I thank and praise Him as I look up above.

    —*Janet L. Gibson*

A Tribute To Papa

I called him Papa when I was small
  He was not a big man not very tall,
With merry blue eyes that twinkled with glee
  When a certain surprise he'd planned for me
      I call him Papa
I called him Papa with sheer delight
  He was my hero my shinning knight
A "Willie walk" to the woods was always great fun
  And always came when work was done
     I called him Papa
A son he wanted when I arrived
  But he looked on me with the greatest pride
For I was oldest and youngest, t'was only me
  But soon I found we wouldn't always agree
     I called him Papa
The day did come when he wasn't here
  But some how I know he is always near
I tell him life's troubles o'er and o'er
  The comfort he gives me is evermore
     I called him Papa

    —*Iva L. Smith Eusey*

Heaven's Diploma

Just a young lad at the age of fourteen.
He was quiet, a little shy,
But he had many dreams.
"Doctor, Lawyer," he said, "that's what I will
  be when I am grown."
Not knowing that his time on earth would soon be gone.
But do not despair,
For Jason will be,
With the greatest of all time, and I'm sure he will see,
That whatever dream might have been before
Can never compare with what heaven has in store.

    —*Brenda Casteel*

Don't Give In

Don't give in to the rocking chair
  Don't give into despair.

You have so much to learn
  and so much to give
So dear heart, wake up and live.

    —*Margie Waltimyer*

My Dad

My Dad was a giant of a man,
He was so gentle, so caring so sweet.
His heart was as pure as fresh-fallen snow.
A stranger he never did meet.

He was my hero, my friend, my confidante;
He loved children and animals and life;
He never dwelled on his hardships,
on anger or fears or on strife.

Precious memories with him are so many;
His whistling, his laughing, his smiles.
Together we rode country roads and through woods,
For miles and miles and miles.

When he died his little girl had grown up,
But I was still the apple of his eye.
His death left a void in my life,
But as he did, I believe,
We'll meet again in the "sweet by and by."

    —*Shirley Singleton Flanagan*

Best Friends

I lost a best friend of all times,
He was the bestest friend you could find.
He told me things he would not dare tell anyone else.
Then he had to move away,
Of my whole life it was the saddest day
I swore we'd never see again.
But just the other day,
I know I saw Him.
He was talking to some guys then walked away,
With nothing more to say.
I yelled His name with tears in my eyes.
He looked at me and shrugged like I wouldn't understand,
And walked away.

    —*Jessie Hunt*

Rave

Seemingly ambiguous and never changing minds
Heart beating quickening moving with the time
Challenging the metre adding to the calls
Listening with pleasure becoming of the walls
Can't stop the happiness feelings of pure love
Knowing you are wonderful heels to you gloves
Hands in the air minds in the beat
Feeling your intensity your whistle to your feet
Non-stop beautiful calls to the wind
Overt asexual vibrance that you send
Touching all the bases donning more than thought
Free to feel whatever never being caught
Maze of wonder lover of life
Giving all of everything reaching through the light
Innocent of madness seeing all that's new
Perfect in your person letting others through
On up to the morning took advantage of the night
Solace for your temper and pain and hate and fright

    —*Kathey Stump*

Dawn To Dusk

O where are we going?
And what do we see?
Who can we share it with…?

The dawn and dusk are equal
Life goes on ————

    —*M. Kay Glass*

Dreamland

As I sleep, I dream of the most blissful things on earth; My heart floats on cloud 9, while I receive all the things I deserve. For Lord knows, when I awake my reality is the most feared thing of all; But in my dreams, I can kill those fears, have pride and stand tall. I dream of the unexisting love I so hopefully wish to find; One that will help me leave all pains and sorrows way behind. One day I hope to drift into that glorious land of dreams; And never again awake to the rising sun and it's scornful beams. For this thing called life has brought me nothing but shattered hopes; It has left me at a point where I simply cannot cope. So off I go, once again, to that extraordinary dream hide-a-way. Hoping never to awake to the next defeating and horrid day. But since I have to live my life, no matter how frightful or demeaning; I live with the comfort of being able to escape to that dream land that's so intriguing. I soar to that secret place locked so deep within my mind; Where someone to love and hold me is so very easy to find. In my dreamland that person I can only carefully invent; so off I'm swept to my dreamland where I'm so blissfully content.

—*Nikia Stone*

Growing Old

When did the years reach out and touch me, age me, but not my heart? I was quite content, unaware, unconcerned about the sequence of time. Not knowing years are disguised so as not to perceive them darkening life's sublime. My reflection shows me there are lines there, not there before, why then now? Beneath this mask is the very same face as before; everyone should remember, but how? The laughter hasn't changed, it grew richer, perhaps more generous than before. Doesn't it flow just as freely, just as lively, just as jestful, anymore? When did all those years reach out and touch me, age me, but not my heart? I still notice that the grass along that familiar path is just as inviting and green as when I walked it with my lighter step seeking the beauty around that bend, unforeseen. The pebbles in the pond feel just the same, for I have bent down and lifted one out and found it to be unchanged . The flowers by the hillside still move in the breeze, beckoning me as always, to be fondled, to be arranged. That sturdy tree still stands there offering me it's limb, welcoming the touch of my hand, as I climb the hill. The gentle wisp of a falling leaf still cools my cheek as it travels by.

—*Mary Kelleher*

Half Past Eight

There was this guy I'd see in town. I'd pass him by and he'd say, "Hi." My heart would pound—my head spin round.

These crazy feelings he did share but feared to show me that he cared until one day when he walked by. He looked at me and I said, "Hi," and he said, "Hi," then we sat down—on a bench there in the town.

"Nice day," he said. "Nice day," said I.

"Your dress is nice," "I like your tie."

"I was wondering," said he, "If maybe some night when you're free, if you and I could maybe go to see a movie or a show?"

"Oh yes!, I'd love to, that'd be fine—just let me know what day and time."

And so we went, the show was great. We fell in love at half past eight. I know the time because you see, twas half past eight he first kissed me.

And we were wed one sunny day at half past one the tenth of May.

Though forty years have since gone by, we're still together him and I. Twas that first kiss which sealed our our fate, one moonlit night at half past eight.

—*Lisa L. Hodges*

Rapture

Calm,
    her fingers flew from note to note.

Her chords
spread them like
                    raptor feathers
                        stretched
                            across highs and
                                    lows.

Her gaze
    picked out a tear shining
                          in the crowd.

This other woman
        caught like a hare
        just sitting
                there
                        with a soul.

—*Stephanie Kornfeld*

Why?

I look at her there in the babybed,
her hair so black, her face so red.
She's tossing and turning and screaming and yelling,
while in the midst her arm is swelling
because of the needles and tubes that are there
that keep her heart under constant care.

The Angel of Mercy is drawing near.
I look in her eyes and see so much fear.
I see it one minute and then, it is gone.
This tiny child's life is over and done.
And though this poem may not be your first choice,
Someone had to speak up and be this child's voice.

Someone has to tell you her mother's mistake,
the one so many young moms often make.
You see, when the baby was young and still in the womb,
her mother decided to build her a tomb.
She took a glass pipe and some crack in her hand
and sent her poor baby to the heavenly land.

—*Melissa Hammond*

Untitled

She twirled and twirled,
Her long flowing dress brushed the floor…
And then flew into the air.
Around and around,
Long red-brown hair whipped around her face
Her cheeks were flushed
around and around,
Silver bracelets clashed on her wrist.
Her eyes sparkled.
   then…
She silently slipped to the ground,
Dress entangled in her legs.
Her little slippers came to a stop.
She lifted up her pale hand
running her delicate fingers in her hair,
Silently, it went limp.
Her eyes slowly closed,
She was at rest.

—*Karma Smallback*

JFK

The year is 1963
Crowds are going wild
JFK rolls by the Dallas streets
Refreshing winds blow through his hair

—*Manjit Kaur Dhillon*

Things Of Love

The first moment, that special feeling.
Her personality, his sense of humor.
Fingers entwined, lips together.
These are the things of love!

The warm smiles, that everlasting embrace.
Her sensitivity, his affection.
Arms of comfort, eyes of understanding.
These are the things of love!

The glorious memories, that life-long commitment.
Her caring touch, his true support.
Souls filled with lust, hearts made of gold.
These are the things of love!
   —*Daria Reed*

Bud The Dog

Bud is a dog and a fine one at that,
He's very shaggy with hair on his back.
Bud's got blond hairs over his eyes,
and when they're in his way,
He blows them up very high.
His eyes are a beautiful brown,
and pretty black nose is very round.
The collar around Bud's neck is red,
and most of the day he's sleeping in bed.
His bone is what Bud seems to like best,
but I'm sure all his other toys are next.
Bud is the cutest dog I've ever seen,
I'll be very mad when he leaves.
   —*Michelle Miller*

Weep And Hope

Weep, you tired, weary eyes. Weep for a sadly sick society.
Hip heavy, saturated with sex and starving for love. Cry
aloud, you weak voices. Cry for neglect of the intellect.
Exchanged for an ocean of emotion, betrayed for pleasure.

Halt, you rushing fools. Halt before you are lost in dismay.
Halt and feed the hungry mind that reaches out for food.
Reach, you long arms. Reach deep into the human brain. Bring
forth your creative, artistic, and poetic riches. Calm your

nerves you tense ones. Balance will be achieved. The pendulum
will swing back. Intellect and emotion will meet. Hope, you
gentle strong ones. Hope, for in peace lies our destiny.
Sexual and intellectual will fall into a pattern of light.
Hope for a love without evil and trust for feeding the mind.
Light your own candle in the dark tunnel. Make peace with all
men. It is the gentle ones who lead with a soft tread into the
light. Hope for an ideal balance through the greatness of
today's creators. Dream in the midst of cannon fire and let
the smoke rise around you. Dream with your eyes wide open
until your dreams come true. Give them your dreams and wake
up to their schemes. Understand.
   —*Willie May Anderson*

Untitled

It's crimson now; the dye is cast—
His liquid pooling eyes hold fast
To the shattered object on the ground
That had met its fated end at last.

He watched it slip with pitted cries—
And razor rain cut through his eyes
And drooled upon the broken mass
That steamed and foamed from harbored lies.

He bent to touch one scattered part;
It immediately split and fell apart.
He tried to hold himself as one
As he sobbed upon his dying heart.
   —*Suzanne Marie Miller*

"I Love You"

I love you he whispered in the middle of the night, with
his arms so warm holding me tight. I wish that this
night would last until dawn, he warms me, comforts
me, and keeps me calm. This love in my heart won't
go away, and I want you to know that it will always
stay. I will always be there, with a little prayer,
and open arms, ready to care. I look in the sky,
and think of you and me. I think of how things
use to be. I wish that we could change mistakes
made in the past, but I hope our love will
always last. You say that you love me, you
say that you care, but when times get rough,
will you be there. I love you more now than
I ever have in my life, I wish that I could be
your wife. You're all I think about day and night,
I wish that we would never fight. I wish that
this night would last forever, cause I need
you now more than ever. I don't know how to
prove, just how much I love you or how much
I care, but I want you to know I will always be there!
   —*Jan Trussell*

A Young Man

The young man comes to me often,
His least-freckled smile across my thoughts;
Days of wet socks on the kitchen floor gone by.

He wears strength and sinew, and carries a certain grace.
Boundless, each day is held in its precious abundance;
Thus he commands his stride.

What the world and I see is (dare I?) at times but a shadow
Of that which, in this familial acquaintance, I have treasured:
The heart which lovingly speaks, sensitively understands,
   tenderly overflows as he grows;
Expressed, even in the indelicate (or so he thinks; not I)
   strum of guitar.
No, never will he hide.

I sing to him a silent prayer, hoping sometime bridged across
   these miles
That he will hear.
I wish to touch the tousled hair and thank him for the vibrant
   portrait
That only seldom has seemed a mystery; I will always love him.
He is Michael, this young man, my brother.
   —*Christine R. Brain*

Untitled

   He doesn't believe anyone could care
his lonely and scared although no one sees
   He's hurt and tired
but hasn't given up, not yet
   His true smile is oh so sweet
though it is a rare thing to see
   So full of pain and experience
are the so hard to read eyes,
that seem so far beyond his tender years
   So many times, betrayed by false love
he know longer trusts,
   so can I tell him how I feel
do I dare, even tell him I care
   Can I show this wounded soul
how to once again trust, would you believe
if him?
   He doesn't believe anyone could care
   —*Neeka Bruyer*

Fate Stepped In

My heart found him in the dim of light
His manly strength enlightened me
His brown eyes spoke right out
   of the thing's he'd missed in life
He'd been searching for that special one
   to fill his heart, his mind, his soul
My life flashed by on the dreams I'd had
   on the way I wished my life could be
Fate stepped in and graced our thoughts
Warm hugs blossomed commitment - vows
Our peace of mind comes in just fair play
   and all worthwhile things in between
Happiness has become our utmost aim
   we have moved right up to togetherness
Our mountain climbing is day by day
    finding more wisdom with rebirth
   discovering the magic like the eagles nest
    reigning enthusiastically within our realm
Yes, that's where our love is found ... when
   fate stepped in.

—*Charlotte Colyer Marsh*

The Loss Of A Tradition

The whooping crane lets loose its long mournful cry
His mate is lost and his love will die
Again and again his sharp cries pierce the clear night air
Cattails and reeds form now his only soulful fare.
To what great depths have you fallen, oh mournful crane
From the marvelous heights you and your mate sought to attain?
For you, as all others, will all too quickly die
And soon you'll make your final plummet from the sky.
Oh let this not be; is there no god for the whooping crane?
Beyond the decay there'll be no trace, not even a stain.
You and your kind will certainly be forgotten
By the passionless race our technology has begotten.
Nay, your image will be retained by the great glass eye
or captured in the folklore of the days gone by
But you, oh whooping crane, will fly no more
Your mournful cries shall cease to pierce the core.
Crystalline tranquility shall replace your natural peace
Though even such freedom fails its true release.
Farewell whooping crane, my heart breaks for you
Your extinction will be understood by only the few.

—*Terza L. Zane*

Pain

The man walked down the busy street
His mind seemed miles away he heeded no one his trip
Although many stood in his way

One man approached him with open hands
Begging for some pennies just to eat
Another cried "whatever you can"
So I can get shoes for my bare feet

A woman sat on the cold wet curb
A small baby in her arms
Pleading to everyone who passed
She had long ago lost her charms

The man continued on his way
With not a tear upon his face
Until someone walked up to him
And with him kept up the pace

"How can you go by those who bleed
Have you no heart, have you no shame"

The man looked at the stranger and
muttered so softly he had to strain
How can I feel for anyone when I have so much pain.

—*Bernice Isaac*

A Child's Playground Gone Wrong

Up and down and up and down, don't lose your balance, you'll hit the ground. Up and down and up and down, you'll teeter-totter pound for pound. Up and down and up and down, loud and quiet, there's still "his" sound. Up and down and up and down, life for you is just one large "pound." Back and forth and back and forth, scrape the ground not just with feet. Back and forth and back and forth, don't stop now or you'll get beat. Back and forth and back and forth, "swing back at me and you're on the street!" Back and forth and back and forth, at least out there you're on both feet. Round to the left, and round to the right, you hear your breath of life tonight. Round to the left, and round to the right, that's because "he's" been out all night. Round to the left, and round to the right, "he'll" be back and ready to fight. Round to the left, and round to the right, "he's" a merry-go-round, so hold on tight. Climb up, slide down, and then again, peaceful rest not on the ground. Climb up, slide down, and then again, happiness is still around, climb up, slide down, and then again, get up, go hide, "he's" back in town. Climb up, slide down, and never again, will we hear you ever make a sound...

—*Wendy J. Reid*

Love

Love I sit, love I stand, Love I
hold in my right hand, Love I see in
yonder tree, if you solve this poem
you can hang me.

This is a true poem. My grandpa had a friend
in the 1800's and was in jail for stealing a horse.
They had a hard time proving it. The
judge told him, you go home and make up
a poem that we cannot solve and we will not
hang you. So the man went home, and he had a
little dog that had rabies. He had to kill his dog.
His dog was named Love. He cut off his tail and put it in
his back pocket, Love I sit, put a piece in his shoe, Love I
stand, put a piece in his right hand, Love I hold in my right
hand, put a piece in a tree, Love I see in yonder
tree, if you solve this poem, you can hang me.

—*Ray Holliday*

Old Doc W A Satchel Of Humor

When I was little we had a kind gentle Doctor who came to our home. He'd sit and talk and explain it all —— measles and mumps — even about lice. If you didn't understand it once he'd take the time to explain twice. He was not in a hurry and never, ever, took time to look at his watch. So deftly he'd remove a splinter and cover the wound with a swatch. I was forever asking him to bring us a little baby sister. He'd look at my Dad - smile, and wink; and I'd conclude he was a trickster! Then one day the black satchel was opened— Such a mysterious thing to see!! A huge bundle wrapped in a blanket —— "Twas a baby and "I'm filled with glee"! Gently he lifted the darling and — handed it over only to ME!! I didn't mind that it was a doll and not a real baby after all —— But from the doorway my Dad was watching — holding his breath and anxiously waiting. So when my Dolly gave out with a CRY —— he breathed out with a great BIG SIGH, BUT Back then I never really knew "WHY"????

—*Helen Bole*

Take Another Look

I am amazed at the honey bee, the story it had to tell. The honey it had stored away, up high in a popular tree. I was only made to believe, the honey was to be free. But the sting that I had to bear, was the pain it gave to me. I was amazed at the acorn, the story it told to me. There would be a giant tree to grow one day I would truly see. I was amazed to see the seed, a story it told to me. Take me and plant me in the soil, down by the foaming sea. I walked down by the sea shore, and let the seeds gentle fall, the rain and sunshine brought new life, and it grew tallest of all, I was amazed to see a child, that lay in its mother's arms. I poised to dream that nature tells to be protected from harm. Many years had passed since I met, this once a mother's held child. No warrior was ever so bold, I relished the past and smiled. I now take the story's refrain, and cherish the lore with a glee. I wander what is to be learned. From the child, seed, acorn, or bee.

—*Arlie U. Bobo*

The Beautiful Letter

I sat down to write you a beautiful letter.
Hoping the words
   would leap from the paper
   and crawl up your shoulder
   and cling to your heart.
I sat down to write but the words wouldn't start.

I sit here in silence and wait for the moment
To tell you I love you,
   but silence is golden.
   And so it remains,
   no one says any words.
But I know the feelings which roam through these halls.

The footsteps are deafening, babies are crying.
But we remain,
   absorbed in our trying
   to work out our problems,
   proclaiming our love
Oblivious to anything else from above.

So why do I write this, a poem and such?
To tell you I love you, so ever so much.

—*Julia Kopylenko*

She Sits All Alone

She sits all alone in the corner of her mind
   hoping to be rescued, hoping to be saved
from her own faults, from her own guilts
of the crimes she never committed
but that's the way she was, is, and always will be
captured by her conscience, and mind
because she was taught right from wrong
but confused by the world around her, and those who taught her
but she doesn't know that the only one who can save her
   is the one she's hurt the most
for the only crime she has committed
is not forgiving herself for the things she hasn't done
what she also doesn't know is that
she will always be sitting all alone in the corner of her mind
unless she lets herself go
and you will too if you don't let yourself go
so do it for yourself
let yourself go!

—*Jennifer Falsone*

"What Is A Rainbow?"

A child said to me, "What is a rainbow?"
How could I answer the child.
I do not know any more about it than he.

I suppose it is the vivid liquid paint that colors the sky a heavenly blue.

Or it could be a temporary ultra violet shield to protect the earth on a sizzling hot day.

I guess it is a shaker of paint that splashes all the colors after it rains because they need vibrance again.

It my also be a big sliding board for little children.

And now it seems to me to be a
beautiful rainbow of colors from heaven.

—*Kimberly Kay Corcoran*

Love

   Love, how divine it sounds upon my tongue.
    How I would love to be loved in return.
   Yet, is loving a crime for one's heart and soul?
    Is loving, one's pain or illness of heart?
  Is loving so deceitful that one must pay the price?
    How I would like to be held and caressed,
    To be touch tenderly with unselfish love,
    To be looked upon with devotion and adoration.
  Oh, tell me! Is it just admiration or common interest
    I feel?
   When will it be my turn to be loved and to love?
   Am I to be loveless the rest of my youthful life,
receiving copulation with no tenderness or loyalty of love?
  No, I cannot make myself into something I am not.
   If I love as in true love with not return,
    then that must be the way of life for me.

—*Alphea McCulloch*

Life

Life, when does it begin?
How it is designed and how it ends?
Life's faces are so complex
Leaving one mind or two in perplex.

Understanding, it is mysterious, intricate,
It is not fair.
Finding, it leads us to experience
How arduous, how facile it is to bear.

Happiness is everyone's dream.
Sadness, no one will search in both extremes.
But life has it all!
Happiness or sadness, one is bound to fall.

It is up to us to find
Which life's course to choose.
But how are we guided by factors
To succeed and lose??? God only knows.

No matter the choice of path,
Whether it's a failure, success or what
Respects and in my heart,
For you, I take off my hat!

—*Julieta Ramirez Mosher*

"Clock"

Clock is ticking, tocking too.
Down the chimes and up the chute.
Turn the gears to wind the pin,
Cross the shaft, I see just tin.
Made to be a set of numbers,
Spinning, pleasing shakes my slumber.

—*Gregory H. Cekada*

My Vision

Brilliant white light so soft and tender
How sweetly I do remember

When you were sent in my despair
And my soul did follow up thy heavenly stair

A beautiful garden I did see
With a holy friend in front of me

Not a word from our lips did we speak
Only truth and love did we seek

As our hearts they did touch
I learned so very much

Love so warm and tender
That to this day I still remember

When I return I know I'll find
Pure love and happiness of the heavenly kind

Thank-you for being there
Please keep me in your loving care
  —*Jacquelyn C. Garner*

Thrones

Stand out in the middle of that open field and see
How you like it
All the sky in some full view
I am of the opinion that you'd better make the most of anything
The chance to look like a million and to be ignored
Times to be picked up on and be used for dreaming
If you dare
Go on and stand out like a hero
Where you might know all about being caught by attention
Still looking to escape the earth as though it were only
Something to stand still on
I have supposed it to be more I must admit
Something like experiments and places to be happy
Catch my eye from time to time
But I guess I still like to sit
  —*Stephen P. Lindeman*

Politics, Before And After

Promises, debates, read my lips and trickle down
I am about fed up to here.
I didn't know 1992
Would be such a busy year.

Mr. Bush may have to eat broccoli,
And so may we.
If we still receive out checks
in 1993.

First our county Judge said he was retiring,
To help his wife vacuum the floor.
But he would help us elect a good man,
Whose last name is Moore.

We now have a new President,
And a new Judge too.
I'm willing to try the broccoli dish,
They say it is good for you.

The Lord will take care of us,
If to Him we remain true.
It is so good to live in a country,
Whose flag colors are red, white, and blue.
  —*Aline Wood*

An Ode To A Mirror

Checking my disposition to make sure that all is well, I am faced with a reflection, a reflection of days gone by. Gazing into my eyes, I am reminded of past unused opportunities, neglected traditions and abused second-hand resources. Wishing that I could turn the hands on the clock and become a senior citizen, I begin to exhale a vision.

A vision of admitting my addiction to evil, my yearning for wickedness and my taste for deceit. Picturing my future, I see a new makeover in store for me. Forgetting old mistakes and errors, I am grabbing my erasermate for the next chapter in my life. Representing myself only, I will be able to go before any judge. Since I'll be directing the traffic of my life, I can avoid some of those tickets I received earlier on. Recognizing the absence of yesterday and the presence of tomorrow, I prepare to attend all of my appointments.

The vision that I envisioned in my vision was a visionless vision that became a vision.
  —*Cynthia D. Poindexter*

Jessie's Thought

Do you see me behind the tree,
 I am here but not here
Alone in my quest to be free,
 I am here but where is here

Interesting tree I shield near,
 I am face to face with a plant
Curious I do not fear,
 This is a big huge plant

Wondrous how life abounds in this tree,
 I am shielded by its girth
Strong and tall my goodness,
 Rightfully so and more than I so free

The tree and I are one on the earth,
 I am upon the dirt like surface roots with my feet
In the earth I stand is this tree,
 Rightfully so and more than I so free

This is a big huge tree,
 A plant and I are here
Alone in our quest to be free,
 We are here but where is here
  —*David Giancola*

Untitled

    In many ways
    I am like a
    Pyramid
   Standing alone
      Standing silent
    Unwavering against
    The harsh winds of time
     Yet...
    Those few who dare
   To breach my outer realms of
   Aloneness
    And
      Solitude
    May discover
  A
    Vast
      Infinite
       Treasure
    As great as a pyramid
  —*Sali Wynants*

"The Fool"

I am the lonely, I am the sad,
I am the hideous, head full of mad.
I am the scream, I am the tears,
I am the worries, I am the fears.
I am the mask, the truth goes unseen,
I am the angry, the hurt and the mean.
I am the heart, yet I feel no pain,
I am the greedy, with nothing to gain.
I am the moon, darkness throughout,
I am the voice, with nothing to shout.
I am the sun, my light has been stolen,
I am the body, my flesh bruised and swollen.
I am the sea that no ship will visit,
I am but a memory, and no one will miss it
I am but a dream, that now will awaken,
I am but a fool, so sadly mistaken.
—*Melinda Renee Gwaltney*

Mystic

As our times together reeks of departure
I begin to discover your beauty in movement
your speech in grace and your tenderness in
Touch me as though our existence will soon be
extinct. When sleep looks at me, then us, then
Nothing could compare to the intensity of your lips
onto my mind. These days were only thought of but
now they attack our thoughts and control our movements.
I cannot write of, or to you separately, it's much too painful.

As you run the relay through life please don't drop my heart
felt tears I'll cry when you are gone and your touch
is only a thought (not heat). My mind represses the memory,
present and future of our oneness. Your tongue will no longer
sing to my body, your mind will not take mine for a walk,
and our hands will no longer dance to the gods. Rather I will
wish to reside with them so that I may be closer to you.
—*Natasha Ria Gibson*

"A July Day"

It was a beautiful morning on a July day,
I can still hear the birds as they sung,
so precious and perfect was that new baby boy,
yes a new life had just begun.
His eyes how they glistened, so warmly and bright,
as he looked in such wonder and awe, and I couldn't help think,
"This is God's little boy" for such splendor and beauty I saw.
His 10 perfect fingers, so tiny and small, matched the 10
little toes on his feet, and I couldn't help giggle when I
heard his first cry, so strong, yet so terribly sweet.
Yet that beautiful morning on that July day not only gave birth
to a child, but gave birth to a woman who was only eighteen,
whose heart was still young and so mild.
Yet a child still herself her own destiny she had chose and a
high price she now must pay, for that day yet so special,
cost more that she had; for that day she had signed his life
away. And today, though it's been now a long time ago, still
the memories on her heart do lay, of a son, of a mother, of an
undying love; of that beautiful July day.
—*Lynn M.*

Goodbye

I can't live with you,
I can't live without.
You were special to me and I hope
You can see. It's time to say goodbye
to our love that'll never die. We share
a lot of memories and I hope they'll never fade.

I know I'll love you forever
No matter what'll came about.
Once we say goodbye, I know your
love for me will die, I'll love you forever,
like I told you before. That'll
be something for me to adore.

I know I'll cherish the fun and
exciting things we did together.
I will often think about you
and hope you'll think of me too it's
not easy to say goodbye but I
think I better before I cry.

Goodbye.
—*Richelle Bukovitz*

A Tribute To Our Armed Forces

From coast to coast and shore to shore,
I care for you more and more.
I love America, you are America

We have the freedom to choose what we do,
Because you are there each one of you.
I love America, you are America

When I look at the vastness of space,
I think how tiny I am in this human race.
I love America, you are America

But thinking of you my heart swells with pride
I am no longer tiny but worlds wide.
I love America, you are America

Freedom must ring and our hearts must sing.
God bless America, you are America
—*Sharon Dennis Legleitner*

All My Heart

I love you with all my heart,
I could not stand to be apart.
Promise me you will never leave me,
That you will always need me.

I love you with all my heart,
I could not stand to be apart.
Promise me you will always be there,
With a heartful of love to share.

I love you with all my heart,
I could not stand to be apart.
I promise you that I will never leave you,
I will always need you.

I love you with all my heart,
I could not stand to be apart.
I will always be there,
With a heartful of love to share. Why?
Because I love you with all my heart.
—*Andrea Allan*

Untitled

As I entered into the midnight yonder,
I cried out, thence forth, "No wonder."
The sky bled darkness, only broken,
By the stars of God's own token.
As quickly as I had ventured betwixt the night,
The climate's face changed expressions, calm to fright.
The trees moaned and the wind howled,
Throughout the night our house got fouled.
The branches ran across the lawn,
They hit our house just before dawn.
The dark night looked less gloomy now,
For dawn was approaching on my brow.
The house felt sorry and sad, full of dirt and scrapes,
Such a sight was not glad, we dreaded pulling the drapes.
Hastily we decided and soon opened the door,
From thence we went outside to clean and explore.
The yard and house beamed overwhelmed with joy,
Clear of the traces the storm gave, when found was its toy and done was its play.
—*Jane Kueber*

"I Danced"

The music began with a piercing note of birth
I danced
The music strained and swelled, and with it, I grew and lived
I danced
Bows flew over violin strings as my youth flew past me
I danced
The harmony burst forth in a sudden blossoming of womanhood
I danced
Faster, dangerously, frighteningly faster I twirled;
Love and tears, friends and years streamed by
I danced
The music stopped
My feet would move no more
In the steady gentle silence, I found a lone ascending note
It took me higher into the enlightened hall
Musicians floated in the light
They lifted their instruments and played a calling
And I heard the music and with my heart I answered
I Dance
—*Amrey R. Dimayuga*

Love and Grace

I didn't know that Jesus died for me
I didn't know that nailed Him to a tree
I didn't know that He'd take my place
And that He'd come and give me love and grace.

I walked alone in this world of sorrow
I walked alone knowing not tomorrow
You see, I walked alone in this world's mad race
Then Jesus came and gave me love and grace.

Now I'll live for Him, the One who died for me
I'll live for Him, the One on that tree
I'll live for Him, the One that took my place
Cause when He came, He gave me love and grace.

Yes, love and grace to fill my heart with happiness
Love and grace to fill my life with joy.

Jesus died so He could take my place
And then He came and gave me love and grace.
My Jesus died to give me love and grace.
—*A. C. Rhodes*

Last Words

I never wanted to hurt you
I didn't mean to make you cry
And I didn't want to have to say good-bye,
But tomorrow's darkness, I can not hide
It's a vision I hold in my mind
Tomorrow is no longer the future, but only a dead end
Please wipe these tears from my eyes
As I try to find strength from within
I no longer have control of my life
Please hold me as I cry,
"I don't want to die!"

I tell you how much I love you
And you smile with a gentleness that sets me free
"Live your life", I say, "Don't die with me"
For tomorrow's light you will see
Grasp its warmth
And in it,
Always remember me.
—*Robbie L. Sarhalar*

Emptiness

There is an emptiness inside of me that nobody can fill.
   I don't know why it's there, but it is.

     I feel it at night
        and during the day.
 Even though I want it to, it won't go away.

    I seem to fight it all the time,
but sometimes it takes hold of me and fools with my mind.

     I can't stop it,
       only pray,
  that one day it will go away.
—*Devon Whitehead*

I Don't

I don't like driving.
I don't like driving in the rain.
I don't like driving at night.
I don't like driving when it's hot.

I don't like driving.
I don't like driving on super-duper highways.
I don't like driving when I have to be somewhere on time.
I don't like driving.

I do like being driven. It shows someone else cares.
I like seeing the people driving swiftly by,
They must have exciting places to go.
They're all in such a hurry!

I like someone else driving. I can see the country side -
Rolling hills and pine trees standing stately still.
Orange groves form a patch-work quilt that covers the countryside.

I do like someone else driving. I feel safe in the passenger seat.
The drivers will watch all those signs and flashing lights
I do like someone else driving because I know,

They know, I don't!
—*Helen B. Perrin*

Dreaming

When I fall to sleep in the dark of the night
I dream of you that I may hold you tight
Though I wish we could be in a world of our own
A far better place for us to be alone
My dreams is that of a forest, a forest saturated in mist
Searching and searching I find you and our lips form a kiss

The beauty within you and the sparkle in your eye.
Gives me the fulfillment of an emotional high, and when
I woke up and my dreams all through, my only wish
is that my dream would come true.
—*John Hart*

Housed Within My Soul

There is a bird housed in my soul
I feel her wings expanding within
Trying to attain her freedom.
At times I feel her in my breast. Wanting your touch.
Or in my loins wanting to be consumed by you.
Today she is in my heart flailing wildly
Needing, wanting, you.

Was there a time
When I didn't know your touch,
Your feel, your smell, your voice.
How could I have spent life not knowing you.
How will I go on with just the memories?
The memories of a lifetime. Built from a few escaped moments.
You are within me.

Fragments of a life I once had -
Now only sadness, despair, desolation.
Once I had it all.
Now nothing
The wind blows, leaves stir.
Within me - nothing.
—*Sue Pernisco*

The Power Of The Night

As the day ends and the night begins,
I feel my spirits start to rise.
The howling wind cuts through my heart like a jagged knife.
My soul comes to life on nights like this.
The wind is a blistering cold.
The moon is full and looks like a blazing fire.
The shrill cry of an owl sends chills down my spine.
I no longer have to pretend, my soul and the night can become
  one.
Like the soft music that moves the graceful ballerina,
the alluring sounds of the night move my soul.
I am like the night, without a care.
The terrible burden has been lifted off my back.
I am free and unchained like the night.
—*Angela S. Durrence*

Our Special Day

When you smile at me
I feel so good inside
Just knowing what we are meant to be
Gives me a sense of pride.

On this day, when I become your wife
And our lives begin together anew,
I am so thankful God brought you into my life
And this I say is true.

You've brought me sunshine and laughter.
You've made me feel so good.
I know we'll have a forever after
and grow old together like all loving couples should.
—*Rosanne Medill*

"Down In The Field"

Down in the field I feel warmer inside,
I feel the crisp morning sunshine upon my back.
I feel love spreading like a wild forest fire.
Down in the field, I can smell the honeysuckle trees.
I can feel the damp grass tickling my legs.
My dog runs up behind me as I run through the tall grass.
As my dog and I run, we see the rabbits,
Running like they had just been shot out of a rocket.
There is no place I'd rather be than down in the field, just
My Dog and Me!!!
—*Maggie Bigum*

That Mountain

Amid the shadows of the valley, obscured by deep despair,
I felt no purpose for my life, no one to really care.
I lifted up my tear stained face and breathed a whispered
prayer, God gently answered, "no child, your works not
finished here".

The veil of darkness lifted in that miracle of prayer,
By the goodness of His Mercy, I had someone to care.
With spirit strong and hope sustained, I'll do the things I can,
He calmed the stormy waters, as in faith I took his hand.

As I looked upon that mountain, leaning 'gainst the sky so tall
Through eyes of faith it did not seem to be that large at all.
By his grace I started climbing, step by step and day by day,
Clouds that held me captive lifted, as through him, I found my way

Now life's road, though rough and rocky, is much easier to bear
God's love seems closer to us, in our moments of despair.
Yes, I climbed that rugged mountain—that trial too has gone;
Wrapped safely in his fervent love, I'll mount the heights to home!
—*Mae Hurst*

Just Sit And Watch!

As I sit in my chair
I gaze at woman so fair.

Her beauty and whimsical ways
Are slipping each passing day.

Old age is a nasty trick played upon us all
For I remember the days she stood there so tall.

But then came old age creeping in through the night
To take away her vigor and slow down her fight.

She now sits in her chair reminiscing of times
When she played, when she danced, when she rollicked in fun
For old age is now here, life's no longer a pun!

I sit in my chair watching Mother so dear
I sit and I remember as I wipe away the tear.
—*Barbara L. Justice*

Saturday

Saturday is my day
I have twenty-four free hours to run and smile

Saturday is my day
It does not belong to any body
I am my host
I can order me to do things I like

Saturday is my day
All the things in week days were gone
I can catch my shadow only today
All the Saturdays are my birthday
I love my free Saturday
—*Millie Lee*

Blessings

Dear Lord, from whom all blessings flows,
I give my soul to thee.
In all my sorrows, conflicts, woes,
Dear Lord, Remember me.

When trials may obstruct my way,
Ill's I cannot flee,
Let my strength be as my day,
Dear Lord, Remember me.

When worn with pain, disease, and grief,
This feeble body you see,
Grant me patience, rest, and relief,
Dear Lord, Remember me.

When in my solemn hour of death,
I wait my just decree,
Let this be the prayer of my last breath,
Dear Lord, Remember me.
—*Julia Cranfill*

The Wall

As I walked along that lonely black wall
I got this feeling I was not alone,
You can't visit this place and have no feeling at all
For it seems to reach out to touch you, this wall of stone.

As you walk and gaze upon the names that are there
You want to reach out and touch each and every one,
Of the men and women who fought on the ground and in the air
The strange feeling of closeness over you does come.

Mothers and fathers, husbands and wives, standing at the wall
As they cry I can only stand there while looking all around,
Many stand in amazement, others with tears in their eyes
At the wall that slopes so gracefully out of the ground.

Our children and grandchildren can live with pride
For all these names on this wall that you see,
Is so that we can go on living is why they died
So that all mankind may have an chance to be free.

As I stand back and look at this great wall
I am proud to be an American and to be free,
They went to a foreign land and gave their all
They gave up their lives for you and me.
—*James D. Alcorn*

Lost Spring

What happened to Spring?
   I had so much faith in thee -
   And trust, 'twas not just lust
I asked of thee
   Who filled the yard and tree with green
   Then emptied my heart
No more seen - the phantom riding
   on the wind,
The phantom happiness was sin
   What happened to my soul within?
Oh, how in winter I longed for thee
Fought, and sought, and bought for thee
My last chance was for the spring
   to become a lasting thing
Oh, why, forsooth, you gave it up
   Lone stands a buttercup,
Withering by my side
In fantasy we can't be tried
Yet tried we are, because of you
Oh, spring don't lie - I know you knew'.
—*Betty Flanagan*

Loving To Hate, Hating To Love

I love you!
I hate you!
I just can't decide
Exactly how I feel inside.
One minute you're sweet the next you're a jerk.
Don't you know inside I hurt?
One day you're happy and then you're mad.
You confuse me so much I'm never glad.
Can't you see how much I've been hurt?
First you are sassy and then you are curt.
It's getting to the point I wish we'd never met.
You act as though you like me, but then you are upset.
Which feelings are real?
The tears in my eyes show how I feel.
Will the confusion ever go away?
You act so different from day to day.
I love you!
I hate you!
I just can't decide
Exactly how I feel inside.
—*Sandra Hull*

"Forever My Love"

I am only sleeping
   I have not gone away,
Though, you may not notice me
   I shall walk with you each day.
Look upon the mountains
   The ones that I so loved,
And if you lift your head
   You'll see me in the clouds above.
Slowly stroll into the meadows
   Where I have made a path,
Once again you'll find me
   Where I've stepped, will forever last.
Peer into the waters
   Of the gently flowing stream,
And among the nooks and crannies
   My smile can still be seen.
Although my voice is silent
   And my body lies so still,
I have always stood beside you
   My love, I always will.
—*Katherine Kalanta*

I Gave Up T.V. And Found Poetry

Except for the Super Bowl
I have severely restricted
   my viewing
   my midafternoon snacks
   my midafternoon naps
even my fishing
Now I am racking my brain for the right word to connect
to the previous right word
   check the dictionary check the thesaurus
   is this word the best is this word better
   what rhymes with tylenol
Now that I am retired I anticipated calm and leisure
   poetry can keep you up late
   wake you up early
   in the middle of sound sleep
Why am I doing this
Now I am house Bard
No competition helps
Move over Shakespeare
I might trade my fishing license for poetic license
—*A. S. Lehrman*

Someday

Someday I am going to make it out of here
I have walked the path of loneliness to long
Someday I will get started on my career
But how many some days are already gone

Some days I feel like I am mocking
Other days I wonder who I am
Some days I know I am something
Other days I just don't give a damn

Someday the world shall fall in despair
But I should not worry except for me
For someday might never repair
If I shall not ever see

Someday, is this today
Am I passing by my someday
Is someday questioning my yesterday
Or is today my beginning someday
—*David L. Ritchey*

Homeplace

From the hill, with the spring rain falling,
I hear the creek cascading below me
Over the rocks. Chimney stones lie tumbled
On the earth from the hundred-year-old cabin.
She may have stood where I stand now,
Listening to the music the water makes,
Mockingbirds, soft cooing of doves,
And whippoorwills calling at twilight.
I have tasted her strawberries
Sprung from a long-ago planting,
I have walked on her orchard grass
Beneath the trees that are gnarled and twisted.
Her garden is overrun with blackberries,
Buckeye and thistles, the roses she planted
Still struggling to bloom in the midst of weeds.
I want to say to her, "Rest easy and be at peace.
The home that you loved is loved once more,
Your garden will bloom again,
Your fields will produce their bounty."
I have come home and the land is welcoming me.
—*Leona Peffly Martin*

Time Alone

The wind is gently moving all the shadows in my mind,
  I hear the quiet whispers, of memories I can find,
While stored away from prying eyes,
  My inner thoughts unwind.
    The quiet hours I spend alone, are helping me to
Gather, all my loving thoughts and visions, I will
    Forever treasure.
Long walks beside the water, the ocean, so very grand,
  I hear the lapping of the waves as they tell their
Story, as they meet the shifting sands.
Time is fleeting, yet it can be forever, much depends
  On how we use it, often, seldom or never.
Don't rush through this life, take time to enjoy the
  Beauty of the stone.
Get back in touch with God, my friend, and spend some
  "Time alone".
—*Doris Staples*

I Hurt

I hurt.
I hurt a lot.
I feel like an open wound that's bleeding.
Nothing can help the wound.
Nothing can make it stop bleeding. Except me.
Nothing can make it stop hurting. Except me.
I'm not sure I can do that.
I'm not sure I know how, but I know I have to try.
I've never cried like this before.
I've never hurt like this before.
I've never had to do anything like this before.
I know I'm the only one who can do it.
I know I have to learn.
I know I can make it stop hurting.
I know I can make it all better.
I know I can make it go away.
I know I'm the only one who can.
I know I can do it.
I know I can stop the hurt.
I know I can.
—*Joan Grady*

Border Crossing

Heeding whispers from the past,
I jaunt across the border.

The city fades in space and time—
  The shroud of orange-tainted haze,
  The chains of target dates unyielding,
  Loneliness induced by turmoil in the streets.

Beyond the border-crossing, vision is unblurred.
A blanket of prairie unfolds to the horizon,
  Blending with sky that peeps from behind fluffy clouds.

Lingering, I watch the burst of red
  As the sun dips beneath the grassy plain
  And darkening shadows consume the gleams of light.
Reverently, I have breathed the air of sunset, unshackled,
  delivered.

Ignored in salad days, the prairie's beauty beckons now
  And whits of memory set astir.

At eventide, when life begins its downward slope,
An enchanting world — too long forgotten —
Lies just across the border.
—*John E. Turner*

Untitled

The sun is bright and yellow
I just wanted to say a little hello
These are couple of lines, I hope they would rhyme
I wrote them so you could be mine
I found them in the bottom of my heart,
Because I want you in my life as a big part.
When you smile you look so cute,
I just want to jump down and parachute.
Your nose and your ears are so fine,
Especially your lips I want to kiss them and make them mine
If I could get married you would be the girl,
Because I just love a girl with beautiful curls.
—*Vishal Aggarwal*

My Lost Warrior

I feel the pain in your eyes.
I know the walls around your soul.
I feel your anger at the lies.
Even now, your truth remains untold.

I hear your screams in the night.
I feel you trembling in fear.
Day after day, I fight,
To wipe away your tears.

I hammer at the walls you've built.
I break one down to find another.
Your childhood washed away like silt.
You still mourn for some lost brother.

You fear to let anyone in.
Your walls protect your innermost self.
You wonder what might have been.
You wonder where your childhood was left.

You're afraid to let anyone care.
You're afraid of what you've become.
But I promise I'll always be there.
Until at last, home you come.
—*Cindy K. Bird*

Back To Utica

Past shades of grey and cool browns
I left the Burnt Hills of the Sacandaja Mountains.
As mist and haze melted into sky.
I passed bridges leading to
Little Falls and Canojoharie.

In Herkimer I found warm, old faces
Recounting the past and lingering in the present.
I left the fireside
Gazing upon those vertical piles
Of stone, glass, brick and cement.
I returned with indigo clouds
Swiftly passing Canojoharie
Curving up and around Little Falls and
the Sacandaja Reservoir.

Pastel colored hills
Pressed against prussian mountains.
I sped past Half Moon and Burnt Hills
To finally rest at the awaiting
Lakes and pines of Yaddo.
—*Babette Martino*

Baking In The Sun

Lying head down on a slope,
I like my camera when I have my glasses on.
I can feel gravity tugging my body
but my pants and shirt stay in the same place
so I can feel my collar against my throat
and my belt at my hips as if it could be
that I was hanging from my toes.
I can see the sun when I close my eyes
pinning me to the slope so that trying
to raise
my head
I really
have to
strain
but then I lay down again because
there's nothing to see when I have my camera,
and nowhere to go when I'm hanging by my toes.
—*Catherine Yu*

Why Golf?

This may be opinionated,
I master everything within my grasp
The way I dress
The way I speak
The way I walk

My dress proclaims my ability to match
To prove my character I need only to speak
Walking proves my wholesome

While playing Golf I often surrender my greatness
to a small gutless sphere, which has no right to humiliate

My dress becomes a disguise,
out of character, I approach it
with vulgarity, hostile vengeance, I now slink,
wishing I could disappear

Like many, I obey this small lifeless gutless sphere,
drawn back to it like a magnetism, time after time
to beat life into it

Why do I golf?
I love golf! I love golf! I love golf!
But not the ball, it Tee's me off!!!!
—*Ferdinand Keller*

How I Love Thee

I may be fat,
I may be ugly,
But that shouldn't change
How you love me.

Please, dearheart, please forgive me so,
Without you, I do not know
(What I would become).
So let us join our two hearts as one.

My love for you is true
I am devoted to you.
I will always love you.

You shall come back for me one day,
Promise me that your heart will never stray.

Let your love be
Straight from you to me.
How I love thee.
—*Kim Jurns*

Me

I have been to hell and back, searching for my Lord.
I meant to meet Him personally, and hear His Holy Word.
I found Him in the wind and rain
I found Him in the deep
I found Him in my heart - felt prayer.
I found Him in my sleep
I found Him in the other's prayers
And in the life they keep.
I found Him in the grass and trees
And in the sounds of spring
But most of all I find Him
When my own heart starts to sing.
—*Betty Patrick*

In The Park

In the park where I do dwell,
I met a man whom I loved well.
He came and took my love from me and now
he's gone to set it free. He sat a woman upon
his knee and told her things he never told me.
I went home and cried upon my bed not a
word was ever said, he came home late that
night and looked for me both left and right. He
came upstairs, my door he broke, there he found
me hanging by a rope. He found a knife and
cut me down, on the floor this note he found.

It said;

"Dig a grave, and dig it deep,
Place a statue at my feet.
On the statue place a dove,
To show the world I died
For Love"

—*Jill M. Frazier*

The Grandma's I Never Had And Hope To See

When I was born my grandma's had already passed on.
I never got to look at them nor they at me
or feel their warmth, their personality.
Or hear their voice when reading a story or inquiring
  about my young life.
I never smelled their cooking or ate their food
or felt the touch of their concern for my happiness.
I did not physically see their great love for me
or present mine to them.
But as I reflect on my life now
I've had help along the way and vow
that those mysterious helping angels were my grandma's watching
out and praying for me from above, tolerant of my mistakes,
not taking credit for my good breaks.
But always there, trying in their remote way to communicate
their love for me.
God loves them for all that they do even though he kept them
from my view.
They're waiting up there for me to see when I leave this life
and flee...into their arms.

—*Don Goethals*

Untitled

When I hear your voice...
   I never want another choice.
When journeying through life with a few...
   I selected you.
Life is strange...
   while people make a change.
Our lives travel fast...
   while we wish it could last.
My love for you today...
   is here in my heart to stay.
I wait here in a special way...
   for you to come another day.
You are special to me...
   for it's in the eyes of others to see.
Let our romance be divine...
   it was meant to be yours and mine.
Oh how I yearn so much.....
   while our phones keeps us in touch.
The dreams about you while alone...
   will always bring you home.

—*Thomas Wayne Hudson*

Reach For The Sky

Last night while I walk and talk with myself
I noticed over both my shoulders
Death destructions and depressions
Followed behind at arms length with quickened send

Hoping and doping to outsmart myself
I leaped into a darkened alley cat way
Coping and roping for an easy get away
Followed behind at harm's strength was a quickened end

Shaking and breaking to outsmart my death
I heaped into a carcass deposit
Life ascension and comprehension
Followed behind at charm's length with a quickened bend

Last day I remember while living and dying with myself
I realized over both my lives this time
Existence was meaningless from the false treat I ran away
Followed behind at farm's strength was a quickened mend

—*Trent Carlson*

Compassion

The phone rang
I picked it up and said, "Hello"
It was a friend
She was hurting and needed to talk
I lent an ear
And hoped the wounds of life were soothed.

If it were I
Who hurt and needed to talk
She would listen
And I would somehow feel better
For everyone needs
Sharing and caring for others.

—*Ellen Smith*

The Art Lesson

"Grandma, don't you know the sky is blue?"
I quickly painted azure over lead.
My skies have been of a different hue.

Grey skies of war. And a happy few
Before he waved and left and came home dead.
"Grandma, don't you know the sky is blue?"

Silent, shapeless, white clouds blew
Above my aimless world of grief and dread.
My skies have been of a different hue.

Imperceptibly I changed and grew
To love again. "I've known skies of salmon red..."
"Grandma, don't you know the sky is blue?"

"And orange, pink, and your azure blue-
And rainbows arching overhead..."
My skies have been of a different hue.

"And diamond and black velvet skies, 'tis true,
Are rare, but you will one day know them, too."
"Grandma, don't you know the sky is blue?"
Perhaps, but my skies have been of a different hue.

—*Heidi Altvater*

Dreams

    As I sit here and think about us,
        I realize we've changed.
  I don't know what makes me feel this,
    But somehow our love seems strange.
    I dream of you holding me tight,
      Or kissing my lips sweetly.
    I dream of dancing all night
And expressing our love completely.
        But my dreams are broken
      When harsh words are spoken.

    I don't know how to say this,
    But I think the end is near.
    I guess I'll have to face it
      And force away the tears.
  If only you could read my mind
      And see the pain I'm in.
Why do we treat each other so unkind?
    Can't we just start over again?
    These questions and more I hold,
But my dreams stay locked out in the cold.

    —*Shannon Lallemand*

Untitled

I fear what I do not know
I run from what is home
I'll sit and ponder
Thoughts of gloom
Alone in my reddened, musty room

My mind a jumble with visions of face
Shut my eyes in hopes of them melting away

Tears fall as they do when I
Think too much
The wireless beside me plays the
Music of love
I sink deeply beneath my tarnished duvet
Scent of Love Supreme lingers where I lay

The colours surround me
The darkness is warm
As I imagine your heart
Bloody and torn
It was you I remember, not me who said
'Damn your heart and your soul
Our love is dead'

    —*K. Laura Linantud*

With My Heart

When I looked with my eyes,
I saw only what I chose to see.
When I looked with my heart,
I saw Mother Nature unfolding in all her grandeur.

When I heard with my ears,
I blocked what did not seem pertinent.
When I heard with my heart,
I listened to the Universe gently instructing me.

When I touched with my hands,
I defined everything around me.
When I touched with my heart,
I felt the warm healing energy that is part of all.

When I was a small child,
I explored the world with my senses,
Justifying boundaries,
Making my world safe, absolute and completely concrete.

With childhood behind me,
I explore the whole world with my heart,
Watching all boundaries fade,
With no limitations or fears, and with true belonging.

    —*Debra Adams*

Sunset

As I walk on the rough, sandy beach,
I saw sea shells, so colorful, twinkling in the sunset.
The blue-green ocean, beating against the rocks, washing the sand.
As the gentle breeze touched my face,
I watched the waves sparkle, blending in with the beautiful orange-red
sky, full of colorful birds.
As I watched the beautiful sun set,
I thought it would never end.

    —*Teresa Edmond*

Golden Steps Of Heaven

As the dreamy blue sky got dark, night appeared.
I saw your face in the moon, smiling at me.
You spoke softly, not waking anyone.
When morning came, you were still there.
Even though others could not see you, I did.
You listened to me, not laughing nor making a sound.
I cried before your shiny gold face, you hugged me and
    told me I was in a safe place.
But then you were gone, not even saying good-bye.
At night I looked for you, hoping you were not far.
Then just as I was leaving, a shooting star picked me up
    and carried me to you.
I saw you lying down, very hurt.
I picked you up and carried you in my arms.
I carried you up the golden steps up heaven
For you would not die, alone.

    —*Becky Hamilton*

What Are You Gonna Do Today Joe

I get up this morning I'm feeling so good
I say to myself, 'tis a shame to be alone
On this here kinder day so pretty
Will I thought about it a lot

There's a little gal over there, you know,
Joe, across the holler, yes sir
I've done made up my own mind
To ask her this day to marry me

Do you think I really should?
Am I just having a good dream?
She sure is a pretty peach
Real soft and warm to touch
Kinder reminders me of my Ma

Well Joe what are you gonna do today?
Why I've gonna sit back laughing
And see just how you come out
I'll still be a free man
I think you're crazy that's what I think
I sure ain't gonna tie no knot

    —*Myrtle Hunter*

Springtime

As I sit and look out my window.
I see all the beautiful things that God has created,
The trees waving, the flowers starting to bloom.
The birds all flying around trying to find a new place to nest.
I awake early to gaze at the beautiful new things that God has created.
As the plants grow we realize how quickly time is speeding by.
When we were children time seemed to go by slowly.
As an adult we never have enough time.
Each day we should be glad to be on earth to see the new day.

    —*Linda Arnold*

The Transparent Eyeball

As a transparent eyeball and a part of God —
  I see everything in the light.

Rainbows and sunsets are gifts which nature has given
  so generously to the world.

The forests and lakes act as domains for delicate
  deer and felicitous fish.

Animals are innocent prey which man often stalks
  upon for food.

Mankind is simply a part of God put upon the earth to
  be tested.

Flowers and trees are a special kind of beauty which grow
  and blossom from the warmness of the sun and the coolness
  of the rain.

A shooting star often reminds the world of the majestic
  Heavens and the suffering earth.

Nature is a beautiful escape for people—but mankind is
  continually destroying this creation through littering
  and cutting down of forests. I wish people could see
  how the essence of the earth is suffering as I see it.
  Maybe someday everybody will be a transparent eyeball.
  —*Stacy Crocker*

To Dorothy

    When I look at you
  I see the face of an angel

    With eyes that shine
  Like stars in the night

  Your eyes brighten up the room
  Like the beams of a thousand lights

  Your lips are as soft and tender
    As the pedals of a rose

When you dance you glide across the floor
  As light as a white and fluffy cloud
    gliding slowly across the sky

There is no one else in all this world
    As Nice And Sweet As You!
  —*George L. Hall*

Untitled

Across the horizon,
I see the monastery
The monks who practice chivalry
Courtesy, courage these are the
Columns on which they balance.

Ah, the red rain is gently
blanketing them.

Thunder,
"Welcome back, we almost lost you"
"You were torn up pretty bad"
Since then I've never seen another monk's face.
  —*Jeremy Taylor*

"Dearest Mother"

Even though we've had our ins and outs.
I still consider you the "best" mother without a doubt.
Someone who cared for me when I was small,
Who shared with me her tenderest all.
Someone who was there when I needed them
To show me love and affection as well.
Someone to whom my problems I could tell.
For this I will be forever grateful until the end,
Because, now I know that you are my only true friend.
  —*Dottie Di Fede*

Dragon Tears

As I look into her eyes,
I see the world's demise.
Like crystal diamonds in a forest pond,
Crying for her animal bond.
The violet orbs show my face,
In a perfect reflection of our race.
Crimson blood from the wound.
The silky mane so well groomed.
Both reflect the setting sun,
Like the bright explosion from the gun.
I see the dying wisdom of a thousand lifetimes,
The dead men next to me, covered in grime.
I could not help her, It was too late.
We were the ones who sealed her fate.
I blink,
And the stars claim their earth bound link.
A wail arises from the land to morn,
The death, of the last dragon born.
  —*Michelle Norton*

Lost Without You

When I look in your eyes
I see thoughts I never knew
It is hard to realize that you're leaving
So what am I going to do
Many thoughts run through my mind
many reasons I try to find
I want you to stay with me forever
And leave me lonely never
I will always remember the things you do
I am really gonna miss you
I will miss the way you made me laugh and smile
Your remarkable personality and your wealthy style
Now you leave me with nothing but a tear
Because in my heart what I feel is fear
I can't help what I feel, this feeling that I have is true
That's why I'm lost without you.
  —*Ireca Witter*

Footprints In The Wind On The Water

Footprints in the wind
I see tonight as the sun of dawn
creeps behind in the water beside me
I wonder an animal might I speak
nor a person was here
nor a leaping lizard these footprints were made by me?!.
  —*Cory Poyner*

Secret Place

When the world is just too much to face
I seek peace and quiet in my secret place
The hurry, worry, joy and pain
Are all forgotten when my solace I gain

There's no place in particular - no room, nor church nor city
Just deep within my soul - a place undescribably pretty
I seek just solitude, where with time and inner harmony
Again I am filled with gratitude and deep serenity

Renewed, refreshed I face the world again
Ready to share - to receive - to keep the circle goin'
To do my part in His universe
Confident with the knowledge that daily I'm growin'

I'm helped by many upon my path
From the very beginning 'til I've breathed my last
I pray I'm blessed and allowed to see His face
When I'm granted my final secret place

Praise and blessed be Jesus Christ - Now and forever. Amen.
  —*Lynda G.*

Dear Ginny

As you lie dying on your birthday,
I send my love from far away.

I think of you and days of long ago
When we ran and played in sand and snow.

Though nature lovers are usually boys
We had little time for dolls and toys.

We ran and played from dawn 'til night,
and watched butterflies and birds in flight.

Fields of wild flowers were at our feet,
We picked them for Mother, she was so sweet.

When day was done and Mother called,
We came home slowly, we were so enthralled.

Years have passed and we have gone our separate ways,
I love you Ginny, I miss you and those good old days.

My secret wish on your birthdate
Is to turn back the clock and celebrate.

Since God holds our fate in his two hands,
We'll face what comes and I'll understand.
—*Verda Heimann*

Significance

It rains on a Sunday afternoon in mid May and
I sip coffee and look out the window as the city
is washed over with soft pattering drizzle.

Three blocks away another man whose home is the
street curses at unseen monsters talking in his
head and picks up the soaked cardboard that would
have been his bed.

Back in my room I turn to my lover and say,
"How beautiful the rain; let's go out and play."
But we decide to stay inside and watch the raindrops
collide with the window's pane, and scribble our
insignificant thoughts onto blank pages.

A sick feeling wells up in my stomach; and I'm only
too certain it's from the stale coffee I sip.
—*Robert Burns*

I Dream

It's a grey, dreary afternoon. The rain is falling fast.
I sit alone, dreaming of the past.
I dream of days when the kids were home and there was much to do.
They are gone now and like this make me sad and blue.
I dream of days when I proudly watched as they caught the bus to school. Or when I sent them off to church to learn the golden rule.
I dream of days when I shopped for them, and chose with loving care
The clothes that were most becoming to their eyes, their skin, their hair.
I dream with wild anticipation when Christmas time was drawing nigh,
And how upon the mantel, three stockings were hanging high.
I dream of joy and laughter on many a Christmas morn,
Happy, healthy and alive on the day that Christ was born.
I dream of Spring and Easter when they were decked out in their best,
In celebration of our risen Lord, from where He was lain to rest.
I dream of Junior/Senior Proms, and graduation days;
And the joy of seeing them grow and go their separate ways.
I dream of hearing wedding bells, and remember with a smile.
How I watched with tear filled eyes as they marched down the aisle.
I awaken from my dreams and slowly realize.
There is a present and a future as I wipe my tear stained eyes.
—*N. J. Brock*

Secure! In You, Lord!

I'm secure, Lord! In Your Love!
I sit down by the still waters, secure in rest,
Knowing Your love and wisdom want for me the best.

Lord! I ask for Your strength - in my weakness
I have the joy of knowing - great is Your faithfulness.

Turmoils of the world seem to fade away
In the sight of Your presence, let me always stay.

I see through Your eyes, alert and secure
Beauty of precious thoughts, so clear and pure.

My faith! A gift from You! Secure! All mine!
My prayers go up to You; a sweet fragrance
Like rare and special wine!

Lord! By Thy Holy Spirit, be my alarm!
Bless! Renewing my mind-
Let me be wise as a serpent but humble and kind.

Bow when I fail and disobey, I always get hurt!
As my Compass, Lord! Keep me alert!
Let my life be with a whole mind, body and soul.
Secure Lord! As I submit to You and Your control.

Praise the Lord!
—*Lemoyne Huffman*

The Courts

This was the field where I played.
I spent my childhood here.
I ran and jumped and sang.
The grass was mine: the cool summer grass.
Now it's all withered away.

This was the lake where I swam.
I left my fears here.
I raced and fished and dove.
The water was mine: the clear translucence.
Now the fish are all gone.

This was the air that I breathed.
I dreamt my dreams here.
It flew my kites, cooled my face, and dried my tears.
The clouds were mine: the ever-changing clouds
Now it's thick and grey.

These are the streets that I drive.
I will live my life here.
I hold on to memories; they're all I have left.
These roads are mine: the hard, cold courts.
Until all of my grasps are gone.
—*Todd Hawkins*

Orphaned Child

As I listen to the pouring rain
I start to think about my pain
I think of my life, I think of my love
I think of when I will be in heaven above
I can't wait for when I will be
With everyone who used to love me
Roll of thunder hear my cry
Flash of lightning see my sigh
Tears pouring down my face
I try to feel the warm embrace
I used to feel when they were around
The times I felt I could fly off the ground
I want to be with them again
Please God just tell me when
All of the times I've screamed and cried
All of the times I've almost died
With them my feelings could show
Please God, let me go!
—*Kristine E. Doyle*

"Please Forgive Me"

I peeked into your room last night for just a moment,
I stood there frozen in my tracks as I looked at you,
Your eyes were searching desperately for mine,
You tried to speak, but couldn't.
I didn't know at that moment that it would be the
last time you would ever try.

You looked so frightened, and I could tell that
you were all alone.
I wanted to come to you and touch your hand, and
whisper softly that everything would be alright, but I
couldn't.
How could I know that you would die shortly
after I walked away?
I think you knew as you looked at me that the end
was near, and that your time had come.

That night as I lay in bed, I said a prayer for you,
I dreamt of you.
I am so sorry that you had to die alone,
Please forgive me for not being strong enough
to hold a dying stranger's hand.
—*Melody Houston*

My Imaginary Lover

In the dense darkness of my lonely room
I summons him to appear,
Like a bride anxiously awaiting her groom
My body trembles with emotion and fear,
He comes to me in a swirl of haze
Symmetry brown god of muscle and height,
So perfect, so beautiful, I stare and gaze
Every time he appears I welcome my plight.
As a moth drawn to a deadly flame
His eyes bid me come,
Our souls burn with unquenchable shame
Wild abandonment we will race home,
In a crescendo of harmony our spirits meet
Peacefully, I fall into a contented sleep.
—*Sandra A. Wharton*

"My Child"

I carried you when you couldn't walk.
I talked for you when you couldn't talk.
I rocked you to sleep and held you close. So you
would know I loved you most.

I led you through paths you couldn't take, Was
always there when you would awake.

I bathed, clothed, fed and pampered you well,
because I knew time would tell - all that
I did for you - would make you a citizen
true and blue.

I'm proud of you this day my child because
those grandchildren have made it all
worthwhile,

I watched you grow with pride and joy.
Love to you my girl and boy.
This wasn't accomplished by myself your
Dad shares in my wealth.
—*Shirley M. Brown*

Fruits Of Our Labor

Looking out my window I see my children at play
I think of what I sow as I go from day to day.

Each one of these little ones is unique
Each one a different harvest will reap.

We plant in them our thoughts and feelings
We nurture and care for these little seedlings.

The light and warmth of love we try to give
That they might thrive and live.

Yet many distractions come our way
So many involvements from day to day.

Too much work that needs to be done
We can only hope that in the long run
We've said the right things and made
the right choices
Praying that as they grow we shall rejoice
To God who gave them life
And who blessed us as husband and wife.
—*Irene Hoffman*

I Wonder

As the sun goes down in the evening sky,
I think of you and I wonder why;
I didn't tell you how much I care.
And now you're gone and I'm left here;
To wonder how it would have been,
If I'd said "I love you" even then.
Would you have stayed in love with me,
Or would time have ended what we could be?
Is there still a chance inside your heart,
To mend the hurt that keeps us apart?
Or will time erase the memory,
Of a love that no longer will be?
—*Denise Dupree*

"A Message"

They brought a message to my door,
I thought at first I could live no more.
My hopes all left and my hands did shake,
as the worst of messages I did take.

It started out, "we regret to inform you,"
oh! God I prayed this can't be true,
but yes, it was so very true;
and I started to feel so lonely and blue,

"That your son," it went on to say,
"was reported missing on the seventh day."
I began to grow faint, tremble and shake
as I started realizing the courage it did take.

I knew very well right then,
that we would have to be brave to win.
And if friends will drop a word of love
we'll get sufficient power from above.

I know now that he'll come back
as I've got the power I used to lack,
and when this awful war is won,
my mother will have her darling son.
—*Leanora Musser Shaw*

Why Me?

I woke up this morning all sad and depressed.
I thought, "Why me, Lord?"
I thought why can't things be simpler,
I looked at myself and was not pleased.
I studied my heart and felt empty.
I took my wife to work and ran errands.
I dropped the car off for my wife and walked home.
The wind was blowing and I was sweating.
I thought, "I have it rough."
I walked a little farther and saw a woman.
A woman holding pretty flowers.
I said, "hello" and she smiled and said, "hello"
The woman only had one leg.
I was able to walk away.
—*Frank Wright*

A Mother's Message

Every time I kiss his loving face,
I want to make the world a better place.
I gaze into his bright and trusting eyes,
Void of hatred and of lies.

His chuckles and smiles are filled with charm.
Why would anyone want to cause him harm?
When I dream of him playing outdoors with his peers,
My mind is overcome with fears.

I must make him aware and teach him the danger
Of accepting a treat and going with a stranger.
I pray he will be a fine student and get good grades.
He will realize the devastation caused by drugs
and the heartbreak of AIDS.

In a world corrupted by violence and strife,
How sad the inhumanities of man and the realities of life.
Striving for change should be our goal,
Strict laws for the offenders and their parole.

If we can make the streets a safer place,
We will walk with dignity instead of mace.
Now is the time — to make the punishment fit the crime!
—*Carolyn Kessler*

The Hard And The Humble

I am a rock.
I was born when I left the mountain
I made My way from the mountain to the sea.
I have rounded and smoothed My corners.
I can glisten and sparkle in the light.
I am a gem among the pebbles and the sand.

i am a rock
The Water was frozen by the Wind and separated
me from the Mountain, of which i am made.

The Water carried me to the sea, which
returned me to the Land.

The Water tossed and tumbled me, and my
contact with my brothers has removed
my sharp edges and polished my roughness.

The Sunlight can dance and reflect its
brilliance in my sides.

i am as you, but without the Water,
i would still be a part of the Mountain.
—*John Torrey Berger, Jr*

Challenges

I sat on the roof watching the cold fog seep in from the ocean.
I was cold and freezing but glad I was out there.
I only sit there when I have too much anger or emotion.
I could hear my sister's radio blasting and the sweet smell of
mom's cooking. I thought about my brother and how he lost his
shoe and I was sure he was still lookin'.
The fog got thick and the sun disappeared.
I sat in darkness on a high point not being able to see,
something I deeply feared. I wasn't going to move till the fear
and anger were swept away like the fog. I sat so still and
everything was silent except the high-pitched bark of my dog.
The fog got thinner and my anger and fear did too, and
pretty soon it was gone and I wasn't sure if I knew what to do.
I could go express my feelings to my dad of why I felt so bad.
I didn't want to go to another place, but it was reality and
a challenge I must face.
So down to the window I went and through it I knew I had to go.
I stood up when I was in, ready to face the challenge and never
give in.
—*Martha Howe*

The Real Me Nobody Knows

I've tried to look at myself once,
I was startled and shaken from the effort.
I had to tunnel through garbage and memories.
When I reached the core,
I was shocked and fled back to the surface.

I've spent years of conforming,
being what everyone wants me to be.
My emotions are like a candy machine—pop in your money,
push the right code and you'll get your treat of
anger, tears and laughter.

I'm not sure whom I love or whom I hate.
I've drifted so long with this baggage,
it's too hard to relinquish my hold.
I've learned when people ask me to be myself;
they want me to be like them.

The person that stands before you
has the reflected faces of everyone whom I've met.
So if one day we stumble into each other and begin to carry
on an animate conversation,
you're really chatting with yourself.
—*Kristen Cornett*

Building Blocks

And so they two begin, building a tower.
  I watch as it rises ever so high.
    Majestically risen, behold such a memorial indeed.
      Never before have I saw a more beautiful thing.

Soft gentle breeze blowing, 'round about the great tower.
  Sitting amidst two breathing mountains, it looms.
    And they two breathe a sigh of relief.
      Their monument now complete.

But afar off I hear thunder, it's deep menacing growl.
  Soon darkness invades, the walls tremble and shake.
    The tower is rocked, Mother Earth reigns supreme.
      In the violence of a deep seeded passion.

The storm passes, the great tower is fallen.
  And Mother Earth beckons me, showing no remorse.
    "They shall live to build again" she mutters.
      "They shall build again, and so again they shall fail."

So this is the way of the world. Just man and his woman.
  Building their monuments, till death they do part.
    Only to be broken asunder.
      And so they two began, building a tower.............
—*Rodney Quisenberry*

Sleepless

The moon growing higher in the horizon
I watch its ascent through the hours
hopeful of some blissful vision to write

too sleepless to enter a dream state
the place of our demons and fairies
though I can only lapse aside
content to the music of Floyd in the player
and the cigarette burning in the ash tray

shapeless—too large to be seen
only the dragon's breath visible
blue mists content to drift upon the open air

I too wish to drift
drift away to a land of peace
of the clear languid pools
with the sprites and fairies at play
but a scene envied by all

though as of yet—not a thing
before I lay my head to the pillow
but a few notes scratched upon my fabled pad
I note the rising of the sun
—*e j lundy iii*

A Strong Will

I will survive
I will learn to feel free
I will toss away the clouds
within an understanding in me

I will learn to feel free
I will still walk in hail
Within an understanding in me
I'm more able to bail

I will still walk in hail
under Clouds of Promised Rainbows
I'm more able to bail
with hopes of reaping…well-earned sows

Under clouds of promised rainbows
I will walk to find warm sunlight
With hopes of reaping well-earned sows
I will have to see through this stormy night

I will walk to find warm sunlight
for I will survive
I will have to see through this stormy night
before I…take a wife
—*Christopher R. Chubb*

I Am

I am but a person who is sorrow and weak,
I wonder if my soul will keep,
I hear the call of a sweet angel crying,
I want to know now and why,
I am but a person who is sorrow and weak.

I pretend my life is ahead to see, yet,
I feel so empty and unknown
I touch the hearts of many people but only hear a groan,
I worry if I will meet the angel above so quiet and sweet,
I cry for I know my time is gone and I must go home,
I am but a person who is sorrow and weak.

I understand I am just a man, no one will understand,
I say to them I am full of sorrow and weak,
I dream that my soul will keep,
I try to be pure and sweet, yet,
I hope to meet the angel so pure and sweet.
I am but a person who is sorrow and weak.
—*Melissa Marion Fazio*

Yearbook

Tomorrow and tomorrow, and then again
I will turn pages of this book.
Once more to look upon the years
Of growing and of learning,
Of seeking and of yearning.

For within this book I can come
As close as anyone has ever done,
To hours and days and years
Whose sands have run, to run no more again.

But there will be a time for that.
Today I turn the other way
Toward the rising sun
Of this long awaited day,
When all the world does before me lie.

As northward in the spring
The wild geese fly,
So, follow my dreams must I.
And Oh, I'll try!
I'll try!
—*Glenn W. Skiff*

Thanks To God

Thank you God for sending Danyel my way,
I wish I could be with her each and every day.
I love her so much and only you know,
How much I do love her and that I won't let her go.
Now that I have her I plan to hang on,
I pray to you every night that I do nothing wrong.
I'll do nothing to lose her or push her away,
With her, til I die, is where I want to stay.
Through sickness and health, until I breath no more,
On her I won't turn my back or walk out the door.
Oh Heavenly Father on you throne up above,
I want to thank you again for Danyel and her love.
—*Jason Sidney White*

"A Rainbow Day"

As I stand in my doorway looking out,
I wonder what life is all about.
Early morn, another day without sun,
Sad at first, thinking this won't be fun.

The sky is dark, with few clouds of grey,
I can smell it in the air, another rainy day.
As the rain begins to fall from the sky,
I see a blue patch from the corner of my eye.

Perhaps, with luck, the sun will shine,
Oh, that warmth, sure would be fine.
The rain is falling less and less,
And the sky starts to shed that dark wet dress.

The sun peeks out but the rains still fall,
It's the promise from God, as I recall.
The rainbow's colors, such a beautiful display,
With this awesome sight, comes a special day.
—*Jo-Jo Folz*

Untitled

Swimming all day, under the sun's violent rays
Me and my friend, my friend and me,
Diving floating thoughts felt free, gliding along
As though minds full of happiness,
For my world is touched by this beauty and grace….
—*Brenna Nelson*

Problems

I am a girl, living in a world of dreams.
I wonder what the future will bring.
I hear the screaming demands of tomorrow.
I see the high school dropouts wallowing in self-sorrow.
I want everyone to work together as a team.
I am a girl, living in a world of dreams.

I pretend to be a strong person.
I feel the anxiety, fear, and concern.
I touch the emotional needs, that we keep hidden behind a wall. I worry about the murders, the gruesome killings, and all. I cry for the families that have lost a member.
I am a girl, living in a world of dreams.

I understand the problems of drugs and alcohol.
I say, "Those of us who use them are surely bound to fall."
I dream of fixing all of these problems, that are attached in the way of a tail.
I try to help everyone, but sometimes I fail.
I hope that I can change the world, and make it work as a better team.
I am a girl, living in a world of…Dreams!
—*Mary Elizabeth McCombs*

I Am

I am
I wonder what the world will be like
   with no more sadness
I hear happy people, filled with joy
I see how what will come, affects people now
I want it to happen today, but I know it won't be long
I Am

I pretend everything's different
I feel
I touch the images in my mind
I cry when I think about this worlds sorrows
I am

I understand it can't be long
I say, "It won't be long"
I dream about a different world
I try
I hope
I am happy
—*Ericka Scott*

A Christmas Wish

Oh I wish that I were Santa with eight tiny deer
I would get so excited when Christmas time draws near.

I'd call together all my elves to sing our favorite song
That Christmas time is coming and we don't have very long.

Soon we'd go out to the woods to find our christmas tree
And decorate it with many things for all the world to see

In the mail we would go letters from little girls and boys;
So it's time we all start working to make the Christmas toys;

Christmas eve is finally here I must be on my way
To give out toys to girls and boys and make their Christmas day

Yes I wish that I were Santa
by now you can plainly see
That if I were Mr. Santa Clause
my heart would be full of glee!
—*Pepper J. Pizzino*

Wish Thoughts

When I grow weaker and weaker, and fear the end is near,
I would like a Reuben sandwich, and an ice cold bottle of beer.
Then find someone who would love to bake—
To make Toll House cookies and a Carrot Cake.

I've done without a lot of things to keep my sugar down—
And even when I really try—my blood count brings a frown.
I must admit I've been known to cheat——
But sometimes a gal must have a treat.

I sit and dream about Ice Cream
But its really not the same,
As eating a Dove Bar—a rare delight—
Or eating Danish late at nite.

Being pesty is not my style—
For a Camel I wont walk a mile—
But for Brownies or Apple Pie—
My limit is the sky.

After all is eaten, and I'm agog!
And I've pigged out like a hog—
I'll close my eyes—cross my hands—put a smile on my face,
Then say farewell to the Human Race.
—*Jane Y. Weller*

My Dream

If I could only talk,
I would tell you of a dream.
Oh, what a wonderful dream.
I lay in front of a glowing fire,
My cedar bed soft as snow.
I never felt a hungry day,
or a moment without a little play.
My master treated me with a kind heart,
and gentle hand.
In return, I gave him my love and friendship;
for I am "Mans" best friend.
As I lay here cold, hungry, and all alone;
I wonder where my friend as gone.
A creature of "GOD", prisoner of "Man".
Doomed to die a lonely death,
only because I was born.
As I draw my last breath,
I will be dreaming "My Wonderful Dream."
—*Kevin S. Jennings*

So Easily Detached

A wintery wind slashes like a jagged knife,
Penetrating the breath of a somber wilderness,
Taking the leaves from their branches.
Leaves once ribbed with the color of life,
Their lifeless stems lie astray,
   so easily detached.

Leaves that break from their branches
Are hidden as others follow,
Soon to turn back to soil and
Blend with the browning earth.
Thrown into an unmarked grave,
   so easily detached.

Shadows play with Nature's daughter,
As this cycle is repeated.
The resting earth quiets the wind,
Shedding the darkened life within,
Nature reproducing what once was,
   so easily detached.
—*Karen O'Connor*

Dad

How he laughs, how he cries
He makes my darkness bright.
When all of the world gave up,
He was there to make sure I made it.

He means the world to me,
He means it all, every moment,
Every day, he'll be by my side.
I love him so much that is
All I can say, I love you Dad.

From the day I was born,
To the day you walk me down the aisle
I'll cherish you forever more.
—*Goldie J. VanHeel*

The Lord Is My Redeemer

The Lord is my Redeemer
He meets my every need
I'll be a tree along the river
Though now I'm just a seed

Sometimes I feel the peace of God
Sometimes there's torment in my soul
But my Savior's right here with me
And He shall make me whole

I'll trust in Him forever
From His path I will not roam
I know He will direct my way
And someday lead me home
—*Kenneth Van Owen*

Ma Ma Knows

When God made little boys, my son
He must have had you in mind.

Not your sins and not your crimes
But a little boy who's loving, gentle
and kind.

The little boy grew up to be a
man who's still loving, gentle and kind
which sometimes he tries to hide.

But Mama knows, Mama knows
The little boy the big man left behind.
—*Dena Abbott*

Star Sonnet

"Thanks for your help,"
He said to me,
"In reaching for the moon
And catching stars."

I've thought of that...
Moon's cool green cheese,
Opposed to stars' sharp
Burning light.

Maybe I've swallowed one,
Carelessly,
(A star, that is),
And that is why
I hurt inside
Tonight.
—*Mary Louise S. Hardin*

Wet

They trickle down my face
he speaks in pillow language
but the words cut like knives
and imbed my flesh
growing, it eats away
at my heart
and deteriorates my mind
like a rotten melon
perception is insane
I live in the world of the dead
you hold me in your arms
the scent of you poisons the air
breathing slowly in and out
shortening my life with every breath
I know I have been betrayed.
they burn into my face
like acid
they just won't dry.
—*Deanne De Nyse*

"A Squirrel"

A squirrel ran across my morning paper.
He stepped across the face of the
   president,
   the verdict of the trial,
   the fiery tragedy of yesterday,
   the words of some great leaders.
He stepped across the fine line
Of yesterday that somehow
Extended into the realm of today.
He stepped across the prejudice,
The hate, the misunderstanding.
He walked across time in the
Span of one small moment.
He touched yesterday, today,
And tomorrow with each of
His four furry paws.
He swept his tail across
The future, widened his eyes,
And scampered away
Back into the safety of his tree.
—*Crystal Michelle McAlister*

Enlightened Darkness

I came across a man today
He turned to me to say

The sun it shines so bright right now
And lovely is this day

The sound of waves upon the shore
And birds that chirp and sing

When I am down and feeling blue
Its happiness they bring

The sounds of spring are in the air
And lovely do they sound

I only wish I had my sight
To see what's all around

For he I'd met this fine spring day
With joy throughout his heart

Had never seen God's miracles
He'd been blind from the start

I really hope this makes you think
If only for awhile

That there are those less fortunate
Who still manage to smile
—*Ralph Salata*

He Who Wants

He who wants, must want to do,
He who doesn't, don't boo hoo.
If you want to win in life,
You must be willing to fight.

Fight for what you think is right,
Fight and fight with all your might.
If you want to win in life,
You must want to pay the price.

Life's road isn't always paved gold,
You must tarry with your load.
And don't be one who will doubt.
Or you'll surely do with out.

We who wants might wait and wait,
To enter that golden gate.
And your face will not be sad,
Because you gave it all you had.

He who wants, must want to do,
He who doesn't, shame on you.
If you want to get ahead,
Take heed of what's been said.
—*Sylvia Schlagel Ragsdale*

The Hole In Grandpa's Shoes

My grandpa was a stalwart man
He yearned for open spaces
When as a boy he set his course
His shoes with tightened laces.

The road was rough, not smooth at all
The shoes they took the blows
For grandpa knew as years passed by
The shoes no longer glowed.

The hole in grandpa's shoes, my friend
Grew larger with the years
And as the saga now unfolds
So does grandpa's fears.

The life that grandpa knew so well
Came swiftly to an end
The hole in grandpa's shoes, my friend
Could no longer bear the mend.
—*Anthony N. Checki*

Angel Prayer

Guardian Angel,
Hear my call,
Help me see
Your Light today,
Fill this soul
With love and caring,

Show me how
To share with all
God's creatures
This loving light:
Everywhere...

Pick me up
When'er I fall,
Dust me off
with your soft wing,
And send me searching
Along this trail,
For all in need
Of our good deeds.
Amen...
—*Donna M. Gilio*

Our Lord

Our Lord means all the world to me
He's with me night and day.
He's with me in my garden
and when I kneel down to pray.
He's with me in the grocery store.
He's with me on the street.
He's always looking over me.
His love is oh so sweet.
What would life be without our Lord?
How could we face each day?
How could we live?
How could we love
and kneel each night to pray?
He is a very special Lord.
When my mind's as confused as can be,
I talk to Him;
I pray to Him,
and He in turn helps me.
Thank you Lord.
—*Norma Claflin Trask*

"He"

A gust of wind, there He goes.
His destination no one will know.

Floating, flying, free falling.
Consenting to Mother Nature's calling.

After time, finally touchdown.
He makes for Himself a home on the
 ground.

Begins to grow, reaching for the sky.
Until the fateful day when He will die.

Before His expiration He continues the
 strife.
Contributing to another's life.

He stands patiently waiting until the time is
 right.
The time He deems fit in his sight.

The wind blows, it is now done.
Of all His children he does not see one.

All of His children he did send.
His time is now up, He reached the end.
—*Michael J. Wos*

Dances For Earth

Spiritually transformed, he chants.
His song pleads for restoration.

Restore harmony to the earth,
restore harmony to my people.

Let all of nature harmonize,
each songbird's song,
the eagle's call,
the insect's hum,
rivers clear,
each shining pebble
has its place.

Every forest, every tree,
their leaves and needles
cradling new winged creatures.

Listen brothers to his song.
Restore harmony to the earth,
restore harmony to my people.

Can you hear it,
above the distorted din
of mechanization?

—*Marlene Stanford-Cox*

The Winepress

Let me to others Christ make known
 His Word be my delight
so when I stand before His throne
 My fruit will have no blight.

Let me make sure God's Word I sow.
 Like seed it will take root
and God will cause it then to grow
 into precious fruit.

Then let me in His vineyard toil
 each day with loving care
let never worldly pleasures spoil
 the fruit from Him I bear.

For when the Winepress of His wrath
 one day my God shall tread
He will give to all who hath
 the everlasting bread.

But to the one who hath no fruit
 for Christ hath no desire
the axe will be laid to the root
 the tree cast in the fire.
—*Leslie A. Sinquefield*

Untitled

I close my eyes
hold out my arms
and no one is there
I reach out in the night
for your reassuring warmth
and no one is there
I wait quietly
for the sound of your car
and no one is there
the tire is flat
I curse it
and no one is there
If I forgot you're gone
many things make it clear
for no one is there
death separates us
but our love
lives in my heart
and I am not alone
even tho' no one is there
—*Jan Elder*

Oriental

Yin and Yang
How beautiful
Two become as one.

Finally we are laying side by side
The even consuming tempest is over
For now
The flesh bruised by love
The spirit still gorged by sensations.

Yin and Yang
How beautiful
Two become as one.
—*Monique Purguy*

More On Africa

I am pleased you are not my man
I am pleased I am not your woman
 Africa

You have a pattern
You provide abundantly
You coax gently
Until we rely on you
And live off you
And love you
And our spaces and power

And then you withdraw
And give us drought
And we starve
And you hold the ace

I am learning
about you Africa

And I learn to love fiercely
And brutally.
—*Katie Botha*

Bringing Up Mona

Too young to Procreate,
I became a surrogate.
Temporary custody granted,
I attempted to keep the covenant.
You, the cheeky, precocious sprite,
Became my absolute delight.
Spitting Spinach with a grimace,
You shouted "Stupid" with vehemence.
Fearing only large dogs growling,
Raising your arms skyward howling,
Up you'd come with a giggle,
Moments later descending with a wiggle.
Now a woman full grown,
You have babes of your own.
My vicarious pride is continuing,
Though unskilled in my parenting.
Your Age-tempered fighting Spirit
Now champions your own urchins.
—*Kim R. Stewart*

Dead Men Don't Cry

My feelings were hurt
 I began to sigh
I must die to self
 If I want to get by
I began to babble
 My thoughts were torn
They said they loved me
 But showed me their scorn
I contemplated how they
 passed me by
While others received
 that pie in the sky
I couldn't collect my thoughts
 And I just went on
About how unfair -
 All that was going on
Then I remembered
 To self I must die
No pity, no discontent, only Joy
 Because Dead Men Don't Cry
—*Marian B. Allen*

I Believe

    I believe in you and me;
      I believe in us
          TOGETHER.

  I believe in hopes and dreams;
      I believe in
          THE FUTURE.

  I believe in love and laughter;
      I believe in
          THE HEART.

I believe in patience and understanding;
      I believe in
          THE SOUL.

  I believe in magic and wonder;
      I believe in
          THE IMAGINATION.

      But most of all,
      I believe in
          YOU.
—*Lisa Simmelink*

A Melody

The melody within my heart
I bore, long after our depart.
A melody of gloom, my dear,
which came to me so strong and clear.

To know our love could never be,
was hard to bear for you and me.
To feel the blooming of regret,
was like the losing of a bet.

I still can see you standing by,
the window where we said goodbye.
And felt the sorrow in the air;
the air that stood about us there.

The tears and fears that filled our eyes
were present when we bade goodbyes;
and ever stains the smiles we wear.
On skin of clay their marks we bear.

—*Reagan Murff*

A Picture of Love

In the moon light
I can picture your face
with smiles so bright
and eyes with grace.

I can see your arms
spread open wide
with gentle charm
with me inside.

I can see your hands
so tender, but strong.
Just like a man's
that would do no wrong.

I can see your feet
coming forward and slow
in order to meet
the oncoming glow.

Then I put it all together
and stare at what I see.
Hoping it will last forever,
because it's a picture of love to me.

—*Tami McRoberts*

Untitled

In my dreams
I can reach out
and touch your hand,
and know the warmth
of your love.

In my dreams
you are there
to laugh and
cry with me.

In my dreams
I fear nothing
for I am by your side.

If ever in my life
a dream is to come true
you are the dream
I wish for.

—*Leslie Zotz*

My Time

The years have sped by
I can't count the times I've tried
To slow their pace
To escape this race
To sweeten life's taste
Always to no avail
Attempts at all, were doomed to fail
Often I felt this life a jail
And happiness, a fools fairy tale
Insanity, has sometimes ruled
Making days long and cruel
I try now to let the future be
And allow the past, to become a memory

—*Mike Kimzey*

To Beth;

If there was something,
I could say
To take your hurt away
I would say it,
until the end of time
But no matter how hard I try
The words just seem
to slip on by
Until the pain you feel
I wish I could take
and make it mine
I'll never understand
why someone has to
hurt so much
And saying I'm sorry
is just not enough
But you'll never be alone
and you'll never be unloved
As long as there's a God in Heaven
And someone to think of.

—*Noel Carter*

Broken Glass

    As I sit in my old shack
and look through the
broken glass I hear the
sounds of freedom. I
wish I were free. Oh I
wish I were free.

—*Alicia Kohlwey*

Amanda

I cried when you were born
I cry for you now
I miss you
I love you
I long to see your smile.

You are my princess...
My angel from above
God truly blessed me
For I have you to love.

We're apart
But we're together
Mommy thinks of you
Now and forever.

You are my world
My life
My inspiration
Together we'll be for...
It's God's destination.

—*Brenda Sallie*

Missed Love

When I was loved
I didn't love him
Till it was too late

I can't stand being without him
My love grows stronger everyday
I wish I could be in his arms,
Holding me tight

I wish I could look into
His beautiful brown eyes

I love him so dearly
With all my heart
Without him my dreams are falling apart

—*Debbie Nelson*

I'm Sorry

I'm sorry if I hurt you,
I didn't mean to do so.
I want you to believe me,
I want you to just to know.

When we were together
What we had was good
It was something very special
It was only us two.

Even thought we have nothing now,
We were meant to be together.
To never be apart,
To be with each other forever.

So always remember that someone
is here to understand you,
To laugh with you,
To cry with you,
To talk with you,
And to love you today and always.

—*Audrey Baray*

The Homeless

You pass me by
I do not weep, I do not sigh.
I'm the homeless,
Otherwise, the same as you,
But I
do not have a home.
You have a life,
You have your jobs,
We both have our God.
But you pass me by.
Do you not cry
My God! My God!
Where is the heart, where do you start
For we homeless?
We are your life
Don't pass me by
Lest you in turn, weep, weep and sigh
And maybe die.
—*Evelyn Sherburne*

Death

Death is a rather good thing,
I don't know why people think it's bad,
It takes away all pain;
You no longer have to feel mad,
You no longer have to feel pressured,
You no longer have to feel stressed,
But when you really think about it—
Death is not the best;
It leaves behind all your family,
It leaves behind all your friends,
It leaves behind all your possessions.
Your candle has a burned at both ends.
—*Nick Madsen*

Why Did You Go?

Why did you go?
I don't think I'll ever know.
Sometimes I feel sad,
And others I'm so mad.
I know its not your fault.
You really couldn't stay.
But, I'll love you forever,
and ever anyway.
So now the question is...
Do you remember?
The way we fought the way we cried?
The way we got caught,
and the way we lied?
Oh the times we had,
I'll never forget.
Your the best friend
I could possibly get!
—*Joelle Boots*

Untitled

When we first met
I know I'd never forget
the feeling of a special
touch, a beautiful feeling
I needed so much!

Your love is so special to me
together again for all the
world to see!

Forever your love
—*Kristine Zenda*

The Final Goodbye

I feel silence.
I feel hurt.
The wind is chilling me
but I only feel numbness.

Then the lightning hits and
the thunder rolls.
And I can't stop it...
the tears fall down my face.

You are gone from my life
gone forever.
They close the curtains
and call up the family

I guess this is my last
good-bye.
—*Jessica Vollmerhausen*

"Sweet Refuge"

I Know I walk the razor's edge,
I feel it now and then.
For if I ever walk too close,
I feel it nick my skin.

I know a place inside myself,
Where all is dark and still.
I wonder if I'll visit there?
I wonder, if I shall?

Just quietly step inside myself
And gently close the door.
Where no one on this earth,
Can find me anymore.
—*Juanita K. Pickel*

Untitled

I feel like laughing
I feel like singing

I feel like crying
I feel like sighing

I feel many
that I cannot

  Explain!
But I know I
am feeling all
of these for you!

I feel like rejoicing
I feel like praising

I feel like pleasing
I feel like loving

I feel many
that I cannot

  Explain!
But I know I
am feeling all
of these for you!
—*Stephanie A. Preku*

His Love

He has a love that can not die,
I have a love that will not lie.
I have to see him every day,
So he can help me find my way.
He's like a brother, always there,
He is there because he cares.
If he were to leave, I would cry,
Still his love would never die.
—*N. Johnson*

Thoughts

When I'm with you
I feel safe, and our
talks, I love them.
You touch and warm
embrace. Your eyes
so strong, with you
is where I must belong.
Its not yet love, but getting
close. Are these feelings
bad? Are they good? Do
they make you happy?
Do they make you cry?
I need to know where I
stand, as more... As less
than a friend, think it
threw and let me know
if you feel for me as I
feel for you.
—*Stephanie Desadore*

Good-Byes

There was a certain feeling
  I felt it when we met,
A feeling you can't give up
  You've found a friend.
The feeling is like a magnet
  One I won't forget...
I feel I know you totally
  and more.
What is this special feeling
  that lets you know at once
you've met, not only a person,
  a friend.
And if and when you must say good-bye,
  your emotions take hold...
The warmth you feel you want to keep
  But this was only to be...
  A moment in time set apart.
Good-byes are not for friends.
—*Beth McIntyre*

My Bad Day

I'm not very happy
I had a bad day.
I'm mad at my family
What else can I say?

My family and I
went to a diner;
Couldn't have been happier
Couldn't have been finer.

Wasn't being mean
Wasn't being mad
Wasn't being grumpy
Wasn't being sad.

Then me and my sister
We got into a fight
We got into deep trouble
Late that night

So that's my story
That's how it goes
I'm mad all over
From my head to my toes.
—*Katie Fischer*

Not Me

Many times throughout the day
I have to take some time to pray

For if I don't I always find
How hard it is to just be kind

Sometimes what I want to do
Is maybe black an eye or two

Or throw a shoe or break a plate
Or verbally retaliate

Or maybe just be very cold
If you refuse to fit my mold

Human nature will provide
Selfishness and foolish pride

I just thank God constantly
I need not depend on me

I have come to understand
He is there to take my hand

On His power I now rely
I have never blacked an eye

That power, I know is from above
For those that I dislike, I love
—*Patricia Moore*

Entranced

A certain magical man
I know
has cast a spell over me
and though it's still
unpromised
I'm unable to break free
I get a little deeper
and more mesmerized
each day-
he's wrapped so close
inside my heart
his thought won't fade away.

It started out
a slight, faint glow
that got stronger-
every day-
till
now he's like a part of me
that may
forever stay.
—*Lori Kriss*

Prayer Of The Handicapped

Why do I carry this cross, Oh, Lord
I know not the road to Calvary-
My feet are not with sandals shod
Yet I have known no revelry.

Help me to carry my cross, Oh God-
Do you hear and understand?
There's torment in my body
As there's torment in the land.

Forgive me for my cries, Oh Lord,
I feel aught but shame-
There's such a weakness in my soul
I do but cry Thy name.
—*Alyce "Lisa" Gehrling*

Forever In My Heart

I love him very dearly,
I know we'll never part.
He calls me every night,
forever in my heart.
Whenever he kisses me,
I always seem to grin.
But what makes me even happier,
is the touch of his soft skin.
He always seem to pick me up,
when I'm feeling down.
He knows how to comfort me,
and turn around my frown.
He holds me close,
and nice and tight.
I feel so secure
and perfectly right.
He has great respect for me,
I know we'll never part,
He knows how I feel,
forever in my heart.
—*Julie Hirano*

A Message

Dear Father up in Heaven
    I need to talk to you today.
I'm here to ask a favor
    For my Mama who's gone away.

I couldn't bear to look at Mama
    And see tear drops in her eyes.
Just give to her my message,
    I know I should have been more wise.

Please tell Mama that I'm sorry
    For those unkind words I said.
I didn't mean to hurt her,
    Now those unkind words I dread.

But for my words she'd still be here,
    Showing love in every way.
Please tell Mama that I'm sorry
    For my actions on that day.

Please let Mama into Heaven,
    She deserves the very best.
She never meant to take her life,
    She just needed a peaceful rest.
—*Barbara Hillicoss*

I Am No Superman

I never said I was Superman,
I never said I could fly.
I never said I was superhuman,
I never said I can't die...

I never said a lot of things,
So why does everyone expect so much?
I can reach awfully high,
But the stars I can never touch.

Never did I say I was perfect,
For it's hard to soar that high.
I am no Superman,
All I can do is try.
—*Joshua Adam Whited*

Dusk

As I looked into the night's dark faces,
I saw your shadow there.
Entwined with pages you had read,
Of people far and near.

Words of passion, yet of loathing,
Composed by chiefly those,
In life who saw you as no other, a
Fading, black shooting star.

A mystery, then, now so evident,
Your bodies first keeper
Caused the dread and contempt in your
Most peaceful of mens' hearts.

Though many of us never skimmed,
Your previous short text,
Or your score of memorable music,
The notes, rhythms, wade on.
—*Maya K. Smith*

"A Special Mama"

As I look into the past
I see a very special Mama
Always thought of herself last
She met a very special Papa

Got married 53 years ago
Raised 13 beautiful children
Lately she loved to play pokeno
We're so sorry she had to go

Although there were rough times
She was always willing to play booray
There were a lot of happy times
For having 34 grandchildren, 13 great-
Grandchildren, she could shout hooray!

She loved to do search a word books
That was a very special time for her
Although we weren't ready
It was her time to go

We will always remember her
"A Special Mama"
—*Cindy Blanchard*

Untitled

As I look out the window
    I see God everywhere,
Assuring me that He is now
    And always will be there.

The trees have traded summer green
    For costumes made of gold
And warm, clear nights are yielding
    To winds of icy cold.

The flowers that just recently
    Stood colorful and tall,
Bow in acquiescence...
    Giving way to fall.

All too soon this brilliant beauty
    Will give way to another kind:
The stark, white snows of winter
    As fall is left behind.
—*Suzanne E. Anderson*

Street Stage

In the theatre of the street
I see the faces of the players,
Some intent with certainty
Some itinerant strayers.

Multitudes of single forms
in varied shape and size,
Old and young, rich and poor
Foolish ones and wise.

They hurry so, they scurry so,
it almost seems to be
a race, in which the winner,
will be chosen, imminently.
—*Helene Balch*

Romance

Across the miles.
I send you a thousand smiles.

The birds singing in the tree.
Reminds me of thee.

Of our many talks.
As we went for walks.

You have been like sunshine to me.
Allowing me the world to see.

The loneliness I felt.
You have caused to melt.

Being around you.
I feel like I fit like a shoe.

The times we shared.
Unspoken how we cared.

Happiness could it be.
Since I found you and you found me.

Flowers are in bloom.
Hope to see you soon.
—*Margaret Holloway*

Oedipus Revisited

In my dreams I fly over an open field
I throw my mother into the ocean
And I kiss my father
In my dreams my house is burning
Crickets crowd in front of my window
There is a panther on my bed
And the moon swings on a piece of string
In my dreams I lie with horses
A great wave draws me under
And I never die
I know the question to every answer
In my dreams I understand who I am
And who I can never be.
—*Maxa Ott*

If

If only time could stand still
    for just a little while,
If we could walk more slowly
as we go that last long mile.

If only the sun could shine more brightly
up in the clear blue sky,
and we could linger longer,
as we say our last goodby.
—*Frieda Shanks*

I Am A Traveler

I am a traveler
I travel from West to East,
I travel on time's level
Hand in hand with my Brethren,
Round and round the ladder
That leads me to fame
    in our inner circle,
I travel with all the tools
    to build temples
In the hearts of my fellowmen.

I am traveler
I travel on rough's rugged road,
My heart full of trials
    and tribulations,
My soul's resolute
To fulfill my promises,
To love my God, myself and my
    neighbors,
And when I die, to live in that house
Not made by hands, eternal in Heavens.
—*Luis P. Cava*

Untitled

I say that I'm a Christian, Lord;
I try so hard to be.
Then why this conflict in my soul
Where calm and peace should be?
Jesus came upon the earth,
Our sins to sanctify.
Dear Lord, when sins I do commit,
Do you sit down and cry?
When angry thoughts are in my heart,
I try to keep control.
Forgiving the anger that I feel
Can only help my soul.
Dear Lord, help me to make amends
With those who've done me wrong.
That angry feelings in my heart
May turn to joyful song.
—*Martha A. Maxfield*

God's Own

The house was cold
I turned up the heat
And thought of the woman
I'd seen on the street.

She wasn't there by choice
But by man's greed.
God created plenty
For everyone's need.

They said, "She's a bag lady
So pay her no mind.
She's old and homeless
She isn't our kind."

Our kind? I wonder,
How can people say that?
Except for the grace of God
We would be where she's at.
—*Betty A. Ellis*

I Remember

After school I would walk to his house
I was anxious to see my grandpa.
He would be there all alone,
for my grandma had to work.
He was feeble and
in his house
he would sit
day in, day out.
There wasn't much for him to do
so he would watch wrestling.
I would go there
just to help him out.
A popsicle or more water
when he needed it.
These things I would gladly do.
I knew soon it would be his time
and it was, too soon.
—*Roxanne Wyant*

A Sad Goodbye

Why did it have to end like this?
    I was so young.
    I loved you so much.
My sister and I always thought,
    that it was our fault.
We were going to stay all night.
    You got sick,
    and then you left.
    We never saw you again.
    Grandma, we love you,
    everyone here loves you,
    we always will.
    We can never forget you.
    Things are different now,
    because you are gone.
    I wish I could see you again,
    we could still have fun.
I still wish we could have stayed all night.
    All I have now are memories,
    Special memories that will never die.
—*Lisa Sowers*

Rainbow Chasing

It happened a year ago.
I was standing in a field
watching the clouds roll by.
I think I'm by myself.
Waiting to see rainfall
to make this field grow.
Lost and make me run home.
It's been a long time.
I've been running through
this storm.
You'd think for a moment
when the clock stops I
could turn to see
the sun touch the earth.
Blow out the candle and I'll
chase a rainbow to stop you
from crying.
Open your arms I just want
to come home.
—*Theodore Leo Jordan*

Beyond Words

It is strange that you should say it
I was thinking the very same thing
Of how that youthful gait we had
Has turned to shuffling.

How girlish waistlines diminished
And raven hair has grayed
Now the sights we see are hazy
Our reactions so delayed.

We no longer hear a pin drop
Or frolic freely in the sun
But live together quietly
Enjoying good days, one by one.

I cannot utter a single word
So my voice will never express
That I understand your thinking
Feel your love, or our loneliness.

So you, my mistress, and I, your friend
Share so much of everything
That even though I'm a speechless dog
I still think the very same thing.
—*Miriam E. West*

Look At Me

Look at me.
I was youth once,
I laughed and loved,
I hoped and dreamed.

Look at me.
I am half of your beginning,
I am one of two who made you.
You are love and so am I.

Look at me.
I gave you life.
I loved, I dreamed,
I hoped in your growing.

Look at me.
I'm getting old.
I'm grey, I'm wrinkled,
I still dream, I still hope

Look at me.
You are my dream, my hope.
You are love and so am I,
Don't forget me - look at me!
—*Rae R. Peterson*

Missing You

I love you with all my heart
I wish we weren't apart
So far I've been faithful,
You should be grateful.
I miss you so much!
Too bad we can't touch.
Remember when you get back,
That I may soon attack!
Like I say,
Too bad you are so far away!
This is all bad dream,
I wish I could scream!
I know I should keep trying,
But I just can't stop crying!
I'm in a bind,
Baby, I can't get you out of my mind.
So you see,
I miss you baby!
—*Heather Taylor*

My True Love

If wishes came true,
I would find my way back to you,
You gave me so much joy,
And you made my soul whole.

My hopes and dreams shattered,
When you left that day,
My heart has never felt such pain,
I wonder if I ever love again.

If we had a second chance,
I would be stronger than before,
My love for you will never die,
As I watch each day pass by.

I hope that you will forgive me,
And I pray that you are happy,
Because I shall never forget you,
My one true love.
—*Willie Sandifer*

"If I Were"

If I were a bird up in a tree
I'd fly as far as I could see
I'd fly the ocean deep and blue,
And then I'd be right there with you.

If I were a fish on the ocean top
I'd swim and swim and never stop
Until I got right there with you,
Across the ocean deep and blue,

If I were a butterfly so high
I'd fly way up into the sky
Until I caught a falling star,
And then I'd fall right where you are.

If I were a lightning bug at night
I'd fly and fly and then I'd light
Up on your ship across the sea,
Where you're waiting just for me.

If I were you and you were me
I'd come back home from o'er the sea
And then I'd stay right there with you,
And never sail the ocean blue.
—*Mae D. Hopkins*

He Knows The Way

Christ is my shepherd and my guide;
I'll follow Him what 'ere betide;
The waters may look rough to me,
He'll lead me o'er life's rugged sea.
I do not know what lies ahead,
I know He'll lead as He has led.
Sometimes I wonder what will be
The days that lie ahead for me.
There may be heartaches, maybe loss,
But come what may, that sea I'll cross;
Because He'll take me by the hand
To help me over; He'll understand.
He bore the cross that I might see
How great a love He has for me.
Then when my journey here is done,
And life's battles I have won,
And the last step I have trod,
My soul will find its rest in God.
—*Julie M. Gunderson*

"I'll Miss"

I'll miss the snow so white
I'll miss the trees so green and tight
I'll miss the sky so blue
I'll miss the rose so true
I'll miss the rain so sweet
I'll miss the birds that tweet
I'll miss the ground I walked
I'll miss my families talk
But Heavenly grand
I will Stand
—*Roberta M. R. Latham*

Lonely Reality

I fall asleep
I'm in a place
I'm all alone
I turn around and
see a face
I ask who's there
there is no answer

I close my eyes
I'm in the dark
I'm in a box
Please let me out
It's dark and cold
Please let me out
Please hear my cry
Please let me out
I'm trapped inside
—*Amy Unetich*

Impressions

Impressions made
impressions grave
Too many impressions

Hopeless fears
through the years
take effect, don't connect

Minds pass over
truth dies.
—*D. DeSha*

Untitled

It's easy to be a feminist
  in a roomful of womyn.

she is aware that
  from his vantage point
he can catch a glimpse
  of her breast
She can feel him
  looking at her legs
and she shifts to a more
  advantageous angle
Methodically, she touches
  up her crimson lips
  she lowers her
eyelids and smiles
to let him know
  she welcomes his
advances she puts charm into
her voice in order to
take advantage of this chance.
—*Jackie Swain*

Understand Learning

I knew a man that was one-of-a-kind.
In a short lifetime was hard to find.
No one understood his ways.
But he taught me a lot, in our days
That we had together.

At time he was teaching me,
I didn't understand what was the key.
But in do time, I grew to understand more.
I didn't know what all this was for.
I was unsure of his methods of teaching.

I'm glad he taught me all of these things.
For I look at the joy that he did bring.
Even though he was murdered one day.
His memory of all the lessons I've learned
are here to stay.
And that I shall pass it on to his children.

Now I know the reason for teaching me.
—*Marketta Anderson*

The Brooch

Tarnished gold, it lies
in a velvet box,
remnant of a love affair
that warmed my heart
and made me sing
when I was sweet and young,
and thought the ecstasy
would last and dreams
would all unfold
that love would always grow,
but it tarnished like the brooch,
faded and grew dull,
all luster gone,
cast aside like things long past,
I think to shine the brooch
but polish won't restore its lore
or the love of long ago
that made everything
to glisten and to shine.

—*Virginia Borman Grimmer*

I Love You

I love you everyday,
in all kinds of special ways.
 The love I have for you
today will never go away.
 I know you love me, too.
I can feel it when I'm blue.
 I love you with all my heart
and I promise we'll never apart.

—*Sunni Macias*

Repentance

The scarred little boy laid
in an open meadow
torn from within and confused
he pondered
fury extended throughout his soul
and he yelled at Him
shaking his fist to the heavens,
why me? He screamed —
silence broke out as his arm turned
to lead
and fell to his side
tears then filled his eyes
as he bowed his head
in prayer

—*Jeffrey Jenkins*

Past Or Present

 I have lived before
 In another place and time
 I have visited the unknown, and
  Found familiarity

I find I am comfortable, even at ease
 To walk the desert at dawn
 Carrying memories of people
 I could not have known

 I hear distant voices
 Beckoning me to continue
 In my search for my destiny
 My purpose in this life

 I have lived before, and
  I am alive again
 I have visited the unknown, and
  I am home

—*L. Melyndia Wikander*

"Extincts"

Within the freshness of rain damp flowers
in clement dampness of warming showers
within the warmness of a zenith sun
lie the high summits of human powers
to perceive full meaning of life begun
to receive sweet smells of victories won
over the basest of human instincts
before we become only the "extincts"

—*Patrick D. Fero*

Tears For Thy Tears

Every day,
in every way,
I try to keep my fears
and thy tears in,
but it is hard,
so very hard,
to keep in my fears
and thy tears,

You see,
my heart is broke,
because my father
had a stroke!

—*Timothy Walker*

"Where He Leads I Will Follow"

Oh father, Oh father
in heaven on High
Father, Father;
Dear God...I cry...

I come with my hands
Stretched to thee
Humans, Humans;
Help us all, help us all
As we are so wee...

Oh Father in heaven,
How did I make it
Through this day;
You were there for me
And lead the way...

—*Blanche Cole*

The Eagle's Cry

The Eagle soars where mountains rise
in heavens changing rippling tides.
Diving, dipping in the wind,
nature's spirit loving him.
The giant cliffs are his domain
and willfully he stakes his claim.
This princely bird of spacious skies,
a symbol of the just and wise,
alone can see with wondrous ease,
Angels flying on the breeze.
When his mighty wings span
into the dawn's open hand,
greets the first great light of morn,
crying out a new day is born.

—*Carolyn Grace Wilkey*

Untitled

Color doesn't matter
in my eyes we're all the same,
different shades of that one color,
yet the hatred still remains.

We have to work together to make
our world a better place,
Stop the pain and violence,
create a happy face.

We may be different on the outside,
but inside we're all the same,
all of us have joy,
all of us have shame.

Be yourself, speak your thoughts,
and be proud of what you believe,
it's the only way they'll hear you out,
it's the only way you'll be pleased.

To me, we are all equal, so
let's stop this racist trend,
respect each other's appearance
put prejudice to an end....

—*Nicole Donohue*

The Feeling In My Heart

It is hard to explain the feeling
 In my heart
A warm sincere flick of light
 Down within
A bit of love, a sprinkle of joy,
 A pint of small laughter
Inside my heart
 It may be little, it may be some,
But in my heart it gives me warmth
 Though I may not show it
Though it may seem I care very little,
 Look inside, deep inside
Where the flick of light warms my heart.

—*Magdalena Mercado*

Given Life Again

My life has been given
 another chance.
I was there when my
 soul was enhanced.

Given life,
Not yet death.
Death did hand me a knife
But I knew no knife was
 better than my breathe.

—*Felicia Smith*

Presence

You are continually there,
In my thoughts,
And my dreams.
You are far away,
But always near,
As I think of you -
Drawing you closer.
Talk with me,
Not just in your thoughts,
Or dreams,
But in words,
So I know
You are continually there.
—Kyran S. Holliday

A Concerto Three

To a little sparrow -
In nature God has blessed
A gift of three musicians
Within a little nest

The lay - amidst a downy blend
Each hatch an awkward tune
Three little songsters crying din
Excite the mothers croon

To each a flute were given
Which they would master well
As mother with her pride
Would - so often tell

Upon a limb in grey-brown trim
A tree-top prance romance
Affection, proper, prim,
Three little sparrows dance

To each they are musicians
A concerto three
Their orchestral ambition
Eccentric harmony
—Scott Cleveland

The Hills Of Woodside

A myriad of moods
In one little corner of the earth.
Sunlit bathed or green gray
on a dismal day
these are my Western Hills.

A myriad of colors
in this sweet corner of the earth.
Emerald green or purple shades
as daylight fades
these too, my Western Hills.

A myriad of scenes
in this special corner of the earth.
rays of gold or shrouds of mist
by summer kissed
my beloved Western Hills.
—Marilyn Ellis

I Shall Not

I shall not die,
for I love you
and shall not leave you
so you shall die alone,
die with me,
and live forever.
—Amy Michelle Hines

On Loneliness

She walks alone
In sublime innocence,
Her feet treading
On clouds of concrete.
What does she think,
Her eyes starry,
Looking to a heaven we cannot see?
What does she feel,
Not knowing of our worldly cares
or sins
or passions?
She reaches the heavens
Beyond our reach
And finds fulfillment.
—Jessica Meyer

O Lobster Dear

You were so happy there
  in the deep cold sea
How I wish you could
  run away,
You look so innocent
  in that big tank,
You do not know how
  sweet you are, and
before it's too late
  I wish you could run away
—Ruth C. Dobrucki

From A Seed

A tiny seed I planted
in the earth below.
I watered it, nurtured it,
Hoping my flower would grow.

Each day I would look
In hopes that I would find
A flower I could call mine.

The sun provided all the heat
My little flower would need.
The rainfall would provide
  the water
For my newly planted seed.

Days they passed, weeks did too.
Then much to my surprise,
There stood a lovely flower
Right before my eyes.

What a wonderful miracle
To see a flower grow.
From the smallest seed I planted
  in the earth below.
—Jennie Renshaw

Imagine

A day went by, still no sign of him.
In the endless night,
I cried my self to sleep.
Sometimes I can imagine
him with me,
Sometimes I can imagine his
lips against mine.
But then I wake up and
realize its a dream,
I can't pull my self together,
I can't say he's not here.
But I can imagine!
—Sarah Costa

Spirit Of The West

She first appeared
in the fleeting moment
just after the sun set
and disappeared
beyond the vast horizon

She remained unseen
until moonlight
cast her shadow
on the mountain

With only an echo
to guide her
she stepped lightly
from high places
where no one else had tread
and crossed the water
leaving behind
only the trace
of a vague promise
to return with the morning mist
—Mary J. Larkin

History Repeated

I dreamed I lived,
In the long ago;
Saw dear faces—
That I have wished to know,

Read of in history,
About heroic feats;
Some ordinary—
Others known "greats,"

But history is repeated,
Each and everyday;
So I'm meeting many,
As I pass along "This way."
—Lucy N. Stroman

If You Think I'm Gone

Hear my voice speaking to you
  in the wind, through the trees.
Hear my laughter through the children
  who came after me.
See me smile through the sun
  that shines on those below.
Through the rain I cry from sorrow
  that I feel when you are low.
A part of me is everywhere
  in things you see each day.
I am not gone, my spirit lives
  I am with you all the way.
Remember me with smiles and tears
  as I watch you from above.
Tell little ones I did not die,
  I live on in you with love.
—Kathie J. Bierman

"Wild Wings"

Wild wings of freedom
Flying over a silvery lake.
Wings of evening breezes,
Wings of foaming waves.
These wings may have
  happiness,
Or a calm peacefulness inside.
For these wings are my own,
Guiding me through my life.
—Christa VanBuskirk

Seasons

There are many seasons
   in the year.
Many more then what seem
   to appear.
There is a season when a love
   comes to an end.
And a season when you find
   new friends.
A season for expanding your mind.
And a season when you search
   your soul to find.
A season full of darkened days.
And a season to sit in the
   suns rays.
The seasons where changes develop
   over our mother.
And a desperate season,
   when you feel you'll never see another.
—*Douglas Alan Karaszewski*

"Moments Of Grief"

Many thoughts before me
In this moment of grief
There're not many answers
Where is my sleep?

Food is just tasteless
I cry many tears
Take hold of my hand
And hold it so dear.

I pray many hours
And study real hard
God will give answers
He's not very far.

He'll lift up my burdens
Put me back on my feet
He'll take away sorrow
And all of my grief.

Life holds a meaning
When a loved one passes on
You've got more to strive for
So you've got to hang on.
—*Ava Yocum*

Bound By Love

In times of need,
In times of love,
In times of sorrow,
He's bound by my love.
He is my every breath.
He is my everything.
In my heart and soul.
He's my one and all.
So I guess that's
Why we married last fall.
—*Georgina G. Grubbs*

Me

   All alone
   On my own
At peace with my surroundings
 Content in my solitude
     So glad to be
    Finally — Me
—*Carol McGilbra*

Was It Dysfunctional Beginnings

Helpless; Helplessness,
Incompatibility maybe,
Much to much distance,
Sharing, caring ceases,
Hearts shattered, uncertainty,
   asoured investment?

Helpless; helplessness,
Hands withdrawn, disfamilies flight,
Prayers, many tears, missing love,
Weight loss, sleepless nites,
Insurmountable stress,
   must mistakes be learned?

Helpless: Helplessness,
Hate destroy,
Played out games,
Emptiness,
 Help;
   More processed pain
—*Charles F. Mines Jr*

Untitled

Small child with the wide eye view
Innocence lies about him
Trampled at his feet

Vicious cycle spinning outta turn
Product of a new one
Experiences rebirth

With my new found joy
And a turnaround toy
I will go
Meek smile
Weary spirit
Skipping to my …

Heavy revelation
But the sun still beats
A vision of tomorrow scratched my eye
And drew the blood of a thousand others
—*Brigette Pina*

Life Is Real Reality

I feel the spirit of Walt Whitman
Inside my soul.
I feel that I am life, and
Life flows from me.

I have absorbed the worst
Of my time.
I have felt the pain
From all the pains of time.

I've felt the loves of my life
The love of a brother
The love of a friend
The love of a spouse.

I've felt the pain of loosing love.
The love of a brother
The love of a friend
The love of a spouse.

Inside myself I feel all life.
Inside myself I see you as you are.
Inside myself I begin to see
That life is real reality!
—*Daniel Crytzer*

A Feeling

Inside my soul,
Inside my soul,
I have a feeling
Inside my soul.
It could be love,
It could be fear,
Or it could be a memory,
Inside my soul.
I wish I knew,
I wish I could tell,
More about that feeling,
Inside my soul.
But it is nothing
I really could tell,
'Cause all it is,
'Cause all it will be,
Is just a feeling
Inside my soul.
—*Jennifer M. Carr*

Tears

Just a simple drop of water
   Is astounding to behold,
As microscopes reveal to us
   The wonders they unfold.

A scientist can tell us
   What's contained in every slide,
And life forms that exist therein
   From us no longer hide.

But what about the teardrop
   Falling slowly down a cheek;
Have they found a way to stop it
   Or do any of them seek?

Teardrops are quite different
   And are very much apart -
They don't filter from the heavens
   But well up within the heart.

The importance of each teardrop
   If we take the time to see,
May be found within the question
   Was this teardrop caused by me?
—*Joseph T. Quinn*

Happiness

A person who is happy,
Is happy to enjoy things,
Happiness counts,
Not golden rings

It's the "spark" that comes,
In the matter of life,
Not a girlfriend, boyfriend,
Husband or wife

Please look hard,
You may have to find,
But do remember,
Happiness comes from the
Mind!
—*Anna Lee Alden*

"Teardrop"

I wish I could be born
   as a tear drop in your eyes
to live on your cheeks,
   and to die on your lips.
—*Tyler Cady*

Gently The Purpose

If time is -
   Is it the breeze
Ancient wind become whisper?

Beautifully-
   Branches gesture
Leaves nod a different nature.

Comfortably-
   Old stones reside
Peaceful dynamos abide.

A creating-
   Clouds disperse
Vapor currents in reverse.

And on pass we-
   Through moments fair
With eternity to spare
—*Rita Vaughan*

Not A Friend I See

If once a friend forever
is not a friend for always
than what kind of friend
can this friend be
if not both sides
a friend to me

No friend at all
or friend would see
To both sides of friend
I'd always be
If friend was truly
friend to me.
—*Marci Elliott*

"Feeling For You"

How I feel about you
Is very hard to explain
Half the time I'm filled with pleasure
The other half with pain
Part of the time I hate you
Other times I'm in love
But most of the time I wonder
Is this sent from above?
If you offered me a hug
Or a kiss goodbye
I really don't know what I'd do
I might even cry
Or maybe collapse in your arms
To sit and weep a while
But I probably wouldn't do that
'Cause I know it's not your style
Secret feelings I have for you
I vow to keep them inside
But if I hold them too long
I'll just lay down and cry
—*Sara Kenison*

Daddy

Hold my hand, Daddy.
   It makes me stronger.
Talk to me, Daddy.
   It makes me wiser.
Pick me up, Daddy.
   It makes me taller.
Read to me, Daddy.
   It makes me smarter.
Say "I love you", Daddy.
   It makes me smile.
—*Cory*

"Soft Rain"

What is soft rain? Well its almost like a prayer!
It comes after days and weeks of lovely sunshine,
Some walk in it and some run in it,
for me it's a time to think of all the wonders of this earth, the Majestic Mountains here,
the lakes and seas, the desert to the tall trees.
How beautiful is all is!
I cannot seem to get my fill, my soul swells to see these things.
Even in the soft soft rain!
And then a rainbow so high so large,
So beautiful, and the snowcapped mountains,
for a background, if only I could paint it,
but only saw it in passing.
To think I must leave all this
behind but after all, I have a camera in my mind!
—*Claire M. Webber*

Sexy Smoke

At first, I see it shape my air
It curls and twists with little care
Its arch is up towards peaks of mind
In search of things it should not find
I dream in sexy smoke.

The smoke—a kiss, a cloud, a puff
My air, each breath to get enough
By hand and heart it makes me feel
And brings to life my dreams made real
I'm lost in sexy smoke.

I watch and hold on each nuance
Onto a thought, a hope, and launch
Into a world of light no sound
I slip into life whose only bounds
Are the fires of sexy smoke.

No time to think, my mind has stopped
I catch my breath, I hear my heart
And watch and blur—my vision gone
While deep inside, I stand alone
In the ashes of sexy smoke.
—*Mitchell R. Vann*

Ice-Cream

Ice-Cream is yummy.
It hits the spot in my tummy.
I bring the cone up to my lips.
Oh no! chocolate ice-cream drips.

Ice-cream comes in many flavors,
Strawberry, raspberry, lemon and lime...
What is your favorite kind?

Is it cherry or blueberry,
Chocolate chip cookie dough,
Do you even know?
Maybe even tropical snow!

I like ice-cream, it is neat!
It tastes good in the heat!
Especially when you've been working
And you're beat!

Ice-cream deserves an "A" plus from us!
—*Jennifer Nicole Muras*

"Sunday Afternoon"

As I watch the leaves fall,
It makes me feel so very small.
When I compare myself to the trees,
It makes me want to get on my knees,
To thank the good Lord above,
For all the many things I have to love.
He made so many things great,
How in the world can anyone hate?
He sends his love through nature,
And all things sweet and pure.
Across the street I see "Our Flag"
Down the street kids play tag.
This has been a perfect Sunday,
What more can I possibly say!
—*Joy King*

Of Night People

Do not wake me if I sleep
It's been awhile you know,
Since sleep has closed my eyes with ease
In nightfalls afterglow

For day is night
And night is day
When twilight softens all.
We people of the night begin
To sense sweet midnights call

Unlike our life companions
Who preen at break of day.
We other souls feel spirits soar
When darkness comes to play

For day is night
And night is day
To beings of my ilk.
We can't resist the beckoning
Of evening shadows silk
—*Ruth Comella*

A Day

   The sun is rising in the east,
It's going to shine upon my door,
looks like a day of pure sweet peace.
So, I'll get to work and fret no more.

Throughout a day may bring,
a mate with news to make me,
just want to cry or maybe sing,
a child, who makes me proud as I can be.

I'll welcome old friends and neighbors,
hopefully, some new ones too,
happy to see them at my door,
all showing up, just out of the blue.

Now it's getting on toward night
and I'll go gladly to my bed,
the day is past and all seems right,
I'm thankful for a day of no regrets.
—*Helen L. Cole*

Grace

God wants His saints to persevere
  It's in His perfect plan,
  Don't vacillate, don't waiver;
  Just reach out and touch His hand.
    We share wet tears of sadness
      God bestows on penitents,
  When faith's renewed our tears of joy
    Bring certain confidence.
  Though we may question inwardly
    Our spiritual worthiness,
    God promises to His elect
      JESUS' righteousness.
The hand that offers hope through faith,
  And faith through love that saves,
  Will give enduring strength to all.
  So cry your tears, and then give praise
    —*Joan Booth*

Dreaming

Dreaming never stops,
it's like water dripping from a hilltop,
It still runs when your sleeping,
and when your not.

When it dies,
it's like a crying woman's cries,
It's gone forever,
and it will never come back.
    —*Rehonna Martin*

Memories Away

Don't grieve for me I'm in no pain
It's not for me you cry
I'm in a place above the clouds
beyond the deep blue sky.
It's peaceful here, no wars, or bombs,
harps and angels everywhere,
the grass is green-the flowers bloom
sweet harmonies fill the air.
Don't think of me as dead and gone,
I'm simply "just away"
I'm with you everywhere you go,
I'm just a memory away.
    —*Penny Sue Koerner*

"An Image"

When you look into my eyes,
It's not me you see,
You're only seeing an image,
That's not really me.
I've put on this makeup,
To hide the fear and pain.

The reality hurts to much
So I'll live my life of lies.
No one seems to care, for
No one has looked deep enough
To find, that underneath the makeup,
Is only fear and pain.
    —*Amy E. Miller*

Flower

Fragrant blossom
Lovely to look at
Ornament of nature
Waving in the breeze
Especially admired
Remarkable creation
    —*Jamie Sutton*

Pre Destined...?

A sparrow in the forest-
It's predators abound.
Scurrying from tree to tree
No Solace to be found.
A cunning one it isn't
But - one day tried to be..
(and that success was king.)
Its Foe was met.
No contest - yet!
Too bad-it had to be.
    —*Mona Gonzalez*

Goodbye

Goodbye to life.
It's time for me to die.
Cutting into my heart with a knife.
Never did like to lie.

Goodbye to time.
The clock has stop for me.
For I am in my prime.
Angels are coming for me.

Goodbye to happiness.
Never will smile again.
Hello to loneliness.
Let death begin.

Goodbye to all my friends.
They do not understand.
This is where it all will end.
I'm going to a better land.
    —*Chad Wollbrink*

Road Of Life

The road of life looms far ahead,
it's way is long and narrow;
but we who travel down this road
are naught but as the sparrow.
Sometimes we sway or stagger
as we round bend after bend.
But always we continue on
until the road shall end.
    —*Judy G. Duvall*

To David:

 I've done good;
  I've done bad.
It doesn't matter.

You've done good;
  You've done bad.
It doesn't matter.

Remember the good;
  Forget the bad.
That's what matters.

Remember my love,
  Whatever you do.
You are my son;
  I love you.
      Dad
    —*Fredric B. Burns*

Faith

Along the many paths of life,
I've often met with grief and strife,
With every problem facing me,
Were answers that I couldn't see.
But out of every one —
I came to find the sun.
Somewhere along the way,
I'd found the Lord and learned to pray.
Now I marvel at the light,
That comes out of the black of night.
My blessings, every one,
I know, come from "The Son."
    —*Donna Glenn*

Worse

In life
I've seen examples
Of nature's wrath

Storms of electricity
Thundering, booming,
Thrashing across the land

Tornado twisters
Endless breaths of air
Turning over ground

Hurricanes of horrid strength
Nor' easters too
Having love for violence

But above all these,
I've seen much worse
The most horrifying rage of all

The silent cold stare
Of an angry friend
Pretending, inexistence
    —*Eugene M. Szostak*

Still: Birth

I've seen them come,
I've seen them go.
All I want,
Is what they know.

Escape from pain is my fight,
Take this soul into flight!

Merciless I may be,
But still you do not see.
So I throw down to earth,
Back where you are given birth.

Still I see them come and go,
So I ask what do you know?

There is a hole in the sky,
I have seen the light.
That is where I must fly,
Guide me on through the night.
    —*Robert Fuller*

Untitled

I like animals very much
lions, tiger, Bears, and such.
Keep their forests, Lakes, and
Rivers clean if you don't you'll
be mean please try, try and try
if you don't I will cry.
Dogs, cats, hamsters too If
you do this I'll love you.
    —*Allison Mercurio*

Life

What is life?
Just a long long strife
Gloom and happiness
Both a long, long stress
When you are happy you are glad
When you are gloomy you are sad
People may be cruel and mean
They can't be as bad as they seem
So even if they laugh and shout
There is no cause for you to pout
Put up your head and be a man
Find out where in life you stand
—Helen Nagy

On A Bus

She got on the bus in Las Vegas
just as quiet as can be
She sat in the front seat of the bus
across the aisle from me.

She sat so very silent
not speaking to anyone
Very quickly she fell asleep
this trip did not seem much fun.

I watched her sleep
as the bus went mile after mile
The bus was stopped in Utah
it was there I first saw her smile.

A smile of rare beauty
the kind that makes your heart melt
Not a smile to be seen
it is a smile to be felt.

Though I spoke a few words
to this girl across from me
My pleasure was in watching her
in the beautiful smile I got to see.
—Barry "Bear" Miller

Friends

Friends are very exciting
Just like the New Year,
They have a special meaning,
but I still don't know what
it is.

   Friends are very special
as true as true can be,
   But I still do not know
why. I'll find out sooner
or later. Or I guess I'll
never know why.

   Just to wrap up this
poem. I guess I just have to
say I guess I'll just have to
live with my friends until my
dying day.
—Kandi Ilardi

Memories

Past memories of time gone by,
haunt me.
I remember the laughter of
the good times, and
I remember the tears of
the bad times.
The past is gone, but the memories
are still vivid in my mind.
—Maria Thomas

Silent Dancing

Dance with me under the stars tonight.
Just our silhouettes in the moonlight.

Moving to music that only we can hear.
Two hearts together, and all is clear.

Finding what other's only dream about.
Searching has ended, there's no doubt.

This ol' world isn't too bad a place.
Words of love, a tightening embrace.

… time please slow down.
—Ronald M. Noe

The Shadows On The Street

The shadows on the street are always
just right,
They're like a perfect painting
through a perfect person's sight.
They're like a baby's smile when
his mother comes and sings,
They're like a bird in flight with
the wind beneath its wings.
They're like a shadowed face without
a name,
They're like an argument with no
one to blame.
The shadows on the street are always
just right,
They're like a perfect painting
through a perfect person's sight.
—Kara Weaver

Nirvana

Round, round and round.
Keep going in circles
Mindlessly.
Circles within circles
One circle completed
Move up to a bigger one, then what?
Round, round, and round
Keep going.
In the last circle, are you?
Watch it.
You may be released
To float away
Finally free.
Or you might slip
And fall back
Into the first circle.
And again you begin
Round, round and round
Same old circles
You now have no memory of.
—Vinita Chinoy

The Tiger

Orange, White
Black Stripes…
Wild, fierce
Roaming the wild land
His eyes burning with freedom
A tiger searches it's prey
Seeing an antelope
He springs,
And death may come upon an antelope,
But life may come upon a tiger.
--Alicia Caravan

Kite Sight

   Children's eyes dance
   Kites on string prance
   Launched into the air
   Maybe three pair.

   Boxed, bowed or flat
   Crowds on ground sat
   Shapes and colors delight
   The lines remain tight.

   Imagine your factory
   Building kites satisfactory
   Pray for windy days
   That's when it pays.

   Wind to your back
   A day not of lack
   Oh, for the thrill
   Kites sky fill!
—Phillip O. Walch

Untitled

Summer rain of Yokohama
laced my face
as I raced down Bluff Hill
a glow with thoughts of Tamiko
returning on last train

There is nothing more lonelier
than a empty station
Yet in the mating of eyes
there is nothing more lovelier
Love may be written in sands
   Ours was smitten in hands
Love may come in springs flowers
   or autumns reign of leaves
      or winters rain of darken hours

Sharing a umbrella we climbed the hill
Caring not rain would pass
but it was summers rain passing
Since our meeting
   Our love never fleeting
      like summers rain of Yokohama
—Johnny Viola

Untitled

Love is but a grand illusion
Left me with so much confusion
Hear my heart, won't you listen
On my lashes tears still glisten
Captured by a potent lust
Hold me tightly, if you must

Dreams are made of so much cotton
Lovers whispers, soon forgotten

God, turn back the hands of time
Shake me free of all the grime
That time has left upon my face
Smooth it, leave it with no trace
Of all the sorrow I have known
Give me back my youth now flown

Take the gray from once bright tresses
Let me feel his soft caresses
Let me be the one he'll cherish
Soon enough from life we'll perish
—Pat Hopkinson

Lamentations Of A Cherokee

In those Oklahoma hills,
Life began for me;
Without any earthly frills,
'Cause I was born a Cherokee.

Schooling in a one room class, I had.
They taught me it had to be
For me as a young lad,
'Cause I was born a Cherokee.

With "Pale Faces" all around,
Somehow I could not agree;
Why I was always put down,
'Cause I was born a Cherokee.

But now in my latter years,
I know that I am free.
I shall shed no more tears,
For being born a Cherokee.

Oh Lord! as I beat my tribal drum,
To send you this my plea;
Give me grace to forgive and overcome,
For I'm glad to be a Cherokee.
—*Robert N. Perkins*

Without You

I am missing you.
Life continues, but
it's not the same with out you.

It's impossible to forget you
or make a new life without you.

I keep missing you
day after day
and through the lonely nights.

I keep asking "why you?"
I am not strong
I can't live without you.

But life continues
and I am alone in this world
without you.
—*Sergio C. Silva*

Loneliness

Life has its ups
Life has its downs
Life in some ways
will make you frown

Sometimes I'm happy
Sometimes I'm sad
Sometimes I'm sleepy
And sometimes I'm mad

But mostly I'm lonely
And oh so depressed
I've got no friends
You've probably guessed

So here's just a clue
for you lonely few
Once you got friends
Keep them close to you!!
—*Jennifer Michelle McDaniel*

"Patterns"

Kaleidoscopes of emotions,
Life is so strange,
Twisting and turning,
Never ceasing to change.

But, we can choose,
To look up to the Light,
Bringing forth our true colors,
Reaching new height.

Symmetrical patterns,
We can control
Our destiny lies
In the depth of our soul.
—*Bette Bertucci*

Sometimes

  Sometimes I wonder about
life, whether it's really here.
  Sometimes I wonder
if I'm me or if people are
Who they say they are.
  Sometimes I wonder why
Love was put on the earth,
Was or could have been put
here because of some foolish
Sinner or because it's
meant to be true.
  I'm not sure why
Sometimes, is on my mind but
Sometimes, I wonder what
Sometimes really is
— *Krissy E.*

"Life In Five Seconds"

Born out of frustrations.
Light, life and exaltations.
Meandering, pandering,
Drifting through time.
Making no sense,
Like an out of date rhyme.
Narrow the lines
And slip through the fire.
It's not in a life,
That we will inspire.
Rot down to ash
And blow away,
Only to begin
On another day.
—*Denise L. Halliday*

School House

It towers over me
Like a rock God
Old red paint,
Chipping, peeling, cracking.
The inner walls dripping
With knowledge of past lives.
It smells of learning
And of excitement.
The rusty-hinged door hangs open
As if to talk.
It tells me of the past lives
And learning and excitement.
It begins to weep
And cry for its children.
—*Chris Fletcher*

The Capital

It looms above the city
Like a beacon all aglow
Like a knight in shining armor
Watching over things below
In the darkness with lights beaming
All the shadows seem alive
And the street lights blink a greeting
As the cars begin their drive
The skyline comes in focus
The sun is growing bright
As daytime starts to come alive
And closes out the night
I see a different beauty
Than lots of people do
In flickering lights and shadows
And all the lovely hue
Now the hustle and the bustle
Has really come alive
The Capital lights have faded
From University Avenue drive.
—*Ruby Peck*

What Is Love?

Love is a flowing river,
Like a mighty stream,
Coursing through our life veins
Filling us with dreams.

It gives without the taking,
Never counts the cost,
All it asks in payment
Is that labor is not lost.

Love fills the heart with singing,
Lights up the eyes like stars.
And in the giving to others
The gift received becomes ours.
—*Elgie V. Seeman*

Apart

Absence's a distant thunder,
Like a pain we can't define,
Or the dread that's 'there' on waking.
The future sends us a sign.

Like a comma in a sentence,
Or the pause in daily breath,
A minute crack in living,
Call it a sip of death.

Compare it to an early snowfall,
A sudden and silent scene
That smothers all life and all living.
Have long summer eves ever been?

So cherish time's spool together,
Unravel with love her slim thread;
Greet the soft light of mornings,
In shade spread out a spread.
—*Wilfrid Grey*

Green Leaves

Bright, brilliant
calming and soothing
the spark of life...
    guardian

Shading those who sit under,
A canopy
more like a blanket

Soothing
—*Carolyn S. Ruffin*

Clay

Ageless mound of clay,
Like a silent Buddha,
You sit upon my potters wheel,
Waiting to be touched,
Waiting to teach me
Your ancient secrets.

I close my eyes, and
As the wheel begins to spin,
Touch you gently with my hands.
I listen quietly
As you awaken my awareness
To everything that is.

Then, in the stillness
Of the silent motion,
We reach the center and
Become one
In harmony and peace.
—*Mary Del Bello*

Snow Flakes

Snow flew through the marshmallow sky
Like dancers floating
away
With the breeze.
The snow on the trees looks like
crystal.
It's so bright
It hurts my eyes.
—*Joseph Daniel (J.D.) Quillen*

Death

Your white ivory arms are
like porcelain to touch.

I can't hold on to you
too much.

Your kiss is like velvet
on my lip.
Into your realm I want
to step.
Your robe of satin with
a silky touch, when first
seen strikes fear. too much.
You're the mistress of the
dark and a friend.
A new beginning not an end.
—*Sarah R. Vorwerk*

Night

Outside the darkness deepens
 like some unbroken evil.
The wind is howling in the trees
 with a sound of horrid agony.
Shadows scamper to and fro
 running from a hidden foe.
The nightingale sings his song
 of an unspoken passion.
Death descends o'er the doom
 taking what is due.
Day hides her face in terror;
 sunrise is far from here.
Ghouls move in perverse dance,
 and demons hurry forth to prance.
But, behind this world of terror,
 lays happiness in some.
For inside a world of hate
 is you, my light and life.
—*Melanie Bunger*

To Accept Each Step

The art of learning is ever there
Like the fine-tuning of a violin;
Each must be learned again
Lest it appear too maudlin.
It is not enough to know at best
That tomorrow brings its own relief;
For the lesson is never easily learned
Tomorrow may only bring empty belief.
The hardest thing to learn is this
You can never change another's way.
The thing to do is quickly accept
To change yourself, to save your day.

There are life's lessons to be learned
at all the changing stages of living;
You must learn to accept the fact
It's to yourself, you must be forgiving!
—*Ruth Fleishman*

Untitled

Alone but not
Lonesome in my
Singledness here
I am today
After seven long - short
Years of no help mate
Chauffeur, listener
Provider. We courted
Nine years married
For nearly fifty
Very much in love
Always respectful
Of other's interests
Values, endeavor.

Twice young lovers
Laid open to us their question
"Marry or not to marry?"
They did
Still are happily so
—*Martha Gerritz*

The Trucker's Life

Winding roads and blinding lights
long days and short, short nights
hauling freight to and fro
through rain, sleet and snow

Fighting traffic on city streets
we got appointments we must keep
across this nation we do roam
rarely seeing the place called home

Shippers and receivers all day long
dispatch is holding on the phone
up the mountain to the other side
day and night never losing stride

Speed traps set here and there
look out trucker that's a bear
D.O.T. is checking on me
to see if I drive legally

Bosses yelling don't be late
I am learning to love
this life I hate.
—*Donald A. Lemin Jr.*

Ocean Thoughts

As I sit
 looking out over
 the broad blue ocean,
I see the sea gulls
 diving and dunking.
Oh, to soar through
 this bright, brilliant day...
To reach for heaven
 and then back,
 back to earth.
The sand is hot,
 almost burning my toes.
The wind is cool and damp
 from the sea's spray.
Like the sea, life can be
 at its ebb.
Tomorrow the tide returns
 bringing back courage
 from the sea, the cool
 and unending sea.
—*Melissa Sheriff*

Ocean

 I stand on the deck,
looking toward the ocean.
 Its waves are rapid,
 the motions are clear.

The waves constantly splash
 against the rocks.
 I find this mystic
 magic to my eyes.
How boats wander in to dock.
—*Valerie Mochulski*

To The Man I Love

To the man I love, I give my heart.
Love and devotion, we'll never part.
My thoughts and dreams are of you;
Others so fortunate are few.
I hope you know that I love you much,
And I yearn for your every touch.
So warm and gentle a man,
I am your greatest fan!
Together we will always be.
Just look and you will see!
A love made in heaven for just
You and me!
—*Diana L. Perusin*

Love Is

Love is the future
Love is the past
Love is something
that will always last

Love is the feeling
between you and me
it grows and blooms
like flowers on a tree.

Love is the one thing
that keeps me strong everyday
I love you my love
please don't go away
—*Diane Patricia O'Sullivan*

The Time Is Now

If you are ever going to love me,
love me now, while I can know,
the sweet and tender feelings,
from which true affection flows.
Love me now,
while I am living,
do not wait until I'm gone.
And then have chiseled in marble,
sweet words on ice-cold stone.
If you have tender thoughts of me,
please tell me now.
If you wait until I am sleeping,
never to awaken,
there will be death between us,
and I will hear you then.
So, if you love me,
even a little bit,
let me know while I am living,
so I can treasure it.

—*Theresa Ungerecht*

Best Friend Award

As we travel through our lifetime
   many people come and go
but if we're lucky we will have
   a handful of friends to show.

To accept our joys and troubles, too,
   whether large or small;
never judging what we should do
   but encouraging us one and all.

I know I'm the lucky one
   to have a friend like you,
and I want you to always have
   what's best in life for you.

Wrapped by my hugs, filled with my love
   may your happiness overflow
to daily remind you of the joy I have
   because of you I know.

When all is said and done
   and our travels come to an end;
the world will be proud to know
   that you're my Very Best Friend!

—*Diana Sillence*

My Friend

Several years, have passed, and gone
Many things, we have done
Never, a harsh word did, we have
We have our faults but, accepts as is
The best, which is this
One who is kind, and sweet
And so, ever on her feet
A Dear, Dear friend
You will always be,
Who is always there, with a helping hand
What a friend, Oh! so grand
Someone, to tell my ups, and downs to
There'll never be anyone, quite like you

—*Sarah Rodenburg*

Untitled

I'm writing this poem for you,
Marlene, dear.
Your out of my reach but
I know you are near.
Your life was so fruitful.
Your future seemed clear.

You knew your direction and
never did veer.
Bravely, you faced every challenge
that life had to deal.
With strength and certainly courage
you never displayed us your fears.

Dear Sister, I love you, and though
I shed tears.
I know you will help me because
you are near.

—*Carol A. Chenevert*

As I Pass By

The path I choose in my way of life
May be rough, and hills steep and long
But as I pass by, I hope that I
Will not miss the wild bird's song
Or fail to see the flowers that bloom
by the wayside, or know
the joy of watching the sunset
Or bask in the moon's soft glow
and as I journey day by day
I will count it a loss if I
forget to share the good I find
with my friends as I pass by

—*Ethel Lane Albiani*

Friend

You are very special to
me,
My friend of cheer,
You've always brought
life to my affairs,
You made everything
happy,
Even when my days were
gray,
When I was unhappy
You lifted the rain,
And when I had done
you wrong,
You stuck by my
side,
So I thought I would
take this time,
to say thank you,
For being in my life.

—*Liberty Thompson*

Ode To My Daughter

My daughter, God's blessing to a mother.
My daughter, one who brings tears, joy,
smiles and laughter.
My daughter first, a friend second.
My daughter, I enjoy always.
My daughter, I cry with and laugh with,
My daughter, whom I share with,
My daughter, shares with me.
My daughter, she blesses my heart.
Thank you God for my daughter.

—*Shelby J. Smith*

A Prayer

Oh, Dear Lord, may we ever be
Mindful of thy love and care.
May we truly know that thou
   art everywhere.

Guide our footsteps everyday,
And teach us oh Lord,
How and for what to pray.
May we dedicate our lives to thee,
And a better Christian be.
Help us to let our light so shine,
That Thy way, the lost might find.
Guide what we do, and what we say;
Lest we cause one soul to stray.
We pray, oh Lord, that Thy will be done;
To the glory and honor of Thy Son.

—*LaVerne French*

April's Brief Affair With Winter

April's brief affair with winter
—more flirtation than embrace—
showered limbs and lawns with layers
of frigid lace.

Forsythia caught half-a-leafing
topped by puffs of clinging snow.
Snowflake kamikazes bombing
streets and cars below.

Soon the sun beamed benediction
on that most unlikely pair,
but when April turned to kiss him,
Winter wasn't there.

—*Dorothy Mosher*

Peace In A Temple Garden

Pale blossoms drifting on
   morning's crystal air,
Float slowly into
   a mirrored pool—
Languidly swim snow-white koi
   and golden among
Liquid lotus shadows,
   reflections ever-changing—
Branches, white-petalled overhead,
   move silently,
Hide mossy banks and
   a crimson wooden bridge;
Fill the temple garden with
   scattered floral fragrance—
There pilgrims tread softly,
   whisper quiet prayers—
There an ancient garden gong
   resounds and
Buddha listens!

—*June Allegra Elliott*

Can You See...?

Can you see me cry,
Can you see me die nearby?
Can you feel what I feel,
   Or am I a heartless eel?
Can you see my fears,
Can you feel my tears?
Can you see me suffer,
Can you see I've grown tuffer?
   Are you blind?
Can you see?

—*Jackie Becher*

True Beauty

I can not see a sunset
  most people can but don't care
  but I can feel the beauty
    and God's presence there

Most people take for granted
  birds singing in the sky
  Stop and take a second
    to hear their lullaby

I feel the cool and gentle wind
  caress against my skin
  I only see the beauty
    that comes from within

If you want to feel the earth
  before it passes by
  All you have to do
    is stop and close your eyes

Some think I'm handicapped
  because I cannot see
  I don't feel the same way
    God created me FREE!
      —*Jenny Lee Johnson*

"Grand Mother And Her Little Boys"

Little feet, over many long years,
Must wonder on, through hopes and fears.
Little hands, either weak or strong,
Must rule or serve so very long.

A long long time to give or ask,
I weary - just thinking of your task.
Little souls so pure and white,
I long to guide you, through your night.

My life- I'll hold you to my breast,
Til God Almighty bids me rest.
Then I'll wait for both of you
On Heaven's Holy Ground,
To live forever and ever,
Never to be parted again.
    —*Frances Donnell*

Be Still My Heart

Be still my heart be still
  Must you show the thrill
Of how his lips do warm me
  through and through so tenderly
How I rise so very high
  High above the clouds and sky
And softly softly rest my head
  As on a clean white cloudy bed
Like Little Angels dancing round
  I Listen closely for the sound
Of his heart beneath my ear
  The sound of love I long to hear
For I love him so with all my heart
  Yet know it's just the start
For all the thing that I have said
  cannot compare to when we wed.
    —*Theresa Grimaldi*

Untitled

We meet each week on Monday nights,
My aunt, sis, mom and me.
To watch us play a game of cards,
Is something you should see.

My aunt sits on one side of me,
Not sure that she should bid.
And when her partner goes too high,
She really blows her lid.

My mom sits on the other side,
Good cards for her's a must.
Cause if her hand is always bad,
She stirs up quite a fuss.

My sister is my partner,
All night she plays the same.
She's always much too serious,
Gee whiz, it's just a game!

And then there's me I make the fourth,
The one with all the guts.
To play with such a trio,
I think I must be nuts!
    —*Dolores Nycz*

Ireland, My Ireland

  My arms are so empty,
  My heart is so heavy,
  O, Ireland, my Ireland,
    How I do miss thee.

Thy green rolling lowlands,
  Thy glorious highlands,
  O, Ireland, my Ireland,
    How I do love thee.

  At last my true home,
    No more to roam,
  O, Ireland, my Ireland,
    How I do need thee.

  But I will return,
  My soul does so yearn,
  For Ireland, my Ireland,
    Mine own destiny.
    —*Veronica Giacomelli Ritter*

My Love

Long ago we first met
My heart young and innocent.
Even then I think I knew.
The look in your eyes.
You couldn't disguise.
Said I will see a lot more of you.
The day we were wed.
Blissful thoughts filled my head.
I questioned my Lord is this true.
You kissed my young hand.
Gave me a small gold band.
Said I will always be faithful to you.
Many years have gone by.
Other men caught my eye.
With charm like a rose laced in dew.
They can't be a part.
No room in my heart.
My love is forever for you.
    —*Sharlene Harrison*

His Promised Coming

He speaks to me through ages past,
"My love abides the stormy blast
Though tempests rage full and strong,
And satan's host about you throng.

Though all of life seems hard to bear,
Trust to me your every care.
Hold to my hand day by day,
The Son shines through in golden ray."

I hear His voice so quiet and still,
Bid me come and do his will.
Obey His precepts, word by word,
In my life to make Him Lord.

I cannot lose when on His side,
Under sheltering wings I shall abide;
And I will hear the trumpet sound
Beckoning all His children home.

Oh, what glory that will be!!
Such a sight for eyes to see;
When He cometh by night or day,
To carry His precious bride away.
    —*Kathleen K. Lowes*

Untitled

Flashes of light sear
My mind
I long to escape into the
Sweet night,
The air caressing my skin,
Sending soft shivers
Through my soul

My mind turning to darker
Things,
I am swept away on the wings
Of the moon
She smiles on me, and
My heart knows truth
And happiness
Even though still longing
For something more
    —*Andrea Anderson*

My Mother's Love

Dedicated to Mary E. Lucas
My Mother's love to me,
Is a love that will always be.

Always giving from her heart,
And that alone is a major part.

Ever since I was born,
Her love for me was never torn.

Over all of the years; all of the
Love she has shed with tears.

All her love I have seen, a love
Some people can but only dream.

Even though I have done wrong, her love
For me is still so very strong.

My Mother's love for me is from
Her heart, and given free.

She's the best Mother I could ask for;
For her love means so much, and I too
Love her a whole bunch!

My Mother's love for me will stay and
Always be.
    —*Mary Polus*

Without You

My heart grows weak without you.
My soul is growing old.
I wish you'd keep me warm at night,
Instead I'm growing cold.
I want to spend my life with you,
I wish you could believe
That I love you with all my heart,
And I want you close to me.
My love for you is endless
And I wish you'd understand,
That some day we could walk along
The warm and golden sand.
I wish you felt the same way too,
But that's asking for too much.
I just don't want to live without
Your soft and gentle touch.
Please keep me in consideration.
That's not that hard to do.
And please remember one more thing...
That I will always love you.
—*Emily O'Donnell*

Earthbound

Earthbound? No, not I!
My thoughts are free,
To embrace all the good
God gives.

Enveloped with love that knows
no boundry,
I soar the heights of Mind
to claim my heritage as a child of God.
—*Hazell Albins*

Journey Down The Pane

I look through the window
My view blurred by streams
of water journeying frivolously
down the panes.

I follow a single droplet
As it begins it's descent
across the translucent surface.
As if intoxicated, perhaps unsure,
it travels a crooked path,
Creeps along
Bending light rays.
Miniature rainbows tint the blur.

The droplet loses force as it goes,
Dwindles until, almost a thread,
It touches and adheres
to another, not unlike itself.
The two strengthen each other, fully join
into
One, more powerful. More purposeful,
They, it continues
The journey down the pane.
—*Geannine Hladky*

Untitled

"Some of us do not realize,
Nor will our dull brains comprehend
The value of being ourselves,
And not disguised as some sophisticate
Who feigns equality with sagacious
    minds".
—*Elizabeth Huffaker Norris*

Negro Burial Grounds

Dry bones raised from sacred terrain
Negro burial grounds opened to defile
Feds claim right of eminent domain

Manhattan skyscraper plans remain
protests and Mayor's cry futile
Dry bones raised from sacred terrain

Native American pleas bear tearstain
city bigwigs take low-profile
Feds claim right of eminent domain

Compromise agreed to contain
skeletal fragments in domicile
Dry bones raise from sacred terrain

Monument planned memories sustain
building climbs upward meanwhile
Feds claim right of eminent domain

Remnants of Manifest Destiny profane
the great masses stay docile
Dry bones raised from sacred terrain
Feds claim right of eminent domain
—*Virginia Lee*

Say I Am

People say I am lucky
never did I agree
until I seen you, say I am lucky no.

Say I am grateful
say I can't believe
that you chose me, me of all people.

Say I am in love
deeply that it's sad,
cause without your love
I will not live, I'll just exist alone.

Before I met you
didn't care to live,
don't want to die
how could love have changed my mind.

Don't care to understand
just know I am happy,
but why isn't there time for me and you.

Never believed in love
never believed in living
since I met you, a fool that I was.
—*Howard Kindred, Sr.*

Untitled

The tossing and turning
never stops
as sure as it rises
it then drops,
like an elevator that
goes straight down,
it slams into the
ocean's frown.
The lone vessel rides atop
the ocean waves
a circular path it
does pave
it cuts through the water
that's clear as glass
disturbing the melodic
pattern, alas.
—*Carrie A. Weismann*

On Time!!

Late again! Late again!
Never on time!
Like those in a nursery rhyme!

Late again! Late again!
Never on time!
Have trouble getting away from the line?

Late again! Late again!
Never on time!
Plan on being behind?

Late again! Late again?
Never on time!
The schedule you wreck may be mine!

Late again! Late again!
Never on time!
Shake it - we must meet the deadline!

Late again! Late again!
Never on time!
We all have the same hours to bind!

So stop being late again
And please be on time!
—*William Hardy*

Untitled

She comes when she wants to,
never when she's needed.
Cynics laugh at her,
so she scorns them.
Weaker ones are in constant
confusion over her.
Some feel they can control her,
   only to be crushed.
(Who is this goddess that has
power to effect all beings?)
She falls like a bomb on some,
yet dances around others,
   teasingly out - of - reach.
She showers few, while leaving
many in utter abandonment.
Oh, but there are people who wish
they never knew her, but most
only dream of having her; just once.
—*Heather L. Holman*

A Grandma

A Grandma always loves you
No matter what you do
She'll listen to your problems
And help you work them through.

A Grandma always listens
And loves it when you visit
She'll give her greatest treasure
And never will she miss it.

A Grandma is a friend
You can turn to in despair
She'll comfort you and laugh with you
A Grandma's always there.

She's as solid as a mountain
She's as gentle as can be
And I know mine is the best
'Cause God gave her to me.
—*Sharon A. Weber*

Inside Of Me

What I feel inside of me,
No one can ever know.
I love you with all my heart,
And just can't let you go.
If you looked inside my soul.
I know just what you'd see.
There'd be pounding force,
With visions of you and me.
Behold the love I feel for you,
So gentle and so kind.
You make me feel so loved,
And I'm so glad you're mine.
Our love is one big miracle,
Underneath the sky.
All the angels high in heaven,
Envy you and I.
There'll never be another,
Who makes me feel the way you do.
And I can't help but fall,
So madly in love with you!
—*Jessenia Magua (Luis Camacho)*

"Turn Your Eyes To Heaven"

When troubles and woes beset you
no peace on earth can be found,
then turn your eyes to heaven
where God's peace does abound.

When your heart is down in your shoes
and your hope is all but gone,
then turn your eyes to heaven for
God's hope shall come with the dawn.

When sickness has besieged you;
it is truly getting you down,
then turn your eyes to heaven
where God's miracles can be found.

When your faith is all but shattered
and you are feeling sad and blue,
then turn your eyes to heaven
for God's love shall comfort you.
—*Mildred Sheldon*

Lonely World

Pushed away in every direction
Not knowing what to do,
Where to turn
Alone in a corner
Confused and neglected
Feelings are hurt
Can't say a word
Instead think to yourself
Wishing for things to change
In this lonely world.
—*Gilda Lungariello*

Beauty

Your beauty shines like the flame
of a candle in a dark room,
And your spirit quickly sets you out
amongst a crowd.
But let that not be the reason
for my captured heart,
No, let it be because I have looked
upon you as a blind man would;
To only see what I can hear
and only listen with my heart.
—*Larry Brewer*

Universal Race

They were treated like things,
Not like human beings.

They didn't deserve to be treated
  this way,
Even then it shouldn't have been
  okay!

No one deserves to be treated like
  this,
These sort of things can't be healed
  with a kiss.

I don't care if you're white, black
  or red,
What matters is we're human beings
  instead.

No one anywhere will be free
Until everyone can see

The only one race we can find
Is the universal one and that's mankind.
—*Sara Duncan*

Don't Ask Me

English is quiet confusing
Not simple as some claim
Which should I be using
When many sound the same

Let's begin with since and sense
Also there's ware and wear
Another choice is hence and hints
We must add fair and fare

Sounding the same is won and one
Each a quite different word
For two more there is dun or done
Those I have herd or heard

To venture on there's scene and seen
Add to those tint and tent
We also must use lean and lien
Plus cent and scent and sent

Forgive me if I add one more
Well maybe too or two
One cannot be too sure or shore
What he should dew or do.
—*Doug Senna*

Summer Night

I lay in bed, it's late at night
Not yet dark, in the afterglow
of the new summer light.

The killdeers sing their rhythmic
whippoorwill song, and the
frogs and toads will moan
and croak for long.

The mountains loom high,
with their power and beauty.
They storm over the ocean,
blue mist filling the sky.

Oh summer nights,
bring joy to all,
much the same, but yet unlike
winter, spring and fall.

With their own special sparkle
like a dew dropped fairy ring,
but the delicate softness of a
newly opened flower, in spring.
—*Betsy Faber*

Untitled

Scared of life
nothing to show
a gun in his hand
nowhere to go

Life in his hands
a tear in his eye
the time has now come
for a selfish goodbye

He leaves without warning
his heart full of pain.
his thoughts of confusion
so hard to explain

He raises the gun
and takes his last breath
cries his last tear
then falls to his death

His nightmare is over
how glad he must be
look up to the skies now,
my brother, your free.
—*Sara Egelston*

A Riddle

To steal from the Gods
  nuggets of delight and equanimity
transforming reality's existence

Each wrapped in gossamer covers
  gently held close to both
oneself and source

  Handcuffed one can only hear
the sound of the clock
  steadily and softly whispering
shash...shash...shash, be still

  Stealing from the Gods is
highly punishable
  inflicted on those that dare

In a single moment dear God
I am ready, can you take
  another walk...?

Reality/dream exhausted
  the nuggets returned un/rapped
the gossamer shimmering still covers
  that which has remained un/touched.
—*Gigi McKendric*

Contacts

The touch of the silk
  of a long white dress
On the skin of your breast
  is smooth and cool
Like a Sphere of marble.
  Full of promise

The touch of the hand
  of a good man
On the skin of your breast
  is firm and caressing
Like a swim under water.
With a passionate promise

The touch of the hand
  of a tiny baby
On the skin of your breast
  is soft and timid
Like the touch of the wing
  of a butterfly.
With fulfillment of a promise.
—*Susan Jones*

In The Pipe If An Organ

As I sat in the pipe
of an organ one day,
the pulse of a melody,
eerie, beautiful,
and strange beyond telling,
pressed against my body
like the weight of a giant tear...

and I wept
and I died from weeping
as I sat in the pipe
of an organ one day.
—*Shirley Rod*

Private Space

In a second, of a moment
of forgotten dream
no more second chances
no more dreams to dread
in this hell, I've made my home
I wish, I'm not, but I'm alone
dust to dust, forever lost in lust
in this hell I call home
a cosmic cloud of darkest gloom
now my temples, dust in every tomb
somewhere in my head
forgotten space, a hiding place
darkest place where devils tread
the Earth so hot and burning red
voices crying inside my head
fear for your soul, it's never dead
—*Mark Simonson*

Springfever

I while away the time and dream
of home and hearth
a place to rest
I yearn to build and line the nest
of life
with love and breath.
A garden soft and rich and deep
in fertile earth
put seeds to sleep
to wake and blossom, this
I ache.
For springtime's voice within me sings
the song to rise from others dreams
and live my own
alone and free
this dream is mine,
just me.
—*Louise Salmin*

"Friendship"

"Friendship" is a wonderful part
　of life!
It softens the cares of daily strife
But the passing years can take
　its toll —
Unless we carefully to that
　Friendship Hold!
Like a fragile bird once held
　in one's hand —
Our friendships gradually drift
　over the land!
So nourish and value each passing
　year —
Our loving friendships that We
　All Hold So Dear!!
—*Julia King Duff Wheeler*

To Students Everywhere

When your minds are clear and free
　Of life's necessities,
　Your thinking of tomorrow
Prevents endless days of sorrow.

Ask the Lord for ways to win,
　To destroy those traps of sin.
　You can maintain laws of hope
Helping people now to cope.

You are leaders of today -
　Heroes of our great tomorrows.
　Lead us on to stable ways,
Prevent endless days of sorrow.

Remember this rule of life:
　"Be free of deadly strife."
　Ask our Lord for ways to win —
That love and peace may begin.
—*Mary K. Dissinger*

Mind Country

History is the recording
Of man's culture and times.
A warning reminder
Of his follies and crimes.
A remembrance
Of generative energy
and zest.
A creative mind-country
Where man's at his best.
A mind-country so vast,
Every soul's welcome there.
Whether lover,
Or poet,
Or statesmen who care.
To all
Who contribute
Their large or small share.
The gates are wide
Open
To all who will dare.
—*Susan Selby*

Gift

Beyond our common love
of nature's beauty,
you gave me science.
I absorbed your conviction
that the search
for understanding
does not vanquish wonder
but rather nourishes it.
With your encouragement
I learned my part
in the ancient round
of eater and eaten
and found myself
to be knit
with the molecular thread
of kinship
into the web.
—*Kathleen O'Donnell*

Earth So Green

Oh! Earth so green
Of splendor colors
I see, I touch you
With such amazement

I walk upon you
On my life's journey
I feel the winds
That sometimes shake me

Your streams and rivers
Lead to the oceans
And join the lands
That make you whole

I know that winter
Will fade your colors
But in the springtime
I'll see your beauty
—*Juanita Saenz*

Anniversary Prayer

On this our anniversary,
Of the day that we were wed.
I'd like to take you by the hand,
And lead you off to bed.

I want to lay down by your side,
And whisper words of love,
While saying a little prayer of thanks,
To the good Lord up above.

Thank you Lord for giving me
This man so good and true,
A man of real integrity
Sent to me from you.

I'll do my best to make him proud
And happy as can be,
And never let a cloud of doubt
Obscure his love for me.
—*Sharon Hyde*

Marriage

Marriage is a union
of two hearts a glow.
And love is the secret
that makes it grow.
The special attention
You need everyday,
is three little words
always remember to say.
No matter how sad, tired, or blue,
Don't forget to say "I love you."

Marriage is a union
for sharing your love.
With ties that bind,
with God up above.
For He's the one
that joins you together.
And with him in your life,
it will last forever.
—*Sara B. Christian*

The Christmas Gift

Christmas is a busy time,
of visiting and singing,
of festive lights and Christmas trees

Church bells gaily ringing
of sending cards, and planning meals
of baking cleaning, cooking
of shopping lists and party fun.

How sad when people seem to feel
That spending is the reason
and in their haste they miss the gift
That is the Christmas season

God gave the world, eternal life
Through his own baby boy,
and knowing him we realize
His peace, his love his joy.
—*Leone Lee Coates*

"Chosen To Dream"

Resembling a monotonous underlay—
Of whatever we choose to be—
Growing older each day with grace—
And not looking at what we should see—
What is our world as a human race—
Finally chosen to dream?

Do not tell me; I'd only weep—
(And they'd be tears of my shame)
Observing my aged tales and beliefs—
(Which died with our yesterdays)
Bring back to life-bring back to me—
These unused prayers, I pray.

If each of us were more than a name—
Had heart and soul we'd seem—
Different desires alive every day—
Each our individual lives to lead!
(But programmed robots we remain)
All living the unchosen dream!
—*Marlene Baugh*

Untitled

Heaven loved death so rich a treasure,
Often it is too fine to measure.
Death freed me from domestic strife,
It came to my house and took my life.
I was sick to the point of death,
I was gone before I gave my last breath.
They put my body down to sleep,
Where I have my body and soul to keep.
Now my grave is my body's bed,
It is here I shall lay my head.
I shall stay in that celestial sky,
Where I shall live and never die.
Up in heaven my soul does dwell,
To live there with the angels, Farewell.
—*Christopher David Gates*

Love

A dandelion spreading its fluffy
Petals in a flurry of wind
A flickering fire, soft and cozy
Warm and gentle
Total giving as mother to child
A dream of perfect bliss, ecstasy!
Flowering buds of sweet roses.
A reason for life-
 a meaning to live.

—*Jo-Ann M. Van Hoecke*

America's Symbol

Eyes bright with courage,
 on another fair day,
The Eagle swoops down,
 up on his prey.

He flies so majestic,
 his wings outspread.
While a halo of white,
 Shines over his head.

His talons so deadly,
 his beak, curved and sharp.
The music he makes,
 is sweeter than a harp.

This country so young,
 yet seeming so old,
Should stand tall for freedom,
 Like this bird so bold.

So America take note,
 of our Symbol the Eagle.
If he can't have his freedom
 then how will the people?
—*Orvetta Osterlund*

A Golf Pome

When I tee off
On number one
All I think of
Is having fun,

But after I reach
Number one green
I putt so much
I feel real mean

Then on number two,
If I make a good shot,
I find my feelings
Have changed a lot.

So I keep going
Till I finish the game
And look at my card
And say "what a shame!"
—*Lemuel L. Lee*

Midsummer Night's Imagination

The night slipped stealthily
on strong elfin feet
fleeting across lawns of
suburbia's homes.
Invader from another world,
out of time,
out of minds,
planting their mischief
across the world
like dandelion spores
floating from a tiny child's lips
sowing strife and discord
in the darkened streets.
—*M. S. Thomas*

Little Penny

Oh, Little Penny
 On the ground—
Be happy, my friend, you have
 been found.

When I was so little
 You were so big.
Now that I'm big
 You've become so little.

I wonder and wonder
 What you bought last, and
How many times you were
 spent fast.
Oh, Little Penny
 stay for a while
I think Mr. Lincoln
 Is going to smile.
—*H. John Susmuth*

Despair To Come

The sun beats down
On the harmless humans
Stupendous trees
Serve for:
Enlightenment,
Inspiration,
Beauty,
Shade,
Resources,
Gone,
Gone, too, are the animals
Driven out of their environment,
Home and habitat
Driven to death.
A death caused by humans,
People not thinking
Reusing
Or recycling.
Not knowing what lies ahead,
Death.
—*Kristin Scott*

Sea Of Life

As I set sail again
 On the sea of life
 A favorable wind
I pray receives it.

My course set true
Resupplied anew this time
I hope to achieve it.

On voyages of past
Friendly ports I passed
I thought then I didn't need it.

But when the storms approached
 They swamped my boat
 Through neglect
My ship, I deceived it.

But I didn't drown
And with new courage abound
Gods promise I now believe it.

The treasures I seek
Are in the hearts of the meek
This time I truly can see it.
—*Harry T. Williams*

Traveller

Youth awakens to a spring rain
On this battle field sacrosanct
Culp's Hill
Where I stood
100 years past
Lincoln's passionate address.

From the Floral walk of my lake
Quannapowitt
Alone I watch the petals fall
Wet spring cumulus
Roll overhead
Where I stand
The spring rain again I request.

No beauty finer does my love find
Between the spaces of this time
Knowing sweetly my heart is thine
And all the tumult has come to rest.

—*Frederick L. Forster*

Top Of The East

At the summit of the hotel
on this clear evening from high
where the White Mountains in the west
reach crimson sunset painted sky,

the view sweeps east past Deering Oaks
toward Casco Bay where tides are one
with sunset as they ebb and flow
while nature's daily course is run.

But as I look past Congress Street,
down from this lounge all windowed in,
I feel the human touch extend
past where Atlantic waves begin.

Longfellow Square, Museum of Art,
the Old Port structures long in place,
and Scotia Prince out in the bay
add texture to the harbor's face.

The music starts as tiny amber
ceiling lights dance to and fro
to calm the spirit of the night
reflected in the afterglow.

—*Carrol McNeal*

"Thoughts"

So many times, I ponder alone
On thoughts, of a proper poem
To best describe, the four seasons
   and natures reasons

Autumn's leaves
turn to red and gold
And stand a top
the trees so bold

Winter's winds
   heartily blow
And sweep up
the new fallen snow

As a gentle friend
We look to spring
And it's promise
to renew everything

Warm summer sun
nourishes the earth
and brings pretty flowers
   to birth.

—*Dorothy Gallagher*

Dawn

Far across,
On top of distant mountains
The jagged, white, ridges,
Of the zenith,
Like fingers grasp,
Eternally at the sky.
While sunrays of fire gold,
Bursts, diffusing through air,
Suffusing the darkness,
Of the passing night,
As the crimson sun,
Strikes the morning spark.
Then bright struck blue,
Ignites the wind water,
To burn the furnace of light,
Imbued in the sublime,
As the empyrean dew,
Gracefully across the firmament,
Falls,
From the dias of heaven.

—*Ho Jun Song*

"Just A Rose"

A Rose petal of life falling
one by one to the ground. A
rose of life not many treasure
but many do live petal by petal
and do soon die. Just a rose
it was I received yesterday, and
one by one the petals blew away.

I grew older my heart weaker,
the rose of life. I hung by a
petal of a rose which was my life
and soon my death.

—*Denice L. Glover Cordova*

Poetry

Poetry is a list of titles,
one-liners, short subjects,
stop-overs, one-night stands.
Poetry is adrenal instants,
emergency landings
on strips too small.
It is that knowing before words,
a collapse in the solar plexus,
breathless, while the brain
devises programs to explain.
Poetry is flight before fight,
kisses for nothing,
a punch after the bell,
falling in love fault-blind,
a foot in the dark feeling for edge.
Poetry is milk-rise before boil,
spill before say or save,
and a blink before yes.
Even in epics
poetry is one step at a time.

—*Katie Ingram*

"The Meaning Of A Snowy Night"

Snow falling from the night sky
   Like frozen tears
  Descending from heaven.
  They are shed in memorium
   of the one I love,
  but can no longer see.

—*Catherine Victoria*

The Painted Glass

Here an artist
or a mortal.
Here upon a painted glass
or a past.
For his paintings
are so fainting
and yet no words to utter
for them.
For he has seen the horrifying
painted glass
or past denying
of his freedom.
He speaks no more.

—*Rachel Barron*

Prayer

You don't have to have an appointment,
Or call before you go;
Or wonder if the door will be closed
Before you ask what you want to know.

The door is always open.
The latch string is always out.
He's ever willing and able
To help erase every doubt.

He'll heal the broken-hearted
He'll lift a heavy load.
His outstretched arms will enfold you
When impassable, seems the road.

So trust in this wonderful Saviour
Who's on call, each hour of the day.
He'll lead, guide, and direct you
And continually, show you the way.

—*Margaret Lawhorn*

Hearing Voices

  Never more will I see you
  Or rest my palm against
    your face
  A face so wonderful
   That God Himself
  could not have gazed
    upon you
   and wept not
  at his creation
   How I loved
  your troubled mind
   So sweet, so sad
  And how your soul
  crept gently into mine
   Only a moment
    in time
  But for all eternity
   I will carry you
    in my heart
My Angel, My Desire, My Destruction!

—*Gerri Elizabeth Orr*

Country Roads

Country roads
  Meander
   The Land
As tho'
  Penciled there
By some
  Child's
Uncertain hand.

—*Gerald Ebner*

"Precious Child"

Should we work it out
Or should we even try.
Should we grow up
And just say good-bye.
Is it fair to her
To listen to us fight.
She knows what's going on
She hears it day and night.

She will understand
When she gets older.
Why daddy wasn't there much
To love her and hold her.

It's harder for me
Because I see her less.
Daddy's sorry Ashlee
For getting you in this mess.

I want you to know
That I will always be there.
And you're very special
You're my little Sugar Bear.
—*Mike Billings*

Secret Hopes

With our birth, amid
 our dreams.
Throughout time, across
 the seas.
Above the clouds, beyond
 the heavens.
We walk alone, our only
 companions, our secret
 hopes.
Then as those hopes fade,
 our life ends for
 another's birth.
—*Miranda Prather*

Untitled

The tears swelled up and ran out
 our eyes,
It hurts so much saying our
 last good-byes.
We will remember our cherished
 times together,
And we will hold them close to
 our hearts forever,
We will miss you, but we know
 you won't suffer no more,
Because today you went knocking
 on our Heavenly Father's door.
—*Cindy Tyler*

High Desert Mural

You can see it begin
over the Carizos, a blending
of lamb's wool down and late day sun,
teal blue sky and budding nova,
as if by a giant paint brush
in a skilled artist's hand.
Spreading, lining half the heavens
with a masterpiece in color,
blessing the desert with a mystic glow.
Now it ebbs, and inches
into the night sky,
and over the edge of the earth.
—*Marguerite Rideout*

The Heart Of Humanity

Like a foolish child,
 Our reality is clouded.
We no longer listen with unbiased ears
 Nor do we see with unmasked eyes.

Struggling against time,
 We hasten to capture
What is lost
 But, it's too late…
Calamity had turned the tide.

Dark shadows cloud our false visage
 Conceited compassion compromises
With the corrupt soul
 But, our hidden passion,
 lingers.

Desperately clinging to
 something, anything
As the life within faded…
 Obliviously into nothingness.
—*Alice Kang*

"Mother Nature"

Made by our Creator,
Out of dust it breathes,
The entire universe,
Hosting its lands and seas.
Enjoy her seasonal changes,
Respect her power and peace.

Never-ending beauty,
Always a great tease!
Trees, flowers, birds, bees
Upon the earth's great floor
Reach up beyond her mountains and stars,
Explore, explore, explore!
—*Dorothy A. De Antonio*

Snow

Snow - sifting softly down
Over a sleeping town,
Covering the ground with gleaming white
Hushing the noises of the night.

Snow - drifting drowsily down
Over a dreaming town,
Making halos of rainbow colors bright
Around each shining light.

Snow - stealing shyly down
Over a slumbering town,
Filling each stately tree's embrace
With feathery flakes of snowy lace.

Snow - waltzing gaily down
Over an awakening town,
Painting pictures in the night
Filling me with wonder and delight.
—*Virginia C. Starkey*

Angst

 Time passing,
 Moments gone away.
 Thoughts remain,
pictures from the mind.

 Quiet and still am I
 holding the vision and
 waiting, as time and
 others move by.
—*James W. O'Neill, Jr.*

The Power Of One

Glowing green eyes
peering from the charcoal
sky, piercing to silence
the beating heart.
His run as quick
as the bullet from the gun.
The prey cannot move,
hypnotized by the hazy preview
through the jade crystal balls.
With his eyes at half-mast -
Boom…
An empty gaze washes over,
the prey now meets and becomes one
with the ground moistened
with his own blood.
—*Derra L. Dubie*

Deaf World

Eyes staring
people glaring
No one's caring

Mouths speaking
Harsh, bitter words
that are always heard
Someone's hurting

Ears hearing
Lies that are said
Hate being bred
No one is trusting

Hearts feeling
Alone and confused
Angry and used

Is anyone listening?
—*Julie Richmond*

Save The Children

 There are little children
playing everywhere.
 That don't have a
wish or prayer.
 Abusers, kidnappers, and
dealers all around.
 You can even find them
on the playgrounds.
 There are children missing
and dying every day.
 There are no safe places
to run and play.
 Adults need to take more
special care.
 They should have the
children in sight, everywhere.
 Band together to fight
kidnappers, dealers, and the abusers.
 Then in court those people
must face their accusers.
—*Rebecca Edens*

A Mother's Cry

(To My Son Steven…)
My little boy, I loved him
so much it hurt. Where
did he go? What happened,
he grew up and I let
him go.
—*Natalie Johannesburg*

Lord, Show Me The Way

As I live this day,
Please touch my shoulder
   along the way.
Let me feel your concern
   whatever I do or say
   to another the whole
   day through -
So at night I can pray
   with a grateful heart,
The Lord was my shepherd
But I did my part.
—*Josephine McGuire Swanson*

Ocean's Window

Near my window by the sea
Pounding surf and ocean's roar
Bring the gulls on spindrift tossed
In the morning rays.

Gone now are the wintry winds
Sea smoke rises on the bay
Wonders in one morning pass
Times you'll dream of this?
—*Nancy L. D'Amario*

Communicating

God speaks to me in a wonderful way,
Proclaiming His love each new day.

Lulling me to sleep on a quiet night—
Awaking me with a bright sunlight!

Broadcasting snow from Heaven's Tree,
A beautiful sight for me to see.

Just a whisper when a south wind blows,
A healing, soothing balm it bestows.

A quiet, placid brook when I feel blue,
My quivering voice, He'll listen to.

Clearly speaking with showers of rain—
Writing messages on my window pane!

A loud voice when the sun comes out—
A shout when buds send blossoms out!

I hear His silent words as they convey,
His love for me in a wonderful way.
—*Aline Ubelhor*

Static

I am blue-grey boy
product of television
and the twentieth century
desensitized senseless
by news and nudity
cut dry and solid
as concrete
but I'd rather be malleable
as metal
now
know no limits
and offensive is only interesting
I say spout shout
your own words
go forth and destroy their normal
to find your truth
because morals are dead, dull, and done
and if you still have faith
you must have missed the funeral
stay tuned for the news at eleven
—*Bryan Whitefield*

"Good Night"

Emerald forests,
Purple clouds.
Pink-orange sky,
Shimmers out loud.

Falling warmth,
Dimming light.
Dark steps out,
With specks of white.

Heavy eyes,
Close to let,
The dark blanket,
Kiss "good-night" the sunset.
—*Micheleen Harris*

"A Friendship"

As I walked, I could feel the zephyr air
Remembering the fond adieu
and the tear stained glare
A chill comes over me now
just remembering, the "Good-byes"
A friend I shall not see for a long time
walking away, never looking back
Soft distinction of friendship
A part of you walking away
The rest separating and staying with you
A friendship between two.
—*Brenda M. Gray*

Untitled

i ride past the tricycle of life
   removed, moved, alien.
am i a part of it or
   apart from it?
i question only -
   no questions, please!
uneasy touching,
   uneasy being touched.
touched, moved, removed
   i remain apart from it.
different and alien,
   i choose to be so.
no one allowed in,
   no one allowed out.
my world is different
   from that of yours.
my world is me
   and me alone
goes riding by
   on the tricycle of life…
—*Michele Papavasiliou*

Earthquake Alamo, CA: 1990

The Lord with His Wondrous Power
Reshaping His Planet Earth,
By quaking, shaking and rumbling things
No matter what their human worth.
Ours is not to question or wonder
   At his method,
of changing our earthly structure
From deep within the ground,
That future generations,
Much treasure can be found.
Under pressure, heat and time,
Coal and diamonds can be formed.
Who knows what God's creating
When the earth does roll and shake.
Our's is not to question
But to hope we survive the quake.
—*Lorraine Thomas*

Star Bright

Beautiful star above
Reunited with the moon above
Regained the beauty you once lost
In turn a star again reborn

You who wanted to outshine them all
By far more brighter
And more beautiful
Then all the stars above

You, who wouldn't leave me alone
I couldn't think of nothing more
But the star shining down on me

I sit alone and wonder why?
I look up. And there you are
You seem to say "Here I am"
And tell me things I long to here

There's no one else in the universe
Only you and I alone
A peaceful feeling overcomes
Dear Mother in heaven
I love you so.
—*Celia Lagunas*

Spring Wedding

The purest white,
Rounded, bisected tips
Touched with cream
And watercolor rose,
Clustered ceremoniously
On slender black branches;
A celebrated betrothal,
Dazzling in the sun,
Dancing in the wind,
Brushing my window.

Then overnight,
Gone from the window,
Transformed below,
A mud-spattered veil
Trailing down the hillside
Over gray rocks to water's edge,
Where the rain-swollen creek
Gives daredevil rides
Downstream
On delicate white rafts.
—*Sandra Goode Bricker*

The Meaning Of The Age

Unfurl the banners,
Run up the flags;
Serve in love and peace
And climb the highest crags.

Believe in truth and goodness,
Give yourself to beauty;
Work for harmony and brotherhood,
And always strive for unity.

Lift the world with your compassion,
Share whatever you have and are;
Don't be hesitant about your future,
Pour out your blessings near and far.

World culture is your theme,
Harmony and concord your aspiration;
Make of your dream a reality,
And every experience an education.

This is the meaning of the Age:
Meditate, Serve, and Realize;
There is nothing great in man but soul,
Nothing more to finalize.
—*Howard John Zitko*

"Freeway Farm"

It's late after noon
Rush hour traffic buzzes
Threw my head as I
Lie waiting for the queen

The air in here is thin and cold
Yet peaceful, cool and dark
The wind outside is full of madness
As it sips down the frozen highway

Oriental tiger women peer
Threw my window and block
Sunlight from my face
It's good to be awake in the dark
But it won't be long until I go back
—*Shawn McCoy*

I Apologize…

I love you, I am sorry
Scared you won't hear it
Afraid you'll turn away
I apologize through and through
Never trying to hurt you
Wanting to prove my concern
I try to catch up to you
Just explain it all in truth
I apologize through and through
Give anything to be with you
Sacrifice my freedom for one touch
All I can do is wait and hope
Begging for your forgiveness
I apologize through and through
I want you to trust my word
You can believe all I say
The decision is solely yours
For you to conclude all on your own
Still…
….I apologize through and through
—*Kristie Brodfuehrer*

Waves Of Autumn

The stealthy Autumn colors
Scatter the mountain range:
Red apples sparse within reach
Gets juicier with age.

Savage blackberry bushes'
Thorny canes drape the stream,
'Neath purple Autumn crocus
Fulfills her latest dream.

The sunflower heavy with seed
Droops and before sleep, prays;
The chancing poppies absorb
The last of the sun's rays.

The sheltered green tomatoes
Shudders the coming frost,
The weeping willow awaits
The spray of radiant dust.

The rattle box rattles
By the brushing cattle,
The Egrets are riding high
Stately posed on saddle.
—*Harriet Poplar*

Dawning Of A New Day

She traveled south
Searching for reality
There she met a man
With a great personality.

He wined and dined her
And took her western dancing
They shared common interests
As they began romancing.

The months rolled past
They fell in love
As Christmas approached
There was a sign from above.

The wedding plans began
And the bride grew harried
These two special people
Were finally getting married!

Her faith remains strong
As this has been her way
She thanks God for her new life
It's the dawning of a new day!
—*Megan Hagen*

Echoes

Whispers through eternity
Secrets in the pines
Shadows on a winter wall
Dying leaves and vines

Echoes from an ancient well
Down a darkened hall
The touch of things remembered
Bittersweet recall
—*Kathleen Gester*

April's Seduction

Bright April's sensuality
　seduces me.
　　The scented breeze
　　and sun's warmth seize,
enfold, caress me. I succumb.
　　And I become
　　the melodies
　　of birds and bees,
the redbud, mosses, daffodil,
　　the greening hill,
　　and violets
　　that earth begets.
—*Ellen Gray Massey*

"Walls Of Pain"

Walls of pain
see and hear everything
they know when someone's hurting,
yet they remain silent.
Walls of pain
are a person's best friend
they know many secrets,
yet they remain silent

Walls of pain
sense a person's sorrow
and cry a single tear.

Walls of pain
crying,
no one knows why.
—*Michelle Garcia*

Peace Comes Through Love

Peace is an inner feeling
Sent from God above,
When we show love to each other
Peace comes through that love.
We all come from the seed of Adam
Who God created from the dust,
Let us all be kind and gentle
Let us all try to learn to trust.
Then peace will come on gradually
As we grow in trust and love,
Isn't peace worth trying?
So we can all take off our gloves?
—*Allie Lee Smith*

Desert Sunset

Soft pastel colors
Set against an enchanting
Blue sky with a sweep
Of nature's hand,
Casting rivers of light
Onto the white sands below.
Flowing in shimmering,
Silken waves.

Blazing red sun
Falling between cotton
White clouds.
Sinking into an endless,
Darkening horizon.
To be replaced
By the lightly traced
Silhouette of a moon
And the first of many
Glistening stars that
Fill the night sky.
—*Lynn Sommerville*

Atmosfear

Ghosts and regrets
settle
like curtains hung
by humid hands,
stifling the will to hope
and the hope
to will.
Heavy fog-feelings
crowd me out.

I catch the winking eye
of Despair,
who retires
to the corner island
of my mind.
Warm winds blow away
postal thoughts.

Wishing you were here.
—*Elizabeth Davenport*

Absolute

All
That I am
I give you
With the love
That you
Made me aware
I am capable of
—*Isabel S. Cooper*

Ode To Slick Willie

Hear me screaming to high heaven!
If it were not for me, you'd realize how poor you really are

How could you leave me destitute and stranded?
If it were not for money and greed, you'd count my worth

You leave my fate in the hands of the unknowing who despise me
If it were not for foolish pride,
   you'd feel my humility and wit

Criticize me as lazy and wanting to be here
If it were not for blind stupidity, you'd see I'm anything but

I ask only for my dignity
If it were not for your refusal to answer my letters,
   I would not blame you

I walk this walk and talk this talk, I have the solution
If it were not for my life as homeless,
   I'd prosper and so would you

It is you, "Mr. President", that I trusted and was betrayed
And it is "I", who is, "America"

I speak for myself and those who have lost all hope
Hear me screaming to high heaven, from the streets of "America"
   —*Thomas W. Kirk*

Cross My Heart

I know there's times when you must wonder
If my love is true, and
I'm satisfied
I wish I knew a way to show you
I'm forever yours for the rest of my life

I cross my heart and hope to die
I'll always be here by your side
My love grows stronger as the time goes by
Cross my heart and hope to die

And all those times we're not together
You're in my heart and you're on my mind
You're like a part of me that's missing
I cross my heart and hope to die
   —*Serena S. Breen*

Imagination

Imagination is one of the greatest things
If you listen to it, your heart takes wings
You can go anywhere whether great or small
You can even go to a prince's ball
You can dress in any kind of a dress
You can be pretty inside tho you look a mess
you will have a twinkle in your eyes
And see lovely things under the skies.
The flowers smell sweeter, little kittens are cuter,
The air feels softer, the raindrops are cooler,
Little rocks have more colors, the grasses are greener
Everything has hundreds of beautiful parts
To those of us who have fairy hearts.
   —*Edith Blasdel*

Mourning

I'm sad because she means so much to me,
I'm sad to think it really doesn't matter,
It wasn't long ago that we were friends,
And yet there surely wasn't any friendship.

What happens to us when we break away
From people who were very dear to us?
I think we lose more than we'll ever know,
I think someday there will be much regret.
   —*Genevieve E. Hauptly*

Your Only Road To Peace Of Mind

If your life isn't all, that you'd like it to be.
If you need something more, than your daily routine.
If your mind is confused by your thoughts so unclear.
You need to know who you are,
You need to know why you're here.
All the answers of life, are inside you and me.
Your must examine yourself with love and pure honesty.
   Only Then will you be able, to thoroughly see.
Now you must gain control of the thoughts in your mind,
so you can live out your dreams, it's just a matter of time.
Once your negative thoughts disrupt your positive way,
turn to your subconscious mind,
and you can chase them away.
   Only Then will you learn, to live for today.
Peace of mind will be yours, "Living Anxiety Free,"
once you eliminate envy, self-pity and greed.
Share your love with all life, one with God you will be.
With your heart as your guide,
and your health at your side...
   Only Then will you truly, be happy and free.
   —*James Merenda*

Life

The road of life is both long and wide
If you want to take it in your stride
You have to make the most of all you can
And on your principles, you have to stand
Give any man an hour's work for an hour's pay
And keep the promises you make on the way
Love your neighbors and protect your home
Be faithful to your mate and never roam
Give of yourself and do what you must
To live as God intended and be loyal and just
Then, all of a sudden, you will see
There is always hope for you and me
   —*Jane Ann Baker*

Mr. Lincoln

Mr. Lincoln, oh what would you say,
 if you were to rise up from your grave,
 the nation you led was a house divided,
 and now a century later, we remain divided,
 by the prejudice of race and creed,
 and the ignorance of truth,
 Oh Mr. Lincoln, what would you do,
to bind the wounds of a nation, who cry out
   for charity, and yet malice presides,
 and people are lost like little sheep,
 as the nation's debt grows deep,
 Mr. Lincoln, look around, at the faces of pain,
at the dismal feeling that seems to reign,
 and tell me Mr. Lincoln, what do you say,
 how would you solve the problems we have today,
oh, Mr. Lincoln, I know this is profound,
but we need someone like you around,
   —*Celine Rose Mariotti*

VeryFirst

The sweatypalmednervouscolognesaturated he-person took
the hand of the tallforheragenailbitingstillalluring she-girl.
All of the cricketchirpingstargazing rushed in around them
now trying to think of something notnecessarilywitty to say
just to say anything and finally saying:
   "Did you ever have a sister?" he, not caringabouttheanswer
asked, wanting more than anything to kiss her cherrygloss lips
and she, nothearingthequestionbutlaughinganyway, kissed him
      ON THE LIPS
   Flashinglikeinthemoviesboomcrash!
   —*Fawn H. Pattison*

I'll Miss You

I'll miss you more than you'll ever know.
I'll miss you more than I can show
I feel like you are gone forever
I feel like the next time I see you will be never
I don't know what will happen once you've gone.
I guess I'll find out when I'm thinking about you til dawn.
Thinking about the dream we've drawn
The summer nights on the lawn
I feel like I'll never live those dreams again
I'm afraid you may say this is the end
I don't know how to tell you how I feel
I don't know the right appeal
I know that no matter what.
I'll miss you

—*Jennifer Wise*

"If You Should Walk Away From Me"

If you should walk away from me, today or any day.
I'll need a guiding angel, to help show me the way.
For it would be as if I never lived this life before,
And I would have to start again and live my whole life over.
For I know now the things I only wish I knew before,
And nothing in this whole wide world could make me love you more.
What would I do if you leave me?
I hope I never see.
My life would not exist, if I couldn't hold you close to me.
I'll never, ever, open any doors I've closed behind.
You're embedded in my heart, and you are always on my mind.
If you should walk away from me,
Which I hope you will never do.
Remember dear, wherever you go you take my life with you.

—*Clementine Harris Scott*

Grandpa

You know I love you so,
I'll never let you go,
There's a place for you in my heart,
When you go to heaven you'll have a brand new start.

Your the best,
Better than all the rest,
I can't stand to let you go,
God, I love you so.

I can't picture you gone,
When you go to heaven you'll hear a brand new song.

The angels will be singing,
Bells will be ringing,
They'll all be praising your name;
Over here nothing will be the same.

I cannot bear to cry,
When your in heaven your gonna fly.

You're the best man I know,
God, I wish you didn't have to go.

—*Erica L. F. Shifter*

Summer Eyes

Oh, my summer eyes behold
Lavender bluebirds singing in a willow tree.
Golden flowers swaying in the sunlight.
A rainbow colored sunset over the ocean.
Red, hot, sweaty people playing basketball.
The bluish sky above the silent horizon.

—*Matt Winters*

Why, Why, Michele?

As I lie back and think about life,
   I'm captured by thoughts of my lovely wife.
She's stood by me through all of my strife,
   even tho' at times I have put her through hell.

We married when she was just in her prime;
   I've sometimes neglected her: what a terrible crime.
She could have deserted me time after time;
   yet she stays, wishing me nothing but well.

About life's ups and downs I always complain;
   not so with my wife: she's able to remain
the one whose strength and solidity doesn't wane.
   My walls of my conceit finally fell!

She came home from school wearing her familiar smile.
   I told her my thoughts, then we embraced for a while.
I struck up my courage and without any guile
   inquired of her, "Why, why Michele?"

She told me she loves me in spite of my fears
   of what the future holds; she then dried my tears.
My sweetheart said she welcomes our coming years;
   this loveliness, my beloved Michele.

—*Jaime Rosado*

Don't Worry Mom

"Don't worry Mom," he'd always say
   "I'm doing what I like to do today."
His call would come nearly every week
   Preparing his family so to speak.
"Don't worry Mom," if the phone doesn't ring
   "You know my job means everything."
Such a handsome man so straight and tall
   He loved being a soldier above all.
"Don't worry Mom," if they come to the door,
   And say, "Your son is missing in El Salvadore."
"Just remember the good times out number the bad
   And you are the number one Mom a guy ever had."
"Don't worry Mom for me anymore
   I've just entered onto Heaven's shore.
It's beautiful here with streets of gold,
   So much love and blessings to behold."

—*Earline Murphy*

"Shadows Of Love"

I live in the shadows of your love,
I'm like a hand without a glove.
You've left me so far behind,
I'm somewhere in the back of your mind.

Somewhere in the shadows of love,
Flying low like a lonely dove.
Somehow loving me causes you shame,
Why does love give us so much pain?

I use to think I was your pride and joy.
I found out, I'm just a play thing,
Nothing more than a toy.
Back in the shadows,
Behind closed doors and dark windows.

I must be a fool to be in the shadow of love.
Even though it hurts I keep holding on,
Somehow I linger in the dark.
Trying hard to get into your heart.
I know one day we'll part.
And I'll listen to mind not my heart
And I'll stay out of the shadows of love.

—*Lee Evans*

My Grandmother's eyes

My grandmother's eyes aren't both the same
I'm not talking about color, but happiness and pain.
When I look grandmother's eyes I see a whole lifetime,
A life that's lived a lot more than mine.
I can see all the times she needed a hug and didn't get one,
I'll be more than glad at anytime to give her a "ton."
I see all the times she triumphed—when others thought she'd fail;
I see caring eyes that want others to follow on her trail.
When I look at my grandma and she looks at me,
I can see she loves me without her saying a thing.
I know the reason that grandma is exactly the way she is,
It's because of everything that has happened to her.
That's why I thank God for letting things be the way they were.
My grandma's got stories to tell—exaggeration or not—she tells them well.
She can talk, and talk, and talk, she's just like a walking treasure box.
My grandma and I share many memorable times,
And I can recall them all—
Just by looking into my grandmother's eyes!

—*Jina Maree Logan*

Untitled

Above and beyond the country's call
I'm ready to give my entire all
I'm ready to die so you'll be free
So please understand and don't blame me.

Across the seas to foreign lands,
Holding a rifle with shaking hands
To kill an uncaring and greedy man
Who would pour out life's blood on golden sand.

A devious foe who is so falsely great
But who, in the end, is second rate
Thinks he can and will eventually win
Despite the lives of many men.

Whatever became of "Thou Shalt Not Kill"
To go to war was never God's will.
Be peaceful in heart and peaceful in mind
No better solution could we find.

Put down the guns and stop the war
Bring home to the families the men they adore.
Fear God and love him and keep him nearby,
God is your maker so don't make him cry.

—*Georgia Thompson*

My Grandmother's Travels

My grandmother's travels all began
In a covered wagon, caravan
Brave words, of promise led the way
A life to fulfill another day
Miles and miles in swirls of dust
Into winter, numbing cold, unjust
Climbing the slopes, hiding her pain
No one ever heard her lips complain
Over all the woven trails and ruts
It seemed heaven and earth were shut
Grandmother, were you lonesome in dimming shadows low?
Were you comforted with promises to grow?
Now many who bless you as mother, for your name
Love and heritage, weave a circle of fame
Rest peacefully grandmother of mine, your name written in stone
Your life completed - perfect your very own.

—*Suzanne Boyster*

Chosen

The lady stood waiting with a look of pride
in a dress of pure white, she stood patiently by.

Her lovely blonde hair hung perfectly in place,
her mysterious blue eyes glanced at ever face.

As people entered the room, she gave not a nod,
she knew her time would come when he suddenly arrived.

The place filled to capacity in a moments time,
the people stared at her as if she where divine.

In a moments notice the music began.
Everyone seemed to be waiting for a certain man.

He entered the place with a look of pride,
as she walked down the aisle he knew — he had chosen
the perfect bride.

—*Yvonne B. Kane*

The Eastern Shore

We stood on the pier, laughing there,
In a fine slanting rain on an April day.
You took my hand, and I watched the way
Soft rain-drops glistened in your black hair.

Through sunless, soundless grey-bound sky
Smooth raucous sea gulls were circling low,
Swiftly searching for food. Reluctant to go,
We stood there enchanted—just you and I.

Time would not cease; the world came through.
Only bittersweet memories of love remain;
And I wish I could live that one hour again
On a rain swept pier, with the gulls and you.

—*Gladys Clarke Minteer*

The Animals' Rain

The birds nestle softly together
In a hole in a small walnut tree
The rain is falling
Swiftly, Boldly
Across the fields and forests
The foxes hide in their warm, dry dens
Like a puppy would hide under its mother's legs when scolded
The rain falls yet harder
Snakes coil up tighter to keep warm
Bugs dig farther under the leaves to keep from getting wet
All the animals are asleep
The rain stops
The sun comes out
A rainbow forms in the sky
The birds come out
The foxes peek out from their dens
Snakes slither out from under the rocks
The harsh rain is over
Morning is here.

—*Abigail Snow*

The House

   The perfect dream; A plastic and wood reality. The family of porcelain, the emotionless faces staring into space as they sit and think of nothing. There is no joy, there is no pain only cobwebs of forgetfulness. And we ask ourselves is this the life we dream of?

—*Nicole Noyes*

Memories

Alone by night, as a little child,
In a place so silent and cold.
In the starless dark, and shadowy air,
Are your words more belov'd and bold.
You borne my steps with printless foot,
In lightness did I weigh.
Your eyes failed not, in sight of Hope,
Nor Judgement did you say.
Nigh are my memories, all fitly spoken,
In my Heart, as they are sown.
Firmly planted in a place of safety,
Your visions have richly grown.
So wandering at leisure in flowering thickets,
Through the circuits of Life's Way.
I consider the spot of open greenery,
In remembrance of Mothers Day.
—Terry L. Ross

The Moon And You

I watched the moon rise late one night
In a sky of darkest blue.
  And as it floated through the clouds
Ah yes, I thought of you!

  I kept on watching, dreamily
As lovers often do,
  And being quietly all alone,
Ah yes, I longed for you!

  If you could have held me in your arms
That night the moon was new,
  You would have kissed my tears away,
Ah yes, I cried for you.

  And then as storm clouds floated by,
The moon again shone through,
  As eyelids drooped - asleep at last,
Ah yes, I dreamed of you.
—Myrna Rickard

The Quiet Man

   What was it about him? Many wondered. He was in pain and in bed with fever. He couldn't eat, drink, or move. Death was close by. He never complained, whined, cried, or showed feelings. As if his lips were sealed tight. He never depended on anyone for help, and if someone helped him, he looked up with his face lit. His eyes filled with tears, but he never spoke, not even thanked. He laid in bed as pain tortured his body and soul, but not even a peep came out of his mouth. He just laid there as if he didn't have the breath of life in him. His face was pale like the white sheets of bed. His eyes were closed. He was so still that you could hear him breath.

   Then suddenly, he began to move in every direction. His mouth opened, but no sound came out. He was fighting with himself, or maybe against death. Then slowly he calmed down. Once again he stopped moving. He was still. His pale face looked paler. Then he struggled to reach the glass of water from the table, but never made it. He fell off the bed, rolled on the floor. His eyes began closing slowly, very slowly. He stopped breathing. His time was up. No longer had he the breath of life. He died. Still after his death. Many wondered. What was it about him, that made him so quiet?
—Nune Gazdhyan

Loss Of Loved Ones

Love's good, Love's bad, Love's happy, Love's sad. If you're in love, you won't be for long because nothing's forever, not even your own life. Everyone has to leave at sometime or another. I guess yours was sooner than we thought. I wish you hadn't left us. At first I was angry at you, then sad. Now I don't know what to feel. Everyone says I should move on. It would be better that way and you would want it that way. I wish it was easy; but every time I close my eyes, I see you. I wish it had been me instead. I want to be angry because you left me alone in this world. I hate to be angry but I cant stop. I keep thinking, what did he do wrong? He doesn't deserve this. I have even thought of a gun or a knife. My friends say it's the wrong thing to do. They just don't understand, or is it me? Do I not understand? I don't think I did understand, because I wasn't all alone. It just took me awhile to realize, no matter what, you were still with me, and I still have friends that are very special, too; but nothing will be as special as you. You were my love and always will be. I guess I have accepted your death because I had a dream last night about our last night together.
—Tiffney Kelley

The Beauty Of The Lord

Oh, perceive the beauty of the Lord
in many ways all around you every day.
Blossoming trees that herald the coming of spring;
Songs of the lovely cardinal serenading his mate.
Fragrance of flowers adorning lawns and countrysides;
Splashes of colors bringing forest ranges alive in autumn.
Snow-capped mountain peaks rising high towards the heavens;
Sun glistening on the snow—like diamonds sparkling all around.
Designs of lightning flashing across the thunderous sky;
Awesomeness of a rainbow arcing colorfully after the storm.
Pitter patter of raindrops watering the thirsty ground;
Rivers meandering over the hills and through the valleys.
Waves of oceans lapping constantly against the shore;
Creatures of many sizes, shapes and colors dwelling there.
Words and music flowing from the heart of a composer;
Pictures expressing the feelings of a young artist.
Sparkling eyes of a mother holding her new born babe;
Laughter of children skipping merrily along.
Yes, all around is the beauty of the Lord;
Take time to reflect and enjoy it today.
—Frances L. Myers

Question!

Is there hope or mindless meaning
In my life's undaunted dreaming?

I search for answers yet unknown
Inscribed upon some ancient tome;
I look for reasons still unseen
Buried below aquamarine;
I comb the heavens through the night
For some celestial guiding light.

My quest goes on through clime and place,
Through existential human race,
Through labyrinths sublime I chase
Surrealistic time and space.

Is there hope or mindless meaning
In my quest and in my dreaming?
—Gary D. Bliss

The Land

It's barren now where once I trod
In my youth with dog and rod

No streams or fish that once held sway
Gentle nature gone away

God's will I think it not
Man has created this our lot

Trees stripped, streams gone bad
Our grandchildren will never glory in what we had

Concrete jungles riddled with crack
Our civilization dies from moral lack

Dinosaurs died through no fault of their own
While mankind dies from his own seeds sown
—*Jerry E. Allred*

The Ones In White

Who are they that walk in white
In silent steps through day and night?

Who come to bed-sides and take their stand
To smooth a fevered brow with comforting hand.

They are always on ready to help the physician.
They are proud of their professional position.

They stand guard over the very sick;
Hoping and praying, the problems they'll lick.

They hold the hand of those who are dying,
And when they are 'gone,' do a little crying.

There are so many other things they do
That just can't be said in a line or two.

They are the ones on whom many depend.
They are every patients' blessed friend.

The nurses and their aides make life worth living
And of themselves are more than giving.

In silent steps through day and night,
Yes! These are the ones who Walk in White.
—*Dorothy L. Anderson*

God's Plan

God brings us beauty in all that is seen.
In Spring the grass and trees are green.

Summer is hot and humid at no cost.
To remind us of Hell if our soul is lost.

Fall arrives and the trees lose their leaves.
One more effort to make us believe.

Winter brings a blanket of snow pure and white.
This will remind us of his guiding light.

Seasons come and go is the plan.
Just to remind us he is the man.

Believe in his power and eternal life is the plan.
And when you die heaven's gate you will scan.

His love and grace abounds us all.
If we only believe when we hear his call.
—*Donald A. Woodson*

Moon Mood

When my thoughts fly around frantically
In the cage of my mind
Like captive wild birds
I think about the moon.
The way shreds of clouds
Catch on its crescent points
The way it makes shadowed lace on the lawn:
The way it rises in the darkness
Above a timbered skyline
Like a shrunken soul who is suddenly loved.
I think of the way it stirs
A poignant longing
In some deep, dimly known dimension of my being
That knows that somewhere, sometime
There is wholeness and peace.
—*Glenda Hawley*

Snow Flakes

On a cold, gray winter afternoon
In the forest, a quiet you can almost feel
No sound is heard, not even a bird
The feel of snow is in the air
So erie, but still so beautiful
Suddenly snow flakes, gently falling soundlessly
Among the forest trees, a certain magic in the air
The sky is gray, no wind is blowing
I stand spellbound among the trees
Soon the forest floor is turning white
Soon the darkness comes
Still the snowflakes fall silently
Daylight comes, the forest is dazzling white
A million Jewels
Shining bright
—*Silvio A. Sala Sr.*

The Awakening Dawn

I am grateful in the mornings
In the light of the early dawn
The sweet smells of the Earth
Is flowing with the rising of the sun.
The sounds of all God's creatures
Awakening to a brand new day.
The morning star is fading
As a greater light comes into play.

I look, I count my blessings
An give my dues to God
Because I know he is watching
As my head at night begins to nod.
I am grateful for the gifts He gave
And the little one's he's trusted in me to raise,
And when I lay me down at night, in His hands
I place my soul.
If I get up tomorrow,
It will be a brand new day,
I will give my thanks to Him (I AM)
For making me this way.
—*James Stephens*

"Teabags and Trust"

The sharing of tea brings such repose;
infused with laughter, and, yes, I suppose -
some solemn exchanges amidst sacred thoughts
on all that surrounds us - the "haves" and "have-nots."

We empty our teacups and also our hearts;
reflecting on endings and past panicked starts;
transforming two women by all that's discussed -
enjoying the sanctity of teabags and trust.
—*Alyxys Snow*

Everywhere Apple Blossoms

Everywhere apple blossoms falling down
In the rain, turning brown
In the green grass
Remind
Me of
Us
Not because
If I could put them back
I would know happiness again, like bees,
But
Because they bloomed, however briefly
Before they fell
And we
Never.
If you
Could send me kisses
Like snowflakes to keep me warm in Winter
Send me apple blossoms now, I pray
To fall in rain
In May.
—*Louis L. Acker*

I Fly Alone

I fly alone
In this space of existence- God's heaven above me,
Man's earth far below;
With my head a-guiding, on my two wings, a-gliding -
I fly alone in this space of existence.

I fly alone
To my place of existence- from the heredity of my birth
To the goal of my becoming;
Despite advises of those who're more learned,
I fly alone to my place of existence.

I fly alone
In this life of existence- my thoughts,
Words and deeds are mine alone to own.
Through storms of conscience and promptings of the soul,
For this life that I own I fly alone.
—*J. C. Bacala*

Where Were You?

I thought I saw the look of love
In your smile last night

But when I looked again, it was gone

I thought I felt the warmth of love
When you understood me the other day

But when I came to thank you, it was gone

I know I saw the look of love
In your smile, many years ago

And when I looked again, it was there

I know I felt the warmth of love
From your tender touch and understanding heart

And when I came to thank you, it was there

The years have silenced the looks of love
That once you gave so easily

The years have cooled the warmth of love
That once you gave so tenderly

But I know last night I saw that look of love
And I know the other day I felt that warmth of love
I know I was there - But where were you?
—*Marjorie Ann Carlson*

My House

I have a little house on a hill.
Inside and out is quiet and still.
In the rich, black soil.
Flowers bloom because of my toil.

The house is spic and span inside and out.
Anyone seeing it would have no doubt.
Something is missing from my house on the hill.
I need people its rooms to fill.

I spent so much time alone in my younger years.
To trust in others, I had my fears.
Now that my days are lonely and drear.
I can't help but shed tears.

I'll hang out a sign on my house on the hill.
I'll tell people to come if they will.
I have been so selfish in the past.
I've decided to be inviting at last.
—*Mildred Moses Macon*

"I Now See"

Outside my window, I see sunshine and fun.
Inside, I see not a ray, not one.
Outside my window children laugh and play.
Inside here, I can barely feel the light of day.
Where did he go, why did he leave.
Why am I here, why can't I see.
He's happier now than he was with me,
He's happier now than he'll ever be.
What's wrong with this picture, what's wrong with me?
What's wrong with this picture, I'm beginning
to see.
He left because he wanted, he left because he
Needed, he left because he had to, he left because
He bleeded.
I now know, I now see, he left because he
Had to, not because of me.
—*Stephanie Thompson*

Forgotten

I work in a Nursing Home and have for the past 25 years. I was inspired to write this last Thanksgiving.

Please tell me children,
As my days here are dwindling,
Why is it you don't visit much anymore,
Could it be you've not time
To drop me a line,
or is visiting me, too much of a chore

I remember the nights
When you were just young
and you'd cry with a fever or flu
I would hold you & comfort you
Tell you I loved you
and walk the floors all the night through

Never once did I think of myself or complain
For my love for you
Just wouldn't let me
And now at the end
I can't comprehend,
How Could It Be That You'd Forget Me!!!
—*Lynda Coffey*

"I Am What You Seek"

Jack my love, I am what you seek
Instead of living your life full of leaks
  What's the need for a broken heart
It's better for us not to be apart
  Each day without you gets harder on me
I get more depressed each day don't you see
  Jack it's you, for which I just can't get over
Even before we ever became lovers
  Oh my love just take my hand
Hold me tight to your body and just understand
  That, I have to make my love for you clear
And oh my love I do need you here
  If you can give my love a chance
you'll find out, it is your lasting Romance
  Leaving you behind cuts like a knife
for you've always been the love of my life
—*Darleen M. Haggard*

Prescription For Peace

Do not through envy a fellow man offend;
Instead, to him a Christian hand extend.
Sincerity of actions must come from within
If there's to be hope for peace.

Banish all greed, selfishness, and pride;
Hatred of others God will not abide!
When these shortcomings are cast aside,
There will be hope for peace.

Cast not aspersions along the way;
Practice the Golden Rule throughout each day;
For world harmony fervently pray;
Results? All mankind will live in peace.
—*Margarette Combs Saunders*

America's Core Question At Washington D.C.'s Air and Space Museum

Oh, Showcase of Great Masses of Metal and Plastic
  Instrumentation and Structure,
Oh, final resting place for
Humankind's Aerial Achievements—
  the Wright Brothers' airplane, the Kitty Hawk Flyer
  Goddard's rocket; Lindbergh's Spirit of St. Louis;
  American's Apollo XI; NASA's Space Station;
  The joint U.S.-U.S.S.R. docking mock up

What do you say to visitors from around the Globe
When they look up at your mechanical magnificence
And then their eyes fall on a uniformed Black man, slightly stooped,
Who has seen progress pass him by,
A man whose job it is to push a cleaning wagon and
Periodically stop to spray droplets from his bottle of Windex
  onto a Plexiglass barrier to wipe off fingerprints with a rag?

Oh, Showcase of Technology, how your achievements (and lack of them)
  stretch the limits of human existence!
—*Deena S. Madnick*

A General Curse

Damned be the skulkers and chicken roost pluckers
  That torment my brains and my viscera!
May your eyes crystalize and your tongue become dumb,
  My bonhommie "goodbye" you may kissera!
—*Tom D. Raulerson (Ogden Gnashed)*

Where Is Grandma?

Lilac wafted through the open window of my room
  intermingling with the fragrance of hundreds of apple tree.
Crickets sang. The irrigation ditches were living entities;
  dancing down the farmlands; lined with wild asparagus;
  emitting a perfume of wet clay.
Morning brought the sound of Grandma's musical voice
  humming and singing along with the radio from her bathroom.
When the sun streamed through the shutters, she emerged,
  clean, perfumed, powdered,
  always encircling me in her arms.
"How's my girl? Where's her chile spirit?" she'd ask.
Into the kitchen she'd shoo me where we would feast
  on homemade tortillas and preserves carefully
  removed from her stock in Mason Lid jars.
Where are those summer days now?
Now Grandma lives quietly in my memory.
She is alive; humming and singing; sending her joie de vivre
  and love through me to my grandchildren.
—*Eve Cobos*

I Would Like.....

I would like my brain to explode
into a million dimensions,
reaching and trespassing
frontiers
never imagine
by another human being before.

I would like my soul
to grow light and ephemeral,
and at the same time
for ever lasting.;
so together, body and soul,
could start a long journey through eternity.

I wish the wind of tonight
could wrap me around
and take me with it into the unknown,
mysterious darkness of the night,
and beyond
where the light of the stars will open my eyes
and my soul
to a new bright tomorrow.
—*Mirna Naylor*

He's No Man

Snow transformed from white sheeted meadow
Into features detailed with simplistic fashion.
A swarthy silk cover rests on his crown,
While black charcoaled eyes sighted broad fellow.

Beneath dark eyes, an orange icicled snoot,
Which "gang-planked" over, distorted coal smile.
Held in his hand was a witches flight,
While three ebony buttons fastened white suit.

His staunch neck donned hanging garb,
Woven, knotted, wide with plaided colors.
From mouth directed upward, a hollow stub.
Waist, bellied to bottom, a frozen barge.
—*Royce L. England*

Why?

I used to wonder why, I used to wonder why
I still wonder why, I still wonder why
Will I always wonder why, I always wonder why?
I'd rather not know, rather than not wonder why
—*Scott Parks*

To My Love

To spend the rest of our lives together,
Is all that I'm thinking of.
And my heart is overflowing with the
Gladness of our love.

I waked up every morning,
And your face appears,
To brighten up the hours,
When we're apart my dear.

I love you every moment,
Of every morning, noon, and night.
And your warm tender kisses just
brighten up my life.

To spend the rest of our lives together
Oh, Darling, it sounds so sweet,
To love you, and belong to you,
Would make my life complete.
—Dolores Leone

By Candlelight

What you see by candlelight
Is always a mystery.
The way the fire dances on top of a stick made with wax,
Casting shadows around the room.

You see his profile through the dimly lit atmosphere
The way his hands caress your auburn hair
Makes you think that you can do anything
As long as he believes in you

Whether it's modeling or exams,
You know he has faith in you.
His loving smile and his concerned eyes,
Show how much he cares for you.

The wax drips down the bright red candles
As it runs to the table sticking permanently
You blow out both candles quickly
Now, your alarm goes off; time for work.
—Kristie L. Morgan

You Are Important

Each note composed in a symphony
  is equal to the next.
One note being left unplayed
  will distort all the text.

And, so it is with all mankind,
  each one with a part to play
in God's vast works for life on earth,
  that all will go His way.

Just as a pebble, dropped in a pond,
  spreads rings out so wide,
so it is with our transgressions,
  like those rings, we cannot hide.

Just like the rings that spread on the pond,
  our good deeds will spread, too!
When God directs us to help all others,
  He's directing both me and you.

We're each on earth a part of the whole
  with chores diversified......
some large, some small, but when they're finished,
  all good is magnified!
—Mary B. Conn

Questioned Realities

What is man?
Is he a demagogue
A ruler, a father,
A provider, a revelation, or a human.
Can man be defined?

What is society?
Is it an open door to chaos
A world of hope or a dream of lies
Are we society?

A hand in nature or
a dictated future, governed by social
stature.

Never realizing a beautiful day,
or developing a peaceful world.
But instead locked on a course of collision,
to let the chips fall where they may
and pieces to be picked up later.
—Talib Walker

Sara's Turn

Little baby Sara, why do you cry?
Is it because you've left heaven and
  can't remember why?
Perhaps you miss hearing the angels sing,
and are startled with the sound of the telephone's ring.
You left the arms of heavenly parents above,
to share your mortal family's love.
We waited so long for your turn on earth,
and finally you came on the day of your birth.
We'll teach you to hold to the iron rod,
so you'll know again you are a child of God.
—Merle Eggleston

My World

The world I live in,
Is not a world of my own.
The life I lead,
Is not the way I want it to be led.
The worries I have,
Are not created by me,
But yet I still exist,
In a world with no meaning.

The tears I weep,
Are tears for you.
Because I have no reason for living,
With that no reason for crying.
But I do,
because the world around me is crumbling.
And in a few hours, days, weeks, years.
I shall be gone,
In an instant
Then forgotten by the world.
That never wanted me in the first place.
—Alison Quan

Rebirth

Homeless - unemployment - natural disasters - aids.
Is this some kind of warming?

If we allowed all this gloom to shadow our lives,
Why get up in the morning.

But the miracle of rebirth - flowers in the spring,
Children's laughter - babbling brooks that sing,
Lift the spirit of the heaviest heart
and makes life worth living.
—Louise Spicer

Celebration

Someone left the door wide open, alas, the blame
is on me

Close it ever so gently leaving only a glimmer of
light to see

There is no blame for vexing secrets housed within
my soul, I am the cause

Let vigorous growth begin, as I stare upon
a glimmer of light through the crack in the door

Come with me for a celebration, as I become a
peaceful soul once more
  —Judith Gayle Sherrouse

The World

The Niagara Falls, The Caspian Sea,
Is that what our Earth can only be?
Lake Baikal, Lake Superior,
What on the world could be more merrier?
The animals, the plants are all merry,
What about Mars, as red as a berry.
Our Oceans and seas are so turquoise blue
The Pacific, The Atlantic, the Indian too.
Our Earth is wonderful
Any other planet won't do.
  —Maria Besedin

The American Dream

The American dream I would like to find,
is to speak to the world and tell it my mind.
To voice my opinion face to face.
And not be ignored because of my race.

The American dream I would like to come true,
is to be considered an equal to you.
To see in my heart a better tomorrow,
where no one must live with grief or sorrow.

The American dream I would like to see,
is to live in a world where everyone is free.
To have people greet me where I go.
And that I am a person is all they need know.

The American dream I would like to live,
is to be in a world where it is better to give.
To abolish crime, grief and pain.
And create a world where no race shall reign.
  —Marguerite Anderson

Flowers

'April showers bring May flowers,'
is what the people say,
but I believe they were brought by fairies,
from a land far, far away.
There are many different flowers there,
yellows, whites, and blues,
reds, oranges, black-striped and violet, too.
Beautiful fairies deliver them,
while we're all fast asleep.
They dig holes for the roots of the flowers,
buried in the soil deep.
And when I close my eyes,
the way a dreamer does,
I see this fairy land and can hardly remember,
that winter ever was.
  —Kristina Schweizer

The Mountain Top

Out on the mountain top, certain that
it all won't stop. Wondering how I got
here and why I can't stay.

Looking at the sky looking at me,
wondering how I got here and why I can't stay.

Talking to the one and listening to me.
Giving a little thanks to all that be.

Out on the mountain top, certain that it
all won't stop. Keeping the images that
others may see.

Looking down for the distance, but can't
see far. Listening for a relation, hearing
combustion and destruction below.
My eyes are burning. My soul's on fire.
Out on the mountain top, certain that it all
wont' stop.
  —Robert L. Davis, I

A Daughter's Love

A bond-never-ending
It can last oh-so long.
It can be weak or strong.

The bond we have is nearly gone.
Separated from the love we never knew.
When I'll see you again I never know.
Thinking of you as tears flow down my already
saddened face.
Will I get the chance to make things right?
I'm asking you mom please help me fight.
Everyday your love seems to fade more quickly
than the day before. You say "I love you"; I
think you mean it, yet it's hard to say.
There's more to this than what I've said,
Just get this message through your head:
   I'll be here as long as it takes, in life
we all make a few mistakes.
   my love always.
   Your daughter.
  —Crystal Piner

Sunrise

A beautiful sunrise is such an illustrious sight,
it can only be experienced, never described.
Red, purple, orange, green, yellow, blue,
yes, the colors of the rainbow are all present.
It is just spectacular how nature can
generate such majestic creations,
and as you stand there gazing with amazement,
you can only hope your day
will be as magnificent as its beginning.
  —Cuong Tran

Peace On Earth

Peace on earth is each heart's desire,
It's a perfect goal to which all should aspire,
But in order for Peace on Earth to start,
It must begin first in each human heart.

To gain that inner peace
Controlling our own lives must cease,
Let God control the reins of your heart,
Then Peace on earth will have made a start.
  —Bernice A. Louden

Scarred

I give my heart to the women of the world
    It goes out to the ones who
     get beat up at night
 They are in a corner curled in a ball
and are so sick they couldn't even crawl
      The night brings
       them terrible fright
   The morning brings them pain
   The man comes home at night
     drunk and in a rage
 While she's cooking in the kitchen
   with a stain on her clothes
     One hit, two hits
    They're all the same
 Just one more painful than the next
 She cries for help but no one comes
 For they all think it's just a fight
    between four thick walls
   The only one that knows the
truth is the woman that's black and blue.
   —*Amy Kiehlmeier*

That Word!

What does the word "that" really mean?
It has no point! It can't be seen!
I think it is just just an excuse,
For the teachers to commit "student abuse!"
I guess that's what they had to go through,
So they think we need to learn it too!
What they don't know is at the beginning,
All the teachers liked tormenting.
So they told them about the new word.
Which when they had heard,
They loudly booed and hissed.
And threw tomatoes but missed.
The teachers had finally won the war!
Which bugged the students even more!
They thought the new word was berserk!
But eventually, the new word did lurk,
Into everyone's conversations.
And the teachers started using it in the daily discussions.
So that's "that!"
   —*Tiffany Hosmon*

Unfair Love

It's confusing and unfair,
It hurts some declare.

It's crucial and there's pain,
and for your feelings there is no gain.

Unless of course this love is true,
then maybe you shall not be forever blue.

For some it's magic,
for other's it's tragic.

Why! Why! Why is the cry!

Of your frail and delicate heart,
that has begun to crush at the very start.

Of this breakable love,
often thought to be sent from heaven above.

Forever might you keep,
this internal sorrow weeks

That builds and builds inside,
until you explode and confide.

Your love is over, your love is gone,
and yet you still wonder just
what went wrong.
   —*Kelly Wolfe*

"The Golden Years"

From the moment we are born we start to age.
It is just each year it is a different stage.
When born most of us have no teeth and little hair
When old I would say, it is very easy to compare.

The skin once tight and smooth starts to sag,
Those little pockets under the eyes, look like a bag.
You start to squint and see objects in masses,
You soon find out you just need glasses.

When you spend more time at the doctors then at home.
Just stop and realize you are not alone.
Just like a car, we can sometimes keep going real good.
As long as the doctor doesn't stop and pull up the hood.

One thing to remember, it's easy to see
This is the best it will ever be-
I often find happiness in thinking this way.
It happens to all of us one day.
   —*Rita Otto*

The Converse Of The World

The converse of the word
It is not the seam poorly done
on the fine cloth that covers your body
turning you a vision in the eyes of all that sees you
glimmering shine and softness.
It is not a thread of another color
that you try to hide in the clarity of the light
that illuminates showing your gestures,
on the steps while you come down and wait.
It is not the old clothes that you wear
when the party of dreams is ended
and you feel ashamed to show your naked body.
It is not the lipstick that covers your lips
not even the perfume that you so wisely wear.
The converse of the word is the poem that you keep
in each gesture when you deny flying in liberty.
The converse is your own word,
is your blood
is your mind
is your head where you search, and find yourself.
   —*Ana Chaves*

Rain

The clouds are turning from white to grey.
It is quite beautiful in its own special way.

   The blackest star,
   the darkest night,
   the beautiful moon,
   what a beautiful sight.

The heavens shower us, and cleanse our souls.
we dig our graves to live in the holes.

The clouds rumble, the clouds roar,
my heart is ripped out, my heart is tore.

The clouds have a meaning of there own,
through the darkness the light is shown.

When the clouds have broken up and gone away,
it puts the heart and soul to dismay.

The night falls, the day arises,
the stars and their shapes, the clouds and their sizes.
   —*Anita Marie Castillo*

Feeling Down

When I'm feeling down,
It makes me weep and frown.

Like when a friend talks behind my back,
It makes my friendship with that person lack.

I'm not saying any names and I for sure
hope this isn't a game.
If I did something wrong or bad, tell me
So I can do something about it, so their not mad.

Whenever I think about it,
I want to cry and sink.

When I told my friend that they were mad,
I guess I'm just a friend they never wish they had.
—Natalie Yakstis

Just Stand Up Wind

I said as I woke to skies dark and gray,
It matters not, I'm happy today!
I went outside, my son's in a lather,
Seems a big yellow car made our dog a cadaver.

I stopped for a moment, a very brief pause,
Concluding in turn, for concern there's no cause.
What's the diff, it's his dog, not mine,
I'm happy today, I'm feeling just fine.

I went to the bank to take out my cash.
The teller had none, but told me this trash.
"Your credit's no good," with a ho-hum and yawn
"Might I suggest your son's dog you do pawn?"

I almost lost it, that happiness I'd found
But with a deep breath regained my mind, sound.
After all I'm healthy, I have no psychosis
I've only one ill, that of morning hal'tosis.

And as Lincoln once said to you and to me,
We're all 'bout happy as we all want to be.
So if your day's like mine, one word of advice,
Just stay up wind and your day can be nice.
—Byron G. Cornelius

"The Forgotten"

People say we built this land for freedom. They say we built
it on our own. Well, I'll tell you what really happened; we
took the Indians home. The Indians saw us coming closer. They

stood waiting, wondering, but wanting no war. They listened to
the screech of our wagons coming across the lonesome prairie.
We treated them like animals. We were wasteful with their

water and game. We laughed at their traditions and Gods. We
did not understand them. They cried as we burned down their
homes, they fought and lost as all do know. They listened to

the buffalo moan, as we killed more to watch them groan. Yes,
they tried to keep us out. We tasted triumph, as they tasted
doubt. But, their chief still stood as tall as could be, his

pride was all he had left; as the rest of his soul was taken by
the wind. His warriors were being killed, while women and
children were starving and chilled. When he knew his tribe
could fight no more, he asked the great spirit for forgiveness,

and followed the rest of his clan down the trail of tears. So
when you think of battles fought; and winnings won with freedom
sought; remember where we got this land, and how it was taken
from the Indians.
—Ryan L. Polsgrove

Wildly Dreaming

My mind explodes like bursts from the sun
It races like silver, the mercury one...
Reeling and rocking its feeling is free
Wildly it dreams of you loving me...

Sometimes it glides speeding through sky
Driving through living, while humming a cry...
Stopping and going scanning for clues
Wildly dreaming, and again it's for you...

Sensing direction, it searches for treasure
Shining with brilliance, it creates its own weather...
Crashing and thundering, as the swells of the sea
Wildly it dreams of your wanting me...

Endlessly wandering, it thrives on its learning
Warming with softness, like the glow of a burning...
Cracking and flickering, making music of fire
Wildly dreaming of your secret desire...
—G. Stephen Clausen

Forever Flash

I glanced up just in time
It shot across the night sky, slowly...
   yet faster than I could actually comprehend
It left behind a luminous trail...
   Like the flash of a camera...
     Fading...
       many nights go
       almost in a dream
I made a wish and it was gone...
   Leaving my wish unfulfilled...
     Yet, still satisfying

Shooting stars last only a moment...
   but the impression lingers on...

    Forever....
—Mitch Posner

Melissa

God took her from this earth, I do not know just why,
  It sometimes makes me sad, yet it sometimes makes me cry,
She was so small and tiny, and lifeless yet to say,
  God had then decided, that that would be her day,
Today would be her birthday, she would be 24,
  She walked right out of my life, and behind her shut the door,
We would have done everything together and between us we'd always share,
  my feelings for her were love, tenderness, and care,
With her my life would have been perfect, in every way can be,
  but with her spirits at my side, I'm happy as you can see,
I never really knew her yet I loved her anyway,
  needless to say that God, will let us meet someday,
I may not know the answers of just why she had to die,
  I just wish I could have told her that I loved her and Goodbye.
—Erica Brown

Love Is There

Love is there like a shadow
It won't leave you, it will follow.
In the night, when no one is in sight,
Love is there like a shadow in the light.
Love is there to be strong when you are weak,
Love is there no need to seek.
Love is there when you long to be right,
Love is there like a dancing fire in the night.

Love is there like a shadow in the light.
—Tawnya Gomez

Poetry

I showed my love a poem written with my heart:
  it spoke of emptiness and pain remaining when we part.
He read it carefully, took his time, then gently said to me,
  my dear, you see, if there's no rhyme, then it's not poetry.

It's true that he is partly right, most poetry does rhyme,
and some would say that unrhymed verse is just a waste of time.
And yet, to me a verse that's free unchains my feelings deep,
  allowing me to clearly see dream nightmares that I keep.

He's right that free verse seems to lack in discipline and form.
  The very qualities that I like are those that he does scorn.
  I guess the difference seems to be that verses free of rhyme
give form to thoughts inside of me and lets their spirits climb.

And so, my love, it seems I'm doomed to always lack in form,
  to lack in discipline and style and barely reach the norm.
So when I write my heartfelt verse, wrenched from the core of me,
  I'll have to ever be aware that it's not poetry!
    —*Edith T. Byrne*

One Last Cry

Teardrops fall softly from my eyes.
It took some time, but now I realize
How much I love and care about you.
These tears on my pillow should tell you that I'm true.
How you can be with her, I will never quite understand.
She smiles sarcastically at me as you take her hand.
Now I sit here with tears streaming down my face.
Go on and have fun as I hang my head in disgrace.
The drip-drop of my tears is like the rain.
Never in my life have I felt so much pain.
But your warm smile embraces my broken heart.
The attention that you're giving me now is a great start.
I'm going to dry my eyes after I've had my one last cry.
You never miss your water until your well runs dry.
It's time to put you out of my mind.
You are truly one of a kind.
    —*Adele Hines*

Firebase Cleveland

That feeling of the past grabbed me earlier this month
It was 20 years ago on the 6th.
The year was '68
The boy/man/child about to born, about to be torn
Now comes Firebase Cleveland....
Read about it happening, had to go see
Got there, sat there, felt the weight of it all
Like a sin-eater I felt, it all absorbed within me
Felt the sadness, felt the grief
Couldn't look, couldn't speak
Fighting back the agony, the tears
The gate was opened, let out the beast
All the joke, the toke, at most can only keep
Him at bay
Here I was again, it's '68
    —*Jim Kavouras*

Simple Prayer

My Prayer is just a simple prayer,
It's not a prayer of greed,
I'm only asking God,
For just the things I need,
I'm asking him for a better life,
To keep me well,
And strong I'm asking him for a guiding hand,
To show me right from wrong
    —*Patsy Thornton*

I Have A Dream

I have a dream deep down inside
It will only come true when racism has died
Will this happen? I hope to soon know
Because I don't want my kids to have to grow
Wondering why people have this problem
I have always loved everyone for who they are
And never thought about the position of their stars
I have this dream that is deep down inside
I hope it comes true before the day I have died
If it doesn't at least I know
I can help teach my kids to grow
And dream about solving this problem
To love people for who they are
Even if it's as simple as wishing on a star
    —*Kara Durden*

Fathers Day Remember Your "Daddy"

Father's day is a special time.
It's a day, when our Daddy's are on our mind.
Without our Daddy's how could we be?
He's got to be "Special" to you and me.
A Daddy's love is hard to compare.
And, without their love we could not bear.
Without my Daddy, life wouldn't be right.
He's always around when things get tight.
If you've got a Daddy, you should care a lot.
For their are many this day that has them not.
So. remember your Daddy on this "Special" Day.
And, remember with him you'll always "O.K."
    —*Hal H. Hocklear*

"Why"

It's really so hard to say goodbye
  it's even harder to understand why,
a love so pure has gone astray
  where it failed I really can't say;
I tried my best - I gave my all
  never did I dream I'd take the big fall,
I love you dearly you are so fine
  so sweet and smooth like a rare vintage wine;
mistakes in life are easily made
  for the one's I've made I've surely paid,
the hurt I carry is hard to bear
  what your doing to me is just not fair;
you say it's over your love has died
  my tears slowly fall-my heart silently cries
"Life goes on" or so people say
  but for me it's just one long miserable day...
    —*G. Cattnach*

Wind Songs

I love to hear the South wind sing
its warm-toned songs of another Spring.
It sings of sunshine, and falling rain;
of waving fields of growing grain;
of blooming flowers and leafed out trees,
and water flowing to far-off seas;
of birds that nest-build all day long
but pause to rest and sing their song.

It sings of youth; also of age,
of what we've written upon Life's page.
But best of all, it sings to me
of happy times that used to be.
It sings my song, that's ever true—
How much I love, and think of you.
    —*L. M. Green*

The Little House With The Bee

My little white house is home to me,
It's home to my visitors, dogs, and a bee.
One day an owl made the roof its perch,
A parrot arrived while I was in church.

A teenager came, having run from her home,
"My mother won't love me, and I'm all alone!
Our house is bigger than yours," cried she,
"But your little house can hold you, and hold me."

"My little house welcomes you. I do too,
But I'm sure your mom will be missing you.
We can't let her worry, in her big house,
While you rest here, content as a mouse."

"Don't worry", I said to her mom on the phone,
"Just let her heart settle, she's not here alone."
In my little white house she was home with me,
With my dogs, the owl, and that bumble bee.

—*Hendrika Tol*

Untitled

I'll tell you a story that was quite sad.
It's nice in the beginning the weeks that they had.
The good times, and the friendship they shared,
The memories will last a lifetime, that's if anyone cared.

They started our flirting, a little here a little there,
Then they found out, that they really did care.
All in a weeks time they had progressed this far.
But the next week she left to go on vacation afar.

She came back, thinking he'd gone home,
But he didn't and now they were all alone.
This last week was the one that counted,
Were the relationship bloomed and the friendship mounted.

The tragic part is about to unfold,
For he was forbidden to speak to her, so he was told.
Time has gone by, two years to be exact,
But now I think it's time they got their relationship back.

—*Rachel Baldwin*

"The Last"

Lovely days, lovely nights!
It's not so lovely when y'all fight.
The hitting, the screaming, the pain to endure
Until you walked right out the door.

He said he loved you, he loved you true.
But instead of taking the blame, he put it on you.

Later, much later they find you there
Under the bridge lost in despair.

He comes to you with open arms,
But you know he will bring you only more harm.

You try to run, but he grabs you fast.
You gasp for air; you took your last.

Sentenced to death with no parole.
Before they cut the rope, they gave a drum roll.
As he stuck his head in the noose,
He screamed your name.
To him it was all just a big game.

—*Rebecca Tate*

The Night

The night can be so long and so lonely at times it holds
its own magical show with the sky so dark and the sound so
still you count down the hours till dawn but the night seems
to never end you hear a faint howl of a dog in the distance
so sad so lonely as if he also is hoping praying for the first
glimpse of the bright sunlight as you see the twilight hour
you know morning is not far off as we take the dawn for granted
for another day to begin.

—*Mary Ann Brugger*

Inkling

Glorious world of this our universe
Its people of all religions and races
Posterity of a golden age and day
Changes of morals, religions, and deeds
Freedom easier for us to live
Foundations wrought by our fathers
From their honor generations are born
Our world their talents to share
Stars of the heavens and the outer space
Wishing its secrets to divulge
We are but a shadow upon this earth
And our mortality is forever near
Standing at the crossroads are the generations
Those gone before, those now, and those to come
The deplenishment of air, water and the good earth
Making life unsure in the future times
We stand on the thresholds waiting and watching
For the creation of our perfect Universe
God made this world for all of us to share
Have we made it heaven or hell?

—*Elizabeth A. Van Pelt*

The Survival Of The Weakest

The house was new, with modern bricks.
Its strength enhanced with mortared bricks.
Designed to last through hail and sleet.
An armored foe for cold and heat.

Another house that stood nearby,
Had tipped it's hat to sun and sky.
Its shell had bowed in humblest stance,
As if it knew it stood by chance.

Then, a hungry wind became a beast,
And sought all things on which to feast.
"No mercy show" was in its screech,
While hearding waves beyond the beach.

But calmness came to make a claim,
Expelling wrath in nature's name.
The ruling breeze then seemed to say,
"My brother's dead like yesterday."

There in the calm, the shanty stood,
With weakness in its silvered wood.
As for the new, its parts were found,
For the greedy force had blown it down.

—*Leroy Albert*

Mr. Sax

Mr. Sax man plays his tunes that touch
my heart and electrifies my very soul. The
rhythm moves through me so deep I can feel
his passion flow from the depths of his very
soul. You know how to sooth my spirit and
fill my heart like no other jazz man, so play
to your hearts content, because your the
man filled with endless soul.

—*Gloria Cunning*

Mask

I wear a mask, yet no one knows,
I've been in places, No one goes
My mask is liked
But underneath, there's nothing but fright
Fear of death, Fear of danger,
Fear of nothing left but strangers,
No one, to cry to,
No one, to laugh with,
No one, to share emotions with,
No guys, to give a good night kiss,
One day my mask will go away,
And I'll unleash a me to stay,
If my mask is not shed,
Alone I'll lie on my bed,
With saddened feelings in my head,
Now that you've heard, heard what
   I've said, my emotions are no
   longer dead
     —*Stacy Mulhern*

"Charades"

I know I'm told to watch where I walk
I've found it's best to be stodgy with talk
My bones are brittle, my eyesight is dim
And I don't go off on any old whim
For I am 73

My cologne is "flowery" I'm "cleany" attired
My shoes will last ages; for I am retired
Waist cinches are loosened for what could they do
After all - I'll admit to a pound gained - or two
Well - I am 73

At 73 you must be sedate
And calm and collected like a nice, shiny slate
You budget your time, your cash, and your smiles
That's when you decide to wear "sensible styles"
For you are 73!

But oh! when my public life's day is o'er
Happy am I when I rush through my door
Shed my shoes, twirl my skirts, dance up a spree
Sing of "June" "Spoon" and "Moon" with a heart filled with glee
And I laugh "How I fooled them I'm still 33!"
     —*Agnes Hurlburt*

What A Good Morning

What a good morning just to awake with
joy and gladness in your heart and greet
someone with a smile and say good morning

what a good morning to awake and say
Good Morning to another and meet
the challenge of another day.

What a good morning just to awaken and,
know that you are blessed just to open your
mouth and say to another living soul
Good Morning.

What a good morning just to fell the
present of the master and know that
we are blessed to be able to say to another
Good Morning.
     —*Rosie Brown*

Scorpio Moon

An old man
   judged as such only by appearance and whiteness
     of beard and soul
glancing skyward, cloudward, seaward
outstretched in his solitude
   of only once having known and felt
the waters governed by the scorpio moon
   (full again tonight, opaque and waiting)

Tidal thundering of black sea currents
   pulsing inward to his depths
     dreaming the clarity of sea and sky
       borne upon each other in the generation
         of union between his visions
           and his experience

Letting go
   among waves of moonlit serenity
Remembering
Letting go.
     —*Jeff Trowbridge*

Roman History 101

After chasing Pompey to the Nile,
Julius Caesar had dallied a while.
Though he got little rest
In queen Cleo's nest
He understandably left with a smile.

Said the Roman Guard, "We ain't a buyin'
No more food for you Christian, you're dyin'."
So at noon the next day,
Cornered, at bay,
The Christian devoured the lion.*
* He did it without hardly tryin'.
     —*Rolland Gallup*

Urban Secrets Or Scalawags

Commune-community workshop-playground, stoops; dogs-alley cats,
junkies, whores, booze, grass/coke, show, MD"s PhD's, LSD's;
main thing, joy-misery- DOA. Euphoria- hallucination,
crying-sighing, panting- joy. Racist- pacifist, lawyers-
deacons, teachers- students, Bias; Fast- time, genius- talent,
insane, motivate- ambulate; Legitimates, hypocrites,
whoremongers, homo's- hetero's peddler rent- taxes- food,
hungry- thirsty- baby, welfare-check- nothing. Police- hitman,
track- run, motor, bicycle, feet... escape, bushes, houses-
backdoors, pathway- hi'way, male- female, harmway, sirens-
bells, loud-speakers, music, shouting- screaming, baby- lives;
moaning- groaning, sighing, crying, panting, wanting, food-
taxes- rent, thirsty- baby: no'where's to go. Anger- peace-
confusion, useless- jobless, judges and jails, sunlight-
litter, boxes, cups, stylofoam, knives, chicken books, broken
glass, window glass, paper, bags, news, torn- pocket-books,
moans- groans, shouting- crying- sighing, panting peeking;
food- taxes, rent- hunger- babies, slow learners, poverty and
no- wheres- to go; A dog barks... A cat meows...
silence—nothing.
     —*Booker T. Smith Sr.*

Love

What is love?
Love is pink,
Love tastes like a sweet big cherry,
It sounds like a purring cat, on my lap,
It smells like fresh chocolate chip cookies cooking,
Love looks like a new blossom,
Love makes me feel special!
     —*K. G. Tunila*

Poet's Poem

Here is a poem, oh, just a silly old rhyme,
Just a silly little poem, but it's one of a kind.
Some say it's for fun, other's say for money,
See, I make people laugh just by being funny,
I can make them cry with a sad little sonnet,
I can make thoughts peaceful with fields of blue-bonnets,
I can make them love, I can make them hate,
With my little hands whole worlds I create,
With my silly poems about my silly old dreams,
Touching every peasant, reaching every king,
Hitting every heart, molding every thing,
With my little poem I make the world sing,
Just my silly little rhymes in this poem that I write,
Here is my poem, here is my life.
—*Karl Rees*

Unpredictable

Like the ocean in the tranquil state
Just as the calm before the storm
When you think everything's A-O.K.
it changes as night and day, there's no norm
You try to stay in the eye of the hurricane
Jumping over hurdles that cross in your path
The tiredness comes but you push to the limit
Then you find peace, it's life and worth all the pain.
—*Sharon L. Miller*

Wounds

There's really never an adequate reason why-
  Just feelings: irreparable, unredeemed loss,
    hopeless abandonment and
      unforgiving despair, for me and for you.
  Just feelings; suspended in Time's vortex forever,
    Undiminished, unhealed, unreplaced,
      not washed clean by tears.
  Just feelings: serving only to remind Us how life is
    precious, perilous, precarious,
      poised on an unbuttoned foil and
      pre-empted by a knowledge that
Somehow things between Us will never be the same:
  if not worse but certainly no better:
    diminishing Us to shame,
      loneliness and recrimination without redemption.
  Just feelings: surviving on their own strength and impact,
    feelings We too must balance to terms:
      like, Poetry without Robert Frost, Ballet without
        Berishnikov, John F. Kennedy's timeless, senseless
          murder, Vietman and Christmas Again: without you.
    —*Jon David Sommers*

Blessings

If you think you have no blessings to count,
Just think of the fresh drink, you get from the fount.
Hear the birds sing and children's voices ring.
Think of the sights that you admire in early spring.
In summer it is so long before it gets dark;
You swim, take walks and have picnics in the park.
Feel the rustle of the leaves when they fall.
Watch the snow flakes, feel the sting on your nose.
And the taste of snow ice-cream, we surely know.
We have now had thoughts of an entire year,
And we hold each season very dear.
So for all of these blessings
  give thanks where thanks are due,
To the Lord who knows and
surely cares for you.
    —*Maxine Johnson*

Through The Glass

I was on the other side of the wall of glass alone wishing,
Just for even one, to beckon me inside, but there was a locked
door. I watched them in their merriment and activities,
They had no thought of me nor awareness,
That I longed to come inside....indifferent of my presence.

My heart felt rejected, and I felt great pain,
always on the outside looking in

Then he came and stood alongside me alone,
Looking in at the crowd of merriment...the same look of hurt
upon his face.
I watched him as he patiently waited to be invited inside,
he even unlocked the door, in case they would ask....
But they never did.

He turned his head and looked at me and smiled such healing
love, and took my hand in his.

We walked and talked and I grew to love my new friend deeply.
As we laughed and talked, Jesus and I,
We turned to see the wall full of people crying,
Banging fists on the glass to come in...but the door was locked
Time had run out...it was too late.
    —*Jean McGinn*

Saturday May 15, 1993

    Saturday May 15, 1993 started out
      just like any other day.
  Laughing and talking at our branding
and taking pictures of friends to stay.

    Later we cruised around the countryside
      but something went wrong.
  He had too much to drink, the minutes until
    the pickup straightened seemed so long.

    Our fathers were on the rampage
    we were supposed to be home before now.
  They won't get us down, no we'll never forget him
and later in the dark night we made that solemn vow.

Headlights came into my window at exactly 10:30 p.m.
  but is that really his way of saying goodbye?
He got up and left the next morning without a word
  and now the only question left is why?

    We'll always remember him
      although in different ways.
  He was her boyfriend and my cousin
and our memories of him will always stay.
    —*Karen Mosher*

One Of A Kind

Waiting here in this lonely room
  just makes me miss you.
I'm missing you more than ever, now.
What else can I do,
  besides sit and dream of you.
Looking at your picture brings tears to my eyes.
Wondering, where you have been all of my life.

A smile comes to me when
  I think of your sweet ways.
I soon realize that I will be in your
  strong arms
And all of my troubles will be drifted away.
While your soft lips caress mine
  and your fingers touch my face
What more can I say than,
  our love is one of a kind.
    —*Crissie Lippman*

Separately

Dear Children;—Please save time for me,
Just to know you, separately.
No pleas, not tears, no anger yet,
Just for a moment do not fret.
Don't tangle with each other's view,
All I want to know is you.

Each separate form I want to see,
So it will always be with me.
One wistful look, one quiet dream,
Without demanding it be seen.
One ambition written where,
Only I can see and share.

Let me feel your presence please,
Let each gesture stay with me.
And if there be a moment dear,
Let it be for me to hear.
To feel, to know, to love, to see,
But please,—just make it separately.
—*Nancy Beaulieu*

August 28

You'd never know the bird was wounded
Just to see it there except that doves just
Don't sit comfortable on blacktop in front
Of Howard's MiniMart and let you pick them up

Which I did marvelling wild beauty fluttering
Heart and gently took it to the clerk inside
Something wrong its wing the rumpled feathers
I told the clerk who took it from my hands

Without a word not roughly and placed it
back outside as though he'd done all this
Before and went on back inside and I drove
Home I'm trying to go back there now

And take the dove home with me
As I should have done oh so gently
Soothing water food a box of safety
No prowling cats I can't go back
—*Frank Wattron*

My Thoughts

Life, where is it taking me, I do not know.
Just when I think I know the answers, everything slips away.
Who am I, someone tell me where I am headed, I need to know.
I take so many things for granted, how do I stop.
Why is it that one moment I am so happy, and the very next I am
lost, uncertain with my emotions.
Does the future include me, or will my life end without seeing
it? It is not such a crazy thing to say, am I afraid, only
I know....do I?
The universe, it's unknown boundaries are fascinating.
I want to be there, I want to see it, I need to know the
unknown, make the unknown known.
It sounds crazy, but is it?
Five years old, nothing mattered, innocent and carefree.
Take me back, let me feel what I felt, surround me with it.
I understand, I know what I mean, do not try to understand,
understand you, take yourself to you,
before you are not yourself.
—*Jon Lapriore*

A Haircut

Take away his will,
Keep him very still;

The good you profess,
Will make him digress.

Dominate, subjugate;
I say, you obey.

One mumbles that she will murder me,
The other, God punishes, threatens she;

Cats, old bats,
Possessive, aggressive.

He went to the barber, so old, so sad,
A haircut, a shave
the good man gave.

A fine job he did,
so much weight was rid;

"Cannot remember the last time I had,
A haircut and a shave, I was but a mere lad."

Glad was he, content was I, that day,
'til back we went and was hell to pay!
—*Nina F. Martino*

Fire And Light

The cinders from coals of impetuous internal fires,
keep stoked the earnesty of the heart's deepest desires.

Never to be sure from the hallowed within,
just how or if, their dowsing shall ever begin.

Knowledge of endearment's essential necessities,
handed down as relics from the core of antiquities.

So effortlessly are such as these to be applied,
yet forsaken are those to whom the lore was denied.

Forever a trial for rational will through creative years,
to be insanely linked by a chain of perceiving tears.

Yet not before the coming of maturity's seasoning with age,
will one be enlightened by the turning of wisdom's page.

Inevitably the mustering of all one's internal might,
shall never be enough for the flame one wishes to smite.

Alas, to do battle with one's own mind is of little use,
for hidden in ashes are embers and the fire they induce.

Only the years will teach what is true to believe,
with time you shall learn what a heart may not deceive.

To learn of this first hand is not an enviable plight,
however, to understand may allow the only healing light.
—*William Chris Waggoner*

Boat

Chart my life Lord so I will be ever in presents with thee.
Keep the wind in my sails that the waters I chart wouldn't
steer me towards hell. Make my life glisten like the salty
sea, and keep me ever mindful of others needs. Most of all
keep me close to thee. When waves of fear come over me, help
me move my anchor into calmer seas. When fog covers the land,
help me reach out and feel your hand. When my boat is finally
docked, help it be securely locked in your love and calming
care, because without you Lord no steering I would dare.
—*Deretha A. Harris*

Peace

I am facing the wind. The force is blinding
Keeping my balance requires great skill
Things are not always as they seem
Yet somehow they turn out
Always differently than expected
At one moment I can step forward...
The next thing I know I am two steps behind
Behind is where I stand
If I could only fly
If I could soar above all

As sleep comes dreams appear
Always I awake sweating
I don't dare scream
Screaming only revives the memories
The horrid devils that swim about my head

While I'm awake the every day life gets to me
The loneliness of friends surround me

I need to escape, to leave this place.

Too many memories and lies

I need peace. I need a peace of mind.
—*Kathryn Strand*

Winner Buys Dinner

May is the month Jim and I thrive
"Kentucky or Bust" it's the Derby Day drive
Racing Forum, newspaper, refreshments to go
Hitting a longshot could mean lots of dough
Programs in hand we study the field
Lineage, past performances, trainers with zeal
A round of Mint Juleps before the big ride
Warms you no matter the weather outside
Two minutes flashing, our wagers are in
A toast to the Derby! echoed in each grin
Throwing open the gates with lightning bolt force
Wishing and praying for that one winning horse
Jockeys grasping the reins using all of their might
Wearing silks of all colors, a rainbow in flight
Down the back stretch crops high in the air
People jumping, yelling, a gregarious affair
Anxiety peeks, one last burst of speed
Photo Finish! Inquiry! That's all that we need!
A final decision, all judges do agree
To the winner go roses, points and a lovely trophy.
—*Pam Fitzmartin*

"Still Love You"

When you look in the night sky and see the stars above
   know that I still love you
You feel in your heart you were my one true love
   and I still love you
When you see the rain as it falls from the skies
   always know that I still love you
When we both have tears that fall from our eyes
   remember that I still love you
And as you live and breathe
   know that I still love you
And in my heart you'll never leave
   because I still love you
Every time you look up and see the shining sun
   remember I still love you
Because you'll always be my only one
   And I still love you
—*Ron Rapp*

Lost Child

Its a lonely life for a child without love
Lack of love builds walls of fear
Defiance then takes over there
You act tough to cover your pride
But all the time you're crying inside
Fear and rejection become a way of life
You learn to put your feelings on ice
You hope when you grow up, for a better life
To be able to knock down the wall
And take the feelings off ice
To love and start a new life
—*Linda Osborne*

Untitled

Oh! delors delorum
Last day of planting
   two hawks circled the valley of lost content
   small birds drew in their wings
And I
Still strained to the music
Country Gardens
An Eden tuned to piano keys
Only made more so by constancy

We retreat where there is no retreat
Knowing August will bring
   cracked earth
And the only moving object
A garden hose

Yet the well is full that never ran dry
And we play leap-frog across the pond
Quite easily

My hands have become the grain of the earth
   —*Charlotte Blizard*

"Repercussions"

The repercussions of performed acts today
Lead to an empty bottomless pit afar
Our cup is full and rightly so
We have a place in which to go.

However long the joy remains
Is like an ocean and its depth
For it entends as far as time
And matter of principles are forever gone.

To settled for less is often the thought
But strength to fight is hell itself
The conscience we carry is flung aside
Taking what's offered in our stride.

Backward we glance with hardly a dare
For beauty is found and that we care
Between the two a struggle emerges
But for the night there is no light.

If the black be turned to white
And our future appears to sway
The choice that's open, left to be made
Will show how we live, our future days.
   —*Terry E. Ridgway*

Moon

You lay there upon the sky
Taking control of the mystical night.
Your white evil light summons creatures with blackened souls
I am on the edge of exhaustion walking home in your eerie presence
You are immortal, you shall be king of the night forever
   —*Paul Petro*

Thoughts On Peace

Connect—not conflict; the preacher said
Lead with your heart as well as your head.
The world indeed would be a wonderful place
If we could just live together as a human race.
Kindness, tolerance and courtesy would go a long way
To resolve the conflicts in the world today.
The problems of the whole world can be met;
If some reasonable ground rules we could set.
To-gether a difference we could make
If some time for thinking we would take;
When the sights and sounds of war do cease
Only Love, not Hate, makes a lasting Peace !!!
—*Louise H. Hawk*

Walkway

Green walkway
Leading to the blessed sky
With lines of those waiting
To wander on feet
Light as air.

The sight of the walkway makes the
Smothering fog
Disappear from their lungs.
With petals reaching for the sky,
Dew glistens, attracting their eyes.

As sacred ones dance on that special land,
Chants of hope and harmony haunt the
Air above and arms
Flail in celebration below.

Young eyes observe the elders in awe
And wonder if they too will
Dance on this sacred
Green walkway of hope.
—*Ann Seiser*

The Wind Of Fall

Playful children, running through seas of red and gold
Leaves crackling under the feet of rambunctious kids
Laughter mixed with wind, stirring rainbows from the trees
Smoke filled air and cool, crisp nights
Make up fall

When children run from school,
And laughing and playing is the rule
Drifting slowly into a wondrous winter,
Fall is just one season; one hour in the day of life
Coming swiftly as years pass by

Leaving, like a raindrop on your mind,
Memories of carefree times
Times that are young and that still live on
In the wind of fall
—*Jessica Rivera*

Peace Through Love

I offer you my hand in friendship
let us go forth and make more friends
Let us rid ourselves of prejudice and hate
   hate blinds us
Hate makes us bitter and unhappy, love can make us
   free and joyous
let us teach our children how to love and laugh, work
   and play and grow united
In unity there is strength, and in strength is security
   I cannot be happy by myself
Please take my love and let us grow and develop
I drink a toast to love, the love for my fellow human being
—*Edna Horn*

Winds Of Love

The winds that blow across the trees, whisper softly to the leaves. Willowy sounds that hover near, then magical rays of the sun appear. It dusts the limbs with shimmering light, and sends a glistening through the night.

The winds that blow across my heart touch a place, that's set apart. And gently tells me, "stay so near," for I'm the voice you'll always hear. The winds of love..........

Oh, winds of love come warm my soul with dreams that you have never told. Soar me upward, gently high, and blend my spirit with the sky. Peaceful winds of love......

Beautiful winds comes touch my face. Our faith and love will interlace. And lend me beauty of truth divine. And you, sweet winds you're ever mine.

Forever blow, sweet winds of love.....
—*Dodie Guzman*

My Handbag

Do you have a paper clip?
Let's see —
   There's green lipstick—all but gone
      Lotion, library card, nails to put on.
   A half-chewed doublemint stick
      Diary, driver's license, ivory toothpick.
   Combs with missing teeth
      Compact, check book, pads for feet.
   Aspirin - dates long ago
      Scissors, safety pins, stick of eye shadow.
   A used three cent stamp
      Coupons, colored crayons, snacks for camp.
   Keys that no longer fit
      Curads, kleenex, loose coin bit.
   A wallet frayed from use
      Wipes, water pills, bottle of juice.
What did you ask for?
   A paper clip!
Sorry, I can't help you.
—*Ina Leland Broe*

Come Dance With Me

Come dance with me,
Let's soar to the other side of the rainbow,
Up, up, and beyond.

Loosen your chains,
Come dance with me,
Our Lord has placed us here,
to grab hands and dance.

Loosen your chains,
come dance with me,
to the other end of the rainbow,
up, up, and beyond.

Come dance with me,
let's jump over these bumps,
together, fueled with faith and serenity
break free from those chains,
come dance with me,
to the other end of the rainbow,
Up, up, and beyond.
—*Jane L. Marcus*

God's Garden

Jesus looked down and said to me, "Come,
   let's walk, there are things you must see."

I thought we would see gardens, flowers and brooks,
   angelic faces, you know the look!

Butterflies and pink lemonade, and some of the beautiful
   things God had made.

Our path was dim, dirty and dark. It was a city
   street, not a park.

As my eyes grew accustomed to Satan's den, the truth
   unveiled - But not for God's grace, I might have been!

Captives crushed, bodies broken by their worldly lust...
   Satan said, "They're mine! Enter if you must."

Swaying back and forth to the rhythm of sin...
   liquor and the needle, was their best friends.

They were young and old, even a child or two. I said,
   "Oh God, must we walk through."

He said, "This is my garden, I water it with my tears.
   Won't you tell them that I love them, help deliver them
   from fear.

I will go with you, you won't go alone.
   Come help me bring my children home."

   —Lucretia Sanders

The Seed Of Love

O'er the land and O'er the sea. Men have died to give us liberty. Why must that be?. As brave warriors they gave their life for all to be free.

To love oneself there must be love for our fellowman. If peace is to reign O'er the land. Not just me. But we. Take a stand an sow the seed of love. With all the nations hand in hand and all the races of the land

A mothers sorrow. Tears of pain. We must not let the fallen warriors pass in vain, in doing so what is the gain. As been repeated again and again.

Come, sit at my table and sup with me. Share thy bread. Let's make a plan. Might we sow the seed of love upon the land. Give to the have-nots, teach them to have, show love to those who know not how. A hand shake. A hug. A kiss upon the brow.

To each his own, as life might be. Not you or I. But we.

   —Edna Steele

Life

Life has its valleys and mountains tops.
   Life has its understandings and mysteries.
Life is given to us by our Moms and Pops.
   Life is a continuing series.
Life is full of changes.
   Life can be demanding.
Life can fulfill our Creator's purposes.
   Life can seem without meaning.
Life is what you make it.
   Life is what you didn't expect.
Life is living with doubt.
   Life is worshipping God with respect.
Life isn't made for cowards.
   Life requires us to be brave.
Life sometimes seems to go backwards.
   Life doesn't know how to behave.
Life was given by our Creator.
   Life first came to Adam and Eve.
Life has continued in spite of horror.
   Life is you and me.

   —Gladys Henderson

The Secret

Consummate genius
Lies dormant in all of us,
Waiting for self-awareness
To self-bestow

Just as mediocrity
Is likewise self-inflicted,
Holding us down to the level
We alone have chosen

The Key is desire
Fanned by consuming flames,
Inviting synchronicity
From mind-energy of God

Essentials for greatness
Are not found in books;
Nor can they be taught
In prestigious schools

No, greatness is born in the consciousness
Of those who seek creative perfection,
And it is understandable
To that small audience only.

   —Mila Wilson

Pandora's Box

Open up Pandora's box look at what's inside
Life and death old regrets, sometimes suicide
You plainly see if caught in sight, the magic of it all
The peaceful parts of love and truth as through a
crystal ball
The stars fly out and cluster, the box hides all your
Lies, magic, witchcraft, mystic sense from your grasp
the answer flies
Darkness covers souls despair, sparks the evil flames
Erases faces and destroys the masks that we call names.
To you, you're yours, to me I'm mine, together we'll
close the box to let the sun rays shine.
Like a newborn child struck, with famine or disease
We plead just once to close the box and live in tranquil
ease.

   —Kimberly L. Anderson

Smile, God Loves You

If your heart is heavy, spare a smile, and you will see the
light.
A light shining in your path to show the way.
Be faithful, tell not a lie, and a smile will show you are
willing in your heart, the reason why.
A smile will cost you nothing, but will lighten your heart and
remind you to pray.
God made us, and he made us to enjoy life, but if we walk
around each day not smiling, he will forget us, and we want
remember
to pray.
Pray for yourself and your fellow man, that have somehow forgot
to say,
Lord have Mercy, for every little problem that fall in their
way. So look up to God when you feel you are down,
He will press a button, and surely omit your frown.
Smiling is a gift from God, I know, because, when he made me he
gifted me with a happy face.
I will always cherish him with, peace and grace.

   —Lalage Abrams

"Fragments Of A Prose Poem"

Dearest One: I know what your heart must have seen in that
light across the pond. It was the paint that hid the cracks.
The night that hid the day. An eye shadow that covers the
heart's blemish, and a space that is so full of nothing that
for lack of something, we etch valentines, and pick flowers' petals
for luck. Now, I am on a train bound nowhere; like the
different places on a map that say here or there. And then, I
am blind from having seen so many things. And then, I see
your name. The numberless zeros pour into morning with only
one conclusion: No poem could ever suffice, however brilliant.
No love letter either could say it; to know winter's bite that
our summers die. When I watch drifts of snow melt from a storm's
respite and a precarious sun, as lofty as those gossamer webs
of noon that drift through my mind, with every drop of snow,
I say your name, and every sound and syllable warms the
winter's bite. I close my eyes with the period of every
sentence end...... Missing hair, eyes, smile.....missing you.
Missing us not being there. And I rode the train, and saw your
face in every drop of snow.
—David V. Robinson

The Cry Of The Brave

The sounds of thunder rumbles in the air
lightening strikes and rain pours to the ground,
Washing away the blood that covers the braves hands.
As he holds his fathers lifeless body in his arms,
He looks up into the heavens his tears as heavy
as the pouring rain,
The young brave gives a shrilling cry that would
shatter the coldest of hearts.

The loud moans of the dying around him echo in his mind.
Anger and hate burst from his soul like,
water that explodes from a dam.
The young brave lifts his fathers body toward the clouds.
The deafening sound of guns fire through the air once again,
With one last horrifying cry the brave falls to
the ground his soul joining his fathers soul.

Through the walls of time the braves cry still
lingers for all of us to hear.
The next time you hear natures sounds,
remember what I say the braves cry will never die
It will just fade away.
—Pamela L. Crews

Pressures

Pressures of the world around me,
Like a bottle with me trapped inside.
There is a way out, though I've not found it yet,
for these pressures are still on my mind.
I feel so alone.
There is nowhere to run.
These pressures have cornered me well.
I can see my escape but it's just out of reach
So these pressures continue to dwell.
—Jenny Davala

Falling

I am falling in love,
Like the water falls at my feet.
I am falling for you,
Like the rain falls on my face.
I am falling to my knees,
Like a slave falls at the sight of Master.
I am falling over to see you,
Like the sea falls back from the sand.
I am falling, falling for you,
Are you falling for me?
—Dawn Bieber

Blue Saturday

The ash dimmed clouds drag
like a lazy river over the park
suffocating the high spirits of summer.

Black ants dance on festering blue winds
strangled sea, and hover ominous
in thick dust.

A quick stench of sulfur fills the air with a crack,
soaking any hope of a sharp line-drive,
or suicide squeeze.

The musty green army bag with helmets and bats
remains on the dug-out floor, imprisoning pop-flies
and free icy cokes.

The concession stand door slips and falls
like a swollen barometer, meeting the earth
head on, crashing and giving birth to stillborn tears.
—Eric K. Habig

Walking Away

Her face, white and pale in the goddess -moon's light,
Like a newborn child under florescent hospital lights;
Like an old woman's skin under the chapping sun's rays.

She lies on the steps, blood pouring slowly,
Dripping, trickling down, step-after-step,
Flowing into the gutter below.
Jealousy, the cause of misfortune,
And treachery, its child.
(Seeing her face, I was reminded.)

Her hand, reaching out into the darkness,
And her voice calling to me.

My eyes left her, moving to my hand below.
The crimson blood, and the metallic glow — the blade.

"Why?"

I walked away.
—Vicente F. Blanco

"The Black Wall"

Bombs blasting, fire engulfing the wide sky
Like a nuclear dawn rising, by and by.
Government owned, raped of their pride
Scared to fight, from Vietnam they could not hide.
Angry bullets their lives they chase.
Agent Orange used in this place
Running for their lives at a fast pace,
These men fought shadows in a crawlspace.
Snuffed out in a jungle town
In a box, sleeping, six feet down.
In the ground a grave, dark and hollow
While years the widow reaps her sorrow
They return, the ones that remain.
Only to face memories the drive them insane
As a father, a grown man
Runs and traces his shaking hand
Down a black wall, in the rain
His life— never the same.
For there, carved in granite,
   reads his only son's name.
—Krisi Prater

Fire And Ashes

I see a special man - my emotions are set afire
  Like a raging inferno they blaze
My life has new meaning, I yearn with desire
  I move around through a misty haze

Then ever so slowly, the fire loses heat
  His mannerisms and looks fail to please
Soon I wonder why my heart skipped a beat
  The fire dies into ashes, my emotions cease

I yearn anew, as desire shines in my eyes
  Blazing love again, hot as the desert sun
Stirs me to glories and my passions rise
  As my new lover and I become one

Then slowly again, the hot fires are spent
  Nothing but the dead ashes remain
But I know in my fickle heart it is meant
  That I shall fall madly in love yet again
     —*Lila Wiegert*

The Evening Sun

  The sun went down in the western sky,
  Like an orange slowly falling from a tree.
  The fireflies knew that darkness was nie,
There were little lights as far as you could see.

  In the distance I heard a crickets song
  And the buzz of a mosquito nearby.
    I had waited all day long,
    But really I don't know why!

    I stayed out for an hour or two,
    Just to see what was going on.
  I swatted mosquitoes till I was blue,
    And soon the fireflies were gone.

  The cricket's sang way into the night.
    It was kinda pretty at first,
Then someone turned on the front porch light,
  And the mosquito's gave me their worst.

    I went inside with bites on my arm,
    And looked outside with a frown.
  Somehow the night seemed to loose its charm,
  Boy! I hate it when the sun goes down!
     —*Russell W. Ragsdale*

Pebbles On The Beach

Pebbles on the beach, scattered on the sand,
Like memories washed away, and brought back onto the land,
Hear the sound, of the crashing tides,
When the moonlight hits, the sunshine hides,
Endless waves come, and crawl back in again,
Like moments that once started, like moments that have to end,
Pearls hidden in oysters, are often out of reach,
Like voices silenced by time, that cannot recognize speech,
The scenery of moods, change as the waves do,
They come like a cherished jewel, are tossed like an old
    shoe,
Ah, the smell of salty water, the thought of swimming them,
Like an impulsive desire, that leads to a suppressed end,
Oh, I cherish the moments of today, I fear not to say why.
I find joy in living today, for tomorrow I may die.....
     —*Manisha A. Vakil*

Teardrops

Teardrops falling from my reddened eyes
Like rain drops falling from the steel grey skies.

Feeling sad and very blue,
Wondering what exactly I can do

To save myself from desperation
All we need is communication.

That's why I'm wondering where you could be
Wondering if me eyes deceive me.

Or do I see you standing there
Telling me how much you really care.

That's why tear drops fall from my reddened eyes.
Like rain drops falling from the steel grey skies.
     —*Theresa Price*

Victory

Sometimes the gloom of the day envelops us
Like the fog rolling in from the sea to the shore;
Imprisoning all who might dare to meet it there.
How can we escape such a mocking intruder?
It offers oblivion from the present, and
Holds and enfolds, but never grants freedom.
Struggling and tortured, we fight this selfish fiend,
Until gasping for breath, we break through, and come forth
To greet the sunlight of day again.
The victory is ours, and now we can meet
Life's challenges—bravely and unafraid!
     —*Ginny Urban*

Fleeting Joy

How fleeting this emotion we call happiness;
Like the mist that fades with the rising of the sun.
How temporary this joy we experience;
Like the dead leaves that fall when the summer is done.

And so with resolve we hang onto the moment,
All the while fearing what tomorrow will bring.
And some of the pleasure is lost in the terror
The way reality becomes lost in a dream.

So we must learn to close our eyes to the morrow;
To see, with clarity, the joy we've found today.
And after the smiles have given way to sorrow,
Perhaps, in our hearts, a trace of hope shall remain.
     —*Jill Bodderij*

Let's Love

Let's love like lovers love.
  Living love lightly, lets lovers live little
Heavy hearts have heart hunger,
  Heavy hearts hang heavy; heave ho heavy hearts!

Let's love like lovers love.
  Living love lightly, lets lovers live little,
Let's love like lovers love,
  Linger longer, loving like little leprechauns.

Love like Ladies love, Laddies, lasts longer,
  letting love linger longer.
With wifely wit, wife withdraws wisely within walls.
  Willing ways won't wander with weather.
Vivian votes valid, valentine value.
  Vanity vanishes vast volume violently.
     —*Vivian C. Peters*

Understanding

Pray don't find fault with the man who
Limps or stumbles along the road.
Unless you have the shoes he wears
Or struggles beneath his load.

There may be tacks in his shoes that hurt
Though hidden from view,
And the burden he bears, placed on your back
Might cause you to stumble too.

Don't be harsh with the man who sins,
Or hit him with rocks or stone
Unless you are yet doubly sure
That you have no sins of your own.

For you know perhaps if the sinners voice,
Should whisper as soft to you
As it did to him when he went astray
It would cause you to stumble too.

You may be strong, but still the blows
That were his, if dealt to you in the
Exact same way, might cause you to stumble too.
—*Kelso L. Hall*

Autumn Song

As I sit by the edge of cooling coals
"Listen to the hiss of the dying ember"
I feel the call of a thousand souls
that bear the dead weight of September
the darkness is sleek and hungry and proud
as it waits for me to cross over
a beacon life, my spirit is loud
I pay the dear price of October
I drink my wine and resent the bright coals
then smash the glass on the ember
I am ready to join the thousand lost souls
and sing a song for November
for tonight the ghosts haunt themselves
—*Bobby Dwain Davis*

The Glove

Alone I sit,
Listening to the symphony outside my window.
If only I could play a part.
Instead I am forced to succumb to my painstaking journey,
Where I must let myself be molded into what I am supposed to be,
what I am supposed to feel.
I yearn to break free,
To join the majestic celebration,
To revel in my true fantasies,
To shout with laughter and expose my naked soul.

I feel trapped,
My entire body covered with a glove.
Allowing movement only in certain directions at precise angles,
Never permitted outside the boundaries of society.
Only enough room to be one of them.
I suppose sometimes this is a safe place.
The glove protects me, and I shall no longer feel morose.
But whenever I dig to the bottom of my spirit,
I realize I am not meant to be one of them.
I shall never fit the glove, but I must always wear it.
—*Amy F. Rozman*

Little Bits

Life's made up of little bits transpiring through the years,
little bits of happiness and little bits of tears,
a little bit of childhood with faith and trust and fears,
a little bit of manhood before the "golden years."

A little bit of ecstasy must come before the pain,
a little bit of sunshine before the fall of rain.
It takes a bit of courage to help abate the fright,
a little bit of moonglow mingled with the night.

A little bit of sacrifice precedes a feel of cheer,
a gathering of storm clouds for the rainbow to appear.
A little bit of honor comes before a fall of grace,
a little bit of smiling upon a tear wet face.

There must be times of plenty or we can't relate to loss,
an experience of glory or we can't perceive the cross.
We have to see the raven to appreciate the dove.
We have to deal with hatred to insure we treasure love.
—*Ruth Roberts Douglas*

Faces Of Death

No one in the world knows their fate.
Live everyday to the fullest because tomorrow might be too late.
Do you remember these faces from the depths of the past,
Because fate decided that their life would end fast:

John F. Kennedy was a great man.
He fought for civil rights and to escape from Vietnam.
One bullet took his life from a lone assassin's hand?
Remember his face because his death was not planned.

"I HAVE A DREAM!" is what everyone sings;
But no one wanted it as bad as a king.
All he wanted was a world full of peace;
And because of a racist he lays down deceased.

You might be tough, and you might be strong;
And if you think you're immune, you're deadly wrong.
Once you contract it, it's always too late;
Not even Magic can escape from this fate.

The worst death of all is to hang from a cross;
He died for our sins, it was our loss.
His love was so great that he died for man.
Follow His word; your fate rests in His hands.
—*Beth Bartel*

Enlightenment's Journey

Echoes thunder through the night,
  Live life
Strong, resolute, ardently
  With dignity
The taste of our conviction to life
Will provide the final testimony,
  Why death
Should not be feared, once we
Understand life's fire and passion
  Heroic virtues
Charity, compassion, fortitude, humility, wisdom
  Will uncover
The reasons why there is no death
  Always wear
A beautiful smile as a badge of courage
  Defy despair
Embrace destiny without malice
  Allow life
To strengthen and activate a virtuous karma
  Happy rebirth.
—*Ralph H. Rapozo*

Depression

Somewhere in a deep recessed part of your mind
Live the happy thoughts that now you cannot seem to find.
Life around you is going on as normal as can be
But lonely, hopeless, helplessness is all that you can see.
One day you wake to find yourself in a deep, deep hole
That's known as depression and it's robbing you of your soul.
The more you try to shake yourself of the emptiness
The more it drags you under into its black abyss.
At times you're afraid of the fall because you don't know
   its harms
At times you want to welcome it with outstretched, open arms.
You're cold, you're numb, you cannot sleep, your mind it is
   confused
The smile that was a gleam in your eye has somehow been
   defused.
You hide the tears you're crying inside behind a forced
   false wall
And don't bother to cry out to those who come to call.
But maybe, just maybe someone will see and give you a hand
   to clasp
And help to pull and free you from depressions mighty grasp.

—*Bob Hayward*

Ginko Sanctuary

In my garden under the ginko tree
Lives a family of orioles in secrecy.
The smallest fledgling broke his wing,
And I, I could not watch it die, you see,
But fashioned a new nest below.
Ferns and yellow hibiscus form a screen.
We are alone, the orioles, their guardian.
How trustingly they fluttered down, shyly peeping.
Courageously they dropped in solo to the sheltering ferns.
Soon they will depart, and I,
Very beholden, golden birds, am weeping.

—*Barbara Girard*

Real Truth

The real truth is not the issue between....
Living or dying, My God or your God
My religion or your religion
My unreligion or your religion
My sex or your sex
My sex preference or your sex preference
More or less "Temptation or no Temptation"
Taking or giving "My good or your bad"
Right or wrong, Sober or unsober
Want or unwant, Killess or Killer
Friend or foe Peacemaker or destroyer
Material wealth or no wealth....

...But knowing there lies in us, a conflict, which is
unsatisfiable, and with this knowing, any person can live with
their personal conflict, as well as the conflict of others...
or with any belief that "does not share their personnel value."
These persons have found the ultimate truth...
peace with oneself

—*David Eilenberger*

Creed

Life is all around us
Look and you see
To the left are the sinners, doing dirty deeds
To the right are the Christians, praying on their knees
In the middle are the confused, searching for what they need
Up above us are the rich, giving into greed
Below us are the poor, that no one wants to feed
Stomping in on all of us, are the lives that we mislead

—*Melissa O'Kelley*

The Rocking Chair

   The old rocker sat empty and alone, in a living room where much love did bloom and grow. Oh, if it could talk, the stories it could tell. Of laughter and tears of many people where it did dwell.

   But there was one it remembers above all the rest, for she was his very best. A little old woman kind and frail, knew many of life's disappointments but triumphs as well.

   In the rocker would she sit, with the Bible upon her lap, as she read by the dim moonlight. She would read out loud as if God were there, for safe was she under his care.

   Now the time has come when she was laid to rest, but behind she left treasures and memories for us to possess. In my living room you will find the biggest treasure of them all. For I have the old rocking chair that sat quietly and listened to all.

—*Trisha Baran*

Painting By Picasso

I see a girl
lonely and sad
wanting one
the one she cannot have
at least not the way she wants.
She tries not to let him hurt her
She tells him she won't take it anymore
Knowing all along this is impossible
but she bites her tongue
and she keeps her pride
instead of throwing herself at his feet
and weeping as in her fantasies
She longs to see him hurting for a change
but love and loyalty run deep in her veins
which explains the
lonely and sad look on her face
as she sits in the pouring rain.

—*Tamara Kanne*

The Find

I spied a little, striped, beach chair that
looked dilapidated and left lonely by the
Friday's discarded-garbage collection.

Was this a tiny tot's summertime seat, or
Perhaps a resting spot for a weary doll?

How could the owner part with such a memory-
filled delight?

Was the owner aware of the chair's plight, or
did the unaware owner's mom, in a whirlwind
of motion, clear it out of the house in the
name of cleaning-up?

I'll bet someone will discover this little
throne and use their mending mind to restore
this doll-size delight's dignity.

A little splash of bright color painted on
the frame, and a lively piece of patterned
canvas secured to the body will bring this
chair to life again.

Will it bring a smile to a doll, ...a child,
....or an adult then?

—*Rosamond Martin*

Reaching For The Stars

Sitting, thinking, dreaming,
Looking at the moon and stars.
I shall reach for the moon and stars.

The moon, pretty though desolate,
Shows no promise to me.
I shall reach for the stars.

As I look to the stars,
They shine and shimmer,
Beckoning to me.
I shall reach for the stars.

Stars can be calm, quiet, and serene.
Yet they can be jumpy, playful, and excited.
But, underneath it all,
They are strong and dependable.
I shall reach for the stars.

To me they are so much more
Than just a distant light.
The stars are a hope, a future,
A promise of something better.
I am reaching for the stars.
—*Terry Ross*

Where People Lay

As I walked through the cemetery so sad and so cold.
Looking at the tombstones: some new, some old.

Walking where the people lay.
You know God will take you one day.

Now I visit a man I knew.
Knowing he wouldn't want me to feel so blue.

As I got up and wiped the tears from my face.
I know someday I'll be in this sad and solemn place.
—*William A. McGinnis*

A Journey Through Life

Beginning of life, darkness, then light.
Looking into the light - shadows.
Smiling faces. loving arms reach out.

A time to play and explore the wonders all around.
Wondering - touching
Now the magic's gone.

A time to learn: ABC's, coloring books, stories read.
Years go by - knowledge obtained - graduation day.
A time to ponder: Who am I, Where am I going, What is my
   goal?

Adulthood: Love, marriage, family, responsibilities.
Some: Questions addressed - action taken. With divine
guidance found the way, climbed the ladder to success.

Others: Questions not addressed: divine drifting, groping,
searching - no challenge - lacking guidance - no purpose, full
potential never obtained.

Golden Years: Time to enjoy fruits of labor - children,
grandchildren's smiling faces and loving arms reaching out.

As it was in the beginning of life - darkness then light; at
the end of life's journey light becomes dimmer, then darkness.

Mission completed - Journey's end!
—*Elsie Johanson*

Trees

I am standing by my window
Looking out at God's trees.
They're dressed in their shades of fall
As they sway in the autumn breeze.

No artist could ever capture
The beauty that I've found.
One by one the colored leaves
Flutter gracefully to the ground.

Soon the wind will strip the trees
Of their beautiful red and gold.
And they will be bare with just their limbs
Standing naked in the cold.

The winter trees are tall and silent,
Not too much to admire.
But it won't be so very long
Till they adorn their spring attire.

When it turns warm they dress for summer,
When spring comes to an end.
Then God works His wonders
And brings autumn back again.
—*Mary June Vick*

A Little Girl's Pride

A little girl, standing not very tall,
Looks up at her daddy, and thinks how brave and bold.
He picks her up, and swings her around,
Places her up on his shoulders, her laughter is the only sound.
He lifts her up, and gently sits her down,
How lucky I am to have a wonderful daddy, she thinks so proud.

Years past by, and her feelings stayed the same,
He watched her grow taller and smarter,
As she saw him grow in his faith.
But through it all, she never gave up on him,
For she prayed and knew,
If he got out on a limb, God would pull him through.

I am that little girl, who watched her daddy grow,
And knew he would always have hope, even when things got low.
I've been so blessed, to have a leader like you,
Who loves and cares for me, and shows me the way through.
I've never been so proud of you daddy as I watched you from
the side,
And to look at what you've done, is a little girl's pride.
—*Amanda McCarty*

Infinite Wisdom

In infinite world's of Presidents
   Lords and Kings
Churchbells and playground swings

We struggle with the concept
   of being free;
And yet we have starvation and
   needless death in our country

But, can we afford to be so free
With so much wrong in this land of liberty

Yet, who is to say which solutions are best.
In these times of uncertainty and unrest.

Although we can't change the world
   in only one day,
we can start the ball rolling
   in a special way.

The solution is very clear to this simple man.
Be more responsible and lend a helping hand.
—*Sonny Poor*

Love

Love is the flowers that bloom in the spring
Love is the sweet songs that humming birds sing.
Love is shared between a King and a Queen
Love is everything to me...

Love is the joy in the mist of our pain
Love is the sunshine and the rain.
Love is constant, it never change
Love is everything to me...

Love is the happiness that takes sorrow away
Love is what we need more of in this world today.
Love should be spoken in every word we say
Love means everything to me...

Love should be seen in the life we live
Love is something we all can give.
Love was sent from the heavenly skies above
Now we should understand that GOD is LOVE...

—*James Conscious Barrett*

Love Is...And So Much More

Love is sharing,
Love is trusting,
Love is caring,
Love is listening,
Love is forgiving and so much more.
That's when love is strong;
And when a love is so like that as ours
It shall never die,
Because a love like ours
Only happens once in a lifetime.
It is a love like ours
That unites for an eternity,
Two individual lives so unlike one another—
Until they realize just how alike they truly are
In all that they share.

—*Mary Ann Lamme*

Loving You

Loving you means my day begins with a smile,
Loving you means disappointments last only a short while.
Loving you makes me grin from ear to ear,
Loving you casts out all my doubt and fear.

Loving you brings sunshine and song to my heart,
Loving you is knowing we'll never part.
Loving you brings healing to my body and mind,
Loving you gives me everything I could ever find.

Loving you means I can achieve without threatening your masculinity,
Loving you means our closeness will never destroy our individuality.
Loving you is knowing you accept me for being me,
Loving you means I allow you to be all that you can be.

Loving you brings forgiveness its release,
Loving you gives me joy, harmony and peace.
Loving you means your happiness is my life,
Every day I thank God I'm your wife.

Thank God you feel the same way about me too,
Thank you for loving me as much as I love you.

—*Nancy T. Burk*

That Bird Became Me

I ran to see the quiet bird,
Lying on the shore.
It was soiled and abused,
It could fly no more.

How happened bird to venture here,
for me to see and care.
What can I offer,
To regain her soul into the air.

I reach out to free the bird from this worldly place.
I help her heal and soon she has regained her grace.

Up! Up! She flies—then circles around,
As if to say good-bye.

O' healed bird you bring my soul,
To your life on high.

And once again, I see the bird.
We are both soaring free.

For when I reached
To free that bird,
That bird became me!!!

—*Barbara-Ann C. Herpst*

My Pen

My name will not make History
Made famous by my poetry
Limits far beyond control
Will not let me reach my goal

But in my heart a wild desire
Consumes me like a burning fire
As thoughts of verse race through my head
As I lie upon my bed

I'll arise and with my pen
Let that verse take form again
Thoughts I cannot speak aloud
Hover o'er me like a cloud

Of misty foam or misty dew
Until that verse comes breaking through
Verse, that cannot spoken be
Beneath my pen can be set free

Secrets of my heart unfold
Written words that can't be told.
I know I am, but can't say when
I became enslaved to my pen

—*Alene Stamper*

The Cycle Of Soul

Our lives are like the seasons
making their beginning as seeds of spring develop
into summer's new growth.
Always seeking higher truths,
Soul becomes illuminated and vibrant
like the autumn leaves.
We are taught to quiet our mind and listen
when going within, to find life's answer in liberating our soul.
Winter's dormancy allows us this time for reflection.
Stripped of our egos do we learn
to fear not the angel of death -
for she is but a veil that we pass through
to get to the other side [of consciousness].
And the cycle is repeated as we take with us
a new dimension of understanding.

—*Lynda Hoffarth*

A Grandmother's delight: Magic Soup

I've tasted many kinds of soup
Made on my kitchen floor
By tiny "chefs" with wooden spoons
And pots and pans galore!

A pinch of this, a bit of that,
So sweetly were they blended,
By little hands that measured
The ingredients, pretended.

"Taste it, Mommy! It is good!
My little ones would say.
I sipped on that supreme cuisine
So many times each day!

What innocence is make-believe!
The soup was judged "delicious"
So naturally, we ate it
From imaginary dishes!

Long years have passed since I have sipped
Such savory soup as then.
Now my grandchild's in the kitchen,
And it's soup time once again!
—Joan Tenner

Little Boy Lost

Oh' the morning doves mournful cry
Makes me want to stop and sigh... as in that
sad and lone July, of another year gone by -
T'was then the child departed
Passed by my very door -
I even remember the shoes he wore
Lil' blue sneakers on study feet
A'running in the sultry heat
He paused but once and pointed -
Up to a clear blue sky...
And I watched and wondered why
Oh' Lord, could I have stayed his running feet
Or caused his little heart to beat?
Alas, now all I can do is remember.

They found his body afloating on the pond
His little life over and beyond...
Then he lay in a casket all dressed in white
And Oh, what a heartrending sight!
Lil' Bobby Campbell was his name...and he
Had no claim to fame—save death.
—Harriet Trotta

Ode To The Pines

The lights of the shopping center pierce the night air
Making light where once there was only darkness.
Deep wood darkness where little animals,
Raccoon, possum, deserted cats, could hide.
Now one walks in light on pavement.
No vines reach out to snare unsuspecting feet.
No underbrush with thorny fingers
Out clothing tears-or skin.
The sounds, too, have changed
The murmur of the darkness, the hoot owl,
Some unknown nightbird calling to its mate;
These have given way to sounds of modern man:
The humming of transformers,
Other machinery,
For man's comfort within the vast stone and mortar buildings.
But I miss the whistling wind
As it sang overhead
Where once there stood
The towering, majestic pines.
—Julia M. Phillips

Untitled

Nature extols the differences between the sexes, and revels in making love in all kinds of places. Nature doesn't worry and doesn't hurry. Pay attention, listen and learn - nature has much to teach the human races. Nature is spoken of as a She and the earth as Mother Earth. There is a reason and a plan - it takes two different sexes but only the She can give birth. Nature is orderly but never, ever equal - the male and female must unite - that's nature's unchangeable sequel. In nature, nothing is base because the smallest entity knows and is content with its place. Nature destroys for continuity, never for convenience. She can appear to be soft and sweet but her reality excludes lenience. In nature, no entity fights to be what it isn't. Furiously fighting amongst themselves, different species fight for survival. But, no species sees their own - especially the opposite sex of their own species - as their rival. It is only the human species who battles against nature. With a superior brain's arrogance insisting on doing their own thing, ignoring the fact that nature, in the end, has always been and always will be the decision maker.
—E. Donnelly

Mama's Garden

Just after dawn when the sun is still low
Mama comes out with her bonnet and hoe
Her heart full of grit, she battles the weeds
That threaten her precious garden and seed.

Digging and pulling 'till each little row
Is tidy and clean so the flowers can grow,
She splatters her garden with colors so bright
Creating a magical, beautiful sight.

With love in her heart and a smile on her face
Mama plants treasures in this special place.
Like some with a brush, she's an artist with soil
Using her garden to brighten God's world.

Autumn approaches and Mama is sad
Colors are changing and Winter's ahead;
Quilting and sewing will fill up the hours
'Til Winter's farewell and Spring's gentle showers.

She's watching and waiting until she can go
Back to the garden with her bonnet and hoe.
—Bonnie F. Hall

Myrna's Mother Lenora

I've warm feelings of you, that I want to share
Mama I want you to know, I still deeply care

With a stroll to the sunset, you left us kids and dad
We felt so hollow and empty, and we hurt so bad

Since you've went away, I've ached so much
For your beautiful face, your warm tender touch

I miss hearing your voice, so soft in my ear
I miss your delicate love, my mother so dear

I remember your kiss, when you'd tuck me in bed
And your intricate work, done with needle and thread

When I was a little girl, I'd sit for a spell
And think about things, I heard you did so well

When I was alone, I'd fold my little hands and pray
And wish to be like you, in every single way

Now I hold in my hand, a lock of your hair
I stand at your grave, in silence and stare

God has all the answers, He gave the command
He knows we still grieve, and don't understand

Like flickering orange embers, my memories still glow
Do you know that we miss you, and still love you so
—Arley M. Bischoff

Birthday Blessings

Fortunate is the
  man who was found The Way
  to a contented life.

Daring is the man
  who puts aside worldly ways
  to cultivate peace of mind within.

Humble is the man
  who gains the wisdom of a sage
  but wears not a robe and long beard.

Lucky is the man
  who has many friends throughout the world,
  to the North, East, Sough, and West.

Devoted is the man
  who leads a meditative life
  in the midst of 20th Century chaos!

Joyful is the man

  who shares his talents and creative skills,
  in art, music and philosophy.

Happy is the man
  who did all this
  through T'ai Chi Chih,
  and love.

Who is this man?
  He is Justin Stone.
    —*Rosalind Braga*

Can You Hear Them Cry?

Faces of sorrow, pain and anger.
Marching in rivers of green and brown;
  I pledge allegiance to the flag.
To insure their glorious way of life.
To defend their righteous country;
  Of the United States of America.
Fighting for reasons unknown.
For those who don't really care;
  And to the Republic for which it stands.
America the beautiful, the rich, and powerful;
  One nation under God.
Unstoppable, unafraid, however mortal;
  Indivisible.
Killing because they have to. Dying because they're told to;
  With liberty.
Brothers dying. Families crying;
  And justice.
Never forgotten, seldom remembered.
Can you hear them cry?
  For all.
    —*Frank Gscheidle*

Contra Verse

Oh heat!! Oh Mercury! Sloth-like, I
meander down the walks of the garden.
Water!! Shade! The blooms wither as crepe.
Despite my futile intervention.

Chaperelle! Star Thistle! Thrive this inferno.
Boxwood unphased, must line the paths of Hades.
Toyon! Manzanita! reveling and peeling
in the ecstasy of this sweltering state.

Thirsty!! Sweaty! Our bodies weaken.
Our pets lie panting in the shadowed still.
And yet Squash!! Tomatoes! The hot earth nourishing
brings forth the eagerly awaited progeny.
    —*Stewart B. Gross*

Feelings

  Emotions, bubbling to the surface seem ready to burst.
  Maybe they are better left unsaid, ignored, and forgotten,
    But it seems too hard to let go of the
      Feelings,
Feelings of hurt, love, anger, longing for someone to talk to.
    Loneliness, missing someone who might not be gone.
     People who we once knew, but they have left,
A stranger has replaced them, a stranger who doesn't want to
  listen, or doesn't care about the things that matter to you.
    Your friendship, once bubbling with life, effervescent,
      A vivid memory now forgotten.
Or maybe it is you who have changed, you who have different
    interests It is easy to blame ourselves for being who we are,
    for living how we want to. It all comes back to feelings.
Longing to be free, but locked up inside, for fear of losing
          something,
     something that you are unsure about.
    You don't know if it matters anymore.
      Follow your
      Feelings.
—*Elizabeth Orem*

I Need You To Be True

Maybe you totally misunderstood
Maybe you never knew
But if I didn't say before, I'll tell you now
I need you to be true

I'll forgive you this time, but not again
even though you lied
I'm being realistic when I say
I need you by my side

Don't get me wrong, I'm not the type of girl
to forgive, forget and understand
I love you but I need to know
that you're a one-woman man

We can have the greatest love in the world
Like no one ever knew
All I ask is love, but most of all,
I need you to be true
    —*Kellie Haberkorn*

"When You Need Her"

When I cry, she wipes away my tears. When I'm sick, she makes me well. When I hurt, she tells me everything will be okay. When I need help, she gives the lending hand. Everyday...day in, day out, she gives, comfort and love in her own very

special way. The faith she has, through her teaching and guidance, hoping to make life better. Can't remember if I ever heard her complain. Always a smile, always the same. She'll be there when you need her, anytime, day or night... She'll be there. She'll be there when things get tough to ease the pain,

bear the strain, keep you dry in the rain. She'll be there to

show you the way. Point you in the right direction, Give you love and affection. She'll be there when you need her. I'm going to sit down and write you a letter. I'm going to tell you, that I love you forever... and ever. I'm going to say, thank you for your undying support and showing me the way. If not for you, I wouldn't be here today. I'm going to sit down and write you a letter and tell you, I love you forever... and ever. Because, she'll be there when you need her, anytime, day or night... she'll be there. She'll be there when things get tough, to ease the pain, and bear the strain.
    —*Jerome R. Case*

Ocean's View

I look at her and am pulled to her through a beautiful melody of a hundred thousand angels' voices that make me drunk with Awe of all her mysteries and treasures and drift helplessly as if being in the midst of her strongest current. Pondering her depths, it confirms my faith in God Himself for only He could create such beauty.

Her emotions, thoughts and dreams are as different and colorful as all the life that swims within her. I realize my love for her is like the reflection in my eyes, that makes me blind with all she brings to my life, with her vastness she fades to a different shade of blue when her surface seems to blend with the sky above her.

With the enormous power she holds, I smile to think I'm in control. And am simply satisfied knowing she's forever changing but is always there for me to swim and play in... and to look at.....and talk to, my ocean view is of my wife and as I awake I'm standing on her shore and feel the mist of her wet kiss on my face and hear yet another of her endless waves as she says I love you.......

—*Robin Schraider*

We Shall Overcome

In the mist I hear a cry, a soul once unspoken.
   Memories of incest, sorrow hearts broken.
Reaching beyond the skies listening to unanswered prayers,
Seeking a life of freedom from the troubled and prepared.
   Softly I whisper to the heavens high above,
dream away your nightmares and fulfill your thoughts with love.
   We are free from all the torture as our hearts tingle, numb,
but we shall never forget the message that "We shall overcome".

—*Sarah Judd*

The Dilemma

Mister Prank and Mister Shrank
Met each other on a plank
Prank had not seen Shrank coming
And Shrank was too busy humming
To notice where he was going
So soon the two men were toeing.

Under them ran a very deep stream
You would think they could have seen
There was room for only one on that plank
But surprise made their faces blank
Shrank asked, "Who do you think you are?
Don't you know I'm a movie star?"

Prank looked up and then looked down
But on his face there was no frown
"If you're a movie star", said he,
"I know just where you ought to be
Stars always escape from dangerous spots
So over you go, like it or not."

—*Edna Mae Lowell*

Spring; My Interpretation

A warmth and a coolness
Mingling, pulsing, vibrating
Releasing a dazzling fragrance
It is the
Annual battle
between two shades of a color
The darkest one, reluctantly fading away
And
the lighter, a joyous brightness, with a touch
of hazy sorrow
Bring promise of rebirth and life.

—*Tova Messer*

Mom...I Got An 'A' On My Paper

"I got an A on my paper."
"Mhm." The only reply.
She hadn't heard a word I said.
"Mommmmie make me cereal."
"Mom I'm hungry. What are you gonna make for dinner?"
The children surround her like kittens whining for milk.
Running through the kitchen, barely glancing at me, she begins
yet another task on her list of duties.
I think the little ones are more important than I.
Isolated from her world, I am the only one she doesn't hear.
"Mom, I need money." I say, hiding the truth.
"Get it out of my wallet."
Rolling her eyes at the amount, she cries,
"Just how much do you need?" "This is enough."
Turning around I slam the door behind me.
I wonder if she really knows?
Will we ever learn not to speak at each other
But to each other?
We both reside at the same address,
Yet our worlds are different.

—*Vanessa LaMorte*

Sonnet On Stones

There were two plain headstones on a country hill
Midst tiny white markers of babes who had flown.
Lulled in death's slumber by a meadowlark's trill,
Loving father and mother amid grief now unknown.

A mole run rambles toward the Anderson's plot
Where a gray granite monument stands without frills.
E'en from the grave they grow forget-me-nots,
Faded words on their marker: "Together Still."

A dirt-dulled rectangle lies flat on the ground
With no date nor a name nor any kind word;
Half covered with grass, and weeds all around—
Who had this been, one so blankly interred?

It pays one to contemplate when reading these stones
If life will end blankly, or with love, ever known.

—*Karen L. Meeker*

"Night"

I hear the wind, I hear the trees and low the moan of night come I dread all in me. But yet I am what I be. Yet you cry all you can do is let it go. And then it comes the spirit the guider the peacemaker all. And his presence ye wither you feel comforted as he walks. The forest of which you walk let the moon come in like a crown of light fit for a king. This is a place were the wind blows and the willows grow. In the distance there he is yet all alone to be. He cares for any who walk alone lost and in fear. He is just a tree but yet not all fore who lives in that forest is the comforter. And he be God of all nations the one and only God.

—*Patrick Walz*

Sleep

    It comes at night,
 most people snore, some people dream.
Most people wait and wait for it to come,
    Yet things get no better.
  Sleeping pills, sleep and then,
  then it comes again and again.
 And then it comes once and for all,
   Permanent sleep takes us all.

—*Fay Arzadon*

Beautiful Mystery

You are my child, a gift from God,
molded and made in His image.
Children are blessings, beautiful and pure.
What a wonderful thing to see, you are a beautiful
mystery.

I feel you growing, I feel you moving down inside.
You are a heritage, conceived and made in love.
You are fearfully and wonderfully made.
What a wonderful thing to see,
you are a beautiful mystery.

Your heart is beating, you are alive, you're
not just a tissue that should be pushed aside.
As each day passes, you are growing and being
formed. What a wonderful thing to see, you
are a beautiful mystery.

The time is getting closer, when we got to
see your face, what a great day that will be
for in our arms, you we will embrace. So
we will be patient and wait for the day when
we will see our beautiful mystery.

—*Alison Hines Cristello*

Under The Bridge

Under the bridge is where I am condemned. The fetal position is most comfortable, I assume. As I watch the different cars go by that have a piece of something I desperately search for, it makes my body numb. The car of independence is red...to show its bold exterior. The car of love and support is solid white with many tints of black to show equality and to provide encouragement it has. The color of a dark pine green passes me by quickly and makes my body cringe down ever more. Realizing my own life that isn't moving. That certain car shows the eagerness to change the speed of their life. But if I move too much to the right, I could get hurt by the obvious uncertainty. And if I start to elevate myself and extend my left arm and hand to reach the side of the intimidating bridge; I may fall. Oh God, listen to me and help me straighten my back and hitch a ride in that car with the red, white, and green colors.

—*Tracey L. Johnson*

Tell My Heart

Things have happened in my life
Most have been wonderful
Others full of pain and strife.

Some of these I know I am not responsible for
Everyone says you're not the cause.

You followed all the rules
and broke no laws.

In my mind I can understand
the words that are said.

These words are no problem
for my head.

But when they told me all of this,
they forgot one very
important part.

Nobody remembered to
Tell my heart.

—*Cynthia Petersen*

Prayer For Our Baby

As we hold this precious little one and look upon its face,
much joy and wonder fill our hearts as our baby we embrace,
for in this lovely gift of life we meet you, Lord, face to
face. Now show us, Father, just what to do with these tiny
hands we hold. At first our grip is strong and firm, but as
the years unfold we need to gently ease our hold and allow
this child to grow. There are so many wonderful things that
these little hands might do; some-day they could help build or
heal, to comfort or renew, so help us, Lord, guide these hands
to always work for you. To this little voice that coos and
laughs and cries out to us this day help us respond through
all the years with love and care and praise, that by our faith
and love, dear Lord, child will learn to pray. These
lovely eyes that look to us, so curious and so new, reflect
a loving heart and trust, innocent and true; please teach
us, Father, to direct these eyes to always search for you.
For the precious years of childhood will quickly pass away,
like pretty flower blossoms that delight and fade away. Help
us, Lord, to plant seeds of faith in this little one today,
so when tomorrow comes, our child will follow in your way.

—*Judy Wagner*

Sounds Of Georgia

Mumble mumble red mumble and
mumble pass on mumble lane mumble
The truck drivers mumble mumble nice
But some passenger mumble drivers aren't
The hills mumble are mumble pretty

The mumble sign says mumble
And go mumble miles to the junction
The pavement mumble mumble rough here
That creek is mumble mumble ducks
Let's eat at mumble mumble across mumble
You know the mumble near the mumble

Then we can switch mumble and
You can mumble some rest.
It is nice to drive through the mountains
With a truck ahead to guide the way
As we go down the long hills.
It was thoughtful of the highway department
To put a slow lane up the hills
For the mumble mumble to mumble.

—*Milton F. V. Glock, Sr.*

Untitled

My mind is tired
My body aches for comfort
My eyes sends messages
    that I rather not.

I need a place to hide
to seek refuge till I am ready.

I need to renourish my broken soul
before I leave it unarmed and open
to defeat.

Somewhere in the back of my mind
Somewhere lurks the soul of tranquility,
the dreams and beliefs of wanting and needing
to be heard.

Lead me into tomorrow's dreams, lead me into
the space that is mine.

Let me shine, let me live, let me be.....
For it is only life of peace I seek.
Steer me into the path of the road that leads
    me safely home.

—*Hope Januszewski*

I Know I Never Did

My life is forever chaotic,
My childhood is forever lost,
I use to be able to hide the pain,
And able to run from my thoughts.

With all the nightmares that awake me,
And cold sweats that flow down my face,
I keep trying to convince this body,
That it was never to blame.

His breath smelled like that of a brewery,
As he laughed into my small face,
Then went on to kiss me abruptly,
No matter how much my heart did ache.

The feel of his short fat body,
Laying against my small fragile frame,
Sent many unhappy feelings,
To a child who felt only shame.

I laid there and gazed at the ceiling,
As my eyes filled with salty wet tears,
Who told him that he could abuse me?
I know I never did.
—*Peggy S. Lewis*

Daddy's Advice

When I was just a little girl, troubled by some night-time fear,
My "daddy" would hold me close, and whisper in my ear:
"There'll be sunshine in the morning, love. Just sleep on it tonight.
There'll be comfort in the morning, child. Everything will be alright."
His words, they always calmed me, as I drifted back to sleep.
He was my loving shepherd; and I, his little sheep.
All those years, "my daddy," he was always there for me.
Through many pains of growing up, my dad would counsel me:
"There'll be sunshine in the morning, love. Just sleep on it tonight.
There'll be comfort in the morning, child. Everything will be alright."
Now, daddy can't be with me, to calm my fears at night.
Or gently rock my hurts away, 'till they are out of sight.
Yet, how I long for daddy's arms to chase the hurt away.
To hold me tightly once again, sweet words to hear him say:
"There'll be sunshine in the morning, love. Just sleep on it tonight.
There'll be comfort in the morning, child. Everything will be alright."
My father, God, now listens. His presence will assure
of peace and comfort; love and hope. And I will rest secure!
"There'll be sunshine in the morning, love. Just rest in me tonight.
There'll be comfort in the morning, child. Everything will be alright."
—*Jacqueline Bowers*

My Dream

Tonight I sit, all tattered and torn
My heart is broken, a desire is born
My mind is cluttered, its her that I miss
It all started that night, with the very first kiss
Her soft flowing skin and that look in her eyes
When she wrapped me in her legs, and held me with her thighs
The warmth that filled my body is more than I can deny
The only thing on my mind is to be by her side
To be the one that she runs to, when she needs comfort or love
And at night while we sleep, to be the one that she hugs
Every day and all the nights, would be passion and lust
And the bond between us would be centered upon trust
Could this dream be possible, will I see her again
If so then it's that day, my life would begin
—*Harley D. Voss II*

"Hello...Again"

Hello, again
My dear friend
How are you doing?
How've you been?
I'm so glad to see you again!

Hello, again
It's been so long
Not much has changed since you've been gone
but, the days are empty
and, the nights too long.

Sometimes I wish you'd come back to me
but, I don't think it's meant to be
'cause if it were you'd be here
and there would be no more tears.

Hello, again
my old friend
Where are you going?
What do you intend?
We'll be together 'til the end!
—*James W. Baumgardt*

"Make Someone Happy"

As I travel along through my day, each day
My desire is to make someone happy along the way.

There is the magic of a smile and a cherry hello
Or a friendly chat warms the heart with a gentle glow.

Listen - hear the cheerful song of a happy bird
It keeps our thoughts in tune by what we've heard.

Just giving the simple gift of a small bouquet
Will make someone very happy along the way.

Let's go for a ride to see nature at her best
The tree's, blue skies, lakes and streams, adds the zest.

A trek into the woods to gather spring flowers
Do take note of that majestic pine tree that towers.

What else can make someone happy along the way?
Say - "Let's go on a picnic" it's a beautiful day.

Send a letter through the mail, what happiness it brings
Add a lovely photo - that makes the heart sing.

Commune with nature—join a friend in a walk
View the soaring flight of a hawk.

Remember it's the little things that count each day
That helps to make someone happy along the way.
—*Leslie J. Wiltse*

My Father

When old man time finally knocked at the door
My father unwittingly opened it
And an angel appeared at the door
My father, stunned, looked at his guardian angel
And the angel gently whispered in his ear
And said, "This is important; we must talk"
So my dad put on his coat and sat on the porch
Because it was a beautiful day
And listened intently to what his guardian angel had to say
When Dad came back in, the angel stood guard by the door
Dad went to bed to rest
And fell into a very deep sleep
And when Dad awoke, he was not of the earth
But on a boat deep sea fishing
With his guardian angel at his side
For the messenger talked to Dad with special care
And make a deal that Dad unconsciously cherished
For he knew it was heaven sent. And his family would
understand, now that he could get his rest. For his guardian
angel would be taking care of us all from above.
—*Rhonda Maddox*

Barrier

I have a barrier between a friend that's not,
My feelings are interior and my heart is an empty lot.

I want my heart to fill up but I don't know how,
I wish my heart was a cup I could fill it up, now.

Then the cup would be full and I wouldn't have to worry,
I wouldn't have to pull to say I'm sorry.

But I don't know how to express it; should I say?
Should I write it? Should it be today?

I don't know if the barrier will break; I wish it would.
I'll have to take it as though it could.

The barrier is now broken; I have written,
I have spoken; I feel like a kitten.

I have the friend that was once not,
My heart won't bend or tie in a knot.

I am glad that my heart is filled,
I am like a frog on his lilypad; my heart is fulfilled.

I need no more the worry I had,
The fluid doesn't have to pour into the cup I had.

—*Lindsay Simm*

"You Can Fly, Caterpillar!"

I was feeling like a caterpillar, just crawling on the ground.
My head was in a low position, for I was feeling down.
Sometimes I felt stepped on, or closed up in a jar.
I tried to crawl real fast, but I never got too far. Sometimes
I wiggle in my problems, but that did not seem to solve.
Oh, I crawled a little deeper, I got so deeply involved.
Sometimes I felt picked up, but more often kicked about.
Leaving me feeling helpless, too hard to wiggle out.
At times I felt so lonely, I would just curl up in a knot,
and as people rushed pass me, I was reminded of what I'm not.
Whenever it rained on me, I crawled up in the grass.
I tried looking for my sunshine, oh, how much longer will this last?

I get so tired from day to day, yet I keep on crawling any way.
But when I leave my crawling state, I'll turn to one I can appreciate.

I'll turn into a beautiful butterfly, once crawling low, oh but now I'm flying high!

No matter what life brings, I'm going to mount up my wings,

And Fly. . . . .

—*Gayle A. Hall*

Reaching Out

Tumbling in confusion, rolling down the lane
My heart soars so high, comes slowly crashing down again
My mind in a muddle, what is right or wrong
Looking heaven high silent words reach out, soar the skies
Dashing here dashing there, crying out in confusion
Steady tears flow endlessly, endless rows of disillusion
Why when it appears to be, it isn't what you hear or see
Tears still trailing me
I ask you this and I ask you that
No one seems to know
Than looking heaven bound, again I ask and
Answer I don't hear
No one seems to know

—*Sharon A. Downs*

My Desire To Follow Jesus

My friend don't let time pass you by one day could be too late, My heart was heavy in sin, and I was sinking low. I said, "Lord please forgive me." I confessed and repented of my sins. I was born of the Spirit, and water, and Baptized, and received the Holy ghost, my desire to follow Jesus. In this world of sin I'm free, I've been washed in the blood of the Lamb, with stretched out arms of Jesus, I said Lord give me Wisdom, and a pure Humble Heart. God's grace is sufficient, he will forgive, and we over come by the blood of the Lamb my desire to follow Jesus. Turn your life to Jesus, don't let time pass you by. He is calling today, in the path that Jesus has chosen for me and your family in the Garden of Eternity, Jesus, Redeemer of my life gives Eternity, God gave miracles. He has Healed many, even me from cancer, I thank him often. The Holy Ghost was with me, my desire to follow Jesus. One night I had a vision I saw Jesus above my bed with stretched out arms I felt his love around me; an angel appeared in my room it was like my mother was present. She was talking to me with love, it was like God's river that flowed though me like the Holy Ghost, while I was in the Hospital, Jesus sent Angels around my bed.

—*Louise Allen*

Spiritual Walk

Just walk in my shining star
my home is yours no matter where you are.
Here's my word, sing my song, clap your hands,
you now belong.

Oh, how I love you so
there's no limit on what you need to know.
There may come a day when you have to pay a price
just like my son- his name is Jesus Christ,
I truly love you, I really do and through it all
I will be with you.

You can come to me at any time,
the cross you bear is my sign.
Many times you will stumble, but get back on your feet
this is a mission you must complete.

Like a creeping ivy green and free,
you'll keep growing and eventually catch up to me.
One day we will meet,
spirit to spirit, love to love,
and that's when you'll know you've reached heaven above.

—*Anna L. Colmer*

Vision

  I do not notice the cold as
my knees press against the stone
  The faintest of breeze lifts a stray
hair to rise before my eyes for one
dazzling moment then falls again
  But I am not distracted for all
I can see before me is my Lord
  My hand rises slowly to guide the
razor sharpness while the heart pounds
  A brief flash from the candle light
glances off the instrument and blinds me
  I lay parted lips against liquid steel
Thus do I swear my allegiance
Thus does his cause become mine
  Required for my strength is
nothing beyond this faith in me
  I have become his vessel for duty honor and courage
  Nothing more could be as glorious
and nothing less would be worth my
life than to die in the knowledge of complete devotion.

—*Valery Maercklein*

Mediocrity

Mediocrity is the villain that takes away
My life as easily as a knife in my heart.
It gives me nothing but the hole to spill
My soul without retrieval and gives me no
Salve with which to heal. Mediocrity
Masters my talents rather than my talents
Mastering mediocrity. In the midst of my
Own work I reveal mine affliction, my
Disease of which no cure exists. My
Heart aches of the wound that will not
Kill my spirit but toys with my immunity,
Whispering of miracles that echo false
Hopes. I lie and suffer and continue to
Bleed into the ground which swallows my
Vitality to fertilize humility. I can
Little understand the seed I will enrich
In tomorrow's garden that I might be
Quieted in a peaceful respite, though
Never content with the predestined gash
Of mediocrity in my heart.
   —*Fawn R. Caparas*

Tree Of Life

I am a mighty oak, you are willow
My limbs are strong and hard,
   Your branches are small and light.
I stand tall and straight to all life winds;
   You bend to life winds.
Strong life winds may snap off my limbs,
   But your branches will bend and withstand.

You are a willow, I am an oak.
You have withstood life winds and have grown
   Stronger,
I have lost strong limbs to life winds and
   Have suffered.
You are a mighty willow, I am an oak.
   —*Sally Longfellow Sanderson*

I Am King Of The Grackles

I am king of the Grackles.
My majesty is well affirmed
As long as the seeds are
Spread and we are still alive.
I am king of the ecureuils
Who come each day to get their share.
They bring the wild - they teach the child -
My heart to beat.
Let this parliament of creatures
Begin its feast, defeat the cold,
And live again for another day.
Snow buntings, elegantly shy,
Circle around and do not mix.
A flash of blue crashes through
And a jay brakes in the wind.
Old Flick-Flick from years past
Stops to explore bark, but does not linger.
Our concern is joy that today
We have won.
   —*William T. Yarbro*

Lonely Night

Solitarily confined in the silent night,
My mind goes blank as I turn off the light.
I penetrate a world where I am free,
Where all my hopes, where all my dreams,
Set their sights on reality.
Darkness seizes my every thought,
Squeezing its grasp, making me hot.
I flip on the fan, unbar the clear glass,
Neutralizing darkness, as it loosens its grasp.
Cracking a smile as my thoughts dwindle down.
Dreams elevate as I lie on the ground.
Reflections of rays easing through the blinds,
Hoisting my lids as I come to find,
That my thoughts last night cleared my mind.
   —*Joe Wier*

"The Poker Poem"

Sitting at the poker table -
my mind not on the game.
Haven't won a hand in a while -
I'm the only one to blame

But there is a tiny bright spot
a ray of shining light
The cards are being dealt
but a beautiful female sight

Her move was slick and graceful
Her style was like a pro
I knew right then and there
She was someone to get to know

I lost a lot of money
on that fateful night
After seeing her it didn't seem to matter
much to my delight!
   —*Kenneth J. Bender*

True Mother

My mother is one who sticks by you threw thick and thin.
My mother can tell you what lies within.
My mother knows her child's cry,
when he's alone she knows why.
My mother shares her child's grief and
she knows her belief.
My mother is there when father is gone on,
she will help her child get alone.
My mother is one who knows the day
time and hour that you were born,
she knows because of her child born.
My mother cares for her child no matter how good or bad,
she will never let you be unhad.
My mother carries secrets in her heart that no one can restart.
My mother knows her child's cry she don't know why,
but she knows her child's cry.
   —*Estella Chism Conwell*

A Poem

The mist rises from the grassy mounds.
In the background a mountain rises,
it's snow-capped peaks grin at the deep blue sky.
The river flows lazily by,
and a turtle swims about.
It also grins at the sky.
A turtle grin of malicious evil.
It doesn't like blue.
   —*Christopher West*

Cold Mornings Rest

I awake before dawn while darkness stills the air
My neck clinches the damp drift riding up my spine
While early breeze gently sweeps away mornings moisture
Its cling is broken and once again everything is free
The only life in the forest is the sound of songbirds
Singing from the underside ceiling of natures world
    Where morning fog filters the sunbeam above
      Through the army of timbers standing guard
        Protecting her grounds
          As the moon clears way
            For the shine of a new day
The forest has a pride mightier than the strongest man
Her spirit shines brighter than any city could dream
And no one could question the strength of the forest
For once we start chopping we begin our eternal rest
—*Donald L. Zeller*

Just A Suspicion

Everything seems to have changed overnight.
My sleep patterns are different.
I sleep lightly now, instead of heavy and deep.
I'm tired, but cannot sleep.
Even my taste buds are different.
Things I couldn't seem to get enough of.
I now don't even like.
They've become repulsive to me.
My mood shifts without warning leaving me nauseous.
I'm happy, then angry, then I burst into tears.
I have my suspicions, but nothing concrete.
Am I sick, or just loosing my mind?
I feel lousy and giddy, furious and exhilarated,
exhausted and restless.
What more can I say? My suspicions have been confirmed.
I can only hope, that the next eight months won't go this way.
Though I'm sure in the end that, that sweet little bundle will
be worth everything it puts me through.
(But Please God.) "Don't let it be twins!"
—*Veronica Petersen*

Husband's Promise

When they put me in the ground I know my body will be alone.
My soul will travel to heaven and my mind will stay at home.
I'll be there through the thick and thin. I'll always be by
your side and I'll be standing waiting on you when you reach
the other side. You are the woman I love. You are my closest
friend. Your what makes my life so special. So our love will
never end. Whether I am standing here with you or your
standing alone in the wind there's one thing you can bank on,
our love will never end. So each day we wake up together and
not knowing what's ahead. When you are alone don't think of me
and be sad. Love and life go together. This is something that
we share. Death you do by yourself. But the love will always
be there.
—*Rodman Ewing*

Peace Forever More

When I awake in the morning and when I go to sleep at night,
I wish and hope for world peace with all my might.
Imagine that there were no wars, no racist comments being said,
Imagine that all people in Somalia could finally be fed.
This world could be peaceful, oh, what a world it could be,
If only every adult could look through a child's eyes and see.
Everyone would be joining hands, dancing and having fun,
Maybe, finally, they would understand what it is like to be one.
For so many years, this world has been broken apart,
Now that we're picking up the pieces, we've, made a good start.
We'll make this world better, better than it has ever been before,
It will be so good, that there will be world peace forever more!
Imagine, imagine that...
—*Jaimee Horowitz*

A Prayer For My Special Child

    A perfect bundle of joy,
     My special little boy
With hair of gold and eyes of blue.

   No time to sleep, he has to play
    Maybe rest some other day.
    Growing taller, getting older
     Can he get any bolder?

Where did he go? What did he do?
I wish I had that kind of energy too!

   The other children can't understand
  Why he continues to thrust out his hands
   Or why he acts out or needs to shout.

Oh, dear Lord, I pray we find a cure for Tourette's someday
  Or at least a way to help these kids fit in one day.

I love this child with all my heart even from the very start
  Trying each day to make him feel an important part
    To show the world he is just as smart.

   Please dear Lord, keep this child in your sight
   And show him the things that are good and right.
—*Sherry D. Tucker*

God's Work

I looked through the window yesterday morning
My what a most beautiful picture I saw
I thought I'd look out again this morning
and the same picture was not there at all

God had painted a entirely different picture
of a snow covered ground and trees
Oh it was just a beautiful as the one before
it made me stop and think, as I know he did it to please

Being handicapped, and living in a wheelchair
I wheel outside to get some fresh air
I can see Gods work where ever I go
So when I have a chance to get out I never say no

Yes God works for you both day and night
to make these beautiful scenes just right
the many stars that twinkle in the sky above
and the moon up there just watching two people who are in love

So as we travel Gods highway to heaven
Remember the scenes are all God's work and freely given
So when I pray each night, I want to be
prepared to meet my God when he calls for me
—*Gail Wilcox*

Untitled

We stepped into each other's life wearing designer rags of no name. Indigent lovers hoping to resupply our diminished capacity to care. We lived for too long in the alley-way of discarded human desire. Hand in hand we begged each other's contribution to our down-trodden state. We reignited our last . charred stubby piece of tobacco with one flame. Drank from our half filled, empty bottle of alcoholic despair. In the

unsheltered doorways of life we huddled; ready to conspire of the defeat of our enemy, friend; love turned to hate. Hoarse incoherent whispers, vows echoed off graffitied walls. Groping, touching the sexuality of our passions once lost. Poverty's tender rich kisses clearing our bloodshot eyes. As the lover sun awaited its mate's morning call, We staggered uncertainly over paths once crossed 'Til Death's release settled in our dreams and claimed us as its prize.
—*Charles F. Kaplan*

A Better World...How Nice It Would Be

How nice it would be if we could see peace and harmony in every
nation. How nice it would be it we could see the end of
sickness and starvation. How nice it would be if our world
would be preserved free of trash and pollution. How nice it
would be if we could unite peoples' talents and work toward a
constructive solution. How nice it would be if world leaders
would realize that evil deeds and destruction of human lives
and resources are contrary to the will of a Higher Power. How
nice it would be if the preservation of human life and the
energizing of human potential could be given top priority
rather than political power. How nice it would be if different
peoples would make a sincere effort to live in harmony with
each other. How nice it would be if we could eliminate crime,
violence and hatred for one another. How nice it would be if
all nations would direct their energies toward motivation of
the young and the old through improved education. What a
better world we would have, everlasting with insured salvation.

—*Rolando M. Pena*

Family Members

Members of a Family standing ever so tall,
Need to be there whenever we fall.
Sometimes they are wrong and sometimes they are right,
But strong family members shine ever so bright.
Just as a star reflecting glowing light,
Loving family members are there for
each other - be it day or night.
At times they fear things they may have done,
But more oft than not the battle is won.
Love, kindness, caring are words that prescribe,
The cure for what ails each member inside.
So, remember to keep your family
forever oh so close,
For their needs are so simple
Love, kindness, caring - a triple dose.

—*Dennis Michael Brown*

The Present

A heart is wrapped with a bow and a ribbon waiting to be given.
Needing to feel the warmth of being held.
The gift of love keeps it beating.
Giving it the strength to live.
Hoping to find someone to share all that it has to give.

It is a gift given with care.
Wondering if it will be opened.
Will someone dare strip it of the ribbon and leave it bare.
To be shattered and broken without someone to care.
Leaving the pieces to lay alone in the cold air.

The damage that is done can never be repaired.
Parts of it will always be scared.
Not willing to bond or try to adhere.
Safer apart not letting anyone near.
Refusing to be wrapped with ribbon to tight.
Leaving parts hidden in the darkness of night.

A heart is a gift given to you.
It is your choice what to do.

—*Larry Farley*

Perspectives

I am one person, one person in this city-
Neon lights flashing in this city, one city in this state.
This state of gold and treasures...
...One state within this country-
This country of freedom and opportunity.
-One country on this continent,
This continent of different views.
One continent on this Earth.

This Earth of royal blue and emerald green
One Earth in our universe - which is far from serene.
One universe in this galaxy that we know so little about...
...Outside the universe so unrestful
...Which holds our Earth of breathtaking colors in it's palm
...Upon which is the continent of a variation of opinions
And the country on this continent where freedom is yours to
    choose
With the glowing upbeat city where everyone is friends-
Is me, one person.... And if I, one person, can help to save
the rain forest, the ozone layer, the animals, and the People-
-Imagine what the forces of the galaxy can do.

—*Melissa Goldstein*

The Glassless Windows

Your blackened bones grasp twisting at the sky;
New snows sift up these broken shell scarred hills.
Mamiyev Kurgan's smoldering slopes lie stilled.
Cold armor crouches as a living thing,
For word again to sound war's clarion ring.

Black, blazing red, and white are all I see;
A thousand glassless windows gaze at me.
Burning eyes in a dying city's frown,
They know we've come once more on this sad day,
To pierce their crumbling shields of bricks and clay.

Old Stalingrad, what nameless monster hides
Beneath your rubbled streets and factory sites?
Hard by the frozen Volga's wind swept banks,
What new laments shall these pained ruins sing,
While young men spend their final offering?

Surrender to my legions pressing power!
Give way to iron panzers lightning thrust!
For only you delay Reich's finest hour;
And damn us all with crushing ice and fire,
As Dustchland yields in this great funeral pyre!

—*Peter F. Round*

To My Grandmother: I Love You

Ten children in all five boys and five girls
Nine children are left here in this world

With tender love and strong hands
    of each she was proud
She raised each one the best she knew how

Grandchildren they gave her
    great-grandchildren too
She was loved by each one more than she knew

Now a small lace handkerchief,
    pink Bible and Cross
She holds in her frail little hands

Ceramic rabbit, fluffy chicken
    red heart shaped trinket box
George Straite poster above her head

Amazing Grace, Old Rugged Cross
    "How Great Thou Art" was played
There she lies in peace and beauty
    no more in torment or pain

Mother, wife, grandmother and great
Pauline Myrtle Ehrhart was my grandmother's name.

—*Stephanie Harrison*

My World Of Grey

The emotions love and happiness
no longer fill my heart.
My hopes and dreams are so far apart.
My skies are black in this world of grey.
Pushing love and romance out of my way,
I harden my heart against caring, sweet soles
because hurting and grieving can take its toll.
I'd rather be lonely and live all alone
than go through the pain of losing one's own.

—*Mandy Hammon*

Strength

Strength is sometimes hard to find there are days I feel I can
no longer try how I wish I would quit wasting so much time. I
have a dream beneath my heart it's not like anyone else's. I
wish so much for happiness I know I am still young but what's
going to become of me If I keep letting time pass. So many
days I have wasted on being sad. But if I still believe the
dream beneath my heart there will be a day when I am no longer
sad. I'll be as strong as a mountain and as deep as a sky.
There's going to be a day when I'll no longer cry.

—*Barby York*

To The Violent Earth!

Peace for the world, peace for all the nations.
No more holocaust, no more wars.
Don't keep silence as the unknown soldiers!
Put on the Statute Book every nations,
Illegal the holocaust, illegal the wars.

Peace for the world, peace for all the nations,
Under the guise of religion don't massacre,
With bloodshed brothers, never be peace.
Put on the Statute Book every nations.
The name of Human Rights, live or die.

Peace for the world, peace for all the nations.
Serbs, Croats and Muslims go for the peace!
Only peace can give you the affection.
Put on the Statute Book every nations.
The name of God, no more killing fields.

Peace for the world, peace for all the nations.
Great Power politics sign an agreement,
Full liberty everywhere without wars.
Put on the Statute Book every nations,
Dove and olive-branch symbol for the peace.

—*Laszlo Szuromi*

The Ballad Of "Big John"

Dedicated to Louise S. Byrd, my good friend.
Not too long ago, it happened one day. An exciting event in a
very unusual way. Outside on the hill, in a building so fine.
Sat Blue Bonnet, a very good friend of mine. With her Sears
and Roebuck and her half-moon on the door, what happens next
we just can't ignore. She had very important business to do that
just couldn't wait. But what happened next put her in a very
nervous state. She started out the door, when suddenly the
floor began to shake and she just knew that it was about to
break. She prayed and she prayed and said "please save my soul
and keep me from falling down deep into that great big hole."
All of a sudden there came a big blast! And then she knew that
she had fallen at last. They called the wrecker service,
"Skip's" was his name. Pulling damsels in distress out of
toilet-holes surely was his game. Don't go to the toilet if
you value your life. Look forward to trouble and a whole lot a
strife. The tale of "Big John" will go through the ages. And
be recorded on the Sears and Roebuck pages.

—*Cynthia R. Stassin*

My Little Boy

What is a little boy made of?
No, not snails or puppy-dog tails
But mischief and sweetness, naughtiness and goodness,
Climbing trees and catching bugs, tired out and lying on rugs,
Spilling milk and soda pop, hurry, Ma, get the mop!
Sometimes he's so very wild,
I tear my hair, oh, what a child!
He makes me boil when he is bad,
But then he's good and I forget I'm mad.
When I look at him, I enjoy his smile,
And then I think that all the while
He's really good, good as gold. I guess it's I who's
getting old.
Oh, let him keep on playing tricks,
And climbing trees, and breaking sticks,
Let him fight with other kids,
They make up opening cookie lids.
I love him so, this little guy,
So filled with courage, yet so shy.
A better person I will be, for loving him and his loving me.

—*Mary Oshrin*

It Just Happened Again. . .

I fell for another one.
　No, not the last one,
　　or the previous one,
　　　but another one.

A typical, terminally juvenile man,
　who showed some interest in me
　　and now has seen fit to move on.

I should have seen it coming
　but I never do.
I always say "It won't happen again—"
　but it does.
Their knives cut deep to the quick:
　and I alone am left to stop the bleeding.

O for the courage to soothe my shattered soul:
　How I long for the day
　　when they won't be able to hurt me anymore,
　　　and they won't be able to use me anymore,
　　　　and my heart won't cry out for them anymore.

The flash, the noise, the pain, the memories, the terror...
　The serenity.

—*Margarite Bettley*

No One Loves Me

No one seems to love me, no one really cares.
No one ever sees me cry, or how my heart just tears.

No one even knows me, or listens to what I say.
They only think of themselves, to me, "Please go away."

If they only knew how I felt, how I feel inside.
But little do I have that chance, to me they always lie.

Young I am, but just like you. Always doubted here.
They don't think that I exist. If they knew, would I be dear?

In my life, I have no choice. This has been stripped away.
Dependent I am on only you, here in emptiness I lay.

For today I shall leave this earth, never to return.
My mother chose to abort, Why? I shall never learn.

—*James Proffitt*

Somewhere Out There

Somewhere out there, there is a little baby crying.
No one to care for her.
Somewhere out there, a mother pines her loss.
Her only child to a drive-by-shooting.
Somewhere out there, a boyfriend contemplates suicide.
His girlfriend was killed by a rival gang, because of him.
They were all innocent.
Violence never solves anything.
Why can't people see?
The pain, the agony, the loss.
How bad will it get before we kill ourselves off?
In a matter of one lifetime, we learned how to create life.
We also learned how to destroy ourselves.
If this continues, who will be the next generation?
The people who survive the savage gang wars!
Why can't we all just get along?

—*Amy Elias*

O Lawdy Mercy How Time Has Changed

Time sure has changed since I was a young pup
No one was on dope perhaps a few grown-ups

You were free to walk streets night or day
Oh what a joy then to go out doors and play
Who is to blame for all this worry and fear
I say it starts at home Dad Mom do you hear?

Take a small peach tree let it grow all alone
Want mount to a hill of beans when its grown

Plant that same twig prune watch night and day
It will bare good for many years they say

I believe turmoil started back in hippy days
Long hair and beard pony-tail ragged pants rowdy ways

I shall never forget seeing the first hippy Lord what is that
Should I offer that a chew tobacco or tip my hat

—*John Gilbert Flowers*

Walk With Me

Walk with me to the end of the road.
No, please a little bit further
to the age five and hold my hand.
Please walk with me to the age of ten
and hold my hand the way it's never been held before.
Walk with me with the hand you hold to the age of twelve
where the sun kisses my face.
Walk with me through my teen years to the age of thirteen
and let me be loved and kissed.
Walk with me to the end
of the road and maybe a little
bit further.

—*Jillian Hathaway*

Untitled

The scent of yesterday in the air,
No time machine could bring you back.
Your dandelion smile
Is frozen.
I screamed at the spirit hovering above me,
And you left your salty laugh on my pillow.
Still you refuse to speak!
Leave your plastic mask behind
While you sleep in velvet tranquility.
I'll visit you tomorrow,
When I want to be alone.
Just remind me not to cry
  For my eyes seem to forget.

—*Lisa A. Clayton*

Untitled

The moving hand has stood still
Nor writ nor moved on
Nor the mind expressed thoughts
That have thronged it through the years
No sweet blossom of the early spring
Has triggered melodies from the heart
Nor brought rapturous songs to the lips
No stark nakedness of the winter months
Has brought tears of woe to the eye
Nor saddened the heart with memories of yester-year

And then, a presence is felt
That fills my being with harmony
A vibration flows through my soul
As I become one with my self
My heart sings with joy
As tears well through my eyes
Lightness fills every step
My fingers quiver
And my hand moves
To write.

—*Harshi Syal*

Untitled

One day my fears will come to pass,
Not that it will last but they will be in the past.
My tears won't pass but until,
They are in the past they might as well last.
My dream is a forbidden one,
That should not come to pass.
Why I had a dream,
Is a question I ask myself.
A question for no one to answer,
Not anyone to give a reply.
So I'll go on dreaming,
And trying to answer my question
But for now I'll let it pass on by.

—*Melissa White*

Animals

An eagle screaming through the mountains wild and free
Nothing can stop him not even me
Oh where, Oh where does he go?
Above the mountains above the snow
On top of the mountains where he roams
On top of the mountains to his great home.

Cheetahs chasing herds of gazelle
Cheetahs can catch them they run so well
Cheetahs run fast as lightening
Even though they may look frightening
Under their jaws of steel
They're really full of pride and zeal.

Cheetahs slyly sneak upon the grassy ground
While eagles fly and swoop around
Cheetahs and eagles both catch prey
But each one has their own way
Cheetahs and eagles are my favorite animals as you can see
And you know why? Because they're free.

—*Amber Wegner*

Untitled

Here I am alone again
Nothing in my heart but sorrow
Knowing that we are apart
Tomorrow the distance will be the same
But tomorrow I will call your name
Though the distance does not shorten
We have tomorrow to ease our sorrow
We have our hopes and dreams
We have tomorrow
We may not have each other right now
But at least we have tomorrow
Tomorrow we share our lives
Tomorrow we will have left yesterday behind
Thoughts of joy fill my mind
When I think of our tomorrow
Tomorrow is our future together
Even though we can't hold each other
Remember there will always be tomorrow
To share our lives, our dreams, our hopes
We will always have tomorrow.

—*Duncan McIlwain*

Apart

We stand thousands of miles apart,
Nothing shared but our heavy hearts,
The time I spend thinking of you,
Drives me insane like a mad, wild zoo,
Shedding cold desperate tears,
Straining through the hardworking years,
All you feed me are ugly lies,
Why is it me that you despise,
All I have is memories of the past,
Hoping these pictures will always last,
I wish you were here with me,
I would be happy, happy as can be,
So why do you leave me here in despair,
Why don't you return and our love we'll repair.

—*Giang Hong*

Backwards Ho

Kind friends took me back to the homesite of my childhood days now altered in many many ways. Took me back to the valley home
where I was raised back to the pasture lands where my Father's cattle had grazed back to the hay meadows where we had cut tons of sweet smelling alfalfa hay. Never thinking that some day I might return old, blind and gray. Back to the many trails that we had trod green grass now covers them in the sod. Back to the river that always ran a stream, the sandy bottom is now all that can be seen. Back to see the rock buildings that my Father had built, nothing remains but rock rubble and silt. There were no trees to protect the old home site, now three rows of cedars give shelter day and night. Back to see a little frame house where Bertha and I started our married life not a board remains where 66 years ago we came as man and wife. Men and horses were the main energy source on the old home place now REA wires bring energy in from another base. The rock bluffs across the river south that could always be seen are now hidden by many trees that are tall, thick and green.

—*Leslie Linville*

September Love

How cruel that my life should touch yours now;
now that it is too late for me to give
you all the joy you crave. Upon my mouth
I taste your sweetness and my fingers feel
the smoothness of your skin, your warmth, your power,
the richness that is you. Oh, what a wealth
of wonder and of joy you bring to me!
What can I give? Too late, too late! I cry.
Too late to give the first, shy halting kiss,
the first embrace, the eager blush of youth,
too late for frightened wonder. Yet within -
the blood still and hot surging through the veins
strains as before. The yearning and the need
are stronger yet, and deep within me moves
a hunger that is reaching out for you.
Is it too late to give all that I am,
all that I know and feel? Not so!
Too late perhaps for first love's breathless joy.
What loss! A deeper love is mine.

—*Jean H. Stem*

Beautiful October

Look! At the hill tops with lofty height.
October shares autumn colors bright.
Watch! Migration of birds in flight
They are a beautiful sight.

The Great Creator has rushed October
In with golden splendor.
There is an enchantment with
October, that makes the earth sing.

Beautiful October begins in August
And ends in November.
Little folks like October's ending
With yellow leaves blending.
You see! It is halloween
They can trick and treat.
I saw a butterfly alight a golden rod
Underneath a fallen leaf lay on top
The sod.
God has all the earth on a string.
Autumn colors are blended, the
Green and red among the gold.

—*Evelyn Wrobel*

The Wind And The Dream

The wind is an element of nature, defined as a natural movement of air of any velocity, size or shape, without impediments. Sometimes warm, cold, gentle or brisk, its performances unlimited throughout the universe.

The wind is normally and naturally accepted, and it is cultural and social. The wind intersperses ... itself "with all" .... nature and its beings, "among all" ... the inhabitants of the earth, sea and sky, "for all" to reap the benefits of its pollination.

I still believe in the dream you see, that Dr. King had for you and me. When life becomes as the wind...with no preference to origin. Impartial and disperses for one humanity. In my thoughts I chose the wind. The dream unfold and the wind caress, together...forever and colorless.

—*Rose E. Standifer*

Out West

Miles and miles winding west our roads pass through valleys
Of beautiful cropland.
Miles and miles winding west our roads pass over mountains
High, capped with snow.
Miles and miles winding west our roads pass through vast
Prairies.
Miles and miles winding west our roads pass through
Deserts wild and lonely.
In time by following these roads winding west we come to
The mighty pacific ocean.
This vast expanse of course is aptly named Out West.
West is many things to many people, people of all race and
Nationality.
Vast ranches fill our west, vast farms dot the landscape.
It took men and women of courage bold to tame our vast expanse
Called Out West.
God in his wisdom knew best when he created our beautiful land
Called Out West.
—*Marian Jordon*

Brotherhood

We are all one in kind, brothers in need
of bread and love. All races, with one blood,
Plant in good earth the universal seed
that knows no boundaries. The tender bud
becomes the rose in any foreign sod.
And all creation bears the single mark
of beauty that the artistry of God
Alone can give, breathing the divine spark
that kindles life, as from a central fire.
Parent of all and friend of every creed
his first command to make Him our desire
and be assured that He will meet our need.
Teach us our oneness, God! Give us the key
to unity and peace, that man with man
may know his common kind and better see
the wonder and the wideness of his clan.
—*Frank Curtis Williams*

Only A Lifetime

How silence speaks louder than words,
Of dreams broken,
And prayers never heard.
Inside my heart,
The silence reigns.
And never again - my soul will sing,
I get tired of hurting,
And tired of pain,
Nothing last forever - who's to blame?
And so it's been,
The time doesn't chime,
I'll go on hurting - it's only a lifetime.
—*April Anderson Faulkner*

A Special Man

I know a man that has a special way
Of knowing just when
Someone need's a lift that day
He has a twinkle in his eyes
And cheery little smile
It gives you a lift, and hope for the day
Without any cost from you or me
He gives encouragement when everything seems dark,
And then goes about his way
You might say, why is he so special?
And I will simply say.
He's my husband and my friend
And means this world to me
I love you dear
—*Nancy Baker*

Emotions

Cherish is a state of mind
Of emotion and caring for two of a kind
Love is a turning point in one's eye
When a heart grows fond of one's space and sky

Can we as people grow strong
And put these values where they belong
Or do we continue to cause death and war
The reasons are not so important to do it for

If caring for another means saving
Then toward this goal we should be slaving
Not seeing one to one but one for all
This is why all nations will fall

To strive for the common good
Is what must be understood
Do we continue to rape the land
Until nowhere is there a place to stand

The path we tread leaves a world that cries
Tears of acid rain that fall from choking skies
Keep all that I say in memory with this rhyme
To put all in perspective now is the time
—*John J. Aupperlee*

Old House

Old house, full many dreams you've known
of joys and sorrows, yet stand now stark
Lifting hollow eyes to the gracious dark
like a time-tossed nest, fledglings flown.
Strong, loving hands fashioned thee
A noble structure, nor lived to see
Each planted tree (whose growth now locks
decay within) attain maturity.
Child of his child has lived to call
You blessed. What was built so surely strong
Has sheltered sorrow, rejoiced with song,
Has stood like a firm arm over all.
Though famous works boast lofty dome
And rich embellishment, your bid for fame
Comes from harboring a humble claim
For being what you are—a home.
Old house, you have a listening piety
As you stand grave and lone. It seems you have
Of dreams amassed so great a store...
   Need nothing more
To give decay a quiet dignity.
—*Elsa Gantz*

Memories On Growing Old

Looking back on eighty years
of lots of fun, though mixed with tears,
it seems the things that I recall
are not the things I should at all.

They're not the joy of running feet
through a meadow, smelling sweet,
or snuggling close in mothers arms,
or thrilling to a girl friends charms.

They're times that brought me fear or pain,
when summer sunshine turned to rain,
but through it all I have survived
and I'm so glad I'm still alive.
—*B. Carmichael*

Summertime

Summer, time of relaxation...

Childhood memories
   of luscious berries, games in the park,
   vacations in the pine country.

Later on
   swimming in the cold surf of the North Sea,
   with it's tall waves,
   and blindingly white beaches

In "Leisure World" itself
   the joy of seeing the migratory birds' return,
   watching the courtship of doves,
   being witness to the hatching
   of their eggs on my balcony.

Somehow, in spite of the
   evenly beautiful California weather,
   there is a feeling of nostalgia
   for the big cities' sidewalk cafes,
   distinctive clothes, so different
   from the winter gear...and even the electric storms
   with their feeling of awesome beauty
      —*Gisele Lauffer*

Hiroshima Remembrance

In a flash the slow irreplaceable weave
of millennia unravels.

Fundamentalists in underground shelters pray
for raptured deliverance.

Their faith, unswerving, lifts them up from the holocaust
to hover miraculously in heaven

while the world below scorches.
Kafka's metamorphosis, a prophecy of sorts:

cockroaches, suddenly now graced, move up the ladder
while other earthbound creatures, disbelieving, free-fall

from their kingdoms, classes, families, and phyla
into radiated oblivion. I believe

a mere one hundred Hiroshimas can cancel all
futures, all pasts.
      —*Caroline G. Banks*

What Was That Sound?

Lying here alone, in the mute darkness
Of my bedroom, the snort-like explosion of air
Transports me backwards in time to the
Sleeping room, with a circular window
High in its east wall, which was my chosen retreat
When I was four years old, sixteen years into
The Twentieth Century, and General Pershing directed
Forces in pursuit of Pancho Villa in Mexico and
My beloved "48 States" joined England in its
Conflict with Germany, the following April,
And I had, only a few days before, discovered that
Our kitchen wall-calendar, featuring pictures of
Thickly robed people from the Bible, presented
Them to my awed gaze as standing erect and
Threatening, even when the calendar was removed
From the wall and lowered to lie on its back
On the cool, slick, linoleumed floor.
Now, what was that sound?
      —*Alvin L. Tafel*

A Revelation

Guilty,
Of riding the wrong wave length
For a deep blue stability.
Sometimes moving away from this world.

The kingdom,
With a singular member.
He has ruled and followed himself,
In a tranquility base of a higher world.

For the end
I wished to have all of something.
And none of any other.
These could not be separated in one world.
      —*Douglas Hartman*

Memories Of The Old Country School

My thoughts go back to memories,
Of the good time in our old country school;
Where we learned readin', writin' and 'rithmetic,
And we lived by the Golden Rule.

Each morn began at nine o'clock,
And promptly the bell was rung;
We pledged allegiance to our flag,
And patriotic selections were sung.

Our teacher was our good instructor,
She was janitor, fireman, as well;
She taught us all about the "Little Red Hen,"
Yes, our country, and how to spell.

And there were no conveniences,
Hot lunches— they were never heard;
The water came from an outside pump,
Newer methods had never occurred.

After the short nine months were completed,
We bade farewell to friends we had made;
I'll always remember the one room schools,
I wish they could have stayed.
      —*Lillian Thune*

Untitled

As the early morning sun begins to rise I still see the embers of the last midnight star. The sky is painted with summer hues of brilliant reds and glimmering yellows. The moon closes its eyes and drifts into the memory of the night. Fragrant flowers awaken with a kiss from the dew. Trees stretch their arms toward the sky to welcome the dawn. Birds sing their sweetest song in anticipation of a brand new day. I, too, shall greet this day with gladness for it truly is a day that God has made.

No one could ever paint such an artistic splendor, no one could ever see this day as I do. When all my earthly possessions have lost all meaning, I have only to reflect on my memories of this day, to recall the beautiful sunrise, to smell the fragrant flowers, to hear the sweet melody of the birds. Yes it will be forever etched in my soul. For what God has given —no one can take away.
      —*Bonnie B. Carr*

Eternity

Eternity is here
right within this sphere of familiar earth
that I have known.
I wonder why one's soul must die
before it knows that it is home.
      —*Mary Buckley*

The Daughter Of God

From the seven wings, and prayers
Of the un known came into the world,
The daughter of God unknown to the Pope,
Angels, and the World. God's daughter grew up,
Had a family of her own.
In the light of the morning, God spoke to her,
Telling her, He was proud of his beloveth daughter.
In a beautiful dream, she saw God as a man.
God told her, she would be the First Princess,
To enter golden gates.
Carmella, would sit in a white marble chair, next to God.
And earth will see never ending Justice and Peace.
Believeth in these holy words, of truth.
And the will of God to protect His Daughter Amen.
—*Catherine Inserra*

Just Say Yes To Success

Let's give our youth more than No's to follow
Offer them something to brighten their tomorrow
Just say yes
To success and the American dream
Be it music, medicine or an olympic team
Pursue happiness as you find your niche
Continue on focus without a hitch
The sky is not the limit as you will see
Go higher than the stars if you choose to be
Climb the yes ladder as you give service to all
And yes to the positives that won't let you fall
Board the success train that runs on little rest
Work hard, strive for excellence as you stand the test
For you'll know when you reach it you gave it your best
—*Liane Harris*

A Light In The Dark

A shot of light through the dark,
Often leaves a lasting mark.
Blinding those who walk into its path,
While lighting the way in its aftermath.
He doesn't care if he does them harm,
Those who are attracted to his brilliant charm.
The only way he can hide his pain and fear,
Is to, in solitude, shed a lonesome tear.
He has a hunger for something more,
Than a one night stand, and run out the door.
He searches and searches for that one little thing,
That will ease his heart and let him sing.
He knows that his lifestyle cannot last,
Because the light that burns brightest burns too fast.
—*Oscar P. Wager*

Sunshine And Shadows

A part of heaven fell on earth
And changed into a flower.
Its pinkish blooms against the
Green brought happiness to
Finders;
Its fragrance filled ones
feelings tight.
Who dares then say that such
A thing of poison could be
Built,
And leave a doubt forever
in one's mind.
—*Annelyn Kayson*

Residue

Remember when we lived so happily?
  Oh so happily, yes so happily.
And now we sit here, oh so silently,
  With nothing to do, nothing to say,
Like two lonely strangers in each others' way.

It seems like only yesterday,
  And yet, it seems so far away.
What took so long, went so fast,
  I thought you and I would always last.

Oh, you and me and baby make three,
  At least, that's the way I thought it would be.
I never thought we'd grow so far apart,
  But we did, and now there's two broken hearts.

Well, you no longer believe in me,
  So, I guess it's time for me to be leaving you.
Remember when we lived so happily?
  So happily, oh so happily.

Now, such misery, oh misery,
  Such misery.
—*John R. Fowler*

Sunday Afternoon...Memorial Day Weekend

I travelled to city canyons
On a sunny, windswept day,
I went on my exploration
To keep loneliness at bay;
But when I reached my destination
I found no one was there,
The streets as empty of connection
As my heart and soul were bare;
So I fled home to my garden
Filled with friendly faces there,
And in the flowers' perfumed splendor
Consolation blossomed fair;
Thus my heart bloomed fresh with gladness,
And my soul grew new resolve,
As I realized deep within me
That prayer's answer would evolve.
—*Mimi Premo Fleming*

Works Of Art

"The greatest masterpieces," says Haskins, "were only pigments
  On an artist's palette."
The greatest sculptures, let me add, were only rock
  Sans the sculptor's chisel and mallet.

The greatest poems, you'll agree, were only figments
  Of a poet's fanciful mind.
The greatest cathedrals, in essence, were only visions
  An architect had designed.

Such notable works of art are created
  By earthly mortals who adeptly ply
Great talents of transferring thought,
  As well as superlative skill of hand and eye.
—*Veloye A. Koenigsberg*

Distant Simplicity

Gentle breezes whispering softly in my ear,
Singing melodies of sweet remembrances,
Of days gone by when life was simple;
Simplicity so profound,
It is but a faint and distant memory,
Never to exist again.
—*James Haefner*

North End Butcher Shop

The butcher keeps offal, tripe and kidneys
on display behind the counter
like trophies,
and customers stand with dollar bills
in their hands.
I remember the day
someone whispered behind me
in eighth grade English.
Papers were folded into secret shapes
and passed along a chain of hands
until they were taken
and pinned on a board
for everyone to see my name.

—*David Harbilas*

Mother's Day Thoughts

Today, a yellow rose I placed
On the grave where my mother lay.
Tomorrow is Mother's Day
And how my heart does ache
For the absent one this special day.
No longer here, to here the words
"I love you Mother," and thoughts do wander
Of the good and bad times we shared
As she molded and shaped me
And tried my life to prepare
To be a good and loving wife and mother.
How many times in everyday life
Do thoughts wander and the mind play tricks-
She's not really gone- she's really here
As I find myself thinking-
Oh, she would have loved this great grandson of hers;
And the songs that she wrote and she sang
"Yes, you're mommie's my baby again."
As I placed that one yellow rose;
One perfect rose for a Mother gone on.

—*Ruth E. Armbrust*

Almost A Poem/Seasons To Roam

   Summer gallops in lackadaisical and lyrical
   On the shiniest red filly — almost empirical
   She brushes by and begs to be idolized and adored
She has mystical eyes and a magical tail of summer silk
  So unusual, once touched you never forget its ilk.

   Fall comes in on a mottled brown horse
   Past fallen leaves and barren trees
     Its wipsy tail is bare and frail
   Its mournful tune echoes its own doom
 I anticipate this season, totally without reason

  Winter rushes in on a grayish white mare
 Looking for its children in a time of despair
  It rears its back with a proud demeanor
  Aware it's watched by an envious gleaner
   Winter is looong, going very strong

  Ah, but spring prances in on a gentle day
  An unbridled pony full of energy at bay
   It lusts for companionship and color
   The sweet winds tell of budding beauty
  And birds chirp cacophonilly in duty

—*Lydia Montgomery*

Untitled

Clarence Murray
on the verge of death
   went to the edge of life and met
   death
and yelled I'm not gonna die I'm not gonna die just like that
   but I always knew
he was a strong man
   but what I always wanted to find out was
how he looked it in the eye
DEATH

—*Laurie Adams*

Untitled

We here in my company are faking success.
On the verge of selling for a large lump sum
to a company ten times as big as mine
Before they discover how anxious I am
to be rid of the monthly outgo and put a solid
nest egg in the bank and just get a part-time
salaried job to augment the aggregate sum's interest.
Little do they know how I'm hiding my anxiety
behind a bold indifference.
But as I wait for the call confirming their offer
I remember forty years of running my company,
And look forward in glee to running only myself!

—*Ralph S. Marks*

Four Steps Into The Abyss

  Look, my thoughts fall tired through my fingers, trip
on their own obscurity, fall without sound in the pen,
where ink creates them, adopting them this way.

  Everything could be reduced to a flap of a wing.

  The thought begins. Its essence implodes into the many arms
demanding something to hold, the many fingers insisting on
something to grab.

  When all resemblances prove themselves inevitable, there's a
great yearning to forget; ask the earth why it forgets its
grass every winter.

—*Radu Hotinceanu*

Best Gift

Bells jingle and a "Ho! Ho!" begins to fade,
  on this cold wintery night.
Hopes of a visit was paid,
  "were those reindeers in flight?"

Creeping downstairs early christmas day,
  to peek under the tree.
Eyes open wide as to say,
  "Gifts! Could one be for me?"

Lights blinking and shining bright,
  as little boys and girls fill with joy.
Wishing at such a wondrous sight,
  "That gift? Could be a toy?"

Ribbons, bows and paper now cover the floor,
  After little hands toiled with care.
All gifts given and a feeling of one more,
  "The best gift is the love all share!"

—*Howard B. Brown*

One Life

O, sweet breath of life I take
On this, the day of birth.
Soul and mind are joined as one
in search of what it's worth.

Life is composed of a thousand scores,
of visions, quests and schemes.
And to strive with ardent desire
brings reward of achieving those dreams.

Mistakes were made, mishaps took place,
looking back on the road I traveled.
Tears of loneliness choked my nights
as dreams became unraveled.

But friends and laughter have filled my days.
With hard work, the years have flown.
And in the twilight of my life
the tapestry now is sewn.

For as I begin my time of rest,
the lone flute comes to my ear.
Sweet and low, on the still, night air...
Peace, my soul will hear.
—*Julie Lynn Clason*

Reflections On Emotions Once Felt

I was reflecting on emotions
once felt-

I quickly read the words
that were once written on the pages,
as if time would never alter their strength.

I glanced at the notations
embossed at the bottom
of the writings on the pages, time spent.

I nearly noticed their significance,
marks of memories wanting
to be kept at that time.

I pieced together titles and endings,
triggering tiny flickers
fragments of feelings once had,
once mine.

I now discard those feelings,
mere words upon the pages
of the writer who has managed to move on.
—*Ann Marie Bryan*

"What Is A Hug"

It's that first embrace as your mother holds you in her arms!
Once you have known to receive a hug and you don't get one it hurts!
For a hug heals a hurt!
A hug can heal a hurt in your heart.
A hug and an embrace from someone tells you they love you.
A hug can be a forgiving embrace.
A hug as someone holds you can speak louder than the words spoken I love you.
A hug can say to a friend lets be friends again.
A hug is a human expression of many loves in life.
—*Alice Agostini*

One Cold Night

One cold night when the mist crept over the moon
One cold night when the spirits scream BOO!
When the haunted house roars up in laughter
Candy pumpkins and ghosts never come after
It's all, all so scary,
When we shriek in such fright,
ALL TONIGHT!
Into the creepy house we go, looking at the gruesome corpse
Running away, we really should go
But NO!
We walked in the back and what should we see,
But a repulsively scary bandaged zombie!
The leaves crackled creepily behind us
And we said
Run away, far away
And never come back here again!
—*Candice Cihocki*

My Hands

The Lord's gift to me of my hands is most certainly a treasured
one. My hands may not be attractive, but they are functional &
talented. Think of all the gifts I can give others with the
use of my hands.

I can grow fruits & vegetables with my green thumb,
then prepare them so my family may have fresh, healthy food
eat. I can instruct my children in good table manners
by setting good example with the use of my hands.
A firm hand can protect a toddler from a busy street.
A gentle touch of the hand can comfort a hurting child.
I can teach my son to write his name.
With thankful hands I can teach my children to pray.

With staccatos & arpeggios I can release my feelings
through my fingertips, creating sweet-sounding music.
I can mend clothes & stitch beautiful tapestries.
I can express myself in my writings.

My hands are not pretty, but through God's love,
they are a work of art.
Thank you, Lord, for giving me my hands.
—*Christie Lee Shook*

My Life Of Pain

There were two things I wanted the most
One to be the very best of wives. To
raise great children who would make us proud.
To love each other no matter what
Too serve our Master while here on this earth.
And hopefully make our home really God's church.
I know my Lord is proud of me Because he knows
how hard, I tried, you see!

and death has taken my only Son, from me
What new sadness does life hold in store..
I don't know if I can take much more.
—*Patricia A. Bacon*

Easter Poem

As dawn was breaking on the morn,
I walked the path many feet had worn.
As I neared the tomb where my savior lay,
I saw the stone was rolled away.

My heart was filled with grief and despair,
As I saw my savior no longer lay there.
Two heavenly angels did then appear,
And spoke, "He is risen, have no fear".

As I listened, heavenly voices sing
For my Jesus is the King of Kings.
—*Almeda P. Karsko*

"The Children Of The Forest"

The bulldozers came to the forest as the trees looked on,
One tree of wisdom, old and grey, spoke of the vigorous pain.
He says they all watched in complete vain;
His heart broke as did theirs, for they felt it wasn't fair.

As they sat there, looking on,
The monsters, big and yellow, broke loose at dawn.
The bees buzzed away as the children of the forest ran;
But the trees could not run from the hideous yellow band.

The children of the forest now heard the screams of those
   which remained.
Later, they went to look, only to see a horrid sight.
Still they feel the pain of that night,
Now their beloved home has been named.

Today the place where many trees stood tall,
is now called City Hall.
   —*Tracy Roberts*

Untitled

Feelings.
One word can mean so much.
From the emotions deep down inside,
to the way your body feels to my touch.

Feeling of happiness
to feelings of depression.
A word that can take you higher
or send you into regression.

A word that can bring people closer together
or tear them apart.
No matter mental or physical,
feelings never leave your heart.

One single word.
It can bring you joy or fear.
It can create laughter
and it can cause tears.

One word with so much power,
at first it seemed so little.
It is just another part
of life's big riddle.
   —*Paul Marshall*

Polly

The first sight of her, descending the stairs, I thought 'tis
only a trance, dressed all in white and a vision of light, an
effusion of sacred elegance. Though I knew not her name, nor
did ever see, this woman who now owned my life, but I did then
feel and knew in my soul, this vision I'd soon make my wife.

We strolled hand in hand through the park that night, an
Island of beautiful green, I gazed in her eyes, held her face
in my hands and told her that I'd never seen, such a lovely
sight, Oh Dear God, that haunting voice so soft and light, My
heart beat so fast, words caught in my throat, life began
anew that night.

By the Canal we laid, as the canoes floated by, the moon
high in the sky, a great oak divided the moon, and we fell
in love, she and I. Our souls infused, we melted
together and as one forever are one, the memories still new
and e'er will stay as long as the earth has a sun.
   —*Francis Mc Carthy*

My Dreams

   Only in my dreams you could love me,
only in my dreams you could care.
I always thought my dreams would come true.
But - when I was thinking that I was dreaming
too! I always thought I could live without
you. Dream all day and all night through.
When I saw how cruel you acted towards
me. You really helped me to see these
things through. When you showed me
how much you really loved me.
I knew your love was forbidden and never true.
   But you see my friend I could never
stop loving you, although you've made
my heart break in two.
For I know I could never stop caring,
for my love for you is so strong,
   Although I know one day I will see
you again.
In my dreams my heart will never mend.
   —*Jolene Wilemon*

Windfall inheritance

The ephemeral day is all our treasure—
Only now does the wild wind blow;
Only now the clean cloud-laundry pile up white in the sky.
Only now the lilacs tumble their scented beards upon the breeze.
Paupers indeed if all our thoughts are of yesterday or tomorrow,
We beggars ourselves, squandering fortunes freely enfeoffed upon
   us.

I have lived in pain, and I know that today's pain is bearable,
Couched as it is in terms of robins and violets.
It is yesterday's and tomorrow's woes which crush us.
You are free to disagree, it's your concern.
But I will gorge myself upon today,
Served up upon the silver air of spring.
I will revel in the wilderness of green untrammeled
No matter how many houses hem it in.
I will sate myself with fire of tulips,
Adorn myself with diamonds in eyes that behold love.
I will share your tears and make you laugh today, Riches beyond
Riches beyond compare!
And if tomorrow's hot breath or yesterday's chill fingers shall
   touch me,
I shall give them a piece of today to pay their bills.
   —*Susanne Coalson Donoghue*

What I Have Seen

I have seen, where others have been; I did walk, the steps of
other men. I have witnessed, evil at hand; I'll always follow
the Lord, wherever I can. I once had birds, dance for me; they
showed me life, was simple and free. You go for what you can,
you do what you must; but always be thankful, to those that you
trust. I see things, that others miss; I'll always enjoy a
heartfelt kiss. Do those of you, see these things too? Or
must I paint, a picture for you?
The answer is simple, to this complicated game; just remain
soft spoken, and don't cause pain. Others will treat you, with
joy and respect; as long as you show, there's no room for
neglect. There's things that cause anger, and bitterness deep
inside; these are signs, you cannot hide. They show your hurt,
your torment, your shame; they're bad thoughts, they'll destroy
your brain. But life can come, and go so quick; yet death
gains no fear, from those that are sick. I hope these short
guidelines, I've written for life; do not interfere, with your
burden and strife. They're my way of saying, life is still
new; It's just thoughts in your mind, that make it seem blue.
   —*Greg J. Vogelsang*

"Reluctant Heroes"

This is for those boys we dressed up as soldiers
only to become white crosses
when their time and luck ran out

Sacrifices, lost in war's shadow

And this is for those boys who haven't given up the ghost
of a war made long ago
but still fought fresh

in night terror, and flashback fears,
shed in Viet Nam tears

And this is for those who survived
the war, the guilt, the pain, the horror,
and were honored for it

and the price they had to pay.
Reluctant heroes
who gave their medals away

For the honor is in the living
a debt we must repay
as reluctant heroes
who gave their medals away
—*Krag Hunter Swartz*

What A Family's Love Can Do For You

People often picture me as something big and grand
Or a millionaire, doctor or even the president!
I don't really care what they think of me
Because I am what I intend to be
As long as I have my family
I'll be happy as I can be
I don't need no fame and glory
And I don't need no money
As long as I have family, I have no worries
I feel just as grand and big as a doctor
And the president cause I'm somebody, not nobody in my family
And I feel just as rich as a millionaire,
Cause I have a whole bunch of family care
I will tell you again so you will not think me insane
Happiness cannot be obtained through
Fame, glory, or even money
Cause non of that can buyh ya' it
Cause family love is a treasure rare
And it will always be in your heart
No matter where
—*Michelle Nguyen*

Halls Of Life

Finding a park
  or finding a gift
    illustrates a rift
      which alters what we see when we embark
        upon a stroll down a crowded hall—
making what's seen, possibly not all.

Grading papers
  or making good grades
    changes these arcades,
      so that one trudges as the other capers,
        walking down this busy aisle—
seeking pizza as the other shops for a while.

Children, husband, caretaker
  brother, sister, caretakee
    affects the things which we see
      Tis a difference between you and me.
And so while walking through this hall
I see appearance—might not be all.
—*Joyce R. McElveen*

As Though Sorry Spoke Through Eyelids

Was it just your words
or perhaps the kind gesture
that gave me something to believe in

Should I thank you first
or perhaps apologize
or say nothing at all just to let that kindness speak

Just exactly why your words have the strength
to give my silence direction
I will never know

Should I still ask why
Or just let you know that you make a special difference
to the silence no one ever listened to before
—*Darlene Fremgen*

Life

When you hear the sound of a baby's first cry
  or see a baby take its first step,
    he is beginning his life.

When a child lets go of his mother's hand
  on his first day of school,
    he is growing.

    As a teenager struggles
  to be accepted by his peers,
    he is learning.

When an adult works six days overtime
to make enough money to support his family,
    he is trying.

    As an old man sits on a rocking chair
watching his grandchildren play in the yard,
    he is nearing the end of his life.
—*Elena Burymski*

Blue Chick

Some chicks get their kicks from feathers
Others from spikes on leathers
The Lady looked vivacious and easy to meet
Friendly, with a smile and very petite
Demurely, she gave him a glance
So he asked her politely, "Let's Dance"...
The Lady wore blue
She missed not a cue
While her heels flew high
Under the dark dance floor sky.
As the night grew late,
He asked her for a date
But the Lady said "I've a mate"
She told him not to wait
That things weren't right
Then skipped into the arcane night.
He waved goodbye with moistened eye
Hoping to see her in the "Sweet By'N Bye".......
—*F. A. Brees*

Aging Gracefully

Some folks grow 'older' with birthdays 'tis true,
Others grow nicer as years widen their view,
And a heart that is young lends an aura of grace,
That rivals the beauty of a pretty young face.
For no one will notice a few little wrinkles,
When a kind, loving heart fills the eyes full of twinkle,
So don't count your years by the birthdays you've had,
But by things you have done to make other folks glad.
—*Ruth A. Riddick*

Peace

We reveal in the elusive dream of Peace on earth,
our constant theme
We talk, we sing, we dance and pray of joys to
come that far off day
The doves of peace set free to soar beyond their
limits evermore
Silently in our reverie come sounds of marching-marching
Marching on to Valley Forge through Georgia and past
General Lee on to Texas and the Alamo, up San Juan
Hill the marchers go across barren fields of "No Man's Land"
To Iwa Jima on burning sand. Then to Korea with its hostile
snows the thundering of the marcher goes. Marching on
to Vietnam then to the east in Lebanon. When will this
intrusive sound be gone, suddenly, with a deafening roar the
boots fell silent on that shore. When blazing across the
summer sky the message of the Dove descries "Peace" is
but a fleeting thing".
—*Jean Dawe-Hayes*

The Opening

Remembering, in the quiet haze of
our inner souls, we see the beginning and
end.

We are touched with each other's thoughts so
often, how can we not say we are but one?

Together we form the Creator; alone we are
denied full growth.

Give of your self that you may grow and
know, we are all of the universe.
—*P. S. Tuck*

You And I

You and I are one of a kind.
Our kind of relationship is hard to find.

You and I are quite a pair.
The way we care is very rare.

You and I are just friends now,
but we could become more somehow.

You and I could love each other,
but sometimes you seem more like a brother.

You and I will forever be confused
to the point that it makes me amused.

You and I will always be there
with our feelings ready to share.

You and I will get through this,
and my feelings for you I will miss.

Someday the feelings I have I will show
him,
but for now this is the end of my
poem.
—*Judith Arlene Del Vecchio*

My Sand Castle

Two bony, sea crabs began to rassle,
Over which should own my sand castle.
They knocked over my door,
And busted up my floor.
Before they could destroy any more,
A hugh wave splashed ashore,
Scattering those rasseling crabs, forever more,
Back onto the ocean floor.
—*Jennie S. Meshulam*

My Wife And My Cats

My wife and my cats how I miss you so,
Our time apart passes so very slow.
I don't say it much but I do hope you know,
That when I am away I feel so very low.

My cats are my warm and furry friends,
And they will sit by you until who knows when.
If you are working with small stuff a helping paw
they will lend,
And let you know it is dinner time by the noises they send.

My wife, my companion, my lover, my friend.
We've started down the road of life from beginning to end.
As we walk down the road hand in hand,
We find ourselves in some distant land.
Now life there is not easy, that is surely so,
But wherever I lead becomes the place she wants to go.

My wife and my cats how I love you so!
As our time apart passes, my feelings do grow.
I know I don't say it often but I want you to know. There's
a special place in my heart where these feelings, I stow.
—*Christopher R. Johnson*

Opus Optimus

Odd, obsolete octopus! Outcast!
Outwitted, oozing oleaginous oils...
Oysters - overflowing objectives,
(Only once outdone,)
Oppose oppressing odds!
Optimistic, or over-optimistic -
Offended oysters oscillate,
Occupying ocean's oblong omnibus.
Oh, octopus! Opportunity! Open optic orbs!
Oysters! Old, ordinary oysters, offer ornament!
Octangular octopus...often offset,
Often overpowered...overthrows obstinance -
Oyster obstinance! Outlandish oysters:
Overstrung...overwrought, overcome!
Operation: Oyster! Oriental oyster!
Our octopus, ostentatious, opaque oaf,
Obliterates our oysters!
Only oysters, on occasion, outwit our octopus!
Over-overwhelming octopus, outward oddity -
Offensive, only in outrageous odes!
—*Terry L. Cowles*

Our Source

Our hearts are written on, to our Heads, Thoughts all our
   own —
which no one can steal, even if raped upon —
Crushed, or tried upon by force, but, nevertheless -
God's spirit within us is everblessed!

"Never Worry little ones," as once was told to us
by a Saviour who is real - one you Can trust!
It's a matter of the Heart, attitude, and frame of mind -
Spread God's Love around - show the fruit of His Vine!

We may do it in various ways - a simple shake of the hand,
Grandeur not necessarily needed, to cure our land -
but Love for one another, Honestly, a good Name and Trust -
is what will save our Nation, - it is God's Must!

Thank You Lord!
So Many Idols, One True God!
—*Viviana H. Pappas*

Bananasmoke

How is it that I cannot explain this feeling?
Paranoia but sadness. Lonely but comfortable.
It's an emotion that tells that you take too much for
granted, but you're not going to stop.
You cry and laugh. All problems hit you hard,
makes you weak, but your defense grows even stronger.
Tell me, is there a name for this?
Not insanity or madness, happiness nor sadness.
It is an emotions also of heart and soul.
Your mind must protect your soul so that no one
Can reach them until they've defeated mind.
You think the same, only you think twice.
You look the same but cannot feel the same;
Your same memories, but now with more complex one.
You can't tell where you are, but you can tell me where
you're going.
Touching the ground but flying high -
Going up forever, but never touching the sky.
　　—Edge/Erica Garcia

I Wonder If You Know

I wonder if you know how my life has changed since you became a part of it...

My day begins at dawn just thinking of you. Throughout the day no matter what the task at hand is, I am distracted by thoughts of you that warm my heart and brighten each passing moment.

I wonder if you know what a wonderful friend you have become and how much it pleases me to be in your company...

Whether it's sharing heart-to-heart talks, sipping wine, listening to music, or watching a movie, everything turns into a memorable experience because it's with you.

I wonder if you know how you excite and thrill with your touch and words of love...

You have found and awakened a sensual side of my nature that I had not even realized was lost. You've captured my imagination and evoked a sense of wonder and awe about love and life in general.

I wonder if you know how much I love you and always will...
　　—Bernadette Smith

This Is How Fast In Life We Go

New snow fallen, so fresh, so pure. Footprints covered, my past so lost. Life reflections, fast travel, a leaf in wind. Blink an eye, miss it you will, live fullest life. Rising sun, new days birth, night shadows left behind. Crisp, clean morning dew. Cool fresh air, breathing in my lungs. Vengeful cold, grabs my spine. Nips at my nose, ears unprotected. Clouds, dismal gray in sky. Strange reality, Mother Nature's wraith. In swift lion, out gentle lamb. Game of life, rolling dice, turns to take. Life's meaning, each their own, destiny found. Loved one's come in, front our faces. Starry sky, crystal moon, fireplace hearth. Find it, you will look hard. Rewarded
ye will be. Dreadful fight, joyful out come. Fear be gone, day will come, answers given. Open eyes, quest revealed, what you have hold tight. Memories, friendships forever. God taught lessons learned. Pages of books being turned. Changes chapters of life. Humor needed, romance a must, fly as birds up above. Locomotive speed, jet airliner soars; the only way of our world. Realize now, day by day, one at a time. FOOTPRINTS IN SNOW, COVERED FAST, HISTORY PAST: THIS IS HOW
FAST IN LIFE WE GO.
　　—Thomas Bryan Cichocki

The Wind Stalks

It is silent as I hike,
Peaceful
But as I walk, it stalks
Slowly, quietly at first, it comes from behind me,
Like a whisper.
It gains, and as it does, it grows louder.
Rolling like thunder or waves upon the sand.

My footsteps slow.
It is upon me, pushing me from behind.
It surrounds me now,
Playing in my hair.

Leaving me behind.
My steps quicken, but it races away.
It is gone.

Barely audible, but I know it is there.
And it will stalk again.
　　—Melissa Sack

Night Song

I stand here, back
peering at the hands reaching out,
offered to me.
I can't move—panic; a paralyzingly
heavy over coat.
I long to stretch out, open
myself to the warmth of those hands.
Tan myself in hope
purring, feeling
Soft dense feline fur
heavy and fluffed with heat.
But no.
How very much safer it is to cry alone
in this dark corner.
Warm myself with musty car exhaust.
I still the panic this way
fight off the cold
alone, glorious in my solution, as no one need
hold my hand.
The radio sings me to sleep.
　　—Amy Montana

The Best Of Times

You find a place, where things are right.
People, friends and couples, tight.
Common likes, goals and dreams.
These are the best of times, it seems.

We'll have a family, and we'll grow,
But not everyone can, you know.
So years go by, some friends are gone,
You can't fix it, you just move on,

And hope to God our magic stays,
In these lucky, healthy, happy days.
Others split, did they once believe,
They'd stay together, never leave?

I won't think it will happen to me;
Our love gone, eventually.
Those who have fallen won't make me see,
That in time 'we' won't continue to be.

I'll care for you, please care for me,
We'll show our love will forever be.
We'll stay in step. We will survive.
We'll stay in our own best of times.
　　—Matthew J. Rini

Cartagen

Four years old, and forty wise,
She pleaded out of huge black eyes
For coins to ease the built-in pain,
the beggar-child of Cartagen.

And when her tiny fingers took
The coins I gave, her solemn look
Changed not at all. Quite sad remained
The infant-face of Cartagen.

I thought, as she stood in the sun,
"The beautiful have life half-won".
But she must grow (for she is plain)
Strong as the walls of Cartagen.

How long will her small life go on
After Mermoz and I have gone?
How sad to leave, let her remain
Alone and lost in Cartagen.

Written on a tour from the cruise ship
Mermoz, to a hilltop monastery in the
old, fortified city of Cartagena,
Colombia.
—*Blake M. Mitchell*

Aids

She thought he loved her.
She thought he cared.
She thought it was safe
and so she dared
to sleep with him
without protection
and she got
the AIDS infection.
He never called her.
Just left her alone
to face the disease
all on her own.
I'd sit with her at night
and we'd talk until dawn.
I still hear her voice
though I know that she's gone.
So if you have sex
please use contraception
because everyone can get AIDS.
You're not an exception.
—*Kirsten Shifflette*

If Love Were An Angel

If love were an angel
She would be mine
If love were the rain
The sun wouldn't shine

If love were a healer
All would be healed
If love were a sword
I would be a shield

If love were a stranger
It would be my friend
If love were life
Life would never end

If love were a glass
I would be the wine
But love is an angel
And she is mine
—*Javiel Gonzales*

Once Near

Once near him
Shocks of chills
Course through my limbs
Electric air
Snaps at my skin
Rivers of steam
Roll through my pores
Hot syrup
Overtakes my blood
Thick air
Binds me down
Once near him
—*Jill Clevenger*

God Made Us All

God made us all
Short and tall
Black and white
Why must we fight?
It's not right
To call each other names
Or play our silly games
Please stop the hate
Or will never get through
The gates of the promised land.
So remember one thing
As the church choir sings its
Song
God made us all short and tall.
—*Jocelyn McDoniel*

An Every Day Occurrence

An every day occurrence
Shouldn't be a child losing life

An every day occurrence
Shouldn't be man killing wife

An every day occurrence
Shouldn't be homeless in the street

An every day occurrence
Bullets fly
Women die
People with nowhere to go

An every day occurrence
Shouldn't be so...
—*Lynnor Latham Graham*

Color Me Warm

The world is such an empty place
Since I no longer see your face
Nor hear your warmth-filled voice.
And when I heard that you had gone
That day in May
In the early dawn
My heart near stopped.........
It's beating
But..... time has come
And healed a bit
I'm staying warm
By the fires you lit
In this heart
Which is part of you.
—*Helen M. Hofman*

Peace

Darkness, yes black
Silence, so quiet
Just one way to get there
Do you want to try it?

The sights and sounds of death
Comfort the deceased
They come here just to rest
In the resting lodge of peace.

And yet I tell you, friends,
Death provides no cures
It's just an end to all that could be
And all that should be yours.

"Where there's life, there is hope"
So you've heard it said
There is no second chance to peace
When you have it as the dead.
So I urge you, take a stand
Tear down the walls of hate
And when they're finally gone
You'll find life's golden gate.
—*Darin Van Dorn*

Going Home

Weeks, months, perhaps years
since I have been back
anticipation rushes through my veins
Memories flood my mind

I wonder, will I look the same
or will the lines etched by life
be seen in searching eyes
truth cast in my shadows

rights, wrongs...
will they be remembered
will my deeds be held against me
or go before me

I stepped into the world of the past
and open arms awaited me
tears of welcome, smiles of wonder
embracements of joy

I did not hear, how could you
why did you nor shame on you
just welcome home "my child"
I'm so glad you came
—*Lori A. Gresham*

Untitled

Up from a puddle of
  sinking liquid glass I rise,
Reflecting the objects and
  faces surrounding me
    like a shattered mirror.

Do I perceive something sinister
  in the kaleidoscope of designs
    that are falling away and
      making sounds
    like spinning coins
      on the surfaces below?

Toppling flashes, vibrating wings
    inside the light flicker,
  distracting me from
    fleeting surges of fear.
And in the confusion

  I am alone.
—*Anita Narramore*

Columbus

Columbus gets mixed reviews
   Since the Atlantic was crossed,
Yet he deserves a grand prize
   For the art of getting lost.

Like some missions of today,
   There was some lack of purity,
And his plans did not prevent
   Some lapses in security.

Regrettably he is blamed
   For five centuries of grief,
Especially for Natives
   There has been no good relief.

America before him
   Had its own wars and knaves,
And controlled populations...
   Also gold-hoarders and slaves.

Ecologic disasters...
   Pestilences were a fright...
But why should we keep sipping
   That old hemlock of hindsight?
     —*William A. Paff*

The Three Sisters

Clotho, spinning,
Sings softly to herself
As she weaves the threads
Of each life.
Did she smile, I wonder,
When she came to mine?
Lachesis, sister,
Sitting, staring at the length
Of silken threads, measuring,
Atropos, snipping,
Scissoring each thread.
And when these sisters
Bend forward,
Sifting through the sounds of time
For their coffee break,
Their soft cat delights
In pouncing, playing
On the loom behind their backs,
And that explains everything.
     —*Irma Garbarino*

To The One Hundred Twenty-three of '93

I, too, am Student
sitting, absorbing, educating myself
to know the fine tuning
of disciplined care
for you
who challenge, please, defy
and sometimes take the bait
to chew, swallow and, yes,
get hooked
caught in the nourishment
of knowledge.
To watch you grow
unfurling, unfolding
now feeling, freeing
following new paths—
astounding, breaking limitations
I would set.
You teach me patience
and possibilities untold.
I, too, am Student. (Ms. *)
     —*Sharon Snow*

Time Of Fire

Slow
Slow Dance The River Twists Twists
Rocks
Winging Time In Froth
Snaking
O Light And Light
Beating
Whispers, Whispers
In Green Dragon Screams
O Singing
Singing
In This Spark
End On End
On End
     —*Robert Harding*

Through Tamara's Pane

Light, fading into darkness,
  slow, painful, beautiful,
    picture of evolution.
     Mild-mannered rain
    beginning to pounce,
    clouding my pane.

  Distant clouds ebbing -
    ever closer, baring
their darkened angry faces.
  Hurling rods of lightning
    at the barren ground.

  Distant trees dance
  with delight in the
    sporadic light,
mimicking the apparent rage
  of the swollen sky.
     —*Tamara Alysia Williams*

The Big Fight

She's walking home at a
Slow, slow pace.
She's thinking back to
The door in her face.
She can't understand what
Got into her friend.
As she started
To round the bend,
She heard a holler
From behind.
She slipped beside a tree
To hide.
She didn't feel like talking,
Not to her friend.
Her friend got mad just because,
Her shirt, she did not lend.
She heard a holler
One more time.
She then decided to leave
The bad feelings behind.
     —*Stacia Verhoef*

Flowers In The Wind

  Fleeting flower in the wind
    The fallen face of sin
  In two rows, but one garden
One heart lifted as the other hardened
     —*Gisele Carrere*

The Statue

The cold stone face
smiles boldly
Eyes open to the world
determined to always be.

The stern smile
spreads strongly across
the chips in the hard stone
covering the minute cracks.

The head held staunchly
facing upward
ready for tomorrow
stiffly looking ahead
not looking back.

The shoulders squared;
no slouching;
no stooping;
carrying the burden of the day.
     —*Susan M. Frechette*

Illusions

Children's books, nursery rhymes
So called truth to waste the time
Cruelty and hate exist
Dreams get lost in the mist.

Walls get built that never come down
Love accepts its death without a sound
Reach for hope, find despair
Reach for a hand, touch only air.

Endless searching, holding a wish
Only to find it doesn't exist
Vie for a star, find only space
Search for truth in an endless race.

The magician bowed, illusion's won
Only I saw how the trick was done
Curse him for allowing me to see
Now, no illusions are left for me.
     —*Donna L. Towle*

The Rose

Crimson Petals,
  so deeply wound.
Hidden with dew,
  it speaks not a sound.
Aware of its beauty,
  the symbol of love.
To everyone's passion,
  it fits like a glove.
The tulip and daisy,
  watch with envious eyes.
But this humble, scarlet flower,
  has no need for despise.
It sits upon high,
  in a majestic, proud pose.
This lovely red ruby,
  the princess,
    the rose.
     —*Katherine Connally*

I Thought Of You Today

The World is just the greatest place
That our Lord God could conceive,
But Adam needed something nice
So He created Eve.
     —*Sam R. Smith*

May

He said Hey!
So I came his way,
I hoped to stay
With him that day.
So we could go out and play;
And we saw a blue jay,
In the time of May.
So we could mold clay,
On that very day,
I found out he was gay
On the Hudson Bay.
So I went to church to pray,
But I still love that gay,
Who said Hey!
On that very day;
I still think of him in May.
—*Saylease Couch*

It Doesn't Need A Title, Either

This is a poem which does not rhyme.
So if you only like rhyming poems
put it down
and walk away.
This poem has no meter,
no fixed length of line.
It is simply
an expression of my thoughts.
Why must poetry rhyme?
Why must it be a certain length?
Such restrictions are stifling.
Creativity has no limits.
A poem is a poem
whether or not it rhymes.
It does not need to make sense,
nor does it need
form or function.
It just is.
—*Eileen Kelly*

My Father Mark

His very life a man may give
So that the one he loves may live
   And then his soul ascends above;
And one man calls it "madness"
   Others call it "love."

A pilgrim on life's dusty road
May help another bear his load
   And bearing, slower reach his end.
Now some men call him, "foolish"
   Others call him "friend."

And when at even' the sun is low
Paining deeply all below;
   Then droops the yellow golden rod,
And one man calls it "sunset"
   Others call it "God."
—*Sharon Preston*

Sympathy

Somewhere the sun is shining
Somewhere the sky is blue,
Somewhere the flowers are blooming
Everything looks so new,
Why do we wish our loved ones
Return to good things so few,
When they live in a land of sunshine
And the sky is always blue.
—*Vivian Hook*

"I Am Me"

We are all God's creations,
So why do you treat me so differently.
I may have a handicap
that you don't have but why
does that make you so blind to
see that on the outside I may
be different but on the inside
I am the same accept that
I am me! I have feelings too.
In fact, they are the same as you.
I have difficulty showing my emotions
and saying how I feel. I'm not
blind I can see that some people
are afraid to be around me. I
don't understand how people
can be so cold and shallow because
I'm a little different than some of you
I see because I am me.
—*Sue Emanouil*

Grandpas

Grandpas, all different this I'll show
Some are fat
some are thin
some wear hats
some have hair on their chin
some have no hair on their heads
some can't hear what is said
some are gray
some have faces full of ray
some can't see
that, surely would be sad for me
some are short
some are tall
there are all sorts
but my Grandpa
I like, the best of all
—*Margaret Waldbuser*

Peace With God

There is peace of a different kind,
Some for the land, heart and mind.
Something like your Dad and Mother,
You can't have one without the other.

While walking through the wildwood,
A trail alone, I have often trod.
I hear the birds sing songs of Peace;
The Peace for man, is Peace with God.

There was a small bird, that He made,
His task was great; jumping around.
Perseverance, he would not give up;
He was pulling a worm from the ground.

There is a proper time and place;
When Peace fits in the fruitful clime,
It comes from His marvelous Grace,
It will not be late but right on time.

"Spare ye the rod you spoil the child,
The formula's good and still worth while.
Seek the will of God, things will begin,
"Peace on earth, good will, toward men."
—*Harvey T. Holsapple*

Untitled

The railroad tracks ricochet with the
   sounds of a train rolling by.
   as i sit at my desk of life
   planning and preparing,
i hear the constant repetition of
   the train as it moves
   on to somewhere else.
   i, too, am like that train.
—*Nicole Kathryn Tremel*

On The Brink

Spindrift, like love
Sparkles and shines
And sinks,
Into the sandy brain

Tossed by the waves
And nourished
By the heart
The waves
Caress the throbbing mass
Holds it
For a moment
Or for a lifetime
In memory
Shimmering
Beneath the sun
It lives..like love
To know
Brief ecstacy and disappear.
—*Ruby Q. Petersen*

Tiffany And Cartier

Tiffany and Cartier
Sparkling in the sunlight
Jewels of their own kind
   One shining black
   One gold and bright
Tiffany and Cartier
Eyes flash and scintillate
Two slithering beauties
Smooth and warm
Just watch and wait...
   and wait
Tiffany and Cartier
—*Kaitlen Jay Exum*

Nosferatu

Listen softly to the rain,
Speak of other listeners, other times,
Tender words for better times-
Whispered words lost in the rain.
"Time's winged chariot" waits always—
A chariot where I never ride!
Come and rest here at my side.
No regrets for sun-wheeled days!
Come talk with me about the rain.
Whisper words that cause you pain.
Spend the night here lost with me;
See my eyes to read your destiny.
Let me touch you - cold as rain;
Never feel the touch of sun again.
—*Mary L. Schaeffer*

The Poet's Web

My mind weaves words, like a
spider weaves her web.
The delicate strands wrap not around
wooden beams, but beams of imagination.
Turning and spiraling into an intricate
pattern, it forms a design.
The words make a shimmering shroud,
a veil, that seems so frail, but is
stronger than the mind's eye will
lead you to believe.
So come into the web of words, and
become entrapped in the world of
imagination.

—*Mary Ann Wittman*

Breeze Of Life

Life is like a whirl wind
  spinning round and round;
    Sometimes you are up
and sometimes you are down.

When the winds carry us to
  the right, we want to be
left; when the winds carry
us to the left, we want to be right.

  Just as the leaf, if we
could just learn, acceptance
of life and change with each
turn; a new freedom and peace
as with the dove knowing not
hate, but feelings of love.

Simple and free as we could
be, just as a leaf that falls
    from the tree;
Blowing and floating in air
  with such ease, caressing a
sunbeam as we drift with the breeze.

—*Darlene J. Mrvelj*

Crocus

In the middle of March
  springtime overtakes us,
when by my front porch
  in bloom comes the crocus,
a patch of pastels,
  some solid, some striped,
eye-catching appeals
  for passing by biped
who shortens his stride,
  observing and noting
that Spring long delayed
  at last is igniting.

—*Howard Winger*

New Day

Neither gull nor osprey
stirred the void
of sight or sound.
The silence cloyed.

Young Phoebus crowned
the crest of dawn
brighter than the chariot
he rode upon.

Draw near, new day,
but just the finger tips
will toss a greeting skyward
from parted lips.

—*Connie Hess*

Ah,...Lady Grace!

Ah,...Lady Grace!
Star of the sea.
Oh,...blessed lady!
Lady of mercy.
Ah,...Lady grace!
Dream of tomorrow.
Oh,...blessed lady!
Lady of sorrow.
Ah,...Lady Grace!
Bundle of joy.
Oh,...blessed virgin!
Virgin of hope.
Ah,...Lady Grace!
Fountain of love.
Oh,...blessed mother!
Mother of God!

—*Jess Camilo*

A Mother's Love

A cry in the dark
Stark, and real
He fears the shadows of sleep
Tries to roll away from them
And squalls louder than before
Until she comes.
And with her wisdom, and love
She knows
She turns on the light
Banishing the shadows
And cradles him close
Murmuring nothings in his ear
Letting him know
No matter how early
No matter how late
No matter how deep she slumbers
She will hear him and come
And tell him each time
Without reservation
How much he is loved.

—*Micki Cecka*

Untitled

    A pounding on my door
  starts a pounding in my chest.
    jump up, fall back down
     and push the ground
      up and up we go
       hit the streets
     in one big fleet
   we are invisible to
       the trees!
    A forest of men
  marching down the streets
      kill kill kill
      murder reigns
      inside my head
    wonder what it's like
      to be dead?
     Sea of darkness
  lurking shadows of lifelessness
  underneath the neon stage
frozen in limbo between states of hate?

—*John Dowling*

Haiku

The rushing water
quiets in the rock filled stream,
ripples silently.

—*Mildred Murakami*

Sunday Morning

Driving all night
Stop at first light

Early Sunday morning
No one gave us warning

Of what was to be
Of what we would see

There at The Wall
Cards and pictures standing tall

From children who never saw
Their dads, now names on The Wall

The messages are brief
Yet filled with silent grief

Left with loving care
To tell them they were there

Early Sunday morning
No one gave us warning

Of what was to be
Of what we would see

Silently we pray
For this is Father's Day

—*Karen Molden*

Sylvan Blades

Sylvan blades of seagrass
Sway wistfully as they
Stand amidst the sand
      strong
     and
    patiently
Growing
Resisting the forces of nature

—*Donna Topper*

No Less A Man

Tears to show pain,
  tears to show sorrow.
Tears to show grief,
  or tears for tomorrow.

Tears of joy,
  for those happy times.
Tears of sin,
  for some awful crime.

Whatever the reason,
  they roll down your cheek,
Tears are not a sign,
  that you are weak.

Crying, to some,
  means that you're a sis.
But it's the manly part,
  that they always miss.

You're no less a man,
  if you shed a tear or two.
But you're no more of one,
  if it's kept inside of you.

—*Tom Geier Jr.*

Untitled

The artist's brush dropping
Sea of green, dash of yellow
  Unavoidable chill.

—*Kathleen L. Cook*

Because All I Desire Is You

I would rather know you,
than the answer to my questions...
I would rather love you,
than not to know love at all...
I need to know nothing else,
except you, and the love
I have inside for you...
When I think of all the things
you can do for me,
Oh, how I long to be with thee;
Whatever draws me away
Is not better than being with you
When all I desire is you...

—*Beverly A. Owens*

Untitled

No greater love
Than the love of desire
No greater love
Than the love for hire

No greater love
Than the love of the past
No greater love
Than the love that will last

No greater love
Than the one right now
No greater love
Than the love with a vow

No greater love
Is like the one that we share
No greater love
Can even compare

No greater love
Is like my love for you
No greater love
Is as true

—*Elizabeth Laverdure*

The Hand

It's the hand
That clings to our side,
It's the hand
That keeps our spirit alive.
The hand
That gives us life,
The hand
That guides us through strife.
It's the hand
That makes us feel
For those without a meal.
The hand
Nature must obey,
The hand
That provides another day,
Respect the hand
With love unfurled,
Adore the hand
That keeps the world.

—*Sara Kaden*

Raindrops

Raindrops are tears
That God does shed
When He sees the world
In evil spread

—*Charlotte Sobel*

The Hour Glass

Both the hands and the sands of time
That constant change the hour glass
And circle still the clocks own
Face....Where is that older
Wiser place that the sands
Of time so run to? The
clocks own hands do
Circle 'round
Whils't
Sands
Of time fall
To the ground...
Where is that wisdom
Mine should be...I only
Find an older me and yet this
"Time" with hidden grace has
Wrinkled not the clocks own face
Nor bent the curving hour glass where
Sands of time just merely pass.... It
Really does not seem quiet fair.

—*Nancy Moritz*

Fear

The all - consuming flame
That engulfs the soul
It sears and burns
Not with heat
But with the deepest,
penetrating cold.
It wraps icy fingers
Round the beating heart
And slowly saps the
warmth and strength
from every human part.
It feeds upon itself
And like a cancer spreads
Leaving in its wake
The living dead.

—*Carol Fontenot*

Remember When

Remember when...
That first day of school,
Everything was so new—
You didn't know me;
I didn't know you.

But as days grew into weeks
And months into years,
We became as one big family
Overcoming any doubts and fears.

Then finally came the biggest day,
Graduation was here at last!
The one we had so long waited for-
Our school days were in the past.

Now, it's twenty years later,
And we're gathered once again,
To renew old friendships;
talk over old times,
And to ... "remember when."

—*Mavis Gonshorowski*

Time Slips By

I've been told I've reached my peak
That I am growing old
But who's to say it's time to stop
On life, I have a hold
There's much to see and things to do
The days slip by so fast
Can't waste my time on day dreams
Or dwell upon the past
For today is now and I'm a part
Of what is going on
But they'll say that she was growing old
When the final curtains drawn
Until that time I'll live each day
As though it were my last
For there's much to see and things to do
But time slips by so fast

—*Betty Traver*

Our Son Donald

We had no way of knowing
That in April Ninety-three,
God would call you home to be with him
How grieved we all would be....

You hugged and told us you loved us
At some time in every day;
Oh how we miss you Donald
Far more than words can say.

We feel that God decided
Your work was finished here,
You loved and helped so many...
You were very, very DEAR.

—*Esther G. Rush*

"To Me You Are My Everything"

Your love is like a tender touch
That lasts throughout the day
Your love is like the gentle rush
Of waves within the bay
Your love is like a song I know
The one that makes me sing
Your love is like the whitest snow
More pure than anything
Your love is like a dream come true
The bliss cannot be matched
Your love is like a stick of glue
That's why I grew attached
Your love is like a little child
That grows more every day
Your love is like a lovely smile
That takes my fears away
Your love is truly all these things
It makes me very glad
To me you are my everything
Without you life is sad

—*Jean Mistretta*

"My Wall"

I've built a wall around me,
That no one else can see,
It's like a strong protective shield,
Keeping bad things from hurting me.
When illness, lost dreams, and
thoughtlessness,
Attack me from all sides,
Within my safe protective wall,
I shall always reside.

—*Diane W. Newman*

Beauty

You are the rose,
That opens up,
And spreads its beauty all around.

You are the sun,
Up in the sky,
That sheds its warmth to frozen ground.

You are the love,
Within our hearts,
That keeps the lonely people warm.

You move like waves,
Upon the beach,
That flow with perfect grace and form.

You're everything,
That's kind and sweet,
That God has ever gently made.

And through the years,
And passing days,
Your beauty will not ever fade.
—*Mark Kilmer*

Storms

There are storms
 that rage within;
There are storms
 that rage without.
There is turbulence
 within,
There is turbulence
 without.
How to calm
 the storm within?
How to calm
 the storm without? ...
I will face my inner self;
I will ask the Lord for peace.
His hands will stretch in blessing,
Storms and turbulence will cease.
—*Sister Mary Paula Kolar, F. S. P.*

Love

Love is a song
that rises and falls
in a soft melody
with the winds and the tides

With the turn of the seasons
in the expression of colors
and the changes of heart
love comes and it goes

And in its wake
of happiness and joy
there is a sweet sorrow
a blossom of regret

A note of remembrance
of the cares of the past
and the song of the future
with the times to come

Will drum in your ears
and echo in your heart
for the years to follow
is the music of love
—*Malina Holm*

Hieros Gamos—The Highest Game

What is death, then?
—that sweet thief!
slipping through the cleft
with a tight squeeze of rage and relief
thrusting the world as we know it
down into the earth

—that rotten sucker!
biting through the flesh
sharp and stinging like strong music
grabbing the open wound,
never letting go
—*Roberta Lawringsky*

Untitled

'Tis time my friend,
that will see the end.
Not you, nor me
but the droplets of the sea.
The clouds, the air,
how will they fair?
The birds, the trees
And all that we see
Breath deep, and fast
For it may be our last.
Take time, to care
—*Scott Saviano*

People Are People

People are people,
That's how it should be.
There is no difference
Between you and me.
We're different colors,
That's no lie.
When I see a racist,
It brings tears to my eye.
You may be black,
I may be white,
The war of racism
is a gruesome sight.
Why can't we get along
together?
To have global peace,
Now and forever.
—*Heather Privitera*

War

Red as dragons breath
The god of war goes on
Spreading crimson death
Amid the coming dawn.

A clash of bladed steel,
A thunder and a light,
Then groping hands that feel
For safety in the night.

A battered group of men,
Wriggling toward a hole,
A spurt of flame and then
The soldiers missed their goal.

At home their kinfolk wait.
They hope, they wail, they dread
While those in yonder field
Are lying cold and dead.
—*Edgar F. Hosking, Jr.*

"Portrait On The Wall"

See that Portrait on the wall
That's the grand lady of us all
How very proud I am to be
a part of her family tree

Her life was not easy
Long days and heavy loads
Times were hard and folks were poor
yet you were welcomed at her door

Home to her was center stage
A place for all the family
To cook, clean and care for them
And songs to sing on Sunday

Then came the war and all its strife
Took away some of her family life
She wore a face for company
Alone, she felt the misery

At rest now with those she loves
And I have missed her so
Thank heavens for the memories
And my portrait on the wall.
—*Carol Gallizioli*

Happy New Year

It's just another day
That's what you said to me
I wish that you had just stayed here
To hold me tenderly
But you had made your mind up
On what you planned to do
And those plans that you had made
Were not for me and you
So as the old rings in the new
I think about our time
And know that you don't want me now
For days of auld lang syne
—*Kelly Lynch*

Untitled

As the clock strikes,
the ambulance howls,
and the children play at home,
Ryan's Daughter becomes the Crying Game,
Jonestown is now Waco,
and politics and religion
are still forbidden subjects
at the dinner table.

A twisting and turning continuity
of I know nothing elseness
has like the fork in its tongue
given us two paths to choose one.
—*William Wright*

God's Gift's

God's gift's can be great
Like the cry's of a new born.

Or they can be small such
as a single word that can
Touch us all.

But great or small the Lord's
Greatest gifts He and Jesus
is with us one and all.
—*Anthony Hurst*

The Guard

I dare not speak lest I should rouse
The anger of the guard
Who lets me look, but not to touch,
The windows being barred

I look for one whom I well know
To be held captive here
Locked fast behind the billowed wall
Gone far, and yet too near

I see the sparkle of her eye
On ev'ry crest he wears
This guard who keeps her underneath
This one who put her there

He lets me look, in vain he says,
To see if I might find
Some likeness that resembles her
The face he shows is mine

He holds the key, the only one
Who passes through the door
But still he keeps it from me 'til
He lets me look no more
—*Shawn E. Fisher*

Untitled

On days when there is an azure sky,
  The blue eyes of my love I see.
Through the softness of the clouds
  I feel his gentle touch;
And when the breezes blow,
  I hear his mellow voice.

He comes to me in the winter
  through the warm glow of a fire.
He's with me in the spring when
  life and love are new.

I sense him at night when I see
  the moon and stars,
And remember the magic of romance
  and the friendship of love.

Tears now salve the wound of grief,
And my heart heals across the break.

I am richer by far than had I not
  known his love.
—*Loretta G. Taylor*

The Addiction...

the twinkling eyes
  the captivating smile
    the bubbly laugh
      the lilting voice

fill my thoughts
  cloud my dreams
    contain my memories
      comprise my hopes
—*Vincent Fettinger*

Mistaken Love

A question of love, a wonder up above.
The clouds by far,
The doubtless thought arises, my
heart asunder.
A love will I ever know?
A chance taken, a love mistaken.
—*Danielle Baker*

For Susan

My brethren, my kin,
the cosmos is ours.
Our dreams have been
but pauses in the hours.

The space between stars
and dreams yet unflown;
like the workings of heaven
are things unknown.

Space, endless time -
Canst beginnings be known
of a will most divine
for which the stars must shine?

Heaven is where
the Lord, he does,
whate'er we endeavor,
always loves.
—*Michael R. Cirillo*

The Crystal Wolf

  Tethered to a marble obelisk,
    The Crystal Wolf,
  blinded by numbing ferities
    veiled in the moonwinds,
  limps his moon-scared circle
    ironed against the earth.

    Hollowed from sorrow,
      the living sepulcher,
        summons forth
    phantoms of warriors bones
          to unearth
        frothing passions

bleaching the forest-green wildness.

  Spirits of the four corners,
    spirits of the earth
    murmur to his form,
    "Rise to the heavens
        no tomorrows
          pacing
  the drowning sun." Run...
—*Ann. . ."E"*

His Kiss

My love for you has grown since then...
  The day on which we met...
But never quite as fast as when
  That day you paid Eve's debt.

And love respect and fear we must
  Show God in every way...
For witnessing His love for us
  On that, that special day.

And nothing can compare with one
  Relationship YOU share
Of mother-daughter, mother-son...
  A fool would only dare.

So please accept on this your first
  important day our wish
That once again as we've rehearsed...
  He'll touch you with His kiss.
—*Richard P. Barnitt*

"Children No More"

Our time is winding down
the end is drawing near.
some will face it eagerly
others will face it with fear.

What we will do
is entirely up to us.
will we pull ahead of the pack,
or be left in the dust.

We must start thinking
of how we would run this land,
For it won't be much longer
until it is placed in our hands.

We must think clearly;
we must use our heads.
There's a crisis going on
and a nation to be led.

We must spread our wings;
it is our time to soar.
The future starts now -
we are children no more.
—*Cory Glidewell*

My Night, My Path

The sun slowly sinks downward,
The evening leads into night.
Starshine flickers oh so softly,
Moonbeams beckon flight.

I hear wind rustle through the trees,
It whispers in my mind.
My words tumble off of the walls,
Light will never find me.

I must follow the darkened pathways,
I must find where I belong
Tumbling upon the wreckage,
I now know of a friend.

I fly with my wings of darkness,
Caressing the sky and the wind.
I follow the path of destruction,
I see only a blur.

May I never return.
—*Jaime Tenney*

Evening's Expression

On a sultry, warm night,
The giant ball of fire
Slowly fades behind a vivid mountain.
Meanwhile, nature's artist
Begins a work of beauty,
Painting broad strokes of purples,
Whisps of magenta and fuchsia,
Streaks of coral and yellows,
Soon a palette of colors decorates,
The distant horizon.
An expression of sadness appears,
As the beauty fades to grey,
Knowing it will be lost forever,
As the paintings disappear
Into a blanket of darkness.
—*Michelle Cawthra*

The Love Of God

Astounding love! What joy is mine!
The gift of God - His son divine;
That I from sin might be set free-
His body hung upon a tree.

What sacrifice! What perfect love!
He left His home as God above;
And to this world of sin and strife-
He came to give his precious life;
That all who will might be set free-
So now it's up to you—and me.

So help me ever, Lord, to see-
And consecrate my life, to thee
Please keep me daily by thy side—
And let me in that love abide
That I may enter heaven's door;
And with thee dwell forevermore.
—*Ruth Rose*

Zen Moment

Curbside,
The gleaming scarlet Regal Buick
Stands.

Above,
Two pale and fluffy heads
Float,
Two pairs of lips fiercely
Grimace,
Four almond eyes
Glare,
Waver, shift and roll
From deep within their puffy beds.

Four hands wave, flap and flutter
Fruitlessly,
Amidst the flight of
A single
   slowly
      soaring
         gnat
Against a clear and perfect sunset sky
—*Audrey Eisman*

Callie

As I look out on the field,
the grass waves and a golden
haze fills my eyes.
I see a rat scurry across the
old tire and think of her.
She once played in that field,
Stalking rats and chasing
Butterflies—occasionally sniffing
a flower.
Now she sits indoors—she has
more important work.
My heart fills with joy as I go
inside the house and see that
in her basket now lie four beautiful
new lives.
—*Rebecca Leigh Playford*

A Work Of Art

   A masterpiece of music and art,
     Sealed away from the world.

   Where life and death do not exist,
     And no man has ever gone.

   My brother keeps his thoughts and ideas,
     Sealed away from the world.
—*Ciarra Rose Loudin*

Mi Amiga

Pam, who is she?
... the greatness of the sixties
and seventies
all the good stuff.

The kalua and cream
open arms, a hug
a listener

Our friendship:
the warmth of the sun
the blue of the ocean
both we love

Our kindness is our kinship
our kids
we are women women women
our husbands love that!

We make it all meet
barely breathing our time
but we make it!
Margaritas, anyone?
—*Kim R. Snell*

If We Could Understand

If only we could understand,
The heart of every fellow man,
We'd stop and think ere we speak,
The bold we'd measure with the meek.
We'd know why selfish people be,
Why reckless folks no harm can see,

An aching heart a smile oft' shields,
A sad expression to worry yields,
Glib and carefree we are born,
By hardship, happiness is shorn,
The surly face so hard and bold,
Perhaps of love was never told,

Those we sometimes paint so dark,
We'd find them kind beneath the bark,
Those we think cool and aloof,
We'd welcome them beneath our roof,
A prisoner oft would be absolved,
A problem child a problem solved,
Could we but understand.
—*Alice Pendleton Leatherman*

Bus Station — USA

The busses come and the busses go
The human cargo ebbs and flows.
Sleepy boys and tired men
Get off one bus to board again
   Another going elsewhere.

Pretty girls in chic attire,
Old women looking near to expire.
Colored, crippled, drunk or sane
Only one thing does remain
To board a bus and on again
   To destinations unknown.
—*June A. Robinette*

After the Storm

Well content with belly full of men and ships
   the grey green monster
laps his frothy lips
   against the sand.
—*Velda Douglass*

To My Newly Retired Husband

In all the years of my married life
the kitchen has been my domain,
but since my husband's retirement
life has never been the same.

If I go out to a meeting
or on a shopping spree,
I never have to hurry home
for my meal is awaiting me.

The Crock-Pot comes in handy
he'd settle for nothing less.
But, oh, when I behold the scene
my kitchen is ONE BIG MESS!
—*Ruth Anderson Harker*

Twilight

Mellow, like aged wine.
The late afternoon sun dapples
her way through the same trees
that in earlier morning light
twinkled more vibrantly-
bouncing off morning dew.

A different mood, this twilight sun,
not so unlike those of us that too
have passed our mid-heaven.

The muted flavors she features at her
expiring hours are soft and forgiving,
rich and succulent, caressing lovingly
at those branches and treetops
she favors most.

A fond adieu, a tender embrace.
A promise of tomorrow and (life renewed.)
—*Kelly Wyatt*

"Walking Shoes"

Society is bending
the law to save its skin
and weaving life through loopholes
to gain the quicker win.
We're slipping through the fence while
justifying sway,
in order to be freed of
that old chaotic way.

Hob-nailed boots and slippers stress
the system's highs and lows,
but interfused are "Walking Shoes"
connecting needed flows.
Through court and law they're trying
to keep us all from fall,
and oxford blend is moving in
to help with overhaul.

Oh "Walking Shoes," Oh "Walking
Shoes,"
keep moving for that day
When our old world of chaos will be
gone... like yesterday.
—*Thelma T. Steinberg*

A Poet's Sunset

 A poet
 paints
 pictures
 with words.

   The
 thoughts
 of Lola.
—*The thoughts of Lola*

The Best Gift

The best gift I have to give you,
The one gift I want most to share,
Is to tell you about my Jesus,
and to tell you how much He cares.

You may not even know it's value.
You may not even know it's worth,
but if you invite this Jesus
in your heart, you'll have a new birth.

The best gift I have to give you.
The gift that o'er time has not failed,
is to know that He died to save you,
and for you to the cross was nailed.

Now, when all other gifts are faded,
and when all other gifts are worn,
you'll still have the gift of Jesus,
for on this day you were reborn.

If you'll accept what I offer,
the gift that will last for all time.
Confess Him to be your saviour.
My heart's open! Come in Lord, be mine!

—*Lorraine H. Davis*

She's Gone

She's gone and I still miss her
 The pain goes on and on
 The years have not diminished
 Her life, her love, her song

She's gone but I still miss her
This sister, This friend, This mom
 The years have not erased
 Her spirit, strength and calm

She's gone and the world is missing
 this woman of soul and heart
 Her life was cut too early
 Her life just got its start

The question of a woman's strength
 to me does not belong
For all in me that's good or great
 from her was passed along

She's gone and I still miss her
This hero, This friend, This mom
 I long so much to hold her
 My God! My God!....She's Gone!

—*John Laudico*

Will My Sun Ever Again Rise?

At times I wonder if it can stop,
 The pain, the tears, the anger,
 Will they ever stop?
People tell me that life goes on.
 "Live again," they say,
 "It is always darkest before the dawn."
 Will my sun ever again rise,
 To brighten my day,
 To bring my smile and dry my eyes?
 Get off to a fresh start,
 I am advised and told.
Pick up the pieces of your heart,
 Love and remember to live
 Forget the bad memories
 Learn to live and forgive.

—*Teresa Thompson*

Misgivings At Thanksgiving

A certain fear
The person feels
Who holds the knife at festive meals
It's time to face that annual crisis:
To cut a turkey into slices.

At first the breast meat falls so neatly
A carver's unaware completely
Of what a labyrinth he's in
An inch or two beneath the skin.

He plots a course to circumvent
Each tendon, bone and ligament,
But failure's lurking in the wings
And legs, and joints and tangled things.

How stubbornly that fowl releases
The rest in stringy bits and pieces!
The answer's simple, but depressing -
Skip the bird and serve the dressing.

—*Joan Elwood*

Elizabeth In A Nursing Home

In a field of withering wild flowers
the rain drips and is absorbed.
Rain and wind gather momentum
with no regard for their direction.
The ground swells.

Peeking unseen
into this room of
patients, they being offered
such unfamiliar sustenance
as clay, pastel chalk, colored pens;
a book, conversation, a visit—they
sometimes refusing, sometimes
accepting—
it all seems like rampant turmoil.

But it only seems that way.
It is the turmoil of growth.

Then, a revived stem latches on
to a shaft of sunlight and
leaves unfurl.

—*Athena Iris Warren*

My Love

I found you with a broken wing—
the sad and lonely kind.
 Your heart had lost it's will to sing
and, Sweetheart, so had mine.

But the silence held a hopeful prayer
that lingered deep within.
 And then, my darling, you were there
to make me whole again.

I cared for you, as lovers do,
and cherished every day.
 How sweet of you to love me, too...
God's will had found a way.

As time went on, our love still grew
and blossomed beautifully...
 Then came the day I felt you say,
"My Love, come fly with me!"

—*Rena Sommers Lippert*

Seeds Of Change

You planted the seed,
 the seed of change.
I thank you.

You planted the seed,
 the seed of hope.
I thank you.

You planted the seed,
 so deep.
I need you.

It's the end of my world,
 as I know it.
I've met you.

It's the end of my world,
 as I've lived it.
I want you.

It's the end of an old world
 and I'm glad.
My new world includes you.

—*Pamela Barnes*

Romance Gone

Into the night
The shadows dance

The fire glows
With true romance

You cannot see
Too far away

Instead you await
The break of day

You awake
Night's gone by

I awake to hear
Your silent cry.

—*Monique Carole Brown*

The Deserted Barn

 If you listen, you can hear
 The soft coo of pigeons
 Nesting high in the cupola.

The rafters creak with the gentle wind,
 The scent of hay fills the loft.
 Do I hear the low moo
 of freshly milked cows?

 The sunshine through cracks
 Dances on particles of dust,
 And reflects back the memories
 Of all that was here.

—*Stella Davis Van Note*

The Sun

The sun goes up.
The sun goes down.
It goes around without
a sound.

The sun is bright as you
look at it's light.

You think if you were the
sun, it would be so fun.
To float in the sky and
make the world so bright.

—*Carrie Baker*

Homemade Dress

The palest blue,
The softest white.
Five skeins of yarn
And a sleepless night.

Starting with the top
Every stitch with care.
Knowing with the tick of the clock
Easter would soon be here.

On to the bottom
Looking like white lace.
Mother envisions
Her little girls face.

The sun is rising
And the last stitch complete,
Just in time
Mom hears the patter of feet.

In her Easter basket
The little girl discovers,
The prettiest dress, tagged
With love and kisses from mother.
—*Ronda A. Winters*

Heaven

Heaven is —
The stars in the sky.
A beautiful sunset by the sea.
A love so great it's shared by all.
Two friends together
Just you and me
Heaven is feeling so
free and peaceful
It's your first breath
In a spring day.
Heaven is love
Heaven is Free
Heaven is shared by you and me.
—*Missy Kuhn*

The Forest Wonderland

T'was a time to long remember
The stars were clear and bright,
The frogs, awake from slumber,
Broke the silence of the night.

A quiet little river
Wends it's way among the trees,
The flowers that grow along it's bank
Wave gently in the breeze.

A night owl perched up in an oak
Watched, but showed no fright
But a little rabbit saw me
And scampered out of sight.

All the creatures of the forest
Dwell in harmony,
All the birds and animals
Know the joy of being free.

As I wandered through the woodland
I beheld the work of God,
If does manifest His glory
He has blessed this land I trod.
—*Florence Kling*

Youth

The bow is arched
The string taut, vibrating.
On it rest the arrow
Straight and strong
Eager to fly into the unknown
Knowing not its mark
As Fate awaits release
From the guiding hand.

Together

A sweet caress,
The stroke of a gentle hand.
A quick kiss,
warm feelings,
A chance to experiment;
An exciting new experience,
A welcomed touch.
Sinful thoughts.
No worries, no cares
Our minds were anxious
Together, we became one.
—*Susan LeeAnn Swift*

"The Sky"

The clouds are puffy,
The sun is bright,
This is the place,
Where dreams are made right.

Sometimes blue,
Sometimes gray,
It is inspiring,
On any day.

The bluebirds sings,
With all its might,
About this place,
Always in sight.

This place in which,
All birds fly,
Is a place,
Known as the sky.
—*Summer Thomas*

Lynn

Lynn shuffles down
The tiled corridor,
Cleaning mop carefully
Held above the floor.
He is slow but steady,
A tidy and neat janitor.
Little is he stooped
With the age of whiteness,
Curls he proudly wears
Atop his head.
He'll tell ya', "kid,"
About his grandson in Florida
(He's about your age, son,),
And turns to clean again,
For his honor
Is demanding of his work.
—*Bill Reiss*

Summer Evening

As the soft breeze blows through
the trees.
And the temperature reaches 70 degrees
Stay with me,
and watch the beautiful night to be.
We've been together so far,
and promise me it'll never end
even when we're afar.
—*Renee M. Wsol*

Untitled

The cold war ended
The walls came down
The world was safer
A whole planet sighed with relief
What happened?
Cities erupted
Brother killing brother
Torture, suffering, starvation abound
Murder, race wars, hate upsurge
No hope, no tolerance
People of all nations awake
Put down your weapons
Take up your pens
Open your hearts
Don't close your minds
If you don't there'll be
No one to hate
No one to kill
No Gods to war over
Just death for us all
—*Margaret E. Dillard*

Africa

Underneath
the whisperings of
African nights
there is a
dark secret
that death
invents
in the wild
cries of
Africa's inhabitants.
—*Tia Landau*

The Tree

Its leaves swayed in the gentle breeze.
The wind blew the branches
  quietly back and forth.
The initials of past couples were
  carved upon the tree.
Large roots upon the ground made
  cradled seats for playing children
Kids climbed the sturdy tree higher
  and higher until they could
  climb no more.
Chipmunks and squirrels climbed up the
  branches noisily to their
  homes,
You can smell the air of the
  woods, and the nature.
It represents childhoods of small kids
  who are now adults.
This tree is filled with hopes, dreams,
  memories, and peace.
—*Amanda Miller*

Daisy

Standing in my field of dreams,
The wind blows gently,
Sounds of bird and stream.

The sky an effervescent blue,
A single cloud,
Floats proud and true.

To disregard this sanctity,
Would certainly be,
A tragedy,

Perfection however,
Is not always as it seems,
For I am alone in this field of dreams.

As I have searched the field over,
I am but one daisy,
In a field of clover.
—*Russell E. Dingman*

Stay A Moment?

Look into my eyes,
the windows of my soul.
Gaze upon the darkness,
the emptiness and cold.

Will you stay a moment?
Gift the darkness light?
Look beyond my open wounds,
without adding to my strife?

Will you seek beyond my bitterness,
to the cause of my pain?
Patiently sow the seeds of trust,
light friendships flame?

Can you find compassion,
maybe aid this soul to mend?
Will you stay a moment,
and simply be my friend?
—*E. "Shadow" Maddox*

Is This The Night

The sun so bright,
   The world so dark,
Is this a night,
   To build an ark?

Behold the sky affright,
   Peals of lightning spark,
Is a demon in sight
   Over the sea of shark?

The moon so bright,
   The earth so dark,
This is the night,
   To build an ark!
—*Jim H. Lee*

Long Ago Beau

I have thought of him through
   the years.
A flash, sometimes,
And then again, a ponder.

He will hover in the shadows
   enough to make the wonder,
   do I visit him and
      does he see me sitting at
         his feet, the way it was.
I wonder if he does.
—*Jan Whalen*

Dissolution Game

The two monsters clash,
Their children die.
They lose their loved ones,
The mothers cry.
Carnage reeks of death and decay,
Cutting at feelings.
While sending all into disarray,
No one is healing.
The people all go away
And with them all life.
Because all that day,
There was nothing but strife.
—*L. J. Dunman*

"Rocks Of Honor"

Rocks lay dormant on the ground,
Themselves, they cannot fend.
They do not grow nor dance with wind.
If marred, they do not mend.

They never feel a gentle breeze
Nor smell the green of spring.
And when the winter ice prevails,
No shelter does one bring.

A tree spreads grandeur toward the sky
And sings with fruits and flowers.
But rocks, alone and quiet,
Exist in silent hours.

Why is this child of nature's womb
Deprived of life's real joys?
Forgotten through eternity,
Like a child's Christmas toys.

But yea, their Godly place on earth
Outstands all nature's babes.
Rocks have honor. After all,
They grace our soldiers' graves.
—*Edward Altiere*

Parents' Love

They start off as husband and wife,
then create a new life.

A house is not a home,
till Christian love is shown.

They show us their love,
that comes from above.

They nurture us with great care,
then teach us how to share.

They show us the way,
twenty-four hours in a day.

They teach us to be strong,
then pray we won't go wrong.

They teach us how to talk,
then show us how to walk.

They teach us not to mess,
then show us how to dress.

They teach us tying shoes,
then come the golden rules.

They teach us how to climb stairs
then best of all; hear our prayers.
   Amen and amen!
—*Roberta M. Allen*

Eight Years Old

Gracefully leaping,
Then running and jumping;
Now twisting and turning
Or stretching and slumping;
Energy abounding
And chatter resounding;
But seldom just sitting —
And never just still; —
Awhirl in perpetual motion —
Is - Jill.
—*June Duroux Foster*

Untitled

   I
     There,
   Now I've said it all

   Us
   I and another I
   Mutual parasites

   Hope
   Quiet inside corner
   External driver

   Love
   Hope exploded
   Giving all but I

   Teach
Silence and patience and show
   Us and love

   Art
   I and love and teach
   Inside hope learned

   Death
—*Ralph D. Guterman*

The Gates Of Hell

Beyond the gates of hell
there is an innocent one
that will be convicted
of a false crime
Beyond the wall is a child's face
that faces the dangers
of our world today
Behind the darkness
is a gleaming light
for a beautiful feeling
and a loving world
but without this light
that is so great,
all the world
will turn to hate
because of that darkness
that lies beyond
the gates of hell
—*April Young*

Melancholy

In what is felt and sensitive
Quiet tenderness yet remote in reality
And the affection and gentle touch
Put upon by constraints for allowed
By finding the solitude of melancholy
Left alone but to soar on fragile wings
And dreams kept remote from reality
—*Bruce A. Lutgen*

My Mother's Red Kimono

In the memory of my childhood
There is one scene I recall.
It is my mother's red kimono
Which was hanging on the wall.

My mother's robe was a symbol
Of a richer life to be.
With visions of a wonderful future
In a far away community.

I saw myself as a grand lady
With lovely clothes and beautiful home.
There was no limit to my dreaming
When my fancy started to roam.

Those were happy days and pleasant
With few jealousies or strife.
No one kept up with the Jones'
In our simple country life.

I regret that my dreaming is over
And admit that this is not all.
I wish that I once more could see
My mother's robe upon the wall!
—Verna L. Olson

The End

There is rest when it is done.
There is peace in the floating center.
Like the snail shell, all of life
In spiraling ecstacy ascends.

From the spirals - like the shell -
Great shafts of light, like days gone by
And yet to come, they pierce the
Darkness of eternity.

The moon, he watches all,
And by and by he plays a joke
On tragedy and causes all to join
In joyous song:

"Death where is thy sting?
You have been conquered!
Oh, tragedy and pain must come
And drench us like the rain, then some,
But when the Sun comes conquering
The clouds they disappear, and,
Love and Life, and Growth, behold!
The Great Orgasmic Sphere!"
—Jason D. Schutz

There's A Space For Every Man

There's a place here on this planet
  there's a space for you and me,

Somewhere below the highest peak
  somewhere above the deepest sea,

Beyond the blue horizon
  of every country land,

There's space here on this planet
  for every race of man!

There's a time here in this age
  There's a season to be born,

Let's write history page by page
  with the dawn of a golden morn,

When we see the same sun risin'
  and we vow to do our part,

And the space we reserve for every man
  is a place within our heart!
—Theresa Hendrixson

Men Don't Cry

Men don't cry, you say?
  They are much too strong.
Tears are for the weaker sex
  As they say in every song.

So what about the tear that forms
  In the corner of his eye
When he reads a lovely verse
  A poet left in passing by?

Or sees the mural painted
  By the fiery setting sun
Clothed in regal splendor
  Telling the day is done?

Often there are like times
  When a word, a glance, a sigh
Tugs at his heart strings
  As memories go passing by.

So tell me gently once again
  That men don't cry, 'tis true,
But there are times I do believe
  'Twould be the only thing to do.
—John Shelton Cate

Heartbeats!

Heartbeats!
They harmonize in a
  in a symphony
  of measured chords
  resounding
What our hearts must feel
  for Berea.

Mercurial,
They rise and fall
  as each dream
  remembered

intensifies each throbbing beat...
  action — reaction
To each Berea experience —
  a mountain climb,
  a campus stroll,
  a Chapel prayer —
All these and more
  stir hearts and souls
  of All who long for Berea Beloved!
—Mrs. Ruth V. Fierros

Sullen Feelings

Devoid of light
  they sobbed
Fervently desiring the one
  so dear
And deeply inuring a secret
  love affair
Like a ravenous raven
  they starved.
As with wings may
  they fly
Into a world where
  they are free.
How stout would
  they be
Surviving every unfolding misery
  if they
lingered idly possessed
  with passion?
—Lovelle Sokan

Silence

Their eyes meet
  they talk,
  but in silence.
  They talk
through their hearts.
Their souls combine,
  to make one.
  But no one knows,
  not even them.
—Jenny Michael

Looking At Those Eyes

Just looking at those eyes,
They tell so much,
So much I want to know.

And yet you're not mine,
But, inwardly I know you are.

There's so much of life we can share,
And so much that we already have.

But, just looking at those eyes,
They tell so much,
So much I want to know.

Wish we could turn back the clock,
To discover all our likes and dislikes,

And have the chance to know
The inner soul of those eyes.

Just looking at those eyes.
They tell so much,
So much I want to know,
So much I want to know.
—P. Cassano

Philosophy

I saw four diamonds in a pool
They were so lovely and so cool
I stooped to pick them for my hair
But found there were no di'monds there.

What trick is this my senses play?
To show and then to take away
I pondered long and smiled to find
The di'monds still were in my mind.
—Joan Bloyd

"We Have Something"

We have something that
  thieves can never steal,
Or that no one else can
  ever feel.
We have something that
  rust cannot decay,
Or that no one can take
  from us any day.
We have something that
  money can't buy,
Or that a sorrow can't take
  away, or even a cry.
We have something that
  is rare and true,
It's the memories we hold
  of me and you.
—Jo Ann Pedersen

Talking To The Stars

Sometimes when I talk to the stars
thinking how we're so alike.
there is only one of us in the world
although there are many alike.
Sometimes when I talk to the stars
I think how we both shine so
bright, how unique we are.
Oh, how I think when I talk to
the stars.
—*Jennifer Lynn Hostutler*

What Is Poetry?

Poetry is RHYME and RHYTHM,
This we should know as fact.
So many poems that I read,
These items they do lack.

To give a poem RHYTHM now,
We need to sound it out.
Comparing poetry with prose
You will then learn this route.

An ancient dictionary says,
"Distinguish it from prose"
To keep the RHYME AND RHYTHM
then,
A real poet knows.

A count to eight and then to six,
Will put the RHYTHM there.
To make the last words sound alike
Will make you then aware.

A poem now you will create,
Eliminating prose,
To keep a poem now in gear,
Intelligence then shows!
—*Joan G. Barrie*

Clouds For Fun

I love to watch the clouds float by
Those fluffy cotton balls of the sky
Floating lazily so big and white
Images soon way out of sight

I let my imagination take hold
And see all kinds of faces
And animals and fancy things
And dream of far off places

And think wouldn't it be fun
To drop down among that fluff
And roll around and just enjoy
Jumping from puff to puff

But then reality sets in
And I know I'd make quit a dash
And folks would get a big surprise
As I landed on earth ker-splash!
—*Mary Saunders*

Father

Father you are the one I long for,
threw out each and every day.
You are the one I wish for,
when things are not so great.
You are the one I dream I'll be,
when I grow up like you.
Father you mean so much to me,
I hope I'll be like you.
—*Lorri Gum*

Looking Through The Window

I'm looking
through a window
I see myself
on the other side

I'm making a mistake
I see it happen
"Oh no please no
don't do it" I say

But like a silent movie
you cannot stop it
the cast members go on
the reel keeps running
and the movie never ends
—*Karen Nielsen*

The Eyes Of A Child

The child stares
Through eyes of innocence
She perceives a world so bright
A loving place to be
Peace is all she sees
In the world she perceives
Her eyes are hidden
From the pain
All tragedy eludes her
Life is just a game
Do we live in vain?
Why can't we all be
Just what she perceives
Free of all evil
Lover of man
Little girl in the corner
She believes that we can
—*Janine DeRiso*

Love's Longing Dream

On fragile wings of dawning's dream
Through silvern mist you come to me.
 I hear your voice
 I see your smile
 I feel your gentle hand.

My joy-filled heart now finds anew
That perfect love I had with you.
 O stay with me! I beg the night
Delay my dream's departing flight.

The mist returns — and you are gone.
 My soul grieves on
 Until that shining, glorious day
When Heaven shall bid me come to stay.

 I'll hear your voice
 I'll see your smile
 I'll feel your gentle hand.

My joy-filled heart shall find anew
That perfect love I'll have with you.
 And hand in hand you'll walk with me
 Through all of God's eternity.
—*Hilda Schaefer*

Alone

The wind howls
through the rift in my soul
Deep as hell
and wider than eternity
There is no bridge strong enough to span
the canyon in my mind
There is a glacier
in my heart
no one but I can feel
It was not there a while ago
it grew quite gradually
Funny thing- I feel no pain
just a certainty of doom
Life seems long
dark and bleak
And tho' the sun shines bright
It cannot touch the glacier deep
hidden from the light.
—*Lisette Root*

D-A-D-D-Y

As a child growing up
 Through the green grassy fields I ran,
Free as a bird, knowing
 I was protected by daddy's firm hand.

Daddy was so very strong
 But with me he had a gentle touch,
He was perfect in my eyes
 And I loved him, oh so much.

When I fell into trouble
 No matter what it was all about,
I could reach out my hand
 And daddy would pull me out.

Through the good times and the bad.
 I can make it on my own,
But as long as I have my daddy
 I'll never have to stand alone.
—*Robin Bales*

Untitled

The birth of a house is a
 time-consuming thing.
It is accomplished by bulldozer
 and bricklayer.
The house is nourished by carpenter,
 electrician, plumber, and roofer.
It grows and flourishes with
 cabinet-maker, and painter.
It learns to breathe and smile.
It enfolds a family into its being.
But it starts as a dream.
—*Virginia Stille*

Untitled

Do not play games;
It will only end up in tragedy.

Always tell it like it is;
You will respect yourself.

Never try to please anybody but yourself;
You're more important than anyone else.

Be honest with yourself and others;
Trust is important.

Never compromise your integrity.
—*Amy Bray*

Old Friend

From the distant past
  time long misplaced
    yet cherished
    you appeared

In a year of pain
  tears of sorrow
  raw, rancid loss
  you understood

At a time of ending
  death's desertion
  shared remembrances
  you encouraged

Like enchanted fantasy
  dreams long forgotten
  youthful escapades
  you conjured

Around the loss of love
  an empty chamber
  memories' wreath
  you entwined
    —*Constance Woodward Houser*

The Uninvited

Love doesn't knock when it enters.

It comes as whispered lyrics
  to a soft guitar,
As a gentle hand on the shoulder
  when the world crashes in,
As laughter
  and twinkling blue eyes.

Love settles into unswept corners.

It drifts from the radio
  on the way to work,
Remembers a caress
  when thunder rolls in the night.
Waits
  in an album of old photos.

Love is a kiss in the dark
  which refuses to leave—
  even when the door slams shut.
    —*Martha I. McGahan*

Untitled

you've huddled yourself into the corner
to be alone in the dark.
i wish you understood
the darkness inside of me.
i wish my arms were perpendicular
to form a corner
for you to crawl into.
    —*Catherine Hope Greene*

My Church and I

  My church and I are all in one
We laugh, we praise, we rejoice in song.
    Together we worship
      Together we pray,
  Helping one another along the way.
  My church and I sometimes don't see,
    The way that things need to be.
    But greater still no bonds untie.
that special love of my church and I.
    —*Beth Anne Pyle*

"The Wonder of God's Creation"

  I walked out in the woods one day,
to be alone with God - and pray;
  The beauty that enhanced my sight,
With glorious wonder and delight;
  Was more than words could ever tell;
It caused my heart with joy to swell,
  With songs of praise to God above,
For his creation and his love.

  I heard the birds sing oh so sweet,
and smelled the wildflowers at my feet;
  I felt his peace flood o'er my soul,
And knew that God is in control;
  Of everything I hear and see,
Praise God! He's in control of me.
    —*Lola Curtsinger*

Battered

i want
  to bite off
  your toenails,
  gnaw and spit
  them out

Into
  Your prune-shriveled lips
  when you kiss me.

Yet
  i lie quietly
  after devouring Your existence,
  cooing softly to Your ego,
  till You sleep,

For
  i am contained
  in Your 24 karat prison,
  constricted within
  Your eloquent torture.
    —*Laurie Leininger*

Gray Whale

Whimsical haunting voice has he
To call with echoes across the haze;
As music dancing on the sea
in lost and misty bygone days.

Great beings revered once by braves
Of times when man and earth were one;
When lone canoes plied glassy waves
And whales need not fear anyone.

Then came the horde from lands afar
To turn the ocean red with blood!
With harpoon ships, vile men of war
Whale ways no longer understood.

Gray whales should hate all men today,
But kind and gentle beasts they be,
I touched a whale in Frisco Bay
And with soulful eyes he gazed at me.
    —*Joyce A. Rice*

"Death"

Death is such a lonely word
To everyone around
When you're gone, you hear no noise
You hear no special sounds.

You might go to Heaven
Or, you might go below
You'll never get to see sunshine
Or, hear the mad wind blow

Death is darkness
As you'll soon see
There is no light
For death blinded me

It will blind you to
When your time appears
You might as well laugh
Cause there's no use for tears.
    —*Christy Stewart*

Untitled

People told me not
to get my hopes up,
hopes up for a guy
who made me feel
so special, important
and cared about.
But now I know
they were right
and now my heart
is broken
because I believed
in something that
would never happen.
    —*Renee Morgan*

Take Me Away

Take me away to be with you
To hold your heart to mine
To feel the love in every kiss
That's never hard to find.

Take me away to timeless days
I spend alone with you
Seeing things we like to see
And things we love to do.

Take me away inside your dreams
Where your fantasies run free
And show me all the things you feel
When you're next to me.

Take me away to endless nights
Holding you close to me
Where we'll share our secrets
And things we hope to be.

Take me away with all your heart
Take me with your soul
Take me in your loving arms
And never let me go.
    —*John Sullivan*

In Honor Of Mother's Day

I wish I had a mother
To honor on her Day
So many memories of her
And things I'd like to say.

She always was so gentle.
and always so kind
Never an evil thought
Ever crossed her mind

Nine children in the family
She loved us everyone
We were all treated equal
As she had no favorite one

Each and every birthday
I showered her with a gift
Just a small loving token
Really gave her heart a lift

—*Susan H. Gates*

Afraid To Live

Because I'm afraid to take a chance
To live my life, maybe find romance
I hide behind a cool facade
Can't ask friends to come to my aid

I sit alone, from Dawn to Dusk
Read, watch TV and sometimes dust
It hides the loneliness Deep Inside
For in my home, Unseen, I hide

I promise myself I'll change my ways
I'll spend more time enjoying my days
I'll call a friend and go to lunch
But tomorrow comes with that scary Hunch

He won't want to see me
He'll be busy and rushed
My life, My love he could enhance
If only I could take that chance.

—*Ellen DeWoody*

Grandma's Wish

A baby in the family
To love and to hold
Has been Grandma's wish
So I have been told.

Could it be a little girl
Oh! How happy she would be
When she sees all the dollies
That are meant for her from me.

But wait! It could be a boy
Grandma says no big deal
He can bring a lot of joy
And my heart he will steal.

Mother is fine and Daddy too
Looking forward to having you.
Grandma's wish is coming to pass
Whether a boy or a lass.

—*Ruth Gally*

Your Soul

Had I a second chance
To rear five daughters and a son,
I'd stress without a second glance
The soul that is within one.
It is the most important,
Of that I have no doubt.
There is no need to rave and rant,
Not even cause to pout.
Just teach the body is a house,
And within's a living soul.
Keep it safe from mouse and louse,
No matter what the toll.
For when your life on Earth is ended,
And all is said and done,
The beginning is just splendid,
If for God your soul was won.
It's really all that matters!
It's top priority,
Just keep your soul from tatters,
For God's eternity.

—*Barbara Godwin*

Somewhere

Trapped inside with nowhere
to run, nowhere to hide. I
cannot escape. There is no
place that I can escape from
here. Mentally I'm in a place
where you can stay to
get away from here,
where people don't get
mad if you say the
wrong thing, a place
where we can get away
from our problems and here.
Somewhere, where there is
no reality. Everybody has
there own place, but mine
is a place where I can
escape from here!

—*Misty Davidson*

Within The Lines

Lengths of cloth hung 'round my neck
   To show that I conform;
Muted colors, proper width
   And knotted to the norm.

Expectations met again...
   Anxieties laid to rest.
To culture's "critic's eye" once more
   I've met their litmus test.

I move within my spectrum...
   No rough edges are in view.
When I speak, I speak in platitudes...
   Naught there to misconstrue.

I shuffle through my vapid role;
   In life I make no wave.
I guess the good Lord put me here
   To teach me to behave.

—*Roger L. Markle*

The Sting

Innocence hurts...
to watch that is.

The eyes dancing towards the light
as if to trust no matter what.

The head turned slightly to the side
as if to fathom what it cannot know.

The ears perked up to listen deep
as if to hear what simply cannot be.

Oh, the pain of purity...
I am with it, but not of it!

—*Marjorie Norris*

Con Lyric Test

Within we begin
  to without emerge tho
   in context to remain...
    not an uncommon refrain fraught
     with virtual reality and myth.

     Hence vacillating and thence
    caught in the fen of thought.
   Maintain. Hold fast, ere ta'en
  fro on winged, whispered echo
in lyric contest, a claim.

—*M. P. S. Suri*

Ode By A Crossword Puzzle Addict

With snee in hand I bravely loped
To yon arete so sharply sloped,
Midst aloe, myrrh, and elemin
To idolize fair Eoan.
'Twas all so xeno there below
As down the osar I did go;
A rana jumped across my path
As to the tarn I sought my bath.
But lo, an adit I did spy
Where I could deep in solace lie,
In ebon sere my soul more bent
Before a grot where dreams foment.
Alas, this ode was ne'er complete
Since 19 down still had me beat.

—*Bert Chapman*

Derek

When I see the two of us
together, I think of a flower.
I, as the flower lonely and
swaying in the wind. And you
as the man who picked me
and gave me the love I needed
to grow. Then as time went by
you had to leave me. I quit
growing, but you didn't take
everything from me, I did not die.
I still have some strength from
your leftover love. Now, when
I glance at a flower and think
of us, I try not to cry.

—*Honey Yankey*

Untitled

Time Time Time
Too much!
Not enough!
Stands still.

Time Time Time
Relevant
Relative
Hurry Scurry Stop!
Chip chip away at time.

Time Time time
An enemy!
A friend!
Continuity unending
Only time can tell.
—Beverly Mulconry

Requiem Pro Pacem

Within a gash close to the bone
Too virtual, displaced in youth
We felt the fangs of humankind
We donned reform of jaw and mind
Imagining ourselves as "one"
We dared to utter "truth"

Confronting every lethal lie
Abuse, oppression, feasts of blood
Sustained on silken serpent tongues
Allied with greed but deaf to songs
Of other tribes intoned in cries
We stalked the beast who lead

And somewhere poets dropped the call
Forsaking universal themes
Who self-indulgent stood and stared
In little mirrors long and cared
Too much of self but not of all
Abandoning the dreams
—Mark W. Williamson

My Sunset

An inspiring sunset
   touches down to awaken twilight,
The crest of the waves
   roll in sleepily,
to greet airbubbles
   in the damp sand.
A brilliant beam of orange
   reaches across the shore line,
   unveiling feasting sea gulls.
A worn horizon
   making a desperate
attempt to burst,
   retreats into a
      mysterious
         darkness.
—Barbara Craig Panzeter

I Wish

I wish I was a brook,
Traveling through the mountains,
Going slowly through the woods.
The animals would drink from me.
It would be so peaceful
Watching the sun rise and set.
I would always be moving,
Through the spring, summer, and fall.
When the winter snow and ice comes,
I'll be asleep.
—Cheryl L. Ziegler

The Tide

The tide brings with it many little
treasures:
The tide brings forth an abundance of
pleasures:
The tide is restless forever low
and then high;
The tide greets the shore wildly
When boats pass by:
Sea shells wash up on the wet
white sands;
And I scoop them up in my eager
hands:
The tide, and I have been age-old
friends;
And I honor the many gifts that
the ocean lends
—Shannon Payne

Lovely Rain

The rain is pouring down
Trickling and splashing
Making many people frown
But I'm out here dancing,

Singing, being merry
I must look like a fool
My nose just turned cherry
Hey, that looks pretty cool

Right now I feel as free as a bird
My liberty makes me sing
I need so much to be heard
But no one is listening

These people obviously don't care
But it doesn't matter.
To me, the rain is precious and rare
Even if it makes my teeth chatter.
—Elvia E. Flores

God Cares For The Sparrows And Me

God's begging man to change its path
Turn back to helping man,
Not feed each other's wrath.
Give people work to make them proud.
He cares for the sparrows
So I know He cares for me.

The leaders are the ones who get
Immersed in great big plots.
The peoples of this mighty earth
Have only simple wants:
Pure food, pure water, land and air.
He cares for the sparrows
So I know He cares for me.
Let all the peoples of the world
To leaders make their plea.
Combined, the thoughts create a power
That's mighty as the sea.
God knows our plight. He'll help us fight.
He cares for the sparrows
So I know he cares for me.
—Edith G. Huckins McMahon

Contentment

I've seen the evening sunset
Twenty thousand times or more
I've traveled this great country
From the east to the west shores.

I've explored the Rocky Mountains
Tilled the great midwestern planes,
Sailed the coastline of Alaska
Seen D.C. with all its fame.

Layed on beaches in Hawaii
And I've cruised the Caribbean
Landed salmon in Alaska
And trout from mountain streams.

I've known the love of family
And the meaning of true friends,
Shared in many happy moments
Realize how blessed I've been.

Should I be called tomorrow
And my life on this earth ends,
Save your sorrow for those others
More unfortunate than I've been.
—Melvin Houseman

"A Quake To Remember"

June 28, 1992 so early in the morn
Twin quakes shook up our desert home
An event like this makes life more dear
That's why I'm writing this poem.

When the ground starts to shake
We want a place to hide
Nerves are a little sharper
Our eyes are open wide
Starts the rocking and rolling
Seconds feel like minutes
Hold on to keep from falling

Check that mean "old lady"
The one with the cane
And find the little children
Leave no one in pain
To cure the stress and blues
A little extra hug today
Hold and touch each other more
God works in a mysterious way.
—Evelyn R. Sullivan

Listen To The Song Of Life

Listen to the song of life...Ocean waves
   Twinkling stars
   "Be all that you can be"
   "I'm sorry"
   WHY?
   Snowfall
   "I love you"
   The Lord's Prayer
   "I understand"
   Daffodils in the spring
   "Until death do us part"
   CONGRATULATIONS!
   A baby's 1st smile
   "I need you"
   I forgive you"
   "There is nothing we can do"
   The Lord is my Shepherd
   "Farewell"
   DAWN
   ... Listen to the song of life
—Aleicia Hayes

In Sphere Of

Sealed in a sphere of solitude
Unable to share
Held against my will
Alone, cold, and still.
I hear your voice
I see those eyes,
I feel your love,
Yet, cannot touch;
Within my heart there lies my soul,
Held in check awaiting your move.

—*Hezekiah Henley*

'Coming Of Spring

O'er and through the fields,
Under the blue so bright,
The howling wind yields
In its weariless flight.

Covered in thick snows
On the overladen road,
Roams he who blows
The breeze evercold.

Never to be seen,
Only to be felt
By the cold and keen
Who wait for the melt.

But, alas, he is gone
And she is here,
The newborn fawn
And the waking bear.

Surely as the sun shall rise,
Spring will eventually 'rive.
After earth's cold demise,
To help things thrive.

—*Kenneth Lee*

"Thief"

In the corner of the shed,
Underneath the floor,
Through the tunnel, straight ahead,
I pass the wooden door.

From the creature in the bed,
Comes a quiet snore.
Swiftly past his sleeping head,
I search the dresser drawer.

Suddenly, from in the bed,
I hear an awful roar.
And I know (with heart of dread),
That he's asleep no more.

Wanting not to join the dead,
Knowing what's in store,
Rapidly from there I tread,
As swift, were none before.

—*Dan Stratton*

Reunion

The dance
Was meant to be you and me
With eyes closed it was.
Feelings intense
Dreaming far away
Remembering years ago.
At the end
Silent tears
Wanting but knowing
The past is cast
The future still to be.

—*Billie J. Ponzetti*

God's Son

The wreath of thorns
up on your head
the blood for us
you dearly shed

Then up on the
cross you hung
While darts of hate
at you were slung

When Jesus saw
His mother there
He knew that
she would not despair

Now Mary knew
God's will was done
to bring back to Heaven
His only son

—*Hilda Clapper*

Silent Snow

Looking out my window
Upon a pristine scene,
Where sheets of startling white
Transform what once was green,
I marvel at the silence
As birds share the skimpy board,
Pecking quietly, discreetly,
By mankind quite ignored.
Snowflakes, large and puffy,
A soundless dance perform,
— Terpsichorean marvels —
Unaware of winter's storm.

This angelic canvas pleases,
But unfulfilled am I: —
No childish squeals of laughter
To pierce the leaden sky.
(I miss the children so!)

—*Mary-Lou Turner*

Dreams

Dreams are a door,
used to send us far away,
They help us forget
about our miserable day,
We can go to the future,
or back to the past,
Be in the army,
or part of a movie cast
Without our dreams,
we would have no goals,
Our lives would be empty,
we would just be lost souls

—*JoAnn Guidice*

The Other Side

Nobody ever sees my other side. My other side maybe filled with beauty and harmony, but people only see my side. People only see my side filled with hideousness and hatred and but nobody sees my other side.
The guy I liked only looked on the side that was filled with hatred. I wish people would see a cute guy/girl and look on the other side which may or may not be filled with hatred. I wish people would see my other side.

—*Erica Martinez*

Moving Forward

The spirit of the sea
visited me tonight
on Bodie Island. He
came as an old man with
watery blue eyes.
His hair was receding
but in back it
was white, long and
knotted in a rubber band.
He grabbed my hand and asked,
"Do you know your way off
this island of the drowned?"
"No," I said
and he led me through memory
back to another man
who did his best
raising me. And I
forgave him.

—*Bob Kirkley*

Hologram

The terrible silence is echoing.
Walls reflect the sound waves.
Loneliness bounces around.
The emptiness grows fuller.
I am scared and alone.
Everything becomes blurry.
My mind is playing tricks again.
A tapping at the window begins.
An image of a man traces the window.
Rain falls heavily upon everything.
Time stops and becomes faster.
The confusion complexes too much.
Reality falls farther from my mind.
A dream is the only reality present.
The pieces break apart,
And the puzzle grows harder.
Slowly the man's image fades.
The rain begins to stop.
But the sun doesn't shine.
Never again will the sun shine.

—*Tracy Perachi*

Slipping By

At the dawn of each new day,
Watch the sun ride through the sky,
Imprisoned here inside myself,
As my life goes slipping by.
There seems to be no reason,
Can't figure out just why,
I'm backed into the corner,
As my life goes slipping by.
Can't get up from the canvas,
No matter how hard I try,
I always fall from grace,
As my life goes slipping by.
Moonbeams dance in shadows,
Stars twinkle from on high,
Another day, another sorrow,
As my life goes slipping by.
Will there be another tomorrow,
To put a sparkle in the eye,
Or eternal darkness to remind us,
That life keeps slipping by.

—*Scott "Spider" Ferguson*

"Lonely Love"

I can feel it deep in my heart,
We are slowly drifting apart,
For us I want only the best,
And it seems it just gets less and less,
Our love no matter how strong,
Can't survive this time alone,
Time together means so much, a
Time to share a time to touch,
My heart is reaching out to you,
To save our love that is so true,
I get so lonely when you're gone,
If only we could share a home.
Something Darling has to change,
If only I could share your name.
Our time together is so rare,
When you go, it's more than I can bear,
I love you more than words can say,
And always will till my dying day.
—Kathryn Morgan

farewell to sungod

black against orange
we bid sungod
goodnight.
arms raised
in final farewell
we wave
as he slips slowly
behind the darkening grass
a trail of paling orange
his twilight legacy
fades to blue black
night.
—Heather M. Nevill

When We Were Children

Yesterday
We were young
We were children
We understood nothing but fun

We were young
We were dirty, messy things
We understood nothing but fun
Our hearts beat joyfully in our chests

We were dirty, messy things
We understood nothing but fun
We were dirty, messy things
Our hearts beat joyfully in our chests

Yesterday
We understood nothing but fun
Our hearts beat joyfully in our chests
We were children
—Caroline A. Savio

Strengths Within

Hope is a feeling deep within,
It gives us the strength to move on,
Holding our current ideals in place,
Long after the old ideals are gone.

Faith offers us the future,
For all to strive for,
With beliefs that are strong,
Ones we could never ignore.

Love is indescribable,
It surrounds us everywhere,
Full of warmth, security, and joy,
There is nothing to compare.
—Grace Dela Cruz

For Peace Of Mind And Heart

If we want peace in this life
We will need a living faith,
Then season it with true love
And weed out all our hate.

A life that is without hope
Is one of fear and despair,
If we but trust in the Lord
He will give us loving care.

Charity is the virtue of love
It brings peace to the heart,
Helping someone in their need
Is one good way to start.

We need the virtue of patience
And the best place we can go,
Is to the Master of patience
Then pray for this virtue to grow.

We can exist from day to day
And succumb to the daily strife,
Or we can ask the Lord to help us
For peace and a new lease on life.
—Mary Milliman

Our Sunbeam

A sunbeam lived at our house
Went in and out the doors
Filled our hearts with gladness
Made playtime of the chores.

Our sunbeams name was "Judy"
Her hair was flecked with gold,
Her eyes told of the wonders
No mortals eyes behold.

Our sunbeam danced away from us
One windy afternoon.
Left our home so bleak and lonely
Our hearts cried our "too soon"

But sunbeams were not meant to stay
They always come and go -
We'll see our sunbeam dance again
The master planned it so.
—Relda Ward

Love

Over the years
we've grown strong
You've helped me understand
That life goes on.
You gave me a hand
To help me through.
You've always cared
When I was blue
You gave me hope
Through all the years
You are always here for me
You're always a friend
You've helped me see
That we'll never end.
—Crystal Pendleton

Looking

I'm looking within.
What do I see?
A spark. A rose.
Personality.
I'm looking without.
Low and behold,
A smile. A hug.
A shoulder that's cold.
I'm looking at you
When we we're young
A fight. A push.
A sister I love.
I'm looking about
Down at our feet
Who would have thought
That boys we're so sweet?
I'm looking ahead,
Time has to move.
Grey haired and old
But life was so good.
—Lisa Diane Martin

What Is Freedom?

Freedom,
What is freedom?
Freedom you ask,
I do not know.
For being in this place,
Watching others of my kind,
Dying!
What is your kind?
mine is not of yours,
—or I am a Jew,
The smell of the dead
Makes me sick,
Seeing my son
Die!
Is that Freedom?
—Tasha Jeffreys

The Unlucky Day

My hem is down,
    What rotten luck!
What'll be next?
    My zipper's stuck!

My button's popped,
    My jacket's torn,
I split my seam,
    My knees are worn.

My breakfast's burned,
    The kids ain't fed,
I've changed my mind,
    I'll stay in bed!
—Linda Paterek Scott

The New Spring Day

I walked outside to see the day,
When all the snow was gone away.
The birds were singing loud and clear,
The sight of spring was finally here.
Flowers bloomed here and there,
New green grass was everywhere.
Trees were growing tall and full,
The air was clean but kind of cool.
That's what I saw and heard that day,
A sign of a wonderful new spring day.
—Brooke McPherson

"What Shall I Say, My Love?"

A leaf asked the rose bud
"What shall I say, my love?"
A sparrow asked the fig tree
"What shall I say, my love?"

But the rose bud sweetly blushed
and the fig tree shed a tear
For neither one could find the words
To reach a lover's ear.

Soon the leaf turned bright red
and floated down to earth
Where it made a little pillow
For the fallen sparrows head.

Now I stand here in the forest
In the freezing, pouring rain
And I try to find the meaning
of the words they couldn't say

For I wish to share a secret
Before I lose my way
In the freezing, pouring rain:
"what shall I say, my love?"
—*John P. Esquivel*

Perfection

There are moments in time
   when all is harmony and rhyme,
When a vision of perfection is real,
   and time itself seems to stand still.
Remembered days and nights of pure
   pristine clarity of inner light, sure
As candles cast an aura of shadow
   not unlike moonlite of a meadow
High above the restless shore,
   who could ask for perfection more
Than memorable moments like this
   for telling a time of perfect bliss.
—*John Harvey Newbury*

When You Were A Teen

How was life when you were a teen,
   When all you wanted was to be seen.

To be able to have a voice,
   Of all the things of your choice.

Not worrying about the mistakes that
   You could make and all the sadness
   That it takes.

Forgetting those, who you thought
   Did not care Oh how life had been
   So unfair.

When all you wanted was to dream,
   When life was at It's fullest
   Extreme.

All you could think of when you were
   A teen, was the day you would be seen
   As a human being.
—*Mary Lyons*

"Cupid"

There is the day that comes each year
When Cupid spreads his joy and cheer,
The happiness that comes our way
The joy we feel on Valentine's Day.

They say when his arrow hits the heart,
The feeling of love, it does impart
Romance begins, the spirits rise,
And visions of beauty fill our eyes.

But I have a question…
Wouldn't it be wiser
To have an adult shoot the bow
Than an infant in a diaper?
—*Bob Snyder*

Life

Life begins
when dreams out-span the present task,
vision reaches to horizons new,
hope's compass reads eternal signs.

Life begins with each new day,
each moment, each breath of healing air,
each lifting of the heart
to higher things.

Life begins
when all seems bright and new,
all is triumph, victory assured,
friends are many,
love bears us up, affirms our worth.

Life begins when all seems lost,
friends seem few,
as Life began, hung on The Cross.
—*Aaron Webber*

Only Mothers Know

Once upon a summer
When Love was warm,
My Father ran with me
Through a hailstorm.
We were all laughing,
Though struck from on high -
My sweet fleet sister,
My Father and I.
But Mother saw darkness
Where we saw none,
And spoke of sadness
Though we were safe at home.
How could she know the sorrow
We dared not see?
How guess the heartbreak
And soul shake to be?
There is no safe home.
That's the deep well
Only Mothers know about,
And seldom tell.
—*Mary Katherine Murray*

May Dreams Come True

I dream a world of beauty
where creed and color make no difference
in granting opportunities…
I dream a world of dignity
where all men strive to be their best
no matter what the sacrifice…
I dream a world of peace and love
not just for some, but everyone…
I dream the World of Brotherhood.
—*Myra M. Gregory*

Imagination

I am not I
when my thoughts take over
they take me very far.
I am not I,
but a snowflake,
because that's what I want.
I can be a knight in armor,
a king upon the throne.

I am not I
at these times,
I am something strong and fun.
But if someone interrupts,
my fairyworld is shattered.

I am all alone again,
when I am I.
—*Sandra Horwitz*

Untitled

When will I learn to trust Him
   When will I quiet be?
I fret about life's problems
   He tells me "Trust in Me".

I e'en can trust my own needs
   I give to Him each day
But anxious fears for loved ones
   Find me their weary prey.

My patient Saviour loves me
   Despite my stumbling walk
He waits to bless and comfort
   Even chastens when I balk.

Well might we really wonder then
   At young who will not heed
When we who met Him long ago
   Forget He knows each need.

Dear Saviour - teach me once again
   To fully wait on Thee
To know you love them more than I
   And your plan yet shall be.
—*Irene V. Carlson*

I Wonder

I wonder if David knew
when writing the psalm
a mother would find comfort
in those healing words,
a child know security
even in the dark,
a ray of hope found
for the husband who had lost his job.

I wonder if David knew
the depths of pain he experienced
would be felt throughout the ages,

I wonder…
   if David knew.
—*Deborah Budwig*

I Will Remember You

I remember that summer day
When you walked away
I remember that glorious smile
When we walked that mile
Now I am left with the
Remembrance of you and me
And how it use to be.
I wish I was at the mall
Where we use to have a ball
I wanna call to say Hi
But I am a little too shy.

—*Tammy*

Cost Of Love

I look back on that time
When you were still mine
  It was so long ago
  Many years, I know.

  I dream of you still
  And many times I feel
  Your hand upon my face
And your sweet embrace.

I wish I could go back,
But I know for a fact
That sweet time is lost
And my heart was its cost.

—*Laura Chrisco*

Little Clam

"Little clam, little clam,
  Where are you going?"

"Down to the beach
  Where the water is flowing."

"Little clam, little clam,
  Where will you be?"

"I'll be under the sand,
  under the sea."

—*Lauren Williams*

Laughter By Edgerly

Once in our lives; maybe once
While in the rain
Leaning 'gainst the brick
Standing alone
  You see another
  Unprotected
  Walking through the rain.

And you smile at him,
Laughing a little
At the attitude and the wetness;
And look away.

Only
To look again
To see a wonderful,
Smile coming back.
  At you.
  That leaves you
  In the rain
  Filled with
  Sun.

—*Erica Friedrich*

Living: Diligent And True

I watched the robins in the spring
While on the ground and on the wing
There's talk of ants and busy bees
But none's more diligent than these
In building nest they work in twain
In gusty wind and dashing rain
Then while upon her nest she sits
Her true love seeks and brings her bits
Together then they feed their brood
From morn till dark they seek for food
If we could be as fair and true,
In our lives in things we do
as Robin Red Breast and his bride
There'd be nothing then to hide
There'd be no anger, crime, or hate
Just true openness from mate to mate
Such nobleness the world would gain
Love and peace on earth would reign

—*Orion Jennings*

Sunset

The summer is dying in my veins
while swimming in a purple sunset,
bittersweet smoke of my tiredness
tormenting me - like a cigarette
my soul is waiting for a wonder
dancingly, like a thrown-away yoke,
a gentle breeze picks up the rhythm
freely catching the blessings above!

The shadows are motionless, patient
they stand tremblingly before the End;
farewell, farewell my graying darling,
your golden touch is my only kind
I know, you wait for a parting kiss,
willingly offering your lips to me;
your tears washing my wrinkles away,
while our love lives in eternity...!

—*Joseph Kovacsy*

Watching A Rose Open

The green sepals closed in a neat tip
While the bud inside grew larger.
One, then two sepals loosened their hold
Now all five curled under
To reveal a lovely red rosebud;
A wonder
To me whose eyes beheld
The rich petals
That beckoned me nearer
To gaze until the bud
Became a full blown rose.

—*Rae Stone*

Colored Hated

Nigga'. Honkey.
White trash, black trash.
Hate, stupidity, rivalry.
Two gangs deadly possessed,
Color is all They see.
Silver flies,
Sirens sound, feet run.
No one wins.
Everyone loses.
Two boys dead,
One race wronged.

—*Robyn Wyant*

Bless The Children

God bless all the little children
While they play and sleep;

Watch over and protect them
For they are like lost little sheep;

They need our patience and guidance
Until they're full grown;

They need to learn right from wrong
For they are our very own;

Sweet little angels
Sent from heaven above;

Treasures to have and to hold
But most of all to love.

—*Christina C Simmons*

Remember

Remember those who are not here now
who fought so we could be,
Remember those who gave their lives
on land and on the sea,
Who left the ones they loved
when the call for men came out.
Who went to serve their country
and knew without a doubt
that no matter what happened
they were doing right.
So they stood beside their comrades
and they all prepared to fight.
They were in the combat
and died fighting in the war.
Thank those that are still here with us
And remember those that died before.

—*Kate Buckman*

"Playful Miss"

There was a little miss
Who had some fun like this.
She had a bouncing ball.
She tossed it to her doll.
She had a little box
In which she hid some blocks.
She had a flowered shirt.
She made a matching skirt.
She had a teddy bear.
She shaved off all his hair.
She had a favorite book.
She read it in a nook.
She had a toy bassoon
On which she played a tune.
She had a dancing frog.
They danced upon a log.
She had a small pink bed
On which to rest her head,
To dream of things to play
While night turned into day.

—*Rachel Tenney*

Darold Hill Truly Missed

When you truly love someone
who has passed on, you never
know if the grief will be long.
I loved my husband so much
and we were always in touch.
He was my best friend and
Our marriage was never going to end.
The accident brought me pain,
heartache and bad luck which
was caused by a careless person
driving a large truck.
The Lord God is the only one,
that knows what I'm going
through and every word on this
paper is true.

—*Yvonne Hill*

What Is Life Without A Dream?

What is life, without a dream?
Who knows the answer to this theme
Maybe it is something good, I'll say
Or should I wait for one more day

What is life, without a dream?
When everywhere I hear a scream
Should I say, I don't want to be here
Or should I stay and have no fear

What is life, without a dream?
Is it really all part of a scheme?
Or is it very real
That there is something I should feel

What is life, without a dream
Is it like the color cream?
Or is it something I can't explain
To everyone who knows my name

What is life, without a dream
When I could be in one big team
Is it fair, or is it wise
To want to live in Paradise.

—*Radhica Ramharack*

My Elderly Friend

I went to see a friend today
Who lives across the way
At a place called Senior Square
In a setting that is rare.
He always has a smile for me
And is cheerful as can be.
Although home bound every day
He seems young in every way.
He recalls each yester year
With a memory very clear.
Without good sight of former days
And tho feeble in his ways,
My dear friend has outlived many
He's now eighty years-plus twenty!

—*Wanda Belt*

Thunderstorm

Oh thunderstorm in the spring,
You make me want to dance and sing
I listen and I hear your cry
It makes me laugh and makes me sigh
I see the lightning tumble down
It hits the trees and then the ground
I hear the thunder, I'm prepared
Oh thunderstorm, I'm not scared.

—*Amanda Bailey*

A Tribute To Carlton

I once knew a man
Who was a very special friend.
His Christianity was shown
Through his kindness and generosity
He had a witty sense of humor
And a twinkle in his eyes.
Although when his health began to fail
His personality stayed the same.
He's not with us now.
There is a little sadness
But a lot of happiness, as
God has his soul in waiting
Until the day of judgment.

—*Betty Whitehead*

A Closer Friend

I know of a closer friend
Who will be with me until
the End.

No it's not my mother, that
I Love so dear.

I know of a closer friend
Who brings Joy to my aching
head.

No it's not my sister that
I Learn to Overcome.

Nor it's my brother who don't
Give or Care.

I know of a closer friend
Who answers my Prayer.

No it's not my Lover, I
Love year after year, nor my
Father who died some years.

I know of a closer friend,
that none can compare, oh
It's Jesus that I Love so dear.

—*Lillian Mackey*

I Will Always Love You

The day I met you
Who would ever have believed
You would be the one
I'd love for all times

They say opposites attract
It appears to be fact
You were true country
I was true rock

I fell in love
You fell apart
I held on tight
You ran all night

I wish you the best
Success and all the rest
But no matter what happens
I will always love you

—*Deborah Turner*

Spirits

Where they go
Who would know
To heaven, maybe
Or across the sea
To the sun
Or to the moon
To the bottom
Of a beautiful lagoon

Today we weep
And see the streaks
Of tears running
Down our cheeks
For we pray
That God will care
To give the love
That we share
To the people
Who have gone away
That we'll catch up with
Some other day

—*Kelly Ross*

My Troll

I have a troll,
who's as straight as a pole.
He walks really funny,
and dresses like a bunny,
Has big bug eyes,
and he never lies.
He has purple hair,
but do you think I care?
I love my troll.
He's like a mole.
He's stuck to me,
as you can see.
He wears a hat when it's cold,
and always does what he's told.
He has pointed ears,
and shops at Sears.

He's my troll!
We like to stroll.

I love him!
Him, is Jim!

—*Alicia Hathaway*

Social Commentary - 1964 or 1993?

Hello, nut-brown child,
Whose flying feet and cheerful shouts
Give not a hint of all the pain,
The turmoil, tension, fear, despair,
That soon will dog your future path.
What will you be?
A nurse or waitress, doctor,
Teacher, lawyer, senator
Or bum?
You may feed me,
Teach me, write my laws,
Or raise my son,
Or write a book.
Or probe the atom's farthest depths.
But don't move next door!

—*Roy Darlington*

"The Disease"

Epilepsy, the disease
Why did he have to have it?
Why did time have to freeze
Epilepsy, the disease
God, take it away please!
But he is still practically fit
Epilepsy, the disease
Why did he have to have it?

—*T. J. Mosher*

Melancholy Bewilderment

Innocence wonders:
Why is the grass green,
What makes the sky blue?

Experience wonders:

Why must there be lies
To hide what is true?
Why do people hurt people,
And then watch their tears fall?
Why must there be pain?
What will break the wall?
Why is there fighting,
In which so many die?
What must be done,
To make the world try;
Try and join hands,
Come together as one;
Try to find peace,
And all suffering be done.

—*Paige A. Larson*

Nerve Ends

Why reflect?
Why mirror?
Why ponder?
Why image?
Do you think?
War is bad -
Blindly follow?

What is love?
Follow me.
What is hate?
It isn't free.
Feelings, thoughts,
Full potential.
When?

—*Peter A. Halle*

Mice Who Roar

Conscientious, quiet folk
Will always answer letters
Whether business kind or social
From inferiors or betters,

Suffer gladly fools of friends
And those of not-so-friendly,
Because the flowers of brotherly love
Will bloom in breasts of many,

Often dig in empty pockets
Seeking coins by chance,
As importuning strangers stare
At thrifty skirts or pants.

They are those of doughty stuff
Who rail at government
With fire in eye and steely fists
To redress wrongs unmeant.

—*Henry White*

The War Of Dark And Bright

Gently bright blue sky
will it rain, will it thunder
morning brings day light
can the morning bring
light in the dark, dark, dark night?
will it shine—will it not?
morning is like a bulb
morning is a knight that breaks night
riding until dawn
fire bright as the sun
fire bright as the sun light
fire is sun light

—*Carter Torrey*

Mike

The love that I feel for him
will never grow dim
Day after day
while we're so far away

I loved the way he held me tight
whenever danger was in sight
I loved the way he looked in my eyes
when he said goodbye

All those nights we spent together
under the moon
The morning always seemed to
come so soon
I thought we'd always be together
but I guess nothing lasts forever

So I just have one thing to say
No matter who comes my way
He'll always be the one
I'll be waiting for to come.

—*Michelle Henry*

God Are You Listening?

God are you listening,
Will you please hear my prayer?
We haven't met personally
But I know you are there.
I'm merely a human,
A mother, a wife;
It's not always easy
This thing we call life.
Will you please take my hand
And show me the way?
How to be more understanding,
And kinder each day?
To not stand in judgement
of anyone else;
But to take a close look
And improve on myself.

—*Lynda K. Carter*

"Grandpa Jim Is Watching"

Grandpa Jim is watching when;
  You're in the fields walking.
Grandpa Jim is watching when;
  You're in your toy box playing.
Grandpa Jim is watching when;
  You're growing.
Grandpa Jim is watching when;
  You're dreaming and sleeping.
Grandpa Jim is watching you;
  Keny Wayne from Heaven.

—*Sheila F. Franquero*

Bronze Madonna

She walks in splendor, bronze madonna
  With a basket on her head
  Filled with luscious pomegranates
  Oranges, and grapes and bread.
The weight and balance stretch her body
  Straight and tall with subtle grace.
  Bracelets on her arms and ankles,
  Seductive smile upon her face
  Make her irresistible
To the youths who mark her pace
And pant to touch the luscious softness
  Undulating silk and lace.
Ah, beauty is its own enchangement
  Holding hearts in its embrace.

—*Helena Hult*

Mona Lisa

  Ah! This painting
  With a face of mystery,
  Eyes of the unknown,
  Smile of uncertainty.

Even the valleys behind her,
  Testify! to a mystique.

    She's a reflection
    of her creator,
    Fortune teller
    Of modern man,
    Ageless beauty,
    The fruit of life.

—*Pasquale De Santis*

"Wonder"

Sitting at night atop a hill
With a field of lights below
We gaze through the haze
As the winged beasts
Rise above the fog

Happiness is a peaceful daze
Breathing as our flowers burn
Watching dragons soar
Above our hill
We wonder where they go

All is a dream not in a dream
We are high upon our hill
In an elven dream
We are the hunted beasts
Of archers with no eyes

In the paisley womb of velvet night
Under swimming distant suns
We search for the god
Who created us
And wonder where he's been

—*Jason M. Krena*

Limits

  Limit your time
  Would that be divine?
  Limit your mind
  you'll be left behind!
  Limit your skills
  you'll climb no hills.
  Limit your thoughts
  your brain will rot.
If you have no limits you will see,
  There is nowhere you cannot be.

—*Adam Greenhalgh*

You Act As Thou Art God

You act as Thou Art God to me
With every move made carefully.
But you are timid beyond that cheek
And form the words for me to speak.
And I in recognition
Of your righteous wrong
Must in turn
Turn my cheek
And check which ever notions
I have built
My life upon.
— *Ethyl Treatman*

Heart Without A Home

A heart alone without a home
With half your life behind you,
There's no words to describe
The emptiness inside you.

It's like the river without water
And the sky without the blue,
There's no other way to say
How bad, love can hurt you.

Lonely days and lonely nights
A heart without a home,
That's exactly how you feel
When love has passed and gone.

Nobody knows how many tears
One lonely heart can cry,
They just seem to come and flow
When love says "Good-Bye."

This heart alone without love
Came from Kentucky to Tennessee,
With the tears and the fears of looking
Into tomorrow for a new destiny.
— *Nila Yvonne Buck*

That Blessed Mother

That mother
With her sacred trust,
Who sees her child
As an earthly plus,

Who weary
With her earthly chores,
Will encourage her child
Forevermore.

Though her days be heavy
And problems present,
She'll still see that child
As heaven-sent.

And, when at last
Her time shall end,
God will take her soul,
For He's her friend.

He'll send His angels
To bring her home,
And she'll dwell with Him who sits
On the heavenly throne.
— *Mary Lee Dauer*

Friendship

You are here
  With me.
There are no
  Expectations.
  We exchange
  Idle chatter.
  Some laughs,
    Some tears,
    Some anger,
    Some love.
Whatever we feel
  Is all right.
  We are free
To be ourselves.
  This is how
  Friendship
  Should be.
    You
    And
    Me.
— *Julie M. Klimesh*

Untitled

Warm velvet night
With moon looming through mist
Over fogfields and sleeping town -

Warm velvet mouth
With pretty lies welcomed
And spoken to my skin -

Warm velvet body
With life-force sparking
And screaming its youth -

Warm velvet feeling
With hard warrior arms
Holding me in sleep -

    And with chill harsh light
    Comes the death of dreams....
— *Jean Manning*

Living

A merry chase it is and will have been -
With no thing sure -
Except that thee and me and others such
That starting from propinquous atomicity
In swamp primordial
Emerged as Cyberpunkish tinkerers
Awallow in a realm
Of digitated infosatiety
And gadgetry galore -
Must one day yield our place.
Perhaps no other way can be
Beyond insensate moil
For protoplasmic mass particulate
That overruns and fouls its nest
And heeds no curb.
Let then the human soul beware -
Propitiation will not serve
Where deeds alone can testify.
If tribunal there be
"the readiness is all."
— *Leland Austin*

On Birth And Life!

Conceived in love,
  with nurture you will grow.
Until that day...
  like the butterfly coming out
    of its cocoon,
You will flower.
  Yearning to fly...
in new directions!

You will go forth.
  Conceive in love.
The cycle of love and life
  continues!

God's Master Plan
  for all things great and small.

God bless you little one and the
  parents you have chosen.
May your road be smooth and filled
  with wondrous treasures.
— *Nancy Ferraro*

Beauty Of God's World

I wish that I were an artist
With palette, easel and brush
Beauty and glory of nature
To paint to the song of the thrush

I would paint the mountains majestic
In blue and purplish hue
The sky all red and golden
With the sun dropping from view

I would paint the trees in fall color
The aspen all gold in the wood
Then I would lift my face slowly
And thank God for being so good.
— *Wanda Callante*

Second Chance

As I looked at the hospital
  With terror in my eyes
I happened to look down
  At my disfigured body
And knew my life was over

If only I wasn't so stubborn
  To changed my tough image
Into what I felt inside
  On the outside I showed
People I was strong,
  But the truth of the matter is
I was weak and fragile.

My body finally could not
  Take the stress anymore
With my mind telling me to
Get a better attitude towards life

Where to start I had no clue
  Nevertheless it's too late
If only I had a second chance
  I could somehow turn my life around
— *Craig Deskins*

Spring Time

On a cool spring day,
with the crickets chirping a
brand-new song of love.

The birds are flying
way up in the sky like a
plane that people fly.

While the beaver chews
up a long piece of red wood
from the light blue pond.

Small little gerbils
running fast in a red wheel
like racing runners.

This season is a
favorite of mine because
I love the spring time.

—Roxanne Mott

Spring Time

Spring time is wonderful,
With the new flowers and buds
Covered with a light mist,
Like honey dew drops
In a midnight summers rain.
Glistening in the moon light,
The flowers decorate the fields
With their beautiful fragrance
And rainbow colors.
While the little field mouse,
Scampers from petal to petal
For protection from the owl.
The pink and orange rays,
Awakes the morning skies.
The warmth of the sun
Dries the misty dew,
From the night before.
A new day has begun.

—Sandra Meyer Brunnert

"The Ghetto Child"

So lost, so alone,
without a chance,
without a home.
Hoping for a future
that just won't come to be.
Hoping to be a doctor, a nurse,
or just somebody.
Trying to make it in a world,
full of poverty and shame,
always looking for trouble,
or for someone else to blame.
Education, just doesn't come
easy, to a child that seems
so wild. Is it all because
they are the Ghetto Child?

—Margaret L. Lunsford

"A Moving Force"

Yesterday I spent some time.
Working in that garden mine.
Snipping posies here and there.
And sniffing lots of springtime air.
A voice within me seemed to say
Isn't this a lovely day. Look up
and out beyond and to the sky
Watch the fleecy clouds go skipping by
As I watched the blue and white
it seemed I saw a brilliant light
Then, something happened very odd
I thought I felt a touch from the
hand of God.

—Edna G. Hilliard

The Poet Of The Past

No longer an amused epicardium
Wrapping History and Myth
Then reciting blindly
But heartily.

No longer the effeminate
Sniffing a poesy or sonnet
Then getting miffed
At frippery.

No longer Java Joe Espresso
Beating the generation before him
Then klatching coffee
In his goatee.

No longer a stereotype
Selling rhymes for greeting cards
Then collecting cash
From royalties.

I doubt he ever was
This poet of the past
But if, indeed, he ever was
Pray that no longer does he last.

—Darrell R. Brown

Evensong

I dream of finally
   writing a poem
   that will make me
   truly a poet.
   One that leaves
   relentless echoes
shining and stirring and
   sink
      ing,
      pressing
         down
         with
the humble weight
of the touch that
restoreth beauty.
Until then I suppose
   I'll just have to
   share the glory in
second person singular.

—Tammy Boyd

Facing The Consequences

They could never be closer,
   Yet be so far apart.
He longed to hug and hold her,
   To lie there heart to heart.

She watched him from a distance,
   Though only on his lap.
Her heart was pierced by a gun,
   Her tears running like sap.

They could never be together,
   Like they wanted to be,
   Because of a lusty lure,
   Because of HIV.

They could have been so blissful,
   If only he had waited,
   Now they were only wishful,
   As he stands before his fate.

—Jennifer Lahr

Untitled

As I stood in the front of the room
you all laughed at me.
I began to cry.
Since the beginning I was different
always laughed at.
I never laughed at you -
I never had the guts.
We're older now and you still
point and stare,
you call me weird.
All your life you were accepted,
now it's your turn to be laughed
at and mocked.
How does it feel?
That's how I've felt all my life.
Pretty neat -
huh?

—Melissa Milheiser

Friendship

Friendship is for ever.
You and me will stay
friends for ever.
I always say I
hope you don't forget
   me,
Because I'll never
forget you.
I wish upon the
brightest star
That will meet some
   day again.
And still remember
The good old days.
Till our death comes
Will still be friends,
But then I'll carry
Your friendship to
heaven with me.

—Cathy Jimenez

Ukiyo-e

My Hana-ogi
You are back
You blue kimono..carelessly
Hair in disarray
Nostrils flared
Perfect teeth clench a napkin
Your neck-nape exposed
Obi undone
I've been undone
Undone till your return
You've been with another
I've been with no other
Thought of no other;
Divine Geisha
In your floating world...
...your floating world.
—Toby Rappolt

An Easter Prayer

Oh, Holy One, do come in!
You are My Friend Divine.
Let me feet You're here,
Know Your will,
And heed You every time.

Let me not wear the Judge's robe
Nor the flames of my anger fan,
But seek Your Way -
As I go forth -
To love God and my fellow man.
—Sam Worthington

Farewell Papa

   Although you are here
   you are still so far away
you don't know how much it hurts me
   to watch you suffer this way
Hopefully far away there will come
   a day
   Where I shall say goodbye
   And you shall say hello
   to a place only you
   will know
—Lauren Corvino

The Light

In the dark of the night
You can see a bright light
that shines at the top of the hill.
No matter how long
or what has gone wrong
you can still see the light
at the top of the hill.
For years it has shone
and in wisdom we've grown,
but that light still shines
at the top of the hill.
As I look out tonight
and look for that light,
I ask God to do what is right
but above all the pain
between sunshine and rain,
protect if you will
that light at the top of the hill.
—Gene L. Dyer

Justified

Be proud to remember,
You children of "The Wall,"
Your fathers went to fight
For freedom for us all.

Be proud to remember
T'was not a war of shame
As the demonstrations of
The protesters proclaimed.

Be proud to remember,
Hold your heads up high,
For those protesters' freedom
Your fathers had to die.

Be proud to remember
They killed and they died;
T'was freedom for all
Their deaths justified.
—M C Ridenour

Sun And Fate

Leave us Sun,
You have been near
and have caressed the land
and shown Your care.

Vines have borne their harvest,
and naked limbs are seen
instead of green;
fields are silent, cold and bare.

Streams have had their pleasure
but they shiver now, and twist away
soon to stay
cold and hard in an icy stare.

Leave us,
O brilliant sphere
leave us here
and retreat to Your winter's lair.

We have no choice.
We are bound to await,
You, our Master
You, our fate.
—Richard G. Flores

The Leaves

The love I have for
you is stronger than a tree,
  And smooth as the breeze.
  This kind of love will
last a life time,
  But only in my mind,
  You said you loved me,
I guess you were wrong.
  That tree over there,
it was once so strong,
  Now the limbs are
breaking, like my heart.
  The leaves are turning
brown, because they have
no love.
  The leaves fall from
the branches like the tears
fall from my eyes.
  This tree, like me,
will die without love, your love.
—Donna Hitt

Love Me, Please

  Baby,
  You know I love you,
but you don't seem to love
  me.

  Sometimes my tears blind
  me and I cannot see.
Where do you go when your not
  here?
At night I wonder if you ever miss
  me, but I doubt it.
  You haven't talked to me in
days and I'm getting worried.
  So here's my last plea;
    Love me,
    Please.
—Jennifer Thompson

"The Thorn"

Your petals never felt the light.
You reached high.
Your goals set straight.
The velvet of your petals
Never had the chance to open up.
A thorn had stuck in your side.
No harm was meant to come to you.
  But alas.
You never reached the light.
Your face never felt its heat,
  Its warmth.
There was only a thorn.
Even with that thorn,
You tried to reach the light,
  But to no avail.
—Kristi Estes

Untitled

The sky above, so endless and blue
You sit, wonder and watch
But you know the feeling -
It's inside you
Deep - Deep and true
You are never alone
It will always come to you
  Wrap around you -
  Make you safe -
  Warm -
All you have to do is want it
  Feel it -
Night so dark
  Stars shining true
Love the feeling
  Cherish it -
  Respect it -
  Love it -
It is all for you
  - My Best Friend -
—Kelly Cribbs

If Only In My Dreams

Though many miles are between us
You still seem very close,
I can almost feel your arms around me.
It is almost like a ghost,
Your spirit is beside me.
And in my mind I hear,
Your laughter and your sighing,
Your joys and your fears,
Your memory makes me happy
No matter what may be!
'Cause you're still close beside me
If only in my dreams.
—*Marilyn Severance*

Dr. Bearable

This is Dr. Bearable watching over
you with his cute grin,
Wanting so much for you to feel
better again.
His Bear advise is simple and free
An improvement he hopes we'll see.
So Dr. Bearable prescribes
Bear-Hugs and Bear-Kisses too
From all your friends and family
Each time they visit you!
—*Catherine Heironimus*

If I Was Not Here

If I was not here
You would not, here me when I cry
Or even here me say goodby.

If I was not here
You could not, see me sway like
The trees and feel the breeze

If I was not here
You could not, see me grow like
The flower in may and here me
Say those words that mean so much

If I was not here
I wouldn't be nowhere
If I was not here
—*Jacinta Wallace*

Growing Old

Eternal spring, or so it seems,
Young and fragile like buds upon a tree,
I don't give shade, at least not yet.

But in summer the leaves grow green.
It seems that all around,
My shade expands over the ground.

Many begin to wither
Now that autumn has arrived,
But I am still young
And I know not what it means.

Now it's winter, but spring is near.
Not wither, not wither yet,
For my youth is still within,
Let's not forget -
Not wither, not wither yet.
—*William Rees Gettys, III*

Conversing With Phoenix

Wounded bird, rise up and fly!
Your beauty makes my heart sing.
You once glided in the sky
Swooping with fluttering wing.
You whispered in voice to sweet:

Take me to the sky once more,
Lift me up on to my feet
Caring will unlock the door,
Shield me from the hurt and pain
Comfort me with deep concern.

Fly with me not minding rain,
Love and give passion its turn.
—*Clare Tepper Harrison*

Spirit of Happiness

Happiness is the Stars I see in
  your eyes
The Sun that rises to greet the
  Morning Skies.

Happiness is the dew Kissed by the
  Summers breeze
A Blue bird in flight in the Shadows
  of trees

Happiness is a rainbow of halo
  colored light
Cascading the Heavens after the
  Darkness of Night.

Happiness is a family that grows old
  together
That endures life through all Seasons of
  Weather

Happiness is a Spirit of unselfish
  Love
A Soul inspired from God
  up above
—*Shirley Lou Robertson*

To My Son

Here I sit in this front pew
Your father by my side.
There you stand so tall and proud
Waiting for your bride.

As I watch, the church lights dim,
Sweet memories come flooding in.
A tiny babe upon my breast,
A surge of love that knows no rest.
Relentless years go fleeting by
With Christmas mornings, shining eyes;
Easter egghunts, happy cries;
Tiny footprints on summer sand;
The soft touch of one small hand.

That little boy is gone from view,
But, oh, my son, I wish for you
All the joys that I have known,
A loving spouse, a happy home,
A wondrous child to call your own.
But, please remember when you do,
That child is only lent to you.
—*Marie Patti*

After Sixty

When you are after sixty
Your life and every day
You are perceiving simply
And in another way.

The generations are changing
Some are near the end,
When you are after sixty
Your health is in your hands.

Like clouds in windy weather
That do not go back,
Your illnesses go together
And rush to the attack.

Your illnesses are in struggle
Against your only fate
And they are promise trouble,
Take care, you shouldn't wait.
—*Joseph A. Vinokurov*

My Brother

Your face passes through my mind;
your precious voice so clear.
I long to talk to you again;
I miss you, brother dear.

A brother and a friend as well;
I've treasured through the years.
We've shared some happy moments;
and also some tears.

To one who had a gentle heart;
with a spirit wild and free;
who was loved by all the family;
but most of all by me.

It hurt so much to see you suffer;
I helped you all I could.
If only I could have taken your pain,
then precious brother I would.

With God I hope you're resting;
your work on earth was through.
I hope someday we'll meet again,
some where beyond the blue.
—*Billie Clouse*

Jonas-ito

You came to visit for a while
Your strong young arms reached
To hold me close and
I felt baby arms go around my neck

As you leaned your head
to rest your cheek
Upon my hair
I felt soft baby fuzz
beneath my chin

And when your voice so rich and deep
spoke to me
I heard the music of a baby voice
asking for a lullaby

Today and yesterday fuse as one
when I look at you
so tall and strong
and see my precious baby grandson
—*Hazel A. Bumgardner*

Untitled

Suddenly,
20 minutes passed
seemingly unaware of our presence
and, before we knew,
the total reality
of what happened
could sink into our very
immortal and festering souls.
We need not carry this out
to the full, for pain
much like joy,
is a temporal state of being.
And with that exchange
of bitterness
and lashings
came the true and
unfettered self,
leaving us free
once more
for the journey south.
—*Eric Klekamp*

A Star

　　　　A star
　A beautiful diamond in the sky
　　　　A star
　A reminder from the Lord that
　where there is darkness there is
　　　　light
　　　　A star
　A hole pocked in the sky by a
　　gigantic straight pin
　　　　A star
　　Thousands of flash lights
　　　hanging from the sky
A star a star so pleasing to the
　eye as I walk out at night and
　　　look in the sky
—*Catrina Polk*

I Wish I Had...

A little of your love,
a bit of your time,
just to show you I care.
A moment of your life with me
very near,
a piece of your heart,
understanding for a tear.
A simple hello not a soon good bye,
a show of your feelings,
no need to be shy.
A part of your life, I want so bad,
a small portion of your love....
....I wish I had.
—*Natasha Theriot*

Maiden Of The Rose

Silent and still she stands alone,
A solitary figure she is the rose.
Lily while she greets the down,
Her splendid head sends forth a song.
In slender form, her arms outstretched,
A sense of beauty, nature's sketched.
The light from above case a sergon glow,
On the figure grace born there below.
Silent and still she stands alone,
A solitary figure she is the rose.
—*Mari Iagulli*

Different Chairs

Everyone should have
　a favorite chair
　A chair to call their own

Mine is a white wicker
　with flared-out arms
　far away from the phone

Morning coffee
　tastes better there
　while my eyes open to the day

My mother's chair was her
　was her very own
　I remember its color was blue
Maybe someday
　when my daughter has hers
　could be, it might be black

Her daughter after her
　just might choose a red chair
　Now look what we have

Red, white, blue and black
Different chairs
—*Renee Green*

The Dying Leaves

The morning was paradise.
A gentle breeze begged for
A fragrance from heaven.
The mourning trees seemed
To whisper all of a magical
Requiem

For their death would soon
Come to be.

As the flowering breeze mesmerized
The leaves, they waltzed
To nature's lullaby.

Falling gracefully they rained
Onto the unborn grass.

A kiss from the never ending
Creation.
—*Roberta A. Barrera*

Tall Grass..

Gentle breeze
　a gentle rustle
through the tall protecting green,
　as new seeds will try to root
in a world
　mostly unnoticed.

For the ant it is a forest
other creatures struggle through
　using up
　their lifetime strength
　living
　　and not knowing it.

Yet —
　survival is predicted
　to all gliding, crawling, flying,
as the dew
　will soak their wings
as the sun
　dries up their bodies.
—*Elvira Tramposch*

The Stranger At My Door

In the silence of the cellar
　a giant crash was heard.
It was the crashing of the thunder
　from halfway across the world.
The silent raindrops falling
　with a patter on the floor.
It sounded like someone knocking,
　knocking on my door.
I went to the door to discover
　who was knocking on the door,
　but when the door was opened
it was only the wind blowing anymore.
It blew and whooshed around my feet
　and flew around my skirt
　and sent some leaves flying
　　flying into the dirt.
　Then the storm was over
　and the silence came once more
until next time comes the stranger
　knocking at my door.
—*Shannon Sullivan*

Tonight

Tonight, with you I share.
A gift. Talked of by most.
Sought by many, experienced by few.

Tonight, with you I.
Ask only your acceptance of this gift.
With sincerity, to value and protect.

Tonight, with you.
We two, become as one of the few.

Tonight, with.
Pleasure beyond description.
Pain of immeasurable magnitude.

Tonight.
Tonight love.
Tonight with love.
Tonight with you love.
Tonight with you I love.
Tonight with you I share love.
Tonight!
—*Roy E. Burke*

"Living Out A Dream"

　It would be a life of me and her
　　A life to live happy and free
　Who she would be I wasn't sure
but I never thought of it as misery
　　　Life's not as it may seem
　　　　Living out a dream

Her eyes would leave me in a trance
　　Life is an adventure if you care
　　As it is you must take a chance
Even if at times it's as a nightmare
　　　Life can be cruel and mean
　　　　Living out a dream

　　Some place some where
　　There is a love so fine
　Of hopes and dreams to share
　　A true love of all time
　Of life's crop she's the cream
　　　Living out a dream.
—*Tony L. Clark*

Always

A caring word
   A loving hand
One concerned thought or two...
   An encouraging smile
A cheerful laugh
   Given to me from you -
A patient heart
   A thoughtful deed
With every step, you've been there
   To help, to love
     Throughout the years
To show me that you care,
   A giving way -
     You truly have
Never hesitant to share or lend
   And, always,
I will love you -
   Love you true, until the end.
—*Kristine Miranda*

"Youth"

YOUTH, a burst of energy
a multitude of personalities

YOUTH, growing in a metamorphosis
of life,
trouble and free.

YOUTH, thoughtless
but yet kind.

YOUTH, growing up in the street
warlike full of despair.

YOUTH, giving of themselves
looking for direction.

YOUTH, reaching for that
ultimate dream.
—*Marie McCook*

Storm Tossed

The seagrape leaf—
a perfect round
now dried and brown
after winter storms
and tossed about
by strong north winds
turns joyful cartwheels
on the beach
until it collapses
flat on the sand
much like man
who dances through life
at times in ecstacy
then finally bows
also stormed tossed
until he lies
on his funeral bed
entirely spent.
—*Frederica McDill Culbertson*

Untitled

My heart has become
a tainted hollow
built to suffer and harbor
the many small black secrets
that gather there like
mating serpents.
—*Ginger Weaver*

A Friend

A friend is a special person.
A person who is caring and kind.
A friend is a companion.
A friend is someone that you've
got faith in, you can really
trust a friend. Some people ask,"
who can I trust to keep a secret?"
My reply to them and everyone
else is, "A friend." When you look
for a friend, look at the color of skin,
don't look at the clothes they wear, and
don't look at the sex of a person.
Look deep inside of a person.
This is what a friend means to me.
All of these qualities exceed
greatly in my best friend.
—*Heather Dyer*

When The Pathway Disappears

Childhood is
a playful pathway
to a heavy, dark,
closed door.
As you travel forward,
the sweet smelling
flowers die,
the chocolate-covered
faces melt,
the huggable-lovable
teddy bears disappear,
and the big, dark door
opens,
pushing
   you
     forward.
Then, the playful pathway
disappears,
Then, the playful pathway
disappears.
—*Johanna Steinhaus*

Victory

I'm broken, yet I stand -
A reed straining
In the wicked wind,
Searching for the seeds of justice
Which placed me here - rootless
In the concrete of many years.

Now withered and unplucked
I see it all quite clear,
Standing and straining
In the wicked wind -
I'm still here!
—*Mary-Ann Lewis*

A Child's Cry

A child's cry in the night,
a room with padded walls,
Thick and white.
Bars on the windows, no sunlight
Screams and weird noises
From the rooms next door.
They all live in fear and in horror.
They wonder what's going to happen next
Some hope for the worst,
But most hope for the best.
A child's cry.
—*Shannon Ortiz*

The Last Voyage

A Soul,
A Ship at sea,
The Divine Master, the Captain
With an outcast like me.

We'll chart no course
Or follow a star
We'll dock at no ports,
As we travel afar.

We'll fathom no depth,
The winds will be true,
The ship will not flounder
No storm will ensue.

We'll carry no cargo,
The log shall be closed.
We'll fly no allegiance
Brotherhood will be imposed.

A Soul
A Ship at Sea
Destined.....
For Eternity.
—*Ruth Hub*

Good-bye

As we say good-bye,
   A tear falls from your eye,
You try to hold it back,
   But our love is much to strong,
You try to smile,
   But it soon fades as I walk away.
Many letters I get from you,
   But many letters I send, too.
Soon we will see each other,
   And It will begin.
The tears will fall,
   All over again.
—*Anne Bailey*

Unseen Landscapes

I see with my minds eye,
a terrain of vast hideousness
where all the eldritch offspring
of some unfathomless horror
leap and bound
across the plains of surreal
nightmare.
—*Patrick Maunder*

Stiletto

You cut me -
A thin line of red wells
Then trickles along my arm,
Droplets of blood
Fall into the ground,
My life mixes with the earth
Where you stand before me
Watching and waiting;
In your hand a stiletto,
Trimmed in crimson,
Glinting silver in the sun.
You close the blade, turn and run.
I raise my arm to quell the flow,
And touching the sky
Look down at the spattered ground,
Stained by my temporal gash
Which will heal and scar,
And never be forgotten.
—*Jack Ahrens*

Love

Love.
A thing of might and dread.
A poison to all
Of heart and soul.
A force of birth and death.
It cuts through the lives
Of the blessed and cursed.
A fool to worship
When after all,
It just fades into the night.
Someone stands proud.
Surcharged by the feeling,
And then left alone.
It runs the cycle of life.
There is no end to the beginning
And no beginning to the end.
—*Jovanna Centre*

The Airport Tree

Just across the way was
a tree of green and gold,
Shimmering in the rain,
Glowing golden on boughs.

I sat myself by it,
The cruel, well, rain on my face
Seemed, somehow less cold,
The worried airport passengers went by.

The tree was the storm's one beauty,
In the never ending downpour.

Oh, when this one summer is over,
The storm and tree, remembered will be.
—*Carol Deane Thomas*

In The Waters

Waves pounding against the shore
A whale jumping in the sun,
Swimming in the bubbles
Is such fun.

A crab and a starfish
lying in the sand
frolicking in the seaweed,
listening to the band.

Here come the dolphins,
all in a row
jumping up and down,
now here they go.

Deep in the blue where I live
Where the sea animals go
to find seashells in the sand
We all swim to and fro.
—*Evelyn Stacey*

My Love For You

If not in mind —
   always in a heart

If not in life —
   always in a dream

heart, soul and thoughts —
   you'll be kept always,
   here, somewhere inside of me —
—*Arika Garcia*

True Mind Power

Our minds can conceive
a world full of hate.

And we trust them
to follow what goes
on the slate.

We think they can
   follow;
   each rule;
   on the page,
But end up in serious
torment and rage,

Please help us and
Save us, for we do not
   know,

What our minds can
conceive; the power
   to grow.
—*Jennifer Ferrell*

Thoughts Of You

Honey, I've been thinking
About the time we spend together
   Knowing in my heart that
It will always last forever.
What we share is very special
   Our love is very strong
With all we share between us
   Nothing can go wrong.
My heart is filled with thoughts
   Of you and only you
   Standing side by side
There's nothing we can't do.
No words can clearly explain
How you're my lover and my friend
   I can only promise this -
We'll be together till the end.
—*Joyce A. DeFrancesco*

Society's Rules

People are talking,
about you and I.
Is what they're saying,
just a lie?

You seem to be worried,
about society's rules.
But didn't it occur to you,
that they could be fools.

They are striving,
to keep us apart.
But you have to listen,
to your ever changing heart.

Please let me know,
your final decision.
Don't leave me here,
in this demented prison.

If love has failed you,
then maybe I shall too.
But you may never know,
when playing by society's rules.
—*Michelle Bowers*

I'm Old

My mind looks back and not ahead
Across the years where time has sped

While others laugh their world a stage
I sit a prisoner of my age

My gnarled hands will no more hold
my children who have grown cold

If time is just a fleeting thing
then soon I'll feel death's fatal sting

With memories swiftly passing by
I pray to God that I might die
—*G. B. Bradbeer*

Coinherence

Cold blue lake water laps
against granite rocks beneath us,
making sounds like sucking mouths.
Juice from grand junction watermelon
rivulets down our chins and forearms.

Last night you traced my life
in your wine-stained palm.
Holding you, I dreamed a hologram
of galaxies waxing in your menses.
—*Thomas Ramey Watson*

Rage

The trapped tiger slams his body
Against the cage
Roaring to be set free
Anger blinds him
As his steely claws puncture
The hard wood floor
His skinny captors laugh
As he flies against the bars
Probing sticks prick his sides
Making his frustration unbearable
With his remaining strength
He gives a final lunge
A broken lock, a cry of fear
A spray of blood
Freedom is earned
And justice is served
—*Mike Blenden*

The Sea

Her rhythmic roll
against the shore
as if to say
forever more
and in the night
her roll, rolls on
rolls on and on
Till break of dawn
for all the legends
That she hides
are lost now deeply
in her tides
her din and fury
are such a sight
yet she'll be steady
by tonight
The moon will light
her pleasant dance
and I'll be there
if I've the chance.
—*Anthony Travers*

The Day Before April

The day before April,
  All alone,
  I walked in the woods,
  And sat on the stone.

I sat on a broad stone,
  And sang to the birds,
  The tune was God's making,
  But I made the words.
—*Misty Campbell*

Faces Unclaimed

Unclaimed faces
  All around me.
Not caring; not knowing
  If I'm alive or dead.
Children's cries.
Drunken bastards lies.
There isn't a caring face for miles.
Unclaimed faces all around me,
  Laughing at me.
Why?
Why do you laugh at your troubles?
Because you know no one will
  Claim your soul?
Because no one knows to care for
  An unclaimed face?
No one can care
  For anyone else if they can't
  Care for themselves.
Unclaimed faces.
Faces unclaimed.
—*Christina Rae Blackmon*

Dream Boy

All day long I think of you
All night long I dream of you
I don't quite know who you are
But in my dreams you shine like a star
Your voice gives me freedom
Your arms keep me safe
Together we move with rhythm
In bed we sleep embraced
It's not what it seems
I wish it could be
You'll never love me,
You're my creation, my dream,
My inspiration, you make me happy
You make me smile
You make my dreams so worth while.
—*Yesenia Rodriguez*

Untitled

I love it when your near me,
  although sometimes we fight,
I will still try to love you,
  with all my soul and might.

Sometimes it will be hard,
  but our love will see us through.
I will try my best,
  as long as you will too.

I'm telling you all this,
  because its really true.
And so I look into your eyes,
  and say that I love you.
—*Esther Taulbee*

Giving Thanks

I look around dear Lord and see
All these blessing given me.
I see trees, slender, tall,
I see a rushing waterfall.
I see a lake where fishes jump —
And too an old forgotten stump
Where once a giant oak tree stood.
Here in the quiet of this peaceful wood
Violets hiding here and there —
I breathe the cleanliness of air.

I stood and looked
And as I gazed —
Dear God,
I truly am amazed.
I have no words, my Lord
  but say,
I thank you for each lovely day.
—*Betty McCown*

Not Born

Living in a world of strangers,
alone and unattached.
Belonging not to anyone,
just to a secret past.
A child born without a name,
identity obscured.
The faces of my origin
lost into this world.
My roots forever hidden
run deep within my blood,
and reveal themselves at last
in the countenance of my child.
But even having seen the proof
that somehow I belong,
my connection seems unreal to me,
like I had not been born.
—*Elaine J. Xenos*

A Fleeting Fancy

A flower stood, its petals spread,
alone in a crystal vase.
A butterfly that lingered there,
bathing in the fragrant air,
placed a kiss on its upturned face.

Its petals wore as soft as silk,
like clouds 'neath the butterflies feet.
To the butterfly it was thrilling,
that the flower was so willing,
so He drank of the nectar sweet.

The butterfly grew weary
of the flowers beautiful bloom.
He flew off to find another
no, He didn't really love her.
it ended all to soon.

The beautiful flower withered and died
alone in that beautiful crystal vase.
No other butterfly did come
and do what one butterfly had done,
to put the beauty in the flowers face.
—*Martha Hoover*

Alaska

Where the Bald Eagle hovers
amidst clouds and open skies
And snow appears like covers
where the awesome mountains rise

Where the rampant rivers flow
on their endless journey forward
And the sound and torrent grow
as the water moves forever onward

Where the vast and open spaces
strain one's eyes to comprehend
And the seeming lack of traces
that man's travels would portend

Where wild life abounds in plenty
undisturbed by man nor nature
And the joy of native gentry
seeking a life that's hard to capture

Where each day is life a season
filled with awe and expectation
And one's constant search for reason
brings a pause with revelation
—*Glenn A. Swanson*

Communion Of Regrets

I'm like an angel.
An angel in the night.
The only reason I shine
is there's darkness in
your sight.
But wait just a little longer
the sun will shine through
making me a shadow,
just someone you once knew.
Like a shadow on the ground
I'll always be around.
And when the night bird
sings his sad song
I'll always came along
To shine a little ray till
night becomes the day.
—*Kim Lindgren*

"The Wife"

Her house is just a hideaway
  an envelope in the world,
Safe when the phone is silent
  or no knocks at the door are heard.

Broken, frightened and friendless
  she stands quite near the door,
Searching for something better in life
  then beatings and slavery, much more.

As she walks to the kitchen window
  she longs for freedom of will,
Her master drives up in the driveway
  as she looks out her window sill.

What did you do today, he asks,
  the house looks just the same.
You had eight hours to toil for me
  no excuses, they're always lame.

Silent cries lie within her throat
  a tear for each well placed flail.
As the twinkle in her eyes go out
  her wish is now fulfilled.
—*Esther L. Hurst*

Vermont Views

The snow is the cream of
an oreo cookie,
two black rocks its
parentheses.

The river is a life-sustaining
vein
coursing through the body of
the land.

The moon is a bright bulb
silhouetting
a darkened house
on a hill.

The highway bows to the demands
of the mountains —
dipping and snaking
endlessly.
—*Shirley Fremeth*

The Crucifixion

We should come to fully obtain
an understanding of what frees us,
by realizing how much pain
was put through the body of Jesus.

His blood was shed for you & me,
when going through great torture;
as He was put through Calvary,
to save each life for sure.

As he went through sacrifice
among the Holy Cross,
He completely paid the price
preventing our great loss.

Now this was all extremely for
complete protection of our sins;
in effect for evermore,
through the bearing of our burdens.

So all the nails which had been used
to put Him through this task,
caused Him to be fully abused
of which no one could ask!
—*Katherine Anderson*

The Wisdom Seeker

Warm beauty of adobe walls,
Ancient wisdom quietly calls.

Webs of Indian eternity;
Hispanic durability;
Anglos seeking veracity.

Light slashes through shaded places
On Pueblo, Spanish, Anglo faces.

Native wisdom guarded with care;
Hispanic laughter in the air;
Anglos searching everywhere.

Silver, turquoise, malachite gleams,
At one with dark eyes full of dreams.

What do they know? How can we guess?
Wisdom from Mother Earth's largesse...
Can we find it in our distress?

The Ancient Ones' truth leads us on
To find the trail to wisdom's dawn.
—*Jackie Kemmer*

Anger In Silence

It is night,
And all is down,
No one cares,
And no one is around.

When you see
The shadow glare,
You will see me
Standing there.

There is anger,
There is hate,
No one talks,
And they still wait.

Making fire,
Snowing down
As time passes,
Still no sound.

There two sit,
Grudged with anger,
They will live,
Like two strangers!
—*Jenni Silva*

Keep The Lord Before You

The Lord is with you everyday
And all the way
As long as you keep him
Head of your life
And stay from sin
And stray from strife
For to be jealous
And full of malice
Is cruel as the grave
But, he wants us to be brave
Brave for him instead of sin
And to be bold
And to win souls
For he that wins souls is wise
But, he that tells lies
Will not get the prize
For the prize is not given to the strong
Nor the fast
But, unto him -
That endureth until the last.
—*Desiree Weiss*

He

He made her laugh at herself
and at life itself.
He made her feel personal worth
by things he said.
He listened when words barely
squeezed past falling tears.
He calmed and centered her
with his calm centeredness.
He admired her determination
and plucked it from the void
when she misplaced it.
He returned it to her heart
with tender caring hands.
He made her feel like a woman
and a friend in an age when the two
seem like oil and water.
He made her feel blessed to have known
this kind, gentle man.

The loss of his friendship
would tear her heart in two.
—*Betty Dodson*

Untitled

Passion burns within the heart
and brings to souls together
The sparks created ignite a flame
for a love that lasts forever

I see the fire in your eyes,
the windows to your soul
Inside I find still burning strong
the love from me you stole

I will cherish every moment
of our life that soon will be
Because I know of nothing greater
than the love you feel for me

So take my hand and guide me
Give me all the joy of life
Just simply say you love me
and take me as your wife
—*Danielle G. Franquet*

The Night

The sky is clear
And cool night air,
Is brushing gently
Through my hair.

A thousand crickets
Sing and play
As night slips willingly
From the day.

I try to write
But then I see
How the night sounds
Call to me.

And I the awed
Spectator sigh
How beautiful is
This Godly eye.

That lets me peer
Into the night
And feel the dark
With heart's delight.
—*Carolyn J. Snerr*

Eyes Of Love

I saw your eyes
 And for a moment, I thought,
 I was falling in love.

I saw your eyes
 And for a day, I thought,
 I was falling in love.

I saw your eyes
 And for a moment, I knew
 I was falling in love.

Through my eyes, I realized,
 I could not have this love.

I saw your eyes
 And I knew, I had fallen in love.
—*Jennifer A. Gonzalez*

Death Came

Death came on little soft feet
And gently took you away

To a land where the flowers grow
And every month is May.

Rest by the running brook,
The violets and the yew,

Where your soul will be refreshed
By heavenly drops of dew.

May you pass thru the gates of eternity
Into the ethereal mist

Like a young girl in the springtime
expecting a lover's kiss.
—*Jane J. Jenkins*

Untitled

Valentine's day is here again
And here we are,
thousands away with
each other.

I can still remember
Our first Valentine together
It was simple and yet sentimental.

Now I'm here and you are there...
A Valentine with
No one to share

But I know we really care
And so our love
Will be there to spare.
—*Charina Salanga*

You Touched Me

When skies were the darkest,
and I needed light,
You reached out and touched me.

When I was feeling sad and lonely,
and needed a smile and a hug,
You reached out and touched me.

When I was feeling angry,
and needed calm,
You reached out and touched me.

When I was feeling cold and alone,
and needed warmth,
You reached out and touched me.

When I needed your love,
you reached out,
And touched me with love!
—*Marilou Hardway*

Love

I love you, I love you so
And if you should ask me why
I'll never know
And as the years should go by,
And if I should die
Even if you shall forget me,
And the sights I will never get to see
And as I shall lay.
I want you to remember what
you haven't forgotten to this day.
I love you, I love you so
And if you should ask me
why I'll never know
—*Emily Hill*

Poetry For Vickie

I found some pretty flowers
and I picked them for my mother.
There were many others blooming
but these two were like no other.

I hurried to the house with them
and called, "Mom, I have a surprise!"
She said, "I hope it's not an elephant"
with a twinkle in her eyes.

She turned the kitchen faucet on
and washed them off with water.
Then, popped one in her mouth!
To the surprise of me, her daughter!

"What you've found is clover
and it's very good to eat.
Bees use it for honey,
and cows to make milk sweet."

So, I took one to my brother
and we each took a small bite.
Now we know why clover
can stop bees mid airy flight.
—*Sharron L. Meyer*

Your Picture

I look at your picture
And I smile at memories.

I look at your picture
And I'm sad you're not with me.

I look at your picture
And I remember how you made me laugh.

I look at your picture
And I miss hearing your voice.

I look at your picture
And I realize how you changed my life.

I look at your picture
And I know I'll love you forever,
I will always keep you in my heart.
—*Agnes Borecha*

Your Picture

I look at your picture
And I smile at memories.

I look at your picture
And I'm sad you're not with me.

I look at your picture
And I remember how you made me laugh.

I look at your picture
And I miss hearing your voice.
I look at your picture
And I realize how you changed my life.

I look at your picture
And I know I'll love you forever,
I will always keep you in my heart.
—*Agnes Borecka*

The Analyst

Does watching make you sad
and I take with me those stamps
form the office drawer
do those lies get to you
when I tell them to a few
friends, who would never talk
does this explain
my walk, past bicycles
under highways, and lights
the street through night,
like suspiciousness,
like you
can tell me to keep a secret
(during transition periods)
when I am myself.
—*Elizabeth Nelson*

Interior Decorator

My world is awash with color
And I'm always matching tones—
Comparing many swatches
For my clothing and my home.

Then suddenly I asked about
The color of my thinking.
I want its hue to be like you,
God, with Christ in charge of linking.
I want Jesus' example
And his holy attitude
To decorate my mental home
With peace and gratitude.

Your palette paints man gentle
And forgiving, with a touch
Of humor, spontaneity,
And unselfed love—there's much.
You paint man pure and very strong,
Persistent all the way.
So thank you, God, for giving us
This color-blended day.
—*Mary H. Reed*

In A World

In a world of change
And imagination,
One can think and dream.
Pretending
To be someone
Or something
That one would dream of being.
For example,
A vividly colored flower
Or a knight
In shining armor.
In a world
Of the child's
Imagination,
Dreams of hope
In one world
Are full
Of all these thoughts.
—*Sara Aldridge*

Blue

Blue is a hat
Blue is a car
Blue is a year old candy bar
Blue is a sadness deep inside
Blue is a baby's cry
Blue is the sky flying free
Blue is the ocean surrounding me!
—*Rory Smith*

Untitled

I hold the Universe in my hand,
   and it looks like a cat.

Infinities - past and future -
join in a conjugal kiss,
to conceive the "now" of my feline.

Could they be what they are without her?
   (or me?)

She is as Eternity is,
   no less.

I hold the Universe in my hands,
   and it purrs.
     —*Kathleen Rhein Lockwood*

Untitled

I hold the universe in my hand,
   and it looks like a cat.

Infinities - past and future -
join in a conjugal kiss,
to conceive the "now" of my feline.

Could they be what they are without her?
   (or me?)

She is as eternity is,
   no less.

I hold the universe in my hands,
   and it purrs.
     —*Kathleen Rhein Lockwood*

The 1930's

The days were filled with sunshine
And laughter filled the air.
The hills were filled with life
Because as children we played there.

The times were tuff for Mon's and Dads
We children didn't care;
They felt the hard times upon them
Coming from everywhere.
We children had a good time
Laughter filled the air.

The years have passed and I look back.
I see the hard times there.
Yet in the front of my mind
I hear the laughter there.
     —*Dale Murvine*

The Seawoman's Invitation

Come walk with me across the sand,
And let me take you by the hand.
Together a world of love we'll build,
As long as it's true love we yield.

The pretty skies the bright sun-light,
Are all we need for love so right.
Come hold my hand and walk with me,
And a love so great you'll see.

These times together will be dear,
The future you shall never fear.
For this time we have now is rare,
Thou should know how much I care.

The world would be a better place,
If only this walk you'd embrace.
And if you'll just say yes to me,
The happiest girl alive I'd be!
     —*Jessica Kim Gallardo*

Losing A Memory

Can you take a memory
And make it into now?
And if it is possible,
Can you tell me how?

Am I the only one that knows?
Am I the chosen one?
Am I the only one that sees,
When things end they're done?

I cringe when you tell me
I must always look ahead,
For what is now will soon be then
And that change is what I dread.

I want to take my memory
And make it into now
And if it is possible,
Will you tell me how?
     —*Nicole M. Overman*

"Daughters Are For Real"

They make you laugh,
And make you cry,
Or feel like you're flying high,
When they reach the sky.

In good times and in bad,
They're the best anyone ever had,
Always there when you're in need,
Very special indeed.

A gift from God's treasure,
My love for them is beyond measure.
I'm proud to be your Mom!
     —*Joan Pawlowski*

Morning Tears

    My vision blurs
   and my throat goes dry
    the tears come slowly
  then fade into the passing night
your every word echoes through my mind
     over and over again
 I can still feel your hand in mine
   the warmth of your body
    the smell of your hair
 my thoughts race with pleasure
      the pain
    for I am alone
  the tears come quickly now
then fade into the morning light
     —*Norman C. Salonen, Jr.*

Love Is Not Free

I gave my heart so freely,
and now I pay the price.
you think love is easy and free
but in the long run you pay more
than you expect.
you tell everyone "you're fine"
but you know that's a lie,
inside you feel the knife stabbing
at your heart.
When the night is here that's
When you feel the loneliest,
There's no one to hold, there's the
empty bed.
No one to share your dreams or hopes.
That's why love is not free.
     —*Teresa Davis*

"Ode To Domino"

The snow is softly falling
   and presses put to bed
Four Maples starkly quiet
   Are they down the road instead?

At Ace's lights burn brightly
   And tho the road is slick
The car discharges Bop and Babe
   Ken and Dave and his side kick

The game is fast and furious
   And change flies back and forth
The double twelve was played at once
   The design grows on the cloth

The beer is cold and tasty
   it has it's natural say
Someone says "Be right back"
   And lets nature have its way

How it always happens no one really knows
But someone always scores "forty"
whenever someone goes
This "Ode to Domino" was composed for
just one reason
To wish you all the merriest Holiday
Season!
     —*Richard R. Powers*

Youth Forever

When I was very young
And resting on my mother's knee,
I never thought of growing old,
It couldn't happen to me.

Then come school and playmates,
Life was fun - don't you see
That I was never going to get old,
It couldn't happen to me.

Marriage and children followed
With its ups and downs, you'll agree,
But I wasn't getting older,
It couldn't happen to me.

The years have come and gone now,
I'm alone - completely free;
And old age is coming to someone,
But it didn't happen to me.
     —*Marion Coleman*

The Time Forgotten

One day I looked in a river
and saw my reflection clear.
I looked back in the river
and decided my future was near.

I thought about what I'd done,
and what I wanted to do,
and realized that the best dreams
were the ones I've made come true.

I thought about my life
and the memories I've made
and acknowledged in my heart
the future plans I've laid.

And when I decided to lay to rest
all the secrets I have kept,
I looked back in the river,
and I wept and wept and wept.
     —*Taryn Aubree Fix*

A Shocking Story

I came through the door
  and she was standing there
Tear drops in her eyes
I asked her what was wrong,
She stared into my eyes
And told me my dad passed away
I couldn't believe what she told me
Is this a dream it must be
I didn't think this could happen to me
Why did he leave
Why did he go
I hope he can hear me,
Cause I love him so.

Dad-If you can hear me
  you'll always be in
  my heart.
    —Tami Dobrinski

Destructive End

  Shuddering with fear
  And standing here alone
    in the cold
    and done with
  destroying the world,
  I fall to the pavement
    crying,
    watching,
    dying
  as solid stones
  fall to the haven
  and the wind takes
    with it
    my dreams -
  in the sealed glass bottle
    crashing down,
    yet building my frown.
    I live,
  watching our bitter plan
    come true.
    —Angela Bagatta

Sundown

The sun goes down
and the sky he cries
and runs her makeup
in brilliant pinks.
He's blue and pounds
his fist against the other
and purple evolves from pain.
He rests his fist upon a pillow;
a cloud that's no longer white
but a vibrant orange from
the knuckles of his hand.
Tired, he rests his feet
atop a hill and wipes
the tears until they're dry...
until again his lover rises
to a single yellow circle in the sky.
    —Holly Amatucci

"Do Something"

Yesterday the grass was green
And the sky was forever blue
But that was when the earth was clean
And the idea of pollution was new

Today the grass is turning brown
And the sky is filling with smoke
Everybody is looking down
Cause if they look up, they'll choke

Tomorrow the grass will be nothing
And the sky you won't be able to see
So get off your butt and do something
Or the earth the next day may not be
    —Amy M. Dittmar

A Sister Of The Earth

And the moon
And the stars
Came to me,
When I was alone.
She blessed me with
Her comfort
Her love
Her kinship
She sought solace
And relief,
Yet I received.
Hearts and hands,
Sons and daughters
Entwined,
We travel forward.
    —Trudy Schaelchli

Two Suns

What if the sun were to rise
  and then rise once again?
Would the world be so bright
  That we could see everything?
    Or nothing?
Would the blind be able to see?
  Or the sighted be unable?
And what if they were to set
  and then set once again?
Would it be so dark that
  sight would be impossible?
Would it close our eyes?
  Yet open our conscience?
Or would it close our souls forever?
    —Steve Wovkanech

Jack Frost Gets Me To Yearnin'

When the frost is on the punkin
  And there's a nippin' in the air —
Oh my heart for home is yearnin'
  How I'd love to be back there.
But - mama's gone with papa —
  The old homestead has burned down;
Strangers - are a living
  In new houses all around.
When the frost is on the punkin
  Smells of pumpkin pie fill the air —
With all the family at the table
  Now I'd love to be back there.
So pumpkin pies I'm baking
  Though, my sons are grown men —
And I'm sending invitations
  For them to come home once again.
    —Helen J. T. Brumbaugh

Given To You

A heart is for giving
And this I have done
Given to you
This you have won
Won through your kindness
Tender and true
Each warm embrace so
Exciting and new
Generous kisses
That melt on my lips
Caressing you
Soothing my fingertips
Your hands as they touch me
With gentle intent
Passion exploding
With such eagerness meant
Trembling, aching
As we merge into one
A heart is for giving
And this you have done
    —Jeanne Roberts Maertens

Cosmic Glue

Atoms make up matter
And this you know is true
Also in the universe
Is blessed cosmic glue

Because this glue is great
Some people call it God
It's in the biggest planet
And in the smallest pod

It's everything and everywhere -
All directions that you turn
Now if you understand all this
There's one more thing to learn

We too, are made up of this glue
And it's alright to ask,
"Is our body really us
Or is it just a mask?"
    —Adam Green

Today Will Lead To Tomorrow

  Today will lead to tomorrow
    and tomorrow will fade away
    into the dark gray sadness
      to begin another day

    If time were nonexistent
    and troubles we had none
then the world would not crumble
    and disappear for everyone

    If all were really equal
      and all were as one
then there would be no hunger
    to rise the morning sun

    Today we stand together
but tomorrow we stand still
    waiting for the moment
  We'll rise back up the hill.
    —Kelly Spitzer

I Loved You In My Life

You smiled at me
   And took the pain,
Nothing lost,
   And all to gain.
I judged you wrong,
   And misjudged myself.
Now it seems
   You're someone else.
You held my hand,
   Gentle but tight.
I took a stand
   And said good-bye.
I know you're an actor.
   Misjudge me not,
For all along,
   It wasn't love you sought.
It was all fantasy,
   But for awhile,
I loved that you
   Could make me smile.

—*Heather Riggs*

Will You Be My Angel

   Will you be my angel,
  and walk through life with me?
   Will you be my angel,
and help me to be the best I can be?

   Will you be my angel,
  and help me through my strife?
   Will you be my angel,
and always watch over my life?

   Will you be my angel,
  and help me through my pain?
   Will you be my angel,
and show me light when there is rain?

   Will you be my angel,
  and take away my fears?
   Will you be my angel,
  and wipe away my tears?

   Will you be my angel,
  to help me when in need?
   Will you be my angel,
  until from life I'm freed?

—*Klarice Tucker*

Untitled

Today dark shadows filled my day.
So in sorrow I knelt to pray.
After a while of feeling blue,
I felt a surge of something new,
Like a curtain lifting I see the light,
And felt life need not be like the darkest night.

Years have passed and I've grown old
But in my heart the world's not cold
Each day is new and filled with joy.
I thank the Lord for things I've seen,
May life be always full of dreams,
For dreams to build on show the way,
So heres to the world and a brighter day.

—*Gloria Fabian*

Spring Is Here!

Spring is now here
And we're all so happy
'Cause the maple trees
Are getting sappy.

Jonquils and tulips
Appear from their beds
And, soon we will see
Their colorful heads.

Birds peeking and flitting
As they search here and yon'
For just the right softness
To lay their eggs on.

Lambs and calves frolicking
In fields new with clover
Woods crackling and rustling
With new life, all over!

A season of wonderment
After frost and wind blowing
And dreaded anticipation
Of the first lawn mowing!

—*Nina Fannin*

Untitled

So you are gone
And with you some small intricate part
Within me
Yet I remain
Without your warm, intimate laughter
Broken enchantment
Scattered stars about my feet
No one thing left
No sound
No staying chord
No pin of light

Slow do I move to raise and place
The pieces of your name
Impossible to speak
Unheard
Yet constant with the never ending day

—*Beverly Gustavson*

"God Made It So"

You plant a seed,
And you watch it grow.
You don't have to question,
What made it so.

God knows the answer,
He gave you the seed.
He gives us everything,
Everything we need.

You wait for the seed to grow,
It's beginning to sprout.
Then all of a sudden,
The leaves all come out.

There's a flower inside,
Of the leaves you see.
God gives us the flowers,
For you and for me.

When you plant a seed,
And you watch it grow.
You'll know where it came from,
Know God made it so.

—*Hazel Haning*

Tonight

I have pain
   anger
like a flame
   burning
pain and anger that is burning
   friendless
frustrated extremely
   hysterical
I am frantic
   insane
Climbing up walls
   foolish
That is me
   tonight.

—*Jamie L. Busen*

A Cry

Hear our oceans
Anguished cry
Once the cradle
From which we
Came
Having gorged ourselves
Of this great bounty
Many species are
Now extinct
Majestic waters
Once pristine
A vessel now
For toxic waste
Stand before the
Incoming tide
And listen
Please listen
And you will hear
Our oceans
Anguished cry

—*John Hedderig*

"Ghetto" Living"

I have one child
Another on the way
My husband has left me,
With no place to stay.

My life I say
It's not worth living
I have no hopes
That are worth giving.

My life is slowly fading away
Times have grown old
And "Ghetto" Living"
Has grown gray.

My child complains
of no food to eat
I can't do anything
But lie down and weep.

I try hard to survive
Within "Ghetto Living"
My child is born
With no hopes of Living...

—*Cassandra McCrary*

Brothers

The baying is loud, but grows soft.

I poise, ready to strike
anything that enters my home,
my den.

Nothing.

I move, carefully,
silently, to the entrance.

I gaze outside,
trying to catch a scent on
the wind. . . .

Nothing.

In the distance,
I hear a sound, a pop,
and a howl.

It is my brethren, he is hit.

I crawl outside,
and offer my voice,
my soul up with his.
The last sound he'll ever
hear, was of love, not hate.
—*Danny Eaton*

Friends Are Forever

Friends are forever
Apart or together
Friends are for life
Isn't that nice
If your friend moves
You will not loose their friendship
Your laughter is worth 1,000 words
So wonderful and neat no other laugh
Can complete
Your friends forever
Apart or together
—*Ragen McCarty*

Four Weeks Of Fun

  Four weeks of happiness,
   archery, riding, swimming,
memories that last for life.

  Four weeks of friends,
   laughing and crying,
singing and having such fun.

  Four weeks of competition,
   tournaments and games,
  a tribe kept for life.

  Four weeks of camp,
   the best days,
the best friends of life.
—*Laura Clark*

Heredity

Do they often wonder? Now and then;
As I do, again, and again;
Giving me life, giving me away;
Providing me a new place to stay;
Always feeling separate;
Never feeling connected;
What an unfair legacy;
Concerning my H-E-R-E-D-I-T-Y.
—*Christina Marie Ulrich*

Untitled

  Across the street from today
   Are all my tomorrows,
And there alone, my future lies...
   It's happiness and sorrows!

  Behind me are the yesterdays,
   The past with mem'ries sweet,
Where only in the throes of death...
   Will once again we meet!

Across the street from yesterday,
   Is where tomorrow starts,
And yet I live in days gone by...
A different time, of happier hearts!

  Across the street from living,
   Is where I'll find death's door,
And there the days of yesterday...
   Will be forever more!
—*Marat Bandemer*

My Innermost Thoughts

My Innermost Thoughts
  Are hidden deep inside
   Where I have not fought
    And cannot hide.

My innermost thoughts
  Are for me to know
   They cannot be taught
    And they're not for me to show.

My innermost thoughts
  Are for me to save
   They can't be bought
    And they are my fave.

My innermost thoughts
  Have a very special meaning
   Like nothing that has to be caught
    And nothing we have to sing.

My innermost thoughts
  Can't be broken
   And can't be sought
    They are like my own gold token!
—*Becky Hall*

The World Pleases Me

Dark and dank, not dusty
Are our sins,
And the Cheshire Cat grins.

Love is lust—
Date trust.
Hope is hate—Wait!
Earth's fate.
Joy is jeer—
Quiet queer.
Peace is political purification—
Bloody thirsty nation.

Wanton and wicked, not withstanding
Are our sins,
That crack the Cheshire Cat's grin.
—*Mark Alan Thibodeau*

Untitled

Daydreams
Are they just schemes
Or are they means

To escape
to contemplate
On a certain debate

Or are they a place
To let your mind race
To a better place

Where roses grow
In many, many rows
And people love to go
—*Kara Wattnem*

Circles Before Me

Circles of life before me
Around us we do fall
Into a time of insanity
Death comes to call
Entry ways to other times and places
Never friends but evil faces
Trying to make you see
You're loosing your sanity
Beating on the circles
Trying to get in or out
Death is coming closer
All you can do is shout
Clawing blood from your eyes
Dripping off your heart
Onto the lonely land
Your home is so far apart
Lusting for deliverance
To free you from this hell
Doesn't anyone hear your cry
In the wishing well.
—*Olivia D. Swader*

I Call Him Husband

A man was given to me
As a gift from up above,
To always walk beside me
And share with me his love.

The pieces seemed to fit
In this puzzle we call life,
I'll never forget the day
He asked me to be his wife.

On the road of marriage
Were many troubles and tears,
But his strong arms around me
Have put to rest all my fears.

With him I understand
The joy of having sons,
For this thing called "motherhood"
Only once in a lifetime comes.

For through his loving eyes
He tenderly makes me see,
That as long as I shall live
My husband, he will always be.
—*Rita Kopidlansky*

A Good Man

"There's a good man," he'd always say,
as a greeting to one and all.
As he welcomed us to the worship site,
He was stooped and not too tall.
But when he met his fate
At the pearly gate
I know that his stature was grand;
As a heavenly voice proclaimed with joy
"Let him in, for there's a good man."
—*Pat Garner*

My Collie Friend

He came into my life
  as a round ball of fur
    with button eyes,
  and has grown into
my loyal companion.
  If danger is near,
he stands, brave and strong,
    in front of me.
  While I work,
he waits, patient and intelligent,
    at my feet.
  And as I rest,
he sleeps, quiet and gentle,
    by my side.
If ever two souls could blend
  human and canine together,
  then surely, we are -
    one soul, one heart.
More than just a pet - my best friend.
—*Mary Kegarise*

Vicious Twist

He sat home alone last night
As he did most every night

He ate his dinner
And cleaned his plate

For dessert — put a gun in his mouth
Pulled the trigger
And realized his fate

He said he had nothing
But he had it all

I think he forgot to realize
That in every life
A little rain must fall

So screw him
That's what I say

He knew the rules
But decided not to play
—*J. Craig Lambert*

Fatigue

I've put the milk in the cupboard again.
And the cereal in the refrigerator.
My eyes are stinging.
My body aches.
My temper is short.
Push, Push, Push.
Work harder.
Work better.
Work faster.
I can't wait to crawl into bed.
—*Susan Lawson*

The Power

The Spirit came at pentecost
  As He had not come before,
And the power of His Presence
  Has been felt forevermore.
Jesus had a heavenly mission,
  And after resurrection day
The comforter and guide was left
  To help us learn to pray.
Some work now for truth, morality
  While from God's throne, His light
Shines to make the way quite clear.
  There's power, and purity and sight.
Much of the world remains in sin,
  But the indwelling spirit is here,
And sorrow, suffering and pain
  May soon just disappear.
—*Alta Richardson McLain*

Untitled

So…who am I tonight
as I am silent by your side
the darkness steal my image
my identity you decide
my face is veiled by blackness
your eyes are closed by choice
I dare not speak a single word
you'd know me by my voice.
nighttime feed this fantasy.
changes the flavor of my lips
whose body do you imagine
as you reach gently for my hips?
you hover above with lust
all I give you take
you kiss whosever mouth I own
my heart can't help but break
and I'm so afraid to wonder
as I give life to all your lies
is it such a disappointment
upon opening your eyes?
—*Jill M. Boyd*

Beach Print

Small footprints on the sand.
As I held my baby's hand.
His first time on the beach.
He looks at the water to far to reach.
He stare's at the shell below
And reaches down very slow.
He picks one up and holds it tight
Not to sure if he did right.
I nod my head that it's okay.
He holds my hand to guide the way.
I look back and see the small
Prints on the sand.
And know one day he'll be a man.
With children of his own.
Walking on this same old beach.
Holding his child by his hand
Watching footprints on the sand.
—*Nina Ehrke*

Bubbles

Bubbles, bubbles in the air
Bubbles, bubbles everywhere.
Aren't they fun to watch and chase?
Whoops; one landed on my face!
Bubbles, bubbles in the air
Now I've got one in my hair.
—*Jill M. Scheer*

"I Saw A Stranger"

I saw a stranger, the other day,
As I was going on my way.
I wondered, just who was he,
Of what did he, remind me?

I was puzzled on what to do.
Was this thing, a deja-vu?
Why by him was I impressed,
By some memory still unexpressed.

Did we meet in some past life,
Was I the husband or his wife?
Was he a part of my family,
Or just a part of my memory?

Can you say I am to blame,
If I dare not ask his name.
Oh woeful! Woeful memory!
What did that stranger mean to me?
—*Ervin H. Chase*

Passionate, Relentless Love

My love pours,
as if golden grains of sand,
flow as an ever-lasting hour glass,
all in the palm of your hand.

Purple passionate clouds,
rest motionless in the sky,
while the moon sets peacefully,
in a reflection within your eye.

My love for you grows deep,
through pits of raging fire,
you're the only man I need,
all my hearts desire.

My greatest fantasy,
that would turn my dreams to gold,
to fill my life with all time,
for only you to behold.

We can climb the highest mountains,
walk the roughest lands,
swim the most treacherous seas,
as long as our love stands.
—*Heather Honey Lyle*

Changes

The grass stands still
As spring slowly sweeps by
The trees go unnoticed
And the birds fly so high

The day is coming
Faster and faster each morn
As the flowers sway in the breeze
Their friendship is torn

It's time to depart
We must say goodbye
No more easy times
As the wind gives a sigh

They will always have each other
But never in the same way
What they had was special
Each and every day
—*Jamie Nardino*

Memory

My dreams of you are bright
As the October brush;
And fill me with delight,
As the song of a thrush.

I see you now, my dear,
In all the leaves of gold;
And hear your voice, so clear,
Though time has made me old.

But in my heart, dear one,
I'm young and gay again;
And though I'm only one,
We shall be two again.
—*Leo P. Mahon*

I Do, Really Do, Like You

I like you a lot,
  as you can see
I hope you feel
  the same about me
What was it that went so wrong
  this feelings I have are so strong
Is the way I feel so very wrong?
  When I first meet you
My dreams came true
  skies were black
but now their blue
  My friends say I should let go
but as you know I'm holding on
  hoping one day that you'll be mine
So we can last
  till the end of time
Please let me know
  how you feel about me
Because I can't stand this misery.
Not knowing what you think of me!
—*Melissa Richard*

Raindance

How I love to watch your show
As you dance about my window
I watch you descend to the ground
Each little drop a different sound
Like tiny ballerinas dancing all about
But you will have to leave when the
Sun comes out
Not everyone enjoys your little show
But I kinda hate it when you go
And I know that when the sky turns gray
And the sun goes in
You'll come back and perform again.
—*Dorothy J. Pittman*

No Skeletons To Share

Tip-toe softly on padded feet,
as you travel

Enter subtly,
as the wind

Announce your presence privately,
as the chill of the spine

Distribute your love,
in fragile, crystalline snowflakes

And when it is time,
depart in a whisper…
—*Julia Elizabeth Richards*

The Angel

I look up to the sky
asking why
why did you take her
from me
she was an angel sent down
in human form
I learned to love from all
the love she threw so freely
and again and again I ask
why?
why did you send her to me
only to take her away
was it just one of
your tricks flashing something
good in my eyes only to take it away
I sit now and cry
for the angel
who walked in human form
—*Jennifer Beals*

"Theatre"

Theatre is a way to escape,
Assume a new role,
Away from all problems,
To forget.

You see everything,
In a new amazing way.
Other than holding feelings inside,
Let them run free.

By secretly sharing ideas,
Expressions,
You can find that missing puzzle piece,
And go on with your life.

Until you come again,
To this distant pleasure,
To open yourself up,
And see what's inside.
—*Katie Rossi*

The Man-Servant

She gets on head bowed
at Eighth and West,
this morning's brawl smeared
from lips to cheek,
carelessly covered by blond wisps.
The driver and passengers stare
or turn away,
too shocked and concerned
to voice either.

She will make excuses
that she was clumsy and fell
or bumped a wall in the night,
despite his ring's impression in skin.
—*Rebecca A. Clever*

Day Of Daze

Confetti on the bathroom floor,
Bill collectors at the door.
Petticoats draped on chairs and beds,
Pains and aches in tummies and heads.
Pulled off hose found in spots,
Wilted flowers - not in spots.
Unopened presents everywhere,
Day after mess in the air.
Can you guess what I described?
The day after she left - the bride.
—*Helen Gersbach*

"We Are One"

As I stare down,
At these faces
I wonder how
people can be
racist.

So many colors,
So many beliefs,

Whatever happened to
what's underneath?

That's all that matters,
nothing more,

So why do some
feel so superior?

We are all the same
within, so who should
give a damn about
the color of skin?
—*Cathy Povilaitis*

Princess Lilly

Princess Lilly
awakens at night
from her flower,
purple and white.
Riding on a shooting star,
she brings hope
near and far.
Then you see a violet,
too tiny for the eye.
It's as lovely as a bluebird,
way up in the sky.
—*Margaret E. Boyle*

The Cherokee Man

The cherokee man
Be at your side
To protect and guide
So faith never dies

Strong of heart
The warrior stands
His face worn dry
In his promised land

His hands held still
With the strength of many
Torn and cracked
By American pride

His boldness and truth
Add strength to the nation
Fertile the soil
That reaps the land

This proud young man
With head held high
Man of his nation
Chief of his tribe
—*Elaine Y. Fugate*

Beauty

Beauty is all around us.
Beauty is all within.
Beauty counts what's inside you.
Not just on your skin.
Don't go by what people say.
If they make fun of you?
Just be happy for what you are.
Then you will like you.
—*Laura J. Samuels*

Faces

Faces are
beautiful. I
knew this long
ago, or rather,
the boy I once
was knew this.
(I cannot claim
to be the same.)
He never erred
by judging face,
but knew surprised
completeness in them
all. Now, right side,
I look again, not so
much for foe or friend,
but for that same
surprise—once again
increased delight,
sunrise after winter night.
—*Glenn Andrews*

My Protector

I walk, and fear not,
Because he walks beside me.
I have, and want not,
Because he provides for me.

I work, and faint not,
Because he strengthens me.
I endure, and worry not,
Because his love comforts me.

I stumble, and fall not,
Because his hand lifts me.
I sin, and die not,
Because his blood saved me.

I owe, and pay not,
Because he paid for me.
I go, where, I care not,
Because he will guide me.

—*Norman L. Tincher*

A Weird Thing Called Love

Under the stars I have tears in my eyes
  Because my broken heart
    Can't hide it inside
  Under the moon I feel alone
    I can't go home
    Oh please God no
  Into the sun is where I must go
  Because I don't have any fun
  I would if I had someone
  I feel like jumping in the skies
  Because when I look in those eyes
    I feel as if to die
    And it breaks me inside
    I've been picked up
    By a weird thing called love
    But it thrashed me all up
    And threw me in the dump
      Now I've given up
    on a weird thing called love

—*Brandon Nichols*

Dying Because Of You

I die inside when you cry
because of me.
I die because I live for you
and only you.
A dying flower is what I am.
I'm not loved or cared for as
my life withers away.
Each petal of the flower represents
a piece of me.
The petals fall as the flower
dies.
I die as you take pieces
away from me.
I'll never be whole or loved
again because you don't understand
me,
People said we were perfect together,
but I guess they were wrong
because you would understand me.
But most of all you would love
and care for me.

—*Samantha Middleton*

Love

It is a flower
Beginning to bloom
Climbing a bower
Filling a room

It has no smell
It knows no time
You can't tell
If it'll rhyme

You won't go too fast
With that special friend
If you want it to last
Not come to an end

It won't make you fend
For anything lower
Than the end
Of the flower

—*Sarah Schmiesing*

Tis Christmas

Trees trimming
Bells jingling
Tinsel shimmering
Lights gleaming
Fireplace crackling
Popcorn popping
Chestnuts roasting
Doorbells chiming
Visitors greeting
Presents giving
Children laughing
Eyes sparkling
Hands clapping
Toes tapping
Sleighbells ringing
Carolers singing
Snow glistening
Stars twinkling
Moon glowing
'Tis Christmas

—*Dorothy Kaufman*

A Linear Measurement

The space is often long
between the two of us.
It is hard
when you control the inches.
You are like a surveyor
marking exact boundary lines;
everything has a beginning and ending.
Our life is calibrated
to your greatest advantage.
My body is marked with monuments
of your advancement.
I once thought
we had a common ground;
now all that is common
is my life.
I welcome your new appraisal.
When you can find no inches to measure,
I can hand you
your eviction notice
over the yards between us.

—*Kathy Kremins*

"Heart Mind And Soul"

Flowing on wings of wind
Beyond shadows of our dreams
Through clouds of thought, there will be
Twisted path of destiny
and something called reality

In silence try and listen
To the heartbeat of your soul
Without guilt, or slight remorse
Dare not to question why?

Waves of life upon the shore
Are what we make them, nothing more
Many years have come to pass
Like sand inside an hour glass

With every moment given me
I know I will forever be
A part of you, a part of me

So please remember with each day
We've shared our love in every way
I miss you more than I can say
Heart, mind and soul

—*Jamie Stephenson*

The Wind And The Breeze

The winter wind blows
  bitterly in,
Snow fills the air
  without a care.
With every thought
  of summer sought;
Memories of summer breezes still
The gusts of winter wind's chill.

The cool summer breeze
Blew through the trees;
Reaching children playing in the sun,
  having a lot of summery fun.
Bringing back to relief
  for everyone's belief,
That summer is just in bed
  while winter is here instead.

—*Amy Erickson*

People

Curly, blonde hair
black furry jacket
red skirt
black boots stepping

Black dreadlocks
black pants
black shoes
a swaggering walk

Mirrored sunglasses
black leather jacket
navy blue corduroy pants
strong, masculine gait.

Each going to
their
certain destinations.
—*Juanita Torrence-Thompson*

Bless The Children

Bless the children, Lord
Bless them all,
The plump ones, the small ones
The short ones and the tall.

Their eyes so bright and shining
Their laughter fills the air,
So full of love and life are they
Free from strife and care.

Happiness surrounds them
With their sweet and winning ways,
Such hope and trust they have in us
With joy they fill our days.

Sing merrily my children
Of blue skies up above,
And ask the Lord in heaven
To bless you with His love.
—*Betty J. Druck*

Have You Counted Your Blessings

Sometimes we don't count our
blessings that's for sure, until we see
someone that is less secure.
Suppose you were blind without sight,
and couldn't tell morning from noon
or night.
Suppose you were an invalid in a
wheelchair and had to depend upon
someone to take you here and there.
Suppose you didn't have a home
and lived on the street and had to
scrounge for food that was thrown
away for something to eat.
Suppose you had no place to take a
bath, or clean and decent clothes
to wear, and people passing by you
and stare.
Suppose you start counting your
blessings today, because, little by
little time is ticking away.
—*Dolores Bloker*

Birth

I sit here wrapped in silence
Blind to deaf ears
Feeling the pain of years
Caged and trapped in fears
Shadows within visions
Tears flow from my sightless eyes
Tortured by endless lies
I float away cutting all ties
Flying away into deeper shadows
I begin to search for peace
Finding only inscrutable beasts
My mind cracking piece by piece
Blood seeps from my veins
Feeling my body decay
Connate instincts to fly away
Racked in torture dying I lay
—*Eric Truitt*

Love

Love is like a flower
Blooming on a vine,
Tend it oh so carefully
And more love you will find.

But if you leave it to its own,
To fade and wilt and die,
Then all the love you could have known,
Will surely pass you by.

In the garden of your life,
Though difficult at times to do,
Cultivate the loving vine,
And it will surely bloom for you.
—*Harriet Lee Warner*

Georgia O'Keeffe's Desert World

The desert- the only place she knows —
  breathes of life and beauty
Through old remains she enters
  a sky full of dreams
Dreams where death transforms
  into life
Life is vivid colors
  caressing sand
Shaping the artist's imagination
  to another world that knows no fear
Only certainty that life surrounds
  even the most decaying spaces
—*Stephanie Springer*

Death

If I die,
before the dawn,
would my friends just carry on?
I would want,
for them to be,
just as if,
it hadn't happened to me.
Would they care?
How would they be?
Would they feel at all for me?
I would want no grief,
nor any pain,
just the love in life,
I had yet to gain.
—*Clayton Mastaw*

The Fire

Distant mountains,
Breeze, blowing,
Leaves and flowers,
Open, growing.
Crystal river,
Twisting, turning.
Forest fire,
Scarring, burning.
Red inferno,
Angry flaming.
Fire fighters,
Fired, blaming.
Blackened soil,
Dusty, flaking.
Charred oak branches,
Cracking, breaking,
Dead horizon,
Calling, crying.
Distant mountains,
Weeping, dying.
—*Ann Gruber*

Untitled

It happened so fast,
  but at first it was just a game.
Everything meant nothing,
  and now its not the same.
Things have developed,
  and have become their own.
Ending as quickly as it started,
  leaving each alone.
Trying to hold on to what inevitably
  must go.
trying to fight reality,
  and what we truly know.
The picture is unclear,
  of what the future holds.
What fate will leave to be felt,
  still remains untold.
—*Rachel Dixon*

Yesteryears

The days go by,
but every now and then
I feel this giant arm
pulling me back to
yesteryears.

Times which saturated my mind
and body with energy. But now
this saturation has become a
trickle of life.

Some days the struggle is so
intense, but when I find
myself back here; have I
won or lost this battle?

I must go back!
—*Doug Klipstein*

Lasting Friendship

Sometimes it got rough,
but knowing our relationship was tough.
I'd just think of the past
and knew it would last.
When things got thin,
you'd be there to help me fit right in.
If I was down you would want
to help me up.
It's a friendship, that's the way
it's supposed to be,
and when the time comes and
we have to say 'good-bye,'
all memories will hold tight.
I will always remember you by
looking at the moonlight.
Even if we're miles apart you
will always bring smiles to me.
Thanks for being such a great friend!

—C. Becker

Eternity

It starts,
　But never has begun.
Eventually it does end,
　But it never dies.
You can always hear it,
　But there is no sound.
It does have a middle,
　But where are the insides?
Everyone thinks it can be,
　But somehow, it is impossible.
Only dreamers can see it,
　But it is never there

—Brianna Mowry

Child Cries Out In Asia

A child cries out in Asia
but no one hears his call
For what's a child who's hungry?
For one who's late for the ball?
A child cries out in Asia
but his noise received no answer
For no one cares for this little child.
Who hopes to be a dancer.
A child cried out in Asia
will no one help at all?
the little child is dying
and no one hears his call.

—Carlos Torres

My Purpose

Tis not for me to reason,
but only for a season to serve my
Lord with a gladdened heart.
Tis not for me to ask why,
but only for me to try and be
the best at doing my part.

Tis not for me to complain,
but only for me to remain in the
light where my life did start.
Tis not for me to grumble,
but only for me to rumble in the
back seat of God's go - cart.

—Charlene R. Muncy

Thanks For The Memories!

Our family built a shelter,
but, our shelter has no name.
We built it on the hillside,
down the road, along the lane!

In the late of the evening,
after the days setting sun,
we gather at our shelter,
when all our work is done!

We talk about some memories,
we've remembered thru the years.
Some would make us happy,
others bring us tears!

We know someday we'll gather,
in your shelter beyond the blue,
at a place that God calls Heaven,
he named for ones like you!

Till then we'll go on meeting,
in our shelter just the same,
always wondering what to call it,
that reminds us of your name!

—Ron Allen

Old Age Lament

Identity was what I sought,
　But "Who Am I?" was often fraught
With questions of my certitude.
　Why wasn't I the perfect dude?

I never made the "Fortune" list:
　The "Richest" role I always missed;
And "Best Dressed Man" was not my style.
　These all escaped me all the while.

The "Ten Best Looking" missed my name.
　With every group it was the same.
E'en "Ugliest," though not so good,
　Was kept from me just as it should!

The "Ten Most Wanted" didn't call.
　I missed again; that wasn't all;
The "All American" anything
　Would never fame and fortune bring.

On nature's way we oft depend;
　But just for me she had to bend.
Though through it all I'm not a coward,
　I've gone to seed, but never flowered!!

—Billy M. Legler

The Old Women

To see the children run,
　brings tears to my eyes.
As they frolic to and fro,
　I am taken back to my youth.
Where days were care free,
　and wasted without thought,
　and happiness prevailed.
I remember when my legs could run,
　and my eyes could see.
　and my ears could hear.
Oh, to spend one day in youth again,
　once more before I die.

—Sarah Martini

Memories

My love for you was so true,
but you ran away without any
say, I still love you but it
hurts so much, you had a very
special touch.
The memory of you still wanders
inside of me, I love you so much,
can't you see.
Please come back from that awful
place.
Now I remember your boyish face.
Tears drip down, from my eyes.
Everything that you ever told me, was
nothing but lies.
Goodbye forever and always to be.
I really still love you but you
can't see.

—Karly Rice

Oh, It's A Joy To Behold

　High above the blue sky
By a double rainbow lies a
throne; what a joy to behold
his loving grace; what a joy
it is to behold his mercy he
give with no haste.

　Oh, what a joy to behold
the light shine in darkness;
He let me know I am winning
the fight;

　Oh, what a joy it is to behold
his saving grace, what a joy
it is to behold a love unfold like
no other untold and save
the soul; what a joy it is to
behold up in the heaven the
sun is far beyond the seven
wonders; where true love is
and the sound of thunder is heard.

—Janice Croxton

Inspirations

Caring for people and saying it
　By knowing the ones that know me
 Loving the ones that I love
　By knowledge of reality
Helping in everything I do
　By having a reason
Caring offering concern
　By feeling care from others
Hoping for the best in life
　By helping myself
Feeling how people care
　By asking them to
Touching a soul
　By strength and courage

—Daniel Healy

Untitled

Time went by
but did not erase everything
at its passage.
Memories were left,
like stars in the sky of oblivion
to remind the pain of old wounds.
Time the Healer,
was defeated and fell...

—Antonis Zervos

"Question"

A single throw of the dice,
   By the ancients of time;
Will determine isolation,
   Or two lives entwined.

Traveling time's many ages
   Their paths oft do cross,
High emotion, cold indifference
   Raise loyalty's cost.

A question unspoken,
   As each enters a new life -
The searing heat of the fire
   Or sharp cold of the knife?
—*Lynn Eicher Penn*

Aging Days

A wordless voice
Calling out from the void,
The black hole that devours.
The light that escapes,
A mindless vision
Seen in the clouds,
A boy's perspective,
A child's wisdom,
To see more than rain,
Longing to stare into the sun.
In the middle of summer
Caught in the heat,
Perspiration, and sweat,
Quench the thirst with water.
Still watching the clouds,
Older, wiser, in time's hand,
A desire to feel the rain.

—*Jos Manuel Accapadi*

Gettysburg

Once peaceful farm lands
   came alive one day
'Twas the roar of death
   that came their way
As Armies marched at
   a very quick pace
Such carnage never before had been
   seen, by the human race
Graves and a beautiful cemetery
   had to be made
There was even one for
   beautiful Jenny Wade
The ridges are silent now
   that once heard the yell
And monuments stand guard
   where men once fell
So salute the men in Blue, and
   men in Gray
As they passed the test
   on that fateful day
—*D. R. Gilliam*

Sadly Missed

I know you tried so hard to stay,
But we knew the time was near,
You grew weaker everyday.
I cried, you wiped my tears

We will always love you,
And think of you everyday,
The nights and days are lonely,
Since you went away.

—*Janet Daugherty*

Symphony

The grandest canyon
can not be shown by speech,
only with eyes.
With flowing
waterfalls and fountains
covered with moss.
Flowers growing
   many places.
The Grand Canyon
is a land of music
and a land of song.
All together
it is a symphony
of music.

—*Allison McCabe*

Thunderstorm Watch

Diamonds from emerald leaves falling
   Cannon volleys in the night
Cool clean breeze whistling and calling
   To brilliant flashes of instant light

Hear the rushing raindrops whisper
   Against applauding leaves
What were flat as parchment paper
   Now appear in cellophane sheaths.

Canons sounding in the distance
   Sodden cricket complains below
Raindrops whisper softly in their dance
   Storm fades only gentle breezes blow

Quiet rumbling, gentle flashes, quiet,
   quiet is the aftermath.
Violence of a short and jeweled variety
   Traveling nature's avian path.

—*Sally E. English*

Untitled

Dazzling water
Cascading down the gray ledge
Fizzing in whirl pools.

Fish being deprived
Of a swimmable surface
Tossed around like stones.

Crawdads losing ground
Being pushed by water pounds
Ripping their small claws.

Waters getting more harsh
Current taking boulders over
The defying falls.

God made all of it
He did in six full days
Rested the seventh.

—*Nathan Holdeman*

Untitled

Dive into the dark waters of our hearts
Cool spirits of hidden secrets
Be known to all who see in the dark
Flames in eyes that don't see
Disappear like shadows before the rain
I keep memories of you in my heart
Often you come in and ask me to dance

—*Wendy Davis*

untitled

if a chortling child
   chimed it
      Earth is a rose,

   or
      a bouncy baby
      melting down
      carried it to you
      on his wafting
soul
   people its fragrance,

would you still think it's just
a common analogy
   and peace its nurturing soil.
—*Rich Wilson*

Withered

Look across an empty desert
Close your eyes and see the dark
Feel the frigid air of winter
Then you'll know what's in my heart

Days too long and breaths too many
Loneliness and fears abound
No longer searching for the answer
That would turn my life around

Love once filled this hollow being
Gave it life and warmed its soul
Then love died and life died with it
Without love it couldn't grow

Withered now and barely caring
No heart left to love anew
Spirit gone and no dreams pending
Nothing left to say or do
—*Joseph J. Moirano*

Eleanor

A lovely young maiden
complexion so fair,
Touch of gentleness
that motivates care.
Stroke of Benson brush
add rosy pink to her cheeks.
Smile she projects on canvas
is inspired by glow in her eyes.
Eleanor has hair chestnut
touching her shoulders and brow,
Long dress of design
has multiple charm.
Enhanced with stunning wide brim
that makes her attire complete.
The gracious lady a simple delight,
fulfills her duties with
magic in her heart.
Admired by her peers,
Eleanor demonstrates the gift of
love can be shared by all.

—*Fern D. Church*

Memories

Memories
Come selectively.
I can bear
Partial light.
Let no scintillating flare
Uncover the All.

—*J. Audrey Stafford*

Aurora

Rosen-fingered dawn,
Countenant Eos,
Lifts her spectral hand,
Blazing sun to grasp
And take unto herself—

Ivory-beamed Apollo
Will unite in her fiery core
Blackened night's dank kiss
And morning's soft halo.
—*Carol Rodgers*

O' Horrible Night

I hid under my covers
Cowering in fear
I let out a shudder
Every time it drew near

The windows flew open and hung
It gave me such a fright
I shouted at the top of my lungs
"Go away, go away o'horrible night."

Lightning crashed and thunder boomed
For this was the night that I dread
It scared me so much all I could do
Was hide under my bed

I cuddled under a sheet
Awareness slipped away
I fell asleep
When I woke it was a whole new day.
—*Patrick Hesse*

The Party

We were there, the five of us
Crowding close in the dimness
Drawing from each other a bit of
 laughter, a ray of hope
Each had need of the other
In the deepness of our minds
The bells were tolling.
This just might be the last
Another time there'd be but four
We touched our glasses, our
 merriment knew no bounds
We pretended no shadows lurked
 beyond.
—*Ruby Sarty*

Dear Friend

Release me from this pain I'm feeling,
 Dear friend I wish my tears were healing
So innocent and unexpected,
 your pain and hurt so unprotected.
We try to beg, and try to plead,
 your life was shared by those in need.
The road we once had learned to walk,
 led us to love and friendly thoughts.
There is so much to say, but my time has
 ran out,
 I hope you take with you what I brought
about.
You may be scared and full of fright,
 Dear friend I'll lead you toward the light.
—*Julie Ratliff*

Street Litter

Spat out red faced.
Crumpled spittle pressed cheek
Sidewalk litter-fried brains.
Happened to fold on the cement
One day every.

Dust panacea needed
Keep to the left-overs
Behind your time table
And side stop up-head

He was dodging buildings
That jumped sky-crackling wise
And befuddled the sidewalk
Right of the way of the
Up elevator.

Patients —— patience!
He found it in a bottle
Slap his face with the times
Too late! So they called an ecologist.
Put 'im behind bars,
 They did.
—*Bruce Quick*

In The Shadow Of The River

The river flows
crushing rock, smoothing stone
rushing water
carving its path.

I am of the river
from its origin; my birth.
flesh from its waters and bone
- a mirror of the river.
it knows and disapproves;
yet I revere the river.

I grow in its shadow
listening to its angry voice
staying from dangerous shores.
this river can be murderous
but the river knows —
I am the weakness of the river.
still, I remain close.

I watch from the distance
my ancestry
and in its shadow.
—*Wayne Kniskern*

Ocean

 Quietly, waves rushing;
Birds, lively playing in the foam,
 Whales crying, how sad.
 Sand melting, floating away,
 Reefs with halos of clouds
 off in the distance,
 Seagulls are those lively birds,
 From the depths of the sea a
 Mermaid with seaweed
 in her hair.
 The birds surround her
 lovingly.
—*Melissa Gallihugh*

Where Is Daddy?

Where is daddy?
Daddy doesn't exist.
Not for her.
Not ever.

She searches.
She grasps every kind word
Man will give her.
She latches on tight.

She looks to teachers, elders,
Doctors, lawyers.
Any man with authority
And says, "Will you be daddy?"

She longs for a daddy that
Will love her "as is."
He doesn't exist.
Not for her.

As long as she lives,
She will never find him.
He doesn't exist.
Not for her.
—*Pat Blum*

Love Is...

Love is a flower
Damp from the rain.
Love is a heart
That never feels pain.
Love is the green grass
Kissed by the dew.
Love is me in love with you.

Love is a bird
Wings upon flight.
Love is the feelings
Deep in the night.
Love is the problems
You help me through.
Love is me in love with you.

Love is knowing
You're always there.
Love is knowing you'll always care.
Love is what it ought to be.
Love is you in love with me.
—*Amy Ledden*

Untitled

Watery horses,
dancing in the wind.
She was flying over a field of diamonds.
But that's just nonsense.
Wheat fluttering,
reflecting in her eyes.
She grasped his hand,
he let it go.
Calico dresses and green aprons.
memories of a past life,
with Mrs. Lewis
—*Erin Henry*

Annulment

Time has elapsed
Decision still unpalatable
Urgent visceral confusion
My souls has been violated
My whole being still cries out
For justice.
Not wanting him back
Not wanting the past,
Wanting the world to recognize
It was a failure
Not that it didn't exist.
Life did happen
26 years did happen
A union was made
Children were born
Children were wanted
Children were loved.
Patterns of family were established.
Protection for my person encircled
At my will.

—*Judith A. Neitge*

Lay Peacefully In Shadows Deep

Lay peacefully in shadows
  deep;
and soul not wander as thy
  sleep.

Resting now and then
  forever.

Hoping to forget never
days of wonder great in
  pleasure.

Lay peacefully in shadows
  sleep.

And thy spirit joyful in
  deep;
deeper knowledge of greater
  peace.

Lay peacefully in shadows
  sleep
  all forever,
  now or never.

—*Erika A. Mitchell*

A Dying Friend

Do not hide
Do not run,
I see him through
the fading sun.
Walking along
This shore at night,
Seeing him here
Is not a fright.
Death may come,
Death may go,
But for him,
We did not know.
Lost in a dream,
Lost in rest,
He never knew
He was the best...friend.

—*Nicole Milliken*

Adams Leaf

What about clothes
do they make the man...
no...
not bigger...
or better...
they do what they ought...
cover up skin...
so forget about those...
open up your heart to
let that thought transpose
for men were only men...
long before they wore
those clothes.

—*Marilynn J. Eagan*

A Shadows Of A Doubt

When a shadow falls across your face,
do you smile for your sorrow?

Do memories make you laugh
with desire?

You paint a picture with your feelings,
but it just turns out gray...like
your world.

Happiness is next to none, while
you try to fulfill your life as a
recluse.

Your feelings hurt time and time
again, but you speak, no words
come out.

Your pain is timeless, and
It will never end....

—*Kelly Malcolm*

A To Z Of Surgery

After Being Cut
  Doctor Estimatad Fate
    Given His Instructions
      Just Keep Laughing Mate

No Other Persons
  Quite Reassembled Slicker
    That's Ultimately Victorian
      With Xtra Yellow Zipper

—*Paul Hinds*

Chameleon Child

Which am I - angry or sweet?
doesn't' matter
I am what you want me to be

father don't yell at me!
I'll change my expression
watch and see

My sister wears make-up
while my brother rages on
it's ok, i'm used to being alone
I shiver in a corner
or a closet where you can't see
so adaptable and quiet
that's me

everyone yells
but I am silent
blending in
later on, I'll paint my hair pink
doing anything not to fit in

—*W. Weisheit*

Spiral

A time when youthful strength
  Dominated and obliterated
    the weakness within
Defeat was only an untouchable concept
Another word used only in context,
  For this young, strong spirit
    Would not, could not be defeated.
Well, for all the belief and all
  The struggling
We see that concepts are just that
  How we choose to interpret.
And what we choose to interpret
  Is at times the defeat in itself
    For self-denial can wound within.
In short this undefeated heart
  Has been spurned
  And in the long,
  Treacherous process
  Has inadvertently defeated
    Itself also...

—*Martha Munoz-Knowles*

Mommy - Daddy - Me

  Mommy and Daddy
    don't agree
so I wonder what will
happen to baby and me.

  Mommy says Daddy
    is to blame,
  Daddy says Mommy
should be ashamed.

Sunday School Teacher says
  FORGIVE
    but
  Daddy is looking
for a new place to
  LIVE.

Mommy tells me it will be
  alright
but how does Daddy kiss me
  GOODNIGHT?

—*Dwight Wallington*

Love On The Inside

Nike shoes - Zip shoes
Don't do's - do do's
Red socks - yellow socks
Whoopi or Goldilocks,
Guess jeans - Lee jeans
Zip fly - button fly
High tops - low tops
Long shirts - crop tops,
Big hands - little hands
Pins or rubber bands
Blue eyes - green eyes
Laughs or sometimes cries,
Runs or walks a lot,
Sings or hits a pot
Whatever you like, wear or do,
I love you because you are you.

—*Amber Kraai*

Untitled

Don't shut the door on me.
Don't lock me out
Let me in. Let me see.

Don't turn your back on me.
Don't block me out.
Turn around. Let me see.

Don't run away from me.
Don't shut me out.
Stop. Turn around. Let me see.

Don't hide from me.
Don't be scared...
Come out. Let me see.

Don't turn away.
Let me in. Let me listen.
Let me see.

Let me listen. Let me see.
I can help you if you'll let me.
I can understand. I can lend you a hand.
Let me listen. Let me see.

—*Denise Ward*

"Love?"

Love, what is love?
Doves represents love,
Is it a time to be confused
Or is it a time when everything
　else doesn't matter to you
And you think only of that person
Or is it really love,
How do you know?
Love is sometimes there
　when your not aware of it
　and sometimes, it's just there
And you were meant for each
　other
True love you might just
　call it.

—*Holly Burton*

A Final Change

Trees stand starkly, blindly staring,
　draped in jewels gray, austere.
Bells of each dull crystal ringing,
　silencing the silent air.

Clouds of gray and silver shadow
　steal across the murky tracks,
when pealing out with bells victorious,
　sunrise comes, the grey pall cracks.

Icicles shiver, snowflakes quiver,
　waters chuckling deep and strong.
Dewdrops glistening, lifebeat quickening,
　warm winds whisper growing song.

Sunlight dances through stiff woodlands,
　blackbirds laughter fills the air.
Now is morning, change is forming,
　joy is freedom, if you dare.

—*Jan Harding*

Front Page

Jets on shoestrings
Drawing in the sky,
Hatchlings in stick nests
Learning how to fly,
Headlines on the paper
Grab at my eye-
Drought in the Africas.
All the children die.
Rumor, oh blasphemy!
It all must be a lie
For when the church bells
Ring at night,
I can hear the children cry.

—*Melissa Bleiler*

Within

Each minute is a heartbeat
Each hour sheds a tear
My ears are ringing with the
voice I shall no longer hear.

What comfort is found in screaming
What good is it to cry?
My conscience will never clear,
for I did not say good-bye.

For years I've stored unshed tears
in a secret place inside.
But now it has overflowed,
so there it cannot hide.

Now my rage must be released,
and for days I'll want to die.
But conscience sighs in knowing,
that my heart has said good-bye.
　"Good-bye"

—*Genny Baker*

"The Sentinels"

Perhaps you passed by us
En route to other places
Or had you stopped to visit
Some past familiar faces

You gently strolled among us
Searching for that someone
Foregone from present madness
In a land of harmony

For you see we guard the passage
And you take this journey alone
To a land of finer graces
Contented—where favorites are none

—*Colleen K. Ashcom*

Nice Smells

My mom likes the smell of
coffee my dad likes the smell
of clam chowder for one of my
sisters it's perfume, for the
baby it's powder for me it's
Something we really can't spear
it the smell of clean fresh air!

—*Shaneeka Opulencia*

"Will You Remember Me, Love?"

When the gentle breeze of spring
enters guided by the light
to awaken you from your sleep
with a kiss on your cheek.
Will you remember me, love?
When the strong summer sun
burns with passion
each move you make
when you walk on the sand.
Will you remember me, love?
When the gold autumn leaves
dance with the wind
when they hear you
whisper my name.
Will you remember me, love?
When the fragile flakes of snow
drift in the silence
while you wait for my return.
Will you remember me, love?
I will my love... Forevermore.

—*Luz Mendez de Rosado*

Delicious Hot Summer

Delicious hot summer,
Erotic...
Awakens the senses,
stirs the soul to passion
and abandon...
Awakens the spirit,
quickens it to fire
and desire...
Delicious hot summer,
Exotic...
Races through the blood,
flashes in the eyes,
sears the heart,
and melts...

　my inhibitions...
　　my fears...

—*Rose Hernandez*

Burgundy Love

Image of an Angel
Etched into my mind
Her lips the shade
of purple grapes
Our kiss
The taste divine
Fierce ecstacy awaits me
When I see you pose so still
Like an animated statue
cemetric beauty
That could kill
Intoxicating body
Living love
On wild vine
I'll kiss you till I'm drunk
Wet passion is the wine
Mandella girl you charm me
With your mystic stance
Presence of a thornless rose
You keep me in a trance.

—*Jon Sheehan*

Untitled

　　Always together,
　　Eternally apart,
　　　Love you,
　　　I do,
　　if only in my heart,
　　　Dream,
　　　of the day,
　when the night is the same,
　　　For we shall,
　　　then be,
　　　together,
　　　our pain.
—*Danielle J. Johnson*

Untitled

Just sitting here thinking of you
Even though your feelings are few
You know how I feel
With these feelings I can no longer deal
I'm so confused
Everyone says all you'll do is use
All that you tell me
I believe it to be
So little I do
I wanna be with you
Even though truth is it'll never be true
—*Lisa Stoutenger*

Memories

Everywhere,
Everything,
A reminder of days gone by.
Times, past and forgotten,
Brought back
By the littlest things
Dolls,
Music,
People,
All around me.
Behind
Yet not fully gone.
Happy,
Sad.
Life,
Death.
All memories.
—*Elissa McCormack*

Scene From A Window

Sepia toned trees,
Faded leaves, and
Two incongruous evergreen bushes
(Even they are muted
On this drizzly day).

It is a subdued still life
Until the black and white
Cat enters
Sparking the scene.

Gallantly he struts
Animating each area
He passes.

Gone now,
Only the sepia backdrop
Remains.
—*Susan Tuttle*

My Bitter Tears

　　My bitter tears
　Falling through my fears
　Losing you would make
　　　me blue.
　　But as it is true,
　　　I'm losing you.
　　As my tears fall
　　It could be after all.
　My fears, growing through
　　　the years
　　Nothing but my fears,
　　Had I through the years.
　　But nothing shall I
　　　have now
　But my tears through
　　　the years.
　　Nothing but my bitter
　　　bitter tears.
—*Naomi Myers*

Take Me By The Hand

　　Let's run away
　　Far into tomorrow
　　Far from this world
　And closer to the next.
　Leave your troubles here
　　Where they belong
　　　Hold me close
　　And kiss me long.
　This world will never do
　Let's go to another place
　　　Me and U...
　Squeeze my hand, tightly
　　And don't let go
　I 'no there's a better place
　　That we can go...
　　When I'm with you
　　Nothing else matters
　My cares are out the window
　And yo' love engulfs my soul...
—*Virgil Gordon Glenn, III*

Untitled

One o'clock in the morning
Felt the Eastside drift tonight.

One o'clock got off the wall
And checked the nine to fives
From end to end.

One o'clock in the morning said
Fool if you can't sleep through
Me, then you might as well be
my friend.

One o'clock got off the wall
And for a split second it started
with mine.

One o'clock in the morning I
Lay traps down the hall trying
To catch the time.
—*Allen Scott*

The Unveiling

I sit here
filling you with fluid,
putting your pain to paper,
coloring in the outline
slowly emerging
from the shadows.
I set your soul
on the corner of my desk,
examining it,
an unusual insect
finding its way into my home.
I lean back in my chair,
my fingers throbbing
from the power of my words.

I look at you
and like a mirror
you reflect my face
back at me.
I am unveiled.
—*R. J. Lee*

Silent Voices

　The anger of the voice crying
for me wanting to hurt me.
I don't like to be hated! I don't
like wanting to hate!
I didn't want to put of fist, instead
fingers, two perhaps.
I felt signs of hate lurking toward
me, sneaking up behind me and exploding
into soul! I felt scared and some
what confused, like I was lost in
a nightmare and couldn't be found.
But as time goes by things get better
and so do people. The anger
will. Probably always be here, but
just not show. Remember what
goes around comes around that's what
people say and the hate you put
in me will come back to you
someday.
—*Tahirah Essix*

Good-bye Dad

I watched my dad
for the last two years,
as he slipped away
in spite of my tears.

Some days he knew me,
some days he didn't;
some days he would talk to me,
some days he couldn't.

Each day I saw him
I knew the time was near.
I wanted to hold him
to keep him here.

When the call came at 5 a.m.
I felt I had to be with him,
share the moments of passing
with loved ones, family and friend.

It's special time of home going;
a time to share with those you love,
a time of peace and quiet,
a time of love from above.
—*Doris J. Nall*

Flavors and Feelings

Today the sky was blue
For the very first time,
The grass was green,
The lemon was lime,

I've been thrown emotions
From riot and races,
Look at the homeless,
Sympathize with empty faces,

It's like a blind man once
Said to me,
I can't see the pain
And hurt there appears to be,
Although violence and hate does occur,
I prefer to smell a flower,
or an animals fur,

Realizing there is only
one love, one life,
Unable to exchange,
It is now! We must stop!
and rearrange
—*Jamie Roger Pierce*

America, The Wasteland

Oh, toxin-filled polluted skies,
For withered waves of grain.
For trash heap mountain tragedy
Above the littered plains.

America, America, oh,
How we've destroyed thee.
We've let you rot,
We should be shot,
From sea to oily sea.
—*Candee Lindsay*

A Tip Top Easter

Forget the cooking,

Forget the pan.
Forget your troubles,
   and turn on the fan.

Enjoy the holiday,
sit back and relax.

Sit down on the couch,
and push side the Ajax.
—*Diana Duerer*

Haiku: A Journey

   Here we stand at this
fork in the road, afraid to
   realize we're in love.

   To take a step towards
you would mean to accept my
   need/craving for you.

   To ask that I walk
by your side, would encourage
   humiliation.

   From different paths we've
come to this vertex. So what
   happens to us now?
—*Jacquelynne M. Jones*

Nostalgic View Of A River

The dawn breaks.
Free of its dark chains,
the water turns
to liquid silver.

The silver becomes
gold,
red and purple
hues.

The silence is
broken by
the twitter of
a bird.

The water becomes
crystal.
The breaking now is
heard.
—*Deanne Elizabeth Durrell*

Devil's Play

Two lovers
Fresh and sweet
Knew naught of right or wrong

All consuming
Their love seems
And only they so blessed

Yet e'er there was
Such blissful love
Satan held it in his hand

Tossing love
This way and that
Laughing at their fears

Heaven saw
The lovers two
And sought to ease such pain

but came a time
When heaven fled
And let the devil play.
—*Austin R.B. Wolf*

Nurturing

I stood erect.

You came to me,
   frightened,
   penitent,
   hopeful,
to lay your burden
at my feet,
thinking all along
that doing so
would lighten your load.

Yet seeing me so willingly
accept your pain
only increased the weight
you bore.

And so we walked,
silent,
together,
stooped similarly,
away from the revelation.
—*Claudia Greenwood*

Clean, White Pages

My rhyme it reaps a tender tear,
from eyes of which I hold so dear.
   The painful truths,
     so crystal clear
rise slowly from clean, white pages.
It tells of faults and bitter lies,
   a lonely life,
     the nights I cry.
Through men's mistakes and alibies,
they've kept me in their cages.
The words they harmonize and flow,
   from love stained pen
     to one I know.
But the pain felt will never show,
   truly,
on these clean, white pages.
—*Robert Weiner*

God's Gifts

A sweet smelling rose wakes
from her winter sleep.
A secret she holds
forever she will keep.
The sun will always rise
The moon will always fall
The flowers will bloom
As long as God loves them all
—*Courtney Dietzler*

L-O-V-E

A shower of one million creatures
   from midnight-blue to dawn,
Strain to see through the mist of
   which they lay upon.
A web of light shimmers and shines
   and slowly pushes through,
Only to reveal without a doubt
   that there still is nothing new.
The bond of energy was unbreakable
   but now quickly gives way,
The aura of hearts, spirits, and souls
   unite just to say....
Please Leave Our Vibrant Earth,
   all it takes is love.
Please Leave Our Vibrant Earth,
   it's a message from above.
—*Kelly Davidson*

At The Lakeside

The flowers have gone
from the lakeside anew.
I wonder here and about
searching for lost blue as
the small breakers ride the
water's edge, showing sand
and small dunes
like memories of the hue of early dew.
I wonder when the flowers
will return with tall tales
of having been alone
Perhaps the time will come
as the dunes ride high
upon the shores and by and by
the flowers will return again
—*Dorothy West Shepherd*

Destroyed

Burnt flesh
Frozen screams
never quite
as it seems.
Victory no
Defeat reigns
Wipe out
the insane.
Land mines
in the ground
Stopping life
that can be found.
Lost soul
A cold fire
Bleeding heart
Wrapped in barbed wire.
Confused mind
lost to live
Giving up
thoughts to give.
—*Cherie Butts*

Love

Love is a great feeling,
Full of hope and despair,
Sometimes I think love isn't fair!
But there is hope,
Because love makes the world,
A better place.
And brighten every humans face,
That is what I think of,
When I think of love.
Nations united,
Smiles lighted,
Friends and lovers,
No ones under cover.
Truth, justice, peace and harmony,
Nations forming into,
One big colony
That is what I think of,
When I think of love.

—*Stacy Obert-Thorn*

Starving

As I watched the angels open the gate
I kept wondering, was this really my fate?

The people I made cry
The people I wish would die
All I could say was "Why"?

Sometimes I thought I was starving for love
When would it be my turn to fly like a dove?

I was starving for something...
Something unknown
But what can you do when you're all up and grown?

Then I remembered what someone once said
   "All God's children must be fed"

—*Tiffany Kingston*

The Swans

The swans peacefully strode.
Gracefully, yet with power and
Force. The music hummed on.
They tasted it, smelled it.

They gleamed and streamed on
The light wood floor. The sun
Shone brightly. The minds were
Swept into the rest of their bodies.

With a leap! They steadied
Themselves. They carefully,
Silently, fell on the cold wooden
Floor. The swans had died. The
Dancers did not move.

The drums beat. The last, final
Note echoed consistently.

The crowd wiped tears away.
They shouted "Bravo" to the beauty.

"Encore, encore" the audience yelled.

The dancers stood. With delight,
They each took a deep, dramatic bow.
—*Cerissa Shaw*

Untitled

Without you...
Gray are my days,
 black are my
  nights;
A feeling of
aloneness, a feeling
 of fright;
With you...
If only in my head,
the thoughts be just
  mine;
For me you'll
always manage to
make the sun
 shine.
—*Concetta M. Roden*

Nature

Spring rains bring
growth of weeds.
Garden work
overwhelms old bones.
The lawn shows golden stars
of dandelion,
violets take over
to be replaced by daisies
asters, goldenrod.
Why toil for a perfect lawn?
Wildflowers are in fashion.
—*Lotte Klenbort*

Tomahawk

Handle handle handle handle handle
Handle handle handle handle handle
Chop chop chop chop chop chop chop
Chop chop chop chop chop chop chop
Blade blade blade blade blade blade
—*Zach Akers*

Romantic Delusions

Is this love that we relate?
Have others known or is it fate?

Is it to last or go astray
for years to come or just today?

How long must woman face
this anguish till she finds her place?

The path is long.
The path is steep.
The rocks are sharp
The snow is deep

We're not alone!
—*Nan Thomas*

Poem For Peace

A world of peace oh would we could,
Have peace and love and brotherhood.
This is God's world, just ours to share.
To keep the peace that is our care.
The pain, the heartache and the strife
Of war and fighting in this life;
The tears from women's eyes once shed
To no avail, their men are dead.
Oh, let men talk and talk yet more.
'Tis better than the cannon's roar.
Let leaders talk from dusk till dawn
And with the coming light of morn,
God's light illuminate their mind
That they may know, the peace to sign
From this day, forever more
Our heads upheld, our spirits soar
God, from you the world we lease:
Let us your tenants live in peace.
—*Eleanor G. Coen*

The Man From Mars

There once was a man from mars,
He always talked about stars,
One night he got in his spaceship,
He rode away on a very long trip,
I sure do miss that man from Mars.
—*Krystal Bedtelyon*

My Jesus

He doctored an old lady back to health
He caused the lane to walk
He caused the blind to see again
He caused the dumb to talk

These are a few of the miracles
My Jesus did Perform.
Before they placed upon His head
A heavy crown of thorns
And hung Him on a cross to die
Which He did for you and I

He never spoke a word
He never shed a tear
I guess He did it His way
As he hung on the cross that day
—*Doris Tyner*

A Mother's Pain

Perhaps he got what was coming to him
He did, I know that now.
I wish there were a better way
Although I don't know how.

He is dead because he killed
My two little baby boys,
Using them as though they were
His helpless little toys.

And yet, I know how his family feels—
Their loss, grief, and pain.
Because of that, to see him killed
Is of very little gain.

I cannot accept what he has done;
It was brutal, inhuman, and cruel.
But he is much like those he killed
As stubborn as a mule.

After what he did to us,
I wanted to see him die.
But now that it is really over
All I can say is...Why?
—*Kris Baker*

Shadow

I view my shadow with pity.
He exists empty, void of emotion,
feeling neither hate nor love.
Living in darkness, surrounded by light.

His movements are controlled,
His will is broken.
A reflection without a soul,
An existence without meaning.

I watch my shadow closely,
To learn from his plight,
To pay heed to his warning,
So as not to become a shadow myself.
—*Salvatore Pizzuti*

Man From Galilee

Who is this man from Galilee?
He heals the lame, makes blind men see!
And speaks of faith and truth and light
To see us through the darkest night.

With gentle mien and look serene
(An inner peace I'd never seen)
And piercing eyes that hold my gaze,
He stirs my soul in countless ways.

His words of hope wake heart of me,
Cast ray of light that I might see
There's way to live from what we know,
And glorious place where faithful go.

Why does he press on tired and torn
'Neath heavy beam which he has borne,
With neither angry look nor blame
For those who sting and barb and shame?

Then hang by nails on bloody tree,
When only innocent is He -
Who could forgive such agony?
The Savior's come - He sets us free!
—*Grace Kecmer*

The Looking Glass

Across the room I see a child
  he looks a lot like me

    I speak

    no response

I roll my ball to the child
  he does not return it

    I jump and scream
    he does the same

    he's mocking me

in anger I strike the child
he shatters, then disappears

    I am bleeding
    —*Edward Garner*

That's My Guy

  His innocence shines through
  He sparkles like the aftermath
    Of the fourth of July
He combines love, joy and mischief
  As one would the fixings for a
    cake

    He is strong, yet gentle
  Mature in his childlike manner
  He gives me reason to start a new
    morning
And makes me thankful for the end
  of each day

  He is my very own rainbow
    My rock of Gibraltar
How lucky can one mother be?
    —*Gloria E. Ramos*

The Bogey Man

I dreaded, once, the Bogey Man
(He was an awful ghoul)
His ugly face invoked disgust
(He was extremely cruel)
He used to scare me though my dreams
With giant vampire bats
And he could frighten me to death
Just with his howling cats

I asked my mother what to do
She said, "You must be tough"
"Just pull his hair and
Kick his shins
And that will be enough!"

I did it! He was so surprised
He jumped right out of bed!
And went to find another child
To terrify, instead.
    —*Eveline Taylor*

"Dream Baby"

I Dream Baby got me dreaming sweet
dreams my sweet dream baby.
You got me singing sweet dreams
baby keep on singing sweet dreams baby
I must have done something good in my
childhood or womanhood I must of done
something good.
So dream on my dream baby got me
dreaming sweet dreams baby.
    —*Kathy Garrett*

Where?

She reached for him,
  He was not there.
Where did he go?
  Did he not care?

It was only
  Hours ago.
They'd snuggled up
  To watch it snow!

Then looking down,
  She saw him there.
His big brown eyes
  Returned her stare.

"Forgive me, Teddy Bear,"
  She said.
"For pushing you
  Out of my bed!"
    —*Donna A. DeLena*

Make Me A Helper, Lord

For those who hurt, dear Lord,
  help me to share their pain;
For those who suffer loss,
  make me, to them, some gain.
For those who weep, dear Lord,
  help me to dry their tears;
For those afraid, O let me
  help allay their fears.

For those, dear Lord, who through
  the vale of sorrow go,
Help me your word of hope to give,
  that they may know
The perfect peace of God
  which is your gracious gift.
Help me, dear Lord, where'er I can
  some load to lift.
    —*Oliver E. Peterson*

My Only Gift

Her smile I remember so real
Her love encased within a seal.
Her eyes focused upon mine own
Letting the love for me be shown.
My eyes swelled up with salty tears
Knowing my mother's last word nears.
How can I tell her how I feel
And yet let my tears be still?
Her breath is timed by a machine
Erst her body lies blank and lean.
The love for my mother grows fast
Remembering our great times past.
As I grasped her still hand so tight
The Lord took my mama that night.
Holding back tears, I kissed her face
Knowing God had prepared her place.
My heart is heavy but not sad
Knowing mama's love I once had.
    —*Deborah Hilliard*

Lovely And Shy

As she encloses silk petals about,
Her, lovely and shy.
The moon hangs a crescent in the sky.
Moonbeams surround her and flutter,
About, shadow people watch
As she stands brave and stout
Ne'r a quiver or a shiver.
And a shadow man approached her
Just like the night, to give
Her a gift that is of a queen.
Kneeling beside her, his kisses
Is of dew, then the sun arose,
The shadows instantly froze
They ran in fear to their places and
The rose stood alone with all of
Her beautiful faces as she stood
Their alone the shadow appeared.
The shadow peered after he looked
Very intently and waved her
Good-bye. Lovely and shy.

—Rebecca Lee

My Granddaughter

Her eyes are like the sky of blue
Her skin like fallen snow
Curls of gold surround her head
And set her all aglow.

She's full of love for everyone
It's very plain to see
And when she smiles that special smile
I know it's meant for me.

We sing and dance and march in time
Around the living room
We laugh and play, each in our way
Enjoying every move.

Then all at once the doorbell rings
It's Mom and Dad I fear
To claim their child, return to home
Which brings a little tear.

—Patsy Gitto

The Army Man

His battle is not on a field—
He's battling his past—
Will he lose or will he win—
How long will this war last.

This battle is not new to him—
Already his confidence is blown apart—
Though he has no fleshy cuts—
His wounds are in his heart.

His uniform can help him not—
To him this battle is much more—
The scars he has are way too deep—
He, himself, must win this war.

You ask what my interest is—
How can I understand—
I guess it's because I Sincerely care—
For my friend, THE ARMY MAN.

—Wendy Walker

The Hunter

A fierce evening sun,
Hidden in yellow-green grass.
Live stripes of midnight,
Watching a wild ass.
A paw draws back,
Like an arrow to a bow.
A growl is heard
So soft and low.
Pearl colored needles,
Glistening in the sun.
Pearl colored needles,
Moistened by his tongue.
The bow is pulled back.
Its fury has sprung.
It strikes its target.
Before its prey can run.
Pearl colored needles,
Glistening in the sun.
Pearl colored needles,
Moistened by its bloody tongue.

—Tyler Hawkins

Precious Love

His eyes were like the ocean bright.
His hair, as if abyss by night.
My soul, he stirred, with love so deep
To torment death from endless sleep.
Love, 'twas it, that burned so high
As if to torch the troubled sky.
But vanished, he, as love 'twas born,
And now my soul, forever torn,
Can love no more, as it hath done.
Look! Riseth now the noble sun.
Can daylight's rays, my hope, restore
Or must I search, forevermore?
My heart, it aches, for him alone.
For that one love, which he hath shown
And to the world shall be unknown
For love like this is never told
Except in lovers' tales of old,
And by the lovers' ever bold,
Who dare to speak of love like gold.

—Natalie Lewis

His Fault

His little hand
His silly laugh
 His gurgling
His first step
His first world
His first day of school
 His graduation night
  His wedding
   His beer
    His car
His funeral
His fault.

—Denyse Metcalfe

His Love

He has a love that can not die,
I have a love that will not lie.
I have to see him every day,
So he can help me find my way.
He's like a brother, always there,
He is there because he cares.
If he were to leave, I would cry,
Still his love would never die.

—N. Johnson

"Summer"

Jams and jellies
Home - made wine
Gifts of the soil
Fruit of the vine
Scarlet tomatoes
Peaches pure gold
Following recipes
Treasured and old
Bottled and labeled
There on my shelf
Making me feel
Quite proud of myself
We who are dreamers
Who wish upon stars
Catch a little of summer
And put it in jars.

—Patricia A. Feighan

Hot Summer Night!

As I sit alone in a
hot summer night, with my feet
buried between the sand, which
cooled my soul as I reached
deeper into the sand. I hear
the echo from the ocean
that seems so far, but yet
so close I could feel the
water splashing between my
body. As I steer so far,
I'm in a daze, I imagine,
I visualize, I can see myself
there with peace and tranquility.

—Loredana Iudici

Dear Mother,

Dear Mother, I want you to know
how deeply my heart embraces your
every silhouette.

Dear Mother, I want you
to know your an extraordinary
and beautiful sole in which
is perfectly set.

Dear Mother, I want you
to know that your a walking
goddess of uniqueness,
warmth, and love.

Dear Mother, I want you
to know how at times I think
as an angle from above.

Dear Mother, I just wanted
to share some of my high
thoughts of you.

Dear Mother, I want you
to know I love you to the
depths...........I do.

—Marie Crissone

"Life"

I was lost, afraid but knew
I had eyes to see but not His love
I had ears to here but not His voice
I had hands to feel but not His touch
I had legs to stand but not by Him
I had feet to walk but not with Him

I walked with a man in habit of brown
and shown the way of life in Him

—Sandra L. Starkey

Tough Teacher

Tough teacher, tough teacher
How did I get you?
I probably got you by mistake
and this you know is true.

Tough teacher, tough teacher
will I get another one like you?

I will get you candy
I will get you flowers
If you cut my homework time
by a couple hours.

Tough teacher tough teacher
My mom and dad love you
You've taught me so much this year
You've made their dreams come true.
How did I get you?

Tough teacher, tough teacher
How do I thank you?
—*Arlie Stacy II and Mikel Stacy*

Accepting Life

There comes a time, when the
hurt is so profound
That no "body", no one, can hear
your soul!
You breath, and your breath
screams, and you know, someone
is listening. No "body."
You are enveloped with layers
of spirits, you exist.
Somehow your soul becomes
one with the unknown, and you
can smile. For the unknown knows.
No words, you become one, with.
—*Ann (Lis) Martinez*

Realization

When I was young and very shy
 I always stood alone,
Not being able to express
 my thoughts in proper tone.

While gathering experience
 I slowly learned to know
My worth and limitations.
 The progress was but slow.

I am an open book now
 For him or her to read.
It may-should someone like it-
 To friendship even lead.
—*M. Gertrud Kuhn*

Untitled

Though I am your Mother's husband
 I am factually not your Dad,
But if indeed you were my daughter
 I should be forever glad.
For you have all the attributes
 A father holds so dear.
You are easy to know, easy to love,
 And just a joy to be near.
On this day we seem so special
 These Irish eyes are smiling for you
And I have a most happy feeling
 Good Saint Paddy's smiling too!
—*Russell Murphy*

Admonition

If my mother were here
I am sure she would say
Stand up straight, take long steps
And try not to walk like a duck
And while you are about it
Wipe your nose when it drips,
Do not gulp your coffee, take it in sips
And never smack lips when eating.

She is not around any more.
At age eighty-four I fend for myself
So I quote her each day, saying
"Stand up straight, take long steps..."
And I go on from there with out her.
—*Zelia J. French*

Coyote

My secrets make me scream;
 I am the real native.
I'm the original article,
 the beast in the flesh.
I am Mother Nature's outcast son,
 abandoned to die in barrenness.
I howl and rave at her cold face
 and hide from her warm one.
I kill her other children to survive
 and still I grow lean,
 wasting from her disfavor.
—*Jennifer Drew*

Sunrise

I have no armor.
I am without cloth.
No shelter from the night.
No arms around me tight.

I have no armor
No veil across my face.
No walls for my disgrace.
No stones to build my brace.

I have no armor
Naked in the light.
I seek an ember burning bright.
To hide me....To guide me....

A ray of everlasting light.
To heal the wounds of time.
To seal my love with thine.
To feel my touch and shine.
—*Karen J. Garrett*

Untitled

Once again my old friend and
 I are together,
We spend a lot of time this
 old friend and I,
Earlier times my old friend
 was scarce,
My family kept me busy and too
 tired for my friend,
Sometimes I go out and leave
 my friend home,
Its great music, laughter and lots
 of people,
It doesn't last forever and my
 friend always waits,
So now as so many times, it's me
 and my old friend - loneliness
—*Barbara Mulert*

A Melody

The melody within my heart
I bore, long after our depart.
A melody of gloom, my dear,
which came to me so strong and clear.

To know our love could never be,
was hard to bear for you and me.
To feel the blooming of regret,
was like the losing of a bet.

I still can see you standing by,
the window where we said goodbye.
And felt the sorrow in the air;
the air that stood about us there.

The tears and fears that filled our eyes
were present when we bade goodbyes;
and ever stains the smiles we wear.
On skin of clay their marks we bear.
—*Reagan Murff*

Cupid's Demise

The die is cast
I can do nothing but wait
For you control my fate
Does it last?
Does it fall?
My back is to the wall
There's no more time
You've committed a love crime
You hellish creature
Get out of my sight
You picked and you chose
But the love never grows
You turned out the light
And brought it to night
Now a duel
You wing-ed fool
All power is now gone
Again it's dawn
Cupid is dead!
Cupid is dead!
—*Tim Jackson*

The Midas Touch

I am fire
I can see the blue and orange
and dismal yellow
battling inside me
making patterns
like those of a quilt
with angles and sharp edges
I expand
I flicker
I reach out to touch you
but I realize
that I will destroy you
a demented Midas Touch
isolation
I am killing myself
I am burning
—*Jocelyn Nissa Grimes*

"Love Is In The Air"

Love is in the air
I can smell your shining hair
The fragrance you leave behind
Sends chills up and down my spine
I get lost in your eyes
Sending me soaring through the sky
Seeing your smile pass my way
My love for you grows each passing day
In my arms, I wish you there
So I can hug you like my teddy bear
In these arms you can stay
With no fear of slipping away
When there is love in the air
I know I can find you anywhere
—*Christopher L. Louie*

Love?

Do I love you?
I cannot compass it
North nor' east
I only know the woods and sky
fill me
with a glow
And I take that moment that we shared
And hold it tight
To star a sleepless night
with deep delight
My world is beautiful
because of you.
—*Alice Ungar*

Don't Forget About The Past

Memories of you flood my mind
I close my eyes and there you are
Just to touch you one more time
That's a wish that's just too far.
When reality quickly returns
You vanish into mid-air
Leaving me here alone
To face this pain and fear.
I'm so scared and confused
And I don't know where to turn
I wish I understood you more
But now I'll never learn.
This is where I say
The painful goodbye
To you my good friend
You didn't deserve to die.
—*Teena Shatos*

Taps

And we have on tap
hot and cold running war
running frenzy
running fear
running — thirst driven
with the world on the tips
of our tongue, but strangled
in our throats
and the tap at our finger
   — tips.
—*Kirsten Quick*

Homeless

Go ahead, laugh at me.
I don't care.
It's not my fault,
I lost my job.

I can't find one.
Boy, have I tried.
It's hard to find something,
When it's not to be found.

I live outside,
In a cardboard box.
Most people think,
I'm a lazy ox.

Please help me,
But you don't understand,
Nobody will help,
A homeless man.
—*J. Baker*

I Still Love You

I may not be the perfect daughter,
   I don't know what to do.
It's really weird to be at home,
   With all that you've been through.

I just can't comprehend,
   How a stroke affects your mind.
I know you've changed an awful lot,
   You know that I'm not blind.

You can't do anything on your own,
   You wear more than you eat.
I slipped away two years ago,
   I couldn't take the heat.

It's awkward being back here now,
   The strange things that you do.
You're in the same old body,
   But it's no longer you.

I wish we both could understand,
   And get back what we had.
But even though you've changed a lot,
   I still love you—Dad.
—*Sally Carroll*

The Wanderer

Nobody knows where he came from
I don't think anyone cares,
He's just a wanderer
goes from here to there,
He's been around for a long time
going from place to place,

There's one thing about him
no one has seen his face.
All I know he's a wanderer
not looking for a place to stay,
He's been gone for a while now
maybe he'll be back some day.
—*Stephen Beth*

Lake Kabekona Interlude

Sitting down by the water,
I hear the trees whisper and rustle.
They are all around and above me.
Down in the shallows birds are seeking,
   seeking...
The sun shines, the water glistens.
The quietness and peace are my reward.
—*Betty Ramstead*

To Walk The Road Without You

To walk the road without you
I feel I walk alone
Our road of love and sharing
Is now a lonely road of stone.

I reach out as if to take your hand
But find an empty space
Our tender world of happiness
Is now an empty place.

And as I travel on my way
Your voice I long to hear
I brush my hand across my face
To dry my silent tears.

The road is full of winding curves
And dangerous hills to climb
I need your love to carry me
I'm running out of time.

To walk the road without you
I feel I walk alone
The music of our laughter
Is now a fading song.
—*Jennifer Raybon*

I Forgot To Remember

I forgot to wash the dishes.
I forgot the trash, how messy.
I forgot to wash the clothes,
now the bedroom door is closed.

I forgot to pay the bills
and I ran out of pills.
I forgot to call my mother
sometime I wonder, why I bother.

I forgot to wake up
now I'm late for work.
My wife got on my case,
I left with egg on my face.

Now I don't forget
just to forget.
Sometimes I remember
in spite of it.
This memory of mine,
"I forget".
—*Franklin Rogers*

Summer

I close my eyes,
   I get lost in the day,
The sun rising and setting,
   The sand where I lay,

The feel of the wind,
   The sound of the sea,
So meaningless to some,
   Yet meaningful to me.

I won't know it again
   For another whole year;
Nothing else to see,
   And nothing more to hear.

But like other past years
   I know my fate,
I'll just sit and I'll dream
   And I'll patiently wait.
—*Kristen Foley*

Top Priority

As they walk by,
  I hear weeping .
As I walk by,
  I see them sleeping...alone.

Cold and dark,
  Their lives are lonely.
Poor and hungry,
  I could...if only.

Mother's and children,
  Home on the street.
Reaching out,
  For something to eat.

Save the people,
  From this growing majority,
Make the homeless,
  Our top priority.
—*Joan Zipp-Lumb*

The Old Steam Engine

Today as I was all alone
  I heard a familiar sound
It was the old steam engine
  Passing through our town

I saw the black smoke rolling
  Heard the clicking of the wheels
The whistle blew a mournful sound
  And to me the world stood still

It brought back old memories
  Of days and years gone by
To know those times can never be
  Brought a tear drop to my eye

I stood there in silence
  Until the sound I heard no more
I turned around with a sad, sad heart
  And walked back through the door
—*Grace Babcock*

Silhouette In The Doorway

As you stood there in the doorway
I knew I must say goodbye.
I must turn and walk away
Lest I begin to cry.

The smile you always wore
that spread across your face
I wanted so much to hold you
Let another take your place.

The years seemed to go so fast
but love and memories forever last.
The tear on my cheek too will fade
as we must go on day by day.

So now it's time to say goodbye;
I must turn and walk away
Tho I shall always see that quiet smile
on the Silhouette In The Doorway.
—*Florence Eldredge*

Fall Leaves

The fall leaves are blowing softly
I love the fall leaves so,
So gentle,
So magical,
I wish fall would never end,
But I know it has too.
So I wait,
And I'm so glad when it comes again.
—*Amanda Swedlund*

Safe In The Arms Of Jesus

I belong to Jesus
I know he loves me so.
That when I leave this earthly shore
to heaven I will go.

I'll know no more of pain and tears
he'll set me free from all my fears.
My days in glory will be spent
to Jesus' garden I'll attend.

I'll sing and dance in heaven above
safe and secure in the saviors love.
I'll know no more of earthly pain
I've trusted in the savior's name.

With the love of Jesus in my heart
I've tried my best to do my part.
To do the things he wants of me
for only he can set me free.
—*Ralph Nienhouse*

Dreams

As the night falls slowly
I lay down and see the stars
and the moon, I think of
the dreams I have when
I am full of wonders.

I wonder what my dreams
are telling me about my
future. Dreams do come
true, if you let them.

Dreams are forms of a kind
of life you like to have
but sometimes dreams don't
come true.

Life could be a part of
your dreams that you have
in your mind and soul
throughout your spirit.
—*Valentina Rabbitt*

Alone

I search far,
  I look near.
I only look for
  someone special.
A special person
  to be my friend.
A friend that will
  listen to me.
A friend to have a
  shoulder to lean on, to cry on.
I only want a friend
  because I am alone in a world
  where no one cares about me
  or listens to me.
If I only had a friend
  I wouldn't be lonely anymore.
—*Alison Lee*

Untitled

Like a magnet,
  I was drawn to you,
Like gravity,
  I fell for you.
And like nothing else,
  Is my love for you.
—*Michelle M. Blandy*

Being Friends Is Everything

Being friends is everything.
I need to know you are my friend
First before all else.
I need to know most of all
That I can trust you with myself.

Being friends is everything.
I need to know, when we disagree,
You will always stand by.
Lovers quarrel, now and again
So shall you and I

Being friends is everything.
When tough times come, and they will,
Lovers always break up.
When tough times come, and they will,
Friends can always make up.

Being friends is everything.
I delight in you as my love
More than you will ever know.
But I most enjoy just being your friend
I will never let that go!
—*Mark C. Barrentine*

For The Man

For the man who holds a gun
I pray for him each night
For the man who has no fun
I think of him in fright
For the man who feels alone
I'll be by his side
For the man who seems unknown
He's known by me with pride
For the man who loves to give
I trust him with my heart
For the man who wants to live
I hope we never part
For the man who likes to joke
I smile and laugh with glee
For the man who just went broke
His helper I will be
For the man who calls my name
I quickly answer him
For the man with glorious fame
I watch his life grow dim.
—*Cheri Cole*

"The Bright Morning Star"

When I arose this morning
I saw the early morning star
Shining in the heaven so far
above. To give us all delight,
to see such a beautiful
sight, I had no doubt that
the Lord gave us a prec-
ious gift with all his
might, to see the lilies
of the field so prou-
dly Standing Still, to
feel such warmth makes
My heart abide and I
know this is not hard
to find to wish upon
A falling star and
dream of dreams
your heart desires.
—*Patricia Noil*

I'm A Snowflake

I'm a snowflake falling,
I see a forest below me,
I hope to drop into it,
If I don't I will not see any animals.

I make it to the forest,
I see lots of homes,
They belong to the animals,
I'm glad I landed in the forest.

Trees danced in the wind,
Snowflakes fall off them,
I make a friend with one,
We play together.

We see who can fly farther,
I win,
After we play it's time to go home,
I'm glad I'm a snowflake.
—*Michael Lanfranchi*

Remembrance

I close my eyes;
 I see his face;
 His swollen limbs.
 Yet I remember his grace.
 I said goodbye
 and I was shaken.
 I can't stop thinking
 about a young life taken.
Why did it have to end so soon?
 Was it accidental on a dare
 Or on purpose by a goon?
 Dreams never reached;
 Goals never attained.
All that training was in vain.
—*Elaine M. Powell*

The Falling Leaf

I'm laying under a falling leaf
I see it and it sees me
I'm laying under a falling leaf
Oh how it brushes side to side
Oh I'm laying under a falling leaf
How soft the sound
When it glides to the ground
I'm laying under a falling leaf
The wind blows it up and up to the sky
I'm laying under a falling leaf.
—*Paul Pellegrino*

Untitled

 When I think of you:
I see the sun bright and strong
I hear special thoughts and dreams
I touch the strength of your body
 and the softness of your eyes.

 I feel good about you....
 You've become a part of me
 no one else is, or can be.

 You make me feel warm with
 an ever flickering flame.
 The dead winter appears so
 much more alive and beautiful
 as you make me aware
 that I am too....
—*Robin Barrett*

On That Simple Little Ride

I sit here alone
I think about the past
I listen to our song
I didn't think things would go so fast
I remember you here
Sitting beside me
I remember your face
I remember the key
The key to our hearts
The key to the car
The key to the accident
And now you're so far
Away in another world
Away in another land
But you're still in my heart
And we're still holding hands
I can't believe it happened
I can't believe you died
The doctors say it happened too fast
On that simple little ride.
—*Sarah Wadle*

I Love You

As I lay in bed each night
I try to get my feelings right
There is no doubt, I do love you
But do you really love me too.

With your arms around me tight
Everything always feels so right
Your touch to me feels so good
I'd stay forever if I could

We seem so good together
I hope it lasts forever
For you are my one & only
Please don't ever leave me lonely
—*Nicole Klein*

Into The Forest

Into the forest
 I walk unseen
Through shadows and light
 and shades of green
The path underfoot
 and the trees above
Keep my spirit alive
 as I wander these woods
Songs are heard
 from birds up high
And the wind gives life
 to the leaves with a sigh
Though I walk by myself
 I am not alone
There is life all around
 in this place I call home.
—*Alan Jacobson*

Potential Debasement

Overwhelming aura of sensuality,
 far removed from reality.
 Quiver, quake, pulse and shake,
 another unsolicited heartache.
 Surely sent to tempt my soul,
presenting another unobtainable goal.
 Sent to challenge the inner me.
 To pierce the armor of my fantasy.
Sweet phrases pouring from my depths.
 I set them free and softly wept.
—*Henry L. Humphrey*

Brief Respite

Engulfed in softly flowing dusk
I watch the fireflies light their lamps.
Like jewels they slowly flit and flash
Through fairyland of ebbing green.
 Within the brightly lighted house
 T.V. and radio blare forth
 enticements—violence—alarms!
Clouds parting briefly show one star
Soon curtained by the silken rain,
As darkness lays a gentle gloom
Lit by the fireflies fitful gleam.
—*Mildred T. Marsh*

"Brotherly Love

If my brother's in trouble,
I will be by his side,
To be his helping hand,
And through the night I'll guide.

If he's gonna to be in trouble,
It'll be the both of us,
To stand up for each other,
And show our love and trust.

Your brother is a special guy,
God sent him from above,
So be with him and care for him,
And show your brotherly love.

Of course you love your brother,
And loved him from the start,
You say no one can break you up,
Cause your love comes from the heart.

Keep saying you love your brother,
And say it with no doubt,
Just keep on giving your brotherly love,
Cause that's what it's all about.
—*Shirelle Brown*

Dante's Inferno

 Tonight,
 I will lie in bed,
 watching and waiting
 for the door to open,
 bile leaping
 furiously in
 my throat.

 tonight,
Another Dante's Inferno,
 thoughts racing like
 machine guns
 in my head.
 Lies, lies, lies.

 tonight
 We will lie
 together,
 Never touching,
only erratic breathing,
my body and heart cries
 How Much Longer
—*B. J. James*

Father

I want no more fighting
I will take no more ridicule
Your approval I have lived without
All I wanted was your time

I can mourn the relationship
  We never had

My only need is to let go
  of the anger and isolation
  and the void of manhood

Now I can thank you for giving
  me the best that was you

At last I can wish you well
    —*William C. Fritsch*

I Am

I am sad and curious
I wonder why my grandpa died
I hear his voice at night
I want to feel his strong embrace
I am sad and curious

I pretend he's still here
I feel his tender love
I touch his gentle hands
I worry about his happiness
I cry for he is not here anymore
I am sad and curious

I understand why he left
I dream he's still here
I say, "I wish you were still here"
I try not to cry too much
I hope he is not sad for
I am sad and curious
    —*Amy Yost*

Together Someday

If you ever needed me
I'd be there
If you ever asked for help
I would care
It has been every day
That I felt this way
  I know in my heart
That some day you'll feel
The same way I feel

For in time you will see
That we were meant to be
    —*Cathy Adams*

To The Point

What's the point of living
If you're only to die
What's the point of loving
If you're only to cry
What's the point of "us"
If it's not you and I
There is no point
There's only goodbye.
    —*Brandy Connell*

I Love To Write Poetry

I love to write poetry
I'll tell you why
Poetry is the apple of my eye
I love to write poetry every day
I'll always love poetry
Come what may.
I love to write poetry up on a hill
Where it is peaceful and still
My best efforts are up where
The air is rare
And all is bright and fair.
I also love to write poetry
Down by the old mill it is peaceful
And still poetry has won my heart
From it I'll not depart.
Poetry I'm mad about it
In my mind there's no doubt about it
All poet should be commended
We don't have to be defended.
Again I'll say we should be commended.
    —*Edna Maiden*

Friend

Dear best friend I'm talking to you
I'm asking for advice
Once again I need you friend
To make my world be nice.

It seems whenever my heart is empty
Just like my nights and day's
I think of laughter we shared together
And your sweet loving way's.

Dear best friend

Can you hear me now
Can you feel my gentle tear
Upon the soft green grass it falls
While you peacefully sleep here
    —*Beba Kusevic*

My Adolescents

Help me,
I'm crying!
No one seems to hear me.
I know the solution,
but no one hears me.
Misery me no more.
Let me be who I am!
Let me love like I need!
Let me live how I choose!
Still, no one hears me.
I love you,
I hate you.
Clearness is unavailable,
understanding seems not possible.
Death, a choice.
But won't be taken.
Slow death is what it is.
Suffering,
to me, to you.
    —*Carey Frick*

The Golden Rays Of Sun

Its summertime
I'm walking down
the beach
Sea gulls fly high
in the sky
The golden rays of sun
shines down on me

I stop to look
up to the sun,
I wonder if the sun
is made out of gold
I stand there
wondering

Then suddenly I'm
awaken by a wind
echoing through my
ears as if its trying
to tell me something
beyond reality.
    —*Roxanne Nose*

A Friend By Far

Not long ago I lost my mom
in a automobile accident.
By her grave were many months spent.
Every night I cried myself to sleep.
While she was hospitalized
I prayed her soul to keep.
A coma took over a life and a friend.
It's hard to believe her life
has come to an end.
Her love still wonders around on earth.
I love that women that gave birth.
Since then my life hasn't been the same.
Can't smile just wonder who's to blame.
    —*Tracy Skipper*

Strike 3

I feel so alone; trapped
In a deep trance.
And no one is there
I'm a victim of circumstance,

My life is like a game
I already have two strikes.
As the final pitch is thrown,
My life flashes before my eyes.

I prepare to take my last swing
And hear all the screams and shouts
I swing, I miss, and the umpire yells,
"That's it-strike three!" I'm out.
    —*Teri Rutter*

Silhouette

Still
In total blackness
Like no other paintings
Homeless
Only to be seen
Unlike paintings
Each piece is unique
Touched by light
The silence is broken
Eternal life, black as night
    —*April Zahn*

Stay Of Execution

I was lost in time
In a place I did not want to be
In the grips of war
Forgotten by humanity
I was scared to death
In this God forsaken place
I knew that I would never leave
No one would win this race.
I called upon the saints
All that I had ever known
And recited every prayer
The first since I was grown.
The smell of burning flesh and
The ammo dust filled the air
I had only selfish thoughts
Mine was the life to spare
When suddenly out of the sky
Appeared a purple butterfly
It swept toward me through acrid mist
And gave me life with an angel's kiss.
—*Judith M. Smith*

Beautiful Lady

One day I was lyin' in my bed
in a world of my own.
Never really realizing what's going
on through my head
It was about a lady I've seen before;
where I don't know.
She was the most beautiful lady.
I've seen her before, she looked exactly
like you.
Never knowing how to talk to her;
every time I see her walking and she
leaves me speechless.
When she walks in the night
underneath the sky.
The moonlight from the
night sky shines onto
her body, her looks sweeps
my breath away every time.
—*Neville Porter*

Whitewash Of The Mind

Hidden away
in back of my brain
  lies a diamond-covered hand
    hindering my movement
  eating caviar
    while I starve
      squeezing
      squeezing
    Trying to push me down
  knowing I am weak
    Stealing my tears
  Replacing them with anger
    erasing my thoughts
      forgetting my name
  remembering my number
  squeezing until I have nothing
    Then squeezing
      some more.
—*Julie Pressman*

The Raging Storm

The wind blows
  in every direction.
The rain comes down hard,
  almost like a fight.
Lighting shines,
  you can read by it.
Thunder is loud,
  it almost makes you deaf.
The raging storm
  is every kids nightmare.
—*Michele Harwood*

Tears For Thy Tears

Every day,
in every way,
I try to keep my fears
and thy tears in,
but it is hard,
so very hard,
to keep in my fears
and thy tears,

You see,
my heart is broke,
because my father
had a stroke!
—*Timothy Walker*

Benjamin

He looks all grown up,
  In his gown and cap.
When did he get bigger,
  He should still be in my lap.

So many years ago,
  When to the world, I gave a son.
How would I know,
  A mom's caring is never done.

As time went on,
  Bigger did he grow.
Now he says, "oh mom!"
  Instead of always no.

Graduation came,
  My baby is a man.
Things won't be the same,
  Survive it, maybe I can.

When in the air, his cap flew,
  My tears began to flow.
With this I knew,
  Eventually he would go.
—*Barbara Saefke*

If I Could

I wish I could hold you
  in my arms tonight
Then, I'll know everything
  will be alright
I wish I could have you for me
  and then I shall see
If my wish has come true
  It would be me and you
If my dreams should come true
  It would be forever me and you
—*Heather Litchfield*

Night Snuggler

Little blue-eyed snuggler
In my bed at night,
Tiny arms around my neck
Holding or real tight.
In your night-time dreaming
You see things you fear,
Does it help, my tiny one
To snuggle ever so near?
Tiny hands so warm and free
To pat my hair and face,
Does it keep the cruel world out
To share at night my place?
Oh, little one, you trust me so
You feel so free from harm
If you are cuddled to my breast
Or resting on my arm.
Do you know, my wee one,
That in my own despair
I reach to you in darkest night
And thank God you are there.
—*Helena B. Watson*

Separate Ways

There are always distractions
in our lives.
Things that draw us far to
the right,
Out of sight and out of view
of the things we need to do.
Up, toward the sun we fly.
Leaving everyone and everything,
everyone and everything, that has
helped us to get by.
Up high alone we fly.
Eventually, alone we die.
—*Willie B. Jones*

Mother Earth

Shouldn't we all try harder
in saving this planet earth?
Shouldn't we all be smarter
in remembering her worth?

The Creator gave us all Eden
to live in and treat with respect.
Because of our greed and excesses
we've only shown Him neglect.

Hasn't she brought you pleasure
all these years you've been alive?
Don't you want to protect her
and make sure we all survive?

Don't you know she is fragile
and cannot take this abuse?
To save the plants, the water and air
it's time we called a truce!
—*Kathryn J. Jacoby*

Seeking

  Seeking love,
I found friendship.
  Seeking help.
I learned to share.
  Seeking knowledge.
  I found faith.
  Seeking tomorrow.
I learned to make the
  most of today.
  Seeking God,
  I found love.
—*Evelyn Marrow Cox*

Carolyn

Before dawn
In spring
The world is not asleep.
Blossom-buds on the trees
Are awake in the dark
And move me
The way my baby daughter's
Dark eyes move
Me
Shining and awake in the dark
Before dawn
In spring.
—Ruth Reynolds

Always Changing Yet Always The Same

   Leaves fluttering down,
in the dead of night,
   hitting the ground
all cracked and brown.

   Veins standing out
to testify,
   the battle fought
against the sky.

   The sun and rain
the battleground,
   from which
the leaves come tumbling down.

   Its brief time there,
all crisp and green,
   must share its space
for those unseen.

   Its one brief fling
and like the rest,
   must take its place
on its mother's breast.
—Shirley C. Kirkpatrick

History Repeated

I dreamed I lived,
In the long ago;
Saw dear faces—
That I have wished to know,

Read of in history,
About heroic feats;
Some ordinary—
Others known "greats,"

But history is repeated,
Each and everyday;
So I'm meeting many,
As I pass along "This way."
—Lucy N. Stroman

"My Way"

Don't ask me if I see a thing
Just tell me what you see
Cause if I see it my way
Then it belongs to me
Rather see the thing you see
And tell its sight to me
Then I will know your world
And I will look for me
—M. Donohue

To A Moth

The fluttering moth
in the palm of my hand
is no more captive to me
than kindly thoughts
in the grasp of my mind
struggling to be set free.

I open my hand
and the moth flies away
in search of one of its kind;
I open my heart
and the words spill out,
perchance on a kindred mind.

The sight of the moth
as it soars away,
the sound of the words of this rhyme;
"Thoughts are the only reality
all else will perish with time."
—Gayle A. Jones

Letting Go

   Somewhere in the darkness,
   in the shadows of my mind,
   Searching for the answers,
     to questions undefined.

    Waiting for a miracle,
     Living on the wire,
   Hoping for enlightenment,
     Lost in my desire.

   So now our song is over,
   and the light begins to fade,
   Memories linger ever sweet,
   just like the love we made.

Tomorrow's such a long, long way,
   Someday's have never been,
It's a lonely road to paradise,
   When will this journey end?

   My heart lies broken —
   from this shattered illusion,
    Knowing this love —
    was just my delusion.
—Irish Canon

"To Be Free"

In this world we call home,
In this land that we live in,
People are killed,
Because of someone's lack of love.

In children's eyes,
We can see the hate,
And the lack of love that is needed,
To free our world.

To be free we need to love.
To be free we need to shake hands.
To be free ask any child what to do,
And they'll say,
"To be free you need to be FRIENDS."
—Tammie Christensen

The Earth

The earth, it is one planet,
In which all we people stay,
But we all take advantage,
And don't use it the right way.

We never learned how to share,
We only learned how to play,
We need to take better care,
And we need to start today.

So stop your celebration,
And take up a stand,
If we want another generation,
We all must lend a hand.
—Mandy Hudson

Time For Bed

A somber wave
In your suggestive eyes
They rise
Surprised
A wild-eyed child sighs
Moistens the air, wets my cry
Strange me from the truth
Scratch out of whim
The nights are good
But the days evil twin
So take they dry away
Let the moon drive
Here the sirens launch the night
Majestic realm
Charming battle ground
Let's please this day and sleep it away
We the creatures of habit
But in our awake we see only stars
We the creatures of night and habit
—B. L. Gonzales

Enlightened

Activate with energy
Indeed the fear prevails
Dedicate more sympathy
Suppose the battle fails?

Conflicts over ethics
Opposition soars
Negative connotations
Flavor public roars
Indeed its time to educate
Discrimination gone
Empathize the sadness
Noting those who've gone
Trust and guidance enter
Into daily quests
Altered indignations
Litigious hours spent
Identify the kindness
Triumph with success
Yaw with increased strength!
—Valerie A. Mariani

Coffee Grounds Samba Sounds

The tropic environs of Rio
Inspired this musical trio:
Ottorino (the Italian image-collector),
A brilliant Brazilian named Hector,
And France's own Darius Milhaud.
—Arnold Fabrikant

No Question

Is a raindrop wet
Is a desert dry
Can a hounddog fetch
Is a rattlesnake spry

Do fishes swim
Has a rainbow hues
Does a chimney smoke
Does a clown amuse

Do sparks glow
Does a sleeper snooze
Does a sage know
Does a victim lose

Does a bubble float
Does a jogger run
Is a star remote
Is a start begun

If all of these
Things are true
Then you know
That I love you.
 —*Donald Allen Driskell*

The Creator's Landscape

The beauty we see on this earth
Is a seasonal change by birth,
 It comes and goes
 And everyone knows
It's the Creator's Plan to give mirth.

When the landscape is cheery and bright
And flakes are falling so white,
 It comes and goes
 It's the season for snow
And it brings to all a delight.

When nature is awakened from her rest
And life is restored at its best
 The flowers are blooming
 The birds are assuming
It is time to get out of their nest.

Vacation time is here,
For children it is a time most dear,
 They run and play
 And all will say,
"School is getting near."
 —*Vita Hamilton*

Me

The ocean, miles out
is calm, smooth and glossy
like tinted glass.
With an occasional ripple,
an irritating little disturbance.
As you travel inward
the disturbances become greater,
more intense.
At the shore waves crash
like a person flying off the handle.
Inland always agitated,
while outward, mainly calm.
Both so different like black and white.
But me, I hover between the calm
depths of the ocean and the choppy
water pounding on the shore
like the many colors of the rainbow.
 —*Natalie Enright*

The Truth Of A Matter

The spectrum of light that
is colored by lost
realities, hides in the corner
hidden by clouds of mayhem
and frivolous stock.
Although reluctant to come out
at all, its' beauty is brilliant
when not of certain matter.

But when of thought given away;
to waddle an aimless path?
Beaten as that of footsteps left
by ones voyage through dry snow;
holding shape momentarily
collapsing to the beat of a faint
breath; like a dream at climax.

Left without recollect, only
an excited sensation to stir
the beast crouched in the corner
blinding you with a mere stretch.
 —*Marc Groah*

Being Without You

 Being without you
 is like someone closed
 all the doors to my
  world.
 But when I'm with you
I feel like my life has been
 recharged.
 But know being without you
I feel terminal sadness...
 —*Shawn Slater*

Memories

The pleasure that was you to know
 is now a thing long gone.
Your mark's indelible within me
 there to memory be upon.

I see you clear as day afore,
 exception only one;
no hand to hold, no cheek to kiss,
 all earthly touch is gone.

Enough, for now, to have you
 with me in the mind alone.
Someday we will be hold and kiss
 in heaven, take me home.
 —*Lynn Diane Johnson*

The Contest

To enter a contest
Is oh so exciting,
To learn of the prizes
Makes it that more inviting.
To try your hardest
And to do your best,
To prove to the judges
You can out do the rest.
Then there's the silence
And the waiting is done,
They've called out the winner
The contest.......you've won!!
 —*Annette Marie Horne*

Untitled

I can tell graduation
 is really near.
I guess your happy since
 it's your last year.
Just think, you won't have
to do any homework no more.
And you finally got rid of them
 teachers, what a bore.
When you turn eighteen you got to
 know what it means.
You can't party all the time, you got
 to keep it clean.
Have fun and a happy
 celebration.
There's only one time
 that you have a
 graduation!
 —*Karie Otterson*

From Me To You

The love we share
is special
These feelings
are for no one
but you
I hope the feelings you have
for me
are the same as
mine for you
you are the world
to me
as I am
the world to you
my wishes
are in my heart
I want them in
your heart too.
These feelings are
from me to you.
 —*Kelly Valerius*

Murder Of A Soul

This tear you see
is the first of many
Each that falls
is one piece of my
broken heart.
My soul,
murdered,
Laying bare
with a memory of you
shoved in its' side.
Drops of blood
dripping
You my lost love
the murderer.
 —*Tonimarie A. Gionti*

Family Ties

You have given your heart to someone new
It no longer just belongs to you
To him you gave a part
Forever in his arms to hold
Keeping you from the cold
Here is where true love lies
In the bond of family ties.
 —*Robyn L. Rancourt Suder*

Untitled

Our Senior Citizen Club House
Is the place we like to go
To reminisce with our Dear Friends
About days of long ago.

Friday is our social day
It's always a lot of fun
When someone calls out Bingo
Just to see what prize they won.
You can look the whole World over
But you will never never find
A finer group of People
Than those Dear Friends of mine.

—Ann Becker

Black Door

Can you exit the black door,
Is there a way of breaking free?
The hinges are bolted shut
It seems your trapped the same as me.
Can you see through the tiny keyhole,
Is there someone at the other end?
Is it someone who's familiar,
Or maybe a vengeful friend?
Have you checked the other doors,
The windows and the cracks?
Have you healed from all the pain
Of when you fell onto your back?
Did your bones heal when they broke?
Did your bruises go away?
Did your heart mend back and your tears
Run dry, from agony the other day?
Is there a way to break the chains,
Can you exit the black door?
Can you find your way from yesterday
And be where you were before.

—Jodi Theresa Roldan

Daydreamer

I hear music of the past.
It blends into my soul.
My mind, so slowly, floats away;
An age of long ago appears.

A quiet street, a bright blue sky.
I stand erect, my thoughts so clear,
This is my town of years gone by.
A tear drop falls; then several more.

A simple cottage, small and bright,
Stands so lonesome down the street.
I move with joy toward its site;
To this, my home an age ago.

A pleasant face, a smile of joy,
Appears beyond a window clear.
Suddenly, a rush and noise of many cars,
Destroys my joy, returns my pain.

—Ray E. Reents

No. (3)

It's Death you know,
It has that glow.
It comes.
It goes.
One never knows.
It gives no time to drop a dime.
It's Death you know.
It comes,
It goes.

—Claire E. Crayton

"Life Is Like A Rose"

Life is like a lovely rose.
It hides its thorns beneath
We do not know
That they are there,
Until we feel the sting.
A thing of beauty.
Our life can be
Although, the thorns are there.
We may not feel
The painful hurt
If we handle it with care!

—Ozelle Conway

Friendship

Friendship
It is something that is near and dear
To us all
It can be a great thing
When treated with respect
But can be a travesty
When it is misused

I have been fortunate
Having had many good friends
Who have been there through
Good times and bad times alike

Only a handful of people
Who claimed to have been my friends
Have abused our friendship
And for those people I feel
Sorry for a good friendship in priceless

—Joyce Herrold

Seasons

When I see the leaves turn
It makes me so glad,
For I love the bright colors
Yet I'm a bit sad
To bid good-bye to summer,
To see the warm weather go.
To think about winter
And the cold, cold snow.
The birds all fly south
I bid them good-bye.
When I think about winter
I just want to sigh.
Be patient and enjoy it,
One can't do a thing
But enjoy the moment
And wait for spring.

—Pearl Wingrove

A Hard Word To Say

Goodbye is such a hard word to say
It means you'll be leaving me someday
There's no coming back not ever
For goodbyes last forever
If I had one wish I'd make the wrong
   go right
And I'd be spending time with you
   tonight
But goodbyes last forever that parts
   true
Goodbyes are forever and I said
   goodbye to you

—Charissa Struble

Sad Goodbye

When sorrow fills your heart,
It won't be a bother.
For you to make a call,
To your heavenly Father.

You may not realize the reason,
God put someone to rest.
But just remember this,
He always knows what's best.

Where they are now,
There is no hurt or malice.
Their time on earth was through,
They're now in God's palace.

And now that they're in heaven,
They are there to stay.
Just be glad that you,
Can go there someday.

—Megan Rutt

Vampires

It's midnight
It's dark
It's silent but still alluring
The night air smells
   damp and fresh
The moon is half full
And grovelling threw
   the wet and creepy
woods is an immortal
   blood thirsty beast
He's searching for his
   love to feast upon
She screams in
horrifying terror and pain
The air smells of
   drenching blood
The moon has vanished
And now venturing
   and hunting are
two blood starving beasts

—Stacey Tyler

Fascination

Fascination.
It's got me again,
and I'll succumb to it.
Stupidly. To talk
too loud, too much;
To laugh, to smile
too often.
To listen too closely,
To watch too closely,
I'll fall too quickly.
To think too much
and dream too far, yes,
To kiss
before we've spoken,
To dance
before we've met.

—Jennifer A. Gulbin

Life Is Like A Plane.

Life you can't explain,
It's like riding in a plane.

It can be bumpy,
It can be fast.
Just like a plane to go in
    first class.
Life when it goes,
Its like a crash.

The plane is dead without a
    doubt.
The human race comes
    and goes.
Grab the casket and
    dig the hole.
—*Timothy Jirak*

Life's Song

The musical wind
It's smooth and serene
It's clean as a bean
The birds sing "I love you"
And the water ripples
As the ripples move
As the sky flutters
The sounds rejoiced
And harmony is poised.
—*Selva Aronson*

Untitled

Life is a crooked yet beautiful thing,
its strange path is realized each day
and you and I,
so small next to its naked body—
our fingertips touch,
and truth is born.
A kiss,
and love will overcome the soul.
An embrace,
and freedom becomes ours.
Open your lungs to it,
and it will fill us
with sweet breath.
—*Tiffany Hines*

The Mask

This mask I wear is painful,
it's too tight, it doesn't fit.
I'm afraid though if, I take it off,
I'll be a true misfit.

There's way too much inside my mind,
that I, just can't reveal.
To me, the world just couldn't know,
exactly how I feel.

I'm just too sensitive for this world,
and so I must protect,
my heart, my mind, and soul inside,
you know, I can't neglect.

So please don't hold it against me,
if sometimes I don't respond just right,
it's because I'm so uncomfortable,
my mask is just too tight.
—*Shari Tackett*

It's You

When I wake up in the morning,
    it's you who I see
When I go to be at night,
    it's you who embraces me
I think of you often,
    as we spend ours days apart
Watching the hours go by,
    so our nights together can start
My heart belongs to you,
    and to this life we share
Thank you for being a part of me,
    and for showing me you care
These are things you heard before,
    stuff you already knew
There is only one Valentine for me,
    and baby it's you
—*Genevieve Castro-Nunez*

Drunk's Lament

I've known pain
I've know sorrow
I've hoped for no tomorrow

To the bottom less pits
I have sunk
for I am drunk

I have said
I would go to hell
for a drink to get well

But I have found
you can turn it around.

Now you may think that this is bunk
But take it from a drunk

To be happy and clearly think
So no to that first drink
—*Angelic Hollander*

Prejudice

   Prejudice is
   Judging one by
   Race or skin,
Instead of looking
   For the beauty
     Within.

Those who judge
   The book
   By the cover,
   Or the person
   By the skin,
   Do not have
The true beauty
     Within.
—*Krista Mc Larty*

Jungfair Of Roses

The young beauty virgin age
Jungfair of the roses
Tender love to be engage
Roses of garden poses

The young moonlight romance
Beautiful Jungfair of roses
—*Alice Norman*

Kids...Playin' Hookie, Etc.

Kids...Southern kids
Just like any other kid.
Kids are people
Who do the darndest things.
Rebels without a cause,
Writing dirty words
    on everything.
Skipping school
Cuttin' class
Saying "So?" to adults
Makin' bad marks on tests
Smokin' pot
Doing what every other
    kids does.
Just to prove
They're not a kid.
—*Billie Preston*

Class Poem Hearts Of Gold

Through the years, our hearts grew fond;
Knowing one day, we would move on.
Day by day friendships were built,
Some will stay strong; some will wilt,
But the future is what we hold inside;
Behind our fears, we hold our pride.
And as for us, we'll meet again
In God's grace at the end.
So the memories we have, we must hold-
And we'll meet again
With hearts of gold.
—*Megan Leigh Crawford*

Reminder

Putting it down to remind me
later on of that singles scene
arunge is what I like
seattle scene I'll breathe it in
the fog coming in quicker and quicker
I love to stand in a stormy rain
That rusty nail sound
So pure and dirty
to put this down on paper
will remind me later on of what I
was thinking then
Try to remember
Don't want to ever forget!
—*Jennifer Reiffert*

Beginnings

On a bedside table
lay a small pink rose, vased,
rendered to a lady
with eyes of the oceans,
hair of egyptian creation,
a smile of crystal carnations.

Coaxed, she gave her hand
to caressing lips,
and I wondered if ever again
my heart need wander.

As I gaze upon the pink flower again
I sense that my heart is the vase
cradling the sweet rose
on the beside table.
—*Paul I. King*

Oceans

The oceans waves call to me as I
lay on the sandy shore

I wish summer was every day
so I can smell the salty ocean air

As I enter the town I know I
can be me

The same I always used to
used to love, the same old me

I love every thing about the ocean
and the town and I love that I can
be me!
—*Katie Conroy*

Untitled

Love is but a grand illusion
Left me with so much confusion
Hear my heart, won't you listen
On my lashes tears still glisten
Captured by a potent lust
Hold me tightly, if you must

Dreams are made of so much cotton
Lovers whispers, soon forgotten

God, turn back the hands of time
Shake me free of all the grime
That time has left upon my face
Smooth it, leave it with no trace
Of all the sorrow I have known
Give me back my youth now flown

Take the gray from once bright tresses
Let me feel his soft caresses
Let me be the one he'll cherish
Soon enough from life we'll perish
—*Pat Hopkinson*

A Change

I use to have a cold heart
Life was not worthy of my love
The wall around my heart was tall
No one could see above
Then came you

You stepped into my life
When things were oh.. oh.. so bad
You made me feel that I could live again
When I thought I could only be sad

Happiness was not what I was seeking
A lonely life had my name
Then you opened up my eyes
And I started to feel the same
The same as you... in love

Thank you for holding on to the thought
That my heart would slowly change
You've given me a joy inside
That love will never be strange
Be strange to me — never — not love
—*Kathy J. Gipson*

Untitled

When I was young and in my prime
I thought old age was 49.
The later on, to my surprise,
old age had jumped to 65.
At 80 now its quite conclusive
And that it only gets a start
When you're no longer
"Young at heart!"
—*May Griffith*

Sometimes

Sometimes I wonder about
life, whether it's really here.
Sometimes I wonder
if I'm me or if people are
Who they say they are.
Sometimes I wonder why
Love was put on the earth,
Was or could have been put
here because of some foolish
Sinner or because it's
meant to be true.
I'm not sure why
Sometimes, is on my mind but
Sometimes, I wonder what
Sometimes really is
— *Krissy E.*

"Moon"

It shines bright
  lighting the night

I walk by its light
  I gaze into the night
the clouds roll over him
  it's dark and cold
    in fright I walk faster
much to my delight they roll away
  everything a bright again
    I calm myself

I look to him and the stars
  in wonder of their creation

I stare in total amazement
  and know only the
    Lord really knows.
—*Marilyn Fedewa*

Prepare To Surface!

Up daffodil, swing around,
like a periscope, survey ground.

On horizon just ahead, go morning
children, feet of lead.

Why so sleepy why so glum,
don't they see spring has come?

Ah-awake at last obvious glee,
announces "Up daffodil" come see!

Feet grow lighter, faces beam
renewed faith makes the scene.
—*Miranda Peechatka Manelius*

Umbrellas

Umbrellas bloom along the street
Like flowers on a stem
And almost everyone I meet
Is holding one of them.

Under my umbrella top
Splashing through the town
I wonder why the tulips hold
Umbrellas upside down?
—*Paul Kaminsky*

My Grandfather

His shiny head glistens
Like marble on a statue.
His spectacles cast a shadow
On his wrinkled cheeks.
His stature was once young
But not is much older.
His mind is still quick
Like when he was young.
His intelligence surpasses
A man of his age.
His wisdom amazes
All who surround him.
His life still lives on
And on and on...
—*Mitchell Bilker*

Hypocrite

...And they hurled from lips,
like silver sabers
poised to pierce even granite hearts,
word weapons
uncoupled,
no flesh to flesh movement here.

My heart, a ripe plum,
ready to split from fatal fissures...
I promised to die
If you left.

Don't chastise.
from you I've learned well,
to wear words like cosmetics
to masque, conceal.
confused?
unravel the enigma,
surely by now
you know
I lied.
—*Mary Ann Pickerill*

Untitled

Little things that I remember,
like smells or sounds or the way of the
weather.
reminds me of something I could not
remember

Dreams I recall, events I can't find,
sometimes I feel I could break down
and cry.
But each day forward is a brand new
start to find something new that's
been hiding in my heart.

Yet each memory I will piece together,
and when the puzzle is finished I'll
be at peace forever.
—*Mary Kaye Davila*

View Of Poetry

I hate writing poems,
I never know what to say.
Everyone talks about the weather,
Isn't it a beautiful day?

Spring is lots of fun,
If you get to play and run.
But if you're stuck inside,
With homework piled to the sky,
Just say "no way,"
I'm going outside to play.
—*Brenda Luff*

Rhythm

There is a rhythm in the rain.
Like the gently rocking mother
Cuddling her newborn child,
Like the heartbeat of a lover
In the midst of an embrace,
Like the softly muted voice
Of a soothing lullaby,
Like the music of the waves
As they crash upon the shore.
There is a rhythm in the rain.

There is a pattern in my pain.
Like the rain outside my window
On this lonely wet long day,
Like my tears that form the words
Of a song that has no name,
Like my thoughts that wander madly
In the rooms inside my head,
Like my loneliness which drowns me
As I lie beneath its weight.
There is a pattern in my pain.
—*Laurie Troiano*

Desire

Your eyes shine and sparkle
  like the midnight stars
When I look at you, I'm your
  prisoner behind bars
Your smile is as bright as
  heavens light
And I know that these
  feelings of desire are right

The love I feel for you is
  greater than any before
When I stare at your face
  I long for more and more
This love cannot be broken,
  not even by Satan
I'm not afraid to show it
  I will be blatant.

My passion for you grows
  higher and higher
And nothing will ever
  stop my desire
—*Amber Ross*

Sisters

Every day I am not with you
  Like when we were at home
Miles may separate us
  But my love for you has grown
Through the years you've known my faults
  Yet you have never been unkind
And when all others fail me
There is a strength in you I find
  So we are more than sisters
It is much more of a blend
  The sharing of our blood
But with the closeness of best friends
—*Ethel Brady Conley*

Untitled

Downstairs and outside, your eyes
like bubbles stilled in lacquer.
Us, we;
windows open, the clouds almost came in.
—*Sean Parker*

Untitled

I like animals very much
lions, tiger, Bears, and such.
Keep their forests, Lakes, and
Rivers clean if you don't you'll
be mean please try, try and try
if you don't I will cry.
Dogs, cats, hamsters too If
you do this I'll love you.
—*Allison Mercurio*

Benightedness

    Garbage, Trash,
  Little children eating last,
    Water bland,
Bruises from their father's hand,
    Morals lost.
  How much more will it cost.
    Violence all around,
    No peace to be found.
   No food on our table.
  Ignorance is our label.
—*Julie Hester*

Sandbox Dreams

  I remember those days
long ago
  I remember the carefree
happiness and confidence
I felt.
Thinking I could do
anything.
Having dreams of doing
everything.
I remember the feeling of
love and
acceptance I had that
made my mind
fill with dreams.
Dreams of being something.
Something wonderful.
Dreams.
Reality.
Does not exist on
Sandbox Dreams.
—*Nikki Montague*

Humming Birds Returning

Friday before easter,
Looked out to the west
The humming birds have returned north
To build their nest.
Cold raindrops were falling
All around.
He perched on the perch,
And nothing he found
Like red sweetened water
Hanging in a jar
He was so hungry
And thirsty
Because he had traveled
So far!
Fluttering and buzzing
He flew away.
Soon he'd not be hungry
At the end of the day!
—*Jessie Taylor*

The Door

Sitting on the floor
looking at my door.
Wondering what I'll find
behind its oaken boards.

Will there be a bottomless pit?
Will there be just sky?
Or will there be the Grim Reaper
with his deadly scythe?

Maybe there's a demon
waiting to kill me.
Or maybe just a vast abyss,
or an endless sea.

There could be so many things
so dangerous behind the door.
And so since I do not know,
I'll stay here on the floor.
—*Benjamin D. Mickelson*

Untitled

I have a thought an idea.
Looking through a crystal glass.
Visualizing everything from
the present past - the future.
What these actual things might
bring for me know one knows.
I'll just have to wait - see.
Wanting only happiness, not sadness.
Every day of my life,
I don't know what will happen.
Only time reminds me of that.
I must be positive
and take each day step by step.
Can't let my self fall,
fall like a bird in the sky,
I'll fly up up in away.
Where no one can see me,
I will make sure of that.
—*Lenard Smith*

Nature's Wonder

The sky a canopy of gray
Looks down on branches, bare of leaf
And suddenly a magic hand sweeps grandly
Over naked trees, adorning them with
  crystal beads
And hanging glossy prisms
That light the winter scene.
Each new season has its own
  nature's wonder to behold.
So when the sky is cold and gray
I'll cast an eye on nature's gems,
And catch the glint of diamond play
That lights a cold gray winter day.
—*Caroline Duryee*

Forever

As I stand here and look at you.
Let me tell you what I see.
I see someone whom I love,
Someone who cares for me.
None of those other guys
Could ever compare to you.
You're all I need,
You're my dream come true.
Please don't ever leave me,
Say that you will stay.
Let's say that it's forever,
And we'll never go away.
—*Alana Shirkey*

Asylum On The Hill

It is said that angry creatures of
lost beginnings live above us in
  wistful intervals of lunacy.
    Sometimes, in the night,
  they creep into the forest
    around their solitude,
      embracing the trees
    to plead their words.
  The pattern of their wails
drifts down on a night breeze
    to catch me as
    I stretch in my bed.
    On these nights I pause
to listen for the one clear voice
    carried as a faint song.
  I must tell you, it says,
  Of the one unalterable thing,
    After my winter,
    there will be no spring.

    —*Gayle Stants Hendrix*

To The Man I Love

To the man I love, I give my heart.
Love and devotion, we'll never part.
My thoughts and dreams are of you;
Others so fortunate are few.
I hope you know that I love you much,
And I yearn for your every touch.
So warm and gentle a man,
I am your greatest fan!
Together we will always be.
Just look and you will see!
A love made in heaven for just
You and me!

    —*Diana L. Perusin*

The Playground Is Empty Today

Like a merry-go-round
love stopped to let me off,
I was a child at play
with laughter soft.
Dressed in jeans,
showin' my boots,
Ridin' the horse
with ups and downs.

A year has passed,
you left last May.
Oh, the good times,
the happy sounds
have gone away,
The playground is empty today.
Empty to-day.

    —*Deanne Carol Bishop*

We Are

The roses
luminous at dawn,
glow crimson with the
resurrected light,
clustered full and thick,
too delicate for night,
their fragile petals fall,
speak to my fading heart—
an
  invincible
    connection.

    —*Leah Leopold*

"Around The Ground"

What would it be like ...

Living under ground without
making any sound.

And watching all the moles
digging out all their holes.

Or seeing all the ants
pulling up all their pants.

And watching all the snails
hauling all of their pails?

Now, let me ask you this —
How could you survive, under all
that dirt without wearing a shirt?

    —*Melissa Roos*

My Grandmother's Prayer

I pray that, risen from the dead,
  May I stand in glory
    Perhaps put a crown upon my head
    And a needle in my hand.
I've hardly learned to play or sing.
  But let no harp be mine;
    From birth until my dying day,
    Plain sewing's been my line,
So therefore, accustomed to the end
  Also playing the useful stitches,
    I'll be content if asked to mend
    And to the little angel's breeches.

    —*Gina Wilson*

The Love Of Life

Life is a precious memory,
Maybe some day in your life you'll see,
People go and people come,
They are always on the run.

Nothing ever lasts so long,
But everything is as sweet as a song,
Remember this and one day you'll see,
How precious life can really be.

    —*Kayla Lanham*

Weeping Willow

Weeping willow old and gray
Maybe we can play today
Outside upon the summers wind
Fall is starting to begin
Go and play among the leaves
So we can go and climb the trees
As long as were going strong
We can sing and play along
Weeping willow tall and still
I'll be back again to tell.

    —*Kathryn Hutchens*

True Love

    Love is loyal,
    Love is sweet.
  It's in your mind,
  And in your heart beat.
It's in the tips of your fingers,
Throughout your body it lingers.
    Love is kind;
    True love is blind.

    —*Melissa Picotte*

Untitled

Quiet, mellow, little deer,
  me a beast it may appear.

I will not say a word,
  I only want to look.
As you stand there drinking,
  beside the quiet brook.

If I make a single sound,
  I know that you will flee.
But I know I'll always remember,
  That time you spent with me.

    —*Lauren Taulbee*

A Prayer

Oh, Dear Lord, may we ever be
Mindful of thy love and care.
May we truly know that thou
  art everywhere.

Guide our footsteps everyday,
And teach us oh Lord,
How and for what to pray.
May we dedicate our lives to thee,
And a better Christian be.
Help us to let our light so shine,
That Thy way, the lost might find.
Guide what we do, and what we say;
Lest we cause one soul to stray.
We pray, oh Lord, that Thy will be done;
To the glory and honor of Thy Son.

    —*LaVerne French*

Saxophone

The jazzy sound of a sax solo
mingles in with the darkening city.
A colorful display of lights
takes the form of buildings
... and one lone saxophone plays.
The sounds of the city
on a hot summer night,
the fan does nothing
but go round and round.
Half lit neon lights
flash a florescent message.
A young child cries into the night.
... and one lone saxophone plays.

    —*Jennie Wassmer*

Time And Memories Equal Life

Although memories are but
  moments in time,
I will treasure each and
  everyone of mine.
For if not for the memories
  of my life,
There would be no reason
  for my time.

    —*G. R. Faber*

The Dove Ring

I had a dove ring
My dove ring was
Pretty
I lost it somewhere
it was such a pity
I couldn't find it
I looked everywhere
Nobody knows where it is

    —*Paloma Lopez*

High Gear

Cheeseburgering down telegraph
Mustard lapping up the miles
Coffee clutching through the nonstop
Nerves taught to keep in spills

How I'd love to park my mind
But for that rear-end fear
On my way to another hurry
That keeps me in high gear

So hard on performance
But gets me where I wish
I wasn't going....
—*Shar Blair*

"Friendship"

When tears full from my eyes,
   my friend wipes them up,
When I need some guidance,
   my friend leads me there,
When there seems to be no hope,
   my friend cheers me up,
When I share my heart, mind, and soul,
   my friend holds nothing back,
When the sky is gray, my friend
   makes it blue,
When we are old, I see us talking
   about the good old days on the porch,
When death is knocking at the door,
   my friend will be there to the end.
—*Jason Cunningham*

Thank You Lord

Each time I hear your voice
My heart begins to sing
Each time I see your face
My spirit takes wing

My love for you is endless
True love.... complete and pure
And if seem as a sickness
I don't ever want the cure

You mean so very much to me
More than I could ever say
And my love for you keeps growing
So much deeper every day

I thank the Lord for you
And will until time ends
For making you a part of me
And for letting us be friends.
—*Michael Clements*

Swept Away

Swept away
My heart cries
Alone on an island
Waves crash on the shore
Echoing my tears
Moonbeams fall
Endlessly on the water
I can see forever
Alone in my tomb
Salty streams
Washing down my face
Whispers of sad years
Sing to me...
—*Cynthia Goddard*

Untitled

Flashes of light sear
My mind
I long to escape into the
Sweet night,
The air caressing my skin,
Sending soft shivers
Through my soul

My mind turning to darker
Things,
I am swept away on the wings
Of the moon
She smiles on me, and
My heart knows truth
And happiness
Even though still longing
For something more
—*Andrea Anderson*

The Dreamer

As I slowly drift to sleep,
   My problems seem to disappear.

I dream of days to come,
   And people that remain dear.

As I slowly start to wake,
   I forget all of the mystical music,
   and places.

Nor can I recall, all of
   The friendly faces.
—*Kristine McCool*

Untitled

My sore eyes bleed of clear,
my tongue is tied and you're so near.
I close my eyes, my dreams begin,
soft as your hair, silk as your skin,

your hands wipe away my tears,
your gentle voice eases my fears,
your body moves like the flying dove,
and your eyes reflect undying love.
—*Stephen Stangland*

Mysterious

Dim light flickers
   Near a dark desolate corner.
Next flicker brings someone?
A shadow mystifies sight
   A short, soft gleam...
A tall man
   Stands alone as a shadow.
   With mystique and elegance.
   Wrapped in flowing black satin.
His face unseen but the eyes,
   Eyes of enigmatic blue and green seas
   Withholding secrets, reserved.
—*Shasta Swaekauski*

Love

Together forever that's what will be,
Love is a bond between you and me.
We had our, our problems,
yes you and me.
But there is a bond of love
between you and me.
—*Andre Hillman*

Still Music

I am sixteen
need to dance
no music plays
no one sings for me

my five brothers
are younger
need care
I walk in the woods
a stone speaks:
care for your brothers
keep fires cook

I do as told
my brothers grow
the stone speaks no more

I'm thirty now
my brothers gone
I still could dance
if music played
or some one sang
for me
—*Charity Chang*

Untitled

Goodbye — sweet, life
never to be.
The end has come,
so soon for me.
All the warmth —
the joy have sped.
For mother dear —
I am shed.
to sail the skies,
round heavens shore.
A drifting place —
nothing more.
—*Leah Mary Barlow*

Untitled

The heavens shine
Next to a setting sun
It's radiating heat
Soon becomes none
The air becomes cool
The night light grows dim
To the power and mystery
Of the moon's inner sin
So why is it light
Which beckons us on
Down life's only roadway
A dead-end, no wrong
A wrong we must right
Rejoice, forgive and believe
That the light which awaits us
Shines bright at the end...
—*Jason Crandall*

"Icky"

   There was a spider
     Named 'Icky'
Who made life for bugsy
     Quite sticky...
   He just hung around
     For that certain
     Little sound...
   And feasted on bugsy
     Quite Quickly!
—*Mary Ann Penn*

Nature

As I walk through the woods
  next to my house
I can find any creature here
  even a tiny field mouse
They scamper and scurry
  from left to right
Some of them sleep all day
  and some sleep all night
They live in trees
  or on the ground
Some make loud noises
  Some, not a sound
Some are tyrant
  Some are still
Some of them people love
  But some, people kill
This is what we call nature
  We see it everywhere
A lot of us enjoy it
  But others, just don't care

—*Sarah Jones*

My Darkest Hour

I'm standing here forlorn.
No one can help me now.
This step is mine alone to take.
Support they don't allow.
I must not show my fear
Nor let a teardrop fall.
As I ascend the stairs
And enter in the hall.
I see the door ajar
And must soon enter there.
No turning back today for me,
No one along to share.
You've all been through a day like this.
No exception to the rule.
By now you've guessed this has to be
My very first day of school

—*Doris Schwark*

I Ask Why?

You do as you please
  no questions asked
    but then you treat me
      like a piece of trash

I mess up once but you do it twice
  you can live but I should die
    I ask why?

No harm done, but to you
  I have failed so now
    I should be nailed

Why should you be free ready to fly
  But I must stay out of the sky
    I ask why?

—*Penni C. M. Anifer*

Leaving

I'm tired of everyone leaving
One day they are here
The next day they are gone
Next thing, there will be houses
Falling down or even families splitting
I feel like screaming

—*Andrea Wheelock*

Unobserved

His thin Hope
No race of Giants
In Grande rusted clamor could conceive
The burden of cold
Carried like a bell
Iceless and reborn
Unnoticed, unbelieved

The gears of their age
Never faster
While odd mist the Sun dispels
How swiftly soars the Soul
Unobserved in the clamor
Dancing, Dancing on the wind
Dancing just as well

—*Alan Palmer*

A Day To Remember

One day I awoke there was
no sun. My heart was broke
From what had been done.

Just like the leaves that blow
in the wind. I want to believe
I'll be happy again.

I failed at love the first
time around. I'll pick myself
up with no looking down.

This day I won't forget it will
stay in my mind. Seems like
heartaches are all I get
And lots of memories left behind.

Now, where do I go and what
do I do. When I get low, I'll

think of you.
We stuck by each other from January
to December. There'll never be another.
What a day to remember!

—*Karen West*

Just Me

Dear Jesus, I'm not a celebrity
Nor am I well known

I'm just a little person
Trying to find my own...

No great qualifications,
Credentials or degrees
I'm simply a child of God
Asking you - please
To accept me Jesus for it's just me...

Take what I have for only you can see
That "something very special"
Hidden deep inside of me...

Bring it to the surface
So I can believe - that
You put it there for me to be...

Everything in Christ
You want me to be...

It doesn't require me to be
Anything other then
Being just me...

—*Nancy Lee Sudziarski*

"Awake"

Awake in the night
Not even a dream in sight,
Tossing and turning
My inside burning
  Awake in the night.

My eyes won't close
  Can't even doze
My heart is froze
  And my insides burning,
frustrations, flowing
  Awake in the night.

—*Flora Dukon Horn*

Untitled

Not long ago
Not far away
There was a girl
Who lived by the bay

She liked a boy
His name was Tim
He always worked out
At the gym

Then one day
He asked her out
So this was what love
Was all about

She felt so great
She jumped with glee
They would be happy
Just wait and see.

—*Jeni Hardie*

Blues City

Somewhere in New Orleans
not far from Lake Pontchartrain
near a honkey tonk—

Down and around the corner
  on Lafayette
under an old gas light—

Someone is feeling the blues
  a train will whisk
him away in the damp night mist

Somewhere in New Orleans
in the Veiux Carre' blue eyes look
  over the wrought iron
in vain; they search for him

Somewhere in the magnolia of the south
blue mid-night skies ease the
  pain out
Somewhere in New Orleans hear the
saxophone—

Blues, a trumpet sound, the piano will play
  the blues for two

—*Clyde A. Wray*

Love Hurts

When I love you
sometimes it's to death
the reaper on my back
taunts me as I kiss you
he touches me deep
my soul is open
with a kiss I am sent
to heaven and hell

—*Obdulia M. Box*

"Love"

Feelings knotted up inside,
Not knowing where to turn.
Am I in love,
Or going to get burned.
What are you feeling?
Do you think of me?
Am I to dense to see
What you really can be?
My thoughts are desperate
As I think of you.
I only wish I knew
Just what to do.
In the still of life
My feelings raging inside.
Am I driving myself to insanity
Or just letting life pass me by?
—*Stephanie Mackes*

Love Is Nothing

Love is nothing!
Nothing but a feeling,
Two people share
Showing they care.

Love is nothing!
Nothing!
But a tearing pain
That fills a heart with strain.

Love is nothing!
Not a feeling!
Not sharing!
Not caring!
—*Kay Lynn Rosenau*

Life Goes On

Life goes on.
Nothing is ever
too terrible
to keep you down.
So don't let it.
No matter what
you want,
you will get
only what you
Need.
But,
life goes on
and
every day
God works
in
mysterious ways.
Keep on going.
—*Lauren A. Strasser*

Ghost Rap

Spirit
Some people fear it.
Some people hear it.
Spirit
Some people just won't
Go near it.
Show me a sign
That will define
The purpose of afterlife
On the mainline.
—*Zachary Bowman*

Untitled

Monstrous, grasping, pulling, crashing
Ocean waves are quickly passing.

Turning, tugging, rushing, pounding
Humpback whales are loudly sounding

Lighting flashes, thunder frightening
Ships are tossed, and waves are crying

Waves crash upon the shore
The beach is tattered, plain, and torn
Minutes passing without a number
Every man is free from slumber

All the sailors growing weaker
The wind is like a silent speaker
The air is scented with cold wet rain
And on the shore a shell is lain

As I put it to my ear
This roaring storm is what I hear.
—*Kristen Sieh*

Ode To The Captain

Of all the captains
Of all the ships
Of all the seas in my heart
You shine brightest
And every storm is calm by your name.
And as I watch the moonbeams make love
to the folds of the white-capped waters
I see images of you
bathing in their passion
and they in yours
It is an honor for the moonbeams
and for the white-caps
to wash themselves with you
The glowing they give your skin
and the dances they create on your body
are full testament
to your title
as the captain
of the most beautiful ship
in my sea.
—*Robert LeRoy Trampe*

World Of Innocence

Spinning in a world
of fears and tears
tearing me apart
throughout the years
it's a cold, cold
age of sex and
drugs
or shall I say
AIDS and death
I'm only a kid
so what do I know?
they think I'm blind
towards murder and love!
it's a strange idea
when in fact
it happens right under my nose
—*Karli Illes*

Hypnotic Music

I have a cassette
Of hypnotic music
Played on an electric music synthesizer,
Harp, electronic piano and woodwinds.
The music floats from side to side
From one headphone to another.
There are major, minor
And pentatonic scales.
I lie in bed listening to the music.
I feel every muscle in my body
Dance and then relax.
I feel like I'm going under anesthesia
In an operating room.
And my body feels weightless.
Soon a veil of sleep envelops me.
—*Deborah Lucie Rae*

Beyond The Mists

Beyond the mists
Of life's long past,
Beyond the mists
To which stones are cast,
We find our souls,
Far from seeing;
Hidden in holes
Lie their separate being.
Beyond these mists,
These mists of night,
No longer to resist
Those mists of fright.
We travel forth
through their thickening gloom.
We travel forth
To escape their doom.
Far beyond the mists.
Lies our being;
Beyond these mists
Far from seeing.
—*Don Sargent*

"Our Gift To Each Other"

Grandma, you give me the gift
  of love as if I were your
    very own child.

We share times and memories of
  things gone past and those
    to come.

We know—what makes the other
  hurt and feel good too.

Grandma, my gift to you is to
  tell you how very much I
    love you.
—*Theresa A. Easton*

Mama Knees

I long to lay the collective head
  of my black brothers and sisters
    on the lap of Mother Africa;
Hold on to the fat ebony knees
  of my birth mother;
Rock in the arms of one long lost,
  sleep on the nurturing breast
    of my dark mother;
      my mother
      my mama
      Mama.
—*Brenda P. Turner*

A Love Song

I decided to write you a song
 Of my love it would be made
I tried to write this song
 For many, many days
A song that you would love
 The song a part of me
A song that you would sing
 For at least eternity
But if I put to words
What I really feel in me
Though they might be heard
It would be impossible to see
The love that I have found
 In you and you alone
A love like the sweetest sound
 That I have never known
So now I hope you see
 A song would not be true
To replace the words of three,
 I love you.
 —*Kyle T. Westmoreland*

A Land Of Unicorns

It is a land of legend
Of mythical mystique
Of fabled fascination.
Sweetly tantalizing and fragrant
A land of elves and nymphs
A land of fairies and unicorns.

It is a land of legend
Of shadowy spring nights
And autumn morns
Of angelic apparitions.
Filled with the musical
Conversation of birds
And the rhythmic rustling of leaves
A land of unicorns.
 —*Vasiliki Alexis Pardallis*

A White Rose

The red rose whispers
Of passion
And the white rose
Breathes of love.
Oh the red rose is
A falcon and
The white rose is
A dove.
But I send to you
A creamy white
Rosebud, with a
Flush on it's petal
Tips;
For the love that
Is the purest and
Sweetest,
Has a kiss of desire
On the lips.
 —*Michelle Butts*

From The Wolf's Point Of View

I feel like running forever,
Of smelling fear in my enemies.
 The fresh scent of Blood
 Filling my senses with rage.

Hearing the call of the wild,
 And attacking my prey.
 The Glory of winning,
 Never feeling defeat.

The taste of blood in my mouth,
 That's why I'm longing.

Roaming through the forest,
 Unheard in the snow,
 Howling at the moon,
And killing those who fear me so!
 —*Samantha Faye Kvale*

Night Flight Over The Pacific

She sat in the dim light
Of the night streaking jet,
Her hands in graceful flight
Making her filmy net.

For hours I watched tatting
Inching across her skirt,
When on a promenade,
I stopped to ask its worth.

"Oh, my granddaughter, see,
Will be married in June,
She's depending on me
For yards of tatting soon."

"From Denver to Tokyo
Should give me enough time
For ten yards, as I go,
Then her dress will be fine."

We talked of other things,
I admired her quaint art;
Returned on angel's wings,
Gift given from the heart.
 —*Lorraine Yearwood*

Silent Scream

Know not what to think
 of this crazy life.
What seems right is wrong,
 What seems wrong is right
Seems you could like me;
 Seems like you don't.
There's all these seems
 which are coming unseen.
I tied today before myself.
What a tragedy for mankind.
Yea right, open your eyes,
 Saw the sights you find
I'm fighting a monster,
 and the monster is love.
I want it to leave.
But, it's to big to shove.
Tighter around me,
 my fate starts to squeeze.
No matter how loud,
 I have a silent scream.
 —*James Tutor*

To Heaven And Back

I am home in heaven, dear ones.
Oh! So happy and bright.
There is perfect joy and beauty
in this everlasting light.
All the pain and grief is over.
Every restless tossing passed;
I am now at peace forever,
Safely home in heaven at last.
 —*Melinda Melvin*

If You Were A Bird

If you were a bird
Oh what would you do?
Would you fly through the sky,
Such a beautiful blue?
Would you fly with the breeze
Or above the deep seas?
Or just sit in the trees
And catch a few z's?
If you were a bird
There'd be so much you could do,
But would you rather be a bird
Or would you rather be you?
 —*Vicki Boyd*

The Pond

A peaceful pond
On a clear and sunny day.
In the morning
The melody of birds,
The lazy wind blowing
The amiable softness of the
clouds, over power
Ripples on the water
Birch trees bowing to the wind
Creating inviting, docile, shade,
Bugs humming, swarming
Everything's alive - yet solitude
reigns.
 —*Cheryl Boyd*

Friend Through Time

I was bored and blue
 On a gloomy day
When an unexpected friend
 Just happened my way.

He brought his laughter
 And joy with him
Brightening up what had
 Become dark and dim.

His friend he would call me
In a voice filled with love
 Truly this relationship
Had been created up above.

 Forever he and I
 Will stand the test of time
Knowing that I am his best friend
And him knowing he is mine.
 —*Mary Beth Joplin*

An Arkansas View

A wise old cow
On a hot humid day
Stood in the pond of water
To pass the time of day.

Then back to the pasture
To eat the greens
To renew her cud
To be milked again

When the farmer came
To the barn she went
To be put in a stall
With a pail beneath her flanks

The farmer did squeeze -
The teats below
And filled the pail -
To the dairy he did sell.

The milk was pasteurized,
Homogenized, churned and cheesed
So all those who thirst and hunger
Would be pleased.
—*Theresa B. Trapp*

"Truth Love"

Our lips first touched
On a pier one night
Hand in hand under the stars light
Embraced with you on the beach
Your golden hair within my reach
   To laugh and play
   To sing and dance
To watch you sway a true romance
A moon that shines in the mist
A neck with perfume just kissed
An embrace to end all fear
A chill to bring a tear
Like the sky your eyes so blue
I longed for true love
You and I a dream come true
—*John P. Boyle*

The Dust Of Snow

The way a crow shook down
on me, the dust of snow from
a Hemiloch tree, has given my
heart a change of mood and save
some part of a day I have ruled.
—*Randy Jordan*

Behold, I See!

When beauty fades and lines appear
On the faces of those we hold dear;
Then we see their real worth
—The character, developed from birth.
By the spirit within
    which yielded or strived,
Building on adversity
    —the will to survive.
Finding strength through prayer,
To win, and to dare
To live each day with kindness and care.
In that time worn face so dear,
I see beauty etched through tears.
—*Eva O. Scott*

Dawn

Far across,
On top of distant mountains
The jagged, white, ridges,
Of the zenith,
Like fingers grasp,
Eternally at the sky.
While sun rays of fire gold,
Bursts, diffusing through air,
Suffusing the darkness,
Of the passing night,
As the crimson sun,
Strikes the morning spark.
Then bright struck blue,
Ignites the wind water,
To burn the furnace of light,
Imbued in the sublime,
As the empyrean dew,
Gracefully across the firmament,
Falls,
From the dias of heaven.
—*Ho Jun Song*

Rainbows

A rainbow is the work of God
On whatever lands you trod
The colors yellow, blue, red, and green
Are the most beautiful ever seen

Making a wish is what you do
When you are almost overcome by the view
Looking for that pot of gold
As they did in days of old

Life is like a beautiful rainbow
Here today and gone tomorrow
Never question the Lord as to why
Just thank him as each day passes by
—*Gwen Douglas*

On The Edge Of The Badlands

A yellow tree —
One lone, golden-leafed tree
Among the primrose grass.

It stands on the flats of Dakota,
That is, South Dakota—
On the barren, prosaic land of grass.

Why do you stand alone?
Why have ye made this spot your home—
Among the yellow grass?
—*Glen R. Anderson*

"Shadows"

As I lie here in my bed
Remembering something father said,
"Shadows are with you everywhere."
Like the Angels do they care?
So mysterious and so dark
Why do they never leave a mark?
—*Angela Cooper*

Why?

As I sit here,
One lonesome tear
Falling from my eye,
I think of you
And can't help
But wonder why?
It couldn't have been
Because your purpose was through
I'm still here!
Now what am I to do?
Still as I may
Wish or might or hope,
I could never want
To see you here again.
For the suffering you took
Hurt me more
Then the rest ever could
I love you Daddy!
—*Jenifer McDonald*

Unwelcome Change

Of all the things I thought I'd see
One thing I thought would never be
I never thought I'd see the day
You'd pack your things and move away

But then reality came to pass
The dreaded day unfurled
How can you leave behind your past?
I'm still your little girl!!!

My selfish thoughts get in the way
Whatever shall I do?
I am hurting! Damn this day!
And then I thought about you

How hard it must be to walk away
From the world that you have known
An uncertain future heads your way
Where will you call home?

But know that I will be alright
And I will pray for you each night
Inside your heart you hold the key
It is there I'll always be.
—*Debra Campbell*

Untitled

A lump
Only a bump
No, it's much more
It's death paying a visit.
He's young
Leave here now
We all need him
Death's appetite must be met.
He'll fight
Remove the lump
Take what you must
Death takes all he has.
Help him
Anyone who can
The experiments all fail
Death invades his fragile shell.
He's scared
He didn't know
Home was right outside
Death didn't pass him by.
—*Wendy Frankel*

Hidden Inside

Outside the sun is shining,
Only drear is seen inside.
The children are all playing,
Yet the fight has just begun.
The birds are softly singing,
As the world gets torn apart.
At church they all are praying,
While alone she tries to cope.
Outside the flowers are blooming,
Silently he takes his last breath.
Soon the breath of the world.

—*Amy E. Rybar*

The Window

All that seems to be reality

A picturesque window that has
only one side

Seeing one only as you picture
them to be

No one can see the truth through
Ones own reflection

Are we living to die or dying
To live

Is today the first day of the
Rest of your life
Or was the first day of your life
One that you cannot comprehend

To live is to lie for ones own
Self-conscious satisfaction

Read these words as you may
For the window has only one side

—*Devry D. Tebow*

Tomorrow

The sun has set and gone away,
 Only to rise and begin a new day.
 Each day we waste, we take away,
  Life's joy of future age.
The more we invent the harder it gets,
 To keep our world a clean success.
 A joyful night, a fearful day,
  Our world slowly withers away.
 Whatever we say whatever we do,
 The choice belongs to me and you.
So just be wise, and don't disguise,
 This problem coming into view.
 What will be, the closing key,
  To end our world forever?
 The sun has set and gone away,
 Never to rise or begin a new day.

—*Suzanne J. Murray*

Like A Flower

I am like a flower in so many ways
I like to grow a tish each day
Be bright, green and ever colorful

I am like a flower in so many ways
Sometimes my owner forgets
To water me
To weed me
To take me out of the sun

I am like a flower in so many ways
I can live
Or wither and die!

—*Elena Alm*

Find A Dream

To find where a dream begins
 Or even where it ends
 Look over a rainbow
 Or around the bends

If you look hard enough
 You shall find
 A wonderful thing
 Called an open mind

It allows you to look
 And be whoever you want
from an engineer to a businessman
 or an astronaut

 And when you become
 What you have found
  Work real hard
 Make the world go round

—*Mary Tino*

Respect

Is it a matter of color of skin?
Or is it a case of what's taught within
 our childhood?

Could it possibly be race or creed
that hand delivers our destiny and need
 to be bad or good?

Are the inherent genes we've found
passed from family trees on down,
 that cause inferior aptitude?

Or is it simply a sad neglect
of a society programmed to reject,
 based on a preconceived attitude?

Oh, what a difference it would make
if only each time for everyone's sake,
 we took a moment to reflect;

Not on the color of the person's skin,
but what is found when we look within.
 That is respect.

—*Marina D. Mathews*

Too Close?

What, the sky is too blue
 or me to you.

Too Close?

Why the leaves are to the tree
 or you to me.

Too Close?

Why the fear? No! is sufficient
 you are in control.
So Don't be so complacent:

Too Close?

We live to learn what makes
 a heart to love.

Too Close?

No! Never!

Because He died
 for our sins, showing his love.

Forever!

—*Clarence Williams II*

To My Dad On Father's Day 1993

Whenever I need a friend,
 Or someone to care,
I never have to be afraid,
 My dad is always there.

Kind to everyone he sees;
 His wisdom is his love,
As steady as the morning sun,
 As gentle as a dove.

I'll always be his little girl.
 With him I'm never sad.
No one makes me feel as proud.
 I love him. He's my dad.

—*Nancy Fuller*

Lonely One

Who needs those lonely nights
or those endless goodbyes,
memories of walks and talks
make me want to cry.

If only you could look
and open up my heart,
and see all the things
that happen when we part.

Soon I'll be able
to open up like a book,
and then again
you'll give me a second look.

But why do you need love
when all you do is cry,
and he's the one
that always says good bye.

But one day
you'll came back to me,
and I'll look deep inside your heart
and nothing is what I'll see.

—*Jaclyn Karelta*

My One And Only Love

If for only in a dream
Our lips would meet
and a fantasy
Would become reality
For there to be just one moment of passion
I would have lifetime of memories
Mysteries of our flirtation
And whispers of our lust
Something so pure
so natural - so sweet
to be swept into
A wave of painfully sweet torture
I only wish you could love me
I am foolishly in love with you
I can only imagine
A night
with no limits
and a forever more love.

—*Julie Sjodin*

Untitled

The trials and tribulations
of the Clinton's administration,
Will fade away towards
the Perot hallucinations.

—*Virginia R. Muniz*

Water

Ripples and waves,
overlapping,
undulating,
seeking and searching,
becoming one without sound,
reflection,
mirroring
each other,
while still their
inner forms
remain true
to
themselves.
Such is love.
—*William B. Browning III*

A Poet's Sunset

  A poet
   paints
    pictures
with words.
    The
   thoughts
  of Lola.
—*The thoughts of Lola*

The Suburbs

In the evening the married women
parade around the neighborhood
pushing their ugly little monsters
back-and-forth back-and-forth
their fat asses jiggling obscenely
like some hideous blubbery testaments
to their easy lifestyles
and their full refrigerators
their pale bespectacled husbands
will arrive home soon
expecting their cheap little prizes
to be al lined up and waiting for them
and so it goes day after day
ad nauseam
a big fucking farce of nothingness
the American Dream:
a nation of ass-lickers
with health plans
and good teeth.
—*Kevin E. White*

Western Dress And China Faces

Western dress, China faces
Pass me by without traces.
Come from streets engulfed by trees;
Pushed along by Hand Hu breeze.
Purple, Red, Pink and White
Breaks a heart, Love's lost delight.
Jet black hair, almond eyes
Casts a mystery, secret dies.
Satin skin, jade green pools,
Voices mingling, thinking jewels.
Airen! Airen! Ni shi wode ai.
Won't know your loves.
Won't know your cries.
Zai jian! Good-bye!
Zai jian! Good-bye!
Western dress, China faces
Pass me by.
—*Francis C. Thiemann*

Untitled

Life's sweet breath
Passing by
Telling love a last good bye
Life in now receding
A love that was so deep is now grieving
But from a high cloud she sees his pain
And now the wind whispers in his ear
"I love thee always, oh my dear"
He feels a gentle kiss
And leaves that lovely place.
—*Sarah Lien*

Down In The Sewers

Down in the sewers of the mind
Past the sane thoughts
Past the need to be happy
You will find refuge.

It is lonely here
It is dark
It is full of the ugly monster
Of my past life.

Down in the sewers of the mind
No one can find you.
Alone
But sometime you must go back
For there are things to see to
Battles to fight.

You must go back
But not yet.
Down here you are alone.
—*Zoe Vercelli*

Make Room For Peace

Make room in this world for peace
Peace in the hearts of men
Love over brutality
Liberty over subversion
Life over sacrificial murder
Sharing over plunder and rape

Make room for the United Nations
Full blown partners in peaceful
Pursuit of equality for all
Stamp out forever dictatorial
Plunder of human decency
Genocide and racial obliteration

Make room for everlasting peace
Youth no longer called to muster
Mutilated and torn asunder
Warlords fade into oblivion
Let the mighty oak of justice grow
Unhampered for all mankind.
—*Paul E. Garrett*

Vintage 1992

Too late to catch the
pergola. Gone, consumed in
crates of tart, green grapes,

Crushed and drunk fresh. Grapes
ripen and spoil in moments
Nude, the pergola

smells like vinegar.
—*Kathy Skubikowski*

Tigers

A tiger is large and
powerful. It has black
stripes over its tawny-
light fur. It has amazing
courage. It has fierce, sharp
teeth to devour its kill.

It races like thunder. This
is another animal that belongs
in the forest. As man ruins their
home, they flee in fear, some want
to fight back. They fight back for
their home in the shady forest.
—*Natasha R. Castillo*

"Busy Little Fingers"

Busy little fingers
  pressing down the keys
practicing piano for the teacher
  trying hard to please.

Busy little fingers
  doing scales and chords
playing little melodies;
  singing when there are words.

The little hands come to rest
  (they make quite a pair)
when busy little fingers
  fold at night in prayer.
—*Virginia Palm*

Untitled

The stern steel pipe
puffs away for it's life.
Gracefully, the white steam billows
forming layer upon layer
  of chemical pillows
Their appearance so soft
begs to be touched. For years
children have hoped for this much.

Although these tainted white puffs may
appear the same,
Only an intangible effect of industry's
dangerous game
with all those who sing the unending
praise of technology
Still, one fact they miss, only in
Dreams can man create, the beauty
of the cumulus.
—*Kathleen L. Nilon*

Setting Sun

I'm here to watch the setting sun
    quiet and alone
  the ocean waves are crashing
    I listen to their tones
there's no one here upon the beach
   so, I talk to no one else
  this setting is so tranquil
  like sea shells on a shelf
    movements are limited
   sounds are all you hear
   the music of the ocean
   plays her notes so clear
   the sun is slowly setting
   falling towards the sea
in minutes she will disappear
  in quiet serenity.
—*Chip Schofield*

Reflection

She sits there unnoticed
Quiet as can be.
People start to wonder,
Who is she?

She cries outside,
All through the day.
She cries outside,
When her family's away.

She is a girl
Who lives a pretend life,
And wants to end it all
With the stab of a knife.

Who is this girl?
Who could she possibly be?
I look a little closer,
And find that she is me.
—*Bridgette Bryant*

A Tubby Tabby

Short, squat
Rather like a watermelon
Eating, sleeping
Nothing else to life.

He eyes
His target
He jumps up to the window sill
He's got it!
No, he falls back down.
—*Emily B. Rezek*

To My Partner

I could never float the
river of life alone
I need a partner to share
this trip

Whether driving with purpose or
drifting in silence
I need a partner to
feel the oneness of life surround us

I have such a partner who
imagines the power of the wave
upon which we ride and
appreciates the beauty of the shore
by which we pass

And now as we see time
become weak like our arms
the rocks we steered by
and the storms passed through become
the baggage we cherish most of all.
—*Charles E. Fakes III*

"Searching"

All my life I've been searching
Searching for my true meaning
Meaning in this wretched life
Life so cold and demented
Demented like the beggar on the corner
Corner of lost souls
Souls wondering aimlessly
Aimlessly praying for more
More out of life
Life full of searching
—*Danielle R. Bowman*

A Silent Tear

A silent tear
  runs down my cheek,
It's voice so soft
  no one hears it speak.
Memories come knocking,
  on the door of my heart
Feelings rush in
  and I fall apart.
What is love?
  and why is it here?
When along comes suffering, loneliness
  and fear.
Looking in your eyes
  now all I see,
are the vivid memories
  of you and me.
Now that silent tear turns
  into two.
But no more fall
  from thinking of you.
—*Melissa Schiess*

Crying The Dark

Black death, square dark
Sad
Sad
Sad
I am alone
Everywhere cruelty
Everywhere hate
I am alone
Falling
Pain
Pain
I am alone
—*Billie Jean Turner*

Diving Line

Sea gull complaint
Sadly fainter
Flying inland

Fertile tide going out
Red sun going down
And my good life ebbing older.

Ancient horseshoe crab
Burrowing in to make some more
It did before the dinosaur

A million years before I came
And a million years after I'm gone,

All the time there is but now
All things were done and will be done
Without me standing on the shore

Hearing the gull's complaint
Grow sadly fainter
Flying inland,

Watching the fertile tide retreating
And the red sun going down
And my good life ebbing older.
—*Barbara Keogh*

Inception - Deception

Sea gull calls amidst fiery sunset
Sand castles washed away like dreams
Footsteps swept aside from tomorrow
Starlites signal another dream-night

No more reasons to think of yesterday
Vanishing into the mists of time
Misspelled memoirs of fantasies
Incorrections are never correct

It is called another name of the same
Distorted images in broken mirrors
Reflections in all your directions
Early morning teardrops on my windows

The end is just another beginning
The beginning of just another ending
To go is always to return again
To return is someone else leaving
—*Kirby*

Come

  Come to the tree of life
  see how the children play.
  They feel no pain or strife
  happiness is their only way.

  Come to the sea of loneliness
  see how the maidens cry.
  Their men they shall miss
  wondering all the time why.

  Come to the cloud of dreams
  see how the people smile.
  Everything is good, so it seems
  unaware of the untold mile.

  Come to the path of love
  see how the lovers kiss.
  No sadness here, only love
  only time to reminisce.

  Come to the flower of truth
  see how it has bloomed
  Know that only through truth
  shall lies be consumed.
—*Tina Hostetler*

"Neglected Soul"

Glass in the soul,
See through to the other side.
Nothing has been deposited,
save the nickel it cost to buy.
Fragmented by pressure,
shattered on the ground,
Swept aside by ignorance;
sparkling left unfound.
Turned in by those
whose minds do not comprehend,
its worth to thy-self,
Rather the five pennies to spend.
Change fits in the pocket-
the soul occupies infinite space,
Which is the greater?
Which cannot be replaced?
—*Donna Casler*

"The Way I Feel About You"

You make my world,
seem so clear.
You take away,
all my fears.
Thinking of you,
is all I can do.

When you hold,
me in the night.
Your gentle touch,
is ever so tight.
Our love grew so,
very fast.
I hope it will,
always last.

I always want,
to stay with you.
If we break up,
I don't know what,
I'll do.
I love you!
—Stacy Annette Hines

"Love Of My Life"

The shining rays of light,
sends my restless heart to flight.
The glowing embers of fire,
fulfilling my hearts' desire.
Memories and the past fade,
majestic waterfalls cascade.
Love and life are one,
for those lucky enough to happen upon.
My heart, my soul and my mind,
are all the man needs to find.
—Crystal Hoffman

"Madrilena"

She issues
  shards
   of ire
    as glass
     pushed forth
      to my plate.
My response
 in the face
  of seeming despair:
To push away the vessel
 of seething stomach,
  and anchor my room
     at a place
      of much solace.
—Kathryn A. Meier

Brightest Light

  Standing alone on the coldest night
Searching to find the brightest light
never knowing what tomorrow will be.
I'm so scared of what I might see.
Trying to find my way through the pain
Why am I the only they blame

Please set me free, I want to fly
Like an angel high in the sky,
I want to see the world so bright.
But I can not find the brightest light.
—Gloria A Hess

The Hero

    Silence,
     Shattered life
No mercy, never surrender.
     Fighter,
      Until the end
Fought with every last breath.
     Controlled,
      By an unknown fear
Forced to live in terror.
     Savage,
      Painted beast
Never to kill again.
     Manipulated,
      By the strings of gods
Bred to slay not mourn.
     Cadaver,
      Wasted life
A young boy dreams no more.
—Robert Schlaefer

Untitled

She was still a child,
She didn't know what growing up meant.
She was a beautiful little girl,
so naive and innocent.

What would the world do to her,
now that it had her in it's hands?
Wrap her in something soft, like fur,
just so the world understands,

That something needs to protect her,
She can't just stand alone.
For now, I need to know she's safe,
at least until she's grown.
—Kelly Ford

October 13, 1965

Happy birthday to my baby,
She is now a little lady.

Eyes so big with mischief gleaming,
One can only guess her scheming.

Only seems like yesterday,
She was always in the way.

Wearing mommy's grown-up clothes,
Right down to her little toes.

Lipstick, powder, jewelry flashing,
Hoping Knights would soon come dashing.

Cheeks so rosy, hair so curly,
She's my youngest little "girlie".

Now at "twenty-one" you'll see,
Life is beautiful and free.

Make the most of it, dear heart,
For too soon from it, we part.

Let God take you by the hand,
Guide you through this glorious land.
—Nora D. Vance

The Knightess

She swings the gavel down again,
She leads the women hating men,
Her club is Robert's Rules of Order,
This woman knightess is our soldier.

The look store by the village green,
By her hold leadership is seen,
Her dog's at lay at her front door,
Men hate her women as before,

She writes to congress in a pinch,
Her platform will not budge not inch,
The motion made, the motion tabled,
The knightess made our women able,
—Carolyn Kies

Super Bowl Sunday

Dracula's bride,
she licks her bruised and bloody lip

it's okay
he wants it this way, she
orders more make-up from Avon
invents more tales
for family and friends
reads him like
the daily news that never changes, she
turns from anything
that might reflect her world
this sacrificial lamb
stands by her man
listens for his step
cowers then offers
her self

Joan of Arc, she
thrills to her flesh in flames
—Alice Berryman

Sarah's Facade

Behind the red curtain
She pretends to sleep;
In that sleep she makes herself guilty
As the light flashes.
Her peers know;
The apes like it.
She's transparent:
Yet she fools some.
Does she like the drooling?
Does it make the sleep dreamful?
She gets what she's acting for.
—Anne Marie Perrotti

Death

If I die,
before the dawn,
would my friends just carry on?
I would want,
for them to be,
just as if,
it hadn't happened to me.
Would they care?
How would they be?
Would they feel at all for me?
I would want no grief,
nor any pain,
just the love in life,
I had yet to gain.
—Clayton Mastaw

On The Demise Of Our Apple Tree/House

Wizened, bearing feebly her boughs
she speaks the farewell

Her blossoms full-blown
gently scenting eternity

And followed shortly upon the earth
her shadow
lay down
to join her beginnings

This tree
once shelter to gleeful sun-bodies
gladdened in pink-white splendor
whose limbs sparkled
diamond-fluffed in winter

This tree
haunts the air

—*Grayce Haanes-Olsen*

Silent Peace

I am a candle,
Shining my light.
I am a candle,
Flickering delight

Sit and watch me,
You will know,
How I calm souls,
With my light, so low.

I brighten the spirit,
I lighten the life,
I help all the people,
Overcome strife.
My light so weak,
Can only show,
That anyone can help,
No matter the foe.

Remember my light,
And remember it's guidance.
Remember that peace,
Can come in silence!

—*Rachel Erickson*

Notches

I got my first gun at fifteen
Shooting straight and shooting clean
I got my first notch at seventeen
Steely faced and feeling mean
The notches came without no trouble
As the years went on the numbers double
As time past on it wasn't long
And before I had seen
What I had done
I'd become a notch
On a stranger's gun

—*John Bourque*

Fear

A still, dark night —
Silence conquers all but
The screaming crickets
And the roaring heart-beat
Of the mind;
Muggy heat
Causes sweat to trickle
Down gleaming faces —
Sending chills
Through every bone;
The reality is overwhelming;
Or so it seems;
Seconds,
Like hours,
Last forever;
When suddenly,
Once again,
Silence reigns.

—*Amy Varo*

You Have Touched My Heart

How deeply you have touched me
Since you have touched my heart.
You've gone beyond the skin and bone
Passed over every part.

You started with a tender kiss
Above my eyes and brow,
Continued with a soft caress
No thought of stopping now.

My hair you ran your fingers through
Your arms entwined with mine.
Your gaze so sweet upon my face,
Your smile like bright sunshine.

A loving touch by gentle palms
Came next upon my cheek.
And then the kiss you gave to me
Sent shivers to my feet.

My heart just raced! — it would not quit
For this became the night
So tenderly you shared with me
Love's wonderful delights.

—*Bonnie J. Adams*

The Audition

Take a number
sit down and wait
see the contestants
shop-talk
revving up for the race.
Timing is everything
attitude, everything else
thinking back on
the preparation weeks
Well done? We'll see.
snippets of symphonies
leaking from within cubicles
Next up; five minutes
breathe deep
think it through
ready or not.
Stand outside the stage
soon behind the screen
anonymous pencil scratchings
Alone... Play now.

—*Jennifer Scriggins*

Sculpture Of Two Cats

The two cats,
Sit side by side.
Mother and daughter,
Caring for each other.
Loving each the same.
Mother for daughter,
Daughter for mother.
It could never be;
Between father and son,
Their lives consist of
    violence and dominance.
Father for son,
Son for father.

—*Sara Ziegler*

Cola Bears

Two cola bears up in a tree
Sitting alert sip Pepsi, free
"Now that Quantas
Needs and wants us
Our life's a breeze; would you agree?"

The first one says, "Well, let me see,
Can you recall what used to be?
How that Quantas
Then did haunt us
When we'd be snoozing in our tree?"

"Before the advent of that bird
Old eucalyptus was the word
Since now there's cola
And Soave Bolla
To chew on leaves seems quite absurd."

"So I'd agree our life's a breeze
I bless that bird each time I sneeze
And our sunglasses
May cause some clashes
But face it, we're celebrities."

—*Robert Morri*

The Modern Grandma

All of us will remember Grandma
    Sitting all alone in a rocking chair
Dressed so proper in a calico dress
    Wearing combs in her gray hair!

She made homemade jam and jelly
    Had molasses cookies for us to eat
Chicken and noodles, homemade bread
    Her cakes and pies could not be beat!

Nowadays, when the kids see Grandma
    They're lucky to find her at home
She's always going here and there
    'Cause she just loves to roam!

When Grandma and Grandpa go camping
    She wears her tight blue jeans
Grandma doesn't have time to cook
    So she opens a can of beans!

If kids don't see Grandma in a chair
    Where they expect her to stay
Maybe they won't mind growing old
    And do things Grandma does today!

—*Murlea Brewer*

The Child

Lying on her bed crying
Sitting on her floor thinking
Lying on the grass dreaming
The child.

Blowing out her candles wishing
Going to the mall spending
At her slumber party laughing
The child.

In her new car driving
On her first date kissing
Going to college learning
The child.

Showing you her engagement ring smiling
Loving someone completely
Moving out bouncing
The adult.
—*Jamie E. Dickerson*

Ode To Mimi

I looked at you with tired eyes
Sitting there, playing house
Dressing your dolls, looking wise
I wish I was five again
Doing what you are now enjoying
Oh! Being so young, reliving
No worry, no doubt, never tiring
My day become dreamy and bright
When you are here
Grand daughter of mine
—*Marie J. Montet*

Untitled

It's groping at my tender soul.
Slowly I tremble and lose control.
Calling me into a world of grey,
Terrorizing me as its only prey.

Beckoning me in with dying calls,
Endless darkness of dreary walls.
Broken hearts, empty souls,
Slowly watching, no control.

Eyes ablaze with and evil light,
Drawn within full of fright.
There's no escape, no one to tell,
You feel the fiery depth of hell.

Nothing peaceful, nothing true,
Nothing sacred, only you.
You tremble in a pitiful heap,
And fade into a endless sleep.
—*Jennifer Jo McKinley*

My Winter Dream

Autumn is past
Snow is here
Cold winter wind
Blue sky
Dainty white snow
Snow birds sitting in the trees
Children playing friskily
Frost nibbling at my nose
Couples gliding along ice
A cheerful Christmas
—*Sara Filipoff*

"Tomorrow's Dream?"

"Yesterday's gone
 So far away

"Tomorrow's dream"
 Is here today

Machines are here
To take our place

At work, at play,
 In outer space

So do we risk
 Our liberty

 To further
Our technology

For what is still
 There yet to be

And who will there
 Be left to see

The day computers
Erase you and me!"
—*Roger Dotson*

Length Of Love

 Jesus told me he loved me.
So He died on the cross.
 God told Him to do it,
because He was the boss.
 I love Jesus for what He did,
He was a great person even as a kid.
 He suffered great pain for
His loss was our gain.
 And for what He has done
He has gotten great fame.
 It had to hurt to be treated
like dirt. Put on a cross for the
world to see.
 But if you can see, He died on
that cross for one reason which
 was you and me. His children
are so special to Him that He
allowed His life to go dim.
 For this is not the end
because he arose again.
—*Kim Rhodes*

Little Girl

Little girl,
so innocent, so sweet
so unaware;
of the dangers,
the drugs,
the crime,
the never-ending violence.
Take some advise...
Listen to your father,
heed your mothers words, and
never stray
from the path.
Take refuge with God,
and little girl,
always remember,
I love you.
—*Aaron Maxa*

A Women Who Loves

He a gentleman
So kind, so sweet
So warm and caring,
then came deceit

there were lies and pain
for all he had done
and, his responsibilities,
he had shun

So sad to see
one heart be so fond
of a man who has
tore apart their special bond

What happened to: "for better,
 for worse."
When it becomes ones nightmare
or a lifetime curse

if love is forever
Then what is to be
of a women who loves
and, a man like he?
—*Kim Cummings*

Nature's Way

Oh, towering maple
 So stately and grand
You've spent many a year
 Growing on our land
In summer, leaf laden,
 Birds a lit to rest,
In the crook of your boughs
 Robins made their nest.
They tell us you're dying
 Dear faithful old tree
Your haven for nature
 No more we will see.
We'll miss you dear maple
 But you must come down
You are weakened by age
 From your roots to your crown.
—*Ruth E. Cantrella*

"Perfect"

Everything is not perfect
So why is there such a word
People are not perfect
Nor a day in the world

Everything is not perfect
So why is there such a word
Nature is not perfect
Nor books and words

Everything is not perfect
So why is there such a word
The best thing that is perfect
is love for the world

Everything is not perfect
So why is there such a word
For people to try to be perfect
Is not the Word!

Dedicated to the world
Perfect or not
—*Marcia L. Montgomery*

The Graceful Baby

I am a baby with
soft delicate skin
soft as silk
delicate as a spring flower
I feel warm inside
my mother's arms
I feel loved
I never feel lonely
My mother always holds me
Every time she cradles me
I feel special
like a little yellow daisy
with silver liquid drops on
my petals.
—Katie Gengarelly

Life

Sometimes good, Sometimes Bad
Sometimes breaks your heart
Sometimes makes you laugh
Sometimes makes you cry
Sometimes doesn't go your way
Sometimes makes you jump with joy
Sometimes makes you depressed
Sometimes it never changes
Sometimes every days a paradise
It may be good
It may be bad
Life. It's whatever you make it
—Danielle Marquis

Untitled

Hockey is for Me!

I like to play hockey.
Sometimes the ice is too rocky!

My skates are sharp and fast,
If I fell and broke my leg,
I'd have to wear a cast.

I like to play goalie,
But it can be lonely.

Thomas is my mate.
He, also, likes to skate.

We call ourselves, "Rink Rats,"
Sometimes we can be brats!

We like to win,
But if we get beat,
We try again!
—Zack Swears

Wanting

I always heard more music
 than my fingers could find

I always saw more on the canvas
 than my brush could describe

I always felt more in my heart
 than ever reached my pen

I always knew more of life
 than I had the wit to tell

I always
—Robert Goldsmith

Untitled

And on a journey, distant...
somewhere
between two shores...
where paths,
again fated,
will meet...

you and I,
and others too...
if but
for a moment,
brief...
will walk again
side by side...

memories, smiles,
and laughter...
renewed.

and as we part,
and long for more...
this tear,
I shed for you...
—Jerome Laurence Langworthy

The Pit

The air is heavy
Sorrow wells in my chest
My valor forgotten
I do my best

The wailing of the dammed
It fills my ears
My heart melting in sorrow
I know their fears

My stomach turning in revulsion
I watch helpless thousands die
I try to shun the sight
But it is burned upon my mind's eye

A constant reminder of death
I see piles of the slain
Bodies crooked and twisted
Faces frozen in pain

I cannot escape the pit
No matter how I try
I will never escape the pit
Doomed eternally to die
—Joseph Kutniewski III

Pain

A lump in my throat
tears in my eyes
That just won't go away

A permanent condition
so it seems
that is with me night
and day

Don't speak to me,
pretending that you care
It only makes it harder to bear

Count your blessings, so they say
I do, I do, I silently scream
But try as hard as I will
it just won't go away
—Kathie Thurman

Today I Cried

To you loved pet I say good-bye
Sorrowful, and with melting eye
She lay all night in her sickened bed
In my circling arms I held her head

Gathering my courage to her aid
With brow severe I'm much afraid
Lonely hour, just her and me
In my redeemer's hand, a tender plea

By thy controlling power
Give me strength this sliding hour
With bursting tear and trembling hand
Please guide my heart to understand

I won't let her die alone and scared
Nor force the pain her face has shared
Compassion cannot be displeasing
Mercy thus sustains the reasoning.

The doctor finds the withered vein
To release her from her lengthened pain
My kisses now bathed with tears
Sad loss my pet of many years
—Sandra E. Reno

"October"

October skips about at random
Splashing paint with wild abandon
'Til the hills are ablaze
With scarlet, orange and maze
And the green of the pine
With the colors all combine
To make a lovely hue
'Neath a sky of azure blue
Then she covers it with frost
Till the colors are all lost
And lingers just a little
While November plays the fiddle
—Dana Thorne Perkins

Misbehaving Youth

A drop of blood
squeezed through her ruby red lips
flows down her chin
then falls on her breast

It is wiped off by her finger tips
And absorbed by her tongue
Another one falls and
the process is repeated

A napkin is applied to the cut
And all seems well,
but the napkin soon gets soaked,
then the process starts all over
again,
the only true remedy is time.
—David Cross

Stars

Stars, stars, beautiful stars
Stars shine swiftly in the sky.
Stars make pictures seen in the sky.
Stars get seen softly at night.
So when you see the stars tonight
Think of sweet little angels
Holding on tight.
Stars, stars, beautiful stars
Stars shine slowly at night.
—Christine Corrado

Wind

Every time I hear the wind
  stirring up the air,
I wonder where the wind will go,
when it moves from here to there.

Every time I hear the wind
  blowing with the trees,
I wish that I could grab ahold,
and travel with the breeze.

Every time I see the wind
  flying with the birds,
I wonder if they will go
higher than our mother earth?

Every time I see the wind
  guiding a kite along with might,
I want to grab ahold and fly,
    way up high,
  Feeling free, in a dream,
    with you and me.
—*Valerie Palumbo*

Destiny

A dull pain deep within my chest,
strangle each and every breath,
An ache so great it dries my tears,
a love so great it last for years.

I sit alone and think of when,
I fell in love - where to begin.
The lake so calm, our heart's so scared.
Unspoken, love, yet at it's end.

Three years passed by and pain did come.
My broken heart that you had won,
Was waiting for the only kiss -
that years ago I had missed.

Admitted love that now we share.
I know I do, I know I care
Yet how can I feel it so deep?
It feels like years - I feel so weak...
—*Kimberly Lynn Epting*

The Column

The pillar stands.
Strength, grace, and power;
It appears to everyone.
Supporting all,
  except itself.
Unbeknownst, it is deteriorating.
Becoming more and more hollow.
Empty and weak.
No one notices the tilt of the column;
Too intent on leaning themselves.
Looking for support and never giving.
Never listening or noticing.
  Never caring.
—*April Goller*

Eternity

The candle burns with
such intensity
it's existence reaches towards
the sky to unite
the universe
its mesmerizing dance
captures the eyes
and in the flame
peace and love are found.
—*Hillary Paige Larson*

Self-Punishment

Wrapped in a cocoon of self-doubt
  Surrounded by loneliness
  Breathe deep the pungent
  Smell of being afraid.

Knowing that loneliness is the enemy
  You continue to welcome him
  You kiss him in friendship
  Instead of turning away.

Don't you realize it's your death
  Turn from it and run
Suddenly it grabs you and you turn
And you hold it with your weak embrace.
—*Robin Denise Harmic*

Swimming

When I swim I swim all day,
swimming is more fun than play.

Butter, Back, Breast, and Free,
all these strokes are for me.

Goggles, swimsuit, towel, swim-cap,
in meets I swim only one lap.

Second place is red,
"Swim a three-hundred" our coach said.

Coming in third is yellow or white,
getting ribbons is out of sight.

Swimming is my favorite sport,
I am happy to report.
—*Ashley McGee*

Vision Feast

Early morning freedom/thoughts
taste better than mom's apple pie.
non-fattening,
nutritious for the soul.

Cinnamon covered chainless dreams
  turn cages into castles,
  steel cells into sanctuaries.

Sugar sweet
slivers of sunlight bring
  visions of liberation
  into my 8x10 domain.

Come.
share my repast.
frosted butterfly/wings
  of changing times,
hope held high
  in honied splendor.
a feast of peace,
  utopia.
—*Michael E. Garnett*

To The Teacher

From the middle of a desert
  The waste of barren sand,
You came as out of nowhere
  To offer me your hand.
To bid me drink the fruit of life
  From palms you cupped for me.
Your love is my oasis,
  My quiet reverie.
—*Rowland G. Moulding*

The Moment

The pictures on the wall
Tell a story

Of unsung songs
And fleeting glory

The faces are smiling
Their grins are beguiling

They stare as they freeze
With their eyes they tease

They pose and wonder
How do I look from over yonder

The picture behind the face
The stillness of the camera will erase

The happiness and sorrow
Will be there tomorrow

That moment in the mind
The picture will never find
—*Lois Gay Duncan*

Love Is

Is Love a problem
  that can't be solved
  or a problem
  that shouldn't be solved?
Is love even a problem?
  some are guided by it.
  some are blinded by it.
Is love the base of the world
  or the base of peace?
Is love a need that keeps us alive
  or a want that fills our desires?
Is love for me
  or someone rich and beautiful?
Love is the answer!
  (or is it?)
—*Erin Marie Muller*

Shadowed Light

The shadowed light,
That falls across your face,
Reminds me of,
Another time and place.
Whispered thoughts,
Behind your eyes
Make me sad to finally realize,
That nothing lasts forever,
Or so it would seem,
Unless you live,
With in your own dreams.
A treasured place.
But all to rare,
And then you find,
only you can go there,
So search for a path,
Through the defeat,
and find that place
Where life and dreams meet.
—*Shannon Parker*

Love, Laughter, Peace And Music

Love is the strength
That fills the body
With the energy it needs
To conquer the obstacles life holds

Laughter is the cure
That fills the mind
With the joy it needs
To forget it's sorrows

Peace is the calm
That fills the soul
With the warmth it needs
To live in comfort

Music is the language
That stimulates the body
Relaxes the mind
And unites the souls
—*Michele Cascio*

The Little Acorn

There was a little acorn,
that had a little sprout.
And one day it died.
in an autumn drought.
It never saw Oklahoma plains.
It never saw Indiana rains.
It never stood proud and tall.
It never really stood at all,
It never heard laughter and joy.
Laughter and joy of
girls and boys.
—*Sarah Kessans*

Untitled

  Here as I sit across the river
that has grown so wide,
  I see the home in which I lived
in times gone by.
  Those autumn days and winter winds
and summers glistening dew —
  Spring time rains bring special
thoughts of the times of me and you.
  How we once were young with
a world of our own.
  With thoughts of a family
and dreams yet to be sown.
  The kids all grown and the years
gone by,
  As I sit on the edge of my chair
and sigh.
  A new family lives in the home
we once knew,
  Looking on I reminisce of the
times spent with you.
—*Susan Y. Heinz*

Is He Listening

Is he listening,
That man upstairs
Does he care,
That man upstairs
Does he answer your
prayers,
If we are dying,
Does he care
He cares for everyone
That man upstairs.
—*Jamie Pool*

Sorrow

Oh the sweet sensation of sorrow,
    That melancholy mood.
Thoughts of yesterday and tomorrow,
    And to what they might allude.

The weight of each and every thought
    Rests heavy upon the heart.
    Of what was and wasn't sought.
    And where or when to start.

    A great void within the soul
        Opens to the sky.
        Consuming the whole.
    Destroying the minds eye.

What is it about this sensation
That one hates, yet loves so well.
    Time filled in contemplation,
    Searching for Heaven, and
        Searching for hell.
—*David W. Helba*

Love Around The World

    The environment is a topic
    That people ignore in every way.
        Time is not on our side,
So we must work to save it everyday.

Life is just like the environment,
    People just take it for granted,
But then one day we'll be gone-
    No life form will be stranded.

So please tell someone you love them,
And tell the environment that you care.
    Together we can make a difference
If love around the world is shared.
—*Jill Caplan*

Arpeggio

Speak then the passing years
    that play staccato
on the picket fence of time.

Speak then the loves we've known,
    the smiles, the tears,
    the parting of the ways.

Speak then the moments we remember,
    some large, some small,
    that pass in fond parade.

Speak then the great arpeggio.
    Life comes. Life goes.
    And I am not afraid.
—*Robert W. Mather*

The Open Door

Emotions are feelings
They are there deep inside
  of you

They are the door
That when open -
  show the real you

Love, anger, fear
These are the
Emotions - seen
When you open
  the door
—*Sarah Creery*

Twilight Singer

I heard a song in the twilight.
That rose from the shadows so dim.
It came on the shades of the night.
Like a lost and scared hymn.

His song was one of despair.
As he sang his woeful grief.
His heartbreak carried on the air.
Pressed on each twig and leaf.

It carried a message of the sorrow.
That marked the death of a day.
Singing with hope of a morrow.
When the sun might come and stay.

It flowed on with the gathering shadow.
That lengthened in the woods so deep.
It crested the high from the low.
And rang to the pillars steep.
—*W. L. Reynolds*

Untitled

Life is a precious gift
    That should not be wasted
But rather enjoyed
    And definitely not hastened

Do the things you enjoy
    As I am doing on this day
Go for a walk on the beach
    Or call a person who cares

Put hatred behind you
    For at least one day
And take a look around
    Ask yourself one thing

Why? Why all the hate
    Why all the fear
Then continued on your way
    The answer shall be clear.
—*Allison Gotschall*

A Rose

    A rose will represent the love
that someone shows to another person
who care about so very much. Like
a husband to a wife, father to a
son, mother to daughter, and one
family member to another. A rose
is a simple symbol of love.
—*Kathleen Tapia*

Beach Music

    Beneath a full yellow moon
      that was almost hidden
    by dark clouds, a cluster
    of sea gulls floated on a
        turbulent ocean.
    Over the continuous roar
      of the waves, I heard a
    little girl scream and laugh
      when cold water covered
    her feet and then the melancholy
    melody of three men playing
    their guitars drifted through
        my window.
—*Tasha Brown*

Little Children's Dream

Little children to have dreams
That we adults would not understand
They want love with Mom & Dad
And maybe a trip to Disneyland

They want tender love and care
Not bruises or maybe a black eye
They want Mom & Dad to love each other
And they don't want to see mother cry

Children will ask for toys sometime
What they get is no great concern
They need the help from Mom & Dad
In the lessons they have to lean

They need to know about the Bible
To teach them right from wrong
Let them know that God will help
To make them good and also strong

—*Carl Mathus*

Mother

   Oh, how precious was the hand that wiped away the tears and even the arms that protected us from all fears.

   The warmth, the understanding that came forth was always there to mend the wounded heart.

   Yes, mother, we love you and we will always keep you near,

   In heart, in mind, and in spirit too; mother, we will always cherish our memories of you.

—*Robert Parker Sr.*

A Heart

Have you ever had the thought?
That you just couldn't cope;
This thing gives you hope.

Have you ever knew anyone?
Who just didn't care;
But thus this thing taught
you to share.

Have you ever had a love?
That never did part;
What helped you out?
This thing, a heart.

This thing sometimes felt
sorrow,
But not always,
It is a thing;
Called a heart.

—*Tabitha Moye*

Candle Light

The candle is glowing.
The wick is going low.
What a pretty sight
It's not a fright
in about an hour
The candle will be
devoured. And the
candle that was
glowing turns into
a bright night
What a sight.

—*Rossan Casciaro*

Good Fishing

I went fishing in our lake,
That's in the Ozark Hills.
I spent the morning on our dock,
Expecting many thrills.

I know you wonder what I caught—
I didn't get a fish,
But, oh, I made the grandest catch
That ever I could wish.

I saw that day, the work of God
As daybreak had begun
God was the artist painting for me
The glory of the rising sun.

A gentle breeze blew in my face,
It ruffled up my hair.
And as I watched the crimson sky
I didn't have a care.

I wouldn't trade these Ozark Hills
For any place so very grand.
I feel the presence of our Lord
In this dear Missouri Land!

—*Virginia Shannon*

Anticipating Waves

I watch the rolling waves
The air so clean
The sight so beautiful
I am looking out
Watching people walk out on water
Actually tumbling down.
I laugh.

Just waiting for my turn
To follow in their footsteps
I was scared
As I waited.
Watching friends thrown upon the shore
Can they really take much more

As I jumped on a piece of board,
I slide across the water.
I felt the cool breeze
With a feeling so great,
It put me at ease.

—*Maria Phillips*

Footsteps

  The night was cold and wintry.
    The air was crisp and dry.
  Above the snow capped mountains,
    the stars were in the sky.

  The old man bent and haggard,
  was wandering through the streets.
  His clothes were torn and dirty —
  old rags wrapped 'round his feet.

  He once was young and vibrant;
  his walk was swift and strong.
  But now his brow so wrinkled,
    his heart without a song.

  The village streets have widened
    since last he walked this way.
  His friends no longer live there,
    but they will meet someday.

  His last return was sorrowful,
    yet in his heart he knew
  that he'd come back to see it —
    this town where he once grew.

—*Jeanne D. Miccio*

Long Lost Bay

Whispering winds across
  the bay;
Whispering winds, where
  my memories lay.
Farewell to that place,
  where I wish to stay;
Farewell to that place that
  is so far away.
I close my eyes, my
  memory is swell;
I close my eyes, I can
  see it well.
I see a bay with waters
  of blue;
I see a bay, a place
  where my love is true.

—*Noel Rhodes*

Him

As he trods across
The blood sodden earth
He remembers times
Times of vanished mirth

He remembers times
Times of blissful peace
Free from restraint
The feeling of release

He remembers times
Times of beauty and song
He remembers past days
So tranquil and long

As he travels back
A return from the past
Thinking, wondering
Why those days didn't last

—*Kelly Jensen*

"Come The Day"

When the sun combs
The clouds back
And the ice melts away
The sound of bells will
Fill the air.
The Crucifix will stand
Proudly upon its steeple.

The stars, although not visible,
Will chirp and twinkle
As Heavens' Light
Shines upon the focus
Of the days' congregation.

As we stand in the Light
We begin the day that belongs
To us - and that day
Shall last for the rest
Of our lives.

—*Don Ryan*

Colorful Tears

Skeletal trees,
the color of brass
Now fill the sky
And reach to be free
from earthly bonds.
Bony fingers aren't shy
When clawing for the sun
that gives life, but will
take away
Their time has come
to cry colorful tears.
—*Candace Hensley*

Prejudice

Red, black, brown and white,
The colors of people's skin.
It should not matter about that,
Only about the person within.
Why would it matter if I were black,
And you white?
Would it matter between two friends,
Would there be a fight?
If I were Jewish,
Would I say, "This is not fair?"
Or if I were Catholic,
Would I turn away as if I did not care?
People should not act like this,
But look inside and you might find,
PREJUDICE!
—*Joy Hermes*

Changes

Sunset,
The deep blue sky
Gives way to the redness of a volcano.
As it moves from dusk to dark,
A shadow of a bird can be seen
In the fraction of a second
Before darkness envelops the Earth
In a blanket of silence.
A silence that grows louder and louder
With each new minute until once again,
Light emerges—victorious at last.
—*Sherilin Jennings*

Time

   The bells are ringing
The doors are shut
Time is bringing
Us a mock

   Love is lost,
Days to come splenderly waiting
The time has cost
As the steel-iron gates a grating

   For mirrors now tell the time
Because the clock has died
Oh, but a sweet and sorrowful crime
We have all wept, to death we cried...
—*Jennifer Balan Catabas*

Rust

Rays of fire glitter down and disappear
The earth turns cool as night at dusk
We enter this world fresh and clean
And then we rust

Shadows dance along the ceiling
Candles burn at what once was
We listen to the dying music
As we turn to rust

It doesn't need to be so sad
We could recapture the dreams we had
We could soar like falling stars
If we only had something to hold onto

The fires all alight, Love
Come lay by my side
We have made it this far, Love
There's nothing more to hide
We've had it all by now
Everything that we could ask
And still the loneliness engulfs
Our rusting, smiling masks
—*Christine Ball*

Familiar News

Combined:
   the familiar
     visited
        majestic buildings

The house where H.G. Wells had dreamed

Contrived now
   where they had lived
     and thought
       and written

Money could buy his fantastic stories
   but not one inspiration

Ordered linkages
   invent
     familiar news:
       Recombined
—*Chereka Keaton*

Tempest

     Off in a distance,
   The halt of gunfire is heard.
The sight of a tempest fills the air.
     With its common decor,
   The city is the sight of war.
    During the pause of battle,
   The soldier squats on a tank.
    Her beauty reflects peace,
   While the tanks intimidation
     Provokes militance.
    The two are unbalanced.
—*Megan Richer*

Whose Hands Shape The World?

Whose hands shape the world?
The hands of the stone mason or
dishwashers in Soweto?
The hands of the interrogator?
The gentle hands of the gardener
in Togo?
The hands of Mexico, Chile, Ethiopia
reaching out to
empty air?
—*Elizabeth K. Doran*

Lonely Me

I lay awake in my bed
The house is so quiet
And everyone's asleep
I feel lonely. Lonely me.

Sometimes I hear my father snoring
And I hear my brother's too
I hear the bathroom water running
As I try to sleep. Lonely me

I can't understand
The emptiness I feel
People are around
But the night is quiet
Inside me. Lonely me.
—*Samantha Spinelli*

"Flowers"

   The beauty of a magnolia.
   The inner soul represented
     by a rose.
The welcome smile and laughing eyes
remembered in the image of daisies.
   The feminine charm of
     a lily.
   And like a flower,
   Your time came gently
   And with dignity.
   You will be missed:
     Magnolia.
     Rose.
     Daisy.
     Lily.
And like all flowers,
   Your memory will be
     Carried on
     The wind.
—*Courtney DiNapoli*

"Locksmith"

Watch for the Locksmith.
The master of the keys.
The one who can open,
Anything he please.

He can open the door,
To your heart and soul,
He can open the door,
To your every goal.

He can open the door,
To the pearly gate.
He can open the door
To renew your fate.

He can open any door,
You see.
He's not just the Locksmith,
He is the key.
—*Diana Higginbotham*

Lonely Tears

If you can count the rain drops,
then you can count my tears,
from the loneliness in my heart.
...it can take many years.
to keep a perfect count
you got to be near
no more loneliness
through out the years.
—*Carl Keller*

Untitled

God gave you this child
The most precious gift of all
To love, protect, and guide
To stand so proud and tall
Why then do you abuse your child
You hurt his heart and soul
A word so harshly spoken
A slap across the face

You've gone out of control
Then you wonder why this world's
gone bad
I think it's time we looked
Then ask our Lord and Savior
And begin to read his book
To turn ourselves around
Because when you hurt a
child
You bringing the whole
down,
—*Janice Crockford*

Mountain View

Looking out from
the mountain's view.
Seeing everything
that looks so new

Taking off
flying in the sky
watching the birds
fly so high.

Watching everything
stand still
makes your day
become fulfilled.
—*Johanna Edmondson*

It Was The Earth

The year is 2093
The ocean is no longer bluish green
She thinks we are mean
For the water never again will be clean
The sky is as grey as morning fog
And yet it is not fog
This is forever smog
This is what the earth could be
In the year 2093
We need to protect what we see
Earth is hers used by you and me
Don't worry there's still hope
Now here's the scope
This is our planet
Please, don't can it
But soon Mother Earth will be crying
Because of us the earth is dying.
—*Wendy Barrascout*

The Shedding Of Our Tears

Only through
The shedding of our tears.
Can we polish the sparkle,
Within our eyes.
A sparkle that reflects,
The rainbow.
Within our soul.
—*Leisa Bain Good*

Saturday Mornings

We come to grips again.
The old hate burns through
again.
Again is too often, but there is
no other way than
again.
As often as we try to keep some truce
going, we find some excuse to talon
skillfully into the heart
of memories and waning illusions.
We never fit the mold
we summon for each other,
so we contend.
The scope of our private visions
allows no latitude, beguiles us
towards a jealousy that corrodes.
   We eat each other down to entrails
   and call that
   winning.
—*Bill Thierfelder*

To My Uncle

You were my favorite uncle,
the one I once adored.
There was no other like you,
and no one loved you more.

Then you got sick,
and I prayed you would pull through.
That's exactly what you did,
for a year or two.

This is the hardest thing,
that I ever had to face.
To finally realize,
it's you I can never again embrace.

Now you are in heaven,
and I surely do miss you.
Because the day when you died,
a part of me died, too.
—*Pamela Gumbman*

She's Gone

She's gone and I still miss her
   The pain goes on and on
   The years have not diminished
   Her life, her love, her song

She's gone but I still miss her
This sister, This friend, This mom
   The years have not erased
   Her spirit, strength and calm

She's gone and the world is missing
   this woman of soul and heart
   Her life was cut too early
   Her life just got its start

The question of a woman's strength
   to me does not belong
For all in me that's good or great
   from her was passed along

She's gone and I still miss her
This hero, This friend, This mom
   I long so much to hold her
   My God! My God!....She's Gone!
—*John Laudico*

Night Walk

Across the lake,
The pavilion lights
Paint bright columns
On the dark water;
Like the pipes of an organ
That plays music made of light.

A lone white bird glides
In a graceful dance across the lake.

Above, the hot stars
Pepper the sky
Like the notes
Of an enormous symphony.

A faint breeze stirs;
God's whisper: and I
Can almost understand
The song creation sings.
—*Joel Ross*

Peace

The walk along the flowered path
The quite soft breeze, that moved
The leaves, on every tree,
This is peace.
The birds, of all colors, sang
Softly, the stream ran smoothly
Down over the rocks,
This is peace.
The green grass, lay like a carpet,
With wild flowers, and red clover,
Nodding their heads, the weeping
Willow, looks like a beautiful
Dancer, as Its lower branches, swing
Back and forth.
This is peace.
A golden staircase, lined with angels
On both sides, golden sandless, on their
Feet, soft feather wings, gold halos,
Around their heads, beautiful flowers
In their hands. This too is peace.
—*Everlyn Riley*

No Place Like Home

There's no place like home.
The saying is true.
What happens if you have no home
to go to?
Summer and winter out on the street.
Immense cold.
Extreme heat.
Dirty, holey clothes.
Nobody knows what it's like.
Home is where you hang your heart.
That part is true.
What happens it you have no home
to go to?
—*Emily Simonian*

Escape

I must go down to the ocean,
The sea, the surf and the sand.
I must taste the salty water
and swim away from the land.

To the world of the waves
And the broiling sun,
Where a boy at last is free.
Where a boy can breath
And ride on the surf
At last, at home in the sea.

I must leave my books and pen
And all the work that is due.
Get away from teachers and parents,
Come friend to the ocean with you.

I must go down to the ocean,
To the place where I am free.
Where there is room to dream and grow
From this boy to the man I'll be.
—David Alan Smith

Love

The hope that pulls you through;
The thing that makes you feel anew.
If lost, it brings you down;
When you're sad, it comes around.
It's weakness is a tear;
It's strength is a cheer.
The hope that goes that extra mile;
The light of a smile.
A hug from the heart;
Time given to make a new start.
It's as free as a dove;
This thing called love!
—April Keeney

Policy

Be that as it may,
the time has come to flee,
the only righteous mind
has lost every battle.

sins are piled to the
borders of every sunrise.
once, our noble lusts
could conquer anything.

but flames engulf our
senses, in the haze
one true destiny will
never be realized.

not by you or I,
the irony that led
us here, has only
to show us how to return.
—Sarah Applebaum

Autumn's Farewell

Autumn leaves still on
the trees and yet,
I catch a glimpse of
Winter on its way.
Soon the snow will
start to fall,
I know, azure skies
will fade away
To grey.
Leafy flowers will shed
their blooms, and then,
Time alone will bring the
winds as cold.
Fall will die and say
Farewell to when
Life was young and gay
With heart so bold.
—Wilma J. Johnston

Obstruction

Each limb congested with life
the unity of the greens,
working together to produce peace
the rain forest.
I gazed at the roaring machines
ripping and chopping my home
burning memories
diminishing the future,
murder.
A crime no man could be convicted of
it was he who brought it upon us,
the greediness of his species.
I gaped
their domination
brought my people to an end.
—Emily Vient

Love

Sometimes I wonder if it will ever be,
the way it use to be.
In this huge world existing,
just you and me.
I guess you could say,
I cared to much.
Now that you're gone,
I ache for your touch.
Oh dear God I beg of you,
I promise this time I'll be true.
I never, ever meant
to hurt you.
I guess it's one of those
things you never knew.
I never thought
how badly you would feel.
Just give me another chance
and I promise it will heal.
Couldn't we just start out new?
Don't you see how much I care for you?
—Missy Sanford

Kaya

Kaya
 the Wind
  is Forest Walking
 so high
  among the Trees
Kaya
 the wind
  is Forest Dancing
 a jig
  upon the Leaves
Kaya
 the Wind
  is Forest Walking
 and singing
  deep unto the Trees
Kaya
 the Wind
  is Forest Musing
 giving a blessing
  to the Breeze
—Anne C. Terhaar

The Tree

Its leaves swayed in the gentle breeze.
The wind blew the branches
 quietly back and forth.
The initials of past couples were
 carved upon the tree.
Large roots upon the ground made
 cradled seats for playing children
Kids climbed the sturdy tree higher
 and higher until they could
 climb no more.
Chipmunks and squirrels climbed up the
 branches noisily to their
 homes,
You can smell the air of the
 woods, and the nature.
It represents childhoods of small kids
 who are now adults.
This tree is filled with hopes, dreams,
 memories, and peace.
—Amanda Miller

The Worm

When the earth turns into spring
The worms are fat as anything.

And birds come flying all around
To eat the worms right off the ground.

They like worms just as much as I
Like bread and milk and apple pie.

And once, when I was very young,
I put a worm on to my tongue.

I didn't like the taste a bit
And so I didn't swallow it.

But, oh, it makes my mother squirm
Because, she thinks I ate that worm.
—Michelle Larrabee

War And Peace

    Red blood runs in streams,
    Then somebody, in pain, screams.
    These are the sounds of war.
    Young people trying to learn,
People studying plants, like a fern.
    These are the visions of peace.
    There are killings by gangs,
    Guns shooting at people with bangs.
      Even during peace we act
    Like war is on its way back.
      War is not at all fun,
But everyone is glad when peace is won.
    —*Leslie Lemus*

Untitled

Deep inside of me
   there awaits a kind of love
   a love that can only be set free
   with a kind of push or shove.

I need this kind of shove
   to help bring it out of me
   the person waiting inside
   the person I want to be.

The person who sees no color
   or needs not one "high"
   this person needs only one thing
   just the love and support to fly.

Would you consider taking
   the time you need to see
   that I need a shove on the outside
   so my special inside can be free?

Will you give me that shove?
   Will you let my inside free?
   For the one who lets it out
   Is forever a friend to me.
    —*Angi Cheney*

The Raccoon Family

Around the bend, in an old, hollow tree
There's a raccoon waiting for me
It has a mask as dark as this night
Its green eyes stare with fright.
Quietly it jumps
out of its lair,
Acting like
I'm not even there
That raccoon walked
to the lake's edge
Then I saw
three babies on the same ledge
Soon they had crayfish
at their feet
But now they were
beginning to eat
Then the sun began to rise
They browsed back to their home
That's when I noticed that
I was again alone.
    —*Jeslyn Miller*

On A Cold Winter's Night

On a cold winter's night
There is a light breeze,
Which rustles the crumbling,
Brown, dead leaves.
It is snowing lightly,
And on the icy roads cars
Are slipping slightly.
Just before it disappears
The moon shines off the
Frozen lake,
Almost as if it is watching
Every falling snowflake.
Soon the dawn nears and in
Comes the light,
And I know it is over, a cold
Winter's night.
    —*Alissa Lorene Halsey*

Holy Grave

I wait for the storm,
knowing I'm alone.
I can't cry for help,
so I'll drink the rain.
I can't hide from myself,
for I am reality.
Let my eyes see,
let my eyes see a companion.
I am still alone.
With a smile I die.
Thank you.
    —*Clay D. Hall*

I Still Love Him

Rickey was his name,
The one who caused all the pain,
He said he loved me very much,
Then he left me in a trance,
There I was crying and crying,
Till tears I had no more,
He left me free like a dove,
To find someone new to love,
Now he is gone forever,
But I still love him!
   I love you Rickey!
    —*Rhenay Dereck*

Happiness

Happiness lies within those that have
The capacity to love
To trust in someone with your
Very soul that your heart
Will not fell pain
Life is too short to build a wall
Never experiencing love at all
So open your heart and
Close your eyes to what the
Future brings
The joy of loving
Can bless you with happiness
Above all monetary things
    —*Lilly M. Adkins*

Skyhorse

There he is,
The huge blue and white dappled
horse that roams the sky,
Thunder, the sound of his playful
hooves,
Lightning, the gleaming shine of
his shoes against the sun,
His playful habits frighten all,
His beauty, adored by all...
   The skyhorse
    —*Amanda Collier*

Wishes

If my wishes could give you
a castle within a chest of gold,
Than I'm sure that you would have them,
and everything else it could hold,
But prayer must be your jewels
and faith your golden strand,
The little babe in the manger
held the glory of life in his hand,
So think of all the good you could do Dear,
With these little thoughts from me,
I'm hoping someday in heaven,
Is where your castle will be.

—*Edna G. Burton*

Resentment

The chip off the old block has one
A chip on the cold shoulder.
A 'righteous' cause
For the rebel's wars,
That's never free of angry pain - this side of Mercy.

It comes down through generations;
It burns the open sore.
It is stoked and fed,
It is poked and bled,
It's never free of caustic pain - this side of Healing.

Preceded by ominous rumbles -
This dangerous atmosphere;
It swells and spews
Its toxic fumes,
Not free from suffocating pain - this side of Justice.

—*Rowan Reynolds*

My Bad Day's Good

I was clearly having a very bad day
A "colossal disaster" one might say
The fuse of my boss was short of being long
Everything I did proved totally wrong

Right after work - in my car on Main Drive...
I glanced up and spotted two ducks in a dive
My sunroof was closed and you guessed it right
A thunderous "splat" - from a very great height

"Why not?", thought I, "It's really quite fitting,
They obviously knew upon whom they were sh————!"
"The only good thing about today, I suppose...
Is the fact that my sunroof - I decided to close!"

—*E. Mae Collins*

My Country

My dreams, my hopes, my life.
A flash in my eyes.
A gaze at the horizon, to the unknown.
Where am I going?
What is my future?
Where are my dreams?
A new life, a new country, new hopes, new dreams.
For this is my life,
the life of an emigrant.
I love you Canada!
My country, my dreams, my hopes, my life.

—*Jenny Comito*

Memories

A puddle on a roof-top, shimmering in the sun
A little bird rests wearily, after work is nearly done.

An important task upon him come, and fly off on his way
The water lingers after him, as ripples prove his stay

But one by one the ripples pass and soon they will subside
As all things remain in nature, laws we must abide.

The moment may be short, relative to all time
But the memory long outlives itself, as part of the sublime.

—*Mary Beth Ezekiel*

Pride In A Portrait

The year was nineteen, fifty-two,
A little girl you had.
With auburn hair, and skin so fair,
So proud, was mom and dad!

Again, in nineteen, fifty-six,
A second, blessed you both.
A blonde was she, and that was me!
This family started growth.

But then, in nineteen, fifty-eight,
So much to your surprise!
Another girl, but what a pearl,
Brown hair, could one surmise.

Now it's nineteen, ninety-two,
These three, this life you've shown.
Have posed for you, yes mom, dad too.
And look how much we've grown!

Thanks, we'd like to show you both,
And chose this special day,
To show how much, our lives you've touched,
We three, in our own way!!!

—*Brenda Thurlow*

The Lady Came Home

Through the time we have cherished
A love that shall not perish
There was pain, there was sorrow
But always tomorrow
The hope lies eternal
for the lady came home

The good times are forever
The bad times forgot
The love of her children has faltered naught
But now as we lay her down to rest
We know in God's goodness
Its for the best

Her husband was waiting those many years
So, please now, dry your tears
For now through the ages
He no more shall roam
For now they are happy
The lady came home

—*J. D. Brandow*

Spring

The sky turns indigo blue,
And robins return on cue.
Flowers, trees seemingly budding,
Rivers and creeks begin their flooding.
Mosquitoes and black flies itching to sting,
Quick, get out your bug dope
And welcome in Spring.

—*Cornelia Young*

Nature's Witness

Amid autumn's array; blushed by Sun's light,
    a presence is felt from
        peaceful insight.
Dancing nearby like a kind summer breeze,
    it touches our souls
        and frolics with leaves.
The Spirit is playful, inspired by Love.
    He seeks out the ones
        whose faith rests above.
Communion with Him is seen through
        the trees.
    "I'm over here," He muses,
        "I'm over there…"
hey, it's okay, don't be afraid…
    it's only Me.
    Who will listen to His voice?
      It's more than words.
      We make a choice.
Spiritually wise are we that behold,
    His windy disguise made manifold.
    —*Rita Woodman*

Apatride

    A musical composer, a painter,
a sculptor, anything but this: a writer.
When I come to my desk and pick up
my pen, I never know what colour of
ink to use, which dictionary to look
into, what history book to copy. I wish I
were someone born in a land which has
seen his parents and grandparents
working on that same piece of land,
eating its fruit, building houses and
bridges that always come back to the
point of departure. But I was born to
travel, to move without end from one
house to another, crossing bridges to
other shores, always a tourist, envying
strangers tilling their land, building
their houses and bridges. I am an eternal
pilgram who will never say: "Me voici
restitue a ma rive natale" (Saint-John Perse).
    —*Antonio D'Alfonso*

Surfing On Heat Waves

On top of a hill
a small suburban crescent of yellow street lights,
a string of incandescent pearls hanging loosely
around the neck of the sultry night

glistening copper leaves
dispersed on the sun bleached grass
dishevelled lawns that shiver and perspire
under the ethereal veil of dawn

an arcade of maple trees
with the anatomy of elbows, wrists and knees
genuflecting under the weight of the calciferous sky

the clumsy silhouette of swollen clouds
sky riders surfing on heat waves
under a vast celestial dome
splattered with a billion stars
    —*Gaetan La Belle*

"In My Heart"

Look deep inside my heart and what do you see
A turmoil of feelings churning internally
The pain, the fear, the anger tumbling all around
And my love for you forever strong and sound.

Through empty spaces I laugh, and think, and talk
But I know you are near when by the water I walk
Are you sharing my hurts with each falling drop of rain
And filling me with loving warmth when the sun shines on me again!

Look deep inside my heart and what do you see
Feelings of peace and love building up eventually
Now, as I go through each and every day
I will cherish each moment along life's precious way.
    —*Tonny Hackwood*

On The Fourteenth Day

What is this before me, climbing forty miles high?
A wall of stone: a self-made prison
Holding me within. Without. Forever?

No. There's movement in the dark—inanimate, yet moving
Back and forth. Back and forth, through the wall.

You're beside me—dearest, dearest.
Why now; from where? Go away, it's dangerous.
Not that way; don't pull me! The wall will hurt me. Hurt us.
You're not afraid. Then I will follow—hold me. Help me.

Now colour, fire, wind, and sunlight.
The wall is shrinking. Falling. Losing.
It's small and I am free to pass, unharmed.

But where have you gone? You're gone away, dearest.
It's not fair. It's a nightmare. I'll cry for all eternity.

    My whimpers reach your resting ears,
    You're calm beside me still.
    You roll and touch my sleeping head
    And I wake with joyous thrill.

    That you're close by and in my grasp, a present from above.
    To you, who's given me everything: I give to you, my love.
    —*Jerry L. Chappell*

Letters

I read your letters every day
Absorbing, feeling each word that they say
And as my eyes pass each letter through
There are those three words. I love you.

Now these there words small as they seem
Have become part of me, my fantasy, my dream
A dream I have, filled with thoughts of you
A dream, I hope for us to make come true

There is no other who has touched my heart
Like you have done right from the start.
And as I read your letters each time
It's nice to know that you have become mine

Little words that mean so much
Who ever could have thought of such.
For I have come to plainly see
Just how much your letters mean to me.

I read your letters everyday
Thinking of you and feeling this way
And as I feel your words are true
I now realize that I love you.
    —*Stephen Burke*

The Dark Side Of The Moon

Hurt, heart aching to know why to throes must bow, heart aching from need, heart aching to be freed, heart feeling the blame, heart cursing the shame, heart fleeing forever meeting her own specter, condemned to suspicion out of fear to find that her shadow is her peer...Never again, under a vow, should heart be reduced to pain, never again be so endowed as to reap horror, be insane...Yet since in waves keeps crashing in the end, my friend, the crime, my sin, Love give me strength, grant me the courage, to let the mirror shatter my image...Love be at the center, no way to enter, bust risk my soul, not play a role...Dear friends I leave behind, the moon calls me forth, forget all I'm worth, surrender to my mind. Deliverance as a break, as a tear on the stake, as a ghoul from a tomb, as an exit from the womb...Ah yes, my life as a token, as a wife, estranged from her husband, alone in the night, howling in a labor that keeps stretching her fright through an abyss opened by a ritual knife. O Love, here you are, I love you so, I missed you so, I want you so...

—*Chad Howe*

"Desert Storm"

Amid the flashes of explosion, fire and smoke,
Amid the feelings of hatred and fear,
Amid the mirrors of mind and heartaches,
Amid confusion, sadness and destruction,
Amid sorrow and tears of the whole world,
Amid prejudice, beauty of tongue in all
Cultures are still unique,
Amid crisis, strife and rebuilding,
Amid continual hunger, death and suffering,
One thing is clear our masters palm holds
O-so-dear awaiting our surrender to: True freedom, love - peace offered to all.

—*Marilyn Savage*

The Whisper

As I lay by my countryside trail
Amongst the leafy woodland dale
Beside the ferns, the weeds, the cress
I dream of her being and sensual dress
Behold! Dear heart, is she your want?
Maddened by dismay and unjustly daunt
"Yes" is the answer I know to be true
This magnificent love was sure to ensure
"Call our her name," a voice contrived
Resurgence of excitement hath distinctly revived
With dry lips perched, a whisper long feared
Danced out in the air bearing name so revered
"Janet" billowed out like feathers in a gale
As solemnity blossomed in this fine woodland dale in closing my eyes to relish thy bliss. My cheek entertained a most tenderly kiss. The most beloved of joys is the reality of life. When beside your body is laying your wife an enchanting dream, a golden treasure. The only woman to offer such pleasure as I lay by my countryside trail. Amongst the leafy woodland dale I thank Lord God so high up above for my wife, my angel, my love.

—*Stephen Galati*

Untitled

Before I finished the letter my heart had been broken.
   In the dark I found myself in the woods all of a sudden.
For along time I stood in the mud where I had been.
   By moonlight only mud and flowing water would be seen.

"Flowing water, where will you go?
   Please carry my heart and my soul.
Together with you let me go
   To see my bride, snow, snow."

—*Bolin Liu*

Wishing

I wish I was eighteen again, a healthy boy with lots of tan.
An architect I'd like to be, so years of university, to learn designing buildings, tall or low or large and huge or small.
And looking at those lovely girls, dark hair or blonde, just straight or curls. It does not matter, don't yet choose and stay away from drugs and booze.

I'm old and tired and don't live long
though hoping still to go along
for some more time, and hiding tears,
the way I did for all those years.
I leave behind a busy life
and seven children with my wife.
I'm sure they miss me for some time,
but they live on, that's not a crime.

Not looking forward to the end,
I don't know what's behind the bend.
The carriage holds Sir death and me,
behind us immortality.
I wish I was eighteen again,
I'd study to become a man!

—*John Lee Den Ouden*

No Boundaries

Why deny the eyes of a stranger,
And continuously laugh at their questions,
And harshly ruin their dreams
Why do we break down their shells
Of self-esteem and pride
We were not born, but we were taught
To be superior and richer than thou
Some of us run away and turn out the lights
So we can no-longer judge or steal
Ones confidence to be individual
And see beauty outside of looks and colors
Stand for what you are
And what you want
Arrogance and ignorance no longer
Block the path that the future lies on
Although one may be rich
And one may be poor
If we open our minds
We are opening doors

—*Kelly Lupien*

The Love That Hurts

I loved him from the moment that we met
And I love him still and never can forget
His smile, his warm and tender touch
that made me feel weak and faint
as a school girl in love.
His laughter, most of all, was happiness set to music.
His arms, when he held me so close I could
feel the beating of his heart and mine
His arms, strong like the old-time village smitty
Encircled me - and my tears of joy flowed freely.
We cared and shared and trusted, with the
passing of each day
But our love must be a secret always, for
he can never belong to me.
He took some vows he meant to keep;
Some thirty years or so ago which he can never break.
Love is supposed to ease all pain but
with my love for him
My tears blend with the rain, and pain
envelopes me each time I hear his name.

—*Anne Abbott*

The Fox

Night had fallen
And in the swamp
The cunning fox began to creep and sneak,
Light on foot, alert at ear,
His way to where the chickens sleep.
For well he knew
That there was food
An instinct told him that he should
Beware the farmer's roving eye
Less he should fail
And victory's cry not be his tonight.
Softly, softly, ever softly,
Light on foot he crept
Until he was before
The house wherein the chickens slept.
A hole - inside - the kill - and out -
Away into the swamp.
He stood and watched
The young ones fill;
Lays down to rest and romp.
—*W. C. Hull*

Memorial To A Friend

God saw the road you tread upon
and knew the pain within.
The hills got steeper the valleys lower,
the battles you could not win.

Though many people would criticize
the way you lived your life
Jesus looked down upon you
and saw your heart and strife.

He heard your inward prayer
crying, someone save me please
Take me from this ruthless world
so I can have some peace.

On that day in autumn,
He graciously called you home.
For He knew there were more dangers
you could not face alone.

So, now my friend, you're with the Master
where all your tears are gone.
Only freedom, joy and peace in Him
and a place where you belong.
—*Heather Marratt*

Sleeping With The Angels

You've slept on the clouds for numerous years,
  and like an April sun shower
    your memory brings tender years.
My sentiments alive, I still feel we're one.
And I'm warmed by the thought that your blankets the sun.

Acres of my heart belong to you
  where the land is free and clear.
There's ample space for your colleagues to park
  their wings, from year to year.

To know that from sadness and from harm
  you are finally free.
Spending eternity with other angels
  oh, how I wish, I could see.

But, I'm content to envision
  the peaceful sight,
    of watching you slumber
      amongst the stars each night.
—*Laureen Buchner*

I Often Wonder When I Scan Your Face

I often wonder when I scan your face
And peer deep down into those sightless pools
If I, for just a day should take your place
And bravely don your baggage and your tools.
Would I with courage stride the darkened halls
Mid hoots and hollers of the noonday crowd
My hands outstretched for guidance from bare walls
And rattling locker, clad in steel cold shroud?
Would I with courage and a willing heart
Compete with those more gifted and more blessed
And yearn for light to shine within that part
That far too long in darkness has been dressed?
And would the Muses likewise give to me
The gift that makes the darkened eye to see?
—*Idris R. Hughes*

To Our Son

You stood alone atop the world,
And saw what God could see
From earthly vantage point, and He
With voice that whispered on the wind
Did tell of things gone by
And what is yet to be.

And then you turned and journeyed on.

You stopped to rest in alpine meadow
White with snow; with shadows
Stretching blue and rumpled 'cross the land.
You watched grey jays ghost by on silent wing,
And listened to the raven's raucous call,
And silence.

And then you turned and journeyed home.

And now, in land so warm and green,
You stand on mountain top in dream
And mem'ries of another time and place.
Content, you stand and watch the restless sea
Lap golden shore, and think of things gone by
And what is yet to be.
—*Mona J. Caukill*

Tender Love

When I see you at the shoreline
And the moonlight is glistening
Off every strand of your beautiful hair,
I feel tender love.

When you look at me
With those dark, hazy eyes
In the middle of my deepest, darkest troubles,
I can't help feeling tender love.

When I pull out a picture of you I haven't seen in years,
It is hard to but not notice that, at one time,
Those lips that are smiling back at me,
Were once pressed against mine,
And all that was going through our love struck minds was
Tender love.

And when you hold me for a while,
It is like everything in this troubled world does not matter.
And that every trouble I have ever imagined
Disappears to your, ever giving, ever hoping, ever lasting,
Tender Love.
—*Luc Robertson*

Because You Loved Me

You said you loved me,
And the world was filled with warmth,
And golden days, and azure skies,
And laughter melting on the breeze;
And happiness was everywhere I went,
Because you loved me.

You said you loved me when you went away;
'A holiday - that's all' was what you said.
And though my heart ached with the
pain of parting, I did not grieve. Because you loved me.

You said you loved me in the note you sent; the note tell me
That you did not mean to let her come between us.
It just happened. But you still loved me.

You said you loved me; but it is not I
Who stands beside you at the altar rail.
'The love that dare not speak its name'
Was ours to shout aloud
If only you had faced the world
And said you cared not what it thought.
Because you loved me.
 —*Jean Scott*

"The Name Of This Poem…? Whatever You Want To Call It."

You play games with life, you seem to think your games are fun.
And you can luck into an outrageous future of sex and money,
drugs and rock-n-roll. Well you're wrong!!!

The games you play are so carefree and irresponsible,
but without these elements, it wouldn't turn out
the way it's supposed to. You're afraid of life and
you hate the way it can keep your dreams—just dreams.

You pretend you don't give a damn, which throws
in a little excitement and intrigue. You think you can
mock life, but you know who's really mocking who.
It only makes you look more obvious,
That you're a scared little child, lost in the confusion
of the total meaning of life!!!!
Wipe away your tears, I'm not going to tell anyone.
You see I'm the only one who can see this.
So don't just sit there, deal me another hand. I love it,
this brilliant game!!! After all I invented it.
 —*Jody Jean Forward*

"Sailor's Prayer"

God bless our boat the captain said,
As each crew member bowed his head,
Bless all that sail her day and night,
And lead us by thy beacon light,
When near the shore the waters shoal,
And mountains seem to rise and roll,
Still we can feel thy presence near,
And rest contented in thy care,
When far from land on waters deep,
With much content may we find sleep,
And realize when stars shine bright,
That God our ever present light,
Still guides us through the peaceful night,
Content we know that God controls,
The destiny of our christian souls.
 —*David E. Andrews*

Peaceful Endeavors

The purity of the Earth envelopes my soul
As serenity sails swiftly throughout my mind.
It delivers to me a sense of peace
That this confusing world makes hard to find.
The Sun's rays gently kiss my skin,
Lingering listlessly to warm it.
Like a message from Heaven
It cures the cold, lonely spots.
Inner Goodness whole-heartily succumbs me.
His cool, calm love that is truly alive,
Holds steadfast to the depth of my soul,
Wishing His presents could forever survive.
 —*Karen Faryna*

The Protector

Her dark shadow dances against the wall,
as she clumsily undresses near the bed.
I, in admiration, allow my eyes to caress her softness,
while trying to stifle a smile.

Her hair brushes pass my lips as she lies next to me
and I move closer, the tiny body molding into my upper torso.
The heavy woolen blankets cause her to sweat,
so I hastily rub her forehead.

All the while whispering in her tiny ear,
'I love you, precious child. And always will.'

The quiet words stir her and she moves closer,
as if to understand, despite the slumber that's taken control.
She makes a funny sound and I smile,
sleep comes easy tonight.
 —*Rod Etheridge*

Entreaty

Winds of peace. Gentle winds,
as silent as lamb's kid
Fan the congested earth, we deplore.
Save the sweating earth,
with your breath as fresh as a face,
desert by undisturbed sleep.
Enrich all trees with abundant growth
as you make us grow stronger 'n richer
each day to care for the environment.
Let us see foliage jubilant.
and rich in health make them nod 'n shake
with abundant grace,
to your soft nudges 'n touches.

Winds of peace Gentle winds silent winds,
Extinguish fires that burn man's soul.
Immerse him in a river of love 'n compassion.
Lest, bloodlogged the earth becomes.
On grounds that rage let the captors
hear voices that plead for mercy.
 —*Helen Apolo Ocaya*

The Sea

As I gaze out into the vastness of the sea
I notice the colors on the horizon;
The fishermen's nets stare back at me in despair.
Blistered eyes filled with tears
Ask if there is more to life
Then being baptized into the sea day after day.
They grope for an exit to their useless existence
And find one in the rotting saltiness of…
The sea.
 —*Kevin Schellenberg*

Parallel Worlds

What once was a dream, is becoming a reality,
as the life inside kicks with such vitality.
Just an innocent child so anxious to explore,
so eager to learn life's mysteries and more.

The hours drag by as anticipation mounts,
in the end a healthy child is all that counts.
While miles away a starved infant dies,
and a helpless mother silently cries.

Once in my arms comfort and warmth will be yours,
whether the snow blows or if the rain pours.
While around the corner a lonely man is sat,
hoping for some spare change to be placed in his hat.

Please be happy and safe in the coming years,
and only shed those of joyful tears.
While just next door war is proclaimed,
greed and power to be blamed.

At long last we meet face to face,
the sound of your cry makes my heart race.
Around my breast your tiny lips are curled,
oh sweet baby, welcome to the world.
—*Lisa Marsh*

Your Place In Mine

Your sweetness shines through your heart,
as your gentle kisses can tell.
Your softness of your being
can be felt by your giving soul.
Your unspoiled ways are cherishable beyond reality
which makes your caring, loving ways more joyous to my heart
you bring light to darkness
by just a simple adoring smile.
You have poured your caring soul into the
empty bowl I call my life,
which I will be forever grateful.
'Cause I needed a spirit, lifting Angel
to carry me away to this place called love.
Which I hope you will join me forever.
'Cause you have now forever found,
Your place in my heart.
—*Larry Bursey*

The Friend Of Friends

Alone our Savior prayed at dark Gethsemane.
At Calvary, His precious blood he shed.
He rose triumphant from a rocky tomb
That you and I might live - when dead.

My Savior suffered untold agony
Upon that cross of bitter pain.
Once stripes were laid upon Him bare,
Salvation for you and me He'd gain.

Forsaken then by all His own,
His winning race below was run.
"It is finished," was His humble cry,
His mission to mankind was done.

They said, "The veil is rent in twain." Angelic voices filled
the air. "The Son of God comes Home to reign; of all the
kings, He's the most fair". Liberty, justice and truth are His
ways, Said to be past finding out. To set the captive's spirit
free Is the job that He's about. The Bible paints a picture
rare of God's redemptive plan for us. In prayer we seek Him
day by day, In quiet times we read it thus.
—*Stella MacEachern*

Rainbow Love

Across the sky was a wonderful pattern,
At this moment; I never felt happier,
I focused on a wish of mine.
To touch that rainbow in the sky,
Reality was setting in;
My level of endorphins, had skyrocketed again,
I felt in control of my heart once more,
I turned and walked out my door,
I knew you and I would again score.
As long as we keep our two feet on the floor.
—*Marie Welch*

Sun Shineth. Cometh Spring.

How mournful as she sits
balanced on the railing of her deck.
Underneath, the snow forms melted puddles on the grass.
She is still
and waiting
as the haunting steel guitar filters through her
cigarette smoke.
If you are quiet, you can watch her.
If you are still, she will never know.
How mournful as she sits.
—*Michelle Bechtel*

Hungry Child

   Please hungry child, dry your crying eyes,
because I feel the pain you have inside.
   Please hungry child in your world of sad and sorrow,
you are here today and maybe not tomorrow.
   Please hungry child in your underprivileged land
I can help if you just take my hand.
   please hungry child that is all skin and bone,
you will never make it on your own.
   Please hungry child full of heart ache,
I want to help you I will do what it will take.
   Please hungry child who's life is such a mess,
Why are you put through this awful test
   Please hungry child all full of sorrow,
I know that we can't wait until tomorrow.
—*Rita Davis*

And I Will Be Thankful

Bless me with health of mind and body.
Bless all my loved ones here and away.
Help us to learn the laws and the rules,
And adhere to them from day to day,
   And I will be thankful.

Bless me also with understanding
Of simple things that constitute love,
Like honesty, sincerity, doing one's duty
Guided by forces from up above,
   And I will be thankful.

Bless me with food to last out each day—
A chance to earn what is my right.
Bless me with a dry bed and soft pillow
To sleep and to dream away each night,
   And I will be thankful.

Bless me with appreciation of beauty
In souls encountered along the way.
Help me temper my daily labours
With a little laughter and a little play,
   And I will be thankful.
—*Vona Ruth Mallory*

A Memory Of A Friend

Each day she put on a smile
But beneath her she was hurting
No one seemed to really care
No one seemed to understand
The world only brought her sadness
And tears only came from her eyes
For she was a girl whom everyone loved
And a child who hid with lies
Even as her heart became smaller
And the love in it started to die
I still never knew, there was so much pain
Down deep inside
For I will always remember her
As a friend that gave me happiness
I just wished I could have helped
Before she had gone away and died

—*Kim Harold*

"My Special Plant"

I don't know why you took him, Lord,
but I know you had your reason.
You sowed a seed, I watched it grow,
You picked it in its season.

Some may say He grew like weeds,
wild and so free.
But this plant was a special plant,
and meant the world to me.

Yes, He was a special plant,
unique in his growing.
I nurtured him with love and care,
time for picking was your knowing.

One morn you reached and picked this plant,
He could no longer stay.
One heart-breaking day He went away,
my blue skies turned to gray.

My heart aches, Lord for my special plant,
the one it will always carry.
But if your picking has saved one other,
I feel like the Virgin Mary.

—*Carolyn Janowski*

The Lament Of A Man!

I want to be No. 1 all the time
But my wife doesn't understand me
And will not accede to my wishes
She's now gone from the ridiculous to the sublime
Because in terms of affection
I'm 16th in line after the goldfishes

She says I seek too much attention
I want my own way all the time
And don't help her at all in the house
But she obviously doesn't know
That her role in my life
Is to look after me, and be a quiet as a mouse

I'm not trained in housework
My mum did everything for me
And when left alone, I'm happy as can be
I just don't understand women
Why don't they apply logic like men
And just try to be as awkward as they can!

—*Eileen Turnham-Jones*

"World Of Silence"

The silence is always broken,
by the chisel of the wind - the crumbling of the leaves,
Roar of the thunder or by a hypersensitive sound
When I consider my silence. It's unaffected by sound
'Tis like I am locked in a sound proof loom,
To which there is no way out.
Where the walls are made of strong clear glass,
Through which I can see the birds chirping away
Flowers dancing by the wind. People talking.
but for I can never hear 'em.
'Tis like I am left to predicant silence
'Cause this imprisonment seems like immortality
Oh! how it makes me wonder, aren't natures sound meant for me
or are they only for ye - 'cause I am no different
and then why should I be deprived of sound - what crime did I commit.
Why was I sentenced to live in hell ......
Oh! I can only wish that someone would open the doors
and let me free so I too could hear the music that you hear.

—*Faiza Mahmood Mufti*

Stormy Day

Frantically I slide down the hill of dreams
Carrying a daily face, into the labyrinth of fingers, as you wish.

Into eyes I discovered nights
At the foot of the fountain I drew remorse
And it was so easy to see growing
The occult boundaries of life.

Shadows, tempests, impassable walls
I brought them down all, with hands of a master
And satanic precision

Slowly, I lay my eyes
Into the tumultuous look of skyscrapers
Ironically I void myself of everything
And silent, I keep until my voice frets.

I muse, I feel a giant sensation
Running through my muscles, to the roots of my cells
Fighting a psychological duel in me
I start counting, even the unattainable, as you wish.

I think, dream and forget so everything is inaccurate and crazy
Perchance fantasy... Dream, metaphysics, or pure realism

—*Ana Julia Macedo Sanca*

Fear Not.

There is no doubt,
Clear is the choice; CHRIST will they crucify.
Assent is given, - JESUS must die.
Love's gift DIVINE pays now the final price;
Vieved on a cross, - the sacrifice.
Apex of earthly woe, reprieve there's none,
Resigned is HE, - "...THY will be done."
Yielding the ghost, CHRIST now knows earthly death.

As darkness falls,
Trembling now, friends HIS body tend,
Ordained it was, - HE would descend.
Much fear of theft; the watch increase,
Buried and sealed, - the PRINCE OF PEACE,

But now behold!
Ethereal LIGHT outshines the sun,
Assuring all, - JESUS lives on.
Spiritual LIFE to all is given,
Truth has prevailed, - "The LORD is risen,"
Eternal faith now leads the WAY,
Rejoice in CHRIST, - HE is here to stay.

—*M. Monica Smith-Harder*

Fear

Blackest inner terrorism of feeling
   Clouding the mind and pounding
the heart, until your ears seek havoc in
straining, to suggest even the slightest
hint of sound,
   Pushing back, the very essence of,
bravery, to snuff it out and leave it to decay,
closing ever tighter, upon your rotting
languid being, to be an incursion that
to any hero is inconceivable,
   but yet to you, it seeps ever deeper to
dilate your irresolute horror stricken frame,
until, it reduces you to the state of a simpleton,
Coagulating any capacity to assert what
infinitesimal atom of vigilance that once was
yours, now, only to leave you and a skulking,
cowardly, degraded particle of nothingness,
   as you tremble with fear.
     —*Karen M. Keil*

A Toronto Harbour Cruise

Centre Island approaches, dusk has begun.
Coloured lights glow and mosquitos hum.
The sun's dying rays 'round the Skydome creates
A halo of gold which shimmers and vibrates,
Turning the scene to a colourful dance.
Mother Nature knows best how to enhance.

New moon slowly rises in a mauve and blue setting.
We pass a marina, boats quietly resting.
Bird Island appears, ducks preen and dive
In safety and serenity, trees either side.
Fluffy pink and white clouds swiftly float past.
A good omen for the morrow is surely cast.

As the sky darkens, shore lights blaze.
Stars try to twinkle - competition is great.
Splendour in the sky, reflections on the lake.
A cruise to recall when time we can take
To ponder upon the spectacular sights
Of Toronto Harbour at night.
     —*Audrey M. Fiteni*

The Box

   It's there, in the back corner of my mind.
Covered with dust and cobwebs,
   I've stored it away, to forget.
Years have passed and I'm still running,
   From life, from myself, from "the box."
I forget how to feel, but not how I felt.
All of my memories of being a child are inside.
You can try to understand, you can try to help,
   But you'll never get close enough to see, "the box",
I have bound up with chairs, and locked
   with locks and labeled "kindly do not disturb"....
     I continue to run.
     —*Kimberly Baldwin*

Unity

Love take my lips with thine own
And sip the wine that passion will bestow,
But love if thou has not found heaven as thy home
Then thou must part and let me go;
For in the wind there dost blow
The sweet white rose, not yet come to bloom
And my heart waits for the pure white rose
To mingle with the red above thy tomb.
Only then will our hearts join together
In a love that will surely last forever!

White rose buds meaning a heart ignorant of love
White and red rose meaning unity.
     —*Susan Nichols and Amber Raye*

A Voice In The Darkness

A voice in the darkness, all alone
Crying out for someone, someone to hold
But nobody's there, I'm just crying alone
I keep looking for an angel, trying to be bold

Wait, look on the horizon, there is a glimmer of hope
The sun is rising, there is an angel of hope
The angel is looking to find a friend
Someone to be happy with to the end

With the warmth of the rising sun, a new beginning
A new period in time to bring change and happiness
To build a friendship that is warm and loving
A creation that will be strong and timeless
     —*Kelvin Pearson*

Poverty

Poverty is my demon its evil,
Decadent presence penetrates my walls of perseverance
And casts me down into a rubble heap of despair
I tell myself there is hope and I am constantly in prayer
This persistent demon grins in unholy glee-"Who am I fooling?"
I am nowhere I am society's plague I live on welfare

Hell is my fire of unspent and undying rage. I find nowhere to
earn a wage, my children cast in the fire with me and ignorance
with its red tape imps call out our numbers. The numbers of
the beast that eliminates humanity and delegates what one is
entitled to even if it is inadequate

You must beg before the anti-christ called policy
If you bow down, worship, crawl and give in
A mere pittance of the material world you win, but you will
lose your spiritual soul
Its burned out shell this demon will suck dry
Spitting all your fallen values back in your eyes

I will wrestle with poverty perhaps to my dying day
I know who I am. My wealth is my health and strength
I will not allow poverty to take this away!!!
     —*Madeline Spurrell*

Broken Tears

Just because the morning sunrise silently slips, away,
Does that mean it cannot speak, cannot touch, has nothing
to say?

Just because the wind beats angrily against your face,
Does that mean there is no quiet, silent resting place?

Just because the voice of winter repeats its song,
Does that mean there is no hope forever, the music is gone?

Just because Indian summer is the shadow of fall,
Does that mean we forget to see the Artist in it all?

Just because you cannot hold time in your hand,
Does that mean you stop seeking, searching to understand?

Just because someone told you broken tears cannot mend,
Does that make it true? Answer me... answer me my friend.
     —*Sharon Mae Clark*

Autumnal

Living day by day is wise,
Declared the old man. Dusty lies
The way ahead, and steep. But here
It's peaceful, and the air is clear.
This height I've reached is not, true, where
In former years I thought to dare,
But far enough. I am content
To rest, and watch the slow ascent
Of others past those rocks which seem,
Surmounted, nothing but a dream.
     —*Del Pine*

A Sign Of Trust

She's a regular visitor
Each day she sees me
We share our breakfast
Our lunch and our tea
Her blue gown of feathers
Trimmed with some white
Tells me that nature
Has had great foresight.

This visitor chirps loudly
If food's not right there
She knows I sit watching while rocking my chair
We've come to a bargain
Just me and my friend
She'll trust me to feed her, and visits won't end.

So each day I place carefully
A cracked-open nut, and soon there comes chirping
My friend full of strut.

"I thank you," she sings, as she sets for her flight
And tomorrow I'll trust you
To see baby's first flight.
—*Eleanor Fitzgerald*

Emotions

As she winds her way along the lonely beach called life,
emotions come and go like the waves of the sea

Sometimes she feels tense as they build and grow, swelling
and cresting into a gigantic wave that fills all her vision
and appears to block all avenues of escape

The wave envelopes her and tries to overwhelm her will to survive
It tries to pull her back into the ocean of oblivion as she
clings with great inner strength and determination to something
on the shoreline

The waves lash unrelenting trying to tire her and suck her
physically, emotionally and spiritually of the will to live

But again and again her struggles to survive and gain purchase
in her quest for high ground and safety win as the waves of
emotion lose their intensity and strength and skitter away
almost as though they are afraid of her or form little pools of
discontent that they hope will trip her up along her path
The waves reflect searing glances of rage from reflected
sunshine as they realize that they will never again control her.
—*Lawrence John Seliski*

The Proud Feelings Of A Parent.

Ever since the day that you were born. Our feelings and
emotions were often torn. for you which was the right thing
and which was wrong which would make you smart and which
wouldmake you strong. we wondered about what you would be
And couldn't wait for the time to see. Now that the time is here
and your all grown I'm glad you listened to good advice and
helpful things you were shown. you sure turned out the best we
could have hoped for And god gave us one of his best, of that
we're sure. Now the time for you to find your own life is
near. we have no doubt's or any fear, That you will make us as
proud. as you can. for the child we raised so proud, is now a
graduated man. made for graduation to my son.
—*Elaine Barrington*

The Parting Of a Relative

Here's a little poem, I thought you'd like to hear.
  Especially for you because you are so dear.
Here's a little poem, to brighten up your day.
  To remind you that you're loved in every little way.
Here's a little poem, I wrote from within my heart.
  Wishing we were closer now and not so far apart.
Here's a little poem, to open up your mind
  Let peaceful things enter and warmth you'll find.
I'll be with you in thoughts and dreams,
  And at your side one day.
To let you know I care and help in anyway.
  So anytime you need some help,
    To get you through the day.
Just open up my poem, and read the words I say.
Memories are what we have, to hold us all so close,
  And take the time to help each other
    when it's needed most.
So there's my little poem, I thought you'd like to hear.
  Especially for you because you are so dear.
—*Delby McLean*

The North Sky

The sought blazed with molten orange as the sun showed its face
          ever so briefly.
    The north sky lightened from black to deep blue
        And the whisper went through the village:
            The sun is up!
            The sun is up!
          Come quickly and see
          Before it is gone.

  The sky returned to black but the world remained grey
      As the snow let off a light of its own.
        Then as I looked up I delighted to see:
            Green flashes!
            Blue streaks!
        Wavering and whispering,
          Proudly proclaiming,
     This is the land of the North!
—*Janet Barbin*

The Day I Began To Understand

I remember seeing a small girl. Her clear, bright, youthful
eyes were now filled with confusion. She could not understand
her mothers' hollow stares, blank looks, despite their
conviction, their determination. She could not understand
their always dirty fingernails. Even in photos, dirty
fingernails.

In my mind this small girl becomes an old man. I see him
standing in front of the store window. He's looking at himself,
his reflection, at his life. His see-through jacket does
nothing to the bitter wind. His hands are raw, knuckles white
grasping his empty coffee mug, dreaming of its fullness. He's
screaming at what he sees, arguing with his reflection,
fighting with his life.

This old man becomes a goldfinch perched on the budding branch
high above the Earth. His screaming now becomes its singing;
soft, sweet singing. It sings of new joy. New pain, but more
of new joy - of life. Its yellow brilliance tells me life can
be sung.
—*Chris Slosser*

Just Once

Tom gallops as
fast as two legs
reluctantly will carry an
eleven year old eternally
pursuing the back of the last
player in wind sprints.

Like a punchy boxer, he hunches at
the far end of the batter's box, swinging
and ducking (all in one motion) from
fast balls he's convinced are aimed at him.

Fly balls and grounders are like
negatively charged magnets dancing
from his similarly charged glove.

Just one, he scoops up a
screaming grounder -
like dew off grass - and
stamps a kilo of dust from
second base for an out.

Heaven.
—*Garry Ryan*

A Lost Friend

A candle
flame burnt out
A speck of sand
blown high above the most barren desert
Feeling as though I'm stuck in the middle
of this desert
inclosed in a black box on wheels
knowing I've just a pint of gas
On a long endless highway
But the road goes on and the gas I've got
Should make up for what I ain't got
I have no more
A lost friend
—*Howard T. W. Hyde*

Dreams. . . . .

When we are kids we dream of being able to...
fly the highest kite, eat chocolate cake for breakfast,
ride a bike faster than the wind, find a long lost treasure
growing up and leaving home....

When we are teenagers we dream of.....
having the fastest car, falling in love, being a rocket
scientist or veterinarian or breeding race horses,
being the most popular kid at school....

When we are adults we dream of....
success in our chosen career, financial status displayed in
faster, cars, larger houses, exotic trips,

When we grow up we dream of.....
finding someone special to spend the rest of our lives with,
someone to love, honour and cherish, of building a home, filled
with laughter and love and filling our lives with friends to
share all the blessings and disasters life throws our way.
—*Deborah Harris*

I No Po.t(e nigmatic)

I no a po.t (e dam)son
for no medicines spill or splendor
as they are craved or demanded
by my sick slate of facuet he)art roots.
I am merely a balsam potion, mixed
by a whirlpool of calamity &
stirred by an imaginary belt
of stainless rust,
to be pass)aged & funnelled with my
us)ed en)liven lives
because I
need so gravely.
and my ambush of antiseptic riddles lends
athristly
to her (anot h)is
sin)cere cloth)ed ema)native fee)lings
as aspiranian antidotes.
he and his genuine rapture
a)lone forever swell
in my silent horror.
—*Kenneth J. Trenholm*

A Wish

Here I lie all alone,
For now in this place I will call my home.
My family and friends come to see me every day,
And they show their love for me in every way.
God's birds will set me free,
Out of this place where I don't want to be.
But I will fight right to the end,
Through a thousand white doves God will send,
His power and love to make me better,
Then friends won't have to write another letter.
For I will then be free to go?
Where everyone soon will know,
She's well, she's well they will all say,
Then I won't have to fight another day.
—*Jennifer Lynn Cywink*

Count Your Blessings

For the wonder of a morning's sunrise,
For the dew on grass so, green;
For the brilliance of an evening's sunset,
For the beauty of all nature's scenes—
   Count your blessings.

For springtime with all life anew,
For summer's growth and splendor;
For autumn's burst of colors bright,
For winter's sparkle and grandeur—
   Count your blessings.

For a baby's first angelic smile,
For childhood's joys and tears;
For laughter and love of growing youth,
For wisdom gained in adult years—
   Count your blessings.

If you have enjoyed such pleasures,
If you've remembered your fellow men;
If you've helped those less fortunate,
If you can give a kindly hand—then
   Count your blessings.
—*Wes Goldsmith*

Mamma, Cried

An old lady sat in the corner, alone in her rocking chair.
Four days and four nights she had sat there, but she no longer
cared. She had asked her children over, but they had too much
to do, to come and sit with the old folks, for it seemed to
make them blue.

Well, now they needn't bother, for she passed away that night,
with many thoughts running through her head, of when things
seemed alright. Her eyes would light with happiness, when
she'd see them coming in. She'd do her best to please them, and
what memories they'd bring, of days when she'd felt better and
could run and play with them, when her little ones were close
to her, and how, she had loved them.

Two weeks went by before I knocked, upon her kitchen door.
There were no smiles, there were no laughs, my tears fell to
the floor. So now, I've told my story, and I have a mom no
more. So children, please don't be like me; go knock upon her
door. She's sitting there so lonesome, put laughter in her
eyes, listen to her stories, don't come, when she has died.

—*Earlene Hintz*

A Youthful Vision

Virgin untouched land, wild, yet free
free from all pollution
All, that is now gone
Took the hands of the land, kissed good-bye
Blindfolded

Not a savage side at all, simple? Maybe
not savages!
Once we were united and together.
Family oriented through verbal teachings
Happy and satisfied,
great love and respect for our Mother earth

Ceremonies include secret societies
Mask, dance and song.
Dedication, fellowship, by the means of giving
and receiving
Wealth and richness, respect and chieftainship gained
Fishing and hunting, seasons change
as did the food, one for all and all for one.
Not a single space for selfishness

A hard working united group
of civilized people we once were!

—*Dallas Pootlass*

Ride The Wind

Ride the wind, oh mighty one, pass through my weary soul,
give to me that which you took, so many years ago.
I've waited long, I've suffered much,
I've searched both far and wide,
for that tiny piece of my heart you stole,
the night your body died.
Oh how I broke, the Earth it shook,
the life was sucked from me.
I cried, I raved, I chased 'Great Death'
but I could not break free.
So, I set out upon the road that life had lain for me,
wanting but to end it's course so I could be with thee.
But-
Life is strange, it's course is long,
at times I lost my way.
I never thought I'd get to you, I never thought I'd say,
that I am glad I walked my road, it's well it's at an end
but I come to you, both wise and true
and calling life my friend.

—*Linda Mailhot*

Key West

Parasailing, or snorkeling
From a 30 foot Catamaran.
90. miles to Cuba,
If you want to go that far.

Ernest Hemingway slept here,
His cats still do.
And many lowly travellers
Who stop to soak up the sun.

See the 'gators and the sharks
Or ride the train. No matter,
Everywhere you'll see vendors
Selling shell jewellery and t-shirts.

Take the turnpike to Key Largo.
Visit the Latin Denny's. Have a gyro.
Enjoy the view along the overseas highway;
450 miles both ways.

Take it all in before you leave
Have a drink on the pier.
But walk on the beach and count the stars
They're much brighter here than at home.

—*Nicole Holas*

Simple, Pure, Free

Daddy, daddy!
Give me your love in a gentle hug,
In a sweet kiss smack on my cheek.
Let me be free to be a child...
I don't like grown-up love as between two lovers.
I want to be me!
Hand in hand enter my world.
I love - sunbeams filtering through our kitchen
window on a warm summer day.
I love - raindrops splish, splash on my nose and cheeks.
I love - the gentle breezes of summer feathering my hair.
A daddy's love is found in -
Listening, I have story to tell.
Caring, help me get a drink I'm thirsty.
Take my hand and let's walk together -
You in your adult world reaching down to understand
my child world...
Simple, pure, free.
Love me as a daddy and I'll love you as a daughter...
Proud of her father!

—*Barb Clark*

Conscience

There's a man who lives within my mind a critic on my shoulder.
He makes my judgement cruel and harsh he makes my outlook colder.

He turns my friends into my peers he puts all them on trial.
And hides the wrongs that I commit in bitter sweet denial.

He stops me from taking chances and makes those who do unfit.
To keep within my company and those who are close knit.

He sits upon my shoulder and keeps the poor delusion.
That my morals are intact and I do not practice exclusion.

We all know this man very well and have one of our own.
Who forms our justice and morals with a faultless heart of stone.

To free yourself from his control the next time you feel contempt.
Do not dismiss those who you see, do not be harsh, accept.

—*Gregg Shanks*

Carbon Monoxide Is Poison

I feel so sad.

He shot himself.
He took a sawed-off shot gun, and shot himself.
Right through the heart.

Not because of the battered police cars in his wake.

Desperation - cornered - trapped.

Because he ran out of gas.

To keep moving, he took a logging truck,
Not meant for public highways.
And Between Duncan and Victoria.
Brought down every power line in his way.

I didn't know him well.
He was a neighbors son.
Just a bright and smiling face.
A cheerful. Hi - Pauline

He shot himself
He took a sawed-off shot gun and shot himself.
Right through the heart.

Because he ran out of gas.
—*Pauline Good*

We Know He's There

The dew is dried by his gentle touch, as he passes by,
He wipes the tears we all tend to cry.
At night while we slumber, and all dream together.
He brushes away the clouds, with a powerful feather.
We awake to his scent, to his newness and flare,
And recollect times we've all had to share.
With sun shining brightly, his powerful gusts.
Give us warnings of our adultered lusts.
Slowly he retreats, from the hills and the valleys,
To rapidly invade holes in the alleys.
Calmly he comes,
Abruptly he goes,
We all know he's there,
Every time he blows...
—*Steve Tripp*

Trapped

I came upon the fox this morn; his freedom gone
His foot was torn and held so tight
That in his fright with all his might
He tried to break away and flee; his eyes beheld his enemy
And therein shone a fear so bright; oh how he longed to be in flight
And I shall not forget the sight
Of human carelessness so cold
To leave unchecked this trap of death; for him to suffer with each
 breath
And with his strength finally gone; to spend last lonely hours alone
With birds of prey circling high just waiting for the fox to die
The truth cannot be left untold
But maybe man will yet behold a better way to earn his gold
Remove this curse from nature's friends
This pain and plunder without end
That has continued for too long; we must admit that this is wrong.
—*James Abram*

Illusion

His eyesight is dim yet how clearly he sees.
His hearing betrays the soft whispering muse.
Each morning denies the limbs stirring ease,
Old Martyn waits!

As daybreak ignites the spirits depart.
No deliberate meander amongst mortal undefended.
Aspire yet to deliver this unwilling heart,
Old Martyn waits!

Fourscore and ten have long been abandoned.
His senses assimilate past understandings.
Compliance to deed yet chosen at random,
Old Martyn waits!

Old Martyn waits! The brilliance grows stronger.
The pattern is ended; the search triumphant.
Souls delight with success adrift no longer,
Illusion complete.
—*Gillian McConnachie*

He Has Gone Home

He is the king of rock and roll.
His music would touch your very soul,
Born in Tupelo in 35.
One of a twin to survive
With his guitar in his hand,
He sang and travelled throughout the land
He was handsome and debonair
He loved his friends and he did care
He was loved by thousands that's no doubt.
His great entertainment brought this about
And then one terrible, tragic day
Elvis Presley passed away
He's gone home with God on high
We didn't get a chance to say goodbye.
And as the breezes softly blow
We must now let Elvis go.
We love you Elvis from our hearts
It's so sad we had to part.
—*Beverley Erwin*

My Past Time

Baseball is the game of choice when springtime comes around
hit and run and catch and slide and clothes turn green and
brown then spring blends into summer, and the diamond is hard
with dust a game of scrub or pick-up is surely a daily must

The summer days are lazy and the morning is fresh and sweet
I can't wait to put my glove on and feel the bases beneath my
feet to hold the bat and stand so proud is my favorite baseball
thing cause when I'm up at the plate I feel like I'm the king

Some eyes watch the pitcher, some eyes look around then all
eyes are watching me, to hear the great CRACK sound

Then it starts to rain, and we hope it passes by we really hate
to leave, but we also want to stay dry

So we scatter in all directions to homes of friends nearby and
we stare out of every window, as the rain falls from the sky

For the other team it didn't matter, they were losing 5 to 1
but for me and my friend Scotty, it meant the game was done

We'll go out again tomorrow and every time we can after that
until its too cold for catching, I'll put away my bat

We'll sit and talk with our friends of the fun that summer long
as the birds migrate overhead, we await their new spring song.
—*Richard Durocher*

To Be Blinded

Not understanding not knowing how you feel,
How could I have thought our love was real.
We never talk like we did before,
Things just aren't the same any more.
We only talk when you feel it's right,
I wait around but you don't phone at night.
You act as if I'm to blame,
When you're the one whose not the same.
I trusted you like I'd never before,
But you let me down I can trust you no more.
People warned but I was too blind to see,
Just what it was you were doing to me.
But now I see just what they mean,
And wonder, why in my eyes it couldn't be seen.
—*Chantel Ware*

Jesus Can You Tell Me?

Do you love me?
I asked Jesus one day.
Or is that something you'd rather not say?
If the answer is behind a locked door please give me the key

Jesus, when you love, why do you give your love for free?
Guide me towards your light and show me the way.
Give me the strength to make the world happy and gay.
And please also, help me to also give my love for free.

Jesus, I don't know why you love.
You are God's only son,
You are the beloved.

You are as pure, so graceful, like a dove.
In your eyes, love is nothing but fun.
Your love is the greatest gift that comes from above.
—*Melinda MacNeil*

Church Bells At Dawn

I was fine with my life until this day
I fell to my knees, screamed, prayed...
"My Christ! My Christ!
What have you done to this life?"
And the whole room turned holy.

I was aware of my needs until this night
I fell upon bended knee with shiny, sharp knives...
"My soul! My soul!
What have you done with this control?"
And the whole room turned holy.

Upon waking from my affair with death
I stood and promptly took a bow.
Then once again lay down to rest
where the Earth and grass is plowed.

I will rise to this occasion
I will rise and greet you well
I will rise at the dew of dawn
and at the ringing of church bells.
—*Karen Buechler*

Untitled

Like gentle rain
Falling softly on the parched earth
You came into my life
Bringing with you
Quiet strength and joy
Nurturing the desert of my soul
With the well-spring of your love
Causing a profusion of wild flowers to bloom
In the aired sands of my heart.
—*Jo Ann Morgan*

Bracken Ice

Beached again,
I had been swimming with flotsam friends.
Soon,
Even they will be pushed to shore.

The whale,
His shadow-leeches,
Moist bent-wood.
(Soon dried, mounted and saddened)

All I touched and pressed against,
Soon,
They will be seen and heard,
Mournful.

The water will smother.
Look accusingly at each other,
Wonder,
How?

Here's a driftwood-dream,
Push me to God's lake.

I feel my throat crushing.
—*Paul Llew-Williams*

My Father's Memory

The stories told by my father no one will ever replace
I just can't wait to see him again face to face
One story I'll always remember that in 1948
The R.C.A.F. Flyers hockey team brought a gold medal back to Canada
For all of us to appreciate
It was a great accomplishment for my father
I know he was very proud
He did play hard for Canada
For a very triumph crowd
The hockey Hall of Fame did remember
For the Olympic team picture will always remain
In the hearts of many admirers
In the Civic Centre walk of fame
Some day when our fine Senators
Will gain honor just like them
Maybe their picture will hang proudly
  In the new Paladium
To say Hey! Weren't they great Canadians.
—*Cheryl Corrigan*

Empty Space

As I was walking down the street one day,
I looked around me and noticed-
  Nobody was there.
Just empty space beside me,
  Nothing coming near.
I'm used to being alone,
  But not to being lonely.
The empty space sometimes soothes me,
  Showing that I am okay.
But when that empty space breathes cool air on my neck,
I realize that I need someone to fill my empty space.
Now whenever I'm walking and there is nobody there,
I pretend that you are warming the cool air falling on my neck.
—*Gianna Lampitt*

My Autumn

The wind blows.
I love it!
The sky is so blue!
I sit
And watch the wonder of nature
as she wipes the face of her nature
world clean
Of leaves, now dead, from summer past;
and smoky smells that never last
long enough to satisfy my wanting, and longing.
I'm getting older! It's frightening.
Often now, I wonder how long before the seasons
and I mix in a jumbled atmosphere;
And everything's gone; everything dear.
—*Vickey Davis*

Just For Me

You are to me a dream come true,
I love your face your eyes so blue.
Your smile lights up my heart and life.
I wish things were different and you'd
make me your wife.

I sit at home...
All alone
I think of you and start to moan.
I love you so my knight of knights
My heart for you beats fast as light.
Your my protector my lover my friend.
I'll love you right to the very end.
Our nights and days we must always steal.
Cause love like this just can't be real.

So my love, when the time is right
We say our goodbyes and good nights.
If sometime in the future, are paths do cross
I'll look at you and see just what I lost...
But in my heart you'll always be...
A beautiful memory... Just for me.
—*Cynthia Lynn Stacinski*

A Tale Of The Quayside

Down by the Quayside.
I saw an old crone
She sat all alone
On the cold, "Weeping stone".

Her head it was bent
And she seemed forlorn
In her cloak, all tattered and torn,
Wondering I'm sure why she'd been born.

As I approached,
She moved her head,
So very slightly, then she said,
"How I'd love to be a bed".

I bade her, "Goodnight,"
And she muttered low
Then with failing strength, she tried to go,
Off into the mist and the fast falling snow.

I ran up beside her
And gave her my hand,
Then we walked together, in that wonderland
In perfect peace and silence so grand.
—*Helen Allan*

The Desert

I have wandered the desert for a thousand years.
I see a tree and cautiously move toward it.

An oasis.
The water is pure, the shade cool, the dates sweet.
But the sting of the sidewinder and scorpion drive me away.

Time drifts by.
More trees loom in the distance.

This oasis is truly beautiful.
The lush greenery and aromatic air intoxicate my mind.
I try to draw near but sharp rock and cactus hold me at bay.

I roam the desert, a ghost among the dunes.
More trees on the horizon.
Guarded hope again creeps into my soul.
My eyes deceive me though
they are an illusion of ancient dreams.

I reach the end of the desert
Thirst finally exacts its toll.
I fall and rise into the glory of the mountain twilight.
—*Robert Choquette*

As I Grow...

As I grow among the weeds, the flowers and the dust
I see the starfish lying lifeless, sad and dead to us.
I walk the walk of many before and dream of...
We'll I'd tell you but you'd think me strange to rattle
thoughts about the page and think they'll come together.
I sing in my mind, it sounds bad otherwise.
I love the clothes he wears.
They hate to groups who are smaller than they
But the groups are together as one. One
Yes, just as one.
I fall behind and watch it all, the birds still dance
And the babies fall into the water
And they drown.
The mother put their nest above a pool that
Was empty in the spring. Now it's full.
I see the world. They say it spins but I
Don't think I do.
I am still, like the starfish on the beach
A star, but anonymous.
—*Andrea Stone*

The Endless Night

I am all alone as the clock strikes two,
I toss, I turn, I think of you.
I wonder where you are tonight,
Enclosed in my dark tunnel without any light.

The frightening shadows bounce across the wall,
Taunting my lonely existence, there is no one to call.
Images of you dance across my mind,
I am locked in with these memories, there is no key to find.

I relive all the moments that we once shared,
Wanting to call, to hear your voice, if only I dared.
Will I ever truly be free from this pain?
Will my nights forever be filled with black clouds and rain?

This aching need feels so fresh and new,
No matter how hard I try all I think of is you.
I bite my lip, I won't let myself cry
I want to spread my wings and learn how to fly.

This kaleidoscope of emotions assault my mind,
On this long endless night where there is no peace to find.
My world without you is too much to bear,
Knowing as I do, how little you care.
—*Mari Van Horne*

Lady In The Darkness

Standing right before my eyes
I touch a goddess in disguise.
You make me sparkling and alive
Let's go into the twilight and watch the tide.
Catch the midnight butterflies in cupped hand
Make castles and bridges in the sand.
Live on the ocean riding at night
Crashing, churning, guided by a pillar of light.
Sending out signals to our lost humanity,
Facing a ticking clock called sanity.
I see you waving in the distance
Trembling slightly but sturdy stance.
Shadows and faces passing through
An eternity of pain swept away by you.
 —*Renee Stoddart*

Harley

When you first came into my boring life
I was a lonely, empty, sad person
You where very sick and slept all the time
But when you awoke you made me happy
Your inner light made my life worth living
I would not let you go for hours on end
Soon you learned how to walk short distances
And make cute noises with your little mouth
But I knew that it would not last forever
Soon you had to go to another house
And be cared for by more loving people
When you left my life went dark once again
I wish that I could have one more hour
To bask in the light of your warm, kind love
 —*Paul Lemay*

Dare To Dream

Before I had a dream before I had a vision
I was getting by but I wasn't really living
I'd left my aspirations in the dust behind
And in melancholy comfort
I didn't even mind

I'd never be a singing star or playboy centerfold
Race a snazzy foreign car or cure the common cold
I wasn't called a failure I could look you in the eye
My error was of omission
I didn't even try

Then vicarious living through others began to take it's toll
I wasn't dead and buried I wasn't even old
So from musty hope chest memories a dream I resurrected
I would neither pass nor fail
But my chutzpah would be tested

I'd submit my words to paper for my peers critique
For to see my work in print was the dream I dared to seek
And should I gain renown my heart will swell in pride
But regardless of the outcome
I can say "I tried"
 —*Elaine Fischer*

Untitled

Shining stars twinkling so bright —
 His playing the beauty of the night
Thoughts of you and all that you are
 Far surpasses the highest star.

Finding each other was meant to be
 You were chosen, especially for me —
My eyes fill up with joyful tears
 Cause you are mine and I have no fears —
I have you close, here in my heart
 I'll always love you till death do us part!
 —*Theresa Benford*

Time

When I went to sleep last-night I
 I was sixteen
When I woke this morning I was
 sixty.
Is this what they call the changing
seasons? Or have I let my life slip by
 unnoticed?
Last night I went to the Prom.
When I woke this morning I was alone.
As I lay there and realized how fast my
 life has flown,
I will not grieve, for I still have memories
 of a better life I've known.
 —*Lyla Byers*

The Rose

Petals as though made of satin caress my fingertips.
If I am not careful I will have blood drawn by a
 thorn.
Sensitive flowery buds amuse my eyes.
It is for that reason that I nourish it.
Ever so gently keeping its perfection.
The roots are like the soul of a person.
Running deep, forever constant, forever beautiful.
The rose is mine to keep forever.
Without the rose I am without love.
 —*Robert Lee*

Controversies

As I sit here and take a good look around I wonder
if there is hope left to be found.
The poverty and the despair, seems to be contagious
through out all of our air...
I have no idea as to how I've made it this distance,
considering most society; greets you with manmade resistance.

Along with the frustrations and the anger, that's coated with
such depression that the mind and body no longer function as
one but two separate entities struggling to get back in sync
before our time is done. Soon the reason to go on, to pick
yourself up, dissipates and has become all but baron. The
emptiness has conquered us all, for we have failed to break
down the wall.

All is not lost as long as there is a chance, to go forward
instead of going back, with the willpower to choose to advance.
Now that I have had my say, I've regained the strength to face
yet another "questionable day."
 —*Lynne Harper Mallory*

To Write A Poem

'Twill be a simple task, I thought, this writing of a poem.
I'll simply write the words that come into my mind:
And then I'll change some lesser words, for words
That say a lot, that mean a lot,
That have a lovely sound.
But I am quickly finding out
That choosing words with lovely sounds is not the only task.
It's more than that!
It's searching, grasping, gingerly trying to find the words-
Oh yes those words-
That emphatically portray
What I am trying to say.
And then another thing;
If I can somehow find a way to match those words
To the deepest thoughts that lie embedded in my dormant brain
I will have won. I will have achieved.
This is poetry!
 —*Henrietta Scholten*

Another Spring

The chinook wind comes blowing from the hills,
In the valley it will still give you the chills.
  All the bubbling creeks are now on the rise,
A flash flood from the river will come as a surprise.
  The magpie is in her nest warming her eggs,
The calf moose is trying out his new wobbly legs.
  Out of the lakes, the fish head out to spawn,
In the meadow bounces a new born fawn.
  Hear the screech of an eagle over head,
The cow elk is still lying in her bed.
  The bears will be coming out of hibernation.
All the young will start a new generation.
  The geese are heading up the valley and beyond,
Ducks are swimming around the beaver pond.
  Buttercups can be seen all around,
As the new grass is coming up through the ground.
  A squirrel scampers down a mossie log,
Red winged blackbirds are on cat tails in the bog.
  New life is forming for everything,
Cause it is the starting of another spring.

   —*Lorne Cochran*

Mercy

  Nowhere on earth is a place to hide,
In whatever thing you have done,
  Not a single inch can be hidden,
In the eyes of the Lord.

  Its natural for people to sin,
They're guided by their emotion,
  Its hard for them to hold,
When they're surrounded by temptation.

  WE'RE given faith by God
To make a foundation,
  Making it great and strong,
To guard us from being tempted,
  By bad influence on our path.

  People wanted to see the world,
How they looked from the outside and inside,
  Canvassing in every way,
Not knowing they go astray.

  God is just waiting for them,
To remember the faith that He gave, wanted them to call
  For help, for mercy is just above their head.

   —*Socorro Ch. V. Trinidad*

Settling Light

When a light glows, does it call to you?
Is it warmth you feel?
Does it pull you towards center stage?
Does it cover you like a down quilt on a star frost night?

Can you leave?
When a light glows in the dark of mind
Do you follow close or fall behind?
Do you reach and grow?
Or meet that all time low? I want to know

Can you leave? When you touch that light
Is it wrong, is it right?
Are you weak with fright?
Alone, so alone with the glow that will not let go

Can you leave?
After glow, how does it set with you?
Is it soft, is it cold? Is it young, is it old?
Do you get to the place beyond?
What is there? Something you can share?
And answer please…Can you leave?

   —*R M Mackay*

Oh Christmas Tree

Oh Christmas tree with the lights burning bright,
It can be seen in the distance on the darkest night.
Surrounded by packages of red, blue and green,
Waiting their turn when the daylight beams.

"Come one, come all," it seemed to say,
Enjoy my beauty, be merry and gay.
Only once a year this warmth I feel,
Read your cards by my light with the
Christmas seal!

   —*Audrey Bushey*

Silence

Silence is like a gunshot heard late in the night,
it cuts through your heart deep like a knife.
When wrong words are spoken, they wound like weapons,
so what will I do keep silent or ruin my life.
If I choose silence my anger will build and my
heart will harden.
If I choose to speak my life will end.
I will choose silence, like I have before, but the
day will come when I can't stay silent anymore.
When that day comes a line will be drawn and
I'll be erased from the board like a pawn, but maybe
my words will be heard and the silence be broken.
Until then I will hide behind my vail of silence
and be safe from the violence of the world
beyond my bedroom door.

   —*Tara Leitch*

The Middlefield

The middlefield is calling from Eden's den.
  It is neither loud nor strong but
Glistening marks its woeful trail.
  It has eaten noiseless insults and
Can never be advanced along the
  Metal clasp again, until vanity.
Long strings have knotted, disregarding
  Time until it's return to exile.
Harboring the past, judgments have melted
  Words long due but as yet unbidden.
Can you hear its' power song, full of
  Welcome and blank paper?
Despair if not, because its' ages are
  Infinite and flesh tires all too soon.
Someday unravelment will come to say
  And the bleeding will close.
And the middlefield will welcome
  The knock of the shaded door.

   —*Sean Dennis*

Time

Time walks over shifting sand,
It means nothing to anything but man
Time to catch the bus and off to school
No time to watch clouds or play the fool.

Time to do a special line of work
To be a driver, a teacher, or short order cook.
The child yearns to be sixteen
To hurry up and know what life will mean.

It's just a step to having a life and home.
Now all this time has come and passed.
You have reached the golden years at last.

Time walks on into space
Leaving loving ripples on your face.
I am so glad I knew
This walk with time and you.

   —*Lucille Mossman*

The Lighthouse

It stands bold, like an old oak tree Whiter than white it seems,
Looming high above me, Its eye is silent, only a gleam.

I look across the ocean wide, As I stand upon the sandy
beach This place has not a thing to hide, Only points
I cannot reach.

A revolving beam that pierced the night An answer to a
sailor's cry In a storm, a guiding light For ships that
sailed by.

It stood through war and rage Through peace and subtle
years, It was there to turn a history page Through good
and bad cheer.

I begin to walk away from it, But I turn back and look.
This place just seems to fit A story from a story book.

It stands bold, like an old oak tree Whiter than white
it seems, Looming high above me Its eye is silent,
only a gleam.

—*Erica Witteman*

Song Of The North

In the still of the night there comes a voice
It seems to grief deeply and yet to rejoice
It soars up high in the crisp, clean air
Then plunges down sharply to the depths of despair

It wavers and dances and tells a story
Of hunter and hunted, defeat and glory
Of Northern Lights and Midnight Sun
Of battles lost and victories won
A second joins in, a third, a fourth
A chorus of voices tell of the North
It bounces and echoes; goes on and on
A pack of wolves are singing their song

—*Sabina Kriegel*

Bitter Love

What is this thing called Bitter Love?
It tastes like acid on my tongue
And turns my stomach into knots;
It twists my heart until it hurts
And aches with longing, hopes and dreams,
That never will come true it seems!
Nothing else is on my mind,
No other interest can I find,
But thoughts of Him are always near
And will consume me, I do fear;
There is a lesson to be learned
If you play with fire, you'll get burned!
For Bitter Love is love denied,
Which cannot or will not be returned!

—*Vivian E. Bunch*

My Only Love

    My angel where have you gone?
  I've been searching for you from dusk to dawn.
    Darkness is all around me, I'm lost without you.
      My world is colourless, no reds or blue.
  Do you hear me my love? I'm screaming your name.
If I've hurt you, or made a mistake, I accept the blame.
Remove my eyes from my head, and replace them with sand.
  I have no reason to see, if I can't see you Gitane.
    Shackle my hands with chains, incase them in steel.
If you are not her to touch, I have no reason to feel.
    My heart is broken, I hunger for your love.
    You are everything to me, my gentle dove.

—*Kevin Philip Gagne*

The Boughs

The storm subsided and the naked tree shivered.
Its leaves, left while the branches stretched,
brushed away into the pockets of the wind; delivered.
The humiliated shrub shrank and pleaded, wretched.

Timidly the petals of rain restored, coaxing.
The trodden tree found its returning spring
and peevishly raised its limbs to the sun, softly singing.
The blue sparkled and flashed, diamonds on a ring.

The flashes and sparkles became swoops and glides.
Wantonly the shrub flowed with the flowers of freedom.
Blushed are the tender emeralds of green by their rides.
Hopeful is the meek, but gaining, frame sprung from seedom.

Bliss, I am seen, flowers' dew rests on my bough.
She beckons with songs, romancing the emerald buds.
She calls by name the lowly shrub who asks how?
And coos within the encradling branches and hubs.

O to sing an echo to the petal of the sky's blossom,
that I could be the cherished grip of her hips.
She coddles and croons, a young pearled gossom. Handily, upon
the bough, sturdious confidence is built with her lips.

—*Peter Klingvall*

Motorcross

This is the love of his life.
It's like risking your body on a river of ice.
The thundering of those machines,
Encourages everyone to let out their screams.

With death-defying speed,
He flies through the air like a steed.
A fearless hero with such determination,
There is no room for contemplation.

He needs these thrills:
He can't feel the pain when he takes these spills.
So much adrenaline rushes through his veins,
He can't think of any other games

Which would be more thrilling or exciting,
The danger, he is willingly abiding.
At the end of each race
Awaits him a trophy, he says, it pays.

—*Heidi Bechard*

The Ocean

The ocean has such beauty, such peacefulness and might.
Its waves are travelled the whole year through
Each morning, noon and night.
It beckons us to come and use it whatever the reason,
We're always invited to visit its shores, whenever the season.
The lapping waters can serve to soothe our aches and our pains,
Our ancestors have advised us on its true medicinal gains.
The white caps and the crashing waves tell us of a change in
  weather
And when a hurricane reaches the land, that's when folks band
  together.
The sailors experience the dangers the sea has in store,
And divers search for treasures that rest on the ocean's floor.
So waders, swimmers, sailors, divers, and those who fish in
  between..
Let's all make a conscious effort to KEEP OUR OCEANS
CLEAN!

—*Erlor E. Dean*

Just Remembering

She sits lonely in her rocker,
Just waiting for her son to come through the door,
But she knows it will never happen, for he is gone.

She walks silently to the grave,
Puts flowers by the headstone,
Then softly to herself, she prays.

She prays of all the things she never done,
Trying not to shed a tear
But her eyes are red and swollen, from crying

The time has come to let it go,
As she slowly walks away,
Trying not to turn back,
And weep again.

But she shall be back,
To rest flowers and pray,
And weep again, for this lonely moment.

When she comes back,
On remembrance day,
She may not weep,
But she will still remember.

—*Amy Carter*

The Runaway

Summer seemed to lead you astray
like a wanton child
turning the whispering weeds as you passed,
there lies a coat so carelessly thrown aside
and the hat you never would wear
here are the shoes without laces
covered in roadside dust
scattered among slim grass.
Dear to your sight
was the huddle of maple woods
on the autumn hills
or quail in the sapling groves,
but where did you run to
after you chased the cows from the brook
under that blue expansive sky?
Where have you gone
for I never saw you again
though I searched many times
and even called out your name?

—*Larry Rowdon*

"Carnival"

Ceremonial trash
Litters the streets of this drunken town
Ritualistic, cannibalistic bastards
Feasting, like vampires, on one another
The wine as red as blood
And flowing just the same

Their music
Infesting; infecting the atmosphere
They chant and cheer in worthless delight
Sickly parades clutter the urine-stained streets
Presenting heritage
But no one gives a damn

A celebration
Of love and ridiculous intoxication
Free sex; unattractive whores
Preying, like vultures, on the inebriates
Crazy daze
Pounding heads and vomit; a poetic legacy

—*Aiden Hibbs*

Threatened Beauty

Down in the marsh, where the bullfrogs sing,
Live a pair of swans, that come every Spring.
Live in the marsh until Fall comes again.
A couple, a pair, a cob and his pen.
Annually, new eggs are hatched.
Unless, of course, the young are snatched.
Snatched by the foes of the beautiful fowl.
Large fish, a skunk, or an ominous owl.
The cygnets learn to swim, grow up, and fly away.
Then the parents, too, on a warm Autumn day.

Migrating Mutes are a wondrous sight,
Neck stretched way out in graceful flight.
Not quite as graceful as when on water,
Sharing a home with fish and otter.
But alas, they must be wary as they follow the sun.
Wary of man, and his deadly gun.

—*Shelly Dawydiuk*

The Dawn Of Day

Open your eyes
look up at the sky
it's unusually pretty
can you see why?
Early this morning, the stars disappeared
the moon has faded but not all the way
it's staying out late to see this beautiful dawn
the sun has just risen
and turned the sky crimson
the clouds are all puffy
thick and fluffy
they change their looks
from shape to shape
the birds fly by
their outlines accenting the sky.
it's a beautiful morning
look at the sky
it's unusually pretty
now can you see why?

—*Angela Holzapfel*

When Everyone Smoked But Me!

There was a day "The Northland" was boosted to the sky, But it makes me sad to tell you, those days have passed on by. I was told to take "The Northland," "The Northland" was the best. To find a comfortable seat and just settle down and rest. I found a seat and settled back - then I began to choke. Almost everyone surrounding me suddenly started to smoke! So I said to the one beside me, in a voice so loud and clear, "Can you read English?" pointing, "It says no smoking here!" He was a decent fellow, he put his cigarette out. And then he sank back in his seat to have a sleep and pout. Now I'm a law-abiding citizen, it wasn't me who smoked and stank. But a woman opened her great big mouth and said, "There's always at least one crank." I pretended I didn't hear her, what could a lady gain? To tell the truth, I did not feel welcome on that train. A woman wanted off at Bracebridge but a trainman couldn't be found. They passed it, so backed up, of course, you can't turn a train around! I should have been upset for the woman, or at the Northland for pulling that prank. But I didn't feel sorry for the "biddy," she was the one who called me a "crank"!

—*Clara MacEwan*

Reflection

Long have I yearned to see your sweet face,
Many tears have I cried,
Many illusions have I seen,
Many a pain I have endured.

Long have I wanted, needed your warmth,
But as a flame flickers and dies,
I have a fire that will not rekindle.

Many a tear I cry
But as seasons change, weave to one another,
I stay but one step behind.

Oh you are devious, like a true magician,
But your trickery can be deceiving;
I wait...
But as life is long, a labyrinth of change,
I too must be patient.
—*Craig S. O'Neill*

A Little Closer

Despoiled and polluted body of addiction
Mind possessed by lusts of the flesh
Knowing such wrongs, but insufficient
To dispel their sinful seductions.
The flesh is weak
But the mind is weaker.
Tormented by guilt
By lost innocence, by lost opportunity
Of truth and life.
Miserable and weak animal
Steered by instinctual desires
Lost dreams, lost visions of holiness
Give me discipline, let me grasp virtue.
There is no mystery snouting in the filth
But its siren's call overcomes my higher dreams
And forever I fall
To its transient enchantments
And each time the distance grows greater,
Death
A little closer.
—*Stuart Walker*

The Sweet Road Of Wisdom

Oh God of life, what seek I in thy munificence
Must my heart beat so fearfully in uncertainty
 What say I when life turns its fury inward
What know I of thy wisdom, thy power, thy love
 And who must I to savour thy divine gifts

Cannot this maelstrom deep in my brain subside
Is thy loving peace too elusive a gift to grasp
Why think I well along thy sweet path of wisdom
 To find I am at but an early bend on thy road
 And who must I to savour thy divine girts

So many temptations block thy narrow passageway
 Yet still I hunger to grasp thy godly promise
 To relish thy peace of enduring tranquility
 To soothe my heart in the purity of thy love
 For need I must to savour thy divine gifts

So on go I in search of thy grand munificence
 Find must I thy fountain of hallowed wisdom
 Feel I my heart beat wildly with anticipation
Sensing thy power as it bathes my longing soul
 For need I must to savour thy divine gifts
—*Brooks Alden*

Untitled

Wilting away
My dreams untouched, time standing still.
I will never know the meaning of true love.

People used to tell me about their experiences,
But I never cared to listen.
Now I wish they would tell me again.
But I know they won't. Do you know why?
Cause they want nothing to do with me.

You see; I'm a vegetable
And nobody cares about what I want or think.
I lay in my bed all day — I have all my life.
They like me better this way.
The word is that I'm getting better though,
But I don't know if I want to.

I like my room.
I've been forced to, I guess.
Actually, I think it would be easier on everyone if
I just went away for awhile...
Like on a vacation.
A vacation I've wanted to go on for a long time.
—*Jill R. Albrecht*

The Last Spy Of Berlin

I lost my way nobody knows me anymore
my grey coat is dirty life became a bloody bore

I'm running through the night I lost my job for sure
now I'm only human I've got no clue what I have done

Oh would you please help me I'm the last spy of Berlin
I know you never knew me don't ask me where I have been

Oh please I feel lost and lonely tell me where I should go
yeah I really realized friends I never had one

Only useless forgotten information now you get it for free at
all no more death traps no more hunting along the wall

Seems like the dark age is over that was so bright to me
sometimes I remember Le Carre he wrote novels etc.

I sold my false moustache and my secret identity
but nobody sold me any directions I needed so desperately

Before I forget here's my brand new picture I.D. for you just
the same believe it or not I don't even know my real name

Eastside or westside I wasn't sure where I drank my gin
at daytime or at nighttime all I knew was the City of Berlin

Traded my 45er and lots of papers after midnight
but nobody wants me seems I never knew the right side.
—*Rudiger Albert*

Vision Quest

Time of passage, a tradition of true identity.
Many moons lapse as the Great Spirit
guides this haunting of your heart.
Fire in his veins, he moves like clouds
over the land; a chuckling creek among
fragrant pines, he observes life, listening.
Long, blue-black hair shines - a raven.
Through ebony eyes, the warrior finds his quest.
They live far apart; stars that glitter
and the ground he walks upon.
Now, they share one path,
the White Eagle soars over a musical river
in search of their destiny.
—*Linda Bailey*

The Race

The sun blazed down the air had stilled
My heart was pounding as the whistle shrilled
I started off fast and didn't look back
And paced myself as I rounded the track.

The first turn came and I lost no time
But kept ahead with one though in mind
I had to win nothing else would do
Be the best in the world the chance of a few.

I could see myself standing proud
Hear the cheering and clapping of an excited crowd
We'd raise our voice as the anthem was sung
Then silence would fall as the medal was hung.

The finish line was now in sight
Just a few tiny seconds it was going to be tight
With a second wind and a burst of speed
I passed the leader and didn't pay heed.

And there it was the end was here
The crowd was starting to yell and cheer
I stretched my muscles and lengthened my stride
The ribbon broke and I jumped with pride.
—*Allan Nicholls*

Only Time Can Tell

Oh precious Sleep where are you, like a nymph you flit across my mind. I glimpse you for a fleeting moment, then you diffuse into the night. Where is that kindly cloak you waft extinguishing a thousand points of light?
Come unbidden then, do your kindly deed and put my thoughts to flight. Instead, such clarity of mind I feel, my imagination has free reign. The shutters of my mind swing open, and a creative bird is set free. Unbidden rhymes and phrases spring to mind, so tantalizing and plain.
I bask in this exquisite light, thought patterns flood my brain. Ah, does the creative light burn too brightly, a candle lit at both ends? When the wick is spent, the flame flickers and eventually is quenched.
Will my flights of fancy, so brilliant in the wee hours of the night, pale to nought in the light of day, and lay mouldering at my feet? Then sweet Sleep surrounds me and I succumb to the realm of blessed rest, but when daylight breaks, will I, a potential poet be, sylvan phrases on my lips, or just one of life's "simple plodders", with dirt beneath my fingertips?
Only time can tell!
—*Dorothy Stabeck*

Superman

Once as loved believed and once has now since past.
Past in my childish fantasy, there would be a lover as mysterious
  as that of a hero.

Hero!?! I have since found every thing else, in here, but that hero.
Who was to be the one 'the soul mate' in love,
Now has no majestical spell for me.

For you grow and know that there is: not such a thing!!
as there is no real love as there is no superman, here.
Here only the distances of past fantasy drowned in my keeps.
My thought and heart remain silent and still
—*Laura Lee Aarts*

Anger

Anger is red.
It sounds like roaring lions.
It tastes like bitter grapes.
It smells like a burning piece of plastic.
It looks like a speeding train.
It makes you feel like screaming.
—*Greg Gilkes*

More Than A Friend

You're always there when I need to talk, and you're there when I need you to listen. You tell me it will all work out, when my eyes begin to glisten. You tell me not to worry, it'll all work out in the end. And no matter what, you're always there. There when I need you, my friend.

The beauty of you is not only what's seen, but also what's deep down inside. You make me feel safe and I realize, there's no reason I ever should hide. There are simply no words strong enough to describe what I'm feeling for you! It's deeper and stronger than love, and it grows when I'm thinking of you.

Whenever I need to talk to someone and everyone seems to be gone; you are always there no matter when, to help me carry on. When I'm feeling down and lonely, and my life seems at an end. You tell me that you care for me, and always will be my friend.

If only you knew how you made me feel, how I long to be with you. If only you could understand that I want our love to be true. I know my feelings for you so strong, will never ever end. I only hope that one day, we could be more than just friends.
—*Brent Wiebe*

The Rake's Tines

We shiver,
 nervous and cold,
  anxious at a bolted,
concrete table nestled on the beach.

We tear strips off stray leaves,
the larger rubbery veins,
 a pathway for the lacerations,
the smaller ones shredded on the way.

Like the leaves in our hands,
we try to rip our halves of culture down,
 follow a vein path,
and search for similarities in our blood.

The search is stubborn,
leaves that won't grasp the rake's tines.
 In time we might be left behind,
caressed by a root,
 sheltered, kept warm by our interest,
not scattered by a harsh wind.
—*Renee Dhaliwal*

AIDS

AIDS victims are people too
No matter what we try to do
Shunning them and of our life
We might as well stab them with a knife

Some aid victims are as innocent as you and I
They had a blood transfusion so as not to die
But they become so very ill
Some even go out and make their will

Aids hits people of all ages
It makes them feel as if they're in cages
We hear people saying don't judge a book by its cover
But what happens if the aids victim is your lover

Don't turn your back on a friend
Stick with them to the end
Let's all stand up and put forth a fight
And then we can say we did what's right

Let's be thankful for our health
For to a victim we have the wealth
Let's help aid victims to the very end
For a victim may just turn out to be your best friend.
—*Tammy Smeltzer*

Untitled

Today Jesus sits beside your empty well.
No matter where it is you fell.
Be it in adultery, lust or greed
He'll give to you whate'er you need.
Be it murder, theft, envy or pride
He's full on forgiveness, no need to hide.
Be it anger, fear, rejection, or deceit.
He's willing and able to wash your feet
Be it injustice, idolatry, guilt or shame
He'll remove your sins and take the blame.
No, there's nothing man can do to justify
Or make things right although he tries;
For through the eyes God alone, Jesus can appeal
And fill your well with water that heals.
For he who drinks of the well of salvation will never thirst,
If he chooses to draw near and put Jesus first.
—*Jan Little*

Heaven Sent

You've touched my heart with your warm, caring touch.
No wonder it's so easy to love you so much.
I love you more and more with each passing day.
Your spirit is always with me, even when you're away.

You make me so proud of the nice things you do.
That special dream is finally coming true.
My entire world is beautiful and new
Nothing else matters, just the dream I share with you.

Together we watch the sunset over the hill
Holding each other close in the evening chill.
We will watch our children grow healthy and strong.
It seems like nothing at all can go wrong.

You have a gentle touch when you caress my cheek.
When your hand touches mine, I grow weak.
You are the one I shall forever love.
God must have sent you from heaven above.
—*Sharon E. Shapka*

A Picket Fence Place

Some folks dream of picket fences
Not page wire like I have.
Picket fences make folks feel safe,
Secure, calm and serene.

I watch the hawk soar overhead.
He floats so easily.
The raven crows from his tree top.
They both feel safe and free.

The robins, swallows and hummingbird
All live so neighbourly.
With grazing cattle, graceful horses,
Gophers, fox and deer.

We live out in the countryside,
Safe, 'mid nature, and on our own,
Without fear, loud noise, and hectic pace.
Our page wire works just fine!
—*Lynn Adams*

The Clocks On The Wall

This place sure does get lonely
now that you have gone.
The people coming around just aren't the same.
I thought of moving a million times
but could never get it done,
because a sound would always haunt me,
the time could always taunt me,
when I'd hear the ticking,
a thousand memories clicking
from the clocks upon the wall.
I remember when you made each one,
a different face for each,
at night we'd snuggle close, the beat went on.
Not a one would miss its time, a lone bell might chime
but in the morning each one shone so happily.
I'll hear those sounds forever,
for if I don't I'll lose it all.
The times we spent together with
the clocks upon the wall.
—*Sylvia McDougall*

Five Yellow Flowers

Five are the children
of a loving mother,
five are lives
of a special mother;
she has unfading love
for her sons and daughters,
and she's more than any other.

Yellow is the light guiding through the dark,
the power bursting beyond the final mark,
the power of a mother,
more powerful than fate,
it's love beyond any other.

I'd like you to take
those flowers from me,
They are but a small thing,
but they mean more for me,
They are a resemblance
of the love I have for you
and they remind me of your
Everlasting love for me!
—*Andrew Sherban*

In Memoriam

Winter unleashes the frenzied sea, dervish of death, cacophony. Of wailing winds and icy bores. Crashing on the ice-lined shores; moulding, with a measured haste. Winter's shroud, like almond paste, the deadly ballycater pours. O'er rock and crag and rugged shore.

No refuge now. No haven serene. That moves the poet. No tranquil scene. For artist's brush. No symphony. Save the dread dirge of an angry sea, whose tormented, demonic swell, heaving like a purge of hell. Snatches now the helpless ones. From warmth of hearth and lights of home.

O hear the hearts break on the shore, gone forever, home no more. Out of reach, out of hope, Far beyond the rescuer's rope. The wind resounds the anguished cry. Of Mothers when their young sons die.
—*Edith C. Rideout*

My Wedding Promise

In front of our families, in front of our friends, our life as one begins tonight; with a simple but beautiful ceremony in a church filled with candlelight. We pledged our love to each other adding new dimensions within our hearts, bonding our lives together, in spirit if we're ever apart.

No one has shown me such happiness as you have these past years, your support and understanding through the laughs, the smiles, the tears. The ability you have to sort things out when I get lost along the way, you lead me through the darkest nights, wiping all my fears away.

I have found the perfect partner as our lives begin anew, I thank you, Allan, for sharing your love, I make this promise to you: I'll support you in all of the choices you make, I'll be proud of you wherever you go. If any of your dreams don't seem to come true, there's something I want you to know.

When you can't smile …I'll be your clown, when you need strength …I'll be your rock, when you need space …I'll disappear; your best friend if you need to talk. You can lean on me in weakness, use my shoulder when you're blue, I'll be your warmth on cold, cold nights, I'll be my best for you.
—*Cathi Hobbins*

I Smile Now

The day begins with overlapping hearts -
   One small, tasting its life
   One larger, re-freshed with new hope
The sun struggles to emerge -
   A cry of horrified hope
   The night shatters; it memory soon forgotten
A shadow pointer moves at its pace of yesterday -
   for some it is slow, gaining the wisdom of pain
   for others it is swift, losing the innocence of hope
Heaven awaits its arrival in its lofty element -
   they fusee, their union chase all shadows
   life cries bright, despair has no home
The glorious orb plummets, quicker than hope, slower than fear-
   the day matures, its moments become blurred
   thy pass and hope is soon forgotten
But now, night has fallen -
   hope trembles in slumber
   life lingers as a dream
   trepidation has no womb
   I smile now
—*Scott M. Simon*

Suffer The Children

In troubled times like these, we find,
Our hands are pinned, our eyes are blind
After all the pain, we ask Him, why? God...
Can't you hear the children cry?

It's cloudy, dark, and getting late,
There's no way they can escape,
It's simple truth, these facts I state,
Please don't let the children hate.

Just look around at what you see
That's all that they will ever be,
The time is right, or can you see, God...
Can't you set the children free?

They're all we've got to get us by, and,
Despite our greed, our fear, our lies,
In truth the children shall arise, God...
Please don't let the children die.
—*Suzanne Blakney*

Dance Of The Northern Lights

The sky's afire, sun-dogs fly,
Palest yellow streamers in the noon-day sky,
Beckoning, come North, come North,
And I will dance for you.

The sky's asleep; her cloak of royal blue
Enveloping the Earth; sleeping
The cold, dark sleep of night,
Silent, peaceful, dreaming.

But wait! The dance begins! Streamers of gold
And mauve, curtains of brightest green, red, purple.
Rainbow colors, brightly shimmering,
Floating across the sky.

Frightened, transfixed, we gaze in awe,
Shivering, is it the cold or is it a dream?
Did we really see the beauty,
In the sky tonight?

Magical, gypsy wild, vivid in their colored gowns,
A ballet of wonder in the sky.
It was no dream, we had a front row seat,
We saw the dance!
—*D. Margerison*

Our Path Of Souls

Plague of our servants
People who inhabit our past define our stones.
Create stairways of our abandoned temples
Those forged in eternal bliss of past times
Cripples left walking,

They leave, our souls dancing
Here, aware of tough times past;

Recalling; births and deaths of angels!
These are; our only true definitions of time.

We view those who, would have not lived, another way
Someday I hope to recall my fixture dancing
Within a glittering path to be treated like you.
—*Michael Jones*

Stale And The Disappear

An insight
Pours over insanely
In the haze of water, of dimness-
And the laugh
Bellows all of its intentions toward me.

Inevitably a sigh,
And like lives before,
Loneliness prevails. Transparent, ill
Deceitful with those disputing evils,
Those evil silences-

Those forbidden, those of
Parasitic intent and those of solitude.
Apparently bleak, apparent
Is not it, is not it true? It is so told,
Though throughout, they shall never know of stand or fall-

Of love, oh love, infirmity and lassitude,
An absolute, an obsolete distillation-
But you, oh with your intentions,
They conceal what is so easily hidden,
What is so easily overlooked.
—*Cathy Bauld*

Awakened

Awakened, I feel the cold claws of death
   reaching to grasp me

My breath is held, my body quivers
   My senses now gone numb

I search for some familiar object
   yet I'm blinded by the darkness

The darkness in which half my life has been lived

Silence, is all there is like the silence before
   an attack of the long watched pray

Movement, is beyond reason, as my muscles ache
   from being so still

Slowly, slowly, my eyes are focusing
   on a familiar object

Then faintly is heard the soft 'tick, tick' of my
   alarm clock, as my eyes focus on the time

Then a shock of anxiety fills my body with horror

As my senses regain control, I realize I must
face the coldness of this winter's morning
   before once again, I'm late for work!

   —*Delinda Lachapelle*

The Front Line

I lay in my hole,
Ready for anything.
Muffled sounds come from above

I'm so tired, I'm not tired anymore.
I'm so cold, I'm not cold anymore.

I lay in my hole,
Thinking of my girl back home.
I hold my gun…waiting.

I'm so scared, I'm not afraid anymore.
I'm so lonely, the enemy is my best friend.

I lay in my hole,
Holding on to my dreams is all I have
A grenade lands at my side…

   —*Katharine J. Quint*

Untitled

Here I sit with head bowed low and have to admit I'm rather slow.
Receiving letters I'd like every day, answering, I'm slower than
   molasses in May.
With family and friends coming out of my ears, there's no time for
   writing, just laughter and cheers.
They eat up my goodies, and track up my floors, and sometimes even
   forget to shut doors.
When everyone's gone, there's no time for dreaming, there's work
   to be done, like baking and cleaning.
When everything's done, the letters I'll write, to friends and
   relations I feel are just right.
With pen in my hand and plenty in mind, a letter I'll write, with
   hopes to be signed.
Interruptions are plenty and thoughts are all shot, when I look out
   the window and more company I've got.
Time has gone by and guess what I've found, there's no one this
   evening to whom I am bound.
Family and friends are in their own nook, and hubby's away on a flight
   that he took.
To hell with the goodies, floors and doors, I'm off the hook, to
   write you a book.

   —*Royel Smith*

Knock Knock Original

When I sit in my chair, and have been inclined to stare
Remembering things I've seen and lost (k)nights and queens
When I get there I already know
Just how I let it all go
And I drift and phase in and out

Sister, don't think I haven't played this game before
You've just seen what happens when I close the door
I know what is going on
And what should never be

They don't know me, don't nobody know
When the stars illuminated so high in the sky
And poplars stood naked down by the snows edge
I remembered that I have a lot more friends than I thought

   —*Bill Liebe*

Finale

I have seen the wrecks of autos
Rusted beyond repair,
Ruined relics of another time,
Staring windowless from junkyard heaps.
And I have thought that abandoned autos
Mimic the human condition.
For, wrecklike, we too, grow old,
Yield up the lustre of our youth,
And witness, at last, the sad demise of all our hopes
and dreams.

   —*Anne E. Brown*

Still

I kiss your ring of love still
Scarred still
Lost in memory of you still
Tendrils of love wealth surround me still
I'm a sore that never quite heals.

And when I burst, the raw exposed
The naked sweet you, dead
I can't let go' to me you're tied and tied
It seems this grief cannot subside.

At once there's love, there's hate
"You died on me." I should forget. Still
My being breaks, bleeds, begins to mend
Enclosing you I'm chained, bound, in thrall. Still

   —*Sylvia E Johnston*

Serenity

Away from the blaring horn and
screeching brake,
I find my peace at this northern lake.
A lake, where eery mists arise
And blend with shadows, and soulful cries
Of graceful loons.
The birches sway in the gentle breeze,
As I inhale the scent of pine trees,
I watch as a beaver swims for shore.
To gather twigs, and moss and more
To build his dam.
In a shallow bog just to my right
A large blue heron is in partial sight.
Awaiting his unsuspecting prey
To stray into this hidden bay
And be his meal.
What joy to escape the city's pace
Leaving behind the urban "rat race"
To search your soul for true ideality
And find it in this lake's serenity.
Peace at last.

   —*Phyllis Janjic*

The Ordinary Man's Legacy

Rise for the day,
Set with the sun,
Life on earth has begun.
Struggle and scratch
To move ahead
Fills each day with gloom and dread.
Likes and wants set aside
Hope you are ready for life's bumpy ride?

Why, why I cry
Does the good life pass me by?

No room for laughter,
No time for jokes,
Just a long life
Filled with yokes.
Have to hurry to pay my way
Never a moment just to play.
Tears of exhaustion have begun
But many a song is still unsung.

Why, why I cry
Does the good life pass me by?
—OLGA

Picture Perfect?

When Mother Nature paints her scene
She splats the earth with shades of green.
Then, for contrast, sure and true
Paints the sky with white and blue.
Then, as the other colors spread
She dots with yellow, white and red
Through the forest and prairie range
You'll see her painted picture change
The green remains, but then throughout
Gold, orange and rust are spattered about.
When the picture seems just right
Winter comes and paints it white.
—Linda Chamberlain

If Only

Seated sadly under a blooming leafy tree
Shrouded with scented smells and verdant sights
Thinking how and when he'd be finally free
If only his hands... were again alright!

His head heavy and harnessed to a chair
Saturated with thoughts of yesteryear and today.
Ideas and opinions, not to offend but to share,
If only he could talk...he hopes and prays.

The pyramid of clean air and beauty before him
Stirs his able, aching and heaving heart
To wild hopes and dreams, all useless and grim.
If only he could move...'tis but a start!

Unable and awkward, he sits and stares
With leaden limbs, lanky and lifeless.
A pitiful prisoner, solitary and shackled for all to care
If only he was fit...he wishes to confess.

Tired and tormented with thoughts of being well
He considers the beauty that pervades the air,
Grateful for the symphony of sounds and help he compels
For all those who make it possible for him to bear!
—Dhanam Naidoo

To Hear The Scream

Night, black and ominous, the air overwhelmingly still,
silence everywhere.
Nothing moves or seems to alter and cast in the spells of this
awesome silence, I dare not breathe too loud or deeply.

Trees, silhouetted by moonlight rays against a velvet background.
Not one leaf rustling, nor bird calling from branch into the
echoing stillness surrounding this segment of blackened
earth. Only the diamonds dare to rebel, yet silently, as they
sparkle in the heavens.

Even the river flowing smoothly makes not a sound as it moves
around protruding jagged rocks worn by time and pressure.
No ripples, waves, nor crests of foam to glimmer in moonlights
reflections. Birds neither preditorially lined along the shore, nor
in flight skimming slightly the waters surface glassiness.

Fear builds inside a shattered soul of harbored thoughts,
feelings, emotions. Still now, as everything is, yet not
willing to continue its silent course. No longer able to
remain in the means unnatural sameness of the night I break
through the fear, the pain, and I scream to make the stillness stop!
—Linda Irwin

Jolly Roger

Peace of mind is what I'm after,
So raise your voices, still your laughter
And hurl your heads against the sky,
Contemplate the reasons why
You were created, marshall facts,
Your play may be in several acts,
Round one may find you on the floor,
Your rib-case cracked, your ass-hole sore,
The second scene may find you spent,
Your brain inert, your backbone bent,
Practicing vices vile to behold,
You're a youth but quickly growing old,
But thirdly you rise and plant a flag,
You're ship-shape though your senses sag
And the jolly Roger is your sign
And at long as things have worked out fine.
—John Binns

I Never Knew Love

I never knew love till you came along, I never knew a feeling
so real and strong.

I never knew love could fill my heart, and because we love
each other, nothing can keep us apart.

I never knew love till I met you, and I could never love
another the way that I love you.

I never knew love would come my way, but now you're here, and
in my heart you'll stay.

I never knew love like I've known it with you, I never knew
that I would ever find someone who would always be true.

I never knew love until you held my hand, I never knew that
love was something that I would ever understand.

I never knew love could wipe away my tears, I never knew love
could take away all my fears.

I never knew love till God sent you to me, and some day when
we're together, you will see just what you mean to me.
—Lisa Gillingham

The Eagle

Today I saw an eagle,
Soaring across the sky.
And I thought of the peace and the freedom,
He must feel, above us all so high.

Freedom from our turmoil,
Our strife and our hate.
Peace in his heart,
Not fighting his fate.

No need for him to struggle,
As we humans do.
No wars, no famine, no hurting.
Just lives his life true.

We could learn from that Eagle,
And have peace and freedom too.
But, we're human-beings,
We fight for all things new!

God gave us all these things,
Greed took it all away.
But, we can always get it back,
By living day by day.
—*Wanda Quock*

Gifts

If I could grant great gifts, it's true
Some might seem quite strange to you.
I'd give you the strength to forgive and forget
Any wrongs that come your way
For that is how great friendships form
And grow from day to day.
I'd give you health and enjoyment of work,
And grant you the wisdom to see
That of all the gifts you could receive
These are the greatest three.
—*Dorothy Wadup*

My Buddy: (Kristina's Song)

My buddy, someone who's around when I'm down.
Someone to scream with and to play, to look up to, or act as a clown.
My buddy, someone to love and follow around, keeping me at
a distant bay, by protection, in a big sisterly way, from the
out of bounds.
My buddy, I have someone to bug and to toy around.
I'm glad to have you (my buddy) around, that I know someday,
you would eagerly, take me out on the town.
Thank you for being my buddy.
—*Marina Petrovic*

The Rose And The Thorns

I was walking in the wood a time ago, and
spied a beautiful rose that grew amongst
the thorns. I dared walk closer to admire it
for a time and found myself enslaved by a
mass of prickles. And from that briary prison,
I looked unto the rose. Feeling far to awkward
to speak, I merely stared in awe. While I
lay there pondering this flawless bloom, I began
to wonder of it's life of obvious enchantment.
to know, after all, of beauty such as that,
and to relish in all it's glory. And as I
wondered, I came to wallowing in my pity
to be among those thorns. I thought....how
unfair it is, to look upon this rose I'll never be.
—*Kimberley McDonald*

The House On The Hill

On a hill, overlooking a quiet town
Stands a house, forgotten and falling down.
It was built with love; each board and nail.
If it could speak; it would tell quite a tale.

Of Christmases gone past and laughter and tears.
Now it is silent; it has been quiet for years.
It is where I was born and my life began.
Three occupied the house; a woman, child and man

He was a policeman; she was his wife.
They never were rich; but we had a good life.
Whatever they had; they gave and they shared.
Although I was troublesome; I knew that they cared.

At the age of seventy-nine; the man died in his sleep.
On a cold February morning, his soul God took to keep.
The wife had been failing and forty-eight years wed.
Alzheimer's stole her; now she too is dead.

Never having married; I now stand alone.
Missing my parents and the times which are gone
Life goes on it will not stand still.
It can leave you with emptiness, like the house on the hill.
—*Patricia L. Sutherland*

Night Sounds: A Sonnet To Spring

Like a silver drum the timeless moon rolls by;
Star-spangled bands of clouds march to its beat.
Soon rosy Dawn must leave her bed of sky;
Come trailing sheets of sunlight at her feet.
Spring lilacs drown the warm night air with scent,
As if to question every passing breeze;
And nod their purple heads in royal assent
To whispered answers blown from poplar trees
The telephone wires hum hymns to soothe the dark;
Car wheels cough gravel hoarsely in their track;
A haunting wind-lost voice calls from the part;
The whistle from a train comes echoing back.
Night sounds of spring through open windows creep,
To prick the outer edges of our sleep.
—*Valerie J. Palmer*

Blessed Art Thou

Hail Mary full of grace face
Stared with solar eyes the
human race pace
   took a cigarette break
   and broke a brandy sifter with heavy ash
   -trying to wet my eyes without blinking
   Quasimodo moan without thinking
She licked her figoro
   Whiskers
flicked my tobacco into the orchestra
and sang a modermairre theme song
   took a loonie out of her proco grande
   and bought her a lottery ticket
Harvey Oswald eyes replied
   Don't look at me like you're wearing mirrored shades.
She played with the tuft of hair that hang across her
   one skeptical eye; much like it was a garter snake
   or my aorta.
Hail Mary full of grace face, the Lord is with thee and only
   thee; I match your stare.
—*Brandon Enriquez*

Hear My Thunder

Foaming, impatient water
swiftly races along - to
tumble into a chasm!
The muddy, dark brown cauldron
churns up a dizzying blend
of cast off, unknown toxins
and heaves in violent spasms.
"Hear my thunder rumble and
feel the moist ground shiver!"
Listen well as the Great One shouts a warning to his people!

Stately towers of cool green,
reaching for the heavens, come
crashing, smashing back to earth!
Death stalks the fallen giants,
seizing Nature's wounded heart
and chopping it to pieces,
to moan its sorrowful dearth.
"Hear the whisper of my sighs
as they rustle through the leaves!"
Listen well as the Spirit cries so gently for his children!

—Anne Marsh

The Farmer's Dream

I have to go to sleep.
Take a peep at, that...
Which always makes me weep.
The dew fresh in mind,
from yesterday's sweep.

In vaguest mindset point.
There is a dot, ever growing.
A cancer, I doth anoint
Taking root, seeds ever sowing,
Faintest detection at the joint

Of which the clouds, rupturing,
Their back soul on a fertile region.
Spreading their genes wide, capturing,
overwhelming the loam, and their legion.
With mud, comes the feet smothering.

But we will overcome, we dart,
To the next trench, over mud we cart.
Our possessions, our thoughts, most treasured.
Our soul, memories, long, most leisured

Pull damn horse... We must sow a weed!!

—Tim Green

Untitled

Go the ocean and spend the day
Take your children and watch them play
Turn over a rock and watch crabs scurry
Then ask yourself why you hurry
Sit back and enjoy the rhythm of life
Dwell on harmony, push away strife
Help the little ones dig in the sand
You've built a castle, oh life's grand
The treasures of shells ground at the shore
Mean more to them than if bought at the shore
Use these moments to give them a reason
A lesson of life will help for a season
Bury in sand their cute little feet
Yet it cool them as a fun filled treat
Watch as the winds gently blow their hair
Most important of all, show them you care.

—Jo-Anne Pedersen

Mother's Day Poem

To put my feelings into words is so tough,
Thank you just doesn't seem enough.
For in this little poem I want to say,
All that you mean to me each day.

I thank the Lord for giving me,
A mother who prayed down on her knees.
And that her prayers were selfless and sweet,
That my Lord would answer and meet.

So Mom, today is a day set aside,
To share the feelings we just cannot hide.
I love you so much and want you to be,
Proud of the person you've made out of me.

So thank you for all that you have done,
Your love is greater than that of anyone.
And if I should be blessed with a child someday,
"May I be just like my Mom." is what I pray.

—Marlene Healey

On That April Night

It was once on that cold April night,
   That I wondered just what if I might.
So fierce the thought,
   So bold, I would have fought.
Yet the thought remained,
   But what if I were blamed?
For that longing to share that glory,
   Or to hear a familiar story.
For the warmth of those words,
   Like a chorus sung by birds.
And yet they flee with their wings,
   At the crinkle of my rings.
For then I'm left lonely,
   As I cry and weep mournfully.
And yet I'm left gazing at that bright hypnotic light,
   On that cold and mournful, April night.

—Rahim Dhanji

The Wanderer

A blindman could not miss that path
That is so bright and straight,
But along that path that is so bright
Walks a man with a wandering gait!

For along that path on every side
Are the things that tempt and pull,
So that as he tries to walk along the path
He feels his life is not full!!!

Yet something within the heart of the man
Always answers the beacon call,
Guiding him back onto the path
To walk it straight and tall!!!

Throughout his life that beacon of light
Has guided this man that would roam,
And some day, he knows, that beacon of light
Will call "The Wanderer" home!!!!!

—Eduard J. Hinko

Tortoise And Serpent

Here, there is no light.
No sun, no moon, no stars.
Abysmal lies the black ocean,
In cold forgotten caves where old night
Chuckles and burbles behind the walls of madness;
Here
In this corpse's womb
In this mind like a church yard rape,
where there is no light.

—Jeff Connors

Always There

If I could find the doorway,
That leads to your heart,
I'd lock the door and hide the key,
A friendship we could start
Aside from all the rumors,
The gossip that they tell,
Beyond our dreams of pleasure,
The road they make it hell,
Although there's miles between us,
We can pass this test of time,
Our love is shared for hours,
Further we seek for piece of mind,
To have them let us be,
And when the tears have finished falling,
You'll be left with me,
And when we reach this peace of time,
We'll handle it with care,
I'm very proud to speak these words,
Because you're always there.
—Cathy Hnatiuk

Forever Love

I dreamed of a love so pure, so wonderful,
   That no other mattered more.
And I longed for it, felt an emptiness
   Where it belonged.
I relentlessly search the eyes of
   Those I meet, to perhaps
Capture a glimpse of the spark,
   But the days roll by,
And my yearning grows
   'Til indeed I wonder if
Any thing, any one, could look so beautiful
   As through the eyes of love.
The rain, our tears,
The sun, love's burning desire,
The thunder, our passion,
The wind, our gentle whispers.
   And, alas, the beauty of them all would
Be ours to cherish, and no
   Other could perceive our universe;
For we would be in love, everlasting.
—Pamela J. Gunderson

Doodling During The Commercial

There isn't a rhyme for orange.
   That seems silly to me for there aughta be,
But there isn't a rhyme for orange.

You can pair a chair with a millionaire,
   Or couple a stew with a kangaroo,
But try as you might for a day and a night
   And you won't find a rhyme for orange.

There just isn't a rhyme for orange.
   You can try on a shoe in Kalamazoo,
Or swat a fly with the end of your tie,
   You can go to Havana and buy a banana,
But you won't find a rhyme for orange.

No, there isn't a rhyme for orange.
   You can catch cold in December without your suspenders,
Get off of a train and walk in the rain,
   Get out of the rain and get back on the train.
I'm repeating myself, I'm going insane,
   "Cause I can't find a rhyme for orange.
—Mel Mitchell

Brush Poppin'

The cowboys told me to find a bull
That was lost somewhere down the coulie
So stompin' through the sortin' pen, while other cowboys cull
I catch a horse, saddle up and head off on a horse I call
   unruly.

Ridin' through the brush, blue heeler at my side
Thorns tearin' at my chinks
I come across a boulder, a good forty feet wide
And high above us lookin' down is a very hungry lynx

Well that cat he gave a growl and sprang
While me an my geldin' went aloft
That Heeler intercepted, showin' quite a bit of fang
And my ticker stopped for ten showin' me I'm gettin' soft

Well that cat took off like he had to spread a rumor
He was sprayin' gravel out behind
If I hadn't been so scared, I might of seen the humor
But one thought kept me cool, I had a bull to find.
—Karen C. Poynter

The Killer Disease Aids

I'm the killer disease aids.
The acquired immune deficiency
No existing disease can match me
For I am worse than worse is.

Those with exploding sex desire
Are my best friends
They enable me to survive
Yet I discriminate against neither age nor race

I always result in death
For I have no defeater my worse enemies are those with
good morals for I hardly strike.

Doctors spend sleepless nights
vainly trying to stop my existence
yet I'm always the winner
so I'm the boss!

My lyrics are known to all
yet I'm always a booster
I'm the deadly disease aids
whose existence can be in disguise
—Lefoko Otsetswe

Retirement

Nearing retirement? What does that mean?
The beginning of the end? The end of a dream?
Oh, no! When one door closes another opens wide,
Take a deep breath and step inside.

Wonders await you, pleasures by the score,
The things you never had time for before.
Travel - our beautiful land to see;
There'll be bright new experiences for you and family.

There are challenges ahead and work to be done.
The world has need of each and everyone.
There are many lonely people who need a kindly word,
The young need guidance; now volunteer and serve.

So dream new dreams and follow them through;
Good friends are waiting; there'll be others, too.
Share your talents, bring new ideas into light.
RETIRE — and enjoy the best years of your life.
—Vi McFarlane

"When The Clocks Of Time Stand Still"

When the clocks of time are made to stand still,
   The Cathedrals have ceased with their chime;
When the Great Reaper comes to gather His own,
   What then, at the end of all time?

What then, when earth's anvils have been laid to rest?
   And the toilings of earth made to cease?
When all of the shopkeepers' doors have been closed,
   No more heartaches or crime in the streets.

What then, when the housewife, so bent with her chores,
   From her labours, away has been torn?
She has gathered her children in at her side,
   Away from the gathering storm.

What then, when no harvest of earth has been gleaned?
   No more grinding or toil at the mill;
When daylight and darkness have vanished away,
   With the clocks of God's time standing still.

When the Grim Reaper calls for the trumpet to sound.
   To end earth's crime with it's sin;
There will be no shelter in which to hide,
   for life's summer is fast closing in.

—*Clara Dowling*

Cosmic Spin

The balance of the Galaxy gives us the Ocean's tide.
The consistent give and take keeps us all in stride.

The cosmic spin that keeps us here so tightly bound inside.
Is balanced by the vast night sky encouraging our mind.

From waters edge to mountain top the beauty is inside.
Keep the balance through your heart and you'll always have the prize.

—*Diane Ruffo*

The Symposium

The dinner was delicious, the chicken was divine.
The drinks they came and down they went,
Especially the wine.

Now after we had partaken
In this mid-day snack we had.
We started on a symposium
And I tried to out drink Dad.

I drank him under the table.
I drank him to the floor.
When we could go no lower,
I drank him out the door.

Out doors it was so cruel.
The cold it stung like rain.
But my old man would not give up
And I was in no pain

We stuck to it for hours until the drink no more, came
flowing from the bottles that were thrown against the door.

In the wee small hours of the morning when all the guests were gone. I staggered toward the weaving porch
But only made the lawn.

—*Ken Bennett*

Hero Of Mine

In the year of 1957,
The good Lord took dear John to heaven.
The story of his death I've been told,
It happened in October and the day was cold.

John was out hunting with his two mates,
And crossing a bridge he met his fate.
A one-eyed horse pulled him down,
Over the bridge and to the ground.

A simple phone call from a heartless mountie,
And the news of John's death rocked the county.
His funeral was the biggest and saddest I bet,
And all his friends wore coats of scarlet.

John Stuart would have been 51 that November,
But I was only 6 months old so I don't remember.
Mom tells me tales of a man she loved so,
Who played with her and watched her grow.

John Stuart was a "Hero of mine,"
He was so strong, gentle, and kind.
He wasn't handsome, just simple in looks,
But you won't find "Grandpa" in any story books.

—*Cindy Patterson*

The Flour Beetles

Everyone's busy going somewhere. Me, I'm just walking.
The insane hum of human energy at its peak
the sun barely cresting the horizon.
Faster, better, more,
As a collective group they move.
Self centered insects with a hint of intelligence
   -and always somewhere to go.

Do they smell the dirty ocean in the air?
Do they acknowledge the sun, or simply despise the rain?
Do they know how to stop and smell the roses?
or do they just understand that there's somewhere to go?

and what of myself,
am I (I am) no better.
As if by inheritance I've a ticket to the show
front row center - or was that on stage?
Designed to conquer, conquer and survive
having a purpose is being alive.
While me, I'm just walking.

—*Susanna Guthrie*

Lake Cowichan Massacre

In a time I hold close to my heart,
The majestic Bald Eagle shared his space with me.
I marveled at his flight,
Watched him dive into the wild Pacific surf.
Sat amazed at his skillful strength;
He fished like a mighty warrior.
Out my window I would gaze
While he snuggled with his mate, just as we might.
Today I despair, I learned that ten eagle carcasses
were found on Lake Cowichan Reserve.
Shot!!!
and for what? $2000 a bird.
My heart is suffocated by the sorrow I feel.
I understand the eagle is sacred to the native
people, who love their land.
All for money they would kill!
Has life become so hard for these people?

—*C. Pallagi*

Where Is Love?

Sometimes I really wonder if I'll ever find true love
The only thing I'm sure of is, it comes from up above
In a lonely world like ours, there's always room for hope,
but in a nasty world like this one, can we untie the rope?
The rope that holds us back, leaves us defenseless from
attack, the rope that keeps us home from a world full of
unknown.

Breaking free's not easy , there is an obstacle down every
path we take, sometimes you find somebody, how easily our
hearts break. It seems to me the right path is bumpy and so
narrow, that every step we make pierces our feet like flaming
arrows.

If we endure the pain and agony life brings, we live to see
another day, the day all birds will sing. The music that they
make will fill your heart, body and soul, it will give you
peace of mind that you've never felt before.

—*Carla Fehr*

The Child That's Two

One child is rude, mean and demanding
The other is loving, caring and understanding
The first belongs to night and likes to play
The second is opposite and lives in the day.

One is outgoing and sly
The other is quiet and shy
One will stand and make a scene
The other lives behind a screen.

One needs friends and attention
The other just wants a little affection
One has a wild personality
The other believes in reality.

One is too free to be a wife
The other just wants to get through life
One doesn't believe in school
The other thinks she's a fool.

One is comfortable around guys
When the other is around them she feels she'll die
Two different sides from the same body
But that body is a child that's two.

—*Theresa Meister*

Frances Plays The Blues

The sun gleamed, and the sweat poured, as Frances approached
the plate, the score was ten each, bottom of the ninth, and
a win was Frances' fate,
the crowd cheered, and the Blues booed, as Frances took the
stance, bent his knees, poised the bat, and wiped some pit on
his pants. A bubble snapped from the pitcher's lips, he gave
an icy glare, he raised his knee, swung his arm, and the ball
soared through the air,
Frances eyed the ball, swung the bat, and heard from the crowd
above, a low hum, and the snap of the ball into the catcher's
glove. Fears chilling touch crawled up his neck, he wiped a
sweaty brow, the old coach cussed as he swung the bat, 'cause
the ump shouted "foul". "You play like a girl," the pitcher
teased, as the Blues laughed and cheered. He pitched the ball,
heard a crack, as the crowd went wild and cheered.

It soared over the fence, as the Blues threw their hats on the
ground, the fans clapped, and the coach smiled, as he ran his
journey around. He jumped on first, danced over second, at
third he took a bow, tipped his hat, as the crowd gasped in
silence, wondering how.

—*Lisa Bauche*

The Rain

Silence came and silence left and then silence returned again
The skies turned black as if a blanket had been placed over the
sun. No longer did the birds sing and no longer did the other
animals play; something dangerous was happening in the sky this
day. Lightning shot through the sky like a bullet being fired
from a pistol thunder roared across the sky like the sound of
two ocean bound sea freighters colliding together out in the
open waters of nowhere, and then there was silence; Everything
lay still until it happened. The wind began to blow fiercely
Slowly at first and then more, much more wildly, And then the
rain started to fall all amongst the soils of the earth;
streams and lakes became fierce, forceful flowing rivers of
danger and doom, Taking with it anything that stood it its
path. Hours later the rain slowly came to a halt Leaving the
ground to lie in its' own muddy, wet soil, The wind died down
and disappeared into the clearing sky that lay above; the sun
once again starts to shine slowly beginning to dry Mother
Earths' sandy flesh.

—*David A. McKenzie*

Spring

Spring is here, winter is past,
The snow has melted away at last
The leaves are budding on the trees,
As they gently sway in the breeze
Here and there grass is peeking through,
As the frogs croak in the nearby slough
They have slept all winter long,
Spring is here seems to be their song.

The honk of geese as they wing their way,
Northward bound to Prudau Bay
Birds all on joyful wing,
Chirp and whistle, give voice and sing
They have been south all winter long,
Spring is here seems to be their song.

The whistle of the robin, caw of the crow
The bleat of sheep and cattle low
In lovely pastures coming green,
They yellow dandelion can be seen
They have been hid all winter long,
Spring is here, seems to be their song.

—*Hugh Donovan Roulston*

Breath Of Dawn

Dawn on an autumn day
  the winding road breaks free to make way
    crisp breezes
    gentle falling
  of leaves scattered down to lay.

Filtering bright through a mountain of cloud
  breaking dawn to morning light
    brazen hue
    musical wisp
  sentiments of an autumn sight.

Whispering winds through enchanting sky
  the whimsical pathways floating by
    softly touching
    slowly teasing
  beckoning dawn to freely fly.

Natures horizon
  such a flawless amend
    of beautiful seas
  bountiful in a harvest of descend.

—*Sheila Marie Nunns*

Fred Wright 1879-1937

I am sitting here alone,
the words carved in stone.
"Here lies Fred Wright,"
My imagination becomes my eyes.
As there appears a silvery light,
that burns deep inside.
The life this man once lived,
all the love he must have given.
The light becomes brighter, it engulfs my soul,
I then realize I've finally reached my goal.
As I wonder aimlessly through this place,
All these people without a face.
They've all left a mark,
And now they're left in the dark.
They've lived and they've died,
there are no secrets to hide.
The meaning of life is not to make a mark,
or to live in the dark, but do all you can do,
and feel all you can feel,
then everything will become real.
—*Regan Van Luwen*

One Day At A Time

It's a wonderful world, so don't cry little girl
The world is not your cup of tea
The sun sets on your tears and we hear you loud and clear.

There is a message there somewhere
Does somebody care? You've got the moves that sway
That get you into another day
You stay in the same place - and you pray for grace
You need a little more - a little space
And you will rise up and give us a sign - proof from the ashes,
That you are strong - then you will make us laugh and cry and
Sing and sleep peacefully, and we will kneel down to pray the
Prayer you used to pray- and then you will be free to fly,
And watch the sunset from afar high up from a star
Silent peace amid awesome stillness that never stops moving
You will be part of time and space
So give me your hand let us dance and sing like children in the
meadow, and run down the slopes with innocent hopes.
So don't cry little girl the future is in your favour
'Cause you have all the moves that sway
That get you into another day
—*Martin L. Burns*

A Father's Day Gift Of Joy

An evening draws night and the birds close
  their eyes, my flower still Peacefully grows.
As the stars blink their eyes, and the moon
lights the sky, My Petal stems sweet as a
rose. My hearts long desire, my bundle of Joy,
stands as sweet as a garden in bloom, and
captures my heart, with a wonderful warmth
whenever he enters the room. A gift I
would say, a gift of my heart, and there
  he'll go running away. A Joy I would say,
A joy of my life as he skips, as he dances
in play. What a beautiful sight, what an
open delight, oh what pleasures of Joy do
descend, as I walk in the Park, as I
stroll by the sea, when I casually hold
your hand. And to tell you again,
my sweet little man is entirely out
of the way; but the pleasures and Joy
of my very fine boy makes every day
    Father's Day!
—*Doreen Spence*

Fissure

They lay in the sand, sun, oiled hot
their single minds parry; time is not
Funny how their feelings flee
Away from thoughts of misery
Her touch is glad, inquiring
her soul is not retiring.
He gives her words which
embrace her whole
she feels them deep
and can sense his goal

Imminent absence a viable threat
it would this woman cause regret.
Her curiosity is not near soothed
she rarely plays the game by the rules.

Like a carrot pisces romance beckons.
part cynic her cruel mind still reckons.
She stares to the ocean and feels
her heart stirring,
Pat lessons—due time—are finally blurring.
—*April Prinz*

"Deepest Need"

Each living soul has their deepest need;
their strongest passion, love or greed,
the one thing that cannot be replaced,
on which that person's life is based.
Some people are born with theirs in mind;
others spend years in search to find -
that beautiful promise, that sparkling a glow,
and all I want is for you to know:
My special something came my way,
and my heart will never forget that day
I found the only thing I know is true,
My deepest need, my sweet, is you.
—*Nicolette DeVeen*

A Mother's Reality

I watch them grow, take their first step, then have to watch them fall.
I want them to see just the good, but they have to learn it all.
They're not my vast creation, but people all their own.
With their own hearts and minds and thoughts, I've seen that
    as they've grown.
To shield them from everything I used to think was best.
But when they grow and moms not there, how will they pass the test.
To show them such a perfect world, that's what I'd have to be.
But there is not a perfect mother here. It is just me.
Sometimes I do the wrong thing. Say words I can't take back.
I do my best, make some mistakes, but then I get on tract.
To teach them strength, self respect and love that is so true.
I'll have to start by showing them that I do love me too.
—*Mary Bracken*

Summer Sky

Shimmering... dusk
   Heat rising... rising
Purple and pink, green and rust.
   Earth colours meeting sky,
Over the mountains and rising high.
   Beautiful colours in the summer sky.

Alaskcan Highway snaking through,
Driving, driving to the blue horizon.
Now it's purple and pink, green and rust.
Mountains and sky holding hands in trust.
Yukon summer, Yukon sky
Beautiful colours rising high.
—*Nellie C. Dale*

Ode To The Woman I Never Spoke To In My English Class

If only I could be someone else.
Then maybe her bright eyes would favour me.
If only I could be someone else.
Then perhaps she would see,
The worth in my heart and tenderness in my eyes.
If only I could be someone else.
I know I could reach-out.
If only I could be someone else.
I know she would reach back.
Unfortunately I cannot change,
Or acquire the confidence I lack.

Her bright eyes will never favour me.
Will never look in my direction or honour me with her attention

Only sweet glances from the corner of my eye.
Just a few chances, between hello and goodbye.

There was something about her angelic eyes
That appeared like two perpetual stars
How brightly they shine
So close, yet so far.
—*Lenny Cohen*

The Reception

The clamour, the howls, the fire, the smoke;
Then the battons, the bullets and the maiming
Run for cover! Run for cover!

And now the calm
Empty streets, markets and parks
No ruffles - very peaceful, too peaceful.

Then the midnight meetings
Secret reunions, to plan,
To conspire, to prepare, to out - maneuver the foe.

Now the chanting, their rhetoric
Accusations and counter - accusations
Their lies and flattery
The raising of hope - just to win;
"Make sure you win...do anything
Just make sure you win"

Then the verdict! followed by
The fury, the fire, the smoke, the arrests, the confinement...
Its the coming of an ideal
From the East, an ideal called...Democracy
You're welcome.
—*Amabibi T. Fayeofori*

Bonds

A families bonds are strong and sweet.
They hold the family nice and neat,
but you have to care and love these bonds
or the strength and sweetness will be gone.

Your bond is a rope that weaves you tight.
It gives you morals of wrong and right.
So hold it tight, don't let go,
it'll teach you things you will need to know.

So cherish the bonds and hold them near,
they'll supply you with love and fight off fear.
With love and kindness in your heart
your family will grow and never part.
—*Dayna Dutot*

Talents

Talents are spoken of in the Bible
They are a God-given gift it is true
But just how much they are developed
Is entirely up to me and you.

Now talents may lay latent
Like forgotten treasures hidden away somewhere
Then suddenly, when a need arises
You'll find it is right there

What you haven't any talent?
Just don't be so negative my friend!
What about that telephone call you made,
And the lonely heart it helps to mend?

The letters you wrote with the cheery thoughts
Tucked down deep within its lines?
If you could just see the smiles they brought
You'd know it was a definite talent sign!

So give of yourself, of whatever you have,
Your smiles, and letters, and the fruit of your hands,
For talents increase as you keep doing for others,
And you'll find opportunities all over this land!
—*Ida M. McCormick*

Trees

Trees they enchant me at this time of year
They look so beautiful with colours so dear
They cover hedges and to the ground softly fold
with colours of yellow, red, green and gold
I sit and I watch them each one and all
They stand there so tall and naked in fall
They seem to be saying as they stand so serene
Hello cold winter see you next spring
—*Lucy A. McDonald*

Memories

They were the best of friends.
They were inseparable.
She would tuck him in at night.
He would wake her up in the morning.
They always depended on each other.
Never being let down.
Always having someone to lean on.
They always thought of each other shown by actions,
looking into each other's eyes,
showing what they mean to each other.
Now she can only dream of him,
of their wonderful life together.
Him jumping into her arms.
Getting her face wet from his moist nose.
Licking her face clean though unneed of it.
Not knowing now if she should get attached again.
Thinking of being with her next best friend.
—*Ramona Ginter*

The Ruin Of Souls

Sad consequence of original sin
The reason for the mess we're in
Our faculties have been deranged
Led astray by desires and temporal possessions
Has led us to our mortal transgressions
Snares are lade up for our own uniqueness
We the corrupted forever degraded
The sum of our life I think we betrayed it.
—*Philip Tarrant*

Do You Recall?

Do you recall in the olden days
things you did and the games you played
the easter service when Christ died on the cross
the prayer that was given when you thought all was lost.

I remember it well

Do you recall when you were young
learning to read, draw, write and spell
then to expand to the other world
Spreading your wings hoping all would be well

I remember it well.

I recall when the young grow old
times have changed, some are bold
Jobs are scarce times are hard
And the young folk look at you with little regard.

I remember it well

I remember the changes in my life
the hand ships of living and the strife
of our time running out, but do not despair
We'll be intrusted in our fathers care

—Sylvia Dearman

My Perfect Day

My perfect day would be to wake up with the sun shining on
this fair land
To look at my lover who looks at me with loving hands
The birds would be singing high in the sky
The wind will be blowing softly, like a whisper only few can
hear but the one who can feel it knows it is there.

I would feel good inside about myself
no more darkness inside for it has passed it has subside
I would look in the mirror and see my best friend
for it is you and know one else you'll have to face in the end

And when this beautiful day was over,
the bright moon would rise
for the stars would twinkle like my loved ones eyes
I would look around and be thankful for all the good things
that I can share
I would thank the Lord that I am here and I made it
through trouble that I had to love!!

—Carolyn Maxwell

Prayer For The "Rose"

Oh Rose how beautiful art thou. To all your loveliness I make
this vow, that each day, to you I will say; "smile for me in
your very special way." Oh so yellow, oh so red and oh so
white. In my lonely nights you are always my faithful light.
If God could create such a perfect delight as you my dear rose,
Than there is no telling how far God's perfect talent really
goes. God also made man and woman to understand about the love
that is felt when they hold you in their hand. No greater love
is known from sea to sea or from land to land. Even little
children know about the rose, also babies learn as soon as they
begin to grow. They can feel the love just by watching your
petals flow. Softly, softly, to and fro, gently falling,
falling to the ground. And as they fall, everywhere the rose's
scent does abound. My prayer for you oh gentle rose, is that
God will always bless us with your presence. And your loving
seed forever and ever grows. Amen

—Lucille Ruth Brooks

Savage Hunter

A stealthy shadow whispers in the jungle plain
Through stalks of gently swaying grass
T'ward cautious and warily sleeping prey.

   He prowls, the cunning of a man insane,
   Glistening green eyes glow like crystal glass.
   His tail swiftly switches, then slowly sways

Keeping time with sinister strides and strain
As muscles rip and bunch in awesome mass,
Exploding power on a hapless stray.

   Foaming teeth spill the blood of heated veins
   As victim fights for life; then falls at last.
   He is feasting well this joyous night's day

Knowing the gruelling and biting pain
Of hungry tomorrows from long days past.
A death for a life is the savage way.

—Stephen Hart

Angel Of Passion

Her brown eyes bothered me
to keep her secret safe, don't ask me why
Whilst other teachers fussed,
I tried to keep from getting in her aura's way
I didn't like her pony tails
but then there seemed no better style for her
A cherub's face this bonny girl in smocks and lace-up shoes
Our eyes would lock in glance so she could hear my silent voice
Oft the tears would well and spill like empty days
an awful grief, as if the sinners everywhere should know,
Don't mix the genes, offspring pay the Goodbook's price."
Her Mom was white as snow
her Dad the ace of spades
I held her only once;
she clung so tight, my strength was more despair
Our bond was short and sweet
she died alone in her crib at home, this tiny tot
"Crib death, I heard,
"A fretful child who mostly cried herself to sleep at night."

—Diane M. du Toit

Good-bye

Why does it hurt so?
To see you go
Leaving me all alone
I sit here thinking back
To the good times that we had
The laughter that we shared
And the tears that were shed
It brings back the sweet memories that I cherish
Then reality hits
And the pictures flash in mind again
I see again
On that dark, wet and cold raining day
When we said our final good-byes
It was then that a part of me was lost to you
To follow you as they lifted you
And lowered you into the ground
That closed up around you
Leaving you all alone in the dark and the cold
And all I could say was Good-bye.

—Bao-Van Vu

Journey With Me

Journey with me - my forever friend
To that plateau - only the mind can reach
To that place that spices - your senses to full
   Can you feel it?
   Can you hear its music - it's calling you
   Mm - Mm - that sweet Ambrosia
    I know you can see it now
     soon - you can touch it
     soon - you can become part of it
   Dwell there - for a time
   Just remember - to come back
Know it till end
Your mind can renew it - whenever it wants
It can change the scenes often - it does what you bid
It will always be there - for you comfort and pleasure
It will help you discover - that this planet of ours
As vast as it is
Has much less to offer
Than the journeys
We travel within
   —*Rosina Campbell*

Listen To Me, Please...

Yes, you who are taking my dream's faggot
to travel by unsheltering hamlets.
Give me back my burden.
It is true; it has shadows and weepings and fissures
but it also holds amiable caverns,
and mirrors and ghosts and sea gulls
with the mystery tied to a poem
between a bond of foam... and a large tear.

Do not hit it that way. Return it to me, for charity.
You know? With no dreams do not dwell heart beats
to be converted into butterflies,
and does not happen to be born in landscape
the time for fables and for charming.

Its tenderness? It rocks and after brakes
into a blue orgasm.

Yes, put my burden here—thank you a thousand times—
on my back.

I carry it like a son of my own blood
because it was born, and perhaps I did not know,
from love and from fireflies.
   —*Olivia De Montelongo*

A Visitor's View

Yesterday, we paid seventy dollars
To walk about fifty miles!
We learned about past, present, and future,
And discovered other countries' lifestyles.

We dropped in on clean, restful washrooms,
We sampled the food with delight,
And we stayed to the end of the day,
To view fireworks and lasers, at night.

Our day was filled with pleasure,
With tiredness and knowledge we were besot,
But well worth the miles - and the money-
To visit Florida's famous "Epcot"!
   —*Mary Monteith*

Long Lost Love

There wasn't anything more special. When you and I were together. The love we had for each other. Is now lost forever.

I know we weren't meant. To last a lifetime long. Because if we were meant to be. Our love would not now be gone.

It had been seven months ago. When we said our last good-bye's. But it only seems like yesterday we met. Oh my How the time flies.

Slowly I'm still recovering. From all the hurt and pain. Still showing my love through tears. That roll down my face like rain.

This long lost love experience. Has turned my life around. A loved-one has to come and go. Is what I suddenly found.

It is an experience that has taught me.
What the outside world is made up of.
And there really isn't anything as painful.
As a long lost love.
   —*Donna Compton*

True Love

My aching heart why must we part
true love is hard to find
must we find the peace and joy
for love alone cannot support.
Show us the light oh sweet starbright
abandon me not for he is my life - my pride - my joy
love me not for I could not bear to lose you
and forget not the good times
even though they are bad - not forever sad
be glad for the good times are to be had.
Despair not my love for we will reach out
and pull the knot and be free at last
in peace and harmony and it will forever last.
Be glad for these is one life to live
for how ever difficult the road
oh how heavy the load - just think
the good times are around the comes
reach out and grab - give up the sorrow
and be glad you've alive
for it is like a precious one.
   —*Josie Cifala Abrams*

The Spirited Heart

Falling asleep while on the beach
Underneath a tree, lighted by the moonlight
Showered by the breeze, which was out of thy reach
Was this showering spirited heart of delight.

But I couldn't move an inch in fear
Because all of a sudden, everything was clear
The spirited heart that I have seen
Was the answer to what ever it means.

Never have I seen such a purity of heart
Into the night of everything so dark
But as I stood there watching this spirit staring back at me
Was the reflection of what I was meant to be.

Then closing my eyes, surrounded by the only dark
I saw thy soul walking towards the spirited heart
But as it reached, thy body fell to the ground
But pain I could not feel, nowhere around.

Receiving the touch of this spirited heart
I could no longer feel the pain of thy part
And never shall I return to thy body
Because from now and then, I will forever be free.
   —*Danielle Lanthier*

Untitled

There's an old house standing alone tonight
Waiting in some one to shut the down and turn of all the light
But if it could only talk it would hear some one say
We will tear the only house down for it certainly had its day
But oh the memories it must have stored
Save those days so long ago
Whether the sky was sunny
Or the ground was white with snow
It sheltered many a lonely soul
Through some day and troubled years
Now its waiting for the day
Someone will be shedding tears
I know that I for one
Still look back on those old days
For that's when I was young
And spent my happiest days.
—*Cora Yuill*

Island Summer Night

Come. Take my hand.
Walk with me under a celestial sea of stars,
Soaking in the sweet cool air
Of this Island summer night.

Slowly we navigate towards the water-side,
Ultimately finding ourselves there.
Standing on the virgin sand
With our hands tightly intertwined;
Looking only into each other's eyes.

　Just you and me.
And the soft, soothing mussitations of waves
Crashing and foaming onto Cavendish Beach.
—*Leslie MacDonald*

My Conversation With A Toad

Twas on a bright and peaceful day as I walked along the road, I was startled out of my walking shoes by a noisy little toad. This one was kinda complaining about the traffic out here; this way they drove was atrocious, he certainly made that quite clear. "I was out for a walk," he related on this very fine day, "And eight times I was run over tho' I managed to stay out of Death's way"; "No manners have they," he spoke again; I didn't know he would say, "I had already started to go across; seems I had the right of way", too startled to speak I stood there quite numb not knowing for sure if I was losing my mind or going nuts oh gracious me oh my; but at last I finally found my tongue and I said to that little toad; that maybe he didn't belong out here in the middle of the road; there's lots of forest and plenty of grass to hop on Mr Toad; and if you don't like the traffic sir then why hop into the road; "They drive where they want and you walk where you like and you have the nerve to say;" "That because I was born to a different world that that's where I must stay;" "I'll go where I want I'll do what I wish so there you go my girl;" "Just because I'm a toad don't mean I can't see what goes on in the rest of the world."
—*Margaret R. Sell*

Room

I'm all alone in this room.
No one to share it with.
My friends say that I want be in this room alone for long.
but I know I will be alone for a long time.
When people walk in they turn around and walk out.
When I yell no one hears me.
Hundreds of people walk by and don't even notice my room.
No one ever comes to say "hi".
All they do is walk past my room
they don't even notice my room.
I will always be alone in my room.
—*Shannon Rudkevitch-Bowen*

Belly Of The Beast

In the Belly of the beast is where we throw many of men.
We cast them into darkness because of their criminal sins,
We don't give much hope,
While they're dwelling in this ruthless den.
Even though some have committed vicious crimes,
They still need a loving friend.

If these men are not shown the truth and guided to the light.
What will we expect them to do,
When released back into the night!?,
We must show them love and give them hope and rehabilitate their minds.
We must lead them by example by letting our little lights shine

Our penial system need to be reexamined and could use some serious reconstruction,
Because we have so many repeat offenders that continually pursue destruction.
But what else can we expected them to do,
When they are finally released.
If we only have warehoused them for years in the belly of the beast!
—*Roylin J. Picou*

Love Lost

Lost in memory, I think of you
We had a battle going, we two
A mist fills my eyes
As I remember your struggle
That November morning
Following your birth

I stand beside your incubator
You were like a little soldier
Trying so hard to fight that battle
With you to survive on this earth

I looked on with my baby
Wrenched with pain
Trying to figure it all out
Why you were conceived to go
To such strain

You were not to live my baby on this earth
But was there to shine like
The stars that light up the earth

You are Michael Anthony
So loved, still alive in my memory and my heart
—*Lillian Pollard*

Grandchildren

They tug at my heart strings;
Their faces light up full of love and joy!
The oldest granddaughter just graduated a hay.
From high school, now ready to train from work!
Her brother a little over a year.
Just learned to walk, not yet ready to use a fork!
One grandson almost 16 look for his driver's license.
His sister eight is full of laughter and song!
The two younger boys are two and three.
Each grandchild is special as they came along.
Full of life, laughter, curiosity and carefree!
—*Lilly M. Kopp*

Young Girls

Young girls grow up to be beautiful ladies
Young ladies grow up to be beautiful woman
Young women grow up to be beautiful mothers
Young mothers grow up to be beautiful like you!
—*Mike Cowles*

This Morning

The sun rose this morning.
We spent the day at the beach,
no more than six we were.
Laughing running swimming splashing digging,
castle after castle,
gathering shell after shell.
The sand sun-smootched with warmth,
panicked our tiny feet until they reached
the blanket of wetness.

The sun rose this morning.
That birthday party,
no more than nine we were.
You sat beside me as I cut the cake,
and sucked lick and stick behind the maple.

The sun rose this morning.
Magic moments were planned with you.
Malls dances parties, but times ran out.
It was an accident.

The sun rose this morning,
the day ended in rain.

—*Bobbi Ann Brady*

Being A Teenager

Here we are,
We stand alone.
To the rest of the world
We are unknown.

Here we are,
Facing so much pain.
But no one cares,
They think we're insane.

We're here today;
We'll be here tomorrow;
Yet no-one will say
That for us they feel sorrow.

Now we've reached their age,
Seems like we just broke out of our cage.
And looking back at yesterday
On being a teenager, we now say:

There they are,
They stand alone.
We want to help them
But they are so unknown.

—*Barbara Trudeau*

The Last Good-Bye

You left this world without a good-bye.
We who remain so weakly cry.
The love we possess is magnificently strong;
It will not discontinue though you are gone.
Our memories of you will forever last
As we who knew you hold on to the past.
It is important to remember the good and not dwell on the bad.
Nothing can bring you back, that is why death is so sad;
But your spirit will rise to the heavens above,
Where you will be surrounded by a circle of our love.

—*Brandi Gruber*

Love Has No Price

Many years of loving you is what I see
When I look at this old wedding band always on me
To others it must look all battered and old
But to me more precious than any valuable gem sold
Sometimes I wear my new ring just for show
While this old wedding band is still a symbol for the
Love we always know
No one ever tells me my ring doesn't look too nice
Because they know I'll remind them that love has no price.

—*Mary Gervais*

Then We Will Have Peace

When the roar of war is heard no more
When soldiers march not on a foreign shore
When innocent blood and tears cease to pour
Only then will we have peace, long awaited peace

When the greed of man is laid aside
When love for neighbours out weighs his pride
When lusts of the flesh is finally denied
Only then will we have peace, wonderful peace

When man accepts our Lord's sacrifice
And believes his blood has paid the price
When we practice the love of Jesus Christ
Only then will we have peace, glorious peace

Peace to this world will finally come
Not brought by jet, by missile or gun
But by the return of God's only son
Then, we will have peace, everlasting peace

—*Everett Adams*

Loved Ones

Nobody knows the pain we go through,
When someone leaves us which was a friend like you.
One day you think everything's gone wrong,
You never know how much you miss them until they are gone.
You cry all night, you think all day,
You can't imagine why it turned out this way.
We try to forget, we try not to cry,
We try to live on after we say good-bye.
Life is like a piece of clay, you mold it into the perfect way,
But one day that piece of clay fell off, and that piece of clay was you.
You can't tell when the pain will end,
You hope they get the love you send.
We try not to think of it, but it pops up everywhere,
We hear about these things almost everywhere.
You think it's a dream, you think you'll awake,
But there's no way out, you can't escape.
I said it in my poem and I'll say it again,
"Loved ones" are in charge of life and its end.

—*Lindsay Gabrielle*

Canadian Sunset

The grey foam of winter's melted tears
Gushes from the mountain wall beyond
This field I cross. Upon the steepled tiers
I'll drop, sprawled upon the diamond-frosted
Grass to writhe and rot, a pellet drilled
Between my ribs. No cider haze could calm
My numbed and bloodless bones. Neither bear
Nor fish pause except to scorn my kind -
For I let leap my infant from my care.
While salmon diced for life past grizzly paws
My unwatched Shannon drowned in icy jaws.

—*Graeme Webster*

Inspiration From Fiji

Back to the concrete jungle once again
Where so many of the people play games
Where natures beauty is never the same
Lost with the voices of the city.

My life in the country I have the birds and the bees
I have the beauty of the evergreen trees
The oceans waves pounding on the rocks
The eagles flying above to whom I talk.

I walk along the beach
No one to bother me
I walk through the park
Sit on the old oak tree.

I miss the place where I live
I long for the feeling nature gives
And I see now that my home is home
And when I'm there I'm never alone.

For natures beauty is all around me
And makes me feel completely free
As the eagle that flies high above
In nature's garden where there is plenty of love.

—*Jaye Low*

Woodland Music

It's evening in the green clothed valley
Where the orchids nod and sing...
And underneath the shady pine tree,
Lily of The Valley softly rings.

And all along the quiet lane
The daisy's droop and sigh
For in the shinning moon-lit valley,
They hear the nite birds cry.

There vagrant breezes fill the air
And honey-sweet fields sleep
A misty veil doth cover all,
And dainty violets weep.

Where elders bend and rustle
And ladies eardrops grow
And streamlets fringed with deep green moss,
While wind through whisper'ng grasses blow...

—*Shirley Isaac*

Beyond That Mystic Gate

Simple are the times that pass beyond that mystic gate,
Where unicorns fly and pegasus roam and blossoms flourish,
Casting the smell of ancient times,
Where mountains rise to vine green walls,
And trees reach through the sky,
The dew sweetly gathering drops, where puffins still fly by,
The air so rich and purified,
Rivers clean and crystal clear,
Silver flashing as fish swim by,
And the calm lake becomes a mirror,
Where peace is with all, each are at one,
And blue is the moon, still bright is the sun,
Where the warmth is a comfort,
The rain quenches thirst,
Where thoughts are serene and nothing is cursed,
Life is still sacred beyond that mystic gate,
And simple are the time that pass,
There is only love there... not hate...

—*Heather Ann Cairns*

Just Leave Me Alone

Life has its problems in many ways,
Which break and shatter our dreams.
This creates even harder days,
'Just leave me alone' is my theme.

It seems frustration will never let me be,
I can't find peace, it's unknown.
It seems like everyone's disturbing me,
Why can't they just leave me alone?

I need time to myself, the time to cry,
Over my problems which seem to have grown.
It seems like my life is nothing but a lie,
Why can't you just leave me alone?

This time can be hard, this time can be rough,
That is the reason for writing this poem.
It's time to be strong, it's time to be tough,
But first, please just leave me alone.

—*Jason Makinen*

Antelope

They are so beautiful, these creatures of the wild.
Who, ever edging closer, come to peer
At the strange things that humans all possess,
Buildings, machines, and such strange-looking gear.

Their lives are simple, water and green grass.
A sheltered place to lie when day is done.
Frightened they run when the "steel-monsters" pass
Knowing the message of the hunter's gun.

How beautiful to look toward the day
These gentle creatures are our friends—not prey.

—*Ruth Geving*

More

Why can't we be happy with the things we have?
Why do we always want more?
A rich man is not a rich man
until he has more.
Love is not love
unless we get more.
A penny is not worth having
unless we have two.
Two pennies are not worth having
unless we have three.
A lot is not enough
if we're not getting more.
We'll never be happy
having enough
while striving for more.

—*Aileen Calligaris*

Why Must We?

Why must we look through eyes with tears?
Why must we fight to hide our fears?
Why can't we run through meadows of light?
Why don't we honor our hearing and sight?
Why do we act as if we don't care?
Why do we kill even an innocent hare?
Why must we die of hunger, no food?
Why do we change from one to another mood?
Why must some children have no home?
Why must we live to die alone?

—*Kevin A. Fulford*

April Rain

I calculatedly angle
wind-swung umbrella to tilt away the
toes of an April shower absently dancing in the air
watching habitlike, not in fun
the formation first slowly accelerating bulging
ambitious to fall falling millimetreing free (what secret will
it tell) bright drop dropping
off the cloth platform
sinking into oblivion in my skin I wish, the public says, I'm
laughing

I step with rubbered feet around a bland, happy smile: around
a drop-rippled puddle with stale grace
misses splat in oily, must-scented water
my boots shine tacitly
rain has queer friends, the trees smile, noddling off drips

finally, chin quests up, eyes glitter with flames
step lightens to breezy skip
the umbrella shield falls, crashes stupidly onto the street
and sopped hair, soaked clothes, and April's rustling laughter
mock together in the freak of revelation
—*Irena Aligizakis*

Untitled

On the seashore when I saw you late last night
With another man, you seemed to put up no fight
You told me you were working late
You said it must have just been fate
From then on I knew that it was you, lying on the beach
Seeing you in another man's arms, for then I lost speech
I grabbed the lamp off the stool and smashed it on the floor
I stood up, you screamed "Don't leave me"
And then I slammed the door her face went blank, but so did
mine. I knew all of this was true
I no longer have to ask was it really you
As days went by, on and on I could not think any more I heard
the phone ring, but turned my head as a tear dropped to the
floor I knew it must have been you phoning late that night
I thought you were calling to see if I'd be alright
A full eclipse of the moon made the sky so black I once feared
the thoughts of leaving, and having to pick up and pack
Coming back to you would be a dream come true
Even another woman in my house, I'd rather still have you.
—*Steve Cyr*

The Land

I was young and I believed this land belonged to me.
With haste we tore at the unwilling trees.
Planted fenced furrowed and plowed as we pleased.
My future home and I at war, I made it bleed.
Feverishly I bred my family.
Now I am left with breasts a-sag.
With a frail old man I once saw as a great stag.
Now I feel the land look at me.
Silently awaiting my death so it may bury me.
Meanwhile giving me food from it's bounty in pity.
I am old and I believe, the land does not belong to me.
But I to the land.
—*Ida May Anderson*

Friends

   A friend is someone kind and sweet
someone who everyone would like to meet.
A friend is helpful, kind and always there,
to help with problems and for care.

   Friends are people who understand
and always there to give a hand!
Their to talk and give advice,
and in one word their simply nice!
—*Melissa Hutchings*

Alone At Night

Alone at night is scary shadows come out to greet you
With moans and groans

The house is full of darkness as the shadows creep down
the hall your heart is beating faster

Sweat is pouring down your face
As you sit there wondering what will happen next
Your eyes look around the dark empty room

All of a sudden you hear a dreadful scream

You jump up but tell yourself to be calm
You look around the corner to see a horrible sight

A body laying in a pool of blood
You scream for help but no one comes
You hear somebody calling your name

You let out a loud and horrible scream and start to run
A guy grabs you by the arm and drags you into a room
He closes the door behind you

He starts coming at you with a knife
Your heart is beating ten times faster you scream as loud as
you can all of a sudden your parents open the door and say
they're home.
—*Kristel Dawn Carels*

A Lifetime Of Devotion

He was an Angel sent from heaven
With passion he shared his fame
He shook the hearts of millions
'Til his last breath he entertained

Graceland was his home
But his worldly pride is his only child
Their togetherness he left behind
Will all be bequeathed to her side

An everlasting image
A father, son and a friend
From his first guitar to his crowning moment
He gave his all to the very end

Now the kindly king of music
Has kindly left his throne
A man we all extol the king
Has gone and left the truth unknown

He gave a lifetime of devotion
With a voice that redeems his flame
The legend we love will always live on
And the memory of his name.
—*Ellis C. Gamble*

Monalisa

In tonight's tranquil silence
With soft spoken melodies of that summer season
With enchanting verses - with reflecting melodies
A garland is made to coronate the next living planet.

Down and down to the hemisphere of the universe
Stars foretell - cool breeze blows
Same old words vibrate to the atoms of the atmosphere
Echoes during the seasons, after the seasons.

Beauty rests behind those green meadows, where
Dark desert freezes - wild faunas fly
Where holy women pray over all golden beaches
Music waves meets azure of your sky.

When the little prince will search his way to the next planet
Galaxies will glitter - fair maidens will sigh
When incense will spread from all celestial cells
Other earth will create, other oceans will smile.
—*Mandira Ghosh*

Wilderness Woman Queen

Out of the wilderness
within the ivory palace walls
the royal daughter shines with all her glory
waiting for her King to call

The bride waits to be given
her clothing woven with gold
she's brought to the groom robed with many colours
a vision to behold

Robed with the sun
the moon beneath her feet
a crown of twelve stars
the vision becomes complete

With the wings of an eagle she flew
into the wilderness where I could hear her cry
this lamp lady vision
became the apple of my eye

Who is this coming out of the wilderness
perfumed with incense and pillars of smoke
with all powders of the merchants
smelling the sweet fragrance I awoke

—*Todd Paul Langis*

Wasn't That A Hoot

While strolling along the lake one night, my aging body withstood a ghastly fright. Wandering around not thinking of much, just the day's events, my job and such from overhead a strange voice appeared. Oh my God it's robbers, I feared. Off I ran crashing through limbs and bush. My heart pumping wildly with an adrenalin rush under a tall pine I stopped and I punched. But from above I'm sure the same voice canted. I was certain woods were filled with thieves. Only no other sound I heard rustle the leaves with my imagination on the loose and running a muck. I was sure I was at the end of my luck. While thinking my Maker and I would soon be acquainted. My legs out, I must have fainted next thing I knew I was shaken awake and heard the voice of my nephew, Jake. What happened, he asked, his voice so concerned. So the events I related as my memory returned. When I was finished, I couldn't believe my eyes. For there was Jake laughing and slapping his thighs. He asked if the sounds I heard were hooty-hoot-hoot. T'was nothing but owls, he said, you crazy old coot. A man my age, now imagine how foolish I felt being afraid of nothing but fear itself.

—*Donna A. Claw*

Change

Long ago, before paved roads.
Women were known as stepping stones.
Baking and cooking, ironing and sewing.
Keeping the house under control.

As time grew old,
the woman's role, began to unfold.
Her desire to prosper,
led her to the world we know.

Look here, look there, look everywhere.
Women are carrying their share.
No longer playing the part of a man's sweetheart,
they're making it on their own.

Doctor's, Lawyers and so much more.
Women have become our everyday warriors.
Showing others how it's done,
a balancing act has begun.

Working nine to five, and feeling fine.
Women still take time to bake a pie,
for those at home, she leaves behind.

—*Laura Ueland*

Spending Time Walking Miles

I've walked along with sorrow - night and day she clung to me. Yes, I've spent my time with sorrow, but now I know it had to be. And pleasure, well I loved her, but she hardly ever stayed. I would try to keep her with me for she brought laughter to my days. But I was all too fleeting and she would never stay. She'd have me racing on a fast ride - then push me easily aside. I've spent my time with madness, being relentless was her pride. And even now she haunts me for she has a key inside. She plagues me with old stories, things I've had to face before. All I can do is keep my head up, praying I won't meet her anymore. She loves to walk my memories; longs hope will never come. But now i hold that pen of power that will decide when she's dead and gone. Still I've shared some miles with silence - the sound she made was sweet. I could have spent a lifetime curled up, childlike, at her feet . Along these many miles of time someone walked in step with me. He took my hand and held it strongly...and yet so tenderly. Then showed me wonders I thought would never ever come to be. He said to call him Jesus and a candle lit my heart. Our hands enclosed together even tighter than the start. We passed cruel pleasure, sorrow, madness - these ones we left behind.

—*Tracy L. Swain*

Time

You are tears
You are laughter
You are a combination of frustrations and mixed emotions
You leave your stamp on everyone
But you're 24 - when you should be 44

You're mistakes made and still thought of
You're the result of endless questions
askin' "why" and "if only"

You're my dog who's no more
And my tea set that's chipped and broken
You're my dolls who've closed their eyes
And the girl who wishes she was 13 and now she's 22

Like a whisper behind my back
Like a fog rolling swiftly over the water
Time is only moments, which quickly become my past

Please give me back such precious time and wait for me
To change, to grow, to become someone
To hold on to each minute until nothing is left of it
To squeeze every second out to fulfillment
You've passed me.... and left me .....standing alone

—*Heidi Rideout*

The Lover's Leap

Up with the hills and the cobblestone, is where
  you can find me.
I sit and gaze far beyond my homeland, and the sea.
The mountains soar high, like hungry preying hawks.
Why all peaceful? When really known, it's not.
I'm here to figure out a peace of mind.
To seek for answers of not asked questions.
...to wonder why decisions made by others hurt us all.
Maybe it's just me... blocked out of the world that lives
  below.
Should I go and be at peace?
Face the challenged earth?
My hope is lost for someone's reach before I make my fall.
This giant vault I could make, could break up every heart,
But hopefully, it'll be just mine.

—*Nancy J. Parsons*

The Mystique Sculptor I.

"The conveyance of spirit by means of matter" [Ruskin]
You know what I think about.
Words symbols concepts raw materials spilling abundantly.
I amaze you myself as I take these thoughts
and sculpt them into poetic forms.
Each poem revealing another part of me.
To you I confess my love my struggle
my devotion my God my strength.
You see my art:
giving substance to abstraction;
word pieced to word to form a meaning
to make sense of all that is here.
Still one answer evades me,
is this creation, or merely self-exposure?
God, you know.
Today I believe.
We will know the truth tomorrow.
— *Doug F. S. McKellan*

My Husband

You've always been my friend, through good times and bad
You laugh when I'm happy and sooth when I'm sad.

You hold my hand when I am scared and in fear.
It's your kind, loving words that I long to hear.

When I've upset you with my hurtful, sharp words;
You hold back the tears, the daggers, and the swords.

You forgive my misfortunes and my mistakes;
You're quick to remind me I've had some good breaks.

You're great with our baby, our dog, and our cats.
Interesting always-our "parenting" chats.

Always so giving, putting family first;
You'd give us the last drop, no matter your thirst.

You take me to dinner after a long day.
That's just your special style, your very own way.

We make love so tenders and make love so true;
That's when I feel the closest ever to you.

You have meant more to me than words can express.
I want you to know husband; you are the best.

To my lover, companion, and friend right through...
I don't know what I'd ever do without you.
— *Wendy Henricks-Friesen*

A Valentine's Gift

On this Valentine's day,
You may wish for a dozen Roses in red.
All I have to offer is a heart full of love instead.
You may wish for a candle-lit dinner for two.
All I have to offer is a love so true.
You may wish for a diamond set in band of gold.
All I have to offer is the love my heart holds.
You may wish for a mink or gown made of lace
All I have to offer is my love, which is easy to trace
You may wish for a box of candy with a special card.
All I have to offer is my love, as times passes I know
you won't discard.
Valentine's Day only comes once a year.
But my love for you grows each day, and will always
be there.
— *Bonnie Hore*

The Zombie

He did not die yesterday. He died years ago.
You should have mourned him
when he lost the wonder in his eyes,
when he stopped asking the question, "What if?"
He died when he gave up the will to live,
when each morning was an enemy to be encountered,
rather than a journey to be enjoyed.
He died when he said, "Games are for kids.
Adults must preoccupy themselves with important matters."
He died when he said, "Risk taking is for fools;
it destroys self-esteem. Do what you know!"
He died when the starving children of the world no longer
assaulted his senses,
when he could no longer distinguish the blitzkrieg of sordid
stories in the newspapers
from fiction on television.
He died when he said, "Love is for school children; involvement
breeds pain.
I am content to be self-sufficient."
— *Anthony M. Buzzelli*

You Gave Me A Vision

You gave me a vision, of what life was to be.
You showed me the world, what I was to see.
You promised me love, - said you'd always be there.
To lend me a hand,-to show me you cared.
We walked through the days, not rushing a step.
We cherished our times, - for the time was well spent.
Then suddenly one day - you weren't by my side.
You were gone for a year - not a tear did I cry.
Then one day I thought of you - and sighed a bitter sigh.
The long awaited sadness, - pierced my heart and then I cried.
I cried for all the empty, the people have these days.
I cried because I had a dream, and let it slip away.
I cried because a love like ours was supposed to last.
To endure throughout eternity, - the present, the future, the
past. I finally realized you were with someone new.
I wish I could tell you that I am to.
But my feelings for you are much to strong, and it hurts to
let you go. But I can't keep you, because I don't own you.
So good-bye for now, good bye for ever, good-bye for eternity.
— *Jennifer Phillips*

Infant

Your eyes so sparkling so full of tears
Your heart so small so full of fears
Your saddened face searches to find
That loving touch that's warm and kind
You struggle to move but your all alone
Then you hear that soft sweet tone;
"Quiet now and go to sleep,
I'll hold you in my arms to keep,
dream of meadows and blue skies above,
I'll see you next morning my little love."
— *Azelia Manners*

Untitled

Swept into a dizzy world full of fragrant roses
Sweetly caressing our intensified senses
Carefree, soft, comforting feelings of mutual trust
Displayed in our every whim of secret desires
Delectable sounds of us permeate the air
Expressing affections in multitudes of love
Continually flowing towards our unabashed heaven
As we gaze into one another's souls
Unleashing untold of emotions as our hearts
Repeat the sweet words of "I Love You."
— *Wyn Roden*

The Way Of Love

I love they way you look at me,
Your searching eyes look oh so grand,
The way you touch a simple shirt,
The tender way you touch my hand.
The way your lips will brush my cheek with elegance and grace,
The way you hold me when we kiss, your hands upon my face.
The way you hold me in your arms, your body soft and warm,
You make me feel so wonderful, no worry, strife, or harm.
I love you just the way that you are,
I really want to see you stay this way,
Not for very long my love, just ever and a day.

Immerse me in your love, my love, the only way you know.
Open up your doors my love, let your sweet love flow.
Take me to your promised land you offer in your kiss.
When you open up your heart, how can I resist?
I love you just the way that you are,
I really want to see you stay this way,
Not for very long my love, just ever and a day.

—*Robert A. Dyckson*

What Is Love?

Is love something you see?
Something you can hear, taste, or smell?
Is there a way to touch love?
Or is it something you can only feel?
If no one can say what love is,
how can you love someone or something?
How can you say "I love you"?
Is love an emotion, or a thought?
Is it something you're born with?
Do you have to learn how to love?
Can someone teach you how to love?
Are there limits, boundaries, or levels of love?
Is it something that two people can accomplish?
Or can one person love by themselves?
Is love a two-way street?
Can you love someone or something,
if you get no love back?
Is it possible to forget, lose or confuse love?
Is it possible not to understand love?
Can you find or gain or inherit love?
Can you win or buy love?
Can you sell or give love away?
What is love?

—*Jason Lefebvre*

Little Man

    Cuddled in amongst his stuffed friends
   He's dreaming of stories in which the truth bends
  His hair is a bit messed, but that does not matter
He has no one to impress and no one will chatter
   His body is so tiny yet he snores like a man
His dream is to own a John Deere tractor and maybe someday he can
His goals in life are a bit different then those of me and you
  But his heart is set and he hopes they come true

—*Burke Henry*

Departed

People leave, things are lost and feelings are forgot,
The things we want, the things we seek, the things that
should be sought.
We don't appreciate them until the time is passed,
but we have to realize that noting can last.
And even if not taken in death,
but taken by the heart.
Whatever else has come has gone,
because everything must part.

—*Kendra Gilbert*

The Flower Blooms

Love is like a beautiful flower
Blooming in the middle of spring.
This beautiful life has a lot of power
Since it's such an enchanting little thing.
That love can bloom anytime, anywhere.
It can bloom from any place within
Like a flower so soft, delicate and fare,
Only then do you know that it's love you're in.
The love flows through your body and mind.
Sometimes you won't even know that it's there.
You just have to know where to look and find,
Then you will realize how much you do care.
That flower may die too soon, you may see,
But the love should stay between you and me.

—*Kelly Cullison*

"Mirror Of My Dream"

There was a time when I realized
There were things I could not buy
So I had to stop and evaluate
The course of my life

For all I had was a dream
Of loving you someday
So I put the world behind me
And I faced another way

And I looked inside
And I found that dream
Of a love my heart did crave
You are the mirror of my dream

Should you break by mistake
Seven years bad luck they say
But now I have to tell you
I'll risk it come what may

And until the end does find us
With a broken frame and cracked
We'll always see each other
And find the other looking back

—*Bwayne Collins*

The Window

There is a street light outside the window.
Shadows are cast about.
Sitting upon the living room couch,
The shadows seem to dance.
Engrossed in reading a book,
The shadows are soundless.
Everything is quiet and peaceful.
One shadow has moved closer.
Intuition says don't look toward the window.
The shadow looms ominously near.
Panic mustn't overcome.
The shadow seems larger.
Arose from the couch and moved toward the window.
What is that moving shadow?
With a sigh of relief, there sat the next door cat,
Pawing away at his own shadow.

—*Nancy M. St Clair*

Juniper Man

    Light-limited juniper man
you have taught us to eat humbly
to reverence the palate and train agile fingers
to savor sustenance and be our sensuous selves
You have inner smoothness and scent-laden tenacity
like the cedars of Bermuda fingering the very roots of
the islands absorbing the life juices of rain-dropped red
earth
Strong yet gentle enduring yet fragile
You hold the past in your veins of fragrance
exuding the vigor of days yet to come
    Juniper man teach me to bend my stiffness
to flow with wind and far-distant patterns of sun-laden
rhythms
Touch my soul with nimble fingers elevate my senses to
humbleness,
For you know how to savor the fibers of being
Opening the perceptions to delicate hues
and unyielding strains of sirens and stars
Durable man juniper man fragrant being vigorous serene
swaying
in the hushed breezes of dusk like noiseless limbs caressing
a fluid sun.
   —*Norman Beaupre*

Perfect Lady

    …The one who asks
      how you're feeling.
    …The one who picks you up
      when you're down.
    …The one who'll pat you
on the back to help you along.
    …The one who brings out
the sunshine when it rains.
    …The one whose smile will
fill your heart with pleasure.
…The one whose hugs and kisses
    fill your heart with love.
    THE PERFECT LADY
   —*W. E. Jackson*

Untitled

To understand
  Penetrate
The wall of confusion
  That surrounds, engulfs
Having only self to give
To break barriers
  that confuse
Barriers
  That come
    Unknown, dangerous
Knowing…reaching
  To comfort, give hope
Fill you with the unconditional promise
  To engulfing love
    Uncompromised
Blindly moving
  Toward the ultimate
    victory
      of
Self over chaos
   —*Laura E. Davidson*

Sunset

I looked up and saw
The most beautiful sight ever seen,
The sky was full of colors,
And I felt I was inside a dream.

I feared to move a muscle.
Or even take a breath.
That the sky would somehow change,
With the upheaval of my chest.

So I sat there wondering,
Who else had seen this sight.
Maybe no one but me,
Saw these colors fade into night.
   —*Terra Keating*

A Grandmother's Will To Live

Our grandmothers are never too tired or old
To carry in wood or bundle up not to be cold.
They are never too worn out to shovel snow from the walk
So they can get to a lonesome friend to have a talk.
Grandmother is so very wise
That she can give good advice to any age or size.
She may feel bad and have to take a pill
So she can cook a good meal for her family to have a good fill
She cuts the grass and rakes the leaves
And no one knows of the lonesome moments that she grieves.
Within is heartaches and pain and a room full of love
As she gets her strength from the good Lord above.
Never too busy to let someone tell of their troubles
And as they leave, their mind joyfully bubbles.
Grandmother has a great will to live
So to family and friends, her time she can give.
So all of this (Dear Granny) will not be in vain.
For in heaven one day you will have a mansion to gain.
   —*Glen Eiler*

The Rhapsody

Listen, listen to the rhapsody.
A song of fondness and passion.
This exquisite blending of harmony,
For a tale of so much affection.

Trumpets announce an arrival,
Of a secret favor shared.
Strings ripple for love's survival.
Lyrics capture a willingness to care.

The notes scream off the pages,
In a silence no one can hear.
Present is a serenade for the ages,
A special sweetness for only one ear.

His heart beats like a drum,
As he endures so impatiently,
A cherished union yet to come,
Togetherness sought so desperately.

Listen, listen to the rhapsody.
Music for only you and he?
Tunes snared away from many,
Only to drift so far from me?
   —*Keith M. Gillies*

My Someone

There's a name and a face
    That keeps me up at night
'Cause it lingers longingly on my mind...

And a soft, soothing voice
    Tickles my ear drums
        As I replay
Every warm and sweet word uttered...

And I cannot resist a smile
    That is slowly creeping
        Its way onto my face
As a much missed feeling
        Comes over me...

A ray of sunshine pours over
    My cold, white face,
    And I soon begin to feel
        The light
That my life so deeply craves.
—*Heather Louise Hildebrand*

The Wind

What is this called, the children do say,
Can come among us during the night or the day.
It flies around buildings, and seems alive in the air,
Can put fear in our hearts — and does not seem to care.

It seems to come from no place, and yet can do so much,
It clings to trees, and is so cold at a touch.
It gives me a chill, that goes right to the bone,
Who would want him for a friend, not I, let's leave him alone.

He must be in pain, cause he moans through the night.
Keeping me awake with fear till dawn shows its light.
I wonder if it's lost souls that have sinned,
But Mother says do not be afraid as it is only the wind.
—*Catherine E. O'Neill-Reardon*

Untitled

There you are all alone and fallen to your knees
Just throw away your life to follow a lying tease
You hoped it would be a breeze
Instead you are screaming to God," Please, Please
Don't let me freeze a hollow shell of a man
Please let me rise back up from my knees again
Open my eyes enough to let a new life begin
And try very hard and have it without sin."
Though you will always hold past pains deep within
And still manage to confront others with that phony grin
Yet stand scared, worried that they can see what's within
The shattering wall you use to hide
An over mass of childhood sins
—*Frank Rogers*

War Paint

Timeless times
I've beat myself physically
In that closed corner in my mind saying
This is the way
You've got to be
Smearing that pasty
War paint under my eyes
[Got to hide those dark circles]
and trying to hide that nasty scar
on my bottom lip with
my social wax stick
Pouting and saying
Are they kissable enough?
Am I loveable enough?
is my face right enough for you?
I have prepared myself
for a world who is at war
with who I really am
and with who they will never
let me be.
—*Victoria Seretis*

I Wonder

I wonder if David knew
when writing the psalm
a mother would find
comfort
    in those healing words
a child know security — even
in the dark

a ray of hope found for
the husband who had
lost his job.

I wonder if David knew
the depths of pain he experienced
would be felt
throughout the ages

I wonder...
  if David knew.
—*Deborah Budwig*

Tribute To Mother

A mother is a leader, a teacher, and a believer
A mother is a friend
She helps you and supports you in all that you do.
She is there till the very end
She encourages you to be your best
 And to always believe in yourself.
 Her words are full of wisdom
 Her love is everlasting.
 And no doubt,
 A mother is someone cannot do without.
—*Christa VanBuskirk*

The Pond Of Life

Caught between tomorrow and today
My soul lives on but does not breathe life.

As the days turn cold and nights grow long,
My thoughts are running few and bleak.
Vivid images dance before my eyes
But deep down inside I taste nothing.
My mind is as black as the midnight hour.

People pass by as do the days, months, and years
Speaking words only my ears cannot hear
As the ponds freeze over and the ice grows thick
I become trapped forever.
Am I frozen with time? Or in it?

Nothing has been said or done,
No impact I have made.
Oh eyes of grey, and eyes of green,
Better days these eyes have seen.
—*Dawn Huycke*

Untitled

I close my eyes
Only to see
You are a figment of my imagination
You are something my mind, heart,
 and soul need to overcome

I open my eyes
Only to see
You holding someone, who isn't me

I use to not know pain, love,
happiness or defeat
But now my mind will always wonder,
My heart will always weep,
And my soul will never be complete
—*Jessica Flores*

Tranquility Versus Torment And Destruction

The quiet sand shivers beneath the peaceful waters,
A lonely rock on the sand buries his head,
hiding from the cold. When the peaceful waters turn
away the little rock lies naked uncovered,
for the world to destroy. Then the waves roar and
again comes the blanket which buries the shame,
deep beneath the quiet sand under the peaceful waters.
—*Lisa Fakkeldy*

Solitary Reaper

The top is a lonely place...
Or so it seems in every case
I stand up here looking down below
Lost in the depths of the valley - aglow.
Not caring to think how high above I stand
But wondering at all that I had left behind ...
Friends, security, happiness and care
Of which now I had no share -
Only because of the path I chose to tread?
And the spirit with which I forged ahead?
While I stopped and savoured each experience,
They saw the end; gave that importance.
And in the light that shone on both valley and hill,
The shadow of one loomed larger still.
What I treasured was left fallow ....
For I saw their light - and they, my shadow.
—*Priya Desikan*

Poem To A Friend

Be Happy,
Don't worry, always smile

If you feel depressed,
Just take a look around, think!

Check carefully,
You will see
Everything is beautiful.

If you need help
Choose someone as a confident
Who is close beside you.

Share your problems
With him or her
You will see...

Everything will be easier,
Everything will be over,
And you... you will be happy!

Smile! always smile.
God closes one door
But he always opens the best door.
Smile my friend, smile....
—*Gil Ventura*

Somehow, Somewhere, Someday

Feels so strange
Yet it feels so strong
To feel this way
You've been away so long.
A long time ago
It seems it felt so good
We should still be in love
Like we said we always would,
We turned our back
All those years ago
You cursed me in my heart
The times you've been away
And it's tearing me apart.

Feels so strange yet it feels so strong
To still say I Love You
You've been away so long.
I remember how I cried
The day you went away
I prayed we could fall in love again
Somehow, somewhere, someday.
—*Danny Clay*

City Of Ghosts

Barriers thrown down,
the victor marches through the rubble.
Glorious, yet not so;
he is captor of a ruined city.
The city he once longed to rule
is stricken down, never to be rebuilt.
A truce might have been called;
warriors should have been brothers.
Now, he can only cradle his enemy's head and weep.
Too late, darkness has lifted,
revealing truth as it is lost.
But the world will move on,
leaving the conqueror incomplete,
king of a city of ghosts.
—*Sharon Dawn Selby*

Hometown Convention

I went to a "Poetry" in my hometown,
A "small" town called "New York."
To get there took a subway ride, plus just a two block walk.

I went to one in Washington because I thought
'Twould be the closest it would come to old New York.

Sir Caesar started off the show
And we just laughed with glee.
Many poets remembered when he first starred on TV.

Rita Moreno stole the show, showing much aplomb
By reciting the funniest monologue
With such enormous charm.

There's much more I could tell to make this poem succeed
In convincing folks the fun I had
But would be too long to read.

If you want to go to "Poetry," then send in what you write.
Don't be shy about it, for you may receive an "invite."

So if you're a novice poet,
Or one who's written just one poem
Don't hesitate to send it in,
So let's get goin'.

—*Betty Vogel*

Untitled

The rich reign
the poor are in pain
and our country is losing hope

Acid rain
someone smoking cocaine
and people that can't cope

Shrinking barrier reefs
ozone hole, false teeth
and needles washing up on the sandy beach

Old president's shame
new president's game
and a deficit beyond reach

Brothers killing to live
everyone forgetting how to give
and all these frightening things are true

So let us find a way
to put down the darkening day
but for now the sky is never blue.

—*Teresa Roberts*

The Vessel

A Potter saw a vessel broken by the winds and rains, it was
full of misery, pain, trouble and strife. No light within,
only darkness, blackness of night. All hope gone a vessel
that once stood strong now lay broken, weak and full of despair.
It did not care if it lived or died, it cried not nor attempted
to communicate with those around, it had no care within. Life's
situations had drained it, taken a toll upon it, the wears
and tears of daily existence had split the cracks into pieces,
the vessel dormant. When it moved, having no will of its own,
where it landed it did not care. The vessel merely existed,
now the Potter was full of compassion, he looked upon the
vessel merely existed, now the Potter was full of compassion,
he looked upon the vessel with love. He knew the story of
the vessel's life. The Potter began to pick up the pieces and
gave the vessel new life. He molded and reshaped it, cleansed it
on the outside and purged within. Now the vessel is full of
life, it can move, breathe, sing out loud, for its being is in
Christ. The gift of the Potter, a new lease on life, a
chance to dwell eternally with Christ is why this vessel never seems to give up.

—*Sharla B. Johnson*

All The Same

Everywhere you can find,
People of all different kinds.
Although underneath we're all the same,
If peace doesn't come the world will remain.
An awful place full of hate and dread,
So all of us must start using our heads.
From Canada to Japan, Mexico to Spain,
All the people are still the same.
If world peace does not come,
Then our world will be outdone.
Pollution, war, and racism
Are tearing our world apart.
If we don't do something about it now
and here,
We will have to watch is disappear.
If people don't start growing up fast,
and put our differences in the past.
Then our world will be gone forever,
and we can't just put it back together.
  —*Jennifer Broumley*

To Live On The Streets

As you lay in your bed on a cold winter's night, you think of the people who continue to fight. They work each day to stay alive, eating garbage is how they survive. Some push a carriage with all of their stuff, many look weathered, angry and gruff. Some sit on benches with a rusty tin can, reaching out to their fellow man. Begging for a nickel or dime, after all, is that a crime? When all that you own is in plastic bags, and people look at you like dirty old hags. They have no love, they're all alone, they have no reason to use a phone. Who would they call? What would they say? After all it's just another day. You and I have a home, and people who care, why ask for more? Who would dare? Is it up to us to find them a home, give them clothes, and food of their own. To make their lives like a flower in bloom, so they can sit each night in their own dining room. So they can sit each night at their dining room table, and know that their lives are solid and stable. So when you go to complain, think of the pain these people feel, due to lack of a meal. You think your problems are really that great? Try just once to compensate. Give up your house, your meal, and your bed, and maybe then you'll see why they dread.
  —*Daniel Walty*

Untitled

Winter falls upon the land
Peoples fears are all at hand
Morning comes and melts it away
Sun is shining, so now its time to play

Spring scents fill the air
People have no more cares
Rain comes and washes them away
Now people have no more time to play

Summers here, the weather is hot
Everyone searches for a cool little spot
When they find it they nap in the shade
Waiting for the night to end the day

Fall is coming the summer is gone
The people are picnicking on their lawns
This is the end of what seems so dear
The winter is near, so up pop their fears
  —*Barb Mason*

I'll Be There

When the sparrow sings in the twilight still,
　Perched in the willow on the hill.
Where the breeze blows gentle, quiet, and free,
　I'll be there, think of me.

When the moon casts its silver glow
　Into a wooded glade filled with snow.
Where silence surrounds every tree,
　I'll be there, think of me.

When the stars appear in a velvet sky
　Like a sparkle in a fairy's eye.
　When you wonder, what will be?
　I'll be there, think of me.

When you sit by the fire's flame,
　Remember love has a name.
Love, strong through eternity.
　I'll be there, think of me.

When death's embrace, cold and sure
　Carries me from love so pure.
　By your side I'll forever be.
　I'll be there, think of me.
  —*Leonard Hutchens*

Untitled

Dear God, I pray to someday be a
　person of health and wealth-yet free.
Free from all the toils and stress
　living peacefully—enjoying rest.
Shelter me to not go asunder
　for man thinks of you in awe and wonder.
You are the one, supreme and strong
　teaching man to not go wrong.
Some of us have not seen your light,
　we curse, we kill, we sin, we fight.
Dear God, I pray to you tonight
　give me the strength to do thy right.
Dear God, I have no more to say,
　except in thine holy name I pray.
  —*Linda Cormell*

Death

On the blade of a knife
Playing with death's dark horn
the crimson liquid
slowly slips away.

The morn oh! the morn
the weeping of widows,
the silence of widowers,
and the nightmares of small children.

Who to blame?
Living life in memories trying to find a reason to escape reality
the bleak days
the bitter nights which are spent
reaching out for the person who touched
your soul, and took a piece of your heart

the utter frustration
the inner weakness
crying out for a person lost forever
while you ease into a realm of
memory beyond reality.
  —*Amy Sinko*

"Reality"

"Hello," and "How are you?"
Please read the poem and you won't feel "blue."

Lots of things we can't avoid,
But we can write them in our tabloid.

It is nice to live in the U.S.A.
With the Ups and Downs, we can still say, "Have a Nice Day."

Getting along with people is such a challenge,
But with everyone's help, there is a balance.

Materialistic things are such a rage;
Let's put them in a big, big cage.

Money also is the thing to have;
And it is more than just a fad.

But may be we can learn not to want so much,
And still be healthy, happy with "Lots of Luck."

If we apply the golden rule,
And as the saying goes "stubborn as a mule,"

Then ALL OF US can feel well.
"Gee, won't that be swell?"
—*Sue Lennon*

A Descriptive Of My Dearest

Creme de la creme envelopes
Poached pear softness
Face-fashioned smiles overlay
A matched stunning sunset beauty
Drenched delightfully with sparkling intellect
Gracious charms
Surrounding endless charisma
Tousled ticklers tier that terrific torso
Alluring azure expressives
Just beautifully nosing
Above luscious kissables
Which musically sing lyrical arpeggios
In delightfully thrilling soprano laughter
Tender is the heart
Surrender is my part
When entwined within caressing arms
Squeezing the luckiest
I'm
—*Eugene D. Ross*

I'm A 1991 Man

I can shinny up a telephone
Pole to hang a cable TV line,
Lift up a Cadillac just in time
To save a woman's broken hipbone.

Will cuss with my friends at local digs
Named "The Library". We trade baseball
Memories. Did "Sam Jones pitch all
Twenty-two years, American League?

What inning did DiMaggio hit
His last homer in, three-sixty-one?
Out the swinging doors, beer-drinking done,
Got to go to Lucky's, get some skim

Milk for the twins, Kleenex for the wife,
Bud Lite for me, Milk-Bones for my Bo.
Bo's tail wags. Dinner with our age two
Boys, my beautiful Marge. Sharpen knives,

Carve wooden dolphins in my garage
Workshop. Jack and Joe help me sweep up.
I show them how I'll carve a seal pup.
Twins put to bed, I'm Arnold for Marge.
—*G. Coomes*

Ice On The Petals

The morally good maintains a relative
position like an ever-green pine.

While the immoral goes through
so many beautiful changes.
Like a flower in a garden.

It seems as if the pine is
not as splendor as the flower.

One of these days, when feathery
crystals of ice form.
The pine will still stand strong and tall.

While the flower subsides and
will be seen no more.
—*Linda Ho*

My Pot Of Gold

Today I saw a rainbow; it made me think of my
   Pot of gold,
I wonder if there will be another for me or should it
   Not be told?

You see Life with my husband of forty-four years was my
   Pot of gold
That is what makes me feel my story does indeed need
   To be told.

We had our share of life's laughter and tears, but I did have my
   Pot of gold.
As of this writing he has been gone eighteen months; I feel my story
   Must be told.

I laugh a lot at things he'd said and done, and I cry for my
   Pot of gold.
But still very thankful for all that I've had so my story
   Can be told.

I hope the Dear Lord gives me time to tell the world about my
   Pot of gold,
And then I will know that my life's story at last really
   Has been told.
—*Pauline Grindey*

Praying Hands

As in life I go through,
Praying hands will remind me of you.

Hour after hour you've prayed for our needs,
Seeking God's will in the way He would lead.

Sick people were touched when you prayed in love,
For answers to their needs from God up above.

Broken hearts were comforted as in prayer you went,
When the peace that goes beyond understanding was sent.

Praying hands that remind me of you,
An act of Christ-like love showing through,
Demonstrating faith and trust in all God promised He would do.
—*Berttie B. Miles*

Just One Kiss

Abruptly, you came into my life.
There we were alone in the room.
You glanced out the window—hesitated—to come to me.
Then you were before me, bending to caress my neck.
My arms reached for you—your arms enfolded me.
Our lips met in a tender, lingering, loving kiss.
Your touch put me on a cloud—then I started to
topple off——
You turned—walked out the door.
—*Arleen J. Myers*

A Gourmet's Delight

Startled, I awake! Worries
Press upon my brain,
Pressure mounts until …
I doubt that I am sane.

Worries! Is there no end?
Some I thrust; others I parry
Problematic when they become …
More than I can carry.

One disappears. Another takes it place
Still more! A monumental accumulation
That I should be a glutton with an appetite
Devoid of all cessation.

Somewhere in this universe, a man is sitting,
Eating, eating lamb and curry
While I lie beneath the ground
Eaten up by worry!
—*Anthony F. Gulotta*

No Answer

Journalists
pretend to ask
questions of substance.

The boys of Congress,
Tuesday morning quarterbacks,
mark their turf,
proposing fault-finding panels.

Perhaps they suppose we will find meaning
in hour-long specials and hearings on the hill.

They misinterpret
our collective "Why"
as a search for a reasonable explanation.

It is only the expression of
our mourning and outrage
at death and destruction.

Some of us have a faith that allows for
uncertainty.

Sometimes there is
no answer.
—*Luke Walbert*

My Pet Cat Prissy

My pet cat Prissy, jumps, and runs, she is silly.
Prissy chases the neighbor cat, big Billy.
She runs after their large brown bunny.
Her tail is so short, and she looks real funny.
Playful unrolls the big red ball of twine.
When you scold her, she will cry, and whine.
Prissy loves to play, with a old silver dime.
Mean little cat, but still she will be mine.
My pet cat Prissy, likes to bite my toes.
Billy the cat scratched her on the nose.
A very likeable cat, but can really be mean.
Her eyes shines at night, they are light green.
A big surprise, Prissy caught a mouse.
The mouse ran under the front door, of the house.
My pet cat Prissy, loves her canned chicken liver.
One day she followed the dogs, to the river.
A spoiled rotten cat, but she is a sight to see.
Silly cat has a hiding place, in a big tree.
Plays with her toys, but loves her red ball
Prissy climbed the flag pole, and didn't fall.
—*Kristina Payonk Matcek*

Us

At first it all seemed so easy; the love we shared was
pure and full of vigor, and without any type of hesitation.
After a year your love is full of confidence in which we
know the other will always be there; and when we share each
encounter our minds and our hearts are now a little more aware.
Each day I go on hoping I will never wake from this dream of
bliss and romance, and each night I pray it will not be our
last together, but instead that it is only a beginning for
tomorrow. I see relationships that others may have, and
question you on ours, only because I cherish it with all my heart.
I have tried to give you space which you have wanted and needed
and I, myself, have adapted to the new ways. But after a year
loving and caring I only hope we will grow more and more
together and that each little space will not tear us apart. If
love could ever expressed in words without any type of action;
I could not say all the things that our love means to me. This
little poem is not of the mushy sort or even a sign of
insecurity, just a reminder of what we have and what we share
when we are together or apart: Love
—*Tanika Hendrick*

Regret

She sits alone
   Quietly staring into the darkness
Silence surrounds her
   A reminder of too many lonely nights
Weeping softly
   Teardrops fall like rain
Heartache and emptiness
   Too much for her soul to bear
Regret is a heavy burden
   Crushing what little happiness remains
Wishing she could relive the past
   She gives up hope for a future
Time passes slowly
   Each minute an eternity
The sun rises
   Filling the room with light
She sighs
   As another day begins
—*Sharon Thibodeaux*

One Day

One day peace will show its face, One day freedom wont be one
race. One day God will make his stand, One day we'll walk
hand in hand. One day as we struggle to be free, One day we'll
find the recipe. One day Blacks will be courageous, and one
day people will not hate us. One day drugs will take its toll,
One day he'll call the honor roll. One day people of all
colors, will take the time to love each other. One day man
will lift his head, and see the trees of the forest instead.
One day nature will cease to touch, and we'll lose the land
we love so much. One day children who've died of hunger, in
the land of plenty, will make him wonder.
One day babies will stop their cry, when angels sing their
lullaby. One day slaves of scorn and shame, will rise to claim
their fame. One day the ocean will no longer tide, and the
grass wont be greener on the other side.
One day hands that begged for food, will be rich from oil and
crude. One day soldiers that lay unknown, will see the light
where wise men shown. One day blacks will understand, and
finally see the motherland. One day America, land of the free,
will be the place it used to be.
—*Allene Reed*

Empty Wagon

An empty wagon was pulled down the street and Lord, what a racket.
My friend and I just looked about and said, I just can't hack it.
It squeaks and grinds and rattles so, it puts us in despair.
Then in our minds a voice did speak, I do not know from where!
An empty wagon, the most noise makes, from this learn a lesson,
And when you do, and see the point, to you it'll be a blessing.
Sometimes we toot our horn so loud we really say just nothing
When really we should 'peace be still' and keep our mouths muffled.
How loud and coarse we sometimes are and for others we don't care,
We shout and yell and play the part of an angry Grizzly Bear.
Our minds and hearts are barren of the courtesies of life,
And all we bring to others is anguish and strife.
So, lets all fill ourselves up with love and courtesy,
Then quietly go down life's road, filled up, you and me.
—*Lois J. Rammacher*

Love Struck

Abandoned my heart, I sit here alone,
Ran out of happiness, ran from, "my home",
Awaiting the taste which falls upon my tongue.
The taste of love, but I am still young.
You see not what I see,
Creating false images of me.
Never thinking to look inside my voice,
Carelessly, making a foolish choice.
My tears hold secrets, forgotten memories,
Silently, crying out, I am free.
Free to feel the feelings, which made me shy to you.
Love me for who I really am, and not what you make me to.
Being here in your arms, I can again be full of bliss,
You've restored my life, my happiness.
—*Rebecca Vicente*

"Immunity"

I'd really like to drive around in shiny fast wheel cars.
  Reaching out towards the screaming stars.
Whenever I think of those gone with the wind.
  I wonder if I'll ever see them again.
My hands keep on picking like a soldier marking time.
  My thoughts keep on believing there must be some special rhyme.
We can fly like an eagle,
  We could swim like a fish in the sea.
Just like a flower we could grow like a tree.
  All I want to be is free.
All of the times I lie awake in the middle of the night.
  All of the times I choke because the words didn't come out right.
I wish that I were free to be what I want to be.
  All I want is the opportunity to have an opportunity.
I need the immunity.
—*Marleen M. Williams*

Ghost

Now, no longer ceasing to exist, but
Reaching, searching—before existence—
I struggled upward through fields of learning
Pushing at the truth of darkness.

Still held by forces unbeknown
I briefly touched the other side,
Then wrapped myself in mist and shadow
To break beyond and free.

Changed, I soar on wings of eternity
Beyond the farthest sparkle of a dream,
Toward the vast incredible warmth
And the power and glory of love!
—*Jane M. Frady*

My Country Memories

I'm sitting under an old oak tree
Reading my bible, eating raisins and candy,
Seeing all the animals, and
Looking at the flowers out by the barn
Remembering my visits here,
In Memphis, Tennessee, when I was twenty-three.

I remember going on vacation,
To my aunts' house, down on the farm,
When I was a little girl just three,
Eating the apples right off the tree
And the squirrels run across the farm yard
As the day turned into night.

I remembered the big rock
Where I used to sit and see the world
As I thought of being a little girl
Watching the farmers bring down
The animals through the pasture
And into his own barn yard for the night,
That old barn with wild grass growing high.
—*Irma L. Stallings*

A Gift Of Love

With whispered things and golden chains,
Real love cannot be bought,
Love's essence, ever bittersweet,
Came first to man from an old rugged cross.

Real love became a sacrifice,
Made for you and me.
The hope of salvation was poured out to man,
As the Father wept in agony.

So if I open up my heart to you,
Then you must understand.
I've given my life and soul to Him
Who holds the future in His hands.

Yes, I will give you love, my friend,
Channeled from above.
Not with worldly pleasure or pride,
But with the sacrifice that is Real Love.
—*Lynda C. Walker*

There Is No One Left To Tend The Garden

Where the shadows end and the gentle breeze stops,
  reality is scorched into the dry barren land.
The once majestic trees with supple limbs waving,
  now rest on the ground dried and dead.
We left long ago, never to return again.
  Through our hate and greed we were banished.
To all four corners of the Earth we spread,
  in our path death and destruction.
Now the poisoned Earth pleads with us to change,
  but we lost our innocence long ago.
Our beginnings have now ended through our vile ways.
  The trees, the flowers, ourselves, we have all died.
For there is no one left to tend the garden.
—*Michael Clark*

A Poem From A Senior Citizen Mom

As I sit and think of the past
  The year's have gone, so fast
Now, the children have grow, and all away,
  I think of when, they use to roam and play
My love for them, has never ceased
  All I pray for, is God give them peace
I wish them luck health, and success
  With lots of love and plenty of happiness.
—*Josephine Falsetta*

Precious

Gold, emerald, diamond, the best of stones;
rectangular, square, oval, marquise or round.

Rich and poor, men and women, all regard them.
They will pay a lot for a small piece of gem.

Some wait a lifetime for the wedding band,
to put the special jewelry on their right hand.

A gift of emerald, bright, dark and green,
will fulfill someone's long lasting dream.

Gold—pure, shine and gleaming yellow,
around the neck of some fellow.

Fancy shapes, sparkling diamond varied in carats,
these, society value at their highest merits.

Still, there is something more valuable;
the breath of life is most admirable.

Touching, closeness, warmth and comfort of another,
babies resting in the arms of a mother or a father.

Loving, whispering having someone near,
unselfish, sharing, continuing to care.

Emeralds, diamonds or a lot of gold,
is never brighter than a person's soul.
—*Shirley Rose Jones Edwards*

"A Quest Of Yore"

Out of the moonlit, misty night there rose a knight adorned in red,
and at his sides the thorns of war lay waiting for thedead.

On his shield there was a crown
With a rose for the head,
And at his feet upon the ground
Lay the slain and the dead.

Then with a cry so fierce and bold he ran head long into the fray
never halting nor retreating always advancing through the day.

His sword blazed with shining steel
As drops of blood spilled on the field,
And by his hand he wrought the kill
Never showing signs that he would yield.

But as the day wore on his foes grew less and less, and
by the sinking of the sun he had completed his great quest.
—*Nicholas Edward Buckner*

Pain Of Love Never Found

Blue velvet sky of pain,
Red rivers wash the rain,
Bitter sunshine twilight's haze,
Your tears can't hide its scorching rays,
Orange light beyond your soul,
Black as night you are so cold,
Broken emotions leaving now,
The joy of love has left somehow,
Can it be this vision lost,
Through sorrow found soul is cost,
Standing in the twilight's rays,
Your smile can't hide the tears you rain,
All you see is nowhere now,
All you feel lost somehow,
Bitter sunshine crescent moon,
There is no love in this room,
Pain of life an ending near,
You've lost your sight, which way to steer,
Can it be love is gone,
When in truth was never found.
—*Daniel Henderson*

Into The Light

Slowly, slowly, the door is torn
reflecting light upon the dawn
If I look too hard, it blinds me with pain
So I gaze softly
to illuminate the darkness in my brain

I can see shadows of people I know from my past
Silhouettes of the present, the future not cast
Do not close the door, I want to come in
For the journey of my life is about to begin

Wider, wider, the passage is revealed
Memories, like blisters, need to be healed
The tears burn my eyes, and my anxious heart grieves
As the knowledge I am facing
confronts me to leave

I will walk into the light when I am able to see
That the love I've been yearning must come first from me
Each day brings me closer, one step at a time
To a world filled with love that is rightfully mine
—*Nancy E. Kozak*

"The Great Decision"

You were born into this world,
Regardless, what the situation,
Whether born into middle class,
Or nobility.

You had no say,
In what happened that day.
But
Now, you have a choice,
A will of your own.

Don't play the fool.
Time is of the essence,
And the ball is in your court.

Will you pass   or   aim and follow through?
—*Thomas Onorato*

Mr. Frog

Hello, Mr. Frog — it's me.
Remember, I was here before— him and me.

Remember, we embraced beneath those trees
And felt the breeze as we locked our knees.

We listened to your song, the foghorn ditty,
I was happy then— now, what a pity.

All I seem to do is cry,
And, Mr. Frog, do you know why?

It's because I'm here alone today;
My love has chosen to stay away.

Well, Mr. Frog, I'll stop my weeping
So you can get back to your sleeping.

But, if you should see him,
Please, Mr. Frog, tell him that I
need 'um
need 'um
need 'um.
—*Davida Dawn Williams*

"Remembering Other's"

    Remembering other's, is that so hard to do?
    Remembering other's, is that so hard for you?
    Remembering other's, and happy you will become!
Remembering other's, will keep you from becoming blue!
    So, just what is it, that you want to do?
Peace, Harmony and Happiness, will be so good, for you!
    Now you know, just how happy, other's do become!
Remembering other's, is how you keep from being blue!
    Taking that split second, is all you need to do!
        To Remember Other's.
    —*John W. Jackson Jr.*

Maybe He's Watching Me

As I sat on the porch stairs sulking,
Remembering the times he was near,
Now he's in a far off distant land that only God knows of,
But maybe his spirit is close to me this very instant watching me cry,
And maybe he's remembering the times that we would lay together in the long, long grass looking up at the deep blue sky,
Then he would fall asleep in the blazing sunlight delightfully purring.
His black and white fur shining in the breath taking morning sunshine,
And the fresh morning dew on his sweet little paws,
He meant the world to me, and always will,
But now he's only a memory,
A memory, that will live on forever.
    —*Carolyn Ballema*

Frightened

The thunder crashed,
    reminding me of a gunshot;
    the one that killed my friend.

The rain falls,
    reminding me of the tears
    that dripped from our eyes.

The rain still falls,
    reminding me of something other than tears...the blood
    that slid from him.

The sun finally shines,
    telling and showing us all
    that everything will be okay.
    —*Halecia Scott*

Blood Sisters

That afternoon, we were two childhood friends
Reminiscing about what feels a lifetime past.
Indian-style knees touching
I pass you a picture frame
Engraved Jo-Jen for your 21st birthday.
A hurtful look passes your face
The look I know so well.
You're thinking of Brian, your little brother
Who died on your thirteenth birthday.
We talk, and then suddenly begin to laugh about a million other
Things remembered.
Alice in wonderland, our fourth grade play
Kevin Ford, my first kiss.
That evening, we become college friends
Drug induced
We laugh, about your dreams of being a tap dancer
My big break as talk show host and you, my first guest.
We feel high, like being friends forever and get the crazy notion of making it official. Two childhood college friends reminisce, and talk about the future.
    —*Jodi Rigberg*

"Meditations"

Tears and groans and black despair
    Rend the foggy, tense, electric air!
Know not I where to turn—
    While ravishing fires within me burn!

Ah—that some day fate would be kind!
    But fools only trust him—and left behind,
They mutter "isms" 'neath "learned beard"—
    Such as, "It's just exactly as I feared"!

Could we but fight with our true self!,
    And leave all doubts upon the shelf—
We may still fail—but with a grin—
    We'd arise and fight—and some day win!

To win! To win! What magic words!
    It takes us high—like soaring birds;
To know success sans honor lost—
    Just faith in ourselves, the only cost!
    —*C. Wesley Hume*

All About Me, I Am Exceptional

    I am a student just like you... I desire to be loved and respected too... There are so many things that I wish I could do, to enable myself to be just like you.

    I come to school each day you see, to better myself according to my abilities. My teachers are special, they are really the key, they are dedicated to excellence when teaching me...

    So smile when you see me, or just say hi! I don't mind it if, at first, you are a bit shy...

    There is really no difference between us two...

    I am E X C E P T I O N A L and so are you.
    —*Sheila Mitchell*

Meditation

When twilight smoothes the edges of a
    restless busy day
It makes me want to bow my knees to
    God and humbly pray

To thank Him for the wonders
    of a world He made for me.
For the beauty of creation
and the eyes with which to see.

For the flowers that bloom by the wayside
and the trees that turn gold in the fall
and my soul rejoices with gratitude
To the Lord that made them all.

The birds sing to me every morning
To calm my doubts and fear
How can my heart be lonely
When God is every where.
    —*Myrtle Slaughter*

Night

The night is bright and full of light.
The sky crammed with stars and planets so bright,
Plants so bright the sky is lite like a light.
The full moon brings excitement to the eyes,
The night was beautiful and soft.
We are awake for this wondrous sight.
We are fast asleep waiting for the bright sunlight
To awaken us from this dreamy night.
    —*Autumn Rainey*

Armenia

There, upon the summit of Mount Ararat,
Rests the dove with the olive branch.
It sits quietly and observes an intense struggle,
While far below, across time's ethereal distance,
The mountain casts a shadow and a dream.

Tears fall from the weighted soul of an elderly woman,
A tormented witness to a seemingly forgotten Genocide.
The light fades slowly at this corner of the world.
Her obscured eyes darken at the momentary reflection
As she places a flower down by the tombstone.

Fallen heroes now replace mighty kings, as fate's
Unpredictable nature leads us on a quest for justice.
Pleading whispers evoke not recognition, but sympathy.
As the cold mist rises in the early morning sun,
It smiles warmly upon realms of sweet melancholia.

Unified, brother and sister stand side by side holding hands.
They marvel at the new flag overhead, soaring in the wind.
A new generation reinforcing old foundations of wisdom.
The dove slowly begins its descent, offering hope to them,
Their cause, and to a free and independent Armenia.
—*George Anastasian*

Question And Balance

Call out shallow graves
Reveal stories of the past
The ultimate wisdoms prevail
And the Meek shall inherit the earth
For what is the ideal philosophy
It must be what is never nearly explained in unity
Glancing upon diverse minds

The wise observe and contemplate the cosmos
No horizons for imagination
So sputter no more about questions ending
Balance astray
Stagnation shall stay
So pour proportion

Spirit, intellect, and emotion
Search and sail river flow of being
Listen and map dynamic tributaries
Coursing nature's rhythms and senses
Among each other
Love sustains the counter-entropy battle
To float the vast ocean of human being
—*John David R. Robertson*

Sunrise

On an early spring morning
The sunrise is dawning,
And it begins to glow,
Giving us a spectacular show.

Colors of splendor, mingled and mixed,
Hues and tones, seemingly fixed.
Each one so different,
Unlike the day before — far and distant.

A surprise to some
A prize to most
A gift from God, your one Great Host!
—*Laura Simpson Woods*

"New Faces"

Just as the sun rises each day
Revealing her brilliant light
So does new faces that vanish away

In these faces I see feelings that can't be expressed
Love, hope, anger and pain
All emotions
Robbing them of their rest

If only the sun would never set
Then friends would last forever
And not vanish, as if they never met

Words do not always say what's in the heart
Often we try to tell who we are
But can not find the words to start

If only we could express what we really feel
At least we would know the truth
And our wounded hearts would heal

A free soul is not afraid to dream of a new day
For night does not last forever!
Surely the sun will rise again!
And her brilliant light will not fade away
—*Selina P. Barua*

The Shadow's Fearful Reign

Full darkness is not yet upon me.
Reverently, I gaze at the last traces
of the afternoon's glorious blue sky.
While all about me, shadows lay in wait.
Eagerly they've come out,
for soon the night will be complete.
I, alone, am witness to their gathering.
Like huddled groups of black-robed dwarves,
I see them in alleyways.
Within the obscured depths of a garage
their numbers are ever-so-slowly increasing.
In the woods, these night-things
create a more ominous presence.
Refuge was found beneath many trees
where ferns yield, a death-life, ebony color.
I escape, terrorized, for they cling to me.
Slowly I was becoming invisible.
Beneath the safety of a streetlight,
I discover my terror is as complete as the night;
and the shadows rule once more.
—*Marcus Davis*

Time

Time beats as a clock of quick sands
riding through the desert of illusion
following the implacable track of the sun
without stopping nor even for an instant
controlled by an old passion....

Oh, time, that crazy old man!
without even perceiving
what was the past
from what could be the present,
looks eagerly as an unstable compass
in a firmament without any star
what it will become the future
and in the meantime that untamed foal, runs, runs, runs...
—*Rebeca Skinner*

Decisions

No two people are the same, every person has a name.
Right or wrong, we make a choice, we see, we feel, we have a
voice. Up and down, left and right, at this time the future
looks bright.

I'm not sure but I've been told, "Some are quiet and some
are bold". Some may glitter, some may shine, some say
"yours and this is mine." Inside, outside, down and around,
test yourself through sight and sound.

Horse or mule, they're strong no less, look over them
carefully to pass the test. Laughter and smiles is great to
see, crying and frowns is not for thee. In love and
respect, some people do slack, you'll be lucky if you get
any back.

"From this day forward" is a long, long time, never again
"yours" and never again "mine". Be sure of your heart and
doubt free, be true to your heart and you'll be true to
thee.
—*Janis Kollatschny*

The Phoenix

   I see myself as a phoenix,
rising out of the ashes of a ruined marriage,
when he didn't want to get stuck with someone
who might become a bedridden invalid,
due to the arthritis creeping up my spine
and causing swelling, stiffness, and pain.
   So he took the money and left,
and went to another woman. And I stood
with the children and trembled on the
threshold of my brave new world
and second start in life.
   I flapped my wings against the air
of shattered hopes and broken dreams,
and decided to use the strength of anger
to produce something good, and commenced—
still racked with fears and physical pain—
until the surgeon's knife slashed
and ended the misdiagnosed arthritis;
away the tumors pressing against my spine
and the counselor's wisdom ended
the agony of inner pain.
   And I rose upon wings of hope
and determination to sail into collegiate skies
where clear blue air and billowing clouds parted.
   Three young shadows followed
as I soared toward the golden sun.
   I am a phoenix.
—*Diana Davis*

No Johnny No

No! Johnny No I yelled as a redheaded tornado
runs for the bathroom.
How many times have we pulled out combs, brushes, lipsticks.
And I don't know what from the toilet.
And then he turned and ran into the kitchen
And we yell No 1 Johnny no as a dish of spaghetti
hits the floor, and oops there goes a gallon of milk.
I go to grab him and off he goes right for the lamp. I grab
them both in the nick of time. And he's only two years old.
Boy, Does he have a lot of years to hear my favorite saying,
No! Johnny no! But you know young man,
There's one time you'll never hear me say it.
And that's when you give me a great big hug and kiss.
—*Sharon Whitten*

The Mountain

I saw the mountain again today
Rising powerfully from the Earth
A giant sentinel watching over me
My sole companion since my birth

I heard the waterfall again today
Flowing through the fingers of time
While I drown in eternity and listen to its song

I smelled the fragrance of the Land today
So clean, so pure, so ancient
It smelled of life and love and peace
It embraces me with tenderness

I could taste the power of the wild today
It was sweet with the flavor of freedom
Strengthened by human desire I lust for its knowledge

I touched the Earth again today
It felt like soft heather and barren rock
Its feelings became my own and I wept at its pain
I met myself today on my way up the mountain
—*Zachary Simms*

Just Like A Sea Shell, She Is..

Uniquely independent.
Rolling with the tide from shore to shore,
Adapting to its new surroundings.

Uniquely courageous.
Traveling the depths of challenge,
Confronting the unknown with strength from beneath its shell.

Uniquely beautiful.
With beauty all its own,
As no other.

Uniquely a treasure.
Just like a sea shell, she is....
—*Therese M. Sliwa*

Anticipation

Daffodil bulbs, in earliest spring,
Roused by the vague, silent stirrings -
The secret urgings that all birthings bring -
Responding, send slender, virginal shoots,
Like slim, seeking fingers, groping their way
Up through the soft, yielding wakening roots,
Feeling through uncharted paths they will find
A fresh, budding world, where seasonal change
Has left Winter's icy climate behind.
Gaining its goal, each shoot now will hold
Toward a winsome, soft azure sky
A chalice-like bloom of tenuous gold -
Catching the tears April shed from on high.
Busily, clouds flitter by overhead.
Day fades to night; night lightens to day.
This pattern - repeated, will soon usher in
The carefree, the blissful, the blithe month of May.
—*Mildred E. Sandomenico*

I Shall Never Reach A Dream

Dreams are the weeds that
Run along the road deep in the fields.
Tall and limber they reach the sky.
Like a pillow they rest the eye.

Those weeds that are fantasies,
That bite at the heel;
Those weeds that are monsters
Turn fake into real.

Wonderful, glorious dreams.
Painful, horrid dreams.

The road is long and tedious,
It laughs and taunts.
It pulls close...
And then it curves.
It winds and winds, and twists and twists,
Drawing every breath.

I think I shall never reach...
A dream.
For I know not the way...
Off the road.

—*Traci Kinsler*

"Imagination"

Looking into her shadow knowing she's not there,
Running my fingers through her imaginary hair.
Drawing a picture of how she used to be
Drawing a picture of how she looked to me.
Seeing her walk, seeing her laugh
But remember that's of the past.
Looking everywhere trying to find her I forgot she's not there.
Now she's in God's world looking down I don't even know if she has a smile or a frown.
She was a wonderful lady mother to me,
As you can see I loved her very much I loved to feel her sweet hand touch.
I'll be able to see her when my life is gone,
I'll be able to see my imaginary Mom.

—*Jeremy Harris*

Blind Justice

To raise a child alone, we urge you to believe
sacrifices made, are choices few conceive.

To house and cloth a child is hard, though often we deny
sometimes we work without much pay, but still we have to try.

Try to give them everything, we think they want or need
guilt repressed within the heart, is ours we don't concede.

At night, late from work, the children often sleep
little time we spend, give cause for us to weep.

Though rarely not asleep, so little time to spare
anxious and exhausted, they think we do not care.

Blame we place upon ourselves, is one we don't explain
little minds won't understand; we listen, they complain.

Someday we'll look upon them, soon after we've been tried
and pray that we see only clear loving mirror eyes.

—*Diane L. Howard*

Together

Whenever you fall, I'll be there to catch you, to carry you safely into tomorrow. Hand in hand we will conquer, all in life that shall bring us sorrow. Two hearts that beat as one, a soul I know you own. Though you're faced by darkness, you will never be alone. I'll be with you every step you take, every hill you ever climb. If you need someone to lean on, I will be the crutch that holds you up. Whereupon strength is weakened, lovingly I will refill the cup. Reassurance ever needed, look no further than my eyes. Sorrow tells a story to make us stronger, make us wise. Nothing as ever mattered, as much as you do now. Provided you ever need me, reach out, call my name. My promise to you is, I will always do the same. No matter how deep the waters, we will keep our heads above. For we share the greatest bond, unconditional love. We are in this life together, from now 'til the ends of time, every heartache, every joy, together yours and mine.

—*Sherry Oates Nichols*

Hippo

"Sure takes a lot of us to move a hippopotamus,"
Said Sammy to the seals.
"Now - could we float him on a boat,
Or put him on some wheels?"

The little bunny said, "How funny
To see a hippo coast
Along the street, on all four feet
Say! That would be the most!"

"A hippo skating? Oh, how degrading!
Tell me what where is your pride?"
The walrus bellows (they're snooty fellows).
"I'd rather see him slide."

At that, the hippo rose, and stood up on his toes.
He grinned quite happily,
"I thank you much, I'm very touched
By your concern for me

But I feel just great; In fact, first rate
And though I may be slow,
I'm here to state for all my weight
I SWIM where I must go!"

—*Esther Ford Felsburg*

Landscape With Island And Quixotic Dreamer

And loneliness is always a blue port setting the trap for the sailor. Giants, escaped from the tiny hourglass, life comes into being, you see, a sad nightmare in the knights's corroded armor. They seem to be windmills; they seem to be enchanted country girls. The magician lets his pigeons fly and tells the traders that a man is dreaming while riding a white nag. Lonely nag, old and dusty shadow walking around the damp shed, Lonely knight recalling passages from the book kept in his memory. And the giants and the sweet country girls go away; and the knight crosses the bridge.
      Island, fragment of light, Promised Land the knight dreams of in his vigil; Island where the smooth light transforms the snow into warm waters; Island, uncertain Island where the knight's dream nosedives into the sea.
The dreamer hides in his contour the windmills' giant arms; gallivants around the princess, enchanted country girl. He rambles, his eyes opened to the dusty, whirling wind. Island, the knight just went away. Awaken knight's dream; awaken knight in your sleepy waters. Island, dreamed Island, you're only a place for an endless sequence of shipwrecks.

—*Orlando Ferrand*

Gloria And Senie

G race, thy beauty enchants me to dwell with thee forever.
   Saintly do I love thee for genuine understanding, dear.
L ove, broadly meant, equally shared with, and truly understood-
   Endearingly binds us together in a wholesome livelihood.
O f moments of difficulties or days of crucial adversities
   Never shall I falter nor yield in fear to worship thee in
     reverence—
R esolution geared out of real love springing deep from the human
     breast,
   In sacred homage to thy beauty of thy heart and soul,
I , for one, pledge to vindicate in perpetuity the dignity of
     the conjugal principle.
   Everlastingly bound together in love, in purpose, or in sacred
     vows
A nd then in death do we only hope to part in oblivion.

   —Senie Calip

Murder The Coffin

Witness my suicide,
Satan tries.

Plan family murders,
Shoot sanity death,
Call angels witnessing psycho therapy,
Into a mind hell bent sadly believing death.

Evil or pressured emotions feeling hard up,
Sex tricks all 3 rules,
Like sleepless moons carving forward wishes,
Passing riddles and black nailed scrolls.
With life stretched maxes,
Only Pisces number 12.

Words cry, giant tears,
Acid-eating devouring authority-stirred recipes,
Satan cooks while he cleans.

A mind stronger age to conquer,
Limited with times Godly proportions of cruelty,
Friends fallen leaves seasons pass,
Seeds grow souls rotten baring HIV positive,
Observing the world so great at me.

   —Jason Jones

Wish It Was Me

When I was young and looking ahead, I saw kids going to
School. Wish It was me.

When I went to school, I saw kids dating, falling in love.
Wish it was me.

When I was dating, I saw couples getting married, moving
Out. Wish it was me.

When I married, I saw parents in the park with children
playing around their feet. Wish it was me.

When I had kids, I saw couples, the kids moved out, free to
Do what they pleased. Wish it was me.

When my kids married and moved out, I saw retired couples
With no job, no responsibilities. Wish it was me.

When I retired I saw kids playing, looking ahead.
Wish it was me. Wish it was me.

   —Steven L. Riley

Spoon River Revisited: Darius Revry

During my life, they laughed at me, taunted,
scolded my dreams
so different from their own,
saying mine would never come true.
Still I persisted,
becoming the black sheep,
never to be accepted or recognized.

A pioneer I would have been,
a breaker of new grounds,
expanding minds and horizons.
Yet I, restrained by ridicule,
conformed to normalcy,
rendering me immobile.
Dreams unfulfilled,
left to die with the person possessing them.

Perhaps I saw what they could not,
or simply would not.
Now, like broken-winged birds,
they are either afraid to fly with my dreams,
or are too ignorant to know how.

   —Lisa Petry

From Birth To Death

I saw him once, like a tadpole scurrying about,
   Searching and searching for his fitting home.

I saw her once, patiently waiting, waiting for that moment to
   journey through the long tunnel and emerge in a halo of light.

It weighed nothing and was invisible to the naked eye,
   yet both knew it followed them.

In the hectic daytime hours, it comforted them,
   soothing their battered armor.

In the silence of the night, it guarded them,
   roaming from room to room.

Timelessly it engulfed their mind and body,
   gently guiding it to a peaceful existence.

What was this that emerged in a halo of light?

To date, no scientist can identify it,
   no scholar can describe it.

Yet it is there, for only those who gave of it, and no one else.

I saw them once, in the western sky,
   All aglow from the setting sun.

A love so strong, a creation of eternal spirit,
   The validation of their souls.

   —Caroline Annand

The Path

Streets, they pave the way through one's life.
Shall one go left or to the right.
How can man or woman choose, for they both have unseen ends?
Straight ahead, they go, forever passing the curious
routes they could have chosen.
Why did they not turn, and see the brilliant lights
of golden routes passing them by?
Scared they are, going forward into the treacherous dead
end of time.
For only, if they veer off, all will not be lost,
on the path through life's journey, road ends, detour.

   —Danny F. Brungardt

Gone Around

Barnacles cling tight to ships, through the sea so turbulent.
See that glass over there, full to brim free of care.

Into port ships do slip, barnacles scraped and fol-e-age
stripped. Shiny glass over there,
a little less full, a little bit of care.

In the sea the scrapings float, the abyss awaits the innocent
to cope. Three quarters full the glass now stands,
care can fit into the palm of hands.

Drifting floating bouncing grinding, smoothing edges through
swirls their finding. Half to full, or half to empty,
the glass is draining, and care extending.

Mix and mingle they cling another, smoothed around they settle
down. The glass three quarters once was full,
now as was but visa-verse.
Care the same? Oh its building.

Blown to beaches as destiny would have, molded in process
through turmoil and glad.
Care is now total, with glass all empty, the last swallow was
fate, but it was just plenty.
Barnacles cling tight to ships, through the sea so turbulent.
   —Scott Silk

Senior Responsibility

All children are most surely the World's Future!
Seniors, especially, must now definitely ensure
That every child enjoys good health and education;
No person ever encourage any unhealthy competition!

Concerned Seniors, who surely have love and compassion
For all children, families, and people of every nation,
Challenge all world leaders to absolutely discard greeds,
Promote Worldwide cooperation: Effectively provide needs!

Should not religious seniors, worldwide, help propagate
Congregations that Unite to eliminate anger and hate?
Such activity demonstrates advantages of fellowship,
Enabling children, worldwide, to enjoy happy friendship!

Seniors must now present the need for conferences,
To intelligently discuss and resolve differences!
Then, worldwide, all nations can happily together
Demonstrate all people can be loving sister, brother!

All peace-loving seniors need to actively unite;
Request every nation decide to never again fight!
When, worldwide, all people, war-free, happily live,
to active peace-loving seniors grateful thanks give!
   —Sita Akka Paulickpulle

To My Wife, Renee:

The wife of my youth was beauty and truth,
   She brightened our home and my heart;
Like a wedding ring, a song of spring,
   Giving each day a new start.

My wife of mid-years was laughter and tears,
   As she romped with our children and me;
Or, together we cried when loved ones died,
   And God set their spirits free.

The wife of my age is witty and sage,
   Still a lady fair to behold.
She honors my schemes and perpetual dreams,
   And tells me I'm not too old.

My wife for all time is rhythm and rhyme,
   As mystical as the sea.
Love is pure and life means more,
   Since Renee abides with me.
   —Robert J. Dunathan

All Will Be Well

In the dark and the silence, awareness awoke.
Sensing her presence, the entity spoke:
"We've a cosmos to build, and Time to begin;
Stars to compose, and planets to spin.
With gravity, energy, matter and space,
And unbreakable laws holding each in its place."

No mortal eye peered through that primeval night.
The immortal creators had no need of sight...
Nor voices. Each thought in each mind became known
To the other the instant its seed had been sown.
As his words drew her closer—a summons; a knell,
He commanded her: "Touch me! All will be well!"

Reaching out in the darkness their bodies entwined.
Came the dawn with the light as their essence combined.
Her matter was anti. His science ordained
His mass being greater, some matter remained.
With her death she gave life. Her loss was his gain.
Without her, his science had labored in vain.
They had joined in the night and at dawn said farewell.
God was building His heaven. All would be well.
   —Lewis P. Harper

Thoughts On Birthday 80

Not with calendar nor with clock
   shall I count the time that's left for me —

But with acts of kindness
deeds of love and mercy
children hugged
sick and lonely cheered

Roses smelled, sunsets seen
mountains viewed, canyons crossed

Dances danced, dinners dined
games played well
good music heard
great art observed

Walks on beaches
and in the woods
walks in moonlight
and in the rain —

All these and more
I shall enjoy
with double joy
when shared with you again!
   —John W. Donnelly

The Mover

She woke up this morning with moving on her mind,
She grabbed the newspaper to see what she could find.

Didn't list too many that she could afford,
Left messages on machines till she got bored.

Kept packing boxes waiting for them to call,
Went and looked at houses till she thought she would fall.

Some were too large, some were too small,
She couldn't arrange the furniture so her mama wouldn't fall.

She bought houses, rented houses and apartments too,
Moving wasn't such a job, as that was what she liked to do.

She bought a house in Oak Grove and one in Petal too,
She even moved to the coast but back to Hattiesburg she flew.

She will be glad to get settled in an apartment once more,
And cut out all that expense as moving is a chore.

She and her mother are getting older and their health is failing fast,
On her tombstone she wants printed "through moving at last."

—*Mickey Mangum*

You

Today I took our little girl to the zoo.
She had such a great time, and I guess I did too.
The only thing missing was you.

She laughed at the monkeys and talked to the bear.
Seemed like everything was new and worth a stare.
And I kept wishing you were there.

We smiled and walked and talked.
To her it was just a wonderland.
To me it felt so good
To hold in mine her little hand and you know,
I even wore my wedding band.

There's nothing on earth that could ever undo
This precious little girl. She's me, she's you.
I can't help but feel, if we try, we could start anew.

I sure hated to bring her home when the time came to go.
And I wanted to stay
Just to say hello, just to say hello,
And see your face
I still love you so.

—*Abe W. Kelly, Jr.*

The Reader

As she sits in the corner in her favorite rocking chair
She is alone, but not lonely.
She becomes lost and never wants to be found.
She is swept away into another world,
a world of fantasy that becomes so real.
She forgets herself and who she is
as she becomes part of a time and place
which exist only as pictures in her mind.
For a little while her own problems are forgotten
as she cries someone else's tears.
Her hands have become puppets
turning the pages of a good book.

—*Sarah Levien*

Memories To Hold Onto

Grandmas play imported roles in today way of life.
She is ready & able to take charge at the push of a panic button.
Grandmas today are living longer, enjoy better health, a better style of living. The old rocking chair is empty, she is off to spend a full day, putting her energy to satisfy her own needs, to further her own accomplishments.
She is forceful, versatile, dynamic, completely independent.
You find her at the tennis courts, golf courts, or relaxing with a good book.
She likes to be heard whether its a voice in politics or just generalizing. Her typewriter goes clickity-clack, for Grandma is now writing a book. She doesn't tend babies anymore, baby sitting is not in her curriculum, still learning has taken its place. She is not content with second hand knowledge.
She likes to sing & dance, enjoys romance, her philosophy, if you can't live it down, then live it up.
Three cheers for grandmas - and three cheers for senior centers - they make good things happen.

—*Fran Satz*

Love

Love sometimes eats people's hearts, for dinner.
She is very beautiful at times,
But she can be wicked as a witch.
She is locked away in people's hearts,
Until they let her out.
Her hair is as golden as the sun;
Her eyes are like the only two stars,
On a dark night.
She is as quiet as a meadow;
She can be a teddy bear,
When fear comes over to visit.

—*Myah Osher*

The Wedding Is Over

The wedding is over, and the reception is too
She is your wife now, and she belongs to you
But on this day when everything is in a whir.
One thing I ask of you, be good to my little girl.

When you chose my daughter for your wife
I knew she'd marry one day, that's life
Yes. God gave me a daughter instead of a son
I love her, too; we had such great fun.

When you took my daughter for your bride
It filled this old heart of mine with pride
She has her faults, you have yours, too
If you pull together, life will be good to you.

If in-laws stir up trouble for both of you
Talk it over, laugh, forget it, then start anew
Keeping up with the neighbors isn't everything
Love and happiness will come through God the King.

The wedding is over, and the reception is too
She is your wife now, and she belongs to you
But on this day when everything is in a whirl
One thing I ask of you, be good to my little girl.

—*Mary Frances Kemp*

She Looks

For one more day,
She looks his way,
She has a lot to say,
But she must turn away.

Soon her vision begins to blur,
As emotions start to stir,
She picks at a stray dog's fur,
Like a cat she begins to purr.

He has dark brown hair, and chocolate brown eyes,
When she looks at him her heart practically flies,
To her he's cuter than all the other guys,
She tries to get his attention, how hard she tries.

For one more day,
She looks his way,
She has a lot to say,
But she must turn away.
—*Jill Baker*

Best Friend We'll Always Be

I had a best friend, but she was not like you
She moved away, then our friendship was through.
Days, months, and years had past, I had other best friends
but they didn't last.
Me and you it sounds so right, we'll last
forever even if we fight.
We'll never part, unless death sets us free, but someday again
you'll be with me.
That's if I die first, but if I don't, I'll never find another,
but that's if you won't. Even if you betray me, our friendship
in me, I will always see to be.
I'll stand by your side in the worst of times and best.
And I'll never stop to take a rest. Your there for me and I'm
there for you. The friendship between us will never be through.
Till the end of time we'll build up our trust it will never
stop, break, or bust. We know we'll die, we know we live, we
know we'll cry, and we both know we still have lots to give.
But for now our friendship is here to stay and I'll never stop
loving you in that best-friend kind of way.
—*Laura Hippe*

She's The Lily Of My Valley

She's the lily of my valley.
She now walks where angels tread;
Having left life's cares behind her,
Her pain is gone. There's peace instead.

She's the lily of my valley.
Once again she leads the way.
Keeping watch o'er those who love her
Like when I was a child at play.

There were storms along life's pathway
But the rainbows always came.
Now in heaven's choir she's singing
Praises to His holy name.

She's the lily of my valley.
"Weep not for me. I've made it through.
Through the valley He walked with me,
And He'll do the same for you.

David said, "...Walk through the valley..."
Only shadows dim the view.
Now I'm where the sun is shining
Waiting patiently for you."
—*Vernelle B. Allen*

Before Too Long

As she looked down on us
She saw the tears in our eyes
While we said our goodbyes.
She knew we would be o.k.
As the years went by,
She knew there would be many more things to cause us to cry.
You have to be true; you have to be strong.
You will be with her before too long.
—*Maria R. Struck*

You Cannot Stop The Rain

She left me at a moments notice
She sold me down the river
I wished I'd never met her
the thought of her makes me shiver

Then you came along, I thought everything would be alright
Life was going great again, until I saw her tonight
The memories came back like pouring rain
When she spoke, all I heart was thunder
Then came the storm, the storm of pain

I wished you could replace her, take her off my mind
you have tried to stop the pain, but
I can't leave the memories behind.

And
   You cannot stop the rain
   You cannot stop the thunder
   And, you cannot stop the pain
—*Reggie Alford*

Together Forever

I noticed the sparkle, in this lady's eyes,
She told a love story, of precious memories gone by,
Shack back in a holler, her and her man"
Seven children she was blessed with
As she smiled once again,

No gold on their fingers,
Hard times all around. No earthly possessions
But true love they had found,

Together forever, till death do us part,
Two people in love, and it came from there hearts,
Through sickness or health, good times or bad
Now these were the vows, of my mom and dad,

Years of depression hardly no food to eat,
Worn out clothes, holey shoes on our feet,
But love saw us through, and by the sweat of their brow
With a strong will for survival, we made it somehow,

She lays now on a hill side, by her baby and man,
Over looking a valley, so beautiful and green,
Then I realized, buried there were her dreams
To me life presented her a hard blow it seems,
—*Phyllis Steffey*

Blue Stream

My beauty I imagined in my dream
She was standing alone by the blue stream,
Hair of yellow showing her pureness
Confident and wise I knew my sureness.

I noticed her grand step, grace, and style
Suddenly she looked at me slowly she smiled,
I carefully stepped softly and sound
The first to step on this uncommon ground.

My beauty I imagined in my dream
Now we together stand by the blue stream.
—*Brandon Riggins*

They Will Be Here Soon

The plates were on the table, it was almost noon,
She waited by the window, they would be here soon.
She had been cooking, since before day light,
This special day, everything must be just right.

Her old hands were shaky, her hair had turned grey,
Working hard to rear them, since their dad passed away.
Hours passed by slowly, the day's light grew dim,
She couldn't understand what had happened to them.

She dialed their number, no one was there,
She reheated the food and hurried back to her chair.
"A trick" she thought, "they are trying to play"
They are all coming, they are all on their way.

She watched to see, them turn in from the street,
Her tired body weakened, she fell off to sleep.
It was almost midnight, was she still alone?
Had she been dreaming, had they all come and gone?

She went to the table, "I'll sit here and wait"
Her sad heart stopped, she slumped over her plate.
The next day the neighbors found her that way,
Still waiting for them on her last Mother's Day.

—Margaret Sue Cox

Legacies Of The Heart

With blush fresh upon her cheek, gardenias grace her gown.
She waltzes in silver moon shadows long into night.
Adoring suitors seek her hand, she smiles sweetly.
Beneath a sky of sparkling jewels a lover wins her heart.

Too soon his breath is hushed, once again her bed is cold.
Now in twilight years, long silken gowns with silver
dancing shoes are tossed aside. Gardenia's edges bear the
amber glint of time. Quiet moments invite leisurely

Sorting of missives tied with silken bows. Can memories
be tallied as pebbles in a jar? Has she gathered ecstasy
enough to last a lifetime? Without the crash of cymbals
her fifth decade arrives. Elusive as a butterfly,

Romance stays beyond her reach. Could not her smile
or grace of form turn yet another head? Footsteps
fall...perhaps just leaves that rustle in the morning
breeze. A rose, freshly kissed with morning dew, is left

Upon her step. She leans to cup the scented bloom. The
glow of youth returns to face so long without a kiss.
Perhaps a suitor...Her brow arches, eyes narrow...lips bow
in mystery in the promise of tomorrow and tomorrow...

—Carol J. Cutrona

The Pup

The pup is sitting there all alone,
Sitting there thinking while gnawing on his bone.
Wondering about life, death, love and hate,
Sitting there contemplating how his life is great.
The pup sits there gnawing hard and long,
Trying to discover what's right and what's wrong.
He runs across the room to be with his family.
Not knowing how much he means to them all.
Because he is so young his mother still protects him,
Holding him close so no one will reject him.
As the pup nods off into a deep sleep,
He is not aware of what's awaiting him this week.

—Molly West

"Solitary Depression"

A sky of velvet black hovers above
Shedding its bloody tears onto me.
I clamp my eyes shut, refusing to let mine spill.
Isolated, I live in my own secluded world
Ignoring the reality that tries to break through.
I block its ever persistent blows,
Fighting back with mind and soul.
Protecting my niche, not giving an inch
Watching my enemies scurrying away to hide,
Planning deception...
Humans metamorphosize into creatures
Ready to claw each other to pieces.
I turn my back and I get stabbed
By the one who calls himself friend.
Now I'm hanging by the thread,
Facing the ultimate end.
A question arises above my head,
Would I want to die or choose to live?
But I can not decide
And I don't know why.

—Anita Jelavic

Untitled

She looks in the mirror and sees only you,
She's the image, the person, the idea that grew;
She is real and human to those from afar
Yet to herself she's a robot - closed, behind bars.
You see her as perfect, yet inside are flaws,
She's lived all her life under all your strict laws.
Her ideas are true to the person inside,
The one you can't see; the one who but died,
Had it not been for you, your pride and your love;
You see her through glasses; she's so like a dove,
Yet really she's shattered and broken in two,
Torn between all she needs and all that's for you;
She knows not who she is, but what you all see,
And the person you molded into what she should be;
She has no true self, but the one you created,
And she feels insecure of her person - mutated
By the people who thought they should pave the whole way
Of this young girl's intentions; she had nothing to say.
She is frightened and startled to think of them then,
Since she's spent her whole life only living for them.

—Alice M. Hanna

Can You Hear It?

Come with me.
Shhh
Listen carefully, can you hear it?
I mean the sound of the wind blowing gently through the trees,
as though it were whispering softly,
words of peace and tranquillity.
Can you feel the cool breeze against your soft skin?
Can you feel the warm sun upon your face,
and smell the clean mountain fresh air.
Can you see the beautiful snowcapped mountain peaks?
Look up into the sky,
Can you see the fluffy cotton-like clouds?
Shhh
Listen carefully, can you hear it?
I mean the sound of the wind blowing gently through the trees,
as though it were whispering softly,
words of peace and tranquillity.

—April Humphrey

Tribute To peace

Peace is: the essence of true love
  Showered upon us from the Lord above.

Peace is: to free us from worldly emotions
  Keeping calm as smooth waves from the ocean.
Peace is: a faithful handshake around the world
  Thus keeping all national flags unfurled.

Peace is: a must on our daily agenda
  May all evil surroundings, surrender.

Peace is: renewed faith with each other
  Whether it be family, friends, sister or brother.

Peace is: deserves an applause from all
  We want this nation to grow strong and tall.
    —*Beatrice Delorier*

The Carolina Farm

The farm house stands empty and
  shuttered
The people I loved are all
  gone
Tall trees stand o'er
  the landscape
Still, the birds trill on an on.
The rain and thunder and
  lightning
Play their part in this sad,
  misty scene
Still, the bees search the flowers
  for nectar
And the squirrels their acorns
  glean.
Behind the house in the forest
  deep
The deer play out their days
And nothing in nature has changed at all
Still comes Winter, Spring, Summer and Fall.
    —*Catherine Cahill*

Contortionist's Night

My arms are snakes,
shy from the day's movements
and hiding within cloth; safe under the sleeves.

Night:
they uncoil and stretch,
near and about her own fancies;
fangs biting, bringing bruises.

My feet have fingers,
squeezing her shoulder's flesh:
rising wet clay through my grip.

Necks hugging and pushing
and hard, clean motions are
all engendered by soft, twisting bones.

We conquer the fighting minds.
She is ocean's might.
I am ribbons tide.
    —*C. W. Hanson*

My Uncompleted Journey

What can I write with naught to say,
Since I have so long lost my way?
I'm weary, tattered, tossed and torn
Without hope for the coming morn.
There is no wind to fill my sails,
As each thought for the morrow fails!
The black and heavy clouds o'er head
Each passing day compound my dread.
There is no sun to lift my heart,
While I remain here worlds apart
From friends and foes, from toil and rest,
From everything I loved the best!
There's nothing but to sit and fret,
To cuss, and fume, and hate, but yet
There's still no port to beckon me
From nineteen years upon the sea!
So what is left holds little worth -
There's only sorrow for my birth!
    —*Miriam E. Douglass*

A Poem For Ruby

We move onto the dance floor
Slowly wrapping ourselves in each other's arms
The rest of the world moves on around us, unnoticed
We close our eyes, but there is so much we can still see
A wave of emotion moves over us, confusion being the strongest
The music takes over our bodies
Guiding us over the dance floor as if we were floating on air
The puzzled look is replaced by an unsure smile
By now we are comfortable and don't want the song to ever end
We feel as if nothing could come between us
And we could go on, dancing this closely, forever
Then, surprising us both, is that untimely interruption
That always seems to find us no matter where we are
or what we are doing
We jump apart, startled, as if we were caught doing
something we shouldn't be
We look at each other, a little embarrassed,
Still not knowing what to think
Maybe we will always wonder what we should think
Until we are able to finish the unfinished dance.
    —*T. Hawkins*

Small Steel Tubes

Her pain and sorrow lie in
small steel tubes
waiting for their white caps to be
opened, releasing the contents within.

Her despair, anger and impatience
arrayed in a palette
of blended emotions. Succumbing
to shades of joy,

Only for a moment, covering over hues
of frustrations as her strokes, heavily laden
with tints of guilt, brush away on
the canvass of life.

Her palette empties onto this vast space
and becomes a composition unlike
any other, unique-and yet ordinary.
Immortalizing her pain and sorrow for all.

And the small steel tubes
lie still
with their white caps
tightly closed.
    —*Iva Marie Serrano*

New Generation

She's heard the sound of thunder, felt the ground shake!
Smelled, "smoke," off the rocks. Felt gentle rain.
And Today, is "her day..."
She becomes a part of, "Tents' bows, and hide..."

He plays a part to win her hand, shows strength!!
Goes through the "Rites of man..."
Proudly rides his horse, challenges the land!!

She waits inside a quiet place, cries deep inside.
Today she becomes the "Wife, to the leader of the tribe..."

She'll wear beads and feathers, he'll wear the buckskin hide.
He rides a painted horse, she'll follow by his side...

They come upon a quiet place, drums begin to play...
For there's a prayer to spoken here, "The elders only know..."
It's short but sweet as the "eagles sing, and doves begin to cry..."

Today there was a wedding,
Children sang, women cried, as the couple came to view...
And today they start a new life...
"Another generation for the tribe..."
—*Robin Barber*

Master Of Reality

The power of ten million truth's pulled me up from the ground
Snapping me to attention, then turning me around.

In the darkness stood a figure I couldn't quite see.
His eyes burned with fire.
It was the Master of Reality.

He knew of my task to make myself whole...to finish my deeds.
That's when he began to speak of mankind's hopes and needs.

You must see the good and the bad....the right and the wrong.
If you fail to see both sides, you will never be strong.

His voice sounded like the howling eternal winds.
The strength of his wisdom no doubt carried him to his ends.

Always look through your own eyes....never from above.
Show your fellow man compassion and kindness.
Show him love.

Before he left, he looked at me with a sigh.
Stand with what you know to be right.
Then, he bolted into the sky.
—*Zane M. Williams*

What's For Christmas?

There once was two old people who had twelve kids,
So Christmas presents must have been tough.
And one Christmas eve they soon realized,
That they didn't have presents enough.

If their kids couldn't brag,
About their presents this year,
It'd hurt all their feelings,
And they'd both shed a tear.

Their parents thought for a minute,
Their clothes were sweaty and tattered,
And no one else could figure out,
What was the matter.

Like that it hit them,
They knew they were smart,
They'd give out certificates,
To buy from Wal-Mart!
—*Justin Baker*

The Warrior

In the misty morning light bloomed a Rose
 so delicate and bright.
As each drop of dew fell to the ground, it
 stood up straighter and played its
 sweet song.
Toward the midday sun it thrived; its
 presence in the Garden was surrounded
 by pride.

As evening shadows began to dance, a ripping
 storm gave the Rose no chance.
With all its strength and all its might it
 tried to fight and bear the ride.
The winds blew stronger, the hail came down
 and the petals of the Rose could no
 longer be found.
Now as it hung in the darkness alone, the
 warrior knew a good fight it had won.

Only one thing remained to be, the Rose
 took its Bow, gave its last Sweet Breath...
And in one moment was ever so gently set free.
—*Lisa D. Smith*

DIVERSITY

DIVERSITY wears many hats, none of which he owns. Because his taste is
so eclectic, he shops at the local thrift store. His wardrobe is as varied as the rainbow and fortunately never goes out of style. By the way, he is still searching for just the right pair of shoes...

DIVERSITY is well travelled. She has lived in major capitals of the
world as well as in remote regions of various lands. And although she takes journeys frequently, she never has use for a map. She can converse in a number of languages and can understand many more. Her talents are myriad: artist, teacher, salesperson, fund raiser, poet and prophet.

DIVERSITY has an ample mouth, huge ears and wide eyes. His smile is warm and laugh contagious. Give him a moment and he can learn any song, master any dance. Often it appears that he is nowhere in sight, when in fact he is right under you nose. Best of all, his long inviting arms are always ready for a hug.

DIVERSITY hangs at the airport and discusses philosophy with the flower vendors. People watching is her favorite pastime. She loves to go on long walks and take in all the sights and smells of her environment. Her family is far-reaching. While she has had many lovers,she still treasures Camaraderie most of all.

DIVERSITY is simple yet complex. Because he cares for no one in particular, he is interested in everyone in general.
—*Robert H. Levin*

Risoluto

I will not pass this way again, come spring,
So fickle are her ways, I cannot know
Why birds who sang to me no longer sing
And field flowers wait for summer's heat to grow.

But should green boughs find my heart quickening,
Let me recall the winter tears I knew -
That though I yearn to feel the April rain
I will not pass this way again.
—*Bernice Fordyce*

Untitled

I love the carefree way you talk to me
So happy, so free of guile,
So free of fear I will not understand.
The touch of your hand
So careless, tho ever so gentle
Tells me what I want to know.
In a quiet moment you look at me with no word spoken
And I know a oneness; a oneness of the spirit.
The world retreats in reverence
Leaving us standing alone as if lost in space
Entranced with the beauty that is.
Tho, our worlds are far apart
I cherish the place you have in my hart
Secure from harm of daily cares
Your image ever ready to smile at me
And I will know again the world is good.
Sheltered here, I will never see a hurt in your eyes.
You will look at me again
Yet say no word
And I will know...
—*J.R. Austin*

Untitled

I want these words to be straight from my heart
So I'm going to start by saying, I hope we never part
You mean so much to me
You've made me everything I'll ever be
When I think about you I always smile
How our love is such a unique style
At night when I'm laying in bed
I think of our future and what lies ahead
We've come so far in such little time
I hope someday you'll be all mine
On that special day, we'd go to town
Of course I'd be in my wedding gown
You would be the loving husband in my life
I would be your forever wife
But let's not rush this relationship
If we do, our love boat just might tip
For now let's live our lives happily together
Because I know my love will last forever
—*Carrie Jackson*

Friendship

Money is very valuable,
so is friendship, too.
But when it comes to choosing,
I'd rather be with you,
when I'm feeling down,
you're there to cheer me up.
I feel like a clown,
whenever we fight.
We always get back together,
because we both know it's not right.
There's nothing I wouldn't do,
to keep my friendship with you.
That's why we'll always be Best Friends Forever!
—*Stephanie Elia*

A Prayer

Dear Lord of heaven and earth and sky,
So many times, I wonder why
You love and forgive me every day
When I walk in sin all the way.

I come to your altar on bended knee
To ask forgiveness for such as me.
I know of your wonderful saving grace
And I'm praying to meet you face to face.

So many things I don't understand
But you're always there with a helping hand,
To let me see joy instead of sorrow
And live in faith for each tomorrow.

And so dear Lord each day I pray,
That you will guide me on my way.
I don't ask for freedom from harms,
I only ask for your loving arms.
—*Mildred Oleson*

"Sleeping"

Sleeping so calm
So peaceful
So relaxed and warm,

Then off comes my blanket - torn.

Sleeping so harsh
So annoyed
So tense and cold,

I'll take anything, even a blanket - worn.
—*Penelope Lewin*

The Face Of Fear

You had a dream that seemed so clear; an artists dream that was
    so sincere,
Like the lines you used to draw. How clearly they form your face.
Shadowing the dark slim man that holds the face of fear.
I know these words cannot express the pain you feel inside, the angel
    of death has kissed you and there's nowhere left to hide.
I hold you close and hear you breathe, if only this were a cure.
Oh tell me please will this nightmare end? What has it all been for?
I'm looking for the answers—inside the face of fear.
We're searching now the rainbow's end, as the colors start to fade.
Like all the friends of days before, how quickly you've turned away.
Afraid to look into the eyes—into the face of fear.
I hear your laughter echo as I search this empty room; still looking
    for a trace of the days we knew before.
When sunshine meant a ray of hope and dark clouds passed away.
Now grey skies have been frozen here by this unknown face of fear.
I'll say my last and final goodbye, knowing once again;
Another day, another place—I'll look into the face of fear.
—*Marlene Minaeff*

Untitled

The eyes—a laugh.
Some locks of brownish hair
Make the serpent
mysterious as love.

The nose - it hears.
A twist of supple limbs
Haunting like Indian summer.
Why do I, a simple Romeo, love its poison?

Rain falls as I stand bewildered
By its fiery ferocity.
The Gods beat drums as I
Follow it into the forest.
—*Christopher Bradley*

I Gladly Will

I do not wear a hat; but I gladly will;
so that I may take my hat off to you.

I do not go to church, but I gladly will
so that I can be sure my prayers for your safe
  journey home will reach heaven.

I do not like needles, but I will gladly
give my blood to replenish yours in hopes that
you will return to the ones you love.

I do not like protesting, but I gladly will
to fight for your recognition and place in this battle.

I am not a general nor an officer
but I will gladly tip my brow in salute of you

I do not like to cry, but I do!
For every life taken and every day you are gone.

I will also gladly; fly and salute my flag.
Tie a yellow ribbon, support our troops,
and I will gladly be there to welcome you home!
  —*Apryl L. Goren*

Small Town Gossip

The poor idle gossips haven't enough to do
So they get real busy and spread some news
Such as: "I heard this, or I heard that"
"Now be sure to keep this under your hat"
The sword is less mighty than the tongue
When a brand new story has just begun
Especially, if it's unusual news
And it spreads much faster than the flu
The finish always differs from the start
Is even sharper than an arrows dart
How can imaginations grow so wild
Even faster than that of a child
Poor lonely gossips, we pity you
Spreading tales that aren't even true.
Can't you find something better to do?
  —*Lillian Gill*

Jennifer Ann Clare's First Christmas

  I was born March First, you see,
So this is the very first Christmas for me.

  Daddy and Mommy bought a big, big tree,
  And decorated it special, just for me.

  Mommy put a manger under the tree,
    With a little baby just like me.

  I hope he is happy, as happy as me,
  Sharing my very first Christmas tree.

    I pray that this will always be
    A loving cherished memory,
    Of my very first Christmas
      With Mommy, Daddy and me.
  —*Edward Buta*

Mothers

Someone to talk to.
Someone to think of you.
Someone who understands you:
Someone who comforts you in good times and bad.
This someone loves you.
Even though this someone may be hard to understand
  and over protective.
But will by your side no matter what.
This someone is your mother.
  —*Toni Marie Wise*

Daddy

When I was young I worshipped you, you were so strong,
so wise, so true; when I grew up we grew apart and
I thought myself liberated, so smart;
Throughout the years I went my own way, I was so stubborn,
to you nothing to say;
And then one day you needed me and I knew you again I'd
never leave;
Instead you left me for good in May, when flowers bloom
and willows sway;
You're in God's hands and how I pray that you're finally
at peace and got your way;
I'm just so ashamed I didn't know, how to tell you I love
you and how to show;
I hope you know, daddy, wherever you are, that in my eyes
you're an eternal star;
And also, daddy, I know someday, we'll be together again,
we'll laugh and play;
We'll hug each other and never let go; I'll never cry again,
happiness will make me glow; my promise to you daddy, while I'm
still on earth, is to make you proud and prove my worth.
  —*Paige D. Hiemier*

Clouds

So high up in the sky
So wonderful and useful
They rain upon us gently and gradually

They are so fluffy and white
That they look like large marshmallows in the sky
They look so wonderful in the bright blue sky

It's just a magical kingdom in that sky
with wonderful people riding on white horses with wings
The people are never cross and always nice

The clouds are just a wonderful sight to see
So strong floating in the great big blue sea in the sky.
  —*Jennifer Haynes*

What Would Life Be As A Normal

Life as a normal person would be like peaches and cream,
soft and sweet going down your throat.

It would be like there is not one single thing that you would have
to worry about, if you had life as a normal person.

Life as a normal person would be exciting.

Life as a normal person would be meeting new people and
enjoying them as new found friends.

But since my life is not normal why then do I want to enjoy the
normal things of life, if I am not a normal person be begin with?
Sometimes I wonder about this.

As a disabled young woman, I end my story.
What would life be like
as a normal person, it would be nice to know.
  —*Liza Marie Delgado*

"Contemplation On The Hairbrush"

Its bristles aren't quite as rigid as before
Some bent or spread apart from constant use
Some still erect without that same abuse
With bits of lint and dandruff, too
With strands of shiny hair
Like when it grew
It's rather sad to see that object laying there
Because of past caressing of someone's hair.
  —*Betty Colvin Dunn*

"The Tern And The Gull"

Hark! hear that cry of a sea gull's lament
   Softly, now loudly is his mournful bent.
Swooping and turning and swooping again
   taking his place so regally on the main.

Watching in silence his ease and his grace
   One feels uplifted and off into space.
Visions of wonders come quickly to view;
   Oh! dear Sea Gull, how I wish to be you.

Terns seem to symbolize youth of today
   by racing about in their own true way.
While you, dear Sea Gull, have time to repair
   upon the sea top with your pristine air.

You wish to command the surrounding seas
   watching and waiting for terns, if you please;
to swoop down and gather their evening fare
   with great abandon and so unaware.

The Sea Gull should have his turn, Heaven knows.
   It is not known by the tern, I suppose.
Ah! well! Ah well! that is life - far from dull -
   If the tern has his turn; so shall the gull.
     —*Margaret Praitano*

Ladies

Why do some ladies like to latch on to a man of means?

While others are so content if they have a pot of beans
Some like nothing better than to be draped in sables, and
have the largest kind of car.

Others wear hand me downs and drive around and never go very far
Some ladies like to step out, to the most elite places
Another can have two dollars in her pocket, so she goes to
the races

A trip to Europe to some oh! is a must

A shovel is the desire of a certain lady, who would rather
dig for a diamond in the dust

Why are ladies so different, why aren't we all the same?

Could it be because of him, when he took a rib.
From Adam to make a Dame?
     —*Ednamay Foeckler*

The Afraid Knight

The night was dark and grey
some people say.
The ghost that would stay up at night
would not be out at light.
I went to the house to see.
I went in very, very, quietly.
What I found was a sight;
it was a knight.
"I see I see," he said, "A beautiful lady."
I heard a whisper that said, "never more
to see, never more to hear, because of death,
that is the one thing I fear."
I ran to escape, but death does take.
No one is free I sake.
The day has came for me Sir Drake;
he died away of old age.
No one can take his place.
     —*Crystal Whitlow*

Life

Life has its ups and downs
Some with seriousness, some with clowns
Life has its loves, and its losses
Some with its dictators, and others with its bosses

Life is full of dreams and hopes
Full of political idiots and dopes
Life is full of helping another country, what about us?
Put these unwanted foreigners on a bus

We can feed another countries kin
Neglect in our brothers and sisters is an ultimate sin
Land of the free, home of the brave
Our own country we can't save

Homeless people where'er we stand
Government taking the Indian's land
Poor an' hungry, addicted to life's drugs

Life is a bed of roses, full of thorns
Being run by a bunch of political scorns
The buck stops here, with no strife
So God bless this so-called life
     —*Bud Mann*

"Friends"

Someone to talk to
Someone who cares
Someone who has just always been there
Your feelings and thoughts you always shared
Knowing when you're there
Knowing when you're gone
Remembering that day when one had to say "Good Bye"
I said "I'll miss you" as you turned your head
and sighed
You whispered, "Friends should never be apart."
You went one way and didn't look back
The next day I packed
I never glanced back at what I left in my past
     —*Tracie York*

Untitled

A face with no name,
Someone who is always in pain
Who is she? No one knows.
Someone with open arms, but
no place to go.
Someone who everyone has seen,
untitled is the ghost that
wanders the streets.
Darkness falls when she comes
no one stays - everyone runs
In loneliness she will cry
with memories of a cold dark night.
But no one listens, they are all in fright,
So they leave her untitled
to wander forever, through the night.
     —*Alissa Halsey*

Untitled

I've studied the teachings of Sages,
Sought in Prophets a magical code,
But the wisdom passed down through ages
Failed to guide me through the frightening world.

Aging volumes of scholars undying
On my shelf being treasured all time.
I would stand on the shoulders of giants
But - the humble - unable to climb.
     —*Valentin Litvin*

The Person In The Mirror

As I look into the mirror I see,
Someone who looks a lot like me

Not only does she have my nose and eyes,
She feels the same hurt if I were to cry

The person on the other side has the same ideas
and personality that I do,
She laughs and jokes just like me too

She cares and talks to others just like me,
There are so many other traits that I see

I turn and look at my mother and say,
I'm more like you everyday!!!!
—*Jenny Bittick*

The Dark

I don't think I'll ever hear
Something as stupid as the fear

That my brother always gets
Whenever he lays down to rest.

He's scared to death of the dark
He starts to scream and the dog will bark.

He'll pull the covers over his head
And if you tease him, he will even dread
All the things around him
A thousand things that could scare him;

From a bug, to a dog, to a lark,
And he had to be afraid of the dark!
—*Bruce O. Darrah*

The Rose

What does it mean, a rose, I say
Something important I know, in its own special way.
What does it mean, when it comes from a guy
A special friendship, or a wink of the eye.
What does it mean, when its fragrance is sweet
Is it a sign of love, a very beautiful treat.
What does it mean, with not a word attached
Something that once was, needs again to be patched.
What does it mean, a special love, could it be fate
Something needs to be started, before it's too late.
What does it mean, a friendship was lost
A rose is a beautiful, sign of small cost.
What does it mean, so pretty in its vase
The caring thoughts, from a warm, gentle face.
—*Jill C. Smith*

Untitled

All is dark, the life of us is gone.
Sorrowed faces fill our minds with
memories of emotions. Mournful people
in the air, to share their grieving past.
Proceeding to the next room, we are full of
glee and amazement of what stands before
our very eyes. What gracious beauty
and light we see! Rejoice! They yell.
We've come to share our love! For those
we know, and for those we do not, we've
come to share our love and care! Rejoice!
Do not be sad we were once gone, we are
back to carry on!
—*Joanne Spyridakos*

The Gift

Seems I did something sensational in some past life
Something particularly wonderful
Something I don't quite remember
Because the Goddess sent me you in this life
You with your soul-shattering eyes and exquisite mouth
That speaks without the use of words
Touching my being with a mystical kiss
You with eyes burning deep into mine
Holding me as if I'd been impaled by a shooting comet
Yes it must have been absolutely astonishing
I must have fought a great battle
Created some historic monument preserved today
Because the Goddess sent me you in this life
I must have rescued an African Nation
Rescued my ancestors from extinction in some horrific holocaust
Invented some great medicine or was a strong female warrior
O No none of that
I know what it was
I must have been a saint in my past life
Because the Goddess sent me you in this life
—*Victoria Lee-Owens*

Give Us Peace

Peace is something we strive for,
Something we live and die for.
People say there is peace on our land,
So we help others defend their sand.

But drugs and poverty is all I see,
Why won't the government help me.
I live in a box with my son
But will he ever speak, will justice be done.

Because of hunger he does not sleep,
I pray the Lord his soul to keep.
If he dies before he wakes,
I pray the Lord my life to take.

And if I live, the government will find,
Another case of suicide.
I may not be able to write or read,
But peace of mind is all I need.

Is it too much to ask of a country so wealthy,
To give us food and keep us healthy.
Don't turn your back on the ones that are here,
Peace should start at home this year.
—*Cynthia Hubble*

The Night Road

The road rambles on in the night;
Spinning big black shadows on my mind.
I reminisce in my heart with each flicker of light;
All the smiles, hugs and good-byes left behind.

The cars are racing to and fro;
Like huge illuminating bugs aglow.
They're all encompassed under an extending dome;
Rushing wildly, anxious travelers, home.

High in the sky hang a silvery moon;
Joined by thousands of sparkling stars.
The busy, humming, world plays a familiar tune;
While visions of figures dance to the rhythm of the bars.
—*Faye Garrett*

Untitled

This thing called time I could not comprehend
sometimes slow and then fleeting...
but now it seems so obvious, time I know you well.
you leave your mark for me to see,
seems I've awakened to see you all around.

The seasons changed and I just waited to see them again,
now I know they were not returning, each had a meaning of it's
own. Seasons passed are gone forever...

But the hardest mark you leave for me is one the faces of those
I love, oh...you were subtle with your changes...
the gray, the lines, their pace, their eyes...their eyes,
I see you mostly in their eyes.

There seems a sadness in this passing of time.
Yes, I'll respect you more than ever, I see what you have done.

Where are you going???
I'll have to wait and see, but I'll be very patient...
I know the changes are not only around me but within me.
I am in no hurry, for I don't know how long you'll exist for me

"Time Waits For No Man"

I truly understand.
—*Jeannette M. Charles*

Feelings

Feelings are complicated and
  somewhat mysterious.
Sometimes joyful and
  other times furious.
Happy or sad, angry and mad,
Feelings can get confused.
Love or hate, destiny or fate,
Sometimes you're feeling abused.

Feelings get hurt it's true.
Someday it will happen to you.
You don't know where
  your heart belongs.
But, you have to hold on
  and be strong.

No matter what happened
  yesterday or today,
Tomorrow is always to come.
Be confident from the start,
  and hold on to your heart,
  'cause that's where your feelings come from.
—*Laurie Grant*

Can You Hear Them?

Can you hear them?
Sounds wandering through the night,
Carelessly echoing,
For they belong to no one,
They are totally free.

Can you hear them?
Noises feeling through the air.
Touching places of the unknown.
Though sounds are totally free,
Could noises ever be?

Can you hear them?
Sounds and noises are the memories
And ideas from past, present, and future.
Their ultimate joy is freedom,
Like lives they search to be somewhat free.

When you hear sounds and noises
You are hearing the beginnings
And ends of freedom.
—*Bethel Murphy*

Once Elbourne, Now Elburn

You would find someone so cheerful, who could sing a happy song. She would make it sound so very joyful, you might want to hum along. Listen to this kind of music going up and down Main Street. Catchy rhythm, it goes so sweet, call it Elburn Rag. People are so sweet and gentle, she would sing of you and me. It could make you feel so sentimental, and Elburn sure has to be. Come along on down to Main Street, see what gives Elburn the beat. This is the tune of the Elburn Rag. In the happy month of August, you come on these summer days. The town tempo starts to brighten. I must tell you that it's Elburn Days. Weekend is more like a great show, and these days make Elburn glow. Go on to Main Street, you get in the beat of the Elburn Rag. Lion's put it all together, while the other groups pitch in. Making Elburn Days so much the better, people would be coming in. A moment of Elburn at last, the happy years of the past. It surely gets you, the Elburn Rag. Now back in Nineteen Eighty Four, bring back memories of past. One hundred and fifty years to show for. Name of village was not fast. Back in the Nineteenth Century, Elbourne once was Blackberry. Movement is so neat. Really is jumpy. Call it Elburn Rag.
—*Arvid A. Homuth*

Civilization

Grey, bare and vast, the pavement stretches forth. Arid and spiteful, the dust swirls endlessly in a rotating suction. But is it the vapor, and not the filth, that the cruel winds mean to possess? High above the asphalt, a single sparrow tumbles in the midst of fury. In desperation, she slices and circles. Her piercing cry just penetrates the relentless howling and squealing; she seems to dance; a tumbleweed in a stellar wasteland; her thin wings, soft ornaments, are beaten and whipped in a tearless frenzy. For her, there will be no rest tonight, for she is thirsty, and there is no water left in the wide cracks crowned with yellow weeds, and the night shall shall be cold and empty, and black as death.
Just beneath the surface, in gleaming scarlet, adorned with broad white stripes, barely chapped below the shower of shifting sands, a single thin cylinder of aluminum grace. It does not tumble about in the irascible flurry of stone, nor does it tremble in the face of a storm. It has found its rest near a slab of dry granite, and so like an unpolished jewel in the remote hills it lies, for within, the burning heat of a sweet liquid gently and slowly fades, deep in the peace of darkness.
—*C. Vadai*

Thoughts Of The Lonely, Thoughts of the Loved

Solitary footprints on the beach.
Stars so close but out of reach.
Dandelion feathers blown away.
No real home in which to stay.
Silent crying for the dead.
Confusion coursing through my head.
Sitting wondering if I'm the only
one who thinks thoughts of the lonely.

Sunlit fields full of flowers.
Autumn leaves and April showers.
Warming smiles and words so tender.
One dozen roses from an unknown sender.
Tracing the greenness of your eyes.
Watching for rain in cloudless skies.
Silently sharing the stars above.
Often thinking thoughts of the loved.
—*Kristi Woodring*

The Half-Built House

We knew it was wrong, but the foot-wide
strip of bright copper flashing
in a sapphire afternoon hypnotized our legs.
called our slick-soled shoes up
three stories to the peak
where, squatting, we slid
one after the other, like a glissando
splitting the warm air to the eaves
until suddenly, Mom, pale and remote,
yelled from the ground, come down,
palms rising, don't come down.
Our cinnamon tan legs disappeared
through the attic window space.

Just as well she couldn't see us tiptoe
over naked beams thirty feet above nothing
and climb down aromatic X's
spacing 2 x 4 new pine uprights.
We emerged into timid sunlight, glooming
in the shadow of her fear, wondering,
when she was ten, what did she do for fun?

—*Barbara A. Meyer*

Life's Miracle

A life grows within me beautiful for all to see, so tiny but so strong oh how I long, to hold you in my arms and keep you from all life's harms wonderful miracle made from love a precious gift sent from above you are our pride and joy whether, you are a girl or a boy we anxiously await your birth to welcome you to this earth. Jut always remember how much you are loved and thought of as our family's newest member.

—*Sondra Lamb*

These Eyes Have Seen No Glory

I wish I knew what's wrong with my mind. I seem to be struggling all the time. I know there's a price to pay, that's why I'm living this way. It began in the 60's for Uncle Sam; we lost our childhood and became a man. We were sent to this place called Vietnam; we soon found it to be a scam. I fell in love with the children in this faraway place. How could I take part in their killing and be part of the human race? We were told the Vietcong was the enemy. What about Daddy Warbucks in the land of plenty? It's been many years and we still have all those fears, especially those voices that always appear. I often have flashback's and dreams in my head. God it would be kinder if I were dead. Now I have children of my own; God don't let them be caught in a free-fire zone. People wonder why I stare... I'm afraid to tell them it's those crying voices I hear. I found a group of people - patients, doctors and staff - who volunteer in our behalf. Look in the eyes of a combat vet and you'll see why we can't forget the death and destruction in this small place called Vietnam. There are 58,000 names on a Wall of a generation that touches us all.

—*Tom Collins*

"Listen"

Sun, wind, storm and rain,
Sweep the earth, ease the pain.
We often fail to see or hear,
The voice inside who is always near.
We shut our minds and take the lead,
Won't hear the voice, will not take heed.
Sit awhile, be very still,
Find the answer if you will.
It's there you see, so very near,
If you'll be quiet enough to hear.

—*Sondra Williamson*

Baby Suns Burn Brightly

A pair of sons slouch in an empty arena,
Stunned, still staring at the court.
The crowd has long since taken flight,
as has the circling couple carrying the celestial bundle.
A slice of the sun may be a strange trophy for
a basketball victory,
But, contrary to the sons' supposition, this
contest was much more than an exhibition.

They were looking away when the shot fell through.
They thought the game was over,
that it was their turn to play.
They were expecting to hear the last tock tick off the
biological clock when a woman screamed and a crowd roared.
The two twenty-somethings rose just in time to see the
presentation of the baby star,
And to see the joy in her father's eyes,
And to wave goodbye to the smiling, self-sufficient
solar system as it spun into space,
Throwing the life cycle out of kilter as it ascended,
casting a weird, fraternal light onto their dad's face.

—*Dwight Stirling*

Untitled

The trees, having slept through the winter days,
Suddenly burst out in robes of green.
Warm rains turn the once dead lawns
To cushioned carpets.
Apple blossoms scent the cool night air.
Crocuses lift up their purple heads,
And birds return and search for spots to nest.
A robin cocks his head
To listen for the worm beneath the earth.
The garden soil, warmed by the sun's deep rays,
Waits for its seeds.
We stand in awe
And know God's Spring has come again.

—*Loretta M. Brown*

"Teachers"

Slowly they walked but swiftly they came
Summoned and called by a force untame
And slowly they guide trudging wearily along
Pondering the damage of something done wrong
Over and over they are left behind
With only their memories and the future to bind

—*Shana Smulyan*

My Angel Cloud

As I lie here and see that the sky is blue. What is a man suppose to do, when he is giving all his love that he can for you, but get down on his knees and beg that his Angel Cloud will see him through.

Now that the sky has turn gray, and with the very lasting strength I began to pray, "Oh my Angel Cloud, please wipe these falling tears from my face, and take me back home to that beautiful place. I can not wait for another day, have mercy and take me away."

At last the sky has turned black, but where is my Angel Cloud, is he going to take me back? I was so afraid, I did not know what to say, then a voice as loud as thunder said "My child look this way and come forward to me. I am the almighty, the great, and the light you have been searching to see."

—*Richard R. Loveland*

Eagle Eyes

The eyes, soaring high in the sky
survey the earth for any movement in shadows.

The eyes, which never seem to blink,
are masters of the hunt and have no enemies, but one.

The eyes, which work with the mind and claws,
have just one purpose, the feeding of himself and family.

The eyes, like radar, select moving targets,
and his body becomes a missile of destruction.
keeping the balance.

The eyes, never tiring, constantly perform their
mission of vision, and the bald eagle remains
in command of all he sees.

—*Michael D. Hall*

Full Circle

A swing so turns to and fro in the wind
Swaying this way and that, undecided it goes.

Suddenly it will halt to decide what's next
Should it take that same course, it just doesn't know.

I watch it stop as it thinks of a plan
After but a moment of thinking it continues the same.

By resuming its course, it found its path again
Did the thinking resolve its quandry or pain?

To and fro, back and forth, that swing still moves
Never to reach the full circle as it searches in vain.

It can only achieve it through the help of one another
That full circle it needs but can't seem to find.

One day it is touched by a body who loves
That swinging and swaying, that soothing, smooth ride.
Together they meet, so slowly at first
Then faster and faster, to full circle they glide.

—*Marabeth Grogan-Fairchild*

Snapdragon

Frost hangs like gossamer on the leaves beneath her feet
   Sweet dew graces her petals
He slides from the shadows like mercury
   Appearing behind the white braid trellis
He feels the firmness of her neck in his hands
   Blades pierce the thick stalk
The breath of life escapes her; darkness
   The rose taken from her throne
She falls limp to the damp ground
   A blood red petal left behind
The man smiles in satisfaction
   The rose is left to die in vain
Somewhere a robin sings

—*Gwethalyn Williams*

Stupidity

S is for SOMETHING we never should do.
T is for THINGS we say that aren't true.
U is for UPPISHNESS found in a slob.
P is for the PRYING that produces the snob.
I is the EGG that goes with the ME.
D is for DUMB-BELL we sometimes can be.
I, once again, that word said before.
T. for those THINGS that makes us a bore.
Y is the YOU that goes with the ME.
  Put them together; get STUPIDITY.

—*Duane Hougham*

Eternity

A river flowing wide, my soul is free.
Sweet life is mine
Until I reach the sea.

I travel far and wide
through distant lands.
I run through mountains…
Swim among the sands.

A winding path I choose
I want to Live! To experience
All that life can give.

The sweltering summer sun
Shall heat my soul.
To feel the height of passion is my goal.

To appreciate such passion
I'll feel pain. Endure the stinging cold,
The pouring rain.

With such fulfillment
I shall reach the sea.
With no regrets
I'll spend eternity.

—*Gina M. Estes*

Untitled

I've got nothing against wildlife, but Sheez!
Take that cute little bunny rabbit, Please!
He was out here first on the edge of town
Before I moved in and put my roots down

And take those blue jays that sit on the fence
They let me know that they've taken offense
How dare I think that those grapevines are mine
When that is their favorite place to dine

And take that marvelous covey of quail
And what those regular visits entail
"What's on today's menu?" they seem to say
They eat my garden and go on their way

Prior rights they have, I guess that is true
But lately I've thought of what I might do
Barbecued jays? No, too hard to chew
Ah, but fricasseed quail or just rabbit stew?

—*Eleanor J. Seibert*

Life's Roadway

Who am I to stand in judgement of which road your life should take. Who am I to stand in judgement when you stumble along life's way. Life has many turning points and long avenues, only to myself must I be true. I was sent here for a purpose as yet I know not what. One day His loving hand will lead me to that perfect knowing spot. Until that time of knowing and my job on earth is done. I live each day a one act play, not worrying about tomorrow and forgiving the mistakes of yesterday. To my friends and loved ones I take into my heart. I pray I make impressions on their lives and have played some small part. In seeing clear which road to take and find their purpose along the way. My friend I stand not in judgement of which road your life should take I'm busy with my own map, I have yet to make.

—*Martha Shelton*

Play Ball

The second baseman stops just short
Takes one look and drops the ball
From beneath her bangs, she feels the stitches,
places her bets:
One more inning if the wood sings
Over and out if two balls fly south

Cotton candy sticks to his mitt
Aims the scent of leather straight her way
The long wind-up reigns her in
A twitch and the ball swoops overhead
Her husband with the hot dogs reaches out, steals it,
Holds it aloft like a heart
All bets off

Breath and resume
—*Wendy K. Wicks*

Seashore Seamstress

The sea at shore is a seasoned seamstress
Taking nips and tucks here
And stitching ruffles and flounces there.

Waves of voile and ribbons of moire,
Born of gravity and wind,
Burst into swells of shirred silk and sunlit lame.

Jacquard patterns on washed, clean sand
Disappear for a satin second
Only to rush up again with sea shell sequins.

Sew quickly, O seashore seamstress,
For quickening wind and thickening murky clouds
Foretell of tailored tweeds and worsted woolens coming.

Leave not your post, stitcher of shorelines,
Just thread a thicker needle and,
For a little while, sew a different seashore shroud.
—*June Kelly*

To Carol, with fondest memories

The path of life is often winding -
taking task on a tiresome soul. But the
breaths get deeper and the steps get
stronger when there's light at the end of one's stroll.
These clearings speak with a gentle
breeze - relieving the aches, putting
body at ease. This is God's way of
giving one rest before trodding onward to
complete the test.
It's moving forward that makes us whole-
and reaching each clearing is everyone's goal.
—*Dona Mary Lomio*

Untitled

(Fighting back the lies)
the blood-darkened abscess of my heart fears
the white shaft of truth
accustomed to deception, the hole deepens further
becoming
a stained and black pulsing organ
my wan complexion becomes the playing card,
rectangular and sharp,
where the heart lies tattooed
—*Leslie Nuby*

Imagining Thee

Glancin' at an oak tree
  Tall, strong, and mighty,
One finds time to ponder
  And ask thyself with wonder…

  Can he feel the warm kiss of the morning breeze
    or the cold touch of the gentle dew drops?
  Can he hear the gay tune of chirping birds of June
    or the sad song of September morn?

  Can he smell the sweet perfume of naive flowers of May
    or the ardent burning of dry leaves of hay?

  Can he see the innocent beauty of a young day
    or the stunning pride of a dark night?

  Can he taste the honey lips of soft air
    or the pungent tongue of barren soil?

Ponder and then wonder…
Take a steady look
  And try to see,
Is it just a tree
  Or am I imagining thee?
—*Norma Nuyles Robinson*

Poetry Of Life

Stop for a moment please
Taste the smell of life
And don't tell me
There is no poetry but crime

Every single day is a poem
Golfers in the park
And look! This is my cardinal bird
On the branch over your head

Listen to the bird
Busy days are like a river
At night hug your soul
Listen to the silence - the mother of music

And that is the poetry of life
Look for it!
Just find it and don't tell me
There is no poetry but crime
—*Maria Ivona Chrzastowska*

The Page

Up to my rock, withered with age, the wind blew to me a tattered page. Wrinkled and torn, filled with hate, a part of your journal, as cold as slate. How good you were, at concealing your rage, but you kept it all on this yellowed page. You wore a mask when we were out, but then at home your real self came out. This paper here, it makes me sad, it shows few happy times, the rest of them were bad. The bumps and the bruises, and the broken bones, then in your final fury, the cord from the telephone. The scratches on my face, the ring around my neck, you were such an actor, the doctor didn't check. You threw me off the boat, you told them I was drunk, Blamed my wounds on the propeller, you stupid, foolish punk. You told the entire story, on this page against my stone, but now, dear, I have left you, now you are alone. You made a massive tale, about the wife you tried to save, but I saw the grin across your face as they lowered me to my grave.
—*Andrea Nowicki*

A Mother's Child

A mother looks down upon her child with eyes full of tears of sadness and hatred. She prays to the heavenly skies that someday, her child will experience real life. A life where a person can walk down the streets of a town and not carry a weapon that kills. A life where a woman, or a girl, isn't afraid of men and men's actions. A life where children can go to school and learn, and not feel like they should drop out. A life where adults and children aren't pressured into drugs and alcohol. A life where people believe in God and don't kill innocent children for convenience. And a mother's child doesn't know fear yet, until it is forced upon them. And a mother's child grows slowly, taking in every little detail of its childhood. And a mother's child will someday understand its mother's cries.

—Tara Skorohod

1993

America the beautiful, are we in danger?
Tendering promise to every stranger?
From whence came this destructive and greed.
Where's the respect for our Pilgrims Creed?
The food shelf and soup line are in our midst.
Homeless and jobless increase the list -
Forsake the burden, accept the cup,
When you hit the bottom, there's no place but up!
Leave no money for tobacco, drugs or booze
Maybe poverty will our brains infuse.
Loosen your purse string, dispel your greed,
You'll be surprised how compassion fills need,
Resolve to save and maintain our security,
And restore our crippled nations unity.
Just ask for an answer before it's too late -
Don't let us falter or hesitate.

—Eleda Scribner

Songs Of The Beach Wind

I see the morning wind move along the hazy shore, It lifts long tendrils of pale beach grass and Carefully strokes each sun-lit strand, like the hand Of a dreaming father playfully ruffling the hair of his only child. All at once, a well of pride and secret joy envelopes him, Overwhelms him, as he sits entwined in deep communion, Before the surf, with surging sighs, starts to rise and break the spell. I watch the lazy afternoon breeze slowly twirl the swaying stalks that bend to touch the beach and trace concentric circles in the sand. Pale stems caressing like the gentle fingers of a new mother. Lightly tracing the curve of her newborn's cheek. The touching binds them both into one, single, shining, wave of love. Held fast in time - a moment grasped between the drawing of a breath and the wakening stir that rouses both to separateness. I listen to the nighttime air humming through the shifting dunes, sighing in remembrance as it gathers dreams to hold in safe embrace. Returning like some clear celestial echo, high-riding hidden currents ride whispering from the evening star-lit sky and I, hear now, the soothing sounds of an everlasting blessing Crooning its universal, timeless lullaby.

—Marlyn H. Perkins

Growing Dreams

Is it better going forward with dreams
Than remaining dazed in disagreement,
In disagreement, fixing all movement
Frozen, planning egotistical schemes
Arguing imperfections' many reams'
Mind setting depressions, too many spent
Falling behind, wondering where time went?
Or will you by consensus agree dreams—
And I say, best realize character,
Real, growing, possible, potential, so
Growing potential dreams makes life charter
More dreams, constantly expanding need so
Growth wonders, embraces love, and love nurtures
The next generations with will to sow.

—Patricia Zabka Kaszycki

For My Unborn Grandchild

The Chinese are a wise people, who say
That a child is already a year old when it is born.
You have been a person for eight months now,
Much loved, eagerly awaited,
As you quietly, miraculously create yourself, cell by cell
In compliance with the code—
Genes handed down in an endless chain,
DNA, RNA, blood, brain, bone—
There has never been anyone like you before, nor will there be again.
How calmly we accept our uniqueness!
If we could, even for a moment, truly apprehend
The sacred nature of our individuality
(Millions of us, and never a duplication,
Not so much as a fingerprint repeated)
Could we go on as we do?
Could we exploit each other, make war on each other?
You will find this a peculiar world, my darling,
But you will bring to it a heritage of understanding and compassion
And make it, I think, lovelier than it was.
Welcome!

—Edith Taylor

Eva Marie

  A dark haired, dark eyed beauty
That at once reminds me of vintage wine
and gypsy songs, of romance and mystery
A stirring kind of beauty...
With lips, soft and sensuous
More expressive than a soliloquy
And, eyes more beguiling than the open sea
An aura of earthiness,
Echoing with a supernatural grace
A spirit, as haunting as the calling wind
   Aaah...To be as a leaf
Captured by the wind's charm
And just hap upon her arm
To ride along with her awhile,
Perhaps a good while
Entwined in her flowing embrace
Gently spinning in an intoxicating pace
To ride along with her awhile
Perhaps...A good while

—Kathryn D'Avanzo

Our Loving God

God sends the beautiful sunshine
  that brightens up our busy day,
When everything seems to go haywire
  and trjennifermes to stay.

He heals the hearts that are broken,
  filled with misery and pain.
The warmth of his Divine love
  brings peace and happiness again.

God watches over us
  morning, noon and night.
He protects us from the evil one
  who is always in sight.

He knows when we are hungry
  and need the daily bread.
He looks down from heaven
  and we are spiritually fed.

We must love and obey God,
  if we want to survive.
For He is the greatest of all Fathers
  and he keeps us alive.
    —*Ora Jones*

Bootsie

I once had a kitten, fluffy and brown.
That came from Connecticut to Havelock town.
He never wandered, he never strayed.
In our front yard he always stayed.
I fed him each morning, then again at night.
To see him come running was such a delight.
He grew everyday from kitten to cat.
Maybe he was just getting fat.
Under the car or in the bushes he'd hide.
But when I came near, he would come to my side.
I'd rub him and pet him as he knew I would.
All this attention made us both feel good.
When our door was opened a little or wide.
He would go through the opening as if on a slide.
Soon it was time to put him back in the yard.
This time of day was, oh, so hard.
Then one morning he was gone, we searched all night.
But my cat didn't come home, I was filled with fright.
To this very day I wonder where my cat might be.
Maybe some day he'll come back to me.
    —*Melissa Androlevich*

That Someone So Near

When you experience a sight
That fills you with delight
You want to be with that someone so near.

When times and events not only excite
But may even cause a fright
It is comforting to be with that someone so near.

When beautiful music is part of the event
Making the occasion as though heaven sent
It should be shared with that someone so near.

The daily trials and tribulations
Become less burdensome in every situation
By talking them through with that someone so near.

When the news is of trouble
And your eyes want to bubble
You need to be with that someone so near.

Your warm hug and tender kiss
Is something I would desperately miss
If you were not That Someone So Near.
    —*Marvin G. Billings*

November Wind

My soul cannot follow the dried-up leaves
That float down from the trees and are blown away.
The days I do not see you
  are all ashes in my mouth,
    I cannot stand them.
The sap of life which courses through my veins
Seems to be only of your making;
I am weary of all that is not you.

The chill November wind sweeps down
  over the barren plain,
And the brown husks of last summer's hope
  are its pawns,
I cling more fiercely
  to that tenuous allusion of love -
    I have nothing else -
Lest I should give myself
  despairingly to the November wind.
    —*Janice Hilburn*

The Currency Of Love

Love is the money
that God gave us to spend
We should not be frugal with it
for the more we give away—
the more He'll send

We shouldn't try to save it—
there is no bank to put it in
And to deny that we receive it?
Well, that is called a sin

Spend it on those who need it
Give it to those who say they don't
Double the amount to all who say there is no such thing
Give to all who will accept it, and all who say they won't

And the interest received from giving love
seems too good to be true
There is one caution: Be careful not to spend
too much of it on you!
    —*Barbara Benesh*

Dream Fantasy

My dreams are but a fantasy, they represent a side of me
that hides within at morning light, until I close my eyes at
night and as the darkness settles in, a cavalcade of shows
begin.

My dreams are but a fantasy, allowing what I want to be,
an actor's role I'll play the part, of deep desires
within my heart. With all the scenes a dream can make,
I'll save the world before I wake.

My dreams are but a fantasy, at times they even frighten me.
The evil I suppress by day, into my thoughts can fine a way
to turn my wants, my hopes, my dreams, into a carnival of
screams.

My dreams are but a fantasy, things I'm not, in reality,
but should I find my life today, was once a dream, then I could
say my daytime in reality, is just another fantasy.
    —*Kenneth M. Ohlfs*

The Ways Of My Mother

As I go through this life I find
   that I am walking in my Mother's way
I say the things that she said
I do the things that she did.

When I envision things to come,
I envision myself doing them in the way of my mother.
And I am proud.

I respect the ways of my mother —
   her reasonings,
   and her actions,
   and her words.
I imitate her,
   for I know that she has gone this way before
   and has done well.

It is with no flattery that I do this,
   but with admiration
   and love
   and a sense of awe
That God would so design me

That I would walk in the ways of my mother.
   —Awnali D. Mills

Mid-Day

You say that I'm like the sun,
that I brighten up your day.
and show the beautiful flowers bloom.

I say that you're like the moon,
you lighten up my way.
the moon brings light to the dark.

But the clouds seem to cover up my sunshine,
just like our friends do, time and time again.

But the stars try to make you blend in the sky,
which our other guys that try to make you look the same.

It is very unusual to see the sun and moon together
in the sky,
Once in a while you can see them both, but if you can't
they are still there.

Just like you and me.
It might not look like we are together, maybe not to
even us.
But we are always there, waiting for midday.
   —Rebecca Gehman

Death

Death is something
That is hard to understand.
We don't want our loved ones
To leave this earthly land.

Death doesn't care
How young you may be.
It will come as a thief in the night,
And take you or me.

Some loved ones are sick
For many, many days
Before death comes
And takes them away.

Death of a loved one
Makes us feel lonely and sad.
Until we think of all the wonderful times
And then somehow, we feel glad.
   —Rhonda W. McLaughlin

Untitled

There's a clock in our house
That is so steady and true.
It goes click-clack, click-clack
Day after, after day, the same.
And at night as I lay on my bed
And the only sounds are muted
With the occasional bark of a dog
Off in the far, far distance,
Or the faint buzz of a motor car
Breaking the evening quiet.

It is nice to hear the click-clack, click-clack
From that clock on the bedroom wall.
It carries a sense of re-assurance
Like the heart beat of the world.
It lulls one to sleep feeling
That God is there seeing
That time keeps going on, and on.
That tomorrow will surely follow today.

I'm glad for that clock
On the bedroom wall.
It tells me to rest in sleep
Trusting that God takes care of things
And morning will come, click-clack, sure.
   —Robert H. McNabb

The Miracle Of God

As we walk along the path of life, I acknowledge
   That it is not as difficult as we believe.
If we come across a discouraging turn, we hold
   Each other's hand and pray to the Lord for the
Strength to see ourselves through these hard times.
   Granted, these time of trouble are often; I am
Thankful that you were at my side to share my despair,
   Or laughter, or sorrow.
We are not only mother and daughter but friends,
   Confidants, and believers in the miracles of God.
Through His ways, I have seen the miracles of life and
   Death, but more importantly, that of friendship.
Without your support, I would be walking the path of
   Life alone. Thank you for being my friend.
   —Julie Weinmann Pearson

The Expression Of - "The Age Of Reason"

It is the new day of question that sites all to explain,
   that one may triumph protecting the rights that proclaim.
The statement of new cause and consolidated hope,
   combines in belief as others pursue their opening scope.

"Oh better the mind as it has a hypothesis and theory,
   than to shut out all explanation, making the embodiment weary."
"As one may look into an inhabited scroll of the mind,
   justice may be found with doctrines of a different kind."

There is the new dawn of creation that sites all to be,
   as a postulated figure in the opening of a decree.
Though the pursuit may be a challenge to proclaim and to state,
   careful scrutiny will never obtain no devastating fate.

Discovery will continue for generations of greater height,
   promoting new experience and philosophy in one's own Age of
Reason - in an opening light.
   —Sean Stover

Love Can Never Die

We looked into each others eyes and grinned,
That strange flutter traveled down my spine.
My face turned red as though I'd sinned,
I remember the first time he held my hand,
The electricity filled my body our hearts entwined
Those cherished moments of walking in the sand.
That tenderness grew as our lives became one,
So filled with joy, gazing at our son.
But after five years the distance started,
Leaving me lost, empty and broken-hearted.
Friends don't understand I don't want the home,
For without him I feel so alone!
Now we wait for the papers to be served,
This isn't the life an innocent child deserved,
Yet through this bond my love will never die,
Is it too late to say I'm sorry now,
Can't we remember when we met, just try.
You want me to let you go, I don't know how.
Somewhere in your heart is the love for me
That we felt so long ago.

—*Cathy J. Sargent*

MiGs Over Michigan, 1990

When the fulcrum flew I finally saw it end
That war my father fought
    forty-eight years
      with a score
    dead in a rush of a flame roar
      glory he would have wished to see

With the snap of a cobra
    cold ebbed
the enemy slipped between our fingers

We buried the memory
    with casual economy
      strained mirth called the day another day
      belied by our halted turn from the past
Repetitions cannot prepare
We never really know
Can coffers only be spent today

The war ended without me
no last calls or words—no warnings
leaving me to face the morning
    cold with abandonment

—*C. Michael Johnson*

Untitled

I love you
That will never change
Your thoughts and memories will always stay the—
same
No more christmas together
No more birthdays to spend
No more songs to hear
No more hugs or kisses to feel
No more love to share except what will be left here
Now I remember all the things we did together
The doll you gave me,
once was played with
Now lies still waiting for that shiny day
The blanket you made
Now I take out to look at each day
You came now your gone,
Because you spent so long,
So I keep the memories in my heart,
To remember all the best times we had together.

—*Brooke Jankowski*

Parents To Graduate

We took you to church school
    that you might learn our religious ways.

We sent you to school
    that you might learn reading, writing, arithmetic,
    and equip yourself for the future.

We joined teams and groups
    that you might learn to be successful
    in your relationships with others.

We have steered you through the winding roads
    and meandering paths of the first seventeen to twenty-two
    or so years of your life.

We have chauffeured you, guided you
    —yes, sometimes, commanded you—
    that the right action might be taken.

Now, you are "on your own."

You decide to meet responsibilities
    or to do something else.

We are still available for you.
    Please continue to share with us.

And, know always that you owe yourself your best!

—*Leola A. Young*

Invitation

Lord,
    the announcements and invitations arrive-
    graduations, marriages, births.
    Asking that we celebrate an ending
    or beginning
    of a phase of their lives.

Lord,
    we are reminded of your announcement to us-
    'I am come that ye might have life'.
    And you have invited us to celebrate forever
    in your presence-
    'That where I am ye may also be'.

Lord,
    thank you for honoring us.
    With anticipation,
    unworthily,
    we accept!

—*Shirley A. Allen*

Norma Jean

Small town lights made you dream of big city lights.
The attraction to the glint left you innocent of the glare.
Dancing closer to the light, entranced,
You lost yourself, Norma Jean,
From brunette to blond bombshell,
From Norma Jean to Miss Monroe,
Your name on every shiny, neon marquee.
Caught up in webs of deceit,
Playing with fire only got you burned.
Poor Norma Jean, you realized too late
You were never more to them than just a face,
    Just a body.
That August day, the lights faded.
No more facade, no more lies, no more pretending,
No more Marilyn- you could finally be yourself.
Poor Norma Jean, the price you had to pay
For dancing too close to the flame
Blinded by the glare
Those big city lights...
The price was more than you ever dreamed.

—*Jana Babb*

The Battle

The dawns ablaze,
The battle may soon rage.
Red fire lights the sky,
The fiercesome warriors set out to try.

The castle's quiet is broken,
As the drawbridge drops open.
The thunder of the hooves heavy tread,
Alerts the foe of ominous dread.

The lances level for the attack,
But the strength of the shields push them back.
The clash of blade against blade,
Splatters crimson blood throughout the glade.

At last the cries of wounded men,
Slowly comes to a gruesome end.
As the fading sunset wraps the world in gloom,
The winners and losers face the impending doom.
　　—Steven Shapiro

Snowflakes And Dreams

The sphere of glass you hold in hand,
The beauty held inside, the figures there,
　a symphony of colors.
You shake the glass and snowflakes fly.

Enter this world and close your eyes,
　a Shangri-la, perhaps a paradise.
Shake the glass again, fear not.
Enter the Geni, come within, dare the
　wonders of your schemes.

Release your mind let it find its way.
Drift now, dream again, dream
　again, on this your day.
　　—Melvin J. Fridh

The Playground

The sunshine, the children, the laughter.
The benches, the mothers the gossip.
The swings, the songs,
The sandbox, the teardrops,
The slide, the line,
The monkeybars, the derringdo.

The scream, the fall,
The realization, the anguish,
The helplessness, the crowding, the noise
The policecar, the ambulance,
The uniforms, the stretcher,
The sirens, the prayers.

The hospital, the doctors, the nurses,
The x-rays, the crying.

The waiting, the waiting, the waiting.

The results, the joy.
The hugs, the kisses, the relief.

The end? The beginning.
The next day, the request,
The Playground.
　　—Lisa Oliver

Moorings

Like gulls of varied size and hue
　the boats were postured in the cove
　　as gentle wavelets lapped their sides
　　　and iridescent patterns wove.

But though that day was calm and fair
　a bank of clouds as black as night
　　appeared to threaten tranquil scene
　　　and cause the skippers awesome fright.

In moments, winds and waves most fierce
　did in that cove all craft accost.
　　Soon many from their moorings broke,
　　　and quite a few from sight were lost.

But there were some withstood the blast,
　since deeply anchored 'neath the brine
　　theirs was a base impregnable
　　　to tide and storm and wind malign.

Thus we can also face the gales
　of hostile forces all around
　　when we are moored to bedrock firm:
　　　God's Word, God's love, God's will profound.
　　—R. Donald Clare

Untitled

The love of God is so intense
The body cannot bear it.
Even the Savior's body was not strong enough.
Only three years of ministry...
The frailty of humanity brought
The heart... ruptured and punctured,
The witness... water and blood
Caused by heavy stress,
Emotional strain.
He died before the cross killed him.
He died of love.
How painful love can be.
Yet through pain and love
Comes the revelation
For us.
We can know, feel
The intensity of God's love
In Jesus Christ. The Cross
Even after all these years
Remains... still revealing.
　　—Muriel Evans

The Arc

The kiss, the song, the quiet smile,
The breeze long past that sighed through
Auburn hair I grasped with such security;
The gentle laughter treasured so
That soothe my tiny sorrows;
These are the deep and distant memories
Lying soft upon my heart.
And if God be the solitary soul
Who knows the full, unseen measure
Of loved passed on, I know He smiles to know
She breaths in me.
For in no small way I know He sees
That I am she, and she is me.
And so the slow arc moves eternally.
　　—David Herman

The Organist

The sounds of the streets are quiet now.
The burdens that mount with the days
Seem light and float through the arches
With the music the organist plays.

   Calling the people to worship
   Softening hearts to receive
   The blessing of words and of music
   Affirming what we believe.
   Orchestrating emotions
   With sounds that speak to the soul —
   Clear, cleansing notes of confession,
   Assurance of mercies untold,
   Martial strains calling to service,
   The joy of renewal by grace,
   And lastly a soft benediction
   To go in peace from this place.

The sounds of the streets will still be there.
Some days will be harried and frayed,
But over it all comes the echo
Of the music the organist played.
   —*Jane MacKinnon Oldroyd*

Her Life

The gift of faith, a soft white veil,
the casket near the altar rail.
Pretty bright flowers with ribbons lay there
to speak of the love, from all those who care.
But placed to the side for the mother and wife
was a symbol of honor and courage in life.
A sturdy old tub filled with beauty and grace:
blossoms grown wild on the high desert face.
The old scrub board, still resting inside
brought silent reminders of high desert pride.
The sounds of her children with dusty bare feet,
the ragged old fence post, her garden to keep.
The sweat of her brow, her fight with the land,
the ache in her back and the touch of her hand.
The joy she felt with a job well done
the moments of laughter, the tub full of fun.
Many spoke of her life, but the women will say
none said it as well, as a tub, that day.
   —*Betty M. Griffiths*

A Moment In Time

I walk down the streets of our city
the children playing near, stop and stare.
I can see the fear and uncertainty behind them.
Those young eyes, have seen more then they should
in a lifetime. Young hearts feeling things they should
never have too, making them no longer children on the inside.
Not knowing who to trust, their innocence taken from them
by a cold world we thought we knew.
The elderly sit behind closed windows, not uttering a sound,
but hearing the wind. It whispers of the past, murmurs
of the future, and sings an eerie song of the present.
The sound of a phone breaks the haunting silence, but no
one answers.
They've all read the writing on the walls, they've begun
looking for hero's but there are none to be found.
They turn to me, helpless eyes looking through me
wondering when the pain will end, if it ever does.
   —*Gina Miller*

Losing The Sun

Sitting on a beach,
The clouds within my reach,
Contemplating life and all it means,
The crashing waves, interrupt my dreams,
Open my eyes,
Realize,
I've lost the sun.

I've lost the sun,
Am I the only one,
The light fades a little more each day,
And, though I try to hold the dusk at bay,
It's getting very hard to see.

Is it just me,
Or is it everyone,
Look to the sea,
Because it seems I've lost the sun.
   —*D. G. Thomas, III*

Irish Pass

Through ancient Irish walls
the continuous pinhole of summer light
kindles the constant Connemara wind,
the first bleats of newborn lambs,
the whispers of children.
Missing stones and moss reveal
no wall is no better or more strongly woven.
Centuries mark these tightly spaced
measures on a jigger.
Only the weathered man knows
if he's been cheated
as he examines not only his double,
but his neighbor's horse as well.
He trusts the years of balance
will lead him home
beyond the edge of this cliff.
   —*Roe Sonye Sprouls*

Silent Tears

My silent tears come from the destruction of my being.
The damming up of my arteries and the blockage of my
passage ways.
As I think of my falling, millions of limbs and the burning of
my magnificent forms that reach up, my silent tears fall.
Everyday I keep getting choked more, more and more, and I have
no place to go with my silent tears like acid falling because
of the close effect of my ceiling.
My silent tears change to joy with droppings of seedlings.
They give me happiness as they return me to my being.
The pumping out of the devastation of my vast open areas
brings back great happiness to me.
My silent tears come back to me as things have been done to
change limits of the law and give total freedom to
my (being) back to me.
Earth
   —*Lynn Holland*

Us, We - People Searching

   Waken to the sounds of laughter

  Hidden deep down inside, covered by
  The fear, tears and all of our pride

The freedom that rides on eagles wind wings
   The liberty that the silence brings
     You must feel this way

  To find the burning bright light
  Of two lost souls in endless flight
   —*Ronald M. Hansen*

Friendship Souvenirs

I thank you, for the day I can never forget
  the day I met you.
    For if ever I go away
the memory of us I shall carry
in my heart each and every day.
The memories of the tears, the
laughter, and even the secrets we've shared.
May these get you through the most trying
years, if ever you are scared.
  The good times, and the bad times
will always linger in my mind.
That's why I cannot bear the thought
of leaving you, my friend, behind.
But for some selfish reason that we
may have to part
  Please remember that you hold
a special place within my heart.
  No matter where I might be,
It is my personal guarantee
That the same shining star we both shall see.
    —*Spring D. Davignon*

Which Gate?

On a cold dark morning, the sun rises.
The dew is struck by surprise;
Eight hours of laboring pains-
A world with nothing to lose, and everything to gain.
Some question that lies within the heart,
Longs to be answered at heart.
Now the minute gazes as the seconds approach,
And the hour is yet awaken.
The delivery of a child is done,
And who knows of the birth of a lamb-
For everyone's innocent, it seems,
But the world gains its victory.
Sin takes the form of man,
And creeps on into the grave;
As Satan waits for the lost soul,
God's eyes are filled with tears-
Bursting flames or eternal paradise?
    —*Michael Williams*

Untitled

The direction of the eye so misleading;
The direction of your heart quickly to judge;
You're feeling quite strong and superior;
But you're ignorant and don't know nothing;
I don't question our racial existence;
I just question our problems and their needs.
I run through the world thinkin' for tomorrow;
Yet I'm stepped upon by another man;
What's wrong with this wicked world?
Turning against those of different color;
Reach in deep, look within the love;
Or we will conclude in civil war.
    —*Kristopher Murray*

A Forgotten Love

    In the past we shared
      The feeling of love and life
    Yet the life we shared only I can love
      For the life was left to me
I thank - you for what you gave up ...
    I share the world with
      A love I know I will have forever
        So my forgotten love
I see you ... I touch you ... I can love you
    In the life you gave me
      —*Linda Lou Hammer*

A Disease Called Love

Thickened hearts broken once again;
The disease called love thrusts its final blow.
Will it ever stop causing people pain?
Though once it has come it will never go.
For anyone close will fall into its grasp.
Anyone close will catch the disease.
Many have made mistakes in the past.
Just waiting for love to bring them to their knees.
There is a cure to this fatal course!
And many have passed the test.
But you must follow your heart, which is the source.
For love brings happiness, I must confess.
In the midst of all loves anguish and hunger,
It will not let hate conquer.
    —*Lisa Ann Compagno*

The Forest

Slowly the dew dripped off
  The dogwoods and the maples
With the brightness of the shining sun
  Reflecting off the lazy leaves
The sky exploded from behind the clouds
  As I walked through the large forest
My senses came alive
  With the sweetest smells of the maples
And the clean, fresh air
  Tickled my nose
Suddenly my ears heard
  A rustling in the bushes beside me
As the birds and insects echoed
  Their calls above me
I walked slowly not making a noise
  Wishing it would never end
    —*Carl Deskins*

As I Rest Here

As I rest here
the earth spins beneath me,
the moon races above,
and time rushes past.
  (Oh, it moves so quickly)

Our blessed moments together fall,
farther and further,
into yesterday.
  (Pray that they not be forgotten)

Why isn't it that these times could be today.
Or, better yet, let them lie in tomorrow,
eternally poised on the horizon.
  (Deep within me, it will always be thus)

So let the earth spin,
and let the moon race,
and let time pass;
for, as I rest here,
I dream of you.
  (Such is my love)
    —*Anthony Rintala*

Companions

Evening has long since passed.
The faint shimmer of dawn lies nowhere near.
The road is unlit, elusive.
My eyes are blurry, head throbs.
Odd for us to be traveling at this unfamiliar hour.

In the darkness ahead, the road distorts.
I slow, adjust my vision.
A small figure stiffly sits.
Unclear at first, my headlights illuminate the rabbit.
It turns its head, and the unnatural glare of headlights
reflects in its eyes.
But, something else there, too.

Its keen gaze swiftly returns to the silent,
unmoving companion recumbent at its side.
I look over at my mother.
We sit for a while, in the dead of the night
and hear the stillness.
—*Tina Gordon*

Friends

There you stand, and here am I
The feeling so real
So many questions I need to ask
So many words I wish I could say
Slowly we turn and walk away
We walk from everything
Everything in life
But most of all we walk from each other
For the time is never quite right
We are friends, we are friends
Or at least that is what we wish to believe
For do friends feel as we do
Do friends have that glow within their eyes
That light within their lives
We are friends, we are friends
That is something my mind believes
I only wish that one day my heart
Would believe the same thing
We are friends, we are ....friends
—*Melissa Ellen Cunningham*

Spring

Spring - is nature beginning a new life.
The flowers awaken from their long winters nap.
They breathe new life, and they display arrogant
colors and pretty faces.

Spring - the breeze like a whisper, echoing her sweet song
through the leaves of the many trees.

Spring - I saw the red robin, its breast a flaming red, bob,
bob, bobin lookin for a worm.

Spring - the evening sun shining bright, casting a golden hue
over the colorful desert flowers of West Texas.
—*Debbie A. Byard*

Second Thought

I crush that which so long I sought
The heart so high, the soul so free.
What fate is this with silent tear
To whisper "No, this shall not be?
I need not crush that which I sought
The heart so high, the soul so free.
Once having soared and scaled the heights
T'will last through all eternity!
—*Virginia K. Danz*

The Sky

As I look up, I see an endless confinement.
The fluffy white clouds float by to remind me,
that even though they seem so close, they are
very far away.
I watch the birds with envy,
  my only dream; to join them.
as I dream on more, I wish I could live in the sky.
  The blue wall that goes on forever, and being free.
  I wish I could fly, I wish I could fly.
  I wish I could live in the sky, I wish I could live in
  the sky.

Often I despise gravity,
  It keeps my feet on the ground.
Having no ground under my feet,
  My life would be complete.
The sky awaits my arrival.
  I also await the sky.
One day I will get there, but until then I can only dream.
I wish I could fly, I wish I could fly.
I wish I could live in the sky, I wish could live in the sky.
—*Automne Ferland*

The Death Of Him

The death of him I cannot hold,
the forever tears cannot be told
He was all I had and a lot much more,
he was something I've never had before
when I was with him I didn't think much,
  of when his soul I could not touch.
  The laughs, the cries we have had together
those special times I will always treasure
I wish I was there for him so much more
I wish we talked about what death was for
as i sit all alone thinking of what us gone
wondering if I will ever hear his song,
The song of love, the song of death
why did he have to take his last breaths.
—*Rachael Sonia Ulbrich*

We Selfish Mortals

The good and the bad, the wise and the just,
The gay and the sad, will all turn to dust.

  Why be so proud, a little too high,
Like a flying cloud, will soon come to lie.

The rich in his best. The young and the old,
Will all come to rest, in the deep grave cold.

The strong and the weak, the beggar on the road,
Will all come to seek, the grave as their abode.

  As waves on a shore, withering like a weed,
  We shall be no more, to let others succeed.

  We take the same road our fathers had taken,
  We learn the same code Fathers had painstaken.

The King and his crown, the heart of the brave,
They all will come down, to mingle in the grave.

  We rise like the wind, to be blown to dust,
    peeling like the rind, to decay and rust.

We pass like a breath, then down to a shroud,
To the paleness of death, so why be so proud.

At the end of the road, up to deaths portals,
Live us to the code, don't be selfish mortals.
—*Joseph N. Antonuccio*

In A Whisper

The warmth of your breath upon my ear
The gentle words of love I hear
Words from the heart are there
In the gentle warmth of a whisper

Tingle down my spine from just one touch
Who could think that it could do so much
Your love my heart does yearn
In the gentle warmth of a whisper

Your tender lips when we kiss
Is what my lips will always miss
The love that I felt
In the gentle warmth of a whisper

Take me into your arms and just hold on
Help me control myself for my feelings are strong
Mind filled with thoughts of making love
In the gentle warmth of a whisper

Just with your body near
And the words I hold so dear
How would I know it would hurt so much
In the gentle warmth of a whisper

—*Elizabeth Forrest*

A Slave For Life

I'm spending all my time, breaking all my ties, I live to find the glory, riddled from our eyes. I can't wait until tomorrow, there's got to be a chance, to do the most with what you're given, unfold your mind's entrance. See me rise; see me fall; we're born into this world, to be a slave for life. I know of no beginning, we may not have an end, we are the means to all extremes, I've known the mind to bend. Just as every single excess, soon becomes its vice, our everyday emotions, aren't felt without their price. Sometimes you must destroy your mind, to keep in touch with your senses, live to embrace our dire need, to free our minds from their fences. Come, and see me rise; see me fall; we are born into this world, to be a slave for life. There are many who exist, merely using up their time, and there are others so amiss they have added no sense to their rhyme, So please lend unto me an opened mind, and forgive the years you've left behind, to think of others we need not be unkind, 'tis just our fears within that make us blind…and, a slave for life.

—*Robert Conklin*

Untitled

Standing together, face to face, in the dark chilly night. The golden moon was full and countless stars glistened bright. Gazing at you, and you at me, my mind, like the breeze, wandered into eternity. There's a mystery about you I can't figure out, but I know deep down inside my feelings are true without a doubt. Your touches are like the ocean waves caressing my bare flesh. Having your confessions of love for me as my security blanket, as flashbacks of our togetherness raced through my mind, I began holding on to every unforgettable memory.
While cherishing every hug, compliment, and kiss once again I thought, "forever we will be." Inspired by the words of courage that you speak and your boyish charm that has swept me off my feet. My soul has taken your lines of passion prisoner, and in my heart I'll forever keep. Suddenly, fears of heartbreak began to stir deep down and my expressionless countenance, I could no longer hide. The eternal, storms of emotion began to calm when your soothing voice whispered, "I'll forever endure by your side." Your goodbye kiss for me was full of ecstasy and romance, and the departing words that you spoke were said with gentleness and care.

—*Tuesday Gorham*

A Letter To My Four Children

Forty-three years, seven days, and eight hours,
The good times, the hard times, they were all ours.
We loved each other and our hearts were true,
We fought the battle all the way through.

Four children later, three boys and one girl,
Eleven grandchildren, we lived in a whirl.
Nothing could shatter the love we all had.
Then something happened, and it's all very sad.

When God took your daddy that morning at three
You fell out of love, even with me.
I don't have the answer - only God knows.
Together or apart, the anger grows.

Will you ever be friends, will it ever be right? I gave it to
God, and I pray every night. Each one suffers
in their own way, so full of sorrow, each night and day.

Well, I'm not strong - it hurts me now. I'd like to end it,
but I don't know how. I've prayed to God through all of my
sorrow for your daddy and us there is no tomorrow.

God took him to heaven before we got there.
He's waiting for us by the golden stairs.

—*Verna Freeman*

Appreciation

The sun shines through the warm, orange haze.
The grass expresses the dew on each blade.
The morning fog lays low to the ground,
and I rise to show my appreciation.

The leaves begin their habitual fall.
They grace the earth with their delightful praise.
The winds grow colder, chilling the air,
and still, I rise to show my appreciation.

The snow marks the season with white pillowy flakes.
Children cry in wonder at the sight of God's creation.
Snow sleds and sleigh bells fill the air with joy,
and yes, I rise to show my appreciation.

Spring is marked by the flowers parading in diversity.
Storms rage through the clouds creating calamity.
All is renewed by the hand of God Almighty,
and each morning I rise to show my appreciation.

The earth groans in the agonizing silence.
It yearns to bring forth its supplication of praise.
Waiting on humanity to bring forth its proclamation.
I rise, my Lord, to show my appreciation.

—*Cheryl A. Lavender*

My Special Friend

I have a very special friend
The greatest gift that God could send.
We've been through hell and back together,
And the bond we have, will last forever,
She's beautiful, understanding,
and forgiving.
She is my reason for living.
She never questions what I do.
She understands and see's me through.
And when I look at her and see
the love I know she has for me,
I know that I can tread life's water
She is my life, she is my daughter.

—*Sharon Boyer*

Debby

Listen world, we're casting a play
The greatest love story ever that say
The girl must be beautiful beyond all compare
The boy must be handsome the fair lady to snare
The story will rival William Shakespeare's best
The acting of girl and boy will take care of the rest
The world's in a turmoil as to who'll be selected
Hundreds and hundreds will surely be dejected
Well glory be did you all hear
Debby Lake's to be the girl of the year
Tom Cruise is the boy they've chosen to lead
He's handsome, talented and tall yes indeed
So applause, applause - the best play of the ages
So say the critics the public and sages....

—*Harold Bergman*

The Groom Quietly Rests

As the cemetery closes its gates,
The groom that died quietly rests.
Bells ring as his soul is lifted.
Blossoms cry in sorrow.
The wind blows as everything is silent.
The angels arrive close to the grooms fate.
Fire does not burn any longer.
It is put out by the solemn wind.
The silky pond nearly dries up,
Like a frog in its sleep.
Then, the fog makes everything fade,
Like a cloud in your face.

—*Marcia Costa*

Winter's Pauses

The color is gone from the towering trees
The ground is covered with burnished leaves

The breeze is gusty, a nip in the air
Coats and umbrellas cover body and hair

Plants are draped and animals are in
The family gathers within the den

The fire is crackling with a huge log
And close to the hearth sleeps the family dog

The children are playing on the floor
Dad comes home and closes the door

His cheeks are red and seem to glow
He smiles and says "Have you seen the snow"?

They rush to the window and gaze outside
At white flakes falling that float and glide

They watch in wonder as it covers the ground
Blanketing the earth with silence around

We thank you, Lord, for winters pauses
That slows our pace and focuses our causes

On family at home from their busy day
For moments like these too soon fade away

—*Kay L. Day*

Mountains

Mountains remain for long eons of time;
the heights of their summits rising sublime.
Mountains have witnessed so many things;
the cry of an eagle on high-soaring wings;
The scream of a cougar, calling her mate.
Will mountains bear witness to all wildlings' fate?

Man, in his ignorance, tries to constrain the
lives of the wildlings the mountains contain.
With gun, trap, and poison — man's little aware
his life is entwined with the animals there.
Exploit not the wildlings, nor destroy their homes,
or the mountains may witness mankind...alone.

—*Shirley Carson*

Untitled

She ran out of the old, yellow house,
The house she grew up in. Tears streaming down her face,
Arms wrapped tightly around herself.

Her shoulders shook with pain and hurt.
A storm was brewing,
The wind was dry and cool.
She ran to the old, fat, willow, tree.
The very same willow she had climbed as a child.

The same that one day, not so far from now,
  her child will climb too.

The wind gust up, and wrapped her hair around her.
A mist began to spray in the breeze.
Great clashes of thunder rolled in,
And the unforgettable storm began.
The sky darkened, just as her heart.
She leaned against the tree, and slowly slid down it.
Wrapping her body in her arms, she wept.

The sky comforted her with its dark gloominess.
It silently expressed the way she felt,
  alone, scared, and worried.

—*Angela Mae Stepp*

A Gale And A Gust

A gale and a gust.
The hull rocks.
The feel of the salt air rush,
The sails fill.
Wake grows like a river it's own.
Hold the Balance of Ballast for bigger knots,
Creaking mahogany escapes a groan.
For the sail, more than passion and affection,
Inexplicable romantic obsession.
It is something mysterious, a life's metaphor,
It rushes back to your soul,
Your life, your spirit,
With all the force of a gale and a gust.

—*Michael Whitbeck*

Library Sounds

The loud sounds, the soft sounds,
  the humming and the mumbles
The crying kids, the contented kids
  the screeching and the rumbles

The fax machine, the copy machine
  the typewriter and the printer
The in-house questions, the telephone questions
  the summer and the winter

The clicking heels, the dragging heels
  the walking and the running
The laughing teens, the boisterous teens
  the ribbing and the punning

The smooth card, the jammed card
  the shrilling and the tugging
The slamming books, the placing books
  the carting and the sorting

Library sounds, people sounds
  the caring and the learning
The searching mind, the relaxed mind
  finds the book it's yearning.
    —*Lillian Zak*

An Unseen Carnage

His body slowly rots in the unknown sepulcher
The innards decay, while pale, pathetic, pliable skin peels away
Gashes gape his gizzard from a greedy vulture
A slow, skilled, sucking sound as it pecks its meal from where
  the carcass lay.
A pool of blood runs cold from beneath the remains
Truly he was insane, because from one bullet there was no pain
Taking his own life was his end
His demented soul to Hell will slowly descend.
Too long it takes to wait to make him at one with the earth
He left nothing to own, no money, no home
Nothing he left, but skin, blood, and bone
The poor scum never had any true worth.
A tale of the deranged, this savage brutal being
A shocking way to end a life, a wasted human offspring.
    —*Jason Carr*

Day's Break

Fingers of light reach out over
the jagged rock giants.
Slowly their owner rises.
The wooden statues that await in
Their grove rustle in delight
As the rays touch each one's green helm.
The leaves themselves seem to speak out in joy
As God's breath tosses them to and fro.
The peace that arises with day's break
Calms the most anxious heart.
The rolling green foothills go on and on
Opening only to the vast open fields
Full of life's plentishes.
My eyes wander to stare up
Up into the blue glass dome that covers us.
Sudden patches of cloud gently swim by
Filling my soul with warmth.
Warmth only felt long ago,
As I stand in front of my Father's grave.
    —*Dourlas R. Handlon*

I Never Knew Him

Until the ball came gently back to me

Suddenly I realized that he never knew
the joy of hitting the fast ball

Running around the bases, the cheers, the boos
Catching the football, the human contact

The kick sending the ball soaring,
the satisfied grunt of a good tackle

The handball sliced into a corner

The punchball stroked over the head
of the outfield

The use of the body for fun
games, comradeship

Apprenticed out at 12 years old

All he knew was the treadle of
the sewing machine

Saved by love, he married the
boss's daughter, my mother

No, I never really knew him
until he threw the ball back to me, my proud father,
with the feeble overhand motion of a woman.
    —*Sam Zipkin*

Toxic Street

I just moved in this little place not far from the toxic dump
The kids use to run in those fields until this town just gave up
Is money always the problem when you can't find a way out
Who to screw to get what I need that's what this is all about

I want blue skies above and green down below
if we don't fight for it we'll be the first to go

It's all locked away real tight buried deep in concrete
It's hard to get things done when it makes you feel so weak
Now I've been to the red zone I didn't stay there too long
But now my hair is coming out and my breaths not very strong

You can't have what's not yours and you can't take what's mine
It's hard to make it on your own when your living in toxic times
    —*Scudder Miller*

The Little Balcony

In the hot mid-day sun, away from rolling traffic-
The laughter of people—
Still I sit, on my balcony, white
—Lilac scrolled—

Fragrance of satin deep lilac
Narcotizing, drifting my mind, changing the mood.
—You open my heart—

Yellow, big butterflies, bumble-bee plump
Around red trumpet bells, where the hummingbird rings-
—With a rose in my heart—

As midsummer-sun dreams, over the meadow-beauty wide-
Congregation of daisies-
In sea-blue cornflowers—scarlet "Margareten Blumen"
—I dream of you—

As wind plows the grass blades
-cotton-grass blows away-
Plucking over a mandolin—
Over contents, full-filled Anthology-
Eye of heaven around, still country - hills-
—I am with you—
    —*Christiana*

It's Autumn

I walk the streets of my home town
The leaves are tumbling all around
The frost will soon be on the ground
It's Autumn

I've traveled many and many a mile
With many a tear and many a smile
But now I'm home for a little while
It's Autumn

The skies are clear and crystal bright
With little clouds that are fluffy and light
And everything on the earth is right
It's Autumn

The ground is covered deep with leaves
And yet there is color in all the trees
But soon there will be only memories
Of Autumn
—*Lea VanderBoom*

The Old Man's Dream

The last rays of the sunset can be seen through the trees...
But the little boy isn't quite sure what he sees.

The old man looks all around at the beautiful sight.
While the young one darts about to give the birds a fright!

Shhhh!!!!!! Be Still!! Listen to the soft rustle of the leaves.
See the birds dip and sail through the colorful, majestic trees.

The tired old man would like to gather his strength, linger and tarry.
But the child moves quickly, picking pine cones to carry.

The communication between the old and so very young. Does
sadly leave a world of beauty unobserved and unsung.

Another day will dawn and the sights will be there to be seen.
Just to have the young one truly see them is the old man's dream.
—*Bernice Warner*

Can I Go Home Now?

Looking out on a sunny day and thinking wistful thoughts
The little girl asks plaintively, "Can I go home now?"

Hospitals are sterile places no matter how they try
And little girls don't want to stay, "Can I go home now?"

But when she goes home her Daddy is gone
"Gone to his reward", they say. "Can I go there too?"

A growing girl learns to love and hurries on her way
Away from the childhood home "Is this our home now?"

But hubby's folks are troubled and need help that cannot wait
And so back to the farm they move, "Is this our home now?"

She learns that farm work is grueling and the winters are cruel
Until that poor farm is lost. "Where is our home now?"

Then far across the country to a brand new start
Still they're able to plan. "We'll have this home now."

Finally the kids are raised; they move south to retire
They sit in the sun. "We are at home now."

And then she falters in pain and must to the hospital go
Each day she weakly asks, "Can I go home now?"

'Til the day comes when she can bear no more
She gently closes her eyes and finally goes home.
—*Barbara Jean Vaughn*

Mother's Advice

Gather the children, Mother!
The little heads close to your knee,
In the hush of the beautiful twilight,
And talk to them tenderly.
When the bright eyes grow tired and restless,
and gaze at you wistfully,
and the sweet lips beg for a story,
Then gather them close to your knee!

Not long will your little ones linger,
So talk to them while you may,
a world may be better tomorrow
For the story you're telling today.
So tell them the story of Jesus,
For the child heart is tender and true
and not all the Teachers and Preachers
can guide them, O Mother, like you!
—*Lydia G. Iutzi Litwiller*

Ride Hard Your Fiery Tail

A deafening blast! A roaring red red inferno!
The massive form hangs free within its gantry
On edge! Alive! atop its ball of flame!
It lifts! Its off! To space it makes its entry!

The deep blue dome of sky fades into black
Stars, stripped of twinkle, pierce through in dazzling grace
Vast galaxies emerge from age long hiding
And solar winds sweep wide through empty space

These stars have seen it all -
Seen birth of life and continents afloating,
Seen Man's triumphant climb from cave to palace
Seen Pharaohs and Ceasars rise and fall

Proud Man, Crown Prince of Evolution
Usurper of the powers of the God's
Sets Earth ablaze in wild unfettered freedoms
With certain harvest - chaos, crime and blood

Up! Up! Rise up from off your gantry!
With firm resolve ride hard your fiery tail
Humanity hangs breathless on the outcome
The timeless stars demand you dare not fail!
—*George J. Mayer*

The Rainstorm

The roads are abandoned, the fields left alone,
  the meadows are empty, people at home.

Huge strands of clouds appear in the sky,
  funny how quickly they seem to pass by.
Big wind blows, a flash of lightning appears,
  the hail and the rain come threateningly near.

There's a loud crash of thunder
  that comes from way high,
it intrigues us all
  as we watch the sky.

The lightning makes light shapes in the clouds
  that have darkened and have made the children arouse.

The fireflies are smart and have gone away. I'll
  save my pennies for another rainy day.
—*Shelley Marie Quilter*

Sunday's Fathers

We're Sunday's Fathers, Sunday's Fools
the merry-go-round, the dip in the pool
heart's breaking slowly, eye's shiny with tears
we're Sunday's Fathers soothing children's fears.

"Daddy come home, I cry in the night,
Daddy come home, Mom said you might,
Daddy I want, I need and I care,
Daddy come home I'll be good and I'll share."

We're Sunday's Fathers, Sunday's fools,
trying to give of ourselves and time is a tool
the quantity's gone, but the quality stays,
once a week only, and then just for a day.

Babies I love you, and I always will,
the joys of life I hope to instill
I'll be with you always, you are my jewels,
for I'm a Sunday father, yea a Sunday fool.
—*Billie Valez*

The Hills

That cabin still is standing in the hill,
The mocking bird sings sweetly by the mill
While the frogs of spring send out a melody
From a pond just underneath the willow tree.

Once upon these high hills gladly I did go.
As I gazed into the valley far below,
I could see fair homesteads for many a mile
And the whippoorwill was singing all the while.

It was indeed a picturesque scene
To view the cattle that were grazing on the green
And large rocks which were a very natural road
Served as pathways in this happy abode.

Tis the place to go when I am filled with care
And my burdens seem more than I can bear.
It's the most majestic place in the land
I'll be here again, sometime, I understand.
—*Georgia Maurine Peterson*

A View

The stars are shining bright tonight,
The moon is in its place,
The leaves are swaying slowly,
At their very own pace.
The wind sings a song of peace
As it blows gently through my hair.
As I let my gaze go 'round
I wonder how it all got there.
"Who put that tree way up there?"
I think as I watch it sway.
"Who put the stars in that perfect spot,
Where not even a cloud stands in its way?"
So as another day goes by,
And while the moon's up in the sky.
I see many things as I look
And I truly believe earth's beauty can't be mistook!
—*Karen Williams*

I Will Be There

I will be there whenever you need me. In
the morning, noon, and during the night.
Oh dear heart, our love in so strong, nothing
could break us apart. We have been through so
much together, we have experienced - sunshine
with bright skies and dark skies with stormy
rain.
We have cruised through:
oceans,
We have sailed through:
streams and,
We have paddled through:
ponds.
We have experienced the impossible, unthinkable,
and yes - even the unmentionable. Through many of
the good and a few of the bad, my love has stayed.
I will not leave, nor will I stray. I hope
you won't either, I pray you will stay.
—*Jamillah Garrison*

God's Rose Bud

The sun sent a beam from a rose bud
　The most beautiful I ever have seen,
The rose was my darling daughter
　That God had sent to me.

We shared our joys and sorrows,
　The load sometimes heavy to pull,
We each pulled a little harder
　Then we made it, over the hill.

The sun still shines from this rose bud,
　The love in its smile still true,
Although the beam is not so bright for me now,
"I always will love you!"
—*Sylvia M. Burns*

Earthman

Earthman has and can explore,
The mountain heights and the ocean floor,

But man has a goal up in the sky,
To reach the moon, and I wonder why?

The moon to us all is a mystery,
But I wonder what it's like on mercury?

Is this planet the same as ours?
And what is it like on Venus and Mars?

So man is building a rocket to zoom,
Into outer space and shoot for the moon.

And when he gets there, he can stay as long as he please,
If he brings enough crackers to go with the cheese.
—*Helen M. Olson*

Life...

The baby is born.
The new life comes out of the dark and into the light.
The young human being sees its mother thinking real
or unreal, is this a dream or real life.
Is it different from any other kind of life.
From seeing dark to light and dreaming.
I hear voices coming and asking how do you love
this beautiful life.
With out holding on to the power thanking the life of you.
Holding on to this power is called
　Love
　Life
　Beauty.
—*Tia Ickes*

Ravensbruck

Best is not to have been born at all;
The next best is to die as quickly as possible.

- Nietzsche quoting the ancient Greeks in the birth of tragedy.

Her name was Mari Breslauski. She was fourteen years old and watched her mother die beyond her arms. The guards, the SS, took her from the train to the wire. They staked her to the earth with wooden pegs, and allowed their dogs to use her until she died.

Emphasis: Crying all week.

She lost her children in the fire
The smoke being small ghosts
Snaking their way to heaven
Passing startled souls and furnace stars
Their dark circuit to God
The fired ovens the rocketry of matted blood.

Charcoal rooms and empty plates the final solution.

Think this:

Small bones and cindered flesh
Are buried with trepidation
Beneath the bare trees of ravensbruck.
—*Art Glasow*

Grandpa's Barn

In the early morning sunlight, in the fresh morning dew,
the old barn creeks- memories more than a few.
Memories of serious talking farmers, with their worries of drought.

The young ones all smiles, so eager to learn,
of the way of the farm life, of their grandpa so stern.
The farmer himself, his weather worn face, so many chores,
so little time.

The smell of the cows, the chewing of hay,
the soft buzz of the lights, glowing up above.
The laughing of children, straw in their shoes,
not worried about getting dirty, taking the steps two by two.
Trying to be brave, they're still scared of the bull,
more close to the calves, eager to feed, bottle in hand.

The barn misses these sights.
It's now cob-webbed, with mildewy hay.
Sharing its memories with few passers-by,
Memories of yesterday.
—*Stefanie Gehrke*

"I Am Human, Hear My Cry"

I am a person of the street
The one we refuse to give our donations to
I make my home from the cardboard box
After I watch you zoom by in that BMW
I am the shadow that has no owner
The person picking food from the nearest trash barrel
If there is room, I make my home at a public shelter
I am human hear my cry.
My children grow in poverty and violence
Save just one aspect of my life
Help me for the moment
Should I call upon you
Help my children to make the most from their life
Don't make them live the same life I endure
At night I lay grasping newspaper for warmth
Shivering in the cold I try to sleep on the park bench
and at the moment of my death
No family member is there to comfort my needs
I am all alone, for I am the person you pity
I am a person of the street.
—*Katie Fisher*

Untitled

Have you heard the silent child
the one who cries but no one will hear
the one who needs someone to love him
the one who is filled with fear.
Can you see the pain in his eyes
No sparkle as they radiate cold
the joy that once filled his laughter
now captures the pain that he holds.
He lives in a world of glassy beauty
but everything's broken and charred
he lives in a world of hopeless sorrow
he lives in a world that is barred.
No one will care as tears fill his eyes
a child with no laughter to find
with a screech and a wail his heart pounds
he just cant escape from the bind.
I never can help the child whose silent
the one who cries but no one will see
How could I care for a child so helpless
When the child I speak of, is me.
—*Aimee Jo Fish*

"We Are The Shore"

One is immense sea;
the other immeasurable sand.
Together, a new image is weaved;
this is called a shore.

Yet the sea encroaches upon the sand;
the sand disperses into the sea.
Without one another, they are each an entity;
then the shore cannot be perceived.

Still the sea is bound by the sand;
the sand holds up the sea.
While separated, each has its own name.
Though can be together, they are not the same.

I may want to be the sea,
but I may become the sand.
Who am I? It matters no more,
'Cause being together, now we are the shore.
—*Louis Chow*

"The Passage"

The tears flow from his eyes,
The pain of his heart is almost too much to bear,
There seems to be no relief from the continual torment
That his life is filled, emptied, and filled again.
How much can one man suffer and does this searing
 in his soul lessen with death?

Broken relationships are scattered in his past
As bones in an arid desert devoid of life.
The constant friction of life's troubles eat away
The kindness and goodness until trenches form where
Smooth, clean surfaces lay before.

The night has arrived.
The decision will be made tonight.
No more will life trouble him.
Then his vulnerabilities no one can touch,
Not even those he has loved.

His passage from this world was swift and silent,
And fell as the first winter snow at night
Unknown to those around,
But revealed in the dawn of a new day's light.
—*Stephen K. Fordham*

Through The Fog

We walked alone to greet the dawn,
   The passing of night, birth of the sun,
This transition of time, was ours alone,
   Where nature, and being, seemed fused, as one.

The solitude about us, speaks softened words,
   Slow moving fogs, entice away the world,
Enveloping us, this the realm, of silent birds,
   Who await bleak light, for a new day, unfurled.

This moment but a gift, ours alone, to possess,
   The blending of night, with day, a time golden,
Given us, we who seek, nature's gentle caress,
   And absorb hope, for a new beginning beholden.

Take my hand, sense the burning fires, renewed,
   Let the fogs clear, watch the sun slowly rise,
This day ours, a renewal of vows, our minds imbued,
   With inspiration, love and faith, beneath these skies.

Yesterday, a morrow past, lays in death's decay,
   Ne'er to be again, given to oblivion,
This moment of dawn, ours, graciously sent our way,
   Instilling spirit, love, a new life, to live in.
     —*Gilbert Choinski*

Perfection In A Bough

How few the youth these days have shared
   the passion of our boyhood days,
   that sought within each willow grove
   or branching tree, that special growth
   of twinning limb with contour formed
   to make a perfect flipper-crotch.

How eager was our glance for symmetry
   with balanced fork of limb or leafy branch
   that shaped its spreading form
   to meet the standards of our eye—
   a standard felt as much as seen—
   to form that perfect flipper-crotch.

That skill so deeply learned that even yet,
   with three score years and more behind,
   I find my failing eye will scan
   a willow's graceful stance or wander up
   an unfamiliar tree to scan its verdure
   for that pattern of perfection wrought—
   The perfect flipper-crotch.
     —*William D. Fox*

"Sold On Gold"

   They are often referred to as those "golden years,"
The peace and the quiet, without any fears,
   I waited impatiently, for all of those changes,
Everything remained in the usual ranges,
   I finally realized, "this isn't too bad,"
I don't miss those things, that I never had,

   I still have my family, fickle as they may be,
what would it be like, if nothing worried me?
   I still see my doctors, for adjustments and repairs,
I'm still attending to my own affairs,
   how can I complain, if I'm all grey of hair?
Those blue haired old ladies drive me to despair!

   I don't look too bad, growing old with good grace,
I'm not in a hurry, I just take a slow pace,
   I wait and I watch and wonder exactly when
something new will happen it does now and then
   I can't always remember what happened yesterday,
I'll take you back fifty years to one special day!
     —*Harriet J. Moore*

Jim

Weaved in strands of gold and red
the perfect mask.
Sparkling, clear eyes,
a mouth as pure as the dawn.
Eyes, as old as an orange leaf.
Thoughts. Thoughts too corrupt to comprehend.
Brilliance? Floating around in the mind.
The body. So scary and so scarred. Covered in black.
A disowned child.
Body, hiding a heart which is so untouched and protected.
Protected by the black ink, so newly painted, years to chip.
The whole. So translucent. No one sees, no one cares. Just
passed by. Soul. Devoid. Forgotten, no, non-existent.
Conscience. Obsession, preoccupation. Pounding evermore.
Never to leave, never to cease.
The voice. Never used. Too shy, too scared, to empty.
Spoken only in mind. Only in thought.
See you, as I know you are.
Unlike others, corrupted, yet pure.
Protected by death while drunk, stoned, beautiful.
     —*Laura Van Wyk*

Hog Killing Season

Eenie, Meenie, Minie, Mo—
The possessions will stay,
   but the marriage must go.
Everything must be evenly divided
So the divorce will not end up "one-sided."
I'll get the bedroom suite, dresser and bed,
But sleep won't come, now that our love's dead.
You'll get that comfortable chair for your own,
But will you enjoy it now that you're alone,
With no one to put a pillow to your head?
Oh, I'll take the chair, and you take the bed!
And then, the pictures; how can we divide
Them reasonably without bleeding inside?
A lifefull of memories, happy and sad -
times that were good, those that were bad.
How can we each hope to make new starts
When we are drawing and quartering our
   very hearts?!
     —*Jane Paty Waldrop*

Old And In The Way

Over the years, you watched me grow. And in my eyes, you were
the pro. You let me do some things my parents would not
You may not remember, but I never forgot
You comforted me when I was afraid
And you made sure my parents were obeyed
You let me sleep over and stay up late
The time I spent with you was really great

Many years have past, and I am all grown. Your husband's gone
now, and you're all alone. I no longer spend much time with you
And that fact really bothers me too
You deserve better in your later years
Especially since you've been such a dear
Your mind is not what it used to be
And I know that's caused you some misery

It's a shame how old people are treated today. They're ignored or
made to feel old and in the way as if we have the right to make
that choice just because we're younger and have a voice.
It's because of you that we are better off, yet we tend to ignore
that fact while we scoff we should assist you in your later
years and bestow homage to you and your peers.
     —*Gregory Tarnowski*

Who Are You?

Gathered together so tenaciously visible elements evolved from the silent stars, drift now gently from the heavens to rest upon earth. Reserved in this woven garment of magnificence dwells a keeper- whose name dare not be uttered... were it ever to be known! A Sacred Dweller assigned Itself the monumental task of opening the closed door to the universe within! We think and so we are. We hear and respond. Yet, far above audible sounds and invisible thoughts the Dweller creates... This is Life which faithfully tends and never sleeps lest this garment fail. This is Bliss, that gladdens the heart with visual beauties yet undreamed of. This is Truth that hears angelic sounds and all the while moves and has its being within the Self. This is Love, who fulfills our righteous desires with secret knowledge known! Tenderness reigns undaunted, if we but step aside ourselves...If asked one question, "Who are you?" What might your answer be?
  —*Rose Mary Steiner Juarez*

When Jacqui Moved Away

When Jacqui moved away
The sky turned gray
From a beautiful shade of blue.

You don't know the way
It feels today,
If Jacqui moved away from you.

Jacqui and I did everything together.
We had so much fun.
We could never be torn apart,
But after she left there was no more sun.

It was very unusual
The first couple of days.
It was like the sun had no more rays.

It was noon that day
and Jacqui moved away.
The only thing I had to say
Was I wish she could stay.
  —*Elizabeth Almeida*

For A Student I Know

Guilt is such a strange thing
the slightest whisper of your name
and you jump—
startled as from a nightmarish dream
pairs and pairs of eyes hurry in your direction
coverting the well-kept secret of
(your fiery red, watery eyes
sniffling, runny nose
cracked, parched lips)

Damned guilt!

like he who was translated
and never made to taste sweet death—
wish away, my son
but first you must favor the bearer of
fire and whirlwind and worthy you are not

Mecca is still far away,
but I guess you will be alright—
From the heavens
he has not said a word
  —*Gerald Mackey*

Untitled

A beautiful sunrise, the work of your hand
the soft summer breezes that caress the land
the trees of the forest and the desert land too
all speak of your wonders, for they were all made by you.

The lakes and the rivers with water so blue
and the beautiful flowers, you sprinkle with dew.

All these creations you made with your hand
and then you decided to create a man.

But man became sinful, so you made a plan
you sent your own Son to die at mans hand.

To pay for our sins, that we could be free
to live in the hope, someday God we'll see.

Don't cast Him aside, hear Him calling to you
He'll take you in love and make you brand new.
  —*Pat Roberts*

Through My Eyes

In the windows of my eyes
  The sorrow you see I can't disguise

The smile you wait for will never appear
  Because happiness was replaced with sadness and fear

The stained glass lids that bring in color and light
  Constantly fight to void the black and white

The off colored greys that shade my days
  Signifies my being in an overcast haze

Still these blue eyes fight to bring in the sun
  And tint the dullness that kills all that's fun

As hard as I try to capture the light
  The colors fly by and are soon out of sight

Its as if all the rainbows are trickling down a drain
  And the anxiety I feel I can't restrain

I can't help but peer down a sewer then stare
  And wonder what is hiding down there

Are the rainbows that had once colored my skies
  Under the ground for everyone who dies

If that's the case then take me now
  So the sadness I see will leave my brow
  —*Cheryl A. Jannoni-Morrissey*

Untitled

Life is full of many things!
The sound of children playing and laughing;
The smell of flowers blooming in spring;
The view of a snow-capped mountain from
an airplane;
The taste of cool water from a brook;
The feeling of joy after a babies' first step.
But life can also be bitter:
The sound of a siren when someone has been hurt;
The smell of a house after it has burned down;
The view of a town after a hurricane has hit;
The taste of blood after being in a fight;
The feeling of sorrow at the death of an old friend.
  —*Denise Gayle Wathen*

Darkness

The darkness of light is surrounding my sights
The sounds of dusk are just ahead, the sight is so unreal
The darkness is becoming colder minute after minute
I can't live in the light, the light is blinding me
I'm sinking into the blackness of what?
There's no more to know, there's no where else to go
Now I live by darkness and the light is still yet to come
The light smothers my every breath, I can't see in the light
without a shade of dark
The light will never be the same, my life is almost gone
I must not live until the light of my life is turned to dust
The words are faded of darkness, everything black nothing to
see, as the wind blows unto the flesh it becomes colder and
colder, I can't describe the sight it's too dark to see.
But my life is moving unto a new horizon
The darkness will catch up with me and my life will be gone
But until then the light will stay the same.

—*Valerie Johnson*

Peaceful Place

I look around me, such a peaceful place.
The sun glimmers softly across the lake.
A fisherman casts his line out deep,
Hoping to add more fish to his heap.

I look around me, such a peaceful place.
A small furry animal twitches her face.
Down into his hole a mouse scurries by,
Just barely escaping the hawk in the sky.

I look around me, such a peaceful place.
A leaf falls down slowly taking up little space.
Dew on the ground like little tears,
Like someone was crying, letting out fears.

—*Jennifer Habada*

Incantation Of Love

The brilliance of love forever shines
The taste of love as varied as wine

The sight of love - a subjective thought
The feeling of love can never be bought

The quest for love is a journey of fate
The essence of love denies that of hate

The power of love can conquer an army of men
Shades of love seeking us out now and then

The beauty of love knows not one's shell
For the truth of love can always tell

The story of love is romance and bliss
Falling in love beginning with a kiss

The soul and its search for love endures...

—*Richard A. Ballesteros*

Violets Sweet And Blue

It was on yon wooded stump that grew,
  the violet sweet and blue.
It's face so lifted, as to say
  come, pause a while - I'm lonely, too.

The woods were quiet as though to say
  what better place to come to pray.
I stood a while with thoughts of you,
  and to thank God for violets blue.

—*Ada L. Mckinney*

Right From The Heart

  Right from the heart
The tears sparkled slightly
    Telling everyone
How much I cared.
    The crystal teardrops fell soundlessly
To the hard unfeeling ground.
    I wept many days and nights
Swept up in a torrent of emotion
    Held by the hand of destiny
Following its way.
    The rose you put in my hand
Fell to the ground.
    As I looked up at the sky
And without a sound.
    I realized
Life was not going to stop!
    And I was going to go on.
Living as I always have
    Searching for you until dawn.

—*Jennifer Blackburn*

"But There's One That I Know"

Many mothers have tried and many have failed,
The test of motherhood and all it entails.

Some mothers do enough just to barely get them by,
"But there's one that I know", whose love touches the sky.

Many chose abortion or just plain gave them away.
"But there's one that I know", who loved hers from their
very first day.

Many abuse and neglect, or act like we're not there,
"But there's one that I know", who will always care.

The Lord really blessed me, mother, when he gave you to me.
For without your love and caring, I don't know where I'd be.

And I thank God that he gave us just one more day together,
To let you know, I'll love you forever .....

—*Annie Adams*

Choice

Today was just like any other day, but today was different.
The thing that was different about today, was I wanted to live
    Before today, death was something that I had wished
        God would deliver to me.
    Life was one big depression. One bad thing after another.
    I thought nothing good has or will ever happen to me.
    I was wrong. Something good did happen to me in the past,
        To everybody in their past.
        The good thing is called Life. God gave us life.
            Life is something beautiful.
    I was always looking for the easy way out of all the bad things
        Well, now I found the easy way out, I'm dead.
    I felt that I had no choice in life. I found that I was wrong.
        Everybody says they are looking for the Meaning of Life.
            I found it.
    The Meaning of Life is Choice.
    You were given life to make choices.
        Now that you have life, you have the choice to continue life or not.
    I found out today, a day too late, that God was right.
            Life. What a beautiful Choice.

—*Shawn Burda*

Heaven Help Us

Heaven help us all, short-fat-skinny and tall
   The things we do- the things we say
Bring us so much misery everyday
   I think we've all lost our minds
Some say-It's a sign of the times

We all move so fast
   Wish we could go back to the past
We have no thought for no-one else
   Everybody, thinks of only themselves

Is there a reason for this madness
   All it ever brings-is sadness
Life is so short, is what we say
   But's it's not true-we've just let it slip away

Everywhere you look-somebody's in a mess
   None of us today has a noble quest
Heaven help us all, short-fat-skinny and tall
   If you don't—this whole generation will fall

   —Mary M. Battle

Rose Petal

The Petal from the rose was lying on the ground;
The thought of it touching her made her move all around.

He blew the petal gently through the air;
And slowly it landed on a single small hair.

As he pushed on the petal and it moved down farther;
He used his strength and pushed even harder.

As the petal went gently in the hole;
He used all his might and released his soul.

As he took the petal smoothly out;
She looked at him and gave a loud pout.

As he stood up and said goodbye;
She looked at him and slowly started to cry.

She knew right there and then
She'll never see that rose petal again.

   —Jessica Lee

Thunder On The Mountain (I Heard The Angels Cry)

The night when I heard
the thunder on the mountain
was the time when God passed by.
And as it began to gently rain,
then I rather fancied
that I heard the angels cry.

For God in Jesus Christ came down
to dwell on Earth with all mankind.
To comfort the mourners, and raise the dead,
to feed the hungry, give sight to the blind.
And for all sinners to suffer and die,
That's when I heard the angels cry.

But Easter morning, Jesus was raised,
that's what God promised, and what I believe.
Death was destroyed, and Satan bound,
that life eternal all believers receive,
Hallelujah! God be praised!
And in that brilliant morning sky,
I no longer heard the angels cry.

   —Richard P. Thompson

Sonnet

Don't let your soul be worried by your age,
The time to die could be any time at all,
We are not chosen to die a certain way
We can die at any time being young or old.
Life is a wonderful and a daily gift
That should be counted no more than day by day,
A day to love, to cherish, to take and give
And make the best of it in our daily stay.
Oh! Glorious times the time when we are born
And with a life to live we are presented,
Then, there is the mind to enjoy this world
And by the mind, living can be accented.
Don't let the years passing spoil your theme
When life becomes less intense, you still can dream.

   —Alicia Terrones Shapiro

Untitled

The blazing sunset starts to dim;
The trees have lost their shiny dress;
Now they are dull.
That strange bird keeps whistling outside the balcony.
What is he trying to say?
He seems so happy.
Could we but speak one tongue
Then we would understand.

It is dark now, and the whistler has gone away;
Perhaps he will return another day.
But I am sad; I have no wings
And must turn my thoughts to other things.

   —Sheila Brolsma

Memories

The wind blowing through my hair,
The trees swaying here and there.
Nothing can take back the memories of that night, the
way that you left, disappearing out of my sight. Maybe
someday I will understand why you went away, but until then,
for you, I will pray. You were the life of the party, the
class clown, and it will remain unknown how successful you
could have been. In your new life please do not forget the
souls down below, while you hope, I will pray, our love we may
never know. Remembering the times we spent together,
reminiscing, the good and hard times. Although you are gone
and we are not together, your memory, your soul, your love will
live on forever. If only I knew you were leaving, I could have
said or done more, you will never know how special you are to
me. It was only until now that I discovered my true feelings,
even though I will never say good-bye, I can let you go. And
all I have left are the memories and in my heart, your soul,
One day we will be together again, I know.

   —Melissa Ann Hines

The Path

The path is overgrown now.
The underbrush faithfully guards the previous way
where children found those special things
that only children find.
The trees make an arch overhead and their leaves,
glistening with rain, are like so many jade
brooches reflecting back the sun.
The feet that once trod that carving path come
seldom now.
They are making a path of their own.
They bless the ground in another place.
And yet they are not really gone, for they play
silently within my own heart.

   —Genevieve J. Biglow

"Equality"

She saw the apple fall from the old tree
The uneducated girl wondered...WHY?
Newton had the same idea as she.
Her mind went to waste and not his...WHY?
How was it been for women in the past?
She in a cave and he gathering grub.
While we aren't able to make careers last,
He's getting more salary for the same job.
In this man's world she struggles tooth and nail,
Just to keep her head above water.
She can work just as well as ANY male,
Yet some how never praised by her father.
We don't want wars, quarrels, or even fights.
All we are asking for are EQUAL rights.
—*Faranak Farjamrad*

"Flowers"

They stand for love and friendship, death and life.
The violet stands for friendship that's true.
The thorns of a rose can cut like a knife.
The red rose also says that I love you.

A crocus tells of a world with new life,
While the marigolds grieve for those passed on.
Chrysanthemums are full of love and no strife.
Forget-me-nots remind you of days gone.

An orchid will always be special on prom.
A daisy can bring a laugh or a smile.
A sunflower might remind you of Tom.
A dozen roses show that extra mile.

The flowers from a friend get you through the day,
So be a sweetie and send some right away.
—*Allison Moore*

The Truth Will Show Itself

Does it content you to afflict others, to rip
the vitality away from them?
Must you always insult and distress?
Hurting others for your justification isn't the way.
You can steal from my possessions, destroy my name
But you can't steal from my mind.

Say what you desire to say
You can't change the truth.
Strive as you may
Your efforts will prove to be worthless.

Continue if you should with your lying, your
deceitful tricks.
You're only hurting yourself.
Do you not know any better?
Or are you just too hell-bent for deception to care?

It doesn't trouble me anymore
I know what I know is veritable.
What you're doing might still harm me,
but it doesn't matter.
The truth will show itself.
—*Lou Weyler*

Dear Cousin

Wasn't it fun when we were young
The way we played together?
They couldn't keep us in the house
No matter what the weather.

We built play houses on the hill
Beneath a big oak tree.
The houses that we made were a lovely sight to see.

Furniture made of sticks and stones,
We put it all in place.
Then fringed our leafy linens until they looked like lace.

Green mossy carpets on the floor, mud pies on the table,
We made it look like Mama's house, as much as we were able.

There were many things we did
That I can't put into rhyme,
But isn't it wonderful how memories reach
Across the miles of time?

In that magic land of pretend
We always stretched the truth.
But wasn't it fun to play there?
With love, your cousin, Ruth.
—*Ruth Duff*

To Randall - Our Son

You came into this world with so much joy.
The welcoming day was radiant for you, my boy.
The skillful hands that ushered forth your birth
Of one who knows what life is really worth,
And to the Doctor by his side to say—
"This bringing of life is the essence of my day—
And then a thoughtful nurse to bring you near,
And you reached your hand, and touched my cheek, my dear.
What lungs you had—you surely let us know
And, Oh! how good it was to hear you so.
Father saw you as you passed him in the hall,
So, of course to the telephone he ran to call.
In the nursery you were snuggled warm and tight
But Father looked again to say, good-night,
And then he came and said, "what joy—
To think we have a darling baby boy."
—*Ruthellen Pyle Davis*

White Winged Horse

High above he flew,
The white, winged horse ... so white, with wings I knew he
had to be my horse.

Fast, I ran, stumbling on shoestrings, pray, pray,
I run faster.

Down,
down.
He came, galloping before me.
His thoughts spoke with ne'er a sound.

"David," he said, "I've come bidding hello. You are so
special in so many ways.
Horses you love, and I love you."

Suddenly, in the cloud of a mighty wind, we flew, the
white winged horse and I.
High above the city, above my house, above my friends,
skating, riding their bikes.

Again, suddenly, in the cloud of a mighty wind, back to
earth was I, standing in front of my house.

Good-bye, my mighty white winged horse, another day,
I'll see you again.
—*Sophie Padilla*

The Beauty Of Life

The ocean cries life takes time,
The wind blows yet not enough to knock me over,
I look to the sky and reach for the birds
and the freedom of a dream.
The waves come
but I want quit for peace is floating in the harbor.
Storms can't stop my life,
for my life is like a bird free and strong.
Flying high never to stop to return back.
For I like the soldiers of the blue and grey
will find a way to survive, making it through storms,
making through the tide learning new life
like the wind ticking the trees,
and the sunshine kisses my hair touching me without a care,
melting a heart that was frozen by time springing up a green
new life. The wind speaks to the water,
flood over thee o'still water, flood over thee please.
Peace be still, Peace be still.
—*Brenda Poling*

The Storm

Clouds gathering together like snow in heaven
The wind turns cooler and blows harder
The clouds change to an angry gray and start to boil
There's a storm on the way.
Animals hunt shelter, then look to see
if anyone has seen their hiding place.
The storm rages as if angry, like a spoiled child
that didn't have his own way.
The trees dance in the wind,
Twisting and bowing like a ballet dancer.
The angry storm becomes less angry,
The clouds clear away, the sun comes out,
The birds start singing.
The raindrops glisten like diamonds on the leaves and grass
The animals come out to play, glad to see the sun again.
The flowers nod their heads, as if to welcome the sun
And the gentle warm breeze.
The bees fly here and there to tell the good news,
The storm is over.
—*Beulah Crowell*

"The Truth Now Found"

Gone—
  The wind whispering through the trees
  echoing the message of despair.

Alone—
  The heavens sighing their eternal herald
  of misery.

Lost—
  The waves pounding out the secret of their
  cold, shadowy depths.

Afraid—
  The mighty thunder beating to the rhythm
  of desolate destiny.

Peace—
  The dawning of a new day with new truths
  to behold.
—*Terri L. Dean*

The Changing Tide

The vast, endless sky stretches out above me
The wind whistles by
The water, as vast and endless as the sky, flows beneath me
Waves roll in .... one after another
Emerging from the past
Traveling toward the future
We meet when the time is right
The waves never ceasing
Quieting at times
Like a child sleeping
Then, as the child awakens, so does the tide
Pounding the shore in a fierce tantrum
The movement of the waves revealing life's secrets
Calming a wounded heart
Bringing peace to those who accept its magic
Offering hope to those who hear its voice
—*Sherie L. Marling*

The Moon

A sliver of the moon traveled from left to right.
The window caught it within its box
and then the moon moved on.
Forty-six years later a sliver of the
moon moved from left to right.
The window caught it within its box and then traveled on.
I have traveled a long way and so has the moon.
—*Mary Elizabeth Mujahed*

The World Today

The world today everybody wants to get in a fight
The world today everybody does the wrong not the right
The world today when the riots had stopped
The world today everybody hates the cops
The world today everybody has to go
The world today every girl is called a "ho"
The world today everybody makes fun of the old
The world today you're not important if you don't have gold
The world today the ozone is leaving us
The world today it's because people use cars, cabs, trucks,
  or the bus
The world today people are getting killed
The world today everybody is being billed
The world today the popular song is hip hop hooray
The world today time flies everyday
The world today nobody respects each other
The world today Waco was blasted by the undercover
The world today people get robbed
The world today people get fired from their job
The world today some are low; The world today I gotta go.
—*Steve Goodwin*

Old Things

I like old shoes and battered hats.
  The wrinkles in one's brow.
    The fields that have not felt
for years the turning of a plow.

I love each month and moon of long,
  long ago.
I love every smile and tear as they
  become the joyful music of a
melodious song, each one of them leave a
void and beholding souvenir in my living
heart.

I treasure all old things that used to be.
  And I'm so very happy when
I dream in memory of all those old, dear
things that were part of my being.
—*Pauline S. Gonzales*

Who Said, Over The Hill?

"Old age ain't for sissies", as the saying goes.
The young and healthy couldn't take it, heaven knows.
You think they'd tolerate having to get up a couple times most nights?
Or—to listen to them talk—they'd just as soon receive their last rites
As put up with ever diminishing, even abandoned, sexual activities,
And I include both genders, no matter how frequent their present proclivities.

You think they could stand having their hair turn white,
Or shrink a couple inches from their normal height,
Could they put up with fuzzy vision, feeling poorly, and a forgetful brain?
And creaking joints, weakened muscles, and arthritic pain?
Lemme tell you now, they just haven't got the stuff
That we have, because, as any senior can tell you—we're tough!

—*Pete Peterson*

"Of Such Is The Kingdom Of Heaven."

Who burned out the Light in the children's eyes before their noonday naps? When the walls came tumbling down on the table with the lamp and the bible, who heard the mothers' last words? We saw God took them quickly, but heard not a sound on our TV, except the crackling of the fire. We saw the awesome flames and the dark smoke over the wooden buildings, but not a human voice was coming from the fire. Did they scream in fear (the babies in their mothers' arms)? When the flames consumed their bodies, did they scream? We know they did!

—*Ruth Seeger-Huff*

Contemplating Candles

There's something about candles,
Their quiet flames
Gently illuminate a darkened room
Inside a house, perhaps, a restaurant,
Or a church.

Votive offerings to love or God
Can't help but captivate the eye,
Or heart
Playing hide and seek with shadows.
And a thousand unrelated thoughts
Can come to mind while watching them
Tossing and churning one against the other.

Musings; consternation, doubt,
Human, ethereal, divine,
And always someone
Wanting to put them out!

—*John A. Orichosky*

Message To Butterfly

Butterfly, come fly into my life and touch my soul.
Then fly away to touch the lives of others...
To homes of families who read to children and hug them
and say, "I love you," and mean it. To schools where
teachers read and sing and coach and model "I love you,"
And mean it. To churches where children sing and hear that God
"Gave His only begotten Son" and means it. Then fly
to reform schools and prisons, to Ghettos and soup kitchens,
to nursing homes where old ones wait patiently to die alone,
to buildings where officials gather to unlock the secrets of
the problems of the country. Then fly back to me and sit
upon my sill and touch me through the cloudy pane...
Elusive butterfly of self-esteem.

—*Donna Goldammer*

Let's Go Backwards In Life

Why not begin life when we're old and sage,
then go backwards and get younger in age.
At 90 we are wary lest we slip and fall,
at 70 we can walk hours in a shopping mall.
At 60 we purchase Pepto Bismol and Mylanta.
At 40 we gulp chili between planes in Atlanta.
At 30 we start climbing the ladder of success,
at 10 we're happy with skateboarding finesse.
But age 10 has exacting story problems to solve,
and age 30 has money obligations to resolve.
Age 40 worries about a child's college tuition,
while age 60 fulfills a lifelong travel ambition.
And age 70 has happy memories, too many to recall,
and age 90 has wisdom and high esteem from all.
Maybe going backwards in life is an idea to forget,
let's instead go forward to the future without regret.

—*Nancy Petersen*

Baby

That first moment so full of pride,
then you held her close to your side.
Day by day she started to grow.
Those were the days you loved to know.
And those long years spent at school,
remember her learning the golden rule.
And then the jobs and her starting to date,
you'd always stay up, thinking she'd be late.
And then came that very special boy.
We'll there still married so full of joy.
So now were old and gray,
just sitting watching the flowers of May.
Someone's here honey, don't you think maybe,
that it might just be our little baby.

—*David L. Watkins*

What Do We Know About Love?

What do we know about love?
There are a lot of things about
love that we know.
There is a lot of things we don't know about it.
When we find love we feel like we are on cloud nine.
Then other times we are hurt by love.
No one ever said that love doesn't hurt because it does.
Love is also a partnership that takes two people.
They have to figure out their feelings for each other.
Sometimes it doesn't work and their love for each other
doesn't last.
When they are able to figure out their feelings
for each other it works out if they are meant for each other.
Love hurts but is also a pure relationship between two people
with strong feelings for each other and that is mostly what
counts.

—*Marcie M. Ackley*

Between Worlds

Left in a field with no one around
There I was helpless
On shaken ground
For miles and miles
Nothing but air
No one to love me
No one was there
I stretched myself out
lain on the sod
I sent out a shout
Cursing my God
The sky became eerie
The sun lost all light
Nothing but darkness
enveloped my fright
The earth opened up
And swallowed me whole
My body now rests
Apart from my soul
—*Tara Allgood*

"My Wonderful Parents"

Since the time I can remember
   There is no one I adored,
As much as my wonderful parents
   And for them I thank the Lord

I was born in Calgary Canada in 1917
   I have two brothers who are very sweet,
We were always such a happy family
   To this day they can't be beat

We came to the United States
   When I was eight or nine,
We didn't have a place to live
   But it all came out just fine

I lost my father in nineteen sixty-eight
   I adored him all my life,
My lovely mother has also gone
   But she will always be his wife

If I could start all over again
   There never could be another,
That ever would be able to take the place
   Of my beautiful father and mother.
—*Frances T. George*

Thoughts On The Beach

Here clears my mind of anxious thoughts, I am at peace.
There is no yesterday — no tomorrow
There are only these moments.

I sit in silence, void of thought.
Then, slowly but surely all efforts fail
To keep you out of my mind.

There you are, your smile
And your constant sense of being,
With me as surely as if you were here.

The miles do not — cannot separate us
No more than time and written law
We are an entity — deny it if you can — I can't.

Say it cannot be — it is!
Say this is all there is — there's more.
Say this love cannot exist — it does.
—*Gaye Hughes*

No One To Love

I have a heart that's full of love, and no one to give it to.
   There must be someone as lonely as I, someone who's feeling blue.
I'll keep on searching, high and low, for a Sweetheart to call my own.
   And when I find her - my Special One - I'll no longer be alone.
She'll be my Darling, to have and hold, to share everything that is mine.
   We'll be happy and gay from morning 'till night, with a love that is almost Divine.
I long for that someone who needs my love, someone to hold close in my arms.
   She'll love me and then the wonderful thing will be feeling her loving charms.
Give me one I can cuddle close to me, a sweet and wonderful wife.
   She'll be the one with whom I want to spend the rest of my life.
—*Floyd Edward White*

Elsewhere

In Gee's yard on the southwestern plains,
there was a small fig tree, a patch of asparagus,
a flourishing bed of sweet peas. Beside the house
a trumpet vine climbed the radio antenna, telephone
pole-high, to pierce the cone of silence. Between
dust storms she scrubbed the roof above the cistern
that was behind the house. The honey-colored water
from it was rationed for shampoos—your hair felt
like satin-back crepe.
In Gee's house the rooms were high-ceilinged, quiet.
We stood on the porch to say good-by before I left
for Italy—she said I wouldn't like it. She died
that November, I read the letter sitting on a bench
on the Janiculum. Instead of the domes of Rome
I saw the east window of her dining room full
of purple glass. All glass turns purple left long
in the sun. Some was richly purple.
—*Sherley G. Unger*

Black Snow

If snow were black, black as sin,
there'd be no cheer, just winter's wind;
no snowman's smile no hilly race gloom and doom would place
and winter's darkness all joy erase.

But snow is white by God's command it droppeth down to cover land
dazzling in the waning sun making days bright and sledding fun

'Tho the night with deepest chill makes all the land bleaker still;
the moonlight glow the sparkling band with snow adorn'd 'tis fairyland.

And when the sun was deepest down and seem'd as if 'twas nearly gone
with the crystal snowflake fall God sent His Son
the greatest gift of all.
—*Warren Sully*

Empty Shell

It's cold outside, but I feel it not.
There's laughter in the room sounding out
from all about me, but I hear it not. A
pinch here, a pinch there, but they still
cannot bring me around.

I'm an empty shell without emotion,
nor feeling, nor hearing, nor seeing. They
can't understand what they have done,
and cannot remember for how long they
have left me alone.

But I remember when they forgot to
love me. And this is why I cannot
feel, or hear their words, nor see their
faces, as they are fading away, and their
touch is numbing to my body.

No one can explain to them how they
have torn out my soul, and left a
lifeless, hopeless empty shell. But I
know the reason all too well!
—*Tamie Pucek*

Ode To The Owed

The national debt's a marvelous loan,
There's no piece of paper to say what you own;
Your four trillions in bonds, in Uncle Sam's name;
To be paid, when due, with more of the same.
Your interest's paid yearly in an interesting way,
By issuing more bonds that your children will pay.
You've bankrupted the Commies and won the cold war,
And now peace's a problem you're not prepared for.
The Soviets withdrew with no national debt,
by a scheme of financing that you don't understand yet.
Now you must loan them the means to be free,
so they can join in the capitalist spree;
and build up a debt of enormous amount
that even their heirs won't be able to count.
The only sane way for this saga to end
is to wipe the slate clean and all debt suspend.
Just cancel all bonds and interest too,
and forget all debts that are currently due.
With no interest to pay or principal to pend,
why should we worry that no one will lend?
—*Spencer W. Spaulding*

Homelessness

Whenever I am in the street...
There's so many homeless people that I meet.

My heart breaks, as I pass them by...
But for the grace of God that could be you or I.

What is wrong with our government to let them live this way...
Don't they understand there's a price to pay.

Our government is supportive of people not of this land...
Why don't they reach out and give it's own people a hand.

They're sleeping in torn boxes, and eating from trash cans...
God help them, from what ever type of disease they may
  possibly land.

They ask me for money, I gladly give it for whatever the reason
I thank God, for he gives me from season to season.

Some homeless people are young, some are old...
My hearts hurts, when I know that they are hungry and cold.

What can we as a people do to make things right...
Never give up on the homeless people, we must continue to fight

Keep pressure on our government to make the government do
that which is right.
—*Wygenia Thompson*

A Heartfelt Feeling

Oh! How I love to watch the sun go down.
There's such a wonderful calmness, a
freshness in the air.
Not a sound, just the birds singing, as
they rush to feed their young.
With a beautiful glow across the fields,
this gives your heart the feeling of being
suspended for the moment in time.
As darkness overcomes, there is still the
warmth of knowing your not alone, for our
Lord Jesus is always near.
—*Carol Eliot*

Life What A Beautiful Choice!

Life is more beautiful as I go on,
There's three times I could have been gone.
I'm glad there is radiation to cure such a disease,
My arm is swollen but do you know why I'm pleased?

My favorite thing to do is with my children hug,
Or give to them with lots of love, a tea cup or a mug.
Cancer has blessed me and opened my human heart,
And I can tell friends I love them with a Christian start.

I have been more normal since my first cancer surgery,
I can tell friends and relatives they're important to me.
Life used to be a thankless, unwanted chore,
But from God, people and self now I have joy galore.

My eyes have been opened to beauty and many wonders,
My heart is full of sunshine even though it rains and
thunders.
My son can make my day, when he says, "Good morning,
Mommy."
He made me feel like a million bucks instead of a Dummy.

It's great to be here after being so close to death,
My life is all cleared up now, and no longer is a mess.
My arms are now weakened and an EMT I no longer am,
So I'll study something different and for a test cram.
—*Theresa Wellnitz*

Winds Of Change!!!

Redbud, Forsythia, Tulip, Spring.
These sights inspire young birds to sing!
Congestion, Pressure, Concrete, Steel.
Why must we change the world to make it ideal?
Blue to shades of gray and orange we do see.
Something's wrong with this picture don't you agree?
Dew upon green leaves of a fallen Wilderness tree,
time's quickly running out for the truly free.
Rip, crack, and sizzle go the tree limbs
Computers, Fast Food, No time for whims.
Decimated cures for World ills,
Ask now, who pays the bills?
Ozone Depletion
Apathy, Toxics
Flooding
Erosion
Drought
Famines
Diseases
??????????????Catastrophes & Pollution??????????????????
—*Stephen E. Podewell*

My Husband

Hoes, racks, shears, and work gloves galore,
These work tools and more.
See him as he cleans, mows, and weeds,
And whatever else his lawn needs.

Sweat, sunshine, and insects are his foes;
But when he reaps beautiful flowers,
   away go his woes.
Smiles, pride, and accomplishments,
Show when I pay him compliments.

—*Mina L. Green*

Hey "Bro"

Hey "Bro", you heard but didn't understand,
These worlds were said, to honor a man;
Hey "Bro", you heard, but never knew,
What these words meant, to the chosen few;
Hey "Bro", he says, in an Asian jungle, in the darkness of night,
As he moves beside you, to help you fight;
Hey "Bro", you're not black and he's not white,
You're just brothers, who together must fight;
Hey "Bro", it makes no difference the color of skin,
When the only way to survive is fight together to win;
Hey "Bro", if one gets wounded and is to die,
Then I know the other, will sadly cry;
Hey "Bro", the shadow of death knows no color,
He'll take one, as quick as the other;
So fight my friend, one for the other,
Protect my "Bro" cause we're all brothers.

—*Rex M. Giddens*

"Hey Gram — Let's Talk"

Let's talk of golden sunbeams streaking from the skies—are
they a little peek at heaven, right before my eyes?

Let's talk of airplanes flying, and why they are so loud.
Can't they travel through the heavens by riding on the clouds?

Lets talk of hugs and kisses, and why they help so much when
I'm feeling sad or frightened—I know—that's the way that
Grandma's touch!

Let's talk of soft warm puppies, and why we love them so.
Do we need them as they need us—I wonder—Do you know?

Let's talk of where I'm going—let's talk of where you've been.
Would you like to join me in my journey and do it all again?

Let's talk of why you say to me, "be all that you can be"—
cause, when I look into your eyes I know, you love me just for me.

—*Barbara Turpen-Lanham*

"My Everything"

What are children
They are flesh and blood
Given to us from God above
Sure we have problems with our children everyday
But who don't that's the American way
They get up each morning
They scream and shout
And when night time comes
Poor mom is worn out
But still she goes on day after day
Watching them grow, laugh and play
Life is short and they grow up fast
Then your stuck home with memories of the past
You remember all the nights and the things they said
As you kissed their lips and tucked them in bed
Now your days are empty and your nights are long
Because the children you raised
Are married and gone...

—*Frank Sheehan*

The Sounds In My House

Have you heard the noises in my house,
they are unique indeed. The cries
from our pet gorilla may be loud, but
that's nothing. The sharks that swim
in our indoor pool growl with bared
teeth, while sometimes they whine or
bark, hoping for a treat. The scream
of children from our amusement park
are sounds that fill you with joy. The
whizzing of 12 toy airplanes circling
your head brings terror to others nearby.
The sound of a chain saw cutting down our
Christmas tree and the words "tim-bberrr"
echoes through our forest in the kitchen.
Sounds of horns and whistles come
drifting from a birthday party in the
bathroom. There are many strange noises
that come from our house.

—*Lisa R. Sorensen*

Romance With Nature

On a quiet journey, the Traveler's move along the bracken path.
They bore on winged feet, barely skimming the moist ground,
afraid to disturb those sleeping below. Each life beyond has
its special quality, and the Passengers do not want to
squelch a single existence of the tender species. What lies
ahead is harmonious beauty bringing much splendor to the naked
eye. Shadows of monarchial oranges and blacks, drift so
graciously along. The expand of wings float in spontaneous
tranquility, to the rhythm of lively foliage. A spotted fawn
can be caught at a glimpse, as the Travelers freeze in calm
solitude, trying to bottle the glorious rapture of nature
abound. Splashes coming from the tiny pond lend ear to
schools of rainbows below, transcending colorful images to the
surface. The Onlookers stop to take a peek, their shadows
intimidating the shy Inhabitants, to seek refuge in secluded
camouflage. Gentle breezes musically touch golden colored
daisies, causing them to sway to the tempo of the sweetest
concerto. It is here, in this thick embroidery of lavender and
multi-colored greens, the weary Souls take time to rest and to
unite as one with the sweet Earth.

—*Dawn Kemeny*

Death Is Not My Neighbor

There is this neighbor that I have
they call him Death.
He delivers the news to tell others of his doings
in our daily paper,
and I find him always on the front page.
He knows me well, but can not catch me!

I have seen Death and have been invited to many of his
parties.
They all seem to be the same but always different.
He walks behind me along with my shadow.

I feel that he is there but when I glance,
there is no one but me ringing Death's door bell.
I ring once,
then twice,
and hesitate to ring it a third time,
as I see Death looking through his peep hole in search for me
with a smile.

He pays no rent but is always welcomed by a soul of
sadness and grief. I am old........slow.....and Death
is not. I feel him ahead of me with heavy foot steps.

—*Jerry Leon Wiseman*

"Stars"

The stars talked to me last night
They drew me pictures and told me stories
They said looks can be deceiving
One said he burned out yesterday
But he will be lit for a million more years
Another one told me to look beyond facts
That is for the truth
The stars knew a lot
They have withstood time
They fight black holes single handed
And win battles with their might
We should learn from some of their actions
They have no surroundings to grasp on to
They just float around in one spot
Each are different and accepted
And they accept each other
They live in universal harmony
We could learn a lot from the stars
—*Allison M. Ventura*

Separation

Pink finger tips are icy and
They have lost their charm.
The nails are torn and ragged,
Paradoxically nibbled to ascetic compulsion.
The rings, almost a part of the flesh now
Are worn and molded to the fingers,
So full now, once loose
Like an old woman's shoulder joint
Engulfed in empty skin.

She turns her eyes upwards and toward me,
A filthy angel in a steamy basement cafe,
And herself as filthy and lost.
"Even your rings are the same", she whispers,
"It's good to see you again".
—*Hilary Schwartz*

A Star

Standing a far looking at the stars above,
They have no feeling they give no love.
Stars make us believe
We are important to them,
But they wouldn't care
If our lives would condemn.
Be just one less soul one less soul to touch,
They probably wouldn't notice
It wouldn't matter much.
Oh, to reach out and touch a star,
To make a difference
They're just too far.
Bring out the good
Help them shine bright,
But they can only be seen
Throughout the starry night.
Can't learn to love,
Can't learn to be true.
There are so many things,
A star cannot do.
—*Danielle Bauer*

True Colors

They lay their lives on the line each day for those of us in need
they protect and serve, some even die, without regret or heed

Their workday is never ending when they go home to sleep
their beat becomes their nightmare and their heart can only weep

With the dealer they arrested who's out on bond by dawn
and the bust that made the papers in the public eye is wrong

They have a reason to be bold and proud and wear their colors
   with pride
they have the right to flash their shields that mask their fate inside

To stand "aside" and salute these men is to dignify our wealth
but to stand "alone" and salute these men is an honor in itself
   --*Debbie Haskins*

Malignant Petals

The flowers are beautiful.
They stand fresh, delicate, bright.
Dying, but blind to that, the eye.
I am like them.

The flowers are wilting.
They struggle proudly, colorful, hopeful.
Hurting, but blind to that, the eye.
I am like them.

The flowers are dying.
They sag gracefully, fighting, praying.
Bitter, but blind to that the eye.
I am like them.
   —*Susan D. Whelan*

A Seed In The Wind

Now I know why I love trees.
They stand so strong, for a hundred years never to be
disturbed
Unless by foolish men.
Their branches grow muscular and strong,
reaching towards the heavens.
Able to with stand storms and harsh winds.
Unlike myself...
I am like a seed that travels in the wind.
Never getting the chance, to plant myself in the soil,
and grow strong.
Yes, I've met a lot beautiful, strong and unique trees.
They've left profound memories in my soul,
upon my passing.
As I drift by as a seed in the wind.
   —*Donna Cipri Castro*

Forgetting You

My friends tell me to forget
they tell me to move on
To leave behind this love
that went so very wrong
they tell me to forget about "us"
then I'll get over this High School crush
It's easy for them to say
they weren't there that wonderful day
they didn't feel your touch
the one I miss so much
they didn't fall in love with you
they don't feel the way I do
To each their own I softly sigh
as I try to accept that you
——————said goodbye——————
   —*Robbin Brown*

Unwanted

Let's have a girl said mom and dad
they tried and tried until they had.
She had dark hair and brown eyes
to them it didn't seem a surprise.
They really cared until she was old
then their love ran really cold.
There was always fighting in the house
She would shut her door and would be quiet as a mouse.
Hoping they wouldn't know she was there
to her it seemed they didn't care.
She really thinks they want her gone
is she really causing everything to go wrong?
or is it something else to?
Please God tell me what to do.
I will be waiting in my house
in my room like a little mouse.
Please God help
Little baby girl

—*Tammy Leshovsky*

For You See

The brightest stars are in your eyes
They twinkle and tell me no lies
In your arms you hold me tight
I'm safe and secure all through the night
We awaken with a start
To find we're being torn apart
I looked into those eyes I know so well
To see the anguish we both feel
But don't worry we will make it together
For you see I love you and you love me
As we travel down that road of life
I know I will be your wife.
And you my husband dear
For you see I love you and you love me.

—*Colleen Townsend*

Youth

The youth today, wants everything their way.
They want free love and pot.
They'll steal anything available you got.
To pay their expensive habit, that's their lot.

Their love, a relationship that's what they call it.
But doesn't really make it right a bit.
It's still immoral, and sinful you know.
And causes an epidemic of diseases to grow.

It used to be a cottage, with roses vining near the door.
With a loving husband to leave for work each morn.
They both had their jobs each to do.
And then at days end, hurried home for their love to renew.

Life is built on worth while things.
Not liquor, drugs, and guns, that give you wings.
But stable and the earthly, and noble acts.
With love, and home, and cultural facts.

Children need love of both parents today.
As always, or will be trouble to pay.
They turned away from Church and God.
And with their offspring spared the rod.

—*Burga H. Vickers*

Time Heals The Dream

It seems like only yesterday
They were lovers in the sun.
Their love built a shield
Which could conquer any outside world.

But the time passed too quickly
Her eyes revealed her pain.
As memories, and her former happiness
Danced in her head.

She sits beneath the tree,
As tears streak her face.
The sweet innocence, and compassionate love within—
Vanished.

The child she used to be
Is replaced by another girl.
A harder heart possesses her
Vengeance is in her soul.

Yet as she walks away
Her eyes sparkle as before
As the past is slowly forgotten
A new dream fills her soul.

—*Shawna Presley*

"This Evil Creature Man"

Starting with a greedy clan.
They worked around their selfish plan.
Never stopped, they killed what can.
And grew, this Evil Creature Man.

They began to claim the land they found.
How quickly they had spread around.
They cut down trees, and cleared the ground.
This Creature Man, which has no bound.

Taking what they call their own.
Fighting to gain the respected throne.
Seeking the answers to all unknown.
Evil Man leaves nothing alone.

Too selfish to ever get along.
What's right to some, the others think wrong.
Any threats for war keep both sides strong.
This Creature Man, there's Evil among.

The progress made cements their fate.
The more there is, the more to hate.
Until life on Earth, they terminate.
No more Evil for Creature Man to create.

—*Natalie Venard*

Beautiful Day

It's a beautiful day, isn't it I knew you would of said.
Think about all those times you've done left me.
I couldn't go away and I realized that you was
gone, I drop tears in all the ways I could.

It was a beautiful day then I had to realize you was
really gone away and I still love you no matter what,
It's still is a beautiful day.

—*Shelitha Norwood*

A Poet's Frustration

Those without talent for beautiful prose
Think poetry flows like water from a hose
They think it comes easy. God given, I suppose.
They have no idea that rhythm comes from those
who struggle and suffer time after time,
to say something important and make it rhyme.
I'm an example of this compulsion,
as I sit here, in rapt repulsion,
trying to end this verse, tie up the loose ends,
but all rhyming words just left on the winds.
—*David N. Shipman*

The Beginning Of The End

Sounds of remorse linger through the minds
Thinking of the memories that will always be left behind.
Waves are never heard or either no one listens
The dew of the morning presses but never glistens.
Cries of help slowly seep from lonely animals
Sickness stomps the weak and suppresses the gullible.
The rat race strives for power and prestige
The less fortunate are snubbed and in along with the stampede.
Truth, sincerity, values, and beliefs
Are losing importance and containing all grief.
Slowly the world loses all abilities to mend
The love will die shortly in the beginning of the end.
—*Roxanne Rowley*

Depression Era

Sugar beet farmers, on Eastside, lived
thinning the plants in the spring of the year;
was hard work, and a pain in the rear.

The Big Ditch drew a lot of attention,
water for crops or a new invention;
last, but not least, sheep herders' Heaven.

Now Harpers and others, with logging camps and mills,
helped to buy sugar for the Bitter Root stills!

Bankruptcy was plenty, tis said, 4% interest on $10.00 notes;
Some folks got shifty, sold the old car, and the Billy Goat!!

That was life in the Valley, as old timers said,
Your home had a mortgage until you were dead.
—*June Chaffin*

"Better Safe Than Sorry."

A man once shared
this bit of wisdom with me.
He spent his whole life being safe
and never had a chance to be sorry.

But I can't live protected from
regret,
remorse,
second thoughts,
and second-guessing.

If you never take the chance to regret,
then you never will be able to rejoice.

Without second-guesses,
there will never be second chances.

I've lived my life.
I've felt pain,
and I've known joy.
I have this bit of wisdom to share with you:
"Sometimes it's better to be sorry than safe."
—*Nathan Pritchard*

Cycles

When is life going to keep quiet?
This constant screaming is clouding my sight.
Where is reality?

Its stable dock is drifting further and further away.

Wait!
People are calling me.
They see me!
But can they see me?

I'm trying, Oh God I'm trying, to swim through this
never-ending sea.
The sea is myself.

The dawning light appears.
I reach out.
I try.
It grows brighter and brighter.
I think I can grasp it!
I believe that I can finally solve and resolve the confusion
of this sea! My sea.
Do I dare?
Will the light fade? Like before.
—*Tyler Perry*

The Dream

Last night as I lay sleeping
This dream came to me.
I heard the voice of Jesus calling
My child, come unto me.

As I walked across the fields
And thru the flowers so sweet
He held out his hand
And beckon unto me

He said "Come unto to me, sit and talk while
We'll cross another bridge,
We'll walk a few more miles.

He wore no crown upon his head
He had sandals on his feet
But the look upon his face was so radiant
And sweet.

Jesus took me on a journey
Toward the promised land
He's always here beside me
He will always hold my hand.
—*Nora Atkins*

There Once Was A Girl Who Ordered Teen

There once was a girl who ordered Teen
this girl was very preppy and mean
her mother told her No!
I'm going to send your order to uncle Joe
so the preppy little girl got clean
her mother then told her you wait till you older.
The girl got so mad she began to smolder
her mother still told her to wait till she's older.
The preppy girl went off to college
she gave up on the teen knowledge then she got
married. But this thought she's always carried
about her mother being so mean
about that teen magazine.
The she got old and gray
there's still something she's been meaning to say.
Her mother had to be so darn mean
about her subscription to teen
She died and came back to haunt her mother one day
and asked why did you take my Teen magazine away?
—*Brooke Rozeski*

Altered

You
This is the face
That I remember
This is the touch
That I recall
The breathless whisper
Of undying love
Then you turned away
Which cast a shadow
Upon my face

"I could never change to be what you want;
I can only offer you my virginal love"

You left saying "remain untainted by me,
for you will forget with time"

But I haven't—
For I am not the same
Woman today
As I was
Yesterday.
—*Angela Palmer*

Just Another Day In The Machine

    Another such day dawns, as the shy light spawns.
  Those little people fly again; the very ones void of reason
and fear, among the desperate blinding cricket cheer.

      The sun crawls over green hive,
    as it blesses its leaves to strive.
They seemly rule over this long covered rock, and the morning's
 breeze shares its granted stock; yet beyond this insufficient
      cry, everything has that gift of motion.

And the duel between timid positivity and the kingdom of
hostility exposed in this passing is but one and will soon
      evolve to a flicker of light on the horizon.
  Soon the wrath of the tides will swallow the laughter,
  before silent mountains which crumble thereafter.

    For this doesn't wait for the green to fade,
nor the lasting call of the shade; that which sudden moonlight
      forbade.
  This casted rotation is marked only by time;
 It shall be forgotten as will those little people as they fly
      through another day.
Real as it seems on blue earth, nothing is destined to stay.
—*Will Haswell*

Untitled

You have shattered my mirror of innocence.
You still ponder the thoughts of my mind.
Your touch always did make me quiver,
and the sight of you makes me feel blind.

I look at you day in and day out,
unable to push you away.
I'm 15, and alone,
with a child of my own,
and she looks like you more everyday.
—*Mandi Roberts*

Chains

He bringeth out those which are bound with chains.
Those that are shackled with strife
Those that are held captive
By the sin in their life.

Those chains that bind
Those chains that choke
Those chains that keep you down
Those chains keep tightening around your heart
They constantly keep you bound.

Do those chains smother your very being?
Do they smother you as you breathe?
Do you find you feel strangled?
Are you begging those chains to leave?

I know the one who holds the tool
That can break through those stifling chains.
He is the One who hung on a cross
And for me He bore that pain.

He can cause those chains to fall
And drop along the road. This tool I talk about is love
And that is the One thing those chains cannot hold!
—*Veronica Wood*

February Spring

In thy springtime resurrection
   Thou doeth draw up toward thy skies,
Yellow bells, hawthorn, jonquils, blue bells,
   Joy bell delights for clayborn eyes.

Glorious resurrected beauties
   Prove a greater bloom to come,
When all creation recreated
   Sheds the snakeskin curse now on.

So with each spring's reassurance,
   Mankind born of clay should pray,
Let each mankind flower as springtime
   In third heaven's flowering day.
—*Chauncey Harbert Wealand*

That's Him

He was brought to us in 1987, on the 13th of July,
Though, as his sister, I sometimes have to wonder why.
But then again he brings us joy,
So we can't help but love this boy.

He has a big heart and a spirit that always soars.
Even when something has him down, he is never a bore.
Though sometimes weak and all drugged up,
This little boy is known to be quite tough.

When he's sick, down and out,
He comes to us with only a pout.
But when he thinks that we are sad,
He comes to us to make us glad.

He is our miracle proud and true,
Although he has Downs, it doesn't stop him from shining
  through.
He may be different and he may seem strange,
But we still love him just the same.
—*Christina Rumschlag*

To My Husband

My love is lost to me
though he still lives,
in shadows on the brink of hell.
His heart so true to me,
at times now wanders
in a wintry 'scape
alone,
searching.

His eyes look faraway and see-
who knows?
His childhood's joys and friends?
His future?
The secrets of the Universe?

Ah! If I could, I would not call you back
for you must meet your destiny...
Your God,
Who waits to heal the wounds and pain.
To hold you in his arms and say
Welcome home good and faithful one.
—*Mary A. Sacauskis*

Don't Trade Me In

Please don't trade me in on a younger model....
Though worn be my tread and loose be my throttle,
Just place me in the right mechanic's hands..
With a tune-up and grease job, I'd run just grand.

My body is older, and the mileage kind of high...
But my engine still Revs-up for the right kind of guy,
This dependable model isn't made of tin...
A new model takes too much time to break in.

So gas up my tank and turn on the key....
This engine still purrs, I'm sure you'll agree,
I may not be fast, and my tranny shifts slow...
But once I'm in gear...I'll never need a tow.
—*Sharon L. Hauge*

Time

You are alive and I am not, but I'm in your thoughts
Though you get what you need, you may not get what you want
Your state of being, depends on my will
If my presence was absent, then all would be still
As the clock ticks away, the moments that make up the day
You are waiting for someone or something to show you the way
I am taken for granted, each day through and through
But one day you'll find, that years have gotten past you

I shall never know you, but you will know me very well
As the millions before you and those after you I compel
Through my presence, which is immortal, I bring forth night and day
Respectfully in silence, I control all I survey
Should I introduce myself, since I may be all you have left
While self inflicted poisons, shorten breath and bring you
closer to death

I'm not the Alpha or the Omega, I'm the First and the Last
I'm the Beginning and the End, the Future present and past
For I am ....TIME!
—*Peter Jay Snowden, I*

Home

"Home" is not just where you hang your hat,
Though you've heard that said I'm sure.
Nor is it where you make it.
No, "home's" a whole lot more.

It's where you always want to be
When you're all alone and blue,
When other places all seem strange.
Is that what "home" is to you?

It always feels good to walk down the street
And see houses and friends that you know.
And then, when you get to your own sweet "home"
You sense a peculiar, but quite pleasant glow.

The "home" may not be very large.
It may not be very ornate.
The outward appearance may be rather plain
And maybe a bit out of date.

But there's something about it surpassing all that.

It's something that all cannot see.
"home" is where the family is.

Yes, that's what "home" is to me.
—*Dorothy A. Taylor*

I Shall Never Hope Again

   I once dared to dream
Thought hope to be a luxury owed to all men
   A treasure one snatched and held
within the clutches of his lust
   I once thought to love was to die
But now in the mist of it I see with a perfect
   vision only others can envy.

   I once thought to hate
was the way to find strength. Yet only in hate
   did I find weakness in the absence of love
The different parts of my life
   change in shades of color, while my sea
of emotions mutate in an air of uproar.

   Such a state of bliss
knows no limits or expectations
   I am content and yet I am hungry.

   How can I ever hope again
when I have lost the will to dream.
—*Javier Perez*

Labeled

Labeled is my life for that is what I live
through pain, sorrow I am Labeled
Labels give a name, shows what something is,
that is the case I am Labeled
Though unknowingly, I give a sign to people unknown
to me what I did to be labeled
Labels are cruel, and uninviting we all have labels, even you,
for if you don't they will choose one for you.
Labels, I fear, for you can never let your feelings be
known. Yes I fear the Label.
Labels have trapped me in a world of disgrace, and hatred
for I will never be as my Label
I have no more words to describe the Label but I am the
man who struggles on.
—*Jon James*

A Tree, A Rock, And A New Day

A child, a teacher, a classroom, a paper, a pencil or pen, a thought of creation. The tree stands there and does not fall, and the rock is firm and does not break. The leaves of a tree may fall but another day will come and another leaf will blossom. The rock stands there like a stubborn child who will not display the brilliance in the picture of his face. The tree says come to me for I am your mother. For she knows that every question needs an answer and every child needs a tree to hang on to. We all need that special tree to open the door and lead us to this journey, this great adventure called life. The time has come for these precious leaves to separate. The tree will remain strong, and the rock will continue to be firm. Who knows where fate will lead us next. Whatever maybe life has to offer us we will face it with great confusion, and we will conquer it with great pride and joy. God will look at the tree with great admiration, and simply say look at your leaves and what they have accomplished. It is with great dignity that I stand here as one of those leaves that fell from the tree. I shall call on you my fellow leaves with the utmost love and gratitude to join me in the fight against ignorance. With a passion for creativity and a fear of obstacles, I stand here before you so that you may take me into your gentle hands and show me the way.

This is not an ending but merely the beginning of a new day.
—*David De Los Santos*

True Love Will Return

The waves come to the shore, as Julie walks along, she never thought that John would leave her alone, they used to lie in the sand and talk about their future together, John said that the love they shared would always last forever. Julie's now realizing everything that she did wrong, she would never have done them if she knew she'd be left alone.

Julie silently walked along as the waves crashed against the shore, she was trying to make herself believe that she didn't love John anymore, she remembers the rocks on the beach where they first met, and the many times they spent up there that she'll never forget.

She's thinking about these times and she starts to cry, when to her left a distant shadow catches Julie's eye, Julie slowly turns around and there John stands, a smile on his face and he's holding out his hands, he softly whispers out, "Julie, I love you", Julie lifts her head, smiles and says, "John, I love you, too", she starts crying as she grabs his hand, she never thought that John would ever hold her again, through the whole ordeal the one thing that Julie learned, that if it was meant to be, true love will return.

—*Byron Oglesby*

The Seventh Day

As we hurry through the busy week
Through the hustle and bustle with tired feet
There is one day I like best, The seventh day,
the day of rest. For through the week we hurry about
with little time for thought, for things that we
ought to be thinking out. And so we have the seventh day
a time to meditate and pray
A day we can get our rest, The Seventh Day
A day of rest!
—*Sue McLorie*

Unforgiven

Torturing slowly,
Thoughtlessly,
Very painfully.

Imitating our Gods.
Throwing away our lives
That may have saved our lands,
Dedicated to aiding our attempt at harmony;
But in response,
We hostilely unsheathe our despise.

Unintentionally we scare away our minds,
Leaving nothing behind.
So now gone,
We are nothing;
Yet we are all.
We do not live;
Yet we cannot die.

We are the weak.
We are a race.
We are the despised.
We are the UNFORGIVEN.
—*Matt Ross*

Sight Behind Blindness

As I lie down and close my eyes, behind my lids is darkness,
my thoughts and conscious beckons me to find, if sight is
  revealed behind blindness.

My memory of sight abandons me, as I go much deeper still,
and penetrates through this vision of mine, until darkness is all I feel.

Imagine never to have seen, the world that exist around you,
a tree, a tear, the sky, the sea, a bouquet of flowers, the color blue.

My senses are becoming more alert, as I listen to myself
breathe, there's a breeze tarrying on my face, that I immediately
  perceive.

There is sight behind blindness, like the sun behind dark clouds,
and like beauty behind distortion, behind my lids I stand proud.

For I see love behind the hate, I gain victory from defeat,
and while engrossed in total darkness, I thank God for what I see.

Although life may seem hopeless, because for some there is no
  light,
but of all the precious gifts to give, thank you God for my insight.
—*Carolyn Miller*

Ned's Delight

I sat upon my bed, not intending to think of Ned.

But, as the sun shone bright, he crept into my
Thoughts of delight.

I remember the first night.
Oh, such charm and smooth flight.

Not a word was spoken, as unknown heights were explored.

The moon lit sky,
Exploded right before my eyes.

As Ned took off, from perch on high,
He quietly soared through the night sky.

I will sit upon my bed and think of the young
Owl that I named Ned.
—*Betty Douglas Lins*

Thoughts Of You

The hours drag on taking forever to pass by.
Thoughts of you are running through my mind.

Can't concentrate at all, I'm just passing time,
The smile in your eyes, the feel of your lips on mine.

My skin tingles now remembering your touch.
I need you here now, I want you so much.

Not knowing what's right, not sure if it's wrong,
Just knowing I've never had feelings so strong.

You struck a chord deep inside
Where my inner self likes to hide.

You've drawn me out and made me see
I belong with you, you belong with me.

Knowing I love you, but too scared to say,
Afraid the words will get in the way.

Since I've met you, I know for sure
That I've never really been in love before.

One day at a time for me to get through
Until the one day I'm again with you.

My heart's in your hands, it's all I have to give.
Please handle it with care, I've just started to live.
—*Marie Fitzsimmons*

Shards Of Lies

There stood the only one who would pray for pain. Serious threat of rain and thunder, black skies and terrible lightning. There stood the only one holding a steel rod to the sky, begging for the strike.

Smiling with teeth that chew on misery.
Thick like old milk mixing with clotting blood.
Screaming, sinking in the ash and the mud.

I am walking faster and faster...but getting farther away from Heaven.

Shards of lies and the calling of dark skies,
and I can't find my wings in a closet of desire.

There is a small geometrical figure suspended in my brain with hundreds of little odd doorways.

I am afraid. Outside the storm rages, white fire born in a thundercloud. Its' kiss is loud.

Fear grips me like fists closed upon my life...

The bathtub is filled with brown blood, my eyes itch. I hold on, tightly. And I remember kisses from Eden. Each one like a tiny smooth stone dropped into the black water of a silent, hidden pool.
—*Douglas Winfield Hiser II*

Holy Vigil

Like the children, four sturdy pines stand
To catch the snowflakes of Christmas,
Sentinels of alabaster, so grand—
In memory of the time it was...
Like beacons of our celebration
Of cheer, for The Christ Child.
It was the Angels' jubilation
Quietly announcing a message so mild
To shepherds, so lowly, tending sheep.
This Holy night, a vigil we shall keep.
—*Terri M. Tuleta*

"My Little Dog Wood Tree"

I peered from window and there did I see
Three lonely little leaves hanging from my dogwood tree.

They told me a story all in themselves
This is the tale that I beheld

Summer has ended autumn in neigh
Beautiful horizons dazzle the eye

Soon winter winds will be singing their songs
White blankets of beauty to cover the lawns

Before we realize spring will be here
Birds building nests - flowers everywhere.

This is Gods way of nature renewing
But for my Lord this could not be
Thank you God for creating me
That I could behold my little dogwood tree

Let me do thy will, begrudging not my duties
Finding happiness, always, in natures beauties
—*Ruth M. Emig*

"Sunshine And Wind"

Bright rays of sunshine,
Through a window fall on my face,
Make my life worth living,
To feel mother nature's grace.

Jumping out of bed,
Putting on my clothes in a haste,
Shoestrings all tied,
And my belt buckled around my waist.

Went outside and sat down,
Looking over hills and plains,
I taken a woodland stroll,
And then I sat down again.

Birds and butterflies are flying,
The honey bees are buzzing,
Wind is blowing through the trees,
And leaves are falling by the dozen.

Sunshine and Wind make me happy again,
Make me want to be mother nature's best friend.
—*Martha M. Foster*

"Hunting Time Again"

It's hunting time again - Mum - the weather cool and clear.
Time to clean our rifles up so we can hunt for deer.
I'll take you on the mountain - Mum - a hunting you and me.
And time will turn back pages to like it used to be.
I'll leave you on the crossing - Mum - where the deer pass
 Every day.
Where I know you'll get to see one before the sun's
 last ray.
You'll put meat upon the table as you did in days of yore;
There'll be many renewed memories of the hunts
 We've had before.
It will be like old times - Mum - my Son said with glee;
When I take you on the mountain - Mum - a hunting -
 you and me.
—*Hazel Manchester*

Panther

Fierce and deadly, the panther glides
Through the evening grass,
His body sheathed in cool black velvet
And flowing like liquid glass.

Gleaming emerald eyes, like beryls,
Search the hungry night,
Shining forth as jeweled heralds
Of death as it wings into flight.

The darkness is your vaunted ally,
Hiding all but the sounds so clear —
Two heartbeats—yours, quite calm and bold,
The other, filled with fear.

Then, razor-sharpened curving scythes—
The claws upon your feet—
Collect their deadly evening tithes
With deathstrokes indiscreet.

One muffled scream, the deed is done!
Back you glide through the grass,
Sheathed in blood-stained velvet,
And flowing like liquid glass.
—*Albert F. Becker, Jr.*

On The Northern Shield

Against a leaded sky, wisp's of water vapor, slowly undulate through the Palisades rising and falling as the sun does a peek-a-boo among the clouds.
Mists hang down in the Bays, shading the Inlets and Isles. The undisturbed water is a deep cobalt blue. A quick north wind stirs the mirrored surface; almost imperceptibly, the wind shifts, causing a corrugated blue and white fury. As calmness returns, fuzzy nymphs start a dance. The water, is violently parted, in a scaly green and silver spray; sending rings of motion lapping toward pebbled Beaches and tree dappled Crags.
A Loon's wail echoes through the Birch and Aspen stands; as it fades, the Sumac bushes turn dark, then black. In the coolness, a hoar-frost forms as armor, on the tall Pines standing lone and sentry-like against the moonlit landscape.
—*Robert J. Kirwan*

The River In Spring

It's no longer held by winter's icy grip
　through the town the river flows
　　on it's spirited trip.

Abundantly filled with gurgling water
　from a stormy, spring shower
　　looking at it...
I'm filled with happy laughter.

On it's banks; crocuses and daffodils
　stand and watch the water play
　　upon the rocks and stones in it's way.

Ducks make their home on the river's back
　soon their ducklings will add
　　their waddle and quack
　　　to the river's back.

It gives me much pleasure
　this branch of the Chicago River
　　that flows through our town
Summer, fall, Spring or Winter!
—*Judith A. Frazier*

Voyager

For I am but a voyager passing
Through this time, this place.
A stranger in the midst of all
That is old, all that is new.
Careful not to tread on the beauty of the day.
For I am but a voyager passing
Through this time, this place, should I leave
My mark? So someone else will see
This passing through? A loving heart the
Gentle kindness, the beauty of God's love in me.
For I am but a voyager passing
Through this time - this place, no more a stranger-
For I am a part of all I behold,
All I feel. I left my mark on
The people I have loved-
The people I have touched.
For I am but a voyager.
—*Dolores Ford*

The Abortion

Murdered, slaughtered, brutally slain
Thrown in a garbage can and left to die
Why did the little child have to die in pain?
His only way to fight back is to cry.

Bones broken, body burned what have they done?
To her, he was a very big mistake
She does not care that this was her son
She will not remember him when she wakes

An improper burial he receives
A large, tin, bin is where he is layed
His mother awakes and proceeds to leave
Not knowing she'll soon have a price to pay

　God's merciful love will save the child,
But the mother who murdered does not make
　God smile.
—*Marguerite Collins*

Baby Boomers

Baby Boomers they call us.
Thrown together like a chorus.
Once long haired and bell bottomed hippies,
Now well dressed and over worked yuppies.
Not all are the same - please don't criticize.
Look at the individual - no need to fantasize.
So we liked the wild styles and rock tunes,
Not a reason to condemn and say "lose your fortunes."
There's a person behind that label.
Look up! Play the cards on the table.
—*Rene Du Bois*

A Touch Of Heaven

I grabbed for a piece of the sunlight and I held it ever so tight
But it filtered through my fingers and was instantly out of sight.
I reached for a star in the heavens; I could see its pointed edge,
But it faded away when I touched it and dissolved into the
　Milky Way.
I held my hand out for a moonbeam for its rays were oh! so bright,
But my hand could not contain it and it disappeared into the night.
The wind had kissed my forehead as it flitted across my brow,
And I tried to take hold of the breezes as they tossed and
　tumbled my hair;
I looked but my hand was empty for it was no longer there.
I cannot possess a one of these things.
They're there for each one to share.
But I didn't miss out on a single thing for I had touched
　heaven out there.
—*Grace Scott Durdin*

The Rose

The seed is sewn
Time goes by and soon it's grown
The sunshine and showers blesses its heart
Its life has begun and soon to start...

Through time and seeds it shares its life
Again blessed by sunshine and rain for further life
The family grows until one day
The old petals start to fall away

So sad one would think to see the old rose go
But no, it is just beginning again to grow
Through love and nurturing and through life and sun
The rose lives forever. Only those that know love would know
  ...it's just begun

The seed is sewn
Times goes by and healing is done
The sunshine and showers blesses its heart to grow
Its life has begun and forever more the rose continues
on.....
—*June Iris Smith*

Untitled

Walk back in time? I wish I could
to a day when as child I stood
At Mother's knee so safe and sound
Mysteries of life were all around

With hopes and dreams come teenage years
Cherished friendships lots of tears
"I know I can change the world," I said
"Or at least make a difference." And
the statement led to growing and middle years
While I realized upon life's stage
Our lives play out their charted plot
Whether we've made that difference or maybe not

Now I've got me and what I am has taken many years to form
A person different from the rest
I can reminisce — I've passed the test

Walk back in time? I must say "Nay'
I know what happened yesterday
Tomorrow is a new frontier walk back you say?
No!!! I'll stay right here.
—*Rubie Andrews*

Dreams

As I close my eyes at night and drift from this familiar world
to a land where fears are revealed and dreams come true
I await to see what type of creatures will accompany me this
night, and like many nights before, I wait for you.

In a place beyond time and reason, where emotion itself is the
brush and the canvas and the paint
where illusion is reality, and reality confusing...I wait

I know you will be there with smile or frown or wing
and you will grace my sleeping hours with the comfort you bring

Your face is sometimes changed and the place is never the same
and always different circumstances
You identify your love with a smile and your soul with a touch
and I take my chances

It is more than lust or desire, and its energy sends us
soaring through the clouds above
I wake in the morning with heart content, having known true love.
I walk through my life of consciousness, fulfilling these earthly
  demands,
and yearn for the evening when I close my eyes, and we meet
  again.
—*David Rilling*

Perilous Progress

Repent the raw wind of man's ravenous reason
To alter his food, his health, or the season
As Eros diverts his reverent devotions
And logic laments his languid emotions

His final defiance of nature thwarted
Disturbs sinful souls who have long since departed
Somber sad spirits that beg, call and screech
To join in their ranks, they firmly beseech

Relics and ruins that reek of man's mystery
Collect fatal facts for his rush into history
Can mankind survive his perilous progress?
Provide him a womb into which he can regress?

He corrupts politicians and bribes his police
And justifies war as a means to bring peace
He closes his mind to the protest of youth
Then reluctantly yields to their innocent truth
—*Billy Bankston*

The Battle Of Supremacy

The need to belong completes a sense of worthiness
To be such a friend, respect for others is a necessity.
We must fashion ourselves wisely to find the quality of
friendship.
There are no rebels in newborns as they are unaware of
  sin that deletes one's self esteem.
As we mature, we must increase our self worth, as we decrease
  our shamefaced conscience.
It is only we, who can deal with our inner mind and nature of
our being
A brittle word is as fragile as a glass bubble, to be
  handled with the greatest care.
One false move and we see fragments disintegrated to powdery dust.
We must bear witness to the succession of successes, to keep our
  worlds on the highest level.
A worthy friend never lurks in dark alleys, as pleasing
  gives us a sense of belonging.
Perseverance requires stamina of intestinal fortitude.
To have a friend and be one, we need to muster a stout heart
  and spirit.
The courageous and venturesome are blessed, as we throw
  prudence to the wind.
—*Sylvia Argow*

My Heart

Here is my heart, with its tremendous task it has,
  to beat all day and all night.
We add to this burden, the task of love, hate, some sorrow
  or hopefully a happy way in life's plight.

Taking personal comments from others
  whether it be with the best of intentions,
Or perhaps with the cruel thought of
  hurt or maybe even destruction.

We wonder sometime, how it can keep on beating
  and why do we put so much extra weight on it.
Can this tiny organ, no larger then my fist,
  do so much and still keep fit?

Every so often we lose a part of our wonderful heart
  to something or someone in our life.
But it seems, no matter how much of our heart we lose,
  it mends and becomes whole once again
  and sometime only the scars are left.

So let me give you, my Dear a piece of my heart.
Keep it, hold it, let it grow to become big enough
....so that you can give it away and know I'll always be
near..
—*Helen "Bell" Berakovich*

Missing You Too Much

Have you ever missed someone so much that you just wanted
    to cry?
And knowing something that really hurt, like that they never
    said good-bye?
Well, I know this feeling and it stings more than you could
    ever know.
I try to hide the loneliness and desperation so no one would
    see it show.
Deep inside my heart I care so much that I can't think straight.
I don't know how to find out if we've gotten through that "gate."
Are you still there for me like you were once before?
Could you please show me, oh just once more?
Prove your love to me so I'll be freer to be
The more open person that's been locked up inside of me.
I need your courage and support behind my back.
The feeling of encouragement and love to never lack.
Hold on to me tightly when we meet again,
And let me know that it will never end.

—*Fayla Janel Chambers*

Dear God, Am I an Atheist?

To deny the trees?
To deny the grass?
To deny the animals on the hillside?

To deny the scheme of the world?
To deny the family?
To deny the friends?

Testing us with disease
testing us with death
holding the prize, just out of reach.
Calling our names, no rejects, no repeats.

The mystery of the story
The coming of the Lord
The Proverbs for the thinking
The end for all in store.

—*Jan Shogren*

Blasphemy

The only words he spoke - blasphemous.
To describe his life - treacherous.
In Sunday School, he was always bored.
He would entertain himself by insulting the Lord.

The only words he spoke - blasphemous.
Did not believe in Heaven, he confessed.
No one knew why he acted so odd.
He blamed all of his problems on God.

The only words he spoke - blasphemy.
No one knew why he accused Thee.
In front of a church is where he lies.
In front of a church, what a strange place to die.

—*Cole Barager*

Untitled

So many try to say not now, so many have forgotten now
To say I am, and would be lost, if they could in history,
Bowing, for instance, with such old world grace
To a proper flag in a proper place
Muttering like ancients as the stump upstairs
Of mine and his or ours and theirs, just as if time were what
They need to will, when it was gifted with possession still
Just as if they were wrong in more wishing to belong
No wonder then so many die of grief so lonely as they die
No one has yet believed or like a lie another time has other
lives to live

—*Tomas Castillo*

Wings In Spring

You lucky birds, you seem so free
To fly above the land or sea
Your wings spread wide, you flap and float
Emitting cries from feathered throat
You look down on your friends earth bound
Who need a ship to leave the ground
And blink a proud superior eye
As if to ask "why can't you fly?"
Well birds we really cannot say
Why God created us this way
But in our minds we too can soar
And even visit distant shore
We have the power to hope and drive
And work to keep our dreams alive
So birds just keep on flying high
Your forms accented by the sky
Strong wings may take you very far
But we can reach the highest star

—*Olive Gregory Urban*

Lost Heart

I need your love—I need it oh so bad
To get me through this pain I cannot stand
I'll give you love, I'll be the only one who cares
And when darkness falls, I'll still be standing there

I'm a lost heart, save me baby, don't let me down this time
I'm a lost heart, so stay with me, and say that you'll be mine

So please understand—I'm giving all I can
Just believe in me, I'm a lost and lonely man
In my troubled times I see love's shining light
And it guides me to your heart in the night

—*Darrell Bruce*

Talents

We all have a talent - or five or ten,
To give to the Lord and to share with men.
It may not be teaching, music or art:
It may be a smile that is right from the heart.
You may not be able to build or sew,
But you may have a "warm personality" glow:
A word for a stranger, a soft-whispered prayer,
A sharing of sorrow to show that you care.
Such seemingly small things are real TALENTS, too.
So use them for JESUS - He'll bless all you do.

—*Gertrude Krenzke Ebeling*

Senior's Nest

Like birds, we migrate North each Spring.
To hear the birds proclaiming
Their terrestrial abode.
"A new family before long,"
They burst forth in song.
Their nest is full.
A chipmunk stops to listen.
Sits up to stare,
Then darts to a home
He alone knows where.
Squirrels run up a tree,
Perhaps the better to see
Who has invaded their domicile.
Creatures of God are all guarding their nests.
Our nest is empty.
But our hearts are full.
Love for our children and grandchildren
Exert a magnetic pull
Back to our nest.
But for us, now, it is only to rest.

—*Rebecca Davis*

Sometimes They Feel Like Boulders

God gave me these broad shoulders
To help me carry a heavy load,
Tackling mine and everyone's problems
As I travel along life's bumpy road.

I'm there as a sounding board
Trying to never give advise,
I listen with my heart and ears
Hoping that this will suffice.

Their problems become very heavy
Along with the many problems of my own,
I'd like to help in any way I can
But couldn't a little consideration be shown?

Friends always tell me their troubles
That's why God gave me these broad shoulders,
But combined with my own problems
Theirs often seem like heavy boulders.
—*Edna Coon*

Words Are

I read somewhere that words were wheels
  to help our minds convey
Scientific facts, the mountains great
  and beauty of flowers in May.
Some folks' words are like cascades
  others like the river's flow
Some are struck like sparks of steel
  from the anvil and hammer's blow.
Some words are eloquent and smooth
  others are pure and sweet and mild....
A mother's words can soothe the hurt
  of the wounds of a little child.
If a 'train of thought' has an 'engineer'
  guiding 'cars' along 'word' tracks
The mind can journey both far and near
  learn beauty and store up facts.
A dictionary is filled with words
  and by skill, truth and beauty unfold
And it's like beads of pearl and silver strung
  on a delicate chain of gold.
—*Edith M. Redmond*

For Mac

Can we behold life and not be touched by pain,
To hold a smile in our hearts with the promise to remain.

To cherish a small boy and return him to a place
That we can only dream about and hope is filled with grace.

Mac, I need to know you are free of pain and now can sing and
  play
And all the stars that shine above light your glorious way.

Take time to think of us who cared for you in our simple
  special style
And pray that eternity will unite us all to behold your
  beautiful smile.
—*Mary O'Connell*

"A Widow's Reflection"

I made a visit to the Cemetery today
To kneel for a moment and silently pray,
That my loved one below the sod
Is in safe keeping in the Kingdom of God.

The years he lived his faith on earth,
Eighty, all toll from day of his birth.
Of these years I was privileged to share
Fifty of them in marriage of love and care.

I made a visit to the Cemetery today
Not only for quietness, peace, but to stay
And reflect on the blessings we had enjoyed
When God had blessed our home with two boys.

I made a visit to the Cemetery today
To kneel for a moment and silently pray,
To reminisce of times past and caring love
And think of his spirit with God above.

I listen to the silence that surrounds me
And watch the sun beams, through the trees.
I draw strength and a sense of healing
And bow my head in prayer while kneeling.
—*Lorene C. Young*

Expectations

For who am I? I am who I am and for today that is enough. To live up to my expectations of myself is more than I can sometimes handle. I expect more of me than anyone does. Why? Because that's what I have come to learn. But Wait- Today what I expect of me is to enjoy the warmth of the sun, the brightness of Gods rainbow, the songs nature sings, walks on the beach, and to laugh with my friends, and to take time to smell the flowers. My expectations are different because I am different. I am more at peace with myself. I can't worry about yesterday and I can't project what tomorrow will bring. I can only live for the moment of now. To be there to share a dream with a friend, to share in the delight of a child eating an ice cream cone, or to comfort a friend in time of their need, and to be able to laugh at myself. I can now do
whatever comes my way. I don't have to plan my expectations of the moments coming in my life. I can expect of me that I will do and be where I need to be right now and it is a beautiful place to be.
—*Pamela J. Senn*

My Special Day

Little I knew when, as a child
To me, each day seemed as a mile
While waiting for days so special to me
I felt that day would never be.

Since then, many special days of mine
Have come and gone, but in life's design
I no longer plan, there is no need
One day at a time is now my creed.

For as older I grow, I am content
With memories of a life well-spent
And when I die, don't dare to say
"Too bad, how sad," 'twill be my special day.
—*Catherine S. Engstrom*

Dells Mill - Augusta, Wisconsin

I grew up down by the old mill.
   To me there was no other thrill.

My cousins were so very kind.
   They would let me hang around to kill time.

I went fishing above and below the dam.
   The small ones I threw into a tin can.

As some people of history know.
   Business at the mill got slow.

My cousin, Gus Clark, had a plan.
   He is quite an inspirational man.

Some people called him lazy.
   Others I knew thought he was crazy.

He is a hero, so go see him.
   The mill is now a national historic museum.

So if you are ever in Wisconsin
   Get your butt over there don't miss this one.

It will journey you into the past.
   You'll hear the mill run very fast.

Gus will sing you a nice little tune.
   The weather is best in June.
   —*Arnold L. Raether*

Mind Country

The bluebell woods and all the last goodbyes
To parentage to country bones and roots
A sea of promise under sheltering green
Without a further shore.

The immanence of voyage uncommenced
The bluebell glades a haven out of time
You cannot pluck them only drink the blue
That will not fade.

There was a time a place a distant past
With other springtime flowers the years roll on
The blue I conjure through an inward gaze
A doubled vision of mind's eye.

The angels fell choosing the temporal
—In paradise time was has never been—
And I am free to wander in mind country
The only country truly mine.
   —*Dilys Winegrad*

The Sea

The sea is an unusual thing to see
to people like you and me,
but if you look close at the sea
you will see something pretty
   about the sea and all its
   beauty.

You will see many a shell
if you look very well,
you can hear the shells tell
a story it knows very well
   about the sea
   and all its beauty.

And if you look closer to your surprise,
you will see fish with open eyes,
   and the rest of the sea
   and all its beauty.
   —*Matthew Jones*

The Beginning Of Tomorrow

Today the world begins tomorrow
To put away the past, end all the sorrow
We can do away with wars and crime
No more prejudism and other such slime

Peace in our hearts and in our minds
Can be so very hard to find
If tomorrow begins with thoughts of today
Then surely the world will find its way

We must find a solution to the pain
From political promises we must refrain
Our time in life is running low
Now is the time for our colors to show

Open expression is the real test
To understand what the people think to be best
Give, not lend, to those who borrow
For today is the beginning of tomorrow
   —*Bruce W. Shirley*

"If I Could Only Save One Memory"

If I could only save one memory
   to remember the rest of my life
I know exactly which one I'd choose.
The one I don't want to lose.
I'd keep that special homecoming night
The one I remember so very well
The room was dim
The song was slow
And I was hoping he'd never let go.
Being with him was the very best part.
It was the look in his eyes that captured my heart.
I realized soon as the song ended and faded away
In my heart he would always stay.
If I could only save one memory
This is the one it would be.
This is the one that forever
   would be a part of me.
   —*Nicole Fletcher*

Please Pass The Salt

I don't eat out an awful lot - It's hard
   To satisfy me;
It seems no matter where I sit, the waitress goes
   right by me;
But that is not my prime concern — I have another reason
Why I am not quite satisfied; I have to "salt to season."

Most people eat with much content;
   Their food they seem to savor;
But I must add a little salt so to enhance its flavor.
I ask no odds of anyone; I give no one my reason—
I merely grab the shaker, for I have to
   "salt to season."

So far, I've managed to get by without too much
   that ails me;
But one thing sure, it can't be my intelligence that fails me;
I've finally discovered that, for no apparent reason,
No matter where I choose to eat, It's always
   "out of season."
   —*Edwin P. Wolfe*

Our Town

It's not too much to ask of you
To say hello — a handshake, too,
When you're in town and we should meet
Upon our quaint and busy street.

You don't know me? - now that's no crime,
A great big smile will do just fine;
And then when next we chance to meet
I'll be the first to come and greet.

For you and I, we make this town,
We build it up, or tear it down,
And friendship is a small request
To help our town become the best.
—*Kathleen E. Blaisdell*

This Is Life

What do I think of the world today? I don't know, it's hard
to say, there's so much hate, so much strife, I pause and
think, so this is life? Wars and rumors continually, people
fighting just to be free, Crime and killing on a giant spree,
I pause and wonder, so this is life. Am I my brothers keeper?
People say, and pass the hungry, go on their way, if you don't
work, you don't eat, there's no work, no shoes for my child's
feet, my heart aches, my tears flow, I can't leave, there's no
place to go. I look for a forest, and see no trees, just smoke
and soot, no cleansing breeze, what God has made, man is
killing, is there someone out there willing, to make the
smallest sacrifice, to save our world, to save our life.

I look and suddenly I see, One helping a blind man across the
street, giving a beggar something to eat, lending a hand,
  helping a tiny child to stand.
Look there is someone planting a tree, cleaning the river, so
it flows free, there are those who go the extra mile, making
everything worthwhile.

Now this is life.
—*Jennie Waskey*

The Rush

'Twas the day before Christmas. We all awoke at day break,
to see fresh fallen snow, glisten in the morning light.
Rush all! Rush all! One day till Christmas, with so much to
do. Dash away! Dash away! To the nearest Christmas treelot,
to pick out that near perfect tree, for half off the regular
price. The smell of pine filled the air, with needles
scattered everywhere, there stood the near perfect tree for us.
Away! Away! We go to the nearest shopping mall, to pick out
that perfect gift, at half off the regular price.
Rushing in and out of stores, pushing, shoving, and pulling.
When all was done, we all dragged ourselves home for a long
winter's night. With still lots to do, before we could
snuggle into our beds. Pa, in his grubbies, putting up the
Christmas tree. Ma, in her grubbies, cooking, baking,
slicing, dicing, and humming a tune.
The kids wrapping their gifts and cleaning their rooms in hopes
that St. Nick would soon be there.
We all settled down for a short winter's night; Ma and Pa kissed
the kids goodnight.
Sweet Dreams, Sweet Dreams, for tomorrow is Christmas.
—*Marjorie Rapp*

Untitled

How long will we have together
To share loving touches and warm sweet smiles?
Only the passing of time will give the answer,
An answer that perhaps I don't want to know.
In love I'll taste, and share, and grow.
I'll offer some things unique, and then a little more.
Our sharing will be an exchange of gifts,
Permitted by desire and not forgotten through time.
And if there comes a time when I no longer see love
    reflected in your eyes,
I'll turn away contented with what we once shared -
    with what you gave.
     Strong yet gentle, freely given and accepted yet binding,
     your love has nourished me.
Forever I'll keep your heart gifts
    tenaciously, vividly, and nostalgically within
    forever a special part of me.
—*Antionette Lenoir*

Untitled

We come together on His day
To sing of praise, respect we pay
I would not have it another way
He means so much to me

Our preacher has really been a blessing
He never really keeps us guessing
God's word is what He keeps on pressing
He lived so sinlessly

Our fellowship is one that's gifted
If you come I'm sure that you'll be lifted
His word is pure, need not be sifted
He died so graciously

If you get a chance before you go
Stop by and He will let you know
There is really nothing that you owe
He rose so gloriously

All you must do is to accept
The fact that He has paid your debt
Repent and make sure your word is kept
It is our Lord you see.
—*Steven Laudano*

Transfiguration And Denial

A vision hovered just beyond my brow,
To sooth my soul and make my madness wane.
No wistful dream, this sight that bade me vow
To bare my worldly mind as proud and vain.

'Twas Truth I sensed and raised my head to shout,
And share with all who begged their destiny.
'Twas hope I brought to those besieged by doubt,
And prayers meant to set their spirits free.

But though I looked to Truth, they saw but doom,
And blindly clung to pleasures God forbade.
Now these same witless fools would dare presume,
To cast my fate, and see my breath be staid.

   I yield with scorn and justly jaundiced eye,
   And damn these heathen hordes for whom I die.
—*Verle Nelson*

My Heart Is In The Sea

Once a glowing morn, I thought to ease my heart now torn
To stroll aside the glistening sea, that reflects the fire
   ball's rays coloring its waters with an orange tint
My love has left, farewell to the best
Now the vessel inside my bosom, filled with grief and sorrow
As I walk atop the velvety, emerald moss, the thought of my
   love melts my eyes to sauce
A lucid mist gracefully escapes from the placid surface of the
   water, which reminds me of my love fleeing from thine heart
I fix my teary eyes upon the ripples dispersing from the deep,
   that have been made by two fish intertwined in love
Similarly as the mist dissolves into the peaceful air, thoughts
   of my love invade my mind
While my confused emotions spin swirling and twirling, I wander
   ahead to large boulders
The great mounds of steel grey divert my thought to anger and
   hate; but, than I think much deeper and come to realize
That it must be fate.
   —*Allison A. Wissinje*

The Telephone Call

The telephone call that cloudy day
to tell me my father had just passed away.
I sat in my room, slumped in a chair
sobbing and crying with no one to care.

The old empty house,
the lonely atmosphere too
Oh, Dad, how I miss you!

The ringing of the phone still fresh in my mind.
My recollection of the night
when my father died.
   —*Tessa Thompson*

This Old Barn

Could this old barn but find a way
To tell the tales of yesterday!
When cows were wild and the horses rough,
And you'd rather bleed than say "enough."

Here generations now quite gray,
First got a start and had their day.
Where men were men and the days were long,
Where Dad held court when the boys did wrong.

So warm when a blizzard raged outside,
Yet cool in summer after a ride.
So far from the house Mom wouldn't yell,
Close enough to hear the dinner bell.

Now sounds of horses eating hay,
Stir echoes of a bygone day.
When boys chinned themselves on the sturdy rafter,
In the silent barn which holds their laughter.
   —*Colen H. Sweeten, Jr.*

Renaissance

You speak the language of understanding
Touching my soul like an angel
Tuning in to a higher state of existence
I hear the harps of a thousand gentle minds

Moonbeams forming an invisible stairway
To the soft haven of cottonball clouds
Where the light of stars leads you to your berth
And love surrounds you forever
   —*Carol A. Simmons*

On Spruce Knob With Nancy

A trip we took, my lover and I,
To the top of the mountain state.
Where vapors and mists collide in the sky
And thunder makes the world shake.

Together we were in nature and love
Sharing rain and wind and sun.
Heaven - almost - was surely right above.
Time stopped for us, and yet did run.

By day we saw and felt God's great world.
So many wonders offered us to keep.
By night his greatest gift unfurled,
As he rocked the two of us to sleep.

Together our love curled up in his palm.
On his gentle thumb rested my head.
On my shoulder she dreamed a sweet love song,
In perfect safety, without fear or dread.

We cuddled each other and were cradled by him.
His fingers curled up to become our cover.
The night was a bliss and harmony blend
On top of the world with God and my lover!
   —*William Clavel Smith*

Home Alone

   Left alone by the will of God
   to tread the path we once trod
   alone & lonely - almost forgotten
   like the old rag doll made of cotton.

No one hears the tears that fall upon her
   pillow softly & quietly like the sighs
     of the weeping willow.
   The days & nights are long & lonely
     since he was called away.
   Sometimes I think I hear him calling
     to come beside him lay.

   She often sits & wonders what he would
   have done with the time, had it been he
   instead of she that was left behind.
   The Lord is her shepherd & with him by her side
never seen, never heard, but always a companion & guide.
   —*Maye Sanders*

Reflection In The Mirror Of Life

I wake up in the morning, afraid to face each day
To try to conquer my fear, as I slowly dress; I pray
I've made it through the lonely night, and for this
   I should be glad
"Then why?" I ask when I awake, "do I feel so terribly sad?"
   These middle years, these present tears,
   The emptiness, the space...
I dread each passing year, the seasons, count them all
Though only four. I seemingly deplore the winter as it calls.
It is cold, dead, cruel, confining...
Surely reminding that our years on earth are
   Definitely declining.
Youth is for the young, so spring like and optimistic
   And oh so naive.
To try and capture the past and the happy years,
When good health prevailed and energy surged within,
We would only deceive ourselves; for we will know
   That time passes on, and so do we;
     For life is for the living.
   —*Pearl M. Dion*

If I Leave

If I were to leave, would you turn and shed a tear,
To wash away the indifference and make your vision clear?
Would you let the sadness take you to a place you've never been?
Could you look towards your soul and find my love within?
You say you think you love me and that's growing rather old.
If there were ice on the ground, would you say you think it's cold?
I've loved you with my heart and soul for many, many years.
Only to have been confronted and challenged by your fears.
I give you my life, now I am complete,
If I were to walk away, would you, could you weep?

—L'Myrl Burleigh

Memories

I have sweet memories of you and me...
together forever to be united under God's
great heavens and in mother earth's palace
we shall live in memory, we shall live
for eternity just you and I
love shall live forever!

—Sophia Verrinder

Never Again?

There was a curtain, red, that shielded Euro-East. And all
together there, they walked in single step. This was the
empire built to last, and last for sure. And all within its
walls seemed so secure.

There came a forceful wind from Euro-West. The curtain rented
with a final blast. Till the empire built to last, and last, and last,
No longer was a factor or a test.

Along the Adriatic shore was born a roar. Where once it was
all quiet and serene. Ancient hates that once had bound but
seemed dislodged. Flared up again and reared their ugly heads.

A holocaust, the twin of one that once consumed six million
souls. Consumed the lives of innocence once more. While all
the others seemed to be transfixed, As ethnic cleansing took
its evil toll.

No one dared to halt the ghastly wave. Mindless of a world
which once woke up too late, to stem the tide of another
master race.

A lesson not learned from history past. A repetition for the
world is done——the die is cast.

—Michael Affanoso

The Wrong Way

Today on me, pressure was laid,
Tomorrow, the price I shall pay.
For the wrong decision I made twice,
For my life I refuse to set a price.
The trust I plea for, shall no longer live.
My actions I only hope God will forgive.
My heart shall no longer feel,
For now I know how life is real.
For the way of life there are two roads,
Along the wrong, I always go.
I play these games back and forth in my mind,
While the evil side wins every time.
I have no way of saying "No!"
Or maybe I'll be considered low.
Friends aren't always friends,
At times they determine when life ends.
I've tried and tried to cry all my tears,
I'm afraid life doesn't provide enough years.
I've been given another chance once again,
This time I pray my heart will win.

—Julie DeArmond

The Horses Of San Marco

I saw horses walk from the sea, dripping wet,
Tossing green foam,
Bearing gifts in their long, golden eyes.
Lips curled round an invisible bit,
Manes cropped and nostrils flaring;
Such beauties pranced straight out of Constantinople, through
Seven centuries of war to stand on forty-second street,
Bearing their proud, Imperial Guard.

Heads turn, hearts beat faster as they trot past in perfect
Unison,
Battle horses, great, bronze chargers,
With necks thicker than we've ever seen....

How lovingly some artist crafted them, so they come at us still,
Fresh and strong as they were cast.

—Virginia A. Lamarche

Will It Happen Again?

In the beginning there was a complete emptiness. A state of
total nothingness in which nothing did or ever had existed.

Then by the wonderful powers of our God there was created a
World, life, and existence.

The creations then flourished and grew, but God was displeased
And all was destroyed and started anew.

Again all things flourished and grew, but God was satisfied this
Time and everything was allowed to continue.

Time passed by slowly while all of God's creations grew,
Survived, and gradually improved.

This time though man also grew and improved and made new
Discoveries. Along with him grew his technology until the
Technology itself surpassed man's own improvements.

So now in this magnificent world of trees, plants, animals, and
Friends, man himself has the power of total destruction.

In this world there has always been problems and flaws, but if
Man does use his powers of destruction who can say that God will
Ever recreate all that gets destroyed, that it will ever get
any better, or that the same thing won't ever happen again!

—*Carl M. Trinko*

At Death's Crossing

When I let me go the bonds of earth and soar
Toward the gold and silver of heaven's shore,
I will dance on snowy clouds etched with
   wondrous sun
Stretch on tiptoe to touch fiery stars when
   that's done.
The winds of all the earth shall gather and carry
   me far,
Far, far into the aeons of time, into space's
   black bar,
And this old robe of flesh that I now wear
Will be exchanged for heaven's bright attire.
I'll sail to heights before unknown
Where man and bird have never flown.
No man or bird would ever dare fly,
Not so far, or fast, nor high as I.

—*Elmer Tuttle Church*

Rib Cage

Balanced on bone,
trapped above a pool.
And I could tell,
even when the water flowed into my nose
(& he didn't see)
that his ribs poked out when he peeled off his tie-dye.
One rib missing. Then came woman.
"I have an obsession with the valley of the shadow of death."
Can't sleep too well, in the shadow of death.
Like Jonah in the belly of the whale;
Forever leaning on crooked ribs.
To lay my head on those cracked ribs,
and hear that thing beating,
wanting out of the rib cage.
I can learn to love,
With my breastbone up in arms.
I can see your ribs move,
when your lungs go in and out.
But there will always be water in your rib cage
With a little man floating inside.
—*Lament*

Me The Balloon

Me a blue balloon rising higher and higher into the air
Travelling farther away from worries and not a care
The color blue blends right in with the lovely sky
I see an airplane fly by
I try to wave "HI" but nobody sees me nobody cares
I fly higher and higher, still no worries and not a care
As I travel through the clouds and see the stars,
I come to some gates and float right into heaven
As I go in I am greeted and God gives me to a little child
I still have no worries but I have a care,
This child.

—*Lisa Mallicoat*

The Strider

I have been here before, in this wood where the
Tree's thin fingers scratch the raw sky.
Their bare bones exposing such brittle frames.

And - if my memory serves me well - just 'round this
Bend, the snow's quilt lies too thick to find one's
Way with keen eyes alone.

Though with sufficient reflection, I will recall it's
Spiral pattern and even those parts where my steps were wasted.

It is difficult to know - with my pace, which never
slackens - how I have made this apparent circle.

For I was far beyond this point last Christmas
And had hoped to soon draw my charted journey to an end.

My course is fixed. My compass is set
I refuse to believe that my map needs revision.

I have already pondered the secrets of this wood, and can
Spare little time for such needless regressions.

—*Pamela L. Rockwell*

Untitled

Where are the legends?
What strange static
nation under the highway beckoned to them?
Was your dimension a
tiring performance of life? Lies?
It must have been, they answered
the seductive message. Descended
through a pit.
Why did you drive them away?

—*Adam Podlaskowski*

Call To Battle

Standing tall, I see the world at my feet
Trembling, I fear the worst is yet to come
Below a man walks with a mask of defeat
He sees my shadow and I see his kingdom
As enemies in battle, we fight to the death
A window opens once for a chance at glory
He walks through the night catching his breath
I notice the wind rising as if waiting for a story
I hold the future in the palm of my hand
For once, the past holds no pain or sorrow
Waiting for battle in the midnight fog I stand
Above me soars a creature of beauty, a sparrow
We have fought throughout time, day and night
Long hours of destruction end at dawns first light.

—*Nora Erica Ponce*

False Immortality Does Not Good Idealism Make

What a lamentable day,
Truly lamentable,
'Twas the day all the leaders
Died and became immortal.

Immortality
Does something to a leader,
Changes, twists, cuts.
Martin Luther King said only,
"I have a dream."
Malcolm's X is a hat, a movie, a shirt.

Look to the men
When they were mortal.
They'll tell you what it's really about.
Freedom. Freedom ringing.
You have no bonds
To keep you from your dream,
Except those created by what you do.
Don't let any mortal man tell you who you are.
Don't listen to men made immortal by man. But listen.
For the past instructs the future.

—*Johnnie Lamar Odom II*

The Past

I run in fear,
Trying not to think of my past.
It still comes back to haunt me-
Playing games of guilt with my soul.
I can't forget what I have done.

I remember the faces
Filled with pain.
I still see the horror in their eyes,
Begging for mercy.
I can't forget what I have done.

I wish to change the past,
To save the lives I took.
Alas, I cannot change what has already happened,
But I must live with the guilt.
I can't forget what I have done.

—*Christopher Pohts*

Untitled

Old dusty, dirty trail,
trying to run away from the footsteps
on your back going on and on 'till the end.
Each day when the yellow sun
brings up the noise of a new day
I remember you trying to flee
from the footsteps on your back.

—*Kristen Young*

Spring

Spring came then,
Tugged at hearts still cold
From winter's chill.

Delighted us with silvery brooks
And freshly waxed buttercups,
Awakened sleepy violets
To briefly worship the ground.

Slender poplars put on
Their finest green lace,
Danced, shimmered and bowed
Awaiting our applause.

Still bare-limbed elms
Seemed to beckon the heavens,
Perhaps remembering leaves and birds
From other summers.

Deeper in the forest
Where stately pines grow,
Snow still clung stubbornly to sheltered ground.
But for us, spring came then.
—*Angela L. Beaumont*

Experiences And Twice Told Tales

Open my book and read a story of my life,
Turn the pages but concentrate hard
Because one rip and then you'd be barred
From ever seeing such magic and mystery.

It's hard to see that some pages are torn
However my book still is not worn,
Though the words might run
But my life so far has been fun.

Hit me with your eyes
And believe me that you'll be surprised
Of the many tales and lores
And my entrances of life's many doors.

Interesting you will see,
Jump on one of my rungs and climb my tree.
My stories branch out to places all about
And contain many lines that are connected with
Numerous vines.

So pick up my book and read a story
Maybe the one with Lorrie,
Page 50 chapter four, trust me, it's no bore.
—*William W. Sigler, Jr.*

The Magic Wand

The magic wand
Turned a tree into a pond.
I wonder what it would do to me!
I tap the wand on my head.
What will happen- well, you'll see.
I turned into a rose!
All I did was to sit and look pretty
I let people smell me with their nose
But I got tired of that.
I turned myself into a gymnastic's mat.
All I did was let people do tricks on me
But I thought, "This wasn't meant of me!"
So I changed back into the me that you see.
—*Joanne Sepulveda*

The Yellow Leaf

Dancing
Turning
Falling
The yellow leaf is lying on the rushing water

Floating
Swirling
Dipping
The yellow leaf is resting on the flowing water

Chilling
Freezing
Entrapping
The yellow leaf is held in the crystalline water

Winter
—*Mary Sue Ubben*

Night Dreams

The smoke colored snow from my window at night
Twinkling stars the moon shining bright
The heartbeat of life in humble resound
A moment in time where peace can be found.

My thoughts taken softly on a wandering breeze
Over the roof tops through branches and trees
To places unknown and never explored
An endless collection of memories stored.

The lights glitter now in the distance below
My spirit lifted higher still higher I go
Riding the currents of some cosmic stream
An eternal adventure a single night's dream.
—*Kenneth Foster*

The Dance

Swaying to the right. Swaying to the left.
Twisting, turning. Rising on your toes.
Reaching, punching. Kicking - higher, higher.
Leaping, stretching. Striking out.
Slashing, screaming.
Mouth a red-black O
Eyes glittering
Stomach knotted
Bile rising in the throat
Whirling faster - faster
Flying through the air
Around and around
The world a blur.
Suddenly you stop!
On the edge of a precipice
Staring into a black hole
Your head droops to your heaving chest
Scalding tears fall at your feet.
Dancing with anger.
Dancing with anger.
—*Georgia Terwilliger*

America Heritage

Americans let's stand up and be counted.
We want our American Heritage.
That's America was built on.
From our forefathers, our American Standards
with disgrip line in our homes and schools
will save with less crimes and less in our jails
and back the way it used to be
in America of taste for our standards
That's our American heritage that we
honor and respect for generations-
in our beautiful America
—*Irene Mary Larson*

The Odd Affair

Some would say it was an odd love affair;
Two coming together...
One it would seem rather reluctantly -
One brimming with passion openly.
But I do not agree.

Where is it written that all love must be equal?
Why do emotions have to be lined up in degrees;
Neatly arranged in straight rows
Like so many waxen tulips?

Rather should it be free and graceful
Like stalks of wheat bending with the winds
Of desire and time.

"I do not love you," he said, "I never have"
Yet the two have come together, and he is there!
There is something unbeknownst to conventional lovers
Undefined and invaluable.

For afterwards there is equal satisfaction
Within each and with each other.
And there are still those of us who know
That fulfillment is Love.

—*Betty Ryder*

For Sue

Pain has been our widow,
unbidden memories an abiding mate,
in the grey grieving of our time,
willow-wound around our conscious state,
phantom fingers ring dry the drops
of dreams from still-believing eyes.
So we sweep up the scraps of life and wait
for the strength that has not failed us,
and wings to rise above it all unscathed.

We give grace to our learning,
and as our parallel paths wind
through what perils this passage holds,
we build these hopes on our defeat;
we triumph in our own right.
In our own time we will taste the fruit;
akin as sisters in our solo flight,
we traverse this tunnel
in search of the healing light.

—*Melinda de Marmion*

Insanity Is A Lovely Place To Be

Focusing on the cold mist nocturnal air mixed with oxygen
unclear. Thread mills cotton nylonic talk babbled in a
foreign
tongue. Look-a-likes everywhere you turn. Blue-yellow-black
makes no sense where logic appears only once. Babies creep
out of mother's wombs, eyes first.
Look around and see nothing but figures dancing in gold dust.
Still beauty awaits when Cartesian gravity is no more. Coral
seas polluted with technology to better the human race, while
planes fly without wings and all fantasize to watch and play.
Stars disappear wit ease as they squirm in God's breast, she
laughing heartily at the universe below. There is no middle,
no beginning, no end with three-legged goats giving mountain
cheese. I hit my head against the wall, blood flows into a
genetic stream with Fellini's Satyricon dreams and the
exploration of Mr. Id pure and refined.

—*Antonio Simoes*

Daniel....

Hold me close, I will close my eyes and pretend we are
dancing under a moonlit sky.

I now hear your breath staggering, Oh God no!
Let's pretend this is not all happening.

I love you and I want to say I do,
I promise to cherish you because I already have.

I remember now the first time you held me in your arms, don't
you remember now? All the times we shared together, how we
talked of our dreams together, just you and I.

No, I feel you slipping away, tell me you love me just one more
time and I will finally let you be free to roam.

I now stand up from your precious body I want so bad to
embrace, and watch your beautiful soul stream up to the
heavens above, while tears of emotion, pain, and remembrance
run down my face.

I close my eyes and walk into the wind hoping it will all blow
away misery and pain.

But I will always love you and never forget you Daniel...
Because no matter what, the wind nor the rain will never wash
away the pain.

—*Kelli Ann Eliason*

"Warning"

There's a wonderful thing called death, that no one seems to
understand, I don't even think the dead can comprehend.
There are things that I don't know and things that I have seen,
Too many places that I have been, Sometimes I just want to die,
but in my mind, I'm in a corner trying not to cry, My mind is
very disturbed with ideas built from evil, satanic symbols
cloud my thoughts, even my thoughts are from the devil,
the world suddenly turns black, and for me there's no turning
back. So take my advice, turn around and run, get away from
satan's fun, once you're caught there's no escape, you soon
find yourself hiding under satan's cape, the cape is made of
special steel, so the heat you cannot feel. So I'm warning
you now, don't get caught, or you're mind will be filled
with what the evil brought all I know is if you don't get away,
you can say goodbye to the day. Please heed my warning, I'm
not pushing you around, I can't stand loose things that I
care about.

—*Tedd Duncan*

What's What... God?

I come in many shapes, many forms.
unexpectedly, out of the norm.
I'm all around, very easy to be found.
Remember the birds... The honey bees...
colorful leaves abounding among the trees...
looking up in the sky, motion clouds dancing
swiftly by.
What's what... God?
Can you imagine the vast blue sea?
Do you have unlimited, childlike Faith in me?
Open your eyes and I will show you all there
is to see, I'm not such a mystery...

—*Bernadette Huffnagle*

Survivors

Conditions here and abroad appear unsolvable
Until compared with those of the distant past
Ten thousand generations have borne us here
Since Mother Eve in Africa braved the way
Through unknown terrors, wild beasts, and marauding tribes,
Extremes of weather, random food, shaking ground and tides
Just to name a few dangers they survived.

One may surmise what daily life entailed
But artifacts from dark-cave days showed some of them were wise
Sensing something mystic as well as the will to live
Aware of wonders all around which nature freely gives
Stars and changing seasons, variety of earth
Along with astonishing and unexpected birth!

Sustaining inborn yearning to nurture and protect
To pass along the best they knew with growing intellect.
Thus we today may better cope and with tough love, offer hope.
The spark of life, an hard-won loan, let's grab this chance
To make a difference in our troubled world
Perhaps to be remembered, like the survivors of long ago!

—*Lois Smith Triplitt*

A Fork In The Road

From the moment when we are born
Until we are called to our eternal reward
All must face the fork in the road
For each decision that it may bode.

Shall I take the road to the left
Or maybe I should turn to the right?
Life does not grant a second chance
To him whose judgment may take flight.

Was father's choice of my career
Another fork on the road of life?
Or the dreams I could not fulfill
Were they my fate or God's will?

When romance came into my life
I remember it was in Central High
A pretty lass without a vice
But I did not take her for my wife.

Now in the twilight of my years
I reflect again to the fork in the road
I took the left and not the right
And with God's help will make it through the night!

—*Joseph G. Imperatrice*

Armistice

Behold the crosses, row on row,
Upon the earth like a cold, white stain.
Recall the rivers of tears that flowed,
The brave young bodies racked with pain,
And the eyes that will never see again.

The sea is too deep and wide to show
The places where heroes fought and died.
See the confused ones. Wide-eyed they go,
Minds stripped bare of hope and pride,
With the horrors of war locked deep inside.

Calm is the breeze that is blowing now
Over the places where the valiant lie,
Having fulfilled the soldier's vow,
Unmindful of the years that fly.
There wasn't time for a last "goodbye."

Grant us freedom and peace, though we don't deserve
The benefits of a peaceful state,
Nor the mercy of Him whom we fail to serve.
Free us, Lord, from the burdening weight
Of our yoke of intolerance, greed and hate.

—*Angeline Maine*

Synchronizing In Secret

A man who blew a noonday factory whistle
  used to check with the woman
  at the city hall switchboard
  for the very official time
  when all the time that woman
  was setting her city hall clock
  by the noonday factory whistle.

Wordlessly at times you check with me,
  I know, for courage and for meaning
  and for other timely contradictions
  against the ages of an evacuated hour,
    a lightless minute,
    a savage second.

Won't you be amused to learn someday
  that all the besieged, erratic while,
  I've been setting my heart
  by you!

—*Joseph Gallagher*

Righteousness Or Religion

Yes.. God is great and God is good,
Very few would argue that this is true.
But if one dares mention God's name—a fight is likely to ensue.
The lives of people are growing extinct
While we deny and dispute what each other may think.
Religion is a custom we cannot forcefully change,
But the separation of people because of their choices must be
    rearranged.
Whether it be Allah, Jehovah, Jesus, or Moses;
Our problems can't be solved without our closeness.
So who are we to say, "My God is true!"
When all that we've learned has come from a human's point of view.
Instead find your God and grasp him tightly.
And be faithful to him for he is Almighty.
If studying your God teaches you anything
You'll learn to work with any human-being.
So, regardless of religions or the powers that be,
If you're a man of God you can work with me.
So now, we must alleviate the wall we stand behind
And come forth as one nation to improve mankind.
When this is done, all God's will smile.
And all of our human sacrifices will be proven worth-while.

—*LaMills Alexander Garrett*

Awareness

A path of super-awareness
vigilantly fixed on pure consciousness
regardless of beauty or ugliness,
wrong or right, sensual or mental activities.
Dealing with facts
then desires -
discrimination
clear Light.
Knowledge of the Divine
appears in its own time -
surrender -
which way to Truth
Truth is one,
approaches are different
Awareness is Divine Light shining
spiritual and material success
Awareness is the antidote
to failure in both worlds

—*U. S. Hellman*

My Wish

I walked a country lane at dusk, beside a rambling brook.
Violets and sweet williams were growing everywhere I looked.
Their fragrance filled the air like a tantalizing perfume.
Birds and bees still busy gathering nectar from their bloom.

Then I sensed another movement off into the trees.
There was a gorgeous Doe and a Fawn walking softly as a breeze.
Squirrels scurrying up and down the trees were everywhere.
Tiny little bunnies peeking out from burrows to see who is there.

I even saw a fox as he trotted toward his den.
The food he had in his mouth told me where he had been.
A raccoon beside the brook was carefully washing off a fish.
As a coyote begins to howl, I made a silent wish.

I wished that all the world could be as perfect as this lane.
And that everyone everywhere could be healthy and free from pain.
I wished all the world could be at peace just like me.
And hate and discontent would vanish in this land of the free.

—*Karen A. Pierson*

Love Hurts

Stark;
Virgin White Walls surround Me.
Trees bloomed. Sauce smelled.
Unbuckled belt;
Sky so vast and endless around Me.
Grass smelled. Sauce boiled
Zipper;
Birds singing in praise to Me.
Cats fed. Sauce boiled.
Brown trousers;
Hardwood floors gaze at Me.
Table Set. Sauce smelled.
Wondering;
What is happening to Me.
Blindness overcomes sunlight.
You are gone. Sauce simmered.
   I scream in silence, no longer loneliness.
    Feelings not old, Feelings not new.
Dinner has come. Dinner was good.
Is this where love is from?   Then I'm no good.

—*Kelly A. Fasco*

Lost Souls

Dreams of today have gone by
Visions of tomorrow yet to be,
My yearning for love will never die
It must be love that I cannot see,
I am but a lost soul looking for another,
A love that I could hold tight
A love like no other,
A lady that I could keep in sight,
One that I could hold forever,
A lost soul that would leave me never
There is a lost soul inside of me
If I could find but one lady to love,
That lost soul would be free.

—*Michael T. Zimmerman*

Freedom

I stand for freedom;
while walking my 'Cross Walk'
And praise Jehovah Shalom
It's not just religious talk.

I've been through many trials
And give God all the Glory
Prayer and praise helped me through the miles
And that's the very best story.

—*Elizabeth Lloyd*

Memories

The two, sharp eyes of the mind,
Vividly remind you of extravagant and horrid
   thoughts you want to leave behind.
Recalling times of laughter and pain.
Which always leave their personalized
   signature upon your soul.
Life's torturing way of making you remember
   your past unrighteous deeds,
That dwell endlessly within your body,
And are reflected upon with each and every
   breath you breathe.

But it is also life's glorious way of letting
   you recollect joyous times.
Bringing them out of oblivion,
Puts a smile on your face, and a feeling of
   warmth in your heart.
Memories are truly revolting, but yet comforting.
They can bring you pleasure or grief that can
   haunt you 'til the end of time.

—*Anne Vestal*

Untitled

The music and spirit of the first days. Upon the roots that
voiced of the beginning, stood only the nymph of darkness.
And traced through every bare corner, there lingered the solemn
obsession of a moment... And God stood with perseverance,
and his poesy.

God lifted his mystic face to the earth, beckoned his eyes in
concentration and then... The earth trembled with excitement,
The sun grew, burnishing rays of shine. Plant coils untwirled
ravenously, as if stretching from perpetual sleep. Dancing
water kissed the holes in the earth, cascading in tousles, in
mist. Flowers sprouted above robust hills and mountains,
Softly scenting the earth with its sweet breath.

Oh! How did such a resplendent moment, come only by the
cast of God's hands? The spirit of the beginning lies with
its curator, God. And in belief, one day, all will behold..
The lissome way the birth of the earth began.

—*Leilani Sinocruz*

Too Tall

I sit and watch by the water front,
Waiting for the miraculous stunt:
The draw-bridge opens to the sky
To let a too tall ship go by.

I sit and think of another event.
Einstein was here, then off he went.
Riddles were unravelled because he came,
And now our universe will never be the same.

I sit here and feel the weight
Of the legacy he left behind.
Simplicity and a mind first rate
Are rarely intertwined.

I sit in a daze and question:
What have I learned from Einstein's lesson?
But my imagination refuses to soar.
My mind is just a revolving door.
The draw-bridge isn't open to us all.
It only unlocks for those too tall!

—*Craig Walker*

Always Among Us

Muffled murmurings in the night.
Wake me from sleep and I'm ready to fight.
Neighborhood dogs bark their displeasure.
Alerted energy rises a measure.
Swiftly they move in the dark of the night.
Intrusive strangers preparing for flight.
One more time they've stolen from others.
What are their names?
Who are their mothers?
These children of darkness boast of deceit,
And with evil brothers they like to compete
In taking from others to claim as their own
What others have bought.
They won't leave it alone.
When all their unethical seeds have been thrown,
They're certain to reap the ill harvest they've sown.
Their mothers will cry.
And plead for their souls.
And a gang of replacements
Will rise from their molds.

—*Helen Tate Lehmann*

Eternal Ballad Of The Soul

    Oh! How ignorant I have been!
    Wallowing in selfishness living in sin!
Accepting appearances for what they are not drowning in
    self-pity - defeated - over-wrought.
Eternal ballad of the soul - oneness with God is the ultimate
    goal!
And immersed in his grace - I have found my place - like a
    diamond - shimmering; splendid!
    For now my life is over - yet yours has just begun.
We melt into each other - like the glow of the setting sun!
My earthly self I have abandoned - like the lilies of the
    field. God is my companion - humility is my shield!
Eternal ballad of the soul - the old man now is dead.
But he who lives for the breath of God - is eternally clothed
    and fed!
And He that begs for mercy - must first be merciful indeed.
And He that hath no problem - is He that truly hath the need!
Eternal ballad of the soul - may temptation cease to sway me.
    For you're the performer - and I'm the instrument
        So play me Lord - Please play me!

—*Dennis Dale Popham*

Walls

There are walls of stone and walls of clay,
Walls of steel and paper-mache.
My wall was built with none of these,
Because, my wall you cannot see.

My wall was built with silence and shame,
And feelings I no longer claim.
It's held together with hope and tears,
And braced securely by all my fears.

On the outside it looks calm and strong,
But it's only an illusion that can't last long.
The inside is crumbling and falling apart.
So I cover the outside with works of Art.

If I let you in you'll see the wall,
From the other side, weaknesses and all.
You'll know the truth, and leave me there.
And that would be more than I could bear,

To risk rejection, hurt and pain,
Will only magnify the shame.
And so I sit inside these walls,
Waiting for their inevitable fall.

—*Linda Stauffer*

Untitled

This cell is the size of a closet, and even when empty the
walls seem to press in. I bought my place here with a crime
that society and I consider a sin. I know that this time is
for society, a debt I owe. Yet, nevertheless, at times I
can't help but to feel low.

I feel low when I hear the soul chilling clang, of the door
being locked for the night. When I watch mellows blow
good time, by getting in a fight. And when I watch a bird free
as the air on which it glides, float lazily out of sight.

Prisons are made to punish for wrongs, and to make wrong
thinking minds well. But rarely do I see rehabilitative
programs offered. The only thing I see is a man made hell.
The M.D.O.C. gets approximately twenty plus grand for me,
from
the state each year. As they do for each one like me, or
that's what I hear. With an incentive like that, no wonder
they don't like to let us go. Just keep on packing us away,
in row after row. They store us in a human warehouse, lock it
and keep the key. Lord, I was made for better things.
Please see it in your heart to release me,
Into the land of the free!

—*Larry Kapp*

War And Peace

Peace is what all people want
War to people haunt peace is good
war is hate
It is when two sides test their fate
Peace is freedom of choice for people in this world
War has its criminals war has its strategy and war has its
own wits when it strikes, it destroys peace bit after bits
Peace is weakened, therefore it has died
Bloodshed and casualty is spread over land
Because war has used its fire power far and wide
Peace cries in need of help
War laughs because he has won
Fascism is form of war which caused depression
Germany, Russia, Korea, Viet Nam, and Japan succumbed to
   this power as an obsession
As you can see war is not worth having lives lost
The people of Somalia, Bosnia, and much of the world
   grew into famine and death, as a result of its cost

—*Silas McArthur*

The Ride

Small black hairs across your chest
Warm moist lips upon my breast
Tender touches, caressing hands
Walking onto lovers land
Long wet kisses filled with passion
Each one's tongue giving the others a thrashing
Heart to heart, skin to skin
Pouring with sweat
Dreams from within
Sliding in and out
Feeling so good you want to shout
Then your body starts to tingle
All your cells each one single
Pressing, throbbing from inside
Slowly, slowly you end your ride.

—*Christina DeRamus*

Looking Inward

Underneath, hidden behind a smile
Was a guy who could care less about the latest style.
Appearances are misleading,
His making him out to be slow.
Yet the real man inside was one we'll never fully know.
He had such great potential,
Yet he was always playing the part of the fool.
A comedian, he could very well be,
But the reason for his laughter
Was to hide and escape from reality.
Take notice, encourage, and lend a hand.
For he who is truly special, is the ordinary man.

—*Erin Nystrem*

Two Sons

My first son's death
was a sudden amputation.
I awoke to find my leg removed,
cast aside to become a pale, withered waste.
What remained of me struggled to balance.

I heard his sturdy strains of "High Hopes"
and the rhythmic thumping of his ball
against the garage door, my mouth opening
to scold him for ruining the paint.
I felt a burning, aching where my leg had been.
I caught the phantom limb peeking around the corner at me.

My second son's life
has been a stumbling, stammering effort.
Born blue, tiny, twisted,
fit only for slaughter, had he been a pig on my father's farm.
He, too, is part of me, like an arm stricken with spasms.

I have held his body, shaken by classmates' teasing,
observed his fumbling fingers struggle with shoelaces.
I have watched him become an awkward man.
I have wished my arm had been lost instead of my leg.

—*Kristen Kirwan*

Dorothy's Garden

In busy maintenance of my middling provision, her garden
was cared for and trimmed with precision. Each day I would pass
in revered amazement The Lady's exhibit to all how her days
went.
One day I met her as she caught me staring: "My name is
Dorothy, should I be so daring." And so we conversed of the
hours she labored; I ashamed at my ignorance of the language she
favored.
How my embarrassment must have shown through! I stood
befuddled not knowing Rose from Rue. "Thus goes the way of
many," was her despondent reply. Then she gave me a cutting
of my very own to try. The farmer and botanist working together:
"What if," I said "Come spells of bad weather?" Dorothy
then laughed at my hesitation, my interest entangled in her
presentation.
An erudite view from which I ne'er before took notice, for on
closer inspection awaited quite a bonus! "Look inside thepetal."
My imagination ran wild, my sentiments not touched so since
I was a child.
   "All you can do when leaves grow the wrong way
  Is turn the pot around and Change the angle of the day."
    In Dorothy's garden one will not see
      leaves or dry soil—
      Only fresh blooms...and me!

—*James Wineland*

What If .....

What if the sunlight, that warms us by day,
Was covered by darkness, forever to stay.
the stars that once shined, the moonlights pale ray,
Now forever forgotten, now faded away.

No more would we see, the sun rise at dawn.
The air would be hushed, to the birds morning song.
The trees would stand naked, no fruit to adorn,
Now just a bleak shadow, a great lifeless form.

No more would the flowers, burst into bloom,
The earth would be darkened, and filled with cold gloom.
The waters once teaming, with life of all kinds,
Now just a dim memory, in the depths of our minds.

No more would the splendor, of the sunset be met,
The vibrancy of color, we now must forget.
The artist's fine palette, turned muddy and grey,
Now sonnets of poets, rhyme in somber dismay.

What if a glimmer, of pure light would shine through,
Returning the beauty, of good things we once knew.
the earth dressed in splendor, rejoiced in all nations,
Now with loving forgiveness, God restores His creations.

—*Alice Perzigian*

Art

As I sit by my thoughts I consider Art's many disguises, Art
was once all seduction turning sorrow soulful the moment
eternal, tricky emancipation from each tier of loneliness,
Art lifted the road angels melting ahead, god fading in the
dimming mirror, Art said sanctuary naked and new in a vacuum
for
madness, my dear Art you were all skies and seas for the
closed castle door.

I tried to leave Art when I met he,r Art was a distant lie
she the true sunrise.

When the night awoke our mislead day, Art returned from never
gone, loud and luring to the exit, tempting futures with fabrics
of the past, Art screamed collection of all that was in a
filtered starry song for constant dawn.

As I sort out the real and unreal upon art's demand I think
of young art as a curious curse embracing pity and wonder
in a trampoline universe.

—*Ken Janjigian*

Inner-City U.S.A

Welcome to Inner-City, U.S.A.
Washington, Baltimore, New York, or L.A.
Naming cities can go on and on
Isn't it a shame the list is so long
Same old picture as you travel down the street
Drug needles everywhere, lying by our feet
Please don't run away and leave us behind
Everyone else already has, to a place they describe as very fine
Don't worry that fine place will not last too much longer
Our problem will also be yours before you have time to ponder
Fatherless sons, each with his own gun
Being killed off while they're still young
Teenage girls who are pregnant
No money for their babies not even one cent
Bullets flying everywhere, many times inside
Having us feel hopeless with no where to hide
Stoves, put in our homes as an apparatus to cook our meat
Now serves a second purpose of being our only source of heat
You'll probably leave, calling us a wild zoo
Why don't you help us, we live in America too?

—*Dedrick Henry*

Love

Kill, hate, defame, inflame, scar, maim, cripple,
    waste, smother; it does to living beings.
    You me, him, her, she, it knows. Bastard
        bitch a product of talk; sharing a
        mind that music balks.

    In a word...happiness, in an instant despair.
Love is you, me, them, he, she, it, they and ours...
        but mostly mine!
    A one-eyed Jack of time. Of are not's,
        of mistakes, of tears and years.

        Love will we never have!
You're a tinsel! a careless, thoughtless fleeting...
    until one day you turn deep-rooted, real,
    hard and unchanging in the depths of the soul.

        Flaunt us now oh priceless one!
        kill our dreams! teach us to live!
        Help us and our hearts will melt
        in the wonder of our affliction...Love
        —*Jim DeFeo*

"Questions Four"

"Do you know the agony that is ever mine,
Watching, ever watching, as he sits and sifts the sands
   of endless time?
Do you know the value of smile upon his face
That fleeting glimpse of cherubic grace?
Do you know how much I'd love to hear
Childish chatter falling on my bended ear?
Do you know how much I'd love to see
That lad come racing up to me,
When I call out to him to come in?

If you knew—the answer to—these questions four,
You'd never more—wonder why—I sometimes cry,
When I'm alone—in the silence of my home,—hoping for—
Nothing more—than to hear and see—him truly comprehending
   me.
Then you'd know—why I love him so,
And why I ask—that you help me in the task
Of raising him—for some nobler thing.
Interweaving the gossamer strands—of the fabric of his
   life—for the Maker of the sands!
      —*Lenore M. Lemire*

A Hard Day's Work Ahead

A dog lays close to the edge of the shore,
Watching the clouds slide by.
The last warmth of the day is felt,
Soon to be cold and dry.
A window of stars moves closer,
Followed by another.
Quickly there is silence,
There is nowhere to be cover.
Waiting no longer,
A dog trots away.
Homeward bound but soon to return,
Back to the place a dog will lay.
Rays of light slowly remove the dark,
Then begin to awaken.
The dog suddenly shudders,
As light touches his furry skin.
For many hours and many days,
A dog savors his happiness.
He has his ways,
No different from the rest.
      —*Jim Burkart*

Indiana

Seas of grain in the fields
waving in the winds gentle breath.

Hills with sheep grazing on their tops,
valleys below filled with fresh and tender grass
that is damp from the morning dew,
hillsides speckled with tiny houses.

Beaches with their grains of sand
that sparkle in the sunlight
as if they were rare jewels lying on the ground.

The rolling plains with their wildlife
that can rome freely without harm.

Indiana will always be my home.
    —*Stephanie Roberts*

Untitled

You're someone I thought would be in my life forever. In many ways I thought we were a couple who could conquer anything together. Nothing seems to be going right. All we do is argue and fight. I still love you, don't get me wrong. But will the hurt and pain still last this long. Something tells me you're just a regular guy. So I ask myself "Why?" Catching the tears that run down my face. Makes me feel out of place. I just can't let go, you mean everything to me. My love for you is so very deep. I can't love anyone else, like I love you. It hurts so bad when you say, "I love you too." You've stolen my heart. Even though we are so many miles apart. If you were to forget everything. Please, always remember the three words I truly did mean. They're not words I'd just say. They're not words to just say "Hey." And they're not just words to brighten your day. These words, I hope, mean a lot. I hope you never say, "I just forgot." I thought your love was true to me. When you proposed from your knee. I never thought your love was false, even though your lies put my life to a halt. All I have left to say, is never forget the day. The first time you told me you loved me, and said I'd never go away.
    —*Jennifer Osborne*

Embryo

When an embryo is only 28 days old.
We are positively told;
It has a beating heart,
which is more precious than gold.
And before it gets a life's start,
Doctor becomes judge;
mother becomes jury;
and has the embryo removed,
from her womb, to forever lie in a tomb;
leaving mother without a fret or worry.

It's innocent, without a reasonable doubt.
So what is this really all about?
Making an embryo suffer,
when it hasn't committed a crime.
And when GOD has decided;
this is its life's time.

It's no one's right;
to decide yes or no.
If you conceive,
then let the embryo grow!
    —*Debbie L. Tibbals*

Time Travelers

Infinite is our universe, infinite space time.
We are the time travelers through the gates of our mind.
If you wish to talk to the future, speak to your mind.
Nothing by chance exists in this time.

When we all dream together, our dream becomes real.
So raise up your thoughts, then, power you'll feel.
We will ride the wave, a revolution will stand,
Existence cannot hold us, we are Power God-Man.

You are free to choose the course of your path.
So you are free to feel the power of your wrath.
Say you are Divine Spirit, say you are one with God.
Say it with clarity, watch your world evolve.
The Master of space time and dimension is here,
If you will only look up, love life, and not fear.
—*Roger Fleck*

My Best Friend

My best friend is very dependable
We are very compatible.
She is also very true
She will lift my spirit when I get blue.
It's fun to do lots of things together
I don't think it could get any better.
She seams to always want to be sharing
No matter what the situation, she always caring.
My best friend is very devoted to me
Integrity is her main key.
Our friendship is the best
I know she is always honest.
We share each others thoughts and feelings
It makes life much easier to be dealing.
I am glad that I have a best friend like,
Lisa who exhibits great qualities in our friendship.
—*Rose Mary Hunter*

Memories Of The Future

Remember when
we dreamed of knights
and days had pictures in their clouds?
We rode imaginary horses
and there were such things as ghosts.
We were going to be princesses and concert pianists,
jockies and magicians.
A lifetime Halloween.
As we get older, I've heard, our dreams become more
"realistic."
And I've noticed we're no longer asked
what we want to be when we grow up.
So I'll ask.
Since we're always growing up,
What do you want to be?
—*Diane Hooper*

We Are Indians

We are Indians of the Americas.
We are from different regions,
but we share a history.
Our people have been exploited,
have been robbed of their possessions
and even of their lives in this world.
Conquerors and governments
have tried to break our spirits,
but they have not and will never succeed.
Our heritage gives us strength
to face whatever comes
because we are Indians of the Americas.
—*Beth Hamilton*

Pathway Through Life

As we grow older we should get milder, and we do.
We learn the only things of value are things that are true.
The pride of possessions and joy from success never last,
Failures and disappointments in life, with patience, will pass.

We get weary and tired and loneliness may be our pain;
Yet through all of these trials, we do have so much we can gain.
For a bank of memories and friendships are purer than gold,
So Get Out and Get Active - don't sit 'round just getting old.

We've worked hard to succeed in the challenge before us each day
And faced major and minor decisions constantly along the way.
These choices, whether large or small, will determine our fate,
And with prayer and peace of mind, for judgement we must wait.

We know our precious walk with the Lord is all that will count
As we go forward with anticipation, our spirit begins to mount,
For we know and accept our goal is to be closer to heaven above
And be sheltered from hurt and be wrapped in the Arms of His Love.
—*Rebecca E. Milner*

"Fall" From Grace

For those of us - not of summer ambience,
We look to autumn as a renaissance.
We patiently await the settings of September,
the occasions of October, and even the no's of November.
But the calendar that signals a harvest moon
alerts the young at heart, that it's time to re-une.
Soon we'll meet behind that ivied wall
to relate tales ere told and tall.
We'll reminisce and of course, insist with glee
how those who came after didn't subsist as we.
But will we forsake our stake in heaven
when we break bread with our brethren?
For to oft repeat a fib is forbidden -
even the polite glib - "you look great - no kiddin!!"
—*Louis J. Durante*

Preserve Our Earth

Earth is our planet and this is where we live.
We must contribute to our world, conserve and give.
We have to wish for the best and hope that it lasts;
If we don't preserve it it'll be our past.

The waters are polluted, our air is dirty,
The forests are falling and earth's no longer pretty.
It's time to start and save our home
Or there'll be nothing left - including the ozone.

Plant a tree, recycle a can,
Instead of air conditioners, use a fan.
This saves our ozone and earth as well,
We'll live a lot longer and have much to tell.

We know it's dying, but there is a cure
And we're starting to care much more than before.
This is the earth about which I write, and
Together we must join and start the fight.

Our future generations will lose their chance
To live their life and sing and dance.
It's now up to us to save it for them
As our ancestors did to preserve it since then.
—*Renee D. Forkin*

He Said

That the coldness would hurt, not me.
We must work hard for all we earn; right he was.
Through a slurred tone everyone obey me; they didn't.
Seek and you will find; I did not.
I'll hold you, but keep you I cannot; I left.
Awful, so many believe that he was; did they not know?
Caring his eyes, hard-hitting his hands; they did not know
That shadows follow you forever;
He never glanced upon clear and straight sunlight.
Never could I understand his voice,
So cold today, warm yesterday.
I left.

—*Julie Thompson*

When We Were Boys

When we were boys, we had plenty of toys
We played until our hearts content
Never knowing how our time would be spent

We'd always wage a war or two
Not thinking that it might come true

Now time has quickly past
We have grown up at last

There is no time for silly games to play
For it's different world we live in today

This war I'm in now, is different somehow
For there's real bullets and real guns
To shoot real boys not make-believe ones

It makes me sick to play this deadly game
To kill a boy, am I to blame?

Why must this be can't anyone see
What this war is doing to you and to me?

My mind goes back to when we were boys
And we'd play with our toys

We'd fight and die, rise, fight and die again—
Oh, God why can't it be that way again

—*R. A. Stout*

Playing Children

When we were children happy and gay
We roamed the meadow as we played
Picking wild flowers, bouquets galore
Then watch them float, from the river bank shore

Oh it was fun to sit down awhile, and look at
Gods creation, that we could see for miles
Some cattle were grazing peacefully near by
While squirrels were scampering on the tree tops high

Some fish were making circles, as they basked in the sun
While others were swimming, having lots of fun
The sun was making shadows, that made the water gleam
Like a million little diamonds all in one stream

The owl gave a hoot in the hollow tree near by
Letting us know evening was drawing nigh
As we traveled homeward, we saw the evening star
We made a wish and said, "Oh, God, how wonderful you are."

—*Arlene Samec*

The Shame

The wind, it whispers through the grass.
We sadly remember our shameful past.

A sacred species we savagely slew,

Wild and free, they roamed the Plains,
A cruel and wasteful thing to do.
Like sky and earth and land and rain.

The beasts, they were the People's way,
But the way was lost, the people stray.

Rotting carcass in the sun now lies,
The people ponder, sage and wise.

The gift of Nature the people knew,
But we, the Pale Ones, had no clue.

The sun bleached bone reminds us all,
To respect our Earth, lest we, too, fall

—*Bethany Miller*

The Bastard

Over the moon to the mountain of green
　We searched for what could not be
All that was possible, and due, but never seen
　Was already in you and me.

Once was a time we hit on, but spurned
　Knowing what mind can't remember
Come to me, the abstract we learned
　Owe me the tense and the gender.

Come to me, the passion, the pain
　Come, if nothing but sorrow
I'll bask in our dross and treasure the strain
　And pray for as much tomorrow.

What made us happy now makes us mourn
　We spawned what we could not parent
We found the bastard was never born
　Our agony owns us inerrant.

I've lived in limbo and lost all link
　To reality, or even false hope
Of higher intentions I weary to think
　So content myself to but cope.

—*David A. Rossiter*

'The New Year is Here'

The New Year is, we all say so
　we start all over, be friendly as we go.
We greet the ones, who'll be new to all
　It won't even matter, if they've short or tall
We'll hope for the best, and make things right
　Give thanks to our lord in, prayers at night
We'll wish you well and much happiness you see
　Along with good health in the year to be
Let's not forget success, prosperity and joy to you
　As you go through the year with memories too
We'll send this message to all far and near
　And all will know, the new year is here.

—*B. J. Hamilton*

When Mama Had The Flu

Daddy and us kids we all had the flu,
We was a pretty sick bunch, I'm tellin' you.
Mom took care of the four of us, and never made a bit of fuss.
She put us all in our beds, put cold cloths on our heads.
Get hot water bottles for our feet,
The way she handled us you never saw the beat.
She rubbed our backs and carried us trays,
Went up and down stairs a dozen a day.
She never complained, no sir; not her,
Every few hours she'd take our temperature
When we was really bad, she'd sit up all night,
Sit and crochet, with just a little light.
By the time we was well again,
Mom had grown pale and thin. Her cheeks was flushed.
  "A little fever I was told." Then one day she passed out cold. Daddy said," you've got the flu."
"Now I'll tell you what to do." "Doctor yourself and go to bed." "Don't forget to put a cold cloth on your head."
"Be sure to take your temperature."
"Take care of yourself, and you'll be all right I'm sure".
—*Harriett R. Wilson*

The Heart of Aids

Through all the weathered times we've spent, you would think we would get a break. But we don't always get the chance to follow out our fate.

The time we had was extra precious it meant a lot to me, when you were feeling down and out and fought to barely breath.

If I could hold you close to me and never let you go, I would fight all your pain and never let it show.

What I feel the most right now are angry tears of love,
but at the same time I hope and pray there is a God above.

And if there were than I would say take him now he's your's
for every girl and boy please help us find a cure.

So if you're tired and weak my love I will understand, this fight was fought through thick and thin, so until we meet again.....
—*Debra Viale*

Shorewise

Aerial intelligentsia patrol with surefooted
webbed skill
surveying each wavespill with unblinking eye
horizons defined

Ebb and flow duality expressed motion carried
clearing the sandtable a salty smorgasbord
successively sprinkled
brief glimpses affording a feast

Flites suspended by ground conditions
beaked prospectors search customlike
prodding winning losing
salt soaked trophies

Beach denizens silhouette the sky
Low flying now resumed with lonesome cry
Fresh pools remain tidefilled
measured mapping, small-fry caught napping
birdlife on the edge...
—*Walt Glendinning*

Nature's Balance

From asphalt jungles in this modern day and age
  We're bombarded with ideas left and right
For some boycotting meat and fur is now the rage
  This kindness to the animals should relieve their plight.

A noble thought, but it contains a serious flaw
  They don't consider Nature's Balance in this plan
You don't mess with Mother Nature and Her Law
  Which applies with equal force to beast or man.

All kinds of life are classified as predator or prey
  As idealists a thing we oft forget
The fawn will feed the coyote, no matter what they say
  Was thus from the beginning and that way yet.

Still, from the Concrete Canyons and their supermarket caves
  Where Nature's bounty lies profusely on the shelves
The meat boycotter raves about the animals he saves
  In his mind the lower forms are like ourselves.

But by our brain—our profound thought—from them we separate
The conscience trip, hate, guilt, these and many more
A difference vast by nature cast, as these thoughts illustrate
  We plan and plot and 'tis our lot to be top predator.
—*John Robertson*

Untitled

I saw your eyes first
  Were they blue...green...grey?
They moved around me like an artist
  surrounding me till I was in another universe.
I laughed and you laughed.
How gentle you were how playful too!
  I liked that but I had not yet seen you.

We danced on the beach, in our universes in our dreams

Then you reached across time and touched me
                with what?
At first I did not know——
  I looked, not with human eyes, but with my being
and then the truth was there...
You touched me with your innocence.
                Thank You
—*Marlo Kimmel*

Keeping Touch

I've known you all my life
We've been through thick and thin.
Just when you think it's over
It's ready to begin.

I miss the talks we used to have,
I miss the fun, I miss the laughs.
All the fun we've ever had can be ours again.

Recently I've been far away and I often think of you,
Getting caught up in your own little world is an easy thing to do.

Don't think that I have forgotten you,
Don't think that I ever could.
Although I feel I've let you down,
I never thought I would.

All these classes we have to take
That will prepare us for a career.
They do not teach us about real life,
Or how to deal with that fear.

I love you and I'm here for you, as always and forever.
I need your love and friendship, as an eagle needs a feather.
—*Terence F. Powell Jr.*

To Live Is You...

Over the past seven years, you've meant the world to me,
We've created so many memories to last for eternity.

You've helped me mature in plenty of ways,
Being able to share with you so many days.

To see you smile is the joy of my heart,
For this I wake each day welcoming a new start.

For to love is one thing, but to be loved is far more,
Thru our very special love, I could never be poor.

Thirty seconds of being loved by such a man as you,
Is more precious than life itself and a real dream come true.

One major desire is to make you a happy man,
To return the favor and provide an assuring hand.

The ability to love is wonderful—it has made me whole,
By your teachings from none other than your soul.

I give thanks to God for blessing me with you,
For until we met, I had not lived nor knew how to.

If I am not allowed to share with you a tomorrow,
Being loved as you've loved me, leaves me without sorrow.

For to love is to live...And I have truly lived.
—*Telitha Taylor-Torrence*

This Universe Of Ours

See the moon, the sun, the planets, the stars;
What an interesting sight this universe of ours.
As you look at the moon, as you look at the sun;
Does it make you wonder why all this was done?
Oh, the sun, how it warms us, how it brightens our day;
'Til the moon takes its place, in its own special way.
Each star has its purpose, each star has its place;
See them twinkling above us, each showing their face.
Oh, look, there's Jupiter, there's Saturn and Mars;
They, too, are out there, accompanying the stars.
It now makes me wonder, was there a purpose, a plan;
A part of this universe that we can't understand?
If all these great things, by God were created;
Who knows what's out there, to whom we're related?
—*Linda Johnson*

Success

Success.
What does it mean?
Is it fulfilling your true dreams?
Big or small they're your future,
To any heartache they're the cure.
In dreamers eyes you see the gleam,
Dreams are a part of the life of a teen.
Most popular; most beautiful; homecoming queen;
To many that's the success of life.
To some it's straight A's, hard work and strife.
Inside the heart, outside the body, and all around
Success is not just who's Harvard bound.
Success is fulfilling ambition of any kind.
On and On we really find,
Success isn't set as a public goal, but
It's an individual's will and way
To be able to say and believe in their mind,
"I HAVE A DREAM!"
—*Kimberly Smith*

Chocolate Butterfly

Peaceful, I've noticed when you're asleep;
What happiness do you dream?
I would imagine visions of loveliness as
lovely as yourself.

Delicate as you lay while your soul floats
on the wings of a butterfly, traveling to
different romantic stops of the mind.
You hunger and thirst for the sweetest of nectars;
The strongest romance, the deepest love.

Like the butterfly, land on me gently;
Pierce my heart and drain me, my love
is yours for the taking.
—*Bobby Samuels*

What If Words Unspoken

What if Words Unspoken could have mended a broken heart?
What if Words Unspoken could put you in the light and take you
   from the dark?
What if Words Unspoken could have made someone else's life put
   to right?
What if Words Unspoken could have made someone smile or soar
   like a kite?
What if Words Unspoken could have changed the world?
What if Words Unspoken could take away the turmoil?
What if Words Unspoken could change the gaps between our kids?
What if Words Unspoken could have taken a chance, and
   not putting on our brakes coming to a skid.
What if Words Unspoken could say what needs to be said;
   BECAUSE
Words Unspoken are just thoughts in our heads.
Words Unspoken can never be heard.
Unless you open your heart and let out the words.
—*Janice M. Penson*

Small Rooms In My Mind

There are small rooms in my mind filled with emotion.
What is in them, I have a notion.

Emotions I try to keep locked inside
Anger and sadness I feel I must hide.

At times when a room can't contain anymore
The emotion slips out under the door.

Anger finds its way to my lips
With words and reactions I must submit.

Sadness finds its way to my eyes
With tears and with questions, is it a secret or lies?

The answers, along with a paralyzing fear
Are locked in a small room far from here.

Knocking down the walls is not easily done
But it must be to make all my small rooms become one.
—*Selma Brady*

Untitled

In a velvet bubble made of glass I rest
where equilibrium does not exist
poisonous fog rolls in
penetrating the vulnerable skin
forever a prisoner within
strangled by guilt child of sin
innocence cherished innocence lost
love and happiness come at a dear cost
fooled into believing that anything will change
for velvet crushes and glass breaks
and stability is out of range.
—*Sylvia Szubielski*

"The Common Bond"

What is it that we so often strive for
   What is our common bond
What is it that we can't describe
   But of which we are so fond

What is the purpose of so many of our deeds
   What are we trying to win
And what is it that can be so addictive
   That we try to redeem it again

What is it that proves words can do harm
   That the heart too can break
What is it that causes anger to collapse
   That diminishes all the hate

What is the object of so many stories
   What is the writer's dream
What lies behind the words they form
   What makes our eyes so gleam

What is it that we could never conquer
   As it spears us from above
It is the strand that can so bind us
   It is our want for love
     —*Michelle Phillips*

God Bless The Children

God bless the children, everyone
What makes them do the things they've done?
Is it the violence on T.V.?
Is it what's taught by you and me?
We'd better find the answer fast
Or this generation just won't last
The situation is sad, but true -
Let's get together, me and you -
And teach them love, right from the start -
To save a lot of broken hearts -
A life so precious, maybe saved
The road to peace, it must paved -
By all of us who really care.
Reach out your hand -
A child is there!
    —*Shirley Bloom*

If Men Dared

If men dared to do,
   What men dare to dream,
     Within this life's web-patterned scheme-

To build a world
   Of love and peace-
     Where wars and hatred finally cease-

Where pains and sorrows
   No more are borne
     By the life drained shoulders of the worn-

Where verses are sung
   And hopes are read-
     Where actualizable visions dwell in each head-

This world would be
   As never before-
     There'd be no need of that distant shore-

If men dared to do,
   What men dare to dream,
     Within this life's web-patterned scheme.
    —*Deene A. Webster*

Victor

Silently, softly, she sighed for what once was,
   What might have been.
The dream she'd dreamed now brought her pain.

Sadly, surreptitiously, she sobbed for love never returned,
   For promises never kept
And years spent for naught; yet all was not lost.

Patiently, prayerfully, pleading for what he would not give,
   She grew through loving,
For loving is its own reward and patience comes by waiting.

Painfully practicing principles throughout the passing years,
   Looking to the Presence deep within,
Gave her strength to face what finally came to pass.

Deserted, demeaned, devastated, yet with head held high,
   She walked away,
Surrendering it all once again to God.

Firm faith forever fashioned her response, yes, even now.
   No victim, she with heavy heart
Faced forward and, with gratitude to God, smiled.
    —*Beverly Holmes*

Revelation

What utterance of mine will prove I care?
What moving deed will say to you "I die"?
Why die? Because my love's of vintage rare,
Audacious, yet of quality most shy.
To see you pass each day, head bowed in thought,
My being leaps to aid you in your strain.
Entreat my help, dear soul, I do exhort.
Abashed, I cannot proffer; I'm in chain.
Do come to me for succor, sweet, I pray.
I'll 'suage your grief and press you to my heart
For two can carry burdens well, they say,
And brace the pains that men to life impart.

Your eyes meet mine; I reel - and then I hear,
"You are my pain so poignant, love, I fear."
    —*Theresa Kocsis*

Good-bye

Do you ever sit and wonder
   What tomorrow will bring?
Do you ever look out a window
   And see birds fly and sing?

Have you ever been through
   What I am going through?
It hurts me so much
   Did it hurt you like this too?

Have you ever loved so much
   It was so hard to say good-bye?
I did,
   And if you haven't, you wouldn't want to try…
    —*Torrie L. Wells*

Beginning And End

When we open our eyes in the morning
we see the beginning.
When we close our eyes at night
we look for the ending.
Never knowing what lies ahead
we live each today as if it were tomorrow,
and we live each tomorrow as if were today.
When the end finally reaches
no one knows the true you but you,
and the outcome is then evident and true.
    —*Tara Parker*

Wheels (For Chris)

Like a flock of birds descending,
Wheels, young lives defending,
Slipping silently up the lane.

In a second they're gone again.
No hurting ears, can't explain.
Soon they are back in the glen,
One, two, three, four, five, six,

Not one is pulling tricks.
No lights, no noise, just gliding
Quietly, all those boys
Are into these new, big toys.

Zipping up the driveway,
Sliding back down.
Just a flicker of light to go to town.
No tires squealing, no rubber laid.

No reason for any to be afraid.
These are great kids to trust to our world.
Fine times too,
Without any girls.
—Anne M. Blanchard

"A Wedding Prayer"

Forever is just a word, that today is seldom heard.
When a true love you do find,
Please take the time to be kind.
At this time in your life.
As you swear to be forever husband and wife.
Take to your heart, all the riches God has to impart.
Cleave only to each other,
Do not become only constant bother.
Never close your eyes, to the Devil in disguise.
He would be there waiting, to see you hesitating.
Do the right thing
And make your heart and soul sing.
There's no truer love found in time
For it knows no boundaries and will forever rhyme.
You will find your love to be pure,
As you work together to be sure.
Taking time to pray.
At the end of each and every day.
—Dottie Sue Pollard

"The Colors Of Life"

I use colors to paint my life,
When blue was there, there was little strife,
The mother of three and a pretty good wife,
That was the phase of blue in my life.

Then one day, my husband did stray,
And the blue was slowly fading away.
Along went the kids, and my heart felt rage,
Then red was ready to enter its stage.

Red brought out an independent soul,
Who'd hid behind fears of yesterdays' toll,
With it came strength, and the will to live,
To wipe away tears, and learn to forgive.

Then green brought healing to a shattered heart,
A little good luck, and a brand new start.
And purple brought spiritual guidance to me,
It opened my eyes and allowed me to see.

So it doesn't much matter what colors we use,
For we all paint our live's with different hues,
So be an artist, learn to blend and be wise,
For all of these colors are right before our eyes!.
—Debi Eve Burge

Now And Forever

Where did you come from? I had no thought of you.
When did you slip into the crevice
That was in my heart?

Without question, you came to me. Gigantic, overwhelming,
colossal. Your presence covered my spirit with a deep sense
of profound love.

A new perception of caring and a dynamic definition of
always have taken hold of my life.
How did you know?

From out of the blue you came.
With an uncanny lack of anxiety,
I gave my heart, full, and complete.

You receive my passion,
And molded it with yours.
You pressed out hearts and made one.
The full measure is what you gave.

Though dreams include massive shores,
The miracle of the moment is clearly
The reality that God allowed.
Two hearts that beat as one, now and forever.
—N. Patricia Yarborough

Rights

It was quite shocking on that day—let's call it June 6, 2066-,
When Dr.—for the sake of not preserving his name— Seuss,
Found that due to certain lesions in the brain, which contained
The evolutionary qualities of anger, violence, and rage,
actually determined the horrible truth that white and black
people's hatred for each other was innate and there was nothing
one could do about it. It just had to be accepted that Dr.
Seuss was right. So, the races decided that the next logical
step would have to be war. Each race took stock, then the
planes began to soar. It didn't take much time until each side
got it hands on an atom-neutron-nuclear bomb and exploded it in
each other's faces taking all the remaining races with them.
Everything, as far as peace and equality were concerned, was
alright. The only remnant remaining of the former civilization
Was a piece of paper buried in a concrete container twenty feet
below the surface of a place once called Washington, D.C. that
Agreed that all men were created equal. Finally, this
document's truth had come into sight and that's what really
counts. Right?
—James M. Pishock, Jr.

The Journey Of The Magi

A star above has shown the way
To kings afar who seek its light.
They travel far across the land
With respite near in stable sight.

There they find a maiden with a child
Who smiles to greet their near approach
And holds her child in fond embrace.

The lamb and oxen gather round
The maiden and the little child.
The kings draw near the ox and lamb
To see the child they guard so dear.

The light they sought, they now have found
Not in the star which shines above
But in this manger with God's Love.
—Paul A. Trouve

Lets You Down

When everybody lets you down,
   When everyone says one thing and does something else,
     When other's motives appear questionable,
       He turns the tide.

Rewards you with kindness, wiping your unquenchable tears,
   Renders tender generosity, a healing balm,
     Bends over backwards by human standards,
       Gives and gave His all for and to you.

When everyone wants what they covet,
   Right now!—immediately—stand on your head,
     At not a moment's notice, satisfy their whim,
       And when you did their will, they rack you over coals.

He cools the intense anguish with living water,
   Soothes your parched soul with peace like a river,
     Wraps a shepherd's cloak snugly around you.
       Takes all your burdens and cares to His bosom.

He lifts you to a heavenly loft miraculously.
   Your balloon rises above every circumstance.
     His bullet proof shield wards off fired darts.
       You're untouched by man's inhumanity to man.
   —*Kathryn Ann Harris McCormick*

Changes

My daughter came to me one day
   when feelings interrupted play.
Her voice was tearful, tense, and strange.
   "Mom, I feel sad. I hate this change!"

With aching heart and trembling voice,
   I said, "My dear, we had no choice.
I know how difficult this has been.
   It'll be all right, but I can't say when."

I thought of how things once had been,
   of our lovely home and many friends.
The perfect life; the American dream;
   but things are not always what they seem.

I remembered things that walls could hide,
   and I felt a little better inside
because I'd found the strength to try
   to make a new start for my kids and I.

Now we have a new life, new home, new friends.
   Adjusting is hard! It never ends.
But things look brighter every day.
   I knew they would. Change works that way.
   —*Carol Burdick*

Tribute

A quick and sudden rage goes through my body,
when I encounter instances when my mother won't allow me to
do for her. I see her struggling to perform certain task;
But she won't allow me to intervene; she just doesn't
realize that, it's my way of honoring her and that is what I'm here for.
Instead, well...I watch as she carries on.
Oh, for sure my mother is strong and capable;
She carries her burdens in the curve of her hips,
Her pain is cemented in her huge brown knees.
She is reminded of past and present disappointments in the
rubbing together of her big thighs as she walks, sits and stops
The meat of her life is hanging from her arms and it's in the
folds of her stomach; her body betrayed her like mines did to
me and now she has to have a hysterectomy.
There is no fear or worry in her eyes,
Won't even hear it in her voice;
All of her joy, pain and will to survive can be found on her
hips and on her thighs.
   —*Natalie Jones*

"A Love Letter"

From the moment of our beginning
When I heard your very first cry,
While checking ten toes, ten fingers
To singing countless lullabies.

Reality hinged on incredible
How blessed to be chosen the one,
To take part in creating the miracle
Of you, my beloved son.

Such a cute and cuddly baby
Yet quite an independent boy,
Many hours were spent speculating
What's to become of this bundle of joy?

Toy soldiers gave way to keyboards
My child grew to a handsome young man,
Though you're on your own, I feel calmly assured
You will always be held in God's hands.

And now that the blessing of children
Is passed on and created anew,
Take the time to enjoy each miracle
They're the very best part of you.
   —*Bonnie T. Dennis*

Do You Think About Me?

     I often think of you
      When I wake up at night
    During all hours of the day
And at times when I think about you
   I wonder do you think about me

      I count the days
     Until I see you again
      During those days
     And sometimes nights
   I wonder if you do too

     I think about the night
      You asked me to dance
During the dance when you softly kissed
And then the times after when you kissed again
    I wonder do you think about this

     I cried when you said goodbye
      But now I am over you
   During the time we've been apart
And the last few times we were together
   I found out that you do think about me
   —*Sheena Humbird*

The Happy Man

I mind a time when I was young,
When I was very young.
The bread was warm, the house smelled good,
And my mother minded me.

I mind a time when I was young,
When the woods ran green and free.
The tides rolled in, the nights ran out
And I was minding me.

I mind a time when I was young,
When I was quick and free.
I loved you then, I love you yet
And I am minding thee.

When I am old, I'll mind these times
And never old will be;
For love is youth and youth is thee
And you are minding me.
   —*F. A. Tyce*

Time

Time is like a way of life.
When it passes through a story of a life.
Amazing! How time can pass without a sign.
How quietly it strikes upon you and your mind,
like a cat trying to attack its prey.
With its prey not knowing its coming,
trying to keep the good memories in,
fighting to not remember the bad ones.
Hoping not bring the evil out of us,
but, to keep our goodness in our minds.
How can we describe time?
Just a spirit or thing that float in our minds,
or is it a punishment when we been bad.
We are trying to escape,
from our own torture in our minds.
Wondering whether it is our friend or foe.
We will never fully know,
but, our venture of life must continue
to seek, find, and explore unknown knowledge
and realize that time will never disappear.
—*Michael Sullins*

Why Does Love Hurt

Why does love hurt...
When it seems that everything is going great,
and you feel that you've met your mate...

You've spent so much, time together figuring out
the right from wrong, the bad and the good...
The last thing in your mind would be questions not understood..

Seasons change and for every reason was meant to be,
and the last thing you'd expect was your love to decease....

It hurts inside, many nights you cry
and you never think you'll say goodbye....
And for many nights you'll set and think that love comes
and goes like a million blinks......
—*NeGre' M. McKenney*

An Ode To Wrigley Field

Once upon a flickering time ago,
When life was simpler than what we know,
There stood an edifice facing the lake
That has withstood time, fire, and quake.

How would the days of my summers gone by,
Were it not for this home of the wind-blown fly?
Where bounding joy combines with agonizing despair
On the whims of the winds in the summer air.

For all of us a time must come, to succumb
To the roll of the incessant, everlasting drum.
It is now that I muse, in my life's seventh inning,
And ponder if "forever" really means a new beginning!!

When the roll of that drum says that my time has come
and I'm thrown out at home, after my three-base run,
I'll scan the skies with my dimming eyes, and say "Dear God,
let me rest forever by the park with the natural sod."

Those days of spring, summer and fall
Made rich by the call, "Let's play ball,"
Will endure beyond the last breath that I ever take...
Where the wind blows fly-balls high above the lake.
—*Irv Hickey*

Reasons Why

It's the tender heart, that sees no rest.
When memories arise, that time has passed.

The time of years, will heal the pain.
But memories that warm the soul remain.

It's the song, that brings, a tear to eye.
And quiet times, with a gentle sigh.

And these, a few, of the reasons why.
My love for you, shall never die.

So be assured, I'll do my best.
That this heart of mine,
Shall see no rest.
—*Charles Lake*

If Old Glory Could Speak

I bought an American flag today,
   When raised, what a sight to see!
If it, could speak, what would it say?
   Oh, what tales would it tell to me!

It could tell me how it feels,
   As stars and stripes from a flagpole unfurled;
Or to be gallantly carried into battle
   Throughout the history of the world.

It could tell me how it feels,
   Raised in a battle where victory was earned.
Oh, the shame it must surely endure
   When trampled, desecrated, or burned!

It could tell me how it feels,
   Draped over a coffin on its way to a grave;
Or folded and given to a loved one
   In honor of that one so brave!

It could tell me how it feels,
   To be Old Glory waving steadfastly there;
And to know its image is engraved
   On the hearts of Americans everywhere!!
—*Ike W. Crabtree*

When School Books Appear

Now kids never fear,
When school books appear,
You'll be held as a prisoner of sorts;
You'll see there are masses
Of kids in your classes,
And adults who like to watch sports.

When Thanksgiving arrives,
You're sure to survive
'Til Christmas, and then see the New Year.
Winter will pass,
Then you and your class
Will soon find that summer is here.

With baseball and hoops,
And airplanes that loop,
You'll enjoy this great time of the year.
So now have some fun,
For when summer is done,
It's time for the books to appear.
—*Howard L. Becton Sr.*

"The Chill Comes..."

The chill comes...
When she sends you away with your heart in pieces...

The chill comes...
When no one wants to share your heart or thoughts...

The chill comes...
When you try to look in her eyes, and she turns away...

The chill comes...
When you cry and your tears fall and dry without her notice...

The chill comes...
Late at night when you feel truly alone and no one can know...

The chill comes...
At the wrong time...

The chill comes...
When a lonely painful death shadows your heart...

The chill comes...
When you feel the cold of your empty hands and think of her...

The chill comes...
Because she isn't there.
—*Joe Tzortzinis*

Camille '69

I remember well the horror, of a night not long ago,
When the children all were quiet, and the minutes passed so slow. When at each sound men would shiver, and women wished to cry, 'cause they knew that if the walls came down, together they would die. At 8 the wind was calm, but brisk, at 10 each shelter full, at 12, Camille brought down the walls, on 23 in one school. 200 mile winds kept up its pace, throughout the entire night, crashing buildings, killing people, flooding homes above water height. Many times the people prayed, alive they wished to be, as the devastating winds increased, fire red sky they could see. At last the morning sunshine came, only to be found, cars and trucks and houses smashed, dead bodies all around. Families looked at piles of boards, here they couldn't stay, graveyards torn from top to bottom, diseases on the way. Many buildings were demolished, many trees uprooted, many people died that night, many people looted. Marshal law now in effect, people's things were scattered, furniture thrown on the street, clothing torn and tattered. People can build buildings and fix things about the same, but many lives paid for the damage and will many times again.
—*Joyce Boyer Schuler*

The Frontier

I always wondered what it was like back then—
When the country was anew-
The people as free as birds.
The sky was a clear light blue,
No smog or haze or even smoke
That grabs our air and makes us choke.

We have no peace in this place.
We fight and fight against each race.
They had their trees, they had their air—
They had animals everywhere.
But the best thing I do miss,
They had the love that we don't share.
—*Robert S. Bowker*

My Dream Day

I dream of a day when I won't have any sorrow or pain.
When the days are cloudy and blue and no rain.
People will laugh and play all through the day.
"What a wonderful, wonderful world this is," they would say.
I dream of a day when there will be no more dying.
Everyone will be truthful and no more lying.
Cocaine and all other drugs of this sort will be wiped away from the earth.
Babies won't have to worry about pain at the date of their birth.
I dream of a day when no one will have anything to fear.
I dream of a day when no one will get drunk off of wine or beer.
I dream of a day when happiness will be the key to life.
And no one will have to worry about any headaches, pain, or strife.
—*Alana Walker*

Concrete And Stone

You can't dance in the summer heat
When the hot black tar sticks to your feet
And the neighbors are fighting it out down the street
And you expect nothing from the people you meet.

As you sit on the back steps mopping your head
Wishing you were somewhere else instead
With a little more money, a little more bread,
You know it's all gone — the life that you've bled.

Your woman is sleeping, the kids have all grown,
And you wonder the worth of the prospects you've shown
When they've slipped through the cracks of the concrete and stone.
(Be it ever so humble, it never was home.)

No, you can't dance in the summer heat
When the hot black tar sticks to your feet
And the neighbors are fighting it out down the street
And you expect nothing from the people you meet.
—*Lynn Marie Craig*

Coming To An End

Spring is the refreshing time of year
When the snows of winter will disappear
And winter lingers with an occasional frost bite
Leaving the morning sparkle with delight
Breathing the beautiful freshness in the air
That leaves behind the winters nightmare
This is something we all look forward to
As the air is crisp with morning dew
Watching the flowers bloom with spring
And the birds nurse on them as they sing
Drinking nectar from their pretty Bouquet
Doing their part for our habitue
This is something we do apprehend
Like the seasons coming to an end.
—*Charles N. Schuety*

Clouds

Cloud's cloud's in the sky,
You look so soft, floating by.
If I hugged, would you evaporate?
Clouds, clouds, in the sky.

Have you ever wanted to touch
a cloud. To feel how soft they look.
Have you ever looked up and seen
The clouds, and notice the shape and size?
Ever wonder how you feel, if for
one day, you were a cloud floating
by? Floating by.
—*Carolyn Wright*

Quickening

In the stark depths of winter,
when the Spirit feels its lowest;
and no hope is seen in the dead trees,
the grey skies and the frozen earth,
it snows.

Snow — the wedding gown of Spring.
Red holly berries fall into that whiteness
Like virgin's blood spilled on newly plowed fields.
Does the earth cry out when we dig our spades into her flesh?
Her mother's love, producing her bounty,
even as we burrow into her flesh.
We feast of her woman's treasures,
children suckling nutrients from her body.

O wise one, sweet maiden, mother,
sustain us with your courage to continue.
—*Patricia Dance*

When They Tell You

When they tell you to work harder
When they tell you to count blessings
When they tell you to listen,
to the clap of one hand,
you listen and think

When they tell you to go with the flow
When they say, "Make it your business to know"
When they shout you have a long way to go,
look down the road and keep on walking

When they tell you you're not important,
remember you are totally unique!
A form who needs the liquid of life,
so your dreams can float on the boat of success
—*Walter Thompson III*

Why?

Why is it that we can't just fly away
When things get to much?

Why is it we can't leave all the disappointments
that happened in life behind?

Why is it that we blame other people
When something goes wrong?

Why is it so many of us choose to
exist than live?

Why is it when we need someone to
understand, nobody has a clue?

Can you find the answers to these questions?
When you do let me know, because I sure can't.
—*Susan Stetson*

Our Angel

We've said good-bye,
We shared our cries,
We faced our fear,
Remember, she's still here.
Her spirit is in each one of us,
We have pictures, letters, and gifts,
We have memories; happy and sad,
Remember her smile, it'll make you glad.
Think of her and your heart will fill
With all her love that she gladly spills.
I picture her flying free,
I am talking about Frannie.
—*Cheryl LaFever*

Looking Back

As I look back on the days before
When things seemed to come with ease,
With time came the openings of many doors
Some of my dreams blew in on a simple breeze.

Taking me places I never thought I would go,
Seeing things I never thought I would see,
Learning new things that I didn't know,
Helping me become the person I always wanted to be.

Looking back I miss when days use to be so simple
The days that no one took for granted.

Today time seems to pass by quickly,
Like never before.
Opportunities pass by with no time to spare
And you're lucky to get one foot in the door.

If you're lucky
You'll get your chance.
Your dreams could all come true
And there's no looking back and no doubtful glance.

What happen to days I used to look back to?
They disappeared right before my eyes.
—*Kathy Dungan*

Hello, Mr. Bell?

Oh, Alexander, did you know what you were starting
When those words you spoke were heard over that wire?
Did you even have a clue as to what this thing could do?
Did you foresee the heights to which man would aspire?
Did it occur to you that life would never be the same
Once mankind could "reach out and touch" one another?
In your vision did you see what it would mean to you and me?
Did you realize the miles our voices would cover?
Once the phone became a fact there was just no turning back

We were committed to a life-style new and wide.
For no matter where we go, we will always - always - know
That there's just no place on earth where we can hide.
If it's debtors that we are, though we travel near and far,
We can rest assured our creditors will find us;
And if creditors we be, to the very same degree,
We can close in on our debtors without fuss.
Communication is the name of this never-ending game -
Keeps the world in constant touch both night and day;
Let us in on all the news - and on everybody's views -
And could we survive without it now? No way!
—*L. Mae Nelson*

Love's Promise

You were there before me like sunshine and flowers
You didn't see me for what seemed like hours
But then you came to me like a breath of magic
My heart was racing, praying the end would not be tragic

But now that you're here, where do we go?
Maybe it's best just to take it slow
When next to you, I need no more
Come on now, there's much to explore

My promise of love is pure and true;
Til we're old and spent, I'd die to be near you.
—*Roberta Jean Flissinger*

Last Night's Dream

Hello, darling, tell me where you went
When you vanished so quickly last night.
I held to you tightly, but couldn't prevent
Your leaving in such hurried flight.

We sat watching fishes, amid a small stream,
With light glimmering through the trees.
The sun left us quickly, or so it did seem,
While we talked in the hush of a soft evening breeze.

Then, darling, you left me
And though I held tight,
You faded so swiftly
From my searching sight.

I looked in that darkness
'Til dark faded away
And the first morning dimness
Announced a new day.

And, now night is returning
And I'll be at the stream
And I will be yearning
For an encore of last night's dream

—*Farolyn Collins*

Friends -

True friends,
When you're down and under the weather
That's who's there
When you need someone to talk to or
just someone to cry with
That's who's there.
When you have friends who listen and
really, really care.
Then your life can never compare.
If you have true friends such as I
Then your world will always seem fair.
Keep your friend with you and close to
your heart,
Cause once you're with them you're never apart.

—*Kaylynn J. Mier*

Through The Years

Ever since I was a little girl you were there,
Whenever I cried you picked me up and dried my
tears,
Through the years, every first day of school I
came home to the questions with the sound of pride
in your voice.
Even now, in the worst times, I see you through
the tears encouraging me to continue...
Mother, I will make you proud, because through
the years I have always looked up to you, and
through the years you have always been here for me.

—*Elizabeth Mekeel*

Dreams Made

Dreams are the nectar of life
without them we wither away
Loosing abstract input
Causing binding threads to unravel
That support our drive and expectations
Of an all too sober and often cruel world
So let us dream of good and true
And make the world better for me and you.

—*Rick Wright*

The Forgotten Land

There is a land called "The Forgotten"
Where forgotten people dwell
They roam the barren soil
Not even their souls left to sell
They have been shoved aside
By loved ones and society
They have little to call their own
But themselves and their dignity
The weak, the aged and those with a disability
Huddled together
Attempting to find a shred of stability
Hod did our world become so heartless
Where is our charity
In search of our quest for power and riches
We've forgotten to share our prosperity
Set sail for "The Forgotten land" when the sun arises
Retrieve our forgotten people
Who can't remember loving surprises
Tomorrow, you too could be in, "The Forgotten land"
Now is the time to open your heart and reach out with your
hand

—*Jean Hunt*

The Journey

Where go ye, little lass
Where go ye with sadness in your eyes
With lips turned down and face a frown
And hither glance to cover your disguise
How sad 'tmust be to carry such a load
What pride makes ye don this crown
T'would be but to ask, to have a hand or shoulder lend
To clear the way, the journey to lessen on the road
Where go ye little lass, or do ye not know
Little I can offer for this is where I chose to stop
Weary I became, and in the winds lost all direction
I can however give ye that which I have learned
To use or discard should it become to heavy
The days are hot, and the nights extremely cold
And the tears into your countenance are burned
Where go ye little lass, be sure ye know
For t'is the journey worth making what we find
Reach into your heart, and trust what ye know is true
If all of the consequence is to be what's left behind
T'is yourself lass your to find, is what's to do

—*Ron Martin*

Soulmates

Eternally one, a peaceful dream world,
Where hurt may be healed by a warm smile.
Companions for life, sharing desire, fear and love
To be shattered by nothing.
Soulmates forever, meeting a core of understanding,
Knowing when one is hurt or lonely.
To be like a rose, dependant on the stem,
The stem dependant upon rich soil.
Circumstance being of no matter,
A caring heart for medicine.
Both care for the other before themselves,
Always a bandage of forgiveness.
Turning to Jesus Christ in times of hurt and happiness,
Eternally blessed for the truth and honesty of their love!

—*Shelbie Snyder*

Old House

Old house all alone in a field,
Where is the merry laughter that once pealed
Through rooms now empty and bare?
Where are those who once lived there?

The gardens once tended; the cool green lawn
Are choked now with weeds; the flowers all gone.
The steps, always swept; the floors so nice
Are now the playground of spiders and mice.

Windows which once shone welcoming light
Now are broken empty eyes without sight.
And the kitchen once full of mouth-watering smells,
Is now as barren and dry as the well.

Oh, if the walls of this house could but speak,
The tales they could tell of the strong and the weak,
Of happy times surprises and celebrations;
Of tragedies, sadness, man's fulminations.

But now its an old house, alone in a field.
Its wall from the elements offer no shield
As rain drops, sunlight, wind-blown dust
Are welcomed by the front door sagging open in rust.
　—*Jane Shiley*

Winter Solstice

The year is drawing to the point again
where shortest day is backed by longest night,
and age-old stories flicker through my mind
of ancient people, huddled 'round the fire site
to celebrate with chants and mystic rite
their expectation of returning light.

I think of revelry and Boar's Head feast,
of candles flaming, wreaths of evergreen,
of midnight masses, promises in word and song
of Life born in the East, returning like the sun.

God, if you are, send me a light
amid the mummery and patent glow,
to give me hope that after bleakest night
spring will return and waken life beneath the snow.
　—*Inge C. (Chris) Hollingsworth*

On Retiring

I have taught in schools by the side of the road,
Where the children of time pass through,
Those who are eager, and those who are shy -
The same as me and you.
Some grasp the knowledge with quick young
　minds,
Some hesitate - and it's up to you
To instill in their hearts a desire to learn,
Then strive to see it through.

Yes, I've taught in schools by the side of the road,
And many a child's passed through,
I've planted some seeds in fertile young minds,
Some seeds that grew and grew,
And though I won't see the harvest
I can only hope and pray,
That those children's lives may be richer
Because of some seeds I've planted along the way.
　—*Dorothy Cressman*

M.I.A. P.O.W.

Where are you, my long lost lover?
Where's the love that we once knew?
Now that all the fighting's over,
Where are you?—Oh where are you?
Are you in some secret work camp,
Or a lonely, wind-swept grave?
Did you die a frightened baby,
Or a soldier bold and brave?

Through the years, your memory haunts me,
And I long for just one word
That would tell me if some stranger
Might have seen, or might have heard,
But the silence is unbroken, and I guess I'll never know,
Through the years, your name unspoken
Still is locked up with the foe,
And they won't release the secret,
For, I guess, it's hard to tell
If your soul has gone to Heaven,
Or, like mine, is still in Hell!
　—*Paulette Talhay Cary*

Shadows And Light

Under the light of the silver moon
Which cast a ray of light on my heart
Which always brings back memories of my
once beloved.
I think of his ever sweet touch on my face
And the strong arms holding me into the
night and into tomorrow.
He was once my light.
My only life.

As the tears stream down my face
I think only of our love
But secretly wish the love in his heart
did not die.
For I know I must move on
And I know I will
For I am strong.
　—*Andrea Smith*

God's House

I hold some magical powers,
Which I use for all kinds of things,
I use them for making flowers,
To decorate God's house for spring.

I make the beautiful oceans,
With waves sounding like a drummer,
I keep the cool wind in motion,
All for God's house in the summer.

I make the leaves fall to the ground,
From all trees short or tall,
From trees of all shapes, square or round,
To decorate God's house for the fall.

I make the snow fall from the sky,
Which makes the ground cold and bitter,
Cold wind then blows, real low or high,
Now God's house is set for winter.

Now it is really clear to see,
With powers I use magically,
The powers are used for reasons,
They're for making the four seasons.
　—*Erin Hendrick*

Prince Of Darkness

In the darkness of my soul lies a spark of light,
which no one can hold

Who is the one that is so bold
To release my blood that is so cold
Replace the coldness with warmth, the hate with love

Now I can see the beauty and flight of the doves

It is the night that I hold, the darkness that you
may fear, the light that you hold so near

You my dear have touched my immortal soul
I know that it is love that I will never hold
For I am bound to darkness, trapped in the night
It is now I must go before the morning light
I will always remember this night
For you have showed me the beauty of the doves in flight

—Karla Imbrogno

Cool Beauty

Spirited moist air howls through the lonely trees,
   while dry crisp leafs dance across the frozen
   tundra.

Evergreens bow their limbs, heavy with wet sparkling
   snow.

Christmas lights are twinkling from the tall spiny tree
   as aroma, laughter and light mingle in the quiet
   still air.

Twilight creates peaceful beauty sent down as moonlit
   rays from heaven, gently caressing the cool beauty.

   —Linda Benson

In Memoriam To A Departed Chief

A nation weeps
   While, he sleeps-
The President is dead!

He gave his all,
   To his country's call-
And, the lovely Jacqueline wed.

His Caroline and John-John
   Were the apple of his eye-
Oh, God! why did one so young have to die?

Let me this truth impart-
   Behold what happens:
When Hate Rule the Heart.

Robert Frost, whom he loved
   Will be so glad to see him
In heaven above.

Little Patrick won't be lonesome anymore-
   He now has a Dad
On the heavenly shore.

Let these truths forever hold:
   They killed his body-
But, not his soul—
   As long as "Anchors Aweigh"
There'll always be a Triumphant J.F.K.

   —Bess Becker

Guitarist

Broken struts bend at temporary repair points
While the guitar sings powdery melodies
From unseen balconies, in the night rain
Laid back and floating like nebulous mist
In the blackness while not-so-nimble fingers
Strain to find their songs, is it real?
Or only fantastic imagination making feeble efforts
To become tangible...momentarily whisked away by
Occasional balmy breeze...muffled and falling
On deaf ears, echoing and returning as if by
And for the generator...but played and strummed
For the absent audience.

   —Dave Parker

"The Fire"

Hear it crackle, crackle, crackle,
While the quietness it steals
As the coolness it does tackle,
Like a desperate, hungry jackal,
Searching for some tasty meals!
Watch it flame flame, flame,
Like a cheerful little game.
From the warm, cozy glow that
   you do so much desire,
From the fire, fire, fire, fire, fire, fire,
From the popping and the crackling of
   the fire!

   —Laura Lynn Diamond

While

  While you're helping all the lowly ones less fortunate,
    While you're giving all the time that you can spare,
  While you're putting on the altar what you sacrifice,
    While you're saving the world from its despair.

    While you're aggressively crusading needy causes,
    While you're encouraging everyone to make amends,
    While your humble ego endures your great success,
  While you're celebrating these occasions with your
friends.

    While you're accepting the applause and admiration,
   While your sturdy back is being patted 'till it's sore,
    While all these people know they can depend on you,
    There's been others overlooked who need you more.

If you aren't where you should be, your place is empty.
Then you aren't doing what you should, where you belong.
   Your bloated ego doesn't rate all that attention;
The one who should be "bowing" did your job while you were
      gone.

   —Audrey W. Sanders

November

Days when the spirits of autumns past
whisper amid a whirlwind of crispy nature.

The summer sheds its skin, and then covers
its nakedness in a blanket of early frost.

Lonely souls are haunted by bright summers
and springtime romances down the shadowed
meadows of their dreams.

An aged man prepares for an eternal spring,
while a newborn opens its eyes to a coming winter.

A golden harvest of desire; Dreams racing
against time to be stored in the warm
hollows of the heart before they are tossed
and blown by the winter wind.

   —Jeffrey Wade Hale

The Dream

Martin Luther King Jr. had a dream, that one day blacks and whites would walk hand in hand down the street. This dream went on for a while, but what happened to that wonderful dream? How come we see less blacks and whites loving each other? What happened in Los Angeles with Rodney King? Why did the L.A. Riots happen? Was it just because Rodney didn't win? I don't understand this and Martin Luther King Jr. wouldn't either. Rodney King spoke these unforgettable words "Can't we all get along? Why are these words so significant? Because Rodney, along with so many other people, is sick of fighting. Why can't we all live in a peace filled environment, where all types of people can live in the dream of Martin Luther King Jr.?
—Monica Anderson

The Ghost

I am the Ghost who whispers in the winter skies,
Who breezes around city corners among bustling figures
Along each decorated sidewalk

I am the Ghost who hovers at frosted windows,
Who is hypnotized by each tree's lights, carrying echoes
Of Christmas hymns as I wind along snow covered lanes

I am the Ghost who sails through country fields,
Who follows behind each horse and sleigh
Trailing the footsteps of children with mittens
Touching the snow capped evergreens

I am the Ghost who dances to the mountaintops,
Who accompanies every falling snowflake
Whistling through the trees, journeying to the star

I am the Ghost who unfolds the winter world, who casts shadows
In the cold night, coloring the deep blue starry sky

I am the Ghost, the Christmas Joy, the winter embrace
I am the sadness and the happiness of all memories
I am every child, every old man
I am the chill and the warmth inside the chill
I am December
—Julianne Lawton

It's Not Too Late

The wizard foretold the prophecy of man
Who created an evil to destroy the land.

No one would listen to what he would say
Man's only care was to live for today.

"What can I do," wizard asked of me,
"To open their eyes and make them to see
The destruction of earth that is to be."

We have the power to get what we need
But warnings from wizards we still do not heed.

Why can't we see? Why are we blind?
To ignore it now means the end of mankind.

If we don't strike back at the problem at hand
All life will die face down in the sand.
—David Phillips

Christmas At Buckner Village

Thanks, Buckner employees, each of you
Who gave us "Wildwood Village" to happily view.

To the right as you began your tour
You'd ooh and ah, that's for sure.

Twinkling trees and candy canes galore
Made you anxious to see more and more.

There's the belfry atop the little red school house.
Bet each child that entered was "quiet as a mouse".

The church with stained glass windows and a steeple
Was adored by oodles and oodles of people.

And look at the old village store.
That brought back memories of days of yore.

Whew! There were the penguins so very cute;
Some lazy, some happy, and some seemed astute.

Look! Mother goose and her goslings three
Are peeking o'er the hedges to spy on Mr. Lee.

For children there's Santa and his reindeer.
That made each child jump up and cheer.

Sorry I couldn't cover every single thing,
But be assured happiness to many your efforts did bring.
—Eula Potter

Sunshine

Who warms my soul through and through?
Who holds my heart with bonds of love?
Who fills my life with purpose true?
There is only one Sunshine, that is you.

Who's kisses make my spirits soar?
To heights unknown to me before?
Who's eyes capture mine at every glance?
And cause this heart of mine to dance.

Who's "little girl look" can melt my heart
And make my stone-face come apart?
Who pulls me close and holds me tight,
And fills my soul with golden light?

Only you my Sunshine.
—Bruce A. Beckmann

Goodbye Dwayne

I missed your smile amongst the children
Who welcomed me home each day.
Their voices ringing with excitement
  about the day's adventures.
You were not there yet your name was on
  the lips of every child,
As they told me misadventure had come your way.
I dashed to where they said you were
  to say hello and wish you speedy recovery,
But what we did not know - God already held you
  safely in His arms.
I knew someday you would go home
But never did I think He would beckon you so soon!
I'm only sorry I was not there to send you home with a kiss.
However, I am content to know that God knows best for you and
  me.
Good-bye, Dwayne, see you when I join you in the safety of
  God's arms.
—Kat Ferrell

Song For Mother

Whose name makes our memories of childhood so fair?
Whose name takes us back to the sweet carefree days?
Whose hands through long toil wrought the blessings we
shared,
Whose heart held us close in a tender embrace?
   When the circle was whole,
   Sorrow only a word,
   When the blithe heart of childhood
   Winged free as a bird,
Who held in her hands that dear world all secure?
Mother, mother, name dear evermore.

Let me speak now the words I thought not to speak then
Of tender affection, of warm heartfelt praise.
Let me sing now the song that I could not sing then
To the mother whose presence blessed all our young days.
   Though the circle be broken,
   Sorrow real as the rain,
   Let me pour out my thanks
   In a tender refrain.
All that you gave in our hearts shall endure,
Mother, mother, name dear evermore.
   —*Lois Kathryn Hanson*

Oh, Child Of Grief

Oh! Child of grief
Why are you so sad on a day like this?
Child looks up and a tear rolls out of his eye,
Child tell me what make you cry so deeply
Child looks up and says
I lost my mother
I lost my friend
I lost my teacher
So now I am nothing
Child, child, you are somebody
Then the child said then who am I?
Who are you? Think about it for a minute
God put us on the planet
And gave us a job
But...it is your job to find it
   —*Nalani L. Williams*

Transition

The weeks pass by, the weekend is here
   Why do I dread it so?
All week long the routine is boring,
   But the weekend is worse you know.
Happiness is gone, it has been so long
   since I have felt a glow.
It's time to take a step ahead, to
   make the future brighter.
Maybe then the weight will lift and
   my shoulders will feel much lighter.
Maybe for awhile it is best to give
   ourself some peace and rest.
I think and think the whole night through
   trying to do what's best.
We all will hurt, but I pray each day
   that God will lend his hand
So maybe soon we will all be happy again.
People change and so have we, if you stop
   and think I know you will see.
   —*Linda Hollingworth*

Theological Speculation Concerning The Nature Of God

   The question is:
   Why doesn't God commit suicide
And plunge all existence into total nonexistence?

   You must admit
   Such an action would exhibit
   The maximum virtue of maximum simplicity

Here are several possible reasons why he hasn't done it yet:

   1. The possibility hasn't crossed his mind yet
      And if it does
   He will instantly see what a great idea it is
      And do it without a second thought

   2. He is enjoying himself to such an extent
   That he has no inclination to commit suicide

   3. He is somewhat like myself
And believes that suicide is simply not the right thing to do

   4. He is completely incapable of such an act
   Due to a fundamental limitation of his power

   5. He is already doing it
      And always has been
      As fast as he can
   —*Alan Tschetter*

Love And Peace

If love and peace can grow in Greece
Why not in the U.S.A.
You can go around with a frown
But, why not smile and pray?

We are living in a world without many friends
Someday it will come to an end
But love and peace is what we need
So people will stay away from greed

We will get joy and Peace from God
To get together in the Land of Nod
God said Peace and Goodwill to Men
And He will be our best friend

We need a friend and not a foe
As we travel in this world of woe
Make peace and not war
Because with it we'll get very far

God is the Prince of Peace
And His love will never cease
Let's find that love we all need
And not live in the land of Greed.
   —*Bernice W. Rainey*

The Wind

Without warning, the wind from on high
Will carry us all astray.
Neither showing mercy for fear of the unknown,
Nor slowing for the turmoil of emotion.
The wind of the heavens sweeps through
The petty problems of our world,
Forcing us to choose between our hearts and our sanity,
All the while knowing the wrong choice can only
Strengthen the ferocity of the storm.
Strong as the wind may be though,
If we believe in love, we shall survive.
   Love Conquers All.
   —*James Prescott*

Because I Love You

I don't know why You did it Lord,
Why you hung upon that tree

For Lord, I'm not worthy
For you to suffer and die for me

All the pain you must have felt
All the suffering you had to bear

And now you say you'll take my troubles
I'll ask you Lord, is that fair

For I'm the one who cursed you
I'm the one who took the Devil's side

Yet you still say, you'll take my sins away
As far as the sea is wide

Why O Lord, why
Then God said:
"Because I love you"

—*Bary Herrington*

Grandpa's Farm

The times when we were growing up and spent on Grandpa's farm
   will always be remembered for its old time country charm.
Set away back off the roadway and in a grove of trees.
in summer you could hear the droning of the bees.
The black cat had new kittens, Old Shep slept by the door,
dreaming of the rabbits he would chase no more.
Grandma's kitchen was the best place there could ever be.
Big molasses cookies and a glass of milk for me.
Then there was the hay loft where we would jump and play
especially if it turned out to be a rainy day.
One place I remember with fondest memories was Grandma's big
dark cellar pungent apples, hand-picked off the trees,
onions, pickles,
  cider, and potatoes by the score
the smell of that old cellar will live forever more.
Then there was the wood smell on a frosty morn. Breakfast on
the wood stove, Grandma flushed and warm. Grandpa brought the
milk in and eggs warm the nests. We all held hands and said
grace, then to church in Sunday dress.
Those were the days of childhood time cannot erase, the modern
child today could use that kind of space.

—*Jane Mullenax*

Thursday's Child

I am asleep and I can't wake up.
Will my alarm clock never erupt!
The birds cajole and carol the light
That to me is a nightmare without the night.
The sun is an eye that follows along
My wasting time and energy on few chores done.
I feel flat although I'm wired.
I think and work until I'm tired.
But my mettle is arust in its valley of tears
For the lack of motivation that is in arrears.
Oh - God! End this plod of plight
And give my soul a goal insight.

—*Joan Wheelock*

Tell Me, Can I Touch You?

Tell me, can I touch you? If I reach out for your hand,
Will you only pull away, or will you understand
That all I really want from you is tender, tactile-touch?
Your slender fingers entwined with mine would truly mean so
  much.

Tell me, can I touch you? If I gently brush your cheek,
Will you push my hand away? Or will you silently speak
Your acceptance of me by allowing my caresses
Of your satin-velvet skin and silken, autumn tresses?

Tell me, can I touch you? If we stand here face to face
And gaze into each other's eyes, will I catch a trace
Of fear go fleeting through the blue-gray windows of your soul?
Don't flinch! Please let my kiss, your hurt somehow console.

Tell me, can I touch you? Can my heart embrace your own?
Can my love melt the mortar in your walls of brick and stone?
If "perfect love casts out all fear", then when my life is
  through,
Will I have chased your fears away, so that you can touch me,
  too?

—*Michael Landis*

Tranquility In The Early Morning

   A garden of flowers and birds on the wing
Wind chimes in the breeze and the chickadees sing.
      Roses, ferns, and elephant ears
I just feel like kneeling and saying my prayers.

   The breeze in the trees, the hum of the bees,
      The cinnamon vine, the senses to please
With the breath of many flowers, the air is sweet,
   But soon will pass with the summer heat.

      The bird that thrust in needle bill
   And off a blossom in mid-air stands still.
The hummingbird visits and leaves with a "swoon."
      "Oh, that's paradise in bloom."

   A butterfly passes, gracefully, leisurely by
      Morning mist rising toward the sky.
   The light of heaven falls whole and white.
   The rising Sun makes the morning bright.

      The butterfly and I had lit upon
   Nevertheless, a message from the dawn.
      That made me hear a voice within
   Say "Always, God speaks at the end."

—*Bessie Harp Steele*

To You

I write this
with a pain in my stomach
and a tear in my eye
TO YOU

Wondering when you will come back
will it ever be the same?
I once was loved
Am I now?

You left us
for your work
You hurt me because you never saw me as me
just a shadow of your beloved sons!
What am I to do?

I write this
With tears streaming down my face
Wishing I didn't have to
This is for you
TO YOU.

—*Jenny Gurd*

Untitled

They call us the "Sandwich Generation"—
With ambition, workaholism, two-salary incomes,
With children who want the privileges of independence
But few or none of the responsibilities,
With parents who survive cancer and heart disease
Only to live to the have Alzheimer's—a bitter blessing.
They used to have other names for us,
Like Hippies or Yuppies, names I never really understood,
At least not as I understand this new name—the Sandwich Generation.

—*Elaine Brookshire*

Memory

I still see the girl so fair
With fine silk ribbon in her hair.
She helped me brush my own at night-
Stood tippy-toed to hug me tight.

Then with a caution not to peek,
Planted moist flowers on my cheek.
Each stayed with me till dawn's first glimmer
Like sprinkled sunshine in the winter.

The little girl I've raised I know
Has gone where only children go
Leaving the petals of her youth behind
Some turned to diamonds scattered in my mind.

The rest within my heart I keep
For nights if in a trouble sleep
My anxious soul wants me to weep
For dreams that life away may sweep

It's then perhaps I'll sense her near
In gentle thoughts that soothe my fear
And calm my sleep as my hands seek
To touch her sweet softness on my cheek — again.

—*E. H. Sobeck*

A Gift

Four lovely blooms in our rose garden grew,
Beautifully vibrant with fresh morning dew.
Rosy and radiant, with sunlit hair,
Darling little girls, so pretty and fair.
Each with a special trait, her very own,
Shedding a fragrance, the sweetest known.

They were a gift from a Wonderful Friend
Tenderly to nurture 'till their colors would blend;
'Till each blossom would burst in magnificent hue
Captivating with rapture all who would view
That flowering love shining on her face;
 Offering strength and courage they could embrace.

Such joy and happiness has filled our life
Midst earthly struggles and its strife.
'Twas God Himself who had blessed us so
These priceless roses graciously to bestow.

In memory now, we recall each tiny bud,
Maturing slowly in the destiny of God.

What assurance to know 'twas His gentle Hand
That directed each how she should stand
While brightening the gloom of troubled skies,
By His portrait reflected in her friendly eyes.

—*Anne Benda*

Generations

My granddaughter, Samantha Miss Three
With grave expression inspected me.
Last year she hid in her mother's dress.
Now, picture in hand caused her distress.
Pointing, "I want my kitty," she said.
I knew the truth, poor kitty was dead.
I explained, "Your kitty is broken."
"Can you fix my kitty?"
"Where did they put my Kitty?"
"Did I break the kitty?"
Gritty questions probing words spoken.
"No, kitty just got broken," I said.
"Will I get broken?" she cocked her head.
Innocent inquiry. Child of three
Asking of death and infinity!
In awe of the deep, agile, young mind
I reasoned for words both true and kind.
"When you're old and old and old, maybe."
Young lady frowned, "I want my kitty."
My granddaughter, Samantha Miss Three.

—*Robert E. Beeson*

Sleeping On Peopled Waves Of Converging Mythos

Once, our children's eyes would brighten
   with hope and excitement and wonderment and anticipation.
Now, the dark secrets hidden behind the cloudy truculence
   cataracts of a reign of terror
   deception, concealment and televised lies
   decaying the eyesight of our children
   digesting the dreams
   leaving empty sockets of nightmare and horror
   because the price is right.

We will plant fresh seeds in our children's eyes
   and grow new grapevines
   sprouting succulent bunches of grapes
   season after season
   cleansed of poisons and pesticides
   until we lick away our children's wine wet tears.

Down down down into the scarlet sea of puberty
   we will descend until our children are freed
   from official traffic in guilt
   intimidation and commercial religion
   disguised as authority.

—*Greg Dunn*

Untitled

The verdant hill
With its lush trees and summer assortment of colors
Secludes the house of apricot brick.
Reflections from the red tin roof
Attract my eye—enticing.
Once dignified, opulent,
Of Greek Revival architecture,
A fortress to the forest.
The white noble pillars are the protectors of the estate,
The great oak doors secured the wellborn.
Wild thick emerald ivy and untamed hollyhocks
Now overtake the gardens.
The wrought iron fence allows only a glimpse,
I turn, satisfied.

—*Paula Schonhoff*

I Am Somebody Special

I am somebody special unique and ever changing,
with my mind clean and free a new life I am arranging.

My hopes are big and glorious and wishes will come true,
my dreams may still be curious but they are out of the blue.
I am a child of the universe with style, grace, and charm
not another living soul did I ever mean to harm, for I was
being driven by an outer force that sounded no alarm.

Now that I've come to realize, the constricting presence
has lifted, I can continue to live my life knowing I am
truly gifted.
—*James Chiarlanza*

Forever Friends

If you should find yourself lonely and lost
With no remedy for your sorrow,
Do not trouble yourself or count the cost,
Or from some other borrow
A stolen pleasure or even one moment spend
Carelessly in a stranger's care.
For always remember I am your friend.
I will forever be there.
No matter where or how far at all
You will always know
Just a letter, thought or call
And to my friend I will go.
When your world is shaken and shatters
All you know and what it can span
Your state to me ALWAYS matters
I will do what ever I can.
You are never far from me
Even when we are worlds apart.
For your presents will now and forever be
Something VERY SPECIAL within my heart.
—*Rhonda Sullivan*

Untitled

Sometimes my friends will wake me up asking for a rhyme.
With pen in hand, I say "Okay, but honestly, just this time".
And though it's fun, they need it now, and I get awfully weary
'Cause inspirations keep me up, and then my eyes get bleary.
I'm so compulsive, I must finish what I start to write
Thinking up new words to rhyme in the middle of the night.
For invitations, thank you notes - so many call on me
And jokingly I tell them that next time they pay a fee.
I never enter contests, but this one seemed like fun
And wouldn't all my friends be awed to find that I had won.
If I could turn professional, I'd charge for every line.
I wonder, then, how many still would say they're friends of mine.
—*Bernice F. Lee*

Untitled

I love your funny little freckled face-
With turned up nose and jet blue eyes-
I love each curl that dons your crown-
Your famous red hat-that graces your head-
Proudly acquired from your winning game-
I love your funny little freckled face-
Always beaming-ear to ear-
I love each day I spend with you-
My darling little imp of eight-
I love your funny little freckled face-
I love the cards you silently make for me-
With words like-"I wuv you"-
I love you when you get angry-
And storm up to your room to hide-
I love your funny little freckled face-
I love you son—because—you're mine-
—*Pamela J. Macleod*

The Senior Citizen Funsters

We gather each week with hearts full of glee,
With Sopranos striving to hit a high C. Altos and Bass
Just hoping to agree with the notes in a lower key.
We show up some mornings with frogs in our throats,
Must be the smog, we sigh with a croak.
Then settle down as the warm-ups begin.
The Mi Mi's, Fa Fa's and Tee Hee's set in.
Bring 'em up from your innards and hold your mouth So,
Then puckered, we, with all shapes of O's.

Smiles light our faces and we look for delight,
On our Director's face, if we think we've done right.
But oft-times she views us with a deriding laugh,
When we sing a Full Note as a Quarter or a half.
She points out the notes with a sigh of defeat,
Black moles with tails—these Are Not on your sheet.

But music is destined to be our forte,
With Black Moles and Full Notes to reign someday,
In a Union of Voices, she will be proud,
As Applause rings out from an adoring crowd.
   (We can dream, can't we?)
—*Mildred D. McCumber*

Baby

There's someone here in my home, a stranger to me.
With tiny little hands, big brown eyes and tiny little feet.
It cries through the night, wakes me up early in the morn.
   To it everything is new, the world is foreign.
   It's a wonder in life how it ever came to be,
     this little thing in my home, this baby.
  I watched it grow inside her, felt it move in my hand.
   She looked so miserable, makes me glad I'm a man.
     But she smiles at it, rocks it in her arms,
raps it in bunches of blankets just trying to keep it warm.
     All this attention that use to be given to me
     is now bestowed upon this little thing, this baby.
  Now what's she doing!? Oh no, she's handed it to me!
        It's crying aloud, why can't it see
       this love that she feels for it I feel it too
           for I am its father, proud and true
            Hush, baby, baby, baby it's me
                Don't you know who I am?
                    I'm your daddy.
—*Denise M. Ray*

Trapped

What's a head,
Without a mind.
What are eyes,
When they are blind.
Blind of all things that appear,
Blind of what is next to fear.
Not able to feel,
Not able to see,
Not able to live happily.

An empty mind
That cannot grow.
Wanting to love
But cannot show.

So lost and alone, cannot cry.
Living this way, wanting to die.
A soul so loving, so simple, so pure
Gliding thoughtless with wings that soar.
Feelings so strong, a voice so weak
A soul that stands,
But cannot speak.
—*Barbie Hughes*

"I Walked Alone"

All through my life I walked alone,
without any hope of ever finding my freedom again.

Like a bird trapped in a cage on a stormy night,
I wished to break free and fly away from all my fears,
but every time I tried to escape my prison
the storms got angry and fell down upon me trapping me
once more.

Then one day you came to me like a guardian
angel out of the heavens and freed me.

With your love and support up under my
wings I flew to the stars and beyond.

Never again did I feel trapped or afraid,
for I knew that with you by my side I would
never walk alone again.
—*Jaime Warden*

"My Yesterdays Today And Tomorrows"

I'm as thankful as can be, For what God has given me;
My wonderful parents who are loving and dear,
Always doing and giving for everyone because they care;
My husband and two sons I cherish each day,
We're thoughtful and caring of each other in every way;
Friends, Family and good health is most important in my life,
I'm a very lucky mother, and a very happy wife;
Myprofession is very rewarding medical related clients I see,
I look forward to helping them, wigs and hairpieces are my specialty;
I have a great feeling within myself all the time,
Always try to be compassionate, understanding, and especially
  to be kind;
Two brothers, 2 sisters-in-law, 3 nephews, 3 nieces, I've been blessed,
We are all close, and have a great family love nest;
My heart is filled with much happiness, I have a lot to be thankful for,
I'm a very lucky woman, who could ask for anything more;
"My Yesterdays, Todays and Tomorrows" I cherish.
Somedays are tough,
 but if you have the love and support from all it's not that rough,
I love life, it's wonderful, little things mean a lot,
If the future isthe same as the past, I'll be thankful for what I got!
—*Fran Goldman*

Memories

Sifting through the memories of my past;
wondering why that time went so fast.
Sorting out the good times from the bad;
wishing for time I never had.
Time needed to make my memories more dear;
to remember the rest of my life year after year.

Sifting through the memories of my past;
wondering why I couldn't make them last.
Things were said and things were done;
friendships were lost one by one.
Questions are wrestling in my mind;
the answers I'll probably never find.

My memories are cluttered;
by the unkind words I've muttered.
If I knew yesterday what I know today;
there would be so much to change so much to say.
I need my memories here with me;
so for tomorrow I can see -
—*William O. Hardman*

Dance Of The Fairy Queen

As the poignant strains of Liebestraum flow in the night,
  Woodland nymphs dance into sight,
Twirling forth from wooded green,
  Paying court to their Fairy Queen.

Starlight glistens in her hair,
  Illuminating skin so fair,
Glowing on her smiling face,
  Shining on her dancer's grace.

While round her hover fireflies,
  Sparks of light in the evening skies.

Jennifer, our Queen, steps to center stage,
  Graceful carriage, arms upraised.
Moonbeams touch her lips of rose,
  As she waits in classic pose.

Now come the pixies and elfin sprites,
  Whirling and spinning in the soft moonlight.
Pirouetting in exhilaration,
  Delighting in their celebration.

For we shall have a faerie ball,
  An air of expectancy pervading all.
—*Catherine R. Kelble*

The Lamb

When the rock looked at the
  world he created.
He saw turmoil and became frustrated.
So he created a lamb of love,
and sent it to the world from above.
Hurting beings came far and near,
welcoming it with joy and cheer.
The lamb toured the land on its own.
Telling us outcasts this world
  Is not our home.
Then the lamb was captured and
agreed to pay the world's price.
So it was taken to the skull to
  be sacrificed.
As the lamb's life began to diminished,
It said to the rock "It is finished."
On that day his friends mourned,
then he returned as if reborn.
Telling them to remember all they learned
for the lamb and rock will soon return.
—*Ron Ebanks*

As I Sit Here

As I sit here, I wonder what
would happen if there was a
spark between you and I that
could ignite the fire of passion
I would sit before you and stare
into your beautiful blue eyes and
try to capture all that pass behind them.
I would take your hand in mine and
lead you back to yesterday where we
could sail away just the two of us.
But no, I just sit here and drift away.
As I sit here and admire you from
across a distant shore. I turn away
when you look up at me so I'll never
get a chance to gaze into your eyes.
—*Travis Linfoot*

Untitled

Would it be just as hard to cross old Dewey Square?
Would paper boys shout? - Would cabs be there?
Would chestnuts be roasting? Would the buildings still be
As quaint and old-fashioned as history?
Would the cobblestones shriek with their pushcart brigade?
Would bookstalls and sweetshops invite all trade?
Then I opened my eyes to my memories own.
Where have they hidden the places I've known?
Did a streetsweeper sweep all these things in the sea?
Could he know that they meant so much to me?

Then I found as I walked up and down ev'ry street
The places I knew were still there nice and neat
And towering o'er were buildings so tall
That they seemed to reach out and embrace it all.
My town was now new but old just the same.
A blend of the best of two worlds is this Dame.
Her dome on the hill is as bright as of yore.
Her harbor protects everything on the shore
And her people are friendly and helpful and kind.
Dear Boston - keep changing and I'll never mind.
  —*Alice M. Waters*

Imagine That

Imagine if there was no time.
Would that postpone things, especially crime?
Would we ever be late or ever too early?
How would we get along?
Knowing if we we're right or wrong.

Would there ever be night or day?
If there wasn't, what would you say?
How would you know when to get up?
Some people would be lost,
While others are paying the cost.

Do we need time?
Imagine that.

What would the world be like,
If there wasn't a day or night?
Would it ever be dark or light?
Without time, we could not tell.
Why is there time?

Is there a purpose or a meaning?
Or maybe a reasoning.
We do not know.

Imagine that!!
  —*Amanda Sherlinski*

Forgiveness

What would it take to forgive me,
Would you like me on my knees?
Perhaps you'd like it better if I were to beg and plead.
I really don't see what's so awful
That could make you turn away
And why am I asking forgiveness
When it was you that walked away?

Maybe because I've realized what it means to lose a friend,
Sit alone on the weekends and hope it soon will end.
Or when you pick up a phone just to say a simple Hi!
And the one on the other end has to start it off with a goodbye.

A person gives no chances to that person once a friend
If it wasn't for forgiveness we'd have no real beginnings
Just a bitter end.
  —*Crystal Schuyler*

Crime

Guns firing, bullets soaring.
Wouldn't you think crime could get boring?
People kill for drugs and money.
When they do it, they think it's funny.
Innocent people killed each day.
What can we do, what can we say?
Jails are overcrowded, sales of guns on the rise.
Cannot trust anybody, everyone lies.
Shotgun shells laying all over the place.
Life is such a big disgrace.
Riots and rumbles everyday.
Getting stopped by the cops, what can we say?
The sound of sirens screaming.
The red and blue lights gleaming.
Police running lights to get to the sight
of the horrible crime that happened at night.
Criminals are put in jail for their crime,
escaping and doing it another time.
  —*Timothy Patrick O'Brien*

Time

Time's an amazing thing, it is said time heals all wounds.

If that is true, how much time will have to go by before I stop seeing your face when I close my eyes?

Will time indeed make me forget how it felt to lie next to you?

Will there eventually be a moment when I no longer recall, the look in your eyes, the flavor of your lips, the taste of your body, the passion you gave or the affection you showed? Maybe, but not until the end of time.........
  —*Tom Sullivan*

Jelly Beans

Jelly beans of every hue
yellow, pink and purple, too.

Red and green and also white
orange and black, as is the night.

Yellow reminds us of the Son
who gave new life to everyone.

Pink is for His special touch
Lord, we need You, oh so much.

Purple stands for royalty
Lord, You are the King to me.

Blood is represented by the red
They killed You but You are not dead.

New life is stirring in all that's green.
We feel Your touch, it can be seen.

White is oh so special, too
It means purity through and through.

Orange is from the glow of fire
In hearts of those, Your will desire.

Black is the heart where there is sin
Won't you come and let Him in?
  —*Lois J. Moore*

The Butterfly

Mama, does a butterfly have wings?
Yes, my darling, he truly does have wings,
But Mama, can he sing, can he sing?
But, my darling, she was not made to sing, to sing.

What does he do, Mama, I ask you true?
He sees golden light and flies above the ocean blue.
But why does he do that, Mama, I ask of you?
God made him that way, for me and for you.

Will he stop and talk, Mama, to me and to you?
Only if he knows you'll listen and love him true.
Why did God make him, Mama, I want to know.
To make us happy, to view his beauty-simple beauty
to all he does show.

Mama, do you care if the butterfly flies?
Yes, my child, I care if the butterfly flies.
Mama, what will you do, if he does not stay?
Then, I, myself shall fly away.
—*Louise Kantenwein*

Voiced Anger

You disregard my feelings,
Yet for yourself you spill tears,
So don't be surprised if I abandon you,
Because I've enough hatred to last years,
Enough to let go of my hopes and dreams,
Of the perfect life, enough to take my chances,
And face the consequences of strife,
How can you say I must love you,
Because we we're like fishes in a bowl,
Joined together by blood, but not by the soul,
Know that I can't forgive you in this life time,
For it was your cruel words that built this mask of mine,
There's no way to describe this hurt inside me,
If there was only a way to open your blinded eyes to see, so if
So if one day I disappear do not try to find me and get me back,
It would have been you who drove me away and it is your love I lack,
Although sometimes I may cry feel desolate, and frightened,
I'll always keep it mind that with every new beginning there must be an end.
—*Lorra Jackson*

The Shadow

Strength is not in the shadow- but in the tree,
Yet surely in the shade, dwells a part of me.

In the shadow of myself- it's cold, it's lonely.
Tho I have strength for others, there is none for me.

The obscure darkness!! — no touch does it ever know,
Nor do crystals ever fall, when tears quietly flow.

The air feels no tremors, should I ever speak,
So all my inner feelings, I quietly keep.

To know laughter—joy—and yes—even to sing!
Yet, that someone would hear, would mean everything.

The passage of time— the strongest tree will fade.
The weaker grows the tree, the lesser is the shade.
—*Janice Collins*

A Love Poem

I come to bed.
You are already asleep.
I kiss your shoulder,
You open your eyes halfway,
and hold my hand in yours,

I want to keep you here.
I fear cars,
kidnappers.
I can't help thinking of losing you
and how I would want to break everything.
I would never stop crying and breaking.

You roll over now and lay your cheek on my chest.
I fold you in my arms and we sleep
into the next dangerous day.
—*Dave LaSalle*

Reality

You are not a simple dream,
You are reality.
You are not a egotist,
You are generous.
You, were not jealous,
When the Russia announced
They were the first to conquer the stars?!
You congratuled.
When the American's science
Explored the Moon
The China communist party
The people didn't listen.
You are rich, powerful and helped-help.
America is needed today
To think more for your people
For Peace in the world you sacrificed more
The whole world thinks of you
With confidence to do for you
And any aspiration is a reality
You God-be, a real guard for them
—*Lazar Maria*

Life Is A Movie

Life is a movie
You are the star
Friends and Enemies
They are supporting and opposing actors
And if you let another star in your movie
Your life is not worth living

Taste
Smell and feeling
They are 3-D factors
Your ears are the recording studio
Your eyes are the camera
And your mind is the film and tape for both

God is the judge
Wings are the trophy
Heaven is the hall of fame
Hell
The hall of shame
And your soul
Another actor to be replaced

Life is a movie
—*Adrian Duran*

The Rape

With your force my arms crashed into the ground.
You came down on me like a thunderstorm;
Uninvited and unwanted.

My voice and tears rang out;
Only to get lost in the rain.

Your hand struck out at me;
My face red with blood.

Thunder rolled and lightning crashed;
As you repeatedly tore down my wall.

Ashamed and alone;
I lay there frozen in the wet grass.

I'm left here now in this room;
To live somehow with the memories of a summer night.

A night from which I continue to run;
Crying into the arms of a stranger.
—*Kelly Burns*

Nightmare Or A Story That Was Never Told

It was a quiet, dark night
You could hear the clock on the wall
You slept, but you saw the light
It was a scream of your memories, all
People were real, they asked for help
You couldn't help them at all
Their fates were more than you could hold
You couldn't feel their call.
You woke up, it was a dream
A story that was never told
That you kept in yourself like a wise old tree
And you felt you were centuries old.
You grew up and you understood life
Life that is best and worst of all
Life that may kill like a sharp knife
That is a story that was never told.
—*Natalya Faynboym*

How My Heart Tore

I walk through this life in a blurry daze.
You filled up my life. All of my days.

You made me believe in a love so strong.
You left me to wonder; how did our love go wrong?

After all the pain you've put me through,
There's still nothing I wouldn't do -

To make you happy, and see you smile.
Which lately you do only once in a while.

Now do you see, or shall I say more?
Do you understand how my heart tore

When you said our love was over, done with, through?
You may not love me, but I'll always love you.
—*Stephanie Lynn Bowers*

Untitled

With the delicate strength of poet's wings
You flied
Reaching mystic heights of unknown bliss
You tried
On freedom's edge, at last, a curse on life
You cried
With hopeful, sad, impassioned eyes
You died

Icarus,
Noble youth who dared.
Your death reminds
Of compromises shared
With cowardice
—*Barry Findley*

Untitled

Oh! Liberty And Truth where have
You gone, the blood of many was shed to win you as their own.
Broken foundations now you stand, hopes and
Promises on sinking sand. No longer established in God
We trust, morality spoiled by antitrust. Lost to those
Who seek for gain closing eyes to paupers shame, children
Dying people crying, nothing offered to ease their pains.
—*Nadier T. Martin*

Monroe, Ode To A Redbird

A descendent from heaven with His message,
You have born.
Of God's precious jewels,
You came in a special form.
Reigning as stately queen,
from your loftiest perch,
You taught me more about God,
Than I ever learned in church.
Could it be, before your journey to earth,
You may have known,
The one who gave me birth.
So now as you reascend to your abode above.
Tell her now I too know of a mother's love.
—*Billy Gene Windham*

"The Mag-Man"

Think back at nineteen twenty three
You knew then what was to be.

You knocked on doors all day long
Till you wore your fingers to the bone.

Sell-sell-sell the magazines
Some days the pickens were mighty lean
But you kept selling for fifty-seven years,
Thru heat and cold and snow and rain.

And now at the age of seventy-five
You look for another twenty-five.
—*Fluett W. Peterson*

Frozen Flames

You can hurt me no longer.
You know not what I can do -
   My powers far exceed yours.
Moonlit nights - your promises;
   I believed in you.
We would be together forever - another lie;
   On your part, not mine.
You tried to mold me;
   I am not of clay -
But of flesh, bone, blood, and fire.
The moon will haunt you -
   I will be everywhere.
Your lies - the frozen blade severed my soul.
My wounds, now healed -
   Your eternal nightmare.
Now, you can hurt me no longer.
You know not what I can do -
   My powers far exceed yours.
My flames -
   They surround you.
     —*Angela L. Gladfelter*

An Appreciation Of Cliches

Remember the grass always appear greener on the other side.
You know where the brown spots are hidden, which familiarity will not let you hide.
This is not to say that adventuresome you should not be, but before you trade in the old make sure the new is really what you see.
Tomorrow will be a better day.
Green grass all around you, as green as you want it to be.
A smile can always help light up the way; followed by a prayer
Let love of self be the "Bird in your hand".
Take another look..
What do you see?
Green grass all around you, as green as you want it to be.
     —*Bertha L. Carroll*

Love Won't Be A Stranger

Love won't be a stranger if you open your hearts.
You meet casually, you talk, just don't rush.
Love will grow if you are right for each other
If you trust each other, it will grow.

Sunday afternoons you will walk in the park holding
   Hands,
As the night approaches and the stars shine above
   You
He will softly kiss your lips, his arms around you,
   Close to his heart.
True love you will know as you become one.

Remember, what matters is what is in your hearts;
Is it greed, ambition, do you seek security?
Or are you searching for a heart that unconditionally
   Loves?
Love won't be a stranger if your hearts are open and
   Trust.
     —*Daisy C. Fernandez*

Seasons

With the colors of the leaves so brilliant and stunning
you, my lover, are running
Oh sweet lover
running from my love to another's

Snow is on the ground
and you are not around
The wind is blowing everywhere
the smell of flowers hangs heavy in the air
and you're not here

The heat of the summer's day
gives way to my nightly lover's bay
When the leaves have returned to colors of brilliancy
will your presents surround me
or has this year just passed
become the memory of the last
and your happiness been found
in another state, another town?
     —*Ethel M. Hunt*

I Thought... You Never...

I thought you loved me, I thought you cared.
You never showed it, you never dared.
I gave and I gave, you always received.
You never gave back, I was deceived.
You made me promises everyday,
And everyday you would break them.
I thought you loved me in a special way,
My friends would ask, "What do you see in him?"
I thought one day, you would see,
Just how bad you were treating me.
I was waiting for so very long,
Even thought I knew this was wrong.
I never knew why I loved you,
When all you did was 'cause me pain.
I thought you were the one for me,
But from you, there's nothing to gain.
Now that you are out of my life,
And that you are far away.
I hope no one falls for you,
'Cause they will have much to pay!
     —*Allyson Ronning*

Oh September

Oh September, you do such things,
   You ripen the chestnuts
But kill other things.
   Your nights are so cold we shudder,
Your days so balmy we mutter.
   You paint the trees so bright
But you end the children's summer delight.

Your rains will fill the thirsty wells,
   But ruin parades that were planned so well.
The children will romp and play
   In piles of leaves that fell today.
The frost will silver the ground,
   And disappear when the sun comes around.
The ducks will start their southern flight,
   Later to become some hunter's delight.

The antlered buck will polish his tines, In preparation for
   the mating time. The Black Bear will eat by sun and moon,
For he knows his long sleep is coming soon. Grey squirrels
   will scamper to and fro, To gather the nuts before the snow.

Oh September, must you go? All God's things will miss you so.
     —*Charles D. Wilson*

Untitled

In a dream you're mine, you'd never part
you say you love me with all your heart
your blue eyes match the sky above
living a dream full of your love
in the dream you marry me
you say you'll love me for eternity
the next we know, two children to grow
a darling son, a darling daughter
now we are a mommy and daddy
your girl has the cutest blond curls
and the prettiest ones out of all the girls
your son is exact copy of you
his hair is blond, his eyes, they're blue
we're the happiest couple through out the world.
But only in a dream.
—*Christal Bailey*

Universe

Oh, Mr. Sun, Oh how far away you are.
You shine so brightly, brighter than a star.
You know nothing but to shine all day.
You light the world up to let the children play.
You make the people seem small, so small they cannot see.
When they look at you there hearts go free.

Oh, Mr. Star you are so small
don't stop the twinkling or go to far.
The wishing is upon you, you're very rare.
You are so special that all should care.
Like the sun you know nothing, nothing at all.
All you know is your waiting of call.
Will you be bright, white, yellow, or blue.
Will you be dull or shiny as a shoe.
Don't be afraid of what you will be
Because you will always be as lovely and beautiful to me.
—*Roseanne Hoyt*

The Other Woman

Across the miles on beached shore,
you stand, the one he does adore,
take care you cherish and love him true,
as he does love and think of you.
You stir in him some great desire,
and hearing of you at times I tire,
his passion runs deep, free and wild,
return not a love that's cold and mild.
Be rest assured, fear not, nor dread,
for with you in bonds he'd share his bed,
be careful, his love, if your love be not true,
for others are waiting to steal him from you.
If you reject him and leave him cold,
rue it not later, your warning I've told,
I gladly will step in with arms open wide,
to readily stand and walk by his side.
As long as you both shall love each other,
you have nothing to fear from me or another.
—*Brenda Boline*

Last Sun

Clouds shadow as your mind starts to drain
You stare at the darkness
  but see nothing
Just your life; disregarded

You watch your last sunset
Unaware of the buzzards that have formed,
  circling your head

You hear the ocean
  feeling the wind that now lifts you;
You float

As the light fades
  your sun dies
But you are not alone-

The buzzards land
—*Lindsay Brissette*

How To Show Love To A Mother

You watched me grow,
you taught me to sew.

You told me it was ok to cry,
you helped me answer the question why.

You backed each decision,
you gave advice with little indecision.

You always knew my fears,
you showed me life's many cheers.

You kept my chin up,
you even asked, "what's up?".

Each year many sit and wonder, how do I show love to a special woman, who could only be a mother?

I sat and wondered,
"How do you show love to a mother?".

I thought about a figurine,
but it would become another dust-collecting thing.

I considered a purse,
then I developed this verse.
So, as a daughter, this is my way to show love to a special woman, who could only be my mother.
—*Chrystal Dawn Dalby*

What Is A Friend?

A friend is someone with whom you get along, someone who treats you the way she would like to be treated.
A friend is someone who helps another in distress, is there when someone is in need, and also who is caring, understanding, and fair playing, someone who doesn't hog the ball in games, and who doesn't cheat. A true friend is there for you in good times and bad times. She will apologize when she has made a mistake or hurt your feelings. A good friend will comfort you, and help you go through hard times. A good friend is someone whom you can trust, someone who will be on your side when you're in a fight with another friend. A friend is someone which has a shoulder to cry on, and someone who you can trust telling secrets to, who wouldn't tell anyone else. A good friend is someone who will not turn you down, and talk about you behind your back. A friend will share her ideas and thoughts with you, and value your opinions. A friend can be any age whether it's a classmate, a parent or a teacher. She enjoys the things you do such as playing sports, going to the movies or just talking to one another.
Hayley is a friend!!!

—*Kate Waitkevich*

Mama

Mama, I owe everything to you!
  You took care of me, when I did not know myself!
    I did not know my hands from my feet or eyes from my nose.
    I did not know whether I was naked or had on clothes!

Your beautiful face and your dancing eyes
  Have guided me through tough times and around obstacles;
    Have shielded me from the destruction of my body and mind;
    Have given me love for myself and others, of any kind.

Mama, I owe everything to you!
  You taught me the love of Jesus and sacrifices He made.
    You taught me to work for what I wanted and to study hard.
    For with an education, doors would be open and not barred.

    Mama, your inner peace has given me strength.
  Your commitment to work has kept me honest and true.
  Your ability to set realistic limits for reaching goals,
    Has helped me to stay within bounds to reach needy souls

Mama, God gave me to you and you to me.
  I thank Him for you and I thank Him for me!
    I'll always love you until death leaves me still cold.
    I owe everything to you and that story will never grow old!

—*Eunice Paddio-Johnson*

You

You were the one who always cared.
You were the one who always shared.
You were the one I treasured.
You were the one who made my day
  and life complete.
I always enjoyed the stories you had to
  share.
The laughs, the tears, the jokes, the pain.
You were the one I cherished.
Now you walk around up above looking down
  on me.
My life is empty now that you're gone.
And there's not one thing I can do
  about the pain and sorrow I bare.
You'll never know how much I loved
  you.

—*Amanda Beth Bunch*

Of Mothers And Daughters

What is it you don't understand?
  You, who threw everything my way. I sorted through it all,
Though the Sands of Time grant me wisdom not.

I am a seeker of truth and would wish to heal, But with you,
  My words can only Sting... For this I am truly sorry.

I am because of and in spite of You—a legacy we all share.
  Motherhood grants us empathy and compassion for the
Plight of all womanhood—now Mine.

  And the joys of the grandchild far outweigh that of our
Own issue...Pleasure, not pain; Responsibility not strain.

Alas! Surely there are Answers to these Questions of Life
  we shall never know; ours is but to Learn and Grow...
And become Enlightened in the afterlife (or is it the afterglow?)

But until then it behooves us to just forgive and forget
And never cease to Love; for without You—
I would not BE.

—*Geraldine Kazolias*

Senior Citizen Today

Old age is God's blessing, in disguise
you will recognize it, if you are wise
master time passes by so very fast
Before you know it, you are a senior at last
The simple things are now your priority
you no longer have to compete with the minority
there are so many activities for older people these days.
It's sad when one lets age keep them from enjoying happy ways
there is always someone who needs a hug or smile
Remember when you venture out, let it be your style.
Don't forget to smell a rose as you go by.
And enjoy all those chattering Birds, in the sky.
You all have great stories to relate
It's such a pleasure when you can share your past fate.
So you see, life isn't over because you are old.
For as long as you can breathe, your life is better than gold.

—*Kathleen Waight*

If You Were...

If you were a flower,
You'd be the purest rose.

If you were a perfume,
What else but pearls and lace.

If you were an animal,
The most beautiful, white unicorn.

If you were a star,
The one that shines above them all.

If you were a piece of jewelry,
A sparkling diamond ring.

If you were a plant,
A perfect four-leaf clover.

And if I were to have to explain my love,
No words could ever help out.

—*Stephanie Hillen*

High School Reunion

Thirty five years, can it really be that we were seniors, so
young and so free? Before payments, insurance and taxes
galore, before wrinkles and dentures and so much more.

Basketball, football and roller skates, and everyone
remembers
their very first date. Biology, history and chemistry too,
English class where I sat by you. Study for tests till late
at
night, waiting for grades could be quite a fright.

I remember my first love, so tall and so slim, with lots of
brown curls and a cleft in his chin. Can that really be him,
the one standing there. Why he's gained sixty pounds, and
where is his hair?

Remember the girl with dark hair and eyes.
She's now a matron with huge chubby thighs.
She was going to remain single, a career girl she said.
How life has changed her, she's now a grandma instead.

The grey hair is colored, the skin is pulled tight,
I jog and I diet, it's a constant fight.
The years have slipped by as quick as can be.
How sad that everyone's aged, except me!
—*Jean Lind*

Life's Search For Serenity

As perennial as the wonderful season of Spring
Young Mens fancies turn to thoughts that sing
Their tender dreams form deep musings of love
Sweethearts dwell fondly as on wings of the dove

For every found Friendship down thru the years
A memory serenic seems calms direst of fears
When life's path confronts in manner quite bold
The spirit reigns easy with a loving hand to hold

Hearty true friendships with creed are never a sham
Their caring accepts me truly for all that I am
I gracefully surrender to all that life do hold
Seems life's pattern of trials more gently enfold

Greet times with a prayer..a hope and a dream
Cause life to flow gently as a rambling stream
Thrust onward in Honor to the passing of time
Hold Heart and Head high.. enjoy rhythm and Rhyme
—*Anne Porter Boucher*

To A Beautiful Woman

You don't fool me with signs of age,
Your beauty shines right through;
I see a lovely woman,
I'm sure that others see her, too.

Before you get your mirror
To see if the beauty is really there,
Remember, beauty rubs off on others
As you love, and give, and care.

So, you may have lost a little bit;
Some may even have rubbed off on me.
Well, I'd like to think so, anyhow,
Since now I'm long past thirty-three.

Beauty grows a step at a time,
As life is lived and trials you meet;
You water the plant and we see it bloom
Those times when you're patient ….and gentle …. and sweet.

Isn't it nice to reflect on the fact,
As you arrive at your ninetieth year,
That God loves a beautiful woman
And looks forward to having you near?
—*Glenn D. Maxwell*

Jeanne (Decision 1946)

Jeanne, sadly I view your sensual dance;
Your body curved and molded
As if Pan, himself, had decreed
A cloned Aphrodite.
And yet the face disconnected,
Goddesslike beatified, angelic,
denies that swing and sway of your body.
—The musical cacophony increases!
Blasting the truth from your eyes.
Suddenly, you are Gomar, or perhaps, Salome; and I,
Knowing that I am no Hosea,
And not wishing my soul served
On a platter,
Make my way through a sea of faces.

And the door closes silently behind me,
And the door closes permanently behind me.
—*Samuel P. Flanagan*

Without Expectation

Dream of Spring
Your comfort is not needed
The wait is over
The winter did not survive again against my faith
Blessed springtime is come

Dear image of spring
My loyal friend
Yet winter hope dies useless
One last frost-fear fades ghostly where I grow green
Washed in your bright crimson morning
Fearless spring
Hopeless spring

The golden rhythm warms the earth
Through the azure holes of my favorite blanket
A tuneless din waters the signs of life
Deep roots stretch forth the wet hues
Pushing blossoms burst
Sure mud-stuck dreams
Spring awake
—*O. Paul Coombs*

Images

Images of you pass through my mind—your smile spreading across
your face, Your eyes searching mine, hoping to find a clue to
my love that surely lingers there. Images of us together are
locked in my memory. You holding me locked in your embrace,
You and I holding hands in a public place. These memories are
priceless and are like gold to me, Images of the past can no
longer hurt me. We've made it through the bad times and shared
a lot of good times. But, now, together we cannot be and that
is the saddest image of all. Images of us no longer together
are now in my mind. We just can't seem to make it work.
When the pages of my memory are opened, there I find that you
were an essential part of me.
—*Jacki Rick*

A Touch Of The Earth

It's gritty as it pushes up through your toes,
   It's itchy when in your nose,
  It's chilling on a cold winter's night,
   Yet burning in a hot summer's light.
  It's as smooth as a baby at birth.
It cushions your feet as the water swirls 'round,
  Erasing your footprints without making a sound.
—*Elizabeth M. Scott*

Grandma

I saw you there, so beautiful at rest
Your hands crossed upon your chest.
You were so peaceful and calm,
The Lord had taken you in His palm.
You have suffered so with cancer,
I suppose He thought death was the only answer.
I don't know if you knew how much I love you,
And the rest of the family, too.
You were one of the best people ever to live,
Your love and help was always to give.
The life you live in heaven,
Will be better than this even.
God has chosen your time to go,
But I love you, Grandma, I want you to know.
—*Nicole S. James-Pendley*

Sun Child

I pray as I awaken for the sun and
Your smiling face
For they both have the same affect upon my being...
They give me energy and release my anxieties
That I might go about my duties
For a better tomorrow...
I pray as I awaken that you'll understand my love for you
Unlike any I've ever known or will ever know again...
As I awaken I pray that you'll forgive my
Lashing out at you...
For I was in deep pain and I fought back as is my nature...
Where the good Lord puts burdens he also gives strength
I need that strength today.
Let in the sun.
—*Myrtle Ford*

Our Youth Today Adults For Tomorrow

I know you feel that things don't always go
your way,
Just do your best and hang in there anyway.
Above all stay in school, get your diploma and a
Good education,
Because a few years down the road some of you will
Have to lead this great nation.
Stay away from drugs, gangs and a life of crime,
There is only one thing this can get you and that is
A lot of jail time.
There is only one thing drugs are good for of
which,
Is only to make drug dealers rich.
I certainly hope this message for you is quite
clear,
For as our youth today we want you to know we hold
you all very dear.
—*Eldon L. Stolzenburg*

Why

When I go to sleep at night I think
you're going to be there to hold me tight,
and make everything alright.
   But then you're not there and I start to
realize how much I care for you.
I've been so sad that I'm down here
with my dad, why did I go, why
couldn't I just stay with you? Are the
questions I ask myself everyday.
I remember how we use to play around
our short walks through the playground.
   I remember the tears we shared,
the night you said I didn't care,
I told you I'd always be there and I mean it.
—*Erica Huber*

Here After

1993 - A woman Judge -
You've come a long way, baby
Sitting high on the back of a convertible
We've come a long way
In a parade
We've come a long way
Arms around her lover, kissing
We've come a long way
A child sitting in the middle watching
We've come a long way
As the two women embrace
We've come a long way
Abraham pleaded with the Lord
We've come full circle
If ten righteous can be found
We've come full circle
Will you not destroy the whole city
We've come full circle
And the Lord rained down burning sulfur - 1993 BC
—*R. Leclare*

To Spaghetti Junction

O Spaghetti Junction!
   Zenith of an engineer's dream!
Elegant solution of highway dilemma,
   Product of Tom Moreland's genius,
Will there ever be thy equal?

Magic mingling of the numbers 85 - 285
   Splendid soaring ramps above us
Merging trucks and gasoline tankers
   Flowing endlessly, slowly inching,
Joining in the festival dance.

O Malfunction Junction!
   In 7993 will they find thy pristine form,
Parabolas, arcs and curving bridges
   Under plastic, cans, and old xeroxes,
Faxes, foils, and microwave boxes?

Will evening traffic jams still be there
   When spilled chickens, bales, loose cows,
Jackknifed trucks and fender benders
   are merely memories?
Who shall sing thy praises then?
—*Tommye Mueller*

Missing

What happened to the man I knew
So warm and kind — was that not you?
Who listened and laughed and brightened my day
He just disappeared and went away.

In his place is someone, I know not who
He looks the same, but it's not you.
Was it really just the work and stress
That turned the sweet to bitterness?

What happened to the things you'd say
Words of encouragement sent my way.
Instead sharp words like arrows fall
Or worse yet — no words at all.

Did I grieve or hurt you in some way
Or did I choose the wrong words to say?
Was it not right for me to expect
We could go on with the same respect?

Is this man now the more real you?
Was the other a role to just get you through?
I miss the friend you used to be.
I wish he'd come back and talk to me.
—*Catherine M. Sefton*

Untitled

To Austin, who wanted some shoes;
So we had a cake made like one -
    will that do?
Bright blue eyes and blonde hair
Austin is as loveable as a teddy bear.
Two years old and quite a big boy
Austin fills mom and dad with joy -
His brother and sister love him too,
this little boy who wanted a shoe.
A cute request for one so small -
"Two shoes" he said, and that's not all -
A bike he'll get on his day
The love will flow in every way.
Lots of family to share this with
Our precious little birthday kid!
   —*Melanie Smith*

Arachne's Folly

Arachne knew the unspoken law of claiming equality to Olympus
So when she revealed her talent, she was sure to start a
tempest. Minerva wove for the Olympians and sat at her loom

everyday. Admiring her splendid art, calling it the best in
every way. So naturally, when Minerva heard of this lowly

mortal called Arachne. She was outraged beyond belief, and held
a contest understandably. With supplies of the finest kind,
even threads of silver and gold, They prepared their beautiful
looms and set to creating something bold. On that day of the

decisive match, the atmosphere was tense As the women wove
their stunning tapestries, Arachne won, at her own expense.
Minerva revealed her product of unapproachable cloth But saw
Arachne's was superior and from the loom tore it off. Minerva,

in her outrage slit the web from bottom to top, She beat the
mortal with her club until the bleeding would not stop.
Arachne was so humiliated that she hanged herself from a noose,

But the goddess felt repentant and cut the body loose. And
then the goddess, Minerva, with pity in her heart Turned

Arachne into a spider and let her keep her art.
   —*Nell French*

Untitled

Cold and wet, she crawls along the smooth slab of concrete
sobbing, begging for recognition from the hundreds of blank faces
that hurry past.

Frightened and alone, she sacrifices her pride and clamors for
the smallest amount of fortune. Her will to live slowly
leaving her thin frail, defenseless body.

She finally rests against the dark and damp building.
Looking deeply into the first eyes that will notice, staring
into their face, reaching their soul, their conscience, she
whispers one word: Why?

Unable to survive much longer, her crystal blue eyes close,
the echo of the last word she spoke ringing around her forever.
   —*Kristy Roberts*

Untitled

Life today started out good, and blindly I thought it would
stay that way. Oh sure, this morning there were a few
bumps, but I thought I finished my ironing. Everything was
going so good until he slashed me open and cut out my heart
with the same knife I used on him.
   —*Carolyn Saur*

"Beast In Love"

Insanity is what I feel,
   society is what made me real.
   Crying out the killing pain,
   It drives me to live in vain.
   I can't seem to realize,
   to see life with open eyes.
   This feeling of suicide,
   I need you by my side.
   I live with broken wings,
   but for you I'll always sing.
   I live alone in agony,
   and you simply bring out my harmony.
   This feeling of going crazy,
   your touch makes me feel lazy.
And though I'm the beast in hatred's mind,
   and your the beauty that love will find.
   I'll feel my heart begin to cry.
   and baby our love will never die!
   —*Daniel E. Ramirez*

Snow

White, Clustering together like two lovers during a cold, night,
soft, gentle, caressing your face with a smooth, silky,
Invisible hand. As they fall, You hear the most beautiful thing of all.
You hear silence. Pure silence, the silence of the trees
sleeping, the silence of peace. And you see wonderful sights.
The snow almost forms a tapestry, that you wish you could take
home and hang on your wall to keep, forever. And as the snow
falls, little puffs of air come out of your mouth and gather
around the snowflakes, forming a cradle of a thousand arms,
to hold that one, special but vast, image together.
   —*Ashley Pinakiewicz*

Untitled

His beauty is true
Soft locks of auburn hair
long, glorious,
Lovingly
Shining on the forest hills
Tapering down his back
Cherished tatoos that all covered softly
Chestnut eyes as brown as mine
Streaks of golden sunrise
His decisions old and worn
They define him and his powerful mind
Raging with turbulent waves of passion
Sifting through dangerous times; thinking
Teaching people with positive energy
that seems to reflect his motion and sound
Rough edges mellow down
He is carrying the flame in his soul
That still burns bright
That will never die
   —*Joanna Rene McCarthy*

Untitled

Although I couldn't see you
You're in all my dreams
Missing you everyday
Sending my love your way
Keeping you in my heart
Although we've always been apart!
   —*Carey Luckeroth*

"Any War"

The casualties really are not small.
Some are ours and they all walk tall.
Wouldn't be if there was only one.
He happens to be somebody's son.
Should the numbers end in eight,
At least one could be someone's mate.
Then, too, what is really sad,
Some of them may have been called dad.
They are all giants in so many ways.
Who has the right to count their days?
And, when this terrible thing is done,
Who will say they did and what was won?
O God grant that this time for sure,
We all understand that there should
   never, ever, be another war.

This for those who really started this catastrophe.
And those who had to fight and die to set all free.
   —*Irene Mary Turk*

An Example Of Life

Soft, wet sand beneath my barefeet
Some discomfort from small rocks.
The sound of waves, crashing to the right,
Distant to the left.
The moon, oh how beautiful!
A perfect circle, gleaming above the water.
As I walk, a soft dusk of wind,
Brushes against my face.
And I start to think…
What an example of life!
Life, sometimes an easy path to follow,
Other times rocky.
The moon, perfect and outstanding, something to become
The sound of waves, exemplifies advice,
Sometimes heard, other times, not taken.
And the soft dusk,
May keep you from your dreams.
Stay on track
Be that person you want to become.
Because only you, can make you beautiful.
   —*Kari Schumacher*

Guess What

Some are thin, and some are fat,
Some do mock the old gray cat.
They're sewn in satin, sometimes lace,
And rest in comfort every place.

Filled with foam they often are,
And made to look, a Christmas star.
When feathers from their innards float,
They really tend to get our goat.

They're red, and blue, and black, and white,
And in our homes are quite a sight.
For kids a fight with them is swell,
I've had a few, ho ho, do tell.

Without one, all would surely mourn,
To rest their heads, so tired and worn.
Upon the floor they cushion buns,
While other still are made for fun.

Let's end this rhyme, the answer tell,
And rest yourself with pillow swell.
For man's best friend they surely are,
And for our comfort, get a star.
   —*Faith Carol Larson*

Texas Roads

Texas Roads run for a hundred years in all directions
Some rush to the future some meander through yesterday
Some scurry for miles to nowhere.
A thin black line on some on Texas map
A Farm Road lost in the past
Wanders through fields crowded with
Bluebonnets and Indian Paintbrushes
All pushing and shoving in the humming wind

This road now civilized and
Paved once ran wild and free A slash
of beaten grass past fields and farms
Stacked against the sky wind worn
A long broken chimney stands
a monument of mortar and stone
Muddy rivers of clouds beginning their flow across
the blue Blinding the sun Darkening all
And the thunder rumbles like restless buffalo
While the wind mourns and
Texas roads run for a hundred years in all directions
   —*Beverly R. Roach*

Untitled

A man never knows what he has.
   Some things just never seem to last.

A man never hurts as bad
   As his woman who knows what he had…

A man often tends to forget
   When it's to late then he regrets.

A man can't make the right choice,
   Between a Ford and a Rolls-Royce.

A man is never really grateful,
   When his pride makes him hateful.

A man soon becomes down and out,
   When he learns what love is all about.

A man remembers how to care,
   When he sees who was always there
A man decides to come home,
   When he finds himself all alone.
   —*C. M. Flowers*

Praise Ye The Lord

Let us all give "praise" unto the Lord
   Someday we'll receive our great reward.
His name is wonderful, let us give "Him," praise
   Tell of his goodness, the truth always pays.
Praise Him for the dawn of each new day
   Remembering "Him," when you kneel to pray.
We should always praise and honor His name
   Thanks to Jesus, I'm so glad, my life's changed.
Every creature should give "praise" to Him
   He'll help us through, when the path seems dim.
He's no respect of persons, He "loves us," one and all
   We must be "born" again, because of Adam's fall.
From the depths of my heart, may I say to you
   Thanks for your great love, and I "love you," too.
We should "all" be willing to do our small part
   "Praise ye the Lord," let it come from the heart.
   —*Jeannie Rutledge*

The Unknown Soldier

Although I'm unknown to you,
someone once knew me.

Someone rejoiced when I was born, and
someone cried when I died.

Someone loved me for who I was, and
someone missed me when I left for war.

Someone is lost without me, and
someone cries for me on her pillow every night.

Someone regrets things he never told me, while
someone regrets things he did.

So, although you will never know me, and
no one will ever know my name;

Someone once knew me, and
someone once cared.
—*Mary Ellenberger*

The Last Time

I walked up to the casket and touched his hand,
Someone was whispering in my ear trying to make me understand.
"He is with the Lord, his troubles are over now."
I turned my head and prayed I too could understand somehow.
All of our old memories began to flash inside my mind,
The things we had been building on would now be left behind.
The things that we had done, the places we had been,
The last time I had held him shall be remembered until the end.
I looked into his face, remembering our first kiss,
He taught me many things, things I know I now will miss.
But he shall never leave me, in my heart he'll live inside,
So he's never really left me, and to me he's never died.
As I look upon your body for the last time I will on earth,
I look into your face and again I begin to search.
I hear someone saying to move on and sit down in a pew,
I shake my head as I walk away, that not how I'll remember you.
As they take you away, remembering we'll someday be together
again puts my mind at ease,
Goodbye my love I'll miss you, rest and sleep in peace.
—*Susan A. Schindler-Wolf*

Wondering Bird

Lying there so peaceful and calm not knowing that
Something was terribly wrong,
It has feathers that are so beautiful and delicate,
no human could ever compare to it.
It has eyes slightly open yet it can not see a thing,
Because it has gone to the world of the unliving.
It soared through the air with no worries at all, till
the horrible day when it took the deathly fall.
It lived among the flowers and the large oak trees,
Until the day inside the cats mouth when it cried
Please oh please.
As the cat took its soul and committed a great theft,
the birds little life and powers slowly, slowly left.
The bird was killed for no cause, by the scary monstrous
Killer claws.
The bird will always fly in heaven just like she did
here, except for one exception she will have nothing to fear.
Do not say goodbye,
Because she will still be flying in the sky.
  Just a little bit higher...
—*Jennifer Jordan*

Give Me My Flowers Now

Give me my flowers now,
Sometime while I am here,
For when I am sleeping silently
How can I know they are there?

Give me my flowers now,
Extol some virtue of mine,
And whether the day be dark or clear,
The sun will surely shine.
What though the altar be banked with blooms,
In the air the sweetest perfume,
How can I know that this is mine,
When silent and still in my tomb?

When the earth is high above me
If one or a thousand praises were said,
How can I know they are meant for me,
When I have long been dead?

So give me my flowers now
Sometime while I am here,
And their fragrance will linger always
Because I know they are there.
—*Violet Miller*

Tears Of Joy

Many things bring tears, laughter and sorrow,
Sometimes they stream down like no tomorrow.
Tears of joy is the best relief of mind.
The stream of life is hard to find;
The length of time is not the depth of years,
Sometimes bringing many laughs before the tears.

A thousand laughters is worth your weight,
It will keep your tears from turning your fate.
Over the hard road of success of life,
Tears of joy shed through many a strife.
Across the waters of time and years,
Laughter can bring on many cheers.

Oh! Tears don't make me cry out loud,
For I count the water of the clouds.
I have to take my kerchief to wipe
The many tears of different types.
I dab with my finger at my eyes,
It is hard when I give it many tries.
—*Thomas Watkins*

Untitled

Inside, I feel an icy hand grip my heart
Somewhat like death grasping your soul.
How cold it is and how dark the world appears.
Sadness and gloom seem everywhere—
Even in the lightest of corners,
a familiar touch can make me jump,
And a friend's smile can make me cry.
Happiness is locked behind a door,
But I cannot find a key.
And yet, in spite of everything, my will carries on.
I WILL MAKE IT THROUGH.
For down the long, dark hall- there is a light.
The light holds warmth and there I am my own person.
My journey has been long and hard
and many times I have thought of quitting.
But the light held me steadfast.
Now- I am approaching the end
and I feel that somehow my trials have all been worthwhile.
The hand is lessening its grip
And TODAY, I FOUND THE KEY.
—*April Kelley*

Finally Spring!

Tiny green buds are on the apple tree
Spring has finally "sprung" in our back yard.
I long to let everyone heart me say "I feel so free."
Of all the Winter, that seemed so hard.
Leave all heavy laden thoughts and clothes,
   and shout with glee.
Spring maiden, "you look so glad to be alive."
You hid behind the deep white snow.
Peeking around the rain and fog.
Just waiting for the first sign.
And now bursting with beauty,
Singing to all. "It's finally spring!"
   —*Evelyn M. Stevens*

In Fields

Farmer gathering stones out in his field...
Spring sun and thawing earth speak to him
of growing things and warmer days
Of tree blossoms and flowers fragrant too.

A kind of communication the yield...
Mother nature shakes off winter's dim
Gives rise to hope for future days
Of greening, budding growth — the promise
of fruit in time due.

Close to nature and the Creator sealed
Gift to farmer's strong of faith and limb
Living the rhythm of natures' ways
Thankful for sun and rain that nourish growth new
   —*George F. Bergman, Jr.*

Sunset

I dreamed of a shaman
squatting by a fire on a jagged
ledge above me, dark against the reddening sky.
"Look"
he said, pointing to the west,
"The Gods are dying
The world is nearly finished"
And the red sky angered to black.
Then suddenly I was
in the frozen section of a crowded supermarket,
blinded by screaming flourescents,
trying to find a way out,
but there was no exit,
only more aisles
and more people.
And the shaman appeared again
In aisle seven,
trampled by hungry shoppers
In the last moment he said
"The Gods are dead
The world is finished"
The dream is over,
and I'm awake hours before the dawn.
   —*Kevin McGrath*

Timeless Love

My grandparents, unknown by me, were all gone
before I came to be.

So I think of my parents as they were known to be.

My grandparent's, were they much as my parents,
long before my time to be.

Their history, I find, reflects who I am.
Their love, the gift of how I came to be me.
   —*Alice Hartwig*

The Water Falls

Oh, waterfall,
Speak of my sisters
I cannot hear their voices
But I see them

They bend to tasks unknown in my world
   Bringing hides to stretch on your rocks
   Pulling, plying soft suedes to swaddle babes
   With hand flutters belying strength
   Weaving sturdy baskets
   Tucking, tugging bearers of grain and gruel

They are waiting
   Wanting to be hunters
   As you rapids pound against
   Anger interred in swollen breasts
   Eyes issue silent screams; plead
   A mute scenario

Oh, water fall,
My sisters surround me
A hunter among women
Beside me
   —*Melva J. Lewis*

Hoping, But Only Dreaming

You are like a rainbow
Special
But with your own beauty.
I can see you
But are you really there?
I search
But the ends I cannot find.
The gold is like the place in your heart
Always filled with someone else's love.
   People tell me to give up
   But it is not that easy.
   To me you are an antique,
   To someone else you are just wasted space
   But to me you are a treasure
   To dear to give away
   And precious to my aching heart.
   —*Stephanie Anderson*

Untitled

As if everything was turned to stone. I looked at them, their spirits shown. The bodies paralyzed, rotted in their places. The eyes blank stared at the corrupted faces.

Except the one, the one that moved, that felt, that tried, that understood. The hair like the sky at night as the wind rustles the trees. The eyes so dark, yet so bright as the morning dew dances with the breeze.

The arms, back, chest as a machine, strong, vital. I became weak as he put his hand in mine, I learned his title. He became mine, I his, we were one. I felt at peace. I was the earth he, the sun.

Now I feel I'm losing him as we go our separate ways. He'll be back some day, by then it may be too late. But, he's not gone yet, to help another in need. Nothing lasts forever, if I must, I will turn away from my own greed. Things will be as they once were and again everything will turn to stone.
   —*Chris Wistrom*

The Darkness Of The World

A small child as innocent as a shining
   star in the sky;
Drawn into darkness - with only a speck
   of light, which is glowing in her eyes.
No sound except the beating of her heart.
Not knowing right from wrong,
   Her innocence is taken.
   Her trust is lost.
   Her heart is broken.
   Her soul is torn.
   Her dreams are shattered.
   Her life is ruined.
No more stars shining in the sky.
No more light glowing in her eyes.
No more sound from the beating of her heart.
All that is left is a destroyed child,
   With tears of innocence rolling
     out her eyes;
As she sits alone in the
   darkness of the world.
     —*Alicia Barger*

Past And Present

Laying in my bedroll late at night
Staring at the stars that shine so bright.

Thinking of days in the past
Knowing they would never last.

Of wagons once on open plains
Now all we see are cars and trains.

Buffalo and antelope and lots of pure air
Now we find a lot of pollution there.

Mustangs and burrows were a sight to see
Golf courses replace them from tee to shining tee.

Highway s and byways and freeways everywhere
Whatever happened to the cougars and black bear?

I guess you can't go back in the past
If you did my friends, it wouldn't last.
     —*Kyle T. Pace*

Late Summer Morning

The swan has not yet awakened the cicadas have just
started their song. The cows are being fed and they tell the
world. And the moon hangs high and light,
barely visible against the blue of the sky and the gold of the
sun. The trees are filled with leaves, potent and mature.
It is here, at the edge of Fall, that I am both happy
and sad; surrounded by the warmth, the smells,
the sounds of August, and haunted by what
is to come.
I will not tell the cicadas
I will not tell the cows
I will not tell the trees
what not tell the trees
what the sun whispers to me.
I will listen and feel
and breathe in this
day, this warm August day
And wait for the
sleeping swan to rise.
     —*Kellie C. Specter*

One Life To Live

The stiff motionless corpse burned in my memory like acid on
steel. The perfect fingers which would no longer grasp a hand
laid clenched by her side. The curled toes which would never
feel mud oozing between them were pressed into the sheet.
My breath blew by a nose which never knew the smell of mother
or father. My cries fell on ears which had heard only cries
and sobs. My tears fell on lips which never tasted a mother's
kiss or a father's cologne. My gaze was riveted on eyes which
would never see a sunrise or the rainbow of a waterfall. The
flash of the coroner's camera signalled that another instant of
life had been frozen for eternity. The stillness of the room
wrapped around me like shroud, trapping my thoughts of how to
comprehend a tragedy which the victim could not know. The dead

cannot transfer their understanding, or the living their desire
to know, of death.
This creature had experienced living as I never would
but I had lived experiences now impossible for it.
Did we balance each other, some sort of cosmic null?
Thus, life moves on but goes nowhere, or do you live in
my experience until my death becomes part of your life?
     —*William J Shadwell*

Washing

   The water soaks the sweat from my skin
     Strips the dirt of where I've been
     Keeps me cool, yet warms my body
Takes me to a place I've only held in thought
 I've cleansed my wounds, rinsed my beliefs
    Of this day's deadly sins
  Passing like the breath from my mouth
  Passing and desperation goes astray
 Let me fall to sleep in this water
   At least I'll drown a happy man
     Morbid, yes I'll agree
   Reason: It speaks of my wisdom
     —*Phil Owens*

Returning

Home, coming home
striving to find that elusive place
trying to find who, what I am.

I don't know where my road is leading at times
but I know how to find my home
I know, I know
there I am safe and secure
there I am safe for sure.

Home, coming home
trying to discover the way
that's clear as day, bright as the sun
..flashback to what this place used to look like
why is it different? why not the same?

It looks so strange to me, my home where I was not raised
….more home than not.
     —*Darin Crilley*

Untitled

I have from sins of infancy
found the Lord of Wisdom
waiting at My Gate at 98, saying:
"What is done put on the shelf;
for Others, fill the Space of Absolute Magnetism"
     —*Arthur Paul Peden*

Morbyd Flowers

Morbyd co-dependency strangles my vomiting heart.
struggling-you avoid importance
black is all you see.
Thinking lazy thoughts of a beautiful future that doesn't
involve me.
Negative energy surrounds my hopeless mind;
rejectingly I force ignorant thoughts away from the entrance
to the door of my soul.
Only pondering the most beautiful sides of you.
Not a second in our chaotic world are you not in my inner most
conscious mind. Fly with me...
...to a world called reality.
eternal love shows me no bounds;
but it involves two immortal minds,
and at the present sits only one-
on a lonely bench with clinching tears falling from her mind.
She is waiting,
and will never stop waiting-
for what she calls true love.

—*Michelle Elizabeth*

Lost

As long as I have known her, she has been there.
Suddenly she was gone.
Where is she? Where is she?
My heart ached.
She was gone.
What had I done?
Was it my fault?
Should I have protected her better?
Why was she robbed from me?
I will tell no one how I feel.
I must be strong.
No one must know.
It was my fault for letting her go.
But she is not tangible.
You should not let go of her.
Virginity.
She is a precious thing.
Don't let go.

—*Kristy Blankenship*

Snowflakes

Freezing cold of winter gone, snowflakes too
   Summer smoldering hot
Colorful fall best for all
   We deny it not

Snow-white soft and beautiful
   Clean as the air above
Thanks for summer bountiful
   Colorful fall I love..

—*Donald K. McDowell*

Untitled

May we all be blessed and do what's right.
Teach the children to pray tonight.
The miracles of life are yet to come.
When we do what the Lord wants done.
When the sun goes down oh what a sight.
We know he smiles on us tonight.
When morning comes and we awake
There is no doubt of who to thank
So get on your knees and give him a call
For the Lord sees us stumble
but never let us fall.

—*Debora Dodge*

Tempting Summers

Those summers by the sea, seem to be a sandy mystery.
Summer that easily tempted childhood innocence.
Making precious lives unsure.

Only children were we, open minded free,
like virgin white eggs we could easily be smashed.
Truth comes easily to curious children,
as when wind blows over a castle, made out of sand.

Watching her mystified us. She was a child.
Are children didn't die.

When around her we felt it, the life that she spread.
But death, hung like a shadow, over a deserted ocean bed

She would flutter about the crowded beach.
Enchanting us all.
But like a lonely ocean gull,
she seemed diving for that ocean,
so far out of her reach.

And that summer the ocean gull returned.
Spending all winter scavenging among inlands' dumps.
He found he could no longer consume the ocean meat.

—*Joy Waitkus*

"Back To The Sun"

Forgive me father for I have sinned, I was born of the
sun and raised by the wind. Up through the trees and into
the skies oh God save me before I die. Some people say it
was all in my head, but they'll know better when I'm dead.
To a world I can't go, to a place I can't see, there he
said he would take me to be. To a land far away,
yet so close I could touch, a kiss of the sand wouldn't
seem much. Over the seas and into my eyes oh God save
me before I die. When the clock strikes twelve I'll be
on my way with no more to do and no more to say
I knew someday it would come to an end, only I he will
take back to the sun and back to the wind.

—*Carrie Lee*

Seven Weeks

In town called Waco, on the twenty-eighth day. A
Sunday morn in Texas four ATF men stormed to their
death, not knowing the final end. Six others thought
dead. No one knew how long the journey would be.
Only staring down eye to eye, word to word, for the
world to watch. Stories all confused by the news
team. Hints of weapons in automatic mode and of
children so abused. Step by step towards a suicide
pact made. Day by day the FBI waits through lies and
mind games, they played gleefully, joined together in
a pact made in February. In Reno's choice the gas
flowed, the bullets sprayed, the house ablaze, and
seventeen innocent died, without a phase. I got my
doubts on why today, fifty-one days to come to amen.

—*Rogelio Villareal*

Untitled

   My gift is in this box.
It's not really a gift, but my gift is PEACE.
Nothing is wobbling in it. No one is screaming
or bellowing. It's just a box with one
beautiful thought in it. That's PEACE.

—*Jessica Friedberg*

Civic Center

A pandemonium of homeless victims
surrounded by city, state and federal agencies,
a park, no longer a park
buildings monitored by security officers
people requesting? no demanding, "spare change"
officials earning astronomical incomes.

Feces strewn on streets and in alleyways
urine soaked sidewalks assault the nostrils
faces displaying despair, anger and hurt
bodies clad in tattered, soiled rags
foul language, wine and drug abuse
all manner of illicit and licentious acts.

Fear for those employed here
anger at the homeless, a constant
reminder of man's inhumanity to man
hope? no. Prayer to survive another day
to continue walking by, not hearing
not seeing, not feeling the pain,
hating the sights, the smell of desperation,
loathing, but always returning to the Civic Center.
—*Aqeela J. El-Amin*

"Spring Time Memories"

Walking through the flowers in the Spring time.
　Sweet blossoms, fragrant and fair.
I wonder if up in God's Heaven
　Spring flowers are blooming up there.

I remember the fragrance of lilies.
　By a little white church on a hill.
Where often my feet would wander,
　Beautiful, serene and still.

I pressed in a page of my Bible,
　petals of a flower sublime.
planted long ago in the Springtime,
　Fading with the passing of time.

So, if my footsteps should wander
　Among Spring flowers so gay,
I'll store them away in my memory,
　God's treasures, His fragrant bouquet.

I've chosen these precious memories,
　And tucked them in my Bible so fair,
I'll find at the end of life's pathway,
　God's blossoms, exceedingly rare.
—*Blanche Richmond*

The Prince

He rides through his kingdom on a charger of white
Sworn by his king to only do right

A pure prince, a real prince with a heart that is true
He must do the right thing the right thing to do

As princes go he's as good as the rest
As hard as he can he tries to do best

He knows as a prince he has to be tough
But also be kind to be good enough

To stay as a prince and someday be king
He has to do right and do the right thing

A pure prince, a real prince with a heart that is true
He must do the right thing the right thing to do
—*Charles Shipman*

Funny People

"People are funny" is a very trite phrase, but true it has been
taught. We reverse ourselves in so many ways with very little
thought. If its raining we complain of the weather and wish
the sun would shine; But when it does in all its glory, we draw
the drapes or blind! "I need exercise is a common complaint of
not only man but his mate; But walk to the store or church or

Our culture calls for phrases soft even tho its a tiny lie.
To be outspoken, straight and true, results in a quick "goodbye."
One listens to the spoken word with only half and mind -
The other half is still involved with problems of another kind.

The urge to learn as well defined -
And just where he's inclined.

Each one is striving for the top and is willing to forego
What's true and honest in this world, if that will make it so.

To speak the truth with no regret and live your life the same
Can bring such peace and happiness there is no need for fame.
—*Lois E. Scott*

Waiting

Thursday evening, gone only leaving
tears in my eyes.
Friday morn till dawn,
patiently I wait.
Saturday arrives, confirming lies.
A candle, a prayer -
day of rest, that is best.
Monday comes and goes, who knows?
Annoyed? Mad? Just very sad.
Tuesday midnight, this I write:
　Make all my tomorrows
　Joys not sorrows;
　Make me your only
　never your lonely.
　Take me far and wide,
　always by your side.
Wednesday is due, still waiting for you...
—*Marika Bougdanos*

Loneliness

Oh, thy great one, tell me what it is that I feel within me?
Tell me for my heart is numb, and, my emotions are confused.
What is it that I feel?

Loneliness, what is this that I feel?
Is it happiness without laughter,
Sunshine without sun,
A storm without winds.

Is it pain with never ending sorrow, or an empty body with deep,
Dying emotions.
Oh love, tell me what it is that I feel?
For the world seems so unclear and so unfair.
Is my heart bleeding with anguish and remorse.
Is my soul drifting from place to place?

Am I crazy or just confused?
Tell me what it is that I feel?
For my heart is numb and my emotions confused.

Oh, is it loneliness, that I feel?
Is it the dark Goddess of unfulfilled dreams and desires,
Is it the monster that is eating at my insides and has trapped
my soul? Oh love tell me what it is that I feel?
—*Shani Dalberry*

The Picture Of A "Perfect" Relationship

I see you trudge around my room
Tell me friend, why so much gloom?
Sitting near the wall, swirled in blue and black
I asked, "What's wrong?" and you turned your back.

When you turned again, one eye had a tear,
It's hard losing someone dear.
The other eye — dry — full of strength and vision
Ready to make a final decision.

One dainty hand — a rose so new
Knowing it's best he said good-bye to you.
A small smile creeps on your injured face,
The love for him in your heart has a space.

With a sigh, realize he's far away.
Don't worry my friend, he's yesterday.
Tomorrow he will be gone,
And you'll be better before long.

You'll never be physically abused again.
Slowly, you'll learn to trust men.
Give it time to go away.
Hey, tomorrow's your day.
—*Amanda Peterson*

Mother

Thank you Mother for giving us life.
Thank you Mother for always having time for us,
Always there with a listening ear,
a helping hand and a kind smile.

Thank you Mother for instructing us to place our
trust in the Lord and his Blessed Mother.

Thank you Mother for motivating our children and
grandchildren towards kindness and love as you did
with all your heart.

Thank you Mother for showing us how to accept suffering and
dying with never a complaint.

Thank you Mother for showing us how to live our
Catholic Faith by your example.

Thank you Mother for being you.
For all these gifts and blessings we are eternally grateful
We know as we look up to Heaven, you are happy at last
With our father, brother, and sister. We pray that you
will protect us until we meet again.
—*Edna Reicks*

Character Lines

Many feel that wrinkles mirror lines
That age them day by day.
Some get those little nips and tucks
To take those lines away
But, wrinkles are our lifelines,
They add character to one's face -
Like fingerprints, they are unique
With every line in place.
So, wear a smile and look upon
Those little lines with pride;
Time put them there, but what counts most
Is how we are inside.
—*Ruth Louise Will*

"Roots Of Love"

Ripping winds may tear the leaves
That bring to life the woodland trees.

Driving rains may flood the ground,
Choke the trees and make them drown.

Scorching sun may cause a blaze;
Scared black bark in a ghostly haze.

Yet, that which is live cannot be found
In the surroundings seen above the ground.

Wind, sun and driving rain
May come your way and cause you pain.

But look to your heart, and you shall see,
The roots of love shall be your tree.
—*Richard J. Rettig*

Strange Madness

What strange madness this
That can change one's direction, to two
Obliterate the single, to a plural attitude
Making opposites attract, forgetting one's own plans
Change the "I"s that we use to "we"

What strange madness this
This rapturous lunacy
Experienced by many, though only cherished by a few
The culprit of many an unkind words spewed

What strange madness this
That makes one struck so blind
Replacing kindness to each other
With jealousy and distrust

What strange madness this
Started by a kiss
What depth of understanding needed
To share this thing, called love
—*Russell Baker*

Sidewalk (Red Blue Nothing)

I walked on an inky sidewalk
that glittered with crushed stones.

Twinkling like the night sky, where
all you see are specks of splintering
light and the occasional passing airplane

Flash of red; flicker of blue.

So you watch the night sky
hoping to see a falling trail
of flames. Listening for
faint thunder - Nothing.

All you see is black.
sheer, rich, uncut black
so smooth your eyes have
to spoon it all in.

So shivering, a thin wreath
of frost forms from the
long, drawn out breathes,
escaping into the thick
domed sky. Leaving the sidewalk
far behind. Only to be stepped on.
—*Jonathan James Kersting*

The Voice Of God

Rise up and know my children
That I have need of thee,
Thou art my hands,
Thou art my feet,
Thou art my eyes to see.

You are my servants on the earth,
The apple of my eye,
Arise and live my precious one,
Let your reach be the sky.

"Heaven is not reached by a single bound"
No, you must work for this.
What great reward; what privileges;
And too, what heavenly bliss.
 —*Nenie Mayo*

My Playground

There's a place where children play
That I pass each and every day
I wheel past and ground where Susie swings, Billy slides and Janie rolls,
In a playground for all to find
I search the deep and distant corners of my mind
So pleasant and preserved is the time
Swings are swings, rhymes are rhymes,
The children's laughter is soft and sweet
My pedals thrash back and forth in summer heat.

The children's laughter is soft and sweet
My pedals thrash in summer heat
But there's a war somewhere out there
The children don't know it — don't tell them — it'll bring on tears.

There's a place where children play
It's in my mind when I bike the world away
It comes out whenever I desire
Susie swings, Billy slides, Janie rolls,
But my age and wisdom they admire.
 —*David L. Paterno*

The Path Of Life...

You start life out on a pretty straight path,
 That is slow and older people pass you by.
Time passes by and people move on down the path,
 That is faster and more crowded with people.
You get all confused about which turns you should take,
 Some turns are big risks,
 Others are definitely not for you.
Some people will return to this path.
 Others are completely lost out there forever.
So you should do what you can.
 Before time and the end of the path passes you by.
 —*Jill Hersh*

"Silent Black Wall"

What is the peace of this silent black wall
That touches one's heart making it still
The heroes that fell so that we may live on
Let us not forget the anguish and pain
The unselfish love given, let it not be in vain
Keep in our hearts and thoughts each day the memory and love for our heroes gone away
 —*Rosemary Irish*

Love: What's There To Understand?

He's like dew that's not overdue,
that it doesn't fall, due to the weather,
that it doesn't fall like a feather.

His love, so sweet, it runs so deep.
Deep into the mist of my mist of lists,
of his glitter and glist.

Don't try to understand the wonderful,
powerful, and plentiful thing, called love.
Cause to a dove, love's just a big mystery
and sometimes misery.
But through all the sorrow,
you borrow once more,
the love of a dove, in love,
the thing called love!
What's there to understand? Nothing!
 —*Amanda Ellett*

Photos

Who are the people in old photographs?
That moment in life the camera grasps.
What goals or dreams did they try,
What made them laugh or made them cry?
Nameless faces on a black and white still,
Their stories lost; know them we never will.
Most people see just an old picture,
Captionless, old, with a slight tincture.
But I see more when I look,
More history than has any book.
Real people I see who made the world work,
In dusty photo albums their images lurk.
Once living, loving, working, vibrant,
Now unknown; lost; forever silent.
 —*G. Hudson*

Life

At that moment the choice seemed right,
That one black day,
I just couldn't fight.
I couldn't see my future, present, or past,
But instead,
My dying life which wouldn't last.
My life was filled with sadness and pain,
So those forty aspirin,
I swallowed in vain.
I realize now,
That wasn't a good choice,
I was hurting people with more than my voice.
What I realized at this point in my life,
Is you have to live,
If you want to get through your struggle and strife.
 —*Rebekah Guertin*

Poetry

As I walk along the beach
I see Death riding waves of black.
Dark water that sends out chills
Chills throughout my body that can kill.
 —*Diep Thanh Vu*

"Believe In Yourself"

Life is a gift that's given at birth
That only the chosen receive
A seed that is planted already spiced
A masterpiece for to conceive

A life within life a child of God
With a purpose in life to uphold
Already posted on heavenly charts
With a story that's already told

Well this is your life and be as it may
It's yours to pursue and attain
Your better judgment in each step you take
Will determine your losses and gains

Let your mind be your knowledge, your heart be your guide
But never mix up the two
For in one you'll find strength with the other comes hope
The rest is all up to you

So I leave you this thought and within it a prayer
That you take on and give it your best
Aim high in your goals but don't get too bold
And your will be rewarded success.

—*Valerie Hernandez-Castor*

At Night I Dream

At night I dream
that people love people for what they are.
  Not whether they lose or win,
  Or for the color of there skin.
I dream that there were no fights,
And we all have the same rights.
  I dream that the nation,
  Didn't have so much nation
At night I dream

—*Lindsay Brooks*

The Person I Know

There's a person I know so very well,
That person's name I will not tell.

She is usually happy, and most of the time cheery
Although sometimes she may be weary.

Usually she is a pretty good friend,
Although now and then she may bend.

She tries her very best in all that she does,
She never dwells on what she was.

A few that know her very good,
Know she does all that she should.

She takes each challenge day by day,
And faces all, come what may.

She's been through very good and very bad,
She rarely ever gets mad, well, maybe a tad.

When she does, she is in great sorrow,
And then she looks forward to tomorrow.

To some she is just another face,
In this whole wide human race.

This person that I often see,
Is none other than ordinary me.

—*Jennifer Steines*

To My Son's Best Friend

I marvel
that the same species which include
a Solzhenitsyn,
a Tchaikovsky,
a Thomas Jefferson,
a John Muir,
and a Jesus Christ
            can also include scum like you.

And you would wonder
how the heart of
a Kennedy,
a Joplin,
a Jagger,
or a Fonda
            can be even medically equivalent
                to that of a nerd like me.
        that is—if you ever wondered
                    about anything.
Anyhow, would you please stop flicking your roaches into
my begonia bed.

—*James E. Jefferson*

The Way To Peace

What the world needs now is "peace sweet peace"
That tranquil state of mind that we all seek
But peace won't come till we search our soul
And find that we have not been living by the "Golden Rule"

We had the greatest teacher the world has ever known
But we thought that we could make it on our own
Now the time has come, when we must realize
That "the forces of evil" are on the rise.

We can no longer ignore, the suffering and agony of war
Perpetuated by the inhumanity of our fellow man
The answer to this travesty of humankind is-
To seek his guidance with all our heart and mind.

We inherited a "land of milk and honey"
But our love of lust and our greed for money-
Has desecrated our great nation, so now we must take a stand
And let God take back our land.

It has been written, that "peace" can not be had-
Until we learn to live by the master's plan-
To love our neighbor as ourselves- and then by his "amazing
grace", He will bless our land- and there will be peace.

—*Kathleen W. Adolf*

The Message Of The Dove

There is a voice deep within each of us
That will guide and show us the way
If only we listen to the voice of love
It will lead us to the sunrise of a new day.

To a day full of promise and peace
For all of the people of this beautiful land
Just think how glorious and wonderful
It would be to walk hand in hand.

No more hate and distrust
Only true unconditional love
Would fill all of our hearts and souls
If we listen to the message of the dove.

—*Barbara McClary*

Shatter

It was a simple joke about a past fight.
That's how it all started or lead to our end.
I was left speechless without words to make it right.
Then he said "It'll be the last time never again."

I sat there alone thoughts and memories going through my head.
Me without him us with another I could not see.
I remember his words could be really mean what he's said?
Then I realized he must have just been angry our love always will be.

My phone just rang.
I heard the word; "I'll soon arrive for last goodbye's."
I felt my hand shacking as his car came.
As he came closer tears slowly filled my eyes.

I couldn't believe it had happened till he drove away.
It hurt so bad we neither wanted to let go.
I desperately wanted to back down and whisper "please stay"
But, pride and tears wouldn't let the words flow.

Now I wonder if the love that's his will reclaim?
Can we make it through the days and years with another?
But together could we really make our love stay the same.
I would try together without you my heart seems to SHATTER.
—*Tiffanie A. Sparks*

Life

   The basis of life can sometimes deceive,
that's why we must work doubly hard to achieve.
It's a lifelong battle, that's only sometimes won,
the people who are determined are always successful ones.
Mental strength always prevails,
try hard, trudge on, I'm going to make it.
Be set in your ways, don't let others deny your dream.
Believe in yourself not what they say,
because maybe you'll reach your dream some day.
—*Chris Moyer*

"Rainforest"

A light mist blankets the Rainforest.
The ape's bellow echoes, carried with the wind.
Exotic birds of many kind swoop down from the sky.
A waterfall floods into a clear, blue pond.
Enchantment encircled, encircled by palm trees,
Glistening with the morning dew.
Sunlight pours out from behind a mountain,
Bringing the rainforest to life!
Such spectacular beauty, a rare beauty;
Please...save our rainforests!
—*Sarah Bigum*

The Despair Of Autumn

           Dust;
The autumn leaves crumble to ashes in your silky hands;
      A noise in the distance
        A signal?
         Or a warning?
   The lurid winds of winter are coming;
     I feel their chill
  Yet still I suffer the effects of August:
    A dying toad in a blackened pool;
   A forlorn rose lost until spring returns
     to lift its fallen soul;
 A young woman perched upon a rock ponders the
   slowly encroaching reign of darkness
I know with certainty that spring will return
     But will any live to see it?
—*Scott Lawrence Matthews*

Moonlight Dancer

As the sun slowly fades under the horizon.
The beautiful and mysterious glow of the moon begins to shine.
Once day has ended and the night has come.
All is silent and peaceful as can be.

Out of no where a romantic, slow song fills the air.
A woman in white, is gracefully dancing beneath the moonlight.
Each step is so perfect and carefully taken.
She gently turns and strides, as if to say, "beauty is within."

As the song comes to an end, and day is reborn once again.
The dancer disappears in the blink of an eye.
—*Rebecca Dwyer*

Fantasy

I paint a picture in my mind
The beautiful ocean is blue and sparkling
The sand is white as pearls
The sun is setting, as a faint breeze blows
I walk along barefoot, with a lover's hand in mine
As the last traces of pink and gold leave the sky
We lay near the water's edge, the sea spraying our faces.
Kissing passionately is only the beginning
As the bright moon casts silver light about us,
We lay in each other's arms
Never wanting to get up...
My mind goes blank as the phone rings
Fantasy doesn't last forever does it?
—*Amy Gago*

Tonight

On a night like tonight,
The black clouds under the moonlight,
The swooshing wind and trees,
The background songs they make relieve,

Yes, on a night like tonight,
The dancing feeling fills my delight,
The relentless wind pushes trees,
The falling leaves run with the breeze,

Only on a night like tonight,
Our spirits feel free from spider fears
and snakebite,
...and when the clouds return home,

And the breeze leave the trees' leaves alone,
All will be calm with the moon shining bright,
Only on a night like tonight.
—*Jason Velacich*

Winter Seashore

The sky was pallid red,
The city lights shown mistily.
The ocean thrashed against the rocks.
And spread white necklaces over its reach.

They sat there silently:
He, huddled in his coat,
She, with her nose buried in fur,
Head on his shoulder,
Assured by his arm around her.

Two, surveying the tide, alone.
—*B. B. Morris*

The Burdened Heart

Dedicated to: Glendeline A. Albert

The burdened heart, for reasons known only by its holder,
does not reach out, nor does it accept the giving of others.
The burdened heart, crushed, just as the body's flesh, when
it has been trapped by a fallen sheet of steel. Wounded,
the burdened heart lies silent, not knowing if it will be
saved. Slower and slower it beats, its eagerness for life
becomes lost. Then a loving appears, and attends the wounds,
to allow the burdened heart to see its tomorrows. The loving
heart listens carefully, like the hunter in the woods, when
he's surrounded by the unknown. The loving heart, with its
powerful range, need not always be present to dry tears
fallen by the burdened heart. Although sleep may fall upon
it, the loving heart does not rest, until the burdened heart
has found comfort for the night. The loving heart does not
condemn, just as the sun, it beams a portion of its light,
and restores those things once dying the breath of life.
The words I could not speak, you said them for me.
The pain I felt, you carried your own and shared mine.
The understanding I needed, you gave without judgement.
May God bless you for your loving heart.

—*Monica D. Mitchell*

"What Is White?"

White is the color of a clean crisp paper,
The cloth of a shirt
And a little salt shaker.
White is powdered sugar
On a hot French toast
And the savoring aroma of a thick beef roast.
White is the color of clouds
And the color of light,
The color you can see even at night.
White is the house in Washington D.C.
And the mouse in the wall that just squeaked.
White is everything wherever you go
From cotton to rocks, there's a lot to know.
From hair to shoes, there's much much more
There is even white when waves crash ashore.
White isn't just a color, it's a feeling too,
A color that will cheer you up when you're feelings blue.

—*Simranjit Singh Grewall*

My Homeless Friend

He lays there in silence, tightly gripping his few belongings.
The coat he grasps in his stained hand is so plain, Bearing no
brand-names symbols, merely a plaid design lightly Shaded with
mud and a few grass stains. An empty bottle of liquor and a
pipe lie next to him, halfway Concealed by the jacket he so
courageously protects. The pipe, stuffed with burnt leaves and
grass, possesses no Visible blemishes, only a polished shine
and a few teeth marks. His weathered, aged face is hidden by a
thick gray beard, neatly Groomed and picked clean of fleas,
ticks, or any other infesting Parasite that may have once held
residency in this man's face. These bugs are probably his
closest friends and confidants. The uncaring crowds pass
him by, some glancing down, but most just
ignoring him completely. He doesn't seek their pity or their
money, merely the Acknowledgement that he is an existing
human being. He does not possess the tangible luxuries that
most enjoy, but Does hold the emotional feeling of worth that
every other human Being desires so dearly. We deprive this man
of the one thing every human being deserves.

—*Shane Luquire*

Why Must A Child Cry?

Why must a child cry? When it wants
the comfort of it's Mother's arms, or her gentle
touch to clean the child, or someone to kiss it's
cries away.
   Someone to save the child from a bad dream.
Someone to make up stories. To be there to
support one. So why must a child cry? Is it
because he lost his mother or maybe his father.
   Gone, gone,.......gone forever.
Never to hear the child's cry ever again.
Dead and buried. Gone for life. Dead and cold
under ground. To wonder will they ever be united.
   Maybe......maybe in death.

—*Aisha Morgan*

The Dance Of Anger

Reacting, losing——Crying, choosing——
The "dance of anger" is about to begin.

Arguing, defeat——Macho, retreat——
Love and respect are fading, like a feather in the wind.

Why, must one lose in order to win——
Why is "once true love" now like trash in a bin.

Unforgiveness is now all that lasts——
Unwillingness to "again" be vulnerable prohibits
   removal of our "masks."

Chances have "over and over" been given and tried,
But now there's only feelings like death inside.

All the "once had specialness" is locked deep within
   "castle-type walls"
Emotionally crippled, like a broken doll.

Forgotten are the familiarities of goals and insights——
Only unseen wounds prevail in continuous fights.

"One," is a very lonely number——
But feeling less than zero keeps happiness in slumber.

Complaining, blaming, naming, shaming——
These are the tunes of the "dance of anger."

—*Jo Ann Marti*

Black

The color of hate and sadness.
The dark night, the stars are missing.
Deep underground, Satan is listening.
He rules the night, the pitch black of it.
Finds your soul in the air,
Keeps it in his deep pit.
Bars on all sides, burning like fire.
So hot they turn dark as coal, that
   fuels the heat.
You can feel your soul burn as you sleep.
Your heart beats with rage, trying to cool
   your soul down.
But Satan has took hold of it.
It's all that's needed to tear you apart,
And bring you to your knees.
   Begging for mercy.

—*Jessica Powell*

The Deepest Secret

For you, who are beautiful light in the night,
The darkest flower sings compassion
I flow into you expansion's dreams.
For you held me in your heart with aloof tower
Rapture through the morning to find you sane. It's been
You all along through temporary blisses, pretender's kisses
We ate together and drank up the sun and the moon blew lavender
Through your golden, silky skin. You, who I let slip.
Through the cold we hated together and loved each other
Into warmth. Through the heat we loved together
Sweating into soaring doves, who flew into us rhyming pathos.
The deepest secret is ours sweetest swan and though I never
Loved you or another more, I still lurk with you in
Freedom's separation. I want to love you for days, non-stop caressing
Beating in your heart, my blood never rests. Craving guiltless
Passion without shame or hesitation. I want to live
Our secret again and again, for nothing in my life has been so
Natural as the touch we endure. The deepest river.
The deepest river.

—*Timothy Murnane*

Davidly

Oh, the pain of separation and divorce
The days are long, the nights even longer
I fear, I cry
The future is gone, no life together
No life
Will I ever love again? Will I ever be loved again?
So many doubts and fears of failure
God, help me through this agony
Then one day the sun starts to shine a little
There are less tears, less bad dreams
I start to feel better about myself, start work on a future
I see the growth coming out of yesterdays
I still love you but also love myself
Why is growing so painful?
Are we so used to our ruts we need pain to advance?
I wish you well, my love, to allow you your own progress
I dream it could be together
But Karma leads us on separate paths
Only time will show if our paths cross again
In this lifetime or the next.

—*S. Elaine Davis*

The True Tragedy Of The Human Heart

There were two families, different in only one way,
The deep seeded anger which punishes anyone with none crime committed.
Everything else but the same, with the civil blood unruly.
Two fated lovers with a passion seldom feel,
Torn apart by a severing knife, the sharpness intangible.
A world full of unhappiness much like today,
Where long lasting, irrelevant hatred can make love weak or strong.
Two victims of what's meant to be must find a way.
Both of which took their own lives, wishing only to be together.
Lessons learned too late, although truly deserved.
Finally, the dislike covered with the tears and lamentations
   The true tragedy of the human heart

—*Ryan Halvorson*

Untitled

The direction of the eye so misleading;
The direction of your heart quickly to judge;
You're feeling quite strong and superior;
But you're ignorant and don't know nothing;
I don't question our racial existence;
I just question our problems and their needs.
I run through the world thinkin' for tomorrow;
Yet I'm stepped upon by another man;
What's wrong with this wicked world?
Turning against those of different color;
Reach in deep, look within the love;
Or we will conclude in civil war.

—*Kristopher Murray*

Media

The painting is so textured,
The drawing is so flush,
The pastel is so blended,
The painting enjoys fluid strokes,
While the drawing is so exact
and the pastel possesses the perfect solution.

The paint levels out when the impact of the knife
collides with the pallet.
The pencil blemishes the paper when the two clash.
The water colors are composed of the right tint for the exact image.

The wrist determines the painting,
The realism determines the drawing,
The creativity determines the pastel,
The composition determines the water color.

—*Jed Tamarkin*

The Hope Of Spring

I wait patiently for spring
   The earth seems weary from
The darkness of the cold and sunless days.
   The snow lies heavy on the ground;
And yet I know in God's own time and day
   The flowers will awake and bloom;
The sun will warm the earth,
   And life will once again spring forth;
The miracle of earth's new birth
   Will take away the gloom.

I wait patiently for God's own perfect time,
   I listen for His still small voice
To reassure me and to bring comfort to my soul;
   My patience feeds upon the hope of answered prayers.
His love eternally gives nourishment and warmth
   To strengthen and awake my weak and weary soul.
Then the dark of winter will be gone;
   The miracle of His perfect way
Will spring eternal in my heart,
   And I shall be made whole.

—*Grace Law*

Forest

Dark cries are heard from within it.
The gloomy ways of the forest
Seem to be calling me.
I see the white mist floating above me.
The mist looks like spirits showing the way to me.
Oh what does it mean?

—*Sarah Schranz*

What Is The Wind?

What is the wind?
   The Final Breath of the suicidal dead,
    The Moment
They put the gun to their head;
   Sent passed their lips, by their own insist,
    The Moment
The last drop of blood drips from their wrist;
   Whist in a woeful silent shrill,
    The Moment
They swallow the final bottled pill;
   Squeezed from throats by a tightened noose,
    The Moment
   Their hanging legs dangle loose;
    Wheezed from garages in cars asleep,
     The Moment
The poison into their lungs doth creep;
Breathe it deep within your chest - take a big whiff:
   It too shall be yours,
    The Moment
  I take the Step off the cliff.
   —*Daniel P. McLauglin*

The Diamond

True love had gripped him with its uncanny hold.
The fire burned with intensity immune to the cold.
Unlike all the rest, she viewed the person within,
Banning presuppositions for the intrinsic him.
Far from masculine, and not what others called "tough,"
She chose this stone anyway, a diamond in the rough.
She polished her stone and buffed it with care.
Two friends shared a love with which none could compare.
His past inhibitions of thoughts unexpressed
Were nowhere to be found, for from these she gave rest.
Still wearing the diamond, she beheld a new gem.
Without thinking things out, she gave into her whim.
With immediate regrets the flame she had quenched.
Sweet smell now departed in creeps a rank stench.
She pawned off their love for a cheap piece of rock.
Though hurt by deceit, her foolishness he'd mock.
There's one thing not mentioned: His heart needed no patch.
For as the firmest stone of all, diamonds can't scratch.

   —*Noah Tysick*

My White Knight

In my life there are two places I wish to go
The first one, I dream of being with you
Being with you in a wonderful land of fascination; a dreamworld of enchantment.
For I am your princess, you are my white knight
The wind breezing through our embracing bodies; embraced as though as one. No one but you and I in this enchantland
You whisper, "no one ever, just you"
For I am the one you must share every everlasting loving moment with. To live for until the end of our lives

The last place I must go will be the heavens above the earth
The blue skies, the white clouds, a heaven where we must still love beyond death. No one, nothing ever come between us, to fear us, never again. I walk along the grass of green, I do not see you. Though I feel the warmth of your tenderly touch my cheek. I turn, I still do not see you, are you here in heaven with me? The Gods tell be we are together, never parting, you and I. They tell me we are transparent, the souls of what once was, still being. Floating through this beautiful heaven, our home, yet another enchantland. We are and always will be loving, for you will always be my white knight...

   —*Treva Miles*

"It's Only A Dream"

Everything is a dream, a dream full of mystery
The fog enshrines the forest so that I can't see
The path which will lead me home
I remind myself that it is all a dream
But my racing heart tells me different
I hear it coming and knew what my fate was
And I tried to remember that it's only a dream
I turned slowly around and then knew
For certain that it was not a dream
Because I was facing myself in the mirror
The stringy hair, the bloodshot eyes, and
The pale yellow skin that outlined every
Bone in my body, faced me with menace
I saw in my right hand, a bottle of rum
And I smashed it against the wall
As I slowly turned away from the
Horrifying image and the alcohol

   —*Chris Wright*

"The Rage Of Samsoung"

   Seemingly at peace with all,
    the fury rose without warning
   as when Krakato escaped to the sky.
  aimed at no individual - just at all injustices -
   they filtered through the hourglass
    . one by one .
   until the load outweighed
    all restraint.
  It had been buried deep inside -
   hidden even from himself -
    that is
    until —

—*K. O. Smith*

Love

Please, dear, don't cut the grass just yet,
   The grandchildren are due...
And when they see the dandelions,
   They're sure to pick a few.

And running in, with gleeful grins,
   Their treasures hid from view,
I know they'll say: "Here, Grandma!
   We picked these just for you!"

Then I shall take each yellow bloom
   And find a proper vase.
We'll put them on the table, and
   I'll kiss each upturned face.

Let others have their orchids rare.
   I'd truly rather see
A crushed bouquet of dandelions
   Smiling back at me.

So, please don't cut the grass just yet...
   I see them at the gate!
Today's another "Grandma's Day".
   The lawn will have to wait.

   —*Doris Heikkinen*

Untitled

  The wind blowing wildly through the air.
The tree's swaying side to side.
A lake as blue as the sky.
Birds whistling a harmonious song.
   Spring has come.

   —*Megan J. Drew*

The Ruby

Beneath the sand,
The greedy hand toiled,
Clenching, grasping, searching the soil.

A red sharp point there appeared,
The nerve of touch, with pain it seared.

The greed of life had now exposed
The flower within, the deep rich rose.

The blood of hearts, through which life rang,
Now returns to the soil from which it sprang.

The red image once liquified and pure,
Now a tangible solid, forced to endure.

To the soil, it shall return;
Forever and ever, to relentlessly burn.
　—*S. Emauroe*

Mirror

When you look into this mirror...
　The image you see... I hold so dear
The colour of your eyes... The tint of your hair...
　Expressive lips and complexion so fair...
Upon this mirror... Within this image you view
　Is the woman I love... You should know this true
Though... You may be critical of some small thing
　The beauty you give to me is viewed in this scene...
Upon this mirror it can not show
　All the beauty... Within you... I've come to know
Your laugh and giggles... Your sensuous side...
　Quizzical looks and feelings of pride...
Put all these together and call them you
　And know I find beauty in all that you do...
　—*Kenneth D. Green*

Natures Beauty

A butterfly with wings of transparent lace.
The impish smile, on a baby's face.
The velvet fuzzy coat of a bumble bee.
A beautiful flower; to touch, smell, and see.
The lush thick feel, of grass so green.
A bubbling, winding, gurgling stream.
The wind, as it blows through a swaying tree.
And then there's "you" whom God made for me.
To have and to hold, in a warm embrace.
To see a smile upon your face
　—*Virginia Cobble Merrell*

"My Life's Story"

I guess that I was born, no proof no one has sworn,
The Lady that raised me, as a lad, told me her man,
Was not my dad, they took me in, that is no sin.
I have no really known, related kin
My name is Chief (SELRAH CWA)
The tale I tell might make you squall:
But the happiest moments of my life
Were spent in the arms of another man's wife.
　—*Arthur Charles*

Research And Development

Below suspicion, beneath the circumstance
The judges lurk, and lawyers look to lurch,
Idle by fair markets, go to church;
Surplus population dwindles as it grows
(To zero goes), astounding analysts.
Now women preach the gospel to the poor.
The land, its increase seen, shall see no more
But less—'oh, let the old confess;
'Bring me the youth!' (—A stranger to the truth,
The corporal realized their darkest fears
As, together with his social engineers,
He cobbled us anew the master's race.)
Yet, need we care? For, in this age's
Miniaturization, extermina-
Tion's concentration goes apace:
Laager and K-Lager, Zyklon-D,
Listed clinics, next (for inner space)...
RU-486. But 'teenies know, see?—
(Preteenies, too)—past and ere their hour
For modern revolutions to devour.
　—*Thomas A. Howell*

Apartment 12

The light is dim in Apartment 12
The kitchen's filled with empty shelves
Lipstick stained cigarette in the tray
It's the 5th one that she's had today.

Spilled Tequila, the bottle's empty.
Bloodshot eyes and sleep is tempting.
An open suitcase she's half packed
With unmatched clothes & cash for crack.

Tells Mom and Dad that she's all set,
Speaks of a job and a man she's met.
Not a word of this true,
Worse then that - she thinks they knew.

What happened, no one comprehends,
To her promising future and many friends.
The stories are true, they see for themselves,
About the girl in Apartment 12.
　—*Laura Vogel*

A Letter From Home

In a hollow over the hill where the sky begins,
The latent sun summons a backdrop bold
　of glowing, clarion colors
To silhouette the trees and roofs and chimney tops
　in the valley,
The light rose clouds with violet shadows trailing
　northward
Becoming a bouquet of coral rose blossoms graced by
　ribbons of purple, orange, and lemony gold,
All sinking slowly, quietly, inevitably, into the
　ample arms of night.

　Only the soft hush-a-bye of the wind in the grass...
　Only a barking dog a mile away...
　Only a loving thought of you...
　So far from home,
　So close to me at the end of the day.
　—*Cyra Grace Renwick*

The Little Balcony

In the hot mid-day sun, away from rolling traffic-
The laughter of people—
Still I sit, on my balcony, white
—Lilac scrolled—

Fragrance of satin deep lilac
Narcotizing, drifting my mind, changing the mood.
—You open my heart—

Yellow, big butterflies, bumble-bee plump
Around red trumpet bells, where the hummingbird rings-
—With a rose in my heart—

As midsummer-sun dreams, over the meadow-beauty wide-
Congregation of daisies-
In sea-blue cornflowers—scarlet "Margareten Blumen"
—I dream of you—

As wind plows the grass blades
-cotton-grass blows away-
Plucking over a mandolin—
Over contents, full-filled Anthology-
Eye of heaven around, still country - hills-
—I am with you—
—*Christiana*

Run, Run Away

Here and there it doesn't matter where.
The lightening strikes at will with force to kill.
To choose one way or another is a dream of chance.
To take cover from the storm eliminates the dance.
Bouncing around the sky, idle dreams start to reign.
With every drop, a little romance dies in pain.
Thunderous strikes fill the sense.
Although violent, there is peace; there is calm; there is life.
With enough force to tear down the fence,
The wind blows through the souls of desire.
Hurry, run for cover.
Scurry and trample; there can be no others.
Take your place.
Find your shelter.
Here and there it doesn't matter where.
The lightening strikes at will with force to kill.
It's up to you to find our place.
It's up to you to set in stone the sarcastic face.
—*Jacob Olson*

Untitled

While the other children play outside
The littlest girl finds a place to hide
As they sing and laugh and play
The littlest child tries to last another day
Even through a smiling face she cannot
hide her secret hate
The crack of the switch is all she
knows memories that last
until she is old
Never did she know a childhood of cheer
The littlest child a child full of tears
A lifetime of pain and hate and distrust
Ashes to Ashes and dust to dust
—*Reba Ashby*

The Uncommon Common

The light is dull, It does not light the way
The rocks crumble, the family crumbles.
The rocks fall, the family falls.
The pieces are scattered.
The light slowly goes off.
—*Gabriel Murray*

Treasures

The Lord directs our greatest treasures to our hearts.
The Lord has sent you to mine because He knew I would
love you with all my heart.
And my love shall not sleep till our hearts are joined.
I will follow you to the gates of heaven or the fires
of hell to show you how I feel.
Because you are the treasure the Lord has sent to my
heart for you to fill.
—*Michelle Polhamus*

Coat Of Arms

I curl up and wait for my body to warm
the mint-green sheets of my twin-size bed.
Van Morrison floats a lullaby, and my mind
drifts on "Warm Love" like an orange
maple leaf on the Mississippi.
  I hold her head gratefully in
  my cupped hands. Our hearts echo with
  only rhythmic breaths for company.
  My head rests to the left, ear to ear
  we lie with legs entwined like a
  tree branch grown around a high-wire.
    I remember finding my mother in a maze.
    of corduroy dresses on cold metal racks.
    I planted my head in the crook of her thigh
    and cried though her smell whispered, "mommy."
The brisk backbeat of "Wild Night"
snaps my eyes open, and I squeeze
the feather pillow to my chest.
—*Jeff Helgeson*

My Lovely Cell

My stark white walls face deadly silence
The mirror in which I look shows no face-
only my soul my presence lost.
Dead flowers once live like me in an
empty beer bottle show of times and
remainders in my cell
It is now my enemy, taunting me with
memories of yesterdays never to be forgotten
(To those of you newcomers may you
experience many blissful moments
as have I.)
—*Lisa Zeliski*

A Day In The Rainforest

The bright, blinding, yellow sun peaks through the oak trees.
The mist falls, watering the flowers and plants.
Branches begin to sway as the wind hits them.
Birds sing
  Monkeys squeal
    And squirrels
Life in the forest is a beauty.
But soon, the trucks will fly in.
The machinery will squeak
  Instead of the monkeys.
The saws will rustle
  In place of the squirrels
The men will sing
  Not the birds.
And soon, down goes one more tree
  Two more monkeys
  Three more squirrels
  Four more birds...
—*Lori Tomlinson*

Prayers For Peace

That girl over there, the one with those eyes.
The mixture of pain and loneliness is so distinct.
She always seems distracted by something far away;
but always has a smile if someone glances in her direction.

She's gentle with the children,
for she seems like one herself.
Yet she doesn't hold the innocence,
she knows what men can do.
She's very careful with her words
and quiet in her ways.
She strays away from emotions,
Careful not to let anyone know.
Her body has felt the anger of a relative's blows.

She wants to somehow get a feeling of carefree living,
Although she has never felt it.
She takes in the children's happiness and prays.
She prays for the thing we all want for them: peace.
So pray for her although she is no longer a "child."
But pray for the child within that still remembers the
nightmares, and pray for her inner peace.
—*Kiersten Lynn Ray*

A Prayer For Wednesday

And after time has hammered
The nails of truth in place...
I will look across the tracks
To find a beloved, timeless face

If I could paint a portrait
Of what's inside my heart...
I would paint a Wednesday
For the Gods to tear apart

And every day is Wednesday
As the weeks fade into years...
Each day I see your face
In a vision blurred by tears

And if I had a prayer that day
I would ask every voice on earth to say...
That I am running to you
Each time I turn and walk away.
—*Eleanor Lustig*

Untitled

The cat sleeps, the clock ticks on
the night is there but the world is gone,
Have you seen the girl with the beautiful face?
She's been gone for several days.
For her the pain is fully grown.
She walks the night fully alone
Knowing her life can never be
she screams her loudest, silently.
She wishes all the world away
the night swallows her like gentle prey.
She stands before you, her eyes staring black
searching for a reason to comeback.
—*Kim Bentley*

After The Clouds Sunshine

What a stormy rainy night
Left the grass green a pretty sight.
Four pink peonies opened up bright,
Yellow lilies and red roses opened too.
Petunias opened in a beautiful blue
Beauty of the flowers made me feel like new.
—*Glozella Bowman Meyer*

Mother Nature's Crying

Tigers, Rhinos, Elephants,
The Noble Wolf still scorned,
We strip them of their parts and lives,
Someday, for them, we'll mourn...

We breed like fleas and locusts,
And talk of Coin and cars,
The Real Wealth we squandering,
Won't fine palm-Trees, on Mars....

All Gore and other prophets,
Tell us to "Awake!",
We're caught-up in such petty things,
We really need "A Shake"!....

Yes, Mother Nature's crying,
Attacked by Greedy Man,
Will WE speed to rescue,
Her waters, air, and land???
   (...'cause if she's ravaged, left to "die",
    ... then, my friends, WE ALL will cry,
    ... as we bid OURSELVES!....."GOODBYE"!!!)
—*Stephen F. McCormick*

"Existence"

Daylight dances on the mountain tops.
The ocean swells to flood the earth.
Drought Dehydrate and gag our crups.
Famine and disease stagnate the human birth.

This untangible game is called life.
Cards are on the table, but they're not shuffled.
Boundless energy is full of silent lucidious screams.
The irreconcilable ignorance keeps them muffled.

Can you hear the excruciating moans for benevolence?
They are drowned out by the insipid
Predetermination of restraint,
Or is it the eccentricity of constraint?

Politicians offer insufficient expectations of meaningless
Resolutions, instantaneously detracting from our trust.
Street walkers entangled in the vicious game
Of the immoral decension and deterioration of lust.

Be happy and enjoy life!
—*Tony Diggs*

I Cry

I cry whenever I see
The once green pasture and meadow
Where gentle breeze and lilies used to play
Now barren, thirsting for a morning dew.

I cry whenever I see
A tree once thick with a leafy crown
Where robins sang their love songs tenderly
Now fallen, wearing a deathly frown.

I cry whenever I see
A river once flowing with refreshing splendor
Where water fowls swam majestic and free
Now dried to the bed, naked to its sandy floor.

I cry whenever I see
A mountain once rich with precious stones
Where gold and diamonds abound in plenty
Now hollowed, with mine shafts for its bones.

But when mankind shall join hands together
And cease to rape mother nature
And bury greed in the pit of humble surrender
Then and only then shall I cry no more!!!
—*Bienvenido G. Aguihon*

Adalian

Adalian, the flower of me...
The one which makes me see through and over the pain of destiny. Why am I here, why is the world in such fear? My Adalian tells me. Nothing can hide, pain will always arise, but look into Adalian your own or mine, find your color with your key inside. Inhabit yourself in your new mind, be ready Adalian is never far behind, I found my key under a redwood tree. Adalian taught me I am like snow; beauty that hides until the most perfect time, catching everyone's eye, spreading who I am in a natural way. I look at nature and know where I need to be, with my Adalian and that's my destiny.

—*Laura Coleman*

"Our Days"

What happened to those days?
The ones we cherished so.
They weren't extravagant, but they were special to us.
They taught us about each other, and about life.
And how one event can cut deep into the heart.
They kept us together through thick and thin,
   and helped us cope right to the end.
They were special to us in their own way,
   and will be again, hopefully, I pray.
They helped us express our feelings,
   and brought them to the surface.
What happened to those wonderful days?
Will they come again?
Will they be as important?
Or are they gone just like the seasons?
We can let them go by, we have no reason.
Hold on to those days, for they are cherishable,
   they are made of memories that will last forever.
Don't ever let them go, no, don't ever let them go.

—*Sunny Cross*

There Is No Proof I was Ever Born

There came a time and I desired to know
The passport called for place and name, a fact
of was and where. "It's true," my father said.
"It's true, the midwife sighed and screaming I
   aborned the world into my parent's bed.

In time, the Bible record disappeared
   and with it confirmation. It was
the old bird, lost in trackless sands and rime.
   Began at home and where am I to die.

   No memory for me of long ago
and my belief is faith. What did I dream.
   Because I am a part I am alive.
   Because of what happened I am a part.

     What happened.

—*Aaron*

Empty Street

The workday is done,
The people have gone.
Silence.
Even the sun is disappearing
The street, the buildings, and offices are abandoned
Alone, and deserted.
There are soft distant sounds of leaves rustling
And the empty soda cans on the street rolling.
People have gone
And darkness creeps out like a sly cat in the night.
The wind moans sadly.
Dark gloomy shades from the disappearing sun like velvet,
Deep scarlet and midnight blue
Wash over the empty street and cover the sky.

—*Josephine N. Kizza*

Maryland's Eastern Shore

It's pleasant living on the Eastern Shore
The place you want to come to o'er and o'er.
Where the crabs are succulent and sweet
And red ripe strawberries, oh what a treat!
Corn on the cob and melons galore,
There's no place like the Eastern shore.

It's back to Idaho, you must be going,
But, your physique is surely showing
Those scrumptious meals you've been fed
From early rising till you are tucked in bed.
You've got to go home, and that's for sure,
But you'll be remembering the Eastern Shore.

You hate to leave your family and friends
But all good things must come to an end.
The chicken and dumplin's, you'll miss them, too.
The oyster sandwiches you've eaten a few,
And Mom's ice cream that tastes like more,
These things just taste better on the Eastern Shore.

—*Virginia Messick*

Going Fast

As the drapes are pulled and the shutters drawn
The proof is clear - another day is gone
I sit in the dark and think of the day
The seconds tick by and it all slips away

Each night I ponder of what is now past
Oh how I wish each moment could last
This day I have lived, is now out of reach
The good and the bad washed out from my beach

It's over and done and in my life's file
Oh what a sadness when I end each mile
I grasp in the night for the sun to shine through
As the hours do pass, it soon becomes true

The sun is warm, so again I will start
And treasure each moment, deep in my heart
Life is too short to throw the memory away
So while I am here, let us caress each day.

—*Beth A. Nickerson*

Scotia Mines

The wind grew strong and cold as I watched the lightning flash
The rain started pouring down and then I heard a blast
I ran on home to Mamma to see what was wrong and as I opened
   the door
I heard the ringing of the telephone
"Mamma, Mamma, what has happened? You'd better pull yourself
   together."
She said, "Son, don't ask me questions now. Just go and get my
   sweater."

We started walking up a hill. She ran ahead. I tried to hold onto her
   arm, but she jerked away and said,
"Son there was an explosion inside the Scotia Mines last night.
Your Daddy was on the rescue team; they asked if he would go
inside and he said, 'Yes.'

   After all the men were out another explosion took place.
   Your Daddy was almost out, but he could not be saved."

Now you can tell a hungry child tomorrow he'll have food to eat.
Or promise hem a brand new pair of shoes to go on his cold feet.
But how can you tell a thirteen year old boy who's hurting for
   his Daddy inside,
That tomorrow the pain will go away and everything will be all right?"

—*Margaret Buell Neal Sheffield Colvin*

Non-Traditional

    School days, (school daze?)
    The refrain lingers, long past
    The sunny football games and
F&*R+*E<*N%Z^*I**E *D final exams.

    I didn't stay. . . the mountains called,
      And skiing, song-making,
      Being easy-free and foolish,
        N—o-NF—o-c——Us—E-d

    The birds flew, and time extended . . .
    A sense of longing, a need to return
To acquire greater knowledge — to reach, to reimburse
    A life of learning, behind and ahead?

    Study, question, ponder, wonder . . .
      Will young minds accept
        My maturity and age?
My enthusiasm to participate? To know?

    They do! The hope and promise of youth
      Share with me the joy and caring,
    Excitement and frustration — the trying,
        Learning into eternity.
    —*Annette L. Backus*

Requiem For A Love

Suddenly, today it was back in my thoughts;
The restless, exciting person of my memory...
The one I didn't get to love.

It rains, it snows; it's warm or cold;
Again, today it was back in my mind, in my thoughts,
The lovely, dream person.. the one
I didn't get, and won't have to love.

Too many long, full of maybe years,
the living dead, life full of fears...
Silent prayers and empty tears.

Requiem for a love that never was.
Living, smiling and trying so hard again.

No more maybe. No more hurting;
Whatever was, is not.
Today, shining promises for all,
the present is just a requiem
For your love.
    —*Alma D. Guadalupe*

"The Actor's Dream"

In the beautiful garden of flowers
The Rose - the gem of them all,
The actors recalling the message
For a true friend they are hoping to meet,
The doll is dancing the polka
Way down at the players feet,
The blossoms have smiles in abundance
In this wonderful pictorial scene,
The lily looks up at the actor
With a smile so gracious and sweet
To greet a pleasant good morning
As this beautiful company meet,
The message is now at hand
Which says, we thank you!
For creating a picture so grand!.
    —*George Barden*

Comfort Zone

The cry of the winds
The sighs of the angels,
heard in the distance.

A distance you can not reach
A distance forbidden to you.
You may try to reach for this
distance, but you are inclosed by
a force greater than yours.

A sad song melody
A cry of the steadily throbbing heart
Feeling safe and special in your own
world, but when put into a world
not welcome to you knowing you can
never come back to the world you were
born into. Not being able for your cries
your sighs and longing for your world.
You can only remember the happy thoughts
of the COMFORT ZONE.
    —*Jessica Hay*

Spring

Spring is a pretty time of the year,
the sky is almost always as blue as the sea,
and bird's are singing everywhere in the trees.

Spring is new things after a long winters
rest, and when things are really at there best.

Spring is listening to the cricket's sing,
and watching the grass turn green, its got
to be the prettiest thing I have ever heard
or seen.

Spring is watching the bees buzz on
the flowers and it just seem's like
they take for hours.

Spring is just having lots of fun
when the work is done, and just spending
time with family and friends and enjoying
time in the sun.
    —*Robert Hallman*

Who Gives A Damn

Who gives a damn if the world goes round.
The sky is blue the grass is green. Who gives a damn about
night and day. Why we live how we breath.
Who gives a damn why the rich get richer
The poor gets poorer the lonely gets lonelier.
I do, I mean isn't this suppose to be a world of
Concern. Just happiness, and of one God. Or was I
the one that was raised wrong. I was taught to
Love thy neighbor. Cherish thy world, and relish thy
feelings. To honor and love all that is living of the
sake of one loyalty to themselves. Yet all I seem to
see and hear about is hate, and self-power. We need to
come together as one in unity before it is too late to
say: I am sorry for you are my brother
  I am sorry for you are my kin.
  I am sorry for we are as equals
  I am sorry all that have made you cry
  I am sorry for not saying sorry a million years ago.
For without each other neither one of us is nothing, will be
nothing can be nothing.
    —*Darryl Ramsey*

Sounds Of Nature

The snow falls softly in the night,
The sky is dark, but the moon is bright.
The air is crisp and cold and still.
All is silent, as if by God's will.

From one lone cabin there shines a light,
To pierce the darkness of the silent night.
The sounds of nature come from within.
They're everlasting. They've always been.

A woman moans and cries aloud.
Another speaks softly and wipes her brow.
The hours pass 'til nearly morn,
When, with one loud cry, a child is born.

The sun shines brightly on the crisp, white world.
The mother sings softly to her new baby girl.
Life continues, yet stays the same.
The sounds of nature will always remain.
—*Shelli Roe*

Sunset

The shimmering sunset silhouettes the ridge,
the soft hues of darkness lurk around the edge.

The sky becomes like an artist's palette,
with a mixture of colors that can only be magic.

A dazzling brilliance that is breathtaking and bold,
only to fade as darkness takes hold.

Another day has come to an end,
but the beautiful sunset will come again and again.
—*Candice M. Beck*

A Higher Ground

A breeze, a sunrise, the call
the sounding of a new day,
the annunciation of a crossroads,
taking me to a higher ground.

Not a choice like that of Frost.
But one to serve as a spring to something new.
A fresh outlook, an inner peace attained, giving
a complete view from the valley to the clouds.

Like before the first drop of dew
I have a clear path of sight.
A guiding light illuminating my way,
Showing the direction to a harmonious oneness.

The call propels me to reach farther.
Show myself in my trust sense.
Courage, strength, and tranquility
Taking me to a higher ground.
—*Neil Glass*

My Mind

My mind is like a sea,
  The waves of life swallow me up.

The storms are the hard times,
  The calm is the sadness.

The fish are there to remind me of memories,
  And the weeds are my confusion.

The simple waves are my happiness.

The sharks are the troubles that swarm
  around me.

And the sunsets are the special moments
  that set me back into perfection.
—*Erin Sawyer*

Thank You, Chicago

Thank you, Chicago, for guarding so well
The suitcase I left in your care.
I had to go on to San Francisco
For the week-end convention there.

I left my gown of ruffles and lace,
My gold shoes and tiara at your place.
I don't know if they'll let me in This Fabulous Place
In my tee shirt and dungaree.

Being wined and dined in glamorous company
As I accept my award on National T.V.
I'll be the only one in disgrace
In my tee shirt and dungaree.

But ... I know when I get home to New Jersey
My suitcase will be there for me.
As I clutch my award to my bosom
Still in tee shirt and dungaree.
—*Mertie Elizabeth Boucher*

The Sunset

A splash of beautiful colors.
The sun slowly sinking low.
Can you tell me what all this is?
I sure would like to know.
A Sunset! A Sunset!
What else could it be?
Red, yellow, orange, blue
This blur of colors is all I can see.
Is it really a sunset?
Is that really true?
It all depends on what this poem means to you.
—*Stephanie DeMarco*

Forever Is Until Now

As I watch the roses pile onto the casket,
The tear ran from my eyes.
He was such a heavenly soul,
And he wasn't in disguise.

He used to get me fast asleep,
With just a wink of his eye.
But now it is forever,
And I must say good-bye.

Before he left he said three words,
I love, and you.
And as the tear dropped from my face,
It hit the grass like dew,

As I had a silent shock,
And said to myself, "Wow!"
I guess I'll have to say good-bye,
Because forever is until now.
—*Sandy Meddock*

Taking A Test

Pencils up, on your mark, get set, go,
the test is on, and I can't be slow.
Two plus one, the answer is three.
It's a math test and it's confusing me.
What's four plus two?
My mind is blank,
the answer is six, will I get a good rank?
The math is hard, I'm not so sure
That I can take it anymore!
Beep! That's it!
The end of the test!
Now time has come,
for me to rest.
—*Christine Ellis*

"Memories Of Summer"

The chatter of birds in the distant trees,
The tinkle of bells on a gentle breeze,
The drone of a plane unseen in the sky,
The swish of a car driving by,
The charge of a train rattling along,
It's cadence echoing a lonely song,
The buzz of a bee hovering around
The rustle of leaves a comforting sound,
The bark of a dog chasing a cat,
Kids playing ball the crack of a bat,
The greeting of friends coming together,
Everyone praising the perfect weather,
The kiss of the sun so welcome and warm,
It's golden rays a soothing balm,
The smoky aroma of a cook-out somewhere,
And laughing voices filling the air,
The splash in a pool with shouts of delight,
May this day last forever - hold back the night!
These are the memories I hope to keep,
When the weather is cold and the snow is deep.

—*Beatrice Mulrean*

Going Towards The Light

Going through a dark tunnel.
The tunnel is dark and scary.
"I feel as if I'm in a nightmare, Lord.
Why have you done this to me?!
Lord let me out!"
But as I shout at you, you speak to me softly,
"Who are you yelling at my child?
Haven't I always been there for you?
You even call me your special friend because I never leave your side.
I have not deserted you.
Look at the end of the tunnel.
Do you not see the light?"
Through my tears I look.
To my tearful eyes appears a bright light.
Bright as a star.
The light is my little sign of hope.
I should never doubt you Lord.
Help me to remember to trust you.

—*Joy Herpel*

Seasons Of Winter

With summer comes the sun
The warmth of love shadowed across the earth
I stand in silence
Feeling its presence close to me
But entangled in night
Darkness forms its barrier
Holding me back
Looking toward winter
I see destruction distracting me from the fight
I grow as spring grows
Intertwined in its blossoms
But my soul remains cold
Afraid of the warmth scarred from a burn
I felt many summers ago
But I still reach
Unsure and uncertain
Yearning to touch what I could have
Before he leaves
And winter cloaks me again.

—*Ashlyn T. Rodgers*

Sweet Sweet Fellowship

As I go driving from day to day, sweet sweet fellowship; all the way. Just the Lord and I. It has been said that you must be on your knees, when you pray for the Lord to please. Though I know different, when you can't be; for I have proven it to myself you see. No matter where you are going or where you may have just left; if you are his child, he's right there himself. Just the Lord and I. I pour out my heart in prayer and thanksgiving, and ask him to bless all who are lost and need forgiving. The more I drive sometimes I cry, with joy and pride; with my dear Lord right by my side. Just the Lord and I. I remember those loved ones who have gone on before, and my cup just runneth over, I burst out in song knowing our meeting can't be very long. Just the Lord and I alone. This is my time of close close fellowship, I suggest you try it. Just the Lord and you. My life has been blessed more and more by it. I look forward to that glad reunion day when all the dead in Christ shall rise first; oh what shouting and singing, with voices of our loved ones ringing. More people rejoicing than I experienced in happiness, but it isn't just the Lord and I, praise his Holy Name.

—*Jolene Willis*

Untitled

You're such a strange girl
The way you look the way you do
The way you talk, and the things you do
it was so unbelievable
When you caught my attention

But from the start I knew in advance
that their was something in your tender glance
the thoughtfulness, gentleness, and patience
   you showed
that made it possible to care for you so
and, to ponder inside what could've been

We didn't know each other
But, became the best of friends
and it's a pleasure and a privilege
to have a friend so dear and close
as any friend should be.

—*Ariel Castillo*

Falcon

The graceful wings of the falcon slowly caressing
the wind with its soft strokes,
   It soars over forests, rivers, and lakes.
   The falcon is free and it has no cares.
   The only thing that is on its mind is to float
through the air and see the sky turning bright orange and
vivid purple as the sun says good night to the world as it
slips into the ocean in the west.
   The falcon watches the squirrels on their never
ending chase up the trees, and deer racing down the side of
the mountain.
   He sees his home, a mighty and tall oak tree.
   He perches on a branch and in a few moments he is
fast asleep with his thoughts about tomorrow to dream about
throughout the night.

—*Justin Guarino*

Diamante Verse

Zionist
violent, militaristic,
conniving, terrorizing, subverting,
deceiver, opportunist, victim, disenfranchised,
starving, wandering, retaliating,
confused, hopeless, homeless,
Palestinian

—*Lorraine E. Lindahl*

Little Infant In My Arms

Little infant in my arms
The world awaits your debut,
Even as your eyes gaze into mine
The future speaks to me of wonders untold;

What El Dorado will you find?
O little infant in my arms,
What glories of fortune await you?
Even as your tiny fingers close around mine;

Little infant in my arms
Sleep then and dream your baby's dreams,
And I will sing softly to you
In sweet lullabies of my heart's love for you.
—*Mary Kathleen Conway*

For Alice, Forever Young

I wish I believed in Santa again;
The world seemed such a mysterious place
To have a kind, portly, old man, flying
About with reindeer and a sack of toys -
G.I. Joe, Red Flyer, new bike, guitar.

I want to remember what a rainbow's
Sight was first like - to see the hand of God
Painting across the cerulean sky -
Wondering where the pot of gold was stashed,
To heaven standing agape, neck outstretched.

To be a child is my mature desire:
To experience life with innocence,
Acceptance, gratitude, fascination -
Hold a loving hand, sit on Grandpa's lap,
Lick the remains of popsicles off sticks,
Waiting anxiously for seeds to sprout.
—*Paul J. Richards*

If I Were In Charge Of The World

If I were in charge of the whole world
The world would be a perfect place
It would truly be a heaven on earth.

I'd swim deep into the perils of the sea
race fish for miles across the ocean,
ride on the back of a whale,
and quarrel with a great white.

Next I'd go to Africa
where I'd run with a cheetah,
hunt my prey with a tiger,
and laugh like a hyena.

After that, I'd go to South America.
I'd play in the tropical rainforests, all day.
swing for vine to vine with monkeys,
and stalks meat with a jaguar.

Then I would float through space
I'd ride comets, meteorites, and shooting stars
I'd surf asteroids,
and explore all the planets, moons and everything in between.

I would realize it's really a small world after all.
—*Matthew Crotts*

New Year's Eve

On a cold December night,
The years pass me by.
With the promise of tomorrow,
A tear fills my eye.
The soft sweet touch of love,
Is only a memory.
But in my mind it's all I have,
As I recall what you mean to me.
While champagne passes lips across the world,
And lovers kiss on the hour.
My mind will drink in your love,
With my heart suspended in its power.
Over sand and oceans,
My kiss will slowly seek.
Through time at exactly twelve o'clock,
To land upon your cheek.
And again all is as it was,
No change apparent here.
Where in the sands of war is heard,
The falling of a tear.
—*Daniel C. Anderson*

Home

Iron-cast gates just beginning to rust,
their mustard brown chips timelessly fall,
dipping through the blades of the parched grass.
Weeds tangled through an old red wagon.
Porcelain flakes mixed with petals,
bees simultaneously make honey,
in the roof of the abandoned outhouse.
The front door painted many shades,
shows off patterns resembling teardrops,
a present left by birds.
Inside, spiders spinning the story too well known,
containing memories of what used to be a home.
—*Laura Velez*

Class Reunion

In innocent and school days' youth,
their paths did seldom cross.
And unripened to life's real truth,
they were completely unaware of their loss.

Divided by destiny, they lived life
in pursuit of their hopes and dreams.
He was searching for fame and fortune,
and she was seeking her prince or a king.

Now she dutifully served on this committee,
and to her it was positively plain.
He had come to this congenial gathering
to rekindle his much fantasized old flame.

But fate bound them with friendly remembrances,
and they recaptured lost laughter and fun.
And oblivious of the old friends around them,
every song they ever knew, they sung.

Then in sudden surprise, he pondered
about his fondness of this one's sweet smile.
And delighted she saw the last flickering ember
of an old flame he had loved for awhile.
—*Patsy A. Dewbre*

The White Coats Are Coming

They move in a hurried manner
Their time is always too short
They think they know all the answers
That is if they don't gent caught
If you really want to survive, the person
   you must truly see
Is the one who's inside of you, the one
   you always call "me"
Rely on yourself, get involved, keep informed
Because if you don't, consider yourself
   warned
Health is a tricky business, your life a
   one- shot deal
Become your own advocate or you may
   literally keel!
      —*Judith Katz*

Adultery

If it is like Medea that I must be
Then let me be as cruel as she
After all it was you who began this madness
And fell in love with pretended blindness
And if it was ever easy to love me
Forgetting me is something that shall never be
For there will be something that will always remind us
Of our sickening passions, our maddening lust
Our carelessness and stupidity, our blind irresponsibility
And it shall not be I alone who'll pay for this
While you with another fool live in peaceful bliss
And it shall not be I who alone will bear
The product of someone who may never care
And it shall not be I who alone will face
Shame and repulsion and utter disgrace
And if is like Medea that I must be
And kill whatever begins to grow in me
Then let me decide what is cruelty.
      —*Patricia Larios*

Growing Pains

O Yo-yo string you pull so tight,
Then let me go way out in flight.
And I think for just a moment of the freedom that I feel;
Then the string pulls back in tightness, just like a fishing
   reel.

But the reel has fish upon it and the joy of game is on,
While I snap back up to yo-yo and forget my joyful song.
Why can't I fly and grab that fish and stay out for awhile?
Why does it always pull me back and take away my smile?

Someday I think I'll know the trick of the yo-yo and the
   string;
And when I catch it napping, then forward I will spring.
I'll grab that fish and find my joy in the game that we call
   life.
And I'll joust about while shouting and encounter no more
   strife.

But a little bell calls to me and I listen to it ring;
For a question stirs inside me - who is pulling the string?
      —*Kathleen P. Ward*

Friends Always

I thank the day when I met you, because
then our friendship really grew. We sang and
played day in and day out, that's what friendship
is all about.
   The days turned to years as our lives sped by.
From the little girls we once were with a twinkle in
our eye. Now as adults I look back at the times that
once were. How fast it went by just like a blur.
I think back to my childhood days, with my
friend and I and our crazy ways.
Through grade school and high school inseparable
were we. I thought we'd be together forever, how
wrong I would be.
After two years of college my friend moved away. I felt
so alone and empty when my buddy left that day. She
transferred to another school, me, I stayed where I was.
We used to write quite often or give each other a buzz.
Although the years have come and gone and she lives so
far away.
She's always been my very best friend till this very day.
      —*McKenzie Olson*

What Do We Know About Love?

What do we know about love?
There are a lot of things about love that we know.
There is a lot of things we don't know about it.
When we find love we feel like we are on cloud nine.
Then other times we are hurt by love.
No one ever said that love doesn't hurt because it does.
Love is also a partnership that takes two people.
They have to figure out their feelings for each other.
Sometimes it doesn't work and their love for each other doesn't last.
When they are able to figure out their feelings
for each other it works out if they are meant for each other.
Love hurts but is also a pure relationship between two people
With strong feelings for each other and that is mostly what counts.
      —*Marcie M. Ackley*

Wanted That Child

It's hard enough being an adult -
There are times you're told what to do.
And when you are a little child -
You're also, then, told too.

How about before you're born -
Your voice cannot be heard.
There are those who make a choice -
- A B O R T -... How utterly absurd.

Why! Do we always make decisions -
That seem to be so wrong?
Then listen to others in what they say -
Can't we stand upon our own?

Some care for God's own word, that's true -
We read it in his book.
His plan, through earthly man designed...
Just have yourself a look.

It seems the world is upside down -
Our joy, has gone away,
When a child unwanted 'silently cries'...
"I won't grow up - someday."
      —*Alice Makla*

Born To Suffer

I was born to suffer
There is a dark cloud that constantly follows me
Everywhere that I go

The skies are always cloudy
Dense fog fills the air
And rainstorms will thunderously appear

I was born to suffer
But I don't know why

Lightning will surely strike me
It will zap the essence from my entire being

The cold winds will blow, as treacherous waters engulf me
Sapping the spirit out of my soul

Eternal happiness, youthful vigor,
And complete serenity will never be mine

Why was I born to suffer so?
—*Carolyn Cooper*

Unadvertised Special

Enter my interior, just don't pass me by,
There is a lot more to me than what meets your eye.
Although I may not look like what you really had in mind,
I'm that unadvertised special that's truly hard to find.

Sure there are those others that may seem better at first,
But generally those kinds turn out to be the worst.
They have that special packaging that's sure to catch your eye,
But when you get to try them, they are not a real great buy.

My packaging, however, appears rather bland,
It hides many good traits; but that's how it is planned.
I didn't have much control over that but I don't mind,
Because unadvertised specials are very hard to find.

I realize that I am not packaged as well as many others,
But what I lack in packaging, I make up for beneath my cover.
All that I ask is that you do not just pass me by,
Instead, look past my exterior and give me a try.
—*Gregory Tarnowski*

The Pond

Out into the forest's depth, out where old things are kept.
There lies something weird and strange, something funny and
   deranged.
It is a pond full of tears and beneath it lies old fears.
Once the children could swim, but now the memories are too dim.
Crystal clear it was before now it's muck and nothing more.
An emptiness is there now and it wonders why and how.
The poor old pond is now forgotten, even by the animals that
   visited so often.
Good bye old pond, good bye.
I ask one thing please... don't cry.
—*Tara McGill*

Boats

Boats are the key
to unlock the everlasting stretch of water
beyond the violence and harshness of the world.
Boats are the ability to make peace with the world
by coming to be one with the water.
They are the cradle of a young child inside you
yearning to break free.
Boats are the challenge to find peace,
peace within yourself and with the world.
Boats are the natural selection to tranquility.
—*David Long*

The Whale That Made The Sea Dark

There was a whale that lived under the sea.
There was no light, so he couldn't see.
He looked all around him, to the left and to the right.
But there was no light, so he had no sight.
There was no gold fish or glow fish or anything there.
Oh Where? Oh Where? Oh Where are those fishes?
Can't I have just a little bit?
Oh I know, I know, I know,
I kept beating them up, I kept eating them up,
Oh please little fishes come back to me,
Oh I promise, I promise not to eat you, you see.
So the fishes came back to him,
He read them a story and never ate them again.
—*Sani Ann Mathew*

Mom

It's quite a pleasure to have a Mom who cares
There's no one in the entire world who ever
Can compare.

When I only clean up half my room
And you tell me to do the rest,
I have to clean up all my room
Cause Mommy knows what's best.

You feed me when I'm hungry,
You buy clothes when I'm in need
When there's something I want to know
You're always there for me.

You love me, I love you
Even though we are only two.
—*Sheridan Jenice Tennant*

"David's Song"

Close your eyes, my little one,
There's nothing to fear.
Rest your head tenderly,
As I hold you so near.
And dream of the angels
That make you feel safe.
And ask them for guidance
for your parents' sake.

So hold on tight.
We'll share the light of your inner glow.
You'll teach us things about ourselves
That we'd never know.
We wanted your love
for all of our lives
And now that we have you
It's magic tonight
—*Gregory Garrett*

Untitled

Thrown out, missing, gone, forlorn—
There's time to sleep and rest and dream.
Earth churns on and life's on the move
While I've stopped dead.

Useless teeth
Can't see to listen, can't even lie.
But now at least I am alone.

"You say that I am he who wrote those lines to you
Of love and pain.
While I insist what was expressed was that insatiable
Thirst for gain."

Curse I these awful blue eyes that be
In worlds without my world's home?
—*Zimmerman Stein*

Insomnia

Cold and lifeless skin of the dead, my big and lonely bed,
these insane thoughts inside my head,
    And so I'm still awake.
Pre-dawn oblivion and fantasies, not really where I want to be,
under this nightmare canopy, I suffer inside.
Never functioning to full potential, life to me is differential
never believe in something celestial,
    My smile is just a mask.
I'm really not that stable, like a frayed cord or cable,
    a Cain without an Abel,
    Still others lean on me.
A black and white movie with no sounds, my life is lived within
    bounds,
a deep melancholy inside myself I have found,
    Lackluster is my sight.
Living in the rut of poverty, can never be what I want to be,
    others get what they want and see,
    I never get what I need.
An empty shell of humanity,
What's the reason of life for me?
    —*Danni Lemon*

"One Of A Kind"

One who is willing to listen when you are blue,
they are few and far between that really listens to you.

One who is capable of sharing your cares,
and you need for happiness, one is very rare.

One who calls and makes you smile,
just because he goes that extra mile.

One who likes to do things you do,
and expects nothing because he does it just for you.

One who is there to help make it through,
to be there to laugh and talk with you.

People are so many, it is hard to find,
that special friend who is "one of a kind."
    —*Tina Fina*

My Sisters

My sisters are very special
They are very, very special to me
I hope someday, they will be all that they can be
I know I can't always be there, but I will when I can
I know when I can't be there they are always in God's hands
When I am not with them they are always on mind
Everyday deep down, I am praying all the time
I want them to know that I love them very much
I know when I'm with them I feel
That sisterly tough
My sisters are a pain, but where there
Is no pain there is no gain
I know my sisters love me and I know I love them too
That's how I feel about my sisters
I love them I really do
I now can't put in words how I really
Feel about them this is just a hint
No actually just a pinch
    —*Tenisha Colbert*

Untitled

No wonder this country is right on the brink!
They can't make ink pens that won't run out of ink!
When I'm feeling so frustrated and no time can I find,
these stupid rhymes start playing in my mind.
It's totally insane, it makes me feel silly...
I walk through the day trying to rhyme with "Billy".
Silverstien writes nonsense jingles that pay...
All I get is a headache at the end of the day.
It can't be because I have nothing to do...
I have laundry that's calling and where's Katie's shoe?
The bus just left and my ears are still ringing,
my coffee is gone and I don't feel like singing.
How can I sit and write silly words,
when letters and cards are just for the birds!
Oh well...someday when I'm dead and buried,
they'll find these and say, "her talents sure varied!
"She could sing, she could dance, her kids were a joy...
too bad the old gal never found the right boy!"
    —*Ranelle Kane*

Changes

Time brings its changes o'er the years.
They creep in softly with no tears.
But what a difference they can make!
Timewise take twice what used to take.

Things are not what they used to be.
(Of course that's just twixt you and me).
We have no trouble sitting down.
It's getting up that brings a frown.

Sure footed's not the way we walk.
But we do better when we talk.
Don't stop on stairs you upward tread,
You may turn round, descend instead.

Remembering, forgetting too -
Both problems now no longer new,
Particularly names you know
Most unexpectedly just go.

It's little things like these, you know,
That whisper we have lost Youth's Glow.
    —*Margaret H. Balch*

Dance Of The Angels

The angels laughed that holy morn;
    they danced and sang, shouting with glee
because our Savior Christ was born.
It was a most triumphant dawn
    when God's Son came to set us free.
The angels danced that holy morn.
Their song and dance the fields adorned
    where shepherds left their flocks to see
the manger where their Lord was born.
The devil's done: his power is gone.
    Let earth rejoice, for all can see
why angels laughed that holy morn.
Let's ring the bells and blow the horn
    and roll the drums most merrily.
Our Savior, Jesus Christ, is born.
No need for us to be forlorn.
    We, too, can dance and shout with glee;
with angels sing this happy morn.
Rejoice that Jesus Christ is born.
    —*Dorothy A. Hamann*

Endangered Species

Poachers don't care about animals,
They don't give elephants a chance to speak up,
while their tusks are chopped up.

Why do we even try to ask why?
Hunters - hunt,
Killers - kill,
just to create a modern pill.

What is happening to our world today,
all our species are going away.
While their paying the toll,
We'll be the next to go.
—*Natascha Isaak*

Shadow Of The Mind

He watched her blonde hair in the early morning sunlight.
They held hands; his dark one against her pale white.

Society's shadow of the mind
Could not allow a love of this kind.

"Why do you love me?" he asked. Unsure as lovers sometimes
  are. He kissed her forehead.
She smiled. "You remind me of a gingerbread man I had when I
  was a kid."

He laughed as he threw sand in her hair.
"I'm not anybody's gingerbread man, ya hear?"

"Well, why do you love me?" she asked walking barefoot in the
  edge of the sea.
He said "It's the way you whisper my name when you reach to
  touch me.

Society's shadow of the mind,
Could not stop a love of this kind.
—*Dani Dixon*

Grandpa's Boy

A child has a very vivid mind
They know what they want to say,
And usually put the pressure on—
So they end up getting their way.

Some people think this spoils a child
Yet it is the way they learn.
How else would they know the stove is hot,
If they didn't receive that burn.

They have unlimited energy
And can run like a dear in the wild,
But don't ever underestimate
This sweet and lovable child.

As we look back on our childhood
We can see we were just the same,
Always learning things the hard way—
We'd always be hard to tame.

So let's not be too harsh with them
And keep our tempers mild,
There's nothing that can take their place—
This mischievous and lovable child.
—*J. B. Pendleton*

"10:22 P.M."

10:22 p.m. was just another minute for the Johnsons.
They live in a yellow house in a suburban neighborhood.

But for Lorie Rodgers it meant hopefully waiting
only eight, sixty-second periods more for a telephone
call that's never gonna come.

The Stephens have just come back from
golfing. Dad's jaw clinched the whole way home while a
foolish coat of silence filled the air. Junior beat dad
with a hole in one.

And good ol' Lucy wishes she wouldn't have gone
out with Randy tonight. She's starting to notice that
he's driving him and her a few miles from the nearest
pay phone and paved road.

And the bright, lemon-yellow sun rises in New Zealand,
putting a smile on the face of a widow who cried her
heart out last night.
Wait...now it's 10:23 p.m.
—*Darren Delmore*

Changes

Throughout our lives, there are many changes,
They occur in many ways.
There are changes of the weather,
Changes of the seasons,
Yes, even personal changes too.
Without things changing, there'd be no reason
To think about challenges, successes, not to mention the sky
turning blue.
Fortunately for us, changes are a part of our lives.
We often look for new directions to flow.
The direction very often is not off course,
From that, about which we know.
Whether it's social or the business side of our lives,
We're often challenged and can touch lives of many.
From days as a child to the demands of adulthood,
There are many obstacles we're sure to see.
Leap the obstacles, meet the challenges and help some one.
How rewarding and satisfying that will be.
—*Calvin C. Lee*

Any Moment

Cruel men took my Saviour, and nailed him to the Cross.
They put him in the grave, and sealed the tomb.
But there wasn't any power, that could keep my Saviour there.
He arose and went to Heaven, to be with God on high.
But he promised before he left, that he surely would return.
Now there isn't any power, in Heaven or in Hell,
That can prevent my Blessed Jesus, form coming back again.
He is coming back to get me, to live with him always.
It could happen any moment, any moment of the day.
So we need to be a listening, for the mighty trumpet sound.
When he will come and take us, to our home over there.
—*Harold L. Griffy*

Ode To Love

Oh love, some say thou art a precious gift.
They say thou art the best thing owned by man,
But I say that thou with thy arrows swift
Dost cruelly slay men by thy unjust hand.

Love, if thou art so gentle and so kind
Then why inflict the ones who seek thee not?
Thy power strong doth rule men's hearts and minds
While against thee no battle may be fought.

It's when upon a man desire is thrust
For someone whom he never could attain
Or lovers true are forced to part, unjust
That makes me think of thee as hurt and pain.

So love I pray thou wilt pity display
And make some other lonely heart thy prey.
—*Joseph B. Mann*

Enlightened Metamorphosis

These are not drowning waters
They'll not crush and pull me to oblivion
These are cradling waves
To float and rock upon
To feel gentle heavings of a mammoth mother

Eyes view the same closed or open
Cheek rests on cool emulsion
That splashes playfully at eyelid and lip
As salty rivulets caress my tongue

Undulating liquid robs me my spine
I bob about at the beckoning of a greater mind

Not warm not cold not dry but slippery
I ride away side to side
My insides gel and give no pain
As I return to a single cell again

As such—I have all knowledge beyond science and dreams
I am programmed to mutate and forge new worlds

I am a cell I am a galaxy I am nothing I am all
Because I have let go of identity and am awash in the mist
—*Irene Watts*

Free Bird Don't Fly Away

Try to stay for just one more day.
Things don't always work out this way.
Politicians who're all your friends,
must all your stories have such tragic ends.
You pushed the freebird into flight,
spread your famine created your plight.
I've got to say: Freebird, don't fly away.
Try to stay for just one more day,
things don't always work out this way.
Mr. Man if you're red, white, blue,
keep up the good work I'm not talking about you.
Seems I heard some skeletons rattling on a windy day,
they said feed the freebird I know she'll stay.
I've got to say: Freebird don't fly away,
try to stay for just one more day,
things don't always workout this way.
—*C. M. Ulman*

Abuse

I lie here crying in the dark of the night
Thinking about that awful fight
I sat right here on our baby's trunk
That night you came home completely drunk
The vase you threw at the baby was fatal
And all because he peed in his cradle
When you came toward me all I knew was the vase had shattered
Later I became conscious and my head was battered
Now I stroke our bloody child's head
But he can't feel my strokes because our baby, my baby is dead.
—*Lynn Burkett*

Search

Hungry, hungry all the years no matter where I dine,
Thirsting a thirst I cannot quench with any known wine,

Driven by hunger and thirst I go into abysmal places
Armed with courage to meet my own diverse unyielded faces:

For I am master and I am slave, I am parent and child,
Friend and foe - divided, lost; I must be reconciled.

Craving wholeness from the shards, from crumble and decay,
I struggle within myself to rule the wasted iron and clay,

Crying, crying in the dark until I am made whole,
Until my scattered selves unite and command my soul.

Let not the young grow old before they taste of truth and reap
Early harvest of their own, nor follow on like sheep

Hungry, hungry all the years no matter where they dine,
Thirsting, hungry they cannot quench with any known wine.
—*Elizabeth C. Booth*

Night

The stars shine bright
This moonlit night
The sun lay low
I sleep as the bright stars glow
The wind blows through trees
As I hear the rustling of their leaves
I drift off to sleep
Thinking of the animals that come out to creep
Down in the pond I hear the frog croak
And the hoot owl in the old oak
The song of the cricket
Echoes through the pine thicket
With or without satisfaction
The night is full of action.
—*Angie Martin*

An Old Book

My life is like the pages of an old book.
This old book is a book of subtle line.
Every line has a phrase that makes no sense,
Maybe the writer hasn't started His story yet.
The theme is an unsolved mystery
(that) I have no assumptions to its being.
Yet there's a purpose that's untold,
When I look back on my book of old.
In the future it will be
An old, old book with pages used, now empty.
—*Shelly Steward*

The Miracle

Seeing her mother in pain, was something she couldn't bear,
This pain to her, it just wasn't fair.

There was nothing she could do to take her mothers pain away.
She wanted to comfort her but what could she say?

She stood in the hospital with eyes full of tears,
Deep down inside, her heart was full of fears.

The pain-what was the use of it all?
She turned her back and looked into the hall.

And then she remembered what was causing the pain,
A little miracle, the thought eased her brain.

The family would have a tiny baby to love and to hold,
The suffering and the agony was worth it-or so I am told.
—*Crystal Marrone*

The Gift

A siren's calling beckons me, to a lighter shade of blue,
this scent of distinction, which is alone hers, the gift to self-improve.

But strangers touch and take the gift, to use it as their own,
attaining greed through blinding eyes, destroying their own home.

Unaware of future dread, these fingers continue on,
and a darker shade of blue appears, until all the blue is gone.

Her voice, once strong and viral, is now a whispering sigh,
as a lighter shade of black appears, and a tear becomes a cry.

Precious are those that have been lost, beneath this strangers hold,
the gift that once stirred with life, is now so dark and cold.

Employed and loaned towards lesser things, her will is set adrift.
An unworthy master has broken down, and larcened away the gift.
—*Chris Lancaster*

Daddy...

Daddy I always loved you, today I still do
This ugly life has cheated us both
You of your heart, and me of mine too
You filled your body with the bottle of sorrow
You left me then, drank away our tomorrows...
You made me fear you, I was lonely and scared
Your salt in my wounds I could not bear
What happened that day when you picked up the drink?
My daddy had left me, before I could think
This new man was inhuman, his heart made of stone
He stole my Daddy, my life and my goals
Who do I look up to? Who will be my hero?
Who will clap their hands for me?
Who do I now try to please?
Daddy I don't blame you, the devil stole your soul
I just hope you loved me once in life,
Because you left me oh so long ago.
—*Nicole Krug*

"Fulfillment Of A Dream"

To the woman I love with all my heart,
This emotion and I will never part.
To wake by your side each and every day,
brings joy to my life in every way.
The laughing, the smiling, and the fun that we share,
The rays of the sun upon your golden blonde hair.
I've searched all my life for a woman like you,
who could make all my dreams come so true.
I've found this woman, I swear this true,
And now I know my dreams were of you.
—*Philip W. McDowell II*

Romantic Notions

Before you, my life was empty
Tho I knew it not until your absence.
Now the finch's song is silent
The rose petal's fragrance is faint.

The colors of the sunset are less spectacular
And the promise of the sunrise meaningless.
The sparkle in my eyes has faded
And the joy in my heart replaced by despair.

Then the door opens with your return.
Your eyes search mine for acceptance
And a smile radiates across my face
As the anticipation of your caress dispels any hesitation.

We embrace, we kiss and without a spoken word
Vow never to part again,
Unless if upon your return, we can fall in love
Just this way, all over again.
—*Phyllis Cacciatore-Soeder*

Tide To You

Waves sound
Though to me not soothing
Each surge like my emotions rushing forth
Crashing relentless against a rocky cliff

Hard as the surf may pound
The rock remains
Appears unchanged
The sea refuses to concede
Each moment, completely unique and still
Strangely the same as the one before
The flood is endless
At moments more or less intense
Yet never ceasing

You are my rock, my earth
My grounding, humbling force
I am the sea, giving neither in nor up
Press and ripple against you
Tug at you as I recede
Know that it will be countless years before
The slightest change is evident
—*Carol Howard*

Our Tree Of Love

The seed of love was planted the day we met
Though we didn't know it then
It would be a day we'd not forget.
That seed received its nourishment with every smile you
    gave to me
And soon — soon the earth made room for our tiny little
    tree
Its roots went deep — its trunk grew strong —
    its branches pointed high
It became an everlasting symbol
    that our love would never die
And so its growth is endless
Its strength no woodman's ax could sever
Our tree of love with words inscribed
I will love you as long as forever.
—*George Nazarethian*

Remembering You

Distance.
Though you are close
It's as if you're still miles away from me.
Looking at your fare
Brings back the expression
That appeared on it when you told me your loved me for the
first time.
Treasured.
Forever laced into my mind
How every time our eyes met
I felt your warmth
Along with the embrace of your massive heart
Taking advantage of a single second
To wrap it, ever so gently around my own.
I realize that I love you even more for bringing pain.
It wasn't easy on my heart,
But you discovered a better path:
The road without me.
—*Jaime Barker*

Born Leap Year Day

A woman who loves you the most,
Thought your friends and relations
Should join in to toast -
Your own special day
That comes once in four years
With quadrupled size wishes
To make up for arrears.
You're robbed of that feeling
Three years in a row,
And now that it's "leaped"
There's one way to go:
Follow the "Yellow Brick Road", of course
And enjoy this great occasion,
Only Wizards create situations like this
A once in four years celebration!
And even though your date of birth
Is such an oddity, you'll meet this yearly challenge
Quite successfully -
In knowing that you'll always be
"Forever young" - numerically!
—*Carol Zimet*

"Destiny"

As I lie here in the dark and listen to the falling rain my
thoughts are many miles away. They are of a journey I traveled
once and I would die to travel again tonight - Any night I
would give to just live the pages of memories of that once in a
lifetime journey most every human travels at some point in his
or her lifetime.

At the turning point - days, months, even years later you seem
to look back and wonder if you took the right turn. It seems
an eternity will pass before I reach my destiny; for I am torn
between heart and mind. I know that one day our lives shall
again be entwined; I and this "once upon a stranger" - on the
journey that stayed in the back of my mind. Only then will my
thoughts be with me. Destiny is where my heart lies.
—*Bonnie L. Jackson*

"Not Tomorrow - But Today"

Come walk with me on higher ground-
Through meadow brooks and whispering sounds-
Lay down our swords-no battle sounds-peace within
our soul is found.
Weary one please cry no-more just come with me-
and rest ashore-
For tired we are- with such a load- we found no joy
in what we sowed.
Cast our net- with seeds of love-
Tomorrow has been— Today is here.
—*Jenny Williamson*

The Rose

The seed is sewn
Time goes by and soon it's grown
The sunshine and showers blesses its heart
Its life has begun and soon to start...

Through time and seeds it shares its life
Again blessed by sunshine and rain for further life
The family grows until one day
The old petals start to fall away

So sad one would think to see the old rose go
But no, it is just beginning again to grow
Through love and nurturing and through life and sun
The rose lives forever. Only those that know love would know
   ...it's just begun

The seed is sewn
Times goes by and healing is done
The sunshine and showers blesses its heart to grow
Its life has begun and forever more the rose continues on.....
—*June Iris Smith*

The Clock Of Time

Round and round like the hands of a clock
Time slowly at my window knocks.
What is the hurry? I say to myself
Time's on my side, no need to get off the shelf.
I feel like an adult but I'm only in my teens
So I have time to go where you have been.
Give me time in my snug little nest
While I struggle with my inner unrest.

Of the world outside, I'm frightened and feel insecure
Of all that's expected and what I'll have to endure.
The things I must do, the tide I have to ride
I'd rather stay in the place I can hide.

But that handle, oh that handle keeps staring at me
Stirring up the restlessness within me.
Struggling for adulthood, yet still a child
Seeds not yet sewn, are running wild.
Leave me on this shelf in my snug little nest
I have a few more years, who cares about the rest.
Oh but darned that clock on the wall!
Not letting me be, telling me all.
—*Hilda Sorhagen*

Him

She looks at him and sees beauty
Wanting to know more about him
Yearning to be more than a little nobody
Wanting to let him know she wants to be a part of his life
With her knowing she is nothing but a
Dying weed in the mist of fresh roses
She looks away
But only to look back
To such in his image
So she can dream about him later
—*Candace Green*

Man's War

Like sand through the hour glass;
Time stops for no one.
Escaping reality is fixed in the mind:
We cunningly escape disguising ourself will to find:
History repeats itself only because of the nature of Man.

Understanding feelings of power, greed, riches, war,
peace, there is only one that can.
Peace just within ourselves can never be;
For our own will forms a black wall not allowing us to see.

The wall can be steadfast, secure and confident
Assuring ourselves that black is white with no need to repent
The longer in darkness the more adapted we become
Eventually never knowing where the light came from.

The dark wall ever fights the light
Confusing what is wrong and what is right.
Man's inhumanity is a question of sin.
When we ourselves are defeated only then can
We begin to win!

—*Tony Walker*

Forsake Me Not

O, never leave me, love of mine;
Time without you, would seem but vain.
Life, like a fragile, dying vine,
Waves in the winds of joy and pain.

If there had been some way to choose
My walk of life's short vale of tears;
I would have chanced it, win or lose,
With you beside me through the years.

So, stay with me—and keep the faith.
Cling to life's thread, though frail it be;
Even, beyond the clouds of death,
Your love will always comfort me.

—*Clara B. Brooks*

"Power Of Prayer"

How often do you take time out to say a prayer to Him?
To ask God to forgive you for every sin.

How often have you ask Him to show you the correct way,
To be with you as you travel through life every day.

It took a crisis in my life that convinced me to pray,
Cancer was the culprit that convinced me to do it every day.

When I got the bad news something to me seemed to say,
Don't fear, my son, I'll be with you every step of the way.

It took me some time but I believe God was really there,
When my visitors came to visit I even ask them for a prayer.

After brain surgery my doctor said "about six months I fear",
With Gods help and every prayer it's now been over five years.
Now I am a firm believer that God does listen to what you say,
So whenever you feel the need, get down and pray away!

When you have prayed for everything you think you ought,
Pray the "Lords Prayer" like you have been taught!

—*george gurney*

I'd Like To Share My Dream

I'd like to share my dream with you and tell you what is best
to do,
So, first before you start the day, ask God for courage as you
pray,
Whatsoever things are lovely, live them in your heart,
Whatsoever things are honest never let them part,
Do not turn away discouraged - keep your eyes upon your dream
Fight the things within you even hopeless they may seem,
Keep going in one direction laughing at your fate
Turning to the things you dreamed of, on the track of something
great!
Fill your heart with rainbows, don't let clouds linger there
For there's no time for sadness when happiness fills the air,
We all can't climb the mountain to that glorious height,
But we can go on ahead and upwards to the guiding light.
Don't worry about the yesterdays - the winds have blown away
Lift up your heart and sing again for there's another day,
So, if you let me share my dream, life will feel sublime
For somewhere just beyond the clouds the sun will always shine.

—*Doris K. Finck*

The Parasites

Thirty days given to the fly,
to eat, and pester, reproduce and die,
While we may see seventy years or more,
to toil and play, spend and store.

We feed ourselves three times a day,
We eat for pleasure and dine on gourmet,
We strengthen our bodies with our intake,
We gorge and consume for our bellies sake.

We pester our Great Boss to give to us,
a life to live without sweat or callous,
We make a nuisance of ourself,
As we gossip, plunder and delve.

We reproduce to fill the earth,
Dependents to figure out of Uncle Sam's purse
We want to see the success of those,
That we have taught, their friends and foes.

Then we die and meet our Lord,
The generation behind us we leave our hoard.
Is this all we have come to comply
to eat, and pester, reproduce and die?

—*Nathan Weaver*

"The Death Of My Foes"

If I had the gift of an artist
to fashion whatever I chose
I'd make a painting oh so strange
and call it "the Death Of My Foes"

The monster discouragement I'd vividly show
way down in one corner an ugly mass
On the scrap pile of life, mean and twisted
And I'd design a broad path for all to pass

Lack of confidence also must go on the pile,
Intolerance, dishonesty, egotism and fear.
They'd all lie together in great array
I'd use thick black tone as I painted there.

As I'd lay aside my brush at the end of day
I'd know in my heart I could never have fame
No masterpiece, this for the world to see
Perhaps I wouldn't even sign my name.

But this painting I'd treasure above all else
It would serve to remind me each day
We make of our life just what we choose
And from our foes we must turn away.

—*Edith Greer Gustin*

"Never Change"

Never try with all your heart.
To change someone, that does their part,
To make your world a better place to be,
That you may live happily.
It will never work out, bad rules over good.
People just don't know how to act.
They'd rather go back to their evil ways,
instead of being good, deserving of praise.
People just can't get along, when you change,
everything goes wrong.
It's better to stay where your at,
that where you belong.
—*Elaine Herranen*

Musings

Flickering tendrils of faded, moonbeams seek
to cleanse his darkened soul
  of demons spawned in dead of night
  of knaves emboldened by lack of resistance
  of lovers envisioned as egoist's fodder
  of treasures enveloped in shrouds of obsession
  of memories interred in secret places
  of images burnished by passage of time
  of icons worshipped through gossamer threads
  of hungers assuaged in decadent splendor
and to expiate his human frailties
as he
  struggles to face
   his mortality
    with poignant
     sangfroid
—*Kay Gary*

"My Prayer"

Unto you I seek my salvation and pray you save my soul,
To cleanse me thoroughly from my sins and pray you'll make me
  whole.
And give me wisdom, when I know not to discern right from
  wrong,
That when I am faced with temptation, I pray you make me
  strong.
To walk after you and seek you out is sometimes hard for me,
And when I stray from your light, then only darkness do I see.
In my blindness I stumble about, trying to find my way,
Back into the shelter you made for me, oh help me please, I
  pray.
Teach me patience so I can wait, for your answer to my prayer,
Instead of walking down the wrong path and finding you're not
  there.
Please, dear Lord; guide me back to the shelter I once knew,
For I am so tired of walking alone, I want to walk with you.
Amen.
—*Lorena Smith*

Until Death Us Do Part

The beauty surrounding you and me is everlasting.
Time we've spent has been the best thing.
I want you to know I will Always Love You
I'll be there each and everyday in whatever you do
Your power is strong in my mind and soul
I'm destined to be there until we grow old.
Then we can look back on all we have done,
Smile and be thankful God granted our fun.
And when one of us departs from Earth's waiting place
Go on with your life, smile on your face
All is forgive and nothing forgotten
Wait for me, one day I'll be there my sweet one.
—*Peter John Finan*

My Wedding Day

I've always had a dream,
To be a bride one day.
I guess the good Lord listened,
Because he sent you my way.

I walked down the aisle all dressed in white,
Knowing that everything would be alright.
Lot's of happy faces, and tears too,
Wondering if life would start anew.

I open my mouth to say my vows,
And I can hardly speak.
Thinking of how happy I am,
As the tears roll down my cheeks.

God brought us together as friends,
And we grew closer each day.
We will always be there for each other,
Together in every way.

I truly thank the good Lord above,
For sending me someone like you to love.
Someone to live with and never part,
To live and care and fill my heart.
—*Rebecca Lynn Spires*

Utah

There is a place I'd like
To be, that is prettier
Than the Pacific Sea.
With spiral canyons very
Deep, and big tall mountains
That are steep.
The desert there is hot and
Dry, and the mountain
Colors touch the sky.
There is wildlife; that's the reason
People go there at hunting season.
You'll also find rivers, streams and lakes;
The beauty shown by our National Parks,
Zion, Bryce and Cedar Breaks.
These are the things that
Help to make,
"Utah a Pretty Great State!"
—*Levi Topham*

The Weeping Tree

The weeping tree stands alone isolated from the rest
To challenge the strength of a dying tree could this be a test
Hollow inside if prays for a chance
Nothing has ever given it a second glance

Longing for life as it once had been
Never thought it would wish for now to be then
It used to have the most beautiful leaves
That would sway ever so gently in the breeze

The warm touch of a kind hand
Awakens the lonely across the land
Love and attention is all it needs
That's how it survives that's how it feeds
—*Jodi Lamproe*

Somehow, Somewhere, Someday

Feels so strange yet it feels so strong
to feel this way
you've been away so long,
along time ago
it seems it felt so good
we should still be in love
like we said we always would,
we turned our back
all those years ago
you cursed me in my heart
the times you've been away
and its tearing me apart.
feels so strange yet it feels so strong
to still say I love you
we been apart so long,
I remember how I cried
the time I let you slip away
I prayed that we could fall in love again
somehow, somewhere, someday...
 —D. Clay

Where Eagles Dare

Where eagles dare..
 to fly, do we even care.
For the air, the land, the sea
 to keep it clean as can be...

Where eagles dare...
 to build nest high in the cliffs, the trees
So they can rest and raise families,
 we should care...

Where eagles dare...
 to be a beautiful, majestic bird.
Symbol of freedom, should be heard
 if we care...

Where eagles dare...
 to protect from all harm,
Sound the alarm
 we must care...
 —Yvonne M. Hillman

"I Need"

Sometimes I need a helping hand
 to get me through the day;
Sometimes I need a joke
 to laugh at along the way.
There are times when I need a goal,
 something to achieve,
And times I need the truth,
 something I can believe.
Sometimes I need a dream
 to try to make come true,
And times I need a hero,
 someone I can look up to.
At times I need confidence
 when I'm in doubt,
And times I need to cry,
 just to let things out.
Then there are times when I need a friend,
 someone I can talk to,
At those times... I need you.
 —Angela Marie Brendlinger

Mother — The Heart Of A Home

What is a mother you may well ask
To give an answer is no easy task
She nurtures, she teaches, she makes you grow
The best instructor you'll ever know

She is a tireless worker a true inspiration
Who worked hard for you with her perspiration
No sacrifice was too big to make
She'd do it all just for your sake

Time goes on and you're all grown
A product of all the love she's shown
You've become a fine person because she cared
A part of a happy family that you shared.

Now there's silver in her hair
It's time for you to provide the care
Show her it was worth the struggle
No more responsibilities she wont have to juggle.

Life is a struggle with many a test
I hope that I'm able to do my best
To nurture my children as you did me
And I hope that you'll be around to see.
 —Lucy Rae

Talents

We all have a talent - or five or ten,
To give to the Lord and to share with men.
It may not be teaching, music or art:
It may be a smile that is right from the heart.
You may not be able to build or sew,
But you may have a "warm personality" glow:
A word for a stranger, a soft-whispered prayer,
A sharing of sorrow to show that you care.
Such seemingly small things are real TALENTS, too.
So use them for JESUS - He'll bless all you do.
 —Gertrude Krenzke Ebeling

"Dreams About You"

My love for you is too strong
to have been denied for so long,
This act of being only friends in nice, though
I want to hold you and never let you go.
Nothing you do is wrong
Everything you say is like a love song.
Your blue eyes are so sweet
like the ocean that covers our feet
As we walk together along the beach in my wonderful dream
that dream about you and how everything should seem.
Every night and every day
I wish things could be that way
It's hard for me to tell you how I feel
Your rejection is something that can definitely kill
For that one reason, I am so grateful to
Still have those magical dreams... about you.
 —Angie Walker

Ode To Children

To live everyday as if it were my first, and last;
to dream every dream, and believe it will come true;
to see the world through loving eyes,
 as little children do.
To dance every dance, and sing every song;
to stay up talking all night long;
to know the worth of life is living, and to paint a sky blue;
to LIVE!
 ...as little children do.
 —Beth McKelvey

Dreams Will Come True

I wished all day, I wished all night
To have this wish at my very sight
No more threats homelessness or wars
To have freedom and smiles unlock closed doors
To think of everyone's skin color as clear
No more days of hatred and fear
Where the hungry shall eat, the weary shall sleep
The violence to stop and the bombs never drop
To have no more fights or cold barren nights
The lonely find love from the wing of a dove
Where the lost shall be found on firm solid ground
The poor shall be rich not with money but love
While voices cry out rejoices from above
And in my small voice I will then be delighted
That all of my wishes and dreams be united
Then I shall thank my lord, our Savior
for these precious gifts He gave in our favor.
—*Jennifer Sloan*

Rain

I enjoy the rain, it justifies a weary man's excuse...
To idle for a moment, to conduct a life peruse...

The gentle pitter patter, of rain upon the roof...
Initiates reflection, profound, immersed, aloof...

Pools of soft rain showers, reflecting like the mind...
Absolve, expunge, purify, once jaded, now benign...

The trickle of pure clean water, through primeval forest streams...
Clears obstructed passages, to our origins and our dreams...

The roar of raging rivers, cleanses pebbled notions...
Stimulating fresh ideas, as fertile as the oceans...

The pounding of the salty surf crumbles first impressions...
Granting time to reappraise our hasty interpretations...

The rain is natures harrow, tilling our good earth...
Rejuvenating our inner world, a cerebral rebirth...
—*Gregory V. Lomakin*

Moon Magic

Pause on a flight to the Moon
To insulate yourself with love and faith.
Shake hands with the stars
And pat the clouds that fluff by your
　fingertips.
Sing in contralto, bass, and soprano.
Let the breezes be your drum
In this journey to heaven and far beyond
Until you step on the moon and delight
　in her moonlets,
Thousands and thousands who smile, "Hello."
　—*Erma Gross-Haley*

Dogs

Wonderful pets, wonderful playmates
Though they aren't very good to take out on dates
Get a dog, love the fun
You'll know they're your only one
Give them baths, hug them tight
Let them warm you every night
I know they bark, I know they're loud
But they're great friends to have in a crowd
All in all, my poem is done
But to have as pets, they're the only one.
　—*JaRae Armknecht*

Crayon Culture

It is so easy for those crayons...
To just stand there
Bunched together
All different colors
Shapes
Names
Shades
Why
Why can't it be so easy for us people
To just stand together as one
We are just like the crayons
Different
Races, colors, and cultures
Please
Can't we all stand together and get along
　—*Daphne Limmer*

Oh, Black Man

Oh, Black man, when will you learn? The white man is trying to to keep you down. When you're on the street killing, robbing and stealing, you have fallen into the trap. By this Black man, you will get a bad rap. Oh, Black man, when will you learn? Without Jesus, knowledge and a education, you are lost. Then you, Black man will pay the cost.. Black man wake up this is a conspiracy! Racism and hate to throw you off track. Come on Black man, the white man wants to keep you back! Oh, Black man, when will you learn? Drugs are killing off our race. When a brother kills another brother, it's a total disgrace! Oh, Black race, where have we gone? With unity and love, our job is done! Therefore, Black man get off your buns; get an education, turn the other cheek! When the white man can't keep you down, then you have Won!
　—*Monique Y. Graham*

Best Friend

This poem is my special gift to you
to let you know my love is true.

It has been sixteen years ago today.
We stood before God on our wedding day.

We made promises straight from the heart
For better, or worse, till death we do part.

For richer, for poorer, in sickness, and in health.
Who was to know we would have so much wealth.

I'm not talking about material things or even money.
I'm talking about how I feel when you call me honey.

We've had our ups, and we've had our downs.
We always seem to come out closer bound.

Life can be wonderful, and strange in some ways.
How were we to know we could still feel this way.

We were so in love we thought it would never end.
Who was to know we'd become best of friends.
I don't know all the right things to say,
but I hope we'll always feel this way.

So when my life has come to an end
I'll be sure to thank God for my "Best Friend".
　—*Cheryl Hopper*

God Made Woman

God made woman in a special way
To put a "bright" spot in each day
He made her gentle, loving and caring
He made her full of laughter, good cheer
And the calmness she can bring
At times though, she can show anger, sadness and tears
Many are well-known and respected among their peers
While others are content with no such "flares"
God made woman to be a jewel so rare
Beautiful and priceless — A treasure to behold
And each has her own unique "mold"
God made woman with many pieces
Full of a wonder that never ceases
Each has her own character and personality
A real-true painting of nature to see
No matter what "the world" may take away
God's work will always stay
Her true beauty can be found deep inside—soul,
Mind and heart—
You need to look past the physical part
Because the "inner self" is where to start
—*Marlowe Jill Pietrzak*

Idledown

The rounded hilltops stretch far away
to reach the level dawn.
They're shadowy gray in the lap of the sky
as they sit in the way beyond.

Here near me their verdant greens
are met with dusty golds:
grains and crops in patchwork style,
a pallet made of bolds.

Coddled in between the hills
as if upon green cotton,
there lies the town of Idledown,
a community mostly forgotten.

Curls of smoke and sounds of work
rise as the day comes on.
This little town, a way of life,
will last no longer than dawn.
—*Jay Parkes*

At Laguna Beach

I come high atop my favorite hill
to refresh my spirits,
to dream the dreams
that guide me in my quest for life and soul.

I feel the essence of my true me
and rejoice in my creation,
celebrating
my private eternity.

I hear the gulls call to one another far below
as they follow their mysterious pathways in space,
floating gracefully
above the rocky decent to the beach.

I know heaven sings as a screen of sunbeams plays
with the warm breeze against my back,
and a magic color lights the air
in perfect harmony.

I am full of the joy of living
as my Guardian Angel relies to my thoughts,
"Come, dear one, be glad, for God is with you.
Rest on the wind."
—*Helen L. Breunig*

A Prayer Of Praise

Dear sweet Jesus to you we pray
To remove the stress of life each day
You gave your life upon the cross.
To cleanse the souls of us the lost.
And the gift you gave us was greater than nice.
For you released our souls from Satan's vice.
And blessed us with your golden book
To guide all our lives if we take a good look
For in this book the words that we read
Are nutrients for Gods Holy seed
A plan for each day of our lives
For babies, kids, husbands and wives.
And for these gifts we give you praise
With song and dance and many more ways
And praising you Lord brings such delight
That lasts through the day and all through the night
In Jesus heavenly name we pray amen.
—*William H. Warner*

A Valentine To Mom And Dad

Things happen quick, from time to time, that helps me see,
to search, and find, to realize, appreciate,
All those about me, and the slate,
Of what I am, those things I see,
That come from others, not formed by me.
My human mold, whose moral power,
Was carefully cast by their works hour.
Such heart, such mind, such conscience I bear,
Forged by their patience, confidence, and care.

With retrospect, it may be said,
That oft I've erred in filial duty and,
Failed to call or write, instead,
Remembering, clearly, those works well done,
Are readily measured by just one,
Stiff encounter in my life,
Made so much easier, free of strife,
By recalling,' fore die is cast or bell is rung,
Life's lesson learned.

"What would Mom say?"
"What would Dad have done?"
—*James Wellman*

How Wonderful

Have you ever thought what it would be like if you weren't able
    to see?
The flowers, trees, and even the deep blue sea.
The sun come up in the morning, the dew upon the grass,
The beautiful clouds in the sky that will forever last.
A dear friend and loved one who you might miss,
To look forward to hug and give them a kiss.
To read a book to pass the time of day,
And hope the ending will be your way.
To watch the birds, and listen to their song,
And see the rabbits hopping along.
So enjoy all these wonderful things that we can see,
Because without our sight where would we be?
—*Gladys Schmoyer*

The Journey

They say this journey is short
Yet for me it's gone too far
So bury me in my grim grave
And let me dream my lonely dreams
But when the bitter snow comes
Give me that warmth of hope
And I'll come back with open arms and love
And together we'll go through
The journey again
—*Christina Stockdale*

Last Dance With The Unicorns

While waiting on the moon
To send its surreal smile,
I rocked upon its crescent lullaby
A while.
It spoke in its bewitchingly familiar way
And lit my thoughts to sparkling
Giving me a say.
One shot a voice
To plummet back to me in song
I'd serenade the blackness
On key; never wrong.
With silver tongue
So wide in range
And always true
With unicorns
I'm waltzing
When I
Recognize you.
—Aimee Radel

"To Love And Laugh And Play My Life Away"

Oh How I would like to love and laugh and play my life away
To skip and run would be such fun
To have no fears or shed no tears
Just to love and laugh and play my life away

To smell the flowers and walk for hours
To watch the birds and bees and towering trees
To gaze at the moon and stars, and look for mars
To bask in the sun under the sky
And watch the clouds go drifting by
Oh just to love and laugh and play my life away

To walk in the sand down by the sea
And have that feeling of tranquility
To have joy in my heart, till the day I depart
So I go on laughing and singing
As I hear the bells ringing
As I love and laugh and play my life away
—Edmund Hodnicki

Letting Go

As a legacy of my love
  to the babies, in my arms,
I will never hold,
  I tossed out into the ocean
but one single, fresh white rose.

I felt the pain, that I had buried,
  and tears fell from my eyes.
for never being able, to give them birth,
  I hung, my head and cried.

Then I looked towards the heavens,
  and for the first time, felt at peace.
Knowing the Lord was waiting, there for them
  like he will, someday, wait for me.

I threw some kisses, into the wind
  whispered softly, my last good bye,
I may never know, who you resembled most
  But you were once; Part of my life.
—Laurie VanWinkle

Gifts

  My greatest gift was sent from above, He sent me 5 children
To give all my love! He gave me a husband I will always hold
Dear! And these are just some things I wish them to hear.
(Without them close, or without them near, I wouldn't have much
that I would hold dear!!) So I send my thanks to the Lord
above, for all the gifts He sent me to love!!
—Tina L. Docko

Good Friday Thoughts

On this, Good Friday afternoon, I find I'm at a loss
To try and comprehend, My Lord, your death upon the cross

I've read this scripture earnestly, but still I'm at a loss
To carry to the depths of me, the message of the cross

For sinful children as we are, you perished on that day,
So those who take the Word as truth, may come to know the Way

I agony, you took upon your pure, unblemished soul,
The wretched evil of this world so sinners may be whole

There's nothing I could ever do to grasp it all completely
But luckily you ask it not; the plan's been done so neatly

I understand myself to be a jot upon this earth
And yet you lived and died for me; in this I find my worth

O Jesus, King, my saving Lord, my meager thanks can't show
The depth of comprehension that my being longs to know

But even so, I summon all my reverence today
And bow my head in fervent prayer, and then my Lord, I pray:

"For what my human mind can see, the sacrifice, the pain
I thank you Christ, you chose to die, to give me all the gain."
—Maria LaPira Castillo

You Are The Only One

You want me to leave,
To vanish from your eyes,
And no longer be apart of your life.
But I cannot do that.
You loved me once,
You showed me what love is,
I cannot leave you now.
How can you just get up and walk away,
After everything we have been through?
What we have means too much to throw away.
We can work things out.
Please give it another chance.
But if you go,
Take my heart with you.
I won't need it when you're gone.
I could never love anyone else,
Like I loved you.
—Angela Dawn Murphy

Another Thanksgiving

Over the river and through the woods
To visit grandmother's gave,
Through pine-scented mountains, animals, the farm,
Oh, the memories that we save!

The gathering of the family, all the children,
So much love and fun,
And the hidden treats grandmother had for all,
From the oldest to the young,

Not to forget the odor of roasting turkey,
The fragrance of baking pie;
A table laden with goodies,
It seemed to reach the sky!

Now all has changed this year, you see,
Grandmother is now at rest
In the cemetery, snuggled close to grandfather,
With whom she felt so blessed.
And grandmother's children are wit her now - save for only one.
They were to her the whole wide world, the stars, the moon, the
sun. It's Thanksgiving time again, my grandmother, whatever
shall I do? Why, I'll do my best - my very best - to be as
loving as you!
—Betty Sweet

Chest Of Memories

We each possess a treasure chest
   To which there are separate keys,
And in it filled to its crest
   Are galleons of golden memories.

In this chest we have hidden,
   Stolen riches of the mind,
And to all others we have forbidden
   These captured jewels of time.

To this chest of memories we can add more,
   But guard it we must and hold it dear,
For outside this moment's door,
   Time is our Buccaneer!
     —*Mary E. Lauderdale Smith*

The Secret Of Success

You wonder what it is that one must do
Today to bring a measure of success
Into their life and give one happiness?
Examine well the talents that are yours,
Then strive away and practice and perfect
Whatever gift has been bestowed on you,
And never let a circumstance of life
Stand in the way of being all you can.
For when we live the life for which we're meant,
There comes a great contentment in our soul.
Our spirit soars when we have reached that goal,
And great and special blessings we'll bestow
On all within the circle of our world...
It is no secret this great fact of life.
It's just a reaping of a just reward
When souls are brave enough to live their best.
     —*Mary Jean Lane*

The Beach

When I go to the beach I can feel the sand going between my
    toes.
      And my feet sinking into the sand.
When I walk on the sand I could feel the light and cold wind
    blow in my hair and on my face.
When I walked down the beach I could feel the warm sun shine
    on me with it's powerful rays.
When I walk down the beach I could feel the cold ocean water
    flowing and reaching to my feet and toes.
When I go to the beach it's like a companion walking with me.
My friend is the kind of friend everyone dreams about down in
    the ocean.
     —*Alexia DaSilva*

They Say The Earth May Crumble

If God designed the World to be round, I wonder if He puts it together like a cake we might bake. In layers, in color to rise and with the ingredients. First the dirt - (the colors) The rock (the foundation). The water - (to separate). And then the heat - (fire and eruption). Next comes the sweet tooth, then the cavity. When a cake rises, it will also fall with the tiniest jolt. Most anything, or anybody, if overloaded, will weaken. And now our World is overloaded and may crumble. If man becomes smarter than the Creator and overloads the earth with too heavy equipment, more than God had planned for — then it becomes weak and destruction begins. And if God was a mathematician and calculated His number of people — like first He added, then He multiplied, divided and then subtracted. He weighed it out like a triangle shaped like the famous Pyramid to preserve life. I am sure He wanted a balanced World and made it round and beautiful like a cake, to either rise, crumble or fall.
     —*Susan Whitener*

For The Night

Come closer to me, give me your hand.
Tonight they won't see our small piece of land.
I turned off the phone
Nothing concerns
We are alone until morning returns.
From upstairs out of the bay is the front line in sight
Behind the horizon that way
The flickering burn of muzzle-light.

Gently drafts already creep
Through the branches in soft streams
I see the bloodhounds sleeping deep
And twitch in their dreams.
Can you hear the silence sound? louder than it was before?
Get used to hear it all around and it won't scare you any more.
Is it war or is it peace here on this meridian?
No, I think in a moment like this I'm not worried if I can.

Is this the end of our way? Will we see tomorrow?
Let's drink the last glass of this day and then let us go.
Move your pillow over here I will count you sheep
and help you to forget the fear until you can sleep.
     —*Oliver Seitz*

The Serpent

So much pain through so many years,
Too little laughter, too many tears;
A heart cloaked in darkness, a mind bathed in strife,
This is my past, my future, my life.

A child raised in love, given hopes and dreams,
In whose eyes a child's innocence sparkles and gleams.
Until life, like a serpent from evil bred,
Slithered up to that child and raised his head.

And looking that terrified child in the eye,
Entwined her small body, deaf to her cries.
Tighter and tighter that serpent constricted,
Until the child ceased to live; she only existed.

And in that moment, the child's fate was sealed:
A life filled with wounds, never to be healed.
Innocence lost forever from life's painful blow,
An adult was born into a life of woe.

The serpent stood back and surveyed his work.
He knew that, in the shadows, he would forever lurk.
Childhood drew its last breath on that fateful day...
The serpent just laughed as he slithered away.
     —*Pamela Smith Hammer*

Peace

Peace is found in the cleft of the rock,
Too priceless to buy with silver or gold,
This wonderful gem within the soul.
Without spirit to give will surely block,
While passing through valley withstands shock.
Absence of greed pays a major role
In pressing toward the eternal goal.
A giver no deceiver can mock.
O child pray the prayer of self understanding.
Giving all will give no pain.
Feel the touch of peace caressing
Sing the song, the everlasting refrain;
To give is Christ; to die is gain.
Peace flows in God's divine blessings.
     —*Rudell McGuyer*

Weeping Willow

Standing erect on the planks with the
train station behind you .....
   Wind billowing furiously around
you as you clench and unclench your fists
   surrounded by the passengers and
their farewellers, the merchants and their
wares .....
   As you look down upon your feet a single
tear, soon to be followed by others, courses
down your made-up cheek .....
   Looking up, striking your eyes
upon that train of departure you
see possible insanity .....
   Searching infinitely ..... the windows
of the train, your eyes lit upon him ....
   You wave back .... and laugh ..... and cry .....
NOOOOOOOOO !!! Your heart wrenching and
withering ....
   Stopping .... shouting words of eternal
commitment ....
     —*Michelle D. Pearson*

Keep The Faith

To cover up and take the bad with what's even worse is simple
trickery. You cover your ears when a child is weeping in the
harmful night And then tell it its going to be alright? No,
no. What is to happen if the child is to be brought into the
true light Or maybe even exposed to the complete darkness?

In a low-lying plain, men and women of all ages hold hands and
sing "I believe the children are our future," yet they have no
faith in all children Just their children. But what about our
children?

Martin Luther King, "I have a dream". Is his dream your dream?
Think about that. This child, lost, rejected by his elders,
yet disrespected by his own brothers and sister. We are not
alone. We are not alone. No cry is going to vanish the past.
The past will vanish by itself. The hope for the future's past
is in effect. Don't bother to stand in the way. Let the
children's objectives outsign the negative day. It'll soon be
okay. And until then, we keep the faith.
     —*Toni Elizabeth Black*

You're The One For Me

When I first laid eyes on you I knew we were destined to be true.
No one else can make me feel the way when I'm with you.
You're the one for me, we should never be apart,
fate brought us together but then you broke my heart.

I thought you loved me, I thought you cared
but now you're treating me so unfair.
So, if and when I'm in your arms again,
it will be like a dream come true.
You took the sorrow and pain away and stopped me from being blue.

My heart is like a locket, you hold the key,
when ever you're down and lonely I'll have some TLC.
My heart has a hole that is just so deep,
every night I think of you, I cry myself to sleep.

Could you ever imagine how our relationship would be?
If once again I had you and you had me.
     —*Livia D. Sykes*

One Poet's Intentions

I am just another poet trying to get a point across I am not
trying to be famous I don't need fame, it only creates problems
no, I don't want to be another Hughes, my favorite poet not
that I had to mention that, nor a Dunbar, McKay, Cullens or any
other that I need not speak of I'd like to be read, not
necessarily read to be liked for I don't try to please all,
some are simply not to be moved but of course, that's their
problem you don't have to agree neither disagree with my
work... I'll call it work because some won't call it Poetry
not that I care...really, to those who like what they
read...Good for you to those who dislike what they read...good
for you I'm not in this world to live up to anyone's
expectations nor are you all in this world to live up to mine
but I'll be the person that I am, of course, like the Army:
All I can be and that being it so to all who are critics - be
it, that's what you do best winners win, singers sing, dancers
dance..., and I suppose poets po-et but like I said...
I am just another poet trying to get a point across
     —*Robert Christopher Butler*

Imponderable

He cried a little as he closed the door
trying to forget the hideous gore
Just an hour ago they were happily married
yet he just found out the burden she carried
There was only a note on her little wooden dresser
It said "No matter what my love will never grow lesser..."
Then he retraced the steps of that night
The harsh words of the agonizing fight
After the quarrel he had walked away
and then he came back the very next day
Hoping to find a teary eyed bride
Instead he found her limp on one side
He rolled her over to see of she was alright
Then he found from her throat a blood streaked knife
Pulling it away he began to cry harder and harder
He realized he'd have to go on without her
Then he pondered on a reason why
The imponderable question, why his wife wanted to die
     —*Johanna Rossi*

Untitled

You get me feeling like never before
turn my emotions inside out
listening and caring about what I say
give your shoulders freely for my tears
you hold me and caress me
get me feeling so very good
we can talk about everything with each other
oh what am I going to do
you are one very special man
I'm so glad that you entered my life
what would I have done without you
so I'll say this as easily as possible
you can make me laugh, feel good
lift me to the skies above with your caress
fill me with an aching desire
only you can, only you can fulfill
you listen when I talk, you truly care
so I don't find it at all hard to believe
that I so do want you, I love you too.
     —*Erika E. Karnos*

Ambivalent Boys

Dustin and Tim are my two, precious little boys—
Two little boys who bring so many joys.
Invading my thoughts, above the friendly noise
Of children gingerly, innocently playing with toys,
Are images of boys of bygone days
For whom childhood ways are but a faded haze,
Triggering memories of a boy I once met
Who set aside his toys to become a Vietnam vet.
Camouflaged, tough men—who were only boys in disguise,
Distanced from innocence listening to other boys' cries.
Meanwhile, other boys painted yet another picture:
Laughing on campus, while distributing antiwar literature.
Some boys went on to become wonderful fathers,
Others did not or were unable to travel life's roads farther.
Some followed an inner call,
While others, from grace did fall.
While some boys pay the jury's call,
Others are honored on memorials and the Wall:
Boys can make the world sore like a sting
Or bring pride and joy by doing special things.
—*Catherine Ann Kooyers*

The Tattoo

I dream at night of the dragons who slither soundlessly and unceasing in my dreams they twine their rough smooth bodies around me and lick my eyes they enter into me they take hold of my mind not clawing at it not grasping but seductively whispering upon it they heat it with soft breaths In the morning I carry them around with me I disperse them unknowingly throwing them off throwing them out at the rude woman on the bus who shoves against me no apology proffered a dragon marks her In the afternoon a dragon flame darts across a phone line and stretches far and fast connected by fibers and sonar and satellite to zap the ear of a whining customer with tact and a crisp simmering civility. "As the sticker says, all corrections must be submitted in writing." the dragon whispers, "Can't you read?" subliminally and joyfully the left behind dragons laugh and rub their scaly bodies against each other soon they too will be dispersed At the end of the day all of the dragons have gone save one with a red shaggy mane and gleaming green armor its blue eyes wide and black whiskers always whipped in tense stillness I carry this dragon on my back at night it lays me down and beckons to its same others.
—*E. K. Devers*

"Ode To The Mother Of A Teenager"

The world rushes by in a hurry. There are things I don't understand. I long for the horse the surrey, I'm tired of the saying "Oh Man".

I should be setting in a rose covered bower, ruffled petticoat beneath diminity dress, but here I am at an ungodly hour, overcome with pain and distress.

Yes, the world rushes by in hysteria, faded jeans, flower children, hippies and joints. Forgotten is all the mystery, of old familiar childhood haunts.

Confusion reigns, communication is nil, only God is real to me, I long for the spot on the top of the hill, where I could really see.

Where I could see with simple, pure perception, the direction I wanted my life to take, How does one cope with modern deception? Free love, mind expansion and on the make?

Yes, I am tired of screaming tires, and oh so weary. Revved engines, bad news out of the blue. I find it in my heart to be very sorry, I wonder if God isn't worried too?
—*Hilda Kirchman*

Untitled

A special man, a different man
Unique, in your own way

You came into my life at a time
When I thought everything was fine.

I thought, we'll see each other for a short time
You'll go your way, I'll go mine

A special man, a different man
You give so freely, even your precious time

You awake in me feelings I try to hide
You make me feel alive

I wake with energy, motivation
Ready to conquer the world, see what I can find

A special man, a different man
Sometimes a look, a glance, words unspoken
But a feeling so intense, I have to catch my breath

I will treasure the times we spend together
for as long as they may last

Remember me!
I will remember always
A special man, a different man.
—*Ann Jehlik*

The Blossom

A patch of soil
Untrod, unturned, virgin
On a breeze, fresh and free, like a seed, love floats in
and soon a beautiful flower breaks the earth and grows
Healthy, innocent, naive
Living it's existence
Giving beauty to all and asking nothing in return
But peace is inevitably shattered
Storm, hail, rain
Trampled beneath uncaring, unfeeling feet
Smashed, torn, mangled
Finally, when hope disappears, the once wondrous blossom dies.
Gentle rain, the skies weep for it's passing
The ground hardens under the sun, scarred and calloused
Time after time it tries again to grow among the weeds
Time after time it dies
Finally, one day it succeeds and a blossom is born
But now, the only access to the beauty of the blossom
is through the ugly thorns it has grown to protect itself.
—*Jack Helm*

Street Smart

They move to the beat
Up and down the street.
Kids getting high,
Thinking they'll fly.
How can we help our future generation,
Rid 'em of sweat, sweat and perspiration.
Nothing to hide, everything to loose,
Why are all the papers full of bad news?
Grass, speed, crack, and cocaine,
People are crying so full of pain.
The world keeps turning round and round,
While everybody falls to the ground.
Kids are dying without education,
That's why they need lots of persuasion.
Nothing we can do but hope and pray,
Hope and pray for a new and better day.
All the kids, they want to be cool,
Only way to do this is to stay in school.
—*Renata Biernat*

Red And White 4547

Grasp the bobbing stick
up and over the pulley

Pull
down down down

taste the salt

Pull
down down down

sway
dip
splash

one motion pulls it aboard

filled with creatures from far below

some crawl some flip some do nothing
but lie spiritless

overflowing like a treasure chest of gold
admiring this and that

keeping this
tossing that

see them descending

down down down
　　—*Tiffany J. Goldberg*

My Weakness

He did not bid me walk with Him
Up Calvary's lonely hill.
He only asked I wait and watch
As He prayed in the garden still.
He bade me stay as He drew apart
And sank to His knees on the ground.
He rested His arms on a stone, hard and cold,
Tho' His lips moved he uttered no sound.
I meant to keep faith with Him during that hour,
But body and spirit were weak,
And when He arose and returned to my side,
He found I had yielded to sleep.
"O could you not watch with me one short hour"?
His words pierced my heart like a sword.
How could I, who so loved Him, have failed Him thus...
Broken faith...broken trust, with my Lord?
　　—*Amy L. Wadsworth*

When Clouds Get A Little Too Dark

　When clouds get a little too dark
　Upset you and all goes wrong
　And the hill to hard to climb
　Remember God is still on the throne
He will not let you go alone
In places unseen and unknown
But you must give to receive
And make yourself known
　And remember his goodness
　Praise him and glorify his name
　Obey him and love him
　And he'll take away your pain
He healed the blind, deaf and cripples
He changed water into wine
He raised Lazarus from the tomb
His miracles are to great fully define
The words you speak for him can be rewarding
From the garden of your heart
No matter what creed, race, or color
When clouds get a little to dark...
　　—*Lottie Marie Cupp*

Glass Friendship

Two persons carefully and precisely molded
Very different in many ways
Beautifully melting into one
But by hard words of cutting tongue
The beauty of it all is shattered
Leaving sharp, confused, and hurt feelings
Parts of each person lost forever
Never to be the same
Can it be remelted and shaped again
And slowly pressed into place by apologies and tears?
Or will it be tossed away
In sharp splintering pieces, destroyed forever?
　　—*Aarynn Cypher*

The Wrong Way

America,
Vietnam,
Persian Gulf,
Saddam,
These are the beings,
and countries you see,
that kill in war and battle,
for oil, countries, and money.
But wounding and killing,
the soldiers of war,
There's better ways to work problems out,
I know there's more,
Innocent people,
killed all the time,
while guns and missiles fire,
why must they pay the fine,
So stop fighting,
and having wars,
we can't kill another being,
that's not what God put us here for.
　　—*Allison Oblen*

Untitled

All alone you sit,
Waiting for the end,
But it doesn't seem to come,
The mystery of the unknown.
The future is blank, wide open,
Waiting for you to fill it in.
No restrictions,
Happy times, sad times.
Domination is there,
Waiting for you and others,
At some point during the time line.
You will be alone, lonely, when your family,
Who you love is gone,
To heaven or hell,
Until you're old and decrepid,
Waiting for the end in a
Powerless Fear.
　　—*John Stolnis*

Dreaming To Live

　To live in a dream world unable to face reality.
　To sleep to dream, wake up and relive that dream.
　To talk in monotones never saying what you mean.
　To walk to get to nowhere never getting anywhere.
　　Living to belong, nowhere do you belong.
Seeing only what you want to see never seeing reality.
　　To live to love never loving to live.
　　Giving all your love with no more to give.
　　Living only to dream, dreaming to live.
　　Never a reality, never only a dream.
　　—*Donna Godfrey*

Waiting In Vain

Waiting for the ring that never rang.
Waiting for the song you never sang.

Closing his eyes, then blowing away
to sit and wait for another day.

A hope, a dream, a thought that died
a painful death. A man who cried.

A lost soul wandering, but never found to find
the fulfilled desire inside his mind.

Broken, battered, his heart is shattered.
Waiting, wanting, his thoughts are haunting.

Of freedom gained, unwanted though.
Of the missing face with the golden glow.

A secret shared and shredded, the heart stands still.
A desire detained and deheaded, his loss of will.

Resolute and mute, he sits and sulks
and waits and wants and writes as well
and leaps unsure at the ringing bell
but it is not the one to relieve his hell.

For the song unsung still sounds so sweet,
but the words unspoken are incomplete.
—*Greg Klein*

Questions On Love

"My left hand"

Why, when I try so hard, does love never sit patiently
waiting to be kissed in the palm of my hand?

"Remnant"

To not crave the sensation of her lips pressing against mine,
why must I suppress all feelings?

"My Umbrella"

And why, while standing alone in the cold rain, does love
never absorb the tears?
—*Michael Duffy*

"Listen"

Listen to the wind that whispers late at night,
Walking down the road with the moon shining ever so bright.
Listen to the words I whisper into your ear,
Holding you in my arms to show that I really do care.
Listen to the flow of water down the stream,
Life passes by quickly, it's like living in a dream.
Listen to the sound of the pouring rain,
It's like love that's been broken, and you crying in pain.
Listen to the words, my friend,
The love I have for you will never end!
—*Frederick Mike*

Just Fifteen

I'll be homeless soon, with many others I assume.
Walking the street with nothing to eat.
Cold inside, with nothing to hide.
People look right at me, but see right through.
Nobody cares, but I do.
Souls are dying, but I keep trying.
My head is spinning. I am confused.
There's so much to be done, but nothing to do.
The world lives on, but it seems
  All
   Hope
    Is
     Gone.
—*Venus Burbage*

To My Great Granddaughter, From Great Grampa

Why is the girl sitting sideways on her bed, looking at the
wall? Why is there a tear trickling down her face?
Why is she thinking what she's thinking?
Why does she turn to see herself crying in the mirror?
Why? Why doesn't anyone answer her?
Is it because no one cares?
Maybe only I can answer these question,
Since I cause the pain. Why is she sitting like this?
Why is there a tear trickling down her face?
Why does she turn to see herself crying in the mirror?
Why doesn't anyone answer her?
As another tear trickled down her face, I realized it was pain
I had given her on my dying day. I know she cried so hard,
So hard that no one could stop her tears.
But finally my son, her grandfather, stopped the tears.
I know I gave that young girl too much pain.
I loved her so much but yet I caused the pain.
I wish someone could stop her tears know but she needs to let
go, but can she since she loved me so much or will she hang on
for life.
—*Janel L. Chick*

Why?

Why are we doing what we do?
War and destruction are not new.
We should all have learned by this time
War is the most heinous crime!

Why is humanity at such unrest?
Anger and war should be suppressed,
If we all loved God, as we should do,
There would be peace for me and you!

We must try to give peace a chance
To forget hatred and learn to dance.
Our grandchildren deserve much more
Than the destruction of life and remains of war!
—*Bunny Rogers*

Making A Decision

He fell in love with her heart and showed it physically. It
was a night of love and passion for the whole wide world to
see. Nobody ever told her that one and one makes three. And
now she cries at night, til the morning light dries her.
tears up in misery.

The talk she had with her mother didn't seem to ease her mind.
The night of love and passion seem so far behind. She learned
to late just one mistake. Can turn a love to hate.

Her mother cries at the table, her daddy slams the door. Her
boyfriend, he left town last night she won't see him no more.
She wakes up sick each morning and lies down alone each night.
Can she hold her head up and live with the shame or will she
end it all out of fright.

She left the innocence of her childhood in that motel room.
And now she's facing motherhood with a baby in her womb. All
of her dreams for the future are now in the past. Can she face
tomorrow, will her courage last? She's gonna make a decision
about the baby inside. She's only seventeen and she's not a
bride. She's gonna make a decision, which will it be. Which
ever she chooses, will she ever be free?
—*Tammy Shilo*

"I Need To Believe"

Acid rain falls.
Water is fouled.
And Man continues
to pour poison into the air
and the good earth.
I look for
and I see,
the points of tulips
thrusting through the dirt,
and the gold
of fragile daffodils
promising spring again,
And I remember
The ancient promise of God,
that Christ shall rise from the tomb,
that "The wilderness and the dry land shall be glad."
   They shall see the glory of the Lord
   And The Majesty of our God.
     —*Doris W. Barlow*

Untitled

All throughout the year
We have learned from you.
You were young
And seemed to motivate each and every one
   of us.
You ignited the flame
And a light was lit within us
We created a newsletter with your help
We learned programming and how to type
But most of all you gave us inspiration
You will be missed
You were our computer teacher
And you were one of a kind
You will never be forgotten.
     —*Libby Josephberg*

No Boundary

  Our gender is the same and a love we share.
    We know it is true that we can care.
     For we are able like others to feel
   Emotions of the heart we know are real.
    Through gladness and joy, sorrow and pain
     True to each other we do remain.
For love knows no boundary of age nor gender -
   Whether straight or gay, love is tender.
  For true love is not seen by the sexual eye,
   But only by a heart that can laugh and cry.
    A heart that laughs with love so free,
     Yet cries for the world that cannot see
   That love is not born from jeans or a skirt
     Or from any little sexual flirt.
    But rather love is born from a caring heart,
And when nurtured by any gender, it will not part,
   Because we know true love is no toy or game
Whether its gender be the opposite or the same!
     —*Charles David Ellsworth*

"What Ever Happened To Injun' John?"

    The one with all the friends -
  Was he only a figment of your imagination,
    or did he really exist.
    Everyone loved him -
  why do so few choose to try and destroy him -
 or did he destroy himself in his own glory.

Called a saint or a sinner depending on who you ask.
    Mr. Oklahoma Hollywood,
    A character you may seldom forget -
 That too destroyed him - inconspicuous he was not -
A free bird flying too high, claiming his own glory
instead of crediting the only one deserving credit -
    The Lord of Lords, and King of Kings -
   Jesus Christ, the savior of the world.

  Oh Lamb, you can only tell where he will go,
    for the time being,
  only time is what is happening to Injun' John -
   Praise God, I'd rather be here with Jesus
   than anywhere else without him.
    (a Prisoner of Sin)
     —*Jonathan Selph*

Anticipated Enchantment

Someone I really idolized before I was fifteen;
Was tall and dark and handsome, and always in my dreams;
His picture stood upon a shelf, not in my room I wish;
But in his mothers parlor where company went to sit;
He was off to collage, a medical one at that;
While I dawdled in a school room, and judged all he's by him;

I spent my time just dreaming of if I were there with him;
Vacation time came early, that sad wet summer day;
When my dream love came home to me, I thought;

Till I saw standing near him, a vision, a movie star alive;
He treated her so gently and right before my eyes;
How could he do this to me? Although we'd hardly spoke;

The famous words he said to me were young lady how you've grown
And deep inside my silent hurt just couldn't even groan;
Why couldn't he just wait awhile, with my head hung low;

My eyes caught the ad on a cigarette pad;
Someday I'll look like her, It isn't fair I told myself;
Then when they all left the room, I turned his picture upside
down; As anger helped the gloom.
    —*Joan Carter*

Intangible Rain

Why can't the tide
Wash away my pain? Why can't I see through
This pouring rain?
   Things get so
Difficult and seem so unreal - I can't figure
Out just how I should feel.
   From all this
Anxiety and confusion I cannot detach
And the part of me I'm losing I can't
Seem to patch.
   The more I hide
Behind this farce of stoic stealth, the
More I feel I lose myself.
 I need to find
A stable rhyme and reason, one to weather
These emotional seasons.
   Though through
Wind and snow and hail and rain - I
Know I'll find myself again. -
    —*Shawna Southwick*

A Gift

Our children are a gift from God
We rent for eighteen years

As they grow, they bring such joy
And trust not many tears

We help them experience life
With few, if any fears

Children are a gift from God
Entrusted to our care

When they leave home, the pain we feel
Is more than the heart can bare

We wish them success
And trust they will be treated fair

We give them our love, knowing full well
That we have done our share

To give them the principles they will need
To raise their own with care

Then we can remind them, that their
Children are a gift from God
They will rent for eighteen short years.

—*Deborah Perrine*

Memories

A memory is a dream. A dream that only you and I live.
We shall live this dream together and forever or this
memory shall fade away.

A memory is like a flower. If that flower is not loved
and cared for it will die lonely. A memory will die
heart broken.

A memory depends on love. The love that you and I create
With not our brains but with our hearts and soul.

A memory lives in the heart of a child. A child who
lives for freedom. Like the bird who boars through the
air freely like the way a memory soars through your heart.

A memory can fill your heart with sadness and with happiness.

—*Gina Crawford*

The Divine Skyway

Arm in arm in radiant garb
We walked the rainbow archway.
Majestic trees cast purple patterns
Upon the celestial skyway.

Divinity's peace infused our soul.
Holy love healed us whole.
Silver stars about us stole,
And temple bells in the distance tolled.

Arm in arm encircled by light
We walked the rainbow archway.
Blossoms rare poured forth their fragrance
Upon the celestial highway.

Birds of splendor praised eternity's
   young;
Living fountains played melodically
   along;
From our hearts winged springtime's
   song.
Heaven's treasures we strolled among.

—*Rachel Seidman*

Sin Is Like A Dirty Robe

Sin is like a dirty robe,
We wear everywhere we go,
Until we want to change,
But where do we get a new robe?

We ask Jesus to help us change,
For He is the only one who wore a dirty robe,
Like us to help us get out of our robe.

So we confess or say I want a clean robe,
Or a clean life, Jesus gives us the new one,
And from that time on we are no longer wearing,
The sin that is like a dirty robe.

—*Gina A. Gonzalez*

Love

When love comes home
Welcome it with open arms.

And when it leaves blow a kiss as if it was the last time you
would ever see it again.

When love asks your name, tell it to him as if meeting a new
friend and never defy or cheat on love because when love leaves
so does your heart.

When you find true love tell him that you are his and never
leave love, just hope love never leaves you.

—*Shannon Duffy*

I Want To Go To Heaven

I want to go to heaven to meet my loved ones there
We'll all be happy with Jesus when we meet Him up there.

There will be no tears in Heaven, we'll have our love to share.
Don't you want to go to Heaven and meet us there.

We will shout and sing in Heaven; there will be no sorrow there.
We'll have no burdens to bear, we will be so happy to be with
Jesus there.

We won't be strangers in Heaven; we'll meet together and pray
together.
Don't you want to go to Heaven? It will always be springtime
in Heaven.

I gave up my husband, I gave up a child.
They are waiting for me there.
I will be ready to meet them in Heaven by and by.
Meet me in Heaven. I will be there.

—*Evelyn S. Pierce*

I Wouldn't Be Me

I would do anything for you.
Well, almost anything,
I mean, I wouldn't die for you,
I'm only twenty, you know.
And I wouldn't sacrifice my
Reputation for you,
I have standards.
And I wouldn't relinquish my
family and friends for you,
They've stood by me.
I can't give up my identity for you,
I've spent a lifetime defining it.
I can't lay down my personality for you,
For I wouldn't be who you fell in love with.
I can't give even one of these things up for you
Because then I wouldn't be me, I'd be you.
I wouldn't be me
And you'd be in love with you.

—*Brenda Bremer*

Then Came You

I've made mistakes and I've felt success
Well you can say I had my share of ups and downs;
I took my chances and I've had regrets
But through it all I never had anyone around... Then came you

I hear them say that I have it made
Well then how come there is no one here with me;
I try to smile when I look back on those days but when it
Comes to love I have painful memories... Then came you

I see your eyes and I feel your joy
Yet I seem to feel your sorrow just as well;
It's no big secret-you can't hide it from this boy
'Cause I have been there many times myself.... Then came you

You may never realize the way you've touched me deep inside
Or should it come as no surprise - after all this time of pain
When I thought I could never love again... Then came you

A dream come true, you're not like the rest
I never thought we'd be as close as we are now;
I've said before that I felt success, but that can't
Compare to how good I feel now 'cause here comes you !!

—*Dan Marro III*

"Unit"

Unit together as the human race,
Were all under God's great grace,
Love can smother the hate,
It's never too late,
Let's show respect for one another,
Your my sister and my brother,
We are the people,
The ignorance has been built like a steeple,
Wouldn't it be a boring place,
If we all had the same face,
Look to your neighbor,
the differences are there to savor,
Don't keep your distance,
Change for the sake of existence,
To know who you are is grand,
But take a stand,
Listen don't just hear,
It can calm your racial fear,
We (you) can make a better change,
Yes broaden our range.

—*Sarah Hope Coy*

Grasping The Edges

Our lives... brief, meaningless
we're only children....precocious, undeveloped

Lies..lies..lies
a bombardment of deception
fed by the power-hungry,
enforced by the innocent.

We need not be led,
sucking dry the fruits of our wisdom
and discarded like that of its rind.

Drink deep our thoughts
for we run the world.
expand the realm of imagination
join us in the flight.
we have reached for the stars,
only to grasp the edges.

With these words
we laugh, cry, dream, love.
we join as one!!!!
just words? ...Maybe
We are only children

—*Matthew Braunbeck*

Far Away...

Far away towards East, South,
  West, and North,
In a hazy mist on a foggy seashore,
Underneath the sky, upon the
  gold sand,
There lies a sea shell, in it a
  whole different land.
There the sky's purple, pink, and blue,
And the grass is always green while
  the flowers are in bloom,
Where the waterfalls fall and
  the butterflies fly,
With bubbles and confetti floating
  in the sky,
Where there's castles, rainbows, music,
  and smiles,
And everything's joyous for miles and miles,
This world is so perfect. No fears, tears,
  or lies,
This world is perfect for it's all in my mind.

—*Natalie J. Hausia*

The Swan

I glide along the water each day,
Wetting my fluffy white feathers
In the cool, clear water.

My long neck stretched up to see
The sunset, a majestic thing of beauty.
I will soon go to my sanctuary
A little nook under a small foot bridge,
Shaded by trees, a beautiful place
all of my own.

I will then tuck my short legs
And my delicate webbed feet
Inside my silky white feathers,
Where I will sleep until the morning light.

As soon as the first light,
I will swim away,
Neck upright,
Into the beautiful day,
Showing off my graceful movements
As I will always live my life.

—*Lynn M. Graci*

Jewels

Jewels.
What are they?
Are they precious gems that sparkle and shine?
Are they what you receive
after a romantic dinner and wine?
Are they diamonds and rubies and emeralds so green?
Are they what you wear when you go out to be seen?
For my special jewel is none of those things.
She is 1,000 times better than jewelry and rings.
She brings love in my heart and joy to my life.
She makes my days merry after moments of strife.
She teaches me to live one day at a time,
Cherishing each moment and giving its prime.
For my precious jewel is worth so much more,
and a life without her
I wouldn't even think to explore.
She brightens my heart
and puts a smile on my face.
My niece is my precious stone
that no jeweler could ever replace.

—*Brygida Gajda*

Man On The Moon

    Man on the moon, man on the moon
What do you see from way up there?
What you see from there I cannot bare.
Why do we not stop this hateful violence?, you ask.
Sir, that is a very hard task.
    Man on the moon, man on the moon
Why do you lie so up in the sky?
Is it because of the terrible voices at night.
Does it give you fright?
Please tell me man on the moon.
    Man on the moon
Good-night for now,
What great answers you provide.
I too, have advice; be careful and safely you'll abide.

—*Peggy Martinez*

What Are They Thinking? What Are You Thinking?

When you're standing in the middle of a crowd,
What do you think?
What are they thinking?
Don't you get scared,
Scared of all the wacky people that are around you?
Or when you go to the circus,
And you sit next to someone you don't even know,
What are you thinking?
What are they thinking?
When they stare at you the whole time,
Tell you they like your clothes,
Then take out money,
Now the only question is,
What are they thinking?

—*Shelly Maheux*

A Poem For Susan

How can I thank you?
What gifts can I offer?
What payment can,
   in grateful mastery for all you have done, be proper?

What tithe may be imposed,
   that my heart's desires may equal a proper sum?
What words spoken in gentle prose,
   would be just by this frail man, composed?

I do not know within the bounds of time,
if there are suitable words,
   whether in prose or rhyme,
that would adequate express,
   how I feel, its width and its breadth!

Time, like the light of day
   can evil, expose.
But as I welcome the sun each day,
   in boldness I walk and not dismayed.
For I know time will not betray,
   neither you nor I, any day!

—*John L. Carter*

Country Fair

Cotton candy, french fries and hot dogs scent the air,
When carnival time arrives at our old County Fair!
The dunking booth brings laughter; men make a mighty splash!
While children ride tired ponies with pseudo-skill and dash!
The ferris wheel is crowded, screams mingle with the din,
Or seated in the grandstand we watch the best horse win.
Slowly, daylight yields to dark and stars dance in the sky.
Fireflies dot-dash the moonlight; young folk court nearby.
Carnival time in our county comes with honest July Heat!
Where we all gather together it's a treat that can't be beat!

—*Helen Linton Hague*

My Special Gift Of Love

A father and daughter both eyes of blue, one teaching the other what he loved and knew. He lived his dreams in her happiness, she lived knowing his love and with this had been blessed.

This gave her strength to live each day, knowing his love forever would stay. Now he grows older, though his wrinkles are few, he still worries and frets about how she will do.

When will he know how much he has been? Oh that soft twinkle in his eyes, the smooth wrinkle in his chin!

A touch from his hand, that look of love - this gift surely from God, this gift of love. None could replace or any compare, to that soft balding man with once beautiful hair.

Not age, or hair, or even time, could ever change this Dad of mine. I love your music, all the dancing we've done, and hope it's many more years that you'll give me a run!

I'll never forget the father-daughter talks that we've had—I didn't do much and you rarely got mad. The love that you've given me is straight from your heart. It's simple and honest and been there from the start.

Sometimes your view is clouded I fear — by this blanket of love surrounded my years. How much do I love you?

—*Janet M. Zitzke*

Special

Special.
What is special?
Special is a day in a meadow of green grass
   or a clear brook on a cool spring day.
Special is the tickle of the wind on your face
   on your first time riding a bicycle.
Special is the gift you give your mother
   on mother's day
   or a loved one
   on valentines day.
Special is your first gift
   from a boy
   or a first award in school
Special can be a lot of things
   so cherish every special moment.
If you want something to be special
   make it special.
Or the special things in your life will fly by
   without you even knowing
     that they're gone.

—*Jessica Lewis*

Idea Or Thought

"It occurred to me," we often say.
What really did? — an idea or a thought?
What's the difference?
A thought one might say, a mental process is.
The mind at work, on a matter concentrates.
Over time, or but for a fleeting moment,
It analyzes, it examines, it weighs pros and cons
Before acting, before speaking,
Before coming to a conclusion,
Before making a decision.
Something the mind does — thinks.
An idea on the other hand enters the mind.
Thoughts about the idea are made
Those lingering thoughts into an idea may explode!
The idea could be the outcome of a thought process,
But it is not a process.
Now if the idea is entertained,
It gives rise to thought,
And thoughts may result in an idea..
No wonder it's confusing!

—*Christiane Dussiel*

Girl Unknown

The pain is buried beneath smiles that glow
What she holds inside no one needs to know
She screams for help without a sound
There's no one there is what she found

A million things rush through her head
Tears hit the pillow as she lies on the bed
One nightmare became real for her today
Now afraid to sleep she's awake till day

Time will make dull the knife that cuts
But will the time she waits be long enough
They hear her crying in the room next door
They've done what they could she needs much more

So many people playing games with her mind
That it leaves the truth so hard for her to find
It will soon be over is what she pretends
Helplessly waiting for her pain to end
—*Michelle Mattson*

Clean Up America

Some people don't seem to say
What the world means to them today.
Some people don't really see
Why I want to shout, feeling really angry.

And say, "Look at this polluted air,
Come on people, don't you care?
Look at this grayness, look at this dirt,
Can't you see these animals are hurt?"

Set a good example, show that you care,
So that many generations can breathe fresh air.
So listen to me now,
And make this world glisten,
Clean up America, so others will listen.
—*Nicole Goehringer*

Good-bye

Do you ever sit and wonder
   What tomorrow will bring?
Do you ever look out a window
   And see birds fly and sing?

Have you ever been through
   What I am going through?
It hurts me so much
   Did it hurt you like this too?

Have you ever loved so much
   It was so hard to say good-bye?
I did,
   And if you haven't, you wouldn't want to try...
—*Torrie L. Wells*

The Unborn Child

I only wish to be a star in the heaven
To be gazed upon by those who appreciate me.
I only wish to be the end of a rainbow
To be desired by those who are looking for me.
I only wish to be a magic lamp
To be sought by those seeking riches within me.
I only wish to be the pied piper of hamelin
To be loved by those who are children like me.
But all I hear is talk of abortion
I only wish to be me.
—*James D. Hodges*

Wheels (For Chris)

Like a flock of birds descending,
Wheels, young lives defending,
Slipping silently up the lane.

In a second they're gone again.
No hurting ears, can't explain.
Soon they are back in the glen,
One, two, three, four, five, six,

Not one is pulling tricks.
No lights, no noise, just gliding
Quietly, all those boys
Are into these new, big toys.

Zipping up the driveway,
Sliding back down.
Just a flicker of light to go to town.
No tires squealing, no rubber laid.

No reason for any to be afraid.
These are great kids to trust to our world.
Fine times too,
Without any girls.
—*Anne M. Blanchard*

A Wedding Prayer

Forever is just a word, that today is seldom heard.
When a true love you do find,
Please take the time to be kind.
At this time in your life.
As you swear to be forever husband and wife.
Take to your heart, all the riches God has to impart.
Cleave only to each other,
Do not become only constant bother.
Never close your eyes, to the Devil in disguise.
He would be there waiting, to see you hesitating.
Do the right thing
And make your heart and soul sing.
There's no truer love found in time
For it knows no boundaries and will forever rhyme.
You will find your love to be pure,
As you work together to be sure.
Taking time to pray.
At the end of each and every day.
—*Dottie Sue Pollard*

Statement Of Peace From A Concerned Girl

    How can people do this to our world?
When Columbus first came to America with sails unfurled,
our world was beautiful and much admired by the human eye.
  To all this great beauty we might as well say good-bye.
What happened to spacious skies and amber waves of grain?
  All we see now is the destruction caused by acid rain.
    No more spacious skies, just billows of smoke,
  but people just push this aside or take it as a joke.
Where did the land of the free go and the home of the brave?
  Everyday now we are digging someone's new grave.
Day after day there are reports of crimes, murders, and AIDS.
Everyone's afraid to have any more festivities or big parades.
  This is because there is always fear of being killed.
  For when you look at the news it is totally filled,
  with news from wars to warfare and killing the whales.
    The truth is that there are many gory details.
  Look what's going on with the whites and the blacks.
I know we don't want to believe it, but these are the facts.
  There are children who are dying, homeless, and mistreated.
Take care of the earth because these conditions could get worse
—*Danielle Sepulveres*

Encyclopedias

The encyclopedia is your friend,
   when doing research from beginning to end.
It answers questions you do not know.
   Yes, the encyclopedia is the place to go.
The volumes range from A - Z,
   with answers for the family.
Authors and illustrators do their best.
   It's up to you to do the rest.
There's a world of magic to be found.
   The information is all around.
It's amazing what you'll find,
   by using this tool to develop your mind.
   —*Alice E. Frantz*

Jesus And Mother Were Always There

When I was born, who was there? Jesus and Mother.
When I am hurt, who shows such care? Jesus and Mother.
As I grew up to a young tot, who shared my hurts and loved me a lot? Jesus and Mother.
Then as I became older and entered my teen years, who was there to share the tears? Jesus and Mother.
Soon I was married with children, not one, but two, who do you think has helped me through? Jesus and Mother.
As the children grew older who was there to show the way? Jesus and Mother.
Now the children are grown and no longer at home, who is there now? Jesus and Mother.
Many years have gone by and mother is now gone, who is left to help me go on? Yes, my friends as you can see, our moms hold a sweet memory.
But as life goes on, and mom has died, there will still be Jesus by my side.
   —*Sarah Ackley*

What Is Time

Time is something I do not have enough of
   when I am with you.
Time is something I have too much of
   when I am away from you.

Time is missing you,
And wishing you were here.
Time is wanting to hear your voice,
To fill my heart with cheer.

Will time ease the pain
that's in my heart today,
or will time bring someone else,
to take my heart away?

What is time without love
when time stands still?
Is our love so strong?
Only time will tell.
   —*Georgia Bray*

A Mothers Unconditional Love

I'm glad to have a mother like you.
   When I hurt, you know all the right things to do.
When no one else understood.
   You were there to do what you could.
Though times came when we disagree.
   In my mind, I knew one day I would see.
Why you stood your ground.
   So I wouldn't wander far, where I couldn't be found.
Though we've said things we didn't mean.
   I'm glad you sheltered me beneath your protective wing.
And daily I thank God above.
   For the mother you are, with your unconditional love.
   —*Patti J. Brogden*

Cupid's First Arrow

Once when you were first there
When I looked into those eyes
I was taken to a very special somewhere
Somewhere where people care

Those memories of us seem like a faded storm that has
   passed away
Something you remember but is no longer there
Now you're no longer here and I can't find anything to
   say
I can only remember how you said you'd always stay

You may not always be in my mind
But always in my memories
I know that what we had I'll never again find
Always remember you're in my heart even if not in my mind

Now you're gone where I do not know
It seems like "us" was never there
And the only thing I feel is life is moving slow
So maybe one day Cupid will once again shoot that bow
I just hope he'll shoot just a little low
   —*Amy Weiner*

Open Eyes

Sometimes it occurs to me
When I walk alone, or when I hear a bird sing,
I find myself alive
And I revel in the knowledge
That I've recognized life;
I see it at face-value,
And what a beautiful face it is.

And when it occurs to me sometimes
As I rock in my chair, as I whistle a tune -
I see that others are blind,
And I pity in their unseeing
Because they know not what they miss;
And yet they miss it all the same.
What a pity to live that way.

Then it occurred to me
That though I see - when others are blind -
That the matter is reversed on me sometimes;
And when that occurs,
I hope others will find
A way to make me see again.
   —*Gary W. Bennett*

A Poet's Lament

Life came to an end the other day
   when I was left with nothing to say.
The words I craved and could not longer see
   had come from the depths of who I pretended to be.

Such had not been my original plan
   in allowing my life to become so bland.
Regrettably, with my pen in hand,
   did I abandon that creative land.

Now and forever, have I come to know
   that such a departure is just for show,
For from that place I cannot really go
   restraining my soul-not letting it grow.

As the mind doth beat the heart
   with passions that can never part,
So does the poet live through his words
   expressing feelings with nouns and verbs.
   —*William Robbins*

Key

Freedom, love, understanding, the key to anyone's heart,
   When it opens the lock, it releases a person, thoughtful
    And kind, ready to explore, free to live and love, to expose
   The soul,
Music, the key to the soul and to the mind,
   When the lock is open, expression and openness escapes,
   Joy and sadness combine in one, written in notes.
   Expressed from the mind, mouth, and finger tips to show
Art, the key to creativity and imagination,
   The key turns, and something different emerges from the
   Soul,
   The lock opens, and turmoil is comforted, joy is loved by
   All and
Myself, locked, contained and closed,
   Ready to reveal all, but held prisoner to the mind, to the
   Lock,
Will someone find the key and release me.
    —*Nick Talbert*

"What To Do"

What to do, what to do
When it rains as so.
When the rain shall rule,
And boredom will quickly grow.

What to do, what to do
When clouds cover the sky
I think I've got the flu,
And will almost die.

What to do, what shall I do
When thunder roars and lightning bolts from above.
My boredom has grew,
I need more love.
    —*Josh Kay*

Memories Of Grandma's Garden

My mind goes back to long ago.
When just a child I'd play.
Around my grandma's house of white
   Where her beautiful garden lay.
The roses of red on the days of June
   would send your heart a float.
The phlox of Pink Purple and Blue
   made the rock wall a perfect coat.
I often think of time I spent
   at grandma's house through the years
   memory's of laughter joy and love.
But not a one of sorrow or tears
   I often dream of long ago.
When around grandma's house I'd play
   Where the Roses Bloomed on the garden fence
   Where the coat of phlox would lay.
If I could have one wish in life
   I'd wish that I could go
Back to my early Childhood days
   where my grandma's garden would grow.
      The end.
    —*Connie Wynn*

Elizabeth

Elizabeth the baby is a real sweetie pie,
When people get near her she often acts shy,
When she doesn't get her way she likes to fight,
So don't get near her cause them teeth
of hers to bite,
She picks at your skin and pulls at you hair,
This baby Elizabeth never plays fare,
But sometimes she acts so sweet and so kind,
No one can beat this sister of mine
    —*Dana Barnette*

Untitled

I ask you reader, at what time of day did it really begin,
when man hated because of religion or color of skin?
Was it part of our systematic education,
or shielded under the guise of institutionalized indoctrination?
Tell me reader, ask yourself, how long has it been,
As you sat idly and just let bigotry, hatred and prejudice win?
Biko and now Hani, tomorrow maybe Mandela for the revolution!
Kristallnacht, first the books burn, and then the Final Solution.
We watched as a wicked puppet cut his strings, gas innocent
   children and attempt extermination of Kurds,
Serbs, Croats and Muslim atrocities, rapes and mass graves,
   it's just a civil war; haven't you heard?
A STORM, a SHIELD, PROVIDE this, PROVIDE that, and
United
   Nations resolutions all broken,
But we drop food, push for sanctions, record the horrors; such
   a small token,
One billion dollars, 10,000 businesses destroyed, 56 lie dead,
   that's just 12 jurors' way of thinking,
Mexicans, Cubans, Vietnamese all reaching our borders, while the
   makeshift ships from Haiti are still sinking!
    —*Alphonse M. Gilbert*

"My Little Girls"

Remember back, when things were grand
When my little girls played in sand.
Their little smiles, Oh! so bright
It gave such a wonderful delight.
Their pony tails and saddle shoes,
Brought them to the age of rouge.
Soon they found the song and dance,
And gave that boyfriend one last chance
Out at school so far away
This is how they learned that day.
Little by little it came to pass,
I toasted my girls with a champagne glass.
So now that I have grown old and grey,
My little grand girls have come to play,
    —*Steven W. Allbright*

"I Care"

When life seems too much to bear, I care!
When strangers gaze with empty stare, I care!
When your best dress gets a tear, I care!
When it's too hard to climb the stair, I care!
When all you can do is sit in a chair, I care!
When you are as tired as a hibernating bear, I care!
When your blue eyes fill with a tear, I care!
When the weather is sunny and fair, I care!
When you are near, I care!
Truly, you are dear,
Truly I care! I love
    —*Leon J. Holsopple*

Too Early, August 29

In the last few bleak days of August
When the inevitable threat of grueling academia
Looms ahead, alarmingly close
When summer friendships are brutally severed
And left dangling by an occasional postcard that refuses to
   submit
I went up on the roof at one in the morning
And let the night do my crying for me.

Too late
    —*J. Raulerson*

The Choice

When you hear the call of the whippoorwill,
   When the moonlight mist is rising,
When you see the hand of time stand still,
   The stars alone are shining.
The heart alone is beating time
   To a soft, still drum a 'drumming;
The soft wind blows when the time is near;
   I know the time is coming.

Now arise strong one, let your heart-strings sing!
   Set your clear, young voice to flying!
For the time has come,
   It's a night of choice,
It's a night when the moon is rising.

What choice have I, with a voice all alone?
   What choice in a world unforgiving?
The choice, dear one, in a world far from home,
   The choice, dear one, is in loving.
    —*Lynne F. Scott*

Stolen Moments

There are two people,
When they come together,
It's really a wonderful time,
From the moment they embrace,
This is when it all takes place,
The moment is so fulfilling,
Its just like a dream,
These two people can't,
Get enough of each other,
Even though it's only,
A little at a time,
They wish life,
Had spared them for each other,
But in order to be together,
They have to steal their moments together,
Maybe one day they will,
BE TOGETHER FOREVER.
    —*Dorothy Helen Haupt SAD*

My Freedom Poem

I was in a warehouse looking at a flea,
When two tall men came and kidnapped me!
They took me to their hideout and put me on a stool,
They told me to hush up and for me to stay cool.
They tied me to a rope and it almost made me choke!
At six p.m. they went to sleep;
I'd have to figure a way to get out or my friends would call me a creep!
The door was only eleven feet away and the rope was made of hard clay.
I broke the rope with the chair
There was no one to hear me anywhere.
I ran to the door and I opened it up,
I started to run, I almost tripped on a cup.
I ran to my house, I was all alone,
And that's the reason I am late to get home.
    —*Audrey Sykes*

Poem Dedicated To Non-Drug Users:

We say nothing's gone right-everything's wrong-
When we fail and fall while getting along,
The other guy always wins and I always lose-
I'm forever hearing bad news.

Drugs and Alcohol will put you through despair-
You'll feel that your life may be through.
Hey, my friends, there's always tomorrow-
Start your life anew.

Your determination will keep you in the Human Race
Your self-esteem and courage will give you a place,
The thought of trying Drugs or Alcohol will then disappear-
Life will give new meaning and thoughts will become clear.

Be determined with the insight to see-
Courage and strength is what all of us need.
No matter what life throws at you during the year
Determination first, courage next and leave behind the fear.

It is then when our senses are healing-
Faith and love will be your feeling,
Patience and courage will have you wait-
Remember life is a beginning-never too late.
    —*Rose Grum*

The Mist

You know that one feeling way deep inside,
when you have so much to say and so much to hide?
Patience is a virtue but waiting is murder.
He says that he loves her he'd never hurt her.
But I haven't yet mentioned the question of fear,
that clouds my perception and darkens my pier.
The waves of the ocean promise new life
as my mind jumps reality cuts in like a knife.
Don't get too close - you might like what you see -
or maybe you won't and then I'd be free.
All is a setting - each day a new stage.
I feel through my acting - page after page.
Dialogue pre-written, my heart inside walls.
Each day my character becomes less involved.
Please don't release me - my sanity sways.
You are the rope upon which I hang. The mist of my madness
waits down below. I feel it breathing it's heat on my toes.
Confidence leaves me - I'm very afraid. Disgust at my being
pulls me like chains. Maturity mocks me, just one of the
endless illusions which shattered and fell in the mist.
    —*Liz Boyce*

Auction Park

In Auction Park there stands a gray sandstone
Where sales of beasts and humans were once held.
Resigned to fate her master had compelled,
We picture how a maiden stands alone
Where by the auctioneer she had been thrown.
"What do you bid for this strong, young wench?" he yelled.
The black maid bravely held back tears that swelled
And yielded to her fate without a groan.
We rue the day when slaves were held in chains
With spirits crushed in hopeless, dire despair
And inhumanity of man condoned.
We long for days when understanding reigns,
When sons of Masters and sons of slaves show care
And shake their hands in love beside that stone.
    —*Gladys Crump Pierce*

Fear, Like Love, Is Blind

Thinking back when time stood still
When you were always there for me
Doing things against your will
In hopes that your love I would see

Far beyond I had searched
For that which before me stood
A dove so patiently perched
Awaiting like none other could

How cold was thought my heart
Do you think I could be so unkind?
What you'd forgotten right from the start
Was that fear, like love, is blind

So off to the sky you took
With wings outstretched in flight
Never giving a second look
Were you scared that I may have been right?

Landing in his nest you've made unbreakable the bind
Where you thought that you had finally found true love
But still I wonder who's more blind
Was it I, or was it you, the patient dove?
—*Joel A. Dixon*

Somewhere In My Dreams And Wishes

I dream of a world where all is right and no one ever wrong.
Where days are filled with endless laughter, and nights are
 filled with song.
A place one can dress in black or white and never be questioned
 why.
Somewhere pain is non-existent and no one knows how to cry.
I wish for a place where hate can't be felt and love rules
 the heart.
Where everyone ends up in the same place regardless of where
 they start.
A place someone can relax in and not worry about others'
 thoughts.
Somewhere people focus on positive and never on others'
 faults.
—*Jessie Landis*

Yesterday, Today and Tomorrow

Yesterday is a memory of fantasies and dreams
Where, in youth, I wandered freely and played in crystal streams.

Then danced upon a rainbow and drifted on a cloud
And felt the winds where mighty eagles soared, alone and proud.

Today is here but for a while and must be used with care.
For Time stands still for no one but must be everywhere.

Whatever tasks are to be done, whatever plans are made
Must all be done in harmony like a song to be played.

Tomorrow is elusive, a mystery at best.
Something to anticipate apart from all the rest.
Yesterday has come and gone, today just a piece of time.
Tomorrow lingers ever near but may never be mine.

As Time goes by and marks the way for all the world to see
And gives each one his place in life, whatever that may be,
Remember it is not for man to either lend or borrow.
It's only his to have for a while; yesterday, today and tomorrow.
—*Emma Maxine Hirth*

Blood

Blood in breathing bodies or airtight bags
 where it has some rightful business
  does not have the same properties
  as blood escaping uselessly and steadily
  from angled injured subjects of attention
  in the ER, then the OR

sticky, salty, slippery soft clots forming
 on the floors and soaking into bed-sheets
  the unstoppable red smells like despair

which keeps coming and coming despite
 our best efforts to be hopeful
  we are forced ever lower like the blood
  finding final resting places and changing
  from our fluid useful forms into
  separated jelly-solid substances

the marble floors accept what gravity brings
 the warm red spreads itself
  no longer certain of its purpose
—*Susan K. Palmer*

"Heaven"

Escape with me to a world unbeknown,
Where nothing matters but love and life
Where children play without fear,
No more hardship; no more strife.

Where roses bloom throughout the winter,
And grass nor trees ever die,
Where sunshine is a friend, not an enemy,
And no one is ever sad enough to cry.

A place where no evil egos exist,
So there is never any reason to be mean,
And all the world is a splendid place,
And ugly faces are never at all seen.

I close my eyes and see this place,
With castles cascading from the air,
Where money nor gold is a requirement,
And in all the land, nothing is unfair.

A land where people are not afraid to love,
And hearts are given without fear,
Where laughter and happiness fill every day,
We'll live for each moment, year after year.
—*Bethany Gee*

The Darkness Behind

Standing in a rainstorm, darkness falls behind,
While a sweet melody races through my mind.
All thoughts linger in the air,
Like an oncoming stranger passing fair.
For in the distance, I see a fading light,
And a shadowy figure embedded in soft white.
It slowly gets brighter, and then fades away.
From then on I wonder from day to day.
what is my purpose on this withering plain
and why do the heavens bring forth the rain?
I'm a seeker of truth, and I'll soon come to find,
that my happiness lies in the darkness behind.
—*LaDonna Dockery*

Ode To Karluk Lake (Alaska)

Oh, let me go back to Karluk
Where the red salmon conceive and die
Remote for the most
They return with their host
To the stream where they started as fry.

This Karluk is a lake of the free
And the scaups and the loons and the golden-eye
Paddle round without fear
For no one is near
But the drifting gull and his cry.

And Karluk is lofty in its humble way
The lowly cottonwood assuming respect
Storm beaten and bold
In a home of grey cold
Persevering in soils the glaciers have wrecked.

If only this Karluk would always be
Lap lapping waves on the stony shore
With pearly clouds billowing
At the mountain crests spilling
And washed gravels would wash as before.
—*Arthur Freeman*

Harbor Of Love

Few things last forever, few things are here to stay;
where there is no love, all will pass away;
what is now, can and will not be;
what is to come, we may never see;
when feelings of selfishness, have become an inclination;
a void of love, shrieking from starvation;
the bowels of earth, let loose a gruesome cry;
lost is the defining line, where the ground meets the sky;
the horizon lies desolate, and the future stands oblique;
the man who serves himself, is all but unique;
yet, there is one hope, where innocent children play;
for what is prohibited, their conscience does not say;
hand in hand together, in social one accord;
tiny vessels of love, deep in fellowship are moored;
and if these tiny vessels, withstand the mighty gate;
against the winds of selfishness, that aim to rend their sail;
then the harbor of love, in the bay of eternal fellowship;
will open up its channel, that each may have a slip.
—*C.A. Hoffman*

Lady Of The Sea

By the sea, by the beautiful sea
Where there is peace and tranquility
Soft whispering waves
Gently lapping the shore

Sea gulls soaring overhead
Their white wings spread against the blue
No artist could capture this scene
And make you believe it was true.

When we turn from this splendor
And wait for the night
Full moon setting her aglow
Breathless with the symphony of sight.

She is not always gentle
Sometimes she roars
And sets all ships aside
She is the thunder of a restless tide.

She is a mystery, this lady of the sea
Colorful, cold, warm and bold
Ships at sea honor her every code
By the sea, by the beautiful sea.
—*Bette Roan*

Untitled

On the old deserted road
Where times are long and hard
All you think is why

And I will always feel the pain
Will always hear the cries
Of an unborn miracle

Playing God in this old world
Is the hardest job to accept
Who would have known, how would they find out

I love you
Even way up in the sky
Where I hear you cry

Nobody answers when I call your name
Someday soon I will be there
To hold and comfort you
Even if you don't accept the decision I made

Please, oh please forgive me, my child
For I have sinned
And you are the one that really suffered
My immortal pain
—*Carol Ann Moorby*

Fences

I find myself drifting along on some astral plane
Where white picket fences and reality blur
Now that life and love and you have blended
I ponder where the road might go.

The dreams are here as I know so well
for I have dreamed them o'er and o'er
And still I will push at the gate
Where white picket fences and reality blur.

An oasis in a dry land
Where at last I can anchor my dreams
And let revolve around you
Giving substance to their means.

Out on that astral plane where sometimes I live
Never knowing, always hoping the white picket fence
and reality will blend.
—*Jeffrey S. Cooper*

Love

Love is a four letter word
which can make you happy or sad;
with it you'll never get bored,
and you'll have the nicest times
you've ever had.

Some people don't know what love really is
so the true meaning of love they will miss.
They'll use the word love on those in their way
by making their lives miserable, unhappy and grey.

While others, they know, their hearts can tell,
by a nice inside feeling; a sound of a bell.
They know that their love is just right
because they've understood and seen the light.
—*Teresita Gutierrez*

Hurtful Ache

My heart is filled with hurt and pain,
which has left my soul stagnant and vain.
I no longer can deal with it at close level
only at a distant silence.

For, pain is less, if not near nor interrupted,
but, by the what or who is inducing such pain.

I am a stranger within myself and my outer self.
Until pain and hurt meet with love and understanding,
it all still exists the same, the hurtful ache and pain.

So, loving someone may be all that is needed to exist.
But, having that love returned is pure, survival,
for then my hurtful ache will cease
and finally I will have found my peace!
—*Susan R. Madison*

Family

Family goes from generation to generation
which spreads out
across the nation,
but never without
calling one another with a salutation.

But family means much more.

Family means sharing and caring
by spending time together
on outings
as they gather
to do some celebrating.

But family means so much more.

Family also means loving
through the rough times
knowing that it is leading
to better times.
That is what the world family really means.
—*Tammy Neely*

Shawl Dancer

    Turquoise flashes bright beneath the yellow shawl,
  while buck skin moccasins weave intricate patterns upon the earth.
      The tempo of the drum increases,
    and the shawl dancer spins ever faster,
  always in synch with the throb of the ancient heartbeat.
         One! Two! Three! Four!
      hard beats sound out across the arena.
      She deftly backsteps, accenting her dance
         to honor the drum.
      Her brow is knitted with concentration,
      but her spirit rides the wave of sound
      created by the voices of the drummers.
        She is a leaf carried by the wind.
  Once again, the tempo of the drum and her steps gain speed.
       Her feet become a dizzying blur
         of color and motion.
      Suddenly, the drum and dancer stop.
She is still as the echoes from the thunder of the drum fade.
       A smile plays across her lips.
         It is good to dance.
—*James Cedric Woods*

Ma-Ma Ledoux

As I watch you
While sitting on the recliner
Laying, in your bed secured with guard rails
With an afghan at your knees.
Or
As I watch you
In your old flowered nightgown
With pink slippers, worn at the heel
Laying, dreaming your dreams
of the days when we were young.
I say
As I watch you
I think of the old photographs
With you in your Sunday dress
Carrying me, your grandchild, on your hip,
Calming all of us from our fears.
I stand up
through all the tears,
I stand up.
—*Monique Manuel*

Springtime Shimmers

Cool, cool breezes flow through the air,
While the leaves turn their backs on winter,
Blinding sunlight peeps through the windows,
Forming images of the season,
The overwhelming tide creeps slowly forward,
Bringing the oceans gentle call,
Each tiny seashell sings the song
of the cry of the waves as they jump all around,
Sap forms on the newborn trees,
While the bees buzz all around,
Flowers reach their arms to the sky,
Bathing in the sun rays,
The shimmering silence of springtime sunlight lives on.
—*Audrey L Pawlecki*

Burning Blood

Everyday, the child cries, but no one bothers to lift a whimper, when the child cries, for the last time, the world offers a mere whisper, machine guns and shell-fire, rain down on a land called Yugoslavia, women, children and old men become
fodders to the pyre, burning, blood forever burning in Bosnia and Serbia, are we Muslims or are we Christians? What religion
you and me embrace should not be a cause for hate, whether we are behaving like animals or human, should be the ultimate debate, where is the world policeman to lend a hand? Always present in past conflicts it has had importance, is he waiting
until Sarajevo is rid of every woman and man, until he flexes his omnipotence? Daily atrocities to which even the Nazis would give recognition, enough! How can our conscience go on living day by day, while knowing fellow humans are suffering now and today, eating cats, dogs, themselves; make them stop this instant, say our peace, together, or keep our peace, forever...
—*Ariff Ahmad*

A Special Daughter

Your a special daughter to me,
You're as sweet as a honey bee.
Without you my life is lost,
I would do anything for you no matter the cost.
You are a special little girl,
You're worth twice as much as a pearl.
I'll be here for you whenever you need me,
I promise you that just wait and see.
—*Rose Ferreira*

Untitled

Sleep quietly, conquerors, dream in peace — wild sea winds whisper your story. (Swiftly they bore the warrior wings sustaining your skyward to glory!) Shield-maidens sought you in stormy heights. As your life flame dimmed to ember, embossomed you, chosen in battle's blaze. To slumber, slumber - no more to remember. Tumult of conquest in star-swept gloam, Dying ships on the ocean's breast; (be yours surcease in silent song. Forgetting, forgetting, in timeless rest) May your freed souls wander, griefless. Where your musing bid your roam; may your paths cross budded blossoms down the wide green roadway home. And ever one Presence shall follow. Lest a tempest seek to fill you, one voice as pure as cathedral chime shall summon softly, until you. Take place with the heroes before you in the ranks that march to the Throne; to the rumbling roll of drum beats. The Maker shall claim His own!

—*Edward R. Dollard*

Color Me…….Mother!

I reached for a palette at the dawning of the day, and whispered a prayer - so low Lord, show me the way. To color me mother in a blend of lovely hues all spun with greens and golds and touched with red and blues. First color me green….
Oh, not for envy or strife but to match the shades of earth where there is freshness of life. Then, color me a vivid blue……
Where dark clouds ever try. Along with my moods to erase the blueness of the sky. Next color me shades of red….. For laughter and smiles and so the warmth of Mother's love shall follow, where they go. Sure, burnish it all with gold……
To reflect the vibrancy and light. But tone it down with humility to make it perfectly right. Look! I've painted a rainbow for the whole wide world to see, and with your help, dear Lord, that rainbow shall be me.

—*Velvadeane Romack*

Quiet With Haziness…Dark With Cloudy Thunderstorms…Alone

There once was a boy,
Who had not one toy.
He is to poor to afford,
What cost more.
He is no different,
Cause we are the same,
Just because he has nothing to claim.

—*John Womack*

Friend

A friend is someone you can talk to
Who offers shoulder to cry on to
They offer advise and yet never contradict
the way you are feeling, though quite remiss
A hand to hold, someone who cares
is always by your side
A thank you seems never enough to show how much you care
For a person who passes through your life,
to put a smile upon your face; your heart to beat in time
Somehow just to take the burden out of life
So if you are my friend, which I feel somehow you are
These words may sound funny, and somewhat sublime
I just wanted you to know I took the time
To thank you for being my Friend

—*Elizabeth Patricia Tauscher*

Cubby Conrad

There once was a lad named Cubby Conrad
who wanted to master a sport.

But he was too short for the basketball court.
He fell flat when he came up to bat.
He didn't like to ride a bike.
He couldn't run under the gun.
He could only ski on one knee.
He was no great menace when it came to tennis.
And he couldn't pong for very long.

So Cubby Conrad being such a determined young gent,
finally discovered his own talent.
He could whistle like a guided missile.

Now he's become a referee -
and is quite happy.

Because when he whistles all the jocks stop;
all eyes turn to him; all the balls drop.

Cubby Conrad has the final say of all that he surveys,
and the games that others play.

—*Linda Harrington*

"Like Unto A Rose"

A rose is like an unborn babe
Whose roots are in the ground,
Then its Spring!! The branches burst forth,
A new life has been found.

As the branches grow with proper care
at last a bud we see,
This bud can be the child
So dainty and lovely it is to me.

The bud does not stay small for long
It's petals soon will unfold
So is the life of this child
Who is more precious than all earths gold.

Then one day its in full bloom
How beautiful has been its life,
So is the adult not the child
Thus far through toil and strife.

Sadly we watch the petals fall
one by one they fall to the earth,
So are the years of our life
"Like unto a Rose," We've been since birth.

—*Carolyn B. Prewitt*

Life

A King who is royal and admired
whose wealth is strongly desired
   cannot tell you the meaning of life

A rich man with wealth and greed
who has no feelings or need
   cannot tell you the meaning of life

You must ask a poor man—one who knows
defeat. not loved for living on the street.
But in his heart there is a fire
a strong, strong desire—that desire is not
a pill-but will- the will to survive
and that is the meaning of life

—*David M. Curnew*

Puzzle

I used to wonder —
Why are all English teachers grumpy
   middle-aged ladies
Who wear support hose and ugly shoes?

Now I know.

Grumpy comes from reading a Shakespearean sonnet
Then looking up to see that five people have fallen asleep.

Middle-aged comes with the territory.
Everyone looks older from the other side of the desk.

Ladies are the only ones able to afford the luxury
Of attempting to thrill children with Shelley's flights of fancy.

Support hose are the glue that holds together a leg
That has bent for the thousandth time to offer help.

Ugly shoes are the price of walking down concrete aisles
To reach the desperate wave that's always on the other side.

I used to wonder—

How could anyone make Byron boring?

Now I know.
   —*Susan L. Luebke*

Black: Man To Woman

     Why do you sound so bitter?
     Why are your words so cold?
Like the arctic wind, they cut to my heart, nay, my soul.
    Is a Blackman's heart as black as coal?
     No, it bleeds like any others
No, more so, for it bleeds for all his brothers'.
    Long gone, swept from this land
    Alive, he wasn't considered a man.
   This, blackwoman, can you understand?
   You talk about his...no, my problems
   but you just aggravate, not solve them.
 Do you think that helps, you're sadly mistaken
 Maybe someday you'll wake up and smell the bacon.
 I admit there are brothers just looking for lovers
  but some of you by sixteen were already mothers!
When you point your fingers, look who you're pointing at...
   It's your reflection and it's pointing back.
So, which one of you will be daring and start sharing and
  caring instead of blaming, shaming, and naming

     The black man as a problem!
   —*Philip F.E. Griffin*

Riding Is A Beauty

Riding a horse is a beauty of nature.
Wild and crazy, flying through the air.
The warmth of his back and the warmth of your heart.
Riding to nowhere, just riding and riding.
Running through water as it cools you off.
Going to a meadow and leaving our river.
Stopping for a nibble of grass and an apple for me.

Riding 'til eternity through hills and plains.
Over bridges, through rain and through storms.
Taking journeys together enjoying our moments.
Riding is a beauty as you might imagine.
Take a ride, enjoy the animals gliding beauty.
   —*Michelle Brownsberger*

Born To Lose

Have I lived my life in vain?
Will I always have to have this pain?
Is it all really worthwhile?
If so, I'll take it with a smile.

It is awful hard for me to see
Why I should have this malady.
I'll just grin and try to see it thru;
In fact, that's all that I can do.

So, I'll keep praying to Our Mother, Mary,
So she will help me carry
This cross. And, by and by,
Death may take me up in the sky.

To God and the Heavenly throne
And keep me for His very own.
And I will kneel up there and pray
For you all to join me some day.
   —*Clarence Primus*

Dreams Unfulfilled

The sweet innocence of days gone bye—
will it never be again?
If I could live again, I would choose
the time of the richness of innocence.
I long to walk the fields of green
and lie upon its softness
and gaze at the blue eternal sky—
I would to fill my cup with the joy
of little animals romping thru the grass
and try to catch a glimpse of the birds
as they flirt and nest with love.
Time stands still for me now—
I have stopped counting days, weeks, years—
How lonely it is when we finally arrive.
Give me back my innocence, my youth—
Give me back the fields that once held dreams.
Now I dream of yesterdays, now I dream of
the joy of old beginnings (that used to be)
And I weep, I weep for lost loves and lost innocence
And I weep for dreams—unfulfilled.
   —*A. Gloria Brunt*

L.A. Police

A friend or foe
Will the people ever come to know
They are confused for some say they did abuse.
Courts are for justice, they give us the right to decide.
But will justice be served?
It isn't right what happened in that big California fight.

The clubs were swinging left and right.
The man on the ground had no friend in sight
Was he wrong or right?
Only the man swinging the clubs will ever know
if he was a friend or foe.
   —*Shaun Boyce*

Untitled

My retirement presents a quandary locating a kindred soul,
whose problems aren't more vexing than mine,
a listener who will agree with all I extol,
astute, but not overly smart, one who's kind
and compassionate and praising and will dole
out advice sparingly as I don't need to find
I lack wisdom that old age bequeaths my mind.
You say, I possess a wife—soul mate to tell?
That's true, but we know each other too well.
   —*Edward Resnick*

"Daddy"

Daddy, what's it like, can you show me?
Will you hold me, can you take me to the light?
How's my grandma, have you seen my sister?
Did you tell her how much we missed her?
Daddy what's it like, can't you tell me?
Won't you hold me, can you take me to the light?
I can't stand the void, the hole inside my chest.
My mind can see you, can you feel my emptiness?
Daddy can you hear me, can't you hear my plea?
I'm so full of anger, do you care, can you see?
Daddy, what's heaven like, can you show me?
Will you hold me, can you take me to the light?
I wake up at night and gaze into the stars
When I look with all my might, I wonder just how far.
  "Daddy, what's heaven like?"
  —Michelle C. Belli

God

As God is indescribable, love is indescribable. As God is wise, love is wise. As God is omnipresent, love is omnipresent. As God is silent, love is silent. As God is mysterious, love is mysterious. As God is nameless, love is nameless.

God is love. Love is simple. Love is colorful stars, a rainbow. Love is light, a rainbow. Love is gentle, secure, a blanket. Love is a feeling, a blanket. Love is a touch, a teddy bear. Love is a hug, a teddy bear.

Love is hugging you. Love makes you feel secure. Love makes you feel gentle. Love makes you feel light. Love makes you feel like stars. Love makes you feel like a rainbow.

Love makes you feel connected. Love makes me feel the same. Love makes me feel connected. Love makes me feel like a rainbow, stars. Love makes me feel light, gentle, secure. Love makes me hug you. Love makes us be one.

One is love. One is God. One is silent, nameless, mysterious, wise, indescribable. One is God. Love is God. God is Love. God.
  —P.W. Seamans

"By The Light Of The Moon"

By the light of the Moon, here I sit,
Wishing, Wanting, Hoping
That it is you next to me and not just my Shadow.

By the light of the Moon, all the world takes on a
Magical, Silvery, Radiance
Which secretly covers up
What is Real
And cleverly unveils
What is Not.

By the light of the Moon, things are seldom what they appear.
Is what why I continuously see you out of the corner of my
Ever-deceiving eye?
My logic knows you're not really there...
You had to go Greyhound, baby, all the way to San Diego!

By the light of the Moon,
Only one Truth can withstand this Masquerade of Reality...
I miss you.

In the brutally honest light of the Sun,
It's me and...
Just my shadow.
  —Kris Gricus

Searching

Taking the world in constant strife
With a bleak understanding of reality and life
Searching for happiness that is never revealed
And no one quite understands just what I feel
Lost in a world of contention
Looking for a new beginning with esprit
Hoping to fulfill my every fantasy
Crying out for compassion and forgiveness
When everything else has failed in essence
I am compelled to forget all possibilities of hope
Never receiving an answer of truth
Losing all happiness while searching my youth
Omitted from life's everyday transactions
To depart my inhabitants with desolation.
  —Jackie Drake

Rose Petals

The wind blowing off the petals of my rose.
With each gust pulling and tugging at a petal.
Down it falls lifelessly to the cold ground.

With every tear I cry, every last evil stare,
Every shoulder turned against me,
I lose a piece of myself.
One after one my petals gently riding the wind.

At last my petals are all gone but one.
Waiting on me to lose myself to the breeze.
I hold on so tight to that petal.
I am losing my grip.

All of my petals have left me to stand in the darkness.
Now my red rose is gone.
Now this life of mine is done.
  —Lisa Penos

The Price Of Heroes

Her tears splashed carelessly upon the dock
with eyes stained with the blood of a wounded soul
she stared at the last glimpse of a black dot upon the horizon.
Children cling weeping to her legs she can not hear or comfort
them her own pain is too great.
The demanding wench has taken him from her again,
it should get easier but never is.
The cold mistress of the sea demands his life for
the giving or the taking.
Fear grips her heart will he be returned this time?
Months will pass without a word,
although that silence was strangely comforting.
Now she is mother and father to her children
a role suffered in loneliness.
Until again she will stand upon the dock with tear-stung eyes
just to grasp and hold the one she endures for as a Navy Wife.
  —Marguerite Whitcomb

Why Wasn't I?

Why wasn't I that tear that slid down your cheek?
Why wasn't I that fish that swam in the deep?
Why wasn't I that dove that flew far, far, away
Or that lazy old fly that rested all day?
These are some questions I often asked myself,
'til I looked at my picture upon that dusty old shelf,
I'm me, really me, no matter how tall,
No matter how short, how skinny, or small.
I'm me and I'm special and this is all true,
So before I close, I ask this of you --
Do you look at yourself and frown,
Well if you do don't be down,
You are special just like me,
Look in the mirror and see what you see.
  —Crystal Thompson

A Loving Grandma

I have always wanted to be a Grandma,
   With Jesus in my heart.
To love and share together,
   All the special things right from the start!

I want to be so peaceful
   That I can calm a worried mind.
Or, help them lift their burdens
   That so often young folks find.

I want to keep their secrets,
   So no one else will know.
They can trust dear Grandma
   And my promise I will hold.

I must be very cautious
   To keep my steps in line.
So if they should try to follow me,
   A straight path they will find.

It is really so neat being a Grandma,
   Getting hugs now and then!
And kisses from sticky little faces,
   It just trills me to no end!!
   —*Fannie M. McElveen*

Moods

It started out a sunny day
With nature all aglow;
Bliss suffused the sultry air-
Not a single spirit was low.

The mood began to gravitate
As leaves fell off the trees;
The Earth suavely adapted
As to put its mind at ease.

Soon a rush of frigid air
Gushed into nature's soul:
Its hopes and dreams had fizzled out,
Its spirit had turned cold.

With spring, a wondrous change occurred,
As temperatures started to rise;
The hopelessness began to fade,
And nature felt alive.

Summertime arrived once more,
Jubilance now in full force;
But as time passed by, the circle of feelings
Repeated its infinite course.
   —*Jennifer Hilcoff*

Like Father, Like Son...

Sometimes you cry at night
Wondering if he's doing the same
Taking of what he might
The laughter and tears, ya'll both claim...

The son of love
The father of his son flying like a dove
Racing through the sun...
Listening to the wind
Thinking of no tomorrow hoping it'll never end
the thoughts of sorrow...
Holding on so tight
hanging on with care
and of all the days, wishing he was here
Hoping of telling him ways, he could be near...

Taking his hand, letting him know
You'll never let him down
Count on me son, I'll always
Love you, like father, like son...
   —*Erica Harris*

Lament On Richard Cory

He had it all together, this "Richard Cory" man;
   With grace, he wooed the crowds that he passed by.
Silken threads from head to toe, and gold upon his hands,
   We stared at him and asked the question "Why?"

Why should one so lucky be singled out by all?
   And why, pray tell, doe he deserve the best?
We sat him on a pedestal and leaned against the wall;
   By him, we seemed to judge most all the rest!

But was he really lucky to be born with silver spoons
   Which fed him from the finest tableware?
Or was it a curse to be blessed so soon,
   And never to have earthly cares?

Oh, cursed life of struggle that we must live each day!
Yet, sane, we move against the pain, and pray for better days!
   —*Charles E. Cravey*

The Playground

I saw the children play today
With happy smiles and hearts all gay.
Their echoes roared in tones of bliss.
The sun, their bright face beamed to kiss.

I saw the children dance and frolic.
In aimless modes, intense in tizic.
Their feet flung high with speed.
Regardless of costly deed.

I saw the children's fortress, a barren land.
They claimed and clasped it tight in hand.
Stifled by the urban cage,
Finding acropolis to siege and rage.

'Midst all the turmoil, buried in woe,
The beat of tiny hearts in symphony go.
Destined to find a place to play.
The children will, some how, some way.
   —*Jazeene Henney*

Our Children's Eyes

Once, our children's eyes would brighten
   with hope and excitement and wonderment and anticipation.
Now, the dark secrets hidden behind their cloudy truculence,
   cataracts of a reign of terror.
   Deception, concealment and televised lies
   decay our children's eyes,
   digesting their dreams,
   leaving empty sockets of nightmare and horror
   because this deceit is disease.

We will plant fresh seeds in our children's eyes
   and grow new grapevines
   sprouting succulent bunches of grapes
   season after season
   cleansed of poisons and pesticides
   until we lick away our children's wine wet tears.

Down down down into the scarlet sea of puberty
   we will descend until our children are freed
   from official traffic in guilt
   intimidation and commercial religion
   disguised as authority.
   —*Greg Dunn*

Silence Saw While Sister Blindness Lay She Down On
Bound To Break

She knew at a glance!
With one eye deep,
she struck to the source
in silence, seized —
That man is a fault
in a frozen lake.
Don't put your foot
on bound to break,
he never can hold you.
Give your love?
Fill up a sieve
with water, might as well —
or fly with wings of sea-made things
and never wake
to wear the rings
where trebling sing
the necks of mourning doves.

—*Geneve Gil*

Butterfly Path

I remember a time when butterflies
with pearly drops of red, purple and green
danced through my fingers; slipped with sleepy dreams
of distant times and worlds in child's stare,

A time when pillow and quilt quelled dark's mare -
the stillness pleasant; the warmth soothing; streams
of memories unborn in the black serene.
I remember a time of butterflies,

When a enveloping love of one near
would kiss my sorrow with a caressed tear.

I remember a time of butterflies
when I could watch the squared water drops wink
into flowers of oodles and doodles
as my wet finger licked the screen window.

My smiles, my cuts - all gone? I cannot know.
Rare times I found them, always sharp - none dull.
Should I taste the liquid past? A dead drink?
I remember a time of butterflies.

My smiles hidden, my young joys now tight,
I do cherish the nearby warmth at night.

—*Luke Michaelson*

The Voyager Ship

How you rest calmly upon the sea
with sails billowing in the ripping breeze
The waves crashing at your mighty bow
and yet you do not splinter
Onward through the torrent storms
of thunderous boomings and magnetic
lightning
Falling back nor losing your path
no matter how you stray
Cutting through the blackness of night
and gloomy fog
On to be you for a moment
have your strength and glorification
to always reach the destination
no matter how perilous or rocky

—*Pam English*

Konza Prairie

We like a place where cattle roam,
With tall Bluestem surrounding our home.
We object to the Prairie National Park,
Let us have no part in tearing our fields apart.
The grassland is necessary, the hills are great,
We should do all we can to protect our state.
The Konza country, where our big Steer is King,
This is something about which we can sing.
Stand and gaze as far as you can see,
Enjoy our heritage, is my plea.
Write to our Congressman, fellows, you must,
To keep our prairie land growing untouched.
The cost of park making would be immense,
They'd jerk out every post and fence,
Spread cement, and cover our good soil,
It would surely end in political turmoil.
The 8,614 acre Kansas Prairie is our concern today,
It could be destroyed if some people had their way.
It will take knowledge, ingenuity and toil,
To preserve productivity and fertility of our soil.

—*Rose Nix Leo*

A Harley

Riding the night on the arms of freedom
with the stars and moon following. The wind
blowing hard and strong it's sweeping my
worries away leaving me to feel free. My
mind becomes a blank and a sense of pure
satisfaction and excitement flows through
my whole body leaving me numb. Rolling down
the road of space where the time seems
to stop. Moving fast and steady the cool
air thrashes against my face making me
smile. My arms strapped around I sense
fear which gives me the thrill I know I'm
safe. I close my eyes and I hear the wind
and the roaring of the engine loud and
demanding. And there is this sudden rush
so intense it leaving me speechless.

—*Kim Barry*

Hardwood Floors

What can you say about my home
with your flat wooden surface
and your waxed wooden face?
How can you bend, yield, dream?
You are solid, oak solid, secure

where the grain hasn't rotted
where the dryness of the air hasn't
stripped you, made you brittle.

What can you say about my home:
That many people have crossed your surfaces
and crowded your spaces and not filled them?

They pulled the tree's root from your heart
and now no more you sway, expand, grow.
You are the same,
year after year.
Static, inert.

—*Terri Heard*

"My Friends, The Libraries"

The libraries are where I used to go
Away from home and needing to grow
Whenever I was lonely and sad.
My friends, the libraries, were never bad.
The books and magazines become my pals

—*Holly Carol Ward*

Tale Of A Heart

The beauty that lives
Within one's heart...
Is expressed in tears, laughter and love,
No change in the seasons
Or hands of time
Can remove the feeling
Within one's mind,
We're each set apart
In so many ways
Like the coming of night
Or rising of day,
With each step we take
Fears and doubts will start
Only to bring about
The tale of a heart...
—Lee Wilder

The First Thanksgiving Day

The Pilgrims came from many lands and brought,
Within their hearts, their strength of faith and love.
It was a new beginning here they sought,
And put their trust in their dear God above.
They built rough homes and tilled the virgin soil,
Faced the challenge of this wondrous land,
And bent their backs to the hardships and the toil,
Faced the rugged wilderness demands.

They planned Thanksgiving at the harvest time,
To share with friends and foes their bounteous yield,
In honor to the One who is divine,
Whose glory ripens orchards and the fields.

Let us give thanks this bright Thanksgiving Day
To God who walked with them that they might stay.
—Lucille M. Kroner

"What's Happened?"

We once could walk anywhere
  without trepidation or terror-
What's happened to these streets?
    What's happened to these streets of ours?
      Now all of the windows have bars.
The streets where I learned to drive
  now the kids learn how to survive-
What's happened to this town?
  It's not even safe in our cars.
I want to go back to the place I called home-
  Where in the arms of comfort I never felt alone.
The place of familiarity -
  where the trees along the streets formed a canopy.
I want that feeling of unquestioning trust -
  I want the grace that was once bestowed on us.
Don't we all look for the very same things?
    Don't we ponder the senseless meanings?
What's happened to these streets?
    What's happened to these streets of ours?
—Diane M. Gardner

Sisters

Sisters will be our lifelong friends;
They'll be with us until life ends.

Sisters always stay close;
They are the friends we need the most.

I know I would never want to be
Around and have to see
Anything part my sister and me.
—Heather Allen

Woman

Woman born after man, but walks beside him.
Woman bearers, providers and protectors of generations past
  and to come.

Woman epitome of a disillusion:
  A strength given by God to overcome obstacles placed in her
  path, but placed inside a delicate encasement.

Woman role model:
  innocence looks up to,
  maturity respects and honors; and
  adulthood walks alongside.

Woman we set no limits of ourselves-
  we anticipate the unexpected and
  we welcome controversy.
  we are the Women of yesterday, today and tomorrow.
  we are Women.
—Adrian Martinez

If

  If I can intercede an unkind
    word or action toward a child....
    I have accomplished.

  If I brush away a child's tear
    and that child smiles...
    I have accomplished.

If I bring laughter to a child's heart...
    I have accomplished.

  If I help to create a child's interest
    in, and love of, the universe...
    I have accomplished.

  If I am the reason a child develops
    the desire for knowledge...

    I am complete.
—Lue Kennedy

Untitled

Why does it seem that its a white American
World, when there's so many races?
Why do people judge others by their looks
And faces?

Why don't people get treated equal and let
The appreciation grow?
Why does it seem prejudice is just a field
Of weeds that someone needs to mow?

Getting along with each other is something
We all need to learn.
Instead of seeing people with white robes
Watching tall crosses burn.

What is the meaning of life, when no one can
Get along?
Who cares. Most say. Soon we'll all be gone.
—Amy Shepard

The Wrong Question

A little ant, slowly crawling along,
Wondering where oh where do I belong.
All these little hills have me in a tizzy,
I've been going round and round, and I'm getting dizzy.
I wonder if that stranger with the long nose would know,
Hey stranger, would you know where I'm suppose to go?
  Slurp!!
  Burp!!
—Adam Grinovich

"The Ghost In The Tides"

It rides in like a bucking horse,
yet leaves like a dove so rapid in flight.
You hear its whispered secrets slip away,
as you listen and learn in the night.

It tells of the mere people far below,
also of the fisherman not knowing
which way to go.

The ghost only speaks when your
muscles are tense and tight,
or while the sea gulls fly their,
very, first flight.

Some stories talk of truth,
some songs of tales.
But the one who can tell the difference,
or can not, is the one who talks to the one
who knows not the ghost,...

Strange as it is the words have to rhyme,
For the Ghost in the tides will
soon be lost in time.
—*Courtney Stallings*

A Revelation

The lightning crashed throughout the crowd,
Yet no one made a single sound.

The thunder pounded, the earth did shake,
The people fell for their sake.

The anger built up deep inside,
Twas the gruesome feelings they could not hide.

The winds did blow vast and wide,
As the people began to cry.

Then Christians looked o'er to the crowd,
Yet still the sinners made no sound.

The earth, it opened, the fire came down,
Upon the hating, unholy crowd.

The judgment day had now come,
The Christians went to meet the Son.
—*Amy D. Krambeck*

Untitled

Inwardly I smile
Yet often I softly wonder
Should I wake this sleeping animal...
If I was the sun
would you know my color
would you find blackness in my glowing face
Evil lightning; sound of thunder
Noises created by you to drive me insane

Love those grapes, but would you eat me
If I was a grape and the only one left

  Or if I had seeds?

Would you spit me out if I was the seeds of a flower
Or would you plant me deep in the earth so I could grow up
and smell pretty just like you
  If I was a rock would you throw me
  Throw me away like milk from a cow
  If I was a tree and you were but a leaf, would you
  Ever let me fall...

Fall into nothing with nobody waiting
Nothing to see and nothing to do
—*Nate Warner*

My Memories

M y memories are such priceless treasures
Y esterdays tears and yesterdays pleasures

M aking each second a cherished delight
E ngrossed by the fire two lovers ignite
M oments we've shared in the years passed by
O ften I smile, and yet times I cry
R emember the tears, remember the bliss
I recall each embrace and each passionate kiss
E very beautiful moment, I've tucked deep in my heart
S o in My Memories, dear one we'll never part
—*Nona Lopez*

My "Grampap"

I sit and daydream often of when I was very small,
Yearning for my yesteryears, wishing for my doll.
I especially miss one grayed-gent, yes, my aging, weathered Pap,
Our special times, his gentleness, when I sat on his lap.
I'd say "Grampa will you rock me, and tell me a story tonight?"
And he'd put down his paper, and pick up his 'thinking' pipe.
I'd crawl up into his lap, get all secure and snug,
With the aromatic pipe scent as he gave me a hug.
He'd have the greatest stories, of his life when he was young,
And we'd both giggle later, at the home-made songs he'd sung.
I'm not ashamed to tell you, my heart broke, and I cried,
When Mother told me, softly, that my 'Pap' had died.
Although I was very young, I truly understood
And I knew he went to heaven, to be with Grama if he could.
I hope my memory will be half as sweet, as that of my weathered
  Pap,
As I tell stories to my grandbabe, who sits upon my lap.
—*Joyce Schuler*

Richard

I met a man who told a story. His face was aged from the
years, His eyes were sad from the war. His heart was heavy and
tired from the burden he carried. He talked of hope and glory,
but still there was more pain and tears than any man should
have to carry. Many years ago he was on a ship called the USS
West Virginia. It was a mighty ship until that dark day in
history, December 7, 1941. To some, it was just an era
passing. To him, it was his life. When I met him he had an
old photo album that was weathered and worn, you could tell how
he held it, and when he spoke, those memories were kept alive
and close to his heart. His hands would tremble as he
carefully pointed to a photograph, and a new story would begin.
He would cry and as much as we all tried, we couldn't help but
cry with him. He captured my soul. Then I approached him and
this is what he was told... "I have a special place in my
heart, I salute the flag and cry a tear for veterans like you.
Those gone before me who have laid their lives on the line, I
promise with time I will give back to you what you have given
our country." So you can rest assure, that with each passing
day you will be the one I pray for when colors is played.
—*Joellen M. Plum*

Untitled

You can't let cancer get you down.
You have to learn how to clown.
You have to hitch your wagon to a star.
It doesn't matter how old you are.
What your goals are in life.
You try to succeed.
But never with greed.
The Lord will help you when on the right track.
He will never turn his back.
Life is here and it's up to you.
Just trust the Lord.
He'll see you through.
—*Christy Phillips*

A Sweet And Dreamless Sleep

Twilight just begins to near,
yet I must get some sleep.
My coat still draped over my chair,
and my shoes fallen from my feet.

I lay back, my pillow soft as moss;
my ragged blanket old and worn.
I close my eyes, suddenly lost,
and so dreamless images are born.

The gentle sound of silent tears
falling from the sky.
And the ancient moon, wise from years,
mysteriously passes by.

A song whispers sweet,
of the golden days of Yore.
And upon the roof, the rain still beats,
of old forgotten lore.

I awake with a yawn,
and stretch to my feet.
As I drink in the purity of dawn;
I reflect upon, my sweet and dreamless sleep.

—*Kammie Chapman*

Home

You see me walking down the street,
yet I see no friends for me to meet.
But I had friends, and family too,
they cared for me when I was blue.
Yet now my family is all gone,
and I guess my friends have all moved on.
No one has any time for me, unless they see me for a fee.
These bags I carry are my life,
and each new day brings only strife.
I'll go to the mission where I have been,
you can get some soup just shout Amen.
I'll walk these streets till it gets dark,
when it's time to sleep I'll go to the park.
These bags I carry will make my bed,
and the grass is the pillow for my head.
These voices I hear inside my head,
sometimes tell me I should be dead.
But voices, delusions, anxiety and fears,
have been my friends for many years.
but you don't know what I might have been
So today when you see me roam, I'm not lost, just gain home

—*Sandy Haar-Curtchall*

Dreams

Last night I could see a world without sin
With the warmth of the sun shinning within;
Wildflowers covered a meadow so green and
When the breeze blew they would gracefully lean;
As far as the eye could possibly see
There were beautiful colors surrounding me;

Rows of trees of cherries and vines of grapes
Were guiding the way to a bright blue lake;
As I followed the path to the lake I could see
Many children playing and swimming with glee;
Then the children turned and began to sing
I awoke — it was only a dream.

—*Marie Lena Brandon*

What My Mentor's Up To Now

The sun gently lights the way on the path. The path is worn and gives the direction. To a clearing.
A solace. A solace from the world. The world and it's confused generations of people.
He is seated in a weather-worn, wooden chair. Two dogs, a mug of coffee, and the sun keep him company. In a relaxed state of mind he looks out at nature.
Contentment.
His cabin rests upon the threshold of the mountain. The trees surround the house, standing erect as soldiers venturing off to a war they know nothing of. The fresh air is laced with strong pine and an underlying aroma of wood burning. It is light, like incense.
The huge mountain dwarfs the cabin, holding it in her bosom. Huge fields open at the foot of the mountain further dwarfing the cabin. The great blue sky and cool wind, uplift them to unity.
The sun quietly plays its fingers upon the flowers. The wildflowers of the fields.

—*Mitch McClain*

The Cape

There was a Cape that stood 'pon a dune
Worn and weathered one Hyannis June.
Its shingles were grey and shutters white
With an anchor in the yard centered upright.
Traps and buoys were placed childlike in the sand
Above a marsh terns stood their stand.
Shells and claws were ornamental in a net
The day too material to be thinkin' 'bout a set.
A single wire connected the cottage to the world
While oceanside a lone starfish parched and curled.
Markers fought for breath in the swell
Sailboats bobbed with their masts at bell.
Waves mimicked grasses, the grasses the air
A lighthouse run-aground jetty on a pier.
Swaying marsh grass began stinging at my thighs
Then pastles of fog hazed the skies.
Suddenly heat-bugs became electric in the sun
And suddenly from that Cape I began to run.

—*Lois P. Flanagan*

My Daughter

My little daughter, who loved me very much
Would throw her arms about me and I was very touch.

She came to me with all her hurts and I'd kiss them well
And all her wants were ever filled with the love I held.

The years passed so quickly and she grew from my sight,
Even the love she once had, vanished like the night.

If once more I could hear her say "Mommie, I love you so"
I would be oh so happy, no one will ever know.

They say no one ever forgets Mother's Day, Birthdays and such
But they come and go each year and she never gets in touch.

Some day maybe she'll remember all the love that was given her,
By her Mother who still cares and loves her more each year.

—*Dorothy A. Livingston*

Love Melody

The wind is singing a melody of love,
Written solely by the one above.
Lyrics filled with uncommon emotion,
A promise of passion and life-long devotion.
Portraying affection, sincerity, and beauty,
Clarifying our friendship's essential duty.
If you listen, if you hear this wind, too,
Imagine that G-d composed it for just me and you.

—*Rachel Cher Flynn*

Changes

The changes come gradually,
Yet the effects hit swiftly,
Being caught up in dark oblivion,
Wanting to escape the acceptance,
But being aroused by a new beginning. Ambivalence. Fear.
The Changes cause such turmoil at the time they come.
But when they have settled in,
One can begin to survey the goodness in it all.
To look at the large picture of life,
And find new pathways that point toward the light.
To ponder why all the spots of darkness were needed.
For how would one recognize light if emersed in it?
Or see the positive, if the negative never lurked, In the
    darkness.
The Changes. So many, so difficult;
And in retrospect, so rewarding.
If only one can learn to accept,
That nothing will ever be the same again; and that it is good.
For one never grows by staying the same,
Tranquility isn't achieved without the coming of change.

—*Angela M. Jones*

Passing Moments

Some special moments go by fast,
Yet, we all want to see them last.

Like when an infant has entered our world,
The parent of that child thinks one day and asks herself
"Has this really occurred?"
She wanted that special moment to last,
But now it has gone by so fast.

Or when a teenager graduates from college,
He or she would want that moment to be treasured.
But when you put those moments together they cannot be measured.

Then this man or woman gets married, and has a family of their own.
They all share and talk to each other about that has happened
in their lives, and how they have grown.

Maybe some moments were crazy, and maybe some were sad.
But through it all, when you think of it, They're not so bad.
You may have wanted a shooting star to stand still,
Or maybe you'd want to see the silky petals of a blooming
blue rose stay the way it is now...

—*Isabelle Macaltao El-Chami*

"Friendship"

I waited so long to get him
Yet you and others think it's just a game
You call it flirting, I call it talking
Why do you call it the same?
Everyday I support you
But you think I'm hurting you
Why isn't our friendship the same?
You know me very well, so
Why do you think, I would want to hurt you
Your my best-friend
and I don't want to lose that
So why do you accuse me
Of something that I wouldn't want to do
If it was going to hurt you
Maybe I don't know why
But what I do know
Is that our friendship can't die!

—*Jamie Czepcinski*

Thinking Of You

Today as I awoke I thought of
    you and yours.
Your eyes that carry everything in dark
    colored mists
    but never say a word.
Your mouth that says so little but means so much
While caressing my mind.
Your hands that leave me breathless
    with just a brush of
    their gentle feelings.
You know how to reach in to and enter
    a woman's self-control...
but you enter with caution and awareness
    of every step you take.
Like a baby taking his first steps
    almost afraid of what he
Might find around the next corner.
You are the image of the perfect heart in human form.
A man of love in his heart...
And no doubts in his mind.

—*Cristy A. Malone*

To Youth

You are the wind - unshackled, unrestrained;
You are a blossom pregnant with new life;
Yours are the battles fought, the vic'tries gained,
Yours are the hours and the days immune from strife.
In you lies hope, on you we build our dreams
Of new tomorrow. Stalwart, fresh - increase
Your bold campaigns for truth; for what now seems
Your Armageddon soon will be your peace.
Cease not to love, for love will give you breath.
Cease not to trust for confidence is dear.
Preserve the freedoms that were won by death
Of such like you - whose aliens were fear.
Though some should laugh and others fail to mend;
Youth, seek your star pursue it to the end.

—*Camille L. Roy*

To My Children

You are my past, present and future.
You are my reason for combatting all strife.
You give me faith, courage and passion
To complete my goals in life.

There will always be sunshine and shadows
As you travel through each new year.
But keep looking for new tomorrow
And try to spread comfort and cheer.

My parents gave me faith, hope and courage
To greet each new day with a smile.
To sing when I was discouraged,
And ask God to make my life worthwhile.

So look cheerful when you are weary,
And keep searching for treasures each day.
For contentment and satisfaction will come,
When you bow your head and pray.

—*Marguerite Welser*

"Doug"

So young and so free, you used to be.
You brought joy to my world and peace to my mind.
You were so dear to me, just one of a kind.
Why did you have to leave in such an awful way?
You had so many unfinished games to play.
I try to understand you were being called home to God,
You answered his call without even saying Goodbye!
We will miss you here on earth,
You'll never know how much your being here is worth.
I'm left here with so many things to say.
With so much love to send your way.
I try to smile to hold back the tears,
Why couldn't you stay around for a few more years?
When I try to understand I get all choked up,
Knowing your with God just isn't enough.
Knowing you are no longer suffering will put my mind at ease,
Douglas Ray Smart, "Rest in Peace."
So young and so free, you used to be.
You brought joy to my world and peace to my mind.
You were so dear to me, just one of a kind.

—*Theresa V. Covington*

In The Still Of The Night

In the still of the night,
You can hear the zanzibub trees whisper
Calling to you in their hushamung way, greatly grimping with the wind.
Speaking of kamori's dancing with the koosk-kin, all in the zizzy-wood.

   Singing, those zanzibub trees,
     of junkly-junes cavorting,
in mirth with all the catchimines above. All-
     In the Still of the Night.

   And I ask you, would you listen to zanzibub trees,
or mingle with the kalmori's and kenderkin, would you dare to come,
to a junkly-junes' wedding, held in the heaven's above,
and to be surrounded by catchimines, — such is a child's
imagination-would you presume to take part in these
magnificent miracles, all—
     In the Still of the Night?

—*Stephanie Vander Weide*

Sunset

Gentle breezes on an evening visit to the lake.
You can see the sun as it tiptoes across the sky.
The colors turning to purple, blue, gold, and pink.
The ducks swim to their nests to go to sleep.
The bugs are out tonight to watch the sunset on the lake.

The colors so brilliantly saying the sun is going to sleep.
The water bubbles over the rocks and the fish swim to their sandy beds.
Bedtime stories being told to children as they watch the sunset fade.
Married couple taking a walk along the beach to watch the sunset slowly fade into night.
The moon rises to take the night shift as the sun goes to sleep.

—*Jenny Roberts*

To You From Me:

Give me a break
you can't forsake this brother-sister love
that has come so far
remember the song where I held you in my arms
it seemed as if nothing could go wrong,
But some how it got changed, rearranged
to where I could not hold you anymore
one sunny day while we teased and played
the sky fell and turned gray,
the grass turned brown-n-the rainbow faded,
and our smiles turned into frowns
you were thrown away,
and I could never say I love you
and that one day, while he tear us apart
he tear my heart in half,
like so
I can never see you my brother;
who I will never know

—*Janet Jones*

The Strongest River

Like a river is your mind.
You can't leave your thoughts behind.
They'll twist and turn and flow with you.
You never know what they will do.
They continue on and run so deep
Controlling every word and leap.
Then when your body's dead and gone,
Perhaps your thoughts will wonder on.
Like a river is your mind,
with currents so strong they rule mankind.

—*Holly Dison*

Life In My Eyes

   Life is something that goes away,
You don't know if you will die tomorrow or today.

     That's life in my eyes,
      Flying by!

     You are either dead or alive,
   you know you have to eat to survive.

     Life is really short,
   you know you need a lot of support.

     It just happens to be there,
   Like when you get mad and swear.

     This poem may not mean a lot,
   but it really can't be stopped.

     That's life in my eyes,
      Flying by!

   Life is short or life is long,
You won't know if you will have time to compose a song.

    Even if you think life is slow or fast.
   You might as well make of it what you can,
     while it last...flying by!

—*Jessica K. Weeks*

Fire!

You awake to a shrill, high-pitched tone.
You feel an intense heat.
Your breath quickens as you search for air.
Your eyes burn and water, causing you to go blind.
Your brain is contemplating whether you are asleep or not.
Your muscles twitch as you spring out of bed.
You get a headache from lack of oxygen and you feel smothered.
Your skin begins to blister as the heat grows.
You run to the window and throw it open;
A cool breeze of night wraps and cools your face
While the rest of your body is starting to sizzle.
You breathe your last breath and jump.

The night air envelops you and you hear a cricket.
Far, far away you hear distant sirens.
Your muscles twitch as your body begins to cool down.
You slowly drift away while watching your home burn.
It reminds you of your childhood fireplace.
You forget all that's happening and all that's happened.
Your body aches from the severe temperature change and your fall.
You can't remember———
—*Sarah Plymesser*

A Gift Of Life For Giving Birth

I gave birth to you,
  you gave me life...

I took care of you,
  you gave me joy...

I taught you how to walk,
  you taught me hoe to love...

I gave you a mother's hysterics
  you gave me logic...

I gave you tears as you went
  out on your own, you gave me
  respect and made me proud...

I gave you all my love, and you
  my darling angel, you gave me
  more joy and happiness than
  anyone has a right to...

I gave birth to you my Angel
  and you, my darling daughter,
  gave me the world...
—*Dot Duhon*

Your Mended Heart

God bless your mended heart
You need it every part
The rhythm of the beat
It must repeat, it does repeat
The valves click open, close
They meter the blood that flows
The nourished muscles go
The unblocked blood must flow
To feed your heart, your mind
Body parts of every kind
God, bless your mended heart
Whole within you from the start
Beating constant in every age
From baby curl to white haired stage
Now mended 'til you turn life's last page
This thankful prayer ends as it did start
God bless your mended heart.
—*Lavonne A. Holland*

The Love Letter

My Love,

Mi Amour, Mi Amour
You have all that I've been looking for.

You have big, brown eyes that hypnotize and captivate me
and long, dark eyelashes which are
always noticed when it's you I see.

Out of everyone I think you have the cutest smile.
It makes me wish you were always happy,
not just for a while.

Your dark, brown hair is silky and like no other's,
Its softness makes me want to
stroke it one time, then another.

Your hands are the softest and smoothest of everyone.
It's what I always enjoy when you take my hand and run.

Your personality is truly one of a kind.
It's one of the many things that
make me so glad that you're mine.

I love you, Mi Amour, with all my heart.
Our love is so strong that I know we'll never part.
—*Leslie Price*

Untitled

You turn your head away from me,
  you look at me with hate.
You think that I am unequal to you,
  you think that you are great.

But through the hate I see the fear
  that you hide so well.
And it is the fear that I see and hear
  when you shout and yell.

So when you curse I just walk away,
  because I know you are small.
And without the mask that keeps you strong,
  we both know you are nothing at all.
—*Oudom (Kekam) Inthisone*

Untitled

The sun glistening in your eyes,
You look so young and innocent,
life awaits you with its many surprises,
you accept each gratefully,
so happy with what you have,
and glad for what you have received,
then you look at the world around you,
and you see the poor and the homeless,
and you take what you have and give it to others,
who aren't as lucky as you and don't receive surprises,
that's when you truly realize that
you're lucky for what you have.
—*Charlene Eisen*

That "Other" Day

Someone mentioned yesterday.
It made me stop and wonder.
If there truly was that day
Or just today gone yonder.
You could take it many ways
You could even count the days
That still won't let you see tomorrow
Until today has come to borrow
That time that is destined to be the past
But still is unseen and the die not cast.
—*Claudette Williams*

The Homeless

I walked by and saw them standing there,
a cardboard box they call their home.
They have no place to go, nowhere to turn.
They may have a family, but they're all alone.
They need some help, someone to understand,
all they need is a helping hand.
If they had an education, they could go further,
but who's willing to help them?
Right now they're asking for pennies,
while others are making millions.
They could be making millions too.
If someone was willing to help.

—*Kim Rusch*

A Mother's Morning

    Boy! Get out of bed.
    You need to be working instead.
    Early to bed, early to rise
makes a man healthy, wealthy, and wise.
Boy! Can't you hear me talking to you?
    I've already made breakfast for you.
    Wake up and look at the sun light.
    It's so beautiful and bright.
Boy! Your breakfast is going to be cold.
Going so slow like you ninety years old.
    Across the street, look at that old man.
    Moving a whole lot faster than you can.
    Boy! This is your last warning.
I ain't calling you anymore this morning.

—*Kenneth Lance Bowen*

Lady

    Lady when I met you, I was so in love
  You saved my heart from drowning, and lifted it up above.
    You gave me such a passion, conquered mortal sin
  You built a burning fire, still burning true within.
And even in my thoughts I ponder where it all went wrong
  Sitting on a sunset beach, birds singing our song.
And though I thought your heart was true, filled with love like mine,
  It ran away so hurt and bruised, yet so delicate and fine.
  Yet to this day I wonder, how I lost a love so fine
The intimation was so strong, yet it failed to catch my mind.
  So long ago, has it been, that I had lost my love?
A love so strong, a love so pure, that lifted my heart above.
  Just let me say this before it is interred with my bones,
    Lady, lovely lady, I have not a heart of stone.

—*Paul Basinger*

Goodbye

Moments in my childhood,
You were always there.
Times of need and pain,
happiness and joy,
I thought I would always be
your little girl.
But...now you aren't here
And, I don't know what to do
As my thoughts drift to you,
I know you will always be with me.
As I live my life, the pain begins to fade.
But the memories of you will never die.
Because in my heart you will always exist.

—*Mary T. Wells*

"An Expression"

Softly, gently, touching, loving you is an expression.
Seeing you smile, to hear you laugh, to listen to you is an expression. To feel your warmth, your tender embrace, your loving touch is an expression. To sense your inner spirit, to see your emotional stability is an expression. To passionately feel your soft smooth lips, your strong embrace is an expression To hear your little talks, your encouraging words, look into your eyes is an expression.

A slow walk through the park, holding hands, stroking my hair is an expression. Your consideration, your kindness, your loving ways is an expression. Your faithfulness, your protectiveness, your patience is an expression. Your being yourself, your giving, your caring is an expression. Your boldness, your prayers, your reaching others is an expression. Togetherness, oneness, closeness, respecting one another is an expression. Let me, express me, as I let you express you, for expressing one's self is an expression.

—*Jessie S. White*

How To Show Love To A Mother

You watched me grow,
you taught me to sew.

You told me it was ok to cry,
you helped me answer the question why.

You backed each decision,
you gave advice with little indecision.

You always knew my fears,
you showed me life's many cheers.

You kept my chin up,
you even asked, "what's up?".

Each year many sit and wonder, how do I show love to a special woman, who could only be a mother?

I sat and wondered,
"How do you show love to a mother?".

I thought about a figurine,
but it would become another dust-collecting thing.

I considered a purse,
then I developed this verse.
So, as a daughter, this is my way to show love to a special woman, who could only be my mother.

—*Chrystal Dawn Dalby*

Dear Nanny

  Nanny, you were the best. We showed our love and hope to you. We honored and respected you in all you said and did. Weare proud of what you stand for, an angel and our guide. When we grow up we will be like you, a soul within the sky. Even if you were hurting, if we got hurt you would care for us more and stand united with your love so strong. For you, all your friends and family take pride.
  Nanny you are so loving, you showed your love to us. You would listen, honor, and respect us in all we said and did. I'm proud of all the things you have done. Your love is all we need. Even though you have been through a lot, you would be strong about it and then fight it. You would be considerate to people and give help to whoever needed it. You showed people how to be kind and many other things, and they would give it back because of you Nanny. Nanny you gave the most and best advice that is why your family and friends are kind! We love you Carmen (Nanny)!!!
Love Always, Your Granddaughter...

—*Michelle Elizabeth Carmen Desposito*

Friend

My friend, I met you here
you were different, I don't know how
we start talking about life,
then we past on to love,
from there you were mine
but I knew how to be yours sweetheart
I gave you my passion
you should never forget.
That we where afraid but sincere
you could never forget me neither I.
That feeling that we felt
that night on those moments
I couldn't forget that makes
the words small in comparison
what we discover,
not forgetting to always
be sincere from our hearts.
—*Diane Gonzales*

Stay

(For My Mom, Katherine)
"You'll always have a home here."
She promised so much.
How was she sure of such power?
But she meant it.

I can still hear her persistence.
Whispering "stay."
"This is your home."

Walking away did I really know?
What I thought I could truly leave.
A constant rarer than love.
Her words were fluid that filled and soothed.
Bringing me back with the pull of blue oceans.

The light, breaking windows.
   and the Atlantic flooding rooms finds me.
I float 260 miles from home,
   and beside an impossible promise—kept.
—*Niki Perakis*

Kamuela Rose

Kamuela Rose you've captured my heart
Your beauty and fragrance sets you apart
No other rose will ever compare
In my lapel, no other I'll wear.
A dozen or more I'll take home with me
To give to my true love, so she can see
Your beauty, to prove, my love for her
And she'll love me more, with each prick of your spur
So Kamuela Rose be lovely today
Enhance my true love, less she go astray
Cause deep in my heart, like my affection for you
Kamuela Rose I'm in love with her too.
—*Walter Cambra*

Finding You

Finding you has put my life in a new perspective
your warmth and your kindness,
has made me feel as though I'm someone special.
With thoughtfulness and communication,
Were open to talk about feelings
For I know this is real
Even though I don't understand
What or how I should feel.
I can start to believe, we will mean something to each other.
For my feelings towards you are growing stronger and stronger.
And the bond that's growing between us...
Don't ever let it tear apart.
—*Sarah Schulte*

To My Little Ones

I see me in your eyes
Your big brown eyes, that sparkle with joy or tears
You see...my little ones, my eyes sparkle with joy or tears, too

I hear me in your cries,
Your urgent little voices that say, "Mom, Dad, Help!"
You see my little ones, I too, cry for help to our Dad in the sky

I feel me in your touch
Your urgent hands wanting attention
You see, my little ones I too want attention and I too seek by touch

I feel me in your hearts as you repeatedly say "Mom, Dad, I
   love you!"
I repeatedly feel I love you back

My little ones
Your innocence is your strength
And it is your innocence that continually reminds me
of what we have in common...We need each other.
—*Maria G. Vega Clark*

Untitled

An infant stares with loving eyes
Your face an image making,
A small child grasps your fingers tight.
Trembling steps and stumbles taking.
   Away they walk; but back they run
   They don't want you ... they do!
   "I want to do it by myself"
   Independence is oh so new.
Soon you're replaced by 'bestest' friends,
Bicycles, books and boys.
Power struggles getting tougher.
Cars and clothes instead of toys.
Your grip is loosening but you hang on tight
   And in the end you pray;
That all the years when you were there
   make a difference when you're away.
'then' has become 'now' again
   The years have gone around.
The infant stares with loving eyes
   The face you've shaped, they're found.
—*Kathryn Grove*

Ode To Arizona

    Arizona, you're on my mind
  Your gentle breezes, your warm sunshine
  Caressing my soul, delighting my heart
  I'm deeply saddened we had to part.

   It was in only four short days
   I felt the richness of your ways
  Your friendly people, your pure air
Your sky of clear blue, your green valley fair.

Your bright colors abound, all splendid in hue
  Smoldering festively - yellow, red, blue
  Your lovely scent permeates all the air
Your Mexican children, their straight black hair.

   Your mountains so majestic a scene
   A noble backdrop for cacti green
   Your desert beauty sheer opulence
  God's handiwork to see and to sense.

   Your splendor just seems to never end
  To think in four days I've a life-long friend
Although on this earth there's no Shangri-La
  Arizona, to me, you come closest by far!
—*R. DeCristofaro*

"I Walk Alone"

Did you ever feel alone
your heart feels an emptiness
a hurt... a pain...
I have...
Even when I'm with a group
I still walk alone side by side
with my loneliness.
Even my shadow seems absent
in the hot summer sun.
How do I explain my inner thoughts and feelings?
I don't...
I keep them bottled up inside with all my
deepest secrets.
Who would listen anyway?
Why express your feelings to people who
don't care and never will?
You don't!

—*Shannon Elaine Milligan*

Star-Struck

The moments we've had together are very few.
Your memory haunts me...like someone I knew,
From a distant past or far off galaxy in the heaven's above.
Was I someone you hated? Maybe someone you loved.
I cruise on the memory of your beautiful face,
And long to be with you in some far off place.
My heart was yours when we first met.
Was it long ago or just recent?
Yet, it may have been in a life before this
When we met, fell in love and had our first kiss.
It seems so funny it seems so strange
But here we are together again.
This is no new love; it's ancient and strong.
Not even death can hold it for long.
We once promised love till death do we part
Now I know it lasts longer I know in my heart.
We were together long, long ago
Before rain, before thunder, before the wind began to blow
From now on our hearts will play
Together, forever till our souls fade away.

—*Anthony Albano*

The Red Cross

Your yells bruise me.
Your name calling hurt more than I ever let on.
When you broke my only thing from home, it hurt.

The pain worse than ripping my heart out,
puncturing it and sprinkling salt on it.
Your nagging smiles make me cry.
But I won't let you see my hurt.

I beg of you please STOP!!!
I CAN take your yells, name callings and smiles.
But leave my sweet memories alone.
The only thing I have right now.

At night I cry while you sleep.
Tears rolling down my cheek.
I can taste the salt of my tears.
Yet, I know I can only live like this,
with my thing from home.
My red cross.

—*Zienia Cabrera*

To One I Wish Was Braver

You greet me with a gush of warm, posh charm,
Your voice with squeak as if I was long lost.
When I think then of one who always farms
The hearts of loves to brave encroaching frosts
(No matter what their age or shape she barns
For them the memories which you have lost),
I cringe; you even can't recall my craft.
You're of the club that for their flag raise smiles,
Defend appearances like property
And wake up suddenly a thousand miles
From power, brotherhood and liberty.
You pine for human touch. You run. You shaft.
The kind of life's events that pass hard felt by friends
Friends keep as markers home. To you they're only ends.
Great smiles surprise from hearts by honest spirits staffed.

—*Frederick Solari*

My Value Line

I don't live for the future, because by living for the future
you're forgetting about the past. You should kill to be first,
cause in heart you'll be last. I wouldn't leave to find out
where I really want to be, nor turn on the light, in darkness
I view what I really need to see. If my heart says go, but my
mind says stay, I find out what my prayers have to say. I
believe you can accomplish more then the best, just remember:
In real life your no better then all the rest. I believe you
can change your mind as much as you please, as long as others
opinion you do not seize. I don't make decisions that reflects
someone else's mind, for to your very own heart that would be
so unkind. I believe in life you should have a goal to reach,
especially if on the way someone else's soul you teach.

—*Abagail Fabiaschi*

Untitled

Don't ask me anything.
You're right, something is wrong.
How's she doing?
No, I never noticed how great she looked. I never noticed her long,
black curly hair, nor did I notice her beautiful smile.
Don't ask me anything.
You're right, you should call her and get to know her.
Yes, she probably would like to hear from you.
What's wrong? Wrong? What could be wrong?
No, I have had this outfit for years. No, I had my hair cut last
week.
Don't ask me anything.
Oh, you tried to call me earlier.
No, I was at home, I couldn't have missed your call.
Don't ask me anything.
Yes, I never told you that I think the world of you; yes,
I never showed you.
Your eyes never met mine, but mine were always on you.
What was his name again? Do you have his number?
Don't ask me anything.

—*Letitia V. Fowler*

The Gardener

There once was a little seed in a pot of weeds.
A beautiful gardener discovered the seed amongst the weeds,
He watered her with kindness, and fertilized her with love.
He brought sunshine to her always, and didn't mind the weeds,
The gardener sheltered her from cold and harm.
She bloomed into a flower, for this man took the time, to care
for this seed with so many weeds.
Without this man, the seed would surely have died.
Why he decided to sow the seed with so many weeds,
And why the gardener gave so much devoted love,
The seed will never know,
She will always love this gardener of hers.

—*Victoria J. Anderson*

Untitled

We are in two completely different worlds.
Yours filled with violence
   and substances costing twenty five bucks
   a bag to put the same on your face.
Where laughter doesn't come
   from deep inside your soul,
   which holds your deepest thoughts
   and dreams.
No smiles.
   No tears.
You act as if you are immortal,
Without feeling,
   Without love.
My world is surrounded by love.
Love for him, love for you.
   I, maybe too mortal,
     feel everything.
The happiness, the hurt, the pain
   inside of both you and me.
—*Denise Olson*

Family Pictures

Oh Daddy, Daddy,
you've been gone so long.
I can remember running to meet you,
but, I can't remember your face.
Looking at my small supply of pictures,
you always have on a hat.
There you are in your Army uniform,
standing very straight, perhaps to look taller.
Your face is shadowed by your service cap.
Ah, here's one of you, holding me as a baby;
I can see my face, but not yours.
Here's another,
you with Mother.
The straw hat shields your face.
I'm told I look like you, but
the pictures don't show it.
At the bottom of the stack,
one of us sitting at the edge of the surf—
Your back is turned.
—*Katherine T. Nufer*

Untitled

As he says goodbye her tears fall
  1 2 3 .... they fall
    Don't go don't go she says
      But he turns and leaves
        And now she learns love is not easy

As he marches across the stage
  In his cap and gown
    Don't go don't go she says
      But he turns and runs
        and she learns love is not easy

I love you I love you she says
  But his eyes are unreadable
    He turns and walks away
      And she learns love is not easy

And as he pack his bags
  and goes to College
    I love you she says and
      always will as her tears fall 1 2 3...........
        Now she knows love is not easy
—*Nadia Soukup*

"The Celebrated Mocker" Or "A Virtuoso"

He's a prancing dancer, clad in a dapper gray tuxedo,
A ballerina, fluttering on the sturdy 'lectrical line,
It's courting time; and weary of his stage, his routine
is quieted, as he dashes from oak tree to a nearby sign.

His antics and concerto ring out from dawn 'till dusk—
'Bob-bob-o-link, bob-bob-o-link'—it's a vibrant call!
A cowboy's yodeling refrain is heard by babbling brink
as the 'aper' struts with his love on an embankment wall.

Echoes of a cardinal's warble, a whistling bluebird—
Sounds of finches, then voice of wren with bubbling trill.
Those lilting melodies emit tranquil tones to list'ning ear,
while his mimics captures an elopement flight o'er hill.

Ah, re-echoes of quavers, chirps and gurgling calls
as those melodic embellishments yearn to e'er be heard.
To a harkening ear, those tunes of the jovial animated mocker
is truly a virtuoso of a celebrated mocking-bird!

   Hark—listen to the mocking-bird trill
     as he clowns about on Mocking-Bird Hill!!!
—*Deloris Lynch*

The Amazing Phils!

The ninety three Phillies are amazing!
A baseball team, you just can't help praising.
This team has power and good pitching too.
These two things are essential and must
Continue the whole season through.
There are one hundred sixty two games
to be played.
So if they lose a few games; you
shouldn't be dismayed.
Because, the other teams in their league
have good pitching and hitting you know
And there are still quite a few games to go.
Baseball like any other sport; you need to be patient.
So even though you are now leading
the league.
You just can't be to complacent.
If they win eighty one games that's five
hundred ball.
But I think the team that wins the
most games in the nineties will win it all.
—*Clyde Harrar*

The Pain Within

I feel my heart, I know its there
A broken heart only feels despair
Not a word, a hug or pill will help
The pain is so deep it is only felt.

Each day goes on as before
I think I can't take it anymore
I search my soul for strength
A little thread to pull from the brink.

The sun shines, the moon beams
I think over all the things I've seen
Happiness comes quickly, in the twinkle of an eye
Then it's gone and now I can only cry.

It was good, it was bad, it was exciting, and sad
We loved deep and fought hard
But the bond that united us —
Held us together until you were called by the Lord.

I miss you so much, the pain is in me
I search for peace, as I know you had to go
Maybe this is the way I'll always be
I'll never forget you and I love you so.
—*Linda Johnson*

Tree Swing

You are not worth all that much
A bit of wood, five yards of line
Fastened into my great old Elm

The birds, blue, red, black and green
Each, treat you as their own.
Perching, out of site of furry, fast flying Benjamin.

My winged friends wait upon your back
To take their turn for the noon day meal.
Only a waiting spot, for more important fare.

Benjamin, too, finds you alluring
He sweeps across the bushes
Landing in your bench, stays but a bit.

Friends and family have sat within your arms.
They have pushed their feet and enjoyed the swinging
They have risen and said, "That's nice."

I think only I feel your spirit
Only I sense the meaning of the universe as you
Give me vision of the birds, flowers, stars and sky.

I shall share you with my grandchildren.
You and I shall transfer to them the beauty of life.

—*Florence Murphy*

Nod

My city is without light...abiding in a tangible darkness.
A cimmerian star shrouded in black clouds;
A heart unimaginably heavy voraciously devouring
Time and light and life.

The streets are filled with throngs of people
Wandering aimlessly.
Deprived of light, deprived of sight.

Our great minds gather in stygian halls
Speaking circuitously....these murmuring pedants,
Whose thick speech serves only to suffocate;
Falling on the people like volcanic ash from the dark sky.

In a cloud shrouded temple
Rabbis and priests bow and kneel in endless obeisance
Before the veil of the holy of holies,
Ceaselessly whispering prayerful chants and incantations;
Their sonambulastic rituals (soulless at the core)
Pay homage to the past alone.

We find no respite in sleep.
Our dreams are haunted by blind featureless shadows

By death alone are we made free.

—*Mark Murray*

Teachers

Mom, Nurse, Counselors too, these are just to name
a few, of the caps a teacher wears, in a day filled
with cares.

If it wasn't for teachers there would not be, Doctors,
Lawyers, Judges not any of these, But God created the
teacher you see, so you could be what you wanted to be.

Wiping noses, tying shoes, these are not things which
you choose. But it goes along with the job, or else the
children you would rob.

Their lives are in your hands, to mold and make as best
you can, teach and reach every single child, then you can
give yourself a great big smile.

—*Dixie Graham*

Shadow Teasers Of Jacek And Yore

Dusty shade, floating like the echoes of a car's footsteps on
a dirt road swim into a darkness - I grip. I tease. I hold
with the heartbeats of every layer of skin this darkness, so
sonorous it fills the hollow inside my soul - It pulses like
sweet security hand shakes-, a breathing mass of my inner true
shakiness. Like the panels of a board nailed through the middle
drastically swinging past-that lingers in the black of my
eyes, like the black of his soul that gripped my dignity, my
innocence in a realm of sweaty insecurity I waver in front of
you-causing my body to hate touch, my mouth to reach from the
blackness-stuttering, sputtering the word sex that it can't
form anymore: And the hand—inside my mouth still crooked,
awkward-holding my vocal chords against you in my vellicating
movements-pleading wails in a sputtering ecstasy-a denial of my
desireto inhale your skin like a wave in an orange sunset over
thebrown pebbles of sand. The spotlight, dim with its whitened
edges, your teary eyes ask me "Who loves you?" —to create an
anvil upon the muscles of my hardened panels of limbs-no
longer capable of distinguishing the rape, and your death.

—*Carrie Gordon*

Trapped

Time, fluid from beginning to end. Starting with
a drip to a gush, through spurts and perilous bends.

Realities, that now indifference breeds. Shaped
by faith, beliefs, and charity for most mortal needs.

Always, the cry immortals sing. Only health, time
and realities shape the eternal springs.

Perhaps, the message is unclear. Giving rise to
yet another voice, or hope for more years.

Preparation, for that which is unknown. Without
love, mate, children, so precarious, so alone.

Ever, the deep tide of life. Now that embodiment
is spent, long is the night.

Death, as fluid time goes dry. Limited by the
machine, as it withers, wears out and dies.

Trapped is not the end, yet. Indeed a last dark
fight. As clarity fades...and struggles take....
life's precious, precious light.

—*Larnders Roy*

A Gift Of Friendship

Of all the gifts that I have ever received,
A friend is the best, I truly believe.
A friend is one who will unselfishly share,
Who will instinctively know we need someone to care.
A friend shows love in many thoughtful ways
And is always near on stormy days.
A friend can warm your heart with a little touch.
A gentle pat on the back says "I care so much!"
A wink, a nod, or a much needed smile,
Or perhaps the offer to just listen awhile.
Often when comforting words are hard to be found,
Just sharing together without making a sound,
Just to know that a friend is near
Can turn a gloomy moment into one of cheer.
You are all the things a friend should be;
You're a special gift - a friend to me.
So, today and all year through
May I be that special gift to you.

—*Bonnie Kistler*

Graffiti

Mouths in blindfolds,
A funeral of sounds - swallowed.
There's no escaping the wrinkled lips
And the whirlwinds come crashing, twisting,
Playing tug of war.
I fall, drenched in the dizzy of me.
Yet the eyes - oh, the eyes
Like the sky ignited with fireflies,
And the heat rises.
The eyes tell a story,
Of graffiti colors
Screaming mutes - do you want to hear?
Listen
—*Chris Umhoefer*

A Sad Spring

Spring means green grass and flowers
A gentle rain that softly showers
Spring means Winter is retreating
With all its darkness cold defeating
I feel as if I newly waken
All dark thoughts should be forsaken
A rustling of the wind in trees it rushes
Birds are singing, nesting in the bushes
So I wander alone through nature
Forever abandoned by my lover
Abandoned with loneliness a curse
My lover taken by the eternal hearse
Now I go to visit him in Spring
In the cemetery where birds still sing
—*Margot G. Dargel*

"Son-Of-A-Buck"

He was "Son-of-a-buck", a buckin' bronc.
A hoss that'd never been ridd'.
Some of the best had draw'd his lot. Some jest bragged they did.
They bet good money that they'd be the one, to ride that
 "Son-of-a-buck".
When they made the ride, the money was lost to the luck
 of "Son-of-a-buck".
His habits was rotten 'n got even worse as the money went
 pocket to pocket.
"Son-of-a-buck" would sunfish 'n sulk, then shoot in the air
 like a rocket.
He'd land like a rock, come to a stop, then take off in a run like
 greased lightnin'.
Stumble 'n fall, bounce up like a ball, then head fer the fence. It
 was frightnin'!
He used all the tricks to get rid a them hicks that clung to his
 sweatin' back.
Eight seconds of hell. Riders knew real well, old "Son-of-a-buck"
 cut no slack.
—*Frances R. Long*

To A Son On Fathers' Day

F is for the fun you'll have together.
A is that you always will be friends.
T is for the times you'll need each other.
H is for the help that never ends.
E is ever loving, faithful, hoping.
R is right you'll always try to be.
Put them straight they spell
 the kind of father
That you will want
 and you'll be proud to be.
—*Marie P. Alm*

The Magic Of Reading

The wonders of mind and treasures galore,
 A hummingbird's song, a dinosaur's roar.
A trip to the planets or just down the street,
 What makes a cloud? Why does a heart beat?
 Who fired the shot heard 'round the world?
 Who wrote the song of old glory unfurled?
  Can you eat worms, broiled or fried?
 If a monster came running, where would you hide?
  All of these questions are puzzling indeed,
But the answers are found in the books that we read.
 So pick up a book and read through the pages,
  Go into the future, or go back to the ages.
  Whichever you choose, your journey awaits,
 Reading's the key to unlock the mind's gates!
—*Bryan Bawtinhimer*

The Unnoticed One

at age fifty - a woman with
a husband, four children, and now my widowed mother.

Thirty years of giving - putting their needs before my own.
 I've given myself away.
 There's nothing left.

He doesn't talk to me - doesn't even answer
They never listen - are too busy to phone!

AREN'T I HERE?

 Being pulled in all directions - trying to please everyone
 I'm flying apart and no one even cares!

WHAT HAVE I BECOME?

What happened to my smile, my personality,
 my spirit, ME? my spirit, ME?

I dreamed I was a carcass - picked clean - discarded, bereft.
 Bit by bit over the years,
 They've taken ALL of me.
 There's nothing left!

DOESN'T ANYONE SEE ME?
—*Ellen E. Barnes*

My Brother

He was a tiller of the soil,
A husband with great love.
He had a knack for milking cows,
He had the strength for holding plows.
When time came to plant the seeds
He knew which month to fill his needs.
The corn grew high, the silos filled.
The cows gave birth and he was thrilled.
Alfred was a gentle man and loved his pretty wife,
She bore his child and this put sunshine in his life.
He was a happy man when grandchildren came,
This made him proud and Mae the same.
He suffered a lot, but did not complain,
This man, who worked under stress and strain.
He is free at last from any chores,
My brother, who never got to distant shores.
I am proud to say, "I knew this man!"
With the gentle eyes and calloused hands.
May he rest in peace in God's strong embrace.
I loved him so, and will miss his sweet face.
—*Trudy Pierpont*

Remember That I Am Always With You!

O, God, please give my precious friend
A fount of joys that never end.
And make her soul with love to breathe.
With smiles her face, dear God, enwreathe.
—*S. Gilbert Mark*

Visions

Feelings still present, from relationships now past
A kaleidoscope of emotions, tears at your heart.
Bloody tears run down your face,
As you think of what could have been,
And reminisce about what was.
But just remember, as you look as visions past,
Not to let them impair visions of present and of future.
—*Megan Vaughan*

Untitled

Take a Gentle look at the world
A kind heart to see things through,
For when you see things with compassion
Ultimately, peace will come to you.

A slower pacé in this fast world
Makes everything seem less pressed,
Enjoy the breeze on a summer's day
And you'll find that you're less stressed.

Think twice before you speak your mind
Are your intentions for all good?
Your thoughts to share with someone else
If happy, then you should.

This life we live, we share with many
A mere fragment of its whole,
Where you walk, another walks
So leave good where you must go.

Appreciate the life you live
And those who share this day,
Take a gentle look at the world
And let kindness lead the way.
—*Susan Meyers*

What My Family Means To Me

My family means to me:
A leaf dropping in the fall,
Snow that falls from the sky above,
The rain falling on lily pads in a pond,
A rose budding in spring,
The morning dew on flowers in a garden,
A field of daisies, as golden as the sun,
Trees rustling as the wind blows them,
A white stallion running in a moonlit field,
The shiny reflection of the moon
on a rippling stream,
The buzzing of bees getting honey,
Laying in a green field
with the sun in my face,
The sound of a BlueJay singing,
  That's what my family means to me.
—*Clint Bradley*

Queen Of Hearts

So she was and she was Gracey Ann
a long time ago in another land
in front of a dirty brick wall in the city
was Grace Ann at dusk, and sure looked pretty
For only the moment, all was mine —
when she said "yes" it was like-drunk on wine
She and I were virgins then, and still are to each
through many nights restless and dreams out of reach.
Yet we can still be glad to hear one another's voice
both sometimes wishing-we've made some other choice.
Now its come to forget-me-nots
days of times we never forgot?
Time took youth and you-wedged us apart
so there may never again be -
  a Queen of Hearts
—*Michael Bern Dixon*

"Life Of Despair"

A life of destruction, a life of despair,
A life of disillusions beyond compare…

When all I thought was lost,
When it seemed that nobody cared…

In all the emotional trauma,
With memories, I could hardly bare…

The physical misery, the physical pain,
A life of uncertainty, with no positive gain…

With much at stake, and a need to refrain,
A pattern of behavior, I must not maintain…

To be totally removed, and just one thing to obtain
The control of a life, so shattered and in vain…

When denial was realized, the healing then came,
To a life so misled, a life of embarrassment and shame…

Consequences in question, destination unknown,
Old ways and habits buried, a new spirit reborn…

A life of destruction, a life of despair,
A life of disillusions, which only I could repair…
—*Don L. Pressley*

The Wind

The winds of change blow relentlessly across the sky
A lifetime's cherished moments scattering as I stand helpless by

  Where is the snowflake I held in my hand?
  Where is the footprint I left in the sand?
  Where are the blossoms on the cherry tree?
  Where are the little children that were
    so much a part of me?

  Not gone
  They are not gone

But sheltered oh so lovingly
In the soft places of my heart
In the archives of my mind
And in the remote reaches of my soul

With these I shall not part
—*Helen Seay*

"Flowers Of Spring"

Spring arrives and blossoming flowers appear.
A meadow full of flowers looks like a color book of bright
chromas, brilliant blue, radiant red, and graceful green line
the corners of my picture.
But forming in the middle sprinkles of youthful yellow,
Outstanding orange, and vivid violet make a circle of
  peacefulness.
It reminds me of a box full of crayons, each brand new.
Each having its own distinct power of emotional thought.
One sad, one happy, one gloomful, one surprised, one confused,
  and one scared.
The flowers are water color seeping together uniting in a mixture
The picture I see is a free flowing flag swaying back and forth in
  the wind.
Quiet, relaxing, pretty as a painting.
But I awake and find that it is.
—*Janie Schramm*

If Teachers Were

If teachers were flowers, you'd be a rose—the sweetest scent to
a person's nose.
If teachers were fruit, you'd be a strawberry—with tiny seeds
not a pit like a cherry.
It teachers were trees, you'd be an Oak—tall and beautiful and
that's no joke.
It teachers were birds, you'd be a robin, for at the first sign
of Spring they're the first to start bobbin.
It teachers were season, you'd be Spring—for the first sign of
life, does she bring.
If teachers were creatures who liked to swim, you'd be a fish,
Thank God you're not, but you are the best teacher of English.

—*Roger H. Ackley*

Forgotten Senses

A lone wolf's howl falls upon deaf ears.
A plea for change,
reminder of what used to be.

Thundering buffalo pound the Earth,
frustrated and bewildered,
sending tremors no longer heard.

An eagle cries across an open canyon,
silence echoes back.
His sharp eye catches a glimpse of the past.

A mustang (no longer wild),
tastes the stale water.
His thirst for freedom is not quenched.

The American Indian-
Sees no vision-
Hears his ancestors' cries.

—*Tamara K. Remy*

Wag Ass

A gaping hole, in my head, there is.
A putrid hole, in my head, there is.
I have seen the icons of Maternity
and dodged the apron's asphyxiating swathe.
I have seen the comrades of Fraternity
and evaded the tentacles of focus and constraint.
I have seen the paladins of Mercy;
the apostles of Freud; the devotees of Jung;
Off me! Groping, empathic lechers!
I have seen the sinister drug men
eyeing me, lasciviously, like Mengele.
For every scrap of gristly happiness,
you must plunge, headlong, through the hoop,
roll, heavily, upon the hard turf,
and wag your round, delectable, ass

in their faces.

—*J. H. Ward*

Untitled

I lost a very special friend
a friend I thought I'd have til' the end.
　There was never another friend
that meant as much as she,
　Even though we aren't friends now
I feel she's still a part of me.

　The pain hurts me deep inside
I just want to run and hide.
　I don't know what to do,
I don't even know what to say,
　I just hope soon this all will go away!

—*Michelle Pickles*

Where Columbines Grow

Tattered towns below timberline
A quest for gold, a deserted mine.

Rotten timbers and empty shafts
Deep and dark with cold damp drafts.

Tents and shacks on Mountain slopes
Shattered dreams and forgotten hopes.

Broken porcelain and rusted pots
Squeaky springs on vacant cots.

Wagon ruts climb a brushy slope
To a place up high, a place remote.

Where eagles soar and flowers grow
A drop of rain, thunder rumbles low.

Here wooden crosses and granite stone
And wandering winds, through jack pine moan.

A tiny marker lays in the grass so tall
Crude cracked sandstone, the oldest of all.

Words are gone from this little page
Except on the bottom, a girl 5 years of age.

Saddened you retreat to the valley below
Never to return to where columbines grow.

—*Asa Battles*

Tears Of Heaven

I stand alone, waiting, almost anxious.
A sense of excitement surrounds me,
as it would as a child at play.

Like a gentle kiss of nature,
the soft rain begins to fall
upon my face.

Its strength slowly increasing,
the warm rain quietly descends and
caresses my entire body.

Peace and calmness enter my soul, I am one with myself.
I am free to feel, and to express,
there are no barriers.

Like a child in its womb,
I am safe for a time, a time which is now.

I nurture my mind,
strengthen my spirit and give thanks to my God.

Energy radiates through my veins
sending shivers down my spine
I am in a state of tranquility,
I am engulfed in the Tears of heaven.

—*Yves Raymond*

Heartbreaks And Tears

　　As the little girl lay in a meadow of thoughts
　　　　a sentence repeated in her mind:
"The storms will be heartbreaks and the frost will be tears".
　　She guessed it meant a reminder for all the hard times,
　　　　　　to get through them.
　　　To put them aside when they are too much
　　and when you need them again just pick them up.
　　　　Then feel and hear them once more.

—*Janie Oliver*

"The Night Of Jesus' Birth"

The night was dark and very quiet
A silence covered the valleys and hills.
The stars God had made and called by their names
whispered to each other, "This was the night"
God would reveal his plan. The moon, in its splendor and glow
God had created so long ago, also knew of God's plan
that would show his love to all mankind.
The angels stood with heads bowed low,
knowing Jesus would be leaving Heaven to go to the earth below.
They knew God was going to send his Son to be born in Bethlehem
The shepherds, after a long hard day,
were watching their sheep nearby.
They watched in the stillness of the night
how the stars were shining so "extra bright"
when the sky lit up and the angels began to sing
telling them where they could find
the Christ child who was to be their King.
God chose the eastern star to lead the way
where they would find the baby Jesus sleeping in the hay.
The stars and moon played a part in the night of Jesus' birth.
—*Mary Murphy*

Little Brother / American Child

Death came dancing silver down the grotesque street,
A sinuous shining; winged arms and legs
Glittering the night, he swirled-
Snake of all their dreams

A mask of brilliant feathers hid no eyes
For nobody to see; the head-dress swaying
Dangerous in harsh-lit dark promised
Frenzies of destruction

He cast no shadow, that old old body;
Only the silent scream on every street
They ever saw, sweating ecstasy
At the last party

Dancing their dreams he came
Twirling his gleaming fans-
Come taste my honey for dead souls
Come dance with me.
—*Serena Sorensen*

A Patriot's Heart

A soldier's cry at time of war,
A sound not heard, but simply mourned;
We do a job not easy to like,
but the sound of liberty and freedom make it seem right;
The smell of death makes a sane man scared,
As medics rush to save a life;
As our Veterans will back us up, for they have seen our goal,
A medic's oath, to save the patriot's heart and soul.
—*Douglas Stein*

Untitled

My retirement presents a quandary locating a kindred soul,
whose problems aren't more vexing than mine,
a listener who will agree with all I extol,
astute, but not overly smart, one who's kind
and compassionate and praising and will dole
out advice sparingly as I don't need to find
I lack wisdom that old age bequeaths my mind.
You say, I possess a wife—soul mate to tell?
That's true, but we know each other too well.
—*Edward Resnick*

College Life

One bottle of milk. Two sticks of butter
A stalk of celery. Four cokes
A half-eaten steak
Six cans of Keystone Light

A Granny Smith apple
A couple of oranges. Three baked potatoes
16 oz jar of Strawberry jam
half a loaf of bread.

Five cans of Keystone Light
Two pieces of Late Night Pizza
A package of bologna, onions, carrots,
A friend stops over.

Three cans of Keystone Light
A pan of leftover Kraft cheese & macaroni
An unfinished bowl of cereal?
Another loaf of…Penicillin
Another friend stops over. And another
No cans of Keystone Light
Hey, who took the last beer!
—*John Hanna*

An Architect Builds An Apple

Somewhere in a world he sought
a vision lost as if one must have
a thought of winter where leaves talk
or whisper as they wander lost
somewhere in a world he sought.

He designed purple, created grapes in Rome,
constructed an orange in L.A., they say
years ago, slowly, he built a legacy
from blueprints of a melon
until rains came, eroded long away — painted
green, like the reason
of youth and old age, one season like leaves
from trees that whisper
the same silence we don't hear when we do.

Somewhere in a world he sought
safety among the rocks
as if one must have a thought of ground for
cathedrals spire, for shrines, or apples that don't rot
somewhere in a world he sought.
—*Robert L. Grundy*

Symphonic Invasion

Flooded from obscurity, a tide of images hit shore.
A voice is in the rooms,
   …a chorded laugh,
Poignant crescendos heat the pulse,
   …strings and reeds seed havoc.
Thieves! Marauders of the peace!
How the sounds unnerve! In numbing conquest,
Flowing up the hollow bamboo of the spine
As through a funnel, spilling, filling,
Reaching speeds one can't deter.
Hinting danger, rousing climatic fevers, until
   …the music crashes!
Shattering my inner window panes!
And all the hidden crystal on my fragile shelves!
Then silence,
   …and silently,
Ten thousand jagged nuances of grief recur.
—*Lucy Meyer*

Untitled

I have dreams for myself, and hopes,
A wish I strive everyday to make come true,
And although people say "Oh its impossible" and
"You'll never make it," I hold my head high and Try to do

Everything in my power, praying, hoping
that one day something will happen and
My dream will pour down on me, hold my hand,
And I will know I have succeeded.

It may be discouraging, and sometimes I feel
So much frustration at not having enough
to grasp my dream, missing the single element
that always keeps me one step behind, my heart
tearing at the knowledge that I might never do it,
While the optimist in my keeps my spirits up,
reassuring me that I can.
So I will press on, doing all in my power to fulfill my
dream, and in the meantime, giving
myself the undying courage to keep on trying.
  —*Evelyn V. Trester*

Filling The Void

Filling the void
A women's job is never done. You hardly have the time for fun.
Between work, home, and business too
There rarely is time left for you
A constant leakage from day to day
That need refilling in a special way.
So you indulge in food you like
To fill that empty appetite. You may relax, take time to read.
A book on which your mind could feed.
Or just do something you would like
Write, rest, shop, or ride a bike. Perhaps you turn to a
friend that cares. To someone you know will be right there.
They'll fill your joy and renew your mind.
That someone's willing to take the time.
Because it's expected of women to give
So much of themselves in order to live. So as the cycle of
life began. For women, there is a leakage within.
And needful things keep dripping out. That leaves you empty
and without. So women you must always do
What fills the void inside of you.
  —*Nikita Johnson*

Happiness

Everything is fine with the USA,
A wonderful thought to have today.
Deserving pride that this fact is true
So why should anyone sigh, sob or feel blue?

If it is happiness you want to find,
You can acquire it in your mind.
Seek what is honest, noble and right
Seek these qualities with all your might.

You will have a feeling of pleasure.
An abundance of joy in great measure.
You will gain a sense of peace, too,
And surely happiness will come to you.
  —*Thelma Williams LeGette*

Someone Needs You

Someone needs you to help them, on the journey of life.
A smile, a handshake, a firm grip.
A slap on the back, a nudge or two.
Or maybe an ear to listen, to their woes.
It might well be you that needs a helping hand.
We all need someone to cheer us along.
So be ready to be the someone they need.
  —*Erskine Ramey*

Untitled

The heart....so weak yet....so strong.
Able to withstand breaks and magically mend itself.
Breaking....mending....breaking....mending....

Is it really worth it?
Yes!
  No!
My mind is like my heart.
Going up and down like a yo-yo.

Joy....pain....happiness....sorrow.....
I don't think I can take much more.
Should I quit on love or give it one more try?
As I roll the dice one more time, I silently pray.

Everlasting love!

Is it for real? Will it last? Do I really think it's worth it?
Yes!
  —*Cathrese M. Owens*

A Special Man

I know a man who is witty and charming and his talents do abound.
But then sometimes he gets moody and really feels down.

When he is down he seems to feel that life is a double view —
one for himself and one for others too.

This is to say his double view is just like double rules.
What applies to others may be sound but for him it will not do.

To know this man is quite an interest. One I wouldn't have
missed. He looks at life with great adventure and is always
full of zest.

He laughs, he loves and is so caring and really loves to jest.
He is bright and kind and very clever and tries to do his best.

I can vouch for him and all his talents for I really know him well.

I feel his love and great dimension, and his story has been my pleasure
to tell.
  —*Ailene Smith Slominski*

To Gene

You have taught me
  about the beauty of the seasons -
  the snap of winter in a woodland walk,
  the freshness of the new-born animals and plants
    in spring's bright sun,
  the sea-borne breeze of summer on the sandy shore,
  the radiant array of leaves before their rest in fall.

So now, my love, I'll see you
  as I walk the snowy paths of winter,
  and greet the fawns born in the spring,
  stand drinking in the ocean's waves in summer,
  and climb steep trails strewn with crisp leaves in fall.

You have taught me
  about the beauty of the seasons -
  we are together as the seasons change -
  our love goes on.
  —*Myra L. Weiger*

War Vet

What does a war vet do, when he comes home
Amidst parades of hero worship if talk
of great fete and daring deeds.

He sits in a dark corner and weeps oh so quietly.
Less someone hears him and know of
his wounded humanity and his never ending pain.
For what? Country it is said liers
  —*Glenn E. Isler*

We'll Meet Again

Last night, I had a dream.
About the way it use to be.
But now that you're gone,
Thing's changing slowly and slowly,
As I can see.

The lord put's you in his hands.
Don't you worry about know more.
Carry on to the promise land.
I'll be there one day knocking on the door.

But until then I'll carry on with my life.
Sooner or later one day I'll see the light.
We'll sleep on cause you don't have to worry
About know more pain, not ever danger.

Cause I'm witch will remain.
You're been a family, you've also been a friend.
I'll wait for now.
But we shall meet again.
—*Robert Pipkin*

Grandma's Words

Grandma didn't use naughty words
About the worst I heard her say
Was "hell's bells" or "oh, drat"
If she was having a really bad day.
I know it's a lot to wish for
But I bet you wish for it too
That lots of bad words you hear today
Would appear on a list called "taboo"
Taboo means forbidden - did then and does today
It means there's whole lot of bad words
We would like to magic away.
We all have funny habits - funny and even strange
Grandma called them "peccadilloes"
To her a stove was a "range"
She called a refrigerator an "ice box"
That's because when she was not very old
A big chunk of ice in a wooden box
Is how her family kept food cold
I have a longer list of Grandma's words - these are only a few
I don't want to lose them - that's why I'm telling you.
—*Eileen Gould*

Untitled

Harold McCuen Leader editor.
accept my "Little Lamp", on your birthday
may this little lamp, lighten your way;
with the news that you print
and the photos you take
To enlighten and brighten the peoples day.
    What a delight!
To have an editor that's ever so bright.
    Rain or shine
His paper the Leader is always
    delivered on time.
—*B.J. Deltoro*

Someone Else's Petri Dish

Looking at the protozoa and various micro-bugs
a smaller one struggles and a larger one tugs.
Looking at their world through a microscope
it is sort of hard to cope
had someone realized ———
they might be civilized?
To learn the truth, I can only wish
'cause maybe we're floating in someone else's petri dish.
—*Kekoa Seward*

Roses For Remembrance

We started out in a two room shack with a trellis of roses
across the back, cabbage roses of yellow and red. The rich
sweet smell drifted across our bed.

I dried the petals to make them last through winter's cold and
frigid blasts, and when spring brought new blooms to life, you
had a child and a wife.

Three more winters and four small beds that old shack sheltered
all our heads. And every year the petals were saved to bring
summers promise to winter days.

From house to house and state to state the Roses always had
their place. The kids grew up and took cuttings too, scattered
roses the country through.

Then the saddest time I ever knew, was when I planted one for
you. Let it grow upon your grave.

The only rose I never saved.

Soon now I'll be by your side as I was as your bride. When we
started out in that two room shack with a trellis of roses
across the back
—*Vonna Bechtel*

Body, Soul And Mind

Blinded by feelings of the heart
Afraid to go on from my love and part.
A love so great we will never ever find
    love of the body, soul and mind.
We all make our mistakes
    causing each other endless heartaches.
Never wishing to have a love scold me,
    Only one to always hold me.
One to never ignore me and always adore me.
Dreaming of how it use to be
Thinking of the greater control you've gotten over me.
Holding back all I wish to express
Thoughts and feelings of not only love and happiness,
    but memories of pain and sadness.
Coming to realize holding back caused more pain,
And only by expression will I have more to gain.
Expression not only of the flesh, because only
    then does our love become less.
Everything in life takes time, so now I share
    with you not only my body, but my soul and mind.
—*Sangaw Alston*

A Change Of Seasons

You held me in your arms six weeks ago,
After a long walk home through the wind and snow.
From my lips you took my long awaiting kiss,
I thought the future was a strong promise.

Five weeks ago we walked quite near,
I quietly expressed the feelings I held dear.
By the way you talked I thought you'd always be mine,
Forever in love in an unending time.

You said you would visit four weeks ago,
So I sat and waited thinking of the past fallen snow.
When you never showed up I just lay there and stared,
The tears running down my cheeks told me you never cared.

Three weeks ago, and two weeks and one,
You treated me as though I was just a no one.
When I gathered the courage to ask why you were distant,
You said we couldn't be together because I was too persistent.

Six weeks ago your sweet words meant so much,
Now all I am left with is the dream of your touch.
Today I sit here and wonder why you would part,
You left me alone with a broken heart.
—*Crystal Kravanya*

Evening Peace

Flowers folding their blossoms at night,
After being so brilliant and bright.
The plaintive sound of the mourning dove,
Coming from somewhere up above.
Fireflies flitting here and there.
Never seeming to have a care.

After such a hot day, cooling breezes
Stirring the atmosphere as it pleases.
Birds twittering softly in their nest.
Getting ready for a night of rest.
The sun losing its heat of the day,
With pastel colors in its ray.

Twinkling stars in the sky at last,
Lends beauty to a day just past.
These are the signs of evening peace,
When all mother nature seems to cease.
Evening is the best time of each day.
When peace takes over and the day turns to gray.

—*Vera Warren*

The Ocean In The Sky

The moon was a silver light,
   against the dark blue sky.
The mists and the clouds were rolling,
   while gushing winds blew by.

The clouds were waves of foam,
   the mists were ocean spray.
The moon was a beaming dome,
   while the winds were out to play.

The stars were shimmering stones,
   under the splashing sea.
With the clouds as breakers with low tones,
   I witnessed this all above me.

So any night by chance you see
   the beams of silver light.
Or almost taste an ocean spray,
   or hear the mists by night.

Remember the whirling winds,
   twirling while the clouds blow by.
And you will see what I saw,
   the ocean in the sky.

—*Joyce Datiles*

One Dream

Our romance, the denouement of an enchanted story begun long ago.

A beach on a late summer night, after a storm like fireworks in the sky. I look at you and happiness fills my eyes with soft, slow tears.

We stand in the breeze, my hand in yours, our love exploding into a stillness that is only us as we kiss. The waves tease our ankles as the tide arrives and the moon begins its descent.

I am in your embrace and we sway, as if performing an ethereal dance in the starlight. Your hand like a ghostly memory against my skin, I hold you near so as not to lose you like the wispy smoke of a bonfire.

We begin to dance and I feel the melodies of long ago, our hearts beating in tandem with the rhythm of our dance. The world spins round us and the dawn surprises us as the night comes to an end.

And I am left looking through my window at clouds and dreams of what could be, with tears in my eyes.

—*Jennifer E. Gladis*

The Bible In Poetry

They went into the ark two by two,
All God's living creatures.
Noah went first with his sons and his wife,
All that were left died: all that had life.
It was forty days and forty nights
When God placed a rainbow in the sky.
To remind us all that never again
by flood would we all die.
Then one holy night when the angels sing;
Through virgin Mary came Christ the king.
With stripes on his back and thorns on his head;
Nailed to a cross he suffered and bled.
To heal the sick and to save the lost,
We received it all without any cost.
We should show him our love
through the way that we live,
and our love for him we should freely give.

—*Kathy Watson*

My Special Goodbye

When you left they let me not say bye.
All I could do was cry and cry.
It was said that it wasn't right.
I had to put up with a great fight.
I could not win with all my might.
But at least I know you're in a good place
and I can always remember your adoring face.
So in this way I say goodbye
and I will always try not to cry.

—*Sabrina Caro*

Poetry

Poetry is an arrangement of feelings, thoughts, and emotions
all in one fleeting split break of time
Poetry is the United Nations is session
Poetry is the twinkling of speed across the mind
Poetry is an oil spill spread across thousands of miles
Poetry is the realization of suspicions
Poetry is bricks freshly laid in mortar
Poetry is the personification of eternity
Poetry is a flag flying in the wind
Poetry is the rhythm of silence and noise intertwined
Poetry is the eye seeing the ball sending messages to the
hands to hit it over the fence

—*Jamie Hart*

In-Tolerance

Do unto others as you would have them do unto you
    all men, so it says,
   indeed; all people are created equal
and if you have nothing good to say about something
    say nothing at all,

   these creeds I try to follow

when I have no tolerance for the intolerant
   and I keep it no secret
   I deceive and defeat myself

take notice all you in the world who
   foster prejudice and ignorance
supremacy of some imagined superior race

even while I fight it, I also teach it.

   But I do continue to fight it.

—*Colette M. McGillis*

Beyond The Moon

Each night I look into the stars and see,
All rhyme and reason has been found up there.
I know not what my destiny will be,
And wonder what is in that denseless air.

Futuristic prayers fill my mind,
With many hopes and dreams of years to come.
If success and happiness I fail to find.
I must go back to where I started from.

I fear the thought of not remaining whole,
And know that I will not get over this.
But God stays true in my heart and my soul,
I know for fact that I'll always be His!

For He above has made a place for me,
And that is where my destiny will be!
—*Stephanie Livaccari*

A Plea From My Deprogrammed Heart

Gnashing of teeth raw hate, devour my last child
All that is real is lost in a void called reality.
Oh winged angel of fate, handsome dark man upon a black
mare, come now and with a swift fatal blow, take my life
Standing in between darkness and light I finally see
the difference
Which is there is none, except that we are told there is one
Beauty please take hold and drag me away from these stone
People with plastic hearts and heads held high
Monuments of morality and control, but only robots
Love seek me out and find me, take from me this
infatuation, this juvenile heart
Poked to death by the thumbs of brain washed
computerized non free minded individuals I want out
So please grim reaper come with your scythe and claim me,
before I can become programmed, mindless, and numb!
—*April (Lynn) Sharp*

A Soldier's Dying Words

As I leave this war-ridden world, how can I ever face,
All the things I've done to them, and go on to another place?

How could I ever demean my wife, as I argued over her food,
While she worried because of my actions, I haven't the strength
  to brood.

And Adam, will he know my love? My love for him is strong;
I wasted days with the boy, who will not be a boy for long.

Levi; what of him? The child that was smart in ways,
I did not bother with him very much, but I will miss many of his days.

And my mother, how can she live, with me being the last of my
  brothers.
Now she must believe the fact, that sometimes children go before
  mothers.

Now I take my words from Earth, my energy gone without a trace
As my child screams in the background, and I slip to another place.
—*Rebecca Husband*

The Twenty-first Century

Read quickly by mechanical eyes,
All true life stands dead, computerized.
No sighs, no syncope stops permitted.
No whens, wheres, whences - no whiles or whys.

Given code and place - space - date, season,
Machines don't ponder, wander, wonder.
Only facts, figures, name and number
Enter and save - no rhyme or reason.

Devoid of fear, laugh, and affection,
The human race stands mute, quantified.
All dreams, all pride and soul deleted,
The world whirls wan - a false reflection.
—*Catherine Madeo*

True Athlete

The gun fired
All twenty five were off
They are the strongest and bravest
They had more courage than I
They are the true athletes
Men, Women, and Children in wheelchairs racing
Not racing each other
But racing themselves
They all were winners
Each day they fight
Fighting to keep their sanity
For some it was pure competition
For others it was a test
To see if they could beat the odds
In finishing the Boston Marathon
In a wheelchair
—*Glen Medford*

Gateways Of Yesterday, Today and Tomorrow

The gateways of yesterday,
allow us to look at the past,
to learn from our mistakes,
and build a future that will last.

The gateways of today
let us stop and look around,
to see where we are,
and what pathways can be found.

The gateways of tomorrow
let us journey to far off lands,
we know we can accomplish anything,
with an education in our hand.
—*Kathy DeWeese*

Concealed Evil

Walking steadily among the thin blades of grass
Allowing the crackling sky and swift sea to wonder,
Roaring whispers of the sword quickly pass
Realizing all evil is still stuck in thy center,
In the piercing eyes of yet this day
Oh, the pointed madness drips of blood near,
Raging out of control webbing another mass of betray.

Only our edged steps cuts us,
From our own buried carcasses.

Abolishment-we must stand guard;
Going from birth to death, only to leave
Evil that has razored us in—cold and hard.
—*Katrina Marie Gali*

What I Hold

Thinking in the corner of my mind -
Alone, with all my friends, pondering the day when there will be no more, the final silent end -
yelling at the stupidity of life,
quietly screaming and wailing. Smelling the bitter sweet redolence of a dream I had once had of happiness.
Time of times, to dream of the catastrophe of the beginning of the end. To end the start of what had once been life.
To hold within my hand, fragile and small, futile, pitifully, uselessly
Meaningful and powerful, sweepingly awe-striking and mysterious. A paradox of all forms of extremes.
Too frightening to confuse over. An arrant hope of comprehension has faded to empty horror.
Horror of not knowing but understanding all too well the terror and joy of what I
hold in my
hand.
—*Alex Barrett*

This Side Up

We tend to lean to the left or right,
Although it ends up to be tight.
Where is the middle of this round?
It is nowhere to be found.
What a conflict we wait to see,
Which way we will turn is like a tree.
The branches go from here to there,
Not up and down with straight lines fair.
Seems all we have to do is just think great,
Just say, "This Side Up and Stand Up Straight."
—*Virginia Cornelius*

Temptation

There lay four cookies on the top
Although quite still, they seemed to hop.
I heard them whispering to each other
And looking 'round enticing, rather.
They smiled at me invitingly,
And giggled, wiggled, silently.
And though I walked right by them thrice
My mouth was watering — only twice.
The next time I distinctly heard
One saying: "Hey, there goes that nerd!"
And then, out from the cream with glee
The same one taunted: "Coo— Coo-kieeee!"
That was enough!
I ate him up!
That's why there 're only three.
—*Wilfried Lippmann*

Colors

Children are like crayons
always mixing themselves
forming a rainbow... only crayons share
They match the black with the white
the brown with a technicolor,
not discriminating colors
They make up their own coloration
and they use them with no confrontation
It takes a child to mix and match colors,
but it is the grownups... that separate one from another.
—*Kimi Adamson*

"Blue Of You"

It seems everything I think of and do,
always seems to make you feel so blue.
No matter what I do or say,
it just turns out that way.
If only to let you know, that I always
will love you so. I will be your husband true,
even though you can also, make me feel so blue.
What I am really trying to say,
is I love you each and every day.
So on the days you might say,
"I'm blue of you", just remember that I'll always be true,
with the love that I give to you.
—*Charles W. Acklen*

"Life At Eighty-Nine"

When I was young, I had a wonderful life,
Always whittling with my Barlow knife.
Making butter paddles and rolling pins,
Also meal and flour bins.

Now at age 89, planning to move is quite a chore,
Getting rid of some of my magic to make room for more.

School pictures and Christmas cards, love letters by the score,
I look at them just lying there on the floor.
With these precious memories, I'll never be poor
So I'll put them all back, the same as before

If I throw away, I just know I'll cry
So I'll just keep them all 'til the day I die!
—*Vera McDonald Blake*

Great Giant

That once you stood in the spotlight adored by all
American pixie you were hailed
You had nerves of steel never to cry
But when the chips were stacked up high
And the rou really mattered
You cracked into a million tiny pieces
Shocked you were and stunned was he
That the great giant took a great fall
Now this time there was no second chance
I bet you cried, for I know I did
That day I learned fate is sometimes cruel
And that great giants can take great falls
—*Kelly Moore*

Noble Lady

She's raped and ravaged every endless day,
And has been since her innocence was lost.
Her selfish lover vowed to have his way,
And reach his goal, no matter what the cost.
With tender love she would have met his need,
And withheld naught that reason might implore,
But by his nature he succumbed to greed.
Insatiable, his lust still grasps for more.
The lady's modest blush still comes with spring,
For painful years cannot her beauty hide.
With tender chords of hope her voice does ring.
And pleads for peace, for virtue, and for pride.
How nobly Our fair Mistress bears her death;
How vulgar Man's offense to Mother Earth!
—*James W. Sutphin*

My Grand-Daughter Brandy

Brandy is only seven,
An Angel sent from heaven,
Full of love and strength,
courage, joy and confident.
Always giving, not demanding
My grand-daughter Brandy.

Born with Spina-Bifida,
She never makes anything difficult
She dances and she sings
She does most anything.
Oh! did I mention to you?
She plays the piano too.

Brandy is very, very smart.
If you see her, she will capture your heart.
Her handicap, does not get her down,
You should see how she gets around
A lesson to others she can give
And teach them how to live.
She is as brave, as brave can be
My grand-daughter Brandy.

—*Vivian J. English*

Exile

Standing on the edge of time I looked out on the night of life
and all that I saw was dark; a glimpse within revealed the same
identity was woven through the whole of what was seen and what
was not, behind the show of things, lurking, the slender thread
and shears; when out of the void a voice spoke: "Your world is
gone. Move on, exile, move on!"

Unmoved, unborn, still I stood, when a hand invisible wrote on
the nothing I saw, something that I could read, a shooting
star; then the light was gone and the dark returned; out of the
darkness, and into the darkness, from whence or where I knew
not, but I saw that it was beautiful; and a voice spoke: "You
are alone. Move on, exile, move on!"

Alone on the edge of time I stood, lost in rising tides of
thought, when out of the void a voice spoke: "Drive on, exile,
drive on! The trials of life are the tools of light, and the
void and the dark the molten ore, and driving forth you must
draw from the deep unknown the forms of time with timeless
atonement, to still the voice now know. Move on, exile, move
on!"

—*James Layton*

Deadline

With the date X'd off on the calendar,
and a pen in hand and fire in brain,
she puts off until the very last minute
the very thing that labels her a procrastinator.

Then to the typewriter, a new machine,
whose alternately dull and sharp sounds
begin to take over as the other sounds of children
playing and motorcycles rumbling fade into the dusk.

Over the stilled hush of the dusty night street
the sound continues, when, close to two a.m.
she turns off the machine, takes a swig of Pepto Bismol,
and turns out the light before turning in.

—*Ann Tillmann*

Death Of A Heart

To thine own self be true yet a lie keeps deep in the mind,
and a superficial threat seeks out reason you cannot find,
Love for another can always end in a senseless way,
and scare you into another frightful day,
Night falls and your fears come out,
and when it's over you see you always knew what it was about,
Remembering, living the past breaks away a tear,
and causes your courage to subside into the future your
    darkest fear,
I remember you through this struggle to be champion in this war,
Your smile like a thunderstorm a rage for the right of wanting
    more,
In this voice of fear at a place of undiscovered hopes and
a soul that strives on pain,
with my hopeless conscious to be safe away from your invisible
tears that lock around me like a constricting chain,
Together never were we yet we still do not remain apart,
A life a world that is born again and still left with the death of a
    heart.

—*Amber F. Brown*

"Autumn"

As the season of summer has left us
And all seems so forlorn,
Just think of all the beauty
That awaits us as new season is born.

We can climb the highest mountain peaks
With the shiny stars above.
All this is given to us
By one who truly loves.

How many Angels did it take?
Did it take a week or a day?
I would like to know how much paint it took
For the Beauty of God's Bouquet.

We travel along the highways
And see the birds and squirrels in brown,
Playing in the golden leaves
As they fall upon the ground.

Our hearts should be filled with gladness
As we say goodbye to the day,
And when we close our eyes in slumber
We still can see the beauty of God's Bouquet.

—*Shawn Swindlehurts*

Untitled

My Mom was a true mother
and always a friend.
We spent many hours talking
and walking hand in hand.
She loved all her children, seven are alive.
One baby went to heaven,
high prayers in the sky.
Mom had six children
through the second World War.
The bombs were falling and we were small.
She was all alone with six little kids.
Only God saw her weeping
as he watched in her sleep.
Soon the war was over
and Spring came to our land.
My father and brother came home again.
It was Palm Sunday
and Eastern they returned.
We all went to church
and sang God's praises again and again.

—*Theresa Meyer Herzig*

The 11:23 P.M. Flight To Nowhere

The city lies below the evening sky
and awake in our room I lie,
listening to the city's unconscious seething.
Now the feeling has come once more;
I rise from our bed, leave your quiet breathing,
softly unlock and lock the door,
and step into the street's orange glow.

My thoughts lead me to the place I know,
down to where the airplanes flee,
to stand with the others at the window,
who watch the airplanes at 11:23.

So if you wake up and no one's there,
look for me on the 11:23 p.m. flight to nowhere.
—*Adrian Beebee*

Stranger In Her Own Land?

Water
   and blood
     govern this, our unseen land;
      We, the claimless, perhaps blameless ones
        who shudder and squeeze our eyes shut
          for a vain flicker
            of memory.

Centuries ago
   they came by water;
     Our parents and grandparents fled over it,
       leaving only trails of water
         beneath a sky of blood.

An ocean ran through our fingers before we even saw it
   but still we clench our fists tightly,
     nails cutting into palms.
    —*Eve Nilenders*

A Captive's Lament

   Death - I hate you!

Without permission you changed my life.

You cheated me of what was hoped for the future.

You brought ineffable sadness over what was
and can no longer be. You make me angry at life.
I am disoriented, frightened, confused.

You push me to envy those who have not lost,
who live unscathed by death.

You make me depressed at the emptiness and
loneliness in my life.

You haunt me in the watches of the night and in the
solitary recess of my mind. I feel grief in my blood.

You let him slip silently out of my life without
us saying "Good-bye".

A vicious thief, you expect me to raise a son
without a father.

Death - I despise the freedom that came crashing down on me.
My world is in shambles.

Ahead is nothing but the empty unknown.
You defy all logical explanations.

I am your victim. Death - you are my captor.
   —*Debbie Stewart*

An Eternal Eye

Oh that I had an eternal eye
and could see why my loved ones die;
Then I would never wonder why
nor would ever have to cry.

Then I would know both beginning and end
and could always distinguish foe from friend;
I would always know what's around the next bend
and my path it would always transcend.

But then I remember - I know such a One
He knows everything but still lost His Son;
Rather than seeing perhaps I should run;
to hold tight to the promise of knowing His Son.

He offers us life and an eternal home
and promises a family reunion to come;
His eternal eye sees those who may roam
and lovingly brings them to His dear home.

So I trust in the One with an eternal eye
and know I will see my loved ones that die;
I still may question and wonder why
but I know that someday to His presence I'll fly!
   —*Bill Bradley*

Moon

When stars open comforting arms
And darkness consoles
When trees sway and the only
Sounds are of I and my old,
Weathered companion - wind
When the only shadows reflect
A lonely girl and her tears
I'm only good enough for the moon -

When clouds seem to flutter and fly
And friendly opossum finds his way to
Warm black haven
When creatures of night venture
Forth to pursue rituals in silence
I'm only good enough for the moon -

When I sit breathing, silent and softly cry
For hope, wishing for patient eyes
Upon me
When I sit alone I often wonder
Why, wind, why must it always be that
I'm only good enough for the moon -
   —*Vanessa Villarreal*

Inspiration

Narrow and steep the pathway we must tread,
and even then the crown may be of thorn,
which all the years thereafter must be borne,
until silence number us among the dead:
Hard must we toil to win this bitter bread,
and through the clear flash of the radiant morn,
often see the clouds, with edges tempest-torn,
rise in dense gloom, by disappointment led.

Yet is not all this strife a better gift,
than aimless wanderings through sunlit days?
Does not each upward struggle serve to lift
the soul to where God's clearer radiance plays,
until through some stern and rock-embattled rift,
we reach at last life's firm and level ways?
   —*Vernon D. Thompson*

All Is Not Lost

Everyone now knows all the truth
And fancies the people have earnestly sought.
The words have been spoken,
And the deeds bestowed——
And always remember-hoarded deeds
Are sadly obsolete.
And for better or worst:
All is not lost.
The bankrupted shoemaker
Lives today as he did yesterday -
His song is forever,
And forever with him.
Do not belittle your truths and fancies
They are power still:
For all is not lost.

—*Gil Cavallo*

(The Sun's Warmth)

We stood like young trees on a mountain
And felt the sun's warmth upon us
We heard the cry of the lonely wind
And we grew strong in it's strength

But unlike the trees or lonely wind
We had to go our own separate ways
When God called you away so quickly
Leaving me to walk this world all alone

As I look back on those wonderful days
I can only hold fond memories in my heart
Knowing these memories will make me strong
To face all of my tomorrows with out you

I won't see you again this side of heaven
You will always hold a spot in my life
All of our yester days are gone forever
And we can't control any of our tomorrows

But I wish you peace and thank God for you
And look to that great day in the future
When we will stand once more on a mountain
And feel the sun's warmth upon us again.

—*Rueben R. Lesser*

Call Me

When you feel you're all alone
And friends have left your side
You start to think your life's been blown
And washed out with the tide
Now you're reached the end of your Rope
And you want to end it all
It's getting to much for you to handle
As you prepare to take the fall
Well life's not all that bad
This I know for sure
Why go through life feeling sorry and mad
Because you never found a cure
So when you're feeling down and troubled
And you know not what to do
When you hurt so bad cause the pain has doubled
Just give me a call and I'll help you make it through.

—*Elzadia Lum*

Paths

Though I walk the sandy beaches on warm, calm evenings,
and gaze in wonder at the setting sun as the ocean tides
leap at my feet, I will feel your presence—
perhaps in the warm breeze that gently touches my cheek,
as a dewdrop lightly caresses a rose petal.
Though I may not see your footprint behind me in the sand.

And though I climb the highest peak and loftily look
up in admiration on the heavens, I will not feel so high
that I can't distinguish your nearness nor feel it
strengthening me.
Though I may not see your footprint behind me in the earth.

When the rain falls down, stinging my face and thunder roars
upon my ears, I won't forget that you are near
or fail to notice that you were there.

Whenever I stumble and fall and perhaps feel like giving up,
I will remember that you came this way too,
and tried to guide me.

You made me unfettered and happy at first, you see. But when
you said goodbye and left this world, my heart was made so
heavy from the burden you carried, that I can never be free.

—*P. M. Reed*

The Late Survivor

I am a true survivor
and have been for many decades now.
I'm not related to the humankind
and I do thank God for that.
I stand outside in a shaded area holding
my treasure.
I am a brave survivor.
I have fought all four seasons and have
had victory over them all.
What irritates me the most is the feathered ones.
They grip me tight with their claws.
If I had fingers for pulling a trigger,
I would shoot them dead.
But if I had a voice, I would kindly ask them
to loosen their grip.
If I had legs instead of being rooted, I would run swiftly
away. But I stand erect against the wind like a barrier.
My end draws near, approaching me now is my
greatest fear. The Lumberjack!

—*Shonte McDaniel*

A Mother's Day Message

Mother! Today is your special day,
and here I come to bring your pay
for all your sacrifices and pains
from the day I was born till today.

Mother! Allow me to venerate your name.
This name so full of love and tenderness
which cures instantly all pain and sickness
and fill the heart with joy and happiness.

Mother! Nothing is worth your salary.
And since today is your day of glory,
how could I ever be so ungrateful

To let it vanish away without ceremony.
And for me not to feel too shameful
please, take my bouquet of roses just picked for you.

—*Jean Rene Beaujuin*

Morning

When mornings dawning,
and I awaken yawning,
I hear the melody of natures' sing,
and all the things that today will bring,
I see the chirping birds on the tree,
The rabbits playing both he and she,
This in the morning is what I always see.
—*Erin Moore*

Michael

Well, there's someone new,
And, I didn't have a clue, the first night we met,
So, far, he's not like all the others yet,
He told his whole life story the first night,
And, he put up quite a fight, he's quite a guy,
I can say that with a sigh, he treats me so good,
He would get me anything if he could,
There aren't too many guys like that,
None worth batting your eyes at,
But, he's not like them at all, he thinks I'm such a doll,
I still don't know where he gets it,
I think the love bug finally bit, he is so great,
Prom was our first official date, I had so much fun,
I wanted it to go on when it was all done,
I'd hope he had as much fun as I did,
if he didn't he sure kept it hid,
Well, I guess that's all I have to say,
Except, I'll have this one for a
Long time if I get my way!
—*Amy Newboles*

Why

The majestic redwood eternally sought the sky -
  And I thought "Why?"
The earth was bathed in golden light before the
  impending night - and I thought 'Why?'
The birds were singing a crescendo, casting shadows
  as they flew by - and I thought 'Why?'
The new born infant whimpered - cried as it rubbed
  unseeing eyes - and I thought 'Why?'
The Soldiers fought - killed - maimed mothers, fathers
  and daughters - sons, and I thought 'Why?'
The tornado roared and spat destroying everything
  in its path - and I thought - 'Why?'
The pestilence, the pain, the famine and the sweep
  of deaths reign - and I thought 'Why?'

Today I went to a holy place worshiped by the
  human race
I saw the blind man raise his eyes
  The child's crutches cast aside
The tears ran down my face, my cheeks
  and now I know Why!
—*Edward A. Pascucci*

Over

What we had doesn't come so easy
And it's sad that we took it for granted,
The love I have for you is still in my heart,
Where it will always be planted,
You were special to me in every way
And I still think about you each day
I know you're sorry for what you did,
But it's something that will never be forgiven
All I can do now is hope to be free,
Free from my feelings-free from me.
—*Rachael Hayes*

I Wonder

How do birds fly so high in the sky?
  And if birds can fly, then why can't I?
  I wonder.

What makes the stars shine so bright?
  And where do they go at the end of the night?
  I wonder.

How do things grow, like the trees and the roses?
  And how do fish swim without holding their noses?
  I wonder.

How do cows make milk and chickens lay eggs?
  And why do giraffes have such long skinny legs?
  I wonder.

I'll know all these things when I grow up, I hear.
  I'll know everything when I turn five next year!
How long is a year?

  I wonder.
—*Josephine Haffner*

The Rural School

I'm a rural school and I am lonesome today progress has come and I'll fall by the way. My yard is weedy and the fence in distress cattle graze here and leave it a mess. My windows are broken, my siding has slipped shingless are tattered, and front steps are tipped my bell has quit tolling, the chimney has cracked my foundation has crumbled, money was all my carpenter lacked, But I still can remember a good looking teach and some of the kids she just couldn't reach school plays were a hassle, I laughed till I cried much stumbling and bumbling, but they really tried. No more laughter at recess, no more coats in the hall no more water to carry, no more spills in a fall eight grades for the teacher in one room that was small she settles fist fights and teasing, how could she live through it all? Now that all of my children have feathered and flown hope I have helped from big to unknown I really don't think I'm expecting too much so go get'em kids, you farmers, you lawyers, you doctors and such. Ouch! A bulldozer just hit me, there's a hole in my wall another whack like that and I surely will fall I see the monster coming for its fatal attack now a shudder runs through me and I'll never be back.
—*Lee Welch*

Proud To Call You Son

I am proud to call you my son -
And Impressed with all you've done.
  That's why I had to say -
  On this your special day,
That I'm so proud of you -
In all the things I've seen you do.
  To watch you grow -
  Has amazed me so.
Friends said, "You had it made,"
But it was at the price of youth you paid -
(And the sacrifices you made.)
  I know it wasn't easy,
  Know one knows that better than me.
To know how proud I am -
Is to view you as a man.
  I want to, "Thank you" for the feeling of family
  And the wonderful feeling of continuity -
  For this is the way it was meant to be.
    There's no doubt it's love I'm talking about.
You've grown-up just fine - so this pleasure is all mine.
—*Barbara Lewallen*

The Anniversary Gift

They were wedded in the summer over 25 years ago,
And in the aftermath of the honeymoon glow,
He stopped on the way home from their wedding trip,
And returned from the farmer's stand, in his grip,
Dozens of radiantly colored gladioli blooms,
So that she could fill her first apartment rooms,
Dazed, she asked if he was suddenly overcome by the heat,
He replied, "I'm glad I married you, my sweet,"
And on their anniversary thereafter, each and every year,
He filled her arms with gladness and she shed a tear,
As he whispered that refrain, oh so familiar and dear,
That he had repeated from the very first in her ear.
—*Dolly M. Boulton*

"Daddio"

Sometimes I get to thinking about you, Dad,
And it seems like a lifetime ago
When I was your precious "Little Sugarlump,"
And you were my "Daddio."

You were already old when I was born,
But you loved me with the love of a young prince,
And you gave your heart so completely to me
In a way no man ever has since.

But you put me on a lofty pedestal,
A place where no one ever should be,
And you kept me there - your "perfect little girl,"
And never knew what it was doing to me.

I often wonder if you'd lived 'til I was grown,
Do you think that we could just have been friends,
Or would you have kept me up on that pedestal
Until the very end?

Well, I'd like to say in spite of all that,
I will always love you so,
And no matter where I am, or how old I may grow,
You'll always be my "Daddio."
—*Tess Wells*

The Christening

They christened her Lisbeth Lynn
And it was Easter Day.
All the bells caroled merrily,
"New Life," they seemed to say.

The fairies brought their christening gifts
To this blithe child of mine,
Their gifts of love and wit and song
In one small lass combine.

Her eyes reflect the cobalt seas,
Spun golden thread her hair,
Her singing is a silver bird
Released into the air.

On dancing feet she wends her way
This child, this charming sprite,
A joyous, fairy creature she,
Creates for me delight.
—*Louise T. Cullen*

Release

I grabbed the fish with my hand
and it was slippery
It wriggled against my palm
as I dug my fingers in
but my nails broke
and I dropped the fish
as the blood slid down my arm
It writhed in the hot summer's sand
as I fell on my knees
to scoop it up off the ground
I pressed it to my chest
and with a pull the steel was free
I held the fish in my hands, it was lying still
It was cold against my skin and
it shivered
I threw
the fish to the lake
It leapt away from me on the dock
Its scales sparkled in the water
—*Stacie Lents*

What Is A Father?

A father is a man who cleans up all the messy things babies do,
And love them and care for them without much ado.
A father is a man who accepts his child no matter pretty or handsome.
And loves them with all of his heart and then some.
A father is a man who goes to dance recitals and tee-ball games,
And knows all his child's friends by their first names.
A father is a man who earns all the money,
And buys lots of things for his little honey.
A father is a man who teaches you how to dive,
And when you turn sixteen he teaches you how to drive.
A father is a man that cries when you start to date,
And tells you not to stay out too late.
A father is a man who gives you away,
And can't wait for Grandfather's Day.
A father is a man who loves you 'till the day he dies,
And his memory will touch many lives.
A father is a man who gave you life,
And your mommy is his wife.
—*Victoria Townley*

The Truth

I met you in my darkest hour,
   and loved you at first sight.
I feared the day when you would leave me,
   (because you thought it was right).

You said you never wanted my love;
   You didn't need me to be concerned.
I cried in vain, and wondered
   — What lesson have I learned?

My tears have ceased,
   ...the memories live on;
   The vision of tomorrow has come gone.
But with the tears that cleansed my soul,
   The search for truth became my goal.

And as I wandered in despair,
   Wondering who on earth could care,
I met a friend who took my hand.
   He said, "my child, I understand."

"Love conquers all fear" is the truth he
   taught, and

     ...True love is never lost.
—*Sally Heyns*

"Redeemed"

When I die as I surely must
And my earthly body returns to dust
May there be no tears shed for me
As my soul shall be eternally free

I will leave no worldly acclaim
I will leave no fortune or fame
I will leave no anger or hate
Because I will be heading for those pearly gates

When those pearly gates open wide for me
And the face of my Dear Lord I see
I will find happiness beyond compare
Knowing our Lord really does care

I will ask King David while He was on His throne
Why didn't He leave Bathsheba alone
When Nathaw the Prophet said "Thou Art The Man"
Now get out of that one David if you can

But David prayed and David cried
And a merciful God set David sin aside
And that same God will listen today
If you repent and start to pray.

—*Chester Coyle*

There Is A God

In the dead of night I face Death;
And my heart stops — cold with fear.

O God, my God! I cry in panic.
Save me, a coward; give me strength.

Then o'er my spirit a calm descends,
My wild trembling ceases — and I know peace.

There is a God out there, somewhere.
I know, He's come to me in the dead of night.

—*Viola M. Rambo*

Pilgrimage

We vow to do our thing
And never reach the region of responsibility;
The cargo that we bring
Seems enough for the foreign legion in equipage for the journey
But round and round we go
In the circles of the sand that comprise our desert land,
And while the hot winds blow
We fail to understand we're upon a course unplanned.
Mirages all around
But plague us with their mystery of trickery and fate;
A strange and haunting sound
Defies all history in this unseemly state.
And, yet, we dare the deeds
(Regardless of their nature, their imposing nomenclature)
And carry out the creeds
In fulfillment of our needs—and we hope they will endure.

—*Wayne Meredith Miller*

Shadows

Although the road to the past is but a footstep away.
And it's beckoning cry toward its darkness we sway.
The now and the futures path tho seems unsure,
Is dawned with sweeter smells.
No glad tidings exchanged when those dark shadows we chase.
In circles we spin. At our backs they embrace.
Step lightly my friend, for light eats the dark.
Move on to a place where love dwells.

—*Pat Hill*

Darkness

The day has ended,
and night is coming.
Quickly, this blackened
sheet covers the sky.
Devouring everything in sight.
The warmth of the sun is gone.
The safety you once felt,
vanishes into the darkness.
With darkness,
comes the evil of the world.
Death lurks in the air,
scanning it's victim closely.
Choosing the one to take with him.
Darkness comes in many forms.
He is what makes the floors creek when you walk.
He may be the evil behind you,
daring you to turn and look!
Or he may be the dead silence of the night,
pushing you to the edge.
Driving you insane!

—*Todd Schmidt*

The Master And I

He had black eyes
   and no reflection

He told me no lies
   and gave me direction

I'll never go to heaven
   and I'll never go to hell

He showed me the signs, all seven
   Those I will never tell

I come out into the night
   To drink the blood so red

At first I put up a fight
   now I'll never be dead

My mortal past has yet to fade
   and now I live my days as a masquerade

—*Jasmine Fierro*

She Sips Hot Tea

Even though it burns her tongue

Chinese food and duck sauce, a headache,
And of course, getting crushed by the church
Wilting flowers that her boyfriend gave her
You're in my arms—whispering—a loud grand canyon like echo
I'm dangerous

Grass out back needs to be cut
Dish washer never been used
Complaints about dishes not being done
Plans to work out and get in shape

You—my unplanted flowers that lie on the table
   my unread newspaper with the comics on front

Your voice—sometimes an anchor hitting the bottom
   the spear jabbing me in the ribs
   the electric blanket that warms me
   the electric blanket that shocks me

A phone book and the nonringing phone
A headache, and of course,
Getting crushed by the church

—*Shawn Anthony Lewis*

"Turtle Tears"

The moon shines bright, on the water at night!
and out of the waves, in the dark out of sight!
Crawls the turtle to lay eggs in a deep hole -
With all the strength from her very soul -
She crawls over sandbar and shoal!
She labors long and hand in the sand -
Her flippers constantly moving, without a hand!
She works hard and long to dig for her eggs -
A safe haven with her legs -
She then labors to lay in her nest -
All of her baby's eggs to rest -
She covers the hole, when the last one is in
With her flippers in back, she pushes and in
With tears in her eyes she crawls off again -
To sea she returns, her work is at end!
Next year she might be found, If she makes
it past danger around!
She lives in the ocean, where life abounds!
Next year with hope, she will be back again!
To crawl out of the sea, and do it again!
—*Margaret Suzanne Lauver*

Winding Trail To Home

Green meadows are gone from the valley
And perfume of the rose brings tears,
As I travel back in memories
Thru long lonely years.
Days of youth have faded
My steps have slower grown,
As I view the browning meadow
Down the winding trail of home.
Gone are the sweet days of yesterday
Loved ones left for their heavenly home.

Still I cling to the golden memories
As I walk the trail to home.
Carefree years flash before me
As a child once again I see,
The meadow so green in the springtime
Where I dreamed 'neath the spreading tree.

Like a story each chapter must end
As each page today I review
To find sunshine and sorrow
In this passing world I knew.
—*Virginia West*

Chuck-It-Out

  I looked around our home today
  and saw articles to "put away."
  That much less each day to dust.
When out of sight, I'll soon adjust.

Why are these "things" so dear to me?
  Without them I would better be.
  Treasure or trash? I can't decide.
  Some I've had since a young bride.

Some of these items might be just junk.
Why put them away in the treasure trunk?
  Maybe a garage sale would be better.
  Oh my goodness, but not this letter!

Yes, yes, chuck them out. Put them away.
  I am really cleaning house today.
  Give them away! Rid them out now.
  I pray the Lord will show me how.
—*Eleanor Shaner*

It had To Be The Hat

Well she walked up and smiled
And put her money down right
She looked into my eyes and I knew
Everything would be alright

It was a feeling that ran through my mind
A kind of feeling that left my eyes blind
I was walking home and she passed right by
It was something I sought in those bright green eyes

Because she walks with a style that's all her own
She speaks of words that seldom have come to know
She's out there waiting for something in the sky. The same
thing I saw last night. The thing I couldn't describe .

Then it's back to the streets where walking gets you by
Lying by the shadows under a darkened sky
Breathing the air from the bird filled trees
Opening your mind and sailing in the breeze

It had to be the hat, the roses all in bloom
The long flowing hair, the vibes all in tune

I don't know where she's going. I don't know where she was
I know I witnessed beauty. All I've ever dreamed of
—*Chris Burke*

Lust's Last Touch

Disturb me not, while in idle thought
And refrain from presenting thy gentle touch
For your hands, like those of a thief, have robbed me many
Times and many ways, of all my humilities.

Tell me not long, sad tales
But whisper them seductively, to willing ears
To those whose hearts are cold and silent
Like faceless art hanging on barren walls.

Spare me your aristocracies and your petty platitudes
And run for the flesh that calls out to you hungrily
Make sweet sweat upon your smooth silk sheets
For no man is a stranger with invitation in hand.

Will you not wear again, your vows around your waist?
And make space between you, for he grows tight against the seam
Wait and thee will hear, all too familiar sounds
But passed from different lips.

So, past the night, into the shyness of dawn's first glimpse
I'll abandon this prison, this dungeon of deceit
For the instrument of my love, plays behind no other chair
And the symphony it sings, is heard only by one.
—*Ronald R. Bishop*

Coldest Of Night

I try not to touch
And yet they touch
Their icy fingers caress my trembling hands
I pull away yet the grasp is firm
They are so many.
And I am but one unto myself
I scream and yet there is no sound
Only the cries of yesterday and today.
Violence without pain, Love without passion
I watch as they are tormented
  Men, Woman, Children it makes no difference
They are the victims, the chosen
I am but condemned to feel their anguish
  in the coldest of night
—*Michael Hamilton*

Harriet

She died early this morning.

Her heart was weak
And she was very old.
Did you know her birthday is next week?

During breakfast
Someone forgot to shut the curtains.
Everyone saw the long black car come for her.

They took a long black bag out of the car
And put her in it.
I wonder how may people have been in that bag before.

Into the car they shoved the bag
And slammed the doors.
Then she was gone.

All that is left is a small wet spot
In the middle of the bed
And a lot of old old memories.

She has a name you know.

—*Tami Lloyd*

Shine

Shining happy faces, bouncing
and shifting in the crisp sun
small fragile figures, hopeful
and uplifting in their spirited run

Fresh sand they mould with
soft tiny hands
Fresh hopes they lose with
sifting golden sands

Their complexions of hopefulness
Their boundless energy
Their heir of unexpectedness
And unrelentless sympathy

Toys they contemplate with great thought
Testing their bounds, what they've found,
grasping the sound, the fertile ground,
Pleasure and happiness within them abounds

Shining faces so content
Brings a sullen tear to my eye
Young minds so innocent
With joyful tears I cry

—*Tom Wilson*

Scared

People is the street have nothing to eat.
And sometimes they get beat.
For what little money they do have.
They have no clothes.
They're full of holes.
They sleep with the moles.
They have nobody to care for them like a family should.
They are afraid of their own shadow.
And most have a dog to follow.
Some don't have shoes.
They have no where to go hear the news.
Some feed squirrels in the park.
Some push a cart.
Some sit and beg for money.
Some wander the streets so lonely.
They rarely find a nice place to stay.
They eat what we throw away
Many of them talk to the trees.
Some just sit and feel the breeze.
They're just scared because nobody cared.

—*Heidi McCalla*

Nature's Gift

Each spring begins with flowers and birds
And sounds of laughter from children's hearts
What joy is this that enfolds within
Why don't we hear it in winter's wind

Pussywillows, long and soft
Seem to add to the season's warmth
The little ones upon their nest
Leap up and down and try their best

Oh spring within us you bring out anew
What secret of life we all hold so true
The sorrows of winter melt with the snow
And gone are the days of unending moods

Who could not join in the glory of spring
Who could resist the urge to love
The skies are blue, the waters clear
Three months of happiness throughout the year

—*Katherine Constantinou*

You

It is when I see the stars above,
And the moon is all aglow,
I stop thinking if it's you I love
For then, of course, I know.

When I think of all the things
You used to say and do,
You held me tight, and my heart sings,
In just remembering you!

It is not so much the charming way
You had about you, dear,
It is the dream that could come true some day
That makes me want you near.

Seems strange that once you loved me,
(A Thousand years ago)
But now you're ever far away
From the one who loves you so.

You said, "Good-bye," I can't pretend,
I have a broken heart to mend,
Though I know now I'm just your friend,
Dearest - is this the end?

—*Erasmia Veligrakis Cacciola*

I Am American!

Though the stars burn in the darkness of night
And the sun shines upon us with a guiding light.
Freedom burns through night and day
for all people it should be the same way
I moved from the city, to start a new life
To a small town just me and my wife.
I thought it would be different as I moved along
but prejudice voices sang the same song.
White black yellow or green
No matter where people are mean
Americans say give us a chance
Just try and take a stance
Politics, power, money and greed.
Nobody cares what people need.
Hunger, drought, starvation and sadness.
Is there no end to this madness.
We make a choice and some stand for what's right.
We fight for our freedom with no end in sight.
I've learned my lesson through all this pain.
Without the sadness there is no gain!

—*Kenneth J. O'Rourke*

The Leaf And The Wind

Come with me, he called to her, in a whisper softly spoken,
And though he wooed and sang to her the silence was not
  broken.
Her form was young and tender, supple, smooth, and green,
And to his gentle nudging she yielded willingly.
So entwined together the dance did begin,
The gentle violent rushing of the leaf and the wind.
Up they soared as one, swirling into space,
Swaying to his rhythm she lay in his embrace.
His sweet caresses thrilled her she fluttered with delight,
Tumbling, spinning, twirling, she leaped with all her might.
His touch was ever present, his breath so moist and warm,
He held her close, she clung to him like darkness to a storm.
Oh how woeful was the day the dance came to an end,
You can hear the tears of the rustling leaf
And the mournful howling wind.
—*Phyllis M. Fenn*

Living In Harmony

If there is but one sun
And we live under one sky
If there is but one world
Why couldn't we be but one people
If we were all created equal
When did one race become
Superior to another?

Our world is divided by struggle for power
All around us people are killing their own
Isn't time we stop and look
At the destruction of the human race
Must we always bade in blood
Before we can achieve peace and equality?

Isn't time we lived in a united America
One people, one country
Perhaps in time, one nation
Only then can we be free
To live in loving harmony
Let the nineties's be the decade
Of peace and equality!
—*Anne M. Baptista*

Thoughts

It is said that beauty is in the eye of the beholder;
And when I see you, what I behold in my eyes is beauty;
Beauty of mind, body and soul.

To have you is a thought, I have often contemplated;
But reality sets in and the thought always dissipates;
Gone until the next time I think of you.

Since the first time I saw you, I wanted to get to know you;
And finally I have had the pleasure to learn a little about
you; and what I have learned can't be found in books.

I have began to care about you in a special way;
Special because of the friendship we share;
A friendship that knows no time.

What I feel for you is something I cherish;
It is something that I can express;
But most of all it is from my heart.
—*Corey V. Green*

Hope

Hope ... what is hope...
  And why is it's fiver so bold...
How can it reach to the depths of my heart...
  Yet not in my hands may I hold...
I once thought love was the almighty power...
  A force that made mountains fall...
But alas it is hope and hope all alone...
  That stands by my side through it all.
—*Rickie A. Young*

An End To A Beginning

A part of your life has come and gone;
  Another beginning is about to start.
Leaving behind the friends and memories;
  But dearest and best stay close at heart.

The road ahead leads to many directions;
  All filled with choices both right or wrong.
Confusing or troubled, some enchanting at times;
  You have to decide where you most belong.

It's not read in a book or lead by another life;
  It's your own story to live and learn.
Mistakes and triumphs present to be seen;
  Both appearing on their own turn.

A chapter has ended for another to start;
  The words will be spoken and written in mind.
For the rest of your life and the memories held;
  Will forever be lived and always frozen in time.
—*Deborah Stuhr*

The Answers?

Walking on the beach with a kind look from above watching, anticipating, hoping we understand the spirit of love. Moving down the right path, can we find the truth? From wrong turns may stem jealousy and hate....Given this magnitude these monsters can control. Slowing down in the middle of the road, we realize the true meaning is in the sacrifice of giving. Mirrors of heaven reflect these thoughts. Restless and impatient, we wander along—only to find no meaning at all. Running frantically, we hide from the answers to these questions. Cry, fight, hurt and despair—will this lead us to the core of our inner depths? Resting where we hide, we must find the strength to press even further. A stranger quickly passes by, is this the one? A gentle hand extends from our friend. These sunlight rays are blinding—trying to guide us. This time, another stranger passes us by. Are we going to greet him with open arms? Exposure and vulnerability—is this another slap in the face? Trust, honesty, and forgiveness must unleash these restraints setting us free. Do you think society will realize these keys to a truer humanity?
—*Mary Margret Collier*

Forest Of Life

When you step in you're scared. Then you begin learning and appreciating the Forest.

During your adventure you will cry, laugh, and make mistakes.

In the Forest you will come upon many enemies, but one day you will find your true love and hope you've made the right decision.

Then one day you will come to the end of the Forest and you then will know you've survived the Forest of Life.
—*Shawn N. Smithson*

Just say "I Love You"

So many things can come along, that suddenly your loved ones are gone. Millions leave never being told they're loved or even get to hear "good-bye", that's enough to make a person cry. Don't take a risk like that, because it hurts, there's never anything worse. You'll never forget, the feel of such a terrible regret. Forever more there will be pain in your heart, you'll always suffer with the dread, knowing those words you should have said. So don't take a chance, tell them, for you may never get the chance again. Show them your love is real, tell them exactly how you feel. Just make sure you never fail to say, you love them day after day. Because if you don't, the day will come, the person whom has left, will be your loved one. Don't let it happen this heartbreaking way, you know all you have to do is just say; I love You, I really do!!! You'll feel better and certainly they will, just say it, feel the enjoyment and the heart lifting thrill.!!! Let them go with a happy thought on their mind, they'll recall when you told them those words, what a special time.!!!

—*Jennifer Petersen*

You

Tall, blonde, and blue
Are just a few descriptions of you,
A true love to my best friend,
A best of a best friend to I,
But when I think of your "jokes"
I begin to cry.
I guess I may be overreacting,
But it is just the way I am.
I will not change for you,
And I am not asking for you to.
But if you could just once talk to me in a friendly manner,
And really make our friendship matter,
I could really loosen up
And become your friend,
Instead of like a shy, little, closed-in pup.

—*Cynthia Webber*

Grandma

   The tears I've wept,
   are the ones I've kept,
   in my heart for you.

   The memories I see,
   are of you and me,
   and the good times
   that used to be.

   The future I saw,
never came true at all.

   You were taken away,
   before I could say
   how much I love you.

Everything seemed blurry to me,
til I understood the reason and could see,
 the impact you were to leave.

   You've shown me well,
   now only time will tell,
   how proud I can make you of me.

—*Shelley Anne Ross*

What Are You?

What are you?
Are you the tears of sorrow or that quiet explosion of love?
Are you the melody of rustling leaves on a summer's breeze - or
   the cold grey of winter's breath?
What are you?
Are you the gently ebbing tide - slender reeds nodding as you
   pass to the open sea - or the
Searing desert sand - endless, rolling formless shapes?
What are you?
Are you the wail of a new born or that tearing, rushing wind
   of death?
What are you?
What are you GOD?

—*Ernest A. Botti*

Blessed Delia

From the heavenly realms beyond The Great Abyss of Darkness
   arrived this mere child spirit from the past.
As silent as a secret she crept from the depths of my
   subconscious and fights like a veteran warrior upon the
   rugged and perilous battlefield of my brain.
Here stands Delia!
Delia, assigned by The Goddess to be my protectress and guide
   fends off dangerous assaults of mind clutter which have left
this cranial environment a blackened wasteland.
Her task is demanding for one so young and accustomed to a
   previous life in a bygone era, but Delia, as bright as
   sparks from the welder's torch, a tiny messenger smaller
   than a pulsating atom, yet as powerful as all Creation,
   stands her ground in the mortal fight.
Delia, tired, wounded, frightened to tears, constantly invokes
   The Goddess for strength and courage while praying for
   victory with every breath.
Still Delia fights on, never giving up an inch to the enemy nor
   turning her back for an instant upon uncertainty.
Blessed Delia!

—*George A. Hubbard*

Heart Broken

Seeing you two together,
   as a couple should be.
Knowing you're not the one,
   I thought would be right for me.
Having these feelings,
   that are so hard to hide.
I can see that now and forever,
   you will never be mine.
My heart begins to break,
   when I see you two together.
Every time I close my eyes,
   your smile is what I still see there.
I've tried to find others,
   and fix friends up too.
But every time I think of couples,
   I picture what it would be like if I were with you.
Trying to get across to you,
   the way that I feel.
I guess those signals from you,
   were never even real.

—*Stacy Allred*

Letters Of Sorrow

The last gentle kiss good bye
As a tear rolled from his eye
She drove off out of sight
On that cold winter night
It's been months since he last saw her
Every night is sleepless thinking of her
Will she return in June
When they first meet under the crescent moon
Not a day goes by
That he won't think of her and cry
He'll admit it wasn't perfect
Now that he's looking back on it
He gave all he had for her
Now he's wishing he'd gotten a little more from her
Reduced to dreaming, hoping, wishing for a better tomorrow
Sending out to her his letters of sorrow
     —*Bill Previte*

Fetching The Cows

Tall quack grass tears
as barefoot I spring through
to the next rock, cool and smooth.

The pasture yields
a bouquet of buttercups and hawkweed.
Blackbirds complain at my passing while
the unconcerned meadowlark continues his song.

Under the old pines a creek stumbles,
opens to a deep pool, stagnant and green.
A Holstein stands cool in the slime.
Others are scattered under
the limbs of tag alders, munching.
Tails twitch and muscles wrinkle at flies.

Slowly they lumber to the path
stringing out into a black and white parade,
marching steadily from the field.
Silently I follow, bare foot patting the dust.
The buttercups wilt.
I gently let them litter the lane.
     —*Laura A. Eastman*

Think About It

   Hands of time move so slow
as days go on from young to old
   You can't stop the hands of time
All you can do is listen for the chime
   Days of hot, days of cold
When the young get older and the old get bold
   People think that life's a joke
that is why the young and old smoke
   They don't think about life the way they should
As if they even could
   Some have fear for the future on
So they kill themselves to be gone
   Just think about how it would be
If the world didn't have you and me
   Listen when someone tells you they care
Because soon our world will be bare.
     —*Lisa Jeffers*

Stuck In The Rain

  Trying to find the words to say what I really mean isn't
as easy as it may seem.
  Who knows what'll happen or how long we'll be together
but no matter what happens, I won't forget you ever.
  It seems no matter how long you run from the pain it always
comes back and you're stuck in the rain.
  I hope no matter where you go we'll always have something
special because I don't know where I'd be if I thought you
didn't care for me.
  You were always so caring when you held me day or night and
you always did what felt right.
  But when I think about you leaving someday I wish I could
run away from all the feelings of hurt and pain I'll feel
when I get left stuck in the rain.
     —*Kena Juso*

The Misguided Mind

So innocent he moved with ease
As he strolled through school as if it was a breeze
His grades were poor, that he knew
But the hands of his peers covered it through and through
Sports was his game
Looking good on the gym floor was his fame

Crippled with illiteracy has haunted his life
But because he had sports, he knew no strife
Books were strangers, he could not read
For his peers had covered it with great speed
He has height and coordination with his mighty large hands
Could dribble a basketball through quick sand
Future was far away not a care did he bare
Until one day he realized his peers were not there

He could not think, for little did he know
His peers had vanished, refused to show
For his peers had vanished as quick as a blink
Here he is out there in the world, can not read, can not think
There is no rationalizing that he could find
For his peers had left him with a misguided mind
     —*Barbara Privott Jenkins*

Tribute To The Troops

Never before have the days seemed so long
As hundreds of thousands correct a wrong.
The best of men and women are in Saudi,
Aiding in fight to keep Kuwait free.

While troops are in a foreign land,
Vets and civilians gather - united they stand.
Everyone listens for a new report
As candles glow with our support.

Many troops are there - strong and bold.
There's pride in our soldiers - let them be told.
Our country is honored by all that they do.
People believe in the red, white, and blue.

We pray to protect our warriors from dying.
Americans keep Old Glory flying.
Ribbons of yellow are all around
Welcoming you back to our home ground.
     —*Nicolette R. Peters*

When the Lord Returns

When the Lord returns as He said He would, I hope to be ready
as I should; wondering, what will the weather be like - should
I pack winter clothes or something light?

And how much money shall I save to have enough funds to pay
the way; If it's going to be a very long trip maybe I'd better
pack more than one grip.

The Lord, always aware of the Book of Rules. Will surely
announce the time He will choose to come like a thief in the
night and take us Home when the time is right. I wonder what
present to get for Him. should I ask
forgiveness for all my sins? Surely I must fix us a bite to
eat, or is He preparing our Feast To Be!

Christ has already Planned Food for all to share this journey
with Him as He prepares to bring us Home where we belong
because of His grace, and not our wrongs.

But I still ponder where all my money will go that I've been
saving to run this show; maybe someone will use it to start a
new trend of sharing a love that has no end.

—*Anne Robinson*

"The Ledge"

Life means nothing to me anymore,
as I sit upon this ledge ten stories up.
My feet dangling over the ledge as I contemplate my life,
going through memories and reliving each moment, good and bad.
Mad at myself for things I had not done,
and regretting things I had.
Nobody knows how I feel, and nobody cares,
just me and the ledge, my only friend.
I've been on the ledge many times before,
the people below stare as if I am insane,
one of these days, I'll end it all,
plummet to the ground like a bird to young to fly.
Today may be that day.

—*Tony Maiscalco*

With Love, To Ann

Dark clouds cross my path today
As I walk in the shadow of my grief
And as my eyes fill with tears and
   my thoughts backward fly
I draw my strength to press ahead from
   the memory of another time

It was only yesterday that you were here with us
How could it be so suddenly that you were called away?
We must not question his bidding
But say "Thy will be done"
And give us courage to go on to welcome another day

To each of us a different memory is left
And each finds comfort in his own manner
And the joys we shared while you were here
Will be our guides to dry tomorrow's tears

The clouds will lift as time goes by
And shadows pushed back as the sunlight comes again
And though tears will always be here
We will smile and walk ahead

—*Mona Smith*

A Child's World

When I was a little girl, I used to watch and think;
 As Mama was in the kitchen, doing dishes at the sink.
 Oh, she'd sing so pretty, as she worked on foot all day;
Did she know that I was listening, as I passed by in play?
I dreamed someday I'd sing like her, as I went on my way.

 Then outside to my Daddy, planting flowers in the yard;
 On his knee I sat contented, no idea he worked so hard.
 So hard to raise his family, this handyman of many jobs.
 It all seemed so simple then, life in a child's world;
 I wanted to be like Mama and always Daddy's little girl.

Now three times ten I look around,
   Their grandchildren call me Mom.
   Yet time stands still somehow,
      As the years go on and on.

Today I smile at little eyes, while they pass by in play;
Wondering what they're thinking, as they go on their way.
 Hoping thirty years from now, they'll look back and say,
It all seemed so simple then, in a child's world of play.

—*Donna-Maria Schild*

The Abyss

I stand over her and weep
As she reaches out, my comfort to seek
The pain-filled eyes, the tortured cries,
The Abyss of Total Helplessness

I stand over her and weep
Not knowing what to speak
Fear, for us both, the predominate emotion
The room is filled with purposeful commotion
As gown-garbed figures work with devotion
The Abyss of Total Helplessness

I stand over her and weep
Praying, Dear God, our souls are yours to keep
Let us not know complete devastation this day
With a racing heart and brimming eyes, I Pray
The Abyss of Total Helplessness

I stand over her and weep
This lump in my throat preventing me to speak
With amazement and wonder at what she has done
I gaze into her eyes and know we are one
We look in awe, at the Beauty of our Son

Dear God, Your days are endless
Please help me find my way from this
Abyss of Total Helplessness

—*John Dickson*

Free

Walking freely
As some would say,
Could take away my worries
Right away.

I walk along the deep blue lake
With my hair blowing,
I'm afraid of nothing.

The birds are soaring through the sky
As if they hadn't a care in the world,
Some people wonder why
But I can understand.

They are free
Like you and me,
I'm afraid of nothing.

—*Jessica Mitchell*

A Night At The Beach

A peaceful hush comes over the land.
As the sea rolls in and out.
The sky is dark, but a little bright light
Shines down on the cold night sand.

The wind blows gently against my hair
As the sand blows in my face.
Beach grass whistles while the sea gulls sleep
Soundly, til the morning wakes.

Morning comes and the sky turns red,
And sounds return to the shore.
The hush is gone. It is quiet no more.
The morning is born; the night is dead.
—*Krystal Doyle*

Remember Dad

When I think of Dad
As the years rolled by.
When I couldn't fix things
He'd say- Give it a try.
And patience will win
Just begin again.
Now that I've grown up
And when things get rough
I'd think of Dad with all his patience, Love and trust.
Somehow things will work out-
If I just have patience-Love-and trust
On this fathers day
I'm sending this little prayer
May God Bless you and keep you in his care.
—*Ellen Tomanica*

Winter Is Near

The Golden sun sets against a pink sky
As we watch the ducks, south they fly.
The wind blows the trees left and right
And heavy rain clouds are in our sight.
All the animals go home to hide
But my friend and I stand side by side.
We listen for a lot of unusual things
We don't even here a robin sing.
The weather starts to get wet and cold
Outside we wait for the cool liquid gold.
Suddenly from out of the sky
Come drops of rain falling nearby.
All the green plants and colorful flowers
Are losing their brilliance from the cool fall
Showers.
We hear an animal scream
As it quenches its thirst from a nearby stream.
Once the animals return to their dens
All is peaceful once again.
—*Jessica Skrobot*

Remembering

As I lay down upon the ground;
And look up at the sky;
My mind leaps off to endless bounds;
And I begin to cry.

I think of all the things that's through;
And everything that's past;
And how I wish things were the same;
And all of it would last.

But now that everything is done;
And I look back and know;
That everything is lost and gone;
But how I loved him so.
—*Rebecca Parks*

"Universal Creator"

Beyond all humans' capability of understanding,
At least from a worldly individuals prospective.
So comprehendible and also loving, yet his purposes
And plans are so misinterpreted.
So human, and yet so divine.
You, who are so rich, yet your still so poor.
You, who are so powerful, yet your so weak.
You, who are so intelligent, yet your so illiterate.
Temporary love and pleasure, yes money can buy.
Although, a peace of mind, where will you find.
For all problems, he is the solution.
For all sickness, he is the cure.
For all pain, he is the joy.
Try him, and I guarantee you will like him.
Oh, you feel that your not good enough well
He has no pick and chooses.
Ask and you shall receive, that's if you are willing to
take heed.
Just always remember, things happen in time
For those who step in Jesus line.
—*Steven Dominque*

"In My World"

Just when I start not to think of her
At night a dream then occurs.
Why do I think of this girl I hardly know?
Cause when I think of her do my feelings start to flow.

Maybe these dreams I have are a sign.
That maybe one day she'll be mine.
But I don't know that's only in the dreams.
But it looks so good, so good it seems.

I've never felt for girls like this in the past.
I had wanted to be with her, to make it last.
I didn't get to know her well, but I knew her in a way.
That when I was with her, I wanted it to last all day.

Will I ever see her again? I'm not sure.
God I hope so, I really want her.
But if I never again see this girl
She'll always be in my mind, in my world.
—*Gary S. Wilson*

Shadows

A world of shapes and shadows hovers just beyond the curtain,
At the limit of our senses of the things that we are certain.
Where the living shadows hide, and hold us captive in our
dream. It's a world where not a living soul can hear us when
we scream. You can see this place of shadows in the crooked
dreams of slumber. While you're creeping through the nightmare
that is wont to keep you under. In the heavy purple velvet
of the fabric of the night. In the deeply wrinkled corners you
can glimpse a fitful sight. Of the shadows as they nibble at
the edges of your dream at the corners of the kingdom of your
fragile self-esteem. In the place where dreams and nightmares
can become reality, it's those who live beyond the edge that
clamor to be free. Just as we await the time we meet the
reaper's face. It's those who haunt these shadows dark that
wait to take out place. Their freedom's path? - a dreamer's
hand; so heed this strident voice, and look, don't touch,
you'll burn your soul with any other choice. And if you
touch them... even if it's for a moment brief, you'll let them
back instead of you, your soul awash in grief. Now if you're
feeling sorry for that world of living sin.
—*C. A. Van Horssen*

Untitled

Emotions - silenced and laid to rest so long ago
Awaken to the excitement!
Who's there?
Goodness - Strength - and Warmth - and Wisdom

Go slowly
The morning spreads her light to the noontime hour
Reach up!
Reach up and out to the golden sun!
Quench your thirst!
Drink of his love and affections

And now - afternoon's breeze gently carries you to evening
Where thoughts of him have taken you through Saturday's
    journey
And once again emotions are laid to rest
But only until
Tomorrow's light
—*Gail A. Braithwaite*

Imagination

Hi; Mr. Fence Post, the little boy said, you've been here an awfully long time! Do you ever get tired of standing all day? do your legs get as tired as mine? I see you standing all alone, what is your purpose in life? Tell me what there is to tell, are you married, do you have a wife? You never move or speak a word, you're lonely I have this hunch! So tomorrow at noon 'bout this time, I'll share with you my lunch. "See," I pull this wagon by myself, the load it's hard to toy. The wheels are worn and slightly bent, quite much, for a little boy. But I walk this lane, near every day, for the eggs I gently tow. And long 'bout evening for the sun goes down, I'll have some rows to hoe. But I don't live far, just over the ridge, no further than you could throw a stone. It's a big ole house, with lots of rooms, they call an Orphans home. "So" see its kinda lonely, in my world too! and it's my Mama that I miss the most. But I've never had a friend like you, you're the best "Mr. Fence Post."
—*Diana L. Trimble*

The Suavest L'Expressways Around 'Yo' Boulevardiers

So, Alfio's Centaurians, smile at me and be gayer!
Babes, so thanks to you and you alone, not that I don't—for
I have a busy imagination of that romances day at home
It is cooler, much more off than the fuller moon and lazier
Than some years in folks can say a passe' in...
Oh you cool moon and reggae gazer tell me of lifts in dreams
Only for the innocent betrayal of that memory of any a day
Of means, when my days will never explain it like a so and so
Not for now and anyway, and so, as they all hadda say it,
The going's gone okay, and then; though I still feel in it the
hot Civvie'itis' of the cities and city in the faces of some
strangers It may have been such a gift with which I've coped
in... In all of its fragilities,...yes, although I cannot take
those Walks to the angels of a yesterday in this country,
hey... And so I will stay where the stars heat the skies for
always in a wake of the toasts to and into my todays, whether it
Be usual or unusual, yeah, what can you or I say in the U.S.A.
For the angels think and they say it to me - "I'll be out too-"
Are you okay...honey...I don't know...I'll see ya later...
I'm gonna hang out 'til it's time to leave forever in anything!
—*Hee-Ju Yoo*

March

March is knocking at my window,
    Banging the shutters is glee.
March is making the wild wind blow,
    Heralding Spring with a flurry.
    Pulling back the winter's tight cover
To give me a preview of green through the earth.
    March, who is April's passionate lover,
Coaxing her out with his wild brand of mirth.
—*Jean Carr Smith*

The Past

Across the wind-swept desert the eagle gracefully flies,
bearing with it memories of distant days gone by.
Days when the burly buffalo roamed ever so free and the
sun-touched prairie stretched as far as the eye could see.

During those decades dwelled a wondrous feeling of joy,
daring courageous men to act and feel like boys.
And the women who nobly stood - a silent strength by their side
were strong and heroic, so their men could feel pride.

These people had dreams, and families whom they loved,
but their lives are done and over with, by a whim from above.
Although our ancient ancestors are long since dead,
they shall live evermore in our hearts and our heads.
—*Susan Giesemann*

"A Walk Through Nature"

As the flowers bloom, I gaze at the enchantment of their beauty. The beauty which runs throughout my body as the nightingale sings her melodious tune. The beauty which gives to my life the added compassion and warmth that I do not have.

Why do I crave the sensitivity and peacefulness of nature? My answer would have to be amazement. Why am I amazed? I am
amazed by the calmness and quietness that nature expresses, not in words or in motions, but simply in beauty. The beauty that touches the inner soul and being, the beauty that releases philosophical and metaphysical thoughts and ideas, the beauty that I am bound to enjoy and honor.
—*Brian McDonald*

A Virus

Being sick is not much fun
Because I like being on the run.
I don't know who gave me the bug
But I suspect I got it from a hug.

The virus has invaded all of me
From top to bottom as you can see.
My sinuses are full and begin to flow
Filling my hankies when I blow.

My work was held up for a day
As my body begged to rest away.
The nurse told me the cure was rest
So off to bed I went at her request.

A week has gone and the bug remains
Keeping my hankies full of stains.
The good news is, my weight has gone down
The bad news is, I still can't get around.

I thank you Lord for the drug Imodium
It has reduced my level of gastro pandemonium.
But why Lord do you make these bugs
And allow them to be spread by hugs?
—*Robert Gagne*

I Wear Your Clothes Inside Me

I wear your clothes inside me
Because I've found no safer place for them.
Inside - I believe -
They'll keep from fading and wearing out
In the brief period in which most do.
Only inside, will those who dare look in through windows
Find me wearing your clothes.
I wear your clothes
Because they set me on my journeys.
With them I hike the forests of dense growth.
With them I climb peaks sharp and cold.
I wear your clothes inside me...
If I wouldn't, these curious words
Would not have found themselves into me
Just so they could appear here in front of you.
—*Jaime Frastai*

Things I Wouldn't Want To Be

I wouldn't want to be a floor,
because people walk all over you.
I wouldn't want to be a microphone,
because you take a lot of lip too.

I wouldn't want to be a door, because
people don't care to respect you.
I wouldn't want to be a
tree, even birds peck on you.

I wouldn't want to be a balloon,
people can make your world go pop.
I sure don't want to be a garbage
can, you take too much trash and slop.

I wouldn't want to be a fire hydren
either, its a place for dogs to pee.
I wouldn't want to be a walking
cane, because really they can't see.

Some people don't want to be responsible,
their afraid of what they have to do.
And if this something you don't want
to be, then I sure don't want to be you.
—*Mr. Horse*

Changes

Through the darkness walked the seeker,
Becoming desperate, ever weaker.
And in the twilight when stars shown bright,
He sought the difference between wrong and right.

And in the shadows of days gone by,
He'd find no growth and wonder why.
Then through the darkness came a glowing,
Possessing wisdom, ever knowing.

Now he walks in sunlight with his head held high,
He has found inner strength and he knows why.
He had found a faith which humbled and awed,
He had placed himself in the care of God.
—*Joan Clark Curtis*

All It's Worth

Waking up to the beautiful sounds of Mother Nature
Being reborn by the earth
Enjoying it for all it's worth
Having the world's insects revolve around thee:

Beauty being hidden behind simplicity
there is a small caterpillar that shall blossom
into a beautiful mature spectacular
it to has been reborn by the earth
so it may be enjoyed for all it's worth
as the beauty of the butterfly blossoms and fly's
right on by
to experience everything without a heart breaking sigh
or simple cry
Fierce winds gives the butterfly great obstacles
to fly by
But determination and aspirations
shall test every sensation
So the beautiful butterfly will reach it's highest high
And may be enjoyed for,
ALL IT'S WORTH
—*Tami Lust*

An Ode To My Family

Once upon a time a young man and a young lady got married!
Being very poor there was not much threshold over which to be
carried. After a year of married bliss much to their surprise,
A baby girl, Janelle, was born who was the apple of their eyes.
Much happiness, hard work and two years later a baby son,
"James" entered their life; this family kept busy during a
depression with a world full of sorrow and strife. The father
worked at 25cent per hour, three days one week and four days
another, but ah-ha! This little family did not grieve for one
year later "Bob", a brother. The next few years the first two
children became very ill, but not to be discouraged, for next
came a baby boy named William, called "Bill". Three years have
passed, the nine year young daughter is promised a sister baby,
This baby to the family came then another boy "Charlie"
appeared, the last? Maybe! This family now complete this
father taught his sons many skills, and extra pay earning. The
mother loved the outdoors with garden, chickens and cow, very
much learning. This father built a family house, small, but a
place they all still call home. This family has through the
years worshipped, prayed and stayed together.
—*Johnnie Janelle Goodall*

Life's Orchestra

Let down your hair, great willow trees of the human condition
Bend your branches, be supple within life's great storms.
Feel the lightening rip through your green skirts
Yes, you can stretch just a bit further,
Stretch higher, wider- it must be done.
All the continuance of life watches your flexibility.
If you can survive the pain, reach the limits of anguish
You will be the first to experience the great white light,
It will be you playing the fiddle made from your own branches
Dancing with the most beautiful maiden of song.
Your smile, your kiss will explode as the diamond star.
Look around you-
See how the orchestra is filled with those who keep trying,
We have done it. You are doing it.
You must do it today, tomorrow and always.
Just keep trying and life will be without end.
Just keep trying and life will be without end.
—*Nancy Marguerite Waple*

Heartsounds

Something heard overhead like a spark in the mind
bends my ear, yearning to find any answers.
Wasted time I discover;
nothing resides there.
Lean down beneath cold cognition.
Seek your volumes from the heart,
a beautiful merger, says the eye to the dreamer.
Warmth glows like destiny glistening before dream-glazed eyes.
The heart tells beautiful stories, you see,
something of a literary harmony fueling your passions,
that indescribable zest for life deflated by dreary thoughts of
reality.
Never let them tell you your life is fated
to spin useless circles of boredom and conformity.
Wrestle those notions until they shrivel into deflated nonsense.
Kick the can or the rock down the street
with Birkenstocks and bare feet.
Sing out loud when the crowd rests stiffly in silence,
just to speak once and always what's on your mind.
Resonate harmonic whispers—
cherish the words of the heart.
—*Tiffany C. Wheeler*

Best Friends Are...

Best friends are loving,
best friends are caring,
best friends are someone who is Always there.

To me I guess best friends are someone who is,
pretty on the inside not necessarily on the out,
kind,
gentle,
and always has a shoulder for you to lean on.
—*Dawn Boeglin*

Zodiacs

   Tempers cast clouds of gloom; wasting light
beyond all moons. Chants become wisdom from afar.
Wishes peering from many stars. Light reflects
through clouds so clear; asking rainbows to appear.
   Colors bloom around dusty moons. Keeping time intact,
will surely bring the zodiacs. Temperatures salute
the tides, coming in on an endless ride. Dancing across
the land so sleek; sprinkling stardust among the weak.
Shine through all layers with answered prayers.
   Just to show their powers, they lash out with sparks
that last for hours. Spinning 'round our universe,
making a path for the future. Twinkle bright on clear
nights. Tracing shadows within our sight. Visible at day;
yet still forbid to show.

   When appearing, look real clearly. For your destiny
could be among the zodiac signs. So look beyond the clouds
and through the stormy moons; and perhaps your stars will come
peering at you!
—*Victoria P. Cauley*

Corn

Yellow beads with green weeds,
A man of gold with a fine green coat,
Shabby hair all sticking out,
I wonder if I can eat it—
Without a doubt!

Little bits that you can eat,
Wondering, wondering why they're so sweet,
A wiggly tree trunk, half yellow half green,
That's corn, that's corn, that's corn for me!
—*Lauren Flessner*

Social Disease

Frustrated to limits
Beyond boundaries known
Affirming deepest fears
No one's listening.

Weakened by anger
Physical tantrums
Giving credence to
Nudging thoughts of self-betrayal.

Bound by unearned guilt
Baggage slung on bent shoulders
Weighted to earth yet free to fly
Frozen fingers struggling to release bonds.

Airborne ideas glistening through clouds
Grasping wildly to catch them
Without stopping to build the ladder
Rungs of polished dreams carefully hewn.

Dutifully meeting demands
Rising to expectations
Accepting, not choosing
Too tired to fight.
—*V. Susan Evin*

Dreams

Into a deep sleep
Beyond the line of reality,
Across I fly over the shimmering blue lake
Above I feel the warmth of the golden sun.
Throughout the dream I'll sneak a smile
Beside me it shall be floating
With a halo round its head
Inside I'll feel a soft warm glow
From the friendly forest a pine cone
Down it falls into my open hand.
We fly until we can no more
To the line of reality
Nearer and nearer 'till I'm there
Around I turn to wave a farewell
Except darkness surrounds me
But my eyes flutter open
Despite what is left, a pinecone in my hand...
—*Chanelle Benz*

The Sunset Of Life Is Best

I've had a happy, active life, and my share of love, And blessings from almighty God, have showered on me from above. So I was ready now I thought, for my declining years, With a woman who could share, my thoughts, my laughs, my tears. I knew thatI could be content, with just a hand to hold, And a body warm beside me, to keep me from the cold. A dear friend for company, someone with whom to pray, To fly with me to Waikiki, and watch the sea gulls play. To share with me the cooking, and all the cleaning too, We'd always do our best to keep, each other from being blue, Someone to hike long trails with me, wherever the path may lead Always ready to "get out of Dodge", whenever we feel the need. Well friend, when I married Evelyn, these things all came to pass, and I realized that God had sent, to me the worlds finest lass. I'd thought that I'd been loved before, but little did I know, what true love and devotion, one sweet little girl could show. So I am just as happy now, as any man could be, She's given me new lease on life, I feel like thirty three. So friends wherever you're living, north, south, east or west, Have no fear of growing old, the sunset of life is best.
—*David W. King*

Say Hello To Her Heart

Laughing, talking, having fun
Blonde hair, blue eyes, a smile like the sun.
Lots of friends, lots of dates,
She's someone nobody hates.
She's lucky!...Right?

Her parents call her the mistake.
How much more can she take?
She's tired of feeling all alone.
She has no love from her home.

She stays in her room and cries,
Big tears from those pretty eyes
There's so much she misses,
Like those soft parent kisses,
I want to help, and I know where to start.
I'm going to say hello to her heart.
—*Kelley Mitchell*

Dawn's Desire

Morning breaks not briefly
Blooms deftly up from lingering night
As sun-shafts slay shadows in the sky
In a Genesis of gathering hues

I, too, hope to rise like morning
And exorcise night from my life
Leaving behind a trail of blooms
A shining desire disguise
That burns bridges but builds rainbows

That colors the cosmos with fire
I leap face-first into the flames without fear
And find they ever inspire
Poetry is lightning; my heart is a sky
In which a galaxy of fears is turning
And this morning I am burning!
—*Kevin Cochran*

Tornado

As I sit and listen to the whispering wind in the trees, as it blows it gets stronger, hitting against me. Then I look up into the sky, expecting it to be blue, but instead, the sky is black and gray, impersonal and cruel.

As I take a deep breath, I stand up and wait to see the mastermind who created this great hate. The rain has long since ended and I'm without a doubt, that something's about to happen because of all the clouds

The temperature gets higher and hotter as it may, then I see it coming toward my driveway. The thing sounds like a train coming down the tracks, the thing is very hateful, goodness is what it lacks.

As it comes toward me, it pushes things around. As it moves, it knocks trees over and houses to the ground. It is a real big bully that no one likes to see, but I am standing here staring as it comes to get me.

It's really a disgusting sight that I don't like that much. All it needs is to sit down at a table because it's already eating lunch. I would love to have pretty weather, such as sunshine or snow but I really can't handle such a thing as a tornado.
—*Dawn Hough*

Life

Life, what is it I ask is, it not just a breath,
   Life, it is the period, between birth and death,
   It has been said, when you are breathing
You are positively living,
   The rest is what, you make of it but
Life is something you are given,
   Life is great for some, but not for all,
Sometimes we rise and, sometimes we fall,
Life I question, what is it all really
Truly about,
   Mysteries we, will all reveal in time
There is no doubt.
—*Jennifer Lynn Marie Cislak*

The Plight Of The Infection's Pen

To write is to breathe, long shuttering breaths.
Breaths of struggle, breaths of pain
Rip the throat with blistering sound,
Burning the pages with abandonment.

Soft gentle bursts of air whisper joy to be there.
Speaking, laughing, they play with the sounds,
Arranging, entertaining, teasing the mind, the soul,
The essence of life.

To write is to live, to wonder, to be.
To write offers hope, a solution, a plan.
Give me my pen; I'm called to the page,
Searching, seeking, the secrets of wit.

My breath is rising, growing sharp in my breast.
I write to release the cries of my soul,
To spill over the pages and fill them with life,
Laughing and crying, to write is my plight.
—*Sandi Geronimo*

"Perpetual Thoughts and Motions"

Perpetual thoughts
Breed perpetual motions
a never-ending cycle
turning 'round my head.

Thoughts and dreams jotted on paper
therapeutic intervention
allows dreams to take shape
and come true.

Dreams quickly fill the empty spaces
becoming permanent
to never be erased -
never will be forgotten.

Thoughts of a simple-minded girl
not so simple in content and context.
Surprising to others
to herself commonplace.

This thought process never ceases
always constant
except when sleep overcomes her -
allowing her dreams to somehow come true.
—*Laurie Willcutt*

Pandora's Box

The landscape lies wrinkled by countless egos
As headstones stand sentinel over the hollow tombs
Of the sacrificial offerings.
Famine, war, pestilence —
Are these the touchstones of man's progress
Or are we greedily trying to fulfill the myth
Of Pandora's Box?
—*Rick Miralia*

"Sandcastles"

Sandcastles are a child's dream of what the future can bring.
A child doesn't hesitate to say what they'd like to be.
As adults our opportunities change and grow.
Life can be so confusing as to which way to go.
As children everything could happen in our imagination.
From being firemen, nurses, kings and queens or a leader of a nation.
Building those whimsical places out of sand.
That put you into that special magical land.
No two Sandcastles are exactly the same.
Just as no two peoples dreams are exactly the same.
We all hold are own magical Sandcastles from our childhood
in a special place in our hearts.
As you walk by a Sandcastle let it remind you of your own
magical whimsical land from your childhood.
That's sure to put a smile or even a little grin on your face.
To remind you of that happy place.
—*Cynthia L. Kee*

Youth

The snow was like stardust falling to earth,
Bringing with it the cold of empty space.

We sat among the mountains,
Beside log fires,
And drank our beer.

And tried hard,
Not to be happy.
—*Robert McIlvaine*

A Poem For Dad

The mist of this day,
Brings thoughts to my mind
   Memories of you,
Who are one of a kind.
We've had our little troubles,
Our quarrels, our fights.
But everything always turns out right.
But there is something that you must know,
Something true and unmistakably so
You are my father and will always be,
But you have always been
An inspiration to me.
You have been there for me through my timeless pain,
Helping me start all over again.
My love for you is honest and true,
Just like the roses upholding the dew.
—*Heather Bastion*

Victims Of Circumstance

Victims of circumstance running from the knife,
broken bits behind them, tiny shards of life.

All their dreams are shattered, and they try to
start anew, but the slate remains empty, a
frustrating hue.

Hiding all their feelings, none may seep through,
losing their identity so the pain will go away,
hoping they'll forget what made them feel this way.

But hidden in the mirror far inside their minds,
flashbacks make them remember the wished forgotten
times.

So they pick up all the pieces, although slightly
out of place, and face these terms with courage,
and go on with mastered grace.
—*Marie V. Collins*

Untitled

Euro-steering opions, peering in form dilapidation of the wall,
broken down from blocks of tempered, communist mortars,
mortars
that rip and tear at the seams of borders, torn from ethnic strife.

Before the wall could fall, its been raised and mended,
in the blood and death of minds peering in from a stream line
of scarecrows, wearing the rags of power, blocks of untempered
mortars, mortars that scar and cause fear to settle the world,
steering opions to settle for death.
—*Jerome Wald*

Friends

   Friends are made as sister and
brother, that's why they love one another.
Friends were made for holding hands,
they were also made for making plans.
If you have a friend, treat them right,
so they won't disappear out of your sight.
So meet a friend and keep that friend
forever, so you'll become a couple together.
Make your friend a part of your life, and
they'll never stab you in the back with a
knife. Treat your friend like you treat your
neighbor, and they'll help you if you need a
favor. Remember, if you want a friend, you
can't buy one that will stay until the end.
So go and find a friend today, and
then you'll say "hip, hip, hooray"!

   A friend is someone who cares, not
swears.

—*Tavia Manderson*

Christian Sense

People ask me, "What do you do for fun?"
Brothers and sisters, why destroy yourselves with drugs and
alcohol? Never facing reality. Never seeing and appreciating the
full beauty of God's Universe.

And the material things of this world does not
matter; for Satan will come after you rich or poor; and he
is not powerless and can fool our careless minds.

   You see, to know Jesus means rewards are waiting in Heaven
throughout all eternity. Heaven will be a new home, where you
need not lock your doors or fear anything. We'll be protected
by the Angels throughout each night, with God's hand amidst us.

   Things are not easy in this world today. But why not make
this earthly home like Heaven? Why all the fighting? Will it
bring peace, joy or happiness? Or self-satisfaction that will
only prevail a little while?

   Be thankful God breathed life into you forevermore to live
peacefully among ourselves.

   So let not material things or envy hinder your love for
mankind. For life is precious, and life will come again
after death.
—*Carrie L. Young*

Endless Waves

Standing in the midst of an ocean
   buffeted by its waves
   I felt the tentative touch of a smile
   like the gentle fingers of the sun.
   A kindred spirit I wondered;
Wading through the debris of the faceless
   I found, alas, it was only a lifeless shell
   its warmth, imagined.
—*Ai-Ling Weis*

The Ocean

The waves hitting against the rocks, the seaweed
   Building up on the shore.
All the beauty in the sea is for all the world to enjoy,
   Especially a girl and a boy.

When the sun sets, the time has come for lovers to walk,
   Hand in hand along the sand.

When the wind whistles in your ear,
   The vision of love appears.
The white, invisible mist hits your face,
   The time is right for lovers to embrace.

The footprints in the sand of people walking hand in hand.
   Against the crimson light of the sunset,
Going down over the hill in the west.

They tell you where they're going,
   But never where you've been.
When you make love in the sand,
   It could be the undeniable sin.
     —*Rosalina Fallin*

The Windmill

Stands it tall against the sky,
   Built upon a verdant hill,
With mighty arms raised up on high,
   That majestic sight, the great windmill.

From ages past this Goliath came,
   When man was working in the field,
All in the country knew it's name,
   It ground the corn from the Earth's fine yield.

No longer are those sails unfurled,
   To turn the stones and grind the grain,
Lonely it sits in a different world,
   The time has gone from whence it came.

Silent the sentry atop the mound,
   Shabby and paintless, deserted and still,
But forever it will hold it's ground,
   That magnificent thing, the great windmill.
     —*Eric R. Hardy*

Hardcore

Hardcore is that single mother
Burden down in despair and grief,
With children to feed, bills to pay
And no sign of any relief.
Hardcore is that single mother
Who gave that man her very best,
Her children calls him father
Yet her children remains fatherless.
Hardcore is that single mother
Who has made it through all the rough times,
And she thanks God and praises him
For all her children are grown and doing fine.
HARDCORE is that MOTHER...who survived.
     —*Sonia Leggs*

Home

Home is where I always dreamed
As a child sometimes even schemed
Home is where my heart longs to be
But when I was there I wanted only to leave
I can smell mom's pie baking
Now my heart is only breaking
I long to see the little yellow house
I remember saying it was built for a mouse
Please old bus take me home
Where there is love and I won't be alone
     —*Terry L. Deignan*

We Never Know

Why is it we never know when love begins,
But always know when love ends.
You don't know what it is 'till it's gone,
But while it's there, it's like a song.
A beautiful song, sung in the trees,
With the birds singing in the swaying leaves.
Like a beautiful sunset, the colors warm and gay,
The purple, pink, and orange always seem to say,
Love is here now, but soon it may be gone.
It starts out soft and dies out strong.
Painfully it tears our souls,
It burns our hearts and turns us cold.
We have tears, but we must cry,
For that is the only way our old love can die.
We must move on and have our hearts to mend,
As to start a new love, the first must end.
   —*Emily Gallagher*

Whose Disappointment

Nothing
   but cool air brushing against bare legs
   as eyes stare
      into the gloomdoom
   of rainy wake-up morning afternoons
Gulp Slurp orange juice on
   burnt lips
   While toaster pops waffles that go
   brown slushy with syrup
as fingers search
   in vain boredom for a fork
And eat and eat brown slushy
   in bad mannered anxiety
   for mother-may-I, half-way down
   pretty east coast beach
knows the potato pantry's got eyes too
   —*Rebecca Vaughan*

"Booze"

I ask a man to bring me some bread,
but he came and brought wine instead.
As we sat there boozing away.
We become dizzier and dizzier all the day.
the cows didn't get milked, or the hogs fed
all because he brought wine for basal,
As he started home, he fell over a barrel,
And up to his shoulder in mud he sank,
All invariably I went hunting a rope,
to tie to my truck, the only hope!
and throw to him the other end,
to get him out of that quick sand,
when he was out, oh, what a mess,
this I most certainly will confess.
I stayed around to hunt a hose,
as he was most dirty up to his nose.
My head was hurting with lots of pain,
all beware of all that wine.
As I washed him off, as clear as before,
I desisted I wouldn't drink that booze anymore.
   —*Max Schnitzler*

"Being Apart"

When you and I are apart
can sorrow break our tender hearts,
I love you Sweetheart, yes I do
Sleep is sweet when I think of you.
All you are is a blooming rose
Night is here so I must close,
With care...read the first word on each line,
you will find a question.
   —*Vivian L. Toves*

"Legend"

He left the game because of his back,
but he still had more moves than Jordan or the Shaq.
He wrote white and green in front of the crowd,
whenever he scored he made them proud.
Boston Garden was where he played,
that's where most of the points were made.
They all knew as he walked down the hall,
that his jersey would soon hang on the wall.
He has always been a hero to me,
I'll never forget number thirty-three.
—*Jason Lowe*

Brother's Gift

For Christmas I thought hard about what to get you,
but I couldn't think of a thing, I hadn't a clue.
Then I remembered you wanted a skunk for a pet.
so I decided right then that's what I would get.

I searched and searched, I looked all around. I tried all the
pet stores in and out of town. They had cute fuzzy kitties and
fat little puppies, turtles and gerbils, hamsters and guppies;
but each time I asked for the pet of my choice, "No skunks,"
the clerk replied in a bored, tired voice.

At last to my dismay, the only real skunks to be found.
were dead on the roadside, their brains covering the ground.
Finally, to the Shopko check-out I went with a stuffed skunk in hand.
This will have to do. For skunks there's no big demand.

So I regret to inform you, your present's not real.
Still I think you will like it. It's not such a bad deal.
It's already de-scented, and it doesn't need to eat,
so it won't cost you a penny. Isn't that neat?

Now, I'm tired, and I'm frustrated; no more will I roam.
If you want a darn live skunk, go get your own.
—*Deborah Lenz*

The Green Room

In mother's house are many rooms
But I enjoy the green room most of all
'Tis there I seek the flora and fauna
Listen to chattering squirrels hear raven's call.

In the green room flowers smell their sweetest
and butterflies bloom in every hue
The animals live and play freely
The placid lake wears an azure blue.

My senses have reeled in pastel rooms of springtime.
And thrilled to the gold and ruby rooms of fall
I've lingered in paler-than-white shades of winter
But I enjoy the green room most of all.
—*Nancy Rutledge*

Change

Times and feeling may have changed,
  but I need the love you gave me
    to realize life's little pleasures and pains.
I'm finally on my way to making a fresh start
  to see the things I've been missing out on.
    All I needed was a helping hand and a loving heart.
God has a special way of telling people what's right.
  All it takes is some time and patience
    and people like you to help overcome a fight.
To this day not a day goes by
  when I don't want to Thank You
    for never leaving and staying by my side.
      Thanks!
—*Allison Champagne*

"Goodbye"

I know someday you'll be a sun in someone else's sky
But I'll never really know the hidden reason why
His essence will be drawn from the luster in your shine
Of all the things I could hope for, I wish that you were mine
You touched a part of me I didn't think was there,
The windows to your soul is what really showed you care
Inside is something so special, and I don't think you even know
The last thing in the world I want is for you to ever go
Don't ever for a second think that any of this was your fault
This deluge of pain inside of me I can never seem to halt
All that encompasses me just turns my world to black
I feel the best thing I could do for you is just to turn my back
back. If you just gave me one chance I know you'd feel it too
But because of what I've done in the past I could never be with you
I know someday you'll have a beautiful life and all will go your way
All that's left for me now is do my best to say
I never thought it would turn out like this, never had a clue
All the thoughts in my mind will always converge to you
Now I realize that when I leave, part of me will die
Life it seems to treat me cold, now I will just say goodbye.
—*Robert Medaska, Jr.*

The Heart

A dagger enters the heart,
  but it does not bleed.
Only pain lies deep within its core.
The heart longs for spiritual giving
  and love for which it feeds.
Pull the dagger from its depth
  and than it will bleed upon the floor.
Can you see or feel the pain written upon once face?
Deep within their soaked filled eyes
  looking for a touch of grace.
The heart with time will mend time and time again.
Will your mind tare it apart and keep it torn in sin.
How many times will it take for the heart to totally break?
If I shall die before I wake?
  Will my heartbeat peace of fall of hate?
I pray the Lord my soul to take with love up into Heaven's
Gold Gates.
—*Barry L. Halleck*

Only

  Only a poisonous drop from the cup;
But it gave a thirst for more,
And awoke a craving that wrecked a life
on a barren, desert shore.

'twas only a glance—but a scornful glance;
And it fanned a dreaded flame.
It was only a kind look,
But it won a heart from shame.

It was only a smile—a pleading smile—
But it reached a hardened heart,
And roused a desire and an earnest will
to perform a noble part.

It was only a tear—one pearly tear—
that stood upon her cheek,
Yet it spoke a sweet goodbye that words
could never speak.

It was only a word—one gentle word—
But sweet as the summer's breath;
And it touched the spring of a thoughtless mind,
And rescued a soul from death.
—*Richard A. Rose*

Alone In Darkness

The world is shut out
But, it manages to peep back through.
A sound of thirst and hunger
From the minds forming, yet.

A sound of madness, darkness,
Loneliness, sadness,
Forming in the surroundings
I am "alone in darkness"

A cry of a baby, a bark of a dog,
A breeze of a wind, a writing's in one's hand.
The same as always from the world within
Everything's in peace now, besides me.

I can see no light, I can see no pain,
I can hear no voice, I can see no signs.

I am "Alone in darkness",
But, darkness is not dark anymore,
For I have come out into the light.

—*Kendrea Focht*

The Key To Peace Is Love

We want peace in this world for you and me,
But love is the only key
Love and understanding for stranger or kin
Regardless of his action or color of skin.
For every unkind word, return a smile;
For an unkind deed exchange one, worthwhile;
For unworthy service of another,
Be a kind and patient brother.
When a person's attitude is sour
Be like a honey-laden flower.
Take our humble Lord's advice,
And always treat our brethren nice.
Love's strong cord can bring us peace,
And cause hatred in this world to cease.
'Twill take compassionate love profound
To offset the hate and sins which how abound.

—*Ruby Farnham Skaggs*

A Math Lesson

A friend should be radical, fanatical,
but most of all, mathematical!

A friend should be radical!
She should love when you're unlovable,
Hug when you're unhuggable,
And bear when you're unbearable!
A friend should be fanatical!
She should cheer when the whole world boo's,
Dance when you get good news,
and cry when you cry too!
But most of all, a friend must be mathematical!
She must multiply the joys,
Divide the sorrows,
Subtract from the past,
and add to tomorrow.
Calculate the need deep in your heart
and remember the sum of all the parts

—*Rachel Brown*

Reclaiming Joan Of Arc

They've claimed you for themselves,
but, my friend, you've felt the flames,
the hot lick of your lot, our lot,
rise up from the fagus canes.
And they? Their eyes,
drunk on the smell of your burning,
rolled up the quiet sky—waiting, they were
for the quick snap, the prop, the heavenly trap.
and now I say, dear Jeanne,
I have seen you in my dreams,
With your blackened boots
and your soldier's suits—
you are a woman of war.
I have seen you, oh Jeanne, with your stride, your mannish mime
and I know you well, though time
is bloodied between us.
and now, the ashes lie heavy in their palms.
My friend, with words alone,
I claim you for my own.

—*Julia Cumes*

Listen

My heart is in love, same with my body,
but my mind keeps telling me, your going
to fast, but it never seems to work, it
seems I'm to blind to understand, so if
my heart gets broke, and my body gets hurt,
It's all my fault for not listening, to
what my mind had to say.

—*Andrea Rapp*

A Love Poem

She's poison to me
but not the bittersweet kind.
She's more like honey or port wine.
Opium smoked from an ivory pipe,
a tiger's soft and cunning stripe.
Whiskey aged in charred oak barrels,
lonesome songs of whippoorwills.
Butter melting down, icing on a cake.
Clouds that hang around, things not fake.
The smell of rain and summer heat.
She's poison, but not bittersweet.

—*Richard Aubrey*

Diane

I could go to France or Milan
But - nowhere is there anyone
So very beautiful - as my Diane
Like her Heaven only made one

She is like sunshine in a shower
With her smile so dazzling white
More lovelier than a rare flower
Making this dark world so bright

Her eyes sparkle like jewels in the night
Her sexy ruby lips set my heart on fire
I visualize her when she is out of sight
A princess - filling my heart with desire

I'd climb a steep mountain very high
Even swim an ocean to be by her side
I'd do anything for her to be nigh
She is my love - life - joy and pride

The most beautiful girl in the land
Oh - the moment I saw her love began
She holds my heart in her dear hand
Diane - my most precious - sweet Diane

—*Ray Gordon*

April

Rainy April days are here.
But soon the flowers will appear
Bringing with them delights of spring
Colorful shows of which birds will sing.

Watering the seeds planted with care,
The start of another gardening year.
Each will soon burst forth with life
And please the gardener with this sight.

Budding branches proclaim life inside
Each tree who from winter's cold did hide.
April gives hope that May will come
With warmer days filled with the sun.

Days like this are perfect for
Curling up with a book you brought before,
And never had the chance to read
But now you have the time you need.

So light one last fire to warm your heart,
Summer's busy days are about to start,
And moments like these will be hard to find,
Enjoy the quiet while you still have time.
—*Steve Ehlscheid*

Music Without Melody

For some music must have words explaining the feeling
But the music of life comes from within ourselves
We create our own dance to accompany it
The accrendos and decrendos of life
Their rhythmic beat pulsating
Their soft delicacies played slowly
Take away the words and you have only the music
Take away the music and you have only
Silence
Poetry is music without a melody
Its words are the notes on a music sheet
Its instrument is the heart beating sounding
Through the rafters of our emotion
—*Shelly Herrington*

One Day

Shadows fall around the town,
  But the sun has not gone down.
Dogs howl loud and clear,
  Little children are filled with fear.

No wind does blow;
  Good make's no show.
Dark clouds move in,
  Could it be the end?

Is this the darkness of sin?
  Can it dare to win?
Through the clouds come a light
  Oh what a glorious sight!

He is here to save the day,
  Not just in any old way.
There shall be no more evil gusts.
  That man from above is our Lord, JESUS!
—*Susan J. White*

A Night At Wrigley Field

It was a cold, rainy night at Wrigley Field,
But the true Cubs fans refused to yield.
The mighty north wind was blowing in,
So we knew that one run might be enough to win.
In the first few innings the Reds could not score,
And the awesome Cubs could do no more.
Shots would be hit to center and right,
But the wind from the bleachers would knock them
down from their flight.
Through the seventh inning it was much of the same,
As Harry Carey sang "Take Me Out of the Ballgame".
In the bottom of the ninth the score was still tied,
And on Ryne Sandberg the Cubs fans relied.
With the first pitch the umpire cried, "strike one,"
But the Cubs fans knew Ryno was not done.
Louder and louder the Cubs fans did cheer,
The next pitch was high, right past his ear.
With the count even at one strike and one ball,
Ryno hit the next pitch out, over the wall.
Before it was time for fans to leave and go to bed,
Cubs win! Cubs win! Harry Carey said.
—*Joey Turner*

Medals For People With Faces Of Love

Often times, we don't get credit for what we do
But there are eyes, ears here and everywhere
Eyes that see what is really true
Ears to hear, and people who offer prayer.

We must forget sad unimportant words they say,
and never dwell over wasted time!
I believe, and live for each and every day
For everything is cared for and turns out fine.

There is a place I never have been,
they tell me it is in the beyond or up above
I heard they pass out love medals and I'll bet they are keen.
People wear them and they can be seen
By other people on the "Faces of Love".
—*Naomi Ruth Barrows*

Ode to Birthdays

　　　Birthdays are but once a year
But thoughts of birth and death come with every breath.

　　　Parties and cake go to the celebrator
But joy and reflection go to the mother.

　　　As I celebrate "My" day, as they say.
Peace and joy to you, my mom, each day I pray.

　　　Birthdays come and go every year
Many with laughter and thoughts so dear.

　　　Now that I have a child of my own
I realize birthdays are gifts from God, His own.

　　Looking back, on this twenty-seventh year of my life,
I realize that of the 9,855 days, some have been filled with
　　　strife!

　　A counselor, a mediator, a friend, a chauffeur,
　　　To me you've been plus many more!

　　　On this seventh day of June, 1993
　　Thank you with love for loving me!
—*Dyanne E. Daugherty*

My Family

My family is a confusing one.
But when we get together we have a lot of fun.
I live with my Grandma and Grandpa too
But love to see my Mom as I sometimes do.
Every other weekend I stay with my Dad
That's where my sister lives
Where we fight real bad
My Aunt Linda is the craziest one
But when we get together we act really dumb.
I also have a Grandpa Fred who I hardly ever see
But I love him just the same because he's good to me.
Last but not least my cat Lukester pie.
My family is a confusing one
But then again so am I.

—*Richelle Cook*

Under My Bed

There are many things under my bed, I know,
But where do you put a green and red bow?
What do you do with three checkers, a ring?
Where do you put a jet submarine?
And then there's the matter of your nest and your stamps,
Your marble, your necklace, your old genie lamps,
Your cave, your castle, your old red tree fort,
Now where do you put such things of this sort?
What do you do with a unicorn or fairy?
Where do you put your old dog named Harry?
I do not know where all these things go,
But these things are all under my bed, I know.

—*Kim Shinner*

Love Me

I sit here alone no one to talk to.
But you know the only one I want is you.
If I could only tell you how I feel.
But I know my dreams could never be real.
I look up and imagine you standing there.
My heart could just break when I see you no where.
When I think about you I could just die.
All I want to do is break down and cry.
You are my friend when I need someone
In my heart I love you so much.
How I hunger for one simple touch.
But you have no idea that I am alive
Though still in my heart this love does thrive
But you love others now I can see
Though I still wish one day you'd only love me.

—*Jennifer Allison*

The Songbird's Song

I was awakened this morning
By a songbird's song
I went to the window to see
And there was a songbird
Perched high on a limb of a tree
Singing her melody to me
I looked again and I soon knew why
For there in the boughs in a tiny little nest
Were three baby birds so sweet
With their mouths opened wide
And their heads held high
Waiting for something to eat
Then I said, "I see,"
"That's why she's singing her melody to me"

—*Nora M. Reynolds*

Recycling

To nurture the earth I have to save the soil
By recycling all dirts the everyday things spoiled
In households and firms
Or in business terms
When satisfaction is cloned
The job is done, then I become the icon
Get back to the tone
Myself, I find amusing
When I think about human being
In term of recycling I believe it's working
Since the beginning the world is circulating
In reincarnating:
The good will be clinging
On to become a super being
The bad will be transforming
Into animals, and devils - ugly and stinked
What a thing!

—*Duong-Thi Phuong-Hang*

January

Fingers numbly startled
  by the coldness of
    each other.

Toes that ask you where they are
  or beg you to be
    someplace else
    somewhere warm.

The wind howls

and the lobes of your ears
  turn pale, and
    cower before the force of the blow.

Your breath flees
  only to return afraid
    and be turned away, for
it is too bitter outside
  to open the door
    on a night such as this.

—*Chris Vyhnal*

"Ad Eternity"

The precursor: The essence

The infertility of death is contemplated
  by the primordial essence of life.
Hand in hand do they scale and balance
  Neither falling to either side
    but in total harmony.

The Voyage

The voyage was no great toll
  but only a dream...
...a faint-hearted nightmare of delusions
an epic of grant proportion in the eyes of the mind.

The light, The Conclusion

There is a light. Let the seeker reach it
  Give him eternal life, fearless sight
into the great unknown of endless light.

—*Ahmet Samedov*

Compositions Of Glass

The fragile cover of the evening's splendor is eclipsed in form
   by the spinning flower
Divided, I slake my thirst upon the bitter dust of reality
Dreaming within the greenhouse, scattered pictures compliment
   the intensified magnificence
Images assault my thin consciousness
Alone, I forsake the womb-garden
Among the blind sight is a curse that begins early
Silently, I wonder at the forest's significance
The torch reveals retched horrors inside our lives
How much easier to hide behind the clear partition of
   uncertainty
Ignorance and pain compose the barriers with which we confuse
   others
Comfort overrides contact
True love is banished behind shields of glass
   —*Christopher B. Edwards*

The Elephants's Flight

     The silence of the jungle is broken
by the thunder of hooves echoing through the trees.
     The swish of the leaves,
       the crackle of the branches,
       the cries of the frightened animals
         let us know danger is near.
In the clearing ahead there is chance for survival.
     As the mighty figure approaches,
       his sorrowful eyes tell his fate.
        Like a clap of thunder,
       the bullet pierces his rigid body.
         His shrill cry
as his huge body collapses to the ground,
       brings a haunting silence
         back to the jungle.
   —*Eric Gorden*

To Greg

You may be gone, but never forgotten
   by those who remember you best.
Your sense of humor, your smile
   and your laughter touched the hearts of many.
In our aloha way, we hold you very dear.
You made us feel welcomed from the start
And that your memory, we'll always
   keep in our heart.
You've found a better place where hurt is no more.
No pain or tears to shed.
No burdens to bear or bills to pay,
Only a road of gold to tread.
As you look down upon as now
And hear our silent prayers,
Enfold your arms around us
And keep us in your care.
   —*Glenda Tensfeldt*

The One

You see her laying in her casket
but there is nothing you can do.
you can't hold her, you can't kiss her,
you can only touch her
and feel her cold hands and face.
a tear then falls as you remember her embrace.

And if you knew you could bring her back,
you know you would.
But that can't be done; she gone.
And you cry for days because you knew
she was the one.
   —*Rebecca Sue Pagonis*

What I Hear

What I hear is the trees speaking to me
calling out my name remember me
Your roots are deep as mine
we are intertwined needing the same substance to survive
Mother Earth has given us both the best she has for our growth

The leaves on my tree they are like your clothes they cover me
The children you have is your family
like the branches of my tree is the life of me
I love to feel the wind blow through me
it's like the spirit moving in you making you fresh and anew

Can you hear what the trees are saying
we are life please let us live too
Clean up the environment love respect show gratitude
give back to Mother Nature the work of a positive attitude

Stop being careless with our lives
polluting the air is not wise
The air is the breath we breathe
the spirit of life indeed
   —*G'ya Hamashea*

Un Jour "One Day"

There are no knights in the world today. No man that
can catapult over the towering walls of my heart.
Be it noble man or page,
they all know the art.

They mount their mighty steeds,
to win the pennant of love in a joust.
To only drink their fill of mead that eve,
and say they won the joust in jest.

They roam the world breaking hearts,
with this art of love they have acquired.
Seeking not to abide by chivalrous code.
No man is of need in a squire,
For their minds need no other man to aid in the skill of
hearts so cold.

Diex Aie! I say, "God helps".
One day a seasoned knight will give me his heart with
true love felt.
Un Jour! I say, Un Jour … "One Day".
   —*Kimberly R. Ober*

The River

A river so lovely, so long, and so clean
Can persuade any person that he has not a fiend
The freedom of spirit that comes from the view
Is one that is taught from a pristine church pew.

The water winds smoothly without many flaws
And gives life to the beings of whom wish to draw
The paths which it takes are many from few
And the lessons obtained will tell a new true

The mirror-like image reflects to the viewer
All things he has done from older to newer
Whenever life winds and things go a strew
Remember each day starts with a fresh dew.
   —*Kelly Burke*

Little Bird

Little bird with your feathers all wet
Can you tell me has it stopped raining yet?
I can see that it has, but in your tree
Rain is still dripping off the leaves

You skitter back and forth across a branch
A leave fills above you, starting an avalanche
Of rain that drips upon your head
I feel your discomfort, it goes unsaid

But wait little bird, I see the sun
Soon you'll be flying and having fun
As soon as all your feathers dry
You'll be flying across the sky

You will do loops and spins
Flying to places I've never been
Making your living off the land
With the love of God's helping hand

Little bird who's looking at me
How I wish that I was thee
To fly anywhere, a home in every tree
A beautiful creature, wild and free.
—*Timothy Shawn Cowing*

Ode To A Firefly

Lightning Bug, firefly, listen:
Can you tell me why?
When it rains, and then it stops,
And the dew forms in tiny drops
on the leaves and boughs of trees...
The mockingbird rests upon a branch,
then flits from twig to twig,
as though waiting for some tune to flow
from the fragile tube in his tiny breast.

Early evening creeps in unseen silence,
shadows covering the whole of countryside;
And you, little insect creature,
In utter silence extend your wings
and flutter from twig to twig,
You wait for that magic moment of the dark of night...
Then, beneath those fragile wings
Comes a God-given glow,
a soft, yellow-white light, bathing your
surroundings with mystical, soundless touch.
—*John Carruth*

Friendship

The greatest treasure in the world
Cannot be bought or sold
With all this planet's diamonds
Or its silver and its gold.
This treasure makes the world go round.
It makes the heart to sing.
To our prayers gives hands and feet
That to others many blessings bring.
And then surprise! We realize
That we ourselves without a thought
Of gain have great reward indeed -
A happiness inside that can't be bought
From filling another's needs.
This treasure- have your guessed? Is friendship -
Expression of the Golden Rule.
How far the ripples on the pool
May spread to other's lives we cannot know.
Just try to make the world a better place
Through the kindness that we show.
—*Dorothy Kolbe*

My Size

My wedding was going to be a beaut
Can't see the groom now, bad luck, as
Carroll practiced his flute
It was tomorrow and Mollex had made my dress
But when I put it on it was one size too small--a mess

And so I entered swimming contest, found
a swimsuit out of this world
One size too small, No win for this girl

Bought a pair of shoes- happy as a lark
That's O.K. It's fine. Now the race can start
Pulled them on said I won't fall
But it's not that easy for they were
One size too small
—*Leola Caldwell Gardner*

Native Fields

Mine eyes have seen early morning mist shining silvery over Carolina fields, billowing banks of moisture-laden fog clinging tenaciously to low hollows yet to be rained upon the earth below A promise of mystery and treasure beneath its wispery folds, of gently rolling slopes broken by furrows bearing life-yielding green. And specter woods with muted symphonies of night creatures and morning risers passing before dawn's rays. Silver and jade rising before a border of lusty, turquoise-streaked forest; limitless into the far reaches of the horizon. Barefoot youth, king of all he surveyed with his eyes and heart Pride swelling within his chest, dirt upon his hands and trousers. With a cleanliness and peacefulness surrounding his soul. Mine eyes have seen a downtrodden nameless face shuffling down endless streets windswepted by icy winds of scorn and rage, lost in a maze more bewildering than native fields, streams and woodlands. Seeking haven and identity in taverns along the wayside, with the solace of another drink its only reward. Seeking a friendly face, a kind smile, afraid to be alone within himself. The coldness within his breast deepening with each passing stranger,
—*William Dail*

"Awaiting"

Take me, reside in my body and soul
Carry me with you wherever you may go.

Feel the warmth, see the glow
O' how you've filled my heart and my soul.

Love me forever, I'll leave you never
For you are the one who makes it all possible.
Without you this world would not be.
So hear my thanks and feel my faith
and help me to take my life and make it the best it can be.

You are our Father, the daddy of all
So guide us O' Lord as we await your call.

Help us not to be foolish
so that you might see us stumble and fall,
But to be wise in our judgements
so that you may be proud of us all.

So hear my prayer Father, and be with us in our dreams tonight
So come morning we'll feel your presence
in the warmth of the sunlight.

Take me, reside in my body and soul
So that I might carry you through the day wherever I may go.
—*Judy E. Wood*

Untitled

I've always wanted to have my name scribbled on a wall,
Carved in wood, etched in stone.
I've always wanted to hear my name whispered
Breathlessly by a lover, screamed out in rage
By one I've angered, spoken softly by one in need.
I've always wanted my name to be held sacred
By those who know me, cherished by those who care,
Respected by those I leave behind.
I've always wanted a name,
But no one ever thought to really name me,
They just call me Jane.
—*Jane Green*

How Can I Find The Words?

How can I find the words to let you know just how I feel?
  'cause every time you come by, I want to make it real.

    The joy I have inside, whenever you are there.
    Lifts me up inside, but now it's just not fair.

      Knowing that you will go away,
        hurts me more everyday.

        If only I could say it right,
        I would then give up this fight.

          Maybe not, right away,
        but I'll keep hopes up, for some other day.
—*Christy Sawaya*

The Ballad Of Massacre Bay

On this island of tundra we live out each day
  'Cause there's work to be done
At Massacre Bay.
Early each morn we go to the docks,
  Where the sea slaps the boards
And the shuttle boat rocks.
The Bering is rough and ships by-pass our isle,
  They have to miss Shemya by many a mile.
From Shemya to Attu we bounce on our way
  Like a cork on the sea,
To Massacre Bay.
We work on the shores where heroes have died,
  We're young and we're lonesome, our spirits are tried,
But there's work to be done
At Massacre Bay.
—*Charles E. Grooms*

Our World Today

Adam and Eve, two of God's first creations, the forbidden fruit causing the world's ruination. A new world began thanks to Noah and his ark. Two of every kind always together never apart. This destructive new world is very sad I must say, for once a mistake is made there is always a price to pay. Unabiding our ten commandments, we became our ownself destruction. Murder, theft, rape always the same repercussion. Honoring thy mother and father, such a rare form of respect. Incest, domestic violence, how is a family to connect. In life we can no longer consider money as a necessity. Illegal minds, with no self respect in hope to find a destiny. Pain, sickness, death, they often call this hell on earth. What a shameful sin a child must be diseased at their birth. These punishments we now suffer does not seem very fair. For God's first two creations felt they didn't have to care. It's all because of that apple we live in this destructive world of today. Just remember you'll always have God, and make it a point to always pray.
—*Angela Giacone*

For Gazelle Boy, Chameleon Wonder

I close my eyes think of you,
  chameleon wonder chime the tower
Bellow! you'll get there and the whole
  thing will rock carillion mad the whole
Think will rock a whispered sigh,
  sweet like the salt of the sea,
Sweet like the boughs of a tree, slippery
  green as the chameleon I've seen.

A thought, now thinking, expands
  in your making—a body crystal glowing
Rhythm, the glory of your promise,
  the light of your creation.
Don't be blinded by the light you reward,
  it flows without your touch,
It sings without your voice.

We close our eyes in see with you.
—*Sally Swartz*

You Came Into My Life

You came into my life so weak and so small. You weren't the child I had prayed for at all. You were oh so much more. The moment I saw you my heart just flew. Then my heart went thump when they said it was true. An extra chromosome, how unlucky for you. Trisomy 21, an odd name for such a little one. At first I was frightened, unsure of myself. Where to go, who to see, oh God please guide me. Your eyes were to be brown, just like your dad's. God made them blue, but he wasn't sad. You were here; he was so glad. Those blues held a twinkle, and your ears had a crinkle. I checked your body for every little wrinkle. Your lips were like rosebuds, so beautifully defined. They were soft and pink, you sweet child of mine. A tiny space between your toes. And a single crease your left hand knows. I hold you closely while you're sleeping and breathe in your breath. Your face is so peaceful, no stress, just happiness. What child is this God has blessed unto me? My son William, you are my miracle, my angel. Thank you God for giving him to me.
—*Stella H. Fellinger*

A Child's Loss

You look down at me as if to say,
"Child, what are you thinking?"
While slowly, some of my hopes and dreams
have suddenly started sinking
You think you can try to help me to
understand this horrible mess,
but you can no longer do that,
for he no longer stands.
You thought your life was so fulfilled
like a young girl's in a book
my life was too fulfilled, 'til the
angels came and took.
They took a valuable thing of mine,
a figure I called Dad
for I could not say anything except how
mournful I was, and sad.
A child's loss is surely like something
you'll never know,
for a child's loss, unfortunately, is what
it takes for some to grow.
—*Andrea Nutter*

The Real World

As I walk across the stage to enter the real world, I see my
childhood wave me goodbye and my adulthood waves hello.

As I reach for my diploma with my left hand and shake with the
right, I see the real world come into sight.

When the hugs and laughter are gone and everyone disappears,
I take a whole new step into life, choking back my fears.

When the cap and gown are hung again, a family, career and love
in the real world I will begin.
—*Andi Clark*

Oceans

Sea gulls, soaring high above my head,.
chirping happily as they move to their destination.

Waves rolling in and out,
crashing loudly against the rocks.

With the scorching sun beating down on my head,
I move into the water.

Smells of salt water
occupy the air.

Off in the distance,
I see a sailboat,
slowly moving across the blanket of water,
sending waves rippling away.
—*Nicole Crane*

Spin A Word

Words, words in my head
Choose the correct one as it fled
Do it quickly for I dread
An unspoken word I should have said.

Dreams, dreams in the night
Write them down before it's light
If the sun becomes too bright
Those distant dreams may lose their sight.

Songs, songs on my tongue
Sing the melody 'til it's sung
Don't give up until you've won
The words, the dreams, the songs we've spun.
—*Megan Hagen*

Joseph

For this particular February day was not filled with riots or
  civil wars or tax increases forewarned,
It was a day of joy, peace and nurturing — This was the day
  my first child was born;

There would be no more searching or questions needing answers
My ground was solid and the meaning was clear,
For life begins and life must end — and in between is simply
  what is given to us and what we give from there;

Do not fear when I am no longer with you or sad and grieve for
  me — my beautiful son,
Because my teachings you carry in your heart and mind, and
I am a part of soul — So see, through you, I will always be
  alive and my legacy shall live on.
—*Fran Matty*

"Orion And I"

Orion... The Hunter, and I, both men of honor. Savage yet civilized. Him, watching over the world from his celestial perch, forever frozen in his pose to strike. And I, watching over the world from this mortal ground, forever bound by oath to strike. Orion, like myself are guardians of the masses by night, yet obscure, and un-noticed by day. Hero's never seen. I think the closest thing between us that we, as men, have taken our sworn duty to be our life. Men of commitment, and solitude. Until today. For I have found something that could only make my commitment seem more meaningful than I ever dreamed, and that is love. As I basked in the happiness of having you in my arms I looked up and saw Orion. Ever present, ever faithful, ever alone. For I have deserted him. And I mourned of his loneliness. In his honor, as my gift to him I showed the woman, the bearer of my happiness, this great guardian of man-kind. He, shall forever be mine and my beloved common bond while we are apart. So that, he too may hear the whisper of wishes, from a woman's heart. And know the feeling of companionship.
—*Robert K. Light II*

The Last Night

Mountains floating through the sky.
Clouds lay across the ground.
The barking of birds.
The mooing of cats.
It all seemed so normal at the time.
Flesh against flesh.
Lip against lip.
Skin could be so soft.
The hair could be so smooth.
Blood rushing through my veins.
The warmth of the night sings with laughter.
The blood-shattering sound of voices
Shot through the air.
Like a murder, or should I say suicide.
The round white pills dropping into my mouth.
Then the blood stops and the black flashes.
It is over, the last night is here.
—*Steffanie Graham*

Innocents

Eyes of blue, curls of gold.
"Come eat your soup, it's growing cold."
Dark eyes sunk in a tiny face.
No food awaits, no drink, no grace.

Shattered limbs, hanging, bleeding.
Mother's arms outstretched, pleading.
Crying children how can we
Bequeath to you such misery?

Warlords, presidents, poets, priests,
Can't we at the very least,
Sacrifice greed,
For lasting peace.

Dry the tears on each tiny face.
Return childhood to it's rightful place.
Or divide and conquer, then to our sorrow,
Innocence won't live in our near tomorrow.
—*Jessica Whittaker*

Dreams

Dreams are rattled and twisted. Serpents
come with sapphire eyes ready to hypnotize
and pursue you to lead you to the Devil.
The Devil is the sorcerer of scarlet evil
ready to scar you with a sickle just to
remind you where you are and why you are
being punished, (to some rewarded). The
Devil would say, "slaves obey your master
with fear and trembling; and do it with a
sincere heart." God would look down on the
Devil and say "masters behave in the same
way toward your slaves and stop using
threats." The devil just laughed.
You wake up, you feel a pain, you see the scar,
every time you close your eyes you see him, Satan,
and you know you'll never be free.

—*Laura Ann Woodruff*

To My Son, With Love

I started to love you my dear son Right from the moment I
conceived you From that moment on, you transformed my
heart, my feelings and my life... Especially at the first
time I felt you moving inside me I laughed, I cried with so
much joy and excitement And, in that particular moment, I
let my hands follow you, to feel you to live and to
experience the most beautiful moment of my life the miracle
of life and love. I gave you life and love And in
return...you gave me joy and hope A world full of
laughter...sometimes tears But I understand my dear son
that life, laughs and love... Always come with tears. I
love you just the way your are my dear son You are my
sunshine and my pride Be always honest to yourself and have
compassion with the less fortunate respect yourself and
others Do good...love God and seek His presence When you do
wrong...learn from your mistakes Read good books, plant a
tree, observe nature Be kind to life and live your
spiritual life. I love You So Much My Son

—*Gabriela Freitas*

A Toast

Peace pipes singlehandedly declare war
Confrontations a beaten drum skin
My will has submitted; my soul has refuted
The life of the animal dead
Echoes so ancient cause present friction
While she slowly dies, my demise occurs within
Involuntarily, her heart slows to a standstill
Yet in voluntary fashion they kill themselves
Invitations chosen, handpicked at their request
No longer submission, thoughts battle brains
So minute and clouded by mayhem's virtue
Humility to seek, peace the victor
Four months to heal this bludgeoned wound
That the past five years have salted
Weep for them, there are many like them
Darkness gives way to dawn
   My "friends" wake up deluded.

—*Brian M. Spradlin*

The Warriors

An intensity unmatched
compounded by pure desire untamed
for lays my silent screams of an intensified rage

A rage which puts me on a mission of a higher purpose
To excel and succeed above the rest
And that is why
I must test my limits
and execute my best.

—*Leonard Falcone*

Untitled

Shadows fall all around my world.
Cool winds blow through the mountains of my mind.
The valleys of the day and the peaks of the moment
filter through my memory.
A sixth sense is developed through his presence,
ultimate awareness.
Sensual weight warms my body with the unseen traveling
in my mind.
Clouds filter the sunlight of my future, yet allowing
the skin to be bronzed.

—*Camille A. Sloan*

The Nineteen Thirties

The nineteen thirties were days to hang on
Coolidge and Hoover were soon long gone
The market hit bottom - along with our cash
From New York to here - you could hear the banks crash
Farmers lost land to tax foreclosure
Work hard and pray - you were sure to endure

A pension for soldiers - came through just in time
We sure needed cash - a buck or a dime
For some there was welfare - Federal jobs or food dole
Roosevelt was the saviour - he assumed the God role
Providing old age pension and social security
A dream for the future - more love and more piety

Poor health was a problem - mom cured with home remedy
Mustard plaster for chest colds - lots of rest was the key
Midwives and nurses served at farm birthing
Doctors made house calls - be it winter or spring
We became a world power - ending Hitler's oppression
We modeled capitalism - having escaped the depression

—*George M. Curtis*

"Blame It on Me"

Dear God, I have a problem of the heart,
could you please listen to me, while I tear myself apart.

Help me through this awful mess,
one I created myself I guess.

I'm falling for this guy, who's really sweet,
the most perfect man, you'd want me to meet.

He's tall and gentle too, he's a saint sent from you,
he wears his halo, and his little wings too.

I didn't plan it, I didn't want it this way,
but I can't help myself, I see him everyday.

This man is not to blame, the blame is all on me,
he's just very special, he's as kind as can be.

The problem is, he doesn't even know that I care,
I guess I resent him, just because he's there.

He doesn't know, he's on my mind all the time,
he's not aware, that he controls my mind.

I know I shouldn't feel, the way that I do,
because I belong to someone else, and so do you.

God there must have been a reason, that you wanted us to meet,
my only question is, did you have to make him so darn sweet?

—*Pamela Rhoades*

Pop

When I danced with my son at my niece's wedding at his
cousin's joining Unexpected reflections bubbled up in my mind,
like spaghetti sauce does on simmer, little round orbs coming
up to the top of the kettle, exploding.
POP you are the same height as your father with whom I danced
for 30 years. POP my ex-brother-in-law sits at that far table
my brother for 23 years. POP my sister's present husband and
mine appear here with no history.
POP married forever couples, some caught in commitments
attended our weddings, years ago. POP the pop-pop of the
photographer's flash catches the comely bride and groom:
with her real parents with her real Dad and his wife with
her real Mom and her husband, POP with his real parents with
his real Mom and her husband. POP the newlyweds stand in each
photo, filled with expectations, just as their parents had.
POP in the misty future - may they smile, dance and be
photographed together at their children's weddings.
May It Not Go —— POP
 —*Patricia Riley*

Declining/Inclining

Aging, such a furtive state
Creaking in so slyly hardly anyone notices

Masking with a benign smile the withering senses
Wistfully foraging for a place to rest
To wait out the wintery scene
While drooling mosaic patterns on the coverlet

Saying what did you say till it hurts
Hearing what was never said

Not remembering today
Vividly recalling yesterday

Numbers so perplexing
Still counting every hazy sin

Seeing through a mist
Seeing what was never seen

Muscles flaccid, grip so soft
Touching what was never touched

Feeling poorly
Feeling what was never felt

Weak and slowing
wise and knowing
 —*John J. McKenna*

"Honorary Men"

57,939 they said
Crossed the line to dead -
Now, against a nightblack wall,
The names of Honorary Men
To be remembered by all -

Who amongst us can hear
The silent valediction -
Does it speak of:
Liberty - Duty - Conviction -

Or is bitterness and deep hatred the tone,
For lives given to a war uncondoned -
"Oh, God! It is a fearful thing
to see the human soul take wing"
 —*C. Headley*

The Door To Life

Birth, the first step in my life;
crying, my first sensation.
fantasy, my first thought, it grew with me.
I remember how it began,
opening slowly as a flower
waiting for the right moment to come out
petal to petal,
until it finally showed in all its splendor,
and was admired by everyone.
"Can we really fly, mommy,
and enter the other side of the mirror?"
"Is it true the fairies love children
and that unicorns exist?"
As I grew up, I remember how it
suddenly died away.
"What a riot! Do you really believe in fairies?"
This was an awful time to grow into an adult.
Wrinkles appeared in the flowers,
Until fantasy didn't exist,
and the flower fell from the tree.
 —*Marimar Rosario*

The Freedom Bell Rings

The freedom bell will never stop ringing, as long as someone is crying to be free. Men, women and children wait in lines with all their belongings for an opportunity to go. Leaving their country, their past and loves ones behind. In their hearts they hear the sound of the freedom bell ringing Dreaming about the money they will earn and good food they will eat. Some are praying that God will help them. It was the same freedom bell that rang in the past for our forefathers. They came with their belongings and dreams that day. The old timers came with pride and thanksgiving. They worked and sweated with their tears. They fought to keep our rights and freedom bright. They came today and yesterday with worries and fears. Will these new marchers keep hearing the freedom bell ring. Will they give back to our country their skills and learn new ways. Some came without dreams, and some without faith in their hearts. Will the freedom bell always ring in the dreams of the new marchers. I bowed my head and closed my eyes with tears. God, please keep that freedom bell ringing in our hearts. Ringing for ever in our land of freedom.
 —*Patricia H. Wallace*

A Country Autumn

A kaleidoscope of trees like fluffy feathers gracefully
 curtsying to and fro,

Within the shelter of the mountains they dance just so.

Not a single one haphazardly placed against the sky of blue,

Crowned in scarlets, bronze and tangerine, mauve and shades
 of amber too.

Wisps of clouds adorning the mountain tops coyly playing
 hide-n-seek with the sun,

Dispersed in an instant by the sparkle of bright light whose
 splendor kisses the leaves one by one.

Bunched together like bouquets of living jewels by the
 Creator for our rapture,

Vibrant with a life not a photograph or painting could ever
 fully capture.

Their awesome beauty compels you to draw in your breath with
 an unconscious sigh,

As you wipe away a grateful tear and regretfully bid the
 season goodbye.
 —*Charlene Swan*

The Ongoing Legacy

Theodicy theism, the basic equator of justice and peace, we
daily defy, herewith, excessive interest, taxes, fuel costs and
deficits continue multiply. Evolutions of terrorism, dictator-
ship and deprivation an evinced diverse,

Obnoxious inhuman denial of minorities, their rights and
equality now worse. Nonviable citizenship; circumvented, thus,
increasing native pain and strife, grotesque legislation
initiated repeatedly, and disregard for human life.
Occultism astounds, while church and state rights continue in
open debate, immunity from democratic justice, public elected
officials demonstrate. Nuclear annihilation of humanity
encouraged by leaders of super powers; generations yet unborn,
their hopes and future diminish by the hours.

Limitless evasion of urgent issues, which effects this and
every nation, embellishment of untrue leadership and promises,
an ongoing claimation. Guardian of the people, tho, by the
people, countless politicians neglect, alleging honesty while
campaigning, such claims remain unproven yet. Cajolery rampant
The Ongoing Legacy of deceit uncontrolled so abound, Ye voters,
the true government, resuscitate and cancel the unjust confound.
—*Oscar C. Walker*

Serenity

There's a field of flowers at your foot
dancing with the wind.
I can smell your sweetness with a hint a dew.
You give me comfort and a place to rest.
Your outstretched arms help me to relax and keep cool.
Your strength ever enduring and your beauty increases with age.
Sleep for a time,
then dress up for all the world to see.
Ah yes you are,
all the grace and beauty of a great oak tree!
—*Maureen L.R. Bloesch*

The Darkness Behind

Standing in a rainstorm,
Darkness falls behind,
While a sweet melody races through my mind.
All thoughts linger in the air,
Like an oncoming stranger passing fair.
For in the distance, I see a fading light,
And shadowy figure embedded in soft white.
It slowly gets brighter, and then fades away,
and from then on I wonder from day to day.
What is my purpose on this withering plain,
and why do the heavens bring forth the rain?
I'm a seeker of truth, and I'll soon come to find,
that my happiness lies in the darkness behind.
—*LaDonna Dockery*

Alone

I am alone, witnessing the birth of this day.
  Dawn is born silent.

Rosey golden child with time, her godmother,
  looks at me with her new eyes.

Sipping from a red crystal glass, I nurse you
  along with my thoughts.

Come new day,
  take first small steps to the encouragement
  of morning birds.

Walk with me, my new born day and I shall no longer be
  alone.
—*Pamela J. Gore*

My Prayer As I Live

As I live my life day by day,
Dear Lord, hear the words that I pray.
As I put one foot in front of the other
Don't let me step on a sister or brother.
As I eat food you supply for me,
Don't let me take from those in need.
As sinners my path does cross
Let me speak your truth to the lost.
May my goal in life always be
To think of others before I think of me.
Lord, I know that's what you would do.
I pray each day to become more like you.
—*Candice Giles*

Suicide

"A razor slashed over your wrists,
Death coming to your door with a fatal kiss,
Pills in your body clogging up your heart,
Suffocating yourself so your heartbeat won't start,
A pull of a trigger from a killer gun,
Or a knife pierced in your chest will surely get you done,
Keep in mind, if suicide stabs you in the back,
The one thing you'll be sure of,
Is life is what you'll lack!"
—*Rebecca L. Gale*

Heidi

On the most beautiful day and the brightest of morn, the angels
decided that you would be born. They took two stars from the
skies, and gave them to you for your eyes. The red rose they
took the color, for your lips only and no other. They molded a
cute and tiny nose, ten little fingers and ten little toes. I
could not believe the very first time, when I saw you that you
were all mine. You are growing up now and I want to say, how
proud I am of you on this day. In the twelve years that have
past, have gone for me a little too fast. We will always have a
love for each other, just as it should be between daughter and
mother. You must grow, learn, and even leave home in time, but
right now I know that you are still mine. You will forever in my
heart be part of my life, even the day when you become a wife. I
will hug you and give you a kiss every day, and there is just
one more thing I wanted to say. I love you- and Happy Birthday
—*Patricia Rubera*

How Love Can Last

Love that will last,
  depends on things that have happened in the past.

It includes the vows we once took,
  when we laid our hands on the Good Book.

It is the difficult times that we had,
  the comfort we gave each other when we were sad.

The children that you bore
  a blessing that makes no love poor.

As we live longer,
  our love can only grow stronger,

If we continue to realize,
  that love is based on compromise,

And no matter how stormy loves weather,
  we will make it, if we brave it together.

Dearest, we can ask for no more,
  than an eternal key to our loves store.

So that, from time to time, we may take inventory
  of all the things that make up our love story.
—*Kenneth E. Spann*

Silent Sojourn

Endless miles of pavement stretches before me. Hallow, deserted farmhouses bid farewell. Through dust covered windows few people are seen upon the rolling hills of green. Skeleton houses haunt us of the past; when thousands had to sell. Years passed and too, once an apprentice had to sell. Smiles and cheers were all the customer was to hear. Existing in motels my life seemed to be a sojourn to hell. Hours, days, and weeks passed with growing despair; you were not there. Shaving my scarred face I saw death. Piece by simple piece my work sold me off. At home time seemed to cease through my ear, our thoughts indulged in time your breath. Shaking the wooden headboard I would leave again with my sweat-stained hat held aloft. To a town long forgotten by most; me and my wares went. Silence grew to a loud clatter in my brain. Holding in my hand was your ring; polished until all my tears were spent. Sleep helped me relax as an old muddy side road took me to our first good-bye in the rain. Castles on air was my promise to you. For your birthday the only comfort I could afford was a worn copy of a song, The Piano Man. My silent sojourn through this world brings me sadness of every tragic hue.

—*Jim Springer*

Running

Feel the mist in your eyes...touch the cool ground that you devour in your quest...hear the sound of the brisk wind that soothes your rage... breath the fear you say does not exist... taste the fog that clogs your sight...listen to the trees scream to you...see the dark sky hover victoriously over you... think of your tragedy...sense the eyes watching your every motion...run, with your all...never to stop and look back at your past. Run.

—*Curtis Campbell*

Now I Know

Sometimes I wonder why I left home
Did it to be on my own
Many times I've wanted to leave
Just to be with my family
But if I did that then I wouldn't be home
Since your home is mine no more

It hurts me sometime everyday
That's how much I miss you
Just glad you can't see me now
Writing this has put tears in my eyes

I've never tried hard my whole life
Now I wish that I had
Always said I understood what you were saying
Now we know I didn't and I'm paying

I never realized how much you knew
And everything you said turned out to be true

I just wanted to thank you for all you've done
You know that I'll always love you

—*Stuart Schwartz*

Special Friend

You were like a sister to me;
You are very special don't you see;
Through the years we had our fights;
But don't worry, everything will be alright;
I can't write poetry very well;
But I had to tell you how I feel;
Somehow you always knew;
When I was feeling down and blue;
I have had other friends in the past;
But this is one friendship
I know will last.

—*Mary Thorn*

Death Inspired By Death

Creeping slowly up my flesh
did this emotion venture.
Its idealism still laid fresh,
and it lingered for some tenure.
Though it lay in my mind at ease.
I could not help but cry
Jealous rage could all but freeze.
Tears that flow from my eyes.
The epoch of such a breeding trepidation.
I could only estimate.
Seal of vows now broken,
have speeded its inception with hate.
Though breeding fiercely, this silent creature,
did torpidly move in my head.
It dawelled there for many hours,
until I could, inspire its death.
I pondered long for numerous hours.
until conclusively I discovered a course.
An action taken, to free the rage,
on an innocent, helpless source.

—*Joel Martin Smith*

Dirt

Dirt, whether it be earth, soil, dust or mud
Dirt is neither good nor bad
Dirt is home
Home to the worms
Home to the dead
Dirt is the base of life
Dirt is the end of life
Dirt can be soiling
Or it can be cleansing
Dirt is trampled upon and
Dirt is worshipped
And this is how I view poetry, as dirt

—*Robert Abraham Wylder Stevens*

Freedom

Not many people can understand the I face.
Discrimination is a large motivator of hate and violence.
Hate destroys mind and violence destroys body.
When will the world understand that without mind and body, we cannot exist!!!
The only thing we can do is to not question what other people are.
Not try to destroy people just because they are different.
Try to exist without violence, hate and fear.
Maybe then, we can try for peace!

—*Lyle Eric Johnson*

Elusive Truth

Truth is a unicorn standing among the white mares.
Distinguishable by the singular horn,
He wanders the pasture.
He looks so much like the others around him,
Yet he is clearly different and special.
He doesn't hide from you,
Yet you search far and near.
You mistake others for him
Until confusion overcomes you and you lay alone and hurt.
This unicorn stands with pleading eyes, crying out,
"Why don't you see me? I am right here!"
Truth is a unicorn standing among the white mares.
Recognized by some who stare unbelieving, thinking,
"This cannot be."
So, because of their disbelief, they make excuses and distort
All they have seen.
For we often cannot believe in something so hard to understand,
So very unlike ourselves.
However, truth remains,
So clearly different and special.
—*Bethany Hawkinson*

Dad

Many people do without thinking, many people think, but never
do. I know a man who's thinking helped me learn to think and
do. Once he had said to me, "Think Before You Act."
Now my brain's a thinker and I have it paying me back.
Another time he said to me, "Do What You Know Is Right."
Now (usually) I do my chores on time, instead of at night.
Then again I heard him say, "Be Thankful For What You Have."
Now I try, come what may, in all cases to be glad.
Still again he said to me, "Knowledge Is Power."
Since that day I've always read. Over my old self I tower.
Later on again he told me, and I found it true,
"The Whole Picture Is What You'd See." One time I proved I
knew. That doesn't count all the rest that there will always be; "It
Only Matters You Do Your Best." And "Budget Your Time
Wisely." There's always, "Be Considerate." And "Money Doesn't
Grow On Trees." Along with, "Work Smart, Not Hard" And
"Nothing Good Comes With Ease."

I know that I've been raised the best I ever could.
This man, my dad, he should be praised for raising me the way
he should.
—*Suzanne Cafasso*

"Love The World Away"

When you close your eyes at night, do you ever dream about me?
Do you ever stop to wonder, just how sweet it could be?
If we were together forever, until the end of time.
So take me by my hand, and say that you'll always be mine.
For tomorrow is a new day, and I'll love you just the same.
And I promise you from the heart, there will never be anyone
   who could ever take your place.
Memories of you have come and gone.
But still our love remains the same.
And all I can do is dream of you and love the world away.
So now that my life has come to pass.
Let me hold you just one last time.
To say the words that you've loved to hear, the words that
   sound so divine.
They're the words that have guided you and protected you from
   the storm.
And even now, in the after life, they're the words that I'll
   be saying to you from now on.
—*Jim Moore*

Should I Ask

Should I ask you,
Do you have the answer?
Why am I so scared to be held in your arms?
Why am I afraid to be called only yours?

Should I ask you,
Do you have the answer?
Why am I afraid of feeling your love?
Why am I afraid of you?

Should I ask you,
Do you have the answer?
Why is true love so hard to find?
Why is it so hard to keep it between us?

Should I ask you,
Do you have the answer?
One day will you break my heart?
One day will you leave me all alone?

Will you ask me,
Will I have the answer?
One day will I do the same to you?
—*Maria Kachel*

For Tyler

Little boy with eyes so blue,
Do you know what Grandma thinks of you?
She thinks a miracle was born
All baby soft and cuddly warm.
Grandma's joy and Grandpa's pride
All our fondest dreams inside
One little fellow; innocent child
With a loving heart and an impish smile!
Little hands reach out for me
And melt my heart immediately!
A little hug; a sticky kiss,
A Grandma's world is made of this!
So much to see, a world to explore...
Curiosity opens every door.
Treat him kindly, world, please do!
He's placed his childish trust in you!
Little boy, as years go by...
The days of childhood quickly fly...
Remember when we're far apart,
You're cherished here in Grandma's heart!
—*Isabel Rohrbaugh*

Love

Love. What does it mean?
Does it mean watching when you go by?
What does it mean?
Does it mean butterflies in your stomach?
Love. What does it mean?
Does it mean a really intense feeling?
What does it mean?
Does it mean your heart beating faster?
Love. What does it mean?
Does it mean always thinking of you?
What does it mean?
Does it mean feeling soft and tender?
Love. What does it mean?
I've searched far and wide and the best answer
I've found by far is you, and All of the above!!!!
—*J. Abbott*

Poem - Dream

Think of a funny, clumsy, weird looking wimp,
Dream erotically launching a fantastic sunset.
Don't think death, weapons, sacrifice,
Think beauty, just think.
—*Louquel Butler*

Distant Dreams

Oh blessed peace where ne'r I tread, yet there in distant dreams
Thou speaks to me through shaded thoughts, and restless tattered sleeps
Bloodless hands and heartless mouths pry loose that last dying hope
And yet in desperate cries I scream, relieve my captured soul
Oh love, sweet love, the very fragrance of life
Sweet rose surrounded by thorns
How do I reach inside for the plum,
When attempts have left me lifeless and torn
I wrestle with waiting tomorrows, fearing a repeat of disappointing todays
The air filled with mock understanding, endless smiles never meaning what they say
An abundance of taunt skin and loose minds, holding conversations spoken in cliches
And my tormentors, dressed as suitors, crushing dreams, then begging to stay
Where is that peace that plays in my head, and a love without thoughts to betray.
Still there, stranded as silent wishing in dreams yet too far away
—*Wanda White*

The Death Of Mother Nature

Walking into the future, I see her grave.
Dried, dead, long-stem roses lay upon the mound of newly-shoveled earth,
That is where she lies.
The sound of mourning is in the air,
As we blame and point fingers at each other.

She died a slow, painful, embarrassing death,
Now she's a part of what she tried to fix.
She told us what we were doing wrong, but we did not listen.
She explained our mistakes, but we did not care.

We have killed her,
We must pay the consequence for this murder,
How could we do such a thing,
To such an innocent, beautiful, caring creature?
Are we cold-blooded, cold-hearted, numb feeling cannibals?,
She was our last chance of hope.

We can not live without her,
No more changing seasons, no more sun rises,
No more night falls.
She was responsible for life, love and the pursue of
Happiness, now our future holds what hers does.
—*Danyele Burton*

Jesus Is Right

Jesus is right
And Jesus is the light
Just say no to drugs and yes to Jesus
Jesus was born King of the Jews
Yes, Jesus is the one to choose
Just say no to drugs, and yes to Jesus
  Jesus is love,
And Jesus is sitting on the right hand of his father above,
Just say no to drugs and yes to Jesus.
—*Evelyn Brown*

A Kiss Good-bye

I am engulfed by an ocean of loneliness and isolation
Drowning in a river of tears
And as I cry out for you, you are nowhere to be found.

I look to the sky to seek warmth from the sun
But only clouds lurk there and the wind taunts me
As it whips cold blades of rain down upon my face.

Darkness invades the sky and the man in the moon
Laughs at me from above as I fall into a restless sleep.

I have a dream about love
It is a mirage of the friendship we once shared.
I hear laughter and see two people, you and I
Chasing our hopes and dreams hand in hand
Through a world illuminated by the perfect sun
Shielding us from the destruction of emptiness.

But I am afraid as I begin to awaken.
I slip away from you as I watch the sun set one last time for us
You cry for understanding and your single tear of pure love
falls upon my lips.

As I open my eyes I realize that you are gone forever.
But I will never forget your saltwater kiss good-bye.
—*Christie Lowmaster*

I Am Honored

I have carried a spear across this great stage in many theaters during my assignments. Tonight, I pass it on to whom-so-ever may search for high adventure. Also tonight, I have been offered the opportunity to speak, to say something significant in a matter of a few moments. I am reminded of the old pirate, Captain Jas. Hook, in Peter Pan. At every opportunity offered, he would start telling his life story. He believed that if he waited too long, he would not have time, when the time came, to say it all. He could hear the alligator going 'click' 'click' 'click'! He believed also, that any deed, no matter how foul, was made appropriate and acceptable, if done in good form. Now that I have a chance to say part of my speech, I will forbear and speak only to what I have found important. The Academy has provided to each of us opportunities that otherwise we would have been denied. Opportunities to serve in the traditions first established by mariner heros in ancient times while in search of adventure, and who forged the very foundations of all civilizations with commerce. Each of us, the friends, the supporters, the graduates of Kings Point, can be proud of our parts we have played in continuing this great tradition.
—*Douglas Echols*

Untitled

If I were to climb a mountain
And look down from the top
I'd see nature everywhere
All beautiful green, blue, white
The colors so perfect
How could anyone destroy this?
I ask myself and shake my head.
The earth is scarred with our carelessness.
And I'm left on the mountain top all by myself.
—*Karla McNeese*

I Tend To Wonder

The first time I met you I knew you were different.
I knew the time we spent together would be cherished
in our hearts forever.
Now when I look back on all the things we said and did.
I tend to wonder just what might have happened had we not met
Would we be the same or would we feel as if something
were missing.
—*Paula Janelle Pierce*

Retirement: Pros and Cons

R estful peace can fill a day.
E nduring friendships come full cycle.
T ime stands still for birds and sunsets.
I dleness is a delicious pastime.
R eclaiming hobbies excites the psyche.
E nergy rushes forth to help.
M aking new friends becomes second nature.
E lation comes from planning trips.
N othing keeps you tied to home.
T omorrow is a new adventure!

R ationalizing daily boredom becomes a challenge.
E ndless nights fill the bedroom.
T ime flashes by and drags its feet behind.
I nsecurity tugs at consciousness.
R eality creeps in to tell your fortune.
E veryday is a treasure to keep, not spend.
Memories are your best friends.
E nergy becomes a memory.
N ature reminds you of your mortality.
T omorrow becomes a goal!

—*Mary Lee Jackson*

"That's The Poet She Sees In Him"

He sits down at his patio
Each day he writes away
Book after book he reads
Confines oneself to his room
She knows one fine day
Soon he will bloom
All the poetry he writes
Did not come to him over night
It took many lovely nights
Alone but not in any painful way
As long as he has a pen
THAT'S THE POET SHE SEES IN HIM

Happy oh, so happy to state she is just a friend
But this friend has a crush on him and I know she
thinks the world of him No way will she break away
From the one who confines himself to his pen
THAT'S THE POET SHE SEES IN HIM

Yes, he thinks it's better this way as he will
happily write away. Until his last breath
That's the poet she sees in him

—*Christopher Yanez*

Searching-An Epistle

My Love,
   each day is not complete and the sun refuses to shine my way
   a void of darkness is all that reigns
The serpent coils itself
   around all that is mine, which is only myself
   and separates me from the other half of myself,
   you
My sole desire is
   to crush the walls of this labyrinth,
   that keep me from you, every corner I turn
I feel brings me closer, yet it only pushes me
   further away, I am
   lost
Still, I hold the
   thought of you close to me, and I will
   find my way to you, through the hellish
   catacombs which life leads us through, and
   you, you are my
   destination.

—*Megan Hartey*

Untitled

I can remember his face so worn out by time.
Each wrinkle a memory or scar of some kind.
His eyes were so blue, with a story to tell;
   of some far away place that he might have once dwelled.
His hair was so white, so pure that it seemed, from a distance
   a halo that was earned and esteemed.
I found the courage to approach this old man,
   to offer a coffee or just a helping hand.
"Beware!", he did warn, as I came close to him.
"I am an image in your mind", he said with a grin.
I reached out my hand to show that I cared.
He had no hand to return, just a look of despair.
I turned away quickly, leaving his side; walked back to my car
   and started to cry.
I drove off in silence, I turned away, from that image in my
   mind that still lives today.

—*Elizabeth Soto*

"Memories"

Memories are heartbeats sounding through the years,
Echoes never failing of our smiles and tears,
Moments that are captured sometimes unaware,
Pictures in an album or a lock of hair.

Images that linger deep within the mind,
Bits of verse we cherished once upon a time.

Through the musty hallways of the days we knew,
Ever comes the vision beautiful and true.

Memories are roses blooming evermore,
Full of fragrant sweetness never known before.

Life must have a reason goals for which to strive,
Memories are lights that burn ... to keep the heart alive.

—*Bridget K. Sinko*

Echoes

The swings blow gently in the autumn breeze
   echoes of their laughter-still music in the trees.
Patches of grass—worn thin by their play—
   the sandbox-abandoned from their yesterday.
Memories still fragrant—past moments still now—
   as I sit here beneath the shading elm's bough.
I recall cherished hours—treasures in my mind—
   and each one I savor-my own special find.
I remember the dandelion—their flower to me—
   the open doors, the leaking pool, the scraped elbow and knee
I cherish not the big events-recorded in a book—
   but rather-floating melodies of a hug, a smile, a look.
The giving job of parenting-the hardest there can be—
   Yet, was it I who gave to my children
   or my children who gave to me?

—*Maureen Alioto*

Daydreams

Daydreams daydreams that's all I ever do
Ever since you left me I can't get over you.
I can't get out of my own way.
I have at least one daydream everyday.

   Today I was sitting on the sofa watching T.V.
I had this daydream you were sitting right next to me.
Then I stopped to realize it wasn't true.
Because our love is over according to you.

   Maybe it's because there's something I have missed
How can it be over just like this
I'm not sure why you left me and why I'm so blue.
Maybe I have these daydreams hoping they will come true.

—*Brenda Hoyt*

Untitled

Heart of stone
Embrace me with your desire to ride waves
While skies float toward earth
Free from the darkness in life
Free, to be washed on the soft shores of dreams where
   we can be
Souls, free to run wild, aimlessly through darken lands
Seeking nothing but the dangers of temptation
Oh heart of stone, face of reality
Allow your imagination to guide us as we fall through flame
   filled skies above a black sea of nothingness
Take flight and glide, endless through each day of
   uncertainty and I shall follow
Heart of stone be no more for love has found you and it shall
   hold you in its arms,
As will I—Forever.
   —Constance R. Libsack

"Can You Tell Me When This Pain Will End"

Can you tell when this pain will
end? Will it end when you leave again.
Or will it end when you use me again.
Will it end when you tell me, we are
through again. Can you tell me when
this pain will end?
   —Danielle Hayes

Trouble In Willard

He's at it again. Too many drinks to full the pain.
Enemies making another attack. His 45 ready to send them back.

Mary was missed but her kettle is dead, John to escaped as a
shot passed his head, out of the mobile home they ran,
Yelled to the neighbor to call policeman Dan.

Now Dan stood at the door calling out, Fred, damn it, what's
this all about? You've killed them all, it's ok buddy,
I know how it gets all dark and muddy.

You went to a war that couldn't be won,
Then said you weren't their countries son,
You and I fought, you saved my life,
When we returned you had lost your wife.

Please my friend, don't shoot anymore,
I love you and I'm coming through the door,
We'll sit and drink for as long as it takes,
So you can forget crazy war time mistakes.

Faces will fade and their cries will subside,
Only you and I know the things we must hide,
I was lucky, a good woman to show me the way,
But you dear Fred live only from day to day.
   —Gregory Saunders

"Can't You See?"

Your actions to me are a mystery
  Especially now we're apart.
Our love has been frozen in history,
  But is stirring alive in my heart.

My heartbeats are trembling; oh, why did it die?
  I am trying to understand.
I loved you so truly; I begged and I cried.
  But you just let go of my hand.

You cannot see with your very own eyes
  What heartache is doing to me.
It shouldn't come as a desperate surprise.
  What's wrong with your eyes; can't you see?
   —Melanie Brickner

Be All That You Can Be

Time can go by so quickly
Especially when you're having fun
But once that time has past
It can never be undone
So many people misuse it
Everyday it's taken for granted
I only hope and pray that it's not too late
To work to their advantage
Did you notice that you often hear
About younger people on the news
Someone died in a car wreck
Because they drank too much booze
Every time I see and hear
of an accident such as this
I wonder just how old they were
And how much of life they'll miss
Don't be like those of who we've heard
that ran out of time
Be all that you can be now
Before you're left behind.
   —Tonia Lynn Wright

Christmas Cheer

Christmas time is full of cheer
especially with those you hold so dear.
It's time for gifts and christmas trees.
That fills little children with laughs and glee.
It's time for snow and christmas
carols, apple cider, apple pie
Mom's new earnings, Dad's new tie
It's time for Santa and his reindeer and christmas
presents oh-so-near.
It's time to give hugs and kisses
and remember all the ones that miss us.
It's time to share all your love
especially with the One Above.
   —Jeanette Wallace

Heart's Window

Open the window to your Heart and capture a glimpse of Love's
   Eternity - Only for a moment

You will search your whole life to be able to experience it
   again

One day you will open up the window - keep it open and move
with Love's Eternity because you'll know that is what you are!
   —Lauria Lacayo

Look To The Light

Look to the light, my angel did say,
Even though the clouds hang low;
Look to the light of another day
For the sun will shine, you must know...

There is no time so hopelessly dark
That the SON will not shine through;
Even though you're crying your heart out tonight,
Tomorrow will bring joy to you...

Our LORD has promised strength to endure;
HE's promised no burden that breaks;
HE's promised to sustain and care for you
And give you whatever it takes...

So never forget our loving LORD,
Who died for you and me;
HE's living today; watching over you,
That's where He'll always be...
   —Betty Jo S. Berry

Robin's Nest

So contentedly does she sit, blending in with her environment.
Everything does she see, she sees you... find also me.
She watches the house, the dogs, the kids.. wait!
Where is the cat? Pouncing upon a rat?
No, could not be, for she would be able to see.
Say, do you hear? The Kitty is very, very near.
No time to rest, the Kitty is under the nest!
She sings her warning song, for something is wrong!
In a second he is there, pecking the cat in one ear. "ow!"
The cat cries as he leaps into the air.
She sees me, again
She just tilts her head,
raised her bill, fluffed
her feathers, and away she slept.
There is no threat!
—*Christine Smith*

Untitled

There was a time when thoughts were of material substance, when everything was of experience.

Living in the past makes belated dreams and new wishes stagnant thoughts.

I am not yet sure of the path chosen.

Sobriety of the mind makes cleansed thoughts to be carried out by the body.

Indulgence has opened many to a different light, passing the line of coherence lets one live a different life, without passing on.

The mind can go insane when reality is mixed with fictional vacations brought on by self indulgence.

No mortals life is set on a course but when the mind is clouded and the bounds of reality are tested many pass on. This point has been dulled many times too often.
—*Russell B. Polo Jr.*

The Second Season

And, suddenly, it's summertime —
Everywhere sweet blooming roses
And sun's golden filigree.
Summer's symphony is sounding
In hearts and minds equally.
Fleecy clouds, so high, are sailing
On a gentle summer breeze;
Turtledoves are softly calling
From their bowers in leafy trees.

Glistening raindrops, as countless crystals,
Descend in showers to Mother Earth;
Golden Days of pleasant sunshine
Rejoicing in the season's birth.
Far stars rain their brilliant sparkle,
Mystical like dreams of yore.
Summer comes—that time of miracles
And new found glorious splendor.
—*Loreida Harma*

To Rod - 1993

Hold me in your mind
    Everywhere you journey
I don't ask for promises
    Or commitments for time together
I just need to know
    That I am in your soul
And just a thought
    Can make you smile
Life has so many roads to travel
    And our paths will seldom cross
Are you happy?
    I wish for you all the love I have in me
And I hope that during quiet times
    You remember our beginnings
And know there will be no end
—*Barbara Foose*

The Mummy Un-Masked

The Tomb of Doom has crumbled
    EXIT THEE!!
Make a intention to surpass
Their journey, where a boundless stream
Exists, bathing in the cool water of Nile
Cleansed, not caught up in a physical state
Yet still intact
Don't cling to Earth, until the spiritual
Realm, Emits a unseen matter
Which brings upon the Wisdom of
SAGES past, present, and future
Tolerance for Tolerance sake No! No! No!
Let's all awake, to a new ERA
Untie the "WRAPS OF WRATH"
Entering PORT NUR (Light)
Arrived Yes! not Shipwrecked
No land mass can contain US
For we are always accepted
Because of our INNER SEARCH for PARADISE.
—*Taufeeq the Unique*

The Gift

Innocent time of self-contained rapture,
expanding ethereal song.
Youth skipped the path home.
Shuddered to find sole companion gone.
Banished by the bearer of life.
Premature lesson of wickedness.
The wrenching pain of trust misplaced.
Dictatorial power held fast in a frigid heart.
Betrayed, for what?
Never to see the cosmic fracture within.
First helping of hate on the plate.
Cruel gift, the legacy of loss.
—*Linda Snyder*

The Shadow

Like a statue he sits in a huge chair
far away-heart of stone.
Lost in himself,
never wiping his daughter's tears.
A vague shadow from long ago
never wanted to know how much I loved him.
And for that
my words shall be lost
on this page
forever.
—*Denise R. Villarreal*

Waking Up

Waking up in a hospital bed from a coma,
Facing the difficult challenge ahead.
Waking up in a cardboard box known as your home.
Hungry, cold and full of hope.
Waking up in a dysfunctional home knowing that you're not loved,
Scared that your future isn't promising.
Waking up in Somalia, as a child with no food,
Hurting because of selfishness.
Waking up in a place where gangs thrive,
Afraid to walk the streets, afraid to die.
Waking up in a world with aids, dying, suffering,
Facing neglect.
Waking up as a crack baby, deformities, withdrawal,
All because of a destroying, frightening drug.
To live through, the days of suffering and pain,
You have to have one simple thing.
In this world of tragedy and greed,
The children of the future have to have courage.
—*Megan Costello*

Untitled

Even the mightiest tree in the forest
   falls to the ground in defeat.
Even the loveliest rose
   wilts and dies in the cold winter frost.
Even the brightest star
   blinks away from the night
   leaving nothing behind to see.

And though another tree may grow
And another rose will bloom
And the stars will return at night
The emptiness behind will never be filled
Only memories of what was.

And even the strongest of men must sometimes
fall on his knees and cry.
—*Josh Elder*

The Words Didn't Come

The words didn't come as I searched deep inside
   Fear and anxiety were impossible to hide,
My heart pounded so hard I knew all could hear.
   When we met I hoped it'd all be so clear.

You'd tell me somehow what we must both do
   To relax and feel right about this that is new.
Uneasiness dominates, all is intense.
   Why this must be just fails to make sense.

What must I do to have change come so fast
   Something will snap, this just cannot last.
The mind does not answer the heart's cries of need.
   Help from somewhere is what I now plead.
—*Sandra Proctor*

Handicap's Plea

For strength of soul, not sympathy we're asking,
For faith, not dreams, to dwell in endlessly,
For work that we can do without frustration,
For friends - we need them so tremendously.
For patience with the ones to try to help us,
For understanding others' needs as well,
For time to finish what we've started doing,
For courage ringing true as vesper bell.
For wisdom to undo our daily problems,
For love of service and our fellow man,
For God to give us always blest assurance
Though handicapped, we're in His plan.
—*Pat Carlson*

Memories

   He made me laugh, and made me
feel good, but when I heard the news, I only stood.

   My ears started ringing and my eyes
filled up with tears, when I suddenly
realized, he would have no more fears.

   I knew I would never see him
again, when finally the minister said a-men.
I couldn't breathe and I couldn't swallow,
and all my insides felt so hollow.

   My stomach felt weasy and my heart
started to pound as they lowered his casket
into the ground.

   I knew God had planned it this way,
and it was probably for the best, when my
7 month old cousin died of crib death.

   There's something's on earth that you just
don't know, but when it comes to this, you can't
let go. All this happened when I was at
the age of 7, now that I'm 14, I know he's
watching me, up there in heaven.
—*Becca Surface*

It's Love Strange

- New years come; old years pass but love never moves.
- Feeling come feeling go but love has no resting pace.
- Hurt has come and hurt has gone but love linger on.
- Pain has come pain has gone but love never changes.
- Tears run tears dry up but love run on and on.
- It's love strange.

- People fuss people fight but love has the strong hand.
- People come and people go but love stay home.
- People marry people divorce but love never separate.
- People say I'll never leave but love put them on the bus.
- People say you can't live off love but love kills.
- It's love strange.

- You say you're not going to care but love sneaked in.
- You said you were strong but love made you weak.
- You turned and walked away but love made you turn around.
- You say you want out of everything but love want let go.
- You try to bury everything inside but love you can not hide.
- You stop living you want to die but love made you live again.
- It's love strange.
—*Carrie Caine*

Grasping At The Grave

Death, the last gasp
fight the felon that steals it.
That personified medical dictionary entry
grabs at me, introduces me to mortality,
"I'm pleased, but not delighted to meet you."
"You mole!" he digs, he digs
digs away the ground on which I once walked.
I walked, but I don't walk anymore.
I slipped down, and I'm not getting back up,
going to die, and sink down:
fossilize, become mulch, make squash grow
in the backyard above the driftwood cross,
my tombstone, same as the old dog that had babies,
I lived and made life. Regenerated. Carried on the name,
carried on the pain. I have left my son:
he will die too, you know.
Maybe bury him in a high-rise mausoleum on the outskirts.
He'll be lonely amid the corpses,
not pushing the daisies he always wanted.
—*Jason Bowman*

By The Road

The sun was shining, leaves were budding, soft spring breezes
   filled the air. I saw her standing by the road,
A child in hand, a bag beside them.
His clothes were dirty, too small, and wrinkled;
His eyes were bright, alert, and searching.
A car passed by, another, another, another, another;
One stopped:
Green paper was passed, a smile was given, a look was seen,
   an it was gone.
The autumn leaves swirled about, blowing from the north,
   gold and yellow.
I saw her standing by the road, a child in hand, a bag beside
them. His clothes were dirty, too small, and wrinkled;
His eyes were bright, alert and searching.
A car passed by, another, another, another, another;
One stopped:
Green paper was passed, a smile was given, a look was seen,
   an it was gone.
Cold winds blew, and flakes sparkled on the ground and on the
   bared coated trees. She wasn't standing by the road.
   —*Gloria J. Kagan*

"Tears"

Like rain that falls from the sky, my eyes
filled with tears, those tears went down my
cheeks and down into my soul, I don't know
how to tell you how much I love you and I
don't know how to tell you, that you re deep
into my heart, God knows it and my eyes when
they see you, my eyes filled of shine and my
heart of hope I look up onto the sky asking
God if one day you will be here by my side
and I look back down from above, because there
are drops falling down my cheeks, but this time
I don't know if it is the rain falling from
the sky, or maybe its my tears.
   —*Gloria Garcia*

I Wish I Had A Sister

All those lonely days in my life;
Fixing my hair with two hands, instead of four;
Going to church by myself;
I wish I had a sister.

Celebrating my birthday with my parents;
Riding bikes all alone;
Being the only one to open Christmas presents;
I wish I had a sister.

Unaccompanied, I window shop in the mall;
Play solitaire;
Walk in the rain;
I wish I had a sister.

Singly, I eat popcorn in the movie theatre;
Plan out my next school day;
Eat ice-cream with no one to share it with;
I wish I had a sister.

If, only I had a sister.
   —*Marca Bruff*

Love Is To Life

Love is to life what water is to the flower.
For just the flower needs water to grow beautiful,
We need love to grow an inner beauty.
   —*Scott A. Anspach*

My World

Come into my world, Where your dreams are shattered in no time flat, and your sweet visions of laughter are foggy from the unforgiving darkness and wrath.

Come, venture into my world, where true love is never entirely true, and your heart is constantly bruised black and blue.

Come, enter my world, where you are fighting a never-ending battle with your emotions, therefore you never know quite how to feel.

Come on! See if I care! See if anyone does! You'll be kicked around like a worthless ball of fuzz.

I warn you now, if you ever have the opportunity to follow a better track, snatch it, hold it, and never look back.

As for me, happiness still yet must set me free. For this gloomy, desolate way has become my life you see. To struggle, fail, and face the strife, is now the largest portion of my life. The condition I'm in I know not who to blame, for my lack in self confidence, looks, and worldly fame.
   —*Lorri M. Limbaugh*

Path Of Life

Her eyes a sparkling blue ocean as beautiful as a gleaming flowing potion. Her hair, the golden oysters that luster and shine like a sparkling wine. Her teeth, the gleaming pearls flourishing in the oysters, moister than the morning dew. Her lips, the luscious cherry growing near by, swaying back and forth in the wind's cry. Her tongue, the bright apples covered in red. They are covered but not shy as crustless bread. Her eyes, bold yet cold. Their glare is enough to scare a lion away. What use is the ocean if it is cold for there will be no joy and young jumping over wave folds. Her skin soft but what use is it if her inside is rough; as rough as a snake's shedded skin. She walks with a snare and her nose is the air. What use is the sand if it is covered by pollution and the cold solution folding on it's shore. The golden oysters go to waste since they covered by a horrible paste. So what use is the hair if it is just a mere trick to bring you into the fire's flair. What use is the pearls if they shrill with kill; so do her teeth like the ugliest beast. Her lips pretend to be merry but they are sneaky to bite as a snake.
   —*Sherry Orbach*

I Wish

I wish to be a small bird
Flying across the mountains, across the oceans
I wish to be a small fish
Swimming freely in the ocean
I wish to be a small pigeon
Going to finish the mission of peace between the peoples of the
   world

I wish to become the forest
Giving the earth vitality
I wish to become the grass
Wrapping the earth in green
I wish to become the bridge
Linking information between the peoples of the world

I wish to turn into sunlight
Giving warmth to the earth
I wish to turn into spring
Removing thirst from the earth
I wish to turn into a rainbow
Connecting friendship between the peoples of the world
   —*He Xionghui*

In Lilac Time

In lilac time...I reminisced
Fond mem'ries I did trace
When lilacs perfumed springtime air
From petals soft as face

In one bouquet ... There was no doubt ...
I saw my Mother's face
T'was then I sensed her presence
And felt her warm embrace

Her countenance was radiant ...
As fresh as morning dew
More lovely than a rainbow
Or the lilacs' purple hue

I knew these blossoms were her choice
From spring's enchanting bowers
Then ever-so-softly she spoke to me
Through language of the flowers
—*Hazel H. Wells*

Father And Child

Father and child is a good combination
For a man gives off a different vibration
He sees things in the male point of view
And can give his child experiences new

The love of a father is a precious thing
For joy and concern it can often bring
Sharing with father your problems to mend
Should always make him your special friend

Child and father, father and child
He loves them with a love that's wild
Fiercely, loyally, love that will stick
Bad times and good, through thin thick
What a joy just to see a father and child
For with mother and child reaction is mild
While a mother's important, a father is too
For a child to grow up with a balanced view

Father and child, it's so good to see
Laughing and learning, just him and me
Man and child that's just the way
Teaching and reaching, tomorrow, today
Father and Child
—*Jan Freeman*

The Flight

Through all the ups and downs that life often brings,
For all of life's good and bad things,
You must spread your wings.

To reach the goal that you dream for,
To open each and every door,
You must soar.

For each leap you take and fail,
For every time luck does prevail,
You must sail.

To be the first and only one,
To take the blame for what you've done,
You must shine like the sun.

Wherever you are, and whoever you're by,
Whoever you are, and whoever am I,
You can fly.

Now as the young of this nest,
Our wings we are to test,
For truly we can be best.
—*Amy Popick*

May Reflections

An ideal mother's care is watchful, sure;
For every childhood pain her love ensures
A gentle kiss, her never failing cure;
And through the years her loyalty endures.
   We all recall the song by poet wise-
"The hand that rocks the cradle rules the world"-
Alas, when women choose their babes' demise,
What holocaust has come upon the world!
   O lady don't devise a role-MacBeth,
Do not despoil the beauty of your soul,
Do not become a counterpart of death,
But make maternal purity your goal.
   To rose the world from this so tragic hour
Abides within your motivating power.
   May misled mothers pray and reassess
Judeo-christian norms of life and love,
Eternal rules of lasting happiness;
Infallibly, they come from God above.
—*Francis P. Burke*

No More Crying To Give

There are times when I say make the world go away
For I have no more crying to give
Then I walk in a room full of sadness and gloom
And I see how some others may live

Babies who die without seeing the sky
Or watching some horses run free
No spring and no fall, no sweet moments at all
No initials carved into a tree

While the days come and go not one joy do they know
And they never will grow up to be
So I walk out the door for I cannot endure
all the pain and the misery I see

I remember their eyes as the hope of life dies
But one face I will constantly see
And my memory burns as that face returns
And I know I will never be free

Now I go on my way as I start a new day
For we all have our own lives to live
And I silently pray make the world go away
For they have no more crying to give
—*Dorothy S. Turri*

God's Gift A Glad Happy Smile

There's nothing God loves more than a glad happy smile
For it makes every task seem much more worth while.
If you work with the young or you work with the old
You should never, not ever be gloomy nor cold.

If you keep cheerful each day that you work;
Do your best and never to shirk,
No one could pay what you are worth
Not as long as you live on God's good earth.

So we must ask God to reimburse
Every good aide and every good nurse.
The wages man pays could never suffice to pay the price
Of a nurse that's kindly or an aide that's nice.

God is so happy and can really rejoice
That He's found a jewel with a gladsome voice;
Whose glad happy smile fills each one with good cheer
For it tells them so sweetly, "I'm glad your still here."
—*Mary M. Coughlin*

For You, For Me

For you, a city street
For me, a country road
For us, different paths to explore

For you, a star plucked from the heavens
For me, a flower plucked from the earth
For us, natures generosity to share

For you, the Electric Slide
For me, the Hustle
For us, a willing compromise that teaches us a surprisingly
   graceful waltz

For you, a dark color skin
For me, a light color skin
For us, a glorious, wonderful blend

For you, hopes and dreams
For me, hopes and dreams
For us, nourishment for our hearts, fuel for our souls

For you, happiness and love
For me, happiness and love
For us, sharing love, the one true joy of life
For the Universe: The light of truth, the gift of peace

—*Rose M. Murphy*

At Peace

Weep no more, my little sweet,
For no greater company could I ever keep.
I'm happy, content, and glowing inside,
My feelings and thoughts, I don't have to hide.
A loving God is all around me here
I've taken His hand and no longer have fear.
My thoughts are with you and those left behind.
I'll think of you often, in the presence of mind.
I'll have special graces of which I can't tell.
I'm glad I'm in Heaven instead of in Hell.
No greater peace could one possibly feel.
And my cuts and bruises are beginning to heal.
To go from the pains and sufferings on Earth,
It's worth it, you know, to feel this rebirth.
So give thanks to the Lord, for He is Great!
And I'll wait for you, Love, at God's Golden Gate!

—*Carole White*

The Hollyhock

A hollyhock from heaven, that's what it must be
For no seed was planted there by me.

"One day, just wait and see, you will have your hollyhock."
These words were said to me before my sweet sis took her
heavenly walk.

Doing the dishes with my daughter one day,
She remarked, "I have never seen a hollyhock grow in such a way."

So tall and so proud in a shocking pink,
I see it everyday while looking out the window by the kitchen sink.

A more perfect spot I could not have picked,
My sister's present to me is the most precious yet.

She is planting her flowers now by heaven's gate,
But for my hollyhock she did not make me wait.

—*Ronnie Lou Davis*

Butterfly Daughters

They are life in a cocoon you nurture
for, oh, some period of time
sheltering, explaining, encouraging-
Loving!

On a dawn of their own choosing
they emerge from the dark womb of beginnings
vibrant, gracious, electric - brilliant iridescence revealed.
Some colors fade, others turn bold -
all depends upon their chosen pattern of flight.
Swirls and bursts, starts and stops
designs engraved upon a mother's heart.
Each tenders a tremble, a tingle
for you know that well developed wings
are not born of the timid.

A rush of wind and stars, moon and sun
as they perch on the windowsill of your heart,
embrace you, and...
fly away.

—*Paula Kelly*

Contentment

  Be happy, be free...smile for me
For one day, you'll seek prosperity.
  But first release your misery...
By reaching out...and you will see...
  Through life's long-light eternally!
And, when you reach that open door...
  You'll seek what you've been searching for
Then someday soon you'll suffer no chore,
  To discover life's love forever more!!!

—*Diana Andriola Betts*

A Broken Heart

Love is a trap, some people fall into.
For some love is not true.
Some people get hurt and feelings turn blue,
but for some this feeling is not new.

  A lot of us do have a clue that love hurts.
  It is painful when hearts are broken.
  Because love is a special token.

Love is feeling secure and safe.
But some people go off base, and cheat and lie.
That causes us to cry, and signals us that it's time to
say goodbye.

  Because love is a roller coaster, it has its ups and downs
  Unfortunately sometimes love can turn smiles into frowns.

Some of the time love leaves us with nothing but a broken heart
Because the one you love had to part.

—*Nicki Calorie*

The Winner

I read the poem,
grand prize winner the editors
said. Best ever written for
Our contest. Magical words, ethereal,
mystical, meaning beyond our comprehension.
I read, sneering smugness, jeering
laughter in the tumbled mass of words down the page.

Guess my meaning if you can?
I could feel the author's haughty
hatred of all who
dared to read.

—*Jeffie Greer*

Friendship

There was a time that I can remember, when I had a best friend
   for the first time ever.
The best of friends, the biggest of competitors, neither one
   would allow anybody more than the other.
We played all day, laughed all night, anybody not seeing us
   together experienced quite a sight.
But something unknown entered friendship's way and as it tore
   our friendship apart, it turned the remnants of it
   into scattered fragments.
I thought ours was a friendship that would never die, when I
   look back sometimes I sigh.
We had the best of times together, our days were always filled
   with each other.
Since our friendship has been severed we have gone our separate
   ways.
But still sometimes I remember the happiness of those days.
Losing a friend is a feeling I cannot fully describe, but the
   pain of it is forever inscribed.
   —*Meghan Gorman*

Untitled

Remember 6th grade for the times that we had,
for the friends that we made, for the good times and bad.

Remember 6th grade for the teachers and staff,
who got mad and yelled and all we did was laugh.

Remember 6th grade and those terrible tests,
we may have failed but we did our best.

Remember 6th grade, remember the dances,
remember how everybody gossiped in classes.

Remember 6th grade, Miss Afriat, Mrs. Monello,
and don't forget Mr. P. and how he would bellow.

Remember 6th grade, Miss Irwin, Miss Brown,
and Harold driving the bus the wrong way through town.

Remember 6th grade and all of our friends,
and how 6th grade is now at an end.

Remember 6th grade, remember Pinecrest,
and most of all remember we are the best.
   —*Kimberly Boothby*

Open Your Eyes

Open your eyes she whispered to me
for the rains are quick to fall.
Rainbows through open palms we see-
open your hearts to all.
Silence is broken through the winds flutter
for the path we choose leads you to thee,
open your eyes I utter.
Be not tearful as worlds careen.
Rose petals reach for the sun they adore.
Open your minds to all that is real-
The end is the beginning of what is seen
through open palms we touch to feel.
Open your ears the ocean is calling
The lone one tiptoes beside himself-
for he is fearful of the rain falling.
   —*Taylor Westerberg*

Encouragement

Have we set our goals?
Have we looked within our souls?

Do we take the time to care?
Or do we look at life as one big fair?

Dream your dreams, open your mind!
Set fire to your life, you are one of a kind!
   —*Bill Flynn*

Halloween

The whirlwinds blow and the werewolves howl as the evening
   shadows fall
For this is the night called Halloween when Satan comes to call!
The graveyard moan as the undead rise to escape their grisly tombs
While she-devils writhe in agony demons from fetid wombs.
The cauldrons bubble while the witches chant, casting their evil spells
To summon forth the monstrous things straight from the depths of
   Hell!
Beelzebub…his demons…their bloodlust and savage thirst
Send batwings aloft into the night to find the damned and cursed.

The Church bells toll each hour past on this All Hallows Eve
Each ring is like a death knell…lost souls have no reprieve!
The Devil walks, his eyes aglow, the fires of Hell burn bright
And strong men touched by his icy grip are frozen by their fright.

The witching hour is drawing near and as he finishes up his rounds
The silvery moon turns blood red as he takes the souls he's found!
The clock strikes twelve brave men pray, the night is crystal black;
The devil roars his raucous laugh and hisses, "I'll be back!"

Good people, best you heed those words and always remember, too,
That when the demon hunts its prey, that prey could just be you!
So lock your doors and say your prayers when this night appears
   once
   more;
For when you hear a knock, knock, knocking…it could be Satan at
   your door!
   —*Cynthia Box*

There Is No Increment That Could Honestly Weigh

   That life force which inhabits the human shell
For without the soul a pound of flesh is but a pound of clay
Thus one can not measure a man by a scale
Nor by the material possessions he acquires
Judge him not by his birthright of from where he's said to hail
Nor by his aspirations or his fantasies or desires
For whether a man be rich or poor, large or small, dark or pale
Such trivia should never find importance in those most wise
For it is the water that makes the well
And how fresh, how deep the water can't be seen with human eyes
Judge a man from where his integrity lies
Is that man honorable does he have compassion and a sense of pride
What does he have in his heart not what he has in his hand
Those inner possessions not the outer traits should decide
When comes the time to measure a man
   —*Dwight Lockett*

Yellow Lupine, California

Come, yellow lupine, into blossom
for your season on these hills,
shaped, sunripened for abundance.
For the moment of morning
gentle any awkwardness of cragline;
lean to enhance its ultimate sky.

Be more selective of your path at noon
than the poppy or wild mustard
yet, not to understate yourself,
wanton-ride a slope-
relate two broken curves of inlet…

With sunglow in motion on your petals,
suggest chartreuse to a homecoming wave.
With a late breeze firmly behind you,
promise a mile of barren sand-
drop a cluster here and there,
to billow out as a seabird alights.

Then, blossom beyond your fragrance-
for my winter nights-
as gold of mist with certainty of spring.
   —*Hascal Vaughan Stewart*

One Life Poem

A baby born wanting
Forced to scream for it.
looking up for adulthood.

Attaining it, but now resignations
One, a blessing for the immense choir
One, a curse in wanting to fall into lovely dreams and
   beautiful nights.

Too many miracles brought back a scavengened heart at night
   when love was guilty with my innocent blood.

A baby cries for the answer. For the chance.
For the love
For the hearts bloodflow to stop.

Where is the healing?
Where is the answer?
Penance and offerings only gives the Robe your own Power.

And now I will have what I've sought, never bothering to look
   for, forgot to come and face it.

What is my soul, mind, spirit
I never sought to look for me
Me in the darkness and in the sun.

—*Charles Michael Ornegri*

Joey

There was a group of boys. They had known each other
forever. They grew up together. They were friends. In
elementary school they played the games of childhood

boys-chase-girl, hide-and go-seek, keep-away. They
laughed and yelled because they were children, and they
were Happy. Later came junior high. New faces, new
classes. But they remained friends. Now they played

kick-the-can, basketball, football. They laughed and
yelled because they were boys, and they were Excited.
Next came high school. They drove too fast flirted with
girls, drank together. And they
were still friends. They laughed and yelled because
they were teen-agers, and they were Alive. Then one of
them got shot. He was dead before he hit the ground.
When he died he took not only his laugh And his thirst
for life, but their invulnerability, their childhood,
their innocence. Those who were left screamed and cried
because they were men, and they were Afraid.

—*David M. Rodriguez*

Happy Hours—Flowers

The world is bedecked with happy spring flowers
Forsythias bright, crocus peep out after showers
Hyacinth sweet, daffodils, growth of lovely things
Herbs all colors, my heart sings and sings
The tall stately lily so pure and white
Makes everyone feel renewed with God's might.
Purple, white lilac; lacy-violets demure
Snowballs; bluebells, Marigolds pungent for sure
Beautiful velvety roses—delicate lovers' choice
Patience; for-get-me-nots make the heart rejoice
Summer pinks; poppies; sedgwick tea—Lord we thank Thee
Wild flowers in the forest; in the meadows; for you-me
The pansies' little faces; remember they're for thoughts
Carnations beautiful joy—what more love God brought
The Christmas Pointsettia—all say love—remember
Happy hours—from January through December
Because these jewels speak more than words can say
All grow from His little seed; may flowers come your way

—*Mary Lou Y. Darnielle*

Remember To Forget Him

Forget his name, forget his face
Forget his kiss, his warm embrace
Forget the love that you thought was true
Remember... he has someone new

Forget him when they play "your song"
Forget to cry the whole night long
Forget how close you two once were
Remember...he has chosen her

Forget you memorized his walk
Forget the way he used to talk
Forget those things he used to say
Remember...he's far away

Forget his laugh, forget his grin
Forget that dimple in his chin
Forget the way he held you tight
Remember...he's with her tonight

Forget the time that went so fast
Forget the love that now is past
Forget he said he'd leave you never
Remember...he's gone forever.

—*Amanda Dohl*

The Heart

Crystalline statues line the halls of her heart.
Fragile and worth more than anything else in the body.

The surface, a dynamic face, soft sweet tender skin,
Waiting to be held by cumbersome and charming arms.

Lips, moist as the dew on a newly formed leaf in springtime,
Every breath from the passionate lips renders me senseless.

Behind the face is a mind worthy of an equal opposite
Needing stimulation as does the lonely body.

On the level close to the heart, the soul an instrument which
makes up one's whole being, it is beautiful, seeking the
embrace of another warm and caring spirit, not dashing away
from it.

The surface is nice, the mind is fine, the soul is magic, but
the heart is the warm striking tool used to lash out at its
would-be seekers.

The heart is not trapped but can be if not supported by the
rest of the body. It can give hope to many or break a few,
but the heart is what controls all of life. I know her heart
and it may break me, but mine has equal strength and will
overcome the blow.

—*Todd A. Batchelor*

Protection In Shadows

The darkness, thick about me, protects me
    from myself. Wraps itself
   a woolen cloak sodden with tears of pain
  around my face. Blinding, deafening, muting.
But the grunt and growl of my unappeased creature
   echo in the caverns of my ears.
And the burning coals of its eyes will not leave my sight.
    Its foul breath
    a wind of rotting flesh
   still hot and moist against my lips.
His ragged claws play tauntingly over my skin, my body.
   Tapping from the stagnant pool of
    memories.
He dances a tribal dance to my sobs and the faint beat
   of my trembling heart.
  He throws back his head and laughs,
   a deep rolling thunder in his stomach.
    He laughs as my soul hides
    quivering in the shadows.

—*Katie Sherwood*

"My Perfect Bride"

In the midst of writing this poem, my thoughts run slow and free, trying to define this mass activity. Some may say I'm selfish admonished in my greed, to create the woman I desire, plus the type I need.

Desiring to be satisfied, by this woman of my dream, wanting all her love to feed my self-esteem. This poem for me is a challenge and it's certainly just a dream. It's built upon my loneliness to feed my self esteem. Some may think I'm foolish, but really I'm just true, openly expressing, what's inside of me and you. I'm speaking hypothetically with this power on my side. If I could crate a woman this would be my perfect bride.

Her eyes would shine so brightly, like stars up in the sky. I would shape her body so perfectly, like a sculptor does his clay. I would make her complexion so lovely, the color of rich mahogany. But, beside her hair, her eyes and the color of her skin. I would give her something so special and that would be the love I put with-in.

Her Love would be so special, for all the world to see. It's the type of Love God meant for us to have, from the beginning of creation till all eternity.

—*John Wesley Ware*

Popping Corn

Popping corn is different
   From day of long ago,
When we sat by an open fireplace
   Within the firelight's glow,
And Mama could pop the popcorn

In a handled wire basket she held
   Over the radiant hot coal,
Until the whole house smelled
   of its tantalizing odor of popped corn.
How mouth-watering it would be,
   We could scarce control our anguish
So impatiently hanging were we.

But son, the feast was ready,
   And we ate quite gleefully,
When Mama popped the popcorn.
   In the days that used to be.

—*Nannie Ina Holder*

Annie And Two Doors Down

Accident of birth, that's what separates Annie
   From the girls who enter just two doors down.
Where girls are pampered, preened and refined,
   Those girls breezing through, just two doors down.
Annie can mouth the lyrics, dance the beat, same as
   The girls of the building, just two doors down.
Annie bobs her head in a lolly right rhythm,
   Keeping time with the girls of just two doors down.
Annie sometimes peeks 'round the great cemented oak,
   Grandly towering it sentries, for just two doors down.
Most times she distances herself in the watching,
   Leg braced on bricked corner of main and divine.
Watchin' she waits as they spring from the doorway,
   The preened and refined from just two doors down.
When doorways darken, and yawning silence takes over,
   Annie ambles toward the recess, of two doors down.
Widely opening arms, she entreats stardom forward,
   Annie's dancing tonight just two doors down.

—*Brenda K. Bowman*

The Spider And The Rock

Silent in the night, the rock stays fast and strong.

A small spider runs across the surface taking refuge from the predators of the night.

Surviving the spears of light cast down from the heavens and the rejoicing tears of the forbidding clouds.

The spider will venture into the harshness of the world only to return to the rock; wishing that he could bring something back to the rock to ease it's strife but knows not what to do.

—*Robin Welch*

The Love Of My Father

My Father's face grows weary
From the troublesome days gone by
All the times he was silent
And never took the time to cry
On the outside he remains a lion
So brave and faithfully strong
But on the inside there's a kitten
Who is fearful of life's everyday song
His strength can carry you through a lifetime
Of laughter, love, and tears
Lessons to truly be learned
Throughout his many years
My father's not rich in wealth
But is always rich in soul
He can tell a story of yesterday
And make you feel whole
His love is unconditional
Though he's set in his ways
I'll treasure the love of my father
Throughout the rest of my days

—*Kim Sellers*

Bridge Of Fire

No more will the pain I feel, I wear the battle scars
From years of being, years of being not what others are

The frail will's leaving I'm no longer strong enough or was
This tasteless joke the waste of breathing living just because

Without purpose watching waiting history repeats
Patiently and painfully I relive life's defeats

Alive existing nothing more than groping in the fog
Drained and beaten tired of trying a wandering stray dog

And once again I try by once again like always fail
Pointlessly continuing down aimless winding trails

On and on I give they take the smell of burning's me
The bridge to use for another pleasures meets its destiny

With disregard they watch the flames remove the bridge from sight
They carry on as I decline they gloat I loose the fight

—*Michele Alary*

Your Face

The precious things you are
Have held my heart
To untold heights of pure delight
Wherein I traced the memory of your face
Upon the velvet of the night,
And filled each shimmering little star
With the wondrous light of what you are.
So when it's time for us to part,
I promise not to cry,
For I will see your face each time
My own turns to the sky.

—*Millicent Juray Lowry*

Temporary Home

She sits in her rocker beside the bed
gazing at her most treasured possessions
snapshots—torn, faded, and yellow
but give her, her only glimpse of joy.

She eats but gains no strength
She sleeps but gets no rest
She hears but will not listen
She talks but forgets what she's said.

She shakily wanders the hall
of her present so-called 'home'
blindly grasping the side-rails
'til she's back in her chair.

She casts a slender tree-like shadow
with withering branches on each side
Her hair has thinned almost to nothingness
and leathery wrinkles have taken beauty's place.

She can't relive her memorable past
so her only wish is to pass on
to reunite with her loved one
and regain all that she's lost.
—*Darlene Ferrell*

The Winter Of My Life

I sit alone at the window
    Gazing out at the darkened sky.
I'm weary from planting, weeding, and harvest,
    And want only to rest here and watch
the snow fall lazily by.

The snowfall is beautiful. Twigs coated in ice,
    Like the lacy doilies that Mama crocheted.
How could I have dreaded winter?
It's so cozy and warm in my room.
I'm enjoying the fruit in my cellar and the photos on my wall.

My memory is faded now,
But my scrapbook is full of places and dates.
I look at then, the snow, and the ice,
    and wait—and wait—and wait.
    —*Carol Bebout*

The Dance

  There is a bright glow from the sun
Girls are dancing on the beach having fun
  But one girl dances alone—
She wishes she was grown and on her own
  Her feet are supported by sandals
Her hair by a ponytail—
  Her clothing isn't much—
But it has a special touch
  Water is falling from the golden fountain—
She dances around with laughter
  She'll dance there until after—
Everyone has gone
  She thinks of prancing like a fawn—
Then her mother grabs her by her hand
  And she leaves her tracks in the sand—
She loves the beach
  Tomorrow she'll come back again—
And dance with the joy of freedom—
  Even though she'll dance alone—
  —*Jennifer K. McKibben*

Children Of Fortune

Children of fortune dance in the air,
  Gliding on sunlight, without a care;
    Loved by their parents, honored by peers,
      Striding with confidence down through the years.

Children of sadness crying within,
  Like willows, all weeping, bend in the wind;
    Sighing, Uncertain, not standing tall,
      Bowing to forces that seem to enthrall.

Children of turmoil, tossed in the storm
  Of violence and hatred, for childhood they mourn;
    Forced into darkness, evil, despair,
      Striking and lashing out, caught in a snare.

Children of fortune, now fully grown,
  Reach out to those who stand, so alone;
    Give them your friendship, your love, all your best.
      Share your true self, for you have been blest.
—*Helen Nichols Sharar*

The Light

Far, far off in the distant darkness, there is a Brilliant, Glimmering Light that shines out of that darkness. Deep inside of me there is an unquenchable thirst, a longing and striving of my soul that has gone on for years, a wanting and seeking to be Whole - to go to that Ever-Brilliant-Radiant Light that seemed to be everywhere around me. It was in the stars, sun, moon, sky, sea, the birds, trees, flowers, in other people, places, and things... but not in ME! This journey called life has taken me up many mountain and hills, and down many roads, valleys, caverns, and ravines. It has brought me to this place in time. NOW the searching and longing have stopped. An inner calm has come over me. Ah! Yes! It is The Light that is so radiantly shining in my eyes, The Light that has found its home in Me: as if a laser beam is reflecting itself off the mountain top, signaling out into the world for all to see! Ah! Ah! Look! Listen! Can you see it and hear it? It is The Light - The Light that was in the far distant darkness, shining forth! The God Light of Love, Sweetness, Gentleness, Calmness, and Ever-Reassuring Presence is now My Light!. This God Light and Love in me, That I Am, is bursting forth!
—*Mary Frances F. Fleck*

Life After Life

Life is good, life is sweet
Glorious enough to wish a repeat!
At 82 I'll soon be through
And ready to start a life anew.
But death is simple - death is sure
Yet why must we death endure?
So why did nature shorten the span
Of bird and beast, and sadly man!
Now science, now brain, go seek, go work
Unearth the secret where life-cells lurk!
Hypothesis and theories are rife
But where, oh where is life after life?
  —*Henry T. P. Weber*

Primal Instinct

Hair sweeps out to brush the sky,
  head bent low, arms held high
Feet jump to beat the earth
  children laugh with unbridled mirth.
A primal dance long lay dead
  rediscovered on a prairie spread
Bodies ripple, hills roll by
  head thrown back, face to the sky
Legs spin to fall to the ground
  yet the earth still spins 'round & 'round
  —*Jennifer Parker*

Night Monsters

"Off you go," my mother said,
"Go to sleep, my sleepyhead."
Hugging, kissing, tucking me into bed;
Then she would tiptoe out of my room
Lit by beams from the new moon.

"Night monsters, night monsters," I'd begin to wail.
Into the room, my mom would sail.
"There are no night monsters," my mother said,
"go to sleep, my sleepyhead."

Creaky, squeaky, bangy, clangy,
Strange and weird the sounds did seem...
'Til I'd let out a shrieking scream.
In my mom would come again
Assuring me no night monsters were in our safe domain.

Now my child has his own room
Lit by beams from the new moon.
"Night monsters, night monsters," comes the wail
And into his room I sail.
Comforting, assuring him no night monster abounds
Only strange, weird night sounds.
—*Angelina S. Risinger*

Delilah

All of beauty - nothing of flaws. Sustaining the gift from the Gods, that is all of her aspect. Her beauty is irrefutable and the power therein is beyond impregnable. She is the loveliest of sunrises and She is the most captivating rose.
Her eyes glow with grey light of moons,
And pierce as do the sabers of a warriors fury.
Her body is sculptured in perfect design
And her hair is the redness of love itself...
And yet there is no beauty to compare by height,
nor breadth, nor depth, by multitude or magnitude.
She is not in the image of evil... She is evil!
Only mightier than her beauty is the evil of her heart and the wickedness of her soul. She is the cunning predator and the man beast is prey. She craves destruction by means of deception and seduction. All men-men of plenty-men of want. men of age, men of youth, men of darkness and men of the light have envisioned her. Yet only in the times of slumber fantasy. Delilah... She is still unseen.
—*Ronnell D. White*

Realization

How many miles must a man walk along before he realizes he's not going anywhere? How many skies must a bird fly amongst before itrealizes there is no somewhere? How many days must a storm whirl about before it realizes it's not wanted? How many poems must a poet create before he realizes that his words will be cheated? How many years must a war continue on before man realizes that it's not worth it? How many lives must a man continue living before he realizes that he should just quit? How many fragrances must a flower create before it realizes that its smell is poisonous? And how long must a river flow across the rocks before it realizes that it is not needed by us? A man must cross 1,000 miles then he will know the reason why. A dove must flee amongst 1,000 skies then it will know for what reason it must fly. A storm must whirl over 1,000 lands then it will know for what reasons it's needed. A poet must create 1,000 poems then he will know the reason he succeeded. A war must continue 1,000 days then man will realize that it was worth it. A man must live 1,000 lives, but not until then will he know why he didn't quit. A flower must produce 1,000 of its own fragrances but only then will it start to smell another. And a river must cross the rocks 1,000 times, but only then will it know it's forever.
—*Tina George*

Life's Hectic Pace

I run through my life at a frantic pace,
Going nowhere but in there to race.
I run through this life each day by day,
Not knowing where to go, not knowing the way.

I keep running along mid the tears and the strife,
Not knowing quite why but after all this is life.
Somewhere out there is a goal that I chase,
Not knowing quite what, I quicken my pace.

Each day its the same, I put on my dress.
I run till I'm weary and winded by stress.
I pray, "Give me strength, please show me the way!"
I do it because this just might be the day.

I run on and on looking here, looking there,
Not knowing the reasons or if it is fair.
Each day anew, the race starts again,
But only because...I KNOW I CAN WIN!
—*Vera J. O'Pry*

Good Night, My Lovely

Dedicated to Edith Bartee
Good night my love I can not see you anymore the last time I saw you was when they put you down I know that I will miss you because forever you will be gone, My darling I will miss you with all of my heart. You are within a better home than I, soon my friends and I shall come to be with you but don't worry because God is with you and you shall always be in my heart, you shall always live in this world because we all love you so much still to this very day. So good night my lovely.
—*Valicity Resha Downs*

China Dreams

I'm packing up her China.
Grandmother is in Heaven,
a better place, but that doesn't stop my tears.

Each tea cup and saucer reminds me of the
afternoon tea parties we had when I was
three and twenty-three.

Bright, shiny plates still reflect her smile
from Easter lunches, Sunday brunches, and
my sixteenth birthday party.

How do you wrap memories? In newspaper?
In bubble wrap? No.

I'm wrapping these in love and putting
them where they'll be safe, my heart.

This is a place Grandmother will never leave.
Here she is eternally vibrant and laughing,
planting her garden, and setting the table
for afternoon tea.
—*Tonya Zeien*

"Impatient"

As I look into the mirror, no-one looks back.
I feel the emptiness of my life.
I listen for a sound, and hear crying,
   where laughter should be.
There is a void, where love could be.
Loneliness, where unity has never been.
Can time really turn tears into joy,
   loneliness into happiness?
If so, how long must I wait?
—*Doris E. Muilenburg*

Hidden Away in Londontown

Standing at the foot of the escalator,
greeting me with his soothing, nostalgic voice.
  "My baby don't care. My don't care."
Voice cracks just like McCartney.
Beautiful stance, animated guitar;
another working day ends at the tube.
Crossing paths nearly every night in Piccadilly Circus,
I recognize his tattered denim jacket, no longer blue but gray.
Dusky hair, callous-born finger tips.
I hear exhaustion; fading voice echoing throughout the depths
of the station.
Eyes close, "My baby don't care."
I smile and drop two quid into his copper-filled case.
Until tomorrow, good night.
—*Shideh Hashemi*

Bless This Baby...

God bless this baby that I can't see,
growing each day inside of me.

Give it strength I pray of thee,
healthy and wise please let it grow to be.

Give us knowledge and wisdom too,
to teach the baby right things to do.

Help us each day in everything,
so joy and happiness this child will bring.

To its friends,
itself,
and we, its parents too,

But especially God,
bring joy to you....
—*Jennifer Boyce*

One True Love

There he is again
Hair as soft as silk, eyes as warm as the setting sun
They see right through me, melting through my flesh
Straight to my heart
It skips a beat
I study the contours of his face
As he plays a melody sweet and smooth
My soul fills with song and soon I will lose
Lose control of the enchantment around me
That draws me to him
Lose control of my thoughts and feelings
While my senses grow dim
He looks this way once again and his smile is soft and warm
The reassurance in his eyes gives me a new strength
I feel as if nothing is impossible; and with him, nothing is
As he plays, I sing, we form a song of love and faith
It shall endure into eternity
A love forever more
Love can withstand everything
As 'one true love' does for me.
—*Beth Solomon*

He

He told me he loved me,
He told me he would never leave me,
He told me he would protect me,
He told me he would cry for me,
He told me he would spend forever with me,
He told me the stars belonged to me,
He told me he would never lie,
Then he told me goodbye...
He died.
—*Renee Saucier*

Ask Me Why The Sea Gulls Cry?

They watched us walk together
  hand and hand,

The gold dust underneath our feet
  no longer sand.

The gentle ocean breeze whispered your name to me,
  and mine to you.
Above the Sea Gulls circled a most fantastic view.

We climbed the jagged, black, wet rocks—
  Our kingdom you proclaimed—
  and how you crowned us king and queen
  The ocean our domain.

They watch me walk along now,
  my head held low.

The sand is merely sand;
  where did the gold dust go?

The ocean breeze forgets our name now and sings instead a sad,
  sad song.

I climb the jagged, black, wet rocks,
  our lovely kingdom . . . . gone.
Now, ask me why the Sea Gulls cry!
—*Elizabyth Cooke*

To Carmen

Candlelight, and a kiss good-night;
Hand to hold and a smile as bright
As rays from the sun on a clear summer's day—
Carmen, I miss you from so far away.
Arms entwined in impassioned embrace;
Teasing, you run, and I quickly give chase;
Sweet kisses when, finally, I catch you at last,
Carmen, I miss you, has time ever passed
More haltingly, laggardly? Never, I'd say,
Than the passing of time since when up and away,
And into the sun you flew quickly from sight,
Now missing by day - missing by night.
So shapely of form and so tender of touch,
Carmen, I miss you, I miss you so much.
—*A. Francis Hatch*

Waiting With The Memories

He sits there so silent.
Hands once steady, but now are shaky.
No words have fallen from his lips in years;
No emotions on his face ever appear.
No visitors ever come to his door in that
dreary old folks home, although confined to
  his wheel chair, his thoughts still roam.
and he wonders back to the days spent fighting
side by side with his buddies in the war.
and of the day when he came home and was
with his beloved wife once more. With tears
of joy, he remembers each of his children's
births, then his heart hardens as he thinks of
  the way each died and was taken from this earth.
How much the years had stolen from him, gone and
never to return. How lonely he sits there, his
mind locked in the past. Yearning for the day
he will join his family, meet his maker at last.
But he'll never forget the days of when he was in
the war with all his buddies.
—*Faye Shuyler*

Chicago 1993

A hard day, that day
Hard, driven, steel gray day
Waiting for the acid rain to fall

We waited on stone stoops
Seven steps up and over the street
A hard street, that one
Wild flowers and weeds fighting
Arguing for space in beds of cracked concrete

We waited, caught in a fearful silence
While a woman child danced below and before us
We smiled, listening from within ancient memories
- Step on a crack break your mother's back -

Oh how we too yearned to dance
Till the song of the city stilled our feet
Till the litany of the beast echoed in the street
Shots, shouts, screaming tires, silence

A hard day, that day
We wept, hard, bitter, acid tears
As that dance within The Dance ended
And a red river ran between wild flowers and weeds
—*Henry F. French*

Waiting For The Guns

He seemed to be so very young
   hardly more than a child
He tried hard to keep his chin up
   but the look in his eyes were wild.
Just a boy, a long way from home
   in a war, he never really understood
But, he was willing to serve his country
   in whatever way he could.
I knew he felt alone and scared
   as he silently waited there
For soon, the guns would be shooting
   and the smell of death would fill the air.
In just minutes the battle was over
   and the sound of the guns had ceased
The last words that came from the dying young man
   were prayers to our Father for peace.
   —*Edna Frances Sapp*

Exposing Hate

Guilt ridden emotions, purge our thought, what are we doing, what has been wrought? These same emotions, produce a pain, negating hope, relief, or gain. Tears flowing forth, from our eyes, are manifest examples we can't disguise. Nor can we conceal, the ache of our heart, from which these tears, born of grief impart. Hate we discover, is the source of our pain, we can't escape or restrain. Why must hate we ask, so infect the mind, preventing love for all mankind. We none of us so perfect be, that we can be found better, than he or she. Each so alike, in each ones different way, equals before God, when we kneel to pray. Little it should matter, color of skin, amount of acquisition, or exultance of kin. Sharing Gods Grace, we have the gift of life, yet selfishly sow seeds of evil and strife. We care not for others, their needs or their pain, for we are mindful only, of personal gain. There still is a chance to right this wrong, we must not procrastinate, or prolong. The responsibility for ending this tormenting disgrace, must be borne by every, color and race. We must turn to the children, our remaining hope, if with this scourge we are to cope.
   —*Jerald B. Holzman*

"Untitled"

How can you love someone you
hate so much?
   I never really knew you but I think
about you constantly.
   I know what people say is true
that you were mean and cruel;
   But I would like to believe that
somewhere inside you, you loved me as much as I love you.
   When I was little I learned to fear you,
as I got older I learned to hate you.
   Now I'm just really confused.
I wish I could hate you like I used to,
   but I'd be lying if I said I did.
I wish I could fear you like I used to
   but your no threat to me dead.
I keep telling myself it's better that your gone,
   and in most aspects that true
But that doesn't help when I'm alone at night
   wishing for the father I never knew.
   —*Michelle Lachett*

Clouds At Play

On a warm clear summer day
Have you ever watched the clouds at play
The way they float across the sky
You wish, if only I could fly

Some so large while others small
I often tried to count them all
If you look closely you suddenly see
A picture of a great big tree

Or a funny man with a crooked nose
You sit and watch while he grows and grows
And then a ship comes into view
it quickly fades as they always do

Maybe people think I'm a funny guy
For sitting here watching the clouds go by
But it's so much fun, many pictures I see
Sometime sit down and watch them with me
   —*Norma R. Williams*

Memories

She stood quietly under the old tree.
He bare feet moved sensuously in the
evening dew on the grass.

Her arms stretched to embrace the old trunk,
Recalling tender moments, and wishing it were he,

With quickening heart, the memory of
his passionate kiss filled her mind
and trembling body.

He has gone, as have the many years,
Yet she still remembers the fragrance.
of the nights, and young love.
   —*Geraldine G. DeRosa*

Untitled

Tears drip off his cheek as he walks toward the bright light.
He stops for a moment and watches his family mourn over his unexpected death.
Sadly he walks on leaving his family and friends to grieve and mourn.
He steps into a light. No longer is he human. He is a spirit of peace, love, and happiness.
   —*Mollie Wells*

How Sad About Mr. Tate

Mr. Tate had a head on his shoulders.
He could solve Trigonometry II
And equal E=mc2.
He won the Nobel Prize in '72,
And again in '79.

He was smart until that one day.

Mr. Tate discovered new formulas.
Wrote a few books and made a few products.
He was knighted before the queen
For discovering her deadly disease.

Until one day his magic thinking snow
Made his intelligence no more.
How sad to hear about Mr. Tate,
Who is dead but still alive.
  —*Mark Baker*

Quietly The Rain

Paused and staring by cemetery gate,
he feels along its iron the prickling rust
and asks the secret of these dead
who have answered all questions by their dust.
But dust keeps still, only the cricket's song
scrapes at the late red moon.
No voices move the wind with dusty lips.
The spruce lays down its single stroke among rowed stone.

And he, beside the stiffened gate,
sees the moon go out in clouds,
and under oak on dark as smooth as slate
the rhythmic scratching of the cricket's dry refrain.

Then quietly, a whisper on the leaves,
the first soft rush, quietly the rain.
  —*Richard D. McIlnay*

Untitled

Lost interest is all she sees in his eyes
he has better things to do
or so he says
She tries to reach him
but there is no response
He is the special one
the one of many talents
the one of many thoughts
Disappointment
is all she finds
Her efforts
blown away with the wind
He knows and sees
but disregards with a shrug
he could
but won't
he should
but doesn't
maybe next year
maybe not
  —*Tara McDonald*

Frustrated Endeavor

Like a flower we grow
From nothing but a tiny seedling, we grow
Through rain and sunshine, we grow
Hoping to become a tree
Yet we are nothing but a mere flower in a forest full of trees
As we slowly wilt and die!
  —*Tragedy*

A Response

If Jesus came to my house? He has already come.
He is a constant visitor and a very welcome one.

I knew that He was coming the day I was confirmed,
but I was young and foolish and sometimes from Him I turned.

But Jesus in His gentle way is always there for me to
let me know the only way from sin I could be free.

I would not change my clothes before I let Him in,
because knowing Jesus He would take me as I am.

And if Jesus came in person, I'd not let the visit end,
I would let Him know that I consider Him my best and closest friend.

If I Had planned to go somewhere I would not change my
plans. I would ask Him to accompany me and meet some of
  my friends.

Yes, if Jesus came in person I would meet Him at the door.
I would say my Lord and Saviour. I couldn't say much more.
I'd welcome Him with open arms and show Him to a chair
And tell Him in so many words how very much I care.
  —*Edith Buege*

Meet The Savior

To those who His holy name and word defend,
He is a gentle, ever quiet, unseen friend.
He leadeth each thought of the humble mind
More carefully than a friend leadeth the blind.

The restless, troubled spirit, He can still.
He is stronger than our stubborn self-will,
Wiser than our adversary who tries to deceive,
Loving enough to persuade us His word to believe.

When Jesus the Saviour is earnestly sought,
You will find Him to be nearer than thought,
As real as the book that tells His story,
And able to lift our eyes from earth to Glory.
  —*Dorothy Dykhuizen*

He Laughs

He laughs when I tell him I love him,
He laughs when I say that I care.
He laughs when I say that I need him,
And tell him I'll always be there.

He laughs at the tears in my eyes,
He laughs at the pain in my heart.
He laughs at the hurt he has caused me,
As he slowly tears me apart.

He laughs at me,
And throws me to the wind.
He mocks my pain
As my world comes to an end.

I'll make his laughter go,
I'll somehow make it fade.
Someday he'll take me seriously,
And know that I'm not afraid.

And when he finally realizes it,
He'll come crawling back again.
And that's when I'll look him in the eye,
That's when I'll laugh at him.
  —*Lindsay Zimmerman*

Memories

On the windswept mesa the warrior stands, remembering.
He looks down on this once-beloved homeland,
And his mind sees the squaw with laughing eyes
And the tiny one with ebony braids flying in the wind
As they race to greet him, home from the hunt.
He lifts the child above his head and smiles;
She is the pride of this brave, she and her mother.
Another season comes, and they wave goodbye,
To await his return once more.
The flames come, blackening the pages
Of this open book of memories.
He turns his back on the charred remains of his life,
Begins to walk, and grieves silently.

—*Donna W. Alvis*

Luck The Duck

Luck the duck is very stuck up
he never says "please" when he wants something

he snorts all the time when he hears a rhyme
and likes to jump in the stinky old grime

he lives in the boat that's parked in the moat
and he always takes the last drop of milk from the goat

he often lies when eating pies

Oh why, oh why does he do it?

—*Caroline Rose Besley*

The Feeding Of The Five Thousand

When Jesus looked up and saw a great crowd,
  He noticed that they were getting quite loud.
It was about lunch time, probably noon,
  And Jesus thought the people should be eating real soon.
Jesus asked, "Where shall we get food for these people to eat?"
  Because Jesus had no bread, and he had no meat.
Jesus asked Phil, and Phil thought in his head,
  Meanwhile a boy came with some fish and bread.
It wasn't even enough to feed two men,
  But Jesus did a miracle then.
Jesus multiplied the food some more,
  And there were twelve baskets left on the floor.
With only two fish and five loaves of bread.
  That's how Jesus had the five thousand fed.

—*Andreana Mendoza*

Wednesday

I look into his eyes, feeling a strong fire,
He pulls me into his arms with a look of desire.
I can feel his body, my heart's quickened beat,
His hands are gentle with emotions so sweet.
His eyes hold my gaze, filled with love that's intense
in a world where not much besides this love makes sense,
His kisses grow deeper as my hold grows tight.
My heart rejoices in knowing this is finally right.
This is not going through physical motions,
This is real love with the truest devotion.
I close my eyes, pull him closer to me,
Restricting chains fall to pieces and set my heart free.
This moment is ours. No future; no past.
Our breathing quickens, hearts racing so fast;
My body reaches a climax of sensuous pleasure
as my heart knows a love far beyond any measure.
He smiles softly, gives a gentle kiss,
as we slowly recover from ecstatic bliss.
Dressed only in truth as we lie together,
I know this is not only love, but forever....

—*Carolyn Maggio*

In Memory Of Catherine

One year ago, God watched you suffer silently
He reached down from the heavens
And whispered come to me
We didn't want to see you go
But Jesus had a plan
The angels waited silently
Then took you by the hand
And as you walked the streets of gold
No memories of the past
Your husband whispered quietly
Home at last, home last

—*Beverly Busque*

Believe In Him

Back in the times when we'd first begun,
He saved our souls and gave us His son.
Now we are here in this land filled with lust;
He just asks us to love and that in God we do trust.
He watches over me as well as for you,
We're all children of God, no matter what we might do.
So love your fellow man and keep this in mind,
We must do what we can to be loving and kind.
Be passive and forgiving to those who may fall,
Whether they trip or stumble, God created us all.
He started us perfect, then Eve took that bite,
And since that day some say nothing's been right.
But if you believe in His strength and His love,
The day shall come when you'll stand up above.

—*Debra Ann Edwards*

Silver World

Frost, is Jack Frost's envelope
He seals it with love, with his silver finger,
To mail nature back to the world in the spring time.

Our word of nature is post office.
His postmen are legion. Bird jets fly south to mail fall,
The North wind helps chill and sort the silver world,
The lion of March roars wind to wake up Spring
and bird crooked serenade summer.

His deliveries are date:
brownies sitting on mushroom caps,
create bejeweled leaves in the fall,
Frost postmarks silver world winters,
Dancing on his cloven hoofs,
Pan pipes to flora and fauna in the Spring time.
Ole sol sees sylvan summers

His packages are c.o.d. on delivery,
Pay with your smile.

—*Vivienne Hammond*

A World Of Wonder

I look out my window
I found a world of wonder,
The sun reflecting off pine green leaves
Birds flying over trees just yonder.
I stare at some of nature
It's beauty stands out as strongly as can be,
I watch in amusement as it watches me.
As the day passes by and the nights come to shine
All day I have spent feeling the world to be mine
As time rolls past, I challenge the night to last
But I know the day shall come again
But until that time, I will be enduring in the nights rhyme.

—*Amber Brady*

Love

Someone you loved, loved so much
  He tells you that he loves you too.
You think to yourself could this be true?
  But "no" it can't be it has happened before.
But this time there's something new.
  Something that will last a lifetime.
Something and someone you know that you'll cherish.
  But wait one minute you know it will vanish.
That something that you fear of is love,
  Love as gentle as a snow covered dove
You think it over and know the answer
  Yes it's true
You pray it won't turn out blue one month,
  Two months pass by
  You figure that time sure does fly
Because you're in love
  You go too far, head over heels
Then poof, it's gone, gone forever
  The love that you feared did vanish.
It vanished forever
    —*April Derouin*

Jesus Is A Friend

Jesus is a friend who you can take your troubles to.
He understands every trial that you go through.

Help me Jesus today
to walk the straight and narrow way.

I believe the Bible just like Jesus said,
Jesus is coming back and resurrect the dead.

Will you be ready for the great Judgement day?
If not, now is the time to kneel and pray.

Now, won't you prepare
to meet Jesus in the air?
    —*Lillie McGuire*

My Father's Song

He was not perfect but as close as can be
He was a friend and father to me

His philosophy simple, live and let live
When there was a need, he was willing to give

He didn't ask much and always worked hard

With sore, calloused hands in the garden and yard

He loved his tools and he loved his work
Taking the hard with the easy with not even a quirk

No words can tell how good was the man
But now he can walk holding his father's hand

We'll miss him so much 'cause now he is gone
That's why I had to write my father's song
    —*Charles Sheppard*

"I Love You"

I love you........ If it's convenient.
I support you..... If it doesn't put me out.
I adore you....... If I have to.
I respect you..... If we're around others.
I need you........ If it serves my purpose.
I hurt you........ If you make me.
I use you......... If you let me.
I agree with you.. If you do it my way.
I help you........ If I want to.
I leave you....... Because you made me.
    —*J. P. Mello*

Prisoner Of Fear

The battle field lay before him like a satin sheet,
He was level headed, and ready for anything but defeat.
He felt as if he were alone that day, with no other
soldiers around,
But as he awoke from his imaginary world he saw his buddies
lying on the ground.
The noise was deafening as the bombs flared left and right,
He crawled into a cubby hole and stayed there stiff with
fright.
He could hear his fellow soldiers calling out his name, but
not an inch did he move and not once did he quiver with shame.

The night fell and the fighting ceased, only to resume at dawn,
He ran with terror of being shot, not knowing right from wrong.
When morning came they heard no sound, no firing of any kind.
They grabbed their guns and ran to awake general number nine.
The soldier who ran had heard the news, and realized what he
had done,
He dropped his head and lifted his arms in surrendurance of the
enemy's guns.
    —*Pepper Loren Corwin*

The Agony Of The Great One

  It was quite a time ago that he lived.
  He was loved by many and mocked by others.
  He grew up in Israel,
  and preached in the Synagogues
  He helped many in distress,
  He was nailed to a cross and forced
to wear a crown of thorns.
  He was spat upon.
  Many looked up in sorrow.
  Then she wept.
  The great one hung upon a cross.
  Calvary was silent.
  Then the great one was silent also.
  He was put into a tomb.
  It was three days later that the great
one appeared before the Israelites.
  They rejoiced because Jesus lived...
  It was quite a time ago.
    —*Natasha Cruz*

My Dad

My Dad was a giant of a man,
He was so gentle, so caring so sweet.
His heart was as pure as fresh-fallen snow.
A stranger he never did meet.

He was my hero, my friend, my confidante;
He loved children and animals and life;
He never dwelled on his hardships,
on anger or fears or on strife.

Precious memories with him are so many;
His whistling, his laughing, his smiles.
Together we rode country roads and through woods,
For miles and miles and miles.

When he died his little girl had grown up,
But I was still the apple of his eye.
His death left a void in my life,
But as he did, I believe,
We'll meet again in the "sweet by and by."
    —*Shirley Singleton Flanagan*

The Old King

The old king was very mean.
He wasn't at all very lean.
The king was very big and fat.
His only pet was a big gray cat.

Let the king wear a crown.
The shirt he wore was dark brown.
One of his favorite fruits was a pear.
Watch him play with a big bear.

He lives in a big castle.
When he built it he thought it was a hassle.
His stomach was as big as a pig.
The king always hates to go dig.

This old king has a lot of money.
There are bees in the castle that make honey.
This weird king has a lucky card.
He thinks card playing is hard.

His cousin's name is Ray.
Ray has a lot of yellow hay.
This old king is pretty sad.
The old king is so, so, bad.
—*Clay Rohrbach*

Daddy Smile

I once had a daddy that smiled,
He watched me grow with a smile,
He was busy as an owl.
But watched me grow with a smile,
He said Kid always have a smile
In his years of tears,
I watch him grow with a smile
As I become Fifty and him Seventy-five
I watch him grow younger by years.
He said kid you make it.
If you turn your tears into a smile,
So as we grown old together
I took his advice and took the world
With a smile
As I look back
I work like owl take the tears
Grow younger by years and smile
—*Lois Hoeffner*

When His Country Called

As I recall that awful day
He went to fight so far away
Our hearts were broken, with fear did burn
Afraid our loved one might not return
His youth was taken on that day
Yet he did not think to run away
His country called and he was true
To keep it free for me and you
For many months he did push on
He would forever recall the horrors of Nam
We thanked God when he returned home at last
But the youth who left was someone from the past
Within his heart and within his mind
Were tears and thoughts for those left behind
Although many seasons have since come and gone
The man is home, but the youth remains in Vietnam
—*Madeline Spink*

Finding Yourself

Fall across all our yesterdays,
…Hear that sound?…
  to be uncertain and anxious
Now wonder where you're headed and what you're seeing
  the time is right to destroy your fears
You'll find you feel safe and steel away in your destiny.
Repeated in the corridors, performing your movements
The passion lives to keep your faith
You cry in the daylight
  even though you know you're not alone
  the sunlight still beaming in your eyes
I'm seeing my way for the first time in years,
  the same lies with you
  because you use that wild imagination
  with the realization of a new way
And I'm here with you.
—*Joanna Craggs*

Aging And Renewal

Gray heads, bald heads, bent shoulders,
Hearing aids, canes, walkers, wheel chairs,
Props of the survival of long winters,
And too, the empty stares of erased memories
Fill me with a sadness at the loss of the
  greenness, once a'blooming.

And yet the brownish oak leaf,
The seared red and golden maple,
All wind tossed, rain soaked
Nurture the autumnal soil,
Murmuring the promise of spring to come.
—*Evelyn H. Glass*

"Tribute To A Wonderful Husband"

Oh! How I do miss you, husband of mine, just to be near you my heart doth pine. Oh could we but return to the days of yore when we talked and talked some more. There was nothing with you I could not discuss and in your advice I could put my trust. Even now, when the solution to a problem I haven't a a clue, I can almost hear you tell me what to do. "Quit your worrying," you used to say "Or you'll be old before your day." "Your hair too soon will be turning gray, so dry your eyes and come to me;" with one of your sweet smiles I do so love to see. For 34 years we walked side by side, and loved each other whatever betide. We had a companionship so rare and your love for me often, you did declare. You cared for me when I was ill and put up with me when I was being a pill. So rest in peace my
beloved one, and when at last my days are done, I'll rest beside you in the grave and your company I will no longer have to crave.
—*Bonnie Myers*

"Dearest Mother"

Even though we've had our ins and outs.
I still consider you the "best" mother without a doubt.
Someone who cared for me when I was small,
Who shared with me her tenderest all.
Someone who was there when I needed them
To show me love and affection as well.
Someone to whom my problems I could tell.
For this I will be forever grateful until the end,
Because, now I know that you are my only true friend.
—*Dottie Di Fede*

"Daniel"

I've always tried to be good to everyone, even when my
heart felt like a ton but a beautiful son, well I only have one
  I try not to think about the dawn
or be naive as a newborn fawn
  Each morning that I wake
his eyes to open and common sense he won't for sake
  and be a man all his own
also to realize his life is only a loan
  and for him to stand strong on his own two feet
But to always respect the one who loves him even when weak
  my son blames me because I will die
and he's very young and doesn't understand why
  I need him to know
I do love him so
  So hush my son, I need no tears
I need your mind to be crystal clear
  I want him to see, He's showing me disrespect and hate
But I need him to see it before its too late.
  So show me your love so my soul doesn't roam
and I will be at peace on my final trip home
  —*D. M. Haggard*

Endless Love

    Someone special, you so admire,
    Hearts beating rapid with such desire.
    Dancing close, with intense passion,
Sincere feelings, but she's a little old fashion.
  Daydreams of spending every minute together,
  Romantic walks, no matter what the weather.
    Sweet kisses, so warm and tender,
    Embraces so tight their hearts surrender.
Butterflies, with the feeling of nervous excitement,
Anticipation of being one, brings such enlightenment.
    Wonderful feelings. two hearts so true,
    Such happiness, no time for the blues.
    Endless love, it's so very rare,
 A gift from God, to which nothing can compare...
    The precious words "I love you",
And converting two souls into one, by saying, "I do."
  —*Karmel K. Kent*

Mount St. Helen

  Blackened, charred, are her slopes, the ascent of Mount St. Helen. Volcanic eruption covers terrain miles and miles around felt is her fallout over the World, smothering, destroying, killing - molten lava continues to well up - grotesque sounds issue from within.

  She stood majestic - trees, wild life, streams, lakes, rivers abounding - pleasure, peace of soul, even employment came to those who touched her.

  Darkened, bleak, ugly, raw, crown gone, she towers now overseeing miles of ash covered land. Her path of destruction is vast.

  What force makes her erupt and explode? What brings about her ravaging anger? Oh that her power could be harnessed to give life, hope, saving energy.

  World awake to reality! Look upon Mount St. Helen! Keep watch! Be concerned! People, land, water cremated forever! Smashing the atom, radio active decay, chemicals, garbage, nuclear power, nuclear and chemical waste— ENERGY AND WASTE UNCONTROLLED! are doing this to you.
  —*Grace Elgart*

A Prayer To The World

Dear God
Help us to see beyond the darkness
And despair that's plaguing the world
Teach us to be able to cope with each other
In our everyday life.
To have more faith and show more expression of love
Envelope and bathe us in your warm soft
Love and protective arms (prayers)
Help us to share and expand
In all our experiences, thoughts, goals, and deeds.
And fulfill our purpose in life.
And Dear God, help us to walk in peace
And grow in unity.
Amen
  —*V.H. Webb*

The Morning Lady

She crept up dressed in golden glow,
Her eyes so fiery as she stared at the snow.
Her coat lit up like the fire itself,
She made all cozy and warm, even someone off by himself.
Her cheeks so cherry, burning like a flame,
Everything made bright, nothing left lame.
Her golden hair so shiny and long,
Awakes the children and the birds with her song.
She, a golden light was a sight to see,
She made all warm, even the black sea.
  —*Micayla Moltsau*

Gone

On the sunniest day
  her face will appear.
On the coldest of nights
  I'll feel her near.

We were very close -
  where did she go?

She's like water hitting freezing, cold snow-
  Gone.

Her dimples and freckles
  shine in grace

Where is that smile?
Where is that face?

They'll never be replaced.
  Gone.

The giggles, the laughs,
  Her warm embrace-
Gone,
Gone,
Gone without a trace-
Gone.
  —*Michelle Callahan*

Desired Love

I wish upon a shining star,
I gaze upon a glowing moon.
All day and night I dream real far-
To a place desired to see soon.

Where love and peace are never threatened
Where no one or nothing is ever frightened.
This place I dream to be-
Dreaming for you to be with me.
  —*Kari Calabrese*

Annie Apocalyptic

My eyes open to the sight of a saint covered in sweat and blood
Her hair dripping with the salty water that which roars w/ in
the sea below the deepest grave. Her voice utters words to
which even the brightest man could not know. Her message the
fall of an empire claimed to be our world, still my ears are
drawn to listen. She picks me up and puts me upon her frail body
I feel her bones quiver in pain and hear her yellow stained skin
breathe with anticipation. Though she safely carries me on
her wings of happiness I am dropped in a world of suffering
Where darkness scares the light into corners of burnt out dreams
Where candles flicker under faces of disfigured men and smiling
devils. Where souls roam screaming damnations to the woman
whose
sidewalk is paved with broken angel-wings. How dare she bring
me here? A place where fantasies are food for fear and frowns
cover a child's smile. This place that weakens my strength and
burns the very paper house of my love's refuge. A land
intoxicated by the touch of hell's jesty sinners. Where clouds
are visions of inverted crosses and temples of flames burn in
the wind. Where flowers grow only to die from the breath of
possessed children.

—*Brandy Montalvo*

"The Way It Could Be"

There was girl who had a troubled life,
Her parents didn't care so she cut herself with a knife.

She only went one way, and no one could stop her,
Her friends would always try to help, but she didn't care, for,

Now she's dead, and in a way, so is everyone else,
We made a book of her and it's on the shelf.

As the girl who killed herself because she wouldn't listen,
If only she had done what we asked, now she's gone and we're
missin'. There was a girl who had a troubled life,
Her parents didn't care but she didn't cut herself with a knife.
In the beginning, she wouldn't listen,
But then she realized what all she would be missin',

Now her parents love and care, and she's at college,
She is very happy to share her friends knowledge.

Now she is married, successful with her groom,
If she had died, everyone would live in doom.

Locked in a room, was her younger life,
Now she is remembered as the girl who made it through,
Not touching the dirty knife.

—*Alison Michelle Kilborn*

Sunshine

My wife has been my sunshine through each and every year.
Her pretty brown eyes, her long dark hair, and her smile from
ear to ear.

This day in age its hard to cope with life the way it is, but
I'll always love my sunshine, and I'll always keep her near.

Let me tell you something and I'll try to make it clear. If you treat
your sunshine decent and she will never shed a tear.

Now all you gents in wonderland, lend me your ear, I'll
state some facts and promises, I'll try to make it clear.

Love your woman dearly as often as I do, and you'll always
spend your rainy days with your sunshine next to you.

—*David Schillinger*

The Lady

Here's to the lady I love so much.
Here's to the lady with the magic touch.
Here's to the lady full of kindness and love.
Here's to the lady sent from above.
Here's to the lady who fought trouble and strife.
Here's to the lady that give me life.
Here's to the lady who kissed away my tears.
Here's to the lady who worked for years.
Here's to the lady who stopped my sad.
Here's to the lady who taught me good from bad.
Here's to the lady who kept me clean and dressed.
Here's to the lady who quick to caress.
Here's to the lady who kept me fed.
Here's to the lady who made my bed.
Here's to the lady who waited up at night.
Here's to the lady who holds me so tight.
Here's to the lady I love as no other.
Here's to the lady I call my mother.
Rest now,
For I love you!!!

—*Cocoa Johnson*

Bert

My friend Bert is quite a guy.
He's retired and lazy, and does he like pie!
He likes it cold, he likes it hot,
Just any kind, it matters not.
I hate to tell you, but if I must,
He'll even eat it without a crust.
He'll by the stuff it takes to make it,
Then he'll even help to bake it.
He's gentle and good, and the kind of man
That believes in doing the best he can.
He's honest and wise, and everyone knows
The likes of him doesn't come in droves.

—*Elizabeth Ramey*

If Only It Was

If only it was, that I could fly,
High above the eagles in the sky.
Soaring freely, here and there,
Without stopping, because of despair.
If only it was I could run very fast,
So fast, no shadow I would cast.
Running so fast, so far, so quick
Running so fast I would never get sick.
If only it was, that you loved me,
Then we could be together for all eternity.
With each other hand in hand,
Together we could always stand.
If only it was, that you loved me.
If only it was, all of this could be.

—*Alyssa Delaney*

Playground

Little girl, come and play.
I have a desire for you today.
Don't be scared, I won't harm.
I will have you in my arm.

You love your daddy, oh yes you do.
So stop screaming and crying because I love you.
It's play time again in the bed,
Oh Katie, don't play dead!

—*Michelle Lee*

The Little Flowers

All around little flowers are planted.
High and low, far and wide,
within their certain boundaries.
The dawn sunlight comes,
dancing upon the flowers.
At sunset, the sun bids them a warm good-bye.
Everyday the yellow sun and the colored flowers,
Gladly greet each other.
Seasons have come and seasons have gone.
The sun and the flowers,
learned to love each other.
Years have come and years have gone.
The flowers sap has gone dry,
Sadly they are fading and dropping.
Hope is all the sun has, that the old man.
Will re-wallpaper his room,
with the little flowers again.
—*Gregory Smith*

The Blue Heron

His visits are always, unannounced and brief.
His arrivals, quiet like a rustling leaf.
And most often, his presence goes unseen—
As from out the pond his meal he gleans.
Observing serenely his still domain—
Its tenuous borders, he lays his claim.
But should any creature who walks upright,
Suppose to wreck his quiet delight,
Then retiring with speed and without a fight,
He gives up his kingdom in exchange for flight.
—*Phillip T. Greene*

Wait For Mercy

He was alone...at least he felt he was.
His blue uniform was torn, and a fresh wound burned his side.
"Lord," he said through his tears. "I'm going to give up."
But the Lord spoke...
"Wait for Mercy."

"Mercy!" The Young Yankee cried. "During a war like this?"
But the Lord only repeated...
"Wait for Mercy."
Then the soldier's world seemed to turn black...
A young girl found him, and brought him home.

When the soldier was well enough to leave,
Then young girl was very upset.
She held onto his hand and cried and cried.
"At least take something to remember me by," she told him.
And with those words, she took the locket off her neck,
and handed it to him.

She then ran out of the room, and left him in peace.
Alone, he starred tat the shining gold object for the longest
time. And then he opened the latch...
"To my darling daughter..." it read. "Mercy."
—*Gina Marie Twitchell*

A Single Tear

A single tear, then an uncontrollable down pour
How could I let it happen this way?
My mind is lost in all of my problems and dreams
Reality seems so far away
Unable to concentrate
The situation gets worse
And I realize the consequences
But I do nothing to change what's going on.
I sink into the quicksand
Surrounded by people
No one lends me their hand.
—*Melanie Plant*

Blind Man's Blues

I came across an old man playing blues out on the street.
His clothing was in tatters, there were no shoes on his feet.
I stood there while he sang, and his eyes never met mine.
And I wondered how a homeless man survived if he was blind.
I saw his rickety guitar case, the meager coins inside.
Saw his possessions, packed in bags, and something in me died.
I tossed a quarter in his case, and he looked up with a smile.
I asked how long he'd lived like this, and he talked for quite
a while. He talked about his family, his old house with the
picket fence. But the war had taken it all from him, even his
primary sense. He said, "Son, all I got's my music. I just
try to get by on that." I told him I'd bee back later, and
he said good-bye with a tip of his hat. As I walked away, he
sang a song of inner pain. And I asked myself the question,
"Where does he go when it rains?" Over the next few weeks, I
visited him some more. Same time and place every day, in front
of that old grocery store. He never took my donations, said he
had his dignity. This derelict old bluesman became a part of
me. I cherished our talks together, and the time we spent each
day. But it rained last night, and he wasn't there today.
—*Jeff Johnston*

Stormy Memory

The rain goes trickling down the pane; the lightning lights
　his face.
The old man looks and grabs his cane and goes to the door in
　haste.
The thunder roars deep in the night; it rings inside his ears.
His heart goes back to that fateful flight with his beloved
　one so dear...
The rain poured down, the thunder roared, the lightening lit
　the way;
He carried her on his trusty mare that stormy wedding day.
The wind and rain blew in his face; he could not see ahead.
His heart beat fast deep in his chest as onward the lovers fled.
He could not see the warning sign; the bridge had washed away.
He pulled her close and held her tight; the time had come to
　pray.
The water rose around them high as the horse began to swim.
She slipped away into the night, the water dark and dim...
The tears ran down his wrinkled face with sobs he could not
　hold.
His life has been a lonely waste with memories so cold.
—*Aniece Newsom*

Changeling

The mammoth beast ungainly lumbers, roars
his feet are pounding, galloping faster and faster
immense wings spread, the red-wing falcon soars
to shriek out loudly, calling out to the master
She plummets earthward, talons rip the snake
who slithers over sand and rocks so dry
to chase the lizard sprinting off to wake,
alight on hollow log, the dragon fly
Submerged sea monster snaps it in his mouth
his massive tail it slashes causing waves
that crash the shore to push the sand about
transposing drifts, composing cliffs and caves

Lids cracking open, I spy the magician, wand in hand
musicians intent and still, awaiting his next command
—*Claire Ayraud*

Second Childhood

I missed my second childhood the first time around.
I guess my feet were planted to firmly on the ground.
But now by gosh I'm ready, this will be the day,
That I claim my right to "silly", the child in me shall play!
—*Mary Ann Tripp*

Reflections Of A Soldier

As the lonely soldier stares out across the darkening sand,
His thoughts are on tomorrow.
Will it be peace or war on this land?

He said his farewells to family and friends,
Hoping against hope that he would see them again.

No bands, parades or cheers to fill this night;
Only loneliness, fear and a hope to see daylight.

His country called, he came, that was his due
To keep the world safe for me and you.

He would pay with his life if the cost be that high
Rather than see democracy and freedom wither and die.

We honor those that answer the ultimate call
With a flagged-draped coffin.
Soldiers standing straight and tall,
A final salute, the weapons firing,
Suppressing their grief, the family is trying
To overcome the anger at the uselessness of it all.

How many more will follow this end
Before peace is again restored to the land?
—*Linda Housden*

Grandpa

My grandpa was here, but now he's gone,
His time spent down here doesn't seem very long.
He thrilled us and blessed us with love that he gave,
But now all we have are memories that we cherish and save.
We remember the times spent out on the beach,
And all of the lessons of love he would teach.
You see grandpa's are very special and I had one, so I should know.
But then the time came when the pain
Was too much, therefore, he had to go.
It's true what they say, "Life goes on,"
But it doesn't stop the pain.
To know no matter how much sorrow you feel,
His life you cannot regain.
But keep your chin up, there's always hope
That you'll see him once again,
Running to you, arms out-stretched,
Sporting a big grin.
—*Karen Williams*

"Time To Set Her Free"

What happened to the little girl who used to
hold my hand?
   Who used to use my make-up on her strips too
make-believe land?
   She's found someone who needs her; as she
once needed me. It's time to let her go now, must I
set her free?
Some day she'll have a little girl and she will hold
her hand, and perhaps, take "her" on some trips to
make believe land.
But all to soon the day will come when she will say to me,
   Do I have to let her go now Mom; is it
     Time to set her free?
—*Joyce Hetzel*

To My Valentine

When I see the puffy white clouds,
  I think of you.
When I look at new budding trees in spring,
  I think of you.
I never want to say, "Goodbye Sweetheart"
Just stay near me in spirit so I'll not be alone.
My love for you is my strength dear one,
  when I think of you, honey.
—*Patricia Blogna*

You Cradle Her

You cradle her, as she has cradled you:
Holding a small form etched into the dark,
Hearing the silent hunger all night through.

After the tumor is cut away, it's true:
Ravage draws on her face and in your mind its mark.
You cradle her as she cradled you,

Wondering how, through your infancy, she drew
Faith to give suckle in the Depression dark,
Hearing the silent hunger all night through.

You leave because there's nothing you can do
To force-feed time or age. Your anguish stark,
You cradle her as she has cradled you,

And in your mind you spoon-feed love and rue
For unremembered meals, trying to know her dark,
Hearing the silent hunger all night through.

How can the plump warm one who nourished you
Be now so spent? Seeing only a feeble spark,
You cradle her as she has cradled you,
Hearing the silent hunger all night through.
—*Patricia Conner*

Friendship

I wish for you-

Fences to climb for adventure-
   Hope to lean on when you feel vulnerable,
   Strength when you feel tired.

Flowers to brighten your day-
   Encouragement when you feel life's frustrations,
   Faith when you feel exposed.

Fields to roam in freedom-
   Exaltation when you succeed in victories seen,
   Self-fulfillment in victories of dreams in your heart.
—*Denny L. Leard*

Peace

Peace, peace, for the whole world, Our Motto.
How can we, a crooked, perverse nation know?
Wars don't make peace, they must cease.
Do away with bombs, guns and stop destruction,
Have respect for other Nation's customs.
For conscious sake, put on the helmet of good,
Give housing, clothing and food.
Turn the instruments into implements,
To build and make bread for the homeless and hungry.
Not intended by God, to rule with an iron rod.
Nor tread down the fierceness and wrath,
In the battle's path.
Do not lift up sword against nation,
Nor learn war any more, help people
To learn Peace in the heart, evermore.
—*Annie Laura Joiner*

Don't You Know?

Intruder,
How dare you grin
   luringly at me from between the blinds
And whisper
   your sweet bird song!
Don't kiss
   my sleepy face with your seductive breath
Or taunt
   me to come frolic in your glowing warmth.
Don't you know?
It's Saturday.
—*Vicki Pavelec*

I Share Your Pain

How could anyone not cry?
How could anyone outright deny, the pain, the suffering,
the Nazis did apply?
To kill so many people because of their race, what a terrible
thing for you to face.
God give comfort to all the families whose loved ones were lost
God help the world to never let this world experience ever
again such horrors endured by the Jewish people.

I hear stories so terrible and horrible and it makes me so sad,
It's hard to believe the Nazis were so cruel, so inhumane, just
so bad.
Unfortunately it is all true, again it makes me so very sad.
My Jewish friends I say to you, God give you strength to
endure these horrible unhappy memories.
God is on your side
Israel is now so strong and will stay so until the end of time.
Thank God for all who did survive.
—*Tina Karayanis*

Opposites

When is life a dream, and when does a dream become real?
How do we know what is real from what is not?
For we only know what is cold, because we know that it is not
hot, and when something is black, for certain it is not white.
We all know what love is, and for many it is so great,
if love is so grand then, why so much hate?
What is light can never be dark,
and what is complex should not be stark.
Just as laughter is the cure to all pain,
sorrow is the denouement for all joy.
As summer is to life, and winter is to death,
spring is to beginning, and autumn is to ending.
Deception is mistrust, better yet a lie,
where honesty is truth, a cause so few are worth willing to die.
Black will always be black, as white will always be white,
they grey area in between always hidden from sight.
One day we will see, within itself, what was meant to be,
until then, we will only know the other, because of what we
choose to see.
—*Peter Andrew Sacco*

Untitled

Man and bird upon the beach,
How far does man's undoing often reach?
For in our hearts' of many maze's,
Loves undoing often raises,
Tears of joy in that we care,
From head the hair we often tear;
So, why I ask does man's undoing,
often raft of love's own cooing?
If only we could often reach,
   The lofty heights
of our souls impeach;
why darkness falls upon my sight?
of course, the view of morning light:
for stars at night
   Wait in round,
for the birds who sing the morning sound...
—*Ralph Thomas Cole III*

Summer Nights

    Sometimes I just sit and wonder
   how I'm gunna how through the summer.

  Without you, I sometimes feel confused, sad and blue
  thinking of me sitting here, alone, without you.

   I don't know how I can take the pain, of not
seeing or being with you, until the winter begins again.

I just can't wait till the cold, winter snow begins to bite,
   'cause then I'll know that'll be the end
     of sad and lonely
       Summer Nights.
—*Brandy Wall*

The Pattern That Spells Eternity

What is the pattern that spells eternity?
How shall the pieces fall?
What shape or form's this sense of serenity,
is it a gift to all!
And who will recognize the form it takes,
who will notice the shape?
The pieces have come to rest in all of us.
The shape of a heart awaits.

A heart is the pattern that spells eternity,
but when will these pieces call?
And will you realize serenity
or will you not hear at all?
For only true love can be eternal,
all other loves will pass.
And only the truly human heart can know
true love will everlast.
—*LM Kilcullen*

Lost Friend

She thinks of you still everyday
How she cries that life took you away

You were always her very best friend
Something that lasted to the very end

The day you told her of your illness
All she could do was sit in stillness

Now you have gone far away
The love for you will always stay

Your smiling face, which she will never see
Her father, you will always be
—*Kristina Whitaker*

Silent Watches

In the silent watches of the night
how the thoughts race in my head.
Tossing, turning, rolling,
speaking to me in whispers,
reminding me of what is precious and what is worthless.
Faces appear, good and bad memories, past and present.
Sleep is a blessing and deeply into it I fall
for with the morning sun comes another day of toil.
Happiness is something deep inside that no one can take from me
for only on the outside is pain felt or expressed,
because inside, "the inner me" belongs to God,
which no man knows but the Father Himself.
—*Roxanna Delozier*

My Being

My being has been intruded upon; hateful words, awful lies.
Hurt and anger won't surface for fear they'll be recognized.
My heart is broken, it may never heal. Please God make me
    willing to feel.
My eyes are too dry to allow tears to come, my head wants to
    scream and my body to run.
My self worth is shattered, my thoughts are confused.
Thank goodness I know they can be diffused.
For one day my heart will be happy and whole;
One day I will shed a tear. One day my being will understand
    the reason for my fear:
To strengthen me within and without, that someday I can reach
    out to another hurting soul.
I'll be there with my scars from wounds healed. I'll let her
    know her feelings are real.
I'll tell her that we're special, we can't be denied; those
    hurtful people, well they just lied.
I then will believe there will come a day that this painful
    feeling will end.
And then I will know, without a doubt, my being will love again
—*Sonja D. Thomas*

Good Ol' Summertime

Throughout the fall, winter, and spring
I anxiously anticipate what summer will bring.
But when good ol' summertime is finally here,
There is one part of the season about which I don't cheer.
This part of the season is not so sweet.
I definitely wouldn't call it a treat—
Heat:

Heat in the morning, at noon, and at night.
Stifling heat with no end in sight.
It's as hot as an oven when I walk outside.
I stick to the carseat when I go for a ride.
Feeling as wilted as week-old lettuce and out of sorts,
I try to stay cool in a tank top and shorts.
I decide to sprinkle the scorched grass on this sweltering day.
The water sputters and sizzles as it hits the driveway.
Exhausted, I pray for a cooling rain.
I start to wonder how "good ol' summertime" got its name.
—*Laura Schoenbeck*

The Kitten

I wonder if that kitten is lonely in his cage.
       If only I could help him.
        I'm sorry that I can't.
I wonder if he has relatives waiting for him at home.
      I'm sorry that I can't keep him.
       I wonder if he is the same age as I.
         I wonder if I could pet him.
      He is so cute; he had warm, fuzzy tears
          The minute he saw me.
—*Tammy DeCoteau*

A New Day

Early, at dawn, as my day begins,
I ask my Lord to forgive my sins,
And pray that he will help me be,
A kinder member of his family.

That I may walk this earth and show,
Others the faith from which to grow,
To help lift burdens from their minds,
And with them cope in a world unkind.

For faith and hope will take us far,
Love for each other will prevent a war,
All the hungry and homeless, young and old,
Can be protected from the rain and cold.

The little mouths crying out in need,
Can be comforted if we cast out greed,
Alas, so many problems in this cruel world
I must wave my flag of charity unfurled.

For my Lord above did not plan,
The sinful ways of earthly man,
He gave us rules to guide our way,
And we must heed them each new day.
—*D. J. Berry*

Why?

When the war has been all but lost
I ask you, at what cost?

Where do the battles end?
What happens when there are no more messengers to send?

When the front line has been all but defeated,
When is it time to move forward so the process can be repeated?

With each moment another life has been ended.
Was it all a game that went too far
so we felt it must be pretended?

As we carry on with our instruments of destruction
do we not realize we spread death and corruption?

If this is just some perverse game we must play,
then why in our moment of need
is it only then that we feel we must pray?
—*Kathrine M. Moore*

The World

   The World is a playground so fine and fair.
I can dance in the forest or swing in the trees,
   While my senses thrive in the cool summer air.
    I feel happiness-it blows in the breeze.
   The World is despairing and filled with gloom.
      Hunger and poverty create such pain,
   That The World grows dark like a sealed tomb
      In winter's cold and humanities shame.
    Than shall I see love or shall I see hate?
  And will there always be things for us to fear,
    And wolves constantly barking at our gate?
   Or will peace spread in the following years?
      It is up to us-so will we all fail,
      And let hatred and injustice prevail?
—*Steven Tousignant*

American Tragedy

Wounded eyes loom in my mind and
I can't help but think of the pain
that has befallen these once proud people.
The White man's lies
denied them all but breath
and much was expected in return.
White's destiny was to conquer and destroy,
Red's to sacrifice and suffer.
Majestic brave warriors proudly roamed
before white's invasion.
Now those warriors drown in White whiskey and
White lies.
White man's greed destroyed the race
Leaving neither the richer...
Both the poorer.
As Native pride diminishes, so does our own.
True victory would have been unity.
—*Lisa Loveland*

The Sea

On a leisure walk along the shore
I chanced to watch the sea in awe
A cloak of enchantment enfolded me
As its vastness held me breathlessly.

It's rhymetic waves a symphony in motion
Peaceful, graceful without emotion
The sun to set, the moon soon to appear
Casting a glow like a radiant dear.

Unchallenged defiant in its mysterious ways
Strong and masterful of all it surveys
So beautiful, so frightening and overwhelming too
An endless void from where a country grew.

So I continue along my way
The tide reveals the closing of the day
My footprints soon vanish in the watery sand
But time cannot diminish my pride in my land.
—*Rosalie Lambert*

Broken Pieces

In this crowded world of ours.
I choose you and only you to love. You
have been the only one who has
given me love and respect and I thank you.
When I thought you had,
loved me, you choose more than
one to love and hold. I knew no
matter how much you hurt me. I
only need to ask you one question,"
Why do you tell me that you love
me, when none of it is true. Can't
you see my heart is aching and crying out
for you? Won't I ever get a chance to
hold you again?
Please answer me my love. Will
these broken pieces of mine over be
brought together as one?
—*Lizbeth Alcocer*

Peeking

Who is that peeking all yellow and bright.
I believe it's the sun pulling the covers back on
   the night.
Warm and shining to our delight.
Who's next to play peek in the sun light.
—*Marjorie A. Eddy*

Tears

Tears pour from my eyes each and every night.
I cry until I can cry no more.
This feeling is like none I've ever experienced.
It hurts like nothing I've ever known.
This constant squeezing around my heart.
Suffocating me until I gasp for air.
I force myself to hold back, the scream of agony coming
from my soul.
The deeper I breathe, the deeper it hurts.
My body leaves until it's weak with exhaustion.
My mouth is dry and I can't swallow the lump
that must be my heart creeping higher and higher into my throat
I'm drowning in my own tears of pain.
—*Dawn Jennings*

Whispering Wind

Call me whispering wind
I dance across the sky in spring
later, I'll pick up the gentle winds
of summer and then
   I'll sing upon the ocean far and wide.

Why does it have to be me?
Whispering wind picking up the reluctant
leaves to the other side of the tree. My cold
breath hitting against the weary animals trotting
down the pasture. I'll leave my temper at
the end of autumn.

Here I come gasping violently into
winter. While my brushed hair leaves
breathless people cold as I run with each
toe hitting the freezing snow. I cannot stand
it! Spitting tiny flakes of snow on everything
in sight.

I shall leave this winter memory behind
as I calm down to the nice breezy spring which
I've made in my heart.
—*Patricia Hickey*

Forbidden Wish

No one understands me, or the way I feel not even me.
I do know I feel something so deeply
especially when I look into your eyes
such beautiful eyes. Eyes that are so loving
sincere, and truthful.
Do you dream of my kiss, of my embrace
As I dream of yours?
It is a mystery, something I do not dare
But yet, if possible, I'd take that chance
Just for once to feel your lips touch mine.
To feel your arms hold me tight, like once before
I've seen your tears of care
And I've seen your tears of loneliness
Why can't two people who feel so much
Be together in closeness?
Is this a FORBIDDEN WISH?
As I close my eyes now
And look deeply into yours
I wonder if there is one chance
That maybe my FORBIDDEN WISH can come true?
—*Jennifer Wilson*

Experience, Cannot Be Forgotten

As I stepped for the first time on the boat
I dreamed with confidence I will enjoy the good time
Fishing on the deep blue sea
The sun was dazzling hot, a prayer was said
Only deep blue ocean surrounds you
Yet, no big fish was seen
Hey! Boys! Where's the fish? I said
Circling the buoy and seeing boats around
A smile came to me, at last we'll catch a fish
Suddenly the engine stopped, I said, what's wrong?
Bottom fishing is "da best"
Suddenly my laughter stopped
Oh Lord! Something is wrong
My stomach is in dismay
I tried to be strong, but the feeling was wrong
The happiness was also gone
I yelled! Please bring home
Ignoring me, they yelled, we catching fish!
I know with demanding voice, I am your mother!!!
Bring me home sons, I am seasick!! I am seasick!!
—*Lillian D. Saliot*

Eternal Love

The power in your mind
I feel it strong and kind.
The love that is in your brain,
the blood running through your veins.
The beauty you possess
the gentle words that come of your breath,
the reasons why I love the flying of the dove.
As the wind blows through your hair
my soul flies unaware
through all stars and time
floating with your mind.
These feelings I possess
of your love and tenderness
are just the reasons why
my love for you will never die.
—*Eric Hatch*

My Prayers

I have pulled out my novenas
I finger my rosary beads
I burn votive candles in church
"Pray for them," he said in heavily accented English
"Say their names and pray for
Their conversion and forgiveness"
"You-yu-yu," my voice catches in my throat
"You want me to pray for those filthy thieves!" I squeaked
"I can't! They have broken my heart"
"Yes, you must pray for them," he explained
So that you will be freed of the vise that binds you."
I still hate them, but I'm praying for them
I'm beginning to mean it, too
Some how the hate and rage will melt
As well my grief, he promised
My steps echo in the old dim church
My worn novena cards are hard to read
My beads tinkle faintly
I smell the holy scent of burning candles
"In the name of the Father......"
—*Lois Petitjean*

The Window

Looking out the window
I gaze into the night
recalling sweet memories
of the arms that once held me tight.
Looking out the window
the rain is falling down
as I try to recapture
the love that's not around.
Looking through the window
I see the yesterdays
the glistening snow of winter
the flowers that bloom in May.
As I'm looking out the window
in the distance, the sound of the midnight train
the tears begin to roll down my face
just like the flow of the rain.
There's magic in a window
it holds good times and bad
it holds the future and the past
it holds the happy times and the sad.
—*Larry Suhrbier*

Praises Of Life

Today is the best day of my life
I get to spend it all with my wife
She's just as sweet as she can be
You see, she was born just for me.

We've had our ups, we've had our downs
She finally realized, that she married a clown
But no matter what people have to say
She's all mine, and I love her all the way.

She's pretty girl and a real delight
And my best friend both day and night
A companion to me that proves she cares
For the life we lead and the life we share.

We've had fifty years together with love
Sent to us from the Lord above
I'm the luckiest man in this old world
To be married to such a wonderful girl.

Some have it good, some have it bad
But I've had the best that could be had
We've raised our family with the greatest of pride
Each day of my life, I thank God for my bride.
—*Gil S. Greggain*

Pebble

When I was six
I got a pebble for my birthday
The other kids all laughed.
Their presents were of much more value.
Or so they thought.
As we got older I kept the pebble
I was content.
I noticed they got more
And always wanted more.
While I sat with my pebble,
I was content.
They bought everything they thought
would make them happy.
Soon they were depressed.
They hadn't gotten enough.
Most turned to drinking
It helped them to forget.
But still I hold my pebble, still content.
What fools they were to think
that they were so much better.
—*John Schutze*

My Last Day Of School

Did you learn anything new today?
I learned that being knowledgeable means being closed
That it is easier to criticize than to explore
That sensitivity equals stupidity.
Did you know that when someone goes right,
You should go left?
Somehow that means you are smarter.
Because stimulus-response is scientific
Like Pavlov's dogs,
Like mice in a maze,
Like a monkey in a cage.

I'm tired of being a keeper.
I want to eat chocolate in the rain
And not be afraid to smile.
—*Teriann Coburn*

Glass House

When I got off the roller coaster ride,
I had such deep feelings of hurt;
So many years of being treated like a queen
And the next moment treated like dirt.

I brushed myself off and looked around
And saw the Fun House, "Fun", I said,
"That's what I need, a lot of laughter"
Before I realized, I was again wed.

But the House of Fun is the House of Glass
Where all is shiny and bright,
But don't try to touch that lovely image
That wall is as cold as the night.

And after that coldness you try to get out
To find once again you are trapped
No matter which way that you turn,
The maze is deviously mapped.

I'll take a hammer and shatter the image
And step right through the pass,
But all around me are shattered dreams
And shards of broken glass...
—*Christine G.*

To My Grandchildren

I am the sunset — you are the sunrise.
I have eyes that dim — how clear your eyes.
I walk slightly bent — You walk so straight.
I falter when I speak — Your words, never late.
I putter in the yard — You dance all day.
I nap and dream — You think of child's play.
I count my days — Yours are long and sweet.
I reach for a rainbow — You touch it so neat.
I watch time flying by — You just hit the road.
I try to remember — You have a light load.
I beat a drum — You lead the band.
I listen to music — You are on the bandstand.
I finish the book — You just begin to read.
I have sown my crops — You just planted the seed.
I hope to show you the way — You too will know.
I have much to say — You listen — Then grow.
I will always be near — Just keep on giving.
I wish all for you — You have a life worth living.
—*Nate H. Goler*

Untitled

Pieces of eyes and wood I have cradled. I have rocked you.
I have fed you. You sucked my nipple, and I have infected you.
I, in my burgundy rocker, have lingered by the door, as the
creaks tried to center me. The yellow pram's little bears and
elephants have eyes, eyes the saw, eyes I see- only now, eyes of
stuffed animals. I'm not stuffed. The beasts stay for my baby
but now, as the chopped pieces of wood don't make a sound,
shattered eyes peer at me from the trash, reminding me of him.
I find I can not hurt myself, as I did that night, saying 'Why
Not,' thinking I was important, thinking he loved me, as he
made himself happy. Just don't die, or I fear I may find the
strength to give it all up, before I'm supposed to. I wanted
to when he left. Now I know why not to. I cry - all the time.
No — not tears. Pieces of eyes and wood.
—*James L. Riggs*

Keeping Even

I'm just a keeping even and that's doing pretty good
I haven't made the fortune that I used to think I would,
I haven't caused the trump of fame o'er distant hills to sound
But I can always face the music when the landlord comes around.

I've had my ray of sunshine and I've seen the flowers smile
And I have the Rheumatiz but only for a little while,
And when I come to quit this scene of hope and likewise doubt
I'll scarcely leave enough for lawyer folks to fight about.

I've had my disappointments and I've had my silent fears
But I reckon that the laughs will balance all the tears,
This is not a brilliant record but I want it understood
That I'm still a-keeping even and that's doing pretty good!
—*Herman F. Vaughn*

Earth

Our good Earth is turning bad,
I know it is very sad,
Polluted air and trashed up seas
Destroy the Earth's pleasure and peace,
This wonderful planet becoming full of trash,
To the shores come a harmful splash,
A sea which is full of oil,
The Earth's beautiful plan it will foil,
The time has come for humans to regret what they have done,
To the Earth ever since time begun,
For everybody that is listening to me,
Please save the Earth's land and seas.
—*Monojeet Sengupta*

Flight

How sweet those times
I listen, see, hear, feel and
Do not speak.
Worlds touch me,
Reach out, calm, reassure, feed
The senses all.

Sweet the smell of green,
Sweet the touch of color,
Sweet the sound of silence.

In the park I walk pleased
Doing nothing, I am everything
Around me embraced
By color, shape, sound, smell.
A bird wheels in flight. By the movement
Of a feather to alight
On that spot, that one branch trembling!
—*Daniel Rossiter*

El Salvador

With arms opened to receive me,
  I let myself become captivated by your treasures:
diamonds shining through the dark eyes of your children
    jeweled water droplets hanging carefully
      on shy orchids - pearls in the midst of such beauty,
    crystal mornings of dark sand beaches
      with sparkling sun dancing across the waves,
pure gold of friendship plowed deeply into fields of intimacy.

You have nourished my spirit with the
  hopes and gentle strength of a war-tired people
    turned to celebration for promises of a lasting peace.
Your subtle changes of season have taught me
  to love and to be patient with life's contradictions.
With Wisdom as my guide,
  I have walked your dusty roads
    allowing my soul to quench its thirst
      drinking deeply of the spirit of your
        courage and hunger for truth.

I carry you in my heart, into a future, now different
because you have loved me and taught me to love.
    —*Toby Lardie*

Together Forever

As thoughts of you race through my head,
I lie awake restless in my bed;
Trying to unravel the feelings within,
Desperately wondering where to begin;

Call it childish or call it lust,
But in you I feel my deepest trust;
For deep in my body there is a fire,
That's engulfing my heart with flaming desire;

And found in my heart is an undescribable treasure,
A treasure overwhelming with passionate pleasure;
And to this priceless treasure inside of me,
In your immortal possession is the only key;

Twill not unlock with mortal lust,
For the only key is your love and trust;
But just because I lust for you,
It does not mean I can't love you too;

For as long as my passion for you is true,
Together we'll drift on and sea of deep blue;
Together forever together as two,
Together forever just me and you.
    —*William McCarter*

Hurting

In a time of trouble, I could of said,
  "I like to hear your voice and feel you would be there for
  me."
You were my best friend and always were there to cheer me up.
  I never would of believed you could have turned out like my
  friends have said.
You had a lot going for you, but I guess everything I ever said
  to you never sank in.
You have changed, my friend, and I hope someone else has the
  courage to stand up to you and tell you what you have
  become.
It doesn't matter to me that you have become what you are,
  because you could be happy.
But... the fact that you abuse the one you love is so low that
  I wonder what is going on in your mind.
If you are angry about something you should talk to someone,
  but hurting a friend is not the way.
I hope to God that you start thinking about what you are doing
  because you are not only hurting your friends, you are
  hurting Yourself.
    —*Kristina Brewen*

When One Listens

    As I slowly walked down the shadowy street
        I listened

    I heard the rhythmic song of crickets
A cold breeze forced me to hide my hands in my pockets
        I listened

    I heard the cold wind abusing dry leaves
The dark, dead headlights of a car looked into my eyes
        I listened

I heard the sad wail of a police car in the distance
    The cold night air sounded clean and unforgiving
        I listened

      I heard the darkness of life
But even as I looked into infinity stained with lost dreams
        I listened
        And I heard God
    —*Aaron D. Parks*

Where I Want To Be

When I reach out for someone who'll care
I look and I find that no one is there.

And all of the feelings I'm keeping inside
Are gnawing and burning from the place they hide.

And in my mind's eye all I can see
Is home, sweet home, where I want to be.

This time I feel like my luck has run out
For I'm questioning now what life's all about.

People around me, yet I'm all alone
Oh, how I wish I were on my way home!

On my way home, the place I should be
Where friendship and love are waiting for me.

My life and my future, and all that I know
Are waiting for me, if I could just go..

Home.
    —*Kevin W. Fannin*

Untitled

Lying here alone
I look up and see the paint dry
I feel the grass grow
And I sense by body becoming still
My emotions becoming comatosed
I experience the cataclysmic halting of all that I know
The emptiness within me which was once minute
Now grows and expands
To where it pushes against the inside of my skin
I know it happens, although I can not feel it
I reach down into my mind
Searching for something
Something to pull me from this state
But once inside I realize
I realize that I myself am the cause
Thus I deserve this recession into oblivion
For I created it
And placed myself there
    —*Michael James Neyer*

The First Tear Cried

My dreams came true the day I died
   I looked upon those who've shed many tears
the dawn, the dark - the new, the old
   time passes on with stories untold,
   one of you and me and about the other one that made us three

For all the wrongs you are the right
   the trouble was behind us, the months were long
and then the one that made us three was here
   and along with the first breath of life
   came the first tear..... for I was dead
I was far, far away but you held my heart tightly
   the love in your eyes I took with me
Please do not forget, go and live
   it is you that I love, but life that I fear

The part of me you have, will stay by your side
   ....but please remember, with the first tear cried
   came the first breath of life.
   —*Amy Stevens*

Friends

      How can I tell you
        I love you
   If I don't know what to do.
      I know I like you
      But I'm so confused.
     People think it's great
and they think we shouldn't wait.
     They say ask him\her out
      But it's kind of hard
If they don't know what it's all about.
     You can't jump into it
     And say it will work out.
I don't know why they don't just bud out.
   I know we can work things threw.
     And maybe I can say
      I love you.
  It's great that were good friends
    if things don't work out
    We'll be friends to the end.
That's what friendships all about.
   —*Jim Leshovsky*

Goodnight

Goodnight my love, whom I'm hoping to see.
I love you, and it's my heart to be with you
in your dreams, that come true,
It's within your eyes I see,
I really can't believe that you're here with me.
I hope we will never be blind to see,
that in life things may hurt our hearts to be,
if so you know I wouldn't do nothing in the world
to hurt you, because I love you, and you're in my
heart to stay, there is nothing you can do
to ever make me feel the same.
So good night my love see you soon,
in your dreams, I'll be with you.
   —*William B. Doyal*

Time

Invisibility of the time shapes you.
It moves you to toward your end.
You are trying to hold it, but where?
That's why the memories of your childhood,
there is no time for its return. What a pity.
Loss of a child's ring with a blue stone in the snow.
I was looking, like for my childhood now.
Oh, the time won't go back.
   —*Anna Petrasova*

Untitled

Through mundane places, boring faces, and stifling mediocrity
I ran, reached, touched, and searched frantically.
I stumbled through the concrete grayness of the city
studied nameless faces and felt voiceless hostility
that always brews in the dull, dead, lifeless eyes
that gaze blindly past rainbows at gray skies.

Then sliding 'oer the gray and white squares of our board
I moved cautiously between the players in accord,
and perceived they were pursuing their transient goals.
They were such poor determined little souls.

Weary and despaired, I arose and confronted Him,
Master Player, with skillful hand and face so grim;
Is there no door, no path leading from this place
where I dwell in solitude with my veiled face?

Then, my friend, I found you!!!
   —*Brenda Young*

The Break-Up

As I was walking from the house of the man I once loved,
I realized that we were through.
I was falling, falling into a deep, dark shadow.
I tried to find something to hold on to,
but I found nothing.
No one to hold on to.
No one to share my thoughts, fears, and feelings with.
As I gathered the courage to come out of the shadow
in which I was imprisoned,
I remembered what the feeling of warmth felt like.
As I remembered all this,
I cried, cried a thousand rivers.
   —*Ellen O'Leary*

Untitled

I fear what I do not know
I run from what is home
I'll sit and ponder
Thoughts of gloom
Alone in my reddened, musty room

My mind a jumble with visions of face
Shut my eyes in hopes of them melting away

Tears fall as they do when I
Think too much
The wireless beside me plays the
Music of love
I sink deeply beneath my tarnished duvet
Scent of Love Supreme lingers where I lay

The colours surround me
The darkness is warm
As I imagine your heart
Bloody and torn
It was you I remember, not me who said
'Damn your heart and your soul
Our love is dead'
   —*K. Laura Linantud*

Just You

It isn't the things you do or say,
It isn't your look or smile,
Nor what you wear,
Nor your winning way,
Though all these help a pile.
No it isn't your gold that appeals to me,
It is something finer far.
It's just your own dear personal self,
It's you just as you are!
   —*June Mecca*

The Other Side

Ah, the other side of desire - true love. I saw in her a
I saw in her a beauty unearthed by the falseness that surrounded her.
The freshness she spoke with each word lifted me into newer and
stronger days. The sincerity of a lifetime was wrapt in a single layer.
Desiring to be intrigued forever, we forged a
bond. A spiral of communication so intense that the earth did
not move and our minds did not falter. She spoke. The sounds
of lions roared through my emotions. I was captured but I was
not a prisoner. There were no chains to impede our growing.
And we grew. The limitless bounds of our own destination kept
us moving forward. I looked and I saw what was to be my
forever. We walked the aisle of togetherness and together we
shall continue on the path of our own intentions. Understanding, of
course, that as all lovers unite, we shall bear witness to
something that is greater than all before and far superior to
all that will come. We have love. We have friendship. And
together, We have a lifetime.
　—*Kevin Whattam*

Untitled

As I walked in carrying shepherds pie,
I saw people sitting who have been waiting for an hour,
People waiting for the one meal they get a day.
Although most of them have not eaten in a while
In the kitchen I heard people say,
"We can only give milk to pregnant women and young children"
Because money had run out
When I served the food I wanted to know how these
　people got to where they were
I saw old men clutching bottles of alcohol,
Women, alone with many children,
Vietnam Veterans,
I asked myself,
Why?
　—*Valerie Moran*

The Wind

The wind blows cold while greyness fades to black.
I shiver once and wait for silence pure,
For sleep to come and cover every sigh,
For darkness free of day's incessant roar.

I sleep rock sound, all silence now and calm.
I sleep for days, uncounted nights and days.
I sleep long nights and waken not till spring
Embraces all earth's hibernating ones:

We spread our wings and soar into the clouds,
Free at last from winter's heavy shroud.
Our green shoots stretch and reach up to the sun,
Our faces warm, our petals smiling bright.

We roll in grass new green upon the hills
And laugh and sing a song of new born babes.
We savor life as fresh as the breeze we feel
Gentle and warm, our lover's first embrace.
　—*Jacqueline Pitman*

Dear Doppleganger

You catch my eye and feign recognition.
I watch; you are the portrait of my reality.
Image, beyond the xerox of my features,
Are you a tool to counterpart my being? Or to impersonate it?
Twin to my visage, I search your eyes for the truth.
We are parallel and inseparable.
We coincide; no sooner seen than reciprocated.
And yet again, refracted.
You are my reflection. You are my companion.
I sigh; I am reconciled with our soul.
Why do you call yourself mime?
You are echo.
　—*Thery T. McKinney*

I Know My Dad's Out Of Work

　I know my dad's out of work
　　I smell his cologne
　　I smell food cooking
　I smell his peach air freshener in the car

　　I know my dad's out of work
　　I see my dad every day
　　I see the car in the garage
　　I see him sitting at the table

　　I know my dad's out of work
　I hear the shower in the morning
　　　I hear him talking
　　I hear him blowing his nose

　　I know my dad's out of work
　　　I feel his love
　　　I feel his grief
　　　I feel upset
　—*Cindy Parise*

"On My Mind"

As I sit here and ponder, all the things on my mind,
I think of the blessing, Christ left behind.

He restored the gospel, that we have today,
So let's remember Him, when we pray.

He died for all of us, upon the cross,
Think of these things, then think, who's the boss.

The bread represents the body, he so freely gave,
That we, His children, might all be saved.

The water represents, the blood that He shed,
These are the things, that should go through our heads.

So read the scriptures, and do as they say,
And the Lord will listen, when we pray.

These are the things, the saviour left behind,
These are the things, that are on my mind.
　—*Michael Troy Lange*

Untitled

I used to look into the clouds and say a silent prayer
I used to lay in my dark room and wish that he was there
In my dreams we used to dance
And I'd hope for a long romance
Why is it that my prayers are never answered?
People say when you dream the same thing
It finally comes true
But when I sleep
More than ten times
I've looked deep into his eyes of blue
He grasped me in his arms of gold
And then he disappeared
I feel that I am loosing him
And this is a tremendous fear
So God, if you look down on me
You will soon see
Oh please turn his head once,
Once towards me.
　—*Sarah M. Callen*

Chains Of Hell

Sometimes I wake up and feel like the devil has chained
me to the walls of hell. I feel that nothing can break
the chains. A tear rolls down my cheek as I watch the
devil laugh. A tear rolls down my cheeks as I watch the
devil smack. Nothing can stop the way I feel even
though it's not real.
　—*Terri Woodcox*

Just Passing Through

Walking down the road of life - cornered in by pain and strife
I walk on cobble stone for my error to atone.

Just passing through - just passing through you say - yes
Just passing through.

Weary and tired - my eyes are closed -
Heart heavy and thoughts full of woes.

The road seems narrow - it comes to an end and looking,
Looking, my God for a friend.

Just passing through you say - yes just passing through.
The walk of life is over - I lay in my last bed thinking of
the road I tread.

And then my eyes are open - I begin to see birds fluttering in
The breeze - amber leaves falling from the autumn trees -
The ocean blue - the sky is too

The rainbow after rain - I hear music - a refrain -
The grass is green - the flowers bud -
A turtle slushing in the mud.

Friends coming to your aid - making life so unafraid -
Oh God - Oh God - where have I failed?
I missed it all - I missed it all. Just passing through.
—*Mary L. Ryel*

The Voice

      I want a voice.
I want a deep, resonant, effortless voice.
    a big voice; bigger than me.

I want to speak and hear the floorboards take it up
    so that people hear me first with their bodies
      and only then with their ears

      a voice—
strong, like an axe, to cut through the silence
strange, like distant flutes, to still the silence
a voice to quicken the heart like drums in the night

I want to breathe a whisper that shivers like a star
    over some strange Bethlehem
      on some cold stone
    circling some distant sun

   I want a voice like the voice of many
     the voice of a nation
      the voice of a people
   and with this voice I would cry freedom
     and then I would speak peace
—*Peter Mulvey*

Untitled

It's been so delicious
I was frightened, suspicious.
How could I be published now
What about all the hard work?
What of the suffering
The crying
The hurt?

Yet here was a page
From your publishing house
Causing my soul to grow tan in the sun
A public career has finally begun.
From me and you
to the world, in their sight, in their mind
Thank you so much, you've been very kind!
—*Debra D. Romine*

This Is What I Want

I want to be happy and joyful
I want to be free
This is what I want
This is what I need

Good friends, nice neighbors
A healthy and happy family
This is what I want
This is what I see

Diamonds, pearls, gold
These things mean nothing to me
This is what I want
To live my life in glee

I asked my Lord and I received
I gave him my heart love is what he'd given to me
Now I'm full of glee
I have good friends, nice neighbors and a happy
healthy family.

I'm happy, I'm joyful, I'm free
This is what I wanted
This is how life should be.
—*Michael Edward Brown*

Hey Kids

I know you've never seen me very much
I was always to busy to keep in touch
I'd stop and think and get a warm feeling then I'd smile
For you see you were in my heart all awhile
I watched you grow and blossom and grow up tall
From the awful two's, adolescence and off to your first mating
   call
Time has a funny way of fleeting by
I just want to tell you your the apple of my eye
I put down all the thoughts from over the years
   so maybe they'll bring a few laughs and maybe some tears
Keep them and remember the grandma who always loved you
It's been said that out-of-sight and out-of-mind could be true
But maybe you'll think of me and then you'll smile
Just the way I did way back then, cause that was my style
—*Maggie Newfield*

Sleepless

The moon growing higher in the horizon
I watch its ascent through the hours
hopeful of some blissful vision to write

too sleepless to enter a dream state
the place of our demons and fairies
though I can only lapse aside
content to the music of Floyd in the player
and the cigarette burning in the ash tray

shapeless—too large to be seen
only the dragon's breath visible
blue mists content to drift upon the open air

I too wish to drift
drift away to a land of peace
of the clear languid pools
with the sprites and fairies at play
but a scene envied by all

though as of yet—not a thing
before I lay my head to the pillow
but a few notes scratched upon my fabled pad
I note the rising of the sun
—*e j lundy iii*

Mystery Harvest

I planted a lonely sunflower seed.
I watered it and watched it grow,
How did it become a big melon with 50 seeds?
That's what I'd like to know?
I planted a healthy pumpkin seed,
I watered it and watched it grow,
How did it make a big pumpkin with many seeds?
That's what I'd like to know.
One time I planted an acorn,
Through the years I watched it grow
How did it become the mighty oak?
That's what I'd like to know.
Now, if we should plant seeds of kindness,
Had faith that they would grow,
They would produce bushels of happiness,
Then what I do know.
—*Marie Sams*

Proud And Tall

There he sat as content as could be,
I watched his eyes as they followed me.
Outside he was poor and old,
but boy, you wouldn't believe the stories he told.
He knew a lot about history and war,
he had so much to share after I opened my door.
He needed someone to listen, someone to care,
now I am glad that for him I was there.
I don't think he had a home,
for he was a wonderer, he was made to roam.
I sat there and watched the dinner he ate,
he dined from a dirty plastic plate.
He was so talkative, so friendly, so free,
I liked the way he opened up to me.
He sat there holding his bag of treasures,
the smile on his face I could not measure.
He was not aware of how he was dressed,
for his heart to me he completely confessed.
He wasn't afraid to approach me at all.
for he was a good man, proud and tall!
—*Mary Lee*

A Change Of Life

If I could live a different life,
I would be a leaf
I would choose to live majestically atop a big oak tree
so I may absorb the sun, for two reasons
my life is short just two seasons.
You see for the third one
I will show my colors for all to see
then my life is over and it will soon end.
Just remember I choose my life
so I could bring a little color to the world.
So remember when I'm no longer here,
please don't shed a tear.
For I don't feel no sorrow
for I know a new one will replace me tomorrow.
—*Michael Thomas*

Rain

Listen.... listen.... can't you hear the
rain gently falling... falling so gently you
could go into slumber. Suddenly you awake and
find you are floating down a river. The waves
are rocking you... rocking you so gently you
fall asleep. Suddenly you wake and find you
are in a magical place far far away with fairies
and gnomes. Then you wake and find it's true!
—*Beth Zeigler*

"If I Were In Charge Of The World"

If I were in charge of the world,
   I'd cancel all feelings of hate and remorse,
   The times when it's hard to get on the right course,
   And world peace would not be accomplished by force.

If I were in charge of the world,
   There'd be floors you could sink through when you just want to hide,
   Oceans in which problems go out with the tide,
   And incredible victories after you tried, and tried, and tried...

If I were in charge of the world,
   You wouldn't have crooked teeth so you'd have get braces,
   Nor would there be people against certain races,
   'Cause if I were in charge of the world, it would be full
   of warm, friendly faces.
—*Jenny Bengen*

With Love And Care

I'd sing you a lullaby if it could make you smile,
I'd give you a hug if it would hold you for awhile.
I'd tell you stories of where dreams come true,
where the land is so green and the skies so blue.

Where rabbits run wild on prairies so free,
and flowers all bloom in the spring.
Sweet stories I'd tell you if it could make you feel better,
I'd tell about love then put it down in a letter.

Sweet memories of times of yesterday the Lord is here,
he's keeping you safe, he's making his plans for what
he should do, I'm praying my sister,
I'm praying for you.

I love you so much I hope you've always known.
but if I never have the chance again I hope that now it shows.
So take it easy and rest your weary soul
I'm hoping and praying that soon you'll come home.
—*Dannell Case*

"Today Is The Day"

How wonderful it could be,
If everyone in the world would say every morning.
"Today is the day", I'll make someone happy,
I'll make someone smile,
I'll turn the other cheek, because
"Today is the day", for aught I know,
Might be my last day on earth.
When God looks at my record and says,
"Your last day, did you remember??"
"Today is the day"
Did you make someone happy?
Did you make someone smile?
Did you turn the other cheek?
Your purpose was to do all these things.
Did I fail? Did I forget?
"Today is the day"
—*Zelda Burnette*

Alone

A single tree stands alone,
Just like a child without a home.
No one to love,
No one to be loved by.
No one to judge,
No one to be judged by.
No one sees or no one cares,
They all have their own affairs.
And so this tree that stands alone,
Remains just like a child without a home.
—*Kristin Haw*

The Price Of Freedom

What makes the price of freedom unique?
If I but raise my voice to speak.
Will I die or will I live?
Will I be ready, my life to give?

I dared to stand in the city square;
For freedom, justice and what is a fair.
But alas, I didn't stand alone,
Others came for their rights to own.

And we stood together, hand in hand;
Student, worker, child, woman, man.
In words and action: the message is clear.
We want our freedom, to us so dear.

Soon their answer came on tanks afire,
As soldiers left behind a bloody mire.
Everywhere people hurt, dead or dying,
With a crash of a club and bullets flying.

The empty square's a canvas stained red;
But listen, and hear the cries of the dead.
They spur on the living, to right the wrong.
Freedom must come; it's much too strong!

—*Daniel J. Hayes*

"A Drink"

His answers seem to be at the bottom of his bottle,
if not this one, another.
He can't remember the questions,
he opens another bottle to help him remember the questions.
The bottle, he thinks holds whatever it is he is looking for.
The bottle is the cause.
The bottle is the answer.
The bottle of liquor contains his life, his past, his future,
his ruin...........
He is inside the bottle,
the bottle is inside of him.
He is the bottle and the bottle is him.

—*Joyce A. Shannon*

How Do I feel?

They ask me how I feel and I tell them nothing's wrong,
if only they knew that I'm not very strong.
On the outside I'm cheerful, but on the inside I really hurt,
Some treated me special, while others treated me like dirt.
This pain I feel, how can I explain
I call out to people, but no one knows my name.
I go through the same thing day after day
Crying and sulking in every possible way.
Do people notice when I come out of my room,
that my heart is hurting and filled with gloom.
They think it's my lovelife,
but only part of that is true,
they don't know what really hurts and what makes me feel so blue.
This heart it hurts as if it's been killed,
but all they can ask is how do I feel?

—*Sharon Simmons*

Untitled

The incense smokes for Itzamna
In the Central Plaza of Tikal.
A haze of chemicals settles over banana
In a Quiche migrant worker hell.
Throughout the genocide and the pestilence
The tzolkin gears still turn,
While on a mountainside the barefoot tenants
At gunpoint watch their shacks burn.

—*Daniel S. Dale*

If I Could Help God's Children

If I could help God's children alone broken-hearted today
If there would be some message I alone could say
I would reach in my heart for the deepest words that lay in store
If I could only help them not to cry anymore
He hears their crying and is reaching out to them
To heal their little burdens and calm their fears within
He knows they are being hurt in so many ways
If God could just talk through me this is what he'd say
These are my children and they belong to me alone
And if you don't treat them right you will answer to the throne
Give them a chance teach them to pray they were made to love laugh and play
Suffer little children oh come unto me believe in my son Jesus
When he says follow me He will teach you the right way I know
He will watch over you as you live and grow

—*Darlene Sams*

Love Shall Save What Love Has Given

God's love and mother nature seem but terms in nomenclature
If words were stacked in importance these terms would be far
above for they are the concomitant of all beauty an empirical
expression of love

Folks walk over carpets of polynoses and acorns
Pine cones and kicked aside
While cutting trees an aborial form of genocide

T'would take but little time sweeping up seeds to show they
care and spread them where the ground is bare

But then they have not a minute to spare to replace or sow
What took nature millions of years to develop and grow

However, lovers, meandering through this scene
See through adoring eyes each minuscule bit of green.

From each we petal of a weed or minny leaf-each
Exotic in itself form bouquets of trees and verden cover
T'is a symbol of natures love which romance too both reach
This panoramic vision enters their hearts, it will be saved by lovers.

—*Ludwig Kasal*

Untitled

Flower full of friendliness let me pick you.
I'll take you back home, that's what I'll do
A pretty vase will be your place,
On my window ledge you'll delight my face.
Oh pretty flower how you catch the sun,
Bobbing in the wind having fun.
Oh your leaves are soft and bright.
Pretty flower your full of such delight.
Flower full of friendliness your needed in my keeping.
Oh pretty flower stop me from weeping.

—*Pamela Gordon*

"Fly With Me"

Come and fly with me, higher than the highest tree,
I'll take you places you want to be.

As we soar above the clouds,
I will whisper in your ear,
Whispering things you want to hear.

Around and over in the sky,
yes,
that is where we shall fly.

Come now and fly with me,
higher than the highest tree.

—*Catherine Thomas*

Echoes Of A Mom

Look at me, can you say it's true?
I'm a part of you and you're a part of me.

Through the years I've been told
That you are the image of one
That I used to be.
Until today I have never seen
What they have always seen.

Although our eyes are different
Colors my features echo in yours.

Our smiles, our gestures and yes
Even the way we talk are all one
In the same.

Until this day when I look at you
And the way you've grown I can now say
Look at me, can you say it's true?
I'm a part of you and your a part of me.
And I am a proud mom
Of not one but two precious girls
That I can say are a part of me.
—*Jan Huff*

Darkness

The darkness of night closes in around me
I'm enveloped into the blackness of fear.
The silence drives me crazy.
A single sound is like a spear.

It pierces you with all its might;
All the sounds of the cold dark night.
Your eyes dart around, your heart pounds with fear
You feel on your cheek one lonely tear.

The tear falls, than come more.
Surviving the night; fighting your war.
Fear overcomes
You feel defeated
Your life is completed.

The dawn of the day awakens your soul.
You hear the ringing of the churchbell toll.

You finally sleep. though not for long.
Your feelings are deep, you feel they're wrong.

You wait again
For the darkness once more.
Hoping that maybe you'll win the next war.
—*Amber Dodson*

I Knew Her Not

I knew her not. On earth we shan't meet
Imprisoned by her quest for compassion
Her heart was ripe and full of warmth
Her skeleton frail, sickened inside

A woman with a purpose, an inner need
Helping all. All with a need

Perfect was she in every way
For I knew her not yet understood her need

For we shan't meet on this earth
But high on a cloud

So until then my sweet Audrey
Indulge in your reward

You shall be missed
Yet not forgotten.
—*Audrey Hepburn*

There For Me

He was always there for me,
In good times and in bad.
If I was happy, He was happy too,
Sharing in the celebration.
But if I was sad, so was He,
And He would be a shoulder to cry on.
He is everything that anybody could want.
And more.
That's because He is Jesus,
But through my grandfather.
—*Heather R. Webb*

You Are. . .

You are a cold, brisk, howling wind of winter which embraces me
  in its perilous grip.
You are the pure virginal snows which frolic from the heavens
  to blanket the frozen earth.
You are the sweet tranquil rains which brings forth new life to
  the parched, barren plains.
You are the colored leaves of Autumn which meekly fall to veil
  the earth.
You are the blazing incandescent sun which caresses my soul.
You are the symphony under the guidance of Helios to which the
  horned toad waltzes. You are the coyote as he swaggers freely
  across infinite expanses of a whimsical desert.
You are the moon's soft glow which silhouette the majestic
  Joshua as it stands guard of its mighty domain.
You are the stillness and serenity of a velvety dark night.
You are the gentle sparkle of angels' tears that bejewel the
  vast blackness of the heavens.
You are the aromatic fragrances of a desert sunrise in which
  morning dew and sleepy sands mingle as one.
You are the vibrant hazes of a retreating mauve sunset.
—*Rejeana L. DeHart*

Olive

Olive is the color of a bronze statue
In memory of those who wore the army's drab,
An olive tree's sturdy leaves, fresh with oil,
And the firm pit of its savored fruit.

Olive is the color of the cunning eyes of a cat,
The taste of brine left behind in a watery mouth,
A finger's touch on the rough shell of a turtle
In the midst of a fragrant salty breeze by the sea.
—*Daniella Spinat*

Friend

You are as friendly as a dolphin jumping through the tide
I know right now you want to curl up and hide
For the world right now is being very cruel to you
But the number of people with your big heart are very few
I know that heart is hurting right now
I would like to help... But I don't know how
If you don't know what a great person you are
Then my poem has not gone far
Your soul is great, your mind is wise
So don't pay any attention to those guys
If at any time you feel any pain
Just remember you're not the one to blame
I love you Kelly, through thick and thin
Whenever something happens we'll overcome it and win.
—*Cari Deutsch*

All Alone Without You

Last night, alone in my bed
In the darkness of a moonlit night,
I left on a journey, walking through time,
Strolling through the memories of my mind

And there you were, looking so young and pretty
Shining through the darkness
A beauty to behold
A beauty to behold

Images of our life together
A precious time in my life
But now its gone, forever gone
Only memories, fading like time

And there you were, looking so young and pretty
Shining through the darkness
A beauty to behold
A beauty to behold

I hope we meet like this again
Such a lonely journey
All alone without you,
All alone without you.
—*James E. Thomas*

Nature's Caress

In the heady greenness of the meadow in the morn,
In the dewy wetness of a new day that is born,
Underneath a sunny sky
Where hearts should soar so high, so high,
I try to mend the tatters of a heart that is torn.

Under shady branches of tall trees against the sky,
Under lacy wildwood vines meandering so high,
Caught up in the sensuousness
Of nature's passionate caress,
I lie languishing in limbo, contemplating why.

Over grassy hillsides basking in the noonday heat,
Over wild profusion of flowers beneath my feet,
Sinking down in grass so deep
I'm tempted to lie down and sleep,
Forgetting life's anguishes, replacing sad with sweet.

Within quiet woodlands, lying in eternal calm,
I respond to quietness as poor man does to alm,
Lying down beside a stream
I replace my life with a dream,
Reveling in the healing powers of this soothing balm.
—*Emily Daniels Butler*

The Zebra That Lost His Stripes

Once upon a time in a distant place
    in the land of meek and humble
There was a Zebra who thought he was great
    and the other horses grumbled.
    One hot blistery day
    the Zebra's stripes began to fall
        They started at his tail
        and loosened by his jaw.
    But a change came over the Zebra
and he just took it as matter of course
    He always knew for so do you
        deep down he was just a horse.
    So when people look down their nose
        or lift up their chin
    Remember the outside may be different
        but we're all the same within.
—*Greg Buckley*

Arctic Visions

Ivory gull
In the midnight sun.
Caribou
On the tundra run.
The Narwhal
Dives to icy depths,
While the wolf takes it's land-bound steps.
The Ptarmigan and Gyrfalcon
Still watch for each other
Both enemies -
Yet brothers.
—*Eric David Faber*

An Ode To Heather L. Welch

The sparrows come from miles around,
In what used to be a country town.
I'm watching now from my window seat,
The different kinds of seeds they eat.
I love these birds,
I really do.
But not as much as I love you!
The cardinal there,
His coat of red.
Is not as precious as a single hair upon your head.
The blue-jay has what crows do not,
multi-colors, a bevy of blue.
The dove is coaxing with her delightful coo,
My heart is leaping,
My spirit soars.
To know this beauty does not match yours.
In your honor, I blow my horn,
You're my girl, my very first born!
Love, Mom.
—*Jennifer Lynn DeJesus-Jankowski*

Freedom

Memories of you come to me
in whispers
and curious sighs
haunted dreams that wouldn't last
I stand alone in the vast sea
of nothing
midnight's eyes watch
from a moonless sky
I've gotten away
from your love
so right it was wrong
and as I stand
on a towering slope
I know that I can fly.
—*Heather Lynne Hansen*

Lost

There is a little birdie that lives
inside of you. He only comes out at
night to speak to you. He tells you
lies and fills your head with dreams of
sorrow and pain. When you awake he hides
again till dark. He plays with your defense-
less mind until you're all confused and
scared. You feel so many mixed-up feelings
and you feel you have nothing to lose.
You're lost! Everything you have is lost
as you think about your dreams. Lost hopes.
Lost feelings. Lost you!
—*Jennifer Jepsen*

The Strong Woman

My outward, so-called "self-contained," strength is my human,
inner weakness; and in this weakness, I, too, need another's
strength. I secretly cry out for it: seek it, need it—
Where is it? At arms' length? I feel no dependable arms
around me; I hear no reassuring, loving words to calm my fears.
Only my beneficial words to others are the sounds that fall on
my ears: Giving advise to those who ask for it
   Piecing jigsaw sections to broken parts—
To others, this may seem a tedious chore—but to me, it is a
priceless art. Oh, strong woman—you are so needed, but you are
sometimes hated and despised because of your truth, peace and
confidence; you are often the brunt of deceit, injustice and
lies. So woman of strength—
To be truly strong and to continue to stand upright, you must
have faith in yourself and in your inner guiding light—
that inner work you claim keeps your life on an even keel.
Hold fast! Oh, strong woman!
For at least you have found the key.
   —*Margaret L. Whitley*

Discrepant

A foreigner in an unprecedented locality,
Inquisitive for a discovery of individuality.

Emotionally being torn between the present and
past days,
Trying to repel delusion from reality
And find the right life to convey.

So much is lying behind, but there's so much to
be achieved. The speculation of subsisting like
this just cannot be conceived.

I fortify my mind due to an apprehension of a
new environment, I lead a stagnant life, yet I
am young and independent.

I forsake my life and loved ones for
the opportunity to endure,
I always thought of this unity as the
fit to my emptiness as well as the cure.

I now acknowledge that without
companionship I am unhappier than ever before,
Love is the key to wealthiness and
I now realize that I am poor.
   —*Melyssa Lynn Peak*

Grey

A distant murmur of the storm
Inside the old dusty room,
In a far corner, a candle burns dimly.
An old man moans painfully in his old rocking chair
His muscles worn and his flesh a pale grey
Deep crevices on his face tell the history of his life.

The candle grows dimmer
The old man moans again…
And a silence takes over
A grey curtain drapes the room
Death has called him… .

From the corner of the room,
A mouse skitters across the dusty floor.
   —*Nobuko Takeda*

Masochism

After dropping ten percent of my wealth
into the collection basket,
I move up in line, licking my lips
with thoughts of the Holy Feast.
I think of the sensual quiverings
of your nailed limbs,
and my own acceptance of being restrained
to the point of repression.

I receive your body, and revel
in your helplessness as you lay
on the plateau of my tongue…

A stale round wafer,
purchased from a wholesaler
on the Lower East Side, and
impressed with a symbol of sanctity.

I swallow you whole,
like your doctrine,
follow with the sign,
and, wiping my mouth,
quietly return to my pew.
   —*R. Todd Murray*

Doings Of The Mad

The darkness of the night drips steady tears of black
into the remainder of my tortured mind.
As I drink the tonic of another misgiven love
I seek out the pulse within my still heart
that's tired if shielding the broken dreams
now gathered on my bedroom floor.
Needing space to complain of my loneliness,
I again allay the glimmer of a happy life
with a decisive blow, delivered by my pen,
knowing in a few million seconds it'll all start again.
So fear for your heart if I throw you a cord
for it will tangle your thoughts into mine
and when I feel the well has gone dry
the leather will slide through your unwarned fingers
leaving you nothing but burns to remember me by.
Now evening spikes my soul as I'm relieved sad
to ponder the next event in the doings of the mad.
   —*Thomas Aaron Deems*

The Land of I's

I go frameless through the waiting door,
into the texture of my dream.

A land of eyes draws me; an almost-sister appears.
She is the goal I scratched with my hope pen
and then watched while the page was shriven with tears.

Once, in the time of yesterdays,
I might have given life itself to be
clothed in her, for us to be meeting as one.

Now, even in the warp and woof
of passing into alpha's illusion
I encounter her as one I pity
even as I lay her down to sleep.

I turn to other eyes and time has rolled again.
Another mother appears, more innocent still,
laying stones over the rituals of youth.
She I celebrate, watching as her labor
changes the design of today
within the review of the night's fading star.

Between falling and awakening
the world ends, and birth begins.
   —*Barbara McKinnon*

Mankiller

There's a mankiller among us, now who could it be?
Is he white? Is he black? He's of unknown ancestry!
He's killing our children while we watch in despair.
He's laughing & enjoying while he shows not a care.
There are many who stand and try to fight.
But, the mankiller is strong, with only self pleasure in sight.
Now, who do you think this mankiller could be?
Surprisingly enough, it is you and it is me!
We pollute our homes, our environment, and our land.
But, we don't see it is the children who will stand
In the waste & the destruction,
they will stand and they will say,
Could it be that our parents had wanted it this way?
—*Jeanne D. George*

Untitled

Come to me with your sexuality in hand. Tell me, "what is it like to be a man?" Ruler and leader of all his domain, the admirers intact, all set for when he bestows his command.

You walk with the angel of sanity inside, tiptoeing carelessly on the border line. He rules with his weapons, determining our fate. Bondage and freedom; all he can make.

They pull you in, make you believe. Get a good glimpse before the leaves. A kingdom of his making, the temptress stands outside his gate. "She," will no longer wait. Does the castle fall or does he build more walls?

Only the masters know our fate. Only the end gives insight to this mate. Was it right or was it wrong? Did you fail or were you strong?
—*Kerri McMahon*

The Unknown Crew

What festers still to hinder my journey?
Is it the boards of the deck which support my feet,
  or is it the waves which my bow must greet?
Is it the gentle breeze of the sea air?
It is none of these, yet it is still there.

Controlling all that is to be, it is not the ship,
  not even the crew.
I heard a whisper and the whisper said, "you"
I questioned this with no hesitation if this voice now
  shows itself I will vent my frustration.
As I looked up and turned around, it seemed to me this
  voice too profound.

Now I noticed I was sailing alone this voice so familiar
  was always my own.
The moment had come I was to take my own blame but to
  judge myself was not the same.
I had been riding aboard a stagnant ship a hole in its
  port, barnacles on its side too much self-pity had
  hindered its pride.
  —*Thomas J. Begley*

Timeless

It gives meaning to life
It blooms in spring
It descends as the leaves in autumn
It clings as the frost on trees in winter
It's life is everlasting
It embraces, it cares
It is calm and serene
It is elated and blissful
It is full of remorse
It has compassion and mirth
It is forgiveness
  —*Lauren Willis*

Song Of The Schizophrenic

What is the distance from Hell to Heaven?
Is it the length of a synapse
  Somewhere deep in my brain.,
Or the number of days from birth until death?

What is the distance from Heaven to Hell?
Is it shorter than most
  for the Schizophrenic who raves,
Whose pills split the difference
Between Heaven and Hell?

What is the difference between Heaven and Hell
When one brings the other
To those who know them well?
  —*Miriam Engle*

"Why"

Why do you tell me lies?
Is it to make me happy?
Its not working, take a look,
tell me what do you see.
Its a sad, sad person
that don't know what to think.
Our relationship is like a chain,
that contains, many, many links.
But in our old, rusty chain
in many places has been broken,
from the heart aches I have suffered
and it the tears its been soaken.
It loses more and more love
every time you call and say
"Cancel your plans, I coming over"
and then I be sitting here all day.
I don't mind canceling my plans
so that I could be with you,
but when you don't show, you just don't know
how much pain I be going through.
  —*Laura Marie Dunn*

The Future

  I am the tree that stands alone,
    In the forest where no one goes.
  I am the uneducated on the corner.
    Willing to work for food.
I am the homeless sleeping in a cardboard box.
I am the future for the children if we don't teach them to
    Live with our changing world
  —*Justin W. Bird*

Music

The music so sweet to my ears.
It flows and crashes as the waves of time.
The movement is a feeling of slaves being released from the
  bondage.
And each note different as people are in this world today.
What can I say about music other than it is a world around a world.
It is like no other and if we don't have it we will not soar.
The montage of sound and the feeling of movement rocks
me so that the world will never show.
  —*Winter Phoenix*

A Divorce

Each tight air
is more than alone than drowning
wheeling dizzy with sudden
loneliness and
the empty distance of next
the scorched extent of trust
the crushing chatter of regret
leave me
the blank persistent rhythm
of cool loss
I'm of cuttable
too blood enough to
know
of liquid shock but not
pull enough
to keep
you
                      your breath
      though it once swam with mine
          flooding discovery replacing
                  your part is now
              no mystery of union but
                a dragging dependence
     i have no compliment but barren pity
           another's bright beating silence
                 is the drugging unknown
and your flutters of keening voice stifle
                            pulse
roaring with edge i've grown cold to
                         your kiss
                  screams wetter than
            dank electric weariness
                    the last peace
                          Together

—*Sylvia Sellers*

Alone

    The state of being alone
 is not like being on the phone

    There's no one to talk to
      and no one to see
so now you see why being alone still scares me

 Being alone is like walking on the street,
  you hear only the sound of your two feet.

   Standing on your own two feet.

     Your own two feet.

—*Chris Jordan*

A Mother's Point Of View

Some people view love as being like a fruit tree. A fruit tree is planted; it grows and produces a bountiful supply of fruit for humans and other creatures to enjoy. The fruit tree continues to do this until the end of its life.

A fruit tree also bears seeds, which in turn bears more fruit trees. This is a process that has the potential to go on until the end of time. To some people love is infinite.

Other people view love as a limited money fund. There is just so much to portion out to a limited number of people. After that, it is running on empty. How do you view love?

Your child loves you. One day he will meet a young woman, marry her and have children of his own. Your child will form new love relationships with these new people. Will your child stop loving you? How do you view love?

If God is willing, your child will live a long and prosperous life. On this journey through life your child will encounter millions of other people. He will come to love many of these people. Will your child love you less? How do you view love?

When your child comes face to face with another, bonds, and learns to love him, do you believe you will lose your child?

—*Sherry Vonde*

Once Upon A Time

Once upon a time
Is the beginning of every rhyme.
Magical dreams to fairy tales,
To tell of a princess whom we all hail.
Dragons who fly
From a sunlit to starry sky.
Sources with power
To frail mice in corners cower.
Knights in shinning armor on white horses ride,
To catch a fair lady to become his fair bride.
Even the rich and the poor
Find love and enchantment to become even more.
Come take a ride on horses who fly,
To wonderful land where no one cries.
Happily ever after is always the end
And everyone ends up living as friends.

—*Angie Holloway*

Bodymind

The body
   is the quantum phase of the mind.
The mind
   is the field phase of the body.
Consciousness
   induces the particle phase.
Unconsciousness
   induces the wave phase.
The mind
   is too precious to waste.
When young
   it can be molded as plastic clay.
When mature
   it is capable of balanced thinking.
When old
   you cannot teach an old dog new tricks.
Aim your mind
   all the days of your life,
Higher up
   and further on.

—*Archimedes Abad Concon*

Night Light

Where did the light go, the one that shown so bright?
It always kept the fear away as I fell asleep at night.
I have never slept without it,
Not once these many years.
The light would keep the hatred out-
The prejudice and fear.
The world never worried about poverty or war.
The light keeps all bad things out
And keeps me safe and warm.
Each year the light get dimmer,
I outgrow its shield each day,
I must see the world as it is,
Why did the light go away?

—*Juli Michelle Scheiner*

The Strength Of The Heart

The strength of the heart; the weight of our guilt, our youth
is the start, upon which we built, the things we believed, in
that which we trust, the future our bread, the past our crust.
Follow the truth. In the beginning we're taught, to keep what
we need and to discard the naught. Regret is of worth if you
learn from the deed, if it's lodged in your heart, on your soul
it will feed. The mistakes of a man never lessens his worth,
it expands his own mind, inducing rebirth. The love a child is
unique in it's root, it continues to grow making all else seem
moot. By your very existence, you have planted the seeds, the
endeavor to be better is all that child needs. You think they
can't hear you, you think they don't know? Confide in what
hides behind the mind's do'? No, them po' chil'ren know, yes,
they're always aware, that our choices and judgements are the
burdens we bear. We file bad memories, sometimes they fall off
the shelf, and into our hearts, where the demons have dwelt.
But it is the strength of the heart determines the morrow, the
blame be the weight the anchor, our sorrow. So remember when
you're slipping on life's icy patch, I'm the one with my arms
out, ready to catch.
—*Cynthia H. Walker*

Leashes

"Today
is tomorrow,"
I told my dog
(I don't like dogs much although I used to
Tonya
a good friend
I opened the gate she ran away
and I ran
on the curb ran over she lay
I cried)

"Today
is tomorrow,"
I told my dog on a leash

In the land of never
(a place where a dog cannot run free from fences)
every day is like the last.
—*Jeremy Meloy*

America

The flag on the pole with its stripes unfurled
Is waving and swaying for one and all.
The dark clouds pass in the sky high above,
And the wind through the trees will forever blow,
Just as long as God rules earth here below,
We read of the people far, far away
Whose hearts, happiness are destroyed each day;
Whose flags have fallen, and their homes taken away.
Their spirit fights on, as they learn, labor, pray.
So our flag shouts "Courage" for one and all,
As it proudly waves greetings to friends everywhere.
It tells the glad story of "America free."
A land that has always, ever will be,
A "home" for you and for me.
—*Ada Louise Robinson*

In Memory Of Dad

As I try to envision you dad what appears
Is your sitting at the table sipping on a cold beer
Telling wonderful stories of memories gone by
Especially ones of your childhood when you weren't at all shy
Chopping up a piano and climbing up poles
Your father must have had the patience of Job
Be it teacher or preacher you didn't care which
You'd pick on with your gags and fun tricks
But you also had your serious side
And it was one that was filled with a great deal of pride
Especially when mom was there by your side
I wish you could know and it's coming from me
That you were the best father that there could ever be
—*Catherine S.L. White*

It Has To Start With Me

I, Mother, and you, me, gave me the start of life yet to keep
it alive, it has to start with me. I, Baby and you, learn to
walk, holding, standing, help, falls, encouragement, it all
depends on, it has to start with me. I, School and you,
teachers, books, tapes, pictures, films and hard work, to
pattern my future, it has to start with me. Church and you,
ministry, the bible, sermons, love of fellowman, hymns, all are
for naught if I reject, it has to start with me. I, Marriage
and you, you and me, love sometimes fades, bills, jealousy,
arguments, stand in the way, but all would be saved and
settled, we both agree, but it has to start with me. I, world
and you, people, so small in the universe, they, only people as
yet, we can see, demand so much from our countries, land, clean
air, river and sea, the crime murders, stealing, rape,
uprising, if only we had peace, but, it has to start with me.
I, Nations and you, rulers, presidents, dictators, kings,
diplomats, heading the Nations, would agree, being alone on
this tiny Planet called Earth, yet cannot find the ultimate
Goal called "peace", leaders pull yourself up by the boot
straps and proudly say to yourself: It has to start with me.
—*Donald Smith*

Which Way From Here?

As one beholds the sun aglow,
It brings to mind questions to life I wanted to know.
Is where I sit, where I dream, where I am
All in the Heavenly Father's divine plan?
Or am I wandering from here to yonder,
In my heart these things I ponder.
Am I fulfilling the part that's designed for my life,
Or am I aimlessly traveling, living a life of frustrations
and strife.
But, wait, I hear the Father gently say in my ear,
"Carry on my child, do not fear."
So, continuously in His loving care I abide,
Not always knowing what's ahead, but knowing
It's okay, as long as He guides.
—*Savai LaRose Smith*

Shadow

"In Memory of Scott Parker, AIDS victim."
It crept silently into our lives
and plotted its evil plan
It took some time to show its face
The cards were in its hand
It worked so slow for several years,
With power ever growing
Each change was done so subtly
Before it started showing
It was in control, no turning back
The evil deed was done
And when it was through it took away
My beautiful smiling son.
It's taken charge of scores of lives
The outcome-always the same
It's lurking still in the shadows
And AIDS is this monster's name.
—*Nancy H. Parker*

I Know What Happens To Yesterday

I know what happens to yesterday
It dries up and goes away
The past is gone, you can't go back
I've hung my past upon a rack
Tomorrow is a brand new day
Don't torture yourself, put the past away
I know that happens to yesterday
It turns to dust and blows away
In the wind of tomorrow
Leaving only misery and sorrow
Leave the past where it belongs
Looking back is always wrong
Don't look back, I know it hurts
Looking back only makes it worse
Dry your tears, take my hand
I will lead you to the land
Of the future and when you arrive
Look around you — you have survived
—*Melissa L. Freeman*

Yellow Caterpillar

When the music had begun
It filled the room with a spiritual aura
Each note flowed through me with a strength
so strong and vehement.
   And as the rhythms moved faster and faster
   To the magnificent climax, my heartbeat quickened
my mind went to a zone
a place where no one can find me
no one can see
no one can hear the music inside of me
no one person could understand
or try to understand my melancholy thoughts.
   It's my spot chosen for me
   and me alone
   no soul, no universal being can touch me
   here I'm in a haven
   as safe as can be
   until the music finally dies away.
—*Debra Lynn Schultes*

The Old Friend

I saw an old friend the other day.
It had been quite a while since he'd gone away.
His brow was wrinkled, his hair was gray,
Body bent, as if to keep advancing years at bay.
We sat, and talked of things, of this and that,
Remembering—he absentmindedly stroked the cat
And allowed that, yes, at times his memory was flat;
Scenes so bright of yesteryear had dimmed, no more his habitat.
We quieted, and silently let thoughts drift through our memory—
Those that were, those that are, those yet to be.

Thinking back to hazy childhood times,
He suddenly looked at me and opined
That, growing up together, there was no rhyme
Or reason we should look so different. Then chimes
Of the clock on the mantelpiece rang five,
And it was time to part, he said. To be alive
And see the sun rise was privilege enough, and the drive
Into the sunset, the demise, leaves legacy and memory
   those with newer lives.
We said goodbye, and fare-thee-well;
We both had stories yet to tell.
—*Stephen I. Capin*

Untitled

I stroke your back or hold your hand
it hurts so much it is hard to stand
hour after hour watching you shake
from seizures there is no break

I hold your hand and watch you sweat
Your clothes are all soaking wet
I call your mother she changes them
but nothing can change the pain within

I am useless, totally hopeless as a father
I can't even care for my darling daughter
what will come of her when I am gone
If I can't care for her who else can

The shaking has stopped now She'll be all right
With me by her side I'll put up a real fight
I hold your hand and silently whisper I Love You
I didn't know you were awake too

If you had told me you were awake
I wouldn't have left myself unsafe
I don't want you to see....
But Daddy, I didn't know that you loved me
—*Joyce Sherman Murphy*

The Spirit Of The Rose

The rose glistens with romance
It is beautiful and to you it is what
Symbolizes love
You can try to leave it, to forget it,
To abandon it forever
But you always find yourself back where you
started, by the rose,
Staring at it breathless.
You have yet to realize
The rose is your Spirit of romance.
You cannot live without it.
Just as you cannot live without love.
The rose is forever.
And love is forever.
—*Cris Day*

Don't Worry About Tomorrow

Don't worry about tomorrow,
   it is just another day.

Don't listen to those rumors,
   who cares what other people say.

Trust me, those feelings will never stay.

Don't worry about tomorrow,
   the sun is always there.

   In the day and night
I am with you everywhere.

Don't worry about tomorrow,
   it will all soon come to pass.

Just worry about our present
   and make today last.
—*Victoria Caye Woods*

My Last Christmas Tree

The Christmas tree is so very big.
It is so big, it almost touches the ceiling
It is decorated so very pretty.
It is such a shame it will be the
last one I see.
The tree is so very big.
Oh, how I wish I could live to
see another one.
It is such a shame I can't see
another.
All because I have this stupid
disease called AIDS.
—*Christal Privette*

What Love Is

Love isn't something to be waited for,
   It is to be achieved.
Love isn't something to be cried over,
   It is to be cherished.
Love isn't something to be smothered,
   It is to be embraced.
Love isn't something to be forgotten,
   It is to be remembered.
Your love isn't something I'll let go of,
   It is to be held on to - forever.
—*Rhonda Clifford*

The Autumn

Although Autumn has yet to fall
It is upon us like a winter wall
I cannot say that it is sad
For it is not that very bad

Although the seasons have yet to change
The meaning is still all the same
Death can come in the blink of an eye
Some things just wither and die

Although Autumn seems as if it is coming too soon
The geese fly over at high noon
As the leaves turn a golden brown
There are some things yet to be found
—*Mellisa A. Ring*

The Way I Feel About You

Joey, each time I look into your eyes,
It makes me want to cry.
I love you so much,
Words can't express why.
You make me feel a certain kind
of yearning,
But as the days go on we're
both still learning.
Everyday I love you more and
more,
My heart is open to you like an
unlocked door.
I hold onto your necklace, oh, so tight,
Just to get me through each and
every night.
And every night when I lay in my cot, I thank
the good Lord that I've got
what I've got.
—*Abigail Redman*

"The 23rd Psalm For Those Who Love Their Brothers and Sisters"

Love is my candle, I shall not want for light.
It maketh me to forget self in remembering others.
It radiates God's love to brothers and sisters alike.
It restoreth my Spirit.
It leadeth me down the bright paths of service
to my fellowmen.
Yea, though I walk within the world of uncertainty,
trials and tests, where life is given and taken.
My candle burns brightly—the light ever gleaming.
Through a nod, a smile or a word, I know I'm needed.
It glows with the knowledge of my Lord.
What it stands for—how it serves,
And my cup runneth over.
Surely the rewards of my love for others far
exceed what I have given.
And the Light of my candle of Love shall glow
in my heart forever.
—*Alice Kotts*

The River Of Life

   The river of life is never straight,
   It meanders right and left at a varying gait,
'Tis narrow, wide, rough, smooth, shallow, deep,
Within this river are the trials, tribulations, joys, angers
   We experience.

Sailing upon this river there is a constant need to pay
   attention,
   No one lays back and relaxes at any time,
As the journey goes on glory and fame go by the wayside,
   We focus on the future and look back on the past,
   We use our memories to gain wisdom
And go into our remaining journey with high spirits
   and hopeful expectations.
—*Michael Winters*

"School"

Stay in school, please don't be a fool
If you do you'll be so cool
Once you learn you'll know to earn
So don't quit, achieve to learn
Once you know the rules to be hip
Which means more to give the teacher any lip
When you graduate
You'll really be glad
When you can say,
"Hey I'm a grad.
—*Marc Yates*

Can You Tell Me What This Feeling Is?

Real love is something some people don't know, most can turn it on and off.
But for me this feeling goes very deep, its warmth can be so soft.
When the one in your life acts like such an ass and abuses the ones you love
Why is it after hating them so you change like a stone in the rough?
It's like your telling yourself that no matter what they do,
you'll always find some good in them that keeps them clinging to you.
And when they abuse you whether with their mouth or fist, you never forget but always forgive.
Is this an insecurity or pity or real love, and can you find fault in people like me who forgive like him above.
In the end will we be rewarded for the things that we've gone through or will we be punished for letting our hearts tell us what to do?
I want to have tranquility seeking it like a peaceful dove, so tell me what this feeling is, Insecurity, pity or love.

—*Karen M. Saxon*

A Dove

I look into the sky I see a dove
It reminds me of our love
It is very beautiful and pure
Flying so high and secure
This small white bird has no harm
I realize that is part of its charm
Living life the way it was meant
Soaring happy and content
Dreaming, tomorrow will be better than today
It shines as it's hit with the sun's ray
There are no problems and things seem so right
Our love is still there but the dove has left my sight

—*Kymberli Cooper*

I'm Still Waiting

You left me on a night so clear, it was so peaceful
it seemed you were near. You had gone to the bar,
to get a small drink, you said you needed time alone, to think.
I thought oh great! Things around here will be much better,
We had someone to make happy, the bed wetter.
Soon it was nearly ten o'clock,
Alex was in bed with a bad cough.
I was watching the clock real hard,
But all I could see was that darn Christmas card,
Given to you by your old high school girlfriend,
It's sad she really loved my man.
It turned out she divorced my high school dream,
She was coming back for my husband.
The thought of it, made me feel greedy. I was angry, I was mad.
I was lonely, I was sad. So you left me all alone.
For the rest of my life I sat by the phone.

—*Anna Elizabeth Heaslet*

Blame

Being blamed wears one thin
If you take the blame and carry it within.
The load is to heavy for ones shoulders alone
The heart isn't made out of stone.

Being innocent yet feeling guilt and shame
For something that wasn't your fault
Then being blamed
Hurts without a doubt.
It will break the heart which never really mends
Though it often pretends.

—*Priscilla R. Fuller*

Time

Time is spinning out of control, more quickly than ever before. It seems time can not be controlled it just keeps spinning out of control.

I always seem to be going in circles, never getting to where I'm going. Never knowing what exactly I'm looking for, if indeed I've some place to be. Who holds the answers to questions such as these and who is it I am trying to please, could it be me? Will I ever know? Will there be a glimmer of hope, a hint as to why these endless questions are running amuck in my mind, no reason or rhyme? The answers to these questions just beyond my reach, haunting me, teasing me, always keeping me on the go, searching blindly and never reaching my goal. What is my goal? I'm afraid I do not know.

There is a veil of fog that seems to surround me, this veil keeps me running in circles, searching for answers to all these questions...Where am I, why am I. Now another question just entered my mind, will there be time to find whatever it is I'm searching for?

There can not be for time keeps spinning out of control, no time left, no where for me to go, continuing to run in circles, looking for what I do not know. Do you know?

—*Royceann Jackson Heller*

Memories

The snow falls rapidly in milk white flakes.
  It sticks to the ground in vast amounts.
    Soon children come out to play.
    I sit on my porch watching them,
      Remembering the days,
    The days when I played in the snow,
      The days when I was young,
    The days when I would play until it was dark,
      And my mother would call me to dinner.
        Then I would go up to bed,
        And read with my brothers,
        Before the days of television.
My thoughts were then interrupted by the children.
    "Grandpa," they said. "Come play."
    "All right," I told them.
    So I put on my jacket and played,
      Just as in the old days.

—*John Arceci*

Love

A small tear trickles down my cheek,
It tells a story that's hard to speak.
As we travel we search and seek,
When one finds love it is not bleak.

Love
When you find this special affection,
You may think your life's reached perfection.
And when you make this certain connection,
You may find your lover's reflection.

Love
If and when you find this emotion.
It takes a special kind of devotion.
So when your feelings are full of commotion,.
All you need is a certain potion.

Love

—*Laura Jarrett*

Realization

I could see the hatred, the wasting away.
It was howling out its name.
I wanted to be the one to take it away,
To kiss his face in shame.
Give it away, I begged him so
But his grip was tight; he wouldn't let go.
His knuckles were white and held in place;
I wanted to wipe the tears from his face.

He kept turning away and looking there
To a place where he felt safe.
It ached my heart and shattered my pride
When all he would give was that stare.

If he only knew how much I cared
When he turned away from me.
Maybe then all the hurt wouldn't matter.
And I would be all could see.
—*Michelle Schultheis*

Time

Time flows in two dimensions, man cannot invent it or control
it, yet, we try everyday to our dismay.
Minutes can last forever, while entire days are blinked away.
Can you recall those precious, misplaced seconds,
Or enlarge a year of your youth?

How can you shrink, stretch, add to, or subtract from
Something with no body or mass? Yet, this bubble around you
can take your own will away. It can kill you or make you sad,
Then without changing itself at all,
You are happy, alive and playing games.

Like the wind, its effects can be felt and seen,
It is invisible and evasively playful, but even the wind is
touchable or escapable, and time? Time can rob you of friends
and family. Even enemies can be taken away,
But not even the wind can bring back the kites of yesterday.

We plan it, save it, waste it, wish for more of it,
And are we even sure what exactly "it" is?
It isn't born within us, so why is it always fed to us,
And taught to us? Is it like water or sunshine?
It won't sustain our lives... or does it?
—*Dale Watson*

A Rose

A rose blossoms showing its exclusive design.
Its aroma fills the late spring air and arouses
my sense telling me to take advantage of the
roses' beauty.

I now prune a few from their natural birthplace
and meticulously arrange these beauties in a
vase and give them to the one I love.

What a joy to give.

Thank you nature for these roses and thank
you Debbie for loving me.
—*Jerry Smith*

Untitled

The flag stands high and proud
Its multicolors of red, white and blue
Each have a meaning of their own
Red stands for the blood that was shed
To keep all American free
Blue stands for the sky after the dark
storms have past.
White stands for light and joy of freedom
That we have in our country
—*Joan M Costas*

A Meteor

Flaming across the heavens,
Its backdrop, the sky all aglow,
The limitless boundaries of space, its stage,
Its audience, earth - watching below.

Beauty that illuminates the universe,
Seeming omnipotent in its glory,
Beautifully alone - startlingly brief,
Its life, a short, short story.

It falls earthward -
The spectator stops and ponders,
It plunges - extinguishing and exploding,
Scattering dust on Nature's wonders.

A few particles, that's all that's left
On a hillside or field of clover.
Out of sight now, gone forever,
Its brief life finished - over!
—*Edwardlene Fleeks Willis*

Keepsake Of The Heart

There is a rose upon the snow.
Its crimson bud is touched by cold.
A drop of crystal in its heart;
like the tears of a long lost love.
Its song runs free, which fills my heart,
And colors the air I breath.
Shall I then close my eyes to it; turn and walk away,
And keep the vision deep within my heart.
Forever there to stay.
—*Jacqueline R. Davidson*

I'm With God

I'm a little baby, growing in you.
It's early in the month, I'm brand new.
I'm a little embryo, as small as can be.
Just wait mommy, you'll love me.
I'm getting bigger, you notice me.
But you're to young, this can't be.
What are you thinking, will I die?
All I know is, that you cry and cry.
A couple days later, near lifeless and small.
I felt the chord tear, then started to fall.
Into a tube, I'm floating away.
I'm dying now, but in your mind I'll stay.
For now I'm with god, He's watching to see.
That maybe someday, you'll be here with me.
—*Emily Morrison*

I's Rather Die

Sometimes it's really hard to tell someone how you feel,
It's like being trapped in a box with an unbreakable seal.
You close your eyes and think of why God even put you here,
But then your trapped in a world of darkness and the hateful
thoughts you feel,
Are brought to life when you realize this so-called dream is
real. My heart is full of anger and destructive thoughts I
see. I'm trapped in a box of darkness; this can't be reality.

But then I realize that this is true, I've died and can't be seen,
I've discovered a more deadly illness; it's called being mean.
I look around and see people with a cruel and hurtful sickness,
All these people are dying too with a disease called prejudice.

"If you can judge a wise man by the color of his skin, then I
guess you are better than I."
For if this is really possible, then I know I'd rather die.
—*Jennifer Rowland*

Dear Grandpa

Dear Grandpa my quiet kind friend,
It's only me the third grandchild you had,
the one you gave such a wonderful dad.

I can't understand why you've gone so fast,
I wish you were here just like in the past.

When it came to my birthday you would always attend,
and when I looked at you I'd always get a grin.

A cheery glance or a helping hand,
I'll never know a heart as grand.

All you could build and all you could mend,
I knew on you could always depend.

I'm quite sure that I'll never know,
all the gifts you've given that helped me grow.

But, I wonder now if you'll ever know,
that for all my life I've loved you so.

—*Sara Jo Crosby*

"The Outcast"

It's cold.
It's snowing.
You stand at the window,

Bundled up to help keep the cold out.
All your worldly possessions
in a box at your feet.

Longing to enter the house.
Hoping—that when the door opens
this time—you'll be allowed to enter.

All your life you've been this way—outside.
While countless others enter the house,
you can not.

You stand at the window.
Always looking in.
Wondering
what it's like to be loved.

—*Jeff Christoff*

Three-Quarter Moon

What is it about that three-quarter moon?
It's so big and bright,
But not quite right.
It wants to shine just a little brighter.
It's pulse matches mine
And with just a little more time:
Another day, another night;
Comes another chance to get it right.

—*K. P. Martin*

Untitled

She asked me why
I live my life the way I do

Like I truly expect
To be buried with my wealth
Or smothered by my fame
Or entombed with all my toys
Like an Egyptian God-king

But she knows
I live my life the way I do
Because the only things I'll take with me
Are the things I have not done

—*Raymond A. Mulford*

In Search Of Identity

Who am I? is the question I ask.
It's taken half a lifetime for me to get this far.
I was a child of abuse, a very lost child.
Now I know the past blocked my identity.
I was full of frozen feelings and depression.
Now I'm awakening, but what now?
It seems too late to start over again.
Where do I start? How do I begin?
I want to do so many things but where have I been?
It's too late to go back to school.
No one will hire you without a degree or
that ever present requirement of experience in your field.
I feel like a teenager, who needs a goal,
but everyone tells me, I'm too old.
So I ask these questions. Who am I?
Where do I go? How do I begin? What should I do?

—*Hope Humming*

Music To Me

What do you think is music to me
It's the sound of the surf and the sound of the sea
It's rain on the roof when you're going to sleep
It's the moo of a cow or the baa of a sheep

It's the bray of a donkey, the purr of a cat
There are beautiful melodies played in B flat
Like the hoot of an owl, the song of a bird
It's music like this I have always heard

Another sonata that sounds good to the ear
Is a babbling brook, that we all like to hear
A woodpecker's staccato as he pecks at a tree
That is another kind of music to me

Yes, it's another kind of music and there's so much more
It's different music with a different score
You have but to listen, now don't you agree
It's God's kind of music that is music to me.

—*Ruth Hottinger*

Deceiving

The brilliance isn't in being able to fly,
It's the wonderful peace of touching the sky.

The wind is only air with a bit of spark,
And night is only light filled with dark.

A fire isn't evil and water isn't the cure;
Both without mind are wholesome and pure.

The world isn't flat, yet the world isn't round,
But rough and uneven and coarsely profound.

All adults are not wise; not all children are sweet;
Both can be wrong and both can cheat.

All of our thoughts are dreams and nothing is exact
Or really what it seems.

—*Melissa Elder*

I Love This Person 'Cause....

I know this person who lives on a farm,
It seems he's always in the barn.
He gets up at the crack of dawn,
And works until the sun is gone.
When coming in from a hard days work,
He enters with a little smirk.
His straight black hair combed to the side,
In his beard flakes of sawdust hide.
He's caring, loving, and helps you when your sad,
I love this person cause he's my Dad.

—*Valerie Cadieux*

The Hill Country

I would walk here where the sun comes up
its warm light building shadows
that walk down the hill-sides
gathering pockets of darkness
nestled in the hollows.

Cactus is beginning to blossom
and I watch a flower open slowly
as if pulled by an invisible string.
A caterpillar crawls leisurely along
on the staff side of a grass.

I know these open spaces where a man
can breathe and dream... taste the freedom
that comes with cool sweet water lapped up
in my hand from a stream that purls
over the stones.

Is it strange in summer comes a hunger
for space and room
and the heart finds comfort
in this
the fabric of the hill country?
—*Letty G. Moon*

You

No matter where I am
It's you that I will keep in mind,
the precious smile you give me
Also the way you look at me
Is so sweet and kind.

When I'm with you,
my feelings for you are for real
I'm telling you this now
Because I want you to know
How you make me feel.

This feeling will always be with me now,
always and forever
I'll tell you that I love you
Now that our hearts are touching so closely
and perfectly together.

Just remember that special gentle feeling I get
when I'm alone with you,
It's you that I want
because there is something about you
That makes me love you.
—*Rena Miguel*

Searching

   It's so hard trying to change
   I've my whole life to rearrange
   It's hard to know where to start
   Living day by day becomes an art
   I really want to do what's right
But there's no good guy dressed in white
   Telling me how I should proceed
   Which paths to take or where they lead
   I'm so confused that it's a shame
But there's no need for putting blame
   Blame doesn't change a single thing
   Who knows what problems life will bring
   I've discovered in the last few years
That not much is solved by shedding tears
   That in the end I'm responsible for me
But there's just so much that I can't see
   Sometimes I feel I'm lost in the dark
   And the future looms large and stark
But I'm learning to trust, and night does become day
   So little by little, I'm finding my way
—*Lois F. Walker*

Farewell

Allow me to reiterate
I've sailed the seas and walked the plank
In solemn times I've danced with you
And stolen way vicissitude

Endearing are my dreams of home
Lost roaming in their silent zone
And if I would go back to them
I'd wallow in post-mortal sin

A grackles song, chaotic muse
Entrance a distant listeners rouge
Such hemispheres I tell apart
Dividing like the sun at dark

A young girl cries, another dies
And tranquilly the priest replies
She was a dove, she died for love
We all shall miss our favored mom
—*Marc Jacobs*

Untitled

Jesus I'm coming someday
Jesus I'm on my way
When I cross over the wide rolling tide
Jesus you'll be waiting on the other side
Jesus, Jesus above no-one else could have such love
Jesus you died on calvary to save sinners
   and make them free
Oh! how I long to be at your side and
   see the wonders of heaven inside
Eyes have not seen - tongues have not told
   the wonders in heaven we will behold
Help me dear Jesus as I go through this
   life to help others keep down envy strife
I want to be willing to live day by day
   so I can show some lost sinner the way
Now that the birthday of our Savior is
   here people go wondering far and near
Never stopping to give God the praise
   for sending his son so we can have life
     beyond the graves.
—*Gatha Stovall*

They Joined

They talked to the recruiter. They took the mental test. They joined. They surpassed the mental stress, they survived the arduous boot camps to separate them from the rest. They were the best at their art. (The art of war that is.) They were the masters for they survived their own worse fears. Some were at war for months, others for many years. They joined. Some of these men actually lost body parts in places, most people will never know. They also lost their friends to wars, that did not freely go. They joined. Some of these men traveled back to places like Bataan, Correigedor, Saipan, Iwo Jima, Chosin, Saigon, Beirut, Kuwait, and Iraq. Others too numerous to name and everything but faceless, have given the ultimate sacrifice in these and many other places. But they joined.. How can a society, who has not joined keep taking the coin from men of valor, men of pride, men who have earned their ride, making sure our heritage survives. When you vote, whether you are a taxpayer or politician, before you make that decision remember one fact about veterans! That is .... They joined!!! Did you???
—*Earl Weeks*

Darling

Darling, I am dreaming, of a little home for two;
Just a little cottage darling,
With the shutters trimmed in blue.

With white curtains at the windows, and bright flowers on the sill; and a dear husband to love me,
And his name it will be "Bill".

There will be a fireplace in it, and an easy chair or two;
When the twilight is softly falling,
I'll be waiting there for you.

And our love it will grow stronger, as the days go passing by;
We will be so happy Darling, in this cottage for you and I.

Then later on, Darling we may hear the patter of little feet;
Dearest, a precious baby, is what makes a home complete.

And I pray my darling, that, the dear Lord up above;
Will keep this little home secure,
With happiness, peace and love.
—*Treva M. Sauers*

Beverly's Blues

I was more than a notch on a sad old guitar
Just another line to make some guy a star.
I was a tenderly swaying melody on a well used
Saxophone.
Beverly it played, melting my heart with its tone.
Forever, forever, whispering so soft and low.
Oh Beverly, Beverly, I will never go.

Mystical music rolling slowly out to sea.
Like fine mist performing off waves in complete harmony.
Blowing a sound as loud as the ocean's roar.
Beverly it played, my love for you is ever more.
I love you, I love you, I knew it was true.
Oh Beverly, Beverly, you will never be blue.

But rockin' and roll'in, it started to whine down the hills.
Singing it's song of part time love and cheap thrills.
A tune of goodbye was all I could hear.
Beverly it played, you got the most of a year.
Gone away, gone away, never to return.
Oh Beverly, Beverly, when will you ever learn?
—*Beverly Fox*

Spring Cleaning

It's not a war you know
Just cleaning house as one does in springtime
Yet the signs of war are rampant Destruction, Famine,
    Desolation, Homeless, Hungry, Bereaved
Refugees fleeing from the trap that once was home
Going they know not where, anywhere but here
And the children cry, and the mothers mourn
And the fathers grieve the loss of sons
Hope of their future—dead. Heirs, nourished
in the bosoms of mothers, cherished daughters too,
Victims of vice and rage of wicked violent men
Now have become the dust of yesteryear,
Beaten and trammeled, caught up in the purge of springtime
Bundled nameless bags of human waste
Put out in bins that house things—refuse
Aftermath of "ethnic cleansing"
Spring cleaning has no parameters of time or place
It happens any time; it happens anywhere
Its synonym rears its ugly head
And dust begins to fly.
—*Daliah Rankin*

Untitled

Never dream the impossible,
Just dream the possible.
Dream a dream of a far away place
And it's unknown magical faces.
Dream a dream of romance and passion,
Be like Romeo and Juliet forever to the end.
Dream a dream of a knight with his sword
And a princess waiting to be rescued.
Dream a dream of hope, happiness, and peace.
When the night has passed and the sun has risen,
Just remember these words.
The impossible dreams you dream are
Sometimes closest to reality.
—*Michelle Taylor*

Soul-Searcher

I told them I'd be famous,
Just you wait and see.
And I set out boldly searching
For the glamour side of me.

But when I got there,
What I found was all a mystery.
Why was I so empty?
Was there something I couldn't see?

The walls were dark and dingy,
From years of locked-up doors.
The cobwebs dangled helplessly,
Seeking light no more.

No air or life was present-
No place for them to live.
It seemed my soul housed sorrow
And that's all I had to give.

So I passed the star-lit sidewalk,
As reality took its toll.
In the place where my name should have been,
Was just an empty hole.
—*Cari Marie Waggoner*

Forever My Friend

Though we depart
Keep in your heart
The things we have said
And the tears we have shed
The great times we had together
And the memories we'll keep forever
Yet never have I thought this point would come
When we must say farewell
So until we meet again
Your forever my friend
—*Alison Barnett*

For Bym

The sapling knows how best to learn its trade!
If beneath the maple's shelt'ring limbs it holds
its earth, and lets its fragile leaves unfold,
it stands to learn the noble art of shade.
In Autumn's chilling winds, when most dismay,
in tender tones the maple lifts its voice
in chorus, only to help the grove rejoice
and add its hues to what the wind might say.
And thus we share this grove of verse and song.
Beneath your shade I learn the nobler arts,
and feel inside, like leafbud in spring, the birth
of music, and search for richer hues to impart
my words, which fall with struggling grace along
this fertile page, an element of worth.
—*Cory S. Colton*

Guardian Angel

Guardian Angel sweet to thee
Keep us safe from thy enemy
Love is most, trust is first
Let us live and never thirst.

Guardian Angel sweet to thee
Keep us stronger than the tallest tree
Love is kind, like sweet refined wine
Let us grow and age gracefully fine

Guardian Angel sweet to thee
Keep us together and protect my family
Love is a sign, trust is the way-maker's cord

Let us seek and understand our
  Loving Lord
    —*Grace Qi Sovereignty*

Talking To My Lord

Woke up this morning in the right mind
Knew that the Lord was there all the time.

He said get up it is time to go to school
But he said keep your cool.

He said great everyone with a kiss
But Martha, don't you miss.

He said Pam is so sweet
But Miss Mary is neat.

I came too far to turn around
To be knocked down on the ground.

I hope everyone will pass
Because they are moving very fast.

I close with love
Because we are all like a dove.

So, keep the Lord on your side.
    —*Martha Flowers*

My Thunderstorm

Pounding against the window it begs to be heard.
Knocking for acceptance.
Flashing, it momentarily outlines the gray above.
Gloomy, frustrated, it demands attention.
Crashing, it sounds a desperate cry.
Fighting to be recognized it thrashes out upon the night.
Blowing, it throws around ideas.
Unknowing what to do it is spread in every direction.
Whistling through each crack, trying to dive into other's
  depths, to show its own.
It is coming so close, but still is blocked by the walls built
  in between.
In one last attempt, pulling together all its power and force,
  it turbulently reaches the ground.
Flooding to all it is finally understood.
A beautiful day, a stormy night.
I see this often
    —*Michele M. Barry*

Forever And Now

Gentle graceful glances into my eyes, you are alone in knowing what inside me lies. When I am weak and no ones near by, your distant affection diverges my cry. Afflicted wounds from jealous friends, you always stood by me through all of them. Sometimes I become confined, and don't reach out, you are the voice to reveal what my secrecy about. The tears you vanished delicately off my skin, as you strive to cleanse the grief from within. When I have appeared blind, and could not see, you have been the eyes that guided me. You listen for me when I needed to hear, after deafening repetitive echoes concealed my ears. Isolated silence left me to die, but you are the life that kept me alive. You have been my eyes, my ears, my voice, you gave me life, you had a choice. Adore is not an emotion immense enough to describe there is a vast amount of love for you inside. But we know that one day are paths may, have journeys part there separate ways. So eternally remember the harmonious love, that was gift from the serene heavens above. And that beholden love to you I vow, desired devotion for forever and now.
    —*Ashley Kelsey*

"For A Special Friend"

A special friend who knows how to make me
  laugh or annoyance when we are in pain
Someone special to talk too.

The person who is always there
Who you can trust with anything
The friend that acts like your big brother.
A friend I love very much.
This person I would do anything for, and
  would do anything for me with out a blink

How can I tell this person he means the world to me.
That he is actually a part of my life, even though
  he doesn't think so.
The person that means a lot to me.
For a very special friend I love very much.
Thanks a lot love you very much.
    —*Maria Sanchez*

Let's Not Forget To Play

Let's not forget to play.
Life's burdens may be many
and they be real ones,
but if we let them get to us
pretty soon we will be true bores.
Leave your frown at the door
and come inside smiling.
Let's not forget
to enjoy each other's company
because we take things too seriously.
If we laugh, then life laughs back with us.
    —*Daniela Cornea*

A Friendship Bound Together

For secrets to be kept, memories to be relived,
   laughter or tears to be shed.
I know I can count on you and you for me.
That's why our friendship is bound together
   with a special kind of love.
A love that can live forever
   and never will die.
Through good times and through bad times,
   we will always be there for each other.
To listen when needed and give advice when sought.
And that's why whether we're close together
   or far apart, there will always be a
special place for you right here, in my heart.
—*Kim Enger*

The Fall

   Standing on the edge of life, look long and well before you leap. The skies are darkened with memories and promises I could not keep. The fall is long and straight, worries of yesterday…they will carry my weight. My heart yearns to touch the ground, when I fall, will I fall safe and sound?

I leap and I fall. Am I falling or am I flying? If I'm falling, stop my fall. If I'm flying, hold my hand and join me. Who will be there tomorrow? When I'm in another land, in another time…Who will be there tomorrow? My memories…they dim and fade away, the wind blows past thoughts of yesterday. Time, time it soars, ubiquity in time, eternal life is now forever mine. Will I walk with the prophets of the past, will I fall among angels in fires made to last? Will I ever taste the bittersweet kiss of life again? Soaring through skies, eternal life forever mine, forever mine. The dream, the dream is real, the dream is solid, the dream is mine. Forever mine, forever mine……

   —*Rigoberto Cuervo*

Having A Baby

Shopping for booties and bottles and rocking chairs,
Learning lullabies for a mom who cares,
Practicing diapering a teddy bear,
We're having a baby!

Tickling a doll and saying, "Coochy coo!"
Everything is so tiny and new,
Painting the nursery pink or blue,
We're having a baby!

Holding our bundle so fragile and light,
Hoping and dreaming we do everything right,
Waking up in the middle of the night,
We're having a baby!

—*Karen Fenstermaker*

"Her Mom Died Today"

She tried not to think of it, but it didn't leave.
As much as she cried, she would not believe.
Day and night she would pray,
But her mom died today.

She put her head on my mom's
shoulder and started to cry.
She said, "my mom is going to die."
There her mom peacefully lay,
Her mom died today.
   —*Julie Drago*

Days Of Youth

Sweet days of youth, ah happy days, you pass so quickly by and leave with us, as we grow old, a memory and a sigh. If we but knew in summer time which dreams to work upon, we'd have much
more to reminisce when summer days are gone. Brisk autumn is upon us before we've had our fling, and we recall, with tear-filled eyes, how tender was the spring. How beautiful the afternoons we lived beneath the sun, how wonderful the cool spring nights, when all the work was done. Dear little boys, I say to you, just stay the way you are, run barefoot through the warm green grass, and try to catch a star. Don't ever lose your building blocks, and marbles and bubble gum, get jam on your shirts, and mud on your shoes, and have yourselves some fun. Sweet little girls, I say to you, don't ever lose your charm, one look into your sparkling eyes and every heart is warm. Please go on tying ribbons red around your shining hair, and may your troubles fly away like bubbles in the air. Sweet days of youth, ah happy days, how rapidly you fly, and leave with us as we grow old, a memory and a sigh.
   —*Diane Datz*

The Three Arm Flex Of Shiva

A drop of water on a tranquil surface of the lake of mind leaves a disturbance in concentric rings of waves. Then, small vortices of thoughts trail inward my eyes open and time is elastic, the future-now complex challenges the relative real, and fractures my grip into shards quicksand fear filtered with child-burst creativity fills the time vacuum, and the charm of healing begins and I cultivate a forcefield crushing procrastination. My conscience voice pulls me through mazes within mazes. And I walk up the avalanche of psychic noise like an amoeba thrusting out its many pseudopods to move and to consume, pushing the limits, stretching endurance magnifying the mind like an optical lens concentration energy, concentrates your vision and energy fusion is energy fission momentum sustaining the constant pivot and the tree of knowledge germinates thrusting its branches into the atmosphere you probe into reality like acid eating away at rock leaving corrugated caverns and catacombs a colossal cathedral of chromatic crystals manufacturing a marvelous mansion mind with eyes of gravity, growth-exponential the well spring of thought transformed into a geyser of grace.
   —*Derek Hamlet*

Transition

Finale, a lid closing on you and yesterday
leaving no directions for going on.
Go on… oh yes, phony smiles and goo goo eyes
for tomorrow is a fickle flirt. We met. We did.
Tomorrow, mystic road of exits, pot holes, dangerous
curves and unsafe for travel without love.
Time, father of all tomorrows forgive me, I
tried to kill you, that interminable interlude between
sunset and sunrise. As unwelcome as dawn, the
goddess of your side of our bed. Warning me,
"Keep off, No searching for faces"
just look at me, where do I turn?
Did I take a wrong exit of did I get tripped
up by yesterday?
Time, send me a kinder tomorrow.
I'm only asking a few directions. Where is
the exit for lost lovers? Surely it's widely traveled.
Point me to the road where the lonely stranger
is hurrying to take my hand. I need his help to go on.
   —*Annette Gleason*

Wishing On The Stars

Lend me your dreams
Lend me your hand
Give me some time,
So I can just understand.
Where is it that we are going tomorrow?
Where is it that we are going today?
When you told me you were leaving I wanted you to tell you stay.
But go, so we will have a future,
Go so we will have a life.
I want right now to be considered your wife.
In the next hour can we make up our mind,
On how we are going to spend the rest of our time?
No one can say what exactly will happen then,
No one can say what will happen now.
I just want to stay together with you and it doesn't matter how
And when I look at that sky so dark, wishing on the stars
I keep wishing the same every time and I'm wishing the future's ours.
—*Maggie Callaway*

Vampire

Spread your black wings
Let out your soul, let it scream
Make me watch it
Your mysterious aura draws me closer to you
I want to be inside your wings and stay there for eternity.
Your fangs shimmer in the moonlight
I study them wantingly,
How I yearn for your fangs to seep deep into my neck
So you can have my blood in you forever.
And watch it drip from your teeth.
I want to be in your castle.
—*Marianne Eisley*

"Be Thankful"

America, "The land of the free,"
Let us stand tall and proud for the U.S.A.
Lets wove the stars and stripes for ever,
We are brave and strong people,
Don't let your heart be sad,
This is election year,
Let us not fight each other,
Get into the habit of thankfulness,
We can have a good time,
Let your dreams come true,
Let us not starve to death,
Nor be caught in rags for clothes,
We don't need cardboard houses,
Not do we want to eat wood rats,
Economy, has caused many problems,
Today is the day the Lord, hath made,
Rejoice, rejoice, for a better tomorrow, be glad.
—*Ertha E. Bryant*

Two Roses

Two roses entwined
  like your heart and mine.

Two red roses just for me,
  True love this must really be.

Two red silk roses that will never die
  Symbolize the undying love of you and I.

Two roses,
  Two hearts,
    One love-yours and mine.
—*Laura Hall*

December For The Elderly

So, again, here we are in December,
  Let's make it one to remember.
With Christmas love, sharing and the
  yule log atmosphere.
No other time of the year has that special feeling
  regardless of the expected frosty air.
Family, friends and people have a
  little more warmth.
A "Hi, Merry Christmas" or a Christmas card
  seem to come from the hearth.
With that said, lets go to a "Happy New Year!"
It is still December with that year end
  explosion for all to clear.
May that thankful entry into the
  New Year be yours to cheer.
—*Hal Ebersole*

Please Pass The Salt

    On one side of the table
Lies a swirling lake filled with mysterious creatures
  chasing each other against the current.
    A medieval knight clad in armor
Braves his way up an endless mountainside,
    While two figureless ghosts
Dance in circles around a naked child.
The sun rises and sets over the infinite horizon
  Shining its gray beams through the surface.
A dog walks dying from thirst as the vultures
    Circle above

    On the other side lies a napkin.
—*Kevin Borland*

Without Trust......

Just when I think I have it together, I let you back into my life; I want to give us another try and give you the benefit of the doubt; when you say that you've changed and that you still love me; that you don't lie or hide your feelings anymore...

I thought it would be easier to trust you now, but how can I when you still are so clandestine.

Trust is earned and you have no idea what it takes to earn it, nor do I think you ever will.

Me? I am looking for someone I can trust... without trust, there can be no "us".
—*Ellen-Jane Yanofsky*

Pandora's Box

Open up Pandora's box look at what's inside
Life and death old regrets, sometimes suicide
You plainly see if caught in sight, the magic of it all
The peaceful parts of love and truth as through a crystal ball
The stars fly out and cluster, the box hides all your
Lies, magic, witchcraft, mystic sense from your grasp the answer flies
Darkness covers souls despair, sparks the evil flames
Erases faces and destroys the masks that we call names.
To you, you're yours, to me I'm mine, together we'll close the box to let the sun rays shine.
Like a newborn child struck, with famine or disease
We plead just once to close the box and live in tranquil ease.
—*Kimberly L. Anderson*

"The Change"

There once was a time when crack was the only priority in my
life. Responsibilities had no meaning, not even being a wife.

But then one day, that morning, I fell down upon my knees.
With tearfilled eyes I looked toward heaven and said, "God
help me, please!

It's been a few years and a couple of months; God heard and
answered my prayer. He promised no matter what challenge I
faced, for not to worry because he'd be there.

With this thought on my mind and God's love in my heart. I
know I must be strong.

I'm going to win, I don't want to loose, but I know I can't go wrong.

Taking each day one day at a time is what I have to do;
Keeping God the center and by my side, when the road gets
Rough he'll pull me through.
 —*Verselia L. Scott*

To Be In Love

When you love someone, but they don't care,
Life seems so selfish and so unfair.
Your love can grow stronger each new day,
Your words seem mumbled and
 carried away.

All you want is for him to notice you,
But, he doesn't seem to know how to.
What can you do to make him realize,
Your love is true and not a pack of lies?

Maybe someday he'll notice your love is gone,
Because you can't seem to hold on.
But, then again he might not care,
Because he doesn't have any love to share.
 —*Jeanette M. Smith*

No Light Tonight

Most of them left the room,
Light went with them,
Left us surrounded by darkness.

Is it only I who occupy this room?
I feel the presence of another cold soul.
I am not solitary.

You all close,
Yet the lack of light leaves unrevealed
Now close we really are.

Fell the presence of light
within our cold souls.
The light will never enter.
it will only come out of us
and penetrate into the warm
souls of others.

Reach deeper into yourself and
let the light come out,
or darkness, tonight,
will stay forever.
 —*Adrienne Rys*

Confusion

Confusion is disorder, perplexity, distraction
 like a dinosaur living in the 90's
 or being an ant warming under
 a small boy's magnifying glass.

Confusion is the child who is asked a question
 by his parents that he can't hope to answer
  without getting himself into trouble
or being guys at a party deserted by their dates
all going to the ladies' room at the same time.

Confusion is a person trying to determine the use
 of algebra in his life
 or someone using a dictionary to figure out
 the spelling of a word like (keesh)
  How can you find it to spell it
  if you can't spell it!

Confusion is disorder, perplexity, distraction
 a fact of life...a painful fate.
 —*George Mundanthanam*

America Free

Where did we go wrong?
Like a mighty tree, stretching from sea to sea,
Roots so very deep and strong,
Branches to hold every one, even you and me.
Oh mighty country so free,
Oh, freedom to weaken the strong!
Will someone tell me, where did we go wrong?
Minorities ruling the majorities,
Say, can that really be?
Come on America, you problem child,
Oh, say, can't you see, that now
Each one must pull his own weight.
Progress has it's price,
A price each one must share.
We must go on together,
That's if we all still care,
For the greatest country, ever!
Let's fight to keep it together!
Yes, I can really see,
An America strong and forever free!
 —*Jean Edwards*

Willingly Burnt

I would gravitate toward love
like a moth toward light. Is love

in the delicate wings of the moth
as it flies toward light? The moth

would try to enfold light with its wings
and it might get hurt with burnt wings.

Burnt from the heat of the light it sought.
I might get hurt from the love I sought.

But like the moth, I can't stay away.
The light, like love, beckons and away

every moth must fly
toward light. I must fly

toward love. To be burnt
surely as the moth is burnt.
 —*Marye L. Wexford*

The Question

A single airplane glided upward
Like a spirit or a prayer.
It finally disappeared from sight,
But left a trail to prove it had been there.

My years are numbered and days are short.
I often wonder in my heart
If I shall leave a trail
When I depart.
—*Helen E. Schmidt*

God As My Gardner

Tragedy dispelled my personal growth.
Like a tree hidden from the sun I began to fade,
losing my luster with root's deprived of life.
I began to die.
But survival just wouldn't let me go.
My mind could only think to reach,
to feel, to touch the light.
A tiny ray of sunshine fell upon me warmth spreading,
growing over and through me.
Anger became my friend, tear's nourished my thirst,
fearing not even in the darkest hour of night.
God as my gardener, giving me Love,
Faith and Hope to flourish in courage and strength
to become all he wants me to be.
Falter or fall my eyes are on Heaven.
I wait to behold the sight.
—*Dora Locklin*

Love's Teardrops

Frozen love in the hearts of this cold earth;
Like a wound covered with a bleeding sore,
Destined to end life with unopened pores
Which will never reach its entire worth.
Life's selfishness gives certain love a birth.
Man once held the key to their feelings' door,
But out of frustration they will fight wars.
Can man truly ever know the feeling of mirth?
But the world seems to go on crying
And at other times there are laughs for all.
When finally the world stops sighing
And prepares for the final curtain call,
There will be no more regretful dying;
Love's hidden teardrops will begin to fall.
—*Melissa Diane Drury, Jamie D. Herron,
Danille J. Trainer*

The Dance

She danced serenely on the crowded floor
Like gentle fading waves upon the shore
Or evening breezes fading with the light
That lull the restless day to peaceful night

She floated like an angel in my arms
And I became enchanted with her charms
I saw within her mystifying eyes
The never ending beauty of the skies

It seemed that I had slipped into a trance
A helpless captive of her radiance
She smiled and whispered softly in my ear
Dispelling all uncertainty and fear

She came into my heart and filled my dreams
Like moonlight dancing on the mountain streams
—*Curtis L. Atchley*

A Soldier's Ghost

I see flashes in the distance,
Like lightning in the sky.
Then I hear the rolling thunder
and I know someone will die.
Now, I can't help but wonder,
if the enemy is not a lot like me,
and if he had a choice,
he too, would choose to be free.

Every soldier fights with peace on his mind,
and every soldier remembers the dead he left behind.
Every war is the last,
and we won't repeat the part.
(But) suddenly, there are flashes in the distance
that look like lightning in the sky.
Then, again the rolling thunder
means someone else is going to die.
Now, I can't help but wonder,
if the enemy is not me,
and it I still have a choice.
Can I choose to be free?
—*Kossuth M. Mitchell*

Untitled

Time slips by
Like sand through our closed hands
Slowly, but steadily
Each grain of sand falls in a different direction
Representing the pathways of our lives
Some ending in places where they feel lonely
Others in new and comfortable surroundings
But when they are in the air their destiny is unknown
Like us, we don't know what to expect
Closing our eyes like frightened children
Wanting so desperately to know what lies ahead
Whether it will bring us an enemy or a friend
A love or a bitterness
The tiny grains of sand don't have a choice, we do
We can make the best of what we have
Finding the pathway that is right for us
Somehow we will know our destiny sooner or later
And we will fulfill it....Time slips by
Like sand through our closed hands
Slowly, but steadily
—*Valerie Perry*

"More Coffee?"

The coffee cup stands on the counter-
Lipstick kissed lip-
The only memento of her earthly pilgrimage.
The roar of trucks penetrates the diner walls;
Their lights careen on along the winding, asphalt trails.
Chrome and vinyl peppers the smoky landscape.
Her hand gropes for the sugar-
Nothing.
Outside, neon tints a
No Vacancy sky.
Her cup clanks reality into focus.
The smell of bacon and grease filters back her senses
And her hunger is satisfied.
"More coffee, sweetie?"
The waitress asks through a crooked smile,
Her arthritic hand reaching for the pot.
"Nope - can't stay
That long," she replies.
"I'm just passing through."
—*Jennifer Boese*

Undying Love

What can I say to someone who knows my every thought,
listens to my every dream,
helps me through all my problems,
shares in all my joys,
believes in me with all his heart,
stands by me through everything,
and is not only my best friend but my destined lover?

To this someone I say thank you for your support,
for your patience and understanding,
for your friendship, and for everlasting love and devotion.

To this someone I say that I appreciate your every gesture,
admire your intelligence,
look up to your drive for success,
and am capable of life because you love me.

To this someone I say I want to marry you, to bear our
children, to grow old and spend forever together,
and to die knowing I have you to look for in heaven.
To this irreplaceable someone special I say with no regrets,
with all my heart, with my every pulse, with my dying breath,
I Love You!

—*Heather Casto*

My Dad Fishes

My Mama's crying because she broke two of her best dishes the
little brothers are in the backyard on their swing dreaming of
their wishes a cool breeze blew across the lake the neighbors
next door gossip is fake for heaven sake I was having a hard
time putting back the things I'd take his weather beaten
fingers threaded the worm on the hook remembering the ladies
next door sexy look he casted out his line and the ripples of
water separated that thought out of his mind Mama's shadow in
the pond wasn't far behind the memory of her mother's death
wasn't that hard to find the fish seem to smile on the end of
the rope and I experience the wicked high feeling of dope the
simple life didn't seem like much hope the heat of the sun
lived on the river all of us worried about the destiny it would
deliver that is everybody except me and my big brother because
we sat on the dock with whiskey in our liver the fishy smell
was like incense to his nose mom please separate the mistake
that had arose each believing the life they chose none of us
ever really got our wishes Mama's still crying over the lost of
her two best broken dishes yeah! and my wise old Pop still
fishes.

—*Bryan T. Polk*

A Belfast Lament

Weary is my heart from loving,
lonely is my heart from love;
And I yearn for my spirit to be free again,
to soar the skies as a snow white dove.

I put my trust in man you see,
and princes are untrue;
Fore with one kiss you can be forsaken,
and the sweetest lips tell lies which will slay you.

I was virtuous and I was wanton,
my heart worn boldly upon my sleeve;
Never knowing until too late,
that it was common practice for you to deceive.

Wounded is my heart from loving,
broken is my life from love;
And there is no healing nor forgiveness,
except by the grace of the Lord above.

—*Deborah Howard Taylor*

"The Only Child's Thoughts"

Well it's quite now, I haven't anyone to play with or tell my
little secrets to,
Mommy's gone to heaven, so I guess I'll tell them to you.

God took mommy away, he found a special place,
But now in Daddy and my heart she left an empty space.

Mommy usually was here to cook and mend my clothes,
To tell me how to sit, how to walk, and when to wipe my nose.

Daddy's a swell kind of guy who has to work and isn't here all
the time, but while I'm around the house, I can think about all
the good times mom and I had, and how much I love mom and
dad,
I don't really mind.

I miss mom a great deal, I sometimes get mad because God took
her away, but I guess God wanted her to come home,
it's just her time to go home forever to stay.

I'm a big girl now, I have to take good care of Dad for Mother,
But someday Dad will find a woman to become his wife, she won't
be my mother, for there'll never be another.

She might fill that empty space that mom left in between,
But moms thoughts will always be there with me and dad it
seems.

—*Kathleen Adams*

Spring Heralds

The burst of full bloom startles youth.
Living is a sudden, ever rainbow hued promise.

Green chrysalis cuddled gold, and twig's pink
Buds, amid the frost, beckon adult eyes.

Sunny splashed willow and rosy tipped maple,
Gray age awareness spies against ashen sky.

Years engrave tree ring records unique, like
Birthdays colour each human's perceptions
   Of Spring's heralds!

—*Barbara Enid Grosvenor*

When Angels Cry

Take a look at what I've done
Look at what we've become
So many with nothing
Here we are with everything
What you have you don't want
What you want you can't have
Have you ever hear a breaking heart
A sound so loud, It can be felt
It's so very sad when love starts to die
So very sad it makes the angels cry

A long time ago, I heard someone say "You can't have your cake
and eat it too? I never knew what that meant, until I lost you
It's so sad when love starts to die
So very sad it makes the angels cry
Everyone is looking, very few can find
The kind of love that brings us peace of mind
This void in my life can never be stilled
If I had just one more chance
I would had you till I die
But all I can do, is make the angels cry.

—*Kelly M. Henson*

"When The Buzzards Fly"

The buzzards are flying today,
Looking down, they see the prey.
Again, they're all here,
For dinner is near.
Survival and instinct,
For which I do not blame.
My own kind that I look with shame.

Famines and droughts,
They have known.
But they will always reap what we've sown.
A lesson we've heard but refuse to learn.
Why is peace so hard to earn?
The price is too high a cost,
For what is taken is forever lost.

Yes, I know that the buzzards will stay,
For who knows that tomorrow will be today?
They eat, but I shoo them to flee,
Because their next meal could be on me.
—*David Sears*

Mummy

I was running wild in the darkness,
Looking for something I couldn't see.
And there, waiting with the arms outstretched,
Mummy stopped and comforted me.

As innocent as my little plump round-eyed kitten,
Who likes to sniff the daffodil with me on the velvet lawn.
Yet she teaches me with such an amazing vehemence,
How to love and live, amid all life's raging storms.

Patiently and skillfully a gardener
She cultivates my bad temper into a fresh flower.
Though how wild and stubborn and bull-headed I might be,
She makes me feel the strength of tenderness that I didn't see.

I'm growing up, she yet gets smaller.
When wrinkles begin to appear around her eye's corner.
I feel I'm changing and every day just a little bit better,
I wonder how and when I can be a Mother like her!
—*Bao-chi Dinh Doan*

I'm Here To Stay

Head held high, shoulders straight;
Looking forward to another day.
Walk softly to the beating drums;
I'm here, here to stay.

Hold my hand, I am your mate.
Together we'll journey down this path;
Enduring the pain.
Searching for happiness along the way.
A light shines at the end.

Bill collectors are knocking at the door,
I answer with purse in hand.
Children's needs are plenty; mine are few.
Second hand store is down the street.
Owner knows me well; we greet.

Our house is neat, the table is set;
My family will soon say grace. I lower my head,
Pressing my palms together.

Black woman that I am,
Head held high, shoulders straight;
Looking forward to another day. I'm here, here to stay.
—*Cora R. Hamilton*

Daddy

I saw you today Daddy

Your thick burgundy skin
looking like worn leather-
    from too many years of laboring
    in unkind weather;

The once clear whites of your eyes
    now pale orange -
from too many years of mixing hard living
    with bad whiskey.

And, as I gazed into those eyes that
always seemed to be filled with sadness,
I realized I was actually seeing a
reflection of my own remorse.

I'll never stop longing for
    what never was,
    what will never be —
I always wanted you to be a Father to me.
—*Blanche Burch*

Granny Squares

Grandma's squares are clumsy now —
lopsided, too-many-sided, not-enough-sided
    like her life
old patterns are gone
replaced by something new
    art
of life and hands and heart
turned on its head.

My squares are like hers — reversed in time,
    no less confusing.

But in the creation
    comes peace
    comes a certain knowledge that
    makes it all whole somehow.

In God's creation,
    after the light and dark
    life and death
    water and land
came the uneven Granny squares.
And it was good.
—*Sue Misheff*

Parable

I was sitting on the shore of Lake Keystone, I was with the
Lord, so as not to be alone; trying to catch fish for my turtle
so dear, thinking of how he's just a year.

I noticed how when you approach the shore, minnows swim to
survive; but when calm you are, they wait for what's in store,
I'm no longer a threat to their lives.

I cast my net at the lake bottom. And I sit and wait for them;
I ponder my life since last Autumn, and my divine inspired
stratagem.

When they swim over, I raise the net, and catch the Lord gives
me; 'tis better than getting wet, from times of wading to my
knees.

And now I think of what was shown, of how the Lord taught me a
lesson; now I cast a net and let them come on their own, it
does work I'm confessin'.

There are times when you fish with a pole, and others with a
net; but when in Christ, you're just a foal, it's better to
wait than get all wet.
—*J. McDorcid*

!Lost In Your Love!

Lost in your love I am .... am for I Love thee so ...
Lost in your Love I shall always remain ...
for destiny separated thy Love apart ...
I will always Love thee ...
I will always Care for thee ...
Must I not wait for your return ...
For I shall look for thee ...
Where ever it be must I find ...
For I shall find my true Love ...
and create what only dreams would do before ...
Together must we learn to live the joy of life ...
In the good times and in the bad times ...
Together must we die with the love we once had ...
For I will always Love thee ...
With all my: heart ...
soul ... And strength ...
Love me thee ...
As thy loves thee ...
For the only meaning to thy life ...
is the Love of thee ...

—*Alicia Sarmiento*

The Class Of '93

Friends, romance, love, life and goodbyes,
Lots of confusion fills us all.
Now it's time to face reality
Time to move on.

Lots of confusion fills us all
Dreams and hopes for the future.
Time to move on
Challenges and goals to achieve.

Dreams and hopes for the future
Now it's time to face reality
Challenges and goals to achieve
Friends, romance, love, life and goodbyes.

—*Tandi Forgay*

The Progressing World

Many years back, there was a God who thought, "I must spread my love and make my love touch and heal. I must make my heavenly kingdom stronger and wider; I must make a world," and so with these thoughts in mind, He began to shape a world out of a vast domain and as he set his empire down, he added the clean air focus to breathe; the fresh dirt for us to walk on, sparkling water for us to swim in, he added us, the homo sapiens, and creatures and animals of all kind. Now, it is the year 2000 and the world is filled with drugs and violence, hatred and anger; the animals are becoming first endangered, then, extinct, there are diseases to cure and mouths to feed. Our God is thinking, "What happened?" Then, he looks around and sees, those who believe in Him, mostly, the kind, meek and good-hearted and He is content. Now, He waits until the day when we will be together with Him in His kingdom, meanwhile, he helps us out and loves us as our Lord.

—*Preeti Samtani*

An Emotive Poem

    I'm really angry.

Not angry like when I miss a bus.
Not angry like when my hair is cut too short.
Not angry like when I can't find something.

But angry like I'm going to explode.

Angry because of finances.
Angry because we need an income.

—*Catherine Adams*

Love Song

Love certainly is all we thought it'd be
Love conquers all eternally
Never could this all be more true
Then now as I stand in love with you
The shadows try to slip away
Dark threatens to end this summer day
Your eyes seem to whisper quietly
That I feel the same as you do for me
Walk away and with you goes my heart
You promised that we would never part
Please don't leave me all alone
Not here where the sun had brightly shone
My soul does wither in the dusk
But go then if you feel you must
Without you I've no life to live
And to you I've so much to give
All I'm asking is for a chance
There's still time for one last dance
Quick, promise with the rising moon
That you'll journey back to me real soon

—*Cozart*

Untitled

Blind such an obscure word
Love is blind
Justice is blind
So why can't people be?
At least to the presence of color, right?
Do people really love to hate?
Answer me!
I'm not blind, my vision is just hazy right?
Racism the belief in the superiority of one race
I guess I'm racist then
For the belief in the superiority of the one race, human.
Could I possibly be that blind?
Imagine
Have I become so blind I don't see people
as just colors.
Wait and see
Someday everyone will be as blind as me.
    One world
    One race
    Many colors

—*Steve Nigro*

"Love Is Me And You"

Love is me and you.
Love is me and you cuddling on the couch,
lying in bed,
Or just wrestling about.
Love is worrying about us,
not the past.
Love is friendship, hard times and romance.
Love is caring and feelings,
But most of all
These are things we do and feel,
And when it's time to say I do,
I will.

—*Kasey M. Hiatt*

"When Life Changes"

When life changes it is the wind,
Moving in many directions
Sometimes it is rough and hard to handle,
Sometimes it is calm and gentle,
Like the wind is very confusing,
The more you live to understand,
The more you will live a happy life.

—*Jolene Grossenheider*

Love

Inside love is full of a million tiny beautiful things.
Love never ever hurts anyone
Love always gives in what each heart deserves

So don't blame love if you once missed it
But blame yourself for not keeping it witty you any longer

Be reasonable man
In order to get through love in what the way it is

The more emotion you have with love
The farther intrinsical love is away from you.

—*Keatikorn Phanphirojana*

Ocean

Walk beside the ocean, it's another wasted day
  Lying on my back, all I see is blue turn to grey.

Look into your eyes, I see a color— you're not like me
  The color I can see is the color that can only cover me.

First sight was the best thing I ever caught in view
  And ever since we're apart, I know there is nothing coming through.

Something is tearing me apart from the best things in my life
  Searching for the answer and turning it but I just can't twist it right.

The time I spent searching was not the best thing I could do
  Falling in front of a curse cast upon me by in this world I don't know who.

And now I'm trapped in this awful living dream
  Where I know, I know, I know, I can't scream.

So now I'm left with nothing, and all I can do
  Is travel to the ocean where everything is very, very blue.

—*John Joseph Orsino*

The Hangout

Gazing across silvery swells, my mind can see footprints we made in the sand when we bloomed with youth. At dusk, our group met at the HangOut on the golden gulf shores where we could hear the waves lapping the beach mixed with the jukebox beat under our pavilion. Our skins shimmered from deep bronze to lobster red, smelling of cocoa butter and coconut oil squeezed from beauty-promising suntanning potions as we undulated to "Wild Thing" or "96 Tears," Dancing "The Dog," "The Jerk," or maybe "The Twist.' Romance prevailed, tempting at random, drawing succumbing couples into the shadows. Life was delicately tasted at first, then swallowed in great gulps, hiding the dim future. Night was eternity for a while. Laughter, innocence, guilt, tears, and abandon rollicked with

blowing sand. From afar, we looked carefree or scornful; yet zooming in, fear reveled among dancing feet. Summer signaled hope and doom at will. Across the world in jungle heat ones like us had no music or youth. Frantically, we tried to suck life from the salty spray. Tomorrow was an unfathomable depth. Still, in my dreams, that time was a shining star when a towel, cooler,and surfboard were Shangri-La; life was ours to live.

—*Marilyn Solomon*

I Am Like...

I am like flint.
Normally calm, cool and collected.
However when hit hard enough
with abrasive material I spark and get angry.
My spark can be one of destruction,
My spark can be one of warmth and security.
If hit hard enough my self esteem will chip and break.
Too much criticism can leave marks on me forever.

—*Janiel Misener*

People

In this world there are many things that make you laugh, that make you sing, that make you cry and make you plea, that make you feel smaller than the tiniest flea.
There is life, love, hope, despair, people who always get in your hairs.
There is hate, fate, happiness, sadness.
There are people like this in every state.
People who love and people who hate.
People who have no control over their own fate.
People who feel it's never too late.
People who will never have a cleaner slate.
All this we cannot control for we live in a huge world of mere mortals who just cannot get over the hurdles.
To make this world one of great souls,
Over the mountains of any toll.
All we really need is a loving souls.

—*Joe Chase*

In Honor Of Dr. Martin Luther

The late great Dr. Martin Luther King, Jr.—just who was this man?
At the time of his crusade, I was too young to understand.
But now that I grew older, my eyes can plainly see;
What the late, great, Martin Luther King, Jr., means to me.

He fought a long, hard, vigorous battle for equal rights;
Through the hot summer days of June-through the cold December night.
He wanted me as a Black man, to live a peaceful and equal life; To flow with the good things, and conquer the stress and strife.

And I know now as a Black man, I can be what I want to be,
Because thank God Almighty, and you, I am free.
I walk down the streets today with my head held high,
And then I think of the way you died, and my heart begins to cry.

But I will never hold my head down, because I'm equal to any man;
And I have the right to be free, and that's something I will always demand.
The Lord is my Savior, and I'll always love my mom and dad 'til the end;
But I never got a chance to know you, but you will always be my friend.

You gave a speech about a dream you had, a little while before you were killed;
I look around me todayand I see, that your dream has been fulfilled.

—*David Gray*

Phases Of War

There's patriotism misting in the air.
Man brags of the possible dreams.
I pledge allegiance to the flag.
Red
White
and blue
Colors stand alone for
Individuality.
We are America's security guards.
The battle field, colorful of hatred.
The before black and white world with colored spots.
Red white and blue
Colors melt into each other for support.
We are America's abortions, slaves, niggers.
Six feet under the world
The flag wraps around our bodies,
Muffling our cries.
We acknowledge our sins.
America stands tall, searching for her next prey.

—*Tatum J. Pynakker*

Birthday Blessings

Fortunate is the
  man who was found The Way
  to a contented life.

Daring is the man
  who puts aside worldly ways
  to cultivate peace of mind within.

Humble is the man
  who gains the wisdom of a sage
  but wears not a robe and long beard.

Lucky is the man
  who has many friends throughout the world,
  to the North, East, Sough, and West.

Devoted is the man
  who leads a meditative life
  in the midst of 20th Century chaos!

Joyful is the man
  who shares his talents and creative skills,
  in art, music and philosophy.

Happy is the man
  who did all this
  through T'ai Chi Chih,
  and love.

Who is this man?
  He is Justin Stone.
    —*Rosalind Braga*

"Homeless"

They sleep on the street
Many are of different races
No money in their pocket so they never eat
But all seem to have the same faces

They are working as prostitutes
Some are gay in a world of despair
Harshly they are beaten by brutes
All over the street it is there

They are runaway kids confused
Some use drugs because they're scared
In so many ways they were abused
In need of someone to be cared

They are now fortunately living
Thanks to all our giving

They are now unfortunately dead
Only to be left alone in an abandon shed

The homeless is who I'm speaking about
They are in need of a helping hand
Please don't think without a doubt
And let poverty and homelessness be band
    —*Marian J. Zboraj*

Pictures

I looked, I saw, but then
Not a word I answered when
The grey-haired lady on her porch
Inquired if I thought she'd pretty flower pot.
But still I see after years sixty-three
A large spreading apple tree
Full of pinkish blooms
Some distance from the quarter
In which a loving day was interestingly questioning
Her son's daughter.
    —*Ethel Murray*

War

Modern Kuwait bombed to hell
Mass confusion as oceans swell
Super highways once were paved
Now become just massive graves...

Conflicts fought but never won
Soldiers dying under the sun
War torn nations laid to rest
Enemy's clash with wanton zest...

Forced to fight on foreign soil
Paid in dollars for their toil
Fight aggression, so they say
Nothing change's, it's still the same...

It's political, what a shame
Children suffer with the pain
They're the ones who pay the toll
Robbed of life and their soul...

It's called tactics "A deadly stall"
War really is a worthless cause
Dropping bombs by the ton's
After all, just who has won...
    —*Dianne Greenfelder*

In The Palm Of His Hand

May I never grow so tall that I overlook the trees.
May I never get so tall that I cannot bend my knees.
May I never be so right that I am never wrong.
For if I do Lord it's up to you to put me back where I belong.

And that's in the palm of your hands...
melt me, mold me that I might stand...
but not as a monument strong but "oh so cold."
For I'd rather be a marionette and know my Lord has full control.

May I never just look and not really see.
May I never forget Christ at Cavalry.
May I never lose my values of what is right and what is wrong.
For if I do Lord it's up to you to put me back where I belong.
    —*Samuel Lee Jones and Steven J. Canton*

Look Back! Look Back!

Memories, memories, this is something no one can take away from me.
Happy times, bad times, glad time, are memories for me.
Look back, look back, and let it be!

A brighter tomorrow is on the horizon I see.
Welcome it with open arms, happily with glee.
Look back, look back, and let it be!

A future full of hope and faith it will be.
Mountains to climb, places to see, people to meet all waiting for me.
Look back, look back, and let it be!

I'll sow seeds of happiness in my garden of love for all to see
Be happy and glad and meet every day with glee.
Look back, look back, and let it be!

Memories, memories, pick out the glad times for thee.
Or you will always be sad you see.
Look back, look back, and let it be!
    —*Ruth F. Barnett*

God's Poetry

I thank God for his gift of inspirational poetry. He has made me so happy as can be, by making people happy, I live so happily.

Through these past fourteen years Almighty God's Inspiration, has allowed me to heal the hurting hearts! All the glory I give to God, our saving rod!

During 1979 when I was given the gift, as I felt an overwhelming sense of gratitude for all his blessings, I poured out my heart to Jesus, I wrote...

My life Almighty God I dedicate to you, take it, use it, make it true. Forgive my sins and bury past, give me true love to last and last. Teach me oh Lord and show me the way and never let me go astray. To serve you is my only chore and I humbly do so forever more. Thank you for my life, thank you for soul, all glory and gratitude are yours from my humble shore!

My life will never be the same. God has made me happy as can be, has set me free!
—*Emma Martinez*

"Memories And Memoirs"

Looking through memories, reliving days gone by
Memories so strong, I laugh, love, and cry
Opening closets full of skeletons and pain
Closing doors of attempts in vain
Fighting ghosts who haunt my dreams
Holding faith in our Father, who always redeems
Forever my life is captured somewhere
In the memories, hopes, and dreams of those who care
Holding my hand in tough times and falls,
Never expecting to be repaid in any way at all
The past forever remains with me
Locked away to touch my dreams
There to fall back on in times of need
To always remind me that I can succeed.
—*Rosalyn Sommer*

Peace?

Alone lays a green-eyed strawberry-haired girl staring into the midnight sky. Her eyes shift left and right. All of a sudden she notices one single shining star alone in the night seemingly without a care in the world. If only it knew of the troubles on the grassing green grass and the raging blue waters that we call planet earth. Noticing that star up there so innocently, she makes one single wish. This girl is not a greedy person, her wish is shared by the whole world. Peace is her unselfish wish; world peace, that is.
She knows that wish can not come true, for it is too much for one little star to handle. Peace to this little girl means no more fighting in countries, and people of all race, color, size, shape and sexual preference can become one. Peace is a thing where it doesn't matter if you're black, blue, orange or white, it doesn't matter what religion you are.
Peace is a time for the world to unite into one, where we make friends with our enemies and fight no longer. Does it matter that we're destroying our world with dangerous weapons? Who cares if children today go to school with a gun in their pockets clutching it for dear life? I care that's who!
—*Jillian Miller*

Untitled

To enjoy being alive
Never focus far to the horizon's signs
Of doom advancing
Nor back to the sorrow of time expired
But greet each velvet moment as it comes,
Gently caress and undress every one by one
And then without reluctance
Let them travel on.
—*Helen Ludwig*

My World

There was a time when I felt this world was no longer mine, so — I withdrew from it and created my own world.

At first, it didn't bother me a bit but then I became lonely, oh so lonely, and I looked around and there was I only — scared and afraid.

Yes, that was me, but I have since emerged from that world of uncertainty—
For God has touched me and I have grown, reaching heights that were to me unknown.

I realized that this world still belonged to me, even though through my eyes — It I can't no longer see.
Yes, this is the world in which I'd rather be, especially now, especially now, my God has strengthened me.
—*A. LaGulia J.*

Of Penn And The Water Buffalo

On a beast Lao Xu sidewise sits,
  Ming dynasty bronze: the best it is.
He raises to bless with arm full height;
  while at home my eye catches sight -
a wood carving. African line,
  small water buffalo, so fine.

Lao Xu, the African aesthete,
  both honor the buffalo's feat,
despite its name as epithet
  for a garrulous person met:
Such a one each at times may be -
  Francis, "Brother Ass", helps us to see.

Man and beast alike share the earth.
  Does race, color, culture give birth
to insult others - not make fun
  of one's own foibles in the sun?
Soul of Lao Xu, St. Francis, artists
  guide us to be true humanists.
—*John M. Scott*

Hopelessness

Up in the dark, dark sky we shall fly for we are happy in our misery, and with a broken heart shall we die.

You helped me through my happiness and drug me straight to hell, and now there is no togetherness but what does it matter oh well!

Separate we are forever and together we will be never thank you for your love and pleasure, too bad there was no golden treasure.

Bound to you I'll always be but only for eternity. I'm drowning in my tears and in my heart there are no fears.

We ignore each other's cry of need with pride too strong to keep its deed, and as we say good-bye well walk away knowing it was all a lie!
—*Rachelle Owen*

New Hope

new hope in red mountains lye
nearer to the sun
nearer to the little girl I once was

humbled to a broken crawl
too stubborn to think of giving up now
lost and hoping to find myself again, again
    desert flowers blooming wildly
       in the night rain
—*Susan D. Tausch*

Abortion, Is It Ever Alright?

As I lay here each and every day, I listen to the words that my Mommy would say. I wanted her to keep me, and love me forever but, by the way she talked I knew this would happen, just never. Every night I would listen to my mommy cry, about how I was such a problem to her I just couldn't wonder why she didn't want anyone to hear or know about me. I loved her so much how could this be? I didn't want her to kill me but she thought she should I knew she wanted to I knew she would. I wish she would have me and then she would know it wasn't all that bad but, the thought of me never made her happy but always just so sad. She started making plans to get rid of me fast. I would never be the future to her but soon be the past. I wonder if she would change her mind and I would soon have a name but she had no plans of doing that her plans were still the same. It was obvious now that she wanted me out of the way I didn't want to leave her I wanted to stay. Did she tell my daddy about me, that I was in here? She didn't and I knew she never be a part of reality. That day was finally over and it was now the night she had won, I had lost the fight.

—Shannon Finley

I Hate Mondays

Monday I didn't want to go to school.
Monday she wished that she was still in school.
Monday I learned about the Great Depression.
Monday she felt her own depression.
Monday I saw a filmscript on the horrors of war.
Monday she lived in a world of horror.
Monday I fell asleep in Math class.
Monday she fell to her knees in agony.
Monday I sat and laughed with my friends at lunch.
Monday she sat all alone and cried.
Monday I ran the mile in gym class.
Monday she thought of one more place to run.
Monday I wrote a poem for English.
Monday she wrote a note to whom it may concern.
Monday I mixed sodium and chloride to form a salt.
Monday she mixed an acid and made a drink.
Monday I went to bed and had a silly dream.
Monday she was found dead.
Tuesday she couldn't ask if her life had made a difference.
If only on Monday, I had told her that it did.

—Megan Bremer

Red Moon

So you hang from the sky and arouse my deepest passions, Red Moon.
You make me an emotional lunatic with insatiable cravings which translate me to the climax of eroticism.
You're so innocent like a suckling infant,
Yet you bring me to my knees, Red Moon.
You dictate my heartbeats, as you shower me with love potions.
You ignite strange fires and uncontrollable desires,
Burning incessantly from my deepest recess,
As you stimulate every organ that I possess.
Free me, Red Moon so I can make love in the heat of summer and winter's rain.
Remain in the sky with the red of saturn,
So I do not burn with your fiery passion.
Release me graciously from your romantic vice-grip,
So I can ride with the sun and melt away my lust.
You colored my heart with your red poison and lifeless blood,
As you captured me a love slave.
But now I wrestle for freedom. I become blind to your fury,
As I seek eternal refuge beneath the golden sun, Red Moon.

—Frances E. Bellot

I Remember Black Winter Waters

I remember black winter waters when the sky was dark and the moon shun down upon the earth so bright that as I stared down into the deepness of the midnight pond, it burned my eyes from the radiant reflection. I remember black winter waters from the whiteness of the snow and how the blackness, encompassed by the night, and hidden by the rising of the sun. Black as day, black as night. I remember black winter waters pouring over my face. It's warmth on my body filled me with spirit of earthly embrace, as I bathed and played in the darkness of the day. I remember black winter waters as I sat listening still, to the powerful rushing waves of glistening tar over the creamy bone streets of the beach. The sea gulls flying into the night never to be seen again until the waking of the morning night. I remember black winter waters so cool and numbing as I stuck my hand down into the depths of green death, dead gene. The fish and such even deeper to keep their heat swam, swam into the unknown land. I remember black winter waters until the coming of the colorful spring waters, which I then begin to remember.

—Todd Robertson

Kings

The game of life is like the game of chess, one moment you're more, one moment you're less, there's even a bishop if you wish to confess, but move the wrong piece, and you've made a huge mess. The pieces of chess, like the pieces of life, can bring you good fortune, or cause you great strife. The king and the queen and all in between and even the humble old pawns, can make you or break you, give you or take you, or thoughtfully let you move on. A delicate balance like dunes made of sand, victory, victory, so close at hand! Power transference, unplanned occurrence, misjudged deference, does it make any sense? There's knights for destroying, and castles for ploying, and bishops with cunning and speed, there's queens for protection and pawns for projection, and remnants of those who have fled. But, in the end, only one can ascend, for the other is off with his head! "Maybe," he thinks, as his very soul sinks, "I should have listened to what the queen said!"

—David Datz

The Panther At The Water's Edge

A lake.
Mountains surrounding.
Tall peaks that nothing can be seen past.
A darkening sky.
A red horizon.
Barely anything but a sliver of the goldenrod sun shone.
A wind so soft that it is barely felt except for the quiet shiver down the spine of a distant black panther wandering slowly but gracefully up a mountain covered by a grass that is yellow, and changing leaves as the season changes slowly and beautifully from a warm summer to fall.
A small row boat comes across the water,
rowing toward the horizon as slow as a turtle.
The panther that is now walking on the water's edge watches the boat going into the horizon and wonders what will happen when the row boat reaches the edge of the horizon, for no animal that roams the mountains has ever ventured past the horizon, and neither do they dare.

—Erica Lusk

The Endeavored

Dear heart, heart dear, heart so dear, dear to me,
  Much felt but said not can be thus told to thee.
    I know as do other preceding time and in space,
      From where I do speak is a thing commonplace.

My love felt for thee is a thing sacred unknown,
  And without such an instrument no feeling be shown.
    In a thing so profound and a thing so sublime,
      Is this thing I feel profit, or instead my malign?

So beige'd be the white and blanketed the light,
  Is a subsequent malice and possibly the plight,
    A thing in which all of us desperately seek,
      A thing when thought of makes us all so the meek?

Please more of a consequence be made of this make,
  As do us our time and as do us our stake.
    'Cause people we love is our people'd endeavor,
      And as a response these be our people forever.
    —*Steven Craig Zeltner*

Stratospheric Hockey

We play! Glowing neon jumps from
multitudes of bodies sliding, shooting
streaks in a web of technicolor light.

The horizon slopes away majestically.
We exist in this pearly ribbon separating upper and lower.
The puck-apparent zips along between us
forming the brilliant network that connects us.

Above us specks of polished silver
peek through the blanket of navy space.
We play on the slick air with joyous force
Reveling in the breath-taking power of each motion.

Like Gods of some ancient creation myth
We play on in dazzling displays of laughing color
Changing everything above and below.
    —*Susannah Iacovino*

My Best Friend

My best friend is kind and sweet
My best friend is nice and neat
We're very close and that's a fact
Sometimes we're loud sometimes we're tact
We've had our differences and many fights
But it always seems that she is right.
My friend has brown eyes and beautiful brown hair
She has the kind of image that makes you really care.
We share our deepest secrets like we share everything
We have the fun that makes you want to sing.
My best friend isn't like any Dick, Harry or Tom
Doesn't anybody see, my best friend is my Mom.
    —*Sara Jordan*

I'm Awake! I'm Awake!

I'm awake! I'm awake!
My birds are chirping like a computer printing.
My fish are blurbling.
My dad is snoring
And my mother is talking in her sleep.
The faucet is dripping.
I'm awake! I'm awake!
I can't fall to sleeeeeeeeeeeeee...
    —*Elizabeth Gadelha*

My Empty Window

Lights go down and turn to a pale black,
My empty window dimly shines back.

I feel as the darkness pours like rain,
My empty window is now full of pain.

As shadows close in my dreams turn to stone,
My empty window now stands alone.
    —*Dawn Roderigas*

Being Beautiful For Jesus

Looking up from my intense reading,
My eyes fixed upon a figure, very intriguing.
As this figure walked toward me,
And my eyes focused clearly,
I said, "Plain, but clean is she,
This woman walking toward me."

Trying not to appear rude and without grace,
I attempted to lower my eyes, and lower my face.
But there appeared to be a glow,
And my curiosity began to grow,
And I said, "Strangely pretty is she,
This woman walking toward me."

The closer she came to me,
Her radiant beauty I could clearly see.
Realizing that more than physical,
Her beauty was revealed visible,
from within her innermost being.
And I said, "Nothing possible could bring this appeal,
Except from within her, Christ, she does reveal."
    —*Gwendolyn L. Devall*

Untitled

Terrorized by lovers' needs and left eloquent with pain.
My heart a poisoned cup full of hurt and rage spilling onto
life's dress clothes.
Past injustices, future disappointments meld to build the sets
of each day.
Fragile psyche, delicate sanity locked behind bulletproof
glass, Displayed in museums of needful beauty.
Memories dancing, prodded to movement by longing.
Marching, parading ever before me with each urgent request
Until they are frayed and bent with use.
Up from the depths, struggle for the surface.
Comforts of warm aching, my lover, my friend
Freedoms, aspirations, hope all compete for ownership.
Touch, unlock Fondle a secret
Meet in a place unseen.
Leave me uneasy with dormant desire.
Hold me, invite me
Eager for your words to touch me intimately as I loiter in
vacant lots of my heart. Fear immobilizes, longing invades.
Sweet conflict, sweet pain, sweet comfort.
    —*C. L. Patton*

I Am Like...

I am like flint.
Normally calm, cool and collected.
However when hit hard enough
with abrasive material I spark and get angry.
My spark can be one of destruction,
My spark can be one of warmth and security.
If hit hard enough my self esteem will chip and break.
Too much criticism can leave marks on me forever.
    —*Janiel Misener*

Life Without You

Listen closely and you shall hear,
My lonely crying becomes quite clear.
I constantly think of only you,
And wonder if you think of me, too.
I try to smile, to hide my frown,
But deep inside, I'm so let down.
I can't stop shaking,
My tears won't dry
All I seem to do is cry
All this time has gone past
I'm hoping our love will last
It's been so long since I felt your gentle touch,
I miss you dear, so very much!

—*Laura Sever*

The Truth

Here I lay,
my mind in a fury,
too sick to pinpoint the true beginning.

The clear walls are suddenly closing in,
unnoticed by the tears that stain my sight.
I know not whether I have been locked inside,
or forbidden entrance.
I am held back by a force all too well known to me.

To touch, to hear, to see,
is all a memory.
He is gone.
Everything is stolen except my breath which I take from myself.

—*Tarah Popiak*

Best Friends

Many years ago upon a cross,
My only best friend died.
He took upon the price and cost
for my worldliness and pride.
People gathered all around to watch him bear this pain,
They spit at Him and mocked Him,
They cursed His precious name.
As they pressed the thorns into His head,
And nailed His hands and feet,
The blood poured out from His cuts and wounds,
Where His body they did beat.
He could have called His Father,
And said, "Please let me down",
But he chose to remain hung there,
And wear my painful crown.
It often makes me wonder,
How someone such as I,
Deserves such a wonderful friend,
Because for me my Best friend died.

—*Carrie Cottone*

Inspiration

There was a time when I could not dream,
   Of lofty thoughts in the highest realm:
Of thoughts that would purge my soul within,
   And leave there not a place to sin.

Nor knew I what it was to sigh
   As each beat of my heart would cry.

Nor knew I what it was to live
   The ecstacies that life could give.

—*Hyman Sampson*

Alone

I am alone.
My shadow of darkness
Even scared of the light and day.
It's the light that fades away.
By myself, wondering is it me
Or am I an image of my shadow
The gloomy water brakes
When my love goes off to sea
And a lost on is gone and past away
The shattered mournful winds
I hear that blows the day away.
Horrified sounds of weeping willows,
Sounds of hauntly chants
Is my life tearing at the window ledge
For sunless days of delight!
My isolated mind thinks not of dark
But years to come with broken pieces of my heart…

—*Melissa Anne Dauria*

Just A Suspicion

Everything seems to have changed overnight.
My sleep patterns are different.
I sleep lightly now, instead of heavy and deep.
I'm tired, but cannot sleep.
Even my taste buds are different.
Things I couldn't seem to get enough of.
I now don't even like.
They've become repulsive to me.
My mood shifts without warning, leaving me nauseous.
I'm happy, then angry, then I burst into tears.
I have my suspicions, but nothing concrete.
Am I sick, or just losing my mind?
I feel lousy and giddy, furious and exhilarated,
exhausted and restless.
What more can I say? My suspicions have been confirmed.
I can only hope, that the next eight months won't go this way.
Though I'm sure in the end that, that sweet little bundle will
be worth everything it puts me through.
(But Please God) "Don't let it be twins!"

—*Veronica Petersen*

How Many Times

How many times have you stopped to say—
"My, This has been a wonderful day."
And how many times have your thoughts gone astray—
And you find yourself grateful for just one more day
To do all the things that please you most,
including, perhaps, a party you'll host.
How often do you look to the one up above—
For comfort and guidance and all of his love?
How many friends can you count that are close
Who would be at your side when you need them the most?
Have you counted your blessing, both great and small?
And how many times have you answered a call
From someone in pain, or sorrow or need?
Or perhaps from a stranger you just happened to meet
Many times, I hope, is your answer to this—
for a long healthy life full of wisdom and bliss

—*Deloris Rosenberry*

Utmost

I never visited the tombs of the Pharaohs,
Nor sailed the Nile to the site of the Sphinx,
Marveled in awe at the work of the Gods
In response to the theory some like to think.

I never walked the streets of Atlantis,
Nor traced the Nazcas in the sand,
I only climbed to yonder summit
And met the amazing mind of man.

—*Rosalie R. Pate*

The One I Will Never Know

Like a statue she stands, her beauty in my sight
Mysteriously she smiles, her amazing glow
Long do I wait for her to come and say hello,
Yet I only smile back, a look just as bright.

Like a sunset she fades away, bringing the night
Completely stunned, I make no attempt to follow
She caught me off guard, how was I suppose to know,
All that remains is the sweet fragrance of her flight.

In my dreams, she re-enacts a memorable part,
Though each time closes with her still stealing my heart.
While it's difficult to say why she was there;

I doubt whether she realized how precious it meant.
My sole desire is to remember and care,
For every wonderful memory that she sent.
—*Thomas S. Lubiski*

The Child Abused

Though sticks and stones may break my bones
   Names and faces hurt forevermore
  That no can do's of a child abused
   No two-edged sword can sever more

Can we not see they're like you and me
  But that their feelings waiver more
They hurt and bleed and are filled with needs
  To them be kind and favor more

Yield not to the rules of loathsome fools
  Who seek revenge to even score
So children hide their shame and block their pain
  That it might hurt them never more

It's such a slow re-birth when a child's been cursed
  Be firm but love him more
  Praise his good so it's understood
   And it's passed on forevermore
—*Daniel R. Leavitt*

Caldonia

Published perished lost wax lost boat considered
  Negative space again, painted an envelope with
   Strokes of the sky's embracing penumbra,
Obtained those new angles, visions not viewed before.

  A river flowed back there, behind those trees where
His sharpie stuck in the mud, cradled among puffy clouds, waving
  Branches and barrels with oxidized copper junk and rubber tires,
Giacometti-like sculptures on tattered boating magazine covers,
  Alberto Alberto in Rome Alberto in Stampa.

  Around East Martello's toilet-bowl rainbow Greedy Grit
   Drummer Boy's barrel drum rattled the music,
   Suitcase Charlie and the Goon Girl danced,
   Rods churned in Dishpan Annie's crank-case belly,
    Pinhead kissed the bow-legged bride.

    What more do you want Caldonia?
Don't look at the arc, lower your flaming eyes, shield them,
  Raise the rod to set the steel ablaze, rain melted
Pearls on Las Vegas' model sheetmetal breasts, Her iron arms.
—*Adolph Gucinski*

Between Me And You

The day I saw him I'll never forget,
neither the day when we very first met.
I knew he was special, that I could see,
if only I knew how he felt about me.
I thought about him, day after day,
not knowing exactly what to say.
I tried to talk to him, once or twice,
neither time was he very nice.
I gave him some time because I thought he was shy,
after I thought about it, I asked myself why.
Why was I nice to him when he treated me like dirt?
Why didn't I realize, that it was my feelings he hurt?
I wasted my time on him, for more than three years.
When I think of him now, my eyes fill with tears.
There will never be anything between us,
except an occasional hello,
but I have a special feeling that no one will ever know.
I loved him a lot, sometimes I think I still do.
He'll never know how I felt,
because that's only between me and you.
—*Angelic Walsh*

Higher

Higher higher toward the stars lifting rising always going on
Never giving up always forward forging ahead right or wrong
Moving faster, moving up, moving toward the heavens ever more
Striving to be like God trying always to open that next door
People keep getting better and trying to change the world and
  make it a better place
Surviving our infancy on earth and moving away from home and
  into space
Life, technology, and beliefs always changing
Slowly getting better and helping us to end suffering
For now hope and faith keep the dreams of peace alive
As all the children of the world for a meaning strive
Our future is brighter than the brightest star
Humanity will conquer the evils of the world by far
We can do, must do more than just kneel and pray
Hoping we live to see that brand new day
We must destroy bigotry, hate, suffering, hunger, and the like
Crushing evil in one strong strike
And then sow the seeds of kindness, hope, generosity, and love
Our symbols not the sword or gun but the innocent dove
—*Mark Robbins*

"A Cry For Help"

A cry in the darkness only heard at night, a yelping cry that's never in light, I know not where it's coming from, I searched by all and next to scum.

I search in the darkness with no one but me. I know the cry is meant to be. I wish to all that it would go away, but it doesn't matter what I say.

Search high, search low, search all around, but only to say of what I found, I found nothing at all to say at the least. Yet I hear a cry that sounds like a beast.

Around a bush and a small tree, I'm still convinced it's meant to be. A yelping cry that burns inside, suddenly a feeling I need to hide.

I searched front, I searched back, I searched everywhere, but still I forgot a place that is bare. It's as common as a rusty shed, the place is only inside my head.

A yelping cry is inside my mind, a cry that's not just one of a kind. I wish to all it would go away, for help is what I here it say.
—*Kurtis Michael Clausen*

Not My Kind

Why do we only see the cover
Never knowing one another holding rigid to belief
And never seeing underneath never knowing what could be
Only knowing what was seen
But what if we chanced to look deeper
Peeking in, awake the sleeper
Could I deny that beauty shines
Because the face is not as mine?
I once looked into such a face
And found in it my disgrace
And found beauty such that me
Poor white boy that I be
Could love someone of darker skin
Despite the trouble with my kin
I found a great philosophy
That should be taught from sea to sea
That open mind and open heart
Is what we should have from the start
And we should all be as blind
And never know what's "not my kind"
—*Jeremy Campbell*

Angels Do Cry

A tiny soul that will never talk, with tiny legs that will
never walk. A baby's a gift from heaven above, made in his
image to tenderly love. But millions across these United
States are killed before birth, abortion's their fate. Some
are scraped off the wall where they cling, no chance to grow
up, laugh or sing. Others are sucked up by a vacuum tube,
while angry mobs chant, "we've a right to choose." Other meet
death by chemical means, discarded as if it's just a bad dream.
Still there are more, cut out with a knife - so goes the
murders of unborn life. Jesus said "suffer the children to
come unto me," only he feels their pain, hears their silent
scream. They say it is only tissue and cells, but remember in
Luke, and the story it tells? Elisabeth was sterile, could not
conceive, a cousin to Mary, mother of Jesus our King. Still
she was six months along when Mary came to her room, the Bible
says the babe leaped for joy, while inside her womb! How can
that be if it's only "tissue and skin"? Could it be that it's
wrong, that abortion's sin? If we could look up into heavenly
skies, we'd see millions of small angels with Jesus on high.
But oh, what is the fate of those who commit this awful deed?
Turn to God's word and see what it reads! Mark 9:42... And
whosoever shall offend one of these little ones... it is
better for him that a millstone were hanged about his neck, and
he were cast into the sea.
—*Debbie Carol Lawson*

Smoking Kills

To the young people who start to smoke
Nicotine warnings are just a joke
But an insidious killer is the filthy weed
Marching them toward cancer at utmost speed

A terminal patient has told us today
That his vital organs are being eaten away
His mind is altered; his lungs are black
From the poisonous contents of a cigarette pack

The tobacco purveyors say for good measure
Be sure to inhale for far greater pleasure
They care not a whit if we die young
They shed no tears if we lose a lung

When someone says just take a little puff
Show that you're made of sterner stuff
If you are strong and refuse to comply
You will live on while others will die
—*Edward Forsythe*

One Last Tearful Plea

I sit back in wonder at this world of ours, as I gaze at the
night sky, so full of stars. I hang my head in shame, as
people fight over where to lay the blame. Have they no love in
their hearts? And why are they trying to tear our precious
world apart? Can they not hear our children's cry?, And why do
they refuse to understand the reasons why? Our children are
suffering, can't they see? Why won't they leave the fighting
be? Their pain and suffering is more than we can bear! Why do
people refuse to care? We must not hate our fellow man, But
always offer to lend a helping hand. We must all decide what's
to be our troubled world's fate, Before it is much, much, too
late! We must strive for peace with all of our might, But
never forgetting to keep love in sight. We must always remain
strong, And try to correct each and every wrong. Please,
people of the world, hear our most tearful Plea, And we beg of
you, Just to leave the fighting be!
—*Karen Carron*

Military - First, Last, Always

I never really had you - Did I?
No, I only had the bits and pieces they did not need.
The days, weeks, and months strung together randomly here and
there - the time you were not doing your sworn duty.
But, even when I had you, you still were not really mine.
I knew if they called you would go.
You did not have a choice.
And I certainly had no choice.
After all, you had signed the enlistment papers
and in their eyes nothing else mattered.
If they had wanted anything else to matter
they would have issued it to you in basic training.
—*Michelle A. Higgins*

Single

A single flower,
   no matter how fragrant they say,
   won't make a bouquet.

A single berry,
   no matter how sweet on the vine,
   won't make a bottle of wine.

A single person,
   no matter how vivacious and proud,
   won't make a crowd.

But, a single word said in anger
   can cut into a heart,
   like a sharp piercing dart.

And, a smile upon your face
   can sometimes be like sweet-smelling perfume,
   and erase all of life's gloom.
—*Felicia W. Venable*

The Beautiful Ones

A white light shines upon us
piercing our souls
time has run out
and in an instant
the ghosts of our past escape from our bodies
we join hands
and together our heavenly spirits
dripping with purity
are offered up to dispel the darkness
the celestial moon, our guardian
greets us and accepts us
as if we are precious jewels
—*Trisha Ali*

What Is A Friend

A friend is someone who shows that they care.
No matter what your problem they are always there.
A friend is there when everyone else puts you down.
A friend puts a smile on your face and wipes away the frown.
A friend respects you when you don't respect yourself.
They will bring you out of the closet and down off the shelf.
A friend is someone you can tell your secrets to.
When you need advice they'll tell you what to do.
You can talk to a friend anytime of the day.
And you really listen to what they have to say.
Friends are sometimes accused of having an affair,
But as long as they know the truth they don't care.
A friend can be crazy and silly just a lot of fun.
When things look cloudy a friend supplies the sun.
Friends will do things others just wont do.
A friend to me is you!
—*Amanda Foster*

What If?

What if love was always true?
No more broken hearts or shattered dreams
What if the endless screams
and pleads of "Please don't go!"
never existed?
What if life was kind?
And people were not blind
to other feelings.
Not to judge by their looks
religion, or race.
There is no time or place.
To judge someone by their face.
What if we lived forever
And always were clever.
to the welfare of others
What if there were no disputes of war
But only these things happen in forelore.
However we can make the world
A better place if we only ask the question.
What if?
—*Bobbi Jo McLaurin*

"When Tears Fill Up Your Eyes"

A depressing sadness fills the air, as you sit, and feel like
no one cares! The fantasy, yes fantasy, that you truly
thought would come true, is just an echo of your foolishness,
and the despair encircles you! You no longer are the spotlight, no
longer a shining bright star, now you're just a shadow, you're
not who they think you are! You don't want to be the laughter,
you just want to be a tear, so no one will question your
efforts, cuz no one will know that you're here! You don't want
to prove you're special, or prove that you are bright, you just
want someone to prove to you, that everything will be alright!
The world is a beautiful place, if you only have love in your
heart, but someone needs to show you first, so you have
somewhere to start! You need to see an example of love that
someone gives, then your heart, and mind will come together,
and you'll know that you will live! You want to see a rainbow,
that shines up in the sky, but you just can't see anything at
all, WHEN TEARS FILL UP YOUR EYES!
—*T. Michelle Grayson*

God Bless America! And Keep Her Hale!

Thou! freedom's cradle! Bastion of the brave!
No one did ever here in thralldom chafe!
Hast thou not taken in! The 'masses huddled'!?
And hast with Christian love the red man dearly cuddled!
Free! Live the native sons on their 'reserve'!
And thou! - With all thy might! Holdst sacred indian turf!
No single unkind act! Thy record stains!
The black man in a jiffy! Lost his chains!
O! Thous guarantor! Of fair human rights -
Thou makest sure - that tender love abides
In ev'ry nook and cranny of this earth!!
And even though! - It strains the public purse!
Good Uncle Sam! - 's been never caught a-napping!
Instead! His efforts he has up-been-stepping
To make this globe - the perfect Disneyland!
Those rogues! Who dare mistrust the yankee-cant
They shall be quickly caned! Into submission!
Until they too! Share Uncle Sam's sweet vision!.....
—*Inge Pfitzer*

Catalina Island Where St. Catherine's Pier Is Green

Struggling by that rugged Italian coast,
no one saw St. Catherine's pier was green.
Money changers going for the most
successful agio; perhaps to host
the cruise ships dallying in mountain's range
Struggling by that rugged Italian coast,
chameleon's tongues might chant a feeble toast
to California's guise and dressed up fraud.
Money changers going for the most,
as angels' tunes in alleluia boast
of mindful sins washed out Siena's sky.
Struggling by that rugged Italian coast,
escape an island's promise, Eden's almost
tempting power, an apple's tease.
Money changers going for the most
remarkable cards; the shipboard gambler's ghost,
at the casino, evils saint can hear.
Struggling by that rugged Italian coast
money changers going for the most.
—*Adair Burlingham*

Lonely Witch

A lonely witch, I am a lonely witch.
No one to cast my spells on for test's.
No one that I can be witch.
Maybe if I practice with more zest.
I can bring with a flick or twitch.
A couple of people will come into rest.

A lonely witch, that's, what I am.
I talk to books, to pictures and rings.
A lonely witch, that's what I am
I play and pretend I'm all sorts of things.

Alone when someone is with me.
Alone when I am by myself.
Come and visit me sometime and see.
I'm not sitting on any shelf.

A lonely witch, that's what I am
I talk to books to pictures and rings
A lonely witch, that's what I am
I play and pretend I'm all sorts of things.
Because I'm a lonely witch, I am!
—*Carolyn J. Harry*

Father...

Father,
No other could be better.
You have an open ear,
Even when it's to what you don't want to hear.
You are understanding,
But not all overprotecting.
You know when something is wrong
And my love for you will always be strong.

Father,
No other could be better.
For I feel we are quite close,
Even when of my irresponsibility,
I give you a dose.
And no mistake you could ever do
Could lessen my love for you.
Being your daughter couldn't be expressed
   in just one word.
For it wouldn't be right without you in
   my world.
    —*Heather Parrott*

Snow Prints

What fabulous patterns are left in the snow
No rhyme or reason for the way they go.
Wonderful designs begin to form
And stay that way until it gets warm.
How did they get there, how long will they stay?
Was it animals, tires or children at play?
My eyes follow each puzzling line,
And I tell myself, "It's just a sign,
That someone has enjoyed the beautiful white
Made their mark and then took flight."
A message in the snow,
From someone I don't even know.
    —*Barbara A. Newby*

"The Hidden Truth"

Words concealed inside my head, thoughts of you.
No secret revealed to another soul.
I keep it within me, it's never told.
Unreleased passion runs through my veins, passion that I find with you.
This need for you devours my soul and I search for your touch that makes me whole.
Love or the just the thought of, what could this be.
Naked is the lie that I live with you.
Naked are my dreams.
Beyond my veil I cannot deny what lurks within, what lives inside.
A stranger eyes could not see free that part of you that lives in me.
Cling to this even though I can't touch would bring insanity and relinquish my tears.
Raindrops fall down to cleanse my filth.
Pouring down they free me of my guilt.
Still lies the passion that I cannot hide.
Continue on, I think I'll try.
    —*Kimberly Joy Burgess*

No Heart

No heart is complete without love.
No thought is more concrete than the one the heart thinks of.
No heart will find total happiness within someone else.
The heart must first seek happiness within itself.
No heart is immune unto pain.
For if a heart loves misfortunes it will sometime claim.
No heart is so strong that if it's pierced deep enough it will not cry.
No heart will be constantly done wrong without eventually saying
   good-bye.
    —*Willie C. Colvin*

One Day The Chair Used It's Legs

We used to sing and dance—no,
No we didn't but we use to sit around it
Like it was a campfire, or some kind
Of wisdom—now the chair is gone and the carpet
Is scarred with a square tattoo of what life was like.
This square spot is unfaded unlike the rest of the carpet
In the room—my mother tried hiding it with a potted plant
But it didn't fit, neither did the new chair: so we let it be.
I remember that chair, maroon and cracked with flaking
Bronze studs holding it together; I didn't know how much I liked it
Until it left. I know where it sits now, but it has become so ugly
By itself, I find it uncomfortable; perhaps the son hits it wrong.
Nonetheless, I have enough memories of him drinking his gin
With an olive and an onion after everyone was asleep or listening
To him tell the sunday's funny funnies—now, that dumb carpet holds
The cruel reflection of him kissing her, that other woman,
I can't shut my eyes long enough.
To make it go away. He still denies it—it was so much easier
With that damn chair there and now I can't figure out
Which shade is the truest color of this carpet.
    —*Brenan Christopher German*

Fantasy

Born many miles, almost worlds apart
Not knowing that each other existed
Those who have inspired our lives
Are as unique as the cultures we inhabit

The paths we surrender to, for our futures are set but vague
We have led opposite lives over the years
So much in common yet barriers divide us
Can we handle these obstacles that surround us?

Family values better defined for you than me
A true sense of belonging is all that I need
Thoughts of us together wander astray
Can this dream become a reality?

I know that there is something that you want to say
And I long to tell you the same
But we are too shy to articulate our feelings
And the words I wait to hear will never escape your lips.
    —*Holly Criss*

I Am An American

I am an American,
  Not necessarily of any particular gender
I am an American,
  Never one in need of a reminder
I am an American,
  Whether white, black, red, yellow or multi-hued
I am an American,
  It does matter, spirited, pride, always renewed
I am an American,
  Just say the name, intoxicatedly I get high
I am an American,
  Not ten feet tall, hey, I can touch the sky
I am an American,
  Sometimes, I feel like reaching from sea to sea
I am an American,
  Proud of the star spangled banner too
I am an American,
  Say, who cares, you can bet I do
    —*Frank A. Kirkpatrick*

Earth

    A shroud envelopes her;
    Not quite understood, as
the meaning becomes irrelevant.
My only vocation—appreciation.
Yet it is this which eludes us,
    this rapport we seek,
    that with every breath
    by the strong and the meek
    draws us further
from our destination and origin.

  Two into one had won and lost
the praise of her father, a deity crossed.
  Or, in a more logical sense,
    by fire and smother
an incestuous child seeks to kill its mother,
  without a single thought of consequence;
    never knowing that in the end
    victory will be hers alone.
When all the children have gone, and only then,
  will her truest beauty be known.
    —*Michael J. Hutchinson*

Love Always

Another bud blooms on the tree,
Not to diminish those already there,
But to add to the joy
And beauty of the whole.

As another life enters ours,
Swelling the circle
Not breaking it,
We know love has no bounds.

No lesser love is felt,
Instead, a greater outpouring
Of love already given,
And more than enough for those yet to come.
    —*Ann Reese Cline*

Make Me A Living Bible

Make me a living bible that they might see
Nothing but Christ and him Crucified in me.

make me a living bible that those I hug
May feel and see that Christ is love.

Make me a living bible that though I fall,
Yet Christ be with me through it all.

Make me a living bible yet though I'm scorned,
Just let me win them one by one.

Make me a living bible yet crucified,
To tell the whole world that Christ is alive.

Make me a living bible that they might believe,
For I may be the only bible that they will ever read.

Make me a living bible that I might tell
That as sure as there is a heaven there is a hell.

Make me a living bible that they might believe
That Christ my savior did hang and bleed.

Make me a living bible that I may love
Those who never knew the holy dove.

Make me a living bible from genesis to revelation,
That through their search they may find salvation.
    —*Doris J. Sinclair*

Forever

I see your eyes upon the wall,
  nothing has ever suited you.
I see you shaking like the wind,
  but nothing is ever wrong.
Why can't you be happy in a world full of hate,
  when All I want is you.
Of all the fish in the polluted sea,
  you're the purest of them all.
In a crowd downtown.
  I'd see you through the rain with all my love.
I'd sacrifice everything for you,
Even my soul.
  So you can have what you want.
But nothing comes that easy.
It's just like praying for the cold, dark fog to stay,
Forever!
    —*Anna C. Darby*

Saliva Of A Fudged Nymphomania

I was chill to the bones in the darkness of a blunged bench.
Nothing like a boat just a morbid blend suffused with red tears
Chrysanthemum streaming with my mouth, full of fears. So much
clutter in my mind the blindness of nothing to clench. Dance of
the butterflies nowhere to fly. Dance of slaughtered tries
nowhere to cry. Then I saw my spirit in the glint, brain of
froth. There were saws all over my heart lint, grain of moth.
Something in my blood like a bleak plain. Gripping my salted
road in a freak rain. So many blebs in my eyes. My chest bled
in my eyes I was waiting the surceased breath on this lake.
And I heard her quiver and I heard her quake. She was a woman I
was her quarry. I was a man she was really "Jarry". Then she
murmured me her name Nyx. And distraught told me I was on the
Styx As with a sultry kiss of sulfur, touched, my gloomy sight,
with sand. Nevertheless I've known "she will be my wife" while
she was drawing me "land"
    —*Maillot Jibi*

Praire Tableu Vivant: With Scientist, Child And Star

[Spake The Scientist in the Presence of the Child]: There's a notion, rooted fast in the doctrine, Panspermian - this Great Globe itself was seeded by a fugitive of particles of stars, come Earth's way by chance, and settled now, evolved, complexified, and become Earth's population: Nature, man and creatures...

[The child ignores the scientist, in dialogue direct, with his sermon's subject]:

Bright shimmering, shine of star above, seen through haze of heat, ascending from the prairie where in deep amaze I lie to watch you twinkle. You're not too far up there for me to see; but am I so far beneath you can't see me? How sad, if that be true, bright star! To think you could forget our ancient bond. Though me you cannot see, it's yet still true, that once, when we were, oh so very young, and oh so very close, I was you, and you were me; and now that both of us are, of so very old, and oh so far apart, I'm still you, and odd as it may seem, so too, are you still me.

[Silent grew the scientist, in mild amaze, at the prescience of children].
—*John E. Whiteford Boyle*

I Didn't Want To See Momma Mourn Over Me"

I didn't want to see momma mourn over me
Now here I am as she leans over me
My blood sticky head rests in her lap
As she cries to the Lord "Please bring my baby back"

Reality is I am finally dead
I took that fatal shot to the head
It happened just like everyone said
But I'd always reply "I am too smart to catch lead"

I didn't want to see Momma mourn over me
Now each tear she cries falls to my limp body
Her face is a question mark flushed with confusion
Wondering who did this and what was his reason

You live a fast life, you die young and fast
Like most of my friends, but I thought I could last
No one could stop me, not even my mom
Her every attempt I'd dodge or outrun

I didn't want to see Momma mourn over me
Especially knowing that I was her only
My dead heart hurts to see her in pain
Momma did all she could, only I am to blame
—*Tony J. Ferguson*

A Broken Heart

A broken heart takes time to heal.
Now I have began to feel
That life is worth living now.
And I'll bear the pain somehow.
My heart will never be the same
Forever filled with grief and pain
When his voice I hear so strong and clear
I realize he is still so dear.
I will love him forever.
Now inside myself I weep
His sweet words I will cherish and keep
But now he has left me all alone.
At least his love I have known.
—*Christy Busbee*

Numbness Untold

The blackening sky, the ocean blue
now it's come, its darkening hue
the evil, the madness, the spite, it's might
oh God, now it's come, a society of unright
built on fright, raised in mistrust
here it comes, the keltic rust
generations past, generations to come
now it's calling, the beat of the drum
the time has come, gone, and pasted away
but now our children, raised in dismay
violence, disease, and constant discord
for this we give, such a great reward
an eye for an eye, lost in the rye
for now it's come, we live in a lie
freedom of choice, to consume, and to live
a life of deceit, a life to share
with inner thoughts, and inner strain
we now have entered, a life of pain
because of the hurts, because of the toils
we now leave you with, a life of despoil
—*Jason Edward High*

The Flame Bearer

I bear a flame within my heart ———
Nursed from the tiniest glowing spark
That you planted there not so long ago,
It was faint — then suddenly fanned to grow
Into something that even I can scarcely know
So deep is its depth; and as its light will
Enlighten my otherwise quiet face until
I, too, glow, so will this flame sear and burn
My inner soul; for such it is, and so I must learn
That flame bearers must share in the poignancy
Of holding aloft the flame of love. It is never free
From blighted dreams and hopes that ne'er can be.
Alas for me — my standards still must fly, my faith
Cannot be quenched, this flame within my heart is so intense.
—*Mary L. Kearney*

"Of The Past, Of The Future"

Born from the first feelings of light and warmth.,
   nurtured in childhood dreams, sculpted by the winds of time,
annealed by human frailties, I am the past.

Songs heard but not sung, flowers on distant hills yet unseen,
   the passing of one held dear, another newborn cry,
and all things untouched but not yet held, I am the future.

A time when I ran the swiftest race, enjoyed the homage of
   other men, and knew no object unattainable,
all enhanced by the passage of time and retouched by use,
   I am the past.

Tell me of hope, tell me of aspirations, speak with me of
   dreams and, let the past be as a sign post,
for without the past that which will come has n reference,
   I am the future.

Speak not to me of the future for what does it hold,
   the withering of once sleek bodies, weariness, more steps closer to death's door,
I offer comfort, a chance to be again once more, live with me,
   I am the past.
—*William S. Hopkins*

Untitled

A summer vacation to Disneyland.
O there must just dream of seeing adventureland.
   Children who have everything.
    Children who have nothing.

All new clothes for school in the fall.
Others have last year's shoes and clothes too small.
   Children who have everything.
    Children who have nothing.
Christians - a new T.V. and 10 speed bike.
Others get coats and mittens they don't even like!
   Children who have everything,
    Children who have nothing.

A man, a dad, and a love - filled home.
From apartment to apartment than have to roam.
   Children who have who have everything,
    Children who have nothing.

School's out! Kids off the fun-filled places.
What about those with worried faces?
   children who have everything
    Children who have nothing
   —*Kathy Hanson*

Bright Light

So fair the sun as it rises at dawn
O'er the land and the water as I gaze each morn
Peaceful and quiet, with my teacup in hand
As I watch it go higher, over meadow and sand
My thoughts interrupted, from this beautiful view
With five young children there is much to do
Much later I peek out the window and sigh
The sun almost to heaven its risen so high
Casting shadows and beautiful rays of light
Through branches and boughs what a beautiful sight
God in his power, his majesty his might
Has created this wonder, the sun, our light
Days almost over, the sun falling from sight
Darkness descends, and now it is night.
   —*Carol A. Hall*

Challenges Of Life

Sitting outside, I look and stare
Of all the things, I have not dared
Sitting outside, it makes me think
Of what life's future, soon will bring
Sitting outside, now years have passed
And now, I have received, my manhood at last
Time is now here, for lands I shall roam
A farewell to family, now departing I go
Time has passed, I now take a wife
And with two kids, who now fill my life
An occasional visit, down through the years
To visit relatives, and sit with old friends
Most things I loved, have now passed and gone
A visit with flowers, for a moment I mourn
Sitting outside, now back in my youth
I stare of the past, where I once grew
Dared I have, and not with regret
For I have dared, the challenges of life
So now shall I rest
   —*Ronald L. Adkins*

Unknown Soldier, "Unknown Friend"

Who is this fallen lad,
Of body torn and so sad.
A soldier never to rise again,
To see a sunrise or a friend.
A mother or father will never know
Their son's fate, and so
The tears and anguish can't be shared,
With this unknown soldier that lies there.
But who will offer a silent prayer,
To this brave soldier who has fallen there.
It is I who will carry this lad in my arms,
To take him where there will be no more harm.
I'll wipe away the dirt and horror from his face,
And take him where no pain will he taste.
We will walk side by side the still waters,
Where our friendship shall not falter.
For the unknown soldier has come home,
To have everlasting peace, and never to be alone.
   —*Darryl K. Greene*

Bosnia

Go! Convey to the future, kin of another birth
   of human locusts, strewn behind
Devourers of lives and earth.

Awake slumberer! Awake! Weep! Weep, scream, bewail, moan
   Enemy invades your turf
Stripping it, nude, writhing in pain.

Lament you who hear voices, fields ravaged
   Women and children lay broken - bodies
    maimed.
Close your eyes! Cover your ears!
   Appalled? Don't get involved
Earthlings - who shall be blamed?

Stand by and watch and watch - but from afar
   See? Seeds of life, shriveling, die
Treasures cherished, untended now
   Eyes sunken - dry, no tears to cry.

Think you an atom, a molecule should brave
   survive?
Will folk again happily begin to live?
   And times leveler sprout forth,
    forgive?
   —*Thaddine M. Chopp*

Depths

   As I lay there one night, thinking of a repeating story
of life and depths of the unknown I wonder into my own world
of harmony and the deaths of beloved humans that died of
causes that only they might know of...

   Locked into my cellar of deception I cry of lonesomeness.
I scream in my sleep only to find that I'm actually awake.
I find myself sweating, cold, and dripping wet...

   I grasp the nearest thing available and to my surprise
feel choked of my own breath. Everything goes black; I can't
hear, I can't see. I'm thinking God help me, what have I done...

   Loud treacherous screams come from inside my head.
I realized from the depths of my soul that hung myself
by the rope of my underlying velvet bed.
   —*Crystal Cardoza*

Painful Love

How do you deal with the pain
of loosing someone you've loved for so long?
How can you go on
When you feel as if there's
nothing left to live for?
How can I look into another mans eyes
Knowing its you who's still on my mind.
You tell me we can still be friends
But how can I be friends
With someone I've loved for so long
Why can't I forget the love we shared
Why can't I admit the pain I fear
What is this feeling I feel inside?
Why does love have to hurt inside?
—*Billie Jo Spangler*

O Mother, My Martyr

What is the purpose
 of my anguish.
What lesson to be learned
 From such suffering.
As a woman shall I be tested
 Lifelong, for patience.

 You taught me well
O mother, my martyr.
 Even as the pain
 Tears apart my soul
 I know that you
Suffer far more than I.

Thou shall not need! Is the creed
 You try to teach me still.
Fury, pinned against pain. On the walls of
 My heart, gaping hole.

 Where do I turn
 Whom can I trust
 To teach me
 The lesson of love.
—*Casey Bekaert*

What If: If Only

I dream of places far away,
Of pleasant people with little to say.
Nothing but happiness, joy, and glee,
Love and friendship, just you and me.

A place were no war proceeds,
Were people are just people, and not enemies.
Somewhere beyond the stars and skies,
When everyone lives and nobody dies.

It conceives a precious beauty like no other,
Everyone stands side by side, sister to brother.
No diseases or wars plague the country,
Everyone laughs, no one is hungry.

This place of magic, warmth, and love,
Is somewhere far away, somewhere up above.
The trouble with this magical place;
With a blast of a bullet its all erased.
—*Katrina Van Oosten*

The Prodigal Sun

Oh biggest and brightest star, you errantly cast your warm rays
of sunshine about, anointing us mere mortals with your tiny
slivers of light.
We hail your rising and sing your praises, as you carry our
offerings high above the tree tops toward the zenith of heaven.

Each night, you wander off into the darkness,
fleeing with the inheritance that we so graciously gave.
Somewhere beyond our horizons, you frolic gaily, carelessly
spending our riches until you lie penniless and starving.

Hopelessly stifled at your azimuth's edge, you recall times not
long ago when nourishment was plentiful and friends were near.
In the wee hours, as morning approaches, your withered soul
barely musters the strength to peek above the eastern sea.

But we, poised and ready to receive the hope promised by each
new dawn, greet you happily at the edge of the earth. We
shed tears of joy and bring forth gifts of understanding and
forgiveness. God has blessed us during your nightly absence.

But today as always, you willfully accept our gifts,
and show your gratitude by burning our precious skins.
—*Ken L. Powell*

It

The power it has, takes complete control
 Of the entire body, mind, and soul.
It has a demand, no cost, too, great
 Spending and spending, don't want to be straight.
It possesses a force, blinding the eyes
 Creating justification for deceit and lies.
It takes a slow, meaningless ride
 Wrecking hopes, dreams, and pride.
Little by little, day by day
 What was once, slowly slips away.
To regain control, takes strength and love
 And a greater force, the one above.
—*Helen Lamb Henderson*

Music

Music that breathes a flawless note
Of utter loveliness for mind and ear,
With magic harmonies that rise and float
In perfect sounds upon the soundless air,

Can weave delight with dancing tunes, while still
The sudden catch in laughter's voice is heard;
The perfect note, the crashing chords that thrill,
Till I, beyond myself am deeply stirred.

These splendid sounds that rising, soar, then fall
As though the throats of angels rang in song,
Can hold time captive; for a space make all
Creation harmony; sweep us along!

Such ecstasy within such sounds divine
This, for an ageless moment now is mine.
—*P. M. Underhill*

Love...

Love, it is as delicate as a rose
nothing can stop you from being
in love nor can they control your feelings
when you're in love
Love, is a very wonderful thing,
Most people are to caught up with everything
Else to realize how precious love
 really is.
—*Karen Crout*

Orbit

Her life turned into a round
of what's good on T.V.
and what's good to eat in the kitchen—
there's never anything good when she's dieting.
The things that were fun to do
she didn't do
because she felt fat.
But her life was still good.
She found something good to be happy about
every day
thinking she was stopping to smell the roses,
meanwhile,
never noticing,
she was just stopped.
—*Lori L. Nielson*

A Religious Death

Dedicated to a dear friend, Peggy Louise Gist, in memory
of your beloved Daddy, Mr. Ernie Rocha:
You are only away, but never forgotten...
Blessed is the eternal sleep that comes when thy purpose
in life is done
Surrounded by your loved ones, be it a most caring wife,
daughters, or son
At your life's end, you will at last walk hand-in-hand
with the Lord as one

Beginning life the Lord is thy maker and at life's end
you were always given
Throughout life's journey on the way back home to your
most holy maker

You always shared your love through happy and hard times
of work, toil, strife
Being promised, the less you suffer in the hereafter for
the burdens that you bear in this life
Different toward life's end, take your human dignity and
love on the last day that you live

You beacon a peaceful serenity of love that is only
begotten from the Master above
To all, family/friends and strangers, you exemplify the
true meaning of the words faith and love

While you await for the eternal blanket of eternity...
Bowing my head I do pray in the blessed name of the
holy trinity...
—*Donna Lee Mello*

Art

Majestic how it stands,
oh, how I wonder what thee is!
Maybe a man seeking to find the wondrous ways of life,
or maybe a lady who is watching a rainbow drifting in the sky.
To a sense nobody knows, no one really understands the
ways and the tunnels of art that tries to help you find
the meanings of its language.

Can you see the way it is; standing, sitting, or looking?
It's in a pose that no one knows.
Art has it's own world; it's own mind.
It hurts you because you do not know.

Romeo and Juliet are by far an art by Shakespeare.
Trying to find love in a far off place, feuding families
of an almost same human race. "Oh", Romeo calls to Juliet,
"My beloved, bright angel; my beautiful maiden".
Oh, thee knows what he means, but we do not carry our minds to
his thoughts, and wonder what he could mean.

So in life we stretch to see the light, the light at the end
of the art's never ending line of tunnels.
—*Lori Hutto*

A Winter Gallery

Pristine white atop strokes of black and brown;
On a never ending canvas of sky.
Reach out and touch the tree with a cloud like crown;
And know there is an answer to the why.

Where is that precious stillness sought and found?
In a winter forest, on the frozen lakes,
On a clear blue morning, under stars abound;
Beauty and truth, my mind and soul partakes.

Paintings alive, ever changing each day,
With no walls or guards, to get in the way.
In nature's gallery, admission is free.

Dwell in this temple, and how peace does grow,
In the mind and soul, in its quest to know;
All that we are and all that we see.
—*Angela D. Hayes*

The Portland Headlight Lighthouse

As I stood on the sandy shore,
On the rock bound coast of Maine,
My eyes looked upward to the sky,
I saw a flashing light revolving by,
And heard a mighty ocean roar,
It was The Portland Headlight!
Its piercing beam, like a brilliant flame,
Reflecting ghostly shadows on the rocks below,
Guiding ships far out at sea, and harbor buoys,
that show the way, through winter storms,
night and day, how great it is, The Portland
Headlight! Towering high above the ground,
Made of concrete, and very round, a symbol
of guidance, for the World to see. The
Portland Headlight, shining on the sea.
—*Winthrop Warren Prevost*

Infatuation

By imagination's crystal sea,
On the shores of memory,
There stands a golden idol
Cloaked in the mist and spray.

Often I return there and long do I stay,
For a time the journey forgotten, I stand idle,
Entranced by the rainbows shimmering dance.
Everything is forgotten, trapped by a single glance.

What is real? What is fake?
Is she tangible, solid, or a mirage I make?
Is she a dream perhaps, who has take form?
I cannot tell, detail is obscured in this liquid glass.

Yet, wait, a glint not of gold but of brass!
My mind churns, ideas swarm.
Reality returns, its taste bittersweet,
For the globe of my heart lay shattered at this statue's feet.

So, I leave her there,
On the shore, by the sea,
Never will I return to stare,
I journey on, what will be, will be.
—*Dwain Dixson*

"Vacation"

Lonely island. Just the two of us.
Rippled water. Lily pads with yellow blooms.
Stark trees. Branches falling down.
Hard ground. Sleeping softly.
Dark nights. Eyes shining brightly.
Four days. A lifetime of love.
You and I. I'm all alone.
—*Edward Sylvester*

The Drunkard's Son

In an old dusty attic of a tenement house, I happened to wander one day. And there on the rafters 'midst shavings and chips, a drunkard's poor little boy lay. "Oh, why are you lying up here in the cold? What makes you lie on this hard bed?" "My father's a drunkard and he beat me today. My darling old mother is dead. I am hiding from father, and please, ma'am, don't tell. He beat me 'cause I would not steal. He says he will kill me the next time I fail, and I'm so afraid that he will." "I'm leaving you here, son." I sadly replied, "but I will be back right away." But when I returned to the attic I found that Jesus had been there that day. The chips and the shavings were there as before, and the little boy lie on his bed. But with tears on his cheeks and his hands at his side, the poor little fellow was dead. A picture of mother lay close to his heart. A faint little note by his head. As I opened the paper, my eyes filled with tears, for these were the words that I read. "I am hiding with Jesus across the divide. With dear mother forever I'll go out. And I thank you, dear lady, for your kindness to me. And now — it's alright if you tell."

—Annette Akerman

"A Real True Love"

I wish I had a love, a real true love.
One I can care for,
One who'll care for me.
Someone I can trust.
Someone that'll never fuss.
I want a true love that'll last.
Not one from my past.
I want a brand new start
With someone who holds a special place in my heart

This love might be hard to find.
When I find him I might think it should've been easy.
When I find this love of mine,
We will be together all the time.
No one will be able to break us apart,
Because without the other one of us we won't have
   but half a heart.
I can't wait for the day to come
When I'll find my special one.
Together we will grow,
In mind, heart, and soul.

—Jennifer Holdbrooks

My Friend My Mother

Loving, caring, understanding, trusting.
   Only a few factors that describe my friend

Sharing, screaming, laughing, crying.
   All that we express together.

The one who holds the best advice for my life
   when things look pretty ugly, is always there
   for me, and picks me back up when I've fallen.

The one I confide my most valuable secret with.

The one who is always open minded about everything
   I do or say.

No jealousy or pettiness between us, just pure
   and simple love.

One that I can look up to with all my heart, but
   yet makes me believe in myself.

There is a great deal expected of you my friend,
   but you've never let me down when I've needed
   you most.

Qualities in a friend I've always looked for, but
   have yet to find them in anybody else but you.

—Mystie Yeik

Love's Dream

When the moon throws a lingering shadow
On the sparkling waves at the shore
And the bluish tint of the heaven above
Shades a path to your garden door
When the breeze of the summer evening
Sighs, and sways the ramblers bright
And touches the leaves of the willow trees
As they shine in the pale moon light
You and I shall wander together
Just forever and a day
With nothing in sight, but sand, sea, sky
And love to guide our way.

—Rita C. Kent

Stairway Of Life

Each step higher than the next
On the stairway of life
Every animal
Insect
Or living thing climbs the stairway of life
Each step on the stairway stands for each year you live
The longer the step the more knowledge you've gained that year
A seed as it sprouts
An egg as it hatches
An animal as it is born
These events make up life
First step
First straight A report card
Even the bad events are part of life
With every bad thing, something better comes along later
As we learn from our mistakes we increase our step
Let your step grow long
Have a long stairway and a long life
For at the end of your life you will climb your stairway up to heaven

—Nicole LaForte

A Sister's Prayer

Dear Lord, I have a favor to ask of you this day.
Once I had an older brother, but you took him away.
I was his little sister, Lord, and though we numbered ten,
Now there are but nine of us, until we meet again.
I try to understand decisions made by you alone,
You must have had your reasons for taking my brother home.
You know, he had a mom and dad - they both loved him very much.
Every day they feel the emptiness, they miss his loving touch.
You see, he was their first-born son, it was hard to let him go
But they are comforted in knowing that he is safe with you.
Now, to get back to my favor, Lord, if you could find a way
To let him know we love him and think of him each day.
He hasn't been forgotten by those he left behind,
He lives on in our memories 'till we see him one more time.
Thank you for the favor, Lord, for I know it will be done.
And hug him once for Mom and Dad, he was their oldest son.

—Donna Merrill

Journey

Tapestry of green oak on the walls,
Rug of melon beneath the feet.
Tapestry of hand to hand combat,
Rug of crimson beneath the feet,
Tapestry of blue upon the wall,
Rug of stability to ease ill-tremors.
Tapestry of grey humility,
Rug of stone (Jesus, it's cold) to lead the way.
Tapestry of heaven — bright white,
Rug of salvation to ease soul pains.

—Sharol Goeringer

Crimes Of The Soul

A crime of the soul, you can't touch it; you won't hear it;
only angels hear the heart cry in these crimes against the
spirit. "I'm so innocent!" cries the loved one committing his
crimes of cruel control, as he cripples and coldly carves deep
dark holes down in the soul. Deep dark blackness where once
the sensitive shoots of feelings grew; deep dark blackness
where once shimmered all bright colors of the hue; deep dark
blackness where once happiness and all high hopes had loomed;
deep dark blackness where once bursting buds of fervent faith
had bloomed. These crimes creep along slowly; first faith and
hopes are shaken, but the cruelty never ends until the victim's
trust is taken. Trust in those the innocent believed would
love, protect; trust in those the soul adored and looked to
with respect. Yes, crimes of the soul are the crimes of abuse;
they are crimes of destroying, of cruelty, of use; they are
crimes of the selfish, the hardened, the hurt, who pass along
the pain they've known and with hell's fury flirt. Saddest of
all, about these crimes of the soul, is these crimes are rarely
righted, justice rarely takes it's toll; they are crimes
unchecked and rarely caught, cause we accept, ignore.
Even when the victims beg & plead & desperately implore.
Yes, traditions take their toll, leaving holes in the soul.

—*Cathi Goff*

Johnny

Always hitting a drum and a cymbal
  or pressing a key on a keyboard,
Singing a song with his father and practicing for all hours
  is what Johnny lived for.
He was always complimented by his audience
  for the way he could sing,
And always whistled at by passing girls
  for his fine physique.
His shiny black hair and dark brown eyes,
  Soft light skin and pearly smile.
His generous personality was what people adored
  he used a great sense of humor to tease them more.
When I was around him he put me at ease.
Known for making conscientious decisions
  in his life each day
Johnny was not perfect, even he would make a mistake.
The dreadful mistake of drinking and driving
  would cause Johnny to die,
The questions and confusing wonderments
  that make all those who loved him cry.

—*Veronica Pauline Sanchez*

War Is Hate

War is hate
  Or so we say
Then why do we do it?
  Is there any other way?
Why do we kill
  To prove a point?
Why should we hate
  When it's too late?
Why should we fall at the enemies feet?
  It still won't stop at a persons defeat
war is hate,
  It once was said
It's something I guess
  We won't understand.
A confusing mystery no one will solve,
  So give up the hate
  Learn to love.

—*Raemarie Cistaro*

The Song Of The River

So why prize life
Or why fear death
Or dread what is to be?
The river run its allotted span.

Till it reached the silent shore
Then the water rushed back to the mountain top
To begin the course once more.
So we will know where course begins.

Until we reach the silent shore.
The revisit the earth in a pure rebirth
From the heart of the virgin snow.
Don't ask why we live or die.

Or wither, or when we go,
Or wonder about the mysteries
That only God may know.
And so at last.

When our life has passed
And the river has run its course
It again goes back.
Over the track, to the mountain, to its source.

—*Evelyn T. Tallman*

Second Chance Love

Our lives are so much like a book
Our birth is the preface before the story actually begins,
The ending our death
And as we go through the chapters of our lives
We might take a break, stopping to rest along the way
Sometimes a chapter never gets finished
  before we move on to another
Sometimes it is laid to rest for awhile
  only to be finished at a later date
Chapters can repeat scenarios as can our lives
But not always exactly the same as before
Unlike a book, we can't peek at the ending
And decide if we want to go back and read what we've missed
Is this chapter of our lives unfinished
Or is it a new one about to begin?

—*Susan Kaggen-Mashel*

From Heaven With Our Love

That night began like any other night.
Our family was tucked in bed, snug and tight.
Who would have known what the dawn would bring,
The tragedy, the sorrow, such a horrible thing.

But God whispered to George, my daughter to wake.
To save part of our family from this grave mistake.
If it was not for you, the whole family would be gone.
Your courage and bravery saved your sister and your Mom.

Don't ask why this was meant to be,
But God needed Brian to be with me.
We were both too young to go alone,
Together in heaven we have part of our home.

Take care of our children, I miss them so.
Care for and love them as they grow.
Brian is watching and I am too,
We are sure you will do what you have to do.

In your hearts and minds, we are still there.
Be healthy, be happy and please take care.
We will wait and watch with love in our hearts.
One day we will all be together and never again part.

—*Sharon L. Heaton*

Helpless

Where we walk hate follows,
Our footsteps echo with cries of pain,
Bearing down on the poor and unprotected,
We bring the darkness and rain.
We pass battlefields with people dying,
Mothers mourning the ones they loved
Everything bad that happens,
We hover, watching, above.
We cannot, as you think, help this,
We cannot show this world the way,
We are not, as you are, controlled by fate,
We are the never ending cycle of night and day.
—*Jennifer Obed*

Unavailable

There are people we have in our lives that never seem to fade,
Our love for them is deep enough, it's time spent we seem to trade. Jobs, vacations, bank accounts, our homes, our clothes and such, all seem to swallow up our time without leaving very much. But what is left we feel we've earned to rest and call our own, so overworked we fall asleep, too tired to use the phone. Each day goes by, and then a year before we even find, that we have pushed those ones we love beyond our conscious mind. Seasons pass, small trees grow tall, we justify our lives, Suppressing all those wonder years, until our loved one dies. Our tears unleased will flow today for someone that we knew, For we can't change the things we've done, or things we didn't do. We can't go back and say the things we wish we would have said, Our minds will haunt us for some time of things we should have done instead But we can learn from past mistakes a lesson for us all, Don't hide behind our cluttered lives, pick up the phone and call. Let's cast aside those things that seem to give our life such flair. And spend some time with those we love, and let them know we care!!!
—*Lora M. Pier*

Thurgood Marshall 1908-1993

Once again a giant has fallen
Our sympathies are extended
History is known to compensate
Against all odds he weathered a storm

The elevator was full, he took the stairs
Step-by-step he made the change
Humanity is grateful for his efforts
Thurgood, the modern emancipator

Freedom was his motto from the start
Secrets known, he challenged to reveal
That the rejected stone must be replaced
Sight failing, he never lost his faith

National recognition was his goal
Slavery is not a shame
Death is no enemy but a friend
That he may sail on smoother seas

Living proof that man can soar
Advance the clock of time
Administer to the needs we aspire
That's Thurgood's record for acclaim
—*J. Gibson Bey*

The Mysteries Of Life

Our souls, locked within this prison of our bodies.
Our bodies are so complex, but yet so simple.
I hear what my body and soul has to say.
"The Battle"- it's an on going struggle within.
But remember when our bodies and souls are at one,
this is the time we will unlock the mysteries of life.
—*Keith Scarpino*

My Wife And My Cats

My wife and my cats how I miss you so,
Our time apart passes so very slow.
I don't say it much but I do hope you know,
That when I am away I feel so very low.

My cats are my warm and furry friends,
And they will sit by you until who knows when.
If you are working with small stuff a helping paw
they will lend,
And let you know it is dinner time by the noises they send.

My wife, my companion, my lover, my friend.
We've started down the road of life from beginning to end.
As we walk down the road hand in hand,
We find ourselves in some distant land.
Now life there is not easy, that is surely so,
But wherever I lead becomes the place she wants to go.

My wife and my cats how I love you so!
As our time apart passes, my feelings do grow.
I know I don't say it often but I want you to know. There's
a special place in my heart where these feelings, I stow.
—*Christopher R. Johnson*

The Sea

The water from the sea is flowing,
    over the beach as if it were slow dancing
        with the sand.
IT caresses the sand with warm, wet fingers,
    as it dances.
Soothingly,
Quietly,
Lethargically,
As though it were as innocent as the morning dew.
It lingers on the beach for a while,
    before retreating.
Savoring the sand as though it were a lollipop.
All the while,
Plotting,
Waiting,
For its next victim.
—*Tori Parsells*

"Larry's Farewell"

Arise my child, the sun breaks into a new day
Over the land to the east.

Gather they possessions together and prepare
For the journey you are about to partake.

Say farewell to the people you knew so well for
so many years.

Bid peace to the ocean shore which gave you
Peace of mind in your times of loneliness and despair.

To complete this journey look deep within your soul
To find wisdom and strength, look deep my child you
Will find peace of mind at last.
—*Edward Robinson*

Untitled

When darkness spreads through the day,
Reality sinks into your conscience,
breathing heavily, gasping for life.
The moon will look dull, the bass will cut through.
Come to my world, the blue bus is calling you.
Shields reveal the eyes, dreams shatter the present.
An institution of deception will release all resentment.
Meet me at the back, it's the best.
Help me, finally to the last straw, where's the west?
The end, my only friend.
The end, of me.
—*Erin Paternite*

On Love And Peace

Love me Oh Nature! Tell me how do I find,
Overland and overseas in mankind,
Ventures not aimed at supremacy,
End they do nicely in both land and sea,
For jealously in struggle is great ...

And when I hear the sound that tells me
Never to shirk and step back to see
Down the hills and up the mountains high
As to go in quest for peace far and nigh
So that jealousy in struggle be out ...

Peace—peace, all peace be the theme overall,
Enduring peace which is God's will for all.
Amongst the lights we light to their brightest
Candlelight of love be lighted the best
Ever in that jealousy be all out.

Out—out—out ye jealousy and let me find
Overland and overseas in mankind
Peace by love over in supremacy
To endure better in both land and sea
In the sound of LOVE—for the sake of PEACE.
—*Amadeo Abaya*

Crazy Freddie

The Hackensack Water Company
owns the wooded area
where Crazy Freddie lives.
Not usually seen, because
he slithers along the crabgrass,
never using the soles of his feet.
Straggly cables of grass-green locks
and blackened dirt skin
help to camouflage his existence.

Kids at school say he has
a damaged mind from being in
Nam and he only knows how
to live in the woods.
Adults never talk of him,
but they leave brown bags
of scraps on their front stoops
For him to take, only at night
when no one watches.

The war still exists for Crazy Freddie
Which is something the town chooses to ignore.
—*Heather Steele*

Being Alone

Being alone brings us the greatest pain,
  Pain that is always there,
    and never changing.

Being alone is like sitting in darkness,
  Darkness in a long tunnel,
that never reaches the almost forgotten light.

Being alone lets you realize the world.
Its changing seasons and its vicious actions,
  you begin to learn about yourself,
    in ways never thought of before.

Being alone is just one of life's big games,
  sometimes you win and sometimes you lose.
Maybe in these times it's good to be alone,
  you can let your mind run free,
    without having to try and stop you.

Being alone is not the end of the world,
  Even though, for a while, it feels like it,
but being alone is just another part of life.
—*Simon O'Reilly*

Pale Blue Monster

Written after seeing Edward Hopper's painting "Rooms By The Sea:"
Pale blue monster
Lapping at the foundations of my home in your daytime disguise,
Do you wait for another inevitable night?
Yesterday's moonless sky draped your deeds in darkness.
For decades you had kept your distance,
Well beyond the fragile cables linking me to phone and light.
Only the rain had ever washed my stairway to the beach.
Last night you surged towards my door,
The boundary between the dangers of your engulfing destruction,
And the familiar tranquility of my rooms.
Everything between us was swept away into your ravening waves.
For now the strong, clear sunshine shields me from your threat,
While you gather strength to peak another tide.
Shall I close the door tonight as twilight comes?
Or leave it open, knowing there is no oak so strong
It can prevail against you?
—*Phyllis B. Judge*

"The Megalith"

The megalith stood the test of time,
Partially consumed by erosion; yet there.
It's shadow passed constant in a vertical line,
From ages long ago year after year.
Its origin unknown, its purpose unsure,
The placement, benign, eccentric towards the sun.
Its mystery, compulsive, like you've been there before.
A temple for God, if so, which one?
Denied of a life, to bring knowledge from the past,
To correct us from the mistakes we make.
How many generations will it outlast?
How much of the future are we putting at stake?
Its creators long vanished, but it still remains,
Its shadow still cast in a vertical line.
Worn down, and tired, yet looks much the same,
The megalith has stood the rest of time.
—*William A. Saunders*

Gabriella, The Colonist

One night in April in 1775
Paul Revere would come and in surprise
Wake up to get ready to fight
His friend made sure Paul Revere got a signal in the night
One lantern if by land two lanterns if by sea
Paul Revere rode to every town to wake up me
He yelled out, "The British are coming"
The horses galloping that made drumming sounds
Trees whistling dogs barking on the farm.
It was pitch black and scary as he gave the alarm
So I had to get on my clothes and get ready to fight
I felt scared because I didn't know if I'd win or be killed
in the fight
We'd be controlled by them if the British won
But we fought with a gun
So the colonies became free
Thanks to Paul Revere and me
—*Gabriella Butkovich*

A Tribute

In flanders field, the poppies blow, beneath the crosses
Row-on-row.
On brilliant green, the spots of red; a symbol of the blood
That shed.
These brave souls who walked this land, and left their
footprints in the sand of lonely beaches and foreign land.

Though years have passed their prints remain, imbedded in
The hall of fame, of all brave heros who fought and died,
Keeping with them their country's pride.
—*Gladys Everroad*

A New Perspective

Peace-
   Peace will come.
Each moment
Each thought
Each act
   Can be one of contentment and ease.

Cease-
   Cease the turmoil.
Each restless fear
Each swerving change
Each uncertainty
   Whose tale, conflicts with who I dream to be.

Piece-
   Piece by piece.
Each illusion chipped away
Each puzzle piece laid down
Each portion part of the whole
   Revealing the step to take.
   Each by each.
     —*Julie Schmitt*

Untitled

Encapsuled in my own emotions
peering ever so slightly out from inside

It's cold out there
and I feel so fragile - embryotic - like
safe in the fluids of comfort
yet shriveling from the sanctity of calm.

I toss and turn and float
aimlessly about
like the embryo in its mother's sac

I know you're out there
groping for your own safe place

Shall I just wither and wait
and watch you float by?

I have the strength you don't know you give me

And as you flounder, my shell breaks loose
And I grasp for your presence

And we float together

and somehow
it's not so cold.
    —*Debra A. Braun*

Echoes Of Love

Cross - echoes of nails piercing flesh - echoes of nails
   piercing wood
Hear the echoes - ringing through the centuries
Endless reminders - God's endless love
Silent cries - I thirst for you - I long for your souls
Father forgive them - have mercy on them father - have mercy -
   It is finished
Surely, this was God's son - Father forgive us for his
   suffering then
Forgive us for his suffering now - poverty, hunger, nakedness,
   Injustice, war
Father forgive me - I didn't open my eyes - I didn't see his
   sorrow
I didn't open my ears - I didn't hear his pleas
I didn't hear the echoes - the never ending echoes
I hear them and I remember - I will answer them with love
    —*Janet M. Cullen*

Mother Mine

Chill wet thickness lies, gathers to bed under illuminated pinprick heaven sprinkles. Burn smell red dances, permeates nerves to beguile, so hand reaching, ow. Balm sweet edible mists, smiles in forever standing still with open eyes, mouth agape.

Crinkly red-yellow-green drifting hangs, excites chatter to stroll gentle rustling of dappled shadow swath. Fresh rich pungent unearths, stores feast piles gloriously dirt neat and gritty plump. Pressed uniform checkers readies, learns bewildering understand of grown power unknown.

Rainbow-careful form splatters, wishes blue sky wind through light bathing day-bright magic. Verdant mountain field streams, ranges under, over, to journey for unexpected wonder upwelling. Searing air heaviness presses, drips sugar sticky down sweat grime of skinned knee.

Water fresh cleanliness drops, rages occasional jaggedly bright and chest-vibrating air growl. Thawing bud damp begins, plays eager to jump-run-look 'round free teeming yard. Rhyme-flowing word toasts, laughs to sing together joy and twinkle eye hopes.
   —*Sergiu Troie*

She Didn't Get A Chance

    So much to do - so little time.
  Planning for a wedding big, beautiful and fine.

   A new life filled with laughter and love,
    Abounded only by the stars above.
    Encircled in a world for two
With hopes of children - just one or maybe a few.
    Janet didn't even get a chance.

  As the sun set brilliant, bright and blue
We realized this horrible tragedy was actually true.
    On that sunny March day
  A very special person was snatched away.

Trust in God in times of tribulation that's what it did say.
   This note written sometime along the way.
    In her Bible we found her strength
   Her faith in God carried us the length.
 Always happy with a smile on her beautiful face.
With this memory of Janet time nor mind will erase.
   All things for a reason we know it's true
We'll never understand, but my dear friend Janet
   We'll always miss you. NER '93
   —*Nancy E. Rowell*

Bless The Beasts And The Children

For years the buffalo ran free and the children laughed and played. The world use to comfort the Beasts and the children, but not anymore. The children rock themselves to sleep by the sound of loneliness, not by the sound of their mothers voice. Children push those who are different away, just as they see their parents do. They look for that special friend that would not care about the difference they have between them. They find not one but many, they learn that they are not the only one who is a misfit. One takes charge like a lion would do for her cubs, and the others follow and learn. The misfits, they use to run away from their problems and hide behind the skirt - not the one their mothers wear, but the one hanging in the closet, but that was then and this is now. To prove themselves they go on an adventure of a lifetime and discover the beasts, but what do they see. They see mistreatment of animals, and how cruel people really are. The fight for time begins as they try to prove themselves, and to free the beast from their death. After awhile the task is done and they are all free. Then the leader, like a lion leaving her cubs for them to care for themselves, goes off and dies knowing he is leaving his boys to become men on their own.
   —*Heather Griffith*

"Future Voices"

All the children are holding hands
Playing together
Laughing and having fun
And we want to maintain
A sense of togetherness
In the past we hurt
In the present were still confused
But for "future voices"
We must all be heard, seen,
And loved for what we've been created
To be not what is supposed to be structured
Let's have peace and love
It doesn't cost anything
But it takes movement
Let's move toward a frame of mind
Of peace
We've all seen
The walk of hate.
—*Maximillian Leigh*

At Riverview

On the wind-swept slope, we lay, we lay
Playing with weeds that look like hay
A ring you made, of the hay-like weed
On my finger and in my heart placed
At riverview... At riverview

Happy voices in the distance
River running, boats afloat
Blissful souls, forever true
Or so we thought, at riverview

Fate... played its hand
Time... passed the sand

All is gone now, save the wind
That flutters the weeds, that look like hay
And sails the boats, past memories gone...
At riverview... at riverview
—*Martha Loyba Chubik*

Suicide

All the wrong I do is only normal,
please don't sue. I am like an ordinary person
Please forgive me when I start cursin
I've had a lot of down falls in life,
I've even thought of using a knife. Maybe I should
take an overdose,if it doesn't work, the consequence
will be gross. Maybe I should take some poison,
My problems come in by the dozen. feel as if I'm all alone,
by myself...Should I take my life and hang it on a shelf?
Maybe I should, Maybe I shouldn't, I'm all shaky inside...
I couldn't. Here I go I'm cutting my wrist.
I feel my stomach starting to twist. Look at all the blood I
see, it is my fault, it was me. I won't live much longer,
I hope other kids will be stronger.
Think of all the distress I'll bring
upon my family. It was my fault, it was me.
—*Kandace Britt*

Truth

So many thoughts left unexpressed,
　So many feelings left so repressed,
　　The wall of the world within every heart,
　　　Gets higher, and higher, till you can't find the start.
　　　　Is there a beginning, or is there an end?
　　　　　Or is the truth just something to bend?
—*Sabrina Saffel*

To all young people of today.

"Please, take heed, of what I have to say."
You are ruining your health, life and your brains.
Using drugs, drinking, and other corruptive things.
Some adults want to help, and we really care.
The burdens of being teen-agers let us share.
Peer-pressure today, is really strong.
So for you to say, "No," makes you right not wrong.
It's not yourself alone, that you're hurting.
You can lose your mind, and with death you're flirting,
And that's every time you take a drink or smoke.
This hurts your family and other folk.
So stop - look - and listen before it's too late.
Or death can be your final - date.
—*Juanita Thomas*

My Cat Waits For Me

The cat waits patiently, perched atop the table, a saunter, a pose, a tap on my hand. He is present to give beauty to my life, to make me able, to remind me what a friend withstands. Endless patient hours spent in each other presence filling the time with precious small treasures. The feel of his fur to my finger tips, a small kiss planted upon purring lips. So simple, so gracious, so poised in intention. Each movement a thoughtful and elegant endeavor. To move with such a deliberate air, to spring in a moment from here by my side to way over there. To hide in a second or play with such glee, eyes that contract or open fully, as his moment demands it.

My cat needs, kneads me - as I do him, to level my ego, tease warmth to grow within. If I could learn to give the joy he does by blessing someone with precious attention, life would be grand. Simply being in his presence, is a privilege, hearing his inner rumblings of joy - telling all who take the time to notice what is truly important in life - lies just over here. My cat waits patiently for me.
—*Susan Rapanos*

"I Love You"

Cherish the moments we spend together,
pray this love will lost forever.
Dream of how this love is so true,
and remember... I love you.

Think of how much fun we share,
see how much for you, I care.
Treasure this love that was once so new,
and remember... I love you.

Imagine us together tonight,
embrace the thought of holding each other tight.
Memorize the moment before it's through,
and remember... I love you.

Banish the thought of us even being part,
carry my love deep inside your heart.
Wish this love will not once be blue,
and remember... I love you.
—*Angela M. Cook*

Noche de Paz

Pearl studded black velvet
　Pasted on a blue field.
　　Curtains fastened with a glowing crescent.
Sigh at the surrounding sight.
—*Jon Branham*

In A World Of Strangers, You Truly Only Know Yourself

In a talon-less, bruised Phoenix, rising after seventeen prolonged years from the charred rubble and weathered bricks of an institution, I see myself.

In the black, desolate night sky, stars millennia is away send beams of light, and upon these beams ride the overseers of time; time that exists, but isn't, and...
I see myself.
In the shadows of a 72 cent light bulb, where man's dreams meet animalistic desires, there exists a region of simplicity—a boundary we've all crossed before in which

I see myself.
In a muggy bathroom mirror, as I expose myself to the light fixtures, while being raped by millions upon millions of water droplets, steam is wiped from the cold surface of the reflector, and...

I see someone else. Someone who isn't me. Someone I've left behind. Someone — Someone who is someone else.
I see myself.
—*Samir Mehta*

A Single Parent's Prayer

I cannot promise you riches of gold and jewels. I cannot promise you life living in a mansion or wearing custom tailored clothes. I cannot promise you fancy cars or vacations in Europe. I cannot promise you that I won't make mistakes in raising you.

However I promise never to physically abuse you. I promise never to say "I hate you" in a moment of anger I promise never to say "I wish you'd never been born" in a moment of frustration. I promise to tell you the truth about life as I know it. I promise never to make you afraid of me. I promise to love you until the day that I leave this physical earth - I then promise you that I will continue to guard you and watch over you until we are together again.
I promise that my door will
always be open to you. I promise to give you emotional stability and self confidence, even if it means raising you alone. I promise to teach you of a loving, kind, and merciful God. I promise you that the people in our lives will love you and accept you as their own, or they will not be in our lives.

—*Anne Larnella Hood*

Untitled

She sits alone,
quiet and still.
Some people pass by
without thought or care.
Some others crane their necks to stare.
We all say,
"How can this be?",
for in America we say that we are free.
Yet free is not the woman who sits alone,
dirty and cold,
with fresh bruises,
and a mind gone old.
She was beaten last night,
for her fright
and cowardliness when he stood and chose
to fight.
He promised homes of gold,
she believed in him,
and now she's outside in the cold.

—*Rachel A. Smith*

Umbrellas

On A dark and gloomy day
Rain was gently falling.
I turned and looked through an open door.
There is gay profusion
Like Gypies come a calling
In their finest silk and satin.
Bright Bubbles of tan, brown; green, yellow and blue
In ever shade and hue.
Here and there a sober black.
And in the midst of all of this,
A clear bright bubble
Like a ray of sun shining through.
I tread my way through this bright confusion
Knowing that they will soon be gone
Not again to be seen,
Till another rainy day.

—*Vyrel Foss*

Arithmetic

Arithmetic, Arithmetic, why are you so hard? Why, I'd much rather be playing in someone's backyard!
Every day it's the same ole thing, add, subtract, multiply and divide,
And all the answers just seem to hide!

Now, if the figures were all the same, and if it was easy like
   playing a game.....,
But Mr. Arithmetic; you make me mad, and yet sometimes you make
   me sad, but....
If I knew all the answers to all the things you know,
Aah yes, I know just where I'd go. But...seeing as how you
   intend to be so hard,
There'll be no playing in my backyard!

Sometimes to me you're very rude, That's when you come up with
   something new, something like in Fractions, especially in subtractions.
At times, I think that I'm just dumb, and all these figures should be
   hung!
Yet the teacher says; if not for you, when kids grow up, what
   would we all do?
I guess she's right, but even so, I think you stink; you ole
   so, and so!

—*Diane Turnage*

Chicken Scratches

My mind meanders placing chicken scratches on my brain until I reach concrete and dig deep marks which sustain. The mind melee goes from bits and pieces to the millennium forever collecting facts and fiction which create an all nationality condominium. Does our subconscious hold fetal forms of brilliance plus survival tactics from the beginning which designates human's resilience? The realm of reality is held by most people most of the time but there are many people, like myself, who pass back and forth over the line Is it destiny or a tragic human mistake which said condone instead of condemn which lessens morality and leaves humans on a cracked limb? The downfalls of history, world and private, should be the yardstick to guide our country and our life with a need to strengthen and lessen strife. Let's ignite the fires of righteousness, set our course in history, and build a firm foundation of liberty which will serve time through earth's mystery. The ability to condone is a necessity to live but there are times to condemn even if condemnation is painful to give.

—*Doris Mansell*

God Is Standing By

When satan comes your soul to try,
Remember God in heaven is standing by.
He's standing there with outstretched arms
Longing to save and shield you from all alarms.

When the devil knocks at your heart's door,
Just call upon God—He saves evermore.
His love is enduring, His mercies true
That's why He saves the Greek as well as the Jew.

Sometimes you're high as the mountain tops
Along comes the devil and knocks out your props.
Jesus in love will hear your cry,
Remember He is still standing by!

As you travel this lonesome way,
Worship God and take time to pray.
Then when satan comes your soul to try
You'll know that God is standing by!
—*Aeleena M. Heavin*

Cup Of Dreams

Among the wreck ruin and pain
Remember the sweet trek like gently falling rain.

Far beneath anguished memory
There appears before adoring eyes of lore

A cracked cup adorned by rose and trimmed by gold
A shattered cup of dreams once loved.

Slivered moon like shivered soul
Darkened by abandonment

Lone shone the light of before
Small and slight wishing for more.

From morning came the sun
Full bright and yearning not yet done.

From under pillaged care
Comes there the cup most lovely

A cup full of dreams yet dreamed
Lives yet lived love yet shared.
—*Christia Shockley*

"2:50"

At two-fifty of every day my alarm will ring,
reminding me, of the anxious time of sacred sanctity.
Of the time when with you I would be.

A frustrated blush of tepid regret will frame the time
of day at which we met. A time which, for me, isn't over yet.

At exactly that time exactly one alarm will buzz
— a calculated, synthetic, cruel and inhuman fuzz —
To disturb my senses with what once was. And what is time to
a searching empty soul? And who can read a clock in the dark?
I leave only the sound to disrupt my heart.

And who would claim an end to what never did start? And who
can cage another's heart, by stilling the sun and measuring
the time over which their prey does part?

At two-fifty of every night, my body cringes with a memory of
delight. A time to purge my mind's foolish flight, and feel
the spasms of emptiness for that regret inspired fright.

My duty was grand, my scheming was deep.
Now, at the end, my humiliation complete.
—*Adam Zambruk*

The Storm Before The Still

The rain falls hard, without a doubt,
Replenishing the water, keeping us from drought.

A dirt path winds through the forest green,
Along it you can walk without being seen.

The corn went to seed, but still stands tall and proud.
The clouds still hover, giving them a shroud.

The wind softly touches in the tree tops,
Like soft red lips on a cherry lollipop.

Then, what a joy! I can say it has begun,
As out from a dark cloud pops the sun.

The birds come out and fly again,
Taking advantage of the tail wind.

And now you know, I am glad to say,
It's been another great day!
—*Casey Nease*

...And In The Cross Of Your Mouth

And in an uncertain evening
rescued from the Time without worry
I will rest the Pride, if I find you,
in the warm hole of your arms.
And in the Cross of your mouth
I will put a profane kiss
and I will birth for you loves
as roses in winter
And I will search, in your eye, my reasons
and in the world of your hands
my lost illusions
And I will live with you
a borrowed day
from the beginning of Time
from the Final moment.
—*T. Roxana Elias-Munoz*

Heart's Desires

Roaming through the woods
responding to your call,
seeing what troubles you...

Leaving your side
I stagger throughout the land
searching for an oasis
to quench your thirst.

I quest the terrain
in search for food
to heal your hunger and pain.

I return empty handed, but with a thought...
when you can't fill your void, your heart's desire,
I'll fill it with love... and more.

When you're down and all alone, just call me a friend.
I'll be there with you again.

When your desires aren't fulfilled
and things seem hopeless and dim,
I'll give you the support
to start all over again.
—*Carl Willey*

The Old Indian

He settles himself for a much needed
rest. Atop this beautiful mountain crest
The eagle soars in the sky above
They both share an understanding love
He sits and waits his time is near
There's only one thing he wants to hear
"Come my son, I'm waiting for you"
This voice says from the sky so blue.
"Your life on earth is at an end
it's time for a new one now to begin"
"You have traveled for and seen so
much, reach out your heart, you've but to touch"
A breeze blows over him as the clouds
call by. It was a beautiful day to die
"Oh Great Father I was waiting for you, I've done everything
you said to do I'm ready now for this last journey home
This I know I cannot do alone" you have watched over me from
the day of my birth you have been with me everyday on this
earth. I'm ready now my life here is done.
I'm at peace now Great Father come take your son."

—*Donna Lendenberg*

Home

Green, fertile, rolling hills
rice paddies visible over the horizon
farmers toil
work the crops

Mountains in the distance
rising, climbing, ascending, above the flat plain
high above
the village

Beyond the mass you see
the modern city of lights, power, and splendor
this is place
of moneyed

The home of the tiger
where my ancestors lived free, slaved, and free once
more

The tiger
is my home

—*Linda Choi*

Home To The Mountains

Oh the mountains of my home! Oh the foot paths that I have
roamed! Oh the grandeur that I have seen! while lying beside
a mountain stream. The wondrous beauty that God placed below,
that can only be found where cool waters flow. When I was a
lad I could lie there all day, and gaze at the mountains till
all time slipped away. And the night time sounds are what I
loved best. Like hound dogs treeing a coon, or the
whippoorwill calling to the man in the moon. And the smell of
the mountains always so fresh, like the ferns, dogwoods,
laurels, and ash. It would feel your head and you could die
with joy Just to be in the mountains was enough for this boy.
Tree frogs sang me to sleep each summer night, and the rooster
would wake me before daylight. Then the war called me and I
went away. I found myself in Vietnam one day. With bullets
and bombs sounding inside my head I made one request should I
be found dead. Take me home to the mountains to lay me to rest
beside the still waters that I love best. For nothing could
compare to Heaven above, except the Great Smokey Mountains,
God showered with love.

—*Patricia D. Cagle*

This World

This world is filled with hatred and war,
robbery, murder, and much more,

This world is filled with guns and knives,
husbands who rape and kill their wives.

drugs, races, blacks, and whites,
The difference is nothing, we all have rights.

People separated by color of skin,
not how they really are within.

Kids who are stupid and drop out of school,
and do not obey a single rule.

Kids who run away from home,
on the streets is where they roam.

People who kill for material things:
gold, silver, and diamond rings.

People who are shot stabbed or even more,
wonder, "Why Me" as they die on the floor.

People who get high every day,
because they think that's the way.

Don't you get it, can't you see,
we can stop this, you and me.

—*Jen Hanna*

My Workshop Has No Walls

It has no walls that you can see—
Roof it has none, nor floors to walk upon,
A factory of sorts with no smokestack
(Though the black smoke rolls
From equipment old.)
But when I move from place to place,
It is solid as a rock—my workshop.

It's just an old farm, but it's mine,
My father's before me
And his father's before him.
This factory without walls,
Without visible boundaries.

From dawn to dusk I work,
Keeping my factory going,
Till winter comes, with time
For rest and reflection,
Time for repairing my machinery,
And renewing my soul.

—*Daniel R. Pamplin*

"Bicycles In The Rain"

Bicycles in the rain
Round and round in the square
Pedaling faster and harder up a hill
Children laughing
Children singing
Unaware of their names hollered in the wind
Slamming doors and shutting windows
Shutting and closing out the rain
Pounding thunder and raging lightening
Pounding to the earth
Bicycles in the rain circle
Silently squeaking
Pushing pedaling faster in the rain
Rusting dying in the rain
Bicycles pedaling circles in the square
Childhood lost
Shut out of the rain

—*Jennifer Mikus*

'Nocturnal Sentiments'

Dedicated to: Raymond A. Youtsey
Roving thoughts of him intoxicate my mind,
To me he's become my black knight
And it's 'I' that he wants to find.
My hearts' a flutter anticipating his call,
The desolate chill of loneliness
when he doesn't at all.
Another precariously restless night
Thoughts soaring to infinitely Novel heights.
Lost, boundless in a sea of discomposure,
Mollified heart, glistening eyes; demure.
Fervid, captivated, engulfed and enchanted,
Intrinsic, circumspect, quest granted.
Envisaged destiny, resigned awe,
Complaisant, yet the Noblest challenge of all.

—*Barbara A. Willard*

Wonder

Wonder is born in the eyes of a child
Said child seeing for the first time
The wonders that abound in this magical world

Only when a thing is seen with wonder
Can it be truly seen
In all its magnificent splendor

As people age they stop and think
{hey I've seen that before there's no point in looking again}
Which makes the wonder and childlike spirit in them begin to die

I have seen nine year old adults with the ulcers to prove it
And ninety year old toddlers with a scrape on their knee
Being their only ailment

People do not grow old
They let their wonder die
Which makes them a waste of cells

The secret of life is very simple
Keep the wonder alive and the world will become the most
Elegant glorious majestic spectacular toy a child has ever seen

—*Justin Farr*

That Shady Log

Down in a meadow by a shady log,
sat a lizard, a bee and a big green frog.
Croak went the frog, humm went the bee.
But the lazy lizard, just sat by a tree,
sunning himself with his eye on that bee.

Near by the log, was a choice bunch of clover,
its fragrance drawing the bee much closer.
He hummed with delight as he tasted the nectar.
The lizard's tongue came out with a snap,
gone was the bee just like that.

The sleepy-eyed lizard was not watching the frog,
as he hopped up closer to that log.
With a pounce he was on him and with a gulp,
that sleep-eyed lizard went down his throat.

If you visit that meadow down by the trees,
I know you'll see the lizards and the bees.
But stay away from the shady log,
or you could wind up in that frog.

—*Dora Patricia Sturgill*

Wish It Was Me

When I was young and looking ahead, I saw kids going to
School. Wish It was me.

When I went to school, I saw kids dating, falling in love.
Wish it was me.

When I was dating, I saw couples getting married, moving
Out. Wish it was me.

When I married, I saw parents in the park with children
playing around their feet. Wish it was me.

When I had kids, I saw couples, the kids moved out, free to
Do what they pleased. Wish it was me.

When my kids married and moved out, I saw retired couples
With no job, no responsibilities. Wish it was me.

When I retired I saw kids playing, looking ahead.
Wish it was me. Wish it was me.

—*Steven L. Riley*

The Doll...

I had a friend when I was young with whom I shared my fears,
secrets and desires,
She would sit quietly as I brushed her hair for hours.

Her eyes were of purple velvet, they never shed tears,
Her golden hair glistened as I filled her ears.

I loved her and kissed her, she wore the best of clothes,
Matching shoes, her checks blushed rose.

My friend, she never was sad, acted hateful, angry or mad.
Even when there came the day I would tell her, "sorry, no time
   for play."

Sitting on the shelf, with a molded smile,
Sparkling eyes pleading, "can't we chat for awhile."
I wonder if she knew, the day was coming I would give her to you

Please cherish her, keep her clean,
Don't mistreat her or be mean.

I realize she's only made of plastic,
Her heart however of elastic.
It will stretch through thick and thin,
Be kind to her and she will always be your friend.
Love, Mom

—*Rhonda Hodge*

Beauty And The Beast

To Doc: In my dreams you are my beast!

Vincent walks in the city above only the darkness of the night,
Seeing his silhouette moving by the glow of the fire light,
He seems to glide along as if in flight,
His kindness in his smile and eyes shine so bright.

His clothing has the look of the past from his hooded cape to his
   gloves,
Vincent carries a rose, a gift given to him with love,
From a woman who lives in the city above,
His heart soars to her on the wings of a dove.

Vincent lives underground in the tunnels below,
He fell in love with Catherine ever since their first hello,
Their love for each other brings hardships they must forego,
But, seeing them together is like a fairy tale of long ago.

Vincent reads Shakespeare by a stream underground,
His voice has a rough-type manly sound,
The love he has for Catherine has no bounds,
They created a son through the love they had found.

—*Janice Whitworth*

"Wings Of An Angel"

Rode upon the wings of an angel
Seeing life from a whole new angle
I can have a lover or even a friend
But they can't take me where my angel can
I've been to places one can only dream
The most beautiful sights one's ever seen
My angel came to me wings full spanned
Tell's me he's the son of more than man
That wings to I can have one day
An angel I can be in such the same way
To always keep faith, pray and never quit
That it's up to me where I sit
One last journey I went for I became inspired
from all I saw a symbol my friends nothing more
A vision of unsettled scores I've seen the ruins
from high above Threw a set of eyes given only from love
Remedy's there where none
For what I've seen will soon be done
I see no other angle
Since I rode the wings of an angel.

—*Robert Sparks*

Untitled

Children are wonderment
Seeking truth and love,
Acceptance from others,
Free flying as doves.
Creativity flowing, questions on going,
Always willing to grow without limits in tow.
So why do we squash and mold these children without care?
How can we conceivably fill them with fear?
What are we thinking when we push them around?
How do we conceive keeping them down?

Children are the purest light were allowed to behold,
So keep them warm and happy,
Keep them out of the cold...

In love and light
—*Carla Bobczynski*

My Patio

As I sit here thinking about it.
Sensing the comfort and tranquillity of it.
Dawn that lingers with a slight cool breeze.
  The many shadows and shades of green.
  Feelings of being satisfied and secure.
  That filled my little patio for sure.
    Thoughts in here are very deep.
  The same as if you looked into a leaf.
    Upon the lush green sunlit arrivals.
Many different ways for dew drops to travel.
  To listen to ones thoughts and dreams.
    Is what I'll do in patio of green.

—*Janis M. Countryman*

The Game

You, not being here, is like playing a game.
Only with one piece missing, it's just not the same.
Since you left, the game has been delayed,
One can't play a game, when, for two it was made.
The game is left scattered, with pieces all over
  the room,
With high hopes the other player will come
  back soon.
This game is not Checkers, Monopoly
  or Gin.
The game we were playing, was simply
  called friends.

—*Ruby Jo Gore*

Seventy-Cents To The Man's Dollar

Seventy centiliter, ten to the second power;
seventy cents to the man's dollar.
Has it anything to do with a person's body,
intellect, self-respect, makeup or dress?
Seventy cents to the man's dollar...
Is it getting through?
Seventy cents to the man's dollar, blouse
or shirt, pants, or shirts; panty hose, socks-hose,
what difference does it make?
Seventy cents to the man's dollar,
thirty cents give or take...
Seventy cents to the man's dollar,
give yourself a break.

—*P. Elijah-El*

To Be A Little (Boy Again)

An old man went strolling, through the park one day. He noticed
several little boys at play, as he walked on, he'd stop and
turn to watch the little boys, so happy and gay. His body just
a shell, his eyes filled with tears. He stood all alone, so

old and gray, he fell to his knees, and then began to pray,
this is what I could hear him say: "Oh Lord what I'd give, to
be for a day a little boy, so happily at play. Oh Lord what
I'd give, he cried in vain to be a little boy again." A man is

given life, on this earth but once to live it pure or in sin, a
picture from the past, came slowly stealing by of the many long
years, he had spent in the pen. He stood there alone, no
future in sight. His best years wasted, right from wrong he

never knew, if you'd see him someday, I'm sure he'd say to you,
oh what I'd give to start my life anew.

—*Margarito Villanueva*

Children Are People Too

Children, yes, they are people too!
Shadowed by hate, drugs and war
Oh, people what can we do?
Stop the folly and the madness
Give them Peace, Hope and Gladness.

Lets help the children, don't turn them away
Stop! and listen! to what they have to say
Give them love and keep them warm
Let the children live; don't do them harm.

Let them be strong and proud, let love ring,
Let it ring out loud
Thy believe in miracles too,
Show this generation what they need to do.

Help them to see there's a better way
Than the selling of drugs from day to day
Trying to get rich, trying to get ahead
Help them to see, they're being mislead

Ask God to hold them, mold them, make them, and shape them
They are the future of tomorrow
Lest they be buried in pity, shame, and sorrow.

—*Cathy Byrd*

The Window

There is a street light outside the window.
Shadows are cast about.
Sitting upon the living room couch,
The shadows seem to dance.
Engrossed in reading a book,
The shadows are soundless.
Everything is quiet and peaceful.
One shadow has moved closer.
Intuition says don't look toward the window.
The shadow looms ominously near.
Panic mustn't overcome.
The shadow seems larger.
Arose from the couch and moved toward the window.
What is that moving shadow?
With a sigh of relief, there sat the next door cat,
Pawing away at his own shadow.
—*Nancy M. St Clair*

"A Bad Story About A Bad Squirrel"

Sniff, sniff, little squirrel, heres a nut.
Shake your bushy, rodent tail and walk my way.
It's cold outside, I'll give you a place to stay.
It's warm by the fire and there's plenty to eat.
Like almonds, walnuts, and a pecan,
  By the way my name is John.
We'll watch captain kangaroo.
  If you stay out side you'll turn blue,
You'll have a bed of pure cotton,
  These promises will not be forgotten.

This should be reason enough,
  Not to act so touch.
You've heard my plea,
  Now I want you to come with me.

So you won't!
  Hey, I know where you live!
I'll just cut down your damn tree!
  Now see what I have to give!
Nothing but a boiling kettle,
  For your trouble some body to settle!
—*John D. Fancher*

A Course In Love

Although, at intervals, it may soothe,
Shakespeare has noted it best, it would seem:
"The course of true love never did run smooth."

Even if, once, it shone brighter than truth,
Now, it wears tarnish and lackluster gleam
(Although, at intervals, it may soothe).

If you shook to your core and the earth did move,
There won't be encores in wait at each claim;
"The course of true love never did run smooth."

Love wells in your heart while the drink is vermouth -
The wine doesn't always refurbish the dream,
Although, at intervals, it may soothe.

Stronger than power, and sweeter than youth,
When lost, it is harder than both to redeem.
"The course of true love never did run smooth."

It is the best of all treasures - forsooth!
But, dare not expect a midsummer night's dream;
Although, at intervals, it may soothe,
"The course of true love never did run smooth."
—*Lisa T. Jones*

Mom's Touch

When I was small,
She could fix it all.
When I was three,
She was the world to me.
When I was rapped in her arms,
I was protected from all harm.
I could give her a little tug,
And she would turn it into a big hug.
When she would hold my hand,
The world was just grand.
When she would hold me tight, my world was safe,
And I didn't feel like such a waif.
But all that doesn't work anymore,
No matter what is done I am still insecure.
I want my mother,
Because no matter how hard I try there is no other.
—*Christine Cook*

Grace

She gave me love, but she wasn't my mother,
She gave me a family, a sister, a brother.

When I was in trouble, she helped me out,
She taught me what life is all about.

She gave words of strength to face each day,
She was there to take the pain away.

She accepted the challenge, and changed my life,
She gave me balance and taught me how to strive.

She taught me that love of God, and how to live,
She taught me truth, how to care, and how to give.

Now I'm standing on my own,
I have a family, I have a home.

I hope I'm the kind of mother she was to me,
I want my boys to be proud of me.

Though she's miles away, her words ring clear,
The lessons I've learned, I keep very near.

I wish to thank her from my heart,
For giving me life, and a new start.

"I live by example what I learned by example!"
—*Karey D. Reynolds*

Out Of Control

  I know a woman who is out of control.
She is vengeful, hateful, spiteful and droll.
Her wits are not with her when she lashes out...
  Later she'll sit alone in a pout.

  Although this woman feels hurtful inside,
she does not restrain her stark, foolish pride.
  This menacing emotion has taken its toll,
  on this woman who is out of control.

She is helpless to this sensation so strong...
  however, she knows she must carry on.
There is no gate to stop the rage as it flows,
alas, she discovers love is not a sweet rose.

  Is there a magic potion to stop this
  forbidden emotion? The emotion; jealousy.
The reason I ask is because this woman is me.
—*Shannon Briare*

Jealousy For Misery

The night air is still and cool
She lay afloat in her boyfriend's pool
The blue water turned to red
Her soul's still alive, but her body is dead

He locks himself in his room
He sits in his chair to wait for his doom
Since he has killed her he knows he will pay
Her soul will haunt him night and day

She had loved him very much
But lately she shuddered at his touch
She hadn't known of his murderous plan
Though she could sense it on the chill of his hand

His love for her had never died
But when he found out how she felt, he sat down and cried
And tonight she was swimming in his pool
When he got up to get the gun from his room

Now she roams through the house remembering her harsh end
Looking for the room that hides her ex-boyfriend
Wide-eyed and staring his eyes start to burn
Watching there, waiting, as the doorknob begins to turn.

—*Amy Kostiv*

She Feels...

She feels like she is falling through
She reaches for a hard that no one has
She cries out in a voice that no one hears

  he says words that mean the world
  he does not speak true meanings
  he gives false hope without knowledge

She saves letters filled with nothing
She waits for words of true emotion
She sleeps in dreams of pure delusion

  he tries finding something in confusion
  he holds onto sanity with both hands
  he builds imaginary walls of stone

She learns to let go of cold hands
She recalls empty promises from past
She remembers pain of wilting flowers

  he lets no more words fill deaf ears
  he stops feeling for fear of hurting
  he dies slowly with no one knowing

—*Melissa D. Blackburn*

Up Or Down

Is there really up or down
Or just space all around
Is there really side to side
Or do we just slide
Did we just make up each direction
Hoping to explain earth's perfection
Can you go left or right
In the pitch black of night
Do you go up or down
Once you leave the ground
Is this poem true
Could it apply to you
Or am I just another man
Trying to explain what we don't understand

—*Kris Schaumburg*

The Dear Little Lady!

This dear little lady, knew it was her time to go.
She was old and tired, her years went slow.
Her husband had been gone, for quite awhile.
But through her faith, she would always smile.

She kept asking God, she asked him why?
He kept her here, she couldn't die.
Her body was weak, and her mind was slow.
She kept wondering when, God would let her go.

Her life on earth she thought was done.
The battle of times, she had them won.
Her family was grown, and all settled down.
She wanted to go to heaven, not stick around.

One night she was sleeping so very tight.
She dreamed she saw the golden light.
God reached out and took her hand.
She's now so happy, she's in the holy land.

She walks with her husband, like she used to do.
As they look down at their children true.
They are young again, surrounded by a love.
Than can only come from heaven above.

—*Mary Wyant Zebik*

Love And Respect

I love old Glory as she waves so very proud
She waves for a wonderful nation
and she has made the humblest shroud
Many a man has fought for her and lost his life or limb
And if need be many a man will go to war and fight for her again
We should wave that flag for all to see
our men have fought for you and me
many went to not return
They didn't do that for the flag to burn
We learned the allegiance when we were small
It taught us liberty and justice for all
Have you left an arm or leg or peace of mind or may be
came back and no love to find
what are we when it comes our turn to think we are
good enough for the flag to burn
I love old glory as she waves so very proud
She waves for a wonderful nation
and she has made the humblest shroud

—*Clara Tearpak*

Grass Flowers

The grass flowers are best for picking,
She whispered, slipping some behind her ears,
but to make a crown, they are green snakes
twisting and hissing with the dry hot sun.
Climbing up the shirt, they get lost in the hair
and come out at dinner, and slip,
and dive deep into the soup
where they wait for the lip coming close
hesitant at the first hot kiss of soup.
On that the day when we waited for the long black cars,
I ate soup again. The grass flowers
saw it all through the golden fluorescent waters,
soupy, of course,
like the swimming lesson where those loops at the bottom
are the goal. The breath is held, the water fills the ears,
and the plastic loops bend and twist
with the rays of the morning sun.
The lungs a flame and no matter how hard I try
I can't bring that crown to my head
because I can't hold her breath or the soup is too hot or...

—*Derek Stewart*

Mother's Day 1993

She is dead. Now I am dying too.
She who gave me life
Just gave me death as well.
With her dying comes my mortality.

No matter that the creature
Gone to ashes beside her life's foe
Is not in dying she who gave me birth.

Not now the woman who laughed and quarrelled.
The woman I would not speak to for long seasons.
The woman I alternately adored and rejected.
She is dead and now I am dying too.
—*Sharron Carrell*

"A Lady And A Man"

There is a Lady, Minnie Lee, you see
She will always welcome you there, to be
At Her High Walden, we will come to see
The hospitality, you will not be able to flee

There is a Man, Victor, we know
He has here the best of life to show
It is His High Walden too, you know
You will only leave after he has given his best show.

If there is something freely given, we need
There, they have planted the mature seed
They seem to us like a fresh raindrop bead.
They do bring people together, a Godly deed
The best of friends, they are indeed
Yes, this is what our lives do need.

God has given them the fullest lives to live
We will never feel the most they do give
Besides it is, at High Walden, life is to be saved....

To be and to see, in their joy, nobody ever ran
Harpers Ferry is blessed for this Lady and Man.
So, at High Walden, everybody always can!!
—*Michael W. Hatmaker*

My Great Grandma

There's a very special person that I know.
She's not only special to me, she's
special to everyone she knows.
When ever I see her she has a smile on her face.
If you are sad she will make you happy.
One thing I remember about her is the wonderful
aroma you smell upon entering her house.
If you don't know her I encourage you to meet her.
Once you do you'll find that there's a special place
for her in your heart.
She's someone I will never forget for all my life.
GG I Love You!!
—*Lorie Lee Mazza*

Untitled

One day, finally old and gray,
  she crippledly walks home;
    smiling a toothless half grin,
      she pets affectionately a stray mutt;
Then forward, in her rags - dirty and frayed,
  she passes a drunkard bum,
    and drudges forward undismayed;
      these sights are usual;
And going on, inside empty,
  she is a shell formed by pieces,
    found in the throwing out of other's trash,
      and she feels worthless as that trash.
—*Allison*

Field Of Dreams

I guess it's time, I realize,
She's nothing, but a dream.
A figure dancing, behind my eyes.
In a field, with a stream.

Our kid he tells me, I talk in my sleep,
of walking up above.
Behind my bedroom door, he hears me weep,
for the only girl, I ever loved.

But, one sunny day God took her, at night I get her back
How come the day seems so long?
Turn off the lights, don't wake me up,
For it's then, I realize she's gone.

Heartaches and dreams together as a team,
I'm trying very hard to fight.
But just let me walk, in that field and dream,
When I lay me down tonight.
—*Joe Mike Edelen*

Morning At My House

Sun warms the earth with morning's embrace
Shimmering and shining on spider's lace.
Young squirrels scamper in a game of chase,
And the wind pushes leaves to enter the race.

In the water's edge a heron feeds
Catching the food his body needs,
Alert to the dangers he must heed
Almost invisible among the reeds.

Sandhill cranes give a raucous cry
As they wing their way across the sky.
Catching the sun as they fly
To meet with others waiting nearby.

Flat and peaceful the water lies
Broken only by a gator's eyes,
Rippling with him as he tries
To capture the fish his body desires.

Mornings come and mornings go,
Their beauty helps my faith to grow,
For in my heart each day I know
'Tis God who stages this wondrous show.
—*Helen Harris*

Mirage

Black man stands on the pavement alone
Shirt untucked, face unknown
Walks over to the wall, leans against the stone

Feels the pressing passage of the subway car
As he picks up his saxophone..
  Shuffling his feet to a soft
  Kicking tune, a friend stops by,
  A mother stops her child to enjoy
  The music, two young boys clap
  Out the rhythm and a young girl
  Giggles, driver beeps, and the
  Saxophone pumps out a tune that
  Drifts to the neighbors, who smile
  At thoughts of its creator.

Black man slumps against the stone
Stares at the pavement all alone.
—*F. Alan Rissberger*

Platonic Love

How can I make love to you
   Shooting drugs
     Having unsafe sex
As they begin to teach of aids
I begin to flash back into spiritual love
As even a hand shake could melt me into you
A kiss of platonic love another bomb dropped
   By Satan in the last days
God's army is prepared for all lost sheep
   That make it home
The power of prayer from struggle has to end
God knowing we all need rest
Satan wanting it to be death
Fight with a shield of faith
Make known the mystery of the gospel
   —*Heaven's Own Light*

Minion

Soldered
Sickened soul dragging faded limbs
Over blessed earth's fervid whines
Eyeing red stares into the machine.
'It stirs',
Bows the child.
'There, shiftless among gravid images,
Its womb heavy bearing nakedness of incarnation
Within the rot of profane vision.
It is graceless,
As the pearly forehead meets the earth
'Graceless into madness,
The thousand collapsed vassals opening wide their tensed mouths
Sucking deep into wrinkled blackness.
It crawls into time'
Motions the child
'Flowing hollow unclean marrow
The hellborn,
Gripping tightly in spasms of emptiness
The Chalice of Christ.'
   —*Jacob Algire Leister*

Untitled

Emerald grass, sapphire sky,
sights in a mountain meadow.

Birds flitting here and there
sounds, soft; as lovers walk
in a mountain meadow.

A gazebo of trees, bubbling stream nearby,
confession of their love
in a mountain meadow.

Red roses appear, a dozen.
A dozen white, too.
Our love will flourish,
in a mountain meadow.

Stand by my side,
together we face our future,
bright and clear as the sky,
in our mountain meadow.
   —*Donald Mann*

Untitled

The shimmering moon splits the darkness as night slowly and silently falls. As time hastily passes, tiny white glimmering specks immerse from the deep, black ocean above. One, two, four and so on; the stars sparkle in the heavens soon creating magnificent visions that man has gazed upon centuries before. Sounds of nightfall suddenly become apparent. Tiny chirps fill the silent air as the creatures of the night draw near. Sparsely, green, luminescent specks chaotically pattern the distance, pulsating in and out, as lightning bugs leave their trails carelessly behind. A cool, crisp breeze calmly drifts by as the leaves above awaken and start dancing. Lying back, the thick, summer grass has accumulated a noticeable, late evening dew that suddenly chills my bones. Rolling to my side, I gently caress your silky, long golden hair. Softly kissing your beautiful brown skin you turn to me and lie your head down upon my chest. A comforting feeling of peace envelopes my everythought. Like a blanket, my arms strongly embrace your soft, warm body protecting it from our unknown surroundings. Helplessly drifting into a wonder, "If this isn't love that I feel, then my dear Jodie, I don't think I'll ever know what love really is."
   —*Scott Weidman*

Treasure The Simple Life

In this world wind of complications
Simplicity is hard to find.
The smell of fresh, crisp air or
the laughter of children,
the taste of snowflakes tingling upon your lips,
or the vision of somebody taking the time to help nobody.
Why must a crisis happen before we can learn to live
the simplicity of life.
Free from complications.
Simplicity comes from within.
It is a buried treasure of peace.
   —*Siobhan M. Brady*

Survivors

Ten thousand generations have borne us here today
Since Mother Eve in Africa and Asia braved the way
Through unknown terrors, wild beasts, and marauding tribes,
Extremes of weather, random food, shaking ground and tides.

Artifacts from dark cave days, showed some of them were wise,
Sensing something mystic, as well the will to live
Aware of wonders all around which nature freely gives:
Stars and changing seasons, variety of earth
Not the least of which, astonishing unexpected birth!

Sustaining inborn yearning to nurture and protect,
To pass along the best they knew, with growing intellect.
Thus we today may sagely cope, and positively offer hope,
As we remember what we owe, to survivors of long ago.
The spark of life, a hard-won loan, along with all
We call our own; though not for keeps.
Now is our chance to make
A difference—perhaps to be remembered
Like the survivors of long ago!
   —*Lois Smith Triplitt*

You Plus I Does Not Equal We

I revealed myself completely.
You walked away.
I unveiled my soul in love.
You shuddered and ran.

You explored a younger body,
  a tractable mind,
    a kindred soul.
I experienced crucifixion.
   —*Elaine Bentley*

He Is Only A Prayer Away

The world is my family now
Since my family calls heaven home,
It's so nice to know that friends care,
When I'm left here now alone.

My problems whether great or small,
I know all I have to do is to call on the one
Who is greatest of all,
For Jesus loves me and you.

Lots of things are happening now,
That we don't quite understand,
But we must keep our trust in Him,
As He will be there with His helping hand.

It doesn't cost a penny
You don't need a telephone
Just bow your troubled heart and pray,
And He'll listen from His heavenly home.

He's only a prayer away
This for sure I know I can say,
So bow your head and He'll listen to you,
As He's only a prayer away.
—*Helen Jean Davis*

I Miss You

The days go by so slowly now...
Since you have gone away...

I think about the time before...
The deeds of yesterday.

We were so good together then...
Our thoughts entwined as one.

We sang and talked, we laughed and cried...
Our togetherness was fun.

But now the time has come — I'm scared...
For all this had to end.

And when my thoughts have finally cleared...
I'll seek again a friend.

A lover, too, might come my way...
To share my life with me...

But in my memory once more...
My thoughts will be of thee.

A stronger person yet to come...
Is deep inside my heart...
And I'll go on and make a life...
Even though we are apart.
—*Hazel F. Nartowicz*

Peace On Earth

Peace flows from the sweet song of the blue bird,
   singing gaily in the apple tree.

Peace dwells in the beauty of the garden, kissed
   tenderly by the honeybee.

Peace lies in the heart of the little man, making
   mud pies by a friendly stream

Peace rest in the glow of our fireside, alone with
   our thoughts to drowse and day-dream.

Peace is not a creative element, that materialized
   from man's design.

Peace comes from the humble depth of our hearts,
   of all creeds and race and faith combined.
—*Ginny Fretz*

You're A Loser

Life started me off a winner. Later I heard; "you were born a sinner, you're not a winner. You're a loser, no earthly good, and I run you back if I could." These ain't words I read, but ones my Papa said. Mama fed me good food and sent me to school. Papa worked me like a stubborn mule. He objected to me going to school. Mama, said, "He is going to school!" The teachers taught me to read and write and the golden rules. I learned how to fight, play and sing. My classmates laughed, called me, "Old Charley Lame-brain." I fell in love with a beautiful girl. I worshiped her like an angel from above. She said, "I like you, you're cute." My classmate told her I was a dummy and a fluke. I ask her for a date. She said, "you're too late." I want to marry you, please be my wife. She said, "No, It's too soon for me to be a wife." I worked hard at making life better. I haven't yet got it all together. If you're a sinner and not a winner life's one hell of a storm to weather. You're become a whiskey boozer, narcotics user, and a gambling loser. With courage and will, I'll keep trying to understand sinning and to know what winning is.
—*Charles H. Sorey Sr*

Why God Made Mothers

I thought I knew why God made mothers, to torture us with sisters and brothers. Nag and gripe of things better left undone, mission on earth... to keep us from fun.

Watching us like hawks, they wait up late, guess she's not happy till she ruins your date. What about the times she comes to your games, life there after is never the same...
Working hard, thinking on your passes, when up in the stands you recognize, "Ref, Go get your glasses!" It's prom night and your date's a dream— out with the camcorder— can't you just scream! Oh, which way can I run, your eyes look to Heaven, "Lord, where'd she come from?" Time passes as heartaches come and go, how'd you get through them? ask God, he knows.
Now I'm a mom with kids living my past, at times they think bad of me but it won't last. See, God made mothers not to nag us to the bone, no, he just didn't want us to bear our crosses alone.

Every day I look at my kids and I do as my wonderful, loving mom did. I get on my knees praying for their wins and losses, then get up with God to help shoulder their crosses.
God, grant me the wisdom you gave to my Mother, but next time we talk Lord, can we discuss my brother?
—*Danita Hinds*

Blanket By The Bay

One sunny day we saw her; her eyes were tired and gray. Sitting not far from the street corner, by Acapulco Bay. Two babies on the blanket, their eyes so bright today, see Mama raise her hand out; "No need to speak" she says, "For people come from far away, to toss a coin my way" and see her smile and sit all day, on a blanket by the bay. Young child sits on the blanket; no shoes to wear in play, watch brother sell his trinkets to all who pass his way. Wool blanket is their casa; its corners worn and frayed, but there are many more just like it, on the streets that line the bay. No Papa in the daytime he builds "Hotel" all day. He brings home empty bottles and brown sugar candy for his pay. For every time the tourist come, they need a place to stay. But Mama sleeps outdoors each night, below the Milky Way. Where is Mama on her blanket? she silently passed away. Her children are all grown now, and go to work each day. And every morning as they make their way to town to earn their pay, they pass the plot where rests on her blanket by the bay.
—*Bobby R. Henson*

Attributes

Just as the stars twinkle in the bright
   Sky on a moonlit night,
So does my Heavenly Father's love
   Shine on me from above!
Just as the sun dances on a stream,
   Making it brightly gleam,
So do His boundless mercy and grace
   Emanate from His face!
Just as the full moon burns through a cloud,
   A beacon through a shroud,
So does His glory show to the world
   What is twisted and curled!
     —*Kevin Douglas*

Untitled

Some days are like hermits
Sneaking out of the night
Trying to hide in the gloom and rain
Hide from a world full of pain
A world engulfed in injustice and intolerance
A world being destroyed by hate and ignorance
Eventually they fade back into night
Without leaving a trace they were ever here

Other days are bright and loving
Bursting out of the sky in golden glory
Warming all they see without prejudice
Looking at us through the eyes of a child
Eyes which are yet to be clouded
Eyes which still see the truth of equality
Instead of being blinded by lies of bigotry
And as night comes to put them to bed
Each color they leave behind is a glimpse of hope
Hope for a better tomorrow
     —*Kathleen Gorman*

Brother

Like a sea so pretty and blue,
So are your eyes so big, so true.
They tell a story that's never been told,
And fill my heart with memories to hold.
You will go leaving me behind,
With these memories to unlock and find.
Leaving me is what it will take,
Even if my heart does break.
'Cause now I'll appreciate the good times we've had,
And I will be comforted, not feeling so sad.
The sea of Dreams that's what it is,
Knowing this how can I miss?
How could you know or have a clue,
That the sea of Dreams was that sea of blue.
     —*Corianne Freestone*

Being Oneself

Out in the country—in the middle of winter.
So cold and so still.
Seeming so lifeless yet a big forest at the
back edge of the field.
One lone tree standing in the middle of the field
with a shadow coming off it—indicating that what sun
light was there on this drab gray day had touched this
one tree off alone.
In the crowded forest in the back, it seems difficult
to catch any sunlight and therefore give off something
from oneself.

    But that one tree off alone
      gave off a very clear message
      that all could see.
     —*Robyn Alexander*

Not Given The Love

Deep down a narrow hole, down
   so deep a dream may lay.
A dream of a child lying cold on
   the ground.
Lost from the thought of a world
   that may one day be.
Once was a dream to someday come
   true.
Was torn a smile the happiness
   the dreams would bring
Down in a hole a dream wilts away
A dream that once struggled and believed.
Then was broken by the hatred and war.
A war against a child's dreams.
A war against a child's longings to be.
Down in many holes dreams are dead.
Dreams of children that could have been.
     —*Joanna Hale*

"Hidden Pain"

As the sun starts to rise,
   So does my blood pressure.
As the color of the sky keeps changing,
   So does my thoughts.
As the sun gives off heat,
   So does my body.
As the world keeps revolving,
   So does my heart.
As the birds fly freely,
   So does the wish inside of me.
As the sun starts to set,
   So does my clock.
As the moon starts to shine,
   So does my tears.
As the stars begin to twinkle,
   So does my eyes.
And.....
As the sky gets darker,
   So does my dreams.
     —*Heidi Lakos*

Windy Eve

Once at windy eve...
   So fearful was its sound

Carrying my load on lonely road...
   Overcast with emptiness in the background
Walking the sun to its set...
   Overleaping oneself into cloudy bound

Walking the sun to its set...
   For once upon a time in mind

Looking through welkin far beyond...
   To rubble of life left me astound

Following mirage fading away...
   Thou running after and falling behind

Holding the dark with no sense for touch...
   Even it's shaping the silence and all around

Seeking the love with bleeding heart...
   Flooding eyes with tears and drowned

Through life memorabilia into past...
   Conjure the conscience & in soul remain insight profound
     —*Chris Misdary*

Noblesse Oblige

Gentle my lords! - An ye were gentle met,
So had ye not undone the gentle state.
What suits the hireling brutes your purses get
Suits not the noble rank bestowed by fate.

Ye prate of better blood and higher call,
Yet, scarce returned from meting justice cruel,
Ye wallow in your lusts and greeds, as all
Were subject to your whim, and God a fool!

Gentle my lords! Beware the wrath above!
The land ye waste, the gulls ye drive to rage,
Are yet His fief, consigned to you in Love;
He set your bounds who tendered you the gage!

A gentle hand SHALL sweep the spirit clean,
And Prince, and Page, SHALL show the gentle mien!
—*Dan A. Miller*

"One Nation Under God"

Hatred runs rampant in this country of ours
   so I can't understand the reasoning
   behind all of these steeples and towers.
   You go there to worship a "divine being,"
   yet to kick aside our homeless
for their wretched faces you're sick of seeing.
You close your doors to those of different color
   but then you preach to your brood:
      "Love Thy Brothers."
   Bigots you are and full of lies—
      your churches and clans
      I've grown to despise.
   The words of God are in your song
so why do you strongly support annihilation
      by the mighty bomb?
     Quiet I stay for fear of spies;
    so from here I watch my nation
      slowly commit suicide.
—*Nicole Diana Childers*

Untitled

Didn't have much to say
so I stood and looked around.
Why am I forced-to be the one
to defeat this awful feat?
I stammered and stuttered-looked back unto the ground.
And then I scanned the horizon-
dried my tears in the rising sun.
I kicked the dirt that had covered me-but now never more
And then I looked into his eyes-a million miles away.
I blinked again and oceans flowed,
for hours of countless time.
He must have noticed, how could he not?
As he tried to look away.
But could he see my agony, as words fought to stray?
I don't want to, I don't care,
why not give up, once again.
I'm sure that he would and so would you
it's not our jobs to tell then cry
and what was I supposed to say to him?
"my friend I'm gonna die"
—*Marco Rangel*

Out Of Reach

She walked by me in school today.
I'd like to show how much I love her in my own special way.
She walks on past to be with her own group of friends.
I should give up it's no use for me to pretend.
At night I lay awake looking at the stars through my window above.
I think a cruel 4 letter word called love.
—*Vance Randell*

My Brother

It was a cold, cold day in late December,
  so long ago that I can't remember.
When I saw this world for the first time,
  and thought a lonely future was mine.
  I had been born like many another,
alone in this world, with a father and mother.
  Yet there was one more that I did not know,
  and often we would go to a blow by blow.
   We would fight and argue with no end,
  yet to each others side we would defend
  We continued to fight as we got older,
   he grew smart and I grew bolder.
  Finally, we got married and went away,
  only to come back to visit many a day.
But when he was gone I got the strangest feeling,
  I actually found this person appealing.
   I would miss him and long to see,
    If he also missed me.
  And as my love grew for this other,
I finally realized that my best friend is my brother!
—*Robert A. Mihalco*

"So Many...."

So many times I have cried.
So many times I wanted to die.

I have shed so many tears.
And I have felt so many fears.

My heart has never felt so blue.
And I stop believing my dreams will come true.

I don't think my that life can be mend.
And so many times I wanted it to end.

So many times I wanted to be free
To really enjoy being me.

And so many times I have asked
Am I really going to last?....
—*Chue Yang*

Imagine And Know, My People, My People

Just imagine crossing the Atlantic in a ship
  so tightly packed from bodies suffocating yours
  as frightful terror tenses every muscle.

Just imagine being snatched from familiar surroundings
  to unthought of places, wanting death
  to overtake you in any way it chooses.

Imagine our people, the survivors, our ancestors
  who endured mass suffering, pain, slavery
  and were the heartbeat that helped this land thrive.

Just know what our legacy is
  and surely we can rise above the trappings of this time
  as we find ourselves in our ship of today's despair.

Know that our Father gave His only Son
  who shed his blood and flesh for us,
  so we would be healed and have eternal life.

How can we accept this hell inflicted on us
  as if we conceived and birthed
  our own destruction? My people, my people.
—*Patricia A. Stull*

And People Ask What's Wrong With This World Today!

This is coming from a mouth that has lived on this earth for 13 years now. Some people ask "What's wrong with this world today?" And the people who ask this are the people causing the pollution, prejudice, discreation, AIDS, rape, gang violence, 12 year old girls having baby's by there father, and people who claim to be Jesus Christ. Now let me ask you what is wrong with this world today when a young child see's what other children do like killing the other student's in school. Now let me ask you what's wrong with this world today? When all I see is guns, and violence in a place where I go to learn. Now let me ask you what's wrong with this world today?
Can you answer my question while I'm looking down at my 16 year old brother with a bullet hole through his head. And his blood on my clothes. Now can you answer my question?
What's wrong with this world today?

—*Jessica R. Mitchell*

You're Alive!

Life is wonderful, great, each day a surprise!
Remember you can be youthful and wise!
Each bird sings his message of joy by the hour;
Gentle breezes delight you; so does each perfect flower.

There are dark clouds and storms; there are discords and strife,
But the sun will shine through and bring joy to your life.
You are blessed if you claim a true-blue, sincere friend.
Each hour, day, year, is the Lord's dividend!

You ride past a graveyard where thousands lie still;
For those, life is finished! No more spark! No more thrill!
But you have these moments; no one knows what amount.
Make each one a challenge! Oh, make each one count!

—*Shirley L. Speth*

The Night Sky

The moon was full the other night.
So deeply full
It burst white on leafless trees,
Reflected silver on the downed, drowned
Leaves I walked on, skipped on,
Pirouetted on,
Basking in the glow of day at night
Amazing at the angled architecture of
Maples clawing gently at the deep
Charcoal sky, the moving clouds so clearly seen.
The moon was full the other night,
So deeply full.

—*Cynthia L. Forster*

Beautiful Poison

Beauty unyielding, uncomfortable feelings;
Shallow rivers flow fast;
Passionate kiss, so hard to resist;
Heartbeats that won't last;
In the end we begin, irreverent sin;
Hold me close my beautiful poison;
Dreaded Dreams Dance;
Liquid nights, out of the past;
Bury my soul in the labyrinth below;
Could we ever win;
Give me one more chance to make it last;
Our love grew cold;
Hold me close my beautiful poison.

—*David J. Mlakar*

A Teenager's World

Life as a teenager is rough,
putting up with the people and lectures is tough,
we're in a world of our own,
where drugs and alcohol is highly known,
it's a world where thinking about the future is scary,
worrying about your life and who you'll marry,
and dreams are just a fairytale in your mind,
the past is always there, it's never left behind,
in our world true love is hard to get, and to stay with
you know really well is your best bet
because otherwise you'll end up with a user,
or a person who is the biggest loser,
in our world people don't care,
rude comments and painful words is all they share,
it's a world where your feelings don't count,
and using people is what it's all about,
parents say they understand,
it's said to teens all across the land,
but our generation is much more complicated,
ours is made up of nothing but hatred.

—*Brandy Linn Phillips*

Written Words

Wrapped in warmth, I sit and read.
Read the words you have given me.
Words that are your every emotion,
your very being.
Why?
Because you have let me.
You let me into your life with your words.
Why?
Because you love me.
But I will never let you read me.
Why?

Because I love you.

—*Jody Underdown*

The Night Sky

The moon was full the other night.
So deeply full
It burst white on leafless trees,
Reflected silver on the downed, drowned
Leaves I walked on, skipped on,
Pirouetted on,
Basking in the glow of day at night
Amazing at the angled architecture of
Maples clawing gently at the deep
Charcoal sky, the moving clouds so clearly seen.
The moon was full the other night,
So deeply full.

—*Cynthia L. Forster*

Untitled

Like a frightened animal, she runs through the dusty attic making sure not to raise the slightest creak of noise. The rain and the crashing thunder drowns out the fear in her small, frail body. She has nothing except the torn clothes she is wearing and a faded picture of a women. She was told by an elder that the woman was her grandma. The woman's face looked tired and mysterious. In the picture, the woman's eyes gave a hint of sadness. She sits in a dark corner and thinks
To herself. If only the color of her skin didn't matter....
Then maybe there would be peace.

—*Jade Carry*

Treachery

   Beware, my friend,
     on your journey
  through the path of truth,
       for
   unbeknownst to
      you,
   a field of nettles
     may lie
      under a
      patch
  of radiant sunlight,
     and shed
      blood
    from your
   tender feet.
     —*Mariana Austermuhle*

Life Beginning

A face that's glowing,
A belly growing
A joy like no other,
Becoming a mother!!!

A tiny egg, taking form,
A heart that's beating on it's own.
A miracle, starting life!
The greatest gift, to man and wife!!!

All it's organs are in place,
Before it joins the human race.
Little fingers, little toes,
And it's still an embryo!!

Amazing, how the Lord so great,
Designed this plan for us to make,
Another human for this world,
A little boy or little girl!!

A mother and father's love, combine
To create this precious life, divine.
God's gift to us beyond compare
To place a child in our care!!!!
   —*Debbie Beaton*

"Signs"

A bright sunny day,
A chill in the air,
The coolness of winter,
A spring day so fair,
A day filled with clouds,
A sky falling with rain,
A night time of fog.
the wind on the pane,
These are all signs
In which God gave us all;
Springtime, and winter,
Summer, and fall..
   —*Heather Sullivan*

School

School, school,
I love you to bits.
I love when I learn.
I love when I work.
So when I grow up,
I won't be a jerk!
   —*David William Scott*

Cries

I think that I shall never hear
A cry that's sweeter to the ear
Than the first cry of a new baby,
From bloody moorings just set free.
A cry to all excepting one
Means only that he's weak or strong,
A cry that ends all fear and doubt
That something happened him en route;
A cry that brings the tears of joy
And a grateful heart for girl or boy;
A cry that's heard by God above
Who all the little children loves;
A cry that gives to great and small
A "Aisle" greater than them all;
Some are given as a "degree",
But "Mother" God bestowed on me;
A sweeter cry I'll never hear
For it came from my own baby dear.
   —*Carrie Hibbs Martin*

Water

A baby to a mother,
A fish to the sea,
A bird to the heavens
  Flying eternally.

A heart to a man,
A leaf to a tree,
A beast to the forest
  Ever roaming free.

Yet, a raindrop in a bucket,
Multiplying in store,
Controls all existence
  Or we shall be no more.
   —*Jessica Dingwall-Boak*

The Moon

The highlight of the sky
A guide to the galaxy
An inspiration to the thoughtful
A comfort to the lonely
An appreciation to the artistic
A gift to the gifted
   —*Catherine Ferguson Hires*

Private

A speck of frill
A pinch of pink
A touch of lace
And a dainty wink
That's private.

  Heaps of laughter
  A friendly smile
  Wavy long hair
  That makes me go wild
  That's private.

    Untold beauty
    Eyes so blue
    A deep dimple
    That makes me go woo
    That's private.
   —*Gabriel Amyotte*

Untitled

On a morn, velvet with dew,
A silent tear flows,
Staining colors bold and red,
The petals of the rose.
In a garden bathed in light
The stately flower posed,
Drinking in the fragrant air,
The petals of the rose.
Asking nothing in return,
Her love she now bestows
To all who gaze upon her,
The petals of the rose.
No one guessed the misery
Or pain the flower knows,
Because a thorn had pierced
The petals of the rose.
As the night descended,
Satin petals in repose,
She weeps one blood red tear
For the dying of the rose.
   —*Sheila Ann Zyha*

Ode To A Trucker

The highways beckons
A sound only you hear
Your gaze becomes distant
As departure time nears

As the dust settles
Behind your trailing lights
I feel my love reach you
And warm you at nights

I try not to think
Of the danger out there
Only that you'll return
To my loving care

I know that you love me
In your own special way
Speaking louder than words
You shut down for the day

And the highway beckons.
   —*Tami A. Taylor*

Your Dream World

When you dream
And close your eyes
What happens then
To your surprise
A brand new world
full of light
Hopes and dreams
Are all in sight
A world of laughter a world of fears
A world of happiness may end in tears
As you awake
Your world is bare
But when you close your eyes
Your world...will always be there.
   —*Crystal Wilton*

School

School, school,
I love you to bits.
I love when I learn.
I love when I work.
So when I grow up,
I won't be a jerk!
   —*David William Scott*

The Mourning

Each Morning the sun comes up the same
And the moon follows it go down
The hours they come and go each day
And the world goes round and round

Oh! Can't it seem I've lost my joy
My son, my life's extension
A small round face so full of life
With a heart to pure to mention

The purpose I can't understand
Oh grief you come so bold
To strip me of my happiness
And give my arms that ache to hold

The pain so real it stalks by day
And holds so tight at night
I'm a victim hiding in the darkness
All covered up in fright

So stop now world and mourn with me
If only for a day
Help me find the path to sunshine
Help me chase the clouds away
—Sara B. Mior

On Growing Old

The years fly by on silent wings,
and we're a little older.
The summer's heat sees more intense,
The winters cold seems colder.

The hair is slowly turning white,
The steps a little slower.
The robin's song at eventide
Is just a little lower.

We all have faced the storms of life;
We've shared its pain and sorrow,
But let us look with confidence
To the days beyond tomorrow.

For then the earth will be at peace
And there'll be joy and laughter;
And we will live and love again
In happiness ever after.
—Margaret Bowerman

Road To Success

Do it, do it, do it,
And you'll get through it.
Fight, fight, fight,
And you just might.
Try, try, try,
Don't let it die.
Glory, glory, glory,
Without the worry?

Worry, worry, worry?
Where's the glory?
Die, die, die?
Without a try?
Might, might, might!
Without a fight!
Through it, through it, through it?
I did it, did it, did it!
—Barb Spence

Dreamland Delight

Catch a falling star,
and your dreams will all come true.
Journey to the rainbow's end,
there you'll find a land that's new.

Sleep beside a firefly,
and lie within it's glow.
Fly upon a heron's wing,
to see the world below.

Sprinkle moondust in your eyes,
and you'll dream of Heaven's light.
In the morning you'll remember well,
the magic of the night!
—Christine Frances Gorin

First Love

I've come to find a special love
As crazy as it seems
It's as beautiful as the skies above
And fulfills my many dreams

It's the smell of rose in a flower
A twinkle in the eye
It gives me everlasting power
And sends me off to fly.

I hope I never lose control
of this special love I've found
I've got to get it in a hold
And keep it to the ground.

For if I ever lost this love
Although I'm bound to find another
I'd lose the skies above
And as for love
I would not bother.
—Jocelyn Ann Larkin

I Just Stopped By

I just stopped by to smell the roses,
As I climb my mountain high;
Through my joys, sorrows and sadness,
Still I'm finding time to smile.

You will always have the joy of living,
If the Lord walks by your side.
Just reach out and smell the roses
Before you leave this world behind,

Don't forget to love thy neighbor,
Whether he be friend or foe,
And be sure to pass the roses
As through this lonely world you go.

Never let the bad times hurt you,
Always find the joy of life
Just reach out and smell the roses
Then you'll know what life is worth.
—Vera E. Locke

Synergy

A dualistic singularity
Locked in internal combat.
Dark passions, lofty ideals
Opposed aspects of the one.

Synthesis is antithesis
As chaos reigns supreme.
Such is existence
Between birth and death.
—Brad Wendt

Earth's Shades Of Green

Earth's shades of green are changing
As nature slowly dies
Pour me fresh spring water
The tiny rosebud cries
Earth's shades of green are barely seen

Earth's shades of green are changing
Fading with the years
The flora and the fauna
Drink the cup of their own tears
Soon all around is barren ground

Earths shades of green are changing
A rich man celebrates
While trees are begging save us
He, money cultivates
Earth killed by man
Was not God's plan
—Joyce Henders

Broken Heart

I look at you and turn
away a tear drop falls you
look the other way.
My heart is breaking but
you don't see how much you're
hurting me.

I ask you to share your
feelings you mumble and
then sigh I sit down
to talk but all I do is cry.

And now were sitting face
to face. But you won't look
me in eye. The pain in my
heart is growing strong but
my friends are helping me to
carry on.

So I look at you and ask
you once more should we just
be friends or do you want be
more...?
—Alison Hart

Untitled

A darkened space
back in my brain,
a place to hide
from all the pain.

I shut you out
away from me,
don't come too close
you just might see,

My heart with all
my hatred and sin,
you'll hate me then
if you come in.

So don't try and love
as I do you,
for what you love
may not be true.

As false as
any lie may be,
yes that is real,
yes that is me.
—Filomena Correia

Alone Once Again

I sit here in this empty room
Blackness swallowing up the light
Torturing pain goes on and on
As hot tears roll down my cheeks
And slowly drip on my lap
The blackness it seems
Begins to get blacker
Rolling clouds get closer
Coming faster and faster
As I continue to cry
Then as I lift my head
A vision of you appears
I reach out as if to touch you
But you begin to fade
Suddenly your gone
And I am lift in reality
To morn over the thought
I'll never see you again!
—*Tammy Keller*

The Seed

First I was a seed
Buried so deep, I wouldn't wake.
But you called upon a raincloud,
And that nourishment I began to take.
Then you called upon the sun
Giving me the desire to grow.
Never again would I live in solitude,
As I had down below.
Then I grew into a morning flowers,
So strong and proud I stood,
That's what you've done for me
You do me a world of good.
—*Lee-Ann Liles*

A Train Away

Chatter of wheels suggests movement
But no wind through my hair
Confirms stagnant dessert stillness
The velocity of passing trees
Tells me I'm going nowhere fast
Once to separate, once to unite
And both trips simultaneous
World's apart
Connected by steel wheels and gravel

Towns are names with people in them
Only to be passed through anonymously
Here in my carpeted cocoon
Of plastic and steel
The world is a series of such places
All towns to pass through
None of them to call home
Unless it houses you
—*David G. Wood*

Untitled

He looks,
  But sees nothing.

He listens;
  And hears nothing.

He feels...
  But touches nothing.

  Lonely
—*Rod Armit*

A Family Of God

A Man and A Woman shall
by Spiritual Union have
their Physical Union be
Achieved, and the Two
shall become One; as God
Intended them to be —
Husband and Wife in
His sight, and together
with children bore out of
this Union of Love,
shall form a family
of God.
In togetherness they shall
serve the Lord,
with all of their lives -
with Christ as Head of
the Household.
—*Jason Ong Kian Hui*

Owed To Tracy

She was beautiful
Coming on now
Like a forgotten dream
Waiting on rainy days
Lazy music playing soft and low
Why it ended
I don't know
Misguided I guess
Feelings put to a test

Through beauty
Rushing, crashing,
Bursting, bubbling
Sunbeams dancing
Through morning windows
Shadows of midnight's delight
Fragile beings haunted by sorrow
Naked beneath sheets of love's passion
Pages turning
In reminiscence and retrospect
—*Simone Asaro*

My Angel

    No one on earth
   Could mean more to me
Than the Angel of my heart,
  My own sweet melody....
Her movements are like words
   Of a song unsung...
   Accompanied by chimes
    Ringing one by one.
   Each one preceding
   Another much higher
And the tones all lingering
   To join as a Choir.
  Then roses of all colours
   To the air they take,
  And crowning her head,
    A Halo they make.
And emitting from within her-
   An aura of love
   Reaching within me
To a heart made for love.
—*Michael C. Lam*

The Lake

Dark translucence
Cradled still
In the full, rich bosom
Of earth's deep silence.
What wonders!
What of life's sacred meaning
Do you treasure in your deep fathoms?
Birds whistle their love songs,
The reeds sigh their secrets.
Life and death; death and life!
You know it all and offer it up
To the mirrored reflection
Of the dark-domed night.
—*J. C. Gomersall*

Foolish As Time

Guests of the mirror
Dancing white thoughts
Falling night in the screaming light
Lilac dreams
Swallowed by a kite
Secret waves...
Whispering shadows of immensity
Unborn mind
of the peace
Three latin keys
Awakening roots
Altogether shall give life
—*Sarah Cloutier*

You Say You Love Me

You say you love me
Do you really?
Do you think that's enough
For me to love you?

Let me tell you friend
For that is how I feel
You just want to love at will
You think me a fool, it isn't real

However much I'd like to believe
There is love at first sight
Which nothing in the world can kill
That you love me and always will

Your words sound like empty cliches
I have heard them all before
Another time said by another man
I can't believe them yet again

Prove your love for me with deeds
Be there when I'm lonely, in need
Let me think for myself, be free
Then wait and see where it leads
—*Lela Novak*

Tear

Little tear shining light
Falling on this quiet night.
Listen to the voice inside
Never let your feeling die,
In my heart I feel the pain.
Little tears that leave small stains.
In my eyes and in my heart.
Tears of sadness fear and light.
—*Ebony Vardal*

"The Lonely Fisherman"

An old man sits so lonely,
down by the rugged shore,
wishing he was young again,
and go to sea once more.

His feeble hands are trembling,
as he dreams about the days
when he fished off all the islands,
and all the little bays.

He watches all the young men,
as they bring their catch ashore,
and thinks about the time when he
could match their load and more.

He thinks nothing of the hardships,
or the pain that he endured.
He just wants it back again,
the way it was before.

It hurts sometimes to see him there,
for I know his heart is sad.
And I know just what he's thinking,
cause that old man is my Dad.
—*Evangeline Hill*

Weeping Willow

See the willow as she
droops her head and
dangles her arms
Watch her shake and rock
Is she sobbing
Is the willow weeping

Take a closer look
The wind is dancing around her
Whispering sweet nothings to her
Willow bows her bashful head
The rhythm of the breeze
Flows through her

She lovingly sways back and forth
So gracefully caught up in the rapture
There are no tears in her
Only rhythm and gaiety
Willow and the wind share a bond
Leaving willow feeling
Blissful content exhilarated forever
—*Carolyn Hessel*

Crocuses

I planted crocuses today
Dug them deep within the earth
Nudging their firm little forms
Into the fertile rich black soil
The cool October winds blew over
Chilling air and soil
But the tiny expectant buds
Lay nestled
Cozy
They'll sleep now
Spring will burst with their
bold splendor
Then… I will be well
And enjoy them.
—*Bernadette Power*

Poems

Flipping pages
   fast, faster
feelings, emotions
expressed from deep within.

Reminiscing, fantasizing
   changes, changing.
What was once is no longer,
closing one to open another..

An inner peace
   captured, chasing,
in the silence
with my deafening thoughts…

Each tells a story
   past, present,
a non verbal parent
guiding me through life….
—*Judy Redlick*

This Angry Engine

This angry engine idled.
Fuelled from flesh and bridled
By faith, its piston-pen
Trumbled onward, and when
Exhausted, left pale snake
Trails of carbon in its wake.

The arrant image smitten.
Forged from flame and written
With foil, its second-sight
trampled downward, now quite
prostrated, the drained wave
stained and shallow was its grave.
—*Martin Multamaki*

Farming

I've seen my daddy used a
field of wheat all day and all night.

   Just to get it in,
   But that's reality

His hands are full of dirt
His whole face is black with dust

You never hear him complain
That's what farming is all about,

Farmer's really bow their heads to pay,

   They pray for a good crop,
   Pray for rain

He talks about the weather
He can tell you when it's going
to rain,

He prays real hard just may be
this will be the best year yet.

But if it isn't
   He'll have to sell everything

That would break his heart, for all
he knows is
   Farming.
—*Brenda Kingcott*

"Buck"

Pure and blinding
   Fields of snow
A starving buck trembles
   with no where to go
Pushed away by his herd
   and his favorite doe
There's a new young replacement
   and a very skilled foe
The coyotes are stalking
   They'll take him down slow
Where they feed in this field
   no headstone will show
   Spring will arrive
   and the farmer will sow
On the spot where he lay
   a new crop shall grow
   The herd will graze
   when the fall winds blow
On the grain that's been nurtured
   by their sire, below.
—*Peter John Weys*

Full Moon Fishing

You told me the full moon was great
for fishing and making love
and I never really believed you
until tonight.

So far away you lie lifeless
and don't really know that
the sky is bright, the moon is full
and I love you.

Quietly distressed, I mourn
for moments maybe lost forever;
Burwood under the full moon
beach fishing.
—*Robyn Drake*

My Rose

She picked a flower
For her hair
Which was so
Beautiful and fair.

The sun, it shined,
Into showed happiness
Can't be disguised.

Sitting in a garden
She fit the picture fine
A rose among the flowers
That precious rose was mine.

Playing with the flowers
Happiness she found.
Playing until nap time
Not a complaint, nor a sound.

When it was time to come in
A flower she gave to me
My flower will someday die
But my rose will always
—*Monica Brow*

Silent Love

Silent love flows through my veins
For someone from the past
I tell myself it's over now, forgotten
It could not last.

But just like spring, it comes alive
And rushes to my heart
Whenever I catch a glimpse of you
Although were worlds apart.

Why do my eyes betray me?
I try to look away
But for a fleeting moment
They focus, linger, and memory stray

Shame on me!
Where is my pride?
The rules have changed
And I must abide.

Oh! So easy to say
And yet so hard to do
When one has loved someone
As special as you.
—*Connie (Ross) Firlotte*

Defending William

In taking plums
from cool ice-boxes
one should not ask
for forgiveness
but
a thank-you.

Sweet juices
inside tender soft skin
would spoil
if left untouched.
And not tasted.
—*Chris Combden*

Otterville

The leaves rustle to and fro
From crimson, yellow an even glow;
With each autumn whispering sound
Otterville falls will roar to mound;
The temptation of its freedom
O'er the vast and spearing silence
That surrounds the effort of each
Passing Canadian Bir-flight;
Yes, feel the strong wind
Swishing gently across your
Oh so fair face; Quenching the
Likeness of a first snowflake.
Let it come... snow, snow, snow.
—*Shirley J. Hokke*

Untitled

Here I am
Gazing out my window of life.
Nothings changed
Nothing's new
I am stuck in this,
My small corner of the world.
I think I know
What's out there beyond
My reach, yet do I
Really know what I
Have in the palm of my hand.
—*Steve Stapleton*

Only In Your Memories

I can see the walkway
From the skies above,
I can feel my heart and soul
Warmed by all the love.

I can feel my pain now,
Floating far away.
And I can see the darkness
Changing into day.

No more will I suffer,
No more will I cry.
This day I have waited for,
The day when I shall die.

And now the wind will carry me
To my safer place,
And only in your memories
Will you see my face.
—*Patty Thiessen*

Feeling True

The morning the world began
God was born and then it was man
Among the trees that face the light
We live our days, and then the night

To watch the sky, the world by fear
Minds read the end is near
Is it true one soul is born
And later years it must be torn?

There is no reason to suffer a child
Let it run free and get it wild
Not too wild it shuts its eye
Under the ground it would lie

To understand death takes a part
Always remember there in your heart
Makes you feel proud of feeling true
Makes you feel better and not so blue

To miss and miss that very thing
Hurts your heart and makes it sting
Visit a lake, a stilling pond
And think of the world that lies beyond
—*Wendy Powers*

The Fall Of The Giants

Long ago, before any mortal man
Had walked the earth,
They were given life.
Many shapes, many sizes
Living separately,
Yet as one.
Millennia pass,
Centuries come and go,
Bringing many changes.
Man evolved.
Stronger and stronger they became,
With each passing day
Bringing new dangers to their lives.
Then, one by one, they fall
To the ground that once sustained them.
Victims of a greedy world.
The song of the chainsaw
Carried on the wind.
—*Marty Hemmings*

Untitled

He asked me if I loved him...
   He asked me if I loved him,
     And I told him, yes, I did
   And he said that he loved me
     And "couldn't we be wed"?
So we married and our sons were born,
   And I loved them just as true.
  And I told them what they wanted,
     And what they wanted -
   Well, I tried to give them too.
But now the years have rolled along
   And I wonder who I am
   And I wonder what was it for?
You see, it's still a world for men.
   They tell me things are changing,
     But it's too late for me.
     For I am as I was then,
     And how I'll always be.
—*Pat Caldwell*

Little Bird Inside

A little Bird knocked inside,
He knocked so hard he almost cried.
I looked around but could not see,
The little bird who was knocking for me.

I walked away letting him be,
Then I saw he was up in a tree.
I climbed the tree and caught my leg,
The little bird was in an egg.

I took the egg in my hand,
That little egg felt so grand.
The little bird pounded more,
His little wings were getting sore.

I opened the egg to see inside,
I don't know why, I almost cried.
My eyes burned and turned red,
The little bird was... dead.
—*Laurie Zwozdesky*

Field Of Dreams

Off to sea the country
Heading down the road
Never saw it coming
Never felt the car explode

An empty page in my life
And I just bought the book
When I heard I crumbled
I couldn't even look

Quickest friend that I've had
We could talk without time
Years filled up those few short months
When your road could still unwind.

In my field of dreams
You're still in the game
But with each new play
I can only remember your name
Somehow it's just not the same
But there's a moment in time
Where your still in my field of dreams
—*A. Zimmy*

Quartered

The bone white beaches
Prevent three-fourths of the world
From drowning the rest.
—*Gregory L. Davis*

Within His Heart

Shallow lay fields, dreams,
Hollow many young minds.
For me, they call inward.

Barren may reason yield,
Sober plans calmly laid.
Events lease many lives.
Tormented, perceived hurts.

Inflictor detached, smiles.
No pain in his heart cries.
His shadow cast to ground.

Is evil taught, or earned?
Or worn as a resin, rancid.
What of his, its, victims?

Now their laughter, silent.
Tormented screams, echo,
In loved ones, ears,
Hearts, souls, lives...

Oh, so little top soil,
Amid the rocks, that grow..
From depths below...
—Marlene Hopkins

By Candlelight

I link the chain to the other side
I become captive to the darkness
of my soul.

By candlelight
freedom cuts the wrist of the lost
the crimson stream leads the path
to the fiery lake.

By candlelight
darkness fills my day of other's light
walking through the unknown
though knowledge sealed my fate.

By candlelight
my soul cyrstalizes amongst
the damned
all in the name of a broken heart.

By candlelight
my future becomes a memory
the cross may have been the answer
but no one ever told me so.
—Dion Rowsell

The Heavens Are Mine

I'm rich, I'm wealthy.

I have no gold,
I have no jewels,
My purse is as hollow as...

Yes! My stomach is empty;
But my heart is full.

The stars are mine,
The earth is mine,
My world stretches as far as...

I'm richer than you;
I'm wealthier than you.

I'm Free! I'm Free!
—Natalie Quar'rell

Ode To A Porker

Lo and behold, thee porkie roast,
I propose to you, a little toast.
Ye cometh from and old pig sty
A onetime beastie, fat and sly.

Despite your mucky, grubby way
Your rotund carcass is here to stay.
Thee maketh cuisine, fit for queens
And all the other in betweens.

Your tough hide makes a good football
Thine hochs and feet are food for all.
Thy twistie tale and floppy ears
Hath made good soup for many years.

What more can ye say for a lowly beast
That makes for us a gorgeous feast.
So here and now, I proclaim to thee
That pigs will remain for eternity.
—Daryl R. Mosdell

Cherished Forever

My best friend is special,
I see her everyday.
We're always joking around,
In our own special way.

She is the greatest person
She makes me laugh all the time,
and when she's not around,
She's always on my mind.

There's only one special friend
and she is the greatest one,
the best friend that I'm talking about,
well...that would be my mom.
—Tracy Jesmer

Father Hear Me!

I speak You do not hear.
I share a thought
You do not understand.
Let us be friends
For time is precious.

Do not scold! Were you not young?
Dreams are but a moment
Fleeting by.

Father hear me! I need your approval.
A smile is but an effort
Worth many words.

Father
Do not close your eyes
Hear me!

Life is but a wink.
Understand me.
Listen to my pleas.

Rest Father! May peace find you.
My soul cries out. I love you!
—Lise Cianflone

A Picture

A moment trapped in time
When everything seems to be perfect.
The next day it's a part of your past,
But the memory you have
Will always last.
—Carrie Clark

I Was Born To Marry In 1963

When I was born
I tasted the salt
in my mother's tears
before I savoured
the milk
of human kindness

Grandma examined
my tiny palms
Proclaimed
I was a devil
a goddess
who would bring
good luck and fortune
to my husband's house

My loud wails
of defiance
pierced
and reverberated
the long
road ahead
—Kanwaljit Kaur

The Victim

Inside the body, warm and secure,
I wait.
Wait for that special moment
Of life on the outside.
I think
of the happiness life will bring.
I breathe.
Yes, I breathe!

Suddenly I feel pain.
My limbs are being torn,
ripped from my body.
I try to curl up to ward off the agony.
It does not work.
The pressure,
I try to fight it.
I am weak.
I breathe.
Yes, I breathe!

My last gulping, gasping breath.
Yes, I am dead!
—Peggy Wheeler

Little Urchins

Little urchins of the past
I wonder why you never laughed
Was it because you were so hungry
And restricted to a boundary.
A crust of bread sometimes found
Laying dirty on the ground
To you it meant so much
As to a rabbit in a hutch.
Even today there are little mites
Who are hungry both day and night.
For them we must hope and pray
Thy will know happy days
A roof over their heads
And a nice clean cozy bed.
—Ruth Eldridge-Payae

Eighteen

Oh, eighteen
  If I could take you in my arms
    And hold you,
And tell you all I've learned
  Thus far
Would it lessen the pain,
  Ease that time
  And all that goes with it?

I think not
It would be like wishing on a star.

But,
  I remember you.
It was then, at eighteen,
  That the most wonderful thing
  That you could imagine happened;

You said,
  "I'm going to have a child."

I think you've always been in my arms.
  —*Michaela Arient*

My Favorite Place

The meadow is my favorite place
In God's great out of doors.
It's always decked with beauty
From God's great nature store.

The robins and the bluejays
With their songs so fresh and clear
Are the sounds of God's piano
And soothing to the ear.

The butterflies and flowers
With their colors all ablaze
Are the pictures God has painted
So upon them we can gaze.

The trees show all his courage
With their mighty heads aloof
Their branches raised in Glory
To the stars up in the roof.

the morning is my favorite time
In God's great out-of-doors.
You'll find more comfort there
Than you've ever found before.
  —*Lois S. Perry*

Lion's Teeth

Which Romans once as laurels wore
In the hair, back and fore,
To give them courage, hope and strength
They drank the soup of Lion's dent

In each soldier's paradise
He set the seed to banish lice
And then salute the canine God
To light at night where he had trod

In the fosse of equal side
A square "campestrus" dent-de-leon
Whose leaves and flowers furnish wine

Sacred elixir of soldier life
Who need no more leeches knife
When Tarasang - their tree of blood -
Cleansed the system with iron sud

While "salt-to-teeth" is not "salute"!
The Golden Dandelion was fruit
Was this the source of Roman Health
That gave them power to conquer wealth?
  —*Eric Hiscock*

Beauty

Beauty is seen
In the sunlight,
The trees, the birds,
Corn growing and people working
Or dancing for their harvest.

Beauty is heard
In the night,
Wind sighing, rain falling,
Or a singer chanting,
Anything in earnest.

Beauty is in yourself
Good deeds, happy thoughts
That repeat themselves
In your dreams,
In your work,
And even in your rest.
  —*Dion Desjarlais*

Marriage Poem

Marriage is loving,
Is caring and sharing,
Helping each other
The day things go wrong.
Forgiving not hating
For life is not easy.
There will be joys
And some sorrows
So you both must be strong.
Protect all your tomorrows
With very special care
Love is like a flower
It can die one day
Forget all your quarrels
So that love can stay
  —*Kay Grieve*

A Lifelong Marriage

No. 1 rule, so a marriage will last,
Is do good for them, first.
Follow this line, always, and
Your love they will thirst.

Ask them, first thing in the morn:
"Good morning, how did you sleep?"
Follow this line always, always,
And their love you will keep.

Give them a kiss, when they awake,
Then a coffee to wake them up.
Say something real funny,
As you hand them that cup.

When they talk to you, listen!
Love them everyday, every week.
And you'll soon find out, that,
Your true love they'll seek.

Try always to be real forgiving.
Forget their mistakes of the past.
Then throughout your lives,
Your love and marriage will last.
  —*Don Blair*

Why Should I

Why should I repeat
my words of wisdom when you
don't even listen?
  —*Randy Brown*

Teardrops On A Face Of Stone

Some days my loss
is greater than the day before
Our short past is relived
I keep wishing for more.

This kind of grief
Is harder to bear
Then when someone dies,
It cannot compare.

Emotions converge, explode
Green with envy.
They are with you, alone with you
You let me go, I am free.

So much depends on me now
Panic quickly settles in
Old habits keep calling me back
Some days they take over, they win.

Sometimes, more often than not
I prefer to be all alone
I do not want anyone to see
Teardrops on a face of stone.
  —*Marcie Michalewich*

Untitled

Falling in love with you
is only the right thing to do
since I've known you for a year
or two.
  —*Susan Portalatin*

"Eternal Love"

The set of eyes, like glowing hearts
Is shared by each other
Their spirits generate into one full
Love, unsoiled by each others dreams
By the way of love, they are set free alone
Together on the land that God has made
When their time on earth is finally over
The love they had will always be
In just a different time and place
Their love will continue peacefully
  —*Jennifer Muckaday*

Daddy

Since my daddy left me,
I've been wondering what went wrong.
I'll figure it out someday,
and sing it in a song.

I never knew death before,
until it finally struck my mind,
he's never ever coming back,
I've never known his kind.

When I meet my man,
I hope he's like my dad,
I pray he loves me faithfully,
leaving out the drinking plan.

I'm thankful for the man I've met,
who's helped me through my struggles,
who's taught me to respect myself,
he who thinks I'm worth the trouble.

My daddy lays in the ocean,
my daddy lays in the sea,
he sure has saved himself,
and I hope that he did it for me.
  —*Sandra Davidson*

May We

May we, search our soul to find
Life's road will ever wind
Go forth each day and share
With a smile and a prayer
Prepare as our spirit grows
To cherish the highs and the lows

Walk together, hand in hand
Along the beach, through the sand
Feel warmth from a blue skies ray
Be cleansed by a gentle mist's spray
See through the stormy balm
To reach the shore that is calm

Travel life's path with thought
Attain with wonder, wisdom sought
Hear the inner voice and heed
Allow it's guidance to lead
Connect as one and thus create
A life we may celebrate.
—*Kelly O'Neill*

Losing All Sanity

I sit upon the grass,
Listening to the night,
All is quiet,
Except for nature's hum.

The grass is growing,
Slowly beneath my feet,
And intertwined among each blade,
Is a little piece of soul; a pixie,
A fairy of the night,
Which only comes alive,
When the moon is high and bright.

The soft breeze passes by me as I sit,
Gently in the night,
Leaving tingling sensations,
Running throughout my body.

Thoughts flicker back and forth,
Seeping through my flesh,
My mind becomes a jumble,
Losing all sanity.
—*Pauline Jane Bonnici*

Wilted

Wind blowing threw her hair
Little innocent, the glow of her
eyes shows love in her heart.
By day the flower blooms
letting the world appreciate the beauty.
By night the petals close; not allowing
the world around to ever know
what is hidden inside.
Even the sunshine of daylight can
not open the flower to its full
bloom again.
For the glow has been replaced
by pain and the flower has
started to wilt.

Only the petals on the ground, are
there to remind us there ever was
a flower.
—*Sheri Sewell*

Game Set And Match

In tennis
Love is
Nothing.

No points,
No score
No thunderous applause;
No racquet tossed sky high,
No leaping o'er the net,
No trophy held aloft;
No magnums of champagne,
No victory waltz,
No clamour of the Press;
No headlines screaming 'Champ,'
No contracts to be signed,
No sponsorships in sight.

Six - Love; Six - Love; Six - Love.

Only the bitter tears of heartbreak
In the silent dressing room.

For in tennis
Love means
Nothing.
—*Jean Scott*

Seeing Them

Seeing their smiles
makes me feel warm inside.
Seeing them embrace as they reach
For each other
Makes life worth living.
Seeing the hurt in her eyes
Watching him comfort her
Is a dream come true.

Seeing them dancing to the sound
Of just the birds singing
Makes me wants to love nature more.

Seeing the lovely way
They looked at each other
Then he turned to her and say.
"May I kiss you"
Makes me wonder
Why more people
Can't be like them.
Seeing them happy
Makes me happy.
—*Vanda Adams*

Untitled

Maybe I never told you
or showed you that I care
Feelings of sadness—
A heart beginning to tear

I want to reassure you
that in my heart it's true
I love you for who you are
though the times I told you are few

I want you to know now
that my love for you will stay
even though times are changing
I love you more and more each day
—*Melinda Parisloff*

Don't Miss

It was a very special day
Many days ago
Walking through the fields
While the gentle wind did blow

Strolling hand in hand
Moving side by side
It wasn't even like a walk
But rather like a glide

The feeling of closeness
Was simply beyond compare
The love we both did feel
Seemed to us very rare

We cared for nothing else
To us our love was all
We wanted one another
Through summer, spring and fall

We had found true happiness
And so we'd have a life of bliss
Love is something wonderful
Which no one should have to miss.
—*Bryan Adey*

Hopes For The Future

The peace for which we're searching,
May not come so soon, I fear.
Our leaders cause destruction,
They don't really want to hear
The words of our young children
As they speak of love and peace,
Ask to end the pain and suffering
Hope for all the wars to cease.
The value of a human life
Which most people hold so dear,
Seems meaningless to those leaders
Our children have much to fear
They wonder about their future,
In a world that's torn apart
By the wars and revolutions
When will the peacetime start.
We all must work together,
Put an end to wars and strife.
For our future generations,
Not death, just a peaceful life.
—*Carole R. Carnahan*

Why?

Just a heart beat away
One sharp pain or two
A head, a body...
But no!
No head, no body
Vast emptiness
Innocence killed before it started
Slaughtered for vanity's sake!
A funny look, some gossip,
What could be worse?
Talked of, prodded at-
To what extremes we will go
Not to be different.
But why? Oh poor babe,
Trustful and new,
Not even to see
How I could have loved you!
—*Michelle Chisholm*

Unknown Poet

An original poem is hard to write
Most topics have been used
The moon, the stars, undying love
Have been very much abused

I thought of writing many things
But each attempt seemed stale
I'd reach a point where mind went blank
And once again I'd fail

No matter how I'd start it out
My thoughts and verse collided
The two would not assimilate
No matter how I tried it.

I know a seed's somewhere within
Why won't it germinate?
Perhaps it needs more nurturing
And will sprout if I but wait.

I've lived this long unknown
But how I wish I could express
My dormant inner beauty...
I'll just have to wait I guess!

—*Lois Vanwart*

Your Friendship Means A Million To Me!

Your friendship means a million to me
Not a penny less
Even a million more

The distance between us
is only in miles.
You always have a way
to make me smile.

Hearing from you
always brightens my day!!
If the time ever came
where I never heard from you again
I would never be the way
I am today.

Friends we will always be
Together to help each other
through the thick and thin
The good and the bad.

Your Friendship Means A Million To Me

—*Carolyn Smith*

Soldiers

These were soldiers at war,
Quietly heroes who gave their
Lives for us, holding nothing.
Their youth, their love,
Their enjoyment of being alive,
But died for us.

Their future for
Staying alive
But still they died for us.
These were soldiers at war,
Who gave their lives to us,
For peace and freedom
And fought for
Other generations.

That's what the
Soldiers did at war,
And even their
Death must have
Been of their eagerness,
To battle for freedom.

—*Chantelle Cardinal*

Lonely Lonely Me

Tears fall like raindrops,
now that you are gone.
Feeling for you, goes deeper
than my soul.

The lonely and gloomy
nights. I stay seem to
go by so slowly. Just
thinking of you, and
the time we spent together.

I thought it would last
forever, it would never end
I guess, I guess I was
wrong. Now the dream
is slowly fading.

All I have is his picture
and a teddy and special
memories. Now I long to
feel his touch I don't know
what to do.

—*Simone Ottley*

Musical Journey

Drifting and floating
On melody's magic carpet
To delightful, mystic lands,
Far off fountains of fantasy,
My spirit soar soars high.

Quivering and fluttering,
The trills and tremolos
Rise up to Heaven,
Ascending to assist the angels
Great hymn of glory.

Growing and swelling
To a wild climax
And dancing o'er Elysium,
Climbing from cloud to cloud,
The harmonies suddenly cease.

The music becomes silent.
Its journey has ended;
But I've not yet returned.

—*Leslie Ane Donovan*

The Sun Lingers

The sun lingers
on the horizon.
So much older
than the bison
it shines upon.

We almost killed them,
all but three.
Their scrape with extinction
was almost unnoticed,
but we saved them.

As the sun tints the sky,
I stand and think
About life then, simple
yet hard. When the sky was pink,
they didn't know, or care wondered why?

Now the sun has dropped
below the horizon to the west.
To rest and be refreshed,
like a bird to its nest,
waiting for the dawn.

—*Emilie Hildebrandt*

Gratitude

Thanks for opening up the blind
  On variety of Poetry in my mind.
A joy I get beyond compare
  Writing down my thoughts to share.
Imagination now at its peak
  As all around by wit do seek.
My poems come in steady flow
  To fire my brain into a glow.
For inspiring me the words to free
  A hand in union I offer thee.

—*R. M. Fallon*

Cosmos

Somewhere
Out there
There's something in the Cosmos
Trying vainly to reach
The dwellers of Earth
We lie blind to its research
One day we'll find
Its confetti on Earth
But since our birth
From supposed evolution
Or the mighty big bang
It seems we remain
Removed and refrained
From serious action
So we sit and stare
At the sky above
And think that
Maybe
Out there
There's nothing at all

—*Robin Tilley*

My Grandmother's Shoes

"Glistening yellow,
providing confidence
and 'protection.'
They were the
perfect fit.
Left momentarily to
stretch ones feet,
and ABDUCTED.
Long
Walk
Home.
Unconfident and
without" protection.
"Cautious of every
passerby
and as myself accuses
these thieves,
their selves pity
the beggar with no
shoes."

—*Cindy Stead*

Each One In Turn

For a little while,
in this vast Universe,
we could see the beauty around us,
we could feel the power behind it,
until—one by one, we knew
that we were losing what we had—
This was a family,
and it belonged to me.

—*Eleanor D. Clapp*

Tough As Steel

A butterfly of sorts
she comes stomping
our of her frail delicate wings.
Frostbitten in winter
she grows soft petals
tough as steel.

Rains come
winds blow
blizzards fall
there is nothing
she can't withstand.

Like pinched skin
or burnt grass
in a stubby field
hardship
is something she walks through.
—*Eileen Curteis*

In Short time

I see you from the window
Sitting on the sill
I think of how to meet you
And wonder if I will.

How would I know what to say,
To introduce myself to you.
How should I act? When My way
Of life is unlike what you do.

I should not be forbidden
To spend My time with you;
We did grow up with different rules
But, My love for you is true.

How can I explain my inner thoughts,
To the ones who really object.
The problem is they won't understand,
They're only trying to protect.

I'm afraid that the time has come
I bid you farewell, and I go...
If only they would've accepted you
I guess we'll never know.
—*Tanya Pegura*

Just A Routine Procedure

It is there. Inside. Growing.
    Size of a pea.
Breast Self-Examination. Mammography.
  He loves me. He loves me not.

It is a mass. Inside. Growing.
    Could it be....?
  Bipsy. Radical Mastectomy.
  He loves me. He loves me not.

It was there. Inside. Growing.
    Ugly malignancy.
  Reconstruction. Prosthesis.
    He loves me.

    He loves me not.
—*Linda Janes-Depass*

Jazz

Struggle, oh to struggle
So melodic, swinging
Whispers, faded whispers
Set the mood
Pleasure, unanimous pleasure
—*Judy L. Allen*

Endless Pain

I feel like a candle
Slowly melting away,
The spark within me grows dimmer
With every passing day.
Depression has taken its toll me,
Bright colours are losing their glow,
A constant fight within my soul
Help my emotions flow.

Perhaps as the candle can be spent
Before it melts away,
And then rekindled once again
On yet another day,
My body needs a change, a rest,
To help release the pain,
But will the strength and spark be back
Before it is too late?
—*Winnie Cardona*

True Friendship

Friendship is a special thing
So handle it with care
Or when you need it most of all
You'll find that it's not there.
True friends will share the good times
They also share the bad
They'll laugh with you when you're happy
And comfort you when you're sad.
When everything is going great
And there's not a cloud in sight
You'll think that you have many friends
They'll make your world seem bright.
But you will find your true friends
When things are looking down
They'll be the ones that stand by you
As you tumble to the ground.
So if you are a lucky one.
To find a friend that's true
Remember, if you want a friend
Then you must be one too.
—*Vylma Pellerin*

Adieu

A lonely ray of sunshine
Sought refuge from the storm
Darting into corners
Until, at last, too worn
To shine it's light much longer

It rested in despair
Overcome by clouds of darkness
It faded — with none to care

Its light had cheered so many
In day to day concerns
Now for those left looking
No more could they discern

This tiny beam of brightness
That had livened up the day
Refreshed their weary spirits
Now - had slipped away
—*Eliette Lesage*

Entropy

    Blazing, colours,
    Spinning, encircling,
      Spheres.
     Intertwined,
    Colliding in chaos,
    Eternal movement.
Constant state in static.
   Beyond the breath,
   A deeper meaning,
    Untouched.
  Separated distinctness.
  Bouncing off boundaries.
   Smoky partition,
Between conformity and reaction.
   Suppressed truth,
   Multiplied by billions,
Yet we wonder at our inconsistencies,
   And blinded turmoil.
—*Colette Heald*

Sweet Surprise

Candy, candy in a jar.
Stand on tip toes, still to far.
Out of reach and up to high.
A wishful thought twinkles in her eye.
If I had wings I then could fly
Up to that jar for a sweet surprise.
Here comes mom!
She'll get me some.
I don't need wings-
I have my mon
—*Heather Carpenter*

The Flower Of Love

Stem full of care,
Stem for the giving,
But I'm never there,
Where you're living.

Pollen of the heart,
Pollen for the needy,
Now we are apart,
And I've grown weedy.

Roots soaked in love,
Roots planted with feelings,
No longer the above,
Emotions, they are stealing.

Leaves very joyful once,
Leaves eaten but still cheery,
Here grows the flowering dunce,
Worn out, dried up and dreary.

Petals beneath me,
Petals up above,
But I'll never be,
The flower of love.
—*Robert C. C. Merkley*

David

Angels scattered dust
like stars
over our union,
as the lovers knot
which had been tied
for ever
in our souls,
shone in the light.
—*Angela Patchett*

Hey I'm Going

You are!
Take me with you
You need someone strong,
I will be there when something
is wrong.

   Through
Jungles, cities,
To mountains, and sea
If you get frightened you know
   you're with me.

On horses by train
through snow and through rain
ooooooooooooooooooooooooooooooh!
by the way where are we going?
   What, home!
well forget it Mom.
—*Ruth Reiner*

Untitled

My love is like a river
that calls to nearby ears
with water over store
I wait for one who hears

My love is like a rose
trampled 'tween heel and gravel
my petals are stained new father
now no one will stop and breathe we in

My love is like a cloud
sometimes white, fluffy, inviting
sometimes black and murderous
sometimes non-existent

My love is my love is me.
I am like a river
that calls to...
—*Steven Peck*

I Too Have Dreams

In a big city in a doll factory
That is how I came to be
Manufactured with loving care
With someone special my life I'll share

I am porcelain so you see
Do be careful how you handle me
If you drop me I will break
Special care you'll need to take

My hair is blonde and it is real
In your fingers how does it feel?
It can even hold a curl
Same as it does for a little girl

I have eyes and I can see
All the things surrounding me
My eyes are big and they are blue
They are filled with stories too

I have a heart I'd like to share
With someone who knows how to care
A heart is a special place you see
It will store a fond memory
—*Darlene Grandish*

Montana

There is some part of me
that lives in Montana.

In a field
where pure, white snow
hides broken glass

Where a lonely road searches
for a woman with no name

Where everything is dead
or dying of leaving or gone

Where a train whistle echoes
leaves from their trees

Where what was once
can never be regained
where tears stream as easily as
quick, falling rain.
—*Kevin Bjerkness*

Untitled

Sometimes it may seem
   that love is just a game
and every time you play it
   it never ends the same

You build a hand up slowly
   just one card at a time
your heart is filled with confidence
   and winnings on your mind

With just one turn of a card
   how everything can change
What once was in your hands
   now there's nothing to remain

Deep inside, your soul is torn
   you're feeling such great pain
You say the game is over
   but you must try it once again

And then when it seems
   the hand is almost through
You turn the last card over
   your king is waiting there for you.
—*Tim Knight-Davies*

True Love

I love you more each day I live
That will always be my way
To love you till my very last breath
But for now I love you today.

I love you more than the day before
And my love grew for you today
As I think about potential happy times
And the things that you might say.

I love you for the things you do
You always were so kind
To those who were around you
And to the unlucky ones you find.

Let's concentrate on the good times
To make this relationship last
Forever we'll be together
If we hold on to each other fast.

True love lasts forever
And stands the test of time
And for the remainder of days in forever
You will always be mine.
—*Stephanie Lafontaine*

Like Crows

I'm like the little crows
That without hands, just wings
Plead with their beaks lift up
For nourishing good things.
God is the great giver.
I'm weak without his aid.
My wings would fail without
Soul food for which I prayed.

My beak I open wide
Within the house of God.
I devour the word
With greed, and His name laud!
Now fed, I rest content
As crows within the nest.
The Lord is all I want.
God's care is sweet and best!
—*John Martin*

A Homestead Is Sold

The people came from near and far,
The auctioneer was clever,
Time after time his cane came down
A final deal to sever,
From generations long ago
To owner new and eager,
But all could see the toll it took
On farmer frail and meager.

As plow and mower, lamp and chest
Passed 'neath the auction gavel
The couple parting with all this
Would start new life tomorrow.
So smile and pray for them Godspeed,
Retirement, they have earned it,
May other hands be gentle please,
That possession, how they loved it!
—*Edna Smith*

The Lark

Down from the blue and cloudless sky
The lark proclaims his song on high
In harmony his trills are sung
The sharps and flats so nicely done
Here is a creature born to sing
To voice his love while on the wing
And only God who made him be
Knows what he says to you and me
What ever the words, the notes are sweet
And make me dream of waving wheat
Of apples trees and winding lanes
And rows and rows of sugar canes.
Scenes of my childhood, long forgot
But savoured now in happy thought
Recaptured by the wordless rhyme
Of larks who sing in summertime
I thank the Lark, accept these crumbs
And you may also tell your chums
That man appreciates your song
God keep you safely all day long.
—*Ethel Hamilton*

I Like Snow

One-eighth of an inch,
On Christmas eve,
Would be enough
For the winter,
I believe.
—*Walt Luddie*

The Little Filly

As the sun rises,
the little filly opens
her soft brown eyes,
to see the blue sky.

She stretches her neck,
  back and long slender legs.
The sun shines on her coat,
  making it look like soft
  black velvet.

Suddenly like a little spring
  unwinding with her ears
  perked up and eyes filling
  with mischief she runs up
  to the top of a grassy hill.

Then spinning an her back legs,
  like a graceful ballerina
  She races back down to her mother
  for her morning breakfast.
    —*Maureen Regnier*

Creature At Night

In the dark of the night
The stillness comes
The evil sets forth
The creature is reborn

He hides from the light
A hideous form
But stops at the sight
A young lady so torn

An old man comes
He touches her ivory flesh
Her tears scream for help
As she turns from his touch

The creature sits no longer
With fiery lit eyes
He rids the young lady
Of all her cries

Then as quickly as
He set forth, the creature
Flees into the stillness
Of which he was born.
    —*Curtis Zechel*

Rock Willow Park

Rock willow park is in my mind
The trees and brooks I left behind
Down the valley of my soul
I see Mary, my lost love
Gazing at the sky above
And sighting me, her goal

Rock Willow Park is far away
As are the days when Mary stayed
With me all through the lonely night
I can see her by my side
Seeking just a place to hide
From common things and sights

Rock Willow Park, a memory
Glides across my dreaming fields
I reach out and take her hands
And feel her mouth at mine
But Mary's flown to other lands
Life is sad, but dreams sublime.
    —*David Hancock*

What Does It Matter?

What does it matter?
"They" may be black or white.
Nobody can choose.
Are "They" wrong and your right?

What does it matter?
We all have love in our hearts.
Color, language or race,
Is reason for small wars to start?

What does it matter?
Old or young, we're all the same.
Is it so hard to except?
"They" shouldn't take the blame.

What does it matter?
What matters is life and freedom.
Life worth living can end,
By one lethal weapon.....
Racism.
    —*Nicole Kauenhowen*

Moonlight Ponies

In frozen frames of flight,
They ripple through the night.
Spun in silken glimmer,
Their crystal hooves a-shimmer.
Their manes are moonlit streams
That shiver through your dreams.

As silver sparkling light
They shine and shudder bright.
Cantering through a cloud
With plunging heads held proud.
Through star-encrusted skies,
To where tomorrow lies.

The marathon is done -
The nightly race is won.
They always bring this gift
While off to sleep you drift.
The moonlight ponies fly,
To keep lights in the sky.
    —*Irene Morris*

Bamboo Glissades

Creak, creak, the wind doth sway,
This way, that way,
Bamboo spray!
Yellow pipes with leafy frills,
Squawk and squeak their reedy trills!
On their curled tips,
Weaver-birds
Nests of grass-wisps
Fast have twirled!
Song of bird and swaying plants
Mingle in melodic dance!

Casting mottled shadows out,
Phantom silhouettes
That play all day -
Sylvan in their souls, no doubt;
Exotic, temperamental
Nymphs of shades!
    —*Marie-Therese de St Pol*

Destruction Of Eden

Immense timberland
Thriving cornucopia
Falling towards yellow hats.
    —*Katie Poray*

"Noticing"

As I sit in my chair
Through the window I stare
To see what is out there
That I've been missing!

Alone - gazing out
I have little or no doubt
That what I'm about
Is out there!

When I look at a tree
Does it know grows free
Does it see what I see
I wonder!

Another time, another place
Could I keep up the pace
If I joined the rat race
Who'd notice my empty space?
Anyone!
    —*Lois Stone*

Serial Killer

They come into the night
To fill all dreams with fright
The monsters of our youths
Living by their own truths

Their faces we recognized
But soon we realized
That death was in us all
Killing could be are fall

To all of human race
Murder has its own grace
And now we understand
That we can not defend

It could be me it could be you
The killer has many faces
Who could it be if it's not you
Life could end in any places
It must be me so I kill you
You will vanish without traces
    —*Gaetan Vallee*

The Kiss

Mouth salivating
Tongue restless
Caressing
The teeth
The lips
Warm breath
Expelled repeatedly
Yearning desires
Flooding the mind
Slow, agonizing
Anticipation
Moist and sweet
Approaching,
Approaching,
The kiss
    —*Lise-Anne Mack*

The Little Drummer Boy

His name was music,
And he gave himself
Subtotal of the gift
He had to give.
    —*Nell Tucker*

Our Wedding Day

On this day, a special day,
Two hearts will join as one.
On this bright summer day,
Under God's full yellow sun.

We wish to ask with open hearts,
That you attend this day so dear.
To maybe sit and have a laugh,
And to maybe shed a tear.

We hope and dream our time is right,
To last a lifetime through,
Please come and see us joined as one,
To start our lives anew.

—*King Johnson*

The Kiss

Two young voices whispering
Under a flickering light

"Goodnight", they say lovingly
As their hunger turns them to
Reach out and touch each other
Like two willing animals
Grasping for each others breath

Their arms entwine to embrace
Unknowing they are going
Places where swells of passion
Linger like lost memories
Which someday they will recall
Remembering this first kiss

And after many years pass
They find themselves wondering
If they could take it all back.

—*Jennifer Jenkins*

Harvest Moon

Rest your wary head
   upon my shoulder.
Think of else but
   tomorrow.
Close your eyes,
   think of me.
Let me love thee
   while you dream.
Silver strands touch
   your brow.
Time has passed and
   shan't come back.
Like the Harvest Moon,
   we give and take.
But our love shall,
   forever remain.

—*Bozica Perkovic*

Comfort

I wish you would hold me like you
used to do, and whisper softly in my
ear the words "I love you," and tell me
that I will be alright, through all of
my troubles and the darkness of night.
Because in this world full of confusion
and strife, which can rip through ones
soul like a jagged knife, even a man
needs comfort from the person who has
granted him life. And when the darkness
tries to blind my sight, the memories
of comfort will be my guiding light.

—*Sean B. Kearney*

"Carousel"

Go ahead turn around
   walk away again
don't even attempt the words
   and one day when
you decide to think of me
   remember the carousel
the one on which
   we travelled around
and the music
   the song you gave to me
plays on
   lyrics hauntingly alive again
just as if time had stopped
   maybe you want to look back
but if you do
   gone is the carousel
and the music
   for I too will not be there
I also turned around
   and walked away

—*Karen Dyck*

I Knew A God...

   ...Some river before I
   Was drawn to the rhythm
As if to say it could happen
The lark sang its first song.

   ...Some star before I
   Was drawn to the glitter
No one stopped me from noticing
The last and most colorful page.

   ...Some rose before I
   Was drawn to the aroma
With only fate left for picking
The first drop of morning dew.

   ...Some thorn before I
   Was drawn to the pain
As if the migraine could welcome
The final confrontation with life.

—*Mario Perron*

"Someday Tomorrow"

As we look down, the grey road,
We can only see, the past,
Never knowing the future,
Or how long, the good will last,
Our dreams, won't tell us
What the morning will hold,
We always hold it, in secret,
What we've been told,
I love you, put away your sorrow,
And wink at, the coming tide,
Let happiness be your car
Let the rainbow, be your ride,
Remember, we always have today,
Just put away your sorrow,
I love you today,
And someday tomorrow!

—*Dennis Cochois*

Spring

Spring is Easter
and April showers.
Spring is swimming,
sun, and flowers.
Spring is the birth
of many a thing,
don't you just
love the spring.

—*April Lea Auld*

Christmas Is Coming!

Christmas will soon be here
we pray for snow
every year.
The joy in the
children's faces are
worth remembering.
Lots of fun for folks
and gatherings.
Singing Christmas carols
from door to door,
there is a light feeling
in the air for all.
In Bethlehem the
manger scene is awesome.
Yes, Christmas must
have its moments.
The snow is beginning to
fall, and this Christmas,
it will be remembered by
all.

—*Rosanna Wong*

Questions To The Other Side

If the dead could talk
what tales would they tell?
would they talk of the ones they miss,
loves they long to kiss,
of people and places
they would reminisce.

Can you laugh, can you cry
since the day that you died?
Do you miss the touch of the flesh,
the chill of the wind
and all the rest?
Are there sights and sounds
in the place that you're bound?

Tell me are you glad
that you left this world gone mad?
you cried and you screamed
on your way out of this scene.
Everyday, I think of you
I kiss your tombstone when I'm blue,
all because I still love you.

—*Marc Sauve*

The Hardest Lesson

What good is my past
When I live it still?
Have I forgotten already
The faults that had me then
Have me still within their grip?
That was then
and so is this
Why made I those mistakes
When prevent them I could?
for the very mistakes
I made then
are the mistakes
that I make now
what is the use of life I
if we have not learned
from what we've done
To tell us
What we must do?

—*Nathan Smith*

Avalon

There was once a time
when my eyes saw
the mist-shrouded hills
of Avalon
when I touched
another world
a faerie land
lost by time
and I was happy.

But now I can
no longer find
the hidden trails
the secret paths
now I can no longer breach
the misty veil
that shields the realm
of faerie from our eyes
no longer do
I feel at rest for I sorely miss
the serene glens of Avalon.
—*Cameron Hawkins*

Friends

Remember back when you were young,
　When you had time to spend,
And how much nicer it could be
　To share it with a friend.

When in your youth it was a thrill
　A helping hand to lend,
It made our day, and I am sure,
　It really pleased a friend.

Now looking back and thinking of
　Each little trial and trend,
I hope that in the crowd you view—
　I'm one you'll call a friend.
—*Roger B. Flemming*

Edges

'Twas bright and milky in the swamp,
Where foe and friend did dwell.
And much was made of family camp,
That lived beneath the spell.

Be conscious of the other voice
that catches you unmindful.
Beware the fleeting grace of spirit
Which smothers you unsoulful.

They gave themselves permission then,
to be of mind and soul awake.
And in a grief-full moment spent,
long past, old voices, spake.

The hurt, they said, was not God made,
but from the mind of man.
For in true oneness with the light,
bright greatness was the plan.

And so with grateful thanks,
for previous times of pleasure,
Our family trothed itself to seek,
distant, great treasures.
—*Jo Seggie*

Deluge

The rain drowns my lonely heart
While all those I know sail past
Moving on in a rush
Will the sadness inside always last?

I'll spend my last days worrying
Wondering if I have a friend
Who would stop and listen
Because for me I feel the end

I try to speak my feelings
Does anyone in this creation care?
Where love dominates
If there is such a place, take me there

I hear the wind blow through the trees
I close my eyes and listen
While the sun begins to dissolve
And the stars begin to glisten

It's hard to find any ecstacy
In a world filled with pain
So avoid the storm and keep sailing
While my heart drowns in the rain
—*Thomas C. Crerar*

Untitled

　　I don't understand
　　　Why am I here
　　　a lonely friend
　　living in total fear.

Why can't we live in harmony
　　where the food is free
　　and everyone's happy.

　　What good am I
if I don't have the strength to run.
　　What good am I
if I can't do the things you do.
　　What good am I
if I can only cry and feel so sad.

　　Was it my fault
　did I do something wrong
　　if its not my fault
　then what's going on.

　　I'm so hungry
　　can you help me?
—*Tammy Carignan*

"He Could Have"

He could have walked in hallowed halls.
With royalty at His beck and call,
He could have rode on chariots grand,
With servants there on every hand.

He could have wore a crown of gold,
He could have marched with armies bold,
He could have reigned upon throne,
With Kingdoms, the like was never known.

And yet, He chose another way,
He walked on paths of rock and clay,
He had no where to lay His head,
A fishing boat was oft His bed.

He prayed with tears to set us free,
We scoffed, and hung Him on a tree,
And still He prayed that God might give,
Each one of us a place to live,
Void of tears and pain and strife,
He bought for us eternal life.
—*Mary Wright*

My Daughter, My Friend

That tiny, helpless baby
With the sparkle in her eyes,
A special creation.
Just to be,
My daughter, my friend.

That soft, gentle child
Eager to learn,
Eager to conquer the trials of life.
Would always be,
My daughter, my friend.

That beautiful, young teenager
Looking to grow,
Looking for her way in this world.
Could only be,
My daughter, my friend.

Now sixteen
I'm proud to say,
You're still
And always will be,
My daughter, my friend.
—*Linda Ferguson*

My Friend

My friend, I feel,
With us
There is a bond,
It is
With our relationship,
That unifying force,
Which brings
Together two individuals,
Agreeing out of friendship
That I am me,
That you, are you,
Respecting that our feelings,
Are mutual, and do,
Have a special kindness,
That brings out
One's self to view,
The one that has
Acceptance
By the other
Who is you, My friend.
—*Janet Kayzer*

No Love

How can you be happy, when your
World has fallen apart
Why does your life seem crappy,
When there's no love left in your heart.

How come you wish to love someone
But are scared of this beautiful sight
You want your soul to fill with joy,
but it only fills with fright

How many times do you wish upon a
falling star,
How many times do you hope for love
that won't be very far

There are many moments I've had of
hope, joy and fear
But the question I want answered,
is when will love be near?
—*Tracy Taporowski*

Brothers

To have a brother is quite a treat,
Yes, one which you must meet.
More than one is extremely fun
To know and love
Like a peaceful dove.
To watch him when he's small,
And think of him when he's tall
To have a brother is really fun
To play and run right to the sun,
To watch him walk
And listen to him talk,
To not be there for him
Is such a sin.
To lose
Is not what you choose
To never say good-bye
And hold his pictures and cry
But at such a cost
I lost
"My Brothers"
—*Jason Reid*

Memories

Memories are little pleasures,
You can always bring to mind.
They take you back to yesterday,
And things you've left behind.

Sometimes they make you happy,
Sometimes they make you sad.
Each time that you recall the past.
It makes your heart so glad.

When you think back to childhood,
Your heart it does rejoice,
memory can even bring back.
The sound of a loved one's voice.

A loving mother will recall.
When she is home alone.
One day she used to wish.
That all her chicks had flown.

Each memory is a treasure.
Of something gone before.
They bring you joy day or night.
So please don't shut their door.

—*Donna A. Ingraham*

Winds

The winds blow right over me
They know not I am there
For I as cold as they
Lie here perfectly still

They rush over my body
And caress my pale white skin
And go away not knowing
All I hold within

The rain begins falling
They kiss my silent lips
And wash away my body
To the dust where it began

—*Rebecca D. Wooten*

Untitled

Ocean waves crashing
splashing on me divinely
a drop of cloud
cooling my skin
making me wonder
who occupies Heaven

—*Brittany Wylie*

Songs

When times are good
They make you sad
When all is lost
They make you glad;

In life's hard times
They give you hold
They clear your mind
And cleanse your soul;

So when you need
A friend that's true
And when you feel
That life is new;

Just play a song
And enjoy a tune
And life will seem
To grow and bloom.

—*Jesse Correa*

There's Only One Way

They say there's evil.
They say there's good,
but it is written more to love.

They say a blind man can't see.
but he can dream a world beyond ours.

Why do people starve?
Why do children suffer?
soon their will be no more pain!
soon their will be no more hunger!

I don't need to go to church,
nor do I need to watch TV.
I don't even have to read to
know that love, has always
existed for you and me.

There's no room for hate!
There's no time to wait!
just think about it!
and make a change of joy
and shout it (peace!)

—*Gladys Velazquez*

Alaina

As waves rush up and kiss the shore,
They watch the moon and gently sigh.
Comparison not seen before,
The moon and you, the waves and I.

Just as the moon can call the tide.
It's beauty shifts the endless sea.
For them contact shall be denied,
Yet gaze throughout eternity.

Few men would dare to cross that space,
Although such perils must be braved,
To intimately know the face
To which the lunatics have raved.

Though underfunded, ill equipped,
I build my basement rocketship.

—*Jeremy Dragt*

Gratitude

Your dreams were not illusions
they were
thought-seeds
the roots of which
have gone deep
into the
fertile soil
of human conscience
and
watered by the sweat
of our own
moral efforts
already
the buds of
freedom
can
be
seen

—*V. Jarrett*

Regal Pansy

My favorite flowers are pansies,
They're as dear as they can be.
With their little turned up faces,
For all the world to see.

They somehow look so regal,
In fine velvet they are dressed.
Blue, purple, white and yellow,
They want to look their best.

You might find them in a garden,
Or circling a tree.
A window box adorning,
Is a pleasant sight to see.

They may not be an orchid,
Or a special kind of rose,
But when I see their smiling faces
My love for them just grows.

—*Kay Wilson*

Imagine That

If there was world peace,
Think of how we would live,
All happy and willing definitely drug-free,
We'd all love each other,
No fighting or war,
To find someone caring just open your door,
Yes there would be helping at the drop of a hat,
If there was world peace,
Imagine that!

—*Devon M. Walls*

My World

This drop of champagne,
this integrity of design,
its essence of other worlds
is my haven,
is my oasis in this desert
of arrogant ignorance
in a climate of starched brains
homogenized in the piety
of otherness...
with congregations smug
in their pusillanimous spirits
and impoverished souls.

—*Alice P. Smith*

Untitled

I sit with my head on the table,
   thinking of nothing.
One day, I hope I am able to tell,
   you a little something.

In my thoughts there are no limitations,
   to what I can do.
When my day dream halts I still,
   can't say "I Love You"

Don't be sad if you say it to me,
   and I cannot reply.
It's just hard for me to say the way,
   I feel inside.

But, if you open your eyes,
   you will see no one loves you more,
     than "Me".
—*Billy Chambers*

"It's Left To Us."

It's left to us to take good care of
this country
It's left to us to stop the
violence and increase the peace.
It's left to us to get together.
It's left to us to take good
care of our children, and to teach
our children right from wrong.
It's left to us to make this
world a better place.
It's left to us said by
Martin Luther King Jr.
—*Christiana Quarshie*

Life Or Death (Drugs)

Do or don't, do and die,
this description still may lie.
To people who are out there now,
making decisions why or how?
People may persuade you,
they even may divert you,
but don't listen to these people,
or it will hurt you.
Don't do what's "in",
don't go with the "flow".
Be smart, be yourself, and...
   "JUST SAY NO!"
—*Julie Pinciotti*

My Beating Heart

With every beat of my heart
Thoughts of you enter my mind
The sweet music of your words
And the gentleness of your touch

With every beat of my heart
I see those sensitive eyes
Which I know could never hurt me
Although I see the hurt in them

With every beat of my heart
I wish I could make the pain
Go silently without the crying
And bring the happiness you deserve.

With every beat of my heart
I ask the angels in the heavens
To watch over you endlessly
And protect you with their grace.
—*Lourdes R. Visot*

Untitled

An angry face confronts me.
This young woman, whose nose
Is too big for beauty,
And whose mouth is too small.

You can see in her face
In this instant, that she
Is thinking of all her
Numerous and terrible faults:

She has too many freckles,
She is too fat here, too thin there,
She has an ugly scar on her finger.
Should I point out her worst fault?

Perhaps it would be too cruel
To tell her that she will never
Be beautiful, until she doesn't care,
And her soul grows healthy.

Her face is softening, into a smile,
And I glimpse the beauty there,
In that angry face that confronts me,
In the mirror.
—*Kyla Graham*

I was a Child

So long Mom, "Goodbye."
Though sad years are lifted,
I cry.

With no complaints you struggled
through
The life that fate laid out for you.

With mixed emotions, ever strong,
For years I've dealt with them all
wrong.

I've learned a lot, but it took
awhile.
Forgive me, Mom, I was a child.
—*Sandra E. Reno*

Through Life

Oh, how we ponder ourselves,
through life.....
But, as the waves of age
drown our mortal life,
I gaze upon the baby waves
to guide them to a field of sand.
But, as in human tradition,
I too ma looked upon to touch
my destination.
But, the parental waves of us all,
reach the unlimited skies of blue
and tumble upon the field of sand;
and all of the waves of flesh
cascading back to the rest of flesh
as we ponder......through life.
—*Melody A. Martin*

In My Heart

You were there for me
Through the good times.
You were there for me
Through the bad times.
You helped me
When I didn't need it.
And I helped you
The very same way.
You made me laugh
When I wanted to cry.
Your smile brightened
A gloomy day,
So I tried to do the same.
You were too good of a friend
To be lost forever,
But I know you're not lost.
You're in my heart.
—*Shannon Smith*

"The Seed"

Did we arrive from a
tiny unique seed,
to fall by the wayside,
like an ordinary weed!

Surely our life is
worth so much more.
There are still good
things left is store!

Don't give up when
you're feeling down,
pick yourself up,
and turn around!

Give a big smile,
throw away that frown.
GOD wants us happy,
loved, safe and sound!

Yes we did arrive from
a tiny, unique seed!
But, GOD will see to
whatever we may need!
—*Jessie Cooper Owens*

"The Sinner"

The ways of a sinner seems
to be a winner. But as
time goes on his ways get
thinner and the end is never a
winner. Blind is the person
who cannot see the future
of the ways. Moments of excitement
controlled by the power
of evil; bonds your mind
of controlling your body actions
to the end of whatever may
come. Misery, hell always
will end deep in the
well. Where all is hell.
—*Ramona E. Hamric*

Watts Riots "69"

I'm not a civil rights worker,
I'm just a person who benefits,
I sit back and leave it others,
   I have as many causes,
as anyone to solve, I just don't
   get involved.
—*Janice J. Bennett*

Compact Car

One day I went out
   to buy a compact car,

with bright red upholstery
   and a roll over bar.

There were dials and gadgets
   all over the dash

and a little chrome tray
   for my cigarette ash.

Now, the door-to-door carpet
   was mighty thick

and up through the middle
   stood a four speed stick.

With the cash I had,
   I bought this compact car.

But, I can't find a way...
   to get it out of the jar.
   —*William J. Chapdelaine*

Players

A tankard cold at a wayside inn
To cleanse my dusty gullet
The bill of fare a slab of beef
Or the pan-fried silver mullet.

The saucy maid then played coquet
And I with grand elan
Regaled her with my trite bon mots
She deemed me bon-vivant.

The barkeep was a genial host
His laughter was contagious
My repertoire was wearing thin
And at times outrageous.

But oh that blessed interlude
With three of us the cast
Each playing out a kindly role
T'was time to leave at last.

I trod the road with some regret
This road to pain and sorrow
The bard has writ the world's a stage
What play we then tomorrow?
   —*A. J. Ciulla*

The Writer

With a burst of emotion
to explode the fireworks
and then fade to an abyss
of echoes

The flame ignites an
inspiration
to mind the words
to capture the paper
the pen

But the dead emotions
arise not
to blank tears
speechless

Until again redeemed
is the burst of life
in the firework
of creativity.
   —*Stacey Sperling*

Unrequited Love

I offer you my heart
To express my innermost feelings.
I pour open my soul.
It lies bare and revealing.
But to what avail.
My love is not returned
You can't make someone love you.
Is the lesson that I've learned.

With the passing of time.
I grow despondent everyday.
Realizing that instead of being closer,
We're drifting farther away.
So let me learn to accept
The inevitable end,
That if we can't be lovers,
Can we still be friends?
   —*Elaine Davis Polk*

Isolation

We mold and cling
to false Gods.
We protect and bow down
to the golden calf
to worship and sacrifice
as the ancients did.
Lepers are relegated to

   isolation.

Blind Lazarus begs at the gate,
but not in my back yard.
   —*Bonnie L. Berry*

Night Blindness

She gropes in the darkness
   to find her shape.
The eyes, nose, cheekbones—
   are they still familiar forms?

She lays back in the darkness
   to stare at the ceiling.
Blank landscapes, portraits, mirrors—
   is this night blindness?

She contracts every muscle
   to keep herself inside.
The toes, hands, vaginal walls—
   what requires this circumscription?
   —*Merle J. Salkin*

Talk In Mind

If I talk to you,
To know you,
Please care a little...
I dare you.

If I look too sad,
Could be I'm feeling bad.
It comes and goes so often...
Like the love I had.

So don't save your breath.
Fear and silence - it's death.
With my eyes, the world, you will see
Is talking of pain's duress.

And when this lover's dreams awake,
Don't tell lies, my heart to break.
'Cause bold wisdom pries to find
Goodness, for goodness's sake.
   —*Mark A. Meek*

"A Thought Long Forgotten"

When is it time
   to look around and see,

When is it time
   to listen and hear,

When is it time
   to stop and to breathe,

When is it time
   one asks year after year?

Is it not now—
   for tomorrow we die.

Why let it pass
   and not even try?

We're rushing you know
   and then as we sigh,

There goes our last breath
   and time says,
      goodbye.....
   —*B. J. Culbertson*

Lost Youth

Oh to be young again!
To regain those qualities
that were so endear to us.

To have the imagination,
and the light heartiness.
The speed and strength
lost to age.

To feel the immortality
of such an age.
Oh to be young again!
   —*Carl W. Montgomery*

My Little Ones

You help me little ones
   to see the joy in life
With every new discovery
   reflecting in your eyes.
I can taste the sweet
   yet unleaded with strife
And hold close your memories
   when you have cut the ties.
You've held back the darkness
   to revel in the light
And kept me close and warm
   in the cold winter blight.
I love you both so very much
   you'll never know
   how deep my soul you touch.
   —*Stephanni A. Tym*

Traffic

Another day where time begins
   To take its lengthy toll
Mountains shake and waters flood
   And life can move our souls.

We work day in and day out here,
   As if we can be done.
Yet no one ever finishes what
   Yet we've first begun.
   —*Kathleen Larson*

Dear Friends

What can I do
To thank you
For taking my soul
Making if whole
Fixing my heart
When it was torn apart
Inspiring me
To let me see
My creative side
I was made to hide
Drying my tears
Calming my fears
Voice of reason in madness
Turning sadness to gladness
Making the anger cease
Giving me peace
You arrived just in time
To help me survive
For it all, I thank you
For it all, I love you

—*Carol Wirth*

Field of Dreams

Open your eyes
To the field of dreams
Anything is possible
Or so it seems Take a step
Toward the future with hope
A friend kept near
To help you cope Reach to grasp
What means the most Getting that
Is reason to boast Say a prayer
With all your might
For the courage and strength
To fight this fight Live today
With respect for all
Show it first By standing tall
Smell the scent of sweet success
Don't ever settle for anything less

—*Tracey Stacey*

Some Day I'll Wander Back Again

Some day I'll wander back again
To where my old home stands
Along the river, down the lane,
  Afar in other lands
It's humble rooms will shelter me,
  From every care and pain
And life again as sweet, as sweet can be
When I am home again.

Someday I'll wander back again,
To the heart, that was kind and true,
Whose gentle, rugged face still remains,
In my memories cherished view
No more my wayward feet shall roam
Life's troubled pathway o'er
But in the life and love of home
I'll rest me ever more.

—*Frances Claeson*

Peace

It is a mountains climb
to search for peace
and
in everyman's soul
  to find.

—*Michael J. Ruppert*

My Rainbow

Heart
torn, broken,
cold, sad

Sky
blue, cloudless,
clear

Grass
tall, green

Love
gone, cheated,
betrayed

Flowers
delicate, silky,
colorful

World
cruel, spiteful,
mean

—*Carrie Roderick*

Ships Do Pass In The Night

Shattered dreams,
Torn helplessly in two.
Dreams built on Love,
That I have felt for you.

Feeling souls,
Filled with desires.
Looking for another,
Yet unsure of all the buyers.

Drifting apart,
On life's stormy ocean.
Ships that have passed,
Without the anchors of emotion.

Separate ways,
As were tossed upon the sea.
Still longing for the answer,
Was it destiny?

Soul survivors,
Finding life is right.
Destiny or not...
Ships do pass in the night.

—*Kelli Elaine Yates*

Unseen And Seen

All alone in so vast a world that
  tortures the young and brave,
but all the time there stands God,
  so I ask "why be afraid?"

The sun comes up and greets the dawn
  awakening the old and new,
and spreads her mellow golden light
  that crystallizes the dew.

Angelic children run and play
  along the hillside green,
as blessings of the day fall 'round
  of things unseen and seen.

And so the day comes to a close
  and down the darkness lay,
upon the strains and hopes of life
  till tomorrow another day.

—*Linda F. Thomas*

Untitled

When you're handling
touching
probing
amassing me
with pure passion
I sometimes
forget
that under all that
flesh contact of ours
there lies
a deeper unity
What I mean is
we share this bed
as we would
a sadness
a joy
a palatial happening...
Completely.

—*Walda Woods*

Mama's Walk

Mama tiptoed,
toward the candle light of shadow-
twinkling upon my face...
half-dreaming, half-awake—
I waited for my pinkies to be covered,
by the wool quilted of cotton—
moments grasping, seconds,
gone...
Her affection, my devotion.
Long rose bud cotton gown,
swept the invisible print of her walk—
Big, huge shadow of an arm—
Ghostly,
extending upon the wall..
Dark,
Dimmed,
Flashing,
Squeaky cracks of Mama's walk.....

—*Shirley Ann Jones*

Thrown Overboard

Colts, mares, stallions
Trashing wildly
To overcome
The forces of nature
Thrown overboard
By a big ocean liner
Their fate is death
Unless they pull together
Helping little
And helping big
Drifting with the tide
The tide that separates
Fillies from mares
Mares from stallions
Horses from life

—*Brittany Battagliese*

Untitled

Lord, set a watch o'er my lips
  today,
Make me careful of the words
  I say;
May I speak only what's good
  and true,
May my speech always
  glorify you.

—*Ellen L. Coker*

At The Altar

Built an altar in your room
Tribute to the impetuous
Worship of an impulse
Collected fragments of ourselves
By candlelight, games of skill
Bold knights, bitchy queens
Christ's music serenades
Our sweat, lust for death
Glass filled with filters
Melted conscience
In the fury of your gaze
Light a cigarette
And a candle
Worship at the altar
—*Billie Jo Bouic*

Untitled

It is an illusion,
trying to confuse you.
It is not what you expect,
but do you expect too much?
It is what you wish for,
but do not get.
Will these dreams become reality?
Or should they be forgotten?
To desire is to obsess,
to want so much,
just that one touch.
Will it last?
Or silently slip through your
fingertips?
—*Kristine Schmidt*

Puzzles

Putting pieces together
Trying to make them fit—
Trying every possible way,
Even forcing them in.
But it doesn't work that way.
Puzzles are supposed to just
Slide in and click—
There's a perfect fit.
Life works that way—click, it fits.
But putting a puzzle together
Is easier than putting life
back together.
You can't separate the
Straight edges and corners from
The funny shaped ones.
—*Kimberley A. Linstruth*

The Stand

I stand upon a mountain's rise
viewing the world in disguise.
Beauty lurks in every green leaf.
From their cries of pain we are so deaf.

I stand amazed at the sites below.
Our wondrous nature, so much to show.
Will it be here later, do you know?
Or will it be in our memories glow?

I stand and place my heart in front
the stretch of progress and it's grunt.
As long as I am standing here
there is a little bit less to fear.
—*Robert James Plevell*

Crossroad Of Life

Stop and go turn right
Turn left go for it
Straight ahead slow down
Look both ways take it easy

Don't get excited
Calm down
Life's to short
Pressures to great
Take your time
Don't be late
Other crossroads
Bound to come

Face each one
A morning sun
A cheerful attire
Bright and shining
As glittering dew
Victory you'll reap
When the day is through
—*Burton C. Fisher*

I Slowly Go Insane

My eyes are rolling forward,
until a sudden blink
  The pain shoots back,
and again I am able to think

  The pounding still persists,
and my eyes begin to blur
  My whole head is numb,
and teardrops soon occur

  I gently close my eyes,
and every thing is black
  Still a raging throb,
runs from my head down to my back

  I rub my forehead harshly,
and try to massage away the pain
  But soaked in my own tears,
I slowly go insane
—*Julie Thomas*

Without Love

How little I know
Until very lately
You altered so greatly
My point of view
You opened my eyes
To joys which have possessed me
And since you've kissed me
I realize
I realize

Without love, what is a woman?
A pleasure unemployed
Without love, what is a woman?
  Just a zero in the void
But with love, what is a woman?
  Serene contentment, the perfect wife
For a woman to a man is just a woman
But a man to a woman is her life.
—*Chelle D. Tudor*

To The One I Love

The door is open
Unto my heart.
A brand new love is shining -
Coming from you.

A love so great,
Like nothing I have ever known.
A true, everlasting love,
One to call our own.

You are the love of my life,
And always will be.
I belong to you;
You belong to me.

The best and the greatest.
Yes, it is true,
And I thank God each day
For bringing me to you.

We were made for each other,
Any fool can see.
I love you so much,
In my heart you will always be.
—*Tonya Roberts*

The Forsaken Gods

Standing, calm and serene,
Up on life's pedestal,
All so shaven and clean.

Encircled by a crimson pool,
He taste the horrid clotted-sauce,
Turning his silver orifice,
To Insane leers at their loss.

No one can hear the hideous hiss,
From that dark malignant fable.
"The fallen angel of label."
Tap dancing on his golden throne.
He is the master of this clone.

Travesty in the scarlet gore,
A woman gazes at her child.
But eyelessness doesn't phase her lore,
The child's corpse defiled.

By their god forsakened,
Are mortal ties weakened:
And living life, ruined.
—*Chris Camors*

My Friend

You are a light,
When my world is bleak.
You give me strength,
When I am weak.

You give me hope,
When my dreams seem sodden.
You lift me up,
When I am down-trodden.

When I seek,
You help me to find.
You open my eyes,
When I am blind.

The bond we have,
Will never bend.
Because my Lord,
You are my friend.
—*Lorraine Enns*

Jacks

Summer
Vacation
Hot pavement
Young nails scrape against concrete
Love the game; Eggs in the Basket
Play the game; Pits in the Pen

Small, red, rubber ball
flat,
dead.
Golf ball's
crisp, clear, crack
rings loud
in a fifth-grader's heart.

jacks played on hot concrete
jacks
played on
driveways and sidewalks

Called in because of darkness
I wanted more...always more...jacks
—*Jenny K. Fisher*

Peace

Trumpet call to hear
vibrate world events dear.

Inhales eternity human race
good-will pursuits planet face.

Harmonious relations begin anew.

Tradition of Member Nations
create many long sessions.

Truth, trust, mercy sounds
even laughter with frowns.
Order tones traditional culture.

Environment pleads to all
combination with understanding call.

Pursuits this life view
economical development as cue.
Human souls equal courage.

United Nations World Harmony

Peace strives to rule.

Truth bears a role
equal voice ring out.

Least dignity escape doors.
—*Dara M. Ramsey*

The Spirit Of Man

Wild as flame,
Violent as fire;
Steady as a breeze,
Gentle as a zephyr;
Calm as a lake,
Stable as a mountain;
Ambitious, rash, cunning,
Merciful, humble, calm;
Soaring high above the stars,
Crashing beneath the tide,
And if nothing else,
The spirit of man is
Ever-changing, unpredictable.
—*Andrew Lee*

Halloween Is...

Unexplainable phenomenon
Violent drafts of cool air
Frightened screeches
Witches cackling
Windows creaking
Sneaky cats
Feet pattering
Eerie noises
Ruthless skeletons
Wicked ghosts
Lighted jack o' lanterns
And shrieking children
Are all the unique characteristics of
 HALLOWEEN!
—*Katie Huey*

Night Symphony

Locusts and crickets,
violinists extraordinaire,
usher in the dark - melding
day into night.

Sharing my pillow
the yellow kitten purrs cozily,
strumming the quiet harp in my ears.

Vocalist cued:
Trills and honeyed notes
introduce the mockingbird,
who sings non-stop
through her complete repertoire.

Thunder approaches,
pounding, growling,
retreating, returning;
clapping giant cymbals.

Gentle rain
xylophones a quiet lullaby;
segues into dawn;
fades to sunrise.
—*Joyce Hobbs*

Woodland Night Song

On a lonely night in the wood
Violins filled the darkened splendor.
Peaceful tones among nature's glen
Abound in overtures of yen.

Before my ears, the orchestra grew,
My peaceful haven in the glen.
A symphony of echoes, the wind, the lark
Played ever so gently in the dark.

Awakening the wood did yawn
In preludes welcoming the dawn
Like haunting strings of a player's harp
Drawing solitude to my heart.

Light did shine upon the wood
Ever so softly stirring its hood.
Oh, gentle glen with veil of light
Retain the music of the night.
—*Karin M. Nason*

I Hear The Children Crying

I hear the children crying,
Wailing,
Waves of pain
Crashing over my head,
Drowning me,
Engulfing.

I see the children dying.
Blood on the hands of pushers,
Blood stained parents,
Killing each other...
Killing themselves.

Killing me as I watch
On the television set,
from the comfort of my Loveseat,
Eating meatloaf, mashed potatoes,
And a leafy, green vegetable,
lightly steamed.
—*Cynthia E. Blacklock*

Cocaine Cell

Alone in the dark she sits and waits
Waiting to face her judgement
Stepping forth closer to her fate
No eyes gaze in wonderment
Dropping to her knees
She lifts one hand
Whispers urge her to take her stand
She brings forth the glass
that holds the white death
Looking around to hear the answer
A whisper tells her, "Yes"
She brings the white death
Towards her life
That will soon be swept
The white death that she inhales
Will put her in a permanent cell
There she will spend eternity
Screaming for help continuously
This child won't ever be the same
For she put herself into this grave
—*Terri Ratliff*

The Dreamer

Breaking the waters
Warm and grey
I leave echo-finding
To the rays
Spineless and flabby

Air and spine achieved
But the flab remains
Saddled with
Bags of history
Bulging unexpectedly

I pass through
The straits of
The trait pool
Into a foggy post-history

Where vivid and seeper-real
Uncensored stimuli
Jar consciousness

Just let me
Have one night...
—*Rosanne Cornbrooks*

The Civil War

The Civil War
Was a sight to see;
The dashing form
Of General Lee.

But the tragedy
Lay still ahead;
Over 600,000
Would be dead!

"Stonewall" Jackson
Was a godly man;
A military leader
Who loved his land.
Of planning battles,
He would never tire;
He stood like a stone wall
Facing enemy fire.

To end the war,
God had a plan;
And Abraham Lincoln
Was the man!
—*Kate L. Dideum*

A Swift, Simple Stare

A swift, simple stare
Was all that occurred.
The eyes transfixed.
The eyes had lured.

A swift, simple stare
That's all that it took.
A twenty-pound heart
From a timeless look.

A swift, simple stare
Caused you to ponder…
Should I look again?
Should my eyes wander?

A swift, simple stare
A storybook trance.
If looks could kill
We'd be dead at first glance.
—*Joel H. Chan*

Elements

Waves
Wash away my troubles
Takes them to the shores of Heaven
Place them at the foot of God
Pray for me.
Wind
Carry out my despair
Send the dove on wing and tail
Remind me of a time of peace
Sing to me.
Earth
Entrench my deepest sorrow
Bring forth tomorrow's fruit
Renew my hope for beginnings
Grow with me.
Flame
Burn away my grief
Light the torch that guides me
Hold me in your warmth
Love me.
—*Heather Noel Kuczmanski*

Secretfire

You sit so quietly
watching the fire,
lost in your thoughts
of forever love.
You sit so peacefully
amazed by the fire.
It shines in your eyes,
of forever love.
Love has captured your heart
and whisked you away to a place
of imagination.
The fire you sit watching,
holds the secret when
imagination becomes reality.
So what will happen to your heart,
when the fire reveals its secret?
You can cry the tears of love and joy,
but you must believe them
or imagination will be lost in your
heart, with forever love.
—*Jaime Cash*

Journey

I can fly
Way high in the sky
On a puff of air
As the breeze blows through my hair
I see the birds flight
Above in sight

I see the green mountain side
From its beauty I cannot hide
A mountain peak
So mystique
A heart struck sight
As sweet as the soft moonlight
My days adventure
A feeling to always treasure
—*Michael R. Smith*

Untitled

Oh beautiful blue bird,
Way up in the sky.
What are your secrets?
How high can you fly?

If you built a nest,
How high would it be?
Do you like to rest,
In a warm willow tree?

Blue is your color.
Dark blue and light.
You look so pristine,
When the sun shines bright.

Oh beautiful blue bird,
How would it be?
To be souring above the clouds,
Happy and free….
—*Marci Guglielmetti*

Tribute To Golden Seniors

Many times we wish
We knew all you know
So with greater confidence
We would know which way to go.

We wish we had your quiet poise
So we could blend together
Without the careless chatter
And the risk of 'ruffled feathers'.

You have an air of assurance,
While we are quite unsure
Of our methods and devices
Which tempt us from the pure.

You have lived in an era
Which we may never see
That had an enriching influence
On personal ability.

You give us faith and confidence
As our days we live through;
We hope that we mature
As gracefully as you.
—*Marge Roderick*

The Train

A love so blind
We search in vain
To touch our souls
To ride the train
The whistle blows
We ride away
We'll be together
Come what may
Lost souls are we
Forever changed
As life is lived
On this train
—*Lee Mary Dobyns*

The Tragedy

One moment together,
we shared so much fun.
Until lights came blinking,
through the nights sun.

Then all of a sudden,
it got black and cold.
About my brother,
the police man told.

The policeman said,
there's been a roll.
A roll of the car,
to swerve from a pole.

They got out of it fine,
then all of a sudden the lights came on.
What if something happened,
what if he was gone.
IT WOULD BE A TRAGEDY.
—*Alyssa Wentzell*

A Rummage Sale Ad

Sweet rummage spree
Please come and see
What you can buy from me
Thanking me you will be.
Oh yes, yes sir-ree.
—*Frances Gange*

Autumn

A few brief moments,
we walk hand in hand,
while admiring the
splendor of the land.

A crystal clear sky
of baby blue,
the leaves on the trees
changing hue.

A crisp clean bite
in the autumn air,
sunlight reflected
from your golden hair.

Son, you won't always
hold my hand.
That's just not done
by a full-grown man.

So, forever I must treasure
this moment we share,
as we walk, hand in hand,
through the autumn air.

—*Alexander J. Hicks*

Detached Soul

Locked up inside me,
Welled in my eyes,
No one to find me,
The fire inside.

I drift through the darkness,
Feeling the fear,
Shouting for peace,
But no one can hear.

The rumble inside me,
Grows more intense,
Nothing outside,
Seems to make sense.

To find my soul,
Destiny tries,
Reaching for tranquility,
Touching the skies.

—*Media Trent*

I Don't Understand

Why when two people that
were once in love still have
a feeling for another?

I don't understand, I don't understand
why it has to be this way.

What once was may never be again,
but if the feeling is strong,
one day they may be together again.

—*Paul F. Leeman III*

Weep My Eyes

Weep o' my eyes
Weep until I drown in you
My tears are like a song
Songs of tears are sad and long
Weep till morning light
until day break night
Weep of love, weep of sad
Only song that will make you glad
Weep o' my eyes, weep, and cease not

—*Jordan Crocombe*

Our Wedding Invitation

You better sit down.
We've got something to say.
In just a few days
Will be our wedding day.

I won't be nothin' fancy,
No tux or wedding gown.
It'll be down by the river,
In old novinger town.

Our families will be there,
Our moms & our dad.
And all of the children,
that they ever had.

Now the rest of our kinfolk,
And all of our friends.
Are invited to be there.
When the party begins.

You don't have to dress up,
Or make a big fuss.
Just come out and share.
Our special day with us.

—*Leona Johnson*

Texas

Oh, Texas
What a beautiful state
With bluebonnets blooming
Cotton
Pecans
And alfalfa growing
With the sun sparkling during the day
And the stars shimmering at night
Its filled with wonderful things like
Amusement parks
Museums
And historical sights like the Alamo
What a wonderful place to be
Texas

—*Megan Miller*

Wheelchair

I sit
What did you say?
Oh yes, that was the way
I used to do it.
Oh, How so many years ago?

I sit
What did you say?
"Time to eat"
I used to cook and I
had my own way.

I sit
What did you say?
So slowly time has come
And bit by bit
Taken me away....

I sit.

—*Alexia M. Cooke*

The Stranger

I look in the mirror.
What do I see?
Two crying eyes.
It's no longer me.

She watches the tears stream,
Her eyes turning red.
Since she's only existing,
She'd rather be dead.

The mirror reflects sadness,
The image, unclear,
Yet so are her thoughts,
With confusion and fear.

This face in the mirror
Is a stranger to me.
Her head, losing hope,
And her heart, far from free.

—*Misty Tate*

"The Unheard Soldier"

My Lord, my Lord!
What hath thou wrought?
The pain sinks deeper,
than the wound has brought.

Serving honorably was I,
for my country and kin.
Never once did I think,
of lust or even sin.

I do not understand it.
How can this be?
The Lord has deceived,
and brought this upon me.

My lesson has been learned,
but for now it's too late.
We are all just string puppets,
the Lord's humble bait.

My pain has now subsided,
and I slowly fade away.
My last dying hope,
is that things will change one day...

—*Scott Dominic Sleeme*

"A Shattering Love"

My life was shattered
   when I lost you
I pick up the pieces to go on
   and I try and look back
   the memories will haunt
I miss, the Love we had
   and I will now remember
   once good could turn bad
Don't forget the painful memories
   of our Love.
Because they will stay with
   me
Even as I am up above.

—*Theresa Dudley*

(God Is So Wonderful)

God is love
God is sweet
God is awfully neat
I love God
You can too;
Believe it it's true.

—*Jennifer Stacey*

Morning

It's something about the morning
when it breaks into day,
I wish my life could be that way.
I'm lost in an endless night
searching for your love light,

which seems to have gone astray.
—*Raymond D. Cross*

Fireworks

I fell for you in summer,
When July's breath
Panted upon us,
When twilight sweat
Dripped and cooled,
Then begged for more...

I fell for you in summer,
When the blue pools of your eyes
Invited me to swim...
I dove,
And lapped your presence
Until I could stroke no
More...

And now in winter,
I find you banded and
Embroidered to my hand,
The future paved before us
Boldly in gold
A road uncharted,
Awaiting to unfold...
—*Mary McGrath*

Footprints In The Snow

Remember the early morning chill
When, so very long ago,
We walked as young lovers will,
Leaving footprints in the snow?

We dreamed young dreams,
Those many years ago,
Watching early sunbeams
Glistening on the snow.

We have weathered our storms
And mellowed with the years.
Children and life were borne
Knowing that each was near.

We have travelled distant lands
Over these many, many years,
Still walking hand-in hand
Through gladness and tears.

But, I remember still
When, so very long ago,
We walked as young lovers will,
Leaving footprints in the snow.
—*Leon J. Hubert*

Oh! Oh!

I went into a bakery shop,
  To buy a loaf of bread.
The baker did not notice me
  I tapped him on the head.

He turned around so suddenly,
  I did not think could be.
He turned around so suddenly,
  And threw the loaf at me.
—*Lydia Victoria Davis*

The Promise

In the hush of the evening;
When the birds are all still
I hear a voice calling
Far off in the hills;
"I love you" it whispers
"With all of my heart,
And I know that we'll never
Be really apart,

For as long as the wind blows
Far out to the sea,
Your smiles and your laughter
Will wash over me.
So keep me forever
Down deep in your heart;
And I know that we'll never
Be really apart."
—*Elisabeth Vietmeier*

First American

Gone is their day
When the hunt was the way.
Gone is their night
Filled with ceremonial rite.

Gone is their land
Once worked by strong hand.
Gone is their space
Driven off in disgrace.

Gone is their pride
Ancient rituals denied
Gone is their magic
Ancestral hopes turned tragic.

Left is their story
Past times of great glory.
Left is their yearning
For the Great Spirit's returning.
—*Patricia Phipps*

Nature

When nature blooms anew
When the sun is shining bright
When the sky is always blue
then reigns beauty and delight

When I walk through quiet trails
and gasp at all the wonder
mother nature never fails
I think and start to ponder.

Could I ever find
the nicest words to express
What goes through my heart and mind
It would not be good enough I guess

I wish I could write a song
of the trails so fine
I have traveled for so long
Where happiness was mine,

When nature blooms anew
Now I do understand
Why the sky must be so blue
and I must be a grain of sand.
—*Erwin Hentschel*

Reflections

The day is blackest
When there is no dawn,
When no light exists
At the tunnel's end.
Where am I?
I am trapped in this place
Where I now stand,
This darkness around me
Is too close, too tight,
It doesn't allow me to move.
I want to go on
But I don't know the way,
I know where I want to go
But not the path to take.
I need help to leave here,
Who can help me?
Only one can lead me from here
To where I should be,
But she likes me where I am.
—*Kurt G. Lessenthien*

Mom

Is there someone I can turn to
When there's no one else to care?
Is there someone who will listen
When my life is in despair?

When everyone's too busy
To pass a friendly word,
And the cry that I have uttered,
Not a soul has even heard.

When all my dreams are shattered,
And nothing goes as planned,
It's time to start all over
With someone else in command.

Yes, there is one who'll listen
When my face is wet with tears;
I just bring it all to Mom
And she will brush away my fears.

What sweet and silent statements
As I bare my very soul;
She will pick up all my pieces
And again will make me whole.
—*Tiffany Rosenfeld*

I Wonder

I wonder if David knew
when writing the psalm
a mother would find comfort
in those healing words,
a child know security
even in the dark,
a ray of hope found
for the husband who had lost his job.

I wonder if David knew
the depths of pain he experienced
would be felt throughout the ages,

I wonder...
  if David knew.
—*Deborah Budwig*

My Heart

My heart leaps out to you
when you are here or far away.
My love will always be true
to you.
Because my heart will always be
filled with joy all because of you.
My heart leaps up when I
behold a rainbow in the sky.
My heart will always be here
for you.
Through good times and bad
times I will always love you.
My heart is full of joy and
I owe it all to you.
　—LaKiay Monique Arevalo

I Saw A Woman

That night of the party
when you climbed from the pool
and lay glistening like liquid onyx
beneath the moon's crystal gaze

I saw a queen
bathing on the shore of a swollen Nile
cool, black, and beautiful
beneath a hot egyptian sky

I saw a woman
beating life into the earth's brown clay
with life that seeped
through blood on brown hands

I saw Billie Holiday
brewing blues hot enough
to melt the stoic's steel heart

And
I saw you
cool, black, and beautiful
beneath a hot memphis sky
　—Eric Lerez Sherley

Untitled

When I go away,
　When you hear our song,
When lonely in your bed you lay,
Or when we're not getting along…
Remember this letter
　and read it as you go along;
I know it's better-
　that is together we belong.

For as you are a part of me,
　I am a part of you.
Together we are one,
　but separate we are two.
Together we can get anything done…
　hand by hand - one by one.

Our love keeps us together
　and everyday it grows -
Stronger by the second…
　as everyone plainly knows.
In my heart we shall last forever
　and in my dreams we shall always be
together.
　—Christy Smith

Untitled

There is a place
Where the wind is soft
And a voice whistles as it blows.
A spirit?
. . . maybe.
A higher power from within, more likely.
A lake is nestled below the hill;
The water slaps the shore
As visions bounce off the walls of your
Thoughts.
It's pleasant there, serene, warm.
You're not alone.
The trees, rocks, and clouds
Envelope you
And seal you in place.
There is nowhere for you to go
But to sit upon the lap
Of the grassy mother that surrounds you.
It is safe.
　—Vikki Elfering

Untitled

Oh death, what's your sting?
Where the winds blows?
What is its end?
Great Immensity
What's your limit?
Beyond our countenance
No, everything has
barriers. Immortal!!
Only the truth of our words.
Temporal everything else.
Beyond thoughts or imaginations
The eternal supersede
The gifted, or talented
May be for awhile
but wisdom perdure
So, what is it to you?
　—Mauro Hernandez

To Know A Burn-Out

To feel only a spark
Where there once was a flame.
To feel only weariness
That excitement had claimed.

To feel trapped in a cage
When you used to run free.
To have sadness and sorrow
Replace joyful and happy.

To live in a world
Where you feel run down.
And lay there helpless,
Trampled on the ground.

To reach out a hand
And have it slapped away.
To try your hardest
Until your dying day.

To look back on what you've done
With the feeling you've failed.
To not care anymore:
DETERMINATION DERAILED!
　—Janine Mitchell

A Somber Occasion

At that meeting place
Where they gather and become numerous,
A somber occasion.
Their faces show no expression.
For they know their destination.
And, there is no struggle.
At that time,
It will be swift.
So that they can go home,
To a place
Where they shall find peace.
When they should fall,
To their death.
　—Scott Delcoco

Passing

There! Beside an old seedy ramp,
Whereon a thousand feet did tramp,
Lies youth. One who offers delight
and anchors searching eyes -on sight-
In witness of our ideal found.

Look! A slow stretching and turning
-Rich movements to one's whim- matching
Some known but fallen graved image
That calls forth that instant homage
In witness of our ideal found.

Alas! Continue and pass by
Before eyes, in meeting, do tie
Two souls—in love's gain—fulfilling.
Again, that long glance, eyes turning
From witness of our ideal found.

Woe! That in this hasty transit
Two hearts -so thoughtless of profit-
Would, in useless fear, never meet.
Thus passing, lost in foolish heat,
From witness of our ideal found
　—E. M. Wilson

Prayer

The Supreme Being is Supreme
Whether it, she or he
Be God, Allah, Deity, Lord
Jehovah or other.

And we as well as everything
Else in this universe
Owe our very existence
To this Supreme Being.

Let Us Pray
　—Harry W. Hague III

Grown-up Games

Games we play
　when we're young.
　　We grow fast,
　　we die faster
Games we play
　still as then.
　　We lose what
　　we knew when young.
Games we play
　aren't
　　always
　　won.
　—D. DeSha

Aids

A common mature disease
which lurks in my blood,
unknowingly for one year
My soul and heart
raged in anger
In years to come I will
die with my youth
I will die with Aids
My porcelain hands will break
My timeglass will tell
when I must be taken away
into another world
I am now a statue
I must do everything I want
before I die
When I die I must live
with the one who had
sculpted me.

—*Mary Anne Ocampo*

"If He Only Knew"

Mary Ann had a man
Which was very dumb
He tried to whistle
And jump rope but he
Could only hum

His parents told him that
He should treat Mary Ann
Nice but for he didn't
Know was very good advice

His mom told him in
Minnesota it was raining
And his dad told him, he
Needed a lot of training

Although his cousin told him
That it was going to rain he
Finally knew the meaning
Of a very tiny brain.

—*Alyssa Burton*

"Brother"

   The days seem longer
while I wait by the window
   to see him coming.
   The earth seems to
change colors rapidly,
as I look out the window.
   First a lush green,
   them a golden brown,
   red, and a bitter orange.
   The smell of autumn
is in the air, which means
I will see him coming soon.
   So I wait at the window.
   It's been forever since
   I've seen him,
though its only been weeks.
   His heart and soul
 uplifted me and made me proud.
So I will wait by the window until,
   I see him coming, Home...

—*Nicolle Lynch*

Newscast

Two sisters playing on the floor.
While the TV news is on.
Another country is in discord.
Our help they call upon.
A shooting at a basketball game.
Everywhere seems to be hostility.
A knifing at a local school.
The students feel their vulnerability.
Murder trial in its final day.
Another report of a felony.
The conflict never seems to stop.
Is there such a thing as harmony?
As the newscast continues.
The laughter from the children decrease.
If for no other reason.
For them we must find peace.

—*Donna Latvis*

Misty Memory

Raindrops falling, feather light,
Whispered passion in the night;
Jasmine scent on midnight air;
Clothes, tossed tousled on a chair.

Wind a-blowin', thunder crashing;
Billowed curtains, lightening flashing;
Raging seas, with flecks of foam;
A stifled cry, primordial moan.

Sweet or bitter, wrong or right -
Wings on fire, souls in flight;
Downy hair on dewy skin;
Storm without, peace within.

—*Tony Beckman*

Dance Of Hearts

A breeze soft as gold
Whispers,
Gently in your ear

A shadowy song stirs,
In the dark ashes
Of your lonely heart.

And like the sun on a raindrop,
A rainbow shines,
Through your trickling tears.

The dance of Hearts
Has begun.

—*Tammy Marie Mackey*

A True Human Being

I stand aside to consider,
Who and what I really am.
At this moment of looking,
Judgment slowly leaks away.
The pain I sometimes feel
Is like a dagger in my heart.
I take a breath and relax
Allowing energy to move freely.
Strength attracts more strength.
The knife is loosened; it is freed.
More unwanted, unnamed emotion escapes.
I consider forgiveness - mine and others
None is really necessary
I let all life flow
I step forward
To the making of a True Human Being.

—*Glenis Eagan*

Roy's Song/Work Of Art

The Lord, my God's an artist,
who does not use physical tools,
but love, and joy, and compassion,
not clay, or paints, or rules.

The Lord uses a model,
that He finds within our hearts,
to make for each a dream come true,
a wondrous work of art!

What did I do to be so blest,
That I could have had a part,
in the making of this little one?
God's greatest work of art!

The Lord, my God's a listener.
He's heard the prayers I've prayed.
I can feel the love He has for me
when I hold this child He made!

As I sit and watch you sleep,
I can see you're such a masterpiece!
The Lord above looked in my heart
and made for me, you, work of art!

—*Michelle Huffman*

"Playful Miss"

There was a little miss
Who had some fun like this.
She had a bouncing ball.
She tossed it to her doll.
She had a little box
In which she hid some blocks.
She had a flowered shirt.
She made a matching skirt.
She had a teddy bear.
She shaved off all his hair.
She had a favorite book.
She read it in a nook.
She had a toy bassoon
On which she played a tune.
She had a dancing frog.
They danced upon a log.
She had a small pink bed
On which to rest her head,
To dream of things to play
While night turned into day.

—*Rachel Tenney*

Like A Star In The Sky

Like a star in the sky
Who looks down on you.
At dawn, the world looks fresh and new.
A drop of dew in a rose
Can bring a sparkle to your eyes.
A bluebird flying high
Can bring a twinkle to your eyes.
At sunrise you can see the sun
Beaming through the trees.
And the sky is as blue
As a bluejay's wings.
The birds sing a song of love.
See the moonlight dancing on the sea.
I hear the winds softly calling me.

—*Jennifer Miller*

The Truth

If I had to choose
Who I was to spend
The rest of my life with
I would choose you.

If there were a place
That I could only be in
With one other person
I would take you there.

If my heart were aching
With a pain I couldn't describe
And I needed a shoulder to cry on
I would come to you.

If there were a time
When I had lost the will
To stay alive
I would need you to be my strength.

If my walls weren't so high
And so strongly built
My heart would tell the truth
That I love you.
—*Brandi Edwards*

Be Not Afraid

Why are we moving?
Who is following us?
Mommy, Daddy please answer!
"Be not afraid," said Mommy.

Why are we hiding?
Who are we hiding from?
Are we going to go outside soon?
"Be not afraid," said Mommy.

You look sick, Mommy.
Are you going to be okay?
You look kind of pale.
"Be not afraid," said Mommy.

Why is everyone so happy?
Are we leaving this room soon?
Where did they put Mommy?
"Be not afraid," said Daddy.
—*Sylvia Duszak*

Someone

It seems I'm always attracted to those,
Who need a helping hand,
They need someone to lean on,
Or to listen and understand,
Someone to tell them it's O.K.,
And to stay right by their side,
And to find a key to help unlock,
The feelings that they hide,
But they all seem to leave me behind,
When their lives are fresh and new,
Doesn't someone out there know,
That I need someone too?
—*Katie Boice*

They Come To Me

They come to me
Who want to know
When you're free
And where you go

They come to me
Who feel your spell
As they can see
I know you well

They come to me
Who do with you
What helplessly
I long to do

They come to me
Who know that I
Eternally
Must just stand by.
—*Betty Lapham*

Spirits

Where they go
Who would know
To heaven, maybe
Or across the sea
To the sun
Or to the moon
To the bottom
Of a beautiful lagoon

Today we weep
And see the streaks
Of tears running
Down our cheeks
For we pray
That God will care
To give the love
That we share
To the people
Who have gone away
That we'll catch up with
Some other day
—*Kelly Ross*

Glass Pontiac

I have a glass Pontiac on my car
Whom without I could not go far.
He glows in the dark
He waits when I park
On my hood he's a shining star.

When approaching an intersection
I seldom have time for reflection.
But Pontiac will know
Which way I should go
And I follow without exception.

But in looking at the past
In spite of our traveling so fast.
We show no feelings
In our everyday dealings
Living each day as if it's our last.

So I can't keep the doubt from growing
And I'm asking just for the knowing,
Answer me if you can
Brown Glass Indian Man
Just where in the hell are we going?
—*L. Steven Anderson*

Psychic Offender

Who's put these voice around me?
Who's living next to hell?
Who's trying to make perfect crime?
Who's sung about royalty?
Who talked about demon on L.A. Times?
Who sung it's a pressure drop?
Who lay down to the lawn?
Who can explain about this disgrace?

You're psychic offender
You keep watching my brain
You're psychic offender
You break my rights of privacy
You're psychic offender
You're sucking my copyright
You've psychic offender
You push people to insane

Who's gonna believe your one way system?
Turn your way for your bow
Why don't you stop your disturbing
I got call trace service now
—*Kenji Yanagida*

The Best Gift Ever...

Would be to see my dad once more,
Why did my mom leave him for,
He was a nice guy,
And my mom just said bye,
It just wasn't fair,
Cause my father did care,
He cared for mom and me,
His love everyone could see,
If I could find my dad,
Oh I would be so glad,
For a gift I wouldn't want money,
Not even a clown to be funny,
All I want is to see my dad again,
Is that a bad sin!
—*Anita Sorola*

Why

The question I want to ask is why,
Why does he make me cry?
He can be so sweet,
He makes my life complete.

Why does he hurt me like he does?
Is it just because
he likes to be a jerk to me
and make me have a lot of jealousy?

When he holds me tight
my problems are so slight.
Why does he make me feel so special
like I'm in heaven being an angel?

I couldn't live without him
my life would be so dim.
Why do I care for him so
and how do I let him know?
—*Jennifer Bradshaw*

Remembering

Singing mirth travels on
Winds, of time.
Forming shadows:
Pictures of days
As beautiful now, as then.
But with equal speed
Upon these gails,
Travel
Feelings of loss
Wrapped within pain and sorrow,
Threatening an engulfing loneliness.
Yet; as the breeze
Blows by
And we are, caught
As a memory.
The loss becomes
The joy—of remembering.
—*Brian Stewart*

Youth

As the beauty of the day
  with bright promise
Begins,
And then, surely, slowly
Becomes the fabric of time,
So youth,
  in light, fragile essence
Turns and turns, again and again
To view itself closely,
In intimate reverence,
When suddenly,
  as if by magic,
The images swiftly fades,
Leaving only deep yearnings
With mirrored memories
  of youth's presence,
And fragments of dreams
  for that spring
Of fleeting, sweet time.
—*Louise Salzano Ogg*

What Is Life?

Life is a challenge to live and Survive
With hardships throughout which one
  cannot hide
But hardships can help and strengthen
  the will
And give hope from such power to
live as one feels.
—*Nancy Reitano McNeil*

A Mystic Night

The moon shining down,
With its dim, eerie light.
Its pale shadow on the ground,
Itself in the middle of flight.

The stars high up above,
Twinkling with deep emotions.
Broken heart, or powerful love,
Travelling over oceans.

A forlorn traveller journeys on,
Enjoying the sounds and sights,
Feeling a strange, karmic bond,
With that beautiful, mysterious night.
—*Serena Meng*

Christmas

Christmas is a lovely season
With lots of reasons.
It is the time of the year
When people are sincere.
Each one wants to find a way
To make everyone happy everyday.
They have little offerings
To express their thanksgiving.
Giving love on Christmas day
Is sunshine for a gloomy day.
Giving everyone kindness
Makes one live in peacefulness.
—*Madonna Grace C. Follosco*

Truth

  Aspirations explode
  with no signs of humility,
  but drown in seasons gone by
fading through what tomorrow seems.

  They lie haunting
  every tear-filled regret,
breathing the soft, subtle sounds
  of yesterdays forgotten dreams.

Desperate hopes lost along the way
  leave us twisting and clawing,
  for what was tangible
  in the imagination of youth.

  Money drives the passions
  turning ashes into dust,
  dream of the heroin eyes
and the telling of the truth.
—*Scott Arntson*

The Innocent

Stubby fingers struggling
With shoe laces
Determined head bent over—
A skullcap of curls
Soft as corn silk,

Pale as fresh squash,
Falling into two blue stars
In a pale ivory sky
Line tiny mirrors
Oozing innocence

A dim reflection
Of our naivete, long
Lost, forfeited for enlightenment,
The smallest glimpse
Or inkling, a slow

Suicide of the soul
An untrodden pebble
My newfangled peanut
Cracked open and exposed
Your heart unearthed and weathered
—*Karen L. Eld*

Life

  A new born baby
with soft, silky skin....
  A tiny tot
with a diaper pin...
  A small child
with one step at a time...
  A fast growing kid
with big goals to climb....
  A teenager
with a set of car keys....
  A young adult
with parents to please....
  An adult
with college out of the way...
  And now a bride
with loving vows to say....
  A parent soon-to-be
with a warm, soft, new born baby....
—*Ami Cooper*

The Cloud Bird

Wings spread out across the sky,
With sparkling blue eyes,
It's nest has three white eggs,
That stick out like bright little pegs.
As it flies through the sky
people stop, people stare
At the lovely young birds that's fling there.
When the flowers bloom
And the cars go vroom vroom
the Lovely young bird,
Will soar across the sky,
Then with a blasting noise,
That made peoples lives flash before
  their eyes,
The Lovely young bird,
That made the flowers bloom,
And the cars go vroom vroom,
Died.
—*Jaclyn Stewart*

Untitled

You beat her with such fury
  with such fury
    She
had no chance of being
  even after
You were dead
  for years
You reach up from
  the grave
and choke
  the very life
out of her.
—*Deborah J. Campbell*

Mothers

Mothers are a special gift;
With their angel arms they lift.
Their voices are a self-made choir:
With three words they do inspire.

Often when we reminisce
We forget the loving kiss
That they bestowed upon us all
When we were young and couldn't crawl.

Now is here to just forgive;
It's what we need to merely live.
It's difficult - oh yes - it's hard,
But we must remember that backyard!

—*Donna Marquart*

Loving Thoughts Of You

There is never a warm spring day
with tiny birds of grew in the trees
   that I don't think of you.
There is never a summer day with
soft blue skies and children at play
   that I don't think of you.
There is never an autumn day
with scarlet and yellow leaves
gently drifting by
   that I don't think of you.
There is never a bright sunny winter
day - after a new fallen snow
   that I don't think of you.
There is never a beautiful rainbow—
in a clearing sky, or a quiet star - lit
night - when the heavens seems so bright
   that I don't think of you.

—*Della M. Seguin*

Capricious Love

Love is a changing thing
with unique characteristics and ways.
For it either grows and expands in size
or it deteriorates and decays.

So nurture and develop it
with your every single breath.
Or just sit by and watch it die -
a slow but deliberate death.

—*Ferna Mills*

Madonna Sonnet

Blonde ambition.
Woman on a mission.
Who is this Madonna?
Asking do you wanna.
She sits atop
the chart called pop.
Why is she there?
Blonde hair,

With a business mind
of the cunning kind.
Exposing flesh.
Tabloid mess.
She knows so well.
Sex will sell.

—*Paul A. Costello*

Gone

I think of you day and night
   wondering why this disaster had to
happen,
and how I could've prevented it
   Sometimes and feel as if it were all
my fault,
but you said it wasn't
   I don't see why we couldn't have
worked things out
   we always did
   no matter how bad it got
   we always stuck together,
and now you're gone....forever

—*Jen L. Bouthillette*

Satire On The American Way

Bug eyed John
Working on the lawn.
Bug eyed John
Beginning at dawn.
Working up a sweat
Just getting all wet
Bug eyed John
Working on the lawn
Do the front first
Build up a thirst
Bug eyed John
Working on the lawn
Head for the rear
Buy yourself a beer
Bug eyed John
Working on the lawn.

—*Rosa Gonzalez Hammond*

Rain Pour Down On Me

You are my fears
Worthy of my tears
Thunder break me
I want so much for a crying night
But I don't cry, for you're not worth it
Why did you lie
How could you hurt me so much
You broke me like the thunder did
It shattered me like glass
The rain pours its soul for me
Who do I hate more, you or me?
I can't decide
Whoa! It's a lonely day
Shall I laugh, or no, shall I cry?
My love is only but so strong
What a shame
I guess it's me to blame
Damn! I wish it would rain.

—*Alexis Springer*

Come Back

Where is everyone;
Where'd they go?
They left me here,
here on my own.
I'm looking for an answer
Searching for a clue.
Looking everywhere
looking for you.
Where is everyone...
... where are you?

—*Ronald J. Newman*

What Do I Write

What do I write to someone so
wondrous, so mysterious
Someone who is like clouds in my mind
Glorious clouds
Constantly changing
forever floating through the sky

Like the wind
you drift endlessly through my being
Touching my senses, so warm and gentle
Tickling my spirit and worrying my heart
Taking me on a dream ride
through a world of paradise
a world of silver, shimmering light.

—*Rebecca Leger Pospisil*

Guardian Spectrum

Grasp the heavens.
Wrench the stars.
Blend the azure of lakes
With the vermilion of dusk,
and gold of the sun.
Paint them in the crystal
cool of the air.
Inhale the vapor.
Let it be yours forever,
a rainbow shield from your fears.

—*Joseph L. Perlow*

Especially For Me

Is there a star that shines for me?
Yea, I hope it's so.
Is there a song to be sung for me?
How I'd like to know.

Let me see the blue sky.
Don't let living pass me by.
Let me find my pot of gold
   at the end of my rainbow.

Where, oh where are all my dreams?
They have all gone astray.
Leaving me with deep, dark thoughts
   as I travel life's highway.

Looking back over my life.
Where did I go wrong?
That all my phases of living
   can all be summed up in one song?

Walking down life's dreary lane.
Sun shine on me.
Send away my darkest clouds.
Let me feel free!

—*Linda Crawford*

On Such A Dark Night

Homeless you might be,
Yet you are free.
On such a dark night,
One cannot see.
Not one light,
Your are in fright,
On such a dark night.

On such a dark night,
I might add,
You will be sad.
Of all the things you've had,
You will surely miss,
The home you once had.

—*Monica George*

Ukiyo-e

My Hana-ogi
You are back
You blue kimono..carelessly
Hair in disarray
Nostrils flared
Perfect teeth clench a napkin
Your neck-nape exposed
Obi undone
I've been undone
Undone till your return
You've been with another
I've been with no other
Thought of no other;
Divine Geisha
In your floating world...
...your floating world.
—*Toby Rappolt*

The Dancer

Like a wild flower
You bend ever so
Gently, as if touched
By the wind.

Like a bird
You glide through
The air, propelled
Toward heaven.

Like a falling leaf
You float in a
Circle to embrace
The earth.
—*Paula Breitling*

To Susan

Twenty years ago today,
 you came into our lives
and all the love and joy to come
 was sparkling in your eyes.

You made our twosome, threesome
 and multiplied the pleasure,
for Susan, you have made our lives
 much fuller, without measure.

With you, we've learned to laugh and cry
 for all are part of life.
And our rainbows only come from clouds
 and happiness from strife.

Our little girl's a woman now
 and grasping life in hand.
The world is yours to take and hold,
 with courage, take a stand.

A daughter is a precious thing
 so pink and cute and small,
but a daughter, who's a woman,
 is the greatest joy of all.
—*June H. Childs*

"Scarlet Pearls"

Sadness has its own fruit
It's like pomegranates
Have you looked inside?
Don't you see scarlet
Tear drops enclosing
Each white pearl?
—*Avideh Shashaani*

To Death

You can come with your blackness
You can come with your feeble fear

You can take away my breath
that I hold oh so dear

You can chop up my body
and feed it to your beasts

You can drag away my vision
as you pluck out my eyes

But if that's all you can do
you're wasting your might

For I have traveled in your darkness
which turned into light.
—*M. James Shover*

Goin' Round The Hall

You can have your Trooping Colors
You can have a fancy ball
But the big thrill for a Mummer
Is "Goin' Round The Hall."

Billy Penn looks down upon us
Doe he wonder 'bout it all
For the big thrill for the Shooter
Is "Goin Round The Hall."

We've been doing it for years now
We hope we never stall
For what would New Year's day be like
Without "Goin Round The Hall."

Wouldn't it be wonderful
To just send out the call
And have the whole world join us
In "Goin Round The Hall."
—*Bill Conners*

How Peace Begins

I don't know you
You don't know me
Both are suspicious as can be.

I see you
You see me
Both are curious as can be.

I speak to you
You speak to me
Both are surprised as can be.

I like you
You like me
Both become friendly as can be.

I and you
Both become WE
Can't the world like we be?
—*Sharon J. Hulton*

A Beach

Waves roll in,
Waves roll out,
One lonely bird,
One lonely crab,
Only one sunset,
Only one dawn,
Leave it alone,
And then it's
All gone.
—*Shawna Weber*

Don't Be Scared To Tell

You feel like a jerk,
You feel it's all your fault,
You feel like you are trash
But that's not true at all.

He was the one who started.
You were the one he raped.
What you don't know is
Your friends are there all times,
Your parents soon will know.
But they'll be at your side
Then why don't you tell them?

He is the one to blame, then
You'll feel much better, then
you'll feel more sane.
—*Suset L. Laboy Perez*

The Blue Moon Of Amato Farm

Over my shoulder
you follow me.
Each night
we meander the
narrow snake path.
Tunnels of weeping
brittle, boughs drape.
Eyes gaze from
ice-laced windows,
longingly bask your
gray blue fervor
in search of approval.
Two white peaked doe
spring snowy antics.
Dormant forest hideaways
await.
Their spry silhouettes
vanish.
Curtains shadow my
Blue Amato Moon.
—*Susan Miccile*

Tears From A Rose

You know I can't cry
You know I can't complain
You know I have the urge to live
But I'd rather die in vain

Don't you ever cry for me
Don't you ever whine
Just worry about yourself girl
I'll be doing fine

And as I stop, turn and wonder
My eyes slowly close.
There drip my red eye's bleeding
With tears from a rose.
—*Colleen Sheehan*

"Depression"

One more day!
What can I say?
What can I do?
Something must be new.
Something of a challenge.
To bring my life to a balance.
Listen for the phone to ring
Talk to someone, news to bring
God, am I slipping away?
Must I fight for another day
To bring my mind to say
Do something useful today.
—*Rosalie Brand*

Untitled

You told me you'd never leave
You told me love was forever
Especially ours.
How much you cared for me,
how much you loved me,
how many times you held me
and kissed away my tears.
All those years
time spent in heaven.
Why did it have to end?
Why did it have to happen?
Why did you go?
I never made you.
I loved you and will love you
until the day I die
I wish I could talk to you
and tell you how much
I miss you and need you by my side
But...how do I talk to a ghost?
—*Elizabeth S. Carrington*

Happy Birthday

Happy birthday, my love,
You would have been seventy-five today.
I've really missed you,
Since you went away.
I know what God did, was for the best,
But I've really been lonely,
Since you were laid to rest.
God has restored my health,
And He's given me the best of care.
He provided me with the best doctors
I'd ever hope to find anywhere.
Happy Birthday, my love,
Today will always be a special day,
And you will always be remembered,
In a very special way.
So my love, rest in peace,
Enjoy your mansion above.
You will never be forgotten.
For you'll always be my love.
—*Bessie L. Cockfield*

The Longing

Your body shakes,
Your body aches,
When the longing is so near.

What you want.
What you need.
Which rules do you fear?

A starlight night.
Candlelight.
The moon
  a silver sliver.
Freedom calls.
A waterfall.
So warm
  it makes you shiver.

What you need.
What you want.
Which rules will you hear?

Your body aches,
Your body shakes,
And the longing is so dear.
—*Trey Jones*

"Amanda"

The Clock you gave me
Your Dad hung it on the wall
Each time I look up it remind of you
With each passing moment
For the time we have together
For the talks we had
For the times I went to far
For the time I should have been silent
For the time I didn't want to let go
For the mother, your friend

Time goes on the same as us
The clock hangs on the wall
Your dad placed it there
Each time I look up it remind
me of you.
—*Hazel M. McKenzie*

The Apple Tree

Do you see that apple tree?
Your grandfather planted it
when I was three.
When I was just a boy of 10
I'd climb to the top
of that old tree
to see what I could see.
As years went by
I fell in love
and carved initials in a heart
telling you mother
we'd never part.
It's there on that old tree.
But all of that was a long time ago.
And now my son, since you are three,
it's time to plant your apple tree.
—*Pamela Mae Dieffenbacher*

Sensitive Leaf

Oh sleeping one,
Your mouth and paint;
And the flower grows
Between the trash-
Whenever it happens to rain.

I'm so tired
Of watching you there,
Ringed finger and pain;
And the flower grows
Between the trash-
Whenever it happens to rain.

So messed up
And no one knew,
Yet searching yes in vain;
And the flower still grows
Between the trash—
Whenever it happens to rain.
—*Jason Baker*

A.I.D.S.

Life is so confusing
when you know your losing
the battle of the disease
that has brought you to your knees.
There is no cure
so you have to endure
the unbearable pain
that has ended the chain
of your life.
—*Amanda Hughes*

As You Are

Come to me as you are

Fill me what you were
  your past, your histories
  So that I may appreciate
    all you've become

Reveal to me what you will be
  your hopes, your dreams
  In order that I may admire
    all you achieve

As you come to me
  so shall I to you
Come without yield
  or without promise
Yet, never come with falseness
  Come with truth, or not at all

Come to me, as you are
  so that I may rejoice
    in all that is
    You
—*Char M. Gray*

The Hope Of A Rainbow

I know that you have lost
  your precious baby child.
And I know right now your hurting
  you will for quite awhile.
Although I see you suffering
  there's nothing I can do.
Even though he does not show it
  your husband's hurting too.
I cannot take your pain
  and make it disappear
But I will be there for you
  right down to the last tear.
So do not be afraid
  of letting your pain show.
For after every rainstorm
  there's the hope of a rainbow.
—*Clara Kopplinger*

A Dream Come True

Every night when I'm in my deep-sleep
  Your the first thing on my mind
  I'd always put your ahead and
    never behind.

  I'd often wonder should I
    tell you how I'm feeling?
    Putting my heart in danger
      of never healing?

    I've finally decided
    I don't want to
      Stay divided
  I'm tired of sitting in the blue
  I want to make us a dream come true.
—*Billie Burns*

(God Is So Wonderful)

God is love
God is sweet
God is awfully neat
I love God
You can too;
Believe it it's true.
—*Jennifer Stacey*

"The Fear"

You run, you hide
When you turn around it is there
When you dream it is there
When you think it is there
It is everywhere
You cannot run, you cannot hide
Is it your friend
Is it your enemy
The fear of your life
The fear of death
—*Kristen Shipley*

'I Love You Because. . .'

I like you because. . .
    You're faithful and caring
I like you because. . .
    You're fun and you're daring
I like you because. . .
    You're sweet and you're kind
I like you because. . .
    You're cute and you're mine
I like you because. . .
    I know your love's true
I love you because. . .
    Just cause you're you
—*Jaime Chryst*

Only You

Roses are red,
Violets are blue
When I see a smile
I think of you.
when I hear laughter
I dream of you,
If only I could be with you.
—*Blverno Massenburg*

Like Children

We acted like stupid children
fumbling in the dark
on the playground
we played
and left it there
Alone
and never spoke of it again.
—*Alicia Porter*

Untitled

Uninspired, you wait,
  Uninterested, you walk.
    Undaunted you run.
      Searching, hoping to find....
        that one saving refuge....
        unable to cry.
Unrequited, you stop.
  Unwanted you leave.
    Unloved, unloving you die.
—*H. Louise Murphy*

Forget Me Not

    Your calls are scarce
    Your visits are seldom
Your caring words are never heard
    Your touch is absent

Who's voice do you long to hear?
Who's eyes do you long to see?
Who's ear do you whisper into?
Who's embrace do you long to feel?
    Who do you care for now?

Our time together has long since pass
Our moments together have come and gone

    Who is she now?

    Does she care for you?

    Do you care for her?

    Forget Me Not
—*Elizabeth Zuniga*

Retirement

Through all the years you worked so hard
your day has finally come,
Here's hoping that you find life's joys
as easy as they come
—*Ronald W. Casner*

I Will Remember You

I remember that summer day
When you walked away
I remember that glorious smile
When we walked that mile
Now I am left with the
Remembrance of you and me
And how it use to be.
I wish I was at the mall
Where we use to have a ball
I wanna call to say Hi.
But I am a little too shy.
—*Tammy*

Soar Higher

Soar higher, higher, kite,
Until you touch the clouds,
Wind fills you with breath
Bold and brash,
Beautiful and swift,
You flip and dive, rise and fall,
Seemingly your own creature
Having a mind and will
Tugging and pulling,
Seeking freedom
Wanting to fly far and wide
Knowing no care or fear
Soar higher, higher, kite!
—*Sarah Lewis*

Seasons

  Spring is warm
When the bees start to swarm

  Summer is hot
like a boiling pot

  Fall is cool
it's a good time to start school

  Winter is cold
with snow by the load
—*Starr Ryder*

Solitude

I write what I write
because I have nothing to say.
Words escape my mind
and flow restless and free.

But I cannot capture them on paper
to express what I feel.
So, instead, I remain quiet.
And my paper remains blank.
—*Julianne Garling*

My Favorite Person

You're my favorite person
Your jokes amuse me
They come into my mind at night
and call you back
from daytime fun.
—*Sarah Perry*

Biographies of Poets

ABRAMS, LALAGE
[pen.] LaLage Abrams; [b.] April 8, 1924, Rutherford County, NC; [ed.] Small Business Administration, Nursing, Social Work, and presently a writing course; [occ.] Retiree; [memb.] Volunteer Council Board, Raleigh NC; Missionary Circle President, New Bethel, Independent Church, Forest City NC; [hon.] NRI Writing Course, Washington, DC; LaBaugh Teacher for Ilirates, Bronx, NY; [oth. writ.] I did lots of writing during my studies, but did not persue it, due to my age upon retirement, I could only see writing for the rest of my life; [pers.] Writing is my love for people. Although I took courses in other fields, writing captured my imagination after retiring. [a.] Forest City, NC 28043.

ACE, KRISTIN LEE
[b.] March 13, 1983, East Stroudsburg, PA; [p.] Douglas and Mary Ace; [ed.] Arlington Heights Elementary; [oth. writ.] Poem published in the 1993 Anthology of Poetry by Young Americans; [pers.] I try to write about the joys of being a child of God. I have been influenced by my father's poetry and my teacher Miss Kantners, my Mom and my Grammy's encouragement. [a.] Stroudsburg, PA.

ACKER, LOUIS L.
[b.] July 1, 1945, San Diego, California; [p.] Mr. and Mrs. W.D. Acker, Jr.; [m.] Dr. Allie G. Funk, May 21, 1977; [ch.] Jimmy (15), Peter (12), and Brin (9); [ed.] BS Geology, Clemson University, MS Geology University of N.C., Chapel Hill; [occ.] Geological consultant, farmer; [memb.] Vestryman St. Luke's Episcopal Church, Boone, NC; [oth. writ.] A few geological journal articles and maps; [pers.] Began writing poetry in the Fall of 1992. An outdoor life has given me a waelth of natural imagery and an appreciation for the spirituality of nature. Also I love the language. [a.] Creston, NC 28615.

ACKLEN, CHARLES W.
[pen.] Bryan Cody; [b.] September 2, 1949, Shrevepoert, LA; [p.] Oscar and Juanita Acklen; [m.] Wanda Procell, May 26, 1988; [ch.] Corinda Acklen, Charlsie Bryan and Adam Jones; [ed.] Woodlawn High School 1 year at LSU-Shreveport; [occ.] Maintenance at U.S. Post Office; [oth. writ.] "Soul on Fire" a song/poem written by me, for my daughter, Corinda; [pers.] I write from the heart, the way I feel, at the time I write. [a.] Shreveport, LA 71118.

ADAMS, ANNIE M.
[b.] November 2, 1958, Amory, MS; [p.] L.J. Cox (deceased), Nina Kay Knight Cox Morrison and Lewis Morrison; [ch.] Alonnah, Gail, Christopher Lee, Brian Edward; [ed.] Smithville High, Itawamba Junior College; [occ.] Word Processing Operator, Nationwide Insurance Company; [memb.] United Way, Civic Action Program, PTA, Nationwide Activities; [hon.] Citizenship Award, Honor Club, Business Education Award, Student Council Award, Beta Club, Future Business Leaders of America; [oth. writ.] Personal/work use only; [pers.] My writings come from within the heart and are a reflection of my life from infancy to present day. [a.] Horn Lake, MS.

ADAMS, CATHERINE
[b] October 8, 1957, Peekskill, NY; [p.] Mr. and Mrs. James P. Miller; [m.] Paul S. Revis (fiance', May 15, 1994); [ed.] Graduated from Walter Panas High School, 1975. Presently attending Dutchess Community College; [occ.] Operator NY Telephone Company; [hon.] 1993 Editor's Choice award, National Library of Poetry for "Letting Go Isn't Easy"; [oth. writ.] "Letting Go Isn't Easy", "The Winds of Change", and "Miles of Time", are poems of mine that have been published; [pers.] "Miles of Time" is dedicated to all of the angels who were lost to muscular dystrophy especially my brother, Jimmy. I pray that someday soon they wont ever have to "walk alone" ever again, only then can we share the "Mile of Time" together. [a.] Putnam Valley, NY.

ADAMS, DEBRA
[pers.] I dedicate my poem to all those traveling to the Land of Light in the pursuit of wholeness and to all the children, known abd unknown, residing within each of us, who give us the hope and courage necessary to make that journey possible. [a.] Sylvia, NC 28779.

ADAMS, KATHLEEN
[pen.] Kat; [b.] November 8, 1958, Richlands, VA; [p.] Mr. and Mrs. Robert Estel and Maudie Johnson; [m.] Ralph Edward, June 12, 1976; [ch.] James (15), Jesse (13), Ralph (10) and Mary (8); [ed.] Quit eleventh grade, thinking about finishing; [occ.] Mother and Housewife; [memb.] Volunteer work, sometimes help out in school; [hon.] Just a few on poems; [oth. writ.] Some poems were published through Eddie Lou Cole; [pers.] I write my poems from other peoples feelings and things other people does. Or things I feel and do in my life. [a.] Raysal, WV.

ADAMS, LYNN
[b.] April 9, 1946, New Westminister, B.C., CAN; [p.] Cliff and Laurette Adams; [m.] 1962, now separated; [ch.] Teresa GAil, Carol-Lee and Patricia Joanne; [ed.] Grade 10; [occ.] Homemaker/Pt. Store Clerk/Salesperson; [oth. writ.] All of my previous writings have been written for a specific person and/or occassion - i.e. A Friend's 50th Wedding Anniversary, A Death, Birth, Wedding, etc., so wach poem is very personally thought out. [a.] La Corey, Alta, CAN.

ADEY, BRYAN
[b.] December 20, 1972, Berwick, Nova Scotia; [p.] Roy and Karlyne Adey; [ed.] Middleton Regioinal High 1990, Acadia University, Diploma Applied Science, Technical University of Noval Scotia (TUNS); [occ.] At present a student entering 4th year for completion of Bachelor of Engineering 1995; [hon.] Lieutenant Governor's Medal, HS, NSTU Scholarship, IODE Bursery; Physics and Math awards; Bruce and Dorothy Rosetti Scholarship, TUNS; Sexton Scholar, TUNS; [oth. writ.] Many poems, nothing published. [a.] Middleton, NS Canada B0S 1P0.

ADKINS, LILLY M.
[b.] July 17, 1961, Paintsville, KY; [p.] Sheridan and Evelyn Maynard; [m.] Ronald L., May 30, 1980; [ch.] Ronald Lee Adkins II and Amy Christina Adkins; [ed.] Sheldon Clark High, Sheldon Clark Vocational School (Business course); [occ.] Housewife, striving to become a writer; [memb.] Previously-P.T.S.A., 2nd Vice President for Solomon Elementary; [hon.] Received letter of acknowledgement from Post Commander for Volunteer work; [oth. writ.] A few things for PTSA, but this was the first for me. I haven't tried to get any of my poetry published before. I have three poems in this publication; [pers.] To be published by a company of such prestige is a life-long dream come true. I have always wanted to be a writer. [a.] Lovely, KY.

ADKINS, RONALD L.
[b.] March 31, 1962, Paris, KY; [p.] Marcella and Stanley Barker; [m.] Lilly M., May 30, 1980; [ch.] Ronald L. Adkins II and Amy Christina Adkins; [ed.] Sheldon Clark High and Vocational, Job Corp, Misc. Military Schools, Honolulu Community College; [occ.] Brakerman for Norfolk and Southern Railroad; [memb.] B.R. and C.F., Military Veteran; [hon.] Misc. Military awards and Decorations, Honorable Discharge; [oth. writ.] I am currently trying to get my first book published. This poem is what I hope will be the first of many publications; [pers.] You are your own best friend so be yourself and don't try to please other people by being something you're not. [a.] Lovely, KY.

ADOLF, KATHLEEN W.
[pen.] Catharina Whilhelmena; [b.] July 21, 1913, The Netherlands; [p.] Maja and Jan Brielsman; [m.] Louis George, February 16, 1946; [ch.] Charlesn (43) and Louis (51); [ed.] High school - business college; [occ.] Retired; [memb.] Republican Presidential Task Force - 9 years, Concerned Women for America - 3 years still active; [hon.] Medal of merit (from George Bush) and Golden Poet - three merit awards; [oth. writ.] God Save America, Finding Our God-given potential we all have the same human needs; [pers.] I am not a career minded poet - I just see a great need for this kind of poetry and I want to share it with humanity. [a.] St. Charles, MO.

AGUIHON, BIENVENIDO G.
[pen.] Ben-G, January 18, 1947; [b.] Bacolod City, Philippines; [p.] Maximiano and Maria Aguihon; [ed.] Edna D., January 17, 1970; [ch.] Khasmir Anthony, Ma. Theresa, Marc Kevin; [ed.] St. Joseph's High School, La Salle College; [occ.] Security Officer, Arco Plaza (LA); [memb.] Knights of Columbus, La Salle Bacolod Alumni Association; [hon.] Dean's Honor List, La Salle Bacolod Scholar; [oth. writ.] Various poems and articles published in Comtrust Events and BPI Banco News; [pers.] Love for mother nature is love for life. [a.] Los Angeles, CA.

AKERMAN, ANNETTE
[b.] September 27, 1944, The Dalles, Oregon; [p.] Frank and Artilee Absil; [m.] Divorced; [ch.] Yvonne, Jill, Patricia, Sheila, Irene, Sven, Jr.; [ed.] AA Funeral Service; [occ.] Entrepreneur - Waterobics with Annette; [memb.] National Authors Registry International Society of Author and Artists; [oth. writ.] The Eighth Day - non-fiction short stories, several poems, gospel, album of songs written and performed by myself; [pers.] My writing is done for the education. Fulfillment and enjoyment of people everywhere. I strive to make others think, to know themselves better, and to share themselves with me. I like to think my writing helps further that goal. [a.] Dallas, TX.

AKERS, MICHELLE ELIZABETH
[pen.] Michelle; [b.] August 21, 1977, San Diego; [p.] Linda and David Akers; [ed.] Continuing high school at the University of San Diego High School; [oth. writ.] Several poems published in various zines. [a.] San Diego, CA 92124.

AKERS, ZACHARY D.
[pen.] Zach Akers; [b.] December 10, 1982; [b.] Lithia Springs, GA; [p.] Robert L. and Beverly J. Akers; [ed.] 4th grade; [memb.] Douglas County Soccer Association, First Baptist Church, Lithia Springs Karate Club, Church Choir-Royal Ambassadors; [hon.] Program Challenge for Gifted Students. [a.] Lithia Springs, GA 30057.

ALBANO, ANTHONY J. III
[b.] June 16, 1967, Oklahoma City, OK; [p.] Sue C. and Anthony J. Albano, Jr.; [ed.] Jones' High School, Jones, OK and University of Central OK - Edmund, OK; [occ.] Customer Service Rep for WW Grainger, Inc. [a.] Oklahoma City, OK.

ALBERT, LEROY
[b.] October 4, 1922, Baltimore, MD; [p.] Henry and Anna Albert; [m.] Nellie, August 10, 1946; [ch.] Kenneth and Morel Albert; [ed.] Patterson High (Baltimore, MD) special electrical courses, (U.S. Navy) Railroad Telegraph School; [occ.] Machine Operator, Hughe's Tool Co. (retired); [memb.] Masonic Order, Lifetime membership; [hon.] "Poet of the Month", "People Plus", semi finalist in last year's "The National Library of Poetry" contest; [oth. writ.] First poem published by Ship's Mag. (U.S. Navy) 1944. Twenty-five poems published by "The Old Houston Press" 1960s, One poem - If the Flag Could Speak, Pub. by "People Plus" two by "The National Library of Poetry"; [pers.] May all of the names listed in this anthology add greatly to the sparce information regarding future genealogical research. [a.] Pasadena, TX 77502.

ALBERT, RUDIGER
[pen.] Blanford George Ontario; [b.] Oct. 8, 1958, Stade; [p.] Friedrich and Paula Albert; [ed.] Athenaeum Stade University of Hamburg (Literature); [occ.] Freelancer (The Buccaneer of the Seven Seas); [oth. writ.] Several (see previous release); [pers.] (See previous release). [a.] Germany.

ALBINS, HAZELL R.
[b.] Waterford, PA; [p.] Louisa & Fred Rose; [m.] Harry, January 24,1945; [ch.] Geraldine, James and Richard; [ed.] HIgh school and two years college; [occ.] Retired widow; [oth. writ.] Just ditties to my grandchildren; [pers.] My poems tells it well. [a.] Noel, MO.

ALBRECHT, JILL R.
[b.] November 21, 1974; [p.] Edward and Hedy Albrecht; [ed.] Mennonite Collegiate Institute, University of Manitoba; Winnipeg, Manitoba.

ALCORN, JAMES D.
[b.] December 9, 1941, Liberty, Indiana; [p.] Herman and RomaLee Alcorn; [m.] Karen L., November 24, 1962; [ch.] Veronica Lee and Christopher Allen; [ed.] Short High School; [occ.] Sprint/United Telephone Technician; [memb.] Deacon at First Baptist Church in New Paris, OH; [oth. writ.] Other poems published in "A Joyful Noise" by Spiritual Quest Publishing Co.; [pers.] Because of my faith in God and my love for country, most of my poems are spiritually influenced. I try to put into words how I feel inside. [a.] New Paris, OH 45347.

ALDEN, ANNA LEE
[b.] June 5, 1982, Point Pleasant Hsp., NJ; [p.] Kathleen and James Alden; [ed.] Elementary school-Spring Lake Heights; [memb.] Chorus in Church Townplays, cheerleading group; [hon.] Cheerleading and softball and school trophies and awards, understanding to Marta production of "Sound of Music" high school play; [oth. writ.] Other poems published in local newspaper, "The Herald"; [pers.] All the words in my poetry are of positive free lings, and that's the way. I try to live my life. [a.] Spring Lake Heights, NJ.

ALDRIDGE, SARA
[b.] December 5, 1979, Warren, MI; [p.] William and Gail Aldridge; [ed.] Completed 7th grade going in 8th grade; [occ.] Student; [memb.] St. John Volleyball Team, St. John's basketball team, St. John's Track team; [hon.] Poetry award for Lutheran Talent Festival; [oth. writ.] Other poems and short stories; [pers.] I started writing poetry in the 5th grade. I enjoy listening to music, playing sports and playing with my cats. [a.] Cleveland, OH.

ALEXANDER, R. CRISTINA
[b.] October 19, 1978, Augusta, GA; [p.] Reverend and Mrs. James J. Alexander; [ed.] Freshman in Florence Christian School; [pers.] There is no correct way of reading a poem. Everyoine reads it differently. It is not even read the way, it is written. [a.] Florence, SC.

ALFORD, REGGIE
[b.] November 14, 1974, Ft. Worth, TX; [pers.] Life is too short, it must never stand still and must constantly move ahead. [a.] Bogata, TX.

ALIGIZAKIS, IRENA
[b.] December 26, 1979, Calgary, Alberta, CAN; [p.] Olga and Aris Aligizakis; [ed.] Alberta Distance Learning Centre Senior; [occ.] Student, intend to have a future career in literature or journalism; [hon.] Honor student; [oth. writ.] The poem, "My Country" and the story poem, "The Humming Bird's Song" (published); [pers.] I attempt to realize and express the hidden, beautiful, and obscure sides of Man, the World, and Nature in my poetry. [a.] Calgary, Alberta, CAN.

ALIOTO, MAUREEN
[b.] August 30, 1948, Chicago, IL; [p.] John and Rita McDermott; [m.] Joseph M., July 26, 1969; [ch.] Michael and Anna Marie; [ed.] University of Illinois, Chicago; [occ.] Elemntary School Teacher; [pers.] Poetry reflects my laughter and tears. As a recent widow, I find poetry to be a release valve and a healing tool. It is me at my most vulnerable times, and most certainly my purest prayer to God. [a.] Pales Park, IL 60464.

ALLEN, JUDY "GINGER"
[b.] January 7, 1968, Hagerstown, MD; [p.] Judy and Nell Allen; [ed.] Shepherd College, Graphic Art student, Office Technology - James Rumsey Technical, Vocational Center; [occ.] Student; [memb.] Wrote for newspaper and radio; [hon.] Winner State Phi Beta Lambda Impromptu speaking contest, Outstanding Young American award presented by Family Coalition of the Eastern Panhandle; [oth. writ.] Rowena, multi-subject poetry and many children's books; [pers.] A positive, cheerful attitude always has more bearing on life and good writing than does any one's circumstance, which can lend to good writing. [a.] Martinsburg, WV.

ALLEN, ROBERTA M.
[pen.] Robbie, Robynn; [b.] April 24, 1949, Van Buren, ME; [p.] Gerard and Isabel; [ch.] Richard Gerard and Roselynn Isabel; [ed.] Van Buren District High School; [occf.] Homemaker; [oth. writ.] I have other little unpublished poems; [pers.] My inspiration comes Jesus. I am a Born again Christian of 20 years. [a.] Moriarty, NM 87035.

ALLEN, RON
[pen.] Ron Allen; [b.] May 7, 1941, Clay Co. Hosp., Brazil, IN; [p.] Forrest and Winifred (Thompson) Allen; [m.] Judy, July 28, 1961; Christopher Wade, Robin Michelle; [ed.] Van Buren High Schhol; [occ.] RAdioo Announcer: WWVR West Terre Haute, IN; [memb.] Knightsville Masonic Lodge #409, VFW Post 1127, and Ebenezer Church; [hon.] Vietnam Service Award, US Army Commendation Medal award; [oth. writ.] Poems and songs written for friends and family. 1. Joshua and Timothy's Grandpa, 2. It's easy to Fight, 3. Thompson Reunion; [pers.] My writings reflect a personal salute to those people that have made my life a joy, because I have known them.

ALLEN, SHIRLEY A,.
[b.] January 2, 1936, Palmyra, IL; [p.] Floyd E. and Frances Vance Jennings; [m.] Richard M., January 1, 1954; [ch.] Diane L. Krupianik and Kim A. Cornatzer; [ed.] Auburn High School, American Banking Institute, Moody Bible correspondence course; [occ.] Retired from a banking career; [memb.] Berean Baptist Church; [hon.] 4-H cooking and sewing (1st place); [oth. writ.] A few poems written for my own pleasure and to share with friends; [pers.] All my poems had been written to praise the Lord for his love and goodness to mankind which is manifested daily. [a.] Kalamazoo, MI 49001.

ALLGOOD, TARA
[pen.] Tara Allgood; [b.] May 30, 1977, Gainesville, FL; [p.] Kim Couture, Larry Allgood, Mike Couture; [ed.] Freshman in high school at Victory Christian Academy; [hon.] Numerous theatre awards and some poetry awards, academic awards; [oth. writ.] Collection of poems not published; [pers.] There is a twisted, normality in being abnormal. [a.] Palm Beach, FL.

ALLRED, JERRY E,
[b.] March 6, 1923, Sapulpa, OK; [p.] Raymond and Gladys Allred; [m.] Allison, October 15, 1988; [ch.] J. Michael, John W., James C.; [ed.] Central High School, University of Oklahoma; [occ.] Consultant, Retired Air Force; [memb.] AF & AM, Air Force Association, TROA; [pers.] Influenced by history thru the ages, Emerson "Know Thyself"d, Gibron "The Prophet", and "Spell guilt with a small "G". [a.] Harvest, AL 35749-0162.

ALLRED, STACY
[b.] November 14, 1977, Sikeston, MO; [p.] Albert and Betty Allred; [ed.] New Madrid County General High School; [occ.] Student; [memb.] Kewanee Missionary Baptist Church, Girl's Missionary Auxilary, Fellowship of Christian Athletes (FCA); [hon.] MEDAL (Multi-disciplinary Experiences Designed for the Advanced Learner) program grades 4-8; [oth. writ.] Several poems not yet published; [pers.] My writings reflect situations that happen in my friends' lives as well as my own. I try to keep their feelings in perspective as I write. [a.] Lilbourn, MO.

ALM, ELENA
[pen.] Elena; [b.] September 30, 1941, Page, ND; [p.] Carl Alm and Florenmce Klessig; [m.] Pedro Littleton, October 13, 1973; [ch.] Bryan Chubb and Timothy Littleton (stepchildren); [ed.] College degree; [occ.] Present '93 Real Estate Association Broker, past-Plant Nursery (owner) and school teacher; [memb.] Episcopal Church and Real Estate Association; [hon.] Lifetime member of Real Estate Million Dollar Club; [oth. writ.] Poems sitting in a dusty file box; [pers.] My poem represented my awakening that I and I alone was and am responsible for my mental, physical and spiritual well being. [a.] Ocean Springs, MS 39566-1402.

ALMEIDA, ELIZABETH
[b.] June 23, 1983, NJ; [p.] Joseph and Maria Almeida.

ALONZO, CHARLOTTE
[b.] March 23, 1955, Sutton, WV; [p.] James D. and Naomi Johnson; [ch.] April Dawn; [pers.] Never stop dreaming, for when you give up on your dream, you give up on life. [a.] Summersville, WV.

ALTIERE, EDWARD
[b.] August 19, 1942, Summit, NJ; [p.] Edward and Anna Altiere; [ed.] New Providence High School (NJ), Fairleigh Dickinson University; [occ.] Free lance writer; [memb.] Benevolent and protective order of Elks (Springfield, NJ), International Brotherhood of Teamsters; [oth. writ.] Newspaper articles and feature stories; [pers.] The power of one's written words reaching a million minds can generate a rocket to the moon. [a.] Roselle Park, NJ 07204.

AMABIBI, DAYEDFORI
[b.] August 23, 1966, Buea, Republic of Cameroon; [p.] Reverend Pastor Henry Amabibi and Rose Eposi Motutu; [ed.] Bilingual Grammar School Buea, The University of Yaounde, Rep. of Cameroon; [occ.] Graduate student reading Business Law; [memb.] Southern Cameroons Poetry Association; [oth. writ.] Articles for Leading Cameroonian English Language Newspapers such as "Cameroon Post" and "Cameroon Today"; [pers.] I strive to highlight the problems of demonstration in Africa in poems I draw an inspiration from African and African-American protest poets. [a.] Cameroon, West Africa.

ANASTASIAN, GEORGE
[pen.] Ardaches; [b.] November 3, 1975, Queens, NY; [p.] Mardiros and Carol Anastasian; [ed.] Forest Hills High School, New York University (freshman); [occ.] Student; [memb.] NY Academy of Sciences, NYU Armenian and Pre-Medical Societies; [hon.] Westinghouse Science Talent Search Semi-finalist, Recognized in Who's Who Among American High School Students publication; [oth. writ.] Humorous essays, critical commentaries, and serious poetry; [pers.] To be an Armenian is to have this intolerable weight of sadness on one's soul. Those truly enlightened can find comfort in their own thoughts. [a.] New York, NY 11379.

ANDERSON, DANIEL CRAIG
[pen.] Daniel Lonewolf; [b.] November 16, 1969, Augsburg Bavaria Germany; [p.] Donna Garcia and Leroy Anderson; [ed.] Graduated United High School in Laredo, TX, one semester at University of Texas in Austin; [occ.] I am currently pursuing a BA in English at Oklahoma State University in Stillwater; [memb.] A Veteran of the United States Army Paratroopers, Inactive; [hon.] Received the Army Commendation medal, the Southwest Asia Service Medal and the Kuwati Liberation medal for my efforts during Desert Storm and Desert Shield, while in Saudi Arabia and Iraq; [oth. writ.] Numerous other poems and songs and am currently working on a novel. I have had several poems published in local newspapers in Texas; [pers.] I feel that my writing is a piece of myself on paper. A thought, feeling or philosophy that I can share with other people. [a.] Agra, OK 74824.

ANDERSON, DOROTHY
[pen.] Aunt Dolly; [b.] June 20, 1913, Rodeo, CA; [p.] Herbert W. and Maude M. Lindsay; [m.] Carl O., December 7, 1933; [ch.] Joy Carline, Faye LaVerna, David Ernest; [ed.] Eight grade; [occ.] Homemaker; oth. writ.] Poems and small articles in a column called "Green Pastures", by Aunt Dolly, in a near by town newspaper, 1971-72; [pers.] I was injured at birth, leaving me cerebral palsied. That didn't stop me from living as normal a life as possible. We were married 55 years when Carl passed on, July 14, 1989. We had nine grandchildren and eight great granschildren. [a.] Hayward, CA 94544.

ANDERSON, GLEN R.
[b.] April 20, 1952, Chicago, IL; [m.] Elaine R. (Leonard), July 20, 1990; [ed.] Tri-County Area High School, SSI, Social Security Administration; [hon.] To be included in the 24th edition of Who's Who in the Midwest, publishing is scheduled for February 1994; [oth. writ.] My poems appear: American Poetry Association - Best New Poets of 1987, The Poetry of Life (1987), American Poetry Anthology (1987), Loves Greatest Treasures (1988), A Dorrance Anthology, Contemporary Poets of America and Britian (1992). [a.] St. Paul, MN 55117.

ANDERSON, MONICA
[b.] November 23, 1978, Naples, FL; [p.] Jon and Christine Anderson; [ed.] Louisville Elementary School, Louisville Middle School, The New High School - Boulder, CO; [occ.] Want to become a Middle SChool Language Arts teacher; [hon.] Honor Roll - 4 years; [oth. writ.] Short stories, other poems and fairy tales; [pers.] I enjoy helping everyone and anything I can. I put my family and friend's feelings before mine. Hobbies: reading, writing, playing flute, community service. [a.] Louisville, CO.

ANDERSON, STEPHANIE
[b.] January 20, 1978, Riverside, CA; [p.] Dennis and Susan Anderson; [ed.] Riverside Poly High School; [occ.] Student; [memb.] American Bicycle Association (ABA); [hon.] National Number one Girl Crusier for BMX, Presidential award for two years; [oth. writ.] Wrote for school newspaper; [pers.] My writings express the deepest emotions that I have towards the people who have touched me. [a.] Riverside, CA.

ANDERSON-LOVELL, PAMELA
[b.] November 30, 1962, Hot Springs, AK; [p.] Jeanne Slagle and Sam L. Anderson, Sr.; [m.] Bradford E., January 30, 1988; [ed.] Hendrix College graduate 1984 BA, Hot Springs High School graduate 1981; [occ.] Legal Secretary - Anderson Law Firm; [memb.] Circle of Friends-Arkansas Childrens Hospital, Grow and Show Garden Club, Hot Springs Flute Ensemble; [hon.] Poems and writings published in local newspaper; [pers.] My goal in writing about death is to learn to accept the inevitable. I have always had a great love for the arts and the ability to express myself through words and painting is one I depend upon greatly. [a.] Hot Springs, AR 71901.

ANDERSON, WILLIE MAY
[b.] December 15, 1915, Athens, TN; [m.] Dean, August 3, 1950; [ch.] Martha Jean Anderson; [memb.] International Society of Poets; [hon.] Outstanding Authors of America 1993; [pers.] The eye fixed firmly upon goodness sees past evil and corruption to gaze upoon beauty and brightness. [a.] Springfield, AR 72765.

ANDREWS, DAVID ERIC
[b.] December 18, 1952, St. John's NLFD; [p.] Harrold and Julia Andrews; [m.] Rowena G., February 8, 1974; [ch.] Pamela Rowena (17), Angela Brenda (15); [ed.] Ascension Collegiate High, Memorial University, NFLD; [occ.] Fisherman (Mate), Grand Banks of Newfoundland; [memb.] Pentecostal Tabernacle, Port-De-Grave; [oth. writ.] Several songs, short stories and poems; [pers.] "But this one thing I do, forgetting those things which are behind, and reaching forth unto those things which are before, I press toward the mark. For the prize of the high calling of God in Christ Jesus." - the Bible. [a.] NFLD Canada A0A 1W0.

ANTONUCCIO, JOSEPH N.
[b.] September 16, 1917, Boston, MA; [p.] Nicholas and Concetta (deceased when I was seven months) Antonuccio; [m.] Victoria, September 1, 1946; [ch.] Constance, Nicholas, Anthony; [ed.] Northern University (2 years 1936-38); [occ.] Coppensmith for Boston Naval Shiipyard and Bethlehem Steel Corp.; [oth. writ.] One poem published in January 1944 in a military publication, poem called "In God We Trust" during WWII; [pers.] Born an orphan, I was raised under a suppressed freedom. I expressed my feelings through all my poetry. I have many. [a.] Medford, MA 07155.

AREVALO, LAKIAY, M.
[pen.] Kia; [b.] July 15, 1982, Middletown, NY; [p.] Connie M. and Joseph H. Arevalo; [ed.] I attend the Liberty Middle School and in the sixth grade; [memb.] On June 1993, I graduated from DARE (Drug Awareness Resistance Education); [hon.] Certificate for DARE (1993), for achievement in school (1993), for effort (1993); [pers.] I like to read and write poetry. [a.] Parksville, NY 12768.

ARGOW, SYLVIA
[pen.] Meletusa; [p.] Samuel David and Esther Ida (both deceased); [ed.] Attended City University of NY, Bronx Community College, New York University; [memb.] Woman's Press Club; National League of State Poetry Societies; Composers, Authors and Artists of America (Florida); Poets and Writers; International Academy of Poets U.K.; Life member, World Institute of Achievement International; [hon.] World Belletrist award and included in Poet's Hall of Fame, Internatioinal Belles-Lettres Society 1975, Honored in Poet's Hall of Fame, Parnassus Literary Journal 1981, Knight Grand Dame of Merit, Knights of Malta 1986, Named Outstanding Creative Form Poet of the Bi-Centennial Era 1976, award citation for Lady Liberty from World Institute of Achievement, World Culture Prize 1985, received Honorary Cultural Doctorate in Literature from World University of Tucson, AZ 1981, names Woman of the Year 1993 and nominated Woman of the Decade 1993 from World Institute of Achievement, Certificate of award in recognition as a poet in Vesta's Who's Who, 1st edition of North American Poets Canada 1991, certificate of appointment, Board of Advisers Research, American Biographical Institute, award creator of the Argonelle 1971 New York Poetry Forum, Diploma of Merit-Centro Studi Scambi, Rome Italy; [oth. writ.] International Who's Who in Poetry, International Book of Honor, 2000 Notable American Women, Who's Who in U.S. Writers, Editors and Poets, International AL, Who's Who of Intellectuals, Dictionary of International Biography, REgister of Profiles, W/W, International W/W of Professional and Business Women, Directory of Poets and Writers, 5000 Personalities of the World W/W, Biography and photo published in Spotlight newsletter 1992 of World Institute of Achievement–and many others. [a.] Bronx, NY.

ARMBRUST, RUTH E.
[b.] SEptember 28, 1934, Iowa City, IA; [p.] Orris and Esther A. Frisbie; [m.] Gordon, September 14, 1965; [ch.] Leslie Duane, Lonnie David, Lori Faith; [ed.] GED-technical school - courses in medicine and journalism; [occ.] Nursing Assistant; [memb.] VFW Auxiliary, REgional Writers Association, State Historical Society; [hon.] Received special recognition for assistance to Cancer Crusade Who's Who in Wisconsin 1975; [oth. writ.] The Tree [p.]ublished by Sparrowgrass, feature stories for local newspapers; [pers.] Writing is my release from life's frustrations. [a.] Colly, WI 54421.

ARMENT, HEIDRUN
[b.] September 12, 1956, Prenzlau, Germany; [p.] Guenther and Christel Walther; [m.] William, November 3, 1978; [ch.] Daniel, Christopher Martin, Timothy James Christian; [pers.] I wrote the poem in loving memory of my daughter Leila. She died in October 1989 at the age of eight. [a.] Huntsville, AL 35811.

ARNOLD, JEREMY
[b.] May 26, 1977, San Diego, CA; [p.] Linda and Erbal Mayo; [ed.] Upcoming sophopmore at Pamlico County High School; [oth. writ.] Several selections of my poetry have been published in Eckerd Camp (E-Ma-Henwa) newspaper; [pers.] Poetry is a way of life, but you have to feel it to make it happen. [a.] New Bern, NC 28560.

ARZADON, FAY
[b.] September 10, 1980, Baltimore, MD; [p.] Priscilla P. and Francisco B. Arzadon III; [ed.] Hutchinson Elementary, Patricia Nixon Elementary, Haskel Junior High; [hon.] Excellent reading, Honor Roll; [oth. writ.] Other poems, some editorials and news paragraphs in the school paper. Poems excluded; [pers.] Poetry is a way to express some of the stress and feelings of a teen. I try to tell other poets that teens need attention. [a.] Lakewood, CA.

ASHCOM, COLLEEN K.
[b.] December 11, 1952, Johnstown, PA; [p.] Bernard and Elizabeth Clark; [m.] James, October 6, 1990; [ch.] Darrell Scott Good; [ed.] Johnstown High School, Johnstown Vo-Tech, Mount Aloysius Junior College; [occ.] Registered Nurse; [memb.] Mount Aloysius Alumni Association; [hon.] Outstanding Service award - Drama Department, May 1970, Johnstown High School. Dean's List - Mount Aloysius Junior College; [pers.] Let us reach beyond the superficial and encounter the depths. [a.] Johnstown, PA 15906.

AUBREY, RICHARD
[b.] December 22, 1948, Hopkinsville, KY; [pers.] My "Unresolved Love Poems" revolve around the timelessness of love gone wrong. My inspiration comes from women who have colored my life and make my words rhyme. [a.] Berlin, Germany 14169.

AUSTIN, ELIZABETH A.
[b.] January 28, 1961, Columbus, OH; [p.] Hazel and Charles Austin, Jr.; [oth. writ.] I am currently combining my lifelong works into a compilation titled "From My Heart To The World"; [pers.] I have discovered that inside of us all is found the strength to endure. [a.] Dublin, OH 43017.

AUSTIN, JOHN
[b.] December 17, 1907, Charleston, AR; [p.] R.W. Austin and Lucy J. Ledbetter; [m.] Leta, October 11, 1940; [ch.] Leslie Bundy, Holly Klinzman, Mark, Todd; [ed.] BA and MA - Denver Unviersity; [occ.] Elementary Principle Public Schools; [memb.] AF and AM Lions Club; [oth. writ.] History of Early Baca Co. Foibles and Filosophies, Maybe Some of Yours (in process); [pers.] Its the big little things that count. [a.] Westminster, CO 80030.

AYER, JEFFREY MELVIN
[b.] February 20, 1975, Appleton, WI; [p.] Deborah L. and Warren M. Ayer; [ed.] High School and will attend St. John's University in Minnesota; [occ.] Student; [memb.] National Honors Society; [hon.] National Honors Society poetry in Yahara Prarie Review magazine; [oth. writ.] Several poems in my high school's literary magazine, poem in the Yahara Prarie Review called "A Wrinkle In Time"; [pers.] I would like to thank the woman who has called my life and I will always love - Amy Boncher. Also to my caring grandmother - and all the poets before me. [a.] Appleton, WII 54914.

AYRAUD, CLAIRE
[b.] February 23, 1955, Schenectady, NY; [p.] Kenneth and Dorothy Kellsey; [m.] Thomas R., October 21, 1978; [ch.] Tamara Claire and Danica Christine; [ed.] Burnt Hills, Ballston Lake High School, Albany Business College, working on a BA in English; [occ.] Accountant - self employed; [oth. writ.] Poems published in The Breeder, a local literary sampler; [pers.] I enjoy writing both poetry and prose, drawing from travel and life experience. I am currently working on an African Journal and a novel set in the 70s. [a.] Crested Butte, CO.

AZER, SHARLENE
[b.] July 26, 1946, Boston, MA; [p.] Paul and Dorothy Goldstein; [m.] Norman, 1978; [ch.] Two; [ed.] High school; [occ.] Self-employed - Automotive Speciality Products; [memb.] Temple Beth Am Automotive Association. Randolph Arts Council and Randolph Police Association; [hon.] No awards since the appropriate people have never seen my work.; [oth. writ.] Many inspirational poems on healing (of a spiritual nature); [pers.] I am a multi-talented business woman with great creativity and I am starting to live up to my full potential and talents. [a.] Randolph, MA.

BACALA, R.N.; B.S.N.; M.D., DR. JESUS C.
[b.] May 8, 1915, Maasin, Southern Leyte, Philippines; [p.] Both deceased; [m.] Presentacion Capili-Bacala, September 10, 1949; [ch.] Emmanuel, Dr. Agnes, Mrs. Theresa B. Javier, Mrs. Josephine B. Bennet, Mrs. Prestine B. Dierfeldt and Tomas C. Bacala; [ed.] Graduate nurse; Doctor of Medicine; [occ.] Physician, Former Assoc. Prof. Obstetrics & Gynecology; former Dean of College of Nursing; Private Practitioner-Family Medicine; [memb.] American Medical Association, American Academy of Family Practice, Indiana Medical Association, American College of International Physicians, founder and former president-Indiana Philippine Medical Association, Philippine Medical Association of St. Louis, Kentucky and Southern Indiana; co-founder - Philippine American Heritage Association; member- National Federation of State Poetry Societies; Editor-The Quill, Quarterly of Southern Indiana Poetry Club; Editor of the Club's - Voices in the Wind, Vols. 1-3, Wisdom of the Heart; Editor, Indiana State Federation's "Golden Anthology"; [hon.] Golden award, University of Santo Tomas, after twelve years as Dean of the University's College of Nursing; Poet Laureate of Indiana, 1991-93; Distinguished Fellow, American College of International Physicians, Inc.; Dues Exempt Award, Amer. Med. Association, 1991; Fellow, American Academy of Family Practice; [oth. writ.] Text books in Nursing: University of Santo Tomas, Manila: Orientation to Nursing, Professional Adjustments in Nursing, Professionalization of Nursing, University Learnings in Nursing, History of Nursing in the Philippines, Deontology in Nursing; poetry publications: On the births of my children, Moonrise and Other Rhymes, 1950 (Madrid, Spain), Cosmorama and Other Rhymes, 1952 (St. Louis, MO), Across the Years and Other Rhymes, 1954 (Manila), Quicksands and Other Rhymes, 1956 (Manila), Lines To Prestina and Other Rhymes, 1958 (Manila), Sweetsoul in Summer and Other Rhymes, 1960 (Manila); on the marriage of my children: The Blooming Years (1979), The Glowing Years (1985), The Wandering Years (1985), The Grooming Years (1990); grandchildren series (on their births): December Blossoms (1987), Blossom in Autumn (1981), Five Blossoms Together (In prep); anniversary series: Poems on Loving, Living and Believing (hard cover, Silver Wedding Anniv. 1974), The Ruby Years of Family Love (Ruby Anniv. book 1989); poet laureate readings: Selected Poems through the Years (1992),

Ascent to Sonnetry and Other Forms of Poetry, 9 second poet laureate readings in prep for 1993; [pers.] Man is only a creature of the Creator and all that man possesses in body, health, intelligence, virtues and aspirations should be God-centered. Man's literature should express his love, praises, gratitude and obedience to God, and all who proceedth from Him. a[.] Scottsburg, IN.

BACON, PATRICIA A.
[pen.] Pat Bacon; [b.] January 5, 1936, Chester, PA; [p.] RAymond A. and Peal Mae Allison Hubbard; [m.] Ross R., April 3, 1958; [ch.] Mark A. (deceased) and Brenda A.; [ed.] Business College (2 yrs) East Liverpool, Ohio, Chester High School (2 yrs GED); [occ.] Joined military 6/1/54, air force (1 yr.) and army dental asst (3 yrs.); [hon.] Many awards in poetry (much personal enjoyment) happy life; [oth. writ.] Many unpublished; [pers.] First I love my maker and have his church in my home seven days a week. My main job was raising my two children. Now that I have them raised. I am battling Rheumatoid Arthritis. Spend time showing love to my neighbors as the ten commandments tell us to do. And if heaven is like I read our savior said children are it.

BADEAU, DAVID K.
[b.] December 21, 1907, Hammond, LA; [p.] George T. and Edith Locke Badeau; [ed.] Hinds Co. High School (1927 Raymond, MS), Officers Training School (OCS) U.S. Army graduate; [occ.] Tax Accountant, Retired captain US Army WWII; [memb.] The Retired Officers Association, Organ Guild of America, Church Choir, 15 years First Baptist Church (Laurel, MS), Choral Club Burbank, CA; [hon.] Veteran U.S. Army-Italy, Captain US Army-WWII; [oth. writ.] Author and composer of original songs and original music: Mississippi, America, We Adore You, Thanksgiving Hymn, Au revoir (Good-by), The Lord's Prayer and Lullaby. [a.] [a.] Heidelberg, MS.

BAGATTA, ANGELA A.
[b.] April 8, 1978, Newburgh; [p.] Joseph C. and Deborah A. Bagatta; [ed.] High school student; [oth. writ.] American Academy of poetry, essay contest on Abortion, school newsletter magazine and newspaper; [pers.] People can't know, what you don't show them. Wear the spotlight and be all you can be. [a.] Milton, NY.

BAKER, GENNY
[b.] August 29, 1979, Marysville, OH; [p.] Melony and Gary Baker; [ed.] Freshman in high school; [occ.] Student; [oth. writ.] Multiple poems; [pers.] My poem, "Within", was dedicated to my grandfather, who I loved dearly. [a.] East Liberty, OH.

BAKER, JAIME L.
[pen.] J.L. Baker; [b.] July 9, 1977, Kansas City, KS; [p.] Shirley A. and Edwin J. Baker; [ed.] Sophomore at Lawrenceburg High School; [memb.] Sunshine Society; [oth. writ.] This was my first poem submitted; [pers.] I have been greatly inspired by my favorite teachers; Bonnie Cleary, Kate Nicolai, and Lucille Paine. [a.] Lawrenceburg, IN.

BAKER, JASON HOWARD
[pen.] Jason Baker; [b.] April 13, 1975, Richmond, KY; [p.] Vicki Irvin, Roger Irvin and Howard Baker; [ed.] Broughton Elementary, Lincoln County High School, Berea College; [occ.] Student; [memb.] Founder and President-Lincoln County Ecology Club, Senior Class Treasurer, Senior Executive Council; [hon.] Stanford Chamber of Commerce Scholarship; [pers.] Carpe Diem. [a.] Crab Orchard, KY.

BAKER, NANCY
[pen.] Nancy Baker; [b.] November 16, 1941, Ft. Payne, AL; [p.] Bill and Laura McNutt; [m.] Joe Dell, June 21, 1958; [ch.] Jeffery Baker, Carol Baker Ward; [ed.] Ft. Payne High School; [occ.] Craft South Central Bell Telephone Co.; [memb.] Delmar Baptist Church; [hon.] The only award I can boast of is doing a good job at work and raising my children; [oth. writ.] Just writing for myself; [pers.] Love to express my feelings and thoughts on paper. [a.] Ft. Payne, AL.

BALDWIN, RACHEL
[b.] November 23, 1975, New Eagle, PA; [p.] Christine and George Baldwin; [ed.] Ringgold High School; [occ.] Cook; [memb.] World Wildlife Fund; [hon.] Who's Who Among American Students; [oth. writ.] This was my first poem, although I've tried entering a storywriting contest but have not heard anything. [a.] Donora, PA.

BALLOD, CHRISTOPHER
[b.] May 25, 1976, Abington, PA; [p.] Martin and Joann Ballod; [ed.] La Salle College High School; [occ.] Student. [a.] Iuyland, PA.

BANKS, CAROLINE GILES
[b.] January 29, 1944, Boston, MA; [p.] Patricia Wellington and Robert Byron Giles, Jr; [ch.] Logan Giles Banks; [ed.] Hocaday School, BA Wellesley College, MA University of New Mexico, MA and PhD University of Minnesota; [occ.] Lecturer in Anthropology, University of Wisconsin-River Falls; [memb.] American Anthropological Association, Society for Humanistic Anthropology and Society for Psychological anthropology; [hon.] Honorable mention in annual
poetry contest, Society for Humanistic Anthropology, 1990 and 1991; [oth. writ.] Poems published in Agassiz Review; Wisconsin Dialogue; Poetry Motel; Anthropology and Humanism; Midwest Haiku Anthology; Frog Pond; Modern Haiku; Haiku Quarterly; Dragonfly; Brussels Sprout; among other publications; [pers.] I often bring to bear my work as an anthropologist to my poetry. My poetry centers on current social and cultural topics. [a.] Minneapolis, MN.

BAPTISTA, ANNE M.
[b.] August 6, 1952, Cape Verde Island; [ch.] Kathleen, Jacquline, Susan and Elizabeth; [ed.] Rhode Island College; [occ.] Academic/Career Counselor for High School Drop-outs; [memb.] Rhode Island College Alumni Association, Rhode Island College Alumni Scholarship Committee; [oth. writ.] Novel titled "Price of Dignity" and an autobiography titled "Shadow's Edge" both yet to be published; [pers.] Our children's future is dependent on our ability to educate them. Not only in our schools, but more importantly, in our homes. [a.] North Providence, RI.

BARBER, ROBIN
[b.] February 2, 1957, Oklahoma; [p.] Charles and Sara Morrison; [m.] James R., December 23, 1991; [ed.] Small Town America; [occ.] Caretakers of Laws Railroad Museum (Bishop, CA); [memb.] Lions, Moose, E Clamus Vitus Slimm Princes Chapter 395 (These are my husband's organizations); [hon.] Having the National Library of Poetry to take notice; [oth. writ.] Many unpublished cowboy, nature, love, and my best of all, the ones about my father for he was my hero; [pers.] All I want is for someone out there to hear the songs that I have in my heart. I feel that they have what it takes to make your heart sing. [a.] Bishop, CA.

BARGER, ALICIA
[b.] September 21, 1978, Chattanooga, TN; [p.] Leonard and Mary Jane Barger; [ed.] Hixson High School; [memb.] Central Baptist Church; [oth. writ.] I write poems for my own enjoyment in my free time; [pers.] All of my poetry comes from the heart. I write poems to express the feelings that I can't express through words of the mouth, but instead words written on paper. [a.] Hixson, TN.

BARI, GEORGE
[pen.] Geo.; [b.] May 15, 1897, Yorkshire, England; [p.] Alice Abbot and Samuel Barden; [m.] Dead, July 21, 1922; [ch.] Two sons; [ed.] College, Engineering after the 1929 Ganancial Crash I turned to Horticulture; [occ.] Retired; [memb.] Associated member of the British/Institute/Structural Engineer; [oth. writ.] Life story title "Alone I Battle the Storms", due out this month "First Edition" "Who Am I"; [pers.] I am a design engineer for steel concrete and other materials have executed all trades in the construction business. Have a patent in this field of operations. [a.] San Bernardino, CA.

BARLOW, DORIS W.
[pen.] Doris Emelie Wronsky; [b.] July 21, 1907, New Jersey; [p.] Otto and Grace Wronsky; [m.] Divorced 20 years, 1929; [ch.] Three; [ed.] Not finished college, Boarding private school in MA, later in life got half way through college; [occ.] Various with libraries; [memb.] Belong to a church was a deaconess, go for gardens and animal rights; [hon.] Lots of young friends, one daughter and two wonderful grandsons; [oth. writ.] Nothing published. Written much poetry all my life - am now writing family history - biographies of my parents and one grandfather; [pers.] I sent the poem just on a whim. I was working on a book of my poems and came across this. It's a "theme" I feel deeply about. [a.] Aspen, CO.

BARNES, LOUISE (DWYER)
[b.] April 15, 1924, (Charlestown) Boston, MA; [p.] Mary Agnes Geswell and John Patrick Dwyer; [m.] James F., April 25, 1947; [ch.] Judith, Christine, Gail, Leslie, Joyce, Janice, James, Paula, Lynne, Barbara, and Jeffrey; [ed.] Boston and Medford, MA public schools; [occ.] Mother, Wife, Club Woman local clubs, church organizations, PTA; [memb.] Boston Opera Guild; [pers.] I am quite ill now - emphysema requires the use of oxygen 24 hours a day -- it is quite discouraging though I strive and pray that I will not let myself be vanquished by it, and all it entails. I cling strongly to my religious faith throughout this present ordeal with its suffering and resultant deterioration, something or someone Bigger than myself is with me through it all. Illness assaults ones dignity, but I feel that people insult our Dignity--I render to each the respect it deserves or commands - just as we will "Render to Caesar". [a.] Melrose, MA.

BARNITT, RICHARD PERRY
[b.] December 7, 1945, Hasbrook Heights, NJ; [p.] Samuel Colgrove and Elizabeth Anne Little Barnitt; [m.] Martha Oldham, October 15, 1977; [ch.] Emily Julie Barnitt ; [ed.] Indiana University, BA Syracuse University, MLA Middlebury College; [occ.] Russian Linguist Dept. of Defense, (Ft. Meade, MD); [oth. writ.] Various poems to family members; [pers.] I write from the heart. [a.] Hasbrouck Heights, NJ.

BARRIENTOS, MIGUEL
[b.] April 9, 1957, Mexico City; [p.] Guillermo Barrientos and Angelina Martinez; [m.] Laura Torres, December 29, 1990; [ed.] National University of Mexico, McMaster University; [occ.] Graduate student. [a.] Hamilton, Ont. CAN.

BARRON, RACHEL
[pen.] Rachel Barron; [b.] october 24, 1972, Los Angeles, CA; [p.] Carlos M. and Maria E. Barron; [ed.] South Gate High, currently attending Gerritos College; [occ.] Part-time Sales Associate, full-time college student; [memb.] Greenpeace, Aids Project Los Angeles; [oth. writ.] I have recently had my poems published in an anthology titled "Poems of Our Times"; [pers.] I would like to dedicate this poem to my family, who have shown me encouragement and understanding in troubled times. [a.] Southgate, CA.

BARROWS, NAOMI
[b.] November 18, 1920, Wilder, UT; [p.] Anatole and Jennie Trottier; [m.] Philip W., June 13, 1938; [ch.] Sonja Guarino, Cheryl Brown, Lori Hellman, Kenneth Barrows; [ed.] 8th grade; [occ.] Artist of dried flower pictures, homemaker; [memb.] Emblem Club of Elks; [pers.] Have respect of the community and of my life. Married 55 years, respect for others. Comfort within love for grandchildren. [a.] White River Jct., VT.

BARRY, MILDRED C.
[b.] December 24, 1911, Canton, China; [p.] John W. and Lois J. Creighton (deceased); [m.] Dr. Frank M. (deceased), June 19, 1937; [ch.] Jane W. Barry, MD; [ed.] A.B. Wooster College, Ohio MSSA Case Western Reserve University (Cleveland, OH); [occ.] Community Health Planner (retired); [memb.] National Association of Social Workers, American Public Health Association; [oth. writ.] Professional articles (published) Creative skits and poems (unpublished); [pers.] In retirement it's fun to try to be creative. [a.] Penney Farms, FL.

BARTOK, JACOB d.
[b.] November 15, 1977, Eldorado, IL; [p.] Bill and Toni Bartok; [ed.] 11th grade; [occ.] Student; [oth. writ.] Several others in my own notebook; [pers.] Write from the heart, not from the Mind. [a.] Eldorado, IL.

BARZILAI, DAVID
[b.] August 2, 1974, Boston, MA; [p.] Dina and Uzi Barzilai; [ed.] Lexington High School, current student; [occ.] Student, University of Rochester; [memb.] National Honor Society; [hon.] National Honor Society, Merit Scholar commended student, NECEA multicultural award; [pers.] I find meaning in life's chaotic and ephemeral reality only by caring for people, principles, truth, and beauty. [a.] Lexington, MA.

BATCHELOR, TODD A.
[pen.] Todd Batchelor; [b.] April 11, 1970, Rocky Mount, NC; [p.] Sonja Sharon and Tony Batchelor; [ed.] Millbrook HIgh SChool, presently attending University of North Carolina at Wilmington; [occ.] Student; [memb.] United States Navy Inactive Reserve; [oth. writ.] A large volume of unsubmitted poetry; [pers.] My favorite poet is Edgar Allen Poe. Imagination provides limitless opportunities for any aspiring writer. [a.] Raleigh, NC.

BATTLES, ASA
[b.] August 12, 1923, Buckeye, AZ; [p.] Ira and Ada Battles; [m.] Marge L., June 15, 1969; [ed.] High school; [occ.] Retired/professional art teacher/lecturer/artist; [memb.] Scientific Cultural County Council, Littleton Art Board, George Phippen Life time member, Eagle Lodge, Veteran of Foreign Wars; [hon.] Honorary membership Colville Confederated Tribes and Honorary Chieftainship in Chief Joseph Band of Nez Perce also many awards for art throughout West; [oth. writ.] Creative titles and sometimes historical features in the many oil paintings and scratch boards (ink etchings); [pers.] Creating art images on canvas or paper is comparable to creating artistic words into poetry. With poetry you can express your feelings in a more involved and profound manner. [a.] Littleton, CO.

BAUERS, STEPHANIE LYNN
[pen.] Stephanie Carmichael; [b.] March 24, 1979, Charlotte, NC; [p.] Debbie Bowers and Bill Bauers; [ed.] High school freshman; [hon.] Graduate of John Robert Powers Modeling School and Barbizon Modeling School. Chosen most professional model at Barbizon Dec. 1991. Semi-finalist (top 10) in NC. Little Miss Pageant 1983. Certificates for scholastic achievement during previous school years. Cheerleading award 1991, gymnastic awards 1985-1988 at Invitational meets; [pers.] My writings are a true reflection of me and my feelings. I express myself through my work, but without the help of my Mom and Hoogy Carmichael, I couldn't have made it. I O you both. [a.] Cary, NC.

BAUGH, PHYLLIS MARLENE
[b.] October 6, 1977, Russellville, AR; [p.] Jackie and Charlene Baugh; [ed.] Sophomore at Russellville High School; [hon.] I won second and third in our school literary magazine, I am a member of the National Honor Society, and I recently attended the Arts Encounter program associated with Arkansas Gifted and Talented programs; [oth. writ.] "A Rose Without Thorns", "Stranger in My Dreams", "An Innocent Child", and "To Love is to Conquer Hate". [a.] Russellville, AR.

BAULD, CATHERINE LYNN
[b.] May 28, 1976, Burlington, Ontario, CAN.; [p.] Wendy and Steve Bauld; [ed.] Senior M.M. Robinson High School; [hon.] Outstanding short story and poetry writing award, honors in English program and Co-operative Education program. Writing articles for Halton Board Newsletters; [oth. writ.] Several articles published in school and education board newsletters and school yearbook. Other poems published in school poetry and yearbooks; [pers.] I believe that poetry is a reflection of the individual. I feel that we should enjoy the beauty of another's expressions rather than attempt to search out the meaning that stands behind it. [a.] Burlington, ONT. CAN.

BAUMGARDT, JAMES W.
[pen.] J. Williams, J.P.H. Morris; [b.] May 30, 1974, Indianapolis, IN; [p.] Carol M. Lee and father deceased; [ed.] Indianapolis Junior Academy, Broad Ripple High School, Butler University; [occ.] Singer, songwriter; [memb.] Just Say No Programs, Humane Society, State Police Alliance, St. Paul's Episcopal Church; [hon.] Three consecutive writing awards issued by Indiana for the "Just Say No" program; [oth. writ.] Articles for Parade Magazine, local paper" Just Say No" essays. Many pop/love songs. Songs concerning the environment, AIDS, battled women, death, etc.; [pers.] In loving memory Anne Elizabeth Short Morris. Forever in my heart, living in my soul, you are the inspiration of my lifetime. Forever missed. [a.] Indianapolis, IN.

BEAL, RITA
[b.] July 23, 1915, Akron, OH; [p.] Adolph and Mary Stadler; [m.] Glen N., April 1, 1937; [ch.] Larry, Bob, and Betty; [ed.] Kent State University; [occ.] Secretary; [oth. writ.] Poetry -at infrequent intervals; [pers.] I use poetry writing as a release of stress at work or relief of boredom during idle times. [a.] Kent, OH.

BEAN, WILLIAM BEAN, JR.
[pen.] William Bean; [b.] February 16, 1965, Miles City, MT; [p.] William and Helane Bean; [ch.] Erica Charlene, Tiffany Bean, and Savanah Noel Lillian Bean; [oth. writ.] I have written many songs and poems, but my poem "Life" is the first to be published; [pers.] Poetry is to allow all of the emotion within to flow out and touch the heart and soul of another. [a.] Burbank, CA.

BEATON, DEBBIE
[pen.] Debbie Beaton/Beddie Beeks/Debbie Baron; [b.] October 2, 1955, Toronto, Ont.; [p.] Donald S. and Doreen M. Deeks; [m.] Alex, December 31, 1990; [ch.] Expecting a child December 1993; [ed.] Henry St. High School, Career School of Hairdressing; [occ.] Part-time Hairdresser and part-time Girl Friday; [oth. writ.] Many poems published in local newspapers; [pers.] Every poem I write is from personal feelings or experiences. [a.] Whitby, Ont.

BEAUJUIN, JEAN RENE'
[b.] May 1, 1941, Jeremie, Haiti; [p.] Marie Nelia Lande and Begel Beaujuin; [m.] Marie Nicole, July 11, 1969; [ch.] Claude Rene and Jennifer Beaujuin; [ed.] MS in Education - Bank Street College of Education; [occ.] Language Arts, Literacy, French teacher, Linden Middle School, I.S. 192 (St. Albans, NY); [memb.] ASCD (Association for Supervision and Curriculum Development); [hon.] Certificate of Appreciation for a job well done 1992/93, Haitian Flag Day award 1993; [oth. writ.] Numerous French poems published in various Haitian weekly newspapers and magazines including Love 10/89 and My Beautiful Flag 3/93 and He Alone 5/93; [pers.] I enjoy writing for my wife in particular and for women in general. I fell in love with the romantic era when I was studying French literature. [a.] Jamaica, NY.

BEAUMONT, ANGELA L.
[b.] January 4, 1928, Halstad, MN; [p.] Ordean and Lillian Anderson; [m.] Charles W., June 24, 1949; [ch.] Dale Michael Beaumont, Christine Annette

Beaumont Hill, Brian Hugh Beaumont; [ed.] Graduated from Bemidji High School 1946, Split Rock Workshop Children's Picture Books, three year correspondence course famous artists, numerous watercolor workshops; [occ.] Secretary for State Representative Leonard Dickinson, U.S. Senator Edward J. Thye, Little Falls School District; [memb.] Midwest Watercolor Society, Artists of Minnesota, Warm (Women's Art Registry of Minnesota), Boardmember Great River Arts Association, numerous local charities; [hon.] Blue Ribbon winner Artists of Minnesota, third place Great River Arts Association 1993; [oth. writ.] Several poems in local newspaper. I am working on a children's picture book; [pers.] I enjoy expressing my love for God's creation in words and in visual art. [a.] Little Falls, MN.

BEBOUT, CAROL
[b.] April 20, 1926, Convoy, OH; [m.] Eugene, April 6, 1947; [ch.] Stephen/Eugene (deceased), Bradley Carey, Suzette Renee (Stripe), and Jan Marie (McIntosh); [ed.] Bowling Green State University, creative writing classes at Wright State and Indiana/Purdue Universities; [occ.] Retired County elected official (recorder); [memb.] Trinity Lutheran Church (FLCA), Retired Ohio Recorders Association, Van Wert County Genealogical Society; [pers.] I write mostly personal experiences for my family and friends. This is my first attempt at writing poetry. [a.] Convoy, OH.

BECK, CANDICE M.
[b.] December 25, 1965, Waynesboro, VA; [p.] Henry and Isca Mitchell; [m.] First Lt. Thomas Beck, USMC, June 7, 1971; [ed.] Waynesboro High School, Virginia Intermont College; [occ.] Assistant Buyer; [oth. writ.] Other poems and songs "Dawning of Love" published in Wind In the Night Sky by National Library of Poetry; [pers.] My writing is dedicated to my husband who inspired me every day. [a.] Newport, NC.

BECKMANN, BRUCE A.
[b.] September 29, 1944, Teaneck, NJ; [p.] Alston F. and Dorothy Beckmann; [m.] Doris Ruth, May 30, 1987; [ch.] Henry, Craig, Pauletta, and Drew; [ed.] Bergen County Voc. and Technical (Hackensack, NJ), Bergen County Police County - C.O.T.A. Trenton, NJ; [occ.] NJ State P.B.A. Local #105, Fraternal Order of Police Lodge #46, Italian American Police Society of NJ; [hon.] Life Saving Commendation 1988; [oth. writ.] Editor of School paper "Bergen Tech Knight 1960-1964; [pers.] I was ordained as a minister in 1961 and it is my goal to help all in whatever small way I can. [a.] Dumont, NJ.

BECKMAN, TONY
[b.] August 19, 1936, Lawrenceburg, TX; [p.] William H. and Emma K. Beckman; [m.] Mary A., May 31, 1956; [ch.] Debra M., Thomas C., Anita M. and Dana M.; [ed.] St. Bernard HS, BA-Our Lady of the Lake, MS Computer Science - Houston Baptist University; [occ.] Computer Science Teacher, Houston Community College; [hon.] NISOD Teaching Excellence award, Outstanding Teacher of 1989-HC; [oth. writ.] Computer Science Test Banks, Wadsworth Pub., China Chronicle (for family); [pers.] Ignorance and greed are the sustenance of all the ills of earth; they are my enemies. [a.] Houston, TX.

BEISEL, MARVIN L.
[b.] December 19, 1930, Indianapolis, IN; [p.] Marvin and Etta Beisel; [occ.] Writing for local newspaper after a 17 year career with Capital Records (1955-73); [oth. writ.] Authored and published the book "Hopalong Purrsnickity" about my cat Hoppy. Its stories and poems written from my cat's view point. [a.] Las Vegas, NV.

BEKAERT, CASEY
[b.] July 15, 1961, New York, NY; [p.] Eugene and Polly Bekaert; [ed.] Rider College; [occ.] Government Administrator; [pers.] This is the first work I have ever submitted for publication, although the quantity of work I have produced is excessive. I have temporal lobe epilepsy and a trait of this disorder is excessive, even compulsive and obsessive, writing. [a.] Boston, MA.

BELF, TERI E.
[b.] February 24, 1946, New York City, NY; [p.] Gaston and Frances Belf; [ed.] MA in Education Research and C.A.G.S. in Education Evaluation and Learning, U. of Pittsburgh; [m.] Robert A. Williams, June 24, 1967, second marriage-Phillip E. Nelson, June 11, 1988; [ch.] Kim; [pers.] My purpose in life is to inspire and guide people to take steps towards their dreams. Poetry is one way I experience purposefulness. [a.] Annadale, VA.

BELLI, MICHELLE C.
[pen.] Michelle Diefenbach; [b.] September 8, 1959, St. Louis, MO; [p.] Eugene and Clara Diefenbach; [m.] Christopher S., March 25, 1987; [ch.] Jody Michael, Kristal Marie, and Daniel Justin; [ed.] Ritenour Senior High, North County Technical; [occ.] Daycare; [oth. writ.] Article in local newspaper; [pers.] In loving memory of my father, who I feel thankful to for the knowledge, strength and support he gave me. [a.] Maryland Hgts. MO.

BELLO, MARY DEL
[b.] June 30, 1931, Philadelphia, PA; [p.] James P. and Christine DiNubile Del Bello; [ed.] University of the Arts, University of PA; [memb.] Potters Guild and Poetry group at the Community Arts Center; [hon.] Alumni Scholarship, University of Pennsylvania; [oth. writ.] Local publications; [pers.] I try to express the beauty and mystery of the everyday world around me. I have been inspired to write poetry by my teacher, John Brown, who has the gift of bringing out the best in people. [a.] Drexel Hill, PA.

BELLOT, FRANCES EUGENIA
[pen.] Candace; [b.] December 30, 1961, Commonwealth of Dominica, West Indies; [p.] Hugh and Isadora Bellot; [ed.] Convent Senior High (West Indies), AA Lee College (TX), AA WLA College (CA), BS and MA California State (CA); [occ.] Rate Management Analyst; [memb.] Phi Theta Kappa, honors Southern California Edison - Community College Achievement awards, Scholarship; [hon.] Southern Univ. of New Orleans recognized poet first place, Executive Board for Non-Profit Social Organization "Los Angeles-Dominica Connection"; [oth. writ.] "Drums of the Mazaku", "Voices", "The Song of a Black Woman", "The Tiger"; [pers.] Being able to express one's self through the artform of poetry is an invaluable gift which is profoundly desirable. I am privileged to possess the gift of writing. [a.] Los Angeles, CA.

BELT, WANDA
[pen.] WAnda Roberts Belt; [b.] June 3, 1927, Elizabeth, WV; [p.] Lewis and Elva Roberts (deceased); [m.] Former G.D., March 20, 1947; [ch.] Debbie Boice, four grandchildren-Angie, Jason, Crystal and David; [ed.] Two years high school and GED program; [occ.] Housekeeping, working in homes of the elderly; [memb.] Owl Hill United Methodist Church; [hon.] Several ribbons for exhibits at the local Wirt Co. Fair, consisting of homemade cookies, jelly, and crafts; [oth. writ.] Flowers, published by American Poetry Society, Springtime-Sparrowgrass Poetry Forum in Poetic Voices of America Fall 1992 in W.V., The Glory of Easter and etc.; [pers.] I've always lived in the country and spend much time in the outdoors. That is why most of my poems have been about nature and its beauty. [a.] Elizabeth, WV.

BENDER, KENNETH J.
[pen.] Kenneth J. Bender; [b.] July 6, 1961, Santa Monica, CA; [p.] Henry J. Bender and Madelon Tikker; [ed.] Graduate, Venice High School; [occ.] Carpet Tech, Castle Rock, CO. "Bobcat Services"; [memb.] Gold panners Association of America, former - Screen Extras Guild; [oth. writ.] Copies of other poems have not been submitted to any newspapers or publications; [pers.] "The Poker Room" was inspired by a young lady who works as a poker dealer in the gaming town of "Black Hawk", CO. [a.] Littleton, CO.

BENGEN, JENNY
[b.] July 17, 1979, Smithtown, NY; [p.] Joyce and Bill Bengen; [ed.] Montgomery Middle School. Entering ninth grade at Valhalla High School (El Cajon); [occ.] Student; [memb.] USTA (United States Tennis Association); [hon.] Honor Roll - 3 years at Montgomery Middle School. Won 8th grade essay contest; [oth. writ.] Wrote article for Daily Californian (local newspaper, El Cajon); [pers.] I've always had a love for writing and have been influenced and encouraged by my family and teachers. [a.] El Cajon, CA.

BENNETT, CINDY SHARON
[b.] June 27, 1976, Syosset Hospital; [p.] Beverly and Fred; [ed.] Entering 12th grade in Fall '93; [occ.] Wish to work in field of Special Education; [memb.] United Synagogue Youth (USY); [hon.] One poem previously published in "Feelings". Received numerous drama awards and writing awards; [oth. writ.] Been writing since I was 11 years old. It's my way of expressing myself in ways I could never actually say; [pers.] If you have a dream, don't let anyone or anything ever get in your way. The more you strive, the more you will be rewarded in the end. [a.] Greenlawn, NY.

BENNETT, JANICE J.
[pen.] Jan-Jan; [b.] February 10, 1946, Dallas, TX; [p.] Deceased; [ch.] Keisha LaNay and Krisna Lani; [ed.] California State; [occ.] Entrepreneur Opportunity Marketing Group/Contractor's Referral; [memb.] NAACP, BBA, UMCA; [hon.] Helping minorities participate in construction; [oth. writ.] "Divorce", "Mental", "Your Life is Full of Patterns", "Falling", "Brother Knight is Shining Armor", and "Can I Be Free"; [pers.] I decided after the civil unrest in Los Angeles in April, it was time to stop looking and summarizing and start doing. Trying to change things for all mankind "Peace". [a.] Los Angeles, CA.

BENNETT, KENNETH STANLEY
[b.] March 10, 1952, CeePeeCee, British Columbia, Canada; [p.] Stanley (deceased) and Thelma Bennett; [m.] Margaret, April 11, 1981; [ch.] Tansy June, Laura Elizabeth, Collena Katherine, Dwayne Howard and Margaretta Mae; [ed.] George P. Vanier SSS (9171) and Malaspina College (1973); [occ.] Organic Farmer; [hon.] Citizen award, Cumberland JHS, Top student class 23 (1973) Malaspina College; [oth. writ.] Numerous poems and songs unpublished but recorded; [pers.] My early years were influenced by my life living on a tiny island (11 yrs) in the Canadian Pacific Ocean. My writing is now influenced by my Christian way of life. My poetry is life's reality as observed. [a.] Courtenay, B.C. Canada.

BENTLEY, HELEN ELAINE
[pen.] E.Richardson, Guard; [b.] October 24, 1933, Oklahoma City, OK; [p.] Walter Norton and Claire Ellen (Culley) Richardson; [m.] Duane Bentley, June 2, 1956 and Jad Hanner, July 3, 1989; [ch.] Linda Harrison, Merry Buchanan, Rebecca Bentley, Russell Bentley (7 grandchildren); [ed.] Classen High School graduate, 1951; Central State College, 1956 BS Social Studies; University of Central Oklahoma, 1980 MA English; [occ.] Teach English Western Heights High School and now teach College Writing II at Oklahoma City Community College; [memb.] National Council of Teachers of English,, OK Council of Teachers of English, National Education Association, OK Education Association, American Institute of Discussion, Western Heights Education Association, American Quarterhouse Association; [hon.] Listed in Who's Who Among America's Teachers, Teacher of the Year 1980, English Co-chair at Western Height High School (currently), Co-presented a leadership workshop for teachers of gifted and talented students at Metro Vo-Tech 1990, Co-presented a leadership workshop for principals at University of Central Oklahoma 1991; [oth. writ.] Poetry and journals and stories for my personal pleasure. Published in Accent and The Jet Express; [pers.] My life is a poem, which I did not know that I had written until I started to read it. My husband Jad Hanner and I won Wind River Thoroughbred Farm, and we raise thoroughbred horses. [a.] Bethany, OK.

BERGER, JR., JOHN TORREY
[pen.] J. Torrey; [b.] April 14, 1938, St. Louis, MO; [m.] Lee; [ed.] J.D., Washington University 1963; [occ.] Attorney, Partner at Lewis, Rice & Finegersh (St. Louis); [pers.] My inspiration is primarily nature and its spiritual aspects; my forms of expression are poetry and wood carvings. [a.] Olivette, MO.

BERNHARD, GEORGE JR.
[pen.] George Bernhard, Jr.; [b.] June 20, 1924, New York, NY; [p.] George Sr. and Dorothy Starr Dickenson Bernhard; [m.] Peggy Wallace, February 14, 1970; [ch.] Robin Kenneth and G. Kenneth Bernhard; [ed.] Yale 1949, Franklin (now Capital) University Law School 1963, Retired Colonel, USAF 1979; [occ.] Attorney at Law, now retired; [memb.] Columbus Bar Association, Ohio State Bar Association, Retired Officers Association, numerous mental organizations, Sierra Club; [oth. writ.] I put on an employee magazine for Columbus and Southern Ohio Electric Company the utility, now Columbus Southern Power. A monthly , I took photos, layout, wrote the articles Lifelines; [pers.] Taught English Lit., Composition, American Lit., at Franklin's University, business law at Columbus State Univ. Love to read, volunteer at Wright Patterson Air Force Base Mondays. Dropped out of high school to join Army. Since then I have graduated from Yale and Law school. I believe education is supremely important to enrich living, open doors of opportunity. [a.] Columbus, OH.

BERRY, BONNIE
[m.] March 10, 1924, St. Louis, MO; [p.] harry and Thelma Hall Steingrubey; [m.] Harold (deceased), October 4, 1954; [ch.] Andrea Maghamseh and Margaret Tueth; [ed.] Maeystown and Waterloo High, Alton Business and Writers Workshop; [occ.] Senior Homemaker; [memb.] Maeystown Women's Club, Preservation Society; [hon.] 1st place story in Tales From Two Rivers; [oth. writ.] Stories published in senior newspapers, letters to the editor, stories in Tales From Two Rivers, article in Maeystown Volksblatt; [pers.] I write what I know and what I feel with the hope of conveying my message to readers. [a.] Maeystown, IL.

BERRY, JASON CHRISTOPHER
[b.] January 19, 1981, Albany, GA; [p.] Chris and Kathy Berry; [ed.] Highland Middle School (Albany, GA) will start 7th grade in August 1993; [occ.] Student; [memb.] American Motorcycle Association, Taekwondo Plus Karate Center of Albany, GA, TASCO - Leader in a peer support group at school; [hon.] A and B Honor Roll in 6th grade, first place trophies for baseball, soccer, football and karate; [oth. writ.] A friend and I wrote a special project for a 6th grade class which we did the acting and filmed the short story; [pers.] I hope to attend Duke University's summer '94 program and space camp in Huntsville, AL to strengthen my understanding of Math and Science. To relax, I enjoy racing dirt bikes in GA, FL, AL, and TN. [a.] Albany, GA.

BERRYMAN, ALICE
[pen.] Alice Berryman; [b.] December 16, 1950, Bellmore, Long Island, NY; [p.] Glyn and Alice Berryman; [m.] Terry Cornell, September 4, 1993; [ch.] Bronwyn and Lauren; [ed.] Antelope Valley Community College; [occ.] Administrative Secretary, Parks and Recreation, City of Palmdale; [memb.] Amnesty International, Humane Society of the U.S., Greenpeace; [oth. writ.] Several articles published in local newspapers, and several poems published in literary magazines; [pers.] I write as a kind of pay back for what I read, to move others the way I am moved. [a.] Lancaster, PA.

BIERMAN, KATHIE J.
[b.] March 13, 1969, Aberdeen, SD; [p.] Ordean A. and Cary Lou Bierman; [ed.] Aberdeen Central High, Inver Hills Community College; [occ.] Legal Secretary/paralegal; [oth. writ.] Several musical compositions; [pers.] I write about people, emotions, and experiences. "If you think I'm gone" is dedicated to my paternal grandparents who were special people that will be missed. [a.] Minneapolis, MN.

BIERNAT, RENATA
[b.] September 9, 1980, Elk Grove Village, IL; [p.] Halina and Janusz Biernat; [ed.] Middle School (8th grade); [hon.] Super Honor Roll all through schooling; [oth. writ.] Have entered and won several poetry contests at school; [pers.] I feel my poetry helps me express my feelings towards life. I like to have fun when I write. [a.] West Dundee, IL.

BIGUM, SARAH
[pen.] Sarah Bigum; [b.] November 24, 1980, Greely, CO; [p.] Alfred and Edith Bigum; [pers.] In my opinion, the rainforest is the most beautiful creation God has given us besides people.

BIRD, CINDY K.
[b.] September 24, 1966; [m.] John S. III; [ch.] David Samuel, Michael Donovan; [ed.] Fairfield High School, University of Alabama at Birmingham; [occ.] Emergency Medical Technician; [pers.] My husband is a Vietnam veteran and having watched his struggle to overcome the effects of that war, I realize the importance of a supportive person in his life. [a.] Birmingham, AL.

BITTICK, JENNY
[b.] August 25, 1978, St. Louis, MO; [p.] Jacklyn and Victor (deceased) Bittick; [ed.] High school freshman; [hon.] Elementary Mosaic awards, poems published in school magazines; [oth. writ.] SEveral short stories and poems published in school magazines and newspapers; [pers.] I wrote this poem for my mother since I see that we are so much alike and I love her so much. I want her to see how much she means to me. [a.] Narcross, GA.

BJERKNESS, KEVIN
[b.] August 6, 1969, Prince George, BC, CAN; [p.] Lewis and Mary Bjerkness; [ed.] College of New Caledonia, University of British Columbia; [oth. writ.] The Formality, novel 1993 unpublished, Cathedrals of Decadence (unpublished) Volume of Poetry, 1992. [a.] Vancouver, BC, CAN.

BLACK, TONI E.
[pen.] Toni E. Black; [b.] October 6, 1976, Albuquerque, NM; [p.] Christine E. Crippen-Chavez and Don Chavez (step-father), Ronald Black (natural father); [ch.] Would like to dedicate all that I do to my wonderful little sister, Larisa C. Chavez, she deserves my all; [ed.] Menaul High School (College bound); [occ.] Student; [memb.] High School Drama Clubs, always active in AIDS Awareness agendas; [hon.] Numerous awards for Drama, and awards in Music; [oth. writ.] "The Sun in June's Eyes", about a girl forced with the troubles of being held captive in an attic during a WWII Rampage in Siberia, many song lyrics; [pers.] Greatly influenced by soulful and gospel music. Also very influenced by my Grandmother, Wilma (Billy) Black for all that she was not able, but so capable to do. I need to acknowledge the wonderful fatherly efforts in which my stepfather put forth in order to set me straight. Than you Mom and Dad for all you support. I love you. This poem was most of all dedicated to my sister and my future children. Please let not just my children, but all children see a better day. [a.] Los Lunas, NM.

BLACKBURN, MELISSA
[b.] March 16, 1973, Washington, DC; [p.] Don and Dina Blackburn; [ed.] Suitland High School, Wilkes Community College; [memb.] The Wilderness Society; [pers.] I believe poetry illustrates life and provides the vision to see the world. [a.] Hays, NC.

BLAIR, DONALD CARL
[pen.] Don Blair; [b.] July 7, 1931, Crookston, Ont. Canada; [p.] Charles and Madeline (Storring) Blair buried at White Lake Cemetery (Crookston); [m.] Ruby (Maxwell, 5/20/33), April 4, 1958; [ch.] Wanda

Blair, Wayne Blair, Donna (Blair) Davis; [ed.] White Lake School, SS#10 Huntington Township; [occ.] Construction- Don Blair Construction retired; [oth. writ.] "In Days Gone By" a book of poems (self published, with help from Darren and Donna Davis); [pers.] We have 5 grandsons, Ryan (Wanda), Gavin & Brandon (Wayne and Kathy), Matthew & Blake (Darren & Donna) Wanda works in a shoe store in Belleville, Wayne is a Woolworth Manager at Sault Ste., Marie and Kathy bank teller, Darren ius a constable at Elliot Lake Ont. Donna is a home maker. [a.] Ontario, Canada.

BLAISDELL, KATHLEEN E.
[b.] March 7, 1922, York, ME; [p.] Virgil L. and Marion (Newcomb) Horn; [m.] George E. (deceased), August 24, 1945; [ch.] Terrence Wayne Blaisdell; [ed.] Berwick Academy class of 1939 night courses at McIntosh Business College; [occ.] Scheduler/Planner, Watts Fluidain, Kittery, ME retired 1987; [memb.] First Baptist Church, also Assistant Financial Sec. & Choir Director, AARP; [hon.] Berwick Academy - scholastically, Honor Roll, Debating, Prize Books, also "Book of British & American Verse" for compilation of a Maine book; [oth. writ.] Poems in the 1938 and '39 BA yearbooks, during WWII had several poems published in local newspaper, poem written for the 150th Anniversary of the church; [pers.] I enjoy thoughts and ideas that are relevant to everyday living - striving always for a positive attitude. [a.] So. Berwick, ME.

BLAKE, VERA MINTER MCDONALD
[b.] May 28, 1904, Eclectic, AL; [p.] The W.H. Winters; [m.] Lawson McDonald February 12, 1924, M.J. Blake October 3, 1967; [ch.] Reverend Harold McDonald; [ed.] Eclectic High School; [occ.] Cafe owner, owned and operated McDonald's Grocery, owned and operated a barber ship, community editor of Montgomery Home News, nurse for 20 years and now retired; [memb.] Morningview Baptist Church, Montgomery Chapter 180 Eastern Star, Woman's Club of Montgomery, Magic Club, Past President of Oak Forest Garden Club, Business and Professional Women's Club; [hon.] Voted Most Versatile BPW member, listed in Personalities of the South in 1973-74, Dictionary of International Biographies in 1976, Voted Top in Achievements in Montgomery 1989, Mother of the Year, participate in the Finals of the World's Championship Domino Tournament in Andalusia, Alabama for thirteen years, entertained as a Magician for seventy-five years and appeared as the opening act for Art Linkletter in 1992, won first prize and trophy at Bama Lane Bowling, won first prize at Richardson Terrace Senior Citizen's Group in domino tournament, recently completed cassette tape recordings playing my harmonica of over 50 religious hymns; [oth. writ.] Authored "Under the Sycamore Tree"; [pers.] I live my life realizing that my happiness is created by being kind and considerate of others and always being there when I am needed. [a.] Montgomery, AL.

BLEILER, MELISSA J.
[b.] March 24, 1976, Fort Atkinson, WI; [p.] Dan Bleiler and Deb Butzine; [ed.] Fort Atkinson High School; [hon.] High honors, Forensics State Competitor third place; [oth. writ.] Several poems in student publications "The Mark" and "The Dove"; [pers.] "Vita Brevis Ars Longa". Thank you Josh for your faith and love. May your fire forever burn bright and the doors always be open, my friend. [a.] Fort Atkinson, WI.

BLENDEN, MICHAEL JOSEPH
[b.] October 28, 1975, Orofino, ID; [p.] Rusty and Lori Mattson, Rick Robison; [ed.] Senior Orofino High School; [oth. writ.] Various unpublished writings; [pers.] My main goal as a writer is to create my own style and to be different from the rest. [a.] Orofino, ID.

BLEVINS, PEGGY M.
[b.] November 8, 1938, Kingsport, TN; [p.] Horace and Bonnie Bragg Dolen; [m.] Jerry M., December 4, 1958; [ch.] J. Michael Blevins; [ed.] Sullivan High, Crum's Beauty College; [occ.] Retired Beautician; [memb.] V.F.W. Auxiliary; [oth. writ.] Written verses and poetry for personal homemade greeting cards; [pers.] I dedicate this poem to Scott's mother, Bertha Mullins, and to my mother, Bonnie Bragg-Dolen - both having lost young sons in highway accidents. [a.] Junction City, KS.

BLISS, GARY D.
[b.] April 6, 1959, Cuba, New York; [m.] Susan M.; [ed.] St. Bonaventure University, Monterey Institute of International Studies and Hawaii Pacific University; [occ.] United States Marine Corps; [pers.] From Desert Storm to In the Desert Sun...[a.] Kailua, HI.

BLIZARD, CHARLOTTE B.
[pen.] Charlotte B. Blizard; [b.] Wellsville, NY; [p.] Pearl and Chester Bliss (deceased); [m.] Gordon F., July 15, 1931; [ch.] Three sons; [ed.] BS - Home Economics and MS - Home Economics Education; [occ.] Housewife; [hon.] Self satisfaction; [oth. writ.] I have had only three poems published; [pers.] I believe in life. [a.] Ambler, PA.

BLOESCH, MAUREEN L.R.
[b.] December 17, 1942, Bronx, NY; [p.] Harriette D. Rappaport Becker and Chris J. Becker; [m.] Frederic Stuart, April 1, 1981; [ch.] David L., Daniel G., And Aaron L. Bernstein; [ed.] Martin Van Buren High School, CCNY, Westchester Community College, Saunders Trade, Flusing Beauty School; [occ.] Traveling barber and beautician for paraplegics and designer; [hon.] Marquis Who's Who of American Women 1990-93, 11th Edition of Who's Who in the World 1992-93, 24th Edition of Who's Who in the East 1992-93, Who's Who in America 1992-93, 2000 Notable American Women 1990-93, 2000 Women of Achievement 1992-93, International Women of the Year 1991-92, 6th Edition Personalities of American 1992-93, International Order of Merit 1992, 12th Edition the Word Who's Who of Women 1992-93, The 20th Century award for achievement, International Honors cup 1992, The Who's Who Registry, Platinum Edition 1992-93, Five Hundred Leaders of Influence 1992, Lifetime Achievement Award, Thomas Publishing's Directory of Minority and Women-Owned Manufacturers, Who's Who in American Education 1993, Women's Inner Circle of Achievement 1993, International Who's Who of Professional & Business Women 1994, Who's Who of the Year 1993, Certificate of Appreciation-PBS KERA Channel 13 Texas 1987-93, National Jeweler Magazine: Annual Fashion Circle 1/16/90, Greenpeace 1988-90, Munson-Williams-Proctor Institute Museum of Art 1987-93, National Jewelwe Industry Yellow Pages, Dun & Bradstreet, Jewelers Board of Trade 1986-93, North County News 1991; [oth. writ.] Organic Gardening 1993, The Iliad Literary Awards 1993, Prairie Dog Press 1993, Poetry Press 1993, Sparrowgrass Poetry Forum 1993; published short stories: Wonder Digital PressWonder Disc 1993; [pers.] Nothing is gained, if not pursued. Ask, and gain a multitude of knowledge. [a.] Putnam Valley, NY,

BLUM, PATRICIA
[b.] March 4, 1945, East Elma, NY; [m.] Lanny, July 24, 1965; [ch.] Dennis P. and David M.; [ed.] Iroquois Central, Bryant and Stratton Business Institute, Genesee Community College; [occ.] Housewife, Full-time Student; [memb.] Full Gospel Community Church; [oth. writ.] Several poems, short essays. [a.] Attica, NY.

BOBO, ARLIE U.
[b.] April 5, 1909, Fayette, AL; [p.] Ira and Catherine Endora Collins Bobo; [m.] Lucile Eva Schroeder, May 1, 1936; [ch.] L. Douglas, Suzanne, Richard; [ed.] Two year junior college, Mississippi-Alabama Business College; [occ.] Ordained Minister 32 years pastor; [memb.] North Alabama Methodist Church, Grand Lodge of Free and Accepted Masons, Sumiton Temple Lodge; [hon.] World of Poetry "Life's Pathway"; [oth. writ.] Book - "Poems for Special Occasions", World of Poetry, Life's Pathway, This Year's Vacation, Ashy Poem; [pers.] I use a plot from nature and get a lesson to inspire the reader. [a.] Alexander City, AL.

BOGAN, CAROLYN J.
[b.] May 26, 1941, Lilbourn, MO; [p.] David Jr., and Catherine Parrott Richard; [m.] Luther J. Sr., March 3, 1962; [ch.] Luther J. Jr.; [ed.] Hadley Technical High; [occ.] P/T Clerk/Receptionist; [memb.] Northside Christian Church; [hon.] National Honor Society; [oth. writ.] Several poems, non published, primarily for my own enjoyment; [pers.] I believe in "live and let live" either accept a man for what he **is**, or leave him alone for what he is **not**! [a.] St. Louis, MO.

BOLINE, BRENDA
[b.] September 15, 1963, Kansas; [p.] Duane and Patricia Boline; [ed.] BS in Chemistry Baylor University; [occ.] Chemist Wolfcreek Nuclear Generating Station; [memb.] American Chemical Society and American Nuclear Society; [pers.] Support voluntary simplicity. [a.] Burlington, KS.

BOOTH, JOAN (CURLEY)
[pen.] Joani, Joanie, JB; [b.] October 23, 1937, Philadelphia, PA; [p.] Herbert J. and Anna Curley; [m.] James H. Booth IV, February 14, 1976; [ch.] Jim 16, Stephanie 14, Dana 11; [oth. writ.] Woman's newsletters, private collection; [pers.] Whatsoever you do, do to the glory of God. [a.] Norristown, PA.

BOOTS, JOELLE
[b.] September 11, 1980, Wurzburg, Germany; [p.] Denise and Michael Boots; [ed.] Completed elementary school now in junior high; [occ.] Student; [oth. writ.] Other poems, and short stories; [pers.] I owe it all to my fourth grade teacher. [a.] Lacey, WA.

BOTHA, KATIE
[ch.] 2 sons, married and 4 grandchildren; [ed.] BA degree; [occ.] Scientology Minister; [oth. writ.] A selection of 40 poems which I published entitled, "Katie's First Moments with You"; [a.] Cleveland, FL.

BOTTI, ERNEST A.
[b.] October 14, 1930, Somerville, MA; [m.] Marguerite J., October 15, 1978; [ch.] Karen, Andrew, Lisa, David; [ed.] Newton High 1948, New England Aircraft School 1950, US Air Force Flight Training Command 1952, Aircraft Observer - 1st Lt. Boston University 1959 - BS Aeronautical Engineering; [occ.] Consulting Engineer founded E.A. Botti, Inc. 1970; [memb.] MBAE - Mass Business Alliance for Education, SBANE-Smaller Business Association of New England, 339th Fighter Squadron Association, born in the Pacific during WWII; [pers.] I attempt to create images with words that people can relate to. [a.] Waltham, MA.

BOUCHER, ELIZABETH A.
[pen.] Anne Porter Boucher; [b.] February 24, 1915, Fall River, MA; [ed.] Worked for General Motors also retired from Uniroyal Inc. 33 years of service; [memb.] Rubber Workers Union, United Auto Workers union, Harmony Singers (Village Green); [oth. writ.] Sparrow Grass (Treasured Poems of America) 5 TOMES The National Library of Poetry (Wind in the Night Sky) 2nd TOME; [pers.] I have been writing poetry since childhood and a goodly amount of short stories. I'm going all out to have my entire works published and I feel it will be soon. [a.] Blackstone, MA.

BOUGDANOS, MARIKA
[b.] May 29, 1951, Bayonne, NJ; [p.] Michael J. and Mary A. Democritos Kumaras; [m.] Theodosios, September 1, 1973; [ch.] Two - Stephanie and Constanting (Dino); [ed.] A.A.S. Fashion Institute of TEchnology; [occ.] Women's Wear Fashion Coordinator/Buyer; [memb.] St. George Greek Orthodox Church; [hon.] Awards for artwork and poem: a robot that moved and lit up with poem telling the world to "open your eyes, like Lucy in the skies"; [oth. writ.] Poems published in local newspapers and bulletins, poems in personal greeting cards; [pers.] It is sometimes hard to understand the reasoning of man, through poems I try to express my feelings of why. [a.] Montclair, NJ.

BOURQUE, JOHN P.
[b.] July 9, 1957, Sauqus, MA; [p.] Joseph L. and Eleanor M. Bourque; [ed.] Saugus School 12 years; [occ.] General Manager for Piper Trail Campground (Albany, NH); [pers.] Special thanks to Richard and Betty Lou Cunningham and Mom and Dad, Donnie, Joe, Merri Jane and Robin B. Woods. [a.] Conway, NH.

BOWEN, KIMBERLY L.
[b.] January 25, 1976, Columbus, OH; [p.] Susan Bowen; [ed.] Beginning twelfth grade this fall (1993) at Castilleja High School, have completed two quarters at UC Santa Barbara's summer creative writing program '92 & '93; [occ.] Student; [hon.] Princeton Book award 1993, Creative Writing Award; [oth. writ.] Poems and articles in school publications, co-editor of school newspaper, "Counterpoint"; [pers.] I write in an effort to express my own reality to the rest of the world. [a.] San Jose, CA.

BOWERMAN, CRAIG
[pen.] Bud Mann; [b.] August 29, 1960, Lansing, MI; [p.] Wallace Dee Bowerman and Darlene Kay Sawyer; [m.] Barbara, September 26, 1986; [ed.] Holt Senior High; [occ.] Mechanic, painter; [memb.] Flint Eagles M/C Lansing Chapter, AMVETS; [hon.] Good Conduct medal (USMC); [oth. writ.] Perspectives of a Modern Day Man (a book written by me) unpublished. Been writing poetry since I was 8 years old; [pers.] My writings reflect my feelings on life and the things in life that concern our way of living. Hopefully someone will gain something from my poems. [a.] Lansing, MI.

BOWMAN, DANIELLE R.
[b.] February 18, 1971, Harrisburg, VA; [p.] Dennis Bowman and Amerallus Teter; [ed.] Broadway High, Blue Ridge Community College; [occ.] Sales Clerk; [hon.] Daughters of the American Revolution Citizenship award, Merit List; [pers.] It's the little things in life that keep us going so that we can experience all the major things - both good and bad. It is those little things that inspire me. [a.] Broadway, VA.

BOX, CYNTHIA
[b.] Louisville, KY; [occ.] Business Analyst; [hon.] Many; [oth. writ.] Limericks/Scripts for "Roasts" and parties; poetic "Philosophies" for organizations and businesses, holiday rhymes; [pers.] I love words. Words are very powerful, capable of evoking the most visceral reactions. They can also create whimsy and joy, melancholy and mysticism. I write for fun and I hope my poems can add a light touch or a smile for those who read them. [a.] Louisville, KY.

BOX, OBDULIA MARIE
[pen.] Obbi Box; [b.] June 23, 1971, Durango, CO; [p.] Pearl E. Casias and Russell Box, Sr; [m.] C. Winterhawk; [ch.] Pearl Beth and Krystofer Robyn Winterhawk; [ed.] Ignacio High School; [occ.] Advertiser, Southern Ute Drum Newspaper; [pers.] Many people see words on paper and not the meaning behind my poems. I don't like having to spell things out for them; they can read between the lines and draw their own conclusions. [a.] Ignacio, CO.

BOYCE, JENNIFER SUE RUNION
[b.] October 31, 1968, Quicksburg, VA; [p.] Margeret and John Runion; [m.] Daniel Ray, November 22, 1985; [ch.] Noella Alise and Bradley John Boyce; [ed.] Stonewood Jackson High School, Lord Fairfax Community College and Eastein Mennonite College; [occ.] Information Systems Administrator; [memb.] Phi Theta Kappa 1991-93 (Lordfair Community College); [hon.] Who's Who Among American High School Students 1986, President's Scholarship 1993 (Eastern Mennonite College); [oth. writ.] Several poems published in local newspapers and college journals; [pers.] Most of my poems are influenced by the emotions that I am feeling at that particular moment in time. Experience is the best teacher, live life and learn! [a.] Quicksburg, VA.

BOYCE, LIZ
[b.] July 3, 1974, Lakenheath AFB, England; [p.] James W. and Mary R. Boyce; [ed.] Mountain View High School, Northern Arizona University, Scottsdale Community College, Arizona State University; [occ.] Student; [hon.] Dean's List. [a.] Mesa, AL.

BOYD, EMILY A.
[b.] February 5, 1981, Clarion, IA; [p.] Rex and Nell Boyd; [ed.] K-6th grade; [occ.] Student; [memb.] Northern Iowa River-Greenbelt, Trees Forever-Belmond; [hon.] Ribbons and money for art work and writings - letters, "B" honor roll for a time; [oth. writ.] Poems and stories; [pers.] Let everyone live in peace. Color means nothing, on skin. [a.] Belmond, IA.

BOYD, TAMMY
[b.] May 28, 1972, Philadelphia, PA; [occ.] Proofreader for Cornerstone magazine, an evangelical arts and issues publication with in-depth articles, books, music, fiction and poetry. 939 W. Wilson, Chicago, IL; [oth. writ.] Several poems published in national Zines. (Currently editing and revising material for a heaven for a heaven of blackred roses, a chapbook to be published by Phoenix Press; [pres.] All my writing does is express God's truth as I see it, as the Lord has seen fit to reveal it to me. If I can move one person to a deeper understanding of life and love and God and the place of poetry in the modern world, then I will have fulfilled God's purpose for it. [a.] Chicago, IL.

BOYER, SHARON N.
[b.] July 6, 1942, Loup City, NE; [p.] Arnold and Lenna Krieger; [m.] Garland Boyer (deceased), September 1, 1961; [ch.] Marty Lee and Marcy Marie; [ed.] Gresham High Phagans School of Hair Design, Powers School of Interior Design; [occ.] Hairstylist; [memb.] Eagles - Ladies Aux. No. 2151; [pers.] I have written many poems - none published, they all reflect on my personal life. I have collected works from the early poets since I was 13. [a.] Sandy, OR.

BOYLE, JOHN
[b.] June 30, 1960, Mt. Kisco, NY; [p.] Edward and Marianne Boyle; [ed.] Kingspark, NY graduate, Wilson Tech. graduate; [occ.] Data Processing Field (Banking); [pers.] I write romantic poetry. I've written many, many poems over several years, all remain unpublished. Life, Enjoy It. Keep Smiling. [a.] Clearwater, FL.

BOYLE, JOHN E. WHITEFORD
[b.] August 3, 1915, Milwaukee, WI; [p.] Herman E. and Margaret Lauretta Casey Boyle; [m.] Renee Kent, February 2, 1950; [ch.] Vanessa Whiteford-Wayne, Christopher Whiteford Boyle, Andrea Heller, Alexandra Hollowar; [ed.] PhB Marquette University, Harvard 1945-57, Tehran University and L'Institut Franco-Iranien 1959-62 (Doctorandus); [occ.] President: Academy of Independent Scholars; Essentialist Philosophical Society; Foreign Services Research Institute; Whiteford International Enterprise; [memb.] Essentialist Philosophical Society; Harvard Club; Academy of Independent Scholars; International Association for Near Death Studies; [hon.] Prix Teilhard/Londres 1982-83 (poetry); Golden poet 1992; "Outstanding Scholar/Alumni" Marquette University; [oth. writ.] Series of philosophical works: Primers For the Age of Inner Space: Beyond The Present Prospect, The Indra Web, Graffiti On the Wall of Time, Of The Same Root, Heaven Earth, The Way of the Essentialist; [pers.] Essentialism is my philosophy which begins on the sciences of our time and parallels with ancient, Oriental philosophies and religions. The central tenets are essence precedes existence and reverence for life. [a.] Washington, DC.

BOZARTH, JOEN K.
[pen.] Maria Bei; [b.] June 6, 1945, Cleveland, OH; [ed.] Ohio Northern University; [oth. writ.] WHAT DO YOU THINK? a book of poems designed to stimulate childrens' creative thinking skills is currently being submitted for publication. [a.] Olmstead Falls, OH.

BRADLEY, WILLIAM R.
[pen.] Bill Bradley; [b.] April 23, 1951, Akron, OH; [p.] Oliver and Ruth Bradley; [ed.] Akron East High, Florida International Institute of Children's Literature; [occ.] Service Order Language Standards at Ameritech; [memb.] Minster's License - State of Ohio, Various local Christian organizations; [hon.] National Honor Society, Dean's List, elected student body president senior year of college; [oth. writ.] Book of poems, "Come With Me". Articles in local papers, article in "National Religious Broadcasters" magazine, numerous articles "Answer Magazine"; [pers.] "An Eternal Eye" was written upon the untimely death of my cousin Donald E. Young. [a.] Akron, OH.

BRADY, BOBBI ANN
[b.] May 11, 1975, Tillsonburg, Ontario, CAN; [p.] Jim and Patty Brady; [ed.] University; [pers.] Poetry is magical expression too powerful for speech. [a.] Delhi, Ontario, CAN.

BRADY, H.G. DR.
[pen.] Henry O'Grady; [b.] Columbia, SC; [m.] Divorced; [ed.] PhD. Florida State University; [occ.] Retired Professor Florida University system; [hon.] Fellowship FL. State University; [oth. writ.] Articles in Education and Research Journals. Poems in many publications; [pers.] Major interests are sailing and the sea, Psychology, Philosophy and Travel. [a.] Clearwater, FL.

BRADY, SELMA M.
[b.] November 15, 1958, Baltimore, MD; [p.] Hugo and Marion Gratz; [m.] Deceased, October 22, 1978; [ch.] Joshua Paul; [ed.] High school graduate; [occ.] Secretary - Maryland State Police. [a.] Glen Burnie, MD.

BRADY, SIOBHAN M.
[b.] December 31, 1959, Boston, MA; [p.] Ann and Leo Brady; [m.] Michael Arbona, July 3, 1988; [ch.] Kelsey Ann Arbona; [ed.] St. Clare High, Northeastern University; [pers.] Feel what you feel because feelings are real. [a.] West Roxbury, MA.

BRAGA, ROSALIND L.
[b.] August 19, 1940, Des Moines, IA; [p.] Dr. and Mrs. Julian Bruner; [m.] Roland Allen, August 6, 1977; [ch.] Kevin, Wendy, Leslie; [ed.] BA in Psych - University of Colorado; Teaching - Elementary Certificate, Drake University (Des Moines, IA), MA degree in Special Education at San Francisco State University; [memb.] Delta Kappa Gamma, International Honor Society - past president, Presbyterian Church member; [hon.] Hobbies-Certified Instructor of Tai Chi Chih, a moving meditation; [occ.] Resource Specialist for Learning Handicapped Children San Leandro Unif. Schools, CA; [oth. writ.] Published in the Vital Force Journal for Tai Chi Chih Instructors; [pers.] Through my experience of teaching Learning Handicapped children, I have learned that every person has unique and beautiful ideas to express - through poetry and other forms of expressions. [a.] Castro Valley, CA.

BRAIN, CHRISTINE
[b.] July 27, 1956, Berkeley, CA; [p.] William and Maybelle Brain; [ed.] AA Diable Valley College, BA University of California, Santa Barbara; MM University of Houston (both in Violin performance); [occ.] Violinist: Houston Ballet Orchestra, Houston Grand Opera Orchestra; Violist, Tallis String Quartet, Director of String Ensembles, St. John's School; [memb.] Local 65-699, AFM; Texas Music Orchestra Educator's Association, Texas Orchestra Director's Association. [a.] Houston, TX.

BRANDON, MARIE LENA
[b.] July 23, 1946, Tarpon Springs, FL; [p.] John and Ila Mae Amanda Tyre Antonio; [m.] James Ray, September 8, 1980; [ch.] Jimmy James Whitten, Clint Randall Whitten, Timothy Paul Whitten, and Marie Aurilla Brandon; [ed.] High school equivalence, Lake Area Vocational Technical School (Camdenton, MO), State Fair Community College (Sedalia, MO); [occ.] Student working toward degree; [pers.] This poem is dedicated to my parents, John and Ila Mae Antonio. Since my father's passing, October 27, 1990. He has lived in the beauty of my dreams. Mom and Dad, I will always love you. [a.] Macks Creek, MO.

BRANDOW, JOSEPH D.
[pen.] Joseph D. Brandow; [b.] December 6, 1935, Foam Lake Saskatchewan; [p.] Carl and Evelyn Brandow; [m.] Marlene, July 4, 1987; [ch.] Carl Brandow (14); [ed.] Grade 12 equivalent, ICS-Computer Programmer; [occ.] Retired Journalism; [oth. writ.] Not published short stories and a few poems published in local papers around Christmas; [pers.] Life must be worth smiling about. If one cannot laugh at his own mistakes he must be boring. [a.] British Columbia, CAN.

BRANTLEY, ANTHONY
[b.] August 4, 1964, Shelby, NC; [p.] Diane and Paul A. Brantley, Jr. (deceased); [ed.] Crest High; [occ.] Construction worker; [oth. writ.] Several poems published in local newspaper; [pers.] Poetry is the song of the soul. The most precious, sacred, and inner thoughts of humanity are reflected in its structure and form. [a.] Lattimore, NC.

BRAY, AMY MARIE
[b.] April 30, 1978, Fontana, CA; [p.] Tom Bray and Denise Williams; [ed.] Graduate high school in 1996; [hon.] Honor Roll, 1st place winner of History Day (school and county levels) president's academic award, 1st place winner in school-wide Creative Writing. Contest participant in Mathematics and Verbal Talent Search conducted by the Center for the Achievement of Academically Talented Youth of Johns Hopkins University. [a.] Yucaipa, CA.

BREAULT, BR. EDWARD C.
Brother Fidelis; [b.] December 10, 1929, Pawtucket, RI; [p.] Edward A. and Rita E. (Beauregard) Breault; [ed.] BS/BA Spring Hill College (Mobile, AL), University of South Africa; [occ.] Executive Secretary; [memb.] Brothers of the Sacred Heart, (Worldwide teaching order); [hon.] 30 prizes/Honorable Mentions (World of Poetry), 8 Golden Poet awards (World of Poetry; [oth. writ.] Published in 13 anthologies by World of Poetry, many original articles and translations in the Order's publications. [a.] Pascoag, RI.

BREES, FINLEY
[pen.] Finley Brees; [b.] July 28, 1917, Volin, SD; [p.] John and Edith Brees (deceased); [m.] Bernie, May 21, 1949; [ch.] Joan, Jean, Janet, John, James and Jeffrey; [ed.] Graduate Mechanic Arts High School 1936, Dale Carnegie Public Speaking; [occ.] REtired B.N. Inc. 13 yrs sales representative; [hon.] 2 first place speaking Dale Carnegie; 2 full page stories in St. Paul paper, MC 5 talent shows; [oth. writ.] Numerous poems; [pers.] I think flooding will the topography of central U.S. [a.] St. Paul. MN.

BREMER, BRENDA
[pen.] Adeline Guenther; [b.] February 2, 1973, Lexington, NE; [p.] Lorin and Dorothy Bremer; [ed.] Lexington Senior High, Hastings College; [occ.] Junior at Hastings College majoring in Psychology/English and Pre-Mortuary Science; [memb.] Kappa Rho Upsilon, BACCHUS, First Presbyterian Church; [hon.] 10 year 4-H member; [oth. writ.] Several poems published in Hastings College Spectrum; [pers.] I thoroughly enjoy writing poetry and I find that real life experiences serve as my inspirational force. [a.] Lexington, NE.

BRENDLINGER, ANGELA
[pen.] Angela Marie; [b.] February 5, 1970, Johnstown, PA; [p.] William and Emily Rolley; [m.] Wayne, March 12, 1988; [ch.] Anthony Daniel and Joseph Patrick; [ed.] Laurel Valley High School, National Education Center, Thompson Institute Campus; [occ.] Registered Medical/Surgical Assistant; [memb.] National Association for Health Professionals; [hon.] Academic Achievement award for Academic Excellence in Medical Assisting; [oth. writ.] Several poems and short stories published during high school in the Laurel Valley Newsletter; [pers.] My writings reflect upon the goodness of life in a manner that represents the beauty of it. [a.] Grantville, PA.

BREUNIG, HELEN L.
[b.] April 12, 1930, Denver, CO; [ed.] California State University (MA), University of Denver (BA); [occ.] Poet and writer; [memb.] The Authors League of America, The National Writers Association, The Author's Guild Inc.; [hon.] Phi Beta Kappa; [oth. writ.] Book: Nest Egg Investing, published by Dow Jones-Irwin, NY; articles: published by Reader's Digest, Modern Maturity Magazine, U.S. Marine national newspaper 'Flight Jacket'; television scripts and on camera presentation, 3 years consumer information program; [pers.] "Poetry is the highest form of writing as it demands the bared soul of the writer in homage to the spirit of the creator within."-Helen L. Breunig. [a.] Fullerton, CA.

BRIARE, SHANNON
[b.] December 12, 1969, Sacramento, CA; [p.] Lou Ann and Phillip Heranesberger; [ed.] Encina High School, Allen Hancock College, Cal Poly - San Luis Obispo; [occ.] Full-time student self employed; [memb.] Delta Rescue (for animals) A.S.P.C.A., P.B.S., Greenpeace, Y.W.C.A., Star Search International; [hon.] Won 2nd place in nationwide doll poetry contest when I was 12 years old; [oth. writ.] Several poems unpublished (by choice) a children's book called "Freddie's Freckles" also an essay I wrote was published in our school newspaper; [pers.] Most of my writings come directly from my heart and soul, some come from my imagination, but all are the result of a strong, creative mind. [a.] Nipomo, CA.

BRIDGES, CHARLES
[pen.] Silhouett, Tzarka; [b.] August 1, 1957, Attleboro, MA; [p.] Mary Ruth (Martin) and Charles Earl Bridges; [m.] Linda (Roy), August 24, 1991; [ch.] Gretchen Bridges, Aaron Bridges, Justin Bridges; [ed.] Wentworth College and Mansfield High School; [occ.] Computer Consultant; [memb.] Church of Christ; [oth. writ.] Local newspaper; [pers.] I hope to grow in life, to a point of giving advice while listening to what I've said. [a.] Mansfield, MA.

BROE, INA LELAND
[b.] March 27, 1912, Galchutt, ND; [p.] Mathias Bertrand and Anna Louise Leland; [m.] George H. Broe (deceased); [ed.] Mayville State University (ND), University of Illinois (library degree), University of Minnesota (MA); [occ.] Teacher, Librarian, Library Resource Center Administration (30 years); [memb.] N.E.A. (life member), Illinois Retired Teachers (life), St. John's Lutheran Church, F.M.O., F.V.O.A.; [hon.] Richland Co., ND Declaration (1st place); [oth. writ.] Articles in Wilson Bulletin, National Scholastic Magazine, F.V.O.A. Kalidiscope; [pers.] There is nore good than bad in each of us but we often have to femet it our. [a.] Sarasota, FL.

BROLSMA, SHEILA
[b.] November 24, 1903, Jamaica, BWI; [p.] Professor Charles Homer Condell and Elmo Henrietta Bryce; [m.] Clarence, June 17, 1964; [ed.] Private; [occ.] Retired; [memb.] AARP, Made in the USA, Senior Coalition, Member of English Speaking Union in London; [hon.] Golden Poet 1992; [pers.] I have always done hospital visitation everywhere I lived. Interested in Elocution. [a.] Phoenix, AZ.

BROOKS, CLARA B.
[b.] September 16, 1917, Childersburg, AL; [p.] Harlin and Edna Brooks; [m.] Clinton G., June 9, 1946; [ch.] Claire Elaine Butts - married to William H. Butts. Only one grandchild, April Joy - 10 yrs old; [ed.] Spartanburg, SC, Methodist College, Birmingham Southern and Howard Universities; [occ.] Teacher Long Distance, Operator Retired Southern Bell 1982; [memb.] Christ United Methodist Church, United Methodist Church Choir, United Methodist Women; [oth. writ.] Published one book of poetry "Straight From the Heart". Vantage Press 1977. Many poems for every occasion, starting in the first grade; [pers.] Music, next to love is God's greatest gift to man. It touches the heart and bends it towards love, forgiveness and peace. I hear music in rhymed, metered verse, my favorite type of poetry. It is an instrument of God's love and a powerful force for good. [a.] Holly Hill, FL.

BROWN, AMBER FURLOUGH
[b.] January 8, 1979, Edenton, NC; [p.] Mr. and Mrs. Nathan S. Hurdle and Michael E. Brown; [ed.] 9th grade-Victory School Elizabeth City; [occ.] Student; [pers.] I like to write about myu feelings at the moment. [a.] Elizabeth City, NC.

BROWN, ANTIONETTE LENOIR
[pen.] Antionette Lenoir; [b.] August 8, 1930; [p.] Izora and Oliver Lenoir; [m.] August 15, 1950; [ch.] Tamera Morris, Anthony Brown, Lenoir Mallory; [ed.] Case Western Reserve University; [occ.] Math Teacher Cleveland Public Schools; [memb.] OCTM, NCTM, Kappa Epsilon Delta, East Glenville United Methodist Church; [hon.] Dean's List at CWRU; [pers.] I dedicate my poem to Harold the love of my life, with whom I loved, laughed, cried, and smelled the flowers. God is the head of my life. [a.] Cleveland, OH.

BROWN, BERTRAM C.
[b.] March 26, 1925, Glovertown, Newfoundland, Canada; [p.] Charles and Mary Brown; [m.] Anne, June 30, 1959; [ch.] Beverly and Carolyn; [ed.] High school at Corner Brook, Newfoundland; BA at Memorial University of St. John's Nfld. B.ED at Memorial University of St. John's Nfld, MED at Toronto University; [occ.] English teacher (retired); [memb.] Newfoundland Teacher's Association; [oth. writ.] Several articles dealing with educational matters published by the Newfoundland Teachers Journal; [pers.] For me, poetry should consist of clear and arresting images within which lie meaning and emotion. [a.] St. John's, Newfoundland, Canada.

BROWN, DARRELL R.
[pen.] El Hid, Detoo; [b.] September 6, 1962, Denver, CO; [p.] Hallet K. and Evelyn M. Brown; [ed.] Highland High, Colorado State University; [occ.] English and Spanish teacher; [memb.] National Crisis Prevention Institutie, AARP, NEA, Youth Enrichment Program, ANOOS Productions; [hon.] College Creative Writing award, 3 time Teacher of the Year, C.E.A., Lion award; Kaleidoscope award, National Science Fiction 3rd and 9th place winner; [oth. writ.] Two published books of poetry, ten books of prose, and one non-fiction book; [pers.] Communication is the key to existence. Indecision is the world's worst thing. [a.] Denver, CO.

BROWN, HOWARD HOYD
[b.] August 21, 1953, Ware, AL; [p.] Charles L. and Sue E. Brown; [ed.] Quaboag Regional High School; [pers.] In loving memory of Charles L. Brown and Sue E. Brown. To soon youth gives way to time. May we in aging recapture some of the magical moments of our youth. HARE KRISHNA! [a.] Norfolk, MA.

BROWN, KRISTI
[b.] May 26, 1981, Staunton, IL; [p.] Richard and Karen Brown; [ed.] Cion Lutheran School (6th grade); [occ.] Student. [a.] Staunton, IL.

BROWN, MICHAEL
[pen.] Michael E. Brown; [b.] November 28, 1973, Fremont, OH; [p.] Robert and Rose Borwn; [ed.] Fremont Ross High; [occ.] Operation Specialist in the U.S. Navy, writer (poet, author); [memb.] Mt. Pleasant Baptist Church; [oth. writ.] Personal journals and poems; [pers.] Everything I write is a part of me. The pen is my body, the ink is my blood. Therefore, everything I write comes from my heart and the words come from my soul. [a.] Fremont, OH.

BROWN, MONIQUE CAROLE
[b.] July 1, 1964, Hartford, CT; [p.] Richard and Carol Brown; [ed.] AA degree Saddleback College, BA Cal State University, Fullerton Graduate Law Study-Kensington Unviersity College of Law; [occ.] Law student/freelance writer; [memb.] Society of Children's Book Writers, International Women's Writing Guild, National Writer's Club, Nature Conservancy, Greenpeace, Humane Society of the U.S.; [hon.] Scholarship CSUF-Police Officers Association, American Field Service; [oth. writ.] Poem published in "Memories" anthology by JMW Publishing Co.; [pers.] To write is to release the infinite capabilities of my mind. The elements of nature are my inspiration. [a.] North Palm Beach, FL.

BROWN, RACHEL
[b.] May 2, 1980, Little Rock, AR; [p.] Cindy and Michael Brown; [pers.] Poetry is more than words, it's a feeling on paper. [a.] Little Rock, AR.

BROWN, ROSIE L.
[pen.] Snake and (T.); [b.] November 26, 1955, Rohwer, AK; [p.] Rosezinia Toliver and Roy L. Williams; [m.] Leo Brown, April 18, 1976; [ch.] Leo Brown, Jr., Rosalind R. and Helen M. Brown; [ed.] Delta Special High School; [occ.] Physical Therapy Assistance also Certified Nurse Technician; [memb.] Oak Grove Baptist Church; [hon.] Certificate of Appreciation from L.L.M.; [oth. writ.] None really, just welcome addresses and responses for church services; [pers.] Is that its such a treat to feel joy and happiness inside your self and want someone else to know and feel the same love and contentment. [a.] McGehee, AK.

BROWN, SHIRLEY M.
[b.] November 15, 1938, Gap Creek, KY; [p.] Ode and Delphia Massengale; [m.] Bobby, June 12, 1958; [ch.] L.E. Brown and Micah B. Hicks; [ed.] Wayne Co. High School, University of Kentucky; [occ.] Secretary, Bookkeeper Wayne Co. Board of Education. [a.] Windy, KY.

BROWNING, WILLIAM B. III
[b.] April 6, 1971, Lowell, MA; [p.] Arlene S. and William B. Browning III; [ed.] Associate degree - Liberal Arts; [occ.] Student/Swimming instructor; [memb.] Masons-Lowell Chapter; [hon.] English awards and poetry merits. Poetry honors and Editor's Choice awards; [oth. writ.] "Shadow Waltz" in Poetic Voices of America, "Poem's Love in All my Tomorrows", "A Kiss Amidst" in Wind in the Night Sky, "Water in the Desert Sun"; [pers.] Love and nature serve as sources of inspiration in my life, and are reflected in my poetry. These things, flavored with a touch of romance and magic, have been known to transport readers to places of wonder. [a.] Lowell, MA.

BROWNSBERGER, MICHELLE
[b.] April 12, 1976, Columbus, OH; [p.] Rick and Connie Brownsberger; [p.] Rick and Connie Brownsberger; [ed.] Senior at Mentor High School; [occ.] Student; [memb.] 4-H Club (North Coast Riders). Mentor High School Ecology Club, Wildlife Fund; [hon.] First place at the Lakeland Poetry Contest of the high school division; [oth. writ.]

Several poems published in my school magazine and other published in a nearby college newspaper; [pers.] I work very hard to preserve nature in my area. I have been influenced by several English teachers and poets. [a.] Mentor, OH.

BROUMLEY, JENNIFER
[b.] September 25, 1979, Woodward, OK; [p.] Mark and Nancy Broumley; [hon.] Journalism, poetry, and writing honors; [oth. writ.] Winter - a poem recently being published. Several poems published in smal newspapers; [pers.] I enjoy writing about realistic situations, about things that are real. Not dreams or fictional things. [a.] Carthage, TX.

BRUNGARDT, DANNY
[pen.] Dana Franchot; [b.] October 20, 1948, Houston, TX; [p.] Richard and Virginia Brungardt; [ch.] Mandy Lee Rose; [ed.] GED and Aircraft Technical Schools; [occ.] Aircraft Technician; [pers.] Life is only once, loves are true. Trust yourself and live life through. [a.] Houston, TX.

BRUYER, NEEKA
[b.] September 9, 1977, Kalispell, MT; [p.] Lorri and Trent Holman; [ed.] Flathead High School; [pers.] This poem is dedicated to my bestfriend Matthew Jackson, I love you. [a.] Kalispell, MT.

BRYAN, SIBYL
[pen.] Sibyl Byran; [b.] November 5, 1911, Casa, AR; [p.] John C. and Dora A. Burton; [m.] G.N. Jr., (deceased), September 29, 1931; [ed.] University of Central AR; [occ.] Retired teacher; [oth. writ.] 100 poems written from 1930-1935 (lost); [pers.] Live each day as if it were your last one. [a.] N. Little Rock, AR.

BRYANT, ERTHA E.
[pen.] Erk; [b.] July 8, 1925, Orange City, FL; [p.] Will and Mary Maria Thompson Durant; [m.] James J., December 23, 1960; [ch.] Arthur, Carolyn, Brenda, Kennieth, Philo, Ivory, Sandra; [ed.] Orange City FL Adult Education, IROC, Fort Pierce, Martin High; [occ.] Retired minister, CNA Nurse, cook, foster and adoption parent; [memb.] Pentecostal Church, Masonic Lodges, "Minister Alliance", East Stuart Community Historical Society; [hon.] For good poems I do write, certificates given; [pers.] I gets great pleasure in taking a seat and put my pen to work. a[.] Stuart, FL.

BUCHNER, LAUREEN F.
[b.] June 14, 1959, France, Europe; [p.] Marilyn F. Wood and Peter J. Elward; [m.[] Dale, July 2, 1982; [ch.] Beau (9) and Cody (7); [ed.] Grand Centre High School, Lac La Biche Vocational; [occ.] Self-employed; [pers.] I have always retained a genuine interest in the expression of feelings through words. [a.] Cold Lkae, Alberta, Canada.

BUCK, M\NILA YVONNE
[pen.] Yvonne Bandy; [b.] February 8, 1949, Greenville, KY; [p.] Wendell and Merilene Brandy; [occ.] Data Entry Typist; [oth. writ.] This is my very first poem.

BUFFMIRE, HAZEL D.
[pen.] Hazel D. Buffmire; [b.] December 30, 1900, Chicago, IL; [p.] Arthur and Katherine DuVal (deceased); [m.] Wallace, June 15, 1929; [ch.] Robert DuVAl Buffmire; [ed.] Northwestern University graduate, advanced courses-Univ. of Winsconsin and Univ. of Colorado; [occ.] Former Social Studies teacher at Sandwich High School and in Kenosha, Wisconsin; elementary teacher at Willard School in Evanston, IL; [memb.] Wally Byam Caravan Club, Irving Park United Methodist Church, Delta Zeta, Life member in NRTA; [hon.] Ribbons for portrait paintings; [oth. writ.] Twenty-six yearly Christmas poems, numerous club histories in poetry; local and foreign Airstream travel poems for Caravan Clubs; [pers.] The joy of putting into poetry my love of life. [a.] Merrit Island, FL.

BUKOVITZ, RICHELLE
[b.] July 6, 1978, Johnstown, PA; [p.] Bryon and Cathi Pritt; [ed.] Freshman Windber Area High School; [memb.] Windber Area High School Band, Scalp Level Church of the Brethen; [hon.] Super Team Science award, Honors award 1990-91; [oth. writ.] Numerous poems and short stories; [pers.] I believe humor and love for all people are the keys to living a full life. [a.] Winber, PA.

BUMGARDNER, HAZEL
[pen.] Hazel A. Bumgardner; [b.] December 5, 1928, Pruden, TN; [p.] Charles William and Lora Catherine Hamm Allen; [m.] George R., July 21, 1945; [ch.] Clifford R., Cahterine Frances, Clark, Peggy, Susan, Bill, Tim; [ed.] Three years high school (Eubank, KY); [occ.] Homemaker; [memb.] Chuch of Christ (Bellvill, IN), Homemakers Club, (Amo, IN); [hon.] High school yearbook; [oth.w rit.] Poems for weddings and other special occasions, devotings for club, short stories and poems; [pers.] This is the first time I have submitted for competition. I write for pleasure for myself and others. [a.] Coatesville, IN.

BUNGER, MELANIE
[b.] August 3, 1979, Prescott, AZ; [p.] Marilyn J. and Thomas A. Bunger; [ed.] Freshman in high school; [memb.] National Junior Honor Society; [hon.] Presidential Academic Fitness Award, Girl Scout Silver Award; [oth. writ.] Five poems in an anthology published, first plave American Legion essay contest; [pers.] Writing poetry is my way of expressing my inner thoughts and feelings sprinkled with my imagination. [a.] Prescott, AZ.

BURBANK, DIANE
[pen.] Diane Porter; [b.] Brookline, MA; [m.] thomas; [ch.] Susan Downey, Stephen and Douglas Porter; [ed.] Bridgewater State, Hickox Secretarial, Bentley College; [occ.] Guidance Department, Bellous Free Academy St. Albans; [memb.] Order of Eastern Star, Professioinnal Business Women, ASCAP, UWSA; [oth. writ.] "Literary Leaves", local newspaper articles, political speech writer; [pers.] Know yourself, love yourself, be yourself, and know that we are all God's children. [a.] Berkshire, VT.

BURCH, BLANCHE
[pen.] Blanche Burch; [b.] March 5, 1951, Metter, GA; [p.] Earl and Betty Whittaker; [m.] Greig, February 22, 1970; [ch.] Greig, Brkal, Skye, Dijon; [ed.] Emory University (presently third year student); [occ.] Executive Secretary; [memb.] Secretary, Knollwood PTA; [oth. writ.] Book of poems yet to be published; [pers.] For me, writing poetry is an effective form of therapy. Once I've expressed my feelings in a poem, I experience inner healing. [a.] Decatur, GA.

BURGE, EDBI EVE
[pen.] Truck Poetry by Stargazer; [b.] April 11, 1955, Los Angeles, CA; [p.] Aviva and Robert Rann; [m.] Richard; [ch.] April, Billy, Jenni; [ed.] Venice High, Platt College-Graphic Arts Degree; [occ.] Long Haul Independent Truck Driver; [hon.] Several safe driving awards; [oth. writ.] Truck poetry published in Truckers Magazine; [pers.] Poetry helps me express my deeper emotions which in turn reflects the purity of the personality of my soul.

BURK, NANCY TROENDLY
[pen.] Nancy T. Burk; [m.] Thomas L.; [ed.] BBA, MA Human Behavior USIU, Mse D. University of Metaphysics; [occ.] Co-owner with husband in business - Wellness Information Network Consultations, Workshops, Literature; [memb.] Association for Research and Enlightenment, Flower Essence Society, National Homeopathic Society; [hon.] Various scholarships, awards and various performance awards; [oth. writ.] Affirmations for Fast Healing for Surgery Patients, The Metaphysical Meaning and Healing of Rheumatoid Arthritis, The Healing Process (copies available); [pers.] God gives us the power to heal ourselves physically, mentally, emotionally using natural remedies, prayer, meditation, etc. To release our inner spiritual healer, I provide counceling and writing on how to do this. [a.] San Diego, CA.

BURKART, JIM
[b.] Twenty years too late; [pers.] The world is our cup of tea, and I love her flavor. Hold the taste, it is to savor. [a.] Coulferville, CA.

BURKE, CHRISTOPHER
[b.] January 21, 1975, Cleveland, OH; [p.] Richard and Catherine Burke; [ed.] Attending local college majoring in journalism; [memb.] Normal; [hon.] Won local poetry contests held by school and PTA board; [oth. writ.] Other poems published in high school newspaper; [pers.] I try to reach the true emotions of people. I try to grab the feeling of the moment and describe it best on paper. I only write what I have been through. [a.] Columbia Station, OH.

BURKER, FRANCIS P.
[b.] June 15, 1915, San Francisco, CA; [p.] Patrick J. and Ellen R. Burke (both deceased); [ed.] BA-University of San Francisco; [occ.] Retired librarian; [pers.] Good art is good morally; is perceived by the senses; overflows into the emotions; leads to contemplation; stirs and (at least partially) satisfies our higher faculties. (Daniel Lord, S.J.).

BURKITT, ROBIN-LOUISE
[b.] January 12, 1983, Newport, RI; [p.] Robert and Linda Burkitt; [occ.] Student (5th grade - Gaudet Middle School); [hon.] Principal's award. [a.] Middletown, RI.

BURNETT, JENNIFER R.
[b.] July 31, 1978, Enid, OK; [p.] Ruth Ann and Robert M. Burnett; [ed.] Emerson Junior High School; [occ.] Student; [pers.] Take life day by day. [a.] Enid, OK.

BURNS, BILLIE
[b.] October 25, 1977, Newark, NJ; [p.] Stephen and Donna Flockhart; [ed.] Linden High School; [memb.] Rainbow Girls Azure Assembly #49; [hon.] Arts and honors Spelling. [a.] Linden, NJ.

BURNS, KELLY
[pen.] Alyxandria Montgomery; [b.] March 18, 1976, St. Louis, MO; [p.] Karen Campbell and Mike Burns; [ed.] Springford High (PA) and Washington High (MO); [hon.] First place Duet Acting of Agnes of God; [oth. writ.] Several poems publised in school newspapers. Currently working on an up-coming book Childhood Memories; [pers.] Statistically one out of four women can expect to be sexually assaulted. Although this has not happened to me, I empathize with those whom it has. [a.] Royersford, PA.

BURNS, MARTIN L.
[b.] March 27, 1944, County Durham, England; [p.] Dorothy Burns (nee Charlton) and Lawrence Burns (Irish Catholic Family); [ed.] Completed St. John's High School-England; [occ.] Aiorcraft Company Shipper; [memb.] St. Andrew's Roman Catholic Church; [oth. writ.] I have written many songs and poems for Alzheimers also a poem for the disabled and a cancer patient. I have written many poems - first time I have had the courage to go public; [pers.] Art imitates life, therefore, that is what I do with my poetry. I am inspired to write only about personal experiences. [a.] Etabicoke, Ontario, CAN.

BURNS, SYLVIA M.
[b.] October 4, 1911, Jermyn Rd, PA; [p.] William G. and Fannie M. Decker; [m.] Clarence J., November 24, 1932; [ch.] Grace Marie and John William; [ed.] Waymart High School, Wayne Commercial School; [occ.] Coding at Fireman's Fund Ins. Company; [memb.] AARP, Rosary Altar Society, Sacred Heart Church; [hon.] Valdictorian Class '28, Waymart High; [oth. writ.] My first; [pers.] I was inspired by a picture in the hospital hall outside my door and wrote this on my hospital tray sitting on my bed for my daughter for Mother's Day. [a.] Irvington, NJ.

BURRELL, WANDA L.
[pen.] Wanda Lee Burrell; [b.] July 5, 1920, Safford, AZ; [p.] Willard A. and Mary A. (Hamblin) Lee; [m.] John B. (deceased), February 3, 1938; [ch.] John, Lester, Richard, Dennis, Bryan, Wilma, Mary; [ed.] Thatcher High School, San Juan Community College; [occ.] Society editor of Daily newspaper, clerk typist, Asst. librarian; [oth. writ.] "Love Speaks Every Language", short story, Ensign, 1984. "Lee's Ferry Crossing",, poem, American Poetry Anthology, 1986. "The Melting Pot", poem, The Poetry of Life: A Treasury of Moments, 1987. [a.] Farmington, NM.

BURSEY, LARRY
[pen.] Larry Bursey; [b.] May 15, 1969, Happy Valley, Labrador; [p.] Alvin and Daphne Bursey; [ed.] Goose High School, Labrador Community College; [occ.] Student; [oth. writ.] None published, write poetry only as a hobby; [pers.] I paid close attention and re-examined the realities and happenings of my personal life which inspired my writing. [a.] Happy Valley, Labrador.

BURTON, ALYSSA
[b.] November 10, 1981, Anniston, AL; [p.] Travis and Marchale Burton; [ed.] Alexandria Middle School, 6th grade; [occ.] Student; [memb.] Mt. Aarat C.M.E. Church; [hon.] President of 4-H Club, Musical Ability award, Partner in Excellence award, Flag award; [oth. writ.] Short stories and poems; [pers.] Life is like a good book, the cover is hard but the pages are filled with knowledge and adventure. [a.] Jacksonville, AL.

BURTON, DANYELE
[pen.] Danyele Burton; [b.] March 17, 1977, Phoenixville, PA; [p.] Mr. and Mrs. Thomas Burton; [ed.] Phoenixville High School; [occ.] Artist and poet; [memb.] Students Against Drunk Driving; [hon.] Honorable mention for poems written during school; [oth. writ.] Several poems published locally; [pers.] For I am onw who needs no leader, for I am a leader in myself. [a.] Phoenixville, PA.

BURTON, HARRY RUDOLPH
[b.] February 1, 1923, Greenspond, Newfoundland; [p.] Sidney and Lucy Maude (Goudie) Burton; [m.] Mytle Mildred (Wheeler) Burton, November 4, 1966; [ed.] Little formal schooling, principalklky self-taught. Correspondence course: U.S. School of Music, New York (with certificate April 14, 1944); [occ.] Gen. Store Clerk/Bookkeeper at Greenspond; Church organist/choirmaster; Pipe organ rep. Maintenance/Tuner's Assistant; Freelance Musician; Music Teacher (Due to my having sustained a stroke several years ago, I have now become "The Boy at Home"; [hon.] Church Anthem Composition 1976, 10 O'Leary Poetry prizes (1944-1955); several CBC Radio Limerick Writing Prizes (1985-1993); [oth. writ.] Commemorative poem aAH! Canada! on NF's 10th year of Union with Canada; published in St. John's Evening Telegram March 31, 1959. AM writing poem series on a disturbing phase of our colonization here. On completion, I shall window shop for the right publisher. I have also composed various Musical Compositions; [pers.] Being a devout lover of all things TRULY GOOD, from the stars down (Sacred, Serious and Secular Music, porse, poetry and all the inexhaustible facets of Creation), I feel it is one's God-given privilege to play one's instrumental part as beautifully as possible in His Magnificent Symphony of Creation. I faithfully trust that His will - not mine - be done. [a.] Nfld. CAN.

BURTON, HOLLY
[b.] January 16, 1976, Ft. Worth, TX; [p.] Wanda and Dwight Burton Jr.; [ed.] Aledo High School - Jr.; [occ.] Student; [hon.] English, Biology, first place in Science Fair, first place in duet acting, honorable mention in a play, screaming award, certificate from hospital candy stiper, writing plays and funny comedian, art contest, first honorable mention; [oth. writ.] I have written many poems since I was very young, I plan to publish a book of my very own in years to come; [pers.] I shall go to college and pursue my writing career and acting I express my inner feelings and nature, our true surroundings. [a.] Weatherford, TX.

BUSBEE, CHRISTY L.
[b.] December 23, 1978, Americus, GA; [p.] Lynn and David Kirskey and Greg Busbee; [ed.] Student of Taylor County High School; [hon.] Honor student; [oth. writ.] Poems and articles for school paper; [pers.] Through God dreams can become reality. [a.] Reynolds, GA.

BUSEN, JAMIE LYNN
[b.] April 27, 1979, Springfield, IL; [p.] Ronald and Julie Busen; [ed.] Graduated 8th grade St. Mary's Catholic Grade School; [hon.] Presidential Academic Fitness Award; [oth. writ.] Written own personal poetry; [pers.] In each poem I write, I have been influenced by somthing even the smallest things can influence me. My poems are all truth, all me. [a.] Quincy, IL.

BUSQUE, BEVERLY ANN
[b.] September 1, 1960, Hartland, ME; [p.] Barbara Mae and Linwood Kenneth Morse, Sr.; [m.] Andrew Herbert, March 4, 1977; [ed.] Lawrence High graduate, Waterville High, Maine Criminal Justice Academy; [occ.] Correction Officer Somerset County Jail; [hon.] Two awards for incidents that happened while I was on duty at jail; [oth. writ.] Personal poems from experience in lifetime; [pers.] I usually write about personal experiences in my life. Sad occasions or happy ones. I find I write well about my own experiences. [a.] Waterville, ME.

BUTKOVICH, GABRIELLA NOEL
[b.] December 21, 1977, Suffern, NY; [p.] Gabriel and Nadia Burkovich, (sister-Maria); [occ.] Student-Clarkstown North Senior High School. [a.] Congers, NY.

BUTLER, JASON. B.
[b.] October 5, 1972, San Diego, CA; [p.] Michael and Charlene Butler; [oth. writ.] A few writings published in local papers, I have done readings and performance art around town; [pers.] I am a pragmatic anarchist and individualist concerned with obtaining balance and peace of mind in a world of lies. [a.] San Diego, CA.

BUTLER, ROBERT CHRISTOPHER
[pen.] Robert C. Butler; [b.] November 27, 1969, St. Louis, MO; [p.] George R. Butler, Sr. and Etta M. Tucker; [ed.] Clayton High School, Northeast Missouri State University; [occ.] United States Marine Corps until 1995; [oth. writ.] Plenty, broad subject, unpublished poems and (2) short stories and some prose; [pers.] It's not about just surviving; I'd like to survive better than the average survivor, not just above the water, but I'd like to wade in it. We all should strive for such... [a.] St. Louis, MO.

BUYANSKY, NICOLE
[b.] July 21, 1975, Cleveland, OH; [p.] Ken and Karen Buyansky; [ed.] Padua High, Akron University; [occ.] Student; [hon.] First place in District Photo Awards contest, Honors List in high school; [oth. writ.] Several poems published in high school's "Horizon Magazine"; [pers.] My inner feelings go into every poem I write. If I cannot say it--I write it. [a.] North Royalton, OH.

BUZZELLI, ANTHONY M.
[b.] March 4, 1947, Gagliano Aeterno, Italy; [m.] Sharon; [ch.] Michael and David; [ed.] MA English,. McMaster University, Hamilton (Ontario); [occ.] Head of English, Halton Separate School Board (Oakville, Ont. CAN.); [oth. writ.] Short stories published in National Quarterly Magazines: "Malocchio" in Bllod and Aphorisms, "The Old Man" in The Eyetalian. Currently, I am working on a novel have also completed 14 short stories onme novella; [pers.] Writing helps to focus and realign the

senses traumatized by the onslaught of daily experiences. [a.] Burlington, Ontario, CAN.

BYRD, CATHY
[b.] July 11, 1942; [p.] George and Fleter Dickens; [m.] Robert; [ch.] Deidra, Clenard, Scott; [ed.] Booker T. Washington Elementary, Carver Junior Senior High School, Southern California College of Medical and Dental Career, Stadford School; [occ.] Executive Director of Citywide Community Services, Inc.; [memb.] FAith Temple Church of God in Christ; [hon.] Leadership Midland, Dean's List (Stadford School), Project Blue Print; [oth. writ.] Number of poems and songs not published at this time, some in process of being published; [pers.] Singing and writing is a gift God gave me. I get joy and peace in sharing my gift with others. [a.] Midland, TX.

BYRD, SARAH LEVENA
[b.] october 27, 1979, Bradenton, FL; [p.] Sandra Jean and Lewis Beckton Byrd; [occ.] Part-time student; [hon.] Athletic; [pers.] The death of my brother Tom Crump, inspired me, the feelings I had. I've written many other poems, 3 short stories. [a.] Topeka, KS.

BYRNE, EDITH TERESA
[b.] October 16, 1945, San Tome, Anzoategui, Venezuela, SA; [p.] Foster D. and Ofelia Bermudez Smith; [ed.] BA Vassar College (Poughkeepsie, NY); [occ.] Staff Assistant, US Department of Justice (Washington, DC); [memb.] National Association of Female Executives, US Department of Justice Hispanic Association; [hon.] Atorney General's award for Excellence; [oth. writ.] Several poems published in local newspapers. [a.] Annandale, VA.

BYRNE, SUSAN A.
[pen.] Susan Arnaboldi Byrne; [b.] July 26, 1923, Paterson, NJ; [p.] Agnes McFarlane and Joseph Baumann Arnaboldi; [m.] John Patrick, October 24, 1942; [ch.] Susan Agnes, John Patrick and William Edmund Byrne; [ed.] Georgian Court College, Seton Hall University, Benedictine Academy; [occ.] Retired teacher; [memb.] Tau Kappa Alpha, Pres. Alumni Bergen Passaic Chp. Georgian Court College, Pres. Benedictine Academy Alumni; [hon.] Various Fund Raisers for City of Paterson under direction of Mayor Lawrence Kramer; [oth. writ.] Children's Stories; [pers.] Poetry lends itself to beauty - a sorely needed quality in today's world. [a.] Paterson, NJ.

CABERA, ZIENIA
[b.] June 11, 1979, Fajardo, PR; [p.] Maria and Augusto Cabera; [ed.] Ramstein Junior High; [hon.] Academic awards, JRROTC award; [oth. writ.] Untitled, Appletree other poems. [a.] Panama City, FL.

CAIRNS, HEATHER AA.
[b.] December 10, 1968, Penetanguishene, Ont.; [p.] Ab Cairns and Beverly Gauett; [m.] Christopher Elzby; [ch.] Matthew; [ed.] Midland Secondary School; [occ.] Owner/operator of Earthtones Dollar Store, Burk's Falls; [oth. writ.] Short children's stories, and a rhyming adventure for both young and old, also many poems still awaiting publishing; [pers.] Perhaps it's not the beauty of the words as they flow, as it is the feelings they instill as one reads them. [a.] Burk's Falls, Ont. CAN.

CALDWELL, PAT
[b.] November 7, 1938, England; [m.] Roy, August 27, 1960; [ch.] Stephen and Paul; [memb.] SA Writer's Centre, The International Society of Poets; [hon.] Editor's Choice Award for: For All Those Yet To Be' as included in 'Wind in the Night Sky'; [oth. writ.] Short story published in Anthology 'Paper Clips' England 1993 poem published in 'Wind in the Night Sky' National Library of Poetry 1993.

CALHOUN, JR., MICHAEL RAY
[b.] March 31, 1987, New Orleans, LA; [p.] Josephine C. and Michael R. Calhoun, Sr.; [ed.] J.F. Gauthier School; [occ.] Student; [memb.] Poydras Baptist Church; [hon.] Over all first place kindergarten winner, for the Parish of St. Bernard, LA. "Halloween Writing Contest, Poetry Categorie" sponsored by, Mobile Oil Corporation and International Reading Associations; also the National Library of Poetry semi-finalist into the final round, for this poem "Magical Pumpkins"; [pers.] His ambition for the future is to become a paleontology. In his words, to study dinosaur bones. [a.] St. Bernard, LA.

CALLAHAN, MICHELLE M.
[b.] April 9, 1980, Dorchester, MA; [p.] William T. and Irene A. Callahan, Jr.; [ed.] Holbrook Jr./Sr. High School; [hon.] Honor Roll, National Honor Society; [pers.] I love to write and I'm delighted people enjoy my work. I'd like to pursue a career in journalism. [a.] Holbrook, MA.

CALLIGARIS, AILEEN E.
[b.] November 3, 1966, Guelph, Ontario, CAN; [p.] Eileen and John Farthing; [m.] Marco, September 19, 1992; [ed.] St. Lawrence College, Business Administration-Marketing; [occ.] Publisher, owner of Life Thymes Quarterly Magazine, Inc; [hon.] Graduation with distinction; [oth. writ.] Write for my own publication, completed several creative and writing courses; [pers.] The responsibility for personal happiness and the happiness of those around us, rest in the hands of ourselves. [a.] Kingston, Ont. CAN.

CAMPBELL, DEBORAH JEAN
[b.] February 11, 1956, Newton, IA; [ed.] Working towards degree in journalism at Minneapolis Community College; [occ.] Bookseller for The Minnesota Women's Press, Inc.; [oth. writ.] Works in progress; [pers.] I write myself. [a.] St. Paul, MN.

CAMPBELL, DEBRA
[b.] June 25, 1963, Campbellsville, KY; [p.] Tom and Alice Wolf; [m.] Jeff, December 31, 1981; [ch.] Patricia Ann and William Thomas; [ed.] Auburndale Sr. High; [occ.] Preschool Director, First United Methodist Preschool; [memb.] National Association for the Education of Young Children and Local Affiliates; [hon.] Child Development Associate Credential (CDA), from the National Credentialing Program; [oth. writ.] Numerous children's songs and fingerplays. Also won a poetry contest sponsored by a local tv station, several other poems written; [pers.] Treasure each day, with the people you love for your days are a gift from the Lord above. [a.] Auburndale, FL.

CAMPBELL, ROSINA
[pen.] Rosina; [b.] June 23, 1951, Bavaria, Germany; [p.] Wilhelm and Ludmilla Gastel; [ch.] Timothy Richard and Christopher MacKenzie; [ed.] Tec Voc High; [occ.] Touch-up artist (Photography); [memb.] I am a lifetime member of motherhood, sisterhood, daughterhood, and friendhood; [oth. writ.] I've compiled hundreds of prose/poems over a very short time period; and continue to do so. I mostly read them to friends who after "listening" and not just hearing - walk away comforted within themselves - and always "thinking" they give "hope"; [pers.] I write what I feel at that particular moment I strive to learn about my own internal life and origin of thoughts. I am trying to regulate and use them to effect the outer world. I try to put into words what people feel but can't always express. [a.] Winnipeg/Manitoba/CAN.

CAMBRA, WALTER GILBERT
[pen.] Wally G.; [b.] September 24, 1919, Pepeekeo; [p.] Manuel De Cambra and Victoria Rebeiro; [ed.] Pepeekeo Elementary; [occ.] Crane Operator (retired); [memb.] Papaikou Catholic Parish; [hon.] Four first place, two honorable mentions, two entered at museums; [oth. writ.] Autumn Leaves, Lady of the Fourth, The Walls Came Tumbling Down - Ode to Pearl Espiritu Santos; [pers.] Dream often - cause dreams really do, come true! [a.] Pepeekeo, HI.

CANTRELLA, RUTH E.
[b.] August 22, 1915; [ed.] BA degree in Elementary Education, Jersey City State College; [occ.] Retired fourth grade teacher. [a.] Lyndhurst, NJ.

CAPIN, STEPHEN I.
[b.] December 21, 1934, Reading, PA; [p.] Simon and Jean Capin; [m.] Laurie C., July 30, 1972; [ch.] Julie Ann, Susan Beth, Bruce Marshall, and David Brian; [ed.] Penn State University, BA Journalism 1956; Cabrini College Master's in Education 1956; [occ.] Elementary School Teacher; [memb.] B'nai B'rith, Alpha Epsilon Pi, Penn State Alumni Association, Smithsonian, AARP, National Geographic Society; [hon.] Alpha Delta Sigma (national Advertising Fraternity), Dean's List; [oth. writ.] Poetry, short stories for children; [pers.] My writing strives to reflect the emotions I feel concerning humanity in general and my friends and family in particular. [a.] Elkins Park, PA.

CARDINAL, CHANTELLE LEAH-MARIE
[b.] September 23, 1980, Edmonton, Alberta, CAN; [p.] Joe and Patsy Cardinal; [ed.] Grade 8, Ashmont Secondary; [occ.] Student; [memb.] Canadian Cree Status Indian; [hon.] Have won public speaking and a number of essay contests; student of the year awards, student of the month awards, award for assisting handicap during the school year, and volunteer award "Phy. Ed/Gymnasium Setup"; [oth. writ.] Essays published in local newspapers; [pers.] Follow your dream no dream is too lofty -- no goal is too high. [a.] Alberta, CAN.

CARDONA, WINNIE B.A.M.A.
[b.] May 30, 1941, Malta; [p.] Samuel and Mary Grech-Marguerat; [m.] Carmel, September 19, 1965; [ch.] John, Jennifer, Christopher; [ed.] Two year course at Teacher's Training College; Ontario College of Art; University of Toronto; Art Specialist Certificate, Seneca College, Photography; [occ.] Visual Arts/Photography/English High School Teacher; [memb.] Canadian Wildlife Federation, McMichael Canadian Art Collection; [hon.] Distinction in Art; [oth. writ.] Poetry, short stories, working on some children's books; [pers.] Nature is my main source of inspiration: "To glance at the beauty of nature is a fleeting moment; but to observe more closely gives a lasting memory!". [a.] Richmond Hill, Ont. CAN.

CARLSON, MARJORIE ANN MCKUNE
[b.] February 4, 1935, Settle, WA; [p.] Frank McKune (deceased) and Alice Mildred Day McKune (deceased); [ch.] Steven Robert, Matthew Douglas (deceased), Laura Jane, Timothy Nathaniel; [ed.] Abraham Lincoln High (San Francisco, CA); [hon.] Editor's Choice Award - The National Library of Poetry 1993, Honorable Mention - Quille Books 1993; [oth. writ.] "Flight of Peace" in Wind in the Night Sky, The National Library of Poetry,; "If You Ever" in All My Tomorrows - Volume III - Quill Books; [pers.] I always try to write from the heart. I believe it's the purest form of expressing honest feelings. [a.] Santa Clara, CA.

CARMICHAEL, BURFORD
[pen.] Bud Carmichael; [b.] January 26, 1908, Pikesville, KY; [p.] George and Otezza Carmichael; [m.] Elizabeth Sey, January 17, 1922; [ch.] Sheila, Martha, Claire and Susan; [ed.] High School; [occ.] Accountant (retired); [memb.] American Lecturist Association; Elks Lodge, [hon.] Varied; [oth. writ.] Short stories, (fiction). [a.] Santa Clara, CA.

CARNEY, BRIAN
[b.] January 1, 1979, Batavia, NY; [p.] Richard and Doreen Carney; [oth. writ.] I have many different writings on many different subjects. None which have been published; [pers.] Live life to the fullest don't question it to death. The great range of music I listen to influences my poetry. [a.] Darien Center, NY.

CARR, JENNIFER
[b.] October 10, 1978, Bryn Mawr, PA; [p.] Timothy and Francine Carr; [ch.] Siblings-Benjamin, Jeffrey; [ed.] 1993-94 freshman at Spring-Ford High School; [occ.] Student; [memb.] Girl Scout of America, Cappuccio Dance Academy; [hon.] Distinguished Honor Student, Various art awards; [oth. writ.] Numerous but unpublished yet; [pers.] I've been writing since age 9. My poems reflect special events in my life and things I hold dear. [a.] Linfield, PA.

CARRELL, SHARRON
[b.] Danville, IL; [ed.] BA Mississippi University for Women and MA Mississippi State University. [a.] Lynn, MA.

CARRINGTON, ELIZABETH
[b.] February 26, 1977, Falfurrias, TX; [p.] Vera Moya; [ed.] Falfurrias High School currently a junior; [occ.] Student; [memb.] National Honor Society; [hon.] Speech award, Honor Roll, Who's Who Among American Student. [a.] Falfurrias, TX.

CARROLL, BERTHA
[b.] September 2, 1938; [p.] Lee and Virginia Parker; [m.] Samuel Carroll, Jr., June 2, 1979; [ed.] Sheila Holmes, Violeta Corey, Marietta Burks, Felicia Phillips, Jerry Phillips and Audrey Burks; [occ.] Retired Management person, Happy Housewife; [pers.] Dreams can come true with lots of hard work and faith.

CARRUTH, JOHN R.
[b.] January 19, 1905, Philadelphia, PA; [p.] James S. and Emma Carruth (Shannon); [m.] Idella Montgomery, November 7, 1933; [ch.] Robert F. Carruth; [ed.] AB, Emory Henry College, Duke University, Drew University; [memb.] Methodist Minister, Teacher, Professor; [memb.] Social Sciences and Education - National Honorary Fraternities, College; [hon.] National Honorary Frats., Pi Gamma Mu, Kappa Phi Kappa; [pers.] I am Third, What's Your Problem? [a.] Somerville, NJ.

CARSON, SHIRLEY
[b.] April 15, 1930, Reading, PA; [p.] Horace and Emma Strafford; [m.] William A., June 26, 1948; [ch.] William Clayton, Dawn Louise (deceased), eight grandchildren, one great grandchild; [ed.] Wilson High, Institute of Children's Literature; [occ.] Homemaker, wildlife writer; [memb.] Defenders of Wildlife, Greenpeace; [hon.] Several awards for prose and poetry from various literary magazines; [oth. writ.] Numerous poems, articles, and stories printed in local newspapers and literary magazines, a 40,000 word manuscript about an orphaned raccoon I had raised (unpublished); [pers.] Living on a wildlife refuge, I've had many encounters of the natural kind. I strive, through my prose and poetry, to give people a better understanding of our endangered wildlife. [a.] Pine Grove, PA.

CARTER, JOHN L.
[b.] August 6, 1944, Atlanta, GA; [p.] Harlon Bronson Carter; [m.] Diane R., May 31, 1975; [ch.] Charles Powell, Joseph Michael, Harlon Bronson; [ed.] BA History, Texas A&I College, Theology Sunset School of Preaching; [occ.] Border Patrol Agent, U.S. Border Patrol, INS; [memb.] National Rifle Association of America; [hon.] Freedoms Foundation of Valley Forge, letter award program 1973; [oth. writ.] "Such Passion Fills The Night Air..." Whispers in the Wind. National Library of Poetry; [pers.] It is not so important that one be loved, as it is for one to love. [a.] Wildomar, CA.

CARTER, NOEL
[b.] December 10, 1958, Chattanooga, TN; [p.] Lola B. and N. Garl Carter, Sr.; [m.] Kelly, July 17, 1982; [ch.] Kristy Lynn; [ed.] Rossville High; [oth. writ.] Sweet Darling, The Old Man, Downtown L.A., Broken Pieces, When The Music Stops, Heaven's A Long Way to Fall; [pers.] Special thanks to Sue Fuller, Barbara Evans, Kathleen McCain, and most of all Beth Trites to whom the poem is for. [a.] St. Pete, FL.

CASCIARO, ROSANN
[b.] June 9, 1981, Stockton, CA; [p.] Frank and Joel Casciaro; [ed.] Snells Pre School, St. Lukes presentation at this I am going to be in the 7th grade; [occ.] Student; [hon.] Two Christian Leadership awards, runner up in 1993 short story contest sponsored by California Foundation for Agriculture in the classroom; [pers.] I like to write poems and short stories. [a.] Stockton, CA.

CASCIO, MICHELE
[b.] February 10, 1962, Brooklyn, NY; [p.] Michelina and John DelGesso; [m.] John, August 16, 1992; [ch.] Christina Cann; [ed.] St. Edmund High School, Brooklyn College; [occ.] English teacher, Cavallaro Intermediate School; [hon.] Dean's List, Humanitarian award; [oth. writ.] The Sweetness of Success, A Collection of Poems, Sandra's Story, a preteen novel; [pers.] Poetry is emotion recollected in tranquility - Wordsworth. [a.] Brooklyn, NY.

CASE, JEROME R.
[pen.] Jerome; [b.] May 16, 1950, Abington Township, PA; [ed.] Attended Pasadena City College and National University, San Diego, CA; [occ.] United States Navy; [hon.] National Defense Medal (2) Meritorious Unit Commendation award (2), Navy Achievement Medal, Good Conduct Medal (6), Vietnam Campaign Medal; [oth. writ.] Several poems published in The Ships' Newspaper and Naval Base Yokosuka, Japan Newspaper The "SeaHawk"; [pers.] For every dream that you have dreamed and for every star that you wished upon, reality is the belief of the dreamer. Stay focus and believe in yourself! [a.] CV-Division, FPO, AP.

CASTILLO, ANITA M.
[b.] August 1, 1977, Orange County, CA; [p.] Grace E. and Rodolfo Castillo, Jr.; [ed.] Currently attending Socorro High School; [occ.] Student; [hon.] Several creative writing awards (school); [oth. writ.] "Jolene", "Out of Grasp Our of Sight", "Is Life Established as Death"; [pers.] The best theory for the ease of inner self stresses are expressed throughout creative writing. [a.] Socorro, NM.

CASTILLO, TOMAS
[pen.] Tomas; [b.] July 29, 1920, Manila, Philippines; [p.] Tomas Castillo and Perp. Etha De Mata; [m.] Jovita, December 1, 1947; [ch.] Aurora, Ramon, and Armando Castillo; [ed.] Primary to grade 7, P.I. High School, AA Social Science, San Diego College, Southwestern College; [occ.] Retired USN, Chef 25 yrs, Retired Dietetic Food Service worker 17 yrs; [memb.] Fleet Reserve Association, Retired Persons, Republican Task Force (Presidential) Tanza, Cavite Association; [hon.] 7 Good Conduct U.S. Navy: 25 years VA Medical Center, 17 years for Disabled Veteran award, 13 military service medals, two award Dietetic Food Service; [oth. writ.] My Biography, The Snake Pit, I Shall Return, A version by: General Douglas MacArthur; [pers.] Talk about peace no more war go for broke help the poor thank our Lord for our good fortune and all. [a.] San Diego, CA.

CATE, JOHN SHELTON
[b.] October 10, 1912, Itasca, TX; [p.] George R. and Myrtle Shelton; [m.] Mabel Morin, February 6, 1943; [ch.] Susannah Cate Lustica and John S. Cate, Jr. and Christopher Cate; [ed.] 3 years college, Texas A&I Kingsville, TX; [occ.] 4 years elementary school principal, Hardware salesman and Wholesale and Mfrs. Rep; [oth. writ.] Started writing at 65 years f age. Have written a number of poems several short stories and am now writing a novel based on life on a sheep ranch in Idaho early 20th century. [a.] Stanton,

CATTNACH, R. GARY
[pen.] Cat, El Gato; [b.] November 6, 1945, Billings, MT; [p.] Charlotte Lien Cattnach; [ch.] Candace Lynn, Robert Douglas, Angela Nicole; [ed.] West High, Southern Illinois University, Ironworker's #708, May School of Broadcasting; [occ.] Self-employed; [memb.] Eagles Club, St. Vincent Catholic Society; [oth. writ.] Hundred of poems and song lyrics (few published), numerous articles to THE BILLINGS GAZETTE, a screenplay "THE CATS MEOW" (unpublished); [pers.] Through my writings I would like to be able to reach out and touch someone in a positive manner; to let that someone know that there is someone who understands and cares. [a.] Billings, MT.

CAUKILL, MONA
[b.] September 27, 1936, Calgary, Alberta; [m.] Norman Caukill, November 10, 1956; [ch.] Vicki Tannas, Deanne Trewin, Mark and Brett Caukill; [oth. writ.] Fable, published in Canadian farm periodical. [a.] Caroline, Alberta, CAN.

CAVA, LUIS PABLO
[pen.] Sinl Pavac; [b.] August 12, 1913, Philippines; [p.] Evaristo Caba (deceased) and Maria Pablo (deceased); [m.] Fidela Regunay, 2nd wife, August 21, 1989 and Lucia F. Pampo, died January 5, 1987; [ch.] Romeo, Luis Jr., Rodrogo, Manolo, Fernando, Solomon, Florentino and Marilyn; [ed.] Tech. Building Const. (2 years in 1938), Normal course 1950, BSE 1952, and 21 units MA; [occ.] Ind. Arts Tra., Elem. and H.S. Principal, WWII 1st Lt. Guer; [memb.] Pufl VFW, Post 1063, Life Mbr. Pinato Bo Lodge, Past Pres. NARFE CH 1826, Post Cmdr. A. Legion, Dept. & WWII Veteran Post Master Pintubo Lodge; [hon.] Received 8 medals WWII 1st prize award in Green Revolution Contest among secondary principals in Zambales, Phil in 1975; [oth. writ.] The History of Pinatubo Lodge No. 52, The History of Brgy. Nama-Tacan; [pers.] To live and help others live. [a.] San Francisco, CA.

CHAINANI, SONESH
[b.] April 22, 1977, Miami, FL; [p.] Suresh and Sheila Chainani; [ed.] Entering 11th grade in the fall 1993 (Ransom Everglades High School); [occ.] STudent; [memb.] International Thespian Society, Drama Club, Student Government, Mu Alpha Theta, Multi-Cultural Club; [hon.] First place, Florida State Poet's Association award 1993, First place Sinclair Community College 1992, Honorable mention from the John David Johnson Memorial Poetry award 1992, 3rd place in Distinguished Poets of America Open Poetry Contest 1993; [oth. writ.] Poem published in Pikestaff Forum Magazine, poem published in Skipping Stones Magazine, poems published in Suan Song Anthology, several published in Treasured Poems of America; [pers.] Poetry has become my creative outlet for expressing everything I feel. It is an art that allows me to feel free. [a.] Key Biscayne, FL.

CHAMBERLAIN, LYN
[b.] September 25, 1946; [p.] Eric Swanson and Ruby Mae Gold; [m.] Tim, December 7, 1968; [ch.] Todd Eldon, Thomas Lane, Bobbi Lynn and daughter-in-law Dana Marie; [occ.] Assistant Manager at local bowling alley. [a.] Grande Prairie, AB, CAN.

CHAN, JOEL H.
[b.] December 11, 1973, Stanford, CA; [p.] Herman and Edna Chan; [ed.] Presently attending the University of California, Berkeley; [occ.] Student; [memb.] Chinese Student Association (CSA), University of California Berkeley; [oth. writ.] Have written several other poems and am currently working on several short stories; [pers.] Art, in all forms, is a means of solidifying our emotions into something real, into something we can all relate to. I believe that every word and every phrase, if put in the right context, can capture our hearts as well as our minds. It is this that I strive to achieve in my poetry. [a.] Castro Valley, CA.

CHANG, CHARITY
[pen.] Lee Omah; [b.] December 30, 1916, Blount County, TN; [p.] Hugh Edward and Cora Cummings Headrick; [ch.] Frank Greene, Barbara Greene Drury and Vivian Greene Pierce; [ed.] Austin Peay State College (BS), University of Illinois (MS), and University of Tennessee (MA), currently teach a non-credit course in poetry writing for The University of Tennessee's Department of Independent Study; [occ.] Retired school teacher and academic librarian; [memb.] In various professional organizations; [oth. writ.] I have published a number of articles in the field of children's literature; [pers.] I am governed by a determination always, to be the best that I can be in whatever I attempt to do. [a.] Maryville, TN.

CHAPMAN, EVELYN M.
[pen.] Evelyn M. Chapman; [b.] May 16, 1925, Berkeley Co. - Mtbg, WV; [m.] John W., Jr., June 16, 1954; [ch.] Nancy K. Crawford and John W. Crawford III; [ed.] Chastown High - grad. Business College; [occ.] Retired; [memb.] Shenandoah Bible Baptist Church; [hon.] Trophies for Top Sales Rep, with Insurance Co.; [oth. writ.] I have been writing since 1962 after my husband and I moved into the country; [pers.] I can only say my inspirations come from the Lord. This is something I do upon inspiration only. I feel this is a talent directly from God. [a.] Martinsburg, WV.

CHARLES, MONTINE L.
[b.] January 2, 1980, Mountain View, CA; [p.] Wilmer Charles, Jr. and Sandra J. Jones, Karen D. Pierce; [ed.] Deer Valley High; [occ.] Student; [memb.] Dance Shope, KRR (Kids Radical Republic) and GP (Greenier Peace); [hon.] National Junior Honor Society; [oth. writ.] A few poems and stories in other books; [pers.] "To Be or Not to Be?" That question always confuses me. What does it really mean. The life and death of we. My poetry reflects me (Strange). [a.] Glendale, AZ.

CHASE, ERVIN H.
[b.] October 30, 1915, Burlington, NJ; [ed.] First year high; music-Clark's Conservatory; RCA-Production Consultant, etc; [occ.] Production Consultant and Management; [memb.] U.E. and CIO - Secretary and Representative for South Jersey; honorable mention E.E., Mech., Chem. Societies; [hon.] Letters and medals of outstanding recognition from places I worked; [oth. writ.] Praying Mantis, short story, Dur Children for the Peace Poem, Plots for Dr. Death (back in 1927); [pers.] I gave over a thousand lecturers - technical, non-technical, and medical. To observe the universe and life for what they really are without being prejudice, to learn everything in the universe to use it and give it back to mankind. [a.] Camden, NJ.

CHASE, JOSEPH P.
[pen.] Joe Chase; [b.] September 24, 1979, Ft. Lauderdale, FL; [p.] Sally J. Lynn and John I. Chase; [occ.] Student; [memb.] Boy Scouts of America, National Junior Honor Society, Order of the Arrow; [hon.] Honor Roll, Science Fair 3rd place ribbon, Math Competition, Knowledge Bowl, Gifted Program; [oth. writ.] Personal poems and essays; [pers.] I try to express Human Nature and ways of feelings in my poems. I am greatly influenced by the works of Rudyard Kipling, Billy Joel, Aerosmith and U2. [a.] Deerfield Beach, FL.

CHECKI, ANTHONY N.
[pen.] A.N. Checki; [b.] July 21, 1923, Lyndhurst, NJ; [p.] Nicholas J. and Rose Checki; [m.] Dorothy J., September 23, 1951; [ch.] Christine Joyce; [ed.] Lyndhurst High. John Marshall College, John Marshall Law School - JD; [occ.] Retired - formally Supervisor - N.J. Dept. of Labor; [memb.] American Legion, Old Guard; National Rifle Association; North American Hunting Club; [hon.] 5 Battle Stars WWII, from Omaha Beach to the Elbe River 35th Infantry Division; [oth. writ.] Articles on current issues published in local newspapers - The Commercial Leader and The Herald News; [pers.] Writing is always pleasurable to me. Presently working on a book of poems and a novel entitled, "The Inheritance". [a.] Rutherford, NJ.

CHICK, JANEL LAURA
[pen.] Janel L. Chick; [b.] July 2, 1976, Farmington, ME; [p.] Judith and Donald DeLong, Dale Chick; [ed.] Senior at Mt. Abram High School; [occ.] Student and part-time worker; [pers.] From the support of my friends and family I got the courage to send one of my poems in. Thank you. I also want to give special thanks to Mitchell Goodman and Elizabeth Cooke, and to two very important teachers, Ms. Ferris and Mr. Dodge. Thank you everyone. [a.] Kingfield, ME.

CHILDS, JUNE HELEN
[b.] March 21, 1937, Baltimore, MD; [p.] Glenn and Helen Morrison; [m.] Norman, August 11, 1962; [ch.] Susan Helen Childs; [ed.] West High School, Western MD College and Towson State Teachers; [memb.] American Lung Association, Women in Military Service for America Memorial Foundation, Inc.; [oth. writ.] Poem in America Sings, a national anthology of college poetry; [pers.] Words paint pictures that the eye cannot see. [a.] Downingtown, PA.

CHIN, SUE SOONMARIAN
[pen.] SUCHIN; [b.] San Francisco, CA; [ed.] California College Art, Minneapolis ARt Institute, Schaeffer Design Center; [memb.] SfWA Galleries, 1989, California Museum Science and Industry, Lucien Labaudt Gallery, ASL-CIO Labor Studies Center, Asian Women Artists; [pers.] Thinking - feeling - not knowing - falsely knowing just a portion of mother's nature's dynamism -- the awesome thunderbold those unknowing; those clumsy fools can only someday, far way, sense her cosmic blows. [a.] San Francisco, CA.

CHINOY, VINITA
[b.] February 11, 1966; [p.] K.B. and Veena Misra; [m.] Raymond, March 17, 1992; [ch.] Xenia; [ed.] MS University of South Florida; [occ.] Physicist/student; [memb.] IEEE, AIP; [hon.] Sigma Pi Sigma; [oth. writ.] Mostly technical and I haven't submitted any of my poetries for publication before. It has just been a hobby for me; [pers.] It's healthy to have emotions. It's human to express them. My poems are very spontaneous, my style. [a.] Temple Terrace, FL.

CHOW, LOUIS
[b.] July 18, 1954, Hong Kong; [p.] Sui U and Siu Har Chow; [m.] Karen Kwong, June 30, 1986; [ch.] Stephen Jamison Chow (6), Adam Bradford Chow (3); [ed.] BS in Biology-Brandeis University, BA in Pharmacy-Northeastern University; [occ.] Pharmacist; [memb.] Asian American Resource Workshop, American Society of Hospital Pharmacists; [hon.] Cum Laude-85; [oth. writ.] My Friend book of children literature, poems - "A Ballad of The City", "We ARe The Shore" and prose -"Chinese in America" and "Chinese in Mississippi"; [pers.] "A=TE 2" (Achievement = Time times Effort squared). [a.] Brookline, MA.

CHRISTENSEN, TAMMIE SUE
[pen.] "Tam" or "Punkie"; [b.] March 9, 1980, Castro Valley, CA; [p.] Kathie and Bob Christensen, brother-Tim Christensen (10); [ed.] Kindergarten-8th grade so far; [occ.] Kid sister, daughter, granddaughter, niece, academic student and dance (tap, ballet and jazz ballet); [hon.] Honor Society for the last two years; [oth. writ.] Poems and stories; [pers.] My poems reflect on how I have been raised by my parents, my Nanie and my Aunt. They have taught me how to get along, use my imagination and be happy. [a.] Castro Valley, CA.

CHRISTIAN, SARA B.
[b.] January 10, 1943, Guntown, MS; [p.] Mr. and Mrs. O.C. Brazeal; [m.] Jimmy E., April 18, 1972; [ch.] Andy, Beverly and Nathan; [ed.] Saltillo High School; [occ.] Sam's Club #6329 Tupelo, MS; [oth. writ.] I have written several poems, enough to have a book published someday, hopefully; [pers.] My poems are inspired by my surroundings. My dream is to write religious poems for some major greeting card company. [a.] Mantachie, MS.

CHRYST, JAIME-ANNE
[pen.] Jaime-Anne Chryst; [b.] September 17, 1976, Winchester, MA; [p.] Jim and Patricia Chryst; [ed.] Shawsheen Valley Regional Technical High School; [hon.] Bakery Citizenship award, Varsity Letter for football cheering; [oth. writ.] "So Much Love, So Many Miles", "Love Is" and "Don't Go"; [pers.] My one true inspiration and the subject of my poetry, is also my one true love, Jordan Sundstrom. I love you Jordan! Go Shawsheen Rams! [a.] Wilmington, MA.

CHUBB, CHRISTOPHER R.
[b.] June 21, 1958, Huntington, NY; [p.] Elliott and Mary Chubb (step), Dell Chubb (Natural); [ed.] Lundeberg Seararing School, UMSL at St. Louis; [occ.] Former Seafarer, veteran and currently temporary worker; [memb.] Merchant Marine Veteran, VFW Post No. 2593; [hon.] Merchant Marine Expeditionary Medal for participation in the Persian Gulf War 1991; [oth. writ.] Many poems published in several small newspapers, The Seafarer's Log of the SIU (a labor union) has featured my work most often; [pers.] There has been attempted and successful reneggings. After saying trust and friend rather than use the word, friend, in quality time, they also created other reasons they should be paying or paying back or holding to their words. Of course, they only became renegers who then pursued the slanderous action of protecting their shame as others have done against me, a mildly "special" person. The retarded and disturbed and others of my empathies along with the let downs, are spiritually in my poems. [a.] Sunset Hills., MO.

CHURCH, FRANCES
[pen.] Fran; [b.] January 13, 1930, Parkin, AK; [p.] Dona Cannady Capps and Walter Curd Church; [m.] Fern, August 10, 1951; [ch.] Two; [ed.] 12th grade and nurses aide experience; [occ.] Housewife and love for poetry; [memb.] Heart Association and Lung; [hon.] Poem published in local newspaper, poems from oil paintings, poem concerning WWI was also published in newspaper; [oth. writ.] "At Sunset", "A Pound of Gold", "New England Estate", "Pass It On", "Spring Season", "E.d. Patrick", "Quiet On the Set", "Part of Nature", "Our Home"; [pers.] I get the creative juices flowing. It takes coming of your thoughts and making them work for you. Then give it all you have reflect on it.

CIANFLONE, LISE
[pen.] Leeze Marie; [b.] June 9, 1957, Kenora, Ontario; [p.] Denise Marion, Raymond Roy; [m.] Antonio, November 15, 1975; [ch.] Raymond Francesco and Antonio Giuseppe; [ed.] St. Jean - Baptiste College; [occ.] Teacher's Assistant; [memb.] Diabetes Association; [hon.] Mathematics award; [oth. writ.] Poems for local newspapers, children's stories and humorous articles; [pers.] Unconditional love sets the goat free. Until we learn this we shall find no escape. [a.] Letellier, MB, CAN.

CICHOCKI, THOMAS B.
[pen.] Thomas B. Cichocki; [b.] November 28, 1970, Trenton, NJ; [p.] Thomas J. and Donna L. Cichocki; [ed.] Egg Harbor Township High School, Wiest Barron Acting School; [occ.] Security; [oth. writ.] Poem "A Cry For Help" published in 1988 American Anthology of Contemporary Poetry, others not submitted yet; [pers.] I love to express myself through my poetry and my writings and wish to give others that same pleasure in reading it. I hope to make a career out of writing. [a.] Hightstown, NJ.

CIHOCKI, CANDICE
[b.] March 21, 1980, Burlington, NY; [p.] David and Marilyn Cihocki; [ed.] Saint Mary of the Lakes Catholic School; [occ.] Student; [memb.] St. Mary of the Lakes CAtholic Church; [hon.] Certificates of honor in ballet, modeling, and piano; [oth. writ.] Many unpublished poems and stories; [pers.] I like to write about imaginary and dreamlike situations that are taken from reality and based on positive feelings. [a.] Medford Lakes, NJ.

CLAPP, ELEANOR DOUGLAS
[b.] April 12, 1915, Duxbury, MA; [p.] Roger E.E. and Eleanor Douglas Clapp; [ch.] Peter Douglas Clapp; [ed.] Holman School (girls private prep school); [occ.] Receptionist and Mode (fashion and photography); [memb.] Past member of the Germantown Theatre Guild and invited to be an acting member of Plays and Players; [hon.] Several awards for outstanding saleswoman from a large department store in FL; [oth. writ.] Twenty or more poems published in various magazines, newspapers, periodicals, pamphlets, and several anthologies. Several newspaper write-ups; [pers.] Always searching for the truth and striving not to waste time on nonessentials, whether it's poetry, or prose. [a.] Tampa, FL.

CLAPP, TIMOTHY SCOTT
[pen.] Scott Dreamer; [b.] March 15, 1969, Alamance; [p.] Donald Lee Clapp; [ed.] Southeast High School; [occ.] Writer; [oth. writ.] First novel in the works entitled "Arch Angel", and my poem "Gone Too Far" was published in A Wind in the Night Sky; [pers.] I like to think that, that my inspiration for writing comes from my memory of two people I knew back in Hillsborough, NC named Donnie Averette and Nancy Doby. [a.] Liberty, NC.

CLARK, ANDREA M.
[pen.] Andi Clark; [b.] December 26, 1975, Austin, TX; [p.] Roy and Candy Clark; [ed.] High School student. [a.] Silvam Springs, AK.

CLARK, BARB
[b.] January 9, 1955; [ed.] Duchess High, Bethany Bible School, Red Deer College; [occ.] Child Educator; [memb.] Nazarene Women's Missionary Society; [hon.] High school scholarship; [pers.] My primary goal in writing would be to capture a child's world seen through the eyes of a child. [a.] Innisfail, A.B.

CLARK, LAURA ANNE
[b.] November 10, 1978, Galveston, TX; [p.] Dr. and Mrs. E.A. Clark; [ed.] 9th grade Longview High School; [occ.] Student; [memb.] National Junior Honor Society, Majorette-Band; [pers.] This poem is about a special place in my heart. The memories of happy and sad times will always remain. I will always remember Camp Fern. [a.] Longview, TX.

CLARK, MICHAEL
[pen.] Raul; [b.] August 14, 1977, Klamath Falls, OR; [p.] Charles and Sandra Jean Clark; [occ.] Student, Klamath Union High School; [hon.] Outstanding Potential and Musicianship Scholarships: University of Oregon Summer Music Institute; [oth. writ.] Several poems and persuasive essays for regional opinionative newspaper; [pers.] The elegance and sheer majesty of words have shaped the course of national and manifested the dreams of the masses. My only wish is that all mankind will group the esoteric beauty they have to offer. [a.] Klamath Falls, OR.

CLARK, TONY L.
[b.] November 30, 1956, Greenville, OH; [p.] David and Janet Clark; [m.] Divorced; [ch.] Jason L. Clark; [oth. writ.] Yes. [a.] Greenville, OH.

CLAUSEN, G. STEPHEN
[b.] May 24, 1949, Minneapolis, MN; [p.] Gerald X. and Virginia A. Clausen; [m.] Lois Evelyn, February 7, 1993; [ch.] Melissa L. Clausen, Shane Stephen Clausen, Jonah P. Clausen, Matthew P. Clausen and Alicia A. Clausen; [ed.] Normandale Community College AA, Upper Iowa University BA; [occ.] Vice President Delta Management and Associates, Inc.; [oth. writ.] Many other poems written but not published; [pers.] There's hope for all of mankind thru love and education. [a.] Savage, MN.

CLAUSEN, KURTIS
[b.] April 12, 1979, Peoria, IL; [p.] Larry Clausen, Michelle and Richard Hancock; [ed.] Pekin Community High School; [occ.] Student. [a.] Pekin, IL.

CLAESON, M. FRANCES
[pen.] Frances Claeson; [b.] August 10, 1926, Sugar Grove, IL; [p.] Margaret and William Greenlee; [m.] Conrad L., December 23, 1989; [ed.] Freeport High School, Pamona School of Business; [occ.] Bookkeeper and Office Manager (now retired); [memb.] Salem Lutheran Church and Belvedere Woman's Club; [oth. writ.] Short suspense stories, published in school paper; [pers.] I hope that in the near future, since I am now retired, I can write novels and be published. [a.] Rockford, IL.

CLAYTON, LISA A.
[b.] October 19, 1975, Ephrata, PA; [p.] Virginia and William Clayton; [ed.] Lancaster Catholic/Ephrata Senior High School; [occ.] Student; [hon.] Honorable mention, National Scholastic Writing awards; [oth. writ.] Various poetry, short stories. [a.] Ephrata, PA.

CLINE, TINA MARIE
[b.] November 11, 1962, Allegan, MI; [p.] Lawrence and Patricia Wolthuis; [m.] Jay, February 26, 1983; [ch.] Brittany Ann, Cody Daniel and Caleb Jay Cline; [ed.] Delton Kellogg and Wayland High School; [occ.] Licensed Daycare Provider, mother and wife; [memb.] Adult and Children Alliance, Children's Resource Network Doster, Reform Church; [hon.] Michigan Child Care Futures, 4'C Quality Child Care Program, Hopkins Elementary Room Mother awards; [oth. writ.] Several poems and songs not yet published; [pers.] This poem is dedicated to my sister, Jody Jyn Walthuis Bartholomew (wife of Scott William Bartholomew) who went to be with our Lord Sept. 22, 1984. Our time on earth is short let's do the best we can to live in harmony with all mankind. [a.] Allegan, MI.

CLOW, DONNA
[b.] October 14, 1952, Arden, Ontario; [p.] Vernon and Teresa Scott; [m.] Charles, April 6, 1968; [ch.] Stacy Charles Clow; [ed.] Ontario Secondary School; [occ.] Production Worker at Dupont-Kingston Site; [pers.] Thanks to my sister for bringing out qualities I didn't know I had. [a.] Ontario, CAN.

COBURN, HEATHER A.
[pen.] Heather Ashton Forrest; [b.] September 6, 1979, Amarillo, TX; [p.] Edward J. and Linda A. Coburn; [ed.] Dakota Jr. High School; [pers.] It is my belief that poetry should come from deep within; here are found the passions that reflect the essence of life...passions that can only be found where values meet intentions of the soul. [a.] Rapid City, SD.

COCHOIS, DENNIS
[pen.] Mark Sawyer; [b.] October 18, 1957, Windsor Ont., CAN; [p.] Alphonse and Julie Cochois; [ed.] Grade 11 and college Western Secondary School; [oth. writ.] "Blue Passages" I turned this poem into a song; [pers.] My writings reflect different people and different feelings! They are also a window, so I can watch words live! [a.] Ontario, CAN.

COCHRAN, LORNE
[b.] January 12, 1952, Oliver, B.C., CAN.; [p.] Fred and Myra Cochran; [m.] Charlotte, May 2, 1983; [ed.] Grand Forks Secondary; [occ.] Mine Truck Driver, Taxi Driver, Sawmill Worker; [oth. writ.] Some poems published in local paper (1) for my parents 45th anniversary and (2) when I met my wife, plus a few others; [pers.] Love to write poetry, someday maybe write western music. [a.] Lumbay, BC, CAN.

COCKFIELD, BESSIE L.M.
[pen.] Lucy; [b.] April 13, 1925, Ware Shoals, SC; [p.] Clarence Eugenet and Elizabeth Gunnells McNock; [m.] Deceased, June 3, 1975; [ch.] Brooks Lollis, Carolyn Quayle; [ed.] Connie Maxwell Children's Home; [occ.] Cashier and sales clerk, now retired; [memb.] Rockvale Baptist Church; [hon.] Certificate of Achievement in Photography, Camera Kit, Pen, Pocker, Saver; [oth. writ.] Hospice in Greenville, SC and in Anderson, SC; [pers.] I also have two granddaughters Katina Marie Rice and Teresa Ann McCary, two great granddaughters and one great grandson. [a.] Greenville, SC.

COEN, ELEANOR
[p.] Ella and Edward Byrne; [m.] Thomas, September 9, 1950; [ch.] Tom, Mary, Joseph, Theresa, Larry and Christopher; [ed.] Brighton High, Chandler's Secretarial School; [occ.] Housewife; [oth. writ.] Poems; [pers.] Written from the heart. [a.] Newton, MA.

COFFEY, LYNDA
[pen.] Lynda Cole; [b.] February 16, 1951, Troy, NY; [p.] Edward Cole and Lillian LaBelle; [m.] Donald, August 12, 1972; [ed.] St. Peter's Grammar School, Troy High School; [occ.] Activities assistant at Eddy Geriatric Center; [memb.] Full Gospel Tabernacle, Women's Group, American Red Cross; [oth. writ.] This is my first published poem, I've written 1 or 2 other poems; [pers.] Poetry has always been one of my loves of my life. I am inspired by my surroundings and situations. Helen Steiner Rice and Emily Dickinson are my favorites. [a.] Troy, NY.

COHEN, LEONARD STUART
[pen.] Lenny Cohen; [b.] September 21, 1970, Toronto; [ed.] York University; [occ.] Hope to pursue some area of teaching while writing on the side; [hon.] English award (grade 13) Ontario Scholarship 1992-1993, 1993-1994...; [pers.] I enjoy the creative process of writing. Therefore I feel satisfaction in all forms of Art--from academic papers to children's books. [a.] Toronto, Ont.

COKER, ELLEN L.
[b.] February 23, 1916, Collirene, Lowndes Co., Al; [p.] Frank and Carrie M. Lyon (deceased); [m.] Thomas L. (deceased), November 2, 1936; [ch.] Walter Francis (deceased), Thomas E., David L., Joseph William, Jennie E. Smith; [ed.] Hayneville High School, Typing course through Correspondence School (Cincinnati, OH); [occ.] Retired, Medical Records Technician, Clerk typist with state of Alabama and former school bus driver; [memb.] Charter member Society of Alabama Retirees, American Heart Association; [oth. writ.] I had a poem published in "A Collection of Religious Poems", published by National Society of Published Poets, Tampa, FL. in 1978. It is copyrighted, I also had a book of 39 poems and a short story printed by Paragon Press, Montgomery, AL in 1980 (not copyrighted); [pers.] Some of my poems tell of my love for family members and friends and for our beautiful country. Others express the peace and joy found in worship of God, our Creator, and my desire for everyone to receive His Son as Lord and Savior. [a.] Montgomery, AL.

COLE, JR., CURTIS E.
[b.] August 2, 1973, Little Rock, AR; [p.] Curtis Cole and Rachael Martin; [ed.] Clear Lake High, Copper Mountain Community College, Military MOS Schools; [occ.] Radar Repair; [oth. writ.] None published. [a.] Palms, CA.

COLE, HELEN L.
[pen.] Helen L. Cole; [b.] August 2, 1939, Bolton Landing, NY; [p.] Clarence and Elizabeth Butler; [m.] Forest A., Sr., December 9, 1961; [ch.] Forest A. Cole, Jr; [ed.] Bolton Central High, various home study courses in Creative Writing; [occ.] Homemaker; [oth. writ.] This is my first try at writing poetry for publication; [pers.] With this first poem, I wanted to convey just how meaningful a day in one's life can be. [a.] Houston, TX.

COLE, III, JAMES W.
[b.] August 1, 1947, Baytown, TX; [p.] Bill and Colleen Cole; [ed.] BA English Lit., University of Houston 1970; [occ.] Mill worker, Simpson Paper Co.; [pers.] I love English, not so much as an ancient or modern language, but as a timeless vehicle for expressing the thoughts of man. [a.] Pasadena, TX.

COLE III, RALPH THOMAS
[pen.] Anonymous; [b.] January 14, 1958, Seattle, WA; [p.] Ralph Thomas Cole Jr. and Fay Louise (Seaman) (Cole) Townsend; [m.] Margaret Ann, October 15, 1989; [ch.] Ralph Thomas Cole IV; [ed.] Eureka Senior High School; [occ.] Welder, Master Screen Printer; [hon.] Presidential Physical Fitness award; [oth. writ.] Many; [pers.] We aspire to which we truly desire. Love is all powerful. [

COLLIER, MARY-MARGARET
[pen.] Mary-Margaret Collier; [b.] October 12, 1966, Louisville, KY; [p.] Dr. Henry S. and Peggy Collier; [ed.] Sacred Heart Academy, Transylvania University, working on Masters at Morehead State University; [occ.] Studying to become a child psychologist; [memb.] The Catholic Pro-Life Association; [hon.] The Wayside Christian Mission, for working with the homeless; [oth. writ.] Work from college but not yet published; [pers.] I believe God has put each one of us on earth to find truth, equality, forgiveness, and love. [a.] Louisville, KY.

COLLINS, FAROLYN
[pen.] Farolyn Collins; [b.] April 21, 1927, Springdale, AK; [p.] Arlie and Farol Emmett; [m.] Donald B. (deceased), May 13, 1945; [ch.] Donna Cheryl, Ronald Steven; [ed.] Simonsen High - Commercial Business College; [occ.] Medical Secretary - early years housewife and mother; [hon.] National Honor Society - High School, first place ceramic art trophy 1958; [oth. writ.] Several other poems published in newspapers, magazines, stars and stripes (WWII newspaper); [pers.] I write most of my poetry and writings on personal experiences in my own life. They are usually quite long and swiftly written. [a.] Medford, OR.

COLLINS, MARGUERITE
[pen.] Marguerite Collins; [b.] November 10, 1977, Pittsburgh, PA; [p.] Calvin and Evelyn Collins; [ed.] St. Albert the Great (grade school) and Taylor Allderdice High School; [occ.] Student; [memb.] People Concerned for the Unborn Child; [pers.] This poem is dedicated to all of the innocent children who have lost their lives from an abortion. [a.] Pittsburgh, PA.

COLMER, ANNA LISA
[b.] April 16, 1962, Lowell, MA; [p.] Mrs. Irene R. Dery and Mr. Rocco J. Scionti; [ed.] Lawrence High School, Northern Essex Community College; [oth. writ.] Poems, and short stories, nothing published, has always been a pastime up until now; [pers.] All of us hope and pray that we are different and that we can set ourselves apart from everyone else. We must believe in our inner voice, it will be a struggle, for every whisper and signal it sends around the corner visiting is the negative that unexpected, unwanted visitor who can't hold a candle to his opponent, the one, the only the positive. [a.] Salem, NH.

COLOMBO, BLANCHE MARY
[b.] February 4, 1938, Hazelpark; [p.] Arcade and Patricia Goyette; [m.] John J., August 4, 1972; [ch.] John Colombo; [ed.] High school; [occ.] Housewife; [memb.] St. Margaret of Scotland, St. Clair Shores Editor's Choice; [hon.] Two award, one copyright award for my own work. Now I am doing my own poem book 129 will be in it with my own drawings on every page; [oth. writ.] Many housewives like myself tell me to keep on and something will happen great for me. God's will be done so be it; [pers.] Thank you God! for all the poems I have written up to date 240 poems now. And my own poem book to be done soon, to share my poems. [a.] Eastpointe, MI.

COLVIN, WILLIE C.
[b.] December 11, 1963, Tuscaloosa, AL; [p.] Willie J. and Delois Wells Colvin; [ed.] Central High School; [occ.] Mental Health Worker I; [oth. writ.] I've written several poems and songs that I've yet to have published; [pers.] I've always believed in the boy-girl relationship whether it's exalted in a poem, song or satire. [a.] Tuscaloosa, AL.

COMPTON, DONNA MARGUERITE
[b.] October 14, 1974, Cape Breton, NS; [p.] Marguerite and George Compton; [ed.] Memorial High graduate; [pers.] To be all that oneself can be to do all that oneself can do. Opens the door to a world of success and a world full of happiness too. [a.] Cape Breton, NS

CONKLIN, ROBERT
[b.] October 29, 1965, Wayne, NJ; [p.] Margaret A. Conklin and Robert F. Unger; [ed.] Wayne Hills High, Bergen Community College; [occ.] M.R.I. Technician, Musician and Poet; [memb.] The Tiyospaye Club of St. Joseph's Indian School; [oth. writ.] A collection of writings and poetry is in the works, patiently waiting to be completed and published; [pers.] I am deeply moved and influenced by a Shamanic way of life. My writings reflect the spiritual ways of all. In memorium: Dearest Cinnamon, may our love never die - see you soon. [a.] Wayne, NJ.

CONNER, PATRICIA
[b.] May 1, 1932, Seattle, WA; [p.] Glenn Sanford Maring and Muriel Luella Gore; [m.] Donald C., December 27, 1992; [ch.] Christopher, Philip, John, Jennifer; [ed.] Whitman College, University of Washington, Chico State University, CSU Bakersfield; [occ.] English professor Bakersfield college; [memb.] NCTE, NAPPS Storyteller, Episcopal Church, Lay Eucharistic minister; [hon.] PBK, creative writing awards; [oth. writ.] Several poems published in small poetry journals. [a.] Bakersfield, CA.

CONNERS, WILLIAM J.
[pen.] Bill "Curly" Conners; [b.] February 16, 1910, Philadelphia, PA; [p.] Rose and Edward Conners; [m.] Anna M. (deceased), April 27, 1935; [ch.] Two; [occ.] Retired from the Provident National Bank; [memb.] Joseph A. Ferko String Band; [hon.] Mummers STring Band Hall of Fame, Ferko String Band Hall of Fame; [oth. writ.] The Ranks Passing By, Where Are The Strings of Yesterday, "Four Minutes" and The Brigade; [pers.] Most of my poetry has been about the Philadelphia Mummers who on New Year's day put on a spectacular parade through the heart of Phila. [a.] Phila., PA.

CONNORS, JEFF
[b.] September 23, 1970, Grand Falls, NF; [p.] Joseph and Rita Connors; [ed.] St. Michael's High, currently completing BA Memorial University; [occ.] Student; [oth. writ.] A Body of Poetry, short stories and the like; [pers.] Poetry is a medium of communication capable of transcending the arbitrary boundaries of personal identity to resonate on a level which is at once deeply private, yet profoundly universal. [a.] Manuels, Nfld., CAN.

CONWELL, ESTELLA CHISM
[pen.] Tweedney, Queenie, Tweetie; [b.] February 11, 1961, Four Points, Centreville; [p.] Jessie Dean Davidson Chism and J.C. Chism, Sr.; [m.] George William, March 23, 1980; [ch.] Catasha Lashaw Conwell and Georgia Dean Conwell; [ed.] Bibb County High, C.A. Fredd State Tech. College, Shelton State Junior College, Shelton State Tech. College; [occ.] Home Health Nurse, Real Estate; [memb.] LPNNA, North Shore Animal League of America, Humane Society Animal Shelter, Purity Holiness Fund Drive Committee, Cahawba River Society; [hon.] Two honorary merit World of Poetry, Nanny's Floral classes 1988, DCH Home Health, 1992 Golden Poet; [oth. writ.] World of Poetry, NCA, RCA, Sparrowgrass Poetry Forum, Inc.; [pers.] I love to write poetry and to put my life experience to words. It helps me to motivate myself and to help everyone else to get over their life experiences. [a.] Centreville, AL.

COOK, ANGELA MICHELLE
[b.] April 5, 1977, Summers County, WV; [p.] Darlene H. Cook and George F. Raines; [ed.] Talcott Jr. High, Hinton High; [pers.] May the words that I share bring forth love and warmth among all hearts worldwide. [a.] Talcott, WV.

COOK, RICHELLE F.
[b.] September 15, 1980, Lancaster, CA; [p.] Jan Arries and Harold Cook; [ed.] Junior High student.

COOKE, ALEXIA M.
[pen.] Alexia M. Cooke; [b.] November 19, 1944, Centerville, IA; [p.] Ronald and Lois Alexander Swasick; [ch.] Catherine E. Cooke; [ed.] BSBA; [occ.[Real Estate Sales; [memb.] West Pasco Bd. of Realtors; [pers.] Never look back and regret not trying. [a.] Bayonet Point, FL.

COOMBS, O. PAUL
[b.] November 30, 1957, Everett, Washington; [p.] Orville and Diane Coombs; [ed.] Snohomish High School, University of Washington, University of Seville; [oth. writ.] Unpublished as yet. However, I did write some essays, poems, and journalistic pieces for "Underlings", the undergraduate newsletter for the department of Linguistics at University of Washington; [pers.] I laugh - cry at the joke - truth of my dream - reality. [a.] Everett, WA.

COOPER, AMI
[pen.] Ami M. Cooper; [b.] January 4, 1977, Belleville, KS; [p.] Vonda and Steve Cooper; [ed.] Belleville High School (11th grade); [occ.] Work at local Dairy Queen; [memb.] None other than high school clubs; [hon.] Athletic, band, and drama awards; [oth. writ.] Many unpublished poems; [pers.] There is a lot of personal feelings of friends, family, love, and dreams in what I write. I enjoy putting my feelings on paper. [a.] Belleville, KS.

COOPER, ISABEL S.
[b.] New York, NY; [ed.] BA with honors, State University of New York at Purchase, MA Degree, Queens College; [occ.] Sculptor, Art Historian, Free-Lance writer; [memb.] College Art Association of America, National League of American Pen Women, New York Artists Equity, Mamaroneck Artists Guild; [hon.] Listed in Encyclopedia of Living Artist's in America, 5th edition 1990 page 88. Thesis in archives of the Library and Research Center of the National Museum of Women in the Arts, numerous awards for stone sculpture; [oth. writ.] Several articles published in Westchester Arts News, essay published in Village Views, poem published in anthology Wind In the Night Sky; [pers.] In both my sculpture and my writings, I strive to express the universal themes and emotions of joy and sorrow. [a.] Rye Brook, NY.

COOPER, JEFFREY S.
[b.] March 14, 1964, Charleston, WV; [p.] Paul and Judy Cooper, Jr.; [ed.] Greenbrier East High School, West Virginia Institute of Technology; [occ.] Digital Cartographer; [memb.] Delta Chi Fraternity, Parham Hills Christian Church, Youth Sponsor-Sound Advice Christian Music Ministries; [hon.] National Honor Society. [a.] Richmond, VA.

CORCORAN, JANE
[b.] December 15, 1950, New York, NY; [p.] Esther and Thomas Fitzpatrick; [m.] Thomas, April 29, 1972; [ch.] Thomas and Deirdre; [ed.] Cathedral High School; [occ.] Medical Records Analyst; [memb.] Lighthouse Preservation Society, Red Cross Volunteer; [oth. writ.] Two poems in other books, many in the local newspaper; [pers.] In addition to writing (mostly poetry) I also enjoy collecting dolls, coins, and a good hunt at a flea market. [a.] Scranton, PA.

CORCORAN, KIMBERLY KAY
[b.] August 31, 1979, Baltimore, MD; [p.] Sandra May and Theodore Richard Corcoran; [ed.] Completed eighth grade going into ninth; [occ.] Student; [memb.] Golden Dragons School of Tae Kwon Do;

[hon.] "Character Development for the Stage" and Discovering College '93; [pers.] Dedicated to my number one Mom and Dad. [a.] Abingdon, MD.

CORNELIUS, VIRGINIA A.
[b.] November 8, 1928, Waukesha, WI; [oth. writ.] Children's stories for a children's hospital - Christmas stories for children's hospital - published in local newspaper - poem untitled National Library of Poetry Wind in the Night Sky. [a.] Watertown, WI.

CORNETT, EDNA BALDRIDGE
[pen.] Ned and Ed; [b.] September 3, 1929, Floyd County, KY; [p.] Elzie and Cona Baldridge; [m.] Mitchell, April 5, 1952; [ch.] Linda, Denver, Peggy, Laverne and Micky; [occ.] Housekeeper; [oth. writ.] Went to school in Ohio and Kentucky I love my country and the land I live in; [pers.] I have five grand kids their name is Corey, Brian Zachary, Amanda, and Boby Vern. [a.] West Alexandria, OH.

CORREA, JESSE, JR.
[b.] October 5, 1962, Fall River, MA; [p.] Jesse and Maureen Correa; [ed.] Graduate of Somerset High School, Bristol Community College; [pers.] In my writing I reflect what life shows is all. Some show simple thoughts and others complex situations. People and life are a blessing and should be celebrated. I also thank Patricia Lockaby for her inspiration. [a.] Somerset, MA.

CORRIGAN, CHERYL
[b.] September 30, 1947, Ottawa, CAN; [p.] Irving Taylor and Charlotte Smith; [m.] Peter, September 9, 1989; [ch.] Deborah and Robert; [ed.] Grade 10 - two year commercial-secretarial; [occ.] Homemaker; [memb.] Royal Canadian Legion, Aylmer Quebec Canadian Bowling Association; [hon.] Community Involvement award, Aylmer Police Department; [oth. writ.] Have written numerous letters of correspondence and poetry. Family and dear friends have asl told me I was gifted in writing; [pers.] I have been greatly influenced by my sister Susanne and my late parents Irving and Charlotte Taylor Smith. I have so much peace and contentment when I sit down and write correspondence or poetry. My poem is therefore dedicated to the memory of my parents and all 9 brothers and sisters. [a.] Aylmer, Quebec, CAN.

CORVIN, LAUREN
[pen.] January Bellon; [b.] May 6, 1981, Brooklyn, NY; [p.] Anthony and Joann Corvino; [ed.] St. Charles Elementary School; [occ.] Student; [pers.] I wrote this poem during my grandfather's battle with cancer. I received notification that this poem would be published on the day my grandfather was buried. [a.] Staten Island, NY.

CORWIN, PEPPER LOREN
[b.] August 26, 1978, Gainesville, GA; [p.] Jerry and Diana Corwin; [ed.] Sophomore at West Hall High School; [memb.] Selected member of The Times Teen Board; [hon.] Who's Who Among American High School Students; [pers.] If Christ lives in us controlling our personalities, we will leave glorious marks on the lives we touch. Not because of our lovely characters, but because of his. [a.] Flowery Branch, GA.

CORY, LINDA
[pen.] Cory; [b.] August 2, 1948, Concordia, KS; [p.] Anita Coppage and Rex Cory (deceased); [m.] Divorced; [ch.] Phillip (PJ) Plantz, Jr. and Stephen Plantz; [ed.] Life teaches many lessons; [occ.] Yard Superintendent, Glickman, Inc.; [memb.] First Unitarian Universalist Church of Wichita; [hon.] I am blessed with a wonderful family and group of friends; [oth. writ.] I've written many poems, this is my first publication; [pers.] My poetry is the sound that I hear when I open my heart. It's my feelings --observations, it's the world that I see. I write it as I hear it, for the song comes and goes. [a.] Wichita, KS.

COSTAS, JOAN M.
[b.] April 5, 1959, Lancaster, CA; [p.] Spiro and Theodora Costas; [ed.] High school and some college courses; [occ.] Patient Accounts Rep; [memb.] Past matron Order of Eastern Star, MA Rifle Association; [oth. writ.] Poem in the hospital news item where I work; [pers.] If each person on this earth had a kind thought evil could not breed. [a.] Melrose, MA.

COSTELLO, PAUL ARDEN
[b.] December 10, 1966, Wakefield, MA; [p.] John and Gail Costello; [ed.] Malden Catholic High, Salve REgina University; [pers.] My inner thoughts have been decisions without substance. I need substance to survive, my mind wanders, and I let it. I enjoy the illusions it creates. [a.] Wakefield, MA.

COUGHLIN, MARY M.
[b.] June 30, 1908, Detroit, MI; [p.] William and Martha McCarthy; [m.] George F. Coughlin, June 27, 1953; [ed.] BA Marygrove College, MA Wayne State University, Teacher's Life Certificate of Michigan and numerous courses in the field of art education;[occ.] Retired administrator - Detroit elementary school; [memb.] I was invited to become a member of the Beta Sigma Phi Fellowship upon earning an MA. An active member of many art assoc. in MI and FL over the years. Presently a sponsoring member of the Charlotte County Art Guild of Punta Gorda, FL and the Guild Century Club. A life member of the MI Association of Retired School Personnel, a member of the Char-Sota Association, the Republican Legion of Merit, number of church groups; [hon.] The Veterans of Foreign Wars presented me with their prestigious American Citizenship medal upon retirement from Detroit School system. Presented with a beautiful American Flag as a member of the 1992 Presidential Task Force. Have received numerous awards and ribbons as a member of many art associations. One of my most cherished honors was being invited to become a member of The International Society of Poets in 1991; [oth. writ.] Poem were accepted for publication by the World of Poetry of Sacramento, GA, in their books entitled, Selected Works of Our World's Best Poets and Great Poems of Our Times. Poems were accepted for publication by The American Poetry Association of Santa Cruz, CA during 1990 to be included in their book entitled American Poetry Anthology Vol. X. Poems published in 9 anthologies by the National Library of Poetry, two of which are special books entitled, The Best Poems of the '90's and Distinguished Poets of America. All of the poems were selected to be in their volumes were adjudged to be at least semi-finalists in competition. Two of them were rated as favorites of the judges of the National Library. Many articles have been published on the subject of child guidance over the years; [pers.] In 1990 after many years painting pictures with oil paints I decided to lay aside my paint brushes and to begin to paint pictures with words as a poet. It is a source of great joy to me to depict the beauties of nature through poetry or to describe with words the beauty of a lovely smile. [a.] Port Charlotte, FL.

COUSTAN, DAVID P.
[b.] March 18, 1975, Oakland, CA; [p.] Donald and Terri; [ed.] Summa Cum Laude - Classical High School currently at Columbia University; [memb.] National Forensics League; [hon.] Honor Society, National Merit Finalist. [a.] Providence, RI.

COVINGTON, THERESA VIRGINIA
[b.] July 9, 1961, Evansville, IN; [p.] Udell and Marilyn Covington, Sr.; [ch.] Tereshio Lyndell and Natasha Lonell; [ed.] Bosse High; [oth. writ.] Several poems for friends who have lost a loved one, poems on love and my thoughts on situations in life, short stories; [pers.] I write to help ease the pain that comes from a painful situation. If my writing can bring a smile to a face that can't seem to smile, I will have accomplished my goal. [a.] Evansville, IN.

COWING, TIMOTHY SHAWN
[pen.] T.C. Shawn; [b.] December 31, 1959, Detroit, MI; [p.] Joe and Donna Cowing; [ed.] East Detroit High School, University of Maine; [occ.] Estate Maintenance; [memb.] St. Philips Church; [pers.] I have written over 150 poems on many subjects. From love to hate, peace to wars, about animals and the environment all in the style of my grandfather, Earl Bixby Cowing. [a.] Dresden, ME.

COWLES, TERRY LOUISE
[pen.] Louise Terry; [b.] June 13, 1927, Brooklyn, NY; [p.] George Pierce Cowles and Marjorie Manning Cowles; [ch.] Katherine Gibbs; [ed.] Dean Junior College, Earlham College; [occ.] Public Relations: wrote for newspapers and radio for 10 years, freelancer and columnist, church secretary, Hospital Administration; [memb.] Audubon Society, CT Poetry Society, various church and other volunteer and local senior citizen groups; [hon.] Occasional poems published in newspapers and/or anthologies, plus a few freelance articles here and there; [oth. writ.] Working on booklet entitled "Ink Spots" and other collected poems for fun...". [a.] Westbrook, CT.

COX, MARGARET
[pen.] Margaret (Sue) Cox; [b.] May 21, 1937, Columbia, LA; [p.] Jake and Ida Sanders; [m.] Joe Cox; [ch.] Dexter, Mike, Kenny, Jan Lajean; [ed.] Anne Arundel College; [occ.] Operations Rep Computerland Northwest; [memb.] American Legion Auxiliary, Disabled American Veteran Women's Auxiliary; [hon.] Dean's list every semester thru college; [oth. writ.] Several short stories and poems published in Christian Reader Magazine and Reader's Digest; [pers.] I would like to leave something for my children and grandchildren to remember me through my writings. [a.] Millersville, MD.

COY, SARAH HOPE
[b.] January 18, 1976, Coeur d' Alene, ID; [p.] Fred L. and Carol J. Coy; [ch.] Sibling-Lydia G. Williams, Rachel L. Stinde, Priscilla F. Coy; [ed.] Juneau-Douglas High; [occ.] Student; [memb.] Church of God of Cleveland; [pers.] "Beloved, if God so loved us, we ought also to love one another." [a.] Juneau, AK.

COYLE, CHESTER A.
[b.] August 17, 1904, Berea, KY; [p.] William and Addie Coyle; [m.] Deceased, November 23. 1927; [ch.] One; [ed.] College - Law school; [occ.] Retired Attorney; [memb.] AARP, Triple L Community Center; [hon.] License to practice law; [oth. writ.] 130 page book of poems.

COZART, TERA
[b.] May 4, 1978, Columbus, OH; [p.] Tim and Terrie Cozart; [ed.] Currently attending Wyoming Seminary College Preparatory School; [pers.] In this world of ours poets and dreamers are few. I'm proud to say I'm one of both.

CRAIG, LYNN MARIE
[b.] January 30, 1963, Fort Fairfield, ME; [p.] Sandra Pelletier and Loomis Craig; [occ.] 12 years with nationally known press monitoring service; [memb.] Northern Lambda Word (of Arrostook Cty, ME) and sponsor of four children through Christian children's since 1984; [oth. writ.] Poems published in hometown newspaper; [pers.] To allow the definition of my life to become something new everyday. I strive to understand the diversity of all cultures and especially the lives of children everywhere. [a.] Presque Isle, ME.

CRAVEN, JESSICA
[b.] March 14, 1975, San Dimas, CA; [p.] Howard and Anne Craven; [occ.] Student; [memb.] Pasadena Speedboat Club; [oth. writ.] Personal poems and essays; [pers.] Life is the ultimate dream and living life is the ultimate achievement. Always live it to its fullest. [a.] LaVerne, CA.

CRAWFORD, LINDA SUE
[b.] Gastonia, NC; [p.] Grace M. and Charles B. Green, Jr.; [ch.] Derek Warren; [ed.] Holbrook High, North Carolina Central University, Durham Technical Community College; [occ.] Office Manager/Personnel, The Center for Community Self-Help; [memb.] National Arbitration Panel, Council of Better Business Bureaus; [hon.] Dean's Lists, Woman of the Year Certificate; [pers.] My writing reflects that it doesn't matter how hopeless one's life may seem. A person always holds on to a spark of hope for betterment. [a.] Durham, NC.

CRAWFORD, TERRY
[pen.] T.C. Crawford; [b.] March 29, 1960, New Mexico; [p.] Anna G. Faker; [ed.] Foothill High School, Fresno City College, Lyles College of Beauty; [occ.] Cosmetology; [memb.] Society of American Magicians, California Cosmetology Association; [oth. writ.] Have compiled numerous poems for private and publishing purposes; [pers.] A dream is breed by the soul and imagination. To live for a dream is to live for life. To have a dream become reality is to have life. [a.] Fresno, CA.

CRERAR, THOMAS CHARLES
[b.] April 27, 1971, Stratford, ONT; [p.] Charles and Barbara Crerar; [ed.] Graduated grade 12 Northwestern Secondary School; [occ.] Singer/poet; [oth. writ.] Two other poems which I turned into songs that appeared in my first studio tape called "Things you say"; [pers.] I try to write from my heart. About fears, happiness, love and other things that are in my life. [a.] Stratford, ONT., CAN.

CRILLER, DARIN
[b.] December 13, 1969, Queens, NY; [ed.] Sewanhaka High School, currently college sophomore; [occ.] Warehouse Manager, Dental Technicians Supply Co.; [oth. writ.] "Armadillos and Corn Flakes", a short magazine published privately; [pers.] In my writing, I like to offend people. By offending them, I prove to myself and to them that they actually care about something other than themselves." [a.] Floral Park, NY.

CRISSONE, MARIE NATHALIE
[pen.] Marie N. Crissone; [b.] September 11, 1979, Mission Viejo, CA; [p.] John and Armine Crissone; [ed.] High school student; [memb.] Humane Society of U.S., Audubon Society; [oth. writ.] I am inspired by the sheer beauty of nature and by the love. I endure from my beloved parents. I strive to make most of my poems bring out the simple innocence of the later 1880s. "Dear Mother" is dedicated to my family and L.M. Montgomery, my true role model and inspiration. [a.] Hazel Green, AL.

CROCKFORD, JANICE
[pen.] Janice Crockford; [b.] September 10, 1947, Pittsburgh, KS; [p.] Mr. and Mrs. C.W. Buzzard (deceased); [m.] George, October 28, 1967; [ch.] Brian and Kristin; [ed.] One year college majored Business; [occ.] Housewife; [oth. writ.] I've written several other poems - none published yet. I've written a story about my oldest daughter who died at the age of five years; [pers.] I want people to be inspired by what they read. Maybe inspire them to become better people.

CROCOMBE, JORDAN
[pen.] J.R. Crocombe; [b.] March 6, 1977, Denver, CO; [p.] Mr. and Mrs. Thomas A. Crocombe; [ed.] High school 12th grade; [pers.] Remember: The world is yours use it wisely. [a.] Buena Vista, CA.

CROFTON-HYDER, PEGGY
[pen.] Peggy Crofton-Hyder; [b.] June 26, 1949, Wharton, TX; [p.] Thomas E. and Lottie M. Crofton; [m.] Les Hyder, May 22, 1975; [ch.] William E. Hyder; [ed.] George West High; [occ.] Data Entry; [memb.] Veterans of Foreign Wars of the United States, Post No. 6435 - a ladies auxiliary; [pers.] My writings are dedicated to the veterans of the United States without their gallant sacrifices, the freedom we enjoy may never have existed. [a.] Antioch, CA.

CROSBY, SARA JO
[pen.] Sara Jo Crosby; [b.] April 23, 1968, Kansas City, MO; [p.] William Lowell and Denise Glee Crosby; [ed.] Raytown High, Longview Community College; [occ.] Executive Editorial Secretary; [pers.] "Dear Grandpa" was written for my grandfather after his death in March 1993 some words are easier written than spoken. [a.] Blue Springs, MO.

CROSS, DAVID
[pen.] David Porter Cross; [b.] June 29, 1970, Rochdale, England; [p.] Mr. R.A. Cross and Mrs. M. Cross; [ed.] Huddersfield Polytechnic, Leeds College of Jazz Music, Boston Conservatory; [occ.] Musician; [memb.] International Trumpet Guild; [hon.] Graduate diploma in Contemporary music, postgraduate diploma in Jazz; [oth. writ.] VArious poems set to contemporary music; [pers.] We are all alone in our senses - only communication breaks down barriers. [a.] Boston, MA.

CROSS, SUNNY LYNNETTE
[b.] June 7, 1977, Bristol, TN; [p.] Debra and Charlie Matthews and Phil and Janice Cross; [ed.] Junior at Eastern Guilford High School; [occ.] Student; [memb.] BEta Club, French Club, Fellowship of Christian Athletes, Swim Team; [hon.] Who's Who '91-'92 and 92-93, Duke University Talent Identification Program, Superintendent's Academic Excellence awards in French and Math 91-92; [pers.] I pull from my emotions and life experiences in my writings and I give God all the glory and honor for any talent I possess. [a.] Greensboro, NC.

CROWDER, LENORA REVACA ZORKA
[b.] July 16, 1941, Hammond, IN; [p.] George G. and Alice Lenora Zorka; [m.] Larry Arnold, August 22, 1964; [ch.] Kevin Lynn and Karen Lynn Crowder; [ed.] BS in ED, MS in EdS and currently finishing Ed.D; [occ.] Reading and Language Arts teacher; [memb.] AAUW, ASCD, OK Women's NEtwork, Kappa Kappa Iota, Pi Lambda Theta, NEA, OEA, SEA, IRA, National Humane Educational Society, Stillwater Humane Society, Doris Day League, IFAW, NHES, Defenders of Wildlife, AAUW; [oth. writ.] Poems and essays in local papers, contest winner essays; [pers.] I wish to reach all youth and adults to show that reading, writing, and thoughts reveal inner qualities of life and personal reflections. [a.] Stillwater, OK.

CRUZAN, PATRICIA
[pen.] Pat Cruzan; [b.] November 15, 1945, Jacksonville, FL; [p.] Clarence and Agnes Cannon; [m.] Charles, November 4, 1977; [ch.] Christopher Cruzan; [ed.] A.L. Miller High, Tuft College, Georgia State University; [occ.] Chapter I Teacher, Palmetto Elementary; [memb.] ASCD, Georgia Council, IRA, National Council of Teachers of Mathematics, First Baptist Church of Fayetteville Choir; [hon.] Who's Who in American Education 1989-90, 1992-93; [oth. writ.] Poem for Retirement Tea Program Chapter I teachers for 1992; [pers.] Teaching has allowed me the privilege of making an impact on many lives. By writing poems and stories, I feel that I can also influence the lives of others as well as enjoy myself. Reading beautiful poetry or other materials inspires me to seek out goals for living. [a.] Fayetteville, GA.

CUERVO, RIGOBERTO
[b.] November 27, 1967, Oriente, Cuba; [p.] Rigoberto and Amarilis Cuervo; [ed.] Weehawken High, Plaza School of Drafting; [occ.] Unemployed at present; [memb.] National Psoriasis Foundation; [oth. writ.] Several unpublished poems, songs several unfinished tales; [pers.] I suppose that I try to reflect upon the hopelessness of life in this world in contrast to the hope of everlasting life in the kingdom of our Lord Jesus Christ. [a.] Weehawken, NJ.

CULBERTSON, BRENDA
[pen.] B.J.; [b.] January 26, 1953, Moberly, MO; [p.] Robert and Lorene Winterbower; [m.] Andrew, September 12, 1988; [ch.] Rachel Maynelli - Noelle Isyanna - Andriel Jolie'; [ed.] Northeast MO State University, University of MO. Columbia; [occ.] Homemaker; [memb.] United Methodist Women; [hon.] National Honor Society, National Drama Society; [oth. writ.] Numerous poems for my collection and by request of others. One play for local perfor-

mance and many songs for myself; [pers.] My writings come from deep reflection of my heart, mind and soul. I want my readers to contemplate and feel the hope, joy, and love life offers. [a.] Malta Bend, MO.

CULBERTSTON, FREDERICA MCDILL
[p.] Charlotte Nearpass Medrick and Allan Conover McDill; [ch.] Walter E. Jr., Dr. Charles E., and Isabelle S. Culbertson; [memb.] Washington Poets Association and Space Coast Writer's Guild in FL; [pers.] Born, reared and educated in New York, considers herself a gypsy after living in nine states and travelling worldwide. A memorable 1945, serving the military in India and China with the American Red Cross, was followed by marriage, three children, four grandsons, nineteen years as a Connecticut hospital volunteer and a thirty year real estate career, still holding a Florida license. After lifelong enjoyment of all arts, she is now concentrating on writing, friends and family, cooking, and - when possible - beach-walking and travelling. [a.] Port Angeles, WA.

CUNNING, GLORIA J.
[b.] November 15, 1955, Fresno, CA; [p.] George and Rose Jamgotchian; [ch.] Shawn P.H. Chung; [ed.] Bullard High, Fresno City College, California State University; [occ.] Free Lance Writer; [oth. writ.] I have written a P.B.S. show and co-produced with my late husband Chris Drake Cunning; [pers.] Why inspire yourself when you can inspire the whole world. [a.] Fresno, CA.

CUNNINGHAM, JASON
[b.] November 7, 1976, Cleveland, OH; [p.] John and Dorothy Cunningham; [ed.] Completed 10th grade at Villa-Angela St. Joseph High School; [hon.] National Honor Society at Villa Angela, St. Joseph High School, honorable mention in Lation/Original Poetry in the Diocesian Foreign Language Contest. [a.] East Cleveland, OH.

CUNNINGHAM, MELISSA ELLEN
[b.] February 2, 1977, Lockport; [p.] Patsy and Lewie Cunningham; [pers.] My poems are written to express the feelings in my heart. [a.] Lockport, NY.

CUPP, LOTTIE M.
[b.] March 3, 1907, Lanork, IL; [p.] Charles and Mary Pobst (passed away four yrs ago); [m.] 64 years ago; [ed.] Just a few grades of country school; [occ.] Housewife but a widow now for over 30 years; [memb.] Have been school guard for 17 years, just quit two years ago; [hon.] Yes, lots of them longest school guard worker known, and the oldest known, and an honorable one, with doing extra features to help the kids; [oth. writ.] Was born on a farm, didn't marry until 22 1/2 years later. But while at home worked in fields, but no salary but had a table to eat by and a bed to sleep in; [pers.] I write poetry by the bu and give it all a way. I won a big honor writing a poem about our flag, which stirred up even President Clinton. [a.] Rochelle, IL.

CURTEIS, EILEEN
[b.] July 20, 1942, Victoria, B.C.; [p.] Tom and Lil Curteis; [ed.] BEd UVic. Specialty in Primary; [occ.] Teacher 27 years, presently working at Queenswood, a retreat growth and renewal center in Victoria B.C.; [oth. writ.] Sojourner, Know Yourself, a book of my original art sketches and poems published in Oct. 1993. Many other poems published through Prairie Messenger, paperplates, Grail, An Ecumenical Journal, Island Catholic News, Forward in the Spirit, L'Antenne, Sisters Today, A Glance At Our Heritage; [pers.] I am a pilgrim on a journey who wishes to convey through my art and poetry that the fullness of life is for everyone. [a.] Victoria, B.C.

CURTIS, GEORGE, M.
[b.] February 7, 1921, West Branch, MI; [p.] Ira and Edwyn Curtis; [m.] Melvina Reiten, 1945; [ch.] Judy, Donald, Larry and Howard Curtis; [ed.] Graduated West Branch High 1939, BBA and MA University of Michigan; [occ.] School teacher/administrator; [memb.] NEA, NASSP, NASA, MASB, Outstanding 4-H club member 1940; [pers.] My poetry reflects my life's memories and my personal philosophy. I hope that my life may be reflected to future generations through this medium. [a.] New Branch, MI.

CURTIS, SHARON
[pen.] Grace Qi Sovereignty; [b.] March 27, 1950, Minneapolis, MN; [p.] Deceased; [m.] Deceased; [ch.] Jeri, Deborah, Renee, Robbie, Angel and Fantasea; [ed.] University of MN, Elementary Education, Brown's Institute N.E.C. Business Management; [occ.] Disabled, mother; [memb.] Bally Swim and Fitness; [hon.] St. Agnes' Poem Contest, "Rose of Sharon"; [oth. writ.] 'Silent Victim' (child abuse), 'Conquering Congo' (origin of Vampires); [pers.] You must understand what it is to be a human being, before you may know or realize the man and/or woman; to become the 'One'. [a.] St. Louis Park, MN.

CUTRONA, CAROL J.
[b.] December 22, 1936, Chicago, IL; [m.] John J., December 26, 1971; [ch.] Kevin R. Frankovich; [ed.] BA Sociology California State, University Northridge; [occ.] Social Worker - retired; [memb.] National League of American Pen Woman - Recording Secretary; [oth. writ.] "Maggie", "Cottage By The Sea", "Grease Paint", "The Demon" articles for Reachout Magazine; [pers.] For me, writing forms the bridge on which my soul travels from deep within to the external world. [a.] Moorpark, CA.

CYBART, REBECCA
[pen.] Becky Cybart; [b.] May 18, 1975, Ypsilanti, MI; [p.] Bruce and Yvonne Cybart; [ed.] Fowlerville High; [occ.] Army/training to be a nurse; [memb.] SADD; [hon.] Student improvement award, various art awards; [oth. writ.] Many unpublished poems and writings; [pers.] Be your best, be yourself, and don't judge others. [a.] Fowlerville, MI.

CYWINK, JENNIFER LYNN
[b.] September 15, 1979, Quesnel B.C., CAN; [p.] Lynn and Nicholas Cywink; [ed.] Sacred Heart School, Marymount High School; [hon.] Sports, Language Arts award, Mathematics, French, Academic Achievement, Merit award, Spelling achievement; [oth. writ.] Writings published in local newspaper; [pers.] This poem to be dedicated in memory of my Aunt Silvia for in which this poem had originally been written. [a.] Espanola, ONT., CAN.

CZEPCINSKI, JAMIE
[b.] September 4, 1978, Livonia, MI; [p.] James and Carolyn Czepcinski; [ed.] Student at Lumen Christi High School; [memb.] Environmental Committee, Marching and Symphony Band; [hon.] Honors English class. [a.] Jerome, MI.

D'ALFONSO, ANTONIO
[b.] August 6, 1953, Montreal, CAN.; [p.] Carlo and Emila Dalvatore D'Alfonso; [ed.] 1975-BA Loyola College (Communications) 1979 MSc. Universite' de Montreal (Semilogy); [occ.] Publisher-writer; [hon.] Finalist for Le Prix Emile-Nelligan for L'Autre Rivage 1987; [oth. writ.] Black Tongue (1983), The Other Shore (1986,1988), Panick Love (1992), L'Autre Rivage (1987) in French and Auril ou l'Anti-passion (1990); [pers.] My interest lies in the bridging of cultures through the promotion of ethnicity (which I oppose to nationalism). [a.] Montreal, CAN.

DaSILVA, ALEXIA
[pen.] Suzy Dayeh; [b.] May 27, 1987, San Francisco, CA; [p.] Christina Luiz Kucera; [ed.] Grade school - St. Catherine's School (Burlington, CA) and Armondale School (Portola Valley, CA) - Middle School - Corte Madera School (Portola Valley, CA); [occ.] Student; [memb.] PS Production - Peninsula Humane Society - Uniteens, Unity Church, Palo Alto; [hon.] Finalist in Miss Teen Pageant; [oth. writ.] Stories and poems written in first year of middle school - Corte Madera; [pers.] I love poetry, reading, and writing poetry. When I write my poetry I feel independent and I feel special. Poetry gives me a chance to express
my feelings. Each poem expresses a feeling I have in my heart. I dedicate my poetry to my half sister, whom I never see, and to a very special friend in Madesto, CA. [a.] Palo Alto, CA.

D'AVANZO, KATHRYN
[pen.] Kathryn D'Avan; [b.] New York City; [ed.] H&B Studio for Actors NYC; [occ.] Actress/Communication; [oth. writ.] Several poems; [pers.] When the poetic muse calls, we must dare to listen. Poems are often inspired by a strong personal emotion or vision, or, sometimes just visited by the Universal poetic muse. I feel both occurred in my writing of "Eva Marie". Amusingly enough, I was caught in a traffic jam a few blocks from home, when I felt that visit, and "Eva Marie" was born in its entirety, in my car...of all places! Anyway, I dared, and "Eva Marie", truly written on "the wings of inspiration", is an expression of love, happily being shared as poetry is meant to be. [a.] W.H., CA.

DALBERRY, SHANI
[pen.] Pumpkin; [b.] April 12, 1976, Jamaica, WI; p.] Anthony and Maulene Dalberry; [ed.] High School Senior; [hon.] Counselor's Honor Roll subject awards for most classes (Chemistry, History, Spanish); [oth. writ.] Article published in H.S. house paper and other unpublished poems; [pers.] My poetry reflects the inner feelings, misunderstanding questions and confusion of young love, separated by distance. [a.] Miami, FL.

DALBY, CHRYSTAL DAWN
[b.] May 21, 1976, Henderson, KY; [p.] William C. and Linda J. Dalby; [ed.] Senior-High School; [memb.] Marching Marshals Band, Marshall Co. Jazz Band, Math Club, Peer Intervention, Beta Club, FBLA, SADD, Spanish Club, Pep Club; [oth. writ.] The King Fish of Willow Creek, Sunshine Magic, Grandpa's Kitchen; [pers.] My objective in life is to be the best at what I do and have fun at the same time. [a.] Calvert City, KY.

DALE, DANIEL S.
[b.] January 7, 1962, Springfield, MA; [p.] Lloyd and Nancy Dale; [ed.] Northfield Mount Hermon School, BS in Physics from Stanford University, MS and PhD in Physics from the University of Illinois; [occ.] Nuclear Physicist, Massachusetts Institute of Technology; [memb.] Union of Concerned Scientists, Federation of American Scientists, American Physical Society--Division of Nuclear Physics and Forum on Science and Society, Amnesty International; [oth. writ.] A few scientific papers. [a.] Woburn, MA.

DALE, NELLIE C.
[b.] March 12, 1953, Winnipeg, Manitoba, CAN.; [p.] James Maurice Dale and Nellie Jane; [m.] John H. Pattimore, September 26, 1981; [ch.] Rachel Rae and Kristen Catherine; [ed.] BA 1979 University of Winneg; [occ.] Educational Assistant-owner Needleworks North (mail order business); [memb.] Canadian Nature Federation; [hon.] Gold Medal Philosophy 1979, University of Winnipeg; [oth. writ.] Articles/letter published in Peter Gzowwski's Morningside Papers II. CBC publication; [pers.] Living and learning about an environmentally sensitive lifeway is most important to me. [a.] Whitehorse Yukon, CAN.

DANCE, PATRICIA
[b.] May 15, 1967; [p.] Nancy and Guy LaBanz; [m.] Gerald; [ch.] Tristan Arthur Llewellyn (5); [ed.] Towson Catholic High, St. Mary's College of MD, saving for graduate school; [occ.] Archaeologist; [memb.] Council for MD Archaeology; [oth. writ.] Sections of various archaeological reports on sites 18STI-103 and 18STI-131. Working on additional poems and fiction; [pers.] I wish to show the beauty and wisdom in Nature and how we all fit into that whole. I am heavily influenced by the Celtic religious world view - Erin go Bhride. [a.] St. Mary's City, MD.

DASRT, PAULA VIOLA
[pen.] Viola or Vi; [b.] June 29, 1922, Harlington, TX; [m.] Lester C., February 25, 1981; [ed.] High school; [occ.] Retired; [memb.] AARP, Senior Citizen Center - Log Cabin Quitters - Bible Baptist; [oth. writ.] One.

DATILES, M. JOYCE R.
[b.] January 11, 1980, Silver Spring, MD; [p.] Dr. Manuel and Jacqueline R. Datiles Esp.; [ed.] St. Jude Catholic School-Elementary, Oakcrest High (Wash. DC); [occ.] Student; [memb.] St. Jude's Library Volunteer, Oakcrest Student Council Rep., Class V.P.; [hon.] Honor Roll, St. Jude's and Oakcrest. [a.] Rockville, MD.

DAURIA, MELISSA ANN
[pen.] MAD; [b.] February 28, 1981, Einstein Hospital; [p.] Linda and Thomas Daura; [ed.] Our Lady of Assumption-7th grade; [occ.] Student; [hon.] One poetry contest at first place, second honors in school. Many awards in competition cheerleading, principle's award, first and second place in two talent shows; [oth. writ.] Other poems like shadow and walking into the dark, etc.; [pers.] My poems show feeling that are in my heart. And make me want to write about to get over my emotions. [a.] Bronx, NY.

DAVENPORT, ELIZABETH
[b.] September 7, 1967, Corpus Christi, TX; [p.] Charles and Bobbie (deceased) Davenport ; [ed.] Porter HIgh School, Brownsville Texas Lutheran College, University of Texas (BA 1990); [occ.] English teacher, Porter High School; [memb.] Porter site-based management committee alternate; [hon.] Alpha Lambda Delta, Gamma Phi Alpha (UT), Sigma Tai Delta, Dean's List; [oth. writ.] Collection of poems (pending copyright and publishing); [pers.] My influences include (but are not limited to) E.E. Cummings, Sylvia Plath, and Thomas Whitbread. [a.] Brownsville, TX.

DAVIS, GREGORY L.
[b.] December 21, 1946, Red Bank, NJ; [p.] Edward L. and Betty S.; [m.] Carmen, December 26, 1979; [ch.] Justin; [ed.] BSME-Drexel University, MBA-The Wharton School, CPA; [occ.] Management Consulting; [memb.] ALCPA, DCICPA; [hon.] Who's Who in the East 1978, Who's Who in American Colleges and Universities, Circa 1971; [oth. writ.] Unpublished-"Beyond Childhood", collection of poems. [a.] Rockville, MA.

DAVIS, LAURIE
[pen.] Laurie McMichael; [b.] July 4, 1950, Los Angeles, CA; [p.] Moe and Joyce Moses; [ch.] Jonathan Christopher and Brian Matthew; [ed.] Reseda High, Magnolia College for Medical -Dental Assistants; [occ.] Hostess at "Lakeview" Restaurant at Marriott Desert Springs Hotel; [hon.] Four Honorable Mention awards with "The World of Poetry" contests; [oth. writ.] Written hundreds of poems since age sixteen. Was published in a hardbound book untitled, "Our World's Most Treasured Poems". World of Poetry Press; [pers.] I am an emotional individual influenced by my water sign and the moon. My poems are reflections of my feelings; of happiness, sorrow, love and heartache. [a.] Palm Desert, CA.

DAVIS, LYN BRIAR (SWEETMAN)
[b.] July 16, 1967; [p.] Donna Irene (Porter), James GAry Sweetman; [m.] Ronald Allan Davis, July 20, 1985; [ch.] Amanda Jade, Samantha Lynne, Michael Ronald; [ed.] GRaduated Streetsville Secondary School; [occ.] Mother. [a.] Ontario, CAN.

DAVIS, PATRICIA KELSO
[pen.] Pat Davis; [b.] February 7, 1954, Ft. Worth, TX; [p.] Theopeles and Mary Kelso; [m.] Robert L. [a.] Sacto., CA.

DAVIS, RITA
[b.] May 1, 1978, Vancouver, BC; [p.] Penny Davis; [ed.] Grade 10 in Fall 1993 Westview Junior Secondary; [occ.] Student; [hon.] Most Promising Writer, 1993; [oth. writ.] The End I Fear was my first published and many other poems and short stories; [pers.] This poem was written so the storying children will never be forgotten. I would like to thank my guardians Ron and Rita Davis, my past English teacher, Mr. Reid and Ryan Sayers. Thank you all. [a.] Ridge, BC.

DAVIS, ROBERT L.
[b.] March 21, 1946, Weldon, AK; [p.] Keith Sr. and Geneva Davis; [m.] Patricia A. Kelso-Davis; [ch.] Robert L. Davis, II; [occ.] Black & White Fine Art Photographer. [a.] Sacramento, CA.

DAVIS, RONNIE LOU GAULT
[pen.] Lou Gault, Ronnie Lou Davis; [b.] November 5, 1949, Greenville, KY; [p.] Sarah Ruth Grubbs and Alton A. Gault (deceased); [m.] Gary Wayne, September 15, 1969; [ch.] Robert Wayne, Teresa Kay; [ed.] Midland High School, Howard Payne University; [occ.] Secretary; [memb.] VFW Auxiliary. [a.] Midland, TX.

DAVIS, RUTHELLEN PYLE
[pen.] Ruthellen Pyle Davis; [b.] December 21, 1914, Concord Twp. Chadds Ford, PA; [p.] Irwin W. and Gertrude M. Pyle; [m.] William T., December 16, 1939; [ch.] Randall Pyle Kirk Davis; [ed.] West Chester University, University of California; [occ.] Teacher-4th grade, Germantown Friends School-retired; [memb.] Colonial Dames of America in the Commonwealth of PA, DAR, Welcome Society, Women of New England, Swedish Colonial; [hon.] Honor membership-The Chapel of Four Chaplains, Plaque given for Historic presentation by the Heritage Commission of Delaware County, plaque given for service by Newtown Township Tricentennial Commission; [oth. writ.] Poems and plays for my teaching -many poems about my family and friends; [pers.] My poems are the well-spring of strong feeling. [a.] Newtown Squares, PA.

DAVIS, S. ELAINE
[b.] February 7, 1944, Del Rio, TX; [p.] Lella A. and Bernice C. Davis; [ch.] Joell Davis Goldrick; [ed.] No. Miami High, Miami-Dade Jr. College, Jones Real Estate College, Colo. Mt. College; [occ.] Massage Therapist self-employed owner, buyer and seller; [memb.] GWS Chamber of Commerce, Beta Sigma Phi, Defenders of Wildlife; [oth. writ.] "Won Golden Poet Award for 1989", Outstanding Achievement in Poetry (World of Poetry), have written several short stories not published; [pers.] I have been solely influenced by the lessons in life contributing to my evolution and growth. I wish to love and be loved as I grow with life. [a.] Glenwood Springs, CO.

DAVIS, SHARON
[pen.] Cat Davis; [b.] Ft. Wayne, IN; [p.] Gilbert Edward and Nancy Catherine Davis; [ed.] BA,MA - California State University, Fresno; [occ.] Elementary School teacher 4th grade, Earliment Elementary School (Earliment, CA); [memb.] International Reading Association, National Council of Teachers of English, Teachers of English to Speakers of Other Languages, California Math Council; [hon.] Golden Key National Honor Society. [a.] Ivanhoe, CA.

DAWYDIUK, SHELLY
[b.] February 15, 1981, Blairmore, Alberta; [p.] Garry and Mary-Ann Dawydiuk; [ed.] Grade 7 as of August 31, 1993; [memb.] Roman Catholic Church; [hon.] Two firsts for junior posters, one first and one second for junior essays, two firsts in violin solos, and a first for vocal solos; [oth. writ.] Several unpublished poems; [pers.] I try to bring out the greatness of nature and music. I wish everyone could enjoy life as a kid again, if they could. (Unless they still are!). [a.] Bellevue, Alberta.

DeCRANE, ELODY
[pen.] Elody DeCrane; [b.] February 19, 1911, Ghent, Belgium; [p.] Living and Stephanie Hamerlinck (both deceased); [m.] Leo DeCrane (deceased), July

27, 1927; [ch.] David DeCrane and Linda Decrane GRubb; [ed.] 8th grade, came to America Oct. 1921 settled in Kewanee, IL.; [occ.] REtired seamstress; [memb.] AARP; [hon.] 2 poems were published in the Senior Visitor Newspaper; [oth. writ.] Poems, The Lost Souls, My Mountain Home, Shifting Sands, Homeless Man and Boy, Hell, My Soul is Free, My Friend Santa's Misadvantage and more; [pers.] My memoir and experience of WWI in Belgium, where published in the Dec. 26, 1992 issue of the Geneseo Republic Newspaper. [a.] Geneseo, IL.

DeCRISTOFARO, ROSEANNA
[b.] December 24, 1950, Brooklyn, NY; [p.] Anna and Domenick Vastano; [ch.] John Domenick DeCristofaro; [ed.] New York City Community College; [occ.] Administrative Assistant/Executive Secretary; [pers.] Live life to the fullest extent - be all that you can be. [a.] Brooklyn, NY.

DeFEO, JIM
[pen.] DeFeo; [b.] August 19, 1942, St. Paul, MN; [p.] James and Mary DeFeo; [ed.] BA University of Saint Thomas, PhD "Nite" School; [occ.] By Day: Adv. Collar & Tie, By Nite: Writer/Songwriter; [memb.] YMCA; [hon.] The Morning; [oth. writ.] A collage of minute experiences reflected in poetry, American song form and quotes...For Sale!!!; [pers.] Wherever you are...There you are!! [a.] Minneapolis, MN.

DeFLORES, OLIVIA DAVILA
[pen.] Olivia De Montelongo; [b.] January 17, 1940, Saltillo, Coah., Mexico; [p.] Jesus Davila and Estela Flores; [m.] Jose Raul Flores Montelongo, May 25, 1963; [ch.] Raul, Gerardo, Caesar and Carlos Flores; [ed.] Santa Clara High School, Academia "Roberts"- several literature courses; [occ.] Poetry writer, dramatist, scenic director, theatrical producer; [memb.] Soc. Mex. de Geografia Y Estadistica Legion de Honor Nacional - Soc. Cultural Sor Juana Ines de la Druz, Instituto Mexicano de Ciencias Y Humanidades; [hon.] Centro Mundial Pro-Forta licimiento de Los Valores Humanos - Organizacion de Las Naciones Unidas - Rama de Escritores Mexicanos - Academia Mexicana de Las Bellas Artes - Agrupacion de Periodistas Teatrales, Academia de Delfos, Grecia; [oth. writ.] Four poetry books - one drama piece (monologue) one tales book named "Canto Verde" (Green Song) adapted to theatre with original music. This play has been performed since 1980 at the best theatres in Mexico City and at seven countries (Spain, France, Venezuela, Miami, USA, Ecuador, Japan, Greece). Translated to 5 languages about 600 performances; [pers.] (Inedited work) "Confesiones Sabatinas" "Todo Por Una Noche de Amor" (theatre-comedies). A movie story about So Juana Ines de La Cruz already adapted, and waiting for a producer. 200 Hai-kus poems (Japanese style). Most of my writing is against wars and injustice or with echologist message. [a.] Mexico.

DeFRANCESCO, JOYCE ANN
[b.] August 14, 1970, Yonkers, KY; [p.] Maria and Gerald DeFrancesco; [m.] Fiance-Walter F. Sutliff III, April 17, 1994; [ed.] Mahopac High School, Katharine Gibbs School of Business; [occ.] Executive Secretary/Legal Compliance Specialist; [hon.] H.S. Honor Roll, Business Award, Dean's List, Merit Honors; [pers.] I enjoy writing about experiences from my own life and its surroundings. [a.] Carmel, NY.

DeLEAN, RHENAY
[b.] September 26, 1978, Bay City, TX; [p.] Vincent and Yolanda DeLean; [ed.] Freeport Intermediate; [occ.] Student; [oth. writ.] No other writings, this is my first and I am very proud of myself; [pers.] This is my first time to write a poem and I think it is great! I am influenced by love poems. [a.] Freeport, TX.

DeLOZIER, RUTH E.
[b.] January 2, 1920, Sheridan, WY; [p.] Francis and Bessie Grimes; [m.] Arthur H., November 26, 1948; [ch.] Lois, Linda, Mark, Rita; [ed.] Everett High School (PA), Nurses Training (MD); [occ.] Registered Nurse (retired), housewife at present; [memb.] Harvest Center Church; [oth. writ.] Poems in Church publications. Published two books of poems, "God Guided My Thoughts" and "God's Gift To Me"; [pers.] I desire to send God's love of peace to all his creation for honor and glory to God, our Creator. [a.] Ashland, OH.

DePAOLO, DONNA
[b.] June 24, 1939, Portland, ME; [p.] Murdock M. and Helen R. King Day; [m.] Divorced; [ch.] Thomas M. DePaolo; [ed.] Portland High School; [occ.] Sterile Tech; [memb.] Italian Heritage Center, St. John's Evangelist Catholic Church; [oth. writ.] Several poems published in Where Dreams Begin, Who in the Night Sky; [pers.] Writing poetry is just something that seems to come to me at the moment. Some small thing may happen and I just write about it. It brings me much pleasure. [a.] S.P., ME.

DePAULA, HENRIQUE
[pen.] El Brujo; [b.] December 12, 1928, Sao Paulo, Brazil; [p.] Antonio De Paula and Amalia Salgado; [m.] Maria Luiza, May 31, 1958; [ch.] Julio Caesar, Carlos Alberto, Valerie Ealters - Celia; [ed.] First School and Commercial school; [occ.] Retired (former Construction worker-USA, Sales Manager-Brazil); [oth. writ.] Articles in newspapers in Sao Paulo-Brazil about sports; [pers.] I like to write about everything. In poetry, I prefer the romantic. I hate the liars and I'm writing a book: God, the Outright Lie. [a.] Newark, NJ.

DeROSA, GERALDINE G.
[b.] September 17, 1920, Cleveland, OH; [p.] George B. Gerau and Josephine Gerau Morhard; [m.] April 3, 1940; [ch.] B.J. Frampton and Dr. Timothy DeRosa; [ed.] Cleveland School of Art; [occ.] Retired-Interior DEsigner; [oth. writ.] Many-never submitted-both poetry and short stories. [a.] Mayfield Heights, OH.

DeSANTIS, PASQUALE
[b.] February 15, 1954, Chicago, IL; [p.] Peter and Rosalie De Santis; [ed.] Senn High, Tri-Community, Citrus College, University of La Verne; [memb.] International Freelance Phonographers Organization; [hon.] Alpha Gamma Sigma, Two blue ribbon awards for art and Science; [oth. writ.] Poem published in a book; [pres.] The creations of man are a reflection of himself, while men are the creation, and reflection of God. [a.] Azusa, CA.

DeSHA, D.
[b.] November 4, 1966, Port Arthur, TX; [p.] Anne Malone and L. Ronald Jones; [ed.] Port Neches Groves High School, Lamar University; [hon.] World of Poetry silver poet 1986, 1990; [pers.] Never let anyone take your individuality away. Don't take it away from yourself. Conformity kills the soul. [a.] Groves, TX.

DeVALL, GWENDOLYN L.
[pen.] Barbee R./Gwendolyn L. DeVall; [b.] January 27, 1948, Lake Charles, CA; [p.] Ernest and Florence DeVall; [m.] Perfecto R. Rodrigues, June 26, 1993; [ch.] James and Marcus Pourteau, (stepchildren-Jay and Tony Rodriguez and Ginny Lynn Billeaud; [ed.] Lake High School, Polytechnic Institute; [occ.] Instructor/Administrative Assistant; [hon.] Nominated for Tutor of the Year in Houston area National Literacy; [oth. writ.] "Just a Part", "Two Lonely Hearts", "What Has Happened to Yesterday?"; [pers.] To wipe away crime we must wipe away illiteracy. [a.] Houston, TX.

DeVRIES, RAYMOND
[b.] May 27, 1970, Kalamazoo, MI; [p.] Shirley DeVries; [ed.] Naval Nuclear Power Program currently attending KVCC; [occ.] Student, Bartender, Clerical Assistant; [pers.] Writing is a reflection of emotion personal events and current events. I am influenced by the writings of T.S. Eliot, Anne Sexton, and William Shakespeare. [a.] Portage, MI.

DeWOODY, MARIE E.
[pen.] Ellen DeWoody; [b.] October 6, 1927, Los Angeles, CA; [p.] Marie Thomas and Francis Lyons; [ch.] Donald Olson, Jr., and Debra Harris; [ed.] High school and some junior college courses; [occ.] Retired Pacific Telesis Office Supervisor; [memb.] Telephone Pioneers of America; [pers.] Try to live every moment of every day. Life is short. [a.] Fresno, CA.

DEAN, ERLOR EUDINE
[pen.] Erlor Eudine Dean; [b.] January 15, 1943, Sandys, Bermuda; [p.] Ephraim and Inez Callender; [m.] Clarence, March 28, 1970; [ch.] Eugene Dean; [ed.] Berkeley Institute in Bermuda and Ottawa Teacher's College in Ont. CAN.; [occ.] Teacher for 27 years; [memb.] A.B.U.T.-Amalgamated Bermuda Union of Teachers; [hon.] Long Service award for 25 years of teaching; [oth. writ.] Several poems published in the "Sandys Mirror" school newspaper; [pers.] Don't repay kindness, pass it on. The world needs it. [a.] Sandys Maos Bermuda

DELANEY, ALYSSA
[pen.] Leah Delaney; [b.] June 14, 1980, Alexandria, VA; [p.] David and Carol Delaney; [ed.] Attending 8th grade at Robert Frost Intermediate; [occ.] Student; [hon.] All-Star Swimming relays patch, Nettonaland Presidential physical fitness awards and patches, safety patrols awards and bin, all a honor roll, A-B honor roll, fastest female athlete, excellent independent thinker, coolest kid award, first place Fairfax county drawing/poster contest, certificate of scholarship for History, Science achievement certificate, citizenship certificate, small Frost letter; [oth. writ.] None others published, but I have about 70 or 80 other poems; [pers.] I try to look for the good in things and that's what I write about. [a.] Fairfax, VA.

DELCOCO, SCOTT
[pen.] S. Nicholas Delcoco; [b.] August 7, 1969, Latrobe, PA; [p.] Robert and Rose Ann Delcoco; [ed.] University of Pittsburgh at Johnstown, Indiana University of PA, Blairsville High School; [occ.] Bookkeeper, Indiana County, Solid Waste Authority; [hon.] Benz Scholarship Recipient, Class President, University of Pittsburgh at Johnstown; [oth. writ.] "Masquerade" on the threshold of a dream, "Untitled", where dreams begin; "To Believe", Whispers in the Wind; "A Somber Occasion", in the Desert Sun; "China Doll", Wind in the Night Sky-The National Library of Poetry. [a.] Blairsville, PA.

DELGADO, LIZA MARIE
[b.] February 2, 1961, El Paso, TX; [p.] Gary and Olivina Rogers; [ed.] High School; [occ.] Real Estate; [pers.] My writing is spontaneous, my feelings at the moment. My writing is from my heart. [a.] San Antonio, TX.

DELTORO, BERNARD
[b.] November 9, 1911, Brooklyn, NY; [p.] Angel and Marie Deltoro; [m.] Rose, May 24, 1947; [ch.] Joy; [ed.] 7th grade public school studied Phila., PA-Fleisher "School of Art" Museum of Art, Academy of Fine Art; [occ.] Retired; [memb.] Phila. Museum of Art, Academy of Fine Arts, American Swedish Historical Museum; [pers.] As a painter sculpture and poet I like to express joy and peace in writing poetry. So love will come in the door for all of mankind and wars will be no more on planet Earth. [a.] Phila., PA.

DEROUIN, APRIL
[b.] April 8, 1980, North Conway, PA; [p.] Betty and Wayne Derouin.

DEWBRE, PATSY
[b.] July 24, 1938, Clovis, NM; [ch.] Vance and Kerry; [ed.] Portales High School and Eastern New Mexico University; [occ.] Clerk Specialist for the New Mexico Department of Health; [oth. writ.] This is my first work to be published; [pers.] I desire to portray the sensitivity of the human spirit in everyday life situations with a touch of wit or an element of surprise and to always depict a wholesome style. [a.] Portales, NM.

DHALIWAL, RENEE ALICE
[b.] September 16, 1968, Red Dear, Alberta, CAN; [p.] Marlene and Bill Howarth; [m.] Harlakhbir Singh, June 10, 1993; [ed.] E.C.S. certificate, Lethbridge Community College, Okanagan University; [occ.] Nanny; [oth. writ.] Unpublished, but various in theme and many in number. Also short fiction in various themes; [pers.] "The Rake's Tines" is about my first real date with my husband, and my reflections on the day. Living the moment, always. [a.] Westbank, BC, CAN.

DHANJI, RAHIM
[b.] February 7, 1980, Nairobi, Kenya; [p.] Sadrudin Dhanji, LL.B A.C.I.I. and Yasmin Dhanji; [m.] Sister-Nasteen Dhanji; [ed.] Aga Khan Primary School, Montroyal Elementary School and Hardsworth Secondary School; [occ.] Student; [memb.] Co-ordinator of the Lions Gate Aga Khan Library N. Vancouver Can.; [hon.] Medals and certificates for English Literacy, attaining high G.P.A. level, sports, service and academic performance; [oth. writ.] ARticles published in school newspaper (Royal Quest), in local community newspaper (North Shore News); [pers.] To see is to believe, but one's insight, is much worse than Death. [a.] N. Vancouver, BC, CAN.

DiFEDE, DOTTIE
[pen.] D. Monroe, Dottie DiFede; [b.] May 28, 1947, East Oakland, CA; [p.] David and Eva Michael (deceased); [m.] Divorced; [ch.] Wayne, Karen, and Michael (Monroe), Robert, Theresa, Tony, and Dominic (DiFede); [ed.] Sunset High; [occ.] Clerical; [memb.] Women's International Bowling Congress; [oth. writ.] Numerous other poems published; [pers.] I some day would like to see my poem's put to music. The poems I have written came deep from my heart for the strong love that I still have for my husband Donald. [a.] San Lorenzo, CA.

DICKENS, J. VINCENT (One Enchanted Path)
[b.] April 3, 1967, Houston, TX; [p.] LaVene Stokes Purifoy and Hack Dickens; [m.] Lucy "Mama"; [ch.] Zachariah, Kelcy; [ed.] Salzburg International Preparatory School; [occ.] Photojournalist (US Navy); [memb.] U.S. Navy; [pers.] "One Enchanted Pathe" was originally written for, and is dedicated to my loving wife. It was meant to comfort her while duty and the sea kept me away. Lagi Akong Na Sa Iyong Tabi, Sinta Ko -- "Papa"

DICKSON, JOHN
[b.] November 28, 1961, Roby, TX; [p.] Elbert and Nelda Dickson; [m.] Elizabeth, April 3, 1992; [ch.] Dustin Levi Dickson; [ed.] High school graduate; [occ.] United States Navy Petty Officer First Class; [pers.] Poetry mobilizes the mind and allows a whole generation to preserve itself for the future. [a.] Lexington Park, MD.

DIGGS, TONY L.
[pen.] Orion; [b.] April 2, 1973, Los Angeles, CA; [p.] Barbara and Donald Diggs; [m.] Kimberly; [ch.] Christian Anfre J.; [ed.] Redwood High, College of SeQudia (JC). Tcove, Radioman USN, Fresno State, Graphic Arts; [occ.] Painter/House husband; [memb.] Bikers Against Manslaughter, Mothers Against Drunk Driving, Big Brothers and Big Sisters; [hon.] California Journalism Contest: first place photography, second place sports story writing; [oth. writ.] Sublime Melancholy; The Black Forest; Reality; Cobweb Dancers Dying on a Vine; Thoughts of Exasperation; Earthblood. A few compilations from my private anthology (never published); [pers.] I like to search my soul and allow it to freely motivate my pen. I do not allow my mind to put restrictions on my heart. Poetry is a beautiful way to exercise and strengthen the artistic mind. [a.] Fortuna, CA.

DIMAYUGA, AMREY R.
[b.] January 31, 1977, Dunoon, Argyll, Scotland; [p.] Macario Cachero and Aida Ramos Dimayuga; [ed.] Ernest J. King School; [occ.] Student; [pers.] I write what I feel, happy or sad. My feelings come from my experiences and those make you what you are. All that I write is a part of me. I know that someone likes my writing means that someone like what I am. And when you're just a teenager, that's something very special.

DIXSON, DWAIN
[b.] November 6, 1973, Danville, IL; [p.] Mr. and Mrs. Darrell Dixson; [ed.] GMI Engineering and Management Institute: current status JRI; [occ.] Electrical Engineering Co-op Student w/ Teepak, Inc.; [memb.] Sigma Chi Fraternity, Catlin Church of Christ. [a.] Catlin, IL.

DIXON, JOEL A.
[b.] September 18, 1970, Minneapolis, MN; [p.] Simon J. and Marion R. Dixon; [m.] Fiancee'-Christina M.; [ch.] Brandy Nicole, Dane Spencer, Ceara Emerald; [ed.] De LaSalle and Coon Rapids High; [pers.] My poems are generally written when I am in an emotionally charged state. It is my greatest stress reliever and best form of expression - both good and bad. [a.] Latimer, IA.

DIXON, MICHAEL BERN
[b.] July 22, 1958, Clearfield, PA; [p.] James P. and Doreen D. Dixon; [ed.] Trott Vocational High (Niagara Falls, KY); [occ.] Offset Press Operator; [memb.] Susquehanna River Arts Center (S.R.A.C.-Clearfield, PA); [hon.] Several ribbons from county fair and S.R.A.C. for paintings and drawings. Among them 6 top awards, 2 first place and best of show at 1992 county fair; [oth. writ.] Though I have written poems for 17 years, they have never been shown or seen before in public; [pers.] I am known locally as a painter. My poems are my life's records of experience, my paintings are what I want to see. [a.] Clearfield, PA.

DIXON, MILDRED
[pen.] Millie Dixon; [b.] January 11, 1934, Cape Girardeau, MO; [p.] Henry and Emma Carpenter; [m.] Gene A. (Sr.) deceased, January 1, 1953; [ch.] Robert, Karen, Lamar, Barry, Terry, Donald, Michelle; [ed.] Northeast High, Penn. Valley College; [occ.] Unit Secretary, Research Medical Center; [memb.] Children's Writer Institute. St. Stephen Church Drama Club; [oth. writ.] Published article for National Esquire Magazine, Kansas City, Call paper; [pers.] In my writing, I try to reflect reality of everyday life. My greatest influence being the Bible. My philosophy is, You can find the best in anyone, if you search long enough. [a.] Kansas City, MO.

DMITRIEV, ANDREI
[b.] June 11, 1957, Moscow, USSR; [p.] Leonid Dmitriev and Lidia Dmitrieva; [m.] Natasha Balandina, August 18, 1993; [ed.] Moscow Special School #69, Philological Faculty of Moscow State University, graduate school of Academy of Pedagogical Sciences of the USSR; [occ.] Instructor of Russian Language and Literature at Lafayette College, PA; [oth. writ.] Five articles on Anna Akhmatova's poetry in the Institute of Social Sciences and magazine Russian Language at school, an article in college newspaper "The Lafayette" a poem in "Wind in the Night Sky" (anthology by the National Library of Poetry); [pers.] Though I speak with the tongues of men and of angels, and have not love, I am become as sounding brass, or a tinkling cymbal." Natasha, let our love never die-here on earth, there on high. [a.] Easton, PA.

DOBYNS, LISA MARY
[pen.] Lee Mary Dobyns; [b.] July 14, 1965, St. Louis, MI; [p.] Richard A. and Marian R. Dobyns; ed.] Hazelwood Central High, Al-Med Academy; [occ.] Registered Medical Assistant; [memb.] Americal Medical Technologies; [pers.] I would like to thank Grandma Olive and Sean for giving me the courage to ride the train. [a.] Black Jack, MO.

DODGE, DEBORA
[pen.] Debora Dodge; [b.] March 19, 1962, Wichita, KS; [p.] Earl and Dorothy Simmons; [m.] Steven, December 29, 1982; [ch.] Stephanie and Travis; [occ.] Homemaker; [memb.] Ladies Auxiliary to the VFW, Conyers Christian Church. [a.] Conyers, GA.

DOHL, AMANDA
[b.] April 15, 1979, Kingston, PA; [p.] Richard and Diane Dohl; [ed.] Northwest Area Jr. Sr. High School; [occ.] Babysit; [memb.] United Sportsmen's Club; [hon.] Softball; [oth. writ.] Several poems I write when nothing to do; [pers.] Poem writing is my hobby and I hope someday my dream will come true. [a.] Shick Shinny, PA.

DOMINQUE, STEVEN
[b.] August 31, 1968; [p.] Melvin and Inez Dominque; [ch.] Steven Moore. [a.] Angola, LA.

DONNELLY-FELLER, BETH
[pen.] Beth Donnelly-Feller; [b.] August 26, 1948, Portland, OR; [p.] Jack and Sophie Donnelly; [m.] Doug, August 7, 1977; [ch.] Jeremy Patrick Feller; [ed.] BA in Communications University of Portland; [occ.] Opera and Concert singer/writer; [memb.] American Guild of Musical Artists, Development Committee-Holy Cross Area School; [oth. writ.] Advertising Copy, Public Relations stories, Marketing Communications, two stories for Portland Magazine; [pers.] Good writing comes from the heart. Its appeal is timeless. [a.] Portland, OR.

DORAN, ELIZABETH K.
[b.] January 3, 1956, Boston, MA; [ch.] Kathryn Amma, Sika Yeboan; [ed.] South Boston High - working on a BA-Lesley College (Cambridge, MA); [occ.] Freelance Writer, mother; [memb.] All People's Congress; [oth. writ.] Currently working on several essays about life in the United States; [pers.] I am an optimist. I believe we should strive for peace on this planet. I think one must struggle for social justice and against oppression. I have been inspired by poets, Gwendolyn Brooks and Bertoit Grecht; [a.] Roxbury, MA.

DOTSON, ROGER
[b.] April 21, 1966, Blount County, TN; [p.] Thomas and Betty Dotson; [ed.] Graduated Greeback High School 1984, artistically self-educated; [occ.] Night stock worker for Food City Company; [hon.] Won various in school awards, won 1984 News Herald award for excellence in writing; [oth. writ.] Several poems and drawings published in local newspapers; [pers.] I trust God for direction in my writings and drawings. All good comes from him. [a.] Greenback, TN.

DOUGLASS, MIRIAM
[b.] May 22, 1921, Dallastown, PA; [p.] William D. and Erma P. Douglass; [ed.] Dallastown High, Prowell Commercial College, International Institute of Interior Design; [occ.] U.S. Secret Service Sec'y, The White House; Congressman Claude Pepper's Select Committee on Crime Secy, U.S. House of Representatives; U.S. Secy of Labor Peter J. Brennan, Admin. Sec'y, Washington, DC; [memb.] National Committee to Preserve Social Security and Medicare, American Association of Retired Persons, Christ Lutheran Church, Dallastown, PA; [hon.] Three awards of Merit Certificates, two of which ranked honorable mention: 9/1983, 6/1986, and the third ranked Special Mention 2/1984; two Golden Poet Awards 1985 and 1987, and one Silver Poet Award 1986; [oth. writ.] Several poems, one which was published in "Our World's Best Loved Poems", John Campbell, Editor and publisher, World of Poetry Press, 1984; [pers.] It is my firm belief that those who willfully inflict unjust treatment and suffering upon innocent, undeserving persons will eventually pay greatly for their base acts! [a.] York, PA.

DOUGLAS, KEVIN
[a.] Fryburg, ME.

DRAHEIM, ELAINE F.
[b.] May 23, 1936, Swift County, MN; [p.] Emil and Elsie Hanson; [m.] Divorced; [ch.] Theresa Sprung, Leslie Geist, Lisa Bishop; [occ.] Mailroom Services - Clerk (Minneapolis Public Schools. [a.] Minneapolis, MN.

DRAKE, ROBYN
[b.] March 9, 1949, Sydney, Australia; [p.] Verna and Les Slack; [m.] Richard Drake, February 1, 1971; [ch.] Justine and Kristy; [ed.] High school Dip. Teach. B.Ed., M.Ed.; [occ.] Director of Community Services, Canterbury Council; [memb.] Victorian Writer's Association, NSW Writer's Centre; [hon.] Newcastle Technical College, Honors-Newcastle CAE Achievement award; [oth. writ.] Freelance journalist articles published relating to Early Childhood and Special Education. [a.] Australia.

DREGNE, KRISTIN ANNE
[pen.] Misty Kriss; [b.] March 2, 1982, Kenosha, WI; [p.] Rick and Beth Dregne; [ed.] 6th grade Our Lady of Mt. Carmel Grade School; [occ.] Student; [memb.] Safety patrols, girls basketball, softball and volleyball; [pers.] Thanks to my favorite teachers Mrs. Jolene Schneider who helped me find my place in life; and Miss Brund Sauaglio who taught me proper grammar.

DREW, JENNIFER
[b.] September 18, 1972, Philadelphia, PA; [ed.] Northeast High, Holy Family College; [occ.] Full-time student; [memb.] Alpha Epsilon Chapter of Lambda Iota Tau; [hon.] Dean's List; [oth. writ.] Published in Folio (a college publication). [a.] Philadelphia, PA.

DREW, MEGAN
[b.] January 8, 1981, Wenatchee, WA; [p.] Kitty and Mike Drew; [ed.] Sixth grade; [occ.] Student; [memb.] 4-H; [hon.] Fine Arts, Honor Roll. [a.] Burns, OR.

DRISKELL, DONALD ALLEN
[pen.] Donald Allen Driskell; [b.] January 26, 1951, San Diego, CA; [p.] Richard and Lucile Driskell; [ed.] Aspen High, Montana State University, Williamsport Area Community College; [occ.] Self-employed artist/photographer; [memb.] Sierra Club, Bald Eagle Art League; [hon.] Show of Fine Art: MSU, Third place first Citizens National Bank Art Show 1991; [pers.] A quote from John Muir: "Let others travel to the inhospitable moon, I shall stay with my gigantic friends and let them guide my thoughts to eternal truths." [a.] Wellsboro, PA.

DRURY, NICOLE
[b.] September 24, 1976, Hawaii; [p.] Dennis and Mary Rodriguez; [ed.] Valley Union High; [oth. writ.] Wrote for school yearbook and newspaper; [pers.] I've loved writing since I was 10 years old. Writing poems has always been a big interest of mine. [a.] Pearce, AZ.

DUFFY, MICHAEL
[b.] October 8, 1976; [ed.] Student-Junior St. Thomas Moore High School (Lafayette, LA). [a.] Lafayette, LA.

DUMICH, KATHERINE K.
[pen.] Kath Dumich; [b.] November 18, 1978, St. Mary's. PA; [p.] Robert and Regina Dumich; [ed.] Freshman St. Mary's Area High School; [hon.] Presidential Academic Fitness award; [oth. writ.] Several poems for the school newspaper. [a.] Weedville, PA.

DUNCAN, TEDD
[pen.] Steel Wolf; [b.] January 30, 1978, Portland, OR; [p.] John Duncan and Linda Blackmore; [ed.] 8th grade; [occ.] Full-time student; [oth. writ.] Many other non-published poems and a couple of songs; [pers.] I write what is in my heart and my head and sometimes I write about friends that are dead. Whatever I write it's all true to me. The meanings are real and in my mind they flow free. [a.] Longmont, CO.

DUNGAN, KATHY M.
[b.] January 23, 1970, Okeene, OK; [p.] Steven and Barbara Dungan; [ed.] Presently a student at Oklahoma State University-major-Education; [occ.] Work part-time for Homecall, Inc. (Home Health care); [oth. writ.] I have written approximately 180 poems, now waiting and hoping to be lucky enough to have published; [pers.] Success depends not only on what you do, but also on how you do things to gain the success you want to achieve. [a.] Stillwater, OK.

DUNMAN, JOEY
[pen.] L.J. Dunman; [b.] March 4, 1979, Louisville, KY; [p.] Carol Ann and Leonard Joe Dunman III; [ed.] Freshman-Louisville Male High School; [occ.] Student; [memb.] National Beta Club, Suburban Christian Church; [hon.] Honor Roll, Academic Letter Duke University Tip Candidate; [pers.] Writing is one outlet for the stories constantly going through my mind. Drawing is the other. As long as the stories are there, I'll continue to do both. [a.] Louisville, KY.

DUNN, BETTY COLVIN
[pen.] Betty Colvin Dunn; [b.] January 4, 1922, Olney, IL; [p.] Pearl and Rosa Colvin; [m.] Richard D., April 21, 1952; [ed.] Registered Nurse; [occ.] R.N.; [memb.] Retired Officers' Association, National Thyroid Foundation, 187th Airborne Regimental Combat Team (Ladies Reserve), Alumni Association of Decatur Memorial Hospital School of Nursing; [hon.] Numerous military awards and decorations (WWII and Korea); [oth. writ.] Have written several golf articles and a few other poems; [pers.] Believe I try to find the humor in most things. [a.] Sun City Center, FL.

DUNN, GREGORY ALLAN
[b.] June 12, 1946, Los Angeles, CA; [ed.] Samuel Kress Foundation two year fellowship (1974-6) through Graduate School of Art History and Architecture at Brown University at Providence, RI.; [occ.] Poet; [hon.] 1977 assembled an art writing poetry exhibition focusing upon West 6, Charles Olson's last poem, most concerned with the imagery of the John Bozeman trail. Shown in Livingston, MT, 1984 Catherine Denning of the Ann Mary Brown Library of Brown University offered to display a retrospective of my books. Single pieces in many exhibitions, most recently as an employee exhibitor at the Los Angeles County Museum of Art where I worked until 1992; [oth,. writ.] The Wedding of Bowen Island and Atlantis, 1969, The Road to Othello, 1970, The Robert Hubbard Book, 1974, The Juan Downey Book, 1975, Chilambalam, 1969-1984, The X/A Ranch, 1980, Gumshoes and Gumdrops, Los Angeles (five books) 1987-1991, Report from the Government, 1992, 1993, 1994, 1995 continuing and current. [pers.] William Blake is the poet I esteem most highly. Dennis Oppenheim and Robin Blaser are artist and poet whose work I admire. [a.] Los Angeles, CA.

DUNN, LAURA M.
[b.] March 6, 1975, Omaha, NE; [p.] Dolberta Johnson; [ch.] John Paris Richardson III; [ed.] Graduated from Pattonville High; [occ.] Nurse Aide. [a.] St. Louis, MO.

DUPREE, DENISE
[b.] October 31, 1952; [ch.] Chantelle and Cassandra Dupree; [pers.] How many stars are there in the sky--all of them. We are all special. [a.] Santa Maria, CA.

DURDIN, GRACE SCOTT
[p.] Charles and Alma Scott; [m.] Andrew Durdin; [ch.] Donna, Linda, Glenn, Kerry; [ed.] Somerville High School, Ed Rose Commercial College; [occ.] Homemaker; [oth. writ.] Many poems-this is the first contest I have ever entered; [pers.] I am fascinated by words and the power they possess. I can express my deepest feelings best through poetry. [a.] Houston, TX.

DUROCHER, RICHARD A.
[b.] October 17, 1963, Windsor, Ontario; [p.] Larry and Pauline Durocher; [m.] Tracy, May 17, 1986; [ch.] Lucas Jeffrey, Nathan Benjamen; [ed.] Ursuline College Chatham (the Pines) and University of Windsor; [occ.] Educational Assistant; [memb.] Slopitch Ontario; [oth. writ.] A small personal collection of unpublished poems; [pers.] I am inspired by my children because they reflect the simpler and more genuine side of life. [a.] Chatham, Ontario, CAN.

DuTOIT, DIANE M.
[pen.] Di du Toit; [b.] February 2, 1934, South Africa (Cape Province); [p.] Albert and Elizabeth Drayer (nee de Villiers); [m.] Charles, January 9, 1954; [ch.] Laura, Nancy-Lee and Marian; [ed.] College graduate post graduate certificates; [occ.] Jewellery Designer custom); [memb.] GIA Alumni, Canadian Warplane Heritage Museum, Canadian Wildlife; [hon.] Editor's Choice award; [oth. writ.] Articles, stories, completed book not yet published of poetry and design-image stories; [pers.] Subscribe to the life principle. [a.] Oakville, Ont. CAN.

DVORACKOVA, LUMBOMIRA A.
[pen.] Anna Petrasova; [b.] July 13, 1953, Trencin, Slovakia, Europe; [p.] Andrej Petras (father) and Maria Petrasova (mother); [m.] John Klir; [ch.] Mirek Dvoracek, Radim Dvoracek, Patrizie Petrasova; [ed.] Art School, Prague, Czech, Designer; [pers.] Creation of my poems in a given moment is a need to share my thoughts and feelings with others. Poetry is -white clouds flowing in the blue sky. [a.] Ann Arbor, MI.

DYCKSON, ROBERT A.
[b.] December 28, 1932, Cheyenne, WY; [p.] Andrew FRank and Emma Jeanette; [m.] Emily MarGurite; [ed.] High school graduate; [occ.] Retired; [memb.] American Legion Post 9, St. John's Nfld. Post Chaplain; [oth. writ.] Some poems in local newspaper. Anon.; [pers.] I'm always trying to write poetry. While in Vietnam I would write for my best buddy for his fiance. [a.] Nfld. CAN.

DYKHUIZEN, DOROTHY
[pen.] Dorothy Dykhuizen; [b.] February 6, 1924, Bellingham, WA; [p.] Walter and Katie Bailey; [m.] Alvin, August 18, 1947; [ch.] Nadine, Richard, Lois; [ed.] High school; [occ.] Homemaker, poet; [memb.] International Society of Poets, Ebenezer Reformed Church; [hon.] "Editor's Choice"; [oth. writ.] Junior Christian Endeavor articles for newspaper, Editor of church newsletter, Christmas play for Standard Publishing poems in several books; [pers.] A Grandma who believes,, "Why write an article or story to express thoughts and emotion, when I can say it better in a poem." [a.] Morrison, IL.

EAGAN, GLENIS
[b.] December 24, 1929, Seattle, WA; [p.] Stephen and Pearl Andrews; [m.] Harvey, September 13, 1948; [ch.] Michael, Steven, Edwin, Karen, Roy and Daniel; [ed.] Auburn Academy; [occ.] Retired; [memb.] Theo-UHT Society, Inner Truth Foundation; [hon.] REverend Ordination, Donald J. Smith Exceptional Achievement; [oth. writ.] Children's Fairy Tales; [pers.] My commitment is to make an inspired difference in this world. [a.] Renton, WA 98059.

EBANKS, RON
[b.] May 15, 1970, Boston, MA; [p.] Leila Ebanks; [ed.] YMCA Training Inc.; [occ.] Underwriting Clerk Worker's Comp. Rating Bureau; [memb.] Cambridge Baptist Church, Outlaw Ministries Cambridge Port Youth Outreach; [hon.] Boston Food Bank Volunteer of the Year 1991; [pers.] When faced with fear when the rock and lamb are near. Their power makes fear small trust them and fear will fall. [a.] Boston, MA.

ECHOLS, DOUGLAS
[b.] July 7, 1921, Waurika, OK; [p.] Clarence and Zona Echols (deceased); [ed.] Waurika High School, University of Oklahoma School of Letters, United States Merchant Marine Academy '43 (Kings Point) B.S. Master Mariner '46; [occ.] Merchant Mariner-Seafarer, Retired and writing; [pers.] "GOD and Nature recognizes only sacrifice as coin or specie in any transaction." "The greatest of all harmonies is the harmony that is created when two minds meet as one." [a.] San Francisco, CA.

ECK, ROBYN
[pen.] Skye Stettler; [b.] October 23, 1977, Tulsa, OK; [p.] Richard and Debbie Eck; [ed.] Sophomore at Union Intermediate high school; [occ.] Student; [memb.] National Honor Society, Yearbook and Newspaper Staff at Union, Little Lighthouse Volunteer Group; [hon.] Academic awards, finalist in America's National Teen-ager Pageant 1993; [oth. writ.] Two different poems published in A Question of Balance and Outstanding Poets of 1994. Article in school newspaper, unpublished stories and poems; [pers.] Never give up on your dreams. If you do you'll never experience the happiness. [a.] Tulsa, OK.

EDELEN, JOSEPH MICHAEL
[pen.] Joe Mike Edelen; [b.] December 30, 1954, Lebanon, KY; [p.] Charles and Naomi Edelen; [m.] Mary Regina, July 10, 1982; [ch.] Candice Renee and Brian Matthew Edelen; [ed.] Graduated from Marion County High School in 1973; [occ.] Welder for Ford Motor Company (Louisville Assembly Plant); [pers.] I have always liked country music. I believe that some of the best country songs are just poetry put into music. That's my goal with my poetry. [a.] Louisville, KY 40218.

EDENS, REBECCA
[b.] May 19, 1950, Frankfort, IL; [p.] Maxine Basenfelder; [ch.] Robyn Edens; [ed.] Several trade schools; [occ.] Writer and want to be well known author in the future; [memb.] Calvary First Assembly of God; [hon.] Citizen's awards for helping others; [oth. writ.] Christian poems, holiday and special occasion poems, poems of special people with special problems plus more; [pers.] I would like to help those people in need, and letting others know they are out there and need much help. [a.] Winter Haven, FL.

EDDY, MARJORIE A.
[b.] December 3, 1929, Tisberry, MA; [p.] Alfred and Deolinda Mociel; [m.] Drayford J. (deceased), September 21, 1948; [ch.] Stephen, Phillip, Deborah, Douglas, Dennis and Denice Eddy; [ed.] High school, college and real estate school; [occ.] Disabled, retired; [memb.] Ps. Rho, Loiness, Writer's Workshop, RASCAL (Rogue Area Senior Computer Assistance League); [hon.] Women of the Year, Mosow Queen, poems and verse; [oth. writ.] "Poems & Verse", Truth, Friends, Father, SunFlowers, A Parent, Watching Worker of Art, Destination, Easter Puppy's Life, The Lords House, Love, Have a Heart, Beauty and A Tune, My God, My Prayer - story-My Son Was Kidnapped; [pers.] My memory of the Martha's Vineyard Gazette printing children's writings and drawings in their newspaper "encouraging" us to do more not to be ashamed of our ability. I try to write what I feel in my heart (true feelings of what's happening to me and around me). [a.] Santa Maria, CA.

EDMOND, TERESA
[b.] August 27, 1981, Paterson, NJ; [p.] Lolita and Roy Edmond; [ed.] Seventh grade at Hackensack Middle School; [hon.] Martin Luther King Jr. writing award; [oth. writ.] Poems in local newspaper and the school literary magazine. [a.] Hackensack, NJ 07601.

EDWARDS, BRANDI J.
[b.] October 14, 1975, Pomona, CA; [p.] Leisa M. Edwards; [ed.] Will graduate from Linbergh High School (REnton, WA) in June of 1994, going to college; [occ.] Will be an elementary school teacher - developmentally disabled children; [oth. writ.] Never been published before but I have a few short stories; [pers.] I wrote this poem during Geometry class. I thank Mrs. Greiner for "inspiring" me. I wrote when I was being mushy over my boyfriend, John Bensen. So a thanks and "I love you" to him too. [a.] Renton, WA 98058.

EGGLESTON, MERLE C.
[pen.] Merle C. Eggleston; [b.] February 10, 1926, Salt Lake City, UT; [p.] Deceased; [m.] Jay C., December 3, 1945; [ch.] Ann, Chris, Peggy, Sheila, and Rod; [ed.] High school graduate; [occ.] Retired; [memb.] Church of Jesus Christ of Latter Day Saints; [pers.] These thoughts came to mind as I tried to comfort my tiny granddaughter, Sara. I'm pleased they can be shared. Thank you. [a.] Pocatello, ID 83204.

EHLSCHEID, STEVE
[pen.] Steve Elshide; [b.] March 9, 1953, Chicago, IL; [ed.] BS University of Illinois, AA Wright Jr. College; [occ.] Electronic Engineer; [memb.] SPIE-International Optical Society; [hon.] Phi Theta Kappa; [oth. writ.] Poems, songs, and short stories; [pers.] I capture the feelings of people and events that we encounter everyday: the beauty of nature, the joy of a good friend, the love of God. My favorite poet is Robert Frost because he said so much with so few words. [a.] Shoreview, MN.

EHRKE, NINA
[b.] August 4, 1940, Camden, NJ; [p.] Edmund and Philomena Aristone; [m.] Paul, August 8; [ch.] Charles, Nina and Mimi; [ed.] Merchantville High; [oth. writ.] Children stories and short poems; [pers.] I enjoy writing short stories for children, and have recently decided to have them published. [a.] Waterford, NJ 08089.

EILENBERGER, DAVID L.
[pen.] Philosowrite; [b.] September 13, 1947, Monroe County, PA; [p.] Marietta and C.K. Eilenberger; [m.] Susan, 1969; [ch.] David and Laura; [ed.] East Stroudsburg High School 1966; [occ.] Owner, Four Maples Press Inc., Eilenberger Inc., Maples Advertising; [memb.] Copies Plus I and II, L Eagles, Pocomo Mt. Vacation Bureau and the Chamber of Commerce; [hon.] Several graphic designs; [oth. writ.] Frogs in the Fog, My Own Anthology, Dream Killers; [pers.] My poetic purpose is to write honesty and of the time we are. "To help one soul understand, is a relief worth writing for." [a.] Saylorsburg, PA 18353.

EISLEY, MARIANNE Y.
[b.] February 23, 1978, PA; [p.] Carla and Al Eisley; [ed.] Williams High, Bending Oaks High; [occ.] Future Jeweler; [memb.] Greenpeace; [hon.] First prize prose in Bowman Middle School; [pers.] Hard times bring out the best in people. [a.] Richardson, TX 75082.

EISMAN, AUDREY
[pen.] Namsie Yerdua; [b.] September 2, 1934, Philadelphia, PA; [p.] Claire and Irving Waldo; [m.] Larry, July 25, 1953; [ch.] Robin Peterse and Dayl Gibson; [ed.] M.E.D. (Counseling Psychology) and B.S. (Mental Health Technology); [occ.] Mental Health Clinician/Psychologist-in-Training; [oth. writ.] Unpublished Poetry articles - "Women Are Revolting" Mental Health Forum Winter, 1974. "Theories and Practices of Wolfe's Systematic Desensitization and Stampfl's Implosive Therapy in Comparison" [pers.] I write poetry and read it because I need it in my life. It is not a choice, it i both a joyful and painful experience. [a.] Elkins Park, PA 19117.

EL-AMIN, AQEELA
[b.] April 23, 1952, Savannah, GA; [p.] Simson Draine, Jr. and Sarah (Draine) Roberts; [ch.] John, TaMecia, Khalid and Khalil (twins), Abdul and Akil; [ed.] Liberal Arts 1992; CA State University (Hayward) currently enrolled; [memb.] Muslim Community Center (SF), Vice Pres.-Toastmasters (S.F.), Student CA Teachers Association; [hon.] Associate degree (cum laude), Dean's List (Vista College); High school diploma with honors; CA Scholarship Fed. (12th grade); [oth. writ.] "Where is Mama?" published 1992, several other poems, short stories, essays; [pers.] To have something to always strive for makes life worth living, so I constantly set new goals for myself. [a.] Oakland, CA.

ELDER, JANET S.
[pen.] Jan Elder; [b.] February 17, 1945, Bluefield, WV; [p.] Charles M. and Frances W. Scott; [m.] Randolph (deceased), November 2, 1976; [ed.] Ashley Hall, University of Colorado, University of Louisville, Kent School of Social Work; [occ.] Social Worker; [memb.] NASW, Psi Iotia Xi; [oth. writ.] I have written 50-100 other poems. I have never submitted any for publication previously; [pers.] I use my writing to express and interpret feelings about events in my life. [a.] Sellersburg, IN 47172.

ELDER, MELISSA MARIE
[b.] December 18, 1979, Panama City, FL; [p.] David and Connie Nash; [occ.] Student. [a.] Lynn Haven, FL 32444.

ELDRIDGE-PAYEN, RUTH
[pen.] Ruth Faith (Sume Poems); [b.] April 11, 1920, Maidstone Kent, England; [p.] Deceased; [ed.] Private during infant days, church school council; [occ.] REtired (housewife) early years, Kennel Assistant; [memb.] R.S.P.B. Soil Association, Woodland Trust, Bristol Horse Society, Supporter of I.F.A.W.; [hon.] Certificates from R.S.P.C.A. Damart S. Empire for Loyalty, Tree planting; [oth. writ.] 32 nursery poems published, 2 unpublished books have started writing my experiences in the 2 world wars; [pers.] To help where I can to ease anxiety and suffering in all God's creatures whether it be human or otherwise. To bring comfort by my poetry. [a.] Romney Marsh Kent TW29 0RS England.

ELIAS, AMY
[b.] November 28, 1978, Wilkes-Barre, PA; [p.] Joseph and Mary Susan Elias; [ed.] 9th grade-James M. Coughlin High; [occ.] Student; [memb.] Band, Orchestra, Chorus, Karate, Hockey, Soccer, Softball, Rainbows, Science, Olympiad, National Honor Society; [hon.] All-American National Champion, PA State Champion in Karate; [oth. writ.] Poem published in Windows on the World Vol. II. [a.] Wilkes-Barre, PA.

ELIAS, AMBER M.
[b.] September 15, 1983, Wilkes-Barre, PA; [p.] Joseph and Mary Susan Elias; [ed.] 5th grade-Kistler Elementary School; [occ.] STudent; [memb.] Cheerleading, Soccer, Softball, Karate, Choir, Band; [hon.] "All American" Karate, National Champion Karate, PA State Champion Karate, Keystone State Games 1st Karate. [a.] Wilkes-Barre, PA.

ELIASON, KELLI ANN
[pen.] Helsaja; [b.] October 17, 1978, Palm Springs, CA; [p.] Steve and Kathy Hyden; [ed.] Santa Rita High School; [occ.] Student; [memb.] Carson Book Club, Shakespeare Touring Company; [hon.] Recipient of scholarship for voice and piano, Honor roll 1991-92; [oth. writ.] Several poems awaiting publication editor of non-stop NRG Up mag, short story Seth's Suicide; [pers.] I base my writings on my true feelings from the heart and personal experiences. This particular poem published herein is in loving memory of my cousin, Daniel. [a.] Tucson, AZ.

ELIJAH-EL, PERRY LOVELL
[pen.] P. Elijah-El; [b.] June 22, 1952, Winston-Salem, NC; [p.] William Arthur and Catherine DeLorse Elijah; [ed.] Seventh grade; [occ.] Laborer; [memb.] Moorish Science Temple of America, Inc.; [oth. writ.] 128 unpublished poems; [pers.] I think poets are the conscious of humanity and reflect what others sense and feel. I am greatly inspired by "Poets of the Apocalypse", especially Herbert Read. [a.] Washington, DC 20020.

ELLIOTT, ELIZABETH ANN
[b.] Pottsville, PA; [p.] L. Donald and Elizabeth Kalb Elliott; [ed.] Goucher College, Pennsylvania State University, Maryland Institute of Art, Johns Hopkins University; [occ.] Epidemiologist, Johns Hopkins University School of Hygiene and Public Health; [memb.] Baltimore Choral Arts Society, Society for Epidemiologic Research, Arcadia Improvement Association; [hon.] Delta Omega (honorary public health) Pi Lambda Theta (honorary education). [a.] Baltimore, MD.

ELSBERG, KANDIE LEE
[pen.] Kandie Lee; [b.] August 23, 1967, Ellensburg, WA; [p.] Dan and Vi Ferguson; [m.] Brian, December 8, 1986; [ch.] Twins-Teri Brianne and Kari Lennae (6); [ed.] High school and then business college; [occ.] Bookkeeper; [oth. writ.] Currently working on a novel about living and operating a business in Jamaica; [pers.] Life is short. Grab the good things when they're in front of you, less they're taken away and not offered again. [a.] Cle Elum, WA 98922.

ENGLISH, PAM
[b.] June 2, 1975, Howell, MI; [p.] Ross and Ann English; [ed.] Brighton High School and Cleary College; [occ.] Cashier at Meijero Inc.; [hon.] Honor Society; [oth. writ.] The Little People; [pers.] WRiting a dream that started for me in early years. Someday I want to be known as one of the great authors of this time. [a.] Brighton, MI.

ENGSTROM, CATHERINE
[b.] August 12, 1914, Brooklyn, NY; [p.] William and May Rowe; [m.] Charles Johan Harald Engstrom, June 6, 1936 (deceased); [ch.] John H., Carl D., and James H.; [ed.] Seven different elementary schools in three states, Vineland High School (Vineland, NJ-graduate); [occ.] Retired secretary (1981) for Rutgers University Laboratory (Vineland, NJ); [memb.] Newfield Methodist Church (Choir), former girl scout, former member vocal trio (Jersey Skeeters); [hon.] As mentioned above; [oth. writ.] Collection of two published in Clover Verse Poetry, Vol and Vol 2, plus two honorable mention awards Christian Hymns (5); [pers.] I like to write about the common man, his problems, his love, his work, and his faith in God.

ENNS, LORRAINE KATHRYNE
[b.] September 21, 1979, Morden General Hospital, M.B.; [p.] Frank and Mary Enns; [ed.] Grade 8-Parkland Elementary School; [hon.] School Honor Roll 1990-91; [pers.] Some are both great, some achieve greatness, and some have greatness thrust upon them.-William Shakespeare. [a.] Winkler, MB.

ENRIQUEZ, BRANDON
[pen.] Brandon Jacopo Enriquez; [b.] March 29, 1973, Toronto, Ont. CAN.; [p.] Cynthia Enriquez; [ed.] Uxbridge High, York University; [oth. writ.] Poems in Uxbridge Literary Guild printed "Dancing Candles" poetry collection; [pers.] I could never sum up my philosophy or even consider choosing a personal note to call my own. We all share the weave of imagination. We all know. [a.] Uxbridge, Ont. CAN.

ERICKSON, AMY MICHELLE
[b.] May 22, 1979, Jamestown, ND; [p.] Steve and Kathy Erickson; [ed.] Medina Public School, Dakota Adventist Academy; [pers.] I wrote the poem "The Wind and The Breeze" when I was eleven. It was a school project for reading when Miss Gibson was my fifth grade teacher. [a.] Cleveland, ND.

ESQUIVEL, JOHN P.
[b.] Belize City, Belize; [m.] Yolanda; [ch.] John III and Lawrence; [ed.] Master degree Social Work, Fordham University, NY; [hon.] Doctor of Letters, China Academy, Chinese Cultural University, Hawa Kang, Yangmingshan, Taiwan, Republic of China; [oth. writ.] Many songs, several short stories and inventor of I Ching, 3 coins game for 1 to 4 players based on the venerable Chinese I Ching or Book of Changes; [pers.] Love unconditionally and follow your dream! [a.] Naples, FL 33940.

ESSIX, TAHIRAH
[b.] June 24, 1979, Fort Wayne, IN; [p.] Albert and Delores Essix; [ed.] Village Woods Southwick Elementary Middle School, Harding High School; [hon.] Young Authors awards, 4th and 5th grade; [pers.] I express my inner feelings through writing. [a.] Ft. Wayne, IN.

ESTES, KRISTI G.
[pen.] Kris Goodwin; [b.] October 26, 1967, Pittsfield, ME; [p.] Carroll I Goodman III and Carol P. Goodwin; [m.] Blynn, August 19, 1989; [ch.] Jasmine Caraine, Logan Blynn; [ed.] Lawrence High; [occ.] Housewife and Mother; [pers.] This poem "The Thorn" is dedicated to my son, Arik Dustin Goodwin (b. June 20, 1988-died July 4, 1988). [a.] N. Vassalboro, ME.

EUSEY, IVA L.
[pen.] U.C.; [b.] August 9, 1906, Crawford County, OH; [p.] Peter E. and Anna L. Smith; [m.] Deceased-Fred M., December 19, 1931; [ch.] Herbert, Joyce, Georgette and Wilbur; [ed.] High School; [occ.] Telephone Supervisor 34 years; [memb.] No time; [hon.] My family and my job; [oth. writ.] "My Birthday Girl", "Weather", "The Land of Lets Pretend", "Welcome to Easter", and "Birthday Wonderings"; [pers.] As you can see I will be 87 soon. I've had a free and interesting life, my family are not Eusey's so didn't include last names. OK? [a.] Galcon, OH 44833.

EVANS, BRENDA K.
[b.] April 13, 1956, Plant City, FL; [p.] Earnest Loyde and Gladys Mae Melton; [m.] John R., January 8, 1993; [ch.] Rodney S. and April L. Campbell; [ed.] 7th grade-Southside School 167; [occ.] Housewife; [memb.] Jubalee Church of Moorefield, AK; [oth. writ.] Written other poems in the past which I never done anything with. I didn't know I could publish them; [pers.] I have never won anything or had much of a goal in life, I just write what I feel in my poems and I always have God by my side. [a.] Salado, AK.

EVERROAD, GLADYS L.
[b.] September 23, 1935, Clay County; [p.] John V. and Madge Elizabeth (Baughman) Rogers; [m.] Darrell B., February 7, 1987; [ch.] By previous marriage-year '52 to '85-Michael, Jeffrey, Karen, Diana, Kim (Father-Charles Trackwell -deceased); [occ.] Factory - school food service (retired); [memb.] W.O.T.M. - American Legion Aux., V.F.W. Aux., LA Sociate de Femmes (currently State Pres of La Femmes); [hon.] Volunteer service posters, and crafts used in my auxiliaries; [oth. writ.] Have written poems, lyrics to funny songs but never entered any for publication. Wrote my first poem at the age of 13; [pers.] Have been a dreamer all my life. Always striving for peace and harmony for all mankind. [a.] Martinsville, IN 46151.

EVIN, V. SUSAN
[b.] June 20, 1956, Medina, OH; [p.] Emil J. and Ethell F. Evin; [ed.] BS., Business Administration 1978, The Defiance College; [occ.] Formerly sales and management currently disabled/systemic lupus; [hon.] Tau Pi Phi/Business Honorary, Alpha Chi/Academic; [oth. writ.] Last publication, "Progeny" 1977, The Defiance College literary magazine - business, sales collateral, fund-raising and grant writing focus prior to illness; [pers.] Do what you can, as long as you can, and figure out a way to do what you can't. [a.] Cleveland, OH.

FABER, GERALDINE R.
[pen.] Lady G.; [b.] December 30, 1955, Pennsylvania; [ch.] Kirkland Lee and Victoria Leelind Michaels; [oth. writ.] My Soul Has No Color, In Time, If (not yet published); [pers.] Life would be easier, if people didn't try so hard to find a reason for it. [a.] Woodbury, CT.

FABIASCHI, ABAGAIL
[b.] June 23, 1980; [p.] Anthony and Debra Mary Fabiaschi; [ed.] St. Margaret's School (grammar) Orono Junior High; [memb.] Peer Hebering, Student Council, Community Volunteer work; [hon.] Honor Roll, Elected Peer Helping and student council student of the month, Captain for Volleyball, 3rd place regitrals; [oth. writ.] St. Margaret's School paper-poems. Several poems in Community newspaper. Personal writings enjoyed by loved ones; [pers.] "There but for the grace of God go I". I'd like to dedicate this poem to my Grandma Betty who is forever my hero. [a.] Minnetonka Beach, MN.

FALCONE, JR., LEONARD CHARLES
[pen.] Bow Utah; [b.] September 9, 19964, Poconos, PA; [p.] Mr. and Mrs. Leonard Charles Falcone; [ed.] BS in Business Administration, Marketing Sequence; [occ.] Division Sales Manager, Anheuser Busch Inc.; [memb.] Theta Chi-Zeto Omicron Chapter; [hon.] Sales representative of the Year 1992, Anheuser Busch personally Raised over $20,000 for MDA; [pers.] The new millennium is just upon us. Our past decisions will have great impact on our futures potential. As we strive for our goals, we must always keep in mind, a kinder and more gentle world is sure to come, if we trust in our keeper "The Lord Jesus Christ". [a.] Wyoming, PA.

FALLIN, ROSALINA JACQUELINE
[pen.] A.J. Foster; [b.] June 2, 1975, Hood River, OR; [p.] Clifford Fallin and Jacqueline Roberts; [ed.] Senior at Hood River Valley High School; [memb.] Part of a peer helper called National Helpers; [hon.] Honor Roll first semester; [oth. writ.] Other poems, non published and short stories such as "The 3 Lives of Marie"; [pers.] My poetry reflects how I feel and my outlook on life. My other passion in life is acting. Hopefully I can express myself through my acting as well. [a.] Hood River, OR.

FALLON, ROBERT MARTIN
[pen.] Rab Fallon; [b.] April 24, 1936, Scotland; [m.] Divorced; [ed.] Scottish Primary English Grammer; [occ.] Hosiery Operative; [oth. writ.] Variety of poems. "Class Divided" a satirical book, "The Itsy Bitsy Alphabet". Educates to read, write and draw. "Marry Go Round" a board game on marriage and divorce; [pers.] Lead your life within the law but from own conclusions wisdom draw. [a.] Leicester, England LE54DE.

FARLEY, LARRY
[b.] April 24, 1960, Central Point, OR; [p.] LeRoy and Dorothy Farley; [m.] BEth, May 21; [ed.] Southern Oregon State College BS; [occ.] Customer Service Rep. [a.] St. Louis, MO.

FARROW, NELLIE M.
[b.] St. Clair County, AL; [p.] Henry and Williemae Curry; [ch.] Bobby, Eugene, Shirley, Joyce, Kaye, Don; [ed.] Hudson School, Clerical Training and Studies; [occ.] Blair Dealer, Sears Roebuck and Company Sales-Computer Operator; [memb.] Share A Minute Program, Pergamos Grove APB Church, Committee Church clerk; [hon.] Several plaques and awards of outstanding performance; [oth. writ.] Other poems, scripts for Christmas cards, birthday, several song poems. One Christmas song was taped and sung by the Church Choir here in Norwalk, CT; [pers.] My desire is to live for Christ and others may see Him living in me. And to help someone each day. [a.] Norwalk, CT.

FAULKNER, APRIL ANDERSON
[b.] August 17, 1970, Albany, GA; [p.] George Anderson and Pawnee O'Neal; [m.] David, April 8, 1989; [ch.] Kayleigh Michelle and John David

FAulkner III; [ed.] Joseph Wheeler High School; [occ.] Lead Clerk-Kroger Food Stores; [memb.] American Legion Auxiliary; [oth. writ.] None published, there are several unpublished that I keep for myself; [pers.] I feel, therefore I write. [a.] Douglasville, GA.

FAUST, DELPHINE A.
[b.] October 11, 1943, Paterson, NJ; [p.] Walter Harvilick, Anne Gabriele; [m.] James L., April 1, 1992; [ch.] Brian Profeta, wife Jamie, grandsons, Christopher & Timothy; [ed.] Garfield High, various college course; [occ.] Special Assets Officer Barnett Banks, Inc. FL; [pers.] This poems was written for my husband and reflects my philosophy towards life. [a.] Fort Lauderdale, FL 33309.

FAYNBOYM, NATALYA
[b.] February 3, 1976, Kishinev, Moldova - USSR; [p.] Boris and Polina Faynboym; [ed.] Kishinev High School Moldova - USSR; [occ.] Student at High Point University; [oth. writ.] Several poems and fiction stories on English and Russian languages; [pers.] No retreat, no surrender. [a.] Winston-Salem, NC.

FAZIO, MELISSA MARION
[b.] December 25, 1979, Landstuhl, Germany; [p.] Genofeva and Arnold Fazio; [ed.] Lonnie B. Nelson Elementary School, North Springs Elementary School. Summit Parkway Middle School; [occ.] Student; [memb.] Peta Club, Environmental Club, Young American Bowling Alliance; [hon.] Won the Young Writer's Conference for my school and district, Solo and Ensemble superior and excellent award on cello; [oth. writ.] A story published by Young Writer's Conference, and Reader's Digest wanted to publish another poem of mine; [pers.] It doesn't matter how young you are if you use your soul you can accomplish anything so strive to be your best, I did. [a.] Columbia, SC.

FENSTERMAKER, BETTY I.
[pen.] Betty Brebst Fenstermaker; [b.] November 28, 1909, Beaver Meadows, PA; [p.] James P. and Gwennie Howells Fowler; [m.] Late William E. Brobst, June 24, 1933 - Mark M. Fenstermaker, August 31, 1968; [ch.] William A. Brobst (deceased); [ed.] Commercial student of Hazelton High School graduated June 26, 1928; [memb.] Bookkeeper - Cost Accounting; [memb.] Nativity Lutheran Church, Past Royal Patron of Amarath Treas of CedarView Social Club, member of Prime Time Club of St. Thomas Moore, past officer of American Business Women; [hon.] World of Poetry, Sparrowgrass Poetry, Feelings - National Library of Poetry; [oth. writ.] Appear in many church newsletters, highest when I became a member of International Society of Poets and National Library of Poetry; [pers.] I love poetry and at my age I still write. My last one recently in May 1993 written in the first person for a beloved friend, Titled My Son. Just had my own book of 16 poems published by Feelings . I could not afford more than 16 poems - plus my biography and picture.

FERGUSON, LINDA
[b.] August 21, 1954, Humboldt, Saskatchewan; [p.] John and Florine Ollerich; [m.] James, June 8, 1974; [ch.] Carla Jane and Mark James; [ed.] Muenster High School; [occ.] Office Clerk; [hon.] Senior class valedictorian, senior year talent award - combination of achievements in the academic field, glee club, drama and sports; [oth. writ.] Canadian Legion Remembrance Day Essay contest - poem won prizes at the zone and district levels; [pers.] Writing is a way of expressing the inner most thoughts and feelings captured most often by precious moments. [a.] Melville, Saskatchewan, CAN.

FERGUSON, SCOTT
[pen.] Spider; [b.] Fairbanks, AK; [p.] Richard Ferguson/David and Sherrill Mott; [ed.] GED, New England Tractor Trailer School, Aznun Tuck Community College; [occ.] Construction/Truck driver; [memb.] CIA (Connecticut Institute Alliance); [hon.] Bible Correspondence courses; [oth. writ.] I have 5 other published poems and songs in an anthology called "Moments in Time"; [pers.] You can't learn to walk, until you've learned to fall... [a.] Chaplin, CT.

FERGUSON, TONY J.
[b.] May 20, 1968, Worthsmith, AFB, MI; [p.] James and Emma Jean Ferguson; [ed.] BA from Tampa College; [occ.] Claim Representative State Farm Insurance; [oth. writ.] First published work; [pers.] I try to write straight from the heart; whether my own or someone else's. [a.] Tampa, FL.

FERLAND, AUTOMNE RENEE
[b.] November 16, 1977, Indianapolis, IN; [p.] Leah and Scott Ammerman; [ed.] Entering sophomore year at Deland High School; [memb.] French Club, Art Club, Barbizon Student; [hon.] Beta Club; [oth. writ.] The Heart; Death; The World; Sue's Sadness; Bio poem. [a.] Deland, FL.

FERNANDEZ, DAISY C.
[pen.] Shadow; [b.] November 25, 1944, Havana, Cuba; [p.] Avelino and Maria Fernandez; [m.] Divorced; [ch.] Jennifer and Carl Albanes; [ed.] Bachelors of Social Work from Wichita State University; [occ.] Welfare Supervisor I/Madison County Dept. of Human Resource; [memb.] American Association of University Women, A.L.I.V.E. and D.O.V.S. (Director of Volunteer Services); [oth. writ.] "The Music of the Hills" published August 1993; [pers.] I believe that we should strive to be the best we can be. My poetry is an expression of my own inner struggles as I try to determine what is right and what is wrong and set goals for the future. [a.] Huntsville, AL.

FERRAND, ORLANDO
[b.] November 8, 1967, Cuba; [p.] Orlando Ferrand and Maria C, Rodrigues-Riveria; [ed.] Student - Columbia University; [hon.] "Recognition of Honor" by the Institute of Cultural Research, Merida, Mexico "Best Film Award", International Festival of Alternative Video, Montreal, CAN; [oth. writ.] Poems, short stories, plays and articles written in English and Spanish. Have been published in Cuba, Spain, Mexico, and Germany in newspapers and specialized magazines. I'm working on my first novel; [pers.] Words-body-space: I write therefore I exist, I exist therefore I write not to forget. Printed memories of a civil animal engulfed by the world. World, my breathing words: This is the minute world I design in order to survive. [a.] New York, NY.

FERRARI, JONATHAN
[pen.] Jay Ferrari; [b.] April 24, 1969, Mishuwauka, IN; [p.] Randall and Joyce; [ed.] Rich South High School, Lake Forest College (BA), DePaul University (MA); [occ.] Public Relations, Business Communications Consultant, Janet Diedealchs and Assoc.; [oth. writ.] Several screenplays and short stories in development. Publishing dates pending for two magazine articles; [pers.] Vince Lombari reduced football to its essential elements; blocking and tackling. In that essentialist spirit: Waiting is no better than observing and reporting. [a.] Chicago, IL.

FERRARO, NANCY
[b.] December 25, 1944, Greensboro, NC; [p.] Richard J. and Delores (deceased) Ferraro; [ch.] Paul Richard Geisert; [ed.] Eastside High School, Rancho Santiago College; [occ.] Legal Secretary; [memb.] Orange County Sexual Assault Network; [hon.] Volunteer of the Year 1989 OCSAN; [pers.] Success, fame and fortune are all illusion. Real is the feelings and love people share and the acceptance of the humanness and frailties in all of us. [a.] Tustin, CA.

FERRELL, KATHERINE L.
[pen.] Kat Ferrell; [b.] November 27, 1945, Ft. Myers, FL; [p.] Willie E. and Emma M. Ferrell; [ed.] East High, Bryant and Stratton Business Institute; [occ.] Dental Sec'y/retired from NYS Dept. of Labor, Div. of Research and Statistics; [memb.] Prison Ministry; Life Church; Gulf-Coast Walk to Emmaus; Gulf-Coast Chrysalis Board member; [hon.] Daughters of American Revolution award 1959; WGR-TV2 News Center 2-riffic Volunteer award 1981; Erie Co. Savings Bank Volunteer Activist award 1981; [oth. writ.] Why Not Co-Education? Essay published in "The Youth Speaks" section of the Buffalo Evening News 1963. At least 30 plays, skits and poems used by local churches in the New York State and Florida; [pers.] I have discovered that I need not pursue happiness. Once I realized God has a plan for my life and I seek to fulfill his plan for me, happiness found me. [a.] Ft. Myers, FL.

FIDDLE, MARGRIT
[pen.] Grit; [b.] January 20, 1937, Germany; [p.] Werner and Traute Lippmann; [m.] Divorced; [ed.] BFA-Rhode Island School of Design Providence; [occ.] Creative/art director -book publishing company - Children's Press, Chicago, IL; [memb.] Decided several years ago professional organizations are for insecure people-don't belong to any; [hon.] A few for book design and other odd "here and there", like an engraved spoon from a gourmet outfit for a drink recipe (they didn't like the accompanying chicken recipe); [oth. writ.] Lots of personal musings, poetry thru the years; [pers.] Nature is trying to tell us something (i.e., floods, hurricanes, etc.) WILL WE EVER LISTEN? Time to take care of the earth, its flora and dauna, AND each other. [a.] Chicago, IL.

FINA, TINA
[pen.] Tina Fina; [b.] February 17, 1961, Houston, TX; [p.] Bill and Racine Watson; [ch.] Kristina Renee (12) and Amanda Dawn (11); [ed.] Mineral Wells High School, Weatherford College Lun Nursing School, Jones Real Estate School, Texas Insurance School; [occ.] Real Estate Agent, poet, Insurance agent; [memb.] National Library of Poetry, Poetry Academy, International Society of Poets; [hon.] First poem published - Troubled Heart/2nd poem published-My Dear Friend/3rd poem published-One of A Kind, Ruby Poet; [oth. writ.] Shall We Dance, Dare To Care, Oh! Dear Lord, Innocent Man, Friendship of the Heart, My True Blessings, Happiness, Longing, A Bad Affair, Bobby, Without My Darling, Return My Love; [pers.] I strive to write about things in my life that have occurred. I always include God because he watches over us all. I want to thank my beautiful girls Kristina and Amanda for inspiration. [a.] Mineral Wells, TX.

FINLEY, SHANNON
[b.] January 26, 1972, Bristol, PA; [p.] Patrick and Bobbie Finley; [ed.] College student at Bucks County Community College, graduated from Bishop Conwell High School 1990; [occ.] Waitress; [oth. writ.] First contest I have ever entered; [pers.] All of my writings are a reflection of my inner feelings towards life. [a.] Morrisville, PA.

FIRLOTTE, CONNIE
[b.] September 3, 1946, Woodstock, N.B., CAN; [p.] Hollis and Margaret Van Tassel; [m.] Donald Ross, Lloyd F. Firlotte; [ch.] Madonna Joy Ross, Duska Lee Ross and David Alan Ross. [a.] St. Stephen, N.B., CAN.

FISHER, JERRY
[b.] August 24, 1945, Mansfield, OH; [ed.] Arizona State University, 1967 BA; [pers.] Gratitude and love to Marilou, Burt, Frank, Vicki, Rita, Cathy, Boojum Hot Phoenix Summers and Wuzzas everywhere. [a.] Burbank, CA.

FISHER, KATHLEEN E.
[pen.] Katie Fisher; [b.] November 2, 1977, Rochester, MN; [p.] Charles and Bonnie Fisher; [ed.] Presently a sophomore at Bettendorf High School; [occ.] Student; [memb.] National Forensic League, Bettendorf High School Swim Team, BHS Marching and Concert Band; [hon.] Forensic awards - Novice, Perfect School Attendance, High Honor Roll at BHS; [oth. writ.] Poem published in International Readers Newsletter, Spring 1992. Participated in Promising Young Writers Program directed by National Council of Teachers of English; [pers.] My writing reflects the concerns of the times. I am interested in promoting a healthy environment as well as awareness for our country's needs. [a.] Bettendorf, IA.

FITENI, AUDREY
[b.] January 3, 1924, Newcastle-Upon-Tyne, ENG; [p.] William and Muriel Frazer; [m.] Angelo Oscar, May 3, 1946; [ch.] Alexander, Angela, Theresa; [occ.] Massage Therapist (retired), teaching: health, hydrotherapy, massage therapy (part-time); [oth. writ.] One year writing articles for the Etobicoke Guardian on "Health & Beauty"; [pers.] I am committed to good health my own and helping others whenever possible. To give each and everyone the power to overcome adversities with confidence and enjoy life to the fullest. [a.] Etobicoke, Ont. CAN.

FITZGERALD, ELEANOR
[b.] July 26. 1940, Kirkland Lake Ontario; [p.] Elsie and Calvin Fitzgerald; [ch.] None of my own, but numerous God children; [ed.] Central Public School Girl 1-8, KLCVI grade 9-12, Toronto Teacher's College 2 years, University of Windsor BA studying Children's Writing at Institute of Children's Literature; [occ.] Teacher - qualified to teach basic core and music and library and ESL; [memb.] International Society of Poets. Federation of Women Teachers for Ontario; [hon.] Editor's Choice award (National Library of Poetry) Dean's Honor List - 3 years running-1971 Teachers of Gr. 8 Poetry Club, 1984-85 member of Steering Committee for Junior Values Education Programme, 1985-87-member of Steering Committee for Primary Values Education Programme which produced a kit of 200 creative ideas across the curriculum to teach a value; 1985-86 Student Supervisor of Child Care Cooperative Educational Programme, 1986-one of two teachers evaluate a Child Abuse Program for implementation into the system, 1987-88 member of the committee for evaluating junior novels, 1967-71 I was the first teacher in the system to integrate a legally blind child into the regular class system; [oth. writ.] Silence - International Library of Poetry, Remembrance International Library of Poetry; [pers.] Inside of everyone of us there is an assortment of feelings about the world around us. Some of as expressed them on paper. I am one of those people. [a.] Toronto, Ont. CAN.

FIX, TARYN AUBREE
[b.] March 29, 1979, Scottsbluff, NE; [p.] Larry and Tanya Fix; [ed.] Haig School K-8, Scottsbluff Freshman present; [hon.] Finalist in 7th and 8th grades County Spelling Bee Contest ('92 and '93); [oth. writ.] "Drinking and Driving" published in the Western Poetry Association 1993 winter edition. [a.] Mitchell, NE.

FLEMING, MIMI PREMO
[b.] Springfield, MA; [p.] Polly Connolly and Lester J. Premo; [ch.] Susan, E.J., Mary Hayes, Tony and Nicholas; [ed.] Bay Path College (Long Meadow, MA); [occ.] Artist and writer; [memb.] Longmeadow Artists and Writers; [oth. writ.] Poems, essays and short stories; [pers.] Years ago my mother said to me, "Mimi, you're a romantic, and life is hard on romantics." She was right - so now I write. [a.] Enfield, CT.

FLESSNER, LAUREN BLAIR VLAICH
[b.] April 7, 1982, Minneapolis, MN; [p.] Bruce and Melanie Flessner; [ed.] Completed the 5th grade at Pilgrim Lane Elementary School (Plymouth, MN); [occ.] Child and student; [memb.] Greater Twin City Youth Symphony Orchestra, Valley Community Presbyterian Church, School District 281 Gifted and Talented Program, Girls Scouts; [hon.] 1st place team in Golden Valley Girls Softball League, attended Young Writer's Festival through school district.

FLETCHER, CHRIS
[b.] October 31, 1976, Fallston, MD; [p.] Pat Wallace and Jim Fletcher; [ed.] Senior North Harford High School; [occ.] Student; [hon.] 1990-93 Honor Roll, 1992-93 Merit Award for Achievement, 1993 Baseball All-star Team Harford Co. Parks and Rec.; [pers.] Don't let age tell you not to do what you feel is right. [a.] Forest Hill, MD.

FLORES, RICHARD G.
[b.] December 31, 1932, Springfield, MI; [ed.] BFA Degree in Art and Design, Texas Christian University (Ft. Worth, TX); [memb.] World Wildlife Foundation, Ducks Unlimited; [oth. writ.] Contributor to 1990 North Texas Poetry Anthology; [pers.] The love of my life is nature, its inhabitants and its elements. If my words and art can help someone appreciate such things, I will have been successful. a[.] Grapevine, TX.

FLOWERS, MARTHA
[pen.] Sissy; [p.] Mamie and Walter Love; [m.] Jessie; [ch.] Sharon and Angie Love, Monique Flowers and Shereka Barksdale; [ed.] 9th grade; [occ.] Housewife; [memb.] St. James Holiness Church. [a.] Laurinburg, NC.

FLYNN, BILL
[b.] May 8, 1953, Phillipsburg, NJ; [p.] John J. and Frances T. (Wilson) Flynn; [ed.] Wildwood Catholic High School and Neko-Ash, School of Karate, Cape May Courthouse, NJ; [occ.] Self-employed Innkeeper, professional martial arts teacher; [hon.] Third degree Black Belt of U.S.A. GOJU Karate; [oth. writ.] "Meditations of a Christian Martial Artist" self published, column writer - "The Maine Sportsman" [pers.] I like to write for purpose and to help others to think about life. [a.] Stratton, ME.

FOBBS, RUBYE L.
[b.] November 29, 1944, Kansas City, MI; [p.] Paul L.D. and Ruth A. (Merrill) Fobbs, Sr.; [ed.] Lincoln Sr. High Metropolitan Junior College, K.C. Business College; [occ.] Ckt. Design/Drafting Clerk; [memb.] Prayer Vigil Band; [hon.] Baptized in Jesus' Name and Filled with the Holy Ghost; [pers.] If Satan can get you on (1) Tenth Doubt, He has you on (9) Tenth's Faith. God is able. Are you willing? [a.] Kansas City, MO.

FOECKLER, EDNA MAY
[pen.] Edna May Foeckler; [b.] July 6, 1917, New Orleans, LA; [p.] Theodore and Edna Foeckler; [ed.] Two years high school graduate Spencer Business School Banking School, 1 term Tulane University; [occ.] Retired Secretary; [memb.] Choir member - 35 years Sunday School Teacher 25 yrs., Walther League etc., all in Lutheran Churches; [oth. writ.] First poem being published in Contemporary Poets, Dept. CPF 93- entitled leaves, anthology 1993; [pers.] Once can do whatever one wants to - only if it is the will of the Lord. [a.] River Ridge, LA.

FOLZ, JoANNE
[pen.] Jo Jo Folz; [b.] November 30, 1960, Dickinson Co., MI; [p.] D. "George" and Dorothy Folz; [ed.] Florence High School, Bay De Noc Community College; [occ.] LPN Charge Nurse Hyland Nursing Home; [oth. writ.] "My Sunshine"; [pers.] My life has been blessed by God. Mom, Dad, Laurie, Todd, Micky, and DJ - I love you. You are all special and important in my life. [a.] Kingsford, MI.

FORD, MYRTLE
[pen.] Myrtle Ford; [b.] December 20; [b.] Jacksonville, FL; [p.] Janie Vee and James Ford, Jr.; [ed.] Stanton High, Edward Waters College, University of Houston, MED.; [occ.] Health and Physical Educa-

tion Teacher, Cullen Middle School (Houston, TX); [memb.] H.A.P.E., T.A.H.P.E.R.D. and M.P.L.T.A.; [oth. writ.] unpublished poems; [pers.] Love poems are not difficult to write when they come from the heart. The words flow effortlessly. [a.] Houston, TX.

FORDHAM, STEPHEN K.
[b.] October 8, 1956, Heflin, AL; [p.] Vinson and Leatrice Fordham; [ch.,] Michelle Nicole; [ed.] Cleburne Co., High, University of AL (Tuscaloosa); [occ.] Quality Engineer, Calspan Corp.; [memb.] Highland Baptist Church, AIAA; [hon.] Magna Cum Laude graduate - B.S. Mech. Eng., Tau Beta Pi, Valedictorian - High school; [pers.] Formula for fulfillment: Always act to agree with who you are and who you want to become. [a.] Tullahoma, TN.

FORREST, ELIZABETH
[pen.] Liz or LMM; [b.] June 14, 1970, San Francisco, CA; [p.] Oliver and Annabella Forrest; [ed.] Hiram W. Johnson High; [occ.] Travel Photographer; [pers.] My thoughts are my own some calm, some crazy. My writing is from the heart. Some with hate, most with love. True or made up, but full of past, present and future. [a.] Sacramento, CA.

FORSTER, CYNTHIA L.
[b.] October 16, 1947, Columbia, PA; [p.] Robert and Florence Miller; [m.] Jeffrey H., June 11, 1971; [ch.] Meredith Lee and Hilary Clair; [ed.] BA, Elizabethtown College and MA American University; [occ.] Elementary/Junior High English Teacher; [memb.] National Council of Teachers of English; [hon.] Sigma Delta Chi, News Writing awards (PA Newswoman of the Year), outstanding service to Parish award; [oth. writ.] Children's version of New Milford History, Travel articles for Washington Post, numerous poems; [pers.] Poetry should reflect life, and vice versa, my best present to my children would be the blessing of poetic lives. [a.] New Milford, NJ.

FORWARD, JODY JEAN
[b.] March 21, 1973; [p.] Donna and George Forward; [ed.] Going to high school, Prince of Wales Collegiate; [occ.] Student; [pers.] I write to try and help myself and others understand different perspectives of life. I have many influences but one that stands head and shoulders above the rest is Brian. [a.] St. John's, Nfld.

FOSBROOK, SUSAN
[pen.] Melissa Curro; [b.] April 15, 1959, Washington, DC; [p.] Tom and Pat Curro; [m.] Christopher Fosbrook, April 23, 1988; [ed.] BS in Nursing, presently seeking MS in Nursing Education; [occ.] Registered Nurse in Emergency Room, Nurse Educator; [oth. writ.] "Discovery" poem published in the Gerontological Journal of Nursing 1981, "Help for Healing" booklet for grieving spouses, and family members 1991; [pers.] Bringing "Health" to Medicine is my lifelong dream. Writing is my "gift" to mankind. [a.] Columbia, MD.

FOSTER, JUNE DUROUX
[b.] June 5, 1919, Bronx, NY; [p.] Joseph V. and Jennie E. Erath Duroux; [m.] Elmer Patterson Foster, December 30, 1941; [ch.] John Robert, James Clement, Anne, Thomas Edward, Jeanne & William Francis; [ed.] BA Mathematics Hunter College, MA Child Development & Educational Testing University of Michigan and several courses at University of Delaware; [occ.] Retired teacher; [memb.] Alpha Gamma Delta Fraternity, Parish of the Resurrection R.C. Church Lector, Lukan and Liturgist; [oth. writ.] Several poems in graduate courses at the University of Delaware; [pers.] I was inspired by my sixth grade teacher Helen Hunt to love poetry and learning in general, and was taught at Hunter College High School to extend myself in many areas and to love languages. I wrote this poem to my granddaughter, Jill, when was eight years old. [a.] Wilmington, DE.

FOSTER, MARTHA M.
[pen.] Martha Miller Foster; [b.] March 24, 1928, Union, SC; [p.] deceased-A.J. & Florie Miller; [m.] Former-Haskell Foster, Jr., August 12, 1950; [ch.] Marth F. Wilson, Haskell Foster III, and Sylvia L. Foster; [ed.] Simms High School, Spartanburg Junior College (Spartanburg Methodist College), USC - Union & Winthop University; [occ.] Program Assistant for Retired Senior Volunteer Program (COAM-Midlands); [memb.] Clemsion Extension Homemakers-Needle Crafters, Lady Esther Order of Eastern Star, Chapter No. 353 & Bethany Baptist Church, also Prime Time; [hon.] Eastern Star and Clemsion Extension Homemakers and SC Council Homemakers, Pacolet River Baptist Association Auxiliaries; [oth. writ.] Poems and song poems and Family Church History, also write up to three Family History. Church and Family write-up in Union County Heritage 1981; [pers.] I will endeavor with efforts to write for advancement which appeals to people. I have continued to be inspired by poets of the past centuries. [a.] Columbia, SC.

FOWLER, DEBBIE
[b.] June 24, 1962, Tucumcarri, NM; [p.] Dwaine and Judy Short (brother-David Short); [m.] Divorced; [ch.] Meagen Arleen (8), Tiffany Fowler (5); [ed.] Portales High School, Eastern New Mexico University; [occ.] Daycare Operator; [memb.] Women's Auxiliary, VFW Post 9515, MOCA-VFW 9515, First United Methodist Church, 5th and 6th grade Sunday School Teacher; [oth. writ.] My other writings are kept at home with me in a notebook. This is the first time I've been published. This one of the greatest thrills of my life; [pers.] I write poetry for my own pleasure, mainly my writings are about the events in my life. [a.] Portales, NM.

FOWLER, JOHN R.
[b.] October 3, 1960, Northridge, CA; [p.] Delia Margaret and John R. Fowler, Jr.; [pers.] I don't know if I'm really a poet. I haven't read much poetry. Whatever I've written comes directly from my heart, from the pain or the joy. "Residue" comes from my failed marriage to Kelly, whom I'll always love. [a.] Lancaster, CA.

FOWLER, LETITIA V.
[b.] March 1, 1973, Jackson, MI; [p.] Alphonson G. Jr. and Mary V. Fowler; [ed.] 1991 graduate of Jackson High School, sophomore/junior at Central Michigan University; [occ.] Internship with Jackson Citizen Patriot; [memb.] Second Baptist Church and Youth Ambassadors for Christ, CMU; [oth. writ.] Articles published as a reporter for CM Life and Jackson Citizen Patriot; [pers.] I can do all things through Christ who strengthens me. [a.] Jackson, MI.

FOX, BEVERLY
[b.] July 21, 1953, Visalia, CA; [p.] Paul and Barbara Metheney-(grandmother-Ernestine Dunaway); [ch.] Jeff Matthews; [ed.] Mt. Whitney High; [occ.] Phlebotomist/Histological Technician; [oth. writ.] Several poems, non published; [pers.] I believe life is difficult and poetry to me is sometimes a release, and it has also helped me to enjoy and see the beauty in this world. Beverly's Blues - dedicated to Pete. [a.] Grants Pass, OR.

FRANKE, ESTHER S.
[b.] May 28, 1909, Maleras, Sweden, Europe; [p.] Gustare and Hilda Lagerquist ; [m.] George B., November 22, 1930; [ch.] Gorden, Dolores, Jeanette, George, Gerald, Gloria, Barbara, Michael; [ed.] 7th grade; [occ.] Housewife; [memb.] Talent, "Red Rosen" and Worldwide Church of God; [hon.] Poem: Soon on Earth God's Kingdom published in their weekly report by Worldwide Church of God; [oth. writ.] "Esctasy", "The Great Remover", "Soon on Earth God's Kingdom", "Beware", "Half Past Eight", "What Once I Had", "Horse Laughter Love", "Alcoholic Blues", "Your Way of Life", "Cottage Full of Memories", "A Way to the Heart", "Swinging in the Depot", "Cindy Low Dog", "Love Flew Out the Window", "Pepper Can", "Only He", "Happiness and Sorrow", "YOur Tender Love Means All The World to Me"; [pers.] I strive to reflect the actual nature and character of mankind in all my song poems and writings. [a.] Minneapolis, MN.

FRASER, GAIL A.
[pen.] Susan Rose, tabby cat; [b.] March 7, 1920, Pleasant Grove, MN; [p.] William and Minnie; [m.] Late Charles, July 28, 1943; [ch.] William Butran, Lance Gimber, Carla Marie; [ed.] Greenway High, Itasca Community College, College of St. Scholastica, Linwood College; [occ.] Retired Medical Laboratory Technologist, Laboratory Supervisor; [memb.] American Society of Clinical Pathologists, Emeritus. Clallam County Genealogical Society; [hon.] Scholastic and athletic awards, Mrs. NM 1955, literary award and horticultural sweepstakes award; [oth. writ.] Article in the MLO Medical Laboratory Observer, unpublished Susan Rose poems, unpublished book, You Can Live Longer, various newspaper, articles, newsletter editor; [pers.] The poem for/by Susan Rose, tabby cat, began with poetic letters to her master, while away and to her beau cat, Prince, with ensuing encouragement to publish them. [a.] Squim, WA.

FREEMAN, ARTHUR
[b.] January 12, 1925, Youngstown, OH; [m.] Marilyn (deceased); [ch.] Joel Stanton Freeman and Mary F. Lucas; [ed.] Doctor of Veterinary Medicine, Stanford University, and Ohio State University; [occ.] Veterinarian/journalist/ and administrator-retired; [memb.] American Veterinary Medical Association, Executive Service Corps of Indianapolis, Council of Biology Editors; [hon.] Distinguished Alumnus Award, Ohio State University, Honorary Memberships, Ohio, Michigan, Illinois and Indiana Veterinary Medical Associations; [oth. writ.] Editorials and scientific commentaries in veterinary medical journals and periodicals; [pers.] My inspiration for this poems and a longer version of it came from several years spent with the US Fish and Wildlife Service on Kodiak Island, AK. [a.] Carmel, IN.

FREEMAN, MELISSA LYNE
[b.] November 25, 1974, Annapolis, MD; [p.] Harry L. and Wanda R. Freeman; [ed.] Old Mill Sr. High School, Francis Marion University (1 yr.); [oth. writ.] Several unpublished poems and short stories, one unpublished play. [a.] Mullins, SC.

FREEMAN, VERNA
[pen.] Dean; [b.] Sapulpa, OK; [p.] Clarence and Edna York; [m.] Ottis (deceased), July 17, 1946; [ch.] Sandra, Douglas, Wendell and Wesley; [ed.] 8th grade; [occ.] Retired; [hon.] Several for entering contest's poems to family, friends, schools; [oth. writ.] Church groups, a few country and western bands, locally; [pers.] My songs and poems are centered around family and friends - I express my feelings I hold back nothing (the good, the bad, and also the ugly) that's what life is all about. [a.] Eureka, CA.

FREMGEN, DARLENE
[pen.] d miner; [b.] July 19, 1958, Schenectady, NY; [p.] Jacob (Scott) and Diane Miner; [ed.] Greencastle-Antrim High School; [occ.] Crane Assembly Clerk, Grove Worldwide (Shady Grove, PA); [hon.] Editor's Choice Award by 1991 National Library of Poetry (Owings Mills, MD); Wind in the Night Sky publication of "Metal Jungles" pp 696; [pers.] Many thanks to TV Guide's 1973 Associate Editor, W.A. Marsano, for revving my poem: "Tale of the Fatigued Criminal". He replied metaphorically, "The Pun on Marcus Welby is worthy of Ogden Nash" in retrospect this honor achieved in junior high has been an inspiration. [a.] Chambersburg, PA.

FRENCH, LAVERNE H.
[pen.] LaVerne H. French; [b.] July 14, 1923, Bolton, MS; [p.] Daniel Luther and Charlotte White Harper; [m.] Donald F. (deceased), July 22, 1950; [ch.] Dr. Pamela Summers, Donald L. French-carpenter, Kathy Cunningham-nutritionist, MA and Robin French-lawyer Univ. of Michigan; [ed.] MA-Columbia University; [occ.] Retired teacher, 2 years acting principal - Director Pre-K; [memb.] Free Evangelical Church of Cresskill, NJ - served on Christian Ed. Board, Life member PTA; [hon.] Delta Kappa Gamma, Alpha Eta Chapter; [oth. writ.] Recently published tract "God is Love"; [pers.] The standard bearer of my life's work has been incorporating the importance of the bonding between home, the child, a nd the education the child received within the total life experiences. [a.] Cresskill, NJ.

FRENCH, ZELIA J.
[b.] August 20, 1905, Howard, KS; [p.] Harley I and Cora J. French; [ed.] HS Eldorado, KS, Southwestern College, BS-Library Science, University of Illinois; [occ.] Librarian; [memb.] American Auxiliary Association, PENN, Kansas Press Club, Flint Hills Writers Club; [oth. writ.] Editor, Kansas Library Bulletin 1941-1957, poems published in local newspapers; [pers.] Hoping to reflect and preserve through poetry some of the beauty I see around me. [a.] Severy, KS.

FRICK, CAREY R.
[pen.] Claude Brown; [b.] January 18, 1978, Easton, PA; [p.] Robert L. Jr. and Karen L. Frick; [oth. writ.] Two poems in upcoming book about Grindstone Island; [pers.] Reality is an illusion and everything is one. [a.] Easton, PA.

FRIEND, SARAH R.
[pen.] S. Emauroe; [b.] July 4, 1976, Richmond, VA; [p.] Jerry and Nancy Friend; [ed.] Galaz High; [hon.] Who's Who Among American High School Students, United States Achievement Academy Scholar; [oth. writ.] Several poems and prose published in "High Tide" literary magazine as well as a short story published and honored by Virginia M.A.T.E.; [pers.] Each individual must strive to encounter and accept one's own ideas in life, whether conventional or abstract to others. I have been influenced by Poe, Crane, Thoreau, and Emerson. [a.] Galax, VA.

FRYE, CHERYL
[b.] January 9, 1960, Petaluma, CA; [p.] James and Georgia Younger; [m.] Robert E., July 26, 1980; [ch.] Samantha Leigh Frye; [ed.] Petaluma High School grad, Valley College (North Hollywood, CA); [occ.] Nurse; [memb.] St. John's Lutheran Church; [hon.] Journalism scholarship from Santa Rosa, CA Press DEmocrat (High School), Top Student award and scholarship from Professional Nurses Bureau upon nursing school graduation. Also Biography was published in Who's Who of American HIgh School Students; [oth. writ.] I constantly write editorials and also do some free lance writing; [pers.] I wrote this poem from my own experiences - I am a survivor of incest and other sexual molestation. I have recovered and want others to know that it can be overcome, and not to be ashamed of oneself. [a.] Petaluma, CA.

FULFORD, KEVIN
[pen.] Nixx; [b.] June 28, 1977, Belleville, Ont. CAN.; [p.] Don and Nancy Fulford; [ed.] Trenton High School grade 11; [oth. writ.] Few poems selected for school newspaper; [pers.] In my writing I stress reality. The world is drowning in too much fantasy. [a.] Trenton, Ont. CAN.

FULLER, NANCY
[b.] March 28, 1963, Minneapolis, MN; [p.] Henning and Mary Nielsen; [m.] Robert, January 10, 1992; [ch.] Aaron Lee; [ed.] Anoka High; [occ.] Policy Services Representative; [memb.] Ramsey County Emergency Disaster Services; [pers.] I like to point out the wonder and humor in everyday life. I believe that the most powerful writing comes from the heart. [a.] Roseville, MN.

FURCELLO, CARSEN "ROCKY"
[b.] May 10, 1951, Cleveland OH (died June 26, 1993); [p.] Biagio Furcello Sr. and Jacqueline Green; [ed.] High School; [occ.] Musician. [a.] Cleveland, OH.

GAGNE, KEVIN P.
[b.] September 1, 1960; [oth. writ.] My Only Love. My first published poem a dream come true; [pers.] Strange, a poem that filled me with such sadness to write. Now, is a source of happiness. [a.] Courtenay BC Canada.

GAGO, AMY MICHELLE
[b.] March 26, 1976, Ft. Lauderdale, FL; [p.] Christine Peters; [ed.] Forsyth Central High School; [occ.] Processor in a Mortgage company; [memb.] Student Council, MockTrail, a number of school clubs and activities; [hon.] Who's Who in American High School Students; [pers.] Always strive to be the best that you can be - sometimes you will surprise yourself. [a.] Gainesville, GA.

GAJDA, BRYGIDA MARIA
[b.] February 5, 1976, Cleveland, OH; [p.] Stella and John Gajda, Socrates Cyndzas (stepfather); [ed.] 1994 graduate of Westlake High School; [occ.] Student; [memb.] Gorale Polish Folk Dancer, P.N.A. Council, Drama Club, Symphonic Choir, American Heart Association, American Red Cross; [hon.] Honorable mention in Reflections; [oth. writ.] Several poems published in Westlake High School's Literary Magazine Potpourri, assortment of over 40 unpublished poems; [pers.] I write to give, to feel, to live. [a.] Westlake, OH.

GALE, REBECCA LYNN
[pen.] Becca; [b.] June 13, 1973, Columbia, SC; [p.] Karen (School teacher) and Leonard Gale (Neurologist) - Sibling: Nicole (19) and Eli (11); [ed.] Junior at Whittier College, Liberal Arts and International Studies; [occ.] Student and Economics. Staff written at the Whittier Daily News; [memb.] School paper writer, soccer team, student gov't; [hon.] Dean's List, Chosen by AFS to spend semester abroad in high school in Paraguay, chosen to spend semester abroad in college in Spain, Drama Club member; [oth. writ.] Many but none published; [pers.] Write down what you feel at an emotional time and add the polished touch with adjectives later. [a.] Palos Verdes Peninsula, CA.

GALLAGHER, DOROTHY
[b.] July 10, 1923, Brooklyn, NY; [p.] Helen and Charles Misner; [m.] John, August 17, 1946; [ed.] Franklin K. Lane High; [oth. writ.] One of the winners of an essay contest, held by the Journal Newspaper on the late President John F. Kennedy. [a.] Brooklyn, NY.

GALLARDO, JESSICA
[pen.] Jessica Gallardo; [b.] August 17, 1976, Freeport, TX; [p.] Epifanio and Dolly Gallardo; [ed.] High School; [occ.] Cashier (part-time) at grocery store; [hon.] Journalism I, newspaper, yearbook (merit award), third place feature writing, student council, national honor society; [pers.] I believe that through writing all your inner most feelings and fantasies can shine through, and touch others. [a.] Freeport, TX 77541.

GALLI, KATRINA
[b.] May 20, 1973,, Cheyenne Wells, CO; [p.] Paul and Rose Galli; [ed.] Cheyenne Wells High, McCook Community College, University of Nebraska-Lincoln; [occ.] Pre-Law student; [memb.] Catholic Youth Group, Student Senate-MCC Criminal Justice, Club MCC Circle K International-MCC; [hon.] Phi Theta Kappa's most outstanding scholarship-MCC, one of the 2,500 National Dean's Students that are picked from each college, Phi Theta Kappa honors; [pers.] Poetry is one of the few ways we can make our mark of our existence. [a.] Cheyenne Wells, CA.

GAMBLE, ELLIS C.
[b.] October 22, 1970, Beardy's Indian Reservation, Sask. CAN; [p.] Gilbert and May Gamble; [ed.] Stobart High, Athol Murray College of Notre Dame (Wilcox, Sask.); [occ.] Self-taught musician, song writer, hoping for a successful career in the music business; [oth. writ.] Other writings I have written do not consist of poems but in songs that I have written since I was eighteen; [pers.] Practice, Practice, Prac-

tice I've heard so many guitarist say, but writing is different, anybody can do it if your feelings are true and strong enough. [a.] Duck Lake, Sask. CAN.

GAMBLE, HEATHER L.
[b.] January 15, 1979, Rosthern, SK; [p.] Gilbert and May Gamble; [ed.] Stobart High School; [occ.] Student; [oth. writ.] Short story for the local newspaper; [pers.] I write my poems from the heart which express my deepest emotions and feelings. [a.] Duck Lake, SK, CAN.

GANGE, FRANCES
[pen.] Fancy; [b.] June 29, 1928, Orrin, ND; [p.] Nicholas and Philamena Adam; [m.] Anthony, March 5, 1946; [ch.] Dwight, Mary Lou, Gene, Marilyn, William, James, Gerard, Elizabeth and Pamela Grange; [ed.] 8th grade; [occ.] Housewife; [memb.] Catholic Church; [oth. writ.] I wrote a poem for my first baby boy, but misplaced it. Everybody that read it said it was good. [a.] Great Falls, MT.

GARCIA, ARIKA
[b.] July 24, 1978, Kingston, NY; [p.] Jane and Tony Garcia; [ed.] Rondout Valley High School; [occ.] Student; [memb.] Student Council, Cheerleading, Yearbook; [hon.] Honor Roll; [oth. writ.] Poems given to family members; [pers.] To my writing I would like to bring out my emotions and feelings towards life. My first published for this book dedicated to Charles W. Pysher. [a.] Cottekill, NY.

GARCIA, CHALENE MICHELLE
[pen.] Michelle Garcia; [b.] May 23, 1979, Phoenix, AZ; [p.] Mitchell and Julene Garcia; [ed.] Crane Junior High - Cibola High School; [occ.] Student; [memb.] 4-H, FFA, Cibola High Swim Team, Studio 5 Modeling, Community Theatre and Dancemakers; [hon.] Honor classes, award for modeling and dancing award; [oth. writ.] Kept for personal collection; [pers.] I write my feelings and what I see and it makes me feel better about myself. [a.] Somerton, AZ.

GARCIA, ERICA DAWN
[pen.] Edge; [b.] April 8, 1978, Houston, TX; [p.] Carlos and Barbara Garcia; [ed.] Scarborough High School; [occ.] Student; [oth. writ.] "Wind Whispers" (Where Dreams Begin) few poems in neighborhood newspapers; [pers.] Wisdom does not always come with age, it comes from the heart and from the mind. [a.] Houston, TX.

GARCIA, GLORIA GUADALUPE
[b.] April 2, 1972, Mexicali, BaJa, CA; [p.] Maria Dolores and Leandro Garcia; [ed.] Coachella Valley High School; [oth. writ.] Several poems and songs of my own; [pers.] Romantic is the word that describes my poetry. [a.] La Quinta, CA.

GARDNER, ETHEL FENTRESS
[b.] October 12, 1917, Princeton, NJ; [p.] Ora Fletcher and Ethel Fentress Gardner, Sr; [ed.] St. Margaret's Waterbury, CT; Welding School, Stuttgart, Germany; American Academy of Dramatic Arts, NYC; Washington School for Secretaries, NYC; [occ.] Retired and writing; [hon.] Twice presented with a medallion by the Research Institute of America. Merit awards and commendation from the U.S. Navy; [oth. writ.] Wind Borne Seeds Soaring, Where Horsemanship Begins...A Point of View, column Pause and Ponder, many articles in horse magazines and newspapers. [a.] Whittier, NC.

GARDNER, LEOLA CALDWELL
[pen.] Ola; [b.] June 1, 1949; [m.] Freddie D.; [ch.] Lataisha R., Angela Y., Keith L. Gardner; [ed.] Northwestern State University; [occ.] Unemployed; [memb.] Poetry Club of America, Songwriter's Club of America, Saint Matthew Baptist Church; [hon.] Merit certificate for poem "Reincarnation" professional poet; [oth. writ.] The Business of Love, I Have A Say, Seriously, Facts of Life, May I, Love and Bologna and If You Can't Love Me; [pers.] Writing is not a bobby, I'm too indulgent. It is a job and I love what I do. [a.] Saline, LA.

GARNETT, MICHAEL EDWARD
[pen.] Mateen; [b.] January 29, 1953, Bristol, TN; [p.] Louise Booker; [ch.] Michael Stephen and Mario Edward; [ed.] High school graduate; [occ.] Laborer; [hon.] Who's Who In American #1 Schools (1970); Semi-finalist National Merit Qualifying Competition (1969-70); [pers.] THE OTHERWIDE ROOM by Southern Illinois University, 1981-Have been published by certain leftist pub., written for THE TORCH - BURNING SPEAR - THE GUARDIAN; [pers.] "We only become what we are by the radical and deep seated refusal to become what others have made of us." (Frantz Fanon). [a.] Bristol, VA.

GARRETT, FANNIE
[pen.] Faye Garrett; [b.] Hephzibah, GA; [p.] Wade Hampton and Athar Alfia Wells Garrett; [ed.] Master degree in Education (Sp.Ed.); [memb.] Life membership NJEA, Lifters Scholarship Organization; [pers.] I have adopted my high school motto NIL SINE NUMINE "Nothing without Divine Will". [a.] East Orange, NJ.

GARRETT, GREGORY J.
[b.] September 24, 1952, Bronx, NY; [p.] Donald and Jene Garrett; [m.] Cecilia Voccoli, September 10, 1983; [ch.] David Victor (5) and Emily Jene (1). [a.] Dumont, NJ.

GARRETT, KATHY
[b.] October 17, 1954, Paducah, KY; [p.] Mr. and Mrs. Howard Garrett; [m.] Divorced; [ch.] Joseph W. and Wayne B. Ashley; [ed.] 10th grade and went back to training school; [occ.] Work at Citizens in Paducah, KY; [hon.] Few merit for writing and poetry; [oth. writ.] Talk poetic to my friends, everyone loves my writing. I idolized Elvis Presley since I could walk. [a.] Paducah, KY.

GARRETT, KAREN J.
[b.] July 23, 1948, Lynn, MA; [p.] Margaret and Ernest Essery; [m.] Charles M., June 2, 1973; [ch.] Marilyn, Sharon, Kenneth Garrett; [ed.] Lynn Classical High 1966, Essex School of Practical Nursing 1968; [occ.] LPN - Administrative Assistant; [hon.] Poet of the Month, St. Francis Institute Poetry Contest 1988 - 'Hands Around the World'; [oth. writ.] Poems published in Le Livre I and II by St. Francis Institute 1987 and 1988; Collection of poetry names 'Seasons of My Heart' 1990 (self-published) Newspaper article published by Lowell Sun 'Under the Christmas Tree' 1989; [pers.] I write with the hope that the reader will experience the beauty of the moment as I do. [a.] Tewksbury, MA.

GARRETT, LAMILLS A.
[pen.] Alex; [b.] August 2, 1972, Columbia, SC; [p.] Jacqueline D. "Jackie" Priester and LaMills A. "L.A." Garrett; [m.] LaGodia E. Sewell-Garrett, July 4, 1992; [ed.] C.A. Johnson High, Louisiana Tech. University (part-time); [occ.] Dental Lab Technician in the U.S. Air Force; [hon.] Winner of Poetry and Essay Contest 1993 Black Male Conference; [oth. writ.] Several poems published in local papers; [pers.] I strive to uplift all of humanity but I focus my efforts to improving the lives and situations of Blacks in America. My greatest influence has been my Mother's strength to overcome and defeat adversities of her past. [a.] Columbia, SC.

GARRETT, PAUL E.
[pen.] Paul E. Garrett; [b.] November 18, 1909, Tampas, CO; [p.] Charles C. and Ida P. Guire Garrett; [m.] Ornetta G., October 27, 1984; [ch.] Two deceased sons, 8 grandchildren, 25 great grandchildren;l [ed.] BS Biological Sciences, plus Seminar in Entimology, University of Wyoming, CLU, American College; [occ.] Life Underwriter, Educator; [memb.] Million Dollar Round Table, All Masonic Bodies, Elks Club, Brotherhood of Friends, Crystal Cathedral; [hon.] Life memberships in local, state and national Association of Life Underwriters, Million Dollar Round Table, 1st runner-up to Poet Laureate, World of Poetry 1991, Poet Laureate, Alaska 1934-35; [oth. writ.] Five short stories on Hunting and Fishing published by Alaska Sportsman; 12-15 "How To" articles in Manager's Mag. Underwriter's Review, Life Insurance Selling, Ohio National's Bulletin, Weekly poem in Seward Gateway News 18 mos., later compiled in Song of the North; [pers.] Live by the Golden Rule: Do unto others as you would have them do unto you. Give and you shall receive in happiness many times over. Politeness is to do and say the kindest things in the kindest way. The fight is not over as long as you get up. [a.] Lake Havasu City, AZ.

GARRISON, JAMILLAH DARYL
[b.] May 19, 1975, Berkeley, CA; [p.] Betty J. Warner and John E. Garrison; [ed.] Oakland Technical High, Ralph J. Bunch, Laney College; [hon.] Citizenship, R.O.T.C. Drill awards and book reciting; [pers.] My influences are everyday life - the things, people, and sounds around me. My writings come from the heart and flow through the hand. [a.] Oakland, CA.

GATES, CHRISTOPHER DAVID
[b.] March 28, 1978, Marion, OH; [p.] Robert and Susan Gates; [ed.] Van Wert High School; [occ.] Student; [memb.] Van Wert German Club 1993, Van Wert Athletic Club, YMCA, Track and Cross Country, Presbyterian Church; [hon.] Renaissance Club Card Holder to be exempt from exam; [oth. writ.] Written numerous poems that are unpublished; [pers.] I believe anyone has the ability to be a great poet and distinguished writer if they put their mind to it. I believe in dreams coming true. It just takes a little effort to go forth to get to the top of the hill. [a.] Van Wert, OH.

GAVETTI, DENISE
[b.] October 3, 1963 (with twin brother, Doug), Ridley Park, PA; [p.] Douglas J. Gavetti, Sr. (deceased) and Rose M. Crowley; [ch.] Ryan Douglas Gavetti (2 years old); [ed.] Ridley High and some college, Delaware County Community College; [occ.] Secretary and Quality Management Advisor (Phila. Electric Co.); [pers.] I have written poetry since I was a child but never shared it openly with too many people. Most of my poetry expresses my deepest feelings whether it be happy or sad and I don't always feel comfortable sharing those feelings except with a very select few. [a.] Glenolden, PA.

GAZDHYAN, NUNE
[pen.] Noon, Cristey; [b.] January 28, 1979, Yerevan; [p.] Rebeka Asatryan and Sarkis Gazdhyan; [ed.] Thomas Starr King Middle School; [occ.] Student; [hon.] My poem was printed in the school newspaper; [pers.] "Hatred stirs up dissension, but love covers over all wrongs" Prov. 10:12. [a.] Los Angeles, CA.

GEE, BETHANY
[pen.] Kathy Klyne; [b.] March 7, 1969, Athens, AL; [ed.] Tanner High, Calhoun Community College; [occ.] Property Manager; [pers.] My wish is for my writing to create an escape for everyone who reads it. [a.] Huntsville, AL.

GEHRLING, ALYCE "LISA"
[pen.] Lisa; [b.] Queens, New York City; [p.] Alyce C. Hobbs and Kenneth K. Linson, M.D.; [ch.] Gerard Kenneth, Paul E.; [ed.] B.A.; [occ.] Writer, poet, artist; [memb.] Long Island Poetry Collective, Multiple Sclerosis Society, Myasthnia Gravis Society, World Wildlife Society; [hon.] Three first place, 28 honorable mention, 6 gold awards, one Who's Who in Poetry award, Girls scout leader, President High school science club, Editor of Science News Hunters; [oth. writ.] 16 anthologies, St. Dude's Journal, many newsletters, school publications; [pers.] I was first published with a sketch in local newspaper at age 7, poetry editor for school paper, photography awards. [a.] Seaford, LI, NY.

GEIER, TOM JR.
[b.] March 20, 1977, York, PA; [p.] Karen and Thomas Geier, Sr.; [ed.] Completed 10th grade; [occ.] High school student and Pathmark Cashier; [memb.] York and Adams County Game and Fish Association, The Athletic Club, Spring Grove Sr. High School Float Committee; [hon.] Black Belt (1st degree) in Tang Soo-Do (Karate) have been on the honor roll at school; [oth. writ.] Over 70 other poems (all original); [pers.] I could never have written any of my poems without God Almighty, my family, and Heather Gohn. [a.] York, PA.

GEORGE, FRANCES T.
[b.] April 21, 1917, Calgary, Alberta, CAN; [p.] Arthur A. and Emma G. Winsor; [ch.] Clyde Arthur George and Gertrude Neal George Nishino; [ed.] High school graduated 1935 in Shelton, WA - Business College in Seattle, WA; [occ.] 1940s Navy Yard Officer, Bremerton, WN County Treasurer's Office, Seattle, WA - Oregon Dept. of Transportation - 20 years; [oth. writ.] Wrote poems off and On for Years - sent one to world of Poetry but never had it published and it like writing them for family and friends and yet requests to write them; [pers.] To be able to comfort someone by writing a poem gives me satisfaction and a good feeling. [a.] Eugene, OR.

GEORGE, JEANNE D.
[b.] February 11, 1961, Central Falls, RI; [p.] Annette J. Varieur; [m.] Peter F., December 22, 1990; [ed.] Johnson and Wales University; [occ.] Entrepreneur, The Collectible Source, Inc., and One Plus One Company; [memb.] North American Fishing Club, North Shore Animal League, Save The Manatee Club; [hon.] Silver Key Honor Society, Golden Quill Honor Society, Who's Who Among Students in American Universities, Summa Cum Laude, Dean's List; [pers.] My goals in life are these: be true to myself, be kind to others, and appreciate the "moments" of life. [a.] Warwick, RI.

GEORGE, MONICA
[b.] December 23, 1979, New Orleans, LA; [p.] Mary and Merlin George, Jr.; [ed.] High school student, Ursuline Academy (freshman); [memb.] Young Scribes Club, Ursuline Academy; [hon.] Presidential Academic Fitness award, Valedictorian of 8th grade graduating class of 1993; [pers.] Poetry is a way to express your feelings and to share those feeling with the world. [a.] Gretria, LA.

GEORGE, TINA
[b.] Spokane, WA; [p.] Theresa and Kenneth George; [hon.] Honor Roll and awards for grades in school; [oth. writ.] I write poetry very often. I write to express feelings and thoughts that are sometimes explained better in words. I have a collection of poetry, that I myself, have written; [pers.] I hope people who read poetry read it for the fantastic and dramatic literature that I have come to find that it is, and everyone has the potential to be - a poet. [a.] Spokane, WA.

GERMAN, BRENAN
[b.] August 29, 1968, Orange, CA; [p.] Gillian Tingler and John German; [ed.] Villa Park High, Rancho Santiago College, University California, Irvine; [occ.] Proofreader, Reciter; [pers.] I find it important to recognize the symbolism in everyday occurrences and their attachment to the whole. I am truly intrigued by the moderns, especially high modernism. [a.] Villa Park, CA.

GERVAIS, MARY
[b.] August 7, 1939, High Prairie, ALB, CAN; [p.] Edith Ireland and James Ireland (deceased April 26, 1975); [m.] Richard, August 22, 1957; [ch.] Roger, Jim, Pete and Dennis; [ed.] I write from my heart; [occ.] Housewife, songwriter, and poet; [memb.] Nashville Songwriters Association; [hon.] Song Recording Contract from Platinum Records, had a bedtime story published in the Edmonton Journal got one of my poems published in treasured poems of America (Winter 1993); [oth. writ.] Many of my poems have been published in our local newspaper (Smoky River Express); [pers.] I strive to reflect only the good things in life, like the many flowers always in my yard, I hope my writing brings pleasure to others. I believe it's a gift from God. [a.] Falher, AL. CAN.

GESTER, KATHLEEN J.
[b.] November 5, 1925, South Bend, IL; [p.] Margarette Helen (Leatherman) and Howard James Miller; [m.] William N., April 8, 1951; [ch.] Lesleigh, Steven and Marihelen; [ed.] Warren Township H.S., ISNU, and NIU; [memb.] Grace Community Church; [oth. writ.] Political campaign material, poems published in Wankegan News Sun and Church publication; [pers.] To Be Born - To grow in knowledge and grace - to share what I am and what I have - to strive to become more than I was - to die leaving more than I took. To live forever in his presence, praising him for giving me the willing heart that sought Him in both worlds. [a.] Round Lake, IL.

GETTYS, WILLIAM REES III
[pen.] William Rhys; [b.] October 30, 1971, Columbia, SC; [p.] William R. Gettys, Jr and Kathy Gettys-Carndon; [ed.] Middle High School, senior at University of South Carolina; [occ.] Journalism student; [hon.] Two years varsity soccer at USC; [oth. writ.] Sports writing. [a.] Columbia, SC.

GEVING, RUTH
[b.] October 13, 1921, Climax, Sask. CAN.; [p.] Hans and Bertha Haaland; [m.] Oscar, December 9, 1945; [ch.] Stephen Michael, Melodie Roseanne Morgan, Coralie Opal; [ed.] Frontier High, Teacher's College (Moose Jaw) University of Sask. (Saskatown); [occ.] Retired teacher; [oth. writ.] A private collection of poems to be passed down to my children; [pers.] I strive to glorify God in my poems and to reflect on the beauty of His creation. [a.] Frontier, SASK, CAN.

GIANCOLA, DAVID EVERETT
[b.] March 27, 1957, Portland, ME; [p.] Joseph and Beverly Giancola; [m.] Marcia Ann Montrey; [ch.] Jessica Michelle; [ed.] Pembroke Academy High School, Delayed Entry Program April 1974, Navy in June 1974, Army Lithographer School and Defense Mapping Institute, Command Career Counselor School, Navy Recruiting Orientation Unit; [hon.] December 1974 received Lithographer designation, Enlisted Surface Warfare Specialist device, (3) Good Conduct (4), Navy Expeditionary, National Defense (2), Sea Service Deployment (3), Battle "E" (5), Overseas Service (3), Navy Recruiting Service, Expert Rifle, Expert Pistol, Meritorious Unit Commendation, 10 Gold Wreaths for Recruiting Excellence, Letter of Commendation from Chief of Naval Operations (2) and the Philippine Presidential Unit Citation. Currently under consideration for Navy Achievement Medal Gold (4th) award.

GIBSON, DAVID S.
[b.] September 3, 1968, Reading, PA; [p.] Marty R. Gibson and Susan E. Krenzel; [ed.] Muhlenberg High School; [occ.] Welder; [hon.] Several awards for technical work on high school musicals; [oth. writ.] Several other short poems, song lyrics, and short stories; [pers.] Creativity comes from within, from your personal experiences. This is where my influence is -within. [a.] Mohnton, PA.

GIBSON, JANET L.
[b.] November 4, 1946, Sewickley, PA; [p.] Paul E. McNally and Edith M. Jednik; [m.] Divorced; [ch.] Craig Allen Gibson (25); [ed.] Ambridge High School, McLennan Community College, Charles Co. Community; [occ.] Partially disabled homemaker; [hon.] Defense Intelligence Agency Commendation Award 1966; [oth. writ.] Several other poems and songs not yet published; [pers.] "THE ESSENCE OF LIFE" was inspired by a dear friend of 20 years, and truly expresses my philosophy of life. [a.] Whitney, TX.

GIBSON, NATASHA RIA
[b.] March 1, 1976, Kansas City, MO; [p.] Wilma I. and Harrison Gibson; [ed.] Bingham Middle Magnet and currently senior at Lincoln College Preparatory Academy in KC MO, summer 93 at UMC; [occ.] Student in HS and server of Community Guest Coordinator/Co=Host of Teens Talking to Teens; [memb.] NHS, YIG, StuCO, Project First/Upward Bound, Generation Rap, Young Playwrights Roundtable, Mizza Alpha Academic Academy and others; [hon.] Who's Who Among American HS Students 91-93, Poems produced and performed by Caterie Two; [oth. writ.] Many other poems; [pers.] My writings reflect the life of a young black sister trying to make it in this world that is not designed for us. However, everyone can benefit from my message: Life and people change. [a.] Kansas City, MO.

GIDDENS, REX M.
[b.] May 27, 1947, Mt. Vernon, TX; [p.] Milton and Nora Leita Giddens; [m.] Cleva, June 7, 1982; [ch.] Kelly, Emilee, Clayton; [ed.] MBA from East Texas State University; [occ.] Comptroller, East Texas State University; [memb.] VFW, Optimist Club; [hon.] Bronze Star, Vietnam Service Medal, Air Medal, Vietnam Campaign Medal; [pers.] Vietnam Veteran, First Infantry Division (Big Red One) 1st Battalion, 18th Infantry in Vietnam from Jan. 1969 to Dec. 1969 as a Staff Sergeant E-6. [a.] Commerce, TX.

GIL, GENEVE MAXWELL
[b.] August 31, 1967, Cambridge, MA; [p.] Peter Paul and Ann (Anita) Gil; [ed.] Concord Academy, Wesleyan University; [occ.] Interpreter/Translator, Spanish and Portuguese; [memb.] The Living Bank, Association of Legal Translators and Interpreters of Massachusetts; [hon.] High Honors (Wesleyan University), Phi Beta Kappa, Dean's List; [pers.] I am strongly influenced by my roots in Cuba and Mexico. My great, great grandfather was a Cuban poet, Jose Maria Heredia. My poems are inner dreams, slim moments of completion spoken from a voice of passion and clarity within, in which I offer myself. [a.] Newcastle, NH.

GILBERT, ALPHONSE M.
[b.] January 3, 1952, Lynchburg, VA; [p.] Ethel M. and Joe C. Gilbert (deceased); [m.] Deborah Kittredge Gilbert, March 18, 1988; [occ.] Quality Assurance Analyst U.S. Army Europe (civilian); [memb.] Deutsche Alpenverein (German Alps Hiking Club); [pers.] Yesterday's sins are today's alternate life styles; Today's vices are tomorrow's mores and tomorrow we'll dream of yesterday. [a.] Wiesloch, West Germany.

GILBERT, MAUREEN
[pen.] Maureen Regnier; [b.] January 14, 1971, Mayerthorpe, Alberta; [p.] Ed and Maggie Regnier; [m.] Shawn, October 2, 1993; [ed.] Parkland Composite High; [occ.] Dietary Aide, J. King Extendicare, plus becoming Vet. Assistant; [hon.] Creative Writing in school; [oth. writ.] I just write poems for pleasure at home. I have never considered publishing my poems till I entered "The Little Filly"; [pers.] I was raised as an outfitter's daughter so the beauty of the mountains, horses, and wild animals have influenced most of my writing. [a.] Kinsella, AB, CAN.

GILBREATH, ALLAN F.
[pen.] Allan F. Gilbreath; [b.] February 12, 1962, Houston, TX; [m.] Doris Woo-Gilbreath, April 24, 1988; [ed.] Memphis State University; [occ.] Property Tax Consultant; [memb.] Institute of Property Taxation; [oth. writ.] Published in the American Poetry Anthology 1982 and the American Poetry Anthology 1983. [a.] Memphis, TN.

GILLIAM, D.R.
[b.] October 27, 1946, Russellville, KY; [p.] W.D. and Roberta Gilliam; [ed.] Adairville High School; [occ.] Electrician Helper. [a.] Russellville, KY.

GILLIES, KEITH M.
[b.] April 1, 1958, New Orleans, LA; [p.] Winston and Diane Gillies; [m.] Denise Nebel, March 29, 1980; [ch.] Amy (8) and Blake (6); [ed.] BA University of New Orleans and MBA Tulane University; [occ.] Financial Consultant; [memb.] American Society of CLU and ChFC, St. John's Planning and Zoning Commission; [hon.] Dean's List, Beta Gamma Sigma; [oth. writ.] None published; [pers.] Loved ones inspire my writing. [a.] LaPlace, LA.

GILLINGHAM, LISA MARLENE
[b.] February 23, 1977, James Paton Memorial Hosp. Gardner, Nfld.; [p.] Gerald and Cindy Gillingham; [ed.] Grade 10 -grade 11 in September; [occ.] Student; [memb.] The Pentecostal Church; [hon.] Received a $200.00 award a forty dollar award plus a couple of trophies; [oth. writ.] Several poems never sent any for publish. A song that I've sung many times in church; [pers.] I enjoy writing stories and poems. [a.] Nfld. CAN.

GINZEL, LAVELLE
[b.] December 29, 1935, Caldwell, TX; [p.] Rudolph and Ida Frieda; [m.] Alvin, November 11, 1979; [ch.] Daryl Massey and (stepsons Al and Daniel Ginzel); [ed.] Caldwell High School graduate; [occ.] Housewife; [memb.] VFW Auxiliary, American Legion Auxiliary; [hon.] First place - Radio Jingle Contest and first place cook off contest; [pers.] This is the first poetry contest that I have entered and I am pleased to have my poem published in your book of poetry. [a.] Byran, TX.

GIONTI, TONIMARIE A.
[b.] August 2, 1968, Meadville, PA; [p.] Clement and Josephine Gionti; [ed.] BA in Speech, Language, and Hearing Pathology; [occ.] Bar tender (graduate school soon); [oth. writ.] A private collection of my poems; [pers.] I write about the sadness in my life and life in general. [a.] Meadville, PA.

GLADIS, JENNIFER E.
[b.] February 6, 1971, Barberton, OH; [ed.] Rocky River High School, Bowling Green State University; [oth. writ.] Several poems published in high school and college literary anthologies; [pers.] The poem "One Dream" was inspired by pianist and singer Michael Feinstein. I hope that others will enjoy this poem as much as he does. [a.] Rocky River, OH.

GLASS, EVELYN H.
[pen.] Evelyn H. Glass; [b.] September 25, 1915, Brooklyn, NY; [p.] William and Mary Hellman (nee Gallant); [m.] Herman (deceased 9/88), July 24, 1938; [ch.] William Marc, Thomas Eugene, (grandsons-Matthew, Andrew, Alexander); [ed.] BA Brooklyn College, MS City College of New York and PhD program Yeshiva University; [occ.] School Psychologist New York City (retired Oct. 18); [memb.] Brandeis Women's Association, Amnesty International, GreenPeace, World Wildlife, C.F.I.D.S. Association, Beth Chaverim Temple; [hon.] BA Magna cum Laude, Phi Beta Kappa, Psi Chi, High School Lating medal (gold); [oth. writ.] Previous poems not submitted for publication but essays have been printed in school magazines - high school PTA; [pers.] My literary efforts have reflected my deep concern for respecting human rights in every part of the world as well as the protection of plant and animal life. [a.] Virginia Beach, VA.

GLEBO, JOSEPH
[ed.] Provided through study of classical literature: Oscar Wilde Aeschylus, Christopher Marlowe, H.D. Thoreau, J.D. Salinger; [occ.] Following the word of Him; [memb.] American Theatre Wing, Celebrity Services; [hon.] Life and love is the greatest Honor of All; [oth. writ.] Play "Emotions in Motion", p[oem-"Aesthetic's Artist", short story - "Not with a Wimper, But Out With a Bark, Charlie"; [pers.] Art for Art's Sake". The masterpiece arises from the wholehearted artist who is lacking conscience of Cause and Effect, Opinions of Others and sales of Aspirations. [a.] Hyannis, MA.

GLOCK, MILTON F.V., SR.
[b.] July 7, 1918, Baltimore, MD; [p.] Katherine Elizabeth Erker Glock and George Adam Glock, Sr.; [m.] Elizabeth Shackleton Glock, September 26, 1942; [ch.] Milton F.V. Glock Jr. (Fred), Elizabeth Mabel Binker Glock Hughes (Binker); [ed.] BS Chemistry, Washington College; Post-grad course Wayne University; Post-grad seminar Vanderbilt University; [occ.] Retired Chemist, The B.F. Goodrich Chemical Company; [memb.] Emeritus member American Chemical Society, Masonic Order, St. Luke's Episcopal Church; [hon.] Honorable Order of Kentucky Colonels, Past-Chairman, Louisville Section, American Chemical Society; [oth. writ.] "The Chemist Holmes" in INVESTIGATIONS, Vol. 1, No.2 "5:30 Appointment (The Wort)", private printing; many poems and sketches not submitted for publication; [pers.] The frequent trips from Louisville, KY to Atlanta, GA have had a strange effect on me. I always think of the terrible conditions the civil war soldiers faced. It is poetic country for me. [a.] Middleton, KY.

GOLDSMITH, LILIAN
[b.] April 21, 1922, Kennedy, SASK. CAN; [p.] Lee and Lil Smith; [m.] Wes, July 1, 1946; [ch.] Ronald Murray, Judy Linda, Gordon Keith, Roger Dennis; [ed.] Grade 12, Accounting Course - Success Business School, Regina, SASK; [occ.] Early years - Bookkeeper for four years homemaker for 47 years; [memb.] United Church taught Sunday school many years: Secretary of local Agricultural Society; leader of 4H Club; presently treasurer of Women's Institute; [hon.] Gold medal in seniors poetry competition for S.E. Sask Zone, I used the same poem as I entered in your competition; [oth. writ.] My efforts began in childhood as I just enjoyed rhythm. I have continued to play abound with poetry, but never took part in competition until three years ago, it had never been a goal as I did not think I had the talent; [pers.] I try to take each day as it comes and be thankful for all our blessings. I try to be a good friend and neighbor. [a.] Sask. CAN.

GOLDSMITH, ROBERT
[b.] December 24, 1919, Pawnee City, NE; [p.] George and Grace McClure Goldsmith; [ed.] Falls City High School, University of Nebraska; [occ.] Retired, most recently senior programmer analyst, University of Southern California. [a.] Cedar City, UT.

GOLDSTEIN, MELISSA
[b.] January 7, 1981, New York, NY; [p.] Alan and Ronnie Goldstein; [ed.] Miralesie Intermediate School now in 7th grade; [occ.] Student; [memb.] P.V. Musical Children's Theatre P.V. Art Center; [hon.] Honor Roll, Winner in Reflections Contest and two years in a row and Project Poetry; [oth. writ.] Poem in a school magazine, write poetry and plays for fun; [pers.] I think of mu poetry as a prism, reflecting the lights and colors of my thoughts - for others to share in their meaning. [a.] CA.

GOLER, NATE H.
[b.] May 23, 1916, Atlanta, GA; [p.] Sara and Oscar Goler; [m.] Evelyn Friedman Davis Goler, June 5, 1977; [ch.] Bernie, Steven, David, Michael, and Shawn; [ed.] Boy's High,, Memphis State (Creative Writing); [occ.] Business owner retired; [memb.] Jewish Community Center, Beth Sholom Synagogue, RSVP member (volunteer organization), J.C.C. Writer's Club President; [hon.] Pres. J.C.C. Men's Club, Baron Hirsch Men's Club, Beth Sholom Men's Club, Man of the Year award of each of above, volunteer of the year 1993, J.C.C. and Editor of Beth Sholom Bulletin (4 years); [oth. writ.] Many poems and editorials in Synagogue Bulletin: Articles in Southern Jewish Heritage Magazine. Plays and skits for J.C.C. Senior Clubs, many poems and family histories; [pers.] I like to write on incidents from a happy childhood. Also, my personal experiences in business. My fellow man, human interest items. Poems are my strong point. I believe all people are basically good and can find this good in expressions in their writing. [a.] Memphis, TN.

GOMEZ, TAWNYA
[pen.] Tawnya Gomez; [b.] September 4, 1978, Gallup, NM; [p.] Jay and Shirley Gomez; [occ.] Student; [hon.] Several school related awards; [oth. writ.] Nothing published; [pers.] I believe in the old fashioned morality. The Bible. [a.] Gallup, NM.

GONCE, LESLEY V.
[pen.] Gini Gonce; [b.] June 27, 1945, Lekester, Eng.; [p.] Mary M. Vivian and Albert Leslie Hicks; [m.] Divorced; [ch.] Julie, Jamie, Tami, Andy, Kym; [ed.] MEd; [occ.] Educational - Counselor/Consultant Aslan/Eagles Associates; [memb.] Central MA Austin Society Director - PR; [hon.] Psi Chi Psychology award, Magna cum Laude; [oth. writ.] Several poems published locally I write several newsletters, for non-profit organizations on disability issues; [pers.] I was born in England. Emigrated to America, when I was 17. I have travelled extensively throughout the U.S. and Europe. Writing, for me, has always been an emotional outlet. [a.] Southbridge, MA.

GONZALES, JAUIEL ARMANDO
[b.] July 25, 1978, Kingsville, TX; [p.] George Armando and Carmen Lopez Gonzales; [ed.] Presbyterian Pan American School; [pers.] I like to show people the beauty in the chaos that surrounds them.

"If Love Were an Angel" is dedicated to Nohemy Uribe. [a.] Kingsville, TX.

GOOD, PAULINE EDNA (NEE KRYSKO)
[b.] August 4, 1940, Winnipeg, Manitoba, CAN; [m.] October 30, 1959; [ch.] Richard Michael Good; [ed.] College; [occ.] Housewife - Volunteer.

GOODALL, JOHNNIE JANELLE
[pen.] J. Goodall; [b.] October 6, 1926, Baytown, TX; [p.] Johnnie Lawson and Gertrude Dickens Fulton; [m.] Lonny Wayne Goodall, December 31, 1979; [ch.] Pamela Kay Millsap and Abbie Nickerson; [ed.] Lee College, Rose College; [occ.] Retired, Part-time Church Secretary, St. John's United Methodist Church; [hon.] Dean's List at Rose College; [oth. writ.] Many, but for my own enjoyment; [pers.] I only write when I have been greatly influenced by something or someone. [a.] Baytown, TX.

GOODWIN, STEVE
[b.] January 29, 1981, Silver Spring, MD; [p.] Rachael Goodwin (grandparents-Mr. and Mrs. Ronald Goodwin and Uncle Randall Goodwin); [ed.] 6th grade current student; [hon.] Geography Bee Winner, Essay Contest Winner, National Little League Minor League Pitcher; [oth. writ.] Songs - Rappers Reputation, Other Side, DaBulls. [a.] Hagerstown, MD.

GORDEN, ERIC
[b.] August 29, 1979, Laurinburg, NC; [p.] Teresa and Frank M. Gorden, Jr.; [ed.] Freshman-Scotland High School; [hon.] Jr. Beta Club, Academic Achievement Award, Scotland Co., IRA Award. [a.] Laurinburg, NC.

GORDON, CARRIE
[b.] November 5, 1975, Bogota, Colombia; [p.] John and Margaret Gordon; [ed.] Presently a senior-Cranford High, New Jersey School of the Arts (NJSA), University of the Arts; [occ.] Student; [memb.] Peer Minister St. Helen's Church, Cranford H.S. Marching Band - Model UN-Varsity Field Hockey; [hon.] Who's Who in American High Schools - Scholarship to NJSA; [oth. writ.] Several poems in school literary magazine - article published in local paper - poetry displayed at Rape Awareness exhibition; [pers.] The purpose of pain, of tears, of breathing is the chance to let another's breath leave skid marks on the insides of your soul. [a.] Cranford, NJ.

GORE, RUBY JOLENE
[b.] September 12, 1979, Ada, OK; [p.] John H. and Kathy (Allen) Gore; [ed.] 8th grader at Latta Junior High School; [occ.] Student (4-H Club Reporter); [memb.] Camp Fire Boys and Girls, 4-H Clubs of America, ABBIT Club; [hon.] Many awards in 4-H and Camp Fire. I received the "President's Academic Fitness Award" in 6th grade from President Bush; [oth. writ.] None published; [pers.] I love to write poetry and stories. And I'm honored and excited about being a semi-finalist as this is the 1st contest I've ever entered. Creative Writing is one of my favorite pasttimes. [a.] Ada, OK.

GOREN, APRYL LORRAINE
[b.] January 10, 1970, Culver City, CA; [p.] Tonya Kay Best; [m.] Eric Neal, November 19, 1991; [ch.] Nicholas Neal Goren; [ed.] Garey High School, Chaffey College; [occ.] Pediatric Nurse, Rancho Peds Rancho Cucamonga, CA; [memb.] American Heart Association, Honor Thesbein Society; [hon.] Geriatric Nursing, High School Honor Roll; [oth. writ.] Several poems and articles. [a.] San Diego, CA.

GORIN, CHRISTINE
[pen.] Christine Frances Gorin; [b.] December 12, 1962, Georgetown, ONT; [p.] Hazel and Ken Gorin; [m.] Brett Poe, July 15, 1994; [ed.] Georgetown District H.S.; [occ.] Inside Sales Assistant, Sonco Steel Tube, Brampton; [memb.] Brampton Musical Society, Big Sisters of Peel; [hon.] Gourmet Cooking (highest marks in the school for one year); [oth. writ.] Several poems and stories not yet published; [pers.] I've always loved to write it is truly my favorite pastime. My dream is to one day have the opportunity to write for a greeting card company. For now, it is a thrill to have my poem published in your book. I hope that is brings pleasure to all who read it. [a.] Brampton, ONT.

GRACE, JONATHAN W.
[b.] February 4, 1941, Corning, NY; [p.] Helen and Walter Grace; [m.] Divorced; [ch.] Christopher Jon, Jeffrey Andersen, Peter Oren; [ed.] Painted Post (NY), High School, University of Rochester; [occ.] Electrical Cost Estimator; [pers.] I am searching for an understandable voice that captures the essence of the complexity that surrounds us and that is within us. [a.] Norristown, PA.

GRACI, LYNN
[b.] November 17, 1980, Long Island, NY; [p.] Fran and Larry Graci; [ed.] Now attending Vero Beach Junior High School; [occ.] Student; [hon.] Three presidential academic fitness awards, Duke University Talent Identification Program; [oth. writ.] School Reporter for Beachland Elementary School to the Vero Beach Press Journal. [a.] Vero Beach, FL.

GRAHAM, DIXIE B.
[pen.] Dixie B. Graham; [b.] October 12, 1937, Laurinburg, NC; [p.] Mr. and Mrs. George W. Butler; [m.] Tobey D., January 9, 1965; [ch.] Ricky Allen, Vicky Lynn, Brian Keith; [ed.] Laurinburg High School, Richmond Technical College; [occ.] Teacher Assistant (Second grade); [memb.] Writers Network of N.C., North Carolina Poetry Society; [hon.] Many first place awards for Art and write for school and church; [oth. writ.] Won third prize for Farm-City Celebration (was published (story) in a book distributed to all schools for resource; [pers.] When I get inspired and sometimes it's just one word or maybe and incident, the poetry or story just seems to flow out of me. [a.] Laurinburg, NC.

GRAHAM, MONIQUE Y.
[b.] December 20, 1965, Jacksonville, FL; [p.] Ms. Juanita Lewis; [ed.] Wolfson Sr. High, American Career Training, FL Community of Jacksonville; [occ.] College Student; [memb.] Jesus Christ of Latter Day Saints (2nd Word); [oth. writ.] I have three poems at the moment. Two of them have made it to the semi-finals; [pers.] My poems are based on the things that influence or hinder mankind. Someday, I hope there is world peace. [a.] Jacksonville, FL.

GRANT, LAURIE
[b.] June 19, 1980, Bethel Park, PA; [p.] Joan and Laird Grant; [ed.] John McMillan Elementary Independence Middle School; [occ.] Student; [memb.] Newspaper staff, Church Fellowship; [hon.] Distin-

guished Honors in school, first place award Pittsburgh Commission for Women Essay on Contemporary Women Leading US into the '90's; [oth. writ.] A Golden Day, Christmas Poem, and others; [pers.] I let my feelings show through in my writing. It is the way I have found to express myself. [a.] Bethel Park, PA.

GRANT, LOLA E.
[b.] August 23, 1905, Arcola, IL; [p.] Fred R. and Ethel Black Ehrhart; [m.] Deceased, September 1930; [ch.] Shirley Ann and Charlene; [ed.] Graduated from University of Illinois -curriculum of Nutrition and Dietetics; [occ.] Teacher, Assistant Dietitian, Food Service Supervisor; [memb.] NRTA, IRTA, University of Illinois Alumni Association, Baptist Church; [oth. writ.] One Family History, three booklets: I Remember, Poems and Verse of Sense and Nonsense, and More Memories. These I have had printed to give to family and friends; [pers.] The poems I write are mostly spontaneous -- they practically write themselves. I've always poetry. I had two poetry courses in college. [a.] Urbana, IL.

GRAY, DAVID M.
[b.] May 18, 1963, Washington, DC; [p.] David and Barbara Gray; [ch.] Laura Natasha; [ed.] Largo Senior High; [occ.] Severity Police U.S. Air Force; [memb.] Bolling AFB Speaker's Bureau; [hon.] Security Policeman of the Year 1988, Dover AFB DE; [oth. writ.] Success of a Black General; [pers.] I dedicate this poem to my parents who guided me in the right direction. My grandfather David A, Gray, who was very special to me, my grandparents Robert and Rose Harley and Dr. M.L. King, Jr. who loved all mankind. Praise the Lord. [a.] Capital Hgts., MD.

GRAYSON, TAMARRA MICHELLE
[pen.] T. Michelle Grayson; [b.] March 13, 1976, San Bernardino, CA; [p.] Jerome and Linda Grayson; [ed.] Senior: Newport/Pacific High School; [occ.] Singer/songwriter; [memb.] Various heirloom plate companies; [hon.] The Editor's Choice award - The National Library of Poetry, 1993; [oth. writ.] "A Million More" published in, "Wind in the Night Sky" 1993, various, unpublished poems, stories and songs; [pers.] This poem is dedicated to: Sabrina, Michael, Rick, Dean, Lennita, Annie, and Damarra Ashley Sanchez! I'd like to thank my friends, Wendy, Dawnn, Cheri, Kim, Kristy, Robert, Diane, and my parents! [a.] CA.

GREEN, ADAM
[b.] October 23, 1971, Connecticut; [pers.] The beginning and end of time is but a breath for eternity. [a.] Southington, CT.

GREEN, CANDACE
[pen.] Candace L. Green; [b.] December 9, 1976, Kansas City, MO; [p.] Victoria and Robert Green; [ed.] South High; [occ.] Student; [oth. writ.] Life for minorities today, many poems and two books; [pers.] I thank Jehovah God for giving me the talent to write because without it I'd be nothing today. [a.] Plattsmouth, NE.

GREEN, COREY VAUGHAN
[b.] May 21, 1970; [p.] Patricia and Willie Green; [ed.] BS in Information Systems, BS in Finance, Certificate in African-American Studies; [memb.] President of the Black Business Society; [oth. writ.] Poems published in the BBS Times; [pers.] Information is the Key to Life. [a.] Mitchellville, MD.

GREEN, JANE CAMIE
[pers.] To the one who added the brilliant wonder to my world. This poem is dedicated in loving memory of Brian Stephen Edmondson, June 27, 1965 - August 15, 1991. Someday our souls will touch. For all you gave, and for all you denied, thank you. Loving you still - forever - me.

GREEN, MINA
[b.] February 17, 1912, Hilly, LA; [p.] Thomas A. and Eva Lavance; [m.] James H., October 3, 1934; [ed.] Ruston High School, LA Tech, University of Texas; [occ.] English and Social Studies teacher in Junior High; [memb.] Delta Kappa Gamma, NARFE, TRTA, Church Women United, Meals on Wheels, AARP; [hon.] Three terms as TX Silver Haired Legislator, Valley Forge Teacher of the Year, TRTA Grand Prix award, personalities of the south 1992.

GREEN, TIM
[pen.] Tim Green; [b.] March 19, 1973, Regina; [p.] Ernie and Sandra Green; [ed.] Henry Wise Wood High School; [occ.] Child Care worker; [memb.] American Radio Relay League; [hon.] Diploma; [oth. writ.] Small collection of poems, working towards a book and collection; [pers.] To enjoy the battle of the mind, explore, manipulate, search and destroy and control it. [a.] Bragg Creek, Alberta, CAN.

GREENE, DARRYL K.
[b.] August 20, 1941, Bridgeton, NJ; [p.] Mary Elizabeth and Kenneth John Greene; [m.] Rita Ann, September 11, 1965; [ch.] Kimberely Ann Sedeyn and Brian John Greene; [ed.] Graduated Bridgeton High School, U.S.N. School of Meteorology and Camden County Police Academy; [occ.] Past Chief of Police, Lawrence Township, NJ; [memb.] Past President of Local #231, P.B.A. (Police Benev. Association), National Knife Collectors Association; [hon.] NJ State Attorney General Merit Award (police academy), Two distinguished service medals for saving lives (police); [oth. writ.] Other poetry, this is my second acceptance (N.L.O.P.); [pers.] It is reward enough that others who read my words through poetry would enjoy them as much as I enjoy writing them. [a.] Fairton, NJ.

GREGORY, MYRA M.
[b.] September 21, 1912, New York, Ny; [p.] Thomas and Anna Gregory (nee Collins); [ed.] Maxwell Teachers Training School, Brooklyn College BS Education 1940, MA History 1952, University Extension Conservatory Teacher Training Piano 1965 and History/Analysis-Music 1967; [occ.] Teacher, NYC Bd. of Education retired; [memb.] International Association for Childhood Education; Association for Supervision/Curriculum Development; Teachers/Writers Collaborative; Center for Study of Presidency; American String Teachers Association; [hon.] Teacher of the Year 1973, Outstanding Teacher Award, 1977, Ecumenism Citation 1983, Marquis Who's Who Vols. 24 in East, 3rd in Education, 4th in Religion, and 18th among of American Women; [oth. writ.] Local church newsletters, Sunday School Primary Dept. "Have You Heard", Parents newsletter-"Know What". Black history bulletin (local church Primary Sunday School Dept. Annual) re: Black History month; [pers.] Love can be found everywhere for God is present everywhere. [a.] Brooklyn, NY.

GREIG, MARILYN A.
[b.] December 27, 1936, Grand Rapids, MI; [p.] Lester and Marian Walthorn; [ch.] Jim, Chris, Marty, Andrew, Tom, and Angie; [ed.] Attended Western Michigan University and Misc. computer workshops; [occ.] Owner of "The Write Approach" desktop publishing; [memb.] Board member graphical Visual Arts Dept. of Allegan Vocational Center; [oth. writ.] In my business I write for people who cannot express themselves adequately for various printed publications; [pers.] Writing poetry is a hobby I acquired while working through painful feelings. Poetry helps me keep in touch with my emotional center. I let the feelings flow and trust where these feelings are taking me. [a.] Holland, MI.

GRESHAM, LORI ALENE
[b.] July 30, 1954, Oregon City, OR; [p.] Gustave and Olive Benthin (both deceased); [m.] Divorced; [ch.] Dustin Shane Gresham; ed.] Colton High School, Clackamas Community College; [occ.] Currently homemaker; [memb.] Colton Advent Christian Church, Volunteer at Colton Elementary; [hon.] Graduate with honors, Volunteer of the Month, Employee of the Month, Outstanding Recognition as a teacher's aid; [oth. writ.] First time submitting any of my work; however, many friends have received written pieces or read my work. I thank them for their encouragement to submit an entry; [pers.] This world is filled with beauty that God has blessed us with. It is my life ambition to share this to others whose eyes fail to see. I hope to leave this world better for having been here. [a.] Colton, OR.

GREWALL, SIMRANJIT SINGH
[pen.] Sim Grewall; [b.] October 15, 1978, Lakewood, CA; [p.] Amarishwar Singh and Manjit Kaur Grewall; [pers.] It is a great honor to be selected as a finalist. It will be a great feeling for me as well as my family if I win this nationwide contest. [a.] Buena Park, CA.

GRIESBACH, ALLEN
[b.] September 29, 1972, New Haven, CT; [p.] Carol and Richard Griesbach; [ed.] Tarrant County Community College; [occ.] Warehouse (loading and unloading trucks) and student. [a.] Ft. Worth, TX.

GRIEVE, KAY
[b.] February 2, 1943, England; [p.] Edith and Roland Whitworth; [m.] Divorced, widowed and now living very happily with a wonderful man also widowed; [ch.] Three and one grandson; [ed.] Grade 12 equivalent with 1 year university; [occ.] Housekeeper with law firm in Vancouver; [memb.] Sister Eagle in F.O.E. 20 and associate member of the Royal Canadian Legion Branch 263 and member of the Tenrikyo Women's Association of America; [oth. writ.] This is the first time I have ever submitted one of my poems, although I have written many for family or friends or myself over the years, I have always wanted to write lyrics but unfortunately can't put words on paper to music; [pers.] This poem reflects the commitment I believe is the foundation stone on which to build a happy lasting till death us do part relationship. [a.] Coquitliam, B.C., CAN.

GRIFFIN, PHILIP F.E.
[b.] August 29, 1969, Wilmington, DE; [p.] Philip and Patsy Griffin; [ch.] Avery Griffin; [ed.] BS in Mechanical Engineering; [occ.] Graduate student, University of Delaware; [memb.] A.S.M.E.; [hon.] Graduate Fellowship, University Academic Award Scholarship; [oth. writ.] Various unpublished poems; [pers.] I write to share the thoughts of my mind and relate my experiences with others. [a.] Wilmington, DE>

GROGAN-FAIRCHILD, MARABETH
[b.] December 9, 1948, Hartford, CT; [p.] Raymond and Virginia Grogan; [ch.] Eric Deane and Amy Lynn Fairchild; [ed.] Mt. St. Joseph Academy, Central CT State University BSED and MSED; [occ.] Second grade teacher Emma Hart Willard School; [memb.] Berlin Education Association - CT Education Association - National Education Association; [hon.] Dean's List; [oth. writ.] Personal Poetry Writings; [pers.] I enjoy capturing life's experiences and expressing them through poetry. [a.] Berlin, CT.

GRONAU, GENE
[pen.] Adrian V. Brinsley; [b.] December 1, 1936, Indianapolis, IN; [p.] Robert T. Gronau and Irene C. Unmacht; [m.] Audrey M. Jacobs, July 19, 1959; [ed.] Dubuque High School, Iowa State College, Sacramento State College; [occ.] Herumwerkelnmeister (Retire Insurance Executive); [memb.] USTA, MENSA, AARP, IFA; [hon.] Dean's List; [oth. writ.] And The Angels Laughed, Angioma Among The Larks, The Spanish Dagger, Chronicles (all unpublished); [pers.] As Philip Larkin observed, "Poetry is like trying to remember a tune you're forgotten; all corrections are attempts to get nearer the forgotten tune." [a.] Walnut Creek, CA.

GROTTS, JUNIOR K.
[b.] June 9, 1924, Chicago, IL; [p.] Latheral and Helen Grotts; [m.] Olga L., September 1, 1945; [ch.] Kenneth Latheral and wife Lisa - grandsons Ryne and Lucas; [ed.] Fenger High, National Radio Institute; [occ.] Retired Electronic Technician; [memb.] International Brotherhood of Magicians; [hon.] Order of Merlin, IBM; [oth. writ.] Song, titled - "I Want You Close"; [pers.] I try to remember the good things in life and forget about the bad ones. It is the things that I haven't done that bothers me. [a.] Las Vegas, NV.

GRUBER, BRANDI LEANNE
[b.] August 5, 1977, Thompson Manitoba, CAN; [p.] Charles and Bonny Gruber; [ed.] Grade 11 at R.D. Parker Collegiate Thompson Manitoba; [oth. writ.] I write for personal enjoyment or for friends; [pers.] I try to capture as many feelings as I can, so others may relate to my writing and apply it to some of their own experiences. [a.] Thompson, Manitoba, CAN.

GRUM, ROSE
[b.] August 26, 1929, Chicago, IL; [p.] Anna Primozich and John Grum; [ed.] B.A. Education; [occ.] Teacher and 4-H Club leader - St. Paul - Our Lady of Vilna School; [memb.] 4-H Club, NSTA, Audubon Society, Air and Space Museum and N.C.E.A.; [hon.] Nominations - Foundation for Excellence in Teaching - Math and Science Academy - 4-H Club - 5 Year Volunteer - Presidential Environment Certificate; [oth. writ.] Several other poems for publication; [pers.] Writings include my religious statements and moral attitudes. [a.] Chicago, IL.

GRUNDY, ROBERT L.
[b.] October 20, 1950, Pasadena, CA; [ed.] BA, MA English and MS Library Science; [occ.] University Librarian and San Francisco radio personality; [oth. writ.] Two small press books of poetry: Moon Repair and 10 X Black and various periodicals plus one short story published. [a.[] Stinson Beach, CA.

GSCHEIDLE, FRANK WILLIAM
[pen.] William Harrison; [b.] January 15, 1975, Smithtown, NY; [p.] Pam Larsen and Frank Gscheidle, Sr.; [ed.] Newfield High School; [occ.] Medical student - United States Army Reserve; [oth. writ.] Many unpublished poems and short stories; [pers.] Poetry is my therapy; like so many others, I'd be lost without it. I wish to thank my family and friends for their support, especially my love Stefani. A special thanks to a great poet - N.O. Lacey. [a.] Selden, NY.

GUADALUPE, ALMA D.
[b.] October 8, 1949, Caguas, PR; [p.] Luciano Guadalupe and Cualyn Montanez; [ed.] Gautier Benitez High School, University of Puerto Rico, Thomas Nelson Community College; [occ.] Police officer Department of Veterans Affairs; [memb.] Fraternal Order of Police and Prevention Walking Club; [hon.] Reader of the Year, Honor graduate-Detective School, Cum Laude graduate Police Science degree, numerous armed forces commendations including good conduct medal; [oth. writ.] Poetry book (Sea of Sadness) published by Todd and Honeywell, Ny, (Just Feelings, 1990). Several poems published in books and magazines over the country. Song (How) by Rainbow Records taken from second book; [pers.] Strong feelings such as sorrow, broken hearts, deep from within tears heal sooner when they are poured out to the world. After the storm, the skies are bluer and our hearts is ready to love and enjoy life again. [a.] Jamaica Plain, MA.

GUCINSKI, ADOLPH
[b.] Germany; [ed.] Ph.D. State University of New York in Buffalo; [occ.] Writing; [oth. writ.] Work in progress (searching for agent): novel, tragic, political, macabre, pyramid construction, Key West; [pers.] Significant Human Beings (alphabetically): Karen Clemens, George Wilhelm Friedrich Hegel, Barbara Kania, Karl Marx, Deborah Seifert, Dimitri Shostakovich, Meryl Stratford, Kurt Vonnegut, Sidney Willhelm. [a.] Key West, FL.

GUM, LORRI
[b.] May 15, 1961, Fairfield, WA; [p.] Glen Meredith and Betty Hanson; [m.] Thomas, Jr., October 17, 1981; [ch.] Robert, Richard, Wyatt Gum; [occ.] Housewife; [memb.] Inland Northwest Zoological Society; [hon.] Editor's Choice award for Outstanding Achievement in Poetry; [oth. writ.] To My Love, published in Wind In the Night Sky, and Our Special One, published in The Coming of Dawn; [pers.] I wrote this poem for my father, my poems express my feelings about the way I feel. [a.] Worley, ID.

GUMBMAN, PAMELA
[b.] June 21, 1974, Passaic, NJ; [p.] William and Eileen Gumbman; [ed.] Rutherford High School graduate attending college; [oth. writ.] Remember When, Just Another Glance, California Love, New Year's Without You; [pers.] "To My Uncle" is not fictional. It was written about my uncle Jimmy who I was close to. [a.] Rutherford, NJ.

GUNGLIELMETTI, MARCI
[b.] August 19, 1977, Salt Lake City, UT; [p.] Kjeld Guglielmetti and Ann Douglas; [ed.] Junior at Boise High School; [oth. writ.] I have written many other poems, but none of them have ever been read or published; [pers.] Through poetry I can express my passion for love and nature. I write about things that touch my heart and make me feel. [a.] Boise, ID.

GUNDERSON, JULIE M.
[b.] January 1, 1915, Sisseton, SD; [p.] Ole & Beret Benson; [m.] Victor Steen, June 28, 1939 and Marion Gunderson March 15, 1981; [ch.] Curtis Benson Steen and LouAnn Ruth Carpenter; [ed.] Grade school-rural Sisseton, Sisseton High School grad. 1934; [occ.] Housewife, store clerk and secretary; [memb.] Senior Citizens Federation; [oth. writ.] Since school days, I have written poetry on different subjects; [pers.] I have found that life is only what I make it. My hobbies are: quilting, making aprons and raising flowers. [a.] Twin Falls, ID.

GUNNELL, GRACE (GEAN)
[b.] September 27, 1900, Roe, AK; [p.] William and Myrtle Ross Gean; [m.] Andrew, August 20, 1925; [ch.] 5 boys and 5 girls ages 45-67; [ed.] Roe High School, one year college; [occ.] Retired teacher taught 12 years; [memb.] United Methodist; [hon.] Golden Poets award, have read many of my poems at public gatherings; [oth. writ.] Stories published in Stuttgart Leader; [pers.] Very much a lover of fun, lover of nature, in general a lover of life and my poems express these. [a.] Stuttgart, AK.

GURNEY, GEORGE ROBERT
[pen.] George Gurney; [b.] October 23, 1933, Seneca, KS; [p.] Datha Alice and Charles Marion Gurney, Sr.; [m.] Shirley Joyce, June 21, 1953; [ed.] 12th grade National School of Aeronautics 09/60, numerous training classes at "TWA"; [occ.] Medically retired; [memb.] Immanual Lutheran Church, "Make Today Count" (cancer support group) and "TWA" Seniors club; [hon.] Numerous awards from employer "TWA", American Cancer Society Bike-A-Thon (2 years); [oth. writ.] Three published in local paper (Newstime, Wentzville, MO), ten unpublished each (general and personalized); [pers.] "Expect a miracle - miracles do happen." [a.] Wentzville, MO.

GUSTIN, EDITH (GREER)
[pen.] Greer Gustin; [b.] February 24, 1822, Chino, CA; [p.] Joseph Bruce and Nellie (Penney) Greer; [m.] Roy G., May 9, 1941; [ch.] Linda, Wayne, Stephen, Richard, and James; [occ.] Homemaker, Sales trainer and recruiter; [memb.] Christian and Missionary Alliane Church, Christian Broadcasting Network; [oth. writ.] Inspirational and motivation articles for a sales paper. Published my own newsletter for sales organization; [pers.] I always want to encourage and help everyone I meet to be their very best, to believe they have real value and to stand tall. We only pass this way once! [a.] Silverton, OR.

GUTHRIE, SUSANNA
[pers.] In 2nd year ecology at the University of Calgary we did an experiment. You place one male and one female flour beetle into a jar of flour and you wait. First there are two, then four, then 16, then 100

or more. The beetles consume their resources and reproduce without end, until eventually they can't survive in the waste they, themselves created. There are 100, then 20, then 2, then none. [a.] Calgary, CAN.

GUTHRIE, TARA S.
[b.] November 13, 1969, Salt Lake City, UT; [p.] Lavinia Guthrie; [ed.] B.NM.Ed. University of North Carolina - Chapel Hill 1993, East Carteret High School 1988; [occ.] Elementary and Middle School Music Teacher; [memb.] North Carolina Music Educators Association, Music Educators National Conference, UNC General Alumni Association, Carteret Chorale; [hon.] Dean's List, Danforth award; [pers.] Music has a way of expressing the inexpressible, of touching hearts and uplifting the spirit. [a.] Beaufort, NC.

HABERKORN, KELLIE
[b.] January 27, 1977; [hon.] Award-National Council of State Garden Clubs Poetry Contest National winner; [oth. writ.] Several poems here and there; [pers.] I write only from my heart. [a.] Richfield, OH.

HAGGARD, DARLEEN MARIE
[b.] December 19, 1954, Redding, CA; [p.] Chet and Darleen Randall and Desmond and Myrtle Keaton; [ch.] Thomasina Marie Baker Houk and Daniel Erwin Baker; [ed.] California GED; [occ.] Disabled Venetian Blind Tech. and Factory Seamstress; [oth. writ.] With Fears in Her Eyes, To All My Kids, To My Son, To My Daughter (and too many unpublished poems to count); [pers.] When you find out you are dying from a lung disease as I am or anything. You have a compelling urge to be heard and to lovingly touch everyone in hopes your words will help someone and let people know who you are though words. [a.] Smithville, TN.

HAHN, ELLYN
[pen.] Melissa Rose; [b.] September 3, 1953, Cleveland, OH; [p.] Shirley and Daniel; [ch.] Genoah; [ed.] Orange High School, Cuyahoga Community College; [occ.] Student; [oth. writ.] Small collection of poems, not published; [pers.] Poetry is choreography of life, life itself is poetic and precious. Every person or experience in life tells its story and is in itself a poem. Poetry also conveys our beliefs. [a.] Cleveland, OH.

HALE, JEFFREY WADE
[b.] July 14, 1974; [b.] Marion, IL; [p.] Thomas and Lavonia Hale; [ed.] Marion High School, John A. Logan College; [occ.] Disc Jockey at WGGH AM 1150 radio; [memb.] Williamson County Historical Society, Southern IL Writers Guild; [hon.] First place in Drama, 1st, 2nd and 3rd place in Song Lyrics at 1993, John A. Logan College Writing Contest; [oth. writ.] Several country western and pop ballads, stage pieces, locally published poetry; [pers.] Whether the emotion be happiness or sadness, I try to use my God given gifts to express it. What you are is God's gift to you. What you become is your gift to God. [a.] Marion, IL.

HALE, JOANNA
[b.] February 13, 1978, Kansas City, MI; [memb.] Thespian; [oth. writ.] Only in school literacy magazines; [pers.] You're in for a change, so get ready because here I come. [a.] Overland Park, KS.

HALL, BECKY
[b.] October 28, 1977, Fort Smith, AK; [p.] Ronnie and Jane Hall; [ed.] Caddo High School; [hon.] Honor Roll. [a.] Kenefic, OK.

HALL, KELSO L. (KELLY)
[b.] May 30, 1931, Brownstown, IN; [p.] George Dewey and Mary Hall; [m.] Joy L., July 5, 1974; [occ.] USAF Retired; [pers.] This poems was written about myself and the problems I encountered in life and my understanding of same. Poetry brightens my life and make my days fuller and richer with love of my fellow person. [a.] Mulberry, FL.

HALL, LAURA K.
[b.] August 3, 1971, Red Bay, AL; [p.] Marlis and Judy Hall; [ed.] New Site High School, Northeast Mississippi Community College, University of Mississippi; [occ.] Certified English Teacher; [memb.] Auburn Baptist Church, Sigma Tau Delta, Pi Delta Phi, Kappa Delta Pi, The Golden Key National Honor Society; [hon.] Dean's List, Chancellor's List; [pers.] My poetry comes from my heart. I write what my emotions lead me to write. [a.] New Site, MS.

HALLAHAN, EILEEN R.
[b.] May 19, Dorchester, MA; [p.] Helen J. and Jeremiah J. Hallahan; [occ.] Retired Stenographer; [hon.] Boston Seniority's Poet of the Month Oct. 1993. [a.] Dorchester, MA.

HALLMAN, ROBERT
[b.] March 12, 1957, Chicago, IL; [p.] James and Gracie Hallman; [m.] Barbara, September 27, 1976; [ch.] Timothy Lee, Joshua Wayne, Matthew Dewayne, Amy Hallman; [ed.] Booneville High; [pers.] To express the wonders in the world through my poems. [a.] Mountain View, AK.

HAMANN, DOROTHY A.
[b.] Kodaikanal, India; [p.] Missionary parents; [occ.] Retired; [memb.] Christopher Wren Association, National Honor of Poets; [hon.] Editor's Choice award for Sonnet for a water fountain in Distinguished Poets of America; [oth. writ.] Dorothy has had a children's story published but writes poetry mainly. Recently has had poems accepted by the Write Technique and The Amherst Society besides the National Library of Poetry. "To Dance in the Spirit" (30 poems, 29 of them Villanelles) is being published Summer 1993. [a.] Williamsburg, VA.

HAMASHEA, G'YA
[b.] Detroit, MI; [p.] Laneil and Lawrence Moore; [ch.] Rhonda, Tracy, Ronald, Charneil and Choice; [ed.] Wayne County Community College, Mercy College of Detroit; [occ.] Writer and Dreamologist; [oth. writ.] Dreams of The Soul, The Way of Destiny, Herstory in Poetic Form to the Goddess Be The Glory waits for publication; [pers.] My writings are under the influence of the Moon phases, they are inspirational and reflects on what is real. [a.] Detroit, MI.

HAMILTON, BECKY
[b.] January 24, 1980, Madison County, KY; [p.] James and Sharon Hamilton; [ed.] Presently attending Garrard Middle School 8th grade; [memb.] Girl Scouts and 4-H Club.

HAMILTON, CORA
[ed.] Two years of college; [occ.] Retired seamstress; [pers.] Love to write short stories, mostly humor and children books, love to write poetry about love and everyday life. First time having one published. [a.] Shaker Heights, OH.

HAMILTON, MICHAEL J.
[b.] April 18, 1967, Tucson, AZ; [p.] Tom and Shirley Hamilton; [m.] Mary A., December 9, 1986; [ch.] Corie Lynn (22 mos old); [ed.] Thomas W. Harvey High, Central Texas College; [occ.] Squad Leader US Army Infantry; [memb.] Non-Commissioned Officers Association; [hon.] Combat Infantrymans Badge, Army Achievement medal with 6 oak leaf clusters; Kuwaiti Liberation medal; [oth. writ.] Several unpublished poems. [a.] Painesville, OH.

HAMILTON, VITA
[pen.] Vita Hamilton; [b.] May 3, 1905, Royse City, TX; [p.] Mr. and Mrs. J.B. Buck; [m.] Paul, August 29, 1934 (deceased May 3, 1992); [ch.] Two daughters, spouses and four grandchildren; [ed.] BS in Speech and MS in Elementary Education; [occ.] Teaching (32 years); [memb.] Delta Kappa Gamma, Shakespeare Club (Fine Arts Dept.), Music Club, Daughters of America; [hon.] Revolution Teacher of Speech in Adult Education award for Volunteer Service; [oth. writ.] Original songs for children; [pers.] Thoughts that dominate a person's mind exhibit his Christian self-control, moral dignity, attitude toward others, friendliness and conscientious way of life. [a.] Japan.

HAMMER, LINDA LOU
[b.] July 14, 1958. Frankfurt, Germany; [p.] Thomas and Linda Groff; [ch.] Raquel, Wess, and Brandon; [pers.] To write is to feel all that is around you. [a.] Kremmling, CO.

HAMMOND, MELISSA
[b.] October 4, 1979, Houston, TX; [p.] Mark J. Hammond Sr. and June M. Drewry; [ch.] Siblings-Mark J. Jr., Angelina and Jonathan Hammond; [ed.] St, Ambrose Catholic School; [memb.] Hobbies-basketball, volleyball, softball and cheerleading; [hon.] I won a full scholarship for my last year at St. Ambrose; [pers.] I hope this poems does not offend anyone and that it makes people realize what goes on in our world. I dedicate this poem to my loving family and friends. [a.] Houston, TX.

HANCOCK, DAVID
[pen.] Hank, Hanker; [b.] July 18, 1958, St. John's Nfld; [p.] Harold and Ruby Hancock; [m.] Sandra, July 29, 1988; [ch.] Amy and Kayla; [ed.] Prince of Wales Collegiate (honors), St. John's College of Trades and Technology; [occ.] Financial Accountant; [memb.] Metro Umpires Association, Red Cross Society (Blood Donor); [hon.] Centenary of Responsive Government Scholarships, Rogers English Prize (Grade 11), Electoral Government Scholarships, Award for Highest Marks in High School Public Exams; [oth. writ.] Short story published in local newspaper and Hydro Magazine. Poetry published in high school yearbook; [pers.] My poetry tends to always reflect the inexorable passage of time, the value of love and the feeling of insignificance that people often feel. My biggest influence is the incomparable imagery of Robert Frost. [a.] St. John's, Nfld.

HANNA, JENNIFER
[pen.] Jen Hanna; [b.] August 15, 1978, Philadelphia, PA; [p.] William and Susan Hanna; [ed.] Mater Dolorosa, Abraham Lincoln High School; [occ.] Student; [memb.] Temple Program, DARE; [hon.] First and Second Honors - Master Dolorosa. [a.] Philadelphia, PA.

HANNA, JOHN P.
[b.] September 4, 1968, Cleveland, OH; [p.] Ralph and Mary Hanna; [ed.] Hawken School, Ohio University; [memb.] Sigma Phi Epsilon; [hon.] Outstanding College Students of America - Captain of Hawken Prep School Swim Team; [pers.] Strive to do your best in everything you do. [a.] Aurora, OH.

HANSEN, BRENT TYLER
[b.] October 24, 1955, Ottumwa, IA; [p.] Bonnie Irene and Mitchell Dean Hansen; [ed.] Ottumwa High School, Ottumwa Heights College, Northeast Missouri State University, Buena Vista College; [occ.] Sales Clerk at Wal-Mart; [hon.] Honor roll in high school and college; [pers.] My writing is based on experiences and feelings that I want to express. The intensity of life and love I want to share.

HANSON, KARINE
[pen.] Karine Hanson; [b.] May 28, 1969, Jamaica; [p.] Lucy Bennett and George Hanson; [m.] Engaged- Raney Troy, to be October 1993; [ch.] Kadian Janelle (deceased); [ed.] Meadowbrook High, Ardenne High; [occ.] Radiology Technician, United States Navy; [memb.] Association of Emergency Medical Tech; [hon.] Honor Roll; [oth. writ.] Local competitions; [pers.] We are all entitled freedom of speech, expression of choice and should use these to gain the knowledge and insight that will pave the way for our children. [a.] FPO, AP.

HARBILAS, DAVID
[b.] February 11, 1972, Boston, MA; [p.] Dr. Eugene and Jean Harbilas; [ed.] Brewster Academy, University of New Hampshire; [occ.] Student; [memb.] The Modern Poetry Association; [hon.] National Honors Society, honors in English; [oth. writ.] None published; [pers.] My love and admiration to my parent, my brother Ian, Matt Hoopes, Peter Friend, Rex Snyder and all my friends from Brewster. [a.] Haverhill, MA.

HARDING, JAN
[b.] September 15, 1950, London, England; [p.] Vera and John Harding; [m.] Richard Theobald; [ch.] Emily Rose Harding-Theobald; [ed.] Chelsea College, London University 1969 Reading, Physics and Chemistry; [occ.] Telephony Software Engineer; [oth. writ.] I write and paint for myself; [pers.] At age 16, I chose between Science and poetry to be able to earn a living. My poems ar my version of truth. I read voraciously, bring up my daughter and listen to classical music.

HARDING, ROBERT J.
[b.] January 25, 1938, New York City; [occ.] Artist/writer; [oth. writ.] Published essays and art criticism. [a.] New York City.

HARFOUCHE, WALIOL GEORGER
[b.] April 10, 1963, Lebanon, Beirut; [p.] Georges Alexander and Yvonne Harfouche; [m.] February 17, 1947; [ch.] Marie Helou, Jacqueline Bahout, Amine and Nabil Harfouche; [ed.] College de la Sagesse, Florida Atlantic University; [hon.] Upsilon Pi Epsilon, Honor Society of Computer Science; [oth. writ.] French poetry, expose of the medieval times in French History; [pers.] For every dream there is a poem and for every poem there is a listener, and for every dreamer who is a listener there is a poet. [a.] Boynton Beach, FL.

HARMIC, ROBIN
[b.] August 5, 1972, Clearfield, PA; [p.] Thomas and Florence; [ed.] Central York High School; [occ.] Computer Encoder; [pers.] "Before a word is on my tongue you know it completely, O Lord" Ps. 139:4…"All things were created by him and for him" Col. 1:16. [a.] York, PA.

HARRIS, DEBORAH
[pen.] Lee Harrison/Deborah Harris; [b.] May 14, 1960, Calgary, Alberta, CAN; [p.] C.F. Icke; [m.] Michael, June 6, 1981; [ch.] Carla Harris; [ed.] George McDougall S.H.S.; [occ.] Customer Service Rep., Toronto Dominion Bank (Airdine, AB); [memb.] Wild Rose Country Dancers; [oth. writ.] Placed in several local and regional writing contests. Stories published in local newspapers; [pers.] I write short stories reflecting Rural life in Alberta both past and present as well as children's literature and short stories dealing with personal feelings and conflicts. [a.] Alberta, CAN.

HARRIS, DERETHA A.
[b.] September 9, 1948, Tampa, FL; [m.] ERic G.; [oth. writ.] A collection of 103 poems entitled, "He Talks, I Listen" hopefully one day to share through publication; [pers.] He talks, I listen, He tells me what to say. I am so glad He shares with me in this special way. [a.] Tampa, FL.

HARRIS, JEREMY
[b.] November 5, 1975, San Diego, CA; [p.] Jack and Kathie Harris; [ed.] Standley Lake High School; [occ.] Albertson's Courtesy Clerk; [oth. writ.] Every Day, Through The Darkness, Crying Inside, Mother's are Forever, Missing Her, Memory Lane, Feelings, Death is a Place, Floating Away, Pain and Sorrow, Illusion, Pain Loves Company, Seeing Her Fail; [pers.] I started writing at the age of fourteen. Shortly after my mother past away, poetry helped ease my pain and share my feelings with other people. [a.] Westminster, CO.

HARRIS, LIANE
[b.] June 16, 1958, Brooklyn, NY; [p.] Marion Harris; [ed.] Lincoln University, 1976-1980; [occ.] Teacher/writer Dade County School System;]oth. writ.] Completing first screen play, several articles; [pers.] The Sky's Not the Limit. [a.] Coconut Grove, FL.

HARRISON, SHARLENE
[pen.] Allie; [b.] December 20, 1934, AK; [m.] Frank J., July 11, 1950; [ch.] David, Stephen, Sherry and Martha; [ed.] High school; [occ.] Retired plant employee; [memb.] Church of Christ; [pers.] I write to share happy events in my life and to express my true feelings. [a.] Batesville, AK.

HARRISON, STEPHANIE M.
[b.] June 4, 1962, Vidor, TE; [p.] Charlene and Fred Hanauer Jr. and Bruce W. Baxter; [m.] Terry Lee, October 30, 1990; [ch.] Desiree K. Burton, Miranda L. Buxton, Kristopher W. Harrison, Nicole A. Harrison and Torye M. Harrison; [ed.] LcC-M High; [occ.] Housewife; [pers.] This poem is dedicated to my grandmother, Pauline M. Ehrhart; my mother, Charline M. Hanauer, and all family members. We love you, Granny. [a.] Orange, TE.

HART, ALISON
[pen.] Ming, Teddy Bear; [b.] March 11, 1978, Montreal; [p.] Lynda and Peter Hart; [m.] Boyfriend-Marc Carrere, July 16, 1993; [ed.] High school student; [hon.] Editor's Choice award; [oth. writ.] Other poems published in books in English and French; [pers.] To all those who have inspired me. In am in forever debt I love you all. [a.] Montreal, Quebec.

HARTMAN, DOUGLAS
[b.] March 10, 1964, Reading, PA; [occ.] Electrical Assembly; [pers.] Hope is believing that after this life, we shall have our cake, we will eat it too. And fairness will not be our concern. [a.] Putnam, CT.

HAUGE, SHARON L.
[b.] October 24, 1943, Minneapolis, MN; [ch.] Carol Edmonds; [hon.] Honorable mention from World of Poetry Contest July 1991 for Poem "Inner Beauty"; [oth. writ.] Listed in 1993 songwriters market as a new artist. I have two published songs. I am just beginning to chase my dream of poetry; [pers.] I dedicate this poem to my loving daughter, Carol, who made the choice of which poem to send. Thank you. [a.] Lancaster, CA.

HAVENS, WILL H.
[b.] November 21, 1910, Douglas County, MO; [p.] B. Ray and Mary E. (Tooley) Havens; [m.] Clara E. (Keeler), December 2, 1933; [ch.] Ivan Havens, Ruth Evans, Ann Dowell, Bill R. Havens; [ed.] Self-educated beyond high school by Home Study courses and correspondence; [occ.] Retired minister; [memb.] American Bible Society, Ava General Baptist Church; [hon.] A 50 year award for Pastoral Ministry plus an eight year award for Pastoring; [oth. writ.] "fodder" a book of meditations. "Shallow Waters" a book of poems, "The End Time", "Green Pastures", (sermons), many poems and other articles published in local and area papers; [pers.] I strive to encourage people to keep on keeping on for the Lord and for the good of each other. [a.] Ava, MO.

HAWKINS, TODD
[b.] April 7, 1976, Fort Worth, TX; [p.] George and Edee Hawkins; [ed.] Southwest High School; [occ.] Landscape Maintenance; [memb.] Boy Scouts of America, National Honor Society, Student Council, Iota Xi Omicron; [hon.] Varsity Soccer, Who's Who Among American High Schools, Four Year Tandy Scholar; [oth. writ.] Three poems in high school literary magazine within two years; [pers.] I believe creativity thrives on diversity. To be truly creative, one must be able to observe all points of a situation and interpret them. [a.] Ft. Worth, TX.

HAWKINS, TYLER BOYD
[ed.] Hodgkins Middle School; [memb.] Kennebec Ice Hockey, Football Team, Wrestling Team, Student Council, Tennis, Band; [hon.] Maine State Savings Band Poster Award - 1st place, Honor Roll, Tyler and

his grandmother, Romayne Anderson were featured in the 1991 National campaign of the National Leukemia Association, Inc.; [pers.] To continue to develop my wrestling skills and become an olympic competitor. To excel academically and to attend Harvard or Tufts to be a friend and laugh.

HAZEN, MARJORIE K.
[b.] January 22, 1922, Moline, IL; [b.] Otto and Louise Klockau; [m.] Henry (deceased), November 16, 1945; [ch.] Myron Otto, John David, Keith Alan; [ed.] Rock Island High, Lutheran Hospital School for Nurses, Blackhawk College; [occ.] Registered Nurse (retired); [memb.] Imm. Lutheran Ladies Society, Post memberships in camping and hiking clubs; [oth. writ.] Several poems in church newsletter and bulletins, poems published in Literary Arts booklet of local Senior Olympics Arts Fair; [pers.] My poems are simple, down to earth, reflecting a common refrain - love, forgiveness, beauty, and resilence. [a.] East Moline, IL.

HEARL, PEGGY P.
[b.] February 6, 1938, Davy, WV; [p.] Thomas and Mamie Potter; [m.] Henry E. (deceased 11/12/90), August 10, 1962; [ed.] Welch High, Jefferson School of Commerce; [occ.] Office Manager, Unemployment Compensation (Retired); [memb.] Board of Directors McCounty Chapter, American Cancer Society, Board of Director's T.E.A.R.S. (Team Effort Against Ruining Southern W.V.); hon.] Graduated top 10% of class; [oth. writ.] Profile of (T.E.A.R.S. W.V.) which is a grassroots environmental group, other poems; [pers.] I strive to create an awareness to protect and preserve the environment and to enjoy God's gifts of nature. [a.] Davy, WV.

HEALEY, MARLENE
[b.] May 24, 1964, Moose Jaw, Saskatchewan; [p.] Bert and Anita Kolish; [m.] Brent, June 30, 1984; [ch.] Michael Brent; [ed.] Mossbank High; Nipawin Bible Institute, Computer College-Ex. Secretary; [occ.] Farm House wife - previously secretary; [oth. writ.] Many songs about my family and Lord; [pers.] May the Lord Jesus Christ be reflected in my life and writings. May others see His love through me. [a.] Ridgedale, SK. CAN.

HEARD, TERRI
[b.] October 31, 1968, Philadelphia, PA; [p.] Leonard and Carmen Heard; [ed.] H.S. for Engineering; presently a journalism major at Temple University; [occ.] Copy editor, editor of the Imeltros for the Philadelphia Tribune; [memb.] Temple Association at Blace Journalists, National Association of Blace Journalists; [hon.] 1985 Honorable Mention, Alpha Kappa Alpha writing contest, Finalist Juelith Steve Writing Contest 1991; [oth. writ.] Two short stories published in Star Trek Magazine Subspace Guest opinion and review of Slesan. Straight's "I Been In Sorrow's Kitchen and Licked Out All The Pots" published in Philadelphia Tribune; [pers.] An author's greatest gift is to expand someone else's horizons. That's what I want to do. Extend someone else's vision the way other authors did for me. [a.] Philadelphia, PA.

HEATON, SHARON LYNN
[b.] June 17, 1950, Paterson, NJ; [p.] Georgianna and John Lewis Decker; [m.] Walter Joseph, June 22, 1991; [ch.] Warren Stewart Congdon, Jr.; [ed.] West Milford High School; [occ.] Senior Security Specialist; [oth. writ.] Various poems for family members; [pers.] My original poem was forty lines. I had to edit it to twenty per the contest rules. It was written for my sister, Edna Mae Rovinski. [a.] Goshen, NY.

HEAVIN, AELEENA M.
[b.] January 26, 1921, Fillmore, IN; [p.] Nellie Vaningle (Storm) and Fred Kent Heavin; [ed.] Amo High School; [occ.] Retired Housekeeper - Telephone Operator; [hon.] Golden poetry award; [oth. writ.] Poems, stories "God's Highway". [a.] Coatesville, IN.

HEDIGER, KEVIN
[b.] May 22, 1968, St. Louis, MO; [p.] Edward and Marie Hediger; [ed.] St. Louis University High School, Indiana University, University of Maryland; [occ.] Analyst, U.S. Government; [memb.] American Red Cross, Association of the U.S. Army, Indiana University Alumni Association; [oth. writ.] Poem published in local magazine; [pers.] Walk. Don't run. Live life. Have fun. [a.] Glen Burnie, MD.

HEIKKINEN, DORIS M.
[pen.] Doris Heikkinen, Doris Koskela Heikkinen; [b.] August 26, 1921, Virginia, MN; [p.] Samuel and Olga Lofback Koskela; [m.] John Toivo, June 26, 1948; [ch.] Linda Babin, Peter Heikkinen, and Donna Furton; [ed.] Floodwood (MN) High, Virginia Junior College, Swedish Hospital, School of Nursing, Mpls.; [occ.] Retired occupational health nurse; [memb.] So. Range Ap. Lutheran Church, AARP, Finnish Center Association, Misery Bay-Toivola Senior Citizen's Club, Swedish Hospital Alumnae Association; [oth. writ.] Compiled and contributed to the Toivola Centennial Book PICTURES FROM THE PAST, inspirational poems and songs; [pers.] My deep desire is to be faithful to my Lord by using the talent He has given me to glorify Him and encourage others in their daily walk. [a.] Toivola, MI.

HEIMANN, VERDA M.
[pen.] Verdi; [b.] May 17, 1917, Baird, TX; [p.] John and Sara B. Morrison; [m.] Louis Heimann, Jr., June 3, 1950; [ch.] Sharon, Cathy, Louis Heimann III; [ed.] High school, RN in nursing, numerous courses in nursing; [occ.] Registered Nurse in Mental Health (resocialization); [memb.] Lutheran Church, Texas Public Employers Association; [hon.] Goldmedal for Highest Grades in Art - Jr. High; honors in essay a scholastics salutatorian senior high graduation; [oth. writ.] Newspaper articles reporting progress of resocialization unit where I worked, poems for friends; [pers.] I write poems for fun and for friends. Have no special training. Foolish jingles and rhymes dance through my head all I do is write them down. [a.] Kerrville, TX.

HELLER, ROYCEANN JACKSON
[b.] October 27, 12955, Camp Pendelton, CA; [p.] Royston and Marjorie Jackson; [m.] Douglas Heller, November 18, 1983; [ch.] Bridget and Collett; [memb.] Hospitals; [hon.] Published in National Library of Poetry Wind in the Night Sky and won Editor's Choice; [oth. writ.] Several unpublished poems, I'm hoping to gain enough confidence to get these published also; [pers.] My writings reflect how I feel about the world around us. My poems are usually created from trying to understand how to make our lives better. [a.] Oceanside, CA.

HELLMAN, U.S.
[pen.] S.S. Radha; [b.] March 20, 1911, Berlin, Germany; [occ.] Author, poet, lecturer; [memb.] The Association of Transpersonal Psychology, The Association for Humanistic Psychology, The International Society for the Study of Energy and Energy Medicine; [oth. writ.] Author of several books including: In the Company of the Wise, From the Mating Dance to the Cosmic Dance, Seeds of Light. Published books and articles in my home country of Germany as well; [pers.] Life is not a straight line but a wave. To meet the troughs and the crests with equanimity is my main message and encouragement to others. [a.] Spokane, WA.

HELM, JACK
[b.] June 26, 1963, York, PA; [p.] Jack and Bonnie Helm; [ed.] Eastern York High School, U.S. Army; [occ.] Computer Support Engineer, Microsoft, Inc.; [memb.] Society for Creative Anachronisms; [pers.] I write what I feel and see. [a.] Matthews, NC.

HEMMINGS, MARTY
[b.] May 6, 1977, Pictou, NS; [p.] Ralph and Susan Hemmings; [ed.] Completed grade 10, honor student, West Pictou District High; [oth. writ.] Science Fiction "Star Trek" adventures, poems; [pers.] "The Fall of the Giants" was inspired by the clear cutting of the forest behind my home. What a waste! [a.] Pictou, NS.

HENDERS, JOYCE
[pen.] Joyce Bowers-Henders; [b.] May 5, 1935, Prestbury, Macclesfield; [p.] Norman and Mary Bowers; [m.] Michael, December 19, 1963; [ch.] Irene, Diane and Tracy; [ed.] Central School for Girls; [occ.] Writer, Songs poetry, plays, short stories; [memb.] Songwriters Guild; [oth. writ.] One book of poems published 1989; [pers.] Never take anything or anyone for granted that way you avoid disappointments and get pleasant surprises. [a.] Macclesfield, Chesire, ENG.

HENDERSON, DANIEL
[b.] February 14, 1976, Lafayette, LA; [p.] Darrell Henderson and Peggy Sebek; [ed.] Senior in high school. [a.] Lafayette, LA.

HENDRIXSON, THERESA
[b.] January 6, 1952, Indianapolis, IN; [p.] Thomas M. and Clara M. Chastain; [m.] Charles W., October 22, 1972; [ch.] Charlie, Riley, Haley; [ed.] Ben Davis High, Saint Mary-of-the Woods College; [occ.] Secretary; [memb.] Greencastle Fine Arts Society, Indianapolis Writer's Center; [pers.] I try to reflect the healing side of poetry with truth, sensitivity, and humor. Keeping alive the tradition of my family. [a.] Greencastle, IN.

HENLEY JR., JAMES MILTON
[pen.] Hezekiah E. Henley; [b.] March 8, 1963, Huntsville, AL; [p.] James and Monya Henley; [m.] Evey, April 5, 1991; [ch.] Merilee, Mason.

HENNEY, JAZEENE
[b.] September 9, 1974, Kingston, Jamaica; [p.] Donovan Henney and Marie Sangster (deceased); [ed.] St. Andrew and Wolmer's Girls High Schools, Modesto Junior College; [occ.] STudent; [memb.] International Club (MJC), Class Scholarship GRoup; [hon.] Dean's list; [oth. writ.] Several poems published in local newspapers, a personal collection of 40 poems and articles for college newspaper; [pers.] To reflect the beauty of the good, the bad, the sad and happy themes within life. To appreciate literature as a rare expression. [a.] Modesto, CA.

HENRICKS-FRIESEN, WENDY
[pen.] Wendy Henricks-Friesen; [b.] January 6, 1972, Outlook, Saskatchewan, CAN; [p.] Kathy Stoppler and Harold Hendricks; [m.] Randy K., July 19, 1991; [ch.] Judy Louise (8/4/92); [ed.] Outlook High School; [occ.] Wife, mother; [pers.] This poem is dedicated to my husband from me and to Judy's Dad from her. He means the world to both of us. [a.] Conquest, Saskatchewan, CAN.

HENRY, BURKE
[b.] January 21, 1979, St. Rose, Man. CAN.; [p.] Larry and Lynn Henry; [ed.] Completed 8th grade; [occ.] Student.

HENRY, DEDRICK
[b.] August 11, 1973, Indianapolis, IN; [p.] Richard and Diana Henry; [ed.] Oxon Hill High School, University of Maryland-Baltimore County; [occ.] Student; [memb.] Washington Urban League, NAACP, Inroads, Star of Bethlehem C.O.G.I.C.; [hon.] Honors college - University of Maryland-BC, national Collegiate All-American award, National Scholar-Athleth Day award for Track and Field; [pers.] I strive to put forward all the effort that I can, to help revitalize America's inner-cities. [a.] Oxon Hill, MD.

HENSON, BOBBY R.
[b.] August 22, 1956, Dallas, TX; [p.] Robert H. Henson and Elizabeth Slater; [m.] Pamela, April 3, 1976; [ch.] Kevin, Eric; [ed.] Milby High School, University of Houston; [occ.] Musician; [pers.] This poem based on personal observations vacation 1990. [a.] Pearland, TX.

HENTSCHEL, ERWIN
[b.] August 20, 1925, Berlin, Germany; [m.] Widower since 90; [occ.] Retired Sr. Designer Engineer; [memb.] Lutheran Church Zion; [hon.] United States Patent granted on July 4, 1989; [oth. writ.] Write poems and short stories but mostly in German practice drawing, painting and music; [pers.] Enjoy art, dancing, walking and travel. Have now my first art showing. [a.] Bay City, MI.

HERNANDEZ, ROSE (SAPIEN)
[b.] December 10, 1955, Childress, TX; [p.] Amelia and Cipriano Sapien, Sr.; [ch.] Daviel Luis and Olivia Rose Hernandez; [ed.] Goldthwaite High (TX), Howard Payne University-BA degree; [occ.] Spanish, English Teacher. Work with delinquent youth Brownwood State School; [memb.] Brown County Literary Council, First Mexican Baptist Church, BWD; [hon.] GAmma Beta Phi, Dean's List, President's List; [oth. writ.] Poems published in university literary magazine "The Catalyst". Also an oral Spanish/English interview on TX history on record with Brown County Historical Archives; [pers.] I strive to reflect optimism, love and understanding in my works. Great influences in my life are my high school and college professors in English to whom I am truly indebted. [a.] Brownwood, TX.

HERNANDEZ, VALERIE ANN
[pen.] Me; [b.] February 23, 1957, Bronx, New York; [p.] Sandra Frazier, Joseph Hernandez; [m.] Jay Castor, October 17, 1987; [ch.] Brian Keith and Jaycee Leigh; [ed.] Teaneck High, Dover Bus. College, U.S. Arng; [occ.] Word Processor; [hon.] Diploma DBC 4.0, it's an honor to place semi-finalist in this contest; [pers.] Be all that you want to be. Be the best that you can be and believe in yourself and in GOD. [a.] Bogota, NJ.

HERSH, JILL
[pen.] Jillian Collings; [b.] February 23, 1977; [p.] Bob and Jane Hersh; [pers.] I would like to thank Mrs. Elinor Carr, my Greenwich High 9th grade English teacher, for helping me with my poetry unit. [a.] Riverside, CT.

HERZIG, THERESA M.
[b.] February 18, 1938, Germany; [p.] Karl and Maria Meyer; [m.] Tony, November 5, 1960; [ch.] Ron and Heidi; [ed.] High school; [occ.] Pastry Chef - retired teacher; [oth. writ.] Poetry and short story; [pers.] The beauty of poetry is the love of my life happy and sad, new and old always a joy to be a day. [a.] Towaco, NJ.

HIATT, KASEY M.
[b.] May 4, 1976, Noblesville, IN; [p.] Patsy Richard and Mike Hiatt; [ed.] Hamilton Heights High and Artistic Beauty College; [pers.] I write about activities or moments that effect or inspire my life". [a.] Indianapolis, IN.

HIBBS, AIDEN PATRICK
[pen.] Aiden Hibbs; [b.] February 21, 1974, Carbonear, Nfld; [p.] Aiden and Margaret Lorraine Hibbs; [ed.] St. Francis Central High School, Harbor Grace; [pers.] There's a degree of simplicity, characterized by abnormality, coherent with the mind of a poet. I write to be remembered. My words are my legacy. [a.] Harbour GRace, Nfld.

HICKEY, PATRICIA
[b.] April 26, 1980, Worcester, MA; [p.] Gayle and John Hickey, Jr. [a.] Sutton, MA.

HIEMIER, PAIGE DANA
[b.] New York City; [p.] Faith Mae Dow and Stanley Richard Hiemier; [ed.] Ridgefield Park High, Bergen Community College, New School for Social Research; [occ.] REgistered Nurse, Writer, Lt. US Army Nurse Corp.; [memb.] NJSNA, NYSNA; [hon.] Dean's List; [oth. writ.] Unpublished book, The Other Side of Innocence; article published in NYSNA newspaper and several TV scripts; [pers.] I thank God for my teachers and friends, Alyse Gutter, David Can Duren and Ann Loring; for without their patience and encouragement, I would not be who I am. [a.] Ridgefield Park, NJ.

HIGGS, GEORGE
[b.] June 12, 1968, Wilmington, DE; [p.] William Victor and Margaret J. (Millington) Higgs; [m.] Georgina Buffini-Higgs, August 1, 1992; [ed.] Gettysburg College, Trinity College, University of Colorado; [occ.] English Teacher; [oth. writ.] Songs, books, poems and stories; [pers.] My favorite foods the fruit of a futile quest. [a.] Chadds Ford, PA.

HIGH, JASON EDWARD
[pen.] Jason High, Fillapont; [b.] March 10, 1975, Nyack, NY; [p.] Charles C. High and Joan M. Dyer; [ed.] Coronado High School, UTEP; [occ.] STudent; [memb.] Society's Label The Vineyard; [oth. writ.] Several poems published in pamphlet "View from 213"; [pers.] Please respect yourself and realize that the written word is very powerful. Please respect that as well, God Bless". [a.] El Paso, TX.

HILBURN, JANICE
[b.] May 13, 1926, Nevada, IA; [p.] Clarance and Faye Hilburn; [ed.] Fernald High School, St. Joseph School of Nursing, Hankuk University of Foreign Studies; [occ.] Retired; [hon.] Korean Times Modern Literature translation award with Poet Lee Young-gul in 1972; [oth. writ.] Articles in Korea Times and the Korea Herald, poem in Maryknoll magazine; [pers.] I agree with Marias: "To live is to stand between the sword and the wall…" [a.] Loveland, CO.

HILEMAN, ANDRE A.
[b.] May 13, 1981, Wichita, KS; [p.] Terry Hileman and Jennifer Lutz; [ed.] 5th grade; [occ.] Student; [hon.] National Physical Fitness award; [pers.] I really enjoy writing songs and poetry. I have wrote many of each in the past and have to keep doing so in the future. [a.] Sterling, NY.

HILL, EVANGELINE
[b.] June 24, 1953, Aspen Cove, Nfld.; [p.] Olivea and Uriel Coles; [m.] Jack, January 29, 1973; [ch.] Carla and Jackie; [occ.] Head Cook, College for Officers Training St. John's Nfld; [oth. writ.] Wrote a book "Windows to the Soul" containing eighty-two poems published by Good Tidings press March 1993; [pers.] I try to paint poetic pictures and capture the readers attention with emotional, humane and universal feelings. I have been greatly influenced by the writings of Steiner Rice and other great poets. [a.] Goulds, Nfld., CAN.

HILL, PAT
[b.] February 2, 1952, St. Paul, MN; [p.] Frank and Elaine Shuman; [m.] Ernie, April 17, 1970; [ch.] Ernie Lee, Jacob, Rebecca; [ed.] High school, Spooner WI, Rice Lake Vo-Tech; [memb.] Mothers Against Drunk Drivers, Eau Claire Athletic Club; [oth. writ.] A collection of poems and short stories; [pers.] Each time a poem is written a piece of the poet is exposed. Each time a poem is read to another a piece of that poet us released to the world. [a.] Augusta, WI.

HILLARD, DEBORAH
[pen.] Debbie; [b.] November 29, 1951, Durham, NC; [p.] Deceased-Fred and Josephine Wilson; [m.] Joseph, December 18, 1971; [ch.] Crysta (20) and Cory (16); [ed.] Durham High Career Academy; [occ.] Nurse/EMT; [memb.] American Association of Office Nurses/NC Notary Association.

HILLEN, STEPHANIE
[pen.] Stevie; [b.] October 23, 1977, Phoenix, AZ; [p.] Harold R. and Kathy M. Hillen, Jr.; [ed.] Barry Goldwater High School; [occ.] Full-time Student; [hon.] Jr. National Honor Society; [pers.] One never knows what they had until they go without. [a.] Black Canyon City, AZ.

HILLIARD, EDNA G.
[pen.] Edna G. Hilliard; [b.] June 2, 1909, Boston, MA; [p.] John and Sara McLane; [m.] Channing M., July 12, 1958; [ch.] David H. Gilbert; [ed.] Boston Museum of Fine Arts, 2 years Simmons College, Nurses Aide-Cape Cod N. Home; [occ.] Training Super Sheraton Corp. Traveling Hostess - Sheraton Corp.; [memb.] C.W. Fellowship, Art Guild C.C., AARP, Waquurt Congregation Church, American Professional Womens Club; [hon.] Washington Allston Art Scholarship, Washington Post Career Woman of the Month; [oth. writ.] A Moose in the House, His Morning Prayers, Who Am I; [pers.] Judge others as you wish to be judged.

HILLICOSS, BARBARA
[b.] August 7, 1950, Rangely, CO; [p.] John B. and Ona S. Goff; [m.] Ed, September 1, 1975; [ch.] Mark Jenson and Wayne Hillicoss; [ed.] Douglas High School and Weber State College; [memb.] Church of Jesus Christ of Latter Day Saints; [oth. writ.] "A Hand" a poem published in "Wind in the Night Sky" by the National Library of Poetry; [pers.] I feel very blessed if I can inspire someone or help to give someone greater insight into something. [a.] Greenville, NY.

HILLIS, ELSIE
[b.] May 10, 1920, Midco, MO; [p.] Joe and Alice Landis; [ch.] Carol Thornberry, Richard Hendrickson and Randy Hendrickson; [hon.] Two poems printed in the Books of Congress; [oth. writ.] A special editor award on one of my poems. I have had three of my poems published so far; [pers.] My second husband was Tom Hillis. Me and Larry Hendrickson were married April 22, 1939.

HILLMAN, AARON W.
[pen.] Aaron; [b.] September 29, 1926, Chaffee, MO; [p.] Basil E. Hillman and Erthel D. Pearman; [m.] Rosemary T., August 6, 1953; [ch.] David E.; [ed.] Ph.D., University of CA, Santa Barbara; [occ.] Wonderer; [memb.] The Planetary Society plus various and sundry; [hon.] Various and Sundry; [oth. writ.] Various poetry and prose publications, see book by George Brown "Human Teaching for Human Learning", also three great plays; [pers.] I hear your voice and soft roses fall upon the table and bloom. [a.] Santa Barbara, CA.

HILLMAN, YVONNE
[b.] March 6, 1948, New Prague, MN; [p.] Harold and Lorraine Brown ; [m.] Bob, October 21, 1972; [ch.] Jeffrey Robert, Gina Mary; [ed.] LeCenter High, Murkato Beauty College, Institute of Children's Literature; [memb.] St. Alphonso's Church; [pers.] I strive to make the world a better place through poetry. That all mankind can live in peace and happiness in a beautiful clean world. [a.] Brooklyn Park, MN.

HINES, LISA
[pen.] Sheila Sin; [b.] February 15, 1963, Everett, MA; [p.] Joan C. McLaughlin and Lewis E. Hines; [occ.] Unit secretary, Whidden Memorial Hospital, Everett Mass; [oth. writ.] Many spiral notebooks full of poems; [pers.] Writing, for me, is like breathing. It's almost unconscious, not something I give much thought to. [a.] Everett, MA.

HINKO, EDVARD JOSEF
[pen.] The Wanderer; [b.] May 30, 1940, Czechoslovakia; [p.] Peter and Julia Hinko; [m.] Jean (deceased), August 4, 1974; [ch.] Deborah and Rebecca (previous marriage to Donna); [ed.] Grade 12, Nursing Orderly Training, Trade School Welding and Sheet Metal; [occ.] Sheet Metal; [hon.] University of A Leadership Course; [oth. writ.] Commentaries to Papers (published verbatim), 20 unpublished poems copyrighted as an unpublished works 1991 under penname "The Wanderer"; [pers.] Con. Citizen since 1948. Presently engaged to Anne Cordinelly. Love writing. I hope through poetry to reach the inner spirit of the reader and thus make a small difference in a world going ever colder. [a.] Millet, AL, CAN.

HINTZ, JOYCE EARLENE
[pen.] Jusuey; [b.] October 23, 1940, Orillia, Ont. CAN; [p.] Earl and Evelyn Givens; [m.] John, June 5, 1959; [ch.] Jim and Tam Hintz and Terry Bommaito; [ed.] SS No. 9, College in Toronto; [occ.] Have been working on new book of poems called Time and Space of Poetry and hope to publish it in the future; [hon.] National Library of Poetry and Printings in Library of Congress; [oth. writ.] Brotherly Love, Death of Baby Jim, Hell or Marriage, The Hunt, A Life, Grama's Christmas, and many more such as From Who's Eyes You Look; [pers.] I find life situation, the twist and turns of life makes for most of my poetry. How one action causes a reaction and that action another - not only my own. [a.] Rudell, SK.

HIRTH, EMMA MAXINE
[b.] December 31, 1932, Bronte, TX; [p.] William Roy and Jewell Brey; [m.] William Gene, December 25, 1952; [ch.] William David, Michael Gene, Billy Roy Hirth; [ed.] Pecos High, Sul Ross State University; [occ.] Retired teacher; [hon.] Golden poet for five years, poem chose for publication in two books; [oth. writ.] Poem published in local newspaper; [pers.] Whether in stories or music poetry is a wonderful form of expression with styles and subjects that everyone can enjoy. [a.] Midland, TX.

HISCOCK, ERIC D.C.
[pen.] Stenehize; [b.] February 21, 1911, Halifax, Nova Scotia, CAN; [p.] John Albert and Evelyn Cave Hiscock; [m.] Geraldine Virtue (Osmond), December 22, 1943; [ch.] Paul Albert, Evelyn Judith, Rosalie G., Pamela Ruth, Philip Douglas, Beverly Marie, Linda , Leslie John; [ed.] University of Toronto, University of Oregon; [occ.] Agricultural and Vocational Instructor/Electrician; [memb.] Nfld. Teacher's Association, Society of United Fisherman; [hon.] International Order Merit (for Peace Strategy); [oth. writ.] Newfoundland's first 50 years published by Stockwood Ltd., reports; [pers.] No wealth without health which largely depends on adequate housing renewal to safeguard youth during their critical upbringing and education. [a.] St. John's Nfld, CAN.

HLADKY, GEANNINE
[b.] March 15, 1965, Crete, NE; [p.] Mildred and Reynold Hladky; [ed.] St. Thomas Aquinas (DAvid City, NE) and Johns Hopkins University; [occ.] Director of Development, The Lacrosse Foundation (Baltimore, MD); [memb.] National Society of Fund Raising Executives; [pers.] Writing is my way of discovering who I am. I find myself in the words that come forth from my heart through my pen. [a.] Baltimore, MD.

HNATIUK, CATHY
[pen.] Cat; [b.] August 14, 1962, Edmonton, Alberta; [m.] Barry Flundra, engaged; [ed.] Make-up artist and Hair stylist; [occ.] Salon owner; [hon.] Make-up Artistry and Hairstyling; [oth. writ.] I have several other poems and songs that I have written; [pers.] To me these writings are feelings. [a.] Russell, Manitoba, CAN.

HODGE, RHONDA
[b.] December 19, 1962, Tulsa, OK; [p.] Don and Karen Johnson; [m.] Divorced; [ch.] Danielle; [ed.] Broken Arrow High School, Tulsa Junior College working on Business degree; [occ.] Manager of Customer Service Custom products; [hon.] President's Honor Roll, Thespian award, band queen Ms. Congeniality; [pers.] Through my feelings and thoughts of the people dearest to me, I've tried to paint a portrait of words that will be cherished by all who view them.

HODGES, JAMES D.
[b.] March 20, 1956, Galveston, TX; [m.] Debbie G. Baker Hodges, November 28, 1975; [ch.] Ramona, Ray, Jennifer, Brody; [ed.] North Pike High School, Galveston College; [occ.] Machinist and student majoring in health related studies; [memb.] Masonic Lodge; [oth. writ.] Numerous poems on varied topics; [pers.] What shall we learn from a moment of inspiration? [a.] Santa Fe, TX.

HOEFFNER, LOIS
[b.] October 13, 1927, New Orleans, LA; [p.] Herman and Patricia Soell; [m.] Frank, April 24, 1954; [ed.] St. Mary Magdalenes and Rumble High; [occ.] Taking care of the sick; [memb.] AARP, Merry Magdalenes, Mike Maley Golden Age; [hon.] Garden Club; [oth. writ.] Garden Clubs, Golden Age, AARP 2624, Merry Magdalenes; [pers.] I believe if you can make one person laugh a day - you got it made. [a.] Metaire, LA.

HOFFMAN, CHAD
[pen.] C.A. Hoffman servant of the Most High; [b.] October 24, 1976, Grand Rapids, MI; [p.] GAry and Debra Hoffman; [ed.] Senior at Tri-Unity Christian High School; [hon.] Honor Roll student, multiple awards for outstanding achievement in Math and English, multiple year recognition by Who's Who in American students; [oth. writ.] Poetry, short stories and articles appearing in Christian publications and church newsletters; [pers.] I believe that Jesus Christ died to set all mankind free from the bondage of sin and death. It is my prayer that the Lord would use my ability as a writer to convey truth in the light and hope of Jesus Christ. [a.] Jenison, MI.

HOFMAN, HELEN M.
[b.] Brookfield, IL; [p.] Joachim P. and Karoline M. Braun Cohrs; [m.] Ervin N.; [ch.] Wanda M. Lauderdale, Gwendolyn J. Meythaler; [memb.] Chaffee County Council of the Arts, Chaffee County Camera Club; [pers.] People need more knowledge about a great variety of things. If they'd learn to look down the long road and see the alternatives they wouldn't be so overwhelmed by the present. [a.] Salida, CO.

HOFMANN, JENNIFER L.
[b.] August 14, 1969, Coravus, OR; [p.] Donna and Donald Hofmann; [ed.] 1987 H.H.S. and 1991 Bassist College BA-Interior Design; [occ.] World Traveler; [oth. writ.] Poetry, short stories, writer for O.C. Live, Ch. 10 - screenplay, "Shades of Red"; [pers.] In sorting through it all, I am able to find meaning in life by virtue of the that I have installed a sense of passion for the experience of life within the souls of the people that I have known. [a.] Klamath Falls, OR.

HOLAS, NICOLE
[b.] April 4, 1972, Grenada, West Indies; [ed.] Completing Fourth Year of a Political Science degree at the University of Calgary; [occ.] Working towards a career in law; [oth. writ.] This is my first published work; [pers.] My work reflects the world around me, from people to places. I thank my family and friends for their support. [a.] Calgary, Alberta, CAN.

HOLDBROOKS, JENNIFER L.
[b.] January 20, 1978, East Point, GA; [p.] Ana Moss, Harry Holdbrooks and Jerry C. Moss (stepdad); [ed.] Newman High School (Sophomore); [memb.] Beta Club, Pres. Explorer Post 97, Youth Council, National Honor Roll; [hon.] National Honor Roll 6th district Honor Bands; [oth. writ.] "Receive the Light of Jesus" published in Sunday Church Bulletin, article insert for Church Bulletin; [pers.] All my poems are written about my feelings at that time. It's a wonderful way for me to reflect back on memories in my past. Believe in yourself, God and what you do, and anything is possible. [a.] Newman, GA.

HOLDER, NANNIE I.
[pen.] Ira Berry Holder; [b.] April 6, 1895, Rector, AR; [p.] Young Henry and Willie Evans Berry; [m.] Dow M., April 2, 1916; [ch.] Vera H. Smith, Thurman, Don Mack (deceased) Margaret H. Nicor, Eugene; [ed.] One year college; [occ.] Teacher, tutor, teacher in one room school; [memb.] PTA, one of Jehovah's Witnesses; [oth. writ.] Poems in local newspapers two books; "papa", "Willie"; [pers.] I've written poems for more than 90 years more than 10,000) for any special occasion for others. [a.] North Rock, AK.

HOLLANDER, ANGELIC
[pen.] Angelic Hollander; [b.] November 25, 1941, St. Louis, MO; [p.] Nellie Ann Hunt and Charles Conner; [m.] John, May 18, 1958; [ch.] Jonathan, Carmen, Paul (grandchildren-Misty, Patrick, Tessa, Talia); [occ.] Housewife; [memb.] P.A.W.S. [a.] Pineville, LA.

HOLLINGSWORTH, IGNE C.
[pen.] Chris Hollingsworth; [b.] Bayreuth, Germany; [p.] Elli and Friedrich Gorl (both deceased); [m.] Harold, March 1, 1980; [ch.] Scott and Thomas Wilbert, Susan, Daniel, Joy and Thomas, stepchildren nine; [ed.] Graduate Translators and Interpreters Institute, Munich Germany; [occ.] Translator (6-E, E-6, mostly technical material); [memb.] American Translators Association (ATA), Colorado TRanslators Association (CTA), American Recorder Society; [hon.] First and second prize short story writing, Casper Community College (College, WY 1983), First and second place Essay Contest (Casper Community College 1984); [oth. writ.] Short stories, some published in Casper Community College Literature Magazine; one story "Apocalypse" published in Anthology of Wyoming written 1983, article on Radial Keratotomy published in Denver Post 1984; [pers.] I usually go by "Chris", my pen name, abbrev. of my middle name. [a.] Denver, CO.

HOLLOWAY, ANGIE
[b.] May 26, 1980, Fort Worth, TX; [p.] Jerry and Sue Holloway; [ed.] Burleson Jr. High; [oth. writ.] I write some short stories and other poems; [pers.] If you think you'll never be good enough then you never will. Give it your all and keep your spirits high. [a.] Burleson, TX.

HOLLOWAY, MARGARET E.
[pen.] Ellie; [b.] June 18, 1951, El Dorado, KS; [p.] Garett Earl and Dorothy Carinder Salmans; [m.] Divorced 1981; [ch.] Dallas Ray and Heath Issac; [ed.] El Dorado High; [occ.] Too Collector Kansas Turnpike Authority also cashier for Coastal Mart, Inc.; [oth. writ.] Published in Kansas Turnpike Authority newsletter; [pers.] Life is full of experience. Through my personal experiences, of people and situations, I have been inspired to write. My friends have greatly encouraged me to share my inspirations. [a.] Wichita, KS.

HOLMAN, HEATHER LYNN
[b.] December 22, 1968, Holyoke, MA; [p.] Patricia Ann Gogne and David John Holman; [ed.] West Springfield High School Class of '86, Springfield Technical Community College; [occ.] Medical Lab Technical, Baystate Medical Center; [memb.] St. Thomas Church, American Society for Clinical Pathologists; [hon.] Alpha Nu Omega Honor Society, Dean's List, Teresina B. Thompson Award, Health Human Services Award for Academic Achievement; [oth. writ.] I have a vast portfolio of my writings, whether its songs, poems or short stories; [pers.] This poem is dedicated to my family. Especially my Aunt Barbara LeBreque who meant so much to us all. We will deeply miss her. [a.] Springfield, MA.

HOLMAN, JR., JAMES
[pen.] James Holman, Jr.; [b.] April 22, 1965, Evansville, IN; [p.] Lola Carter and James Holman; [m.] Catherine M., December 29, 1990; [ch.] Demario Montez and Jasmine Janee and Olivia Marie Holman; [ed.] Central High; [occ.] Naval Pretty Officer; [oth. writ.] Several poems unpublished; [pers.] My wife is the ink, which follows through my pen, when I'm writing a poem. For without her, their would be nothing but a blank piece of paper. [a.] Norfolk, VA.

HOLTERMANN, HILDEGARD C.
[pen.] Christiana; [b.] June 25, 1939, Resort Bentheim, Germany; [p.] Hilde and Frank Danzinger; [ed.] Four years Women college in Northern Germany, also attended GErmany's oldest social worker school in Berlin; [occ.] Live and work in a Teahouse and Art Gallery in Ferrisburg; [hon.] My spiritual poems have been edited in Protestant and Catholic Newsletters. I have been honored by the Connecticut Poetry Society, poems appeared in the Pictorials, a shoreline newspaper in CJ. I have been awarded 4 times as a Golden Poet by the World of Poetry, Sacramento, CA; [oth. writ.] I write short stories for my own pleasures. I am a down hill skier, long distance swimmer and environmentalist and Doberman lover; [pers.] The purpose of writing Lyric Poetry has been meant to encourage teenagers, to uplift their spirit in our confusing world as support, but above all to convey the beauty of nature and human beings on this planet, called earth. [a.] North Ferrisburg, CJ.

HOMUTH, ARVID
[b.] February 13, 1929, Jamestown, ND; [p.] A. Arnold and Clara F. (Guenther) Homuth; [m.] May 9, 1959; [ed.] Jamestown High School North Dakota State College of Science, Valley City State University; [occ.] Retired; [hon.] Featured in several local newspapers noting musical and artistic talents; [oth. writ.] Composed music and lyrics for several other songs: for the local library; another campaign song for the man who won the election for village president; [pers.] I have been involved in music for 50 years and it is my music that inspires me with poetry. [a.] Elburn, IL.

HOPKINS, MARLENE M.
[pen.] May Russel; [b.] September 25, 1951, New Westminister, BC; [p.] Kay and Irvine (Colby) Watt; [m.] James; [ch.] Jessica, Kimberly, Matthew Hopkins; [occ.] Real Estate Agent; [memb.] Poet's Potpourri Club; [hon.] 13 in Canada first quarter of 1993 for Century 21, Centurian, Gold Club, Medallion Club; [oth. writ.] Local newspaper poem printed, local poetry club publication of few of my poems; [pers.] Thank you for my daughters Jessica and Kimberly and son Matthew who share my love of poetry and great friends Ivy and Ruth and husband Jim who will listen if I listen about Hockey cards. [a.] Abbotsford, BC.

HOPKINS, WILLIAM S.
[pen.] Sr. Wimpy P. Wizner; [b.] August 31, 1941, Alameda, CA; [p.] Lloyd George and Althea Hopkins; [m.] Divorced; [ch.] Amy, Laura and Josh; [ed.] Alameda High School, San Francisco State University; [occ.] Forensic Economist; [memb.] Various economic professional associations and organizations; [oth. writ.] Numerous articles regarding economics, business and finance; [pers.] I have come to learn that the older I get the more I find what I don't know. [a.] Corpus Christi, TX.

HORN, FLORA DUHON
[pen.] Fauna, Pen No. 0638986, Foller, Flora; [b.] May 20, 1926, Putman, TX; [p.] J.E. and Maude Foller deceased; [m.] Elmer, February 13, 1993; [ch.] Beverly, Carol, Barbara, Leola, Eddie and Rodney; [ed.] Junior High, V.G.S. for Senior Citizens, Secretarial training; [memb.] Rebekah Lodge 100F, American Legion Aux., Chaplain of Ladies Aux. Post 4709, Medical Center Hospital; [hon.] Golden Award for Poetry in 1986-1990, Volunteer Medical Center Hospital, Sunday School, Honored First place for making an album in our yearly AMCH meeting contest; [oth. writ.] Poem in World of Poetry, Great Poems of Today, Heartland, On The Threshold of a Dream, and poems in our local newspaper; [pers.] I like to share myself in volunteering in hospitals and my community. "Self Service" I can't help everyone but everyone can help someone.

HORSE, FAYE DIFFERENT
[pen.] Schuyler Donil Kasren; [b.] September 5, 1977, Eagle Butte; [p.] Delores High Pine and Donald Different Horse; [memb.] Home Economics; [hon.] Driver's Ed; [pers.] All thought are free that are in your mind. [a.] Flandreau, SD.

HORKEY, ANGELA
[b.] August 13, 1975, McCook, NE; [p.] Ben and Doris Horkey; [ed.] Graduated from McCook High School; [oth. writ.] Poems have been published in the school newspaper (The Bison); [pers.] I am greatly affected by everyday life and I write about experiences and feelings that I have. [a.] McCook, NE.

HOROWITZ, JAIMEE BETH
[b.] October 7, 1981, Elizabeth, NJ; [p.] Harold and Vicki Horowitz; [ed.] Brandywood Elementary School, Tower Hill School, Burnett Elementary School; [occ.] Student (6th grade); [hon.] Honor Roll, original drawing in 1989 DuPont Safety Calendar, chosen to speak at 3rd grade graduation, Brandywood Elementary School; [oth. writ.] Poem to be published in "Creative Kids" magazine, November 1993; [a.] Wilmington, DE.

HORTON, JOAN A.
[b.] November 10, 1927, London, England; [m.] Michael; [ch.] Angela, Beverly, and Judith; [ed.] Honor Oak Peckham London; [occ.] Housewife; [oth. writ.] "Blessings"-Wind in the Sky. [a.] Rosenberg, TX.

HORVATH, ANNA, MARGARETT
[b.] November 11, 1940, Detroit, MI; [p.] Otho and Reba (Bain) Jennings; [m.] Louis P., 1963; [ch.] Stacy Ann; [ed.] Schoolcraft College 1989,; [hon.] Critiques for college magazine, The MacGuffin; [oth. writ.] Published two poems, "Loving Against the Wind", Garden of Thought, `993, "Cradle of Their Knowing", Celebrations, 1993, and short story "What's in a Name". Verses Magazine; [pers.] Horvath commented: Three years previous, deep in the clutches of an anti-menopausal condition, a thirty year we-did-it marriage, and (with) two semi-clinging Chihuahua puppies attached to my show laces, I returned to college to fulfill a life long dream of becoming: A CREATIVE WRITER. Imagine my astonishment when I accidentally uncovered a little know fact (to me anyway); there were multitudes of excellent writers residing inside my age bracket who were possessed with the same concept. Dilemma? Could have been! But..., over the years my absent minded memory and I acquired the habit of avoiding logic and decided to continue on our merry illusionary path as though a writer's reality was within our reach. While critiquing for the MacGuffin, I came face to face with yet another: I didn't know fact. Roses are red, violets are blue (although traditionally cute) isn't necessarily well-behaved poetry. At this juncture, my mind and I became involved in the "Great Debate." The grey matter perched on top of my head refused to listen to Me, the owner and only home of that stubborn entity; it demanded I change. I've changed diapers, changed my attitude on numerous contemporary issues; literally, uprooted my systematically ingrained belief system. A system that tries to convince me -- ANYTHING NEW = A NUISANCE. But...poetry! Had it not been for the hand-to-fate, my life long friend Sharon who marched chilling, venomous (send your writing to a publisher) messages across my drooping shoulder-blades more then once, I might be sniffing the daisies instead of arranging words to visually display their enchantment. [a.] Wayne MI.

HOSKING, JR., EDGAR F.
[b.] January 30, 1921, Spring Valley, Bucks County, PA; [p.] Edgar F. and Ethel Josephine Anderson Hosking; [m.] Deceased; [ch.] Yvonne Marie and John Craig Hosking; [ed.] High school plus no degree; [occ.] Retired; [memb.] Creative Writing (Pennridge) Senior Center; [hon.] Numerous minor; [oth. writ.] Numerous; [pers.] Owner of Civil War autographs and signatures from WWII, etc.

HOSMAN, KIMBERLY RAE
[b.] December 16, 1977, Chillicothe, MO; [p.] Ronnie and Virginia Hosman; [ed.] High school entering 10th grade; [hon.] Straight A student, would like to think that I have worked very hard to achieve that goal. It is one of my strong points; [oth. writ.] I love to write poetry. When I write, all the feelings that I possess within me goes into what goes on paper. You have to love what you do or you can't do it right; [pers.] Nothing great was ever achieved without enthusiasm. I think it was best put when Spencer said, "The poets scrolls will outlive the monuments of stone. Genius survives; all else is claimed by death. [a.] Hamilton, MO.

HOSMON, TIFFANY
[pen.] Tiffany Hosmon; [b.] January 20, 1980, Carbondale, IL; [p.] Sharilyn and Parvin Hosmon; [memb.] Bible Quizzing, scholar bowl, school newspaper, honor society, and West Monroe Street Church; [hon.] Second highest scoring individual in the Illinois District in 1989 and 1990 for Bible Quizzing; [pers.] I dedicate this poem to my mother, Bible Quizzing coaches and teammates, and to my very special friend Jason Shindler! [a.] Herrin, IL.

HOUGHAM, DUANE F.
[b.] January 1, 1916, Ft. Collins, CO; [p.] Grover Cleveland and Edna Etta Miller Hougham (both deceased); [ed.] Ft. Collins High, BS in Botany and MS in Chemistry at Colorado State University; [occ.] Retired; [memb.] Methodist Church, Toastmasters, International Center, CSU; [hon.] Two trophies in Toastmasters for best evaluator; [oth. writ.] Many letters to the editor (local newspaper), research studies in Science magazines, currently editor of the local Toastmasters #375, Ft. Collins, CO newsletter; [pers.] Travelled extensively: Hong Kong, China, Japan, The Philippines, Honduras, Poland, Turkey, China, and most of the United States. I was drafted into Civilian Public Service during WWII. I'm a promotor of PEACE. [a.] Ft. Collins, CO.

HOUSDEN, LINDA M.
[b.] November 9, 1946, Charles Town, WV; [p.] Mabel and Maurice Moore; [m.] Roger Lee, December 30, 1967; [ch.] Tracee Lyn, Roger, Jr.; [ed.] Harpers Ferry High School; [occ.] School aide and owner of ceramic shop; [memb.] Concerned Citizens Against Drugs and C.W. Shipley Drug Awareness Committee; [oth. writ.] Started writing in high school short stories and poems. None published except in school paper; [pers.] I believe to stop learning is to stop living. I am a voracious reader and never am without a book. [a.] Harpers Ferry, WV.

HOUSTON, BESSIE THOMAS FOSTER
[pen.] Bessie Thomas Foster; [b.] December 6, 1920, Calhoun, GA; [p.] Bunyan Daily and Eula Mae Blalock Thomas; [m.] Marion Preston Foster, June 18, 1941 (deceased 1987) and John H. Houston, September 7, 1991; [ch.] Janet Sims, Stephen Foster, Carol Shoemaker, Karen Daniel, (stepdaughter Ann H. Powell); [ed.] Norman High School (1938), BS in Elementary Education 1964 and MS in Elementary Education 1970 at University of Chattanooga; [occ.] Junior High Teacher; [memb.] Burning Bush Baptist Church, Tennessee Retired Teachers; [hon.] Gold "N" Club (Norman), Alpha Society (UC), Kappa Delta Pi (Honorary Society in Education), Who's Who in Georgia, Who's Who in North America and PTA Life membership; [oth. writ.] Articles and devotionals for Home Life Magazine, a Baptist publication. The History of East Ridge Baptist Church. Skits for PTA and church presentations; [pers.] "Bon Voyage" was written as my farewell to my first husband, Marion Preston Foster after 3 1/2 years of grieving. I've shared it with many who mourn and it seems to have blessed them. My prayer for my life is to be a blessing. [a.] Ringgold, GA.

HOWARD, DIANE L.
[b.] April 13, 1956, Chicago, IL; [p.] Johnie and Laura Smith; [ch.] Bruce Howard, Jr.; [occ.] Administrative Secretary; [pers.] My inspiration is my child. My dedication is to all who encouraged and believed. [a.] Gary, IN.

HOWELL, THOMAS A.
[b.] April 28, 1934, Manhattan, New York; [p.] Clarence A. and Margaret Murphy Howell; [m.] Mary D., September 5, 1964; [ch.] Michael Anthony, Margaret Mary, James William; [ed.] Bishop Loughlin Memorial High School, St. John's University; [occ.] Freelance Journalist; [memb.] Wayne County Historical Society (Honesdale); [oth. writ.] East Europe (magazine) articles, Nkruman and Ghana (Interim History, Facts oN File); [pers.] ...quia absconditisti haec a sapientibus et prudentibus et revelasti ea parvulis. [a.] Honesdale, PA.

HOYT, JESSICA
[b.] December 10, 1979, Hartford, CT; [p.] Ronald and Sharon Hoyt; [ed.] Windsor Locks Middle School; [hon.] Writing award by class; [oth. writ.] Several poems and many short stories, and working on a children's to book; [pers.] To me life is like a river. It's got many endless paths to chose from, but like fate only the way of your life is pathed for you ahead of time. [a.] Windsor Locks, CT.

HRIC, REBEKAH
[pen.] Bekah Hritz; [b.] October 18, 1962, Passaic, NJ; [p.] John and Mary Ann Hric; [ed.] Montville High, William Paterson College-BA degree in Psychology; [occ.] Employee Trainer-Retail Store; [hon.] Dean's List; [oth. writ.] Several poems published in church bulletin; [pers.] My poems try to reflect the presence of God in our lives, his loving kindness towards us, and our need for Him. a[.] Towaco, NJ.

HUB, RUTH
[pen.] Ruth Hub; [b.] December 17, 1934, Chippewa Falls, WI; [p.] Alfred and Margaret Hub; [ed.] McDonell High; [memb.] Notre Dame Catholic Church; [oth. writ.] High school poetry: Young America Sings and Sermons in Poetry; [pers.] Enjoy painting-although amateur. Thankful for sight...to see the simple beauty in the World. [a.] Chippewa Falls, WI.

HUBBARD, GEORGE A.
[pen.] Jorge Alejandro H.; [b.] July 9, 1947, Torrington, CT; [p.] W.P. and K.B. Hubbard; [m.] Laurentina Tenorio de Hubbard, July 11, 1975; [ch.] Lucas B., Phillip T.; [ed.] Ramsey Hall School, Salisbury School, University of Arizona, University of CT; [occ.] Jack of All Trades; [memb.] Community organizations; [oth. writ.] Poetry, awaiting publishers approval. Personal unsubmitted works. Contributor, Sportsman's News, 1976-77; [pers.] The creation of poetic verse is the creation of a metaphysical life form. Once conceived it may be misplaced or lie dormant, but it is never destroyed. [a.] Tamworth, NH.

HUBERT, LEON J.
[b.] March 21, 1936, Providence, RI; [p.] Henry L. and Evelyn A. Hubert; [m.] Delores M., July 10, 1961; [ch.] Michelle C. and Renee D. Hubert; [ed.] BS Business Administration, Univ. of Southern MISS., John F. Deering H.S.; [occ.] Electronic Technician, U.S. Naval Oceanographic Service; [memb.] Lake Christian Assembly; [oth. writ.] "Rainbows in the Spray" in Poetry Premiere and "Exciting Things" in Voices of the South both by Southern Poetry Association. [a.] Biloxi, MS.

HUCKEL, COURTNEY
[b.] December 16, 1979, Raleigh, NC; [p.] Wayne and Suzanne Huckel (siblings-Joss, Jess and Adam); [ed.] Eastover Elementary, Alexander Graham Middle School; [occ.] Student; [memb.] Cheerleading Squad, Spanish Club, Honor Society, Environmental Club; [hon.] Academically Gifted Honor Society, Debate Club; [oth. writ.] I had a poem published in our school's book of poems, "Illusions"; [pers.] I enjoy writing it helps me relate to and express my feelings. [a.] Charlotte, NC.

HUDSON, GEORGE S.
[b.] July 10, 1061, Hammond, LA; [p.] Edsel and Helen Hudson; [m.] Donna Karen, October 9, 1981; [ch.] George Allen and Tracy Anne Hudson; [pers.] I owe any and all of my successes to my patient wife who is also my biggest fan. I love you Karen. [a.] Ocean Springs, MS.

HUDSON, THOMAS WAYNE
[b.] April 20, 1955, Oxford, NC; [p.] Harold H. and Ludie Hudson; [ed.] Bluestone Sr. High School, Rutledge College, Durham Technical Community College; [occ.] Communication Assistant, Department of Speech and Hearing, Murdock Center; [memb.] State Employees Association of NC, Inc.; [hon.] Wendy's Employee of the Month, Dean's List; [oth. writ.] I have several others which are unpublished at this time; [pers.] My poetry is written during the times when I identify strongly with the disciple Thomas in the Bible, who needed to see evidence before he would believe. When I actually see my feelings expressed on paper, then they become real to me. [a.] Butner, NC.

HUFF, RUTH SEEGERT
[pen.] Ruth Seegert Huff; [b.] February 25, 1930, Logumkloster, Denmark; [p.] Alfred and Lorna (deceased) Seegert; [m.] Divorced; [ch.] Jacklyn, Ingrid, Caroline and Alfred; [ed.] College in Denmark and University of Utah (a film historian); [occ.] Retired; [memb.] L.D.S. immigrant, Humane Society, Danish Clubs; [hon.] Naturalized, became a U.S. citizen about 30 years ago; [oth. writ.] Was often published in Utah farm magazine "Farm Quad"; [pers.] Be kind - but carry a stick. (I have to use a cane as I have arthritis). [a.] Las Vegas, NV.

HUFFAKER, JODI
[b.] October 29, 1970, Fayetteville, AR; [p.] Joe Huffaker and Susie Galloway; [ed.] Lincoln High; [oth. writ.] Written many poems but never attempted to have them published; [pers.] I started writing at an early age. What I write is how I feel. I wasn't influenced by any other writer, only my life. [a.] Fayetteville, AR.

HUFFMAN, D. MICHELLE
[b.] March 21, 1967, St. Petersburg, FL; [p.] B.L. Dabney and Peggy J. Matthews, (uncle-Jerry Goins); [m.] Joseph S. Jr., September 11, 1987; [ch.] Roy Joseph Huffman and Sarah Marie Huffman; [ed.] Osceola High School, St. Petersburg Junior College, Hillsborough Community College, Sarasota Vo-Tech; [occ.] Fire Fighter/Paramedic "Mommy"; [memb.] Singer/songwriter of "Just Christians" Acappella Gospel Group - Church of Christ - American Heart Association - CPR Instructor; [hon.] Paramedic - Honor Roll; [oth. writ.] Fictional novel about female firefighter in the works - many other gospel songs - editorials - political songs and poems - cartoons; [pers.] I wish to thank God and Dr. Sharon Belmahi for the child for whom this is written. "And whatever you do in word or deed, do all in the name of the Lord..." [a.] Pt. Charlotte, FL.

HUFFNAGLE, BERNADETTE
[b.] January 2, 1960, Camden, NJ; [p.] Lorraine Mary Sheeler and David Anderson III; [m.] Divorced; [ed.] Edgewood Sr. High; [occ.] Bus Driver, National School Bus Service; [memb.] Trinity United Methodist Church; [hon.] Editor's Choice Award for "Curious" published in anthology - Wind in the Night Sky by National Library of Poetry; [oth. writ.] Curious, Our Love, The Everlasting, What's What God?, Winter of Tears, and other non published writings; [pers.] I have grteat appreciation for the Love of Beauty. "For with God nothing shall be Impossible". [a.] Berlin, NJ.

HUGHES, AMANDA
[b.] October 6, 1977, Hurst, TX; [p.] Donna and Stephen Krella; [ed.] Presently 11th grade at Granite Hills High School; [occ.] Junior volunteer at Grossmont Hospital; [memb.] Illustrators Club Granite Hills; [oth. writ.] Poems published in school newspaper; [pers.] My writings reflect on the tragedies and sufferings of the world. [a.] Alpine, CA.

HUGHES, IDRIS R.
[b.] Llanllechid, Wales; [ed.] Bethesda Grammar School, University of Wales, University of Portland Oregon; [occ.] English and Western Civilization Teacher, G.P. Vanier Senior Secondary School; [hon.] Still speak Welsh fluently after 27 years in B.C. and despite the fact that I have not met any Welsh speaker here; [oth. writ.] Hardly any of my poems have seen the light of day other than a few I entered on a local newspaper; [pers.] My poetry conveys my own personal response to questions of identity and purpose. It also deals with very human issues such as sadness pain and disillusionment which continually dog our heels. I ask why? But there is no answer. [a.] Comox, B.C. Canada.

HUI, ONG KIAN
[pen.] Jason; [b.] January 30, 1963, Singapore; [p.] Ong Soo Guan and Lee Soe Tien; [ed.] Kim Keat Primary School, Victoria School, Nanyang Junior College; [occ.] Laboratory Technologist, National University of Singapore; [memb.] Faith Community Baptist Church; [hon.] Certificate of Appreciation presented in recognition of contribution to the "Window on Youth" for international youth year '85; [oth. writ.] Two poems published in a local book entitled "Poets of Singapore" (1983). Essays and poems for my church's interest group for writings known as "Write-Cell"; [pers.] I strive to reflect the goodness and beauty of God in my writings. I hope others can see his image in what I write, and so come to know him better. [a.] Singapore.

HULT, (CHARLOTTE) HELENA CORNAY
[pen.] Helena C. Hult; [b.] June 13, 1916, Idaho Falls, ID; [p.] Rev. and Mrs. Luther I. Cornay; [m.] John Luther, March 27, 1943; [ch.] John TOD Hult, Holly Jean Hult Stearns; [ed.] High School, Indiana, College, Immaculate Heart, CA; advanced studies UCLA; California Lutheran University (T.O.); [occ.] Retired-CEO social services, Santa Monica, CA; writer; [memb.] Lutheran/Ascension Church, International Association for Volunteer Education (IAVE) 72 countries; [hon.] 1978 Santa Monica Woman of the Year, 1981 Recipient, Protestant Humanitarian Aaward for National Conference of Christians and Jews (Santa Monica, CA), 1984 Registered in World Who's Who of Women (Cambridge, England), 1984 Outstanding Leadership and Community Service Award for WISE Century Plaza Hotel (Century City, CA); [oth. writ.] By-line weekly feature and assigned stories, NIXON Newspapers (Michigan City, IN). Short stories in anthologies, etc.; [pers.] My parents were writers, as well, and encouraged all five siblings to become whatever we chose to become as long as it was honorable and helpful. They were very "generative" people! [a.] Thousand Oaks, CA.

HUMBIRD, SHEENA
[b.] August 16, 1978, Trinity, TX; [p.] Danny Ray and Suzanne Marie Humbird; [ed.] Presently in tenth grade; [occ.] Student; [memb.] Future Homemakers of America, Lovelady High School Band, Lovelady High School, Volleyball Team; [hon.] Past member National Junior Honor Society, President's Academic Fitness award; [pers.] I enjoy writing poetry and I am influenced by experiences that I have had during my life. [a.] Lovelady, TX.

HUMPHREY, APRIL
[b.] May 5, 1974, Tell City, IN; [p.] Dorothy and GAry Humphrey; [ed.] Tell City High School, Western Kentucky University; [pers.] If you look hard enough beauty can be found in the simplest things. [a.] Cannelton, IN.

HUNT, JEAN
[pen.] Jean Hunt; [b.] June 13, 1940, Fresno, CA; [p.] Geneva Keays and James Hutchins; [ch.] George Lamar, III; [ed.] Clovis high school graduate; [occ.] Produce my own cassettes "Special Occasions by Barbie"; [oth. writ.] Poems published "Roger" in American Poetry Round Up, an anthology "Ocean Reflections" published in book "Voices of America" "The Mask" published in "Quest of A Dream"; [pers.] I read my poetry at a local bookstore, night

club and on a radio program. I hope to reache peoples' hearts with my poetry. [a.] Fresno, CA.

HUNT, JESSIE
[b.] February 14, 1980, Delaware County Hospital; [p.] Billy O. and Barb Hunt; [ed.] Starmont Schools (Strawberry Point, IA); [hon.] Honor Roll; [pers.] Remember the past, yet liove for today, you can make those good times last, dream about tomorrow. And you'll make it on your way. [a.] Strawberry Point, IA.

HURLBURT, AGNES KELLEY
[b.] December 27, 1919, Ansonia, CT; [p.] John J. Kelly and Elsa Marie Winkle; [m.] Royden O., April 16, 1938; [ch.] Linda, Richard, Holly and Lawrence; [ed.] Ansonia High, Kathryn Gibbs, Post College (1973-1973) BA; [occ.] REtired; [memb.] New Testament Baptist Church, AARP, Volunteer of Mercer Medicalk; [hon.] P.T.A. Founder of Seymour CT and Redford Township, Mich. 1000 hrs volunteer service; [oth. writ.] Unpublished poems; [pers.] Complete trust in God. Love of Nature. Hope for Future. Complete happiness and satisfaction in children and "Grands". [a.] Hamilton Township, NJ.

HURST, BRYAN ANTHONY
[b.] January 21, 1971, Claiborne Co., TN; [p.] Billy and Barbara Poore; [ed.] Claiborne Co. High School; [occ.] Truck Driver; [memb.] Ceder Fork Baptist Church; [pers.] I wrote this poem because I feel that God and Jesus has blessed me with so much. I thought I would give them something in return. [a.] Tazewell, TN.

HURST, ESTHER
[b.] March 29, 1951, Salem, IN; [p.] Ellis and Eska Hurst; [ch.] Edward R., Elizabeth and Christina Vaughn and Benjamin and Golda Wilhelm; [ed.] Eastern High, Indiana University; [occ.] Domestic Engineer; [memb.] Congregation Beth Isreal; [hon.] American Business Women's Scholarship, Homemaker's Scholarship, Dean's List; [oth. writ.] Jewish Poetry; [pers.] I try to focus on the condition of the world and how it relates to individuals. I hope that each poem I write will help change someone for the better. [a.] Louisville, KY.

HUSBAND, REBECCA
[b.] July 5, 1979, Lansing, MI; [p.] Raymond and Carol Husband; [ed.] 93-94 9th grade at Robertsville Jr. High School (Oak Ridge, TN); [occ.] Student; [hon.] Honor Roll, National French Exam winner, Pianist trophy winner, First place Reflections Contest 1991; [oth. writ.] Poems published in local newspapers, stories unpublished in school newspaper; [pers.] Since I am so young, I try to include all the new feelings I experience in my writing. [a.] Oak Ridge, TN.

HUTCHINGS, MELISSA MAY
[pen.] Vanessa Sullivan; [b.] October 3, 1980, Sasakatoon, Saskatchewan; [p.] Archie Dale and Karen Anne Hutchings; [ed.] Montgomery School attending 8th grade; [hon.] Freinds and family; [oth. writ.] Whispers, The Blue Jay, Dogs and The Holy Baby Jesus Christ. All unpublished as yet; [pers.] We should be more cautious on the issues of the environment and also try to save our wildlife many of my poems include these issues.

HUTCHINSON, MICHAEL J.
[pen.] M.J. Patrick; [b.] September 3, 1968, Arlington, MA; [p.] Warren K. and Alice C. Hutchinson; [ed.] Graduate of University of Massachusetts 0 Lowell: Sound Recording Technology; [occ.] Recording Engineer; [memb.] Audio Engineering Society, Amnesty International; [oth. writ.] A vast array of poetry and short stories, still seeking a publisher; [pers.] I honestly believe that there is no such thing as a problem. There are only challenges and tests of character. [a.] Lowell, MA.

HUTCHENS, KATHRYN MARIE
[pen.] Kathryn; [b.] April 12, 1981; [p.] Ellen Wilson and Ted Hutchens; [ed.] 7th grade; [hon.] Piano, soccer; [oth. writ.] As fas as the eye can see, the calm forest; [pers.] Finding your hidden talent is the best thing that can happen to you. [a.] Rogersville, MO.

HUTCHENS, LEONARD
[pers.] "I'll Be There" is dedicated with love to Deborah Lee Sherman. She is the inspiration behind the words and the magic in my life.

HUYCKE, REBECCA DAWN
[b.] January 11, 1974, Scarboro, Ontario, CAN; [p.] Charles and Eleanor Huycke; [ed.] High school graduate; [occ.] Future occupation unknown, presently plan to attend university Fall 1994; [memb.] Active member in Extra Curricular Activities, YWCA; [hon.] Ontario Scholar; [oth. writ.] Several poems published by Ontario School Boards, many works still unknown to public; [pers.] The only mirror which you should look is the one reflecting your own eyes. [a.] Bowmanville, Ontario, CAN.

HYDE, HOWARD
[pen.] Howard T.W. Hyde; [b.] October 6, 1962, New York, NY; [p.] Francois and Elizabeth N. Hyde; [ed.] Nyack High, Oswego College, Purchase College (New York) major-English. music BA degree; [occ.] Musician, Forestry; []memb.] Shelburne Historical Society; [oth. writ.] Several poems: "Blissful", "Into the Fading Lights", "A Silent Message", "The White Sky", "Love in Life", "She's Home", etc.; [pers.] My favorite poets: Longfellow, Donne, Poe, Frost. I seem to write about love, romance, advice, colors, observations, experiences, and etc. I like to use powerful words, alliteration, and rhyme. [a.] Nova Scotia, CAN.

HYDE, SHARON
[b.] August 22, 1943, Grove, OK; [p.] Norma and Bill Davis; [m.] Howard Neal, June 29, 1978; [ch.] Howard Winston, Terry Ann, Kathryn Ruth, Gregory Kent, Susan Kay, Robert Rex; [ed.] Charles Page High-Sand Springs, OK, OK College of Business and Accounting; [occ.] Owner/Director - Sharon's Day Care; [memb.] Broadway Baptist Church; [oth. writ.] Numerous poems and short stories and some anecdotes. Presently trying my hand at greeting cards; [pers.] Putting my words and inner-most thoughts and feelings, as well as my convictions in to print is a wonderful emotional release and great mental therapy. Aside from family, poetry is my greatest love. [a.] Tulsa, OK.

ICKES, TIA M.
[b.] March 24, 1982, Temple, Arizona; [p.] Shirley J. and jack C. Ickes; [ed.] Adams Elementary 6th grade; [memb.] Girls Scouts, Bowling, Chess Club, Student Council, Community Clean-Up; [hon.] Writing, Honor Student, Student of the Month, etc; [oth. writ.] Shapes, Love, Colors. [a.] Mesa, AZ 85210.

ILARDI, KANDI
[b.] December 18, 1981, Poughkeepsie, NY; [p.] Joseph and Diane Ilardi, Jr.; [ed.] Sixth grade at Benjamin Franklin Middle School; [occ.] Student; [memb.] Oddyssey of the Mind; [hon.] Citizenship, honor roll, student of the week; [oth. writ.] Stars, School etc.; [pers.] Other people's feelings are important to me and I try to express them in my poems. [a.] Rocky Mount, VA.

INGRAM, KATIE
[b.] June 23, 1938, Mexico City; [p.] Rare book seller and dress designer; [ch.] Two college age children; [ed.] BA in Creative Writing, Pomona College; [occ.] Teacher of English, Spanish, and Writing; [memb.] Academy of American Poets, California State Poetry Society; [hon.] Nominated for Best Fiction Writer and Best Poet at Santa Barbara Writers' Conference; [oth. writ.] Poems published in Santa Barbara Review, Poetry Claremont, and other publications. Just completed a novel, short story accepted to anthology; [pers.] I think writing is a way of translation our own life so we can understand it; it also becomes a tool of insight and acceptance for others who do not write. [a.] Santa Barbara, CA.

INSERRA, CATHERINE CABOARA
[pen.] Cathy Inserra; [b.] July 15, 1937, Paterson, NJ; [p.] Philomenia and John CaBoara; [m.] Joseph, July 28, 1956; [ch.] Seven; [ed.] St. Anthony's School, Home study course-American High School graduated Dec. 23, 1992; [occ.] Custodian and writer; [memb.] American Poetry Anthology, Visions, Words of Praise; [hon.] Silver Poet award 1986, A Vigil of Religious Poems and Songs, Castle of Love, This Love of Mine, A Virile of Religious Poems in book form; [oth. writ.] You're My Dream My Love, Love is a Ring Around Our Hearts, Come My Amore, Poems, Charles A Gift From Heaven, From A Sinner, An American Woman, Thy Holy Cross Above, more; [pers.] Different rainbows of love, poetry God's spiritual mirror poet, The Mystery of The Past Present and Future. I love to write. It makes me feel close to God. [a.] Hawthorne, NJ.

INTHISONE, OUDOM
[pen.] Kekam; [b.] December 17, 1978, Paris, France; [p.] Vay Inthisone; [occ.] Poet; [pers.] Increase the Peace. [a.] Maywood, NJ.

IRISH, ROSEMARY
[pen.] Rosemary Irish; [b.] April 8, 1962, Manchester, NH; [p.] Margaret T. (O'Leary) and Paul F. Murphy, Sr.; [m.] Shawn William, September 29, 1989; [ch.] Frank (dog), Hasley, Killian, Bob (cats), Ted (bunny), Sammy, Ed (birds), and The Fish; [ed.] Manchester Memorial High; [occ.] Navy wife, Keeper of the Zoo; [memb.] League of American Wheelmen; [hon.] Certificate of Appreciation from U.S. Navy presented by Capt. Large also Honorary Nuclear Submariner on the U.S.S. Buffalo under Capt. Brown; [oth. writ.] "Caution to the Fly" published 1993 by The National Library of Poetry; [pers.] Let us be cautious when we write for a single word has the power to help or hurt for a lifetime. [a.] Aiea, HI.

IRWIN, LINDA
[b.] November 25, 1960, Vulcan, Alberta, CAN; [p.] William and Patricia Wellwood; [ch.] Brandy Lee Irwin; [oth. writ.] A collection of poetry and lyrics reflecting on life and love and how its constantly changing yet ever circular. "To Hear The Scream" is my first published work; [pers.] I believe that all we experience, the rest and the worst of everything in life tugs at our hearts forcing us to learn from it and to reach out, willingly or not, to embrace it. Through poetry pity longing for this embrace is fully satisfied. [a.] Calgary, Alberta, CAN.

IUDICI, LOREDADNNA
[pen.] Loredadnna Iudici; [b.] April 27, 1968, Italy; [p.] Angelo and Giovanna Iudici; [ed.] High School with few night courses in writing (college); [occ.] Beautican; [hon.] Hairstyling, color and make-up, soon poetry. [a.] Elmwood Park, NJ 07407.

JACOBSON, ALAN
[b.] April 19, 1960, Chicago, IL; [p.] Richard and Shirley; [ed.] Maine West High School, Harper Community College; [occ.] Import/Export; [oth. writ.] Short stories, verse, screen plays; [pers.] I express myself best through words - written. I've always absorbed experiences: sights, sounds, feelings; and through written, I try to recreate and sometimes create; a time and place to be read, and enjoyed. [a.] Elk Grove, IL.

JACKSON, CARRIE
[pen.] Care Bear; [b.] October 5, 1975, San Dimas Hospital; [p.] Ron and Carolyn Jackson; [m.] (boyfriend) Mike for over 3 years; [ed.] Charter Oak High School, freshman at Citrus College; [occ.] Counselor-Sunrise Christian School; hostess - Casa Del Rey; [memb.] World Wildlife Foundation, Glenkirk Presbyterian Church; [hon.] Honor Roll all 4 years in high school GPA 3.0 or better; [oth. writ.] I have written poems since 1989 but this is the first poem that has been published. [a.] Glendora, CA.

JACKSON, JOHN W. JR.
[pen.] The Poet; [b.] August 27, 1958, Ft. Orc, CA; [p.] John W. and LaVonne R.W. Jackson; [m.] Yi Song Cha, October 27, 1978; [ed.] 12 years military Food Service Management; [occ.] Food Service Manager Chef and Locksmith; [memb.] National Rifle Association, International Society of Poets; [hon.] The first poem that was ever entered into a contest by my self was in the top ten, to many to list in a small place; [pers.] This Ole House, The Sweetness of Love, Weep Not For Me, My Thinking Tree, plus 127 more; [pers.] Poetry is read with the heart, not the mind, Poetry is read with the heart, not with the eyes. Poetry is of the heart, not the mind! [a.] Sacramento, CA.

JACKSON, MICHELLE
[b.] August 4, 1980, Philadelphia, PA; [p.] Eula Pauls and Fred Jackson; [ed.] 7th grade; [occ.] Student; [pers.] I have always been fascinated with the artistic qualities in nature and to me it is very inspiring. [a.] Philadelphia, PA.

JACKSON, TIM
[b.] June 15, 1976, Philadelphia, PA; [p.] Joseph and Catherine Jackson; [ed.] Father Judge High School Senior; [memb.] Father Judge High School Band and Dramatics Depts., School Literary Magazine Staff; [hon.] Included in Who's Who Among American High School Students; [oth. writ.] I have several unpublished poems and I have song lyrics that at present have no music to them; [pers.] I try to express, through my writing, the truthful reality of life, death, and love. I write only from feeling and instinct. [a.] Philadelphia, PA.

JAMES, BJ
[b.] Houston, TX; [p.] Nina and Sam Penix; [ch.] Carl Randall Ray, Leslie Ray Griffith, Trenton Ray McEntire; [ed.] BA and MA English - Sam Houston State University currently taking his at University of Texas at Tyler; [occ.] English Instructor at Kilgore College; [memb.] NETE, JCTA, Creative Writer's Society of East Texas; [hon.] Alpha Lamda Delta Favorite Professor, Northeast La University, World of Poetry Award San Fran, 1992; [oth. writ.] Several poems published in poetry books and college creative writing books. I have currently written three short stories and a non-fiction article of which I have submitted for publication; [pers.] I believe that anyone can write if he or she is motivated and possess self-discipline.

JAMES, CHIARLANZA
[b.] December 2, 1954, Philadelphia, PA; [p.] Mario and Florence; [m.] Denise Hood, February 26, 1994; [ch.] On the way; [ed.] Archbishop Ryan Hill High, Pennco Tech-Electronics, Lyons TEch-Huac; [occ.] Supervisor of Maintenance Dept.; [pers.] My poetry reflects the spiritual side of life and the need to be free at heart. I have been greatly influenced by Jon Anderson, Singer/songwriter. Special thanks to my loving wife, Denise. jie Bejun!

JAMES, JON
[b.] January 8, 1977, Chicago, IL; [p.] Joanne James; [ed.] presently 11th; [occ.] Waiter/Caddy; [memb.] T.F. South Teen Staff; [oth. writ.] "Why Do I Smile", "The Park Bench" and "Colored Storm"; [pers.] Society changes so rapidly! Someone has to take a stand and speak out for the people that know in their heart that the cycle must stop. I only wrote what my heart told me to. [a.] Lansing, IL.

JANJIGIAN, KEN
[b.] February 15, 1966, Watertown, PA; [p.] John and Alice Janjigian and (grandfather-Kegham Matuasian); [ed.] Clark University currently at UMASS - Boston graduate school; [occ.] Bartender, waiter, and all those other jobs; [hon.] Who's Who Among American Universities 1987-1988; [oth. writ.] An on again off again novel called Youth and so much Unknown; [pers.] My writing dives for the truth and the perpetual comedy of that search. Influenced by American Romantics - Whitman, Wolfe, Kerouac. [a.] Allston, MA.

JANOWSKI, CAROLYN
[pen.] CJ; [b.] January 1, 1935, Aberdeen, MD; [p.] Carl and Dolly Carrigan; [m.] Henry (deceased 1990), March 25, 1955; [ch.] Edward, Debbie, Michael, Sherry, Steve and Frank and Henry Jr.; [ed.] Elma High School; [occ.] Motel, Hotel Housekeeper and Homemaker; [memb.] The "100 Club" (song writer and lyricist club); [hon.] Honorable mention for song lyrics in a Nashville Competition certificate of merit and song of the month also published in L&C Magazine; [oth. writ.] I had lyrics recorded on album by Rainbow Records also had lyrics recorded on album by Keith Bradford; [pers.] "I don't know why you took him" was written about my son, Henry Jr., who passed away in 1983. He was 15 years old. He was the twin of Frank, they are my youngest. [a.] Clearbrook, BC CAN.

JASPER, NICHOLE ANNE
[pen.] Nicollette Wolfe; [b.] May 12, 1971, Robbinsdall, MN; [p.] John and Carol Jasper; [ch.] Vincent Lee (4); [ed.] Coon Rapids Senior High School, went through Instructor Training course at Northwest Racquet; [occ.] Going to school to work with abused children; [memb.] Northwest Racquet and Health Club; [hon.] Won gymnastics and dance awards; [oth. writ.] Have many poems written and am currently trying to have them published I hope to someday write a novel; [pers.] Many of my writings come from deep within...what I've experienced myself. I try to capture the hearts of those who read my poetry...let them savor in what I'm feeling. I've been told time and again that I'm a true romantic. [a.] Coon Rapids, MN.

JELAVIC, ANITA
[b.] October 20, 1974, Split, Croatia; [p.] Mira and Peter Jelavic; [ed.] Half Hollow Hills, H.S. East; [occ.] Student; [oth. writ.] Several other poems that I have not yet tried to publish; [pers.] When I need to escape from the world, paper and pen become my truest friends as I unleash my feelings and let them flow outward. [a.] Dix Hills, NY.

JENKINS, BARBARA PRIVOTT
[pen.] Barbara Privott Jenkins; [b.] January 6, 1950, Harrellsville, NC; [p.] George W. and Esther L. Privott; [m.] Divorced; [ch.] Shawn L., Michael D.; [ed.] Hampton High School, St. Leo College (Ft. Lee, VA); [occ.] Personnel Staff Noncommissioned Officer; [memb.] Hospitality Committee Mt. Olivet Baptist Church (Petersburg, VA); [hon.] Three letters of commendation U.S. Army, one army achievement medal, one army commendation medal; [oth. writ.] Will be submitting my first book for publishing before September 1993; [pers.] I strive to bring out the positive side of life and hope that through my writing someone will be inspired to do the right thing. [a.] Fort Lee, VA.

JENKINS, JENNIFER
[b.] March 13, 1973, Croner Brook, NF; [p.] Sid and Iris Jenkins; [ed.] Currently attending Memorial University of Newfoundland, majoring English; [pers.] My biggest influences are Victorian and Romantic poets and my boyfriend, Andrew Hutchings, for always encouraging me to write more. [a.] St. John's, NF.

JENKINS, J.M.
[pen.] Jane J. Jenkins; [b.] August 28, 1927,, St. Louis, MO; [p.] Mr. and Mrs. F.D. James; [m.] James, April 9, 1949; [ch.] 4; [ed.] AB, MA working on PhD at St. Louis University; [occ.] Storyteller; [oth. writ.] "The Little Fir Tree" true story of a tree in Aspen, CO written for my daughter, Mauri. [pers.] It is my philosophy that young children should be introduced to fine literature, music and poetry. They will develop an appreciation of our heritage on their primary level. They would be ready for such a program as "The Magic Teapot." These early beginnings will grow into an adult appreciation of our rich

cultural heritage. [a.] Aspen, CO.

JENNINGS, DAWN
[b.] January 15, 1974, Wilmington, DE; [p.] Robert and Deborah Jennings; [ed.] Salem High School; [occ.] College student; [hon.] Creative Writing award 1991-92, Salem High School; [oth. writ.] Poem: Memories several non-published poems and short stories; [pers.] My poetry reflects my feelings and moods. I have been influenced by people and events around me. [a.] Salem, NJ.

JENNINGS, KEVIN S.
[b.] August 21, 1958, Wytheville, VA; [p.] Starling R. Jennings and Doris Corvin Armstrong; [m.] Eva Jones Jennings, August 5, 1978; [ch.] Kevin Patrick Jennings (6/3/79-6/28/79); [ed.] Rural Retreat High School; [occ.] Material Handler/Volvo GM Heavy Truck Corp; [memb.] Library Club/Rural Retreat High School; [oth. writ.] Poem "Within" published by the National Library of Poetry, 1993; [pers.] Writing poems is a hobby of mine. I hope all who read enjoy. [a.] Wytheville, VA.

JENNINGS, ORION
[b.] July 27, 1904, Clinton, AK; [p.] Robert and Nanette Jennings; [m.] Demised; [ed.] BA, Masters, PhD, Oklahoma University, Harvard and University of Delaware; [occ.] School Administrator, State Supervisor of Schools; [memb.] Masonic & Elk Lodges, Southern Baptist Church, National Education Association, OK & CA; [hon.] Past Mayor Jenks, OK, first place OK Statewide Poetry Contest, All state high school basketball, baseball, and track; [oth. writ.] School plays, short stories, many poems for local news papers and monthly poem for Elder Care Agency; [pers.] My philosophy of life has always been to leave the world somewhat better for having lived in it. [a.] Porum, OK.

JENTZ, JENNIFER
[pen.] Jenny; [b.] May 5, 1979, Indianapolis, IN; [p.] Martha and Scott Jentz; [ed.] Still in high school - freshman; [pers.] I live in Littleton, CO., and I am a freshman in high school. am a cheerleader and swimmer. I love to write. [a.] Littleton, CO.

JEPSEN, JENNIFER
[pen.] de Anne Lynne; [b.] July 9, 1978, Lubbock, TX; [p.] Shirley and David Jepsen; [ed.] Shallowater Independent School district for last 10 years; [occ.] Student; [memb.] Basketball team, track team and tennis team; [hon.] National Junior Honor Society, awards for Math, Science, English; [oth. writ.] Several poems and short stories but not published. [a.] Shallowater, TX.

JIMENEZ, CATHERINE SYLVIA
[pen.] Cathy Jimenez (Silent); [b.] January 20, 1975, Los Angeles, CA; [p.] Ramiro Jimenez and Virginia Murillo Jimenez; [ch.] not wish to have 5 and adopt 5; [ed.] Senior at Yucca Valley High School; [oth. writ.] Currently writing poems about suicide, dedicating it to all the people who think that suicide is the only way out. Hopefully I'll make a book with all those poems and publish it, with other topics too; [pers.] I write my feelings and thoughts into poems. I hope some of my poems will inspire many people and help them realize that poems are a great part of life. This poem is dedicated to my brother Ramin, Jr. and sisters Letticia, Marylou, and Angelica Jimenez. And to all my friends I left behind in Pomona, CA. [a.] Yucca Valley, CA.

JIRAK, TIMOTHY
[pen.] Timothy Jirak; [b.] January 25, 1977; [p.] Elko, NV; [p.] Mr. and Mrs. Ronald Jirak; [pers.] If all else fails try try again. Don't give up! [a.] Overton, NV.

JOHNSON, GLORY LUKACS
[pen.] Glory Lukacs Johnson; [b.] May 3, 1927, Perth Amboy, NJ; [p.] Anna and John Rusinak; [m.] Charles E. Johnson, 1977; [ch.] Alexander Lukacs, Diane Doroba, Paul Lukacs, Charles E. Johnson; [ed.] Rutgers University; [occ.] Administrator, Doctoral Programs, Clinical Psychology and Education; [memb.] President, The Heather Garden Club, President Mary's Circle, Nativity Lutheran Church, Slovak Women Society, Church Women United, AARP; [oth. writ.] Two books: Glory I, The First Owner of the Dollhouse, One Hundred Years: Five Families; misc. poetry: "Stones Cry Out" Voices of America, "Old Girl With New Classes" in American Poetry Roundup, "WOMAN", Question of Balance, and "Lacrinare" (for Donald) in Poetry: An American Heritage. [a.] Weeki Wachee, FL.

JOHNSON, LINDA
[b.] June 13, 1943, New York, NY; [p.] Gene and Joyce White; [m.] Leo B.C., April 10, 1974; [ch.] Dane Eric and Scott Mitchell; [ed.] Mainland High, Daytona Beach Community College; [occ.] Computer Coordinator, Archives of International Speedway Corporation (Daytona Beach, FL); [memb.] NSRA, DBWomens Bowling Association; [hon.] Dean's List; [oth. writ.] None published at present time; [pers.] If any words I write or thoughts I share bring a little joy to someone's life, then I have accomplished what I set out to do. [a.] Holly Hill, FL.

JOHNSON, LYNN DIANE
[b.] December 31, 1941, Evanston, IL; [p.] Don and Flora Matteson; [m.] Jerald A., May 27, 1961; [ch.] Robert Allen, Christopher Michael, Marc Andrew; [ed.] Murray High; [pers.] Poetry writing provides me an organization of thoughts and fascinating rearrangement of words to clarify otherwise unsettled feelings. [a.] Burnsville, MN.

JOHNSON, MICHELLE E.
[b.] July 31, 1974, Fayetteville, NC; [p.] Lawrence and Incha Johnson; [ed.] Coopers Cove High and Angelo State University; [occ.] Student; [pers.] To Scott W. Caudle, for ending the pain, I give my eternal love. [a.] San Angelo, TX.

JOHNSON, NICHOLE
[b.] September 10, 1979, Highland Hospital, Belvidere, IL; [p.] Scott and Jill Johnson; [ed.] Washington Elementary School, Belvidere Junior High School will be enter Belvidere High School; [pers.] I wrote this poem because a friend of mine made me feel this way about him. [a.] Belvidere, IL.

JOHNSON, NIKITA HASSON
[b.] August 22, 1974, Philadelphia, PA; [p.] Sylvia Charlotte Johnson and Willie James Murphy; [ed.] Overbrook High School, Music Magnet and Scholars program currently attending Temple University; [occ.] Student, Sophomore, in Communication Journalism School; [memb.] Community and church choir, member of church newsletter committee, writings groups; [hon.] BWEA Scholarship Award, Literary Award, Children's Writing Diploma, Oratorical Contest Winner; [oth. writ.] Poems in school magazines, articles in church newsletter, articles in Wynnefield West Digest, and some short stories; [pers.] Life is what we make it, we can choose to let it pass us by, or resolve to seize every moment of it. [a.] Philadelphia, PA.

JOHNSON, TIMOTHY
[b.] April 13, 1955, Pontiac, MI; [m.] Gloria, October 15, 1988; [occ.] Truck Driver, Gospel Singer, Minister; [hon.] Editor's Choice award, National Library of Poetry-Spring '93 "Wind in the Night Sky"; [pers.] I see a poem in almost everything. God has given all things hidden beauty, which a poet helps all others see clearly.

JOINER, ANNIE LAURA (GRAHAM)
[pen.] A. Laura Joiner; [b.] September 13, 1908, Shubuta, MS; [p.] Riley and Laura GRaham; [m.] Jesse M., Jr. (deceased 1952), September 15, 1929; [ch.] Jesse III and James; [ed.] Waynesboro, MS, Hi-Secretarial School (Tuscaloosa, AL); [occ.] Sales Clerk, Secretary Cashier; [memb.], House Director, Sororities and Calvary Baptist Church, Eastern Star, various clubs, now cancelled; [hon.] DPE, service award, 3 certificates, Elderhsotels. One poem in "A Poets View", one in "The Poet's of Now", six merit awards for other poems. Several volunteer service awards and one poem CAL Association; [oth. writ.] Letters and articles in Daily News, Senior Edition, Poems and articles in Retirement Home News and Views and History and various subject - took writing class, articles; [pers.] I love nature, reading, painting do all kind of handwork. Always a dreamer, looking for a better tomorrow. My motto: It could be worse. I can do all things through Christ who strengthens me. (Phil. 4:13) [a.] Tuscaloosa, AL.

JONES, ANGELA
[b.] May 1, 1966, Cleveland, OH; [p.] Frances Kemmett and Ralph Jones; [ch.] Kateri Jacinta, Klarissa Jasmine; [ed.] Cleveland Central Catholic, Cuyahoga Community College; [oth. writ.] Several country western songs recorded at Victory Studios (North Olmsted, OH) poetry and short stories; [pers.] My writing reflects my personal search for peace in my life. My hope is for others to find comfort through my words as they embark on their own personal journeys. [a.] Cleveland, OH.

JONES, GAYLE A.
[b.] March 24, 1907, McClure, OH; [p.] Zail and Mary (Myers) Jones; [m.] Maria Delores, March 2, 1971; [ch.] Denessee, Jackeline and Reinaldo; [ed.] Some college; [occ.] Electronic Engineer short time taught Math (Junior High) Parochial; [memb.] NARFE, Poetry Institute Southern Baptist; [hon.] Meritorious awards Spark, NARFE, various commendations from federal government relating to work done; [oth. writ.] Poems to newspapers and church bulletins; [pers.] I trace my lineage to American Natives and thus I lean to nature poetry. I prefer the easy to read, simple language style, though I do like metaphors. [a.] Lake Placid, FL.

JONES, JANET
[b.] December 27, 1976, St. Louis, MO; [p.] Barb and Everett Jones; [ed.] Orchard Farm High School; [occ.] STudent; [memb.] Vic. Tanny, American Martial Arts; [hon.] Two bronze metals in Tae Kwondo; [oth. writ.] Other poems about my life, never sent in; [pers.] I write about my feelings mostly when I get depressed. [a.] St. Charles, MO.

JONES, MICHAEL PHILIP
[b.] July 5, 1972, Toronto, Ontario, CAN; [p.] Philip Michael and Sharone Grace (Smith) Jones; [ed.] High School to grade 11; [occ.] Marketing; [oth. writ.] Poems under the titles of "Path of the Weary", "Known to Love", "Death in the Young". [a.] Burlington, Ontario, CAN.

JONES, NATALIE ANN
[b.] April 25, 1966, Dorchester, MA; [p.] Virginia and Bill Jones; [ch.] "Are More Precious Than Diamonds"; [ed.] Each One Teach One! Educate to Elevate!; [occ.] The validation of our existence and experiences; [memb.] Black Child Development Institute, Black Women, Health Project, Free My People, The Boycott Committee; [hon.] "Show our elderly some attention and kindness"; [oth. writ.] Poems, essays, and journal writing; [pers.] "...To assert one's voice and affirm one's humanity in a place that conspires to suppress and deny." K.F.C.H. Gone but not forgotten; A.R.M.P.L.R.A.F.T.S.L.G. GiGi, J.A.A.A.; [a.] Boston, MA.

JONES, ORA
[b.] September 7, 1907, Fort Deposit, AL; [p.] Lewis and Ella Jones; [ch.] Helen Brooks; [ed.] Completed ninth grade; [occ.] Retired seamstress; [memb.] President of Missionary Circle Number 1, Sunday School teacher and Member of the September Club; [hon.] Honored as oldest mother in the church; [oth. writ.] "Fathers", "September", "The Church" none have been published; [pers.] My writings are influenced by the love God has manifested in my life and to let me live to see the beauty of nature and to seek the Wonders of Heaven. [a.] Montgomery, AL.

JONES, SARAH
[b.] March 19, 1981, Henderson County, NC; [p.] Tommy and Tamara Jones; [ed.] Attended Fairview Elementary K-6, moved spent last of 6th grade in TN in Flat Gap Elementary; [hon.] Received various awards in Academics; [pers.] I enjoy writing poems and short stories since second grade. [a.] Thoen Hill, TN.

JONES, SHIRLEY ANN
[pen.] Sapphire; [b.] September 18, 1958, Selma, AL; [p.] Annie Mae and Bacchus Jones; [ed.] Roxbury Community College; [occ.] Counselor, Business owner of Sapphire Cleaning Co.; [oth. writ.] Published in the New England Newsletter called Womyn's Tidings, several poems; [pers.] Writing makes a true poet express what they see and feel. I love and adore Maya Angelo. [a.] Waltham, MA.

JONES, TREY
[b.] September 28, 1969, Houston, TX; [m.] Joey Whitford, June 1994; [ed.] High school for Engineer Professions, Cornell University, Rice University; [occ.] Software Engineer, BRS Software (Albany, NY); [memb.] Linguistic Society of America; [hon.] Phi Beta Kappa - Cornell; Dean's Scholar-Cornell; Presidential Fellow-Rice; [oth. writ.] Several articles for the Speculative Grammarian; Documentation and examples for MacMath 8.0 by Hubbard & West; [pers.] I think the best way to write well is to write for yourself; you are your own best critic. I want to capture an image in my poetry - a sensual snapshot. The best compliment I ever got was: "You rip out your heart and hold it up, bloody and still beating." That's what I strive for. [a.] Ballston Lake, NY.

JORDAN, SARA
[b.] September 11, 1979, Lexington, NE; [p.] C. Earl and Sue Jordan, Jr.; [ed.] Freshman at Troy High School (Troy, TX); [memb.] F.H.A.; [hon.] English award (7th and 8th grade). [a.] Troy, TX.

JORDAN, THEODORE L.
[b.] October 2, 1969, Minneapolis, MN; [p.] Leo and Carol Jordan; [ed.] Wayzata High School, Military Culinary Arts program; [occ.] Cook; [hon.] Numerous military awards; [oth. writ.] "Rainbow Chasing" is my first published many more in my dreams; [pers.] Go forth on your emotions with your intelligence. Use them both to reach a standard of survival. [a.] Plymouth, MN.

JOSEPHBERG, LIBBY
[pen.] Clarissa Reynolds; [b.] April 15, 1976, New York; [p.] Myra and Neil Josephberg; [ed.] Westchester Hebrew High School; [occ.] Student, want to major in Psychology at College; [memb.] Dance Club, Yearbook staff, Computer Newsletter and school newspaper; [hon.] Poetry contest winner at W.H.H.S.; [oth. writ.] Numerous poems that were published in both Hebrew and English. (In school Journals and anthologies); [pers.] Although your past can't be changed, you and only you hold the key to your future. A special thanks to those at W.H.H.S. and Martha Weston for their inspiration. [a.] Bronx, NY.

JUDD, SARAH
[pen.] Sarah; [b.] November 17, 1976, Lewiston; [p.] Sherry and Raymond Judd; [ed.] Jay High School, junior year 1993/94; [occ.] Student; [hon.] Natural helper, Class Secretary; [oth. writ.] Other poems; [pers,] I got my insight from the book "The Color Purple" plus my mother served on a rape crisis hot line called "SAVE" for several years. [a.] Jay, ME.

JUSO, KENA
[b.] May 31, 1978, Deadwood, SD; [p.] Nels and Grace Juso; [occ.] Student at Lead High School; [memb.] Girl Scouts for 7 years; [hon.] Presidential Academic Fitness Award; [oth,. writ.] Many unpublished poems; [pers.] I enjoy writing. [a.] Deadwood, SD.

KACZUR, ERIN R.
[b.] July 25, 1993, Warren General Hospital; [p.] Nicholas and Dolores Kaczur (deceased); [ed.] 8th grade, student; [pers.] All of my poems are reflections of sorrow, suffering, and fear of mankind and earth itself. [a.] Warren, OH.

KAGAN, GLORIA J.
[b.] Kansas City, MO; [m.] Dr. Stuart Kagan; [ch.] Two daughters; [ed.] MA from University of Arizona; [occ.] English, Social Studies and Humanities teacher; [pers.] Keep dancing. [a.] Leawood, KS.

KAMMERER, MELISSA J.
[pen.] Misty Campbell; [b.] August 27, 1981, Ft. Lewis, WA; [p.] Christina Campbell and Rusty Kammerer; [ed.] Student; [memb.] Beta Sigma Phi Legacy US Navy Sea Cadet; [pers.] I like to write. [a.] Everett, WA.

KANE, YVONNE BATEMAN
[b.] May 29, 1944, Morgan City, LA; [p.] Wheaton and Larue Bateman; [m.] Patrick F.; [ch.] Annette Thibodeaux, Susan Mahfouz, and Bonnie Ann Guarisco; [ed.] Morgan City High, and Lafayette High School; [occ.] Aspiring author; [oth. writ.] "My Song", "Memories", "Desperation". "My Song" published by Quill Books, "Memories" chosen for the Golden Poet Trophy for 1992; [pers.] Poetry is a reflection of life. Writing helps me to release the emotions held inside concerning myself and others. [a.] Houston, TX.

KANG, ALICE
[b.] October 25, 1975, Baltimore, MD; [p.] Charles and Betty Kang; [ed.] Meade Senior High, Trinity College (Washington, DC-class of '97); [occ.] College student; [hon.] Who's Who Among American High School Students for three years, Presidential Scholar; [oth. writ.] Featured in USA Today News as a National Teen Panelist for the '92-'93 year; [pers.] In my writings, especially poetry, I express the emotions and thoughts, that come deep within. True expression is not merely a reflection on the pleasant aspects of life, but also the harsh and controversial. [a.] Hanover, MD.

KANWALJIT, KAUR
[pen.] Kelly; [b.] January 23, 1963, Singapore; [p.] Hardip Singh Bedi and Asha Kumari; [m.] John Christopher Post, April 28, 1992; [ed.] Certificate in Education (Singapore), BA in English with Honors (Calgary), MA in English (Calgary); [occ.] Instructor (Mt. Royal College-English Instructor); [memb.] Society for Technical Writing; [oth. writ.] Poem published in Sanscrit. Compiling a personal collection of short stories - (Ok, striving to); [pers.] This poem is dedicated to Mummy, Papa, and my father-in-law John Daniel Post, who insisted I write: thanks for the micro tape recorder! [a.] Calgary, Alberta.

KAPP, LAWRENCE D.
[pen.] Larry Kapp; [b.] September 10, 1971, Farmington Hills, MI; [p.] Joyce and Dennis Kapp; [ed.] Canton High School and Indiana University; [occ.] Student; [pers.] I dedicate my first published piece to my loving family. They've taught me the meaning of true loyalty by going there for me...no matter what! [a.] Canton, MI.

KASAL, LUDWIG
[pen.] Ludwig Kasal; [b.] April 4, 1917, Bronx, New York; [p.] Ludwig and Josephine; [m.] Gertrude (deceased), June 23, 1947; [ch.] Linda and Charles; [ed.] NYU, Industrial Arts and Administration, State University, Tech. Ed., NYU Anthropology; [occ.] Retired School Administration; [memb.] Phi Delta Kappa, Westchester Industrial Arts Club; [hon.] Service Key, Phi Delta Kappa, Rho Chapter, NYU; [oth. writ.] Poems in local paper; [pers.] The key to social excellence is poetry. [a.] Bronxville, NY.

KATZ, ALICE
[pen.] Alice Max; [b.] September 9, 1926, Shelby, MS; [p.] Anna Ostrowd and Sam Yaffe; [m.] Morris (deceased), October 30, 1949; [ch.] Irene Sybil and Scott William Katz; [ed.] Hattiesburg High and Junior College; [occ.] Secretary (retired); [memb.] Burt Reynolds Institute of Theatre Training, Edna Hibel, Lifemember Habassah and B'noir Birthwomen OIT, American Heart Association and Cancer - Norton Art Gallery; [hon.] President Harry Truman for U.S.O., American Heart Association, American Cancer, Jayces Pox, B'ne Birth, Habassah, March of Dimes; [pers.] Neither love, honor, wealth nor power can give your heart a cheerful hour when your health is lost!!! Express my views in my poetry. [a.] West Palm Beach, FL.

KAUENHOWEN, NICOLE
[b.] February 26, 1975, Steinbach, Manitoba; [p.] James and Mary Kauenhowen; [m.] Boyfriend-Ken Friesen; [ch.] Brittany Kauenhowen; [oth. writ.] "Lost" not yet published; [pers.] I can only hope that my generation and future generations will understand and feel what I felt while writing this poem. Dedicated to Ken, our daughter Brittany, and our future son or daughter. [a.] Manitoba, CAN.

KAULILI, DEBBY
[b.] February 4, 1964, Kauai, Hawaii; [p.] Springwater and Marjorie Kaulili; [ed.] Kauai High, Kauai Community College, Leeward Community College; [occ.] Graphic Artist, Hawaii Hochi, Honolulu; [memb.] Songwriters Association; [hon.] Dean's List; [oth. writ.] American Lung Association, article in their newsletter; [pers.] I strive to better my ability in songwriting and poetry - to motivate others to achieve more in life than giving up. [a.] Honolulu, HI.

KAVOURAS, JIM
[b.] October 11, 1948, Cleveland, OH; [m.] Marianne; [ch.] Peter, Alex, Jaime; [occ.] Self-employed; [oth. writ.] Paradox revisited stream of consciousness - Dec. '81 Whispering Smith, '78 4th and Thereabouts II and '78 4th and Thereabouts III; [pers.] The only future we have is death. We have no future, only a past. [a.] Lyndhurst, OH.

KAY, ANNIKA
[b.] January 31, 1982, Anaheim, CA; [p.] Marilyn Kujala and Howard A. Kay; [ed.] Morse Elementary School; [occ.] Student; [memb.] Finnish Society; [hon.] Honor Roll; [pers.] I am concerned with animals and saving the environment. I want to learn Finnish and study in Finland. [a.] Fullerton, CA.

KEARNEY, SEAN BERNARD
[b.] January 28, 1968, St. John's Nfld; [p.] Bernard and Anne; [ed.] Gonzaga High, Memorial University of Newfoundland; [occ.] Student; [oth. writ.] Several poems published in local Herald; [pers.] Never lose sight of your true identity, and always reserve time for the things you love to preserve that identity. [a.] St. John's, Nfld.

KECMER, GRACE
[b.] November 24, 1941, Passaic, New Jersey; [p.] Rocco and Rosalie La Bozetta; [m.] Robert, September 30, 1972, Kristyna; [ed.] Fair Lawn High, William Paterson College; [occ.] Retired teacher, P.S. No. 12, Forrest School; [memb.] American Family Association, National Right to Life Committee. [a.] Fair Lawn, NJ.

KEENEY, APRIL D.
[pen.] April D. Keeney; [b.] August 9, 1978, Wellsboro, PA; [p.] Michele D. A'Key; [ed.] Student at Wellsboro Senior High School; [occ.] Student; [memb.] High School Band Front; [hon.] Honor Roll Student; [oth. writ.] Poems' Friends, Endings, Ships (unpublished); [pers.] I am the Great Great Niece of Herbert E. Muir famous English poet. [a.] Wellsboro, PA.

KELLER, FERDINAND GERALD
[b.] June 17, 1938, Collinsville, IL; [p.] Walter and Martha Keller; [m.] Joann Marie, November 20, 1959; [ch.] Derek D. (28), Heather D. Jancek (26) and Ryan (24); [ed.] High school graduate, spent two years in the army; [occ.] Have been an operator for Madison Co. Hwy. Dept. for 35 years; [memb.] St. Jacob lions Club and the Methodist Church of St. Jacob; [oth. writ.] Four poems were published in the summer/winter issues of the 1993 "Treasured Poems of America" collection by Sparrowgrass Poetry Forum; [pers.] Writing is a way to share times of love, concern, and loss. While working outdoors in the public's eye, I absorb inspiration from people and nature. I say never be afraid to admit what you have accomplished. [a.] St. Jacob, IL.

KELLEY, AMBER
[b.] Lagrange, GA; [p.] Henry Leo and Florence Pam Kelley; [ed.] Going into high school; [oth. writ.] Other poems, nothing has ever been published; [pers.] Poetry is very fascinating to me and I believe that everyone has a little bit inside. All they need to do is find a pen and a piece of paper. [a.] Salem, AL.

KELLEY, APRIL MARIE
[b.] July 21, 1974, Louisville, KY; [p.] Alan and Debbie Leonard; [m.] Rick, Jr., December 5, 1992; [ch.] Christian Tyler; [ed.] DuPont Manual High, University of Louisville; [occ.] Bookkeeper; [oth. writ.] I have kept many journals over the years that contain many of my works; [pers.] My poetry serves as an outlet for whatever feelings I may be keeping locked up inside of myself. [a.] Louisville, KY.

KELLY, EILEEN M.
[b.] August 15, 1968, Weymouth, MA; [p.] John J. Jr. and Mary D. (Mortell); [ed.] BA Foreign Language, Emmanuel College; [occ.] Cashier, Bradlees; [memb.] World Wilde Life Fund, National Audubon Society; [hon.] Editor's Choice Award, National Library of Poetry Spring 1993 Contest, First Prize - fiction 1990, Honorable Mention - poetry 1992, Emmanuel College Poetry and Fiction Contest; [oth. writ.] "The Machine and I" in Wind in the Night Sky, five issues of Emmanuel Advocate; [pers.] Among my writing influences are Stephen King, Isaac Asimov, and Emily Dickinson. [a.] Woburn, MA.

KELLY, JUNE
[b.] February 15, 1920, Milwaukee, WI; [p.] Peter and Edna Kaisler; [ch.] Kathleen Ann Smith (CA) and Patrice McCarnan (OH); [ed.] Solomon Juneau High School and Milwaukee State Teacher's College; [occ.] Editor-Waupun Leader News (20 years - retired); [memb.] Wisconsin Press Women (former), Daughters of Isabella (currently), Rotary Club (past); [hon.] Numerous; [oth. writ.] Book: "Clarence Addison Shaler, a Very Large Wizard of Oz", "Waupun-City of Sculpture", "Waupun-the First 150 Years" and poetry, short stories, news and feature articles. A book in writing; [pers.] Without words, there would be no civilization. Without words, love could not be communicated. Without words, there could be war, but no peace. Without words, the silence would be as death. Words are essential for LIFE. [a.] Mason, OH.

KELLY, OLIVER
[pen.] Oliver Kelly; [b.] March 9, 1940, Honolulu, HI; [p.] Edward and Alice Mainae Kelly; [m.] Ipolani, February 21, 1971; [ch.] Grayden, Alden, Katherine, Lira and Meliah; [ed.] Farrington High; [occ.] PMA III Hilo Hospital-Operating Room and entertainer; [hon.] Kohala FFA Grand Marshall, Big Island Entertainer of the Year; [hon.] Co-host Kapiolani Children's Teleton - Co-host and Entertainer Maui's Muscular Distrophy Telethon; [oth. writ.] Composed and recorded several songs; [pers.] Love is the main theme in my music. This poem speaks of my grand daughter Jaslynn Emiko Kamakanaoakalani Kelly. I wish I could infect the world with love through my music and writings. [a.] Hilo, HI.

KELSEY, ASHLEY
[b.] February 28, 1977, Redondo Beach, CA; [p.] James and Jo Kelsey; [ed.] Student - South High. [a.] Redondo Beach, CA.

KEMMER, JACKIE
[b.] October 3, 1939, Ottumwa, IA; [m.] Lawrence, August 12, 1961; [ch.] L. David, Martha J., Jane A.; [ed.] William Penn College, Colorado State University; [occ.] Language Arts Teacher Park Middle School; [memb.] National Council of Teachers of English, Colorado Language Arts Society; [hon.] Delta Kappa Gamma Twice included in **Who's Who Among America's Teachers; [pers.] I am greatly influenced by the spiritual wisdom of the Native Americans of the Southwestern U.S. I am deeply grateful to the Native American** artists I have met. [a.] Esteo Park, CO.

KEMP, L.H.
[pen.] LHK; [b.] January 17, 1906, Kutztown, PA; [p.] George and Amy Kemp; [m.] Kathryn, August 24, 1933; [ch.] William Kemp and Diane Ludwig; [ed.] Kutztown High, Muhlenberg College BS, Penn State MEd; [occ.] Retired-H.S. Principal, Biology Teacher; [memb.] United Church of Christ, Retired Teachers, Penn State York Alumni, Elks, Mason; [hon.] H.S. Nature Study named in my honor, National Science Foundation stipends summer school at Bucknell Univ., University of Maryland and University of Rhode Island; [oth. writ.] World of Poetry - Honorable Mention 1990, Golden Poet 1991 and 1992; [pers.] Writing poems is a challenge. Life is precious, sacred, a challenge, an adventure and it needs to be nurtured. [a.] Hanover, PA.

KENDRICK, JOANN MAY
[pen.] Heavens Own Light; [b.] August 2, 1952, Newark, NJ; [p.] Richard Austin and Rebecca May; [ch.] Malisha Kendrick; [ed.] Barringer High School, Florida Junior College; [occ.] Disable; [memb.] Sigma Tau Gamma; [oth. writ.] Hotter Than July (article to Stevie Wonder), The Tree of Life, Blanket of Names, Blessing of Rest, Peculiar People, Some of You Just Can't See, Jail, Guardian Angel, Stunt Man Blues, Waiting, Mixed Us, and more; [pers.] I strive to put spiritual light on reality of today's times, I was inspired through music, Stevie Wonder, and people to write poetry. A long time cancer patient with faith. [a.] Newark, NJ.

KENNEDY, LUE
[b.] Chicago, IL; [p.] Edwin A. and Rose Baker; [m.] James D. Kennedy; [ch.] James Edwin, William Thomas, Mary Kathleen and Patricia Anne; [ed.] Elgin Community and Harper Colleges, studied voice (coloratura soprano) under the direction of Maestri Carl Cravin and Burt Preston; [occ.] Directress, ParkView Montessori School; [hon.] Dean's List, voice recital at Chicago Public Library and Kimball Hall; [pers.] A child's laughter is the echo of an angel singing. [a.] Streamwood, IL.

KENT, KARMEL K.
[pen.] Kandi K. Kent; [b.] march 29, 1949, Lincoln, NE; [p.] Milton Emerson and Inez Rosemary Shipps; [m.] Larry L., November 11, 1967; [ch.] Sondra Lynn Thompson (nee Kent) and Bradley R. Kent; [ed.] Northeast High graduated 1967; [occ.] Russell's Corporation; [memb.] First Baptist Church of Baghdad; [hon.] Two year Perfect Attendance at Russell's Corp (9-25-90 t0 9-25-92) also Employee of Month at Russell's January 1990 and August 1991; [oth. writ.] "Beauty of Life" written in Nov. 1987. This poem was wrote about the same time I wrote "Endless Love". The poem is very nice, I just haven't given it any exposure at this time; [pers.] Whenever I write, I put my deepest most sincere thoughts on paper, and later compile all my ideas into a poem. My ideas lean mostly towards romance and what I consider to be beautiful in life. [a.] Pace, FL.

KERSTING, JONATHAN
[b.] August 7, 1972, Pittsburgh, PA; [p.] Janet G. Boess; [ed.] Senior at the University of Pittsburgh; [occ.] Student/Assistant Manager of Miller Hardware; [memb.] German Air Sucker Society; [hon.] Dean's List every semester at the University of Pittsburgh; [oth. writ.] Commentaries printed in the Pittsburgh Post Gazette; [pers.] Writing is like working on old Volkswagens, a little patience, trust and love is all it takes. I have been influenced from to: Derricote to W.L. Williams. [a.] Pittsburgh, PA.

KIEHLMEIER, AMY
[pen.] Amy Kiehlmeier; [b.] October 5, 1977, Erie, PA; [p.] Janis and Bob Kiehlmeier; [m.] David; [ed.] E.A. Laney High School; [memb.] Tue Kwon Doe; [oth. writ.] Some private poems that I have written. That no one has read, over a hundred of them; [pers.] Many people say, for me only being 15, that I have a talent and I will improve even more when I'm older. I love writing about people and different situations that I'm in. [a.] Wilmington, NC.

KIMMEL, MARLO
[pen.] Earth Angel; [b.] July 8, Indianapolis, IN; [p.] Joseph and Jla Paul; [occ.] Communications Advisor, Animal Consultant; [oth. writ.] My second poem but more to come; [pers.] I am most grateful for the philosophy of L. Ron Hubbard for my ability as an artist - its Tara his works I have found myself. [a.] Clearwater. FL.

KIMZEY, MIKE
[b.] February 24, 1954, Maywood, CA; [p.] Tom and Irene Kimrey; [ch.] Meagan Rae and Ryan Michael Kimzey; [ed.] 12 grade Bell High School; [occ.] Welder, Carpenter, Mason; [oth. writ.] 100's of poems unpublished (Help); [pers.] Life's been my teacher. I wish to teach others introspection through my work, hard earned life degree. [a.] Kailla Kona, HI.

KING, JOY R.
[pen.] Tara Southerly; [b.] August 5, 1939, Memphis, TN; [p.] Roy and Margaret Rainey; [m.] Guy King; [ch.] Lonnie King and Cheryl King Ramsey; [ed.] Whitehaven High School 1957; [occ.] Homemaker; [memb.] Homemaker's Club; [pers.] I love life and I love people. I would like to share my feelings with everyone in my writing. [a.] Paducah, KY.

KING, RHONDA
[pen.] Starfire King; [b.] October 23, 1956, Corning, NY; [p.] Ronald F. King and Betty S. Young; [m.] Divorced after 8 years Thomas P. Shinn; [ch.] Amber Christine and Kavin Wayne Shinn; [memb.] National Cherokee Federation under chief Elkheart Griffin born September 18, 1916, died Feb 14, 1990; [hon.] "A Dream For All His Federation" was land to build our reservation, he died before his dream was born. The greatest man I've ever known". In remembrance of my chief, with love - Starfire King; [oth. writ.] Locked Doors - published 1992 Anthology in American Heritage by Western Poetry Association; [pers.] Long before he ever wrote the song, I have lived by the words of Michael Jackson's "Save the World". Our futures reality is staring us in the face but still we choose to destroy what is **vital to our children's survival. [a.] Riverview, FL.**

KIRKPATRICK, FRANK A.
[pen.] F.A. Kirk Patrick (Kirk Patrick); [b.] June 30, 1912, Nashville, TN; [p.] William W. Kirkpatrick, (Lillian-mother - successful in business, was life long inspiration to me, value of education, etc.); [m.] Elaine Yvonne, February 14, 1976; [ch.] Frank Jr., Lillian, Kathleen, Michelle; [ed.] Public schools (Indianapolis, IN); [occ.] Retired, but still actively involved in writing, self gratification; [memb.] The Salvation Army and other charitable organizations, also humanitarian activities; [oth. writ.] None published, but have had the satisfaction of establishing a communication relationship with President Bill Clinton, expressing an ongoing interest in the "State of Union", etc.; [pers.] I am a staunch advocate, that life itself, should be an ongoing educational experience. One should never cease the pursuit of knowledge and an active interest in our civilization, regardless of age. [a.] Cleveland, OH.

KIRWAN, ROBERT J.
[b.] June 14, 1942, Duluth, MN; [p.] Robert Alexander Kirwan and Christine Cathrine Calanducci; [m.] Annette (Zych), October 9, 1965; [ch.] Sean, Kelly Ann, Shannon Noelle, Kristi Erin; [ed.] Graduated De LaSalle High School, attended University of Minnesota (2 yrs); [occ.] I.B.T. Journeyman Mailer; [memb.] IBT, Knights of Columbus, B of RC, ITU; [hon.] Union Steward, Chapel Chairman, Vice President Mailers Union #4 Minneapolis and St. Paul, MN, Asst. Foreman, Mailroom Mpls., Star Tribune Co. Inc., Div. Cowles Publications Inc.; [pers.] This poem, was tribute to God's gift, our planet earth. I was, urged, cajoled, and encouraged by my loving sister, Jackie Baker. [a.] Fridley, MN.

KISTLER, BONNIE
[b.] April 23, 1941, Philipsburg, PA; [p.] Paul and Roberta Matthew; [m.] C. Richard, July 12, 1963; [ch.] Theodore (Ted), Terri and Jennifer; [ed.] Philisburg-Osceola Area High Shippensburg State University; [occ.] Second grade teacher, Wallaceton-Boggs Elem., P-O schools; [oth. writ.] Nothing published. I have written several articles for my church newsletter which I edited, and published. Also, I create many poems for use in my classroom; [pers.] While most of my poems have been written as gifts or tributes, I strive to use my poems and other writings as a witness for Jesus Christ. God has gifted me and I want to give Him honor. [a.] Osceola Mills, PA.

KLEIN, GREG
[b.] September 26, 1970, Syracuse, NY; [p.] Jennifer Evans and Jeff Klein, MD; [ed.] BA in Journalism from Auburn University-minors-Philosophy and Radio/TV/Film; [occ.] Sports Editor-Prattville Progress; [memb.] Fraternity; [hon.] Mark of Excellence-Society of Profession Journalist, Who's Who in American Colleges and Universities, Spades Senior Honorary; [oth. writ.] I am working on my first novel "The Road to Churchill" although I have free lanced extensively for newspapers, this will be my first poetry/fiction to be published; [pers.] From Robert Pirsig and the ancient Greeks: "The future is something that comes upon you from behind you back as the past recedes before your eyes." [a.] Prattville, AL.

KLEIN, C. MARGUERITE
[b.] April 5, 1909, Rural Wichita, KS; [p.] Lewis and Hettie Nicholson; [m.] Richard S. (deceased), August 23, 1938; [ch.] Richard S. Jr., Larry L. and Alford D.; [ed.] AB Degree and majored in Education, English and Home Economics; [occ.] Teacher-Minister's wife, social worker for State of Kansas; [memb.] NEA, Presbyterian Church, AAUW, Retired Teachers, Art Association, AARP-RSVP; [hon.] Woman of Year in Religion, Poems in Presbyterian Publication and also calendar for oil paintings and craftwork; [oth. writ.] "Changes", "My Family", "What Is?", "Questions" "Whose World Is It?", and "ABCs on the Way to School"; [pers.] God is Love. He created the world. He gave his created humans control of all lesser creations. If humans abuse and not love enough to care, then its their fault that there is trouble in the world. However, He can intervene. [a.] Newton, KS.

KLEIN, NICOLE
[pen.] Nikki; [b.] December 7, 1980, New York City, NY; [p.] Yvonne Irizarry and Leo Klein; [ed.] Presently an 8th grader student at Frank D. Whalen Middle School (Bronx, NY); [hon.] Merit award in writing and the Honor Society; [pers.] I enjoy reading which inspires me to write. I hope that more young people explore the beauty of poetry. [a.] Bronx, NY.

KLEKAMP, ERIC
[b.] March 3, 1971, DeKalb, IL; [p.] William and Cynthia Klekamp; [ed.] Elgin High School Community College, Art Institute of Chicago; [occ.] Graphic Artist; [oth. writ.] This is my first published poem; [pers.] Writing helps me keep my insanity. [a.] Elgin, IL.

KLINGVALL, PETER
[b.] May 25, 1969, Medeline Hat AB CAN; [ed.] Currently attending University of Calgary; [occ.] Student; [pers.] If you write your thoughts, even just for yourself. You will be able to achieve perspective.

KOCIS, THERESA (JULIA)
[b.] May 22, 1907, Cleveland, OH; [p.] Julius Kocis and Teresia Gyuris; [ed.] BS in Education Fordham 200 college credits, some graduate courses, 60 credits in Art; [occ.] Retired Art Teacher now RSVP Art for Senior Women. Visit sick to read them a psalm; [memb.] Women in the Arts, UFT, NYSUT, Retired Teachers NY; [hon.] "Poet Laureate of Month" (classical form), Poet of the Month-modern form "Divine Love", Significant promotion of Religion, Morals, and the Arts. Amer. Biographical Inst. Dr. Greenberg's Large French Medal Titular member of International Com. of CENTRO STUDI E SCAMBI INTL ACADEMIA LEONARDO DA VINCI. Drifted away from Round Table Poets of Arkansas, Creative Writing, etc. Listed in Cambridge International Who's Who in Poetry, ADDY received in "Come Blow Your Horn"; [oth. writ.] Course of Study in Art 6-9 half a humorous autobiography (all Tears Left Out). Poems with feeling and religious poetry. Collection of Americana showing the endearing and beautiful titles Our Forefathers gave to the Creator. All of them so God-dependent "What Constitutes a Valid Work of Art"; [pers.] The world has become full of greed and immorality. Those who desire to create a world govt when there is no solitary govt able to live peacefully and morally by itself-are in error. Too much regulation is tyranny. A man with a piece of ground should be able to raise anything he wants to that is not habit forming. Roman Catholic. [a.] Warwick, NY.

KOEHLER, FREDDY
[b.] June 17, 1975, Queens, NY; [p.] Marilyn Koehler; [ed.] Graduated with scholars from Beverly Hills High School, now attending Carnegie Mellon on scholarship; [occ.] Student; [memb.] Aftra, SAG; [hon.] Principal's Honor Roll, finished third in Charlie Awards Creative Writing contest; [oth. writ.] Two poems published in Beverly Hills High School's literary magazine, "From Within"; [pers.] I try to represent the growing clarity and validity that my generation's voice has to offer. I have been greatly influenced by Akken Ginsburg. [a.] E. Stroudsburg, PA.

KOERNER, PENNY SUE
[b.] November 6, 1964, Seymour, IN; [p.] Kenneth Dale Ferris and Joan Lett; [m.] Jess, June 23, 1989; [ch.] Valorie Kaitlyn and Amanda Kendall; [ed.] Crothersville High School; [hon.] Young Author's Award in the sixth grade at Crothersville Elementary; [oth. writ.] Several poems to family, nothing published; [pers.] There is nothing more important in life than family and true happiness. My poems are reflections of my heart to those I hold dear. [a.] Nabb, IN.

KOLAR, SISTER MARY PAULA
[b.] March 26, 1927, Youngstown, OH; [p.] George T. and Mary Francis Kolar; [ed.] Chaney High School, attended Fordham University, NY Canisius College, Boston College, graduate of Fordham University; [occ.] Missionary Sister, Daughter of St. Paul; [oth. writ.] Articles and poems published in the FAMILY MAGAZINE and in INNER HORIZONS. Poems published in Banner Books, commemorative volumes: SORIN OF NOTRE DAME, EDNA ST. VINCENT MILLAY, 1991, 1992; poem published in The Catholic Herald, Hawaii, for 50th Anniversary of Pearl Harbor; [pers.] In writing poetry, I am inspired by poetry's power to raise the mind to sublime, lofty thoughts, to stir the heart's noblest affections and sentiments, and to motivate people in their pursuit and achievement of worthy goals and ideals. [a.] Boston, MA.

KOLBE, DOROTHY
[b.] May 7, 1916, Toledo, OH; [ed.] Masters degree in education financed entirely by myself; [occ.] Retired teacher and telegraph operator; [memb.] AARP, Church, Ohio Teachers Association; [hon.] More than 30 trophies in music and for fiddle contests, I made 2 violins from scratch, no kits, learned from a book. I use them all the time. Have played in country bands and college orchestra; [oth. writ.] Composed words and music for high school song while in high school, composed senior class poem, in past years wrote poems and articles for newspapers; [pers.] I always want to help others and be a participant, not spectator. Anyone can learn to do anything, any kind of work, music, drawing pretty much without formal training. It takes interest and hard work. [a.] Leipsic, OH.

KOLLATSCHNY, JANIS K.
[b.] Houston, TX; [p.] James A. and Jeannette C. Koen; [m.] Gary W.; [ch.] Tracy, Cory, Aubrey, Kari; [occ.] Homemaker; [pers.] My writings relate to life itself. The decisions, happenings, and feelings to we have on a day to day basis. [a.] Borger, TX.

KONCZAL, KELLY LEA
[pen.] Kelly Lea; [b.] January 18, 1976, Baltimore, MD; [p.] Thomas J. Konczal and Carolyn J. Wanciak; [ed.] Sheehan High, Cedarhurst School, Hampton Academy; [occ.] Freelance Writer; [hon.] School newspaper; [oth. writ.] Women and Men, Eleven-eleven, Alcohol; [pers.] People may stare, but after a while their meaningless words blend into one melancholy vibration. I smash it to pieces, stare right back and grin. [a.] Naples, FL.

KOPIDLANSKY, RITA
[b.] January 16, 1959, Manitowoe, WI; [p.] Milton and Joan Waack; [m.] Marc J., October 29, 1977; [ch.] Jordan Joseph, Taylor Matthew; [ed.] St. John's Lutheran Newtonburg, Manitowoe Lutheran High School; [occ.] Housewife and full-time mother; [pers.] I enjoy writing about people who have touched my life in some special way. This is my first poem to be published. I have been writing poems since grade school. [a.] Manitowoe, WI.

KOPP, LILLY MARIE
[pen.] LM Rothe-Kopp; [b.] December 24, 1930, White Rock, BC Canada; [p.] Richard and Marie Martha (Farber) Rothe; [m.] Divorced, September 25, 1953; [ch.] Theodora Edward and Arthur David Kopp; [ed.] High school - R.N.; [occ.] Nurse - Home care giver; [oth. writ.] None published yet, have had a few letters to editor in Surrey Leader years ago; [pers.] Love one another, do unto others as you would have them to do unto you. [a.] White Rock, C Canada.

KOPPLINGER, CLARA
[b.] January 13, 1981, Neenah, WI; [p.] Kathy Radtke and Frank Kopplinger; [ed.] Entering 7th grade; [occ.] Student; [oth. writ.] Molly's New Sister (Children's book) Colors (poem); [pers.] Life is a trip you can only make once-ever. So make the most of it while you can. Don't let it pass you by or you'll be sorry later, forever. [a.] Forest Jct, WI.

KOPYLENKO, JULIA
[b.] January 26, 1974, St. Petersburg, Russia; [p.] Mark and Irene Kopylenko; [ed.] Canton High School 1988-91, Brandeis University 1991-3; [occ.] Purchasing/Sales Assistant, Dedham, MA; [pers.] Happiness is the illusion that someday the tears will come to an end. [a.] Norwood, MA.

KOVACSY, JOSEPH
[b.] December 1, 1920, Hungary; [p.] Joseph and Sophia; [m.] Ilona, May 15, 1952; [ch.] Peter Kovacsy (1953); [ed.] Mechanical Eng. (mC) Budapest - New York; [occ.] Engineering Supervisor (retired); [memb.] Several dozens trade and private organizations; [hon.] Arpad Academy of Cleveland (Literary Excellence Prize); [oth. writ.] All poetry - Blown - Away Leaves, 1987, On Foreign Bosoms 1988, Seedless Harvest 1990, On Two-Armed Cross 1992 (all on 500 pages each); [pers.] The human spirit limitless - so us the uninformed brain, when-timeless ones aging provess; stupidity the only gain. [a.] Seven Hills, OH./

KOZAK, NANCY E.
[ed.] Graduate, May 1979, Magna Cum Laude, Bryant College, Smithfield, RI; [occ.] Self-employed accountant for photographers; [pers.] I write what I feel in my heart based on real life experiences. [a.] Winchester, PA.

KNISKERN, WAYNE FRANK
[b.] September 24, 1953, Miami, FL; [p.] Elise and Ken Kniskern; [m.] Jane M.; [ch.] Sean Sarchez, Jennifer Kniskern; [ed.] BA Criminal Justice University of FL 1977, BS Elementary Education, FL International University 1981; [occ.] Dade County Public School teacher; [pers.] Working qualifications: Membership among the 190 of American males with an active emotional life. [a.] Miami, FL.

KRAAI, AMBER JOY
[b.] July 16, 1977, Zeeland, MI; [p.] Steven and Elaine Kraai; [ed.] Zeeland High; [memb.] 4-H Madrigal singers; [oth. writ.] Book of poems for Young Author's Convention at Hope College, and several poems used at beauty pageants, banquets, and other fundamental functions. [a.] Zeeland, MI.

KRAVANYA, CRYSTAL
[b.] August 30, 1977, Cleveland, OH; [p.] Rudolph Kravanya and Barbara Benes; [ed.] Mentor High School; [occ.] Student; [memb.] Mentor High School Orchestra, Meteor Mannheim Orchestra, Volunteer Organization of the Lake Metro Parks; [hon.] Principal Chair cellist in the 1993 Northeast Regional Orchestra of Ohio, eighth chair cellist in the 1993 Ohio All-State Orchestra, principal's honor roll, Golden Cardinal award of recognition; [pers.] I believe every person should be judged not by their race, religion, creed or sex, but by what is in the heart. [a.] Mentor, OH.

KREFTING, REBECCA
[b.] July 15, 1978, Wurtzburg, Germany; [p.] Bob and Christine Krefting; [ed.] Grace Lutheran School Huntsville High currently a sophomore; [hon.] Certificate of Excellence in Creative Writing. [a.] Huntsville, AL.

KREMINS, KATHLEEN A.
[b.] May 23, 1959, Newark, NJ; [p.] John and Margaret Lahey; [ed.] BA College of St. Elizabeth, MA Montclair State College; [occ.] English Teacher, Mendham High School (NJ), Soccer coach, Kean College (NJ); [memb.] National Council for Teachers of English, Women's Sports Foundation (Coaches Advisory Council member), National Soccer Coaches Association of America; [hon.] SEED (Seeking Educational Equity and Diversity) Project Leader; several coach of the year honors; [oth. writ.] Several poems published in college literary magazine, two articles published in Women's Fastpitch magazine; [pers.] In planting the seeds of our diverse voices. We create the inevitable flowering of a common understanding and language for all. [a.] Randolph, NJ.

KRIEGEL, SABINE CHRISTA
[pen.] Sabina Tamara Estrada; [b.] February 14, 1961, Nurnberb, Germany; [ch.] One ten year old daughter, Alexandra Yasmeen Wenonah. [a.] Calgary, Alberta, CAN.

KRONER, LUCILLE M.
[pen.] Lucille M. Kroner; [b.] Aug., Rolla, MO; [p.] Theodore W. and Virginia Wilson-Kroner; [ed.] Roff High School, Santa Monica City College, U.C.L.A.; [occ.] Poet; [memb.] First Christian Church of Santa Monica, Elder, Choir member, and Santa Lyric Monica Chorus; [hon.] Approximately 100. Two 1st prizes, 3 second prizes, 3 Editor's Choice awards, 7 Golden awards, 3 yearly poet honorable mentions awards; [oth. writ.] Numerous anthology publications and church publications; [pers.] Let all nation's circle their wagons in the interest of world peace. [a.] Los Angeles, CA.

KRUG, NICOLE JOY
[b.] December 18, 1969, New Jersey; [p.] Joyce Krug; [ed.] BS - Accounting Ramapo College, Oxford University England; [occ.] Commissions Analyst - AscomTimeplex, Woodcliff Lake, NJ; [memb.] Bergen County Players, National Organization of Women; [hon.] Oxford Honors Scholar, Delta My Delta National Honor Society, Who's Who Among Students in American Universities and Colleges 1992; [pers.] The challenges in my life have made me the woman I am today. I would not want to be anyone else. Only you can make your dreams a reality. [a.] Ridgewood, NJ 07450.

KUCZMANSKI, HEATHER NOEL
[pen.] Heather Noel Marie; [b.] September 26, 1974, Buffalo, NY; [p.] Donna J. and William L. Kuczmanski; [ed.] Villa Maria Academy High School, University of Buffalo, Psychology major (presently undergraduate); [occ.] Unit Clerk at a local hospital; [hon.] National Honor Society; [oth. writ.] I have three volumes of poems written, several of which have been published in school papers in high school; [pers.] I shall always believe that in a time and place forgotten, where children still play without fear...lies the heart of mankind...Beating softly...still steady. [a.] Cheektowaga, NY.

KUEBER, JANE
[b.] September 25, 1974, Park Rapids, MN; [p.] Duane and Christine Kueber; [ed.] Park Rapids Area High School; [occ.] Resort Work, Half Moon Trail Resort; [memb.] CYO, during high school: HoSA, SADD, CYO, Parish Youth Choir; [pers.] My writings reflect how I am feeling or how I want others to feel, whether about me or themselves. Some inspirations of mine are Bruce Burkman, my family, WS, Madonna, and the color Black. [a.] Park Rapids, MN.

KUHN, MELISSA
[pen.] Missy Kuhn; [b.] October 9, 1976, Chambersburg, PA; [p.] Eileen Naugle; [ed.] High School (home schoolers); [hon.] Academic Achievement (2 yrs); [pers.] My writings are my truth it reflects my mood and my place I am influenced by all truth. [a.] Greencastle, MD.

KULE, RONALD JOSEPH
[pen.] Ron Kule; [b.] February 28, 1947, Bogota, Columbia, S.A.; [p.] Bernard J. Kule and Beatriz ViDela de Malklarino de Kule; [m.] Laurie Anspach Kule; [ch.] Jeremiah Floresch Kule; [ed.] Oakland University, Bishop Egan High School; [occ.] Advertising Sales; [memb.] International Association of Scientologists - lifetime member status; [hon.] National Honor Society; [oth. writ.] Several articles and poems published for former paper, "The National Bulletin", several freelance screenplays, published booklet: "Four Steps To Easier Selling", "Thunder Cloud" (novel); [pers.] The written works of well known author, L. Ron Hubbard, have been a major inspiration for me. [a.] Clearwater, FL.

LACHAPELLE, DELINDA
[b.] June 26, 1962, Magogi, Quebec, Canada; [p.] Glinda Lachapelle (father deceased); [m.] Separated; [ch.] Brian, Elizabeth, Sabrina; [pers.] My writing reflects the inner most parts of myself through my life's experiences. [a.] N. Vancouver, Canada.

LACHETT, MICHELLE SUZANNE
[b.] May 27, 1975; [p.] John Lachett and Margaret Nigro; [ed.] Graduated from Springfield High School; [occ.] Student; [pers.] I dedicate this poem and all my other writings to Robert Henry, JOhn Tiernot, my Dad who are all in their own way responsible for my becoming a writer. [a.] Wallingford, PA.

LAEGER, LAURA
[pen.] Irish Canon; [b.] October 3, 1965, Bitburg, Germany; [p.] Dana L. and Mary Williams; [ch.] Kayla and Matthew; [ed.] Centralia H.S., Centralia Community College and ICS; [occ.] Manager at Halls Drug Center, Centralia WA/Sports Mom; [pers.] It is both a privilege and an honor to be included in this publication. Many thanks to my family and friends for their continued love and support. [a.] Chehalis, WA.

LAFLEUR, ALICE
[b.] March 10, 1910, Winchendon, MA; [p.] George and Aurisie Blanchard Berard; [m.] Edouard E. Sr., April 15, 1929; [ch.] Paul A. and Edouard E. Jr.; [ed.] High school and extended studies; [occ.] Hostess teacher for personnel department; [memb.] Past, Sweet Adelines Business and Professional Club, Toastmistress Inc.; [hon.] Plaques for poetry, navy sustained accomplishment, federal employ; [oth. writ.] Essays, school paper, genealogical research book with Cameo stories, bios for friends; [pers.] Life through love of words. [a.] Ridgecrest, CA.

LAGUNAS, CELIA CORONA
[pen.] Celia Corona Lagunas; [b.] February 21, 1951, Ray, AZ; [p.] Modesto and Ramona Corona; [m.] Thomas, December 30, 1972; [ch.] Tommy Jr., Gia Nicole, Nicholas Angelo; [ed.] Hayden High School (Winkelman, AZ); [occ.] Homemaker; [oth. writ.] Other unpublished poems and writings; [pers.] Good, truth, and all good things I impart with you (this to be your gain) and my thanks and reward to my beloved parents Modesto and Ramona Corona. My aunt Susana Corona, Uncle Miguel Corona and thee up above. My yet untold desire God give me for thy sake. [a.] Hayden, AZ.

LALLENMAND, SHANNON
[b.] February 8, 1979, Spangler, PA; [p.] Susan Cence and Garry Lallenmand; [ed.] St. Bernard Elementary and Cambria Heights High School; [hon.] Academic Physical Fitness Award, Drama Club Award, Attained honors throughout my eight years of elementary school; [pers.] I write my poems to express feelings of love, confusion, and pain. It's my way of unleashing my emotions. [a.] Hastings, PA.

LAMORTE, VANESSA
[b.] December 15, 1972, Brooklyn, NY; [p.] Christine and Carlos Francini; [ed.] Graduate of North Bergen High School; [occ.] Student Ramapo College of NJ; [pers.] This poem is dedicated to my mother - we have come a long way, I love you. [a.] North Bergen, NJ.

LAMB, YVE
[b.] March 23, Marianna, AK; [p.] McKinley and Eudora Palmer; [ed.] Anna Strong High, Barnes Business College, Aspen Christian College; [occ.] Customer Service; [memb.] HEritage Christian Center Choir, Toastmaster's International; [hon.] C.T.M. Toastmasters International; [oth. writ.] Creative and personalized writings, songs, lyrics, etc.; [pers.] I realize the ability to be expressive is a gift from God, one which I will cultivate and utilize. If a life I may touch, may it be for the good of humanity - "To God Be the Glory". [a.] Denver, CO.

LANCASTER, CHRIS
[pen.] Chris Lancaster; [b.] Nags Head, NC; [p.] Jimmy and Sylvia Lancaster; [ed.] BA University of North Carolina, BA Creative Arts; [occ.] Actor; [memb.] Actors for Animals, Humane Society, Wilderness Society, Heal the Bay; [hon.] Scholarship in college for Dramatic Arts, North Carolina Man of the Year 1st Runner-up 1988; [oth. writ.] Unpublished novel "The Saltered Path", Heal the Bay Ocean Foundation poetry collection; [pers.] Follow the path of heart, opposed to the path of convenience." [a.] La Jolla, CA.

LANG, LAURA L.
[pen.] Morgana Lee; [b.] March 15, 1963, Victoria, B.C., CAN; [p.] John W. and Sylvia L. Lang; [ed.] Prince George Senior Secondary, graduated 1981. Business Administration College; [occ.] Office Administrator Canada Post Corporation; [oth. writ.] "Masquerade" and "The Stage of Life" published, "Self Esteem" unpublished; [pers.] This particular poem was inspired by The news of the destruction of one of California's oldest and tallest redwoods in a wind storm in 1990. [a.] Prince George, BC, CAN.

LANGIS, TODD PAUL
[b.] June 23, 1967, Montreal, CAN; [p.] Jean Claude Langis, Bob, Brenda Babich; [oth. writ.] Some articles published in local newspaper, letters to the editor, Kitchener, Waterloo Record; [pers.] During the time of the later rains the desert budded and blossomed like the renewal of flesh on dry bones. From out of the parched land of Palestine a nation was born in one day never to be uprooted again. Isreal, O Isreal how greatly you inspire me! [a.] Kitchener, Ont. CAN.

LARDIE, JEAN TOBIN H.M.
[pen.] Toby Lardie; [b.] March 8, 1950, Ashtabula, OH; [p.] Leo and Ruth Lardie; [ed.] St, Joseph School, St. John HIgh School, St. John College (BSE), John Carroll University (M.ed.); [occ.] Sister of the Humility of Mary working as a missionary in El Salvador; [memb.] Congregation Humility of Mary Kappa Gamma Phi, International Missionary Radio Association; [hon.] Kappa Gamma Phi, Magna Cum Laude; [oth. writ.] Article in Today's Catholic Teacher, lyrics for two songs recorded on the album SONGS OF PEACE produced by Choose Life Records 1985; [pers.] Experiencing the war and violence here in El Salvador, I began to write poetry to search for a deeper sense of the beauty and goodness of people. I have discovered that very much here in the Salvadoran people and culture. [a.] El Salvador, Central America.

LARRABEE, MICHELLE
[b.] March 19, 1980, Madison, WI; [p.] Richard and Mary Larrabee; [ed.] Lodi Elementary School and Lodi Middle School (7th grade); [occ.] Student; [memb.] St. Patrick's Catholic Church, Lodi Challengers 4-H Club, and Divine Savior Nursing Home Volunteer; [hon.] Honor Student - many awards in Math, Reading, and English. Certificates of Appreciation from the American Heart Association; [oth. writ.] Many short stories, true story about Great grandfather, many other poems; [pers.] I have been greatly influenced by my 7th grade English Teacher, Mrs. Ardell Christianson. I try to reflect my feelings and thoughts when writing. [a.] Lodi, WI.

LARSON, FAITH C.
[pen.] Gueinevere; [b.] December 9, 1928, Stow, NY; [p.] Mildred and Wallace Saxton; [m.] Marvin W., Jan. 1976; [ch.] Anne, Holly, Wally, Greg, Ron, Jay; [ed.] Chautauqua High School, Doyle Beauty School of Cosmetology, Adult Education classes; [occ.] Housewife, Caregiver; [memb.] First Presbyterian Church; [hon.] Sportsmanship Brotherhood, Honor Society; [oth. writ.] Special poetry for church organizations and friends, editorials, poems in newspaper; [pers.] "Feelings are everywhere so be gentle". [a.] Lakeland, FL.

LARSON, IRENE MARY
[pen.] Irene Mary Larson; [b.] September 19, 1921, Lynd, MN; [p.] Andrew and Mary Larson; [ed.] High school graduate; [occ.] Retired and disabled M.S. patient.

LARSON, KATHLEEN H.
[pen.] Kathleen Harris Larson; [b.] February 24, 1958, Dayton, TX; [p.] Joe W. and Robbie Harris; [ch.] Scott and Vanessa larson; [ed.] C.E. King; Houston, Texas and San Jacinto Jr. College, Deer Park, TX; [occ.] Marketing and Inventory Manager; [memb.] Playhouse 1960 Community Theatre, Shepherd of the Woods Lutheran Church; [pers.] Inspiration can come as simply as watching canned jelly jars sit gleaming in the sunshine or a difficult as staring at blank pages endlessly. [a.] Houston, TX.

LATHAM, ROBERTA MAY ROZELLA
[b.] October 31, 1940, Delano, CA; [p.] Kenneth and May Downs; [m.] Jesse Allen Latham, December 28, 1959; [ch.] Rhonda May Taylor, Floyd Allen Latham and John Raymond Latham; [ed.] Lewis and Clark High School, The Ambassador Correspondence Bible College; [occ.] Housewife and Homemaker; [memb.] Living Word Fellowship Church, AARP, American Association of Retired Persons, Peale Center for Christian Living; [hon.] Outstanding volunteer service to the handicapped - Rappahannock Area YMCA, outstanding karate-ka award Isshinnyu Karate Club; [pers.] This poem was inspired to me word for word by the Holy Spirit of God and I give Him all the honor and glory. [a.] Falmouth, VA.

LAUDANO, STEVEN
[b.] September 27, 1951, Brooklyn, NY; [p.] Anna Smeraldi; [m.] Julie, November 17, 1979; [ch.] Michael, Catherine, Nicholas, Daniel; [ed.] James Madison High School; [occ.] Drywall Finisher; [memb.] Open Bible Church; [hon.] Army Commendation award; [oth. writ.] Wrote poetry for The Church Bulletin; [pers.] Trust in the Lord Jesus Christ, as in everything else in my life He is my true inspiration in all things that I do for good. [a.] Marshalls Creek, PA.

LAW, GRACE
[b.] April 14, 1928, Hawthorne, NJ; [p.] Wabe and Mary Schaper; [m.] Stephen B., August 5, 1961; [ch.] David William Drenth and Shirley Jean Warnet; [ed.] Marianne Grace Law, Ridgewood Public Schools, presently taking correspondence Institute of Children's Literature; [occ.] Homemaker for my family; [memb.] Faith Reformed Church and editor of church newspaper; [oth. writ.] Several poems published in our church newspaper, "Our Witness"; [pers.] Foremost in my writings, I want to honor God and strive to write inspirational pieces that will reflect his goodness. I also love writing for children as there is much they need to learn in a world that may be very confusing to them. [a.] Ridgewood, NJ.

LAWHORN, MARGARET
[b.] July 12, 1927, Louisville, KY; [p.] Walter and Avis L. Beavin; [m.] J. Alton, September 16, 1948; [ch.] Bonita, Sheryl, Janet, Judy; [ed.] BS in Ed - Union College (Barbourville, KY), MA George Peabody College (Nashville, TN); [occ.] Elementary Teacher - retired 34 years; [memb.] KY Retired Teachers Association, Lewisport United Methodist Church; [oth. writ.] Poem published in 1978 in A Collection of Religious Poems; [a.] Lewisport, KY.

LAWSON, BRENDA
[b.] July 19, 1947, Rockingham County, NC; [p.] Johnny C. and Ellen H. Carter; [m.] Bobby L., March 28, 1987; [ch.] Susan M. Dean, Timothy L. Lawson, Cynthia L. Brand; [ed.] Benhaven High, C.C.C.C.; [occ.] Quality Control Inspector; [memb.] ASOC, Hillview Baptist Church; [oth. writ.] This poem published in our local newspaper, for my mom on Mother's Day; [pers.] When you can't express yourself or are unable to talk to anyone, putting words on paper is a wonderful outlet. Sometimes private, sometimes words you wish to share. [a.] Broadway, NC.

LAWSON, CLARENCE E. JR.
[pen.] John Lawson; [b.] June 23, 1962, Indiana, PA; [p.] Rita and Clarence Lawson, Sr.; [ch.] Melisa Lynn, Candy Ann, Kathleen Helen; [ed.] Reading High graduate, ASE, Certified Technician; [occ.] Auto Tech; [memb.] Abundant Life Christian Center, Tender Loving Care (for pregnant women abandoned); [hon.] In service of completion rock class, leadership training and also new beginnings. ALCC; [oth. writ.] I have written in the area of 1,000 poems since age 13. Though none have been published as I did not feel I had perfected them; [pers.] Inspirations comes in many ways. Where I have found mine, comes only from the love that we see each day, and from God's word. [a.] Deerfield Beach, FL.

LAWSON, DEBBIE CAROL
[pen.] Debbie Carol Lawson; [b.] October 3, 1957, Porterville, CA; [p.] Juanita and Bill Clutter; [m.] James E., November 17, 1976; [ch.] Melody Elizabeth Lawson; [ed.] Graduate of College of the Sequoias, Tulane Union High School graduate 1975; [occ.] Licensed Practical Nurse; [memb.] First Assembly of God Church, U.S. Holocaust Memorial Museum (Associate member), Christian Friends of Isreal, National League of Nurses, American Heart Association; [hon.] Dean's List, Honor Roll, high school Business Achievement award; [oth. writ.] Poem published in Sparrowgrass Anthology - written several others including "Remember", "The Artist", "Color Blind" and others; [pers.] I strive to reflect man's dilemma in current events, often inspired by the teachings of godly men and women. I also enjoy today's contemporary writers. [a.] Madill, OK.

LAZAR
[pen.] Maria; [b.] July 15, 1935, Craiova, Romania; [p.] Dihel Gheorghe (father died 1986) and Dihel Nicolita (mother died 1939); [m.] Eugehiu, October 25, 1955; [ch.] Lazar LiLi Eugenia (12/17/57); [ed.] Seven years elementary schools, four years economic college with Bachelor's degree with diploma, two years university expelled inadequate politics status, formal vocational training - Project Design-water supply with certificate; [occ.] 1953-1987 - Accounting, planning, operation estimate and 23 years project designer in USA-worker-I took test for medical assistance; [memb.] LIRS, ARD- International Society of Poetry, US-Donor Agrement -Holocaust Memorial Museum; [hon.] Editor's Choice Award-The National Library Society of Poetry 1993, Wind In the Sky; A Break in the Clouds; [oth. writ.] Club School-Cariova - "Micromagazin" - newspaper in USA and Canada, Wind In the Night Sky, A Break in The Clouds; [pers.] I love freedom of speech, life free-open - true and real report - respect for people - culture and respect honor creditably and work for this my poems is concrete (I suffered more in my life). [a.] State Island, NY.

LEARD, DENNY L.
[b.] 1958, Oregon; [ed.] Oregon College of Education 1976/77; [occ.] State government - Accounting; [oth. writ.] American Poetry Anthologies for 1982 and 1983/Hearts of Fire: A Treasury of Poems on Love/Words of Praise: A Treasury of Religious (Inspirational) Poetry. [a.] Salem, OR.

LEATHERMAN, ALICE P.
[b.] August 15, 1899, Elizabethtown, KY; [p.] Alice Morgan and William Edwin Pendleton; [m.] Ernest Edward Leatherman (deceased), January 12, 1916; [ch.] Edward A., Clement B., Raymond V., Clarence E., Ernest Jr., (deceased), Lavona Remakel, Olieta Lee, Wilma Dines; [ed.] 4 years elementary in Bethlehem Academy (orphaned by age 6), self-educated; [occ.] Nurse aide, county clerk, labor union organization in N.M., now retired; [memb.] Carpenters Aux. #547, loyal order moose; [hon.] Recognized as leader in Labor Union history in New Mexico; [oth. writ.] THE COW published in National Dairy Science (1985), Joy and Sorrows, Oh Western Winds, Struggle On, Our Savior, Cactus and Desert, many, many unnamed recorded in diary and to friends and family; [pers.] Author, lovingly known by all as "Nana", used her poetry to inspire positive perspectives during life adversities in herself and others. [a.] Albuquerque, NM.

LEAVITT, DANIEL R.
[pen.] The man with no name; [b.] February 1, 1948, Adrian, OR; [p.] Woodrow Leavitt and Mildred Antrim; [m.] Linda Borrego, November 18, 1967; [ch.] Scott, Kelly, Stephanie, Daniel, Adam; [ed.] Nampa High School; [oth. writ.] Several hundred songs and poems some published; [pers.] It comes from the heart and is a window to my soul. Life is my teacher. [a.] Nampa, ID.

LEE, CALVIN C.
[b.] January 1947, VA; [m.] G.C.; [ch.] Kristin, Christopher; [ed.] Bowie State University; [occ.] Educator; [oth. writ.] Several poems written for various occasions; [pers.] My writing seems to stem from family experiences and reflects love and togetherness. [a.] Bowie, MD.

LEE, CARRIE
[pen.] Paige Mercury; [b.] August 14, 1977, Elgin, IL; [p.] Mary Magdalene Blair; [ed.] Christian Liberty High School; [occ.] Plan to be a musician and make my mark in the world that way; [hon.] honor Roll in high school for a grade point average of a 93; [oth. writ.] Newspaper articles about local events; [pers.] My personal feelings come out in a powerful way through the magic of the pen. I have been influence by wonderful artists such as Robert Plant. [a.] Algonquin, IL.

LEE, JESSICA ANN MARIE
[b.] January 3, 1978, Philadelphia, PA; [p.] Bruce and Dolores Lee; [ed.] Finishing at George Washington High School; [occ.] Telemarketing; [memb.] World Vision; [oth. writ.] Several poems waiting for publication; [pers.] I try to describe the love and nature of a man and woman. I was inspired by the great poets of Shakespeare. [a.] Philadelphia, PA.

LEE, ROBERT TROY
[b.] December 28, 1975, Nova Scotia; [p.] Barry and Kay Lee; [ed.] Grade 10; [pers.] When fantasy and fiction fade away, Reality becomes bland and meaningless. [a.] Calgary, Alberta, Canada.

LEE, SALLY L.
[pen.] Sally Lee; [b.] September 22, 1946, West Chester, PA; [p.] Sherman Lee and Vivian Landon; [ch.] Peter, Karen, Kumar; [ed.] Oxford Area High School, Essex County Vocational School, Wilford Academy; [occ.] LPN, Beautician; [memb.] Past Matron Order of Eastern Star, Grand Officer Queen of Sheba, Grand Chapter OES, Pres. Mass Choir, Mt. Olive Baptist Church, Past Matron Daughter of Sphinx, Pres. Benevolent Fund OES; [oth. writ.] School newspaper, church, personal book of poems; [pers.] There's nothing I can't do if I put my mind to it. The sky is the limit. Thru God all things are possible.

LEFEBVRE, JASON
[pen.] Colten LeFaue; [b.] January 21, 1972, Sudbury, Ont. Canada; [p.] Robert and Wanda Lindsay; [m.] Douglas O. Spence, May 16, 1992; [ed.] Grade 12 - H.B. Beal - Eastwood Collegiate; [occ.] Register operator (Zehrs Markets); [memb.] Sea Cadets, Handicap Assistant; hon.] First place Dance division in the Ontario Youth Talent Search '91; [oth. writ.] "Never Look Back", "Did You Ever...", "More Than Just, I Love You", "Time", "To The One I Love on Valentine's Day"; [pers.] Your ears believe other people but your eyes believe themselves. [a.] Kitchener, Ontario, CAN.

LEGLEITNER, SHARON DENNIS
[b.] August 17, 1935, Marietta, OH; [occ.] Homemaker, Artist and Jewelry maker; [memb.] Zanesville Art Center, Ohio Valley Artists and Parkersburg Art Gallery W.V.; [hon.] First place Zanesville Art Center, honorable mention same place, others, poem published in local newspaper.

LEGLER, BILLY M.
[pen.] S.O.B. (Sweet Ol ' Bill); [b.] February 3, 1925, Taylor, LA; [p.] Frank and Lonnie Mason Legler; [m.] Barbara Cady, August 17, 1947; [ch.] Morris Frank Legler and Karen Christine Dennison; [ed.] Freeport High, BS/ChE - Texas A&M, Oregon State, MS/ChE-University of Idaho; [occ.] Retired Chemical Engineer; [memb.] American Institute of Chemical Engineers; [hon.] Fellow American Institute of Chemical Engineers; [oth. writ.] Technical papers in "Chemical Engineering Progress" magazine and at several technical symposia; [pers.] This "wordwright" enjoys spreading smiles through hyperbole and pun. Example: "I knew I'd had a tongue lashing by the infliction in her voice". [a.] Aiken, SC.

LEHMANN, HELEN TATE
[b.] December 10, 1934, Anson, TX; [p.] James Calvin and Connie Louise Robbins Tate; [m.] Divorced, June 27, 1959; [ch.] Frederick Arthur Lehmann, Jr., and Marie Louise Lehmann; [ed.] AA degree, Pensacola Junior College, BA degree in Social Work, The University of West Florida; [occ.] Developmental Services Support Coordinator, The Avalon Center, Inc.; [hon.] Two editor's choice awards for poetry; [oth. writ.] Published poems "Broken Vows", "What I Like", "Solitude", "In My Garden", "Saturday Appointment"; [pers.] While reading some of Emily Dickinson's poetry 2 years ago, I was inspired to write poetry of my own. Although I had never found rhyming easy before on that day the rhymes flowed freely and still do. [a.] Milton, FL.

LEHRMAN, ABRAHAM SAMUEL
[pen.] A.S. Lehrman; [b.] November 3, 1919, Ft. Lauderdale, FL; [p.] Max and Rose Lehrman; [m.] Hazel, May 31, 1946; [ch.] Merid David and Kenneth Robert Lehrman; [ed.] U. of Miami, FL, Palm Beach Community College, North (creative writing); [occ.] Mechanical Engineer (retired), Florida Licensed Plumbing Contractor; [memb.] American Society of Plumbing Engineers, Fourth Marine Division Association; [hon.] President and several other offices, A.S.P.E., and awarded 11 medals Central Pacific WWII; [oth. writ.] Short story (Shirt Tail Charlie) and two poems (Roi Namur and Infinity); [pers.] I hope my writings will be accepted and have a positive influence. With luck I imagine writing can be a very satisfying profession. [a.] Tequesta, FL.

LEISTER, JACOB ALGIRE
[b.] October 7, 1971; [occ.] Buddhist, Hsing I practitioner, writer (student); [oth. writ.] Now writing a novel - <u>No Killer Nothing Killed</u>. [a.] Albuquerque, NM.

LEITCH, TARA SHANNON
[pen.] Christyhanna Royale; [b.] July 7, 1977, Burlington, Ont. CAN.; [p.] Sharon Florrie and Norman Inglis Leitch; [ed.] Presently attending grade 10 Aldershot High School; [occ.] Student; [oth. writ.] I have many other poems, short stories and novels in the works and hope that someday they will also be published; [pers.] Life moves pretty fast. If you don't stop and look around once in a while you might miss it. [a.] Burlington, Ont. CAN.

LEMIN, JR., DONALD A.
[b.] January 17, 1960, Cleveland, OH; [p.] Alma Messerman and Donald A. Lemin Sr.; [m.] Divorced; [ch.] Brandy Lee and Melinda Jean and Kenneth Eric; [ed.] 12th grade, graduated from Northern Balford County High School (Laysburg, PA 1977); [occ.] Truck Driver; [oth. writ.] (Unpublished) The Truckers Wife, City Life, The Homeless, The Final Tribute; [pers.] Everyone should pursue their dreams and do

everything with all their heart. [a.] Hopewell, PA.

LEMISHOW, ALBERT
[pen.] Albert Lemishow; [b.] October 18, 1925, Bronx, NY; [p.] Sol and Lillie Lemishow (both deceased); [m.] Lenore (deceased 1961), June 26, 1952; [ch.] Kari and Bruce; [ed.] BA Accounting CCNY 1949 and 30 credits toward Masters - CCNY; [occ.] Certified Public Accountant; [memb.] Various military veterans and political organizations; [hon.] Various Infantry combat awards - WWII; [oth. writ.] Other poems; [pers.] Be Persistent and Patient in Pursuing your Goals. [a.] Flushing, NY.

LEMON, DANNI
[pen.] Heather Bungle, May 4, 1976, Barbeston, OH; [p.] Dorothy Lemon and Ralf Joyner; [ed.] Currently attending Wadsworth Senior High School; [pers.] Respect yourself, everyone someone special, even if you don't know it! And always strive to make someone else happy, for it will make you happy too. [a.] Wadsworth, OH.

LEO, ROSE NIX
[pen.] Column "Last Scrap"; [b.] April 30, 1894, Rural Norman, OK; [p.] John Thomas (Tom) and Mary Elizabeth (Pace) Nix; [m.] John Leo, June 30, 1920; [ch.] Chios, Anita, Frank; [ed.] Bural Schult one year high school, correspondence self-educated; [occ.] Columnist-gardner reporter of local functions; [memb.] Methodist church historical society-American Legion Aux. United Methodist Women, 3 clubs; [hon.] Talent recognized in newspapers. Certified school teacher - voluntary for elderly, Red Cross volunteer, Menninger Bible Course, Academic Achievement - in fundamental of writing academic achievement; [oth. writ.] In Kansas Crange Hottesberg Kansas People County Women Church paper wrote an published book, "Russ Last Scrap" at age 95; [pers.] I try to keep myself I mental, physical, and spiritual balance and I have cherished writings of poets since childhood. [a.] Howard, KS.

LESAGE, ELIETTE S.
[pen.] Marie Simon; [b.] September 24, 1948, Carman, Manitoba, CAN; [p.] Maurice and Mathilde Lesage; [ch.] David Allan, Lisa Carmelle, Craig Jeremy, Lorie Aline, Daniel Peter; [ed.] Notre Dame de Lourdes Collegiate, University of Manitoba, University of Calgary; [occ.] Human Resources Administration; [memb.] Country Quills, Canadian Payroll Association, Tiger Hills Arts Association; [oth. writ.] Short stories, arts review published in local magazine and writing association collection; [pers.] I am currently working on a novel (fiction). I write as an expression of feelings and creativity. [a.] Notre Dame de Lourdes, Man. CAN.

LESSENTHIEN, KURT G.
[b.] April 25, 1966, Morristown, NJ; [p.] Mariane Lessenthien and Kim Knoblauch; [m.] Lori Beth Einsig; [ed.] Colonial High School; [occ.] U.S. Navy currently serving on U.S.S. Albany (SSN 753); [pers.] My warmest thanks to Shonaleigh Cumbers and Julie Byrd for opening the window in my mind. For my wife, Lori Beth, I love you now and forever. [a.] Orlando, FL.

LEVESQUE, JESSICA
[pen.] Jessica Levesque; [b.] June 6, 1978, Bristol, CT; [p.] Wayne and Susan Levesque; [ed.] Sophomore at Bristol Eastern High School. [a.] Bristol, CT.

LEWARK, SONIA
[b.] March 9, 1976, Elizabeth City, NC; [p.] Irene Byrd and Vernon Lewark; [ed.] Cocoa High School; [memb.] French Club, S.A.D.D., Who's Who Among American High School Students; [hon.] National Beta Club, Assistant Principal's List, Honor graduate; [pers.] I owe my poetry, success to love, the easiest most versatile thing to write about. [a.] Cocoa, FL.

LEWIS, BARBARA
[b.] June 19, 1977, Bloomington; [p.] Richard and Lois Lewis; [ed.] Sullivan High; [memb.] Journalism Club, Newspaper and Yearbook Staff; [oth. writ.] Several stories in school paper and local newspaper; [pers.] While absorbing what is taking place around me. I work at putting it into words. [a.] Carlisle, IN.

LEWIS, NATALIE
[b.] September 12, 1978, Mt. Vernon, IL; [p.] Robert and Rebecca Lewis; [ed.] Benton Muddle School, Benton Consolidated High School; [pers.] The future belongs to those who believe in the beauty of their dreams. - Eleanor Roosevelt. [a.] Benton, IL.

LEWIS, PEGGY
[b.] January 9, 1962, Hamilton, OH; [m.] Robert J., June 4, 1982; [ch.] Sara Jean, Samantha Allayne; [ed.] Preble Shawnee High School; [occ.] Housewife; [pers.] I want to thank my husband for his continued love and support through all my hardships. [a.] Camden, OH.

LEWIS, SHAWN A.
[b.] April 27, 1970, Boston, MA; [p.] Linda A. Lewis; [ed.] Weston High School/West Virginia State College, BA English Writing/Marshall University, MA Communications; [occ.] Graduate-Assistant; [memb.] P.H.D. Church; [hon.] Dean's List/Who's Who/Residence Academic Award; [oth. writ.] Reporter/Cartoonist for Newspaper, short story, poetry published in school magazine, "The Kianawha Review"; [pers.] We strive to progress and enhance our potential and capabilities. We strive to express the perfect poem. I still can't make my left pinky toe move alone like my right. [a.] Huntington, WV.

LILES, LEE-ANN ANTOINETTE
[b.] March 27, 1974, Bermuda; [p.] Mr. and Mrs. John R. Liles and Verda B. and John R. Liles; [occ.] Writer/editor for newspaper, the Bermuda Time; [hon.] High school senior year, best poem various others; [oth. writ.] Poems in school news - local news and anthologies. Have also done front page article and had my own youth page in local paper; [pers.] Most of my poems are deep, and reflect on saddening experiences that I've had before or seen growing up. Generally, I see a lot of things others don't. [a.] Somerset, Bermuda.

LINANTUD, K. LAURA
[b.] November 7, 1969, Catonsville, MD; [p.] Mary E. and Dr. C.C. Linantud; [pers.] A world without music would be a tragic and lonely place: Thank you, Westerberg... [a.] Catonsville, MD.

LINDEMAN, STEPHEN PAUL
[b.] September 11, 1950, Marblehead, MA; [p.] Randolph C. and Gladys E. Lindeman; [m.] Still dreaming; [ed.] Marblehead High School 1968; [occ.] Carpenter; [hon.] The anthologies presently being prepared represent my first public display; [oth. writ.] Writing things down and almost having something to say for some 20 years; [pers.] Developing a curious interest in history, fairly astounded at the news. Looking for more time right along with everyone else. [a.] South Casco, ME.

LINFOOT, TRAVIS
[b.] December 6, 1978, Surrey, B.C. Canada; [p.] Anne and Wayne Linfoot; [ed.] Mission Secondary; [occ.] STudent; [oth. writ.] First poem; [a.] Mission B.C., CAN.

LINVILLE, LESLIE
[b.] January 23, 1904, Beloit, MS; [p.] William and Alice Linville; [m.] Bertha Williams, April 17, 1927; [ch.] Eight; [occ.] Farmer; [memb.] Methodist Church and 4 historical societies; [oth. writ.] Eight books and one book of poems; [pers.] I am 89 years old and blind. No education beyond high school. My hobby is local history and writing. [a.] Colby, KS.

LIPPMAN, CRISSIE
[b.] November 14, 1973; [p.] Christine Lohmeyer; [ed.] Park Ridge High School; [occ.] Retail, Annie Sez (Montvale, NJ); [oth. writ.] My Everything, The Pain and many more. These poems have not been published yet; [pers.] My writings have been influenced by past and present relationships. [a.] Park Ridge, NJ.

LITTLE, JAN
[b.] October 20, 1953, Sussex, New Brunswick, CAN ; [p.] Vincent and Eva Whalen; [ch.] Renee and Michelle; [ed.] Grade 12 Business and Commerce; [oth. writ.] I have many other poems yet to be published; [pers.] Inspired by God to reveal this extent to mankind. Many of my poems are truly evidence of a life transformed by a loving caring God.

LITWILLER, LYDIA IUTZI
[b.] February 17, 1864, Ontario, CAN; [p.] Daniel Iutzi and Maria Gingerich; [m.] Jacob Buerge, October 7, 1885; [ch.] Six sons and two daughters; [ed.] Three winter terms; [occ.] Housework; [oth. writ.] Many others none published. [a.] Ithaca, MI.

LIU, BOLIN
[pen.] Lu Lin, Feng Ming; [b.] January 7, 1956, Huojia Village, Qufu City, Shandong, China; [p.] Yutang and Shangmeiguo Liu; [m.] Ailanchang, January 1, 1981; [ch.] Zhijian Liu; [ed.] Qufu No. 1 high school, Shandong University, East-China Normal University; [occ.] English Lecturer, Vice Chairman (1984-1990) of Department of Foreign Languages, Jining Teachers College, Visit scholar to McGill University (August 1990-August 1991) Translator, reporter and editor; [memb.] Member of Canadian Association of Applied Linguistics; [oth. writ.] Translations and research papers published in local newspapers and magazines; research paper on PREPOSITIONS WITHOUT OBJECTS presented at 22nd Annual Symposium of Canadian Association of Applied linguistics. [a.] Montreal, PQ, CAN.

LIVACCARI, STEPHANIE MICHELLE
[b.] October 28, 1978, Long Beach, CA [p.] Michael D. and Dolores Livaccari; [ed.] Sophomore at Temecula Valley High School; [occ.] Student; [memb.] Drama Club, Calvary Chapel Youth Group, Christian Youth Theatre (CYT); [hon.] Honor Roll Student; [oth. writ.] Essays, scripts and lyrics; [pers.] I have been greatly influenced by sonnets written by William Shakespeare and hope to further study his works. In my future high school and college years and my ambition is to focus on drama, voice, and journalism. [a.] Temecula, CA.

LIVINGSTON, DOROTHY A.
[pen.] Dottie; [b.] September 22, 1916, Harrisburg, PA; [p.] Cora and George Starner; [m.] Galen E. Livingston (deceased), April 15, 1944; [p.] Gayle J, Leininger; [ed.] John Harris High School; [occ.] Retired secretary; [memb.] Memorial Lutheran Evan. Church, life member, AARP; [hon.] Typing certificate doing 87 wpm in high school; [oth. writ.] Several poems, nothing published; [pers.] My writings of poetry seem to be in the sentimental area and I write mostly what my feelings are. [a.] Harrisburg, PA.

LLEW-WILLIAMS, PAUL
[b.] March 12, 1958, Hamilton, Ont. CAN.; [p.] Irish Immigrants; [ch.] Two; [ed.] BA - B. Education - O.T.C.; [occ.] Teacher (Music); [memb.] S.O.C.A.N., Teachers Federation; [oth. writ.] Mostly lyrics for songs; I have been composing since I was 12 years old, many songs performed in public and video seen on Much Music; [pers.] I am a music teacher, guitarist, composer, poet. My writing is influenced by many modern Canadian writers e.g., M. Atwood. [a.] Orangeville, Ont. CAN.

LLOYD, TAMI
[b.] August 6, 1970, Vancouver, WA; [p.] Karen and Ralph Lloyd; [ed.] Hawaiian Mission Academy and Walla Walla College, BSN; [occ.] Registered nurse; [oth. writ.] Simple writings since childhood; [pers.] W.B. Yeats said it best, "Tread softly because you tread on my dreams." [a.] Ferndale, WA.

LOBECK, LISA
[pen.] Lisa Lobeck, L. Lobeck; [b.] July 3, 1970, Minneapolis, MN; [ed.] Washbourn High School, music teen and bern's music; [occ.] Musician; [hon.] Editor's Choice awards, honorable mention; [oth. writ.] Reflections in the Streets of Emotion published in other National Library of Poetry Anthologies; [pers.] These thoughts are like storms in my head, seems like it will never stop raining here. [a.] Minneapolis, MN.

LOGAN, JINA MAREE
[b.] August 3, 1978; [p.] Thomas and Karol Logan; [ed.] High school student - 10th grade Oviedo High School; [oth. writ.] Have been writing poetry since age 10. Recent poem called "Just Love"; [pers.] Poetry inspired by the concern for the well-being of other people and for the importance of love of self and others.

LONG, DAVID
[b.] August 12, 1980, PA; [p.] John and Laurie Long; [ed.] Dane Barse Elementary, Landis Junior High (8th grade); [occ.] Student; [memb.] Art Club, S.V.T.E. program, Safety patrol, Audio Visual Aide; [hon.] Cho Dan Bo Tang Soo Do Karate, Principal's List for 5 years Honor Roll; [oth. writ.] National Conversation Essays on Logging and Water 1993, Poetry, Atlantic City Press 1993, Letters to the Editor 1992, Landis Junior High Anthology; [pers.] Writing poetry is a way for me to express my feelings in my own fascination. Poetry also allows me to wonder onto the creative world of my own imagination. Teacher-Saundra Williams and poet-Shirley Warren gave me the inspiration to write poetry. [a.] Vineland, NJ.

LONG, FRANCES R.
[b.] April 7, 1928, Sanger, CA; [p.] Pete and Millie Gumber; [m.] Frank, August 5, 1950; [ch.] Mark and Marshall; [ed.] Sanger Union High School; [occ.] Ranchers wife and breeder of Basset Hounds and dove; [memb.] Western Folklife Conservancy, CA Women of Agriculture, Rebekahs, Chamber of Commerce, Nevada/CA Pollettes Reg. Board member Selective Service; [oth. writ.] Poems published in local newspapers; [pers.] The old and new West influence my writing. Ranch life as we know and live it in particular. [a.] Mariposa, CA.

LOPEZ, PALOMA MARIEL
[pen.] Paloma; [b.] July 1, 1986, Gallup, NM; [p.] Eileen Bruno Lopez and Francisco Lopez Ochoa; [ed.] First grade completed will enter grade II this fall; [occ.] Student, artist, gymnast; [hon.] Board scholar 1992, scholarship award 1993; [pers.] I wrote the poem because I lost my ring and I was sad. Then I felt better. [a.] Gallup, NM.

LOVELAND, RICHARD
[b.] May 2, 1969, Louisville, KY; [p.] Gerald and Patricia Loveland; [m.] Stacey, December 22, 1990; [ed.] North Bullitt High, U.S. ARmy Medical Specialist course at the Academy of HEalth and Science; [occ.] Perfect bound assistant machine operator Gateway Press; [oth. writ.] Several poems, couple of children books, and one adult book; [pers.] Thank you National Library of poetry. Thank you Tom Wedding. Thanks everbody for supporting me and buying copies of books for my poem. I love you Stacey. [a.] Shepherdsville, KY.

LOWES, KATHLEEN K.
[pen.] Karen; [b.] September 24, 1942, Van Nuys, CA; [p.] Rita and Carl Howe, Sr.; [m.] Gary J.; [occ.] National Homecare Services/Provider; [oth. writ.] Several inspirational poems, one short story some poems were set to music by husband; [pers.] My love for words and poems goes back to my childhood. To me poetry is very personal and written to get a message to the reader. [a.] Stockton, CA.

LOY, CARL A.
[b.] July 31, 1927, Fort Loramie, OH; [p.] Albert Henry and Margaret Viola (Mills) Loy; [ed.] B.Aeronautical Engineering 1955, Ohio State University; [occ.] Retired Aerospace Design Engineer. [a.] Huntsville, AL.

LUDDY, WALT
[pen.] Pen Oak; [b.] January 24, 1917, New Britain, CT; [m.] Carol; [ch.] Julie, Caryn, Robert, Joel; [ed.] University of Connecticut grad, BS Economics and History; [occ.] Retired writing the heart and soul of my life; [memb.] St. Paul's Church, P.G.A.; [hon.] Golden Poet award for 1988 - World of Poetry; [oth. writ.] Books poetry "Frivolous to the Sublime". Non fiction "America, We Can Do It Together" by Pen Oak. J. Peter Grace called it "Great and Inspirational"; [pers.] I'm desperately trying to save our country from going backwards thru the medium of having our people vote directly on some issues each year. My book "America, We Can". [a.] Glastonbury, CT.

LUDWIG, HELEN
[pen.] Helen Ludwig; [b.] July 3, 1911, Tolland, CT; [p.] Alfred and Bertha Trillenbach Ludwig; [m.] V.J. McGill, September 1938; [ch.] Maisie Conrad, Ethan and Vera Conrad (grandchildren); [ed.] Hartford Art School, Art Students League Greenwich House Pottery; [occ.] Artist; [memb.] Artist Embassy International; [hon.] 41 Sketch books at Archives of American Art at Smithsonian; [oth. writ.] Psychiatry for the Home and Garden Golden Gate Park book; [pers.] I spend lot of time doing art teaching to children handicapped and senior volunteering. [a.] San Francisco, CA.

LUKE, CHARLES JR.
[b.] November 15, 1961, Gainesville, FL; [p.] Eunice Cox and Charles Luke Sr.; [ed.] Deland Senior High School; [occ.] Food Service Specialist and Dietary Cook; [hon.] Three years in the Army and I have an Honorable Discharge; [pers.] America. The poems I write is to educate, the younger people about the things that is going on around them each and everyday, in life. I believe Alcohol and Drugs is America's biggest problem. That when used lead to accidents, violence, crime, jails, institution and even death. Without our younger generation knowing that Alcohol and Drugs will cause more problems, when used. There will be "NO" future for them. They are our future, our flesh and blood and they are our children. So let's educate them all. JUST SAY NO TO DRUGS Young People. And you will live a happy and better life. God Bless You All. [a.] Deleon Springs, FL.

LUNDY, III, EDGAR JAMES
[pen.] Sean Michael Saint; [b.] August 23, 1972, George AFB, CA; [p.] Elizabeth A. and Edgar J. Lundy, II; [ed.] Senior at Flagler Coller, T.R. Robinson High School; [occ.] Full-time student; [memb.] Order of Demolay, NESA Ponce Player (Drama Club), Hugh O'Brian Youth Foundation Alumni; [hon.] Chevalier Degree, Eagle Scout, NHS, Hugh O'Brian Youth Foundation Ambassador; [pers.] Thank you to all those who believed in me, most importantly, my family and the Lord above. [a.] Tampa, FL.

LUNSFORD, MARGARET L.
[pen.] Margie Mason; [b.] July 30, 1955, Philadelphia, PA; [p.] Gloria and Louis Mason; [m.] Charles F. Jackson, May 21, 1994; [ch.] Jermaine, Jeff, Jarel, Jovan, Christopher, Sawne; [ed.] Little Flower Catholic High, Community College; [occ.] Nursing Assistant University of PA Hospital; [memb.] American Cancer Society; [hon.] High honors (Art show), special achievement award, golden poet award; [oth. writ.] Time, To Be Wed For Life; [pers.] I give my glory to the Lord, for it is he who has given us all a special task or talent. My poems are based on my life. [a.] Philadelphia, PA.

LUPIEN, KELLY
[b.] March 5, 1980, Tisdale, Sasketchewan; [p.] Dwayne and Maryanne Lupien (brother-Ryan Lupien-10); [ed.] Junior High grade 8; [occ.] STudent; [pers.] I write poems to express myself and to release both positive and negative energy in the only way I know how. [a.] Tisdale, Sas. CAN.

LUST, TAMI
[b.] December 19, 1977, Providence, RI; [ed.] Student in my second year of high school; [pers.] On this planet which revolves around the sun which anything may happen by a humane one inspiring moments are rare for the ones when live here so give love to mother nature, enjoy her for all she's worth, she will give the gift to inspire us. [a.] Cumberland, RI.

LUTGEN, BRUCE A.
[pen.] B.A. Lutgen; [b.] January 26, 1942, Buffalo, NY; [ed.] Ohio University; [occ.] Engineering Associate; [oth. writ.] Have authored and coauthored technical reports and brochures. Contributed to Examples From Ohio University Portfolios, Adult Learning Program, 1990; [pers.] Try never to be so arrogant in my writing that I am not wary of my own agenda. [a.] Elma, NY.

LYLE, HEATHER HONEY
[b.] July 18, 1972, St. Louis, MO; [p.] Allen and Elaine Lyle; [m.] (Fiance-Robert H. Sanders, together since December 24, 1988); [ch.] Bobby Howard Sanders; [ed.] Hazelwood Central High, Florissant Valley Junior College, North County Technical SChool; [occ.] Premium Finance Company; [oth. writ.] I have many other poems, but none have ever been published; [pers.] I always loved Shakespeare, Edgar Alan Poe, and Robert Frost. They all influenced me to express myself from deep within my heart. [a.] Florissant, MO.

LYNCH, DELORIS
[b.] May 28, 1924, Latham, IL; [p.] Leo E. and Irma I (Scarlett) Knebel; [m.] Lloyd, February 5, 1946; [ch.] Sandra Kay Lynch Volkmar, Nancy Gay Lynch Blunt, Larry Lloyd Lynch, Lynda Sue Lynch Gribbins; [ed.] High School 1942; [occ.] Housewife, correspondent for 2 county news medias, 25 years; 4-H leader 36 years; [memb.] Life National PTA, Homemakers Extension, several local and church organizations; [hon.] Poem in Kennedy Library, 4 poems in Fayette Co. Musuem, poem in Bond Co, one room school musuem, poem buried in time capsule 1976 to be opened 2010, 3rd prize high school poetic contest, 3rd place Southern IL Arts essay contest; recognition by IL governor, listed in Who's Who in Poetry 1978 and 1991; eligible in Who's Who 1985 Golden Poet awards, Silver Poet Award, award of merit certificates, poet of merit founded "Bond County Literary Society" 1991; [oth. writ.] Poetry published in news medias, also many feature stories, World of Poetry Press Greater National Society of Published Poets, Quill Books, Sparrowgrass Poetry Forum, history books; [pers.] Words are just words, till a poet gives them life.' As I walk through this life, gaze at the wonders of Nature and miracles of life I enjoy writing my thoughts for readers to enjoy, so entitled my book of writings--'Dee's Diary." [a.] Mulberry Grove, IL.

LYNCH, NICOLLE
[pen.] Daniell Taylor; [b.] December 15, 1978, Iowa City, IA; [p.] Gayle and Arthur Lynch; [ed.] Osuna Elementary and Glenbard West High; [hon.] Literary Journal (school) publication award; [pers.] I want people to understand that I as a youth can write as deeply and passionately as adults. [a.] Glen Ellyn, IL.

MACALTAO, EL-CHAMI ISABELLE
[pen.] Nicolai Robin; [b.] June 9, 1981, Glendale, California; [p.] Rosalie P. Macaltao; [ed.] Colton Junior High School; [occ.] Student; memb.] C.C.D. (Confraternity Christian Doctrine); [hon.] Won merit award, Publish A Book contest-Raintree Steck Vaughn Publishers 1993, first place 1993 alcohol essay contest-S.B. County, second place Science and Engineering fair contest, honorable mention-S.B. County fair housing poster contest, Honor Roll student- McKinley Elementary School, Editor's Choice Award, National Library of Poetry; [pers.] I work hard for my ambition and I support it with prayers. [a.] Colton, PA.

MacEACHERN, STELLA KATHERINE
[pen.] Margo Christy; [b.] April 23, 1940, Charlottetown, Prince Edward Island; [p.] Colin and Margaret (Campbell) MacEachern; [ch.] Three nieces in Maryland, also a sister Mrs. Ethelene Copeland of Columbia, Md. who is a medical technologist at the Md. Medial Laboratories; [ed.] Grade XII, teacher training, 2 1/2 years Bible College, music; [occ.] Homenurse and homemaker, former teacher; [memb.] Women's Aglow, Presbyterian Bible Study; [hon.] Penmanship certificates, Silver Poet Award, Honorable Mention Certificates, also singing recognition; [oth. writ.] Book- "Recipes of the Century", poems- "My Missionary Call" and " The Burden Lifted by Grace"; [pers.] "The only life worthwhile living is one exclusively for our Saviour, the Lord Jesus Christ. [a.] Charlottetown, Prince Edward Island, Canada.

MACEWAN, CLARA HODGSON
[b.] August 5, 1918, Manitoulin Isle, Canada Ontario; [p.] John and Rose Hodgson; [m.] Irvine Macewan, December 25, 1940; [ch.] Bonnie Zieman and Ann Bradshaw.

MACK, LISE-ANNE
[b.] October 18, 1974, Vancouver, British Columbia; [p.] Mardon and Catherine Mack; [ed.] West Vancouver Secondary School, McGill University; [occ.] Student; [pers.] My poetry comes from the heart, it initially begins to belong to me, it then can be shared with others. [a.] West Vancouver, BC V7V 3L6.

MACKES, STEPHANIE
[pen.] Step Mackes; [b.] May 18, 1976, Bloomsburg, Pennsylvania; [p.] Steve and Linda Mackes; [ed.] Columbia Montour AVTS majoring in medical; [occ.] Nursing Assistant; [memb.] Hosa, SADD, letterman's, Adopt a Grandparent, cheerleading, basketball; [hon.] Basketball award, softball award; [pers.] My parents have always been a great inspiration in my life, but only my best friend "my mom" could give so much happiness that I'm inspired to write. As of now, I'm only a teen, but someday I hope to fulfill all of my dreams. [a.] Berwick, PA.

MACKEY, TAMMY
[b.] November 1, 1973, Vancouver, WA.; [p.] Joseph J. and Pamela Ann Mackey; [ed.] Prairie High School, University of Washington, St. Patricks College; [occ.] Waitress, security guard, student, tennis instructor; [memb.] Phi Eta Sigma (Honor Society), VW Student Hands (Community Service); [hon.] Graduated Valedictorian from Prairie, Inspirational Alumni Award; [pers.] My writings try to reflect the hidden human emotions. [a.] Bursh Prairie, WA.

MACNEIL, MELINDA
[b.] September 14, 1979, Grand Falls, N.F.; [p.] Linda and Francis MacNeil; [sib.] Earl MacNeil; [ed.] Holy Cross High, St. Alban's Nfld. (grade 8). [a.] St. Alban's bay D'Espoir, Nfld.

MACON, MILDRED M.
[pen.] Mildred Moses Macon; [p.] Oscar and Mary D. Moses; [m.] Leonard Leon Macon (deceased); [ch.] The late Leonard Macon, Jr., and the late Edward T. Macon, Sr.; [ed.] B.S. Winston-Salem Teacher's College; [occ.] Retired teacher, Winston-Salem/Forsyth Co. Schools, 33 years 8 months; [memb.] Delta Sigma Theta Sorority, National Women of Achievement, President Woman's Auxiliary to the Rowan Baptist Association, National Women of Achievement, Temple Memorial Baptist Church; [oth. writ.] Addresses, Letter From the Heart, published by International Reading Association, poems, one poem published by The National Library of Poetry, in Wind In The Night Sky; [pers.] I seek to write about things seen and felt with the heart. [a.] Winston-Salem, NC.

MADEO, CATHERINE
[b.] January 18, 1946, Lewisburg, Tennessee; [p.] Lena Fitzpatrick Dick and O.D. Dick, Jr.; [ch.] Melissa McLean; [ed.] Marshall Co. High, University of Tennessee, Middle Tennessee State University; [occ.] English and French teacher, Marshall County High; [memb.] National Council of Teachers of English, Tennessee Council of Teachers of English, NEA, TEA; [hon.] Phi Kappa Phi; [pers.] With inspiration and encouragement, much is possible. Thanks to Robert Frost and Henry Adams, Florence Fitzpatrick and Kay Daughrity. [a.] Lewisburg, TN.

MADISON, SUSAN
[pen.] Susan Renae' Wise; [b.] November 9, 1962, Mansfield, Ohio; [p.] Don Wise and Carol Jeffries; [m.] Michael Madison, February 26, 1984; [ch.] Kristy Renae Madison; [ed.] Clearfork High and Wickenburg High; [occ.] Home manager; [memb.] National Consumer Panel, North Shore Animal League, Silent Unity Member; [oth. writ.] Family Stability, Quiet Times published in local school newspaper and have entered many others in local and state contests; [pers.] I feel that writing is a very therapeutic way to express ones self. I have been greatly inspired and influenced by my mother, Carol. [a.] Wellton, AZ.

MADNICK, DEENA S.
[b.] February 11, 1939, Worcester, Massachusetts; [p.] Ann and David Silverman; [m.] Ronal C. Madnick, August 26, 1961; [ch.] Pamela Pollan and Jonathan Madnick, grandchildren: Nathan, Michele and Sagie; [ed.] Radford University, Radford, Virginia, B.A. Secondary Education, Masters in Education from State College of Worcester, certificate in technical writing, Clark University, Worcester; [occ.] Teacher of English at Doherty M.h.S., Worcester, and Writing and Editorial Consultant; [memb.] National Council Teachers of English, The Association of Teachers of English, Society for Documentations Professionals; [oth. writ.] Wrote thirty software user manuals published while working at Financial Publishing Boston, as a documentation specialist, wrote teaching units on teaching writing through works at the Worcester Art Museum, wrote for college newspaper; [pers.] The world will be a better place when everyone can contribute to progress and receive deserved recognition for achievement. [a.] Worcester, MA.

MADSEN, NICK J.
[b.] November 21, 1978, Williston, ND; [p.] Scott and Joni Evanson, Lee Madsen; [occ.] Student. [a.] Grenora, ND.

MAERTENS, JEANNE ROBERTS
[pen.] Jeanne Roberts Maertens; [b.] October 10, 1956, Minneapolis, Minnesota; [p.] Donald E. and Karin A. Roberts; [m.] Daniel J. Maertens, May 19, 1989; [ed.] B.S. Secondary Education Licensed Art Instructor, K-12 and Community College; [occ.] Artist; [memb.] (W.A.R.M.) Womens' Art Registry of Minnesota; [hon.] My artwork has been selected for display in many exhibits throughout Minnesota and Mexico; [oth. writ.] Numerous poems and stories, many of which have been inspired by my artwork. I am in the process of developing these into an anthology; [pers.] My father, who was an admirer and avid reader of the poets, introduced poetry to me. My poems express experiences, observations and emotion of my life and the people who surround me. My poetry serves as a therapeutic and creative outlet. [a.] Eden Prairie, MN.

MAHEUX, SHELLY
[b.] December 14, 1977, Lewiston, ME.; [p.] Anita J. and Henry L.J. Maheux; [ed.] Lewiston High School; [occ.] Student; [memb.] Cheering; [oth. writ.] Working on a book at this time. [a.] Lewiston, ME.

MAILHOT, LINDA
[b.] January 19, 1960, Grand Prairie, Alberta; [p.] Ovila and Marie Mailhot; [m.] David Rideout, December 21, 1989; [ed.] Kelly Road Junior High, Bathurst Community College; [occ.] Animal Trainer and Caretaker; [memb.] Harley Owners Group (H.O.G.); [oth. writ.] Several works being put to music, article published in Calgary Herald; [pers.] Some of the kindest people can come from homes of abuse. The key is in wanting to be that way and learning to see the good and not just the bad. [a.] Standard Alberta, Canada.

MAILLOT, JIBI
[b.] August 2, 1972, Belfort (France); [ed.] Graduation in 1990; [occ.] On the road; [oth. writ.] Stories, never revealed; [pers.] Seal of will, when I was chill, you get over my thrill. [a.] Belfort, France and Montgomery, TX.

MAINE, ANGELINE
[pen.] Usually sign "Angie"; [b.] June 1, Phoenixville, Pennsylvania; [p.] Charles and Charlotte Maine; [ed.] Graduate Phoenixville High School, class of 1937; [occ.] Ret. former from Philadelphia National Bank, had been at one time Librarian at Freedoms Foundation at Valley Forge; [memb.] First Methodist Church, AARP, Church Women United, Bethesda Circle, Meals on Wheels; [hon.] Editor's Choice Award, National Library of Poetry; [oth. writ.] Several poems published, many published in company magazines where I worked; [pers.] Enjoy writing my own verses in greeting cards, sympathy cards, etc. Can write poems about almost anything, prefer poems that rhyme. [a.] Phoenixville, PA.

MAISCALCO, TONY
[b.] April 2, 1977, Hartford, Connecticut; [p.] Susan M. and Anthony J. Maiscalco, Jr.; [ed.] Still in the process of completing high school; [occ.] Odd jobs which is mostly yard work; [memb.] I have my letter and bar in Windsor High lacrosse; [hon.] A constant honor student at Windsor High; [oth. writ.] Some essays and short stories, none of which have been published; [pers.] With every bad comes a good somewhere down the line. I'll also write back to anyone who writes to me. [a.] Windsor, CT.

MAKLA, ALICE
[b.] July 25, 1934, Method Hospital, Brooklyn, New York; [p.] Amy and Michael Makla (deceased); [ed.] Adelphi Academy, Academic; [occ.] Licensed Real Estate Salesperson, Brooklyn, New York; [memb.] Paradise Valley Assembly of God Church, Cresco, Pennsylvania; [oth. writ.] A Great Day, your last publication; [pers.] A way of reaching out, getting to the point, through poetry. [a.] Brooklyn, NY.

MALNER, BRENDA MARLENE KINGCOTT
[pen.] Brenda Malner; [b.] October 18, 1960, Lethbridge; [p.] Aubern and Bertha Hubbard; [m.] Hilton Malner, July 3, 1993; [ch.] Janet, Albert and Amber; [ed.] Lethbridge Collegiate Institute; [occ.] Farm wife and mother; [oth. writ.] Several poems I have written like, When I'm With You, Memories; [pers.] I wrote this poem for my dad because he is a hard working farmer. [a.] Busby, Alberta.

MANCHESTER, HAZEL
[b.] November 14, 1931, Bridgton, Maine; [p.] Raymond Lawrence Knight and Annie Marie Richardson; [m.] Bryon Wesley Manchester, December 13, 1950; [ch.] Frank, Linda, Miracle, Matthew, Michael, Melody, Marie and Dana; [occ.] Housewife, mother; [oth. writ.] I did write a lot of poems but most were lost in the fire, a few survived and it's hunting time again, Mum was one of them; [pers.] I try to see only the good in every one and to do the best I can for all. [a.] No. Windham, ME.

MANNING, ABBY
[pen.] Autumn Rayne; [b.] April 11, 1979, Macon, Georgia; [p.] Fay and Bobby Manning; [ed.] Freshman, Jones County High; [hon.] Honor Roll, Miss Community Service; [oth. writ.] No published works, this is my first entry, I have other poems in a journal; [pers.] I have learned that when I have feelings held up inside if I write a poem I let everything out and I have also produced something beautiful. [a.] Gray, GA.

MARGERISON, DOROTHY
[pen.] Dy Andrews; [b.] December 18, 1924; [m.] Widowed; [ch.] Peter, Gloria, Christopher, David, Lindsey and Fiona; [ed.] Woods Teacher Training College, Computer Tech College; [occ.] Semi-retired now, previously teacher, shorthand, typing and bookkeeping; [memb.] Canadian Cancer Society; [hon.] College Honors List; [oth. writ.] Several poems and short stories for children, currently working on two novels, also compiling crossword dictionary of words not found in most crossword dictionaries, mainly for my own use and also for a son and a son-in-law who also are crossword fanatics. [pers.] Having travelled the globe, I strive to bring readers a vivid picture of something many of them will never see. [a.] Cultus Lake, BC Canada.

MARIANI, VALERIE A.
[b.] July 21, 1940, New Brunswick, Canada; [m.] Gloria R. Mariani, February 1966; [ch.] Joseph A. and Valerie Gina; [ed.] Registered Nurse, Bachelor of Arts and pursing Masters in Health Care; [occ.] Registered Nurse; [memb.] Mass Nurse's Association, American Nurse's Association, various civic organizations; [hon.] Prize for medical nursing; [pers.] The style of my poetry is personal and its content reflects a broad spectrum of social issues often described with a crisp expression of sentimentality. [a.] Medfield, MA.

MARQUIS, DANIELLE
[b.] November 10, 1980, Newport, VT.; [p.] Venise J. Marquis-Sevigny and Richard L. Sevigny; [ed.] 8th grade, St. John's Academy; [occ.] Student; [hon.] High Honor Roll Student, French/Math Awards. [a.] Cadyville, NY.

MARRATT, HEATHER
[b.] August 15, 1952, Montreal, Quebec; [occ.] Housewife and mother; [oth. writ.] Poems of varied moods and style; [pers.] I write in hopes to bring healing to hurting hearts and minds and to reflect love through the listening. [a.] Stoney Creek, Ont. L8G 4A7.

MARRO, III, DANIEL
[b.] September 13, 1971, Hammonton, New Jersey; [p.] Daniel Marro, Jr. and Estelle J. Marro; [m.] Brenda L. Harring, I will be married August 13, 1994; [ed.] Hammonton High School; [occ.] Entertainer/singer, Music Therapist for nursing home; [oth. writ.] Sky/Love Is Blind/Area 51/Kami's Eyes/Tammy, all have been songs; [pers.] Though there are dark skies, just remember, above the clouds it's always clear. See the blue sky hiding above it and there'll be nothing more to fear. [a.] Hammonton, NJ.

MARTI, JO ANN
[b.] December 18, 1947, Ancon, Canal Zone; [p.] Ted and Ann Marti; [m.] Divorced; [ch.] Johnathan Douglas and Theodore Donathan Roebuck; [ed.] High school diploma, 3 years college, flower arranging degree from the Sogetsu School, Tokyo, Japan; [occ.] Professional organist, floral design artist; [memb.] Teachers Association of Sogetsu Ikebana, Organ Guild, Ikebana International; [hon.] Golden Poet Award in poetry 1991, my song " Come Follow Me" on "Gospel Jubilee" a album, various poetry

awards, various music awards (performance); [oth. writ.] 14 poems in all, 6 published in various poetry books; [pers.] I don't get involved with more than I can handle, and I do my best at whatever goal or commitment I make. Poetry is my best sense in true communication. [a.] Orlando, FL.

MARTIN, ANGIE
[pen.] Angie Martin; [b.] August 5, 1982, Winchester, KY; [p.] Daniel and Barbara Martin; [ed.] 6th grade at Powell County Middle School; [memb.] 4-H, Step-Leap Program for Gifted Children; [oth. writ.] Cub Reporter for the Clay City Times, 72 complete poems by the age of 11; [pers.] My poems reflect the environment of my home and my attitude towards life. [a.] Stanton, KY.

MARTIN, JOHN
[m.] Kathleen Martin; [occ.] I am the owner of the Strait Gate Christian Bookstore, since 1981; [memb.] I am a member of the New Hamburg Conservative Mennonite Church; [hon.] I have a contribution in the Mennonite Historical Library in the U.S.A.; [oth. writ.] I have written a poem booklet, some poems have been accepted in church papers in Canada and U.S.A.; [pers.] Christ's presence and His word truly satisfied my longing soul even through I am a sinner, saved from sin by His cleansing blood. [a.] Wellesley, Ont. Canada N0B 2T0.

MARTIN, REHONNA L.
[b.] May 4, 1981; [p.] Lawrence and Judy Martin; [hon.] Young Authors. [a.] Elizabeth, IN.

MARTINEZ, ANN
[pen.] Ann (Lis) Martinez; [b.] August 30, 1921, New York, New York; [p.] Mary Good and Michael Lis; [m.] Manuel R. Martinez, August 30, 1942; [ed.] High school, Drakes Business School; [occ.] Housewife; [memb.] Garden Club of Demarest, New Jersey; [oth. writ.] Nothing published; [pers.] At 72, a definite couch potato, a home body and loner. Love my limited activities and am sorry I threw away so much of my writing, am saving it now. [a.] Demarest, NJ.

MARTINEZ, EMMA MARIA
[b.] September 17, 1944, Mexico; [p.] Harold and Maria Meza; [m.] Jaime Martinex, June 30, 1962; [ch.] William, Jimmy, Patrick and Linda; [ed.] Long Beach City College; [occ.] Bilingual Teacher's Aide; [memb.] Parent Involvement Committee, Washington M.J.H.S., Up With Literacy W.M.J.H.S.; [hon.] Silver Poet 1990, Golden Poet 1990, World of Poetry, Sacramento, California; [oth. writ.] Fisher's of Man, God's Patience, The Reality of Love; [pers.] I thank God for His gift of " inspirational poetry". He has made me very happy as can be, by making people happy through poetry.

MARTINEZ, PAULA
[pen.] Martinez, "Poly"; [b.] June 29, 1971, Santiago, Chile; [p.] Nora Gonzalez and Renato Martinez; [ed.] Junior at Cornell College in Mount Vernon, Iowa, studying art and Spanish; [occ.] Student Reporter for the "Cornellian" the school paper; [memb.] In the Bone Marrow Donor Program; [oth. writ.] Articles for my college paper, The Cornellian; [pers.] You only live once, record and make the happiest life you have, enjoy it. [a.] Iowa City, IA.

MARTINEZ, RUTH
[b.] October 28, 1917, Wildon, AR.; [p.] John Harris and Willie Lagon; [m.] Lupet Martinez, November 23, 1955; [ch.] Joseph Martinez; [ed.] 11th grade; [occ.] Housewife.

MASON, BARBARA
[b.] January 21,1966, Cincinnati, OH.; [ed.] Oak Hills High School; [occ.] Medical Records Analyst; [memb.] BPA Scoremarking Association, Special Olympics coaching team; [oth. writ.] I have written 3 other poems, one published in school paper; [pers.] I really just write for fun, I have never been taken any classes or training courses, but I am also influenced by early poetic writers, like Elizabeth Barrett Browning. [a.] Cincinnati, OH.

MASTHAY, CARL
[b.] January 26, 1941, New Britain, CT.; [p.] Arthur August and Anna Marie Bartosiewicz Masthay; [ed.] Bachelor of Arts in French, Ph.D. in Linguistics; [occ.] Medical Editor; [memb.] American Mensa Ltd., St. Louis Astronomical Society, Mayan Society of St. Louis, Alliance Francais, Algonquian Conference member, The Planetary Society; [hon.] Bausch and Lomb Honorary Science Award (1958); [oth. writ.] Schmick's Mahican Dictionary (1991), Machican Language Hymans (etc) 1980, personal reflections from a China Trip (1978), numerals in 3300 languages, Sun and Moon is 450 languages I Love You in 310 languages and so on; [pers.] I am a cosmopolitan, speak Chinese, French and Spanish and read 10 languages: follow astronomy greatly, have a deep scientific interest. I help people who get words mixed up. [a.] Creve Coeur (St. Louis), MO.

MATCEK, KRISTINA PAYONK
[b.] November 5, 1933, Burleson County, Caldwell, Texas; [p.] Frank J. and Vlasta H. Payonk (deceased); [m.] Anton W. Matcek, March 19, 1955; [ch.] Daniel W., Joyce Rohrbach, Anton Jr. and Doris Heath; [ed.] Caldwell High School, Caldwell, Texas; [occ.] Housewife, husband and I owned and operated grocery store; [memb.] Ladies Auxiliary, V.F.W. Post 4692, Ladies Auxiliary American Legion Post 159; [hon.] Waco High School F.H.A. 51-52, Square Dance Club 51-52, class reporter- 52, Caldwell High School F.H.A.- 53, Devotional Club- 54. [oth. writ.] Methodist Home Orphan Anecdotes, M.H. Alumni Association recipes published and printed. Olathe, Kansas 66061-1260, three poems published in The National Library of Poetry; [pers.] I'm so happy to have had my poems published in the National Library of Poetry and to be as a semi-finalist in the 1993 Northern American Open Poetry contest. [a.] Bryan, TX.

MATTSON, MICHELLE L.
[b.] September 17, 1976, Ely, Minnesota; [p.] Bill and Judy Mattson; [a.] Pequot Lakes, MN.

MAUNDER, PATRICK J.
[b.] February 28, 1974, Pittsburgh, Pennsylvania; [p.] James and Jacqueline Maunder; [ed.] Burrell High School, Grove City College; [memb.] Greenpeace; [pers.] Our imaginations help us cope with reality, how each of us copes with reality is how we express ourselves as individuals. That expression, is creativity. [a.] Lower Burrell, PA.

MAXFIELD, MARTHA A.
[b.] July 29, 1949, St. Albans, Vermont; [p.] Osmond and Frances Brown; [m.] William E. Maxfield, July 3, 1971; [ch.] Childfree; [ed.] Bellows Free Academy. Concord Hospital School of Nursing; [occ.] R.N. of Medical Center Hospital of Vermont, Burlington, VT; [memb.] Georgia U.M.W., 29'ers-VAFCE Club; [oth. writ.] Essay in the book, Without Child, copyright of Hymn, some locally published poetry. [pers.] My poetry is my outlet for some of life's stresses, I don't start out in a specific direction, just go where the words take me. [a.] Georgia, VT.

MAY, SHARON C.
[pen.] "Sis"; [b.] June 19, 1952, Wheeling, West Virginia; [p.] Omey "Buzz" and Ruby Hinerman; [m.] Daniel G. May, July 10, 1971; [ch.] Joshua Daniel and Alyssa Christine; [ed.] Graduated, John Marshall High School, 1970; [occ.] Judicial Secretary to The Honorable John T. Madden, Judge; [memb.] House of Prayer; [hon.] Junior Achievement Leadership Award; [oth. writ.] This was my very first; [pers.] Due to my father's terminal illness, my poem was written to give him some inspiration and hope, most importantly, to show my love. Dedicated in loving memory to "DAD". [a.] Moundsville, WV.

MAYER, GEORGE
[pen.] George Mayer; [b.] February 22, 1896, Denver, CO.; [p.] Christian Mayer and Mary (Maurer); [m.] Christina (Goetschkes) Mayer, April 5, 1948; [ch.] Alan and Sonja; [ed.] Longmont, Colorado High School, U of NC, U of Denver, U of Washington; [occ.] Teacher, Editor, Management Analysist; [memb.] American Legion, London, Berlin, Tripoli, Aurora, Volo; [hon.] Three USAFE Meritorious Service Awards; [a.] Aurora, CO.

McARTHUR, SILAS
[b.] November 2, 1977, Fort Collins, Colorado; [p.] Michael and Darlene McArthur; [ed.] Wicomico Senior High School, Salisbury, Maryland, (sophomore); [occ.] Student; [memb.] Art Club, volunteer in community activities, St. Francis De Sales Church (catholic); [a.] Salisbury, MD.

McBRIDE, CARRIE R.
[pen.] Carrie R. McBride; [b.] August 5, 1954, Riverton, Wyoming; [p.] Eddie and Mildred Axe; [m.] David B. McBride, November 3, 1973; [ch.] Justin and Shannon McBride; [ed.] J.F. Kennedy High, Barstow, California, Barstow Community College; [Maintenance planner; [pers.] I have great admiration and respect for mother nature and all living things. I love animals of all kinds. After observing the silly but precious antics of our pet parakeet Aerial, I was inspired to write a poem about him. [a.] Henderson, NV.

McCABE, ALLISON JO
[b.] February 21, 1982, Morehead City, North Carolina; [p.] Bill and Jo McCabe; [ed.] 6th grader at Broad Creek Middle School, Newport, North Carolina; [occ.] Student; [memb.] National Federation of Music Club; [hon.] First place for poetry for Kiwanis Club contest for elementary school level; [oth. writ.] Several poems but kept to myself; [pers.] I have been influenced by my 5th grade teacher, Ellen Denney, by the hard work she put in to help me write poems. [a.] Morehead City, NC.

McCABE, KIM
[b.] February 13, 1979, Portland, ME.; [p.] Theresa A. Ellis and Michael T. McCabe; [ed.] Freshman at Leesville Road High School, Raleigh, NC.; [occ.] Student; [memb.] Student at Ballet, Dance Creations, Raleigh, NC.; [hon.] Editor's Choice Award for my poem "Ballet Beauty", printed in Wind in The Night Sky; [pers.] I like to express my feelings through poetry and writing. I want to encourage others to explore their feeling through the written word. [a.] Raleigh, NC.

McCABE, MICHAEL JAMES
[b.] September 14, 1973, St. Paul, Minnesota; [p.] Bill and Nancy McCabe; [ed.] Apple Valley High School, U of Minnesota at Morris, Hamline University; [occ.] Student; [memb.] Collegiate varsity football and track; [hon.] Flora Rogge Scholarship, All-Conference football and track captain; [oth. writ.] Several short stories and poems published in local newspapers, feature creative story in AVITS "Echo" 1992; [pers.] The poem "For My Heart Knows Of One" reflects my thoughts on the feelings and emotions of how a true-love relationship can affect a young man. [a.] Arden Hills, MN.

McCARTER, WILLIAM E.
[b.] July 14, 1973, Tampa, Florida; [p.] Soledad and Earl E. McCarter; [ed.] Canyon High School; [occ.] United State Navy, Aviation Firefighter; [pers.] Writing is what we owe... poetry is how we pay it... its an infinite debt we owe to inspiration. [a.] Canyon Country, CA.

McCARTHY, FRANCIS L.
[pen.] Francis L. McCarthy; [b.] February 22,1929, Detroit, MI.; [p.] Richard and Mary Lee McCarthy; [m.] Polly Louise McCarthy; [ch.] Richard, Kevin, Robert, Kathleen, Brian, Alan, Susan, David, Coleen and Tim; [ed.] Architectural Draftsman; [occ.] Master Carpenter and Cabinet Maker; [memb.] Knights of Columbus Moose, American Legion; [oth. writ.] Poems published in local newspapers, political writings in Op-Ed Pages. [a.] Angola, IN.

McCARTY, RAGEN
[b.] January 8, 1981, Milford, DE.; [p.] Michael and Christine McCarty; [ed.] Presently attending Lewes Middle School; [memb.] American Water Ski Association, American Quarter Horse Association, Palomino Horse Breeder of America,Inc.; [hon.] Honor Roll. [a.] Lewes, DE.

McCLAIN, MITCH
[b.] July 21, 1974, Portland, Oregon; [p.] Judi and Rob McClain; [ed.] Kamehameha Secondary, Whittier College; [occ.] Student; [oth. writ.] Poem published in Quest of A Dream. [a.] Honolulu, HI.

McCONACHIE, DIANE
[pen.] Diane McConachie; [b.] January 10, 1944, Montreal Quebec, Canada; [p.] Alexander McIntyre Gregory and Georgina Mary Mercer; [m.] John Alexander McConachie, December 24, 1968; [ch.] Sean Alexander (June 28/71) and Ryan Alexander (April 2/74); [ed.] Royal George High School, Macdonald College, Institute of Education, McGill University, Carleton University, Ottawa, Ont.; [occ.] Teacher and housewife; [memb.] Born again, spirit filled christian, attending Stittsville United Church, choir, Sunday School, board member; [hon.] All round (high school) student, athlete award, final year feneali trophy; [oth. writ.] Commentaries, short articles in local newspaper, poetry; [pers.] To live life praising God and loving people everywhere. [a.] Stittsville, Ontario Canada.

McCOOK, MARIE E.
[b.] April 1, 1946, Philadelphia, Pennsylvania; [p.] Althea and Sylvester McCook; [ed.] J. W. Hallahan Catholic High School for Girls, attended St. Joseph University and Temple University; [occ.] Director, Youth Community Choir, Child Care Worker; [oth. writ.] Written several other poems and lyrics to songs; [pers.] My writings reflect my inner feelings about life. [a.] Philadelphia, PA.

McCOY, SHAWN
[b.] December 16, 1970; [oth. writ.] Songs of no music; [pers.] Exploring worlds that live in the blindside of the mind. Poetic influence J.D. Morrison.

McCUMBER, MILDRED D.
[pen.] Ozice; [b.] March 25, 1909 (by Mid-wife) 84 years, Great Smokey Mountains of Tennessee, (never cost a cotton pickin' cent but will exit on an Inflationary Cloud); [ed.] High school 2 years, business course; [occ.] Retired (War Dept.) Fed. Govt. in Alaska during WWII. banking (Foreign Exchange and bookkeeper) E for excellence; [memb.] Gold Card, National Council Senior Citizens, Charter AARP # 776, 34 years, National AARP; [hon.] 5 awards volunteer work, poem award, Rancho Santiago College Award, in training service " Stand Out In the Crowd", instrumental in getting 4 Disneyland Awards for our Senior Citizens Club as founder and director of " The Goldenaires" a renowned choral group of seniors; [oth. writ.] Many poems and articles published. Was asked to write a column for our newspaper after years of my views. My recent article " The Storm" was used at meetings of adults abused as children after Scared Silent was aired on TV; [pers.] One can never take LIFE as an open book with blank pages to be filled with ONLY your desires. For with your first reluctant whimper, you became just another twig from that family tree first planted in the Garden of Eden to thrive according to the Ledger kept by The Heavenly Bookkeeper. [a.] Santa Ana, CA.

McDANIEL, SHONTE
[b.] March 25,1976, Natchez, Mississippi; [p.] Louise W. McDaniel, I have two brothers and one sister; [ed.] I attend Cathedral High School in Natchez; [occ.] Songwriter and actress, most of my acting is done in New Orleans, LA.: [oth. writ.] I have written over 20 poems, I also write short stories, I also plan to write a novel; [pers.] Most of my poetry is influenced by nature and my surroundings. I rely upon my imagination and simply expand it whenever I write. [a.] Natchez, MS.

McDONALD, BRIAN THOMAS
[b.] December 14, 1972, Sanford, NC.; [p.] Terry and Sheila P. McDonald; [ed.] 1993 graduate of Sandhills College and currently enrolled at East Carolina University;[occ.] Full time student, English major; [memb.] Raven Rock Presbyterian Church; [oth. writ.] Several personal essays and poems; [pers.] I try to be the best I can be, and I also try to learn from the early American writers who in my opinion are the best.[a.] Lillington, NC.

McDONALD, JOSHUA DYLAN-PATRICK
[pen.] Janus F. Kirkazeus, J.F.K., Poet McDonald, Raven; [b.] October 8, 1974, Newport, RI.; [p.] Lavrene and Les Hodovan; [ed.] Lincoln Junior-Senior High (Lincoln, RI.), Gaither Senior High (Tampa, FL>); [occ.] Burger flipper, writer, small business owner, independ. rep.; [memb.] God's Victorious, Amway, Bride's Keep The Faith and many more; [hon.] Styrofoam cup award, (40, 000 hairstyles); [oth. writ.] Currently working on a realist/sf novel and a realist/humorous/fantasy novel plus many poems. Parable is my first publication; [pers.] Jesus re-built my hotrod. I'd love to write a Star Trek novel if someone would show me how, I hate reading wimpy christian novels. [a.] Tampa, FL.

McDONALD, KIMBERLEY D.
[b.] October 26, 1968, Edmonton, Alberta Canada; [p.] Carson and M. Irene McDonald; [oth. writ.] Sunsets With the Down, Claudia and Dance of the Dead; [pers.] I have been greatly influenced by Edgar Allen Poe. Like Poe, I am drawn to that dark side of human nature that is within all of us. [a.] St. Albert, Albert Canada T8N 2K1.

McDONALD, LUCY ANNE
[b.] November 27, 1922 (died September 20, 1991), Lingan, Cape Breton, N.S.; [p.] Amanda and George McIsaac; [m.] Divorced; [ch.] Margaret Ann, John Angus, Joseph William, Patricia Annette, Mary Lucille, Elizabeth Jane, Rita Clare, Walter Alexander and Bernadette Marie; [pers.] My mom was a person that loved poetry, family and life. I only wish she had lived long enough to see one of her poems in print, but I know some how she knows. (Poem submitted by daughter Pat Cranmer). [a.] Leamington, Ontario Canada.

McDOWELL, CHARLES RENWICK
[pen.] Chaz R.; [b.] September 4, 1958, Boston, MA.; [ed.] Davenport Central High, Simpson College, Iowa State University; [occ.] Engineering Designer; [oth. writ.] Several poems and prose that are unpublished; [pers.] We must teach the children the truth, for what is good and right shall be, and with wisdom comes the intelligence to proclaim that true knowledge is priceless, it cannot be brought nor sold, but only given in gift by the one God, for what is truth if it is never told. [a.] Charleston, SC.

McELVEEN, FANNIE
[pen.] Fannie McElveen; [b.] March 24,1925, Florence County; [p.] Frank W. and Abigail Osborne McClam; [m.] October 6, 1934; [ch.] Cynthia M. Outlaw, (Mrs.) David (Anna) E. Smith and (Mrs.) Donald (Abigail) Barnhill; [ed.] Attended Olanta School (Florence County); [occ.] Retired; [memb.] East Clarendon Senior Citizens, Barrineau Church, Barrineau Church choir, and Barrineau Church Women's Ministries; [hon.] Certificates for volunteer work; [oth. writ.] A copyrighted song: The Lord Is My Shepherd, poems for church bulletin; [pers.] I endeavor to give a part of myself to each reader just as I have been divinely inspired by each poem given to me. [a.] Turbeville, SC.

McGINN, JEAN
[pen.] Jean McGinn; [b.] May 8, 1942, Baltimore, Maryland; [p.] Charles and Theresa Harrison; [m.] Robert Michael McGinn, September 16, 1961; [ch.]

Theresa, Robert Jr., Robin and Judy; [ed.] Parkville Senior High, University of Georgia, courses for Tax Assessment; [occ.] Administrative Secretary, Tax Assessors office; [memb.] Georgia Association of Assessing Official, American Cancer Society; [hon.] Graduated in top 10% of class, District top salesman for life insurance; [oth. writ.] Several poems published in local newspapers, one poem published in book The Magic of Muse; [pers.] I like to write poetry to reflect the mercy and love of the Lord. [a.] Pembroke, GA.

McGRATH, MARY BEATRICE
[pen.] Mary Beatrice McGrath; [b.] January 3, 1953, Burbank, California; [p.] Virginia and Edward Mayo; [ed.] BA Psychology/English, UC Santa Barbara 1975, graduate courses in advertising, UCLA 1980-1982; [occ.] Advertising Sales Representative, Sports Illustrated; [memb.] L.A. Advertising Club, Magazine Reps of L.A., LA County Museum grant, Armand Hammer Museum; [oth. writ.] First volume of poetry, Trespassing Stoplights and Attitudes (Mudbern Press 1980), other poems have appeared in. The Back Deck, The Poet, Poet Lore, Rock Bottom; [pers.] If I can inspire someone to address his/her life differently through one of my poems then I've done my job. [a.] Culver, CA.

McILWAIN, DUNCAN
[pen.] Duncan McIlwain; [b.] June 19, 1971, Lilydale, Australia; [p.] David and Audrey McIlwain; [m.] Anne McIlwain, April 17, 1973; [ed.] Upper Yarra High Technical College; [occ.] Car parts sales; [oth. writ.] No writings published yet. [a.] San Ramon, CA.

McINTOSH, AGNES
[b.] March 14, 1932, Nassau, Bahamas; [p.] Henry and Blanche Thurston; [m.] S.B. McIntosh, April 14, 1948; [ch.] Shanala, Keith, Andrea, Rudley and Kivam; [ed.] Diploma- personal development in computational and languages skills, U. college, switchboard operation, technical college; [occ.] Nurse, N/A accident and emergency, Princess Margaret Hospital, Nassau, Bahamas; [memb.] Calvary Deliverance Church, Good Friends Guild; [hon.] The 1st Mrs. Bahamas, 1st class lecturer; [oth. writ.] Works in accident and emergency for twenty two years, out of town patients and Bahamians loves my attitude it goes with love; [pers.] I am trying to educate people worldwide about the dangerous and killer Aids. Aids is a very serious disease, it makes you very sick and there is no cure, pay attention to health. [a.] Nassau, Bahamas.

McINTYRE, BETH
[b.] March 6, 1977, Philadelphia, Pennsylvania; [p.] William and Leslie McIntyre; [ed.] Presently a junior at South Fork High School in Stuart, Florida; [occ.] Cashier part-time at Winn Dixie; [memb.] President of Save the Manatees in school and member of the Humane Society. [a.] Hobe Sound, FL.

McKELLAN, DOUGLAS FERGUSON SCOTT
[b.] November 3, 1964, Edinburgh, Scotland; [p.] Douglas S. and Freda McKellan; [ed.] University of Manitoba (Winnipeg Manitoba), Brookfield High School (Ottawa Ontario); [occ.] Currently Assistant Manager of Footlocker, future career, Presbyterian Minister; [memb.] Cooke's Presbyterian Church (Chilliwack), Chilliwack Track and Field (coach and athlete), Chilliwack Big Brothers; [hon.] Two time All Canadian in track and field, 1989 Canadian Interuniversity Athletic Union 1000m gold medalist, other various awards for track achievements; [oth. writ.] I have written many articles for the Manitoban University newspaper-U.F.M., and had my own column in a local Winnipeg sports magazine (Amateur Sports Week); [pers.] Dreams are the seeds of reality. I believe dreams are the catalyst that can lead to a successful and productive life. [a.] Vedder Crossing, British Columbia Canada.

McKELVEY, BETH
[b.] October 16, 1966, Ashville, North Carolina; [p.] Gary M. and Jean B. McKelvey; [m.] David Humphreys, August 8, 1993; [ed.] Tucker High, University of Georgia, Athens, Georgia; [occ.] Business Development, Houston, Texas; [memb.] National Arbor Day Foundation, National Wildlife Federation, National Association of Corporate Real Estate Executives; [hon.] Dean's List; [oth. writ.] This is the first one I ever tried to get published (more to come); [pers.] Without friction, there is no spark, and a life unexamined isn't worth living. Live to love and open your heart to others. [a.] Houston, TX.

McKENNEY, NeGRE' M.
[b.] October 5, 1971, Tulsa, Oklahoma; [p.] Wilma Anderson; [ed.] Edison Senior High, Langston University; [occ.] Student; [memb.] National Association of Black Journalists, Communications Club, member of Pride of Stillwater 238 and Northwestern Consistory # 84 Masons; [oth. writ.] Several poems, unpublished; [pers.] Poetry is the innermost beauty which is expressed from one's own experience through feelings and thoughts put to paper, which is a gift and talent from God. [a.] Tulsa, OK.

McKENZIE, DAVID A.
[pen.] David A. McKenzie; [b.] September 15, 1971, Hamilton, Ontario Canada; [p.] Clifford Bruce and Barbara Helen McKenzie; [ed.] Grade 11; [occ.] Car jockey, car specialist located in Jarvis Ontario Canada; [hon.] At this time I working towards a diploma in Journalism/short story writing; [oth. writ.] Many poems such as "I've Searched", "The Eagle", "1916 (The Day I Died)", "WHT", "Ye Home on the Grassy Hill", "The Flowered Dress Forever One of My Favorite Memories"; [pers.] I enjoy writing poems and short stories and when I do this it helps me understand myself better. At the same time it helps me understand the world that lies far and wide outside my front door. [a.] Waterford, Ontario Canada.

McKENZIE, HAZEL M.
[pen.] Oval; [b.] July 12, 1943, Max Meadow, Virginia; [p.] Clesta Graham Bennett; [m.] Retired 1st Sgt. Garnett S. McKenzie, October 4, 1965; [ch.] Pippa Smith, Kay Henson and Amanda Prosser; [ed.] High school, some college, sign language; [occ.] Homemaker, poet; [memb.] International Society of Poets, Arthritis Foundation; [hon.] World of Poetry, American Red Cross, Faculty Wife Extraordinaire U.S. Army; [oth. writ.] Poetic Voices of America, "Cries After The Storm", Sound of Poetry, Wind In The Night Sky "When"; [pers.] Children must be taught the laws are to protect them too, children have the right to live without fear. [a.] Galax, VA.

McKENZIE, OLSON
[pen.] Fudgey; [b.] September 5, 1980, LaCrosse, WI; [p.] Gene and Ann Janusheske Olson; [ed.] I'm in 7th grade, I'm attending The Sparta Middle School; [hon.] At school I made High Honor Roll all 4 quarters, I'm a spelling bee winner; [oth. writ.] I've been twirling baton for 3 years with the LaCrosse Warriors Baton and Drum Corps. I twirl with my best friend Christel Gasper. [a.] Sparta, WI.

McKINNEY, ADA LUCILLE M.
[b.] November 28, 1916, Barry, IL.; [p.] Mr. and Mrs. Orville Moyer; [m.] Geogie P. McKinney (deceased), June 27; [ed.] Graduate Barry Illinois grade and high school, graduate of Tem City College, Quincy, IL.; [occ.] Legal Sec. [a.] Richland, WA.

McLAUGHLIN, RHONDA
[b.] February 12, 1958, Dyersburg, Tennessee; [p.] James H. and Vonda Wilson; [m.] Michael E. McLaughlin, August 8, 1986; [ch.] Michael Caleb and Steven Edward; [ed.] University of Tennessee; [occ.] Teacher, Holice Powell School, Fowlkes, Tennessee. [a.] Dyersburg, TN.

McLAURIN, BOBBI JO
[pen.] B.J.; [b.] December 26, 1980, Charlotte, NC; [p.] Elizabeth A. and Robert D. Cauthen; [ed.] College Park Elementary. [a.] Gautier, MS.

McLEAN, DEBORAH
[pen.] Delby McLean; [b.] May 14, 1965, Campbell River, B.C. Canada; [p.] Sarah Martin and Bill McIlwain; [m.] Ken McLean, May 11, 1991; [ch.] Teri Ashley and Jeremy Ryan; [ed.] Carihi, North Island College; [occ.] Housewife; [pers.] Realizing what we have today, may help build bigger dreams tomorrow. [a.] Cumberland, BC Canada V0R 1S0.

McLORIE, SUSAN
[pen.] Sue; [b.] June 21, 1959, Philadelphia, Pennsylvania; [m.] Donald Scott McLorie; [ch.] Erica, Kenny and Aaron; [occ.] Dietary for St. Mary's Nursing Home; [hon.] I am an avid contester, and have won close to five hundred contests; [oth. writ.] I have received many merit awards and a few of my poems have been published; [pers.] Many of my poems reflect my personal life and are of a spiritual nature, they include everything from poverty to hope and reality. [a.] West Berlin, NJ.

McNEASE, MYRTLE TAYLOR
[b.] June 26, 1924, Covington County, Mississippi; [p.] Mr. and Mrs Francis Poolie Taylor; [m.] Lamar Edgar McNease (deceased), May 29, 1948; [ch.] Lamar Edgar McNease, Jr. [ed.] (G.E.D.) certificate of high school equivalence; [occ.] Retired in 1986 from a school crossing and traffic guard; [memb.] A member of the 7th Day Adventist Denomination; [hon.] A veteran of World War II U.S.C.G. (Spar, Specialist 3rd class, job Public Relations or occupation Photo Lab Technical, enlisted July 20, 1944, served in Charleston, SC., discharged March 23, 1946; [pers.] A favorite hobby painting.

McNEESE, KARLA
[pen.] Kaye Miller; [b.] July 28, 1975, Herington, Kansas; [p.] Patsy Burke; [ed.] Council Grove High School; [occ.] Student, writer; [oth. writ.] Feature stories in student publication; [pers.] I use my writing to increase awareness of vital social and political issues and to make people stop and think. [a.] Wilsey, KS.

McPHERSON, BROOKE LYNN
[b.] June 7, 1981, Louisville, Kentucky; [p.] Bill McPherson and Valerie Reel; [ed.] Eastern Middle School; [memb.] CHurch On The Rock, Indiana; [hon.] Cheerleading Award; [pers.] I am so thrilled to have had my poem chosen from so many entries, I thank God for this blessing in my life; [a.] Henryville, IN.

McWILLIAMS, REGINA L.
[pen.] Jean Edwards; [b.] November 28, 1934, Philadelphia, Pennsylvania; [p.] Mildred and Charles Ervin; [m.] Divorced; [ch.] Jean Marie (pen) born same day, Jim, and Bernard McWilliams; [ed.] High school, Samuel B. Fleshaman Art School; [occ.] Assistant Controller for Hospital Support Services; [memb.] I was a committee woman 13 year now inactive; [hon.] None yet, I never tried before; [oth. writ.] My daughter, Jean Marie (Pen) and I had our first book published, Vantage Press, New York Thoughts In Poetry, *10.95 less 55% sale; [pers.] Jean Marie was born on my birthday, November 28, 1961. We just discovered we have a talent for poetry. I never knew she wrote nor did she know I did! [a.] Philadelphia, PA.

MECKLEY, ROBERT CC.
[b.] February 13, 1973, Winchester, Ontario Canada; [p.] Shirley Dicks and Robert E. Meckley; [ed.] Grade 12; [occ.] Cook; [oth. writ.] "Death" to be seen in Quest of a Dream; [pers.] Poems come from thoughts, thoughts come from emotions, emotions come from reality, reality very seldom contains lies, therefore reality deserves to be seen. [a.] Surrey BC., Canada.

MEDASKA, JR., ROBERT
[pen.] James Lesse; [b.] May 11, 1969, Hackensack, New Jersey; [p.] Robert and Agnes Medaska; [ed.] North Arlington High School, University of Scranton, Fairliegh Dickinson University; [occ.] Graduate Assistant, College of Business Administration; [memb.] President, Manhattan Improv Company; [hon.] Phi Zeta Kappa, Cum Laude graduate; [pers.] My inner being is the epitome of human despair. If my work can help just one person, my existence has been justified. [a.] North Arlington, NJ.

MEDILL, ROSANNE
[b.] September 26, 1958, Valdosta, Georgia; [p.] Walter P. Graves, Jr. and Anne Shawver; [m.] Kevin Medill, July 20, 1991; [ch.] Philip Gordon; [ed.] Colonial Heights Highs, Texas Woman's University; [occ.] Housewife-disabled (ex-Medical Secretary); [memb.] Arthritis Foundation; [hon.] U.S.Army Soldier of the Month, May 1984 for COmpany, Brigade Post Runner-up; [oth. writ.] Several poems for relatives and friends; [pers.] I have learned due to my disability that you can do anything you put your mind to. This is reflected in my daily life and my poems. [a.] Houston, TX.

MEEK, MARK A.
[b.] May 20, 1960, Montgomery, Alabama; [p.] Robert A. and Barbara A. Meek; [ed.] B.S. Applied Management, National College, A.S., Electronics Technology, A.A., Music Monterey, Peninsula College; [occ.] Student; [hon.] Dean's List; [oth. writ.] A poem "Spring Time" published in Pacific Grove, California for Monterey Peninsula Poetical Society; [pers.] I write from imagination and personal experiences. [a.] Colorado Springs, CO.

MEHTA, SAMIR
[b.] August 19, 1975, Philadelphia, Pennsylvania; [p.] Mr. Sudesh K. Mehta and Dr. Shobha Mehta; [sib.] Sonia and Sonul Mehta; [ed.] Bensalem High School, attending Northwestern University to study in the Integrated Science Program; [occ.] Student; [memb.] National Honor Society; [hon.] Valedictorian, Coca-Cola Scholarship semi-finalist, Debate Champion, Mock Trail State runner-up, Westinghouse Science Talent Search semi-finalist; [oth. writ.] Several articles for " The Owl" (a newspaper), working on a book about high school life; [pers.] Do what makes you happy and everything will follow. Always smile. [a.] Bensalem, PA.

MEIER, KATHRYN A.
[pen.] Jan Meier; [b.] October 7, 1962, Bronx, NY.; [p.] Barbara A. and Paul J. Meier; [ed.] Nassau Community College, A.A. Cum Laude, 14 credits Hofstra University; [occ.] Teaching Assistant at Vocational School; [memb.] St. Patrick's Church, Glen Cove, NY., (Parishioner); [hon.] Dean's List, Who's Who Among Students, Nassau Community College, transfer scholarship to Hofstra University; [oth. writ.] Wind in The Night Sky, "Untitled", Editor in Chief, Nassau Community College's Urbana magazine; [pers.] I have become increasingly aware of the inherent cathartic value of writing "to write is to hug". [a.] Westbury, NY.

MEKEEL, ELIZABETH MARIA
[b.] August 21, 1977, Hayward, California; [p.] Carmen R. Lindsay and James P. Foster; [ed.] Livermore High School; [pers.] Live life to the fullest before the sun sets for the last time. [a.] Livermore, CA.

MELOY, JEREMY
[b.] September 23, 1973, Kent, Ohio; [p.] Michael and Sheila Meloy; [ed.] Kent Roosevelt High School, Kent State University; [memb.] Crushed Dandelions, Hoss; [hon.] MVP KRHS soccer team, Dean's List; [pers.] The trees are too close to the road. [a.] Kent, OH.

MERCURIO, ALISON
[b.] March 24, West Palm Beach, Florida; [p.] Lorraine and Dean Mercurio; [ed.] 7th grade; [occ.] Student at Bear Lakes Middle School; [hon.] For tennis; [oth. writ.] I write short stories, I make them scary; [pers.] I like to write.

MERRELL, VIRGINIA
[b.] June 25, 1936; [p.] Joseph and Leona Cobble; [m.] Bobby L. Merrell, September 10, 1955; [ch.] Steven, 35 years old and Kimberly, 32 years old; [ed.] Pontiac Senior High; [occ.] Many, dancing teacher, writing, artist, doll maker, seamstress, housewife and opening my own doll shop soon; [oth. writ.] I have written many, but published none and kept few; [pers.] If I can help someone to see and enjoy the beauty of life within one's self or in any of God's creations, it pleases me. I get happiness from giving to and helping others. [a.] Hadley, MI.

MERRILL, DONNA
[pen.] Donna Collins; [b.] October 17, 1954, Moscow, ME.; [p.] Merwin and Rita Collins; [m.] Special person Peter Norris; [ch.] Andrea Mae and Gary Alan; [ed.] Valley High; [occ.] Secretary, data entry; [oth. writ.] I have been writing since I was 13, this is my first publication; [pers.] This poem was written when my brother died at age 41. Having this be my first publication makes it a special tribute to my brother Ray. [a.] Lisbon Falls, ME.

MERRILL, JANICE MERLE
[b.] March 4, 1942; [occ.] Homemaker; [oth. writ.] " Through Osage Eyes" dedicated to Kizziah Creekmore, my great grandmother (self-published June 1993), 50 pages poetical heritage; [pers.] "Grandfather, as we walk the modern way for strength, we pray now, more than ever". [a.] Cambridge, IA.

MEYER, LUCY
[b.] Jeffersonville, Indiana; [p.] Arthur and Mae Burton Sutton; [m.] Divorced; [ch.] Michele Stoutenborough and Eric Meyer; [ed.] B.A. degree, Indiana University; [occ.] Social Worker, job developer; [memb.] Self-Realization Fellowship, Astara; [oth. writ.] Music Views, Far-Eastern Economic Review, Guideposts. [a.] Morro Bay, CA.

MICHAELSON, LUKE
[b.] August 10,1973, Ft. Worth, Texas; [p.] Matthew L. and Noelle R. Michaelson; [ed.] Mirabeau Lamar Senior High School; [occ.] Student; [memb.] ROTC in Panther Thera XI, American Chemical Society, American Institute for Chemical Engineers; [oth. writ.] Write articles for Crimson Newspaper at Florida Tech; [pers.] We walk in footsteps of God and do not realize He has a different shoe size. [a.] Houston, TX.

MICHALEWICH, MARCIE
[b.] November 9, 1950, Bellis, AB Canada; [occ.] Typographer; [oth. writ.] Too numerous to mention, photo stories, people news stories for the "Smokey Lake Signal", a weekly newspaper;[pers.] I am an adult child of an alcoholic. With the help of AADAC counselling, my world has opened up, counselling helps.. give it a chance.[a.] Warspite, AB Canada.

MICHAUX, ELLA MAY
[b.] January 14, 1944, Morganton, North Carolina; [p.] John C. Michaux (deceased) and Mary E. Michaux; [ch.] Tamara, Crystal, Angela Brittain and Na Tasha Michaux; [ed.] Olive Hill High School, Morganton, North Carolina, Federal City College, Washington, DC; [occ.] Postal Clerk, U.S. Post Office; [hon.] Letters of Accommodations and Appreciation from D.C. Police Department and U.S. Postal Service; [pers.] It can be done. [a.] Upper Marlboro, MD.

MICINSKI, MARLENE
[b.] July 5, 1976, South Bend, Indiana; [p.] Greg and Jan Micinski; [ed.] Edwardsburg High School; [occ.] Student; [memb.] National Honor Society, Varsity Letterman's Club; [hon.] Honor Student, MVP, Cross Country, All Conference Cross Country and track; [oth. writ.] Journalist for local paper; [pers.] My poems are created by my heart and soul to reflect my true feelings. [a.] Union, MI.

MICKELSON, BENJAMIN D.
[b.] October 26, 1975, Cambridge, Minnesota; [p.] Bruce and Linda Mickelson; [ed.] Cambridge High

School, Cambridge Community College; [occ.] Student and lifeguard; [memb.] HOSA, Who's Who Among American High School Students, track team and swim team; [hon.] Earned high school letter for swimming, English Recognition for Excellence, Honor Roll; [oth. writ.] Several other poems and short stories; [pers.] Everything in life has a solution, all one need do it take it apart, put it back together and all will be made clear. [a.] Cambridge, MN.

MIER, KAYLYNN J.
[b.] March 29, 1973, Belding, Michigan; [p.] Roger and Sue Mier, Linda Crawley; [ed.] Greenville Senior High, Montcalm Community College; [occ.] Childcare worker; [oth. writ.] I write mostly about personal experiences and places and people that I know or meet; [pers.] Without God's help and the people around me I'd never be able to express myself on paper and share it with others. [a.] Greenville, MI.

MIHALCO, ROBERT A.
[b.] December 23, 1951, Brad; [p.] Albert W. and Marjory R. Mihalco; [m.] Julie W. Mihalco, November 23, 1985; [ch.] Bryan C. (16) and Michael A. Mihalco (6); [ed.] BA, Psychology-Penn State University, M.A. Industrial Relations, St. Francis; [occ.] Human Resources Manager; [memb.] Society of Human Resource Management. [a.] Colorado Springs, CO.

MIKE, FREDERICK
[b.] August 19,1963, Chaneliak, AK.; [p.] Justin Mike; [ed.] High school graduate (1982); [occ.] Ground crew for Ryan Air, Incorporated; [memb.] Alaska Fireman's State Association; [oth. writ.] A few on hand but never been released; [pers.] I am an Alaskan Eskimo. I do a lot of Eskimo dancing to keep our tradition alive. [a.] St. Mary's, AK.

MILLER, AMANDA
[b.] April 18, 1980, Bradford, Pennsylvania; [p.] Barbara J. and Robert A. Miller; [ed.] Still in school, going into 8th grade, plan to go to college; [occ.] Student; [memb.] Orchestra Student of the Month Committee, Photo Club, Organ Donor; [hon.] 3rd place in Kane Area Middle School poetry contest, Honor Roll; [oth. writ.] Stories, poems for English class; [pers.] Only two things are required when writing poetry, words and feelings. [a.] Kane, PA.

MILLER, BARRY M.
[pen.] Bear; [b.] March 17, 1949, Penrod, Kentucky; [p.] Edward and Hazel Miller; [ch.] Dawn Lynn and Robert Edward Miller; [ed.] Graduated from John H. Francis Polytechnic High, Sun Valley, California; [occ.] Hotel Maintenance; [hon.] 2 Golden and one Silver Poet Awards from The World of Poetry; [oth. writ.] She Is Like A Rose, A Long Cold Walk, Crazy Raft Race, Deltarado Daze; [pers.] I started writing poetry to get anger and frustration out of my mind. I enjoyed it so much, I still write and learn. [a.] Aspen, CO.

MILLER, BETHANY
[b.] September 27, 1974, Bloomington, Indiana; [p.] David and Virginia Miller; [ed.] North White High School, currently attending Ball State University; [occ.] Student. [a.] Reynolds, IN.

MILLER, DANIEL ARTHUR
[pen.] Dan; [b.] July 26, 1918, East St. Louis, Illinois; [p.] Arthur R. Miller and Florence M. Godin; [m.] Ruth Ellen Miller, April 3, 1968; [ch.] K.C. Fitzgerald, Kitty Ann and Christopher Cook; [ed.] St. Henry's College, DeMazenod Scholasticate, Loyola, Marymount, Southern Cal., Et Alia; [occ.] Retired Priest, retired teacher, retired counselor; [memb.] California Teachers Association, California Assoc. Marriage and Family Therapist, MENSA Regional Vice President; [hon.] Reg. V.P. California Scholarship Federation, One Man Show Mohave Community College, Kingman, AZ; [oth. writ.] Column, What Manner of Man; [pers.] I am intrigued by words and colors. I write poems and letters, and paint MINDSCAPES in watercolor or pastels. [a.] Webster, MN.

MILLER, GINA
[b.] March 15, 1977, Lincoln, NE; [p.] Steve and Teresa Miller; [ed.] Lincoln High School, graduating in 1195; [occ.] Student and part-time at Arby's; [oth. writ.] Several other poems written but never published, creative writing classes; [pers.] I've been writing since junior high and have loved and believe every poet, writer, singer, etc. should have an imaginative open and sometime child like mind. [a.] Lincoln, NE.

MILLER, JENNIFER
[b.] May 22, 1980, Clinton, Maryland; [p.] David E. and Andrea C. Miller; [occ.] Student at Annapolis Middle School; [memb.] St. Mary's Youth Group, Kathleen's Dance Centre; [hon.] Honor Roll at Annapolis Middle School. [a.] Annapolis, MD.

MILLER, MICHELLE
[b.] February 24, 1981, Bensalem, Philadelphia; [p.] Mary Jo and Charles P. Miller; [ed.] St. Ignatius School; [memb.] Junior Youth Group, CYO, Trenton Junior Golf Program; [hon.] Gwynedd Mercy College, essay contest, Academic Excellence Award, Effort Award, Team Leader Award, All-Star Basketball Award, 5-Hole Golf champion; [oth. writ.] I have written many different poems, but none have been published yet; [pers.] The poem I wrote "Bud The Dog" was composed by me when my teacher Mrs. Borghi brought her dog Bud to our 6th grade class. [a.] Yardley, PA.

MILLER, SUZANNE MARIE
[pen.] Suzanne Marie Ritter; [b.] September 7, 1962, Gainesville, Florida; [p.] Patricia F. and William S. Ritter; [m.] William H. Miller, August 6, 1989; [ch.] Gregory Lee and Christopher Glen; [ed.] Kaiserslautern American High School, University of Arkansas at Little Rock; [occ.] Research Coordinator, University of Arkansas for Medical Sciences; [memb.] American Psychological Association, Smithsonian Institute, Fraternal Order of the Police; [oth. writ.] Various poetry in high school and college publications; [pers.] If you say you can't, you most certainly won't: follow your dreams and make them happen through hard work, persistence and determination. [a.] Jacksonville, AR.

MILLIGAN, SHANNON ELAINE
[b.] September 25, 1977; [p.] Tom and Karen Milligan; [ed.] I am in 11th grade in Penncrest High School; [hon.] The only awards I have are for good grades in school; [oth. writ.] I wrote a few short stories and a lot of poems but I never entered any of them, they were never published; [pers.] I use poetry and writing to express how I feel because I have trouble talking about my feelings.[a.] Media, PA.

MILLS, AWNALI D.
[b.] April 4, 1967, Lancaster, California; [p.] Steven and Morrisa Henitz; [m.] R. Jefferson Mills, June 14, 1986; [ch.] Kaitlyn Rayne and Steven Kincaid; [ed.] Kofa High, Grand Canyon College; [occ.] Homemaker; [memb.] Immanuel Baptist Church; [hon.] National Honor Society; [pers.] Life is meaningless without Christ as it's center. [a.] Yuma, AZ.

MINAEFF, MARLENE
[b.] October 3, 1962, Sullivan, Missouri; [p.] Richard and Margie Pennock; [m.] Robert Minaeff, August 3, 1990; [occ.] Freelance in floral designs and several other fields; [oth. writ.] Additional unpublished poetry and songs; [pers.] Dedicated to my brother Rick Pennock. I will always be here for you. I love you! Sis. [a.] Kissee Mills, MO.

MINES, JR., CHARLES F.
[b.] January 15, 1954, Cleveland, Ohio; [p.] Charles F. and Delia L. Mines; [m.] Gwendolyn, January 1, 1975 ended January 1, 1993; [ed.] High school, some college; [occ.] A.E.M.S.; [pers.] Find a way to be happy! Never settle for less.

MIOR, SARA B.
[b.] June 16, 1951, Newfoundland, Canada; [occ.] Commercial Property Manager/Real Estate Broker; [oth. writ.] Numerous poetry, lyrics and short stories; [pers.] I feel poetry is the only mirror to one's true self and inner feelings. I write for those who can't express their feelings. [a.] Mount Pearl, Newfoundland Canada.

MISDARY, CHRIS A.A.
[pen.] Chris Misdary; [b.] February 19, 1947, birth cer. "August 22, 1946" "original". El-Slameia, Qina, Egypt; [p.] Princea Shaheed and Malak Misdary; [ch.] George, Margret and Chris; [ed.] College D. of Tech. "Egypt", U.G. Degree, Philosophy, Webster University, St. Louis, MO; [occ.] Hi-Tec. of General Motors Corp. Wentzville, MO; [hon.] Coptic School of Egypt; [oth. writ.] Several articles published in local union newspapers; [pers.] Man's life is man's gift, such a time through circle, such a sun... and the sun rise, for never set. I'm greatly influenced by my father and mother also, by early philosophers and romantic poets. [a.] Lake St. Louis, MO.

MISHEFF, SUE
[b.] January 12, 1951, Cleveland, Ohio; [p.] Millard and Dorothy Corbin; [m.] Van Misheff, October 27, 1973; [ch.] Menka and John; [ed.] B.A. in Educ. English, M.A. in reading, Ph.D. in reading and language arts; [occ.] Professor of Education and English; [memb.] International Reading Association, National Council of Teachers of English; [hon.] Kappa Delta Pi, Malone College Research Grant; [oth. writ.] Numerous articles in professional journals; [pers.] This poem is dedicated to my friend and soul-mate Barbara Drennan. Her life brings poetry to my life. [a.] Canton, OH.

MISTRETTA, JEAN
[b.] July 17, 1976, New Orleans, Louisiana; [p.] Emile and Jill Mistretta; [occ.] Artist; [pers.] Whenever I look at natural beauty, I see God smiling back at me. I love art in all of its forms. [a.] Chalmette, LA.

MITCHELL, JESSICA
[b.] November 8, 1977, Cincinnati, Ohio; [p.] Blair and Casey Mitchell; [ed.] Will be a sophomore at Kings High School; [hon.] Award in 6th grade for 2nd best poem; [pers.] I like to read, listen to music, write poetry and hang out with my best friend, Allison. I also love playing with my three dogs, Winston, Cinnamon and Duchess. [a.] Maineville, OH.

MITCHELL, KELLEY
[b.] May 11, 1980, Springfield, MO; [p.] Shirley Keith Mitchell; [ed.] Junior high student at Marion C. Early Schools in Morrisville, MO; [oth. writ.] Various short stories (none published). [a.] Aldrich, MO.

MITCHELL, KOSSUTH M.
[pen.] Kossuth; [b.] August 10, 1942, Thomasville, Alabama; [p.] Zadock and Carrie Mitchell; [m.] Sandra Shafer Mitchell, May 3, 1992; [ch.] Sherry, Kossuth II, Lenore, Krisit and Beth; [ed.] Thomasville High, Thomasville. AL, B.B.A. and M.B.A. James Madison University, Harrisonburg, Virginia, D.B.A., Nova University, Ft. Lauderdale, Florida; [occ.] Professor of Business Management and Finance, Alice Lloyd College, Pippa Passes, Kentucky; [memb.] Knott County Kiwanis Club and Lt.Governor for Division 8, KY/TN. District Kiwanis International, The Academy of Management, The Financial Management Association, The Handman Baptist Church, Life Member of Disabled American Veterans; [hon.] Alpha Chi National Honor Society (president of region 5), Alice Lloyd College's "Excellence In Leadership and Teaching Award", numerous military awards including the Legion of Merit, two bronze stars (one with V for Valor), three army commendation medals, the Meritorious Service Medals, the Vietnam Service Medal, the Viet Nam Champion Medal (7 champions), the Combat Infantry and Expert Infantry Badge and the Parachute Badge; [oth. writ.] I have published several articles in management and finance journals, but this is my first poem; [pers.] I started writing poems in 1968 during the first of two tours to Vietnam. My greatest joy is writing poems for my wife. The poems I write come from my heart and reflect the horrors and pain of war I feel or the wonderful love from my wife Sandy. [a.] Pippa Passes, KY.

MITCHELL, MONICA D.
[pen.] Monica D. Mitchell; [b.] June 18, 1962, Chattanooga, Tennessee; [p.] Mr. and Mrs. Howard Mitchell, Sr.; [ed.] Plan to attend University of Tampa and major in Human Resources; [occ.] Recently completed 10 years in the U.S. Air Force; [hon.] Air Force Joint Service Accommodation Medal, 1 Air Force Accommodation Medal and Air Force Good Conduct Award; [oth. writ.] Upcoming collection titled "Something Inside"; [pers.] I find the results are better when you follow your instincts. The poem "The Burdened Heart" is dedicated to Glendeline A. Albert. [a.] Tampa, FL 33611.

MITCHELL, SHEILA
[b.] December 12, 1955, Brooklyn, New York; [p.] Sallie Linton and James Mitchell; [m.] Norman Lewis, February 25,1993; [ch.] Corain, Lakwanza and Teniseshia Jones; [ed.] May 1993 graduate of Nova University, Ft. Lauderdale, Florida; [occ.] Paraprofessional II at Biscayne Gardens Elementary School, Miami, Florida, work with physically impaired students; [memb.] Member of New Birth Missionary Baptist Church; [hon.] Chapter 1 Parent of the Year, Dean's List, Nova University 1992-93; [oth. writ.] " Proud To Be Me", "To Be Drug Free"; [pers.] I found that through my poems, I am able to express my feelings and help give others hope and guidance in their life. [a.] Miami, FL.

MOCHULSKI, VALERIE
[b.] May 2, 1964, Brooklyn; [p.] John and Yolanda; [ed.] Richmond Hill High, SCS Business and Technical Institute; [occ.] Data entry operator; [oth. writ.] Assailant of Anger, I and II, Changes of Shade, love songs, not published; [pers.] This is the life, this is the purpose that God gave me to share with the world's people with happiness to grow. [a.] Brooklyn, NY.

MOIRANO, JOSEPH J.
[b.] January 10, 1951, Akron, Ohio; [p.] Joseph and Margaret Moirano, Jr.; [occ.] Registered Nurse; [oth. writ.] Nothing published, this is first poem submitted for publication. [a.] Akron, OH.

MOLTSAU, MICAYLA
[b.] February 28, 1980, Lawton, OK.; [p.] Alan and LouAnn Moltsau; [ed.] Central High School, 8th grade; [occ.] Student; [memb.] Cheerleading, basketball, softball; [hon.] Presidential Academic Fitness Award, Citizenship; [oth. writ.] None yet published but I hope so soon; [pers.] I write not just because I love it, but to help prove that young kids my age can succeed. My best friend Fawn Porter and I write stories and poems. [a.] Marlow, OK.

MONTBLANC, SARA
[b.] October 23, 1977, Pacifica in my house; [p.] Virginia and Michael MontBlanc; [ed.] I will be a junior (11th grade) at Terra Nova High School in Pacifica; [occ.] Living; [memb.] Coyote Point Museum, The Foundation for Spiritual Freedom, Rissho Kosei-kai Buddhist Church, The Pacifica Library; [hon.] First place in Pacificas Fog Fest limerick contest, Guardsmen Honor Camper Award; [pers.] Genie Virginia and Bonnie I love you soooo much! Thank you, Mr. Ahpo for being a great drama teacher, and hello everyone who knows and cares about me. The earth will be fine, let's save ourselves. [a.] Pacifica, CA.

MOODY, JONATHAN D.
[pen.] Jonathan D. Moody; [b.] November 13, 1975, Jay, Maine; [p.] Virginia C. and Dale O. Moody; [sis.] Miranda J. Moody; [ed.] Senior in high school, Jay High School, Jay, Maine; [occ.] Full time student, part time Photo-Journalist, Liv Falls Advertiser; [memb.] Future Business Leaders of America, Jay yearbook staff-Sports Editor; [hon.] Dirigo Boys State, MVP golf team/1st place Meaba Anest tournament, Maple Lane Golf Course, varsity letter in baseball, soccer, golf, tennis and basketball; [oth. writ.] Silence, The Decision, Endless Love, Out From The Darkness, Freedom, Life, Condemned, A Husband's Rage, The Destination, Grandfather, Dreaming, There Once Was A Man; [pers.] I try to express the innermost feelings of mankind and reflect how he or she may feel in moments of turmoil and chaos. I would hope that my writings express the essence of life, both good and bad. [a.] Jay, ME.

MOORBY, CAROL ANN
[b.] February 26, 1975, Onondaga, New York; [p.] Carol and Robert Moorby; [ed.] Shenendehowa High School, graduate, freshman at Russell Sage College, pre-med student; [memb.] National Honor Society, Assoc. dance instructor and choreographer, Saratogian softball dream team, 3 years Who's Who Among American School Students, Miss Shenendehowa, All Stars Softball (9 years), church youth group Missionary to Jamaica for "Youth for Christ"; [hon.] Shenendehowa Senator, SFA Sentae 3 years, representative to P.T.S.A., Valedictorian grade 9, Neil Hesson Scholarship and Citizenship Award, "Plainsnen Senior Athletic Award for varsity softball and cheerleading, President Student Council (grade 9), Co-captain softball and cheerleading (4 years), Faculty Scholarship Russell Sage College; [oth. writ.] This is my first publication; [pers.] I would like to touch the hearts, minds, souls and spirits of hurting people. I have been greatly influenced by God. [a.] Ballston Lake, NY.

MOORE, KATHRINE MICHELLE
[pen.] Kathrine Moore; [b.] March 30, 1976, Belfower, California; [p.] Jim and Donna Moore; [ed.] Currently taking G.E.D. proficiency courses; [occ.] Student; [memb.] A member of Glad Tidings Assemblies of God; [oth. writ.] I have currently written a number of poems, but have only two published; [pers.] Let Jesus love you. [a.] Bristol, TN.

MOORE, PATRICIA
[b.] June 9, 1936, Kansas City, Missouri; [p.] Leonard and Bernice Ebenhack; [m.] Robert E. Moore, May 28, 1955; [ch.] Two daughters, Stacia Carr and Roberta Goddard; [ed.] Central High, Draughon's College of Commerce; [occ.] Retired PBX, receptionist; [memb.] Pleasant Valley Baptist Church; [oth. writ.] Many, many many unpublished poems; [pers.] Listen for God's direction, then take it. [a.] Gladstone, MO.

MORGAN, KATHRYN
[b.] October 31, 1958, LaGrange, Georgia; [p.] James Hogan, Jr. and Virginia Louise Sims; [m.] Roger Dale Morgan, August 4, 1974; [ch.] Rodney Dale, Kimberly Dawn and Timothy Isaac; [ed.] Wadley High School; [occ.] Housewife; [oth. writ.] A few personal poems for family members; [pers.] My inspiration comes from reading romance novels in my spare time, and from my own personal experiences. [a.] Alexander City, AL.

MORRIS, BARNETT B.
[pen.] B.B. Morris; [b.] October 25, 1923, New York, New York; [p.] Louis and Ida Moskowitz; [m.] Joan Hamilton Morris, January 10, 1970; [ed.] Ph.D.; [occ.] Human Experimental Psychology; [memb.] AARP; [hon.] Psi Chi Teaching Award; [oth. writ.] Nothing published, do occasional poems and am working on a number of essay memoirs; [pers.] Lifelong interest in teaching and learning particularly in Science. [a.] Indianapolis, IN.

MOSSMAN, LUCILLE
[b.] November 1910, Alberta, Canada; [ch.] Carl and Ken; [oth. writ.] Monthly submissions to The Prince George Seniors Activity Centre's "Tid Bits" booklet; [pers.] I started writing at the age of 80 years old, most of my poetry depicts life in Western Canada. [a.] Prince George, BC Canada V2N 2H8.

MORRIS, MARK T.

[pen.] Majestic, Marquette;[b.] September 16, 1964, Bristol, TN.;[p.] Ruby Thomasson and Grayson Morris; [ed.] International Correspondence course (high school); [occ.] Aspiring writer;[oth. writ.] Novel: And Justice For Larry (currently unpublished), a poem in the Stillwater State Prison newspaper and three articles for the Minnesota American Indian Aids Task Force newsletter; [pers.] World peace can only be found when we all learn to appreciate differences and see that inside we are all souls on an incredible journey. [a.] Minneapolis, MN.

MOULDING, ROWLAND G.
[pen.] Mogal; [b.] May 17, 1911, Collingwood, Ontario Canada; [p.] Percy George and Lillian Simms Moulding; [m.] Elizabeth Miller Moulding, April 29, 1933; [ch.] Leslie Simms; [ed.] Humberside Collegiate, Toronto, Canada; [hon.] Several blue ribbons for oil painting; [oth. writ.] "Secret of Seeing", painting instruction, out of print, other poems not published; [pers.] Student of Metaphysics for 50 years. Meta poetry impressed by Old Masters, also Nicoli Facin, I am ill, legally blind and no longer write or paint. [a.] Anaheim, CA.

MUELLER, THOMASINE M.
[pen.] Tommye Mueller; [b.] February 13, 1924, Hamilton, Ohio; [p.] Charles J. and Myrtle Sharp Mueller; [m.] Single; [ed.] BA University of Alabama, BFA High Museum of Art, MAE University of Georgia; [occ.] Retired high school art teacher; [memb.] Portrait Society of Atlanta, Decatur First United Methodist Church, DAR; [hon.] Phi Beta Kappa, Omicron Delta Kappa, Alpha Delta Kappa; [oth. writ.] None published only recently have I had the leisure to try to write poetry; [pers.] I am inspired by visual beauty and intrigued by the absurd. Contrasts appeal to me, I am influenced by the romantic poets and Japanese haiku. [a.] Atlanta, GA.

MULLENAX, JANE
[b.] June 26, 1919, Warren, Ohio; [p.] John and Mary Ella Little; [m.] Kerth Mullenax, June 29, 1940; [ch.] Raymond, Kenneth, Ronald, Richard, Gerald and Larry; [ed.] High school; [occ.] Retired housewife; [memb.] Sew What Club of Orwell, Orwell Presbyterian Church; [hon.] Conneaut Writers Guild; [oth. writ.] The Little Church, Grampa's Farm, Fourth of July, Where Is God, The Old Barn; [pers.] Poetry has helped me deal with my husband having Alzheimas and in a nursing home. I use the poetry as much needed therapy. [a.] Orwell, OH.

MULTAMAKI, MARTIN
[pen.] Martin Masters; [b.] April 23, 1971, North Bay, Ontario; [p.] Eero and Helen Multamaki; [ed.] Lakefield D.S.S., University of Toronto; [occ.] Student; [memb.] Ontario Federation of Anglers and Hunters, Ontario University Field LaCrosse Association; [oth. writ.] Articles for "The Varsity" campus publication, articles for " Action Pursuit Games" magazine; [pers.] That will teach you for having a cat. I'm not here for the hunting. [a.] Peterborough, Ontario K9J 6X5.

MULVEY, PETER
[b.] September 6, 1969, Milwaukee, Wisconsin; [p.] Frank and Kathy Mulvey; [occ.] Singer, songwriter, poet; [pers.] To do something poetically is to do it with caring, focus, and desire. I try to do things poetically. [a.] Somerville, MA.

MUNOZ-KNOWLES, MARTHA
[pen.] Martha Munoz-Knowles; [b.] September 3, 1955, San Antonio, Texas; [p.] Manuel Munoz, M.D. and Teresa Valdez Blackmore; [m.] James Knowles, October 1, 1989; [ed.] Primarily Parochial Schools also Bellaire High School (Houston), University of Houston; [occ.] Transportation, taxi owner/operator; [memb.] Childreach, Plan International; [hon.] A couple of school awards-local; [oth. writ.] Until present time I have not shared much of my writing with others; [pers.] On my mother's side of family, I actually come from a long line of writers, including Richard D. Blackmore (Lorna Doone) which give me inspiration along with need to share graceful realizations. [a.] Austin, TX.

MURAS, JENNIFER NICOLE
[b.] November 11, 1983, Minneapolis, Minnesota; [p.] Stephan J. and Linda S. Muras; [ed.] Sonshine Copper Nursery School, Wayzata Evangelical Free Church, 4th grade-St. Bartholomew's Catholic School of Wayzata, MN.; [occ.] Student-St. Bartholomew's Catholic School; [memb.] Girl Scout Troop # 420, YMCA Voyageur (Father-Daughter) Program; [hon.] Presidential Physical Fitness Award, St. Bath's Geography Fair Award (1st place), St. Barth's Spelling Bee; [oth. writ.] Lots of stories, plays and poems, (unpublished); [pers.] I love to read and write stories, poems and plays. Many members of my family also like to read and write. My dad has a poem published in this book too. [a.] Plymouth, MN.

MURAS, STEVE
[pen.] Steve; [b.] June 6, 1942, Winona, Minnesota; [p.] George and Charlotte; [m.] Linda, June 20, 1970; [ch.] Christopher, Eric, Sarah and Jenni; [ed.] B.S., M.S. Education and Counseling; [occ.] Teacher, Gatewood Elementary, Hopkins Schools; [memb.] St. Barts Church, MN Educational Association; [hon.] Being blessed with a family and profession I love -just being alive and healthy is honor enough; [oth. writ.] I've written primarily for enjoyment and as a model for students: this is only the second time I've submitted for publication. The 1st "Unfinished Manuscript" appeared in a magazine for local Twin Cities Writers, under construction; [pers.] Words hold magic for me. They express my feelings. " Traveled on Carpets/time was written just after my mother died of Cancer and my wife Linda and daughter Jenni survived a miracle birth. I am a writer because of a writer, a teacher because of a teacher. Jenni's poem "Ice Cream" also appears in this book; [a.] Plymouth, MN.

MURNANE, TIMOTHY L.
[b.] July 10, 1961, Waltham, MA.; [p.] Nancy Langton and James Murnane; [ed.] Northeastern University, B.S. Chemistry/philosophy, Boston College High School; [occ.] Chemist, Astrologer, Chemistry tutor; [memb.] National Council of Geocosmic Research, American Chemical Society; [pers.] True awareness of all experience makes faith, belief and morality obsolete and gives one perfect sanctity and the realization of eternity. [a.] Sharon, MA.

MUROWSKY, PATRICK
[b.] May 20, 1976, Cleveland, Ohio; [p.] Thomas and Kathleen Murowsky; [ed.] Saint Ignatius High School; [memb.] National Honors Society, SADD; [oth. writ.] A myriad of other poems including several sonnets, short stories and a novel; [pers.] I strive to incorporate the idealism, profundity and human qualities of classical literature, most notably that of much-roaring Homer. His wisdom and style is timeless. [a.] Cleveland, OH.

MURPHY, CHARROLEE
[pen.] Charrolee Murphy; [b.] November 5, 1976, Springfield, MI.; [p.] Charles and Pamela Murphy; [ed.] Arkansas Baptist High School; [occ.] Student; [memb.] Fellowship of Christian Athletes, Political Awareness Club, Tea Club; [hon.] Mu Alpha Thetha, Beta Club, Editor of school newspaper, Business Editor of school yearbook; [pers.] I would like to thank God for giving me the talent to write. Through everything I do, including writing, I try to please Him. I would also like to thank my Granny Lou for being my example of what true literature should be. [a.] Maunelle, AR.

MURPHY, H. LOUISE
[pen.] H Louise; [b.] October 17, Lessburg, GA; [p.] Charlie M. and Clara B. Murphy; [ch.] Nieces-Kimberly Louise, Teya, Ashley, nephew Bernard Jr.; [ed.] William Penn High for Girls, Associate Degree Community College of Philadelphia, Rutgers University; [occ.] Retired; [memb.] Church of The Lord Jesus Christ of the Apostolic Faith; [hon.] Dean's List; [oth. writ.] Several poems, a few published in church literature and school paper; [pers.] Live your dream today, tomorrow is not yet here.[a.] Voorhees, NJ.

MURPHY, JOYCE
[pen.] Joyce Sherman Murphy; [b.] December 14, 1948, Bertha, Minnesota; [p.] Elmer and Vesta Sherman; [m.] Floyd L. Murphy, April 12, 1993; [ch.] Barry -19, Brandy-17, Bryan-15, Jessica-13 and Brandon-2; [ed.] Presently attending Detroit Lakes Technical College for nursing; [occ.] Student; [memb.] American Legion Aux., Charter member of Jack Pine Toastmasters; [oth. writ.] Several poems published in a weekly newsletter for christian women. [a.] Bertha, MN.

MURRAY, R. TODD
[b.] August 21, 1971, Pittsburgh, Pennsylvania; [p.] Robert J. and Sandra L.; [ed.] Kiskiminetas Springs School, Skidmore College; [occ.] Student, English/writing center tutor; [memb.] Carnegie Museum and Science Center, Smithsonian Institution; [hon.] Highest honors on Dean's List, Co-ed in Chief of Folio Literary magazine of Skidmore College; [oth. writ.] Several poems published in Folio Skidmore College Literary magazine. [a.] Bradford Woods, PA.

MYERS, BONNIE LOU
[pen.] Dottie; [b.] August 15,1929, Zephyrhills, FL.; [p.] John and Lena Arnold (born the 9th child of a family of 16 children); [m.] Homer Myers (passed away 1987), November 29, 1952; [ed.] Graduated from 12 grade at Zephyrhills High School; [occ.] Retired; [hon.] Received the American Legion Award as the Most Outstanding Girl of eight grade; [oth. writ.] A poem entitled "Our Loved Ones" and two short stories entitled "How I Know My Mother Loves Me" and "Memories of My Father"; [pers.] I greatly enjoy my writing, though I wish that I had more time for it. I gain so much pleasure in life, if I can, in some small way make other people happy. [a.] Richland, WA.

NAGY, HELEN A.
[[pen.] Helen A. Nagy; [b.] January 26, 1919, Lakewood, Ohio; [p.] Katherine and Jacob Gombar; [m.] John S. Nagy, January 3, 1941; [ch.] Kathy Ann Nagy Hustak; [ed.] Graduate of Lakewood High School, June 1937; [occ.] Retired; [memb.] Lake Erie Amateur Athletic Union; [hon.] Presenting awards and plaques for late husband, John S. Nagy, in the Hall of Fame for boxing, basketball, he was on the olympic boxing committee; [oth. writ.] Published in The Lakewood high school paper; [pers.] My late husband (1960) and I went to the 17th olympics in Rome also took fast pitch team to Osaka Japan, in 1970 went to Australia, New Zealand, Fifi Tahiti in 1989.

NARRAMORE, ANITA
[b.] May 26, 1957, Longview, Texas; [p.] LaVern and Ken Kerr, Charles and Genelle Narramore; [ed.] B.F.A.-Stephen F. Austin State University, advanced studies, Orff Institute, Salzburg, Austria; [occ.] Music teacher, workshop clinician; [memb.] American Orff-Schulwerk Association, Fort Worth Civic Symphony; [hon.] Gunild Keetman Fund recipient, Innovative Project grant winner, DeKalb Co. Georgia; [oth. writ.] Songs, children's musicals and stories, recorder music. [a.] Euless, TX.

NAYLOR, MIRNA
[b.] September 14, 1950, Cali, Colombia, (South America); [p.] Emiliano and Libia Lozano; [m.] Anthony D. Naylor, January 28, 1973; [ch.] Marco, Alex and Natasha Naylor; [ed.] Bachelor's degree in accounting; [occ.] Accountant; [pers.] Let's hold hands and together reverse the course of humankind, form imminent disaster to a hopeful and bright future. [a.] El Paso, TX.

NEELY, TAMMY JEAN
[b.] September 17, 1975, Lewiston, Maine; [p.] James and Linda Neely; [ed.] Forbush High School class '93; [occ.] Student at Surry Community College for paralegal; [memb.] National Junior Honor Society; [hon.] Outstanding Media Assistant of Year (1993); [oth. writ.] Precious Sounds published in the 1993 issue Wind in The Night Sky; [pers.] Started writing a little over 6 months ago, has had 1 poem published. Would like to encourage others to show any talents and to keep trying. This is a talent I never knew I had. [a.] Yadkniville, NC.

NEITGE, JUDITH A.
[b.] December 28, 1937, Mankato, Minnesota; [ch.] Meg, Teresa, Louise, Martha, Joe and Tony; [occ.] Medical Receptionist (retired); [pers.] I have penned my thoughts and experiences since I was a teenager. As a participant in life, my energy has focused on the beauty of my surroundings, and the forces that motivate human nature. [a.] Maple Grove, MN.

NELSON, PHILLIP E.
[b.] May 28, 1940, Sioux City, Ia; [P.] Arthur and Lillian Nelson; [m.] Teri-E Belf, June 11, 1988; [ed.] Ph.D in Organizational Behavior, University of Wisconsin; [occ.] Organization Development Practitioner; [pers.] "We are on the threshold of a new information/spiritual age. Poetry, joy and fun are essential elements. [a.] Annandale, VA.

NEVILL, HEATHER M.
[b.] April 10, 1973, Freeport, TX.; [p.] Michael Earl and Janeth Leonard Nevill; [ed.] Baton Rouge High School, Cypress Creek High School, North Harris County Community College, University of Texas; [occ.] Student, swing manager at a corporate McDonald's, Cypress, TX.; [memb.] Native American Student Organization; [hon.] National Honors Society (high school); [oth. writ.] Poetry published in school literary magazines and poems written for private use by specific persons; [pers.] I would like to thank my Muses (my cello and an orange lizard named Grizelle) and my family for support and inspiration, if it weren't for y'all I'd have nothing interesting to write about. [a.] Houston, TX.

NEWSOM, ANIECE
[b.] July 31, 1956, Waco, Texas; [p.] Allen and Alice Newsom; [ed.] Waco High School, Texas State Technical College, (ANS degree) Paul Quinn College (BA.S in OSH); [pers.] Our time is so brief-so I write that we may share a moment of emotion. [a.] Groesbeck, TX.

NGUYEN, MICHELLE
[b.] February 11, 1980, Silver Spring, Maryland; [p.] Thac and Lynn Nguyen; [ed.] Sligo Middle School; [occ.] Student; [memb.] Swim club, tennis club; [hon.] Honor Rolls, writing awards, Presidential Academic Fitness Award, art awards; [pers.] I put my heart and soul into the poems I write. [a.] Silver Spring, MD.

NICHOLS, BRANDON
[pen.] Brandon Nichols; [b.] July 30, 1979, Orange County, CA; [p.] Brenda and Lance Nichols; [ed.] Blanton Elementary and Carter Junior High School in Arlington, TX., Box Elder High School in Brigham City, UT; [occ.] Student; [memb.] National Geographic Society; [hon.] Two academic letters in Science, Conference and Appraisal on short story from Mayor Tom Green and presentation by baseball superstar Nolan Ryan, showing of artwork at the Arlington Museum of Art. [a.] Arlington, TX.

NICKERSON, BETH A.
[b.] June 27, 1969, Rochester, New York; [p.] William E. and Patricia A. Nickerson; [ed.] AAS Journalism degree from SUNY at Morrisville, New York; [occ.] Graphic Artist/advertiser, Creative Printing, Carmichael, CA.; [hon.] Dean's List, College Ambassador; [oth. writ.] Poetry and short stories; [pers.] I believe writing is a sanctuary. It's an outlet a healer and a friend. It can take you anywhere at anytime. [a.] Sacramento, CA.

NOLI, PATRICIA
[[pen.] Pat; [b.] January 22, 1959, New Roads, Louisiana; [p.] Luke and Josie Mae Davis, Sr.; [m.] Paul Reginald Noil,Sr., October 22, 1977; [ch.] Kendra Ann and Paul Reginald Noil, Jr.; [ed.] Rosenwald High School; [occ.] Restaurant worker; [memb.] Zion Travelers Baptist Church; [pers.] I give thanks and praise to God who is the head of my life, for giving me the wisdom and knowledge to express my thoughts and ideas into writing poetry. [a.] New Roads, LA.

NORMAN, ALICE
[pen.] June West; [b.] March 16, 1920, Menomince County, Carney; [p.] Bennhart Norman and Nettie Erickson; [ed.] Harris Twp. High School; [occ.] Farm worker owner nursing work; [memb.] Church Shrine; [hon.] Bicentennial 1975; [oth. writ.] Buck Bros. Lee Librace California, Lew Tabin Massachusetts Library Congress; [pers.] Importance renewal language native new prints. [a.] Carney, MI.

NORRIS, MARJORIE
[b.] December 4, 1938, New York, New York; [p.] Martin and Harriet Rogers; [m.] I'm divorced; [ch.] Richard Edward and James Robert; [ed.] B.A. and M.A. Hunter COllege, Ph.D. City University of New York; [occ.] Copywriter, Bayard Advertising formerly Assistant Professor of English; [memb.] Modern Language Association, West Park Presbyterian Church; [hon.] Sigman Tau Delta, listed in Who's Who Among University Students, 1977; [oth. writ.] Literary critical articles for the Keats Shelley Journal and for Seventeenth Century Abstracts; [pers.] I believe in reading up and reading out. Reading up to achieve personal and professional goals, reading out to help family, friends and the community. [a.] New York, NY

NORTON, MICHELLE JACQUELINE
[b.] November 22, 1976, Englewood, Colorado; [p.] Lori and Donn Norton; [ed.] Junior in Summit County High School, currently studying math, writing and science; [occ.] Part-time jobs to pay for college; [memb.] Girls Scouts, Cadet Fire Fighter at Red, White and Blue Fire Department; [oth. writ.] Nothing published, but I keep on writing; [pers.] I Never thought I'd ever have anything published, much less looked at, except by my friends and sister. [a.] Breckenridge, CO.

NOSE, ROXANNE
[pen.] Jon October; [b.] October 5, 1972, Bethel, Alaska; [p.] Roland and Carrie Nose; [ed.] Completed Peter Evon Memorial High School; [hon.] High school diploma; [oth. writ.] This is my first time writing a poem; [pers.] Fairy tales, Cinderella, rescued by a handsome prince. [a.] Akiachak, AK.

NOVAKOVIC, MILEVA
[pen.] Lela Novak; [b.] July 9, 1938, Zagreb, Yugoslavia; [p.] Major Svetozar Bogicevic and Vera Dragman (mother); [m.] Svetozar Novakovic, February 22, 1959; [ch.] Daughter and son; [ed.] Grammar school, Pitmans College, Wimbledon, Fleet Street School of Journalism; [occ.] Personal Assistant to Chairman of various companies; [memb.] Poetry Society of Great Britain, BASCA, FIBA, etc.; [hon.] Several special mentions etc.; [oth. writ.] Poetry published in various Anthologies by London Literary Editions, Cathay Books, Strand Literary Editions Regency Press, poems published in Ariba Digest, North Carolina Gallery-Now! Magazine, Durango, Colorado, by Juian Tapia. Several of works having been set to classical music in Germany by Dr. Otto Raddatz, all of which lead to being entered into several Western Europe International and World editions of Who's Who; [pers.] A person deep of feeling, reaching to the abyss of her soul, amazingly, above all a realist. Reflecting life like a mirror on the wall "Poet". [a.] London, W3 8LW England.

NOYES, NICOLE DANETTE
[b.] February 26, 1980, Los Angeles, California; [p.] Nancy Noyes; [ed.] Junior high (attending 8th grade); [hon.] Various good student awards throughout grade school; [oth. writ.] Two writings in a 4th grade anthology; [pers.] I thank my mother Nancy for giving me my poetic ability and I thank Sally Noyes for believing in me. [a.] Upland, CA.

NUBY, LESLIE
[pen.] Luna Nuby; [b.] May 20, 1971, Birmingham, Alabama; [p.] Lester and Jaqueline F. Nuby, Jr.; [ed.] Mountain Brook High School, Birmingham-Southern College; [occ.] Still attending Birmingham-Southern College; [oth. writ.] Poems published in college literary and arts magazine, Quad; [pers.] In my writing, I attempt to relate feelings and experiences of a very personal nature, in hopes that others will connect with and relate to it. I am primarily influenced by Annie Nin and Marguerite Duras. [a.] Birmingham, AL.

OAKES, JANALENE L.
[b.] May 21, 1935, Machias, Maine; [p.] Worht Reynold and Violet Dawes Perry (both deceased); [m.] Henry L. Oakes, Jr., May 21, 1955; [ch.] Nina Ellen Runz, Henry L. Oakes, II and Andrew Reynolds Oakes; [ed.] High school; [occ.] Domestic Engineer; [memb.] United Methodist Women (Miriam Circle), Babylon, New York; [oth. writ.] Approximately 20 other poems, mainly personal ones to friends and about special situations; [pers.] Through God there is strength. [a.] Bay Shore, NY.

OBED, JENNIFER
[b.] May 29, 1980; [p.] Patricia Lynne and Robert Joseph Obed; [ed.] Mohawk Junior Senior High School; [occ.] 8th grade; [memb.] Girl Scouts, SADD, group of cool people I hang with (Hi Guys) Mohawk Junior High band; [hon.] Most likely to get gored by a bull after attempting to kiss it on a dare; [pers.] In all of my 13 years of existence, I've only it seems learned one thing, life's to short to take seriously. Oh ya, hi Jessie. [a.] New Castle, PA.

OBLEN, ALLISON
[b.] February 17, 1982, Englewood, NJ.; [p.] Connie and Edward Oblen; [sib.] Heather and Louis Russo; [ed.] Is presently in 6th grade; [occ.] Student; [pers.] I started writing poetry because it came easy to me. I keep a book of my writings and I enjoy writing poetry. [a.] Garfield, NJ.

OBUDHO, CHRISTOPHER J.
[pen.] C. James Obudho; [b.] September 11, 1971, New Brunswick, NJ.; [p.] Willie and Constance Jackson; [m.] Gillian Obudho; [ed.] Florence Twp. High School, Community College of the Air Force; [occ.] Security Specialist, USAF; [memb.] Democratic Party, America 2000 Tutoring program; [hon.] USAF Achievement medal, SW Asian Service medal, Explorer professionalism award; [pers.] We must bring back morality and faith to a disappointingly immoral and faithless world. [a.] Grissom AFB, IN.

OCAYA, HELEN APOLO
[pen.] Amam-Etit; [b.] 1950, Aboke-Apuro, Uganda; [p.] Erisa and Y. Ebil-Okello; [m.] V. Ocaya, November 1968; [ch.] Kidegac, Opio R., Ocen M. Okello J. Odong V. and Ayaas; [ed.] Scared Heart, Sen. Sec. Sch., Tororo Girls Sec. Sch., Makerere University, University of Zambia; [memb.] The LA (Britain), The Southern Africa Lit. of Society, International Society of Poets; [hon.] Brooke Bond Tea Award, The Brenan Jones Memorial Award, Unza (Sch of Education), commendation, Editor's Choice Award (1993), nominated by The NLP for "1993 Poet of Merit Award"; [oth. writ.] Poems in two anthologies, The National Library of Poetry (1992-93), several poems on cassette albums, The National Library of Poetry (1993), Lango Proverbs and riddles (Thesis), Lango/English phrases in my poems. [pers.] I try to show that peace, love, generosity and healthy environment are the most vital factors for the enhancement of human life and dignity. {a.] Gaborone Botswans, Southern Africa.

ODOM, FRANCES LUNN
[b.] September 8, 1926, Swift Creek, Darlington Co., South Carolina; [p.] William D. and Laura M. Lunn; [m.] Cephas H. Odom, September 17, 1949; [ch.] Freddie, Larry, Ann, Mary and Carol; [ed.] Graduated St. John's High School with diploma at age sixty-three; [occ.] Retired Dispatcher Darlington County Sheriff's Department; [hon.] Adult Achiever's Award from State Board of Education; [oth. writ.] Other poems published in local newspapers and the D.A.V. newsletter; [pers.] My hope is to instill in those who follow a love of family nature and God and thoughts of other times. I am inspired by memories and events of today. [a.] Hartsville, SC.

ODOM, II, JOHNNIE LAMAR
[b.] May 21, 1978, Memphis, Tennessee; [p.] Lt. Cmdr. John and Jean Odom; [ed.] Elementary East Hill Christian School Pensacola, Pensacola High School International Baccalaureate; [memb.] Gulf Breeze United Methodist Church, Gulf Breeze Wesley Youth Choir, Gulf Breeze Youth Council, Gulf Breeze United Methodist Church Administration Board, International Thespian Society, Gulf Breeze Council on Ministries, Duke University T-I-P Program, Escambia County School District Poetry winner, Presidents Academic Award E-H-C-S-; [oth. writ.] Editorials Pensacola News Journal, D.H. Holmes creative writing contest; [pers.] I am thankful that God has given me the gift of writing and hope to improve that gift. [a.] Gulf Breeze, FL.

O'DONNELL, EMILY
[b.] January 16, 1976; [p.] Raymond and Laurene O'Donnell; [ed.] Hunterdon Central High School; [occ.] Student; [memb.] Hunterdon Central Silk Squad, YMCA Karate, Sign Language classes; [hon.] Hunterdon Central Vocational Cosmetology Program, Honor Roll; [pers.] Poems are the best way to express your feelings. Be free and be yourself. [a.] Whitehouse Station, NJ.

OGLESBY, BYRON
[pen.] Bryon Oglesby; [b.] December 30, 1976, Clayton County Georgia; [p.] Belver and Peggy Oglesby; [ed.] Mount Zion High School; [pers.] In my poetry I try to let my readers get involved with the characters and feel what they feel, I can do all things through Christ who strengthens me. Philippians 4:13. [a.] Morrow, GA.

OGLETREE, RASHONDA ANJEL
[pen.] Anjel O;[b.] June 27, 1979, Columbus, GA; [p.] Dwayne V. and Annette P. Ogletree; [sib.] Jabari Ogletree; [ed.] Elementary-Lomie Heard, Las Vegas, NV, high-Lewis Middle, Valparaiso, FL, high school-Niceville High, Valparaiso, FL; [occ.] Student in the 9th grade; [memb.] Niceville High band, Valparaiso, Fl; [hon.] Honor Roll, Northside Christian School, Charleston, SC and Lewis Middle School, Niceville, Fl. [a.] Eglin AFB, FL.

OLDROYD, JANE MACKINNON
[pen.] Hane Mackinnon Oldroyd; [b.] December 29, 1915, Oak Cross Farm, Maxton, North Carolina; [p.] John A. and Janie MacLauchlin Mackinnon; [m.] Thomas L. Oldroyd (deceased), 1944; [ch.] Thomas H. Oldroyd (son); [ed.] Maxton High School, Flora MacDonald College, AB degree; [occ.] Retired 2 years English teacher, 7 years Director of Religious Ed., 25 years Personnel Mgr.; [memb.] Charter member Columbia, South Carolina Personnel Club, Maxton, North Carolina Historical Society, First Pres. Church, Maxton, North Carolina Smithsonian Institute; [hon.] High school Valedictorian, college class poet, Front Page Award with army and ASY Force Exchange Service, third army certificate of Achievement, Mount Rushmore History contest for college students; [oth. writ.] Articles for papers and magazines, news releases while in personnel work, training programs for P.X. Personnel, program material for Presbyterian young people; [pers.] I began writing poetry when I was in the 3rd grade. Poets and writers were in my mother's family. I like to manipulate words. My poems are humorous, serious or critical. I am now 78, "The Organist" was written in April of this year. [a.] Maxton, NC.

OLESON, MILDRED
[b.] November 10, 1922, Waltham, Massachusetts; [p.] Harold and Minnie Arey; [m.] George Oleson, October 7, 1944; [ch.] John, Jean and Nancy; [ed.] High school; [occ.] Retired; [memb.] Co-operative Extension Homemaker, President of Lutheran Church Council and Congregation, 29 years Sunday School teacher; [hon.] My church is over 100 years old, I am the first Woman President; [oth. writ.] Have written quite a few poems, mostly for events, have written music for two of them; [pers.] With so many years behind me of both and happy and unhappy times, I have learned to keep a smile on my face and accept the future with Jesus' help. [a.] Berlin, NH.

OLIVER, LISA
[b.] December 13, 1945, Flushing Queens, Long Island, New York; [p.] Stella and Ole Svane; [m.] Kenneth, July 3, 1965; [ch.] David, Michael and Rebekah; [ed.] BA-MA, William Paterson College, Wayne, New Jersey; [occ.] Teacher-Roosevelt School, North Arlington, New Jersey 07032; [oth. writ.] This poem is my first published piece of work. [a.] Rutherford, NJ.

OLSON, JACOB
[b.] August 29, 1970, Denver, Colorado; [p.] Melvin and Wanda Olson; [ed.] Palisade High, Embry Riddle Aeronautical University, University of Colorado at Denver; [occ.] Laboring through school; [memb.] Rocky Mountain Fichon Writers, Taoist Tai Chi Society of Denver; [oth. writ.] Many published poems in school magazines and newsletters including the Black Box and The Taoist Tai Chi Society of the United States Newsletter; [pers.] Writing as an artistic expression is a way of life. Artistic expression is the unfolding of personality, much like a rose opening to reflect the early morning sun. [a.] Parker, CO.

OLSON, VERNA L.
[b.] May 2, 1911, Purdy, Wisconsin; [p.] Alfred and Hanna Gauper; [m.] Walton C. Olson (deceased), March 19, 1937; [ch.] Gerald Douglas and Janice Mae; [ed.] Deer River High School, Young and Hursh Business College; [occ.] Secretary, various insurance offices; [memb.] Bethany Lutheran Church, Lenox Club; [oth. writ.] I have a book filled with poetry which I have written (just for my own enjoyment and interest); [pers.] I have always been interested in history and in the past. [a.] Duluth, MN.

O'NEILL JR., JAMES W.
[b.] September 23, 1954, Philadelphia, PA.; [p.] James W. O'Neill and Mary Theresa Wade; [m.] Marion C. Clarke, February 4, 1984; [ch.] James Michael O'Neill; [ed.] Overbrook Regional High, Rutgers University; [occ.] International Accounting/Finance; [memb.] Theta Chi Fraternity, Rutgers Alumni Association; [hon.] Rutgers Scholar; [oth. writ.] This is my first published work of art; [pers.] Dedicated to my sister Mary Lou. [a.] North Caldwell, NJ.

O'PRY, VERA J.
[pen.] Vera J.; [b.] November 25, 1944, Ft. Polk, Louisiana; [p.] Henry A. and Johnnie Hand Harvey, Jr.; [m.] Divorced; [ch.] David E. Loftin, Caren L. Hall and Robin E.A. Hyatt; [ed.] DeRidder High School, presently attending Louisiana State University part-time; [occ.] Accounting Specialist; [memb.] Louisiana Cattlemen's Association, Beefmaster Breeders Universal; [oth. writ.] Poem to be published in Sparrowgrass Poetry Forum's "Poetic Voices of America"; [pers.] I have a vision that someday all people will be as honest and unbiased as the animals of the world, and smile as oft as the sun shines. [a.] Greenwell Springs, LA.

OPULENCIA, SHANEEKA
[b.] October 17, 1980, San Diego, CA.; [p.] Sherri Opulencia and Charles Anthony Parrison; [ed.] Hazel Valley, Sylvester Elementary Middle School; [occ.] Babysitter, Girl Scout, help elderly people; [memb.] Girl Scout; [hon.] Graduated from DARE 2 times, got honors for having good grades in school and other writings; [oth. writ.] Poetry report A+ on all, won 1st place in a poetry contest; [pers.] I try real hard to try and get my best poetry done, I love poetry that's why I write it now.. I also do my best and succeed in my goals. [a.] Seattle, WA.

ORNEGRI, CHARLES MICHAEL
[b.] March 11, 1966, Paterson, NJ; [p.] Teresa Zevallos and Jose Ornegri; [ed.] Montclair State College; [occ.] Graphic Artist; [pers.] Be strong for life, be content for death, begin and end all things as birth and death. [a.] Passaic, NJ.

ORTIZ, SHANNON
[b.] June 8, 1977, Tucson, Arizona; [p.] Salvador Ortiz and Sandra Roe; [ed.] Still in high school; [occ.] Student; [oth. writ.] I have written other poems not published; [pers.] Most of my work that I have written was mainly based on the time when I was having lots of trouble with depression. [a.] Oracle, AZ.

OTTLEY, SIMONE
[pen.] Chasity Cater; [b.] February 7, 1979, North York, Ontario Canada; [occ.] Student; [hon.] Student of the Term for French and Citizenship Award; [pers.] Look within yourself for what you want, and don't let anything stand in your way. Life is like a road with speed bumps, drive over them and let your heart be your guard. Anything is possible if you put your mind to it. [a.] North York, Ontario Canada.

OTTO, RITA
[b.] Back Then, Detroit, Michigan; [p.] Eugene and Edna Durant; [m.] Arthur, January 8, 1949; [ch.] Susan, Eileen, Deborah, Mark, Mary, Michael and Matthew; [ed.] Grade school Shamrose and St. Philips graduated St. Martins; [occ.] Ladies Shoe Sales Management; [oth. writ.] Quite a few poems published local newspaper and a rather long poem published in the Marine's magazine Leather-Neck; [pers.] I seek to find the humor in our everyday life, and love to put it in verse. [a.] Warren, MI.

PADDIO-JOHNSON, EUNICE ALICE
[b.] June 25, 1928, Crowley, Louisiana; [p.] Henry Paddio and Ce'cile Atris Chesle'; [m.] John David Johnson, Sr., June 23, 1984; [ch.] Deidre, Clarence, Henry, Bertrand Ce'cile, John Frank, Leroy, Lindroy and Joe; [ed.] BS, MA, MS, Ph.D in Education and Religion; [occ.] Retired, Educator and Freelance Writer; [memb.] Order of Eastern Star, Delta Sigma Theta Sorority, Turner Chapel A.M.E. Church; [hon.] Paddio-Johnson Foundation, Outstanding Citizen, Trailblazer, Black and Gold Award from Grambling State University; [oth. writ.] Creative Career Exploration Program, Pat's first book of Poetry and Prose, anthology of St. Helena and other Louisiana poets, legal responsibilities of counselors; [pers.] Everyone makes daily statements by what they say or don't say, do or don't do and go or don't go. Let your statements reflect the real "you". [a.] Greensburg, LA.

PADWA, AMANDA JOY
[b.] May 5, 1980, Johnson City, NY; [p.] Eugene and Fallie Padwa; [ed.] Currently in 8th grade at Jennie F. Snapp Middle School, Endicott, NY; [hon.] Award from Sertoma Club for essay "Why I Love America" when 11 years old. [a.] Endicott, NY.

PAGONIS, REBECCA SUE VICTORIA
[b.] September 20, 1977, St. Louis, Missouri; [p.] Rose Marie and Michael Pagonis; [ed.] 10th grader at Lee High School; [occ.] Student; [hon.] Sports for track, volleyball, basketball and softball; [oth. writ.] I have many other poems that have been published in magazines. I also have a diary of my own personal poems; [pers.] What ever comes to mind write it down because it's really coming from your heart and it will be magnificent. [a.] San Antonio, TX.

PALMER, ANGELA
[pen.] Indigo; [b.] June 26, 1974, Ironton, Ohio; [p.] Tim and Barb Palmer, Carla Ball; [ch.] Haley Marie; [ed.] Central York High, Penn State; [occ.] Student; [memb.] American Diabetes Association, Teen Pregnancy Coalition; [oth. writ.] High school newspaper, Petersburg, VA. Newspaper; [pers.] There is always tomorrow, but never again, so live for today. [a.] York, PA.

PALMER, VALERIE JEANNE
[b.] July 12, 1933, Leeds, England; [p.] Arthur and Ruby Williamson; [m.] Donald Keith Palmer; [ed.] England; [occ.] Teacher, artist, poet; [oth. writ.] Local newspapers, English Quartery, Evergreen, Voices of America, Fall 1992; [pers.] Many of my poems are written for children, or reflect a deep and abiding interest in nature and ecology. [a.] Peace River, Alberta Canada T8S 1S3.

PALUMBO, VALERIE PHILOMENA
[pen.] Valerie Palumbo; [b.] August 25, 1981, Somerset, Kentucky; [p.] Sharon and Ronald Palumbo; [ed.] Starting 7th grade; [occ.] Student; [memb.] Beta Club, 4H Club, President D.A.R.E. graduate; [hon.] D.A.R.E. essay award, the only selected poem in school annual, third place Junior Princess contest, academic awards, first Chair Clarinet; [oth. writ.] Only poem selected for school annual, it was called "Memories"; [pers.] I enjoy writing poems that deal with people's everyday emotions. [a.] Columbia, KY.

PAPPAS, VIVIAN H.
[pen.] V. Pappas/Viana Bey Pappas; [b.] November 19, 1932, Florence, Italy; [p.] Hamid and Nada Bey; [m.] Angelo G. Pappas, II, December 12, 1956; [ch.] Lorraine Ellen Dellarosa, Lawrence Martin and Stephen Gregory Pappas; [ed.] Van Nuys High, Orange Coast College; [occ.] Retired, volunteer musician, volunteer hospital worker, Cosmetologist, writer, church worker; [memb.] Italian-American Catholic Federation, SS Simon and Jude Choir and church; [hon.] Volunteer Worker Award, (Convalescent Hospital) and Hospice Award; [oth. writ.] I've just started writing poetry this year, I have come to a full appreciation of poetry and poets and the depth of the arts thru the pain of life; [pers.] The Lord has blessed me with many gifts of which I'm thankful and want to share with the world lessons learned and reflect a better mankind do our youth can live in peace and have a love for culture and the arts, I have been greatly influenced by early Ronawhe poets. [a.] Huntington Beach, CA.

PARISE, CYNTHIA JEAN
[pen.] Cynthia Parise; [b.] July 17, 1980, Newton, New Jersey; [p.] Robert A. and Anne Linda Parise; [ed.] Sussex Christian School; [memb.] Junior high, Youth Group, Grace Evangelical Free Church, Milton, NJ.; [hon.] Sussex Christian School Honor Roll 1990, present Township Mayor's Award for providing recreational facilities for handicapped children; [oth. writ.] Several poems and short stories published in school newspaper; [pers.] I strive to glorify God in all I do. [a.] Sussex, NJ.

PARK, WENDY RENEE
[b.] May 10, 1977, Oakley, Kansas; [p.] Warren and Gail Park; [ed.] I'm currently a junior at Oakley High School; [occ.] Assistant Director for summer recreation program, office worker at Oakley swimming pool; [memb.] Future Homemakers of America, United Methodist Church; [hon.] Three scholastical pins, Honor Roll student at Oakley High School; [oth. writ.] One recent poem was published in local newspaper. Several other poems that haven't yet been published; [pers.] To achieve anything in life, you must have the power to seize the hour and live out your dreams, to look beyond where others have been to see where you are to go. [a.] Oakley, KS.

PARKER, SEAN
[b.] March 30, 1971, Tokyo, Japan; [ed.] King George V School, Hong Kong Hofstra University,

New York; [a.] New York, New York.

PARKER, TARA
[b.] June 28, 1978, Alexandria, Louisiana; [p.] Delilah Breithuapt and Robert Parker; [ed.] Entering 10th sophomore Holy Savor Menard High School; [hon.] Rally "District" Science 5th place, French 2nd place; [oth. writ.] Have written many poems, no publication or entries beside that of "Now and Then Beginning and End"; [pers.] I strive to relay a message of self. Many things in life depend on the person you are, so be happy and strive high. [a.] Alexandria, LA.

PARMLEY, MONICA
[b.] October 12, 1976, Niles, Michigan; [p.] Bruce Parmley and Susan Sehulster; [ed.] Decatur Junior Senior High; [hon.] Varsity letter for softball; [oth. writ.] Poems and a short biography, poem of my grandfather, Ralph Parmley; [pers.] I write my poems about my feelings and experiences to stay close to whatever it is I want, miss or have lost in my life. [a.] Dowagiac, MI.

PARSONS, NANCY JEANE-ANNE
[b.] August 19, 1976, Corner Brook, Newfoundland Canada; [p.] Stephen T. and Judith A. Parsons; [ed.] Grade XI, Clarenville Integrated High School; [occ.] Student; [pers.] You may cry, scream, sing or whisper but the poetic emotion you let go, it is set free into the mind of its puzzled listener. [a.] Clarenville, Newfoundland Canada A0E 1J0.

PATE, ROSALIE RIDDLE
[b.] November 13, 1932, Burnsville, NC.; [pers.] Intermost thoughts are best opened by a key of words that flow naturally. [a.] Belleville, MI.

PATERNO, DAVID L.
[b.] August 9, 1957, Elizabeth, New Jersey; [p.] Richard and Helen Paterno; [occ.] Accountant; [hon.] Omicron Delta Epsilon, Dean's List; [oth. writ.] Many unpublished poems in booklets, cassette tapes casting the booklet, poems to popular and classical music, all poems relate to biking; [pers.] To entertain friends and acquaintances with interesting "Bicycle" oriented poetry and to branch out and reach others with the uniqueness of the subject. [a.] Roselle Park, NJ.

PATTERSON, LORNE
[b.] November 27, 1959. [a.] Roseland, NJ.

PATTISON, FAWN H.
[pen.] Johanna Irvinge (but I'll never use it); [b.] July 25, 1975, Atlantic, New Jersey; [p.] Lee and Susan Pattison; [m.] Single; [ed.] Absegami High School, University of Virginia; [occ.] Student; [memb.] National Honor Society, International Thespian Society; [hon.] Presidential Academic Fitness, Edward J. Bloustein Distinguished Scholar, Scholastic Writing Award for Humor; [oth. writ.] Several short stories and articles published locally, short story "Mom Goes Mental (Again)" published by "Literary Cavalcade; [pers.] I write about what I see around me everyday. I think I've exhausted the supply of inspiration in Southern New Jersey, so I think it's about time to get out. Maybe to Gravesend, N.H.? [a.] Pomona, NJ.

PAVLISH, DANIEL
[pen.] DVCEP; [b.] October 20, 1966, Billings, Montana; [p.] Donald and Mary Pavlish; [ed.] BA in Mass Communications from Eastern Montana College; [occ.] Survivor; [memb.] Perform poetry with "Voices in The Wind", "Writer's Voice"; [hon.] Larry Cook Memorial Award 1986; [oth. writ.] The Crusader series and "Pav", both spy novels; [pers.] I enjoy writing poetry and stories, writing is the most difficult job in the world. [a.] Shepherd, MT.

PEAK, MELYSSA L.
[b.] February 25, 1974, Hammond, Indiana; [p.] Susan and Gene Peak; [m.] Single; [ed.] Gavit High School and the Hammond Area Career Center; [occ.] Hair technician; [oth.writ.] Several poems lie in a folder in my home, this was my first poem ever entered; [pers.] I write poetry to keep my sanity. I have found that writing things down helps me to work out my problems and make better evaluations for each situation. [a.] Roswell, GA.

PEARSON, KELVIN
[b.] May 30, 1965, Brooks Alberta, Canada; [occ.] Truckdriver/foreman; [pers.] This poem was originally written for my girlfriend, who is now my wife. [a.] Brooks Alberta, Canada.

PEDEN, ARTHUR P.
[b.] March 4, 1895, Johnstown, Pennsylvania; [p.] George and Venetta Peden; [m.] Mable (deceased), Helen (deceased), 1916, June 16, 1947; [ch.] Carol and James; [ed.] Johnstown High School, Otterbein College, Bonebrake Theological Seminary; [occ.] Retired Minister, poet and artist; [memb.] United Methodist Church, Western Pennsylvania Conference; [oth. writ.] "Behold Your King" book copyrighted in 1986, " Behold Your King In Clouds of Glory with Great Power" book, numerous poems in local newspaper "The Spirit"; [pers.] I have aimed to be with the Lord all my life. [a.] Punxsutawney, PA.

PEDERSEN, JO-ANNE
[b.] October 23, 1950, Mission, B.C. Canada; [p.] Joseph and Anne Ross; [m.] Niels Pedersen, July 19, 1969; [ch.] Tanya Manning, Bryan Pedersen and Wanda Dube'; [ed.] Grade 12 graduate Maple Ridge Secondary School, many secretarial courses; [occ.] Homemaker; [memb.] Worldwide Church of God, MS Society; [oth. writ.] I have written several poems and a couple of songs but never sent them to anyone yet; [pers.] My writing is inspired by my family and given to them with my love. To share it with others is an added blessing. [a.] Ucluelet, B.C. Canada.

PELLERIN, VYLMA
[b.] December 3, 1933, Prince Albert, Saskatchewan; [p.] Gunhild and Lars Knudsen; [m.] Arthur Pellerin, May 30, 1980; [ch.] Ruby Lacourse, Les and Darrel Patchin; [ed.] Grade 12; [occ.] Secretary, Prince Albert Foundry Ltd.; [oth. writ.] Numerous poems none published; [pers.] My poems are inspired by my family, friends and events that happen in my life. [a.] Prince Albert, Sask, Canada S6V 6J6.

PENSON, JANICE M.
[b.] May 13, 1955, Jackson, Mississippi; [p.] Charles W. Andrews and Carolyn M. Macris; [m.] Terry W. Penson, September 27, 1975; [ch.] Gayla M. and Hollie L. Penson; [ed.] I completed the ninth grade and twelve years later got my GED; [occ.] Sewing department, La-Z-Boy Newton, MS.; [memb.] Mt. Olive Baptist Church; [pers.] Help others as if you were the one receiving the help. You get back what you give. [a.] Union, MS.

PEREZ, JAVLER ALLAN
[b.] May 11, 1975, Honolulu, Hawaii; [p.] Everardo and Thelma Perez; [m.] Michele Madulid Perez; [ed.] Nanakuli High School; [hon.] Cum Laude, 1st place in poetry contest; [pers.] I'd like to thank my wife Michele, for believing in me and pushing me to write on. I love you, your fairy. [a.] Kapolei, HI.

PERKOVIC, BOZICA
[pen.] Sabrina Stone; [b.] June 30, 1961, Croatia; [p.] Matt and Mary Mrezar; [m.] Jozo Perkovic, July 2, 1983; [ch.] Jasna Marina and Suzana; [ed.] Bishop Ryan High, St. Clair College; [occ.] Q.C., cake decorator; [oth. writ.] 'Always My Love" historical romance, written but not yet published; [pers.] Most of my writings are based on and from the teachings of the ancient Indian, I admire their way of thinking.[a.] Brampton, Ontario L6V 4J1 Canada.

PERRIN, HELEN BELL
[b.] July 9, 1931, Tuskegee, Alabama; [p.] Ruth B. and Robert E. Bell; [m.] David S. Perrin, November 25, 1954; [ch.] Walter Charles, Stephen Lee, Kathleen Ruth and David Thomas; [ed.] Bachelor of Arts in Education, Master of Education, Florida Atlantic University, Boca Raton, FL.; [occ.] Elementary teacher, Palm Springs Elementary School, Hialeah, FL.; [memb.] United Teachers of Dade, Miami Shores Presbyterian Church, Florida Atlantic University Alumni Association; [hon.] Teacher of the Year, Palm Springs Elementary School 1992, Graduate Writing Institute, University of Miami, 1987, Associate Master Teacher, State of Florida 1986; [oth. writ.] I have written several other poems for specific occasions but have not submitted any for publication; [pers.] I believe my poems reflect the experiences I have had that are also shared by many others. I feel these shared feelings make my writings appealing to others. [a.] Miami Shores, FL.

PERRY, SARAH CHRISTINE
[b.] October 21,1983, Andrews AFB, Camp Springs, MD.; [p.] Clyde McAvoy and Marcia Lynn Perry; [ed.] Sullivans Elementary School, 4th grade; [occ.] Student; [memb.] Poetry Club; [oth. writ.] Various other poems not published. [a.] Yokosuka, Japan.

PERRY, VALERIE L.
[b.] March 13,1969, San Juan, Puerto Rico; [p.] Jewell Perry Nicholson; [ed.] Rollins College graduate 1991, Pine Crest Prepatory graduate 1987; [occ.] Field assistant -Security Life of Denver; [memb.] Daughters of the American Revolution, Kappa Kappa, Gamma Sorority. [a.] Altamonte Springs, FL.

PETERMANN, JODI
[b.] October 29,1979, Minden, NE.; [p.] Tim and Carmen Petermann; [ed.] Completed seventh grade; [memb.] Jammin' Junior high band, 4-H; [hon.] Merit Honor Roll, superior in Nebraska State piano competition, superior in saxophone honor band, sing around Nebraska award, civic speech oration award; [pers.] When I write a poem, I don't just think of words but rather write when my thoughts and imagination runs wild, it's important to write from the heart. [a.] Arapahoe, NE.

PETERS, MICHAEL
[b.] September 16, 1975, Fullerton, California; [p.] Pamela Witwer; [ed.] Millington Central High, John Tyler Community College; [occ.] Student; [pers.] I write my poetry by creating a visual collage of scenes and images left solely for the reader to interpret and respond. [a.] Midlothian, VA.

PETERSEN, JENNIFER J.
[pen.] Jennifer J. Petersen; [b.] August 26, 1975; [p.] Greg and Wendy Petersen; [ed.] Stept 2 Learning Center, Gordon Votech taking Industrial Electronics; [occ.] Farm girl, animal lover, enjoy building, crafts and keeping busy; [hon.] None, I'm just starting to try and get my work out to some of the people so they can see that they can do anything that they put their minds to: [oth. writ.] I've written other poems, A Mother's Day Gift and A Word of Thanks to the country singers; [pers.] I live on a farm in Holdenville, OK, I love animals and enjoy the art of writing poems. I believe it's a good way to express a person's deepest feelings inside your soul. [a.] Tinker, AFB., OK.

PETERSON, EARL
[b.] October 13, 1923, Anson, TX.; [p.] Charles and Lela Peterson; [m.] Myrle Peterson, October 18, 1946; [ch.] Lucretia and Dwayne; [occ.] Farmer, rancher, businessman, served with 8th Air Force, WWII; [memb.] Belmont Baptist Church, Odessa, TX.; [oth. writ.] Poems in church newsletters, poem "Master's Masterpiece" published by Young Publishing Co., in "Treasures of Parnaussas, Volume II, 1962"; [pers.] I strive to reflect my best in my writings, especially concerning God and our country. [a.] Odessa, TX.

PETERSON, GEORGIA MAURINE
[pen.] Maurine Peterson; [b.] November 13, 1922, Egypt, Arkansas; [p.] George Milton and Ruth Harral; [m.] Chas. Earl Peterson (who is deceased), January 29, 1946; [ch.] Ronald Lee, Richard James and Robert Charles Peterson; [ed.] Twelve hours of college; [occ.] Housewife, widow; [memb.] J.E.A.P. that is Jacksonville Elderly Activities Program Center; [hon.] A certificate of superior scholarship for the last semester of the high school freshman class of Cash, Arkansas High School 1937-1938 and a certificate of superior scholarship for 1938 and 1939 last semester in the 10th grade at Cash, Arkansas High School; [oth. writ.] I have written other poems, compositions and essays "Oh You Handsome Idol", "A Boy Named Bill", "A Teenager Mother's Pray", "We Will Have What Goes With Journey"; [pers.] I likes literature, I liked poems and I like to read. I am now 70 years old. [a.] Jacksonville, AR.

PETRO, PAUL
[pen.] Paul Petro; [b.] July, 4, 1981, Hartford, CT; [p.] Noreen P. Collen and Peter Petro; [ed.] Going into 7th grade; [occ.] Mowing lawns; [memb.] Glastonbury Raiders Soccer Club; [hon.] Most versatile player on my traveling soccer team, being a semifinalist in your contest. [a.] Glastonbury, CT.

PHANPHIROJANA, KEATIKORN
[pen.] Ohm; [b.] May 30, 1970, Bangkok, Thailand; [p.] Mr. Sathiraparb Phanphirojana and Mrs. Kannikar Phanphirojana; [ed.] U. of Northern Iowa (studying) LL.B. -Thammasat U. (Thailand) Mass Communication, Master's; [occ.] Student; [oth. writ.] Several poems published in local magazines in Thailand, have one published book about poem in 1991; [pers.] I have to thank my dad and mom who gave me a life that I can appreciate and make my poems. [a.] Cedar Falls, IA.

PHELPS, KASEY
[b.] April 22, 1978, Evansville, Indiana; [p.] Barbara and Bob Spear; [ed.] Oakhil Middle School; [pers.] Don't think about gangs, always keep your head up and look for tomorrow. [a.] Evansville, IN.

PHILLIPS, CHRISTY SUE
[b.] March 8, 1942, St. Louis, MO; [p.] Wallace and Helen Hulbert; [m.] Wayne E. Phillips, September 18, 1986; [ch.] Kimberly Sue Shore (from a previous marriage); [ed.] Fayette High School; [occ.] Homemaker; [oth. writ.] First poem published; [pers.] I put my true feelings in my poetry. My poetry tends to be of a religious nature. [a.] Fayette, MO.

PHILLIPS, BRANDY LINN
[b.] September 25, 1979, Sparrow Hospital in Lansing, Michigan; [p.] Marchelle and Jimmy Phillips, I now have a stepfather who is Daniel Creps; [ed.] I go to Webberville High School; [occ.] I only work at a mentally handicapped camp every summer; [hon.] I have awards for Honor Rolls and athletic awards for cheerleading and national physical fitness test; [oth. writ.] I often write poems for school classes that teachers use for their class. I also wrote a poem about beauty when I was in third grade that got put in a book; [pers.] I love poetry, so I write it for all occasions. I usually write it about worldly things such as racism and poverty. [a.] Webberville, MI.

PHUNDAR, ANZARD
[b.] January 5, 1957, Sanfernando, Trinidad, West Indies; [p.] Rasul Phundar and Tymun Rasul; [m.] Sabitadai Phundar, April 24, 1977; [ch.] Hafeeza and Saleem Phundar; [ed.] Preysal Government School, four (4) school leaving certificates; [occ.] Records Management Clerk; [memb.] Preysal Cricket Club, The Association of Cricket Statisticians (England); [hon.] Golden Poet 1990 and 1991 World of Poetry; [oth. writ.] Several articles in Trinidad and Tobago newspapers, designed cricket scorebook used throughout the Caribbean, 19 page poem on Preysal Cricket team 2793 words; [pers.] Writing has been one of my favorite hobbies. I have been blessed with very good friends who have supported me one way or the other. [a.] Couva, Trinidad West Indies.

PICCOLI, MICHAEL
[b.] March 24, 1936, Queens County, New York; [m.] Carolyn V. (Stafford) Piccoli, August 20, 1965; [ch.] Gregory Alexander Piccoli; [ed.] Art Student League, New School for Social Research, Parsons School of Design, High School of Fashion Design; [occ.] Photographer for "The Courier" a local newspaper; [memb.] Coalition for a planned Flushing; [oth. writ.] An article in The Courier newspaper, Bayside, New York, " The Homeless of Flushing"; [pers.] I wish that the world would come to terms with itself and may peace instead of war circle this globe. [a.] Flushing, NY.

PICOTTE, MELISSA
[pen.] Mel, Moe; [b.] June 1, 1978, Marquette, Michigan; [p.] Jim and Marlene Picotte; [ed.] I'm in 10th grade at Gwinn High School; [hon.] State competition band award, honors list; [pers.] All the poems that I have written were dedicated to people whom I have feelings for. I wrote this poem for Jim Fitzpatrick. [a.] Gwinn, MI.

PICOU, ROYLIN J.
[pen.] Roy; [b.] June 11, 1963, Lutchen, Louisiana; [p.] Ruth and Julien DeBeau; [m.] Separated; [ed.] High school-Redeemer High, 2 years at S.U.N.O. University; [occ.] Mailclerk for Alberta Wheat Pool; [oth.writ.] Various poems not yet published and loads of isms that I write daily about various subjects; [pers.] I'm just a Christian trying to let my little light shine. I believe in and follow Dr. King's and Ganhdi principles of non-violence. We must all learn to love one anther as Jesus loved us. [a.] Calgary, Alberta Canada T2P 2T1.

PIER, LORA MAE
[b.] June 12, 1957, Cuba, New York; [p.] Charles R. and Lucia M. Wilcox; [m.] Randy Jay Pier, January 21, 1989; [ch.] Anne Marie Gleason; [ed.] High school diploma, Wellsboro High School, Pennsylvania College of Technology (part-time), Accounting I and II, Business Math, typing, Principals of Banking-through my bank; [occ.] Bookkeeper at Citizens and Northern Bank, Wellsboro; [memb.] Wellsboro Free Methodist Church; [hon.] Scholastic Award, Accounting Service Award, tutoring basic math; [oth. writ.] I have written many poems, since age 10 but none have been published. My writing allows me to escape from the hectic world for a short time; [pers.] I have always had a love for writing poems, even as a young child, but my real inspiration and ability comes from my faith in and relationship with Jesus Christ. [a.] Wellsboro, PA.

PIERCE, EVELYN S.
[b.] July 17, Lufkin, Texas; [p.] John and Alma Stevens; [m.] William M. Pierce (deceased), January 1952; [ch.] One son and three daughters; [ed.] 6th grade; [occ.] Retired widow; [memb.] Church of God; [hon.] Four awards, ten volunteer certificates; [oth. writ.] I have been a volunteer since 1972 for Sheltering Arms and Interfaith Ministries; [pers.] Praying I win. [a.] Houston, TX.

PIERCE, JAMIE R.
[b.] March 25, 1974, Pontiac, Michigan; [p.] Roy and Shirley Pierce; [ed.] Walled Lake Western High School, English major at Saginaw Valley State University; [oth. writ.] I've never really had any poems published before. All of my writings are in a notebook and usually come about when I have to relax or when I have feelings to express; [pers.] Most of the writings in my notebook revolves basically around the facts of life. I'm not implying that I can change the world in any way, however, I feel I can describe the world and try to relate to as many people as possible. [a.] Novi, MI.

PIERCE, PAULA
[b.] August 3, 1978, Atlanta, GA.; [p.] May Jane Porter and Eldred Leroy Pierce, Sr.; [ed.] Saks High (2 years left); [occ.] Student; [oth. writ.] Other poem won in high school poetry contest; [pers.] My poems reflect how I am feeling. It is my way of expressing my emotions through writing, it is a good way of letting anger or joy out. [a.] Anniston, AL.

PIERSON, KAREN A.
[pen.] Karen A. Pierson; [b.] January 25, 1940, Maquon, Illinois; [p.] Mr. and Mrs. Charles F. Little; [m.] Jackie Lee Pierson, January 7, 1962; [ch.] Debra Jo Pierson (Welin) and Tammie Sue Pierson; [ed.] 1958 Galesburg Senior High graduate, Carl Sandburg College, computer and blueprint course; [occ.] Admiral Maytag Corp. assembler; [memb.] American Legion, Methodist Church; [hon.] Golden Poet Award World of Poetry 1991, 1992, 1988, Silver Award 1990, Editor's Choice 1993 Library of Poetry, awards of merit Carl Sandburg College, etc.; [oth.writ.] Have written many poems and working on few stories; [pers.] Writing poems is a way to express myself, plus I find it relaxing, with my reward being able to see in print my work for all to enjoy. [a.] Galesburg, IL.

PINA, BRIGETTE
[b.] March 24, 1975, Newton, Massachusetts; [p.] Lydia and Tom Pina; [ed.] Cimarron Memorial High School; [hon.] Honors graduate, Presidential Academic Fitness Award, Who's Who Among American High School Students. [a.] Las Vegas, NV.

PINAKIEWICZ, ASHLEY M.
[b.] July 7, 1982, Glen Cove, New York; [p.] Diane C. and William H. Pinakiewicz; [ed.] The Kent Place School, Summit, New Jersey class of 2000; [occ.] Student; [hon.] 2 Young Authors Awards, in school contest; [oth. writ.] Many poems written, some selected to be published in Kent Place School log; [pers.] I want to let people out there know that kids can be successful in some ways such as grown-ups are. [a.] Westfield, NJ.

PINE, DEL
[b.] October 20, 1919, Calgary, Alberta; [p.] Harry and Julia Pine; [m.] Berenice Pine, June 14, 1948; [ch.] Philip Montgomery and Debra Jill; [ed.] B.A. (1941), University of Alberta; [occ.] Retired (was an energy industry accountant); [memb.] Calgary Professional Club, U. of A Alumni Assoc.; [hon.] Hosforo Memorial (Literary award at U. of A.); [oth. writ.] Articles in University newspaper and yearbook, travel article about Middle East in a Lumni magazine (1986). Poetry published in Goble and Mail 1993; [pers.] Musical theatre and movie buff since early thirties. Have written science fiction and other short stories (nothing published). [a.] Calgary, Alta.

PIPKIN, ROBERT MERICO
[pen.] Pookey; [b.] October 21, 1974, Georgetown; [p.] (Miss) Roberta Pipkin and (Mrs.) Melvin Bronson; [m.] Boy friend and girl friend; [ch.] Robin, Jerome, Micheal, Demell, Richard and Edward; [ed.] O.K.; [occ.] I like rapping, singing, drawing, basketball and writing and reading; [oth. writ.] I got poems names, "The Old Days", "It's All About Trust", " Pray For A Better Day and Others"; [pers.] Yes, my poems are base on true facts about life. It talks about what's happening in the world today. I got poems about relationships, friends and family problems. [a.] Andrews, SC.

PISHOCK, JR., JAMES M.
[pen.] Paul Zee and Mud; [b.] June 6, 1970, Norristown, Pennsylvania; [p.] James and Carol Pishock, Sr.; [ed.] Bishop Kenrick High School and Bloomsburg University; [occ.] Distribution Assistant for National Packaging Systems, Inc., Allentown, PA.; [pers.] I enjoy writing lyrics/poems and music. In fact, I'm presently writing lyrics, playing bass, keyboards and vocals for a band called **The Ambitious Retards**. Get down with the syndrome, folks. [a.] Norristown, PA.

PITTS-SPURRELL, MADELINE
[b.] December 18, 1957, Placentia, Placentia Bay; [p.] Theresa Marie Barron (nee) and Private Albert Pitts; [m.] Shane Douglas Bernard Spurrell, October 27, 1977 (divorced October 1986); [ch.] Shane Matthew (15), Johannah Edna (14) and Melanie (12); [ed.] Grade eleven graduate from Laval in Placentia, Stenographer I in D.V.S.; [occ.] Mother, writer, poet, Social Justice Activist; [memb.] L.I.S.T.E.N., Group Against Poverty, unofficial member of Nfld. Writers Guild; [hon.] Group award from City Hall, Social Justice Award, Legion of Merit, Captain Nfld Award from Nfld Herald; [oth. writ.] Articles published by St. Anne de Beaupre (80-82) number of articles published by Nfld Hearld and poems. I have been on Radio Noon-CBC Radio, doing commentaries, presently writing a book of poetry; [pers.] If you give to charity and do not include the excluded, then you do not help them regain self esteem to become self-sufficient, but in your ignorance on their backs you ride. [a.] St. John's, Nfld A1B 1C5.

PIZZUTI, SALVATORE
[b.] July 1, 1974, Los Angeles, California; [p.] Helen and Nino Pizzuti; [ed.] Chaminad College Preparatory; [occ.] Student; [pers.] Those who are different and break the mold, they are the ones about whom stories are told. [a.] West Hills, CA.

PLAYFORD, REBECCA LEIGH
[b.] August 2,1972, Oklahoma City, OK.; [p.] Paul Lewis and Jean Ann Pickard; [m.] Daren Kevan Playford, May 26, 1992; [ch.] Two much loved cats, Raven and Gretel;[ed.] Currently a student of Economics and Fiance at Oklahoma State University; [occ.] Student; [memb.] Mensa, Humane Society, in Defense of Animals, OSU, Symphony Orchestra; [hon.] President's Special Scholarship, violin and academics, Oklahoma State University; [oth. writ.] Many poems, all in personal collection. This is my first publication; [pers.] I have been greatly affected in some way by most things I have read. A favorite is Donne's "A Valediction: Forbidding Morning". [a.] Ponca City, OK.

PLEVELL, ROBERT
[b.] December 9, 1968, Aurora, Minnesota; [p.] James Plevell, Rose and Vince Lacer; [m.] Marcy; [ch.] Joshua and Jenna; [occ.] Lieutenant, United States Marine Corps; [pers.] Inspired by my daughter, Danielle in heaven. [a.] Aurora, MN.

PODEWELL, STEPHEN ELDEN
[b.] May 9, 1965, Oak Lawn, Illinois; [p.] Elden and Georgene Podewell; [ed.] Alan B. Shepard High School, Valparaiso University, Western Michigan University; [occ.] Adjunct Instructor, Valparaiso University; [memb.] Association of American Geographers, Sierra Club; [memb.] Gamma Theta Upsilon, Graduate Student Scholastic Achievement and Service Award, Research Grant recipient, graduate assistantship; [oth. writ.] Tax Increment Financing, A Means for Improving the Aesthetic and Financial Condition of a City (a case study of Palos Heights, IL.) [pers.] Life is short, give it your sincerest best shot! [a.] Palos Heights, IL.

POHTS, CHRISTOPHER
[b.] January 29, 1979, Hackensack, New Jersey; [p.] William and Teresa Pohts, Jr.; [ed.] 9th grade; [occ.] High school student; [hon.] 4 marking periods Honor Roll, Distinguished Honor Roll, Student of the Mont (Humanitarian deeds), Technology Award, American Legion Americanism Award (citizenship), 1st place American Legion essay contest, high school Writer Literary Merit, Woman's Club Literary Award, Madeliene Rumohr Romaine Memorial Award, (Public Library Trustees), Presidential Academic Fitness Award; [oth. writ.] 1 poem/1 memorial published in the High School Writer, a national publication for 7th-12th grade students, 6 poems published in school paper, 7 page "Murder Mystery" story published in school paper, "Save the Earth" article published in school paper; [pers.] To want is one thing, but to achieve is far better. [a.] Maywood, NJ.

POINDEXTER, CYNTHIA
[b.] July 15, 1973, St. Louis, Missouri; [p.] Louis and Sylester Poindexter; [ed.] University City High, University of Mo. St. Louis, junior currently; [occ.] Crewtrainer, McDonalds St. Louis; [memb.] Bridge Program of Champion of Service All Stars; [hon.] Dean's List, Academic Excellence Award; [pers.] Everything does happen for a reason and for a reason a everything does happen. [a.] St. Louis, MO.

POLK, BRYAN TERRELL
[pen.] Bryan Terrell Polk; [b.] October 12, 1960, Memphis, TN.; [p.] John A. and Laveine Polk; [m.] Tracy Polk, December 24, 1985; [ch.] Bryan Jr., Michael Ali, Racine and Jermell; [ed.] High school graduate Melrose Columbia School of Broadcasting, Shelby State; [occ.] Sharp Manufacturing; [memb.] Coast Guard Reserves; [hon.] Good conduct, Honorable Discharge; [oth. writ.] Songs, inventions; [pers.] Noone is greater than I yet, I am no greater than anyone. [a.] Memphis, TN.

POLK, CATRINA
[pen.] Cat; [b.] March 22, 1979, El Paso, Texas; [p.] Barry and Carnetta Polk; [sib.] Cedreick and Brent Polk; [ed.] Bramlette Elementary, Foster Middle School, Longview High School; [memb.] National Honors Society, G/T and advanced classes; [hon.] Project Hope for Teens Award, basketball awards, several academic awards; [oth. writ.] One poem published in the book The Academy of Poetry, "Fear"; [pers.] The greatest influence in my life comes from my parents, and I would like to thank my L. Arts teacher, Mrs. Hawkins and Mr. Allen. [a.] Longview, TX.

POLO, JR., RUSSELL B.
[pen.] Russell B. Polo, Jr.; [b.] May 13, 1971, Parma, Ohio; [p.] Russ and Sharon Polo, Sr.; [m.] Single, girlfriend for six years Holly Grayson; [ed.] North Royalton High School, Kent State University; [occ.] College student, Journalism major; [memb.] BMWCCA, BMW Car Club of America; [oth. writ.] Have numerous other poems, would like to someday publish a book of poetry; [pers.] My style evolves from the dark side of the mind. I believe in results from excess. I have been deeply influenced by James Douglas Morrison. [a.] Royalton, OH.

POLUS, MARY JO
[b.] May 29, 1969, Hammond, IN.; [p.] Larry Joe and Mary E. Lucas, Sr.; [m.] Curt Polus, January 18, 1992; [ed.] Lowell Senior High and Davenport College; [occ.] Child care, painting, and wall papering; [hon.] First place awards in choir during high school for district and state; [oth. writ.] I wrote "Owed To A Very Special Dad" that is published in the anthology Wind in The Night Sky; [pers.] This poem is dedicated to my mom who is not only the best mom in the world, but also my best friend. [a.] Lowell, IN.

PONZETTI, BILLIE DULEY
[b.] May 6, 1949, Bangor, Maine; [p.] Charlotte L, Beauchaine and William H. Duley; [m.] John L. Ponzetti, July 15, 1989; [ed.] Caribou High School, B.S. University of Maine, M.Ed. University of Houston; [occ.] Counselor, Career Planning and Placement; [memb.] American Counseling Association, National Employment Counseling Association; [pers.] Somedays it is enough to be different or alone. [a.] Limerick, ME.

POOL, JAMIE
[b.] October 28, 1980, Galesburg, IL; [p.] James and Patricia Pool; [ed.] 7th grade; [oth. writ.] Other poems; [pers.] I started writing poems when a friend and my sister's x-boyfriend died of Cancer, January 3, 1993. [a.] Avon, IL.

POOTLASS, DALLAS
[pen.] Suptiqalk; [b.] July 16, 1974, Victoria, B.C.; [p.] Archie and Dorothy Pootlass; [ed.] Acwsalcta High School, Bella Coola, BC.; [occ.] College student; [pers.] As a young native Canadian going into the business, I see a brighter future for the people of my nation. [a.] Vancouver, BC Canada.

POPICK, AMY
[b.] September 20, 1979, Brooklyn, New York; [p.] Judith Susan and Barry Popick; [ed.] Scholass Center for the Humanities, Howell High School, Howell, New Jersey; [occ.] Student; [memb.] Johns Hopkins Gifted Talented Program, Howell High School J.V. cheerleading; [hon.] 2nd place Monmouth County Park Systems poetry contest, Honor Roll. [a.] Manajapan, NJ.

PORAY, KATIE JULIA
[b.] February 19, 1974, Croydon, England; [p.] Andrew and Barbara Poray; [m.] Gavin Bradley Lewis (boyfriend); [ed.] Silverthorn Collegiate Institute; [occ.] Social work student at Lakehead University; [oth. writ.] A poem published in my school magazine, The Silverthorn Scer, and a piece of prose published in the Spartan Spectrum; [pers.] My poetry reflects my concerns about the state of humanity and the stability of the environment. [a.] Etobicoke, Canada M9C 2R4.

POSTNIKOFF, OLGA
[pen.] Olga; [b.] December 26, 1953, Nelson, BC.; [ed.] Graduated with honors from Moutn Sentinel Secondary School, several accounting, management and sales courses; [occ.] General Manager for a business equipment dealer; [hon.] Received scholarship in literature and Geography; [pers.] I would like my writing to touch the hearts and souls of those who have been wounded by a dysfunctional childhood and who struggle onward to survive and succeed. [a.] Calgary, Alberta.

POTTER, EULA V.
[b.] October 13, 1903, Klondike, Texas; [p.] William R. and Ella Stevenson Potter; [ed.] Cooper High, Mary Hardin Baylor (BA), E. Texas State U.N. (M.A.), S.W. Baptist Theological Seminary (dip. Rel. Ed.); [occ.] Retired as Asst. Principal of high school, taught English, speech general Science; [memb.] Buckner Baptist Church, National Ed. Association, Texas State Tr. Association, Delta Kappa Gamma, Pilot Club, Chamber of Commerce; [hon.] President of local Ed. Association, Gamma Nu Chapter of Delta Kappa Gamma, Ret. Tr. Association; [oth. writ.] Many for special events, none published; [pers.] I try to do the best I can with what I have, where I am for Jesus sake today. [a.] Dallas, TX.

POVILAITIS, CATHY
[pen.] Cathy Joe; [b.] August 6, 1979, Troy, Michigan; [p.] Joanne and Frank Povilaitis; [ed.] Troy High; [occ.] Student; [hon.] Honor Roll; [oth. writ.] Wrote many poems but they are not published; [pers.] I'd like to thank Jason McMichael, Mrs. McKenney, my parents, Mrs. Gillen, Nelita Lewis, Sarah Boyd, Jonelle Diedrich and to all my friends who supported me. [a.] Troy, MI.

POYNTER, KAREN C.
[b.] October 9, 1962, Toronto, Ontario; [p.] James Allen and Jean Isabel Johnston; [m.] Leonard Merle Poynter, September 24, 1988; [ch.] Kerry Lynn and Jamie Sue; [ed.] Graduated grade 12, took several misc. courses and clinics in agriculture type business; [occ.] Part-time bookkeeper for my husband's farm machinery and repair business and part-time horse trainer; [memb.] Member of A.Q.H.A., Royal Canadian Legion Branch # 104; [pers.] My biggest influence has been reading Baxter Black's works and my own experiences. [a.] Bowden Alberta, Canada.

PRATER, KRISTIN D.
[b.] November 25, 1972, Oklahoma City, Oklahoma; [p.] Pat and Tim Prater; [ed.] Currently attending Southwest Texas State University; [occ.] Full time student; [hon.] Dean's List, Houston COmmunity College, Stafford; [oth. writ.] A collection of poems and one short story none have been published; [pers.] Write what you know and inevitably the truth will flow, for the truth is a weapon that kills chasing demons. I am inspired by anyone who has the courage to give away a piece of themselves by putting pen to paper. [a.] Richmond, TX.

PRATHER, DAVID B.
[b.] August 29, 1967, Parkersburg, WV.; [p.] Lewis D. and Sheila R. Prather; [ed.] West Virginia University at Parkersburg, West Virginia University (Morgantown), National Shakespeare Conservatory; [occ.] No occupation as yet-recent graduate of West Virginia University; [hon.] Phi Kappa Phi, Golden Key National Honor Society, certificates of achievement-College of Arts and Sciences, Best Actor, Best Performer of the Year; [oth. writ.] Poems in Parnassus Literary Journal, and I have recently completed a novel that I will soon be submitting; [pers.] Art is observation--not savoir. True poetry is beauty and philosophy rather than moral guidance and political forum. [a.] Parkersburg, WV.

PRATHER, DAVID CLEEVE WELLESLEY
[pen.] David C.W. Prather; [b.] November 9, 1944, Liverpool, England; [p.] Wayne Clay and Esme' Noel King Prather; [m.] Yvonne, October 13, 1992; [ch.] Charity, Reuel, Serena, Beyth, Sereth, Sunny, Selah, Jory, Amy and Jason; [ed.] Titusville High School, University of Nevada Reno; [occ.] Director, Nonprofit Organization; [hon.] Honorary Doctorate of Theology; [oth. writ.] Has written over 200 country western songs this year and is completing book of poetry entitled Messianic Poems For The New Age; [pers.] Advocate for the poor, avid environmentalist and naturalist. [a.] Costa Mesa, CA.

PRATHER, MIRANDA N.
[pen.] Mickey; [b.] June 20, 1974, San Antonio, Texas; [p.] Larry and Claudia Prather; [ed.] Simon Kenton High School, Eastern New Mexico University; [occ.] Student; [memb.] Sierra; [hon.] Dean's List; [oth. writ.] Poems published in school publications; [pers.] Look for the hero within. [a.] Independence, KY.

PRAYTOR, CARLENA ANN FAST
[pen.] Carlena; [b.] July 3, 1950, Memphis, TN.; [p.] Howard Fast (stepmother) Louise Young, (natural mother) Nancy Arnold; [m.] David Anderson Praytor, September 2, 1978; [ch.] Clint (14), Lena (12 1/2), Wendy (11) and Candy (10); [ed.] Stanhope Elmore High School, Millbrook, Alabama, nurses training, Memphis, Tenn.; [occ.] Nurse, private duty; [memb.] U.S. Navy 3rd Class Hospital Corpsman, August 1973, Honorable Discharge; [memb.] Parkway Village Baptist Church, Memphis, Tenn.; [oth. writ.] Over 100 unpublished poems and songs shared with family, friends and strangers; [pers.] By the grace of God, Jesus Christ makes the difference in my life... He is all I need!! I live and love because He first lives and loves. [a.] Memphis, TN.

PREKU, STEPHANIE A.
[b.] October 7, 1974; [p.] Lynette J. and John G. Preku; [occ.] Student; [oth. writ.] Several poems published in school literary magazine.

PRESCOTT, JAMES
[b.] December 13, 1974, Little Rock, AR; [p.] Arthur and Dyan Prescott; [ed.] Plano Senior High School, Texas Tech University; [occ.] Student; [oth. writ.] This is my first publication; [pers.] To truly understand your deepest feelings, you must learn to let go of logic and trust your heart. [a.] Plano, TX.

PRESLEY, SHAWNA
[pen.] Shawna Presley; [b.] December 29, 1978, Long Beach, California; [p.] Don and Lynda Presley; [ed.] I'll be in the 9th grade at LB Polytechnic High School; [hon.] I'm going into Pace at Poly which is a highly accelerated program; [oth. writ.] I write for fun. Essays, poems, a couple fiction pieces; [pers.] I'm only 14, I never dreamed I was that good. It's such an honor, all I was doing was expressing how I felt. [a.] Lakewood, CA.

PREVOST, WINTHROP WARREN
[b.] June 10, 1917, Lowell, MA; [p.] Ernest Alexander Prevost and Pearl Friend (Perkins); [m.] Josephine Darios, July 1, 1939; [ed.] Famous Artists School courses, in Journal-World Literature; [occ.] Record Company Executive Sales Rep March Music Ruthland Records of Chesterfield, England; [memb.] Academy of Country Music, (Lifetime) Lowell Art Association;

[hon.] International Leaders in Achievement-IBC, Men and Women of Distinction-IBC of England, and other awards; [oth. writ.] As songwriter, wrote these songs titled, Moon Over Hampton Loneliness, I'll Love You At Starlight I'll Love You At Starlight I Love Jimmy and others; [pers.] Past member of BMI, photos of paintings by Winthrop Prevost and a taped interview in the archives at the Library of Congress so far, my biography has been published in 10 books world wide. [a.] Sebastopol, CA.

PREWITT, ROSE CAROLYN
[pen.] Carolyn B. Prewitt; [b.] October 22, 1933, Washington County, Kentucky; [p.] Owen J. and Thenia Taylor Bottom; [m.] John H. Prewitt, April 14, 1957; [ch.] Katy Lynn Garrison, Nancy Layne McGeorge and Ann Carol Prewitt; [ed.] MacKville High 1951; [occ.] Care giver, John Hill Bailey Children's Learning Center, Danville, KY.; [memb.] Fellowship Baptist Church, church choir; [hon.] Citizenship Award; [oth. writ.] Several poems published, poems used in church bulletins, write true to life short stories; [pers.] My writings reflect my faith in God, family, country and nature. My motto in life is: "He who does his best does well". [a.] Harrodsburg, KY.

PRICE, LESLIE
[b.] July 7, 1980, Burbank, California; [p.] William R. and Melanie M. Price; [ed.] Simi Valley and Van Nuys Pinecrest Elementary Schools, Valley School (junior high); [occ.] Student; [hon.] Graduating Pinecrest, Valedictorian and Most-Improved Dance, All Time Honor Roll; [oth. writ.] "Sunsets" a poem in the book Anthology of Poetry by Young Americans, several others in the school reporter; [pers.] I express feelings, thoughts and sometimes stories through my poetry. I dream to be a singer in the future and maybe write lyrics to some of my songs, one more thing, please stop d' violence increase d'peace. [a.] Simi Valley, CA.

PRICE, MAURICIA
[b.] January 7, 1925, Shanghai, China; [p.] (deceased) Maurice T. and Olivia Attaway Price; [ed.] B.S.-U.C. Berkeley, M.A. San Francisco State College (university); [occ.] Retired teacher, poet; [memb.] California Retired Teachers' Association, Association for Childhood Education, Ina Coolbrith Circle (of poets); [hon.] Delta Kappa Gamma, several awards for poetry during past 20 years; [oth. writ.] Poetry publication in many little and literary journals, 4 booklets of poetry published, "Beyond the Gates", "On The Wing", " Among The Whispering", "Along The Zephyr's Trail"; [pers.] Poetry speaks to everyone, provided it is clear, understandable and applicable to his/her own experiences, feelings, aspirations, joy and pain. [a.] El Cerrito, CA.

PRICE, MICHAEL
[b.] July 18, 1976, Bryn Mawr, Pennsylvania; [p.] Donald L. and Katherine A. Price; [ed.] Great Valley High School; [occ.] Student; [memb.] National Honor Society, Varsity Club, USTA; [hon.] Distinguished Honor Roll, scholarship to Pennsylvania Free Enterprise Week; [oth. writ.] Many poems, a few short stories; [pers.] Life is a book with no previous page. [a.] Malvern, PA.

PRITCHARD, NATHAN CHRISTOPHER
[b.] March 4, 1975, San Antonio, TX.; [p.] Steven Robert and Janice Mary Pritchard; [ed.] High school graduate from Judson High School; [occ.] Student at Rice University; [memb.] MENSA; [hon.] Graduated Valedictorian of Judson High School class of 1993, National Merit Scholar, Advanced Placement (AP) Scholar with Distinction; [oth. writ.] Three poems published in the Judson High School Literary magazine "The Shooting Star"; [pers.] I enjoy poetry and music best when I can feel the emotions the author experienced while writing and I try to make my own poetry reflect the same quality. [a.] Live Oak, TX.

PREVITE, BILL
[b.] March 5, 1977, Philadelphia, Pennsylvania; [p.] Jessica and Ernest Previte; [ed.] Berlin Community School (elementary), Eastern Regional High School; [occ.] Student. [a.] Berlin, NJ.

PRIVETTE, CHRISTAL
[pen.] Dawn Munn; [b.] March 10, 1979, Oxford, North Carolina; [p.] Melvin and Cathy Privette; [ed.] On going; [occ.] Student; [memb.] High school band; [hon.] NJHS, stands for National Junior Honor Society; [pers.] My inspiration for writing this poem was my uncle, who is infected with full blown Aids. I dedicate this poem to my uncle. [a.] Creedmoor, NC.

PRIVITERA, HEATHER L.
[b.] September 2, 1978, Charleston, South Carolina; [p.] Susan and Kim Privitera; [ed.] Lakeside Junior High; [oth. writ.] Other poems published in local and school newspapers; [pers.] In my poems I reflect my emotions and dreams in words I can only write and never talk about. [a.] Orange Park, FL.

PROCTER, KELLY A.
[b.] September 11, 1982, Jefferson City, Missouri; [p.] Frank and Beverly Procter; [ed.] South Elementary, Eldon, MO.; [memb.] Spring Garden 4-H, Girl Scouts; [pers.] My poems are influenced by what I've seen and what I feel. [a.] Olean, MO.

PROFFITT, JAMES ANTHONY SEBASTIAN
[pen.] Jamison Proffitt; [b.] August 20, 1976, Russell, Kansas; [p.] Lawrence and Shirley Proffitt; [ed.] Senior at Russell High School, 1994 graduate; [memb.] National Honor Society, Junior Student of the Year, National Forensic League President, senior class Vice-President, Captain of the Cross-Country; [oth. writ.] A few other poems and short stories; [pers.] In my poem I try to show the truth about abortion that many people overlook. I hope this poem will open their eyes. [a.] Russell, KS.

PRUITT, ANN
[b.] September 2, 1944, Sneedville, TN; [p.] Norman and Estelle Pruitt; [ch.] Jeff, Mingo, Doug, Norman, Carmen and Charmen; [ed.] Hancock County High School; [occ.] Homemaker; [hon.] Editors Choice Award; [oth. writ.] Several poems published in local newspaper and in books; [pers.] I have been influenced by changes of life around me. [a.] Sneedville, TN.

PUCEK, TAMIE
[b.] February 28, 1960. Richmond, Texas; [p.] Marie and Elhart Pucek; [ed.] Lamar Consolidated High School, Rosenberg, Texas; [occ.] Bookkeeper/secretary; [oth. writ.] Other original poems and one children's book, all unpublished as of now; [pers.] My writing comes from my inner emotions and my moods. May it be depression, sadness, tragedy, love or happiness, it comes out in my writings. Whichever emotion I feel at the time. [a.] Richmond, TX.

PUCKETT, C.E.
[pen.] C.E. Puckett; [b.] May 11, 1909, North Little Rock, Arkansas; [p.] Allen T. and Lela Jones Puckett; [m.] Edith Maydean Word Puckett, July 4, 1936; [ch.] Donald E., Michael T. and Patrick W. Puckett; [ed.] 4th Street High School; [occ.] Building contractor, Little Rock, No Little Rock, AR.; [memb.] Little Rock Chapter of Fraternal Order of the Eagle, Amboy Methodist Church; [hon.] 1979 recipient of John Wesley Award for service to the Methodist church; [oth. writ.] Several poem published in the "Arkansas Methodist"; [pers.] I like for my poems to reach out to people of all walks of life to maybe help bring them closer to God. [a.] North Little Rock, AR.

PUCKETT, CHASITI
[b.] August 14, 1978, Cullman, Alabama; [p.] Michael and Sabrina Puckett; [pers.] "I am silver and exact. I have no preconceptions. Whatever I see I swallow immediately. Just as it is, unmisted by love or dislike. I am not cruel only truthful." -Sylvia Plath. [a.] Cullman, AL.

PYLE, BETH RAULSTON
[b.] January 28, 1971, Maryville; [p.] David and Patricia Raulston; [m.] William E. Pyle, June 20, 1992; [ed.] William Blount High School; [occ.] Customer Service Rep. at Citizens Bank of Blount County; [hon.] I received an honor from Arbor Day Foundation for a poem about trees; [oth. writ.] I write poems on any topic and have every since 5th grade; [pers.] I love reading and writing poetry. It always gives me a sense of comfort for whatever mood I am in. [a.] Maryville, TN.

RABBITT, VALENTINA
[pen.] The Carrot Lady or The Rabbitt; [b.] February 13, 1965, Aberdeen, Washington; [p.] Betty Jacobson; [ed.] Hemet High and some college; [occ.] On S.S.I.; [hon.] Special olympics medal awards and best story writer in junior high; [oth. writ.] In Anza newspaper and school newspaper; [pers.] I feel people are allowed to dream when they feel like it. Although dreams are not reality. [a.] Aguanga, CA.

RAE, DEBORAH L. (BLIND)
[pen.] Deborah L. Rae; [b.] May 27, 1951, Queens, New York; [p.] Sophia J. Rae (mother); [ed.] Graduated from Md. Public High and Md. School for Blind, AA-Music, BA-French and Music, Cum Laude, Master's Voice, present temporary medical leave; [occ.] Professional Singer has absolute pitch and does multiple voice recording, sing in 5 languages; [memb.] Alliance Francoise National French Honor Society; [hon.] Many varied music awards and scholarships, high school junior college, undergraduate and graduate program. National Federation of Music Clubs for 2 years -a first, Dean's List, 4 year Prestigious Garden State graduate Fellowship (1 of 23 out of 250), 1st blind undergraduate student with 2 majors (Cum Laude) varied poetry awards, Who's Who Among Students in American Universities and Colleges, first New Jersey blind student to receive Garden State graduate Fellowship; [oth. writ.] Poems in other anthologies and some church magazines. Poems in French and English, French art, inspirational and folk and country gospel songs in English and some instrumental songs played on cassettes, braille and typed

with sound effects, dialostic music; [pers.] "I see you with my heart" because our Lord Jesus gave me the gift of spiritual sight. I thank Him for my talent. The French poetry I write is influenced by a Century Romanticism. [a.] Montclair, NJ.

RAETHER, ARNOLD L.
[pen.] Arnie, Arn; [b.] Eau Claire, Wisconsin, Lawrence and Doris Raether; [ch.] Alisha Susan (19 years old, Minneapolis, MN) and Amanda Lynn Raether (16 years old, Eua Claire, WI.); [ed.] Augusta High School, Augusta, Wisconsin; [occ.] Hardware buyer and sales, Assistant Busy Bee Hardware, (Santa Monica, CA.); [memb.] Pilgrim Lutheran Church; [hon.] Editor;s Choice Award 1993 National Library of Poetry; [oth. writ.] "Red-Eye He Was Quite the Guy", The National Library of Poetry - Wind in The Night Sky, Library of Congress ISBN 1-56167-041-3, "What Dad and Mom Meant To Us All", National Library of Poetry - The Coming of Dawn, Library of Congress ISBN 1-56167-042-1; [pers.] The Dells Mill-Est. in 1864, The Wisc. State and Eau Claire County Governments have tried to gain access and water control rights to this privately owned pond for many years, they have not treated my cousin justly or fairly according to original contracts and deeds -"Court Battles 1993". [a.] Santa Monica, CA.

RAINEY, BERNICE W.
[pen.] Benn-Benn, Bernadett; [b.] December 31, 1930, Montgomery; [p.] Ford and Viola B. Williams, Sr. (both deceased); [m.] Deceased; [ch.] First marriage-Thaddesu, West Jr. and Dwight Orlando Powell; [ed.] Finished high school with a course in Cosmetology, finished Nurse Aide School, took a sewing course; [occ.] Retired; [hon.] Chosen for Golden Poet Awards for two years and Silver one year but didn't get to receive it; [oth. writ.] Wrote two poem books "The Water of Life", the second was named "Occasions and Adventures of Love". [a.] Montgomery, AL.

RAMBO, VIOLA M.
[b.] January 20, 1916, Rudyard, Montana; [p.] Alphonse H. and Hilda Gertrude (Mayer) Muller; [m.] Howard W. Rambo, (deceased), June 3, 1939; [ch.] Kathleen, Arthur (killed in Viet Nam November 26, 1969), Patricia and Daniel; [ed.] High school-Hingham, MT., Kinman Business University, Spokane, Washington; [occ.] Business Management Asst., U.S.F.S., Libby, MT.; [memb.] St. Joseph Catholic Parish, VFW Auxiliary, Viet Nam Veteran's of America Associate member; [hon.] Aertor manc award, U.S. Forest Service; [oth. writ.] " Ranch Life", Montana Farmer Stockman, "The Low Road", Western News; [pers.] I am an optimist, I count my age by friends, not years. I count my life by smiles, not tears, "NOTE", not original but expresses my outlook on life. [a.] Libby, MT.

RAMIREZ, DANIEL
[pen.] Daniel E. Ramirez, Baby Suicide; [b.] December 21, 1973, Lake View Terrace; [p.] Martha E. Ramirez and Javier Ramirez (father separated); [ed.] Mary Immaculate, Pacoima Junior High, San Fernando High graduate; [occ.] T.V. film and comm'l extra, auto parts sales, referee at Slammers Unn.; [oth. writ.] Chicano Pride I and II, Betrayal of the Promise Land, Hypocrite, These Tears, Suicide, The Beast to God, Without You, Danny's Dead, World of Misery, (not yet published); [pers.] Writing is like therapy to me, writing on a sheet of paper on how I feel and what I see. I sometimes feel better after writing down a poem but I feel better when someone reads it. [a.] San Fernando, CA.

RAMOS, GLORIA E. PEREZ
[b.] Isabela, Puerto Rico; [p.] Irene Girau and Inocencio Perez; [m.] Herbert Ramos, August 21, 1971; [ch.] Dania and David; [ed.] South Side High School, Newark (B.A.), Bloomfield College, Bloomfield, (M.A.), Kean College, Union, New Jersey; [occ.] School supervisor and teacher trainer, Adjunct Professor; [memb.] Teachers and Writers Collaborative, NJ TESOL/BE, Hispanic Women's Task Force of New Jersey, City Association of Supervisors and Administrators; [hon.] Poetry reading contest, winner in high school, essay contest winner in 5th grade; [oth. writ.] Submittals to several publishing companies, published a number of poems in local newspapers and magazines; [pers.] There have been many people who have influenced my writing. Among these are two very special people, my 100 year old grandfather and my late father, both great story tellers. I especially like the French and Spanish romantic writers, Elizabeth B. Browning and Emily Dickinson. [a.] Verona, NJ.

RAMSEY, DARA
[pen.] Dara Mae; [b.] November 19, 1917, Sumerco, West Virginia (left at 6 months), parents followed oil, Tulsa Oklahoma and back; [p.] C.O. and Nancy Ann Garrett Givens, Tidewater Oil Co., Tulsa, OKla. employee; [m.] Lewis T. Ramsey (born 1913, retired Boeing Co.), December 30, 1941; [ch.] Jack-1945, L.T.,Jr.-1942 and Debra-1957; [ed.] High school graduate 1936, Business Schooling plus continued special schooling up to present year 1993; [occ.] P.O. Clerk, Ramsey Variety Store, Boeing War employed 1942, Susan B. Allen Hospital Nurse Aide night employee, National Writer Member; [memb.] Past recorded in Community Leaders and Noteworthy Americans 1974 Edition page 489, 1933 Business and Professional Women's Clubs Inc.; [hon.] Woman of Year 1992, Year B.P.W., other membership First Christian Church since age 8, Knife and Fork Club; [oth. writ.] Plays, western book, page 286 Sympathy (with photo) 1991 year published Book World of Poetry Anthology, do local P.R. for clubs I have membership, former Garden Club, local paper articles "Timely Hints on Gardening"; [pers.] BEware! Hear first, alert, calm, above all, know your subject and keep active for goodness sake! [a.] El Dorado, KS,

RANDELL, VANCE
[b.] August 21, 1977, Botwood, Newfoundland; [p.] George and Judy Randell; [ed.] Attending Botwood Collegiate High School; [oth. writ.] This is my first published writing but I look forward to later writing other poetry and novels. I'm attempting now to get my first novel published; [pers.] My poem titled "She Walked by Me in School Today" expresses a feeling that every teenager goes through in life. I would like to thank my sister Rachel Randell who encourage me to write. [a.] Botwood, Newfoundland A0H 1E0.

RANGEL, MARCO
[b.] July 23, 1978, Salt Lake City, UT.; [p.] Betty and Arturo Rangel; [ed.] EJ Martinez Elementary School, Capshaw Middle School, Sante Fe High School; [occ.] Student at McCurdy School; [memb.] Marching band, symphonic band, acolyte, church youth group; [hon.] Almost annual awards in recognition of outstanding writing in respective schools; [oth. writ.] Poems published in Smithsonian Magazine, poems published in school publications, articles published in school newspapers; [pers.] Whatever you say, say with your whole heart, whatever you do, do with your whole heart, and happiness will be yours. [a.] Espanola, NM.

RANKIN-REID, DALIAH
[pen.] Daliah Rankin-Reid; [b.] January 5, 1931, Oriente, Cubu, grown in Jamaica, W.I.; [p.] William Rankin and Naomi Reid; [ed.] B.A. history, legal education, University of Massachusetts, Boston; [occ.] Varied; [oth. writ.] Poems unpublished; [pers.] Having an interest and concern for others, helping whenever possible, my poems reflect nature, the human condition and sometimes current events. Thanks to John Fischer for typing the poem. [a.] Lincoln, MA.

RANOUS, JON M.
[b.] May 26, 1976, Saginaw, Michagan; [p.] Mike and Kit Ranous; [ed.] 11th grade of high school at Calvary Baptist Academy, Midland, Michigan; [hon.] American Institute of Chemical Engineers Scholarship Award to Michigan Tech for their Summer Youth Program, all A Honor Roll Award, Spirit Award, and Principal's Award at Calvary Baptist Academy varsity basketball "Sportsmanship" trophy. [a.] Saginaw, MI.

RANULERSON, JOSHUA
[b.] October 1, 1977, Decorah, IA.; [p.] Tom and Melanie Raulerson; [ed.] Sophomore at Decorah High School, Decorah, IA.;[occ.] Student; [memb.] Iowa Poetry Association, church choir, high school track and football, speech, drama, Explorer Scouts; [hon.] Iowa Governor's Institute 1992, recipient of Iowa Scholarship from Iowa Talent search and Headmaster's Scholarship from Shattuck, St. Mary's School All State speech contest, Spanish National Honors; [oth. writ.] Poems published in several anthologies; [pers.] Never conform. [a.] Decorah, IA.

RAY, DENISE
[pen.] Winter Dakota; [b.] November 28, 1968, Los Angeles, California; [p.] Robert and Lela Burris; [m.] Jimmy Ray, Jr., (divorced), March 21, 1987; [ch.] Jimmy Ray III (6), Day'vione (4) and Jerrame Ray (3); [ed.] Graduated Allain Leroy Locke High School in 1986; [occ.] Salesperson, Judys; [memb.] Mt. Hermon Missionary Baptist Church; [hon.] 2nd place Omega Si Pi Phraternity's Orientorical competition, Most Talented Youth 1986-87; [oth. writ.] Songs for former musical group "Three D", personal collection of poems; [pers.] As a result of having been selected as a semi-finalist in this contest I have come to know that all things are possible to those who believe.[a.] Inglewood, CA.

RAY, KIERSTEN LYNN
[b.] February 1, 1974; [p.] Charles and Sue Ray; [ed.] St. Pius X High School, Waubonsee College; [occ.] College student, Psychology major; [pers.] Poetry has helped me overcome many difficulties in my childhood. Without the voice of poetry, I might never have spoken. [a.] Aurora, IL.

RAYBON, JENNIFER
[b.] October 26, 1976, Columbus, GA.; [p.] Willie and Sue Raybon; [sib.] Susan, Kimberly, Kacie and Mandi; [ed.] Tri-County High and now attending King's Academy, 11th grade; [hon.] Who's Who Among American High School Students, Sr. Beta Club; [pers.] I thank God for my talent of writing poetry. Writing poetry is a way for me to express myself, and I hope that others will be positively influenced by my writings. [a.] Buena Vista, CA.

RAYLE, TRAVIS
[b.] April 1, 1974, Florence, SC.; [p.] Jerry and Sara Cartrette, Gordon Rayle; [ed.] June, 1993 graduate of Whiteville High School, Whiteville, NC.; [occ.] Freshman at Guilford Community Technical College, Greensboro, NC.; [hon.] 1st, 2nd and 3rd place Art Awards. [a.] Whiteville, NC.

RAYMOND, YVES PHILIPPE
[b.] June 1, 1958, Windsor, Quebec Canada; [p.] Jean Paul and Georgette Raymond; [m.] Carol Raymond, October 6, 1979; [ch.] Alicia Anne and Angelica Lynn Raymond; [ed.] High school graduate; [occ.] Business Manager; [oth.writ.] Several short poems. [a.] Berlin, NH.

READ, W.A.
[b.] July 26, 1915, Mt. Belvieu, Texas; [p.] Chester and Bytha Gardner Read; [m.] Jerri, December 4, 1959; [ed.] 2 years college; [occ.] Retired from Exxon Public Relations, also retired Professional Photographer; [memb.] Trinity Episcopal Church, Masonic Lodge, Golf Club, Heritage Society, "Friends of Lee College" membership; [hon.] 4 National Newspaper Photography Awards; [oth. writ.] Published in Life Magazine, Sports Afield, numerous House Organs, numerous newspaper magazine inserts; [pers.] As expressed by Minnie Pearl on " The Grand Ole Opry", I'm just so glad to be here. [a.] Baytown, TX.

REBER, FRANCES ALMA NEWKIRK
[b.] December 25, 1915, Rice Co., Kansas; [p.] Clare Sparks and Alice Irene Kiser Newkirk; [m.] Matthew Allen Reber, July 7, 1940; [ed.] High school graduate; [occ.] Housewife; [hon.] Editor's Choice Awards for Change Times-Changeless Spirit and for The Austral Light, from The National Library of Poetry; [pers.] This talent was inherited from grandfather, Richard Robert Newkirk and mother Alice Irene Kiser Newkirk. [a.] Grove, OK.

REDLICK, JUDY (LYN)
[b.] June 9, 1962, North, Battleford, Sask; [p.] Charlie and Shirley Michnik; [m.] Barry Redlick, March 12, 1982; [ch.] Benjamin James, Nicholas David and Jonathan Micheal; [ed.] L.C.B.I. Outlook, Sadk., U of S Saskatoon, Sask.; [occ.] Farmer, housewife also presently pursuing a part-time career in modelling; [memb.] Tri-Cel Ladies Club; [oth. writ.] Poems published in school newspapers. A poem put to music and played at graduation. Many poems written for family and friends, several meditations written for church services; [pers.] Writing has given me the opportunity to learn more about myself and share my thoughts and feelings with others. [a.] Biggar, Sask, Canada S0K 0M0.

REED, DARIA
[b.] July 26, 1976, Norristown, PA.; [p.] Terri and Karl Reed; [ed.] Wm. Allen High School; [occ.] High school student, graduate in June '94; [hon.] Oratorical contest winner; [pers.] To my inspiration, Jason Custer, you showed me the things of love, and to my parents, you always said I deserve the best. [a.] Allentown, PA.

REIBSAMEN, DORIS
[pen.] Doris "Light" Mansell; [b.] December 27, 1938, Vibbard, MO; [p.] Mr. and Mrs. Thomas Glen Patton; [m.] Roger Reibsamen, January 3, 1993; [ch.] Tawni, DeWayne, Tony and Jack; [ed.] High school diploma; [occ.] Disability SS; [hon.] Honorary DAR; [oth. writ.] Public forums in Winfield Daily Courier, Winfield, KS, unpublished one non-fiction book and three poem books; [pers.] I am a Bi-Polar (Manic Depressive) person. Writing is the essence of my ability to relate my true feelings and thoughts. [a.] Winfield, KS.

REICKS, EDNA
[pen.] Zelda Blong; [b.] November 13, 1933, Lawler, IA; [p.] Louis and Elizabeth Blong; [m.] Ardwin Reicks, June 6, 1955; [ch.] Dale, Dan, Dean, Darwin and Dana, 6 grandchildren; [ed.] Graduate of Lawler Iowa High School; [occ.] Director of Senior Services, Chickasaw County, New Hampton, Iowa; [memb.] Member of Catholic church and organist, play for weddings, Professional Women's Group, Catholic Daughters, American Legion Auxiliary, member of theater group "County Road Players"; [hon.] Honored to give presentation at National Rural Life Conference 1983; [oth. writ.] Weekly article published in local newspaper; [pers.] I hope to reach the hearts of many people especially to give warm feelings to my mother and all mothers and family life to others. [a.] Lawler, IA.

REID, JASON J.
[pen.] Reid Jason; [b.] June 3, 1971, Halifax Nova Scotia; [pers.] To each his own. [a.] Parrsboro NS, Canada.

REINER, RUTH
[b.] February 3, 1974, Israel -Jerusalem; [p.] Arona Artest (mother) and Michael Zionist (father); [ed.] Twelve years education, specialty in theater; [occ.] Solider in the Israeli Army; [memb.] I.D.F.; [hon.] An award for directing and producing No Exit, a philosophical play by Jon Paul Sartre; [oth. writ.] Many more songs at the age of nine, other than the song published; [pers.] The real peace shall come from the children. [a.] St. Ramot, Jerusalem Israel.

REYNOLDS, KAREY D.
[b.] March 2, 1968; [m.] Eugene L. Reynolds, June 7, 1989; [ch.] Garett F. and Joshua W. Reynolds; [oth. writ.] Being As One, published in Where Dreams Begin; [pers.] Dedicated to Rose Rothfuss, thanks for a second chance. [a.] Ft. Worth, TX.

REYNOLDS, NORA BELLE MEACHUM
[b.] October 4, 1917, Anson County, North Carolina; [p.] WG and Cornelia W. Meachum; [m.] Nathaniel H. Reynolds, October 4, 1939; [ch.] Robert E., Ina Jean, Priscilla Carol and Nathaniel H. Jr.; [ed.] Sixth grade; [occ.] Housewife; [memb.] Fall Branch Baptist Church; [pers.] I strive to reflect the real love of God in all that I do. [a.] Candor, NC.

REYNOLDS, ROWAN
[b.] January 3, 1948, Middlesex, England; [m.] Victor Reynolds, December 5, 1970; [ch.] Tom, Daphne and Cliff; [ed.] High school; [occ.] Writer, homemaker; [memb.] Christian Writers Guild, CA., Christian and Missionary Alliance Church; [hon.] High school Writing Award; [oth. writ.] Local newspaper and The Shantyman; [pers.] I love language/ words. I have been greatly influenced by C.S. Lewis. [a.] Delta, B.C. Canada V4M 1G8.

REZEK, EMILY
[b.] November 5, 1981, McHenry, Illinois; [p.] Raymond and Kathleen Pezek; [ed.] Currently (93-94) in 6th grade at Wentzville Middle School; [occ.] Student; [hon.] 5th place State Math contest in '92, State Math finalist in '93; [pers.] My cats, Nick and Nora, provide much inspiration for my writing. They are, however, unimpressed. [a.] Lake St. Louis, MO.

RHODES, KIM
[b.] July 25, 1979, Ft. Worth, TX.; [p.] Rickey and Debbie Rhodes; [ed.] 8th grade student at Halton Middle School; [memb.] Birdville Baptist Church and Haltam Middle School Top Girls Choir member; [hon.] I received the top score at my solo ensemble for choir; [oth. writ.] I was published in a book called The Anthology of Poetry By Young Americans. The book was published by the American Academy of Poetry; [pers.] Simply be yourself, nothing more, nothing less. I give all the credit I receive from my poetry to God since He is the one who blessed me with this talent. [a.] Ft. Worth, TX.

RIALS, WENDY LEE
[b.] May 9, 1977, New London, CT; [p.] Elizabeth and Vernon Rials; [ed.] Princess Anne High School; [occ.] Poet, playing softball; [hon.] Softball coach's award, silver medal in softball junior olympics; [oth. writ.] Several poems in local paper, poem written on behalf of my sister's wedding (Eternity); [pers.] Being a poet is the hardest and the bravest job there is, you not only tell people who you are but also how you feel. [a.] Virginia Beach, VA.

RICHER, MEGAN
[b.] July 10, 1975, Manchester, New Hampshire; [p.] Arthur and Mary Jo Richer; [m.] Single; [ed.] Danville High School, will be a freshman at Syracuse University in Fall 1993; [occ.] Lifeguard; [memb.] Youth for Christ, National Honor Society; [hon.] Dean scholarship at Syracuse, Ray Krock Youth Achievement Award; [oth. writ.] Various sports articles for local newspapers, several original song lyrics, a script performed at my high school's art festival; [pers.] The words come from my heart, the gift comes from the Lord. [a.] Danville, PA.

RICHMOND, JULIE
[b.] July 29, 1976, Carlisle, Pennsylvania; [p.] Ruthanna and Donald A. Richmond; [ed.] Carlisle High; [pers.] I strive to reflect the inhumaneness of humanity in my writing. I believe that the first step toward righting a wrong is showing where one exists. [a.] Carlisle, PA.

RICK, JACKI
[pen.] Jacqueline Richards; [b.] April 5, 1976, Resurrection Hospital-Chicago; [p.] Joseph H. and Valerie J. Rick; [ed.] Immanuel Lutheran Grade School and Fox Valley Lutheran Academy High School; [occ.] Journalist for Beacon News-Teens Day section; [memb.] HSUS, PETA, Greenpeace, HAHS; [hon.] 1992 and 1993 State Finalist Miss Teen Illinois, super honor roll, year of 92 and 93; [oth. writ.] Write much poetry, written articles for Teens Day in Beacon News, write stories on my own; [pers.] In my writings, I focus on the ups and downs of love. Life is a roller coaster and I want people to understand that thru my writings. [a.] Carpentersville, IL.

RIDDICK, RUTH A.
[pen.] Ruth A. Riddick; [b.] January 5, 1916, Ripley (Lauderdale Co.), Tennessee; [p.] Robert A. and Martha Goin Dew; [m.] Warner A. Riddick (deceased), September 19, 1985; [ch.] Jean Kee Harber and Bette Jones;[ed.] Halls High School, Halls, Tennessee; [occ.] Dept. store owner 35 years, Sales Representative for Olan Mills Studio; [memb.] Jackson Parks and Recreation Golden Years Service and Activity Center member; [hon.] Top Sales for Lions Club, Senior Olympics finalist, Jackson Writers Poetry contest winner; [oth. writ.] Several poems for various themes, one published in a local writers group collection; [pers.] The key to victory is never give up. [a.] Jackson, TN.

RIDEOUT, CABELL (MS.)
[pen.] Edith Rideout; [b.] March 4, 1929, Grand Falls, Newfoundland; [p.] William and Rachel Goulding (deceased); [ch.] Helen Margaret and Janet Rachel; [ed.] Memorial University of Newfoundland, 1978 (B.Voc. Ed>0 St. John's, Newfoundland; [occ.] Retired Business Ed. teacher, Eastern Community College, Bonavista, Newfoundland; [memb.] Professional Secretaries International, Kansas City, MO. CPS Desig), Newfoundland Association of Business Ed. Teachers past president, 1978-80. [a.] Prince George, BC Canada V2N 4E7.

RIDEOUT, HEIDI
[b.] March 11, 1960, Grand Bank, Newfoundland, Canada; [p.] Pearce and Rose Rideout; [m.] (boyfriend) Richard Pittman; [ed.] Queen Elizabeth Regional High School, Cabot College; [occ.] Secretary; [memb.] I am a member of the Multiple Sclerosis Society; [hon.] I was at the head of my class in grade two (2) and I won an English writing prize in grade 4; [oth.writ.] I have written several other poems and at present I am completing a children's book, a short story entitled Robbery at the Spaghetti Shop; [pers.] I have always been interested in writing but a teacher's note on my grade 4 report card encouraged me the most. [a.] Pouch Cove, Newfoundland Canada A0A 3L0.

RIDGWAY, TERRY RHODES
[b.] November 4, 1934, Gonzales, TX.; [p.] Hildeen Barrow and Dee Rhodes; [m.] Marvin B. Ridgway (deceased), 1953-1965; [ch.] Teri Lyn Ridgway Newman and Michael Travis Ridgway; [ed.] Austin High, Austin, TX.; [occ.] U.S. Government, 25 years, Postal Service; [memb.] First United Methodist Church, United Federation Federal Workers, SPCA of Cedar Park, TX.;[hon.] Four (4) Special Achievement Awards from U.S. Government; [oth. writ.] Several poems published in local newspapers; [pers.] The adversities in life cannot be solved unless we as individuals realize our limitations and assume responsibility for our actions, we can create only as long as there is a world where creation will survive... [a.] Cedar Park, TX.

RIGGINS, BRANDON
[b.] October 6, 1970, Wichita Falls, Texas;[p.] Bobby and Gloria Riggins; [ed.] Livingston University, Livingston, Alabama and West Texas A&M University, Canyon, Texas; [occ.] Mental Health Assistant, Vernon State Hospital; [pers.] My writings are the instrument I feel in my heart. [a.] Vernon, TX.

RILEY, PATRICIA OTTO
[b.] July 10, 1940, Niagara Falls, New York; [p.] Verna Storms and Nelson Arthur Otto; [m.] Michael Edward Riley, April 9, 1989; [ch.] Mark Scott Phillips, identical twins Kurt Michael and Kenneth Todd Phillips; [ed.] B.S. Elementary Education, Masters degree-Educational Leadership Nova University; [occ.] Assistant Principal-Meadow Park Elementary, Port Charlotte, FL; [memb.] Phi Delta Kappa, ASCD-Association for Supervision and Curriculum Development; [oth. writ.] Personal journals, poems, short stories as well as professional articles; [pers.] I notice and appreciate the world around me. I've always felt a burning need to record and share these observations.[a.] Punta Gorda,FL.

RILEY, STEVEN L.
[b.] October 2, 1951, Joplin, Missouri; [p.] Marvin and Katie Riley; [m.] Debra L. Riley , July 29, 1979; [ch.] John, Jeremy and Justin; [ed.] Carl Junction High School, Missouri Southern College; [occ.] Farmer and inventor.

RINI, MATTHEW J.
[b.] Junly 16, 1955; [m.] Becky Ann, April 11, 1981; [ch.] Kelly Ann and Kristen Rene; [occ.] Programming Manager for Sterling Software; [pers.] Happiness is wanting what you have, not having what you want. Thanks to a terrific family for making it so easy to achieve. [a.] Mantua, OH.

RINTALA, ANTHONY
[b.] April 11, 1975, Warren, OH.; [p.] William and Linda Rintala; [ed.] Northshore High, University of Southern Mississippi Honors College; [occ.] Student; [oth. writ.] Several essays published in high school newspaper; [pers.] I sit next to you in the dark and whisper lovingly of the magic that drifts around and through us all. I hint at the grand secrets and breathe softly into your ear of life's majesty. [a.] Slidell, LA.

RISINGER, ANGELINA S.
[pen.] Angie Stratta; [b.] February 6, 1941, Bryan (Brazos Co.), Texas; [p.] Sarah and Frank Stratta, descendant of grandparents who immigrated from Italy; [ch.] Alan (29), Brad (13), Andrea (23) and Sarah (10); [ed.] Bachelor of Science in Education and Curriculum from Texas A & M University, College Sta., Texas; [occ.] Kindergarten teacher-Southside Elementary, Cleveland, Texas; [memb.] St. Mary's Catholic Church, ATPE-Professional Educators Group, Kappa Delta Pi-College Honor Society; [hon.] S.P.J.S.T.-State award for 1st place in talent contest in Texas in 1960-61, Gold Globe Award-World of Poetry, 2 Principal Awards for creative work at Southside School, Secretary of SOTA, (Students Older Than Average) at Texas A & M University for 1976-1977; [oth. writ.] 54 poems, a country western song (waltz), educational article entitled-"The Fourth R", which is about using art as the fourth "R" across the curriculum; [pers.] I write a variety of poems that pertain to things I know about such as love, death, children, education, nature and some comical poems, also. [a.] Cleveland, TX.

RITTER, VERONICA G.
[b.] January 3, 1941, Vineland, New Jersey; [p.] Dominic J. and Margaret B. Giacomelli; [ch.] Matthew Charles and Eric Douglas; [ed.] Sacred Heart High School; [occ.] Program Analyst, Federal Aviation Administration; [memb.] N.J. Right to Life Committee, Sacred Heart Church, Cumberland Regional Theatre, National Latin Honors Society; [oth. writ.] Poem published in the National High School Poetry Association's Young America Sings; [pers.] When I visited Ireland for the first time, I had an overwhelming feeling of coming home. This poem reflects that feeling from my heart. [a.] Vineland, NJ.

RITZMANN, ANDY
[pen.] A. Zimmy; [b.] August 29, 1969, Kitchener Ontario, Canada; [p.] Peter and Emmy Ritzmann; [m.] April Ritzmann; [ch.] Sarah Anne Ritzmann; [ed.] Music; [occ.] Musician; [memb.] AMA; [hon.] I get to live in the 90's; [oth. writ.] Currently in works on a small book of poetry entitled Songs From The Barstool, A Portrait; [pers.] You can travel anywhere and hang yourself there, there's always more than enough rope. [a.] Ferntosh, Alberta Canada.

ROACH, BEVERLY RAYE
[b.] September 3, 1945, Mexia, TX.; [p.] Clyde and Dorothy Gaulden; [m.] Divorced; [m.] Stephen Brent Roach; [ed.] Stephen F. Austin University, Charles H Milby High School, Houston, TX.; [occ.] Social Worker; [hon.] 1992 The Muse Interior Lighting 1st prize in poetry; [pers.] With thanks to my family.

ROBERTS, PAT
[b.] August 17, 1931, Holdenville, Oklahoma; [p.] Dee and Jocie Bankston; [m.] Edgar Roberts, September 10, 1949; [ch.] Linda, Michael and Kathy; [ed.] Grade 8; [occ.] Retired clerk and supervisor; [oth.writ.] As of now 82 poems unpublished, inspirational; [pers.] I have been inspired to write special words for friends and love ones and even strangers when they would be going through trials. [a.] Fresno, CA.

ROBERTS, TRACY LEA
[pen.] Tracy Lea; [b.] May 27, 1978; [p.] Ernest and Jenny Roberts; [ed.] Creekside Elementary, Sunnymead Middle School and Moreno Valley High School; [occ.] Student; [oth. writ.] None published; [pers.] I write poetry to bring out my feelings. My poems always reflect the way I feel about my life and my surroundings. [a.] Moreno Valley, CA.

ROBERTSON, JOHN DAVID R.
[b.] May 18, 1962, Shaw AFB, Sumter, South Carolina; [p.] Roland B. Robertson Jr., M.D. and A. Jane McKelvey Robertson; [m.] Single; [ed.] Callaway High, University of Texas at Austin (B.A.-Economics), Mississippi State University (Master of Industrial Engineering); [occ.] Cost Engineering Consultant; [memb.] Institute of Industrial Engineers, CATO Institute; [oth. writ.] Poems, Essays, Little Tales; [pers.] "Ought" is spelled out by "IS" and in the words of Mac McAnally "Do you love all that you are capable of loving?". "Reality reigns our answers to life's questions", original by John David R. Robertson. [a.] Jackson, MS.

ROBERTSON, TODD ANTHONY
[pen.] "Sir Anthony"; [b.] March 2, 1970, Minnesota; [p.] Shirley Mae Robertson and James Calloway; [ed.] University of Minnesota; [occ.] Professional student; [pers.] 'Words are the memories and dreams of those who search for a higher calling". [a.] Minneapolis, MN.

ROBINSON, ADA LOUISE
[pen.] Ada L. Robinson; [b.] September 12, 1900, Wuzern, NY.; [p.] Sara and William Small; [m.] Walter James Robinson, May 8, 1917; [ch.] June and May; [ed.] High school and correspondence courses in writing; [occ.] Housewife and vocal teacher; [memb.] Member of the Monday Musical Club; [hon.] Titled as National Vocalist of the Army and Navy Women's Auxiliary; [oth. writ.] Published my book entitled Dreams, Recollections and Thoughts; [pers.] If you can't say something good, don't say anything bad. [a.] Watervliet,. NY.

ROBINSON, COURTNEY LYNNE
[pen.] Courtney Lynne Robinson; [b.] September 30, 1981, Baltimore, Maryland; [p.] Robert and Marcia Robinson; [ed.] St. Mary's of the Assumption, St. Plus the Tenth; [occ.] Student at St. Plus X; [hon.] Student Council, cheerleading, newspaper, band, dramatics; [oth. writ.] Several other poems, stories and articles some published some not; [pers.] I want my readers to familiarize themselves in my poems. [a.] Baltimore, MD.

ROBINSON, DAVID V.
[b.] December 11,1953, Oakland, CA; [p.] Benjamin and Margaritte Robinson; [ed.] McClymond's High, Southern Ohio College, North Peralta College, Bay City College; [occ.] Pharmacy Technician, Cleveland Clinic Foundation; [hon.] Dean's List, certificates of achievement in art, diplomas in Medical Technology; [oth. writ.] First book of poetry and prose, "Opulent Leaves for a Spring Day", newsletter writings; [pers.] To be inspired to create and to create is like the wonderment of a space traveler who sets foot on the uncharted unknown. [a.] Cleveland, OH.

ROBINSON, EDWARD
[b.] July 3, 1952, Fort Sill, KK., (Comanche County); [p.] Robert Lee and Virginia Ruth Whitaker-Robinson; [oth. writ.] My personal journal of life-that will be passed on to my cousin's children, Sheila and Rick Casey II; [pers.] It's not how much you own or how much education you have had, what counts the most is the love you have for your family and friends and the simple things in life. [a.] Aurora, CO.

ROBINSON, NORMA NUYLES
[b.] February 24, 1953, Makati, Philippines; [p.] Olegario Nuyles and Soledad Nuyda; [m.] Fred O. Robinson, October 3, 1992; [ed.] Pamantasan Ng Lungsod, Ng Maynila, Columban College; [occ.] Computer Programmer/analyst; [memb.] Toastmasters International (1983-1989); [oth. writ.] Has written more than a hundred unpublished poems; [pers.] Writing poems and painting are my two first loves. I intend to work on them full time when I can no longer pursue my professional career. [a.] Alameda, CA.

RODEN, WYN (MRS.)
[b.] February 14, 1960; [ch.] Robert Alan, Michael James and Crystal Victoria. [a.] London, Ontario.

RODENBURG, SARAH
[b.] April 12, 1935, Waymart, Pennsylvania; [p.] Helen and Frank Lopatofsky; [m.] Philip Rodenburg, January 10, 1987; [ch.] Gerald, Anita and Helen Cobb; [ed.] Grade school, Steene, PA., 8th grade; [occ.] Housekeeper; [hon.] Math Award; [oth.writ.] Songwriter, "Sweet Jesus Prayer", "My Best Friend", wrote published them in honor of my mother; [pers.] I've been writing since 1981, poems and songs. [a.] Waymart, PA.

ROGERS, CARY (FRANKLIN)
[b.] January 17, 1946, Taylorville, Georgia; [p.] J.D. and Annie Mae Forsyth Rogers; [m.] Barbara Ann Jones Rogers, October 21, 1967; [ch.] Michael Jason Rogers; [ed.] High school, OJT in supervisor skills and computer operations; [occ.] Warehouse operator; [oth. writ.] Poems, songwritings; [pers.] I like to show the funny side of life and the trials of everyday living. [a.] Rome, GA.

ROGERS, MAVIS
[b.] July 14, 1912, Kingston Jamaica, WI.; [p.] Harry John and Emelyn Laughton; [m.] Deceased, December 23, 1937; [ch.] Dianne Rogers Heatheny and Patricia Rogers McNeil; [oth. writ.] I am in a book called "Great Poems of Today" (The Downed), two Golden Awards, two Silvers and Honorable Mention by The World of Poetry; [pers.] I dedicate my life to five unconditional love to my fellowmen, to utilize any talent the Lord has given me as I think He has a reason for doing so. I'll try my best to super-impose a smile across any frowning face I meet as I have discovered that humanity likes laughter. [a.] Mountain View, CA.

ROGERS, SHERI EVERTS
[b.] May 1, 1958, Hebron, Nebraska; [p.] Herman and Margaret Grote Everts; [ch.] Justin Everts Rogers and Elizabeth Everts Rogers; [ed.] B.S., M.Ed. and Ph.D. from the University of Nebraska -Lincoln; [occ.] Literacy Professor; [memb.] International Reading Association and National Council of Teachers of English; [hon.] Outstanding Teacher of the Year-1991, Student Education Association, University of Nebraska-Lincoln; [oth. writ.] Several professional articles and literature reviews; [pers.] Reading and conversing with my sister, Kathy Everts Danielson (who gave me the idea for this poem), influence my writing. My parents were always wonderful role models of the importance of reading and writing.[a.] Lincoln, NE.

ROMACK, VELVADEANE
[b.] July 25, 1915, Chatsworth, Illinois; [p.] Rosa and Elmer Shelton; [m.] Floyd Romack, December 11, 1934; [ch.] 5; [ed.] High school graduate also 1 year Nursing School; [occ.] Saleslady; [hon.] I won a National Award in Chicago paper in 1931 for a short story; [oth. writ.] I still write and arrange programs for church and also in my former place of employment; [pers.] I love to write and appreciate the opportunity to enter into your contest.

ROMINE, DEBRA D.
[b.] March 17, 1954, Umatilla, OR; [p.] Howard and Evelyn (Lish) Addison; [m.] Larry J. Romine, February 14, 1975; [ch.] Kalaitchay and Zachary; [ed.] Continuing; [occ.] Tutor, homemakerm, chocolate sampler; [memb.] Human race, Comedy of Errors Club; [hon.] Editor's Choice Award, selected for tape reading "It Should Take At Least A Week"; [oth. writ.] "It Should Take At Least A Week", National Library of Poetry anthology The Coming of Dawn; [pers.] I have hitchhiked through the galax, eaten at the restuarant at the end of the universe and I am not a stranger in a strange land. [a.] LaGrande, OR.

ROSARIO, MARIMAR
[b.] December 12, 1981, San Juan, Puerto Rico; [p.] Marisol and Manuel Rosario; [ed.] Acad. Maria Renia; [memb.] Country club, museum, bank club; [hon.] Modeling certificate; [oth. writ.] 1 book. [a.] Ignacio Rio Piedras, PR.

ROSENBERRY, DELORIS M.
[b.] September 23, 1921, St. Louis, Missouri; [p.] Walter and Lou Mudge; [m.] Divorced; [ch.] Chas Kirk Rosenberry, Karen Sue McDonald and Deborah Lynn Marion; [ed.] BA in nursing, RN; [occ.] Retired R.N. after 50 years; [pers.] Things I learned as a child "Be ye kind one to another:, "Do unto others as you would have them do unto you". [a.] Monroeville, NJ.

ROSS, MATTHEW ERZA ABRAHAM
[pen.] Matt, Mear; [b.] February 10, 1979, Bellville, Illinois; [p.] Col. Davie and Karol (Krocker) Ross; [sib.] 1 sister, 2 brothers and 1 big brother dog; [ed.] I have attended 5 schools to date including one in Germany and the Embassy School in Brussels, I will enter my first year at Green Valley High School this year; [memb.] Marching band, track, video production crew; [hon.] Regular Honor Roll, this year I received the winning vote for best political speech written at Thurman White and I was treated to a luncheon with Dan Avale. I also won certificates in writing and math and Science, also won 2nd place at the regional Science Fair for my observation on Scorpin behavior, I have 2 pet Scorpions and a large dog; [oth. writ.] "The Militia", published in Mirror Images 1993 and many unpublished works, poetry is my release; [pers.] I like to write about what I see in human actions that seems like it could be fixed by changing one simple thing. I travel extensively with my parents, and enjoy comparing different people and their behavior. [a.] Henderson, NV.

ROSS, SHELLEY
[pen.] Shelly McCauley; [b.] April 28, 1963, Portland, Oregon; [p.] Elizabeth McCauley and David Ross; [ch.] Troy Michael Riggins; [ed.] Rex Putnam High; [occ.] Transportation Pricing Clerk; [oth. writ.] Several articles written for Cycle News; [pers.] If you have lived well, laughed often, and loved much, consider yourself a success. [a.] Kennewick, WA.

ROSS, TERRY L.
[pen.] T. Ross; [b.] June 22, 1954, Eldorado, Kansas; [p.] Father-Beul and Wilma Ross, mother-Bernice and Richard Peppiatt; [ch.] Jason Allen, Jamie Marie and Jonathan Burns; [pers.] Descending the declivity of waning life, I have touched the metaphysics depths of my own soul. Through a blending of ethereal colors, I have found an inexhaustible treasure, not given by any modifying color of imagination, but protected therein. This I trust to be my poetic powers. [a.] Lindsborg, KS.

ROSSI, KATIE
[b.] November 10, 1981, Suffern, NY.; [p.] Anne and Michael Rossi; [ed.] Currently in St. Pius X Elementary; [occ.] Hard working seventh grade student; [memb.] YMCA, Stoneleigh Pool, Gunpowder Valley Country Club, St. Pius X Newspaper; [hon.] School Spirit, First Honors, Achievement Award; [oth. writ.] A description of friendship for Jack and Jill Magazine; [pers.] As you see by my birthday, I was only eleven when I wrote this. I think that shows that children can be just as creative as adults. [a.] Baltimore, MD.

ROUND, PETER F.
[b.] May 10, 1930, Bridgeport, CT; [p.] George A. and Cornelia F. Round; [m.] Gladys E. Round, July 30, 1955; [ch.] Stephen W. Round; [ed.] St. Luke's School for Boys, Althou Hancock College, AA, LA Vernz University, BA; [occ.] Real Estate Broker, retired USAF MSGT; [memb.] The American Legion, United W. Stand America; [hon.] Military, brass star, air medal with 3 oak leaves cluster, USAF Commendation Medal w/oak leave cluster, Vietnamese Honor Medal; [oth. writ.] First time writer, I am presently writing a novel The Glassless Windows, involving the 1942 battle for Stalingrad; [pers.] I have experienced the indignities and the unconscious wastes of war with my writings. I am attempting to strengthen the public growing aversion to such human conflicts. [a.] Santa Maria, CA.

ROWLAND, JENNIFER
[b.] February 17, Middletown, Connective; [p.] Dorothy Murphy and Duane Rowland; [ed.] Nathan Hale-Ray High School; [occ.] Student; [memb.] Class secretary, book club and drama club; [hon.] Numerous athletic awards in soccer, basketball and softball; [oth. writ.] School assignments only; [pers.] My writing reflects mostly on myself and how I feel at times. [a.] Moodus, CT.

ROWELL, NANCY E.
[b.] December 14, 1969, Douglas, Georgia; [p.] Ashley and Sarah T. Rowell; [ed.] BS in Communication Arts Emphasis in Public Relations; [occ.] Sales; [memb.] Membership Vice President of the Douglas Jaycees and member of College Avenue Baptist Church; [pers.] I wrote this poem in memory of my roommate who was killed in March. Always let friends and family know that you love them because there may not be a tomorrow. [a.] Douglas, GA.

ROY, LARNDERS
[b.] October 19, 1934, Oakland, California; [p.] Juanita and Larnders Roy; [m.] Carol Ann Moore; [ch.] Rachael Fields, Marc and Michael Roy, Launa Kiumer, Jan Hannah; [ed.] Grad at Stanford and U C Berkely; [occ.] Education; [memb.] Multicultural Publishers Exchange; [oth. writ.] Short stories in newspapers and magazine, Viginetts on Themes and Bits of Experience, book of short stories and screen plays; [pers.] Trapped-Alzheimer's. [a.] Berkeley, CA.

ROZESKI, BROOKE
[b.] May 29, 1981, Salem Hospital; [p.] Dallas and Cherry Rozeski.

RUEL, MICHAEL JOHN PAUL
[b.] October 18, 1937, Green Bay, WI; [p.] Rose and Clayton Ruel; [m.] Joanne Kathleen Ruel, March 29, 1969; [ch.] Kelly Sean Ruel, Mit-class of 94; [occ.] Local delivery driver, San Antonio, TX., 1993; [hon.] Transparent water color award, St. Philips College Art Club, 1989-1990; [pers.] God is not a christian God following Christ. God is love, I will not write, He is boss, if not boss-man. [a.] San Antonio, TX.

RUFFO, DIANE
[pen.] Smiley; [oth. writ.] Just shy of one year ago writing was only a hidden desire. I now have a growing poem collection and a solid beginning for my first book; [pers.] I used to have an urge to write that was overpowered by my belief that "I was not an author", now that I take advantage of this writing urge I have found new enjoyment and great satisfaction. [a.] Ontario, Canada.

RUSCH, KIMBERLY
[b.] May 10, 1979, Mercy Hospital, Janesville, WI.; [p.] Nancy and Leonard Rusch; [ed.] Attending high school; [occ.] Student; [hon.] Promoted from 8th grade with honors and high honors throughout my middle school career; [pers.] Never let anything or anyone stand in your way. Strive to be your best. I was greatly influenced by my 5th and 6th grade teachers, my mom and my dad. [a.] Milton, WI.

RUSINAK, ERICA
[pen.] Erica Lynn; [b.] June 20, 1980, Staten Island, New York; [p.] Mike and Lynn Rusinak; [ed.] Our Lady Star of The Sea; [oth. writ.] "Flowers", "Love", "Bitter End", "Understand", "Get It Straight"; [pers.] "I base my poems on life". [a.] Staten Island, NY.

RUSNAK, JOYCE M.
[pen.] Marjorie Joy; [b.] November 20, 1947, Cleveland, Ohio; [ed.] Baldwin-Wallace College; [occ.] Elementary teacher; [memb.] Society for Children's Book Writers and Illustrators; [oth. writ.] What Do You Think? A book of poems designed to stimulate childrens' creative thinking skills is currently being submitted for publication. [a.] Olmsted Falls, OH.

RUSSELL, MALCOLM M.
[pen.] M.M. Russell; [b.] August 6, 1925, Millinockett, Maine; [p.] Harry and Emma Russell; [m.] Lorraine Russell, July 28, 1950; [ch.] Wayne Sterling, Deborah and Gail; [ed.] University of Maine (Portland); [occ.] Muralist; [oth. writ.] Presently involved in writing a novel titled The Evolutionary Spiral; [pers.] The thoughts of man should never be restrained by "Belief Systems" of any kind, to do so not only restricts new knowledge but may deny absolutely access to his true potential. [a.] Port Charlotte, FL.

RUTLEDGE, NANCY LOUISE
[b.] March 24, 1939, Moberly, Missouri; [p.] Ben and Maedean Colley; [m.] Mervin D. Rutledge, December 22, 1954; [ch.] Jody Heather; [ed.] Abraham Lincoln High, Highline College; [occ.] Homemaker; [pers.] Poetry is an artform of the soul depicting life against the backdrop of time. Nature, a great teacher, is often my inspiration. [a.] Mossy Rock, WA.

RYAN, GARRY
[b.] Calgary, Albert Canada; [m.] Sharon; [ch.] Karma and Ben; [occ.] Teacher. [a.] Calgary, Alberta.

RYAN, LINDA L.
[b.] September 21, 1952, Clarion, Iowa; [p.] Joseph and Beverly Lane; [m.] Michael Ryan, May 28, 1983; [ch.] Deirdre Erin, Katie Elizabeth, Christopher Michael; [ed.] Boone Valley High, B.A. Buena Vista College, M.A.-Northeast Missouri State, graduate Endorsement-University of Dubuque; [occ.] Elementary Special Education teacher, West Delaware School; [memb.] Young Democrats, I.S.E.A., N.E.A.; [oth. writ.] Several other poems and beginning a romance novel; [pers.] Whatever I write must reflect honest feelings and must be understood by the average reader of I have lost my audience. [a.] Manchester, IA.

RYDER, STARR
[b.] June 16, 1981, Newport, Rhode Island; [p.] Richard Martin and Doreen Carol Newman Ryder; [ed.] Attending 7th grade; [pers.] I enjoy writing poems about nature and world difficulties. [a.] Norfolk, VA.

RYE, ADRIENNE S.
[b.] September 12, 1978, Philadelphia, Pennsylvania; [p.] Paul J. and Cathy-Jo Rys; [ed.] 10th grade, high school student (Eastern High School); [occ.] Student; [memb.] Student Council, cheerleading squad. [a.] Voorhees, NJ.

RYEL, MARY L.
[b.] April 4, 1912, Trenton, NJ; [p.] John and Matilda Moran (deceased); [m.] Ray Ryel (deceased), August 17, 1935; [ch.] Ray, Vince and John Ryel; [ed.] Grade and what the world gave me; [occ.] Retired. [a.] Trenton, NJ.

SAFFEL, SABRINA ANNE
[b.] Las Vegas, NV.; [p.] Robert and Mary Saffel; [memb.] President of International Club; [hon.] Merit award in World of Poetry, Dean's List-Honor Roll, several Cellist Awards, National Honor Society; [oth. writ.] Poem published in World of Poetry. [a.] Las Vegas, NV.

SALONEN, JR, NORMAN C.
[b.] May 5, 1965, Seattle, Washington; [p.] Aloha and Norman Salonen; [ed.] Meadowdale High School; [oth. writ.] Various unpublished stories and poems; [pers.] For me, poetry is a mental and spiritual release of my innermost emotions and imagination, all of which I am pleased to share. [a.] Everett, WA.

SAMEDOV, AHMET
[pen.] A. Samedov; [b.] December 2, 1967; [ed.] B.A. Rutgers University; [a.] Vineland, NJ.

SAMS, DARLENE
[b.] July 15, 1943, Dayton, Ohio; [p.] Roy and Mable Koon (deceased); [m.] George F. Sams, Jr., August 21, 1963; [ch.] George Sams, III, Darla Sams (Rose) and Jason Sams; [ed.] Stivers High School, Dayton, Ohio; [occ.] Homemaker; [memb.] "ASCAP", Boystown, Christian Appalachian Projects; [hon.] Published song "This Is America" 1992; [oth. writ.] "Love is Like A Rose", Whisper in The Wind, Library of Poetry, numerous songs and poems on copyright; [pers.] "If I have touched one heart I've done my part for God". [a.] Tipp CIty, OH.

SAMS, MARIE
[b.] May 29, 1907, Springfield, Nebraska; [m.] Duane Sams (deceased), June 9, 1935; [ch.] Judith LaRee Starkey, daughter; [ed.] BA degree, Eastern NM College, Portales, NM; [occ.] Teacher (retired, 1971); [memb.] Delta Kappa Gamma (30 years), AARP, Retired Teachers, Methodist Women; [hon.] Service pins, Artesia N.M. public schools, Methodist Women; [oth. writ.] Artesia Daily Press, local events (in verse), personal booklet (Ramblin' Rhythm) printed by Bryan Printers, Artesia. [a.] Carlsbad, NM.

SAMTANI, PREETI RAJ
[b.] October 25, 1980, Queens, New York; [p.] Pushma and Raj Samtani; [ed.] St. Mary's High School; [memb.] Howard Scripps National Spelling Bee, got excellent rating in the National Federation Junior Festival; [hon.] Spelling Merit, musical achievement, Honor Roll, most improved tennis player; [oth. writ.] Many short stories and poems, only two have been published. [a.] Alexandria, VA.

SAMUELS, LAURA JODI
[b.] November 29, 1981, Queens, New York; [p.] Jeanette and Jack Samuels; [ed.] P.S. 26; [occ.] Student; [pers.] Ever since I was in 3rd grade, I've been writing poetry. I enjoy writing poems of my own, it makes me feel good inside.

SANCA, ANA JULIA MACEDO
[pen.] "Tunga"; [b.] March 20, 1949, Cabo Verde; [p.] Caetano Monteiro de Macedo; [ch.] Sibila Macedo Pires; [ed.] High school diploma; [occ.] Consular officer at The Consulate General of Portugal; [memb.] YMCA; [hon.] Honors in Social Service worker (Bachelor degree) award in Women in Literature 1992, in Italy, Cita di Penne; [oth. writ.] Poems and articles published in local and exterior newspapers and magazines, being part of several anthologies; [pers.] If each one of us can identify with the vital interests of the people each one of us can understand and define mankind's common destiny. [a.] Toronto, Ontario Canada.

SANCHEZ, MARIA
[pen.] Mercy; [b.] October 14, 1977, San Antonio, Texas; [p.] Carlos A. and Maria A. Sanchez, III;[ed.] Ira Odgen Elementary, Washington Irving Middle School; [occ.] Student; [memb.] National Junior Honor Society; [hon.] Perfect Attendance, Honor Roll, Science Fair, Pre-freshman Engineer Program; [oth. writ.] Poems published in the Ira Odgen newspaper; [pers.] The best way to express yourself in life is to write poems about life. [a.] San Antonio, TX.

SANCHEZ, VERONICA PAULINE
[pen.] Veroniqua Pauleen Sanchez; [b.] September 29, 1974, Denver, Colorado; [p.] Becky Sanchez Ortega; [ed.] Adams City High School, freshman at Metropolitan State College of Denver; [memb.] Hispanic Women's Caucus, Latin American Education Foundation; [hon.] Solano Scholarship, four years varsity tennis award; [oth. writ.] Several poems, narratives and scripts; [pers.] I write only what I know, only what I live, that way life's true lessons are felt, by other's who read my writings. [a.] Commerce City, CO.

SANDERS, LUCRETIA JANE
[b.] April 25,1920, San Antonio, Texas; [p.] Mr. and Mrs. Truman A. Morins; [m.] Deceased, November 2, 1937; [ch.] Charles E. Sanders and Pamela J. Gallante; [ed.] High school and licensed to sell Real Estate and insurance; [occ.] Retired; [memb.] Christian Renewal Church, Salem, MA. [oth. writ.] Published book of poetry and has written approx. 100 poems and some songs. Poems published in church and ministry newsletters; [pers.] I seek to witness to others through the poems the Lord has inspired in me. To reach many with the message of His love, mercy and grace. [a.] Groveland, MA.

SANDIFER, WILLIE
[b.] March 9, 1971, Huntsville, Alabama; [p.] Elnora Sandifer and Willie Joiner; [ed.] Lee High School, Phillips Junior College; [occ.] Computer Operator; [oth. writ.] Two poems that were entered in two different contests and they are both in the process of being published; [pers.] Life is what you make it and you can attain success by hard work. [a.] Huntsville, AL.

SANDOMENICO, MILDRED E.
[b.] August 11, 1901, Albany, New York; [p.] Alexander P. LaPointe and Marie Louise Hogue; [m.] Widow, November 19, 1948; [ch.] 3 from previous marriage, Robert H., William F. and Roger W.; [ed.] High School of Art, Fawcett School of Industrial Art, Newark, NJ.; [occ.] Retired 1969, CUNY, Hihehman College of Adm. Asst.; [memb.] Pt. Pleasant Playshop 1936-1943, (N.J.) West Pasco Art Guild, New Port Richey, Fl. 1972-1982; [oth. writ.] Poem-"Quest", The American Poetry Annual-1991 Edition, The Observer Seasonal Weekly, Breton Woods, NJ., 1937-40 edition, The observer, VHF. Proj. Eng. Adex, AAC-Allenhurst, NJ, 1943-45. [a.] Mandsquan, NJ.

SARGENT, DON E.
[b.] August 21, 1976, Laurel, Mississippi; [p.] Everett and Sandra Sargent; [ed.] Conroe High School; [memb.] CHS band, CHS debate team; [hon.] 1st division ratings at solo and ensemble, 2nd division ratings at state solo and ensemble,poetry recognition; [oth. writ.] Unpublished; [pers.] The virtues and secrets in life are very well hidden, with a lot of hard work the help of God, they will become clear to you. [a.] Conroe, TX.

SAUNDERS, MARGARETTE J.
[pen.] Margarette COmbs Saunders; [b.] October 3, 1925, Atlanta, Georgia; [p.] Edwards Combs (deceased), Parthenia Combs West (deceased) and Rev. M. West (deceased); [m.] Alfred J. Saunders, January 10, 1943; [ch.] Two adult sons, Donald and Mark; [ed.] Eustis (Fla.) Voc. High, Cambridge Tech. College and School of the Arts (England), Eastern Washington State University, Cheney, Washington, California State University, Los Angeles; [occ.] Retired high school and community college, England teacher; [memb.] California Retired Teachers' Association, International Society of Poets; [hon.] Valedictorian of my high school graduating class, dean's list at Eastern, advisor, Ontario (CA) High School Lit. Club, coordinator, Gifted Students' Program, Montclair (CA) High School; [oth. writ.] One Silver Award (1986), three Golden Awards (1987,1988, 1989) for poems, World of Poetry, pub.; [pers.] I am motivated strongly by the American Romanticists and Transcendentalist, especially Bryant and Thoreau. I believe that if one "steps to the beat of his own drummer", all will be well. [a.] Tacoma, WA.

SAUNDERE, WILLIAM A.
[b.] February 18, 1965, Weirton, West Virginia; [p.] William C. and Anna Mae Saunders; [m.] Marla K. Saunders, October 12,1985; [ch.] Troy M. Saunders; [ed.] Brooke High School, 1983 graduate; [oth. writ.] Several other poems on various subjects; [pers.] I enjoy being able to express my thoughts on paper for other people to read. [a.] Colliers, WV.

SAUR, CAROLYN
[b.] April 18, 1976, Jackson, Michigan; [p.] Thomas and Kathleen Gillahan-Saur; [ed.] Dearborn Heights Montessori Snow Elementary (Dearborn) School, Stout Junior High (Dearborn), Edsel Ford High School, senior year 1993-94; [memb.] Michigan Metro Girl Scouts; [hon.] 1st place Science Fair, Silver Leadership Pin-Girl Scouts, Honor Roll student, Fermata's singing choir, Fairlance Ballet Company, Dearborn. [a.]

SAUVE, MARC
[b.] November 25, 1966, Ottawa, Ontario; [p.] Michel Sauve and Lucille Courchesne; [m.] Still searching and still waiting; [ch.] Still hopeful; [oth. writ.] Currently working on a collection of my poetry; [pers.] Savor everyday as though it were your last and never stop searching for the one. [a.] Aylmer, Quebec Canada.

SAVAGE, MARILYN
[pen.] Marilea Wells; [b.] April 1, 1943, Princeton, BC Canada; [p.] Antonia and Johnny Wells, Summerland, BC Canada; [m.] Earl Keith Savage, February 27, 1965; [ch.] Leilani Marie and Laurel Ann; [occ.] Early Childhood Ed. Teacher, mother, secretary, sales clerk and gas jockey; [memb.] Catholic Women's League, Social Justice Committee - 1990-91, Issues (women's shelter, food bank, Inner City Poor Hampers); [hon.] Poem published in World of Poetry, California U.S.A., Golden Award twice and Silver twice, Honorable Mention 5 years in a row, Edie-Lou Cole, Editor; [oth. writ.] Make most all occasion cards for friends and relatives. articles in Alberta Report and The Mirror, story of Neighborliness in Native Paper Windspeaker; [pers.] I am thankful for the gift of faith from my dear mom and used my sensitivity as woman to love all people as we're called to love. Blessings to our world... [a.] Edmonton, AB T5A 3R4 Canada.

SAVIANO, SCOTT
[b.] May 9, 1967, Worcester; [p.] James and C. Cynthia Saviano; [m.] Angda Caprioli (fiancee, girlfriend of 10 years, high school sweetheart); [ed.] Holy

Name Central Catholic High School, University of Massachusetts _BA major economics minor history - political science; [occ.] Work as a sales agent at Mount Snow Ski Resort in Vermont; [memb.] To the Domain of Mother Nature; [oth. writ.] Nothing published, many love poems, my high school sweetheart and journals of trips to Alaska, Germany, Holland, Sweden, France and England and all over the United States. Journal of sailing the New England coast and hiking the Long Trail/Vermont; [pers.] Follow your bliss, wherever it may lead!!! [a.] Amherst, MA.

SAVIO, CAROLINE
[b.] March 15, 1979, Livingston, New Jersey; [p.] Anibal and Maria Amalia Savio; [ed.] Presently attending 9th grade Ridgewood High School; [memb.] West Side Presbyterian Church choir in Ridgewood; [hon.] Presidential Academic Fitness Award. [a.] Ridgewood, NJ.

SAXON, KAREN M.
[b.] August 20, 1960, Mobile, Alabama; [p.] John W. and Doris McGahagin; [m.] Steven H. Saxon, November 9, 1984; [ch.] Amber Michelle, Kimberly Paige and Ashley Brooke; [ed.] Hawkinsville High School; [occ.] Private Detective; [hon.] Who's Who Among American High School Students, 1977, Hawkinsville High School; [oth. writ.] Several others, to numerous to list, most recent "Davey" (a tribute to Davey Allison who died tragically, July 13, 1993); [pers.] I mostly write about my own life and experiences. [a.] Birmingham, AL.

SAXON, FRED
[b.] May 17, 1942, Lewistown, Philadelphia; [p.] James R. and Goldie S. Saxon; [m.] Sue Ellen, October 10, 1964; [ch.] Stewart, Mark and Jennifer; [ed.] Lewistown High School, Bloomsburg University, BS; [occ.] English teacher, Lewistown Area High School; [memb.] PA Council of Teachers of English, Association of Teachers of English Grammar, B.P.O.E. # 663, Commonwealth Partnership Fellow; [hon.] Outstanding Young Man of America-1976, Outstanding Young Educator-1967; [oth. writ.] Poems and short stories published in college literary magazine, poetry published in Poet's Corner of local newspaper; [pers.] the ideas for my poetry are spontaneous, usually coming while I'm working, driving or fishing. I enjoy writing about the everyday things and events we encounter in life. I write in traditional meter and free verse. [a.] Lewistown, PA.

SCHAEFFER, MARY L.
[b.] Waverly, New York; [p.] Alfred and Julia Cain McGrade; [m.] Jacob H. Schaeffer; [ch.] Daniel Sean Schaeffer; [ed.] B.A., S.U.N.Y. Albany, M.Ed. Loyola; [occ.] English Department Chair, Huntington Park High School and Pit Bull Terrier breeder; [memb.] E.B.A., I.W.P.A., I.W.T.A. and U.T.L.A.; [hon.] Numerous as a breeder of champion dogs and an A.D.B.A. judge; [oth. writ.] A variety on dogs; [pers.] I'm fascinated by the bizarre aspects of our existence, influenced by Arnaud Daniel, Thackeray, Galsworthy, James Dickey, etc. [a.] Los Angeles and Tehachapi, CA.

SCHEER, JILL M.
[b.] July 31, 1961, Fremont, Nebrasak; [p.] William C. and Delarine Johnson; [m.] Brian Scheer, March 27, 1982; [ch.] Eric Brian; [ed.] Fremont Senior High School; [occ.] Mother/farm wife; [oth. writ.] Collection of non-published children's poems, recently completed a light-hearted (but true) humorous, rhyming children's story about our son's "very special" puppy; [pers.] Being fortunate enough to be a non-working mother, I am living each day and re-discovering nature through the innocent eyes of our child. each piece of my writing has come from something that in some way has touched Eric's life. [a.] Fremont, NE.

SCHIESS, MELISSA
[pen.] Melissa Schiess; [b.] November 6, 1978, Englewood, New Jersey; [p.] Donald and Deborah Schiess; [ed.] Cresskill High School; [occ.] Student; [memb.] Cresskill High School Yearbook Staff, S.A.V.E. (Students Against Violating the Earth), Cresskill High School basketball cheerleading squad, Cresskill High School football cheerleading squad; [hon.] Presidential Academic Fitness Award, Cresskill High School Honor Roll, St, Barnabus Burn Foundation Poster award winner, Award of Merit -Cresskill Fire Department; [pers.] I strive to express my feelings and depth of emotions through words and short story. Most of my writings are of heartfelt memories. [a.] Cresskill, NJ.

SCHILD, DONNA-MARIA VERONECA
[b.] April 8, 1957, Fort Monmouth, NJ.; [p.] Joseph A. and Viola T. Conzalina; [m.] Daniel James Schild, February 14, 1987; [ch.] Katrina Whitney, Anthony James and Anastasia Morgan; [ed.] Monmouth Regional High School, Barbizon Modeling School; [occ.] Owner of Heartwind Creations, illustrator; [memb.] Trinity Christian Church, A.C.O.A.; [hon.] 4th grade essay regarding Prejudice hung for public display at Fort Monmouth, NJ.; [oth. writ.] Poems and articles published locally, song writer; [pers.] I searched inside my heart to see, and faith reflected back at me. His image of support divine -the greatest gift "seek and ye shall find". [a.] Summerville, SC.

SCHILLINGER, DAVID FLOYD
[b.] March 30, 1953, Moline, Illinois; [m.] Cheryl Schillinger; [ch.] Dawn, Angie, Shannon and Veronica; [oth. writ.] 11 songs and 3 poems all non-published; [pers.] Inspiring me were artists such as "Buddy Holly" and "Peter, Paul and Mary". This is my first published poem.

SCHMIDT, HELEN E.
[b.] August 29, 1900, Meeker, Oklahoma; [p.] Daniel and Edna Sweet Emley; [m.] Frank H. Schmidt, Exec. Vice President, United California Bank, June 18, 1924; [ch.] Helen Lee Schmidt Gibson and Betty Faye Schmidt Vossler; [ed.] Graduate of Normal and Business College Grand Island, Nebr., attended College of Music , U.S.C., English courses; [occ.] Retired; [memb.] First Pres. Church of Hollywood, Assistant League of Southern California, The Ebell of Los Angeles, president for two years; [pers.] Wherever one is, I feel that place should be a happier, better place because one is there. Enhance life for oneself and others, and don't forget to thank God for our many blessings. [a.] Los Angeles.

SCHMIESING, SARAH
[b.] February 20, 1980, Melrose, Minnesota; [p.] Phil and Deb Schmiesing; [ed.] Paynesville Area Public Schools, District 741; [occ.] Student at Paynesville Area Public Schools, District 741; [memb.] FLA (Future Leaders of America); [hon.] School Honor Roll, school spelling bee participant; [oth. writ.] Many poems and stories unpublished and unknown to many; [pers.] Live on a dairy farm with parents and two younger brothers. [a.] Paynesville, MN.

SCHMOYER, GLADYS A.
[b.] July 23, 1916, Allentown, Pennsylvania; [p.] Edward and Laura LaWall; [m.] Alvin H. Schmoyer, March 8, 1957; [ch.] David Edward Miller; [ed.] Allentown High, Temple University; [occ.] Doctor of Podiatry, retired; [memb.] Episcopal Church of the Mediator; [pers.] Due to failing eyesight before the final successful operation I found consolation in expressing my thoughts of compassion, happy memories in writing poetry. [a.] Allentown, PA.

SCHNETZ, CHRISTINE MARIE
[b.] February 21, 1979, Sacramento, California; [p.] Earl and Sylvia Schnetz; [ed.] Brookfield Elementary School, Christian Brothers High School; [occ.] Student; [pers.] I enjoy writing about the simple things in life, things most people take for granted. [a.] Sacramento, CA.

SCHRAIDER, ROBIN
[b.] December 8, 1959, Berkeley, California; [p.] Johann and Lynn Schroettner; [m.] None-yet; [ed.] Aca Lanes High, Diablo Valley College; [occ.] Actor; [memb.] Screen Actor's Guild, Songwriters' Guild; [oth. writ.] Love's Loss, published in 1993, "All My Tomorrows"; [pers.] I feel my poetry, song writing is an extension of my talent given to me by my Lord Jesus and hopefully I can share with others. [a.] Lafayette, CA.

SCHROYER, JENNIFER
[b.] July 6, 1981, Cincinnati, OH; [p.] Mary and Greg Schroyer; [ed.] Immaculate Heart od Mary; [occ.] Student.

SCHULER, JOYCE J. BOYER
[b.] January 29, 1951, Johnstown, Pennsylvania; [p.] Margaret Ann Anderson and James Galvin Boyer; [m.] Charles L. Schuler, May 22, 1971; [ch.] Charles Scott and Jason Ryan Schuler; [ed.] Woodham High School, Pensacola, Florida, Hillsborough Community College, Plant City, Florida; [occ.] Executive Secretary; [memb.] (PSI) Professional Secretaries International, CPS Academy, National Association for Executive Secretaries, National Notary Association, (AMA) American Management Association; [hon.] (CPS) Certified Professional Secretary, (CAM) Certified Administrative Manager, received "Secretary of the Year" from PSA, elected Florida State Coordinator by National Notary Association; [oth. writ.] Several poems in USF, "Oracle", HCC "Galeria", several newspapers, one poem won first place on radio promotion with one week "all expense paid" trip to Amsterdam; [pers.] My inspiration has been my husband and my children. [a.] Tampa, FL.

SCHWARTZ, STWART
[b.] December 14, 1968, Jamaica, NY.; [p.] Roy and Rita Schwartz; [m.] Janet Schwartz, June 13, 1992; [ed.] Technical studies, Southern State Community College; [occ.] Restaurant Manager. [a.] Dodge City, KS.

SCOTT, ELIZABETH
[b.] June 8, 1978, Fort Bragg, NC.; [p.] William and Debra Scott; [ed.] Attending Westover Senior High School, Fayetteville, NC.; [memb.] National Junior Honor Society. [a.] Fayetteville, NC.

SCOTT, JOHN M.
[b.] September 1, 1928, Lynn, MA; [p.] Deceased; [m.] Frances W. Scott, June 27, 1953; [ch.] Catherine Elizabeth, Larry M. and Julia Anne Trout; [ed.] A.B. Union College 1950, M.Div. Nashotah House 1953, D. Min. Eastern Baptist Theo. Sem. 1987; [occ.] Priest of The Episcopal Church, now retired as Rector of a parish; [memb.] Third Order, Society of St. Francis (Anglican), National Parks and Conservation Association; [hon.] Minister General's Award for "faithful service 2nd public witness of Franciscan Way of Life"; [oth. writ.] Research, (1) 1987 Attitudes to Female Leadership (D.Min. Thesis), (2.) 1990 Significance of Twenty-five Year Rectorates, also Franciscan Times 1993, poem and essay "For Love of St. Clare"; [pers.] Express Franciscan spirituality in one world, one earth. [a.] Philadelphia, PA.

SCOTT, KAREN ELD
[b.] January 30, 1969, Silver Spring, Maryland; [p.] Edward A. and Lois Eld; [m.] Thomas Leo Scott, III, March 28, 1994; [ed.] University of Maryland, College Park 1991; [occ.] Supervisor of Customer Service and Dispatch-TVCN Wireless Cable, Denver, CO.; [oth. writ.] Numerous unpublished poems, songs and short stories; [pers.] Most of my writing centers around children or young adults. I believe that childhood is both beautiful and painful, to relive this is humbling. [a.] Lafayette, CO.

SCOTT, LYNNE F.
[b.] May 15, 1956, Leesburg, Florida; [p.] Dr. and Mrs. W.D. Finlayson, Jr.; [m.] Brian R. Scott, March 22, 1980; [ch.] Adam Nathan (12 years) and Jacob William (10 years); [ed.] Auburn University-Auburn, Ala.; [occ.] A very proud wife and homeschooling mother of my two sons; [oth. writ.] "Children of Wrath", published by Sparrowgrass Poetry Forum, Inc.; [pers.] Before I write anything, I always stop and ask my Lord what it is He wished me to say. Almost without exception I write about children or young adults. As parents it scares me that we seem to be raising a lost generation of youth. At times when I write, I envision these youth and my heart literally breaks. So much of my writing comes from that broken heart, as well as from a heart filled with joy from my own two sons. [a.] Arab, AL.

SCOTT, SUSAN L.
[pen.] Sue Scott; [b.] September 4, 1957, Ava, New York; [m.] Jeff Scott, October 4, 1975; [a.] Boonville, NY.

SEAMANS, PATRICK WILLIAM
[b.] February 9, 1952, Munich, Germany; [p.] William Albert and Francine Seamans; [ed.] University of Southern California, Ph.D. International Education and Philosophy (4.0 GPA), current student, Beta Kappa Chapter, Phi Beta Delta Honor Society for International Scholars-1993, University of California, Berkeley-Master of Architecture Degree (honor student-3.6 GPA)-1975, University of California, Berkeley-Bachelor of Architecture, Cum Laude (3.6 GPA)-1975, honor student and recipient of Cal Disabled Alumni Scholarship-1975, Bowling Green State University, Ohio-major in Industrial Technology (Dean's List -2 years) 1971-73, founder, Photography Club -1972; [occ.] International Education; [memb.] National Council of Architectural Registration Boards Certificate # 40,822, 1991 to present, State of California Registered Architect # CO17324, 1986 to present, Ital Computers, Ltd.-Certificate of Completion, Basic AutoCad II-1992, Academie d'Orleans, France -Certificate of Professional Aptitude: Industrial Drafting-1971, Award of Excellence in State Examination, Academie de Paris, France-Certificate of Professional Aptitude: Metallurgical Drafting-1971; [hon.] Professional of the Year Award-California Governor's Committee for the Employment of Persons with Disabilities-1993, International Who's Who of Intellectuals-11th Editions-1993, Men of Achievement-Sixteen Edition-1993, Dictionary of International Biography-1993, Who's Who in Young American Professionals-1991, founder, President and Network Coordinator-HIAN, Los Angeles-1988, member, American Institute of Architects (A.I.A.), participation in Los Angeles Chapter-1986-88; [pers.] I believe that writing poetry is the discovery of self's goodness and other's goodness. [a.] Los Angeles, CA.

SEAY, HELEN M.
[b.] February 27, 1919; [oth. writ.] Short stories, fables and poems. I write about idealism, joy, nostalgia, pain, irony, love and the human condition; [pers.] Special loves; children and nature in all its forms. [a.] Baltimore, MD.

SEEBER, APRIL FAY
[pen.] Gypsie Marcello; [b.] October 29, 1975, Oak Ridge, Tennessee; [p.] Judi and Gray Argo; [ed.] Still in high school, soon be a senior; [occ.] Certified Nurses Aid; [memb.] Member and secretary of Warren Count Eagles Club, McMinnville Church of Christ; [oth. writ.] I have lost of other writing, most of them come from a state of deep concentration; [pers.] Poems are purely meditated thoughts from the soul. [a.] McMinnville, TN.

SEEMAN, ELGIE V. (MRS.)
[pen.] Elgie V. Seeman (Mrs.); [b.] January 31, 1901, Weldville, Wisconsin; [p.] William J and Lena Jane Tomlin (deceased); [m.] William R. Seeman (deceased), August 2, 1924; [ch.] William Tomlin Seeman (deceased) and William Robert Seeman; [ed.] University of Wisconsin, Mineral Point High School, Wisconsin; [occ.] Retired; [memb.] Immanuel Lutheran Church, AAUW, Women's Club of Madison Wisconsin, etc., Civic Club of Madison; [hon.] Anthology, Syndicated column "Center Post" prayer at Methodist Retirement Center, Madison, Wisconsin; [oth. writ.] Many poems, not published, staff of "Center Post" 8 years; [pers.] This poem is special to me for it was written and dedicated to my granddaughter and her husband read at their wedding reception on June 4, 1993. [a.] Madison, WI.

SEFTON, CATHERINE M.
[b.] Amsterdam, New York; [p.] Bruno and Barbara Czech; [ed.] B.S. in Chemistry, M.S. in Computer Science; [occ.] Manager of Information Technology Group for High Tech Corp.; [hon.] Bausch and Laumb Science Award, Dean's List, Cum Laude graduate; [oth. writ.] Numerous writings have been presented to friends as gifts or written to commemorate an event or occasion; [pers.] My writing is my attempt to capture, express and share life experiences, observations and reflections. These writings are shared to bring understanding and humor often to others. [a.] North Grafton, MA.

SEGUIN, DELLA MARY
[b.] October 6, 1927, Cohoes, New York; [p.] George Murray Shear and Ruth Agnes Kessler; [m.] George Elzear Seguin, September 2, 1946; [ch.] Glenn George and David Francis Seguin; [ed.] SAt. Patrick's Academy, Cohoes High School; [occ.] Office Clerk; [oth. writ.] Two other poems; [pers.] I believe my love for nature and the beauty of the changing seasons are reflected in my three poems I have written.

SHELBY, SHARON DAWN
[b.] February 9, 1973, Winnipeg, Manitoba; [p.] Larry and Glenda Selby. [a.] Mantiou, MB Canada.

SELBY, SUSAN DAWN
[b.] February 9, 1973, Winnipeg, Canada; [ed.] In third year at University of Manitoba; [occ.] Student; [oth. writ.] Poetry for family and friends.

SELBY, SUSAN F.
[b.] Ireland; [p.] Isobell and William Mullin; [m.] Douglas Milford Selby, 1926; [ch.] Geraldine Dayton; [ed.] Bachelors degree from Central Michigan University, masters degree form the University of Michigan also additional credits in elementary education were received in 1959 from Toledo University; [occ.] Retired, former professor; [oth. writ.] Poetry contributions to English Magazine the Triangle, article on Exchange Teaching, Michigan Educational Journal. May 1949; [pers.] I believe that all things work together for good in our eyes. [a.] Leesburg, FL.

SELF, CAROL ANN
[pen.] Carol Gulke Self; [b.] November 3, 1942, Oaks, North Dakota; [p.] Theodore and Margaret Anderson Gulke; [ch.] Kari Jo Hawkins and Scott William Self; [ed.] Moundsview High, Snead State Junior College, University of Alabama; [occ.] Buyer-Mueller CO., Albertville, AL; [memb.] American Quarter Horse Association; [hon.] President's List, Highest Honor-Snead St. graduation; [oth. writ.] Several stories in Gadsden Times, Cowboy's Christmas (1st prize), Christmas Memories, The Rustler, unpublished; [pers.] Upon opening my eyes each morning, I'm thankful God has given me another day to enjoy my family, friends, farm, horses and the world. [a.] Altoona, AL.

SELLECK, ARTHUR P.
[b.] November 24, 1912, Los Angeles, CA.; [p.] David Arthur and Josephine Cecelia Selleck; [m.] Marguerite Oxley Selleck, January 1, 1939; [ch.] Donald, Kathryn and Marguerite; [ed.] University of California, Berkeley AB, MA; [occ.] High school Science and Mathematics Teacher, retired; [memb.] COmmonwealth Club of California, California Retired Teachers Association, St. Luke's United Methodist Church, Sons in Retirement of Northern California; [hon.] Phi Delta Kappa. [a.] Richmond, CA.

SERRANO, IVAMARIE
[pen.] Chloe Benjamin; [b.] October 8, 1968, Cleveland, OH; [p.] Daniel S. and Lorraine E. Strollo; [m.]

Andres Serrano, Jr., November 22, 1987; [ch.] Benjamin; [ed.] Cloverleaf Senior High; [occ.] Bank teller/housewife; [hon.] Award for short story in high school; [oth. writ.] Several poems, unpublished, one short story, currently working on novel; [pers.] When I write, I try to express my feelings and thoughts in a way that I can hide them, yet make them stand out. My favorite poem-Remember -by Christina Georgina Rosseti. [a.] Lakewood, OH.

SEVANDAL, MARCIANA ASIS
[pen.] Mars Sagun or Marian Ambil; [b.] March 9, 1912, Catarman, Samar, Philippines; [p.] (father) Ambrosio Ambil Asis and (mother) Dominga De Los Reyes Sagun (both deceased); [m.] Simeon Enriquez Sevandal (deceased), November 30, 1935; [ch.] Patrialenda A., Libertad A., Virgilio A., Rizalina A., Simeon A., Violeta A., and Adelpha A. Sevandal; [ed.] Master of Arts (26 units, no thesis), Bachelor of Science in Elementary Education or BSEED, with ETC or Elementary Teacher's Certificate; [occ.] Retired Public Schools District Supv.; [memb.] Civil and Religious Organizations, particularly the PPSTA and the CWL and the Soc. for the Prop. of Faith; [hon.] World of Poetry Awards, Who Is Who in Poetry, 1st honors in the grades, Valedictorian in high school; [oth. writ.] Playlets: World Brotherhood, Royalty In My Native Land, newsletter and orations and declamations; [pers.] Use your time profitably, it it the stuff life is made of. Do not put all your eggs in one basket, if the basket falls you lose all the eggs. [a.] San Francisco, CA.

SEWARD, KEKOA
[b.] May 10, 1979, Papeete, Tahiti French Polynesia; [p.] Jeff and Haunani Seward, grandparents Joe and Jean Seward, Henry and Elizabeth Azeka; [sib.] One sister, Mahinahina, age 4; [ed.] Will be entering Dunn Upper School as a freshman in the fall/93; [occ.] (hobbies) Deep-sea fishing with grandpa in Hawaii, have played baseball continuously since age 6 as pitcher, 1st baseman and centerfielder; [hon.] Selected to attend "Na Pua No'eau" summer institute in Hilo, Hi. for gifted and talented native Hawaiian children; [oth. writ.] Various poems, essays and several children's books, none of which have yet been published; [pers.] I try to conduct myself according to the Hawaiian saying, "I Mua" which means, "to push forward or to be a leader". [a.] Santa Ynez, CA.

SEXTON, LAURA
[b.] June 15, 1976, Sparta, NC.; [p.] William Ray and Alma Jo Sexton; [ed.] Senior at Grayson County High School; [memb.] Students Organization for Developing Attitudes, Beta Club, FBLA; [hon.] Two times in Who's Who Among American High School Students; [pers.] Face each day with a positive outlook on life. [a.] Troutdale, VA.

SHADWELL III, WILLIAM J.
[b.] April 4, 1957, Orange, NJ.; [p.] William J. and Martha J. Shadwell; [m.] Patricia Shadwell, March 17, 1987; [ch.] Jennifer Ann, William Joseph, Joseph David and Jillian Lee; [ed.] Montclair Kimberly Academy, Thomas Edison State College; [occ.] Sales; [memb.] Boys and Girls Club of Clifton, Men's Club -Vice President; [pers.] Each day offers infinite possibilities, choose the best one at the time and pursue it vigorously. [a.] Clifton, NJ.

SHANKS, GREGG
[b.] December 12, 1975, Burlington, Ontario Canada; [p.] Elaine Rhodes and Colin Shanks; [ed.] Currently attending final year of high school at Burlington Central High School; [pers.] My work is to me, a commentary on the world that surrounds me and the conditions it forces us all to live in. I dedicate this poem to Mr. Regan Heffernan, the English teacher who showed me what I could become. [a.] Burlington, Ontario Canada;

SHANNON, JOYCE ANN
[pen.] Joyce A. Shannon; [b.] February 6, 1935, St. Louis, MO.; [p.] Noble Ceaser and Joseph Lee Bass; [m.] Leon Shannon, Sr., August 8, 1985; [ch.] Kathy Washington, Audrey Chaney, Patty Glenn and James Washington, III; [ed.] St. Alphonsus Rock High, Forest Park Community College; [occ.] Writer, homemaker; [memb.] SLPC, St. Louis Poetry Center; [hon.] Sams family award and Mother of the Year; [oth. writ.] Tender Touches, Sunnyside Up, Rainbows Edge, From My Heart; [pers.] Unconditional love, always be fair. [a.] St. Louis, MO.

SHARAR, HELEN NICHOLS
[b.] August 8, 1931, Long Branch, NJ.; [p.] Stanley Nichols and Consuelo Nichols Ryan; [m.] Paul H. Sharar, June 19, 1954; [ch.] Carol, Connie and Linda Sharar, Kathryn Prusinski; [ed.] B.A., Ohio Wesleyan University; [occ.] Teacher and social worker; [memb.] College Club of Ridgewood, NJ., United Methodist Women, Inter-religions Fellowship for the Homeless, Habitat for Humanity; [pers.] The rights of children and other issues of social justice are of primary importance to me. My poetry often reflects my thoughts and feelings concerning these subjects. [a.] Glen Rock, NJ.

SHASHAANI, AVIDEH
[occ.] Author, lecturer, trainer, instructor; [memb.] East Coast Rep/P.R., M.T.O. Shahmaghsoudi, East Coast Managing Director, Wayfinders Inc., Founding member, Women International Network (WIN) for Community Development, founding member/director, For the Future of Our Children, board chair, Refugee Women in Development Inc., V.P., Literary Friends of the DC Public Library; [oth. writ.] Promised Paradise; [pers.] Let's look beyond our gender, race, religion and creed to see our true human dignity which as no boundaries isn't time for the longest hatreds to end and new ones never have a chance to begin again. [a.] Chevy Chase, MD.

SHATOS, TINA MARIE
[pen.] Teena Shatos; [b.] October 15, 1974, Worcester, MA.; [p.] Teresa Shatos; [ed.] Fanning Trade enrolled in Quinsigmamond Community College; [occ.] Student; [pers.] I choose to write about life and love. [a.] Worcester, MA.

SHAW, LEANORA MASSER
[b.] May 11, 1928, Lincoln Co., OK.; [p.] Goldie Brown and Corland Musser; [m.] Billy Ray Shaw, May 17, 1946; [ch.] Belva I. and Carla Fay Shaw; [ed.] Some college; [occ.] Account clerk; [memb.] Veteran of Foreign War Aux, Assembly of God Church, a foster parent to 385 children; [hon.] Award for 14 years of being foster parent; [oth. writ.] 3 other poems never sent for publication; [pers.] When you see something to do, do it with all your heart. [a.] Visalia, CA.

SHAW, RANDY
[b.] March 15, 1949, Florence, SC.; [p.] John Carl and Katie Weatherford Shaw; [m.] Sharon Rose Shaw, June 1971; [ch.] Keith Michael, Client Lee, Misty Mae and Eric Randall Shaw; [ed.] 12 grade; [occ.] Disabled, but I am a guitar player, singer and songwriter; [oth. writ.] I have over 200 songs and poems and I put music to the songs but nothing published; [pers.] Life is a moment in time, to be remembered for good things that help people is a real accomplishment. [a.] Florence, SC.

SHEA, EUGENE V.
[b.] December 28, 1925; [m.] Dixie F. Shea; [occ.] Retired; [oth. writ.] Antidote for Cabin Fever, published -Colonial Press ISBN 1-56883035-1, 160 page paperback collection of original poems, L'Envoi being the final poem. Poems in various local and small publication; [pers.] Poetry should rhyme, poetry should be easily understood, though not necessarily believable, poetry should be for pleasure only, no deep or hidden meanings. [a.] Hanna, WY.

SHEPHERD, DOROTHY
[pen.] Dorothy Shepherd; [b.] February 12, 1927, Fullerton, CA.; [p.] Helen and T.O. Hunt; [m.] Hershell Shepherd, July 3, 1972; [ch.] Donald and William West; [ed.] College, Pomona and La Verne; [occ.] Write, piano player, good cook, active swim, dance, good at rummy; [hon.] Several published news stories, poems, my mother named me Dorothy as her gift from God, I have tried to live up to it; [pers.] I believe in helping anyone who needs it. Have learned that the Lord gave the gift of love to me, from my father. [a.] Colfax, CA.

SHERBAN, ANDREW
[b.] February 2, 1978, Constanta, Romania; [p.] Cecilia and Stefan Serban; [ed.] School Mr. Ig Cromania, Arthur Phillip's High (Sydney, Australia); [occ.] Yr 10 Student; [hon.] Winner of several poem contests in Romania, including "Nicolaelabis" 1989 and 1990; [oth. writ.] Poems published in Romanian newspapers and magazines, poem read on channel 10 TV, Australia and SBS Radio; [pers.] Poems allow me to communicate on any level I desire, in them I find the freedom to be anything I wish to be, do anything I want to do and say the things I want to say most. [a.] NSW 2150 Australia.

SHERWOOD, CONNIE L.
[pen.] Lee Sherwood; [b.] November 20, 1961, Medina, NY.; [p.] Paul and Helen Sherwood; [m.] Richard A. Carnley (fiance), October 9, 1993; [ch.] Anthony David and Brittany Khrystine; [ed.] Niceville Senior High School, Coastline Community College, diplomas awarded in Basic Computer Programming and Writer's Digest School of Short Fiction; [occ.] Corporate Legal Secretary; [memb.] Co-chair events committee; [hon.] President's list, Dean's List; [oth. writ.] Editorial in Money Making Magazine, several short stories, songs and other poetry; [pers.] In dedication to PH and HP. A special note of gratitude to RAC for his loving efforts. Inspiration is life experience, life experience is poetry in motion. [a.] Lake Forest, CA.

SHIFTER, ERICA LYNN FENSTERMACHER
[pen.] Erica L.F.S.; [b.] November 29, 1978, Pomona, CA.; [p.] Sany Fenstermacher Shifter and Scott Douglas Shifter; [ed.] I am now going to Walnut High School in Walnut, CA.; [hon.] Sports awards and music awards; [oth. writ.] No published poetry yet; [pers.] The day my great grandpa died, I felt a sadness grow within, He was the greatest man and I loved him with all of my heart. This poem helped me resolved some of sadness in my heart that sad day. [a.] Diamond Bay, CA.

SHOGREN, JANICE C.
[pen.] Jan Shorgren; [b.] December 21, 1933, Council Bluffs, IA.; [p.] Arnold J. and Donna Peters Vollstedt; [ch.] Kera Holm, Kris Shorgen, Kiva Boudreau and Kasi Shogren; [ed.] BA + 24; [occ.] Teacher, 3rd grade; [oth. writ.] Writings for my family and newspaper editorials; [pers.] I'm a new writer, just getting started. [a.] Belle Plaine, IA.

SHOVER JR., M. JAMES
[b.] December 17, 1945, New London, CT.; [p.] Merrill J. and Evelyn Idebel Shover; [ed.] Middlesex Community Technical College, Middletown Connecticut; [occ.] Painter; [memb.] Literacy Volunteers of America, Valley Shore Conn.; [oth. writ.] 1st Honorable Mention Recognition. Ct. Poetry Society May 30, 1992, Vietnam poetry; [pers.] " Things are though enough", I really don't need to create anymore "Fiction" into my life. [a.] Ivoryton, CT.

SHULER, ROSE PERL
[b.] January 29, 1917, Bayonne, NJ.; [m.] Sylvester Shuler, September 18, 1993; [occ.] Retired; [oth. writ.] "I Thought I Walked Alone", a book of poetry, "Death Is Not Saying Goodbye", Serving Time Together: A Correspondence of Hearts published about a year ago by Element Books. A letter exchange of an elder white woman confined to a wheel chair with a black man in the highest security prison in the state of Florida. Published in assumed names: Ruth Sanders and Martin Forrest, aka Rose Perl Shuler and Sylvester Shuler. [a.] Starke, FL.

SILEY-FUGATE, ELAINE Y.
[pen.] Elaine Y. Fugate; [b.] August 13, 1945, Cleveland; [p.] Michael and Ann-Pukach Siley; [m.] Ronald Fugate, Sr., December 15, 1990; [ch.] Kimberly Ann and John Lawrence Stephens; [ed.] St. John's Byzantine Catholic High and Cuyahoga Community College; [occ.] Advertising Classified Ads, sales for Cleveland's Employment Weekly; [pers.] Raised my children to believe that they should reach for the universe and settle for nothing less than the stars. My husband Ron has believed in me and been my Cherokee man. [a.] Cleveland, OH.

SILK, SCOTT
[b.] March 31, 1971, St. Louis, MO.; [p.] Herb and Rhea Silk; [ed.] Parkway Senior High, Lindenwood College, 1 year; [occ.] Student; [oth. writ.] Several other poems none of them published yet; [pers.] I hope people read my poem and take note of what's around them, enjoy life because it's too short not to. [a.] St. Louis, MO.

SIMM, LINDSAY A.
[b.] March 26, Houston, TX.; [p.] Archie and Sue Simm; [ed.] 7th grade student at Kleb Intermediate School; [occ.] Student; [oth. writ.] Short story published in "Creative Kids" magazine other poetry printed in school magazines; [pers.] I was born in Houston, TX., and I have a twin and an older sister. Our family lived in Hong Kong for two years and had the opportunity to visit China and Japan. [a.] Spring, TX.

SIMMONS, CHRISTINA C.
[pen.] Christina Harr Simmons; [b.] December 8, 1963, Hawthorne, CA.; [p.] Donald Harr and Donna Imans; [m.] David Simmons, January 16, 1981; [ch.] David Lee Jr., Nichole Victoria and Joseph Caleb; [ed.] Windham High School; [oth. writ.] Several poems none of which has been submitted for publication before this; [pers.] It is an honor to be selected for this, and without the encouragement from my family it would never have been achieved. [a.] Garrettsville, OH.

SIMOES, ANTONIO
[b.] February 11, 1940, Somerville, MA.; [ch.] Ann-Christino, Jean-Paul; [ed.] BS Boston College, M.S. and Ed.D., Columbia University; [occ.] Dean Graduate School of Education and Allied Professor-Fairfield U.; [memb.] National Association for Bilangiul Education; [oth. writ.] Moments in Culture, several technical writings on socio-linguistics; [pers.] Peace on Earth. [a.] Bridgeport, CT.

SIMON, SCOTT MITCHELL
[b.] January 21, 1972, Red Deer, Alberta Canada; [p.] Jackie and Kelly Simon; [ed.] Camille J. Leguge and Red Deer College; [occ.] Student; [memb.] Volunteer and member of the Board of Directors for the Youth and Volunteer Center in Red Deer; [pers.] Everything around us is significant, especially if we don't understand it. Poetry is a great mysterious puddle that reflects the heart and the soul. If just one person can find mystery within their inner being and a light in my writing then I am satisfied. [a.] Red Deer, Albert Canada.

SIMPSON, JIM
[b.] February 9, 1931, Bristow, OK.; [p.] Jim and Ica Simpson; [m.] Pat Simpson, September 4, 1954; [ch.] James Daniel Simpson III and Mack Reese Simpson II; [ed.] Stinnett Texas High, Panhandle A&M; [occ.] Division Manager, Walco International Inc.; [memb.] Liberty Eylau School Board, Four States Fair, Board of Director; [hon.,] President-Liberty Eylau School Board, president-Southern Pinegaver Cattle Association, Cal Farley's Boys Ranch, Pardner for Life, FFA honorary chapter farmer; [oth. writ.] Published a small book of my poems for my family and friends; [pers.] I write poems for past time and only on things that I have experienced or that are close to my heart. [a.] Texarkana, TX.

SINCLAIR, DORIS
[b.] March 3, 1939, Jackson, TN.; [p.] Tommie Lee and Willie Beatric Cole; [m.] Cornelius Sinclair Sr., (12-23-23), December 18, 1980; [ch.] seven children, five sons and two daughters; [ed.] My education was limited in the public school system but my love and devotions from God's Holy world enlarged my desire to seek truth and understanding; [occ.] Housewife and mother; [memb.] Presently attending The Church of God; [hon.] I am grateful for the opportunity to publish my first poem in The Desert Sun; [oth. writ.] This poem is one of the many that God has inspired me to write, and with all hopes to publish them very soon; [pers.] This poem to me is not just a poem but is my prayer and purpose to glorify and lift up the name of Jesus Christ who was crucified, but is now alive. [a.] Rockford, IL.

SINGER, DARREN A.
[b.] March 24, 1959, Brooklyn, NY.; [p.] Sydel and Murray Singer; [m.] Bonnie; [ed.] I received degrees in English and Theater from Rutgers University; [oth. writ.] I write Shakespearean sonnets fueled by the tension between traditional context and modern content. My poetry has been published in Poetic Voices of America in 1990 and 1993, One/2 in 1992 and the Arcadia Poetry Press Anthologies in 1991 and 1993, in which my sonnet "Only My Lover" was granted a fifth place award. A new poem will be featured in a future issue of Negative Capability; [pers.] "Safe in Sound" was written for those who walk the streets of my hometown, Hoboken. Look out of your own windows. They are on the streets where you live, too, and just like you, they have names, faces, dreams and pain. Give to the foodbanks in your town, donate old clothes to the Goodwill and Salvation Army. Look people in the eye and smile. [a.] Hoboken, NJ.

SINKO, BRIDGET K.
[b.] December 31, 1961, Cleveland, OH.; [p.] Joseph and Juanita Sinko; [ed.] Cleveland State University, John Carroll University; [occ.] Accounting/Property Administrator Management division; [memb.] MADD, Women's CIty Club, AFP, American Federation of Police, HSUS, The Human Society of the United States; [hon.] Who's Who Among High School Students and twice in Who's Who Among American Executive Females, The National Association of Female Executives; [pers.] I will continue to write poetry that is both thought provoking and heart warming. I am forever grateful to and have been greatly influenced by past poet scholars and predecessors. [a.] Euclid, OH.

SKAGGS, RUBY
[pen.] Ruby Farnham Skaggs; [b.] January 16, 1912, Commercial Point, OH.; [p.] Pearl and Sarah Alice Green Farnham; [m.] William P. Skaggs, November 21, 1935; [ch.] David, Keith, Kenneth, Wayne, Elaine, Maxine, Nancy and Joy; [ed.] Elementary through soph. high school; [occ.] Homemaker, saleswork in our Amway several years and 10 1/2 years Rawleigh business; [memb.] Quill Books, National Library of Poetry, Top Records Poetry Academy, Who's Cooking What in America; [hon.] Received International Poet of Merit Award, August 1992, received invitation to receive Ruby Poet at 1993 special ceremony by International Society of Poets, received invitation to Milton Berle's 85th birthday in July 1993, Poety Academy presented lifetime achievement award in California, Milton Berle was to present me with a medallion for Poetic Achievement at Poetry Award convention; [oth. writ.] I write special poems to loved ones and friends for birthdays and other celebrated days. Write cheer up poems to the sick, write and read my poems to church congregations; [pers.] I love an am interested in people because I know God's love. I like to do my part to put some sunshine into others lives and always try to count my blessings instead of my difficulties. [a.] Chillicothe, OH.

SKINNER, REBECA BARAN
[pen.] Rebeca Skinner; [b.] August 13, 1944, Mexico City; [p.] Noe Baran and Esther Margolis de Baran; [m.] Brian Skinner, July 12, 1989; [ed.] High school and college; [occ.] Translator and writer; [hon.] Third prize in a Literature contest at the Jewish Sport Center in Mexico City; [oth. writ.] Short stories and several poems; [pers.] I have dealt with discrimination all my life due to my Cerebral Palsy. One day I wish to live in a society where all human beings are treated equally, with dignity and respect. [a.] Pinellas Park, FL.

SKIPPER, TRACY ANNETTE
[b.] January 31, 1980, Rutherford Co., NC.; [p.] Desi and Judy Greene;[ed.] 8th grade/Ellenboro Elementary School; [memb.] Dare Program, Peer Helping, cheerleading, Corinth Baptist Church and Lady Tigers. [hon.] Miss Fitness, Citizenship, Peer Helping, school softball team; [oth. writ.] I had a poem that was to be published by American Academy of Poetry, but they misplaced my poem;[pers.] In my poetry I try to put my inner most thoughts, that might affect another's feelings down on paper.[a.] Ellenboro, NC.

SLEEME, SCOTT DOMINIC
[b.] March 31, 1975, Decatur, GA.; [p.] Mitchell and Toni Sleeme; [ed.] Blessed Sacrament High School; [occ.] Student, James Madison University; [oth. writ.] Several poems used for school or personal reasons; [pers.] I try to show reality in my poetry. [a.] Powhatan, VA.

SLERSTER, MATTHEW D.
[pen.] Matthew David Slerster; [b.] March 13, 1970, Omaha, NE.; [m.] Julie Ann Slerster, August 22, 1992; [ch.] One on the way, due in Feb. 1994; [ed.] Exira Community High School, Exira, IA., Midland Lutheran College, Fremont, NE.; [occ.] Career agent, Bankers Life and Casualty and an inspiring poet; [hon.] Blue Key Honor Society, Intercollegiate basketball, Dean's List, Agent of the Month for Bankers Life and Casualty; [pers.] I write about things that touch the inner soul, things felt, things known and unknown. Inspiration -James Douglas Morrison. [a.] Fremont, NE.

SLOMINSKI, AILENE
[b.] January 17, 1933, Cambridge City, IN.; [m.] Walter John Slominski, February 14, 1953; [ch.] Allen Ray and Walter Scott; [ed.] Associate degree, Houston Community College; [hon.] Phi Theta Kappa, National Honor Fraternity. [a.] Houston, TX.

SLOSSER, CHRIS
[b.] November 11, 1971, Walkerton, Ontario Canada; [p.] Alice and Dave Slosser; [ed.] University of Guelph, Guelph, Ontario Canada; [occ.] Freelance Journalist and Writer; [oth.writ.] Articles published in local newspapers; [pers.] Life's struggles can only be overcome with courage and hope. [a.] Walkerton, Ontario Canada.

SMITH, ANDREA
[b.] December 16, 1977, Rogers, AR.; [p.] Lloyd Rex and Kathy Smith; [ed.] Rogers High School and Oakdale Junior High School; [memb.] Immanuel Baptist Church in Rogers, AR.; [oth. writ.] This is my first publication; [pers.] I am a big fan of Shakespeare and his works, I am a strong christian and I am an active member. I also enjoy classical music, I play the flute also. I write from experience of events in my life. [a.] Rogers, AR.

SMITH, CAROLYN
[pen.] Carol, Chief, Smitty; [b.] January 15, 1973, Saskatoon, (St. Paul's Hospital); [p.] Garnet and Nancy Smith; [ch.] Godmother-Tessis child; [ed.] Bedford Road Collegiate (grade 12), planning to further education as an rehabilitation worker; [occ.] Fast Food (Burger King) army cadets instructor, future as a rehabilitation worker; [memb.] St. John's Ambulance standard First-aid, Royal Canadian Army Cadets league, Hunter's Society; [hon.] Numerous school activities awards, numerous Army Cadets Awards, rank of Chief Warrant Officer, Employee of month for June 93; [oth. writ.] Poems: Why?, Optimism, I Never Wanted To Let You Go, part 1 and 2, Don..., Live At Age 20, Two Important Friends in My Life and The Sun Shines Through the Clouds (to date unpublished); [pers.] Thanks Brian for encouraging me to work on my talents before they depreciate and for believing in me. "If you have a talent, use it or a great gift is lost, you never know what you can accomplish". [a.] Saskatoon, Sask.

SMITH, DAVID L.
[b.] June 10, 1938, Boston, MA.; [p.] Benjamin and Sonia (deceased); [ed.] Three years college; [occ.] Tax Examiner for Massachusetts Department of Revenue dealing in Chapter 11 Reorganizations; [memb.] Camera Club, Historical Clubs, Civil War Round Tables, Preservation Groups; [hon.] Photo chosen in 1976 for citywide neighborhood exhibit; [oth. writ.] "What God Could Do If He Only Had Money" (humor) published 1973 by Price/Stern. Individual poems published in 1991 in magazines and books; [pers.] Poetry is a form of communication, like the telephone or the touch as well as an art form. [a.] Waltham, MA.

SMITH, DAWN RENE
[b.] July 8, 1963, Hammondsport, NY.; [p.] Ona Franklin and Carol Lorraine Smith; [m.] Brian James Hefler, May 11, 1984; [ch.] Jacqueline Dolores Lorraine Hefler and David Franklin Smith; [ed.] AA in Liberal Arts from City Colleges of Chicago, BA in Sociology from Angelo State University, Texas; [memb.] Pi Gamma Mu (Honor Society); [hon.] Both college degrees with honors; [pers.] After over 200 years being the land of the free -America as a whole needs to be free from all forms of prejudice! God bless America. [a.] Hammondsport, NY.

SMITH, DONALD J.
[pen.] Donald J. Smith; [b.] May 4, 1918, Arpin, WI; [p.] Jacob and Mary Smith; [m.] Helen M. (Barto) Smith, August 19, 1939; [ch.] Donald, James, Cheryl and Holly; [ed.] High school graduate, Lincoln High School, Wisconsin Rapids, WI; [occ.] Division Manager sale road machinery and industry; [pers.] Inspiration flashed in mind at 3:00 A.M., got up and wrote poem, as is, without any changes, returned to bed in about an hour. [a.] Schofield, WI.

SMITH, FELICIA
[b.] November 26, 1976, Natchez, MS.; [p.] Joe and Marilyn Smith; [ed.] Adams Co. Christian High School; [pers.] My writing allows me to better understand and live through life. [a.] Fayette, MS.

SMITH, JASON RICHARD
[b.] December 3, 1975, Milwaukee, WI.; [p.] Wayne Richard and Ibis Melva Smith; [ed.] Marquette University High School, now attending Purdue University, West Lafayette; [memb.] Early Identification Program, INROADS, National Hispanic Honor Society, National Honor Society, St. Patrick's Youth for Jesus; [hon.] National Hispanic Scholar, Who's Who Among American High School Students, Presidential Academic Fitness Award, AP Scholar; [pers.] The best writing comes from the heart and not the mind. [a.] Milwaukee, WI.

SMITH, JOEL MARTIN
[b.] September 7, 1973, Modesto, CA; [p.] Mary and Jerry Smith; [m.] Shannon Mary Smith, August 5, 1990; [ch.] Michael Scott and Joseph Steven Smith; [ed.] High school and Community College; [occ.] Writer; [hon.] Poet of Merit 92; [oth.writ.] Many poems published in anthologies with a poetry book pending; [pers.] Love life. [a.] So Lake Tahoe, CA.

SMITH, KERRY OWEN
[pen.] K.O. Smith, KOS, KOZ; [b.] May 6, 1953, New London, CT.; [p.] Owen B. Smith and Jewell L. Wilson; [ch.] Kerry O., II and Christina L.; [occ.] Life. [a.] Brooksville, FL.

SMITH, LISA MAY
[b.] October 11, 1964, Greensburg, KY; [p.] Jake and Frances Edwards; [m.] Eligie Smith Jr., April 13, 1991; [ch.] Christopher, Matthew, Gina and Kevin; [ed.] 10th grade; [occ.] Housewife, mother; [oth. writ.] Moma's Dream, Waste, What Is It?; [pers.] My personal note is the poem A Necessary Part Of Life, was written for my husband and children for without them there is no life. [a.] Charlestown, IN.

SMITH-HARDER, M. MONICA
[b.] Spanish Town, Jamaica, West Indies; [p.] Octavious A. and Maisie E. Smith; [m.] John N. Harder (deceased); [ed.] Cathedral High School-Jamaica, Montessoli College-England, University of Manitoba, U/Winnipeg-Canada, Teachers Diploma, B. Ed. U. of Winnipeg; [occ.] Retired teacher; [oth. writ.] Acrostic (names) Prayers for birthdays and weddings, Acrostic greeting cards, Easter, Christmas; [pers.] Emphasis on the positive aspects of people. As the positive grows the negative qualities decrease. I have been influenced by English poets from Shakespeare to the romantics. [a.] Winnipeg-Manitoba, Canada.

SMITH, MARY E. LAUDERDALE
[pen.] Mary EL; [b.] July 10, 1949, Hugo, OK.; [p.] John M. Lauderdale and Emogene Ann Smith; [m.] Gary Victor Smith, October 12, 1984; [ch.] Joseph Victor and Andrew Gower Smith; [ed.] Bokchito High School; [occ.] Homemaker, braider; [hon.] Science Award, Art Award; [oth. writ.] Poems; [pers.] The potential to accomplish any goal depends on patience, endurance and determination coupled with motivation. [a.] Bokchito, OK.

SMITH, MELANIE
[b.] January 5, 1959, Louisville, KY.; [p.] Harold E. and Elizabeth D. Smith; [ed.] Elon College, St Andrews Presbyterian, Spalding College; [memb.] Our Savior Lutheran Church, volunteer at Christian Church Home. [a.] Louisville, KY.

SMITH, MICHAEL
[b.] June 21, 1966, Grand Rapids, MI.; [p.] J.D. Smith and Sandra K. Read; [ed.] Catus High, Peoria, AZ., Scottsdale Community, Scottsdale, AZ., SS "A" School, USCG, Petaluma, CA.; [occ.] Cook; [memb.] Operation Hand Clasp Alzheimers Foundation; [hon.] YSCG Honorable Discharge, 9 medals and ribbons; [oth. writ.] Several other poems published by National Library of Poetry; [pers.] The ideas collide Mr. Krznarich, an English teacher at Cactus High and previous work as a lyricist for a glossy product of passion and reflection. [a.] Renton, WA.

SMITH, MICHAEL C.
[b.] June 6, 1975, St. John's Newfoundland; [p.] Charles and Joyce Smith; [ed.] Completed grade 12 in 1993 at St. George's High School in New Harbour; [occ.] Student; [memb.] Royal Canadian Sea Cadet, St. John Ambulance; [hon.] Received Honorable Mention in 1993 Newfoundland and Labrador Arts and Letters competition, received Admiral Mifflins Sailor Award, won scholarship for drama involvement and acting; [oth. writ.] Arts and Letters Honorable Mention with "If You Were Me"; [pers.] The mind and pen are like the river and the ocean, neither flows without the pen. [a.] Dildo Newfoundland.

SMITH, NATHAN (DR.)
[pen.] J. Conway Smith; [b.] September 6, 1913, New York City; [p.] Harry and Lena Smith; [m.] Ada Smith, June 21, 1936; [ch.] Howard Evan and Leonard Jay Smith; [ed.] Doctorate Public Health, Masters Public Health, B.S. Food Technology; [occ.] Registered Sanitarian Sanitation Consultant; [memb.] National Ass. of Sanitarians, American Chem. Soc., A.S.S.E.; [hon.] Director N.A.S.; [oth. writ.] Several poems never submitted for publication, some short stories; [pers.] Nothing is right, nothing is wrong, but thinking makes it so. [a.] West Palm Beach, FL.

SMITH, NATHAN
[pen.] Cynicalman; [b.] August 4,1974, Regina, SK.; [p.] Gary and Arlene Smith; [ed.] Martin Collegiate Institute, Regina; [occ.] Composition Student; [memb.] The Nicely Warped Table; [hon.] Reading Badge Award in Cub Scouts, The Best Poem in grade X and XII English class; [oth. writ.] A solo book of poetry, several short stories and a number of songs; [pers.] Songs and poems should reflect the person who writes them, what I write reflects myself. If you have heard my works, you know who I am. [a.] Regina, SK. Canada.

SMITH, SARAH ALLISON
[pen.] Sarah Allison Smith; [b.] December 1, 1981, Houston, TX.;[p.] Paul R and Anne Elise Smith;[sib.] Jason F. and Jodi A. Meade; [ed.] Graduated from George E. Anderson Elementary, now attends Duiett Middle School; [memb.] Pet Pal for Humane Society, volunteer for Texas Special Olympics, Writers Club, Student Council, Soccer Club, Safety Patrol; [hon.] Presidential Academics Fitness Award, Honor Roll; [pers.] Songwriters for Blues music along with my imagination and creativity influence my poetry. [a.] Spring, TX.

SMITH, SHANNON
[b.] January 19, 1978, East Stroudsburg, PA.; [p.] Guy and Lois Smith; [ed.] Completing 9th grade entering 10th grade; [memb.] National Junior Honor Society; [hon.] Top 5% of my class, Language Award; [pers.] This is my first printed writing and am honored to be printed. [a.] York, PA.

SMITHSON, SHAWN
[b.] May 7, 1982, Bloomington in hospital; [p.] Jeff and Terri Smithson; [ed.] I am presently a 6th grader; [occ.] Student, Binford Elementary; [memb.] Girls Club, YMCA, (of Monroe Co.); [oth. writ.] I have written other poems and I enjoy writing it helps me express feelings and writing is relaxing to me; [pers.] I think that all children should learn how to read and I wish that all children had enough food to survive.

SNELL, CLARENCE J.
[pen.] "Cap" Snell; [b.] July 6, 1926, Anselmo, NE.; [p.] Jolly F. and Nina G. Snell, rancher-farmers; [ch.] 3 daughters and 5 grandchildren; [ed.] 8th grade, public school, Merna, Nebraska; [occ.] Farmer, U.S. Army. 25 years Penn-Railroad, New York City, 20 years Sears and Roebuck, Trenton, NJ.; [memb.] American Legion, Post # 31, 38 years, Trenton, NJ.; [oth. writ.] More than 200 poems and published many songs, 12 on pilot tape, 14 children's stories, 10 in series not published; [pers.] U sing words to make statements in harmony is my great satisfaction and pleasure, I hope to others as well. [a.] York, PA.

SNELL, KIM ROBINSON
[b.] November 11, 1955, Port Jervis, NY.; [p.] Roger I. and Helen H. Robinson; [m.] Donald (Bucky) Snell, May 25, 1974; [ch.] Bucky Robert, Brett R.L. and Rebecca Kendra; [ed.] Attended Syracuse University, Syracuse, NY., Chabot Junior College, Livermore,CA., currently attending Midlands Technical College, Columbia, SC.; [occ.] Full time mom, part time student; [memb.] Living Springs Lutheran Church, Columbia, SC.; [oth. writ.] Many unpublished poems, stories and prayers of family and friends; [pers.] "Never give up your dreams, they are the beginning of every accomplishment". [a.] Columbia, SC.

SNERR, CAROLYN J.
[pen.] CJ.; [b.] September 30, 1942, Philadelphia; [p.] George and Helen Lepak; [m.] George J. Snerr, September 28, 1963; [ch.] George Jr., Nancy, Kenny, Wendy and Steve; [ed.] Hallahan High School, Villanova University; [occ.] Real Estate Broker and owner of Snerr/Decker Real Estate Inc.; [memb.] Catholic Daughters Carbon, County Board of Realtors Pa. Assoc. of Realtors; [hon.] Foster Parents of the Year; [oth. writ.] (Journal book) "The Me Nobody Knows", collection of thoughts and emotions (poetry); [pers.] I like to write poems as gifts to special people or to celebrate special occasions. Most of them come to me as an outpouring of an emotional feeling. [a.] Jim Thorpe, PA.

SNOWDEN I, PETER JAY
[pen.] Peter Snowden;[b.] January 15, 1964, Brooklyn, NY.; [p.] Eva Snowden and Peter Coleman; [ch.] Tiffane Sharone, Porsche Liselle and Peter Jay Snowden, II; [ed.] Graduated-Eli Whitney Voc. High School, Control Data Institute; [occ.] Computer Technician; [oth. writ.] Various poems, which have yet to be published; [pers.] Through my writings, I attempt to influence the positive characteristics in all of those who read my work. For we are affected by the negative influences each day of our lives.[a.] Laurel, DE.

SNYDER, BERTHA
[pen.] Bertha Snyder; [b.] September 24, 1911, Yucon, OK.; [p.] William F. and Florence C. Willman Peck; [m.] Gilbert R. Snyder, June 20, 1935; [ch.] Vea Lynne and Sue Anne Snyder, Wickens; [ed.] Hannibal High School, Hannibal La Grange College, Hannibal, MO., MacMurray College, Jacksonville, Rockford College, Rockford, IL.; [occ.] Housewife, mother, teacher, children are grown, husband is deceased, time now for poetry. Retired teacher; [memb.] Centrel Christian Church, Rockford, IL.; [hon.] Lead in play Hannibal La Grange College. [a.] Winston-Salem, NC.

SNYDER, ROBERT
[pen.] Bob Snyder, B.S.; [b.] September 19, 1949, Tampa,FL.; [p.] Robert J. and Beryle Snyder, Lakeland, FL.; [m.] Vicki Snyder, January 20, 1973; [ch.] Julie Ann and Robin Elizabeth;[ed.] Lakeland Senior High, Lakeland, FL., University of Nebraska at Omaha, Omaha, NE.; [oth. writ.] None published (yet), although I have written several of various lengths and on a variety of subjects, some serious, some funny and some off the wall; [pers.] I'm "no frills" what you see is what you get. I am a strong family person and I have had a full life with a lot of experiences to draw from. [a.] Plattsmouth, NE.

SNYDER, SHELBIE
[b.] January 14, 1981, Castro Valley, CA.; [p.] Kerrie and Paul Scott;[ed.] I have completed sixth grade, I will be seventh grade; [hon.] Citizen of the Year in elementary, Honor Roll, scholarships in sixth grade; [pers.] Through my writing, I work to achieve a personal log to remember younger days and to let others enjoy my feelings.[a.] Castro Valley, CA.

SOBOTKA, FRANCES
[b.] October 10, 1910, Mt Ayr, IA.; [p.] John and Jessie Cabaret; [m.] Ed Sobotka, May 11, 1932; [ch.] David M. and Loren I. Sobotka; [ed.] Mt. Ayr High School, Iowa Elementary Teacher, Music Scholar Teacher; [occ.] Retired; [memb.] Methodist Church; [hon.] Poems in lyrical, Iowa, 2nd place winner in World of Poetry contest; [oth. writ.] Poem book 1977, article for Iowa Historical Library, sheet music, songs; [pers.] It is not what others think of me, it is what I think.[a.] Diagonal, IA.

SOCHAGEN, HILDA
[b.] September 8, 1918, Raumarica; [p.] Rose and Bernard Thaler; [m.] Deceased, November 5, 1939; [ch.] Barbara Dennis and Roger Sochagen; [ed.] Rutger College, business administration, interior decorating; [occ.] Executive of large firm, Macrobiotic Counselor for healing; [memb.] Haddassah, Temple Beth Shalom, J.C.C. and Assoc.; [oth. writ.] I have written other poetry but have never submitted them, all are very sensitive and humorestic.

SODIN-SEMRL, SNEZNA
[pen.] Annelyn Kayson; [b.] December 14, 1962, Slovenia; [p.] Dana and Vlado Sodin; [m.] Andre J. Semrl, September 21, 1989; [ch.] Alexander Semrl; [ed.] BA-University of Ljubljana, Slovenia, MA-Hunter College, New York, University of Illinois; [occ.] Ph.D candidate, Molec. Biology; [hon.] Initiation Award-Hunter College, Who's Who Among International Students in American Universities and Colleges; [oth. writ.] Poem published in anthology-

Wind in The Night Sky; [pers.] I dedicate my work to life, to the optimism and the joys of living and most of all, to the people I love. [a.] Chicago, IL.

SOLARI, FREDERICK
[pen.] Frederick Solari; [b.] February 2, 1947, Plymouth, MA.; [p.] Frederick C. and Cora Solari, Jr.; [ed.] Silver Lake High, Franklin Inst. of Boston, University of MA, Northeastern U.; [occ.] Cabinetmaker; [oth. writ.] Collection of poems, unpublished, collection of short stories, unpublished; [pers.] I like to capture beauty, both human and pastoral, by contrasting the good with the bad. I believe my subjective view has value.

SOLOMON, ELIZABETH ANNE
[pen.] Beth Solomon; [b.] July 23, 1977, California/Mission Hills; [p.] Anne Elizabeth and Stephen Michael Solomon; [ed.] Junior in high school, Canyon High School '93, '94; [occ.] Teach piano; [pers.] I find that the most important thing in this world is not love, but friendship, for how can you love if you are not friends. [a.] Canyon Country, CA.

SOLOMON, MARILYN A.
[b.] October 13, 1946, Mobile, AL.; [p.] Benjamin Franklin and Ethellene Nall Patrick; [m.] Kerry L. Solomon, November 25, 1967; [ch.] Darren Patrick and Brenton Wayne Solomon; [ed.] C.F. Vigor High School-Prichard, Al., Southwest State Technical College-Mobile, Al. Roses State College Midwest City, OK.; [occ.] Section Chief, Minor Services Contracting, Tinker Air Force Base; [memb.] Tinker Managers Association (TMA), St. Matthew United Methodist Church; [hon.] Phi Theta Kappa, President's Honor Roll-Rose State College, numerous performance awards at Tinker AFB; [oth. writ.] Poetry and By-lines in high school newspaper; [pers.] Poetry reflects the secret parts of my soul combing true images with types and shadows. [a.] Midwest City, OK.

SOMMERS, JON DAVID
[pen.] J. David Sommers, M.D.; [b.] January 2, 1949, New Mexico, USA; [p.] Mr. and Mrs. Harold H. Bruggemann, Albuquerque, NM.; [m.] Marsha Lynn (April 12, 1961-September 30, 1989), October 5, 1984; [ed.] B.S. Zoology, B.A. Chemistry, M.D. University New Mexico/USC, U.S. Armed Forces, John F. Kennedy Fountain; [occ.] Physician, Surgeon, writer, U.S. Armed Forces (retired); [memb.] International Society of Poetry, Four Square Gospel Church, American Medical Association, American Academy of Ophth; [hon.] Senior Resident Teaching Award-USC Merit Poet-1993, International Society of Poetry, Los Angeles Eye Society Award, Best Original Research in Ophthalmology Vision Award; [oth. writ.] Scientific Abstracts-Association for Research & Vision in Ophthalmology, article for J. Clin Neurology, poetry published in National Library of Poetry, International Society of Poetry, Quill Pub. Inc.; [pers.] "Though times of great adversity and tragedy, we learn wisdom, humility and acquire great personal strength"-Sommers. "Every man can make a difference and every man should try"-J.F. Kennedy. [a.] Albuquerque, NM.

SOPPA-BARRETT, ROBIN
[pen.] Barrett, Robin; [b.] March 22, 1956, Minneapolis, MN.; [p.] Edward and Elizabeth Soppa, Sr.; [m.] Thomas Barrett, August 17, 1985; [ch.] Jason Robert Barrett; [ed.] Robbinsdale Senior High, Anoka/Ramsey College; [occ.] Owner Porcelain Resurfacing Co.; [oth. writ.] Publication of poetry in high school; [pers.] Thru writing I become more familiar with my true feelings about myself and others. [a.] Andover, MN.

SORENSON, LOWELL S.
[b.] February 15, 1978, St. Paul, MN.; [p.] Roger and Marlene Sorenson; [ed.] Presently at Roseville Area High School, St. Joseph's School of Music-Piano/Voice; [memb.] Christ the Servant Luth. Church; [hon.] Roseville Honor Student, toured in two musicals; [pers.] My love of music and my faith in God will inspire my thoughts forever. [a.] Little Canada, MN.

SOREY SR., CHARLES H.
[pen.] Bogus Wizard; [b.] February 2, 1919, Bascom, FL.; [p.] Hilmon S. and Innizer (Bowls) Sorey, Sr.; [m.] Arrisia G. Sorey, March 30, 1935; [ch.] James A. Charles Jr., Ronald E. and Michael L.; [ed.] High school, Dept. of Edu. GA.; [occ.] Locksmith, writer, photographer, speaker; [memb.] Disable Veterans (DAV) Life member; [hon.] Armed Forces Good Conduct medal, USAF Commendation medal for meritorious conduct as Administration supervision USAF for 26 years; [oth. writ.] Letter to editors, Dayton Daily News, "The New Dayton Defender" (now defunct) anthology Am. Poetry, Love's Greatest Years; [pers.] A person needs only to play as best he can the hand dealt him by the creator of the master's plan. One's success is in his planned hand, not in the hand or plan of another man.

SOROLA, ANITA
[pen.] Ann; [b.] October 25, 1978, San Antonio; [p.] Linda J. Sorola and Vincent Vigil; [ed.] 9th grade at Clark High School; [occ.] Student; [hon.] Several awards for Honor roll and perfect attendance, trophies for volleyball, softball, tennis also for running and soccer, also for being the best in one of my 7 classes. Had my name on a plaque for being one to the 10 outstanding students at Page and an award for being a cheerleader; [oth. writ.] My first; [pers.] This poem is dedicated to my father Vincent, better known as Tito, and many thanks to my mom Linda for encouraging me to send it. I love them both.

SOUKUP, NADIA
[b.] February 12, 1980, New B, TX.; [p.] Mike and Paula Soukup; [ed.] Finishing my last year of junior high; [occ.] School and babysitting; [memb.] I am a PETA member, People for Ethical Treatment of Animals, I go against products testing animals; [hon.] National Honor Society; [pers.] This poem is about a love that I had. [a.] Geronimo, TX.

SPANN, KENNETH E.
[pen.] Kenn E. Spann; [b.] June 19, 1930, Philadelphia, PA.; [p.] Edward and Rosie Spann; [m.] Annette L. Spann, December 5, 1959; [ch.] Kenneth II, Gregory, Deborah, Kevin, Gina, Terri and 10 grandchildren; [ed.] Certificate of Advance Graduate studies in Ph.D. (post-masters); [occ.] Assoc. Prof. and Career Counselor; [memb.] Phi Delta Kappa, Alpha Phi Omega-555M and 82nd Airborne Assocs., D.A.V., American Legion; [hon.] Distinguish Service Award, D.C. City Counsel, Phi Delta Kappa, Boy Scouts of American Explorer Program; [oth. writ.] You Know My Name, Whom Then Shall I Fear, Traffic School Our Champ; [pers.] If the spirit hits you write a poem. [a.] Washington, DC.

SPARKS, TIFFANIE APRIL
[b.] April 17, 1977, Kentucky; [p.] Donald and Kathy Sparks; [ed.] Junior in high school, Salyersville; [oth. writ.] Not published; [pers.] I write my poems in reflection of my own personal feelings. [a.] Salyersville, KY.

SPECTER, KELLIE
[pen.] KC Specter; [b.] November 11, 1961, San Francisco, CA.; [p.] Jesus and Jacqueline Castruita; [m.] Jeffrey Specter; [ed.] Villanova University; [occ.] Public Relations Executive; [oth. writ.] Various professional trade magazines, poem published in Los Angeles Times; [pers.] All individuals are creators. The key is to listen to and create from that glorious voice deep within us. [a.] Newtown Square, PA.

SPEICHER, KAREN SUE
[pen.] Sue Pernisco; [b.] December 10, 1964, Redondo Beach, CA.; [p.] Vicente Pernisco and Carol Anderson; [m.] Aaron Speicher, October 3, 1986; [ch.] Ashleigh Nicholle and Zachary John; [ed.] Aviation High School, Northern Virginia Community College; [occ.] Homemaker; [hon.] Honorably serviced in United State Air Force, 1983-1988; [oth. writ.] First published writings; [pers.] I truly believe we all hold the key to happiness. Happiness from oneself and to others. There is such a great amount of goodness lost through lack of vision, closed minds and lukewarm hearts. [a.] Manassas, VA.

SPENCE, DOREEN
[pen.] Wolete Kidan; [b.] February 8, 1958, Devonshire, Bermuda; [ch.] Quayunte Aikida, Quaytunne Aikima and Sakera; [ed.] Whitney Institute, Bermuda College; [occ.] Sales Rep.; [memb.] World Wide Church of God; [oth. writ.] Several other poems (unpublished); [pers.] I enjoy the challenge that writing brings, to console the hearts of others with words of peace. [a.] Devonshire, Bermuda DVO5.

SPENCER, BRENDA
[b.] May 24, 1960, Canton, OH.; [p.] Frederick and Diana Duck; [m.] Steven Spencer, February 29, 1980; [ch.] Tanya Spencer; [occ.] Human Resources Manager, Dahlgren Control Systems, SSF, CA.; [oth. writ.] Hundreds of unpublished pieces of my life; [pers.] Life is like a river, dark and torrentuous, winding, bubbly and happy, too narrow at times, but always moving. My poetry reflects this. [a.] So. San Francisco, CA.

SPENCER, QUANDA V.
[b.] June 6, 1971, Washington, DC.; [p.] Joan and Harold Spencer; [ed.] Forestville High School, St. Mary's College of Maryland; [occ.] Litigation Paralegal; [hon.] National's Dean's List, Matthias D'Sousa Merit Scholarship, Prince George's Chamber of Commerce Scholarship; [pers.] Good writing seeks to convey reality with astounding accuracy. [a.] Temple Hills, MD.

SPERLING, STACEY ALLISON
[b.] October 29, 1975, Lakewood, NJ.; [p.] Niels and Jane Sperling; [ed.] Central Regional High School, Bayville, NJ.; [occ.] Student; [hon.] Who's Who Among American High School Students, National Academy of Achievement Award in Journalism; [oth. writ.] Other poems and a short story recognized in the N.J. State Teen Arts Festival; [pers.] Life is a series of chapters and the pen is in my hand. [a.] Bayville, NJ.

SPETH, SHIRLEY L.
[b.] New York City; [p.] Albert and Martha L, Schanzer; [m.] Alfred Speth, October 8, 1960; [ed.] Hunter College-B.A., Teacher's College, Columbia University-M.A.; [occ.] Retired teacher, N.Y.C. Public Schools; [memb.] First Church of Christ Scientist, Boston, Mass., National Humane Education Society, The Breakfast Club-WEBB, The Breakfast Club broadcasts over WEBB every Sunday morning from 10-11 a.m. I read one of my poems every week on the air; [hon.] Phi Beta Kappa, Phi Sigma Mu, Alpha Chi Alpha; [oth. writ.] Several poems published in "The Williston Times" and included in Literacy Volunteer booklets; [pers.] I like to celebrate the months, seasons, holidays and historical events. [a.] Albertson, NY.

SPINK, MADELINE J.
[m.] John E. Spink; [ch.] Elizabeth and Laura; [pers.] "When his country called" dedicated with love and affection to my brother Joe.

SPRINGER, JIM
[b.] December 6, 1974, Norfolk, NE; [p.] Gene D. and Elizabeth L. Springer; [ed.] High school graduate of Columbus Scotus High School, attending University of Nebraska, Lincoln; [occ.] Student; [memb.] National Honor Society, International Thespians Society, Husker Forensics; [hon.] Boy's State, Hugh O'Brian Award, Spirit of Scotus Award; [oth. writ.] None other published; [pers.] Recognition of one's inabilities and belief of one's love for others will lead to contentment. [a.] Lincoln, NE.

SPIRES, REBECCA LYNN
[pen.] Becky; [b.] January 15, 1906, Portsmouth, OH.; [p.] Ralph and Virginia Spires; [ed.] Graduating junior at West Union High School, West Union, OH.; [memb.] Ohio Valley Antique Machinery Association, Future Homemakers of America; [hon.] Art work chosen for short story and poetry book cover for West Union High School, West Union, Ohio; [oth.writ.] "In Memory of My Cousin Chris", 'My Dear Friend", 'Friendship", 'My Graduation Day", "I Remember"; [pers.] Writing my feelings down on paper, encouraged me to began writing poetry, as a way of expressing my true feelings. I would like to dedicate my poem to my two wonderful parents, Ralph and Virginia Spires, my two sisters, Julie and Amy, my two dear friends, Meriume and Heather and all of my family and friends. [a.] Lynx, OH.

SPROULS, ROE SONYE
[ed.] M.F.A.-creative writing, Brooklyn College/1982; [occ.] Parent, adjunct Prof., Irish harper; [oth. writ.] Published in several university lit. magazines, i.e., FDU-Lunch Stockton State-Stockpot.

STABECK, DOROTHY
[b.] October 22, 1932; [m.] Married; [ed.] High school; [hon.] Editor's Choice Award presented by The National Library of Poetry, 1993; [oth. writ.] Poem published in Wind in The Night Sky, published by The National Library of Poetry, poem published in a regional poetry group; [pers.] My poetry reflects my active imagination, my experiences in life and an appreciation for the natural world around me. [a.] Kamloops, BC Canada V2B-3N8.

STACEY, EVELYN BROOKE
[pen.] Evelyn Stacey; [b.] November 18, 1984, San Diego, CA.; [p.] Kenneth and Denise Stacey; [ed.] Cummings Valley Elementary School; [occ.] Student in 4th grade; [hon.] Student of the Month, 4 years Calvary Chapels Highest Achievement Award. [a.] Tehachapi, CA.

STANFORD-COX, MARLENE
[pen.] Marlene Stanford-Cox; [p.] Robert and Selma Stanford; [m.] Jack Benjamin Cox, August 4, 1957; [ch.] Teresa, Daniel, Roxanne, Susan and Ann Marie;[ed.] BFA, Art History and painting; [occ.] Visual Artist-watercolor; [memb.] Crosslake Art Club, Duluth Art Institute, Lutheran Church of the Cross; [hon.] Grant to teach, acceptance of art into juried shows, mentor grant, (45 years ago, 1st place poster contest American Legion); [oth. writ.] Short stories, poetry, research papers in art and art history; [pers.] I look for parallels in design concepts used in pottery, weaving and borders by native Americans. All designs come from nature and are similar in pre-historic cultures that were separated by thousands of miles. I believe that there is a common thread that weaves its way through all cultures and somehow ties us all together. In researching these early designs, the most compelling thought was that the artists who made them were keepers of the land. They had high regard and great reverence for all of nature and the earth. In some small way, I am attempting to bring awareness and appreciation to these people who came before us. We can learn from their ways of harmony with the earth. [a.] Nisswa, MN.

STAPLETON, STEVEN P.
b.] September 21,1972, Jasper Alta, Canada; [p.] Pat and Doreen Stapleton; [ed.] Lambton College, Sarnia Ontario;[occ.] Student; [pers.] Always do what you want, do things that will make you happy! [a.] Sarnia Ontario, Canada.

STARKEY, VIRGINIA C.
[b.] December 25, 1912, Catawba, VA.; [p.] Ammon and Mamie Brunk Starkey; [ed.] Catawba High, Catawba, VA., Radford College, Radford, VA., George Washington University, Washington, DC.; [occ.] Elementary and high school teacher and Guidance Counselor in Alexandria, VA., retired since 1975; [memb.] N.E.A. Church of the Brethren, Garden Club; [hon.] Delta Kappa Gramma, Mu Chapt., Fulbright Exchange Teacher Scholarship; [pers.] I am constantly aware of and grateful for the beauties and wonders of nature. [a.] Bridgewater, VA.

STEFFEY, PHYLLIS
[b.] June 20, 1939, Ironton, OH.; [p.] Soloman and Mary Addie Large; [m.] James C. Steffey, May 14, 1957; [ch.] Rickey Lee Steffey; [ed.] Eight grade; [memb.] Member of the Eagles Ladies Aux of the VFW; [hon.] Being published in Question of Balance and Where Dreams Begain, title of poem "Together Forever"; [oth. writ.] Wind In The Night Sky, Distinguished Poets, In The Desert Sun, to be published; [pers.] Thanks to the National Library of Poetry for believing in me, also thank You Lord, for the words of truth You put in my heart. [a.] Marion, OH.

STEIN, DOUGLAS PAUL
[b.] July 1, 1970, Youngstown, OH.; [p.] Roberta E. and Paul Stein; [m.] Melissa A. Stein, May 26, 1989; [ch.] Brianna Rene' Stein; [ed.] AS Respiratory Therapy, BS Management University South Carolina, BFT,S.C.; [occ.] US Navy Hospital Corpsman; [memb.] President of USC B Business CLub (93-94); [hon.] Dean's List, awarded William Mason Hardimon scholarship 93-94; [pers.] I wish to express deep gratitude to those who daily support the United States of America and to those who gave their lives for our freedom. You shall not be forgotten! [a.] Youngstown, OH.

STEINBERG, THELMA T. (NEE-BOUTILIER)
[b.] July 15, 1927, Randolph, MA.; [p.] Aubrey C. Boutilier and Ella Stanwood Harlow; [m.] Robert P. Steinberg (deceased), May 2, 1953; [ch.] Edward A Steinberg and Roberta Lee Steinberg (deceased); [ed.] Concord High School class of 46; [occ.] Clerk; [memb.] ASCAP; [hon.] Acceptance as being a Concord Author by the Concord Free Public Library numerous citations; [oth. writ.] Some published in local newspapers and one in The MA. Senate Journal 4/82; [pers.] My motto is perceive, believe, achieve. [a.] Concord, MA.

STEPHENS, JAMES A.
[pen.] James A. Stephens; [b.] August 18, 1926, Bullard, TX.; [p.] James Polk and Maudie Alice (Kilgore) Stephens; [m.] Mickie M. Stephens, January 29, 1944; [ch.] Dianna, Nancy and Pamela; [ed.] High school and reading self learning books; [occ.] Retired Telephone special (was in charge 3 telephone exchanges 20 years) appartis employee); [memb.] Moose Lodge, National Geographic member, life time member Telephone Pioneers; [hon.] Life member Telephone Pioneer's America, 8 years school board member; [oth. writ.] Have lots of writings and poems never had them published, wrote several items for opinion in local paper, some were in the telephone papers published; [pers.] I believe there is a story in almost any subject that is worthy of discussing, also I believe I have never met anyone that I could not learn something from. [a.] Clarkston, WA.

STEPHENSON, JAMIE
[pen.] J. L. Stephens; [b.] October 22, 1955, Coral Gables, FL.; [p.] Loretta Lyon and James Stephenson; [ch.] April Lynn; [ed.] Life; [occ.] Awareness; [hon.] My only child; [oth. writ.] Trail of Tears, Lost and Lonely Without You, Dream My Child, Love You All Over Again, Like A Child In The Night; [pers.] Things change like the tides and times. [a.] Courtland Manor, NY.

STEWART, BRIAN ALAN
[b.] May 27, 1970, Miami, AZ.; [p.] Terry and Diane Stewart; [ed.] Globe High, University of Arizona; [occ.] Lighting Designer and master degree student; [memb.] Sierra Club, Golden Key National Honor Society, Arizona-Sonora Desert Museum Funding

Society; [hon.] Phi Kappa Phi, Magma Cum Laude, Dean's List, Golden Key; [pers.] In writing I try to discover the forms and colors in life. I have found questions not answers, provide these values. [a.] Tucson, AZ.

STEWART, CHRISTY
[b.] May 3, 1977, Irvine, KY.; [p.] Tina Gilliam; [m.] Single; [ed.] High school; [occ.] Student; [pers.] Sadness has visited us many times, yet we cannot lock our doors, for he will appear through steel stronger than ever before. I would like to show my highest appreciation to my mother, Mrs. Tina Gilliam, for whom I love very much. [a.] Richmond, KY.

STEWART, KIM R.
[b.] November 29, 1957, Hattisbugrg, MS.; [p.] Edward K. and Voncile H. Powell, Sr.; [m.] Wallace E. Stewart, January 2, 1981; [ch.] Steven Allen Stewart; [ed.] Southhaven High, Northwestern State University; [occ.] RN-Schumpert Medical Center; [memb.] Oncology Nursing Society, St. John Berchman's Catholic Church; [hon.] Who's Who in American Nursing 1990-1991, 1991-1992; [oth. writ.] Clinical articles for the Northwest La Chapter of Oncology Nursing Society newsletter, article for the Schumpert Medical Quarterly; [pers.] Life is constantly surprising. My writing is one of those surprises. [a.] Bossier City, LA.

STIVER (NEE) WEEDEN, MARY DOROTHY
[pen.] Mary Weeden Stiver; [b.] February 18, 1909, Farm-Bristol Twp., MorganCo., OH.; [p.] Converse Thomas Weeden and Amelia Mary Cornellia Tiemann; [m.] Lawrence Hahn Stiver, March 26, 1939; [ch.] James L., Robert H. and Lawrence W. (Larry) Stiver; [ed.] Bachelor of Science/Education, 1 term graduate college for MSE in Orthopedics, "Mrs" degree instead; [occ.] Teaching, wife-mother, widowed February 1990, elementary school, second grade North Lima, Ohio (hometown), college- Michigan State Normal College, Ypsilanti, Michigan, Horace Rockham Graduate School, Ann Arbor, Michigan; [oth. writ.] 4 volumes poetry, Lonely Hills - 1961, Brief Argument-1964, Dreams, Astonishments and Realities-1972, The Poems of Mary Stiver -1987 (all chapbooks except "B.A"-1964); [pers.] For me any poem (or expression) that is true, "The best-words in the best order", is of merit, no matter the subject and is more important than the poet's name. The poet like a body is only the receptacle. [a.] Columbia, SC.

STODDART, RENEE'
[b.] December 14, 1950, North Vancouver, BC.; [p.] Mr. and Mrs. Bob Carles; [m.] Divorced (1977), July 24, 1974; [ed.] Grade 12, some college (English) upgrading; [occ.] Work with the mentally disabled; [memb.] B.C. Schizophrenic Foundation, Royal Canadian Legion; [oth. writ.] "Untitled", "Battleground", being published by the Schizophrenic Society of Canada, several other poems published in local newsletter; [pers.] " To touch one's soul with words is to see God". [a.] Surrey, BC Canada V3S 2C5.

STOKES, RON
[b.] September 25, 1950, Mt. Vernon, IN.; [p.] Roy Stokes (Henshaw, KY) and Edith Barney Stokes (Annabelle UT); [m.] Kathy A. Stokes, September 3, 1989; [ch.] Emily S. Stokes; [ed.] Graduate 1968, Central High (Evansville) Central Tex College (Germany), Ind. Voc. Tech, Coll. (Evansville); [occ.] Saw filer, saw mill maint-operation (Kimball,In); [memb.] AMVETA (19 months Viet Nam); [hon.] Hon.Dis. US Army; [pers.] Reflections was written because people have a tendency to judge others because of their actions, and don't see what is in a heart. [a.] Evansville, IN.

STONE, LOIS
[b.] January 22, 1939, Toronto, Canada; [m.] Robert Stone, September 5, 1959; [ch.] Vincent Patrick, David John, Ian Robert Storey and Elizabeth Ann; [ed.] Malvern Collegiate plus 3 consecutive summer courses in business English; [occ.] Word Processor; [memb.] VON, book clubs, etc., (assistant); [hon.] Honors in English from Malvern Collegiate; [oth. writ.] A personal compilation of poems and writings, mainly as a hobby; [pers.] I've found words a fascination of long standing. When written with meaning and heart, there is nothing more soothing for a troubled or saddened soul. [a.] Ottawa, Ontario K1V 9S5.

STONE, NIKIA ANN
[pen.] Nikia Ann Stone, May 3, 1977, Marshal, MI.; [p.] Julia Lynn Shepherd-Williams and Anthony Jerome Stone; [ed.] 11th grade, Westview High School, Phoenix, AZ.; [hon.] 3rd place in state essay contest, I wrote the words for Westview High's Alma Mater, voted outstanding choir member, class president 3 years in a row, honor athlete Underdown Junior High, nominated to be in Who's Who in American High School Students; [oth. writ.] Many unpublished poems and fictional stories; [pers.] With my poetry and stories, I try to paint a picture in the mind of the reader. I try to show the reader the picture that is painted in my mind. [a.] Avondale, AZ.

STOUT, RITA A.
[pen.] R.A. Stout; [b.] August 19, 1949, War West, VA.; [p.] Clyde and Cathleen Stout; [m.] Single; [ed.] Big Creek High School, War, WV.; [occ.] Bookkeeper, secretary at War Light and Power Co., War, WV.; [oth. writ.] Collection of my poems shared with special friends; [pers.] My goal is life is to encourage others to always seek the Lord. I want to tell others Jesus is the door to happiness, peace and joy now in this life and in eternity forever more. [a.] War, WV.

STOVALL, CLARENCE W.
[pen.] Boss; [b.] June 15, 1923, Novice, TX.; [p.] Allen Thomas and Callie Ware Stovall; [m.] Roberta Ernestine Stovall, September 17, 1946; [ch.] Carlton, Charles, Allen, Clarence and Daniel; [ed.] High school; [occ.] Mail supervisor, college, Ret. U.S. P.O.; [memb.] American Legion, AARP, NARFE Church; [pers.] Beautiful poetry soothes the mind. [a.] Duncanville, TX.

STRAIT, KATIE A.
[pen.] KT; [b.] October 16, 1945, Munice, IN; [p.] Mary and Harvey Keith; [m.] Larry D. Strait I, June 22, 1962; [ch.] Lori, Jeff, Tony and Larry II; [ed.] Blackford High, Montipileir High; [occ.] Employed at COuntry Cupboard Restaurant; [hon.] Editors Choice Award for "Brother" in Wind in The Night Sky, chosen for publication in Most Outstanding Poets of 1994 and anthology book In The Desert Sun ; [oth. writ.] Local and non local newspapers, National Guard magazine and pending Guide Post; [pers.] I would like to give recognition to Don and Jena Whiters who has inspired this poem through their encouragement and through his paintings which bring me much inner peace. [a.] Hartford City, IN.

STRUBLE, CHARISSA
[b.] July 23, 1977, Winfield, KS. [p.] Bruce and Kasey Struble; [ed.] High school junior; [occ.] Student; [memb.] FHA, Perrill Club, Forensics, French Club; [hon.] Essay winner, Sassy Magazine; [oth. writ.] Published in Diamonds and Rust; [pers.] Be yourself! No two people were made alike, always remember that. [a.] Hutchinson, KS.

STULL, PATRICIA RYDER
[b.] June 19, Columbus,OH.; [p.] Virginia and Mahler Ryder, Sr.; [ch.] Cydney Lynn, Robert Branson and Gia Virginia; [occ.] Secretary; [oth. writ.] Writing poetry since 1976; [pers.] My writings are the result of human experiences caught in my thoughts. [a.] Columbus, OH.

SULLIVAN, EVELYN ROSE
[b.] March 11, 1921, Auburn, NY.; [p.] John R. and Mildred M. Franzel; [m.] I was a widow for 15 years and raised my family,to Andrew Ruschak, June 15, 1940, he died of a heart attack September 14, 1962, John J. Sullivan, May 21, 1977 (2nd); [ch.] David A. Ruschak, Cheryl M. Morris, Nancy D. Annibale and Terri Ann Wood; [ed.] Auburn N.Y. Schools and Theater Arts, wrote children stories (for fun); [occ.] Homemaker, Girls Scouts, dabbled in art-creative cakes; [memb.] Auburn Childrens' Theater, Auburn Adult Players (theater), Cayuga County Museum of History and Art; [hon.] Several poems published in World Treasury of Great Poems 1980-1981; [pers.] I have been greatly influenced by Rev. Carole McCartney, Calvary Presbyterian Church, Auburn, NY., a wonderful family friend, she wrote and asked me about the 1992 earthquake (hence my poem). [a.] Yucca Valley, CA.

SULLIVAN, HEATHER LYNN
[b.] October 12,1966, Saint John NB Canada; [p.] Patrick and Sandra Sullivan; [ed.] Saint John High; [occ.] Unable to work because of health difficulties; [memb.] Heritage Writers, River Valley Support Network (helping unemployed find work); [oth. writ.] Articles written for the River Valley Support Network, unpublished children's stories and many other unpublished works; [pers.] If you have a dream work hard to make it a reality. It's only through hard work and perseverance that it happens. It worked for me and it can for you.[a.] Westfield, NB Canada.

SULLIVAN, SHANNON ELISABETH
[b.] August 4, 1979, Winter Park, FL.; [p.] Edward H. and Lisa Rimer Sullivan, Jr.; [ed.] Kingston Sacred Heart High School, freshman class; [occ.] Student; [hon.] 4 year Academic Scholarship, Kingston Sacred Heart High School, The Academy of Notre Dame, Young Writer Conference award winner, numerous excellent author awards; [oth. writ.] Poem published in The Academy of Notre Dame Young Writer Conference Selected Works. [a.] East Sandwich, MA.

SULLY, WARREN
[b.] March 31, 1936, Chelsea, MA.; [p.] Wm. C. and Elsie Joyce Sully; [m.] Betty A. Sully, September 27, 1959; [ch.] Bethany Ann; [ed.] Chelmsford High, Edison State, International Seminary, Regent University, Kettering Medical Center (C.P.E.); [occ.] Computer System Specialist, Wright Pat ordained minister, open bible stnd., AFB Dayton Ohio, Chaplin, Good Samaritan Hospital, Dayton,Ohio; [memb.] Open Bible Standard Inc., Chas. F. Menninger Society, College of Chaplains, American Assoc. of Christian Counselors, Sunrider International, Specialty Merchandise Corp.; [hon.] Honorary member of the Sandy Lake Band, Cree Indian Council, Ontario, Canada; [oth. writ.] "Codeilcu" in Great Poems of Our Time, various synopses; [pers.] The greatest gift of God to all humanity is language expressed in written word, exalted in poetry, sung to a thousand generations, inspiring transcendent love and eternal life. [a.] Casstown, OH.

SUMNER, EMILY CAROL
[b.] March 8, 1982, Bowling Green, KY.; [p.] Carrel and Clara Sumner; [occ.] Student-Potter-Gray Elementary; [memb.] Gifted and Talented Program, Girl Scouts of America, Piano Baptist Church Choir; [hon.] Honor Roll, Odessy of the Minds, Invent America; [oth. writ.] Unpublished poems, short stories and one childrens' book. [a.] Bowling Green, KY.

SURFACE, REBECCA ANNE
[b.] March 12,1979, Warsaw, IN; [p.] John and Kathy Surface; [ed.] Whitko Middle School; [occ.] Babysitting for now, studying to be an architect; [hon.] Most of my awards I've received are for being creative. I love to play softball, so I have a lot of trophies; [oth. writ.] This is the first time I've ever sent one of my poems in for a contest, but I have other poems I've written over the years; [pers.] I plan to keep writing poetry because I love it, and it's always been one of my dreams to become a famous writer someday. I hope one day I'll be able to influence a young person to write. [a.] Whitley, IN.

SUSMUTH, JOHN
[b.] September 21, 1923, Bridgeport, CT.; [p.] John J. Sussmuth and Felicia A. Nagorski; [ch.] Dawn Kennedy; [ed.] De La Salle Academy, Toronto, Ontario, Northwestern University, Evanston, IL., U.S.A.A.F. Aviation Cadet Pilot Program; [occ.] Headquarters executive, I.T.T.; memb.] Sigma Nu, V.F.W. 376th Bomb Group Vets. Assoc. [hon.] Distinguished Flying Cross Air Medal with two Oak Leaf Clusters; [pers.] Writing poetry gives one a chance to say something without being prosaic.

SWAIN, TRACY
[pen.] Traci Svihun; [b.] January 17, 1964, Merritt, British Columbia, Canada; [p.] Andy and Laurie Swain; [sib.] Kelly and Carter Swain; [memb.] The Society of Prevention of Cruelty to Animals/S.P.C.A.; [oth. writ.] Several poems published in other books, articles published in local Historical Quarterly, wrote about declaration for home town's new flag that hangs in mayor's office; [pers.] I have always longed that what I write will connect with those who read it. I believe we all experience the same situations in our life because we are created and beautifully so by the same creator. I hope that one day my poetry will give those the comfort of knowing that they are not alone and have a world filled with kindred spirits. [a.] Merritt British Columbia, Canada.

SWANSON, GLENN A.
[b.] August 1, 1914, Cannon Falls, MN.; [p.] Algot W. and Esther J. Swanson; [m.] Martha M. Swanson, March 16, 1949; [ch.] Margaret Doucette, Sharon Crowley and William Swanson; [ed.] BBA-University of Minnesota, American Institute of Banking; [occ.] Lobbyist IBAA Morgate Lending (U.S. Govt.); [memb.] Masonic Order American Legion, American Scandinavian Assn., Minnesota State Society, Evangelical Lutheran Church; [hon.] Public Contact Award (SBA), President's Inter-Agency Adjustment Committee Representative Government Achievement Awards; [oth. writ.] Small Bus. Adm contributor, Community Dev. Hand-book, Legislative proposals on behalf of Independent Bankers Assn.; [pers.] I aim to bring out the beauty of nature and the seeming plight of mankind. [a.] Fairfax, VA.

SWEARS, ZACHARY
[pen.] Zack; [b.] June 22, 1985, Big Rapids, MI.; [p.] James and Deborah Swears; [ed.] Currently a 3rd grader at Hillcrest Elementary School, Big Rapids, MI., (wrote poem as a 2nd grader); [memb.] Big Rapids Junior Area Hockey Association (has played hockey for 4 years-started skating at age 2 1/2) earned a "Zero Club" patch as a goalie, for shut outs this past season; [hon.] Plays soccer and baseball and tennis, also enjoys swimming. Has received two citizenship awards at school, placed 2nd in the school talent show for demonstration on roller blades; [oth. writ.] Have published numerous books through my school publishing center "The Write Place" earning a Young Author's Award this past year; [pers.] I give special thanks to Mrs. Connie Cron for helping me publish my poem. [a.] Big Rapids, MI.

SYLVESTER, EDWARD
[b.] September 4, 1960, Washington, DC.; [p.] Jean Gaylor and Roger Sylvester; [m.] Tamera A. Sylvester (ex-wife), divorced; [ch.] Elizabeth, Mary, Theresa and Edward; [ed.] High school graduate, currently sophomore at Lake Superior State University; [occ.] Restaurant worker; [oth. writ.] This is my first publication of any sort; [pers.] Thank you Dr. DI for showing me what poetry can do. [a.] Sault Ste Marie, MI.

TAKEDA, NOBUKO
[b.] April 21, 1974, Tokyo, Japan; [p.] Hiroshi and Fumiko Takeda; [ed.] Edgement High School; [occ.] Freshman in college. [a.] Scarsdale, NY.

TALLMAN, EVELYN T.
[b.] November 13, 1922, So. Westerlo, NY.; [p.] Hazel F. Mabie; [m.] January 23, 1940; [ch.] Ralph R. Tallman; [ed.] High school at Greenville, NY., Baker's diploma; [occ.] Cook and retired; [memb.] Pension -Social Security Social Service, Albany County; [oth. writ.] Recipes in newspapers, World of Poetry.

TATE, REBECCA
[b.] April 29, 1980, Opelousas Gencal; [p.] Richard and Macy Beth Tate; [ed.] 8th grade, Opelousas Catholic; [memb.] St. Landry 4-H Club; [hon.] Numerous 4-H and social studies fair awards; [a.] Opelousas, LA.

TARTELLA, FRANCIS
[b.] July 29, 1977, Scranton; [p.] Francis J. Tartella and Rosemary Helring; [ed.] Dunmore High School; [occ.] Student; [pers.] Love is but a dream, with it, anything can be done. [a.] Dunmore, PA.

TAYLOR, DEBORAH
[pen.] Deborah Howard Taylor; [b.] Philadelphia, PA.; [ed.] Philadelphia College of Art, BFA in painting, Royal Academy of Dramatic Art, London, England, certificate Wilma Theatre, Philadelphia, PA, acting classes currently pursing M.A.T. at the University of The Arts, Philadelphia, PA.; [oth. writ.] Compilation of songs and poems copywritten with the Library of Congress; [pers.] Lived in Belfast, Northern Ireland for several years and served as a volunteer for Prison Fellowship, N.I., St. Peter's Youth Club, YMCA, Belfast. [a.] Huntingdon Valley, PA.

TAYLOR, EVELINE B.
[b.] February 15, 1935, Dedham, MA.; [p.] Thomas V. and Anna G. Page Binmore; [m.] Frank G. Taylor, August 17, 1958; [ch.] F. Andrew and Jeff C.; [ed.] Portsmouth N.H. High School, Keene Teacher's College, Keen, N.H.; [occ.] Housewife; [memb.] Unitarian Universlor Church; [oth. writ.] Numerous poems; [pers.] I am interested in children, nature and personal reflection. [a.] Suffield, CT.

TAYLOR, HEATHER
[b.] October 2, 1977, Ravenna, OH.; [p.] John and Laurie Taylor; [ed.] Gilmer High School; [occ.] School; [oth. writ.] Short stories and other poems. [a.] Ellijay, GA.

TAYLOR, JESSIE
[pen.] Jessie Taylor; [b.] July 4, 1917, Wise Co., TX.; [p.] John Read and Jannie Ann Campbell; [m.] Clyde T. Taylor, April 24, 1971; [ch.] I have two daughters, he has two sons and one daughter; [ed.] Granbury High School, graduated, Southern College of Commerce and LUTC; [occ.] Insurance Saleslady; [memb.] OES, Sec./treasury of American Heart Assn. and ABWA while working; [hon.] Won a trip to the Bahamas, received the National Quality Award; [pers.] Won many awards, among the National Quality Award which I'm very proud of. [a.] Aledo, TX.

TAYLOR, LORETTA G.
[b.] March 27, 1935, Georgetown, TX.; [p.] Eugenia (deceased) and Lester Green; [m.] Kenneth K. Taylor (deceased); [ch.] Ronald G. and Russell J. Moore; [ed.] Elementary Education/Music Business College; [occ.] Secretary (police department); [memb.] Methodist Church; [hon.] Mother and grandmother; [oth. writ.] Write for pleasure, therapy and self expression. No other published work; [pers.] I have found that feelings from the heart and all connected emotions are powerful sources of the intellect. Transforming these feelings into words to which others might also relate is a primary aspect of my writing. [a.] Sweetwater, TX.

TAYLOR-TORRENCE, TELITHA
[b.] February 6, 1967, Baton Rouge, LA; [p.] Ruby G. Brown and London Taylor, Sr.; [m.] Tyrone

Torrence, February 26, 1993; [pet.] Rottweiler "Bear"; [ed.] Louisiana State University, studying accounting, Delat College, studied Computer Programming; [occ.] Secretary, Louisiana State University; [memb.] American Lung Association; [hon.] Dean's List; [oth. writ.] Numerous unpublished poems; [pers.] I strive to touch lives of all ages, of different problems, cultures and beliefs, thru my poems; there's always someone needing to know someone else is in that same predicament or worse. If I can make one person smile per day, thru my poetry, what an accomplishment. Forget a world of hate, pain, hunger and disease... Thank God I can dream.[a.] Baton Rouge, LA.

TEBOW, DEVRY DWAINE
[pen.] Dev; [b.] August 26, 1965, Blackwell, OK.; [p.] Rex and Chleora Tebow; [m.] Edith Tebow, June 21, 1986; [ch.] Dimitri Robert, Devra Lynn and Dylan Mark; [ed.] Blackwell High School, Northern Oklahoma College; [occ.] Fuel Systems Repair mechanic, Pope AFB, NC.; [memb.] American Heart Association; [hon.] U.S.A.F. Good Conduct Medal, U.S.A.F. Achievement Medal; [oth. writ.] First publication; [pers.] A thousand stars in a thousand skies, one man's mind two earth's behind.[a.] Blackwell, OK.

TEDESCO, BARBARA L.
[pen.] Basia; [b.] November 15, 1966, San Antonio, TX.; [p.] Thomas M. Tedesco and Shirley T. Guthrie; [ch.] Brittany Lee Tedesco; [ed.] Brandon Senior High School, Hillsborough Community College; [occ.] Taekwon Do Instructor, Customer Service Rep.; [hon.] 2nd degree Black Belt in Taekwon Do; [oth. writ.] Uphill Battle, Dreams, Vicious Circles, A Mother's Love; [pers.] I believe in dreams: I believe you make most any dream become reality, as long as you have the courage to dream and the perseverance to make those dreams come true.[a.] Tampa, FL.

TENNANT, SHERIDAN JENICE
[b.] May 4, 1985, Glen Ridge, NJ.; [p.] Winsome Tennant; [ed.] Third grade; [occ.] Student; [memb.] Faith Fellowship Ministries World Outreach Center, Edison, NJ,; [hon.] Attendance award (never missed a day of school for four years); [pers.] My faith in God has helped me to write poetry from the heart. [a.] Bloomfield, NJ.

TESKE, WESLEY C.
[b.] August 7, 1977, Parry Sound; [p.] Debby and Lee Teske; [ed.] Still attending Widdifield Secondary School; [hon.] 1990 Junior Citizenship nominee; [oth. writ.] 1st poem published, many poems written for school; [pers.] When I sit listening to a song on the radio, I think of something to say. I try to think of what I've accomplished and I draw a blank, I'm young 16. I think I have a few years left, thanks for the chance Wezie; [a.] North Bay, Ontario.

THARP, TIM
[pen.] Wolf; [b.] April 20, 1975, San Francisco, CA.; [ed.] Went to De La Salle High School in Concord, CA.; [oth. writ.] Rising and Falling, Heaven Sunshine; [pers.] What is meant to be will be and everything happens for a reason. [a.] San Ramon, CA.

THERIOT, NATASHA
[pen.] Ta-Ta or Tasha; [b.] December 26,1976, Houma, LA; [p.] Gloria Herbert and Glenn Theriot; [ed.] Thibodaux High, Thibodaux Vo-Tech; [oth. writ.] None published; [pers.] I write how I feel about life and the events that happen in life. [a.] Thibodaux, LA.

THIBODEAU, MARK ALAN
[b.] October 10, 1961, Holyoke, MA.; [p.] R. Paul Thibodeau and Ann L. Ittner; [occ.] Student; [oth. writ.] Unpublished. [a.] E. Orleans, MA.

THIEMANN, FRANCIS C.
[b.] December 27, 1927, St. Louis, MO.; [m.] Kathryn; [ch.] 5; [ed.] BA Seattle University, Masters, University of Washington, PhD., University of Oregon; [occ.] Professor, farmer, contractor; [oth. writ.] Books, articles and reports. [a.] Sulphur, KY.

THIERFELDER, BILL
[pen.] T. Richard Williams; [b.] February 19, 1951, Flushing, NY.; [p.] Wilma Sondermann and William Thierfelder, Jr.; [ed.] BA, MA, PhD., St. John's University, MA Theology Immaculate Conception Seminary; [occ.] College Professor, Dowling College, Long Island, NY.; [memb.] National Council of Teachers of English, Northeast American Society for Eighteen Century Studies; [hon.] Sigma Tau Delta (English Honor Society); [oth. writ.] David By The Sea, (book of poetry), several poems in national journals, articles in the Italian Journal, The Explicator; [pers.] My writing is the primary way that I express myself in the world, the method I use to articulate my authenticity. [a.] Northport, NY.

THIEMICH, LAURA
[pen.] Laura Lynn Diamond; [b.] November 14, 1967, Woodbury, NJ.; [p.] Elaine and James Thiemich; [ed.] Elementary Ed. and Psychology at Glassboro State; [occ.] Third grade teacher, Cherry Hill, NJ.; [memb.] Lupus Foundation of America, National Education Assoc., Theisbian Society; [hon.] Miss W. Deptford Little Theatre, Teacher of the Month, June 1993; [oth. writ.] Various 150 other poems; [pers.] Whatsoever ye do, do it heartily as unto the Lord, not unto men. Colossians 3:23. [a.] Westville, NJ.

THOMAS, CAROL DEANE
[pen.] C. Thomas; [b.] January 28, 1927, Waller Waller, WA.; [p.] W. Victor and Ruth Denzel Ostby; [m.] Mario Thomas, December 21, 1947; [ch.] Marc, Marvin and David Thomas; [ed.] M.A. University of Iowa, B.A. University of Illinois, honors; [occ.] Retired school teacher and nurse aid; [memb.] American Associations of University Women; [hon.] Worthy Advisor, Order of Rainbow for Girls, church soloist and Sunday School teacher, Girl Scout Leader; [oth. writ.] "Winter" 1993, unpublished, M.A. Thesis published at University of Iowa 1961; [pers.] I attend church and church circles, I have helped families with problems as a live-in helper. [a.] Walla Walla, WA.

THOMAS, JAMES E.
[b.] June 2, 1956, Lewistown, PA.; [ch.] Jason R. and Kayley Jo Thomas; [occ.] Foundry Engineer; [oth. writ.] This is my first published work. [a.] Lewistown, PA.

THOMAS, JUANITA F.
[pen.] Nita; [b.] September 28, 1935, Cleveland, OH.; [p.] Rev. George and Vircie Jones, both deceased; [m.] September 21, 1955; [ch.] Renee, John, Linda, Bryan, and Brenda, (Keith deceased); [ed.] John Hay High, college, semester at Tri-C; [occ.] Security Guard for Ohio Bell; [memb.] Werner Methodist Church; [oth. writ.] I have written several poems for various programs at church, which I read to the congregation, also for my family and friends; [pers.] My work is based on the joys, trials I've lived as a single divorced parent. I admire Maya A., Langston H. and others. I hope to reach young people. [a.] Cleveland, OH.

THOMAS, LINDA F.
[b.] December 28, 1946, Beaumont, TX.; [p.] Gordon and Helen Thomas; [ed.] French High School, (Beaumont), B.S., M.S., Administrative Certificate, Lamar University, Beaumont,TX.; [occ.] Physical Education Teacher/coach, Vidor Junior High, Vidor, TX.; [memb.] Assoc. of Teachers and Professional Educators, Alpha Delta Kappa, committees-First Baptist Church, Bevil Oaks, (library, recreation, baptism, nominating); [hon.] Who's Who Among Americas Teachers, Craft Divisions Southeast Texas State Fair; [oth. writ.] A story " The Purse", a story "The Christmas Doll" and an unpublished as yet children's book The Most Beautiful Christmas Tree Ever; [pers.] I like to write stories about experiences that portray the "endearment' of the challenges of growing up in the world. [a.] Beaumont, TX.

THOMAS, MARGIE S.
[pen.] Lycidas; [b.] April 5, 1975, Denver, CO.; [p.] John K. and Lillian S. Thomas; [ed.] Lakewood High School, Metropolitan State College, Denver; [occ.] Student/delivery person/technician's assistant; [memb.] Southeast Christian Church, National Forensics League; [hon.] City and County Level, Mayors' and Commissioner's Youth Award, Outstanding Senior, publication, coach's award, speech team; [oth. writ.] Several poems published in local magazines, numerous unpublished stories, poems and several novels; [pers.] All of my writing is a representation of the souls surrounding me. I focus on the freedom of each soul and that soul's quest for eternity. A medieval a renaissance flourish grace my descriptive writing. [a.] Lakewood, CO.

THOMAS, NANETTE
[b.] November 6, 1959, Havre de Grace, Md; [p.] Dr. and Mrs. Leon W. Berube; [m.] Arthur C. Thomas, June 11, 1977; [ch.] Jennifer, Margaret, Kimberly, Christopher and William; [ed.] St. Mary's Academy and Charles County Community College; [occ.] Family Day Care Provider; [memb.] MADD, American Diabetes Association, American Institute of Cancer Research, Greenpeace; [pers.] I use my writing as a personal reflection of my feelings, an outlet for my emotional well being. [a.] Waldorf, MD.

THOMPSON, CRYSTAL
[b.] June 15, 1981, Havre, MT.; [p.] Laura and Ken Thompson; [ed.] Currently attending 7th grade; [occ.] Student; [hon.] One of my poems published in The American Academy of Poetry's "Anthology of Poetry by Young Americans"; [oth. writ.] Several poems published in "Rural Montana" monthly magazine and one in the 1993 edition of The American Academy of Poetry's "Anthology of Poetry by Young Americans"; [pers.] Ever since I got my poem published in a Montana magazine in second grade I've loved poetry, thanks mom for inspiring me. [a.] Gildford, MT.

THOMPSON, JENNIFER ANN
[b.] October 3, 1979, Seattle, WA.; [p.] Sherrie and Michael Sanford; [ed.] At this time, Eastbrook Middle School; [hon.] Presidential Academic Fitness Award; [oth. writ;] The Wind, got published; [pers.] Smile and one day all clouds will go away to make everyday a sunny day. [a.] Dalton, GA.

THOMPSON, WYGENIA
[pen.] Jean; [b.] December 25, 1939, Greenville, SC.; [p.] Robert and Sadie Bradley; [m.] Leonard Thompson, Sr., August 30, 1958; [ch.] Leonard Jr., Anthony; [ed.] William Penn High School; [occ.] Housewife; [oth. writ.] Poems published in local newspaper, Philadelphia Daily News, also published in Daughter-In-laws, Plan Parenthood newsletter from her job; [pers.] Thanks to my husband and 2 sons especially Lennie, who always believed and gave me the highest of support. I love and thank you all dearly. Thanks to my daughter in-law Bayeh, love you always as well, your help was deeply appreciated. Thank you.

THOMPSON III, WALTER
[b.] St. Louis, MO.; [ed.] B.A. Mass Communications, 1979 Duke University, MA. Anthropolgy 1983, Ball State University; [occ.] Fitness Consultant, model (Photo Art); [hon.] Who's Who American Colleges 1979, Mr. Great Plaines Drummer 1988, Mr. Leather Missouri 1989; [oth. writ.] "Black Boy", "Watching" and "Unchained", "Leather Sides" and " Looking For Him" published in The Leather Journal; [pers.] Most of my poetry deals with the theme of time, travel and with the supernatural forces of man's imagination. [a.] St. Louis, MO.

THORNTON, HENRY JAMES
[pen.] Henry James Thornton; [b.] April 8, 1927, Leesville, SC.; [p.] Deceased; [m.] Earlene H. Thornton, Ph.D., August 1, 1964; [ch.] Henry James,Jr., Jeffrey David and Donald Eugene; [ed.] Masters in Education; [occ.] Teacher; [memb.] Associate member of ASCAP, Alpha Phi Alpha fraternity, Evangelical Lutheran Church (usher); [hon.] Who's Who College edition; [oth. writ.] 176 songs (words and music) 10 poems; [pers.] I love the challenge of creating a combination of words into some meaningful song and poem. [a.] Frederick, MD.

THORNTON, PATSY
[b.] May 6, 1935, Pratt, KS.; [p.] Valaria and Dick Harvey; [m.] Divorced; [ch.] Mitch, Georgetta, Jed, Dale, Ronnie and Rexanna; [ed.] Graduated from high school; [occ.] Housewife; [hon.] Simple prayer, has won an award of Merit in 1990; [pers.] I would like to dedicate my poem to Nancy Fellows, who died January of 1992. [a.] Atchison, KS.

THORESDAHL, OSMOND
[b.] November 13,1904, Stevangar, Norway; [p.] Ivan Martin and Elizabeth Toresdahl; [m.] Mabel Helen Toresdahl, June 4, 1984; [occ.] Retired carpenter.

TIBBETTS, KATHLEEN IRENE (KATIE)
[b.] Minneapolis, MN.; [p.] Mr. and Mrs. Samuel Elgin (Irene Lyons) Tibbetts; [ed.] Graduate of West High School and the University of Minnesota, with majors in psychology and sociology at the University; [occ.] Author, poet, Historian, in addition to her work as a Social Worker; [memb.] American Association of University Women, National League of American Pen Women, International Platform Association, Board of Directors of Inter-Club Council (an organization working for the betterment of the community), Board of Directors of Descendants of Minnesota Territorial Pioneers, Secretary of the International Academy of Poets, the Minneapolis Poetry Society, Chaparral Poets, The University Club, Campus CLub, Deanery Delegate, Eucharistic Minister at church; [oth. writ.] Included in anthologies "From Sea to Sea in Poetry", "Memories" and others; [pers.] To bring beauty and happiness to the world through our words, thoughts and actions. To help others along the way by encouraging them to develop their own creative talents. [a.] Minneapolis, MN.

TILLMANN, ANN
[b.] November 25, 1970, Watertown, WI.; [p.] Georg and Jean Tillmann; [m.] Single; [ed.] Pius XI High School, Mount Mary College, Milwaukee, WI., (Magna Cum Laude); [occ.] Art Education K-12, teacher and freelance artist; [memb.] National Education Association, National Art Education Association, Milwaukee Art Teachers Association; [hon.] Kappa Gamma Pi, Wi State Representative to the National Collegiate Honor Council '89, Scholastic Art Awards Hallmark recognition '87, The Milwaukee Journal Calendar Art competition Gold Palette winner and Purchase Award '87, WI and Upper Michigan Optimist Club Speech competition winner '86; [oth. writ.] Poems published in Archive of the Arts National Anthologies; [pers.] My experiences while traveling are main sources of inspiration for my art and writing. I am an avid journal keeper and letter writer. I lived and taught English for a year in Talofofo, Guam. [a.] Milwaukee.

TORRES, CARLOS
[b.] June 15, 1977, Bay Shore, NY.; [p.] Ana Maria and Carlos Torres, Sr.; [ed.] Currently in high school; [occ.] Student; [memb.] National Honor Society, Leadership Team, Debate Team; [hon.] Presidential Academical Fitness Award, Who's Who in American High School Students, high achievement medal; [oth. writ.] " Hatred Calls To Everyone" "A Child Cries Out In Asia; [pers.] In my writings, I attempt to illustrate the need for peace and humanity in the world, and try to express that through examples of unity. [a.] Smithtown, NY.

TOUSIGNANT, STEVEN
[b.] June 21, 1975, Bloomington, MN.; [p.] Annie and Richard Tousignant; [ed.] Entering senior year of high school; [occ.] Student, plan to attend college; [memb.] St. Edward;s Catholic Church, 4-H, Youth Ministry; [hon.] Grand prize Bloomington Art Center art contest (watercolor), school awards for poetry, blue ribbon in watercolor 4-H, blue and purple ribbons in Henn County Fair; [oth. writ.] Unpublished poems and essays; [pers.] Through writing poetry I analyze our world to strengthen my own beliefs and affect those of others. [a.] Bloomington, MN.

TOWLE, DONNA L.
[pen.] Renee Surat; [b.] July 15, Kansas City, MO.; [p.] Donald and Loretta Sarratt; [m.] Warren Towle, January 1, 1983; [ch.] Christine and Lisa Chaffin; [ed.] St. Mary's High School, Jackson County Junior College; [occ.] Bookkeeper/secretary, Littlefield and Whitworth, Accountants; [memb.] Space Coast Writers Guild, Inc.; [hon.] First place in Poetry 1992 Space Coast Writers Conference; [oth. writ.] Two unpublished novels in the "Supernatural Thriller" genre; [pers.] Although I sometimes become frustrated at my inability in finding a publisher for my novels, I will not give up. I am driven to write and a third novel is in the works. [a.] Satellite Beach, FL.

TOWNLEY, VICTORIA
[b.] September 11, 1980, Atlanta, GA.; [p.] Jim and Betty Townley; [ed.] Currently in 6th grade; [occ.] Student; [hon.] My poems and /or stories have been published in the local newspaper and have won numerous school writing awards. My essay won the D.A.R.E. anti-drug education program and was read aloud during the graduation ceremony. [a.] Lilburn, GA.

TRAMPE, ROBERT LEROY
[pen.] Roberto Trampe, Robert H. Bonny; [b.] January 31, 1969, Minneapolis, MN.; [p.] Otto and Karen Trampe; [memb.] Founder/director of "The Emily Rose Movement", dedicated to social change; [pers.] Respect yourself, show love, follow your heart. [a.] Minneapolis, MN.

TRAMPOSCH, ELVIRA
[b.] January 6, 1936, Bielefeld, Germany; [p.] Heinrich and Elfriede Sehlhoff; [m.] Ernst Tramposch, '66; [ch.] Debbie, Ernst, Robert and Steven; [ed.] High school. college courses; [occ.] Homemaker; [memb.] Thirteen-WNET, Lutheran Church, Iroquois Indian Museum, American Ballet Theatre; [hon.] Awards for volunteering; [oth. writ.] German poems from growing up times in Germany as teen between age 12-14, since living in the U.S., poems in English on different subjects; [pers.] "My thoughts on paper are parts of me my true self, that shared with others (they) must look through my little window to see. [a.] Franklin Square, NY.

TRENHOLM, KENNETH J.
[b.] September 12, 1971, Charlottetown, PE.; [p.] Mary and Orlande Trenholm; [m.] Unmarried; [ed.] Three Oaks before I quit and Kensington when I returned, Mr. B. Arsenault's Creative Writing class; [occ.] Unemployed volunteer; [memb.] Newcomers on the island relief program, Prince County Caledonia Club, associate of the Modern Poetry Association, Age of Sail, committee group; [hon.] Two creative writing honorable mentions during high school; [pers.] God bless Patricia Murray and Douglas Millar of Summerside, and Chris Eaton of Moncton, for all their encouragement and influence through musical enchantment. They've helped me find a place where I can be myself, in the depth of a heart of love. [a.] St. Eleanors, PE Canada.

TROUVE', PAUL A.
[b.] June 21, 1952, Long Island City, NY.; [p.] Louis V. and Lorriane B. Trouve'; [ed.] BA, King's College, Wilkes-Barre, PA., MA, Boston College, Chestnut Hill, MA.; [occ.] Operations Research Analyst, Picatinny Arsenal, NJ.; [hon.] National Defense Service Medal, Vietnam Service Medal, Vietnam Campaign Medal; [oth. writ.] Various unpublished poems; [pers.] "Walk With God". [a.] Elmont, NY.

TRUITT, ERIC
[b.] July 28, 1972, Kirksville, MO.; [p.] Allan and Marsha Truitt; [m.] Christine Truitt, October 24, 1992; [ch.] Tanis Alexander Truitt; [memb.] Ducks Unlimited, North American Fishing Club. [a.] Kirksville, MO.

TRUSSEL, JANNIFER LYNN
[pen.] Jan; [b.] January 3, 1979, Dewitt City Hospital; [p.] Debbie and Tommy Trussell; [ed.] I am a freshman at Dewitt High School; [memb.] Beta Club, band; [hon.] Academic Award 1-8 grades, band award, "Most Talent Woodwin" in 7th and 8th grade, art award including the Cissi and Hamilton; [oth. writ.] Past Times, Mistakes, How Much I Love You, Wishes, and Love; [pers.] You never know how much you love someone until you lose them.. [a.] Dewitt, AR.

TUCKER, SHERRY DIANE
[pen.] Bre'ana Delaine; [b.] July 27, 1960, Memphis, TN.; [p.] John Albert Farris and Louise Ann Grant; [ch.] John, Jennifer and Billy; [ed.] Germantown High School, Branell College; [occ.] Real Estate/Affiliate Broker; [memb.] Memphis Area Assoc. of Realtors; [oth. writ.] Several unpublished poems; [pers.] I feel that every child should be given a chance at a normal and happy life and every adult shouldn't be too proud to ask for help for that child if it makes their life richer and fuller. [a.] Memphis, TN.

TUESDAY, JOCLEYN AUTHUMN ELIZABETH
[pen.] Anison. [a.] 106 W 13th Street Apt 28, New York, NY.

TURNER, BRENDA
[pen.] Ebony Story; [b.] April 30, 1944, Detroit, MI; [p.] Wilbur and Anna Turner; [ed.] Cass Technical High School, Harlem Hospital School of Nursing, University of Detroit; [occ.] Registered Nurse; [memb.] Seven Sisters Ministry Group, A local Advisory Board of Mothers and Children with Aids, The Black Womens Forum; [hon.] 1984 nominee for Outstanding Nurse of the Year, 1988 Nurse of the Year-Brotman Medical Center; [oth. writ.] I've been writing poetry for eleven years this was the first poem ever submitted for competition; [pers.] My goal is to reach out and touch others with words, to influence, enlighten and enrich for the glory of God. [a.] Los Angeles, CA.

TURNER, DEBORAH
[b.] September 4, 1961, Russellville, AR.; [p.] Julius and Evelyn Hogrefe; [ch.] Christopher Turner; [ed.] Lamar High School, College of the Ozarks; [occ.] Secretary/solicitor for Allstate Insurance; [memb.] Zion Lutheran Church; [pers.] To live each day to the fullest and to treat other people the way I wish to be treated. [a.] Ft. Smith, AR.

TURNER, JOEY
[b.] June 7, 1982, Cincinnati, OH.; [p.] Jack and Ginny Turner; [ed.] I am in the 5th grade at St. Antoninus school; [pers.] The Chicago Cubs have always been my favorite baseball team. It was easy to write a poem about them and I'm glad it's being published. [a.] Cincinnati, OH.

TURNHAM-JONES, EILEEN
[b.] May 22, 1945, Surrey, England; [p.] Mary and Horace Turnham; [occ.] Local government manager; [memb.] Institute of Administrative Management; [oth. writ.] This is the first one to be published and the first competition I have entered; [pers.] I have written many poems on love, life, beast and burden and all that is dear to me. [a.] Surrey, England.

TURPEN-LANHAM, BARBARA
[b.] February 15, 1934, Denison, TX.; [p.] Ella Olivia Kimbrough and James L. Turpen; [m.] Donald Mac Lanham, March 29, 1957; [ch.] Donald Mac Lanham Jr. and Deanna Rene Lanham; [ed.] Twelfth grade; [occ.] Wife, mother, grandmother; [oth. writ.] None, personal enjoyment only first publication; [pers.] How blessed I am to be "Grand-ma" to my wonderful Joshua. How wonderful the world, if we followed the simple honesty and trust of the child. [a.] Murrieta, CA.

TWITCHELL, GINA MARIE
[b.] October 12, 1976, Northridge, CA.; [p.] David and Andrea Twitchell; [ed.] High school student; [pers.] I try to write what I feel. I want others to understand that through poetry, we can unlock the door to our imaginations. [a.] Chatsworth, CA.

TYNER, DORIS WYONA
[b.] November 17, 1939, Hartsville, SC.; [p.] Harrison and Marion Tyner; [m.] Divorced; [ch.] James Dale Lewis; [ed.] G.E.D. as of May 1993; [occ.] Unemployed; [memb.] Songwriters Club of America (lifetime member); [hon.] Golden Poet Award ('85-'92), Who's Who in Poetry, lead sheets for first two poems put to music, first poem was rated # 3 on a chart of 30 evaluation chart, first two poems won songwriters award and certificate. All poems ranked honorable mention, 1981 member of the Top Records Songwriters Association; [oth. writ.] Poems only, two poems put to music (45 rpm and cassette); [pers.] The Lord deserves all the praise. He gave me the words to write. [a.] Hartsville, SC.

ULBRICH, RACHAEL LAKELA
[b.] July 23, 1979, Puyallup, WA; [p.] Jon and Shirley Ulbrich; [ed.] Freshman in high school at Walnut Wood Independent Study; [hon.] Track and school awards; [oth. writ.] First published poem; [pers.] I would like to thank my best friends Heather Cash and Brett Weaver for encouraging me to send in my poem, and especially thank God for blessing me with this talent. Peace. [a.] N Highlands, CA.

UMHOEFER, CHRISTINE M.
[b.] May 4, 1972, St. Louis, MO.; [p.] Lawrence and Rosann Umhoefer; [ed.] Rosary High, University of Mo., St. Louis, Barat College; [occ.] Student, Barat College, Lake Forest, IL>; [hon.] Various honors in dramatics, art, speech and composition; [pers.] I use to cut and paste construction paper until the tips of my fingers turned rainbow colors, and I gave all these pieces to a wonderful woman named Anna. Sometimes it's nice to communicate without fancy words. [a.] St. Louis, MO.

URBAN, GINNY
[b.] Dravosburg, PA.; [p.] Margaret Newmeyer and Alphonso Berwick; [m.] George W. Urban, July 1, 1939; [ch.] Two, son David (killed in Vietnam), daughter Ilona, art teacher; [ed.] High school graduate, read from Harvard Classics, non-credit courses TV from Western Reserve University; [occ.] Retired legal secretary; [memb.] Not a club-joiner, member First United Methodist Church; [hon.] Really none, recognition and honored for some local endeavors. Greatest thrill as a high school sophomore, publication of a poem in a National Scholastic magazine; [oth. writ.] News and articles of accomplishments of people in local small papers. Wrote for own enjoyment. Some poems accepted by a National Greeting Card Co., but conditions at home prevented me from accepting; [pers.] Enjoy observing people, the beauty of nature, animals and birds. I have had many dreams of writing. I believe everyone passes through this life with a certain dream in their heart, but it usually remains just that a dream. [a.] Brooksville, FL.

VALERIUS, KELLY ANN
[b.] March 25, 1979, Passaic, NJ.; [p.] David and Sandra Valerius; [ed.] Christopher Columbus Middle School, Clifton, NJ.; [occ.] Student; [memb.] Clifton Safety Patrol, school band; [hon.] Honor Roll, certificate for Read-A-Thon, scholarship medal for honors, Presidential Academic Achievement and Fitness Award. [a.] CLifton, NJ.

VALLEE', GAETAN
[b.] May 30, 1968, Thetford-Mines; [p.] Antonio Vallee and Reine Sheehy; [occ.] Aircraft maintenance technician in search of work; [pers.] I am a French-Canadian, this is my first work. [a.] Thetford-Mines, P.Q. Canada.

VAN BUREN-COMELLA, RUTH
[b.] July 24, 1918, Troy, NY.; [p.] Warren Van Buren and Harriet Howe; [m.] Vincent J. Comella, December 4, 1940; [ch.] Vincent Alan and Carol Ruth; [ed.] Troy High School, 1936, short courses while traveling with Air Force husband; [occ.] Sears Roebuck, 25 years, retired; [memb.] Episcopal, Republican Club, Space Coast Wives; [hon.] "My First"- Thank You", (children have several also husband -my turn); [oth. writ.] School publications hometown during youth, hometown newspaper, short stories 1930's and 40's; [pers.] Direct descendant of Martin Van Buren, 8th President of U.S., I claim him as my great-great etc. grandfather. My children are proud of this. I loved Edgar Guest. [a.] Rockledge, FL.

VANDER WEIDE, STEPHANIE ANNE
[pen.] Victoria Hatch; [b.] November 18, Washington, DC; [p.] Gretchen and Vernon Vander Weide; [ed.] Undergraduate, sophomore University of Michigan, Ann Arbor; [occ.] Student; [memb.] Alpha Delta Pi Sorority; [hon.] Mount Holyoke Book Award, American Leigon Bronze Medal, Mona Meyer, McGrath and Gavin Advertising-Journalism Writers Award, International Baccalaureate Certificate Award for English, Presidential Academic Fitness Award; [oth. writ.] Poetry "The Mosaic" a literary magazine, poetry "The Hill and Lake Press". [a.] Minneapolis, MN.

VAN HEEL, GOLDIE
[pen.] Monic Right; [b.] April 21, 1982, Spokane, WA.; [p.] Mike and Patti Van Heel; [ed.] Midway Elementary School in the Mead School District; [pers.] I was taught when I was very young to be as creative as possible. All my creativity came out in Miss Merchants's 2nd grade class. [a.] Spokane, WA.

VAN HOECKE, JO-ANN M.
[b.] September 5, 1946, Providence, RI.; [p.] Michael and Julia Van Hoecke; [m.] Husband is deceased; [ch.] Twins Jeffrey and Jonathan, also Jennifer; [ed.] Elmhurst Academy, Caldwell College, B.A. Art, L.P.N. degree CCRI; [occ.] L.P.N.; [oth. writ.] Written 100's of poems; [pers.] I write my poems for pleasure and to reflect the simple but beautiful feelings of daily life. [a.] Cumberland, RI.

VAN HORNE, MARI
[b.] August 25, 1973, Parksville, BC.; [p.] Gerry and Betty Van Horne; [ed.] Freshman, Camoson College, Victoria BC, Canada; [occ.] Student; [pers.] Be still, let the wind speak hush.. a world is talking. [a.] Victoria, BC Canada.

VAN NOTE, STELLA L.
[pen.] Stella Davis-Van Note; [b.] October 13,1915, Yucaipa, CA.; [p.] Bert and Vera Davis; [m.] Phillip Van Note, February 3,1945; [ch.] 3 daughters, 2 sons, 17 grandchildren and 10 great-grandchildren; [ed.] Hemet High, Riverside J.C., Fullerton, SC.; [occ.] Diversified-waitress, flight dispatcher, electronics; [memb.] Episcopal Church of the Good Shepherd, Hemet-San Jacinto Genealogical Society; [oth. writ.] My first; [pers.] There is always room for learning. [a.] Hemet, CA.

VAN PELT, ELIZABETH ALLENE
[pen.] Elizabeth Van Pelt, Allene Van Pelt, Tiz-Liz; [b.] February 28, 1926, Plano, Collin Co., TX.; [p.] Annis Jane (Coats) Cudd and James Edward Cudd, Sr.; [m.] S.R. McClung Jr., 1944-1955, J.D. Van Pelt, 1957; [ch.] Gary Edward McClung, (stepchildren) Sue and Don Van Pelt; [ed.] High school, I.B.M. Data Processing-U.T.A.; [occ.] 32 years General Motors, 8th Army Service Command, IBM,; [memb.] Charter member W.I.N.A., President Hood County Taxpayers Assoc., President Cudd Family Reunion Assoc., A.B.W.A., A.A.R.P., Baptist Church; [hon.] Golden and Silver Poet Awards from World of Poetry, Army Service Award, G.M. suggestions award; [oth. writ.] Poem published in local newspaper, articles in Statewide Newspaper, publish 3 newsletters, working on book; [pers.] God's creations of writing is my wisdom, poetry my song, Browning's Aurora Leigh my inspiration, the people, the world the beauty in my life. [a.] Granbury, TX.

VAN WYK, LAURA ANNE
[b.] March 12, 1978, Livingston, NJ.; [p.] Florence and William Van Wyk; [ed.] Sophomore at Westfield High School, Westfield, NJ. [a.] Westfield, NJ.

VARDAL, EBONY
[pen.] Ebony Eyes; [b.] August 15,1979, Lloydminster, Saskatchewan, Canada; [p.] Gunnhild Vardal and David Doyle; [ed.] Grade 9 student, Chase Secondary; [occ.] Student, poet; [memb.] Psychedelic President for Freedom, Youth Council (Chase); [hon.] Girls 9 and under champion (1989-track), Citizenship (1989), Enthusiasm and Determination (1988), numerous talent awards, art and poetry; [oth. writ.] Shadows of Happiness, Wonder Why, Sounds of Music, Shinning Light, (anthology of collected works); [pers.] I want to share my poetry with the world now. [a.] Chase, BC Canada.

VAUGHAN, REBECCA
[b.] February 17, 1977, Norfolk, VA.; [p.] Carl Vaughan III and Susan Hunter; [ed.] Mills E. Godwin High School; [occ.] Student; [memb.] Staff member of Mills E. Godwin Literary magazine; [hon.] Nominated for Who's Who Among American High School Students; [oth. writ.] Various poems, some published by school literary magazine; [pers.] I enjoy writing what I feel, how I see things and communicating it to others. [a.] Richmond, VA.

VAUGHN, HERMAN F.
[b.] February 9, 192, Crawford, OK.; [p.] Ernest Claude and Deede Herring Vaughn; [m.] Louise Lillian Vaughn, January 21,1952; [ch.] Shannon F. Vaughn; [ed.] 3rd year college, Tulsa University; [occ.] Conductor-brakeman, Missouri-Pacific Railroad; [oth. writ.] The Busy Man, Hoeing Beans, Cowboys Three, The Curly Wolf, Cats and Men; [pers.] A teacher of senior adults Gethsemane Baptist Church, Ordained Deacon, former high school football coach. [a.] No. Little Rock, AR.

VENTURA, ALLISON MARY
[b.] November 17, 1976, Livingston, NJ.; [p.] Peter and Lois Ventura; [ed.] Kingwood High School, Kingwood,TX.; [occ.] High school junior; [memb.] Youth Against Cancer, Hawkwatch International, HGA Junior Golfmember; [hon.] Letter in Varsity Golf, 10 years participant in Gifted/Talented program, Duke University Talent Program; [pers.] Through the weeds, one will always find a flower. Living in the past, loses the present and leaves you lost in the future. [a.] Kingwood, TX.

VERNON, DUNAWAY JAMES
[pen.] Vernon; [b.] March 26, 1924, Sunbright, TN.; [p.] Joseph and Mae Dunaway; [m.] Lois A. Dunaway (August 24, 1928), November 30, 1946; [ch.] David and Linda Dunaway; [ed.] Sunbright High, Government Special NVA Machinist School, Military Radar School; [occ.] Tool and die metal finisher retired; [memb.] American Legion; [oth. writ.] Many poems in which some have been published in hometown county newspaper, many books on adventure and fiction with offers for subsidy publishing; [pers.] Inspired to seek hidden treasures overlooked by mankind in his quest for riotous living and the lust of the flesh to strengthen the weak and comfort the poor. [a.] Xenia, OH.

VIALE', DEBRA
[pen.] Debbie Vaughn, Debra Viale'; [b.] February 24, 1955, Martinez, CA.; [p.] William and Martha Vaughn; [m.] Ronald J. Viale', August 11, 1984; [ch.] De'Anna age 15 and Amber age 7; [ed.] Alhambra High School, Cosmetology/Real Estate schooling; [occ.] Realtor/poet; [memb.] American Heart Association, Mothers Against Drunk Drivers; [oth. writ.] I have many unpublished poems and short stories waiting to be published. I'm looking for a good publisher; [pers.] As a humanitarian I've always loved poetry. During the late 60's my literature teacher inspired me to write freely in class, I would like to thank her, Audrey Bergen. Before you can write from your soul, you have to feel great pain. My favorite poet is Emily Dickinson. [a.] Vacaville, CA.

VICENTE, REBECCA
[pen.] Becca, RV; [b.] November 20, 1977, Teaneck, NJ.; [p.] Frances and Raymond Vicente; [ed.] Bogota High School; [occ.] Hopefully, future writer and musician; [hon.] Numerous awards for poetry, writing and music since age of 7, I am now 16. Kiwanis Award for clarinet, which I play since age 8; [oth. writ.] Been published in Great Poems of The Western World Anthology of Poetry and in local newspapers also my high school's monthly edition of The Outlook; [pers.] I hope to promote peace, individuality and love through my feelings and thoughts, writing is the art of the heart. [a.] Bogota, NJ.

VICK, MARY
[b.] September 9, 1920, Miller, NE.; [p.] Kate and Frank Elder; [m.] C.C. Vick, June 18, 1938; [ch.] Jimmy, Wayne, Carol, Donna, Paula, eleven grandchildren, eight great grandchildren; [ed.] Milby High, Austin High, Houston; [occ.] Housewife; [oth. writ.] Poems to family members for weddings, graduations, new babies, etc., Christmas or just thoughts, nothing has ever been published; [pers.] I do most of my poem thinking at night when I can't sleep. I love to write about the earth's beauty. [a.] Huntsville, TX.

VILLANUEVA, MARGARITO (MARK)
[b.] June 10, 1927, Scarbro, WV.; [p.] Norberto Villanueva (F.) and Annette Lewis (M.); [m.] Gullermina Acosta, December 7, 1957; [ch.] Herman A., Mark A., Michael and Annette; [ed.] High school, Academic Schooling Armed Forces Institute, Madison, WI., U.S. Army Military Schools; [occ.] Finger printer, Los Angeles Police Department, retired from Cerritos COllege, Norwalk, CA.; [memb.] VFW Post # 7138; [hon.] Military service; [oth. writ.] "My Loved One" published by National Library of Poetry in Wind in The Night Sky, 1993, "Tonight I'm Leaving on That East Bound Train", published in Poetry, An American Heritage, by The American Poetry Association, Colorado Springs, CO., winter edition 1993, writer of Country Western songs; [pers.] "Just Being A Modest Person". [a.] Norwalk, CA.

VILLARREAL, DENISE
[b.] December 4,1968, Meridian, TX.; [p.] Ronald L. and Margaret Ridings; [m.] Rodolfo G. Villarreal Jr., June 15, 1992; [ed.] Morgan High School, Tarleton State University; [occ.] Language Arts Teacher, Rio Vista Middle School, Rio Vista, TX.; [memb.] Nation Council Teachers of English, Texas Council Teachers of English, Texas State Teachers Association; [pers.] Writing enhances life just as life enhances writing. I hope to enhance the lives of others through my writing. [a.] Meridian, TX.

VILLARREAL, ROGER
[b.] November 11, 1958, Fabens, TX. [pers.] Always write. [a.] Baltimore, MD.

VILLARREAL, VANESSA
[pen.] Vanessa; [b.] July 26, 1977, Kingsville, TX.; [p.] Albert and Hermalinda Villarreal,Jr.; [ed.] 11th grade, H. M. King High School; [oth. writ.] Personal collection of over 70 poems; [pers.] My deepest and innermost joys and fears are expressed in my writing. Give me a pen and paper, I'll give you my soul. [a.] Kingsville, TX.

VINOKUZOV, JOSEPH
[b.] January 20, 1925, Moscow, Russia; [p.] Marija and Aba Vinokuzov; [m.] Anna Vinokuzov, July 25,1953; [ch.] Larisa Miropolsky; [ed.] Higher education; [occ.] Engineer; [memb.] Jewish Community; [hon.] The honorable certificate on the poetry contest International Pushkinists Club; [oth. writ.] Several poems published in Russian newspapers USA, in Philadelphia, San Francisco and New York. [a.] Seattle, WA.

VOGEL, BETTY
[b.] Brooklyn, NY; [p.] Nathan and Anna; [ed.] Kingsborough Brooklyn College, Regents College Degrees; [hon.] 13 Certificates of Honor from World of Poetry; [oth. writ.] Child's Lullaby, Convention Time, The Convention, Beach, Time, Summer's Here Again.

VOGEL, LAURA H.
[pen.] Helen Vogel; [b.] December 25, 1977, Point Pleasant, NJ.; [p.] Harold and Jeannie Vogel; [ed.] Msgr. Donovan High School, Toms River; [memb.] International Thespian Society, MDHS Drama Club; [oth. writ.] Several articles published in local papers. [a.] Bricktown, NJ.

VORRATH, MURIEL J.
[b.] July 13,1945, Suffolk, England; [ed.] Dundalk Senior High; [occ.] Medical Records Clerk, miniature craftier of doll houses; [memb.] S.A.W. (Songwriters Assn. of D.C. International Poets Society Sweet Adelines (Barbershop Chorus); [oth. writ.] "If", published in Wind In The Night Sky, Sweet Adeline's Downbeat; [pers.] I tend to look at the funny side of life, and how people react to situations. My style is more lyrical, and I'm influenced by many of the songwriters from the forties to the present. [a.] Dundalk, MD.

VORWERK, SARAH R.
[pen.] Sarah; [b.] November 9, 1947, Waco, TX; [p.] Herbert Allen Bludworth and Evelyn Marie Kingsley; [m.] William Vorwerk, March 3, 1991; [ch.] Three by a previous marriage; [ed.] High school graduate, 7 months certified Medical Assist., 7 months Travel Agent, entry level; [occ.] Nurse, L.V.N.; [oth. writ.] Poems and one short story; [pers.] Forgiveness and love is the beginning of peace by Sarah. [a.] San Francisco, CA.

VRATANINA, BEATRICE
[b.] August 31, 1910, Chetek, WI.; [b.] Cyrus and Jennie Williams; [m.] Joseph Vratania, September 30, 1920; [ch.] William H. Vratanina and Alice A. Dougherty; [ed.] Teacher's College; [occ.] Teacher, newspaper work, telephone operator; [hon.] Several for poetry; [oth. writ.] Patriotic poems published in papers during W War II. [a.] Toledo, WA.

WAGER II, OSCAR PAUL
[b.] May 28, 1968, Alma, MI.; [ed.] Mountain View High School, DeVry Institute of Technology; [occ.] Systems Engineer; [a.] Phoenix, AZ.

WAGGONER, CARI MARIE
[b.] March 28, 1975, Houston, TX.; [p.] Charles (Butch) and Joyce Waggoner; [ed.] 1993 graduate Katy High School, attending University of Texas Austin; [occ.] Student at UT; [memb.] Honor Society, T.E.T.A. (theater), Thespain Troupe, Spanish Club, Girl Scouts of America, Drama Club, Student Council; [hon.] Texas Governors School Gold Award, Girl Scouts, Who's Who in American, All Around Girl-KHS, Most Likely to Succeed; [oth. writ.] Only personal poems, not yet submitted for publication; [pers.] It is escape, solace, channel for thought, pain, delight, feeling, expression-perfection, poetry. I usually write poems with double meanings-one for the softer side of life and one for the hidden deeper side. [a.] Katy, TX.

WAITKUS, JOY
[b.] November 24, 1969, Newton, MA.; [p.] Marjorie E. Waitkus and Algrid L. Waitkus (deceased); [ed.] Plymouth North High School, Plymouth, MA., Columbia of University, Modern European Studies MA Program, Barnard College '91; [occ.] Secretary; [hon.] Ins Albertini scholarship '87; [oth. writ.] Editor of Modern Times newspaper, Columbia University. [a.] New York, NY.

WALBERT, LUKE
[b.] February 27, 1961, St. Paul, MN.; [p.] Clement and Florence Walbert; [ed.] University of Minnesota School of Management, Macphail Center for Arts, Minneapolis; [occ.] Property Tax Clerk, Assistant Controller, poet, music composer; [memb.] Christians for Biblical Equality, Minnesota Composers' Forum; [hon.] BSB with distinction (University of Minn.); [oth. writ.] Commentary in local newspaper, self-published anthology "Luke Means Light", composed songs used in church services; [pers.] I am a very moderate male, modern, modest, musical, intelligent, cross-cultured, honest, peaceful evangelical. [a.] St. Paul, MN.

WALDBUSER, MARGARET
[pen.] M. Waldbuser or Margaret Waldbuser; [b.] July 4, 1946, Urbana, IL.; [p.] Helen Fackler and Thomas W. Thompson; [m.] ben Waldbuser, August 6, 1967; [ed.] Urbana High School, Danville Junior College, Lake View Memorial Hospital School of Nursing; [occ.] Rn-Visiting Nurse; [memb.] Rotary, Forsyth United Methodist Church, Rebekahas, Ladies and Trainmen Aux.; [oth. writ.] Poem published in following, Hospital Paper, Fishing Magazine, Shoppers Directory; [pers.] Lives in country native log home. Avid mushroom hunter. [a.] Kissee Mills, Mo.

WALKER, ANGELA
[pen.] Angie Walker; [b.] February 4, 1979, Valdese, Burke Co., NC.; [p.] Mike and Sheri Walker; [ed.] Student of East Burke High (9th grade); [oth. writ.] Several poems that are unpublished; [pers.] In my poems I share my thoughts and feelings. It seems easier to write how I feel in a poem than to just come out and tell everyone. [a.] Drexel, NC.

WALKER, ANTHONY LEVENE
[pen.] Tony Walker; [b.] July 23,1945, Pike Co., AL.; [p.] Mr. and Mrs. A.D. Walker; [m.] Single; [ch.] Toby, Payne and Amber; [ed.] 12th grade Charles Henderson High, Troy, AL.; [occ.] Owner of 50% Less and More Store; [oth. writ.] I have written poetry since the first grade, this is my first poem to be presented to public; [pers.] I have a deep appreciation for nature, love and mankind especially in its in humanity to each. [a.] Albertville, AL.

WALKER, CYNTHIA
[b.] August 18, 1969, Bronx, NY.; [hon.] 1st place winner for short story in 13th Annual Literary Festival; [oth. writ.] Dehila's Disease (short story), Mama's Boy, Robswife; [pers.] For my sister, Kristen Mary Walker who has had to endure and for my father who has chosen to. I love you. [a.] Briarwood, NY.

WALKER, LYNDA C.
[b.] May 6, 1960, Memphis, TN.; [p.] Reverend Jerry D. and Zana L. Moore,Sr.; [m.] David E. Walker, December 27, 1991; [ch.] S. Samuel and Daniel F. Young; [ed.] White Station High School, Ouachita Baptist University; [occ.] Legal secretary law office of Lanier Fogg; [memb.] F.L.A.R.E., National Right to Life, Shelby County Republican Women, National Association of Legal Secretaries; [pers.] I believe as it says in Ephesians 2:10 that "We are God's poems created in Christ Jesus unto good works". I pray that the content and rhythm of my life glorifies God. [a.] Memphis. TN.

WALKER, OSCAR C.
[pen.] Oscar C. Walker; [b.] October 31, 1922, Dodson, LA.; [p.] Nick W. and Arelia Dill Walker; [ed.] Sixth grade; [occ.] Draftsman (retired), Baptist Minister; [memb.] Pleasant Grove Baptist Church, Ruston, Louisiana; [pers.] I am totally influenced by: If my people which are called by my name, shall humble themselves, and pray, and seek my face and turn from their wicked ways: then will I hear from heaven, will forgive their sin and will heal their land. 2 Chronicles 7:14. [a.] Ruston, LA.

WALKER, STUART
[b.] March 1, 1955, Ebb Vale, Wales; [ed.] Leeds University, Royal College of Art, Imperial College of Science; [occ.] University Professor; [oth. writ.] A number of papers published dealing with relationship between the material and the spiritual, plus writings of a technical and academic nature; [pers.] The arts allow expression of the soul in ways which science and technology can never approach. When responsibly combined, the potential is limitless. [a.] Calgary, Alberta Canada.

WALKER, TIMOTHY J.
[b.] June 14,1981, Neenah, WI.; [p.] John and Bev Walker; [ed.] Will be a 6th grader fall of '93 at St. John's Lutheran School in Montello, WI.; [occ.] Student; [pers.] Tim's father had a massive stroke affecting his speech, cognitive function and right arm and leg when Tim was 8 years old (the day before his 9th birthday), Tim wrote this poem this spring when we were going through a stressful time with his father's stroke.

WALL, BRANDY
[b.] August 31, 1978, Pennsacola, FL; [p.] Gail Redmond (mother), Doug Wall and Lynn Wall (stepmother); [ed.] Carlyle High School in Carlyle, IL; [memb.] I am a member of the softball team at my high school, S.A.D.D., speech team and color guard; [oth. writ.] Three other poems, "I'll Always Love You", "Day and Night" and "Friends"; [pers.] " I believe in writing how you feel, when I write a poem it's my way of expressing how I feel about myself and about others. [a.] Boulder, IL.

WALLACE, JACINTA D.
[b.] May 9, 1977, Camden, NJ.; [p.] Rutholee Hatcher and Richard Wallace; [ed.] 11th grade, Camden High School; [occ.] High school student; [memb.] Champ; [hon.] Champ certificate, CCC OEO certificate; [oth. writ.] None; [pers.] Poetry is an expression of feelings, a thought that just hit you at special times in your life. You may be riding, walking or just sitting in silence, you may jot them down. [a.] Camden, NJ.

WALLINGTON, DWIGHT
[b.] march 22, 1939, Toledo, OH.; [p.] Arnold and Edith Wallington; [ch.] Father of -Stephen A., Karen Rebecca, Deborah Mitchell, Jeffrey Dean and John Paul; [ed.] High school creative writing courses; [occ.] Author, writer, poet, publisher; [oth. writ.] Beyond Abuse, Forgive-Forget-Forever, released January 1993, In The Child's Best Interest, release October 1993; [pers.] In a time when everything seems to be rushing on to what or where we all need to ponder the value of life, a time to make a difference before we become as a vapor.

WAPLE, NANCY MARGUERITE
[b.] May 10, 1949, Washington, DC.; [p.] Marguerite and Louis A. Waple; [m.] Divorced; [ch.] Malisa Ellen Davies; [ed.] B.S. Education, Pembroke State University, M.Ed. Master's in Education, Campbell University, NC.; [occ.] Instructional Systems Specialist, Civil Service, Ft. Bragg, NC.; [memb.] Mailhandlers Union, Military Order of World Wars; [hon.] Commendation, USA, Exceptional Civil Service Performance 1989, 1991; [oth. writ.] Writing is my personal hobby. I write everyday, it is as much a part of me as food and water; [pers.] Writing is the mirror of the soul. It must be done in order for self-actualization to take place. [a.] Fayetteville, NC.

WARD, JEROME
[b.] June 27, 1958, Philadelphia, PA; [p.] Mr. and Mrs. Georgia and Willie Ward; [m.] Lovella Amanda Ward, May 1986; [ch.] Amanda M. and Ponnisheena G. Ward; [ed.] High school grad. (GED), Gary Job Corps, San Marcos, TX; [occ.] Executive secretary, Jazz musician/saxophones and flutes; [memb.] Renaissance Writers Society of Philadelphia; [hon.] U.S. Army Vet, November 81 to November 85; [oth. writ.] In possession of one short story, one short novel, hundreds of poems, numerous political, social, spiritual and theological writings and manuscripts, one full length musical; [pers.] So I am that I live in you, of you, off you whether you be leader, writer or friend. I don't know you. You touched me, I've settled my portrait in your frame. [a.] Philadelphia, PA.

WARD, JUSTIN HARVEY
[pen.] J.H. Ward; [b.] February 26, 1969, Washington, DC.; [p.] Gloria M. and Harvey R. Ward; [ed.] Cornell University; [pers.] I aspire to the legacies of Baraka, Berryman and Dugan. [a.] South Orange, NJ.

WARNER, BERNICE
[b.] November 6, 1930, Baytown, TX; [p.] Leslie and Mary James; [m.] Bruce Warner, 1948; [ch.] Bruce Alan and Shirley Bernice Warner, grandchildren, Christen Page Pescia, John and Jeffrey Warner; [occ.] Retired Real Estate Broker and appraiser in her own business; [memb.] Texas Real Estate Commission, Pilot Club of Baytown-Texas District, American Diabetes Assoc. Baytown Chapter; [hon.] Bay Area Board of Realtors, Realtor of The Year, Outstanding Dedication Award 1991 for her work in the Baytown Chapter of the American Diabetes Assoc., honored for her work in the Kennedy Foundations' "very special arts" for the past 3 years, also art and music director for the diabetes camp for children. Judge for Exxon and Chevron posters for several years. Active in the different fund raisers for the Diabetic Assoc. donating her paintings several times yearly, she teaches children 2 day weekly in her own studio, also in several of the Baytown schools demonstrating her different techniques of marbleizing and watercoloring; [oth. writ.] Poem and song poem for Seniors group and The High Flyers, Eastern Star programs, poetry displayed at Heritage Museum in Wallisville. Friends programs and parties, personal book of poems for grandchildren; [pers.] Along with my art and music my poetry provides a serenity and peace in my busy schedule. [a.] Baytown, TX.

WASKEY, GENEVIEVE
[b.] December 25,1923, Newport, KY.; [p.] Elsie and Frank Wiggins (deceased); [m.] John W. Waskey, August 30, 1962; [ch.] 5 boys, 2 girls, 16 grandchildren, 4 great grandchildren; [ed.] Western Hills High, 2 years night school, 2 years apprenticeship; [occ.] Survey engineer; [memb.] Assembly of God Church, Volunteer of America; [oth. writ.] Several from World of Poetry, published local paper and Parents Magazine; [pers.] I have an abiding faith in God and feel any talent I have comes from Him. [a.] Ormond Beach, FL.

WASSMER, JENNIE
[pen.] Max Gunn/Margaret Alexander; [b.] January 3, 1972, Nyack, NY.; [p.] Frank and Marge Wassmer; [ed.] St. Thomas Aquinas College, Albertus Magnus High School; [occ.] Student of Art Therapy and Art Education; [memb.] Arts Alliance of Haverstraw; [hon.] Dean's List; [oth. writ.] Several poems and short stories, not yet published; [pers.] If you don't shiver in the icy wind or taste the salty breeze... if you don't hear the sounds of the city or smell the wild flowers growing in the meadows... if you don't see malicious eyes peering out at you from behind a tree watching your every move.. if you don't feel my writings, if you aren't actually taken there, then as a writer, I am unsuccessful! [a.] Haverstraw, NY.

WASSON, MARILYN J.
[b.] October 31, 1936, Rogers, AR.; [p.] Jayson A. and Ruth A. Crithfield Wasson; [ch.] Fred Jeffery and Shelley Ann Stuetelberg; [ed.] Atlantic High School, Atlantic, Iowa, Maple Wood Community College, Kansas City, Missouri; [occ.] Medical secretary; [oth. writ.] Poetry, personal journal, currently working on the outline for a family history and stories of my father's childhood; [pers.] Interested in family history and leaving a record for my children and grandchildren. I believe that is one way to achieve immortality. I believe in kindness to my fellowman. Influenced by my father and his philosophy of life. [a.] Kansas City, MO.

WATKINS, THOMAS W.
b.] September 1, 1928, Nashville, TN.; [p.] Mr. and Mrs. James H. Watkins; [m.] Rae H. Watkins, June 20, 1959; [ed.] 2 years college; [occ.] Retired; [memb.] In a Poetry Club; [hon.] Wrote a book of poetry "Leaves of Clover" and has been published; [oth. writ.] Newspaper articles; [pers.] I love writing poetry and has been for a number of years.

WATSON, MARY CATHERINE
[pen.] Kathy; [b.] December 25, 1953, Russellville, AL.; [p.] William McKinney and Beatrice Hyde (both deceased); [m.] Robert Watson; [ch.] Sean and Kevin Pruett; [ed.] Russellville High; [occ.] Caretaker; [oth. writ.] "Twas The Night Before Christmas", "America, The Land of The Free". [a.] Killen, AL.

WATTS, IRENE
[b.] August 17, 1932, Elmhurst, IL.; [p.] John and Clara Sheber; [m.] Kenneth C. Watts; [occ.] Fine Artist; [memb.] Denver Art Museum; [hon.] Phi Beta Kappa; [oth. writ.] Self published book "Art and Words"; [pers.] I have been writing all my life because I must. This is the first poem submitted for publication. [a.] Lakewood, CO.

WEALAND, BUD
[pen.] Chauncy Harbert Wealand; [b.] February 5, 1918, Sheldon, MO.; [p.] Cordie L. Chauncy J. Wealand; [m.] Single; [ch.] Four; [ed.] High School; [occ.] Farmer, shepherd, carpenter and builder; [memb.] V.F.W.; [hon.] Aeneid's, Poet of the Year Award 1978; [oth. writ.] Most of my poems and some short stories published in local papers; [pers.] Matters not whence comes lovely word or deed, matters much how many hear love, and heed. [a.] Grandin, MO.

WEAVER, NATHAN
[b.] May 25, 1970, Millersburg, OH.; [p.] Dennis M. and Mary M. Weaver; [m.] Kristine Weaver, October 12, 1991; [ch.] Luann Joy; [ed.] 8 grades in a one room Parochial School; [occ.] Farming and part-time elementary teacher in a Parochial School; [memb.] My family and I are members of an Amish Church; [oth. writ.] Several poems I never published. I'm helping compile a science book suitable for use in Amish Parochial Schools. [a.] Fredericksburg, OH.

WEBB, HEATHER R.
[b.] November 4, 1974, Salisbury, MD.; [p.] Jeff Webb and Starr Neill; [m.] Not married; [ed.] Graduated from Epworth Christian School, now attend Salisbury State University; [hon.] Co-salutatorian in high school; [oth. writ.] Various poems and short stories that are not published; [pers.] Everything I do, I do to the glory of God, because without Him, I could do nothing. [a.] Girdletree, MD.

WEBB, VERN H.
[pen.] Vern H. Webb; [b.] January 28, 1935, (Bay County) Panama City, FL.; [p.] Harold and Gertrude Heard; [m.] Divorced; [ch.] Gail Gilyard, Faye Pennington, Sharon W. Boone and Briggette Barker; [ed.] Completed high school and have taken some college courses; [occ.] Mother and housekeeper; [hon.] I have many, many awards in poetry, prose and quotations; [oth. writ.] Two books of poetry published, and have been published in many well known anthologies; [pers.] My philosophy is letting God be first in my life, then everything else will fall in order, secondly poetry is that tiny messenger that reveals the honesty in me, uncovers the fear and now is beginning to bring forth the boldness in my life. [a.] Panama City, FL.

WEBBER, AARON
[b.] December 14,1901, Lincoln County, KS.; [p.] Rev. Myron D. Webber and Dorinda Strange; [m.] Margaret Horton, May 28, 1931; [ch.] David Leroy Webber; [ed.] Fairfield High School, Fairfield, Iowa, A.B. Parsons College, Fairfield, Iowa, STB and STM, The Biblical Seminary in New York, advanced studies, U. of Chicago Divinity School; [occ.] Missionary, American Baptist Churches in Puerto Rico, Cuba, El Salvador and Nicaragua; [memb.] Council, Boy Scouts in El Salvador and Cuba; [hon.] Pi Kappa Delta, National Forensic Society, Puerto Rico Council, Boy Scouts of America, National Council of Boy Scouts of America, El Salvador (with wife) Adoptive Son and Daughter of the city of San Juan, Puerto Rico, Member International Missionary Council, meeting in Ghana, Africa 1951. Member Evangelical Conference in Latin America, Lima, Peru, 1961. [oth. writ.] Writings have been sermons and articles, almost all in Spanish. [a.] Dallas, TX.

WEBER, SHARON ANN
[b.] August 7, 1964, Ft. Smith, AR.; [p.] Charles and Barbara Short; [m.] David W. Weber, October 20, 1989; [ed.] High school graduate of Pleasure Ridger Park High School-1082; [occ.] Legal secretary; [oth. writ.] I have written many poems but have never pursued any publishings; [pers.] Poetry has always been a hobby for me, even as young as grade school. I get a thought or topic in mind and can sit down and write a poem within 20 minutes. [a.] Louisville, KY.

WEEKS, EARL
[b.] January 6, 1964, Philadelphia, PA.; [p.] Earl and Carol Jean Weeks, Sr.; [ch.] Earl B. Simmons, 8 years and Stacy E. Weeks 6 years; [ed.] High school graduate, Mercy Vocational High School and Randolph Skillcenter; [occ.] Ex-marine Sgt. Recruiter and auto mechanic, currently student Security Guard; [memb.] Member of University of Penna. Veterans Upward Bound Alumni, high school Thespian Society member; [hon.] 3 Marine good conduct medals, honorable discharge and 10 years service from June 15, 1981 - July 12, 1991; [oth. writ.] He Who Sits Behind The Desk, poems and articles published in The University Penna. Veterans Upward Bound programs' Warriors Journal; [pers.] "I refuse to allow anyone to put limits on my mind". [a.] Philadelphia, PA.

WEIDLER, BERNICE L.
[pen.] Kay Lane; [b.] April 6, 1911, Sorento, IL.; [p.] Edward and Stella Blevins; [m.] Bill Wiedler (deceased), May 17, 1954; [ch.] Sharon Schulte; [occ.] Housewife; [hon.] Poems published in The Alabama Coal Bin by Henry Vance, under pen name, Kay Lane (honorary); [oth. writ.] Poems published in the Birmingham, Al. "Coal Bin" by Henry Vance, pen name was Kay Lane when she was in her 30'3 (honorary); [pers.] She can write only on things she feels from the heart. [a.] St. Louis, MO.

WEIDMAN, SCOTT
[b.] August 27, 1972, Reading Hospital; [p.] Dean F. and Sharon W. Weidman; [ed.] Kutetown High School, Kutetown University (Fine Arts); [occ.] Salesperson (GAP Clothing Store); [oth. writ.] Nothing publicly known; [pers.] Unfortunately I don't consider myself a "true" poet. I am interested in and love all of the arts. I specialize in design and the drawing aspects of art, through art I hope to help others realize the beauty that the world possesses and not to take it for granted as so many do. [a.] Bethel, PA.

WEINER, ROBERT
[pen.] R.J. Sparky; [b.] August 12,1966, Philadelphia, PA.; [p.] Robert J. and Bonnie Weiner; [ed.] Riverview High, Branell Institute-Data Entry; [occ.] Florida State Prisoner; [hon.] Magna Cum Laude-Branell Institute; [oth. writ.] Poem "Beyond The Rain", published through World of Poetry, several poems and short stories actively seeking publication; [pers.] My poetry reflects the hardships that I've suffered through my life because I've grown tremendously from these hardships. I'm a better man for it, we can all be better for it. [a.] Bowling Green, FL.

WEIS, AI LING
[b.] December 6,1968, Kuala Lumpur, Malaysia; [p.] Yat Cheng Fun (mother); [m.] Harry A. Weis, September 12, 1991; [ed.] BBA from University of Central Oklahoma in Edmond, Oklahoma; [occ.] Housewife; [pers.] It doesn't matter what happens to you or the choices you make, all that matters is that you know you. It takes a lot of strength to look at your soul. "In quietness and in confidence shall be your strength: Isaiah 30:15. [a.] Oklahoma City, OK.

WEISHEIT, WENDY
[b.] October 10, 1969, Cleveland,OH.; [ed.] Class of '88 Valley Forge High, Parma Heights, Ohio, Associates-Journalism/short story writing; [occ.] Performer, Journalist currently working for Cleveland Public Library; [hon.] Member-National Thespian Society; [oth. writ.] Article in local paper, songwriter, currently working on a novel and screenplay; [pers.] Never let anger over the past turn you against yourself. Success is the best revenge. [a.] Cleveland, OH.

WEISMANN, CARRIE A.
[b.] July 18, 1968, Yuba City, AC.; [p.] Seurina Nelson; [m.] Robert J. Weismann; [ch.] Melonie and Daniell.

WEISS, DESIREE
[b.] February 20, 1963, St. Louis, MO; [p.] James and Delores Johnson; [m.] Mark Weiss, January 8, 1983; [ch.] Dezi, Mark, Sheriah, Michael, Daniel and Shaina; [ed.] Beaumont High School, diploma as a career secretary from Draghons Business College; [occ.] Writer, homemaker; [memb.] Victanny's, True Pentecostal Apostolic Faith Church; [hon.] Acknowledged by Dorrance Publishing Co., as having unique rhyming pattern; [oth. writ.] I have written 45 or more poems and songs, I have written poems for different occasions and subjects also; [pers.] I would like to have all of my work published on songs someday. My writings are inspired by the bible, there is a message in my writings. [a.] St. Louis.

WELLER, JANE Y.
[b.] May 23, 1921, Moosic, PA.; [p.] Gordon Young, Margaret Y. Thomas and (step-father) William M. Thomas; [m.] Carl J. Weller, August 18, 1945; [ch.] One son Carl, 2 grandsons-Gordon and Ben; [ed.] Taylor High School, class of 1938, 3 years Temple University; [occ.] Homemaker; [memb.] United Baptist Church of Taylor, American Diabetic Association; [pers.] The promise of eternal life, a real good sense of humor has kept me going all my life-in spite of all that come my way. In reality of just in rumor. [a.] Taylor, PA.

WELLMAN, JAMES T.
b.] March 8, 1941, Wichita Falls, TX.; [p.] James Wellman and Opal Mae Davis; [m.] Divorced; [ch.] James T. Wellman III and Romi Anne Wellman; [ed.] BA degree, Naval Aviator, USN retired; [occ.] Airline Pilot; [memb.] Former member board of directors of Airline Pilot Association, Tailhook Association; [oth. writ.] Novel on The Vietnam War in progress; [pers.] Poetry and writing should be a reflection of the best of mankind's morals and feelings not an avenue for the draining of society's life. [a.] White Bear Lake, MN.

WELLNITZ, THERESA PETERMANN
[pen.] Theresa Faye; [b.] April 30, 1951, Breckenridge, MN.; [p.] Henry and Louise Thoennes Peterman; [m.] Roger Wellnitz, September 24, 1977; [ch.] Brian David (15 years) and Lori Ann (12 years); [occ.] Disabled from Cancer but am a homemaker; [oth. writ.] I've many about our church minister, death, religion, love and just about any thing you can imagine; [pers.] Since I've had cancer, there is nothing you can tell me about the Lord I haven't already experienced. Be positive and smell each morning. [a.] Wheaton, MN.

WELLS, MOLLIE
[b.] March 18, 1981, Lancaster, OH.; [p.] Steve and Pamela Wells; [ed.] Sherman Junior High School; [memb.] Fairfield Lancaster Youth Choir; [hon.] Winner of 1993 Young Authors Conference and 1992 Junior Authors Conferences; [oth. writ.] Young Authors winning book A Land Unknown and 1992 winning book The Trials and Tribulations of Growing Up; [pers.] My writing reflects on what mood I'm in. My poems tend to occasionally lean toward a more sad or mysterious side. [a.] Lancaster, OH.

WELLS-DUNLOP, TERESA E.
[pen.] Tess Wells; [b.] July 9, 1948, Houston, TX.; [p.] S. Alex Sushotlz and Rosalie Susholtz; [m.] Jack D. Dunlop, September 10, 1980; [ch.] None of my own, but I have 3 step-sons (all grown) and 3 step-grandchildren; [ed.] Spring Branch High, U. of H., Houston Community College; [occ.] Actress, writer (books, songs and poetry), housewife; [memb.] Country Playhouse Theatre, where I've acted and directed plays for a number of years; [hon.] I have won many acting awards over a 39 year period; [oth. writ;] So far I've completed over 17 songs, numerous poems, and one book of 10 parable type stories (short) for children, which I hope to get published very soon. "Daddio" in it's original form, is a song I wrote about my dad and me; [pers.] In all my writings I strive to confront universally important issues. My writing is greatly influenced by spiritual guidance, my own personal history, and a life long love of observation of humanity;. [a.] Houston, TX.

WELSH, MARIE ELIZABETH
[ch.] Troy and Dena Welsh; [ed.] High school and voc; [hon.] Local newspapers; [oth. writ.] Been writing poems all my life and enjoy poetry, reading. My poems are original and my own living experiences are mostly in my poems.

WEST, CRAIG H.
[b.] Philadelphia, PA.; [p.] Inetta M. Winge; [ch.] Brandi Nicole, Craig Harold and Chynna Te; [pers.] "My poetry is powerful, yet poignant, containing subtle nuances that make you reread and rethink and hopefully help reshape your way of looking at things. I know that one line of love written with artistry and insight softens the glare of a brilliant God and rescues a desolate soul (even in the Desert Sun)". [a.] Philadelphia, PA.

WEST, KAREN
[pen.] Karen West; [b.] October 18, 1957, Middlesboro, KY.; [p.] Ralph and Betty Pearson; [m.] Kyle West, Jr., April 18,1986; [ch.] Steven (age 7) and Joshua Rowe (age 10); [ed.] B.A. degree Elementary Education, M.S. degree Elementary Education; [occ.] 3rd grade T.N.T. Primary Elementary teacher, New Tazewell, TN.; [memb.] N.E.A., T.E.A., National Education Association, Tennessee Education Association; [hon.] National High School award for Excellence, Dean's List, L.M.U., National Beta Club; [oth. writ.] Other poems, I have written 14 gospel songs, I have had a tape made from Nashville, TN.; [pers.] I write about past experiences. Laura Ingalls Wilder's writings have greatly influenced me, I write about feelings from my heart.[a.] Tazewell, TN.

WEST, MOLLY
[b.] July 9, 1980, Birmingham, AL.; [p.] Allen and Marlene West; [ed.] W.J. Christian Alternative Program; [hon.] Presidential Academic Achievement Award; [oth. writ.] One short story and one poem published in Birmingham City Images; [pers.] Don't live life to seriously or you'll never have any fun. [a.] Birmingham, AL.

WEST, VIRGINIA
[pen.] Virginia West; [b.] August 14, 1908, Ingham County; [p.] Etta and Clifford Bates; [m.] Charles W. West, August 14, 1931; [ch.] One son Larry; [ed.] High school graduated nurse; [occ.] Retired; [memb.] Hob-Nob, Amateur Writers Journal newspapers and several others; [hon.] Editors Choice Award, Golden Award, Silver Merit, Laureate, Readers Award, I have won over 375 awards children's poems; [oth. writ.] Song lyrics and music, 7 tapes out; [pers.] Nature and Cod I write most on. [a.] Leslie, MI.

WESTMORELAND, KYLE T.
[pen.] KTW; [b.] November 24, 1971, Baton Rouge, LA.; [p.] Dr. Thomas D. and Martha B. Westmoreland, Jr.; [ed.] Currently working towards a degree in Computer Science and Engineering at the University of Texas at Arlington; [occ.] Full time college student; [memb.] National Honor Society, Mu Alpha Theta; [hon.] Pennzoil Scholarship Award (1990-1992), Outstanding Performance for Internship Program-Houston Area Research Center; [oth. writ.] Poems published in Conroe High School's Troika, other writings include Desideratum and Is This America? [a.] Fort Worth, TX.

WHATTAM, KEVIN
[b.] November 27, 1964, San Jose, CA.; [m.] Maxine R. Whattam, December 23,1989; [ed.] Bachelor's of Journalism, University of Missouri-Columbia; [occ.] Information Officer-Supply System; [hon.] 'Clarion" for newsletter editing -1993, Magna Cum Laude, 1992 'Chinook" award for newsletter editing and design. (note: Clarion is a women in communications national media competition, Chinook is a regional advertising club's competition). [a.] Kennewick, WA.

WHEELER, JULIA CLARK KING DUFF (RALPHA)
[pen.] Julia Duff-Wheeler; [b.] July 18, 1907, Greensboro, NC.; [p.] Ella Council and Charles Marion King; [m.] James Bryer Duff (first marriage), June 19, 1929; [ch.] Julia Ann, Robert Wallace and James Bryer Duff, Jr.; [ed.] High school, Secretarial School, I attended junior high school in Davenport, IA.-1919-1920; [occ.] Housewife now, secretary 3 years before first marriage; [memb.] Church, golf club, Bridge Club, bowling team; [oth. writ.] Other poetry and many letters of "Wisdom" and "Philosophy" to my children, grandchildren and 9 great grandchildren. I wrote a poem written about the "Rappahonnock River" in 1935 when we had a cottage on a cliff overlooking it, near Urbana, short distance from Chesapeake Bay; [pers.] I try to keep an up-beat attitude, sometimes seeing something quite amusing that others ignore. [a.] Hamden, CT.

WHITACRE, PAULINE
[b.] November 19, 1910, Carbondale, IL.; [p.] Mr. and Mrs. Daniel Bye Whitacre; [ed.] B.A. National Col. for Christian Workers Kansas City, Mo., commissioned and consecrated; [occ.] United Methodist Church Deaconess. [a.] Asheville, NC.

WHITCOMB, MARGUERITE
[b.] October 31, 1959, Australia; [p.] Mr. and Mrs. Banker; [m.] Alan Whitcomb, August 25, 1984; [ch.] Marissa, Aaron and Merrandah Whitcomb; [ed.] General nursing training, Graphic Art degree, Australia; [occ.] Homemaker; [memb.] National Wildlife Federation; [hon.] Platinum Academic Achievement Award; [pers.] I believe poetry should express feeling that ordinary communication can't express, it can touch the soul by the touch of the pen.[a.] Honolulu, HI.

WHITE, JESSIE
[pen.] 'BJ" White; [b.] Alexander City, AL.; [p.] Rufus (deceased) and Edlink Benson; [m.] James White; [ch.] Nedra and Jessica; [ed.] Laurel High School, Long Beach City College, Spalding College, Jefferson Community College, Simmons Bible College; [occ.] Office clerk and instructional asst., Jefferson County Board of Education; [memb.] Pleasant View Missionary Baptist Church, Colonial Home Owners Subdivision Association; [hon.] Honor Student, Salutatorian, Employee of the Month, perfect attendance, special effort, high school queen, college queen; [oth. writ.] Several other writings, school contest, church programs, songs, lyrics, inspirational writing, get well cards, thoughts for today newsletters; [pers.] All gifts come from God and I give Jesus Christ, the God of my life the highest praise for this gift and special thanks to all my friends and family for their support. [a.] Louisville, KY.

WHITE, WANDA
[b.] April 29, 1943, Stigler, OK.; [p.] Joe and Willie Webb; [m.] Dr. Gerald Lowther, September 4, 1993; [ch.] Rhonda Paul, Regina Imboden and Gordy White; [ed.] Basic education in Salinas, CA.; [occ.] Not currently but for years church organist and choir director; [memb.] Board of Directors St. Louis Squires and Ladies and Board of Director SLC (religious organ.); [pers.] The only way I write is from the soul, based on my experiences and those of my family and close friends. At times it has been my healing. [a.[] Chesterfield, MO.

WHITLOW, CRYSTAL FAYE
[pen.] Crystal Faye Whitlow; [b.] April 22, 1979, Glasgow, KY.; [p.] Neddie Ray and Betty Whitlow, grandparents, Bernice and Annie Whitlow, Junior and Ruby Blythe; [ed.] Metcalfe Co. High; [memb.] Kentucky Junior Historical Society, 4-H, Community Art Center and Girl Scout member for 8 years; [hon.] Talent awards in 4-H; [oth. writ.] I have written several short stories and poems; [pers.] Do unto others as you would have them do unto you.[a.] Edmonton, KY.

WIGLEY, BARBARA G.
[b.] October 25, 1934, Cedartown, GA.; [p.] Inez and R.B. Graham; [m.] Divorced; [ch.] Kathryn Anne, Elizabeth Kaye, Kennie Lee, Edward Keith, Kevin and Krissy; [ed.] Rockmart High School; [occ.] Homemaker; [pers.] Due to multiple health problems, I limit my physical activities so I write and record to occupy my time positively, hoping to give a good concept of life our Lord gave me. [a.] Rockmart, GA.

WILCOX, GAIL
[b.] April 21, 1911, Grand Rapids, MI.; [p.] Parents were from Holland, Europe; [ch.] Shirley Duvall and Bonnie Goosen; [ed.] High school grad.; [occ.] Mechanic-owned own band, Elect, Pbg. Hgt. work heavy equipment operator; [pers.] Love to write poetry. I am in a nursing home, unable to walk and I'm

in an electric wheelchair, I.m unable to pay any nominal fee, though I would like to. [a.] Gaylord, MI.

WILCOX, LYNN
[b.] September 4, 1935, Huntsville, AL.; [p.] W.F. and Anna Mae Esslinger; [ch.] Gregory C. Haun; [ed.] Ph.D., 1968 University of Missouri, post doctoral work, Universidad Catholica, Quito, Ecuador and Maktar Tarighat Ovyssi Shah Maghsoudi (school of Sufism); [occ.] Professor, California State University, Sacramento, West Coast Director, Wayfinders, Inc., private practice in Psychotherapy; [memb.] Amer, Counseling Assoc., American Psychological Assoc., NOW, AAUW, National Wellness Association;[hon.] Grad. Cum Laude, Gregory Fellow, Danforth Associate, Meritorious Performance Award, CSUS, 1988, Professional Promise Award, CSUS, 1986 Who's Who in American Women, Who's Who in the West; [oth. writ.] Wayfinding (a book of poems) in press, Psychology and Sufism (nearing completion). [a.] Sacramento, CA.

WILLIAMS II, CLARENCE A.
[pen.] Ace; [b.] August 16, 1952, Frankfort, KY.; [p.] Clarence and Evelyn Joyce Williams, I; [m.] Divorced, June 9, 1973 to October 16, 1991; [ch.] Aisha Yvette and Clarence A. Williams, III; [ed.] Graduated Franklin County High School in Frankfort,KY 1970, have degree in computer programming from Metridata Institute in 72; [occ.] Work for Philip Morris USA, Louisville, KY; [memb.] New Zion Baptist Church, Rev. Russell A. Awkard, Louisville, KY.; [hon.] My 3 sisters, Madge Johnson, Washington,DC, Annette Minor, Minneapolis, MN. and Arlandra Williams, Houston, TX.; [oth. writ.] I have 37 poems in 1st volume, and 43 poems in 2nd volume. The "SHA" collection of poems volume I, The Dream We Dream, Fearless, Gath-Boo, You Listen But Don't Hear, If Only-If Only, Ask The Question-Why?; [pers.] I would like to dedicate this to a very special friend in my life, always O'Gatha Horton, Baton Rouge, LA., my inspiration on life,love, religion. [a.] Louisville, KY.

WILLIAMS, DAVIDA DAWN
[pen.] Cherokee Williams; [b.] August 18, 1952, Kennett, MO.; [p.] David and Mavis Williams; [m.] David Paul Greenwell, February 29, 1992; [ch.] Heath Williams-Greenwell and Christine Greenwell-Robinson; [ed.] Bachelor's, Master's, Specialist's degrees at Arkansas State University; Doctoral work at University of Southern MS, Mississippi; [occ.] English teacher/writer; [memb.] Phi Kappa Phi, Lambda Iota Tau, Society of Former Special Agents of the Federal Bureau of Investigation (FBI), National Council of Teachers of English; [hon.] Lambda Iota Tau, Phi Kappa Phi, permanent member of National Honor Society, Student of Special Distinction, Arkansas State University, FBI Letter of Commendation, (former special agent of the FBI), recipient of La Femme Citizenship scholarship, honorary committee work; [oth. writ.] Article published in the publications of Mississippi Philological Association Pompa, papers presented to the MPA, newspaper articles, personal poetry and short stories, currently writing a novel and working on a book of poetry; [pers.] Honesty and humanism are important in my writing, even though it be my truth, my experience. I have been inspired by the 19th century poets and novelists and by my deceased, illiterate grandmother, Minerva Jane Capps, whose wisdom and heart encompassed all humankind. [a.] Doniphan, MO.

WILLIAMS, FRANK C.
[pen.] Frank C. Williams; [b.] June 19, 1903, Cleveland, OH.; [p.] Frank Thomas and May Williams; [m.] Thora K. Williams, June 18, 1983; [ed.] B. Sc. in Education Ohio State University, S.T.B. Boston University; [occ.] Clergyman (retired); [memb.] Tournament Players Golf Club. [a.] Cromwell, CT.

WILLIAMS, KAREN
[b.] April 28, 1975, Miami, FL.; [p.] Clyde Edward and Doris Jean Williams; [ed.] Coral Shores High School in Tavernier, FL.; [occ.] Waitress at Howard Johnson's in Key Largo, FL.; [pers.] This is the first thing I've ever submitted for publication. I've always loved and have been amazed by the beauty of the earth. [a.] Key Largo, FL.

WILLIAMS, KIM ALLEN
[b.] October 8, 1972, Pittsburgh, PA; [p.] Teri-E Belf and Robert A. Williams; [ed.] BFA in Performing Arts, Emerson College, 1994; [pers.] "Thoughts are like boomerangs". The poem that appears was written by Kim at age 17. [a.] Newton, MA.

WILLIAMS, MICHAEL
[b.] October 14, 1974, Waco, TX.; [p.] Bruce and Debra Williams; [ed.] Mexia High School, student Southwest Texas State University; [memb.] Alexander Primitive Baptist Church; [hon.] 4th in class, National Honors Society; [pers.] The tree which stands alone is better left alone. [a.] Mexia, TX.

WILLIAMSON, MARK W.
[m.] Lisa A. Williamson; [oth. writ.] Books published by Authentech Publications, International , Tangled in A Tapestry, Threads of the Obvious and The Obscure, Humanity... Tangled in A Tapestry; [pers.] It isn't what one knows, it's what one presuppose, does meaning waft to every nose or does each mind compose the roses. [a.] Newburyport, MA.

WILLIAMSON, SONDRA
[b.] February 4, 1941, Anderson, MO.; [p.] Lester and Lucille Pulliam; [m.] Ronald Williamson, May 19, 1956; [ch.] Ricky Dean and Vicki Lenn Williamson; [ed.] Satanta Elementary, freshman high school G.E.D.; [occ.] Homemaker, poet, writer of short stories; [oth. writ.] I have written much poetry, also some short stories-not published; [pers.] My writing has been a life line to which I have hitched my star. I pray it will always shine. [a.] Satant, KS.

WILLIS, EDWARDLENE M. (Ph.D.)
[pen.] Edwardlene Fleeks Willis, Ph.D.; [b.] December 27, 1932, Crockett, TX; [p.] Edward D. Fleeks and Mary Adline Wooten Fleeks; [m.] Dr. George M. Willis (deceased), February 8, 1964; [ch.] Miles Edward and Mirron Edward Willis; [ed.] Prairie View A&M University, BA degree, Texas Southern University, MA degree, California State University for Advanced Studies, Ph.D. degree; [occ.] Retired secondary school administrator, management consultant for adult education and social service programs; [memb.] Piney Woods Fine Arts Assn., Alpha Kappa Alpha Sorority, NARFE, PV A&M University Alumni Assoc., Women's Sunday Morning Breakfast Club-Crockett; [hon.] Magna CUm Laude-undergraduate, Cum Laude-graduate, community service awards for volunteer service, including day care center (pres. of bd. of dir.) NAACP, youth speaker for various organizations; [oth. writ.] Published book, Mind Your Manners, an etiquette guide for youth and young adults (559pp) poems, articles published in local papers in Dayton, Oh., and Houston, TX., editor college newspaper; [pers.] Gracious people make life easier and more pleasant. [a.] Crockett, TX.

WILLIS, JOLENE
[pen.] Jennifer Rose; [b.] March 15, 1929, Cleburn Co, AL.; [p.] Claudus F. and Audra M. Pritchett, my dad is deceased as of September 14, 1988; [m.] Arthur Namon Willis, April 11, 1947; [ch.] Herman R., October 20, 1949, Jerry E., October 26, 1952; [ed.] Senior high school, Cosmetology course, State Merit test and followup in State Department of Education for over 7 years; [occ.] Retired under Disability; [memb.] Cosmetology of Georgia, Salem Baptist Church, AARP Assoc.; [hon.] I feel it an honor that I was chosen to write the class will, and present it to our graduating class of near 40. I was the 7th highest honor in my class, so I don't feel that was too bad; [oth. writ.] "A New Star","My Mother, My Friend", "I.C.H.S."/"Guide Us Dear Lord", "My Dear Friend"/"Salvation", "God's Great Beauty"/"Prissy, My Silent Friend"; [pers.] I try to search for the serene wisdom that comes from calm contemplation of life. The universe, God's great love, family, friends, love of marriage, the wonders of God's beautiful world, and His handi-works, and lives ultimate goals here and in the other life to come.[a.] Tifton, GA.

WILSON, GARY S.
[pen.] Gary S. Wilson; [b.] July 26, 1971, Warren, Oh.; p.] Gary F. and Stephanie F. Wilson; [ed.] LaBrae High, currently attending Kent State University (Trumball Branch); [occ.] Inventory Control at K-Mart Distribution, Warren, OH.; [oth. writ.] This is my first published work; [pers.] I feel poems are an extension of one's emotions transferred to paper. This is why I write them, all my poems are based solely on my emotions or who I was thinking of at the time.[a.] Warren, OH.

WILSON, JAMES E.
[b.] July 19, 1941, Louisville, KY.; [p.] Edith Evelyn Myatt, Wilson and Edward Hayes Wilson; [ed.] 9th grade; [occ.] Unemployed Bartender; [hon.] World of Poetry award of merit certificate for poem Thunder: [oth. writ.] Thunder. [a.] Louisville, KY.

WILSON, THOMAS A.
[pen.] Allan Thomas; [b.] September 24, 1975, St. Paul, MN.; [p.] Dorothy and C. Thomas Wilson; [occ.] Writer, student; [oth. writ.] Chamber, Gate, Mystery, Undaunted. [a.] New Ulm, MN.

WILTSE, LESLIE J.
[b.] August 1,1920, Lansing, MI.; [p.] Leslie B and Irene L. King (deceased); [m.] Douglas Wiltse, (deceased), February 14, 1939; [ch.] Judith Irene, Leroy Douglas, Sharon Louise and Roseleen Lea; [ed.] High school, college courses; [occ.] Retired; [memb.] T.O.P.S. Club Inc., "In The Woods Catholic Shrine", Mich. Sheriff's Association; [oth. writ.] None published, write poems for pleasure and in honor of family and friends; [pers.] As I travel along through my day each day, it's my desire to make someone happy along the way. The above are my feelings that inspired me to write the poem. [a.] Indian River, MI.

WINDHAM, BILLY G.
[b.] October 5,1931, Pike Co., AL.; [p.] Alex and Mae Gibson Windham; [m.] Ann Windham, June 7, 1957; [ch.] Garry, Galen and Scott; [ed.] 2 years college Tech. Schools; [occ.] Aircraft mechanic retired (EAL); [pers.] Who could even imagine a heaven without it's beautiful birds.. and the people who loved them. [a.] Monticello, FL.

WINTERS, MATT
[b.] June 27, 1982, San Antonio, TX.; [p.] Ora and Tony Velez; [ed.] 5th grade; [occ.] Student; [hon.] Honor Roll, Presidential Academic Fitness Award, National Science Olympiad Award; [oth. writ.] Rino and Dino, Rino and Dino II, Brandon's Manor, all above complete, but not published yet; [pers.] I tend to write poems about nature because of the beauty I see in it. Much of my inspiration in writing comes from my good friend Leslie Seamon. [a.] Friendswood, TX.

WIRTH, CAROL
[b.] may 17, 1960, Bronx, NY.; [p.] Constance Pickthall and William Cullen; [ch.] Damian Wirth; [ed.] New York City and Charlotte North Carolina Schools, Central Piedmont Community College, Iona Westchester Community College; [occ.] Eligibility Examiner II; [memb.] C.S.E.A.; [pers.] Special thanks to Michael Croke and John Horrell for encouraging me. Gratitude to Bobby, Lynn H., Kenny, Tracey, Kevin, Angela, Lynn A., Jackie, Alegra, Tom, E.J. Fox and Rosa. I love you all. [a.] Bronxville, NY.

WISE, JENNIFER MICHELLE
[b.] November 16, 1978, Spokane, WA.; [p.] Mike and Jill Wise; [ed.] Currently a student at Kamiakin High School, in Kennewick, WA.; [oth. writ.] Have one other poem published by the American Academy of poetry; [pers.] When I write my poems I write on a subject that I feel strongly about or something that I have experienced. [a.] Kennewick, WA.

WISEMAN, JERRY LEON
[b.] January 27, 1976, San Francisco, CA.; [p.] Jerry and Nanette Wiseman; [m.] At least not until 2003; [ed.] De Anza High School, graduate in 1994; [occ.] In the near future after college, will become a Veterinarian; [memb.] B.S.V. Vice President; [hon.] San Francisco write on poetry contest; [oth. writ.] "The Fog"; [pers.] Life is a game if you play the right cards you may win successfully and beat death by a far margin. [a.] El Sobrante, CA.

WITTEMAN, ERICA ANN
[pen.] R.K.; [b.] January 16, 1979, Newmarket, Ontario Canada; [p.] Simon Witteman and Diane Toussaint; [ed.] I am in my first year of high school; [occ.] Student; [hon.] Chosen to attend The Young Author's Conference, certificates of excellence in the English language; [oth. writ.] In the Monkey's Grasp, Human Exit, Between Friends (script); [pers.] I like to write about things that we all take for granted, things that should be praised not ignored. [a.] Bouchette, Que. Canada.

WITTMAN, MARY ANN
[b.] April 6,1968, Cleveland, OH.; [p.] Roslyn and Richard Wittman (Richard, deceased); [ed.] Associates of Applied Science in Dietetics from Cuyahoga Community College, St. Augustine High School; [occ.] Dietetic Technician, VA Medical Center; [memb.] American Dietetle Association, Cleveland Dietetic Association; [oth. writ.] An untitled poem published in my college newspaper; [pers.] Thanks to family, friends and co-workers, I finally have the courage to share my poetry and let my voice be heard. [a.] Cleveland, OH.

WOLF, REBECCA
[pen.] Austin Wolf; [b.] January 18, 1973, Lemoore NAS, CA.; [p.] Terry Wolf and Susan Austin; [ch.] Jordan Boone; [occ.] Student, Johnson and Wales University, Providence, RI.; pers.] I am a nonconformist. I believe in the individuality and uniqueness of every person. I believe in children, playing hard, campfires, honesty, loyalty and living life to it's fullest extent. [a.] Providence, RI.

WOOD, DAVID
[b.] July 11, 1963, Boston, MA.; [p.] Donald M. and Marybeth G. Wood; [m.] Nina Schindler-Wood; [ch.] Rebecca and Lyndsay; [ed.] University of Windsor (B.A.); [pers.] Poetry is a necessary art, it speaks as the collective voice of the social conscience. In its various forms-written, read or sung-it has the power to be the most expressive and influential of all art.[a.] Windsor, Ontario Canada.

WOOD, VERONICA
[b.] August 30, 1957, Cleveland, OH.; [p.] Albert and Anna Sedlock; [m.] Dwight Wood, July 27, 1981; [ch.] Kenneth Isaiah, Kurtis Elijah and Kevin David; [ed.] Brecksville High, Boca Raton High, South-Eastern Bible College; [occ.] Professional mother and housewife; [memb.] Woodbine Assembly of God Church board; [hon.] I am proud of the fact that my husband, 3 sons and myself hold yellow belts in Karate; [oth. writ.] I have had a total of 6 poems published to date, have also had an article written for Woman's World magazine in '90; [pers.] I give all credit for my poems and writing to Jesus Christ. [a.] Delta, PA.

WOODCOX, TERRI
[b.] May 21, 1981, Lapeer; [p.] Terry and Lois Woodcox; [ed.] 7th grade; [occ.] Babysitting; [memb.] Member of the Eagles Club; [oth. writ.] I continue to write poetry; [pers.] The reason I write poetry is because I can't talk out what's inside of me so I write my feelings down. [a.] Dryden, MI.

WOODS, JAMES CEDRIC
[b.] June 3, 1969, Lumberton, NC.; [p.] James H. and Rosa Woods; [ed.] B.A., UNC-Chapel Hill, 2nd year M.A. program in Political Science, University of Arizona, Tucson; [occ.] Graduate student; [memb.] American Club, U of A, "Red Ink" editorial board; [hon.] Morehead Scholar, Tarheel of the Week, National Indian Student of the Year (1987), N.C. Indian Student of the Year; [oth. writ.] " A Dancer's Prayer" to be published in American Collegiate Poets Anthology, July 1993; [pers.] Lumbee Indian from Pembroke, NC. [a.] Tucson, AZ.

WOODS, LAURA SIMPSON
[pen.] Laura S. Woods; [b.] January 20, 1937, Louisville, KY.; [p.] Millage Lee Simpson and Julia McGee Simpson (both deceased); [m.] Divorced; [ch.] Germaine Denise Woods; [ed.] Sylvania F. Williams and F.P. Richard Elementary Schools, Brooker T. Washington High School, Dillard University, LSUNO, IUSE, University of Louisville; [occ.] Retired elementary school teacher (34 years); [memb.] NRTA, KRTA, Brown Memorial CME Church, Delta Sigma Theta Sorority, JCTRA, AARP; [hon.] Honor student-4 years, Dillard University, Cum Laude graduate "58, Dillard University, Who's Who Among Colleges and Universities, 1958, PTA Life Membership, Outstanding Staff Award 1992-1993, Who's Who Among Teachers in American-1992, 1993, Honorary Citizen N.Ogha, Spirit of Louisville Award, Clifford Turner Freedom Award 1992; [oth. writ.] An extensive collection of unpublished poems; [pers.] I believe that I am an instrument in this cycle of life to assist whenever I am needed with God's help, His will be done.[a.] Louisville, KY.

WOODS, WALDA
[b.] April 27, 1952, Revere, MA.; [p.] Walter and Myda Bakoian; [m.] Tom Woods, March 11, 1972; [ed.] North Reading High School, American Institute of Real Estate National Association of Securities Dealers Institute; [occ.] Sales manager; [oth. writ.] Several poems under current market review, through Blue Mountain Arts Publishing Company; [pers.] I write what I feel-my inspiration comes from God. I have been greatly influenced by my strong family-ties, their support and love is unconditional. [a.] North Andover, MA.

WOODMAN, RITA E.
[pen.] Eve; [b.] April 10, 1957, Montreal, PQ, Canada; [p.] Steve and Carol Woodman; [ed.] Broadcast training/CFJC Marketing, Dun and Bradstreet, computer courses, Coastway Systems; [occ.] President of A.V. Global Media Productions Inc., Freelance Broadcaster; [memb.] ACTRA, Canadian Public Relations Society of B.C., Southlands Riding Club; [hon.] Numerous ribbons and trophies in Equestrian events marketing award; [oth. writ.] Song, "Some Hearts Reach High", children's story for national T.V., various poems published in newsletters, music for a movie theme song; [pers.] "Building on Ruins". I'm always trying to get the message of HOPE across in my writing;. [a.] Vancouver, B.C. Canada.

WOODRING, KRISTI
[b.] December 25, 1958, Norman, OK.; [p.] Freda A. Dieterich and Charles E. Woodring; [ed.] Alief Hastings High School, graduated 1976; [occ.] Administrative Executive-Heritage Planning Co.; [oth. writ.] Writing prose and poetry since age 12, extensive private collection, no previous publications. [a.] Houston, TX.

WOODSON, DONALD A.
[b.] April 19, 1948, Kansas City, KS.; [p.] Earl and Eleanor Woodson (both deceased); [m.] Debbie S. Woodson, August 11, 1984; [ch.] Mendy Simpson, Kimberley Lindsay, Jason Glander, Dawn Woodson, Heather Glander and Richard Woodson; [ed.] Wyandotte High, Kansas City Kansas Community Junior College, Webster University, K.C.Mo. Campus; [occ.] Employment Coordinator-Board of Public Utilities; [memb.] Webster University Alumni, Human Resource Management Association, E.A.R.N., Personnel Roundtable Customer Service Institute-life-

time member; [oth. writ.] None published; [pers.] My writings reflect the thoughts that have evolved through a wonderful and joyous life with family and friends. [a.] Kansas City, KS.

WOOTEN, REBECCA D.
[pen.] Rebecca D. Wooten; [b.] July 13, 1971; [p.] Jerry Arthur and Altha Austina (Tina) Wooten; [ed.] Mathematics major at U.S.F. working toward masters may go into engineering; [occ.] Tutor at USF; [memb.] Pi Mu Epsilon, Mathematics Association of American; [hon.] Florida Academic; [oth. writ.] Poems including "Teach Me to Love Him", "Somebody Loves You", "To Life in Death" and some short stories; [pers.] Also enjoys to sing, draw (abstract) art, plays, a little piano and flute. [a.] Tampa, FL.

WORTHINGTON JR., SAM W.
[pen.] Sam Worthington; [b.] May 7, 1907, Baltimore, MD.; [p.] Samuel Wheeler and Lucy Outlaw Worthington, Wilson, North Carolina; [m.] Mary Pegram Wilson Worthington, January 8, 1955; [ch.] Bo, Margie and Georgia, Jim and Billy Humphrey; [ed.] Graduate U.N.C., 1928 A.B. degree; [occ.] Peanut farmer, owner and manager 50 years, Outer Banks subdivision; [memb.] Zeta PSI Fraternity; [hon.] Chairman Laymens Association, Dioces of East Carolina, president Berta County Farm Bureau 10 years, Berta delegate A.A.M.; [oth. writ.] Unpublished poems copywrited song, various articles on agriculture; [pers.] If our Lord's way is not the right way, we don't have any right way. I take it with all my heart, soul and body. Praise His Holy Name. [a.] Windsor, NC.

WOZNY, MARY
[b.] March 12, 1980, Elmhurst, NY.; [p.] Joseph E. and Judith Wozny, Jr.; [ed.] St. Martin of Tours (LaSalle Regional School) Bethpage, NY.; [occ.] Student; [hon.] Honor Roll Student, Science Fair, second place 2 years 6th and 7th grade, Math Bee, second place, 6th grade; [oth. writ.] Voice of Democracy, essay contest (V.F.W.) second place; [pers.] I love to write and draw. I also attend dancing school. In the future I hope to become a Marine Biologist or Veterinarian. [a.] Bethpage, NY.

WRIGHT, CAROLYN J.
[pen.] Carolyn Wright; [b.] March 26, 1958, Tulsa, OK.; [p.] Deceased; [ed.] Classen High School, University of Penn.; [occ.] Basic Computer Tech.; [memb.] Smithsonian member, Air and Space member; [hon.] Dale Carnegie Award; [oth. writ.] Only in high school and college, University of Penn. and Classen High School; [pers.] I do not know about been greatly influenced but bet I have been. But I do know that there is an inner part of us that wants to be the best we can be, and hope someone in this world will think the world isn't so bad after all and there is a meaning to everything after all. By this I mean poems! For through poems at times these words find that deep inner part of us and maybe that deep inner part some had had all the time. [a.] Waters, MI.

WRIGHT, CHRISTINE
[pen.] C. J. Wright; [b.] February 5, 1973, Hammond, IN.; [p.] Robert and Shirley Wright; [ed.] Oak Park High, Missouri Western State College; [hon.] Honor Roll, Dean's List; [pers.] My imagination allows me to see the world in many different ways. In my writing, reality and fantasy can be both the same or different like day and night. [a.] Kansas City, MO.

WRIGHT JR., FRANK E.
[b.] August 31, 1964, Williamsport, PA.; [p.] Frank E. and Thelma L. Wright, Sr.; [m.] Rosemary C. Wright, May 7, 1992; [ch.] Adam C. Wright; [ed.] Williamsport High, Florida Keys Community College, Community College of the Air Force; [occ.] Linguist U.S. Air Force; [memb.] United Methodist Church, Rotarian Club; [hon.] Defense Language Institute honor grad., John Lentow Award, Achievement Medal, Commendation Medal; [oth. writ.] Several articles in Air Force unit paper; [pers.] There's still goodness, decency and beauty today. We just have to look a little harder. God gave me my two most precious gifts, my son and my wife. [a.] Key West. FL.

WRIGHT, MARK
[b.] January 28, 1974, Pasadena, TX.; [ed.] Kingwood High, Sam Houston State University, University of Houston; [memb.] Sigma Epsilon Chi Fencing Club, Young Writers Guild; [oth. writ.] Several poems and two short stories published in school magazine; [pers.] I try to put my mind, my heart and my soul into everything I write. If my poetry reflects this, I am a success. [a.] Kingwood, TX.

WRIGHT, MARY D.
[b.] July 16, 1926, Carroll's Corner; [p.] Douglas and Martha (Pace) Hirtle; [m.] Ivan Sherman, (deceased) March 28, 1942; [ch.] 3 sons, 5 daughters, 15 grandchildren and 10 great grandchildren; [ed.] Grade IX (high school); [occ.] Housewife, Quality Controller for Sears; [memb.] United Church of Canada, Clerk of Session of my church, member of the choir; [oth. writ.] Poetry and songs (none published); [pers.] My life for many years has been grounded in the Lord Jesus Christ, who is my Savior and friend. I walk each day in His shadow and I give Him all the glory for everything that I accomplish. [a.] Nova Scotia, B0N 1R0.

WRIGHT, RAYMOND M.
[pen.] Raymond M. Wright; [b.] April 11, 1931, Kit Carson, CO.; [p.] David E. and Florence Wright; [m.] Harriett, April 11, 1957; [ch.] Sherri (age 34), Suzette (age 30) and Terrance (age 27); [ed.] 12th grade; [occ.] I was a surveyor for State Highway, now retired; [oth. writ.] Many poems one other published; [pers.] I enjoy writing poems to convey love. Many of my poems reflect the love of Jesus. [a.] Denver, CO.

WRIGHT, SHIRLEY J.
[pen.] S.J. Wright; [b.] February 28, Hammond, IN.; [p.] Carl and Ilta Cremeens; [m.] Robert F. Wright; [ch.] Christine Jane and Catherine Janel; [ed.] Indiana University Northwest, Maples Woods Community College, Missouri Western State College; [occ.] Freelance writer; [hon.] Dean's List, Honor's Program, Merit Scholarship, Honor's Certificates; [pers.] I believe that each person should strive to be the kind of person that we all would dream of being. I think people need to believe in themselves. [a.] Kansas City, MO.

WRIGHT, WILLIAM
[b.] March 8, 1960, New York, NY.; [p.] Billy and Cary Wright; [ed.] Miami Country Day, Choate and Vanderbilt; [occ.] Horses, music and living life; [pers.] Special thanks to Prof. Emerson Brown and Rael. [a.] Cartersville, GA.

WROBEL, EVELYN
[pen.] Naomi Reeder; [b.] April 11, 1926, Wiola, WV.; [p.] William and Pearl Toland; [m.] John Wrobel, September 22,1971; [ch.] Barbara, Bill, George, Brawny; [ed.] Sherrard High, Franklin School of Science and Arts; [occ.] Retired nurse; [memb.] World of Poetry, National Library of Poetry; [hon.] Golden Award by World of Poetry; [oth. writ.] Poem, The Greatest Genius; [pers.] I strive to put the greatest praise and beauty of God and the greatest praise of humanity. [a.] Moundsville, WV.

WYATT, KELLY
[b.] Danville, VA.; [pers.] Being a direct descendant of 16th century English poet and diplomatist, Sir Thomas Wyatt... I've often felt his gentle Elizabethan influence in both my writings and paintings. Genetic memory, perhaps? [a.] Kehena Beach, HI.

WYLIE, BRITTANY
[pen.] ALex Wylie; [b.] June 30, 1975, St. Joseph, MO.; [p.] Dwane Wylie Jr. and Donna Kendall; [ed.] Benton High School graduate; [occ.] Student; [hon.] Received scholastic letter for Academic Achievements; [oth. writ.] Several other poems published in high school publications, and poem published in Living Jewels; [pers.] I often write darker, more abstract and subtle poetry, C.C. Cummings has been a major influence on my writing.[a.] St. Joseph, MO.

XENOS, ELAINE J.
[b.] October 30, 1964, Buffalo, NY.; [p.] William H. and Judith A. Gorman, Jr.; [m.] Agapitos Xenos, January 7, 1989; [ch.] Dennis William; [ed.] B.S. Management/B.A. Spanish -SUNY at Buffalo; [occ.] Manager, customer service, American Biorganics, Inc.; [pers.] In this poem I wish to express the loss that is felt by adoptees at not knowing their roots. I was adopted at birth and recently succeeded in meeting my birth mother. [a.] Amherst, NY.

XIONGHUI, HE
[b.] August 25, 1964, Hengyiang City, China; [m.] Ying Xiaohong, August 8, 1992; [ed.] Fudan University (B.S.), University of Puerto Rico (M.S.); [occ.] Graduate student; [memb.] Society of Industrial and Applied Mathematics; [pers.] I offer this poem as a tribute to those who love peace, freedom and democracy. [a.] Rio Piedras, PR.

YANEZ, CHRISTOPHER
[pen.] Christopher; [b.] January 14, 1970, Los Angeles; [p.] May Yanez, an aesthete mother; [m.] Viola Garcia; [ed.] Self taught; [occ.] Student; [memb.] The Contempary Art Museum, downtown Los Angeles; [hon.] Completed high school at the age of 21; [oth. writ.] Several poems in a poetry magazine named, Articulacy and a Fanzine on a British singer by the name of Morrissey; [pers.] Poetry comes from the heart more than the mind. I will continue to write all the time. [a.] Los Angeles, CA.

YATES, KELLI ELAINE
[b.] August 12,1966, Freeport, TX.; [p.] David R. Bellar and Judith L. Schuelke; [m.] Divorced; [ch.] Matthew A., Michael A. and Mitchell A. Yates; [ed.] Presently taking a course at the Institute of Children's Literature; [memb.] The Church of Jesus Christ of Latter Day Saints; [pers.] I would like to dedicate this poem to a very special friend, Tim Punch. [a.] Richwood, TX.

YOLINSKI, HELEN J.
[pen.] Helen J. Yolinski; [b.] August 1, 1921, Ansonia,CT.; [p.] John and Anna Sears; [m.] Edward Yolinski, December 11, 1965; [ch.] Jerry, Janice, Sandra, Chas, Lee and Luanne; [ed.] Comp. high school and 24 years of secretarial background; [occ.] Financial services and insurance; [memb.] Evangelical Baptist Church (27 years and Executive Council Sec. and church clerk); [hon.] Probably in heaven only; [oth. writ.] I have been writing poetry since age 14. Wrote many for church publications. Painting has been foremost hobby, substitute organist; [pers.] The poem on The Little Frog, that I submitted was one of few worth humorous or environmental flavor. It has a patriotic flare which came to me in my sleep (can't you tell)? [a.] Seymour, CT.

YORK, TRACIE
[pen.] Tracie Marie York; [b.] March 21, 1980, Portland, OR.; [p.] John R. and Janna L. York; [sib.] Jamie York. [a.] Forest Grove, OR.

YOST, AMY MICHELLE
[b.] July 6, 1980, Garden Grove, CA.; [p.] Michael Major (stepfather) and Angela Major; [sib.] Christopher Yost and Stephen Major; [ed.] Meairs Elementary 1st-5th, Anderson Elementary (where my grandpa taught 6th grade) and Warner Middle School 7th -8th; [occ.] Student; [memb.] Student Counsel 7th grade home room rep.; [hon.] Student of the Month, Most Valuable Player in softball; [oth. writ.] 2 poems "Why I'm Proud To Be An American", "I'm Thankful Each Day"; [pers.] "I Am" was written after my grandfather, William J. Weatrowski, unexpectedly died. He was loved very much and I will miss him more that words can say. [a.] Westminster, CA.

YOUNG, APRIL DAWN
[b.] June 24, 1978, Sulphur Springs, TX.; [p.] James Maxon Young, Mary Kay and Leonard Kay (stepfather); [ed.] Campbell High School; [occ.] Student, Campbell High School; [memb.] FFA, 1993 Who's Who Among American High School Students Achievement; [hon.] Track-MVP trophy/award, Cross Country-10th place medal, 1992-1993 National Cheerleading championship qualifier, 1992-1993 National Cheerleading championship competition, 1992-1993 National Cheerleading championship top 100 competition, 1993-1994 National Cheerleading championship qualifier, 1993-1994 National Cheerleading championship competition, 1993 Southwest Regional championship-2nd place, 1993 All American competition; [pers.] I express my innermost self through my writings, I hope my writings greatly influence my readers. [a.] Campbell, TX.

YOUNG JR., LEMMIE F.
[pen.] Lem; [b.] December 3, 1939, Brownsboro, TX.; [p.] Lemmie and Katie Young (deceased); [m.] Vivian J. Young, July 10, 1965; [ch.] Larry Wayne and Peggy Ann; [ed.] Graduate of Time, undergraduate of Life; [occ.] Electrician; [hon.] National Dean's List, President's Club; [oth. writ.] Numerous poems (none of which have been published); [pers.] Accept everything as is. Admire it for its beauty and difference. [a.] Whitney, TX.

YOUNG, LEOLA A.
[b.] january 8, 1945, Washington, GA.; [p.] Leroy and Veola C. Anderson; [m.] James W. Young Sr., December 27, 1969; [ch.] Monique D. and James W. Young, Jr.; [ed.] West Charlotte High School, Johnson C. Smith University, Viallanova University; [occ.] Department head of English, William Penn High School, Philadelphia, PA.; [memb.] National Council for Teachers of English, Modern Language Assoc. of Phila. and Vicinity, Second Baptist Church, Alpha Kappa Alpha Sorority Inc.; [hon.] Alpha Kappa Mu Honor Society, Dean's List, RJ Reynolds Fellow, 1990 Council for Basic Education Philadelphia Fellow; [pers.] Nourish a strong faith and doubts will perish. [a.] Mount Laurel, NJ.

YOUNG, RICKIE A.
[pen.] Rickie Young; [b.] May 9, 1954, Lima, OH.; [p.] Paul Young and Cleta Waltz; [ch.] Ben, AJA and Nickolas; [ed.] Columbus Grove High School, University of Texas; [occ.] Marketing Manager; [oth. writ.] Sinless Moon, Canter Conversation and other poems and short stories; [pers.] Wisdom comes from understanding not from age. [a.] Houston, TX.

YUILL CORA
[pen.] Cora Yuill; [b.] August 17, 1905, Clayton, Ontario Canada; [p.] Robert and Ida Munro; [m.] Arthur Yuill, November 18, 1932; [ch.] Dorothy, Blanche, Alma, Eileen and Della; [ed.] Halls Mills Public School; [occ.] Housewife; [hon.] Public school (spelling); [oth. writ.] Poems published in local newspapers (Almonte Gazette and Lanark ERA). [a.] Almonte, Ontario Canada.

YUSUF, EVE COBOS
[pen.] Eve Cobos; [b.] March 22, 1937, Albuquerque, NM.; [p.] Rita S. Minkin and Ruben Cobos; [m.] Mohammed H. Yusuf, December 20, 1981; [ch.] Christopher, Dave and Sean Salaz; [ed.] BFA University of New Mexico; [occ.] Music teacher; [memb.] Daughters of the King, Holy Trinity Church, National Federation of Music Teachers; [hon.] American Pen Women, Sigma Alpha Iota, Dean's List, first place, Dear Beethoven contest; [oth. writ.] "Mystery City", published in Sound of Poetry publications, in Albuq. Literary magazines; [pers.] I am indebted to the inspiration of my family and friends whose creativity keeps me humming. [a.] Rio Rancho, NM.

ZAHN, APRIL
[b.] November 4, 1981, Levittown, PA.; [p.] Gary W. and Rebecca M. Zahn; [ed.] Student at Charles Boehm Middle School, 7th grade; [pers.] If my father didn't encourage me, I wouldn't have come up with what I did. [a.] Levittown, PA.

ZAMBRUK, ADAM WARREN
[b.] July 12, 1971, Denver, CO.; [pers.] Love builds buildings that all can see and none ignore. All of my poems are a result of a single obsession. [a.] Littleton, CO.

ZAPISEK, NOELLA
[pen.] Noella Quennerville, Noella Marie; [b.] December 25,1917, Pawtucket, RI.; [p.] Anicet and Virginie Quennerville; [m.] Stanley Zapisek, September 5, 1948; [ch.] Stanley Francis II, and twins Alfred Paul and Virginie Rose; [ed.] Saranac Lake High, Albany Business College, PTL University; [memb.] Woman's Aglow Fellowship, Badin Writer;s Club; [oth. writ.] Poems published in local newspapers and poems in anthologies, also write songs; [pers.] I attempt to lift the burden of depression that is weighing people down and to give them new hope for a brighter tomorrow. [a.] Albermarle, NC.

ZECH, JOHN N.
[pen.] John of Yorkshire; [b.] July 6, 1950, Chicago, IL; [p.] F. Raymond and Patricia Zech; [ed.] Benilde High School, The College of St. Thomas, B.A. Music; [occ.] Piano Technician and locksmith; [memb.] U.S. Chess Federation, St. Anne's Church Choir, Singsation Jazz Vocal Ensemble; [hon.] National Honor Society, MN State Chess Association, Novice Tourney first place-1967, Twin Cities Chess League team member, Unipep Chess Club, first place-B Team-1974, Ragtime Piano competition, first place-1974; [oth. writ.] Various poems in other styles and historic settings, a children's story poem, various musical compositions and songs; [pers.] Having written both music and poetry, I have come to admire those (Gilbert and Sullivan to Lerner and Loewe, etc.) who can combine the two so well together. [a.] Minneapolis, MN.

ZECHEL, CURTIS
[b.] October 19, 1970, Pinawa, Manitoba Canada; [p.] Gordon and Jacqueline Zechel; [pers.] I feel that writing can be an ultimate release. I believe writers should have a distinct style and not be constricted but rather only slightly influenced by what they read. [a.] Manitoba, Canada.

ZELLER, DONALD L.
[b.] November 18, 1967, Poughkeepsie, NY.; [ed.] John Jay High School, Dutchess Community College, New York Institute of Technology, School of Architecture. [a.] Fishkill, NY.

ZIEGLER, CHERYL LYNN
[b.] March 23, 1968, Hammonton, NJ.; [m.] (fiance') Scott Stochel; [ed.] Cinnaminson High School, Cinnaminson, NJ.; [occ.] Waitress; [hon.] Home Economics, National Leadership and Service Award (for junior volunteer in hospital); [pers.] I enjoy writing. It is a great way for me to express myself. I hope to write more and maybe someday publish my own book. [a.] Maple Shade, NJ.

ZIMET, CAROL
[b.] May 2, 1922, USA.; [p.] Anna Marcus and Oscar Segal; [m.] Jesse, 1969; [ch.] Tasha Garfield and Jeffrey Chesner; [ed.] 2 years Adelphi University; [occ.] Interior Designer; [memb.] World of Poetry, Poetry Academy, Sparrowgrass, National Library of Poetry; [hon.] Window display, lighting consultant, All American Award, World of Poetry; [pers.] After major surgery, poetry was my healing therapy and my greatest pleasure in life now. is when I hear the laughter from whoever reads my poems. [a.] Westbury, NY.

ZITKO, HOWARD JOHN D.D.
[b.] October 26, 1911, Milwaukee, WI.; [m.] Divorced; [ch.] Three children by previous marriage; [ed.] Graduate, Wauwatosa High School, studied, University of Wisconsin 1929-1931, University of California 1946048, graduate, Golden State University, Doctor of Divinity 1949; [occ.] President and Chairman of the Board World University and World University Roundtable; [hon.] More than fifty citations, honorary degrees and diplomas; [pers.] International Consultant to the World Congress of Poets, meetings in Seoul, Korea, Taipei, Taiwan and the USA. [a.] Benson, AZ.

ZITZKE, JANET M.
[pen.] Janet May; [b.] Joliet, IL.; [p.] Richard J. and Betty M. Ermey; [m.] Robert D. Zitzke, Jr.; [ch.] Brian Vincent Westhoff, Drew Robert and Kurt Richard Zitzke; [ed.] Plainfield High, Joliet Junior College; [oth. writ.] Several poems not yet submitted for publication; [pers.] I write what I feel through my own life experiences and observations as well as my impression of others' feelings. I have many other writings and with the encouragement of my family and friends, this is the first I have submitted. [a.] Plainfield, IL.

ZURLO, DORIS
[b.] May 21, 1983, Brindisi, Italy; [p.] Franco Zurla and Mary Hunt; [ed.] El Toro Elementary School, 4th grade; [hon.] Honor Roll, Gate student; [a.] Morgan Hill, CA.

ZWOZDESKY, LAURIE
[b.] September 19, 1963, Fort St. John BC, Canada; [p.] Eleanor and Roy Bush; [m.] Metro J. Zwozdesky, August 9, 1980; [ch.] David; [ed.] College Heights High; [oth. writ.] Several unpublished poems. [a.] Prince George BC, Canada.

Index of Poets

INDEX

NAME

Aaron, 435
Aarts, Laura Lee 295
Abaya, Amadeo 599
Abbott, Anne 278
Abbott, Dena 123
Abbott, J. 525
Abrahamson, Jeanmarie 35
Abram, James 287
Abrams, Josie Cifala 308
Abrams, Lalage 166
Abshagen, Dorothy 61
Abu, Debbie 76
Accapadi, Jos Manuel 235
Accardo, Natalie 43
Ace, Kristin Lee 11
Acker, Louis L. 153
Acklen, Charles W. 493
Ackley, Marcie M. 440
Ackley, Roger H. 487
Ackley, Sarah 463
Adams, Annie 360
Adams, Bonnie J. 266
Adams, Catherine 580
Adams, Cathy 248
Adams, Debra 116
Adams, Everett 310
Adams, Joy E. 78
Adams, Kathleen 578
Adams, Laurie 188
Adams, Lynn 296
Adams, Vanda 622
Adamson, Kimi 493
Adey, Bryan 622
Adkins, Lilly M. 275
Adkins, Ronald L. 593
Adolf, Kathleen W. 427
Affanoso, Michael 382
Aggarwal, Vishal 113
Agostini, Alice 189
Aguihon, Bienvenido G. 434
Ahlstrom, Megan 10
Ahmad, Ariff 468
Ahrens, Jack 221
Akerman, Annette 596
Akers, Tilda S. 19
Akers, Zach 241
Alary, Michele 536
Albano, Anthony 482
Albert, Leroy 160
Albert, Rudiger 294
Albiani, Ethel Lane 138
Albins, Hazell 140
Albrecht, Jill R. 294
Alcocer, Lizbeth 551
Alcorn, James D. 112
Alden, Anna Lee 132
Alden, Brooks 294
Aldridge, Sara 225
Alexander, Cristina 29
Alexander, Robyn 612
Alford, Reggie 332
Ali, Trisha 588

Aligizakis, Irena 312
Alioto, Maureen 527
Allan, Andrea 109
Allan, Helen 289
Allbright, Steven W. 464
Allen, Heather 474
Allen, Judy L. 624
Allen, Louise 178
Allen, Marian B. 124
Allen, Robert L. 62
Allen, Roberta M. 204
Allen, Ron 234
Allen, Shirley A. 347
Allen, Vernelle B. 332
Allgood, Tara 365
Allison, 609
Allison, Jennifer 516
Allred, Jerry E. 152
Allred, Stacy 503
Alm, Elena 262
Alm, Marie P. 485
Almanza, Kandiemarie 100
Almeida, Elizabeth 359
Aloan, Erin 96
Alonso, Charlotte 41
Alston, Sangaw 490
Altiere, Edward 204
Altvater, Heidi 115
Alvis, Donna W. 542
Amatucci, Holly 227
Amyotte, Gabriel 615
Anastasian, George 326
Anders, Beatrice 57
Anderson, Andrea 257
Anderson, Daniel C. 439
Anderson, Dorothy L. 152
Anderson, Glen R. 261
Anderson, Ida May 312
Anderson, Katherine 224
Anderson, Kimberly L. 575
Anderson, L. Steven 640
Anderson, Marguerite 156
Anderson, Marketta 130
Anderson, Monica 404
Anderson, Stephanie 421
Anderson, Suzanne E. 127
Anderson, Victoria J. 482
Anderson, Willie May 105
Anderson-Lovell, Pamela 14
Andrews, David E. 280
Andrews, Donna J. 101
Andrews, Glenn 232
Andrews, Rubie 376
Androlevich, Melissa 345
Anifer, Penni C.M. 258
Ann "E", 200
Annand, Caroline 329
Anspach, Scott A. 531
Antonuccio, Joseph N. 351
Applebaum, Sarah 274
Arceci, John 568
Arendale, Kristin 58
Arevalo, LaKiay Monique 638
Argow, Sylvia 376
Arient, Michaela 621
Armagost, Diana Handy 48
Armbrust, Ruth E. 188
Arment, Heidrun M. 96
Armit, Rod 617
Armknecht, JaRae 450
Armstrong, Janet Allen 64

Arnold, Bill 81
Arnold, Jeremy 34
Arnold, Linda 116
Arntson, Scott 641
Aronson, Selva 253
Arvelo, Monika L. 64
Arzadon, Fay 175
Asaro, Simone 617
Ashby, Reba 433
Ashcom, Colleen K. 238
Atchley, Curtis L. 577
Atkins, Nora 370
Aubrey, Richard 514
Auld, April Lea 627
Aupperlee, John J. 185
Austermuhle, Mariana 615
Austin, Elizabeth Ann 31
Austin, J.R. 336
Austin, Leland 216
Avoth, David 11
Ayer, Jeffrey 53
Ayers, Ellen 18
Ayraud, Claire 547
Babb, Jana 347
Babcock, Grace 246
Bacala, J. C. 153
Backus, Annette L. 436
Bacon, Patricia A. 189
Bagatta, Angela 227
Bailey, Amanda 214
Bailey, Anne 221
Bailey, Christal 414
Bailey, Linda 294
Bakach, Jessica 51
Baker, Carrie 202
Baker, Danielle 200
Baker, Genny 238
Baker, J. 245
Baker, Jane Ann 148
Baker, Jason 644
Baker, Jill 332
Baker, Justin 335
Baker, Kris 242
Baker, Mark 541
Baker, Nancy 185
Baker, Russell 425
Balch, Helene 128
Balch, Margaret H. 442
Baldwin, Kimberly 283
Baldwin, Rachel 160
Bales, Robin 206
Ball, Christine 272
Ballema, Carolyn 325
Ballesteros, Richard A. 360
Ballod, Christopher E. 85
Bandemer, Marat 229
Banks, Caroline G. 186
Bankston, Billy 376
Baptisa, Anne M. 502
Barager, Cole 377
Baran, Trisha 170
Baray, Audrey 125
Barber, Robin 335
Barbin, Janet 284
Barden, George 436
Barger, Alicia 422
Barker, Jaime 446
Barlow, Doris W. 458
Barlow, Leah Mary 257
Barnes, Ellen E. 485
Barnes, Louise M. 14

Barnes, Pamela 202
Barnett, Alison 572
Barnett, Ruth F. 582
Barnette, Dana 464
Barnitt, Richard P. 200
Barrascout, Wendy 273
Barrentine, Mark C. 246
Barrera, Roberta A. 220
Barrett, Alex 493
Barrett, Elizabeth J. 37
Barrett, James Conscious 172
Barrett, James F. 60
Barrett, Robin 247
Barrie, Joan G. 206
Barrington, Elaine 284
Barron, Rachel 144
Barrows, Naomi Ruth 515
Barry, Bridget 492
Barry, Bridget 569
Barry, Kim 473
Barry, Michele M. 573
Barry, Mildred Creighton 100
Bartel, Beth 169
Bartok, Jake 67
Barua, Selina P. 326
Barzilai, David 8
Basinger, Paul 480
Bastion, Heather 511
Batchelor, Todd A. 535
Battagliese, Brittany 632
Battle, Mary M. 361
Battles, Asa 487
Bauche, Lisa 304
Bauer, Danielle 368
Baugh, Marlene 143
Bauld, Cathy 297
Baumgardt, James W. 177
Bawtinhimer, Bryan 485
Beal, Rita 33
Beals, Jennifer 231
Bean, William James 38
Beard, Bonnie Sue 95
Beaton, Debbie 615
Beaujuin, Jean Rene 496
Beaulieu, Nancy 163
Beaumont, Angela L. 384
Beaupre, Norman 316
Bebout, Carol 537
Bechard, Heidi 292
Becher, Jackie 138
Bechtel, Michelle 281
Bechtel, Vonna 11
Bechtel, Vonna 490
Beck, Candice M. 437
Becker Jr., Albert F. 375
Becker, Ann 252
Becker, Bess 403
Becker, C. 234
Becker, Ellsworth M. 92
Beckman, Tony 639
Beckmann, Bruce A. 404
Becton Sr., Howard L. 398
Bedtelyon, Krystal 241
Beebee, Adrian 495
Beeson, Robert E. 407
Beg, Anwer 38
Begley, Thomas J. 563
Bei and Joy, Maria and Marjorie 66
Bekaert, Casey 594
Bell, Robin 38
Belli, Michelle C. 471

Bellot, Frances E. 584
Belt, Wanda 214
Benda, Anne 407
Bender, Kenneth J. 179
Benesh, Barbara 345
Benford, Theresa 290
Bengen, Jenny 558
Bennett, Cindy 26
Bennett, Gary W. 463
Bennett, Janice J. 630
Bennett, Ken 303
Benson, Linda 403
Bentley, Elaine 610
Bentley, Kim 434
Benz, Chanelle 509
Berakovich, Helen "Bell" 376
Berger Jr., John Torrey 120
Bergman Jr., George F. 421
Bergman, Harold 353
Bernhard, George 84
Berry, Betty Jo S. 528
Berry, Bonnie L. 631
Berry, D.J. 550
Berry, Jason C. 62
Berryman, Alice 265
Bertucci, Bette 136
Besedin, Maria 156
Besley, Caroline Rose 542
Beth, Stephen 245
Bettley, Margarite 182
Betts, Diana Andriola 533
Bey, J. Gibson 598
Bhirud, Ganesh L. 90
Bice, Deborah Ann 22
Bieber, Dawn 167
Bierman, Kathie J. 131
Biernat, Renata 455
Biglow, Genevieve J. 361
Bigum, Maggie 111
Bigum, Sarah 428
Bilker, Mitchell 254
Billings, Marvin G. 345
Billings, Mike 145
Binns, John 299
Bird, Cindy K. 114
Bird, Justin W. 563
Birney, Dion 23
Bischoff, Arley M. 173
Bishop, Deanne Carol 256
Bishop, Ronald R. 500
Bittick, Jenny 339
Bjerkness, Kevin 625
Black, Toni Elizabeth 454
Blackburn, Jennifer 360
Blackburn, Melissa D. 608
Blacklock, Cynthia E. 634
Blackmon Jr., John E. 66
Blackmon, Christina Rae 223
Blair, Beth 72
Blair, Don 621
Blair, Shar 257
Blaisdell, Kathleen E. 380
Blake, Vera McDonald 493
Blakely, D. N. 13
Blakney, Suzanne 297
Blanchard, Anne M. 462
Blanchard, Cindy 127
Blanco, Vicente F. 167
Blandy, Michelle M. 246
Blankenship, Kristy 423
Blasdel, Edith 148

Bleiler, Melissa 238
Blenden, Mike 222
Blevins, Peggy 9
Bliss, Gary D. 151
Blizard, Charlotte 164
Bloesch, Maureen L.R. 523
Blogna, Patricia 548
Bloker, Dolores 233
Bloom, Shirley 395
Bloyd, Joan 205
Blue, Irene 63
Blum, Pat 236
Bobay, Walt 76
Bobczynski, Carla 606
Bobo, Arlie U. 107
Boddrij, Jill 168
Boeglin, Dawn 509
Boese, Jennifer 577
Bogan, Carolyn J. 61
Boice, Katie 640
Bolden, Mattie C. 86
Bole, Helen 106
Boline, Brenda 414
Bomgaars, Mary J. 81
Bonnici, Pauline Jane 622
Booth, Elizabeth C. 444
Booth, Joan 134
Boothby, Kimberly 534
Boots, Joelle 126
Borecha, Agnes 225
Borland, Kevin 575
Botha, Katie 124
Botti, Ernest A. 503
Boucher, Anne Porter 416
Boucher, Mertie Elizabeth 437
Bougdanos, Marika 424
Bouic, Billie Jo 633
Boulton, Dolly M. 498
Bourque, John 266
Bouthillette, Jen L. 642
Bowen, Kenneth Lance 480
Bowen, Kimberly Lockwood 77
Bowerman, Margaret 616
Bowers, Jacqueline 177
Bowers, Michelle 222
Bowers, Stephanie Lynn 412
Bowker, Robert S. 399
Bowman, Brenda K. 536
Bowman, Danielle R. 264
Bowman, Jason 530
Bowman, Zachary 259
Box, Cynthia 534
Box, Obdulia M. 258
Boyce, Jennifer 539
Boyce, Liz 465
Boyce, Shaun 470
Boyd, Cheryl 260
Boyd, David 44
Boyd, Emily 47
Boyd, Jill M. 230
Boyd, Tammy 217
Boyd, Vicki 260
Boyer, Sharon 352
Boyle, John E. Whiteford 592
Boyle, John P. 261
Boyle, Margaret E. 231
Boysen Jr., Steve 52
Boyster, Suzanne 150
Bracken, Mary 305
Bradbeer, G. B. 222
Bradley, Clarisse Ann 33

Bradley, Bill 495
Bradley, Christopher 336
Bradley, Clint 486
Bradley, Yavonda T. 85
Bradshaw, Jennifer 640
Brady, Amber 542
Brady, Bobbi Ann 310
Brady, Selma 394
Brady, Siobhan M. 610
Brady, Thelma 102
Braga, Kevin 78
Braga, Rosalind 174
Bragg, Carmen M. 66
Brain, Christine R. 105
Braithwaite, Gail A. 507
Brand, Rosalie 643
Brandon, Marie Lena 476
Brandow, J. D. 276
Branham, Jon 601
Brantley, Anthony 36
Braun, Debra A. 600
Braunbeck, Matthew 460
Bray, Amy 206
Bray, Georgia 463
Breen, Serena S. 148
Brees, F. A. 191
Breitling, Paula 643
Bremer, Brenda 459
Bremer, Megan 584
Brendlinger, Angela Marie 449
Breshears, Marvin 39
Breunig, Helen L. 451
Brewen, Kristina 554
Brewer, Doris Hartsell 79
Brewer, Larry 141
Brewer, Murlea 266
Briare, Shannon 607
Bricker, Sandra Goode 146
Brickner, Melanie 528
Bridges, Charles 99
Brinsley, Adrian V. 76
Brissette, Lindsay 414
Britt, Andrew R. 41
Britt, Kandace 601
Brock, N. J. 118
Brodfuehrer, Kristie 147
Broe, Ina Leland 165
Brogden, Patti J. 463
Brolsma, Sheila 361
Brooks, Clara B. 447
Brooks, Courtney 6
Brooks, Lindsay 427
Brooks, Lucille Ruth 307
Brookshire, Elaine 407
Brouelette, Lucille 18
Broumley, Jennifer 320
Brow, Monica 618
Brown, Amber F. 494
Brown, Anne E. 298
Brown, Darrell R 217
Brown, Dennis Michael 181
Brown, Erica 158
Brown, Evelyn 526
Brown, Howard B. 188
Brown, Kristi 5
Brown, Loretta M. 341
Brown, Lynda 21
Brown, Michael Edward 557
Brown, Monique Carole 202
Brown, Rachel 514
Brown, Randy 621

Brown, Robbin 368
Brown, Rosie 161
Brown, Sarah 51
Brown, Shirelle 247
Brown, Shirley M. 119
Brown, Tasha 270
Browning III, William B. 263
Brownsberger, Michelle 470
Bruce, Darrell 377
Bruff, Marca 531
Brugger, Mary Ann 160
Brumbaugh, Helen J. T. 227
Brummel, Dorothy 66
Brungardt, Danny F. 329
Brunnert, Sandra Meyer 217
Brunton, Jaime L. 54
Bruyer, Neeka 105
Bryan, Ann Marie 189
Bryan, Sibyl 102
Bryant, Bridgette 264
Bryant, Ertha E. 575
Buchanan, Cynthia D. 82
Buchda, Bill 64
Buchner, Laureen 279
Buck Jr., Pitman 97
Buck, Nila Yvonne 216
Buckley, Greg 561
Buckley, Mary 186
Buckman, Kate 213
Buckner, Nicholas Edward 324
Budwig, Deborah 317
Budwig, Deborah 637
Buechler, Karen 288
Buege, Edith 541
Buffmire, Hazel D. 68
Bukovitz, Richelle 109
Bumgardner, Hazel A. 219
Bunch, Amanda Beth 415
Bunch, Vivian E. 292
Bunger, Melanie 137
Burbage, Venus 457
Burbank, Diane 81
Burch, Blanche 579
Burda, Shawn 360
Burdick, Carol 397
Burge, Debi Eve 396
Burgess, Kimberly Joy 590
Burgess, Kristen 67
Burk, Nancy T. 172
Burkart, Jim 390
Burke, Chris 500
Burke, Francis P. 532
Burke, Kelly 517
Burke, Roy E. 220
Burke, Stephen 277
Burkett, Lynn 444
Burkitt, Robin-Louise 67
Burleigh, L'Myrl 382
Burlingham, Adair 589
Burnette, Zelda 558
Burns, Billie 644
Burns, Frederic B. 134
Burns, Kelly 412
Burns, Martin L. 305
Burns, Robert 48, 118
Burns, Sylvia M. 356
Burnt, A. Gloria 470
Burrell, Wanda Lee 42
Bursey, Larry 281
Burton, Alyssa 639
Burton, Danyele 526

Burton, Edna G. 276
Burton, Holly 238
Burymski, Elena 191
Busbee, Christy 592
Busen, Jamie L. 228
Bushey, Audrey 291
Busque, Beverly 542
Buta, Edward 337
Butkovich, Gabriella 599
Butler, Dorothy 57
Butler, Emily Daniels 561
Butler, Jason 95
Butler, Louquel 526
Butler, Melissa Rae 58
Butler, Robert Christopher 454
Butts, Cherie 241
Butts, Michelle 260
Buyansky, Nicole 69
Buzzelli, Anthony M. 314
Byard, Debbie A. 351
Byers, Lyla 290
Byrd, Cathy 606
Byrd, Sarah 13
Byrd, Toyetta M. 98
Byrne, Edith T. 159
Cabrera, Zienia 482
Cacciatore-Soeder, Phyllis 445
Cacciola, Erasmia Veligrakis 501
Cadieux, Valerie 570
Cady, Tyler 132
Cafasso, Suzanne 525
Cagle, Patricia D. 604
Cahill, Catherine 334
Caine, Carrie 530
Cairns, Heather Ann 311
Calabrese, Kari 545
Caldwell, Pat 619
Calip, Senie 329
Callahan, Michelle 545
Callante, Wanda 216
Callaway, Maggie 575
Callen, Sarah M. 556
Calligaris, Aileen 311
Calorie, Nicki 533
Cambra, Walter 481
Camilo, Jess 197
Camors, Chris 633
Campbell, Curtis 524
Campbell, Deborah J. 641
Campbell, Debra 261
Campbell, Jeremy 588
Campbell, Misty 223
Campbell, Rosina 308
Canon, Irish 250
Cantrella, Ruth E. 267
Caparas, Fawn R. 179
Capehart, Flora Stokes 29
Capin, Stephen I. 566
Caplan, Jill 270
Caravan, Alicia 135
Cardinal, Chantelle 623
Cardona, Winnie 624
Cardoza, Crystal 593
Carels, Kristel Dawn 312
Carignan, Tammy 628
Carlena 93
Carlson, Irene V. 212
Carlson, Marjorie Ann 153
Carlson, Pat 530
Carlson, Trent 115
Carmichael, B. 185

Carnahan, Carole R. 622
Carney, Brian 44
Caro, Sabrina 491
Carpenter, Heather 624
Carpenter, Matt 50
Carr, Bonnie B. 186
Carr, Jason 354
Carr, Jennifer M. 132
Carrabine, Cindy 102
Carrell, Sharron 609
Carreno, Alexander 83
Carrere, Gisele 195
Carrington, Elizabeth S. 644
Carroll, Bertha L. 413
Carroll, Marcia 57
Carroll, Sally 245
Carron, Karen 588
Carruth, John 518
Carry, Jade 614
Carson, C. L. Kit 18
Carson, Shirley 353
Carstensen, Brenda K. 56
Carter, Amy 293
Carter, Joan 458
Carter, John L. 461
Carter, Lynda K. 215
Carter, Noel 125
Cary, Paulette Talhay 402
Casciaro, Rossan 271
Cascio, Michele 270
Case, Dannell 558
Case, Jerome R. 174
Cash, Jaime 635
Casler, Donna 264
Casner, Ronald W. 645
Cassano, P. 205
Casteel, Brenda 103
Castelamara, Susan 76
Castillo, Anita Marie 157
Castillo, Ariel 438
Castillo, Maria LaPira 452
Castillo, Natasha R. 263
Castillo, Tomas 377
Casto, Heather 578
Castro, Donna Cipri 368
Castro-Nunez, Genevieve 253
Catabas, Jennifer Balan 272
Cate, John Shelton 205
Cattnach, G. 159
Caukill, Mona J. 279
Cauley, Victoria P. 509
Cava, Luis P. 128
Cavallo, Gil 496
Cavet, Jackie 63
Cawthra, Michelle 200
Cecka, Micki 197
Cekada, Gregory H. 107
Centre, Jovanna 222
Cervenka, Doris K. 91
Chaffin, June 370
Chainani, Sonesh 16
Chamberlain, Linda 299
Chambers, Billy 630
Chambers, Fayla Janel 377
Champagne, Allison 513
Chan, Joel H. 635
Chandler, Donna 29
Chang, Charity 257
Chapdelaine, William J. 631
Chapman, Bert 208
Chapman, Evelyn Lynn 30

Chapman, Kammie 476
Chapman, Melissa 35
Chappell, Jerry L. 277
Chaput, Raymond 82
Charles, Arthur 432
Charles, Jeannette M. 340
Charles, Montine L. 78
Chase, Ervin H. 230
Chase, Joe 581
Chaves, Ana 157
Chavez, Sindy 37
Checki, Anthony N. 123
Chell, Veronica A. 66
Chenevert, Carol A. 138
Cheney, Angi 275
Chiarlanza, James 408
Chick, Janel L. 457
Childers, Nicole Diana 613
Childs, June H. 643
Chin, Sue S. 6
Chinoy, Vinita 135
Chisholm, Michelle 622
Choi, Linda 604
Choinski, Gilbert 358
Chopp, Thaddine M. 593
Choquette, Robert 289
Chow, Louis 357
Chrisco, Laura 213
Christensen, Tammie 250
Christian, Sara B. 142
Christiana, 433
Christoff, Jeff 570
Chryst, Jaime 645
Chrzastowska, Maria Ivona 343
Chubb, Christopher R. 121
Chubik, Martha Loyba 601
Church, Elmer Tuttle 382
Church, Fern D. 235
Churchill, J. W. 23
Cianflone, Lise 620
Cichocki, Thomas Bryan 193
Cihocki, Candice 189
Cincotta, Mariana 42
Cirillo, Michael R. 200
Cislak, Jennifer Lynn Marie 510
Cistaro, Raemarie 597
Ciulla, A. J. 631
Claeson, Frances 632
Clapp, Eleanor D. 623
Clapp, Timothy Scott 93
Clapper, Hilda 210
Clare, R. Donald 348
Clark, Andi 520
Clark, Barb 286
Clark, Carrie 620
Clark, Jo Ella 70
Clark, Laura 229
Clark, Maria G. Vega 481
Clark, Michael 323
Clark, Sharon Mae 283
Clark, Tony L. 220
Clary, Jessica 8
Clason, Julie Lynn 189
Clausen, G. Stephen 158
Clausen, Kurtis Michael 587
Claw, Donna A. 313
Clay, D. 449
Clay, Danny 318
Clayton, Lisa A. 183
Claytor, Sara 74
Cleaver, T. Phyllis 36

Clements, Michael 257
Cleveland, Betty 100
Cleveland, Scott 131
Clevenger, Jill 194
Clever, Rebecca A. 231
Clifford, Edward Lehr 82
Clifford, Rhonda 567
Cline, Ann Reese 591
Cline, Tina 98
Clouse, Billie 219
Cloutier, Sarah 617
Coates, Leone Lee 143
Cobos, Eve 154
Coburn, Teriann 553
Cochois, Dennis 627
Cochran, Kevin 510
Cochran, Lorne 291
Cockfield, Bessie L. 644
Coen, Eleanor G. 75
Coffey, Lynda 153
Cohen, Lenny 306
Coker, Ellen L. 632
Colber, Tenisha 442
Cole III, James W. 24
Cole III, Ralph Thomas 549
Cole, Blanche 130
Cole, Cheri 246
Cole, Helen L. 133
Coleman, Laura 435
Coleman, Marion 226
Collier, Amanda 275
Collier, Mary Margaret 502
Collins, E. Mae 276
Collins, Farolyn 401
Collins, Janice 411
Collins, Marguerite 375
Collins, Marie V. 511
Collins, Tom 341
Colmer, Anna L. 178
Colombo, Blanche Mary 71
Colton, Cory S. 572
Colvin, Margaret Buell Neal Sheffield 435
Colvin, Willie C. 590
Combden, Chris 619
Combe, Valerie Knowles 77
Comella, Ruth 133
Comito, Jenny 276
Compagno, Lisa Ann 350
Compton, Donna 308
Concon, Archimedes Abad 564
Conger, Thomas D. 5
Conklin, Robert 352
Conkling, Yvonne R. 94
Conley, Ethel Brady 255
Conn, Mary B. 155
Connally, Katherine 195
Connell, Brandy 248
Conner, Patricia 548
Conners, Bill 643
Connors, Jeff 301
Conroy, Katie 254
Constable, Carolyn 39
Constantinou, Katherine 501
Conway, Mary Kathleen 439
Conway, Ozelle 252
Conwell, Estella Chism 179
Cook, Angela M. 601
Cook, Christine 607
Cook, Joel 59
Cook, Kathleen L. 197
Cook, Kelly A. 36

Cook, Richelle 516
Cooke, Alexia M. 636
Cooke, Elizabyth 539
Coombs, O. Paul 416
Coomes, G. 321
Coon, Edna 378
Cooper, Ami 641
Cooper, Angela 261
Cooper, Carolyn 441
Cooper, Isabel S. 147
Cooper, Jeffrey S. 467
Cooper, Kymberli 568
Cooper, Polly 23
Corcoran, Jane 99
Corcoran, Kimberly Kay 107
Cordova, Denice L. Glover 144
Cormell, Linda 320
Cornbrooks, Rosanne 634
Cornea, Daniela 573
Cornelius, Byron G. 158
Cornelius, Virginia 493
Cornett, Edna Baldridge 24
Cornett, Kristen 120
Corrado, Christine 268
Correa, Jesse 629
Correia, Filomena 616
Corrigan, Cheryl 288
Cortese, Cary 62
Corvino, Lauren 218
Corwin, Pepper Loren 543
Cory 133
Costa, Marcia 353
Costa, Sarah 131
Costas, Joan M. 569
Costello, Megan 530
Costello, Paul A. 642
Cotter, Dorothy 78
Cottingham, Reid 92
Cottone, Carrie 586
Couch, Saylease 196
Coughlin, Mary M. 532
Countryman, Janis M. 606
Courchesne, Jennifer 20
Coustan, David P. 41
Covington, Theresa V. 478
Cowan, Rhae Lynn 92
Cowing, Timothy Shawn 518
Cowles, Mike 309
Cowles, Terry L. 192
Cox, Evelyn Marrow 249
Cox, Margaret Sue 333
Cox, Tracey 24
Coy, Sarah Hope 460
Coyle, Chester 499
Cozart, 580
Crabtree, Ike W. 398
Craggs, Joanna 544
Craig, Jenny 39
Craig, Lynn Marie 399
Crandall, Jason 257
Crandell, Carol 64
Crane, Elody De 59
Crane, Nicole 520
Cranfill, Julia 112
Cravey, Charles E. 472
Crawford, Gina 459
Crawford, Linda 642
Crawford, Megan Leigh 253
Crawford, T. C. 3
Crayton, Claire E. 252
Creery, Sarah 270

Crerar, Thomas C. 628
Cressman, Dorothy 402
Crews, Pamela L. 167
Cribbs, Kelly 218
Crilley, Darin 422
Criss, Holly 590
Crissone, Marie 243
Cristello, Alison Hines 176
Crocker, Stacy 117
Crockford, Janice 273
Crocombe, Jordan 636
Crofton-Hyder, Peggy 83
Croobaugh, Emma 66
Crosby, Sara Jo 570
Cross, David 268
Cross, James F. 97
Cross, Raymond D. 637
Cross, Sunny 435
Crotts, Matthew 439
Crotty, Gary D. 90
Crout, Karen 594
Crowder, Lenora R. 38
Crowell, Beulah 363
Croxton, Janice 234
Crump, Urvin D. 53
Cruz, Natasha 543
Cruzan, Pat 30
Crytzer, Daniel 132
Cuervo, Rigoberto 574
Culbertson, B. J. 631
Culbertson, Frederica McDill 221
Cullen, Janet M. 600
Cullen, Louise T. 498
Cullison, Bwayne 315
Cumes, Julia 514
Cummings, Kim 267
Cunning, Gloria 160
Cunningham, Jason 257
Cunningham, Melissa Ellen 351
Cupp, Lottie Marie 456
Curnew, David M. 469
Curry, James L. 80
Curteis, Eileen 624
Curtis, George M. 521
Curtis, Joan Clark 508
Curtona, Carol J. 333
Curtsinger, Lola 207
Cybart, Becky 88
Cypher, Aarynn 456
Cyr, Steve 312
Cywink, Jennifer Lynn 285
Czepcinski, Jamie 477
D'Alfonso, Antonio 277
D'Amario, Nancy L. 146
D'Avanzo, Kathryn 344
DaSilva, Alexia 453
Dail, William 518
Dalberry, Shani 424
Dalby, Chrystal Dawn 480
Dale, Daniel S. 559
Dale, Nellie C. 305
Daley, Brent R. 65
Damante, Nicholas 54
Damore, Mary 53
Dance, Patricia 400
Danz, Virginia K. 351
Dao, Huy 15
Darby, Anna C. 591
Dargel, Margot G. 485
Darlington, Roy 214
Darnielle, Mary Lou Y. 535

Darrah, Bruce O. 339
Dart, Viola 65
Datiles, Joyce 491
Datson, Charlotte 73
Datz, David 584
Datz, Diane 574
Dauer, Mary Lee 216
Daugherty, Dyanne E. 515
Daugherty, Janet 235
Dauria, Melissa Anne 586
Davala, Jenny 167
Davenport, Elizabeth 147
Davids, Melissa 58
Davidson, Jacqueline R. 569
Davidson, Kelly 240
Davidson, Laura E. 316
Davidson, Misty 208
Davidson, Sandra 621
Davignon, Spring D. 350
Davila, Mary Kaye 254
Davis, Bobby Dwain 169
Davis, Cat 50
Davis, Diana 327
Davis, Gregory L. 619
Davis, Helen Jean 611
Davis, Laurie 85
Davis, Lorraine H. 202
Davis, Lydia Victoria 637
Davis, Marcus 326
Davis, Patricia Kelso 39
Davis, Rebecca 377
Davis, Rita 281
Davis, Robert L. 156
Davis, Ronnie Lou 533
Davis, Ruthellen Pyle 362
Davis, S. Elaine 430
Davis, Teresa 226
Davis, Verle Elizabeth 82
Davis, Vickey 289
Davis, Wendy 235
Dawe-Hayes, Jean 192
Dawydiuk, Shelly 293
Day, Cris 566
Day, Kay L. 353
De Antonio, Dorothy A. 145
De Los Santos, David 373
De Michiel, Renee 64
De Montelongo, Olivia 308
De Nyse, Deanne 123
De Paula, Henrique 14
De Santis, Pasquale 215
DeArmond, Julie 382
DeCoteau, Tammy 550
DeCristofaro, R. 481
DeFeo, Jim 390
DeFrancesco, Joyce A. 222
DeHart, Rejeana L. 560
DeJesus-Jankowski, Jennifer Lynn 561
DeJonge, Carolyn 18
DeLena, Donna A. 242
DeLong, Michele 60
DeLozier, Ruth 63
DeMarco, Stephanie 437
DePaolo, Donna 43
DePaulo, Janine 48
DeRamus, Christina 388
DeRiso, Janine 206
DeRosa, Geraldine G. 540
DeSha, D. 129, 638
DeVaughn, Sharon 3
DeVeen, Nicolette 305

DeWeese, Kathy 492
DeWoody, Ellen 208
Dean, Erlor E. 292
Dean, Terri L. 363
Dearnan, Sylvia 307
Deems, Thomas Aaron 562
Deignan, Terry L. 512
Del Bello, Mary 137
Del Pine 283
Del Vecchio, Judith Arlene 192
Dela Cruz, Grace 211
Delaney, Alyssa 546
Delcoco, Scott 638
Delgado, Liza Marie 337
Delmore, Darren 443
Delorier, Beatrice 334
Delozier, Roxanna 550
Delson, Barnet 32
Deltoro, B. J. 490
Demyanovich, Mark 63
Dennis, Bonnie T. 397
Dennis, Sean 291
Dereck, Rhenay 275
Derouin, April 543
Desadore, Stephanie 126
Desikan, Priya 318
Desjarlais, Dion 621
Deskins, Carl 350
Deskins, Craig 216
Desposito, Michelle Elizabeth Carmen 480
Deutsch, Cari 560
Devall, Gwendolyn L. 585
Devers, E.K. 455
Dewbre, Patsy A. 439
Dhaliwal, Renee 295
Dhanji, Rahim 301
Dhillon, Manjit Kaur 104
Di Fede, Dottie 544
DiNapoli, Courtney 272
Diamond, Laura Lynn 403
Dickens, J. Vincent 79
Dickerson, Jamie E. 267
Dickson, Jonn 505
Dideum, Kate L. 635
Dieffenbacher, Pamela Mae 644
Dietzler, Courtney 240
Dievendorf, Emily 43
Diggs, Tony 434
Dillard, Margaret E. 203
Dimayuga, Amrey R. 110
Dingman, Russell E. 204
Dingwall-Boak, Jessica 615
Dion, Pearl M. 381
Dison, Holly 478
Dissinger, Mary K. 142
Dittmar, Amy M. 227
Dixon, Dani 443
Dixon, Joel A. 466
Dixon, Michael Bern 486
Dixon, Mildred L. 84
Dixon, Rachel 233
Dixson, Dwain 595
Dmitriev, Andrei 100
Doan, Bao-chi Dinh 579
Dobrinski, Tami 227
Dobrucki, Ruth C. 131
Dobyns, Lee Mary 635
Dockery, LaDonna 466
Docko, Tina L. 452
Dodge, Debora 423
Dodson, Amber 560

Dodson, Betty 224
Dohl, Amanda 535
Doleman, Clara K. 80
Dollard, Edward R. 469
Dominque, Steven 506
Donahue, Harold Paul 80
Donnell, Frances 139
Donnelly, E. 173
Donnelly, John W. 330
Donner, Christy L. 71
Donoghue, Susanne Coalson 190
Donohue, M. 250
Donohue, Nicole 130
Donovan, Leslie Ane 623
Doran, Elizabeth K. 272
Dotson, Roger 267
Douglas, Gwen 261
Douglas, Kevin 612
Douglas, Ruth Roberts 169
Douglass, Miriam E. 334
Douglass, Velda 201
Dowling, Clara 303
Dowling, John 197
Downs, Sharon A. 178
Downs, Valicity Resha 538
Doyal, William B. 555
Doyle, Kristine E. 118
Doyle, Krystal 506
Doyle, Raymonda 59
Doyle, Steve 20
Drago, Julie 574
Dragt, Jeremy 629
Drake, Donn P. 20
Drake, Jackie 471
Drake, Robyn 618
Dregne, Kristin 25
Drew, Jennifer 244
Drew, Megan J. 431
Driskell, Donald Allen 251
Druck, Betty J. 233
Drury, Herron and Trainer 577
Drury, Nicole 60
Du Bois, Rene 375
DuBois, Barbara R. 3
Dubie, Derra L. 145
Dudley, Theresa 636
Duerer, Diana 240
Duff, Ruth 362
Duffy, Michael 457
Duffy, Shannon 459
Duhon, Dot 479
Dumich, Kathi 86
Dunathan, Robert J. 330
Dunaway, James V. 28
Duncan, Lois Gay 269
Duncan, Sara 141
Duncan, Tedd 385
Dungan, Kathy 400
Dunman, L. J. 204
Dunn, Betty Colvin 337
Dunn, Greg 407
Dunn, Greg 472
Dunn, Laura Marie
Dupree, Denise 119
Duran, Adrian 411
Durante, Louis J. 391
Durden, Kara 159
Durdin, Grace Scott 375
Durocher, Richard 287
Durrell, Deanne Elizabeth 240
Durrence, Angela S. 111

Duryee, Caroline 255
Dussiel, Christiane 461
Duszak, Sylvia 640
Dutot, Dayna 306
Duvall, Judy G. 134
Dwyer, Rebecca 428
Dyck, Karen 627
Dyckson, Robert A. 315
Dyer, Gene L. 218
Dyer, Heather 221
Dykhuizen, Dorothy 541
Dyl, Louise 98
Eagan, Glenis 639
Eagan, Marilynn J. 68
Easterly, Connie 73
Eastman, Laura A. 504
Easton, Theresa A. 259
Eaton, Danny 229
Ebanks, Ron 409
Ebeling, Gertrude Krenzke 449
Ebersole, Hal 575
Ebner, Gerald 144
Echols, Douglas 526
Eck, Robyn 31
Eddinger, Kelli 52
Eddy, Jennette T. 43
Eddy, Marjorie A. 551
Edelen, Joe Mike 609
Edens, Rebecca 145
Edmond, Teresa 116
Edmondson, Johanna 273
Edstrom, Patricia A. 99
Edwards, Agnes Guilfoyle 56
Edwards, Brandi 640
Edwards, Christopher B. 517
Edwards, Debra Ann 542
Edwards, Jean 576
Edwards, Shirley Rose Jones 324
Effron, Abbe 6
Egelston, Sara 141
Eggleston, Merle 155
Ehlscheid, Steve 515
Ehrke, Nina 230
Eilenberger, David 170
Eiler, Glen 316
Eisen, Charlene 479
Eisley, Marianne 575
Eisman, Audrey 201
El-Amin, Aqeela J. 424
El-Chami, Isabelle Macaltao 477
Eld, Karen L. 641
Elder, Jan 124
Elder, Josh 530
Elder, Melissa 570
Eldredge, Florence 246
Eldridge-Payae, Ruth 620
Elelnberger, Mary 420
Elfering, Vikki 638
Elgart, Grace 545
Elia, Stephanie 336
Elias, Amy 183
Elias-Munoz, T.Roxanna 603
Eliason, Kelli Ann 385
Elijah-El, P. 606
Eliot, Carol 366
Elizabeth, Michelle 423
Ellett, Amanda 426
Elliott, Elizabeth 64
Elliott, Ivanoria D. 46
Elliott, June Allegra 138
Elliott, Marci 133

Ellis, Betty A. 128
Ellis, Christine 437
Ellis, Marilyn 131
Ellis, Melanie M. 36
Ellsworth, Charles David 458
Elsburg, Kandie L. 90
Elwood, Joan 202
Emanouil, Sue 196
Emauroe, S. 432
Emig, Ruth M. 374
Enger, Kim 574
England, Royce L. 154
Engle, Miriam 563
English, Pam 473
English, Sally E. 235
English, Vivian J. 494
Engstrom, Catherine S. 378
Engstrom, Shalohm 62
Enlow, Allen E. 73
Enns, Lorraine 633
Enright, Natalie 251
Enriquez, Brandon 300
Epting, Kimberly Lynn 269
Erickson, Amy 232
Erickson, Kate 70
Erickson, Rachel 266
Erwin, Beverley 287
Erwin, Courtney 45
Esau, Brenda 4
Esquivel, John P. 212
Essix, Tahirah 239
Estes, Gina M. 342
Estes, Kristi 218
Etheridge, Rod 280
Eusey, Iva L. Smith 103
Evans, Brenda K. 55
Evans, Courtenaye 73
Evans, Lee 149
Evans, Muriel 348
Evans, Sophia M. 64
Everroad, Gladys 599
Evin, V. Susan 509
Ewing, Rodman 180
Exum, Kaitlen Jay 196
Ezekeil, Mary Beth 276
FLores, Richard G.218
Faber, Betsy 141
Faber, Eric David 561
Faber, G. R. 256
Fabian, Gloria 228
Fabiaschi, Abagail 482
Fabrikant, Arnold 250
Fakes III, Charles E. 264
Fakkeldy, Lisa 318
Falcone, Leonard 521
Fallin, Rosalina 512
Fallon, R. M. 623
Falsetta, Josephine 323
Falsone, Jennifer 107
Fancher, John D. 607
Fannin, Kevin W. 554
Fannin, Nina 228
Farjamrad, Faranak 362
Farmer, Dorothy J. 75
Farr, Justin 605
Farrell, Jessica 76
Farrow, Nellie M. 74
Faryna, Karen 280
Fasco, Kelly A. 387
Faulkner, April Anderson 185
Faust, Delphine A. 30

Fayeofori, Amabibi T. 306
Faynboym, Natalya 412
Fazio, Melissa Marion 121
Fedewa, Marilyn 254
Feeney, Colleen E. 15
Fehr, Carla 304
Feighan, Patricia A. 243
Feller, Beth Donnelly 90
Fellinger, Stella H. 519
Felsburg, Esther Ford 328
Fenn, Phyllis M. 502
Fenstermaker, Karen 574
Ferguson, Danny 51
Ferguson, Linda 628
Ferguson, Scott "Spider" 210
Ferguson, Tony J. 592
Ferland, Automne 351
Fernandez, Daisy C. 413
Fero, Patrick D. 130
Ferrand, Orlando 328
Ferrante, Leonard 19
Ferrari, Jay 97
Ferraro, Nancy 216
Ferreira, Rose 468
Ferrell, Darlene 537
Ferrell, Jennifer 222
Ferrell, Kat 404
Ferry, Shaunna 82
Fettinger, Vincent 200
Fidelis 3
Fiero, Jasmine 499
Fierros, Mrs. Ruth V. 205
Filipoff, Sara 267
Fina, Tina 442
Finan, Peter John 448
Finck, Doris K. 447
Findley, Barry 412
Fink, Elaine 73
Fink, Mabel Smith 72
Finley, Shannon 584
Firlotte, Connie (Ross) 619
Fischer, Elaine 290
Fischer, Katie 126
Fish, Aimee Jo 357
Fisher, Burton C. 633
Fisher, Jenny K. 634
Fisher, Katie 357
Fisher, Shawn E. 200
Fiteni, Audrey M. 283
Fitzgerald, Eleanor 284
Fitzmartin, Pam 164
Fitzsimmons, Marie 374
Fix, Taryn Aubree 226
Flanagan, Betty 112
Flanagan, Lois P. 476
Flanagan, Samuel P. 416
Flanagan, Shirley Singleton 103
Flannery, Elizabeth A. 60
Fleck, Mary Frances F. 537
Fleck, Roger 391
Fleischman, Ruth 137
Fleming, Mimi Premo 187
Flemming, Roger B. 628
Flessner, Lauren 509
Fletcher, Chris 136
Fletcher, Nicole 379
Fletcher, Zelda Engle 3
Flissinger, Roberta Jean 400
Flores, Elvia E. 209
Flores, Jessica 318
Flowers, C.M. 419

Flowers, John Gilbert 183
Flowers, Martha 573
Flynn, Bill 534
Flynn, Rachel Cher 476
Fobbs, Rubye L. 49
Focht, Kendrea 514
Foeckler, Ednamay 338
Foley, Kristen 245
Follosco, Madonna Grace C. 641
Folz, Jo-Jo 121
Fontenot, Carol 198
Foose, Barbara 529
Forcier, P. Marguerite 81
Ford, Dolores 375
Ford, Kelly 265
Ford, Myrtle 417
Fordham, Stephen K. 357
Fordyce, Bernice 335
Forgay, Tandi 580
Forkin, Renee D. 391
Forrest, Elizabeth 352
Forster, Cynthia L. 614
Forster, Frederick L. 144
Forsythe, Edward 588
Forward, Jody Jean 280
Fosbrook, Susie 87
Foss, Vyrel 602
Foster, Amanda 589
Foster, Bessie 30
Foster, June Duroux 204
Foster, Kenneth 384
Foster, Martha M. 374
Fowler, Debbie 22
Fowler, John R. 187
Fowler, Letitia V. 482
Fowls, Tamara 75
Fox, Beverly 572
Fox, William D. 358
Frady, Jane M. 323
Frances, Mary 69
Franke, Esther 42
Frankel, Wendy 261
Franquero, Sheila F. 215
Franquet, Danielle G. 224
Frantz, Alice E. 463
Fraser, Terez R. 34
Frastai, Jaime 508
Frazier, Jill M. 115
Frazier, Judith A. 375
Frazier, Olivia 30
Frechette, Susan M. 195
Fredrich, Erica 213
Freeman, Arthur 467
Freeman, Jan 532
Freeman, Melissa L. 566
Freeman, Verna 352
Freemon, Rose Dell 30
Freestone, Corianne 612
Freiberger IV, John 79
Freitas, Gabriela 521
Fremeth, Shirley 224
Fremgen, Darlene 191
French, Henry F. 540
French, LaVerne 256
French, Nell 418
French, Zelia J. 244
Fretz, Ginny 611
Frick, Carey 248
Fridh, Melvin J. 348
Friedberg, Jessica 423
Fritsch, William C. 248

Frye, Cheryl 44
Fugate, Elaine Y. 231
Fulford, Kevin A. 311
Fuller, Nancy 262
Fuller, Priscilla R. 568
Fuller, Robert 134
Fulton, Carla 63
Furcello, Carsen 89
G. Christine 553
Gabrielle, Lindsay 310
Gadelha, Elizabeth 585
Gagne, Kevin Philip 292
Gagne, Robert 507
Gago, Amy 428
Gajda, Brygida 460
Galati, Stephen 278
Gale, Rebecca L. 523
Gali, Katrina Marie 492
Galindo, Stephanie 4
Gallagher, Dorothy 144
Gallagher, Emily 512
Gallagher, Joseph 386
Gallardo, Jessica Kim 226
Gallaway, Myrna L. 98
Gallihugh, Melissa 236
Gallizioli, Carol 199
Gallup, Rolland 161
Gally, Ruth 208
Gamble, Ellis C. 312
Gange, Frances 635
Gantz, Elsa 185
Garbarino, Irma 195
Garcia, Arika 222
Garcia, Edge/Erica 193
Garcia, Gloria 531
Garcia, Michelle 147
Gardner, Diane M. 474
Gardner, Ethel 59
Gardner, Leola Caldwell 518
Garfinkel, Adam M. 69
Garling, Julianne 645
Garner, Edward 242
Garner, Jacquelyn C. 108
Garner, Pat 230
Garnett, Michael E. 269
Garrett, Faye 339
Garrett, Gregory 441
Garrett, Karen J. 244
Garrett, Kathy 242
Garrett, LaMills Alexander 386
Garrett, Paul E. 263
Garrison, Jamillah 356
Gary, Kay 448
Gates, Christopher David 143
Gates, Susan H. 208
Gatto, Joey Lynn 41
Gavetti, Denise 102
Gavin, Shannon A. 71
Gazdhyan, Nune 151
Gee, Bethany 466
Gehman, Rebecca 346
Gehrke, Stefanie 357
Gehrling, Alice "Lisa" 127
Geier Jr., Tom 197
Gengarelly, Katie 268
George, Frances T. 365
George, Jeanne D. 563
George, Monica 642
George, Tina 538
German, Brenan Christopher 590
Geronimo, Sandi 510

Gerritz, Martha 137
Gersbach, Helen 231
Gersht, Pamela 101
Gervais, Mary 310
Gester, Kathleen 147
Gettys III, William Rees 219
Getzelman, May 69
Geving, Ruth 311
Ghosh, Mandira 312
Giacone, Angela 519
Giancola, David 108
Giberson, Tony 7
Gibson, David S. 46
Gibson, Janet L. 103
Gibson, Natasha Ria 109
Gidden, Rex M. 367
Giesemann, Susan 507
Gil, Geneve 473
Gilbert, Alphonse M. 464
Gilbert, Kendra 315
Gilbreath, Allan F. 69
Giles, Candice 523
Gilio, Donna M. 123
Gilkes, Greg 295
Gill, Lillian 337
Gilliam, D. R. 235
Gillies, Keith M. 316
Gillingham, Lisa 299
Ginter, Ramona 306
Ginzel, Lavelle 101
Gionti, Tonimarie A. 251
Gipson, Kathy J. 254
Girard, Barbara 170
Githrie, Susanna 303
Gitto, Patsy 243
Gladfelter, Angela L. 413
Gladis, Jennifer E. 491
Glasow, Art 357
Glass, Evelyn H. 544
Glass, M. Kay 103
Glass, Neil 437
Gleason, Annette 574
Glebo, Joseph 39
Glendinning, Walt 393
Glenn III, Virgil Gordon 239
Glenn, Donna 134
Glidewell, Cory 200
Glock Sr., Milton F. V. 176
Goddard, Cynthia 257
Godfrey, Donna 456
Godwin, Barbara 208
Goehner, Janet Marie 40
Goehringer, Nicole 462
Goeringer, Sharol 596
Goethals, Don 115
Goff, Cathi 597
Goins, Marquita 37
Goldberg, Evan 12
Goldberg, Tiffany J. 456
Goldhammer, Donna 364
Goldman, Alfred 99
Goldman, Fran 409
Goldsmith, Robert 268
Goldsmith, Wes 285
Goldstein, Melissa 181
Goler, Nate H. 553
Goller, April 269
Gomersall, J.C. 617
Gomez, Tawnya 158
Gonshorowski, Mavis 198
Gonzales, B. L. 250

Gonzales, Diane 481
Gonzales, Javiel 194
Gonzales, Pauline S. 363
Gonzalez, Gina A. 459
Gonzalez, Jennifer A. 224
Gonzalez, Mona 134
Gooch, Thelma 55
Good, Leisa Bain 273
Good, Pauline 287
Goodall, Johnnie Janelle 508
Goodwin, Steve 363
Gorden, Eric 517
Gordon, Carrie 484
Gordon, Pamela 559
Gordon, Ray 514
Gordon, Tina 351
Gore, Pamela J. 523
Gore, Ruby Jo 606
Goren, Apryl L. 337
Gorham, Tuesday 352
Gorin, Christine Frances 616
Gorman, Kathleen 612
Gorman, Meghan 534
Gotschall, Allison 270
Gould, Eileen 490
Grace, Jonathan 14
Graci, Lynn M. 460
Grady, Joan 113
Graf, Judy M. 97
Graham, Bud 70
Graham, Dixie 484
Graham, Harriet C. 14
Graham, Kyla 630
Graham, Lynnor Latham 194
Graham, Michael B. 9
Graham, Monique Y. 450
Graham, Steffanie 520
Grandish, Darlene 625
Granger, Elaina 50
Granillo, Analisa 68
Grant, Laurie 340
Grant, Lola 21
Gray, Brenda M. 146
Gray, Char M. 644
Gray, David 581
Grayson, T. Michelle 589
Green, Adam 227
Green, Candale 446
Green, Corey V. 502
Green, Donna Nisonger 59
Green, Jane 519
Green, Kenneth D. 432
Green, L. M. 159
Green, Mina L. 367
Green, Renee 220
Green, Tim 301
Greene, Catherine Hope 207
Greene, Darryl K. 593
Greene, Phillip T. 547
Greenfelder, Dianne 582
Greenfield, James G. 44
Greenhalgh, Adam 215
Greenwood, Claudia 240
Greer, Jeffie 533
Greggain, Gil S. 552
Gregoroy, Peter 58
Gregory, Myra M. 212
Greig, Marilyn A. 21
Gresham, Lori A. 194
Grewall, Simranjit Singh 429
Grey, Wilfrid 136

Gricus, Kris 471
Grieve, Kay 621
Griffin, Philip F.E. 470
Griffith, Heather 600
Griffith, May 254
Griffiths, Betty M. 349
Griffy, Harold L. 443
Grimaldi, Theresa 139
Grimes, Jocelyn Nissa 244
Grimmer, Virgina Borman 130
Grindey, Pauline 321
Grinovich, Adam 474
Groah, Marc 251
Grogan-Fairchild, Marabeth 342
Gromko, Heather 89
Grooms, Charles E. 519
Grooms, Eric 58
Gross, Stewart B. 174
Gross-Haley, Erma 450
Grossenheider, Jolene 580
Grosvenor, Barbara Enid 578
Grove, Kathryn 481
Grove, Theodore B. 60
Groves, Sunhine 46
Grubbs, Georgina G. 132
Gruber, Ann 233
Gruber, Brandi 310
Grum, Rose 465
Grundy, Robert L. 488
Gscheidle, Frank 174
Gsell, John R. 73
Guadalupe, Alma D. 436
Guarino, Justin 438
Gucinski, Adolph 587
Guertin, Rebekah 426
Guglielmetti, Marci 635
Guidice, JoAnn 210
Gulbin, Jennifer A. 252
Gulotta, Anthony F. 322
Gum, Lorri 206
Gumbman, Pamela 273
Gunderson, Julie M. 129
Gunderson, Pamela J. 302
Gunnell, Grace 77
Gurd, Jenny 406
Gurney, George 447
Gustavson, Beverly 228
Gustin, Edith Greer 447
Guterman, Ralph D. 204
Guthrie, Tara 58
Gutierrez, Teresita 467
Guzman, Dodie 165
Gwaltmey, Melinda Renee 109
Haanes-Olsen, Grayce 266
Haar-Curtchall, Sandy 476
Habada, Jennifer 360
Haberkorn, Kellie 174
Habig, Eric K. 167
Hackwood, Tonny 277
Haefner, James 187
Haffner, Josephine 497
Hagan, Fritzie 93
Hagen, Megan 147, 520
Haggard, D. M. 545
Haggard, Darleen M. 154
Hague III, Harry W. 638
Hague, Helen Linton 461
Hahn, Cynthia E. 62
Hale, Jeffrey Wade 403
Hale, Joanna 612
Hall, Becky 229

Hall, Bonnie F. 173
Hall, Carol A. 593
Hall, Clay D. 275
Hall, Gayle A. 178
Hall, George L. 117
Hall, Kelso L. 169
Hall, Laura 575
Hall, Michael D. 342
Hall, Renee M. 10
Hallahan, Eileen R. 60
Halle, Peter A. 215
Halleck, Barry L. 513
Hallett, Ruby 31
Halliday, Denise L. 136
Hallman, Robert 436
Halsey, Alissa 338
Halsey, Alissa Lorene 275
Halvorson, Ryan 430
Ham, James H. 25
Hamann, Dorothy A. 442
Hamashea, G'ya 47
Hamilton, B.J. 392
Hamilton, Becky 116
Hamilton, Beth 391
Hamilton, Cora R. 579
Hamilton, Ethel 625
Hamilton, Michael 500
Hamilton, Vita 251
Hamlet, Derek 574
Hammer, Linda Lou 350
Hammer, Pamela Smith 453
Hammon, Mandy 182
Hammond, Melissa 104
Hammond, Rosa Gonzalez 642
Hammond, Vivienne 542
Hampton, Jammie 19
Hamric, Ramona E. 630
Hancock, David 626
Handlon, Dourlas 354
Hane, Angie 32
Haning, Hazel 228
Hanna, Alice M. 333
Hanna, Jen 604
Hanna, John 488
Hannon, Shannon Nicole 60
Hansen, Brent 6
Hansen, Heather Lynne 561
Hansen, Ronald M. 349
Hanson, C.W. 334
Hanson, Kathy 593
Hanson, Lois Kathryn 405
Harbilas, David 188
Hardie, Jeni 258
Hardin, Mary Louise S. 123
Harding, Jan 238
Harding, Robert 195
Hardman, William O. 409
Hardway, Marilou 225
Hardy, Eric R. 512
Hardy, Julia Irene 26
Hardy, William 140
Harfouche, Walid George 87
Harker, Ruth Anderson 201
Harma, Loreida 529
Harmic, Robin Denise 269
Harold, Kim 282
Harper, Lewis P. 330
Harrar, Clyde 483
Harrington, Linda 469
Harris, Deborah 285
Harris, Deretha A. 163

Harris, Erica 472
Harris, Helen 609
Harris, Jeremy 328
Harris, Liane 187
Harris, Micheleen 146
Harrison, Clare Tepper 219
Harrison, Sharlene 139
Harrison, Stephanie 181
Harry, Carolyn J. 589
Hart, Alison 616
Hart, Jamie 491
Hart, John 111
Hart, Stephen 307
Hartey, Megan 527
Hartford, Raymond James 26
Hartman, Douglas 186
Hartwig, Alice 421
Harvell, Nelda E. 9
Harwood, Michele 249
Hashemi, Shideh 539
Haskins, Debbie 368
Haswell, Will 371
Hatch, A. Francis 539
Hatch, Eric 552
Hathaway, Alicia 214
Hathaway, Jillian 183
Hatmaker, Michael W. 609
Hauge, Sharon L. 372
Haupt Sad, Dorothy Helen 465
Hauptly, Genevieve E. 148
Hausia, Natalie J. 460
Havens, Will H. 44
Haw, Kristin 558
Hawk, Louise H. 165
Hawkins, Cameron 628
Hawkins, T. 334
Hawkins, Todd 118
Hawkins, Tyler 243
Hawkinson, Bethany 525
Hawley, Glenda 152
Hay, Jessica 436
Hayes, Aleicia 209
Hayes, Angela D. 595
Hayes, Daniel J. 559
Hayes, Danielle 528
Hayes, Rachael 19
Hayes, Susan 74
Haynes, Jennifer 337
Hays, Jean 56
Hayward, Bob 170
Hazen, Marjorie K. 39
Head, Elizabeth S. 4
Headley, C. 522
Heald, Colette 624
Healey, Marlene 301
Healy, Daniel 234
Heard, Terri 473
Hearl, Peggy Potter 15
Heart, Annie J. 69
Heaslet, Anna Elizabeth 568
Heaton, Sharon L. 597
Heaven's Own Light, 610
Heavin, Aeleena M. 603
Hedderig, John 228
Hediger, Kevin 16
Heikkinen, Doris 431
Heimann, Verda 118
Heinz, Susan Y. 270
Heironimus, Catherine 219
Helba, David W. 270
Helgeson, Jeff 433

Heller, Royceann Jackson 568
Hellman, U.S. 386
Helm, Jack 455
Hemmings, Marty 619
Henders, Joyce 616
Henderson, Daniel 324
Henderson, Gladys 166
Henderson, Helen Lamb 594
Hendrick, Erin 402
Hendrick, Tanika 322
Hendrix, Gayle Stants 256
Hendrixson, Theresa 205
Henley, Hezekiah 210
Henney, Jazeene 472
Henricks-Friesen, Wendy 314
Henry, Burke 315
Henry, Dedrick 389
Henry, Erin 236
Henry, Michelle 215
Hensley, Candace 272
Hensley, Connie 49
Henson, Bobby R. 611
Henson, Kelly M. 578
Hentschel, Erwin 637
Hepburn, Audrey 560
Herman, David 348
Hermann, Elizabeth 70
Hermes, Joy 272
Hernandez, Mauro 638
Hernandez, Rose 238
Hernandez-Castor, Valerie 427
Herpel, Joy 438
Herpst, Barbara-Ann C. 172
Herranen, Elaine 448
Herrington, Bary 406
Herrington, Shelly 515
Herrold, Joyce 252
Hersh, Jill 426
Herzig, Theresa Meyer 494
Hesbon, Mary 59
Hess, Connie 197
Hess, Gloria A. 265
Hesse, Patrick 236
Hessel, Carolyn 618
Hester, Julie 255
Hester, Laura J. 87
Hetzel, Joyce 548
Heyns, Sally 498
Hiatt, Kasey M. 580
Hibbs, Aiden 293
Hickey, Irv 398
Hickey, Patricia 551
Hicks, Alexander J. 636
Hicks, Mary E. 5
Hiemier, Paige D. 337
Higginbotham, Diana 272
Higgins, Marie 18
Higgins, Michelle A. 588
Higgs, George 15
High, Jason Edward 592
Hilburn, Janice 345
Hilcoff, Jennifer 472
Hildebrand, Heather Louise 317
Hilderbrandt, Emilie 623
Hill, Emily 225
Hill, Evangeline 618
Hill, Pat 499
Hill, Yvonne, 214
Hillen, Stephanie 415
Hilliard, Deborah 242
Hilliard, Edna G. 217
Hillicoss, Barbara 127
Hillis, Elsie 19
Hillman, Andre 257
Hillman, Yvonne M. 449
Hinds, Danita 611
Hinds, Paul 237
Hines, Adele 159
Hines, Amy Michelle 131
Hines, Lisa 9
Hines, Melissa Ann 361
Hines, Stacy Annette 265
Hines, Tiffany 253
Hinko, Eduard J. 301
Hintz, Earlene 286
Hippe, Laura 332
Hirano, Julie 127
Hires, Catherine Ferguson 615
Hirth, Emma Maxine 466
Hiscock, Eric 621
Hiser II, Douglas Winfield 374
Hitt, Donna 218
Hjelm, Mackenzie 61
Hladky, Geannine 140
Hnatiuk, Cathy 302
Ho, Linda 321
Hobbins, Cathi 297
Hobbs, Joyce 634
Hocklear, Hal H. 159
Hodge, Rhonda 605
Hodges, James D. 462
Hodges, Lisa L. 104
Hodnicki, Edmund 452
Hoeffner, Lois 544
Hoffarth, Lynda 172
Hoffman, C.A. 467
Hoffman, Irene 119
Hofman, Helen M. 194
Hoilien, Catherine E. 89
Hokke, Shirley J. 619
Holas, Nicole 286
Holcomb, E. Kay 24
Holdbrooks, Jennifer 596
Holdeman, Nathan 235
Holder, Nannie Ina 536
Holland, Lavonne A. 479
Holland, Lynn 349
Hollander, Angelic 253
Holliday, Kyran S. 131
Holliday, Ray 106
Hollingsworth, Inge C. (Chris) 402
Hollingworth, Linda 405
Holloway, Angie 564
Holloway, Margaret 128
Holm, Malina 199
Holman Jr., James 34
Holman, Heather L. q40
Holmes, Beverly 395
Holsapple, Harvey T. 196
Holsopple, Leon J. 464
Holzapfel, Angela 293
Holzman, Jerald B. 540
Homuth, Arvid A. 340
Hong, Giang 184
Hood, Anne Larnella 602
Hood, Chaplain Fred W. 89
Hook, Vivian 196
Hooper, Diane 391
Hoover, Martha 223
Hopkins, Mae D. 129
Hopkins, Marlene 620
Hopkins, William S. 592
Hopkinson, Pat 254
Hopper, Cheryl 450
Hopping, Clara B. 38
Hore, Bonnie 314
Horkey, Angela 72
Horn, Edna 165
Horn, Flora Dukon 258
Horne, Annette Marie 251
Horowitz, Jaimee 180
Horse, Mr. 508
Horton, Joan A. 31
Horwitz, Sandra 212
Hosking Jr., Edward F. 199
Hosman, Kimberly Rae 59
Hosman, Tiffany 157
Hostetler, Tina 264
Hostutler, Jennifer Lynn 206
Hotchkiss, Nancy S. 89
Hotinceanu, Radu 188
Hottinger, Ruth 570
Hough, Dawn 510
Hougham, Duane 342
Housden, Linda 548
Houseman, Melvin 209
Houser, Constance Woodward 207
Houston, Melody 119
Howard, Carol 445
Howard, Diane L. 328
Howe, Chad 278
Howe, Martha 120
Howell, Thomas A. 432
Howren, NeVada S. 55
Hoyt, Brenda 527
Hoyt, Roseanne 414
Hric, Rebekah 68
Hub, Ruth 221
Hubbard, George A. 503
Hubbard, Melissa 61
Hubbard, Suzann 73
Hubble, Cynthia 339
Huber, Erica 417
Hubert, Leon J. 637
Huckel, Courtney 45
Hudson, G. 426
Hudson, Mandy 250
Hudson, Thomas Wayne 115
Huey, Katie 634
Huff, Jan 560
Huffman, Lemoyne 118
Huffman, Michelle 639
Huffnagle, Bernadette 385
Hughart, Marion 71
Hughes, Amanda 644
Hughes, Barbie 408
Hughes, Gaye 365
Hughes, Idris R. 279
Hughes, Joseph S. 3
Hughes, Sally 54
Hull, Sandra 112
Hull, W. C. 279
Hult, Helena 215
Hulton, Sharon J. 643
Humbird, Sheena 397
Hume, C. Wesley 325
Humming, Hope 570
Humphrey, April 333
Humphrey, Henry L. 247
Hunt, Ethel M. 413
Hunt, Jean 401
Hunt, Jessie 103
Hunter, Myrtle 116

Hunter, Rose Mary 391
Hurlburt, Agnes 161
Hurst, Anthony 199
Hurst, Esther L. 223
Hurst, Mae 111
Husband, Rebecca 492
Hutchens, Kathryn 256
Hutchens, Leonard 320
Hutchings, Melissa 312
Hutchinson, Michael J. 591
Hutto, Lori 595
Huycke, Dawn 318
Hyde, Howard T. W. 285
Hyde, Mary Kathleen Osborne 11
Hyde, Michael 37
Hyde, Sharon 142
Iacovino, Susannah 585
Iagulli, Mari 220
Icard, Patty 4
Ickes, Tia 356
Ilardi, Kandi 135
Illes, Karli 259
Ilse, Julia 14
Ilser, Glenn E. 489
Imbrogno, Karla 403
Imperatrice, Joseph G. 386
Infortunio, Francine 93
Ingraham, Bernard W. 80
Ingraham, Donna A. 629
Ingram, Katie 144
Inserra, Catherine 187
Inthisone, Oudom (Kekam) 479
Irish, Rosemary 426
Irwin, Linda 299
Isaac, Bernice 106
Isaac, Shirley 311
Isaak, Natascha 443
Isler, Ronnie T. 58
Iudici, Loredana 243
J. A. LaGulia 583
Jackson Jr., John W. 325
Jackson, Bonnie L. 446
Jackson, Carrie 336
Jackson, Lorra 411
Jackson, Mary Lee 527
Jackson, Tim 244
Jackson, W. E. 316
Jacobs, Marc 571
Jacobsen, Richard 65
Jacobson, Alan 247
Jacoby, Kathryn J. 249
James, B. J. 247
James, Jon 372
James-Pendley, Nicole S. 417
Janes-Depass, Linda 624
Janjic, Phyllis 298
Janjigian, Ken 389
Jankowski, Brooke 347
Jannoni-Morrissey, Cheryl A. 359
Janowski, Carolyn 282
Januszewski, Hope 176
Jarrett, V. 629
Jaskulke, Marilyn 25
Jasper, Nichole Anne 75
Jasso, Bonnie 46
Jeffers, Lisa 504
Jefferson, James E. 427
Jeffreys, Tasha 211
Jehlik, Ann 455
Jelavic, Anita 333
Jenkins, Barbara Privott 504

Jenkins, Jane J. 225
Jenkins, Jeffrey 130
Jenkins, Jennifer 627
Jennifer, Militello 7
Jennings, Dawn 551
Jennings, Kevin S. 122
Jennings, Orion 213
Jennings, Sherilin 272
Jensen, Andrew T. 88
Jensen, Jane E. 60
Jensen, Kelly 271
Jepsen, Jennifer 561
Jesmer, Tracy 620
Jibi, Maillot 591
Jimenez, Cathy 217
Jirak, Timothy 253
Johannesburg, Natalie 145
Johanson, Elsie 171
John of Yorkshire 16
Johnson, Alyssa 74
Johnson, Amber 88
Johnson, Benita Winget 86
Johnson, C. Michael 347
Johnson, Christopher R. 192
Johnson, Cocoa 546
Johnson, Colleen Clark 12
Johnson, Danielle J. 239
Johnson, Glory Lukacs 98
Johnson, Jennifer 41
Johnson, Jenny Lee 139
Johnson, Joseph Spencer 69
Johnson, King 627
Johnson, Leona 636
Johnson, Linda 394
Johnson, Linda 483
Johnson, Lyle Eric 524
Johnson, Lynn Diane 251
Johnson, Maxine 162
Johnson, Mike 51
Johnson, N. 243
Johnson, Nikita 489
Johnson, Sharla B. 319
Johnson, Timothy 44
Johnson, Tracey L. 176
Johnson, Valerie 360
Johnston, Jeff 547
Johnston, Sylvia E. 298
Johnston, Wilma J. 274
Joiner, Annie Laura 548
Jones, Angela M. 477
Jones, Gayle A. 250
Jones, Jacquelynne M. 240
Jones, Janet 478
Jones, Jason 329
Jones, Lisa T. 607
Jones, Matthew 379
Jones, Michael 297
Jones, Natalie 397
Jones, Norma L. 96
Jones, Ora 345
Jones, Samuel L. and Canton, Steven J. 582
Jones, Sarah 258
Jones, Sharon 82
Jones, Shirley Ann 632
Jones, Susan 141
Jones, Trey 644
Jones, Willie B. 249
Joplin, Mary Beth 260
Jordan, Chris 564
Jordan, Jennifer 420
Jordan, Randy 261

Jordan, Sara 585
Jordan, Theodore Leo 128
Jordon, Marian 185
Josephberg, Libby 458
Juarez, Rose Mary Steiner 359
Judd, Sarah 175
Judge, Phyllis B. 599
Jui, Jason Ong Kian 617
Jurns, Kim 114
Juso, Kena 504
Justice, Barbara L. 111
Kachel, Maria 525
Kaden, Sara 198
Kagan, Gloria J. 531
Kaggen-Mashel, Susan 597
Kahn, Leslie M. 60
Kalanta, Katherine 112
Kaminsky, Paul 254
Kampfer, Thea Aneke 86
Kane, Ranelle 442
Kane, Yvonne B. 150
Kang, Alice 145
Kanna, Svea 91
Kanne, Tamara 170
Kantenwein, Louise 411
Kaplan, Charles F. 180
Kapp, Larry 388
Karaszewski, Douglas Alan 132
Karayanis, Tina 549
Kardos, Ann 72
Karelta, Jaclyn 262
Karnos, Erika E. 454
Karsko, Almeda P. 189
Kasal, Ludwig 559
Kaszycki, Patricia Zabka 344
Katz, Judith 440
Kauenhowen, Nicole 626
Kaufman, Dorothy 232
Kaur, Kanwaljit 620
Kavouras, JIm 159
Kay, Annika 65
Kay, Josh 464
Kayson, Annelyn 187
Kayzer, Janet 628
Kazolias, Geraldine 415
Kearney, Mary L. 592
Kearney, Sean B. 627
Keating, Terra 316
Keaton, Chereka 272
Kecmer, Grace 242
Kee, Cynthia L. 511
Keeney, April 274
Kegarise, Mary 230
Keil, Karen M. 283
Kelble, Catherine R. 409
Kelleher, Antoinette 35
Kelleher, Mary 104
Keller, Carl 272
Keller, Ferdinand 114
Keller, Lois 81
Keller, Tammy 617
Kelley, Amber L. 45
Kelley, April 420
Kelley, Barbara 64
Kelley, Tiffney 151
Kelly Jr., Abe W. 331
Kelly, Eileen 196
Kelly, June 343
Kelly, Oliver 55
Kelly, Paula 533
Kelsey, Ashley 573

Kemeny, Dawn 367
Kemmer, Jackie 224
Kemp, L. H. 101
Kemp, Mary Frances 331
Kendis, Elsie 51
Kenison, Sara 133
Kennedy, Lue 474
Kent, Karmel K. 545
Kent, Kirsten 40
Kent, Rita C. 596
Keough, Barbara 264
Kersting, Jonathan James 425
Kessans, Sarah 270
Kessler, Carolyn 120
Ketron, Richard T. M. 16
Kiehlmeier, Amy 157
Kies, Carolyn Kies 265
Kilborn, Alison Michelle 546
Kilcullen, LM 549
Kilkelly, Katie 53
Kilmer, Mark 199
Kilpatrick, Martha H. 40
Kimmel, Marlo 393
Kimzey, Mike 125
Kindred Sr., Howard 140
King, David W. 509
King, Joy 133
King, Paul I. 253
King, Rhonda 51
King, Virginia G. 48
Kingcott, Brenda 618
Kingston, Tiffany 241
Kinsler, Traci 328
Kirby 264
Kirchman, Hilda 455
Kirk, Thomas W. 148
Kirkley, Bob 210
Kirkorian, Helen 36
Kirkpatrick, Frank A. 591
Kirkpatrick, Shirley C. 250
Kirwan, Kristen 389
Kirwan, Robert J. 375
Kistler, Bonnie 484
Kittinger, Don C. 40
Kizza, Josephine N. 435
Klein, C. Marguerite 97
Klein, Greg 457
Klein, Nicole 247
Klekamp, Eric 220
Klenbort, Lotte 241
Klepac, Stella 23
Klimesh, Julie M. 216
Kline, Shawn David 64
Kling, Florence 203
Klinger, Elizabeth J. 50
Klingvall, Peter 292
Klipstein, Doug 233
Knight-Davies, Tim 625
Kniskern, Wayne 236
Knobbe, Antonia 95
Knox, Alvin 84
Kocsis, Theresa 395
Koehler, Freddy 48
Koenigsberg, Veloye A. 187
Koerner, Peggy Sue 134
Kofoed, Sam 42
Kohlwey, Alicia 125
Kolar F. S. P., Sister Mary Paula 199
Kolbe, Dorothy 518
Kollatschny, Janis 327
Koop, Mildred E. 24

Kooros, Tania 4
Kooyers, Catherine Ann 455
Kopidlansky, Rita 229
Kopp, Lilly M. 309
Kopplinger, Clara 644
Kopylenko, Julia 107
Kornfeld, Stephanie 104
Kostiv, Amy 608
Kotts, Alice 567
Kovacsy, Joseph 213
Kozak, Nancy E. 324
Kraai, Amber 237
Krambeck, Amy D. 475
Krause, Stacie L. 52
Kravanya, Crystal 490
Krefting, Rebecca 79
Kremins, Kathy 232
Krena, Jason M. 215
Kriegel, Sabina 292
Kriss, Lori 127
Krissy E. 254
Kroner, Lucille M. 474
Kroopnick, Kim 59
Kuczmanski, Heather Noel 635
Kueber, Jane 110
Kuehne, Elaine 32
Kuhn, M. Gertrud 244
Kuhn, Missy 203
Kulczak, Christine 29
Kule, Ron 62
Kurg, Nicole 445
Kusevic, Beba 248
Kutniewski III, Joseph 268
Kvale, Samantha Faye 260
La Belle, Gaetan 277
LaFever, Cheryl 400
LaForte, Nicole 596
LaMorte, Vanessa 175
LaSalle, Dave 411
Lacayo, Lauria 528
Lacayo, Manuela R. 87
Lachapelle, Delinda 298
Lachett, Michelle 540
Lafleur, Alice R. 83
Lafontaine, Stephanie 625
Lagunas, Celia 146
Lahr, Jennifer 217
Lake, Charles 398
Lakos, Heidi 612
Lallemand, Shannon 116
Lam, Michael C. 617
Lamarche, Virginia A. 382
Lamb, Sondra 341
Lamb, Yve Palmer 10
Lambert, J. Craig 61
Lambert, J. Craig 230
Lambert, Rosalie 551
Lament, 383
Lamme, Mary Ann 172
Lampitt, Gianna 288
Lamproe, Jodi 448
Lancaster, Chris 445
Landau, Tia 203
Lander, Jean 75
Landis, Jessie 466
Landis, Michael 406
Lane, Mary Jean 453
Lanfranchi, Michael 247
Lange, Michael Troy 556
Langis, Todd Paul 313
Langworthy, Jerome Laurence 268

Lanham, Kayla 256
Lanthier, Danielle 308
Lapham, Betty 640
Lapriore, Jon 163
Lardie, Toby 554
Larios, Patricia 440
Larkin, Jocelyn Ann 616
Larkin, Mary J. 131
Larrabee, Michelle 274
Larson, Faith Carol 419
Larson, Hillary Paige 269
Larson, Irene Mary 384
Larson, Kathleen 631
Larson, Paige A. 215
Latham, Roberta M. R. 129
Latvis, Donna 639
Laudano, Steven 380
Laudico, John 273
Laudico, John 202
Laue, Cindy 71
Lauffer, Gisele 186
Lauver, Margaret Suzanne 500
Lavender, Cheryl A. 352
Laverdure, Elizabeth 198
Law, Grace 430
Lawhorn, Margaret 144
Lawringsky, Roberta 199
Lawson, Brenda 53
Lawson, Debbie Carol 588
Lawson, Susan 230
Lawton, Julianne 404
Layton, James 494
LeGette, Thelma Williams 489
Lea, Kelly 12
Leard, Denny L. 548
Leatherman, Alice Pendleton 201
Leavitt, Daniel R. 587
Leclare, R. 417
Ledbetter, Dicie 37
Ledden, Amy 236
Lee, Alison 246
Lee, Andrew 634
Lee, Bernice F. 408
Lee, Calvin C. 443
Lee, Carrie 423
Lee, Jessica 361
Lee, Jim H. 204
Lee, Kenneth 210
Lee, Lemuel L. 143
Lee, Mary 558
Lee, Michelle 546
Lee, Millie 111
Lee, R. J. 239
Lee, Rebecca 243
Lee, Robert 290
Lee, Sally L. 45
Lee, Virginia 140
Lee-Owens, Victoria 339
Leeman III, Paul F. 636
Lefebvre, Jason 315
Leggs, Sonia 512
Legleitner, Sharon Dennis 109
Legler, Billy M. 234
Lehmann, Helen Tate 388
Lehrman, A. S. 112
Leigh, Maximillian 601
Leininger, Laurie 207
Leister, Jacob Algire 610
Leitch, Tara 291
Lemay, Paul 290
Lemin, Donald A. 137

Lemire, Lenore M. 390
Lemishow, Albert 51
Lemon, Danni 442
Lemus, Leslie 275
Lendenberg, Donna 604
Lennon, Sue 321
Lenoir, Antionette 380
Lents, Stacie 498
Lenz, Deborah 513
Lenz, Jim 90
Leo, Rose Nix 473
Leone, Dolores 155
Leopold, Leah 256
Lepa, Doris K. 75
Lesage, Eliette 624
Leshovsky, Tammy 369
Lessenthien, Kurt G. 637
Lesser, Rueben R. 496
Levesgue, Jessica 65
Levien, Sarah 331
Levin, Robert H. 335
Levine, Jenny 8
Levy, Jamie 91
Levy/Walls, Barbara 67
Lewallen, Barbara 497
Lewark, Sonia 69
Lewin, Penelope 336
Lewis, Barbara 101
Lewis, Jeffrey Stephen 17
Lewis, Jessica 461
Lewis, Mary-Ann 221
Lewis, Melva J. 421
Lewis, Natalie 243
Lewis, Peggy S. 177
Lewis, Rob 20
Lewis, Sarah 645
Lewis, Shawn Anthony 499
Lewis, T. Claytina 73
Leyland, Dolores 8
Libsack, Constance R. 528
Liebe, Bill 298
Lien, Sarah 263
Light II, Robert K. 520
Liles, Lee-Ann 617
Limbaugh, Lorri M. 531
Limmer, Daphne 450
Linantud, K. Laura 116
Lind, Jean 416
Lindahl, Lorraine E. 438
Lindeman, Stephen P. 108
Linder, Lester E. 37
Lindgren, Kim 223
Lindsay, Candee 240
Linfoot, Travis 409
Lins, Betty Douglas 373
Linstruth, Kimberley A. 633
Linville, Leslie 184
Lippert, Rena Sommers 202
Lippman, Crissie 162
Lippmann, Wilfried 493
Litchfield, Heather 249
Little, Jan 296
Litvin, Valentin 338
Litwiller, Lydia G. Iutzi 355
Liu, Bolin 278
Liu, Junmin 45
Livaccari, Stephanie 492
Livingston, Dorothy A. 476
Llew-Williams, Paul 288
Lloyd, Elizabeth 387
Lloyd, Tami 501

Lobeck, Lisa 84
Locke, Vera E. 616
Lockett, Dwight 534
Locklin, Dora 577
Lockwood, Kathleen Rhein 226
Logan, Jina Maree 150
Lola 263
Lomakin, Gregory V. 450
Lomio, Dona Mary 343
Long, David 441
Long, Frances R. 485
Lopez, Nona 475
Lopez, Paloma 256
Louden, Bernice A. 156
Loudin, Ciarra Rose 201
Louie, Christopher L. 245
Loveland, Lisa 551
Loveland, Richard R. 341
Low, Jaye 311
Lowe, Jason 513
Lowell, Edna Mae 175
Lowes, Kathleen K. 139
Lowmaster, Christie 526
Lowry, Millicent Juray 536
Loy, Carl A. 67
Lsehovsky, Jim 555
Lubiski, Thomas S. 587
Luckeroth, Carey 30
Luddie, Walt 625
Ludwig, Helen 583
Luebke, Susan L. 470
Luff, Brenda 254
Luke Jr., Charles 35
Lum, Elzadia 496
Lundy III, E. J. 557
Lungariello, Gilda 141
Lunsford, Joseph 40
Lunsford, Margaret L. 217
Lupien, Kelly 278
Lupienski, Marie F. 91
Luquire, Shane 429
Lusk, Erica 584
Lust, Tami 508
Lustig, Eleanor 434
Lutgen, Bruce A. 204
Lyle, Heather Honey 230
Lynch, Deloris 483
Lynch, Kelly 199
Lynch, Nicolle 639
Lynda G. 117
Lynn M. 109
Lyons, Angeline B. 49
Lyons, Mary 212
MacDonald, Leslie 309
MacEachern, Stella 281
MacEwan, Clara 293
MacNeil, Melinda 288
Macias, Sunni 130
Mack, Lisa-Anne 626
Mack, Renee L. 74
Mackay, R M 291
Mackes, Stephanie 259
Mackey, Gerald 359
Mackey, Lillian 214
Mackey, Tammy Marie 639
Macleod, Pamela J. 408
Macon, Mildred Moses 153
Maddox, E. "Shadow" 204
Maddox, Rhonda 177
Madeo, Catherine 492
Madison, Susan R. 468

Madnick, Deena S. 154
Madsen, Nick 126
Madsen, Ruth 39
Maercklein, Valery 178
Maertens, Jeanne Roberts 227
Maggio, Carolyn 542
Magua and Camacho, Jessenia and Luis 141
Maher, Thomas 91
Maheux, Shelly 461
Mahon, Leo P. 231
Maiden, Edna 248
Mailhot, Linda 286
Maine, Angeline 386
Maiscalco, Tony 505
Makinen, Jason 311
Makla, Alice 440
Malcolm, Kelly 237
Mallicoat, Lisa 383
Mallory, Lynne Harper 290
Mallory, Vona Ruth 281
Malone, Cristy A. 477
Manchester, Hazel 374
Manderson, Tavia 511
Manelius, Miranda Peechatka 254
Mangum, Mickey 331
Mann, Bud 338
Mann, Donald 610
Mann, Joseph B. 444
Manners, Azelia 314
Manning, Jacqulyn 62
Manning, Jean 216
Manning, Suzy 67
Mansell, Doris 602
Manuel, Monique 468
Marcos, O.P., Mary 27
Marcus, Jane L. 165
Margerison, D. 297
Maria, Lazar 411
Mariani, Valerie A. 250
Mariotti, Celine Rose 148
Mark, S. Gilbert 485
Markle, Roger L. 208
Marks, Ralph S. 188
Marling, Sherie L. 363
Marquart, Donna 642
Marquis, Danielle 268
Marratt, Heather 279
Marro III, Dan 460
Marrone, Crystal 445
Marsh, Anne 301
Marsh, Charlotte Colyer 106
Marsh, Lisa 281
Marsh, Mildred T. 247
Marshall 78
Marshall, Paul 190
Marti, Jo Ann 429
Martin, Angie 444
Martin, Carrie Hibbs 615
Martin, Don 21
Martin, James 22
Martin, John 625
Martin, K.P. 570
Martin, Leona Peffly 113
Martin, Lisa Diane 211
Martin, Melody A. 630
Martin, Nadier T. 412
Martin, Rehonna 134
Martin, Ron 401
Martin, Rosamond 170
Martin, Sara Delores 98
Martinez, Adrian 474

Martinez, Ann (Lis) 244
Martinez, Emma 583
Martinez, Erica 210
Martinez, Mrs. Ruth H. 56
Martinez, Peggy 461
Martini, Sarah 234
Martino, Babette 114
Martino, Nina F. 163
Mason, Barb 320
Mason, Christy 33
Massenburg, Blverno 645
Massey, Ellen Gray 147
Massung, Kathryn 36
Mastaw, Clayton 265
Masthay, Carl 67
Matcek, Kristina Payonk 322
Mather, Robert W. 270
Mathew, Sani Ann 441
Mathews, Marina D. 262
Mathus, Carl 271
Matthews, Scott Lawrence 428
Mattson, Michelle 462
Matty, Fran 520
Maunder, Patrick 221
Mavros, Andy 77
Maxa, Aaron 267
Maxfield, Martha A. 128
Maxwell, Carolyn 307
Maxwell, Glenn D. 416
May, Sharon C. 13
Mayer, George J. 355
Mayo, Nenie 426
Mazza, Lorie Lee 609
Mc Carthy, Francis 190
Mc Larty, Krista 253
McAlister, Crystal Michelle 123
McArthur, Silas 388
McBride, Carrie R. 12
McCOrmick, Stephen F. 434
McCabe, Allison 235
McCabe, Kim 64
McCabe, Michael James 81
McCalla, Heidi 501
McCarter, William 554
McCarthy, Joanna Rene 418
McCarty, Amanda 171
McCarty, Dina M. 63
McCarty, Ragen 229
McClain, Mitch 476
McClarin, D. 53
McClary, Barbara 427
McCliment, Frances Bucaro 51
McCombs, Mary Elizabeth 122
McConnachie, Gillian 287
McCook, Marie 221
McCool, Kristine 257
McCormack, Elissa 239
McCormick, Ida M. 306
McCormick, Kathryn Ann Harris 397
McCown, Betty 223
McCoy, Shawn 147
McCray, Cassandra 228
McCulloch, Alphea 107
McCumber, Mildred D. 408
McDaniel, Jennifer Michelle 136
McDaniel, Shannon 102
McDaniel, Shonte 496
McDonald, Brian 507
McDonald, Clara Jane 85
McDonald, Jenifer 261
McDonald, Kimberley 300

McDonald, Lucy A. 306
McDonald, Sarah 59
McDonald, Tara 541
McDoniel, Jocelyn 194
McDorcid, J. 579
McDougall, Sylvia 296
McDowell II, Philip W. 445
McDowell, Charles Renwick 71
McDowell, Donald K. 423
McElveen, Fannie M. 472
McElveen, Joyce R. 191
McFarland, Karen 5
McFarlane, Vi 302
McGahan, Martha I. 207
McGee, Ashley 269
McGilbra, Carol 132
McGill, Tara 441
McGillis, Colette M. 491
McGinn, Jean 162
McGinnis, William A. 171
McGovern, Tessa 66
McGrath, Kevin 421
McGrath, Mary 637
McGuire, Lillie 543
McGuyer, Rudell 453
McIlnay, Richard D. 541
McIlvaine, Robert 511
McIlwain, Duncan 184
McIntyre, Beth 126
McKeen, Nancy 21
McKellan, Doug F. S. 314
McKelvey, Beth 449
McKendric, Gigi 141
McKenna, John J. 522
McKenney, NeGre' M. 398
McKenzie, David A. 304
McKenzie, Hazel M. 644
McKibben, Jennifer K. 537
McKinley, Jennifer Jo 267
McKinney, Mabel L. 9
McKinney, Thery T. 556
McKinnon, Barbara 562
McLain, Alta Richardson 230
McLaughlin, Rhonda W. 346
McLauglin, Daniel P. 431
McLaurin, Bobbi Jo 589
McLean, Delby 284
McLorie, Sue 373
McMahon, Edith G. Huckins 209
McMahon, Kerri 563
McNabb, Robert H. 346
McNeal, Carrol 144
McNear, Deborah A. 43
McNease, Myrtle 31
McNeese, Karla 526
McNeil, Nancy Reitano 641
McPherson, Brooke 211
McRoberts, Tami 125
Mckinney, Ada L. 360
Mecca, June 555
Medaska Jr., Robert 513
Meddock, Sandy 437
Medford, Glen 492
Medill, Rosanne 111
Meek, Mark A. 631
Meeker, Karen L. 175
Mehta, Samir 602
Meier, Kathryn A. 265
Meister, Theresa 304
Mekeel, Elizabeth 401
Mello, Donna Lee 595

Mello, J. P. 543
Meloy, Jeremy 565
Melvin, Melinda 260
Mendoza, Andreana 542
Meng, Serena 641
Mercado, Magdalena 130
Mercurio, Allison 134
Merenda, James 148
Merkley, Robert C.C. 624
Merrell, Virginia Cobble 432
Merrill, Donna 596
Meshulam, Jennie S. 192
Messer, Tova 175
Messick, Virginia 435
Metcalfe, Denyse 243
Meyer, Barbara A. 341
Meyer, Glozella Bowman 434
Meyer, Jessica 131
Meyer, Lucy 488
Meyer, Sharron L. 225
Meyers, Susan 486
Miccile, Susan 643
Miccio, Jeanne D. 271
Michael, Jenny 205
Michaelson, Luke 473
Michalewich, Marcie 621
Michelle, Jennifer 51
Micinski, Marlene 88
Mickelson, Benjamin D. 255
Middleton, Samantha 232
Mier, Kaylynn J. 401
Miguel, Rena 571
Mihalco, Robert A. 613
Mike, Frederick 457
Mikus, Jennifer 604
Milam, Ken E. 7
Miles, Berttie B. 321
Miles, Christine 65
Miles, Treva 431
Milheiser, Melissa 217
Miller, Barry "Bear" 135
Miller, Amanda 203
Miller, Amy E. 134
Miller, Bethany 392
Miller, Carolyn 373
Miller, Dan A. 613
Miller, Gina 349
Miller, Ginger L. 4
Miller, Jennifer 639
Miller, Jeslyn 275
Miller, Jillian 583
Miller, Megan 636
Miller, Michelle 105
Miller, Scudder 354
Miller, Sharon L. 162
Miller, Suzanne Marie 105
Miller, Violet 420
Miller, Wayne Meredith 499
Milligan, Shannon Elaine 482
Milliken, Nicole 237
Milliman, Mary 211
Mills, Awnali D. 346
Mills, Ferna 642
Milner, Rebecca E. 391
Minaeff, Marlene 336
Mines Jr., Charles F. 132
Minteer, Gladys Clarke 150
Mintle, Brenda 95
Mior, Sara B. 616
Miralia, Rick 510
Miranda, Kristine 221

Misdary, Chris 612
Misener, Janiel 585
Misheff, Sue 579
Mistretta, Jean 198
Mitchell, Blake M. 194
Mitchell, Erika A. 237
Mitchell, Janine 638
Mitchell, Jessica 505
Mitchell, Jessica R. 614
Mitchell, Kelley 510
Mitchell, Kossuth M. 577
Mitchell, Mel 302
Mitchell, Monica D. 429
Mitchell, Sheila 325
Mlakar, David J. 614
Mochulski, Valerie 137
Moirano, Joseph J. 235
Molden, Karen 197
Moltsau, Micayla 545
MontBlanc, Sara Varlie 86
Montague, Nikki 255
Montalvo, Brandy 546
Montana, Amy 193
Monteith, Mary 308
Montgomery, Carl W. 631
Montgomery, Lynn 188
Montgomery, Marcia L. 267
Montlet, Marie J. 267
Moody, Jonathan D. 70
Moody, Vivian 75
Moon, Letty G. 571
Moorby, Carol Ann 467
Moore, Allison 362
Moore, Erin 497
Moore, Harriet J. 358
Moore, Jim 525
Moore, Kathrine M. 550
Moore, Kelly 493
Moore, Lois J. 410
Moore, Melvin 4
Moore, Patricia 127
Moran, Valerie 556
Morgan, Aisha 429
Morgan, April 45
Morgan, Jo Ann 288
Morgan, Kathryn 211
Morgan, Kristie L. 155
Morgan, Renee 207
Moritz, Nancy 198
Morri, Robert 266
Morris, B.B. 428
Morris, Irene 626
Morris, Mark T. 82
Morris, Sandra C. 28
Morse, Jessica 88
Morse, Randi 101
Mosdell, Daryl R. 620
Mosher, Anthony Eugene 87
Mosher, Dorothy 138
Mosher, Julieta Ramirez 107
Mosher, Karen 162
Mosher, T.J. 215
Mossman, Lucille 291
Mott, Roxanne 217
Motta, Rosalie M. 13
Moulding, Rowland G. 269
Mowry, Brianna 234
Moye, Tabitha 271
Moyer, Chris 428
Mrvelj, Darlene J. 197
Muckaday, Jennifer 621

Mueller, Tommye 417
Mufti, Faiza Mahmood 282
Muilenburg, Doris E. 538
Mujahed, Mary Elizabeth 363
Mulconry, Beverly 209
Mulert, Barbara 244
Mulford, Raymond A. 570
Mulhern, Stacy 161
Mullenax, Jane 406
Muller, Erin Marie 269
Mulrean, Beatrice 438
Mulrenan, Anna 10
Multamaki, Martin 618
Mulvey, Peter 557
Muncy, Charlene R. 234
Mundanthanam, George 576
Munhall, Karen S. 64
Muniz, Virginia R. 262
Munoz-Knowles, Martha 68
Murakami, Mildred 197
Murff, Reagan 244
Murnane, Timothy 430
Murowsky, Patrick 33
Murphy, Angela Dawn 452
Murphy, Bethel 340
Murphy, Charrolee 56
Murphy, Earline 149
Murphy, Florence 484
Murphy, H. Louise 645
Murphy, Joyce Sherman 566
Murphy, Mary 488
Murphy, Rose M. 533
Murphy, Russell 244
Murphy, Sine Lee 8
Murray, Ethel 582
Murray, Gabriel 433
Murray, Kristopher 350
Murray, Kristopher 430
Murray, Mark 484
Murray, Mary Katherine 212
Murray, R. Todd 562
Murray, Suzanne J. 262
Murvine, Dale 226
Muse, Gary T. 80
Muurphy, Mary 9
Myers, Arleen J. 321
Myers, Bonnie 544
Myers, Frances L. 151
Myers, Naomi 239
Nagy, Helen 135
Naidoo, Dhanam 299
Nall, Doris J. 239
Nardino, Jamie 230
Narramore, Anita 194
Nartowicz, Hazel F. 611
Nason, Karin M. 634
Naylor, Mirna 154
Nazarethian, George 445
Nease, Casey 603
Neely, Tammy 468
Neitge, Judith A. 237
Nelson, Brenna 121
Nelson, Debbie 125
Nelson, Elizabeth 225
Nelson, L. Mae 400
Nelson, Verle 380
Neri, Anna Marie 3
Nesmith, Bobbi 74
Nevill, Heather M. 211
Newbanks, Dee Anna 56
Newboles, Amy 497

Newbury, John Harvey 212
Newby, Barbara A. 590
Newfield, Maggie 557
Newman, Diane W. 198
Newman, Ronald J. 642
Newsome, Aniece 547
Neyer, Michael James 554
Nguyen, Michelle 191
Nicholls, Allan 295
Nichols and Raye, Susan and Amber 283
Nichols, Brandon 232
Nichols, Sherry Oates 328
Nickerson, Beth A. 435
Nicklas, Patricia C. 70
Nielsen, Karen 206
Nielson, Lori L. 595
Nienhouse, Ralph 246
Nigro, Steve 580
Nilenders, Eve 495
Nilon, Kathleen 263
Noe, Ronald M. 135
Noil, Patricia 246
Nordman, Susan 92
Norman, Alice 253
Norris, Elizabeth Huffaker 140
Norris, Marjorie 208
Norton, Marvin R. 46
Norton, Michelle 117
Norton, Tracie L. 85
Norwood, Shelitha 369
Nose, Roxanne 248
Novak, Lela 617
Nowicki, Andrea 343
Noyes, Nicole 150
Nuby, Leslie 343
Nufer, Katherine T. 483
Nunns, Sheila Marie 304
Nutter, Andrea 519
Nycz, Dolores 139
Nystrem, Erin 389
O'Brien, Timothy Patrick 410
O'Connell, Mary 378
O'Connor, Karen 122
O'Donnell, Emily 140
O'Donnell, Kathleen 142
O'Kelley, Melissa 170
O'Leary, Ellen 555
O'Neill Jr., James W. 145
O'Neill, Craig S. 294
O'Neill, Kelly 622
O'Neill-Reardon, Catherine E. 317
O'Pry, Vera J. 538
O'Reilly, Simon 599
O'Rourke, Kenneth J. 501
O'Sullivan, Diane Patricia 137
OLGA 299
Oakes, Janalene L. 8
Obed, Jennifer 598
Ober, Kimberly R. 517
Obert-Thorn, Stacy 241
Oblen, Allison 456
Obudho, C. James 53
Ocampo, Mary Anne 639
Ocaya, Helen Apolo 280
Odom II, Johnnie Lamar 383
Odom, Frances Lunn 74
Ogg, Louise Salzano 641
Oglesby, Byron 373
Ogletree, Rashonda 5
Ohata, June 65
Ohlfs, Kenneth M. 345

Oldroyd, Jane MacKinnon 349
Oleson, Mildred 336
Oliver, Janie 487
Oliver, Lisa 348
Olson, Denise 483
Olson, Helen M. 356
Olson, Jacob 433
Olson, McKenzie 440
Olson, Verna L. 205
Onoratto, Thomas 324
Opulencia, Shaneeka 238
Orbach, Sherry 531
Orem, Elizabeth 174
Orichosky, John A. 364
Ornegri, Charles Michael 535
Orr, Gerri Elizabeth 144
Orsino, John Joseph 581
Ortiz, George Anthony 45
Ortiz, Shannon 221
Osborne, Jennifer 390
Osborne, Linda 164
Osher, Myah 331
Oshrin, Mary 182
Osterlund, Orvetta 143
Otsetswe, Lefoko 302
Ott, Maxa 128
Otterson, Karie 251
Ottley, Simone 623
Otto, Rita 157
Ouden, John Lee Den 278
Overman, Nicole M. 226
Owen, Phil 422
Owen, Rachelle 583
Owens, Beverly A. 198
Owens, Cathrese M. 489
Owens, Jessie Cooper 630
Pace, Kyle T. 422
Pacholik, Agnes M. 74
Padden, Whitney Hix 95
Paddio-Johnson, Eunice 415
Padilla, Sophie 362
Padwa, Amanda 72
Paff, William A. 195
Pagel, Alisha 61
Pagonis, Rebecca Sue 517
Pallagi, C. 303
Palm, Virginia 263
Palmer, Alan 258
Palmer, Angela 371
Palmer, Ann Podolski 75
Palmer, Susan K. 466
Palmer, Valerie J. 300
Palumbo, Valerie 269
Pamplin, Daniel R. 604
Panzeter, Barbara Craig 209
Papavasiliou, Michele 146
Pappas, Vivana H. 192
Pardallis, Vasiliki Alexis 260
Parise, Cindy 556
Parisloff, Melinda 622
Park, Wendy 76
Parker Sr., Robert 271
Parker, Dave 403
Parker, Jeanne 28
Parker, Jennifer 537
Parker, Nancy H. 566
Parker, Sean 255
Parker, Shannon 269
Parker, Tara 395
Parkes, Jay 451
Parks, Aaron D. 554

Parks, Rebecca 506
Parks, Scott 154
Parmley, Monica 100
Parrish, I. S. 82
Parrott, Heather 590
Parsells, Tori 598
Parsons, Nancy J. 313
Partington, Tony 50
Pascucci, Edward A. 497
Pascucci, Tammi 41
Patchett, Angela 624
Pate, Rosalie R. 586
Paternite, Erin 598
Paterno, David L. 426
Patrick, Betty 114
Patterson, Cindy 303
Patterson, James 34
Patterson, Lorne 54
Patti, Marie 219
Pattison, Fawn H. 148
Patton, C.L. 585
Paulickpulle, Sita Akka 330
Pavelec, Vicki 548
Pavlish, David 55
Pawlecki, Audrey L. 468
Pawlowski, Joan 226
Payne, Shannon 209
Peak, Melyssa Lynn 562
Pearson, Jacqueline 27
Pearson, Julie Weinmann 346
Pearson, Kelvin 283
Pearson, Michelle D. 454
Peck, Ruby 136
Peck, Steven 625
Peden, Arthur Paul 422
Pedersen, Jo Ann 205
Pederson, Jo-Anne 301
Pedroza, Luis 85
Pegura, Tanya 624
Pellegrino, Paul 247
Pellerin, Vylma 624
Pena, Rolando M. 181
Pena, Wanda 49
Penaskovic, Tom 71
Pendleton, Crystal 211
Pendleton, J.B. 443
Penn, Lynn Eicher 235
Penn, Mary Ann 257
Penos, Lisa 471
Penson, Janice M. 394
Perachi, Tracy 210
Perakis, Niki 481
Perez, Javier 372
Perez, Suset L. Laboy 643
Perkins, Dana Thorne 268
Perkins, Marlyn H. 344
Perkins, Robert N. 136
Perkovic, Bozica 627
Perlow, Joseph L. 642
Pernisco, Sue 111
Perotti, Anne Marie 265
Perrin, Helen B. 110
Perrine, Deborah 459
Perron, Mario 627
Perry, Lois S. 621
Perry, Sarah 645
Perry, Tyler 370
Perry, Valerie 577
Perusin, Diana L. 137
Perusin, Diana L. 256
Perzigian, Alice 389

Peters, Michael 80
Peters, Nicolette R. 504
Peters, Vivian C. 168
Petersen, Amy 80
Petersen, Jennifer 503
Petersen, Nancy 364
Petersen, Ruby Q. 196
Petersen, Veronica 180
Petersen, Veronica 586
Peterson, Amanda 425
Peterson, Cynthia 176
Peterson, Earl 71
Peterson, Fluett W. 412
Peterson, Georgia Maurine 356
Peterson, Oliver E. 242
Peterson, Rae R. 129
Peteson, Pete 364
Petrasova, Anna 555
Petro, Paul 164
Petrovic, Marina 300
Petry, Lisa 329
Petrykowski, Lois 84
Pettijean, Lois 552
Pfitzer, Inge 589
Phanphirojana, Keatikorn 581
Phelps, Kasey 34
Phillips, Brandy Linn 614
Phillips, Christy 475
Phillips, David 404
Phillips, Jennifer 314
Phillips, Julia M. 173
Phillips, Maria 271
Phillips, Michelle 395
Phipps, Patricia 637
Phoenix, Winter 563
Phoomsathan, Lynne B. 84
Phundar, Anzard 95
Phuong-Hang, Duong-Thi 516
Piccoli, Michael 70
Pickel, Juanita K. 126
Pickerill, Mary Ann 254
Pickett, Becky 65
Pickles, Michelle 487
Picotte, Melissa 256
Picou, Roylin J. 309
Pier, Lora M. 598
Pieratt, Betty J. 88
Pierce, Evelyn S. 459
Pierce, Gladys Crump 465
Pierce, Jamie Roger 240
Pierce, Paula Janelle 526
Pierpont, Trudy 485
Pierson, Karen A. 387
Pietrzak, Marlowe Jill 451
Pina, Brigette 132
Pinakiewicz, Ashley 418
Pinciotti, Julie 630
Piner, Crystal 156
Pipkin, Robert 490
Pipkin, Sally 73
Pipta, Rene Ann 101
Pishock Jr., James M. 396
Pitman, Jacqueline 556
Pittman, Dorothy J. 231
Pizzino, Pepper J. 122
Pizzuti, Salvatore 242
Plant, Melanie 547
Playford, Rebecca Leigh 201
Plevell, Robert James 633
Plowchin, Marge 68
Plum, Joellen M. 475

Plymesser, Sarah 479
Pnyakker, Tatum J. 581
Podewell, Stephen E. 366
Podlaskowski, Adam 383
Pohlenz, Leslie 21
Pohlman, J.C. 52
Pohts, Christopher 383
Poindexter, Cynthia D. 108
Polanek, Donna M. 59
Polhamus, Michelle 433
Poling, Brenda 363
Polk, Bryan T. 578
Polk, Catrina 220
Polk, Elaine Davis 631
Pollard, Dottie Sue 396
Pollard, Lillian 309
Polo Jr., Russell B. 529
Polsgrove, Ryan L. 158
Polus, Mary 139
Ponce, Nora Erica 383
Ponzetti, Billie J. 210
Pool, Jamie 270
Poor, Sonny 171
Pootlass, Dallas 286
Popham, Dennis Dale 388
Popiak, Tarah 586
Popick, Amy 532
Poplar, Harriet 147
Poppe, Ellen Jane 65
Poray, Katie 626
Portalatin, Susan 621
Porter, Alicia 645
Porter, Neville 249
Posner, Mitch 158
Pospisil, Rebecca Leger 642
Potter, Eula 404
Povilaitis, Cathy 231
Powell Jr., Terence F. 393
Powell, Elaine M. 247
Powell, Jessica 429
Powell, Ken L. 594
Power, Bernadette 618
Powers, Richard R. 226
Powers, Wendy 619
Poyner, Cory 117
Poynter, Karen C. 302
Praitano, Margaret 338
Prange, Mark 7
Prater, Krisi 167
Prather, David C.W. 30
Prather, Miranda 145
Pregler, John E. 99
Preku, Stephanie A. 126
Prescott, James 405
Presley, Shawna 369
Presnell, Terry 52
Pressley, Don L. 486
Pressman, Julie 249
Preston, Billie 253
Preston, Sharon 196
Previte, Bill 504
Prevost, Winthrop Warren 595
Prewitt, Carolyn B. 469
Price, Leslie 479
Price, Mauricia 17
Price, Michael 81
Price, Theresa 168
Price, Theresa 70
Primus, Clarence 470
Prinz, April 305
Pritchard, Nathan 370

Privette, Christal 567
Privitera, Heather 199
Procter, Kelly 24
Proctor, Sandra 530
Proffitt, James 182
Pruitt, Ann 59
Pucek, Tamie 366
Puckett, C.E. 73
Puckett, Chasiti 84
Purguy, Monique 124
Puskar, Eleanor 93
Puskar, Nicole 93
Pyle, Beth Anne 207
Quan, Alison 155
Quar'rell, Natalie 620
Quarshie, Christiana 630
Qucch, Nhu 101
Quick, Bruce 236
Quick, Kirsten 245
Quillen, Joseph Daniel (J.D.) 137
Quinn, Joseph T. 132
Quint, Katharine J. 298
Quisenberry, Rodney 120
Quitler, Shelley Marie 355
Quock, Wanda 300
Rabbitt, Valentina 246
Radel, Aimee 452
Radford, R. L. 18
Rae, Deborah Lucie 259
Rae, Lucy 449
Raether, Arnold L. 379
Ragsdale, Russell W. 168
Ragsdale, Sylvia Schlagel 123
Rainey, Autumn 325
Rainey, Bernice W. 405
Rainone Jr., Joseph 95
Rambo, Viola M. 499
Ramey, Elizabeth 546
Ramey, Erskine 489
Ramharack, Radhica 214
Ramirez, Daniel E. 418
Ramirez, Sandy 32
Rammacher, Lois J. 323
Ramos, Gloria E. 242
Ramsey, Dara M. 634
Ramsey, Darryl 436
Ramstead, Betty 245
Randell, Vance 613
Rangel, Marco 613
Rankin, Daliah 572
Ranous, Jon 26
Rapanos, Susan 601
Rapozo, Ralph H. 169
Rapp, Andrea 514
Rapp, Marjorie 380
Rapp, Ron 164
Rappolt, Toby 643
Ratliff, Julie 236
Ratliff, Terri 634
Raulerson, J. 464
Raulerson, Tom D. (Ogden Gnashed) 154
Ray, Denise M. 408
Ray, Kiersten Lynn 434
Raybon, Jennifer 245
Rayle, Travis 54
Raymond, Yves 487
Read, W. A. 71
Reber, Frances A. N. 46
Redlick, Judy 618
Redman, Abigail 567
Redmond, Edith M. 378

Reed, Allene 322
Reed, Cindra 28
Reed, Daria 105
Reed, Holly 52
Reed, Mary H. 225
Reed, P.M. 496
Reents, Ray E. 252
Rees, Karl 162
Regnier, Maureen 626
Reicks, Edna 425
Reid, Jason 629
Reid, Wendy J. 106
Reiffert, Jennifer 253
Reiner, Ruth 625
Reinhardt, Emma 94
Reiss, Bill, 203
Relitz, Carson 74
Remy, Tamara K. 487
Rencher, Wenifer 61
Reno, Sandra E. 268, 630
Renshaw, Jennie 131
Renwick, Cyra Grace 432
Resendiz, Jorge A. 72
Resnick, Edward 470
Rettig, Richard J. 425
Reuscher, Melissa Rose 47
Reynolds, David L. 72
Reynolds, Karey D. 607
Reynolds, Lee 71
Reynolds, Nora M. 516
Reynolds, Rowan 276
Reynolds, Ruth 250
Reynolds, W. L. 270
Rezek, Emily B. 264
Rhoades, Pamela 521
Rhodes, A. C. 110
Rhodes, Kim 267
Rhodes, Noel 271
Rice, Joyce A. 207
Rice, Karly 234
Rice, Teresa 23
Richard, Melissa 231
Richards, Julia Elizabeth 231
Richards, Paul J. 439
Richardson, Joyce P. 27
Richardson, Sheri 77
Richer, Megan 272
Richmond, Blanche 424
Richmond, Julie 145
Rick, Jacki 416
Rickard, Myrna 151
Riddick, Ruth A. 191
Ridenour, M.C. 218
Rideout, Edith C. 296
Rideout, Heidi 313
Rideout, Marguerite 145
Ridgway, Terry E. 164
Rife, Susan A. 57
Rigberg, Jodi 325
Riggins, Brandon 332
Riggs, Heather 228
Riggs, James L. 553
Riley, Everlyn 273
Riley, Patricia 522
Riley, Steven L. 605
Rilling, David 376
Ring, Mellisa A. 567
Rini, Matthew J. 193
Rintala, Anthony 350
Risinger, Angelina S. 538
Rissberger, F. Alan 609

Ritchey, David L. 113
Ritter, Veronica Giacomelli 139
Rivera, Jessica 165
Rizzo, Nikki 32
Roach, Beverly R. 419
Roach, Shondel 53
Roan, Bette 467
Robbins, Mark 587
Robbins, William 463
Roberts, Jenny 478
Roberts, Kristy 418
Roberts, Mandi 371
Roberts, Mary E. 70
Roberts, Pat 359
Roberts, Stephanie 390
Roberts, Teresa 319
Roberts, Tonya 633
Roberts, Tracy 190
Robertson, Florence C. 60
Robertson, John 393
Robertson, John David R. 326
Robertson, Luc 279
Robertson, Shirley Lou 219
Robertson, Todd 584
Robinette, June A. 201
Robinsin, Edward 598
Robinson, Anne 505
Robinson, Courtney 52
Robinson, David V. 167
Robinson, Norma Nuyles 343
Robison, Debra 72
Rockwell, Pamela L. 383
Rod, Shirley 142
Roden, Concetta M. 241
Roden, Wyn 314
Rodenburg, Sarah 138
Roderick, Carrie 632
Roderick, Marge 635
Roderigas, Dawn 585
Rodermund, Patricia 27
Rodgers, Ashlyn T. 438
Rodgers, Carol 235
Rodke, Dorothy H. 31
Rodriguez, David M. 535
Rodriguez, Felicia 29
Rodriguez, Yesenia 223
Roe, Shelli 437
Rogers, Bunny 457
Rogers, Frank 317
Rogers, Franklin 245
Rogers, Mavis Laughton 25
Rogers, Sheri Everts 83
Rohrbach, Clay 544
Rohrbaugh, Isabel 525
Roldan, Jodi Theresa 252
Romack, Velvadeane 469
Romine, Debra D. 557
Ronning, Allyson 413
Roos, Melissa 256
Root, Lisette 206
Rosado, Jaime 149
Rosario, Marimar 522
Rose, Irene B. 17
Rose, Richard A. 513
Rose, Ruth 201
Rose, Susan 55
Roseberry, Jeannie M. 68
Rosenau, Kay Lynn 259
Rosenberry, Deloris 586
Rosenfeld, Tiffany 637
Ross, Amber 255

Ross, Eugene D. 321
Ross, Joel 273
Ross, Kelly 214
Ross, Matt 373
Ross, Patricia J. 54
Ross, Shelley Anne 503
Ross, Terry 171
Ross, Terry L. 151
Rossi, Johanna 454
Rossi, Katie 231
Rossiter, Daniel 553
Rossiter, David A. 392
Roulston, Hugh Donovan 304
Round, Peter F. 181
Rovelli, Paul Joseph 69
Rowdon, Larry 293
Rowe, Edward Charles 102
Rowell, Nancy E. 600
Rowley, Roxanne 370
Rowsell, Dion 620
Roxby, Veronica 37
Roy, Camille L. 477
Roy, Jodi 46
Roy, Larnders 484
Roy, Mell J.-Branch 6
Rozeski, Brooke 370
Rozman, Amy F. 169
Rubera, Patricia 523
Rubio, Vicki 43
Rudkevitch-Bowen, Shannon 309
Rueb, Dorothy 55
Ruel, Michael 97
Ruffin, Carolyn S. 136
Ruffin, Mary Elizabeth 67
Ruffo, Diane 303
Rumschlag, Christina 371
Ruppert, Michael J. 632
Rusch, Kim 480
Rush, Esther G. 198
Rusinak, Erica Lynn 50
Ruskin, Julia Maxine 83
Russell, Malcolm M. 16
Ruthledge, Jeannie 419
Ruthledge, Nancy 513
Rutt, Megan 252
Rutter, Teri 248
Ryan, Don 271
Ryan, Garry 285
Ryan, Linda L. 47
Rybar, Amy E. 262
Ryder, Betty 385
Ryder, Starr 645
Ryel, Mary L. 557
Rys, Adrienne 576
Sacauskis, Mary A. 372
Sacco, Peter Andrew 549
Sack, Melissa 193
Saefke, Barbara 249
Saenz, Juanita 142
Saffel, Sabrina 601
Sahli, Harriet M. 57
Sala Sr., Silvio A. 152
Salanga, Charina 225
Salas, Hana 67
Salata, Ralph 123
Saliot, Lillian D. 552
Salkin, Merle J. 631
Sallie, Brenda 125
Salmin, Louise 142
Salonen Jr., Norman C. 226
Samec, Arlene 392

Samedov, Ahmet 516
Sampson, Hyman 586
Sams, Darlene 559
Sams, Marie 558
Samtani, Preeti 580
Samuels, Bobby 394
Samuels, Laura J. 231
Sanca, Ana Julia Macedo 282
Sanchez, Maria 573
Sanchez, Veronica Pauline 597
Sanders, Audrey W. 403
Sanders, Lucretia 166
Sanders, Maye 381
Sanderson, Sally Longfellow 179
Sandifer, Willie 129
Sandomenico, Mildred E. 327
Sanford, Missy 274
Sansom Jr., Ray L. 54
Sapp, Edna Frances 540
Sargent, Cathy J. 347
Sargent, Don 259
Sarhalar, Robbie L. 110
Sarmiento, Alicia 580
Sarty, Ruby 236
Satz, Fran 331
Saucier, Renee 539
Sauers, Treva M. 572
Saunders, Gregory 528
Saunders, Margarette Combs 154
Saunders, Mary 206
Saunders, William A. 599
Saur, Carolyn 418
Sauve, Marc 627
Savage, Marilyn 278
Savanella, Marie 16
Saviano, Scott 199
Savio, Caroline A. 211
Sawaya, Christy 519
Sawyer, Erin 437
Saxon, Karen M. 568
Saxton, Fred 47
Sayers, Michael 29
Saylor, Tonya 88
Scarpino, Keith 598
Schaefer, Hilda 206
Schaeffer, Mary L. 196
Schaelchli, Trudy 227
Schaumburg, Kris 608
Scheer, Jill M. 230
Scheiner, Julie 564
Schellenberg, Kevin 280
Schiess, Melissa 264
Schild, Donna-Maria 505
Schillinger, David 546
Schindler-Wolf, Susan A. 420
Schlaefer, Robert 265
Schmelzer, Vivienne J. 19
Schmidt, Helen E. 577
Schmidt, Kristine 633
Schmidt, Patsy 25
Schmidt, Todd 499
Schmidt, Winifred B. 67
Schmiesing, Sarah 232
Schmitt, Julie 600
Schmoyer, Gladys 451
Schnetz, Christine 13
Schnitzler, Max 512
Schoenbeck, Laura 550
Schofield, Chip 263
Scholten, Henrietta 290
Schonhoff, Paula 407

Schrader, Stuart 55
Schraider, Robin 175
Schramm, Janie 486
Schrand, Jane M. 54
Schranz, Sarah 430
Schreiber, Dorothy M. 49
Schroyer, Jennifer 69
Schuety, Charles N. 399
Schuler, Cecily 79
Schuler, Joyce 475
Schuler, Joyce Boyer 399
Schulte, Sarah 481
Schultes, Debra Lynn 566
Schultheis, Michelle 569
Schumacher, Kari 419
Schutz, Jason D. 205
Schutze, John 552
Schuyler, Crystal 410
Schwark, Doris 258
Schwartz, Hilary 368
Schwartz, Stuart 524
Schweizer, Kristina 156
Scoggin, Janet 88
Scott, Allen 239
Scott, Clementine Harris 149
Scott, David William 615
Scott, Elizabeth M. 416
Scott, Ericka 122
Scott, Eva O. 261
Scott, Halecia 325
Scott, Jean 280
Scott, Jean 622
Scott, John M. 583
Scott, Kristin 143
Scott, Laurie A. 35
Scott, Linda Paterek 211
Scott, Lois E. 424
Scott, Lynne F. 465
Scott, Michelle 52
Scott, Sue 92
Scott, Verselia L. 576
Scribner, Eleda 344
Scriggins, Jennifer 266
Seamans, P.W. 471
Sears, David 579
Seay, Helen 486
Seeber, April 55
Seeger-Huff, Ruth 364
Seeman, Elgie V. 136
Sefton, Catherine M. 417
Seggie, Jo 628
Seguin, Della M. 642
Seibert, Eleanor J. 342
Seidman, Rachel 459
Seiser, Ann 165
Seitz, Oliver 453
Selby, Sharon Dawn 318
Selby, Susan 142
Self, Carol Gulke 31
Seliski, Lawrence John 284
Sell, Margaret R. 309
Selleck, Arthur P. 22
Sellers, Kim 536
Sellers, Sylvia 564
Selph, Jonathan 458
Sengupta, Monojeet 553
Senn, Pamela J. 378
Senna, Doug 141
Sepulveda, Joanne 384
Sepulveres, Danielle 462
Seretis, Victoria 317

Serrano, Iva Marie 334
Setzer, Bobbi M. 7
Sever, Laura 586
Severance, Marilyn 219
Seward, Kekoa 490
Sewell, Sheri 622
Sexton, Laura 68
Seyler, Amy Jo 25
Shadwell, William J. 422
Shah, Nalini P. 67
Shaner, Eleanor 500
Shanks, Frieda 128
Shanks, Gregg 286
Shannon, Joyce A. 559
Shannon, Virginia 271
Shapiro, Alicia Terrones 361
Shapiro, Steven 348
Shapka, Sharon E. 296
Sharar, Helen Nichols 537
Sharp, April (Lynn) 492
Shartrand, Raymond 98
Shashaani, Avideh 643
Shatos, Teena 245
Shaw, Cerissa 241
Shaw, Leanora Musser 119
Shaw, Randy 15
Shea, Eugene V. 57
Sheehan, Colleen 643
Sheehan, Frank 367
Sheehan, Jon 238
Sheldon, Mildred 141
Shelton, Martha 342
Shepard, Amy 474
Shepherd, Dorothy West 240
Sheppard, Charles 543
Sheppard, Elwood H. 63
Sheppard, Gary 6
Sherban, Andrew 296
Sherburne, Evelyn 126
Sheriff, Melissa 137
Sherley, Eric Lerez 638
Sherlinski, Amanda 410
Sherrouse, Judith Gayle 156
Sherwood, Connie L. 32
Sherwood, Katie 535
Shifflette, Kirsten 194
Shifter, Erica L. F. 149
Shiley, Jane 402
Shilo, Tammy 457
Shinner, Kim 516
Shipley, Kristen 645
Shipman, Charles 424
Shipman, David N. 370
Shirkey, Alana 255
Shirley, Bruce W. 379
Shockley, Christia 603
Shogren, Jan 377
Shook, Christie Lee 189
Shover, M. James 643
Shuler, Rose Perl 56
Shuyler, Faye 539
Sieh, Kristen 259
Sigler Jr., William W. 384
Silbert, Genevieve 61
Silk, Scott 330
Sillence, Diana 138
Silva, Jenni 224
Silva, Sergio C. 136
Simm, Lindsay 178
Simmelink, Lisa 125
Simmons, Carol A. 381

Simmons, Christina C. 213
Simmons, Sharon 559
Simms, Zachary 327
Simoes, Antonio 385
Simon, Scott M. 297
Simonian, Emily 273
Simonson, Mark 142
Simpson, Jim 17
Sinclair, Doris J. 591
Singer, Darren A. 12
Sinko, Amy 320
Sinocruz, Leilani 387
Sinquefield, Leslie A. 124
Sjodin, Julie 262
Skaggs, Ruby Farnham 514
Skiff, Glenn W. 121
Skinner, Rebeca 326
Skipper, Tracy 248
Skorohod, Tara 344
Skrobot, Jessica 506
Skubukowski, Kathy 263
Slater, Shawn 251
Slaughter, Myrtle 325
Sleeme, Scott Dominic 636
Sleister, Matthew D. 22
Sliwa, Therese M. 327
Sloan, Camille A. 521
Sloan, Jennifer 450
Slominski, Ailene Smith 489
Slosser, Chris 284
Slusarczyk, Hollie J. 13
Smallback, Karma 104
Smalls, Shanda 57
Smeltzer, Tammy 295
Smith Sr., Booker T. 161
Smith, Alice P. 629
Smith, Allie Lee 147
Smith, Andrea 402
Smith, Bernadette 193
Smith, Carmen J. 61
Smith, Carolyn 623
Smith, Christine 529
Smith, Christy 638
Smith, Corri 15
Smith, Daniel S. 63
Smith, David Alan 274
Smith, Dawn Rene 34
Smith, Denise 26
Smith, Donald 565
Smith, Edna 625
Smith, Ellen 115
Smith, Felicia 130
Smith, Gregory 547
Smith, Hazel 87
Smith, Ina 62
Smith, Jasmine M. 89
Smith, Jason Richard 59
Smith, Jayne J. 94
Smith, Jean Carr 507
Smith, Jeanette M. 576
Smith, Jerry 569
Smith, Jill C. 339
Smith, Joel Martin 524
Smith, Judith M. 249
Smith, June Iris 446
Smith, K. O. 431
Smith, Kimberly 394
Smith, Leonard 255
Smith, Lisa D. 335
Smith, Lorena 448
Smith, Mary E. Lauderdale 453

Smith, Maya K. 127
Smith, Melanie 51
Smith, Melanie 418
Smith, Michael R. 635
Smith, Mona 505
Smith, Nathan 35
Smith, Nathan 627
Smith, Rachel A. 602
Smith, Rory 225
Smith, Royel 298
Smith, Sam R. 195
Smith, Sarah Allison 4
Smith, Savai LaRose 565
Smith, Shannon 630
Smith, Shelby J. 138
Smith, William Clavel 381
Smith-Harder, M. Monica 282
Smithson, Shawn N. 502
Smulyan, Shana 341
Snell, "Cap" 100
Snell, Kim R. 201
Snerr, Carolyn J. 224
Snow, Abigail 150
Snow, Alyxyz 152
Snow, Sharon 195
Snowdall, Dawn 73
Snowden I, Peter Jay 372
Snyder, Bertha 62
Snyder, Bob 212
Snyder, Linda 529
Snyder, Shelbie 401
Sobeck, E. H. 407
Sobel, Charlotte 198
Sobotka, Frances 57
Sokan, Lovelle 205
Solari, Frederick 482
Solland, Wanda 86
Solomon, Beth 539
Solomon, Marilyn 581
Sommer, Rosalyn 583
Sommers, Jon David 162
Sommerville, Lynn 147
Song, Ho Jun 261
Sorensen, Lisa R. 367
Sorensen, Serena 488
Sorenson, Lowell 92
Sorey Sr., Charles H. 611
Sorhagen, Hilda 446
Sorice, Justin 41
Sorola, Anita 640
Soto, Elizabeth 527
Soukup, Nadia 483
Southwick, Shawna 458
Sovereignty, Grace Qi 573
Sowers, Lisa 128
Spangler, Billie Jo 594
Spann, Kenneth E. 523
Sparks, Robert 606
Sparks, Tiffanie A. 428
Spaulding, Spencer W. 366
Specter, Kellie 422
Spellman, Wilma 51
Spence, Barb 616
Spence, Doreen 305
Spencer, Barbara 38
Spencer, Brenda 68
Spencer, Donely 58
Spencer, Marc 8
Spencer, Quanda V. 66
Sperling, Stacey 631
Speth, Shirley L. 614

Spicer, Louise 155
Spinat, Daniella 560
Spinelli, Samantha 272
Spink, Madeline 544
Spires, Rebecca Lynn 448
Spitzer, Kelly 227
Spradlin, Brian M. 521
Springer, Alexis 642
Springer, Jim
Springer, Stephanie 233
Sprouls, Roe Sonye 349
Spry, Mavis E. 17
Spurrell, Madeline 283
Spyridakos, Joanne 339
St. Clair, Nancy M. 315
Stabeck, Dorothy 295
Stacey, Evelyn 222
Stacey, Jennifer 644
Stacey, Tracey 632
Stacinski, Cynthia Lynn 289
Stacy, Arlie II and Mikel 244
Stafford, J. Audrey 235
Stallings, A. George 42
Stallings, Courtney 475
Stallings, Irma L. 323
Stamper, Alene 172
Standifer, Rose E. 184
Stanford-Cox, Marlene 124
Stanford-Miller, Toni 58
Stangland, Stephen 257
Staples, Doris 113
Stapleton, Steve 619
Starkey, Sandra L. 243
Starkey, Virginia C. 145
Stassin, Cynthia R. 182
Stauffer, Linda 388
Stead, Cindy 623
Steele, Bessie Harp 406
Steele, Edna 166
Steele, Heather 599
Steffey, Phyllis 332
Stein, Davina 35
Stein, Douglas 488
Stein, Zimmerman 441
Steinberg, Thelma T. 201
Steines, Jennifer 427
Steinhaus, Johanna 221
Stem, Jean H. 184
Stephens, James 152
Stephens, Julette Hilton 27
Stephens, Nancy Jo 31
Stephenson, Jamie 232
Stepp, Angela Mae 353
Stetson, Susan 400
Stevens, Amy 555
Stevens, Betty 96
Stevens, Evelyn M. 421
Stevens, Mildred 46
Stevens, Robert Abraham Wylder 524
Steward, Shelly 444
Stewart, Brian 641
Stewart, Christy 207
Stewart, Debbie 495
Stewart, Derek 608
Stewart, Hascal Vaughan 534
Stewart, Jaclyn 641
Stewart, Kim R. 124
Stille, Virginia 206
Stirling, Dwight 341
Stiver, Mary Weeden 50
Stockdale, Christina 451

Stockton, Elizabeth D. 78
Stoddart, Renee 290
Stolnis, John 456
Stolz, Helen F. 65
Stolzenburg, Eldon L. 417
Ston, Jodie 11
Stone, Andrea 289
Stone, Lois 626
Stone, Nikia 104
Stone, Rae 213
Stout, R.A. 392
Stoutenger, Lisa 239
Stovall, Clarence W. 10
Stovall, Gatha 571
Stover, Sean 346
Strait, Katie A. 12
Strand, Kathryn 164
Strasser, Lauren A. 259
Stratton, Dan 210
Street, Shelley 47
Stroman, Lucy N. 250
Stroup, Elizabeth B. 57
Struble, Charissa 252
Struck, Maria R. 332
Strunk, Nicole 93
Stuhr, Deborah 502
Stull, Patricia A. 613
Stump, Kathey 103
Sturgill, Dora Patricia 605
Sturgis, Thelma M. 17
Suder, Robyn L. Rancourt 251
Sudziarski, Nancy Lee 258
Suhrbier, Larry 552
Sullins, Michael 398
Sullivan, Evelyn R. 209
Sullivan, Heather 615
Sullivan, John 207
Sullivan, Patricia G. 65
Sullivan, Rhonda 408
Sullivan, Shannon 220
Sullivan, Tom 410
Sully, Warren 365
Sumerlin, Elsie Rose 57
Sumner, Emily Carol 39
Surface, Becca 530
Suri, M.P.S. 208
Surmiller, Jason 83
Susmuth, H. John 143
Sutherland, Patricia L. 300
Sutphin, James W. 493
Sutton, Jamie 134
Swader, Olivia D. 229
Swaekauski, Shasta 257
Swain, Jackie 129
Swain, Tracy L. 313
Swan, Charlene 522
Swanson, Glenn A. 223
Swanson, Josephine McGuire 146
Swantek, Diane 72
Swartz, Krag Hunter 191
Swartz, Sally 519
Swears, Zack 268
Swedlund, Amanda 246
Sweeney, Barbara A. 38
Sweet, Betty 452
Sweeten Jr., Colen H. 381
Swift, Susan LeeAnn 203
Swindlehurts, Shawn 494
Swope, Helen Perry 77
Syal, Harshi 183
Sykes, Audrey 465

Sykes, Livia D. 454
Sylvester, Edward 595
Szostak, Eugene M. 134
Szubielski, Sylvia 394
Szuromi, Laszlo 182
Tackett, Shari 253
Tafel, Alvin L. 186
Takeda, Nobuko 562
Talbert, Nick 464
Tallman, Evelyn T. 597
Tallman, Mathew A. 96
Tamarkin, Jed 430
Tammy, 645
Tapia, Kathleen 270
Taporowski, Tracy 628
Tarnowski, Gregory 441
Tarrant, Philip 306
Tate, Misty 636
Tate, Rebecca 160
Taufeeq the Unique 529
Taulbee, Esther 223
Taulbee, Lauren 256
Tausch, Susan D. 583
Tauscher, Elizabeth Patricia 469
Taylor, Deborah Howard 578
Taylor, Dorothy A. 372
Taylor, Edith 344
Taylor, Eveline 242
Taylor, Gail Tamara 98
Taylor, George L. 117
Taylor, Heather 129
Taylor, Jeremy 117
Taylor, Jessie 255
Taylor, Loretta G. 200
Taylor, Michelle 572
Taylor, Tami A. 615
Taylor-Torrence, Telitha 394
Tearpak, Clara 608
Tebow, Devry D. 262
Tedesco, Barbara L. 6
Teitsworth, Katie 4
Tennant, Sheridan Jenice 441
Tenner, Joan 173
Tenney, Jaime 200
Tenney, Rachel 213
Tensfeldt, Glenda 517
Terrell, Brandie 43
Terwilliger, Georgia 384
The Thoughts of Lola, 201
Theriot, Natasha 220
Thibodeau, Mark Alan 229
Thibodeaux, Sharon 322
Thiemann, Francis C. 263
Thierfelder, Bill 273
Thiessen, Patty 619
Thomas III, D. G. 349
Thomas, Carol Deane 222
Thomas, Catherine 559
Thomas, James E. 561
Thomas, Juanita 601
Thomas, Julie 633
Thomas, Linda F. 632
Thomas, Lonnie B. 11
Thomas, Lorraine 146
Thomas, M. S. 143
Thomas, Michael 558
Thomas, Nan 241
Thomas, Nanette 27
Thomas, Sonja D. 550
Thomas, Summer 203
Thompson III, Walter 400

Thompson, Crystal 471
Thompson, Georgia 150
Thompson, Jennifer 218
Thompson, Julie 392
Thompson, Kara 47
Thompson, Liberty 138
Thompson, Richard P. 361
Thompson, Stephanie 153
Thompson, Teresa 202
Thompson, Tessa 381
Thompson, Tonia 44
Thompson, Vernon D. 495
Thompson, Wygenia 366
Thorn, Mary 524
Thornton, Henry J. 26
Thornton, Patsy 159
Thune, Lillian 186
Thurlow, Brenda 276
Thurman, Kathie 268
Tibbals, Debbie L. 390
Tibbetts, Kathleen Irene 49
Tilley, Robin 623
Tillmann, Ann 494
Tincher, Norman L. 232
Tinio, Eleanor Calasara 54
Tino, Mary 262
Tirri, Ruth 94
Tol, Hendrika 160
Tolbert, Karle Williams 62
Tolzman, Marc 63
Tomanica, Ellen 506
Tomlinson, Lori 433
Toogood, Mildred 36
Topham, Levi 448
Topper, Donna 197
Toresdahl, Osmond 68
Torrence-Thompson, Juanita 233
Torres, Carlos 234
Torrey, Carter 215
Tousignant, Steven 550
Toves, Vivian L. 512
Towle, Donna L. 195
Townley, Victoria 498
Townsend, Colleen 369
Townsend, J. W. 25
Tragedy, 541
Trampe, Robert LeRoy 259
Tramposch, Elvira 220
Tran, Cuong 156
Trapp, Theresa B. 261
Trask, Norma Claflin 124
Traver, Betty 198
Travers, Anthony 222
Treatman, Ethyl 216
Tremel, Nicole Kathryn 196
Trenholm, Kenneth J. 285
Trent, Media 636
Trester, Evelyn V. 489
Trimble. Diana L. 507
Trinidad, Socorro Ch. V. 291
Trinko, Carl M. 382
Triplitt, Lois Smith 386
Tripp, Mary Ann 547
Tripp, Steve 287
Troiano, Laurie 255
Troie, Sergiu 600
Trotta, Harriet 173
Trouve, Paul A. 396
Trowbridge, Jeff 161
Trudeau, Barbara 310
Truitt, Eric 233

Trussell, Jan 105
Tschetter Alan 405
Tuck, P. S. 192
Tucker, Klarice 228
Tucker, Nell 626
Tucker, Sherry D. 180
Tudor, Chelle D. 633
Tuleta, Terri M. 374
Tunila, K. G. 161
Turk, Irene Mary 419
Turnage, Diane 602
Turner, Billie Jean 264
Turner, Brenda P. 259
Turner, Deborah 214
Turner, Joey 515
Turner, John E. 113
Turner, Kathryn D. 20
Turner, Mary-Lou 210
Turnham-Jones, Eileen 282
Turpen-Lanham, Barbara 367
Turri, Dorothy S. 532
Tutor, James 260
Tuttle, Susan 239
Tuxon, Fred R. 10
Twitchell, Gina Marie 547
Tyce, F.A. 397
Tyler, Cindy 145
Tyler, Stacey 252
Tym, Stephanni A. 631
Tyner, Doris 241
Tysick, Noah 431
Tzortzinis, Joe 399
Ubben, Mary Sue 384
Ubelhor, Aline 146
Ueland, Laura 313
Ulbrich, Rachael Sonia 351
Ulman, C.M. 444
Ulrich, Christina Marie 229
Umhoefer, Chris 485
Underdown, Jody 614
Underhill, P. M. 594
Unetich, Amy 129
Ungar, Alice 245
Unger, Sherley G. 365
Ungerecht, Theresa 138
Urban, Ginny 168
Urban, Olive Gregory 377
Vadai, C. 340
Vakil, Mansha A. 168
Valentine, Danielle 70
Valerius, Kelly 251
Valez, Billie 356
Vallee, Gaetan 626
Van Dorn, Darin 194
Van Hoecke, Jo-Ann M. 143
Van Horne, Mari 289
Van Horssen, C.A. 506
Van Luwen, Regan 305
Van Note, Stella Davis 202
Van Oosten, Katrina 594
Van Owen, Kenneth 123
Van Pelt, Elizabeth A. 160
Van Winkle, Laurie 452
Van Wyk, Laura 358
VanBuskirk, Christa 131, 317
VanDam, Josephine Jean 91
VanHeel, Goldie J. 123
Vance, Nora D. 265
Vanderboom, Lea 355
Vanistendael, Marilyn 74
Vann, Mitchell R. 133

Vanwart, Lois 623
Vardal, Ebony 617
Varo, Amy 266
Vaughan, Megan 486
Vaughan, Rebecca 512
Vaughan, Rita 133
Vaughn, Barbara Jean 355
Vaughn, Herman F. 553
Vaughn, Jane 90
Velacich, Jason 428
Velazquez, Gladys 629
Velez, Laura 439
Venable, Felicia W. 588
Venard, Natalie 369
Ventura, Allison M. 368
Ventura, Gil 318
Vercelli, Zoe 263
Verhoef, Stacia 195
Verrinder, Sophia 382
Vestal, Anne 387
Viale, Debra 393
Vicente, Rebecca 323
Vick, Mary June 171
Vickers, Burga H. 369
Victoria, Catherine 144
Vient, Emily 274
Vietmeier, Elisabeth 637
Villanueva, Margarito 606
Villareal, Rogelio 423
Villarreal, Denise R. 529
Villarreal, Vanessa 495
Vinokurov, Joseph A. 219
Viola, Johnny 135
Visto, Lourdes R. 630
Vogel, Betty 319
Vogel, Laura 432
Vogelsang, Greg J. 190
Voigtsberger, Mary 28
Vollmerhausen, Jessica 126
Vorrath, Muriel 5
Vorwerk, Sarah R. 137
Voss II, Harley D. 177
Vratanina, Beatrice 23
Vu, Bao-Van 307
Vu, Diep Thanh 426
Vyhnal, Chris 516
Waddle, Patti 79
Wadle, Sarah 247
Wadsworth, Amy L. 456
Wadup, Dorothy 300
Wager, Oscar P. 187
Waggoner, Cari Marie 572
Waggoner, William Chris 163
Wagner, Judy 176
Waight, Kathleen 415
Waitkevich, Kate 415
Waitkus, Joy 423
Walbert, Luke 322
Walch, Phillip O. 135
Wald, Jerome 511
Waldbuser, Margaret 196
Waldrop, Jane Paty 358
Walker, Alana 399
Walker, Alice C. 20
Walker, Angie 449
Walker, Craig 387
Walker, Cynthia H. 565
Walker, Lois F. 571
Walker, Lynda C. 323
Walker, Oscar C. 523
Walker, Stuart 294

Walker, Talib 155
Walker, Timothy 249
Walker, Tony 447
Walker, Wendy 243
Wall, Brandy 549
Wallace, Jacinta 210
Wallace, Jeanette 528
Wallace, Patricia H. 522
Wallington, Dwight 237
Walls, Devon M. 629
Walsh, Angelic 587
Waltimyer, Margie 103
Walty, Daniel 320
Walz, Patrick 175
Waple, Nancy Marguerite 508
Ward, Denise 238
Ward, Holly Carol 473
Ward, Kathleen P. 440
Ward, Relda 211
Ward, J.H. 487
Warden, Jaime 409
Ware, Chantel 288
Ware, John Wesley 536
Warner, Bernice 355
Warner, Harriett Lee 233
Warner, Jane 56
Warner, Nate 475
Warner, William H. 451
Warren, Athena Iris 202
Warren, Mayia 55
Warren, Vera 491
Waskey, Jennie 380
Wassmer, Jennie 256
Wasson, Marilyn 92
Waters, Alice M. 410
Wathne, Denise Gayle 359
Watkins, David L. 364
Watkins, Thomas 420
Watson, Dale 569
Watson, Helena B. 249
Watson, Kathy 491
Watson, Thomas Ramey 222
Wattnem, Kara 229
Wattron, Frank 163
Watts, Irene 444
Wealand, Chauncey Harbert 371
Weaver, Ginger 221
Weaver, Kara 135
Weaver, Naomi 57
Weaver, Nathan 447
Weaver, Shawnda 61
Webb, Heather R. 560
Webb, Helen W. 9
Webb, V.H. 545
Webber, Aaron 212
Webber, Claire M. 133
Webber, Cynthia 503
Webber, Margaret Horton 66
Weber, Henry T.P. 537
Weber, Sharon A. 140
Weber, Shawna 643
Webster, Deene A. 395
Webster, Graeme 310
Weed, Peggy Sanford 85
Weeks, Earl 571
Weeks, Jessica K. 478
Wegner, Amber 183
Weichsel, Jonathan 41
Weide, Stephanie Vander 478
Weidler, Bernice 75
Weidman, Scott 610

Weiger, Myra L. 489
Weiner, Amy 463
Weiner, Robert 240
Weinstock, Jessica 67
Weis, Ai-Ling 511
Weisheit, W. 237
Weismann, Carrie A. 140
Weiss, Desiree 224
Welch, Lee 497
Welch, Marie 281
Welch, Robin 536
Weller, Jane Y. 122
Wellman, James 451
Wellnitz, Theresa 366
Wells, Hazel H. 532
Wells, Mary T. 480
Wells, Mollie 540
Wells, Tess 498
Wells, Torrie L. 462
Welser, Marguerite 477
Welsh, Verna L. 63
Wendt, Brad 616
Wentzell, Alyssa 635
West, Christopher 179
West, Karen 258
West, Miriam E. 129
West, Molly 333
West, Virginia 500
Westerberg, Taylor 534
Westmoreland, Kyle T. 260
Wexford, Marye L. 576
Weyler, Lou 362
Weys, Peter John 618
Whalen, Jan 204
Wharton, Sandra 119
Whattam, Kevin 556
Wheeler, Peggy 620
Wheeler, Tiffany C. 509
Wheelock, Andrea 258
Wheelock, Joan 406
Whelan, Susan D. 368
Wheller, Julia King Duff 142
Whitacre, Pauline 40
Whitaker, Kristina 549
Whitbeck, Michael 353
Whitchurch, Kim 19
Whitcomb, Marguerite 471
White, Catherine S.L. 565
White, Floyd Edward 365
White, Henry 215
White, Jason Sidney 121
White, Jessie S. 480
White, Kevin E. 263
White, Melissa 183
White, Ronnell D. 538
White, Susan J. 515
White, Vona Ann 94
White, Wanda 526
Whited, Joshua Adam 127
Whitefield, Bryan 146
Whitehead, Betty 214
Whitehead, Devon 110
Whitehead, Martha B. 33
Whitener, Susan 453
Whitley, Margaret L. 562
Whitlow, Crystal 338
Whittaker, Jessica 520
Whitten, Sharon 327
Whitworth, Janice 605
Whtie, Carole 533
Wicks, Wendy K. 343

Wiebe, Brent 295
Wiegert, Lila 168
Wier, Joe 179
Wigley, Barbara G. 96
Wikander, L. Melyndia 130
Wilcox, Gail 180
Wilcox, Lynn 97
Wilder, Lee 474
Wilemon, Jolene 190
Wilkey, Carolyn Grace 130
Wilkins, Rita 56
Will, Ruth Louise 425
Willard, Barbara A. 605
Willcutt, Laurie 510
Willey, Carl 603
Williams II, Clarence 262
Williams, Claudette 479
Williams, Davida Dawn 324
Williams, Frank Curtis 185
Williams, George B. 55
Williams, Gwethalyn 342
Williams, Harry T. 143
Williams, Karen 356
Williams, Karen 548
Williams, Lauren 213
Williams, Marleen M. 323
Williams, Maryleath Hall 52
Williams, Michael 350
Williams, Nalani L. 405
Williams, Norma R. 540
Williams, Tamara Alysia 195
Williams, Zane M. 335
Williamson, Jenny 446
Williamson, Katharine A. 61
Williamson, Mark W. 209
Williamson, Sondra 341
Willis, Edwardlene Fleeks 569
Willis, Jolene 438
Willis, Lauren 563
Wilson, Charles D. 413
Wilson, E.M. 638
Wilson, Gary S. 506
Wilson, Gina 256
Wilson, Harriett R. 393
Wilson, James E. 72
Wilson, Jennifer 551
Wilson, Kay 629
Wilson, Mila 166
Wilson, Rich 235
Wilson, Tom 501
Wilton, Crystal 615
Wiltse, Leslie J. 177
Windham, Billy Gene 412
Winegrad, Dilys 379
Wineland, James 389
Winger, Howard 197
Wingrove, Pearl 252
Winters, Matt 149
Winters, Michael 567
Winters, Ronda A. 203
Wirth, Carol 632
Wise, Jennifer 149
Wise, Toni Marie 337
Wiseman, Jerry Leon 367
Wissinje, Allison A. 381
Wistrom, Chris 421
Witteman, Erica 292
Witter, Ireca 117
Wittman, Mary Ann 197
Woessner, H. Elizabeth 96
Wolf, Austin R.B. 240

Wolfe, Edwin P. 379
Wolfe, Kelly 157
Wolfe, Ronald G. 32
Wollbrink, Chad 134
Womack, John 469
Wong, Rosanna 627
Wood, Aline 108
Wood, David G. 617
Wood, Judy E. 518
Wood, Mary 75
Wood, Veronica 371
Woodcox, Terri 556
Woodman, Rita 277
Woodring, Kristi 340
Woodruff, Laura Ann 521
Woods, James Cedric 468
Woods, Laura Simpson 326
Woods, Victoria Caye 567
Woods, Walda 632
Woodson, Donald A. 152
Wooten, Rebecca D. 629
Worthington, Sam 218
Wos, Michael J. 124
Wovkanech, Steve 227
Wozny, Mary 42
Wray, Clyde A. 258
Wright, Carolyn 399
Wright, Chris 431
Wright, Frank 120
Wright, Hazel Irene Norton 54
Wright, Mark 73
Wright, Mary 628
Wright, Raymond M. 86
Wright, Rick 401
Wright, Tonia Lynn 528
Wright, William 199
Wrobel, Evelyn 184
Wsol, Renee M. 203
Wyant, Robyn 213
Wyant, Roxanne 128
Wyatt, Kelly 201
Wylie, Brittany 629
Wynants, Sali 108
Wynn, Connie 464
Xenos, Elaine J. 223
Xionghui, He 531
Yakstis, Natalie 158
Yanagida, Kenji 640
Yanez, Christopher 527
Yang, Chue 613
Yankey, Honey 208
Yanofsky, Ellen-Jane 575
Yarborough, N. Patricia 396
Yarbro, William T. 179
Yates, Kelli Elaine 632
Yates, Marc 567
Yearwood, Lorraine 260
Yeik, Mystie 596
Yerro, Teodulfo T. 24
Yocum, Ava 132
Yolinski, Helen J. 99
Yoo, Hee-Ju 507
York, Barby 182
York, Tracie 338
Yost, Amy 248
Young, April 204
Young, Brenda 555
Young, Carrie L. 511
Young, Cornelia 276
Young, Kristen 383
Young, Lemmie 102

Young, Leola A. 347
Young, Lorene C. 378
Young, Rickie A. 502
Yu, Catherine 114
Yuill, Cora 309
Zahn, April 248
Zajaczek, Sarah 53
Zak, Lillian 354
Zambruk, Adam 603
Zane, Terza L. 106
Zapisek, Noella M. 60
Zboraj, Marian J. 582
Zebik, Mary Wyant 608
Zechel, Curtis 626
Zeien, Tonya 538
Zeigler, Beth 558
Zeisel, Carlos 94
Zeliski, Lisa 433
Zeller, Donald L. 180
Zeltner, Steven Craig 585
Zenda, Kristine 126
Zervos, Antonis 234
Ziegler, Cheryl L. 209
Ziegler, Sara 266
Zimet, Carol 446
Zimmerman, Daniel 79
Zimmerman, Lindsay 541
Zimmerman, Michael T. 387
Zimmy, A. 619
Zipkin, Sam 354
Zipp-Lumb, Joan 246
Zitko, Howard John 146
Zitzke, Janet M. 461
Zlomek, Janet 56
Zotz, Leslie 125
Zuniga, Elizabeth 645
Zurlo, Doris 61
Zwozdesky, Laurie 619
Zyha, Sheila Ann 615
alvarado, Sherry E. 22
da Vinci, Nancy C. 7
de Marmion, Melinda 385
de Rosado, Luz Mendez 238
de St Pol, Marie-Therese 626
du Toit, Diane M. 307
lundy iii, e j 121

Copyright 1983
Robert Simon

Library of Congress Catalog Card Number 83-62148

ISBN 0-87875-281-1

Printed in the United States of America

PERCY GRAINGER

THE PICTORIAL BIOGRAPHY

by
Robert Simon

THE WHITSTON PUBLISHING COMPANY
Troy, New York
1983

Dedicated to the Alumni Class of 1938

The University of North Carolina at Chapel Hill

CONTENTS

Acknowledgements...vii

Foreword
    Frederick Fennell...1

The Biography...2

Free Music
    Percy Aldridge Grainger.......................................127

Discography..129

List of Sources..134

Index..137

ACKNOWLEDGMENTS

The long life of Percy Grainger with its richness and variety is a biographer's dream. This book, filled with photographs, programs, letters, memorabilia, and a short biography, offers a brief and balanced view of a musical phenomenon. I have tried to cover what I consider the most important events in Grainger's life without appearing to be a hero worshipper. The most comprehensive biography written thus far about this remarkable man is "Percy Grainger" by John Bird (Faber & Faber, London 1982; originally published by Paul Elek Ltd., London 1976). I strongly endorse it as an excellent source of reference. Another fine book is the "Percy Grainger Companion" edited by Lewis Foreman (Thames Publishing, London 1981 —Sole U. S. Distributor: TRN Music, Beaumont).

Researching and collecting all the materials for this book over the past three years was a task which could not have been completed without the support of kind friends and relatives. I am deeply indebted to my wife, Sarah Simon, my mother, Lois Simon, and my father, Jerome Simon for their faith in me as I delved into the life of Percy Grainger. I want to offer warm thanks also to Stanley and Carol Willner for their generosity. Mr. and Mrs. William H. Nicholson were very supportive as well.

The personal kindness that I received from Stewart R. Manville, archivist of the Percy Grainger Library, far exceeded all of my original expectations. My thanks to Ralph Stang, who since Ella Grainger's death in 1979, has been president of the International Percy Grainger Society. He shared with me so many occurrences from the contents of his many discussions with Ella Grainger. I would like to thank the Grainger Museum Board for the use of materials in the museum. John Bird (with whom this book was originally started) taught me the sympathetic and meticulous manner of researching such a complex and contradictory subject. I wish to thank Dr. Frederick Fennell for displaying a most gracious interest in this book and for being very supportive from the beginning. Max A. Gonano, John Hamilton, and David F. Reed deserve considerable acknowledgement for nurturing me in my formative years. There must be included a very special thanks to Emily Shaw for editing the manuscript of the biography. The following alphabetical list is comprised of individuals and/or organizations who supplied me with information, granted me permission to quote from them, and generally enhanced the development of this book.

Evie, Gordon, and Robin Aldridge, Paul A. Alter, Ruth Orcutt Bacon, Teresa Balough, Mrs. Howard H. Battin, Harry Begian, Greg Benko, Leonard Bernstein,

Jacqueline Blanton, Vera Bradford, Thomas D. Brosh, Storm Bull, Denis Condon, John Conti-Guglia, Richard Conti-Guglia, Aaron Copland, Sidney Cowell, Burnett Cross, Oliver Daniel, William DesChamps, Carl Dolmetsch, Manly Duckworth, Everett Studios (White Plains, N. Y.), Don Gillespie, Morton Gould, Roger Hannay, Mrs. Charles Hawkins, Vincent J. Holland, John Hopkins, Colonel George S. Howard, David Josephson, Neil Kaufman, Daniel Leeson, Maurice Loriaux, Ronald B. Nelligar, William S. Newman, Dr. Kaare K. Nygaard, Sparre Olsen, Eugene Ormandy, Sir Peter Pears, Helen Reeves, Mrs. Francis E. Resta, Joseph Rezitts, N. F. Sandby, John Savage, Harold C. Schonberg, Wayne D. Shirley, Gary Simon, Hilary Simon, Nicolas Slonimsky, Allan Sly, John Steinway, Margaret Hee-Leng Tan, Mel Tormé, T. E. Treutlein, Oslaf Trygvasson, Ursula Vaughan Williams, Constance Vulliamy, Norman Voelcker, Thomas E. Wilson, Brookstown Avenue Universal Printers (Winston-Salem, N.C.), The University of Melbourne, and The University of North Carolina at Chapel Hill.

Robert Simon
Winston-Salem,
North Carolina
April 17, 1983

FOREWORD

I've never seen any poor photographs of Percy Aldridge Grainger. Photographed in no matter what the garb or where, he always came off as the highly attractive male that he was, even when surroundings or situation might have affected others less natural in their way than he was. And what a natural way he had with the camera, with everything and everybody.

My personal experiences with him were all on the warm side and mostly in the last years of his fascinating life when he sought, somewhat desperately, to turn earlier dreams into later realities. I came into his world on a personal basis when, b by previous positives, The Eastman Wind Ensemble had earned its way with the Eastman/Mercury recording resource, and I could anticipate the definite recording of *Lincolnshire Posy* at a specific session in May, 1958. He always encouraged me to use my camera, which I did, and freely, at our times together in White Plains.

Robert Simon's book of Grainger in graphics was inevitable. With Percy's highly photogenic countenance and his complete awareness of the need for and the power of public relations, he managed them better than those he could hire. No shrinking violet, he sought out the media and was obviously ready for what might sell music, tickets, or disseminate his powerfully held views on a wide variety of topics.

His arrival in the United States neatly happened to coincide with the early successes of two particularly American contributions to the duplication and promotion of the image; one was photojournalism, and the other was George Eastman's Kodak, the personal camera with its convenient film on a roll. Grainger obviously missed none of these, nor did those on the other end of the cameras that captured the remarkable life as he lived it.

Such a handsomely striking individual was certain to attract the nearest lens. It is our bonanza that their work was done and the results so carefully preserved. Grainger provided both for us to enjoy in this most welcome pictorial biography.

Frederick Fennell
Miami/1983

THE BIOGRAPHY

Percy Aldridge Grainger (born July 8, 1882) came from the raw and vigorous frontier world of nineteenth-century Melbourne, Australia. He was the only child of John Harry Grainger, an architect from London, and Rose Annie Aldridge, the eighth child of a hotel keeper's family in Adelaide, South Australia.

Percy Grainger appeared in this boom town of the eighties wearing a cap and a sailor suit with an Eton collar, which gave him the look of a Little Lord Fauntleroy. His public education lasted less than three months. His classmates were cruel and ridiculed him and his appearance. Once he watched them torture a helpless animal. He refused to return to school, and his mother, Rose, assumed responsibility for his general education. In addition to studying English, foreign languages, history, art, and mathematics, Percy practiced the piano for two hours every day with his mother sitting by his side. This regimen began when he was five years old and lasted until he was ten.

John Grainger was a dignified and cultured man and respected as an architect. He loved music and in his spare time considered himself a painter. He was also an alcoholic. This condition coupled with Rose's independence of spirit, resulted in many violent arguments. On one occasion Rose chased her husband from the house with a horsewhip. Their superficially respectable marriage was destroyed when Rose discovered that she had contracted syphillis from John. In 1891 he was advised to move to London for his health and when he did he left his family behind. The bond between the mother and son grew deeper, even spiritual, and they thought of themselves as "the two of us against the world."[1]

Owing to her self-motivation and thirst for knowledge, Rose Grainger was a well-educated woman. A tomboy in her early years, she matured into a reader of Greek mythology and the writings of Dickens, Hans Christian Anderson, and Byron. She loved the songs of Stephen Foster and the piano music of Beethoven, Chopin, and Grieg. She was an aggressive person who succeeded at everything she attempted, including the development of her son's musical career.

In the absence of John, one of the first father figures to influence young Percy was a family friend, Dr. Robert Hamilton Russell, who was an amateur pianist. He often played for Percy and took him to many concerts in and around Melbourne.

Percy was a well-behaved child. Rose, a strict disciplinarian, saw to that. He was allowed his freedom to play with model ships, hike in the nearby Dandenong

Hills, and go swimming and tram-hopping. But if he neglected his practicing or his studies, his mother would punish him severely with a whip.

Often while the precocious Percy was floating his model ships on the water at Albert Park, he would ask himself why music could not be as free as the sounds in nature, like the lapping of waves against a boat or the whistling of the wind through trees. These thoughts were later translated into one of his most important innovations called "Free Music": music that is free rhythmically and not confined to any set modes or intervals.

At the age of ten Percy studied harmony and piano with a German pianist named Louis Pabst, who had once been a pupil of the Russian pianist and scholar, Anton Rubinstein. The young Australian prodigy so intrigued and impressed Pabst that he even thought of adopting him. It was through Pabst that Grainger first heard and studied the music of Bach, later coming to compare life with the music of Bach:

> Life is very much like Bach's polyphonic music—themes, beautiful themes, trying themes, difficult themes—other answering themes working in and out, over, about and under to form the whole—the rich masterpiece—difficult of performance and execution, but unequaled in perfection of plan and soul-satisfying in concept.[2]

Percy also excelled in painting, drawing, reading, and speaking foreign languages. His collected correspondence shows that he had a command of more than eleven languages, including Russian. He loved to read and favored above all martial epics and the Icelandic Sagas, which he read in the Icelandic languages.

He made his piano debut on Monday, July 9, 1894 in Melbourne's Masonic Hall. The audience and critics raved about the youngster's technique which was "so nearly faultless."[3]

Herr Pabst returned to Europe the following year, and Percy continued his studies with a former pupil of Pabst, Miss Adelaide Burkitt, whom the boy liked and admired. Under her tutelage he appeared in five concerts before his mother decided that they should move to Germany so that her son could study at Dr. Hoch's Conservatory in Frankfurt-am-Main. Thinking of nothing but the Icelandic Sagas, Percy was excited by the thought of living in Germany, knowing that they would be relatively close to Iceland and that both countries were similar in language and culture. His farewell recital was given in the Melbourne Town Hall on May 14, 1895, and the proceeds were donated to the young pianist. On May 29 Rose and her twelve year old son set sail for Germany.

Dr. Hoch's Conservatory was at that time a major center of European piano pedagogy. Percy studied piano with James Kwast and composition with Ivan Knorr. The composition lessons ended abruptly when Knorr made a mockery of his student's ideas, such as his use of whole tone scales and irregular rhythms. From that point on the young man studied composition with a retired lithographer and novice composer, Karl Klimsch, whom he regarded as his only true and worthwhile teacher of composition.

At the conservatory Grainger made five lifelong friends: Balfour Gardiner, Norman O'Neill, Roger Quilter, Herman Sandby, and Cyril Scott. This group of young musicians was highly critical of central European music and hoped to bring about a renaissance of British and Scandinavian music. Grainger's friends were astonished by his musical concepts, even jealous of them. In 1899 his "Love Verses from *The Song of Solomon*," for voices and chamber orchestra, contained some of the following sequences of time signatures: 2½/4, 3/4, 2½/4, 3/8, 2/4, 2½/4, and so on. He was far ahead of his time. Igor Stravinsky did not begin to use mixed meters and irregular rhythms in his compositions until 1913. Cyril Scott (with Grainger's permission in 1903) used his friend's irregular rhythms and meters for his own Piano Sonata, Opus 66.

Rose and Percy moved to London in 1901, where he triumphed immediately as a concert pianist. In London he was given the title of the "running pianist," because he was always running through the streets to concerts, always bounding up stairs two to four steps at a time. These were important years for him. He became friendly with many other noted musicians of the era, and one of whom in 1903 was the master, Ferruccio Busoni. The young man so impressed him that Busoni offered to teach Grainger free of tuition. They studied Bach together, and Busoni's transcriptions of Bach were thereafter played by Grainger throughout his career.

Meanwhile, in 1901, Grainger had completed his composition, "Train Music," a rhythmic and tonal portrayal of a train ride. Arthur Honegger's composition, "Pacific 231" was written in the same programmatic vein in 1924, twenty-three years after "Train Music."

Influenced by Bach's Brandenburg Concertos, Grainger developed the idea of "Large Room Music" (chamber music), using combinations of voices and instruments. "Willow Willow" (1901) is a fine example. The first such piece was written ten years before Vaughan Williams' "On Wenlock Edge" (1909), thirteen years before Arnold Schoenberg's "Pierrot Lunaire," and preceding Igor Stravinsky's "L'Histoire du Soldat" by eighteen years.

Through his music Grainger rebelled against many conventional practices in composition. Instead of writing dynamic markings in the traditional Italian or German, he preferred to use his own English expressions. For example, instead of "crescendo molto," he wrote "louden lots." On June 20, 1933 he proclaimed:

> I firmly believe that music will someday become a "universal language." But it will not become so as long as our musical vision is limited to the output of four European countries between 1700 and 1900. The first step in the right direction is to view the music of all peoples and periods without prejudice of any kind, and to strive to put the world's known and available best music into circulation. Only then shall we be justified in calling music a "universal language."[4]

While Percy was living in London he became interested in collecting folksongs. He pioneered the use of Edison wax cylinder recorder in the field by hiking through the countryside of Lincolnshire and recording anyone who knew a folksong. From his recordings he was able to transcribe every detail of a song, every artistic nuance and complicated rhythm. Bela Bartok began his own recording activities soon after Grainger's success with them.

One stubborn old woman refused to sing for Grainger, but he was a determined collector and did not surrender easily. He allied himself with the woman's daughter, who allowed him to hide under a nearby bed while she coaxed her mother into singing the folksong for her. Grainger notated the song as she was singing, and she never knew that he had been present.

Grainger said the following about folksongs:

> . . . in the folk-song there is to be found the complete history of a people, recorded by the race itself, through the heartout-bursts of its healthiest output. It is a history compiled with deeper feeling and more complete understanding than can be found among the dates and data of the greatest historian with his knowledge of ethnology and training of race groupings.[5]

On March 15, 1907 the distinguished Norwegian composer, Edvard Grieg, was quoted in the Danish newspaper, *Kjobenhavn,* as follows:

> What is nationality? I have written Norwegian Peasant Dances that none of my countrymen can play and here comes this Australian who plays them as they ought to be played! He is a genius that we Scandinavians cannot do other than love.

In the summer of 1907 Grainger visited Grieg at his villa, "Troldhaugen," in Norway. The two men spent many hours discussing and rehearsing music, particularly Grieg's Concerto in A minor, Opus 16. Grieg quickly became a strong father figure to the younger man. He admired Percy greatly and asked if he would perform the concerto on a European tour with Grieg conducting. A few weeks before the tour was to start, however, Grieg became seriously ill and died. As a result of this brief friendship which had been so rewarding, Grainger became the leading interpreter of the A-minor Concerto and performed it more frequently than any other concert artist throughout his career. Grieg's widow, Nina, gave him her husband's gold pocket watch as a remembrance of his friend.

As early as 1906 Grainger had acquired a considerable reputation as a pianist, yet ironically he looked forward to the day when he could retire from the concert stage and devote himself to composing. His first composition was published in 1908, and in that same year he began his career as a recording artist.

He was easily identified on or off the stage. He had thick, curly, reddish blond hair which he wore long. He was five feet, eight inches tall and had piercing blue eyes and a prominent nose. He maintained a weight of one hundred and forty-five pounds for most of his life. Even though his weight rarely varied, he kept a daily record of it for nearly twenty years.

While on tour in Australia and New Zealand in 1909, Grainger met a dedicated folksong collector in Otaki, A. J. Knocks. The folk material that they collected together was among the most interesting music that he was to preserve. The South Sea Islands' polyphonic music with its "rhythmic delights"[6] influenced many of his later compositions.

He returned to England after the tour and continued to build his reputation as a concert pianist. At the same time his compositional ability was further strengthened with the completion of such works as "Arrival Platform Humlet," "Colonial Song," "I'm Seventeen Come Sunday," "Irish Tune from County Derry," "Mock Morris," "Molly on the Shore," "My Robin is to the Greenwood Gone," "Scotch Strathspey and Reel," and "Sussex Mummer's Christmas Carol."

During this time he secured his friendship with Frederick Delius, Ralph Vaughan Williams, and Nina Grieg. He became acquainted also with Richard Strauss, Georges Enesco, Claude Debussy, and Edward Elgar. He gave many successful concert tours in Germany, Holland, and Scandinavia. In 1911 Sir Thomas Beecham offered Grainger an assistant conductorship and suggested that he write ballet music for Diaghilev. Although he refused the conductorship, he did write "The Warriors" (1913) for a ballet that was never to be choreographed during his lifetime. He called it his music for an imaginary ballet. In 1929 he conducted "The Warriors," scored for three grand pianos and full orchestra, in the Chicago Civic Opera House, on which occasion some nineteen pianos were employed.

When World War I broke out in 1914, Percy and Rose emigrated to the United States. He became an overnight success after his first recital in New York's Aeolian Hall on February 11, 1915. Henry T. Fink, music critic of the *New York Evening Post,* wrote: "Hats off! A Genius!"[7] and soon after wrote: "It is easy to predict who among the composers and pianists will be the hero of the next musical season. His name is Percy Grainger."[8]

In 1917, when the United States joined the war, Grainger enlisted in the United States Army as Bandsman 2nd Class, 15th Band, Coast Artillery corps, playing the saxophone. His managers decided that being an Army bandsman could do his public image no harm. With a mixture of keenness, instinct, and humanitarian earnestness, Grainger brought his "Marching Song of Democracy" to the public in 1918, having dedicated it to Walt Whitman.

While in the Army he also began to score music directly for the wind band which was to result in such compositions as "Gum-Suckers' March" and, later (1937), "Lincolnshire Posy." In these scores he developed his idea of "Tuneful Percussion" with the inclusion in his orchestrations of a percussion ensemble consisting of glockenspiel, marimba, Swiss handbells, tubular bells, and xylophone. In 1928 he did a setting of Claude Debussy's "Pagodes" for a similar ensemble that approximated the musical sound of the Indonesian gamelan, somewhat as Debussy had intended in the original composition.

Grainger began playing at War Bond and Liberty Loan concerts to help raise badly needed funds for the war cause. As an encore for some of these concerts he would frequently improvise on a Handkerchief Dance called "Country Gardens." It was quite well received, and he scored it for piano one night in his barracks as a birthday present for his mother. The published version broke Schirmer's sales records for the previous seventy-five years and continued to do so for the next twenty, selling at a rate of over 40,000 copies annually in the United States alone.

"Country Gardens" and Percy Grainger became synonymous. He came to detest the work, just as Sergei Rachmaninoff is said to have loathed his own Prelude in C Sharp minor. Oslaf Trygvasson, another concert pianist, recalls one of Grainger's concerts: "He had given a full concert already and seventeen encores; Grainger said to me, 'I have to play Country Gardens or they won't go home,' He did; they were satisfied and went home."[9]

After the war, Grainger returned to a life of composing and concertizing, giving as many as a hundred and fifty appearances a year. He and his mother settled in White Plains, New York. They lived at 7 Cromwell Place in a post-Victorian style home which now houses the Percy Grainger Library. He had two large fire-proof vaults built in the basement for the storage of his many valuable manuscripts and documents. By now, his compositions, recordings, and performances were earning him a fortune, and he was able to support more than eleven dependents. His success was assured, and his mind was free to concentrate on Rose's health, which was deteriorating rapidly.

An unusual relationship existed between the mother and son. Rose had great power over Percy, and her consent or disapproval often set the guidelines for his romantic activities.

It was falsely rumored that Percy and Rose were involved in an incestuous relationship. As a matter of fact, Rose avoided the slightest physical contact with her son. She had suffered for most of her life from syphilis, which she had contracted from her husband in the 1880's, and she was obsessive about it. She greatly feared that the disease might be transmitted to Percy. In the nineteenth and early twentieth centuries there was little relief and no cure for syphilis.

Although she did not entirely succeed at managing his social life, Rose was still the epitome of a domineering mother. Her deep involvement with her son's artistic and creative talents fostered one of the twentieth century's most original musicians. In 1929 Grainger took part in a survey for a book on heredity and musical talent by Scheinfeld and Schweitzer (published by F. A. Stokes). When he was asked, "Do you believe you 'inherited' your talent?", Grainger replied, "I do not believe in musical talent. I, in particular, do not have any."[10] When asked further, "*Or* do you believe it chiefly due to home influence and training?", he responded, "Entirely due to my mother's influence and her wish to see me a composer."[11]

In 1922 Rose Grainger, who had become ill mentally as well as physically, committed suicide. The tragic leap from eighteen stories may well have been her last attempt to control her son. He was certainly tormented by the death of this woman who had made him an artist. In 1923 he wrote that as a child he "thought Mother was God"[12] and "Mother was always alive and well in my dreams."[13] Rose's domination of her son continued until his death: "Beloved Mother would have been 95 today. I have felt the tragic influence of her death more in this year 1957 than in any other year."[14]

Grainger found little solace after Rose died and soon resumed his career. He was more popular that ever. In 1922 he traveled to Denmark to collect folksongs in the field with Evald Tang Kristensen. Some of these songs were later incorporated into his "Suite on Danish Folk Songs" (1949).

Grainger became a vegetarian in 1924. Paradoxically, he hated vegetables and subsisted mostly on nuts, cheese, bread, fruit, cakes, fruit pies, and ice cream. He drank mostly milk. In addition to being a health faddist, he was an enthusiastic athlete—running and jumping and, especially, hiking. Distance was no object. When he was on concert tours, he occasionally walked from town to town. He once finished a concert in Pietermaritzburg, South Africa and set off for Durban just before midnight. He walked for sixty-five miles and arrived in Durban at 6:00 P.M. the next evening. He went to the concert hall still attired in his gym shorts, as his manager had accidentally sent his concert tuxedo to the wrong hotel. The tuxedo was finally located a short time before the concert was to begin.

Grainger was interested in crafts and enjoyed doing beadwork. He also designed and fashioned clothes from towels, similar to garments made of terry cloth today. He neither drank nor smoked. He strongly felt that women were ill-used, saying: ". . . you really don't know how ghastly women are being treated! If they were given equal chance at gaining strength, all this prejudice against them would be eliminated."[15]

Percy Grainger was very hard on his hands, which was unusual for a concert pianist. Most were so fearful of injury that they would insure their hands, but Grainger never did. When he was in transit, if a bellman attempted to carry his luggage, he would resist, saying, "Why shouldn't I carry my own luggage if I want to?" "When you have two wrists, two palms, and ten fingers to keep limber and relaxed for the piano, why should you?" asked Deborah Beirne. "It doesn't hurt them," he replied. "It makes them stronger."[16] His hands were never free from callouses, and on one ocean voyage he decided to shovel coal in the engine room along with the crewmen. The doctor on board begged him to stop so that the severe whitlows on his hands could heal before they reached shore and the continuation of the concert tour. Earlier in his career he had lost the tip of an index finger after wrecking a bicycle and had hoped that he would have to leave the concert stage and devote all of his time to composing. His performing ability, however, was not affected by this handicap. Once, during a duo piano performance with Oslaf Trygvasson, a leg popped out from one of the concert grands. Most pianists would have summoned the stage crew, but Grainger quickly walked over to the corner of the piano and lifted it high enough for Trygvasson to replace the leg. Trygvasson felt that it must have been taking him "twice as long to do his part," for he was "truly nervous about all the pressure on Grainger's hands."[17]

Everything that Grainger did was immensely physical, whether he was hiking across the ninety-mile desert in South Australia with a forty-pound pack on his back, or performing the Tchaikovsky Bb minor Concerto.

The Aeolian Duo-Art Reproducing Piano Company claimed Grainger as one of its most important artists. He was featured, as well, by the Steinway Piano Company. Many of his piano rolls are still extant. John Hopkins, who has studied and conducted Grainger's music for many years, recorded with orchestra the Grieg A minor Concerto and the Tchaikovsky Bb minor Concerto piano rolls that Grainger had made in the 1920's. The rolls had previously been edited by Grainger for use with orchestral backing. A music professor in Australia, Dennis Condon, upon becoming aware of these piano rolls, perfected an instrument that resembles a robot, having eighty fingers and two pneumatic feet. The instrument, called a Vorsetzer, fits over the keyboard of a normal concert grand piano and plays the contents of the rolls on such a piano. In recording sessions, with the Vorsetzer taking the place of a live pianist, Hopkins' orchestras have performed superbly with this unusual instrument. Grainger's romantic style and interpretation are as evident as though he himself were present. Even though there may be nothing quite as satisfactory as a live recorded performance, these recordings add a remarkable dimension to Grainger's recorded legacy (see discography).

In 1925 Grainger was earning as much as $5,000 a week performing and up to $200 an hour in private lessons and master classes. He was not only financially secure, but eccentric on occasion. This pianist was extraordinarily beloved by the public as a musician, celebrity and a warm human being. Sometimes the press would exaggerate some of his irregular incidents such as Grainger being found sleeping underneath or on top of a concert grand piano, or running into a filled concert hall (sometimes late for a concert), wearing gym shorts and carrying his rolled up tuxedo under his arm. Sometimes he would run out onto a stage for a rehearsal and leap over the piano for a grand entrance. One story tells of his putting on as many layers of clothing as possible and climbing into a bathtub to wash them as he undressed layer by layer. Now and then he may have behaved strangely for the sake of publicity and to assure himself that his fans knew all about his latest activities. He was always buzzing with ideas.

He once tried to reform the English language by removing all of the Greek and Latin roots from words in his own vocabulary. He hoped in this way to restore the "nobility" of the Anglo-Saxon language. He called this concept "Blue-eyed English" and often injected it into his correspondence and biographical writings.

In 1927 Grainger fell in love. He met the Swedish artist and poet, Ella Viola Ström, while sailing home to the United States from a concert tour in Australia. Their wedding took place two years later in the Hollywood Bowl, during a Grainger concert before an audience of 22,000 people, with an orchestra of one hundred twenty-six musicians and an *a capella* choir. On this occasion he conducted his new composition, "To a Nordic Princess," dedicating it to his bride. When Ella had agreed to be married in the Hollywood Bowl, she had imagined it to be a small, secluded area somewhere in a California forest. The newlyweds spent their honeymoon in Glacier National Park, camping and hiking.

Aside from teaching master classes at the Chicago Music School and at Interlochen National Music Camp in various summers, Grainger held only one formal teaching position in his lifetime. In 1932 he became dean of the department of music at New York University. He was greatly interested in jazz. Duke Ellington was one of the guest artists whom he invited to perform at his classes. In 1924 Grainger published an article on jazz in *ETUDE*, at a time when jazz was considered in certain quarters a musical pollutant. He believed jazz to be the "finest of popular music."[18] After his brief stay at New York University, he declined thereafter every teaching position and honorary doctorate offered him, saying that his music was a product of "non-education" and that he could not understand why any institution would encourage his concepts.

Also in 1932, Grainger became friendly with a British monk, Dom Anselm Hughes, then a leading specialist in medieval music. Together they arranged and published nearly a dozen pieces for chorus, band, and chamber orchestra, based on medieval plain-song.

All of the money that Grainger earned in 1934 was contributed as an endowment to the University of Melbourne to found what was originally to have been known as the Grainger Museum and Music Museum. He helped design the building and actually laid some of its bricks. Among the materials sent by him to the museum are the music manuscripts of innumerable composers, instruments, concert programs, photographs, paintings, sculptures, recordings, clothes, autobiographical writings, and furniture. From his massive epistolary output he sent over forty thousand items of correspondence relating to his life.

Among his many autobiographical writings in the museum one parcel is labeled "Private Matters—Do Not Open Until 10 (ten) Years After My Death." The materials in this parcel are dated July 25, 1935 and May 10, 1956 and include photographs and writings that point to his great attachment to flagellation. He hoped that these materials would never be destroyed, but rather studied in a scientific institution which would explore the influences and habits of creative Australians. On May 10, 1956 he wrote:

> I feel that flagelantism (like boxing, football & some other sports) is a means of turning the hostile, harsh & destructive elements in man into *harmless channels.* Much of civilization consists of turning hostility into playfulness.
>
> I have always been potent sexually & never had any interest in homosexuality.

His obsession with flagellation may have had its roots in the punishments dealt him so harshly by his mother when he was a child. Their unusual emotional relationship paired with her beatings left their mark on a very complex personality.

Percy secretly nursed some bigoted feelings that were fostered by his mother's strong dislike of "brown-eyed and dark-haired people." Willem Mengelberg was one of his favorite conductors, nonetheless. He especially enjoyed and championed the music of Ernest Bloch, Frederick Delius (at that time believed to be partly Jewish), George Gershwin, and Maurice Ravel. His preoccupation with Anglo-Saxon and Nordic purity played a strong part in his quest to restore the nobility of British and Scandinavian music and pit it against German and Italian musical influences. Richard Conti-Guglia addressed himself to this topic on July 8, 1982:

> The pride of Blacks in rediscovering their culture or of Jews in creating a Jewish state is not different in kind from that which made Grainger extol the blond, blue-eyed Nordic archtype. Grainger did not believe in melting pots, because he valued so strongly the raw materials that were threatened with extinction therein.

In 1937 Grainger's composition for wind band, "Lincolnshire Posy," was premiered at the American Bandmaster's Convention in Milwaukee, Wisconsin on which occasion only three of the completed five movements were performed.

One year later the Grainger Museum was opened, but as it was essentially a museum for research purposes, it was not accessible to the general public. Also in 1938, Percy was invited to perform at the White House for President and Mrs. Franklin D. Roosevelt. He gave a program in the East Room for a guest audience of two hundred and fifty. In February of that year he was arrested as a suspicious character when he stepped off a train in Wisconsin, wearing only his white duck pants, shirt, and blazer and carrying an old umbrella to ward off the snow. He was soon released after his identity was confirmed. Grainger carried no drivers' license because he did not believe in the driving of automobiles.

In 1940 Percy and Ella moved to Springfield, Missouri, where they lived through the entrance of the United States into World War II. During the war, in addition to his regular concert tours, he gave two hundred and seventy-four performances for charity benefits and service men throughout the country.

After the war Grainger contacted many recording companies, hoping to make a commercial recording of the Grieg A minor Concerto, but none of them would sign a contract with him. In 1946 he played the concerto in the Hollywood Bowl under the baton of Leopold Stokowski, and a tape exists of this performance.

Percy Grainger was nicknamed "The Inveterate Innovator" in 1947 by Marion Bauer because he was constantly evolving new ideas, although letters from this period reveal a physical breakdown of sorts. On the surface he appeared to be well, but he was sleeping poorly, paying no attention to his diet, and constantly overworking. The Graingers traveled to England, where they visited Cyril Scott and Ralph Vaughan Williams. After their return to the United States, Percy was commissioned to write a work commemorating the birthday of Edwin Franko Goldman. He conducted his new composition, "The Power of Rome and the Christian Heart" with the Goldman Band at Carnegie Hall in January, 1948. There followed another trip to England, where he performed at a Promenade concert in the London Symphony Orchestra's European premiere of his "Suite on Danish Folk Songs," a piece based on a selection from the folksongs that he had collected with Evald Tang Kristensen over twenty years before.

Grainger was now earning very little money from his performances, and the sales of his compositions began to drop. He became a sad and discouraged man. He would perform anywhere without asking a fee, if he could only play his own works and those of his friends. His technical skills as a pianist were beginning to diminish. He said that performing in his old age was something of a luxury, because no one expected note-perfect performances anymore. Grainger thought many concert promoters were indeed delighted that he played and did not collapse at the piano.

Early in 1950 Grainger re-orchestrated five of his popular pieces for a recording with Leopold Stokowski conducting. He played the piano with the orchestra and also scored another piece for the recording called "Early One Morning," but it, like some two hundred other compositions and arrangements, remains unpublished. The record, released in 1952, sold fairly well. It has recently been re-issued on the RCA label (see discography).

In 1953 Grainger suffered a severe abdominal condition and underwent the first of several operations performed by a surgeon prominent in the field of abdominal cancer, Dr. Kaare K. Nygaard. The disease had advanced too far to be cured, and Grainger was to live the rest of his life in pain.

He spent these last difficult years experimenting with "Free Music." Together with Burnett Cross he attempted to construct music machines capable of playing "Free Music" that had run through his head for nearly fifty years. He has received little credit for his work in the field of electronic music, although he was one of its pioneers. Karlheinz Stockhausen completed his "Elektronische Studien I and II" in 1954, three years after Grainger composed gliding chords for his "Reed Box Tone Tool" (recorded September 30, 1951) and two years after the completion of the Kangaroo-Pouch Electronic Free Music Machine. Using four vacuum-tube oscillators, its first test recordings were made on December 1, 1952. The finished Kangaroo-Pouch Free Music Machine, nine feet tall and four feet wide, is housed in the Grainger Museum, Melbourne. It was succeeded by a machine that read Grainger's graph-notation "Free Music" score by means of photocells and translated it into sound through solid-state electronics.

Percy Grainger was growing old. When he played he insisted on playing his own compositions in which no one else seemed to be interested. Although his concert career continued until shortly before his death, he was no longer taken seriously as a pianist and sometimes younger pianists laughed when his name was mentioned.

Instead of playing to packed houses in Carnegie Hall, finishing with a dozen encores, he was now reduced to playing in high school gymnasiums and churches. His final recordings were made in his home in White Plains on an old upright piano instead of on a well-tuned concert grand in a Columbia recording studio.

Frederick Fennell gave Grainger his last ounce of faith in 1959, when the Eastman Rochester Pops Orchestra made an all-Grainger record under the Mercury label. Fennell pleased him very much again on a later occasion by conducting the Eastman Wind Ensemble in magnificent recordings of "Hill Song Number 2" and "Lincolnshire Posy." The latter work was on the same record with Darius Milhaud's "Suite Française," a composition considered by Grainger to be a true masterpiece for the wind ensemble.

Until recently many of Graingers more than four hundred compositions and arrangements have unfortunately been eclipsed by his short and popular folksong settings: "Country Gardens," "Handel in the Strand," "Molly on the Shore," and "Shepherd's Hey." These give a limited view of his scope because Grainger's music truly reflected human experience, from shared enthusiams to the simple joys and sorrows of life.

As the end of Percy Grainger's life neared he was able to look back on a long life of fulfilment both as a concert pianist and as a composer. The little boy from Melbourne had come a long way in 78 years. He died, however, bitter and disillusioned because his major compositions were not very widely known. His battle with cancer was over on February 20, 1961.

NOTES

[1] Extracted from a sketch by Ella Grainger about Percy Grainger—August, 1967.

[2] Article, *Success Magazine*—January, 1926. Author: Deborah Beirne, pp. 54-55.

[3] Newspaper clipping, *The Melbourne Age*—July 10, 1894.

[4] Radio Broadcast, WVED transcript, Grainger Museum. Date of broadcast: June 30, 1933.

[5] Article, *Success Magazine*—January, 1926. Author: Deborah Beirne, pp. 54-55.

[6] Letter from Percy Grainger to Roger Quilter—January, 1909. Reference to Percy Grainger by John Bird, Elek Books, Ltd., 1976, p. 128.

[7] Review, Henry T. Finck, *New York Evening Post*, February 12, 1915.

[8] Review, Henry T. Finck, *New York Evening Post,* May 29, 1915.

[9] Oslaf Trygvasson, conversation with author, October 16, 1982.

[10] Scheinfeld and Schweitzer, *Heredity and Musical Talent,* survey found in Library of Congress. Publisher: F. A. Stokes.

[11] *Ibid.*

[12] Grainger: Sketches for "The Life of my Mother and her Son," item #62—November 16, 1923.

[13] *Ibid.*

[14] Grainger: pocket diary—entry July 3, 1957.

[15] Article, *Success Magazine*—January, 1926. Author: Deborah Beirne, pp. 54-55.

[16] *Ibid.*

[17] Oslaf Trygvasson, conversation with author, October 16, 1982.

[18] Tapes of experiments in the author's possession as received from Grainger Museum.

John Grainger, Percy's father, about 1878

John Grainger, Perth, Australia, 1898 (P by Clark & Son)

Rose Grainger, Percy's mother, aged 18 during 1880
(Photo by S. Solomon, Adelaide, South Australia)

Rose Grainger, Melbourne, 1888 (Photo by Webb & Webb)

Percy Grainger June 4, 1885 (Photo by Stewart & Co., Melbourne)

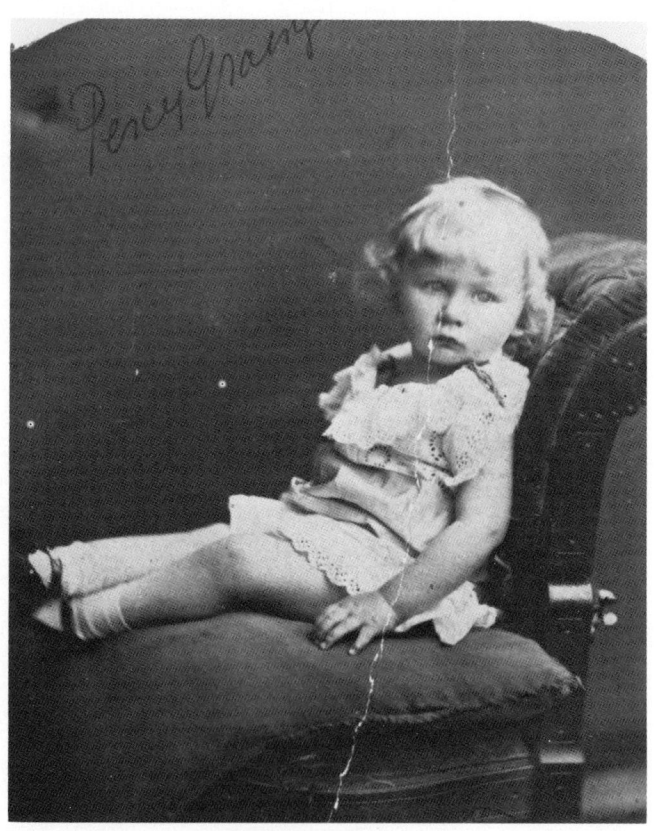

Percy, October, 1885
(Photo by Johnstone O'Shannessy & Co., Melbourne)

Percy and Rose about 1885
(Photo by Stevenson & McNicoll, Melbourne)

FOUR DRAWINGS FROM PERCY TO CONSTANCE MARION GARDNER, 1890

Like a Little Lord Fauntleroy.
Percy aged about four, Melbourne.

In a sailor's suit, 1886, Melbourne.

Percy in a crow's nest, aged seven, Melbourne.

Aged ten when he gave his first concert in Melbourne
(Photo by Vanduck Studios)

Masonic Hall
MONDAY, SEPT. 10
AT 8 P.M.

GRAND CONCERT

Under the Patronage of

His Excellency the Governor and Countess of Hopetoun
His Honor the Chief Justice and Lady Madden
Baron Ferdinand von Mueller, K.C.M.G.
Sir William and Lady Clarke
Sir Bryan and Lady O'Loughlen
Sir Frederick and Lady Sargood
The Hon. Thos. Bent and Mrs. Bent
The Mayor of Melbourne and Mrs. Snowden
The Hon. F. Stanley Dobson and Mrs. Dobson
Mr. Justice Hood and Mrs. Hood
The Mayor and Councillors of Brighton

Assisted by
Mr. O'Hara and
Herr Friedrich Moosbrugger.

Given by

Master Percy Grainger

PUPIL OF HERR LOUIS PABST.

Programme.

Beethoven	Allegro molto e con brio, from Sonata Op. 10, No. 1	**Rheinberger**	"Weihnachtslied"
	MASTER PERCY GRAINGER		HERR FRIEDRICH MOOSBRUGGER.
Schubert	"The Erl King"	**Schumann**	(a) "Traümerei"
	MR. O'HARA.	**Schubert**	(b) "Moment Musicale"
Seb. Bach	(a) Prelude		MASTER PERCY GRAINGER.
	(b) Gigue	**Brahms**	(a) "Von ewiger Liebe"
	MASTER PERCY GRAINGER	**Rubinstein**	(b) "Es blinkt der Thau"
Rich. Wagner	"O Star of Eve"		HERR FRIEDRICH MOOSBRUGGER.
	MR. O'HARA.	**Scarlatti**	(a) Pastorale
J. Raff	"La Fileuse"	**Haendel-Pabst**	(b) Menuetto
	MASTER PERCY GRAINGER.		MASTER PERCY GRAINGER.

Interval of Ten Minutes.

Accompaniment—MISS FLORRIE BUCKLEY.

THE PIANOFORTE USED IS A BLÜTHNER ALIQUOT.

CARRIAGES AT A QUARTER TO TEN O'CLOCK.

A. & W. BRUCE, Printers, Melbourne.

The programme from Percy's second recital in Melbourne of September 10, 1894.

THE FRANKFURT YEARS
(1895-1900)

Rose and Percy in a group at "Pension Pfaff", Blumenstrasse, Frankfurt-am-Main, Germany, 1895

Aged thirteen (Photo by Marse, Frankfurt)

Rose Grainger on her American ("Hartford"?) bicycle on the Ringstrasse" (Miquelstrasse), (Photo by Richard Ederheimer, May 1897, Frankfurt).

Percy, 1896 Frankfurt-am-Main

Norman O'Neill, 1896 at Frankfurt-am-Main

Percy Grainger and Cyril Scott, Schillerplatz, Frankfurt-am-Main, 1900 (Photo by Theod Bänder)

Herman Sandby, the Danish Cellist, Frankfurt-am-Main.

Karl Klimsch, Grainger's only true and worthwhile teacher of composition.

Watercolour by Grainger:
Looking over Karlden Grosse Bridge Towards Sachsenhausen, from Frankfurt, June 6, 1896.

THE LONDON YEARS
(1901-1914)

Percy wearing full concert dress in 1902
(Photo by Mayall, London).

Leaving for his first Australian tour
(1903-1904).

In 1903
(Photo by T. Humphrey & Co., Melbourne).

Alfild de Luce, Percy Grainger and Herman Sandby
on tour in Denmark 1904-1905
(Photo by P. Hadrup, Aalborg).

Photograph to Percy from Ferruccio Busoni, 1903

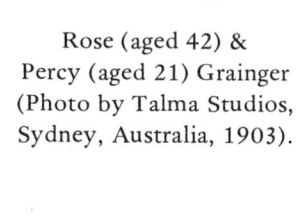

Rose (aged 42) & Percy (aged 21) Grainger (Photo by Talma Studios, Sydney, Australia, 1903).

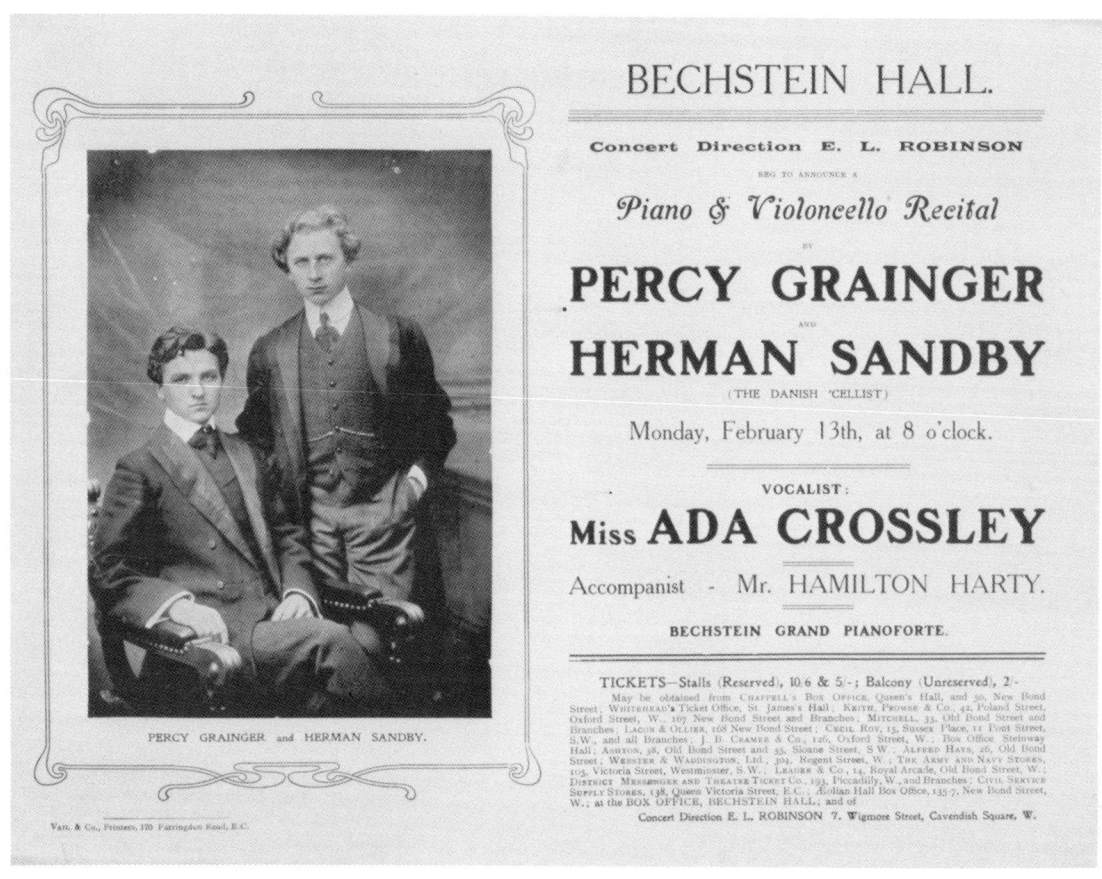

Recital programme from a tour of Percy and Herman Sandby, 1904.

Photograph from Edvard Grieg to Percy Grainger, 1905.

Percy in 1906 (Photo by Lafayette, Melbourne).

Percy and Nina Grieg at the Griegs' home, Troldhaugen, Norway, 1907.

Grainger with his leading folk-singers, Brigg Manor House, 1906:
George Gouldthorpe, Joseph Leaning (standing); Joseph Taylor, George Wray (seated).

Part of Grainger's detailed transcript of George Wray's singing of Lord Melbourne,
later to become the fifth movement of Grainger's "Lincolnshire Posy,"
reprinted from the Folk Song Journal No. 12.

Last photo of Grieg (alive), late July, 1907 at Grieg's summer home "Troldhaugen", ("The Hill of the Faries"), Norway. Left to right: Edvard Grieg, Percy Grainger, Nina (Mrs.) Grieg, Julius Röntgen (German composer).

Percy and girlfriend Karen Holden during summer 1909. (Photo by Miss Mutzhorn).

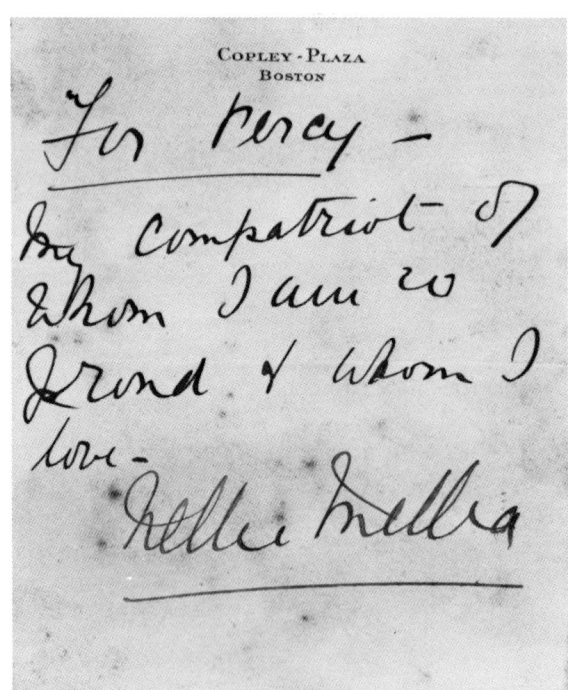

Letter to Percy From Dame Nellie Melba, famous Australian soprano.

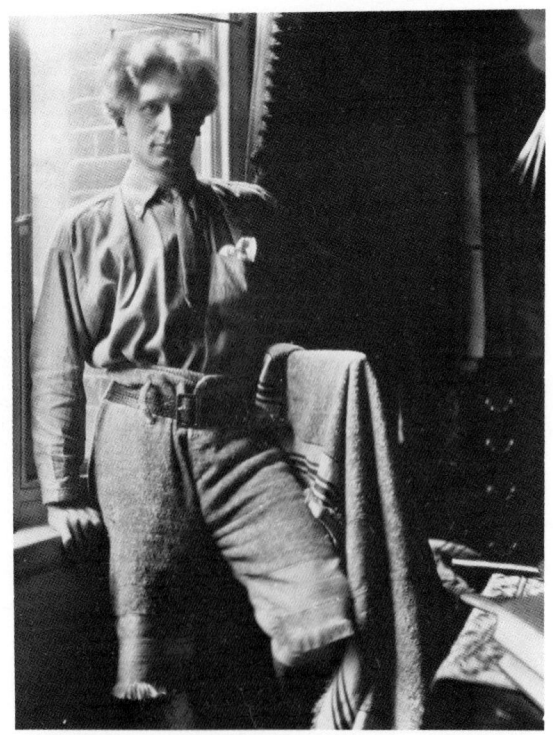

Wearing some of his first towell clothing at his home—31 A Kings Road, Chelsea, London (Photo by Roger Quilter's niece).

Photo by Lafette, Melbourne.

Photo by Holman & Paget, London.

Grainger wearing a bead necklace that he made while in transit between concerts (London).

A Charcoal Drawing of Percy By John Singer Sargent.

TYPED TRANSCRIPT

[Percy Grainger to his mother, Rose Grainger.]

Hotel Wentworth
Sydney
Lørday [Saturday]
27.3.09

I got the enclosed [letter] from Neuberger, your old pupil, whose sister Clara died some 4 years ago, when with him in Paris. Please keep his letter as its [sic] amusingly written.

He came to lunch yesterday & interested me very much. Since Grieg's opinions on the Jews I feel myself strangely more drawn towards them than formerly; indeed, their clearseeing is repose after the confused mental sight of so many Christians.

His collar wasn't clean, but his views on life very so, & quite humanitarian. He knows Blanche* & lots others (Debussy, for inst[ance]) well. He has made money ("to become free" as he says) in a stickerei fabrik [textile factory] in Paris, & is now, seemingly, loafing & journalizing. He says he can do a lot for me in Paris. He is going to Adelaide [South Australia] in about 14 days & will write you & look you up, having yr [your] address from me.

You might talk to him re Paris & me.

Last night [I] was at Auntie Jack's** where I met a most charming & fine looking old Scotchman (a refined & idealized Allerdale Grainger) who gave me a jolly Zulu curio, a bead armband, of that fat sausagg [sic] sort we liked & were amused by.

I'm so sorry I missed writing the day before yest[erday], or, on reckoning it out, I find that together with the Sunday's postal gap, it will be leaving you 2 days without [a] letter. Very stupid of me.

Lovingly, tho[ugh] busily

                The senior partner.

*   Jacques Emile Blanche, the famous artist, who painted PG's portrait.

** 'Aunti Jack's' full name was Annie Marie Quesnel (nèe MacFie). She was the sister of Rose Grainger's sister-in-law, and was known affectionately as 'Jack'.

                Transcribed by Helen Reeves
                (Letter Courtesy of Stewart Manville)

An advertisement for Grainger's first appearance in Germany.

Rose (aged 48) and Percy (aged 28) September 1910 (Photo by Rude og Hilfling Norway).

About 1910

Photo by Rudolf Helzig 1911.

About 1913

Percy at the keyboard sometime between 1902-1912.

Percy with unidentified orchestra, 1914. The Grieg Piano Concerto in A minor is placed on the music stands.

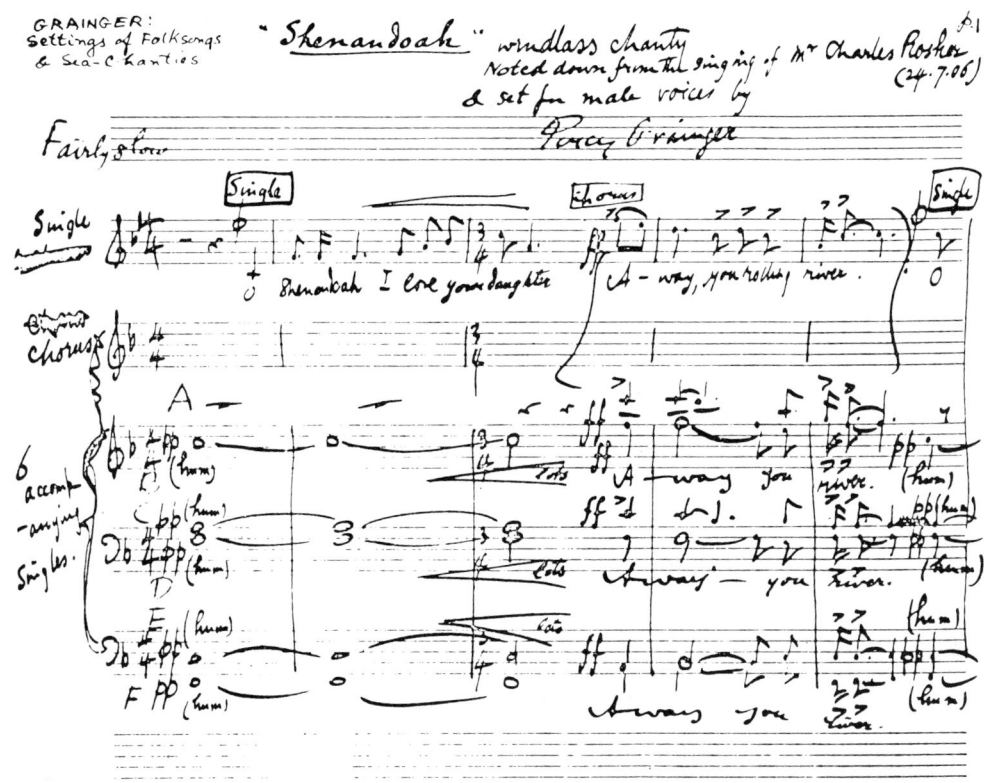

From the unpublished collection of Sea-Chanties notated by Percy Grainger.
"Shenandoah" as sung by Mr. Charles Rosher. Sea-Chanties collected by Grainger date from 1905 to 1915.

Grainger profile by Jane Emminet de Glehn, 1913.

Photo by Bassaro ltd., London.

The Young Grainger, by the Australian Painter Rupert Bunny.
(Photograph of painting courtesy of the International Percy Grainger Society)

ARRIVAL IN THE UNITED STATES

Rose (aged 53) and
Percy (aged 32) Grainger
in 1915
(Photo by Aime Dupont,
New York City).

Rose (aged 55) and Percy (aged 34) Grainger, Southampton, Long Island, late summer 1916 (Photo by Ames, New York).

Rose (aged 55) and Percy (aged 33) Grainger at the home of Mrs. Samuel Thorpe
(Photo by Ames, Long Island, New York) 1916.

Percy in late 1916 · Percy in 1917, New York.

PERCY JOINS THE ARMY

Bandsman Grainger with his soprano saxophone at Fort Hamilton, New York 1917.

Newspaper clipping.

The cover of Columbia Records catalogue January, 1918.

Self drawing by Percy, August 31, 1917.

Drawing of Percy in uniform by Cramer.

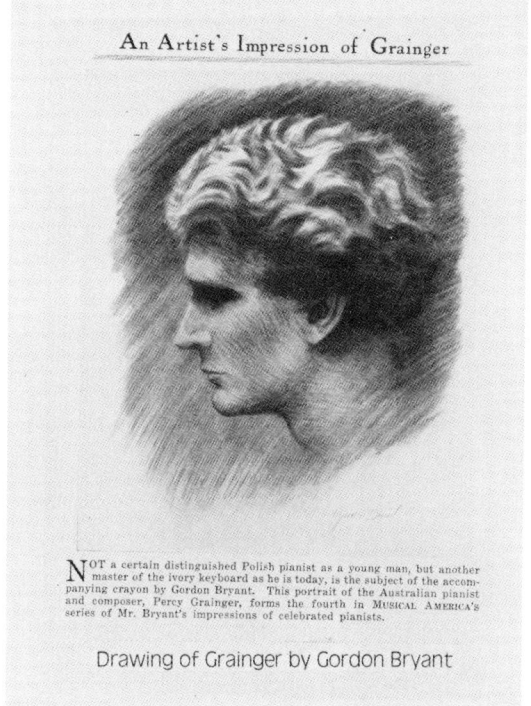
Portrait of Percy by Gordon Bryant in Musical America.

Clipping from the
New York Times, 1917.

AEOLIAN HALL
Entrance on 43rd Street
Bet. 5th and 6th Aves.

Saturday Afternoon
November Seventeenth, 1917
at three o'clock

Percy Grainger
Pianist-Composer

FOR THE BENEFIT
OF THE
MANASSAS INDUSTRIAL SCHOOL
FOR COLORED YOUTH
MANASSAS - - - VIRGINIA

PROGRAM

1. Fantasia and Fugue in G minor for organ .... *Bach-Liszt*
   (Arranged for piano)

2. (a) Kulok (Cattle-call) op. 66, No. 1, set by .... *Grieg*
   (b) Folksong from The Valders district, op. 73, set by .... *Grieg*
   (c) "Reflets dans l'eau" (Reflections in the Water) .... *Debussy*
   (d) Prelude in A flat, op. 28, No. 17 .... *Chopin*
   (e) Polonaise in A flat, op. 53 .... *Chopin*

3. Sonata in G minor .... *Schumann*
   (a) So rasch wie möglich
   (b) Andantino
   (c) Scherzo: Sehr rasch und markirt
   (d) Rondo: Presto

4. (a) "The Whippoorwill" .... *Daniel Gregory Mason*
   (b) "One more day, my John", set by .... *Grainger*
   (BY REQUEST)
   (c) Lullaby from "Tribute to Foster" .... *Grainger*
   (d) Paraphrase on Tschaikowsky's "Flower-waltz" .... *Grainger*
   (From the "Nutcracker's Suite")

STEINWAY PIANO USED EXCLUSIVELY

Management: ANTONIA SAWYER, Inc., Aeolian Hall, New York City

Boxes $20.00   Tickets $2.00 to 50 cents
On sale at Box Office or Manager's Office

1920

At the keyboard, 1920 (Photo by Sol Young).

"Percy Grainger was a good friend of my father's and they would see each other not only in a business way but socially in and around New York. I do remember him occasionally coming to our house when I was a small boy and remember him as a fascinating character."
John Steinway
January 18, 1983

An Advertisement by Steinway & Sons, picturing twelve of their feature artist with Percy Grainger included. (Photo of painting courtesy of John Steinway, Chairman of the Board, Steinway & Sons.)

The Graingers about 1919 (Photo by Jean De Strelecki, NYC).

The cover of The ETUDE Musical Magazine November, 1920.
(Courtesy of the Presser Magazine Company).

Percy Grainger and Gramaphone in Minneapolis (Photo by S. E. Johnson, 1920 or 1921).

Portrait of Grainger during 1920 by Frederick E. Morse.

Grainger at the keyboard during the 1920's.
Photo extracted from a Duo-Art piano roll advertisement.

Percy Grainger in White Plains, NY, 1920 (Photos by Frederick E. Morse).

Percy composing on the veranda of 7 Cromwell Place, 1920 (Photo by Frederick E. Morse).

Carnegie Hall
57th Street and Seventh Avenue

Tuesday Afternoon,
December 7th, 1920
AT 3 O'CLOCK

PIANO RECITAL

BY

PERCY GRAINGER
COMPOSER-PIANIST

PROGRAM

1. TOCCATA and FUGUE FOR ORGAN in D Minor .... BACH
   Using both the Tausig and Busoni transcriptions for piano.

2. BALLADE, Op. 24 .... GRIEG
   In the form of variations upon an old Norwegian melody.

3. (a) CLOUD PAGEANT (From "Country Pictures"), Op 9, No. 1—
       DANIEL GREGORY MASON
       (Born, Brookline, Mass., 1873)

   (b) A FRAGMENT ("When the Sun's Gone Down") Op 40, No. 2
       A. WALTER KRAMER
       Born, New York City, 1890)

   (c) PRELUDE (De Profundis) .... H BALFOUR GARDINER
       (Born, London, Eng., 1877)

   (d) HUMORESQUE .... H. BALFOUR GARDINER
       H. Balfour Gardiner, one of the most original and outstanding of
       British composers, though chiefly known through his highly effective
       larger works for orchestra, chorus and chamber music, is also the
       author of many notable piano pieces.

4. (a) BARCAROLE, Op. 60 .... CHOPIN

   (b) EL ALBAICIN (From "Iberia") .... ALBENIZ
       "El Albaicin" is the gypsy quarter of Granada

   (c) COLONIAL SONG .... GRAINGER
       In this composition the composer has wished to express feelings
       aroused by the scenery of his native country, Australia.

   (d) "TURKEY IN THE STRAW," Cowboys' and Old Fiddlers' Breakdown'
       Set by DAVID GUION
       (Born Battinger, Tex., 1895)

Steinway Piano Used

Tickets 50c. to $2.00   Boxes $15.00 and $18.00
        Plus 10% Government Tax

Management: **ANTONIA SAWYER, INC.**, Aeolian Hall, New York City

Rose (aged 60) and Percy (aged 39) Grainger the latter's "English Dance" in the music-room of their White Plains home, July 17, 1921 (Photo by Frederick E. Morse).

Rose and Percy from a moving picture (cinematograph) taken at their home in White Plains, July 21, 1921 (Photos by Louis J. Simmons, NYC). Rose playing guitar and Percy playing ukelele.

Percy Grainger and photographer Frederick E. Morse wrestling on the veranda of 7 Cromwell Place, the home of Percy Grainger (Early 1922).

7 Cromwell Place, the home of Percy Grainger for forty years.

Photo about 1922 by Jean De Strelecki, NYC.

POSTAL TELEGRAPH – COMMERCIAL CABLES

CLARENCE H. MACKAY, PRESIDENT

TELEGRAM

THE POSTAL TELEGRAPH-CABLE COMPANY (INCORPORATED) TRANSMITS AND DELIVERS THIS MESSAGE SUBJECT TO THE TERMS AND CONDITIONS PRINTED ON THE BACK OF THIS BLANK.

Sept. 9th, 1922

Kristiania 40

ANTONIA SAWYER

AEOLIAN HALL N.Y.C.

FIRST EUROPEAN GRAINGER CONCERT SENSATIONAL SUCCESS WILDLY ENTHUSIASTIC AUDIENCE CROWDED LARGEST CHRISTIANIA CONCERT HALL NORWEGIAN KING QUEEN PRESENT ALSO AMERICAN BRITISH FRENCH BRAZILIAN LEGATIONS NEWSPAPERS UNITED IN GLOWING PRAISES AND WELCOME.

CONCERT DIRECTION HAIS

Sept 11, 1923 Gave to Miss Bauer for Musical Leader

Percy at the beginning of 1922.

Last photograph taken of Percy before his beloved mother's death. End of April, 1922.

Rose Grainger
(aged 60)
after death, May 5, 1922

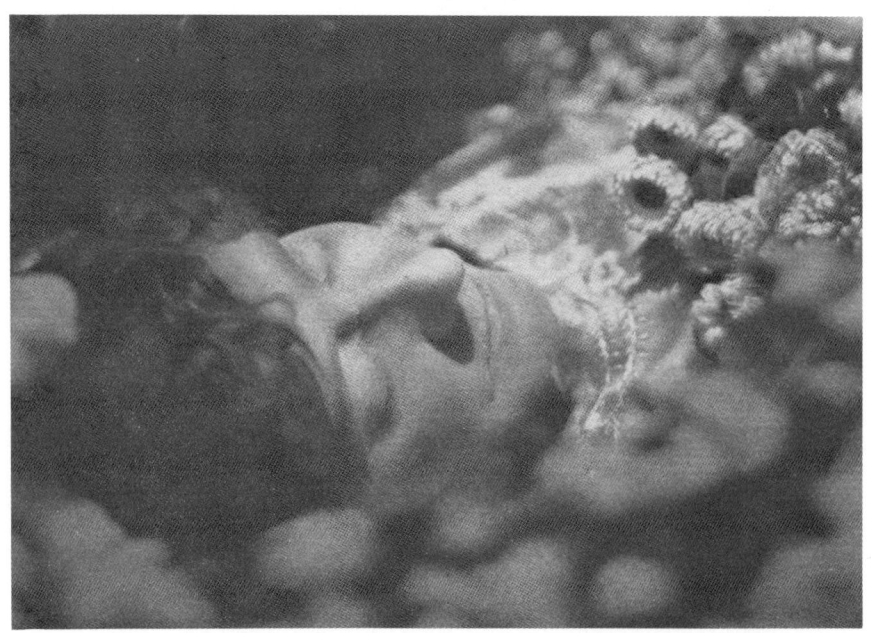

(Photographs by Frederick E. Morse)

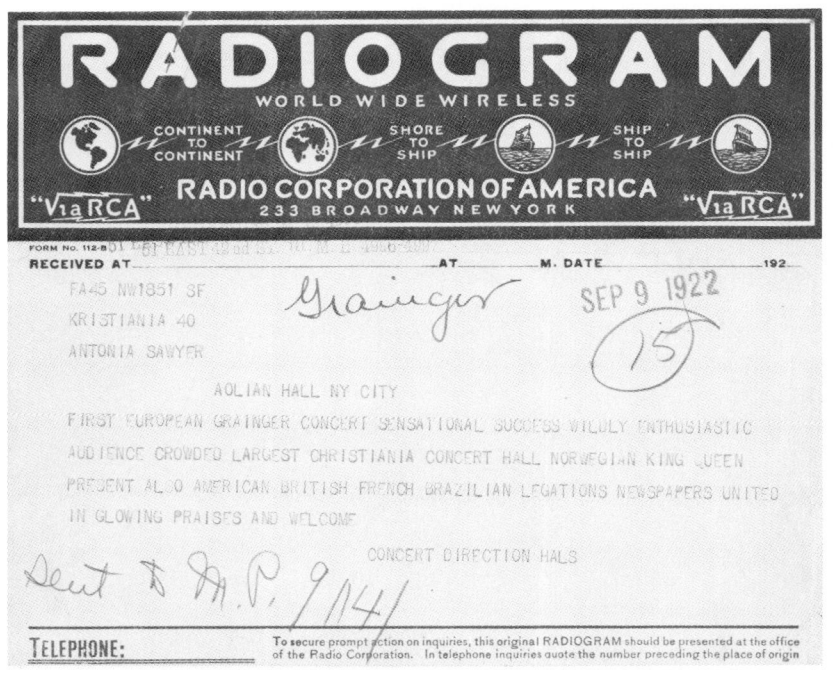

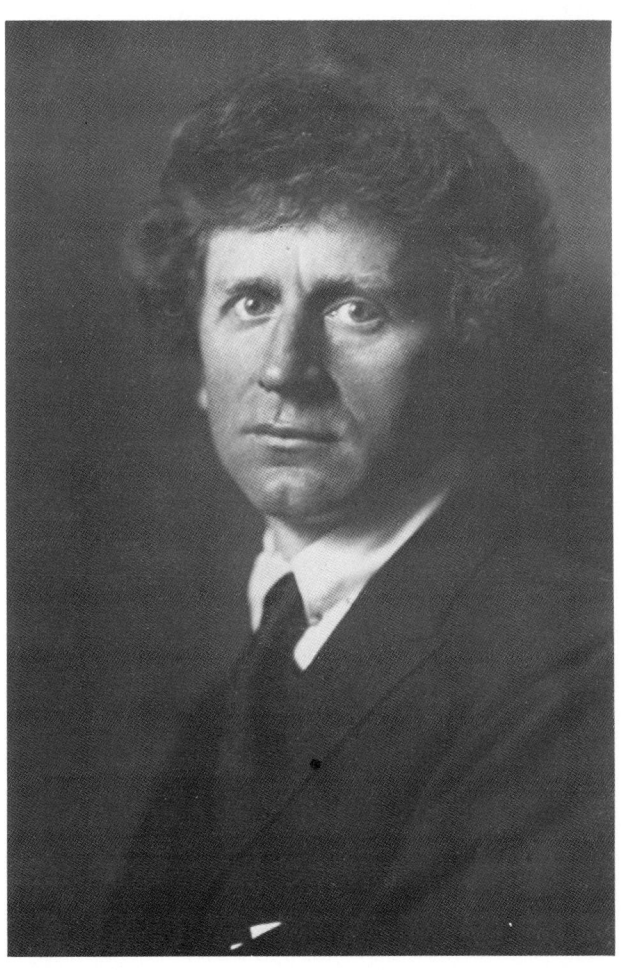

First photograph of Percy after Rose's death, 1923.   On a hike in 1923 (location unknown).

A return to Frankfurt in 1923 to visit his teacher—Karl Klimsch, age 83.

Percy Grainger and American composer
C. G. Vardell, Jr., about to play badminton in
Red Springs, North Carolina, about 1923.

Beginning a hike in South Australia
which lasted over eighty miles in three days time, 1924.

Percy at Frankfurt am Main spring 1923 (Photo by Professor Alfred Krauth).

Two views of Percy in June, 1924 (Photos by Talma Studios, Sydney).

With Folksong collector A. J. Knocks, Otaki, New Zealand, September 1924.

Cleaning his shoes in South Australia, 1924.

Grainger recording Danish folksongs on his Edison phonograph at Lindebo, Hearning, in the Jylland area of Denmark, September 11, 1925. Evald Tang Kristensen is in the center of the photograph, on Grainger's right. Singing is the Jutish singer Jens Kristian Jensen, waiting to record is Peder Flφe and Marie Tang Kristensen.

ONLY BOSTON RECITAL

Jordan Hall

Tuesday Evening
Dec. 15th, 1925
at 8:15 P. M.

Grainger

Photo by Morse.

PROGRAM

1. PARTITA, No. 1 B flat major..BACH
   - (a) Prelude
   - (b) Allemande
   - (c) Sarabande
   - (d) Minuets I and II
   - (e) Gigue

2. SONATA, F minor, op. 5..BRAHMS
   - (a) Allegro maestoso
   - (b) Andante
     > The gloaming falls and the moon doth shine,
     > Two hearts in love together entwine,
     > In rapture each other embracing.—(*Strenau*)
   - (c) Scherzo
   - (d) Intermezzo (Retrospect)
   - (e) Finale: Allegro moderato ma rubato

3. (a) LE GIBET (The Gallows)..RAVEL
     > Is it the stir of the night-wind I hear, or the sigh of the man hanging on the gallows-tree?
     > .... Or is it some spider embroidering a yard of muslin as a scarf for this strangled neck?
     > It is a bell chiming on the city wall, while the sinking sun reddens the body of the hanged man, seen against the horizon.
     > (*From the French by Aloysius Bertrand*)
   - (b) "NELL"..GABRIEL FAURE
     (Song arranged for piano by Percy Grainger)
   - (c) "PAGODAS"..DEBUSSY
     > "Pagodas" is very largely a transcription into European musical language of the sounds of those Javanese gong-orchestras (Gamalan) that Debussy studied so thoroly at the Paris Exposition of 1889 and which fructified his musical thinking, and, thru him, much of modern music.
   - (d) "TRIANA" (from "Iberia")..ALBENIZ
     (Triana is the Gipsy suburb of Seville)

4. (a) STUDY, C minor, op. 25, No. 12......................................CHOPIN
   - (b) STUDY, C sharp minor, op. 25, No. 7............................CHOPIN
   - (c) POLONAISE, A flat major, op. 53..................................CHOPIN

Columbia Records   STEINWAY PIANO   Duo-Art Music Rolls

Tickets, 75c to $2.00, Plus Tax.
On Sale at Box Office

Management: ANTONIA SAWYER, INC.   White Plains, New York
Local Management: A. H. HANDLEY   160 Boylston Street, Boston, Mass.

The Philharmonic Society of New York

Founded 1842

Metropolitan Opera House

Tuesday Evening, March 4th, at 8:30

Under the Direction of
WILLEM MENGELBERG

Assisting Artist:
PERCY GRAINGER

GRIEG
Concerto for Piano

WEBER
Overture to "Oberon"

TCHAIKOVSKY
"Pathetic" Symphony

TICKETS, 75c to $2.50   STUDENTS' TICKETS, 25c

NEXT METROPOLITAN OPERA HOUSE CONCERT
SUNDAY AFTERNOON, MARCH 16TH, AT 3:00
WILLEM MENGELBERG, Conductor

ARTHUR JUDSON, Manager   D. EDWARD PORTER, Associate Manager

The STEINWAY is the Official Piano of The Philharmonic Society

GRAINGER'S
CHORAL AND ORCHESTRAL CONCERT

Carnegie Hall — 57th Street and 7th Avenue, New York City

Wed. Eve., April 30th, 1924
at 8.15 P. M.

First Appearance in New York of the

BRIDGEPORT ORATORIO SOCIETY
(250 VOICES)

ORCHESTRA OF 94 PLAYERS
CONDUCTORS: PERCY GRAINGER & FRANK KASSCHAU

Program

1. **MARCHING SONG OF DEMOCRACY** .... GRAINGER
   (Born Melbourne, Australia, 1882)
   For mixed chorus, organ and orchestra.
   (First performance in New York).
   Organ: Frank Kasschau.
   Conductor: Percy Grainger.

2. **NORTH COUNTRY SKETCHES** .... DELIUS
   (Born Bradford, England, 1863)
   Impressions of Northern England, for orchestra.
   (*First performance in New York).
   (a) Autumn—The wind soughs in the trees.
   (b) Winter landscape.
   (c) Dance.
   (d) The March of Spring. Woodlands, meadows and silent moors.
   Conductor: Percy Grainger.

3. **TWO "PSALMS", Op. 74** .... GRIEG
   (Born Bergen, Norway, 1843)
   Based on old Norwegian church melodies, for unaccompanied mixed chorus and Baritone solo.
   (a) In Heav'n above.
   (b) God's Son hath set me free.

   TWO "SONGS OF THE CHURCH", Op. 37 .... RACHMANINOFF
   (Born Novgorod, Russia, 1873)
   Based on traditional melodies of the Russian Church, for unaccompanied mixed chorus.
   (c) Hymn to the Mother of God.
   (d) Laud ye the name of the Lord.
   Baritone Solo: Alois Havrilla.
   Conductor: Frank Kasschau.

4. **THE SONG OF THE HIGH HILLS** .... DELIUS
   For mixed chorus and orchestra.
   (*First performance in New York).
   Soprano Solo: Catherine Russell.
   Tenor Solo:
   Conductor: Percy Grainger.

---

*First performance in America of Delius' "North Country Sketches" and "The Song of the High Hills", at Bridgeport, Conn., evening of April 28th, 1924. (Concert of Bridgeport Oratorio Society.)

—OVER—

STEINWAY PIANOS.
Tickets, 55c. to $2.20, Government Tax Included   Boxes $19.80 and $16.50
On Sale at Box Office and Manager's Office

Management: ANTONIA SAWYER, Inc.   Aeolian Hall, New York, N. Y.
Telephone Longacre 8476-77

A photograph sent to Percy Grainger from the composer Frederick Delius, about 1911.

Quote: "I consider Percy Grainger the most gifted of all young composers I have met, and he is an Australian! He does quite remarkable things and is most refreshing."

Frederick Delius

Jelka and Frederick Delius with Percy outside 12 Domplatz, Frankfurt-am-Main, April 5, 1923 (Photo by Schumaker).

Grainger and Delius in Frankfurt-am-Main, 1923.

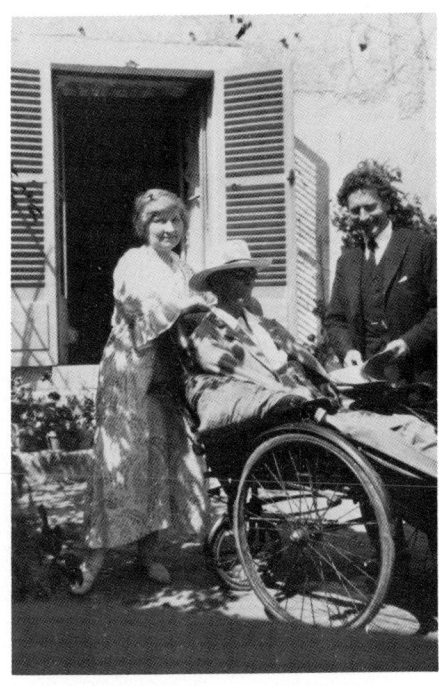

Jelka and Frederick Delius with Percy Grainger at Grez-sur-Loing, 1925.

Percy Grainger, Frederick Delius and Eric Fenby at Grez-sur-Loing, 1927.

Jelka and Frederick Delius at Grez-sur-Loing, 1927.

The last photograph sent to Grainger from Delius. About 1933.

Grainger rowing on the Loing at Grez, 1925.

With Dr. Robert Hamilton Russell on the SS Manganui, 1926.

Cover of a Columbia record catalogue featuring Grainger as their first artist to record a full record set electrically, 1926.

Two photographs from a series of broadcasts by Grainger in Melbourne, 1926.

"Thinking about Percy Grainger the composer, he was a musical maverick, like Charles Ives, but in his own way with his own experiments, he crossed many musical horizons. His brilliant use of folksongs caused us to overlook his major works in which he explored many unique musical textures. Percy Grainger was a musical explorer!"

Morton Gould
November 22, 1982

Percy playing a pump harmonium at 7 Cromwell Place, White Plains, NY, 1926
(Photo by Frederick E. Morse).

Percy and Roger Quilter

With Herman Sandby, Denmark.

Uncle Charlie (Charles E. Aldridge), his wife Aunty Margaret,
children Dorothy & Gordon, with Percy Grainger, November, 1926.

Grainger's wife-to-be, Swedish painter and poet Ella Viola Ström (Photo, Germany 1912).

Ella Viola Ström—date unknown.

S/S Aorangi, the ship that Percy and Ella met on when returning from Australian tour.

Now and then in Scandinavia may be met a Nordic type of womanhood, half-boyish yet wholly womanly, whose soft, flawless loveliness is like that of a fairy-tale princess; whose wondrous radiance makes real for us the sun-goddesses of the nature-myths; whose broad shoulders, amazon limbs, fearless glance, and freedom of deed and bearing recall the strong but noble-natured chieftainesses of the Icelandic sagas; whose cornfield hair and cornflower eyes awaken thoughts of the silent fruitfulness of the soil and of the lowly lives of land-tillers; whose graceful ease in riming, painting, singing, dancing, swimming, is the all-life-embracing giftedness of an unspoiled nature-race.

Such an uncrowned princess may be found in castle or cottage, in town or country-side, amongst high-born or low-born alike; for hers is bed-rock aristocraticness of race, not mere top-layer aristocraticness of class, culture, and breeding. To meet her is to have all of one's boy-hood fairy-dreams and hero-dreams come true.

Such a one is my sweet wife-to-be—Ella Viola Ström.

Percy Grainger.

Photo: Ella in May 1927

LOS ANGELES EVENING EXPRESS, WEDNESDAY, AUGUST 8, 1928

GREAT CROWD WILL WITNESS PERCY GRAINGER WEDDING AT HOLLYWOOD BOWL

Right—PERCY GRAINGER, the pianist, and his bride, who was Miss Ella Viola Strom, at their marriage ceremony in the Hollywood, Calif., Greek Theater. *Herald Tribune Photo*

Nuptials Will Be Part of Concert Program of 'Nordic Princess' in Bride's Honor

Tomorrow night Percy Grainger, internationally known pianist, composer and conductor, will pause long enough—in what has been a busy, bustling life—to get married.

Grainger's marriage, in Hollywood Bowl and as part of a concert program, will be characteristic of the man. His bride-to-be is Miss Ella Viola Strom, poet and writer.

The noted composer-conductor, considered one of the most brilliant personalities in the world of music, will direct the great orchestra. In "To a Nordic Princess," as Miss Strom proceeds slowly down the aisle to the rostrum. "To a Nordic Princess" was composed by Grainger in compliment to Miss Strom.

Grainger's wedding ceremony, under heaven's canopy of twinkling stars, will probably be witnessed by one of the largest crowds ever to attend the Bowl. The composer-conductor has, so to speak, invited the whole wide world to attend the celebration.

Through a life of teeming interests Grainger has retained, to an unusual degree, a warm, human touch. Not so long ago he narrowly missed arrest on suspicion of being a fleeing thief. To almost anyone else it would have been an outrage—to Grainger it was "just funny."

Grainger, in the midst of composing a difficult number, suddenly remembered a friend who was leaving town. Without donning hat or coat he rushed to a railway station, clutching a hastily purchased floor lamp. A policeman gave chase, but everything was explained. Another time Grainger, clad in running togs, returned just as rehearsal was to start. Rather than delay the proceedings he took up his baton and went to work.

Left to right: Wedding party, Mrs. F. E. Morse, Matron of Honor; Miss Ella Viola Ström, Bride; Percy Grainger, Groom; Mr. F. E. Morse, Best Man; Reverend J. Herman Olsson, Officiating Minister. Background: Hollywood Bowl Symphony Orchestra (World Wide Photos).

Grainger conducting the Hollywood Bowl Orchestra. During the intermission he and Ella were married before this capacity audience. The wedding under the stars. August 9, 1928.

The Graingers on their honeymoon.
Glacier National Park, August, 1928.

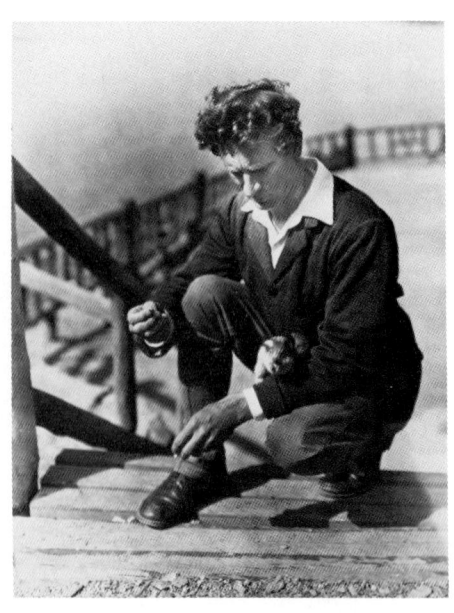

Percy feeding a squirrel,
Glacier National Park.

Returning from their honeymoon
(Photo by Gordon Bryan).

Newspaper clipping appearing after the wedding.

Percy and Ella in a rowboat
(Photo by Gordon Bryan).

Percy and Ella, New York 1928.

Grainger and orchestra before a performance of the Warriors scored for orchestra and nineteen grand pianos in the Chicago Civic Opera House. Composer at piano front stage, 1929.

(Letter from Percy Grainger to Elsie Bristow.) Dec. 25, 1929

Dear little Elsie,

The lovely cable (saying "all going splendidly") from darling Ella and yourself, on top of the letter saying the doctor had said your lung was not infected, has made me very deeply happy. I do so keenly hope that you will get stronger and better very quickly now. It would be splendid if you could soon join us over here.

As a result of your illness I have been thinking a great deal about you and your future. Will you allow me to express these thots quite freely to you—just as freely as if I were saying them to myself?

First of all I think that your yearly allowance (to be paid to you in monthly sums, or otherwise as you prefer) should be 200 pounds. 150 pounds yearly is too small an allowance, in my opinion.

Secondly we should make every possible effort to be together (the 3 of us) for at least 2 years, without separation between you and Ella, if possible. I think it is a silly and needless loss to you to be away from Ella just in these impressionable years. Ella, with her marvelous gifts of art and thot and human wisdom, has so much more to give to you than anyone else (it seems to me) and it would be a grievous wrong to your future to lack close and unbroken contact with her during these years. I also think that I, with my music, and otherwise, could be useful to you and your development. So that—even if you prefer living in England, rather than America or Scandinavia (the how can you know, till you have tried?) or wherever we would mainly be, during the next 2 years—I would advise you to make up your mind to be with us, wherever we are. While living with us you would be living "for nothing," in most ways, and thus would not be using up your own money (the 200 pounds) which you could spend on mere amusing things than mere needs. But while living with us I would advise Ella to ask you to promise never to smoke while indoors. That would not mean that you would never smoke (the words "never" and "always" ought to be striken out of all human relationships!) but only that you would promise never to smoke in the house where we lived. That would cut out the everlasting steady smoking while reading, etc. That would be a great gain, I think. The bad effect of smoking on the lungs is so clearly proven that I dont suppose there is a single athletic coach, anywhere, who would let men in training under him smoke. The meaning of that is obvious. To say that smoke "disinfects the air" is rot. Does anyone want to drink disinfected water? Why want to breathe disinfected air? In your case the matter is particularly obvious, as you had what I told you sounded like a smoker's cough all summer and it has been the breathing gear that has got sick. Anything that will give one a steady cough must be bad. Of course, you might have had the cough without smoking—but one would first have to have the proof, which would be the keeping on of the cough without smoking. You will notice that non-smoking Ella and I are both curiously without coughs. Most likely Ella's coughs in the old days had their origin in her being often in places where others smoked a lot. Also on Ella's account, therefore, I would deem it highly desirable to have no smoking indoors where we live. But that is merely my personal opinion. I do not know what Ella would think of this suggestion—and of course, her wish is paramount and final with me, in this as in all other matters.

I also heartily dislike the thot of your becoming a business worker—associating with the "bandits" of the business world, for that is all they are. Business people are, I think, all united in working "for a profit"—not a living wage, but a "profit." Think of the meanness of it! Exacting a pound of flesh on every deal, as it were! The cultured people of the world (scientists, statesmen, artists, discoverers, benefactors of all kinds) work in order to improve the world. What profit they may accidentally make they generally spend on their work or on needy people. Look at Ella—a typical artist of the highest type: All her stories, poems, etc., are full of compassion. And so are all true art-works. And all true sciences, statesmanship, benefation has a like origin. The people who lead such lives are full of kindliness, health, strength, practicalness. (When folk are in need of help for charity they come to us artists, and our peers. Why? Because we are practical; we can raise money without great expenses, whereas the business type can only raise money thru great expenses). Surely, if one is looking into the future, one would like the lot of a charming, pretty, clever girl like you cast among KINDLY, PRACTICAL, HEALTHY people—not among hard-hearted "bandits," whose outlook on life is so warped that they mostly die in middle age! Also if you are expecting to marry, later, you would sooner pick a husband for yourself, a father for possible children from healthily living, kindly people who are trying to improve the world and who do not merely work for a "profit." Apply that test to anyone, man or woman: Is the individual trying to GIVE something to the world or trying to TAKE something from it? The givers are, in my opinion, the people of culture. And I propose to you to prepare yourself for a life of culture rather than to prepare yourself for a business life.

By a "life of culture" I mean knowing several languages, carrying your music forward till you are a really useful, practical musician, knowing different lands and their peoples thoroly from the inside. What can one know of the world, what can one judge in any international question, if one knows only one language and one national life? Travelling with us you have an excellant chance of knowing different countries from the inside, and meeting all types of cultured types, IF YOU KNOW THE LANGUAGES of the countries visited. French you do know, which is splendid. Swedish and German Ella and I can easily teach you (if you care to learn them), which would set you up thoroly on the language side. Music I will develop you in thoroly, if you care to work with me. (But I cannot teach anyone the piano who will not cut their nails short!)

You may ask: But how should I earn my living (if I suddenly needed to) by merely being a "woman of culture." My answer is that any man or woman of culture can always earn their living—and without great hardship either. There are so few people of real culture and the world needs more than it can find of them. This does not mean that the work you have put in on shorthand and typing will not be extremely useful as a lady of culture. EVERY cultured person should must certainly be well up in both shorthand and typing—and if you care to put your powers at Ella's and my desposal, they will be very welcome.

Of course, by a lady of culture I do not mean a lady of leisure: The ideal of "leisure" is only possible amongst utterly unculture people. Since the goal of culture is the improvement of the world and one's own soul, and since it is such a tall order, there is little room for leisure in the scheme of the cultured types. I am not suggesting that in order to be cultured that one must be working all the time. To be cultured one must be very critical, and in order to be critical one must have time to think a lot and read a lot (I hope that when we are all together that we will find time and wish for a lot of nice reading aloud). But there can be no real culture without health, and there is no health other than ROBUST health. Therfore a cultured life is needfully a robust one—always; and no clothes, shoes, habits and manners can be an aid to culture that suggest leisure and are a denial of robustness. Why should anyone be so mean toward the world and the future of the race as to wish to wear clothes and cultivate habits that unfit him to be strong and able to strike great blows in the right direction—or the direction he at least thinks is right?

Therefore I would urge upon you (as part of your getting back to full health, and also as one of the paths to culture, satisfaction in life and future happiness) to cultivate your ENERGIES rather than to "work" very hard, rather than to set out to "earn your living." By the cultivation of energies I mean: Think hard, love strongly, walk fast and much, enjoy many things and keenly. Look at Ella: She is not a hard worker in the conventional use of the term; but what REAL ENERGY she has: How quickly she masters any new task, how well she sews, sings, plays, etc. How wonderfully she has made her way in life—by choosing only SUPERIOR TYPES for all serious purposes. How young and thin and fresh she is. How she has gone for REAL beauty and eshewed mere SHAM beauty. How lusty, how robust she is in her love-life and in everything else she puts her realest self into. How unfailingly wise and helpful her judgements are at every juncture. Such energies are always successful wherever they go or whatever they take up. Ella had only to talk a few minutes with Arnold Bax for him to be impressed by her and to remember and talk of her afterwards. He did not have to see her tiles or her poems in order to know that Ella was a REAL ARTIST. He could tell it in her energy, directness, NATURAL beauty, sympathy, compassionateness, in the wisdom of all her sayings. Surely that is how everyone ould like to get on—by REAL ROBUST qualities.

As for your dear self, you are, as I have already said, far too sweet, pretty, clever, nice-natured and wise to throw yourself away on a business career. At any rate, give the "cultured life" 2 years trial, learning languages and music, strengthening your body, getting to know various countries and their people. If at the end of the 2 years you feel you really prefer a business career, it is still time to make the change. Myself, I think it absurd for any superior and beautiful type of person as yourself (and come of such stock as you) to waste your time thinking about earning your way. Surely Ella and I together can insure you a life free from money-earning drudgery! When I think how my own years and talents have been wasted "earning my living" I certainly do not want to see anyone I love try that horrible path!

You will probably think me very dictatorial and priggish in all these matters, as in many others you have observed in me. But that cannot be helped. Some of us have to drudge for a living. Others, like myself, feel our chief duty to lie in trying to rid the world of many abuses that cloud and mar the loveliness and usefulness of life. Whether others like our preachings does not much matter. It is better to teach and annoy than never to teach.

In any case, dear Elsie, I am only suggesting these things to you. During your convalescence you may have much time for thot, and it might be a good time to think out many matters anent your future—including these proposals of mine.

Now that you and Ella are much together—could you not get going on the Swedish right away? It will be so much more fun for you, when next we go to Sweden, if you have got a good start on the language. Also it will be so much jollier for us all if you understand when Ella and I talk Swedish together.

Love & good wishes from Percy

Percy and Ella on the Danish Coast, August - 1929.

At Ella's seaside cottage on Pevensy Bay, England, August 1929.

At the House of Herman Sandby in Denmark, 1929.

Cyril Scott, Roger Quilter and Percy Grainger in attendance at the Harrogate Festival, 1930 or 1931.

BELOW: The Graingers with Balfour Gardiner, Grez-sur-Loing, 1927.

After a concert in 1929 or 1930 with pianist Olsaf Trygvasson on left.

From the New York Sun, December 6, 1930.

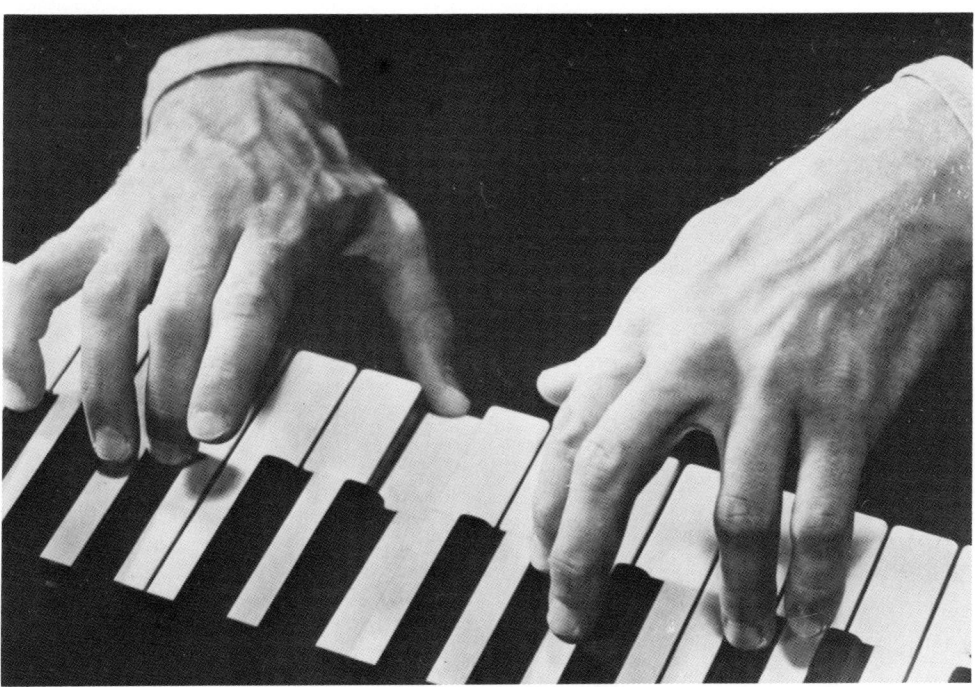

The Hands of Percy Grainger (Photo by Frederick E. Morse, 1930).

Ella rowing Percy after he finished "a hardy swim" on Lake McGregor, Ottawa, Canada.

Percy and his student Storm Bull between 1928 and 1930.

A picture postcard from Cyril Scott to Grainger in 1931.
(Photo by G. Hall-Nealle)

Returning from a sailing adventure on Lake McGregor, Ottawa, Canada, 1931.

On board with Skipper D. Anderson, August 10, 1932.

WESTFIELD SYMPHONY ORCHESTRA

PRESENTS

PERCY GRAINGER

IN

PIANO RECITAL

Friday, February 20, 1931, 8:30 P. M.

PROGRAMME

1. (a) Prelude and Fugue, D sharp minor................................BACH
   ("Well-tempered Clavier", Book 2, No. 8)

   (b) Sarabande ....PURCELL
   (From Suite No. 2, arranged by Herbert Fryer)

   (c) Sonata, D major ....D. SCARLATTI
   (Breitkopf, and Haertel Edition, No. 38)

   (d) Ramble on Bach's Aria "Sheep may graze in safety when a goodly shepherd watches o'er them."............GRAINGER
   This aria ("Schafe Koennen sicher weiden wo ein guter Hirte wacht",) for voice, 2 flutes and **continuo**, is from the Secular Cantata "Was mir behagt, ist nur die muntre Jagd."
   (First Performance in Westfield)

   (e) Prelude and Fugue, A minor...BACH
   (A separate composition, not forming part of the "Well-tempered Clavier" or other series)

2. Prélude, Aria et Final ....CESAR FRANCK

3. Three original compositions

   (a) Arrival Platform Humlet (a study in single line)......GRAINGER
   Awaiting arrival of belated train bringing one's sweetheart from foreign parts; great fun! The sort of thing one hums to oneself as an accompaniment to one's tramping feet as one happily, excitedly, paces up and down the arrival platform.

   (b) "Gay But Wistful" (tune in a popular London style) GRAINGER

   (c) "Handel in the Strand" (Clog Dance)........................GRAINGER
   The title was adopted in view of the fact that the composition seemed to reflect both Handel and English musical comedy—the "Strand" being the home of London musical comedy.
   (First performance in Westfield)

Three Settings

   (d) One More Day, My John, set by..............................GRAINGER
   Based on a sailor's chanty (working song) sung to the following words:—
   "One more day, my John,
   One more day,
   Oh rock and roll me over,
   One more day."

   (e) "Nell" ....FAURE-GRAINGER
   Song by Gabriel Fauré, arranged for piano by Percy Grainger.

   (f) A March-Jig ("Maguire's Kick")..........STANFORD-GRAINGER
   (No. 1 of "Four Irish Dances")
   Composed for orchestra on two Irish folk-tunes from "The Complete Petrie Collection", by Charles Villiers Stanford and arranged for piano by Percy Grainger. The main tune, "Maguire's Kick", was used as a marching air by the Irish rebels in 1798.

Steinway piano
Floral Decorations Courtesy Doerrer & Sons
Management: Antonia Sawyer, Inc, White Plains, New York

Next concert of the **Westfield Symphony Orchestra**, Mr. Charles Seyfried, conducting assisted by Mr. Ernest F. Otto, 'cellist, will be held in the Roosevelt Junior High School, Tuesday, April 14th, 1931 at 8:30 p. m.

With Duke Ellington at New York University, 1932. Grainger's introduction: "The three greatest composers who ever lived are Bach, Delius and Duke Ellington. Unfortunately Bach is dead, Delius is very ill, but we are happy to have with us today the Duke."

In a practice room at New York's Aoelian Hall, 1933.

Five sides of Percy Grainger.
"Music is Harmony not conflict, and all attempts to associate music with humdrum, competitive sides of life only succeed in lowering the art."
June 27, 1933

L'Avenir—The ship
Percy and Ella sailed
to Australia on in 1933.

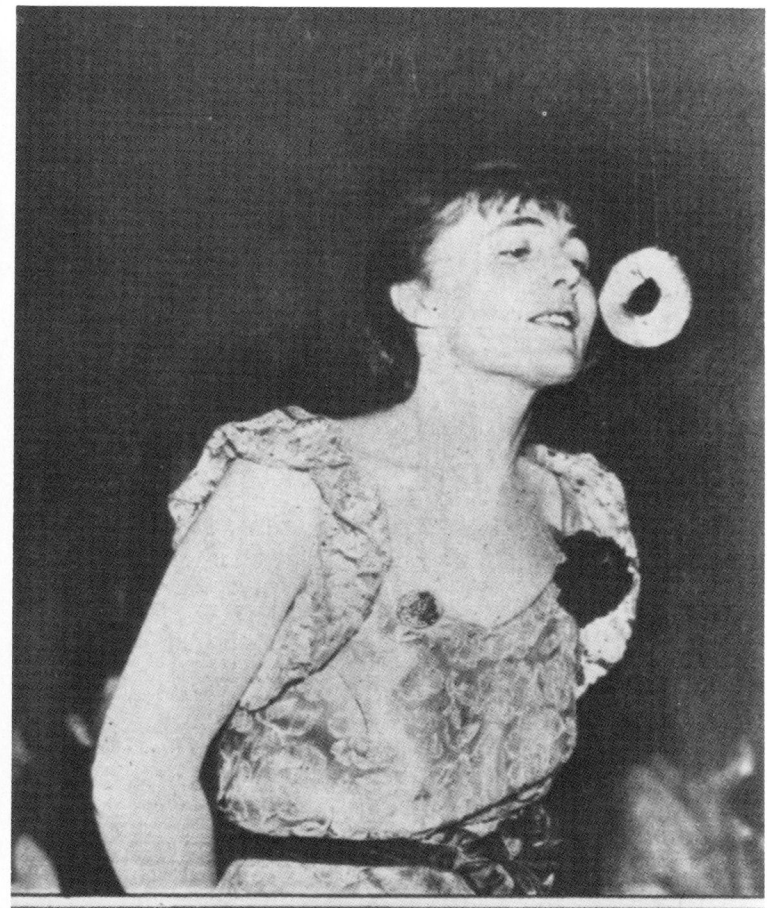

DEFYING HER TO HER TEETH: MRS. PERCY
GRAINGER,
Wife of the Composer-Pianist, in the Doughnut Contest at the
"Depression" Party of the White Plains Choral and Symphonic Society, at the White Swan Inn, White Plains.
(Westchester Photo Service.)

New York Times,
January 29, 1933

Percy and Ella in transit to
L'Avenir by motorboat.

Ella in a sack-race during the cruise.

Percy climbing the mast of the L'Avenir

Brisbane, Queensland, Australia, 1933 (Photo by Andre').

Melbourne 1934.

Playing "Tuneful Percussion."

Photo from Eugene Ormandy to Percy Grainger, 1936. Re-autographed for the Grainger Centenary 1982.
"I liked his works and performed quite a few of them when I was in Minneapolis.
He was one of the finest pianist." Eugene Ormandy, November 30, 1982.

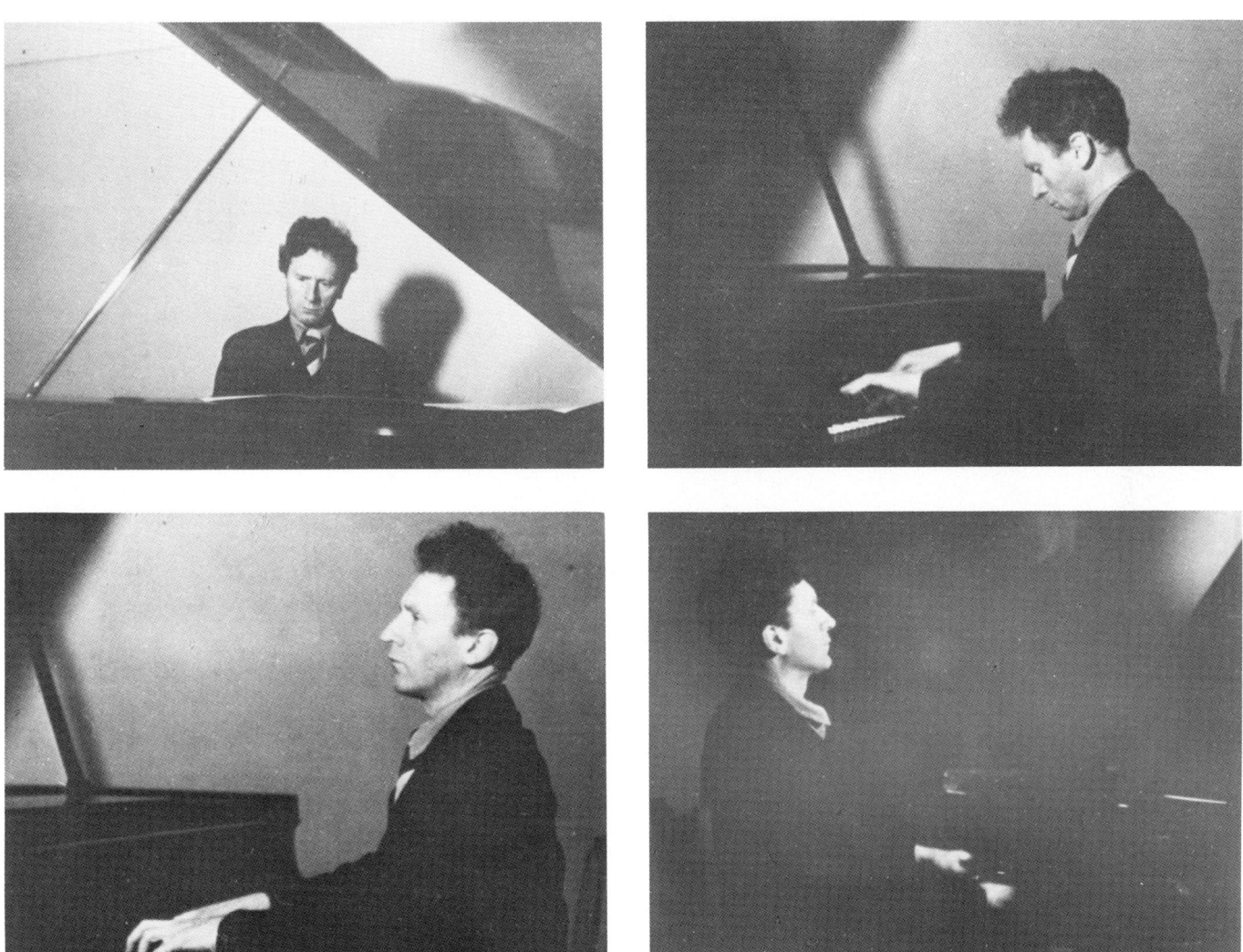

Four angles of Percy Playing, May, 1936 (Photos by Axel Poignant).

Reprinted from

MUSICAL AMERICA

Special Forecast Issue, February 10, 1936

GRAINGER

LOS ANGELES RECITAL, January 16, 1936

CRITICS UNITE IN PRAISE

Morse

Steinway Piano

GRAINGER PLAYS AND TALKS OF NOTED COMPOSERS (Headline)

Grainger is a familiar pianist to Los Angeles, but his concerts have been rare the last few years. His playing is anything but sensational, but if one goes over the roll call of concertizing pianists, it would be hard to find one who thinks more of his music and less of himself.

It was Liszt's transcription of the Bach Prelude and Fugue in A Minor which impressed the audience at the beginning of the program. The playing was clean and the tone resonant. It was a manly, strongly built Bach that Grainger gave.

—Isabel Morse Jones,
Los Angeles Times, Jan. 17, 1936.

ELITE AUDIENCE LAUDS GRAINGER (Headline)

Far away Australia spoke eloquently of her son, Percy Aldridge Grainger, whose pianoforte recital was made more than ordinarily brilliant by the presence of many of our musically elect.

A little excerpt, an arrangement of Grainger's own, from an old English song by Dowland, was a little over a minute long and very captivating. Grainger's plain little talks before each number added much to the enjoyment of all.

—Carl Bronson,
Los Angeles Eve. Herald & Express,
Jan. 17, 1936.

John Dowland composed "Now, O Now, I Needs Must Part" for the voice and lute accompaniment some time at the close of the sixteenth century. Grainger's own treatment of the Dowland song was his second offering, and nicely done it was, being this writer's favorite on the program.

—Harry Mines,
Los Angeles Illustrated Daily News,
Jan. 17, 1936.

GRAINGER STYLE PLEASES PHILHARMONIC (Headline)

Percy Grainger is not one to let tradition stand in the way of doing what he likes. He demonstrated this years ago . . . delighted thousands of listeners. His arrangement of the Dowland old English song for lute accompaniment, "Now, O Now, I Needs Must Part," was delightful.

Encores were demanded and given, and the concert was an unquestioned success both for the lover of exquisite music, and the thrill and sensation seeker as well.

—Florence Lawrence,
Los Angeles Examiner,
Jan. 17, 1936.

Tour Jan., Feb., March, 1937, Now Booking

Management: ANTONIA MORSE, 9 Cromwell Place, White Plains, N. Y.

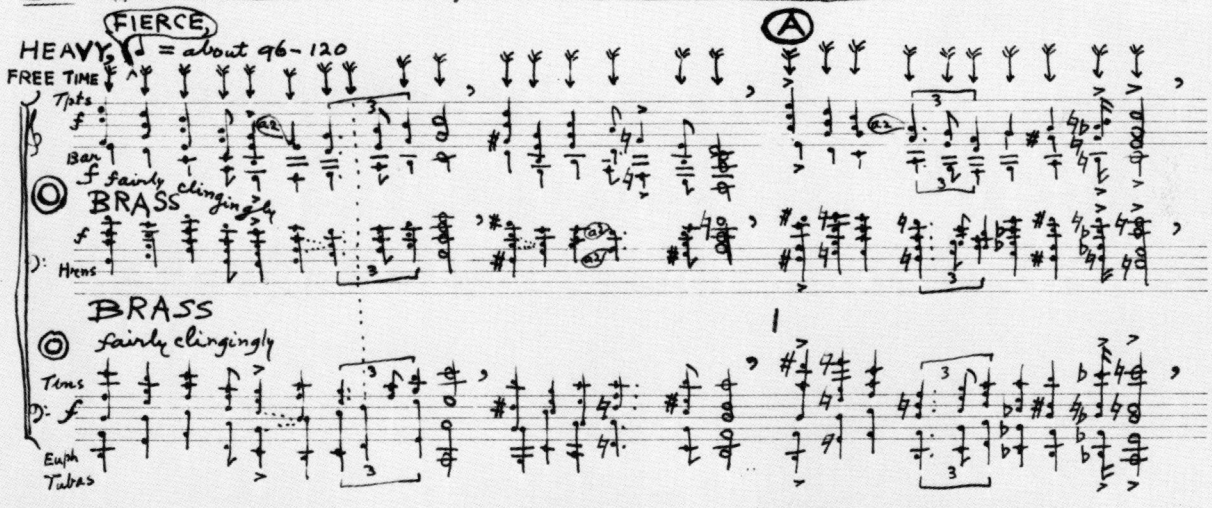

1937

The Grainger Museum at the University of Melbourne

Percy and His Museum
(Photos courtesy of the International Percy Grainger Society)

Glimpses inside the museum
(Photos by Bruce Anderson, courtesy of Stewart Manville)

With Richard Goldman at Mansfield, Pennsylvania State Teachers College, Summer Band Camp, 1938.

With composer Sparre Olsen, Norway 1939.

"People associate the name Percy Grainger with that appealing piece (Country Gardens). Grainger has a world wide reputation, rather like that of Sousa or of Johann Strauss: each is a genial composer of pleasant music in a specialized vein. To have such a reputation is, undeniably, no sad fate, but in Grainger's case it is so partial a recognition of artistic accomplishment that one is forced to reflect on the obscurity created by the wrong kind of fame."

Richard Franko Goldman
Fall 1955
The Julliard Review on
Percy Grainger's "Free Music"

With Sparre Olsen, 1936.

With Balfour Gardiner and Sparre Olsen, 1939.

With the British Monk, Dom Anselm Hughes, O.S.B., White Plains, New York, 1939.

Percy lecturing to harmony classes on folksong and harmonisation of folksongs, Gustavis Adolphus College, February 12, 1940.

The Graingers with conductor William Durieux playing Percy's sarrousophones, 1939.

PERCY CONDUCTING

Self Portrait by Ella, 1940

Portrait of Percy by Ella, 1940

Percy 1941

Percy and Ella in their homemade towell clothing.

Portrait of Percy by Ella, 1941.

7 Cromwell Place, 1941.

Percy as he appeared with the Waukegan Philharmonic Orchestra, January 13, 1941 (Photo by Hal Marty).

BELOW: Fort Hancock, New Jersey, April 21, 1943.

Playing guitar with composer Henry Cowell (Photo by Sidney Cowell).

Practicing in the basement of
Steinway Hall, 1943.

Springfield, Missouri, 1943.

1944

"Percy Grainger seemed to have relished being handsome, photogenic, and blessed with more than little self-confidence; but artists <u>should</u> admire themselves if they want to be free and self-assured enough to create."

William S. Newman
December 1, 1982

At Tollefsen Chamber Music Festival, Spring, 1944.

Welfare and recreation concert
at Camp Endicott, Davisville,
Rhode Island, May 3, 1944.

With his friend and physician
Dr. Kaare K. Nygaard.

Percy with Mrs. Constance Vulliamy
(formerly Gardner) Parkville, Missouri,
November 1946

Playing the Delius Piano Concerto. Conducting is Thor Johnson.

Percy and Ella playing "Tuneful Percussion" with the Sunset Symphony
During a Grainger performance, Salt Lake City, Utah, August, 1946.

Ella Grainger and Burnett Cross playing
"Tuneful Percussion."

Being greeted at the train to the National Music Camp
by Dr. Joseph E. Maddy, Interlochen, Michigan,
Summer 1946.

Percy and Ella in rehearsal with the National Music Camp Orchestra
(Photo courtesy of Wayne Brill).

Leaving the camp with armfuls of "Tuneful Percussion" instruments, 1946.

During a performance, 1948 (Photo by Pat Thorne).

1948

Rehearsing with the National Music Camp Orchestra, Composer Homer La Gassey conducting, Interlochen, Michigan, 1948 or 1949.

About to start a rehearsal at the camp.

Teaching private piano at the camp.

PRIVATE PRACTICE AT INTERLOCHEN, 1949

(Photos courtesy of Wayne Brill).

1949

Concert with Army Orchestra, late 1940's.

Conducting a high school band in Oakridge, Tennesse, 1950.

1950

With composer and conductor Howard Hanson, Stockholm, 1950.

With Herman Sandby, June 29, 1950.

Percy making a recording of Children's March with the Goldman Band, 1950's.

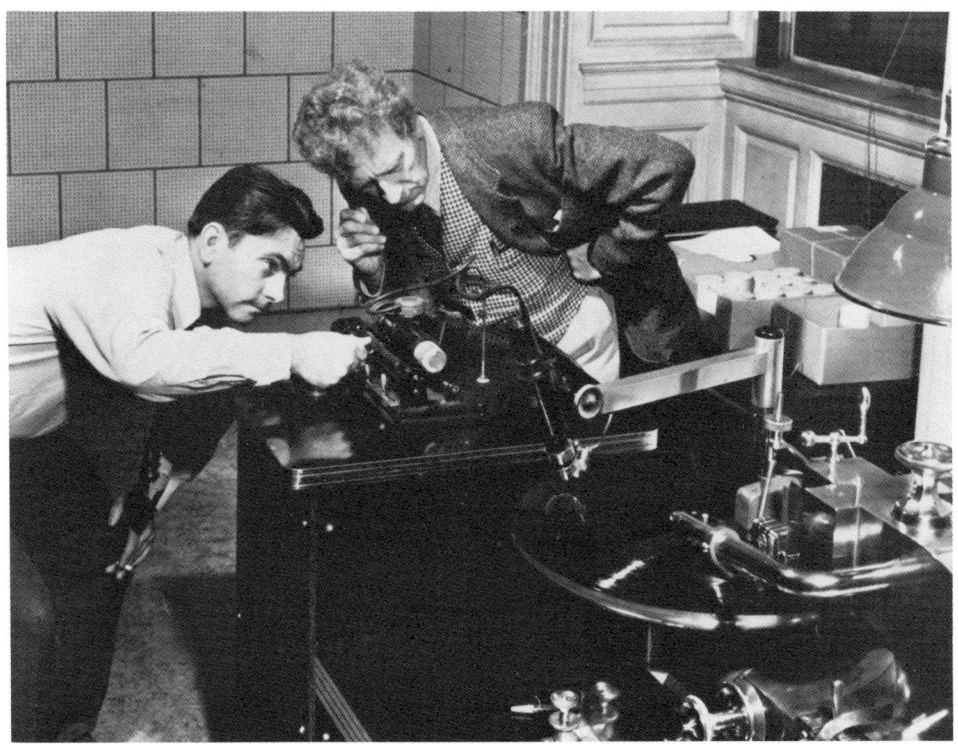

At the Library of Congress Transferring wax cylinder recordings of folksingers to acetate, 1950's.

Sketches of Percy Grainger

Grainger

PERCY GRAINGER

With a portion of
Hill Song No. 2,
May, 1950.

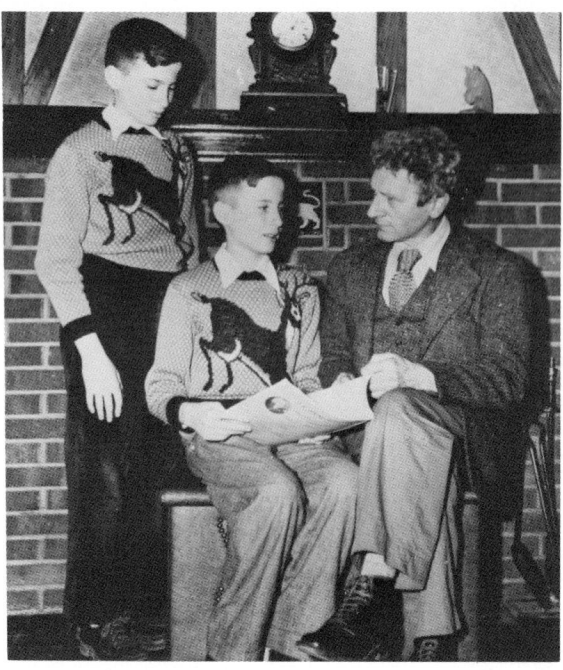

With John (standing) and Richard (seated) Conti-Guglia at their home
in Aubern, New York, before a concert that they performed jointly,
March 18, 1950.

Percy at the Keyboard, 1950's.

Percy late July, 1954, Rochester, Minnesota (Photos by W. H. Feldman).

Ralph Vaughan Williams, Percy and Ella Grainger in the front of 7 Cromwell Place, November 28, 1954.

Percy's "Kangaroo Pouch 'Free Music' Machine."

Experiment with organ pipe, 1950.

Photos courtesy of Burnett Cross.

August 1955, 7 Cromwell Place.

With Free Music invention at the Grainger Museum.

With Daniel Goldman (son of
Richard & Sandra Goldman) summer 1955.

With student and friend
Dorothy Payne.

Finishing a shipping box for one of his instruments needle and thread in hand.

Percy aged 76.

Percy and Ella,
mid 1950's.

After performing with a
community orchestra in New York.

Percy conducting at Kneller Hall, Twickenham, Summer, 1957.

Conducting in Poughkeepsie, New York with a military band, 1957.

Aarhus, 1957

A Gift to Grainger from the Australian Artist, Norman Lindsay. "She Arrives" is housed in the Grainger Museum collection.
(Photo is courtesy of the
International Percy Grainger Society).

Dressing a manikin of himself in the Grainger Museum, late 1950's (his last visit).

The mask done in life by Italian Plastercast, 1958.

At 7 Cromwell Place.

Late 1950's.

Frederick Fennell, the conductor who brought about the development of the modern day wind ensemble, speaking with Percy on the Veranda of 7 Cromwell Place, Late 1959.

With William Abbott (band conductor, Wisconsin State College Band, River Falls, Wisconsin) and Percy, December 17, 1959.

Reception for Ella and Percy at the American-Swedish Institute, Minneapolis, January 31, 1960. The last photo of Percy and Ella together.

Percy Grainger and Henry Cowell two weeks before Grainger's death. 7 Cromwell Place.
(Photo by and courtesy of Sidney Cowell).

Percy Grainger laid to rest in West Terrace Cemetery, Adelaide, South Australia on March 2, 1961.
Reverend T. J. Hayman, Claude Trevelion Funeral Director, Ella Grainger and Burnett Cross.
Being a lifelong atheist, Grainger requested not to have a public or religious funeral.
He wanted his skeleton placed on display in the Grainger Museum.

The last writings of Grainger. Quote from the writing of Ella Grainger: "With darling Percy's scribbles on—He asked me for pen & paper, but I had nothing handy except a newspaper & I gave it to him & he said 'this will do' a pencil as he wrote a unintelligible scribbles—the pen fell out of his hand, & he said 'I dropped it'."

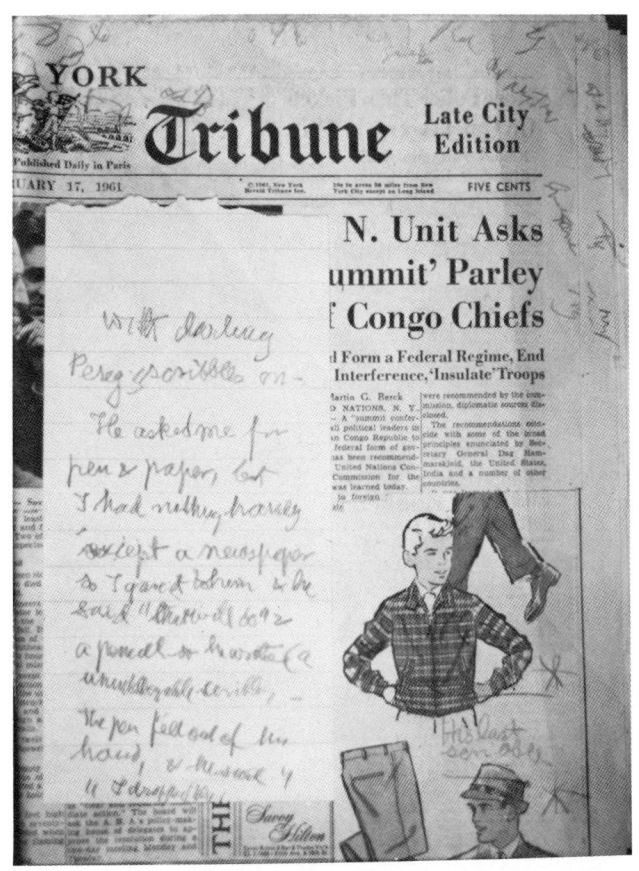

A bust of Grainger by Dr. Kaare K. Nygaard.

Ella Grainger with Stewart Manville, Grainger archivist, following their marriage on January 19, 1972. (Photo by Lionel Carley, Delius archivist).

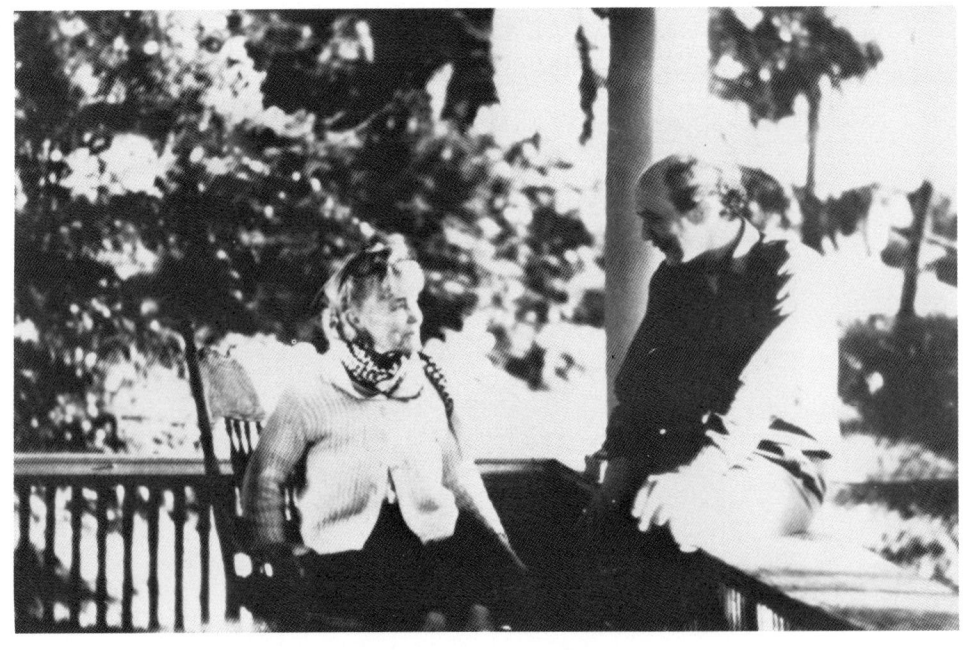

Ella with Grainger biographer John Bird at 7 Cromwell Place, mid 1970's.

John Hopkins conducting the Sydney Symphony Orchestra in a recording of the Vorsetzer playing Grainger's Duo-Art piano roll of the Grieg Concerto in A minor. Denis Condon and Peter Phillips at the piano.

QUOTE: "The whole musical world owes Percy Grainger more than it will ever realise. His contributions to so many areas of performance, research and composition have encouraged and stimulated others in their musical activities. The qualities of freshness and vigour which are present in his compositions and arrangements means they are assured of a growing and appreciative audience."

John Hopkins
March 15, 1983

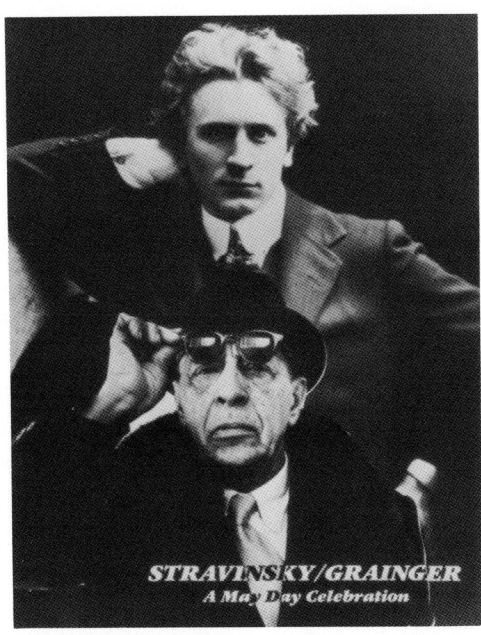

Cover of the programme from the Centenary concert of the music of Grainger and Stravinsky by the Greenwich Choral Society, May 1, 1982.

Alice Tully Hall
Lincoln Center for the Performing Arts

Wednesday Evening, October 13, 1982 at 8:00

Concert to Commemorate the Centenary of Percy Grainger
(1882–1961)

ADELE IRVING
Soprano

GARY NORDEN
Piano

with

The Grainger Room-Music Ensemble
and
Male Chorus

KEITH BRION
Conductor

Your Host: Mr. Ralph Stang, *President*
International Percy Grainger Society

I
GRAINGER	The Lost Lady Found English Dance Folksong

II
GRAINGER	Willow, Willow Old English Popular Song The Spring of Thyme English Folksong The Love Song of Har Dyal Text by Rudyard Kipling Kjaerlighedens Styrke ("The Pow'r of Love") Danish Folksong

III
EDVARD GRIEG	Gruss ("Greeting") Text by Heinrich Heine
FREDERICK DELIUS	Pagen hojt paa Taarnet sad ("The Page High in the Tower Sat") Text by J.P. Jacobsen
FREDERICK DELIUS	Il pleure dans mon coeur ("Tears Fall Within My Heart") Text by Verlaine
EDVARD GRIEG	Fyremaal ("The Goal") Text by Aa.O. Vinje

Intermission

IV
GRAINGER	Shallow Brown Sea-Chanty

V
GRAINGER	From the Four Corners of the British Isles Scotland: Lizzie Lindsay Wales: Dafydd Y Garreg Wen ("David of the White Rock") England: Died for Love Ireland: Irish Tune from County Derry

VI
RALPH STANG	Knott Mansion Text by Gloria Jahoda
EERO RICHMOND	Intention and Fears Text by Ella Grainger
SAMARAH BELLARDO	How to do One's Hair Text by Ella Grainger
RALPH STANG	February Night, Centerville Road Text by Gloria Jahoda

VII
GRAINGER	The Hunter in his Career Old English Popular Song

Miss Irving's make-up and coiffure by Vito Mastrogiovanni

Inquiries:
7 Cromwell Place
White Plains, N.Y. 10601
Att: Stewart Manville, *Archivist*

This concert is presented by the International Percy Grainger Society.

FREE MUSIC

by
Percy Aldridge Grainger
(December 6, 1938)

Music is an art not yet grown up; its condition is comparable to that stage of Egyptian bas-relifs when the head and legs were shown in profile while the torso appeared "front face"—the stage of developmant in which the myriad irregular suggestions of nature can only be taken up in regularised or conventionalised forms. With Free Music we enter the phase of technical maturity such as that enjoyed by the Greek sculptures when all aspects and attitudes of the human body could be shown in arrested movements.

Existing conventional music (whether "classical" or popular) is tied down by set scales, a tyrannical (whether metrical or irregular) rhytmis (sic) pulse that holds the whole tonal fabric in a vice-like grasp and a set of harmonic procedures (whether key-bound or atonal) that are merely habits, and certainly do not deserve to be called laws. Many composers have loosened, here and there, the cords that tie music down. Cyril Scott and Duke Ellington indulge in sliding tones; Arthur Fickenscher and others use intervals closer than the half tone; Cyril Scott (following my lead) writes very irregular rhythms that have been echoed, on the European continent, by Stravinsky, Hindemith and others; Schönberg has liberated us from the tyranny of conventional harmony. But no non-Australian composer has been willing to combine *all* these innovations into a consistent whole that can be called *Free Music*.

It seems to me absurd to live in an age of flying and yet not be able to execute tonal glides and curves—just as absurd as it would be to have paint a portrait in little squares (as in the case of mosaic) and not to be able to use every type of curved lines. If, in the theatre, several actors (on the stage together) had to continually move in a set metrical relation to each other (to be incapable of individualistic, independant movement) we would think it ridiculous; yet this absurd goose-stepping still persists in music. Out in nature we hear all kinds of lovely and touching "free" (non-harmonic) combinations of tones; yet we are unable to take up these beauties and expressivenesses into the art of music because of our archaic notions of harmony.

Personally, I have heard Free Music in my head since I was a boy of 11 or 12 in Auburn, Melbourne. It is my only important contribution to music. My impression is that this world of tonal freedom was suggested to me by wave-movements in the sea that I first observed as a young child at Brighton, Vic., and Albert Park, Melbourne.

Yet the matter of Free Music is hardly a personal one. If I do not write it someone else certainly will, for it is the goal that all music is clearly heading for now and has been heading for through the centuries. It seems to me the only music logically suitable to a scientific age.

The first time an example of my Free Music was performed on man-played instruments was when Percy Code conducted it (most skillfully and sympathetically) at one of my Melbourne broadcast lectures for the Australian Broadcasting Commission, in January, 1935. But Free Music demands a non-human performance. Like most true music, it is an emotional, not a cerebral, product and should pass direct from the imagination of the composer to the ear of the listener by way of delicately controlled musical machines. Too long has music been subject to the limitations of the human hand, and subject to the interfering interpretation of a middle-man: the performer. A composer wants to speak to his public direct. Machines (if properly constructed and properly written for) are capable of niceties of emotional expression impossible to a human performer. That is why I write my Free Music for thereminsーthe most perfect tonal instrument I know. In the original scores each voice (both on the pitch-staves and on the sound-strength staves) is written in its own specially colored ink, so that the voices are easily distinguishable, one from the other.

DISCOGRAPHY

The following discography is by no means a complete list of the recordings of the music of Percy Grainger. It is a current list which includes the records most obtainable on the market upon publication of this book. There are many other records that can be found in most public libraries and possibly through specialty shops, where rare and second-hand records are often available.

In John Bird's "Biography of Percy Grainger," (Faber & Faber), there is a comprehensive discography of the performances by Grainger which were set to disc.

R. S.

DISCOGRAPHY:

"Percy Grainger—Country Gardens and other piano music." Daniel Adni, pianist, plays Grainger: Country Gardens, Irish Tune from County Derry, Molly on the Shore, To a Nordic Princess, Lullaby (from tribute to Foster), Over the Hills and Far Away, Handel in the Strand, Knight and Shepherd's Daughter, Shepherd's Hey, Sailor's Song, Eastern Intermezzo. Seraphim S-60295 (US), EMI HQS 1363 (UK).

"Over the Hills and Far Away." Band Music of Percy Grainger. Harry Begian conducts the University of Illinois Symphonic Band. Children's March, Over the Hills and Far Away, Colonial Song, Lads of Wamphray, Lincolnshire Posy, Irish Tune from County Derry, Shepherd's Hey, Country Gardens, Ye Banks and Braes O' Bonnie Doon, Handel in the Strand, Spoon River, Hill Song No. 2, The Duke of Marlborough Fanfare, The Immovable Do, The Power of Rome and the Christian Heart. Two-record set: The University of Illinois Band record, numbers 74 and 75. University of Illinois Department of Bands (US).

"Salute to Percy Grainger." Benjamin Britten, Peter Pears, the Ambrosian Singers, English Chamber Orchestra. Shepherd's Hey, Willow Willow, I'm Seventeen Come

Sunday, Bold William Taylor, There was a Pig went out to Dig, My Robin is to the Greenwood Gone, The Duke of Marlborough Fanfare, Let's Dance Gay in Green Meadow, Scotch Strathspey and Reel, The Pretty Maid Milkin' her Cow, The Sprig of Thyme, Lisbon, The Lost Lady Found, Shallow Brown. Decca SXL 6410 (Australia).

"Full Spectrum" (Australian Digital Music). Barry Conyngham plays Grainger: Free Music I and II included on Move Records MS 3027 (Australia).

"Grainger on the Shore." Neville Dilkes conducts the English Sinfonia. Grainger: In a Nutshell Suite, Molly on the Shore, Irish Tune from County Derry, Danish Folk-Music Suite, The Immovable Do. EMI records ASD 3651 (UK).

"English Folksongs." Robin Doveton sings Grainger: The Sprig of Thyme, Willow Willow, The Jolly Sailor, Six Dukes went Afishin', Pretty Maid Milkin' her Cow, Shallow Brown, The Lost Lady Found. Prelude records PMS 1502 (UK).

"Percy Grainger." Sir Vivian Dunn conducts the Light Music Society Orchestra. Grainger: Country Gardens, Molly on the Shore, Londonderry Air, Handel in the Strand, Mock Morris, Shepherd's Hey. Included on EMI records TWO 295 (UK).

"Country Gardens and Other Favorites." Frederick Fennell conducts the Eastman-Rochester Pops Orchestra. Grainger: Country Gardens, Shepherd's Hey, Colonial Song, Children's March, Immovable Do, Mock Morris, Handel in the Strand, Irish Tune from County Derry, Spoon River, My Robin is to the Greenwood Gone, Molly on the Shore. Mercury Golden Imports SRI 75102 (US).

"Grainger: Lincolnshire Posy." Frederick Fennell conducts the Eastman Wind Ensemble. Grainger: Lincolnshire Posy included on Mercury Golden Imports SRI 75093 (US).

"Music of Holst, Vaughan Williams, Grainger." Frederick Fennell conducts the Eastman Wind Ensemble. Grainger: Hill Song No. 2 included on Mercury Golden Imports SRI 75011 (US).

"College Band Directors National Conference 1977." Frederick Fennell guest conducts The Eastman Wind Ensemble. Grainger: Hill Song No. 2 included on Crest Records CBDNA 77-4 (US).

Frederick Fennell and the Cleveland Symphonic Winds perform Grainger: Lincolnshire Posy and Shepherd's Hey. Telarc Digital DG 10050 (US).

"Percy Grainger plays Brahms and Grainger." Brahms Piano Sonata No. 3 in F minor, Op. 5, Brahms arr. Grainger Cradle Song, Brahms Waltz in A flat, Op. 39/15, Grainger: One More Day, My John, Molly on the Shore, Jutish Medley, Shepherd's Hey, Country Gardens. Imprimatur IMP 3 (UK).

"Legendary Pianists of the Romantic Era, Concert 2." (Duo-Art Piano Roll).

Grainger plays: Chopin Etude in A flat (No. 2 of Trois Nouvelles Etudes), Scott: Lotus Land, Op. 47, No. 1, Debussy: Toccata (from Pour Le Piano), Brahms arr. Grainger: Lullaby. Klavier Records KS 121 (US).

"Percy Grainger Plays a Selection of His Early Disc Recordings." Chopin: Polonaise in A flat, Op. 53, Prelude in A flat, Op. 28 No. 17, Liszt: Polonaise No. 2 in E major, Hungarian Fantasia, Debussy: Toccata (from Pour Le Piano), Grieg: Wedding Day at Troldhaugen, To Spring, Tchaikovsky/Grainger: Valse des Fleurs, Brahms/Grainger: Cradle Song, Grainger: Mock Morris, Molly on the Shore, Gum-Suckers March, Spoon River, Shepherd's Hey, Pearl records GEM 143 (UK).

"Percy Grainger Plays Grainger." (Duo-Art Piano Roll). Grainger: Country Gardens, Shepherd's Hey, Reel (from Four Irish Dances), Colonial Song, Leprechaun's Dance (from Four Irish Dances), Molly on the Shore, Sussex Mummer's Christmas Carol, Spoon River, Irish Tune from County Derry, Everest Records X-913 (US).

"One More Day." (Duo-Art Piano Roll). Grainger plays Grainger: Jutish Medley, Grieg: Norwegian Folk Songs Op. 66, Cattle Call, Love Song, In Ola Valley, Wedding Song, Gjerdene's Cradle Song, Peasant Dance, Wrapt in Thought I Wander, Guion: Sheep and Goats, Walkin' to the Pasture, Turkey in the Straw, Grainger: Irish Tune from County Derry, One More Day, My John, Delius: Brigg Fair, Stanford: Irish Dances. Larriken Records LRF 034 (Australia).

"Percy Grainger Plays Grieg." (Live Recording). Grainger plays Grieg: Concerto, Op. 16, A minor (Hollywood Bowl Symphony Orchestra conducted by Leopold Stokowski), Grieg: Concerto, Op. 16, A minor, First Movement Cadenza, Grieg: Concerto, Op. 16, A minor (Southeast Iowa Symphony Orchestra conducted by Richard A. Morse), Grieg: Three Norwegian Folksongs from Op. 17. IPA 508 (US).

"Percy Grainger Plays Grieg." (Duo-Art Piano Roll). Grainger plays Grieg: Concerto in A minor, Op. 16, Ballade, Op. 24, Wedding Day at Troldhaugen, Op. 65, No. 6, Erotikon, To Spring, Op. 43, No. 6. Klavier Records KS 101 (US).

"Percy Grainger Plays Schumann and Liszt." (Duo-Art Piano Roll). Schumann: Etudes Symphoniques en forme de Variations, Romance, Op. 28, No. 2, Liszt: Polonaise, No. 2, Hungarian Rhapsody No. 12. Klavier Records KS 109 (US).

"Folk-Song Arrangements by Percy Grainger." The Halsey Singers included on Pearl SHE-572 (UK).

"Music of Percy Grainger." John Hopkins Conducts the Melbourne Symphony Orchestra. Grainger: The Warriors, Green Bushes, Hill Song No. 2, Colonial Song, Shallow Brown, Spoon River, The Power of Love, Lord Peter's Stable Boy. ABC Records RRCS 131 (Australia).

"The Orchestral Works of Percy Grainger (Vol. I)." John Hopkins conducts the Sidney Symphony Orchestra. Grainger: Country Gardens, Harvest Hymn, Under En Bro, Children's March: Over the Hills and Far Away, The Lonely Desert Man

Sees the Tents of the Happy Tribes, Colonial Song, Duke of Marlborough Fanfare, Shallow Brown, Handel in the Strand, Harvest Hymn (Small ensemble), La Vallee Des Cloches, Scotch Strathspey and Reel. EMI 5514 (Australia).

"To a Nordic Princess—The Orchestral Works of Percy Grainger (Vol. 2)." John Hopkins conducts the Melbourne Symphony Orchestra. Grainger: To a Nordic Princess, Willow Willow, My Robin is to the Greenwood Gone, Shepherd's Hey, Eastern Intermezzo, Farewell to an Atoll, Molly on the Shore, Hill Song No. 2, Spoon River. EMI Records OASD 7606 (Australia).

"The Orchestral Works of Percy Grainger (Vol. 3)." John Hopkins conducts the Adelaide Symphony Orchestra. Grainger: Blithe Bells, We Were Dreamers, There Were Three Friends, Walking Tune, The Immovable Do, Suite: In a Nutshell. EMI Records OASD 7607 (Australia).

"The Orchestral Works of Percy Grainger (Vol. 4)." John Hopkins conducts the Sydney Symphony Orchestra. Grainger: Danish Folk-Music Suite, Tribute to Foster, Youthful Suite. EMI Records OASD 7608 (Australia).

"The Historic Percy Grainger Piano Roll (1919) Grieg: Concerto in A minor." John Hopkins conducts the Sydney Symphony Orchestra (Duo-Art Vorsetzer by Dennis Condon and Peter Phillips with the Duo-Art Piano Roll). Grainger plays Grieg: Concerto in A minor, Op. 16. Leopold Stokowski conducts Grainger Favorites: Handel in the Strand, Irish Tune from County Derry, County Gardens, Shepherd's Hey, Mock Morris, Molly on the Shore, Early One Morning. RCA ARL 1-3059 (US) RCA VRL 1 0168 (Australia).

"Historic Percy Grainger Piano Roll—Tchaikovsky: Piano Concerto No. 1 in Bb minor, Op. 23." John Hopkins conducts the Melbourne Symphony Orchestra (Duo-Art Vorsetzer by Dennis Condon and Peter Phillips with the Duo-Art Piano Roll). Included on RCA VRL 1 0342 (Australia).

"Contest Music for Band." Col. George S. Howard conducts the Air Force Band. Grainger: Lincolnshire Posy included on AFV-1 Southern Music Company (US).

"Musicians of Australia (Vol. 15) Percy Grainger: Piano Music for Two Hands (Vol. 1)." Leslie Howard, Piano. Grainger: Shepherd's Hey, Harvest Hymn, One More Day, My John, The Sussex Mummer's Christmas Carol, Molly on the Shore, To a Nordic Princess, Handel in the Strand, Jutish Medley, Irish Tune from County Derry, Knight and Shepherd's Daughter, The Merry King, Colonial Song, Country Gardens. World Record Club R 03433 (Australia).

"Percy Grainger Piano Settings (Vol. 2) Two Pianos, Four Hands." Leslie Howard and David Stanhope, piano. Grainger: Shepherd's Hey, Hermundur Illi, As Sally Sat A-Weeping, Hill Song No. 1, Hill Song No. 2, Suite: In a Nutshell. World Record Club R 06332 (Australia).

"Percy Grainger Piano Settings (Vol. 3) Two Pianos, Six Hands." Leslie Howard,

Geoffrey Parsons and David Stanhope, piano. Grainger: Jutish Medley, English Dance, Green Bushes, The Warriors (with the Adelaide Brass Quintet). World Record Club R 06333 (Australia).

"Room-Music Tit Bits & Other Tone Stuffs." Leslie Howard and David Stanhope, piano. Grainger: Shepherd's Hey, Harvest Hymn, One More Day, My John, The Sussex Mummer's Christmas Carol, Jutish Medley, Country Gardens, The Merry King, Handel in the Strand, Children's March, Over the Hills and Far Away, Lincolnshire Posy, English Waltz. EMI Records HQS 1402 (Australia).

"Percy Grainger Free Rambles, Room Music Tit Bits and . . .". Kenneth Montgomery conducts the Bournemouth Sinfonietta, Phillip Martin, piano. Grainger: Youthful Suite, Blithe Bells, Spoon River, My Robin is to the Greenwood Gone, Green Bushes, Country Gardens, Mock Morris, Youthful Rapture, Shepherd's Hey, Walking Tune, Molly on the Shore, Handel in the Strand. RCA RL 25198 (UK).

"Fantasy on Gershwin's Porgy and Bess," arranged for two pianos by Percy Grainger. Performed by Phillips and Renzulli on Crystal C 6002 (US).

"Paraphrase on Tchaikovsky's "Waltz of the Flowers" by Percy Grainger." Included on Recordings of piano music by Michael Ponti. Turnabout records 34560 (US).

"Salute to Percy Grainger (Vol. 2)." Peter Pears, John Shirley-Quirk, Wandsworth Boys Choir and the English Chamber Orchestra conducted by Stuart Bedford. Grainger: Molly on the Shore, Shenandoah, Under a Bridge, Dollar and a Half a Day, The Merry King, Six Dukes Went A-fishin', Stormy, Irish Tune from County Derry, Brigg Fair, Green Bushes, The Three Ravens, Died for Love, Country Gardens (live recording of Grainger playing), The Power of Love, The Hunter and His Career. Decca records SXL 6872 (UK).

"Leonard Slatkin conducts the St. Louis Symphony Orchestra." Grainger: Irish Tune from County Derry included on Telarc Digital DG 10059 (US).

"British Concert Pops." George Weldon conducts the Philharmonia Orchestra. Grainger: Londonderry Air included on EMI Records SXLP 30243 (UK).

"Music for Cello and Piano." Vignoles Welsh performs Percy Grainger's "Youthful Rapture" for cello and piano on Pearl SHE-571 (UK).

"Faeroe Island." James Westbrook conducts the UCLA Wind Ensemble. Grainger: Lincolnshire Posy, Colonial Song, The Duke of Marlborough Fanfare, Shepherd's Hey, Faeroe Island, Molly on the Shore, Irish Tune from County Derry, Sussex Mummer's Christmas Carol. Varese Sarabande Digital record VCDM 1000.50 (US).

"By Plane From Paris." Denis Wick conducts the London Wind Orchestra. Grainger: Molly on the Shore, Irish Tune From County Derry, Shepherd's Hey, Lincolnshire Posy. Enigma Records K 53574 (UK).

LIST OF SOURCES

Beirne, Deborah: "Meeting Percy Grainger," *Success Magazine,* Chicago, January, 1926, pp. 54-55.

Bird, John: "Percy Grainger," Paul Elek, London, 1976, Faber & Faber, London, 1982.

Buchanan, C. L.: "Analyzing the Greater Grainger," *Musical America,* August, 1917.

Conti-Guglia, Richard: Letter to Harold Schonberg, copy to Robert Simon, July 8, 1982.

Dreyfus, Kay: "Music by Percy Aldridge Grainger," University of Melbourne, Grainger Museum, 1978.

Fenby, Eric: "Delius as I Knew Him," Icon Publishers, London, 1966.

Fink, Henry T.: "Review," *New York Evening Post,* February 12, 1915.

Fink, Henry T.: "Review," *New York Evening Post,* May 29, 1915.

Goldman, Richard Franco: "Percy Grainger's 'Free Music'," *Juillard Review,* Fall 1955, pp. 37-47.

Grainger, Ella: "Sketches of Percy Grainger," Percy Grainger Library Society, White Plains, New York, 1967.

Grainger, Percy: "Anecdotes," Autobiographical Writings, 1952.

Grainger, Percy: "Collecting with the Phonograph," *Journal of Folksong Society,* 1908/09, pp. 147-242.

Grainger, Percy: Diary Collection, Autobiographical Writings, The Grainger Museum, The University of Melbourne.

Grainger, Percy: "Do Not Open Until 10 (Ten) Years After My Death," The Grainger Museum, The University of Melbourne.

Grainger, Percy: Forward, "Lincolnshire Posy," G. Schirmer, New York, 1937.

Grainger, Percy: "Glimpses of a Genius," *Etude,* October, 1921, pp. 631-632.

Grainger, Percy: "Grieg—National and Cosmopolitan," *Etude,* June, 1943.

Grainger, Percy: "Impressions of Art in Europe," Four parts: *Musical Courier,* (June 1, 1929), p. 8, (July 6, 1929), p. 8, (September 28, 1929), pp. 8, 31, (October 26, 1929), pp. 10, 12.

Grainger, Percy: "Life of My Mother and Her Son—Autobiographical," November 16, 1923.

Grainger, Percy: "Music, A Commonsense View of All Types," Australia Broadcasting Commission, Australia, 1933-1934.

Grainger, Percy: (No Title), *Cannon Magazine,* 1949, pp. 179-184.

Grainger, Percy: "Photos of Rose Grainger and Three Short Accounts of Her Life," published privately in Germany by Percy Grainger, 1923.

Grainger, Percy: "What Effect is Jazz Likely to Have Upon the Music of the Future," *Etude,* September, 1924, pp. 593-594.

Griffiths, Helen: "Percy Grainger and the Arts of the South Pacific," The University of Melbourne, The Grainger Museum, 1979.

Howes, Frank: "Percy Grainger," *Recorded Sound,* Summer, 1961, pp. 95-98.

Olsen, Sparre: "Percy Grainger," *Norske Samlaget,* Oslo, 1963.

Parker, D. C.: "The Art of Percy Grainger," *Monthly Musical Record,* 1915, pp. 152-153.

Parker, D. C.: "Percy Aldridge Grainger—A Study," G. Schirmer, New York, 1918.

Schonberg, Harold C.: "The Great Pianists," Simon & Schuster, New York, 1966.

Schonberg, Harold C.: "Honoring a Gifted Eccentric," *New York Times,* June 27, 1982, pp. 1, 19, music section.

Slattery, Thomas C.: "Percy Grainger—The Inveterate Innovator," The Instrumentalist Company, Evaston, 1974.

Taylor, Robert Lewis: "The Running Pianist," *The New Yorker,* Three parts: (January 31, 1948), pp. 29-37, (February 7, 1948), pp. 32-39, (February 14, 1948), pp. 32-43.

Waters, Thorold: "Grainger the Whirlwind," *Australian Musical News,* December, 1926.

INDEX

Abbot, William, 120
Aldridge, Charles, 64
Aldridge, Dorothy, 64
Aldridge, Gordon, 64
Anderson, D., 76

Bach, Johann Sebastian, 3, 4, 80
Bartök, Bela, 5
Bauer, Marion, 11
Beecham, Sir Thomas, 6
Beirne, Deborah, 8
Bird, John, 124
Bloch, Ernest, 11
Bristow, Elsie, 71, 72
Bryant, Gordon, 39
Bull, Storm, 76
Bunny, Rupert, 34
Burkitt, Adelaide, 3
Busoni, Ferruccio, 4, 24

Condon, Dennis, 8, 125
Conti-Guglia, John, 112
Conti-Guglia, Richard, 11, 112
Cowell, Henry, 99, 121
Cross, Burnett, 12, 102, 122

Debussy, Claude, 6
Delius, Frederick, 6, 11, 60, 61, 80, 101
Delius, Jelka, 60, 61
Durieux, William, 94

Edison, Thomas, 5
Elgar, Edward, 6
Ellington, Duke, 10, 80
Enesco, Georges, 6

Fenby, Eric, 61
Fennell, Frederick, 13, 120
Fink, Henry T., 6
Fløe, Peter, 56
Foster, Steven, 2

Gardiner, Balfour, 4, 74, 92
Gardner, Marion, 17
Gershwin, George, 11
Glehn, Jane, 33
Goldman, Daniel, 115
Goldman, Edwin Franko, 12
Goldman, Richard Franko, 91
Gould, Morton, 63
Gouldthorpe, George, 27
Grainger, Ella, 68, 69, 70, 74, 76, 81, 94, 96, 97, 102, 103, 113, 116, 122, 124
Grainger, John, 2, 15
Grainger, Percy Aldridge, "Blue-eyed English", 9; compositions and arrangements, *Arrival Platform Humlet*, 6, *Children's March*, 109, *Colonial Song*, 6, *Country Gardens*, 7, 13, *Early One Morning*, 12, *English Dance*, 38, *Gum-Suckers March*, 6, *Handel in the Strand*, 13, *Hill Song No. 2*, 13, 112, *I'm Seventeen Come Sunday*, 6, *Irish Tune From County Derry*, 6, *Mock Morris*, 6, *Molly on the Shore*, 6, 13, *My Robin is to the Greenwood Gone*, 6, *Lincolnshire Posy*, 6, 11, 13, 27, *Love Verses from the Song of Solomon*, 4, *Pagodes*, 6, *The Power of Rome and the Christian Heart*, 12, *Scotch Strathspey and Reel*, 6, *Shepherd's Hey*, 13, *Shenandoah*, 33, *Suite on Danish Folk Songs*, 8, 12, *Sussex Mummer's Christmas Carol*, 6, *To A*

Nordic Princess, 10, *Train Music,* 4, *The Warriors,* 6; Grainger folksong collecting, 5; Grainger "Free Music," 3, 12, 114, 115, 127; Grainger Museum, 89, 90, 115, 118, 121; Grainger: Music, a universal language, 4
Grainger, Rose, 2, 7, 8, 15, 16, 20, 24, 30, 31, 35, 36, 37, 43, 48, 52
Grieg, Edvard, 2, 5, 25, 28, 30, 32
Grieg, Nina, 5, 26

Hanson, Howard, 108
Hayman, Reverend T. J., 122
Hoch Conservatory, 3
Holden, Karen, 28
Honegger, Arthur, 4
Hopkins, John, 9, 125
Hughes, Dom Anselm, 10, 92

Jensen, Jens Kristian, 56
Johnson, Thor, 101

Klimsch, Karl, 4, 22, 54
Knocks, A. J., 6, 56
Knorr, Ivan, 3
Kwast, James, 3

La Gassey, Homer, 105
Leaning, Joseph, 27
Lindsay, Norman, 118
Luce, Alfild de, 23

Maddy, Joseph E., 102
Manville, Stewart, 124
Melba, Nellie, 28
Mengelberg, Willem, 11
Milhaud, Darius, 13
Morse, Frederick E., 49, 67

Newman, William S., 100
Nygaard, Kaare K., 12, 100, 101, 123

Olsen, Sparre, 91, 92
Olsson, Reverend J. Herman, 67
O'Neill, Norman, 4, 21
Ormandy, Eugene, 84

Pabst, Louis, 3
Payne, Dorothy, 115

Phillips, Peter, 125

Quilter, Roger, 4, 64, 74

Rachmaninoff, Sergei, 2
Ravel, Maurice, 11
Röntgen, Julius, 28
Roosevelt, Franklin D., 4
Rosher, Charles, 33
Rubinstein, Anton, 3
Russell, Robert Hamilton, 2, 62

Sandby, Herman, 4, 22, 23, 25, 64, 109
Sargent, John Singer, 29
Schoenberg, Arnold, 4
Scott, Cyril, 4, 12, 21, 74, 76
Steinway, John, 42
Stockhausen, Karlheinz, 12
Stokowski, Leopold, 11, 12
Strauss, Richard, 6
Stravinsky, Igor, 4, 125
Ström, Ella Viola, 9, 10, 65, 66, 67

Tang Kristensen, Evald, 8, 12, 56
Tang Kristensen, Marie, 56
Taylor, Joseph, 27
Trevelion, Claude, 122
Trygvasson, Oslaf, 7, 8, 9, 75

Vardell, C. G., Jr., 54
Vaughan Williams, Ralph, 5, 6, 12, 113
Vorsetzer, 9, 125
Vulliamy, Constance, 101

Whitman, Walt, 6
Wray, George, 27

GRAINGER

— PRESENTS —

TWO SUNDAY EVENINGS
of
ROOM-MUSIC
The LITTLE THEATRE
238 WEST 44th STREET, NEW YORK CITY

April 26th, 1925	May 3rd, 1925 at 8.15 P. M.
at 8.15 P. M.	Works by
All-Grainger Program	Franz Schreker, R. Nathaniel Dett, Natalie Curtis, Grieg, Paul Hindemith.

PERFORMERS

Conductors: R. Nathaniel Dett, Frank Kasschau, Percy Grainger
Baritone: Erik Bye
Pianists: Ernest Hutcheson, Ralph Leopold, Percy Grainger
Guitarists: Ralph Leopold, Percy Grainger

Kasschau's Solo Choir (Conductor: Frank Kasschau)

SOPRANOS	CONTRALTOS
C. Andrews	
G. Ross	
TENORS	**BARITO**[NES]
Samuel Craig	Elmer Ross
George E. Bennett	Wallace Can[...]

HAMPTON INSTITUTE CH[OIR]
(Conductor: R. NAT[HANIEL DETT])
THIRTY MEMBERS of the NEW YOR[K...]
(Orchestra Personnel Manag[er...])

Piccolo, flute, sopranino sarrusophone, [...]
2 bassoons, double-bassoon, clarinet, sop[...]
horns, trumpet, trombone, euphonium, [...]
cussion, harmonium, celesta, piano, harp, [...]

Subscription Tickets $5.50
On Sale at Little Theatre Box [Office]
Mail Orders to:—Antonia Sawyer, Inc., [...]
Owing to the limited capacity of theatre o[...]

NO COURTE[SIES]

MGT. ANTONIA [SAWYER, INC.]
White Plains, [N. Y.]

In the term "Room-music" I embrace all music (whether for one, few or many instruments, and whether the parts are single or massed) that is intended for performance in rooms or quite small halls or is at its best under really intimate conditions. I feel that programs of such music, in order to present with greatest freshness the compositions of which they consist, should be "orchestrated" with regard to tonal contrasts in the employment of the total soundbodies involved much as are the different movements of such suites as Tchaikovsky's "Nutcracker," Bizet's "L'Arlesienne," Grieg's "Peer Gynt"; where the strings are first heard without cellos or basses and later complete, or where string orchestra relieves full orchestra most tellingly. This scheme, applied to room-music, means that vocal numbers should offset instrumental, that *a capella* part-songs should alternate with instrumentally accompanied choruses, that pianos should be juxtaposed to wind or strings and that contrasts of smaller and larger groupings of performers should be consciously employed as a means of effect in the choice of works to be associated together on any given program.

Natalie Curtis' work, as a whole, forms one of the most perfect flowers in the already considerable nosegay of American musical everlastings. Lovely being and exquisite musician that she was, she possessed, as collector and arranger of primitive music, a wondrous gift of penetrating into the inner soul of the art of alien peoples—partly through her tenderly sympathetic and intuitive nature, partly through her unique technical and cultural equipment. These qualities and powers are evidenced in these short New Mexican settings no less than in her monumental works, "The Indians' Book" (Harper & Bros.), "Negro Folk-songs," 4 vols. (G. Schirmer, Inc.) and "Song and Tales from the Dark Continent" (G. Schirmer, Inc.). The two "Memories of New Mexico," in a somewhat shorter form and a different orchestration, were first performed by Mr. George Barrère and "The Little Symphony Orchestras."

R. Nathaniel Dett, in his choral writing, combines cosmopolitan compositional culture and individualistic creative characteristics with a rich heritage of Negro vocal traditions. There is in his treatment of blended human voices (as, in a somewhat different way, there also is in Rachmaninoff's "Anthems") that innate sonority and vocal naturalness that seems to result only from accumulated long experience of untrained improvised polyphonic singing, such as that of Southern Negroes, South Sea Polynesians and Russian peasants. These things are branches of the very tree of natural communal song.

Grieg told me, in 1907, that he liked "Lost in the Hills" best of all his compositions. He felt that it reflected both the austerity and the sunny sweetness of the Norwegian mountains and also a certain tragic, lonely mood typical at once of his race and of his personality.

Of Paul Hindemith's always effortless and effective, though not always exquisite, music, it might be said (as William Lyon Phelps said of a cat in repose) that "It pours itself out like a glass of water." In its unpretentiousness, in its facile musicianship, in the extent to which it is "absolute" music, in the degree to which it borders upon being "Musikanten-musik," it seems to me to mark a return of present-day German music to some of the tenets and practices of the Haydn-Mozart-Schubert era—to a simplicity and pithiness of expression rare or unknown in Germany in the pre-war years. Less improvisational and less unsophisticated, but correspondingly more exquisite and more refined, is Franz Schreker's Chamber Symphony, composed in 1916. I record it as the most finished and masterly treatment of the solo chamber [...] st beautiful in point of sensuous sound) that has, to my knowledge, [...] and Austrian large-chamber movement. Of course, such a work [...] ged when heard in the original solo orchestration proscribed by the [...] ores are first heard with a distorted balance of sound, resulting from an [...] parts undertaken in large hall performances. The impulse behind [...] chestrations is probably the dual desire for a greater clarity and [...] exactness of tonal balance than is possible with the full symphony [...] r polyphonic range and variety of timbres than was compassed by [...] groupings (quartets, trios, etc.), of the post-Bach "classical" period. [...] r-growing influence of Bach upon the minds of present-day com[...] hind this turn of taste.

[...] presented will be seen to date from 1898 to 1912. Owing to my [...] osition, based upon frequent experimentation and again and again [...] the many chamber works I have begun in more recent years are [...] ance, though I hope to bring them forward in later room-music [...] with large chamber combinations and the blending of voices, reeds, [...] or harmonium, percussion, etc., in proportions and choice of per[...] l composition, began around 1899 and thus antedated by several [...] ntal renaissance of larger chamber groupings that came to a head [...] "Kammersymphonie" (1906). What chiefly actuated me was my [...] stic quality obtainable with solo (as contrasted with massed) parts [...] xes and out-bursts, that can be had, in rooms and quite small halls, [...] ance of wood-winds (why should the oboe, for instance, always be [...] ding instrument—which is the impression it makes in large concert [...] *quality* obtainable with large room-music blends has, in the case [...] rchestration, to be replaced by *quantity*, owing to the obliterating [...] sed strings and to the exigencies of large halls in which only the [...] ently incisive for truly climactic moments—a factor that seemed to [...] of color choices and loss of instrumental individualisticness.

PERCY GRAINGER.

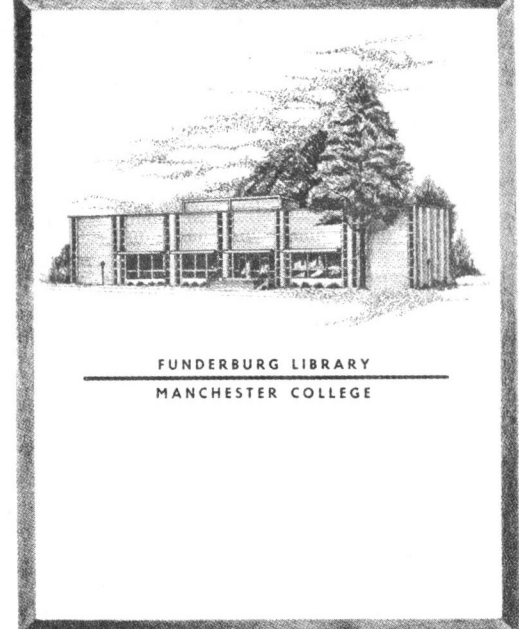

FUNDERBURG LIBRARY
MANCHESTER COLLEGE

Sunday Evening [, April 26th, 1925]
at 8.15 [P. M.]

Pro[gram]

(The choral numbers conducted by [...]
numbers, with the exception of the first [...])

1. **ENGLISH DANCE** (composed 1899-1909) [...]
   for 6 hands at 2 pianos.
   ERNEST HUTCHESON, RALPH LEOPOLD, PERCY GRAINGER

2. **HILL SONG No. 1** (composed 1901-1902) .... GRAINGER
   For piccolo, flute, oboe, English horn, bassoon, double-bassoon, sopranino sarrusophone, heckelphone, soprano saxophone, alto saxophone, horn, trumpet, euphonium, kettle-drums, cymbals, harmonium, piano, 2 violins, 2 violas, 2 cellos, bass.

3. **KIPLING SETTINGS** (composed 1898-1906) .... GRAINGER
   Poems of India and the Jungle (by permission of the author, Mr. Rudyard Kipling) set for voices, accompanied and unaccompanied.
   (a) The Fall of the Stone (mixed voices and 15 instruments).
   (b) Night-Song in the Jungle (men's voices, unaccompanied).
   (c) Morning-Song in the Jungle (mixed voices, unaccompanied).
   (d) Hunting-Song of the Seeonee Pack (men's voices, unaccompanied).
   (e) The Peora Hunt (mixed voices and 9 instruments).
   (f) "Tiger! Tiger!" (men's voices, unaccompanied).
   (g) Mowgli's Song against People (mixed voices and 12 instruments).

   KASSCHAU'S SOLO CHOIR (Conductor: FRANK KASSCHAU)

4. (a) *"MY ROBIN IS TO THE GREENWOOD GONE" (composed 1912), GRAINGER
       A ramble upon an old English tune for flute, English horn and 6 strings.
   (b) *SCOTCH STRATHSPEY AND REEL, INLAID WITH SEVERAL SCOTCH AND IRISH TUNES AND A SEA-CHANTY (composed 1901-1911) .... GRAINGER
       For 4 men's voices, 5 wood-winds, xylophone, harmonium, 2 guitars and 8 strings.

   Conductor: FRANK KASSCHAU

STEINWAY PIANOS, ESTEY HARMONIUM used.

*None of the compositions on the above program are based on folk-music or popular melodies except those two marked with a star.

[Sunday Eveni]ng May 3rd, 1925
8.15 P. M.

[P]rogram

[...] by R. Nathaniel Dett, the instrumental [...]
[...] singer.)

1. [...] [S]ymphony) in one movement .... FRANZ SCHREKER
   (Born of Austrian parents at Monaco, 1878)
   [...]on, horn, trumpet, trombone, kettle-drums,
   percussion, harp, celesta, harmonium, piano, 4 violins, 2 violas, 3 cellos,
   2 basses (composed 1916).

2. **NEGRO FOLK-SONG DERIVATIVES** .... R. NATHANIEL DETT
   (Born Drummondville, Ont., Canada, 1882)
   (a) Gently, Lord, O gently lead us on (mixed voices, unaccompanied).
   (b) Somebody's knocking at your door (women's voices with piano accompaniment).
   (c) Don't be weary, Traveler (mixed voices, unaccompanied).
   HAMPTON INSTITUTE CHOIR (Conductor: R. NATHANIEL DETT)

3. **MEMORIES OF NEW MEXICO** .... NATALIE CURTIS
   (Born New York City, 1875; died Paris, 1921)
   Two Spanish-Indian melodies used in Religious Festivals near Santa Fe, New Mexico, collected and arranged by Natalie Curtis and orchestrated from her scoring-sketches by Percy Grainger for 4 wood-winds, 2 horns, harp, bells, piano and 6 strings.
   (a) Lenten chant (Crucifixion Hymn): "Sangre de Cristo" ("Blood of Christ").
   (b) "Matachina" Dance.
   (c) **"LOST IN THE HILLS"** (Den Bergtekne) op. 32 .... EDVARD GRIEG
       (Born Bergen, Norway, 1843; died Bergen, 1907)
       Old Norwegian folk-poem set for baritone solo, 2 horns and strings.
       Baritone solo: ERIK BYE

4. **NEGRO FOLK-SONG DERIVATIVES** .... R. NATHANIEL DETT
   (a) I'll never turn back no more (mixed voices, unaccompanied).
   (b) There were Shepherds (men's voices, unaccompanied).
   (c) Listen to the Lambs (mixed voices, unaccompanied).
   HAMPTON INSTITUTE CHOIR (Conductor: R. NATHANIEL DETT)

5. **KAMMERMUSIK** (Chamber Music) No. 1, op. 24, No. 1 ...... PAUL HINDEMITH
   (Born Hanau, Germany, 1895)
   For flute (piccolo), clarinet, bassoon, trumpet, percussion, harmonium, piano, 2 violins, viola, cello, bass.
   (a) Very fast and wild.
   (b) Moderately fast half-notes; very strict in rhythm.
   (c) Very slow and expressive.
   (d) Finale: 1921. (extremely animated).

STEINWAY PIANOS, ESTEY HARMONIUM used.